AMERICAN NATIONAL BIOGRAPHY

AMERICAN
NATIONAL BIOGRAPHY

Published under the auspices of the
AMERICAN COUNCIL OF LEARNED SOCIETIES

General Editors

John A. Garraty

Mark C. Carnes

VOLUME 9

OXFORD UNIVERSITY PRESS

New York   1999   Oxford

OXFORD UNIVERSITY PRESS

Oxford   New York
Athens Auckland Bangkok Bogotá
Buenos Aires Calcutta Cape Town Chennai
Dar es Salaam Delhi Florence Hong Kong Istanbul
Karachi Kuala Lumpur Madrid Melbourne Mexico City
Mumbai Nairobi Paris São Paulo Singapore
Taipei Tokyo Toronto Warsaw
and associated companies in
Berlin Ibadan

Published by Oxford University Press, Inc.,
198 Madison Avenue, New York, New York 10016
http://www.oup-usa.org

Funding for this publication was provided in part by
the Andrew W. Mellon Foundation, the Rockefeller Foundation,
and the National Endowment for the Humanities,
a federal agency.

Library of Congress Cataloging-in-Publication Data

American national biography / general editors, John A. Garraty, Mark C. Carnes
p.   cm.
"Published under the auspices of the American Council of Learned Societies."
Includes bibliographical references and index.
1. United States—Biography—Dictionaries. I. Garraty, John Arthur,
1920–   . II. Carnes, Mark C. (Mark Christopher), 1950–   .
III. American Council of Learned Societies.
CT213.A68   1998   98-20826   920.073—dc21   CIP
ISBN 0-19-520635-5 (set)
ISBN 0-19-512788-9 (vol. 9)

Printing (last digit): 9 8 7 6 5 4 3 2 1

Printed in the United States of America
on acid-free paper

G

CONTINUED

GILBERT, Anne Hartley (21 Oct. 1821–2 Dec. 1904), actress, was born in Rochdale, Lancashire, not far from Manchester, in England, the daughter of Samuel Hartley, a provincial printer; her mother's maiden name was Colborn, but her first name is unknown. After disagreements with his own father, who owned the printing business, Samuel Hartley decided to move his family to London, where they soon found themselves financially strapped. To relieve the family's stress, twelve-year-old Anne was enrolled at the Ballet School of Her Majesty's Theatre in exchange for appearing as an extra in crowd scenes in the ballets performed at Her Majesty's and later at Drury Lane. She spent her days in rigorous training; her nights were spent at the theater. Although she worked up through the ranks of the ballet corps, she never achieved the status of being first or solo dancer.

In 1846 she married George H. Gilbert, a dancer and manager with whom she formed a company and appeared as its solo dancer. They toured the provinces in England and Ireland accumulating a small fortune. After deciding that they were "thoroughly tired of talking through [their] toes," the Gilberts emigrated to the United States hoping to acquire a tract of land and settle down as farmers. They landed in New York in 1849 and made their way west in a covered wagon to the frontier beyond Milwaukee where they invested their entire fortune in land. Leaving their interest in the hands of friends, they returned to Milwaukee after the birth of the first of their two children and went back into the theater to make some money.

In 1851 the Gilbert family went to Chicago to join the company managed by John B. Rice, who controlled the only theater in town. Rice had hired Anne for her dancing, but he also cast her in her first speaking roles. It was then that she decided to become an actress. Her husband, who had sustained serious injuries in a fall on stage, never danced again but worked as a prompter and stage manager for the rest of his life. Under Rice and other managers, Gilbert and her husband traveled the Midwest circuit, which embraced the important theater towns in Illinois, Ohio, and Kentucky. This was excellent training for her as an actress, and she acquired a wide repertoire of character roles along the way. In 1857 she appeared in John Brougham's *Pocahontas*, scoring a hit that brought her to the attention of important managers. When Edwin Booth came to Louisville, she appeared as Lady Macbeth to his Macbeth. During the Civil War, she remained in Louisville until 1864, when she received several flattering offers to join stock companies in the East.

In 1864 she accepted the invitation of the actress-manager Mrs. John Wood to appear with her company at the Olympic Theatre in New York. She spent three years in this excellent company and left only when Mrs. Wood disbanded the company to return to London. Gilbert then went with the company at the Broadway Theatre, first under the management of George Wood (no relation to Mrs. Wood) and later under Barney Williams. While at the Broadway, she played opposite Edwin Forrest, acting Emilia to his Othello (among other roles). In 1869 she joined Augustin Daly's company at the Fifth Avenue Theatre and remained with him until 1877. When he relinquished the theater, she went over to his rival, A. M. Palmer, at the Union Square Theatre, then toured the country with the actor James Lewis under the management of Henry E. Abbey. Finally, she rejoined Daly at his own theater in 1879 and was a prominent member of his company until his death in 1899. With Ada Rehan, John Drew, and James Lewis, Mrs. Gilbert became one of a quartet of actors known as "The Big Four," celebrated on both sides of the Atlantic for their ensemble acting. (Daly's company played in London in 1884 and in Germany and France in 1886.) After Daly's death, Gilbert joined Charles Frohman's company and played prominent character roles in his productions. In 1904 Frohman starred her in *Granny*, a French comedy by George Michell, adapted by Clyde Fitch. The New York audiences, by whom she was much loved, gave her a roaring ovation on her opening night (24 Oct. 1904) at the Lyceum Theatre. After her New York engagement, Frohman sent her on a farewell tour with the first stop in Chicago. She died in her Chicago hotel room four days after opening at Power's Theatre.

A tall and slender woman with a long, thin face, Gilbert did not have the looks to become a leading lady; instead, she contented herself with taking character roles, which she came to love because of their infinite variety. She played old women, harridans, witches, kindly grandmothers, cooks, drudges, and grande dames in comedies, tragedies, melodramas, and farces. Thanks to her training as a dancer, she could act with her entire body, dance a jig, execute eye-catching exits and entrances, and do anything else that would enhance the character she was playing at any given time in any given production. Ada Rehan declared that Gilbert had no equal among actresses, and all of the managers for whom she worked knew that she was incapable of doing anything but the finest and most dedicated acting, no matter how small or insignificant the role. In private, she was a kind and generous woman who harbored no grand illusions about either her acting or her status in the theater.

1

• The series of "Stage Reminiscences of Mrs. Gilbert," ed. Charlotte M. Martin, that ran in *Scribner's Magazine* was later collected into a book and published in 1904. It represents the best source of biographical information. The Robinson Locke Scrapbook, ser. 3, no. 412, New York Performing Arts Library, is a valuable collection of reviews and articles. A more personal assessment is by the actress Ada Rehan, "Some Famous Characters I Have Known," *Madame* (Jan. 1905). Also see Marvin Felheim, *The Theater of Augustin Daly* (1956). Obituaries are in the *New York Sun, New York Herald,* and *New York Tribune,* all 3 Dec. 1904.

MARY C. HENDERSON

GILBERT, Cass (24 Nov. 1859–17 May 1934), architect, was born in Zanesville, Ohio, the son of Samuel Augustus Gilbert, a coast guard officer, and Elizabeth Fulton Wheeler. His father died shortly after the family moved to St. Paul, Minnesota, in 1868. At sixteen Gilbert began his architectural training as an apprentice in the St. Paul office of Abraham Radcliffe. In 1878–1879 he studied at the Massachusetts Institute of Technology (MIT) under William Robert Ware and Eugène Létang, who instilled in him the historicist discipline emanating from the École des Beaux Arts in Paris. After a year of travel to examine and sketch European architectural monuments, he joined the New York firm of McKim, Mead & White as an assistant to Stanford White.

In 1882 he returned to St. Paul to open practice, and in 1884 he entered into partnership with James Knox Taylor, an MIT classmate. When Taylor departed for a government post in Washington, D.C., in 1892, Gilbert became the head of his own firm and remained so for the rest of his life. The Chicago World's Fair of 1893 confirmed his affection for classical models, although he also worked with great skill in the Gothic (the Woolworth Building in New York City, for example) and picturesque traditions (for example, his Oberlin College buildings and the Seaside Sanitarium in Waterford, Conn.).

In 1895 his winning entry in the design competition for the Minnesota State Capitol gained him national attention, and another competition victory in 1899, for the U.S. Custom House in New York City, made possible his move to Manhattan, then the center of the American architectural profession. Thereafter, Gilbert's artistic talent, efficient office organization, and widening network of influential friends and clients lifted him to the inner circle of his profession. In 1908 he was elected president of the American Institute of Architects, and thereafter Theodore Roosevelt (1858–1919), William Howard Taft, and Woodrow Wilson named him to succeeding terms on the National Commission of Fine Arts, the body charged with planning public architectural development in Washington, D.C.

Gilbert won international fame for his neo-Gothic Woolworth Building in New York City, the world's tallest building for seventeen years after its completion in 1913, inspiring the phrase "cathedral of commerce" to describe the skyscraper. His West Virginia Capitol, completed in 1932, was the last state capitol to be rendered in the domed, neoclassical tradition dating back to Charles Bulfinch's 1798 statehouse in Boston.

The political and cultural upheaval of World War I, together with the stir of architectural modernism during the 1920s, inspired a deepening conservatism in Gilbert's mood and practice. When his friendship with Chief Justice Taft won him his last great commission in 1929, for the new U.S. Supreme Court building, Gilbert strove to create a climactic citadel for the beleaguered neoclassical tradition. Completed in 1935, the building promptly became the symbolic focus of the great Supreme Court fight over the New Deal, which Gilbert strenuously opposed. He died in Brockenhurst, England, as the building neared completion. Survivors included his wife, Julia Tappan Finch Gilbert, whom he married in 1887, and four children, one of whom, Cass Gilbert, Jr., tried without success to carry on his father's practice.

• The Cass Gilbert Papers in the Library of Congress contain his important personal correspondence. The larger body of his office papers, including plans and drawings for his major commissions, is in the Cass Gilbert Papers in the New-York Historical Society. Papers relating to his career in St. Paul are in the Minnesota Historical Society. A collection of his personal letterbooks, 1896–1930, is on deposit in the Oberlin College Archives. Sharon Lee Irish, *Cass Gilbert's Career in New York, 1899–1904* (1985), analyzes his office practice during the early New York years. Geoffrey Blodgett, "Cass Gilbert, Architect: Conservative at Bay," *Journal of American History* 72 (Dec. 1985): 615–36, stresses the political and social dimensions of his career. An obituary is in the *New York Times,* 18 May 1934.

GEOFFREY BLODGETT

GILBERT, Felix (21 May 1905–14 Feb. 1991), historian, was born in Baden-Baden, Germany, the son of William Henry Gilbert, a physician whose English father had settled in Germany, and Cécile Mendelssohn Bartholdy, a granddaughter of composer Felix Mendelssohn. When Gilbert was nine months old his father died, and his mother moved to Berlin. After graduating from the Friedrich Werdersche Gymnasium in Berlin in 1923, he entered the University of Heidelberg, but financial uncertainties caused by escalating inflation led him to interrupt his studies. For two years he worked as an assistant in the program of publishing documents in the Foreign Office archives, where he was eventually given responsibility for the early history of the Baghdad Railway.

In the fall of 1925 Gilbert resumed his studies in Munich. After a year he transferred to the University of Berlin, drawn there by the presence of Friedrich Meinecke.

Increasingly since the 1930s, Meinecke has been criticized for a bloodless, aestheticizing approach to the history of ideas, but at the time his exploration of the links between ideas, political theory, and culture was innovative, even revolutionary, and he was an exacting teacher. Gilbert soon combined Meinecke's subtle analyses of texts with his own particular interests in the connections between foreign policy and domestic politics, and in the study of society, economics, and war (in his youth Meinecke had also written a significant work on Prussian military policy). An expansive sense of the interaction of diverse historical phenomena came to characterize Gilbert's writings.

Another of Gilbert's pronounced interests was the methodology of history. Otto Hintze, whom Gilbert regarded as the most important German historian of the time, had retired some years earlier, but Gilbert immersed himself in Hintze's institutional and comparative studies and decades later introduced Hintze's work to the Anglo-American reader by editing *The Historical Essays of Otto Hintze* (1975). An even earlier member of the Berlin faculty, Johann Gustav Droysen, attracted Gilbert as a subject of research, both for his theory of history and for his political liberalism. In 1929 Gilbert prepared the index for the two-volume edition of Droysen's letters, and two years later he received a Ph.D. for a dissertation on Droysen's politics and concept of history in the 1830s and 1840s, which appeared as a *Beiheft* of the *Historische Zeitschrift* (1931). Finally, in 1933, he brought out an edition of Droysen's published and unpublished political writings—a remarkable record of achievement for a scholar then barely twenty-eight years old.

Between 1930 and 1933 Gilbert lived primarily in Italy and worked in the Florentine archives and in the Prussian Academy in Rome. His prospects for a career in Germany were nullified by the National Socialist coup d'etat, and he moved to England in the fall of 1933. After two years a temporary teaching appointment at Scripps College enabled him to come to the United States. At the time, a partly Jewish German immigrant encountered great obstacles in the academic world, and he earned his living with occasional journalism and teaching summer school until in 1939 he became an assistant to Edward Mead Earle, the professor of modern history at the Institute for Advanced Study in Princeton. Gilbert helped Earle conduct a seminar on power and foreign policy, out of which grew the widely used volume of essays *Makers of Modern Strategy* (1943), with Gilbert and Gordon Craig serving as Earle's associate editors. Forty-three years later they served as associate editors for the work's revised edition.

In 1943 Gilbert became an American citizen and joined the Office of Strategic Services, serving in England and occupied Germany from February 1944 to the beginning of 1946. After returning to civilian life he accepted a professorship at Bryn Mawr College. In 1956 he married Mary Raymond, who shared his scholarly interests and assisted him in his research and writing. In 1962 he was appointed to a professorship in the School of Historical Studies of the Institute for Advanced Study, where he remained for the rest of his life.

By the time Gilbert began to teach at Bryn Mawr, he had successfully negotiated the transition from European to American academic life, and his scholarly interests, some stimulated by recent events and personal experience, had settled on four often overlapping areas

of research. One thematic line connected his early work on Droysen with *History* (1965), which he wrote with John Higham and Leonard Krieger, his edition of Hintze, and with his last book, *History: Politics or Culture?* (1990), a collection of essays on Leopold von Ranke and Jacob Burckhardt. A second theme—foreign policy—began with his editorial work in the 1920s and continued with a collection of essays, *The Diplomats*, which he and Gordon Craig edited in 1953, leading to a monograph, *To the Farewell Address* (1961), an investigation, combining European and American sources, of the beginnings of American ideas on foreign policy. The tension between idealism and realism, Gilbert concluded, was the basic issue: "Settled by men who looked for gain and by men who sought freedom, born into independence in a century of enlightened thinking and of power politics, America has wavered in her foreign policy between Idealism and Realism, and her great historical moments have occurred when both were combined" (p. 136). The book won the Bancroft Prize of the American Historical Association. A third thematic line dealt with war, running from *Makers of Modern Strategy* and *Hitler Directs His War* (1951), one of the earliest serious investigations of the interaction of strategy and ideology in the Third Reich, to essays on Machiavelli's ideas on politics and war. The fourth theme consisted of Renaissance studies, a field in which Gilbert had originally wanted to write his dissertation and in which he had published articles since 1935.

Gilbert's major articles and two monographs on Italy in the fifteenth and sixteenth centuries are generally considered the most influential of his work. But they are not necessarily superior to his other writings. His studies of German historians, in particular, are masterpieces of textual and contextual analysis; these works, however, responded more to the author's interest than to that of his American colleagues, most of whom did not take much note of the methods of Ranke, Droysen, or Hintze. Gilbert's writings on Italian history, on the other hand, were a major force in advancing Renaissance studies in the United States.

Machiavelli and Guicciardini (1965) studied the political ideas and concepts of history of two contemporaries of different ideologies in relation to the politics and society of Florence and—an expansion typical of the author—read their works as expressions of a declining political culture that at the same time point to the coming centralized state. Fifteen years later, *The Pope, His Banker and Venice* opened up new areas of research in Venetian fiscal policy and used a complex commercial transaction to illuminate the relationship between economic and political power in the Renaissance.

When Gilbert came to the institute, his influence expanded beyond his writings. He encouraged the application for visiting memberships of scholars, among them many young Germans, representing a broad spectrum of fields and methodologies, including some whose work he found unpersuasive but interesting nonetheless. He was remarkably tolerant. During the ideological conflicts of the 1960s and 1970s he maintained collegial relations with people in every camp, and he always paid less attention to personalities and politics than to the quality of the work. Not only the distinction of his writings, but also his unselfish commitment to the discipline of history led the American Historical Association in 1985 to give him its first Award for Excellence in Scholarship. Gilbert died in Princeton in his eighty-sixth year, continuing to study and write up to his last months.

That a school of historians did not develop around Gilbert has been linked to the diversity of his interests. There are other reasons as well. At Bryn Mawr he had few graduate students. He was undogmatic and took the value of methodological pluralism for granted. Although unusually supportive of young scholars, he concentrated his energies primarily on his own work. Finally, his writings reflected his cultural roots and personal strengths too closely to be easily emulated. Beyond the results of his research, his significance for American historical scholarship in the second half of the twentieth century lies primarily in his bringing together American and European values and methods and in the example that he gave of a professionalism equally creative in the old world and the new.

• A part of Gilbert's papers is privately held. Another part, closed to scholars until 2020, is in the Archives of the Hoover Institution at Stanford University. The selection of his essays, *History: Choice and Commitment* (1977), includes a bibliography of his work to 1976. His recollections, *A European Past: Memoirs 1905–1945* (1988), give an evocative account of his formative years. An interesting memoir is Gordon Craig, "Reflections on the Work of Felix Gilbert," in *Felix Gilbert as Scholar and Teacher*, Occasional Paper of the German Historical Institute (1992). Informative obituaries are in the *New York Times*, 16 Feb. 1991; *The Times* (London), 28 Feb. 1991; and the (Manchester) *Guardian*, 8 Mar. 1991.

PETER PARET

GILBERT, Grove Karl (6 May 1843–1 May 1918), geologist, was born in Rochester, New York, the son of Grove Sheldon Gilbert, a painter, and Eliza Stanley. Bonds forged in "the Nutshell," as Gilbert fondly referred to his family home, remained strong throughout his life. Studious from an early age, he attended the University of Rochester and graduated in 1862. His course work emphasized languages and natural philosophy; later, he remarked that he had found engineering more interesting than the solitary course he took in geology. Upon graduating, he tried teaching in Michigan, failed, and in 1863 took a job at Ward's Scientific Establishment under the direction of a former professor, Henry Ward.

In 1869, having continued his studies in natural history independently, with some direction from Ward, Gilbert secured an appointment as a volunteer assistant to John Strong Newberry, then chief of the Ohio State Geological Survey and an outstanding explorer with the army's pre–Civil War expeditions. For the next two years Gilbert worked as a field geologist in Ohio during the summer and assisted Newberry at Columbia University's School of Mines over the winter.

In May 1871, with Newberry's help, Gilbert joined the U.S. Geographical Survey West of the 100th Meridian, popularly known as the Wheeler Survey after its commander, Lieutenant George Wheeler. That first year's reconnaissance through the West, including a July traverse of Death Valley and an attempted ascent by boat up the western Grand Canyon, covered more than 6,000 miles and forged Gilbert into one of the premier exploring geologists of his day. He returned for field expeditions in 1872 and 1873, then spent most of the 1874 season writing his reports. In November 1874 he married Fannie Porter, sister of the wife of Archibald Marvine, the Wheeler Survey's other geologist and Gilbert's closest friend. In December 1874, disgruntled with Wheeler's authoritarian style and increasingly mesmerized by John Wesley Powell, Gilbert transferred to Powell's U.S. Geological and Geographical Survey of the Rocky Mountain Region, centered in Utah. He served Powell until all the western surveys were consolidated into the U.S. Geological Survey in 1879.

Gilbert remained with the USGS for the duration of his career. He promptly became chief of the Division of the Great Basin, located in Salt Lake City. After Powell assumed directorship of the survey in 1881, Gilbert became a valued assistant, later accepting responsibility for the Appalachian Division (1884). In 1888 he represented the survey at the Fourth International Geological Congress in London. A year later he became the survey's first chief geologist, a post he held until Congress temporarily abolished the position in 1892.

Throughout, Gilbert remained active in scientific societies. He was elected to the National Academy of Sciences (1883), served as president of the Cosmos Club (1904) and the Philosophical Society of Washington (1892), and presided over the American Association for the Advancement of Science (1900) and the Geological Society of America (1893, 1909). After a politically embattled Powell was forced to resign in 1894, Gilbert was reportedly offered the post of survey director for himself but declined. Instead he assumed fieldwork in Colorado.

Events gradually freed Gilbert for major changes. In 1899 his wife, long an invalid, died. Both Fannie and Karl had suffered painfully from the death by diphtheria of their first child at age seven. The episode had caused Karl to dismiss any lingering religious sentiments, but Fannie recovered poorly, a condition reputedly worsened by coal-gas poisoning and not erased by the subsequent birth of two sons. Soon after his wife's death, Gilbert ventured north with the Harriman Alaskan expedition. Gilbert's final ties to the Nutshell ended with the death of his brother in 1901. That summer he resumed long-deferred studies in the Basin Range province only to be interrupted when his notes disappeared mysteriously in a fire. Powell died in 1902; Gilbert served as executor of his will and as his first biographer. He then moved permanently to

California, joined the Sierra Club, cultivated new companions, and in 1905 requested the assignment that framed the final phase of his scientific career.

Political attempts to revive hydraulic mining sent Gilbert into the Sierra Nevada to study the legacy of past decades of this practice and inspired him to establish a set of flumes on the University of California campus—the USGS Hydraulic Laboratory, the first facility dedicated to experimentation on fluvial transport. He was in Berkeley when the San Francisco earthquake struck in 1906 and was soon enlisted for both the federal and state investigations. In 1909 a stroke proved nearly fatal. Slowly, methodically, he rebuilt his health, published both his field and laboratory research, made plans to remarry (to Alice Eastwood, a California botanist), and returned once again to the topic with which he had begun his western career, the Basin Range. Before either that monograph or his remarriage could be completed, however, he died while visiting his sister in Jackson, Michigan.

Gilbert's scientific accomplishments were both robust and varied. He first explained (and named) two forms of mountain-building, the laccolith and the Basin Range structure. He made original advances in concepts of isostasy, the graded stream, cycles of sedimentary deposition, glaciated landscapes, lake deltas and shorelines, and the recession of Niagara Falls. He wrote the first scientific paper on earthquake prediction (1909). His "Moon's Face: A Study of the Origin of Its Features" (*Philosophical Society of Washington Bulletin* 12 [1893]) began the modern study of lunar morphology as a product of impact cratering. His labors on the lake levels of the Great Salt Lake were critical to Powell's famous conservation tract, *Report on the Lands of the Arid Region of the United States* (1878). Among his extensive publications, four monographs endure as classics: *Report on the Geology of the Henry Mountains, Utah* (1877), *Lake Bonneville* (1890), *The Transportation of Debris by Running Water* (1914), and *Hydraulic-Mining Debris in the Sierra Nevada* (1917). Two essays remain fundamental contributions to the scientific philosophy of geology: "On the Inculcation of the Scientific Method by Example" (*American Journal of Science* 3d ser., 31 [1886]: 284–99) and "The Origin of Hypotheses" (*Science* n.s., 53 [1896]: 1–13). Gilbert argued that in geology—as in other sciences—ideas came from analogies, that methods were learned by example, and that all conclusions were tentative. "In the domain of the world's knowledge there is no infallibility," he wrote in "The Origin of Hypotheses" (p. 12). Additionally, Gilbert was among the first to bring laboratory methods to bear on geologic problems, cultivating experiments on cratering and flumes, and joined early pioneers in boldly extending mechanical models to geologic processes. For these achievements Gilbert is widely recognized as a founder, in particular, of geomorphology and structural geology, and became one of the outstanding American scientists of the nineteenth century.

Gilbert's scholarly character impressed itself powerfully on his beloved survey, that "great engine of research," as he called it. It radiated through geology overall, influencing not by authority or pronouncements but by example, which is how Gilbert believed science was best communicated. More subtly, it informed his view of an even-tempered, book-balancing nature, best understood by analogy to conservative sciences like mechanics. Landscape represented a balance of forces and resistances, and geologic history became the record of events initiated under the impress of some disequilibrating force and terminated once equilibrium was restored.

Gilbert's biography is an apt cross-section through the heroic age of American geology. In 1900 he received the prestigious Wollaston Award from the London Geological Society, the third American so recognized. The Geological Society of America twice elected him president, the only man to date to be so honored. The National Academy of Sciences bestowed on him one of its longest biographical memoirs. To celebrate its centennial in 1979, the USGS chose to host a symposium on the legacy of the man it considered the outstanding scientist of its first century, Grove Karl Gilbert.

• Gilbert's papers were assembled by William Morris Davis for his memoir, "Grove Karl Gilbert, 1843–1918," National Academy of Sciences, *Biographical Memoirs* 21 (1926); those papers have since disappeared. The family reclaimed some, Donald Coates others. Accordingly, Davis's memoir must remain the primary repository of Gilbertiana. Several useful memorials were published after Gilbert's death: E. C. Andrews, "Grove Karl Gilbert," *Sierra Club Bulletin* 11 (1920–1923): 60–68; Joseph Barrell, "Grove Karl Gilbert: An Appreciation," *Sierra Club Bulletin* 10 (1919): 397–99; T. C. Chamberlin, "Grove Karl Gilbert," *Journal of Geology* 26 (1918): 375–76; Henry Fairchild, "Grove Karl Gilbert," *Science*, n.s., 48 (1918): 151–54; C. Hart Merriam, "Grove Karl Gilbert, the Man," *Sierra Club Bulletin* 10 (1919): 391–96; George Otis Smith, "Grove Karl Gilbert," USGS *Annual Report* 39 (1918): 11; and W. C. Mendenhall, "Memorial of Grove Karl Gilbert," *Geological Society of America Bulletin* 31 (1920): 26–64, which contains a comprehensive bibliography of Gilbert's publications, lacking only *Studies in Basin-Range Structure* (1928), which was published posthumously. A modern biography, more exposition than narrative, is Stephen Pyne, *Grove Karl Gilbert* (1980). A recent review of Gilbert's science is available in Ellis L. Yochelson, ed., "The Scientific Ideas of G. K. Gilbert: An Assessment on the Occasion of the Centennial of the United States Geological Survey (1879–1979)," Geological Society of America *Special Paper* 183 (1980).

STEPHEN J. PYNE

GILBERT, Helen Homans (29 Oct. 1913–26 Sept. 1989), college trustee and community volunteer, was born in Quincy, Massachusetts, the daughter of Robert Homans, a lawyer, and Abigail Adams. True to her Adams and Homans antecedents, she carried on a tradition of public service that dated back to the beginnings of the republic. She was, she said, "a New Englander with a family conscience who inherited community responsibility." Robert Homans decided that both his daughters should attend college to prepare for careers as teachers "since no Homans woman in living memory had ever married."

Helen Homans went to Radcliffe College intending to train as a laboratory technician and earned her A.B. in biology in 1936. However, she confounded family tradition by her marriage immediately after commencement to Carl J. Gilbert, later chief executive officer and chairman of the Gillette Company; they had one child. When World War II broke out and her husband went overseas, Helen Gilbert put her training to good use by working on burn research under Cecil K. Drinker at the Harvard School of Public Health (1942–1944) and with Joe V. Meigs, confirming the work of George Papanicolaou on the Pap smear test for uterine cancer, at the Vincent Hospital (1944–1945). The return of her husband at the end of World War II and the birth of her son in 1947 ended Gilbert's professional career.

With her appointment to Radcliffe's board of trustees in 1950, Gilbert began a new career that came to symbolize what is best about volunteer leadership in higher education. She was a member of the board until 1976, serving as chair from 1955 to 1972. During this time she guided two searches for presidents of Radcliffe and led two successful capital campaigns, in 1956–1966 and 1967–1976, which raised funds for the Cronkhite Graduate Center, the Jordan cooperative houses, Hilles Library, and Currier House. She served as acting president, without salary, during 1964–1965, while President Mary Bunting was on leave with the Atomic Energy Commission in Washington, D.C. Later, she helped President Bunting steer the college through negotiations with Harvard that led to coresidential living and opened all Harvard's resources to women undergraduates. This new agreement, dubbed the "non-merger merger," did not lead to the corporate merger of Harvard and Radcliffe that Gilbert and President Bunting had intended. Instead, it formed the basis of a new institutional relationship, ratified in 1977, whereby Radcliffe reaffirmed its corporate independence, retained its own postgraduate programs, and, while retaining an informal advocacy role for women, delegated to Harvard all responsibility for the academic, residential, and extracurricular activities of Radcliffe undergraduates. This agreement illustrated Gilbert's views on higher education for women, which were pragmatic and specific to the two institutions, Harvard and Radcliffe, that she knew best. Commensurate with women's capabilities, she believed, was that they should have equal access to Harvard and should ultimately be equally represented on Harvard's faculty, administration, and governing boards.

In 1970 Helen Gilbert was elected to the Harvard Board of Overseers. She was the first woman and first non-Harvard alumnus to serve and the first to become its president (1975–1976). The Gilbert Report (1978) reviewed the governance of Harvard University and streamlined the role and responsibility of the board of overseers. Gilbert also served on several hospital boards, the United Fund (Boston), Boston United Community Services, and the Boston Permanent Charity Board. She was director of the Boston Fenway Program, Inc., and trustee of Westover School.

Radcliffe College recognized Gilbert for her years of service by naming one of the halls of Currier House for her. She was also given the Radcliffe College Achievement Award (1965) and was the first recipient of the Helen Homans Gilbert Distinguished Volunteer Service Award (1978). She received the Westover School's Westover Award (1966) and the Harvard Medal (1976).

Helen Gilbert practiced her own brand of feminism. She believed women to be equal to and as capable as any man and broke down barriers for women by ignoring them. Once described by *People* magazine (5 Apr. 1976) as "an elegant liberation movement all on her own," she joked about the impact of the women's movement on the Gilbert household. "Making the beds one day, it suddenly dawned on me, 'why should I be the one to make the beds?' Now the beds are sometimes made by the President of the Harvard Board of Overseers, and other times by the retired President and CEO of the Gillette Company" (*New York Post*, 17 Apr. 1976).

Gilbert once said, "Working for Radcliffe is one of the most satisfactory occupations there is and I intend to keep on doing it for the rest of my life." She returned in 1981 to chair the advisory committee of Radcliffe's Schlesinger Library (1981–1986) and continued to work in the archives of the college and to record and transcribe oral histories with members of the college community right up to the week before her death (in Boston).

When Helen Gilbert retired from chairing the Radcliffe Board of Trustees in 1972, President Bunting said, "No one is more aware of how much Radcliffe owes to Helen Gilbert. The time, energy, wisdom, wit, and the love that Helen has given to Radcliffe have bound us all. Helen has kept us all in motion and on target by sheer force of character, yes but such a lovely character, not grim, but joyous, not dutiful but truly generous." "Helen Gilbert's devoted service to the college," said President Bunting in 1976, "is a shining example of the way in which an educated and concerned volunteer can make a highly creative, very significant, and lasting contribution to an institution and to society."

• Gilbert's speeches, correspondence, clippings, obituaries, oral histories, tributes, and photographs are in the Radcliffe College Archives. Her correspondence as acting president (1964–1965) is filed with the papers of President Mary I. Bunting and is restricted. She contributed to two scientific publications: W. W. Glenn et al., "Treatment of Burns by Closed Plaster Method with Certain Physiological Considerations Implicit in Success of This Technique," *Journal of Clinical Investigation* 22 (July 1943): 609–25; and M. Fremont-Smith et al., "Cancer of Endometrium and Prolonged Estrogen Therapy," *Journal of the American Medical Association* 131 (July 1946): 805–8. She also wrote several articles: "Trusteeship at Radcliffe," *Radcliffe Quarterly* 39, no. 4

(1955): 4–6; "Radcliffe's President Elect," *Radcliffe Quarterly* 43, no. 3 (1959): 4–5, a brief biography of Mary Bunting; "Confessions of the First Woman President of the Harvard Board of Overseers," *Radcliffe Quarterly* 62, no. 2 (1976): 42–44; and "Reminiscences of a Boston Brahmin," *Radcliffe Quarterly* 70, no. 3 (1984): 42–43, about her upbringing, college experience, and volunteer work. The Gilbert Committee's "Report from the Committee on the Structure and Function of the Board of Overseers Concerning Harvard's Governmental Structure" (Dec. 1978) is at the Harvard University Archives. The oral histories recorded and transcribed by Gilbert form part of the Radcliffe College Oral History Collection in the Radcliffe College Archives. An obituary is in the *New York Times*, 1 Oct. 1989.

JANE S. KNOWLES

GILBERT, Henry Franklin Belknap (26 Sept. 1868–19 May 1928), composer, essayist, and musician, was born in Somerville, Massachusetts, the son of Benjamin Franklin Gilbert, a bank clerk and musician, and Therese Angeline Gilson, a noted soprano. At the age of ten, inspired by the playing of Ole Bull, Gilbert determined to study violin—his first fiddle was made for him by his father from a shingle and a cigar box. Impressed by his commitment, his parents arranged for professional instruction and bought him a violin. By the time he was sixteen, Gilbert was playing violin professionally in theater and dance orchestras.

Gilbert studied piano with George Elbridge Whiting and harmony with George Henry Howard at the New England Conservatory in 1886–1887; he also studied violin with Emil Mollenhauer. In 1889 Gilbert became Edward MacDowell's first American pupil in composition and orchestration, and he studied with MacDowell until 1892. He later spent eight summers between 1912 and 1926 at the MacDowell Colony for American composers in Peterborough, New Hampshire.

Convinced that nationalistic music must incorporate native melodies and rhythms, Gilbert assiduously studied folk songs of all countries, even working as a bread and pie cutter at the 1893 Chicago World's Fair in order to hear and notate the folk songs heard in the Midway Plaisance.

In 1894 Gilbert published his first work, *A Group of [8] Songs*. During the summer of the next year he went to France and England, working his way across on a cattle boat, to collect scores for Josiah D. Whitney, a Harvard geology professor who contributed extensively to the music library at Harvard. Gilbert returned to the United States after contracting typhoid fever. In 1897 he published his first composition based on African-American rhythms, *Negro Episode*, op. 2; the work was highly acclaimed by Jules Massenet and hailed by the French as the first indigenous American orchestral composition.

In 1901, fascinated by reports that Gustave Charpentier had incorporated famous Paris folk songs into his opera *Louise*, Gilbert traveled, again by cattle boat, to hear the opera in Paris. During his two-week stay he was so inspired by the production that he vowed to continue composing "American, and un-European music: music which shall smack of our home-soil, even though it may be crude" (Boardman, p. 34). Returning from Europe, he lived for several months in a barn, looking after a cow and a horse, while he composed such works as *Salammbô's Invocation to Tänith*, especially well received in Russia, and *The Pirate Song*, recorded by David Bispham and later used in the film *The Sea-Hawk* (1924).

After meeting composer and publisher Arthur Farwell in 1902, Gilbert became involved with Farwell's Wa-Wan Press, which specialized in the publication of American music, including many of Gilbert's own songs and piano compositions. For a decade, Gilbert was a driving force behind the success of the press. Also during this period Gilbert selected, edited, and arranged public school music songs for Clarence C. Birchard, who published *One Hundred Folk Songs of Many Countries* in 1910. Gilbert also transcribed American Indian music for Edward S. Curtis's *The North American Indian* (1911) and composed short orchestral pieces to accompany Curtis's lectures. As an authority on native American music, he subsequently made significant contributions to *The Art of Music*, edited by Daniel Gregory Mason (1916). Most importantly, he continued to compose whenever circumstances permitted: *Americanesque*, op. 5 (c. 1903), based on the minstrel tunes "Zip Coon," "Dearest May," and "Don't Be Foolish, Joe"; *Comedy Overture on Negro Themes* (c. 1906), which drew upon the riverboat song "I'se Gwine to Alabammy, Oh" and the spiritual "Old Ship of Zion" as well as ragtime; *The Dance in Place Congo*, op. 15 (c. 1908; rev. 1916), inspired by George W. Cable's description of New Orleans Creole dances, especially the "bamboula"; and *Negro Rhapsody* (1912). Originally titled "Shout," *Negro Rhapsody* is based on two spirituals, "Listen to the Angels Shouting" and "I'll Hear the Trumpet Sound." In 1906 Gilbert married Helen Kalischer of Rumania; the couple had two children.

The first performances of the *Comedy Overture on Negro Themes* by the Boston Symphony Orchestra under Max Fiedler in 1911 established Gilbert's international reputation as a composer. According to the *New York Times* (29 Apr. 1928), Gilbert had successfully "fused negroid themes in the fires of his creative impulse, shaped them into eloquent and artistic forms, and produced a music alive with qualities of this people and this environment." In 1914 the work was performed to great acclaim by Reinhold Glière, the revered Russian composer and conductor of the Russian Imperial Symphony, in Feodosiya and Odessa, Russia.

In 1918 *The Dance in Place Congo* was given five performances as a ballet at the Metropolitan Opera House. Although the ballet was favorably reviewed in the *New York Times* as "the most artistic piece of negro ragtime rhapsody Broadway has shown" (24 Mar. 1918), and in the *Brooklyn Eagle* as "the best American music the Metropolitan has ever accepted for its own use" (24 Mar. 1918), the orchestral version proved even more successful. This version was selected for performance at the International Society of Contemporary Music Festival held in Frankfurt, Germany, in 1927, when Gilbert and Aaron Copland were the two American composers honored by the society.

Gilbert's later significant compositions include music for the Plymouth Tercentenary Pageant (1920), the film score for *Down to the Sea in Ships* (1922), *Jazz Study* (1924), *Symphonic Piece* and *Nocturne, from Whitman* (1925), and *Suite for Chamber Orchestra* (1926–1927). These compositions are noted for their mature, original style that assimilates various indigenous elements.

Gilbert made a unique contribution to the establishment of a nationalistic American school of composition not only as a composer but also as an essayist whose articles appeared in many journals, including the *New Music Review* and the *Musical Quarterly*, the latter of which he helped to found in 1915. Gilbert continuously advocated that American composers emancipate themselves from European domination. Called the "Mark Twain of American Music," he believed that if American composers used the melodies and rhythms of folk music as a source of inspiration, they could successfully compose compositions that reflected the American spirit of optimism, youthfulness, and buoyancy. He was also instrumental in the founding of the American Music Society (1905) and the New Music Society of America (1906). Olin Downes observed in the *New York Times* (27 May 1928) that Gilbert "was an artist who filled a place that no one else could fill, at a time when this was the most necessary of all things for an American composer to do. More than measurably did he accomplish his purpose. He stands in his generation alone and incomparable."

When Gilbert died in Cambridge, Massachusetts, at the age of sixty, he made medical history by having lived twenty-three years longer than any other person who had been diagnosed with tetralogy of Fallot, a very serious congenital heart defect. Gilbert became one of the most significant pioneers in the development of indigenous American music by initiating the use of spirituals, jazz, and ragtime in orchestral works.

• The Henry F. Gilbert Papers, including music manuscripts, correspondence, notebooks, sketches, pamphlets, programs, photographs, published books, and music from his library, are housed in the Beinecke Rare Book and Manuscript Library at Yale University. In addition, some of his manuscripts and correspondence are housed at the Library of Congress, Harvard University, the Boston Public Library, and the New York Public Library. The two most complete modern assessments are Sherrill V. Martin, *Henry F. Gilbert: A Bio-Bibliography* (1997), and Katherine E. Longyear, "Henry F. Gilbert: His Life and Works" (Ph.D. diss., Univ. of Rochester, 1968); each contains a biography, complete list of works, extensive bibliography, and notes on sources. See also Olin Downes, "An American Composer," *Musical Quarterly* 4 (1918): 23–36, and "Henry Gilbert: Nonconformist," in *A Birthday Offering to Carl Engel*, ed. Gustave Reese (1943); Elliott Carter, "American Figure, with Landscape," *Modern Music* 20 (1942–1943): 219–25; Katherine E. Longyear and Rey M. Longyear, "Henry F. Gilbert's Unfinished 'Uncle Remus' Opera," *Yearbook for Inter-American Musical Research* 10 (1974): 50–67; H. G. Sear, "Henry Franklin Belknap Gilbert," *Music Review* 5 (1944): 250–59; and Herbert R. Boardman, "Somerville's Composers and Musicians" (unpublished paper, Somerville, Mass., 1941). An obituary is in the *New York Times* 20 May 1928; related articles by Olin Downes and James Philip Dunn appear in the 27 May issue of the *Times*.

SHERRILL V. MARTIN

GILBERT, John Gibbs (27 Feb. 1810–17 June 1889), actor, was born in Boston, Massachusetts, the son of John Neal Gilbert and Elizabeth Atkins. His interest in the stage began while he worked at his uncle's dry goods store in Boston. He was an avid theatergoer and took opportunities to perform while attending Boston High School. Gilbert became involved in the professional theater, without his uncle's or mother's approval, when he was eighteen. He gained the theater manager's permission to audition for the Tremont Theatre company and won the part of Jaffier in Thomas Otway's tragedy *Venice Preserved*. Gilbert then won parts in *The Iron Chest* as Sir Edward Mortimer and as Shylock in Shakespeare's *The Merchant of Venice*.

In the fall of 1828 Gilbert moved to New Orleans to join James H. Caldwell's company at the Camp Street Theatre. He stayed there until 1834 performing in towns along the Mississippi River. It was likely that his performance as an old man in *The May Queen* steered him to play such roles repeatedly. His portly build and sober demeanor may have contributed to that type. In William Winter's *The Actor and Other Speeches* Gilbert is quoted as saying, "I went to the theatre where, to my great disgust and indignation, I was cast for an old man—at the age of nineteen" (p. 10). Nevertheless, he soon realized that his strength and popularity lay in performing older parts, which he did for the majority of his 1,500 different roles.

Gilbert married actress Maria Deth Campbell in 1836; they had no children. In 1846 they traveled to Europe for rest and relaxation. Gilbert was persuaded to perform at London's Princess Theatre in the role of Sir Robert Bramble in *The Poor Gentleman*. He was so well received that he continued at the Princess for a year. His stay in Europe provided him the opportunity to see some of the great actors of the day, including England's fiery and gifted William Macready. He also visited Paris, where he studied at the Théâtre Français. Gilbert's time in Europe served him well; though he was only there a year, his talents seemed to mature. On his return to the United States, he joined New York's Park Theatre, where he continued to perform until that theater burned in 1848.

Following his stint at the Park, Gilbert had a nomadic career in the Northeast. He played at Boston's Howard Athenaeum and Philadelphia's Chestnut Street Theatre and, in 1854, returned to Boston to perform in the opening production of the Boston Theatre. He gave the dedication address, written by poet T. W. Parsons, and played one of his famous comic roles, Sir Anthony Absolute in Richard Brinsley Sheridan's *The Rivals*. Gilbert stayed in Boston for four more years, playing such diverse roles as Caliban in *The Tempest* and Bottom in *A Midsummer Night's Dream*.

In 1858 Gilbert returned to Philadelphia and performed at the Arch until the eminent actor James William Wallack opened his theater in New York on Broadway and asked Gilbert to join the company in 1861. Gilbert stayed even when the group's management passed from the elder Wallack, upon his death in 1864, to his son Lester. After Gilbert's first wife died in 1866, he married Sarah H. Gavett. They had no children. Gilbert's thirty-year association as an actor and stage manager for the Wallack company ended in 1888.

The later part of Gilbert's professional life was spent with Joseph Jefferson's company. Jefferson, the third actor of his name and renowned for his performance as the title character in Dion Boucicault's *Rip Van Winkle*, employed Gilbert in a production of *The Rivals*. Gilbert reprised his Sir Anthony Absolute to Jefferson's Bob Acres and Mrs. John Drew's Mrs. Malaprop. It was Gilbert's last role. He and Jefferson argued about the loose interpretation brought to the production, demonstrating Gilbert's conservative attitude about the theater. As Winter said of him, "The profession of the actor was, in his esteem, sacred. He allowed no levity on the subject, and his anger was quickly aroused by any trifling with the dramatic art" (p. 52). Gilbert's aesthetic was to be true to the profession and true to the script. In his own account of his life, printed in the *New York Herald* (5 Dec. 1878), Gilbert said,

Only a little while ago I saw nine gentle men on the stage all dressed alike, from the waiter up to the hero. What illusion was there in this? If we are going to play the *School for Scandal* we must play it according to tradition, for there can be no such character as a modern Sir Peter Teazle or Sir Oliver Surface. I believe in adhering to tradition and to the coloring of nature that attaches to a given dramatic period.

Gilbert died in Boston.

• William Winter, *The Actor and Other Speeches* (1891), is a primary factual source about Gilbert and includes useful commentary. Similarly, Winter, *A Sketch of the Life of John Gilbert* (1890) and *The Wallet of Time* (2 vols., 1913), offer personal glimpses of the subject. T. A. Brown, *A History of the New York Stage* (3 vols., 1903); F. E. McKay and C. E. L. Wingate, eds., *Famous American Actors of Today* (1896); and Gerald Bordman, *American Theatre: A Chronicle of Comedy and Drama, 1869–1914* (1994), provide a broader context.

KENT NEELY

GILBERT, Mercedes (1889–1 Mar. 1952), actress and writer, was born in Jacksonville, Florida, the daughter of Daniel Marshall Gilbert, the owner of a furniture business, and Edna Earl Knott, the owner of a dressmaking business. In an unfinished autobiographical manuscript, Gilbert wrote that because of her parents' jobs, she was cared for and educated by a nurse. She enrolled in the Boylan Home, a seminary for girls in Jacksonville, when she was in the fourth grade. After her family moved to Tampa, Florida, Gilbert attended a Catholic school and the Orange Park Normal and Industrial School. She went to Edward Waters College in Jacksonville and after graduation taught school in southern Florida before deciding that she wanted a different profession. She then entered the Brewster Hospital Nurses Training School and graduated three years later, staying on the staff for two more years as the assistant superintendent.

After moving to New York City in 1916, with possibly some time spent in Chicago, Gilbert searched for a nursing job. She found, however, that her hospital in Florida did not have the appropriate qualifications to make it a Grade One training school, so she would have had to spend three more years in postgraduate training at Lincoln Hospital. As she had been writing poems and plays with some success for most of her life, in the early 1920s Gilbert began to take seriously the advice of friends who told her to find a songwriter to collaborate with her in setting some of her poetry to music. Though she may have worked as a private nurse for some periods of time in New York City, in 1922 Gilbert began to achieve status as a songwriter. She notes in her autobiographical manuscript, "Strange to say, the first was a song about the 'sport of kings,' horse racing, titled 'The Also Ran Blues.' This song became quite a hit and was recorded by most of the record companies" (Roses and Randolph, p. 123). Gilbert managed an eight-piece jazz band and a blues singer who recorded the popular "The Decatur Street Blues" and "Got the World in a Jug," both of which she wrote in the early 1920s. In 1922 she married Arthur J. Stevenson.

Her marriage did not interfere with her blossoming career in the arts. Though she had been successfully composing songs and writing for the Associated Negro Press, she got her first significant part as an actress in *The Lace Petticoat*, a Broadway musical comedy in which all the members of the cast were white, "except the singers and myself" (Roses and Randolph, p. 123). She subsequently appeared in many Broadway shows, including *Lost, Bomboola, Play Genius, Play, Malinda, How Come Lawd?, The Searching Wind*, and *Carib Song*. Of special note is her performance as Zipporah, the wife of Moses, throughout the five-year run of *Green Pastures*, which played in New York City and on tour during the early 1930s. Her obituary in the *New York Times* notes that her portrayal of Zipporah and her performance as Cora Lewis in *Mulatto* are her most notable. The role of Cora Lewis, the wife of Colonel Norwood in Langston Hughes's *Mulatto*, is especially significant not only because it contains excellent monologues that would highlight any actress's skills, but also because she unexpectedly had to take over the role previously played by Rose McClendon, being handed the script on a Saturday evening and being onstage by Tuesday. A reviewer in the *New York World Telegram* notes on 8 May 1936 that "Mercedes Gilbert pinchhits successfully. . . . Hers is a perilous part and she makes hay with it" (quoted in Roses and Randolph, p.

122). She played the role on Broadway for a year, the rest of the 1935–1936 season, and on tour for seven months. Another contemporary reviewer notes, "Miss Gilbert, as Cora Lewis . . . is performing so remarkably and being so well received by different audiences that both author Langston Hughes and producer Martin Jones predict a long run at the Ambassador Theatre . . . where 'Mulatto' has now been running more than eleven months" (Stewart, p. 7).

Gilbert also appeared on radio, television, and in such silent pictures as *The Call of His People*, *Secret Sorrow*, and *Body and Soul*. In *Body and Soul*, which was directed by one of the most famous black filmmakers of the 1920s, Oscar Micheaux, Gilbert worked with the popular black actor Paul Robeson. Also of note are her performances in the all-black productions of *Lysistrata* and *Tobacco Road*. In the 1940s, she began to tour the United States and Canada in a one-woman show consisting of recitals of her work. During this time she also toured colleges performing and lecturing on black history. A collection of her work, titled *Selected Gems of Poetry, Comedy, and Drama* (1931), contains comments on the dust jacket stating that Gilbert's monologues were performed on national radio. The publishers note that "the work is mainly in Southern dialect, because the direct appeal of this soft speech is intriguing and amusing to readers both North and South" (Roses and Randolph, p. 123). She was also a member of the Olympic Committee for the 11th Olympiad (1936). Her only novel, *Aunt Sara's Wooden God*, was published in 1938 with a foreword by Langston Hughes. The novel, like much of Gilbert's other work, has fallen into undeserved obscurity. She also wrote three plays, *Environment*, *In Greener Pastures*, and *Ma Johnson's Harlem Rooming House*; the last was first produced by the Harlem YMCA in 1938.

The last record of Mercedes Gilbert in the Schomburg Collection is an invitation to her and her husband's twenty-fifth wedding anniversary on 19 July 1947. There is no information available that indicates children or further public activity after 1947. Her obituary in the *New York Times* states that she was living in Jamaica, New York, when she died in the Queens General Hospital in Jamaica.

• Along with an autobiographical manuscript and other information available through the Schomburg Center for Research in Black Culture of the New York Public Library and through Gilbert's publisher, Christopher House, the most thorough accounting of her life is Lorraine E. Roses and Ruth E. Randolf, *Harlem Renaissance and Beyond: Literary Biographies of 100 Black Women Writers, 1900–1945* (1990). This four-page biography is the most complete summation of Gilbert's life to date. A short piece, "The Poet-Actress: A Personal Interview with Miss Mercedes Gilbert" by Harry T. Stewart, was published in *Education: A Journal of Reputation* 2 (Sept. 1936): 7. Hugh Morris Gloster, *Negro Voices in American Fiction* (1948), also mentions Gilbert. An obituary is in the *New York Times*, 6 Mar. 1952.

SHARON L. BARNES

GILBERT, Ray (15 Sept. 1912–3 Mar. 1976), lyricist and composer of popular songs, was born in Hartford, Connecticut, the son of Jacob Kalin, a Russian-Jewish immigrant, and Mina Freeman, a Swedish immigrant. During his childhood the family moved to Chicago, where he graduated from Senn High School in 1930. After graduation Gilbert became a sketch writer for various vaudeville talents, including Carmen Miranda, Harry Richman, Buddy Rogers, and Sophie Tucker. For a time he was a nightclub performer with Sidney Miller, with whom he collaborated on a few songs. One of their efforts, "Send Me a Man Amen," was sung by the Andrews Sisters in the 1944 film, *Moonlight and Cactus*. In 1939 Gilbert moved to Hollywood to write a musical score for the Earl Carroll Restaurant. From 1940 through 1942 he worked for the J. Walter Thompson company as a comedy writer.

Gilbert's importance stems largely from his association with Walt Disney Productions, where he was contracted from 1943 to 1946. He wrote thirty song lyrics while there, usually for tunes by Charles Wolcott and other contract composers but occasionally receiving joint credit for the music. Sixteen of these songs were used in various animated features, notably *The Three Caballeros* (1945), *Make Mine Music* (1946), and *Song of the South* (1946), for which he wrote "Zip-a-Dee Doo-Dah" (with music by Allie Wrubel) and won an Academy Award. Another song, "You Belong to My Heart" (with music by Augustin Lara) for *The Three Caballeros*, enjoyed hit status through a recording by Bing Crosby and was later used in three non-Disney films.

It is not known why Gilbert left the Disney studio. According to the studio he was "laid off," but the impetus may have come from Gilbert himself. The early Disney films were full of great songs by unknown writers who left the studio in the midst of success. Often, as was the case with Gilbert, the score for a film was written by three or four composers and lyricists, usually working on three or four projected films at a time. The last of his efforts to be used by Disney was "Merrily On Our Way" for *The Adventures of Ichabod and Mr. Toad* (1949). Of the fourteen unused efforts, two had been intended for *Lady and the Tramp*, which was released in 1955.

While Gilbert continued to work steadily after the Disney years he never regained the same level of success. Subsequent films with his contributions include *A Date with Judy* (1948) and *Nancy Goes to Rio* (1950). In 1959 he wrote most of the music and lyrics for the record album *The Nina, the Pinta and the Santa Maria*. (The score was rerecorded in 1971 as "We Think the World Is Round.")

A brief return to animated films resulted in at least one critical success with "Vene, Veno, Vena" for the film *Hey There, It's Yogi Bear* (1964). His last work of significance included some collaborations with the popular Brazilian artist Antonio Carlos Jobim, notably "Dindi" and "She's a Carioca," both in 1965. He married twice: to Dorothy Downey of Peoria, Illinois, with whom he had one child, and later to the actress

Janis Paige. Gilbert died in Los Angeles following heart surgery at the University of California Medical Center.

Ray Gilbert was a journeyman lyricist who occasionally benefited from being the right person in the right place at the right time. There is no question that while a few of his studio songs are meritorious, he benefited from the glory years of the Disney animators through "stars" like Brer Rabbit, Mr. Toad, and Donald Duck. On the other hand it can be said that Gilbert's best work could inspire an entire cast and crew to greater heights. Apart from the politically dated aspects of *Song of the South*, "Zip-a-Dee Doo-Dah" sets up the warmhearted humor of the entire movie in the best tradition of Broadway. Other Disney songs by Gilbert that are still cited by critics for their "theatrical" value include "Baia" (1944), with music by Ary Barroso; "Everybody Has a Laughing Place" (1946), with music by Wrubel; "All the Cats Join In" (1944), with music by Eddie Sauter and words with Alec Wilder; "Two Silhouettes" (1945), with music by Wolcott; and "Blame It on the Samba" (1948), with music by Ernesto Nazareth.

These tunes display two traits to which Gilbert would continually return. One of these is shown by the songs that appeal to the child in all of us and the other was his predilection for Latin American melodies. As early as 1939 he had supplied English lyrics for the 1925 Marcos A. Jimenez song, "Adios, Mariquita Linda." During the 1930s and 1940s the American public had a particular interest in Latin music, which was temporarily reborn with Jobim's performances in the 1960s. Gilbert was an experienced choice to help the Brazilian composer expand into the American market, and it paid off for both men.

At least two other previously written tunes have become associated with Gilbert: Don Redman's 1928 standard "Cherry" and Edward "Kid" Ory's 1926 jazz classic "Muskrat Ramble." For this last title Gilbert supplied lyrics nearly thirty years after its original composition, and subsequent performances helped rejuvenate Ory's career.

Gilbert was at his best in a collaborative "theatrical" assignment. If there was a weakness in his career it was his failure to develop a long-standing partnership with any one composer. (He may have had a desire to be his own man: there are a few songs for which he supplied his own music.) In general his output is noted for the wide number of collaborators with which he worked, including Lou Busch, Hoagy Carmichael, Frank Churchill, Ken Darby, Osvaldo Farres, Vincius de Mores, Ted Fiorito, Doug Goodwin, Buddy Greco, Arthur Johnson, Donald Kahn, Paul Nero, Ben Oakland, Bob O'Brien, Louis Oliveria, Gabriel Ruiz, Bob Russel, Eddie Sauter, Marcos Valle, and Bobby Worth. Other Gilbert songs that met with success were "The Hot Canary," "Cuanto le Gusto," "I Want a Zoot Suit," "Sooner or Later," and "Without You."

• Some personal information on Gilbert is housed at the Walt Disney Archives in Burbank, Calif. A useful listing of his works is in Roger Lax and Frederick Smith, *The Great Song Thesaurus* (1989). He is mentioned in the *ASCAP Biographical Dictionary of Composers, Authors and Publishers* (1980) and in Donald J. Stubblebine, *Cinema Sheet Music: A Comprehensive Listing of Published Film Music from 1914 to 1989* (1991), although each book suffers from inaccuracies and contradictions. Two very fine books about Disney films that include critical commentary on Gilbert's work for the studio are Leonard Maltin, *The Disney Films* (1984), and David Teityan, *The Musical World of Walt Disney* (1990). Obituaries are in the *New York Times*, 5 Mar. 1976, and *Variety*, 10 Mar. 1976.

JAMES K. AAGAARD

GILBERT, Rufus Henry (26 Jan. 1832–10 July 1885), surgeon and rapid transit pioneer, was born in Guilford, New York, the son of William Dwight Gilbert, a county judge; his mother's name is unknown. After completing his elementary education, he worked briefly as a druggist's clerk and then became an apprentice machinist. When his apprenticeship expired six years later, he moved to Corning, New York, where he studied medicine for a year with a local physician. He then attended New York City's College of Physicians and Surgeons for a year, after which he worked for two years in the office of the physician in Corning to raise enough money to complete his education. In 1853 he received his M.D. from the college and again returned to Corning, where he opened a highly successful surgical practice. He also married a Miss Maynard (the year of the marriage is unknown); they had no children.

By 1857 Gilbert's wife had died and his own health had declined so precipitously that he closed his practice and went to Europe to study hospital management in London and Paris. While there he became convinced that a major contributor to the generally poor health of city dwellers was the unsanitary and overcrowded living conditions in industrialized urban areas. He also determined that the solution to the problem involved constructing rapid transit facilities to permit the dispersal of urban populations throughout the adjacent countryside, where living conditions were much more healthful.

In 1861 Gilbert returned to New York and became a surgeon in the Duryée Zouaves, a voluntary infantry unit; he is credited with performing the Civil War's first amputation under fire at the battle of Big Bethel, Virginia, later that year. He eventually served as medical inspector for Union forces in Baltimore, Maryland, and Fortress Monroe, Virginia, and as medical director for the Army of the Cumberland's Fourteenth Corps. When the war ended, he held the rank of lieutenant colonel and was serving as medical director and superintendent of all Union military hospitals.

After the war Gilbert married a Miss Price (the year of the marriage is unknown); they had two children. Partly because his health had been overtaxed during the war and partly because he wanted to develop more fully his ideas about rapid transit, he became assistant superintendent of the Central Railroad of New Jersey in 1865 and played an active role in upgrading its lines. Two years later he resigned in order to concentrate on designing a workable rapid transit system for New York City. In 1870 he obtained two patents for a pneumatic-tube arrangement through which a fully loaded passenger car could be propelled by a huge blower. Shortly thereafter he conceived of running an air-driven railroad above the city's streets by supporting the pneumatic tube on a series of arches placed perpendicular to the street. These ideas were undoubtedly inspired by the "pneumatic dispatch" system for transporting parcels, the specially designed passenger cars that Alfred E. Beach had demonstrated at the city's American Institute in 1867, and Charles T. Harvey's West Side and Yonkers Patent Railway, a cable-driven elevated road that operated briefly in the city in 1868.

In 1872 Gilbert incorporated the Gilbert Elevated Railroad Company and received a charter from the state legislature to construct a line above Sixth Avenue (later renamed Avenue of the Americas) from Trinity Church near the southern tip of Manhattan Island to Fifty-ninth Street, which forms the southern boundary of Central Park. Because the panic of 1873 precluded the raising of enough money to build the pneumatic arrangement, Gilbert modified the concept so that his elevated railroad employed conventional steam locomotives and passenger cars. He also entered into an agreement with the New York Loan and Improvement Company, the firm that constructed and equipped the line, whereby the company received a controlling interest in the endeavor.

Construction on the line began in 1876, and two years later it opened for business; however, no sooner was it made operational than New York Loan asserted its control over the enterprise by renaming it the Metropolitan Elevated Road and ousting Gilbert from his management position. He was apparently swindled out of his financial position in the company as well, and his attempts to obtain legal redress failed utterly. Although he stayed on as chief inspecting engineer, his health, which had not been good since before the war, deteriorated to the point that he could no longer work. Abandoned by his wife and children in 1883, he lived out his remaining years in a squalid apartment overlooking the elevated line that he had helped bring into existence. He died in New York City.

• Gilbert's papers have not been located. His role as an urban transit pioneer is discussed in James Blaine Walker, *Fifty Years of Rapid Transit* (1918), and his military career is discussed in *The War of the Rebellion: A Compilation of the Official Records of the Union and Confederate Armies* (128 vols., 1880–1901). Obituaries are in the *New York Times*, 11 July 1885, *Medical Record*, 18 July 1885, and *Scientific American*, 1 Aug. 1885.

CHARLES W. CAREY, JR.

GILBRETH, Frank (7 July 1868–14 June 1924), motion study and scientific management expert, was born Frank Bunker Gilbreth in Fairfield, Maine, the son of John Hiram Gilbreth, a hardware store owner, and Martha Bunker. He graduated from English High School, Boston, in 1885 and apprenticed himself to a local construction company, rising to general superintendent by 1895, when he started his own construction firm, first in Boston (until 1904) and then in New York (until 1911). Before meeting the father of scientific management, Frederick Taylor, in 1907, Gilbreth built his reputation on efficient systematic management techniques—which he detailed in *Field System* and *Concrete System* (both 1908)—coupled with mechanical innovations such as cement mixers and an adjustable bricklaying scaffold.

His conversations with Taylor, however, stimulated Gilbreth's interest in motion study. As a result of his experiments, described in *Bricklaying System* (1909) and elaborated in *Motion Study* (1911), he soon claimed to have reduced the motions necessary for laying brick from eighteen to as few as four. Buoyed by his success but distressed by the building industry depression of 1911–1912, Gilbreth decided to become a consulting engineer, dedicating himself full time to Taylorism and motion study in industry. He bolstered the efficiency movement by organizing the Society for the Promotion of the Science of Management (later the Taylor Society) in 1911, while Lillian Moller Gilbreth, whom he married in 1904 (they had twelve children, one of whom died in infancy), wrote the *Primer of Scientific Management* (printed under Frank's name in 1912) and *Psychology of Management* (1914), arguing that Taylorism was the only management method consistent with the health and development of workers.

In 1912 Gilbreth undertook his first and most successful motion study and scientific management installation at the New England Butt Company of Providence, Rhode Island. Though the foundation of the installation was orthodox scientific management, Gilbreth augmented Taylor's model with industrial betterment programs such as a lecture series, a suggestion system, and a promotion plan. More importantly, he began inventing cinematographic motion study techniques that challenged the stopwatch time study that Taylor considered the keystone of scientific management.

Gilbreth's 1912 invention was micromotion study. This involved filming a worker's operations against a cross-sectioned background while a chronometer recorded the time. By examining the film through a magnifying glass, Gilbreth could determine the time of each of the worker's motions to one-thousandth of a second. He could then compare methods and working conditions and synthesize the best elements into a method that would become standard for that job.

Subsequent inventions enhanced Gilbreth's range of motion study techniques and strategies. In 1913–1914 he perfected the cyclegraph, which involved mounting a miniature electric light on a ring that could be slipped onto a worker's finger, showing on the back of his or her hand. The movement of the light created a bright line on a single time-exposed photograph. Twists and turns in the line bespoke inefficient movement, wasted time. The worker's tools, equipment, and motions could then be altered until the shortest, smoothest line was developed. Gilbreth improved on the basic technique with the chronocyclegraph, which interrupted the flow of current to the light in order to obtain, in the resulting sequence of flashes, a record of the time and direction of the motions. A stereo-chronocyclegraph created a three-dimensional image of motion by using two slightly offset cameras.

Gilbreth's last invention was probably his most important. By 1915 he had formulated a basic alphabet of work motions, naming them "therbligs." All work motions, he contended, could be reduced to sixteen categories: search, find, select, grasp, position, transport loaded, assemble, use, disassemble, inspect, preposition (for next operation), release load, transport empty, wait (unavoidable delay), wait (avoidable delay), and rest (for overcoming fatigue). By analyzing micromotion or chronocyclegraph film, Gilbreth could identify the therbligs and plot them on "simultaneous cycle motion" or "simo" charts, which listed on a horizontal axis parts of the body (arms, legs, trunk, head) and on a vertical axis elapsed time. A reading of these charts enabled him to discern whether, for instance, one arm was actively holding an object while the other was merely passively holding it during the motion cycle. If so, he could redesign the operation to employ both arms simultaneously, while shortening the times for movements by placing tools and parts closer to the worker's grasp.

These inventions, Gilbreth argued, could not only make workers more efficient, thus increasing industrial output to the benefit of factory owners; they could also reduce fatigue and lead to increased earnings, benefiting workers. With Lillian Gilbreth he publicized his claims in *Fatigue Study* (1916), *Applied Motion Study* (1917), and *Motion Study for the Handicapped* (1920), as well as in dozens of magazine articles.

Though these inventions became the keystone of Gilbreth's industrial identity, their explicit challenge to Taylor's stopwatch methods led to a rift with Taylor and his orthodox disciples. This rift deepened because Gilbreth failed to put his expensive motion study techniques into efficient practice for the companies that hired him to improve their productivity. Only after Frank's death from a heart attack near their Montclair, New Jersey, home was Lillian Gilbreth able to close the rift. Her efforts, accompanied by Eastman-Kodak's development of a small, spring-driven 16 mm camera, which made motion study cheaper, secured the future of Frank Gilbreth's contributions to industrial engineering.

In 1930 Horace King Hathaway, Taylor's orthodox disciple, extolled Frank Gilbreth for "refining and developing [motion study] technique along truly scientific lines, for reducing and codifying its fundamentals and setting, by years of persevering effort, a new standard which industry is just beginning to understand and make an effort to attain." In 1931 the Society of Industrial Engineers created the Gilbreth Medal (named for Frank Gilbreth) and made Lillian Gilbreth its first recipient. Developed years before their signifi-

cance was realized, Gilbreth's motion study techniques and therblig units of motion remain fundamental not just to subspecialties like ergonomics, but to the theory and practice of industrial engineering and management as a whole.

• Frank Gilbreth's papers are at Purdue University, West Lafayette, Indiana, as is the Gilbreth Library. Important biographies and assessments of his work are Lillian Gilbreth, *The Quest of the One Best Way: A Sketch of the Life of Frank Bunker Gilbreth* (1926); Margaret Hawley, "The Life of Frank B. Gilbreth and His Contributions to the Science of Management" (master's thesis, Univ. of California, Berkeley, 1929); and Edna Yost, *Frank and Lillian Gilbreth: Partners for Life* (1949). See also Brian Price, "One Best Way: Frank and Lillian Gilbreth's Transformation of Scientific Management, 1885–1940" (Ph.D. diss., Purdue Univ., 1987). Frank B. Gilbreth, Jr., and Ernestine Gilbreth Carey discuss Gilbreth's extension of his efficiency principles to his family life in *Cheaper by the Dozen* (1948) and *Belles on Their Toes* (1950). Gilbreth's importance to the development of scientific management and his troubled relations with Frederick Taylor are discussed in Milton Nadworny, "Frederick Taylor and Frank Gilbreth: Competition in Scientific Management," *Business History* 31 (1957): 23–34, and Nadworny, *Scientific Management and the Unions, 1900–1932* (1955). Horace King Hathaway's laudatory article is "Methods Study," *Bulletin of the Taylor Society* 15 (Oct. 1930): 210–43. Allan Mogensen, ed., *Common Sense Applied to Motion and Time Study* (1932); Ralph M. Barnes, *Motion and Time Study* (1937); and S. M. Lowry et al., *Time and Motion Study and Formulas for Wage Incentives* (1927; 2d ed., 1932; 3d ed., 1940), demonstrate the posthumous significance of Gilbreth's inventions for industrial engineering and management, while a collection of papers sponsored by American Society of Mechanical Engineers, *The Frank Gilbreth Centennial, 1868–1924* (1969), suggests his influence on ergonomics as well.

BRIAN PRICE

GILBRETH, Lillian (24 May 1878–2 Jan. 1972), industrial psychologist, was born Lillian Evelyn Moller in Oakland, California, the daughter of William Moller, a partner in a large retail hardware business, and Annie Delger. Lillian was tutored at home by her mother until she was nine, after which she attended public elementary and high schools. In high school she studied music with John Metcalfe, for whose song "Sunrise" she wrote the verses. Her lifelong interest in poetry began at this period. She attended the University of California in nearby Berkeley, receiving a B.Litt. degree in 1900. She was the first woman commencement speaker at Berkeley. She then moved to New York to begin graduate studies in English literature at Columbia University, but she soon left before getting a degree and returned to Berkeley, where she received an M.Litt. in 1902. Her thesis was on Ben Jonson's *Bartholomew Fair*. She was admitted to the doctoral program but decided in the spring of 1903 to tour Europe. Before her departure from Boston she met Frank Bunker Gilbreth, a cousin of her chaperon. They were married 19 October 1904.

Frank Gilbreth was a self-made man who had risen from apprentice bricklayer to become a prominent builder and contractor. Thirty-six years old at the time of the marriage, he had already invented Gilbreth's Gravity Mixer for cement as well as a moving scaffolding that kept bricklayer, bricks, and wall in the same relation to one another. He was well on his way to acquiring a nationwide reputation for efficiency in building and to becoming a key figure in what came to be called motion studies. The couple established themselves in New York City, where at her husband's urging Lillian joined him in his contracting business. Since they had twelve children in seventeen years, eleven of whom lived to adulthood, during much of this part of her career she assisted her husband mainly by editing his many publications. She also managed the business in his absence since he traveled extensively as a consultant. Though her name did not appear on his first book, *Motion Study* (1911), which she coauthored, it was included on succeeding books, beginning with *A Primer of Scientific Management* (1912). As their reputations and his consultations increased, he closed his contracting business, and the family moved to Providence, Rhode Island, where they founded Gilbreth, Inc., a consulting engineering firm. While in Providence, Lillian completed a Ph.D. in industrial psychology at Brown University in 1915.

In their attempts to achieve greater efficiency, the Gilbreths undertook detailed studies (using motion pictures) of each part of a work process. Their aim was to discover the best way to do a particular task. "Best" for them meant the way that required the least expenditure of energy. The Gilbreths proved to be popular lecturers, particularly in schools of engineering and business. They also encouraged managers of businesses to visit them in Providence and, later, in Montclair, New Jersey, where the business was eventually headquartered. On her own, Lillian also wrote *The Psychology of Management* (1914) and other books. To relieve Lillian of some of the housekeeping duties, Frank's mother lived with the family and oversaw the children and the servants.

Frank died in 1924, but Lillian had little time to mourn, since shortly after the funeral she sailed for Europe to take his place at several European congresses. She was determined to continue the business but soon discovered that the factory owners to whom her husband had served as consultant were not willing to take advice from a woman. Many canceled their contracts. She still continued to lecture, however, and to offer special courses in the laboratory that the Gilbreths had built. Eventually she managed to rebuild the business. Its nature changed somewhat, however, since Gilbreth began concentrating on reaching other women. Home economists and businesses trying to sell their products to housewives were interested in applying the Gilbreths' efficiency methods to household tasks. Her research on homemaking was published in *The Home-Maker and Her Job* (1927) and *Management in the Home* (1954). Some of her research was on contract, and one of the more important projects was a study she conducted on the design, packaging, and naming of sanitary napkins. The study was a major factor in improving product design and in determining ways to advertise.

Purdue University, where her husband had served as an occasional visiting lecturer, asked her to fill his position in 1924 and in each succeeding year until she was appointed a professor of management there in 1935. Her visits to Purdue were a major factor in the establishment of a motion study laboratory. She also held the title of professor of management at Rutgers University, and from 1941 to 1943 she was a member of the faculty of the Newark College of Engineering.

Gilbreth continued to break new ground throughout her career. In her sixties she turned to designing special equipment and methods to make housework easier for handicapped persons. Her most significant work in this respect was a book coauthored with Edna Yost, *Normal Lives for the Disabled* (1933). She also did significant work with veterans and, with Yost, wrote a pamphlet, *Straight Talk for Disabled Veterans* (1945).

For all her emphasis on efficiency in housework, she never modernized her own kitchen, where she appeared only infrequently. Either her servants opposed the change, or she did not want to spend the money.

During her lifetime she received many accolades. In 1921 she was made an honorary member in the Society of Industrial Engineers, the first woman to be so honored. In 1931 the same society created the Gilbreth Medal in honor of her husband and named her its first recipient. In 1936 she was chosen by *American Women* as one of the ten outstanding women of the year; in 1940 she became an honorary life member of the Engineering Woman's Club; and in 1944 the American Society of Mechanical Engineers awarded her (and, posthumously, her husband) the Gantt Medal.

During the 1930s she served on the President's Emergency Committee for Unemployment Relief, and during World War II she was a member of a subcommittee on education of the Manpower Commission. She also did volunteer work with the Girl Scouts of America, with several organizations that served the handicapped, and with various community and religious groups. She was still doing research in the 1970s and continued to lecture and write in her eighties. Her family and the application of management theories were popularized through the writings of two of her children, Frank Gilbreth, Jr., and Ernestine Gilbreth Carey, who wrote *Cheaper by the Dozen* (1948), which was made into a popular motion picture, and *Belles on Their Toes* (1950). She died in Scottsdale, Arizona.

• A Lillian Gilbreth Collection is in the Department of Special Collections and Archives, Purdue University Library. The collection includes personal correspondence, reprints of articles, unpublished studies, newspaper clippings, conference records, films, slides, and photographs. Some material in the Frank Gilbreth Collection in the same library is pertinent. For an example of the unpublished studies, see Vern L. Bullough, "Merchandising the Sanitary Napkin," *Signs* 10 (1985): 615–27. Some of her published writings were brought together by William R. Spriegel and Clark E. Meyers, eds., *The Writings of the Gilbreths* (1949). Her biography was written by her friend Edna Yost, *Frank and Lillian Gilbreth: Part-*

ners for Life (1949). A more personal and anecdotal account is by her son Frank Gilbreth, Jr., *Time Out for Happiness* (1970). See also A. A. Potter, "Reminiscences of the Gilbreths," *Purdue Alumnus*, Feb. 1972, pp. 4–6. An obituary is in the *New York Times*, 3 Jan. 1972.

VERN L. BULLOUGH

GILCHRIST, Raleigh (8 Jan. 1893–26 Oct. 1966), chemist, was born in Windsor, Vermont, the son of Hugh Gilchrist and Ella Renfrew, both newspaper people. In 1896 the family moved to Great Falls, Montana. After his graduation from high school in 1910, Gilchrist worked at the Montana Reduction Works of the Anaconda Copper Mining Company, where he learned fire assaying and earned money to attend college. He attended the University of Montana in Missoula from 1911 to 1915, receiving his B.A. in chemistry in 1915. He earned his expenses by waiting on tables (1911–1914) and by serving as a chemistry storeroom assistant (1915).

Gilchrist became a graduate student at Cornell University in September 1915, majoring in inorganic chemistry with a minor in physical and analytical chemistry. He was an assistant in qualitative analysis, and one of his students, Elizabeth Hodgson Reigart, later (in 1925) became his wife. (The couple had no children.) On 12 November 1917, seven months after the United States had entered World War I and after he had begun his doctoral research on germanium compounds, Gilchrist was drafted into the U.S. Army. On 28 January 1918 he was transferred to the Inorganic Chemistry Section of the U.S. National Bureau of Standards (NBS) in Washington, D.C., where he was assigned the task of determining the effect of differences in the composition of platinum alloys on the efficiency of the Ostwald process for oxidizing ammonia to the nitric acid needed for explosives. The analysis of platinum metal alloys was then an exceptionally difficult problem, and Gilchrist devoted his entire career, almost forty-five years at the NBS, first briefly as a soldier and then as a civilian, to this challenging work, on which his reputation is based and for which he was later awarded the Chemical Society of Washington's Hillebrand Prize (1938).

On 15 January 1919, the same day he was discharged from the army as a sergeant, Gilchrist—known to his colleagues as Gil—joined NBS as assistant chemist, in his own words, "to engage upon a program of investigation of the refining and analytical chemistry of the platinum group metals." He simultaneously continued his graduate work at Johns Hopkins University in nearby Baltimore, Maryland, where he began a new research problem (he was not required to take any classes) leading to his doctorate on 13 January 1922 with a dissertation, "The Preparation of Pure Osmium and the Atomic Weight of Osmium." He was on the faculty at George Washington University from 1927 to 1928 and again from 1929 to 1934, lecturing on thermodynamics and advanced inorganic chemistry. He also lectured on chemistry at the NBS Educational Schools. At NBS he continued to be promoted, becoming chemist in 1936, chief of the Platinum Metals and Pure Substances Section of the Division of Chemistry, and chief of the Inorganic Chemistry Section (1948–1961). After retiring on 30 November 1962, he became a consultant to the Chemistry Division.

The U.S. Assay Commission invited Gilchrist to be a member in 1936, 1938, and 1948. He was an official U.S. delegate to a number of international conferences, and the Gilchrists traveled widely, for both business and pleasure. He played an active role in the work of many honorary, scientific, and fraternal organizations. He was a member of the American Chemical Society for almost a half-century, and for thirty-two years he held continuous office in the Chemical Society of Washington, being secretary (1925–1928) and president (1929). He received the U.S. Department of Commerce's Meritorious Service Medal Award (1950) and the University of Montana's Alumni Achievement Award (1966).

Gilchrist's colleague William K. Wilson described him as "a dour Scotsman" but with "a remarkable sense of humor and a huge collection of stories, which he was very gifted at telling." He was said to be indifferent to convention and was apt to come to work in shorts. He was fond of birdwatching and astronomy and was an avid hobbyist. Of Scottish descent on both sides, Gilchrist was proud of his heritage and served terms as secretary and second and first vice president of the St. Andrew's Society in Washington, D.C. For many years he and his wife transcribed Braille for the American Red Cross. He died in Washington after a short illness.

Gilchrist's initial duties at NBS involved developing methods of preparing each of the six platinum metals—ruthenium, rhodium, palladium, osmium, iridium, and platinum—in pure form and determining their chemistry. He also analyzed materials—particularly when they contained the oxidation-resistant metals known as noble metals—for other governmental agencies. He improved methods of preparing titanium halides, a group of catalysts important in industry, and advanced the analysis of insulators classed as ceramic dielectrics. In many cases he developed entirely new methods of performing his analyses. He also developed the purification process, a chemical problem related to analysis, for sulfur, nickel, zirconium, barium, strontium, and the rare earths (lanthanides).

Before Gilchrist, industrial and analytical work with the platinum metals was expensive and complicated, and their chemical behavior was poorly understood. Some of his methods were improved by future researchers, but it was Gilchrist who first uncovered reliable analytical procedures for this group of metals and thereby dispelled the mystery that had surrounded them. Because his procedures were based on simple reactions comparable to those used for more common metals, his results led to the development of many important practical applications for platinum metals in aeronautics, dentistry, and industry.

• Typical articles by Gilchrist include the results of his dissertation, "A New Determination of the Atomic Weight of Osmium," published in *National Bureau of Standards Journal of Research* 9, no. 3 (1932): 279–90; his write-up in collaboration with Edward Wichers and William H. Swanger of the purification of the six platinum metals in *American Institute of Mining and Metallurgical Engineers Technical Publication No. 87* (1928); and his description (with Wichers) of the procedure for the separation and gravimetric determination of the platinum metals in *Trabajos del IX Congreso Internacional de Química Pura y Aplicada* (Madrid) 6 (1932): 32–49, and in the *Journal of the American Chemical Society* 57 (1935): 2565–73. Gilchrist published several review articles on the platinum metals in books, encyclopedias, and journals, two examples of which are in *Chemical Reviews* 32, no. 3 (1943): 277–372, and *Analytical Chemistry* 25, no. 11 (1953): 1617–21. Information about Gilchrist is found in William K. Wilson, *Capital Chemist* 6, no. 5 (1960): 158–60. Accounts of Gilchrist's life and work with a listing of his most important articles are given by George B. Kauffman in "Raleigh Gilchrist (1893–1966)—American Pioneer in Platinum Metal Research," *Journal of the Washington Academy of Sciences* 65, no. 4 (1975): 140–47, and in *Platinum Metals Review* 21, no. 2 (1977): 59–63. An unsigned obituary is in the *Capital Chemist* 17, no. 1 (1967): 6–7.

GEORGE B. KAUFFMAN

GILCHRIST, William Wallace (8 Jan. 1846–20 Dec. 1916), composer and conductor, was born in Jersey City, New Jersey, the son of William Gilchrist, a businessman, and Redelia Ann Cox. In 1855 his family moved to Philadelphia, where he lived most of his life. During the Civil War Gilchrist was too young for the draft, but he enlisted in the army at age seventeen. Returning to Philadelphia two years later, he decided on music as his vocation after exploring business, photography, and law. For three years he studied voice, organ, and composition with Hugh Clarke, who later became a professor of music at the University of Pennsylvania. This was his only formal musical education.

Gilchrist began his musical career in 1867 as conductor of Our Music Society, a semiprofessional ensemble of singers and instrumentalists, and as a baritone soloist at Holy Trinity Episcopal and Saint Mark's churches in Philadelphia, while singing light operas at the Amateur Drawing Room and oratorios with the Handel and Haydn Society. In 1871 Gilchrist moved to Cincinnati with his wife, Susan Beaman, whom he had married on 8 June 1870, and served as organist and choirmaster in her father's Church of the New Jerusalem.

In 1874, after a brief stay in Cincinnati, Gilchrist became organist and choirmaster at Saint Clement's Episcopal Church in Philadelphia, published two songs dedicated to his wife, and founded the Mendelssohn Club. Originally comprising eight men from Gilchrist's church choir, the Mendelssohn Club became a mixed chorus. It expanded and flourished under his leadership for thirty-nine years, performing with the Philadelphia Orchestra and in several all-Gilchrist concerts. He moved to Christ Church in Germantown as organist in 1877 before assuming the position of organist and choirmaster at the Church of the New Jeru-

salem in Philadelphia, where he remained choirmaster until his death. Other choral organizations that Gilchrist conducted include the Harmonia; the choral societies of West Philadelphia, Germantown, and Harrisburg in Pennsylvania; the Tuesday Club of Wilmington, Delaware; and the Melody Club of Woodbury, New Jersey.

In about 1881 Gilchrist began teaching at the Philadelphia Musical Academy and became quite active in the Music Teachers National Association. Under its banner, he helped establish the American College of Musicians as an agency for certifying professional proficiency of teachers in piano, organ, voice, violin, theory, and public school music.

In 1882 Gilchrist received the Cincinnati Festival Association competition prize of $1,000 for his setting of the Forty-sixth Psalm, for soprano solo, chorus, and orchestra, in a competition judged by Camille Saint-Saëns, Carl Reinecke, and Theodore Thomas. Earlier compositional awards included the Abt Male Singing Society of Philadelphia award for best male chorus piece in 1878 and three prizes from the Mendelssohn Club of New York in 1881. In an attempt to expand his musical horizons, Gilchrist traveled to Europe in 1886, visiting England, Belgium, Germany, Switzerland, and France.

To encourage the composition and performance of new music in Philadelphia, Gilchrist founded the Manuscript Music Society in 1891. Active until 1936, this organization of composers and professional musicians held monthly meetings and presented two public concerts each year. The Symphony Society of Philadelphia was organized the following year, with Gilchrist as its conductor. Composed entirely of amateur musicians, the society laid the foundation for the formation of the Philadelphia Orchestra in 1901. Gilchrist resigned from the Symphony Society in 1899 to devote his time to the Mendelssohn Club.

Gilchrist edited the hymnal that in 1895 was officially adopted by the Presbyterian Church in the United States and *The Hymnal for Use in Congregational Churches* in 1902. In 1896 he was one of the founders of the American Guild of Organists, an organization for the encouragement of high standards in church music. Gilchrist also coedited several music readers published by Ginn and Company and was credited with suggesting the use of the movable-*do* system of solmization when music was introduced into Philadelphia's public schools.

As a composer, Gilchrist wrote church music, cantatas, oratorios, songs, chamber music, solo works for piano and organ, and two symphonies. His Symphony in C Major, written in 1891, was performed by the Philadelphia Orchestra during its inaugural season and again in 1910 and 1925. It was also performed at the Philadelphia Sesquicentennial Exposition in 1926 and by the Chestnut Hill Symphony during the American bicentennial celebration in 1975. The full score of Gilchrist's Symphony in D Major is lost, but a former student, William Happich, reconstructed it from sketches in 1933. Rupert Hughes has praised the No-net in G Minor and the Piano Quintet. Among his choral works, *The Legend of Bended Bow*, written in 1888 for mezzo-soprano solo, men's chorus, and piano, four hands, is noteworthy, as are the cantata *An Easter Idyll* (1907) and the Passion oratorio *The Lamb of God* (1908), both for mixed chorus, soloists, and orchestra. A catalog of Gilchrist's compositions includes over 500 vocal works, many of which were issued by important American publishers such as Theodore Presser, H. W. Gray, and G. Schirmer. Although most of his instrumental music has been performed, little of it has been published.

Gilchrist's music, like that of many from his generation, reflects European models rather than something distinctively American. The influence of Robert Schumann and Robert Franz in his songs has been noted. Overall his compositional style may be described as conservative, with traditional harmonies, motivic development, and conventional use of contrapuntal techniques. Martha Furman Schliefer has concluded that "Gilchrist was a well-trained composer who applied his knowledge competently, and was probably most inspired when writing sacred choral compositions. Unfortunately he did not have the spark of genius to make him the great composer he so wished to be" (15). Nonetheless, he made numerous contributions to the musical life of Philadelphia and was honored with testimonial concerts in 1882, 1886, 1899, 1914, 1915, and 1916. Gilchrist died in Easton, Pennsylvania. A memorial bas-relief was created by Philadelphia sculptor Louis Milione in 1921 for the Academy of Music.

• Gilchrist's manuscripts are in the collection of the Free Library of Philadelphia, and the scores of his larger choral works are located in the Library of Congress. The most complete documentation of Gilchrist's life and work is Martha Furman Schleifer, *William Wallace Gilchrist 1846–1916: A Moving Force in the Musical Life of Philadelphia* (1985), summarized as "William Wallace Gilchrist: Philadelphia Musician," *Diapason* 5 (1981): 1, 3, 15. An assessment of the composer by his contemporaries is found in Rupert Hughes, *Contemporary American Composers* (1900), and William Henry Hall, "W. W. Gilchrist: An Appreciation," *New Music Review* 16 (1917): 470–71. See also Robert A. Gerson, *Music in Philadelphia* (1940); William Wallace Gilchrist, "Philadelphia Singing Societies," *Musical Courier* 29 (1899): 33–34; Salter Sumner, "Early Encouragement to American Composers," *Musical Quarterly*, 18 (1932): 75–105; Lucy Ellen Carroll, *Three Centuries of Song: Pennsylvania's Choral Composers 1681–1981* (1982); William Treat Upton, *Art Song in America* (1930); and Francis A. Wister, *Twenty-five Years of the Philadelphia Orchestra, 1900–1925* (1925). An obituary is in the *Philadelphia Public Ledger*, 21 Dec. 1916.

H. G. YOUNG III

GILCREASE, Thomas (8 Feb. 1890–6 May 1962), oilman and art collector, was born William Thomas Gilcrease in Robeline, Louisiana, the son of William Lee Gilcrease and Mary Elizabeth Vowell, farmers. When Tom was an infant, the family moved to Indian Territory where his mother, who was one-quarter Creek, was entitled to live. As the eldest of fourteen children, Gilcrease grew up working on the family farm and attending school only sporadically. In 1896, when the federal government ordered the Five Civilized Tribes to compile membership rolls in preparation for an allotment of land, Gilcrease became an official member of the Creek tribe by virtue of his one-eighth blood heritage. In 1899 he was awarded his 160-acre plot of land. It proved an immensely lucky piece of property. Located twenty miles south of Tulsa, the land was in the middle of the Glenn Pool, one of the most profitable oil fields in Oklahoma.

Gilcrease at first leased his property, and with income from his early royalties he briefly attended Bacone College, an American-Indian school in Muskogee, Oklahoma. There he met and in 1908 married a fellow student, Belle Harlow, a member of the Osage tribe, with whom he had two children. Gilcrease spent his first years of married life as a farmer, but increasingly he became involved in the management of his property and in the oil and gas business. In 1922 he founded the Gilcrease Oil Company, and by 1929 he had parlayed the initial income from his land allotment into a personal fortune worth an estimated $2.3 million. While his business prospered, his personal life grew tumultuous. Gilcrease's first marriage dissolved in 1924. A subsequent marriage in 1928 to eighteen-year-old Norma Des Cygne Smallwood, Miss America 1926, produced one child but ended in a bitter and very public divorce in 1934.

On trips to Europe in the 1920s and 1930s Gilcrease visited major museums, and he toyed briefly with the idea of starting a comprehensive art collection of his own. But by 1939 he had decided to focus on the art of the American West, a field then of little interest to major American collectors. Though Gilcrease left scant record of how he came to this decision, his friend Dr. Robert Lee Humber took credit for the idea. Gilcrease's friend and biographer David Milsten speculated that Gilcrease "was determined to let the world see the American Indian in all his glory, not as a matter of retribution, but as a means of redemption and release from the persecution he felt they had endured."

Gilcrease collected voraciously, acquiring between 1939 and his death nearly 360,000 objects, including 10,000 paintings, prints, and drawings, 100,000 manuscripts and books, and some 250,000 ethnographic objects. He relished the pursuit of objects for his growing collection and tracked down and purchased most of the material on his own, without the assistance of a full-time art adviser. "If my father had given the same attention to the oil business as he did to collecting art," said Thomas, Jr., "he might have been among the wealthiest men in the nation." The 636 works by western artists, including Frederic Remington and Charles Russell, that Gilcrease purchased in 1944 from the estate of collector Phillip Cole became a cornerstone of the collection. Other acquisitions included the studio collections of Thomas Moran and William R. Leigh and significant collections of work by George Catlin, Alfred Jacob Miller, John Mix Stanley, William de la Montagne Cary, and Edward Deming. Gilcrease's interest in Indian cultures also led to the purchase of more than 500 works by Native American artists.

In 1942 Gilcrease established a foundation "to maintain an art gallery, museum, and library . . . of the artistic, cultural and historical records of the American Indian." The following year he opened a museum on the top floor of his office building in San Antonio, Texas, where he had moved his oil company in 1940. Discouraged by the lack of public response, Gilcrease moved his collection back to Oklahoma and in 1949 opened a museum on the grounds of his Tulsa estate. By 1954 Gilcrease faced seemingly insurmountable financial problems due to a depression in oil prices coupled with his obligations to art dealers. Reluctant to break up his collection, he offered to give it to anyone who would assume his debts. The citizens of Tulsa voted overwhelmingly in favor of a bond issue that would allow the city to acquire the collection. Gilcrease lived the remainder of his life in his home adjacent to the museum, continuing to fund projects and acquire art on a more modest scale. He assigned his oil royalties to the city of Tulsa, and in the early 1980s, some two decades after his death there, the bond money raised to purchase his collection was repaid. Now supported with both public and private funds, the Thomas Gilcrease Institute of History and Art is one of the country's premier institutions for the study of the art and culture of the American West.

• Gilcrease's business papers are in the possession of the Thomas Gilcrease Foundation in San Antonio. Scattered personal records, pertaining mainly to art acquisitions, are in the collection of the Thomas Gilcrease Institute of History and Art. The only full-length biography, *Thomas Gilcrease* (1969), written by his friend David Randolph Milsten, contains useful information gleaned from family and associates but lacks scholarly documentation. An obituary is in the *New York Times*, 7 May 1962.

MARTHA A. SANDWEISS

GILDER, Helena de Kay (14 Jan. 1846–28 May 1916), painter and cultural reformer, was born Helena de Kay in New York City, the daughter of Commodore George Coleman de Kay, a naval officer, and Janet Halleck Drake. As a granddaughter of poet Joseph Rodman Drake and the great-granddaughter of shipbuilder Henry Eckford, Helena de Kay enjoyed great social and cultural prominence in New York City. Her father died in 1849, and ten years later Janet de Kay moved her family to Dresden, Germany, where Helena and her brother Charles absorbed both a love for the arts and a love for things German. When they returned to New York around 1864, Helena continued her education at a boarding school in Middletown, Connecticut. In 1866, fulfilling an old ambition, Helena enrolled in painting classes at the Cooper Union, where she entered into lifelong friendships with Molly Hallock (later frontier-author Mary Hallock Foote) and flower painter Maria Oakey (later Mrs. Thomas Wilmer Dewing). In 1869 she began drawing from plaster casts in the antique class at the National Acade-

my of Design; two years later she was one of ten female students when the academy finally let women draw from live models. In the antique class she met Albert Pinkham Ryder, and her respect for his spirituality caused her to secure for him his first commissions and the support of dealer Daniel Cottier. With her encouragement, Charles de Kay became Ryder's first critical champion once Charles joined the *New York Times* in 1877 as its art reporter, later its art editor. During her student years at the National Academy of Design (1869–1875), Helena de Kay also studied intermittently with John La Farge, who became her mentor, and to a lesser extent with Winslow Homer, who painted a portrait of her modeled after *Whistler's Mother*.

Helena married poet Richard Watson Gilder in 1874. Gilder was then assistant editor of *Scribner's Monthly*, the predecessor of *Century Magazine*. In his role as editor in chief of *Century* from 1881 until his death in 1909, Richard Gilder became America's preeminent arbiter of educated tastes. Soon after their marriage, the Gilders opened their home at 103 East Fifteenth Street, an old stable renovated by their friend Stanford White, to artists, writers, and other creative individuals dissatisfied with reigning styles and institutions. The illuminati who graced the Gilders' Friday evening salon included Mark Twain, Walt Whitman, Augustus Saint-Gaudens, and Joseph Jefferson. The still-ostracized Walt Whitman wrote of the Gilders, "At a time when most everybody else in their set threw me down they were nobly and unhesitatingly hospitable." Artist Will H. Low spoke for many just back from study abroad when he called their home "an oasis" in the desert of New York culture.

In 1875 the jury of the National Academy's annual exhibition rejected two of the three still-life paintings Helena Gilder submitted and several works of Oakey, Ryder, and other artist friends. Gilder concluded that the jury rejected their work because it was too modern: painterly rather than narrative and lacking precise detail and polished finish. She responded by organizing a protest show featuring La Farge, Oakey, Ryder, herself, and numerous women students of Boston painter William Morris Hunt. Held at Cottier & Co., this exhibition was the first to challenge the National Academy's traditional role as the exclusive showplace for new American art. That same year she participated in a student secession from the academy and helped establish the Art Students League to provide more systematic art training. Gilder became its first women's vice president and made sure that during its first decade women retained a strong voice in school administration.

Two years later Gilder responded to the National Academy's refusal to exhibit a sculpture by Saint-Gaudens by agitating for the establishment of an institutional alternative to the academy. On 1 June 1877 she hosted the organizational meeting of the Society of American Artists and became one of its four founding members. The society thereafter sponsored its own art exhibitions, shows deliberately different from those at the academy, emphasizing works in painterly and pastoral styles inspired by modern European movements like the Barbizon school, aestheticism, and Munich realism. Gilder exhibited regularly at the society until 1886.

Gilder and her friends were not hostile to the idea of academies but disagreed with the National Academy's leadership over the proper way to fulfill its duty to educate and elevate public taste. The academy's annuals tried to encourage the progress of art by letting art lovers compare the best works in rival styles. Gilder, by contrast, shared with associates like J. Alden Weir and William Merritt Chase the European idea that popular taste improved only when people followed the lead of a natural elite endowed with inborn sensitivity to genius and beauty. Gilder believed that painterly styles that stimulated the viewer's imagination were so inherently superior to narrative styles that continuing to exhibit traditional works perpetuated bad taste and impeded America's cultural development. Thanks in large measure to the Gilders and Charles de Kay, this philosophy and the artists they championed, including La Farge, Ryder, Dewing, and Chase, came to dominate critical and genteel tastes at the turn of the century.

After 1880 Gilder devoted most of her time to raising her five surviving children (one child died in infancy). One of her daughters, Rosamond Gilder, later edited and published her father's letters and became New York's foremost theater critic. Despite her family and social responsibilities, Gilder continued to paint and sketch. She also translated several books, including Alfred Sensier's *Jean-François Millet, Peasant and Painter* (1881), wrote occasional articles on art and literature, and carried on a voluminous correspondence with Mary Hallock Foote in Montana. She campaigned for reform movements like international copyright and urban beautification. Gilder helped her husband and brother win copyright protection for foreign publications. Doing so helped their author friends by ending publishers' preference for reprinting unprotected English novels in lieu of publishing American fiction. Like her friend Maria Griswold van Rensselaer, Gilder became an outspoken opponent of woman suffrage because she deemed it inimical to the sacred boundaries between women's domestic duties and men's public responsibilities.

During the last decades of her life Gilder divided her time between the Fifteenth Street house and a summer home in Tyringham, Massachusetts. She died in New York City.

• Vast archives of Gilder's papers remain in the possession of a descendant, including thousands of letters, her diaries, many of her paintings, numerous photographs, and a journal kept jointly by the Gilders between 1874 and 1878. Her letters to Foote are in the Huntington Library, San Marino, California. Contemporary reviews of her paintings were often short and superficial but are still of value, such as Susan N. Carter, "First Exhibition of the American Art Association," *Art Journal* 4 (Apr. 1878): 126. The best contemporary account of her life focuses on her hospitality, Will H. Low, *A Chronicle of Friendships* (1908). Excellent information about the Gilders is found in Rosamond Gilder, ed., *Letters of Richard Watson Gilder* (1916). Gilder is a central figure in Jennifer A. Martin Bienenstock, "The Formation and Early Years of the Society of American Artists: 1877–1884" (Ph.D. diss., City Univ. of New York, 1983). See also Thayer C. Tolles, "Helena de Kay Gilder: Her Role in the New Movement" (master's thesis, Univ. of Delaware, 1990). Gilder is discussed in Rodman W. Paul, ed., *A Victorian Gentlewoman in the Far West: The Reminiscences of Mary Hallock Foote* (1972). Information can also be found in Charlotte Streifer Rubenstein, *American Women Artists* (1982), and Doreen Bolger Burke, *In Pursuit of Beauty* (1986). Obituaries are in the *New York Times*, 29 May 1916, and the *American Art Annual* 13 (1916): 315.

SAUL E. ZALESCH

GILDER, Jeannette Leonard (3 Oct. 1849–17 Jan. 1916), editor, literary critic, and author, was born in Flushing, New York, the daughter of Reverend William Henry Gilder, the principal of a Long Island seminary for girls, and Jane Nutt. Because of frequent changes in employment, Reverend Gilder moved about considerably during Jeannette's childhood; he left the seminary in Flushing to take Methodist congregations in Redding and in Fair Haven, Pennsylvania, then later opened another school in Yonkers, New York. Jeannette's childhood years were spent in Flushing and in Bordentown, New Jersey, the home of her mother's family; there Jeannette received most of her erratic education. The Gilders settled permanently in Bordentown after the death of Reverend Gilder, in 1864, from smallpox contracted while he served as a Methodist chaplain in the Union army.

When her brother Richard left the military to support the family through newspaper reporting, fifteen-year-old Jeannette determined to help him, despite objections from her other siblings. Forty years later she recalled this characteristic decision in an aptly titled autobiographical novel, *The Tomboy at Work* (1904): "It was not in me to stay at home and weep, while the men 'went sailing out into the west.' I wanted to sail into the west, too, and to catch fish as well as they" (pp. 3–4). Initially, however, the catch was small and varied—historical research for New Jersey's adjutant general; handling gold in the Philadelphia mint; clerical work for an account.

Gilder's career in letters began in the late 1860s, when she became a reporter for the *Newark (N.J.) Morning Register*, which her brother Richard had cofounded, and was hired also as Newark correspondent for the *New York Tribune*. Richard soon departed the *Register*, but Jeannette continued on, reviewing books and theater and writing an occasional editorial, until she too left, after a tiff with one of the owners over complementary opera tickets. Soon thereafter she was fired by the *Tribune*, the publisher having discovered after several years that "J. L. Gilder" was a woman.

Despite these setbacks, Gilder had found her calling. In 1875, at the recommendation of journalist Kate Field, Gilder began writing book reviews for the *New York Herald*. Her column, called "Chats about Books," centered around an ostensible family conversation, wherein each member took a different stance toward a given text. The dramatic context caught on, and Gilder was made the *Herald*'s review editor for literature, drama, and music, a position she held for six years. But more than success she wanted independence. Using the $750 she had earned for editing an Appleton giftbook, *Jeannette and Joseph*, then the *Tribune*'s night editor, began to publish a magazine of their own, the *Critic*. It would become her life's work.

Primarily a journal of literary criticism and reviews of books, art, music, and theater, the *Critic*, throughout its 25-year existence (1881–1906), maintained an intellectually conservative, highbrow stance, one that was distinctly pro-American: Jeannette and Joseph Gilder made their magazine a vehicle for the nation's burgeoning sense of its own cultural identity. They touted the writings of Henry James and William Dean Howells as perfect examples of cultivated—and moral—literature; paintings by John Singer Sargent, John La Farge, and Childe Hassam were praised for their refinements of technique. British and continental artists, however, sometimes received tougher treatment. Alfred, Lord Tennyson, for example, was criticized for self-absorption in *In Memoriam*, and Thomas Hardy was accused of plagiarizing the southwestern humorist A. B. Longstreet. Truly vituperative blasts were leveled at "Indecent French Fiction," particularly that of the naturalist Emile Zola. "There is nothing more unnatural than his naturalism," the *Critic* proclaimed on 12 August 1882; "the lowest . . . readers must often recognize in his disgusting pictures the *chic* that betrays the inferior artist" (p. 215). Such earnest Victorian ire was generally confined to the literary notices, however; in assessing music and theater the Gilders usually were more liberal, and more kind to British and European artists. As Jeannette had learned while she was review editor at the *Herald*, the musical and dramatic arts in America had only begun to develop. The journal staunchly defended Wagner's operas, reviewing their New York performances favorably; the plays of Henrik Ibsen were praised as well.

Reviews were not the sole source of the magazine's appeal; Jeannette and Joseph Gilder also provided essays, fiction, and poetry written by an array of established and rising authors, among them, Walt Whitman, E. C. Stedman, Edward Eggleston, Joel Chandler Harris, H. H. Boyeson, and Theodore Roosevelt. From the 1880s on, Gilder herself contributed a column entitled "The Lounger," a potpourri of literary and intellectual gossip and small talk.

Gilder found time for other professional pursuits as well. Even after Joseph's departure, in 1901, when she became the *Critic*'s sole editor, Gilder wrote for magazines and newspapers in the American northeast and in London. She authored two thinly veiled autobiographies, a novel, and several plays, and she edited or coedited various giftbooks. From 1895 until her death, in New York City, she also served as New York agent for writers throughout the country.

But the *Critic* was Gilder's foremost achievement, one that merits lasting recognition, particularly in light of the era's prevailing attitudes regarding gender.

When Gilder began her career, "You could have counted the women journalists on the fingers of one hand," she recalled in a letter to *Harper's Bazar* (19 May 1894). "Nowadays you could not find fingers enough in a regiment." Yet she was no suffragist; in the same letter, Gilder asserted that political involvement would endanger a woman's essential roles as wife and mother. "Give woman everything she wants, but not the ballot . . . The ballot cannot help her, but it can hurt her." Such comments from a self-proclaimed "tomboy" may seem paradoxical, but they also reveal the deeply personal foundations of her journal's aesthetic and intellectual conservatism. To her credit, however, Gilder never allowed the *Critic* to become a mere mouthpiece for her particular agendas. Throughout its history the journal was acknowledged as an important organ for American evaluation of art and culture—the nation's own as well as those of other countries. In 1887 the *Boston Post* placed it "at the head of the critical journals in this country," and the *Boston Globe* deemed it "the best literary review in the United States." Such kudos from New England's literary center—and America's for most of the nineteenth century—are high praise indeed. Jeannette L. Gilder's magazine represented a significant response to the nation's need for cultural self-assertion during the later nineteenth and early twentieth centuries.

• Significant collections of Jeannette Gilder's papers are in the New York Public Library; the American Academy of Arts and Letters, New York City; Columbia University; and the Schlesinger Library, Radcliffe College. In addition to *The Tomboy at Work*, Gilder wrote another book based on her life, *The Autobiography of a Tomboy* (1900). She also wrote a novel about newspaper and artistic life in New York, *Taken by Siege* (1887), and she edited or coedited the following volumes: *The Homes and Haunts of Our Elder Poets* (1881), *Essays from "The Critic,"* with Joseph Gilder (1882), *Representative Poems of Living Poets, American and English, Selected by the Poets Themselves* (1886), *Pen Portraits of Literary Women, by Themselves and Others*, with Helen Gray Cone (1887), *Authors at Home: Personal and Biographical Sketches of Well-Known American Writers*, with Joseph Gilder (1888), *Masterpieces of the World's Best Literature* (1905), and *The Heart of Youth: Young People's Poems, Gay and Grave* (1911). She also wrote two plays that were produced: *Quits* (Philadelphia, Chestnut Street Theatre; 1876) and *Sevenoaks*, an adaptation of the novel by Josiah G. Holland (John T. Raymond's traveling theater company; 1878).

For additional biographical data see her brother Joseph's sketch in *Biographical Cyclopedia of American Women* (1928) and Julia R. Tutwiler's article on Gilder in *Women Authors of Our Day in Their Homes* (1903). Frank Luther Mott, *A History of American Magazines, 1865–1885*, vol. 3, pp. 548–51, provides a valuable description of the *Critic* and Gilder's part in its history. Obituaries are in the *New York Times* and the New York *Evening Post*, both 18 Jan. 1916; *Nation*, 27 Jan. 1916, p. 105; and the *Dial*, 3 Feb. 1916, pp. 102–3.

WILLIAM J. HUG

GILDER, Richard Watson (8 Feb. 1844–18 Nov. 1909), editor and writer, was born in Bordentown, New Jersey, the son of the Reverend William Henry Gilder, a

Methodist minister and headmaster of a "Female Sem-inary," and Jane Nutt. Most of Gilder's early educa-tion took place in another school for girls run by his family in Flushing, New York, but all the evidence suggests a normal and happy boyhood, which includ-ed precocious interests in things literary. When only twelve, he frequented the offices of the Flushing *Long Island Times* and learned something of the routines of publishing, from writing and layout to the setting of type. Following the death of his father in 1864, Gilder worked for some time as paymaster on the Camden & Amboy Railroad, got a job as a reporter on the *Newark Daily Advertiser*, and then, in 1869, joined Robert Newton Crane, an uncle of Stephen Crane, in the founding of the *Newark Morning Register*.

To make ends meet, Gilder got a second job as an editor of *Hours at Home*, a house organ for Charles Scribner and Company. The *Morning Register* sur-vived until 1878, but Gilder soon left it to concentrate on *Hours at Home*, becoming sole editor for 1869–1870, the last year of its life. Scribner then replaced the magazine with the much more ambitious *Scribner's Monthly Magazine*, hiring Josiah Gilbert Holland as editor in chief and retaining Gilder as his assistant. The magazine grew steadily from its beginnings in No-vember 1870, until it changed its name to the *Century Monthly Magazine* in November 1881, when Gilder became editor in chief. For the next twenty-eight years Gilder held one of the most powerful and prestigious positions in American publishing, as the *Century* over-took *Harper's* and the *Atlantic Monthly* as the most popular of the taste-setting triumvirate of American monthlies.

In many ways Gilder was responsible for the maga-zine's success. It was he who conceived the series of personal accounts of the events of the Civil War, writ-ten by the participants, from soldiers in the skirmish lines to Generals Grant and Lee, and published as "Battles and Leaders of the Civil War" (1884–1889). That publishing coup was followed by the serialization of John G. Nicolay and John Hay's biography of Abraham Lincoln (1890), which further contributed to the increased popularity of the magazine. With the enormous success of those series, the editors of the *Century* took it upon themselves to help in the develop-ment of the "New South" by publishing a series under that general title by Edward S. King (1848–1896) and then seeking out the next generation of southern writ-ers, including Thomas Nelson Page, Joel Chandler Harris, and George Washington Cable. Indeed, Gil-der seemed to view the revitalization of the South as something of a personal duty for himself and his maga-zine, leaving western writers to the *Atlantic* and Eng-lish writers to *Harper's*.

Gilder's literary tastes were always eclectic, howev-er. He sought the best works by the best writers of his day wherever he could find them. He took on the greater part of William Dean Howells's fictional out-put when Howells briefly disengaged himself from the *Atlantic*. He pursued Henry James (1843–1916) for

contributions until the hugely unsuccessful serializa-tion of *The Bostonians*. He agreed to publish excerpts from Mark Twain's *Huckleberry Finn* as a "teaser" in the months before it was published. And while most of literary New York turned its back on Walt Whitman and his Camden coterie, Gilder welcomed his poems to his magazine and even carried around a battered copy of *Leaves of Grass* to read to unsuspecting philis-tines.

Gilder's own poetry was less successful, never rising much beyond the general mediocrity of the poetry of the day. His first volume of poems, *The New Day* (1875), was written under the influence of Dante's *Vita Nuova* (as popularized in Rossetti's English trans-lation), and it helped him woo the young painter Hele-na de Kay, who became his wife in 1874; they had at least two children. Incredibly, *The New Day* had four editions between 1875 and 1887, several requiring more than one printing. Gilder's first collected edition of poems, *Five Books of Song*, had four editions be-tween 1894 and 1900. Then, in 1908, Gilder was cho-sen as the first living poet to be included in Houghton Mifflin's projected series of "American Household Poets."

Gilder's position as the *Century*'s editor and the re-spectability of his poetic output placed him in the cen-ter of the intellectual and artistic circles of New York. From their various addresses in lower Manhattan and their summer residences, first at Marion and later at Tyringham, Massachusetts, the Gilders exerted con-siderable influence on artistic matters. They were founding members of the Society of American Artists in 1877 and the Author's Club in 1882. Gilder was also important in many of the various reform campaigns opposed to the influence of Tammany Hall. As a per-sonal friend of Grover Cleveland, and through long and significant participation in the American Copy-right League, he was instrumental in the successful in-troduction of copyright legislation. Yet despite his best political intentions, Gilder sometimes found himself unable to accept the harsh realities in the world around him. For example, Gilder played an important role in cleaning up the slums of the East Side of New York City, serving in various capacities, including the chair-manship of the Tenement House Committee in 1894. Yet when Stephen Crane asked him to consider the manuscript of *Maggie, a Girl of the Streets* for publica-tion in the *Century*, Gilder protested that it was "cruel" and gave examples of excessive detail. Crane inter-rupted, "You mean the story is too honest?" To his credit, Gilder nodded agreement, but Crane had to publish *Maggie* at his own expense. Gilder died in New York City.

• The major manuscript sources for Gilder are the Gilder pa-pers, Gilder letterbooks, and *Century* papers in the Manu-script Division of the New York Public Library. Some of Gil-der's letters were edited by his daughter, Rosamond Gilder, in *Letters of Richard Watson Gilder* (1916). A critical biography by Herbert F. Smith, *Richard Watson Gilder* (1970), includes a complete bibliography.

HERBERT F. SMITH

GILDER, Rosamond (7 July 1891–5 Sept. 1986), theater critic and administrator, was born Janet Rosamond de Kay Gilder, in Marion, Massachusetts, where her parents had a summer home, the daughter of Richard Watson Gilder, a poet, social reformer, and editor of the *Century Magazine*, and Helena de Kay, a painter. She was brought up in New York City where she attended the Brearley School. The greater part of her education, however, was received in the intellectually stimulating Gilder household, which was a meeting place for a wide range of turn-of-the-century luminaries such as actress Eleanora Duse, writer Mark Twain, and Presidents Grover Cleveland and Theodore Roosevelt. Deciding not to attend college, Gilder set to work while in her late teens editing the letters of her beloved and recently deceased father. The volume was published by Houghton Mifflin in 1916. The following year she went to war-ravaged France as a secretary with the Children's Bureau of the Red Cross. Returning to New York in 1919, she translated into English the autobiography of French opera star Emma Calvé, who was a Gilder family friend. The Calvé autobiography, titled *My Life*, was published in 1922.

Gilder's long and productive association with *Theatre Arts* magazine began in 1924 when she filled in as a proofreader for a sick friend. She stayed on at *Theatre Arts*, the most highly regarded theatrical periodical of the mid-twentieth century, writing book reviews and occasional articles for the next several years, and became a protégé of the magazine's editor, Edith J. R. Issacs. A number of Gilder's articles dealing with women in theatrical history were collected in her *Enter the Actress* (1931). Keeping a part-time position at *Theatre Arts*, she became the editorial secretary of the National Theatre Conference (NTC) in 1932. The NTC fostered noncommercial, regional American theater and the production of new plays by unknown playwrights. Recognizing the need of smaller cities for written and visual material on theater history and practice, Gilder compiled the annotated bibliography, *A Theatre Library* (1932). A complimentary volume by Gilder and coauthor George Freedley, *Theatre Collections in Libraries and Museums*, a guide to locating nonbook material such as programs, photographs, and newspaper clippings, appeared in 1936. Gilder also led a successful campaign while at the NTC to exempt nonprofit theaters from potentially bankrupting minimum-wage requirements.

Gilder's work at the NTC and her growing reputation as an expert administrator led to a job offer from Hallie Flanagan, director of the newly formed Federal Theatre Project (FTP), a division of the Works Progress Administration. In 1935 Gilder gave up her position at the NTC and took a leave of absence from *Theatre Arts* to become head of the FTP's Bureau of Research and Publications. Frustrated by the government's inadequate funding and unclear primary mission, Gilder lasted less than a year at the FTP, but her tenure was not without accomplishment. Under her direction extensive research on the American theater was conducted, approximately 1,300 plays were analyzed and cataloged, and numerous subject lists of plays were prepared.

In 1936 Gilder returned to *Theatre Arts*, which always held her "first loyalty." Aware that the ephemeral nature of theater made historical study difficult, Gilder stressed the importance of keeping a verbal and photographic record of performances. With this goal in mind, she published *John Gielgud's Hamlet: A Record of Performance* (1937). The following year Gilder was made *Theatre Arts'* associate editor and primary critic. During the next decade she became an increasingly influential voice in the American theater and was, for a time, the only woman member of the prestigious New York Drama Critics Circle. Reflecting the general tone of *Theatre Arts*, Gilder's writing addressed the intelligent lay reader, avoiding lowest-common-denominator gossip and wisecracks as well as dry, academic abstractions. She drew a clear distinction between a reviewer, who gave an immediate, personal reaction, and a critic, who strove to measure fairly an individual's achievement against "the highest standards of art." Gilder's peak years of influence as a critic coincided with World War II. Although she believed that playwrights should not ignore contemporary events, she conceded that the overwhelming subject of war did not easily translate into theatrical terms. The numerous war-themed plays of the era were sincere but dramatically inferior efforts, unlikely to be of lasting value as drama. At the war's end, Gilder asserted that the theater could and should play an important role in creating an improved society. She objected to plays with a totally pessimistic tone and felt that wallowing in despair was as destructive to the theater as too much mindless escapism.

Rosamond Gilder, a shy but witty woman with dark hair and bespectacled brown eyes, became editor in chief of *Theatre Arts* following the retirement of Edith Issacs in 1945 and increased the magazine's coverage of foreign theater. Her refusal to work for a new owner, who, in her opinion, wanted to turn the magazine into a mouthpiece for big-time Broadway producers, led to her resignation in 1948. Although her career as a critic had come to an end, Gilder remained extremely active during the next two decades. She lectured on drama at Barnard College, studied in Paris on a Fulbright research grant (1955–1956), served as president of the International Theatre Institute (ITI), and was for a long period the director of ITI's U.S. Centre. To many around the world, her name was synonymous with the American theater. Gilder never married and led a quietly sociable private life, residing from adolescence to old age on Manhattan's Gramercy Park, where her parents had moved in the early part of the century. She died at the Gilder family farm in Tyringham, Massachusetts.

- Material relating to Gilder is in the Sophia Smith Collection at Smith College. The most complete source of information on Gilder is Caroline Jane Dodge, "Rosamond Gilder and the Theatre" (Ph.D. diss., Univ. of Illinois at Urbana-Champaign, 1974). A useful biographical essay on Gilder, also by Dodge, is in *Notable Women in the American Theatre: A Biographical Dictionary* (1989). An obituary is in the *New York Times*, 9 Sept. 1986.

MARY C. KALFATOVIC

GILDERSLEEVE, Basil Lanneau (23 Oct. 1831–9 Jan. 1924), classicist and founding editor of the *American Journal of Philology*, was born in Charleston, South Carolina, the son of the Reverend Benjamin Gildersleeve, editor of religious newspapers, and Emma Louisa Lanneau. Born at the height of Charleston's eminence in American life, Gildersleeve, who could read Greek at age five, led his life according to values of independence, high culture, and regionalism that he felt were shared by ancient Greece and the old South.

He entered the College of Charleston in 1844 at the age of thirteen, attended Jefferson College (now Washington & Jefferson), and in 1849 graduated from the College of New Jersey (now Princeton University). By this time he had been overcome by what he called his "Teutonomania," a love of German culture, particularly Goethe. In the hope of completing a novel and roaming his holy land, he joined contemporaries like William Dwight Whitney, Francis James Child, and George Martin Lane in Germany. But while at Berlin, Bonn, and Göttingen between 1850 and 1853 the examples of the great German classicists August Böckh, Friedrich Ritschl, Friedrich Wilhelm Schneidewin, and Karl Friedrich Hermann converted him into a serious classicist. He later said, "To Germany and the Germans I am indebted for everything professionally, in the way of apparatus and method, and for much, very much, in the way of inspiration." He received his Ph.D. from Göttingen in 1853 on the Ides of March and returned to a land that scarcely knew how to use him.

After three years spent mostly as an unpaid assistant to his father, he was elected in 1856 to the Chair of Greek at the University of Virginia, a position he held for the next twenty years. In 1861 he enlisted in the Army of Northern Virginia and during his summers served on the staffs of Generals Fitzhugh Lee (1861 and 1862) and John B. Gordon (1864). He also defended the cause with his pen, writing some sixty-three editorials for the fire-breathing *Richmond Examiner* in 1863 and 1864. In September of 1864 near Staunton, Virginia, he was wounded in the leg, and he bore a limp for the rest of his life. While recuperating at a private home outside Charlottesville, he met and in 1866 married Eliza Fisher Colston, the daughter of the owner, with whom he had a son and a daughter.

After the war, to support his growing family, he began to write textbooks. He embarked on a Greek syntax but adapted his outline to Latin and produced his *Latin Grammar* (1867). Though based on a German model, it is free from German theories of metaphysical or comparative grammar and instead contains Gildersleeve's fresh, idiomatic translations of examples supported by a clear arrangement of categories with many fresh examples and original analyses. It spawned the popular Gildersleeve Latin series, including an exercise book, a primer, and a reader, all aimed at the needs of southern students. The 1894 revision remained in print and use a century after its publication.

In December 1875, Gildersleeve met with the president of Johns Hopkins, Daniel Coit Gilman, in Washington and was subsequently offered the new university's first academic appointment, after it had been declined by William Watson Goodwin, Lane, and Whitney. The situation was ideal: Baltimore was sympathetic to the South and Johns Hopkins's will had earmarked scholarships for southern students. The university was to follow the German model that Gildersleeve had so admired twenty-five years earlier: a graduate *seminarium* and a university press to publish the research of faculty and others in professional journals and books. With this move Gildersleeve became a national rather than a regional voice and, with the founding of the *American Journal of Philology*, an international figure who put American classical scholarship on the world stage.

After setting the curriculum and enrolling his first seminary, he began his forty-year career at Hopkins with one word of advice from Gilman, "Radiate." He finished his commentary on the *Apologies* of Justin Martyr (1877), hosted the American Philological Association in Baltimore in 1877 and served as its president in 1877–1878. In 1880 he founded the *American Journal of Philology*, which he edited for the next four decades. To review books for whom reviewers could not be found, he initiated a column ultimately called "Brief Mention," a vehicle for reminiscences, argument, and opinion that was the most popular part of the journal and demonstrated the special combination of erudition and literary élan that made him unique.

Between 1876 and 1888 he gathered the fruits of his reading and lecturing into a series of detailed grammatical articles that would lead to his *Syntax*, and in 1885 he published his *Pindar*, but this great burst of original work seemed to drain him. For the next decade he devoted himself primarily to the needs of his journal. In the 1890s he wrote two articles in the *Atlantic*, "The Creed of the Old South" (1892) and "A Southerner in the Peloponnesian War" (1897), defending and explaining the sense of duty, local patriotism, and "civil liberty, not human slavery" that led southern intellectuals to fight in the Civil War. The former article was called by the Scottish playwright and translator of Ibsen, William Archer, "an elegy—so chivalrous in spirit and so fine in literary form that it moved me well-nigh to tears." Both articles were used by James Ford Rhodes in his histories of America (1904) and the Civil War (1917) as important historical accounts.

Gildersleeve felt that teaching, by passing on information from generation to generation, was permanent, while scholarship was inevitably superseded and forgotten. He was a demanding teacher who taught only the authors of Attic Greek, principally the orators and Sophocles, since the most was known about their language and times. His scholarship arose from the principles and examples he developed in his teaching, and these commonly appeared as notes in his commentaries or principles in his *Syntax of Classical Greek*. His edition of Pindar, *The Olympian and Pythian Odes* (1885), shows the nature of his mind. Gildersleeve sought to comprehend this most difficult poet through an understanding of the structures and themes running through his poetry as a whole rather than through minute analysis of the individual poem. "No truth stands alone," he wrote, "and the most effective work is done by those who see all in the one as well as one in the all." His approach was similar to that of his teacher Böckh, and he traced the evolution of Pindar's thought noting the correspondence of form and content. The *Syntax of Classical Greek* was begun following the *Pindar* in 1885, and the first part was completed in 1900. Treating the syntax of the simple sentence in Attic Greek, the work is distinguished by its clear arrangement, abundant examples, and lucid explanations. The publication was exasperatingly delayed by his associate C. W. E. Miller's time-consuming checking of references, and the second part did not appear until 1911, when Gildersleeve was eighty. Nevertheless, Gildersleeve's work, along with that of his Berlin colleague W. W. Goodwin and his student Herbert Weir Smyth, gave America clear superiority in the study of Greek grammar. "No nation is quicker than ours to take in the point of a situation and there is no reason discernible why Americans should not excel in the solution of the most subtle problems of antique manners and politics," wrote Gildersleeve.

His physical appearance—over six feet tall, a robust 200 pounds, his face adorned by a great white beard—justified his students' nickname for him, "Zeus." He tempered his imperial bearing with a gentle self-irony and an attractive avoidance of careerism. Claiming as his motto "grow, not climb," he liked to quote the line of Ovid that that man has lived well who has lain well hidden (*Tristia* 3.4.25). He received honorary degrees from Harvard (1886), Yale (1901), Cambridge (1905), and Oxford (1905). He lost the use of his eyes and ears in his eighties and retired from teaching in 1915 at age eighty-four, though he continued to edit the *American Journal of Philology* through volume forty (1919). He died in Baltimore and was buried at University Cemetery, Charlottesville, Virginia.

• Gildersleeve's letters and papers are at the Milton Eisenhower Library of Johns Hopkins University and the Edwin O. Alderman Library at the University of Virginia. A selection has been published in Ward W. Briggs, Jr., ed., *The Letters of Basil Lanneau Gildersleeve* (1987). He wrote a number of autobiographical articles, including "Formative Influences," *Forum* 10 (Feb. 1891): 607–17; "The College in the Forties," *Princeton Alumni Weekly* 16 (26 Jan. 1916): 375–79; and

"A Novice of 1850," *Johns Hopkins Alumni Magazine* 1 (Nov. 1912): 3–9. The closest thing to a biography is Ward W. Briggs, Jr., and Herbert W. Benario, eds., *Basil Lanneau Gildersleeve: An American Classicist, American Journal of Philology* Monographs in Classical Philology 1 (1986). Other sources include F. G. Allinson, "Gildersleeve as a Teacher," *Johns Hopkins Alumni Magazine* 13 (Jan. 1925): 132–36; E. H. Griffin, "Professor Gildersleeve as Friend and Colleague," *Johns Hopkins Alumni Magazine* 13 (Jan. 1925): 126–29; C. W. E. Miller, "Gildersleeve the Scholar," *Transactions of the American Philological Association* 56 (1925): xix–xxii, xxviii–xxxii; John Adams Scott, "Gildersleeve the Teacher," *Transactions of the American Philological Association* 56 (1925): xxii–xxviii; Paul Shorey, "Gildersleeve the American Scholar and Gentleman," *Johns Hopkins Alumni Magazine* 13 (Jan. 1925): 136–48. A complete bibliography of over 500 items appears in Ward W. Briggs, ed., *The Selected Classical Papers of Basil Lanneau Gildersleeve* (1992): 326–36. *Essays and Studies* (Baltimore, 1890; repr. 1924, 1968) is a collection of his writings on literary and educational topics. Many of his popular columns in the *American Journal of Philology* were reprinted in C. W. E. Miller, ed., *Selections from the Brief Mention of Basil Lanneau Gildersleeve* (1930). Books by Gildersleeve not mentioned in the text above include *The Satires of A. Persius Flaccus* (1875; repr. 1979); *Hellas and Hesperia; or, The Vitality of Greek Studies in America* (1909); and *The Creed of the Old South* (1915). The two volumes of the *Syntax* were reprinted (1980) with an index of passages cited.

WARD W. BRIGGS

GILDERSLEEVE, Virginia Crocheron (3 Oct. 1877–7 July 1965), college administrator and international affairs expert, was born in New York City, the daughter of Henry Alger Gildersleeve, a judge, and Virginia Crocheron. She received her early education at home and was affected by such experiences as attending court with her father and visiting the Columbia University library. The death of her much-loved brother, Harry, Jr., when she was fourteen devastated her. In part to distract her from her grief, her parents enrolled her in New York City's exclusive Brearley School.

After graduation in 1895 Gildersleeve entered Barnard College, finishing first in her class as well as class president in 1899. Her professors included Emily James Smith Putnam at Barnard and Nicholas Murray Butler, Franklin Giddings, and James Harvey Robinson from Columbia. She received a fellowship and earned an A.M. in medieval history at Columbia. After teaching English part time at Barnard for several years, she was offered a full-time position. Gildersleeve declined but, realizing that she would need a doctorate, took a leave of absence and completed her Ph.D. in English and comparative literature at Columbia in three years (1908). Her dissertation was published as *Government Regulation of Elizabethan Drama* (1908; repr. 1975). She was appointed a lecturer in English in 1908 by Barnard and Columbia; by 1910 she had become an assistant professor.

Gildersleeve's ability led Butler, now president of Columbia, to offer her Barnard's deanship in 1910 after the college's trustees insisted that a woman be appointed. Gildersleeve accepted the offer in 1911 after the position was rewritten to include appointment and budgetary authority. She remained at Barnard until her retirement.

Gildersleeve proved an able administrator, whose strong relationship with Butler assisted Barnard in maintaining its semi-independent status. Finances and academic reputation improved, and Gildersleeve instituted academic advising. She encouraged community by expanding college traditions, building more residence halls and student facilities, and helping end sororities. She expanded enrollment after World War I with national recruitment and ties to preparatory schools such as the Spence School in New York City and the Masters' School in Dobbs Ferry, New York, both of which she served as a trustee. In 1922 she negotiated a new agreement with Columbia that gave Barnard's students more access to university resources and its senior faculty greater prestige.

Gildersleeve's relationship with alumnae was generally good. Faculty responded more ambivalently; many perceived her as distant, though lauding her managerial ability. Her belief in women's abilities existed within what she perceived as a pragmatic leadership style. Her main strategy was to put competent women into important positions to showcase them and to maintain rigorous requirements because she believed it "still necessary for women to do rather better work than men in order to get ahead." And while she persisted, despite criticism, in filling junior posts with women, she offered most senior positions to men. She later wrote of her appointments record, "Perhaps this was discrimination against women, but it was, I am sure, for the good of the college." Her approach probably kept her in power, but it may have alienated those desiring greater change.

Other gender inequities Gildersleeve addressed head-on. She worked for years to open each Columbia graduate and professional school to women. When single female faculty members were the norm, she pushed Butler to grant paid maternity leaves and encouraged mothers to keep teaching. By the end of her life she lamented that the pendulum had swung the other way, prejudicing colleges against hiring unmarried women.

Like other women's college leaders, Gildersleeve believed in higher education for the able few. Like her contemporaries she advocated for general college education as the best foundation for all further training. Her elitism led her to the edge of—some believe beyond—prejudice, particularly in the case of Jewish students.

In common with many contemporaries, Gildersleeve distinguished between long-assimilated Sephardic and German Jews and more recently arrived Ashkenazic Jews, whom she once referred to as "crude and uneducated." Many believed that she maintained an admissions quota for Jewish students and that she was reluctant to promote Jewish faculty. Although there is no direct proof of either, wider recruitment inevitably led to the admission of fewer Jewish students. Later she would publicly oppose the creation of Israel as ex-

treme. Aware of her reputation, Gildersleeve carefully cited her regard for such Jews as Barnard founder Annie Nathan Meyer and her willingness to heed criticism by recalling a Barnard circular that referred to Jews as a "race." Her record on this subject was mixed at best.

Gildersleeve involved herself in numerous women's causes. She was a founder in 1919 of the International Federation of University Women (IFUW), which she served as president, and of the Seven College Conference of Women's Colleges in 1926. She also served as president of Reid Hall, a French residence for visiting women scholars, and was on the boards of the American College for Girls in Istanbul, the Near East College Association, and the Institute of International Education.

Following World War I Gildersleeve pursued peace work through the League to Enforce Peace and the League of Nations Association. She developed interests in European and Middle Eastern issues, serving on committees and advisory boards. She campaigned for Al Smith and Franklin D. Roosevelt, and during World War II she chaired the Advisory Council of the navy's women's unit, the WAVES.

Gildersleeve's contributions and ability led to her appointment to the United Nations Charter Committee in 1945 as the only American woman delegate. At the Dumbarton Oaks and San Francisco conferences she contributed to the preamble and the proposal for the United Nations Educational, Scientific, and Cultural Organization. In 1947, at the invitation of General Douglas MacArthur, she joined the American Educational Mission to Japan and helped oversee the rebuilding of higher education there. She received numerous accolades for this work, including France's Legion of Honor.

Gildersleeve had lived with her parents until their deaths in 1923. Thereafter she worked and lived part time with Caroline F. E. Spurgeon, professor of English at the University of London, who collaborated with her on such ventures as the IFUW. Following her 1947 retirement Gildersleeve lived in "happy companionship" in Bedford, New York, with Elizabeth Reynard, a Barnard alumna and English instructor who was instrumental in organizing the WAVES and who served as Gildersleeve's assistant at the United Nations conferences. Though Gildersleeve had planned to expand her internationalist activities, she was "grimly afflicted with recurrent physical ills." She did complete her autobiography, *Many a Good Crusade* (1954), and wrote essays, some widely circulated, on such topics as the "flabby state" of pre-Sputnik American education. Following Reynard's death, Gildersleeve moved into a nursing home in Centerville, Massachusetts, where she died.

Gildersleeve saw herself as having "lived fully in the main events of my time." Indeed her career largely confirms that self-evaluation. She was Barnard's consolidating leader, expanding a favorable relationship with Columbia and giving the college a more communal focus. Her interest in women's rights and education and in international affairs placed her squarely within that generation of women's college leaders who undertook a broad agenda of institution-building, reform, and inspiration. Though hewing a middle course made her objectionable at times to both Barnard's conservatives and its radicals and though her leadership style was often hierarchical, her power was uncontroverted and her influence undoubted. Though sharing in the prejudices of her times, Gildersleeve also had a wider vision that led to important contributions to the post–World War II order. Her life exemplified for many the possibilities of professional women's contributions to their world.

• Gildersleeve's personal papers are in the Rare Book and Manuscript Library of Columbia University. Her papers as dean are in the Barnard College Archives and include official correspondence, articles, clippings, and photographs. In addition to her autobiography, she published a collection of her postretirement essays, *A Hoard for Winter* (1962). See also an article in *Newsweek*, 25 Oct. 1954. Her Barnard career is covered in Alice Duer Miller and Susan Myers, *Barnard College: The First Fifty Years* (1939), and Marian Churchill White, *A History of Barnard College* (1954). Helen Lefkowitz Horowitz, *Alma Mater: Design and Experience in the Women's Colleges from Their 19th Century Beginnings to the 1930s* (1984), considers her contributions and her alleged anti-Semitism, as does Judith Mae Walters, "Perceptions of Leadership Roles: Women in Barnard College, 1889–1939" (Ph.D. diss., Yeshiva Univ., 1984), who also analyzes Gildersleeve's leadership comparatively. Her contributions to other causes appear in Marion Talbot and Lois Kimball Mathews Rosenbery, *The History of the American Association of University Women, 1881–1931* (1931), and Edith C. Batho, *A Lamp of Friendship: A Short History of the International Federation of University Women* (1969). An obituary is in the *New York Times*, 9 July 1965.

CYNTHIA FARR BROWN

GILES, Chauncey Commodore (11 May 1813–6 Nov. 1893), educator, pastor, and author, was born in Charlemont, Massachusetts, the son of John Giles and Almira Avery, farmers. Young Giles attended Mt. Anthony Academy in Bennington, Vermont, and Williams College in Williamstown, Massachusetts (1832–1835), with the hope of becoming a Congregational minister. Ill health, however, led him to abandon this goal during his junior year. Williams College later awarded him A.B. and M.A. degrees (1876) and he is listed with the class of 1836.

In the late 1830s and early 1840s Giles drifted aimlessly from one teaching post to another in Vermont, New York, Pennsylvania, and Ohio, and he was often plagued with severe headaches and bouts of depression. While teaching in Palmyra, New York, he met Eunice Lakey, whom he married in 1841. They raised a family of two daughters and four sons.

While principal of a school in Hamilton, Ohio, in 1843, Giles and his wife were introduced to the theological writings of Emanuel Swedenborg through their landlord, a tailor. Swedenborg was an eighteenth-century Swedish nobleman, scientist, philosopher, and religious visionary. Swedenborg's numerous theological writings described the inner meaning to the Bible, the spiritual realms of heaven and hell, and the creation of a universal "new church." These and other teachings formed the basis of the Church of the New Jerusalem (also known as the New church, or Swedenborgian church), which views itself inaugurating a new era of Christianity. Giles continued to teach in Lebanon, Ohio, where he also briefly studied law, and in Pomeroy, on the Ohio River. In 1852, as his religious convictions became more well defined, Giles was licensed to preach in the New church. Because he had no formal theological training, Giles expected that he would read the published sermons of other Swedenborgians, but he soon found himself preparing his own messages. He was ordained in 1853 and became pastor of the Cincinnati Swedenborgian society. At age forty he had found his true vocation.

His reputation in Ohio as an educator, however, prompted an offer for him to join the faculty of Urbana University, which had been chartered in 1850 as a Swedenborgian school. Giles remained fully committed to pastoral work in Cincinnati, but he gave Urbana's first commencement address in 1854 and officially served as nonresident president between 1857 and 1870.

In 1864 Giles and his family moved to New York City, where he became pastor of the New York New Jerusalem society. At Cooper Union Hall he delivered a series of popular Sunday evening lectures that explored the reality of the spiritual world, later published as *Lectures on the Nature of Spirit, and of Man as a Spiritual Being* (1867). In lucid and flowing prose Giles described humans as essentially spiritual creatures, destined for eternal existence in a "state of happiness or misery according to their characters." A Swedenborgian classic, the book went through numerous printings and was translated into several languages.

Although an accomplished speaker, Giles came to believe that the most important tool for spreading the doctrines of the New church was the written word. Following the success of *Nature of Spirit*, he authored a series of children's stories, including *The Magic Spectacles; a Fairy Story* (1868) and *The Wonderful Pocket, Chestnutting, and Other Stories* (1868). His love and concern for children may also be seen in his *Our Children in the Other Life* (1872). Between 1871 and 1878 Giles was the editor of the *New Jerusalem Messenger*, the official publication of the General Convention of the Church of the New Jerusalem, and he wrote most of the copy. His articles reflect a keen desire to expand the small denomination through a logical presentation of Swedenborg's teachings and the development of stable New church institutions. Giles was elected to the position of president of the General Convention in 1875, the highest office within the Swedenborgian church. He held this position until his death eighteen years later.

Giles's last pastorate was the Philadelphia New Jerusalem society, which he served from 1878 to 1893. A controversy with the Young Men's Christian Association (YMCA) in 1879 helped him become one of the most well-known and influential ministers in the city. Because of inadequate facilities, he sought permission from the YMCA to use their building for New church youth meetings. The request was rejected, however, because Swedenborgians were not viewed as "evangelical." A Baptist minister promptly offered the use of his church's building, and the newspapers picked up the story. Giles used the incident to give a well-publicized series of lectures on Swedenborgian beliefs that drew large crowds. During his pastorate a large and imposing church edifice was completed in 1883 at a cost of $150,000.

In Philadelphia Giles also continued his publishing career. In 1885 he became president of the American New-Church Tract and Publication Society, which operated out of the library and reading room of the Philadelphia church. By 1890 this organization was distributing an average of 12,000 tracts a day. The requests for Giles's printed sermons became so great that in 1888 they began to be issued as a periodical titled the *Helper*.

Throughout his long career, Giles became one of the best-known and most well-loved leaders of the New Jerusalem church. He died at his home in Philadelphia.

• Giles's personal papers have not been preserved although some of his correspondence; most of his published works, including sermons; and a complete run of the *New Jerusalem Messenger* may be found in the General Convention Archives at the Swedenborgian School of Religion, Newton, Mass. His major publications not cited above are: *Lectures on the Incarnation, Atonement and Mediation of the Lord Jesus Christ* (1870); *Heavenly Blessedness* (1872); *The Second Coming of the Lord* (1879); and *Perfect Prayer* (1883). Several books were also published posthumously, including *Progress in Spiritual Knowledge* (1895), *The Sanctity of Marriage* (1896), and *Consolation* (1904). The most complete biographical treatment is Carrie G. Carter, *The Life of Chauncey Giles as Told in His Diary and Correspondence* (1920); other sketches may be found in J. A. Vinton, *The Giles Memorial* (1864); and W. L. Worcester, *New Church Review* (Jan. 1894): 1–51. His work as a church leader is treated in Marguerite Beck Block, *The New Church in the New World* (1932; rev. ed., 1984). Obituaries are in the *New Church Messenger*, 15 Nov. 1893, and the *Philadelphia Press*, 7 Nov., 1893.

DAVID B. ELLER

GILES, Warren Crandall (22 May 1896–7 Feb. 1979), baseball executive, was born in Tiskilwa, Illinois, the son of William Francis Giles, a paint contractor, and Isabelle Slattery. Giles grew up in Moline and attended prep school at Jubilee College in Oak Hill, Illinois, in 1912–1913 and at the Staunton Military Academy in Virginia from 1914 to 1916. After one semester playing freshman football at Washington and Lee University, he joined the U.S. Army in 1917 and served during World War I as a lieutenant of a mortar company. He left the military after being wounded in France, joined his father's business in Moline, and began refereeing basketball and football games in the Missouri Valley Conference. In 1919 the stockholders of the last-place and financially struggling Moline baseball club called a meeting to discuss the future of the Class B team; Giles attended and, on the basis of his comments and enthusiasm, was named president of the Three-I League franchise.

Although Giles had no administrative or playing experience in professional baseball, his keen business sense and fortuitous hiring of Earle Mack, son of Philadelphia A's owner Connie Mack, as manager quickly reversed the team's fortunes. Moline won the pennant in 1921, and the next year Giles became part owner and general manager of the St. Joseph, Missouri, club in the Class A Western League. There he established a close relationship with Branch Rickey, manager and vice president of the St. Louis Cardinals, and in late 1925 accepted Rickey's offer to become president and general manager of the International League's Syracuse Stars, the Cardinals' top farm team. In 1928 the franchise moved to Rochester, where Giles changed the team's nickname to "Red Wings," pressed Rickey for top-flight players, and won four consecutive championships from 1928 to 1931. An astute judge of personnel, Giles surrounded himself with an outstanding support staff. Managers Ray Blades, Eddie Dyer, Bill McKechnie, Burt Shotton, and Billy Southworth all eventually advanced to the major leagues, as did Gabe Paul, who remained with Giles as an administrative assistant for twenty-three years. In 1936 Giles was elected president of the International League, but he resigned after one season to become vice president and general manager of the Cincinnati Reds of the National League. In 1932 he married Mable Skinner; they had one son, William, who became president and co-owner of the Philadelphia Phillies baseball team.

Giles, who in 1937 took over a debt-ridden, cellar-dwelling club, quickly brought the Reds not only financial stability but also improved fortunes on the field. Giles was named "Major League Executive of the Year" in 1938 by the *Sporting News*. His hiring of manager Bill McKechnie as manager and his acquisition of third baseman Billy Werber and pitcher Bucky Walters were critical to the Reds winning the league championship in 1939 and the World Series in 1940. No team suffered a greater manpower shortage during World War II than Cincinnati, in part because Giles privately urged his players to enlist in the armed forces as a patriotic duty. In June 1944, faced with a depleted roster and an inept team, he signed a local high-school pitcher, fifteen-year-old Joe Nuxhall, who became the youngest major league player in the twentieth century. Giles became president of the Reds in 1948 and three years later found himself stalemated with National League president Ford Frick in the contest to succeed Albert B. Chandler as baseball's commissioner. Giles withdrew after seventeen ballots, stating that the deadlock was "harmful to the game" and that "my first interest in baseball is the welfare of baseball itself." Frick thus became commissioner and Giles became president of the National League after securing permission to move league offices from New York to Cincinnati.

The prototype of the modern business-oriented baseball executive, Giles oversaw far-reaching changes during his eighteen years as league president, the longest tenure in National League history. An admirer of both Kenesaw Mountain Landis and Branch Rickey, he attended to the business of baseball in ways that would protect the integrity of the game and increase its popularity. Jovial, unflappable, and scrupulously honest, Giles was a strong leader who was willing to make hard decisions. His most famous—and controversial—decision was to impose a $1,750 fine and an eight-game suspension on San Francisco pitcher Juan Marichal for hitting Los Angeles catcher John Roseboro on the head with a bat during a game on 22 August 1965; to those who criticized the penalty as too lenient, Giles replied that he did not want Marichal's punishment to affect unduly the close Giants-Dodgers pennant race. He supported franchise relocation, witnessing the Braves' move from Boston to Milwaukee in 1953 and then to Atlanta in 1966 and the Brooklyn Dodgers' and New York Giants' moves in 1957 to Los Angeles and San Francisco, respectively. A proponent of expansion, he presided over the league's increase from eight to twelve teams divided into two divisions with the addition of Houston and New York in 1962, and of Montreal and San Diego in 1969. He urged the construction of new, large-capacity, multipurpose stadia and strongly endorsed the signing of black and Latin American players, which led to the competitive dominance of the National League over the American as evidenced by a 17–4 margin in All-Star game victories. His tenure saw the unionization of umpires and players. Though frequently critical of umpires while he had been with Cincinnati, Giles, as league president, staunchly defended the arbiters in disputes with players and lent his personal support to the formation of the Major League Umpires Association in 1964. An opponent of interleague play and performance bonus clauses in player contracts, he sympathized with the collective bargaining efforts of the Major League Players Association but opposed the hiring of outside counsel to represent them in contract negotiations. Weary from increasingly bitter confrontations with the players' union, he retired after the 1969 season. Thereafter, Giles resided in Cincinnati, where he died a few weeks before his election to the National Baseball Hall of Fame. At the time that Giles took office, the National League had been inferior to the American League in talent, facilities, attendance, and public recognition; when he retired, the Senior Circuit was superior in each respect. He listed as his proudest accomplishments the National League's superiority in All-Star games, the greatly increased attendance, and the construction of new ballparks, and declared: "We are a game of tradition. The right kind of tradition has made baseball what it is, but blindly following tradition may lead into a rut. Baseball must always keep pace with the times" (*New York Times*, 8 Feb. 1979).

• The National Baseball Library in Cooperstown, N.Y., has an extensive clippings file on Giles. Also see Gerald Holland, "Honest Warren Giles: He Always Strives to Please," *Sports Illustrated*, 10 June 1963, pp. 32–34, 39–41, and Lowell Reidenbaugh, *Cooperstown: Where Baseball's Legends Live Forever* (1983). For his administrative career, see Lee Allen, *The Cincinnati Reds* (1948) and *The National League Story* (1967). The Roseboro-Marichal incident is detailed in Jack Mann, "Battle of San Francisco," *Sports Illustrated*, 30 Aug. 1965, pp. 12–15, and the *Sporting News*, 4 Sept. 1965. Obituaries are in the *New York Times* and the *Cincinnati Enquirer*, both 8 Feb. 1979; and the *Sporting News*, 24 Feb. 1979.

LARRY R. GERLACH

GILES, William Branch (12 Aug. 1762–4 Dec. 1830), congressman, senator, and political writer, was born in Amelia County, Virginia, the son of William Giles and Ann Branch. He attended Hampden Sydney College, then the College of New Jersey (later Princeton University), from which he graduated in 1781. He studied law under George Wythe at the College of William and Mary and was admitted to the bar, and in 1786 he began his practice in Petersburg, Virginia. He was elected to Congress four years later. In the House of Representatives he worked with James Madison in building the Republican party in opposition to the administration or Federalist party. He quickly established a reputation for hard-hitting political attacks on individuals in the executive branch. He was not content merely to criticize the Federalist policies of Alexander Hamilton but also accused him of misconduct in office. He presented resolutions in Congress to launch an inquiry that could have led to an impeachment, but they failed to carry. He continued his condemnation of the Federalists into John Adams's administration. After Adams and the Federalist majority in Congress enacted the Alien and Sedition Acts, Giles left Congress in protest. He thought that, through these acts, the Federalists were attempting to make it a crime to criticize and to oppose them. He believed the acts clearly compromised the First Amendment right to freedom of speech and, by extending the legal jurisdiction of the federal government, threatened states' rights. He entered the Virginia House of Delegates, where he supported Madison's famous Virginia Resolutions of 1798 that declared the Alien and Sedition Acts unconstitutional.

Giles returned to Congress during the "Revolution of 1800," the election in which the Republicans won the presidency and both houses of Congress. In 1804 he was elected by the General Assembly to serve in the U.S. Senate. He was a leader in the Republican party. When Justice Samuel Chase was impeached and stood trial in the Senate, Giles led the movement to remove him from office. Giles, like many other Republicans, believed that the Federalists—including Supreme Court justices—had engaged in unconstitutional activities, such as the passage and enforcement of the Alien and Sedition Acts, that the people of the United States had voted the Federalists out of office, and that the Federalists were trying to use the judiciary as a stronghold from which to thwart Republicans in the executive and legislative branches. Against Chase, Giles argued that when a majority of the representatives of the people believed that government officials, executive or judicial, had violated their trust to uphold the Constitution and to look after the people's best interests, then they could and should be removed from office. Giles failed, however, to persuade his fellow senators to remove Federalist Supreme Court justices on political grounds instead of for "high crimes and misdemeanors."

Federalist judges were not removed, and many Federalist policies continued after 1800. Giles, like more extreme Republicans such as John Randolph, did not believe the Republican administration was active enough in furthering the "Revolution of 1800." By the time of the James Madison presidency, Giles led a Republican party faction in the Senate that was critical of the administration. He was once again in the opposition.

Giles got the reputation for being overly inclined to criticize and oppose the executive branch. For example, he criticized President Madison for not calling for war with Britain, then he turned around and criticized him for how he led the country into the War of 1812. After the war, Giles retired from Congress. He served one term in the Virginia House of Delegates (1816–1817), again representing Amelia County, then left active politics.

Giles continued, however, to write and publish political essays, particularly in the main newspaper in Virginia, the Richmond *Enquirer*. He regretted that during the Era of Good Feeling the country was being swept up in a progressive mood, and, as he saw it, seeking change for change's sake. He opposed the expansion of banking, national internal improvements, and protective tariffs. He contended that these projects would not bring about real improvements but would lead only to corruption and higher taxes, dangerously concentrate power in the national government, and drive farmers into debt and poverty in order to pay for an industrial buildup. He returned to active politics in 1826, once again representing Amelia County in the House of Delegates. In 1827 the General Assembly elected him governor; he served three one-year terms.

In 1827 Giles began publishing his political essays and some of his speeches in the House of Delegates. In pamphlet form, they included *"The American System" So Called; Or the Anglican System in Fact!* (1827), *Political Disquisitions* (1828), and *Political Miscellanies* (1829).

Giles ended his political career as he began it, opposing what he saw as British-style policies and corruption. For him, little had changed except the names of his opponents. Hamilton and John Adams had been replaced by Henry Clay and John Quincy Adams. But, while he condemned what he saw as tyranny at the national level, he represented the establishment in Virginia. He was governor and a major leader of conservatives who opposed change, including a democratic adjustment in state apportionment that would allow more power in the legislature for the mountainous western region of the state. In the General Assembly,

as governor, and as a member of the state constitutional convention of 1829–1830, he stood for localism and states' rights, agrarianism, and preserving the interests and power of the gentry.

In 1797 Giles had married Martha Peyton Tabb; in 1810, after his first marriage ended, he wed Frances Ann Gwynn. He died in his home, known as the "Wigwam," in Amelia County.

• The William Branch Giles Papers are at the Virginia Historical Society. The *Annals of Congress* printed Giles's speeches and resolutions in Congress, and the *Journal of the House of Delegates* his speeches as a state legislator, as well as his messages to the General Assembly when he was governor. A biography is Dice Anderson, *William Branch Giles: A Study in the Politics of Virginia and the Nation from 1790 to 1830* (1914).

F. THORNTON MILLER

GILL, Irving (26 Apr. 1870–7 Oct. 1936), architect, was born Irving John Gill in Tully, New York, the son of Joseph Gill, a farmer, carpenter, and building contractor, and Cynthia Scullen. Gill was one of six children born on the family farm located some twenty miles from Syracuse. Gill's parents and ancestors were Quakers who had originally settled in New Jersey. His formal education was limited to attending high school in Syracuse. In 1887 he was working as a gardener and by 1889 had listed himself as a draftsman, employed in the Syracuse architectural office of Ellis G. Hall.

In 1890 Gill ventured west to Chicago and obtained a position in the office of Joseph Lyman Silsbee, one of the Midwest's most successful domestic architects. It was in Silsbee's office that Gill met Frank Lloyd Wright and George Grant Elmslie. He worked in the Silsbee office for a little over a year and then joined Wright and Elmslie in 1891 as a draftsman in the office of Dankmar Adler and Louis H. Sullivan. These were the years that the Adler and Sullivan office was producing a number of its major works, including the Schiller Building (Chicago, 1891–1892), the Wainwright Tomb (St. Louis, 1892), and the Transportation Building at the World's Columbian Exposition (Chicago, 1893).

Because of ill health Gill left the Adler and Sullivan office, and in early 1893 he went to San Diego, California. His reasons for selecting San Diego remain unknown. It may have been owing to the reputation the city had for its dry, healthful climate, or it could have been a recommendation by Sullivan, who had visited the city in 1889. Gill immediately set up his own architectural practice there. Though published sources at the time mention that he was working on a number of projects, only a few of these are fully documented.

In the early fall of 1894 Gill entered into partnership with the established San Diego architect Joseph Falkenham. Together they designed some twenty buildings between 1893 and 1894. Their commercial work tended to combine the late Queen Anne Revival with the fashionable classical designs associated with the Beaux-Arts tradition. In domestic architecture, their preferences were for the Colonial Revival, as in the

Miles Moyan house (San Diego, 1894), a simplified version of the Shingle style.

Gill's partnership with Falkenham lasted through 1894. By the following year he was once more on his own. During these two years of independent practice, 1895 and 1896, he ranged far and wide in his use of fashionable architectural styles: the Colonial Revival, English Tudor, the late Shingle style, and the regional Mission Revival. The general tendency in all of his designs was toward a marked simplification of volumes and details. The most abstract of these was the shingle-clad Granger Music Hall (1896) in National City. Equally simplified was his first essay in the Hispanic mode, the stucco-covered John H. Kleine house (1896–1898) at Lakeside.

In 1898 Gill and William Sterling Hebbard formed a partnership that lasted until 1907. Their most successful domestic designs were in the English mode (the A. P. Stephens house, Coronado, 1898), often with a strong Arts and Crafts overtone (Waldo Waterman house, San Diego, 1900). Some of their larger commissions, such as the State Normal School (1898–1904) in San Diego, were pure classical Beaux-Arts. Like a number of California architects of these years, Hebbard and Gill produced dwellings that were externally Mission Revival in style but within tended to express the woodsy Arts and Crafts tradition. Surprisingly, their most out-and-out commitment to the Mission Revival was not in California, but in Newport, Rhode Island. This was the Ellen Mason house of 1902.

For a very brief period of seven months in 1907, Gill formed a partnership with Frank Mead. Mead had traveled extensively in Moorish Spain and along the Islamic Mediterranean coast of North Africa. His interest in the vernacular pristine stucco-covered houses was transmitted to Gill and helped him to formulate his own highly personal version of the cubic stucco-sheathed box. His first design entailing this rationalist anti-ornament mode was the Allen house (1907) in Bonita. This house was based on the American vernacular four-square dwelling, coupled with references to Islamic North African houses and to the revival of California's Mission architecture.

During the years 1908 through 1916 Gill solidified his approach to design, consisting of stripped-down interiors, and to construction, employing reinforced concrete and hollow tile, thus producing his now famous cubic buildings. Gill's interest in fireproof construction led him to adapt in 1912 the Aiken Tilt-slab method of construction, where entire walls of reinforced concrete and hollow tile, together with framed window and door openings, were laid out on a horizontal flat table and then lifted into place. This was a method developed at the end of the 1890s that then began to be employed in southern California by architects and contractors. He used the Tilt-slab method of construction in such classic designs at the Mary Banning house (1913–1914) in Los Angeles, the La Jolla Women's Club (1913–1914) in La Jolla, and the La Jolla Community Center (1914–1916).

In an article in *The Craftsman* ("Home of the Future: The New Architecture of the West: Small Homes for a Great Country," 30 [May 1916], pp. 140–51), Gill wrote of his approach to design, "We must boldly throw aside every accepted structural belief and standard of beauty and get back to the source of all architectural strength—the straight line, the arch, the cube and the circle." The form of the pristine stucco-sheathed cube served as the basis for his varied experiments in low-cost housing, such as the Bella Vista Terrace (Lewis Court, 1910) in Sierra Madre. It was also the governing approach to design in his larger Ellen Scripps house (1915–1916) in La Jolla, in his well-known Walter L. Dodge house (1914–1916) in Los Angeles, and in his various commercial and residential buildings for the new city of Torrance (1912–1916).

In 1912 Gill moved his main office to Los Angeles so that he could be close to his many projects in Torrance, leaving his San Diego office in the hands of his nephew Louis Gill. In 1914 Gill and his nephew formed a partnership that lasted until 1918. Like other exponents of the American Arts and Crafts and Prairie movements, Gill saw his fortunes diminish appreciably after the First World War. To a considerable degree Gill's career in Los Angeles in the 1920s remains somewhat of a mystery. In 1918 or 1919 he formed his own company, the Concrete Building and Investment Company. In 1921 the projects from his firm were listed as being by Gill and Pearson, though no record is known to exist of who Pearson was or even his first name. In 1922 Gill worked briefly for the architect Horatio Warren Bishop on the design for houses in the newly established west Los Angeles suburban development of Carthay Center.

The decade of the 1920s was a boom period of building activities in and around Los Angeles, but Gill did not receive many commissions during these years. In part this may have been owing to his personal puritanical style, which by then was out of fashion; in part it was an economic issue owing to his insistence on using the much more expensive reinforced concrete for small buildings. His lack of commissions may also have been an outcome of his own view of himself as an artist-architect. His largest projects of these years were the courtyard-oriented country house for Chauncy Dwight Clarke (1919–1922) in Santa Fe Springs and his design for the First Church of Christ Scientist (1927–1928) at Coronado.

In 1928 Gill married Marion Waugh Brashear, and, because of his health problems, they moved in 1929 from Palos Verdes to an avocado ranch that his wife owned north of Carlsbad. Once settled, Gill associated himself with the San Diego architect John Selmar Siebert for the design of four public schools (none of which, because of the depression, was built). Between 1929 and 1934 Gill designed a number of projects for Oceanside, including a civic center, but the only segments built were the fire and police buildings (1929–1931) and the city hall (1934). At the nearby Rancho Barona Indian Reservation, near Lakeside, he designed twelve cottages and a small church (1932–

1933). Gill's last building was the small Blade-Tribune building (Redondo Beach, Calif., 1936), in which he incorporated Art Deco detailing. Gill was preparing several designs for public buildings in San Diego when he died in Carlsbad.

With the triumph of International Style modernism after 1945, Gill's puritanical designs were rediscovered. Decades later his pioneering efforts, along with those of his Viennese contemporary Adolf Loos, were looked upon as seminal to the development of America's twentieth-century modernism.

• The drawings and records of Gill's office are in the Architectural Drawing Collection, University Art Museum, University of California, Santa Barbara. Other records of his practice are in the archives of the San Diego Historical Society. For contemporary views of his work, see "A New Architecture in a New Land," *The Craftsman* 30 (Aug. 1910): 140–51; "Concrete Curves and Cubes," *The Independent*, 28 Aug. 1913, pp. 515–16; Bertha H. Smith, "Creating an American Style of Architecture," *House and Garden*, July 1914, pp. 17–20, 46; "Garden Apartment Houses of the West," *The Touchstone* 5 (Apr. 1919): 23–29; and E. C. Bartholomew, "The House That Will Not Collect Dust," *Country Life*, July 1920, pp. 50–51. Gill's Dodge house in Los Angeles was presented in Eloise Roorbach, "A California House of Distinguished Simplicity," *House Beautiful*, Feb. 1921, pp. 94–95, 142. One of Gill's many three-room concrete houses was presented in Mrs. R. M. Cassiday, "A Fire-proof Home of Moderate Cost," *Keith's Magazine*, June 1924, pp. 288–91.

After World War II Gill was rediscovered as a precursor of the modern. See, for example, Wayne Andrews, *Architecture, Ambition, and Americans* (1955); Esther McCoy, *Irving Gill 1870–1936* (exhibition catalog, Los Angeles County Museum of Art, 1958); and McCoy's chapter on Gill in *Five California Architects* (1960). William H. Jordy, *American Buildings and Their Architects: Progressive and Academic Ideals at the Turn of the Twentieth Century* (1972), includes a long chapter on Gill. On Gill as an exponent of the Arts and Crafts movement, see Timothy J. Andersen et al., *California Design 1910* (1974; repr. 1980). Obituaries are in *Southwest Builder and Contractor*, 16 Oct. 1936, p. 12, and *Architect and Engineer* 127 (Nov. 1936): 65.

DAVID GEBHARD

GILL, John (17 May 1732–25 Aug. 1785), printer and newspaper publisher, was born in Charlestown, Massachusetts, the son of Captain John Gill and Elizabeth Abbot. He served his apprenticeship with Samuel Kneeland, an established Boston printer who also owned the *Boston Gazette*. Gill married Kneeland's daughter, Ann Kneeland, in January 1756. It is likely that Gill met Benjamin Edes, of the same age, while both were learning their craft under Kneeland. Early in 1755, Gill and Edes sent out subscription notices for a weekly newspaper, the *Country Journal*, but before the new venture got off the ground, Kneeland announced that he would soon discontinue his *Gazette*. Gill and Edes took over operation of what they named the *Boston-Gazette and Country Journal*, first issued on 7 April 1755, the third newspaper to carry the title of the *Boston Gazette*. Edes and Gill bought the paper on 5 April 1755, beginning a partnership that would last twenty years.

In the summer of 1755 Edes and Gill moved their place of business to a recently vacated shop on Queen Street. They printed books, broadsides, and pamphlets on a variety of subjects, including the early sermons of Charles Chauncey and Jonathan Mayhew, a lecture on earthquakes by John Winthrop, other theological tracts, polemics, a Latin textbook, and Thomas Prince's *Annals of New-England*. They also continued the *Gazette*, which regularly carried lucrative public notices, but which also contained articles increasingly opposed to the newly enacted British laws, especially the Stamp Act of 1764.

More and more the *Gazette* reflected radical views. Its office became a meeting place for patriot leaders and from there, it is said, the Boston Tea Party set out. Edes and Gill acquired the reputation of "foul-mouthed Trumpeters of Sedition" responsible for "raising that Flame in America." But Isaiah Thomas said of Gill that he was a "sound whig, but did not possess the political energy of his partner." There was at least one exception to this view, after an exchange of heated words between the *Gazette* owners and John Mein, publisher of the pro-British *Boston Chronicle*. Mein spied Gill on the street and laid his adversary low "with force of arms, to wit, with a large club." Gill won a court judgment of £130, later reduced to £75.

After the fighting at Lexington and Concord and the establishment of martial law in Boston by the British, Edes and Gill ended their partnership in April 1775. Edes, however, reopened a printing office in nearby Watertown and resumed the *Gazette* on 5 June. Gill, who stayed in Boston, was arrested on 4 August "by martial authority" for "printing treason, sedition and rebellion," but was, on 2 October, "so far liberated as to walk the Town." On 30 May 1776, Gill, alone, started the *Continental Journal and Weekly Advertiser*, a conservative sheet compared to the *Gazette* (which Edes resumed in Boston and continued to publish until 17 Sept. 1798). Meanwhile, Gill, who had become official printer again, continued his business but ceased publication of the *Journal* on 28 April 1785, in protest against the state stamp act. He died poor.

• For more information on Gill, see Clarence S. Brigham, *History and Bibliography of American Newspapers, 1690–1820* (2 vols., 1947); Joseph Buckingham, *Specimens of Newspaper Literature* (1850); Maurice R. Cullen, Jr., "Benjamin Edes: Scourge of Tories," *Journalism Quarterly* 51, no. 2 (Summer 1974): 213–18; and O. M. Dickerson, "British Control of American Newspapers on the Eve of the Revolution," *New England Quarterly* 24 (1951): 453–68. Also see Peter Force, *American Archives*, vol. 2 (1840); Edmund S. Morgan, ed., *Prologue to Revolution: Sources and Documents on the Stamp Act Crisis, 1764–66* (1959); Arthur M. Schlesinger, *Prelude to Independence: The Newspaper War on Britain 1764–1776* (1957); and Isaiah Thomas, *The History of Printing in America* (1810; repr. 1970).

RICHARD F. HIXSON

GILL, Laura Drake (24 Aug. 1860–3 Feb. 1926), educational administrator and reformer, was born in Chesterville, Maine, the daughter of Elisha Gill and Hulda

Capen. Following the death of her father in 1873, Gill's maternal aunt, Bessie T. Capen, brought her to Northampton, Massachusetts, where she matriculated at Smith College, graduating in 1881 with a degree in mathematics. For the next seventeen years, Gill taught mathematics at her aunt's school for girls. While teaching at Miss Capen's School, she earned a master's degree in mathematics from Smith College and in 1893 pursued additional graduate study at the Universities of Leipzig and Geneva and at the Sorbonne.

Anxious for adventure and for administrative service, Gill was one of the first women to seek executive work with the American Red Cross after the outbreak of the Spanish-American War in 1898. Among the first unit of nurses dispatched to Cuba, Gill worked close to the front lines. Following her battlefield service, she spent the remainder of the war stationed at Montauk Point, New York, selecting and training nurses. For the first two years after the war Gill placed her administrative skills at the service of the Cuban Orphans' Society, working with General Leonard Wood to reform Cuban schools.

In 1901 she began an eight-year tenure as dean of Barnard College, the women's college of Columbia University. Active in various aspects of institutional life, Gill initiated an undergraduate degree in science, advocated student self-government, increased the size of the campus, and oversaw the construction of dormitories. These latter two achievements were of special importance to Gill, whose own experience at Smith had made her cherish the campus life that women enjoyed outside the classroom. She was eager that Barnard students, most of whom commuted each day, have the chance to enter more fully into the life of the college. The central accomplishments of Gill's tenure as dean were her securing from wealthy benefactor Elizabeth Milbank Anderson both valuable real estate adjacent to the Barnard campus and generous financial support for the construction of an on-campus dormitory. Gill also maintained close ties with Smith, serving in 1901 as president of the Smith Alumnae Association of New York City.

Because of her own life as a professional woman and her involvement with women's career issues, both in the Red Cross and at Barnard, Gill became progressively more concerned with work opportunities for women. Gill left Barnard in 1908 to work for the Vocational Bureau for College Women under the auspices of the Women's Educational and Industrial Union in Boston. In this capacity she tirelessly encouraged women to seek the best preparation for their careers, and she encouraged employers to compensate women adequately. Her term as the president of the Association of Collegiate Women (c. 1908–1912) reaffirmed her dedication to enhancing career options for women. Between 1911 and 1914 she continued her efforts on behalf of women's vocational opportunities at the University of the South and at Trinity College, the coordinate college of Duke University in Durham, North Carolina.

Following the outbreak of the First World War Gill again offered her organizational skills to the federal government, this time with the U.S. Employment Service in the Department of Labor. At the end of the war her interests changed drastically. After a lifetime of dedicating herself to the advancement of college women, Gill spent her last years involved with the mountain boys of Appalachia. Between 1919 and 1922 she worked with the Pine Mountain Settlement, a school for mountain children in Kentucky. She then accepted a position as teacher and housemother to approximately 100 mountain boys at Berea College, a coeducational, nonsectarian institution dedicated to the education of Appalachian Americans, in Berea, Kentucky. That a reform-minded person such as Gill ended her career at Berea reinforced the institution's reputation for attracting women of exceptional strength to its faculty and administrative ranks. Following several years of recurring heart problems, Gill died in Berea.

• For a discussion of Gill's maternal ancestors, see C. A. Hayden, *The Capen Family* (1902). To understand Gill's service during the Spanish-American War, see L. L. Dock et al., *History of American Red Cross Nursing* (1922). For an examination of her contributions to Barnard College, see Helen Lefkowitz Horowitz, *Alma Mater: Design and Experience in the Women's Colleges from Their Nineteenth-Century Beginnings to the 1930s* (1984). For accounts of Gill's entire career, see her obituary in the *New York Times*, 5 Feb. 1926.

CAROLYN TERRY BASHAW

GILL, Mother Irene (25 Mar. 1856–22 Dec. 1935), educator and Roman Catholic religious, was born in Galway, Ireland, and baptized Lucy, the daughter of Joshua Gill, a small-businessman, and Catherine Fox. Forced to migrate by economic conditions, in 1868 Lucy with her mother, sister Elizabeth, and a brother joined three sisters already living in New York City. Her father emigrated with another son to join children living in Australia. It is uncertain whether the elder Gills were ever reunited. Catherine Gill and her children lived on the Lower East Side, where Lucy attended St. Catherine's Academy, run by the Sisters of Mercy, the religious community that two of her elder sisters had joined.

As a young girl Lucy played at being a nun, indicating the beginnings of a religious vocation. When the Gill family moved uptown, Lucy came into contact with another teaching order, the Ursulines, who ran a day and boarding school in East Morrisania in the Bronx. This was the convent to which Lucy applied for admission and into which she entered on 31 May 1876. She received the religious name of Sister Irene and made profession of vows on 27 December 1879. She then joined other East Morrisania sisters in teaching at St. Teresa's parish on Henry Street in the Bronx. When this group became the independent Ursuline community of St. Teresa's, incorporated June 1882, Sister Irene elected to remain a member.

Gill's abilities eventually led to her appointment as head of the community's academy and director of the "Board Classes," a program begun in 1883 to train teachers according to the requirements of New York City's board of education. So closely connected was Gill to the program that some referred to it as "Mother Irene's School." (She had become Mother Irene after about ten years in the sisterhood, in recognition of her longevity as a professed religious.) The Board Classes involved the St. Teresa's sisters with adult education and professional training of women, including training at the college level after the mid-1890s. Together with the academy's educational reputation, these ventures sparked Gill's dream of a liberal arts college for women.

Elected superior of St. Teresa's community in 1893, Gill embarked on an expansion of the convent's projects, meeting Irish-American demands for increased educational opportunities. The Henry Street neighborhood had been changing for a decade, leading to declining academy enrollment but also to greater demand for the Board Classes. The combination necessitated a search for new quarters for both convent and academy closer to the school's constituents, who were moving uptown and into the suburbs. By 1897, despite grinding poverty at the St. Teresa convent, Gill had opened a second academy at Ninety-third Street and Park Avenue as well as the Ursuline Seminary (school) at the former Leland Castle hotel in New Rochelle, New York, a town in which the St. Teresa community also conducted a parochial school.

Gill's term as superior ended in 1899, just at the time she became involved in negotiations for the community to accept Pope Leo XIII's proposal for all Ursulines to unite under a central government as the Roman Union of the Order of St. Ursula. Over the next two years Gill concentrated her administrative talents on this project.

Following reelection as superior of St. Teresa's in 1902, Gill realized her vision, announcing her intention to open a four-year women's college in New Rochelle on 4 July 1904, the date she received the incorporating charter from the state Board of Regents. She was beginning without endowment or funds, relying on the living resources of Ursulines and the advice and support of a group of friends, men and women, secular and religious, who supported her idea of higher education for women. Gill's project met some resistance, even direct opposition: Archbishop John Farley of New York considered it a "wild" idea, while some called the college "Mother Irene's folly." The College of St. Angela opened on 12 September 1904 as the first Catholic college for women in New York State. Later, on the advice of friends and to distinguish the college clearly, Gill petitioned for a change of name to the College of New Rochelle, a request granted by the Board of Regents on 31 March 1910.

As first dean, later first vice president, and de facto chief executive officer of the college, Gill pursued the twin goals of academic excellence and recognition by both Catholic and secular authorities. Using a network of clerics, educators, lawyers, and businessmen, Catholic and non-Catholic, to advise and assist her, Gill devoted increasing resources to the college, selling the Park Avenue academy to help underwrite the college, and hiring the best faculty she could recruit.

Gill shared administrative duties with several St. Teresa community members. One close collaborator was her sibling Elizabeth Gill, who had joined the Ursulines in 1885. As Mother Augustine she handled much of the college's day-to-day administration and served three terms as superior, succeeding Gill each time.

Under Gill's leadership the College of New Rochelle grew from a one-room, nine-student institution into the largest college of its kind in the United States by the 1920s. At her death the college enrolled over 850 students. The college combined a liberal arts focus with mandatory teacher training well into the 1920s, and a large percentage of New Rochelle graduates pursued paid work in teaching and other professions. Recognized early by the Board of Regents, the college later offered extension programs that gave women, lay and religious, valuable opportunities to earn degrees and meet teaching licensing requirements as well as Gill's own exacting standards. These unusual factors propelled New Rochelle into a class by itself, where it served as a model for other Catholic colleges in New York and beyond.

Gill continued to be active in her order. In 1905, when the Roman Union of the Order of St. Ursula was divided into provinces, she became councilor to the provincial prioress of the northern region of the United States, with houses from New York to California. In 1909 Gill was herself elected provincial prioress, an office she held until 1927 except for the years 1915–1918. As provincial she promoted the Roman Union, bought and refurbished two novitiates, reorganized business operations, and encouraged the Ursuline mission among Native Americans in Montana.

Following her last term as provincial, Gill was again elected superior of St. Teresa's. She became severely ill with pneumonia in 1930 and retired to the community's Walden, New York, country home, where she died. She was buried in Calvary Cemetery in New York City.

Contemporaries describe Mother Irene Gill as both gentle and firm, ruling her domain with exacting attention to detail, deeply religious but also mindful of earthly ways by which to gain her ends. Demanding of others, she was also demanding of herself, and was therefore respected. Gill took great pride in the achievements of her order and of the Ursuline foundations she shepherded, particularly the College of New Rochelle, which she considered the culmination of her life's work. In the centuries-old tradition of Ursuline founder St. Angela Merici, Gill placed the highest priority on education and on the training of teachers, embodying her ideals and those of the Ursuline order to a degree unprecedented in previous foundations but giving these ideals a flexibility that encouraged the experimentation and change that would continue to mark the College of New Rochelle.

• Few of Mother Irene Gill's personal or official papers have survived. Some are gathered at the College of New Rochelle archives. More numerous are letters sent to her, as well as early records of the college. There is a folder of correspondence at the provincial archives of the Ursulines in the Bronx, New York. The *Annals* of the St. Teresa community may also be helpful. Of several biographical sources in the college archives, the most useful are an untitled sketch of the history of Mother Irene by Sister Gertrude Farmer (1968) and the college's official obituary, "Reverend Mother Irene Gill" (1935). An interpretation of Mother Irene's life and career, which, unfortunately, relies on some mistaken assertions, is Tracy Mitrano, "Against the Odds: Mother Irene Gill and the Founding of the College of New Rochelle," *History of Higher Education Annual* 7 (1987): 79–97. There is no full-length history of the College of New Rochelle. An unfinished master's thesis by Sister Jane Frances Cuddy (College of New Rochelle, c. 1941) provides many keen insights and firsthand information. Information about both Gill and the college is also presented in Sister Justin McKiernan, *It Is Well to Remember* (n.d.; 1963?). Gill's work in the Roman Union of the Order of St. Ursula receives attention in the unpublished manuscript held at the College of New Rochelle of Sister Mary Russo, "A History of the Eastern Province of the United States of the Roman Union of the Order of St. Ursula, 1535–1989" (1989).

CYNTHIA FARR BROWN

GILL, Theodore Nicholas (21 Mar. 1837–25 Sept. 1914), zoologist, was born in New York City, the son of James Darrell Gill and Elizabeth Vosburgh. Gill's father was the son of a merchant in Newfoundland, and the family appears to have been moderately wealthy. Gill's mother died when he was nine years old. He attended private schools in New York City and took an early keen interest in the fishes at the Fulton fish market and in other natural history subjects.

Although his father wanted him to become a clergyman, Gill chose to study law in the office of S. W. and R. A. Gaines in New York City, one partner of which was his aunt's husband. He continued to spend time at the fish market and among the port's sailing vessels to look at the sailors' curios. In New York he became acquainted with several wealthy men who were interested in natural history. He requested and received a scholarship from the Wagner Free Institute of Science in Philadelphia soon after its founding in 1855. Gill later told a friend that the grant "was the deciding factor in his resolve to devote himself to scientific studies" (Dall, p. 314).

Gill began compiling a report on the fishes of New York that came to the attention of Spencer Fullerton Baird, the assistant secretary of the Smithsonian Institution. The report was subsequently published in the Smithsonian's annual report of 1856 when Gill was only nineteen years old.

In 1858 Gill joined an expedition of several months to various islands of the West Indies, which was sponsored by wealthy amateur conchologist D. Jackson Stewart of New York City. In addition to collecting marine fishes, Gill discovered three species of unusual freshwater fishes on the island of Trinidad. This was his only collecting expedition. After working on the

specimens in Washington, D.C., and in Philadelphia, Gill published the results in several papers in the New York Lyceum of Natural History (later the New York Academy of Sciences).

Through Baird's sponsorship Gill began work in Washington about 1860 on the zoological collections of the Northwest Boundary Survey. He was officially employed at the Smithsonian Institution in 1861, and the next year he was appointed its librarian. Although Secretary Joseph Henry arranged for the extensive library to be transferred to the Library of Congress in 1866, Gill continued to be in charge of it until 1874.

Gill was also an adjunct professor of physics and natural history at Columbian College (later George Washington University) beginning in 1860, although he himself did not have a college education. He was a lecturer at the college from 1864 to 1866 and from 1873 to 1884, becoming a professor of zoology in 1884 and a professor emeritus in 1910.

For many years Gill lived in a room in the Smithsonian Institution building, where he carried out his researches. His primary interest was fishes, which are the subject of more than half of his publications. Ichthyologist David Starr Jordan dedicated his *Guide to the Study of Fishes* (1905) to Gill and called him a "master in taxonomy." Gill's approach was to determine the relationship of families or genera of fishes and present his conclusions in short papers. He based the classification especially on the bone structure; this became the format adopted by Jordan and later researchers, although European ichthyologists were slower than Americans to accept the concept. Some of his analysis was given in "Arrangement of the Families of Fishes; or, Classes *Pisces, Marsipobranchii,* and *Leptocardii*" (*Smithsonian Miscellaneous Collections* 247, no. 11 [1872]: 1–49). In other papers Gill described the life histories and habits of fishes, primarily from scattered observations in the literature. Gill's "knowledge of the biological literature of all countries and all times was amazing and profound" (Dall, p. 320). A significant paper on distribution was "A Comparison of Antipodal Faunas" (National Academy of Sciences, vol. 6, 5th Memoir [1893], pp. 91–124).

Gill also published descriptions of new species of mollusks and their classifications in his article "Arrangement of the Families of Mollusks" (*Smithsonian Miscellaneous Collections* 227, no. 10 [1873]: 1–49), but his findings have been generally superseded by later work. He also wrote on marine and land mammals in works such as "Arrangement of the Families of Mammals, with Analytical Tables, Prepared for the Smithsonian Institution" (*Smithsonian Miscellaneous Collections* 230, no. 11 [1872]: 1–98). He published papers on birds, but not all of his views on the relative taxonomic value of certain characters were accepted by contemporary ornithologists. His help on the Committee on Nomenclature of the American Ornithological Union was appreciated by that group.

In his prodigious output of approximately 500 papers, Gill was usually the sole author. He published in the *Proceedings of the Academy of Natural Sciences of*

Philadelphia and in various series of the Smithsonian Institution. Beginning in 1899 he edited an ornithological publication, *Osprey*, and published some papers in it.

Gill was noted as being especially helpful to colleagues, by providing information from his "encyclopedic knowledge and phenomenal memory." Except for the West Indies trip in 1858, his only trip abroad was in 1901 to Scotland, where he represented the National Academy of Sciences and the Smithsonian Institution at the 450th anniversary of the founding of the University of Glasgow. Gill was a member of many scientific societies. He was elected to the National Academy of Sciences in 1873 and was a founder of the Cosmos Club in Washington. He served as the president of the American Association for the Advancement of Science in 1897. Gill was a sociable person, but he never married. His lifestyle was frugal. He died in Washington, D.C.

• The primary biography of Gill is William Healey Dall, National Academy of Sciences, *Biographical Memoirs* 8 (1919): 313–43. It has an extensive but incomplete bibliography. A brief account of Gill's life and work is in George Crossette, *Founders of the Cosmos Club of Washington* (1966). Descriptions of Gill's role in ichthyology are in Carl L. Hubbs, "History of Ichthyology in the United States after 1850," *Copeia*, no. 1 (Mar. 1964): 42–60. An obituary is in the *Washington Evening Star*, 25 Sept. 1914.

ELIZABETH NOBLE SHOR

GILLARS, Mildred Elizabeth (29 Nov. 1900–25 June 1988), radio propagandist known as "Axis Sally," was born Mildred Elizabeth Sisk in Portland, Maine, the daughter of Vincent Sisk, a railroad yardman, and Mae Hewitson. When Mildred was seven her parents divorced, and shortly after, her mother married Robert Bruce Gillars, a dentist, who moved his new family to Conneaut, Ohio. From her early years, Mildred was a stagestruck child whose mother encouraged her desire to be an actress. She appeared in a number of theater productions at Conneaut High School and at Ohio Wesleyan University, which she entered in 1918. In preparation for a career on the stage Gillars majored in English and oratory and minored in voice and piano. At Ohio Wesleyan Gillars's performances were highly praised. She was an erratic student, however, and because of several incompletes and failures, she left the university in 1922 without graduating.

Hoping for success on Broadway, Gillars moved to New York, working at temporary jobs while she studied acting at night. During the 1920s she toured with little-known road companies and acted in regional theaters in the United States and Canada. Success as an actress eluded her, however, and in 1929 she decided to try her luck in Europe. There are conflicting reports about Gillars's life as a prewar expatriate; she apparently took whatever jobs she could find—as a dressmaker's assistant in Algiers, as a model in Paris, and finally as an English teacher at the Berlitz School in Berlin, where she settled in 1934. To make ends meet,

Gillars also tutored privately and translated at least one book into English.

The disruptions surrounding Germany's invasion of Poland in September 1939 left Gillars temporarily jobless. She apparently did not seek repatriation, and in 1941, after she found a job as an announcer on Berlin radio, she claimed that an American vice consul confiscated her passport. Stranded and utterly dependent on her small salary as a broadcaster for survival, Gillars took an oath of allegiance to Nazi Germany after the attack on Pearl Harbor and Germany's declaration of war against the United States.

Early in 1942 Gillars's life took a dramatic turn when she met and fell in love with naturalized American citizen Max Otto Koischwitz. Koischwitz had taught German literature at Hunter College in New York from 1928 to 1939 and had written a subtle defense of Hitler and Nazi Germany, *A German-American Interprets Germany* (1935). Disgruntled at his failure to receive a promotion at Hunter, the controversial Koischwitz resigned and returned to Germany in 1939. At the time Gillars met Koischwitz, he was an important official in the German Foreign Office and was the top person at the Reich Rundfunk, the German radio system. As a result of his influence, Gillars became a star of German radio overnight. After years of obscurity and grinding poverty, Gillars achieved fame on two continents and commanded a monthly salary of 3,000 marks (about $1,200), the second-highest-paid employee of German radio.

In 1942 Koischwitz and Gillars cohosted a show, "Home Sweet Home," which was beamed to American servicemen in North Africa. In 1943 this was followed by the even more popular "Midge at the Mike." GIs in North Africa and Europe eagerly awaited Gillars's nightly broadcasts, for "Axis Sally," as they soon dubbed her, played nostalgic love songs such as "Never in a Million Years," "Kiss Me Again," "I Surrender Dear," and "Somebody Stole My Gal." In a sultry voice, Gillars read scripts written by Koischwitz that tried to persuade the homesick soldiers that Germany was unbeatable, that their chances of surviving death or mutilation were slim, and that some draft dodger back home was probably stealing their gal. "Hello gang," began one of her broadcasts, "Throw down those little old guns and toddle off home. There's no getting the Germans down."

German radio, she explained later, gave her "the outlet for the dramatic expression I had always sought." Unlike other Americans who broadcast for Nazi Germany out of ideological conviction, Gillars appears to have drifted into treason because of her love for Koischwitz as well as her desire for the fame and fortune she had craved much of her life. The Nazis offered her a "chance to be somebody," as William Shirer observed in 1943 of other American radio traitors. It offered her a career.

However, Gillars's career as a radio traitor lasted barely two years and cost her dearly. By early September 1944 Germany was headed for defeat, and her lover Koischwitz was dead of tuberculosis. Stranded once again, Gillars survived by pawning whatever valuables she had accumulated during her brief stardom. Fully aware that she had engaged in treasonous activities, Gillars eluded the American occupation authorities for nearly a year after the war in Europe ended in May 1945. Finally, in March 1946, a counterintelligence agent found her, ill and emaciated, living in Berlin cellars. Since the authorities lacked sufficient evidence at the time for a conviction for broadcasting Nazi propaganda, Gillars was released with orders to report regularly to military authorities.

Two years later, on 20 August 1948, Gillars was flown to the United States on a military aircraft. The following day she was arraigned, charged with giving aid and comfort to the enemy from 11 December 1941 to 6 May 1945. Three weeks later she was indicted for treason on ten counts, but because of illness her trial did not open until 24 January 1949. The *New York Times* and other newspapers from coast to coast provided extensive coverage of the trial. By mid-February there was hardly a person in the United States who had not heard of Axis Sally.

Ultimately Gillars was convicted of treason for one broadcast she made on 11 May 1944, on the eve of the Normandy invasion. In "Vision of Invasion," a radio play written by Koischwitz, Gillars played the role of a distraught American mother whose son dies in the invasion that actually began only three weeks later, on 6 June 1944. "Vision of Invasion" tried to frighten and demoralize American troops by predicting in graphic and horrifying detail that the only results of their efforts would be doom, defeat, and death.

The tape of "Vision of Invasion" was played several times at Gillars's trial, and on 10 March 1949 the jury of six men and six women, after seventeen hours of deliberation, found her guilty of treason on one count. Two weeks later she was sentenced to ten to thirty years' imprisonment and fined $10,000. After exhausting all appeals, in August 1950 Gillars entered the Federal Reformatory for Women in Alderson, West Virginia. Iva Toguri D'Aquino, also known as "Tokyo Rose," who was convicted of treason months after Gillars's trial, served time in the same prison.

Gillars proved to be a model prisoner, tutoring other prisoners and conducting both the Catholic and Protestant choirs at the reformatory. In 1960 Gillars converted to Catholicism, and after her parole on 10 July 1961 she spent the rest of her working days teaching French, German, and music at a convent school in Worthington, Ohio. By 1973 Gillars had accumulated enough credits at Ohio State University and two nearby colleges to receive her B.A. degree in speech at Ohio Wesleyan University. She never lost her love of the theater and in the early 1970s was a member of a Shakespeare Readers' Theatre Club. After her retirement from teaching, Gillars lived a secluded life. In the years after her release from prison, Gillars, the first woman in American history to be convicted of treason, found a measure of acceptance and forgiveness among those who knew her. She died in Columbus, Ohio.

• Sources on Gillars fall primarily into two categories: books on treason, especially radio treason, and contemporary newspaper and magazine articles. The earliest work on treason to examine the role of Axis Sally is Nathaniel Weyl, *Treason: The Story of Disloyalty and Betrayal in American History* (1950). See also Jules Archer, *Treason in America: Disloyalty vs. Dissent* (1971), for a shorter account. John C. Edwards, *Berlin Calling: American Broadcasters in Service to the Third Reich* (1991), contains a chapter on Max Otto Koischwitz that includes an invaluable evaluation of Gillars's broadcasts. Also informative is Richard Lamparski, *Whatever Became of . . . ?* (1968). Gillars received considerable attention from the press before and during her treason trial in early 1949, at the time of her release from prison, her graduation from Ohio Wesleyan in July 1973, and her death. The index of the *New York Times* for those years provides a long list of articles about Gillars. An interesting analysis of Gillars's trial is by Richard Rovere in his "Letter from Washington," in the *New Yorker*, 26 Feb. 1949, pp. 74–82. For an excellent contrast between Axis Sally and Tokyo Rose, see Masayo Duus, *Tokyo Rose: Orphan of the Pacific* (1979). An obituary is in the *New York Times*, 2 July 1988.

ANNA MACÍAS

GILLEM, Alvan Cullem (29 July 1830–2 Dec. 1875), soldier, was born in Jackson County, Tennessee, the son of Samuel J. Gillem. His mother's name is unknown. In 1851 he graduated from the U.S. Military Academy, ranking eleventh in a class of forty-two. That same year he married Margaret Jones. They probably had at least one child. For the next decade he served in a variety of assignments, including duty in the Third Seminole War and on the Texas frontier.

Shortly after the outbreak of the Civil War, Gillem was promoted to the rank of captain and dispatched to Fort Taylor, Florida. In August 1861 he wrote Senator Andrew Johnson of Tennessee, offering his services "to support the loyal citizens of my native state." Johnson promptly became his patron and helped secure Gillem's transfer to a division commanded by Brigadier General George H. Thomas. After a stint as division quartermaster, during which he participated in the battle of Mill Springs, Kentucky, in April 1862 Gillem was reassigned to the staff of the Army of the Ohio, commanded by Major General Don Carlos Buell, where he served as inspector general of the Quartermaster Department and inspector of artillery. In this capacity he participated in the Shiloh and Corinth campaigns.

In May 1862 Johnson, now military governor of Tennessee, appointed Gillem colonel of the First Middle Tennessee (later Tenth Tennessee Volunteer Regiment [Union]). From August to December 1862 Gillem served as provost marshal of Nashville. Then until August 1863 he served as commander of Camp Spears near Nashville. On 1 June 1863 Johnson appointed him adjutant general of Tennessee. In mid-August Johnson persuaded President Abraham Lincoln to make Gillem a brigadier general.

Soon afterward Gillem oversaw construction of the Nashville and Northwestern Railroad, an unfinished rail line between Nashville and the Tennessee River that was badly needed to improve the strained supply lines of the Union Army of the Cumberland. From August 1863 to March 1864 he supervised more than 1,000 black laborers, guarding them against guerrilla incursions with about 3,000 troops. In April 1864 he was also placed in charge of a small cavalry division.

Gillem's units operated under the direct control of Governor Johnson. As a result, Union general William T. Sherman scorned them as "a refugee hospital for indolent Tennesseeans." He added that he had "never reckoned them anything but a political element" (letter to Joseph D. Webster, 6 June 1864) and refused to involve them in his Atlanta campaign. Instead Johnson converted part of the force into a brigade-sized "Governor's Guard." In the summer of 1864 Johnson sent Gillem and the guard into eastern Tennessee with orders to root out the Confederate cavalry and secessionist guerrillas operating in that region. From August through December 1864 Gillem carried out these instructions with mixed success. At Greeneville in September 1864 his troops trapped and killed the famed Confederate cavalry raider General John Hunt Morgan. In November they suffered an embarrassing defeat at Bull's Gap. Rescued by a large force under Major General George Stoneman, Gillem's brigade accompanied Stoneman on a raid into southwestern Virginia in December 1864.

By the end of the Civil War Gillem had compiled, at best, a modest wartime record, but he had become a prominent figure in Tennessee politics. In January 1865 he served as vice president of the state convention that restored civil government to Tennessee. Three months later he became a member of the Tennessee House of Representatives. He also remained a favorite of Johnson, now president after Lincoln's assassination. In July 1865 Gillem, now a brevet major general, took command of the District of East Tennessee, a post he held until September 1866, when he left the volunteer service with the permanent rank of colonel in the U.S. Army.

In the meantime Johnson, Gillem's political patron, found himself increasingly isolated by his conservative policies toward the defeated South. By 1867 Congress overthrew the Johnson program and inaugurated Military Reconstruction. Faced not only with a hostile Congress but also a hostile secretary of war, Edwin Stanton, and general in chief, Ulysses S. Grant, Johnson found that one of the few means of influence left to him was his presidential power to appoint commanders to the five military districts in the South. Accordingly, on 9 January 1868 he placed Gillem in charge of the Fourth Military District, embracing Mississippi and Arkansas. Consistent with Johnson's wishes, Gillem pursued a conservative policy and usually appointed Unionist former Whigs to fill vacant civil offices in preference to outright southern Republicans. The loyalty of Gillem's appointees was sometimes open to question, one Republican complaining that they "had to have the oath [of allegiance] greased to make it go down easy" (quoted in Harris, p. 53). Gillem was also accused of thwarting the Republican-dominated Mississippi constitutional convention of 1868, undermining efforts to strengthen the Republican party in the state, and treating freedmen with a marked lack of sympathy, as in his insistence that unemployed African Americans should be arrested for vagrancy.

Upon Grant's accession to the presidency in 1868, Gillem was relieved from duty in the Fourth Military District and sent to the far West. On 15 December 1870 he received command of the First U.S. Cavalry. Three years later he was placed in charge of the District of the Lakes in northern California, where he saw action in the Modoc War. When his immediate superior, General Edward R. S. Canby, was assassinated by a Modoc leader, Gillem became interim commander of the Department of the Columbia. While Canby's permanent replacement was en route from the East, Gillem organized a new offensive against the Modoc insurgents. Although initially successful, his expedition sustained a severe reversal in April 1873. Shortly thereafter, the *Army and Navy Journal* characterized Gillem's command as "demoralized by mismanagement." Gillem nevertheless remained on active duty. While stationed in Texas he became ill, and he died at "Soldier's Rest," his home near Nashville.

Although a professional soldier, Gillem possessed only modest military ability and owed his high rank principally to his political allegiance to Johnson. Like Johnson, he was a loyal Tennessean whose firm wartime adherence to the Union cause was matched by an equally firm commitment to conservative home rule in the South after the war.

• For general background, see George W. Cullum, *Biographical Register of Officers and Graduates of the United States Military Academy*, 3d ed. (1891); and Mark M. Boatner III, *Civil War Dictionary* (1959). On Gillem's wartime career, consult *The War of the Rebellion: A Compilation of the Official Records of the Union and Confederate Armies* (128 vols., 1880–1901); Clifton R. Hall, *Andrew Johnson: Military Governor of Tennessee* (1916); and LeRoy P. Graf and Ralph W. Haskins, *Papers of Andrew Johnson*, vols. 5–7 (1967–). William C. Harris, *The Day of the Carpetbagger: Republican Reconstruction in Mississippi* (1979), deal with his tenure as Fourth Military District commander. See also *Annual Report of the Secretary of War, 1867–1868* (1868). For his service during the Modoc War, see Robert M. Utley, *Frontier Regulars: The United States Army and the Indian, 1866–1891* (1973). Obituaries are in the *Nashville Daily American*, 3 Dec. 1875; and the *New York Times*, 5 Dec. 1875.

MARK GRIMSLEY

GILLESPIE, Dizzy (21 Oct. 1917–6 Jan. 1993), jazz trumpeter, bandleader, and composer, was born John Birks Gillespie in Cheraw, South Carolina, the son of James Gillespie, a mason and musician, and Lottie Powe. Gillespie's father kept his fellow band members' instruments at their home, and thus from his toddler years onward Gillespie had an opportunity to experiment with sounds. He entered Robert Smalls public school in 1922. He was as naughty as he was brilliant, and accounts of fighting, showing off, and mischief extend from his youth into adulthood.

From mid-1927, when Gillespie's father died, the family lived in poverty. Gillespie studied trombone in the third grade but began to double on trumpet, borrowing a friend's instrument. He became Cheraw's best musician, playing trumpet or cornet. A long-standing feature of Gillespie's playing was evident even then, as a teenage companion, trombonist Norman Powe, recalled: "It was a very fast style. . . . He didn't have a tone. He doesn't have a good tone now, but his execution outweighs all that."

In 1933 Gillespie graduated from the ninth grade at Robert Smalls and received a full scholarship to play trumpet at the Laurinburg Institute in Laurinburg, North Carolina. He studied agriculture and played on the football team, until he realized the danger it presented to his mouth and hands.

In the spring of 1935 Gillespie's family moved to Philadelphia, Pennsylvania, and without finishing school, he joined them that summer and began playing professionally. He practiced piano and trumpet with Bill Doggett, each taking turns on the other's instrument; this activity exemplified his relentless devotion to music and to pushing his abilities forward. In 1935 he joined Frankie Fairfax's band, in which he began to be called "Dizzy," a name that obviously suited his behavior and musical ideas. In 1937 he moved to New York City. After sitting in with bands at the Savoy Ballroom, he replaced Frankie Newton in Teddy Hill's big band on the strength of his ability to imitate the playing of Roy Eldridge, whom Newton had replaced. Gillespie recorded and toured Europe with Hill's orchestra and also performed with pianist Edgar Hayes's big band, the Savoy Sultans, and flutist Alberto Socarras's Latin band.

On the recommendation of trumpeter and Cuban expatriate Mario Bauzá, who stimulated Gillespie's later interest in bringing Afro-Cuban dance music into jazz, Gillespie joined Cab Calloway's band in the summer of 1939. In September he recorded with Lionel Hampton, contributing a muted solo on "Hot Mallets." His unmuted solos on Calloway's recordings "Pickin' the Cabbage"—which Gillespie also composed and arranged—"Bye Bye Blues," and "Boo-Wah Boo-Wah," all from 1940, give early evidence of the continuous velocity and harmonic brashness that would characterize his mature soloing.

On 9 May 1940, while with Calloway in Boston, Gillespie married Lorraine Lynch, a dancer who in their fifty-two years together provided a rock-steady foil for Gillespie's impetuousness; they had no children. That same year he met alto saxophonist Charlie Parker in Kansas City. While participating in jam sessions at Minton's Playhouse in Harlem, Gillespie entered a close friendship with pianist Thelonious Monk, with whom he traded ideas. These and similar jam sessions at Monroe's Uptown House in Harlem served as venues for the development of bebop. "Stardust" and "Kerouac," homemade recordings from Minton's and Monroe's in May 1941, document Gillespie's experiments with a new improvisational style, although their value is perhaps more historical than musical.

In the fall of 1941 Gillespie got into a fight with Calloway and knifed the bandleader in the posterior, thereby ending their musical affiliation. Gillespie performed in Boston with Chick Webb's big band, which had continued under Ella Fitzgerald's leadership after Webb's death in 1939; in New York with Coleman Hawkins's band and Benny Carter's band; and in Toronto with Charlie Barnet's big band. While with Carter, Gillespie composed "A Night in Tunisia." He next joined Les Hite's big band, with which he recorded a solo on "Jersey Bounce" in June 1942. During the summer he was a member of Lucky Millinder's big band. "Little John Special," recorded by Millender in July, features Gillespie's trumpeting; its arrangement incorporates a melody that became the bebop theme "Salt Peanuts."

Gillespie led a small group at the Down Beat Club in Philadelphia, and Parker—who by that time had also become active at Minton's and Monroe's—began sitting in; no recordings survive to document how far they had progressed toward the bop style. Gillespie and Parker then joined pianist Earl Hines's big band late in 1942. In September 1943 Gillespie returned to New York to play with Coleman Hawkins and then, very briefly, in Duke Ellington's big band.

Over the winter of 1943 to 1944 Gillespie co-led a bebop combo with bassist Oscar Pettiford at the Onyx Club; Max Roach played drums. On 16 February 1944 Gillespie composed and recorded "Woody 'n' You," its theme based on a harmonic progression that he had learned from Monk. After a dispute among the leaders, Gillespie moved across Fifty-second Street to the Yacht Club (soon renamed the Downbeat Club), where he co-led with tenor saxophonist Budd Johnson; Roach remained as the drummer. Gillespie also served as music director for Billy Eckstine's big band; his arrangement of "Good Jelly Blues," recorded by Eckstine in April 1944, incorporated rapid, nervous, spiky accompaniments exemplifying a new conception of big-band instrumental countermelody superimposed on an otherwise largely conventional big-band blues performance. The trumpeter toured with Eckstine during the latter half of 1944, and he may be heard soloing above the ensemble on "Blowin' the Blues Away," recorded in December.

Gillespie's seminal bebop performances and recordings emerged in 1945 and 1946, largely in collaboration with Parker. Their quintet appearances at the Three Deuces Club in April and May 1945 had a strong impact on the New York jazz community, but it was of course their recordings that quickly generated a stylistic upheaval nationally and internationally among a whole generation of musicians and listeners. These recordings demonstrated an audaciousness and freedom from convention that at the time had no parallel in jazz. Joined in the next few years by further notable sessions from Parker (apart from Gillespie), Monk, Bud Powell, and Tadd Dameron, the first full-blown bop recordings possess a quirky originality that was (perhaps necessarily) lacking in the bop revival predominant in jazz from the 1980s onward, and thus the path-breaking sessions remain, permanently, among the central documents of the style. These tracks include "Groovin' High," "Dizzy Atmosphere," "Salt Peanuts," "Shaw 'Nuff," and "Hot House," all from 1945, and "Confirmation," "52nd Street Theme," "A Night in Tunisia," "Anthropology," "Oop Bop Sh'Bam," and "One Bass Hit" (pt. 1), all from 1946 and without Parker.

Even as Gillespie was creating historic small-group performances, he sought to lead a big band. His first orchestra, formed in the summer of 1945, met with little success, and he returned to combo work at the Three Deuces (Dec. 1945), Billy Berg's in Los Angeles (Jan.–Feb. 1946), and the Spotlite in New York (Mar. 1946). By this time bebop had acquired some popularity, and in Gillespie's case the impact of his recordings and musical performances was furthered by extramusical considerations: his talent as a comedian and his fashionable appearance, incorporating goatee, beret, and sunglasses. Despite his flamboyance, he remained passionately dedicated to developing an emotionally high-charged but nonetheless intellectually challenging style that would be accepted as serious concert music, not dance music.

In June, while still at the Spotlite, Gillespie formed a new big band to which Gil Fuller, Gillespie, and pianist John Lewis contributed arrangements; in addition, Eckstine lent several of Tadd Dameron's arrangements, including "Our Delight," recorded in June. In July the orchestra recorded a sloppy attempt to have the trumpets perform wildly difficult bebop melodies in unison, "Things to Come"; Lewis's "One Bass Hit" (pt. 2); and a clever put-down of the incompetent hipster, "He Beeped When He Shoulda Bopped." Soon thereafter they made the film *Jivin' in Bebop* (1947).

Gillespie's big band toured from mid-1946 through 1947, with Ella Fitzgerald joining late in 1946 to help make the band more acceptable to southern audiences. In August 1947 the big band recorded "Two Bass Hit" and one of Gillespie's funniest bop nonsense lyrics, "Oop-pop-a-da." With the hiring of conga player Chano Pozo that fall, Gillespie made substantial progress toward uniting jazz and Afro-Cuban dance music, although conflicts between the band's swing rhythms and Pozo's rhythmic conception were not resolved. Recordings from December include Dameron's "Cool Breeze" and "Good Bait"; "Cubana Be, Cubana Bop," co-composed by George Russell, Gillespie, and Pozo; and "Manteca," by Fuller, Gillespie, and Pozo.

In 1948 Gillespie's Afro-Cuban bebop orchestra toured Europe and the South. After Pozo was shot to death in a brawl, Gillespie hired other conga players but found it impossible to re-create Pozo's musicianship and showmanship, although he never stopped trying. He retained a lifetime love for Afro-Cuban rhythms.

By 1949 the novelty of bebop was wearing off, and many swing-era big bands were failing. Gillespie tried to make his group more commercially acceptable by emphasizing rhythm and blues and comedic elements of his repertoire, but the quality of his performances and recordings declined substantially. He disbanded in May 1950. He led a sextet in New York early in 1951 and then in Detroit recorded his blues theme "Birk's Works" for his new label, Dee Gee Records, cofounded with Dave Usher. The label was active mainly in 1951, recording Gillespie's band and Milt Jackson's quartet.

The early 1950s brought occasional reunions with Parker. In June 1950 their quintet recorded "An Oscar for Treadwell" and "Bloomdido," and in March 1951 they appeared at Birdland. At year's end, or early in 1952, they performed "Hot House" with Parker on television for *Down Beat* magazine's jazz awards. On 15 May 1953 Gillespie participated in an acrimonious reunion with Parker, pianist Bud Powell, and Roach for a concert at Massey Hall in Toronto. Their bassist, Charles Mingus, recorded the quintet. Despite its extremely low fidelity, the album *Jazz at Massey Hall* captures brilliant playing by Gillespie, who was never daunted by a clash of egos.

The same year, the bell of his trumpet was bent upward when it fell off its stand. Gillespie liked the resulting sound and had a new instrument designed in this manner. A bent horn and bulging cheeks—this facial characteristic had begun to emerge in 1947—became his unique trademark thereafter.

Through the 1960s Gillespie continued to be busy with recording dates and tours, both in the United States and abroad. In July 1954 he played at the first Newport Jazz Festival, and two years later he led a big band at the initial New York Jazz Festival. He had taken the big band on tours sponsored by the State Department earlier in 1956 to the Near East and Central Asia and to South America, after Congressman Adam Clayton Powell, representative of the New York district encompassing Harlem, had proposed that jazz, with Gillespie as its spokesman, represent the United States as a cultural vanguard in the Cold War. Meanwhile, Gillespie taught at the Lenox (Mass.) School of Jazz and toured with Jazz at the Philharmonic (both 1956–1958).

Among recordings of note during this period are the album *Diz and Getz* (1953); *Afro* (1954), which included Gillespie's composition "Con Alma"; *Dizzy Meets Sonny* (1956), with Sonny Stitt; *For Musicians Only* (1956); and *Duets with Sonny Rollins and Sonny Stitt* and *Sonny Side Up* (both 1957), the latter featuring a virtuosic romp through "The Eternal Triangle" ("I Got Rhythm").

Gillespie became involved with films, too. In 1956 he and his quintet made a film short titled *Date with Dizzy*. In 1962, again with the quintet, he appeared on the television program "Jazz Casual." The group then made soundtracks for the Academy Award–winning cartoon *The Hole* (1962), the film *The Cool World* (1963), and the cartoon *The Hat* (1964). *Dizzy Gillespie* (1965) illustrates his work with Stan Kenton's Los Angeles Neophonic Orchestra, and in 1967 he appeared with Carmen McRae in the documentary film *Monterey Jazz Festival*.

His energy never seemed to flag, and in 1964, while still immersed in music, Gillespie ran for president. Fully aware of the problems of being an African-American star in the world of entertainment, he had over the years approached this predicament in an ambiguous way, taking actions that ranged from clowning to the expression of a near-revolutionary artistic temperament. In this presidential bid, by far the most overt expression of his politics (which were usually private), his principal motivations seemed to be a desire for publicity, to help sustain his career at a time when bop was being overwhelmed by free jazz and rock music, and, of course, a desire to express his dedication to civil rights issues at a climactic time in that movement. Later, in 1968, he adopted the Baha'i faith.

Also in 1968 he formed a big band for a performance at the Newport Jazz Festival and a European tour. While a member of the Giants of Jazz, which toured in 1971 and 1972, he received the Handel Medallion from New York City for his work with schoolchildren. In 1973 his quintet made yet another film, *Dizzy in Brazil*. But that same year Gillespie collapsed during a nightclub performance from an unidentified stimulant, and at the hospital he was pronounced dead on arrival. He recovered, however, and resumed touring.

In the mid-1970s Gillespie was routinely taking part in the ever-expanding international jazz festival circuit. In 1974 he recorded the album *Dizzy Gillespie's Big Four*, including Joe Pass and Ray Brown. He was featured on the public television program "Soundstage" in the 1976 show "Dizzy Gillespie's Be Bop Reunion." He entertained President Jimmy Carter and the shah of Iran at the White House in November 1977, and the following June, in an unforgettable moment at the White House Jazz Festival, he persuaded Carter to sing a duo on "Salt Peanuts." Over the next decade he made the documentary film short *A Night in Tunisia* (1980) and, still leading a quintet, was the focus of a documentary filmed by John Holland at the International Cuban Jazz Festival, *A Night in Havana: Dizzy Gillespie in Cuba* (1987).

In 1988, when he founded the United Nation Orchestra, he brought together probably his greatest ensemble since the 1940s, including not only Americans but also musicians from the Caribbean and South America. Although his endurance and power as a trumpeter had declined over the previous ten years or so, he was still a force to be reckoned with and clearly the group's most profound soloist. Proof of that can be heard on the disc *Dizzy Gillespie and the United Nation Orchestra: Live at Royal Festival Hall* (1989). Another disc of the same period, *Max Roach and Dizzy Gillespie, Paris, 1989*, captures the drummer and the trumpeter reminiscing as well as performing.

By 1990 Gillespie had won recognition of all kinds, including a plaque presented to him by President Dwight D. Eisenhower in 1956. In 1989 he was named a Nigerian tribal chieftain. The next year he received the National Medal of Arts, he was made a French Commandeur des Arts et Lettres, and he was awarded the Kennedy Center Honor.

While performing at Kimball's nightclub in San Francisco early in 1992, Gillespie collapsed, reportedly from exhaustion and a flare-up of diabetes; it later became known that he was suffering from pancreatic cancer. He performed for a month at the Blue Note Club in Manhattan in honor of his upcoming seventy-fifth birthday, but he was unable to attend a tribute concert given at the JVC Jazz Festival in New York in July. He died in Englewood, New Jersey.

Gillespie brought to trumpet playing an unprecedented ability to play fast-moving melodies, both written and improvised, above complex chord progressions. In the classic recordings with Parker, a succession of nearly perfect unison statements of extremely difficult themes testifies to his uncanny knack for matching his trumpet to Parker's alto saxophone. He coupled this facility with an audacious imagination that made his improvisations a musical revelation, rather than merely a technical exercise, as it would become in the hands of disciples such as Jon Faddis and Arturo Sandoval. Gillespie achieved this aim at the expense of timbral nuance, and in this regard he was surpassed by Miles Davis and by a chain of stylistically related trumpeters stretching from Fats Navarro, Clifford Brown, Donald Byrd, Lee Morgan, Freddie Hubbard, Woody Shaw, and Wynton Marsalis onward, although all of these players (Davis excepted) owed their basic improvisational approach to Gillespie's innovations.

The tone of Gillespie's voice had far less to recommend itself than his trumpeting, and yet he made himself into a credible bebop scat singer. Repeatedly he outshone "better" singers on the strength of his timing and his ability to select appropriate nonsense syllables, translating twisting and jagged bebop instrumental sounds into idiomatic vocalized melody.

Gillespie's most memorable and widely performed composition is "A Night in Tunisia." His lesser-known "Con Alma" deserves special mention for its harmonic ambiguity, whereby a pretty theme moves in a little chordal labyrinth back and forth between two keys without ever settling on either. Far more so than Parker, Gillespie as a composer was deeply concerned with bringing diversity into the sound of his ensembles. This is obvious in his work with big bands amalgamating musical elements of the swing era, bebop, and Afro-Cuban dances. It is also a factor in his conception of small combo bebop, as demonstrated in recordings such as "Groovin' High," in which he ornamented the basic song form with an introduction, two changes of key coupled to breaks in the rhythmic accompaniment, and a dramatic new ending at half the original tempo, and "Salt Peanuts," with its introduction, interludes, and ending. He also created a well-known introduction, interlude, and ending to Monk's "'Round Midnight."

Gillespie was the most influential jazz trumpeter after Louis Armstrong, the most significant figure in bebop after Charlie Parker, the driving force behind the most successful early efforts to incorporate Latin music into jazz, and—despite his comic excesses—a pivotal figure in the transformation of jazz from dance music to concert music.

• Dizzy Gillespie with Al Fraser, *To Be, or Not . . . to Bop: Memoirs* (1979), is excellent for reminiscences from Gillespie and colleagues but lacking in musical insight and highly inaccurate regarding affiliations and chronology. An excellent concise biography of his most significant years is Michael James, *Dizzy Gillespie* (1959), repr. in *Kings of Jazz*, ed. Stanley Green (1978). Other biographies include Raymond Horricks, *Dizzy Gillespie and the Be-bop Revolution* (1984), with discography by Tony Middleton; Juergen Woelfer, *Dizzy Gillespie: Sein Leben, seine Musik, seine Schallplatten* (1987); Barry McRae, *Dizzy Gillespie: His Life and Times* (1988); and Laurent Clarke and Franck Verdun, *Dizzy Atmosphere: Conversations avec Dizzy Gillespie* (1990). Surveys and interviews include Leonard Feather, *Inside Be-bop* (1949; repr. 1977 as *Inside Jazz*); Richard O. Boyer, "Profiles: Bop," *New Yorker*, 3 July 1948, pp. 28–32, 34–37; repr. as "Bop: A Profile of Dizzy," in *Eddie Condon's Treasury of Jazz*, ed. Condon and Richard Gehman (1957); Feather, "John 'Dizzy' Gillespie," in *The Jazz Makers: Essays on the Greats of Jazz*, ed. Nat Shapiro and Nat Hentoff (1957; repr. 1979); Ira Gitler, *Jazz Masters of the Forties* (1966; repr. 1983); George Hoefer, "The Big Bands: The Glorious Dizzy Gillespie Orchestra," *Down Beat*, 21 Apr. 1966, pp. 27–30, 47; Ralph J. Gleason, *Celebrating the Duke, and Louis, Bessie, Billie, Bird, Carmen, Miles, Dizzy, and Other Heroes* (1975); Cab Calloway and Bryant Rollins, *Of Minnie the Moocher and Me* (1976); Stanley Dance, *The World of Earl Hines* (1977; repr. 1983); Gene Lees, *Waiting for Dizzy* (1991); and Wayne Enstice and Paul Rubin, *Jazz Spoken Here: Conversations with Twenty-Two Musicians* (1992). For iconography, see Lee Tanner, comp. and ed., *Dizzy: John Birks Gillespie in His 75th Year* (1990); and Dany Gignoux, *Dizzy Gillespie: Fotografien, Photographs* (1993). For musical analysis, see Gary Giddins, *Faces in the Crowd: Players and Writers* (1992); Barry Kernfeld, *What to Listen for in Jazz* (1995); and Thomas Owens, *Bebop: The Music and Its Players* (1995). Jan Evensmo comments on early recordings in *The Trumpets of Dizzy Gillespie, 1927–1943, Irving Randolph, Joe Thomas* (n.d. [1982?]). A catalog of recordings is by Piet Koster and Chris Sellers, *Dizzy Gillespie*, vol. 1: *1937–1953* (1985) and *Dizzy Gillespie*, vol. 2: *1953–1987* (1988). An obituary is in the *New York Times*, 7 Jan. 1993.

BARRY KERNFELD

GILLETT, Emma Millinda (30 July 1852–23 Jan. 1927), lawyer and educator, was born on a homestead in Princeton, Wisconsin, the daughter of Richard J. Gillett, a lawyer and justice of the peace, and Sarah Ann Barlow. After her father's death in 1854, Gillett's mother took her two daughters back to Girard, Pennsylvania, to be near her own family. Gillett graduated from Lake Erie Seminary in Painesville, Ohio, in 1870 and became a teacher. She taught for ten years but grew increasingly discontented with her situation. Describing herself as "tired, nervous and unhappy" in her work and dissatisfied with the "mere pittance" she earned, she resolved to leave teaching and to follow her long-held dream, the study of the law.

Against the advice of her friends and family, in 1880 Gillett took her life savings and went to Washington, D.C., where she lived and studied law with Belva Lockwood, the first woman admitted to the bar of the Supreme Court of the United States. While working with Lockwood, Gillett looked for a law school that would admit her. Lockwood's alma mater, National University, had closed its doors to women after Lockwood's graduation because of the controversy that her presence had provoked. Howard University, however, admitted students regardless of race or sex, and Gillett enrolled in the law department and received an LL.B. and LL.M. in 1883. While studying law, she was appointed the first woman notary public in the District of Columbia by President James A. Garfield in 1881.

Gillett was admitted to the bar of the District of Columbia in 1883 and joined the law practice of Watson J. Newton, a supporter of women lawyers. She built a successful career in realty and pension law, increased her income well beyond her salary as a teacher, and rose to a position of prominence in the area of real estate. She eventually served as vice president and treasurer of the Realty Appraisal and Title Company from 1908 to 1913.

In her legal practice, Gillett adhered to a philosophy that emphasized strictly professional concerns at the expense of philanthropy. "Charity clients should be shunned unless in extreme cases," she wrote. She advised other women lawyers to do the same, warning them that if they taxed themselves with the legal needs of unpaying clients, they endangered their own health and in doing so threatened the cause of women lawyers. "When one takes charity clients to any extent she lowers her professional tone besides using her capital of time and strength. If she drives herself beyond her strength and fails in her work it concerns us all" (Equity Club letter, 27 Apr. 1889).

In contrast to her strong views regarding women lawyers' professional practices, Gillett willingly volunteered her time and effort on behalf of women's political causes. In 1913 she campaigned with Alice Paul for the passage of the Nineteenth Amendment and served in various capacities for the National Woman Suffrage Association and the Congressional Committee. Following the passage of the suffrage amendment, she served as chair of the legal branch of the National Woman's Party, which worked for equal rights for women.

Gillett's greatest contribution to women linked her professional interests in the law with her political commitment to expanding women's opportunities. In 1896 she and Ellen Spencer Mussey, another Washington, D.C., attorney, started a law class for women. They formalized the program in 1898, when they opened the Washington College of Law. Initially, Mussey held the public role of dean, while Gillett took responsibility for the administrative work. In 1913, after Mussey's failing health forced her to resign and Gillette's law partner died, Gillette became dean. She held that position until her retirement in 1923.

Washington College of Law was a curious blend of racism and feminism. Although it was open to men and women alike, Gillett and Mussey founded the school specifically to provide women with opportunities for legal education. At the same time, Washington College of Law provided white women in the District of Columbia with an alternative to the primarily black Howard University, and Gillett and Mussey advertised their school as the only all-white law school open to women in the District of Columbia. Under their direction, Washington College of Law attracted hundreds of women and helped to create a generation of women lawyers for the twentieth century.

As dean of Washington College of Law, Gillett became a strong advocate of women in the law. She also took advantage of her positions as founder and president of the Women's Bar Association of the District of Columbia and vice president of the Washington, D.C., chapter of the American Bar Association to speak out on behalf of women lawyers' collective struggle in a male-dominated profession. She strongly favored the modeling of women lawyers on their male colleagues. "If we take up work that has been monopolized by men we should study the manner in which they have accomplished the work and how they have spent the hours not occupied by their profession, and follow the general line of their experience," she advised (Equity Club letter, 27 Apr. 1889).

In 1908, having established herself financially and professionally, Gillett invited her sister and niece to live with her in Washington, D.C., where they provided home and family for her until her death. Representatives from nearly every national women's organization attended her memorial service, which was organized by the National Woman's Party.

• Many of Gillett's papers are in the Mary Earhart Dillon Collection, Schlesinger Library, Radcliffe College. Gillett's Equity Club letters as well as a biographical essay are in Virginia G. Drachman, ed., *Women Lawyers and the Origins of Professional Identity* (1993). Her work with Ellen Spencer Mussey is described in Grace Hathaway, *Fate Rides a Tortoise: A Biography of Ellen Spencer Mussey* (1937). Obituaries are in the *New York Times*, 24 Jan. 1927, and *Women Lawyers Journal*, Apr. 1927.

VIRGINIA G. DRACHMAN

GILLETT, Frederick Huntington (16 Oct. 1851–31 July 1935), politician and Speaker of the U.S. House of Representatives, was born in Westfield, Hampden County, Massachusetts, the son of Edward Bates Gillett, a lawyer, and Lucy Douglas Fowler. Gillett studied a year in Dresden, Germany, where he developed an interest in history. Entering Amherst College in 1870, he studied political science and constitutional law with Professor John W. Burgess, won prizes for oratory and writing, and was president of his junior and senior classes. Following graduation in 1874, he completed a three-year course of study in the law department of Harvard University in 1877.

Gillett was admitted to the bar in Springfield, Massachusetts, in 1877. Two years later he was appointed assistant attorney general of Massachusetts. In 1882 he entered private practice in Boston, returning two years later to Springfield, where he maintained a law office

until his retirement from Congress in 1931. He served two years in the state legislature before running for election to the U.S. House of Representatives as a Republican candidate in 1892.

The Massachusetts Second Congressional District, which included Springfield, had been redrawn before the 1892 election and contained parts of districts that had been Democratic in the previous election. Gillett won election to the House of Representatives for the Fifty-third Congress, although Democrats won control of both the House and the Senate for the first time in fourteen years. He was reelected to fifteen succeeding Congresses.

Well known in his home state for his speaking ability, Gillett earned the attention of party leaders for his spirited defense of African-American voting rights in the South. Just three days before the end of the Fifty-third Congress, he made his first speech on the House floor to oppose the Democrat-led repeal of all laws providing federal supervision of elections.

Beginning with the following Congress, Republicans regained control of the House for the next sixteen years (1895–1911). Gillett was appointed to important committees, including Judiciary, Military Affairs, Foreign Affairs, and Appropriations. Speaker David Bremner Henderson named him chairman of the Committee on Reform in the Civil Service, a post he held from 1900 to 1911. Chairman Gillett successfully opposed efforts by Republican opponents of the civil service system to strike out its appropriations.

On the Appropriations Committee from 1902 to 1918, Gillett rose to ranking minority member. He criticized the lack of a centralized federal budget agency and the inefficient and wasteful manner in which appropriations bills were developed by multiple congressional committees. He advocated returning jurisdiction over all spending bills to the committee, an action the House took in 1920. Gillett also championed the establishment within the executive branch of a bureau of the budget that would prepare budget estimates based on previous and current years' revenues and expenditures. Later, as Speaker, Gillett pushed through the Budget and Accounting Act of 1921, which created the Bureau of the Budget to centralize administration of the budget within the executive branch and the General Accounting Office to assist congressional oversight of federal funds.

During World War I, Gillett and the aging Joseph G. Cannon were the two Republicans on the five-member Appropriations subcommittee that considered all war expenditures. Gillett sided with the committee's chairman, John J. Fitzgerald (D.-N.Y.), to oppose a single lump sum appropriation for the War Department. Because of Cannon's age, Gillett bore most of the burden of reviewing the details of military spending bills. When the Republican minority leader, James R. Mann of Illinois, became ill in 1917, Gillett's colleagues chose him to fill the vacancy.

When the Republicans won a fifty-seat majority in the Sixty-sixth Congress (1919), Gillett was elected Speaker of the House over a strong challenge from

Mann in the Republican caucus. Although Mann had been floor leader since 1912, his opponents linked him with the autocratic rule of former Speaker Cannon. A coalition of insurgents and followers of rising Republican leader Nicholas Longworth of Ohio accordingly rallied behind Gillett's candidacy to elect him by a vote of 138 to 69 in the party caucus. Gillett's election to the Speakership reflected the importance of seniority and length of service as well as party loyalty in determining party leadership in Congress. He was an "insider," well steeped in the rules, written and informal, by which Congress operated. By 1919 he had the longest continuous House service (twenty-six years) among Republicans, and he was second in total service only to Cannon.

In the internal maneuvering that followed Gillett's election, however, Mann regained much of his influence. Republican committee assignments had previously been made by the Speaker. The caucus instead chose to create its own Committee on Committees to exercise that function. Mann succeeded in formulating the committee in such a way that, although he did not chair it, he still controlled its decisions through his influence over the larger state delegations. Through this control, Mann, not Gillett, dominated the selection of the Republican floor leader, whip, and Steering Committee.

As a result of Mann's greater influence, Gillett was not able to approximate the strong Speakership of Cannon. According to his own statements, he had no desire to do so: "I pledge you it will be my aim to exercise the powers you have conferred upon me fairly, impartially, judicially and with scrupulous regard for the rights and feelings of every member of the House"—a direct reference to the charges that had brought about the insurgency against Cannon. By all accounts, Gillett presided with fairness, tact, and dignity.

During Gillett's first term as Speaker, the party enacted most of its legislative program under the leadership of Mann, floor leader Frank Mondell, and Gillett. Republicans had an even larger majority in the Sixty-seventh Congress (301–131), and Gillett was easily reelected Speaker. In the Sixty-eighth Congress, however, the Republican majority had fallen to just twenty seats, and the balance of power rested with some twenty Republican progressives, who held up Gillett's election for three days and nine roll call votes until they received concessions on rules revisions.

In 1924 Gillett ran for the Senate. His reasons for doing so remain unclear. The usual explanation given is that he bowed to President Calvin Coolidge's insistence that he was the strongest candidate. In his farewell speech to the House, Gillett professed his own preference, "I would rather be Speaker of the House than hold any other position in the world." In his one term in the Senate, he supported the World Court (even though he opposed the League of Nations) and endorsed Prohibition, the Eighteenth Amendment, and the Volstead Act. He retired in 1931, at the age of

seventy-nine, with the characteristically elegant explanation, "I would not lag superfluous on the stage."

A bachelor until age sixty-four, Gillett married Christine Rice Hoar in 1915; they had no children. During his retirement, Gillett wrote a biography of his wife's first father-in-law, *George Frisbie Hoar*, published in 1934. He began work on his own reminiscences, but the effort was cut short by his death in Springfield.

Gillett was never dominant within his party in Congress, even as Speaker. He was a skillful legislator whose lengthy career and whose attention to detail, specialized committee and subcommittee work, and legislative procedure exemplified the emerging professionalization of Congress in the late nineteenth and early twentieth centuries.

• Gillett destroyed most of his papers. A few letters are in the Massachusetts Historical Society and the Houghton Library at Harvard University, and some forty-five letters are in the Warren G. Harding Papers at the Ohio Historical Society. The most informative biographical treatment of Gillett is Henry B. Russell, "Frederick H. Gillett: American Statesman," *Amherst Graduates' Quarterly* 21 (Nov. 1931): 3–16. Gillett's Speakership is placed in historical perspective in Ronald M. Peters, Jr., *The American Speakership* (1990). Obituaries are in the *New York Times*, 31 July and 1 Aug. 1935, and the *Springfield Union*, 1 Aug. 1935.

DONALD R. KENNON

GILLETTE, King Camp (5 Jan. 1855–9 July 1932), inventor and social theorist, was born in Fond du Lac, Wisconsin, the son of George Wolcott Gillette, a hardware wholesaler, and Fanny Lemira Camp, later the author of the bestselling *White House Cookbook*. Shortly before the Civil War the family moved to Chicago, where he graduated from high school. Gillette clerked in a hardware store and then became a traveling salesman. Like his father and two older brothers, he delighted in inventive tinkering, and in 1879 he was granted his first patent, for a water-faucet component. In 1890 he married Atlanta Ella Gaines; they had one son.

In 1891 Gillette took a sales job with the Baltimore Seal Company. When company president William Painter began reaping a fortune from his invention of the crimped tin bottle cap, he advised Gillette that the road to riches lay in inventing a similarly disposable item. Gillette became almost obsessed with Painter's advice, but at the same time he was obsessed with a grand scheme of social reform. Drawing on his own observations and the utopian and populist literature of the day, he presented his ideas in a book, *The Human Drift* (1894), which blamed all social, economic, and political evils on competition. The solution, Gillette wrote, was a publicly owned worldwide corporation, which would own and manage all means of production. He also proposed that the population of the United States—about 60 million at the time—be concentrated in towering apartment buildings located near Niagara Falls, which would supply the needed electrical power.

The editors and many readers of the radical magazine *Twentieth Century* urged Gillette to lead a grassroots reform movement, but his attention soon turned to other matters. One day in the spring of 1895, shortly after he had moved from New York to Boston, it occurred to him that it might be possible to make thin, disposable razor blades and clamp them in a holder that would keep them rigid. Numerous experts assured him that it would be impossible to sharpen such thin steel blades, but the single-minded Gillette, who knew nothing of metallurgy, pressed on. By 1901 the MIT-trained William Nickerson, who had considerable manufacturing experience, had attacked the problem and devised machinery to hold ribbons of steel rigid enough for sharpening. In 1903 the fledgling Gillette Safety Razor Company sold a mere 51 razors and 168 blades, but aggressive marketing soon made the company dominant in its industry. Made wealthy by his enterprise, Gillette retired from active management in 1913, moved to southern California, and spent much of his time investing in real estate and traveling abroad.

Though the competitive system had been good to Gillette, he continued to campaign against it. He subsidized two books about his economic theories: *Gillette's Social Redemption* (1907) and *Gillette's Industrial Solution* (1908), both by his close friend Melvin L. Severy. In *World Corporation* (1910), which he wrote himself, Gillette announced that he had formed a corporation to achieve his goal of global consolidation, and he offered ex-president Theodore Roosevelt (1858–1919) $1 million to serve a four-year term as its president. Roosevelt declined, but Gillette, undaunted, wrote yet another book, *The People's Corporation* (1924), with editorial assistance from the muckraking novelist Upton Sinclair. Gillette justified his contradictory social theories and business activities by noting that in a capitalist system only a fool would fail to invest his assets to maximum advantage. He also maintained that industrial monopolies were precursors of the socialist world corporation that he envisioned. In the end, though, capitalism proved his undoing. By the time he died at his rambling estate at Calabasas, just north of Los Angeles, Gillette's fortune had been virtually wiped out by the 1929 stock market crash and a collapsing California real estate market.

• The most comprehensive biography is Russell B. Adams, Jr., *King C. Gillette: The Man and His Wonderful Shaving Device* (1978). Useful information is contained in the twenty-fifth anniversary issue of the Gillette Safety Razor Company's house organ, the *Blade* (Sept. 1926). Obituaries appear in the *New York Times*, 11 July 1932, and the *Los Angeles Times*, 11 and 14 July 1932.

RUSSELL B. ADAMS, JR.

GILLETTE, William Hooker (24 July 1853–29 Apr. 1937), actor and playwright, was born in Hartford, Connecticut, the youngest of six children of Francis Gillette, a politician who once filled out an interim term as a U.S. senator, and Elizabeth Daggett Hooker. He early displayed histrionic abilities and was a leading orator in high school. Some uncertainty exists about his subsequent education. He claimed at one time or another to have studied at numerous colleges and universities, including Yale, Harvard, the Massachusetts Institute of Technology, Boston University, and the City College of New York, but records show he was graduated from none of these. In his later years he did receive several honorary degrees, however, including one from Yale.

To avoid embarrassing his conservative family, he sought his earliest theatrical work away from Connecticut. His first professional assignment may have been a part in *Across the Continent* with Ben De Bar's company in New Orleans in the first half of 1875. Some sources claim that his family's neighbor and friend Mark Twain soon obtained a position for him with a Boston theater, but Twain more likely lent a helping hand in securing the young actor a small part (Mr. Duff) in Twain's own dramatization of *The Gilded Age*, referred to more generally as *Colonel Sellers*. A return engagement of this once popular play to the famous Union Square Theatre marked Gillette's New York debut on 16 August 1875. The debut caused no stir, and he was soon back in Boston. Over the next several seasons he also accepted employment in Cincinnati and Louisville.

Fame came to Gillette when he assumed the title role of the unworldly pedant in his own comedy *The Professor* (1881). His skills as a playwright even then were hardly negligible, but what critics and audiences admired most were his appearance and style as an actor. They saw a tall (for the time), slim, aristocratically handsome young man who eschewed the velvety, rolling enunciation and the fist-on-the-forehead-to-show-grief gesticulation still so accepted among players of the day. Instead, his movements were sparing, and he spoke in a clipped, staccato manner with a hint of a drawl. He remains one of several actors of his day credited with advancing the cause of modern underacting. Even in his early years he was an instinctive master of timing.

Because he clearly understood that his talents, however undeniable, were severely limited, throughout the rest of his career of more than sixty years he craftily worked within his own limited range. *Esmeralda* (1881), which he wrote with Frances Hodgson Burnett, was a tremendous success, though he did not act in it. After playing in Bronson Howard's *Young Mrs. Winthrop* (1883), he next starred in another of his own farces, one adapted from Gustav von Moser's *Der Bibliothekar*. Gillette initially called his version *Digby's Secretary* (1884), but after coming to an agreement with the British actor who, unbeknownst to Gillette, had bought the English-speaking rights to the farce, Gillette rechristened it *The Private Secretary*, the name by which it became famous.

Having established himself in farce and, to a lesser extent, in contemporary social drama, Gillette turned to melodrama. His success with this genre was so immediate and so pronounced that to many he is remembered only as a writer and player of grippingly theatrical claptrap. Apart from his farce *Too Much Johnson* (1894), his remaining triumphs as an actor-playwright came in his two Civil War melodramas, *Held by the Enemy* (1886) and *Secret Service* (1896), and in his most celebrated vehicle, his adaptation of Sir Arthur Conan Doyle's stories in *Sherlock Holmes* (1899). To Americans of his generation he personified the legendary sleuth, and he returned to the part regularly for over thirty years. Thereafter his own plays were failures, but he gave notable performances in James Barrie's *The Admirable Crichton* (1903) and *Dear Brutus* (1918) and in a comedy by Clare Kummer, *A Successful Calamity* (1917). His last appearances were in New York in a 1936 revival of *Three Wise Fools*.

His marriage in 1882 to Helen Nickles was cut short by her death in 1888. Subsequently he built a huge castle in Hadlyme, Connecticut, where, despite increasing charges that when away from the theater he was becoming a recluse, he entertained guests on the three-mile-long miniature railway he constructed on the castle's grounds. Further proof that he was not reclusive was his association with The Players, for many years New York's leading theatrical club, of which he was not only a charter member but an active one whenever, in his later years, he was in New York. He died in Hartford, Connecticut.

• The lone biography is Doris E. Cook, *Sherlock Holmes and Much More* (1970). Gillette's papers are widely scattered and can be found at the Library of Congress, the Connecticut Historical Society, the Stowe-Day Library (Hartford), the Van Pelt Library at the University of Pennsylvania (Philadelphia), and The Players (New York), among other locations. An obituary is in the *New York Times*, 30 Apr. 1937.

GERALD BORDMAN

GILLIS, James Martin (12 Nov. 1876–14 Mar. 1957), evangelist and editor, was born in Boston, Massachusetts, the son of James Gillis, a machinist, and Catherine Roche. Raised in a working-class Irish-American family, Gillis attended St. John's Seminary at Brighton for the archdiocese of Boston from 1896 to 1898 and achieved a baccalaureate. He later joined the Paulist Fathers at St. Thomas College in Washington, D.C., and was ordained in New York City on 21 December 1901. He immediately matriculated to the Catholic University of America, where he earned an S.T.L. in historical theology in 1903.

Gillis entered active ministry in 1904 as a member of the Paulists' Chicago mission band. For three years he traveled throughout Illinois, Indiana, and Missouri, preaching sermons that emphasized the dutiful life of Christians. He proclaimed that the interior human struggle to avoid sin and live Godlike lives could be described as "the Jekyll and Hyde, the angel and the animal, the man and the brute-beast," which exists in every person. Gillis's preaching, his interaction with the marginalized of society, and his constant encounters with human depravity corroborated this dualistic worldview, which he had developed in his youth.

Between 1907 and 1910 Gillis served at St. Thomas College as director of novices and superior of the local religious community. In 1910 he returned to the mission band, operating from the Paulist mother Church of St. Paul the Apostle in New York City. He crisscrossed the nation several times preaching missions and giving retreats and lectures. His pace of work bordered on obsession, a pattern that repeated itself throughout his career. During his years in New York, a time when he developed a strong antiwar ethic as a consequence of World War I, Gillis solidified the belief that his vocation was to preach to America a message of individual freedom, personal conversion, and a return to moral rigorism.

In October 1922 Gillis was appointed as editor of the Paulist monthly the *Catholic World*. He used the magazine to continue his mission to preach to America; the editorial page became a new "pulpit." During the 1920s, in his books *False Prophets* (originally a series of sermons preached in 1925) and *The Catholic Church and the Home* (1928), Gillis called for a return to an earlier (although never specified) time when the concepts of moral righteousness, smaller government, and personal accountability were respected. America in the 1920s was, in Gillis's mind, living a "false prosperity" where moral degradation, as seen in the rise of divorce and easy-access birth control, was destroying the family. Gillis also criticized the pessimism he perceived in the writings of such literary giants as Sinclair Lewis, Eugene O'Neill, and H. G. Wells. In 1928 Gillis increased the audience of his message when he began to write a weekly syndicated column, *Sursum Corda* (Lift Up Your Hearts).

The darkness of society in the 1930s was manifest for Gillis in the development of what he perceived to be the leviathan state and the destruction of individual liberty. The principal object of Gillis's critique and the one who personified for him the world's evils was Franklin Delano Roosevelt. Like his fellow priest Charles Coughlin and Catholics in general, Gillis enjoyed a honeymoon with Roosevelt and his New Deal. By 1936, however, Gillis had rejected the president and his program of recovery and reform, which he believed jeopardized individual rights. He argued that the state, which existed solely to safeguard the basic liberties of the individual citizen, was subservient to humanity, who drew its rights directly from God.

Gillis's editorials during the period between the wars touched on nearly every major issue. He criticized Roosevelt's refusal to act against Mexico's persecution of Catholics in 1934; was neutral in the Spanish civil war, perceiving error on both sides; and, as a vocal member of the America First Committee, was a strong advocate of nonintervention. When Roosevelt ran for a third term in 1940, Gillis's hostility and emotions overflowed when he wrote,

I confess I don't understand the man. But I do think him inconsistent and unpredictable. A 'dangerous,' 'reckless,' 'audacious,' inconsistent, unpredictable man is no man to be three times President of the United States. . . . To perpetuate in office a man with a mania for power who asks, obtains and holds all that he gets, and demands ever more and more would be as great a political blunder as that of Hindenburg and the Reichstag that handed over all liberties of the people to Hitler. (*Catholic World*, Nov. 1940)

In the postwar period Gillis turned his pen against communism, deceptive government, and his perception of America's imperialist intentions. He rejected the Truman Doctrine and the Marshall Plan as wrongful U.S. intervention. As with the League of Nations a generation earlier, Gillis could not support the United Nations since its incorporation was devoid of God. After his retirement from the *Catholic World* in 1948, Gillis continued his commentary rejecting communism in general and supporting Joseph McCarthy in particular. Gillis, however, opposed U.S. involvement in Korea by saying the nation had no reason to fight the battles of other countries.

Gillis must be seen as a Catholic figure who promoted a legitimate conservative, yet often minority, viewpoint. He was recognized in his day as a commentator, but his historical significance lies in his uncompromising method, which demonstrated that his ideas and opinions were held as convictions of faith. Gillis's message was well received in his day, but his hope to safeguard America from its destiny as a defender of world freedom was not fulfilled. One fellow Paulist described Gillis as "a hero of the first magnitude, a champion of the Church in the first lines of battle, in the pulpit, in the lecture hall, the market place, in the press and on the radio." Gillis did not use spiritual grounds for his political critique of America, as he perceived no problem in the Church. Nevertheless, he was criticized for his staunch conservatism by Catholic social progressives such as Monsignors John Ryan and George Higgins. "Using to the best possible advantage the extraordinary talents God had given him, a brilliant mind, a rich and powerful voice, a superb literary ability, he worked tirelessly for the Church and the salvation of the country he loved." Gillis died in New York City.

• Gillis's papers, including sermons, personal diaries, retreat notes, correspondence, essays, radio talks, and editorials are held in the Paulist Fathers' archives at St. Paul's College, Washington, D.C. Important books by Gillis include *Christianity and Civilization* (1932), *The Paulists* (1932), *So Near Is God* (1953), and *This Mysterious Human Nature* (1956). A popular biography of Gillis is James Finley, *James Gillis—Paulist* (1958). For a more critical and detailed look at Gillis's life and career, see Richard Gribble, "The Life and Thought of James Martin Gillis, C.S.P." (Ph.D. diss., Catholic Univ., 1995). Several books and monographs describe Gillis's views on events, peoples, and ideas. Donald F. Crosby, *God, Church and Flag—Senator Joseph R. McCarthy and the Catholic Church 1950–1957* (1978), describes Gillis's support for McCarthy. George Q. Flynn, *American Catholics and the Roosevelt Presidency 1932–1936* (1968) and *Roosevelt and Romanism: Catholic and American Diplomacy, 1937–1945* (1976), outline Gillis's views on Roosevelt. Teresa Hruzd, "The Northeast Clergy Conference for Negro Welfare" (M.A. thesis, Univ. of Maryland, College Park, 1990), tells of Gillis's support for black Catholics. Donna Merwick, *Boston Priests, 1848–1910* (1973), describes some of the early influences on

Gillis. David O'Brien, *American Catholics and Social Reform—The New Deal Years* (1968), describes Gillis's attitude toward the New Deal and Roosevelt.

RICHARD GRIBBLE

GILLISS, James Melville (6 Sept. 1811–9 Feb. 1865), naval astronomer, was born in Georgetown, District of Columbia, the eldest son of George Gilliss, a federal government employee, and Mary Melville. A midshipman from the age of fifteen, James Gilliss performed the usual sea duty, first on the *Delaware*, then on the *Concord* and *Java*, before receiving the grade of passed midshipman in 1831. By Gilliss's own account, a seminal experience in his life took place shortly thereafter, when members of Congress were told in his presence that naval officers were incapable of performing scientific duties. Determined to disprove this statement, Gilliss spent a year at the University of Virginia beginning in 1833 but left because of ill health that included severe eye inflammation from excessive study. Following a cruise ending in October 1835, Gilliss once again resumed studies in Paris, where he remained for six months.

In November 1836 Gilliss was ordered from the U.S. Navy Yard in Philadelphia to the Depot of Charts and Instruments in Washington, D.C., a fledgling institution then entering its sixth year and headed by Charles Wilkes. Located about 1,200 feet north of the Capitol Building, the depot was responsible for the navy's chronometers, charts, and other navigational instruments and gave ample opportunity for Gilliss to display his scientific talents. Astronomical observations were necessary to "rate" the chronometers (determine how fast or slow they ran), and Gilliss proved himself to be an excellent astronomical observer. In June 1837 he was named officer-in-charge of the depot, and the following winter he began an extensive series of observations of the moon and reference stars for the purpose of longitude determination. In late 1837 he married Rebecca Roberts of Alexandria, D.C. (now Va.). They had six children. Gilliss was made lieutenant in February 1838.

When Wilkes departed for the U.S. Exploring Expedition in 1838, Gilliss succeeded him as head of the depot, and the secretary of the navy ordered Gilliss to make certain observations that would enable Wilkes to determine the longitudes of locations visited on the expedition. Giving a liberal interpretation to these instructions, Gilliss began a series of celestial observations that resulted in a volume entitled *Astronomical Observations made at the Naval Observatory, Washington, under orders of the Honorable Secretary of the Navy, dated August 13, 1838* (1846). This volume, containing the positions of 1,248 stars, was the first star catalog published in the United States. Gilliss also made regular magnetic and meteorological observations, which resulted in a companion volume of data on those subjects in 1845.

Gilliss's most lasting achievement, however, was in almost single-handedly building the institution that became the U.S. Naval Observatory, the first national observatory in the United States. Beginning in 1841 he proposed a new depot and by August 1842 had pushed a bill through Congress appropriating $25,000 for the depot and "a small observatory" to be attached. But with the approval of the secretary of the navy, Gilliss used the funds to equip the new building with astronomical instruments far beyond the needs of the navy. These instruments included a 9.6-inch achromatic refractor telescope, a 5.5-inch transit instrument, a 4-inch mural circle, and a 5-inch prime vertical telescope. He personally went to Europe to purchase the instruments and books for the observatory, mostly from German instrument makers, and by October 1844 the new observatory was ready. In part because of internal navy politics, however, Lt. Matthew Fontaine Maury was named the superintendent rather than Gilliss (the secretary of the navy was from Maury's native Virginia).

Following this action Gilliss was assigned to the U.S. Coast Survey, where he analyzed longitude observations. In August 1848 he succeeded in obtaining $5,000 from Congress for a naval astronomical expedition to Chile. The chief purpose was to determine the solar parallax—and thus the scale of the solar system—by observations of Mars and Venus. From August 1849 until its return in November 1852, Gilliss headed this expedition, again making observations far beyond the original purposes of the expedition and leaving behind the foundation for the Chilean National Observatory. Although the success of the solar parallax work was limited because Maury made an insufficient number of complementary observations at the Naval Observatory, Gilliss spent much of the 1850s preparing the elaborate multivolume set of results of this expedition. The six published volumes of *The U.S. Astronomical Expedition to the Southern Hemisphere* are remarkable for including not only astronomical observations, but also studies of broader interest to science, geography, and politics. The first volume, for example, described Chile as a nation and included a detailed narrative of the voyage. In volume 2 eminent scientists described the animal, mineral, and fossil collections returned by the expedition. And volume 6 was devoted entirely to magnetic and meteorological observations. Gilliss subsequently led parties to observe the solar eclipses in Peru in 1858 and in Washington Territory in 1860.

At the outset of the Civil War Matthew Maury joined the southern cause, and in April 1861 Gilliss was appointed the new superintendent of the Naval Observatory. At about the same time he became a founding member of the National Academy of Sciences and was raised to the rank of captain in July 1862. During the Civil War years Gilliss devoted himself not only to providing a vastly increased number of charts and instruments to the U.S. Navy, but also to restoring astronomy to a preeminent place in the Naval Observatory and publishing a large backlog of observations.

The morning after his son James returned from a Confederate prison, Gilliss collapsed and died from a stroke. His contemporary, the American astronomer Benjamin A. Gould (1824–1896) called him "the first representative of practical astronomy in America." His astronomical observations have proved remarkably accurate for the technology of his time, and his work lives on both in his scientific achievements and in the institution that he founded.

• The best source for Gilliss's life is Benjamin A. Gould, *Biographical Notice of James Melville Gilliss* (1867), which is reprinted in *Biographical Memoirs, National Academy of Sciences* 1 (1877): 135–79. His professional life is documented in the Naval Observatory records of the National Archives, Record Group 78, and is also apparent in his *Report of the Secretary of the Navy, Communicating a Report of the Plan and Construction of the Depot of Charts and Instruments, with a Description of the Instruments*, 28th Cong., 2d sess., S. Doc. 114 (1845), which is reprinted in *Aspects of Astronomy in the Nineteenth Century*, ed. I. Bernard Cohen (1980). His personal life is illuminated in his correspondence (1849–1864) with congressman, diplomat, and philologist George Perkins Marsh, preserved at the University of Vermont.

STEVEN J. DICK

GILLMORE, Quincy Adams (28 Feb. 1825–7 Apr. 1888), soldier and engineer, was born in Black River, Lorain County, Ohio, the son of Quartus Gillmore and Elizabeth Reid, farmers. Gillmore attended a local high school, then taught for three years before his twentieth birthday. His scholarship, especially in mathematics, won him an appointment to the U.S. Military Academy in July 1845. Gillmore graduated first of forty-three cadets in the class of 1849. At this time he married Mary Isabella O'Maher. The couple would raise four sons.

As was typical of the graduates of high merit, Gillmore received his commission in the Corps of Engineers, with the rank of brevet second lieutenant. His prewar service was varied: assistant engineer in the construction of Fortress Monroe, Virginia, 1849–1852 and 1856; assistant instructor of practical military engineering at the Military Academy, 1852–1856, with concurrent duties as treasurer and quartermaster of the academy; and officer in charge of the supply and shipping of fortification materials at the New York engineering depot, 1856–1861. Regular promotions elevated Gillmore to the rank of captain by 6 August 1861.

Gillmore's Civil War experience began with the Port Royal expedition, which he accompanied as chief engineer. He constructed fortifications on Hilton Head Island, South Carolina, until January 1862. His first major accomplishment of the war came during the siege of Fort Pulaski, Georgia, February to April 1862. Gillmore proposed the use of rifled cannon to breach the walls of the fort despite the widely held opinion that the structure was impervious to artillery barrage. After two months of exhaustive work on nearby Tybee Island, much of it done under concealment of darkness, Gillmore had established eleven batteries, consisting of thirty-two heavy cannon and siege mortars. The bombardment, which Gillmore closely directed, began on 10 April and lasted some thirty hours. The fort surrendered after the facing wall had been shattered and the magazine exposed to direct fire. Gillmore was brevetted to lieutenant colonel in the regular army on 11 April and appointed brigadier general of volunteers on 28 April.

Because of an illness, the nature of which is not recorded, Gillmore withdrew from field service until September, when he was then assigned to division command in Kentucky. He fought an action at Somerset, Kentucky, on 30 March 1863, for which he was promoted to brevet colonel in the regular army. From June 1863 to April 1864 he commanded the Department of the South, which comprised the southeastern coastal areas, and concurrently commanded the Tenth Army Corps.

During this time Gillmore was called on to take part in operations against Charleston, South Carolina. After first landing troops on Morris Island on 10 July, Gillmore faced the formidable task of capturing Battery Wagner near the north end of the island. Two unsuccessful and costly attacks over narrow tidal flats that led to the fort proved the folly of direct assault. Gillmore then reverted to a slow and tedious approach by means of trenching. Together with these exertions, he directed the placement of heavy artillery on the island, including the infamous "swamp angel," which was used to shell Charleston. Seven weeks of trench digging brought Union lines to the outer ditches of Battery Wagner and thus forced the Confederates to abandon the redoubt on 6 September. Artillery barrages against Fort Sumter led to its virtual demolition, but Gillmore's efforts could not dislodge the Confederates garrisoned there.

Gillmore himself was proud of his accomplishments and those of his command, but the campaign on Morris Island had disappointed many northerners, for it had cost the Union over 2,300 casualties but had produced little in the way of strategic value; Charleston remained firmly in Confederate hands. Rear Admiral John A. B. Dahlgren, whose squadron had cooperated with Gillmore, privately commented that the engineer lacked the administrative and organizational qualities required of a successful general. Nevertheless, Gillmore had 400 bronze medals struck to reward enlisted personnel who had distinguished themselves in the operations, requesting regimental commanders to submit names of soldiers deserving of these medals, which unofficially were called "medals of honor." And the operation brought Gillmore promotion to major general of volunteers, effective 10 July, as well as a brevet promotion to the same rank in the regular army one year later.

With his Tenth Corps, Gillmore next saw action in Virginia. He was assigned to the Army of the James, commanded by Major General Benjamin F. Butler (1818–1893), and took part in the Bermuda Hundred campaign and the ensuing battle of Drewry's Bluff, 16 May 1864. Although the Tenth Corps halted the enemy advance during the battle, Gillmore's reputation suffered because of association with Butler's inept handling of the campaign.

Gillmore commanded two divisions of the Nineteenth Army Corps during Confederate Major General Jubal A. Early's raid on Washington, D.C., June–July 1864. In pursuit of Early on 14 July, Gillmore was severely injured in a fall of his horse. He served the rest of the war in administrative positions.

Gillmore's postwar career was long and productive. He was conferred a Ph.D. in mathematics by Rutgers College in 1878. Various appointments as superintending engineer of fortifications and of river and harbor improvements along the Atlantic Coast occupied him until ill health forced his semiretirement in 1885. Among his many important offices, Gillmore served from 1879 until 1888 as president of the Mississippi River Commission. At the time of his death in Brooklyn, New York, he was married to a widow, the former Mrs. Bragg.

Gillmore was regarded as the preeminent military engineer of his day. He had been the first to demonstrate the power of rifled cannon against masonry works. Having proven the vulnerability of masonry works, he wrote extensively on the subject, with special emphasis on the compressive resistance of building and bonding materials. He was variously described as a brilliant and profound thinker—scholarly, persistent, and courteous.

• The official papers of General Gillmore are found in the Records of the Adjutant General's Office, Record Group 94, in the National Archives. Much of this has been published in *The War of the Rebellion: A Compilation of the Official Records of the Union and Confederate Armies* (128 vols., 1881–1901). Individual letters from Gillmore are widely scattered in several archival collections listed in the *National Union Catalog of Manuscript Collections* (1959). Of his two greatest wartime feats, Gillmore wrote, "The Siege and Capture of Fort Pulaski" and "The Army before Charleston in 1863," both in *Battles and Leaders of the Civil War*, ed. Robert U. Johnson and Clarence C. Buel (1884–1887). Confederate General P. G. T. Beauregard takes issue with some of Gillmore's statements in an accompanying piece to the Charleston article. Detailed biographical and obituary materials are found in the *Nineteenth Annual Reunion of the Association of the Graduates of the United States Military Academy* (1888) and George W. Cullum, ed., *Biographical Register of the Officers and Graduates of the Military Academy*, vol. 2 (1891).

Herman Hattaway
Eric B. Fair

GILLON, Alexander (13 Aug. 1741–6 Oct. 1794), merchant and politician, was born in Rotterdam, Holland, the son of the wealthy, middle-class Alexander Gillon and Mary Harris. Gillon, who was fluent in several languages, received an initial taste for the shipping business as an apprentice to British and Dutch firms courtesy of his family connections. Besides his lineage, Gillon's other major trading commodity was his handsome appearance and the veneer of social graces, which he used as collateral for the next thirty years.

Gillon's first direct contact with the American colonies came in December 1764, when, as master, he docked the Philadelphia-owned brigantine, *Surprize*, in its home port. The ambitious Gillon established a base in Charleston and during the next two years moved into foreign trade and dealt in real estate. He soon adapted to local customs and imported five cargoes of slaves between 1765 and 1774.

Gillon happily surrendered command of the brigantine *Free Mason* in 1766 when he married the wealthy relict of William Cripps, Mary Splatt Cripps, and disembarked for the life of a Charleston merchant. The marriage not only brought Gillon a new source of funds but two stepsons, William and John Splatt Cripps, with whom he went into business in 1773 when they formed Alexander Gillon and Company. Despite the success of the business, which sold various goods, including food and wine, Gillon sold his share to his stepson, John, and to Florian Charles Mey, and retired in 1777 with a personal wealth that he estimated at £30,000. Gillon intended to enjoy his considerable interests in real estate, including fifteen lots in Charleston and 5,500 acres on the Congaree River, but he soon turned to a full-time career in state politics.

Gillon's political views and open declaration of revolutionary principles were tainted by a strong resentment, which had crystallized in 1770, when he was accused of violating the Non-Importation Association and was brought before the Liberty Tree Committee. Reluctantly, Gillon pledged to stockpile his goods until full importation was legal, but his outrage simmered for decades as Gillon waited to recover the money from the state. Gillon put on his revolutionary makeup with the practiced hand of any actor preparing for a long running performance, Meanwhile, he began his official political career as Charleston's delegate to the Committee of Ninety-nine in 1774. He demonstrated an eye for the main chance when serving in South Carolina's Second Provincial Congress from 1775 to 1776 by securing a munitions supply contract (1775–1776) with the Continental Congress. He also helped to muster the German Fusiliers and served as a captain throughout 1777, amid claims that men of learning were rejected and only the unprincipled and ill bred of the colonists commanded the militia and volunteers.

Gillon's personality and perceived commercial skills were well enough regarded to win another lucrative contract from the Continental Congress to oversee the provision of European goods for the war effort. However, Gillon was soon captivated by Rawlins Lowndes's dream of an independent state navy and rejected Congress's venture in favor of Lowndes's offer of a commission in February 1778 as the sole commodore and commander of the shorebound South Carolina navy. Before he sailed to Europe in November 1778 to borrow money from European sympathizers and exchange South Carolina goods for three frigates, Gillon served as a volunteer on the *Defense* and the *Volant* out of Connecticut and participated in the capture of two English privateers.

The venture to Europe that had seemed so promising proved a financial disaster for South Carolina. Gillon arrived in Brest on 19 January 1779 but soon moved to Amsterdam to make use of his Dutch connections. Armed with fine references from Benjamin Franklin, even though Franklin regarded Gillon as a parvenu diverting valuable funds, he approached Minister Sartine to acquire South Carolina's frigates on credit from the French government. In support of his cause, Gillon revisited a proposal rejected by the Continental Congress in 1776 to use naval forces to defend the southern states. Gillon proposed that either the three new frigates or a combined French and American force attack the British in Georgia. The proposal was supported by John Adams, then a close acquaintance of Gillon. Gillon's momentum faltered when he fell out with Franklin and earned the personal animosity of John Paul Jones, who was furious when Gillon commandeered the new ship promised to him. Gillon had struggled for over a year to lease this one ship, the Dutch-built forty-gun frigate, *L'Indien*, one of the finest ships of its class, from Ann Paul Emanuel Sigismund de Montmorency, Duke of Luxembourg. The price for South Carolina was high: Gillon was forced to agree to a three-year contract and surrender one-third of his prizes to the duke. Gillon renamed his ship the *South Carolina* in a calculated display of patriotism. Then began a series of events known variously as the Luxembourg settlement or claims.

The affair began when Gillon was prevented from sailing by bad weather and ficunary predicaments. Unable to control the climate, he sought to resolve his financial difficulties by pledging his personal wealth and that of South Carolina to pay for his private debts and to outfit the ship. Only through the personal intervention of a fellow South Carolinian, the equally brash Colonel John Laurens, who was then a Continental Congress agent, was a suspicious Franklin persuaded to advance £10,000 to Gillon. On the understanding that the money would buy naval stores destined for South Carolina, Gillon was able to sail in August 1781, but he abandoned the stores, and an embarrassed Adams and Franklin were forced to find other means of transporting them to America. Adams's low opinion of Gillon plummeted further when the young Charles Adams and others, appalled by Gillon's unprofessional conduct, abandoned ship in Spain. Henry Laurens, foreshadowing the immense financial loss to South Carolina, blamed Gillon's failure on his overweening self-confidence and his unjustified belief in his own ability to achieve anything by the force of his own powers.

Gillon arrived in Philadelphia in May 1782, after a journey that took him to the United Kingdom, Spain, Cuba, and the Bahamas, where the *South Carolina* aided a Spanish expedition to capture the islands from the English. Gillon attracted significant self-promoting publicity by capturing the five prizes, but in November 1782 he rejected the Duke of Luxembourg's offer, which would have rid Gillon and South Carolina of their respective debts and returned the *South Carolina* to the Chevalier. Although in May 1783 a joint legislative committee absolved Gillon of any wrongdoing, the matter was not settled to the satisfaction of the French until 1855.

Undismayed by the accusations and convinced of his place in South Carolina affairs, Gillon reentered local politics. Throughout his foreign adventures he had relied on his reputation in state affairs. He represented the parishes of St. Philip and St. Michael in the Second Provincial Congress (1775–1776) and served in the First General Assembly (1776). His return marked the beginning of continual service in the state legislature until 1793. He represented his former parishes in the Fifth General Assembly (1783–1784) and was elected to the Privy Council (1783–1785). Gillon served in each of the general assemblies until 1792. He was elected lieutenant governor twice (1783 and 1789) but refused to serve on both occasions, citing ill health on the second. Two years after Mary's death in 1787, Gillon married Ann Purcell, who bone him three children. Instead of accepting public offices that only carried nominal power, Gillon turned on his mentor, Lowndes, and opted for real power. Gillon built his later political career on an intense anti-British stance, which fitted the backcountry planters' opposition to the resident British merchants, who were seen as the cause of a disastrous postrevolutionary debtor crisis. Gillon's animosity was also personal. The British had expelled his wife and confiscated his property during their occupation of Charleston. Although Gillon represented the middle-country interests of Saxe Gotha during the majority of his tenure in the general assemblies, he won the allegiance of the backcountry interests against the Anglophile Charleston planters with his role in founding the Marine Anti-Britannie Society, dedicated to expelling foreigners. He opposed trade with Britain and supported confiscating loyalists' property. He also supported the currency controls in the Constitution proposed by the Federalists, which prevented debtors from delaying their obligations.

Gillon, who understood the machinery of state affairs, held the important financial post of commissioner for the speedy settlement of public accounts and returned the state to solvency. However, he also used the opportunity to increase his own wealth. His management style revealed a pathological inability to manage state money, believing that he deserved to be compensated for the property he lost under the Confiscation Act.

On his second attempt, in 1793, Gillon was elected to the United States House of Representatives and served until his death at Gillon's Retreat on his beloved Congaree River, where he had proposed building a new state capital.

• Gillon's life is a sub-plot to the tales of other, more famous men, beginning with "Letters from Commodore Alexander Gillon in 1778 and 1779," *South Carolina Historical and Genealogical Magazine* 10 (1909): 131–35, which describes Gillon's attempts to secure a loan from the French and his plans to attack the British in Georgia; Gillon's progress in France and his relations with Adams, Franklin, Jones, and the Adams family are described by Franklin in *The Papers of Benjamin Franklin*, vols. 26–30, ed. Barbara B. Oberg (1992–):

Charles Francis Adams, *The Works of John Adams*, vols. 7 and 9 (1852); *The Adams Papers*, ser. 1, *Diaries; The Diary and Autobiography of John Adams*, vol. 2, ed. L. H. Butterfield (1961); *The Adams Papers*, ser. 3, *General Correspondence and Other Papers of the Adams Statesmen*, ed. Robert J. Taylor (1985); and *Diary of John Quincy Adams*, vol. 1, ed. Taylor et al. (1981). Differing views on the *South Carolina* saga include the established authority of D. E. Huger Smith, "Commodore Alexander Gillon and the Frigate South Carolina," *South Carolina Historical and Genealogical Magazine*, 9 (1908): 189–219; Phillips Russell, *John Paul Jones: Man of Action* (1927); Louis F. Middlebrook, *The Frigate South Carolina* (1929); and the partisan Samuel Eliot Morison, *John Paul Jones: A Sailor's Biography* (1959), which derides Gillon as a poseur. Gillon's later political adventures are described in Jan Willem Schulte Nordholdt (trans. Herbert H. Rowen), *The Dutch Republic and American Independence* (1982); Rachel N. Klein, *Unification of a Slave State: The Rise of the Planter Class in the South Carolina Backcountry, 1760–1808* (1990); John Hammond Moore, *Columbia and Richland County: A South Carolina Community, 1740–1990* (1993); Carl J. Vipperman, *The Rise of Rawlins Lowndes, 1721–1800* (1978); and Michael E. Stevens, "Legislative Privilege in Post-Revolutionary South Carolina," *William and Mary Quarterly* 46 (Jan. 1989): 71–92.

RICHARD GROVES

GILLULY, James (24 June 1896–29 Dec. 1980), geologist, was born in Seattle, Washington, the son of Charles Elijah Gilluly and Louisa Elizabeth Briegel. The boy was raised mostly in Seattle and also spent time on the ranch of his mother's relatives in eastern Washington.

Gilluly attended the University of Washington from 1915 to 1920, with interruptions to earn money to continue his education. He enlisted in the U.S. Navy during World War I and was commissioned ensign at the end of the war. In college he shifted his major from civil and mechanical engineering to business economics before settling on geology. His first interest in that subject had come in high school, but he had then assumed that there was no future in that field. A college friend convinced him to make geology his major in his senior year, and Gilluly then studied intensively under George E. Goodspeed, Jr.

Before graduation Gilluly took the civil service examination for junior geologist, and in 1921 he accepted a temporary position with the U.S. Geological Survey. His first field work for the USGS was in eastern Montana in the summer of 1921, and he spent the next winter at the USGS offices in Washington, D.C. There he wrote his first technical paper, with Kenneth C. Heald, describing a new technique for determining geologic sequence in an oil field from cuttings taken by rotary drilling.

Gilluly began part-time graduate studies at Johns Hopkins University in 1922, then went to Yale University from 1922 to 1924. He later identified Adolph Knopf and Herbert Ernest Gregory as his most influential teachers at Yale. His summers were devoted to field work for the USGS in northeastern Colorado and eastern Utah. The geological work in Utah became the subject of his doctoral dissertation at Yale (Ph.D.,

1926). In 1925 he married Enid Adelaide Frazier, who joined him promptly in his Utah field studies of that year and accompanied him on almost all his trips over many years. The couple had two daughters.

For the USGS Gilluly carried out geologic studies in Alaska, Colorado, Utah, New York, the Panama Canal Zone, Oregon, and Arizona. In 1931 he spent a month at the laboratory of Austrian geologist Bruno Sander at the University of Innsbruck, learning about the structural arrangement of the components of rocks, and he followed that with a tour of Eastern Europe.

While Gilluly's early publications were primarily on the geology of the specific areas in which he did field work, they were also recognized as thoroughly detailed and broad in coverage. The work in Utah, eastern Oregon, and Arizona included significant information on ore deposits.

In 1938 Gilluly accepted a position as professor of geology at the University of California at Los Angeles; this work was interrupted by the advent of World War II. During the war he devoted his time to USGS projects concerning strategic minerals, and from 1944 to 1945, in the Military Geology Unit, he assisted the U.S. Army Corps of Engineers with preparations for the campaign in the Pacific. He advised on water supplies, airstrip locations, and suitable beaches for troop landings. As part of this effort, Gilluly landed with U.S. troops at Leyte in the Philippines.

At the end of the war in 1945 Gilluly resumed his professorship at UCLA. When the university during the McCarthy era imposed a loyalty oath, Gilluly considered it a personal and professional insult, so he resigned from UCLA in 1950 and returned to full-time service with the USGS until retiring in 1966.

With A. O. Woodford and Aaron C. Waters he completed the textbook *Principles of Geology* (1951). Its intent was to "concentrate on the analysis of processes that are at work upon and within the earth." It became widely used; the fourth edition (1975) was revised by Gilluly alone.

In the 1950s Gilluly did field studies in what he called the "fascinating geology of north central Nevada," where, said a colleague, he "set a pace in the field that was difficult for many to match." He held various administrative positions for the USGS and was also an active member of a committee to set standards for geologic mapping. From 1952 to 1956 he was the USGS representative on the American Commission of Stratigraphic Nomenclature.

In the publications of his later years Gilluly went beyond single-area papers into fundamental aspects of structural geology. He presented ideas on the origin of granite, on the nature of volcanic rocks and their water content, and on geologic structure and crustal deformation in the western United States. At the end of his term as president of the Geological Society of America in 1948 he presented a significant address titled "Distribution of Mountain Building in Geologic Time" (*Bulletin of the Geological Society of America* 60 [1949]: 561–90). In it he questioned the idea that mountain building occurs in short periods separated by long quiet times. In various papers he proposed that currents in the earth's mantle must have been involved in dramatic movement such as the uplift of the Colorado Plateau. By measurement of geologic maps of North and South America he demonstrated that the geologic record becomes more incomplete with time, so that theories of mountain building and erosion having increased in more recent periods are not valid. Unlike some of his contemporaries in the field of geology, Gilluly accepted the concept of sea-floor spreading and continental drift as it was developing during the 1960s. On one point of geology he did an about-face. When J Harlan Bretz proposed in the 1920s that the scablands and environs of Washington state had been carved by an enormous discharge of water when an ice blockage broke in a glacial period, Gilluly was a major opponent of the idea. Through the years, various other geologists came to accept Bretz's theory, and Gilluly finally visited the region. He immediately acknowledged the accuracy of Bretz's observations.

Gilluly was elected to the National Academy of Sciences, and he received several significant scientific awards. He died in Denver, Colorado.

• In addition to his textbook and his address to the Geological Society of America, Gilluly published more than fifty papers. He was chair of the group of authors who compiled *Origin of Granite* (1948), published as Geological Society of America Memoir 28, and was also a major contributor to it. One of his summary papers was "The Tectonic Evolution of the Western United States," presented as a lecture and published in *Quarterly Journal of the Geological Society of London* 119 (1963): 133–74. Gilluly wrote a somewhat autobiographical account and analysis of geology, "American Geology since 1910: A Personal Appraisal," *Annual Reviews of Earth and Planetary Sciences* 5 (1977): 1–12. Biographical accounts are A. C. Waters, "Portrait of a Scientist: James Gilluly: Pioneer of Modern Geological Ideas," *Earth Science Reviews/Atlas* 5 (1969): A19–A27; J. Fred Smith, Jr., "Memorial to James Gilluly," *Geological Society of America Memorials* 12 (1982); and Thomas B. Nolan, "James Gilluly," National Academy of Sciences, *Biographical Memoirs* 56 (1987): 119–32, with bibliography.

ELIZABETH NOBLE SHOR

GILMAN, Arthur (22 June 1837–28 Dec. 1909), educator and author, was born in Alton, Illinois, the son of Winthrop Sargent Gilman, a banker, and Abia Swift Lippincott. At the time of Gilman's birth, his father had already accumulated a substantial fortune in the wholesale grocery business. His father's wealth allowed Gilman to receive his early education in private schools in St. Louis, Missouri, and Lee, Massachusetts. When his family moved to New York in 1849, Gilman was sent to the Chrestomathic Institute in Rye, New York, a nontraditional institution that supported the equal education of boys and girls. From 1851 to 1853 Gilman attended Mr. Leggett's school in New York City. In 1857 Gilman went to work for his father's banking firm, Halsted and Gilman, in New York City. The firm was later renamed Gilman, Son, and Company.

Gilman married Amy Cooke Ball, of Lee, Massachusetts, in 1860; the couple had four children. In 1862, because of bad health, Gilman was forced to leave New York and the banking firm and moved to Lenox, Massachusetts. There he became interested in public education and was a member of the local school committee, visiting and evaluating schools in the area. During this time Gilman also began writing. In 1869 he published *The Gilman Family Traced in the Line of Honorable John Gilman, of Exeter, N.H.*, and in 1870 he published *First Steps in English Literature*, a textbook. In addition to writing, Gilman became editor for the American Tract Society in Boston in 1871, and when he moved to Cambridge, Massachusetts, in 1872, he was enlisted as a literary adviser for the Riverside Press.

In 1876 Gilman was married a second time, to Stella Houghton Scott, of Tuscaloosa, Alabama, with whom he had three children. (It is not known how his first marriage ended.) Before her marriage, Stella Scott had received her education at Ingham University in Leroy, New York, and was head of the English literature department at Bradford Academy in New York. Some months prior to the summer of 1878, Gilman and his wife became interested in the possibility of the education of women at Harvard University. In *Cambridge Sketches by Cambridge Authors*, Gilman states that the idea "became a personal matter with [him] on account of the interest that [his] wife and [he] took in a certain young lady at the moment attending one of the schools for girls in Cambridge, who seemed to have reached the limit of the advantages that it offered." Gilman "conceived a plan" whereby women would receive instruction from the professors at Harvard, "but outside of the college and without responsibility to it." In November 1878 Gilman presented the idea to one of the professors at Harvard, who also supported the plan. Having received this endorsement, Gilman wrote a letter outlining his proposal to Harvard president Charles Eliot on 23 December 1878. Eliot approved, and Gilman, along with his wife and several other women, began working to set the plan in motion. Once an appropriate number of Harvard professors agreed to participate in the project, Gilman and these women officially formed the Private Collegiate Instruction for Women in 1879. The circular issued in February "announced in rather vague terms that some of the professors of Harvard College had consented to give instruction to properly prepared women of a grade not below that which they gave to men" (Merrill, p. 190). For the first three years this program was run entirely on a volunteer basis by Gilman and several women. But in August 1882 a need for more money and space necessitated a more formal organization, and the program became known as the Society for the Collegiate Instruction for Women. Gilman based the success of the project on the fact that the organizers "were exponents of no 'cause,' and were known only as persons interested in the best instruction of women" (Merrill, p. 193).

During the time Gilman conceived and instituted this plan, he continued to publish his writings. In 1879 Gilman's *Shakespeare's Morals* appeared. Also in that year, Houghton, Osgood, and Company published *The Poetical Works of Geoffrey Chaucer* in three volumes, which Gilman edited, being the first to use the Ellesmere manuscript of Chaucer's *Canterbury Tales*. In addition, Gilman compiled the index for the 1884 edition of Harper's *Complete Works of Samuel Taylor Coleridge*. Along with these, Gilman wrote, edited, and collaborated on numerous works included in the Story of the Nations Series published by G. P. Putnam's Sons in New York between 1885 and 1904; he also edited *Theatrum Majorum: The Cambridge of 1776* (1876) and wrote *Tales of the Pathfinders* (1884); and *Short Stories from the Dictionary* (1886).

In March 1894, when the Society for the Collegiate Instruction for Women became Radcliffe College, Gilman was appointed regent of the school and remained in that position until 1895. Over the years Gilman's role in creating Radcliffe College has become overshadowed by the parts certain women played in the project. Gilman continued to write on a variety of topics until his death in Atlantic City, New Jersey.

• Gilman's papers are in the Radcliffe Archives, and his letters are in Harvard's Schlesinger Library. Other works written or edited by Gilman include *First Steps in General History: A Suggestive Outline* (1874) and *Magna Charta Stories* (1882). Although there are no comprehensive indexes to all of the writings of Gilman, the *Dictionary of American Biography* provides an ample list. Any writings not included there may be found in the libraries of Harvard University. A short history of Gilman's life is in *The Gilman Family* (1869). For Gilman's account of the events that led to the incorporation of Radcliffe College, see Estelle M. H. Merrill, *Cambridge Sketches by Cambridge Authors* (1896). Obituaries are in the *New York Evening Post* and the *Boston Transcript*, 29 Dec. 1909.

JESSICA LEXIE HOLLIS

GILMAN, Arthur Delavan (5 Nov. 1821–11 July 1882), architect and critic, was born in Newburyport, Massachusetts, the son of Arthur Gilman, a prosperous merchant, and his third wife Elizabeth Marquand, widow of Samuel Allyne Otis. After attending Dummer Academy, he entered Trinity (then Washington) College in Hartford, Connecticut, in 1838 but withdrew in 1840 due to difficulty with his eyes. After recovering, he briefly studied law, developing the trenchant debating and writing style that shortly emerged in three brilliant articles for the *North American Review* in 1843–1844. His initial article reviewed A. J. Downing's *Landscape Gardening* (1841) and *Cottage Residences* (1842). Confirming Gilman's position on the cutting edge of picturesque theory, this article was wholly American in scope, but the second and most important, "Architecture in the United States," revealed an extraordinary knowledge of European, largely English, buildings. He brought the theories of Loudon, Pugin, Leeds, Bloxam, Britton, and Gwilt to the attention of American architecture.

Gilman argued fluently for discrimination and theoretical consistency in design, declaring architecture "beyond question, the oldest and most impressive of the Fine Arts." He denounced Edward Shaw's *Rural Architecture* (1843) and design by artisans from pattern books. In his vision, the quality of American architecture would improve only through gifted architects who "combine a love of beauty with the advantage of thorough education." The dazzling precocity of the 23-year-old Gilman's articles, which were copied and published abroad, secured an invitation to deliver twelve Lowell Lectures in 1844 and established him as the primary intellectual force in Boston architecture. Lauding the picturesque and the natural linkage of building to site, he confessed personal enthusiasm for A. W. N. Pugin, whose Gothic principles he embraced in two church designs, St. Paul's in Dedham, Massachusetts (1845; demolished), and St. John's in Clifton, Staten Island, New York (1869; demolished). Yet Gilman was no ecclesiologist, rather, he promoted the ideal of a single style for each building, appropriately selected and literately applied. Gilman's practice began in Boston in 1845 with "Fernhill," the William P. Winchester House (demolished) in Cambridge, resembling Sir Charles Barry's picturesque Italianate country houses in England. Of Gilman's villas outside Boston, the Hollis H. Hunnewell House (1850) in Wellesley still remains on exquisitely landscaped grounds.

Gilman's extended sojourn abroad in 1853–1854 expanded his international perspective on architecture that was unique among his peers by 1850. He had met William Thackeray in 1852 in Boston, and through him joined the literary circle in London, where he met Charles R. Cockerell, gold medalist of the Royal Institute of British Architects, Professor Donaldson, and Sir Charles Barry, who accelerated Gilman's enthusiasm for Renaissance design. In France, Gilman witnessed construction of the new Louvre and the redesign of Paris under Baron Haussmann.

Returning to Boston in 1854, Gilman designed a plan for filling in the Back Bay based on that of Second Empire Paris. Boston's Commonwealth Avenue, still considered one of the world's great boulevards, was laid out according to Gilman's plan. With his partnership in 1858 with Gridley J. F. Bryant, Jr., he created the largest architectural office in Boston. His monumental Boston City Hall (1862–1865), based on the Louvre, was the first mansard-roofed civic building in America. The Boston City Hospital (1861–1863) extended the French mode to a larger bay and link system. In 1859 he married Frances Juliet Raynor; they had no children.

Horticultural Hall (1865) on Tremont Street featured a raised attic with sculptural figures by Martin Milmore, reflecting the Ashmolean Museum, Oxford (1844–1845) and St. George's Hall, Liverpool (1851–1854) by C. R. Cockerell. Gilman designed the first public building in the Back Bay, the Arlington Street Church (1858), and more than eighty houses, establishing French academic facades for the first section of the district. The most notable were for John Bates (1860) at 12 Arlington Street, the S. Hooper and Oliver Peabody Houses at 25–27 Commonwealth Avenue, and the attached Brewer and Beebe Houses at 29–30 Beacon Street (1863). Gilman aligned American colonial buildings within the English baroque tradition, lauding Peter Harrison's King's Chapel (1749) in Boston, and led an unsuccessful campaign to save the legendary Thomas Hancock House (1737) on Beacon Hill from demolition 1858–1863. Utilizing James Gibb's St. Martin's in the Fields, London (1726), as inspiration for his Arlington Street Church (1858), the interior of which was drawn from Santa Annunziata in Genoa, Italy, he established a monumental scale for Boston architecture.

Gilman consulted with Alfred B. Mullett on the Federal Post Office Building in Boston (1869), where a high budget allowed for lavish Second Empire design, a five-part bay and link facade, multiple paired columns, and elaborate allegorical statues at the attic. The enormous popularity of the new French style drew Gilman to New York City in 1865. There he collaborated with Thomas Fuller on designs for the New York State Capitol in Albany in 1867, but withdrew from the political storms that dominated the project for two decades. Gilman's innovative Equitable Life Assurance Society Building (1873) in New York had a mansard roof and was the first to use passenger elevators. One of his last works was the great Butler Exchange Building (1878) in Providence, Rhode Island. During the 1870s Gilman also worked closely with Mullett on the State War and Navy Building in Washington, D.C., America's largest application of the French mansard mode. His most enduring legacy is the plan of Boston's Back Bay. He died in Syracuse, New York.

• There is no known collection of Gilman's papers or office records. Gilman's importance nonetheless emerges from his own publications "Downing on Landscape Gardening," *North American Review* 56 (Jan. 1843); "Architecture in the United States," *North American Review* 58 (Apr. 1844): 436–80; and "Landscape Gardening," *North American Review* 59 (Oct. 1844): 303–29. A critical assessment of these articles is given in Phoebe Stanton, *The Gothic Revival and American Church Architecture, an Episode in Taste 1840–1856* (1968). Biographical information can be found in *Sketches of Men of Mark* (1871), pp. 817–21. See also Bainbridge Bunting, *Houses of Boston's Back Bay; An Architectural History, 1840–1917* (1967); Margaret Henderson Floyd, "A Terra-Cotta Cornerstone for Copley Square: Museum of Fine Arts, Boston, by Sturgis and Brigham (1870–1876)," *Journal of the Society of Architectural Historians* 32 (May 1973): 83–103; and "Measured Drawings of the Hancock House by John Hubbard Sturgis: A Legacy to the Colonial Revival," in *Architecture in Colonial Massachusetts. Proceedings of the Colonial Society of Massachusetts, Boston*, ed. Abbott Cummings (1979); Gilman's leading role introducing the Second Empire French mansard style is found in George Wren, "The Boston City Hall, Bryant and Gilman Architects," *Journal of the Society of Architectural Historians* 21 (1962): 188–92; Henry-Russell Hitchcock and William Seale, *Temples of Democracy* (1976); and Walter E. Langsam, "The New York Capitol

1863–1876" (M.A. thesis, Yale Univ., 1968). His innovative role in the development of the New York skyscraper is noted in Winston Weisman, "A New View of Skyscraper History," in *The Rise of an American Architecture*, ed. Edgar Kaufmann, Jr. (1970), and Sarah Bradford Landau and Carl W. Condit, *Rise of the New York Skyscraper 1865–1913* (1996). A list of his buildings is included in Floyd, "Arthur Delavan Gilman," in *Macmillan Encyclopedia of Architects*, vol. 2 (1982), pp. 208–10. Obituaries are in the *New York World*, 17 July 1882, and *American Architect and Building News* 12 (July 1882): 33.

MARGARET HENDERSON FLOYD

GILMAN, Caroline Howard (8 Oct. 1794–15 Sept. 1888), writer and editor, was born in Boston, Massachusetts, the daughter of Samuel Howard, a prosperous shipwright who had participated in the Boston Tea Party, and Anna Lillie. Her father died in 1797 and, after her mother's death in 1804, Gilman spent the rest of her youth with relatives in Concord, Dedham, Watertown, and Cambridge, Massachusetts. At a series of local schools she received the education typically given to young women of the time, although she was taught Latin, which she later recalled as "a great step for that period." During these years she gave early evidence of literary talent with the composition of an epistolary novel and the publication, when she was sixteen, of a poem, "Jephthah's Rash Vow."

In 1819 Howard married the Reverend Samuel Gilman, a Unitarian minister well known as an essayist, poet, and translator. Moving to Charleston, South Carolina, where the Reverend Gilman had assumed the pastorate of the Second Independent Church, the first Unitarian church in Charleston, the young couple soon became leading figures in the city's literary circles. By 1831 Caroline Howard Gilman had given birth to six children, the youngest two of whom died in infancy. In 1832 she began publishing the *Rose-Bud*, a children's weekly, one of the first in the United States. It is interesting today chiefly as it reflects contemporary taste in children's reading material and the sobering facts of nineteenth-century childhood life. It featured moralistic stories and poems, including "Mother, What Is Death?" "The Shipwrecked Emigrants," and "Lines on Anna Playing in the Graveyard." The weekly also featured children's obituaries and an advice column responding to young readers' questions on topics ranging from the spiritual to the hygienic. The *Rose-Bud* grew into the *Southern Rose-Bud* (1833–1835) and the *Southern Rose* (1835–1839), directed at readers of all ages. As an adult publication, it occasionally featured the work of well-known writers such as Harriet Martineau; Nathaniel Hawthorne also contributed a short story, "The Lily's Quest," in 1839.

In an autobiographical sketch that appears in John Hart's *The Female Prose Writers of America* (1855), Gilman recounts her life almost exclusively in terms of her literary accomplishments: she does not mention the death of her parents nor the births or deaths of her children. It is difficult to know, therefore, whether her decision to close down the *Southern Rose* in 1839 had

anything to do with the birth that year of the Gilmans' seventh and last child, who also died in infancy. On the other hand, the quality of the magazine (as seen in the amount of material borrowed from other publications) seems to have been in decline for some time.

Although Gilman maintained that her "only pride" was in the children's miscellanies she later published, she also recognized that her domestic novels, originally serialized in the *Southern Rose*, represented "the first attempt, in that particular mode, to enter into the recesses of American homes and hearths." Gilman was innovative in her introduction of women's concerns into mainstream American fiction. In her novels, she provided a valuable chronicle of middle-class American domestic life; equally important, she enhanced the stature of her women characters by exalting their function as moral centers within the family and as administrators of logistically complex household structures. Her work on the *Rose-Bud* reflected her serious regard for the maternal role and for the educability of children. In her intensely active life as writer, wife, mother, and publisher, Gilman—like Louisa May Alcott, Margaret Fuller, and Harriet Beecher Stowe—offers a dynamic model of the intellectually and relationally engaged nineteenth-century American woman. Her first novel, *Recollections of a Housekeeper* (1835; later published as *Recollections of a New England Bride*) appeared under the pseudonym Clarissa Packard. *Recollections of a Southern Matron* (1836) and *Love's Progress; or Ruth Raymond* (1840) were published under her own name. From 1835 to 1859 Gilman also published eight collections of verse, stories, and "oracles" (used in popular fortune-telling parlor games) for children and adults. She also edited the *Letters of Eliza Wilkinson* (1839).

Samuel Gilman died in 1858; Caroline Gilman's *Inscriptions in the Cemetery and Building of the Unitarian . . . Church . . . Charleston* (1860) is a tribute to him. When the Civil War broke out, Caroline Gilman affirmed her allegiance to the South and moved inland, following the shelling of her house in 1862. Upon her return, she discovered that many of her belongings, including her papers and books, had been stolen or destroyed. Despite such dislocation at an advanced age, she embarked on what she called a "new era" in her life, publishing three more collections of poems, stories, and oracles (two in collaboration with her daughter, Caroline Howard Jervey) and a book of recollections in honor of the centennial of the Boston Tea Party. She died in Washington, D.C.

• Gilman's 1810–1880 correspondence is located at the South Carolina Historical Society in Charleston. A selection of her letters from the Civil War period was published in the *Atlantic Monthly* (Apr. 1926) as "Letters of a Confederate Mother: Charleston in the Sixties." A selection of letters and miscellaneous writings appears in Mary Scott Saint-Amand, *A Balcony in Charleston* (1941). William Stanley Hoole, "The Gilmans and the Southern Rose," *North Carolina Historical Review* (Apr. 1934), provides much information on Gilman's literary life in the 1830s. More recent critical treatments of Gilman's contribution to American literature appear in Mary

Kelley, *Private Woman, Public Stage: Literary Domesticity in Nineteenth-Century America* (1984); Nina Baym, *Woman's Fiction: A Guide to Novels by and about Women in America, 1820–1870* (1978); and Helen Waite Papashvily, *All the Happy Endings: A Study of the Domestic Novel in America, the Women Who Wrote It, the Women Who Read It, in the Nineteenth Century* (1956). Contemporary estimates are featured in Mary T. Tardy, *The Living Female Writers of the South* (1872), and Mary Forrest, *Women of the South Distinguished in Literature* (1861). An obituary is in the *Washington Evening Star*, 15 Sept. 1888.

DIANE PRENATT

GILMAN, Charlotte Perkins (3 July 1860–17 Aug. 1935), feminist critic and author, was born Charlotte Anna Perkins in Hartford, Connecticut, the daughter of Frederic Beecher Perkins, a man of letters and librarian, and Mary Ann Fitch Wescott. Her great-grandfather was theologian Lyman Beecher, and she was the great-niece of Harriet Beecher Stowe and Henry Ward Beecher. Frederic Perkins left his family soon after Charlotte's birth and thereafter provided little financial or emotional support. She and her mother and older brother lived on the edge of poverty. As a child Charlotte attended school for a total of four years, which was not an uncommon amount of schooling for girls in her class, or declassed, position. She went to seven different schools, her formal education ending when she was fifteen.

As a young woman Charlotte studied art for a time at the Rhode Island School of Design and later earned her living by designing greeting cards, teaching art, and, for a brief period, tutoring children, an activity she did not enjoy. In 1884, after much painful vacillation, she married Charles Walter Stetson, a local artist. Katharine Beecher, their only child, was born a year later. Almost immediately Charlotte Stetson became so deeply depressed that she consulted S. Weir Mitchell, the well-known neurologist who specialized in women's nervous disorders. His famous "rest cure" forbade Charlotte Stetson ever to write and sharply limited her reading time. She rejected his regimen and fled to California, where she eventually divorced her husband. He married Grace Ellery Channing, Charlotte Stetson's closest friend, and the three remained friends throughout their lives. Charlotte Stetson sent Katharine to live with her father and new stepmother, which freed her to concentrate on her work but which also left her with permanent feelings of guilt about this decision. She supported herself, if often precariously, as a lecturer and writer.

Gilman came of age at the time of struggle over the ideas of Charles Darwin and their applicability to human society. She identified with the reform wing of Social Darwinist thought espoused by Lester Frank Ward, who argued that humans, unlike other animals, determined the social laws under which they lived. Convinced of the plasticity of human nature, Gilman believed that women, as a collective entity, could choose to be the moving force in the reorganization of society. The most important fact about men and women, she argued, is the humanity they shared, not the differences that distinguished them. But women were denied autonomy and thus were not given an environment in which to flourish. Men, too, suffered from personalities distorted by their age-long habits of dominance and power. A healthy social organism for men and women, therefore, required the autonomy of women. That autonomy could be achieved if women led the struggle for a humanized-socialized world.

Her body of thought, expressed in hundreds of articles, essays, and poems and thousands of lectures, combined a Fabian version of socialism and what we today would call feminism, although she did not call herself a feminist. The world is "masculinist," she insisted, and she wished to create a humanist world. She sought to define a humane social order built on female nurturing and life-giving values. She constructed an analysis to explain human behavior, past and present, in order to project the outlines of a future vision. Her theoretical structure encompassed anthropology, history, philosophy, sociology, and ethics. Through these cosmic efforts she created a social analysis that is largely coherent internally and formidable in its proportions.

Gilman's international reputation was initially achieved with the publication in 1898 of her famous book *Women and Economics: A Study of the Economic Relation between Men and Women as a Factor in Social Relations* (repr. 1970). She argued in it that the major influence in our lives is the way we earn a living, a view built on classical economics, but we are different from *all* other animals, she said, because in the human species alone the female depends on the male for food. Thus the sex relationship is also an economic relationship. She built on many traditional ideas but extended them by infusing the perspective of gender. What she called the "sexuo-economic" relationship is fundamental to all her subsequent ideas. Women at the service of men underlies all social imbalance, she asserted.

In later studies she extended and deepened her original formulation. In 1900 she published *Concerning Children*; in 1903, *The Home: Its Work and Influence* (repr. 1970); in 1904, *Human Work*; in 1911, *The Man-Made World or Our Androcentric Culture* (repr. 1970); and in 1923, *His Religion and Hers: A Study of the Faith of Our Fathers and the Work of Our Mothers*. She alone wrote the articles for the *Forerunner*, her monthly magazine, which appeared from 1909 to 1916. Three of her novels were serialized in it: *What Diantha Did* (1910), *The Crux* (1911), and *Moving the Mountain* (1911). *Herland: A Feminist Utopian Novel*, originally published serially in 1915, was printed as a book in 1979. This utopian fantasy of a world inhabited solely by women, along with Gilman's chilling short story "The Yellow Wallpaper" (1892) based in large part on her experience with Mitchell's regimen, are the works for which she is best known today. Her autobiography, *The Living of Charlotte Perkins Gilman*, appeared in 1935 shortly after her death and was republished several times, most recently in 1990.

In 1900, after a long and complicated courtship, she married George Houghton Gilman, her first cousin, also a descendant of Lyman Beecher. They lived happily until 1934, when Houghton Gilman died suddenly. Charlotte Gilman, aware that she was dying from inoperable breast cancer, ended her own life in Pasadena, California, leaving behind a note that was incorporated in her posthumously published autobiography. It read, in part: "When all usefulness is over, when one is assured of unavoidable and imminent death, it is the simplest of human rights to choose a quick and easy death in place of a slow and horrible one."

Gilman's great contribution to intellectual and social thought was making gender the central part of her analysis. That focus made the invisible visible and thereby advanced social thought. Like other Social Darwinists she used the theory of evolution to insist on the desirability of change. What she wanted changed, however, was women's work, home, marriage, and child rearing. Gilman located the source of the subordination of women in the home, society's most venerated institution. She exposed the facade of the sentimental home by demonstrating how it was a limiting place, a place in which patriarchal power was used against women and children, and she did it with theoretical formulations that explained how it came about and why and how it must and will change. She took the ordinary matters of everyday living for most women and put them into a larger context, making them appropriate subjects for intellectual inquiry. The central work assigned to women, the rearing of children, she saw as being of social importance equal to the public work of men, although she proposed doing it collectively and not privately. She called for the expanding of options for men and women, and she proposed ways of reconstituting society to make those options possible. Her work addresses the issues still current today of how to resolve the tension between love and work, intimacy and autonomy. Charlotte Perkins Gilman created the rudiments of a theory of gender.

• Most of Gilman's papers are in the Arthur and Elizabeth Schlesinger Library, Radcliffe College. They are listed and described by Eva Mosley in *Charlotte Perkins Gilman Papers, 1846–1961* (1972). The letters of Charles Walter Stetson are in the Bancroft Library at the University of California in Berkeley. Some correspondence between Gilman and Lester Ward is in the John Hay Library, Brown University. Other Gilman letters are in the Rhode Island Historical Society in Providence, the Stowe Day Foundation in Hartford, and the Vassar College Library.

Gilman's major published work not mentioned in the text includes a book of verse, *In This Our World* (1893), *The Captive Imagination: A Casebook on "The Yellow Wallpaper"* (1992), and *The Charlotte Perkins Gilman Reader* (1980), a collection of her fiction. Among her nonfiction published work is a collection titled *Charlotte Perkins Gilman: A Nonfiction Reader* (1991). Gilman wrote, edited, and published all copy for the *Forerunner: A Monthly Magazine*, which was reprinted in its entirety in 1968. An indispensable guide to her work is Gary Scharnhorst, *Charlotte Perkins Gilman: A Bibliography* (1985).

There are several full-length studies of Gilman: Ann J. Lane, *To "Herland" and Beyond: The Life and Work of Char-*

lotte Perkins Gilman (1990); Sheryl L. Meyering, ed., *Charlotte Perkins Gilman: The Woman and Her Work* (1989); Polly Wynn Allen, *Building Domestic Liberty: Charlotte Perkins Gilman's Architectural Feminism* (1988); and Mary Armfield Hill, *Charlotte Perkins Gilman: The Making of a Radical Feminist, 1860–1896* (1980).

An obituary appears in the *New York Times*, 20 Aug. 1935.

ANN J. LANE

GILMAN, Daniel Coit (6 July 1831–13 Oct. 1908), educator and university president, was born in Norwich, Connecticut, the son of William Charles Gilman, a prosperous nail manufacturer, and Eliza Coit. His father and mother were socially prominent in the community and devoted considerable time to educational and charitable activities. Gilman, after primary school, attended Norwich Academy, an elite school where one of his classmates was Timothy Dwight, a future president of Yale University. When he was fourteen, Gilman's family moved to New York City.

Gilman had shown an early interest in librarianship and cataloging. In the summer of 1848, before entering Yale University, he worked at the Mercantile Library of New York, and during the same summer he was employed by Henry Stevens, the rare book man, to prepare a card catalog of the 300-volume library of George Washington's books. The collection was later sold to the Boston Athenaeum. Upon his graduation from Yale in 1852, Gilman attended Harvard College and resided with the eminent geographer Arnold Guyot. In September 1853 Gilman attended a conference of libraries in New York City, and he was actively engaged with indexing journals for William Frederick Poole's *Index to Periodical Literature*. Late in 1853 the U.S. secretary of state appointed Gilman and Andrew Dickson White, later to become president of Cornell University, attachés to the American legation at St. Petersburg. Gilman remained in Europe for two years, traveling in England, France, and Germany. These years were influential in the formation of Gilman's ideas about higher education. While abroad, he served as a correspondent for a number of American periodicals, particularly *Norton's Literary Gazette*, and many of his early views on education are reflected in the articles he wrote for these journals.

On his return to the United States in late 1855, Gilman was employed at Yale University. From 1856 to 1865 he served successively as assistant director of the Yale College Library and then as its director. As Yale's librarian, Gilman clearly saw the need for expanded facilities, and he continually worked toward creating a library that would facilitate research as well as advanced studies. Most of his reforms were published in three reports in 1862, 1864, and 1865 to the Yale Corporation. In these, he complained that the library was hampered by lack of funds and that many regulations and the lack of staff restricted its use. When it became apparent that nothing would be done, Gilman resigned as Yale librarian in July 1865. In 1869, after his resignation, he wrote, "It is scholars who make a college; not bricks and mortar. It is endowments which secure the time and services of scholars. Next to scholars, books are essential, but Yale College has not a dollar on hand to buy books for the next two years, its scanty library income having already been expended in advance" (*Norwich Bulletin* 3 [July 1869]: 80). In 1861 Gilman had married Mary Ketcham of New York City; they had two children before her death in 1869.

Gilman first became affiliated with Yale's Sheffield Scientific School (founded in 1847) in 1856, when he was hired as a fundraiser for the school. In 1863 he was appointed professor of physical geography at Sheffield. As fundraiser and faculty member, Gilman served as apologist and educational theorist for the new science education. From 1866 to 1872 he was secretary of Sheffield's governing board. As Yale historian George W. Pierson has observed, "Gilman transferred his ambition and fertile imagination from the stagnant librarianship of the College to the teaching of modern subjects and the particular promotion of the Scientific School" (p. 51). By 1872 the Sheffield Scientific School was flourishing. Gilman had seen the Ph.D. instituted, and some progress had been made in achieving a coordinated university at Yale. However, when Noah Porter became the eleventh president of Yale in 1871, the graduate work at Yale and that at the Sheffield Scientific School was seriously arrested, and instruction in the new sciences was now regarded with suspicion. Gilman was apprehensive and uncertain about the future for Yale.

By 1870 Gilman was known throughout New England both as a geographer and as the Sheffield School's secretary. More importantly, however, he was associated with progress in general. He left Yale in September 1872 and accepted the presidency of the University of California at Berkeley. His departure from New Haven in October 1872 "was the cause of universal regret to his friends [who] felt not only their personal loss but also the loss the College sustained in his removal from its activities" (Franklin, p. 108). Gilman's plans for the University of California were revealed in his inaugural address. He had previously gained experience at the Sheffield Scientific School and in his study of the "great changes [that had] been made in the higher educational systems of this and other lands" (Gilman, *University Problems in the United States* [1898], p. 153). Gilman turned to the clarification of two points that embodied the essence of his "university idea" as well as his philosophy of advanced, or graduate, education. These two points were the definition of the "university" (and how it differed from other educational institutions), with its focus on advanced and "liberal culture in all the great departments of learning"; and the required indigenous character of any proposed university, "adapted to this people." Gilman's inaugural address proposals remained unfulfilled during his tenure. In one sense Gilman failed, although some gains were made. These gains were recorded in his *Statement of the Progress and Condition of the University of California* (Mar. 1875), which he prepared at the behest of the regents. His statement was largely a progress report that outlined the basis for future growth. The growth of the university between 1875 and 1900, if slow, was largely due to the careful foundations that Gilman had constructed. He had quietly indicated to Andrew Dickson White as early as 12 May 1874 that he might resign as university president if the right situation presented itself. By the end of 1874 overtures reached Gilman to consider the presidency of the Johns Hopkins University, soon to be established in Baltimore as the result of the munificent gift of Johns Hopkins, the Quaker merchant who in 1867 had formed two corporations, each with an endowment of $3.5 million, one to endow a university and one to maintain a hospital. In 1877 Gilman married Elisabeth Dwight Woolsey; they had no children.

Later Gilman reminisced, "Before a university can be launched there are six requisites: an idea; capital to make the idea feasible; a definite plan; an able staff of coadjutors; books and apparatus; students" (*The Launching of a University*, p. 9). Gilman might well have added a seventh: the proper leader, an individual who provides the university with the needed direction and force. The Hopkins trustees, following the death of Hopkins and the proving of his will in 1873, began a long series of conferences that culminated in the election of Gilman to the presidency of the new university. Trustee Reverdy Johnson was directed to offer the presidency to Gilman, and this was done officially on 23 October 1874. Gilman accepted on 10 November and arrived in Baltimore in late December. He became president of Johns Hopkins University with his formal acceptance on 30 January 1875.

Gilman remained president of Johns Hopkins until 1902. In his long tenure, Gilman touched many of the leaders in American higher education. Two factors in the history of American graduate education in the last quarter of the nineteenth century are indisputable. One is the tremendous growth of American graduate education in the period defined; the second factor is the constantly reiterated acknowledgment of the influence of Gilman in the promotion of the growth of graduate studies in America. Clark University and the University of Chicago were founded in the historical shadow of Johns Hopkins and their first presidents acknowledged Gilman's model, but the influence went beyond the new enterprises; it touched the older establishment, whose leaders publicly declared their indebtedness to the Baltimore experiment. In 1896, when the newly created Federation of Graduate Clubs met at the University of Pennsylvania in order to set up graduate school standards, it outlined the same minimum requirements for the Ph.D. that Gilman had initiated twenty years earlier. The standards approved by the newly minted Association of American Universities for the doctoral degree in 1900 were largely the same standards that had been adopted at Johns Hopkins in 1876. As early as 1886 English historian James Bryce had lamented what he envisioned in American education as "this enormous total [345] of degree granting bodies very few [of which] answer to the modern conception of a university." Johns Hopkins, however, received from him only praise.

Gilman's first contribution to American graduate education was the Johns Hopkins Ph.D., which by definition contrasted the difference between undergraduate and graduate study. The Johns Hopkins doctorate became the ideal that other institutions strove to match. It was carefully defined where little definition had previously existed, and its emphasis was on gainful research. In Gilman's own words: "Investigation has thus been among us the duty of every leading professor, and he has been the guide and inspirer of fellows and pupils, whose work may not bear his name, but whose results are truly products of the inspiration and guidance which he has freely bestowed" (*The Launching of a University*, p. 135).

Yet even a carefully defined Ph.D. that stressed research was no guarantee that the Johns Hopkins graduate experiment would succeed. The history of antebellum American graduate education proved that these factors alone did not gain the day for American graduate programs. Ancillary problems had to be solved, the most important of which being the relation of graduate education to the traditional curriculum of the American undergraduate college with its heavy emphasis on classics. Nor could the impact of German universities be overlooked, for it was there that many American students had found "an ineffaceable impression of what scholarship meant, of what a university was and of what a long road higher education in America had to travel before it could hope to reach a plane of equal elevation" (Nicholas Murray Butler, *Across the Busy Years*, vol. 1, p. 127). Gilman's resolution of the "college problem" was a practical one. His "group system of studies" provided for the continuance of classical undergraduate curriculums with only minor changes; a dynamic, flexible curriculum allowed the undergraduate school to complement, rather than impede, the graduate department. Given his experiences at Yale and at California, Gilman carefully avoided any sense of rivalry between undergraduate and graduate programs; rather, he sought to promote a mutual interdependence that provided for simultaneous development and growth. If the Johns Hopkins undergraduate college received equal attention in Gilman's *Annual Reports*, it was because he regarded it as a vital component in the success of the graduate program. If Gilman can be regarded as "the patron saint of the American graduate school," surely his contributions to undergraduate education have been overlooked.

By assembling the core of a strong graduate faculty (with supplemental nonresident lectures to boot), Gilman solved the problems of a new university and the problem of student migration as well. In Baltimore, the Johns Hopkins graduate student found talent enough to bring research projects to completion, while Gilman's support of scholarly journals ensured that worthwhile results were disseminated. Nicholas Murray Butler viewed Gilman's fellowship program there as one of the great innovations in early education. "Gilman . . . threw the Johns Hopkins Fellowships to general competition; and it was this step . . . which fixed the relation of the new university to the colleges of the country and which attracted to it at once the most promising of the young scholars" (Butler, "President Gilman's Administration at the Johns Hopkins University," *Review of Reviews* 23 [Jan. 1901]: 54). Without doubt, the program solved what had been felicitously termed "the need and demand for advanced studies."

Pleading old age, Gilman formally notified the Johns Hopkins trustees in November 1900 of his retirement, effective at the end of the academic year. His formal resignation is dated 22 February 1901. Gilman's career in education, for all intents and purposes, was over. He soon found, however, that he was unable to refuse an additional service into which he was practically forced. Although Andrew Carnegie had decided on making a benefaction to the District of Columbia, he was unsure as to its form. After consulting with President Theodore Roosevelt, Secretary of State John Hay, and Cornell University president Andrew Dickson White in mid-1901, Carnegie met with Gilman at White's instigation to discuss the gift. The first meeting took place in November 1901, and while Carnegie still held no firm ideas as to the nature of the gift in mind, he did propose to Gilman and John Shaw Billings (the architect of the Johns Hopkins Hospital, whom he had also summoned) that he was "willing to give ten million for an institution the purpose of which shall be the advancement of learning." In leaving a record of this first meeting, Gilman reported Carnegie as saying that

it is proposed to found in the city of Washington an institution which with the cooperation of institutions now or hereafter established, there or elsewhere, shall in the broadest and most liberal manner encourage investigation, research, and discovery; show the application of knowledge to the improvement of mankind; provide such buildings, laboratories, books, and apparatus, as may be needed; and afford instruction of an advanced character to students properly qualified to profit thereby. (*The Launching of a University*, p. 111)

During this initial meeting Carnegie insisted that Gilman become the organization's president. The Carnegie Institution of Washington was formally incorporated on 28 January 1902. At the first board of trustees meeting on 29 January, Gilman was elected its president. Although the Carnegie Institution's work was envisioned as going beyond the scope of graduate schools, Gilman stressed the logical ties between the new organization and American graduate education. Significantly Gilman, the architect of a pure research endowment, found his greatest challenge in differentiating between his new institution and the graduate educational concepts that he had promoted for over a quarter of a century. This task was far from easy, and Gilman saw its resolution in his promotion of the research institute as a valuable adjunct to the universities.

Gilman's presidential tenure at the institute was brief, lasting only until December 1904. While the brevity of his leadership precluded any great achievements, it appears that the initial design of the institution was his; this design, however, was never implemented. Its students as conceptualized never appeared, and the institution has only marginally concerned itself with "facilities for higher education." More than anything else, the institution has concentrated on scientific research, emphasizing "larger projects." As such, it never did become the adjunct to the graduate school that Gilman had envisioned. Possibly its original aim had been defined so loosely that no one could have successfully predicted its development. In terms of substance, Gilman's recommendation that the institution promote knowledge, develop talent, and publish findings had been achieved, albeit not on the close association with graduate schools that he had envisioned. Certainly, it did not come close to matching the programs at Johns Hopkins. Gilman's final service to the institution was in modifying its by-laws in order to permit its president more power in basic policy formulation.

During the period of almost thirty years of Gilman's presidency of the Johns Hopkins University, and of the Carnegie Institution of Washington, he was engaged in a multitude of other educational activities. He was the president of the American Social Association in 1879. In 1882 he was made one of the original trustees of the John F. Slater Fund, an office he held until his death. In 1893 he became a trustee of the Peabody Education Fund, and in 1903 a member of the General Education Board. In 1907, in his seventy-sixth year, he was appointed a trustee of the Russell Sage Foundation. Gilman authored many articles and books, the most important of which include *Our National Schools Of Science* (1867); *James Monroe in His Relations to the Public Service during Half-a-Century* (1883); *The Life of James Dwight Dana* (1899); and *The Launching of a University, and Other Papers* (1906). He was also the editor of *The Miscellaneous Writings of Francis Lieber* (2 vols., 1881).

Gilman died in Norwich, Connecticut, the city of his birth. Only four years after his death, he was eulogized in Paul Monroe's *A Cyclopedia of Education* as responsible for "the establishment of full-fledged graduate schools, the naturalization of research as a leading element in American universities, and the development of a great scale of scientific and scholarly publications [that] date from the foundation of Johns Hopkins University" (vol. 3, p. 112).

• The Daniel Coit Gilman Papers are at the Johns Hopkins University Library and include correspondence, clippings, reports, and manuscript drafts of speeches. The Gilman Family Papers at the Yale University Library contain letters both to and from Gilman. Letters to Gilman are in the Daniel Coit Gilman Papers at Doe Memorial Library at the University of California, Berkeley. The Will S. Monroe Collection of Henry Barnard Manuscripts at New York University contains letters from Gilman to Barnard in 1856–1857. Also useful are the following Johns Hopkins University publications:

Addresses at the Inauguration of Daniel Coit Gilman as President of the Johns Hopkins University (1876), *Annual Report of the President* (1876–1902), and *Celebration of the Twenty-fifth Anniversary of the Founding of the University and the Inauguration of Ira Remsen as the President of the University* (1902). See also Nicholas Murray Butler, *Across the Busy Years* (2 vols., 1935); Francesco Cordasco, *Daniel Coit Gilman and the Protean Ph.D.* (1960; rev. ed., 1973); Abraham Flexner, *Daniel Coit Gilman* (1946); Fabian Franklin, *Daniel Coit Gilman* (1910), which is a memorial biography commissioned by Gilman's widow; Paul Monroe, ed., *A Cyclopedia of Education* (5 vols., 1911–1913); W. Carson Ryan, *Studies in Early Graduate Education* (1939); George W. Pierson, *Yale College: An Educational History, 1871–1921* (1952); and Andrew Dickson White, *Autobiography* (2 vols., 1907).

FRANCESCO CORDASCO

GILMAN, Frank Patrick (14 Dec. 1853–4 Dec. 1918), missionary, was born in Sparta, New York, the son of James Scott Gilman and Jane R. Galbraith, farmers. Gilman taught at Geneseo Academy in New York for several years following completion of secondary school. In 1875 he enrolled at Princeton University, where one of his classmates was Woodrow Wilson; they graduated together in 1879. Gilman then moved west and, from 1880 to 1882, served as professor of science at the Territorial University in Seattle, Washington.

While in Washington he decided to enter the ministry and returned to the East and entered Princeton Theological Seminary. Like many of his generation he felt the need to spread the gospel to foreign lands, and while in seminary he applied to the Board of Foreign Missions of the Presbyterian Church for appointment as a missionary to China. He graduated from the seminary in 1885 and was appointed to the mission in Canton (pinyin, Guangzhou), Kwangtung (Guangdong). Gilman traveled to China via India where, at Landour in December 1885, he married Marion McNair, also of Sparta, New York, who had taught in India for a year at the Woodstock School for missionaries' children while Gilman was finishing his seminary studies; three of their five children survived to adulthood.

After their arrival in Canton, the Gilmans were assigned to Hainan Island, where they hoped to expand mission work. The Canton missionaries thought that because the aboriginal Miao (now identified as Yao) seemed to be less influenced by superstitions and prejudices than were the Han Chinese, conversions on Hainan would be more numerous than they had been on the mainland. The Gilmans and Henry M. McCandliss, a physician who arrived in 1885, were the first Americans to reside on the island. There they joined Danish sea captain Carl C. Jeremiassen, who had interested the Presbyterians in establishing the new mission.

During their first year on Hainan the Gilmans lived in part of an abandoned temple, as they encountered intense opposition from the Chinese when they expressed an interest in purchasing property and building western-style houses and a church. Marion Gilman was required to leave the island for Hong Kong or

Canton whenever the examinations for Confucian scholars were scheduled, lest the presence of a foreign woman in the capital city incite a riot. Eventually the missionaries were permitted to purchase a house and land that had belonged to a German coolie trader; it was adjacent to the British consulate on the coast in Hoihow (Haikou). The missionaries were also permitted to purchase land for their mission in the adjoining capital city of Kiungchow (Ch'iungshan), between the execution ground and the cemetery—a site thought by the Chinese to be very unlucky.

Gilman disliked being carried by sedan chair and preferred not to ride the small local horses, so he became known on Hainan as the foreigner who traveled extensively on foot. Periodically he journeyed to the interior sites of Nodoa (Nada), established as a mission station in 1888, and Kachek (Jiaji), established in 1900, as well as to the mountains, where the Miao practiced slash-and-burn agriculture.

Gilman published an article about Hainan and its people in the *Chinese Recorder* in 1890, and for several years after 1891 the Gilmans lived at the Nodoa station before being reassigned to Hoihow/Kiungchow. Gilman made frequent trips to the nearby Liuchow (Liuchou) peninsula on the China mainland, where he wanted to establish mission stations, but the hope was never realized due to a shortage of funds at the Board of Foreign Missions in New York. Gilman baptized several hundred converts, but because relatively few Chinese were interested in Christianity at the time of his death, the church in Hainan still counted fewer than 2,000 members.

Described by his colleagues as an extremely patient man who could find good in every person, Gilman also had a reputation for being a capable mediator and on at least one occasion was summoned by French Roman Catholic missionaries who also worked on Hainan to settle a dispute they were having with the local Chinese officials. Fluent in Hainanese, Gilman was well liked by many Chinese, both Christian and non-Christian, and earned for himself the Chinese nickname "Uncle Good."

Marion Gilman died in Sonyea, New York, in September 1899 while her husband was in Hainan. In 1903 Gilman married Mary Martin White, the widow of a Canton missionary, in Amsterdam, New York. They then returned to Hainan to continue their work. No children were born to this marriage, and the second Mrs. Gilman died in 1917 in Hackensack, New Jersey. Gilman's daughter Janet joined him as a missionary in Hainan in 1917.

When Chinese troops, engaged in fighting that was part of the aftermath of the 1911 republican revolution, tried in 1918 to enter the mission compound at Hoihow, the missionaries disarmed them. After sitting atop the compound wall and handing their weapons to the British consul, Gilman jumped down, injuring his knee. He died at Hoihow three days later, presumably from a blood clot.

• Gilman's papers, letters, and diaries are at the Presbyterian Historical Society in Philadelphia. His article, "Hainan and Missionary Work" appeared in the *Chinese Recorder* 21 (1890): 271–80, and an obituary is in the *Chinese Recorder* 50 (1918): 68 and 480.

KATHLEEN L. LODWICK

GILMAN, John Taylor (19 Dec. 1753–31 Aug. 1828), merchant, treasurer, and governor of New Hampshire, was born in Exeter, New Hampshire, the son of Nicholas Gilman, a shipbuilder, merchant, and state treasurer, and Ann Taylor. Following his education in the local schools, Gilman learned the businesses of shipbuilding and finance from his father. Throughout his life he resided in Exeter; there he married Deborah Folsom in 1776, and the couple would have three children.

Gilman went with the militia to Lexington, Massachusetts, in April 1775 but served in the military only briefly. When the Declaration of Independence arrived in Exeter in July 1776, Gilman read it aloud from the town square. He represented Exeter in the state legislature—known as the General Court—from 1779 to 1781, and he was a member of the state's Committee of Safety, which functioned as the executive body during legislative recesses. In addition, Gilman served as New Hampshire's delegate to the Hartford Convention of New England states in 1780. This meeting, to discuss land embargoes in New England, evaluation of currencies, war emergencies, and defense tactics, followed a 1779 meeting in Hartford and preceded a 1781 meeting in Providence. The General Court also elected Gilman to represent New Hampshire in the Continental Congress by resolutions of 15 January 1782 and 14 September 1782, and he served there from June 1782 through March 1783. There he was, according to contemporary William Plumer, the youngest delegate. When his father died in the spring of 1783, Gilman accepted the legislature's appointment to the position of state treasurer.

From the family house in Exeter, which included a vault that served as the state's treasury, Gilman executed this office until 1788. From then until 1791 he served on the federal board of commissioners for settling accounts between the federal government and individual states. In 1788 Exeter elected him to the convention considering ratification of the Federal Constitution. Gilman voted with the majority, making New Hampshire the ninth and deciding state to put the Constitution in force on 21 June. In 1791 Gilman resumed his former duties as state treasurer serving under Governor Josiah Bartlett. That same year his wife died, and in 1792 he married Mary Folsom Adams; they had no children. In the early 1790s Gilman also served as a selectman of Exeter and in later years as the town moderator. He was the leader of a group of prominent citizens, including Jeremiah Smith, Oliver Peabody, and Samuel Tenney, known as the Exeter Junto, one of whose purposes was the support of Federalism. During his years as federal commissioner, and later as governor, his younger brother Nicholas

Gilman maintained the state treasury within the Gilman family.

In 1794 Bartlett declined another term as governor, instead supporting Gilman for the post. Gilman was elected that year and was reelected to consecutive one-year terms until 1805. A staunch Federalist, he apparently seldom swerved from that course as governor. During this time the state's economy prospered. He oversaw the refurbishment of Fort William and Mary in Portsmouth harbor, the completion of the naval ship *Crescent*, and the addition of the medical school to Dartmouth College in 1798. He also maintained that taxes should remain at wartime levels so that state services and military defenses could be strengthened.

Around 1800 local issues, particularly banking, served to consolidate an opposition party centered in Portsmouth. Gilman's bank, the New Hampshire Bank, was the only chartered bank in the state, and Gilman used his powers as governor to maintain that exclusivity. Eventually this group, wanting reforms in banking and tax legislation, succeeded in electing John Langdon to the governorship in 1805.

After his defeat Gilman continued his business in Exeter. He returned to the legislature, by then sitting permanently in Concord, for the sessions of 1810 and 1811. Following a spirited debate led by Gilman in the House regarding the foreign policy of President James Madison, the Federalists consolidated behind Gilman's candidacy for governor in 1812. Defeated by William Plumer, Gilman rallied to win the governorship in 1813, 1814, and 1815. He also served as an elector on the presidential ticket of the Peace party in New Hampshire in 1812, only to witness the defeat of candidate DeWitt Clinton. In 1813, owing largely to the growing ineptness of the court system under a series of Republican appointees, the Federalists, having won control of the legislature and having Gilman in place as governor, revised the court system by eliminating many judicial positions and creating new ones to which Gilman dutifully appointed Federalist supporters. Although philosophically opposed to war with England, Gilman supported the military effort once war was declared. He intended to send delegates to the Hartford Convention in December 1814, but the Republican-dominated Executive Council blocked authorization for the delegates to attend. His second wife having died in 1812, he married Charlotte Peabody Hamilton in 1814.

Gilman retired from the governorship in June 1816, about a year after Dartmouth College president John Wheelock had precipitated a dispute about turning the college into a university. As governor, Gilman had served as an ex officio trustee of the college, and in 1807 he had been elected to the board in his own right. In 1815 he appointed a commission of three Federalist legislators to investigate the matter. As a trustee of the college he remained neutral through the legal controversy, giving up his trusteeship only after the dispute was settled in 1819. Gilman also served as a trustee of Phillips Exeter Academy from 1795 to 1827, including

a term as president of the board, and in later years he donated land to the school.

Gilman died in Exeter, having assured himself a respectable place in both state and national history by his diligent attention to detail while holding many public offices of trust. The Society of the Cincinnati maintains the Gilman house in Exeter.

• There is no known collection of Gilman's papers, although many official documents that he signed as governor are part of the New Hampshire State Archives (Division of Records Management and Archives) in Concord. Papers referencing him are among The Papers of the Continental Congress Collection, National Archives and Records Administration, Washington, D.C. Gilman receives significant attention in Arthur Gilman, *The Gilman Family Traced in the Line of Hon. John Gilman, of Exeter, NH* (1869); Alexander W. Gillman, *Searches into the History of the Gillman or Gilman Family* (1895); and Charles H. Bell, *History of the Town of Exeter* (1888); but very little in Robbins Paxson Gilman, *The Old Logg House by the Bridge* (1985). A contemporary and complete biographical portrait of Gilman, written by William Plumer, is in the Plumer papers at the New Hampshire State Library in Concord, as well as in the Library of Congress; it was printed in Nathaniel Bouton et al., eds., *The New Hampshire State Papers* (40 vols., 1867–1940). Gilman plays a prominent role in Lynn Warren Turner, *The Ninth State: New Hampshire's Formative Years* (1983), which deals principally with the period 1785 to 1820, the prime of Gilman's career. Treatments of specific periods may be found in W. F. Whitcher, "New Hampshire in the Continental Congress and in the Congress of the Confederation," *Granite Monthly*, June 1883, pp. 275–81, and Mark D. Kaplanoff, "Religion and Righteousness: A Study of Federalist Rhetoric in the New Hampshire Election of 1800," *Historical New Hampshire* 23 (Winter 1968): 3–20.

FRANK C. MEVERS

GILMAN, Lawrence (5 July 1878–8 Sept. 1939), music critic and scholar, was born in the Flushing section of Queens, New York, the son of Arthur Coit Gilman, a tea and coffee broker, and Bessie Lawrence. Gilman was educated in the New York public schools. As a boy he learned to play piano and organ. His formal training was not in music but rather in art at the Collins Street Classical School in Hartford, Connecticut. In 1896 Gilman launched a journalistic career, working as an illustrator for the *New York Herald*. During his free time he taught himself music theory, composition, and orchestration. In 1901 Gilman joined the staff of *Harper's Weekly*. Here he began writing music criticism and also served from 1903 to 1911 as the assistant editor and from 1911 to 1913 as managing editor. In 1915 Gilman moved on to the *North American Review*, where he wrote drama, literary, and music criticism.

Between 1904 and 1915 Gilman wrote several influential books on contemporary music. The new and dramatic innovations in form and harmony exhibited by such composers as Arnold Schoenberg and Igor Stravinsky seemed to bifurcate the music world. Many critics reflected the conservative tastes of their readers. This hardened lines between composers and audiences; the majority rejected the moderns and turned almost exclusively to the past. Never before had this been the case in the world of concert music. Gilman sought to bridge this gap of sensibility and tried to explain contemporary music to audiences he knew to be apprehensive. In *Phases of Modern Music* (1904) and *The Music of Tomorrow* (1907), Gilman extolled the virtues of many innovators, demonstrating how their breakthroughs were achieved by building on the treasures of the past rather than by discarding them. As one who came to music via training in other arts, Gilman valued music that expressed extramusical ideas and philosophies. This was evidenced by his enthusiasm for the music of Richard Wagner, Richard Strauss, and Claude Debussy. Gilman was particularly lucid in three explications and analyses of new operas: *Debussy's "Pelléas and Mélisande"* (1907), *Strauss's Salome* (1907), and *Aspects of Modern Opera* (1909). Later he wrote a highly regarded study of Wagner entitled *Wagner's Operas* (1937).

Gilman also wrote *Edward MacDowell: A Study* (1908), the first work to promote the neglected American master, a man Gilman knew and greatly admired. A striking feature of Gilman's writings on his contemporaries is that virtually all of the composers he championed have come to be regarded as giants. Very few he praised have turned out to be lesser figures; his instincts were remarkable.

Gilman wrote some music himself, but it was not of the highest quality, as he readily admitted. However, his piano pieces and songs, notably several settings of the new poetry of William Butler Yeats (another artist whose greatness Gilman anticipated), underscored his efforts at promoting the modern artistic styles, which he felt the public need neither fear nor disdain. Through his music Gilman also promoted art that grappled with the complexities of modern life rather than merely seeking escape through superficial beauty or the indulgence of ego. Gilman's quest to render art an interpretation of modern life came forth in his other musical analysis and criticism. He wrote the program notes for the concerts of the New York Philharmonic from 1921 to 1939. During the 1930s he broadcast several important radio programs, thus becoming one of the first regular commentators of musical performances and recordings.

Gilman's importance lies chiefly in his position as one of the leading music critics of his day. In addition to writing for the *North American Review*, Gilman was the chief music critic for the *New York Herald Tribune*, a post he held from 1923 to 1939. He scrutinized both the moderns and the classics, with his ear always attuned to the composers' and performers' ability to communicate and not merely express. This emphasis on communication over expression was critical in Gilman's desire to ensure that modern artists and audiences did not ignore one another. To that end in music the performer was crucial. Here Gilman's praise of Arturo Toscanini was effusive. He wrote of the maestro's "mysterious and inexplicable power of communication." Some felt this was a reflection of Gilman's own strength as a critic. His prose always revealed great care. His interpretations were sensitive to history as well as to music itself. Many contemporary composers gained greater popularity through Gilman's efforts to push the public ever forward aesthetically, efforts that he continued until his death at his summer home in Sugar Hill, New Hampshire.

• There is no biography of Gilman. Gilman, *Toscanini and Great Music* (1938), is a collection of some of his best music reviews. His monographic works are valuable explications of early twentieth-century music. More broadly chronological in scope are three works by Gilman intended for the general symphony listener, *Nature in Music and Other Studies* (1914), *Orchestral Music: An Armchair Guide* (1951), and *Stories of Symphonic Music* (1907).

ALAN LEVY

GILMAN, Nicholas (3 Aug. 1755–2 May 1814), congressman and senator, was born in Exeter, New Hampshire, the son of Nicholas Gilman, a merchant, and Ann Taylor. He received a common school education and until 1776 worked in his father's store. In November 1776 Gilman was commissioned regimental adjutant in the Third New Hampshire Regiment of the Continental Line, with Colonel Alexander Scammell commanding. When Scammell became Continental Adjutant General in January 1778, Gilman became assistant adjutant general; in June he was made a captain. Gilman transferred to the First New Hampshire Regiment on 1 January 1781 and served until war's end in 1783. That same year he was a founder of the Society of the Cincinnati.

Gilman returned to the family store in Exeter, but in 1785 he formed a mercantile partnership with James McClure to establish a wholesale store in Baltimore, Maryland. The business failed quickly. A member of a prominent political family, Gilman turned to politics, becoming a professional politician. He resided in Exeter and never married.

The New Hampshire legislature appointed Gilman a delegate to the Confederation Congress in June 1786, but he did not attend. In September Gilman commanded a company of volunteers in Exeter that helped to rout a mob of insurgents trying to intimidate state legislators into issuing paper money. In January 1787 he was appointed state adjutant general with the rank of brigadier general, a position he held until 1789. In June 1787 Gilman was named a delegate to the Constitutional Convention, called to meet in Philadelphia to revise and amend the Articles of Confederation. Gilman attended the Convention on 23 July, about two months after it had convened. A fellow delegate described him as "modest, genteel, and sensible," without anything "brilliant or striking in his character." Gilman, who did not take part in the debates, favored a strong central government, with Congress having exclusive power over commerce, and he opposed the assumption of the state debts. He was on the grand committee on unfinished business and signed the Constitution.

Reelected to Congress in June 1787, Gilman voted in late September 1787 to transmit the Constitution to the states. From this time until November 1788 Gilman, reappointed to Congress again in June 1788, attended that body regularly. In particular, he kept New Hampshire's political leaders informed about the progress of the ratification of the Constitution. His many letters illustrate his impatience with extremists on both sides. Gilman especially feared that if the Constitution was not ratified, America would "probably pursue the track of nations that have gone before us and establish a Government or Governments by the sword and seal it with blood." When he ended his stay in Congress, the modest, sensible young man of the Constitutional Convention had become "a pretentious young man," disliked by his colleagues. A political enemy later described him as "proud, haughty, and overbearing" and one who "flattered the meanest of voters" when seeking reelection.

In January 1789 Gilman was elected to the U.S. House of Representatives. He was reelected three more times, serving until 1797. In eight years he made only one recorded speech, but he was an active committee man. A supporter of President George Washington, Gilman had an independent streak that sometimes pitted him against the Federalist party, of which he was a moderate member. He favored the establishment of the Bank of the United States and an extensive network of federal courts but opposed assumption of state debts and Jay's Treaty. Attuned to the interests of his constituents, Gilman supported commercial legislation benefitting New Hampshire. He beat back an attempt to prevent Exeter from being the site of a federal district court but failed to stop Exeter's removal from the general route of the post. Fearful that New England might lose influence, Gilman opposed the creation of new states in the West and even voted against providing funds for the defense of the region, although he was an acknowledged expert on military matters.

By 1796 Gilman's independence had so alienated his Federalist constituents that he did not seek reelection. Even Gilman's brother, John Taylor, the popular Federalist governor, could not help him. Gilman drifted toward the Republican party, and in 1802 Republican president Thomas Jefferson appointed him a commissioner of bankruptcy for the district of New Hampshire under the federal bankruptcy act of 1800. New Hampshire's Republican party nominated him to run for the U.S. Senate in 1802, but he was defeated by arch-enemy Federalist William Plumer, whom Gilman publicly accused of fraudulently obtaining election. Gilman became president of the New Hampshire Senate in June 1804, resigning that position in December upon being elected to the U.S. Senate as a Republican. He was narrowly reelected in 1810, after refusing a nomination to be the state's governor.

Initially a supporter of Jefferson, Gilman became one of the President's critics, opposing both the embargo and enforcement acts. From the beginning, Gilman criticized the administration of Republican president James Madison and was one of the "malcontent" Republican senators who often embarrassed Madison.

In June 1812 Gilman was among the few Republican senators who voted against the motion for immediate and unrestricted war against Great Britain, and later that year he supported De Witt Clinton for president against Madison. In 1814 Gilman died in Philadelphia returning to his New Hampshire home from Washington, D.C., an opponent of Madison's war policies to the end.

• The papers of the Gilman family are in the Massachusetts Historical Society and Phillips Exeter Academy. Many of Gilman letters are in vol. 8 of *Letters of Members of the Continental Congress*, ed. Edmund C. Burnett (1936); *The Documentary History of the Ratification of the Constitution*, eds. John P. Kaminski and Gaspare J. Saladino, vols. 13–18 (1981–1995); and *The Papers of Josiah Bartlett*, ed. Frank C. Mevers (1979). The fullest biography is in *Documentary History of the First Federal Congress*, eds. William Charles diGiacomantonio et al., vol. 14 (1995). Also useful is the sketch by William Plumer in the *Early State Papers of New Hampshire*, ed. Albert Stillman Batchellor, vol. 21 (1892). For Gilman's mercantile pursuits, see Elwin L. Page, "Two Sea Captains of Exeter," *Historical New Hamshire*, June 1945, pp. 7–28. For his politics, see Lynn Warren Turner, *The Ninth State: New Hampshire's Formative Years* (1983); and J. C. A. Stagg, *Mr. Madison's War* (1983).

GASPARE J. SALADINO

GILMAN, Samuel Foster (16 Feb. 1791–9 Feb. 1858), clergyman and author, was born in Gloucester, Massachusetts, the son of Frederick Gilman and Abigail Hillier Somer, merchant investors. The family lost a substantial part of its fortune as a result of French depredations on American shipping during the Quasi-War with France, 1798–1800. After the death of his father, young Samuel was placed in the home of Stephen Peabody, a Congregational clergyman of Arminian theology and the brother-in-law of President John Adams (1735–1826), to prepare for college. (In later years, Gilman gently satirized Peabody in "Reminiscences Pertaining to a New-England Clergyman . . . " [1847]). Gilman attended Harvard College and was graduated in 1811. For the next few years he worked in a bank, taught school, and contributed pieces to the *North American Review*. In 1817 he returned to Harvard where he tutored mathematics and read Unitarian divinity in preparation for a career in the ministry. In 1819 he married Caroline Howard (Caroline Howard Gilman), also a writer.

The same year Gilman accepted a call to minister to the Second Independent Church (renamed the Archdale Street Unitarian Church in 1834) in Charleston, South Carolina, the only Unitarian congregation in the state. Unitarianism in Charleston, as in New England, represented the outcome of a gradual liberalization of Calvinist theology within the urban merchant and professional community. This Charleston community included a number of men of New England birth who organized a local "New England Society" that Gilman joined. In South Carolina, unlike New England, the urban merchant and professional class was overshadowed by the great landowners. Caroline Gilman accurately described her husband's congregation as "highly respectable, but engrossing little of the fashions and aristocracy of the place." The merchants of Charleston deferred to the political leadership of the plantation owners and avoided discussion of slavery. Within the constraints imposed by this context, Samuel Gilman sought for almost forty years to re-create something like the moral and cultural leadership that Unitarian clergy practiced in his New England home. He defended rationalism, tolerance, and cosmopolitanism in a setting where these values were suspect.

Gilman's writings display the range of a nineteenth-century gentleman of letters. They include poetry and humor, philosophy, theology, and literary criticism, translations from the classics and temperance tracts. The best are invocations of New England local color, such as *Memoirs of a New England Village Choir* (1829). His "Union Ode" (1831) was provoked by the nullification crisis. Despite his persistent Unionism, Gilman also wrote the ode sung at the funeral of John C. Calhoun in 1850. He contributed to the *Southern Literary Messenger* and the *Southern Quarterly Review* as well as to the Unitarian organ, the *Christian Examiner*. In 1848 he delivered the Dudleian Lecture on Revealed Religion at Harvard.

Samuel and Caroline Gilman bridged the worlds of New England moralism and South Carolina aestheticism. Of the little band of Yankee missionaries who tried to nurture the Unitarian denomination in the antebellum South, they were the most successful. Exercising discretion as well as cultural leadership, they identified themselves with their adopted city and section. Together, they were respected as the leading literary lights of Charleston; the Gilman house there is still preserved. Among their five children was Caroline Howard Gilman Glover Jervey, author of *Vernon Grove* (1859) and other works. Samuel Gilman died unexpectedly at Kingston, Massachusetts, while visiting his son-in-law.

His most famous poem, "Fair Harvard," was composed when he and his wife attended the celebration of the Harvard bicentennial in 1836, at the home of Caroline's sister Harriet Fay in what is now the Radcliffe Yard. The occasion brought out the best in Gilman's literary talent, and the lyric (set to the music of Thomas Moore's "Believe Me If All Those Endearing Young Charms") became the university alma mater. The song, in marking Harvard's transition "from the age that is past to the age that is waiting before," typifies Gilman's combination of respect for tradition with open-mindedness and tolerance. The close of the first stanza, a paean to "calm rising through change and through storm," exemplifies the author's value system. As both writer and literary critic, Gilman exemplified the standards of what was called the philosophy of common sense.

• The Samuel Gilman Papers in the Harvard University Archives include reading notes and drafts for uncompleted work. Gilman's principal writings are collected in his *Contributions to Literature* (1856) and *Contributions to Religion* (1860). See Daniel Walker Howe, "A Massachusetts Yankee in Senator Calhoun's Court: Samuel Gilman in South Carolina," *New England Quarterly* 44 (1971): 197–220; *Unitarian Historical Society Proceedings* 17, no. 2 (1973–1975): 45–72; and William B. Sprague, *Annals of the American Pulpit*, vol. 8 (1865). Obituaries are in the *Charleston Daily Courier*, 11 Feb. 1858, and the *New York Tribune*, 13 Feb. 1858.

DANIEL WALKER HOWE

GILMER, Elizabeth Meriwether. *See* Dix, Dorothy.

GILMER, Francis Walker (9 Oct. 1790–25 Feb. 1826), lawyer, scholar, and author, was born at "Pen Park," Albemarle County, Virginia, the son of Dr. George Gilmer, a prominent and well-educated local physician, and Lucy Walker. Dr. Gilmer died in 1795, and Lucy Gilmer died in 1800, leaving their ten children as orphans. Francis, the youngest in the family, remained in Albemarle, shuttled as a child from one local family to another. Consequently, he was largely self-educated, having read widely in the classics, science, and other disciplines under the guidance of a number of his father's friends and neighbors, including Martha Jefferson Randolph. He also came under the influence of the brilliant eccentric, James Ogilvie, a traveling Scottish educator and orator whose instruction greatly influenced Gilmer's own view of and contributions to the field of forensics.

After attending school briefly in Georgetown, D.C., Gilmer entered the College of William and Mary in 1809 and graduated the following year. He then read law in Richmond, Virginia, under the direction of his brother-in-law and lifelong friend and mentor, William Wirt, one of the state's premier attorneys. During this period he also joined a group of aspiring attorneys in Virginia's capital city in a moot court society organized by Chancellor Creed Taylor.

For a time Gilmer considered practicing law in Kentucky, but on the advice of friends he remained in the east. He moved to Winchester, Virginia, where he began his legal career solidly but half-heartedly. Although always feeble in health, he briefly joined an artillery regiment raised by Wirt during the War of 1812, but he spent more of his time with a new friend, the Abbé Jose Francisco Correa de Serra, a Portuguese philosopher, scientist, and diplomat to whom he was introduced by his father's old friend, Thomas Jefferson. Although nearly fifty years separated the two men in age, they shared mutual interests, especially in the field of botany, and began traveling through the eastern United States together. Correa brought Gilmer into learned society, most notably in Philadelphia, where the young man acquitted himself well. Later, the two joined Jefferson at his Bedford County, Virginia, home, "Poplar Forest," for continued studies and discussion and then visited the Cherokee Country in the Carolinas and Georgia. From observations made on that trip, Gilmer would later compose a lengthy article, "Reflections on the Institutions of the Cherokee Indians . . . ," a piece rather critical of the culture of the Native Americans that appeared in the *Analetic Magazine* in 1818.

Upon his return to Winchester in 1815, Gilmer settled into law practice and began to develop a strong local reputation. He also devoted time to other pursuits, including the composition of an essay, "On the Geological Formation of the Natural Bridge of Virginia," read before the American Philosophical Society in February 1816, and a book, *Sketches of American Orators*, published anonymously in Baltimore in 1816 but widely recognized at the time as Gilmer's handiwork. Appended to his observations of the lives, careers, and oratorical styles of such prominent attorneys and public figures as John Marshall, Thomas Addis Emmett, William Pinckney, and Patrick Henry, Gilmer's own remarks on oratory and the practice of law in this volume advanced a theme held commonly by a small circle of intellectuals (including Wirt, Jefferson's nephew Chancellor Dabney Carr, and another brilliant eccentric, John Randolph of Roanoke) that the postrevolutionary leaders had fallen short of the standard set by the founders of the nation and that Virginia in particular was losing its power and influence in national councils as a consequence. A skilled orator, though one who preferred an overwhelming grasp of facts and theory presented in a crisply logical and articulate manner to other rhetorical techniques, Gilmer himself refused to enter politics, convinced that dividing his attention between two professions might damage his reputation as a premier advocate at the bar. Ever an unrelenting critic of friend and foe alike, Gilmer was equally hard on himself, convinced that he had a great potential always yet to be fully realized.

After toying briefly with the idea of moving to the prosperous seaport town of Baltimore, Gilmer relocated to Richmond to pursue his law practice. With Wirt's appointment in November 1817 as U.S. attorney general, the younger man took over much of his mentor's legal business and quickly found himself in comfortable circumstances. He again turned his attention to letters, publishing editions of John Smith's *General Historie of Virginia* and *True Travels* in Richmond in 1819 and the following year anonymously issuing his *Vindication of the Laws, Limiting the Rate of Interest on Loans*. In the latter, according to Jefferson, he successfully took to task both Jeremy Bentham and his own local nemesis, attorney George Hay.

A pronounced critic of earlier court reporters, Gilmer accepted the job of gathering and editing the arguments in and decisions of Virginia's Court of Appeals and General Court in 1820 but tired of the task within a year or so. In the meantime, he also began work on a new edition of his *Sketches of American Orators*, which appeared posthumously as *Sketches, Essays, and Translations* (1828) and included new or revised observations of the careers of John Randolph of Roanoke and Henry Clay, along with a translation from the French of Francois Quesnay's treatise on natural rights.

During the last years of Gilmer's short life he helped Thomas Jefferson establish the University of Virginia in their native Albemarle County. Although Gilmer's concerns about his failing health caused him on three occasions to decline the offer of the first law professorship in the university, he did agree to serve as Jefferson's personal representative in Europe in 1824 to procure books, supplies, and professors for the new school. These tasks Gilmer completed successfully, to the great relief and pleasure of the university's patron, but at the cost of his own fragile health. After returning to America and realizing that he no longer had the strength to practice law actively, Gilmer finally accepted the law professorship but never set foot in the classroom. He died at "Farmington," a few miles west of the site of Mr. Jefferson's university, having never married.

In a frequently quoted letter to Benjamin Rush, Jefferson once called Francis Gilmer "the best-educated subject we have raised since the Revolution, highly qualified in all the important branches of science, professing particularly that of law." Although he accomplished much in his short life, his consistently poor health kept Gilmer from realizing fully the great promise of his own talents and relentless quest for learning.

• A number of small but significant collections of Gilmer's papers are at the University of Virginia Library in Charlottesville, in the personal papers collection of the Library of Virginia in Richmond, and at the Virginia Historical Society in Richmond. Two large groups of letters are contained in the Thomas Jefferson Papers at the Library of Congress and in the William Wirt Papers at the Maryland Historical Society in Baltimore. Richard Beale Davis's dated but sound biography, *Francis Walker Gilmer: Life and Learning in Jefferson's Virginia* (1939), remains the most valuable treatment of Gilmer's life, which can be supplemented by Michael A. Lofaro's brief but useful sketch in *The Virginia Law Reporters before 1880*, ed. W. H. Bryson (1977). Gilmer's role as Jefferson's educational emissary on behalf of the University of Virginia is the best-covered aspect of his career: see Dumas Malone, *Jefferson and His Time: The Sage of Monticello* (1981); Philip A. Bruce, *The History of the University of Virginia, 1819–1919: The Lengthened Shadow of One Man*, vols. 1–2 (1920–1922); William P. Trent, *English Culture in Virginia: A Study of the Gilmer Letters . . .* (1889); and Davis, ed., *The Correspondence of Thomas Jefferson and Francis Walker Gilmer, 1814–1826* (1946). On Gilmer's literary endeavors, see also Davis, *Intellectual Life in Jefferson's Virginia* (1964). An obituary notice, probably written by John H. Rice, appears in *Literary and Evangelical Magazine* 9 (1826): 269; *Sketches, Essays, and Translations* (1828) contains a memoir of Gilmer purportedly written by William Wirt.

E. LEE SHEPARD

GILMER, John Adams (4 Nov. 1805–14 May 1868), state senator and U.S. and Confederate congressman, was born in Guilford County, North Carolina, the son of Robert Gilmer, a farmer and wheelwright, and Anne Forbes. Both parents were of Scotch-Irish descent; their families had come from Ireland to North Carolina via Pennsylvania. His father and both grandfathers fought against the British in the American Revolution. John Adams Gilmer's name reflected his father's Federalist political predilections. Young Gilmer worked on the family farm and attended a local subscription school a few months during the winter. When he was nineteen, he enrolled in the Reverend Eli W. Caruther's school in Greensboro, where he excelled in classical languages and mathematics. For three years afterward (1826–1829), he taught school in Laurel County, South Carolina, to pay debts resulting from his education. In 1829 he returned to Greensboro to study law in the office of Archibald D. Murphey. In 1832 he married Juliana Paisley; they had six children, five of whom survived childhood. One son, John Alexander Gilmer, became a Confederate lieutenant colonel and superior court judge. Also in 1832 Gilmer was admitted to the bar, and he gradually built a lucrative practice. He was listed in the 1860 census as an agriculturalist and lawyer who owned fifty-three slaves and property valued at $112,000.

Gilmer served as chairman of the Greensboro Town Board and as county solicitor, then in 1846 he was elected as a Whig to represent Guilford County in the North Carolina Senate. He held that position for ten years. A man of moral and intellectual probity, he quickly became a leader in the legislature. He spoke eloquently in support of humanitarian reforms, such as the establishment of an asylum for the insane. He promoted improvements in the public schools and was especially active in planning state-sponsored internal improvements. He was instrumental in routing the North Carolina Railroad from Raleigh to Charlotte through Greensboro and became a large stockholder in the corporation that built and operated the railroad.

In 1856 Gilmer, who had joined the American or Know Nothing party after the demise of Whiggery, ran for governor against the incumbent Democrat Thomas Bragg. He stumped the state but was badly beaten; however, his popularity actually rose. He was elected to the U.S. House of Representatives in 1857 and 1859. Long concerned about the consequences of the slavery imbroglio, Adams became a leader of the southern Unionists in Congress who opposed antislavery and proslavery agitators. His vote against the Lecompton constitution, which would have allowed slavery in Kansas, alienated some North Carolinians, but the congressional district he represented was uncommonly liberal on the slavery issue because of Quaker and Wesley Methodist antislavery sentiment therein. When the House Speakership was disputed in 1859–1860, Gilmer was the candidate of the "South Americans," the Know Nothings of the South, but he never polled more than thirty-six votes. Because of his moderation on the slavery issue, southern Democrats considered him little better than an abolitionist. He sought to minimize the slavery issue during his unsuccessful campaign for the Speakership, and consequently his reputation as a southern Unionist was firmly established. In the election of 1860 Gilmer joined other conservative men in the abortive attempt of the Constitutional Unionists to preserve the Union.

The election of Abraham Lincoln presented Gilmer and Unionists of all sections with vexing prospects. Even before South Carolina seceded on 20 December 1860, steps were proposed to forestall widespread disunion. On 10 December 1860 Gilmer wrote Lincoln seeking a clarification of his views on slavery in hopes of reassuring the South that the president-elect antici-

pated no interference where slavery already existed. Lincoln declined to provide additional clarification lest he appear to repent for the "crime" of gaining election "and was anxious to apologize and beg forgiveness." Instead he urged Gilmer and other southern suppliants to reconsider their previous pronouncements on the slavery issue and clearly reiterated his firm commitment to free soilism. Meanwhile, William H. Seward and Thurlow Weed implored Lincoln to include a respected Upper South Unionist in his cabinet as a means of strengthening unionism in the slave states. Gilmer was prominent among those suggested, and Lincoln invited him to Springfield to discuss the national dilemma and a cabinet appointment. Without a prior meeting of minds, Gilmer declined to visit Springfield, but he continued to seek ways to preserve the Union. On 26 January 1861 he delivered a powerful speech in the U.S. House of Representatives pleading for compromise. In February 1861, when North Carolina voters considered the call for a convention to debate secession, Gilmer sent thousands of copies of his speech to the state at his own expense. His efforts helped temporarily stem the secessionist tide. On 28 February 1861 North Carolinians narrowly defeated the call for a convention. Gilmer also supported the Union by embracing and promoting the Crittenden compromise. Its failure increased his despair.

Throughout the weeks before and after Lincoln's inauguration, Gilmer corresponded with Seward and encouraged the New Yorker to pursue his conciliatory policy toward the South. Gilmer advised the abandonment of Forts Sumter and Pickens, predicting prophetically that a clash of arms would provoke secession in the Upper South. All Gilmer's efforts failed, and after the firing on Fort Sumter he faced the dilemma of all southern Unionists. As a delegate to the North Carolina secession convention, with his son already in Confederate uniform, he decided that his only option was to join the majority who, after rejection of a proposal that separation be based on the right of revolution, voted for disunion.

Gilmer took no active part in public affairs prior to his election to the Confederate Congress in August 1863. By that juncture, particularly in light of Confederate defeats at Gettysburg and Vicksburg, the prospects for Confederate survival were dim. The North Carolina delegation, including Gilmer, was strongly antiadministration, but he did not support his colleague James T. Leach's proposal that the quest for independence be abandoned. Instead he agreed with Governor Zebulon B. Vance that honor required North Carolina to persist in the war effort so long as feasible. Gilmer opposed the 1864 gubernatorial candidacy of William W. Holden, who ran on the proposition that the state should seek a separate peace. Gilmer did have hopes that the Hampton Roads conference on 3 February 1865 might result in peace with independence. When those hopes were dashed, he proposed a dual government or "American diet," in which separate United States and Confederate governments would function independently but in a coordinated manner. This idea gained little support. Late in the war Gilmer became identified with those who wished to continue fighting to the bitter end, when most North Carolinians favored a negotiated peace.

After the war Gilmer remained in Greensboro practicing law and caring for his former slaves, whom he supplied with land, food, farm implements, and medical care. He favored Andrew Johnson's Reconstruction policies, received his presidential pardon late in 1865, and attended the National Union, which met in Philadelphia in August 1866. Subsequently his health deteriorated, and he died in Greensboro.

Gilmer is little known to late twentieth-century scholars, but it should be remembered that he worked valiantly to save the Union. Perhaps all such efforts were doomed to failure. Had he become a Lincoln cabinet member, the fears of the Upper South might have been assuaged, and North Carolina, Tennessee, Arkansas, and Virginia might have remained loyal to the United States.

• No substantial collection of Gilmer papers exists, but two Gilmer letters are in the North Carolina State Archives, Raleigh. Other important letters are in Frederic Bancroft, *The Life of Seward*, vol. 2 (1899; repr. 1967); *The Collected Works of Abraham Lincoln*, vol. 4, ed. Roy B. Basler (1953); and *The Papers of William A. Graham*, vol. 5, ed. J. G. deRoulhac Hamilton and Max R. Williams (1973). Notable secondary accounts are Daniel W. Crofts, *Reluctant Confederates . . .* (1989); Marc W. Kruman, *Parties and Politics in North Carolina . . .* (1983); Joseph Carlyle Sitterson, *The Secession Movement in North Carolina* (1939); and Wilfred B. Yearns, *The Confederate Congress* (1960).

MAX R. WILLIAMS

GILMER, Thomas Walker (6 Apr. 1802–28 Feb. 1844), politician, was born in Albemarle County, Virginia, the son of George Gilmer, a planter, and Elizabeth Anderson Hudson. Gilmer was privately educated and studied law under his uncle Peachy R. Gilmer. He moved to Missouri in 1823 to practice law, but his father's insolvency led him to return the following year to Charlottesville, where he passed the Virginia bar and set up practice. Gilmer married Ann E. Baker in 1826; they had four sons and two daughters.

A skillful lawyer known for his fine oratory, Gilmer quickly gained prominence in Charlottesville. His support for the African colonization movement, state-funded internal improvements, and reform of the Virginia constitution gradually drew him into the political arena. While still practicing law, Gilmer became one of the editors of the *Charlottesville Central Gazette* in 1825. Two years later he bought the *Gazette*, renamed it the *Advocate*, and strongly supported Andrew Jackson in the 1828 presidential election. He abruptly sold his share of the paper in May 1828, claiming it was not lucrative and prevented him from tending to his legal practice.

In 1829 the voters of Albemarle County elected Gilmer to represent them in the Virginia House of Delegates. He served ably in that capacity and earned the respect of both his constituents and fellow legislators by working tirelessly to improve economic conditions in Virginia. Gilmer also developed a reputation as an outspoken advocate of states' rights. President Jackson's actions during the Nullification Crisis and the Bank War so outraged Gilmer that he abandoned the Democratic party in 1834 and joined the Whigs. This change of political affiliation cost Gilmer his place in the legislature in 1834. He recaptured the seat the following spring, lost it in 1836, and regained it once more in the election of 1838. With the Whigs in control of the House of Delegates, Gilmer was elected Speaker in 1839 and served in that capacity for two sessions. Gilmer's abilities and his growing political influence were recognized when the legislature elected him governor in February 1840.

Gilmer's administration, though short-lived, was marked by activity and controversy. He toured the state at his own expense to inspect its public works and to emphasize the need for Virginia to increase funding for internal improvements. Gilmer also became embroiled in a growing controversy with Governor William Seward of New York. In 1839 Seward refused to extradite three free black sailors from Virginia charged with helping a slave escape from Norfolk. The New Yorker's carefully worded and legalistic explanation for his actions did little to satisfy either outgoing governor David Campbell, who called Seward an abolitionist bent on destroying the Union, or the Virginia legislature, which drafted a series of resolutions condemning Seward and requesting once again the return of the fugitives. One of Gilmer's first official duties as governor was to forward these resolutions to Seward. In his cover letter Gilmer explained that Virginia had a "perfect and exclusive right to regulate her own domestic affairs" and would tolerate no interference from outsiders (*Message of the Governor of Virginia*).

For the next six months Gilmer sent a steady stream of letters to Seward, each one stressing the rights of Virginia and demanding that he return the three fugitives. The New Yorker finally replied in November 1840, again refusing to honor the extradition and explaining in a lengthy letter that his actions were intended to preserve the rights of the citizens of his state and not to interfere in Virginia's affairs. The controversy intensified in early 1841 for two reasons. First, the Virginia legislature appealed to other southern states for support and enacted punitive legislation against New York. More importantly, Gilmer refused to honor an extradition request from Seward for a forger apprehended in Virginia. The forger would be returned to New York, Gilmer explained, only if Seward sent the three black sailors to Virginia first. The legislature did not support Gilmer's bold move to end the crisis. Gilmer interpreted this as a vote of no confidence and resigned in March 1841. The dispute between New York and Virginia continued throughout the 1840s and was never effectively resolved.

If Gilmer's pride had been wounded by the legislature's actions, his political career did not suffer. He was elected to Congress almost immediately, where he was appointed chairman of the Standing Committee of

Ways and Means. During his tenure in Washington, D.C., Gilmer earned a reputation as a fiscal conservative and as the Tyler administration's chief spokesman in the House. His unwavering support for the president was rewarded when John Tyler nominated Gilmer to be secretary of the navy in February 1844. Gilmer had served in this new position for less than two weeks when he was killed in an explosion aboard the U.S. Navy steamer *Princeton* near Washington, D.C.

Gilmer's death cut short a promising political career devoted to rebuilding Virginia and defending the doctrine of states' rights. The Old Dominion lost one of its most powerful leaders and the South one of its ablest and most energetic spokesmen.

• No extension collection of Gilmer's papers exist, but the William Cabell Rives Papers and the John Tyler Papers at the Library of Congress contain numerous letters. An important source is Benjamin Magruder's unpublished sketch, completed in 1853, at the University of Virginia. See also Robert A. Brock, *Virginia and Virginians, 1606–1888*, vol. 1 (1888), pp. 180–94; Lyon G. Tyler, *Letters and Times of the Tylers*, vol. 2 (1885); and M. Boyd Coyner, Jr., "Thomas Walker Gilmer, 1802–1836: Origins of a Virginia Whig" (M.A. thesis, Univ. of Virginia, 1954).

Gilmer's involvement in the dispute with Seward is documented in *Message of the Governor of Virginia, Communicating a Correspondence between the Governors of Virginia and New York, in Relation to Certain Fugitives From Justice* (1840). Paul Finkelman presents a thorough overview of the controversy, and of Gilmer's role in escalating it, in "The Protection of Black Rights in Seward's New York," *Civil War History* 3 (1988): 211–34.

WADE L. SHAFFER

GILMORE, James Roberts (10 Sept. 1822–16 Nov. 1903), author and unofficial envoy for President Abraham Lincoln, was born in Boston, Massachusetts, the son of Turner Fales Gilmore and Mary Ann Roberts. He was educated in Utica, New York, and was preparing for college, but he gave up those preparations to enter business, becoming, at age twenty-five, the director of a very profitable shipping and cotton concern in New York City. In 1857, after many trips to the South, whose society and people he admired, Gilmore was successful enough to retire from business and to devote himself primarily to lecturing and other literary pursuits. He published several articles in the *New-York Tribune*, which brought him into close contact with its famous editor, Horace Greeley. Although Gilmore admired the South, he despised slavery, and when the Civil War broke out in 1861 he decided to launch the *Continental Monthly*, a periodical devoted to the antislavery cause, suspending its publication in 1863 after the Emancipation Proclamation was issued.

While pursuing publication of the *Continental Monthly*, Gilmore dedicated himself to the writing of novels and magazine articles, most of which were based on his own experiences and travels and nearly all of which he published under the pseudonym Edmund Kirke. *Among the Pines; or, South in Secession-Time* (1862) and *My Southern Friends* (1863) chronicle the business travels of Edmund Kirke in the South, where he finds the social fabric being slowly torn asunder by violent overseers and corrupt masters. For instance, *Among the Pines* chronicles the life on "Colonel J——'s" South Carolina plantation, where Kirke finally learns the truth that the plantation matron, "Madam P——," who runs the plantation's domestic concerns for the colonel with grace and gentility, is actually the colonel's slave concubine and has borne him two sons while the colonel's wife purposely absents herself from the plantation to avoid the whole matter. Perhaps the most memorable incident in these novels occurs in *My Southern Friends*. It involves Kirke's son Frank, who falls in love with southern belle Selma Preston only to find out, after the death of the heroine's father, that Selma—in a typical occurrence of the tragic octoroon motif—is in fact a mixed-blood slave. After a closed-door exchange, Selma commits suicide and Frank goes insane. This incident is paired with the tragedy of Mr. Preston, who forces a slave into a miscegenetic affair and then sells their daughter, with whom his young son Joseph unknowingly commits incest when he takes her as his slave mistress. Preston, thus, dies with his son's sin of incest plaguing his conscience.

Gilmore's acquaintanceship with Horace Greeley made him the editor's choice as the *Tribune*'s May 1863 envoy to General William Rosecrans, to see if the general might be a presidential candidate who the paper could support against Lincoln, but the trip proved unfruitful in all but one aspect. It was on this trip that Gilmore met Colonel James Jaquess, the Illinois Methodist parson turned soldier who became convinced that God intended to use him as a minister of peace to persuade Confederate president Jefferson Davis to end the war. Jaquess induced Gilmore to intercede on his behalf with President Lincoln in hopes of securing a furlough allowing him to visit the Confederate president in June 1863. Gilmore did this, but Jaquess's trip was a failure, and he returned from Richmond without having been granted an audience with Davis, ostensibly because the mission was not officially sanctioned by the Union. However, Jaquess enlisted further aid from Gilmore, who, after meeting with Lincoln on Jaquess's behalf, displaced Jaquess as the primary, though still unofficial, emissary, and in July 1864 both Gilmore and Jaquess traveled to Richmond, where they succeeded in meeting with Davis in the Custom House on 17 July. In the September 1864 issue of the *Atlantic Monthly* Gilmore describes what he calls "Our Visit to Richmond" and acknowledges that they journeyed to Richmond because they "hoped to pave the way for negotiations that would result in peace." He repeats much of the same story in the last chapters of his novel *Down in Tennessee, and Back by Way of Richmond* (1864). However, in "A Suppressed Chapter of History," which appeared in the April 1887 issue of the *Atlantic Monthly*, long after the war was won, he admits that a much more politically charged agenda generated the mission. Gilmore explains that in 1864 there was "the universal impression existing at the North that some honorable peace could be made with the South" and that he and Lincoln knew that Davis would refuse even the most generous terms if they excluded the Union's recognition of the South's sovereignty and independence. Hence they plotted to use the meeting (Jaquess's honorable intentions notwithstanding) to extract some such absolute, unequivocal statement from Davis, which Gilmore succeeded in doing. As a result of the trip, Gilmore quickly published Davis's implacable response first as a "card" in the *Boston Evening Transcript* on 22 July and then later in a much more extensive version as "Our Visit to Richmond." Gilmore's most extensive rendition of this episode appears in his *Personal Recollections of Abraham Lincoln and the Civil War* (1898).

After the Civil War, Gilmore found his circumstances considerably reduced. He reentered business in 1873 while maintaining his intense interest in literary and political matters, publishing *The Life of James A. Garfield*, a campaign biography, in 1880, the year he married Laura Edmonds, the daughter of Judge John W. Edmonds of New York. They would have at least one child. Gilmore permanently retired from business in 1883 but continued to devote himself to works on various historical topics such as *The Rear-Guard of the Revolution* (1886) and *John Sevier as a Commonwealth-Builder* (1887) and popular novels such as *A Mountain White Heroine* (1889) and *The Last of the Thorndikes* (1889). Gilmore died in Glens Falls, New York.

Gilmore is not as widely known either for his writing or for his political exploits today as he perhaps was during his lifetime. Lincoln evidently thought enough of him to entrust him with a highly sensitive and potentially explosive mission to Confederate Richmond, and his interview with Davis did help to quell the "peace party" movement in the North and to assure Lincoln's reelection to the presidency. In addition, many of Gilmore's "Edmund Kirke" novels reveal an interesting love/hate relationship with the South that transcends the mere propaganda characterization that is often assigned to them.

• A few of Gilmore's letters and other correspondence may be found in the Special Collections of the Research Library at the University of California at Los Angeles, in the Houghton Library at Harvard University, and in the Butler Library at Columbia University; however, the largest collection of Gilmore material, numbering nearly 1,200 items, is located in the Milton S. Eisenhower Library at Johns Hopkins University. In addition to the novels mentioned above, he edited Henry L. Estabrooks's *Adrift in Dixie* (1866). That work, along with Gilmore's *On the Border* (1867), make interesting reading from both a sectional and a historical perspective. Among Gilmore's editorial efforts, *The Gospel History* (1880), with Lyman Abbott, deserves mention. Although he cautiously but mistakenly names Gilmore as an African-American novelist, Blyden Jackson's commentary on *Among the Pines* in *A History of Afro-American Literature*, vol. 1 (1989) is valuable, as is James Kinney's on *My Southern Friends* in *Amalgamation!: Race, Sex, and Rhetoric in the Nineteenth-Century American Novel* (1985). While Gilmore's own writings provide by far the most extensive treatment of his Civil War exploits, *The War of the Rebellion: A Compilation of the Official Records of the Union and Confederate Armies* (128

vols., 1880–1901) provides material on the Gilmore/Jaquess trip through the war zone. The effort to end the war peacefully, including the Gilmore meeting with Jefferson Davis and the politics behind it, is extensively treated in Edward Chase Kirkland, *The Peacemakers of 1864* (1927). Obituaries are in the *Boston Transcript*, 17 Nov. 1903; the *Albany Evening Journal*, 17 Nov. 1903; and *Outlook*, 28 Nov. 1903.

VERNON G. MILES

GILMORE, Patrick Sarsfield (25 Dec. 1829–24 Sept. 1892), bandmaster, was born in Ballygar, County Galway, Ireland, the son of Patrick J. Gilmore, a stonemason, and Mary Sharkey. His flamboyant personality and grandiose musical schemes enhanced his meteoric career, bringing him worldwide recognition as the most celebrated bandmaster in the second half of the nineteenth century. Gilmore's early years were spent in Ballygar, where he mastered the fife, drum, and any other instrument he could lay his hands on. His musical abilities came to the attention of Patrick Keating, a retired British bandmaster who offered to teach him the rudiments of music. Gilmore's rapid progress won him a place in the Athlone Amateur Youth Band.

Since musical opportunities were limited in Ireland, Gilmore emigrated to the United States. He arrived in New York City in October 1849 but settled in Boston, where his older brother had located the previous year.

Shortly after his arrival, Gilmore was employed by John P. Ordway, a publisher and music dealer. Within the year, Gilmore authored the text of "Music Fills My Soul with Sadness" and convinced Ordway to form a minstrel group, Ordway's Aeolian Vocalists, for which Gilmore played the tambourine, sang in a vocal quartet, performed occasional cornet solos, and acted as the group's agent. His ability as a cornetist subsequently earned him the position as leader of the Charlestown Band and then the Suffolk Brass Band. In 1853 he became leader of the Boston Brigade Band, the oldest and one of the best bands in the city. Two years later, he succeeded to the leadership of the Salem Brass Band. In 1858 he married Ellen J. O'Neill; they had one daughter.

As his musical reputation grew Gilmore began to influence the promotional and business end of the music profession. Through his initiative several of the best bands combined in 1857 for a giant Fourth of July concert on Boston Common, the success of which made it an annual affair. Again using several Boston bands, he established a series of popular promenade concerts at the Boston Music Hall, which attracted audiences of thousands. In December 1858 he resigned his Salem post to form a new band. From its inaugural concert on 9 April 1859, the Gilmore Band enjoyed wide public acceptance and praise.

With the outbreak of the Civil War, Gilmore and his band became attached to the Twenty-fourth Massachusetts Infantry Regiment and saw action under General Ambrose Burnside in North Carolina. For financial reasons, however, all regimental bands were mustered out of service during the summer of 1862. At the request of Massachusetts governor John Andrew, Gilmore then organized a number of bands for regular army brigades. In January 1864 he accompanied two of these bands to Louisiana for service in the Department of the Gulf.

In March 1864, for the inauguration of Michael Hahn as governor of Louisiana, Gilmore staged the first of the monster concerts for which he is preeminently known. The New Orleans concert featured a 500-piece band, a chorus of 6,000 children, a battery of fifty cannons fired on signal, forty soldiers striking anvils, and the simultaneous ringing of all church bells in the city. These proportions were dwarfed in 1869 in Boston, where Gilmore conceived and staged the National Peace Jubilee, a mammoth festival lasting five days that utilized a chorus of 10,000, a 1,000-piece orchestra, 100 anvils, cannons, chimes, church bells, a huge bass drum and a gigantic organ built for the occasion. He eclipsed even those figures in 1872 when he presented an eighteen-day World Peace Jubilee, doubling the forces of the 1869 festival by incorporating the leading bands of Ireland, England, France, and Germany, plus Johann Strauss, Jr., and his orchestra.

In 1873 Gilmore moved his band to the Twenty-second Regiment of New York where, in addition to the prescribed number of obligations to the regiment, he was free to present concerts and to go on tour. One of his undertakings was the lease of Barnum's Hippodrome Museum, which he converted into an indoor pleasure garden complete with floral arrangements, trees, walkways, and waterfalls. He renamed it Gilmore's Garden and presented several seasons of successful promenade concerts there. Gilmore became the first to take an American band on an extended tour when, in 1876, they traveled by train from New York to San Francisco. Two years later he embarked on an international tour with concerts in the principal cities of England, Ireland, France, and Germany. In 1879 the Gilmore Band opened the summer season at Coney Island's newly refurbished Manhattan Beach, the success of which led to their reengagement each year into the 1890s.

Although not particularly remembered as a composer, Gilmore wrote a number of short pieces, the most famous being "When Johnny Comes Marching Home," which he published under the pen name Louis Lambert. His anthem "Columbia," which he claimed was given to him in a vision by an angel, also garnered substantial public attention. Hoping to make it the country's national anthem, he presented it as "his gift to the people of the United States" in a special Christmas day concert in 1879 (*New York Herald*, 25 Dec. 1879).

Businessman, bandmaster, promoter, musician, Gilmore set an enduring standard of excellence for bands to follow. Public adulation and a sympathetic press paid him the ultimate compliment by converting his middle initial to the name Sarsfield, after a heroic Irish general, and to this day he is known as Patrick Sarsfield Gilmore. He died suddenly while completing his annual engagement at the St. Louis Exposition.

• Few official documents on Gilmore's life and career exist, for he burned or discarded many of his business papers. However, much information can be found in the collections of the Essex Institute (Salem, Mass.), Boston Public Library, New-York Historical Society, New York Public Library, Library of Congress, and the National Archives. Writings of note include: "P. S. Gilmore, Bandmaster," a series of twenty-three articles by F. C. Damon that appeared in the *Salem Evening News* (Apr. 1936-July 1937); Frank Leslie, *Illustrated History of the Great Peace Jubilee* (1869); "Patrick S. Gilmore," *The New Grove Dictionary of American Music* (1986); Frank J. Cipolla, "Patrick S. Gilmore: The Boston Years," *American Music* 6, no. 3 (1988): 281–92. Gilmore's own book, *History of the National Peace Jubilee and Great Musical Festival* (1871), includes a short biographical reprint from a Philadelphia newspaper. M. Darlington's biography of Gilmore, *Irish Orpheus* (1950), contains errors and is not authoritative. Obituaries are in the *New York Times*, 25 Sept. 1892, the *St. Louis Post Dispatch*, 25 Sept. 1892, and other major newspapers.

FRANK J. CIPOLLA

GILPIN, Charles Sidney (20 Nov. 1878–6 May 1930), actor, was born in Richmond, Virginia, the son of Peter Gilpin, a laborer in a steel-rolling mill, and Caroline White, a nurse in the Richmond City Hospital. Gilpin attended St. Francis School for black children, where Sister Jerome inspired him to seek a stage career by training and encouraging him in amateur theatricals. However, at the age of twelve, he went to work as a printer's devil (apprentice) for the *Richmond Planet* and from 1890 to 1903 held numerous jobs, including printer, elevator operator, and Pullman porter while performing on stage sporadically as a song-and-dance man at fairs, restaurants, and variety theaters and as a minstrel in vaudeville. In 1897 he married Florence Howard, who appeared with him in vaudeville at various times. The couple had one son.

Gilpin became employed full time as a performer in 1903 when he joined the Canadian Jubilee Singers of Hamilton, Ontario. After playing in Williams and Walker's *Abysinnia* and Gus Hill's *Smart Set* in 1905 and 1906, he received his first chance to act dramatic roles with the Pekin Stock Company of Chicago. Along with playing black roles, he also appeared in plays as white characters in white makeup. Over the next few years, the actor worked with the Pan-American Octette (1911–1913), the *Old Man's Boy* Company (1914), and on vaudeville stages (1915). In 1916 he became director of the first African-American dramatic stock company in New York, the Lafayette Theatre, which was located in Harlem. During this time, when stage work became scarce, he returned to work as a porter for the railroad.

On 15 December 1919 Gilpin played his first Broadway role—William Curtis, the black clergyman in John Drinkwater's *Abraham Lincoln*. He was then chosen to play the titular role in the premiere of Eugene O'Neill's *Emperor Jones*. In auditioning for the part of the black Brutus Jones, Gilpin had to compete with white actors. The play opened in New York City at the Provincetown Playhouse on MacDougal Street on 1 November 1920 and was then transferred to Broadway's Princes Theatre on 29 January 1921, with its run continuing until 1924. The role received unanimous praise for the actor's "thrilling performance" and the "gorgeous natural quality" of his voice.

In playing Brutus Jones, the former convict emperor who is hunted by his subjects and eventually killed, Gilpin gave a virtuoso performance, which featured him alone in six of the drama's eight scenes. In 1921 he was one of ten to earn a Drama League award for his distinguished contribution to the theatrical season and in 1926 the National Association for the Advancement of Colored People presented him with the Spingarn medal for distinguished achievement. Of his work critic Kenneth Macgowan said: "Mr. Gilpin's performance is the crown to a play that opens up the imagination of the American theatre."

Although Gilpin seemed destined for continued success, an increasingly serious drinking problem caused him to lose work. Paul Robeson replaced him for the London production of *Emperor Jones* in 1925. Gilpin played the role again for the 1926 Broadway revival and, despite a failing voice, was cast in *The Front Page* in 1928. However, when the play was in rehearsal he was fired for drunkenness and never appeared on Broadway again. His final performance was of Brutus Jones on 29 June 1929 in Woodstock, New York. It was reported that the actor suffered a general breakdown after this appearance and never recovered. He died in Eldridge Park, a suburb of Trenton, New Jersey, and was buried six days later in a quiet ceremony in Lambertville. After hearing of his death, friends provided a second ceremony on 1 June 1930 at the Duncan Brothers funeral parlor on Seventh Avenue. The overflow crowd listened to numerous tributes from actors and friends, including an emotional address by actor-writer Jesse A. Shipp.

As a performer, Gilpin possessed the power and ability to transcend the black stereotypes of the generations that preceded him and created one of the first serious roles played by an African-American actor on Broadway.

• For a review of *Emperor Jones* see Kenneth Macgowan in *Theatre Arts*, 21 Jan. 1921. For an insightful interview on Gilpin's life in the theater and his craft see Helen Bishop, "Gilpin Wants to Play Comedy," *Boston Transcript*, 1922. Playwright and director Moss Hart encountered Gilpin at the peak of the actor's fame. Hart's perceptive assessment of Gilpin is recounted in his *Act One* (1959). Obituaries are in the *New York Times*, 7 May 1930 and 2 June 1930.

PAUL MROCZKA

GILPIN, Laura (22 Apr. 1891–30 Nov. 1979), photographer and author, was born in Colorado Springs, Colorado, the daughter of Frank Gilpin, a rancher, and Emma Miller. Though living at the foot of the Rocky Mountains, Gilpin received much of her education in the East. She attended eastern boarding schools from 1905 to 1909 but returned home before graduating from high school. She later studied briefly at the New

England Conservatory of Music (1910–1911) before going back to Colorado to work on a family farm on the western slope of the Rockies.

Gilpin's interest in photography began as a child when, in 1903, she was given a Brownie camera and developing tank. In 1909 she began making Lumière autochromes and quickly mastered this early color photographic process by following the directions that came with the materials. Although Gilpin was self-taught, her talent was evident in the sensitive portraits and still lifes that she produced working around her family home. With money saved from her turkey farm business, Gilpin moved to New York in 1916 to study at the Clarence H. White School of Photography, one of the country's leading photographic schools. The school promoted photography as both a commercial tool and a medium for artistic expression. Studying with prominent photographers and artists such as White, Max Weber, and Paul Anderson, Gilpin acquired the technical skills and principles of composition that would prove the underpinning of her work for the next sixty years.

After she returned to Colorado Springs in 1918, Gilpin went into business as a commercial photographer specializing in portraiture and architectural work. At the same time she began photographing the southwestern landscape, a subject that would soon become the focus of her most compelling work. A review of these early landscapes in a one-woman show at the Art Center in New York in 1924 called Gilpin's work "delightful" and praised her pictures, "which give most successfully the sense of the vastness of the plains." As Gilpin's interest in the landscape extended to include the past and present inhabitants of the region, she began working both at archaeological sites and the Pueblo Indian communities of northern New Mexico. Her first photographic booklets, *The Pike's Peak Region* (1926) and *The Mesa Verde National Park* (1927), explored ways of using photographs as expressions of regional culture, a theme that would become the central concern of her later books.

Gilpin discovered the most important subject of her work by chance. In 1930, while on a camping trip with her lifelong companion, Elizabeth Forster, Gilpin ran out of gas in a remote section of the Navajo reservation in northeastern Arizona. While she hiked to a trading post for gas, Forster stayed behind with the car and was soon surrounded by curious onlookers. Deeply impressed by the experience, Forster left her nursing job in Colorado Springs in 1931 to become a field nurse in the Navajo community of Red Rock. For the next two years Gilpin visited frequently, making a valuable photographic record of this small Navajo community that was yet to be transformed by federal aid and the impact of World War II. She worked slowly and deliberately with her 8″ × 10″ camera, making pictures that documented the strong connection between the Navajo people and the landscape and the empathy she herself felt toward her Navajo subjects.

Further into the depression, Forster lost her job in Red Rock, and Gilpin was forced to abandon her Navajo work to concentrate on the difficult task of earning a living. Withdrawing from the national and international photographic exhibition scene because of financial problems, Gilpin again turned to turkey farming and to commercial publishing projects for support. During the 1940s, while pursuing a variety of jobs—including a wartime job as a public relations photographer for the Boeing Company in Wichita, Kansas—she published three books. The first, *The Pueblos: A Camera Chronicle* (1941), established her as a regionalist who, like other writers of the time, was attracted to the Southwest as the site of America's most ancient history. The Pueblos, Gilpin argued in her romantic text, bequeathed to all Americans a heritage of peace. In *Temples of Yucatán: A Camera Chronicle of Chichén Itzá* (1948), Gilpin likewise used photographs of archaeological sites and modern-day peoples to stress the ancient history of the Americas and the considerable artistic talents of the area's native peoples. Her third book, *Rio Grande: River of Destiny* (1949), focused more on the present. The result of more than 27,000 miles of travel along the river, the book integrated landscape views with pictures of the people whose lives were shaped by the river. Written in Santa Fe, New Mexico, where Gilpin moved in 1945, it established Gilpin as a cultural geographer and reconfirmed her standing as the most significant woman landscape photographer in the history of American photography. Critic and scholar John Brinkerhoff Jackson noted that "Miss Gilpin's camera, like the sundial, records only the sunny hours" (*Arizona Quarterly* 4 [Winter 1949]). But he praised her book for its accurate economic, social, and agricultural data and concluded, "It is far more than a picture book, therefore; it is a geography for adults."

From 1950 through 1967, with frequent interruptions for financial reasons, Gilpin again turned her attention to the photographic documentation of the Navajo world. While revisiting many of her old acquaintances, she began to conceive of a more ambitious photographic project that would chronicle the Navajo world view, chart the changes that had taken place in Navajo life during the past few decades, and discuss the economic and political future of the Navajo tribe. *The Enduring Navaho* (1968) became Gilpin's most significant publication. It was, as photographer and anthropologist John Collier, Jr., noted, "a work of LOVE not ANALYSIS," which conveyed Gilpin's deep sense of identification with the Navajo people. Focusing on the importance of tradition in Navajo culture, she predicted a rich, long future for the people that photographer Edward Curtis had once called the "vanishing race."

Though Gilpin had a distinguished exhibition record as a young woman and was accepted as a member of the Royal Photographic Society of Great Britain in 1930, she subsequently worked many decades without much outside recognition from the photographic community. During the 1970s, however, as the interest in collecting photographs increased, Gilpin again began to earn recognition for her work. She received a Gug-

genheim grant in 1975 to make hand-coated platinum prints, a process that had long interested her, and saw her work included in several national exhibitions. Still, at the time of her death in Santa Fe, her work was not widely known. Subsequent publications and exhibitions, drawn from the photographic estate that Gilpin bequeathed to the Amon Carter Museum in Fort Worth, Texas, have drawn broader attention to her sixty-year career and her important contributions as a landscape photographer and chronicler of the Southwest.

• Gilpin bequeathed her personal papers, photographs, and negatives to the Amon Carter Museum in Fort Worth, Tex., which has cataloged them for public access. The only biography of Gilpin is Martha A. Sandweiss, *Laura Gilpin: An Enduring Grace* (1986), which includes an extensive bibliography that documents publications by and about Gilpin as well as chronicling her exhibitions record. In addition to Gilpin's own publications, researchers should also consult Elizabeth Forster and Laura Gilpin, *Denizens of the Desert* (1988), which gathers together the letters Forster wrote while working on the Navajo reservation from 1931 to 1933.

MARTHA A. SANDWEISS

GILPIN, William (4 Oct. 1815–19 Jan. 1894), geopolitician, soldier, and land speculator, was born in New Castle County, Delaware, the son of Joshua Gilpin, a manufacturer of fine paper, and Mary Dilworth. He was educated at home until age thirteen, when he was sent to Settle, England, for preparatory school. Two years later he returned home, and after an examination, he was admitted to the University of Pennsylvania as a junior. He received his A.B. in 1833 at the age of eighteen.

While at the university, Gilpin lived with his bachelor brother Henry Gilpin, who was U.S. district attorney for Philadelphia and a rising member of the Democratic party. Fascinated by tales of the frontier, William Gilpin determined to seek a military career. He secured an appointment from Andrew Jackson to the U.S. Military Academy, effective 1 July 1834, but Gilpin found West Point too "confining"; the cadets were "cooped up" all day, studying academics and not the more exciting tactics. Within six months he had resigned.

Back in his brother's home, Gilpin commenced reading for the bar, but in 1835, when the Second Seminole War broke out, he obtained from Jackson a commission in the Second Dragoons. His first duty was to recruit men in the area west of the Alleghenies then train them at Jefferson Barracks, Missouri. Promoted from second to first lieutenant, Gilpin commanded troops in several small skirmishes in the Florida swamps. He resigned in April 1838.

Gilpin served his nation in two other wars. In the Mexican War he held the rank of major in Stephen Watts Kearny's Army of the West. In the bitter winter of 1846 Gilpin led several companies into the mountains of New Mexico to force large numbers of Navajos, Pueblos, and Utes to sign new treaties designed to keep them from molesting the ranchers of the territory. He received considerable acclaim for marching his men more than 700 blizzard-filled miles in less than a month to round up the American Indians. After securing the treaties, Gilpin returned to the main command to help Lieutenant Colonel Alexander Doniphan in two overwhelming victories over the Mexicans in the campaign to take Chihuahua.

Only weeks after his discharge, while suffering badly from malaria, Gilpin was asked to lead the Separate Battalion of Missouri Volunteers against Comanches and other plains tribes, whose raids had closed the Santa Fe Trail. In one year of hard riding, boring encampments, and government neglect, Gilpin's companies of totally untrained farm boys and German immigrants succeeded in opening the trail but achieved little else. This time Gilpin returned home seriously ill with cholera, his body wasting some 60 pounds down to 100.

Gilpin did not think of himself as a career officer, but rather he used his military experience to add to his fame and his knowledge of North America and to continually publicize the West. When not in uniform during the 1840s and 1850s, Gilpin practiced land law and wrote treatises. Described as a "fiercely" partisan Democrat, he edited the *Missouri Daily Argus*, twice getting his publishers into duels over his editorials. Gilpin had hitched his wagon to the star of Thomas Hart Benton (1782–1858) and with the senator campaigned equally for the Democratic party and the great West.

From 1841 to 1861 Gilpin made Independence, Missouri, his home, practicing law, writing, and speaking of the opportunities for American pioneers. Predicting great wealth for those who came west to mine or to farm, he touted the cities of the West—Cairo, St. Louis, Independence (once called Gilpintown), Kansas City, and Denver—and foresaw brilliant futures for them all. He built a reputation as an authority on the West, its topography, its resources, and especially its opportunities. He made dozens of public speeches, sometimes to crowds of thousands, containing some nonsense but a great deal of appeal as he glorified the "untransacted destiny" of the American West. He predicted great trade with China and India and spoke of the millions yet unborn who would one day live in the Mississippi Valley. The *Kansas City Star* recalled: "He spent most of his time making maps, reading and making speeches about the West. His enthusiasm over the future of the West was almost without limitation."

Gilpin acquired greater recognition after an 1842 journey to Oregon with the explorer John C. Frémont and expeditions with Kit Carson, Tom Fitzpatrick, and other frontiersmen. He was credited by contemporaries with planning and laying out Independence, Missouri, and Portland, Oregon.

Gilpin's politics changed during the 1850s. The Democrats of the West were becoming the party of slavery, and Gilpin joined the new Republican party sometime between 1856 and 1859. Increasingly he encouraged railroad networks, and he spoke of the great

mineral deposits to be found in the Rockies. Some of the "Pikes Peakers" who failed, in fact, blamed him personally when they "busted."

When Colorado became a territory in 1861, President Abraham Lincoln was besieged with requests to make Gilpin the first governor, because he was the leading authority on the region. The two men had met only once, when Gilpin helped protect the president's inaugural trip to Washington, but the appointment was made nevertheless, effective April 1861.

Gilpin served but one year. His civil administration was sound, but to finance troops for the defense of the Union in New Mexico, he borrowed too much without federal authority and was replaced by Lincoln. Time proved him right; all the vouchers were ultimately paid, and the military victories he ordered and financed were crucial to the defense of the West.

In his last three decades, Gilpin made a fortune in land deals in Colorado and New Mexico and continued to publish books about the great West. In spite of a number of strange ideas in his writings, he has been proclaimed by authors such as Bernard De Voto and Henry Nash Smith as America's first geopolitician for his advocacy of the United States as destined for world power by virtue of its geographic position and size. In 1874 he married Julia Pratte Dickerson, a widowed mother of four. She and Gilpin had three more children. Their marriage was stormy, but they were still together at his death in Denver, Colorado.

• No single collection of Gilpin papers exists. A few of the many repositories having manuscripts concerning him or his family include the Historian's Office, Church of Jesus Christ of Latter-day Saints in Salt Lake City; Colorado State Archives; State Historical Society of Colorado; Denver Public Library; National Archives; Historical Society of Delaware; Bancroft Library, Berkeley, Calif.; Missouri Historical Society; Oregon Historical Society; and the Library of Congress. The oldest biography is Hubert Howe Bancroft, *History of the Life of William Gilpin* (1889), which, though frequently cited, is somewhat suspect because it was dictated by Gilpin to Bancroft and contains many clear errors. More reliably documented is Thomas L. Karnes, *William Gilpin, Western Nationalist* (1970). Herbert O. Brayer, *William Blackmore* (1949); William E. Connelley, *Doniphan's Expedition* (1907); Henry Nash Smith, *Virgin Land* (1957); Wallace Stegner, *Beyond the Hundredth Meridian* (1962); and many local, military, and explorers' accounts add dimensions to Gilpin. Representative pertinent articles include Bernard De Voto, "Geopolitics with the Dew on It," *Harper's Magazine* 188 (1944): 313–23; Charles N. Glaab, "Visions of Metropolis: William Gilpin and Theories of City Growth in the American West," *Wisconsin Magazine of History* 45 (1961): 21–31; Thomas L. Karnes, "Gilpin's Volunteers on the Santa Fe Trail," *Kansas Historical Quarterly* 30 (1964): 1–14; and Kenneth W. Porter, "William Gilpin: Sinophile and Eccentric," *Colorado Magazine* 37 (1960): 245–53.

THOMAS L. KARNES

GIMBEL, Bernard Feustman (18 Apr. 1885–29 Sept. 1966), retailer, was born in Vincennes, Indiana, the son of Isaac Gimbel, a retailer, and Rachel Feustman. He grew up in Milwaukee, Wisconsin, and Philadelphia, Pennsylvania. Educated at the William Penn

Charter School in Philadelphia, he graduated from the University of Pennsylvania's Wharton School of Business in 1907. In 1912 he married Alva Bernheimer. They had five children.

Gimbel's grandfather Adam had emigrated from Bavaria to the United States in 1842 and had founded a lace and pots store in Vincennes, Indiana. His son Isaac expanded his father's business, founding department stores in Milwaukee, Wisconsin, and Philadelphia, Pennsylvania. Gimbel went to work in the Philadelphia department store in 1907 and became a vice president of the store in 1908. He persuaded his father and uncles to open a New York City store and became head of it when it opened in 1910. The New York store, one of the largest in the city, had one million square feet of selling space located on thirteen floors, including three floors below ground. Located next to the terminals of the Pennsylvania Railroad and the Long Island Railroad, the site became the center of retailing in New York City. A block from Macy's, the two stores engaged in a fabled retailing competition.

Gimbel took over from his father as president and chief executive of the Gimbel's corporation in 1927. Under his direction, the store empire expanded. Even before taking full command, in 1923 he acquired Saks Fifth Avenue, which specialized in higher-priced goods, allowing the Gimbel's chain to sell to all classes of consumers. He also converted the business into a corporation, although he continued to keep control of the stores in his own hands.

As with most other businesses, the Gimbel's chain suffered greatly during the depression, and the company showed losses for most years. Because it catered to the upper class, Saks was the only part of the operation to show a profit during these years. Financial difficulties led to some turmoil in the management of the stores, leading to a revolt against Gimbel that he put down. With the return of prosperity in 1941, the retail clerks, attempting to gain recognition and secure higher wages, struck against the New York City store, forcing Gimbel to recognize the union.

Anticipating the entry of the United States into World War II, Gimbel purchased $20 million worth of consumer products. During the war, the Gimbel's stores had large quantities of scarce merchandise, even a supply of nylon stockings that lasted three years into that conflict.

After World War II, the Gimbel's Company pioneered the development of suburban shopping malls. At the time of his death, the chain had twenty-seven Gimbel's department stores and twenty-seven Saks Fifth Avenue outlets with 24,000 employees. When Gimbel joined his father's business, it did a $15 million annual business. At his death, the Gimbel's organization had sales of $600 million.

A strong merchandiser, Gimbel pioneered the bargain basement along with Edward Filene of Boston. The basement with its inexpensive goods brought people into the department store who had not shopped there before. Gimbel also was a pioneer in the introduction of private brands to compete with national brands and the establishment of boutiques or special shops within the department store. Gimbel belonged to that generation of merchants who built great department store chains. Gimbel's competed with the Federated Department Stores, operating stores throughout the United States. In building his organization, Gimbel modeled his expansion upon the work of Julius Rosenwald and General Robert E. Wood who expanded Sears Roebuck into the suburbs and decentralized operations. With his new mall stores, Gimbel appealed to the affluent shopper of the era. In the 1950s and 1960s the Gimbel's chain enjoyed high profitability.

Like the other great retailers of his era, Gimbel was a showman. The rivalry with Macy's was carefully planned to promote the images of both stores. He held a golf tournament on the store's fourth floor and put up $5,000 for an air race between New York and Philadelphia. He sold millions of dollars of art for William Randolph Hearst through the store, attracting the attention of newspapers from coast to coast.

As a longtime resident of New York City, Gimbel was active in civic affairs. He was a member of many city boards and was an active participant in the New York World's Fairs in 1939 and 1965 and headed the New York City Convention and Visitors Bureau. Among his philanthropies were large contributions to the University of Pennsylvania, donating money for the building of a gymnasium, and the creation of the Gimbel Marketing Center in the Wharton School. As a businessman he was a director of the Coca-Cola Company and the Burlington Mills Corporation.

Gimbel was 210 pounds and six feet tall and was very athletic in his youth, playing on the University of Pennsylvania football team. While in college he led a rescue crew that saved a group of men whose boat had capsized near Atlantic City, New Jersey, in a storm. After college, Gimbel remained an active sportsman. President of the Madison Square Garden sports arena, Gimbel was active in horse racing and was a longtime promoter of Gene Tunney, the world champion boxer.

Gimbel's son Bruce became president in 1953 and chief executive of Gimbel's in 1961, the fourth member of his family to lead the retailing concern. But Gimbel remained chairman of the board until his death in New York City. The Gimbel's empire did not survive long after his death. In 1983 during one of the periodic upheavals in the retailing business, Gimbel Brothers closed its doors for the last time although Saks continued to operate under new owners.

• For information on Gimbel see the clipping file at the Urban archives at Temple University and the *New York Times*, 10 Apr. 1929, 22 Sept. 1935, 22 Feb. 1963, 18 Mar. 1945, 9 Apr. 1955, and 3, 15 Oct. 1966. Also see *The Dry Goods Economist*, and Leon Harris, *Merchant Princes: An Intimate History of Jewish Families Who Built Great Department Stores* (1979). Obituaries are in the *New York Times* and the *Washington Post*, both 30 Sept. 1966.

HERBERT B. ERSHKOWITZ

GINGRICH, Arnold (5 Dec. 1903–9 July 1976), editor and author, was born in Grand Rapids, Michigan, the son of John Hembling Gingrich and Clara Alice Speare. After public schooling in Grand Rapids, Gingrich earned Phi Beta Kappa at the University of Michigan (B.A., 1925). In 1924 he married Helen Mary Rowe, with whom he had three children. She died in 1955.

From 1925 to 1928 Gingrich wrote advertising copy for Chicago clothing manufacturer B. Kuppenheimer. There in 1928 he joined David Smart and William H. Weintraub's Men's Wear Service Corporation, publishers of literate men's fashion booklets and trade newspapers. At Smart and Weintraub's suggestion, in 1931 Gingrich began *Apparel Arts* (later *Gentleman's Quarterly*), a trade paper in his words "both cool and cultural" that included in ad copy such touches as e.e. cummings's poetry. In a 1933 promotional booklet Gingrich envisioned another publication "telling middle class men what to eat, drink, wear, play and read. . . . an adult magazine, amusing, cynical, flippant, superficial, brashly sophisticated."

Under Gingrich's editorship, *Esquire: The Quarterly for Men* made its debut in October 1933. Large and glossy, with full-page color cartoons and stylish advertising (Gingrich claimed it ran the first automobile ad that did not show a car), *Esquire* sold the 100,000 copies of its first issue in record time. With its next issue (Jan. 1934) it became a monthly; within three years it sold 700,000 copies per month, despite its fifty-cent price.

Although *Esquire* remained true to its breezy origins during Gingrich's forty years there, it also quickly established a claim to literary excellence. Gingrich met Ernest Hemingway in a Chicago bookshop in 1933 and persuaded him to write for the first issue. "A Cuban Letter" dealt with fishing, their mutual passion. Hemingway was joined in the first issue by novelists John Dos Passos and Erskine Caldwell, detective writer Dashiell Hammett, humorist George Ade, and critic Gilbert Seldes. Hemingway became one of Gingrich's regulars (he eventually wrote more than thirty pieces for *Esquire*), in 1935 beginning a series of long stories that became the novel *To Have and Have Not.*

Gingrich also sought out novelist F. Scott Fitzgerald, whose *Esquire* connection began in 1934 with two articles credited to Fitzgerald and his wife Zelda. It was later accepted that they were exclusively Zelda's. Fitzgerald contributed more than forty pieces to *Esquire.*

Gingrich's only novel, *Cast Down the Laurel* (1935), was an unusual work combining social and literary satire with roman à clef. It begins with an unnamed narrator presenting "material" to an unnamed novelist, continues with *Apollo's Young Widow: A Romance by Wakefield Speare*, the novelist's published use of the material, and concludes with the narrator telling the novelist where he went wrong.

Also in 1935 Gingrich encouraged Fitzgerald, unable to "write stories about young love any more," to write "anything that came into his head, as automatic writing." A brilliant series of autobiographical essays by Fitzgerald, "The Crack-Up," appeared in *Esquire* in 1936. Other autobiographical essays by Fitzgerald such as "Afternoon of an Author" followed. Starting in 1939 Gingrich published Fitzgerald's comic stories of Pat Hobby, a broken-down screenwriter; over the last three years of Fitzgerald's life, most of his income came from *Esquire*, the only magazine not closed to him.

In 1936 Smart, Weintraub, and Gingrich introduced *Coronet*, a beautiful pocket-sized monthly arts magazine that usually lost money, and edited it until 1945. He later wrote that it was twenty-five years ahead of its time. Under competition from the new pictorial *Life*, *Esquire* became a public corporation in 1937, awarding Gingrich a 5 percent interest. In 1938 Gingrich acquired the editorships of *Verve*, an arts quarterly, and *Ken*, a mildly left-wing monthly for which Hemingway wrote thirteen pieces. Both magazines died as war broke out in Europe in 1939.

During World War II *Esquire* became noted for its stylized, barely clad "pin-up girls," drawn by George Petty and Alberto Vargas, supposedly to cheer up soldiers, sailors, and marines. The pin-ups nearly cost *Esquire* its mailing privileges, when the Catholic postmaster-general attacked the pin-ups on the grounds of morality. Losing second-class mailing privileges would have cost the company $500,000 yearly, so for the next couple of years Gingrich took dummy copies of every edition to Washington, D.C., for approval. Eventually, Thurman Arnold of the court of appeals saw no immorality in this kind of morale boosting; William O. Douglas of the Supreme Court agreed, and in 1945 the Court upheld *Esquire.*

In 1945 Gingrich resigned his editorships (though he kept his shares) and moved to Switzerland. By 1949 he was in New York, editing the magazine *Flair* for Cowles Magazines. Smart talked him back into the company in 1951, and upon Smart's death Gingrich became publisher and senior vice president of *Esquire* in 1952. He remained in those capacities and wrote a monthly column until his retirement in 1974, after which he continued as founding editor. In 1955 Gingrich married Jane Mason Hamilton Kendall. They had no children.

Under Gingrich during the mid-1950s, *Esquire* was threatened by *Playboy*, a "swinging lifestyle" creation of Hugh Hefner, who had worked for *Esquire* while Gingrich was away. *Esquire* de-emphasized pin-ups, moving toward youth and topicality. Gingrich recruited at colleges for editorial talent more in touch with a new generation. Fiction editor Rust Hills renewed the magazine's reputation for discovering major new talent. Another editor, Clay Felker, who subsequently founded *New York* magazine, credited Gingrich with "the successful rescue of his own magazine" (Felker, p. 7). In 1958 came the first of several *Esquire* anthologies edited by Gingrich, *The Armchair Esquire.*

Between 1958 and 1964 Gingrich helped revive the career of another early idol, the witty Dorothy Parker. Her comments on more than two hundred books probably aided *Esquire*'s rejuvenation. Parker's biographer admired Gingrich's "success rate at prying copy from her" (Meade, p. 357). Gingrich defended Parker against right-wing accusations and continued to pay her even after she stopped writing her column in 1962. In 1962 Gingrich edited and introduced *The Pat Hobby Stories*, noting that the book restored Fitzgerald's concept of a "collective entity."

During the 1960s *Esquire* became identified with the "new journalism" of Tom Wolfe, Gay Talese, and others employing fictional techniques to revivify reportage. In 1968 Gingrich received the Magazine Publishers Association's Henry John Fisher Award for individual achievement. A lifelong advocate of leisure pursuits, he wrote in his 1969 booklet *Business and the Arts* that if the arts lack support, "the result can only be a general impoverishment of the spirit that will depress the values that sustain our society."

An avid fly fisherman who wrote *The Well Tempered Angler* (1965), *Toys of a Lifetime* (1966), *The Joys of Trout* (1973), and *The Fishing in Print* (1974) as well as edited two books on fishing, Gingrich was also an enthusiastic violinist who wrote *A Thousand Mornings of Music* (1970). In 1971 Gingrich's autobiography, *Nothing but People: The Early Days of Esquire, a Personal History 1928–1948*, was published.

Gingrich appeared on the cover of *Esquire*'s fortieth anniversary edition (Oct. 1973), short and trim, bald and bespectacled, nattily dressed with a red carnation in his buttonhole. Gingrich died in Ridgewood, New Jersey. An innovative editor so close to his authors that he helped Hemingway finance the rebuilding of his fishing boat and prescribed a hangover cure for Fitzgerald, Arnold Gingrich lived well. When Hemingway told him in the mid-1930s that he had heard Gingrich's salary for the previous year had been $75,999, the editor replied that he did not know but "sure as hell had spent that much."

• Aside from Gingrich's own works, including years of columns for *Esquire*, he can be glimpsed in biographies such as Marion Meade, *Dorothy Parker: What Fresh Hell Is This?* (1987), Carlos Baker, *Ernest Hemingway* (1969), and Matthew Bruccoli, *Some Sort of Epic Grandeur: The Life of F. Scott Fitzgerald*, rev. ed. (1991). He figures in Bruccoli, *Zelda Fitzgerald: The Collected Writings* (1991), and Sheilah Graham, *Beloved Infidel: The Education of a Woman* (1958). Clay Felker's article "Life Cycles in the Age of Magazines," *Antioch Review* 29 (Spring 1969): 7–13, is useful, as is Harold T. P. Hayes, "Arnold Gingrich, Esquire," *New Republic*, 14 Sept. 1976, pp. 33–37. The *New York Times* obituary, 10 July 1976, is comprehensive.

JAMES ROSS MOORE

GINN, Edwin (14 Feb. 1838–21 Jan. 1914), publisher and peace advocate, was born in Orland, Hancock County, Maine, the son of James Ginn, a farmer who also had interests in lumber and shipbuilding, and Sarah Blood. Growing up in relative poverty and poor health, he attended local country schools on an intermittent basis. At the age of twelve he went to work as a cook in a logging camp that his father had established,

and he later worked on a fishing schooner on the Grand Banks of Newfoundland. After returning from his fishing voyage, he attended the local high school in Orland and also attended the seminary in nearby Bucksport in order to learn Latin. Ginn finished his college preparatory work at Westbrook Seminary, during which he supported himself by teaching in local schools during the winter, fishing in the summer, and working intermittently on the family farm.

Originally interested in the ministry as a career, Ginn entered Tufts College (now Tufts University) in 1858 at the age of twenty. Although he developed eyesight trouble during his course, he managed to finish his work with the aid of classmates—who often read his assignments aloud to him—and graduated in the upper half of his class in 1862.

After graduation, Ginn took a position as a traveling schoolbook agent. Working in lower New England and Pennsylvania, he achieved great success in convincing local school boards to adopt his texts. After turning down an offer to manage the *North American Review*, he accepted another proposal—from one of his employers, the firm of Crosby, Ainsworth & Company—to publish Craik's *English of Shakespeare* on his own. Excited by the sales potential—Ginn knew that Shakespeare was becoming increasingly popular as an academic subject in schools—he quickly accepted the offer. He followed this first effort with the publication of W. F. Allen's *Latin Grammar*, which enjoyed great success. Other books, including Madwig's *Latin Grammar* and Luther Whiting Mason's *National Music Course*, soon followed. With the publication of Goodwin's *Greek Grammar*, Ginn, who had formally established his business (with his brother Frederick) as the Ginn Brothers in 1867, gained an entrance for his books in the best schools of the country, and his reputation was firmly established.

Bolstered by the success of his business, Ginn married Clara Glover of Lawrence, Massachusetts, in 1869; they had three children. Other notable titles soon emerged from his firm's presses, including a three-volume set of Shakespeare's plays by Henry N. Hudson, a geometry text by Professor Wentworth of Exeter, Allen and Greenough's Latin Series, and the Athenaeum Press Series. By the mid-1880s both George A. Plimpton and Daniel Collamore Heath had joined the firm, which became Ginn, Heath & Company in 1881. After Heath departed in 1885 in order to found his own company, the firm became known as Ginn & Company. Ginn attributed his success in the school book trade to a careful attention to quality, seeking "books . . . a little better than anything that had yet appeared on the subject, and, whenever possible, to avoid duplication" and always giving preference to "The superiority of the book rather than the influence . . . of the author" (Ginn, p. 21).

A man of wide interests and deep concern for humanity, Ginn was the first Boston employer to offer a profit-sharing plan to his employees. Concerned about the often-wretched living conditions of late nineteenth-century laborers, he also developed "Charlesbank Homes," a fireproof five-story building that provided decent, reasonably priced accommodations for the poor.

Following the death of his first wife in 1890, Ginn married Marguerita Francesca Grebe of Philadelphia in 1894. Two additional children resulted from the marriage. Although he possessed a beautiful home in Winchester, Massachusetts, and a secure fortune, Ginn was not content to spend his later years in idle enjoyment. Turning like so many of his contemporaries to philanthropy, he made his greatest contribution in the movement for world peace.

As early as 1901 Ginn became interested in the world peace movement, which underwent a rebirth of sorts after the turn of the century. Appearing in 1904 before the Thirteen Universal Peace Congress in Boston, Ginn lamented " . . . the indisposition of the people to grapple with the subject in a business-like way . . . Any change in the existing order of things . . . must be effected by education" (Moritzen, p. 291). Sensing a lack of leadership, Ginn set aside one million dollars (a third of his fortune) in 1909 with the goal of setting up his own organization. The International School of Peace, founded in 1909, was led by men such as David Starr Jordan, the president of Stanford University and Edwin D. Mead, a leading peace advocate. Shortly after its founding, the school, which was organized along the lines of a university, became the World Peace Foundation (1911). Although dwarfed in size by the Carnegie Endowment for International Peace—which was founded with an endowment of ten million dollars shortly after the World Peace Foundation made its appearance—the new organization set out to educate the public through literature and speeches about the perils of warfare. Originally focusing its efforts on the young, the foundation later branched out in its outreach efforts to the business community.

Although well funded, the foundation suffered from a lack of clear delineation of authority among its leaders, some of whom were chosen more for their personal prestige than for their experience in social movements. Ginn, who favored direct evangelization of the public over scholarly research into the causes of war, also clashed with his fellow workers over the organization's focus. After suffering a stroke in December 1913, Ginn never regained his heath and died in Winchester. Unfortunately for the cause of world peace, his foundation did not long survive him. The outbreak of World War I in 1914 was a devastating blow, and infighting erupted among the remaining leadership. After 1915 most of the foundation's resources were diverted to the League to Enforce Peace, an organization of which original foundation trustee (and Harvard president) A. Lawrence Lowell was also a member, and it ceased to be an effective organization.

Ginn rose from relative poverty to become a widely known and successful leader in the publishing industry. Although his death left his other great endeavor, the World Peace Foundation, in a state of chaos from which it never recovered, his generosity and drive in the cause of world peace are surely worthy of remembrance as well.

• The papers of Edwin Ginn are widely scattered; some correspondence can be found among a variety of manuscript collections at the Massachusetts Historical Society. Additional correspondence is in the Andrew Carnegie Papers in the Manuscript Division of the Library of Congress in Washington, D.C., while still more can be found in the World Peace Foundation Papers in the Peace Collection at Swarthmore College, and the A. Lawrence Lowell Papers at the Harvard University archives. Ginn's autobiographical *Outline of the Life of Edwin Ginn* (1908) is useful regarding his early life and publishing activities, but ignores his work with the WPF. His activities in the publishing business receive attention in Hellmut Lehmann-Haupt's *The Book in America: A History of the Making and Selling of Books in the United States* (1951). The best contemporary source of his work with the WPF is Julius Moritzen, *The Peace Movement of America* (1912), while the best (and most extensive) modern treatment is in C. Roland Marchand, *The American Peace Movement and Social Reform, 1898–1918* (1972). Ginn also receives attention in Merle Curti, *Peace or War: The American Struggle, 1636–1936* (1959); Charles DeBenedetti, *The Peace Reform in American History* (1980); and John Whiteclay Chambers II, ed., *The Eagle and the Dove: The American Peace Movement and United States Foreign Policy, 1920–1922* (1991). Obituaries are in the *Boston Transcript*, 21 Jan. 1914, and the *Boston Herald*, 22 Jan. 1914.

EDWARD L. LACH, JR.

GINTER, Lewis (4 Apr. 1824–2 Oct. 1897), tobacco merchant, was born in New York City, the son of John Ginter, a grocer, and Elizabeth (maiden name unknown). His father died when Lewis was an infant, and his mother died a few years later; his older sister Jane raised him. Ginter received little formal education, but through self-education he acquired a love of art and music, became an accomplished pianist, and attained fluency in French and German.

He accompanied an uncle to Richmond, Virginia, on several business trips and decided to relocate there at the age of eighteen. Opening a household furnishings retail store in 1842, Ginter used his artistic sense to attractively display his wares to gift wrap the merchandise, talents that garnered him a sizable clientele. Ginter became friends and business partners with John F. Alvey, who convinced him to shift to wholesale notions and dry goods. For the Ginter & Alvey firm, Ginter traveled throughout Europe selecting and buying linens, white goods, and woolens for resale to rural customers in Virginia. Ginter's nephew George Arents became a partner in Ginter, Alvey & Arents when partner James Kent retired.

At the outbreak of the Civil War, Ginter set aside his business and enlisted in the Confederate army and in June 1862 became commissary of subsistence for Georgia regiments under General Edward L. Thomas. Ginter earned the nickname "The Fighting Commissary" during the battle of Second Manassas and rose to the rank of major. When the war ended in 1865, Ginter could not rebuild his business in economically depressed Richmond. He relocated to New York City, where he established a banking and brokerage firm with his former Richmond clerk, John H. Colquitt. The brokerage firm failed in 1869, and at age forty-five Lewis Ginter sought a third career.

Returning to Richmond, Ginter joined his friend John F. Allen to open a tobacco factory, John F. Allen & Co. (At some point the firm's name changed to Allen & Ginter.) Ginter traveled extensively promoting and selling their smoking and chewing tobacco. At home he booked orders, kept accounts, and designed advertising. On business trips to New York, Ginter noticed people smoking cigarettes, and in 1875 the firm began manufacturing hand-rolled cigarettes. Ginter developed "Richmond Gems," "Virginia Brights," and other brands and promoted the new cigarettes with painted advertisements, beautiful packaging with lithographed labels, enclosed picture card series, and coupons as prizes and premiums.

Seeking northern and foreign markets, Ginter exhibited the cigarettes at the 1876 Philadelphia Centennial Exposition, winning prizes, accolades, and smokers. With his contacts in Europe from his former wholesale business, Ginter expanded the tobacco firm's clientele in major European, Australian, South African, and Indian markets. The sultan of Turkey boosted sales of "Richmond Straight-Cuts" when he declared them his favorite cigarette. Allen & Ginter's offer of $75,000 for a practical cigarette machine prompted James Bonsack's 1881 patented invention. By 1883 the firm employed about 500 laborers, 80 percent of whom were white women and girls, for whom Ginter provided a library.

After twelve years of partnership, Allen retired in 1881, and John Pope took over Allen's interest in Allen & Ginter. The business became one of the top five tobacco manufacturers in the country, incorporating in 1888 with 1,000 employees. Rejecting a proposed tobacco trust, Ginter instead sold Allen & Ginter as a branch to the newly chartered American Tobacco Company in 1890 for $7.5 million; he declined the presidency because of his age. On the board of directors until resigning in April 1897, Ginter retired from active participation in the company and devoted himself to philanthropic pursuits in Richmond.

From extensive traveling, Ginter realized that Richmond lacked a first-class hotel and contracted with architects John Merven Carrère and Thomas Hastings to design and build the Jefferson Hotel in 1895 for $1.35 million. He purchased the *Richmond Times* newspaper in 1886 and gave it to his friend and attorney Joseph Bryan in 1887. The elegant brownstone house he built in 1888 became the social center of Richmond where Ginter entertained friends with games of whist and poker.

On a trip to Australia around 1887–1888, Ginter noticed that urban businessmen maintained weekend country estates. He began buying acreage in north Richmond for his own suburban home, "Westbrook," on 163 acres; in Henrico and Hanover counties for Bloomingdale stock farm on 280 acres and Maplewood farm on 750 acres; and to develop Ginter Park and Sherwood Park residential tracts of land on which he

built landscaped roads as president of the Sherwood Land Company and Brook Turnpike Company. In 1884 Ginter developed the ten-acre Lakeside Wheel Club for bicycling and Lakeside Park, a popular natural area with a lake, clubhouse, casino, zoo, professional nine-hole golf course, and bowling alley. Ginter's involvement with other local companies included being vice president of the Virginia Dredging Company, principal owner of the Richmond Locomotive Works, and a director of a local bank.

As a philanthropist, Ginter confined his charitable work to Richmond, disposing of $10 million of his estimated $12 million fortune before his death. He supported individuals on pensions, educated many Richmond children, financed local hospitals, and donated land to relocate the Union Theological Seminary from Farmville, Virginia, to Richmond. Richmonder John Stewart Bryan remarked that "Major Ginter was one of those generous men who regarded wealth as a means of public service and not for private indulgence." Although he never married, Ginter's sister, nieces, and nephew lived with him. Ginter died at Westbrook. After the funeral, one of Ginter's friends said, "He was one of the gamest men that I ever knew; a profound philosopher and one of the most thoroughly well-balanced men that I have ever met."

Ginter's advertising and marketing skills made cigarettes a national habit. He first used Virginia tobacco in cigarettes and pioneered brand identification with attractive packaging. He converted his tobacco fortune into civic improvements by developing beautifully landscaped suburban residential tracts, building an extensive road system, and constructing the magnificent Jefferson Hotel.

• The Valentine Museum, Richmond, Va., maintains files on Lewis Ginter and Allen & Ginter that contain a copy of his will, correspondence from Thomas F. Jeffress, secretary and treasurer of Allen & Ginter, and a letter to a newspaper editor clarifying Ginter's Civil War service record, among other biographical materials. The Valentine and the Library of Virginia Archives Division, Richmond, both have examples of the cigarette advertising cards. The Virginia Historical Society owns a scrapbook compiled by Jeffress about Lewis Ginter, particularly of obituaries from Richmond newspapers, *State*, *Times*, and *Dispatch*, all 3 Oct. 1897. The most complete account of Lewis Ginter's life and legacy can be found in David D. Ryan with Wayland W. Rennie, *Lewis Ginter's Richmond* (1991). For background on Ginter and tobacco, see Nannie May Tilley's *The Bright-Tobacco Industry, 1860–1929* (1948).

SUSAN HAMBURGER

GINZBERG, Louis (28 Nov. 1873–11 Nov. 1953), Talmudist, was born in Kovno, Lithuania, the son of Isaac Elias Ginzberg, a well-to-do merchant who traced his ancestry to fifteenth-century Italian Jewish scholar-bankers, and Zippe Jaffe, great-granddaughter of the brother of the Gaon of Vilna, the greatest Talmudist of all time. Both were paradigms of Lithuanian Jewish aristocracy.

Because young Levi (his European given name) early demonstrated a profound understanding of Talmudic argumentation, his parents sent him to yeshivas beginning at age eleven. In three years at the Telshe and Slobodka yeshivas he mastered most of the rabbinical literature. Illness forced him to leave the yeshiva world, but he later received rabbinic ordination on his own. He migrated to Germany where he completed the curriculum of the European Gymnasium and was admitted to the University of Berlin; he later transferred to Strassburg and then to Heidelberg, where he studied Semitic languages and literature with Theodore Noeldeke and philosophy with Kuno Fischer.

In 1899, shortly after receiving his Ph.D., Ginzberg emigrated to the United States, landing in New York City where, almost immediately, he became a writer for the *Jewish Encyclopedia*, contributing 406 articles to the twelve-volume work. In 1902 Solomon Schechter, making his first faculty appointment at the recently reorganized Jewish Theological Seminary of America, named Ginzberg professor of Talmud, a position he would hold for more than half a century. Ginzberg married Adele Katzenstein in 1909; they had two children. In his younger years, Ginzberg was active both in the synagogal organization of the Conservative movement and as a defender of the Jews against calumny. He later withdrew from the public arena, however, in order to concentrate on scholarship.

Ginzberg's primary goal as a scholar was to create a Jewish learning environment in the United States. He pursued this objective through personal example, exemplary teaching, and by establishing a support structure for the study of Jewish law, culture, and religion. His own area of expertise was what he called "Jewish law and lore." Building on his dissertation, which traced Jewish legends found in the writings of the early church fathers, and on his articles in the *Jewish Encyclopedia*, Ginzberg produced *Legends of the Jews* (7 vols., 1909–1938), a compilation of all the legends and parables about all the major biblical figures into one uninterrupted narrative.

If Ginzberg cherished Jewish lore for its beauty and its insights, he also freely acknowledged that every nation produces legends, myths, and stories. The uniqueness of Judaism, in his view, lay not in its narratives, but in its legal system. Thus, to his students and before public audiences he argued that Jewish law (Halakhah) has always been "the really typical creation of [the Jewish] people," its best expression of "active religiousness," the cornerstone of Jewish life. Most of his research dealt with the development of the rabbinic legal system. By applying the philological-historical approach of German critical scholarship, and by examining recently discovered texts from the Cairo Geniza, he traced the sources of Jewish law in such seminal studies as *Geonica* (1909) and *Studies into the Origins of the Mishnah* (1920). Most rabbinic scholars were steeped in knowledge of the Babylonian Talmud, completed in Mesopotamia around 500 C.E., but had little firsthand knowledge of the Palestinian Talmud, produced in Palestine a century earlier. Filling in the gap, Ginzberg labored to produce *A Commentary on the Palestinian Talmud* (3 vols., 1941), his magnum opus, which remained incomplete at his death and was later completed by David Weiss Halivni. Ginzberg also investigated antirabbinic trends in a pioneering study of the Damascus sect, *Eine unbekannte juedische Sekte* (An unknown Jewish sect) (1922), and analyzed the Karaitic controversy in *Geonic and Early Karaitic Halakah* (1929).

Ginzberg explicated his philosophy of Judaism in two collections of essays. Some of the pieces in *Students, Scholars and Saints* (1928) and *On Jewish Law and Lore* (1955) had been lectures originally delivered to audiences as diverse as a colloquium at the Hebrew University in Jerusalem (1929) and the celebration of Harvard's Tercentenary in 1936. The choice of Ginzberg as the Jewish scholar selected to speak at the Harvard event indicates the respect he engendered within the American scholarly community.

Many of Ginzberg's students became scholars as well as rabbis. The first group of seminarians included Louis Finkelstein, Boaz Cohen, Solomon Goldman, Judah Goldin, and Arthur Hertzberg, scholars who taught the next two generations of rabbis and university students. Pulpit rabbis often solicited Ginzberg's advice on matters of Jewish law. Ginzberg answered them freely but also called on them to further the goal of scholarship. He wrote thousands of letters to congregations, soliciting funds to underwrite the publication of rabbinic studies by European scholars such as Benjamin Lewin, Chaim Kosovsky, and Abraham Schreiber.

Ginzberg was founding president of the American Academy of Jewish Research, established in 1920 to support Jewish scholarship in the United States, and he served the Hebrew University of Jerusalem in various capacities in the 1930s, as academic adviser, visiting professor, and consultant. Also in that period, he was active in efforts to save Jewish scholars who were fleeing Eastern Europe and to find them academic positions in the United States.

As the preeminent American Talmudist of his day, Ginzberg was asked to grapple with many religious questions related to modern life, for example, permission to use grape juice for sacramental purposes during Prohibition, safeguarding women from eternal grass widowhood should their soldier-husbands remain unaccounted for at the end of World War II (according to Jewish law, a widow could not remarry unless her husband's death was confirmed by a witness), and the issue of artificial insemination (to which he was opposed). Ginzberg avoided innovation in Jewish law. In the years since his death in New York City, Ginzberg's contributions have remained an important source for scholars eager to comprehend the many strands of Jewish law and lore.

• The Louis Ginzberg Papers are in the Archives of the Jewish Theological Seminary Library in New York City. They contain letters, published and unpublished manuscripts, faculty memoranda, and policy statements; there also are many queries about Jewish law and some responses to the questions. There is no full-scale biography. Eli Ginzberg, his son, wrote a charming memoir, *Keeper of the Law: Louis Ginzberg* (1966). David Druck sketched Ginzberg's scholarly career to 1934 in *Reb Levi Ginzberg* (Yiddish). For a festschrift on the occasion of Ginzberg's seventieth birthday, Solomon Goldman wrote "The Portrait of a Teacher," *Louis Ginzberg Jubilee Volume* (1945); the same volume contains a bibliography of Ginzberg's writings by Boaz Cohen. See also Louis Finkelstein's essay in the *American Jewish Year Book* 56 (1955), pp. 573–79, and Hebert Parzen's chapter in *Architects of Conservative Judaism* (1964).

BAILA R. SHARGEL

GIOVANNITTI, Arturo Massimo (7 Jan. 1884–31 Dec. 1959), poet, journalist, and labor leader, was born in Ripabottoni (Molise), Italy, the son of Domenico Giovannitti, a physician and pharmacist, and Adelaide Levante. Raised in a family of middle-class professionals in southern Italy, Arturo Giovannitti was educated at the Collegio Mario Pagano in Campobasso, the regional capital, where he first demonstrated his literary ability by winning a national contest for poetry. Rather than attend university in Italy, Giovannitti decided to "visit the world," immigrating to Canada by himself at age sixteen or seventeen. Little is known about Giovannitti's activities in Canada before he enrolled in a theological seminary affiliated with McGill University in Montreal and became a pastor's assistant at a Presbyterian mission for Italians. His early attraction to Protestantism has never been adequately explained.

Giovannitti went to New York City in 1904. Unemployed and homeless, he slept on a bench in Mulberry Park, later memorialized in a poem. Soon he joined a Presbyterian mission for Italians in Brooklyn and began studying at Columbia University's Union Theological Seminary. After a year or so, he moved to Pennsylvania to become assistant pastor at a Presbyterian mission for Italians in a town near Pittsburgh. There he abandoned Christianity and embraced revolutionary syndicalism. His conversion resulted from a combination of influences: exposure to the poverty of the Italian workers; reading *Il Proletario* (The proletarian), organ of the Italian Socialist Federation (ISF); and personal contact with Carlo Tresca, the charismatic labor agitator and newspaper editor who lectured regularly in the mining and mill towns around Pittsburgh. Returning to New York City in 1906, Giovannitti worked as a bookkeeper while immersing himself in the Italian radical milieu. He joined the ISF in 1908. The first of Giovannitti's poems and political writings (some under the pseudonym Nino Gavitti) appeared that year in *Il Proletario* and in Tresca's *La Plebe*. Recruited by *Il Proletario*'s editorial committee in September 1909, he quickly became the newspaper's principal contributor, with articles and poems appearing in almost every issue. A superb orator, Giovannitti now became active in the labor movement, lecturing to striking Italian workers in and around New York City. At the ISF's national conference in April 1911, Italian-American syndicalists elected Giovannitti editor in chief of *Il Proletario* and national secretary of the federation.

Recognizing his reputation among Italian immigrants, the Industrial Workers of the World (IWW) asked Giovannitti to help lead the Italian textile workers who constituted the backbone of the great textile strike that had begun in Lawrence, Massachusetts, in January 1912. Giovannitti's rousing oratory and the organizational genius of Joseph Ettor, IWW chieftain in the East, were so effective in generating support for the walkout that mill owners and local authorities resolved to eliminate the two Italian leaders in hope of breaking the strike. When an Italian woman picketer was shot and killed by a policeman, the authorities used the incident as a pretext to arrest Giovannitti, Ettor, and an Italian striker named Joseph Caruso on 30 January, charging them as accessories to murder for having "incited to riot" with their speeches. The frameup was so transparently contrived, however, that the Ettor-Giovannitti case became an international cause célèbre while the strike ended victoriously in March. After a trial in Salem lasting nearly two months, the three defendants were acquitted on 25 November 1912, the verdict influenced in no small measure by the powerful courtroom statements Ettor and Giovannitti delivered in English on their own behalf.

Giovannitti's eight months in jail had proved to be the most creative of his literary career. Besides translating Emile Pouget's *Sabotage* into English for the IWW, he wrote about a dozen poems in English, including "The Walker" and "The Cage," that were published in *Current Literature*, *Atlantic Monthly*, and other prestigious magazines. They established his reputation as a major poet of social protest. "The Walker," considered Giovannitti's best poem in English, was later praised by Louis Untermeyer as "one of the most remarkable things our literature can boast," a personal document of a man in prison "unrivaled even by [Oscar Wilde's] *Ballad of Reading Gaol*." A collection of Giovannitti's English poems, *Arrows in the Gale*, was published in 1914, with an introduction by Helen Keller. Other poems and essays by Giovannitti then began to appear in *The Masses*, the principal magazine for American leftwing intellectuals, edited by Max Eastman.

After Lawrence, Giovannitti concentrated more upon his literary and journalistic endeavors than labor agitation. His speaking appearances for the IWW became less frequent, and he participated only briefly in the strikes of the Paterson silk workers and Akron tire workers in 1913. He gave even *Il Proletario* less and less attention, as he delegated most of his editorial duties to Edmondo Rossoni, the future fascist labor leader. Giovannitti resigned as editor in chief in June 1914, to pursue a more independent course of journalism based in New York City. Three months later he founded *Il Fuoco* (The fire), an eclectic political-literary biweekly, together with Onorio Ruotolo, a noted Neapolitan sculptor and liberal nationalist. Giovannitti relinquished *Il Fuoco* to his partner within less than a year and published *Vita* (Life), whose brief existence (Sept. to Nov. 1915) closed with a poem to console his mother over the death of her eldest son Aristide, recently killed fighting on the Italian front. Giovannitti had scarcely participated in the debate between interventionists and neutralists that fractured the ISF prior to Italy's joining the Allies in May 1915. But with his moral opposition to war now reinforced by personal tragedy (his younger brother, Giuseppe, would later die in the fighting as well), Giovannitti campaigned in speeches and writings vigorously against the slaughter. His antiwar play, *Come era nel principio* (As it was in the beginning) was staged in New York City, both in Italian (1916) and English translation (1917).

After revolution swept Russia in 1917, Giovannitti supported the Bolsheviks and opposed the interventionist campaign waged by the Allies and their "White" surrogates to restore the old order. He escaped prosecution during the American government's antiradical crusade in 1918 only because he had never officially belonged to the IWW and because he obtained a severance of his case from that of the 101 Wobblie leaders ultimately convicted, a strategy that caused a permanent breach with many old comrades. During the "Red Scare" of 1919–1920, Giovannitti remained unmolested despite his continuing support for the Bolsheviks and his contributions to procommunist publications such as *The Liberator* and *The New Masses*. Too antiauthoritarian to join the Communist party, Giovannitti nonetheless held Lenin in great esteem and would still rank him among his favorite historical personages forty years later.

Giovannitti became more active in the labor movement after the war, aligning himself with the Italian locals of the Amalgamated Clothing Workers of America (ACWA) and the International Ladies Garment Workers Union (ILGWU), led by Social Democrats. In November 1919 Giovannitti was chosen general secretary of the newly created Italian Chamber of Labor (ICL) in New York City, and in 1922 he became head of the ILGWU's educational department; he retained both positions throughout the 1920s. The ICL, largely unsuccessful as a labor institution, provided Giovannitti with a base for the antifascist activities that became the raison d'être for most Italian-American radicals. In April 1923 he was elected secretary general of the Anti-Fascist Alliance of North America (AFANA), founded with the help of the ICL and various Italian-American unions. After the Communists gained control of the AFANA by 1926, Giovannitti sided with the Social Democrats who seceded to form the Anti-Fascist Federation for the Freedom of Italy. Journalism also played a significant part in his antifascist activities. From March 1924 to February 1925, Giovannitti published *Il Veltro* (The greyhound), an organ financed by the ICL; briefly in 1930 he served as editor of *Il Nuovo Mondo*, the antifascist daily newspaper published with union support from 1925 to 1931. And like many Italian radicals in the 1920s, Giovannitti worked actively in the defense of Sacco and Vanzetti.

Giovannitti's career as a labor activist and journalist almost ended in 1931, when he was hired by Metro-Goldwin-Mayer (MGM) to write dialogue for movies dubbed in Italian. But Mussolini's government, fearing Giovannitti might use this position for antifascist propaganda, prevailed upon powerful Italian-American supporters in California to convince MGM to discharge him. Back in New York City, he joined the ILGWU's information office and then became director of the Italian Labor Education Bureau, founded by the ILGWU, the ACWA, and other unions in 1934. He held this post until 1940.

The previous year Giovannitti had separated from Carolina "Carrie" Zaikaner, his Russian-Jewish companion of almost thirty years and the mother of his two children. (A previous marriage, which produced a daughter, had ended in divorce.) The demise of his relationship with Zaikaner, who had endured years of verbal abuse and repeated infidelities, was rooted in Giovannitti's disenchantment with life and lengthy depression. He believed himself a failure because the creativity that won him great acclaim twenty years earlier had seemingly deserted him. In fact, he produced little poetry of note during his last twenty years, and it was mainly through the efforts of old comrades that some of his Italian poems were published as *Parole e sangue* (Words and blood) in 1938. Many of these poems were included in a larger collection, *Quando canta il gallo* (When the cock crows), published by his comrades in 1957.

For his last ten years Giovannitti was bedridden by a paralysis of the legs that doctors could neither diagnose nor treat, a malady that his family believed was psychological in origin. Giovannitti died of heart failure in New York City. In tribute to the departed "poet of the proletariat," Giovannitti's comrades issued *The Collected Poems of Arturo Giovannitti* (1962), with an introduction by Norman Thomas. The volume reproduced *Arrows in the Gale* and other poems in English published earlier.

• The four collections referred in the text do not include Giovannitti's complete output of poetry. Dozens of other poems, in Italian and English, can be found mainly in the radical and labor publications to which he contributed, sources also indispensible for a study of his career in the labor and antifascist movements. Besides the newspapers mentioned in the text, see *Il Lavoro* (New York) and *Giustizia* (New York), organs of ACWU and the ILGWU; and *Il Martello* (New York), published by Carlo Tresca. Also important is the dossier on Giovannitti compiled by the Italian police, the *Casellario Politico Centrale*, available at the Archivio Centrale dello Stato in Rome. Giovannitti was the subject of numerous articles in popular magazines during the Lawrence strike and Salem trial of 1912. Of more specialized interest are Justus Ebert, *The Trial of a New Society* (1912), and the IWW's *Ettor and Giovannitti before the Jury at Salem, Mass., November 23, 1912* (1912). Personal reminiscences by Italian comrades are given in "Omaggio a Arturo Giovannitti," in *La Parola del Popolo* 10, no. 44 (Feb.–Mar. 1960): 1–25. For more substantive discussions of his life and literature, see Joseph Tusiani, "Ricordo di Arturo Giovannitti," in *La Parola del Popolo* 24, no. 124 (July–Aug. 1974). Secondary sources in English are few. See Robert D'Attilio, "Arturo Giovannitti," in *The American Radical*, ed. Mari Jo Buhle et al. (1994), pp. 135–

42; Olga Peragallo, *Italian-American Authors and Their Contribution to American Literature* (1949), pp. 124–28; Wallace P. Sillanpoa, "The Poetry and Politics of Arturo Giovannitti," in *The Melting Pot and Beyond: Italian Americans in the Year 2000*, ed. Jerome Krase and William Egelman (1987). Personal information regarding Giovannitti's family life is given in the autobiographical novel by Len Giovannitti, *The Nature of the Beast* (1977). An obituary is in the *New York Times*, 1 Jan. 1960.

NUNZIO PERNICONE

GIPP, George (18 Feb. 1895–14 Dec. 1920), college football player, was born in Laurium, Michigan, the son of Matthew Gipp, a carpenter, and Isabella Taylor. A member of a large family of modest means, Gipp grew up in the Keweenaw Peninsula of Michigan, a cold, remote strip of land forming the northernmost part of the state's upper peninsula. A loner and extreme individualist, he enrolled in high school at nearby Calumet, but distaste for academic matters kept him in constant trouble, often facing expulsion with school officials. As an adolescent Gipp was an undisciplined prankster who spent time in such dubious activities as pool, poker, and other forms of gambling. Fortunately, the quest for entertainment included participatory athletics. As an adult he stood 6′2″, weighed approximately 185 pounds, and ran the 100-yard dash in 10.2 seconds—equal to the best recorded time for both 1917 and 1919. He excelled at every sport he tried, but because temperament and academic problems kept him out of high school athletics, organized competition came through amateur teams or the local YMCA (Young Men's Christian Association).

It was as a baseball player that Gipp established an identity beyond his immediate surroundings. The nation's best-organized and most popular participatory sport—at least outside of college—baseball occupied Gipp's summers throughout his life, even after football had given him a national reputation. An excellent outfielder and a good hitter, he attracted the attention of both the Chicago Cubs and the Chicago White Sox, and had he not died as a young man he might have played center field in the major leagues.

Baseball, in fact, led Gipp to football. He became aware of Notre Dame University, and the school of him, through friends who had played baseball there. Three years out of high school (he did not graduate), he appeared on the Notre Dame campus in the fall of 1916, bringing the contemporary equivalent of a baseball scholarship—the promise of a job that would pay expenses. Admitted as a conditional student, he was expected to make up academic deficiencies either during his first year or in summer school.

At Notre Dame Knute Rockne, then assistant football coach, detected Gipp's general athletic talents, especially an ability to kick a football. On the freshman squad in 1916 he drop-kicked a field goal of 62 yards, an astonishing feat. He made the varsity in 1917, but for reasons never explained he showed up two weeks after the season had started and missed five more games at the end with a fractured leg.

During the 1918, 1919, and 1920 seasons Gipp was the team's star performer and an emerging figure in collegiate sports. Primarily a running back, he demonstrated speed, agility, intelligence, and power in carrying the ball from scrimmage as well as in returning kickoffs and punts. He was an excellent passer, the team's primary kicker, and, during an era before the platoon system had become common, he often played defense. In his varsity career he compiled a total of 4,833 yards—2,341 rushing, 1,700 as a passer, and 723 in return yards and interceptions. The crowning glory came during the 1920 season, when Gipp, although ill for the last few games, rushed for 827 yards in 102 carries, an average of 8.11 yards per carry. On 30 November he learned while in the hospital that he had been named fullback on Walter Camp's prestigious national team, thus making him Notre Dame's first All-American.

Gipp's lifestyle formed his identity almost as much as his accomplishments in sports. Football did not stand in the way of his personal habits. He smoked and drank heavily, often staying up nights pursuing women and other means of entertainment or making money. Through poker, pool (he excelled at pocket and three-cushion billiards), and betting on football games he provided himself with a comfortable standard of living. In the heralded game with Army in 1920 members of the team raised $2,100 to bet on themselves, $400 of it from Gipp. He practiced sparingly and was a college student only in name; he ignored academic requirements, and in some semesters he received no grades at all. Rockne protected and patronized him, and though school officials, out of four years of exasperation, finally expelled Gipp in March 1920, they cancelled the expulsion a few weeks later. Reason for the reversal remained a mystery, although pressure from alumni, influential townspeople, and Rockne has remained the best answer. At the time there was no league or national organization to police how colleges managed their athletes.

At the end of the 1920 season Notre Dame received national recognition (a rank of second in most polls) as they recorded an undefeated season. The most striking victory came at West Point, a perennial power, in a game that attracted the attention of influential eastern sportswriters. Gipp accumulated 385 yards of offense (150 rushing, 123 passing, 112 in returns) in leading Notre Dame to erase a halftime deficit and defeat the Black Knights 28–17. A few days later Gipp contracted a sore throat and a bad cough, causing him to play sparingly in the following games and to miss the final game altogether. He entered a South Bend, Indiana, hospital on 23 November. The illness turned into pneumonia, a dreaded and deadly disease, especially in that time before the introduction of antibiotics. With the campus absorbed in Gipp's condition and the world of sports paying close attention, he died three weeks later.

In death as in life, Gipp remained a man of mystery. Controversy persisted over the source of his illness, responsibility for his medical expenses, a report that he had converted to Roman Catholicism during his illness (a priest administered last rites, but his Protestant family denied the conversion), and the true measure of his talents. Gipp's reputation became both a contributor to and a benefactor of the mystique of Notre Dame football as it progressed under Rockne and his successors. Rockne, the most admired coach of the 1920s, heralded his fallen star in many ways, including a 1930 article, "Gipp the Great," that introduced the "Gipper" story—that Gipp on his deathbed had urged his coach to use his death to inspire the team in a future game. What became known as "the speech" (Gipp's admonition to "win one for the Gipper") reappeared in the film *Knute Rockne: All American*, released in 1940. In a remarkable turn of events the election to the presidency of Ronald Reagan, who had played Gipp in the movie, gave the memory of Gipp (and the Gipper story) another life, extending the legend and prompting in the 1980s a new round of inquiry into Gipp's brief life.

To say, as did Rockne, that Gipp was superior to his illustrious contemporaries, Red Grange and Jim Thorpe, is at least subject to argument. To contend that he ranked among the best in the history of college football ignores the modesty of the competition with whom and against whom Gipp played. He was, however, an exceptionally gifted athlete who—through exploits on the field and in the mystique that followed his life—probably contributed more than any player to the emergence of Notre Dame as a force in college football.

• There are no papers of George Gipp, and so accounts of his life and legend rely much on recollections by people who knew him, newspaper coverage, and material in collections of related individuals, such as Rockne. Rockne contributed heavily to the legend, either through his efforts or those of his ghostwriter, John B. Kennedy, in "Gipp the Great," *Collier's*, 22 Nov. 1930, pp. 14–15, 63–64; some of this information was repeated in Rockne's autobiography, published the following year. Gene Schoor, *A Treasury of Notre Dame Football* (1962), contains Jim Beach's essay, "Gipp of Notre Dame," and Gipp's account told to Walter Kennedy, "My Greatest Football Game." Biographies include James A. Peterson, *Gipp of Notre Dame* (1959); Patrick Chelland, *One for the Gipper: George Gipp, Knute Rockne, and Notre Dame* (1973); and George Gekas, *The Life and Times of George Gipp* (1987). The 1980s sparked new interest in Gipp, as was exemplified in Red Smith, "Winning One for the Gipper," *New York Times*, 21 Jan. 1981; and James A. Cox, "Was the Gipper Really for Real? You Can Bet He Was," *Smithsonian* 16 (Dec. 1985): 130–50, an essay condensed in *Reader's Digest* the following year. A recent volume that challenges many aspects of Gipp's legend is Murray Sperber, *Shake Down the Thunder: The Creation of Notre Dame Football* (1993).

ROSS GREGORY

GIRARD, Charles Frédéric (9 Mar. 1822–29 Jan. 1895), zoologist and physician, was born in Mulhouse, Haut-Rhin, France; his parents' names are unknown. He received his education at the College de Neuchâtel in Switzerland, beginning probably in 1839. There he was a student and later an assistant to Louis Agassiz for at least eight years. In 1847 Agassiz joined the faculty at Harvard; Girard accompanied him, continuing in the capacity of both student and assistant. The Boston Society of Natural History published his first scientific paper, "On the Genus *Cottus*," in its *Proceedings* in 1849. At some point in 1849 or 1850, a staff disagreement involving Girard developed among Agassiz's staff at Harvard. Agassiz concluded that Girard was not sufficiently grateful when Agassiz supported the younger man in the dispute. Soon thereafter the zoologist Spencer F. Baird, just beginning his duties as assistant secretary of the Smithsonian Institution, invited Girard to work with him as his assistant in Washington, D.C. Girard accepted, a move that angered Agassiz, who considered this evidence of his former assistant's disloyalty and broke off their friendship. Agassiz was also very patronizing toward Baird, whom he regarded as something of a scientific rival, and he was subsequently sharply critical of all publications coauthored by Baird and Girard.

From 1850 to 1860 Girard assisted Baird in several areas. One involved planning for the new U.S. National Museum, which began operations in 1857. Essentially a "closet naturalist," as laboratory scientists were then known, Girard was also handed a substantial number of assignments entailing the identification and description of invertebrate and vertebrate specimens. This decade would prove his most productive period of scientific research. Among his early publications at the Smithsonian was an article on "Mammalia" in the *Iconographic Encyclopedia of Science, Literature and Art* (1851), and *Bibliographia Americana Historico-Naturalis; or, Bibliography of American Natural History for the Year 1851* (1852). Girard's first major study, "Contributions to the Natural History of Freshwater Fishes of North America: Part I. Monograph of the Cottoids," also appeared in 1852. This was followed by collaboration with Baird on the first of what was projected as a multi-part "Catalogue of North American Reptiles in the Museum of the Smithsonian Institution." "Part I: Serpents," appeared in 1853, but no more were ever published. Girard's "Researches upon Nemerteans and Planarians I: Embryonic Development of *Planocera elliptica*" was published in 1854. Other tasks entailed descriptions of invertebrate and vertebrate specimens for publication by the Smithsonian or in various scientific journals. In 1854 Girard became a U.S. citizen and in that same year began medical studies at Georgetown College in Washington, receiving his M.D. in 1856.

Girard's multifaceted zoological talents were exhibited in the many papers, articles, and reports he completed on his own or in collaboration with Baird. Girard did virtually all the work on most of their coauthored projects, as Baird's time was almost wholly taken up with his own research on birds and mammals and his increasingly heavy administrative duties. Girard's publications primarily concerned various insect groups, spiders, worms, crustaceans, fish, and reptiles. Published for the most part between 1852 and 1860, they were based on specimens brought back by a number of federally sponsored expeditions and surveys, including the Wilkes Expedition (1838–1842); the U.S. and Mexican Boundary Survey (1848); army explorations of the Salt Lake Valley (1849), Zuni and Colorado Rivers (1851), Red River (1853), and Nebraska and the Dakotas (1856); two naval expeditions to Chile (1849) and the La Plata River in Paraguay (1853); and the Pacific Railway Surveys to the western United States (1853–1859).

Girard began working on volume twenty of the Wilkes Expedition reports, dealing with reptiles (*Herpetology*, 1858) in 1851. The Joint Congressional Committee on the Library of Congress insisted that Baird's name appear on the title page as having prepared and superintended this work, although Baird made it clear that Girard had done the work and was the more knowledgeable concerning herpetology. Appropriately, a commercially published edition, issued the same year, was credited exclusively to Girard. Three years later Girard was awarded the Cuvier Prize by the Institute of France for this accomplishment. Girard also completed *Fishes*, a massive 400-page report, as part four of volume ten of the Pacific Railway Survey Reports in 1859. In addition, he published other articles on fish specimens from the Pacific Railway Surveys in the transactions of several scientific societies. Most of these accounts entailed the description of substantial numbers of new species and genera, and Girard's work on fishes and reptiles was considered particularly noteworthy.

Girard left Washington for an extended visit to his homeland from 1860 to 1863. Sympathetic to the Confederate cause, he agreed to bring back much-needed medical supplies and drugs for the Confederate army. He arrived back in America with the supplies, although he had some trouble in doing so, and he visited Virginia and the Carolinas for some weeks during the summer of 1863. His account of this wartime journey in the South was published in Paris in 1864 as *Les États Confédérés d'Amérique visités en 1863: Memoire adresse a S.M. Napoleon III*. Following the war, he made a final trip to Washington, at which point he evidently concluded that he no longer wished to live in the United States. Returning to France in 1865, he practiced medicine in Paris for several decades and served as chief physician for a military ambulance there during the Franco-Prussian War. His account of his dealings with typhoid fever during the war was published as *L'Ambulance Militaire de la rue Violet, No. 57* in 1872.

Returning to his old interests in zoology after more than a quarter of a century in 1888, he spent several years compiling a bibliography of his scientific publications while publishing a number of papers concerning fish. A final paper, published in 1891, dealt with North American flatworms and was regarded as an important contribution to that field. He died in Neuilly-sur-Seine, France, near Paris. He never married.

• Biographical sketches are in Clark A. Elliott, ed., *Biographical Dictionary of American Science: The Seventeenth through*

the *Ninetenth Centuries* (1979), and in Kraig Adler, ed., *Contributions to the History of Herpetology* (1989). See also the article concerning Girard by D. S. Lamb in *American Medical Biographies*, ed. H. A. Kelly and W. L. Burrage (1920). Girard's role in writing the volume on fishes for the Wilkes Expedition Reports is discussed in Herman J. Viola and Carolyn Margolis, eds., *Magnificent Voyagers: The U.S. Exploring Expedition, 1838–1842* (1985). For mention of Girard's relationship with Agassiz and Baird, see Edward Lurie, *Louis Agassiz: A Life in Science* (1960), and E. F. Rivinus and E. M. Youssef, *Spencer Baird of the Smithsonian* (1992). Information concerning Girard's scientific publications may be found in George B. Goode, "The Published Writings of Dr. Charles Girard," *Bulletin of the United States National Museum* 41, (1891); Max Meisel, ed., *A Bibliography of American Natural History: The Pioneer Century, 1769–1865* (1926); and Daniel C. Haskell, *The United States Exploring Expedition, 1838–1842, and Its Publications, 1844–1874* (1942). W. S. Hoole, trans., *A Visit to the Confederate States of America in 1863: A Memoir Addressed to His Majesty Napoleon III* (1962), is an English translation of Girard's 1864 memoir concerning his trip to Virginia and the Carolinas.

KEIR B. STERLING

GIRARD, Stephen (20 May 1750–26 Dec. 1831), merchant, banker, and philanthropist, was born in Bordeaux, France, the son of Pierre Girard, an officer in the French navy, and Odette Lafargue. He was blind, or partially sighted, in one eye at birth and, therefore, probably received less formal education than his peers. At age fourteen he signed on as a cabin boy for vessels sailing to the West Indies. His first American port of entry was New Orleans. After receiving a license to serve as a ship captain at age twenty-three, Girard was named an officer on a voyage to Port-au-Prince, Saint Domingue (now Haiti), in 1774. He departed the West Indies and set sail for New York with a consignment of sugar and coffee. Rather than returning to France, Girard remained in New York and became an employee of the shipping firm of Thomas Randall & Son. He purchased a half-interest in the ship *La Jeune Babé*, and on the return trip from St. Pierre, Martinique, in 1776, Girard encountered rough seas and sailed up the Delaware River to Philadelphia, then the largest American port city; it became his new home port. He married Mary Lum, the daughter of a local shipbuilder, in 1777. At some point in their marriage, his wife became mentally ill, and he placed her in an institution, where she remained until her death in 1815. There were no children.

From the American Revolution through the War of 1812, a span of three decades, Girard was actively engaged in the foreign trade sector. He initially emphasized trade with the West Indies but later extended his horizons to Europe and Asia. During his lifetime, he owned a total of eighteen ships but never more than six at any time. He named three of his finest vessels after French philosophers: *Montesquieu*, *Rousseau*, and *Voltaire*.

In 1810 Girard joined a group of merchants in drafting a memorial that urged Congress to recharter the First Bank of the United States. The bill failed on a close vote in the Senate. The bank then went into liquidation, and Girard seized the opportunity to acquire the bank's headquarters, investing $1.2 million in the institution. The Bank of Stephen Girard was a private, unchardered bank that competed with several large incorporated banks in Philadelphia. Private banks were technically prevented from issuing banknotes, but the law was never enforced against the Girard Bank. The bank was liquidated after the proprietor's death.

When the U.S. Treasury experienced problems in floating loans during the War of 1812, Girard, David Parish, another Philadelphia merchant banker, and several New York businessmen recruited by John Jacob Astor (1763–1848) agreed to form a syndicate to help sell government bonds to investors. This was the first occasion that the federal government used investment bankers in raising money in the capital markets. After the war, Girard was an important promoter of the movement to charter the Second Bank of the United States, and he subscribed for $3 million of the bank's $35 million in capital. President James Madison (1751–1836) appointed him as one of five government directors, but Girard was dissatisfied with the managerial policies of William Jones (1760–1831), the bank's president, and he soon resigned his directorship.

Girard was generous toward his adopted city with his time as well as his money. When the yellow fever epidemic struck in 1793, he volunteered to supervise the hospital at Bush Hill. At his death on a farm on the outskirts of Philadelphia, Girard—the most successful private banker in American history—left the bulk of his immense wealth (over $6 million) for the establishment of a school to serve the educational needs of poor white fatherless boys. Certain heirs contested the will in the famous case of *Vidal v. The City of Philadelphia*, but the Supreme Court upheld the terms, thereby contributing to American law concerning the rights and powers of charities. However, in the 1950s the courts permitted Girard College (a misleading term according to modern usage) to admit boys and girls aged six to eighteen of all races, mostly from Philadelphia and surrounding areas plus some children from New Orleans and New York who were orphaned or living in severely dysfunctional families.

• The originals of Girard's voluminous correspondence are held at Girard College and are not open to the public. A microfilm version with over 600 reels is available for research at the American Philosophical Library in Philadelphia. The most recent biography is Harry E. Wildes, *Lonely Midas: The Story of Stephen Girard* (1943). A two-volume biography is John B. McMaster, *The Life and Times of Stephen Girard* (1918). A scholarly book that examines his banking career is Donald Adams, *Finance and Enterprise in Early America: A Study of Stephen Girard's Bank, 1812–1831* (1978). An obituary is in the *National Gazette*, 29 Dec. 1831.

EDWIN J. PERKINS

GIRARDEAU, John Lafayette (14 Nov. 1825–23 June 1898), Presbyterian clergyman and educator, was born on James Island, South Carolina, the son of John Bohum Girardeau and Claudia Herne Freer. His mother died when he was seven years old; his father, when he was ten. Sent to live with relatives in nearby Charleston, the boy attended a school administered by German Quakers until he was fourteen. Such training prepared him adequately for advanced studies, and in 1844 he graduated from the College of Charleston. During the next year he performed tutorial duties at a plantation in the vicinity and became engaged to the estate owner's fifteen-year-old daughter, Penelope Sarah Hamlin. Girardeau nurtured that relationship during the next three years while he pursued ministerial training at Columbia Theological Seminary in the state's capital. He graduated in 1848 and was licensed to preach from the local presbytery. The following year he married Penelope; they had ten children.

Girardeau served a number of rural congregations between 1848 and 1853. Since few of them continued the old practice of mixed seating, he usually conducted services for white members and then repeated everything in a second session for slaves who had come to worship. In 1853 Zion Church, a black congregation in Charleston that had separated from Second Presbyterian, called him to become its pastor. Having no prejudice against ministering to African Americans, Girardeau accepted the invitation and made that church a notable presence in the city. His activities increased membership rolls several times over, and his pulpit oratory attracted large audiences. The preacher's reputation for personal piety, sound learning, and stirring eloquence brought scores of visitors to the church; their frequent return and applications for membership confirmed it. Girardeau was comfortable with blacks forming congregations and directing their own affairs, but whites asked to join Zion Church, too, and the expanding membership soon comprised adherents of all different backgrounds found in cosmopolitan Charleston. The influx of numbers and wealth made it possible to build a larger sanctuary, more in keeping with the church's status and its leader as one of the foremost preachers in the city. In addition to expanding his own church, this energetic clergyman also participated in numerous revivals and conducted regular missionary journeys to coastal plantations.

When his state seceded from the Union and civil war broke out in 1861, Girardeau served as chaplain in the 23rd Regiment of South Carolina Volunteers in the Confederate army. He performed pastoral duties for troops throughout the four-year conflict and was present at such epic conflicts as Malvern Hill and Second Manassas, plus the constant skirmishing during the siege of Petersburg. Toward the end of that last engagement he was captured and held as a prisoner for more than three months. Released in July 1865, Girardeau returned home, intending to resume his pastorate. But he found that Zion Church had been confiscated by agents of the Freedmen's Bureau, and so he was forced to work as a minister at large for several months. Within a year, however, his black parishioners once again formed a new congregation, retaining the name of Zion, and asked him to resume his pastorate among them. This he happily did for another decade.

In 1875 Girardeau turned his interests to higher education. That year he became professor of didactic and polemic theology at Columbia Theological Seminary. For twenty years he instructed ministerial candidates according to traditional, conservative canons that regarded Calvinist doctrine as derived from divine sources but compatible with reason. He insisted that the familiar truths of total depravity, unconditional election, limited atonement, irresistible grace, and perseverance of the saints were manifestly superior to any Arminian claims about free will and human effort. Since his ideas had been formed largely before Charles Darwin's publications, Girardeau was sharply opposed to evolutionary theories and through his writings influenced many others to think likewise. As a regular contributor to the religious press, he argued bitterly against many innovations in thought or social practice. In the latter case, for instance, he zealously advocated church-sponsored education as preferable to public schools. Gravely formidable in the classroom and pugnacious in polemic writings, he retired in 1895 on the principle that one should not teach after reaching the age of seventy. He died in Columbia.

• Girardeau's writings include *Calvinism and Evangelical Arminianism: Compared as to Election, Reprobation, Justification, and Related Doctrines* (1890), *The Will in its Theological Relations* (1891), *Discussions of Philosophical Questions* (1900), and *Discussions of Theological Questions* (1905). See also George A. Blackburn, ed., *The Life Work of John L. Girardeau* (1916); and Douglas F. Kelly, *Preachers of Power: Four Stalwarts of the South* (1992). An obituary is in the *(Charleston, S.C.) News and Courier*, 24 June 1898.

HENRY WARNER BOWDEN

GIRARDOT, Étienne (22 Feb. 1856–10 Nov. 1939), actor, was born in St. John's Wood, a suburb of London, the son of Gustave Girardot, a successful portrait painter; his mother's name is not recorded. Étienne served as his father's apprentice, but although he studied painting for several years and seemed to show artistic promise, he was lured away by some satisfying experiences in amateur theatricals and decided to devote himself to an acting career.

Girardot's first professional appearance was with a provincial company at the age of seventeen. It took him eight more years to achieve his first London success in *The Yellow Dwarf* (1883). During the next few years he made versatile appearances in numerous Shakespearean productions, reportedly taking as many as fifteen parts in a week and playing eight roles in a single play. He portrayed Antonio in the Lyceum production of *Much Ado about Nothing* in which Ellen Terry first gave her celebrated interpretation of Beatrice, and he toured during 1884 and 1885 with Squire and Mrs. Bancroft.

Girardot's big break came in 1893 when he was selected by playwright Brandon Thomas to play the central role of Lord Fancourt Babberley in the first American production of Thomas's farce hit, *Charley's Aunt*,

which had opened in London on 21 December 1892 and was destined to have an original run there of almost 1,500 performances. The comedy of Oxford undergraduate life established itself as an equal favorite in the United States after its Broadway premiere on 2 October 1893. Girardot scored a personal triumph in the role of a student impersonating the aunt of the title. He played it for several years in the original production and in a 1906 Broadway revival, as well as in other revivals on the road.

Girardot appeared in *Miranda of the Balcony* (1901) and in the comedy hit *The Diplomat* the following year. He continued to be active on the American stage for decades, associated with a number of successful Broadway plays. His final period of work on Broadway included *Becky Sharp* (1929), *Lysistrata* (1930), and *Twentieth Century* (1932).

Between 1912 and 1914 Girardot appeared in a series of two-reel silent films for Vitagraph, notably *The Violin of Monsieur* with Clara Kimball Young. Later he made other films for Tannhauser and Universal. He also appeared in several features with Dustin Farnum. He is best known as a screen actor, however, for his work in sound films. The dapper little actor with the birdlike face, aquiline nose, small moustache, twinkling eyes, pixyish smile, and carefully-brushed wisps of hair at the back of an otherwise bald head became a familiar figure in numerous films between 1933 and his death.

Girardot began this period of his film work with a performance as Dr. Doremus, the New York medical examiner, in *The Kennel Murder Case*. Investing the role of Doremus with distinctive personal touches, Girardot created an effective characterization that he would repeat in its sequels, *The Dragon Murder Case* and *The Garden Murder Case*.

In 1934 Girardot repeated the role of the religious zealot that he had created on stage in the film version of the screwball comedy hit *Twentieth Century*. During the remaining years of his screen career he was seen in a variety of supporting roles in films for MGM, 20th Century-Fox, and Warner Bros., including *Clive of India*, with Ronald Colman (1935); *In Old Kentucky*, with Will Rogers (1935); *Curly Top*, with Shirley Temple (1935); *The Bishop Misbehaves*, with Edmund Gwenn (1935); *Professor Beware*, with Harold Lloyd (1938); *The Hunchback of Notre Dame*, with Charles Laughton (1939); and *The Story of Vernon and Irene Castle*, with Fred Astaire and Ginger Rogers (1939). Girardot died in Hollywood. He was survived by his wife, Violetta Shelton, a physician.

Girardot was an accomplished character actor who left the imprint of a distinctive personality on a body of work fondly recalled by those who had the pleasure of seeing his performances at the time he created them. They remain a pleasant minor legacy of the 1930s, an important period in the history of American film.

• For information on Girardot's film career see Sol Chaneles and Albert Wolsky, *The Movie Makers* (1974); James Robert Parish, *Hollywood Character Actors* (1978); and Alfred E.

Twomey and Arthur F. McClure, *The Versatiles: Supporting Character Players in the Cinema 1930–50* (1969). An obituary is in the *New York Times*, 11 Nov. 1939.

ALBERT O. WEISSBERG

GIRDLER, Tom Mercer (19 May 1877–4 Feb. 1965), industrialist, was born in Clark County, Indiana, the son of Lewis Girdler, a part-time farmer and manager of a family-owned cement plant, and Elizabeth Mercer. After attending a one-room country school and the Manual Training High School in nearby Louisville, Kentucky, Girdler obtained the needed funds from a wealthy aunt to enroll in Lehigh University, where he received a degree in mechanical engineering in 1901. After graduation he was employed by the Buffalo Forge Company and was sent to England as a sales engineer.

Eager to return home, Girdler left London in 1902 to accept a position as foreman for the Oliver Iron and Steel Company in Pittsburgh. The following year he married Mary Elizabeth Hayes; they had four children. At Oliver, Girdler found his proper milieu in the steel industry, even though he was to change jobs frequently over the next several years. He took managerial positions with the Colorado Fuel and Iron Company (1905–1907), the Atlantic Steel Company in Atlanta (1908–1914), and Jones & Laughlin in Pittsburgh (1914–1929).

At Jones & Laughlin, Girdler rose rapidly in management. He became general superintendent of the company's major plant at Aliquippa, Pennsylvania, in 1920. There he built a model town in which, as he later boasted in his autobiography, he established "a benevolent dictatorship" with himself as an "unofficial caliph" who ruled without the restraint of any democratic process. His workers would agree that it was most certainly a dictatorship, though they might question the word "benevolent." They more commonly described it as "Little Siberia."

Girdler's success at Aliquippa made him the crown prince of J & L, and in 1928 he ascended the throne as president of the company. As head of a well-established and highly successful steel company, Girdler had seemingly reached a position of preeminence within the industry. It therefore came as a surprise when only a year later in 1929 he announced his resignation in order to join forces with Cleveland financier Cyrus Eaton to create Republic Steel Corporation. This was generally regarded as a foolhardy move, for the steel mills that Eaton had secured by merging four small companies were mostly old and inefficient plants centered in the Mahoning Valley of east central Ohio, where the cost of producing steel was considerably higher than in the main steel centers at Pittsburgh and Cleveland. Girdler, however, was eager to build a new company that would be truly his own. He, moreover, had no intention of remaining bottled up in the Mahoning Valley trying to compete with only a scattering of antiquated mills.

Girdler had entered on this new venture at the moment the country was sliding into the greatest depression in its history, but he saw this not as a time for timid retraction, but rather as an opportunity for expansion. He promptly began negotiations for the acquisition of two additional steel companies, Corrigan-McKinney and Trucson. The former company could provide Republic with some much-needed assets: a modern steel plant in Cleveland, fifty million tons of iron ore reserves in Minnesota and Michigan, dock facilities on Lake Erie, and a steel sheet mill at Monroe, Michigan, only twenty miles from its chief market, the automobile plants in Detroit. Trucson could also make its contribution as the largest fabricator of steel alloys in the Midwest.

Girdler had the vision to see that the nineteenth-century Carnegie age of steel was ending. The major markets for steel would not be in railroads but in automobiles, in airplanes, and in home products. Republic would specialize in lightweight steel alloys for everything from plane fuselages and auto fenders to home window sashes, doors, and tableware. As *Fortune* (Dec. 1935) pointed out, Girdler was giving a new interpretation to integration within the steel industry—by controlling not the raw materials but the finished consumer products.

The fulfillment of these expansive plans did not come easily. Girdler first had to convince his own company of the wisdom of his proposals, and then he had to sell the idea of merger to the owners of the other two companies and persuade them to accept Republic shares in lieu of cash, which he did not have. Finally, he had to fight in the courts the attempt of the federal government to block the merger. Not until 1935 did Girdler emerge as victor. In the meantime, Republic continued to lose money. Its stock dropped from an initial value of $80 a share in 1930 to $2 a share in 1932. By 1934 the company showed a net loss of $30 million, and its mills were operating at only 20 percent capacity. Girdler, however, never hesitated to mortgage the present in the expectation of future gains, and he continued to issue annual bullish statements that the greatest age of steel lay just ahead.

Girdler's optimism was bolstered by the establishment of a national steel code under the provisions of the National Industrial Recovery Act of 1933. Although a lifelong Republican, Girdler became an enthusiastic supporter of this New Deal program. He saw in the NIRA an instrument by which industry-wide standards would prevent the giants of the industry from crushing the smaller companies with unfair competitive practices. Republic was one of the first to sign the steel code, and even after the Supreme Court declared the NIRA unconstitutional in 1935, Girdler continued to urge the industry to comply voluntarily with the code.

One provision of the NIRA legislation, however—Section 7A of Title I setting labor policies within each industry—did not have Girdler's stamp of approval. He was willing to accept a code calling for higher wages and an eight-hour day as long as every other steel company was held to the same standard. What he would not accept was the principle that labor had a right to organize and bargain collectively with management. To offset a resurgent unionism that had lain dormant since the failure of the great steel strike of 1919, Republic along with several other companies established the Employees' Representation Plan. Labor, however, quickly saw it as a euphemism for the hated company union because the final arbiter in any dispute would be Chairman Girdler. The workers found their delight in the National Labor Relations Act of 1935, which enabled John L. Lewis, as head of the newly created Congress of Industrial Organizations (CIO), to proceed with plans for an industry-wide union to be organized by the Steel Workers Organizing Committee (SWOC), chaired by Philip Murray.

A progressive in his vision of a new era for steel in the twentieth century, Girdler nevertheless was a reactionary in respect to labor policy. He drew his inspiration directly from the nineteenth-century world of Henry Clay Frick. "We are not going to recognize any professional union," he told the American Iron and Steel Institute in 1934. He fully expected the entire industry to present a united front against the CIO. He was caught off guard in March 1937 when the giant of the industry, U.S. Steel, without a struggle, signed a contract with Murray. Many other smaller companies, including his former firm Jones & Laughlin, followed suit.

In this crisis four major steel companies, Republic, Bethlehem, Youngstown Sheet and Tube, and Inland Steel, refused to capitulate to unionism. Girdler became the spokesman for these companies, now dubbed "Little Steel." He delivered their manifesto of defiance: "I won't have a contract, verbal or written, with an irresponsible, racketeering, violent Communist body like the CIO" (*New York Times*, 25 June 1937). When Murray on 26 May 1937 called for a strike against the holdouts, Little Steel responded with lockouts. The American Iron and Steel Institute promptly gave its blessing to this action by electing Girdler its president. The stage was set for the showdown that came on 30 May at Republic's plant in South Chicago. Striking workers, attempting to establish a picket line around the plant, were fired on by Chicago police. Ten workers were killed and 100 more were injured. "Remember the Memorial Day Massacre" became as much of a rallying cry for labor in the late 1930s as "Remember Homestead" had been in the 1890s.

Undeterred by the public outcry, Girdler and his allies stood firm as violence quickly spread from Chicago to Michigan and Ohio. Girdler employed new tactics to support old doctrines of rugged capitalism, including futile attempts to drop food from airplanes to employees supporting management by remaining in the plants. A more successful tactic was the arousal of public opinion against the strikers by playing up the communist menace and by threatening to move mills to other communities. With the support of local chambers of commerce, city police, vigilante groups, and ultimately with the protection of the National Guard of Ohio, the mills were again opened to nonunion labor.

By November 1937, the strike was broken. Girdler had become the very symbol of hard-nosed, unreformed capitalism. In the final speech of his 1940 campaign for the presidency, delivered in Girdler's hometown of Cleveland, Franklin Roosevelt depicted as his enemies "the two forces of dictatorship in our own land—on the one hand the Communists, and on the other the Girdlers" (*New York Times*, 3 Nov. 1940).

Girdler's victory over unionism, however, proved to be of short duration. With the entry of the United States into World War II, the newly created National Labor Board in early 1942 decreed that government contracts would be granted only to companies that recognized the right of collective bargaining. NWLB offered a far more powerful inducement to unionize than had the NLRB. Faced with either accepting unionism or having no market for its goods, Little Steel quickly capitulated. By August 1942, virtually the entire industry, including Republic Steel, had signed contracts with the United Steel Workers of America.

Girdler throughout his business career seemed to thrive on controversy. Nor did he find much tranquility in his domestic life after his first marriage was terminated by the death of Mary Girdler in 1917. In 1918 he married Clara Astley, who divorced him in March 1924. One month later he married Lillian Compton Snowden. This marriage was also dissolved by divorce on 28 November 1942, and on 2 December of that year he married his secretary, Helen Brennan. There were no children of these subsequent marriages.

In December 1941, with the permission of the directors of Republic Steel, Girdler accepted invitations to head two California aircraft companies, Consolidated and Vultee, with the stipulation that he would remain the chief executive officer of Republic. In San Diego he quickly demonstrated the same managerial skills that had brought success to Republic. He merged the two companies into Convair, introduced the assembly-line technique, and produced in mass quantity two of the most renowned planes of the war, the B-24 *Liberator* bomber for the army and the PBY *Flying Boat* for the navy.

In April 1945, with victory over Germany assured, Girdler resigned the chairmanship of Convair and returned full time to his duties at Republic. At the conclusion of the war, there was no economic slump as after World War I. Pent-up consumer demands and the exigencies of the Cold War kept the nation's steel plants running at capacity. Girdler took full advantage of the situation by aggressively pushing plant expansion and by continuing to find new consumer products for his steel alloys. In 1955 he was given the Gary Memorial Medal, the steel industry's highest award. By 1956 Republic reached the zenith of its prosperity. Its employees numbered 70,000, and its net income for the year was at an all-time high of $90.4 million. On that triumphant note Girdler at the age of seventy-nine retired to his estate, "Harleigh," near Easton, Maryland, to engage in the breeding of race horses; he died at his estate.

An implacable critic of labor unions to the end, Girdler nevertheless earned the respect, however grudgingly given, of foe and friend alike as one of the most effective managers in the history of the industry. As chief executive he knew how to delegate responsibility while still holding on tightly to full authority. He once astounded a Senate investigating committee when asked how many persons reported directly to him as chairman. He replied, "One president, two secretaries and an airplane pilot." This simple chain of command gave him throughout his career the absolute power he always demanded.

• No known collection of Girdler papers is available to the public. In 1943 Girdler, with the collaboration of Boyden Sparkes, published *Boot Straps: The Autobiography of Tom M. Girdler.* Major addresses by Girdler to the American Iron and Steel Institute can be found in the *Yearbooks* of the institute for 1934, 1935, and 1936. An excellent assessment of the first five years of the Republic Steel Company's development under Girdler's administration is in "Republic Steel," *Fortune,* Dec. 1935, pp. 76–84. An evaluation of his program for the aircraft industry is also presented in "Tom Girdler's Truce," *Fortune,* Sept. 1942, pp. 88–92, 154–162. Three critical evaluations of Girdler's labor policies and practices in the steel industry are Louis Leotta, "Girdler's Republic: A Study in Industrial Warfare," *Cithara* 11 (1971): 41–66; Philip L. Cook, "Tom M. Girdler and the Labor Policies of Republic Steel Corporation," *Social Science* 42 (1967): 21–30; and Michael Speer, "The 'Little Steel' Strike: Conflict for Control," *Ohio History* 78 (1969): 273–87. An obituary is in the *New York Times,* 5 Feb. 1965.

JOSEPH FRAZIER WALL

GIRTY, Simon (1741–18 Feb. 1818), British Loyalist and frontier warrior, was born near Harrisburg in colonial Pennsylvania, the son of farmers. One of at least four children born to Simon Girty and Mary Newton, young Simon was raised in modest circumstances. He received no formal education and remained illiterate. When only ten years of age, his father was killed by an Indian. Girty later maintained that his stepfather met a similar fate. In the course of the French and Indian War, Simon was captured by the Seneca and held captive for thirty-six months. During his captivity, Girty became familiar with the language of his captors.

Following his release in 1759, Girty became an interpreter for the British at Fort Pitt. He lived with native tribes at times, and in 1774 during Lord Dunmore's War he accompanied the Virginia militia, serving as a scout and translator.

When the colonists took up arms against Great Britain in 1775, Girty initially supported the rebels. He worked with American officials to secure the neutrality of the Native Americans, served as a recruiter for the frontier militia, and was briefly employed by the Continental Congress as an interpreter. However, in March 1778 Girty, together with Alexander McKee, a former Crown official, and five others, defected to the British. All were suspected—with good reason—of loyalty to Great Britain, suspicions that increased during 1776, when it was discovered that McKee, with whom Girty had worked, had been in correspondence with royal officials. When the Delaware, Shawnee, and Mingo tribes in the Ohio country took up arms on Britain's side late in 1777, the Continental army commander at Fort Pitt issued orders for the arrest of Girty and several other Tory suspects. Soon thereafter, Girty and his confederates fled to Detroit and joined the forces of British lieutenant governor Henry Hamilton. Long suspected of loyalty to the British, Girty likely fled to avoid capture by frontier patriots. His brothers George and James later joined him, while Thomas, another sibling, supported American independence.

Girty immediately participated in Anglo-Indian diversionary raids that set the frontier ablaze from near Fort Pitt to the Kentucky River. Britain's objective was to destroy supplies and deplete American manpower. In 1779 Girty joined Mingo and Wyandot Indians in an attack that decimated a party sent to relieve beleaguered Fort Laurens on the Tuscarawas River in the Ohio country; later in the year, he and his Indian allies repulsed a Kentucky attack on the Shawnee village at Chillicothe; and in October he and 130 Indians destroyed a flotilla transporting munitions up the Ohio River to Fort Pitt. By year's end, the Patriots had abandoned three installations below Fort Pitt.

The greatest British victory in which Girty participated occurred in August 1782. Following a raid south of the Ohio River, the British-Indian force of which he was a part lured the pursuing frontier army into an ambush at Blue Licks in present-day Kentucky. Caught in the ravines along the Licking River, seventy of the 210 men in the Patriot force were killed.

Girty was feared and hated by frontiersmen, who abhorred his Indian manners and the Native American style of warfare—including scalping—that he embraced. His most infamous act followed the capture of Colonel William Crawford during a raid on Sandusky villages in 1782. Girty allegedly refused to intercede to save Crawford from burning at the stake. A generation of backcountry settlers believed that Girty was amused by Crawford's terrible ordeal.

Following the war, Girty received a British pension and in 1784 married Catherine Malott, who had earlier been taken captive by the Indians. He settled in Canada, near Detroit, but he was active in cementing a confederation among the Wabash and Ohio tribes. When frontier warfare erupted during the administration of George Washington, Girty again took up arms with the Indians. He participated in the destruction of General Arthur St. Clair's army in 1791. He was also present when General Anthony Wayne defeated the Indians in the battle of Fallen Timbers in July 1794.

Girty spent his final years in Canada, continuing to serve the British as an interpreter. During the U.S. invasion of Canada in the War of 1812, Girty fled to a Mohawk village to escape capture. Blind and crippled with rheumatism, he returned to his home near Amherstburg following the war, where he died.

Simon Girty was remembered by nineteenth-century frontier residents as a man given to cruelty and inhuman acts. He was loathed not just for his Toryism but for having fought alongside the Native Americans. Yet his was a life of complexities and contradictions, for he served as both a patriot and a Loyalist, and was a victim of and a participant in Indian attacks. Finally, his reputation on America's western frontier suffered because he chose the losing side in the War of Independence.

• No satisfactory biography of Girty exists. Older works include C. W. Butterfield, *History of the Girtys* (1890) and Thomas Boyd, *Simon Girty, the White Savage* (1928). The best sources on Girty are secondary works on frontier warfare. See George M. Waller, *The American Revolution in the West* (1976); Jack Sosin, *The Revolutionary Frontier, 1763–1783* (1967); Dale Van Every, *A Company of Heroes: The American Frontier, 1775–1783* (1962); and James A. James, *The Life of George Rogers Clark* (1928).

JOHN FERLING

GISH, Dorothy (11 Mar. 1898–4 June 1968), actress, was born in Dayton, Ohio, the daughter of James Lee Gish, a confectioner, and Mary Robinson McConnell, a part-time actress and full-time stage mother. When their parents separated, Dorothy, age four, and her sister, Lillian Gish, age eight, were thrust from a comfortable middle-class life into the nomadic world of the child actor. "Those were the days of the good old melodramas," Dorothy observed, "where the villain pursued the heroine and in the end 'a little child shall lead them.'" Dorothy debuted in 1902 as Little Willie in Rebecca Warren's company of that ten-twent'-thirt'-cent (the prices of touring melodramas) standby, *East Lynne*. The "dimpled darling," as her family called her, made a hit in the classic boy's part but reverted to her own gender in other provincial favorites. In Joseph Le Brandt's *Her First False Step* (1903), Gish was literally thrown to the lions with only a screen—invisible to the audience—to protect her. No wonder the *Boston Transcript* observed that Gish "played so childlikely well that [she] evoked the evident sympathies of the house." When she originated a role in George Broadhurst's *The Coward* (1906) in Chicago, the *New York Dramatic Mirror* correspondent judged her "surprisingly sure, accurate and easy." In 1907 she made her biggest hit with Irish singing comedian Fiske O'Hara in *Dion O'Dare*. As Little Gillie Machree, the inevitable waif found on the hero's doorstep, Gish took New York and the road by storm. A reviewer in New England's Hibernian stronghold called her "one of the most natural and exquisitely dainty little children that have ever danced across a Boston stage."

As Gish continued to tour, a newfangled entertainment was diminishing the ten-twent'-thirt' audience. For a nickel in storefronts and makeshift theaters, the public, without barriers of language or class, could see silent pictures that moved. In 1912 the perky fourteen-year-old ventured down to that nursery of motion pictures, the American Mutoscope and Biograph Company in New York, where Director General D. W. Griffith cast her, along with her sister, in her first one-reeler, *An Unseen Enemy*. Over the next two years

Gish made at least twenty films for Biograph both in New York City and during winter excursions to California, playing mostly dainty ingenues as Griffith shaped the "flickers" into an American art form. She followed the innovator to Mutual, appearing in forty-odd bread-and-butter features such as *Home Sweet Home* (1914) and *How Hazel Got Even* (1915), while Griffith made *The Birth of a Nation*. Although Gish did not appear in that landmark film (except possibly as a soldier in battle scenes), she continued to star under Griffith's supervision in popular romances, including *Old Heidelberg* (1915). In 1917 she traveled to war-torn England and France to film Griffith's World War I epic, *Hearts of the World*, which catapulted her to major stardom as the comic Little Disturber. "She was that rare thing, a comedienne," wrote Linda Arvidson Griffith, D. W. Griffith's wife, in 1925, "and comediennes in the movies have been as rare as hen's teeth." Spirited and comely, with an instinctive ability to translate verbal wit into visual humor, Gish was called the "female Chaplin," occupying a unique niche in silent films that only Mabel Normand challenged.

Paramount signed her to star in fifteen comedies supervised by Griffith with such jaunty titles as *Battling Jane* (1918), *Peppy Polly* (1919), and *Flying Pat* (1920). Another 1920 vehicle, *Remodeling Her Husband*, was directed by her sister and featured the dashing Broadway actor James Rennie, whom Gish married in December of that year. (They had no children and after fifteen years together divorced amicably in 1935.) Following a three-year run of increasingly similar Paramount vehicles, she costarred with her sister in one of Griffith's most prestigious productions, *Orphans of the Storm* (1922), making a decided hit in a complete change of pace as the blind sister lost in the turmoil of the French Revolution. Perhaps because of the similarity of her Paramount comedies, Gish's starring career languished somewhat until pioneer British producer-director Herbert Wilcox brought her to England to star in the title role of *Nell Gwyn* (1926). Its success galvanized Gish's career and the British film industry, becoming the first made-in-England production to find a world market and contributing significantly to the erection of the Associated British Studios at Elstree. Gish's three subsequent films with Wilcox, notably *Tip Toes* (1927), with Will Rogers, and *Mme. Pompadour* (1927), found success, but she disowned their last collaboration, *Wolves* (1930), her first (and, according to Wilcox, England's first) "all-talkie." This rudimentary effort found only limited U.S. release as *Wanted Men* (1936).

In 1928 Gish returned auspiciously to Broadway, to the road, and later to London's West End in Samuel Raphaelson's comedy, *Young Love*, supported by her husband. Devoting the next three decades almost exclusively to the theater, she appeared, often for the Theatre Guild, in acclaimed revivals of Nikolay Gogol's *The Inspector General*, George Bernard Shaw's *Getting Married*, Henrik Ibsen's *The Pillars of Society* (all in 1931), and William Congreve's *Love for Love* (1940). She concurrently excelled in modern light comedy, while originating dramatic roles such as Emily Dickinson in *Brittle Heaven* (1934), the wife of Jesse James in *Missouri Legend* (1938), and the title character in *The Story of Mary Surratt* (1947). She won particular acclaim as Mrs. Oliver Wendell Holmes opposite her longtime lover, Louis Calhern, in *The Magnificent Yankee* (1946). She retired from the stage in 1956 after a final summer theater tour in Enid Bagnold's *The Chalk Garden*, playing Mrs. St. Maugham to her sister's Miss Madrigal.

One of the first stars to try live television drama, which she likened to the pioneering days at Biograph, Gish appeared frequently on the new medium throughout the 1950s. But she only accepted four film roles after 1930, playing mother to younger stars in box-office winners such as *Our Hearts Were Young and Gay* (1944) and *The Cardinal* (1964), her final professional appearance. "Today it's more like an assembly line," she said of filmmaking in 1951. "Whatever you play—a windshield or a mudguard—you are somehow detached. You miss the old feeling." Gish died in Rappallo, Italy.

Dorothy Gish reached early success in the last days of touring melodramas. She participated significantly in the development of U.S. film art and industry, as well as triggering international acceptance of British films. She contributed to the rebirth of a substantive American theater with the Theatre Guild and others during the depression-drained 1930s and helped to create the so-called Golden Age of Television with her early appearances on that fledgling medium. Her career, spanning seven decades, stands as a barometer of the entertainment industry from 1900 through the 1960s.

• Lillian Gish wrote two autobiographical works: *The Movies, Mr. Griffith and Me* (1969), with Ann Pinchot, includes a comprehensive survey of Dorothy's life; *Dorothy and Lillian Gish* (1973) offers a pictorial survey of their careers with fine film and stageographies. A biography of Lillian, Albert Bigelow Paine, *Life and Lillian Gish* (1932), includes Dorothy's life to a large extent. The best studies of her vital years with D. W. Griffith are Mrs. D. W. Griffith, *When the Movies Were Young* (1926); Anthony Slide, *The Griffith Actresses* (1973); Robert Henderson, *D. W. Griffith: The Biograph Years* (1970); and Richard Schickel, *D. W. Griffith: An American Life* (1984).

JAMES KOTSILIBAS-DAVIS

GISH, Lillian (14 Oct. 1893?–27 Feb. 1993), actress, was born Lillian Diana Gish in Springfield, Ohio, the daughter of James Lee Gish, a candy merchant, and Mary Robinson McConnell. Her father moved the family to New York and then deserted his wife and children when Lillian and her younger sister Dorothy were only a few years old. Their mother, who supported them by running a candy stand and a theatrical boardinghouse, also had occasional roles as an actress under the stage name Mae Bernard.

Gish's first role was in a 1902 production of *In Convict's Stripes* in Rising Sun, Ohio. She played other child roles as "Baby Lillian" with touring companies across the country. Her sister Dorothy soon joined the stage, and occasionally the two sisters and their mother worked in the same production, although usually they were on separate tours. Gish's formal education was minimal and consisted of brief stays at schools between her road tours. She taught herself to read and write and developed an autodidact's love for books. In her memoir, written with Ann Pinchot, *The Movies, Mr. Griffith, and Me* (1969), she stated, "I never wanted to own anything but books."

One of the Gish's boarders was a Broadway actress named Gladys Smith, who became the movie actress Mary Pickford. In 1912 Lillian and Dorothy visited her at the Biograph Studios in New York and caught the attention of director D. W. Griffith. He immediately cast them in *An Unseen Enemy* (1912), which began a ten-year collaboration between Griffith and Gish. Gish began to phase out her stage roles and devoted an increasing amount of time to performing in Griffith's films, which included *The Musketeers of Pig Alley* (1912) and *Judith of Bethulia* (1914). When Griffith left Biograph and joined the Mutual Film Corporation, Gish accompanied him and starred in his two landmark films, *Birth of a Nation* (1915) and *Intolerance* (1916). She also appeared in his *Diane of the Follies* (1916) and *True-Heart Susie* (1919).

Griffith became Gish's mentor, urging her to take lessons in voice, dancing, and fencing. He had her visit insane asylums and prizefights to observe the extremes of human experience. After his laboratory technicians taught her about developing and splicing, Griffith often had Gish help edit his films. After designing a new movie studio, he had Gish oversee its construction. Eventually he allowed her to direct one of his films, *Remodeling Her Husband* (1920). Griffith's greatest influence on Gish was in the shaping of her film persona, of which she later stated in her memoir, "The essence of virginity—purity and goodness, with nobility of mind, heart, soul and body—is the stuff out of which, under his prompting, I created heroines."

After U.S. entry into World War I, Gish and Griffith made several propaganda films, including *Hearts of the World* (1918). They continued to collaborate on three final hits, *Broken Blossoms* (1919), *Way Down East* (1920), and *Orphans of the Storm* (1922). By that time, however, movie theater owners and audiences were attributing the success of the films to Gish's performances rather than to Griffith's direction. Griffith, who believed that he was personally responsible for Gish's success, became jealous and asked her to leave his studio. He then tried to build up Carol Dempster as her successor, but he failed to have another large box-office success after Gish's departure.

Having grown wealthy as well as popular, Gish became a financial backer of Inspiration Films, which produced her next two films, *The White Sister* (1923) and *Romola* (1924). A legal dispute with the firm's president, who tried to divert her investigation into its finances by proposing marriage, resulted in her signing up with Metro-Goldwyn-Mayer. She starred in *La Bohème* (1926), directed by King Vidor, followed by

The Scarlet Letter (1926) and *The Wind* (1928), both directed by Victor Sjöström. By then, film production had become dominated by large studios, and Gish disliked their depersonalized, assembly-line production methods. She appeared in *One Romantic Night* (1930) and *His Double Life* (1933), but her wholesome waiflike image was going out of style. Movie audiences now preferred flappers like Gloria Swanson and Joan Crawford and foreign exotics like Marlene Dietrich and Greta Garbo.

Gish returned to the stage and won critics' praise for her work on Broadway and in the national tour productions of *Uncle Vanya*, *Hamlet*, *The Star Maker*, and *Life with Father*. During this time she formed a close friendship with writer George Jean Nathan, who introduced her to intellectuals such as H. L. Mencken and Scott and Zelda Fitzgerald. She occasionally tired of long-run stage performances and returned to Hollywood during the mid-1940s for supporting roles in several films, including *The Commandos Strike at Dawn* (1943), *Top Man* (1943), *Miss Susie Slagle's* (1946), *Duel in the Sun* (1947), for which she earned an Academy Award nomination, *Portrait of Jennie* (1948), and *Night of the Hunter* (1955).

In the late 1940s Gish began working in television, starting with "The Late Christopher Bean" in 1948 for the National Broadcasting Company's "Philco Playhouse." During the following four decades she played leading roles in numerous other televised dramas and several made-for-television films, including *Arsenic and Old Lace* (1969) and *Hobson's Choice* (1983). She also appeared as a guest star on several television series, including "The Defenders" (1962, 1964), "Mr. Novak" (1963), and "The Love Boat" (1981). Her final television appearance was on ABC's "Happy Birthday Hollywood" (1987). Gish also helped write "Silver Glory," a televised biography of Griffith. She added another dimension to her career after the death of her sister Dorothy in 1968, when she narrated a lecture and film series produced by Nathan Kroll, *Lillian Gish and the Movies: The Art of the Film, 1900–1928*, at Columbia University's McMillan Theatre in 1969, which then went on tour in the United States, Canada, and Europe. She also published *Dorothy and Lillian Gish* (1973). Gish never married.

In 1971 the Academy of Motion Picture Arts and Sciences honored her with an honorary Oscar. In 1984 she received the American Film Institute's Lifetime Achievement Award. Gish's last Broadway appearance was in *A Musical Jubilee* in 1975, and her last film roles were in *A Wedding* (1978), Hambone and Hillie (1984), *Sweet Liberty* (1986), and *Whales of August* (1987). She died in New York City. Her will contained a provision funding a $200,000 prize award for a performing arts contest.

• Some of Gish's correspondence is in the D. W. Griffith Papers, Film Study Center, Museum of Modern Art, New York City. "Reminiscences of Lillian Gish" is an oral history transcript at the Oral History Research Office, Columbia University. Albert B. Paine, *Life and Lillian Gish* (1932), focuses on her silent film years. Her relationship with Griffith is mentioned in Adela Rogers St. Johns, *Love, Laughter and Tears: My Hollywood Story* (1978). She is discussed in Ralph Haven Wolfe, "The Ohio Roots of Dorothy and Lillian Gish," *Journal of Popular Film and Television* 22 (Summer 1994): 58; and Richard Dyer, "A White Star," *Sight and Sound* 3 (Summer 1993): 22. She is mentioned in Anthony Slide, *The Griffith Actresses* (1973), Mary Pickford, *Sunshine and Shadow* (1955), and King Vidor, *A Tree Is a Tree* (1953; repr. 1977). Her will and award bequest are discussed in "Lillian Gish's Largesse," *New Yorker*, 15 Aug. 1994. Obituaries are in the *New York Times*, 1 Mar. 1993; *Variety*, 8 Mar. 1993; and *America*, 20 Mar. 1993.

STEPHEN G. MARSHALL

GIST, Christopher (c. 1705–25 July 1759), explorer, surveyor, and Indian agent, was born in Baltimore Country, Maryland, the son of Richard Gist, a judge, and Zepporah Murray. His grandfather was Christopher Guest, but the surname was changed to Gist around 1700. Gist was highly educated for his time and place. During his youth in Maryland he acquired literacy and other skills that enabled him to develop a vocation as a cartographer and explorer in the service of the Ohio Company. In 1750, while he lived in North Carolina's Yadkin Valley (where he knew Daniel Boone), Gist agreed to work for the Ohio Company. He negotiated agreements with several native tribes for land on behalf of the Ohio Company of Virginia (1750–1752). On his two expeditions for the Ohio Company, Gist wrote detailed journals and drew some of the earliest maps of the Ohio-Kentucky region. Gist first entered Kentucky in March 1751. He later kept an important journal covering his service as George Washington's protector and guide during the 1753 military expedition to the Ohio country. Gist's varied occupations included fur trader, ranger, soldier, and Indian agent as well as surveyor and explorer.

In 1728 Gist married Sarah Howard, the daughter of an affluent Tidewater Maryland family. The couple had four boys and two girls. Sarah died around 1755 and Gist never remarried. One son, Nathaniel, who accompanied Gist on several expeditions in the 1750s, followed his father's vocation but failed to achieve similar distinction. Though not overly religious, Gist regularly attended church as a young man in Baltimore and remained a lifelong member of the Church of England. He is reputed to have performed the first Church of England service in the Ohio country, the event taking place at the Indian town of Muskingum on Christmas Day 1750.

Thanks to his years as a fur trader, Indian trader, and land operator, Gist also became a notable expert on Indian affairs. During 1752–1753 Gist attended two important diplomatic conferences with Indians at Logstown, Pennsylvania, and Winchester, Virginia, where he served as Virginia governor Robert Dinwiddie's agent and adviser. Gist's negotiations for Indian land were directed mainly toward strengthening the Virginia land company's claim to the west and opposing South Carolina's rival claims.

Taking advantage of his position in the Ohio Company, Gist built a home called "the Plantation" in 1752, located on a fine tract of land east of the Forks of the Ohio, near the Monongahela River in western Pennsylvania. On land that Indians had granted to the Ohio Company, Gist built a short-lived fortified settlement populated with a few families from Maryland and Pennsylvania. In 1754 French soldiers burned Gist's Plantation, but some of his family reoccupied the place after the French and Indian War ended.

Gist also played an important role, and had a busy career, in military affairs surrounding the French and Indian War, 1756–1763. In 1753 Gist accompanied George Washington's expedition to warn the French to leave the Forks of the Ohio region. It was this expedition, embracing military and land speculation objectives, that helped spark the war. In 1755 Gist served in several military capacities. He was Major General Edward Braddock's personal guide during the failed campaign to conquer Fort Duquesne. Gist's Plantation was the staging area and temporary headquarters for General Braddock's expedition. Later in the same year Gist became captain of the company of scouts in Virginia's colonial militia, under the overall command of his friend Washington. Gist recruited about seventy men from Virginia, Pennsylvania, and Maryland for his company of scouts.

Gist simultaneously served as a commissary for the Virginia colonial militia, but the complexities of purchasing and forwarding army supplies was an occupation for which he was not suited, and some officers viewed him as dishonest or incompetent. In May 1757 the Virginian militia was reorganized, and several supernumerary captains, including Gist, were slated for reduction to the rank of lieutenant. Gist resigned from the militia, and two months later, with the strong support of Washington and the Indian superintendent of the Southern Department, Edmond Atkin, he was appointed deputy agent of Indian affairs of the Southern Department. In this capacity Gist dealt mainly with the Catawba and Cherokee nations, with whom he had formerly traded. The Catawbas were especially fond of him and honored him with the title of "Father" Gist.

Gist continued in his duties as an agent for the southern Indians for two years, his major roles being to keep peace on the frontier and to persuade natives to assist Britain's war effort against the French. Gist died suddenly from smallpox while accompanying a band of pro-English Catawbas on the road from Williamsburg to Winchester, Virginia.

Gist was important as one of the first Anglo-Americans to probe the Transallegheny region, as a diligent and faithful promoter of Virginia's western land claims, as a scout and soldier, and as an able frontier diplomat who labored to preserve peace and boost trade, especially for Virginia's benefit. Though he was identified for many years with the Ohio Company, Gist never became wealthy; rather, he was constantly strapped for money, and he died in relative poverty. With his ability to influence the opinions of the Tide-water elite as well as native tribesmen, Gist was uniquely suited for his frontier careers.

• The Gist Family Papers and other relevant documents are in the Baltimore County Hall of Records. The best printed source for Gist's expeditionary journals is William M. Darlington, ed., *Christopher Gist's Journals with Historical, Geographical, and Ethnological Notes* (1893; repr. 1966). A useful biography, containing an extensive bibliography, is Kenneth P. Bailey, *Christopher Gist: Colonial Frontiersman, Explorer, and Indian Agent* (1976). Another biographical and genealogical work is Jean Muir Dorsey and Maxwell Jay Dorsey, *Christopher Gist of Maryland and Some of His Descendants, 1679–1957* (1969); also of interest is Lawrence A. Orrill, "Christopher Gist and His Sons," *Western Pennsylvania Historical Magazine* 15 (Aug. 1932): 191–218. Much useful information on Gist's association with the Ohio Company of Virginia and with George Washington can be found in *The Writings of George Washington, from the Original Manuscript Sources, 1745–1799*, ed. John C. Fitzpatrick (39 vols., 1931–1944).

BARTON H. BARBOUR

GIST, William Henry (20 Aug. 1809–30 Sept. 1874), governor of South Carolina, was born in Charleston, South Carolina, the son of Frances Fincher Gist, a planter. His mother's name is unknown. As a young child Gist moved with his parents to Union District, South Carolina. He attended South Carolina College, a center of southern rights doctrine during the 1820s, but left in his senior year. He later studied law and was admitted to the bar, deciding soon after to supervise the substantial plantation of his family. Gist married Louisa Bowen in 1828. After Louisa's death, Gist married Mary Rice in 1832. He fathered twelve children. As a young man Gist killed Samuel Fair in a duel.

Gist distinguished himself as an attorney and a leading lay Methodist in Union District. He contributed substantial funds to the church and promoted temperance and restrictions on the sale of liquor. From 1840 to 1844 he served Union District in the lower house of the South Carolina state legislature. He enters the state senate in 1844 and remained until 1856. In 1858 the states' rights faction in the legislature elected him governor, and he remained in that office until December 1860.

An exponent of the states' rights doctrine of Senator John Calhoun, Gist played a part in the efforts of South Carolina's intellectual and political elite to mobilize the entire South for independence. As governor, he applauded southern leaders, such as writer William Gilmore Simms, theologian James Henley Thornwell, politician James Henry Hammond, and newspaper publisher Robert Barnwell Rhett, as they attempted to build a relatively autonomous intellectual and cultural life. Gist believed that, without a viable proslavery culture, the region would gradually succumb to antislavery ideas. As he put it in a letter to Hammond, "He who doubts is damned." While the attempts of Gist and the proslavery newspaper, the *Charleston Mercury*, to fund a $.5 million southern publishing house proved abortive, they helped build secessionist solidarity within the South Carolina.

The efforts of proslavery politicians from 1858 to 1860 to demand secession in the event of the election of a Republican president were successful in Gist's South Carolina. However, southern rights doctrine was not nearly as strong in many areas outside of South Carolina, especially in the mountain and border regions of the South less integral to the slave economy. Gist believed that South Carolina needed to lead the other slave states into secession in the event of a Republican victory in 1860. As he declared in a letter to Mississippi governor John J. Pettus in November 1860, he hoped to thwart "the inclination of our weak brethren to dodge the issue."

In a series of messages to the South Carolina legislature, Gist forecast the inevitability of secession. In October 1860 he sent a confidential circular letter, carried by his brother, the appropriately named "States Rights" Gist, to the governors of other southern states, declaring that his state would secede in the event of the election of Abraham Lincoln. As Lincoln's election began to look increasingly certain, Gist called on the legislature to stay in special session through the fall and winter crisis, arguing the need for special action for the "protection of the State." The day before the election of Lincoln, Gist called for a state convention to consider secession. Within a week the convention was approved by the legislature, and on 20 December 1860 South Carolina's convention delegates, who included Gist, signed the first southern ordinance of secession.

Gist encountered little opposition in leading his state to secession. Widespread ownership of slave property and a pervasive cotton culture throughout the state made South Carolina the leader in southern rights. Unlike most other southern governors, Gist did not have to deal with recalcitrant Unionists in mountain districts relatively distant from the slave economy. South Carolina's secession sparked a series of state referendums and conventions throughout the cotton South during the "secession winter" of 1860–1861.

Gist left office the day his state's secession convention convened. With the beginning of the Confederacy, Frances W. Pickens replaced Gist as South Carolina's governor, and the secession convention appointed Gist to a five-member Executive Council, which played a crucial role in administering the state during the first two years of the Civil War. The body was given not only the ordinary gubernatorial power but also nearly unlimited war powers, such as the power to arrest the disloyal, to seize private property, to declare martial law, and to draw money from the treasury. The formation of the council met little opposition in the secession convention. The Executive Council placed Gist in charge of both the Department of Treasury and Finance and the Department of Manufacture and Construction.

The five members of the council, Gist, James Chesnut, I. W. Hayne, Pickens, and W. W. Harlee, initiated state-level conscription laws in March 1862 to meet Confederate requisitions. The council faced more difficulties in its efforts to appropriate slaves for use in building fortifications, because planters complained vigorously that they would have difficulty bringing in crops. The council received many letters accusing citizens of disloyalty but made few arrests. In his role as head of the Department of Manufacture, Gist sought to establish a "State Works" turning out shot and shell by the fall of 1861. He obtained skilled workers from Nashville and Charleston to work in an armory in Greenville.

The appointment of the council, with its centralized powers, marked the high-water mark of proslavery southernism in South Carolina. By late 1861 many South Carolinians resented the council as an oligarchy with too much central power. Friends of former governor Pickens became instrumental in a campaign to call a new convention and repeal the council. Public opinion opposed the council, and the legislature abolished it on 19 December 1862. Gist returned to planting, and he died at Rose Hill, South Carolina.

• Gist's papers are in the South Carolina Library in Columbia, S.C. Steven Channing, *Crisis of Fear* (1970), relates the secession crisis during Gist's term to a fear of slave insurrection. Lacy Ford, *Origins of Southern Radicalism* (1987), and Stephanie McCurry, *Masters of Small Worlds* (1995), provide contrasting views of antebellum S.C. political culture and Gist's place in the history of secession. Charles Cauthen, *South Carolina Goes to War, 1860–65* (1950), discusses Gist's involvement in wartime government.

WALLACE HETTLE

GITLOW, Benjamin (22 Dec. 1891–19 July 1965), founder of the American Communist party, was born in Elizabethport, New Jersey, the son of Louis Albert Gitlow and Katherine "Kate" Golman, Russian-Jewish immigrants. His father operated a sewing machine in a New York shirt factory, and his mother took in boarders and did piecework at home. He attended Stuyvesant High School in New York City before becoming a clothing cutter. Growing up in dire poverty in Manhattan's Lower East Side, Gitlow heard tales of the Russian Socialist movement. He frequented Frederick C. Howe's forum at Cooper Union and in 1909 joined the Socialist party, becoming the first native-stock member in his Harlem branch. Within a short time Gitlow was named branch organizer and was a member of the party's county and state committees. He also headed the Retail Clerks Union of New York. Drawn to the ranks of the radical union, the Industrial Workers of the World, Gitlow drew the line at violence. He studied law for two years and in 1917 was nominated by his Socialist party district in the Bronx to run for the state assembly. A stirring orator, he was one of ten Socialists elected to office that year, and he adopted an antiwar stance. The outbreak of the Russian Revolution in November 1917 proved catalytic for Gitlow, who became a leader of the Socialist party's militant left wing. Initially Gitlow refused to heed the call, largely emanating from foreign-language federations, for a Communist party, believing that the Socialist party could be radicalized. Consequently, Gitlow, along with John Reed, in 1919 established the

Voice of Labor and that year attended the Socialist convention. Disenchanted by the Socialist party's disavowal of revolutionary change, Gitlow and Reed formed their own organization, the Communist Labor party (CLP), in 1919.

Serving as the business manager of CLP's manifesto, *Revolutionary Age*, Gitlow, in the midst of the antiradical scare of the post–World War I years, was arrested for advocating communism. Gitlow and James Larkin from the CLP, along with Charles Ruthenberg and Isaac Ferguson of the Communist party, were indicted in 1919 for purportedly violating New York State's Criminal Anarchy Act. The National Civil Liberties Bureau provided legal counsel and famed attorney Clarence Darrow assisted in their defense. Darrow attempted to rely on the NCLB defense strategy that one should not face criminal prosecution because of political beliefs, but Gitlow insisted on speaking in his own defense. He defiantly proclaimed "that capitalism is in a state of collapse, that capitalism has brought untold misery and hardships to the working man." On 5 February 1920 Gitlow was pronounced guilty and was sentenced to five to ten years at hard labor.

After being released from jail pending appeal in early 1922, Gitlow was reimprisoned but released once more as his conviction was scheduled for review by the U.S. Supreme Court. The following January New York governor Al Smith pardoned all the defendants except for Gitlow, who allowed the American Civil Liberties Union to use his conviction as a test case challenging the constitutionality of New York's antiradical law. In 1923–1924 Gitlow was managing editor of *Freitheit*, the communist-run Yiddish newspaper. He was also the running mate of William Foster on the 1924 presidential ticket of the Workers party, the name temporarily assumed by the American Communists. Gitlow promised that, if elected, "We will use our room in the White House to turn the rest of the mansion into apartments for the workers and poor farmers." In 1924 he married Badana Zeitlin; they had one child.

In June 1925 the Supreme Court upheld the lower court's ruling on the constitutionality of New York's Criminal Anarchy Act. A celebrated dissent by Justices Oliver Wendell Holmes, Jr., and Louis D. Brandeis declared, "Every idea is an incitement." Although the Court, through Justice Edward Sanford, affirmed Gitlow's conviction, it also accepted Darrow's argument that the First Amendment freedoms of speech and the press should be incorporated, thereby restricting state legislative actions. In November Gitlow was returned to Sing Sing Prison to complete his sentence. However, on 11 December, the day of his first wedding anniversary, Gitlow received word that the governor had pardoned him.

In February 1926 Gitlow was invited to join the board of directors of the newly founded Garland Fund, which allocated grants to left-wing organizations. The fund's board members included other prominent civil libertarians and socialists, notably Roger Baldwin, Norman Thomas, Scott Nearing, and Elizabeth Gurley Flynn. Gitlow remained heavily involved with the Communist movement, helping to orchestrate trade union campaigns. During May 1927, in the midst of party strife at home, Gitlow, wielding a Canadian passport obtained under a pseudonym, traveled to the Soviet Union with Communist party leader Jay Lovestone. Gitlow returned to the Soviet Union in 1928 and later admitted receiving Soviet funds for the U.S. Community party's upcoming presidential campaign, when he was once again the vice presidential candidate.

As the 1920s neared an end, the Communist movement was riddled with divisions, which the Soviet Communist leader Joseph Stalin was determined to eradicate. As a member of both the executive committee of the Communist International and the Presidium, Gitlow again traveled to Moscow in April 1929 to defend Lovestone against charges he had erringly propounded the notion of an American path to communism. Speaking before the Presidium, Gitlow, then serving as general secretary of the American Communist party, insisted that the Lovestone faction best represented their American comrades. Stalin rejected his argument, and the Comintern demanded the expulsion of Gitlow, Lovestone, and Bertram Wolfe from the American Communist party.

In response, Lovestone and Gitlow established the Communist Party, U.S.A. (Majority Group) in 1929, comprised of some 200 members. Gitlow broke with Lovestone in 1933, condemning Stalin's practices in the Soviet Union that were resulting in the starvation of millions. Although he still viewed himself as a committed Communist, Gitlow believed that the Stalinist regime was criminal, the communists' dual unionism in the United States was disruptive, and the united front was "a necessity," not merely a tactic. Gitlow's attempt to bring the opposing Communist factions together proved unavailing, and in 1934 he determined to rejoin the Socialist party. However, disturbed by the emergence of young militants in that party, Gitlow soon withdrew.

Gitlow drifted rightward and eventually appeared as a friendly witness before several congressional investigative committees. He also delivered a series of lectures denouncing what he deemed the evils of communism. In 1940 Gitlow published his autobiography, *I Confess: The Truth about American Communism*, which was largely an embittered condemnation of the movement to which he had earlier devoted himself. He subsequently wrote a number of anti-Communist tracts, notably *The Whole of Their Lives: Communism in America—A Personal History and Intimate Portrayal of Its Leaders* (1948). He viewed communism as leading to "this enslavement of the human mind, this proscription of independent thinking." Gitlow died in Crompond, New York.

• Manuscript collections on Gitlow are at the Atkins Library, University of North Carolina at Charlotte, and the Hoover Institution, Stanford University. Gloria Garrett Samson, *The American Fund for Public Service: Charles Garland and Radi-*

cal Philanthropy, 1922–1941 (1996), contains a brief but illuminating biographical sketch of Gitlow. A good deal of information pertaining to Gitlow is in Theodore Draper, *The Roots of American Communism* (1957) and *American Communism and Soviet Russia: The Formative Period* (1960); and in Harvey Klehr and John Earl Haynes, *The American Communist Movement: Storming Heaven Itself* (1992). A lengthy obituary is in the *New York Times*, 19 July 1965.

ROBERT C. COTTRELL

GLACKENS, William (13 Mar 1870–22 May 1938), painter and illustrator, was born in Philadelphia, Pennsylvania, the son of Samuel Glackens, a clerk for the Pennsylvania Railroad, and Elizabeth Finn. Glackens graduated from Central High School in Philadelphia in 1888, and it was while he was still in high school that his skill as a draftsman was first recognized. His paternal grandfather had founded several newspapers in Pottstown, Pennsylvania, and Glackens began his career as an artist-reporter, first with the *Philadelphia Record* in 1891 and then, in 1892, with the *Philadelphia Press*, where he worked with John Sloan (they had known each other in high school), George Luks, and Everett Shinn. In the evening Glackens attended painting classes at the Pennsylvania Academy of Fine Arts in Philadelphia, where he received instruction under Thomas Anshutz. Also in these years, Glackens came under the influence of the painter Robert Henri, who emphasized individuality and the development of an artist's particular style and point of view.

In the fall of 1896, after spending fifteen months bicycling through France, Belgium, and Holland, where he and Henri worked on their own art and visited museums, Glackens returned to Philadelphia but soon moved to New York, where he shared a studio with Luks and executed illustrations for the *New York World* and later the *New York Herald*. In 1898, as a special correspondent for *McClure's Magazine*, Glackens covered the Spanish-American War, producing images of the fighting in Cuba that are now considered historically accurate representations of the war. Afterward, Glackens joined Henri in New York and supported himself by working as an illustrator for Joseph Pulitzer's *New York World* and the *New York Herald* in addition to doing book illustrations.

In 1904 Glackens married Edith Dimock, also an artist-illustrator and the daughter of a wealthy Hartford silk manufacturer. The marriage produced two children, a son and daughter. It also afforded Glackens financial security, which enabled him to travel frequently to Europe and to work almost exclusively on his own paintings. Glackens's early works, such as *Figures in the Park* (1895, Kraushaar Galleries, N.Y.) and *Girl in a Black Cape* (c. 1897, private collection), reveal the stylistic influences of the European masters Diego Velázquez, Frans Hals, and Édouard Manet as filtered through the teachings of his mentor and friend, the artist Robert Henri. By 1905, however, Glackens's work was beginning to change. Works such as *May Day, Central Park* (1905, Fine Arts Museum, San Francisco) and *Breezy Day, Tugboats, New York Harbor* (before 1908, Santa Barbara Museum of Fine Arts) reflect the influence of impressionism in the brightened color and use of abbreviated brush strokes. Henri was by then the leader of a group of artists comprising himself and Glackens and Glackens's peers Sloan, Luks, and Shinn as well as Maurice Prendergast, Arthur B. Davies, and Ernest Lawson. In 1908 the group came to be known as The Eight after they staged a protest exhibition—against what they viewed as the discriminatory selection process of the National Academy of Design—at the Macbeth Galleries in New York. Some critics viewed The Eight as radical artists, but comparatively, the modernism exhibited in some of their paintings—for example, realistic renditions of city life—was not revolutionary. The radicalism of The Eight, as reflected in their flaunting of artistic conventions, was as much social as artistic, though the group did have a hand in introducing modernism to the American public.

In 1910 Glackens was an organizer of the first Independent Exhibition of American Artists. Held in New York City, the exhibition featured hundreds of paintings in a multitude of styles. In 1912 Glackens returned to Paris with Alfred Maurer and set about buying pictures for pharmacologist and art collector (as well as another classmate from high school) Albert C. Barnes. Traveling throughout Europe, Glackens bought work by Renoir, Degas, Cézanne, Van Gogh, and others, paintings that formed the nucleus of the famous Barnes Collection in Merion, Pennsylvania. In 1913, upon his return to New York, Glackens chaired the Domestic Committee of the historic New York Armory Show, the first large-scale exhibition of European modern art in the United States. In 1917 Glackens became the first president of the recently formed Society of Independent Artists, a group that originated in the juryless, prizeless independent exhibition held at Grand Central Palace in New York in April 1917.

While Glackens continued to paint, there were no notable developments in his work after 1917. Between 1925 and 1932 he spent his time in New York and Paris, from which he also traveled to London and Vence to paint and relax. The last six years of his life he remained in New York. At the Paris Exposition of 1937 Glackens was awarded the highest prize accorded to an American, the Grand Prix. Glackens had been an associate of the National Academy of Design since 1906, and in 1933 he became an academician. He also was elected to the National Institute of Arts and Letters and twice was awarded the Temple Gold Medal of the Pennsylvania Academy of Fine Arts (1914 and 1933). He died while visiting friends in Westport, Connecticut, and was buried at Cedar Hill Cemetery in Hartford. That same year a memorial exhibition was held at the Whitney Museum of American Art in New York.

Glackens is remembered primarily as one of The Eight, a group that, under the continuing influence of Robert Henri, promoted the "ashcan" school of social realism, as the style was frequently dubbed. This independent movement in American art, one of human engagement, prolonged the humanist tradition of Daumier and Courbet and initiated a flowering of native art in America. Glackens shared with most of his fellow New York realists early training as an illustrator, and this equipped him to represent with objectivity and economy the drama and humanity of urban life. Yet the social realism depicted by Glackens was limited to the city as a middle-class spectacle, a collection of parks and gardens, stores and sidewalk cafés, as in, for instance, *Hammerstein's Roof Garden* (c. 1902, Whitney Museum of Modern Art), *Battery Park* (1902–1904, private collection), and *Shoppers* (1907, Chrysler Museum). His subject matter tended to be more upbeat and elegant than that favored by his friends, and his preference for glowing luminous color is evident in his many outdoor scenes as well as in his portraits, nudes, and still-lifes. More than the others in Henri's circle Glackens identified with the cheerful outlook of such French impressionists as Pierre-Auguste Renoir and Claude Monet, and particularly after 1905, he increasingly employed Renoir's high-keyed palette and feathery brushwork. As a result, in some respects Glackens's work more closely resembles the joyful art of the American impressionists than the tougher paintings of his American realist peers.

• Scholarly sources on Glackens are numerous but focus primarily on his years in New York. The most important sources include *William Glackens Memorial Exhibition* (exhibition catalog, Whitney Museum of American Art; 1938); Ira Glackens, *William Glackens and the Ashcan Group: The Emergence of Realism in American Art* (1957); and *William Glackens: The Formative Years* (exhibition catalog, Kraushaar Galleries; 1991). Also useful is Elizabeth Milroy, *Painters of the New Century: The Eight* (1991). Obituaries are in *Art News* 36 (28 May 1938): 20, and *Art Digest* 12 (June 1938): 12.

BRITT STEEN ZUÑIGA

GLADDEN, Washington (11 Feb. 1836–2 July 1918), Congregational clergyman, was born Solomon Washington Gladden in Pottsgrove, Pennsylvania, the son of Solomon Gladden and Amanda Daniels, schoolteachers. As a result of his father's premature death in 1841, he was raised by an uncle on a farm near Owego, New York. The family's circumstances were meager, but, by working as a newspaper apprentice and preparing himself locally at Owego Academy, he was able to enter Williams College in 1856. After graduating in 1859, he returned home to teach but quickly abandoned teaching for the ministry. Though without formal theological training, in 1860 he was ordained at the First Congregational Methodist Church of Brooklyn, New York, which under his leadership became State Street Congregational Church. That same year he married Jennie O. Cohoon, a fellow student in Owego, with whom he had four children. A nervous collapse forced him in 1861 to take a less demanding church in the suburban New York village of Morrisania, where he remained until 1865. While at Morrisania, he attended lectures at Union Theological Seminary but did not complete a degree.

Except for the years 1871–1874, when he was religious editor of the *Independent* in New York, Gladden spent the years after 1865 as pastor of Congregational churches in North Adams (1866–1871) and Springfield (1875–1882), Massachusetts, and in Columbus, Ohio (1883–1918). A gifted administrator and persuasive preacher, he became during the years in Columbus a nationally known leader of progressive religious and social causes, a prolific author, and a role model for younger ministers.

Gladden's manner was genial but formal; his seriousness discouraged easy intimacy. Whether because of shyness or his sense of ministerial propriety, he avoided self-revelation. Perhaps symbolically, parishioners rarely saw him without his Prince Albert coat. Yet he had a razor-sharp sense of humor and often used mimicry, caricature, and irony with telling effect against what he considered social injustice and ignorance.

Gladden's youth was marked by a religious milieu of intense revivalism, pietism, and Calvinist orthodoxy, against all of which he soon rebelled. His most important guide in his struggle to find a flexible, satisfying faith was Horace Bushnell, whose understanding of language as suggestive and symbolic freed him from the binding authority of creeds. Beginning in the 1870s, Gladden argued for openness to theological diversity and associated himself with dissenters who questioned prevailing evangelical views of the atonement and eternal punishment. Two of his early books, *Being a Christian* (1876) and *The Christian Way* (1877), presented Christian salvation in nondoctrinal and practical terms as simply a matter of accepting God's love and exemplifying it in daily life. One of his most enduring legacies, the popular hymn "O Master, Let Me Walk with Thee," originated in the theological controversies of the late 1870s.

As American Protestants confronted the implications of evolutionary science and the higher criticism of the Bible, Gladden emerged in the 1880s as a leading proponent of theological reconstruction. Far from threatening anything essential to Christianity, evolution, he argued, provided evidence of a purposeful universe guided by an immanent God toward eventual perfection. Evolutionary motifs became central to virtually all his thinking. Similarly, he welcomed the historical and literary studies of the Bible that were making their way to American shores from Europe. Even though the higher critics challenged traditional views of the Bible's composition and identified errors and contradictions in it, they did not destroy its spiritual and moral authority. In fact, like the evolutionists, they enhanced its value by giving Christians a more realistic understanding of its nature.

A popularizer rather than a seminal thinker, Gladden did much to win acceptance for theological liberalism through frequent addresses at leading colleges, seminaries, and religious gatherings and such books as *Burning Questions of the Life That Now Is and of That Which Is to Come* (1890), *Who Wrote the Bible?* (1891), *Seven Puzzling Bible Books* (1897), *How Much Is Left of the Old Doctrines?* (1899), and *Present Day Theology* (1913). Though Gladden unabashedly challenged traditional Protestant views of the Bible, his liberalism was strongly Christo-centric and evangelical. He believed that God's supreme self-revelation to humanity occurred in the ministry and sacrificial death of Jesus Christ and that this revelation could best be expressed by the terms "the fatherhood of God" and "the brotherhood of man." In his view, God effected reconciliation with men and women through Christ's demonstration of the supremacy of love over sin and evil, and men and women achieved reconciliation with each other as they emulated Christ's example of selfless love. This message was especially appealing to well-educated, middle-class Protestants who wished to embrace modern thought without surrendering their evangelical faith.

One of the first clergymen to address the social, economic, and political problems of a rapidly industrializing and urbanizing nation, Gladden helped to lay the foundation for the Social Gospel movement and to win its formal recognition within American Protestantism. He insisted that no aspect of human life was beyond the purview of the church. The church's task was to work for the Kingdom of God by teaching that, as children of God, all people must live as brothers and sisters.

Of all social issues, labor-management relations drew Gladden's earliest and most sustained attention. Achieving economic justice was, for him, the fundamental problem of industrial capitalism. Though from first to last he sought to be even-handed and sharply condemned employers' attitudes and practices, in the 1870s and 1880s his attitude toward industrial workers was patronizing. He sympathized with their grievances but counseled thrift, temperance, and patience. When a shoe company in North Adams imported Chinese strikebreakers in 1870, he proferred educational and religious services to them but nothing to the beleaguered strikers. In *Working People and Their Employers* (1876), the first important Social Gospel book on labor issues, he rejected the closed shop and concluded that strikes usually did more harm than good.

By the mid-1880s Gladden had become convinced that employers' intransigence was at the root of many strikes and that workers must be free to organize in order to equalize the struggle. Still, like most reformers of the period, in such works as *Applied Christianity* (1886) and *Tools and the Man: Property and Industry under the Christian Law* (1893), he lamented the necessity of struggle and held up the palliative of profit-sharing in the spirit of the Golden Rule as an alternative. The savage industrial struggles of the early twentieth century, and especially his unsuccessful mediation of a streetcar strike in Columbus in 1910, disillusioned him, however, and he became increasingly pro-union. In *The Labor Question* (1911), he endorsed the program and tactics of the American Federation of Labor. In subsequent sermons he explained the radical Industrial Workers of the World as the natural result of exploitation and frustration.

Gladden's Social Gospel included an expanded role for government at all levels: national, state, and municipal. Government, like the church, would be instrumental in establishing the Kingdom of God. He told his parishioners in Columbus to look to the statehouse across Broad Street, rather than within the church, for signs of God's activity. He deprecated the anti-statism of Herbert Spencer and William Graham Sumner, which, like anarchism, he considered an expression of antisocial selfishness. An individualism that denied the organic nature of society was, he insisted, a cause of America's social problems. In 1885 he joined Richard T. Ely, Woodrow Wilson, and other younger scholars to organize the American Economic Association, which had a platform that explicitly repudiated laissez-faire principles.

Gladden's discussions of the state often included an assessment of socialism, which he carefully distinguished from anarchism and communism. Though acknowledging that socialism appealed to many of the same ideals and motives as Christianity, he rejected it on practical grounds: it undervalued the talents of exceptional individuals, required an unwieldy bureaucracy, and neglected the development of individual character. He considered these flaws especially serious in Edward Bellamy's utopian *Looking Backward* (1888). His most comprehensive statement on the subject was *Christianity and Socialism* (1905).

A regulated capitalism seemed to Gladden the best protector and balancer of individual and social interests. He favored regulatory commissions to oversee corporations and protective legislation for industrial workers and consumers. Virtually the entire reform agenda of the Progressive Era after 1900 received his optimistic support. A lifelong Republican, he supported Theodore Roosevelt's (1858–1919) Progressive campaign in 1912 and Woodrow Wilson in 1916.

Urban problems also engaged Gladden's attention. While working for the *Independent* in the early 1870s, he used his pen to help bring down the corrupt Tammany Hall "boss" William Marcy Tweed. It was in Columbus after 1883, however, that he made his greatest mark as an urban reformer. The First Congregational Church's location downtown and the presence in its membership of many business, professional, educational, and cultural leaders gave Gladden a unique perspective on the city's affairs and unusual opportunities for civic leadership. He went beyond typical Protestant moral crusades for the enforcement of antigambling and liquor laws in the 1880s and 1890s to work for municipal home rule, nonpartisanship, and a stronger executive; municipal ownership of inherently monopolistic facilities and services; and expansion of social, cultural, and recreational opportunities. A founding member of the National Municipal League in 1894, he was a frequent participant in its proceedings and those of its Ohio affiliate. From 1900 to 1902, as an independent alderman on the city council, he was in the forefront of negotiations with interurban, streetcar, gas, and electric companies. His activities on behalf of civic betterment earned him the sobriquet "The First Citizen of Columbus."

A fervent believer in the theological openness and democratic polity of Congregationalism, Gladden worked to advance its interests in varied ways. He gave leadership to the founding of four new congregations, as well as a social settlement, in Columbus. He was a principal figure in the National Council of Congregational Churches' establishment of a series of committees on labor and industry, culminating in 1913 in a permanent Commission on Social Service. Beginning in the 1870s, he actively promoted the American Missionary Association's work among African Americans in the South, and he served as its president from 1901 to 1904. He received the denomination's highest elective position in 1904, when he began a three-year term as moderator of its National Council.

While proud of Congregational traditions, Gladden displayed a broad ecumenical spirit. He led his denomination in unsuccessful merger negotiations with the Methodist Protestants and United Brethren from 1903 to 1907 and worked for many years to reduce denominational competition in rural areas. He was involved in the creation of the Federal Council of Churches in 1908 and served on its commissions on international relations and social service. On a broader scale, he befriended Catholics, Jews, and Unitarians. Though his public attacks on the anti-Catholic American Protective Association probably cost him the presidency of the Ohio State University in 1892, he became the first Protestant to receive an honorary degree from Notre Dame three years later.

In 1914 Gladden entered semiretirement as minister emeritus of the First Church. Surprised and distraught by the outbreak of war in Europe, he took up the cause of peace in his final years. He joined his voice to the Wilson administration's search for a negotiated settlement without victors and endorsed the work of the League to Enforce Peace to establish a postwar system of collective security. Had his health permitted, he would have joined the delegation that sailed for Europe on Henry Ford's peace ship, *Oscar II*, to press for an end to hostilities. During the struggle over "preparedness" in 1915–1916, he vigorously opposed increased military appropriations and any thought of American intervention. He served as president of the Ohio Anti-Militarist League, lectured on behalf of a national Anti-Preparedness Committee, and helped bring William Jennings Bryan to Columbus to speak against preparedness. His anti-interventionist *The Forks of the Road* (1916) was the prize essay of the Church Peace Union, an organization with which he had been closely associated since its founding in 1914. Following Wilson's logic, however, Gladden became convinced in early 1917 that American entry was necessary. Thereafter, he emphasized the war's democratic possibilities at home and abroad.

After a long illness, Gladden's wife, Jennie, died in 1909. Gladden died at home in Columbus following a stroke from which he never regained consciousness.

• The Washington Gladden Papers at the Ohio Historical Society in Columbus (microfilm ed., 1972) is one of the most complete collections of sermons and correspondence (mostly incoming) of any American clergyman. The First Congregational Church Archives in Columbus contain a small amount of supplementary material. Gladden's two major fictional works, *The Christian League of Connecticut* (1883) and *The Cosmopolis City Club* (1893), describe ecumenical ventures in social service. *Social Salvation* (1902) and *The Church and Modern Life* (1908) are broad statements of his Social Gospel. His autobiography is *Recollections* (1909). Jacob H. Dorn, *Washington Gladden: Prophet of the Social Gospel* (1967), is the most complete biography. See also Robert T. Handy, ed., *The Social Gospel in America, 1870–1920: Gladden, Ely, Rauschenbusch* (1966), and Richard D. Knudten, *The Systematic Thought of Washington Gladden* (1968).

JACOB H. DORN

GLASGOW, Ellen Anderson Gholson (22 Apr. 1873–21 Nov. 1945), writer, was born in Richmond, Virginia, the daughter of Francis Thomas Glasgow, an industrialist, and Anne Jane Gholson. "Born without a skin," as her family said, she was delicate and educated largely at home. She was antagonistic toward her Scottish father's staunch Presbyterianism and his comparatively dictatorial methods of running his household. When her mother discovered her husband's long-term affair with a black woman, the breakdown she experienced alienated Ellen still more from her father, and she stopped all religious practices. After her mother's death in 1893, Glasgow suffered depression and hearing loss, which gradually worsened. She also destroyed the novel she had been writing, though she soon began another—against her family's wishes. Women of her class neither went to college nor had occupations.

Glasgow learned about Darwin, Malthus, Spencer, Mill, and other contemporary thinkers from Walter McCormack, her sister Cary's husband. But, McCormack committed suicide after only a few years of marriage, a loss that stunned both Cary and Ellen. Their grief was a bond between them, and they lived together frequently until Cary's death in 1911 from breast cancer.

Glasgow's reading and her early experiences fed her tendency to pessimism. The brooding skepticism of her first novel, *The Descendant*, which appeared anonymously in 1897, led critics to believe it was the work of Harold Frederic, author of *The Damnation of Theron Ware*. Glasgow was delighted with this attribution; at this point in her life, she wanted to be identified with men and male attitudes.

When *Phases of an Inferior Planet* (1898) and *The Voice of the People* (1900) were published under her name to equally good reviews, her career was made. The young Glasgow was a "realist," intent on presenting real characters—unconventional women as well as strong, often impoverished men—in a quasinaturalist paradigm. As her 1900 novel demonstrated, Glasgow could write about the South without romanticizing it, an unusual accomplishment for the time. As Glasgow recalled in *A Certain Measure: An Interpretation of*

Prose Fiction, the collected prefaces to her novels (1943): "I was, in my humble place and way, beginning a solitary revolt against the formal, the false and affected, the sentimental, and the pretentious, in Southern writing."

During the next six years, Glasgow traveled frequently to New York, Maine, and Europe. In England she became acquainted with Thomas Hardy, Joseph Conrad, Hugh Walpole, Henry James (1843–1916) and others. Because of her hearing impairment, she usually traveled with either Cary, another sister, Rebe, or friends from Richmond. She made some money from her novels, but she was still dependent— as she always would be—on her family for support. She had fallen in love with a married man, and some of these trips were opportunities for them to be together circumspectly. According to her memoir, *The Woman Within*, her lover died suddenly, and she learned of his death in a European paper. The novels from this period, *The Battle-Ground* (1902), *The Deliverance* (1904), and *The Wheel of Life* (1906), are romances, with strong women protagonists winning out over circumstances to lead happy lives in marriage. Betty Ambler, the spirited southern woman of *The Battle-Ground*, resists the terror of Civil War conditions and waits for her beloved to return; Christopher Blake, in *The Deliverance*, finds his promise in life through Maria Fletcher, the daughter of an enemy who breaks with her family to await Blake's return from prison, Laura Wilde, the poet of *The Wheel of Life*, faces a doomed love and finds solace in Eastern thought and a definition of "love" that is universalized rather than romanticized.

Glasgow continued to write and publish a novel every few years, always to acclaim. *The Ancient Law* appeared in 1908, *The Romance of a Plain Man* in 1909, and *The Miller of Old Church* in 1911. Following the literary practice of serious fiction focusing on male characters, the two later novels provided readers with strong, yet sensitive, male protagonists, rewarded with the love of women above them in class. *The Miller of Old Church* is also a sketchbook for unconventional southern women characters, and one of its primary themes is that friendship among women is essential. Glasgow had grown bitter because of her personal circumstances—including the deaths of her favorite siblings, Frank, a suicide, and Cary—but one of her best novels, *Virginia* (1913), was written in memory of her sister and mother. Although she began the novel as an ironic treatment of the traditional woman's life, giving up everything for the love of a good man, it became a moving account of Virginia Pendleton, a young southerner married to and finally abandoned by a playwright who grew past his wife's dedicated existence as wife and mother.

When the novel appeared in 1913, Glasgow was living in New York City, still trying to sever ties with her father in Richmond. She remained in New York until 1916, but she wrote best in Virginia and so returned to Richmond. Her quiet life sometimes hid her feminism, but Glasgow was active in the suffrage move-

ment, and in 1916 she published *Life and Gabriella*. Modeled on the character of the independent Susan Treadwell from *Virginia*, Gabriella marries and has children but divorces her husband and moves to New York, where she raises her family, earns a living, and eventually remarries. Subtitled "The Story of a Woman's Courage," the novel attempted to show women, empowered by their own intelligence, directing their lives successfully.

Once Glasgow moved back to Richmond, she was courted by Henry Anderson, a lawyer and politician. Although the two became engaged, after Anderson went to Europe with the Red Cross during World War I, Glasgow realized that she could not marry him. He cared a great deal for the image he presented, but he also cared for flirtations with much younger women— and Glasgow did not want to spend her life worrying about his fidelity. There is evidence that she took an overdose of sleeping pills upon his return, but she survived, and the two remained lifelong friends. Neither married.

Glasgow's *The Builders* (1919) included a fond portrait of Anderson as David Blackburn. Her 1922 novel *One Man in His Time* describes the beautiful, if aging, Corinna Page, who decides she does not want to marry; several of Glasgow's stories from this period, as well as ghost stories, echo the theme. By 1925, when Glasgow published *Barren Ground*, the novel some critics think her most important, she understood fully the relative power of men and women in the love relationship. The betrayed Dorinda Oakley's vengeance leads to her economic and social triumph as a farmer. But her sense of herself as nonsexual disappointed some readers.

Glasgow wrote out all sides of her *angst* in the three novels, usually considered comic, that followed. The relentless irony of *The Romantic Comedians* (1926), *They Stooped to Folly* (1929), and *The Sheltered Life* (1932) brought her new critical recognition. *The Romantic Comedians* was a Book-of-the-Month Club selection, *They Stooped to Folly* was a Literary Guild choice, and *The Sheltered Life* was fifth on the bestseller annual list in 1932. Glasgow's shocking denouement to this Queenborough trilogy—with the anguished southern lady shooting her betraying husband—was softened in her 1935 novel, *Vein of Iron*, where both male and female protagonists triumphed by living moral, upright lives. She won the Pulitzer Prize for fiction in 1942, for *In This Our Life*. Its short sequel, *Beyond Defeat*, was published posthumously in 1966.

Glasgow was incapacitated for much of her old age with a heart ailment. Her autobiography, *The Woman Within*, was published after her death. Her fiction dominated best-seller lists in the United States for decades after the turn of the century. She was the sixth woman member of the American Academy of Arts and Letters; she received the Howells Medal for Fiction and a special award from the *Saturday Review of Literature*. She was the only American writer whose fiction was reissued in two special matched sets, the 1929–

1933 *Old Dominion Edition of the Works of Ellen Glasgow* and *The Virginia Edition of the Works of Ellen Glasgow* in 1938. For the latter publication, she wrote the prefaces to the novels that comprised *A Certain Measure.*

Known by her peers as a southern writer, who chronicled the South from various historical periods and geographical areas, Glasgow is more accessible for today's readers as a woman writer who cared about families, community, and strong individual women and men. Her best fiction reflects the passion, and endurance, of all human life. In her writing, Glasgow moved beyond whatever geographical constraints her southern subjects might have imposed on her imagination.

• Glasgow's papers are in the Alderman Library, University of Virginia, Charlottesville, Va. Critical and biographical materials regarding Glasgow may be found in: Blair Rouse, ed., *Letters of Ellen Glasgow* (1958); Frederick P. W. McDowell, *Ellen Glasgow and the Ironic Art of Fiction* (1960); E. Stanly Godbold, Jr., *Ellen Glasgow and the Woman Within* (1972); Julius Rowan Raper, *Without Shelter: The Early Career of Ellen Glasgow* (1971), *From the Sunken Garden, the Fiction of Ellen Glasgow, 1916–1945* (1980), and, ed., *Ellen Glasgow's Reasonable Doubts* (1988); Linda W. Wagner, *Ellen Glasgow: Beyond Convention* (1982); and Lynette Carpenter, *Haunting the House of Fiction: Feminist Perspectives on Ghost Stories by American Women* (1991). See also William W. Kelley, *Ellen Glasgow: A Bibliography* (1964).

LINDA WAGNER-MARTIN

GLASPELL, Susan Keating (1 July 1876–27 July 1948), writer, was born in Davenport, Iowa, the daughter of Elmer S. Glaspell, a feed dealer, and Alice Keating. She began her journalistic career upon graduating from high school in 1894, working first for the *Davenport Morning Republican* and then writing a society column for the *Weekly Outlook*. She resigned in 1897 to pursue a bachelor of philosophy degree from Drake University, and she was awarded the degree in 1899. She returned to journalism upon graduation, serving as a statehouse and legislative reporter for the *Des Moines Daily News* for a little under two years.

In 1901 Glaspell decided to devote herself entirely to creative writing. She began work on a series of short stories, many of which are set in the fictional town of "Freeport," modeled on her own community. These early pieces, based on her firsthand knowledge of both state politics and midwestern life, helped establish Glaspell as a local colorist, and from 1903 on she published her work in such national magazines as *McClure's, Booklovers,* and *Harper's.* Glaspell also enrolled in postgraduate courses in literature at the University of Chicago during 1902. She published a collection of her short stories in the volume *Lifted Masks* in 1912.

Glaspell's first novel, *The Glory of the Conquered* (1909), garnered some critical attention, primarily because of her established reputation as a short-story writer. Following her introduction to other Davenport artists and thinkers through the Monist Society (a religious and philosophical group), her writing demonstrated an increasingly sophisticated blend of intellectual and social themes. Her next two novels, *The Visioning* (1911) and *Fidelity* (1915), exemplify the fusion of these concerns with a focus on women's lives, a technique at the heart of all her subsequent work.

In 1913 Glaspell married George Cram Cook, a writer whom she had met through the Monist Society. The couple decided to join a number of other midwestern artists who had relocated to Greenwich Village in New York City, a community that would have a profound effect on twentieth-century American culture. Along with a number of their bohemian friends, Glaspell and Cook vacationed in Provincetown, on Cape Cod. During the summer of 1915, they decided to stage some of their dramatic writing, including Glaspell and Cook's one-act farce on Freudian psychology, *Suppressed Desires.* The performances proved so successful that Cook convinced the group to expand the following summer, encouraging friends to provide scripts. They discovered another writer living there, Eugene O'Neill, and decided to produce one of his works. They called the new company the Provincetown Players.

For this second summer season, Cook announced a new play by Glaspell, then told her she had to write one to fulfill his promise. Drawing on material she later used for the short story "A Jury of Her Peers" (1917), Glaspell wrote *Trifles* (1916), her best-known and widely anthologized one-act drama. At the end of the summer, Cook determined to make the theater a year-round venture, and the group started producing plays in Greenwich Village. The amateur company soon received attention for its innovative and experimental work that rejected the commercialism of the professional theater.

Between 1915 and 1922, eleven plays by Glaspell premiered with the Provincetown Players: seven one-acts (two written with Cook) and four full-length dramas. The scripts demonstrate Glaspell's humor, her commitment to the social and political issues of her era, and her stylistic range. *Woman's Honor* (1918) comically reveals the hypocrisy of social conventions of gender roles. *Inheritors* (1921), a historical epic, dramatizes opposition to a number of governmental policies from the Civil War through World War I and exposes the decline of democratic principles. *The Verge* (1921) uses elements of expressionist and symbolist dramaturgy to explore a woman's descent into madness. Although critical response to Glaspell's work varied, a number of reviewers found her plays both compelling and important. During this period of great productivity, critics ranked her equally with O'Neill as a dramatist of great talent and significance for the American theater.

In 1922 Cook became disillusioned with the company, which he felt had succumbed to the pressures of commercialism, and decided to fulfill a lifelong dream of living in Greece. Glaspell accompanied him there, where he unexpectedly died in 1924. Although Glaspell remained close to Cook's two children from a previous marriage, they were unable to have children of their own. Glaspell's letters from this period reveal an ambivalence she had felt toward the theater for some time, and she expresses some relief at the possibility of turning her attention to fiction once more. The shock and grief from Cook's death prevented her immediate resumption of writing, but through the publication of her biography of him, *The Road to the Temple* (1927), she was able to regain productivity.

With her new companion, the writer Norman Matson, she wrote another drama, *The Comic Artist* (1927). She decided to return to Cape Cod, where she composed two more novels, *Brook Evans* (1928) and *Fugitive's Return* (1929). In 1930 she approached actress Eva Le Gallienne with her latest drama, *Alison's House*, based on the family of Emily Dickinson. Le Gallienne's Civic Repertory Theater produced the work, which received the Pulitzer Prize for drama in 1931.

Many New York critics disliked the play, however, and their disparagement may have prompted Glaspell to turn again to fiction. She published a children's book, *Cherished and Shared of Old* (1940), and the novels *Ambrose Holt and Family* (1931), *The Morning Is Near Us* (1940), *Norma Ashe* (1942), and *Judd Rankin's Daughter* (1945). She returned to Chicago in 1936 to serve as the director of the Midwest Play Bureau for the Federal Theater Project but left in 1938 to move back to Provincetown. Her last dramatic work, "Springs Eternal" (1944), reflecting conflicting responses to World War II, was neither published nor produced. Glaspell died in Provincetown.

Although Glaspell's work was virtually forgotten following her death, the rediscovery of "A Jury of Her Peers" by feminist critics since 1973 has led to a reevaluation of Glaspell's writing. The story, with its detailed examination of male control and undervaluing of women's lives, has become a central text for these critics, but it is important to place this work in perspective with all of Glaspell's writing in order not to misrepresent the concerns and thrust of her work. Glaspell stated her commitment to a range of social and political issues, including women's roles in society, and her work must be examined in the context of the diverging cultures in which she developed as a writer: her midwestern birthplace as well as the progressive Greenwich Village and Provincetown communities of her maturity.

• The largest archival holding of Glaspell materials, including manuscripts, letters, clippings, and photographs, is in the Berg Collection of the New York Public Library. The typescript of her 1922 play *Chains of Dew* resides at the Library of Congress, and the drafts of "Springs Eternal" are in the Berg Collection. One-act plays and the full-length *Bernice* were collected in *Plays* (1920); a shorter selection, including a critical introduction, is *Plays by Susan Glaspell*, ed. C. W. E. Bigsby (1987). A comprehensive bibliography of Glaspell's writing and of criticism of her work is in Mary E. Papke, *Susan Glaspell: A Research and Production Sourcebook* (1993). A bibliography of dramatic criticism compiled by Gerhard Bach appeared in the *Great Lakes Review* 3, no. 2 (1977):

1–34. General biographical and critical works include Marcia Noe, *Susan Glaspell: Voice From the Heartland* (1983), and Arthur E. Waterman, *Susan Glaspell* (1966); the latter, however, contains some factual errors and omissions. Information on Glaspell's early theatrical career is in Robert Károly Sarlós, *Jig Cook and the Provincetown Players* (1982). Veronica Makowsky, *Susan Glaspell's Century of American Women* (1993), focuses on her fiction. Useful obituaries are in the London *Times*, *New York Herald Tribune*, and *New York Times*, all 28 July 1948.

J. ELLEN GAINOR

GLASS, Carter (4 Jan. 1858–28 May 1946), newspaperman and U.S. senator, was born in Lynchburg, Virginia, the son of Robert Henry Glass, a newspaper publisher and editor, and Augusta Christian. Glass attended public and private schools until precarious family finances caused him to terminate his formal education at age fourteen and seek work as an apprentice printer. He rose to journeyman in two years, half the normal time, and subsequently worked as a compositor, pressman, and occasionally as a reporter for a number of newspapers, including the Petersburg *Post*, one of his father's papers. He continued his education by reading the classics, his major form of recreation in addition to cockfighting. Returning to Lynchburg in 1877, he worked for three years as a clerk in the auditor's office of the Atlantic, Mississippi, and Ohio Railroad. He joined the Lynchburg *Daily News* as a reporter in 1880 and became the paper's editor in 1887. He bought the *News* in 1888. Seven years later, he acquired the Lynchburg *Virginian* and merged it with the *News*. He also purchased the Lynchburg *Advance*, an afternoon publication. Glass married Aurelia McDearmon Caldwell in 1886; they had four children. She died in 1937; he married Mary Scott Meade, a widow, in 1940.

Glass's editorial voice became increasingly influential in Democratic party politics in Virginia. He consistently espoused a states' rights position, decried what he believed was mistreatment of the South during the post–Civil War period, and crusaded against corruption in politics and in industry. He supported state regulation of corporations and espoused educational and labor reforms. Claiming that politics suffered from the enfranchisement of ignorant and greedy voters, he advocated restricting the suffrage by literacy tests and poll taxes. He intended these limitations to be applied equally to blacks and ignorant whites.

Glass first entered elective politics in 1894 as a candidate for mayor of Lynchburg but withdrew before the election. He attracted attention at the 1897 Democratic State Convention with his speech nominating J. Hoge Tyler for governor. He was elected to the Virginia Senate in 1899 and again in 1901. He was a delegate to the 1901–1902 Virginia constitutional convention, pressing successfully for the poll tax and literacy test.

In 1902 Glass was elected to the U.S. Congress; reelected seven times, he served sixteen years. Named to the House Banking and Currency Committee, he quickly became one of its most knowledgeable and influential members and its chairman in 1912. With the assistance of economist H. Parker Willis, Glass was the primary author of the 1913 law that set up the Federal Reserve System. The act established an elastic currency that could expand or contract in response to the needs of the economy. Although Glass initially proposed a decentralized system under private control by bankers, President Woodrow Wilson insisted that the twelve Federal Reserve district banks be controlled by a central public board. Glass joined the Wilson administration as secretary of the treasury on 16 December 1918, remaining until February 1920, when he resigned to fill the Senate vacancy caused by the death of Thomas S. Martin. He won reelection to the Senate and served there for the rest of his life. He was elected president pro tempore of the Senate in 1941.

Active within the national Democratic party, Glass was a delegate to every national convention from 1892 to 1940. As chairman of the convention's Resolutions Committee in 1920, he drafted the platform plank that endorsed American membership in the League of Nations. Unlike many southerners, he supported nominee Alfred E. Smith in 1928, campaigning vigorously against religious intolerance. He helped to craft the party's "sound money" plank in 1932. In 1920 and 1924 the Virginia delegation unanimously endorsed Glass for the presidential nomination. He was also a member of the Democratic National Committee from 1916 to 1928.

Although unsympathetic to the fiscal policies of Herbert Hoover, Glass responded to the president's plea and joined with Representative Henry Steagall to secure passage of the 1932 Glass-Steagall Act, which kept the United States on the gold standard at a time when many European countries, including Great Britain, had been forced to abandon gold. Glass's concern for sound money also prevented his accepting Franklin Delano Roosevelt's invitation to become secretary of the treasury in 1933 and precipitated his break with Roosevelt when the president devalued the gold content of the dollar.

Glass, again in company with Steagall, sponsored the Banking Act of 1933, which required the separation of commercial from investment banking and established federal insurance of bank deposits. Two years later, however, Glass opposed the Banking Act of 1935, which shifted effective control in the Federal Reserve System to Washington.

That concern about increasing influence and control by the federal government and his lifelong advocacy of states' rights led Glass to vote against the New Deal 81 percent of the time. He was particularly opposed to deficit spending, expenditures for public works and other relief measures, and Roosevelt's attempt to "pack" the Supreme Court. When he ran for reelection to the Senate in 1936, Glass denounced the New Deal. He opposed Roosevelt's nomination for a third term but accepted the verdict of the convention; however, he took no active role in the campaign.

Conversely, Glass could be counted on to support most of President Roosevelt's foreign policy, which he viewed as consistent with Wilsonian internationalism. For example, with the outbreak of war in Europe in 1939, Glass advocated repeal of America's neutrality legislation, castigated isolationists, joined the Fight for Freedom Committee, and backed active American intervention in the war eleven months before Pearl Harbor. Once war was declared, Glass, as chairman of the Senate Appropriations Committee and a member of the Foreign Relations Committee, supported the funding of administration war measures.

Advancing age and poor health curtailed his active leadership, however. Never robust, Glass's health declined so badly that he was unable to appear in the Senate chamber during the last four years of his life, although he retained his seat. He died in Washington, D.C.

His private circle regarded Glass as a sensitive and somewhat erudite man. He liked to argue that Francis Bacon had written the Shakespeare plays. As a hobby, he raised Jersey cattle. In public, he displayed a volcanic temper, occasionally challenged Senate colleagues to fistfights, and employed rhetoric so colorful that he is said to have reduced even Huey Long to silence on one occasion. Describing himself as a "Jeffersonian Democrat" and an "unreconstructed rebel," Glass was especially proud of the title "Father of the Federal Reserve System," a designation that appropriately fixes his place in American history.

• The University of Virginia library holds Glass's papers. He published his account of the Federal Reserve Act under the title *An Adventure in Constructive Finance* (1927). Two popular biographies published during Glass's lifetime are James E. Palmer, Jr., *Carter Glass: Unreconstructed Rebel* (1938), and Rixey Smith and Norman Beasley, *Carter Glass: A Biography* (1939). Glass's role in the 1932, 1933, and 1935 banking laws is explored in Susan Estabrook Kennedy, *The Banking Crisis of 1933* (1973). His vehement opposition to the New Deal is discussed in James T. Patterson, *Congressional Conservatism and the New Deal* (1967), and Ronald L. Heinemann, *Depression and New Deal in Virginia: The Enduring Dominion* (1983). An obituary is in the *New York Times*, 29 May 1946.

SUSAN ESTABROOK KENNEDY

GLASS, Charlie (187?–1937), cowboy, was apparently born in the Indian Territory (now Oklahoma). Little is known about his parents or early life. According to "The Ballad of Charlie Glass," by William Leslie Clark, Glass was "one quarter Cherokee" (Wyman & Hart). Legend has it that Glass moved to western Colorado after shooting the man who had killed his father. What is certainly factual is that Glass was working as a cowboy for the S-Cross Ranch in western Colorado by 1909.

Glass was, by reputation, a colorful character. He was known for going to town in fancy silk shirts and enjoying the saloons, card games, and brothels of the "Barbary Coast," the red light district of Grand Junction, Colorado.

By 1917 Glass was employed by Oscar L. Turner, a cattleman with large ranch holdings in the counties of Mesa, Garfield, and Rio Blanca in western Colorado and Grand and Uintah counties across the state line in Utah. Glass was reputedly well respected by neighboring ranchers and cattlemen, cowboy and owner alike. African-American cowboys were not all that uncommon on the Colorado range, but Glass was extremely exceptional in being advanced to foreman on Turner's ranch.

Except for one fateful incident, Glass might have faded, like most cowboys, into unremarkable obscurity. The Colorado-Utah border was still largely open range in the early 1900s, although agreements were reached by ranchers on who would graze where. Ranchers usually "homesteaded" the water resources on the arid pasturage and had their cowboys do the same, who then assigned their rights to the ranch owner. Glass was no exception; he established a homestead under the Homestead Act and later surrendered his property rights to Turner.

Range wars between cattle and sheep ranchers were very much a part of this period in Colorado history, and it was this conflict over grazing rights that gave Glass his claim to fame. According to later court testimony, sheepmen routinely "trespassed" their stock onto traditional cattle ranges near the Colorado-Utah border. This led to confrontation, and during one such incident, Glass shot and killed a trespassing Basque sheepherder by the name of Felix Jesui.

The trial of Glass for this killing provides the little historical evidence of his existence. Though the court records of the Moab, Utah, Courthouse in this trial were mysteriously lost, the *Moab Times-Independent* carried a close account of the trial. Glass never denied shooting Jesui, but he claimed it was only in self-defense. Local antisheep sentiments made Glass a folk hero for taking a "might-makes-right" stand against what the ranchers saw as a violation of grazing rights.

Testimony transcribed into the newspaper account of the court proceedings revealed several facts about the case: Felix Jesui was with sheep near the Turner Ranch on the morning of 23 February 1921. Jesui was in possession of a rifle and a .25-caliber automatic pistol. Witnesses heard four shots. Shortly after the gunfire, Glass rode into the Turner headquarters and asked Oscar Turner and Alvee Field, a sheepman, to come out to the scene of the shooting and witness the body and the guns.

What happened during the shooting will never be known for sure. Field, the sheepman, testified that he saw a rifle in Jesui's possession, but he saw no other gun. The county coroner testified that three .32-caliber shells, from Glass's automatic, were found "some twenty-five feet from the body" (*Times-Independent*, 24 Nov. 1921). The sheriff, J. B. Skewes, testified that he found the rifle and the .25-caliber automatic on Jesui's body and that "he also found one .25-caliber shell about fifteen feet from the body" (*Times-Independent*, 24 Nov. 1921), which, with the three shots fired by Glass, would account for the four shots heard by Fields and Turner.

Testifying on his own behalf, Glass said that he confronted the Basque sheepherder, Jesui, about trespassing on the Turner range. Glass stated that Jesui "was armed with two guns, a rifle and a pistol, and was very defiant" (*Times-Independent*, 1 Dec. 1921). Glass says he decided not to argue with the sheepherder, but turned to his horse in order to take the matter up with the herder's boss. Glass said that as he reached his horse to leave, the herder fired his rifle. According to Glass, by the time he was able to draw his pistol, Jesui had fired his pistol twice more. Glass then shot the herder in self-defense, returned to the Turner Ranch, and surrendered himself to the sheriff upon his arrival.

The trial lasted more than a week, but the jury's deliberation took less than two hours. A verdict of acquittal was felt appropriate by the entire community, who saw the killing as an appropriate solution for trespassing sheepmen. Glass returned to his job as Turner's foreman and might have faded again into the sunset except for his mysterious death.

Sixteen years after the killing of Felix Jesui, Glass was involved in a poker game in the Denver and Rio Grande Western railroad town of Thompson, Utah. Members of the game suggested that the group travel to nearby Cisco and play in a high-stakes poker game there. Within a couple of hours, two Basque sheepherders, Andre Sartan and Joe Savorna, who had left with Glass, returned to Thompson with Glass, dead of a broken neck.

The two sheepherders insisted that they had been drunk and rolled a pickup truck, killing Glass. Many local cattlemen were sure Sartan and Savorna, cousins of Jesui, staged the accident to kill Glass, the man who shot their cousin sixteen years earlier. Even in the 1960s, area residents who had known Glass were reluctant to speak to historians Walker Wyman and John Hart, who wrote a short history of Glass.

Whether Glass killed Jesui in self-defense or as part of a deliberate murder to scare sheepmen off the open range will never be known. Nor will it ever be discovered whether Jesui's cousins killed Glass in retribution, some sixteen years later. What is known is that Glass was rare, an African-American foreman on a cattle ranch, responsible for giving orders to Anglo cowboys as well as African-American and Hispanic. Although much of Glass's life remains the subject of speculation and legend, it is significant that he is recalled at all, for very few of the legendary cowboys are remembered by name, and even fewer of those were of African-American heritage. According to a newspaper tribute at Glass's death, "cattlemen, former employees and acquaintances of Glass all agree that fiction could produce no more colorful nor picturesque character than Glass" (*Grand Junction Sentinel*, 24 Feb. 1937).

• The definitive book on Glass is Walker D. Wyman and John D. Hart, *The Legend of Charlie Glass, Negro Cowboy on the Colorado-Utah Range* (1970). The book is taken from Walker Wyman, "The Legend of Charlie Glass," *Colorado*

Magazine of History 46, no. 1 (Winter 1969): 40–54. For those interested in the archival account, the *Moab Times-Independent*, 3 Mar., 14 Apr., 24 Nov., and 1 Dec. 1921, will provide interesting reading, as well as the tribute to Charlie Glass upon his death in the *Grand Junction Sentinel* from 24 Feb. 1937.

For more on African-American cowboys, see Phillip Durham and Everett L. Jones, *The Negro Cowboys* (1965) and *The Adventures of the Negro Cowboys* (1966). Those interested in African American influences on cattle ranching should consult Terry Jordan, *Trails to Texas: Southern Roots of Western Cattle Ranching* (1981).

J. C. MUTCHLER

GLASS, Hugh (?–c. 1833), was a fur trapper. Few facts are known for certain about his early life. His place of birth is unknown. According to the historian and novelist James Hall, who published an account of Glass in *Port Folio* (Mar. 1825), Glass was of Irish ancestry. The fine literary quality of the only known communication from his pen, written in 1823, permits the conclusion that he was reasonably well educated. His early years have become the stuff of legend. According to reminiscences of a fellow fur trapper named George C. Yount (edited by Charles L. Camp, *California Historical Quarterly* [1923]), Glass was a sailor in the Gulf of Mexico, was captured by the famous buccaneer Jean Lafitte and his gang, became a fellow pirate to avoid being murdered, and later escaped onto Texas soil, went inland, and was captured by Native Americans identified as Pawnees.

It is certain that Glass joined the fur-trading expedition organized by William Henry Ashley, the lieutenant governor of Missouri, to proceed from St. Louis up the Missouri River to the Rocky Mountains. On 16 January 1823 Ashley advertised for a hundred men to accompany his Missouri River expedition. On 7 March 1823 the group began their adventure. Among their number were Ashley, his partner Major Andrew Henry, James Bridger (then only nineteen but later a famous guide and trader), the celebrated keelboatman Mike Fink, John S. Fitzgerald, the ill-starred explorer Jedediah Smith, and Glass.

The event by which Glass achieved heroic stature soon followed. Ashley's party built a post—called Fort Henry—on the junction of the Missouri and Yellowstone rivers in Montana and sought in early summer to trade with the Arikara Indians for horses to replace some they had lost, but in July they were attacked instead. Eleven Americans were killed and thirteen were wounded, including Glass. On 16 August 1823 Henry began to lead a thirteen-man party, Glass among them, overland to seek reinforcements for the endangered post. Perhaps four or five days later, near the location of present-day Grand River, South Dakota, Glass while a little distance from immediate help was badly mauled by a grizzly bear. Since the group had to keep moving, two volunteers—Bridger and Fitzgerald—stayed behind to watch the lacerated victim die and then bury him. But he lasted too long. So the volunteers, whom he could hear discussing his case, took his rifle and other equipment, abandoned him, caught up with their comrades, and reported his demise.

Glass told his story to all who would listen, they told others, and the legend steadily grew. The four most detailed accounts of the bear attack and its aftermath, based partly on second-hand information and differing in some of their details, are by Hall, by Yount, by soldier-memoirist Philip St. George Cooke (*St. Louis Beacon*, 2 and 9 Dec. 1830), and by journalist/travel writer Edmund Flagg (*Louisville Literary News-Letter*, 7 Sept. 1839). It seems that Glass's anger sustained him as he crawled 150 to 300 miles down along the Grand River to the Missouri, eating berries and meat from decaying buffalo carcasses on the way. Aided by some friendly Sioux, he finally reached Fort Kiowa, near the confluence of the Missouri and White rivers, in what is now South Dakota. Seeking revenge against Bridger and Fitzgerald, Glass went back up the Missouri River with some traders on their boat, happened to go ashore minutes before they were attacked and killed by Arikaras, visited some friendly Mandans, and got to Fort Henry in October, only to find it deserted. He pressed on up the Yellowstone to the Big Horn, found Bridger—and seems to have promptly forgiven him on account of his youth. Learning that Fitzgerald was at Fort Atkinson, across from Council Bluffs, Iowa, Glass and four friends pursued him by way of the Powder and Platte rivers. On the Platte River, the party was attacked by Arikaras, and only Glass and one other escaped death. (Glass was erroneously reported killed in the *St. Louis Enquirer* on 7 June 1824.) According to the most reliable account, when Glass finally got to the fort he learned that Fitzgerald had enlisted in the army in April 1824 and was therefore safe. Another report adds that Glass found Fitzgerald still at the fort, recovered his rifle, and forgave the man. It is estimated that Glass walked and paddled more than 2,000 miles from the time of the bear attack until he finally reached Fort Atkinson.

Next Glass went into partnership to trade mass-produced American goods, including tinware, for embroidered textiles, furs, leather goods, and silverware, and in the process traveled from the western settlements of the Missouri as far down as Santa Fe. After several unsuccessful months on the dangerous trail, he led a trapping party, probably beginning in spring 1825, from Taos north into Ute Indian territory. Another adventure occurred soon thereafter, in 1825 or perhaps 1826, on an unidentified river, perhaps the Snake, near Oregon. Glass and his companions generously sought to give some of their excess beaver meat to a Shoshone squaw on the shore but upon approaching her were shot at by braves nearby. In the exchange, one trapper was mortally wounded, and a brave was killed. Glass sought to comfort his wounded friend and had a metal arrowhead buried in his back, near his spine, for his pains. The surviving white party escaped by river, and Glass allegedly traveled some 700 miles before finding a man back in Taos knowledgeable enough to cut out the arrowhead with a razor. Glass returned to trapping and hunting, probably in 1826. He attended the 1827 trappers' rendezvous at Bear Lake, Idaho.

In the fall of 1828 Glass spoke for his fellow independent trappers at a meeting with price-fixing representatives of the American Fur Company, at Fort Floyd, by the mouth of the Yellowstone River. Later he became a meat hunter out of the fort (by then called Fort Union), until toward the end of 1832, at which time he and some friends went trapping along the Yellowstone near Fort Cass and below the mouth of the Big Horn. The party was attacked by Arikaras. Glass and two companions were killed. Whether Glass ever married or had any children is not recorded. It has been said that his only tangible legacy was his favorite rifle, now lost.

Myth-making about Glass began at once, and the full truth will never be known. He has been accorded spectacular twentieth-century treatment, most notably in two superb works of literature. *The Song of Hugh Glass* (1915), by John G. Neihardt, is a vigorous poem in praise of the Missouri River, the heroes of the American fur trade, and especially Glass, the brave, silent, and aging hunter. *Lord Grizzly* (1954), by Frederick Manfred, is a partly fictional narrative of Glass's spiritual growth away from a desire for revenge.

• The only known letter by Glass, concerning the Arikara attack of July 1823, was stolen from the South Dakota Historical Society, but John G. Neihardt published a photograph of it in his *Splendid Wayfaring* (1920). Stanley Vestal, *Jim Bridger, Mountain Man: A Biography* (1946), devotes a chapter to Glass and his treatment by and of Bridger. Dale L. Morgan includes much incidental information on Glass both in *Jedediah Smith and the Opening of the West* (1953) and in *The West of William H. Ashley, 1822–1838* (1964). John Myers Myers begins his *Pirate, Pawnee and Mountain Man: The Saga of Hugh Glass* (1963) with a careful survey of oral and written foundations of the Glass legend and also treats its detractors. Aubrey L. Haines's "Hugh Glass," in *The Mountain Men and the Fur Trade of the Far West: Biographical Sketches of the Participants . . .* , ed. LeRoy R. Hafen, vol. 6 (1968), pp. 161–71, is a succinct biographical essay. Lucile F. Aly in *John G. Neihardt* (1976) and Joseph M. Flora in *Frederick Manfred* (1974) discuss the treatment of the Glass legend by their respective subjects.

ROBERT L. GALE

GLASSFORD, Pelham Davis (8 Aug. 1883–9 Aug. 1959), army officer and public safety official, was born in Las Vegas, New Mexico, the son of William Alexander Glassford, an army officer, and Allie Davis. He ranked eighteenth of 124 graduates in his West Point class (1904), leading all cadets in Spanish and drawing. Commissioned in the field artillery, he spent three years on the faculty at West Point and was a captain when the United States declared war on Germany. Arriving in France in an early echelon of the American Expeditionary Force, Glassford instructed at artillery schools until July 1918, when he gained command of the 103d Field Artillery. That October he took over the Fifty-first Field Artillery Brigade, making him the country's youngest general. His troops fought in the Marne defensive and the St. Mihiel salient. He was wounded by shellfire and decorated with the Distinguished Service Medal and the Silver Star.

In the postwar army Glassford reverted to the rank of major and held a series of staff appointments, broken by a tour of duty as commanding officer of the First Field Artillery. He served at the General Service Schools (1919–1922) at Fort Leavenworth, Kansas; attended (1923–1924) and then taught (1924–1927) at the Army War College, Washington, D.C.; and, in his penultimate army post, served from 1929 to 1931 as chief of the Mobilization Branch, G-3, on the General Staff. He voluntarily retired in July 1931. At that time he was being divorced from his wife, Cora Carleton, whom he had married in 1906 and with whom he had four children. He married his secretary, Lucille K. Painter, in 1934.

In November 1931 Glassford was appointed major and superintendent of police of Washington, D.C., in effect the city's chief of police. Named by the three-man Board of District Commissioners (presidential appointees who then headed the capital's government), he was immediately the target of criticism. Senior police resented him as an outsider and liberals were disturbed by his military background. Seeming ubiquitous as he rode everywhere on a large blue motorcycle, Glassford quickly caught the attention of the press and public. Within a month he made controversial decisions that caused political problems for Washington's establishment. Participants in a December 1931 hunger march, openly organized by the Communist party, demonstrated at the opening of Congress. Delighting liberals and confusing the protestors, Glassford insisted that even Communist demonstrations on public property should enjoy police protection. Similar marches in other cities had experienced harassment and sometimes police brutality.

Just before Memorial Day 1932, World War I veterans began arriving in Washington seeking advance payment of their "bonus" checks (formally "adjusted service compensation"), which had been approved by Congress and President Calvin Coolidge just before the 1924 elections but were not payable until 1945. These "bonus marchers" vowed to stay in Washington until they were paid, and they set up encampments in the capital's parks and in building sites along Pennsylvania Avenue. Glassford was the only district official to treat them sympathetically. Arguing that they ought to go home but also insisting that they had a right to stay, Glassford helped them organize into a Bonus Expeditionary Force and arranged for public donations for their sustenance, giving $600 of his own money for food and shelter. After Congressman Wright Patman's bill for immediate bonus payment failed in the Senate and Congress adjourned, a majority of the approximately 20,000 marchers left Washington, but several thousand remained.

Obeying orders that came to the district commissioners from Herbert Hoover's White House, Glassford reluctantly began evicting veteran squatters from federal building sites on or near Pennsylvania Avenue on 28 July 1932. Disregarding orders about holding fire, a policeman shot and killed two veterans during a brick-throwing melee, the first serious violence of the two-month demonstration. Even before the deaths, the president had ordered the army to take over. Under the personal supervision of Chief of Staff Douglas MacArthur, a force of infantry, cavalry, and tanks, using bayonets and tear gas, drove the marchers from the district without serious casualties on either side. The commissioners called for and obtained Glassford's resignation on 30 October; his publication the next week of a series of articles in Hearst newspapers criticizing Hoover's treatment of the veterans may have contributed to the president's loss to Franklin Roosevelt.

Glassford served the New Deal as an unsuccessful labor mediator in California's Imperial Valley in 1934. Briefly in 1936 he was police chief of Phoenix, Arizona, and an unsuccessful congressional candidate there. Recalled to active duty in February 1942, he served in the provost marshal general's office until a second retirement on Christmas Day 1943; he was still wearing the single star he had won in 1938. Thereafter he lived in Laguna Beach, California, where he stayed active as an amateur painter, a volunteer in civic groups, and a participant in the United World Federalist movement, and where in 1948 he organized a MacArthur for President club. He died in Laguna Beach.

• Glassford's papers are at the University of California, Los Angeles. Documents about his police career can be found in the papers of the District Commissioners, National Archives; at the Herbert Hoover Presidential Library in West Branch, Iowa; and in the papers of Patrick J. Hurley, University of Oklahoma. Secondary accounts of his career are in Irving Bernstein, *The Lean Years* (1960), and Roger Daniels, *The Bonus March: An Episode of the Great Depression* (1971).

ROGER DANIELS

GLATZER, Nahum Norbert (25 Mar. 1903–27 Feb. 1990), scholar and editor, was born in Lemberg (Lvov), Galicia, the son of Daniel Glatzer, a merchant, and Rosa Gottlieb. When he was twelve his family moved to Tetschen, a German-speaking town in Bohemia. At age seventeen he went to Frankfurt am Main to study for the Orthodox rabbinate at the famed Breuer Talmudical academy. While pursuing his studies he was drawn to a local rabbi not affiliated with the academy, Rabbi Nehemiah Nobel, who had developed a novel approach to the study of the Talmud, bringing traditional Jewish wisdom to bear on the most exigent human questions—questions that were often first articulated in the context of secular culture, especially by critical scholarship and literature. A charismatic teacher and preacher. Rabbi Nobel gathered around him, in addition to observant Jews, many erstwhile assimilated members of Germany's Jewish intelligentsia. In this circle Glatzer met the philosopher Franz Rosenzweig, who would inspire a veritable renaissance of Jewish learning and faith in Germany, and Glatzer became a disciple. Abandoning his studies at the academy, he joined the *Freies Juedisches Lehrhaus* (Free House of Jewish Study), a school for adult education

that Rosenzweig founded in Frankfurt in 1920. Taking his key from Rabbi Nobel's Talmud lessons, Rosenzweig developed a unique dialogical method for reading religious texts and facilitating the encounter between the reader and the text. With this method the *Lehrhaus* was designed to help Jews find their way back to Judaism as a spiritually engaging reality. This task was to be facilitated not by experts—whether professors or rabbis—but by members of the *Lehrhaus*, who were committed to supporting one another in their common struggle with the existential questions of faith and religious knowledge. The ethos of Rosenzweig's *Lehrhaus* had a profound affect on Glatzer's conception of his life task.

Through Rosenzweig Glatzer met the religious philosopher Martin Buber, who employed him as a research assistant on *Corpus Chassidicum*, a compendium of Hasidic stories and maxims, a never completed project that Buber was then working on with the Hebrew writer S. Y. Agnon. Glatzer also assisted Buber and Rosenzweig in their monumental translation of the Hebrew Bible into German. It was also under Buber's supervision that Glatzer wrote his doctoral dissertation, *Untersuchungen zur Geschichtslehre der Tannaiten* (Investigations of the *tannaitic* doctrine of history). In this work, submitted to the University of Frankfurt in 1931, he maintained that the rabbis, the *tannaim*, of the first and second centuries C.E. retained their faith in the God of history in the face of the apocalyptic tendencies of the period and the attendant denigration of their world. He elaborated this thesis in several monographs and essays and would later consider modern Jewish attitudes toward history and historiography. In 1932 Glatzer succeeded Buber in the lectureship on Jewish philosophy and ethics at the University of Frankfurt. Due to the rise of National Socialism (Nazism), he left Germany the following year for Palestine, where he taught at a secondary school in Haifa. Also in 1932, he married Anne Stiebel, with whom he had two children. In 1938 they emigrated to the United States, where he taught at the College of Jewish Studies in Chicago (1938–1943), Hebrew Teachers College in Boston (1943–1947), and Yeshiva University in New York City (1947–1950). In 1950 he joined the fledgling faculty of Brandeis University in Waltham Massachusetts, founded in 1948. It was at Brandeis, where he taught until 1973, that Glatzer left his distinctive mark on Jewish studies in North America. Together with Simon Rawidowicz, he established the first comprehensive undergraduate and graduate program in Jewish Studies in the United States. The academic rigor and excellence of the program contributed immeasurably to the legitimation of the field in the curricula of the U.S. university.

Glatzer also served as an editorial adviser to Schocken Books, from its establishment in New York in 1946 until his death. Having been associated with Schocken since 1931 when his first book, *Sendung und Schicksal* (Mission and Destiny), which he coedited with Ludwig Strauss, inaugurated the publishing house in Germany, he became its first senior editor in the United

States, a post he held from 1946 to 1951. Under the imprint of Schocken Books he published many of his two dozen anthologies of Jewish thought. Reflecting the teachings of Rosenzweig, these works make the ancient sources of Judaism available to the contemporary reader, encouraging a thoughtful encounter with the varied and often complexly interrelated impulses and views that constitute Israel's ongoing dialogue with God.

In the last two decades of his life—during which, upon his retirement from Brandeis University, he served as University Professor of Jewish Studies at Boston University—Glatzer's work increasingly focused on the writings of Franz Kafka and the Book of Job, disparate voices that not only reflect the span of his interests, but that, for him, were primary documents of Israel's restless search for wisdom in the face of the "terrible paradox of existence." He died in Tucson, Arizona.

Glatzer will be remembered as a leading figure in the small corps of scholars who successfully transplanted into American soil the finest traditions of European Jewish studies, traditions that represented an awesome focus on learning, a meticulous and reverential attention to detail, and a profound appreciation of the most compelling existential and religious questions facing humanity.

• Many of Glatzer's papers are housed at Brandeis University. For biographical details see Alexander Altmann, "Nahum N. Glatzer, the Man and His Work," *Judaism* 12, no. 2 (1963): 195–202, and Paul Mendes-Flohr, "'Knowledge as Service': An Appreciation of Nahum N. Glatzer," *Jewish Studies* (Journal of the World Union of Jewish Studies) 31 (1991): 25–45. A bibliography of his works up to 1973 is found in *Texts and Responses: Studies Presented to Nahum N. Glatzer on the Occasion of His Seventieth Birthday by His Students*, ed. Michael A. Fishbane and Paul Flohr (1975). Among his more than 200 publications are *Franz Rosenzweig, His Life and Work* (1953; rev. ed. 1961), *Hillel the Elder* (1956), *The Rest Is Commentary* (1961), *Faith and Knowledge* (1963), *Dynamics of Emancipation* (1965), *The Dimensions of Job* (1969), *The Judaic Tradition* (1969), and *The Loves of Franz Kafka* (1986). Among his edited volumes are *On Jewish Learning* by Franz Rosenzweig (1955), *A Jewish Reader* (1961), *Parables and Paradoxes* by Franz Kafka (1961), *A History of the Jewish People in the Time of Jesus* (1961), *Hammer on the Rock* (1962), *The Essential Philo* (1971), *Twenty-One Stories* by S. Y. Agnon (1970), *The Way of Response* by Martin Buber (1966), *On Judaism* by Martin Buber (1967), *Modern Jewish Thought* (1977), *I Am a Memory Come Alive* by Franz Kafka (1974), *Passover Haggadah* (1979), and *On the Bible* by Martin Buber (1969). An obituary is in the *New York Times*, 28 Feb. 1990.

PAUL MENDES-FLOHR

GLEASON, Jackie (26 Feb. 1916–24 June 1987), actor and comedian, was born Herbert John Gleason in Brooklyn, New York, the son of Herbert Gleason, an insurance company clerk, and Mae Kelly. Gleason's parents drank heavily and quarreled frequently but instilled in him strong Catholic sentiments. His overprotective mother kept him out of school until the age of eight. The best times of Gleason's childhood occurred when his father took him to neighborhood theaters. Vaudeville shows and silent film comedies captured the boy's imagination. He began to perform for his schoolmates and was master of ceremonies for the graduation show staged by his eighth-grade class. In December 1925 Gleason's father disappeared; his mother took a job selling tokens for the BMT subway.

Gleason only briefly attended high school before setting out at sixteen to become an entertainer. He was a regular in amateur contests at local theaters, worked for carnivals as a stuntman and barker, and earned money as a boxer. By 1933 he had caught on as master of ceremonies at the Halsey Theater in Brooklyn. When Gleason's mother died in 1935, he moved to Manhattan. His earliest bookings, however, were in such places as Reading, Pennsylvania, and Budd Lake, New Jersey. His act included impressions, songs, soft-shoe dancing, ad-lib material—mostly insults directed at the audience—and jokes stolen from Milton Berle, then the reigning cabaret comedian.

On 20 September 1936 Gleason married Genevieve Halford, a dancer. They had two daughters, but the comedian's heavy drinking and philandering undermined the marriage. They separated in 1941 but reconciled in 1948. Gleason left again in 1951. Because of their Roman Catholicism they did not divorce until twenty years later.

During the late 1930s Gleason continued his apprenticeship in New Jersey nightclubs and burlesque theaters. He also wrote jokes for the *Jersey Observer* newspaper and performed on radio stations in Jersey City and Newark. His breakthrough came in 1940 when he appeared at Manhattan's Club 18, a favorite spot of Broadway notables and influential newspaper columnists. Movie producer Jack Warner saw him there and offered the comedian a contract. Before leaving for Hollywood, Gleason had a minor role in *Keep Off the Grass* (1940), a Broadway revue starring Jimmy Durante, Ray Bolger, and Jane Froman.

In Hollywood Gleason portrayed minor characters in eight low-budget productions, including *Navy Blues* (1941), *All through the Night* (1942), *Larceny, Inc.* (1942), *Orchestra Wives* (1942), and *Springtime in the Rockies* (1942). Warner Bros. did not renew his contract, but Gleason remained in Hollywood for a highly successful booking at Slapsie Maxie's nightclub. After returning to New York he found steady work—and fame—at Club 18. Gleason's act was, as critic Gilbert Seldes described it, "a bomb that exploded ten times a night—a bomb made up of commonness and noise and insult and a roaring impropriety which was altogether exhilarating."

During the remainder of the 1940s Gleason augmented his cabaret work with musical comedy roles. He made a brief appearance in *Artists and Models* (1943), starred in the touring company of *Hellzapoppin'* (1943–1944), and was a hit as Goofy Gale in *Follow the Girls* (1944–1946), which ran for 882 performances. Lewis Nichols of the *New York Times*, writing in 1944, predicted a bright future for the comic actor: "Mr. Gleason is rotund, with a fat man's beaming face; some day when he gets the words he will be wonderful instead of just very good." During his Broadway run Gleason hosted the "Old Gold Radio Show." In 1946 he headlined at Billy Rose's Diamond Horseshoe nightclub.

Gleason launched his television career in 1948 with a guest appearance on Ed Sullivan's "Toast of the Town." He created his memorable madcap playboy, Reggie Van Gleason, for the Broadway revue *Along Fifth Avenue* (1949), then went to Hollywood to play the lead in "The Life of Riley," a television series based on the popular radio program. But his manic, bug-eyed portrayal of Chester A. Riley did not catch on, and the producers dropped him after one season (1949–1950).

In July 1950 the DuMont Television Network hired Gleason to host its Saturday night variety show, "Cavalcade of Stars." The comedian soon became DuMont's biggest star. His personality and talents were perfect for the program's loose structure and the exigencies of live television production. He introduced the guest performers, sang, danced, and mugged, did monologues and impressions, and, when necessary, improvised—all this with a unique blend of aplomb, verve, and brashness. It was a mark of his rising popularity (and the emerging influence of television) that his catchphrases "And awayyy we go" and "How sweeeet it is" found their way into the American vocabulary.

"Cavalcade of Stars" gave viewers their first opportunity to see Gleason's comic characterizations: irrepressible Reggie Van Gleason, meek Fenwick Babbitt, the silent and sensitive Poor Soul, philosophical Joe the Bartender, loudmouth Charlie Bratten, and blustery Ralph Kramden of "The Honeymooners" skits. (Gleason often said that Ralph and Reggie were his alter egos, but his daughter Geraldine thought the Poor Soul personified her father. She believed that through this sadfaced character Gleason expressed the sorrowful memories of his troubled childhood.)

Gleason also made several guest appearances on singer Frank Sinatra's CBS-TV program. On the strength of his DuMont ratings and his work with Sinatra, CBS signed the comedian to a two-year contract for $11 million and gave him control over all creative aspects of his program. In addition, the network built him a mansion in Peekskill, New York, that served as production and rehearsal headquarters. This deal made Gleason television's highest-paid performer.

CBS enabled Gleason to reach a much wider audience, but in most respects "The Jackie Gleason Show," which debuted in September 1952, was very similar to the star's DuMont program. He retained the variety format, the June Taylor Dancers, and his familiar skit characters. Versatile actor Art Carney, the perfect foil to Gleason on "Cavalcade of Stars," also joined the venture. The major addition was Broadway actress Audrey Meadows, who replaced Pert Kelton as Alice Kramden in "The Honeymooners" segment. The program did not immediately earn high ratings,

but *TV Guide* named Gleason comedian of the year (1952).

Gleason occasionally redefined the variety format, as when he presented "Tawny" (1953), an original ballet based on his own musical composition. He also composed "Melancholy Serenade" (1953), which became the show's theme. In the same year Gleason recorded "Music for Lovers Only," an album of mood music with himself as conductor. The orchestra featured the mellow sound of cornetist Bobby Hackett set against a string section augmented by forty mandolin players. The formula proved successful. The Jackie Gleason Orchestra recorded more than thirty albums that sold in the millions.

In June 1954 *Look* labeled Gleason the fastest-rising star in television history. His show had climbed into ninth spot in the A. C. Nielsen ratings; it rose to second place during the 1954–1955 season. CBS rewarded the star with a new $7 million annual contract.

In 1955 Gleason abandoned the one-hour variety format and transformed "The Honeymooners" skit into a regular half-hour series. The thirty-nine filmed programs became television classics. Each episode took place in a dreary tenement apartment modeled after the one where Gleason had lived with his mother. Gleason invested great feeling and the full measure of his considerable talents in his portrayal of Ralph Kramden, a frustrated New York bus driver who yearned for success, recognition, and a better life. His long-suffering wife, Alice (Audrey Meadows), offered no encouragement to Ralph's ambitions and ridiculed the impractical schemes they spawned. But Kramden could usually cajole his inept neighbor Ed Norton (Art Carney) into helping him, always with disastrous results. Ralph's ensuing outburst marked the climax of each episode, which invariably ended with Alice forgiving her contrite husband, who proclaimed, "Alice, you're the greatest."

From this simple formula Gleason, Meadows, and Carney extracted pathos, comedy, love, and hostility. Year after year local stations rebroadcast the 1955–1956 episodes, inspiring a nationwide fan club called RALPH (Royal Association for the Longevity and Preservation of "The Honeymooners").

Gleason returned to a full-hour variety format in 1956. Carney and Meadows departed when the season ended, and Gleason abandoned his Ralph Kramden character. When Carney became available again, Gleason cast singer Sheila MacRae as Alice and restored "The Honeymooners" skits to his repertoire (1966–1970). The new episodes hardly resembled the classic efforts of the 1950s. Some were musicals, complete with large production numbers and original songs. Typical story lines contrived to have the Kramdens and Nortons on vacation in foreign lands. By transforming Ralph and Alice into bland innocents abroad, the format deprived "The Honeymooners" of its energizing force: the aspirations and frustrations of working-class life.

In 1985 Gleason released videotapes of Honeymooners skits from "The Jackie Gleason Show."

These so-called "lost" or "hidden" episodes from the 1952–1957 era prompted new critical and historical assessments of Gleason's contributions to television. Historian John Patrick Diggins labeled Gleason a comic genius and surmised that during the 1950s, when memories of the Great Depression remained strong, viewers must have found in the poor, but proud, Kramden a particularly poignant hero.

The Gleason of "The Honeymooners" was a superb comic actor. He could handle serious roles as well. He began with appearances on the CBS drama program "Studio One," but it was his work in William Saroyan's *The Time of Your Life* ("Playhouse 90," 1958) that drew widespread attention to the full range of his acting skills. In 1959, after CBS canceled his television show, Gleason scored a major hit as bibulous Uncle Sid in the Broadway musical *Take Me Along*, adapted from Eugene O'Neill's *Ah, Wilderness!* He made a triumphal return to film with his surprisingly subtle portrayal of pool champion Minnesota Fats in *The Hustler* (1961), for which he received an Academy Award nomination as best supporting actor, and a much-praised performance in *Requiem for a Heavyweight* (1962).

Gleason's most creative period lasted from 1950 through 1962. Although his later work was often redundant and uninspired, he remained one of America's favorite entertainers. His variety program returned to CBS (1962–1970) and achieved consistently high ratings. He did occasional specials for the network during the 1970s. From 1963 through 1986 he played starring or supporting roles in thirteen feature films. A few, such as *Smokey and the Bandit* and its sequels, were successful, but none tested his talents. In 1985 Gleason was named to television's Hall of Fame.

In his personal life Gleason was fun-loving and extravagant. He once chartered a train for a coast-to-coast party. He was devoted to his friends and never forgot those who had aided him early in his career. Gleason spent his later years in Lauderhill, Florida, where he had a mansion at the Inverrary Country Club. He moved there in 1973 to pursue his passion for golf, and for several years he lent his name to the Inverrary Classic professional golf tournament. He had divorced Genevieve in 1971 and married Beverly McKittrick, a country club acquaintance. Their marriage ended in 1974. Gleason then married Marilyn Taylor, sister of his long-time choreographer, June Taylor, in 1975. She had been a dancer on his television show during the 1950s.

Late in life Gleason often reflected on his accomplishments and good fortune. "Believe it or not," he told an interviewer, "the whole thing is like a vacation. Everything I've ever wanted to do I've had the chance to do." Gleason died in Fort Lauderdale, Florida.

• Jim Bishop, *The Golden Ham: A Candid Biography of Jackie Gleason* (1956), appeared too early to survey the full range of Gleason's accomplishments. James Bacon, *How Sweet It Is: The Jackie Gleason Story* (1985), covers most of Gleason's career but contains some inaccuracies. Mainly based on interviews and anecdotes, it effectively conveys a sense of Gleason's personality. William A. Henry III, *The Great One: The Life and Legend of Jackie Gleason* (1992), and W. J. Weatherby, *Jackie Gleason: An Intimate Portrait of the Great One* (1992), are more complete and less flattering. More thoughtful assessments of Gleason's work are in *Demographic Vistas: Television in American Culture* (1984) and *Comic Visions: Television Comedy and American Culture* (1989), both by David Marc. For an astute early critique, see Gilbert Seldes, *The Public Arts* (1956). Also see Donna McCrohan, *Prime Time, Our Time* (1990), and Tim Brooks, *The Complete Directory to Prime Time TV Stars, 1946–Present* (1987). David Inman, *The TV Encyclopedia* (1991), summarizes Gleason's television credits, while James Monaco, *The Encyclopedia of Film* (1991), lists his films. Peter Crescenti and Bob Columbe (cofounders of RALPH) assembled *The Official Honeymooners Treasury* (1990). Selected visual recordings of Gleason's television work are accessible at the Museum of Television and Radio in New York City or on home video compilations such as *The Great Gleason* (1987). Many "Honeymooners" episodes are available on home video, as are most of Gleason's feature films. An obituary is in the *New York Times*, 25 June 1987.

WILLIAM HUGHES

GLEASON, James (23 May 1886–12 Apr. 1959), film and stage actor and writer, was born in New York City, the son of William Gleason and Mina Crolius, both actors. Theater was always the center of Gleason's life. Born just a few blocks from Broadway, he was first seen by audiences at the age of two months, carried in his mother's arms in Aristophanes' *Clouds*. At age five he was cast in the melodrama *Stricken Blind*, and when not on stage he learned all facets of behind-the-scenes play production. With his parents' work keeping the family on the road, Gleason had little or no formal schooling. He gave a false birthdate and joined the army as a teenager, serving overseas in 1902 at the end of the Filipino insurrection. Back in civilian life around 1905, Gleason married Lucille Webster, an aspiring actress. They had one child, Russell Gleason, who became a film actor, best known for his featured role as a schoolboy soldier in *All Quiet on the Western Front* (1930).

James Gleason made his Broadway starring debut in September 1914 in *Pretty Mrs. Smith*. He easily found parts in other plays until 1916, when he joined U.S. troops on the Mexican border in pursuit of the outlaw-revolutionary Pancho Villa. When the United States entered World War I, Gleason served in government intelligence.

With the advent of the Roaring Twenties, Gleason again became active in the New York theater. In addition to acting, he wrote plays, and an early effort, *Is Zat So?* (written with Richard Taber), was produced in 1925 to become one of the decade's major hits. The show ran in New York for three years, played a London engagement, and eventually toured U.S. cities. Its combined productions grossed more than $1 million, a phenomenal sum at the time. Gleason "reached a zenith of fame and wealth," according to the *New York Times*, which added that *Is Zat So?* hatched "the hardboiled yet soft-hearted" character who became his "variation on a theme for the remainder of his acting career."

Gleason wrote, starred in, and produced several more shows over the next few years: *The Fall Guy* (co-authored by George Abbott), *The Shannons of Broadway* (written in collaboration with his wife), and *Rain or Shine*. In another play, *Puffy*, he created parts for a score of elderly actors, a gesture that the *New York Times* called "typical of his desire to share his good fortune."

By 1929, when sharply worded scripts were much in demand by Hollywood studios, Gleason was hired by Metro-Goldwyn-Mayer to create dialogue for *The Broadway Melody*. He wrote dialogue for seven other films in 1929–1930 and was dialogue director for *Oh Yeah!* (1929). In five of the pictures, he played leads or featured parts. A film version of his own stage play *The Shannons of Broadway* was produced in 1929 and was remade as *Goodbye Broadway* nine years later.

Throughout the 1930s Gleason worked steadily in Hollywood "B" pictures, appearing in more than fifty films during those years. He nearly always played sardonic, sour-faced, wisecracking New York Irishmen. Probably because of his years of stage experience, he was a master of verbal timing and the comic double take.

Starting with *The Penguin Pool Murder* (1932), Gleason embarked on the popular Hildegarde Withers series of six lighthearted whodunits for RKO. He was cast as Lieutenant Oscar Piper, a New York police detective whose deductive skills usually trailed a step behind the heroine's ingenious sleuthing. Edna May Oliver played Hildegarde in the series' first three films, followed by Helen Broderick and ZaSu Pitts. An observer noted years later that "the comic badinage and the hints of middle-aged romance . . . give the series much charm" (Steinbrunner and Penzler, p. 425).

Probably inspired by the great success of MGM's homespun Andy Hardy features, Republic Pictures cast Gleason with his wife and son as the fictional Higgins family. Although later critics dismissed the inexpensive programs as no better than hectic sitcoms, the Higgins family films were popular enough for five of them to be produced from 1938 to 1940.

The 1940s marked a new phase in Gleason's screen career. He stepped up from "B" films to make a number of notable motion pictures. In 1941 Frank Capra directed him in *Meet John Doe*. That same year he achieved a personal triumph as prizefight manager Max Corkle in *Here Comes Mr. Jordan*, the comic fantasy of a young boxing contender who dies in an accident and is reprieved for a final brief return to Earth. The picture's zany premise and corkscrew plot allowed Gleason to display all of his well-honed talents for verbal and visual comedy; his efforts earned him an Academy Award nomination for best supporting actor.

In 1941 and 1942 Gleason made pictures with Mickey Rooney, Judy Garland, and Rita Hayworth, as well as with a roster of major stars in *Tales of Manhattan*. In

A Guy Named Joe (1943), a major box-office hit of the World War II years, he was featured as Colonel "Nails" Kilpatrick playing opposite Spencer Tracy. Gleason performed in supporting roles in *Arsenic and Old Lace* (1944), with Cary Grant, and the memorable *A Tree Grows in Brooklyn* (1945). He was actually endearing as a milkman cupid to the romantically involved Garland and Robert Walker in *The Clock* (1945).

Gleason faced a personal tragedy in 1945 when his son died in a plunge from a New York hotel window. His wife died two years later. Yet after 1946, when he turned sixty, he appeared in another forty films.

Among the best of Gleason's remaining movies were *The Bishop's Wife* (1947), again with Cary Grant; *The Life of Riley* (1949), with William Bendix; the Frank Sinatra sleeper, *Suddenly* (1954); and the classic *Night of the Hunter* (1955), starring Robert Mitchum and Lillian Gish. Gleason's final film, director John Ford's *The Last Hurrah* (1958), appropriately cast him as one of fictional Irish-American politico Spencer Tracy's retinue of colorful cronies. During the 1950s Gleason ventured into television with appearances on various shows, including the comedy series "The Life of Riley," based on the film of the same title. He died in Woodland Hills, California.

Among supporting actors during his three active decades, Gleason stood out for his impeccable comic timing, his acerbic but somehow likable characterizations, and his ability to hold his own with the finest actors in American films. In all, he was featured in more than 130 motion pictures, always dependable, usually funny, and sometimes inspired.

• Highlights of Gleason's stage career and especially his film years can be gleaned from Ephraim Katz, *The Film Encyclopedia*, 2d ed. (1994); Leonard Maltin, *Leonard Maltin's Movie Encyclopedia* (1994); and the *International Directory of Films and Filmmakers: Actors* (1992). No listing by year of Gleason's featured film parts is comprehensive, but the filmographies in the *International Directory* and David Quinlan, *Quinlan's Illustrated Registry of Film Stars* (1991), are the fullest available in public libraries. A brief survey of Gleason's career up to the early 1930s can be found in the *New York Times*, 19 Dec. 1932. Chris Steinbrunner and Otto Penzler, eds., *The Encyclopedia of Mystery and Detection* (1976), offers helpful comments and details on Gleason's role as Lieutenant Piper in the Hildegarde Withers whodunits. An obituary is in the *New York Times*, 14 Apr. 1959.

ROBERT MIRANDON

GLEASON, Kate (25 Nov. 1865–9 Jan. 1933), businesswoman, was born in Rochester, New York, the daughter of William Gleason, an industrialist, and Ellen McDermot. She was educated in the parochial and public schools of Rochester. At the age of eleven she began assisting her father in his machine shop after school and by the time she was fourteen worked regularly as a bookkeeper. In 1884 Gleason enrolled at Cornell University to study engineering but left before the end of the academic year to rejoin her father's business.

When the Gleason Tool Company was incorporated in 1890, Gleason became secretary-treasurer, a post she held until she left the company in 1913. She ran the office and also played a major role in marketing. She convinced her reluctant father to permit her to go out on the road as the company sales representative, the first woman to do so in the field of machine tools. Gleason proved an effective sales agent; her knowledge of machines gained from years in her father's shop amazed many customers and gave rise to anecdotes that credited her with engineering accomplishments far in excess of reality. In 1894 she traveled to Europe, soliciting orders in Scotland, England, Germany, and France.

The depression of the 1890s dried up demand for machine tools, and in response the Gleasons decided to concentrate on the production of gear-cutting machinery. William Gleason had invented the first machine that could replace hand methods in the production of bevel gears in 1874; over the years he and his two sons accumulated related patents. Use of bevel gears, which transmit power between intersecting shafts that meet at angles, grew after the Gleason machines permitted mass production of standardized gears. The popularity of automobiles resulted in an explosive growth of demand for such gears and for machinery to produce them. When the firm needed to build a huge foundry in 1904 to cope with expanding business, Kate Gleason suggested basing the design on the nave of the Pisa cathedral, since its high roof would facilitate the movement of traveling cranes; when new offices were built she copied the facade of the impressive Pan-American Building in Washington.

After leaving the family firm, where her two younger brothers now played the major role, Gleason was appointed on 1 January 1914 as receiver in bankruptcy for another machine tool company, the first woman to hold such an office. Under her management, the firm repaid its outstanding debts and was returned to its stockholders as a profitable concern before the end of 1915. She became attracted to the village of East Rochester where she helped finance and build eight factories. When the president of the First National Bank of East Rochester was called to war service in 1917, Gleason replaced him for three years, becoming the first woman president of a national bank.

While she was president of the bank Gleason's interests shifted to home construction. Her own palatial home had been designed to her specifications in a Spanish style inspired by the Alhambra, but in East Rochester she began to focus on more modest houses. One of the bank's problem loans was to a local builder who failed to complete the workers' houses he had begun. Unable to find anyone to take over the loan, Gleason finished the houses herself and paid off the loan. She then began to experiment with the use of concrete to mass-produce fireproof homes at an affordable cost; before she was done she had erected a community of nearly one hundred houses of varied architectural styles, along with a golf course, a clubhouse, and several apartment houses.

Attempts to create a colony of concrete homes in California proved less successful but did not end her building activities. In the 1920s she began to spend three months every autumn in Septmonts, France, where she rebuilt for herself a castle that had been ruined in the war. In addition she constructed a public library and motion-picture theater as a memorial to the First Division of the American Expeditionary Force. At her winter home, a large estate in Beaufort, South Carolina, she planned to establish a community of garden apartments where northern professional people and artists of limited means might spend their winters, but only ten apartments and a hotel were completed at the time of her death.

Gleason claimed to have been inspired by Susan B. Anthony, who had been a friend of her mother. She was very proud of the number of times she had herself widened women's roles and was especially pleased by her own election as the first woman member of the American Society of Mechanical Engineers in 1914, an honor that validated her claim to engineering skills. She was also the first woman elected to membership in the Verein Deutscher Ingenieure in 1913.

Gleason never married. She died in Rochester, to which she had returned to spend the holidays. After specific bequests to her sister and various charitable and educational institutions, her will left the residue of her estate, estimated at more than $1 million, to establish a Kate Gleason Fund to be used for the welfare of employees of the Gleason Works and other philanthropic purposes.

• The Rochester Institute of Technology archives has photographs, newspaper clippings, and articles relating to Kate Gleason. Two interviews contain useful information: Eve Chappell, "Kate Gleason's Careers," *Woman Citizen*, n.s., 10 (Jan. 1926): 19–20, 37–38, and Helen Christine Bennett, "Kate Gleason's Adventures in a Man's Job," *American Magazine*, Oct. 1928, pp. 42–43, 158–75. Three celebratory publications of the Gleason Works contain information on the firm: *Fourscore Years of Bevel Gearing* (1945), *The Gleason Works, 1865–1950* (1950), and *The Gleason Works, 1865–1965* (1965). Obituaries are in the journal of the American Society of Mechanical Engineers, *Transactions* 56 (1934): RI–19, and in the *Rochester Democrat and Chronicle* and the *New York Times*, both 10 Jan. 1933. Provisions of her will are in the *Rochester Democrat and Chronicle*, 14 Jan. 1933, and the *New York Times*, 15 Jan. 1933.

MILTON BERMAN

GLEASON, Rachel Brooks (27 Nov. 1820–17 Mar. 1905), sectarian physician and health reformer, was born in Winhall, Vermont; her parents' names and occupations are unknown. She attended local schools, including Townsend Academy. In 1844, following a brief teaching stint, Rachel married Silas Orsemus Gleason, M.D., a recent graduate of Castleton Medical College; the couple had two children.

In 1847 the Gleasons opened Greenwood Springs, a water cure establishment near Cuba, New York. Mentored by Silas, Rachel familiarized herself with the fundamentals of orthodox medicine and the principles of hydropathy. The latter, a medical sect, held that internal consumption and external application of cold water, utilized in combination with dietary reform, fresh air, exercise, and a rejection of urbanizing society's "artificial habits," would prevent illness and cure disease.

The Gleasons moved to central New York in November 1847. Forming a partnership with James Caleb Jackson and Theodosia Gilbert, they established Glen Haven Water Cure on Skaneateles Lake, near Scott, New York. Rachel acted as physician to the women patients. Desirous of formal medical study, in November 1849 she became a member of the first class of Central Medical College, a coeducational, Eclectic school in Syracuse, New York. She received her M.D. from the renamed Syracuse Medical College in February 1851, becoming the fourth woman in the United States to hold the degree.

Differences with the Jacksons led Silas to sell his share of Glen Haven, and the Gleasons briefly found employment at the Forest City Water Cure on Cayuga Lake, near Ithaca, New York. There Rachel received women patients daily and required that they report symptoms and progress directly to her. In 1852 the Gleasons moved to Elmira, New York, where they established the Elmira Water Cure. Known from 1893 to 1903 as Gleason Sanitarium and from 1904 on as the Gleason Health Resort, it was for many years a family-controlled business. Among the patients at the cure were Catharine Beecher, Susan B. Anthony, and Harriet May Mills.

Rachel's eclectic training had introduced her to a variety of medical systems. She used water as a primary agent but not as a panacea. In treating patients she augmented water therapy with a "judicious combination of medicinal remedies." In her popular "parlor talks," Gleason emphasized the themes of self-esteem, personal responsibility, and the important connection between sound mental and physical health.

The success Gleason enjoyed in treating a wide variety of "female complaints" caused many women who previously had "suffered . . . from disease or debility during pregnancy and after delivery" to elect to spend this period at the water cure (Gleason, *Talks to My Patients*, pp. 104–5). Gleason's postpartum regimen is noteworthy in that she did not equate childbirth with invalidism. In place of the extended bed rest physicians usually prescribed for privileged women, she encouraged early ambulation. Her own birthing experiences were characterized by very short periods of convalescence. One week after the birth of her second child she resumed her medical practice, and the following week she attended another woman's delivery.

A supporter of abolitionism and free public schooling, Gleason also championed women's emancipation without aligning herself with the more radical women's rights advocates of the Seneca Falls group. In a series of *Water Cure Journal* articles she advanced the cause of clothing reform. Patients at Glen Haven, Forest City, and Elmira were all encouraged to wear loose, uncorseted costumes similar to Quaker dress. "Rather than make your form fit the dress," she suggested, "make your dress fit your form" ("Woman's Dresses," *Water Cure Journal* 11 [Apr. 1851]: 81).

Rachel Gleason was an important role model for women interested in medical careers. Her daughter, Adele, and her sister, Zippie Brooks Wales, were among the succession of protégés who earned M.D.s and gained clinical experience at Elmira before and after taking their degrees. In a period when medical education for women was controversial and not easily obtained, mentoring in the supportive atmosphere Gleason provided was invaluable. Moreover, by encouraging women to abandon restrictive clothing, take responsibility for their own health, and develop confidence in their multiple capabilities, Gleason articulated early the activist principles later associated with modern feminism. Following a long life of service, Gleason died at her daughter's home in Buffalo, New York.

• The only known collection of Gleason papers is in the Chemung County Historical Society, Elmira, N.Y. It contains "In Memoriam 1820–1905: Rachel Brooks Gleason," a biography written by her daughter, original matriculation and lecture cards from Central Medical College, and secondary articles and assorted clippings, including an obituary copied from an unidentified newspaper. Gleason wrote one book, *Talks to My Patients: Hints on Getting Well and Keeping Well* (1870), which went into seven printings. Among her articles are "Hints to Husbands," *Herald of Health* (Apr. 1885): 97–101; "Hints to Women," *Water Cure Journal* 15 (Jan. 1853): 7–8; "Treatment of Anteversion of the Uterus," *Syracuse Medical and Surgical Journal* 6 (Nov. 1854): 285–88; "A Visit to the American Water Establishments," *Water Cure Journal* 9 (Jan. 1850): 13–15; and a series of articles on woman's dress reform in the *Water Cure Journal*: vol. 11 (Feb. 1851): 30–32, (Apr. 1851): 81–82, and (June 1851): 151–52; and vol. 12 (Sept. 1851): 58–59.

Catharine Beecher included "Communication from Mrs. Gleason" in *Letters to the People on Health and Happiness* (1855). Some useful secondary sources are Susan E. Cayleff, *Wash and Be Healed: The Water Cure Movement and Women's Health* (1987); Jane B. Donegan, *"Hydropathic Highway to Health": Women and Water Cure in Antebellum America* (1986); Kate C. Hurd-Mead, *Medical Women of America* (1933); Regina Markell Morantz-Sanchez, *Sympathy and Science: Women Physicians in American Medicine* (1985); and Harry B. Weiss and Howard R. Kemble, *The Great American Water-Cure Craze: A History of Hydropathy in the United States* (1967).

JANE B. DONEGAN

GLEASON, Ralph Joseph (1 Mar. 1917–3 June 1975), journalist and music critic, was born in Brooklyn, New York, the son of Ralph A. Gleason and Mary Quinlisk. Gleason traced his devotion to jazz music to a day when, suffering from a case of the measles that kept him home from high school in Chappaqua, New York, he heard the music of Louis Armstrong and Fletcher Henderson on the radio. "There were no fan magazines for music in those days, not even *down beat*, and all I knew was what I heard, and what I heard gave a thrust to my life which has never left it" (*Celebrating the Duke*, p. xvi). While a student at Columbia University, where he served as the news editor of the *Specta-*

tor, a collegiate daily, Gleason became a familiar figure at the jazz clubs along Fifty-second Street in Manhattan. In 1939 he cofounded, with Ralph de Toledano and Gene Williams, *Jazz Information*, the first jazz magazine published in the United States. The magazine would close in 1941. In 1940 he married Jean Rayburn; they had three children. In World War II Gleason served overseas with the Office of War Information. In 1946 he moved with his family to San Francisco, California.

Between 1948 and 1960 Gleason worked for an insurance company while writing jazz criticism and columns for the jazz magazine *Down Beat*. In 1950 he began his long career with the *San Francisco Chronicle*, where he established a precedent by reviewing concerts of folk, pop, and jazz artists with a seriousness normally reserved for classical music. Gleason's enthusiasm for his favorite performers—especially Duke Ellington and Miles Davis—set him apart from journalists with a more detached posture. He called Ellington "the most important and greatest composer ever to have lived in North America." Of Davis he wrote "Miles is unique in jazz except for Ellington in that he is not only a superb instrumentalist (trumpet), but a composer/arranger/leader and a figure who sets personal style with his followers as well as in music."

In the late 1950s and early 1960s Gleason founded a short-lived scholarly publication, *Jazz: A Quarterly of American Music* (1957–1959); worked as a jazz disc jockey on radio stations KHIP and KMPX in San Francisco; produced and hosted "Jazz Casual" for National Educational Television, one of the few regularly scheduled television programs devoted to jazz; produced an Emmy-nominated documentary on Ellington, "Love You Madly" (1967); and lectured on jazz at several colleges in northern California.

Gleason also responded enthusiastically to the "Beat Generation" of artists and writers who congregated in San Francisco's North Beach area. He promoted and befriended such controversial performers as the comedian Lenny Bruce. Like many jazz critics of his generation who viewed rock and roll as an esthetically deficient but commercially potent threat to jazz, Gleason initially expressed disdain for such figures as the folk-pop singer Bob Dylan. Yet six months after dismissing Dylan's performance at the 1963 Monterrey Folk Festival, Gleason changed his mind, apologized to Dylan, and compared him to Shakespeare in the *San Francisco Chronicle*. While other jazz critics now turned against him, Gleason began a second career as a bridge over the generational divide.

In 1967 Gleason cofounded *Rolling Stone* magazine with Jann Wenner, a twenty-year-old dropout from the University of California at Berkeley. Wenner was an aspiring journalist who had long admired Gleason's columns. An elder statesman among music critics in 1967, Gleason both named *Rolling Stone* and provided editorial guidance to what became the most influential chronicle of the rock and roll youth culture of the late 1960s and 1970s.

Gleason wanted to educate younger readers about the jazz tradition. Writing of a new release by Miles Davis in 1974 he warned readers of *Rolling Stone*: "Miss him at your loss. He is amazing." Yet where Davis had alienated many jazz fans for seeming to emulate rock and roll, Gleason, his newfound enthusiasm for youth culture notwithstanding, could not always conceal his fear that the new music had pushed jazz to the periphery. In 1971 he wrote that the ascendance of rock and roll took "from in front of jazz the mass audience it almost had and made it again a truly underground art form in its best and most creative sense."

Gleason's efforts to bridge the generations were not always appreciated by younger music critics, including a significant faction at *Rolling Stone*, where one editor referred to him pejoratively as "an aging hipster" (Draper, p. 163). Gleason, for his part, often objected to Wenner's editorial and business practices, and his influence at *Rolling Stone* diminished considerably after 1968. In 1970 he became vice president of Fantasy-Prestige Milestone Records in Berkeley, a jazz label. In 1973 he won his second Deems Taylor Award from the American Society of Composers, Authors and Publishers for a *Rolling Stone* tribute to Louis Armstrong. Gleason died in Berkeley.

Shortly before his death Gleason, who was raised in an Irish Catholic family, wrote that as a result of his early exposure to jazz "I had irrevocably aligned myself with those who had abandoned the formal aspects of religion and found their idols and their inspirations and their saints in the nightclubs where, refugees from a society built on the standards of advertising agencies, they were bravely struggling with the mixed blessings of truth." His beliefs were shared by a small but influential cohort from his own generation. By the 1960s masses of young Americans shared his conviction that "the great musicians are . . . the true shamans, the religious and the secular spokesmen, the educators and the poets." Gleason made it his vocation to establish a continuity between generations of such artists and those listeners who set their lives to the rhythms of American popular music.

• Some of Gleason's columns and reviews are collected in *Celebrating the Duke: And Louis, Bessie, Billie, Bird, Carmen, Miles, Dizzy and Other Heroes* (1975). Gleason's role in the founding and development of *Rolling Stone* are treated in Robert Draper, *Rolling Stone Magazine* (1990). Obituaries are in the *New York Times* and the *San Francisco Chronicle*, both 4 June 1975. A lengthy tribute to Gleason from friends and musicians is in *Rolling Stone*, 17 July 1975.

JAMES T. FISHER

GLEAVES, Albert (1 Jan. 1858–6 Jan. 1937), naval officer, was born in Nashville, Tennessee, the son of Henry Albert Gleaves, a bookseller, and Eliza Tannehill. Gleaves was educated at the U.S. Naval Academy, graduating in 1877. During his early career he had extensive sea duty, serving in both sail and steam-powered warships. His first assignment was on the screw sloops *Hartford* (1877–1879) and *Plymouth* (1879), followed by service on the gunboat *Nipsic* (1879–1883), steam frigate *Trenton* (1883–1886), unarmored cruiser *Dolphin* (1889–1891), and protected cruiser *Boston* (1891–1893). In 1889 Gleaves married Evelina Heap; they had two daughters.

Promoted to lieutenant in 1893, Gleaves spent the following three years on shore duty before again serving at sea in a sequence of ships, the monitor *Monadnock* (1896), the torpedo boat *Cushing* (1897–1899), the battleships *Alabama* and *Indiana* (1899–1901). Although he commanded the *Cushing* during the Spanish-American War, he saw little action, though he did become close friends with the assistant secretary of the navy, Theodore Roosevelt, when the future president made an on board trip. Subsequently, Gleaves gained the command of two presidential yachts, the recommissioned *Dolphin* (1901–1902) and the *Mayflower* (1902–1904).

Between 1904 and 1915 Gleaves alternated shore duty with sea duty. Promoted to commander, Gleaves supervised the Newport, Rhode Island, torpedo station (1904–1908) and then served as commander of the cruiser *St. Louis* (1908–1909) and the new dreadnought *North Dakota* (1910–1911). In succession he commanded the Second Naval District (1911–1912), the New York Navy Yard (1912–1914), and the battleship *Utah* (1914–1915). Advanced in rank to captain in 1910 and then to rear admiral four years later, Gleaves was appointed to command the Torpedo Flotilla (later the Destroyer Force) of the Atlantic Fleet, which, in April 1917, became activated when the United States entered the First World War.

During the early months of the war Gleaves saw his command severely weakened as most of his destroyers were deployed in European waters, leading him to complain, "this robbed me of all my force except [the flagship] *Seattle*." In July, however, Gleaves was appointed commander of the fleet's Cruiser and Transport Force. In this capacity he personally oversaw the convoy that carried the first units of the American Expeditionary Force to France. For the remainder of the war he headed the powerful force that convoyed troop transports and supply ships to Europe. Although German U-boats sunk supply ships, tankers, and several transports, Gleaves could claim that not a single American soldier lost his life while under the protection of the cruiser force. Shortly after being appointed to the cruiser command, Gleaves confided in his diary, "if only they would make me Vice [admiral] I would be content." In December 1918, a month after the war was over, his wish was granted, and he was promoted to vice admiral.

In September 1919 Gleaves was advanced to admiral and ordered to the Far East to command the Asiatic Fleet. He was assigned in 1921 to supervise the Boston Navy Yard but retired as rear admiral (his permanent rank) shortly thereafter in January 1922. In retirement he served as governor of the Naval Home in Philadelphia, Pennsylvania (1928–1931). He died in Haverford, Pennsylvania.

Although Gleaves served in wooden sailing vessels, professionally he matured with the advent of steel warships. He identified with Stephen B. Luce and other naval reformers of the period, proselytizing for a navy of well-trained, highly disciplined officers and men. He was not an intellectual but did write an impressive number of articles and four books, including biographies of Luce, James Lawrence, and William H. Emory. A capable if not brilliant officer, Gleaves is scarcely mentioned by his naval contemporaries in their accounts of the period. His outstanding achievement, and the one for which he did receive acclaim, was his masterful handling of the troop convoys during World War I.

• The Albert Gleaves Papers including an unpublished diary are in the Library of Congress. His memoir, *The Admiral*, was published in 1985. A brief sketch of his life may be found in Clark G. Reynolds, *Famous American Admirals* (1978). In addition to the biographies mentioned in the text, Gleaves's published works include *A History of the Transport Service* (1921).

WILLIAM N. STILL, JR.

GLEN, James (1701–18 July 1777), royal governor of South Carolina, was born in Linlithgow, Scotland, the son of Alexander Glen, a provost, and Marion Graham. In preparation for a career of public service, James, like hundreds of other Scots, went to the University of Leiden in the Netherlands to study Roman law, which was more applicable to the legal traditions of Scotland than was the common law of England. As the eldest of eight children, he inherited his father's estate in 1722. Following a family tradition, James served on the Linlithgow council and was its provost from 1724 to 1726 and again from 1730 to 1736. He gained experience for imperial duties by this service, which also introduced him to national politics when he participated with other municipal leaders in selecting members of Parliament in London. These associations with prominent leaders in both Scotland and England contributed to his appointment as royal governor in 1738. Even more important was his connection to Spencer Compton, the earl of Wilmington and lord president of the British Privy Council at the time of Glen's selection: for Glen acknowledged that Wilmington had "procured for me the Government of Carolina." Glen's marital status was most likely an important factor in gaining assistance from Lord Wilmington. Though *Burke's Peerage* identifies Elizabeth Wilson, granddaughter of Sir William Wilson, as the wife of Glen, the gossipy diary of the earl of Egmont reported that Glen married the illegitimate daughter of Lord Wilmington and that one of Glen's sisters was the mistress of Sir Robert Walpole, the prime minister at the time of his appointment. Extensive research has not revealed the name of Lord Wilmington's daughter. They had no children. Glen received other appointments as well: keeper of the royal palace of the Stuarts in Linlithgow, keeper of the castle of Blackness on the Scottish shore, watchman of the salt duty at the port of Bo'ness, and inspector for Scotland of seizures of prohibited and uncustomed goods.

Glen delayed his departure for South Carolina until 1743, primarily because of protracted negotiations over salary. The Crown finally provided £800 but left the governor to depend upon the local assembly for an additional stipend as well as a housing allowance. This dependency undermined Glen's efforts to uphold the royal prerogative. Arriving in Charleston, he "found the whole frame of Government unhinged." Past governors had permitted the lower house of the assembly to gain powers at the expense of the Crown, and the council, which acted as the upper house, had excluded the governor from its legislative deliberations.

The three-way contest for power among the governor, council, and Commons House persisted throughout Glen's administration. He never achieved full influence over the council as executive adviser. Some of his recommendations for council membership were implemented by imperial officials, but other appointments resulted from patron connections in England. Governor Glen used his power to veto legislation and to prorogue the assembly in exerting his influence. In 1748 he vetoed a bill for a coast patrol because the Commons funded the expense by paper money, a practice prohibited in the governor's instructions. A second veto was imposed on a bill that modified an earlier justice act without including a required suspending clause for imperial approval. At the same June meeting, when the Commons refused to improve the governor's salary and threatened to cut off his housing allowance, Glen prorogued the assembly to August.

The governor had other disagreements particularly with the Commons over appointments, the term of legislative sessions, the requirements for a quorum, the nature of jury selection, control over fortifications, jurisdiction over ministers of religion, and administration of Indian affairs. Glen attempted to get along with the Commons, but he refused to follow the suggestion to approve legislation without consent of the upper house. He tried to mediate conflicts between the two houses of the assembly over issues such as tax bills and the selection of agents for England. In efforts to maintain a good working relationship with the Commons, he agreed to some provisions for revenue and for control of Indian affairs that violated the strict requirements of his instructions. Criticism for this failure to uphold the royal prerogative greatly increased after the appointment of Lord Halifax as president of the Board of Trade in 1748.

During the 1740s Glen had attempted to follow a neutral course among political factions that often pitted the planters against the merchants, but by the 1750s he pragmatically made peace with the influential Bull family, a leader of the planters. He also established connections with the prominent Drayton family when his sister, Margaret, became the third wife of John Drayton of Drayton Hall in 1752.

Indian affairs were among Glen's most successful efforts and at the same time included one of his greatest failures. He cooperated with Governor George Clinton of New York in promoting peace between the Iroquois Indians and the Catawbas of South Carolina, sending Lieutenant Governor William Bull, Jr., to New York to negotiate in 1751. He also persuaded the Catawbas to ignore the traditional law of blood revenge against the Natchez for murders. He negotiated land purchases from the Cherokees in 1747, 1753, and 1756. He supervised in person the building of Fort Prince George among the Lower Cherokees in 1753 and at the time of his recall as governor in 1756, was en route to build a fort among the Overhill Cherokees (later constructed as Fort Loudoun). His efforts, however, to bring the Choctaws under English influence failed with the collapse of the Choctaw revolt against the French in the 1740s. Carolina traders failed to supply the Choctaws with adequate goods, and Glen was guilty of attempts to monopolize this trade in a secret company with associates, including his brother, Thomas Glen.

Glen, nonetheless, consistently displayed a conscientious approach to the duties of his office. In response to a request from the Board of Trade, in 1749 he wrote his *Description of South Carolina*, which was published in 1761. It is the most valuable, comprehensive, contemporary commentary on colonial South Carolina. Glen vigorously championed the role of the colony. He was adamant in upholding the priority of South Carolina in Indian trade and Indian diplomacy in bitter conflicts with both Virginia and Georgia, and he persistently pressed the interests of the colony in the perennial boundary dispute with North Carolina. Glen clashed sharply with Lieutenant Governor Robert Dinwiddie of Virginia by claiming control over negotiations with the Cherokees and Catawbas when Indian allies were being sought for General Edward Braddock in his ill-fated campaign against Fort Duquesne in 1755. These controversies and concern over his compromises of the royal prerogative led to the recall of Glen as governor in 1756. Other prominent appointees of the Walpole-Wilmington era were also terminated with similar criticisms about the royal prerogative: Governor George Clinton of New York in 1753 and Governor William Shirley of Massachusetts in 1756, the latter also accused of incompetent military leadership. Remaining in Carolina until 1761, Glen was able to accompany his cousin, Brigadier General John Forbes, on his 1758 campaign against Fort Duquesne. He then served as the executor of the estate of Forbes after the general's death in 1759.

After Glen's return to Great Britain he took an enthusiastic interest in arrangements for the education of the sons of John Drayton, two of whom were his nephews. He also had Drayton manage his small rice plantation near Charleston, but the relationship deteriorated when Drayton failed to continue regular interest payments on loans from Glen. Glen died in either England or Scotland and was buried at St. Michael's Church in Linlithgow.

Glen served the longest term of any colonial governor of South Carolina. He was most successful in the administration of Indian affairs, despite the failure of his efforts with the Choctaws. He made conscientious efforts to uphold the royal prerogative, but his experience was a prime example of the inability of British imperial officials to reassert colonial dependency through instructions to governors when those governors were left dependent in part on local assemblies for salary and housing.

• The Public Record Office of Scotland in Edinburgh contains the Register of the Great Seal (*Registrum Magni Sigilli*) with Latin documents of Glen's property inheritance and royal appointments in Scotland. It also has the local town council minutes for his years as provost of Linlithgow and the Dalhousie Muniments with his letterbook as royal governor. The South Caroliniana Library in Columbia acquired 101 Glen manuscripts in 1974 with information on his financial activities, his familial relations with John Drayton, and accounts of the Choctaw affair. Indispensable for the study of Glen as governor are vols. 19–27 of transcripts of Records in the British Public Record Office Relating to South Carolina in the possession of the Department of Archives and History in Columbia. This archive also has the unpublished manuscripts of the journals of the council as executive adviser and of the council as upper house of the assembly for the period of Glen's tenure. *The Journal of the Commons House of Assembly* for the same period has been published in ser. 1, *The Colonial Records of South Carolina*, ed. J. H. Easterby et al. James Glen's "Description of South Carolina," may be found in Chapman J. Milling, ed., *Colonial South Carolina: Two Contemporary Descriptions* (1951). The only study of the full career of Glen is W. Stitt Robinson, *James Glen: From Scottish Provost to Royal Governor of South Carolina* (1995). Mary F. Carter completed a dissertation "James Glen, Governor of Colonial South Carolina: A Study in British Administrative Policies" (Univ. of California, Los Angeles, 1951), but it has no coverage of Glen's Scottish and English experiences. Other information on the Glen family is available in Joseph G. B. Bulloch, *A History of the Glen Family of South Carolina and Georgia* (1923), and Charles Rogers, *Memorials of the Scottish Family of Glen* (1888). The most valuable secondary studies of South Carolina during Glen's administration include M. Eugene Sirmans, *Colonial South Carolina: A Political History, 1663–1763* (1966); Jack P. Greene, *The Quest for Power: The Lower Houses of Assembly in the Southern Royal Colonies, 1689–1776* (1963); Robert M. Weir, *Colonial South Carolina: A History* (1983); and David Duncan Wallace, *The History of South Carolina* (4 vols., 1934–1935), vol. 2, pp. 1–20.

W. STITT ROBINSON

GLENN, John Mark (28 Oct. 1858–20 Apr. 1950), advocate for social reform, was born in Baltimore, Maryland, the son of William Wilkins Glenn, a lawyer, and Ellen Mark Smith. Glenn earned a B.A. in 1878 and an M.A. in 1879 from Washington and Lee College in Lexington, Virginia. He then studied law at Johns Hopkins (LL.B., 1880) and the University of Maryland (LL.B., 1882). In 1882 he was admitted to the Maryland bar and began to practice law in Baltimore. In time, like his great-grandfather, grandfather, and father before him, he became prominent in Baltimore legal, business, church, charitable, and social circles.

Beginning in the 1880s Glenn actively participated in the work of various Baltimore social service agencies, such as the Baltimore Charity Organization Society (1881), and served on several charitable boards, often in a position of leadership. Like other socially

concerned people of the time, he no longer attributed poverty, disease, and unemployment to vice, laziness or an unjust social order, but to poorly managed but improvable industry. A practical man of action, Glenn prescribed "scientific" charity as the remedy. Speaking at a meeting in 1898, he pointed out that "the phrase 'scientific charity' sounds very bad to people who do not think what it means. It means that we must be thorough and accurate and know the best way to help people. We must do only what is right and good and not let feelings run away with us." He regarded careful analysis of factual knowledge as the key to dealing effectively with social problems.

Nationally Glenn became involved with the National Conference of Charities and Correction (later called the National Conference on Social Welfare), serving as treasurer in 1894 and president in 1901. He believed this sort of forum offered an efficient way to identify social problems, particularly those related to poverty, ignorance, and crime; debate means of their alleviation; and provide a platform to inform the public about their discussions. He also thought that an informed public would support social change to overcome injustice and demand higher standards for social work.

In 1902 Glenn married Mary Willcox Brown, general secretary of the Baltimore Charity Organization Society. In 1907 Glenn was invited to become the first general director of the newly created Russell Sage Foundation, an offer that he enthusiastically accepted. Thus, at the age of forty-nine, he made a major career change from lawyer to social welfare professional.

The Russell Sage Foundation, with headquarters in New York City, was formed "for the improvement of social and living conditions in the United States of America." With such a broad mandate and with a board of trustees who thought as he did about scientific charity, Glenn was now in a position to encourage on a national scale the ideas that were so important to him, especially the social survey movement. A social survey combined statistical analysis to reveal information about the causes and consequences of poverty, reporting data in such a way as to suggest possible cures and to bring about change.

Glenn was particularly concerned about the effects of industrialization on labor. Although he was a firm believer in progress, he recognized that economic gain harmed some groups at the same time that it benefited others. To investigate this problem he became a leader in funding studies "of the conditions under which working people live and labor." By 1915 the foundation, with Glenn's wholehearted approval, had published fifty-five studies on this topic. Some compared wages with the cost of living to show that wages often were too low for workers to afford decent housing or an adequate diet. Others showed that long working hours had an adverse effect on workers' health and were a significant cause of industrial accidents.

Equally important, Russell Sage Foundation published the results of these studies in books, pamphlets, and public exhibitions. By so doing, Glenn and his associates expected to demonstrate the responsibility of management to labor, educate the public, solidify public opinion about social problems, and persuade communities to come up with plans of action for local reform. Glenn also intended to encourage the poor to work for improvement. Sometimes the publishing of facts did result in needed change: tenements were razed, sanitation systems were provided, and pure water was piped into homes that had none. Other reports, however, generated controversy and efforts by business leaders to suppress them. Nonetheless, if in Glenn's judgment the reports proved accurate and in the public interest, he authorized publication.

Glenn first became interested in the professionalization of social work in the late nineteenth century. Even then, he foresaw the need for trained workers and better agency management. Through the foundation, he continued to foster innovative social service teaching, the development of professional schools of social work, and the use of modern managerial techniques by social service agencies.

Glenn served as general director of the Russell Sage Foundation until 1931. Under his leadership, the foundation initiated and became a leading institution in the United States for the systematic study of labor and industrial relations, women in industry, unemployment relief, child welfare, small loan associations, loansharking, housing standards, recreational opportunities, statistical analysis of social problems, and the improvement of social casework. Even after Glenn retired, his involvement in the foundation and in social welfare continued. He remained an active member of the foundation's executive committee until 1947 and a board member of the National Conference on Social Welfare, the New York School of Social Work, and the Community Service Society until his death in New York City.

Glenn lived a purposeful life. Amidst a time of rapid change, he pioneered and made significant contributions to the social reform efforts of his day. More than most, he recognized that an increasingly technological world added new challenges to economic and social welfare and that these challenges needed to be understood and addressed.

• The Columbia University Library has the most useful collection of papers related to Glenn, including a 401-page typescript biography by Shelby Harrison, "John Mark Glenn" (1966). This document includes several chapters describing Glenn's youth and career in Baltimore as well as a detailed account of his role in the development of the Russell Sage Foundation. See John M. Glenn et al., *Russell Sage Foundation, 1907–1946* (1947), for a description of the development of the foundation from Glenn's perspective. An obituary is in the *New York Times*, 21 Apr. 1950.

JANE L. ANDREWS

GLENN, Mary Willcox Brown (14 Dec. 1869–3 Nov. 1940), social worker, was born in Baltimore, Maryland, the daughter of John Willcox Brown, a Confederate colonel and banker, and Ellen Turner Macfarland. She was raised in a devout Episcopalian family.

While the men in her family distinguished themselves in business—two brothers were executives in the Du Pont and General Motors corporations—the women were active contributors to social reform. Her sister, Eleanor Brown Merrill, served as executive head of the National Society for the Prevention of Blindness.

Educated at Miss Hall's School in Baltimore, Mary's earliest work in social welfare began when she became a home visitor for the Henry Watson Children's Aid Society of Baltimore. She served as general secretary of the organization from 1897 to 1900. In 1900 she became general secretary of the Baltimore Charity Organization Society. After her marriage on 21 May 1902 to John Mark Glenn, a lawyer also active in social welfare (they had no children), Glenn continued her volunteer work with the Charity Organization Society as well as with Episcopal church activities.

When John Glenn became the director of the Russell Sage Foundation in 1907, Mary centered her social service work in New York City. As the director of the Sage Foundation's Charity Organization Department, Glenn, along with such pioneers as longtime friend Mary E. Richmond became one of the leaders in the development of the casework method as a vehicle for promoting family welfare. In New York she also took a leading role in the Charity Organization Society of New York, where she served on the central council and was a member of the national council of the Episcopal church's Mission of Help, a service organization for troubled girls.

Glenn's efforts on behalf of social welfare took her well beyond the local scene; she traveled nationwide and abroad, becoming part of a national and international network of pioneers in the area of social work. Glenn helped found the National Association of Societies for Organizing Charities in 1911, which later became the Family Welfare Association of America. The association served as a coordinator for various charity relief efforts in urban areas across the country. From 1920 to 1924 she chaired the association's executive committee; from 1924 to 1936 she served as the association's president. In 1915 Glenn succeeded Hull-House's Jane Addams, becoming the second woman president of the National Conference of Charities and Correction (later known as the National Conference of Social Work). Glenn helped found the International Migration Service, which provided such social services as funds for transportation and health care to newly arrived immigrants. In 1928 Glenn chaired the committee on casework of the International Conference on Social Work in Paris.

The course of Glenn's career exemplifies some of the most crucial developments in welfare work in the late nineteenth- and early twentieth-century America. Her home visits were typical of charity work in nineteenth-century cities and emphasized the importance of providing sympathy for those in poverty, as well as normative instruction to enable poor families to better themselves. By 1900 Glenn's effort to professionalize social work was part of a national trend toward making family charity work more scientific and less sentimental. Like many of her day, Glenn came to appreciate environmental factors in understanding the cause of family problems. Through the casework approach, social workers attempted to help families by cataloging the economic (lack of jobs or job training), social (alcohol abuse), and environmental (poor housing) areas that might be causing family problems. With regularized procedures, professional caseworkers in the early twentieth century channeled the resources of numerous local charity organizations to poor children, the ill and disabled, widows and deserted women, and individuals and their families. Glenn and her co-workers thus emphasized that goods and services, along with moral instruction regarding the value of hard work, learning how to save money, and proper home life, could be used to lift the poor out of poverty.

Glenn was in the forefront of organizing training schools for professional charity workers, now called social workers. She was a faculty member of the New York School of Philanthropy, which later became the New York School of Social Work of Columbia University, and she lectured at the Chicago School of Civics and Philanthropy, the forerunner of the School of Social Service Administration of the University of Chicago. Like many women among the first generation of social workers who came out of the charity movement, however, Glenn worried that the emphasis on the professional caseworker would leave no room for those untrained volunteers, who could, she believed, provide what the increasingly specialized caseworker could not. She still saw a large place for the sympathetic, friendly ear of the untrained who might better be able to see the client as a "whole being, the family to be viewed as congeries of whole beings."

Like many activists who came from private charity organizations, Glenn often opposed state-funded and state-regulated entitlement programs to deal with poverty. State aid, she argued, would undercut the role of private organizations, which she believed were superior because they placed a greater emphasis on improving the ability of the poor to help themselves. Although a number of women activists in the early twentieth century, notably Jane Addams, Edith Abbott, and Florence Kelley, crusaded on behalf of mothers' pensions (relief funds provided by the state to widowed mothers so that they could care for their children at home rather than send them to orphanages), Glenn, like most charity workers, argued against their implementation. She worried that the financial responsibility for the care of children would thus be shifted from the mother to the state. And in the last years of her life, during the Great Depression, she argued against the increasing tendency of the United States to join European countries in regularizing social welfare through the initiatives of the federal government.

As the New Deal took hold in 1933, Glenn pleaded for a return to self-reliance, which she argued, prevents the need to cure all economic problems with political solutions. She noted that the new large-scale relief programs were "calculated to establish the right of relief in the minds of potential claimants." Whether or not one agrees with Glenn's efforts to return to nineteenth-century notions of self-reliance, the historian examining the second half of the twentieth century cannot help but be impressed by her keen insight that the long-term effects of the welfare state would establish a sense of entitlement on the part of growing numbers of Americans.

Glenn devoted her life to charity work on behalf of the urban poor; she became a champion of the casework methodology as American social work came into its own in the early twentieth century. As the welfare state took hold in the 1930s, Glenn continued to plead for the importance of private welfare institutions.

Mary Willcox Brown Glenn died in New York City.

• Glenn's papers are in the Mary Richmond Archives, New York School of Social Work, as well as in the files of the Family Service Association of America, the Community Service Society of New York, the Episcopal Service for Youth (all in New York), the Baltimore Charity Organization Society, and the Henry Watson Children's Society, Baltimore. Among the numerous articles published by Glenn in the American Family Welfare Association's journal are "The Volunteer—an Appeal on His Behalf," *Family* 5 (Dec. 1924): 205–10, and "On Consolidating Social Gains," *Family* 14 (May 1933): 67–69. See also "Common Welfare," *Survey Midmonthly* 76 (Nov. 1940): 332, and "Congratulations to Mrs. Glenn and the Family Welfare Association," *Social Service Review* 10 (Dec. 1936): 666–67.

MIRIAM COHEN

GLENN, William Wilkins (20 July 1824–24 June 1876), newspaper publisher, was born in Baltimore, Maryland, the son of John Glenn, an attorney and federal judge, and Henrietta Rebecca Wilkins. He graduated from St. Mary's College in Baltimore with a degree in the classics in 1841. On graduating he entered the counting room of William Howell & Sons, Baltimore shippers, and in 1844 was sent as supercargo to South America, where he kept a detailed journal of his voyage. Soon after returning to Baltimore he entered into the iron commission business, in connection with his father's Curtis Creek Furnace.

After a year's grand tour of Europe in 1848–1849, he took an active role in managing the family's extensive real estate holdings. On his father's death in 1853, he became responsible for the large fortune in real estate, stocks, and mining operations that the judge had bequeathed to his widow. The management of the family property became Glenn's major concern. Glenn married Ellen Mark Smith of Philadelphia in 1857. Of their two surviving children, one son, John Mark Glenn, became the first director of the Russell Sage Foundation.

In early 1861 Glenn purchased the Baltimore *Daily Exchange* in partnership with Francis Scott Key Howard and later William Carpenter. An independent newspaper, its editorial policy opposed the Lincoln administration. Although it did not support secession in Maryland, the paper strongly backed states' rights and advocated reunion by negotiation. Its antiadministration editorials, written largely by Severn Teackle Wallis, landed both Wallis and Howard in prison. Glenn was also imprisoned at Fort McHenry on several occasions because of his editorials, particularly those opposing censorship. His family's friendship with Senator Reverdy Johnson, however, helped prevent long prison stays.

In September 1861 the *Exchange* was suppressed. Glenn arranged for Carpenter to begin publication of the *Maryland News Sheet* as its successor, but without editorials. Because public opposition to the Lincoln administration was now illegal he turned to covert operations to publicize the Confederate cause. Having connections with the British embassy, Glenn began to smuggle newspapermen and prominent British subjects into the Confederacy and to pass their dispatches on to England. Among these were Francis Vizetelly of the *Illustrated London News*, author George Alfred Lawrence, and Lord Edward St. Maur. In July 1863 his subversive activities became known to the federal authorities, and he was forced to flee his home late at night from a cavalry patrol and escape to Canada. Glenn then embarked for England, where he spent the better part of a year in London. Returning in 1864 he was still subject to arrest in Maryland and thus spent most of the rest of the war in exile in New York.

After the war the publication of the *Exchange* (as the *Daily Gazette*) was resumed, and Glenn continued in an active role with the paper until he sold his share in 1872. He also aided in the defense of Confederate president Jefferson Davis, raised money for southern relief, and involved himself in land development and railroading. He was a founder of the Maryland Jockey Club, and his postwar racing stable became well known, although it lacked champions. After the sale of the paper, Glenn purchased the Cold Stream Mine in Georgetown, Colorado, and for the next five years tried to make the silver mine pay while fending off claim jumpers. His health deteriorated, however, and in 1876 he returned to Baltimore, where he died.

• Glenn's extensive collection of letters, journals, and accounts is in the Maryland Historical Society in Baltimore. He prepared a journal of his war activities that was published posthumously as *Between North and South, a Maryland Journalist Views the Civil War,* ed. Bayly Ellen Marks and Mark Norton Schatz (1976).

BAYLY ELLEN MARKS
MARK NORTON SCHATZ

GLENNON, John Joseph (14 June 1862–9 Mar. 1946), Roman Catholic archbishop and cardinal, was born in Kinnegad, County Meath, Ireland, the son of Matthew Glennon and Catherine Rafferty. He first attended the diocesan seminary, St. Mary's College at Mullingar, then Dublin's missionary College of All Hallows, whose graduates are recruited for dioceses around the world. Bishop John Hogan enlisted Glennon for work in his diocese of Kansas City, Missouri. In 1883 he arrived in Kansas City, where he was ordained a priest in December 1884. He was first assigned to St. Patrick's Church in Kansas City. After a year's leave to learn German at Bonn, Germany, in order to conduct a more effective ministry among Missouri's German Catholics, Glennon returned to Kansas City to become successively secretary to Bishop Hogan, cathedral rector, diocesan vicar general, and, in 1896, coadjutor bishop. In 1903 he was appointed coadjutor to Archbishop John Kain of St. Louis. When Kain died in October 1903, Glennon became the third archbishop of St. Louis.

Typical of American bishops of his time, Glennon pursued the institutional development of his archdiocese through major building projects. He fulfilled his predecessors' dreams with the construction of St. Louis Cathedral between 1907 and 1926, then the country's largest Catholic church. He completed the new Kenrick Seminary in 1915 and the St. Louis Preparatory Seminary in 1931. As a strong advocate of Catholic education, he started an archdiocesan office of education and built a network of high schools. A growing Catholic population required the opening of ninety-five parishes during his tenure. As administrator of a large archdiocese, he encouraged St. Louis's religious orders in their educational and social service work but did not centralize control of their activities as did many Catholic bishops of the era.

Glennon cultivated a national reputation as an orator with his polished and graceful addresses. He was invited to preach at Catholic events of national importance such as Cardinal James Gibbons's funeral, the consecration of New York's St. Patrick's Cathedral, and many anniversary celebrations. His St. Louis flock knew him as an eloquent supporter of temperance but opposed to national Prohibition, woman suffrage, child labor amendments to the U.S. Constitution, and Socialism. Typical of many religious leaders of the time, he spoke out against plays, movies, and dances.

Glennon's name is not associated with national Catholic causes except for the Catholic Colonization Society, which encouraged European Catholic immigrants to settle in farm communities. This movement appealed to Glennon's romantic ideas about the virtues of rural life. Among local urban problems, he encouraged charitable efforts for newsboys and homeless men. He supported the status quo in St. Louis's segregated racial relations and thereby embittered advocates of racial equality. Although St. Louis University, run by the Jesuits, was integrated, other Catholic institutions remained segregated while Glennon was archbishop.

With a secure reputation as a builder of Catholic institutional life in a major city, Glennon's career was crowned with promotion to the College of Cardinals. He traveled to Rome to be invested in this dignity in February 1946. While traveling in Ireland en route back, he took sick and died in Dublin.

• Glennon's papers in the Archives of the Archdiocese of St. Louis consist mostly of addresses and sermons, but a few letters have survived. Nicholas Schneider, *The Life of John Cardinal Glennon* (1971), a popular biography, brings together many undocumented stories. Richard Joseph Heman, "The Social Views of Archbishop John Glennon in the Context of the Family" (Ph.D. diss., St. Louis Univ., 1979), is a study of his speeches and public statements. John Rothensteiner, *A History of the Archdiocese of St. Louis* (2 vols., 1928), and William Barnaby Faherty, *Dream by the River: Two Centuries of Saint Louis Catholicism, 1766–1980* (1981), treat Glennon's career in St. Louis. Since Glennon is not likely to be the subject of a scholarly biography, such essays as Elizabeth Kolmer, "John Cardinal Glennon's Contribution to Catholic Secondary Education," *Social Justice Review* 60 (Apr. 1967), and Donald Molitor, "The History of Glennville and Adjacent Catholic Colonization Ventures in Southeast Missouri: A Study in Changing Rural-Urban Patterns" (M.A. thesis, St. Louis Univ., 1965), are useful explorations of his views.

JOSEPH M. WHITE

GLIDDEN, Frederick Dilley. *See* Short, Luke.

GLIDDEN, Joseph Farwell (18 Jan. 1813–9 Oct. 1906), farmer, inventor, and capitalist, was born in Charlestown, Sullivan County, New Hampshire, the son of David Glidden and Polly Hurd, farmers. His family moved west to Orleans County, New York, when he was an infant. After attending local district schools, he studied at Middlebury Academy in Genesee County and at the seminary in Lima, New York. He taught school in the area for several years, but farming was always his first love. In 1837 he married Clarissa Foster in Clarendon, New York. Lacking funds to buy land in New York, he headed west in about 1840 with two crude threshing machines, doing custom threshing and general farm work. In 1842 he settled in De Kalb County, Illinois, where he purchased 600 acres of prairie land on the edge of De Kalb village. The death of the Gliddens' three young children, followed by the death of his wife in 1843, left Glidden alone until 1851, when he married Lucinda Warne of De Kalb. They had one daughter.

Fencing was a difficult problem for pioneer farmers on the Illinois prairies. The lush grasslands lacked plentiful supplies of native timber, and the rich soil did not contain abundant stones that eastern settlers had used for cheap, readily available fencing materials. Imported wood was too expensive, thorny hedges were unreliable, and smooth wire proved ineffective in containing livestock.

At the De Kalb County Fair in 1873, Henry M. Rose exhibited an armored wire fencing, consisting of "wooden strips with metallic points." Three men from De Kalb, Joseph Glidden, Isaac L. Ellwood, and Jacob Haish, all later regarded as pioneers in barbed wire fencing, were inspired by the exhibit to invent a more practical and effective fence. Glidden twisted short lengths of wire into barbs, which he then strung along a strand of smooth wire, but the barbs loosened and would not remain spaced along the wire. To solve this problem, Glidden added a second wire, which, when twisted about the first, held the barbs firmly in place. A four-rod section of this new fence erected on Glidden's farm proved very effective in controlling livestock.

Glidden applied for a patent on 27 October 1873, but his patent was not issued until July 1874. Inventors in New York and Ohio had patented several early forms of "armored wire" in the 1860s. But Glidden's second twisted wire was eventually recognized as the fundamental novelty that made Glidden's patent a "bottom," or an original patent in the legal struggles that eventually decided the question of who would profit from the manufacture of barbed wire. Even Haish, a De Kalb lumber dealer, though applying later than Glidden, received a patent for an "S barb" before Glidden's application was approved.

Ellwood, a hardware merchant in De Kalb village, decided that Glidden's fence held greater promise than any Ellwood could invent. After a short negotiation, Ellwood purchased a half interest in Glidden's patent for just $265. The new partners began producing barbed wire as the Barb Fence Company of De Kalb, selling the new fence at Ellwood's store as fast as they could make it.

The surge in orders for smooth wire from this small village in Illinois inspired the Washburn and Moen Manufacturing Co. of Worcester, Massachusetts, to investigate. The company's vice president, Charles F. Washburn, was impressed by what he discovered and initially tried to buy the Haish patent. Haish's excessive demands led Washburn to approach Glidden and Ellwood. The 63-year-old Glidden, always a farmer at heart, quickly agreed to sell his half interest. He received $60,000 in cash and a royalty of twenty-five cents on each hundred-weight of barbed wire manufactured by Washburn and Moen, which he collected until 1891. His invention made him a wealthy man.

In the years that followed the acquisition of the Glidden patent, the Washburn and Moen Co. systematically acquired all significant earlier patents and initiated litigation to prove that they held all the "bottom" patents to barbed wire, of which the Glidden patent was the most important. The U.S. Supreme Court eventually ruled that Glidden's innovation was "a new combination and arrangement of known elements . . . , evidence of invention" (*Washburn and Moen Manufacturing Co. v. Beat 'Em All Barbed Wire Company*).

In the years following the sale of his patent, Glidden bought more farms, built and operated the Glidden House, a hotel in De Kalb, purchased the *De Kalb Chronicle*, which he published until his death, operated the De Kalb Roller Mills, and served as vice president of a local bank. He became a silent partner in a Texas ranch of some 250,000 acres, fenced in with 150 miles of Glidden "Winner" fencing and stocked with 15,000 cattle. His only remaining connection with the fence he had invented came when he occasionally testified in legal proceedings regarding his patent. A staunch Democrat, he served one term as sheriff of De Kalb County, the last Democrat to be elected to any office in De Kalb County for some time, and he served a term as mayor of De Kalb village in 1881. Glidden, Ellwood, Haish, and Clinton Rosette, editor of the *Chronicle*, joined in persuading the Illinois legislature to locate a new state normal school in De Kalb. Glidden donated 64 acres from his original homestead for the campus and, with Ellwood and Haish, helped break ground for the new institution in 1899. A friend said that "no man in the community enjoyed in a greater degree the respect, esteem and confidence of his neighbors and associates." Glidden died in De Kalb.

• There is no collection of Glidden papers, but the Ellwood Family Papers in the Northern Illinois University Library contain some references to Glidden. Biographical information on Glidden can be found in George W. Chamberlain, *The Descendants of Charles Glidden of Portsmouth and Exeter, New Hampshire* (1925), and *The Biographical Record of De Kalb County, Illinois* (1898). Henry D. McCallum and Frances T. McCallum, *The Wire That Fenced the West* (1965), and Earl W. Hayter, "Barbed Wire Fencing—A Prairie Invention, Its Rise and Influence in the Western States," *Agricultural History* 13 (Oct. 1939), discuss the development and impact of barbed wire. Hayter, *The Troubled Farmer, 1850–1900: Rural Adjustment to Industrialism* (1968), examines Glidden's contribution in a historical context. An obituary is in *Farm Implement News*, 18 Oct. 1906.

LEONARD F. RALSTON

GLOVER, John (5 Nov. 1732–30 Jan. 1797), merchant and army officer, was born in Salem, Massachusetts, the son of Jonathan Glover, a house carpenter, and Tabitha Bacon. When he was four years old Glover's father died. Some time thereafter the widowed mother moved with her four sons to nearby Marblehead. Glover became a shoemaker and then entered into the fishing business. He married Hannah Gale in 1754; they had four children. With profits from fishing Glover purchased a small coasting vessel and began trading with the West Indies and the Iberian peninsula. By 1774 Glover had accumulated considerable property and had become one of Marblehead's leading citizens.

In 1759 Glover received a commission as ensign in the Third Military Foot Company in the town of Marblehead. During the years before the American Revolution he remained an active member of the militia, rising to the rank of captain.

As a merchant and trader Glover suffered from the effects of British policy in the 1760s, including the Sugar Act of 1764, which affected his business in the West Indies. His experiences pushed him to the patriot side and he became a strong supporter of the American cause. In January 1775 he was elected second lieutenant colonel of the Marblehead militia regiment. When the colonel of the regiment, Jeremiah Lee, died in the spring of 1775 Glover succeeded him in command.

Following the battle at Bunker Hill (17 June 1775) Glover marched his regiment to Cambridge and joined the army besieging the British in Boston. On taking command of the American army (2 July 1775) George Washington decided to tighten the siege by intercepting British supply vessels. He sought Glover's advice in this matter and in August Washington chartered Glover's schooner *Hannah*. She was armed and sent to sea, becoming the first of several vessels Washington would use for this purpose.

Because Glover's wharf was located in Beverly, *Hannah* was outfitted in that town. Washington's other vessels also used the port. To ensure its security Washington detached Glover's regiment from the main body of troops in Cambridge and ordered them to the port. Under Glover's command the regiment fortified and defended the town. On 11 July 1776, following the British evacuation of Boston, Washington ordered Glover's Marbleheaders to join him at New York.

Washington had divided his army and posted a sizable force on Long Island. General Sir William Howe took advantage of Washington's mistake. In a series of maneuvers he outflanked the Americans driving them back against the East River until they were nearly surrounded. Their only hope was to somehow escape across the river to Manhattan. During the night of 29–30 August Glover and his Marbleheaders ferried Washington's troops to safety. It was a bold stroke that caught the British by surprise. Later at Kip's Bay (15 Sept.) Glover's regiment again distinguished itself by helping to hold off a British assault.

Glover and his men remained with Washington as he retreated across New Jersey. Late on Christmas night (26 Dec. 1776) Glover's troops undertook the task of manning the small boats used to carry Washington and his army across the Delaware River to attack the Hessians at Trenton. Dodging ice flows and maneuvering against a swift current the boats made the crossing at night, delivering the American troops in time to launch a successful surprise attack.

The crossing of the Delaware was the regiment's last act in the Revolution. With enlistments expiring at the end of 1776, the regiment was disbanded. Glover went home to tend to family and business matters. He found his affairs, personal and financial, in a shambles. His wife was ill and his business was failing. In February 1777 the Congress offered him promotion to brigadier general. He declined the appointment, pleading that his family affairs prevented him from rejoining the army. On 26 April 1777 Washington wrote a personal letter to Glover asking that he return to duty. Glover agreed and took command of a brigade at Peekskill. Glover served in the Saratoga campaign under General Horatio Gates. Following the surrender of Burgoyne's army Glover accompanied the prisoners of war to Cambridge.

In the summer of 1778 Glover and his brigade were sent to Rhode Island to participate in a combined American–French attack on the British at Newport. When the French elected to withdraw, the campaign failed. Glover remained for a time in Providence as commander of the American forces; while he was there his wife died. From Providence he was posted to the Hudson River highlands where he served with units assigned to watch the British in New York City and, if necessary, to block their movement up the river. He remained there until early 1782. He married Frances Fosdick in 1781.

In the spring of 1782 Glover returned to Massachusetts. His health was poor and on 22 July 1782 he retired from the service. After the war Glover returned to the business of fishing and trading. He did reasonably well and reinvested his profits in local real estate. Glover tried but failed to secure appointment as collector of customs for Marblehead in the Washington administration. Although he did not receive a post in the national government Glover continued to be active on the local level. He served as a selectman of Marblehead, delegate to the Massachusetts ratifying convention, and representative in the general court. Glover died in Marblehead after a short bout with hepatitis.

• The most definitive biography of Glover is George Billias, *General John Glover and His Marblehead Mariners* (1960). An older work is William P. Upham, *Memoir of General John Glover of Marblehead* (1863). Samuel Roads, Jr., *The History and Traditions of Marblehead* (1897) provides a detailed view of Glover's hometown. The best view of the Revolution is Christopher Ward, *The War of the Revolution* (2 vols., 1952).

WILLIAM M. FOWLER

GLOVER, Samuel Taylor (9 Mar. 1813–22 Jan. 1884), lawyer, was born in Mercer County, Kentucky, the son of John Glover and Fanny Taylor. Educated in the local schools and at Bardstown College, Glover moved in 1835 to Knox County, Kentucky, where he won admission to the bar. In 1837 he removed to Palmyra, Marion County, Missouri, where he quickly established himself as a successful lawyer. In 1843 he married Mildred Ann Buckner; they had nine children, seven of whom lived to adulthood. In 1849 he formed the first of two law practices in St. Louis (with John C. Richardson, who was later appointed to the state supreme court, thereafter with John R. Shepley), through which he achieved prominence in the profession and in public affairs.

In the sectional crisis Glover became a powerful voice for the unconditional Unionist cause in Missouri. A moderate Whig with close personal and political ties to Edward Bates, Glover initially stood with the antiabolitionist supporters of the American Colonization Society. The society's goal, he explained in *An Address to the Colonization Society of Marion County, Mo. by Samuel T. Glover, Esq.* (1847), was to hasten the immigration to Liberia of the nearly 500,000 free blacks in the United States and to promote gradual emancipation "with the *free consent* of the master."

After moving to St. Louis, Glover allied himself politically with Free Soil Democratic leaders Francis P. Blair, Jr., and B. Gratz Brown and, thereafter, with the Republican party. Echoing Blair's Negrophobia, Glover insisted that slavery extension amounted to opening a place for a black man and denying one to a white man. By bringing slaves to the new communities of the West, he argued in his *Speech of the Hon. Samuel T. Glover, of the St. Louis Bar. Delivered at Turners' Hall, July 26, 1860* (1860), "You injure the community in that degree. . . . If you hold them in slavery they are hurtful to the progress and prosperity of the community[;] if you set them free they are not desirable

citizens." Initially a supporter of Bates for the 1860 Republican presidential nomination, Glover soon advised his friend to support Abraham Lincoln. In 1860 and again in 1864, Glover energetically campaigned for Lincoln, identifying the Republican party, as he did in his *Remarks on the Existing Rebellion . . . by an Original Republican* (1865), with "the cause of law, of liberty, of humanity." To resist the southern rebellion, Glover insisted, "was a duty not of *revolution*, but of *conservatism*."

Glover's Unionism was unconditional but staunchly conservative. A member of the St. Louis Committee of Safety during the secession winter, Glover advised Captain Nathaniel Lyon, the Unionist commander of the Federal arsenal in St. Louis, to proceed cautiously in his dealings with the Missouri state militia encamped near the city. Glover advocated the time-consuming approach of securing a writ of replevin to recover from the militia military property that had been seized from the Federal government. Lyon disregarded Glover's advice and acted forthrightly to disarm the state troops.

Glover was cautious as well on the subject of emancipation. With Blair and other conservative Unionists, Glover opposed General John C. Frémont's emancipation order for Missouri and warmly welcomed Lincoln's decision to rescind it. Although Glover became convinced that the Civil War heralded slavery's imminent demise, he continued to support gradual, compensated emancipation in Missouri even as Radicals pressed successfully toward immediate, uncompensated emancipation. Glover also supported Andrew Johnson's conservative program for the restoration of the Union and joined with Blair to welcome the president to St. Louis during Johnson's controversial "swing around the circle." An implacable foe of radicalism in Missouri, Glover helped to secure Federal support to disband the state's black militia units.

Glover enjoyed his greatest influence in the fight against the test oath requirements of the Missouri Constitution of 1865. The oath required citizens to swear that they had been loyal to all past Missouri governments. As an unconditional Unionist, Glover had acted to repudiate the pro-Confederate Missouri state government led by Claiborne Jackson, and he cited this act of disloyalty to challenge the constitution's test oath provisions and the laws passed to enforce them. In *Blair v. Ridgley* (1867) Glover argued for the plaintiff (his friend Francis P. Blair, Jr.) that the test oath as it applied to suffrage violated the U.S. Constitution's proscriptions against ex post facto laws and bills of attainder. When the Missouri Supreme Court, dominated by Radicals, upheld the oath as a legitimate function of the state's police powers, Blair appealed the decision to the U.S. Supreme Court, where his brother Montgomery Blair employed Glover's arguments. An evenly divided Supreme Court allowed the Missouri test oath to stand.

Glover also challenged the test oath as it applied to state licenses for lawyers, physicians, and members of the clergy. Although the U.S. Supreme Court narrowly upheld Missouri's test oath for lawyers in *Missouri v. Alexander J. P. Gareschè* (1865), it narrowly overturned the state's test oath for the clergy in *Cummings v. Missouri* (1866). In 1867, as the political will to maintain the test oaths had begun to fade in Missouri, Glover's suit, *In Re Murphy and Glover*, reached the Missouri Supreme Court. The justices accepted Glover's arguments and, citing the U.S. Supreme Court's decision in *Cummings*, reversed its earlier decision in the *Gareschè* case. In February 1870, following the ratification of the Fifteenth Amendment to the U.S. Constitution, the Missouri legislature repealed the features of the test oath for suffrage against which Glover had contended.

Glover's fight against the test oaths helped to forge a coalition between Liberal Republicans and Democrats that brought defeat to the Radical Republicans in Missouri. In his speech on *The State Campaign* (1868), Glover denounced a "Radical party" that sought to perpetuate the passions of the war and to suppress the vote of their opponents: Radicals held to power by sowing the seeds of insurrection. After the defeat of the Missouri Radicals, Glover remained active before the bar but withdrew from political affairs. He died in St. Louis, Missouri.

• Although no collection of Glover's private correspondence exists, many of his letters survive in the papers of his friends and coadjutors. See, for example, the James O. Broadhead Papers, Missouri Historical Society, St. Louis, Mo. In addition to those mentioned, the most substantial of Glover's published speeches are *Slavery in the United States—Emancipation in Missouri. Speech of Samuel T. Glover, at the Ratification Meeting Held at the Court House, in St. Louis, July 22d, 1863* (1863); and *Missouri Test Oath. Argument of Samuel T. Glover, Esq., in the Circuit Court of St. Louis County* (1866). See also *The Diary of Edward Bates, 1859–1866*, ed. Howard K. Beale (1930; repr. 1971); William Ernest Smith, *The Francis Preston Blair Family in Politics* (1933); Harold M. Hyman, *Era of the Oath: Northern Loyalty Tests during the Civil War and Reconstruction* (1954); Marvin R. Cain, *Lincoln's Attorney General: Edward Bates of Missouri* (1965); Norma L. Peterson, *Freedom and Franchise: The Political Career of B. Gratz Brown* (1965); and William E. Parrish, *Missouri under Radical Rule, 1865–1870* (1965). The most complete of Glover's obituaries is Thomas T. Gantt et al., *Proceedings of the Bar of St. Louis. In Memoriam. Samuel T. Glover* (1884).

LOUIS S. GERTEIS

GLOVER, Townend (20 Feb. 1813–7 Sept. 1883), entomologist, was born in or near Rio de Janeiro, Brazil, the son of Henry Glover, a merchant, and Mary Townend. Glover's parents died when he was young, and he was educated by relatives in Leeds, England, where he demonstrated an aptitude for art and natural history. Upon receiving his inheritance at age twenty-one, he left his apprenticeship with woolen merchants in Leeds to study art for two years at the Munich Art Gallery. Despite extreme myopia, he excelled in painting still life in oil. Returning to England, he opened a painting studio, but in 1836 he visited the United States, where, captivated by the natural beauty, he remained. As a sportsman-naturalist he roamed from New Rochelle, New York, to the Carolinas, Louisiana, and Texas, with rod and gun, on horseback and on foot.

After Glover's 1840 marriage to Sarah T. Byrnes, he managed his father-in-law's estate at Fishkill-on-the-Hudson (later Mount Beacon) until 1846, when he purchased his own farm. With advice from horticulturists Andrew J. Downing and Marshall P. Wilder, Glover transformed his estate into a showcase of fruit culture, meanwhile indulging in taxidermy, natural history, and painting. With Downing he conceived a project of illustrating American pomology by crafting over 2,000 models of fruit, accompanied with etchings showing the insects that attack fruit and fruit trees. His collection won acclaim at the New York State Agricultural Society, the American Institute in New York City, and in Washington, D.C. The latter exhibit, in 1853–1854, coincided with the establishment of a Bureau of Agriculture in the U.S. Patent Office, and on 14 June 1854 Glover was appointed special agent "for collecting statistics and other information on seeds, fruits, and insects in the United States." Glover's appointment and the appointment of Asa Fitch as New York State Entomologist the same year mark the beginnings of professional entomology in the United States.

While engaged at the Patent Office, Glover investigated the insects injurious to cotton, and he traveled to Central and South America, where he purchased sugar cane to replace depleted stocks in Louisiana. In 1859 he took a position as professor of natural sciences at Maryland Agricultural College (now University of Maryland), where he began a project of engraving illustrations of American insects on copper plates, a work that henceforth dominated his life.

In April 1863 Glover was appointed entomologist in the recently established U.S. Department of Agriculture. As federal entomologist, he gathered and disseminated information on insects harmful to agriculture and initiated an agricultural museum. At the same time, he intensified his engraving of insect illustrations. Glover's artistic temperament and unusual working style tended to frustrate the high goals he set for himself. While incorporating pedagogically advanced methods in his museum exhibits, featuring plants, birds, mammals, and insects in their relation to agriculture, Glover seemed oblivious to the opportunity to assemble a central research collection with insect types based on specimens sent to the department by explorers in the West and by agriculturists across the nation. While his contemporaries placed the highest priority on the assembling and preservation of specimens in museums, Glover held to the belief that well-executed illustrations could serve entomological researchers as well or better than preserved specimens. Despite the wealth of unnamed specimens at his disposal, Glover did not publish a single description of new species.

Glover craved recognition but avoided criticism, which may explain why he declined to contribute to entomological journals and thus missed valuable opportunities for interaction with his peers. Most remarkable of all, he prided himself on doing the engraving of insects on his own time. The combination of official duties and near superhuman effort after hours eventually affected his work. In an era when the number of new specimens, descriptions, revisions, and discoveries about insect habits increased in quantum proportions each year, Glover's plan to encompass all American entomology was inevitably frustrated. Undecided about whether to address primarily specialists or a popular audience, he constantly revised his text to include all the latest findings, thus delaying publication while others discovered and published findings that lay hidden in his notes.

Between 1872 and 1878, Glover distributed five separate volumes, in limited proof editions of fifteen to fifty copies each, of his *Illustrations of North American Entomology* and *Manuscript Notes from My Journal* to colleagues and institutions. Three volumes embraced one or more insect order(s), one treated insects affecting cotton, and one was an index of scientific names in Glover's official reports. The complete set of illustrations published in 1878 comprised 273 plates with 6,179 figures of insects. Glover's illustrations generally received high praise, but Baron C. R. Osten-Sacken (a dipterist) and other specialists concluded that the accompanying notes had been rendered outdated by great strides made in the period since Glover had begun.

Glover's official reports provide a valuable record of insect pests and remedies during a critical phase of entomological development. As federal entomologist, however, he lacked the flair for public relations and the boldness to request the appropriations necessary to meet the insect emergency in post–Civil War agriculture. When in the 1870s great swarms of locusts decimated agricultural settlements in the West, Glover was criticized for not directing field investigations of locusts and other destructive insects. Charles V. Riley, Glover's replacement, overshadowed his predecessor by expanding the division and reorienting it toward field investigations.

In 1878 Glover's failing health forced him to retire, and he died five years later in Baltimore at the home of his adopted daughter, Mrs. Daniel Hopper. He had lived separately from his wife for many years, and they had had no children. Although Glover's hesitancy in publishing his work prevented him from achieving greatness in the context of American entomology, his illustrations have been highly regarded by succeeding generations and constitute a fitting legacy of the first U.S. entomologist.

• Glover's notebooks for the years c. 1850–1878 are located in the Smithsonian Institution Archives, Washington, D.C., and are described in the *Guide to the Smithsonian Archives* (1978). They contain extensive notes and illustrations and include final copies of projected publications that were never printed. The copper plates for Glover's illustrations were purchased by the U.S. government in 1879 and deposited in the U.S. National Museum.

The primary source for Glover's career, including a bibliography of his writings, is the biography by his assistant, Charles Richard Dodge, "The Life and Entomological Work of the Late Townend Glover," U.S. Department Agriculture, Division of Entomology, *Bulletin No. 18* (1888), pp. 1–69. There are only fifteen known copies of the complete set of illustrations issued in 1878, six of which are located in Europe and nine in the United States. Glover's insect illustrations are evaluated by Herman Hagen, "Illustrations of North American Entomology by Townend Glover," *Entomologische Zeitung* 48 (Apr.–June 1887): 131–42, and W. R. Walton in the *Proceedings of the Entomological Society of Washington, D.C.* 23 (1921): 86–89.

For a modern treatment of Glover in the context of his times, and for reproductions of several previously unpublished plates from his notebooks, see W. Conner Sorensen, *Brethren of the Net: American Entomology, 1840–1880* (1995).

W. CONNER SORENSEN

GLUCK, Alma (11 May 1884–27 Oct. 1938), lyric soprano, was born Reba Fiersohn in Iasi, Rumania. Her parents, Israel Fiersohn and Anna Zara, had recently emigrated to Rumania from Russia. They had hoped to go on to the United States, but Israel, a buyer and seller of farm produce, died about 1886. Anna, said to have been about forty-nine when Gluck was born, was a hunchback of unstable character and was unable to manage the family. The oldest daughter, Cecile, earned her way to New York City as a seamstress and by 1890 was able to send the remaining family enough money for their passage to join her. Gluck went to public school on New York's Lower East Side, later taking a course in stenography and working in an office. In 1902 she married an insurance agent, Bernard Glick (an Anglicization of the German *Glück*). In 1903 they had a daughter, Abigail, who later became known as the writer Marcia Davenport.

Gluck had not seriously studied music or voice, but her chief joy was singing. In 1906 a business friend of her husband heard her sing at home and arranged for her to study voice with the noted Arturo Buzzi-Peccia. From 1906 to 1909 she studied in New York, Como, and Paris. The payoff came in 1909 when she auditioned for Arturo Toscanini, chief conductor of the Metropolitan Opera in New York and later her devoted friend, and Giulio Gatti-Casazza, general manager of the Metropolitan. Her first appearance with the Metropolitan company was a concert performance at the New Theatre in New York on 16 November 1909, singing Sophie in Massenet's *Werther*. Her success there led to her first operatic role in the Metropolitan Opera House itself, as the Happy Spirit in Gluck's *Orfeo ed Euridice*, in December of that year. For the 16 November performance she had taken the name Alma Gluck—the last being the preferred spelling of her married name, the first being simply a name she liked. Thereafter she was known as Alma Gluck.

At the Metropolitan Opera Gluck continued to sing minor roles for three seasons. Her voice and personality, however, were not those of a great prima donna, and she had little love for acting. Her place was on the recital stage, in oratorio, and on the phonograph records—the old acoustical recordings—that were just becoming important in the second decade of the twentieth century. From 1911 through 1920 she sang upwards of 100 recitals and other appearances each season, mostly in the United States. Her recordings were extremely popular in their time (her "Carry Me Back to old Virginny" is said to have sold almost two million copies); they put her as high in the public's eye as Enrico Caruso or Geraldine Farrar. Gluck's voice was a fine lyric soprano, but in addition she seems to have charmed everyone with her beauty and what the music critic Henry Krehbiel called her "exquisite taste." *Glück* is German for good luck, and it is hard to think of another musical performer who better personifies the "rags to riches" theme in American life.

Her rags-to-riches journey was, alas, a short one. In 1910 she was just beginning to rise from New York's Lower East Side; by 1920 her years of travel in her private railroad car, "Pioneer," had reached their peak. After 1920 Gluck appeared less often in public as a result of digestive disorders and also of conflicts between her career and her parental responsibilities. In 1912 she had been divorced from Glick and in 1914 married the eminent Russian violinist Efrem Zimbalist, whom she sometimes joined in recitals and on recordings. They had two children: Maria Virginia (born 1915) and Efrem Zimbalist, Jr. (born 1918; he became a successful actor and a motion picture personality). Gluck retired in 1925. In 1930 she was struck by a severe illness, later diagnosed as cirrhosis of the liver, from which she died in New York City. Yet almost until her death she continued her many sociomusical activities, including founding roles with both the American Guild of Musical Artists and the American Woman's Association.

• The Music Division of the Library of Congress has a collection of twelve scrapbooks and envelopes with clippings of reviews and other matter related to Gluck. Among that division's books about Mozart is a presentation copy of Marcia Davenport's *Mozart* (1932) to her mother; the flyleaf is inscribed "To my Mother—the greatest singer I shall ever hear and the finest woman I shall ever know. With my lifelong love, Marcia." Davenport's autobiography, *Too Strong for Fantasy* (1967), provides the fullest printed account of Gluck, as perceived by her oldest daughter from age two to thirty-five. See also Paul E. Eisler's informative biographical sketch of Gluck in *Notable American Women*, vol. 2 (1971). Starting in 1917, the Oliver Ditson Co. of Boston published four sets of "favorite songs" chosen and with introductions by Gluck. Obituaries are in the 28 Oct. 1938 issues of the *New York Herald Tribune* and the *New York Times*.

WILLIAM LICHTENWANGER

GLUECK, Nelson (4 June 1900–12 Feb. 1971), archaeologist and president of Hebrew Union College–Jewish Institute of Religion, was born in Cincinnati, Ohio, the son of Morris Glueck, a customer peddler (merchant), and Anna Rubin. Raised in Cincinnati, Glueck entered Hebrew Union College in 1914 to study for the rabbinate. He earned a bachelor of Hebrew letters degree in 1918. Glueck simultaneously at-

tended the University of Cincinnati, earning a bachelor of arts degree in 1920. In 1923 he received his ordination.

Following his ordination, Glueck was awarded the first Henry S. Morgenthau Traveling Fellowship, which allowed him to continue his biblical studies in Germany. Beginning in 1923 he studied at the universities of Berlin, Heidelberg, and Jena, where, in 1927, he received his Ph.D. His dissertation, "Das Wort 'Hesed' im alttestamentlichen Sprachgebrauche" (The word "grace" in Old Testament usage), was later published in English under the title *Hesed in the Bible* (1967).

After further study in Assyrian and Ethiopic at the University of Berlin, Glueck traveled to Jerusalem to study archaeology at the American School of Oriental Research under Professor William F. Albright. From 1928 to 1929 he traveled throughout Palestine, mostly on foot, visiting nearly every excavation, gaining experience in the methodology and techniques of archaeological work.

Glueck returned to Cincinnati in 1928. That year he joined the faculty of Hebrew Union College as an instructor in Hebrew language and the Bible. He advanced quickly, to assistant professor in 1931, to associate professor in 1934, and to full professor in the Bible and biblical archaeology in 1936, a position he held until his death. From 1932 to 1936 Glueck was also a visiting lecturer in biblical archaeology at the University of Cincinnati. In 1931 he married Helen Iglauer, a medical student from a prominent Cincinnati family; they had one child.

Throughout his years at HUC, Glueck took frequent leaves of absence to return to the Middle East to continue his archaeological work. He developed a lifelong association with the American Schools of Oriental Research, serving as director of its Jerusalem school in 1932–1933, 1936–1940, and 1942–1947 and as annual professor and field director at its Baghdad school in 1933–1934 and 1942–1947. Glueck also developed a deep personal attachment to the land of Israel. In his 1967 book, *Dateline Jerusalem: A Diary of Nelson Glueck*, written in the aftermath of the Israeli-Arab war in June of that year, he commented, "I practically cry each time I leave this country and this city. I have spent a large part of my life in this part of the world and it has never, from the first moment on, ceased to grip me."

In 1932 Glueck began extensive surface and excavative surveys of Transjordan. Working across the territory from the Syrian border to the Gulf of 'Aqaba, he based much of his work on sources in the Bible, a technique many of his contemporaries believed to be unreliable. Glueck remained undaunted, however, saying later, "No archaeological discovery has ever controverted a Biblical reference. I just followed what the Bible said and dug." Combining his reliance on biblical sources with a systematic methodology using modern techniques (such as pottery identification to determine chronology), Glueck made many important discoveries. In 1934 he unearthed the remnants of copper mines in the Wadi al-ʿAraba, dating them to the time of King Solomon. In 1938 he unearthed a portion of Ezion-geber, which he identified as a seaport and fortress at the time of Solomon. Later research, however, and the gathering of comparative data prompted scholars to revise Glueck's dating of these excavations to two centuries before the time of Solomon, a reassessment he readily accepted after seeing the new evidence. Still, Glueck was hailed for uncovering two important sites that had been buried for almost 2,700 years. During this time Glueck also clarified the boundaries of the ancient kingdoms of Edom, Moab, and Ammon. In all, it was work that Harvard archaeologist G. Ernest Wright rated as "one of the two most important individual contributions to the field of Palestinian archaeology in our generation," the other being the work of Albright at Debir.

In 1942 Glueck was named executive director of the Union of American Hebrew Congregations, the organizational arm of the American Reform Jewish movement. But he never took office. A few weeks after his appointment Glueck returned to Palestine in order to become a field agent and adviser for the Office of Strategic Services (OSS) at the request of the U.S. government during World War II. At first the UAHC granted him a leave of absence. However, in 1943 Glueck was asked to resign his position, and Rabbi Maurice Eisendrath of Toronto was chosen to take his place. Glueck reveled in his OSS appointment. In effect, he was a spy. "I had the best cover of any spy," he said later. "I knew all about the country, so I would have been invaluable if we had landed troops there. But we did not" (quoted in Karff, pp. 200–201). His many contacts in the area also provided him with connections to local sources of militarily important information.

Glueck's call to Palestine during the war enabled him to return to the American Schools of Oriental Research and to continue his excavations. By 1947 he had mapped more than 1,000 ancient sites in Transjordan, spanning the Neolithic to the Byzantine periods. He published many articles and books on his archaeological findings, including *Explorations in Eastern Palestine* (1934–1966), *The Other Side of the Jordan* (1940), *The River Jordan* (1946), *Rivers in the Desert* (1959), and *Dieties and Dolphins: The Story of the Nabataeans* (1965).

In 1947 Glueck was named president of Hebrew Union College, succeeding the retiring Julian Morgenstern. Soon after this appointment, Rabbi Stephen S. Wise of New York City selected Glueck to be his successor as president of the New York City–based Jewish Institute of Religion. The two schools merged in 1950, and Glueck became president of the new Hebrew Union College–Jewish Institute of Religion, overseeing campuses in Cincinnati and New York City. In 1951 the institution's board of governors elected him to a life tenure. In his 1948 inaugural address Glueck envisioned the school as "the equivalent of a great university in Judaism." As president, he directed a period of unprecedented growth. In 1954 the

HUC-JIR established a campus in Los Angeles that featured prerabbinic courses and programs in teacher education. The New York City campus added schools of sacred music and Jewish education; the Cincinnati campus added the American Jewish Archives, the American Jewish Periodical Center, and a graduate school in Near Eastern and biblical studies that enabled Jewish and Christian scholars to interact and study together in an academic environment. In 1963 the HUC-JIR fulfilled Glueck's long-standing dream with the establishment in Jerusalem of the Hebrew Union College Biblical and Archaeological School.

In 1952 Glueck returned to Israel for more archaeological excavation. Working in the Negev, he traced signs of civilization back to 4,000 B.C.E. He studied Nabataean and Byzantine agricultural settlements through their irrigation methods. He also discovered evidence of the existence of hundreds of churches in the Negev during the Byzantine period. Glueck was often at risk during these expeditions, traveling in areas that were the sites of skirmishes between Israelis and Arabs in the tense years immediately following Israeli independence. He developed good relations with many Arab tribesmen, earning the nickname "Rabbi with a Rifle." "I always carried a rifle," Glueck said. "Whenever we stopped we set up a machine gun. We figured that if the Arabs were going to attack we wanted a fighting chance."

In recognition of his leadership role among American Jewry, Glueck was asked to deliver the benediction at the 1961 inauguration of President John F. Kennedy. He also appeared on the cover of the 13 December 1963 issue of *Time* magazine, which featured an article on Glueck and his work entitled "The Search for Man's Past."

Although quiet and reserved, Glueck was a vigorous advocate of the need to maintain Jewish identity and traditions. A lover of Israel, known by its leaders and citizens as "the Professor," he received honorary citizenship from two Israeli cities, Beersheba and Elath. An educator, he ordained hundreds of rabbis and developed the Hebrew Union College–Jewish Institute of Religion into an international, interfaith center of learning. An archaeologist, he "advanced the cause of archaeology," according to Professor George M. A. Hanfmann in a seventieth-birthday tribute. He "carr[ied] to the general public, especially in America, something of the adventure, excitement, and joy of archaeological discovery." Glueck died in Cincinnati.

• Glueck's papers are located at the American Jewish Archives, Cincinnati. Two full-length works on Glueck's life are Gary M. Klein, "Nelson Glueck: A Leader of Liberal Jewry" (Ph.D. diss., Hebrew Union College–Jewish Institute of Religion, 1975), and Ellen Norman Stern, *Dreamer in the Desert: A Profile of Nelson Glueck* (1980). A Glueck festschrift, James A. Sanders, ed., *Near Eastern Archaeology in the Twentieth Century: Essays in Honor of Nelson Glueck* (1970), contains reminiscences of Glueck by contemporaries, a bibliography of his writings, and assessments of his archaeological and biblical scholarly work. Glueck is also discussed in S. E. Karff, ed., *Hebrew Union College–Jewish Institute of*

Religion at One Hundred Years (1976). Other articles on Glueck while in Palestine and Israel, including his work with the OSS, include Eleanor K. Vogel, "Negev Survey of Nelson Glueck: Summary," *Eretz-Israel: Archaeological, Historical, and Geographical Studies* 12 (1975), Nelson Glueck memorial volume; Stan Sulkes, "The Secret Life of Nelson Glueck: Author, Scholar, Rabbi, and Spy," *Cincinnati Enquirer Magazine*, 11 Jan. 1987; and Floyd S. Fierman, "Rabbi Nelson Glueck: An Archaeologist's Secret Life in the Service of the OSS," *Biblical Archaeology Review*, Sept.–Oct. 1986, pp. 18–22. Obituaries are in the *Cincinnati Enquirer*, 14 and 15 Feb. 1971.

ALFRED GOTTSCHALK

GLUECK, Sheldon (15 Aug. 1896–10 Mar. 1980), professor of criminal law and criminology, was born in Warsaw, Poland, the son of Charles Glueck, a small steel shop owner, and Anna Steinhardt. Facing bankruptcy, the family moved to the United States in 1903. They settled in Milwaukee, Wisconsin, where his father was a street peddler. Glueck attended public school in his youth.

While working for the U.S. Department of Agriculture, Glueck attended Georgetown University Law School at night (1914–1915). His study was postponed for two years when he joined the "Rainbow Division" (Forty-second) of the Allied Expeditionary Force in France during World War I. He served as a translator at the rank of sergeant. On his return Glueck transferred to George Washington University, graduating with an A.B. in humanities in 1920. In the same year he was awarded an LL.B. and LL.M. by the National University Law School, was admitted to the New York Bar, and became a U.S. citizen.

Glueck put aside his plans to practice law when he met and fell in love with Eleanor Touroff. She was a student of his brother, Bernard Glueck, an eminent prison psychiatrist and an early influence on Glueck's academic career. He followed Touroff to Boston, where she took a job as head social worker in a settlement house. They were married in April 1922 and had one child.

Unable to qualify for entrance into the doctor of juridical science program at the Harvard Law School, Glueck enrolled in the Department of Social Ethics and received his A.M. in 1922 and his doctorate in 1924. His thesis, which drew on the fields of psychiatry, law, and sociology, was later published as *Mental Disorder and the Criminal Law* (1925). Eleanor Glueck also received a doctorate from Harvard in educational sociology in 1925.

Glueck spent the rest of his academic life at Harvard. From 1925 he was an instructor of criminology in the Department of Social Ethics until moving in 1929 to the Law School as an assistant professor of criminology. He became a full professor in 1932. In 1950 he was appointed the first Roscoe Pound Professor of Law, and on his retirement from teaching in 1963 he became professor emeritus.

In 1926 the Gluecks were given the opportunity by the Harvard Law School to work together; this marked the beginning of more than four decades of joint ventures in criminology. Their remarkable intellectual partnership produced a series of studies on correctional institutions and, later, on the causes, early detection, and prevention of delinquency. After four years of work the Gluecks published *Five Hundred Criminal Careers* (1930), a study of the recidivism of 510 former inmates of the Massachusetts Reformatory for Men that was the first important large-scale study of the effectiveness of such an institution. The lives of these inmates were further traced in *Later Criminal Careers* (1937) and *Criminal Careers in Retrospect* (1943), and a similar study was conducted with offenders released from a women's reformatory in *Five Hundred Delinquent Women* (1934). In that same year, *One Thousand Juvenile Delinquents*, an assessment of the Boston Juvenile Court and the Judge Baker Foundation Guidance Center, was published as part of the Harvard Crime Survey. The study, continued in *Juvenile Delinquents Grown Up* (1940), promoted closer links between the juvenile court and social agencies.

After fifteen years of pioneering studies, the Gluecks demonstrated that the recidivism rates of graduates of various institutions were far higher than claimed. Their work also illustrated how the conduct of former inmates improved with the passing of time.

In 1940 the Gluecks initiated what was to be their best known study, *Unraveling Juvenile Delinquency* (1950), which examined the causes of delinquency. They rejected unilateral theories of crime, using instead an eclectic, methodological approach to establish a multicausal explanation of delinquency. "We are scientists," Glueck commented in *Think Magazine* (Mar. 1960, pp. 2–6), "concerned with the studiable." Using a team of physical anthropologists, psychologists, statisticians, social investigators, and a psychiatrist, 500 delinquent boys were matched case by case with 500 nondelinquent boys from underprivileged areas of Boston.

Extensive and meticulous statistical comparisons in this monumental study identified forty "highly decisive" factors used to formulate a series of "Prediction Tables." The most influential of these was known as the "Glueck Social Prediction Table," which "spotted" potential delinquents by examination of a child's family environment. "Nature as well as nurture" was also identified as a factor affecting delinquency. The Gluecks believed that mesomorphs (those with predominantly muscular, solid builds) were at greater risk of becoming juvenile delinquents. Recommendations that the tables be used by legal and social agencies were widely criticized, especially by sociologists who claimed the tables unfairly labeled children as "potential delinquents." The work was extended in *Physique and Delinquency* (1956) and *Family Environment* (1962). The 1,000 boys were followed up to the age of thirty-two in *Delinquents and Non-Delinquents* (1968).

Alongside his collaborative labors Glueck had an interest in war crimes. He wrote extensively during and after World War II about the future trial and punishment of the Axis war criminals. Two of his books on the subject are *War Criminals: Their Prosecution and Punishment* (1944) and *The Nuremberg Trial and Aggressive War* (1946). He was a member of the Commission on War Criminals for the League of Nations and acted as consultant to Justice Robert H. Jackson, chief American council at the Nuremberg Trials.

Glueck was active throughout his career in reforming criminal justice administration, serving on two different Supreme Court committees to revise the Federal Rules of Criminal Procedure (1943–1965). He also proposed the establishment of "Legal Interdisciplinary Institutes" in publications such as *Crime and Justice* (1936), *Crime and Correction: Selected Papers* (1952), and *Roscoe Pound and Criminal Justice* (1965).

Glueck was a fellow of the American Academy of Arts and Sciences and the International Academy of Law and Science. He also served as vice president of the American Society of Criminology. In 1961 he received the Isaac Ray Award of the American Psychiatric Association. The Gluecks jointly received the August Vollmer Award of the American Society of Criminology (1961) and gold medals from both the German Society of Criminology and of the Institute of Criminal Anthropology at the University of Rome (1964).

Sheldon Glueck's nonprofessional interests included writing plays, children's stories, and short stories. After his wife died in 1972, Glueck remained in Cambridge, Massachusetts, until his death there.

• The papers of Sheldon Glueck are located along with the joint papers of Sheldon and Eleanor Glueck in the Harvard Law School Library. For a bibliography of their work see Sheldon Glueck and Eleanor T. Glueck, *Ventures in Criminology* (1964). An autobiography including tales of the Gluecks' travels is *Lives of Labor, Lives of Love* (1977). Also see Noah Gordon, "Five Signs on the Highroad," *Saturday Review*, 6 Apr. 1963, pp. 49–52, a personality portrait. Modern appraisals are Robert J. Sampson and John H. Laub, *Crime in the Making* (1993), and Laub and Sampson, "The Sutherland Glueck Debate: On the Sociology of Criminological Knowledge," *American Journal of Sociology* 96 (1991). Obituaries are in the *Boston Globe* and the *Washington Post*, both 12 Mar. 1980; the *New York Times*, 13 Mar. 1980; and *Newsweek* and *Time*, both 24 Mar. 1980.

ANDREW CHAPPEL

GMEINER, John (5 Dec. 1847–11 Nov. 1913), priest and author, was born in Baernau, Bavaria, the son of Sebastian Gmeiner and Caroline Fritsch. With his parents, he immigrated to Milwaukee, Wisconsin, in 1849. In 1859 he enrolled at St. Francis de Sales Seminary in Milwaukee. Ordained a Roman Catholic priest in 1870, he served as pastor of various German immigrant parishes in Milwaukee, Cassville, Platteville, Oshkosh, and Waukesha. He edited the *Columbia*, a Milwaukee Catholic weekly, from 1873 to 1876. In 1883 Gmeiner returned to St. Francis de Sales Seminary to teach ecclesiastical history and canon law and to serve as editor of the German-language weekly *Der Seebote*.

A widely read, progressive thinker and writer, Gmeiner is remembered for his efforts to synthesize traditional faith and modern thought. In particular, he sought to reconcile evolutionary theory with Christian theology by constructing positive theistic interpretations of Darwinism that "acknowledged the ideas of liberal Protestant theologians and scientists" (Appleby, p. 24). Gmeiner went beyond the accommodationist claims of his contemporaries to insist, in *Modern Scientific Views and Christian Doctrines Compared* (1884), that St. Augustine had actually taught evolutionary theory and that Catholics should be grateful to Darwin for provoking a reexamination of Roman Catholic theology.

Gmeiner's best-known work, however, is his contribution to the German question, *The Church and Various Nationalities in the United States: Are German Catholics Unfairly Treated?* (1887). This work ignited a tempest in the Midwest and earned him the disparagement of fellow German immigrants, along with the gratitude of Bishop John Ireland of St. Paul, Minnesota. In the latter half of the nineteenth century, vast numbers of immigrants arrived on American soil each year. Each particular group had to decide whether to cling to its native language, traditions, and customs or to embrace those of the New World. Gmeiner urged his fellow German immigrants to conform, as far as prudence and conscience dictated, to their American environment.

In 1887 Father Peter M. Abbelen submitted grievances of German Catholics to the Sacred Congregation of the Propaganda in Rome. The petition charged that American bishops, especially the Irish, were insensitive to the German language, customs, and traditions. It asked that German parishes be independent of Irish parishes and rectors, that immigrant children be catechized in the language of their parents, and that all European newcomers be assigned to churches that used their native language.

The petition placed the Irish-American bishops, including John Ireland, in an awkward position. They were relieved when Gmeiner came to their defense. As one German immigrant to another, he asked the petitioners, "Shall the authorities of the Church be called upon to perpetuate by their authority as long as possible the baneful confusion of language existing in our midst? Shall the unity of the Catholic Church in this country be practically illustrated by separating authoritatively our Catholics, according to their nationalities?" (*The Church and Various Nationalities*, p. 33).

Gmeiner argued that the sons and grandsons of German immigrants would soon consider themselves fully American. Church-based efforts to postpone the inevitable were misguided and would have a detrimental effect on the faithful when Americanized Germans eventually dispersed to other cities. Gmeiner saw that the issue was not just one of church authority or of German national identity but dealt with the essence of the church. A church divided by language and custom was not united and catholic.

Because he stood with the Irish, fellow Germans tended to regard Gmeiner as a traitor to his nationality. This probably accounted for his 1887 transfer from the Archdiocese of Milwaukee to the Diocese of St. Paul. However, he taught at St. Thomas Seminary in St. Paul for only two years. For the remainder of his life he served as pastor at various small parishes at Mendota, South St. Paul, Buffalo, Springfield, Hampton, and Richfield, Minnesota. Gmeiner kept intellectually active. In May 1888 he delivered a paper on evolution to the International Scientific Congress of Catholics in Paris. In 1893, at the World's Parliament of Religions, he delivered an address on "The Primitive and Prospective Religious Unity of Mankind." In November 1895 he lectured on Egyptology to the combined student bodies of St. Paul Seminary and the College of St. Thomas.

Although his writings have fallen into disuse, Gmeiner is remembered for the role he played helping to fashion American ecclesial identity. His support of the Irish bishops with regard to the German question came at a crucial time. With remarkable vision he helped the American Catholic church build a unity that transcended cultural and linguistic boundaries while helping successive waves of immigrant groups assimilate into the wider American culture. Gmeiner is also noted for his part in American efforts to make Christian theology intelligible to modernity.

• In addition to works cited in the text, Gmeiner wrote *Die katholische Kirche in den Vereinigten Staaten* (1875), *Sind wir dem Weltende nahe?* (1877), *The Spirits of Darkness and Their Manifestations on Earth, or Ancient and Modern Spiritualism* (1886), *Emmanuel, the Savior of the World* (1880; repr. 1888), *Medieval and Modern Cosmology* (1891), *The Church and Foreignism* (1891), and numerous contributions to Roman Catholic periodicals. For biographical information see R. Scott Appleby, *Church Unite!* (1992); Joseph B. Connors, *Journey toward Fulfillment* (1986); Albert Nelson Marquis, *The Book of Minnesotans* (1907); Marvin R. O'Connell, *John Ireland and the American Catholic Church* (1988); and Roger C. Roensch, *Studies in the History of St. Francis Seminary*, vol. 30 (1955).

JAMES P. KEANE

GOBRIGHT, Lawrence Augustus (2 May 1816–14 May 1881), journalist, was born in Baltimore, Maryland, according to most sources. However, one source, an obituary in the *Washington Evening Star*, states that he was born in 1813 in Pennsylvania. Little is known of his childhood, and the names of his parents are unknown. He was the editor of a Van Buren campaign newspaper, the *Sun*, in Batavia, Ohio, sometime during 1837–1838, but the exact date of his entry into journalism is unknown.

Sources indicate that Gobright began his long tenure as a correspondent in Washington, D.C., during the latter months of the Jackson presidency. Also, he was the capital correspondent for the *Baltimore Clipper* before 1840 and was a reporter for the *Washington Globe* in 1839–1840. Between 1840 and 1845, he edited two Washington newspapers, the *Republic* and the *Union*. During the summer of 1845, he edited the *Washington Daily Bee*, a penny paper he owned with two partners that lasted one month. Before 1853, he worked for the *Washington Star*. Gobright cannot be linked to the Associated Press until 1853, although he may have been associated with it earlier as an independent reporter or as an employee of the telegraph company.

Gobright is listed as the agent of the New York Associated Press, a cooperative news-gathering association of New York dailies founded in 1848 as the Harbor News Association, in a congressional directory for 1853 and was placed in charge of the Washington bureau after it was organized in 1856. By this time, Gobright was an intimate of many leading political figures in the capital. His tenure with the Associated Press lasted approximately twenty-five years, during which time the Associated Press replaced the official newspapers, such as the *National Intelligencer* and the *Washington Globe*, as the medium for transmitting the complete texts of official documents, as well as daily start-to-finish accounts of congressional proceedings. Because the Associated Press served newspapers of various political affiliations, Gobright's reporting of government news avoided the partisanship that was a common feature of journalism in his day.

Speaking before a House Judiciary Committee investigating censorship of news early in the Civil War, Gobright described his method of reporting in words that define "objective journalism" today:

My business is to communicate facts. My instructions do not allow me to make any comment upon the facts which I communicate. My dispatches are sent to papers of all manner of politics, and the editors say they are able to make their own comments upon the facts which are sent to them. I therefore confine myself to what I consider legitimate news. I . . . try to be truthful and impartial. My dispatches are merely dry matter of fact and detail.

Samples of his reporting indicate that he proved true to his claim to be impartial, even though it is likely that he was a Democrat.

For most of his career Gobright covered the Washington news scene alone, with only occasional help from one or two assistants. He developed strong working relationships with the federal departments and was often called upon to help with the preparation of proclamations. Also, during the Civil War, he often submitted stories about government war policy to the respective departments for approval before releasing them. When the federal government imposed strict censorship of telegraphed news out of Washington in the early days of the war, Gobright was the only correspondent specifically exempted from censorship by the State Department.

His most memorable work is his coverage of the Lincoln assassination. Gobright was working late at his office when a friend rushed in with the news that Lincoln had been shot. Gobright filed a brief dispatch and then rushed to Ford's Theater, six blocks away, by hack. His oft-quoted bulletin read:

WASHINGTON, FRIDAY, APRIL 14, 1865—The President was shot in a theater tonight, and perhaps mortally wounded.

Gobright was allowed to enter Lincoln's theater box, where he was handed John Wilkes Booth's pistol by a theater employee. He turned the pistol over to a police officer and walked across the street to the house where Lincoln lay dying. There he wrote a long and detailed version of the events. Gobright accompanied Lincoln's body to Springfield, Illinois, and wrote a number of moving accounts of the journey.

In 1866 Gobright covered President Andrew Johnson during his infamous "swing around the circle," a national speaking tour during which he delivered harangues that alienated the Radical Republicans in Congress. In May 1867 Gobright testified about Johnson's sobriety before the House Judiciary Committee during its impeachment hearings. He was elected president of the short-lived Washington Correspondents Club in the spring of 1867. By this time Gobright, who was the senior correspondent in the capital, was called "Pops," or "Father Gobright" by his peers.

By early 1878, dissatisfaction with the coverage provided by the Washington bureau began to emerge, especially within the Western Associated Press, which represented newspapers throughout the midwestern United States. It seemed that Gobright was finding it increasingly difficult to meet the expanding needs of a post–Civil War America for news. Servicing both the New York Associated Press and the Western Associated Press (which had entered into a cooperative news gathering and sharing contract in 1867) involved satisfying a wider spectrum of regional interests and journalistic tastes than Gobright was able to manage alone. Just before June 1878, he hired two young reporters to assist him full-time. Nevertheless, he was displaced as the Washington bureau chief by Walter Polk Phillips soon afterward. His retirement from the Associated Press was announced publicly in August 1879. He was involved with the *Telephone*, a weekly Washington newspaper, for a short time after he left the Associated Press, but his career as a Washington correspondent, which had spanned four decades, was at an end.

The Dictionary of North American Authors lists Gobright as a poet for the children's verse he wrote. His two collections of children's verse, *Jack and Jill* (1873) and *Echoes of Childhood* (1879), are noteworthy. No records of his family life exist except for an obituary in the *Washington Evening Star*, which states that he was survived by a daughter and grandchildren, and that his wife had died before him. No names or other details are given. Gobright died at his home in Washington, D.C.

• Gobright's autobiography, *Recollections of Men and Things at Washington, during the Third of a Century* (1869), contains numerous insights and personal reflections covering the most important part of his tenure with the Associated Press. Highly informative histories of Washington correspondence and the role played by the Associated Press are F. B. Marbut, *News from the Capital: The Story of Washington Reporting* (1971); Donald A. Ritchie, *Press Gallery: Congress and the Washington Correspondents* (1991); Stephen Hess, *The Washington Reporters* (1981); and Culver H. Smith, *The Press, Politics, and Patronage: The American Government's Use of Newspapers, 1789–1875* (1977). Gobright is treated at length in a comprehensive history of news services in the United States, Richard A. Schwarzlose, *The Nation's Newsbrokers*, vol. 1, *The Formative Years: From Pretelegraph to 1865* (1989), and vol. 2, *The Rush to Institution: From 1865 to 1920* (1990). Note also the obituary and tribute in the *Washington Evening Star*, 16 and 25 May 1881.

JOSEPH P. McKERNS

GODDARD, David Rockwell (3 Jan. 1908–9 July 1985), plant physiologist, was born in Carmel, California, the son of Pliny E. Goddard, an anthropologist, and Alice Rockwell, a teacher. His early life was spent in Leonia, New Jersey, where he attended public schools. In 1922 Goddard was stricken with influenza and, quarantined for weeks in his father's library, was inspired to read the works of great authors. This, combined with his studies to prepare for examinations, taught him the valuable lessons that he could learn outside the classroom. When he was fifteen, his father bought a secondhand greenhouse that he and his brothers assembled. Growing plants and flowers greatly interested the young Goddard, and he spent most of his spare time growing plants and selling nursery stock.

Goddard enrolled in the University of California at Berkeley; in his sophomore year he was admitted to a graduate seminar. He spent the summers on field trips, collecting and preparing specimens for courses. Goddard remained at Berkeley for graduate studies, writing his Ph.D. thesis on the metabolism and nutrition of the dermophyte fungus *Trichophyton*. After receiving his Ph.D. in 1933, he worked with Fred Uber on the killing of neurospora by X-ray irradiation. This treatment resulted in the formation of many mutant spores, which were later used as markers in genetic studies. This work set the stage for the development of the one-gene, one-enzyme hypothesis of George Beadle and Edward Tatum.

In 1933–1935 Goddard received a National Research Council fellowship to work with Leonor Michaelis at the Rockefeller Institute. Michaelis was not interested in Goddard's neurospora work, but he was interested in Goddard's finding that keratin proteins (hair, feathers, and wool) could be digested by enzymes after they were treated with reducing agents such as sodium sulfite, sulphydryl compounds, potassium cyanide, or thioglycolic acid. An important finding was Goddard's demonstration that digested keratin gave a positive sulphydryl reaction after treatment with nitroprusside. Based on this work, thioglycolic acid and other thiol compounds became the basic ingredients of permanent-wave solutions. Because of the commercial implications of this discovery, Goddard was urged to apply for a patent, but he demurred.

After two years at the Rockefeller Institute, Goddard accepted a position in botany at the University of

Rochester, where B. H. Willier was assembling a remarkable staff in the biology department. At Rochester Goddard extended B. O. Dodge's work on dormant neurospora spores and established the temperature required for their germination. He also demonstrated that respiration was completely inhibited by cyanide and that germination proceeded if the cyanide was subsequently removed. An important finding was the large increase in oxygen consumption accompanying germination of spores. This finding channeled Goddard's interest to plant respiration. He and Paul Allen studied the respiration of plants infected with powdery mildew and found that the fungus induced a change in the plant's respiration system that was inhibited by cyanide, indicating that respiration in plants was similar to that in animals. With Paul Smith, he demonstrated that dormant spores in an anaerobic atmosphere produce no carbon dioxide, but carbon dioxide is produced on activation of the spores, revealing that they ferment. Goddard extended these studies to other plants and found that their respiration was inhibited by cyanide and that cytochrome oxidase was their terminal oxidase. Goddard and Allen Brown were able to isolate cytochrome oxidase from wheat embryos and to demonstrate that respiration was inhibited by carbon monoxide; this inhibition was reversed by light, establishing that cytochrome oxidase also participated in plant respiration. In subsequent work on respiration in fungi, Goddard showed that glutathione and dehydroascorbic acid could function as electron acceptors when cytochrome oxidase was inhibited by cyanide.

In 1946 Goddard accepted a professorship of botany at the University of Pennsylvania. He negotiated for funds to renovate the old botany building and encouraged the chairman to improve the faculty. In addition to continuing his research on plant respiration, Goddard took over most of the administrative duties of running the department as well as organizing the courses.

In 1950 Goddard received a fellowship to study at Cambridge University for a year. At a conference where Leslie Mapson presented his work on glutathione, it was asked, since most of the glutathione in the body is reduced, what is the mechanism by which it is reduced? Goddard pointed out that no suitable electron donor was yet known and suggested that TPN (coenzyme I, NADH) or TPNH (coenzyme II, NADPH) were likely candidates. The next day Goddard and Mapson tested this hypothesis and found that TPNH (coenzyme II) served as the electron donor. They named the enzyme that catalyzed the electron transfer glutathione reductase.

In 1952 Goddard returned to Pennsylvania and became chairman of the botany department. He felt that the academic separation of zoology and botany was artificial, and partly through his efforts the botany and zoology departments were consolidated as the Division of Biology. Goddard also enlarged the faculty, and his appointments were responsible for the distinguished reputation of the Pennsylvania biology department in the 1950s. Later Goddard led a successful drive to raise money for a new biology building, eventually dedicated as the Goddard Laboratory.

Goddard became increasingly involved in administration. When the university undertook an educational survey in the early 1960s, Goddard played an important role. In 1961 Goddard accepted the position of provost. He wrote an "Integrated Educational Plan" that was adopted by the trustees in 1962; it led to a $93 million fundraising campaign and guided the further development of the university. During Goddard's tenure as provost, the faculty was improved and the physical plant of the university expanded. In the turbulent years of student unrest during the Vietnam War, the question of the ethics of military research was raised. Goddard worked out a plan that all research conducted at the university be promptly published, and that neither government or industry could dictate when or by whom the results were published.

While Goddard was provost there was a six-day sit-in to protest the razing of homes to build the University Science Center. Each morning Goddard walked by the sit-in on the way to work and cheerfully greeted the participants; the students asked him to keep their support funds in the safe in his office. Goddard resisted the urging of the students to take a stand on the Vietnam War, and he persuaded the students not to fly the U.S. flag upside down by promising to erect a peace monument on the campus: it now stands in front of the VanPelt Library. In 1970 he retired as provost.

In 1975 Goddard was elected home secretary of the National Academy of Sciences; he also served in numerous other positions for that organization. Goddard was twice married, first in 1933 to Doris Martin, with whom he had a son and a daughter, and then in 1952 to Katherine Evans. Afflicted with Alzheimer's disease in his last years, he died in Philadelphia, Pennsylvania.

• A collection of Goddard's papers is at the University of Pennsylvania. Rockwell's unpublished autobiography is held by his second wife. A biographical sketch is Ralph O. Erickson, "David Rockwell Goddard (January 3, 1908–July 9, 1985)," National Academy of Sciences, *Biographical Memoirs* 67: 179–99. Goddard's understanding of plant respiration is discussed in detail in "The Respiration of Cells and Tissues," a chapter of *Physical Chemistry of Cells and Tissues*, ed. Rudolph Höber (1945), and in a review by Goddard and James E. LuValle, "The Mechanism of Enzymatic Oxidations and Reductions," *Quarterly Review of Biology* 23 (1948): 197–228.

DAVID Y. COOPER

GODDARD, Dwight (1861–1939), was a Buddhist popularizer and author; details of his family background and early life are obscure. Of his early life, we know that his first experience with living Buddhism occurred while he was a missionary with the American Board in Foochow, China, and consisted of a visit to a Buddhist monastery at Kushan. As a result of this experience, he began reading the available materials and immersed himself in Buddhism as a discipline to be studied and experienced. Following some time spent at a Christian-Buddhist monastery in Nanking, he lived for nearly a year at a Japanese Zen monastery (in 1928) in Kyōto, where he practiced zazen (sitting meditation) and was given the title of monk-novice by the abbot, Taiko Yamazaki-roshi. From his personal experience with Buddhism in China and Japan, Goddard concluded that the leading Zen masters of the time were wrong in their approach of presenting a style of Buddhism that emphasized primarily lay practice.

Following his return to the United States, Goddard in 1934 established an organization known as the Followers of Buddha, initially at his farmhouse in Thretford, Vermont. In this organization his critique of earlier Buddhists on the American scene was emphasized, especially with reference to Zen practitioners, focusing on the fact that their followers and disciples received oral instruction and engaged in actual zazen only intermittently, usually totaling no more than several hours per week. Goddard's response was to institute an American Buddhist monastic order that would provide continuing training on a firm foundation. His model was the Asian Buddhist counterpart, a professional monastic unit composed of adepts supported by a devoted laity. To this end, he used his apparently substantial personal resources, and some lay support, to establish his farmhouse in Thetford and a forty-acre retreat in Santa Barbara, California. The original plan, coincident with the organization's founding in 1934, had been to bring over a Chinese meditation master to provide the critical instruction, but this was never carried out. There was little interest among American Buddhists in developing a monastic tradition in the 1930s, a condition that persisted in subsequent decades.

Goddard is perhaps best known as an author of books devoted to Buddhism. His *A Buddhist Bible*, first published in 1932, was one of the very early attempts to provide an anthology of Buddhist scriptures that cut across sectarian and geographic lines. Goddard included works from the Indian, South Asian, Tibetan, Chinese, and Japanese traditions and spanned the Hīnayāna, Mahāyāna, and Vajrayāna schools of Buddhism. This work has been reprinted many times. He also began publishing a modest journal from his Vermont home in 1930, first called *Zen: A Magazine of Self-Realization* and later reduced to *Zen: A Buddhist Magazine*. He is known for a number of other publications, especially *The Buddha's Golden Path: A Manual of Practical Dhyana Buddhism* (1931), *Followers of the Buddha: The Ideal and Rules of an American Buddhist Brotherhood* (1934), and his translation with Bhikshu Wai-Tao called *The Diamond Sutra, A New Translation from the Chinese Text of Kumarajiva*.

Goddard's efforts to develop an American style of Buddhism, through his publishing and his popularizing, and including a strong emphasis on the diligent practice of Buddhist ideals, have influenced a wide variety of well-known individuals ranging from scholars such as Huston Smith to writers such as Alan Watts,

Gary Snyder, and Jack Kerouac. Smith says in the preface to the twentieth edition of *A Buddhist Bible*: "No other collection has quite taken its place. . . . I know no alternative that is its equal" (p. vii).

• Other major publications by Goddard include *A Vision of Christian and Buddhist Fellowship in the Search for Light and Truth* (1924), *The Principle and Practice of Mahayana Buddhism: An Interpretation of Professor Suzuki's Translation of Ashvagosha's Awakening of Faith* (1933), *Self-Realisation of Noble Wisdom: A Buddhist Scripture Based upon Professor Suzuki's Translation of the Lankavatara Sutra* (1932), and *A Simple Method for Practicing the Seventh Stage of the Noble Path* (1937). Rick Fields treats the author affectionately in *How the Swans Came to the Lake: A Narrative History of Buddhism in America* (1981). There is a brief note on Goddard in William Peiris's *The Western Contribution to Buddhism* (1973).

CHARLES S. PREBISH

GODDARD, Henry Herbert (14 Aug. 1866–18 June 1957), psychologist, was born in East Vassalboro, Maine, the son of Henry Clay Goddard and Sarah Winslow, farmers. His father, injured in a farm accident, gradually sold off all of the family's land and earned a meager living as a day laborer; he died in 1875. Goddard's mother became a traveling missionary for the Society of Friends (Quakers). With his father dead and his mother away, Goddard received scholarships to attend Quaker boarding schools. In 1887 he received his B.A. from Haverford College in Haverford, Pennsylvania. The following spring he taught Latin, history, and botany at the University of Southern California while also coaching the school's first football team. In 1889 he earned an M.A. in mathematics from Haverford. The same year he married Emma Florence Robbins, a schoolteacher; they had no children. Goddard and his wife spent the next seven years teaching together in small Quaker academies in Ohio and Maine. In 1896 Goddard entered Clark University to study psychology with G. Stanley Hall. He earned his doctorate in 1899 after writing a dissertation exploring the psychological principles behind faith healing.

After graduating Goddard became professor of pedagogy and psychology at the State Normal School in West Chester, Pennsylvania. Hoping to introduce a scientific spirit into American education, he started a child-study association for Pennsylvania schoolteachers. Through this work he met Edward Johnstone, superintendent of the Training School for Feeble-Minded Girls and Boys located in Vineland, New Jersey. In 1906 Goddard accepted a new position as director of psychological research at Johnstone's institution. Seeking new ways to study children suffering from the condition then called "feeblemindedness" (later termed "mental retardation"), he toured Europe in 1908 and learned of the new "intelligence tests" first developed in 1905 by French psychologist Alfred Binet and his assistant, Theodore Simon. Using Binet's tests to assess the mental abilities of the Vineland children, Goddard became the first American intelligence tester.

Between 1908 and 1918 Goddard was America's most successful disseminator of Binet testing. In 1910 he convinced doctors in the American Association for the Study of the Feeble-Minded to adopt intelligence testing to gauge different degrees of mental impairment. He also invented a new term for the most mildly impaired individuals: "moron," a word that he coined from a Greek root meaning "foolish" and that at the time had no English connotation.

Goddard soon turned his attention from institutions to schools. In 1910 he became the first American to test the intelligence of public schoolchildren. His efforts to promote special education proved especially influential. In 1911 Goddard helped New Jersey legislators pass the nation's first law mandating special classes for deaf, blind, and "feebleminded" children in public schools. He also studied New York City's special education program as part of its school survey of 1911–1912; his report was later expanded and published as *School Training of Defective Children* (1914). In addition, Goddard trained many educators, both at Vineland's summer school for special-class teachers and at New York University's School of Pedagogy, where he was a visiting lecturer.

Goddard also grew increasingly interested in studying the causes of mental impairments. In 1909 he met biologist Charles Davenport, leader of the American eugenics movement, who introduced him to the theories of Gregor Mendel. Such theories, Goddard argued, could explain the inheritance of feeblemindedness. In his first and most famous book, *The Kallikak Family: A Study in the Heredity of Feeble-Mindedness* (1912), he traced the relatives of a Vineland resident, pseudonymously named Deborah Kallikak, back to her revolutionary war ancestor, Martin Kallikak. Goddard reported that Martin had produced two distinct lines of descendants: a "normal" line, begun with his wife and consisting of generations of "respectable citizens"; and an "illegitimate" line, started when the soldier met "a feeble-minded girl by whom he became the father of a feeble-minded son" and containing paupers, criminals, prostitutes, and other moral and mental failures (including Deborah).

To Goddard, these two lines constituted a "natural experiment" illustrating the dangers of a "feeble" biological inheritance. He epitomized his argument in the family's pseudonym; "Kallikak" came from two Greek roots meaning "good" and "bad." In his next study, *Feeble-Mindedness: Its Causes and Consequences* (1914), Goddard traced the family histories of over 300 Vineland children. Alarmed by his findings, he suggested that society consider new means of reducing feeblemindedness, including sexual sterilization or permanent institutionalization. Low intelligence was probably a single trait inherited according to Mendelian ratios, Goddard concluded, and it was linked to just about every grave social problem of the day, including crime, poverty, truancy, prostitution, and alcoholism.

Goddard also used intelligence tests in other ways. In 1914 he became the first psychologist to present Binet's tests in court—experiences that he chronicled in *The Criminal Imbecile* (1915). Goddard also visited Ellis Island to see if such tests could diagnose feebleminded immigrants. In 1917 he served on the Committee on the Psychological Examining of Recruits for the U.S. Army. Two of his books included army data: *Psychology of the Normal and Subnormal* (1919) and *Human Efficiency and Levels of Intelligence* (1920). By this time, Goddard's psychology had evolved into a broad political philosophy. Intelligence, he proposed, was a biologically inherited, socially unchangeable, and psychologically measurable trait with immense significance for restructuring education, explaining antisocial behavior, and justifying class differences. In the following decades these ideas, as well as those of other testers, would contribute to an increasingly explosive debate between scientists emphasizing the importance of man's inherited "nature" and those stressing "nurture," or social environment.

In 1918 Goddard left Vineland to direct the Ohio Bureau of Juvenile Research, describing his work in *Juvenile Delinquency* (1921). Personnel conflicts, however, led to his resignation. In 1922 he became a professor of clinical and abnormal psychology at Ohio State University, where he remained until his retirement in 1938. While at Ohio State he published two monographs: *Two Souls in One Body?* (1927), which examined a case of multiple personality; and *School Training of Gifted Children* (1928), which described Cleveland's classes for the gifted.

Although by the 1920s Goddard had left the field of intelligence testing to others, his prewar writings became increasingly controversial in the postwar era. A new generation of geneticists began to overturn his ideas about feeblemindedness, while anthropologists challenged his theories about "nature" by elaborating new theories of "culture." By 1928 Goddard had conceded that many of his earlier ideas had been in error. By the 1930s he had become an avid New Deal Democrat whose writings largely focused on improving education. Yet his Kallikak study continued to be disseminated by the American eugenics movement; and the book's warnings against mixing good blood with bad proved useful to Nazi propagandists in the 1930s and to opponents of school integration in the 1950s—associations that cast a pall over Goddard's reputation. His last book, *How to Rear Children in the Atomic Age* (1948), emphasized kindly childrearing and the need to learn from one's mistakes. In 1947 Goddard moved to Santa Barbara, California, where he died.

Goddard lived to see most of his theories not only rejected but often ridiculed by prominent scientists. During the second half of the century his writings were often cited as illustrations of the ways that social biases can distort scientific judgment. Even so, Goddard left a complex legacy, for his studies of mental retardation proved profoundly influential in encouraging research in child development, special education, clinical psychology, and human genetics, and in promoting the use of psychological testing within American medicine, education, and law.

• Goddard's papers are in the Archives of the History of American Psychology at the University of Akron. His correspondence with Davenport is in the Charles Benedict Davenport Papers at the American Philosophical Society in Philadelphia. A full-length biography is Leila Zenderland, *Measuring Minds: Henry Herbert Goddard and the Origins of American Intelligence Testing* (1998), which includes a bibliography of Goddard's publications. Goddard's theories are analyzed in Mark Haller, *Eugenics: Hereditarian Attitudes in American Thought* (1963); Daniel J. Kevles, *In the Name of Eugenics: Genetics and the Uses of Human Heredity* (1985); Peter L. Tyor and Leland V. Bell, *Caring for the Retarded in America: A History* (1984); James W. Trent, Jr., *Inventing the Feeble Mind: A History of Mental Retardation in the United States* (1994); and Raymond Fancher, *The Intelligence Men: Makers of the IQ Controversy* (1985). Goddard's Ellis Island research is assessed in Steven Gelb, "Henry H. Goddard and the Immigrants, 1910–1917: The Studies and Their Social Context," *Journal of the History of the Behavioral Sciences* 22 (1986): 324–32. Also see Michael Sokal, ed., *Psychological Testing and American Society, 1890–1930* (1987). Ian Hacking, "Two Souls in One Body," *Critical Inquiry* 17 (Summer 1991): 838–67, considers Goddard's multiple personality research, and J. David Smith, *Minds Made Feeble: The Myth and Legacy of the Kallikaks* (1985), explores the history of Goddard's most famous book. Obituaries are in the *New York Times*, 22 June 1957, and the *American Journal of Psychology* 70 (Dec. 1957): 656–57.

LEILA ZENDERLAND

GODDARD, John (20 Jan. 1723–4 July 1785), cabinetmaker, was born in Dartmouth, Massachusetts, the son of Daniel Goddard, a shipwright, and Mary Tripp. Shortly after John's birth the Goddards moved to Newport, Rhode Island. There John was apprenticed to cabinetmaker Job Townsend, Sr., in about 1743; on 3 April 1745 he became a freeman of Rhode Island. In 1746 he married his master's daughter, Hannah Townsend. The Goddards had sixteen children, three or four of whom became cabinetmakers. Relatively little is known about Goddard's personal life. On 22 August 1748 he bought a house lot for £250 on Easton's Point, later Washington Street, where he erected his house and shop. In the 1760s he held town offices, including viewer of lumber and justice of the peace, and apparently was a respected citizen.

Goddard, along with John Townsend, was a leading member of the extended Quaker Townsend-Goddard family of woodworkers who created some of the most beautiful examples of American eighteenth-century furniture. His patrons included Nicholas Brown, Moses Brown, Governor Stephen Hopkins, Jabez Bowen, James Atkinson, Captain Anthony Low, Benjamin Hazard, and many other wealthy and influential Rhode Island residents. Three letters between Goddard and Moses Brown in 1763 provide an unusual look at the relationship between client and craftsman in the eighteenth century. On 30 June Goddard wrote to Brown, "I send herewith The Tea Table & common Chairs which thou spoke for with the Bill. the other Work is in good forwardness hope to compleat in a short time. I Recd. a few lines from Jabez Bowen whom I suppose this furniture is for, Requesting me to

make a pre. Case of Drawers" (Isham, pp. 14–15). Goddard wanted Bowen to wait "till some time in the fall which will be as soon as I can finish them as I have but little help. . . . I would know whither he means to have them different from what is common, as there is a sort which is called a Chest on Chest of Drawers & Sweld. front which are Costly as well as ornimental" (Isham, p. 15). Brown wrote back in an angry tone, accusing Goddard of working on furniture for other clients first, as well as selling objects (for more money) that were supposed to have been made for Brown and leveling other charges. Goddard replied defensively, justifying his actions and explaining that Brown "must have expected I should (have) Engag'd work to keep my Boys Imploy'd if it Should a little Retard thy work, for we must do so or we Should be out of Imployment" (Isham, p. 16). The letters also contain details concerning Goddard's patrons, repertoire of forms, pace of work, and shop size.

The British occupation of Newport in 1777 caused a hiatus in Goddard's work and forced him in 1782 to open a sales warehouse on Moses Brown's wharf in Providence for the firm of Goddard and (William) Engs. (There was gossip that Goddard was a British sympathizer, but apparently the rumors were unfounded.) Goddard's business never recovered from the effects of the war, and he died insolvent in Newport. He left his shop tools and materials to his woodworking sons, who were to look after his widow and their younger siblings. A reference to five joiner's benches in Goddard's estate inventory gives an indication of the relatively small size of his shop.

Goddard is especially known for his fine walnut and mahogany furniture, especially blockfront shell-carved desk and bookcases and bureau dressing tables, high chests of drawers with claw-and-ball feet, tables, and chairs. Although Goddard owned a copy of the third edition of Thomas Chippendale's *Gentleman and Cabinet-Maker's Director* (1762; now in the Museum of Fine Arts, Boston), his furniture was not significantly influenced by Chippendale's version of the English rococo style. Rather, he produced sculptural, bold furniture of high quality that represents a distinct regional aesthetic. Unlike John Townsend, Goddard did not make a practice of labeling his furniture, and only a few signed pieces and others documented by correspondence or bills of sale are known to exist. Among them are two important desk and bookcases, now in the Museum of Art of the Rhode Island School of Design in Providence, one of which is inscribed "Made by John Goddard 1761 and repaired by Thomas Goddard his son 1813." Several authors have suggested that Goddard introduced the block-and-shell mode to Newport, but more recent scholarship indicates that he was one of several craftsmen working in the style in Newport during the third quarter of the eighteenth century. As a group, these craftsmen produced some of America's most visually pleasing furniture. These objects, many with crisp, tightly drawn outlines embellished sparely with beautifully carved shells, scrolls, and claw-and-ball feet, have a stately, massive quality that constitutes an American contribution to the history of design. Although relatively few examples documented to his shop are known, Goddard was clearly a significant practitioner of this Newport regional style.

• The Goddard-Brown letters are in the Rhode Island Historical Society, Providence. Goddard has been profiled by many authors. The earliest and most detailed study is Norman M. Isham, "John Goddard and His Work," Rhode Island School of Design, *Bulletin* 15 (Apr. 1927): 14–24, which includes transcriptions of correspondence between Goddard and Moses Brown, along with excerpts from Goddard's will and other primary documents. Studies of the Goddard-Townsend family include three articles by Mabel Munson Swan: "The Goddard and Townsend Joiners, Part I," *Antiques* 49, no. 4 (Apr. 1946): 228–31; "The Goddard and Townsend Joiners, Part II," *Antiques* 49, no. 5 (May 1946): 292–95; and "John Goddard's Sons," *Antiques* 57, no. 6 (June 1950): 448–49. Other relevant studies include Ethel Hall Bjerkoe, *The Cabinetmakers of America* (1957); and Hugh Honour, *Cabinet Makers and Furniture Designers* (1969). For other genealogical details, see three articles by Wendell Garrett: "The Newport Cabinetmakers: A Corrected Check List," *Antiques* 73, no. 6 (June 1958): 558–61; "The Goddard and Townsend Joiners, Random Biographical Notes," *Antiques* 94, no. 3 (Sept. 1968): 391–93; and "The Goddard and Townsend Joiners of Newport: Random Biographical and Bibliographical Notes," *Antiques* 121, no. 5 (May 1982): 1153–55. Goddard's work is examined in Ralph E. Carpenter, *The Arts and Crafts of Newport, Rhode Island, 1640–1820* (1954); and Joseph K. Ott, *The John Brown House Loan Exhibition of Rhode Island Furniture* (1965). Christopher Monkhouse and Thomas S. Michie, *American Furniture in Pendleton House* (1986), includes entries on two important desk and bookcases attributed to Goddard (cat. nos. 39–40). The characteristics of Goddard's furniture are discussed most thoroughly in Michael Moses, *Master Craftsmen of Newport: The Townsends and Goddards* (1984), which provides a conservative methodology for attributing work to Goddard and other Newport cabinetmakers. The characteristics of Rhode Island furniture are discussed and placed in context in Morrison H. Heckscher, *American Furniture in the Metropolitan Museum of Art*, vol. 2, *Late Colonial Period: The Queen Anne and Chippendale Styles* (1985).

GERALD W. R. WARD

GODDARD, Mary Katherine (16 June 1738–12 Aug. 1816), printer, newspaper publisher, and postmaster, was born in Groton, Connecticut, the daughter of Giles Goddard, a physician, and Sarah Updike, a printer. Growing up in New London, Connecticut, Goddard received an exceptional education for a woman in the 1700s, most of it from her mother, who had been taught by a French tutor. Little else is known about her early life.

Goddard entered the printing business in 1762, when she and her widowed mother moved to Providence, Rhode Island, to help her brother, William Goddard. While aiding her brother, Goddard learned the printing trade, knowledge that would prove useful throughout the rest of her life. In 1765 William Goddard moved to Philadelphia to start a new printing business. Sarah and Mary Katherine Goddard remained behind, managing the printshop and continu-

ing the publication of the weekly newspaper, the *Providence Gazette*. In 1768 William Goddard sold the Providence business, primarily because of political and financial troubles. His mother and sister moved to Philadelphia to join him in his enterprise there.

Goddard quickly became the office manager of the Philadelphia printshop. Once more, she helped produce a newspaper, this time the *Pennsylvania Chronicle*. Also once more, a wanderlust struck William Goddard. By 1773 he had lost interest in the Philadelphia business, and in May he moved to Baltimore to begin a new venture. Goddard remained in Philadelphia, continuing to run the printshop until it was sold in February 1774. She then followed her brother to Baltimore.

In Baltimore, Goddard firmly established her reputation as a capable printer. William Goddard very quickly became involved in plans to establish a national post office, and he left Goddard in charge of the Baltimore printshop. Most important among the productions of the business was the *Maryland Journal*, which William had established shortly after his arrival. Goddard assumed management of the newspaper and printing office in 1774, but her editorial control of the *Maryland Journal* was not acknowledged until May 1775, when her name began to appear as the publisher of the newspaper.

Although not always easy to do because of the impact of the war, Goddard managed to publish the *Maryland Journal* on a regular basis throughout the Revolution. Although sometimes published on small-sized sheets of paper, the publication continued to appear. From 5 July 1779 to 16 May 1783, it was the only newspaper published in Baltimore. By the time Goddard left the paper in 1784, it had become one of the most widely circulated newspapers in the United States. Throughout her career as editor and publisher of the *Journal*, Goddard maintained a level of excellence in appearance and content that few printers could challenge.

Goddard's printing activities involved more than just the weekly newspaper. She also produced a variety of blank forms, broadsides, pamphlets, and books. Her most famous publication appeared on 18 January 1777, when she printed the first official copy of the Declaration of Independence with all of the names of the signers attached to it. She realized the significance of this event because she spelled her name in full as printer rather than using her initials as she generally did on other projects.

Throughout the ten years of Goddard's management, the Baltimore printshop prospered. Her brother William came and went, occasionally working in the business but engaging in a number of other ventures as well. The two siblings managed to tolerate each other for several years, but they finally had a bitter quarrel that resulted in Goddard's leaving the business. William apparently bought out his sister's interest in the printshop on terms that she greatly resented. Goddard would have nothing to do with her brother after this argument. She even refused to attend his wedding in

1786. The argument marked the end of Goddard's printing career.

Goddard also engaged in activities beyond the business of printing. In 1776 she began bookbinding, a venture that proved successful for the rest of her life. A year earlier, she had accepted the appointment as Baltimore's postmaster. She was one of only a handful of women to hold public appointments during the 1700s and the first woman to serve as a postmaster in the United States. She continued as postmaster until October 1789, when she was replaced by a man because the job increasingly necessitated widespread travel, which was inappropriate for a woman to attempt to do. More than two hundred businessmen protested her removal in a petition to the government, but to no avail. Goddard continued to live in Baltimore, where she operated a bookshop from 1784 until 1809 or 1810. When she died in Baltimore, she freed the slave woman who helped her in her last years. This woman, Belinda Starling, also inherited all of Goddard's property.

Goddard, who never married, was a very successful businesswoman. She continually stepped in, took over businesses established by her brother, and made them into profitable enterprises. Although she was a successful publisher, bookbinder, and bookseller, as well as a competent postmaster, her greatest success was as a printer. Isaiah Thomas, in his history of American printing, praised her abilities in running her brother's printshop in his absence. Her brother William, who gave her the chance to succeed because of his own wanderlust, described her as "an expert and correct compositor of types." Her printing accomplishments ranged over a variety of publications, but her newspapers provide the best evidence of her abilities. While being produced by her, the *Providence Gazette*, the *Pennsylvania Chronicle*, and the *Maryland Journal* all met with great financial success and developed reputations for quality that reached far beyond the city of publication. Mary Katherine Goddard deservedly received high praise from her contemporaries for the quality of the work she produced.

• Most information about Goddard can be found in studies of her brother's printing ventures. See, for example, Lawrence C. Wroth, *A History of Printing in Colonial Maryland, 1686–1776* (1922), and Joseph Towne Wheeler, *The Maryland Press, 1777–1790* (1938). See also Susan Henry's study of Goddard's mother, "Sarah Goddard, Gentlewoman Printer," *Journalism Quarterly* 57 (Spring 1980): 23–30. Other discussions of Goddard's contributions to printing can be found in Caroline Bird, *Enterprising Women* (1976); Gay Walker, "Women Printers in Early American Printing History," *Yale University Library Bulletin* 61 (1987): 120–21; and Leona M. Hudak, *Early American Women Printers and Publishers, 1639–1820* (1978).

CAROL SUE HUMPHREY

GODDARD, Morrill (7 Oct. 1865–1 July 1937), journalist, was born in Auburn, Maine, the son of Charles William Goddard, a Maine state senator, jurist, and postmaster, and Rowena Caroline Morrill, daughter of Maine governor Anson P. Morrill. Goddard attended public schools in Portland and enrolled in Bowdoin College. A sophomore prank led to his expulsion, and he transferred to Dartmouth.

Goddard's father had plans for him to attend law school, but immediately after graduating from Dartmouth in 1885 Goddard ventured to New York City, determined to land a job with a major newspaper. Noticing that the daily papers had no reporters routinely covering the city morgue, Goddard stationed himself there and befriended an attendant. Simply by being present when corpses were brought in, Goddard was able to generate exclusive stories and sell them to the dailies, including Joseph Pulitzer's *New York World*. Soon Goddard latched on at the *World* and scored a journalistic coup during President Ulysses S. Grant's funeral procession through New York in August 1885. Dressed in a black suit, Goddard brazenly approached the cortege and climbed into the first carriage, next to the grieving Mrs. Grant. Assuming he was the undertaker's assistant, the police and the widow left him alone. Goddard covered the procession for the *World* from that central vantage point. He exhibited the same boldness in June 1886, when President Grover Cleveland was married. Goddard was part of a pack of reporters that trailed the newlyweds from the White House to the honeymoon camp in Deer Park, Maryland, and even spent the night outside the couple's cabin.

Pulitzer promoted Goddard to city editor, and following a whirlwind of staff changes in 1893 he placed Goddard in command of the Sunday *World*. Goddard became infamous for specializing in stunts and for reporting "crime, underwear, and pseudo-science." One of his first tasks was to rehire Nellie Bly, who in an earlier stint as a *World* reporter had feigned insanity to expose conditions at the asylum at Blackwell Island. He also persuaded a prominent Episcopal pastor to live in a tenement in the immigrant slum of Hell's Kitchen for six weeks and keep a journal. Goddard dressed up his content with lavish illustrations and banner headlines.

In 1894 Goddard took advantage of the *World*'s new four-color rotary press to print the Sunday comics in color. Also in that year his staff hired artist Richard Outcault, whose "Hogan's Alley" cartoon for the *World* featured children from the tenements. Staff printers experimented in early January 1896 with a new quick-drying yellow ink and tested it on the dress of the central "kid." The bald ragamuffin was from then on known as the "Yellow Kid" and became a hit with New Yorkers.

The *World*'s innovations and success under Goddard captured the eye of publisher William Randolph Hearst, who had moved from San Francisco and bought the fledgling *New York Journal* in 1895. In January 1896 he met with Goddard to try to lure him to the Sunday *Journal*. Though tempted by a staggering offer, Goddard protested. "I need my writers and my artists," he said. "All right," Hearst replied. "Let's take the whole staff." Hearst gave a spot cash bonus of

$15,000 to Goddard, who along with his staff vacated the *World* building for the *Journal* offices across the street. When Pulitzer, off the coast of France, learned of the mass defection, he was shocked and outraged. "Hire back at any cost," he cabled. The *World* management enticed Goddard and his staff back to the *World*—but for just one day. Hearst dangled yet another offer, and Goddard, Outcault, and the rest of the Sunday crew were gone for good.

Pulitzer replaced Goddard with Arthur Brisbane, who strove to outdo his new rival at his own sensational game. The *World* also defiantly continued to run "Hogan's Alley," with the "new" Yellow Kid being drawn by George B. Luks. With both papers dishing out sensationalism and boasting the yellow waif—even plastering him on posters all over town—the term "yellow journalism" became popular by the end of 1896.

Goddard thus began a four-decade reign as a Hearst editor. Employing the same colorful strategies he had used at the *World*, Goddard boosted the Sunday *Journal*'s circulation from fewer than 100,000 to 450,000 in 1896. Hearst changed the name of his paper to the *American* in 1901 (after the paper drew criticism for inflammatory passages preceding President William McKinley's assassination), and Goddard spent the rest of his life with the *American Magazine*, renamed the *American Weekly* in 1911.

Goddard's *What Interests People—and Why* (1935) provides insight into his editorial philosophy. Goddard prided himself in studying psychology to learn what interested the human mind. Comparing himself to a composer who blends eight notes in two octaves for the human voice, he devised sixteen elements of human interest—love, hate, fear, vanity, evil doing, morality, selfishness, immortality, superstition, curiosity, veneration, ambition, culture, heroism, science, and amusement—and infused them liberally into his *American Weekly*. Lavishly illustrated stories accompanied headlines such as "Photographed—The Lovers as They Attempted Suicide," "Little Annette, Her Snakes and Her Monkeys," "Mystery of the Tourist Who Vanished in the Desert," "Battle with Giant Baboon on Edge of Precipice," "Confessions of a Fashionable Drug Addict," and "Prettiest Legs in Hollywood?"

To Goddard, reporting science ("modern miracles," as he called them) was a service, and readers naturally wanted to know about sex. He took pride in the sensationalist label. "Because a thing is sensational it is not necessarily objectionable or unfit to print," he said. "The more extraordinary, unexpected and sensational, the more likely to be interesting." Besides, he argued, the great news events throughout history, including the wonders and miracles of the Bible, were sensational. Americans, he said, "react to emotional appeal of word or picture, but fall asleep when you present something requiring them to think."

Ironically, the editorially flamboyant Goddard was a very private man. He married Jessamine Rugg in 1899; they had five children. In addition to living in New York City, he spent summers at Naskeag, Maine, where he died. As historian Frank Luther Mott has pointed out, Goddard has been called "the father of the American Sunday paper." By the time of his death, the *American Weekly*'s circulation had reached 6 million, the most widely read publication in the world.

• The *World* Papers, including documents from the *New York World* and correspondence of Joseph Pulitzer, are held in the Rare Book and Manuscript Library, Columbia University. The Library of Congress also has a Pulitzer collection. *What Interests People—and Why* (1935) reprints six addresses delivered at annual conferences in New York. For contemporary reflections on Goddard by a coworker, see Walter Hugh McDougall, *This Is the Life!* (1926). Frank Luther Mott, *American Journalism: A History, 1690–1960* (1962), and Willard Grosvenor Bleyer, *Main Currents in the History of American Journalism* (1927), shed light on the yellow journalism era. Biographies of Goddard's contemporaries include James Wyman Barrett, *Joseph Pulitzer and His World* (1941); Oliver Carlson and Ernest Sutherland Bates, *Hearst: Lord of San Simeon* (1936); Allen Churchill, *Park Row* (1958); and Brooke Kroeger, *Nellie Bly: Daredevil, Reporter, Feminist* (1994). Goddard's obituary is in the *New York Times*, 2 July 1937.

JAMES FOY MCCOLLUM, JR.

GODDARD, Paul Beck (26 Jan. 1811–3 July 1866), pioneer in photography, physician, and anatomist, was born in Baltimore, Maryland, the son of John Goddard and Mary Beck. He received an A.B. from Washington (later Trinity) College in Hartford, Connecticut, in 1828. The same year he entered the Medical School of the University of Pennsylvania, where in 1832 he completed his M.D. with a thesis titled "The Anatomy and Physiology of Mucous Membrane." Goddard did not find the day-to-day practice of being a physician in Philadelphia particularly satisfying. After a few years in private practice, he became the assistant to Robert Hare, a professor of chemistry at the University of Pennsylvania.

The announcement of the discovery of photography in 1839 caused a great deal of excitement, and many young scientists in Philadelphia became involved in the new art. Goddard was no different from his peers in this respect, except that his experimentation led to one of the few improvements ever made to the actual processing of daguerreotypes. He teamed with Robert Cornelius, also of Philadelphia, and the two discovered that bromine vapor could greatly accelerate exposure times for daguerreotype plates. This discovery, along with an elaborate lighting system, made portrait photography practical. Goddard became a silent partner when Cornelius opened the second American photographic portrait studio in the spring of 1840. Goddard and Cornelius kept their discovery to themselves as a trade secret and in fact made an attempt to corner the bromine market. (In 1840 bromine suppliers were very few, and the first and only commercial use for bromine was in making daguerreotypes. The bromine market crashed in 1856 as the daguerreotype began to be replaced by other photographic methods. Not until the 1860s was bromine widely used in medicine or as a disinfectant.) John Frederick Goddard, an English optician of no relation to Goddard, published the description of the use of bromine in photography in December 1840. The fact that both men shared the same surname and that Paul Beck Goddard did not formally publish a report on his use of bromine (although he did subsequently describe the work that he and Cornelius had done) has meant that the latter is not generally credited with this discovery in some circles. However, modern empirical evidence has confirmed Goddard and Cornelius were routinely using bromine in early 1840.

After working for Hare, Goddard became a professor of anatomy at the University of Pennsylvania. Goddard had been Joseph Leidy's preceptor during part of his college training, and Leidy lived in the Goddard home during 1844. Leidy went on to become a leading paleontologist. In addition to his work as an anatomist and professor, Goddard was a skillful surgeon and microscopist. In medical circles, Goddard is most remembered as a contributor to the production of medical texts and reference works. He wrote or published many noted medical texts and anatomies, including *Plates of the Cerebro-Spinal Nerves, with References* (1837); *Plates of the Arteries, with References* (1839); Erasmus Wilson's *System of Human Anatomy* (1843); *The Anatomy, Physiology and Pathology of the Human Teeth, with the Most Approved Methods of Treatment* (1844), in conjunction with Joseph E. Parker; Wilson's *The Dissector; or, Practical and Surgical Anatomy* (both the 1844 and 1851 editions); the pictorial section of P. Rayner's *Theoretical and Practical Treatise of the Diseases of the Skin* (1845); the first American edition of Samuel Ashwell's *A Practical Treatise on Diseases Peculiar to Women* (1845); and Philip Ricord's *Illustrations of Syphilitic Disease* (1851).

Goddard was married to Louisa Bonsell; they had three children. He was a lifelong member of the American Philosophical Society, and he maintained an interest in the different forms of photography as they developed. He died in Philadelphia and is buried in the Laurel Hill Cemetery in that city.

• A complete discussion of Goddard's role in the evolution of photography can be found in William F. Stapp et al., *Robert Cornelius: Portraits from the Dawn of Photography* (1983), and M. Susan Barger and William B. White, *The Daguerreotype: Nineteenth Century Technology and Modern Science* (1991). An obituary is in the (Philadelphia) *North American and United States Gazette*, 6 July 1866.

M. SUSAN BARGER

GODDARD, Pliny Earle (24 Nov. 1869–12 July 1928), ethnologist and linguist of American Indian languages, was born in Lewiston, Maine, the son of Charles W. Goddard, a minister in the Society of Friends who supplemented his meager salary by selling home-grown produce and flowers, and Elmira Nichols. The fourth born in a family of seven children, Goddard learned self-reliance and frugality at an early age. These traits served him well, as he paid his own way to Oak Grove Seminary, a Friends' academy in Vassalboro, a remote fifty miles from home. When the principal of the school was transferred to the Oakwood Seminary in Union Springs, New York, Goddard transferred, too. He graduated in 1889 and immediately enrolled at Earlham College in Richmond, Indiana. Here he demonstrated interest in language by taking a full curriculum in Latin and Greek. He graduated with an A.B. in classical languages in 1892.

Upon graduation, Goddard entered the service of Friends as principal at a series of impoverished Friends' secondary schools in the Midwest. He married Alice Rockwell in 1893; they would have six children. In 1896 Goddard finished his M.A. at Earlham but was forced to seek additional employment to support his family. Eventually, in 1897, he took a position as a missionary with an interdenominational organization headquartered in Philadelphia called the Women's Indian Aid Association, which sent him to live with the Hupa Indians in California.

The small family entered Hoopa, California, in March 1897, ending their long journey from Kansas by riding the last two days on horseback over a rough trail, presumably through a pass in the Siskiyou Alps. Hoopa offered them a life of tranquility, and here Goddard arrived at the idea of making ethnology his life's work. Visiting in the summer of 1900, Stewart Cullin, curator of the Brooklyn Museum, encouraged Goddard in his ambitions, with the result that Goddard enrolled in 1900 as a doctoral student at the University of California in Berkeley. There Benjamin Wheeler, a prominent linguist and the president of the university, took Goddard under his wing and helped him win scholarship money. Goddard was such a success that he was given a job as instructor in the new Department of Anthropology, funded by donations from Phoebe Apperson Hearst. He completed his Ph.D. in 1904 and was promoted to assistant professor in 1906.

During the period from 1903 to 1909 Goddard secured his future; the dissertation (on Hupa grammar) for his Ph.D., the first ever granted in linguistics by an American university, represented the most comprehensive study of a single American Indian language yet produced. His method of recording ethnographic and linguistic data became the standard for the discipline, and he became the leading scholar of American Indian languages, particularly those of the Athabaskan family. Goddard's method provided a multidimensional and thorough representation of Hupa language and culture through the combined use of standard linguistic and ethnologic forms: phonology, morphology, and notes on material and social culture, and a new method of recording data, the linguistic text. The linguistic text, Goddard's major contribution to the discipline of anthropology, gave Indian people a forum to record their own lives in their own languages, something never accomplished before. Goddard also undertook field studies in the Southwest, lured there by an opportunity to translate a Navajo linguistic text, written by Washington Matthews, later published as

"Navaho Myths, Prayers, and Songs with Texts and Translations" (*University of California Publications in American Archaeology and Ethnology* 5 [1907]: 21–63), in which he also recorded data from the Sarsi and Jicarilla Apache.

Berkeley, whose support of anthropology was shifting to state funding, lost its attraction for Goddard, and in 1909 he accepted a position in New York City as assistant curator at the American Museum of Natural History. There his excellent scholarship earned him an immediate promotion to associate curator, and in 1914 he was installed as curator of ethnology, intermittently heading the Anthropology department. From this position he published many pieces, including his famous handbooks *Indians of the Southwest* (1913) and *Indians of the Northwest Coast* (1924). In New York he became a friend of anthropologist Franz Boas, whose ideas on race (the interrelatedness of all humans) were compatible with Goddard's own Society of Friends background and whose conservative linguistic views on the genetic relationship between languages and how they should be classified complimented his own. In 1915 Goddard secured both a lectureship at Columbia University and the position of editor of *American Anthropologist* (1915–1920). In 1917, with Boas, he founded the *International Journal of American Linguistics*, for several decades the major publication on American Indian languages.

In the years between the founding of the journal and his death, Goddard continued to conduct field work among Athabaskan-speaking peoples in the Southwest and California and continued to influence anthropological thinking. He and Boas constituted a formidable team—they maintained editorial and administrative control over collections, publications, research, and education. But Edward Sapir was to appear on the scene in the early 1920s with his revolutionary theories of "Na-Dene," which proposed a relationship between the Haida, Tlingit, and Athabascan languages. After Goddard's death in New York City, Sapir succeeded Goddard as the leading linguist of American Indian languages.

• Many of Goddard's early papers are in the Bancroft Library of the University of California, Berkeley. His Hupa work published in the *University of California Publications in American Archaeology and Ethnology* includes "Life and Culture of the Hupa" 1 (1903): 1–88; "Hupa Texts" 1 (1904): 89–368; "The Morphology of the Hupa Language" 3 (1905): 1–344; and "The Phonology of the Hupa Language, Part I: The Individual Sounds" 5 (1907): 1–20. Others of his articles are in the *Anthropological Papers of the American Museum of Natural History*, the *Journal of American Folklore*, and the *American Museum Journal of Natural History*. A. L. Kroeber published "Goddard's California Athabascan Texts" in the *International Journal of American Linguistics* 33 (1967): 265–79. An incisive look at Goddard's relationship to Edward Sapir is Michael Krauss, "Edward Sapir and Athabaskan Linguistics" in *New Perspectives in Language, Culture, and Personality: Proceedings of the Edward Sapir Centenary Conference*, ed. William Cowan et al. (1986). Obituaries by A. L. Kroeber are in *Science*, 17 Aug. 1928, pp. 149–50, and *American Anthropologist* 31

(1929): 1–8; the latter includes a list of Goddard's publications. An obituary by Franz Boas is in the *International Journal of American Linguistics* 6 (1930): 1–2.

DEBORAH S. DOZIER

GODDARD, Robert Hutchings (5 Oct. 1882–10 Aug. 1945), physicist and pioneer of rocketry and spaceflight, was born in Worcester, Massachusetts, the son of Nahum Danford Goddard, a businessman, and Fanny Louise Hoyt. After Goddard's mother was diagnosed as suffering from tuberculosis in 1899, Robert, who had been attending Boston public schools, remained at home in Worcester until 1901. Fascinated by science, he filled his days with a variety of experiments ranging from plans for a mechanized frog hatchery to the manufacture of aluminum balloons and synthetic diamonds. He was particularly intrigued by speculative fiction, notably H. G. Wells's *War of the Worlds*, which was being serialized by a Boston newspaper. The exciting details of the story were still fresh in his mind on the afternoon of 19 October 1899, while he trimmed the upper branches of a cherry tree in his backyard. He recalled many years later that "as I looked toward the fields at the east, I imagined how wonderful it would be to make some device which had even the *possibility* of ascending to Mars. . . . In any event, I was a very different boy when I descended the tree." Goddard viewed the day as a turning point, and for the rest of his life he kept a meticulous diary in which he remembered 19 October as Anniversary Day.

Goddard graduated from Worcester's South High School in 1904, at the age of twenty-one. He then graduated from the Worcester Polytechnic Institute in 1908 and earned an M.A. in 1910 and a Ph.D. in 1911 from Clark University. His dissertation, a pioneering investigation of solid state physics, earned him an honorary fellowship at Clark in 1911–1912 and a research instructorship at Princeton University in 1912–1913. Following a bout with tuberculosis, he accepted in 1914 an instructorship in physics at Clark, where he was named a full professor in 1920 and served as director of physical laboratories from 1923 to 1943. In 1924 he married Esther Christine Kisk.

Goddard never lost his boyhood enthusiasm for spaceflight. An examination of his early notebooks reveals speculations regarding ion propulsion (6 Sept. 1906); the use of rockets composed of multiple stages to be discarded as propellant was exhausted (24 Jan. 1909); and continuous rocket propulsion through the use of a variety of pressure-fed liquids, including liquid hydrogen and liquid oxygen (June 1909–Aug. 1910). In July 1914 he was granted the first of his 214 patents, all but six of which were directly related to rocketry and spaceflight. By 1914 Goddard had begun experimenting with solid propellant rockets in the physics laboratory at Clark. In 1915 he received $5,000 from the Smithsonian Institution to study the rocket as a means of boosting scientific instruments into the upper atmosphere.

With U.S. entry into World War I, Goddard was awarded a $20,000 Signal Corps contract for work on rocket-propelled weaponry. By the fall of 1918 he was ready to demonstrate a lightweight, tube-launched infantry weapon. The project came to a halt with the end of the war, but later researchers carried Goddard's work to a successful conclusion with the development of the anti-tank bazooka of World War II.

After the war, Goddard turned his attention to experiments with liquid propellants. The Smithsonian published the most influential and important of Goddard's scientific papers, *A Method of Reaching Extreme Altitudes*, in its *Miscellaneous Collections* for 1919. The short treatise offered detailed mathematical proof that solid propellant rockets were capable of boosting modest instrument packages into the upper atmosphere. Determined to underscore the serious nature of his work, Goddard relegated his notes on the possibility of achieving spaceflight to the end of the paper, and he covered the possibility of multistage rockets and high-energy liquid propellants in appendices. The Smithsonian publication established Goddard as one of the three great, pioneering figures, along with the Russian Konstantine E. Tsiolkovskii and the Transylvania-born Hermann Oberth, in the history of spaceflight.

Goddard's work sparked a mild flurry of interest in the press. An intensely private man, he was dismayed to find himself referred to as the professor with the "moon-going rocket," to see the validity of his work questioned in the pages of the *New York Times*, and to receive batches of letters from volunteers for a trip to Mars.

By 1921 Goddard was conducting experiments with rockets propelled by liquid oxygen and gasoline. On 16 March 1926 he flew the world's first liquid propellant rocket from a site near Auburn, Massachusetts. The ten-foot rocket, with the engine mounted on the nose, reached an altitude of 41 feet, traveled 184 feet over the ground, and landed 2.5 seconds after lift-off. Over the next few years he achieved marginal increases in performance. The fiery conclusion of a test launch on 17 July 1929 led to renewed news interest in his work and a ban on further launches in the area.

Goddard received permission to continue his work at Ft. Devens, Massachusetts, and was about to conduct his first launch at the site on 22 November 1929, when he received a telephone call from Charles A. Lindbergh. After a single conversation the famous aviator became determined to help Goddard achieve the goal of spaceflight. Lindbergh helped convince philanthropist Daniel Guggenheim to offer Goddard a $50,000 grant, the first of $188,500 in Guggenheim grants awarded to Goddard between 1930 and 1941.

These funds, together with smaller grants from other organizations, enabled Goddard to take long leaves of absence from Clark (1930–1932, 1934–1942), during which he devoted himself full time to rocket research. He selected Roswell, New Mexico, a relatively isolated spot offering cloudless skies and flat terrain, as the ideal test site. Working with a small team of assistants, he set to work designing, building, and testing the complex systems that make up a modern rocket. He developed a variety of motor types and sizes; reduced operating temperatures and increased efficiency through the use of new methods of cooling; pioneered rocket stability and control systems based on gyroscopes and other sensors; employed both movable vanes operating in the exhaust stream and fully gimballed engines to guide his rockets during ascent; and labored to perfect high-speed propellant pumps and other essential components.

Goddard made significant progress, but he was never able to achieve more than a modest level of performance. The best altitude attained by one of his rockets was under 10,000 feet. Nor was he able to provide such performance on demand. Each of his attempts to arrange a launch for Lindbergh and for Guggenheim's son Harry ended in failure.

Fearful that his ideas would be stolen by unscrupulous rivals, Goddard refused to share the details of his technology with other experimenters. His most significant publication after 1919, *Liquid Propellant Rocket Development*, which appeared in a March 1936 issue of the Smithsonian *Miscellaneous Collections*, contained so little specific information that it was of limited value to other rocket experimenters.

In 1941 U.S. Navy officials asked for Goddard's help in the design of a variable-thrust liquid propellant rocket motor to help boost heavily laden aircraft into the air. By 1942 Goddard and his staff had been transferred to the Naval Engineering Experiment Station in Annapolis, Maryland. While their specific design for a rocket-assisted take-off unit did not go into production, their work influenced the design of a postwar rocket engine for a manned research aircraft.

Goddard's health declined rapidly in the spring of 1945. In June he was diagnosed as having cancer of the throat. He died two months later in Baltimore and was buried in Hope Cemetery near Worcester, Massachusetts.

Goddard's research legacy is found in his patents, which covered virtually every aspect of rocketry and spaceflight. In 1960, in an effort to avoid patent infringement, the U.S. government settled all claims with Esther Goddard and the Guggenheim Foundation for $1 million—a clear indication of how thoroughgoing his contribution had been. But Goddard's predilection for secrecy makes it difficult to assess his impact. According to rocket pioneer and Caltech professor Theodore von Karman, "not listening to, or communicating with, other qualified people hindered his accomplishments." Consequently, said von Karman, "There is no direct line from Goddard to present-day rocketry." As Lindbergh recognized, however, there are other ways in which to gauge the accomplishments of an individual. "When I see a rocket rising from its pad," Lindbergh wrote in 1974, "I sense Goddard standing at my side, his human physical substance now ethereal, his dreams substantive."

• The bulk of Goddard's papers is held by Clark University. The Archive of the Smithsonian Institution and the Library and Archive of the National Air and Space Museum preserve smaller collections of Goddard papers. Esther C. Goddard and G. Edward Pendray, eds., *The Papers of Robert H. Goddard* (3 vols., 1970), contain the most important letters and notebook entries as well as key published papers and autobiographical fragments. The *Papers* also include a complete bibliography of Goddard's writings. Milton Lehman, *This High Man: The Life of Robert H. Goddard* (1963), remains the standard biography. Also see the tribute to Goddard by G. Edward Pendray in *Science*, n.s., 102 (23 Nov. 1945): 521–23.

TOM D. CROUCH

GODDARD, Sarah Updike (c. 1700–5 Jan. 1770), printer and newspaper publisher, was born at Cocumscussuc, near the village of Wickford on Narragansett Bay, Rhode Island, the daughter of Lodowick Updike and Abigail Newton, prominent landowners. Her paternal grandfather, Gysbert op Dyck, had emigrated from Germany to Long Island, New York, where he had purchased what later became Coney Island. Her father moved from New Amsterdam to Rhode Island and anglicized his name to Updike.

Because of their family's wealth and social position, the Updike children had superior educations for the day, with Sarah learning French and Latin from a tutor in the household. She was married in 1735, to Dr. Giles Goddard of Groton, Connecticut. The couple moved to New London, Connecticut, where he was a physician and postmaster. Both were members of the Church of England. They had four children, but only two, Mary Katherine Goddard and William Goddard, lived to adulthood. She is believed to have taught both of them. At her husband's death in 1757, she was left in comfortable circumstances.

Her affluence allowed her to provide capital for William, who had been apprenticed as a printer, to set up the first printing and publishing business in Providence, Rhode Island. She and her daughter moved to Providence to assist in the business, which produced the first issue of the *Providence Gazette; and Country Journal* in 1762. The firm also printed forms, broadsides, and other staples of colonial operations and sold books and stationery. When William Goddard, who had been named postmaster in 1764, encountered business difficulties the following year, he suspended the newspaper and left the printing business and post office in the hands of his mother and sister while he sought opportunities elsewhere. He also left them to manage his share of a paper mill in which he was a partner.

At first using the imprint "S. and W. Goddard," Sarah Goddard carried on, thus becoming the second printer in Providence. In 1766 she revived the weekly *Providence Gazette* under the auspices of "Sarah Goddard and Company." The newspaper, which carried both informative and entertaining items as well as advertising and poetry, became increasingly pro-Whig politically. When news reached Providence of the unpopular Townshend Acts, passed by the British to tax imports, the *Gazette* criticized them. In addition, it reprinted articles from Boston publications attacking British policies.

A capable manager, Sarah Goddard also published almanacs, a popular item for colonial publishers. In 1766 she brought out the first American edition of the letters of Lady Mary Wortley Montagu, who first introduced the practice of inoculation for smallpox into England and who was considered its leading woman epistolary writer on the basis of her accounts of life in Constantinople. Publication of her letters indicated sympathy with efforts to elevate the status of women. That same year Goddard hired an assistant, Samuel Inslee, who was replaced the next year by John Carter. By 1768 she had made the business profitable.

Nevertheless, William Goddard, an individual of disputatious nature who had become embroiled in financial and personal problems in connection with a Philadelphia printing operation, insisted that she sell the business. Although she told him she did not want to move to "a strange part of the world" during her old age, he prevailed upon her and Mary Katherine to leave Providence and join him in Philadelphia to assist in his venture there. Once there, the two women experienced difficulties with William's partners, who failed to provide them with a house as promised.

While William Goddard continued to travel to try to raise money to get out of the partnership, his mother and sister ran his print shop and newspaper, the *Pennsylvania Chronicle, and Universal Advertiser*. In December 1769 Sarah wrote William that the number of subscribers was increasing. In her letter she said, "I shall exert myself to preserve its credit. . . . I daily mourn for your hard fate, and while I live, which cannot be long, I shall be striving to promote your interests here . . ."

Shortly thereafter she died in Philadelphia. An obituary in the *New York Gazette* praised her for running the Providence newspaper, saying that "the credit of the paper was greatly promoted by her virtue, ingenuity and abilities." It further recognized her "uncommon attainments in literature," "sincere piety," and "unaffected humility" as well as her "sensible and edifying conversation."

Although relatively little is known of her personal life, it is apparent that Goddard was a woman of great competence, loyal to her family and committed to printing and publishing. While it was not uncommon for women to assist male relatives in printing and publishing ventures during the colonial era, Sarah Goddard's career showed that a woman was quite able to take charge of an enterprise on her own.

• A letter of Sarah Goddard is at the Providence Public Library, while files of the *Providence Gazette* are in the Rhode Island Historical Society. Imprints of William and Sarah Goddard are listed in John E. Alden, *Rhode Island Imprints, 1727–1800* (1949). An account of the Goddard family's difficulties in Philadelphia appeared in William Goddard, *The Partnership; or the History of the Rise and Progress of the Pennsylvania Chronicle* (1770). Biographical information can be found in Nancy Fisher Chudacoff, "Woman in the News 1762–1770—Sarah Updike Goddard," *Rhode Island History* 32 (Nov. 1973): 98–105, and Susan Henry, "Sarah Goddard,

Gentlewoman Printer," *Journalism Quarterly* 57 (Spring 1980): 23–30. Her obituary is in the *New York Gazette*, 22 Jan. 1770.

MAURINE H. BEASLEY

GODDARD, William (20 Oct. 1740–23 Dec. 1817), printer and newspaperman, was born in New London, Connecticut, the son of Giles Goddard, a physician and village postmaster, and Sarah Updike (Sarah Updike Goddard), a printer. He began his apprenticeship in July 1755 with James Parker (1714–1770), postmaster in New Haven and owner of a press there. The apprenticeship ended on Goddard's twenty-first birthday in October 1761. Parker, a native of New Jersey and himself once an apprentice to William Bradford (1663–1752) in New York, had started the *Connecticut Gazette* on 12 April 1755. Upon achieving journeyman printer status, Goddard sought next to become a master printer, which meant owning his own shop. To accomplish that, he moved to Providence in 1762, becoming its first printer. With his widowed mother, Sarah Goddard, and his sister, Mary Katherine Goddard, he started on 20 October its first newspaper, the *Providence Gazette; and Country Journal,* "opposite the Court-House." On 21 September 1765 he was responsible for the first printed newspaper in New Jersey, a one-issue attack on the Stamp Act called the *Constitutional Courant,* issued from James Parker's printing shop in Woodbridge, New Jersey.

Goddard left Providence in 1766 to create in Philadelphia a newspaper on the grandest scale ever before attempted in the colonies. There he established a secret partnership with Joseph Galloway, Speaker of the Pennsylvania Assembly, and Thomas Wharton (1735–1778), a wealthy Quaker merchant. They issued the first number of the *Pennsylvania Chronicle, and Universal Advertiser* on 26 January 1767, while Goddard's mother and sister stayed on in Providence to manage the *Gazette.* The *Chronicle* was considered the best-designed newspaper yet produced in Philadelphia and perhaps in any of the colonies. It had a cleaner appearance than either of the other Philadelphia papers, Benjamin Franklin's (1706–1790) *Gazette,* edited since 1766 by David Hall, and William Bradford's *Journal.* Its pages were folio size, with four columns instead of the customary three, a feature that supposedly cost Goddard an additional $200 a year for paper. The *Chronicle* was patterned after the *London Chronicle,* and, interestingly, Goddard numbered the pages consecutively from issue to issue, confident that his readers would compile their own annual volumes.

The *Chronicle* was the first newspaper to carry, for three months in 1767–1768, John Dickinson's (1732–1808) *Letters from a Pennsylvania Farmer,* a series of twelve essays against the right of Parliament to tax the colonies in any form. Because Galloway and Wharton favored the continuation of British rule, the publication of the inflammatory *Letters* marked the beginning of the end of Goddard's partnership with the two men. From the Goddard shop came not only the regular printing each Monday of the newspaper, but numerous blanks, handbills, and pamphlets as well.

Perhaps Goddard's most important contribution to eighteenth-century America was the Constitutional Post, which he organized to supplant the Royal Post Office System and which eventually became the U.S. Post Office. Starting with the first issue of the *Chronicle,* Goddard had instituted a system of postal riders. During the six months that he was simultaneously publishing the *Chronicle* in Philadelphia and the *Maryland Journal; and the Baltimore Advertiser* in Baltimore, which made its initial appearance on 20 August 1773, the riders between the two cities greatly concerned Goddard. Plotting a countrywide system of postriders on the order of the one he established between Philadelphia and Baltimore, the ever-restless printer closed down the *Chronicle* on 8 February 1774, turned over management of the *Journal* to Mary Katherine Goddard, who published the newspaper all during the revolutionary war. William, meanwhile, headed north to enlist support for his plan from the Committees of Correspondence. On 26 July 1775, because of Goddard's efforts, the Continental Congress adopted a postal system in defiance of the British. Goddard had expected to be appointed secretary and comptroller of the post office under the continuing leadership of Benjamin Franklin, but Franklin instead named his son-in-law Richard Bache to the position and made the disappointed Goddard surveyor of post roads.

Disputes seemed inevitable for Goddard throughout his career. In the spring of 1777, for example, the patriotic Whig Club of Baltimore bullied him for refusing to divulge the real name of the author of an article that ran in the *Journal.* In the summer of 1779 he withstood more public abuse for having published in the *Journal* a piece by the recently court-martialed General Charles Lee (1731–1782), so punished for his role in the battle of Monmouth in 1778, who had taken to writing in his own defense. Goddard married Abigail Angell of Providence in 1786, and the first of their five children to live to adulthood was born in 1790. William Goddard sold his interest in the Baltimore printing facility in 1792 to his partner, James Angell, his wife's younger brother, thereby ending a thirty-year career. Upon his death, in Providence, Goddard's only son, William Giles Goddard, wrote in his father's obituary: "The first years of his long life were passed amid the turmoil of useful activities—the last in the bosom of domestic quiet."

Goddard was an outstanding, if combative, newspaper editor, militant defender of freedom of the press, and, not least, founder of the nation's postal system. Shortly before the Revolution his *Pennsylvania Chronicle* had the largest circulation of any paper in the colonies; immediately thereafter his *Maryland Journal* had the largest circulation in the new nation. Goddard, according to friend and fellow printer Isaiah Thomas, was "ingenious and enterprising" as a printer, and "few could conduct a newspaper better" (*The History of Printing in America* [1970], p. 322).

• *The Partnership; or, The History of the Rise and Progress of the Pennsylvania Chronicle* (1770), is William Goddard's history of the newspaper, his partnership with Galloway and Wharton, and a refutation of their charges against him. Ward L. Miner, *William Goddard: Newspaperman* (1962), the standard biography, includes much on Goddard's mother and sister. Lawrence C. Wroth, *A History of Printing in Colonial Maryland, 1686–1776* (1922), an annotated bibliography of books, broadsides, and newspapers, includes biographical information on William and Mary Goddard. See also John E. Alden, *Rhode Island Imprints, 1727–1800* (1949), and Charles R. Hildeburn, *A Century of Printing: The Issues of the Press in Pennsylvania, 1685–1784* (2 vols., 1885–1886). Isaiah Thomas, *The History of Printing in America* (1810; 2d ed., 1874; repr. 1970), the standard reference on the colonial period, includes biographies of printers and accounts of newspapers in all colonies and some new states.

RICHARD F. HIXSON

GODEFROY, Maximilian (1765–7 Apr. 1848), architect, was born in Paris to a Hungarian father, Stephen Godefroy, and Marie Catherine Boulnez. Baptized Jean Maur, he assumed the name Maximilian during military service (1794–1795). His employment in engineering during the 1790s and his later use of literary quotations testify to a good education. His figural, landscape, and architectural compositions attest to training in drawing, and about 1802 he began to study architecture from books. Under suspicion of harboring thoughts inimical to the regime, he was held by Napoleon's secret police from September 1803 to March 1805, then released on condition of exile to the United States.

Godefroy reached New York City on 26 April 1805, soon moved to Philadelphia, and in December 1805 to Baltimore, where until 1817 he taught drawing, architecture, and military engineering at St. Mary's College. In March 1806 he designed and commenced construction of St. Mary's Chapel (1806–1808), the first Gothic Revival–style church in America. On 29 December 1808, he married Eliza Crawford Anderson, a writer and editor.

Although several of Godefroy's buildings of the next years have since been demolished, his gates and vaults (c. 1813–1815) for the First Presbyterian churchyard, Baltimore, and St. Thomas's Church (1812–1816) at Bardstown, Kentucky, still stand. As partial reward for his strengthening of Fort McHenry (1814), the city commissioned him to do the Battle Monument (1815–1825) to commemorate Baltimore's repulse of the British attack. Following an unsuccessful collaboration with Benjamin Henry Latrobe (1764–1820) on the latter's Merchants Exchange (1816–1822), Godefroy visited Richmond, Virginia, from July to September 1816, where he presented designs for a courthouse, a front uniting two banks, and landscaping around the state capitol, all now gone. Back in Baltimore, Godefroy raised the Unitarian Church (1817–1818) and began a wing on the Exchange for a Bank of the U.S. branch (1818–1819), which was completed by others and later demolished.

Godefroy introduced the United States to modern French Romantic Classicism, which conveyed allegorical meanings through architectural forms. The Gothic Revival, as it is used in St. Mary's Chapel, evokes mystical faith and the femininity of the Virgin. The Battle Monument possesses historicizing details popular around 1800: its tall base with Egyptian motifs commemorates those who fell in battle, a tall Roman fasces symbolizes unity, and a neoclassical figure represents victorious Baltimore. The plain walls and geometric shapes of the Unitarian Church—Greek cross plan, cubical body, hemispherical dome—derived from the French architecture that developed during the 1770s and 1780s, parallel with rationalist philosophy, making it an appropriate house for the modern intellectual religion.

Convinced that the depression of 1819 and the loss of political and economic power by his supporters left no prospects for employment, Godefroy sailed for England in 1819. His few works in London were destroyed during World War II. Returning to France in January 1827, he received an appointment at Rennes and for a year (1827–1828) carried out minor works. Named architect for the department, or administrative district, of Mayenne in 1828, he built an asylum, prefectural buildings, and a new wing for the Palais de Justice, all still standing.

Godefroy's letters reveal a passionate nature capable of sustaining bitter hatreds as well as warm long-term friendships. His wife's death in 1839 crushed him, and nine years later Godefroy died in Montmartre.

• Primary collections of Godefroy's letters, documents, and drawings are in the Maryland Historical Society, the Archives Nationales in Paris, and local archives in Rennes and Laval. See also Dorothy M. Quynn, "Maximilian and Eliza Godefroy," *Maryland Historical Magazine* 52 (1957): 1–34, and Robert L. Alexander, "The Drawings and Allegories of Maximilian Godefroy," *Maryland Historical Magazine* 53 (1958): 17–34, and *The Architecture of Maximilian Godefroy* (1974).

ROBERT L. ALEXANDER

GÖDEL, Kurt Friedrich (28 Apr. 1906–14 Jan. 1978), mathematical logician, was born of German-speaking parents in Brünn, Moravia, the son of Rudolf Gödel, a textile manufacturer, and Marianne Handschuh (also from a family engaged in the textile industry). As a child Gödel suffered from rheumatic fever. His early education was in a Lutheran school in Brünn, although his brother Rudolf later recalled that they were brought up as "freethinkers" and "had no proper relation to religion." Later, from 1916 until 1924, Gödel went to the German *Staats-Realgymnasium* (a government secondary school emphasizing technical subjects).

In 1924 Gödel entered the University of Vienna, where he initially studied physics. But he soon found that he preferred the exactness of mathematics and the clarity of logic. Among mathematicians at the university, Hans Hahn was the most influential on Gödel's mathematical future. Hahn introduced him to Moritz Schlick and the "Vienna Circle," a group of philosophers best known for their dedication to logical positivism. Ultimately, Gödel's own philosophical commitments diverged dramatically from those of the Vienna Circle, especially from this group's restriction of truth to probable, verifiable experience and the thesis that metaphysical problems are meaningless (Wang, p. 653). Nevertheless, when Schlick was assassinated by a Nazi student in 1936, Gödel (according to his brother) suffered a "nervous crisis."

Crucial to Gödel's development as a mathematician at this point in his career were lectures he heard in Vienna by Rudolph Carnap on mathematical logic, along with his reading of David Hilbert and Wilhelm Ackermann's *Grundzüge der theoretischen Logik* (1928; translated as *Principles of Mathematical Logic* in 1950), in which the completeness of the axioms for first-order predicate calculus (where quantifiers range over individuals rather than sets or relations) was raised as an open question. This became the subject of Gödel's dissertation, for which he received a Ph.D. in mathematics from the University of Vienna in 1929. Gödel's thesis, published in 1930, established that indeed the axioms for first-order predicate calculus were complete.

Gödel next set out to do the same for Hilbert's program in general, which sought to establish the consistency of mathematics itself, viewed as a formal system. To show the internal consistency of a formal system, it suffices to show that it does not contain two propositions P and not-P, one of which is the negation of the other (or a proposition from which *any* proposition can be derived). What Gödel eventually found was that any mathematical system containing arithmetic is incomplete—that it is possible to generate statements that cannot be proven to be either true or false. Gödel published his incompleteness results in 1931, and these became subjects of immediate mathematical interest. They also comprised his *Habilitationsschrift* (inaugural dissertation) in 1932, entitling him to teach as a Privatdozent at the University of Vienna.

In the late summer of 1933 Gödel sailed to the United States, where he was a visiting member of the Institute for Advanced Study at Princeton, New Jersey, then in its first year of operation. Away from family and friends, he apparently suffered psychologically, and on his return to Vienna, in 1934, he spent several months in a mental hospital recovering from a nervous breakdown. A second visit to Princeton in the fall of 1935 ended in another mental breakdown.

Meanwhile, Gödel began to concentrate on one of the major open problems in mathematics, Georg Cantor's Continuum Hypothesis, intimately related to the Axiom of Choice. Finally, he succeeded in 1937 in establishing the consistency not only of the Axiom of Choice but of the Continuum Hypothesis as well (within the framework of Zermelo-Fraenkel axiomatic set theory, a version of set theory based on axioms first introduced by Ernst Zermelo in 1908 and later modified by Abraham Fraenkel in 1922).

Cantor, the founder of transfinite set theory, defined the first transfinite cardinal number $\aleph_0$ (aleph-null) as the cardinal number representing the number of elements in "denumerably infinite sets" like the set of all integers N. He also showed in 1884 that the set of all real numbers R (which includes the rational and irrational numbers) was of a greater order of infinity than N. Cantor's famous Continuum Hypothesis is the conjecture that R indeed represented the next largest infinite set, that there was *no* set X whose cardinality was greater than that of N but less than R. Although Cantor was never able to prove this conjecture, it was closely related to another proposition that every set, including R, can be well ordered (i.e., counted, or arranged in a definite sequence). This was proved by Zermelo in 1904, but the argument Zermelo used depended on another controversial assumption, the Axiom of Choice, which asserts that for any collection of sets it is possible to pick arbitrarily a representative element from each member of the collection.

In 1938 Gödel married dancer Adele Nimbursky; they had no children. That same year Gödel made his third visit to the Institute for Advanced Study, where he presented his major findings related to the consistency of the Continuum Hypothesis and the Axiom of Choice. By the time he returned to Vienna the following year, World War II was looming on the European horizon. Threatened with induction into the army and uncertain about the stability of his position at the University of Vienna under the Nazis, Gödel obtained visas for the United States. Given the dangers of transatlantic travel, however, the Gödels took the Trans-Siberian Railway across Asia. From Japan they sailed for San Francisco and eventually arrived in Princeton by train in March 1940.

Having established the consistency of both the Continuum Hypothesis and the Axiom of Choice, Gödel concentrated his first efforts at the institute on trying to show that they were also independent, results that only in 1963 were successfully established by Paul Cohen of Stanford University. At about this same time, Gödel's interests began to change, turning increasingly from mathematics toward equally esoteric philosophical issues. In 1944 he published a study of Bertrand Russell's mathematical logic in which he also made clear his own views on the foundations of mathematics. Basically, Gödel favored a version of Platonism that affirmed the abstract reality of mathematics, a view that he later explained in a major popular article about his philosophy of mathematics in the *American Mathematical Monthly* (1947).

From 1947 to 1951 Gödel began to toy with cosmological models in which time was bi-directional, that is, mathematically, time travel back into the past and forward into the future was assumed to be logically possible. Surprisingly, by his own account, this work was not motivated by discussions of relativity theory with his colleague at the institute, Albert Einstein, but by Gödel's interest in Immanuel Kant's views on space and time (Wang, p. 658). Related to this work, he lectured on "Rotating Universes in General Relativity Theory" at the International Congress of Mathematicians held at Harvard University in 1950.

Among the many awards conferred on Gödel after the war was the first Einstein Award in 1951 (which he received jointly with Julian Schwinger, the American theoretical physicist who, noted for his contributions to quantum mechanics, won the Nobel Prize in physics in 1965 for his work on quantum electrodynamics). Gödel was elected to membership in the National Academy of Sciences in 1955, the American Academy of Arts and Sciences in 1957, and the Royal Society of London in 1968. He was also a corresponding member of the Institut de France (elected in 1972) but declined honorary membership in the Austrian Academy of Sciences when it was offered in 1966. Gödel was awarded the U.S. National Medal of Science in 1975.

By then, Gödel's health had become increasingly precarious, made worse by his hypochondria and distrust of doctors. Incredibly, he kept meticulous records of the fluctuations of his body temperature and could often be seen at the institute, even on the warmest days, bundled up in a thick black coat. He refused surgery for a prostate condition and was fanatic about maintaining a very restricted diet, fearful that he was in danger of being poisoned. When his wife Adele suffered a mild stroke in 1977 and entered a nursing home, Gödel's depression intensified, and he became dangerously reclusive. Eventually Gödel was admitted to the Princeton Hospital, where he died, according to his death certificate, of "malnutrition and inanition [exhaustion and a general lack of strength] caused by personality disturbance."

Kurt Gödel revolutionized logic and made some of the most fundamental contributions to the foundations of mathematics in the twentieth century. He not only showed how to prove the completeness of first order logic but established the incompleteness of number theory (as well as higher mathematical systems). He also demonstrated the consistency of both the Continuum Hypothesis and the Axiom of Choice (within the context of axiomatic set theory). Philosophically, however, his views have been of more limited impact. Basically, Gödel was an adamant defender of Platonism (also known as "mathematical realism"), which holds that mathematical objects exist independently of the human mind, having a real, abstract existence of their own; Platonists also believe that even infinite collections may be considered as completed, self-contained, mathematically consistent totalities.

Although he was essentially a solitary figure and never enjoyed the influence that greater contact with students might have ensured, Gödel did attract the most promising and gifted logicians to the Institute for Advanced Study, which has served to stimulate the further development of mathematical logic both in the United States and internationally. As Stanford University mathematical logician Solomon Feferman has emphasized, Gödel's "were among the most outstanding contributions to logic in this century, decisively settling fundamental problems and introducing novel and powerful methods that were exploited extensively in much subsequent work" (p. 32).

• Gödel's papers, including correspondence, drafts of papers, and other miscellanea, are in the archives of Firestone Library, Princeton University, and may be used with the permission of the Institute for Advanced Study. Among Gödel's own publications, four are translated from the German in Jean van Heijenoort, *From Frege to Gödel: A Source Book in Mathematical Logic, 1879–1931* (1967), pp. 582–617 (with historico-critical introductions and notes by van Heijenoort). See also works by Gödel translated in Martin Davis, ed., *The Undecidable* (1965), in addition to Gödel's *The Consistency of the Continuum Hypothesis* (1940) and "What Is Cantor's Continuum Problem?" *American Mathematical Monthly* 54 (1947): 515–25. A useful overview of Gödel's publications is John Dawson, "The Published Work of Kurt Gödel: An Annotated Bibliography," *Notre Dame Journal of Formal Logic* 24 (1983): 255–84, and 25 (1984): 283–87. The most authoritative biographical study is Solomon Feferman's introduction, "Gödel's Life and Work," to vol. 1 of Gödel's *Collected Works* (1986), pp. 1–36 (followed by "A Gödel Chronology" by Dawson, pp. 37–43). See also Georg Kreisel, "Kurt Gödel," *Biographical Memoirs of Fellows of the Royal Society* 26 (1980): 149–224, 27 (1981): 697, and 28 (1982): 718. For additional technical reading, see Paul Cohen, "The Independence of the Continuum Hypothesis," *Proceedings of the National Academy of Science* 50 (1963): 1143–48, and 51 (1964): 105–10, as well as Cohen's "Comments on the Foundations of Set Theory," *Proceedings of the Symposium on Pure Mathematics* 13 (1971): 9–15. Reminiscences by Rudolf Gödel, "History of the Gödel Family," and by Olga Taussky-Todd, "Remembrances of Kurt Gödel," are both in *Gödel Remembered*, ed. Paul Weingartner and Leopold Schmetterer (1987). For additional historical studies see John W. Dawson, Jr., "Kurt Gödel in Sharper Focus," *Mathematical Intelligencer* 6 (1984): 9–17, as well as Hao Wang, "Some Facts about Kurt Gödel," *Journal of Symbolic Logic* 46 (1981): 643–59, and *Reflections on Kurt Gödel* (1987).

JOSEPH W. DAUBEN

GODEY, Louis Antoine (6 June 1804–29 Nov. 1878), editor and publisher, was born in New York City, the son of Louis Godey and Margaret Carel, French immigrants with Royalist sympathies who fled to America during the French Revolution. His family had little means to provide formal education, and Godey was primarily self-taught, gaining significant training in writing and editing through newspaper work.

At the age of fifteen Goden became self-supporting, having used his savings to open a newsstand and bookstore. In the late 1820s he moved to Philadelphia, where he worked for two years on a newspaper, first in the composing room, later in the business office. In 1830 he began to publish, in partnership with Charles Alexander, the *Lady's Book*, a magazine for which he also served as editor. It featured fashion discussions and engravings, as well as stories and poems. Much of the material that appeared in this magazine was reprinted from British periodicals, since no international copyright existed to discourage such practices. In 1833 Godey married Maria Catherine Duke of New York; they lived in Philadelphia with their five children.

Godey's career as publisher and entrepreneur expanded in 1837 when he purchased the *Ladies Magazine* from Sarah Josepha Hale of Boston, incorporating it into his own publication. He persuaded Hale to continue as editor of the new publication, and together they launched the most successful magazine of the nineteenth century. Godey discontinued the practice of reprinting primarily British selections and instead solicited work from American authors. He attracted contributions from almost all the major writers of his day, including Ralph Waldo Emerson, Nathaniel Hawthorne, Henry Wadsworth Longfellow, Edgar Allan Poe, and Oliver Wendell Holmes, by paying them generously and consistently for their work. In addition, Hale, who crusaded for women's education in her editorials, published leading women writers of the day such as Anne Stephens, Caroline Lee Hentz, Lydia Sigourney, Catherine Sedgwick, and the young Harriet Beecher Stowe. Much of the work that appeared in the magazine, renamed *Godey's Lady's Book* in 1840, was sentimental and emphasized moral themes, which appealed to its primarily female audience. The magazine reflected and supported the ideals of the "Cult of True Womanhood," featuring stories of piety and maternal responsibility, as well as illustrations that depicted women in genteel domestic settings. Godey himself claimed that his *Lady's Book* "brought unalloyed pleasure to the female mind," and its circulation reached 150,000 copies before the outbreak of the Civil War.

The success of *Godey's Lady's Book* made it a model for other magazines, including its two biggest competitors, *Graham's Magazine* before the Civil War and later *Peterson's National Ladies Magazine*. It also shaped middle-class tastes in literature, fashion, art, and music. An important feature of the magazine, its hand-colored fashion plates were prized by readers; Godey sent his fashion artists to Paris and other European capitals for inspiration. Some of the plates they designed were offered as premiums for subscription drives, and many were colored by young women doing work at home. The engravings, many depicting children or a mother and children, were also popular features.

Godey was a self-promoter of the first order and regularly used his own column in the magazine to apprise readers of the magazine's success. In his column he also answered readers' mail, addressed their concerns and circumstances, offered advice, and created a sympathetic bond with his subscribers. Godey's paternalistic attitude toward his readers also led him to omit material he thought unsuitable, including discussions of political strife and any mention of the Civil War. Godey claimed that it was his "business and pleasure to please [the ladies]," but he was also an innovator in publishing practices. In 1845 he was one of the first to copyright his magazine, incurring the wrath of many other magazine and newspaper publishers who had been accustomed to reprinting work from *Godey's* without penalty. He also sought a national audience for his periodical before nationwide channels of distribution were facilitated by the railroad. Godey and his sons published the *Lady's Book*, with Sarah Hale as editor, until 1877. After Godey and Hale retired, Godey's sons reorganized management and the editorial

staff to combat declining circulation, but they lost ground to their competitors as audience preferences and journalistic practices changed. In 1883 the Godeys sold the magazine to J. H. Haulenbeck, but he, too, was unable to revive its popularity. The magazine changed ownership several times in the course of fifteen years; its last issue appeared in August 1898, after which it was merged with Frank Munsey's *Puritan*.

In addition to his most successful venture, Godey also published the *Saturday News and Literary Gazette*, a weekly magazine begun in 1836 in partnership with Joseph Neal and Morton McMichael. With McMichael, he also published the *Young People's Book, or Magazine of Useful and Entertaining Knowledge* in 1841 and the *Lady's Musical Library* in 1842; he held financial interests in the *Lady's Dollar Newspaper*, edited by Grace Greenwood, and between 1852 and 1867 in *Arthur's Home Magazine*.

Throughout his life Godey enjoyed travel and social interaction; he made three trips to Europe and counted among his friends many authors and public figures. He was described as susceptible to flattery, but Poe said of him, "No man [had] warmer friends or fewer enemies." In his later years, declining health caused Godey to winter in St. Augustine, Florida. He died at home in Philadelphia, leaving an estate worth more than one million dollars accrued entirely from his publishing enterprises. As publisher of *Godey's Lady's Book*, he profoundly influenced the tastes and values of middle-class women in nineteenth-century America while furthering innovations in magazine publishing. A friend of P. T. Barnum, Godey shared a talent for promoting his own ventures and pleasing his audience; during his lifetime, his name was literally a household word.

• Two sources of biographical information are Frank Luther Mott, *A History of American Magazines*, vol. 1, *1741–1850* (1930), and Ruth Finley, *The Lady of Godey's: Sarah Josepha Hale* (1931). For commentary on *Godey's Lady's Book*, see Laura McCall, "'The Reign of Brute Force Is Now Over': A Content Analysis of *Godey's Lady's Book*," *Journal of the Early Republic* 9 (1989): 217–36; Isabelle Lehuu, "Sentimental Figures: Reading *Godey's Lady's Book* in Antebellum America," in *The Culture of Sentiment: Race, Gender and Sentimentality in Nineteenth-Century America*, ed. Shirley Samuels (1992); and Nicole Tonkovich, "Rhetorical Power in the Victorian Parlor: *Godey's Lady's Book* and the Gendering of Nineteenth-Century Rhetoric," in *Oratorical Culture in Nineteenth-Century America*, ed. Gregory Clark and Michael S. Halloran (1993). Obituaries are in the *New York Times* and the *Philadelphia Inquirer*, 30 Nov. 1878.

MELISSA MCFARLAND PENNELL

GODFREY, Arthur (31 Aug. 1903–16 Mar. 1983), broadcaster, was born in New York City, the son of Arthur Hanbury Godfrey, a writer and lecturer, and Kathryn Morton. He was raised on the streets of the city's Irish-American ghettos. Following the death of his father, Godfrey left school at age fifteen. He traveled across the country for three years, working as a truck driver, an office boy, and a coal miner. He later recalled having earned his diploma in "the school of hard knocks" during this period. He joined the navy in 1921, serving as a radio operator until his discharge in 1924. He returned to civilian life still unsure of what he wanted to do with his future. Once again he drifted from one job to the next. He had a natural affinity for sales, and one of the jobs he took, selling cemetery plots, provided him with commissions of approximately $10,000. He had taken up the banjo while still in the navy; eager to perform, he invested this bankroll in a vaudeville troupe that went under in California in 1927. Broke, Godfrey hitched a ride to Chicago. One of the fares he picked up while driving a cab there was a shipmate from his navy days who had just enlisted in the Coast Guard. With nothing more promising before him, Godfrey enlisted as well.

Subsequent to his tour in the Coast Guard, Godfrey entered the radio business in 1929 as "Red Godfrey, the Warbling Banjoist" at WFBR, an NBC affiliate in Baltimore, Maryland. Sponsored by the Triangle Pet Shop account, he earned five dollars per show. He became an announcer on NBC's local Washington, D.C., staff a year later. In 1931 he was hospitalized after a head-on collision with a truck that immobilized him for six months. Godfrey later credited this hospitalization with enabling him to have such a long career in broadcasting. He had nothing with which to amuse himself but radio, and he decided that much of what was broadcast, particularly the advertising that was financing the shows, was too arch and formal. He changed announcing jobs in 1933, moving across town to CBS's WJSV (later WTOP) and beginning an association with that network that would last for decades.

Godfrey lobbied for a position at CBS headquarters in New York, finally getting his chance on the variety show "Manhattan Pee-rade" after famed gossip columnist Walter Winchell gave Godfrey's Washington show attention in his column. Godfrey was a success, but "Manhattan Pee-rade" was a failure. In 1941 a New York station later known as WCBS began carrying his Washington broadcasts. This attracted the attention of network executives, and on 4 October 1942, after some eighteen months of New York exposure, he made his national debut as an announcer on Fred Allen's "The Texaco Star Theater"—only to be dropped in mid-November. Undeterred, Godfrey offered himself freelance for any CBS assignment that might give him air time nationally. His big break came on 14 April 1945, when he was assigned to cover the funeral of President Franklin D. Roosevelt. He did the broadcast tearfully, as if his voice and sentiment were perfectly in tune with a mourning America.

Within days, Godfrey was made a part of CBS's daytime lineup. On 30 April 1945 the morning show "Arthur Godfrey Time" premiered. During the next three years he added local shows to his repertoire, doing three daily shows in all: his network performance, an early-morning show that WCBS broadcast for the metropolitan New York audience, and a repeat of that broadcast for WTOP in Washington, D.C. He rapidly became one of the highest paid radio entertainers in the country. His often-repeated boast that he made

hundreds of thousands of dollars each morning before most workingmen got to their offices was an exaggeration, but not by much. He was behind a microphone some fifteen hours each week, reaching an estimated 40 million listeners. Such a following led CBS to move him into prime time through a weekly nighttime show, "Arthur Godfrey's Talent Scouts." Sponsored by Lipton Tea, the show was broadcast first on Tuesday nights, then, beginning in its second season, on Mondays. The overhead was low, the revenue was substantial, and the concept was simple: important show business "scouts" brought young professional entertainers to America's attention. A studio audience chose their favorite through applause. The favorite then appeared on Godfrey's morning show for the rest of the week. Within weeks of its premiere the show found—and later held—its place among the top twenty broadcasts in the nation.

Godfrey came to television in the 1948–1949 season on 12 January 1949 with "Arthur Godfrey and His Friends," a blend of talk show and variety formats. He also did its companion show, "Arthur Godfrey's Talent Scouts," each Monday night. The first ran from January 1949 through June 1957 from 8:00 to 9:00 P.M. each Wednesday; from September 1958 to April 1959 it was shortened to half an hour, airing each Tuesday from 9:00 to 9:30 P.M. "Talent Scouts" was the number one–rated show in the 1951–1952 season; the next season, "Talent Scouts" and "Friends" were numbers two and three in the country respectively, bettered only by "I Love Lucy." For almost nine full seasons, Godfrey had the singular distinction of two top-rated programs running in prime time simultaneously, with the slightly more popular "Talent Scouts" feeding "Arthur Godfrey and His Friends." He returned to radio after his television shows were finally canceled ("Talent Scouts" in 1958, "Friends" in 1959), continuing his morning broadcasts until his retirement on 30 April 1972.

Godfrey was a wealthy retiree with a variety of interests. Some of them were socially conscious, such as his work for land conservation and ecology, and others were more personal, such as aviation (he was an avid helicopter pilot). But he was restless in retirement. Despite recurring respiratory problems that left him worn and depleted, he continued to do commercials, and until his final months he spoke of returning to the limelight. He died in New York City.

It is perhaps fitting that Godfrey's last appearances were in commercials. Long before he came to broadcasting, he had made his living as a salesman, and as a salesman through the nation's mass media he was top-drawer. He is often mistakenly remembered for mocking his sponsors' products, particularly on radio. There were a few radio personalities who specialized in belittling the products they peddled, most notably Henry Morgan, but Godfrey was not one of them. What Godfrey did mock was the timbre and tone of broadcast advertising, something that occurred to him early in his career during his convalescence from his automobile accident. Much of the advertising copy he listened to on radio struck him as being insincere and cloying. One of the first things he did when he returned to the air was to mock a moth-eaten stuffed bear that stood in front of the store of a furrier who sponsored him. The sponsor was angry until his sales soared.

This suggests what set Godfrey apart from his contemporaries. Godfrey could not sing, dance, act, or tell a joke, and while much has been made of "the old redhead's" charm, there were personalities more charming than his. Nevertheless, he became one of the most popular broadcasters of his generation—and deservedly so. Godfrey was one of the first broadcasters to appreciate that radio and television were not simply a poor man's version of stage and screen; they were more intimate media with dynamics all their own, and it followed that they invited a more personal relationship between performer and fan. Perhaps Godfrey explained the difference most succinctly. There was no "radio audience," no "ladies and gentlemen," he insisted, but just two people in the room: he and his listener. "If the audience is Ladies and Gentlemen," Godfrey explained, "they have better things to do than hear me on the radio."

• The most complete and accessible of Godfrey's television work is found at the Museum of Broadcasting Library in New York City. The most memorable of his radio shows are at the Motion Picture, Broadcasting, and Recorded Sound Division of the Library of Congress in Washington, D.C. Tim Brooks and Earle Marsh, *The Complete Directory to Prime Time Network TV Shows, 1946–Present* (1979), offers useful information on Godfrey's television career: For his much more prominent radio career, see John Dunning, *Tune in Yesterday* (1976).

JAY BOYER

GODFREY, Thomas (10 Jan. 1704–Dec. 1749), glazier, mathematician, and astronomer, was born in Bristol Township, Pennsylvania, the son of Joseph Godfrey, a farmer and maltster, and Catherine (maiden name unknown). His father died when he was one year old; his mother later remarried, and at the age of twelve Thomas was apprenticed to a glazier. When he came of age in 1725, he inherited his father's property in Bristol; at this time he established himself in business in Philadelphia, adding the sideline of plumber to his trade of glazier. He glazed windows for the state house in 1732 and 1733 and later for Andrew Hamilton's residence at Bush Hill. He also served as one of the city's "measurers of superfices," supervising the digging and removal of earth in public projects.

Becoming greatly interested in mathematics during his apprenticeship, Godfrey taught himself with borrowed books. He became acquainted with Benjamin Franklin, and seeking others with similar interests, in 1727 he joined the Leathern Apron Club (also known as the Junto), founded by Franklin. He later was closely associated with Franklin as a founding member of the Library Company of Philadelphia, the American Philosophical Society, the Pennsylvania Hospital, and the Philadelphia Contributionship, a fire insurance

company. When Franklin and his partner Hugh Meredith established their printing shop in lower Market Street in 1728, Franklin rented part of the building's first floor to Godfrey for his glazier's shop and the upper floor for his family, where the Godfreys provided Franklin and Meredith with room and board. Godfrey compiled the ephemerides for Franklin's new single-sheet almanac "in the London manner" for the years 1729 to 1731, but from 1732, following a domestic quarrel with Franklin, Godfrey compiled ephemerides for almanacs published by William Bradford.

In addition to pursuing his trade, Godfrey was constantly involved in scientific activities in his community. As Franklin later wrote in his autobiography, Godfrey "worked little, being always absorbed in his mathematics." Godfrey's subsequent career was strongly influenced by wealthy Quaker merchant James Logan, former secretary to William Penn, whom he first met while glazing the windows of the Logan residence at Stenton. Logan became interested in the self-taught man and lent him Isaac Newton's *Principia* and other scientific works.

Godfrey's fame rests on his invention of the octant. Although his circumstances rendered him remote from maritime problems, he is traditionally claimed to have been given to intemperance and to frequenting waterfront taverns. From discussions with seamen he met there, he became familiar with navigational problems. One day while working at Stenton, he observed the double reflection from a piece of glass that had fallen and realized that by means of reflection, it would be possible to draw the image of the sun down to the horizon. Accordingly, he designed an instrument for observing the altitude of the sun or a star from a moving ship at sea, by means of which it was possible to establish the ship's latitude. According to surviving documents, in late October 1730 Godfrey borrowed a backstaff from his acquaintance George Steward, mate on the sloop *Trueman*, and temporarily attached several pieces of wood and mirror to create a new instrument, which tested successfully. He had a working model made from his design by a fellow worker at the state house, house carpenter Edmund Woolley. The instrument, taken to sea by Steward and the *Trueman*'s shipmaster John Cox, was tested successfully on voyages to Jamaica in November and December and to St. John's, Newfoundland, in February 1731. Godfrey's reflecting quadrant—or octant, as it was later named—was commercially produced and sold in New York during the next few years by Godfrey's acquaintance, mathematical instrument-maker Anthony Lamb.

Logan, greatly impressed with the invention, in 1732 reported it to Edmund Halley, president of the Royal Society of London. At about the same time, however, the society's vice president, John Hadley, announced his claim to the same invention. He demonstrated his instrument before the society and had it patented. Logan's letter was received but not acknowledged, and later that year Godfrey addressed a letter to the society on his own behalf. Godfrey's letter and Logan's earlier letter were read before the society on 31 January 1733 and recorded in its *Minutes* but not otherwise acknowledged. Godfrey's report to the Royal Society of improvements he had made in another navigational instrument, the mariner's bow, was published in its *Philosophical Transactions* but not his description of his octant. His invention, however, is now acknowledged to have been made independently, almost simultaneously with Hadley's invention, or possibly slightly before it.

In October 1740 Godfrey began to teach classes in navigation and astronomy at his home during the winter months. He was also actively engaged with local surveyors, making observations of occultations and eclipses of Jupiter's satellites for fixing meridians for maps. In 1748 or 1749, shortly before his death, Godfrey employed his instrument for making astronomical observations at Cape Henlopen and Pea Patch Island, working with Philadelphia merchant Joshua Fisher, who recorded the observations on the chart of Delaware Bay and Delaware River that he published in 1756. In July 1748 Godfrey published his calculations for a forthcoming eclipse of the sun in *Bradford's Journal*, stating, "As Eclipses of the Sun are useful in determining the Difference of Longitude of Places, if accurately observed, the following Calculations may perhaps be an agreeable Amusement to your Astronomical Readers."

Godfrey died in Philadelphia, survived by his wife and two sons. (The date of their marriage and her name are not recorded.) Godfrey's obituary notice, probably written by Franklin, appeared in Franklin's *Pennsylvania Gazette* on 19 December 1749, describing him as having "an uncommon Genius for all kinds of *Mathematical Learning*, with which he was extremely well acquainted. He invented the New Reflecting Quadrant, used in Navigation."

• Godfrey's life and career are described in John Fanning Watson, *Annals of Philadelphia and Pennsylvania, in the Olden Time: Being a Collection of Memoirs, Anecdotes, and Incidents of the City and Its Inhabitants* (1898), vol. 1, pp. 530–31, and vol. 2, p. 474; H. Hastings Weld, *Benjamin Franklin, His Autobiography: With a Narrative of His Public Life and Services* (1859), pp. 104n, 116–17; "Letters Colonial and Revolutionary," *Pennsylvania Magazine of History and Biography* 42 (1918): 75; and "Early Documents of the Library Company of Philadelphia 1733–1734," *Pennsylvania Magazine of History and Biography* 39, no. 1 (1915): 450–53. Godfrey's mathematical and astronomical activities are reported in the *Pennsylvania Gazette*, 15 Dec. 1730, and *Bradford's Journal*, 7 July 1748, and described in Harrold L. Gillingham, "Some Early Philadelphia Instrument Makers," *Pennsylvania Magazine of History and Biography* 51, no. 3 (1927): 291–93; George H. Sargent, "Almanacs with the Flight of Time," *Antiques*, July 1922, pp. 33–35; and Frederick B. Tolles, *James Logan and the Culture of Provincial America* (1957), pp. 202–5, 213. Godfrey's claim to the invention of the octant is discussed in the *Philosophical Transactions of the Royal Society* 7 (1733–1734): 441–50, 669–73; the anonymously written "On the Invention of What Is Called Hadley's Quadrant," *American Magazine and Monthly Chronicle* 1 (July 1758): 475–80, 527–

34; Thomas Coulson, "Godfrey's Invention of the Reflecting Quadrant," *Journal of the Franklin Institute* 266, no. 5 (Nov. 1958): 336–37; and Silvio A. Bedini, "At the Sign of the Compass and Quadrant: The Life and Times of Anthony Lamb," *Transactions of the American Philosophical Society* 74, pt. 1 (1984): 37–47.

SILVIO A. BEDINI

GODFREY, Thomas (4 Dec. 1736–3 Aug. 1763), poet and playwright, was born in Philadelphia, Pennsylvania, the son of Thomas Godfrey, a glazier, and his wife, whose name is unknown. The senior Godfrey was a member of Benjamin Franklin's Junto and one of the inventors of the navigator's quadrant, but at his death in 1749 his son was apprenticed to a watchmaker. However, with his gift for verse, he soon attracted the notice of William Smith (1727–1803), the energetic provost of the new College, Academy, and Charitable School of Philadelphia, who in effect became his patron. Smith obtained Godfrey's release from his indenture to the watchmaker, praised his "pertinacity in acquiring knowledge," and introduced him to a talented company of young writers and artists in Philadelphia, including Benjamin West (1738–1820), Nathaniel Evans, Francis Hopkinson, and Jacob Duché. Although records to prove his attendance do not survive, Godfrey may have studied at either the charitable school or the academy in order to improve on his earlier education. He certainly profited from the tutelage of Smith and from his friendship with one of the most important literary coteries in 1750s America. Smith encouraged his writing, publishing some of his poems in 1758 in the *American Magazine*, which he edited, and fostered a public milieu in which Godfrey and other young writers could exercise their talents. Godfrey may have participated in Smith's 1756 production of *The Masque of Alfred*, which included music by his friend Hopkinson and may have stimulated his ambition to write a play of his own.

Godfrey's friends often viewed him as a poet of native ability rather than as a writer polished by a formal education; introducing the poems in the posthumous 1765 collection of Godfrey's work, *Juvenile Poems on Various Subjects*, Nathaniel Evans described him as a "natural genius struggling over all obstacles and soaring, by starts, into the brightest tracts of Poesy." Godfrey was not a graduate of Smith's schools, but in 1758 Smith helped him obtain a commission as an ensign in the Pennsylvania militia. Although he took part in the campaign against Fort Duquesne, the main action passed him by as he spent most of his service in the frontier garrison of Fort Henry. However, he apparently made the acquaintance of some of the North Carolinians serving in the campaign, and at its close in 1759 he took a position as a factor in Wilmington, North Carolina. When the merchant who employed him died, he made a voyage between Philadelphia and New Providence Island as a supercargo, before returning to Wilmington. Distance from his friends seems to have stimulated his commitment both to the theme of friendship and to the power of the imagination. His

1758 "Ode on Friendship" and "Epistle to a Friend: From Fort Henry" as well as drinking songs like the "Dithyrambic on Wine" exemplify his poetry of sociability. Firm in the belief that humans are social animals, eighteenth-century writers like Godfrey developed a public sphere in which the pleasures of conversation became a central feature of civic life. Such sociability is the subject of one of his last poems in which he invited his North Carolina friends to escape from Wilmington's heat to "Masonborough's grove, . . . Where blooming Innocence and Love, / And Pleasure crown the day." His taste for conviviality may have led to his death; on a hot day in 1763 he rode out with a friend into the country where he caught the fever to which he succumbed in Wilmington a few days later.

While in Wilmington he also published *The Court of Fancy*, a poem celebrating Fancy's warrant to the poet to use Truth, Beauty, Nature, and Art against such forces of Delusion as Superstition, Affectation, Flattery, and Spleen. In this poem, based on Chaucer's *House of Fame* and Pope's redaction of it, "The Temple of Fame," as well as in his "Assembly of Birds," based on Chaucer's *Parlement of Foules*, Godfrey became the first American poet to show a Chaucerian influence, reaching beyond the conventions of eighteenth-century verse. *The Court of Fancy* attracted favorable attention beyond the circle of his own coterie that undoubtedly helped justify the posthumous publication of his writing.

His most important work in these years, however, was his play, *The Prince of Parthia*, which he began in Pennsylvania and completed in Wilmington in the hope that it would be staged in Philadelphia by David Douglass's American Company, a group of professional actors. In a letter to William Smith of 17 November 1759 Godfrey feared correctly that his manuscript would arrive too late for that season, but when Douglass returned to Philadelphia several years later to play in the Southwark theater, he produced *The Prince of Parthia* on 24 April 1767, four years after its author's death. Godfrey's play became the first tragedy by a native-born author to be staged professionally, and it is one of a handful of eighteenth-century American plays to be performed again in the twentieth century. Godfrey's most direct models were Joseph Addison's *Cato* and, especially, Nicholas Rowe's *Tamerlane*, and, like theirs, his verse tragedy combined heroic oratory, patriotic sentiment, and Whig ideology as it explored a complex plot of love, treachery, and virtue in ancient Parthia. Godfrey's play holds its own in comparison to other examples of eighteenth-century verse tragedy, but none of them have shown much appeal to audiences or readers of later centuries. After Godfrey's death his poetry and his play were collected by his friend Nathaniel Evans and published in 1765 under the title *Juvenile Poems on Various Subjects. With the Prince of Parthia, a Tragedy*. Although Godfrey's poetry demonstrates some talent for exploring the possibilities of the poetic language of his time, it is probably more interesting for its ambition than for its accomplishment. *The Prince of Parthia*, however, a serious play written for a professional company, is a landmark in the development of early American theater.

• The best biographic account of Godfrey is in Archibald Henderson's introduction to his edition of *The Prince of Parthia, a Tragedy* (1917). Thomas Clark Pollock, "Rowe's *Tamerlane* and *The Prince of Parthia*," *American Literature* 6 (1934): 158–62, and Henry Bosley Woolf, "Thomas Godfrey: Eighteenth-Century Chaucerian," *American Literature* 12 (1941): 486–90, discuss Godfrey's literary antecedents. C. Lennart Carlson, "Thomas Godfrey in England," *American Literature* 7 (1935): 302–09, examines his recognition in British magazines of the time. Walter J. Meserve, *An Emerging Entertainment: The Drama of the American People to 1828* (1977), discusses Godfrey's play and its place in the history of American drama, and the fullest treatment of the play is Frank Shuffelton, "The Voice of History: Thomas Godfrey's *Prince of Parthia* and the American Revolution," *Early American Literature* 13 (1978): 12–23. Also useful is William McCarron's introduction to *A Bicentennial Edition of Thomas Godfrey's "The Prince of Parthia"* (1976).

FRANK SHUFFELTON

GODFROY, Francis (Mar. 1788–1 May 1840), Miami war chief also known as Palonzwah, civil chief, and entrepreneur, was born François Godfroy near Fort Wayne, Indiana, the son of Jacques Godfroy, a French trader, and a Miami woman (name unknown). Godfroy was reared at Kekionga, the Miami village near modern-day Fort Wayne. He married Sacachequah, a Miami woman, around 1809 and took a second wife, Sackahquettah, during the 1820s. The marriages produced at least nine children.

Although he was rumored to have fought at the battle of the Tippecanoe (7 Nov. 1811), there is little evidence to substantiate such a claim. He did take an active role at the Battle of the Mississinewa (18 Dec. 1812), in which he rallied Miami warriors and forced an American expedition led by Colonel John B. Campbell to abandon its campaign against Miami villages and retreat back into Ohio.

In the quarter-century after the War of 1812, Godfroy was closely associated with Jean Baptiste Richardville, another Miami metis civil chief and entrepreneur. In 1818, at the Treaty of St. Mary's, the U.S. government granted Godfroy six sections of land on the Salamonie River, where he established and operated a trading post until 1836. In the mid-1820s he opened another post on tribal land along the Wabash, near the mouth of the Mississinewa. At this second location Godfroy dominated the Indian trade in the region and, with federal assistance, later erected a large, two-storied, well-furnished frame house and extensive outbuildings. Called "Mount Pleasant," Godfroy's estate became famous as a center for both commerce and hospitality throughout northern Indiana.

Although the Miamis ceded most of their remaining tribal lands to the federal government at a series of treaties between 1826 and 1838, Godfroy used his influence with federal Indian agents to obtain additional sections of land for himself and for his children. He also purchased land from other Miamis, which he farmed or resold at a profit. In 1837 federal officials acknowledged that Godfroy, Richardville, and Metchinequa (a chief from the Eel River) were "the legitimate Chiefs whose authority is universally acknowledged by the Miamis. . . . Any agreement entered into by the above will be implicitly conformed to by the tribe." Godfroy died near Peru, Indiana, six months prior to the treaty (28 Nov. 1840) in which the Miamis agreed to remove west to Kansas (the 1840 treaty awarded his heirs an additional $15,000). The treaty also exempted them from removal and promised that although they remained in Indiana, they would receive their proportion of all Miami annuities.

Godfroy exemplifies the complexities of the mixed-blood or metis leadership that emerged among the eastern tribes in the years following the War of 1812. Unquestionably he cooperated with federal officials in the cession of Miami lands, and he used his position as a trader and mediator to increase his own personal wealth and influence. Yet he was renowned for his generosity, providing food and shelter to all Miamis or other travelers who visited his estate. Described by George Winter in correspondence as an imposing physical presence ("over six feet in height, and weighs about three hundred pounds"), Godfroy functioned as a "village chief," sharing much of his wealth with his followers. Ironically, after 1840 many of the Miamis who refused to remove or who returned to Indiana from Kansas were given refuge on the private lands still held by Godfroy's heirs along the Wabash. The descendants of these refugees, in addition to Godfroy's and Richardville's heirs, form the nucleus of the modern Miami population in Indiana.

• There is no collection of Godfroy's private papers, although correspondence regarding him can be found in the National Archives, RG 75, Letters Received by the Office of Indian Affairs (M234), Fort Wayne Agency, Indiana Agency, and Miami Agency. Also see Nellie A. Robertson and Dorothy Riker, eds., *The John Tipton Papers*, vols. 14, 15, and 16 of the *Indiana Historical Collections* (1942). Godfroy's will is published in Arthur L. Bodurtha, *History of Miami County Indiana* (1914), which also contains the most extensive account of his life and career. Also see Otho Winger, *The Last of the Miamis* (1935). Both Bert Anson, *The Miami Indians* (1970), and Stewart Rafert, *The Miami Indians of Indiana: A Persistent People, 1654–1994* (1996), discuss Miami history and the events in which Godfroy participated. Sarah E. Cooke and Rachel B. Ramadhyani, eds., *Indians and a Changing Frontier: The Art of George Winter* (1993), contains Winter's portraits of Godfroy and two of his children and Winter's sketch and description of Mount Pleasant.

R. DAVID EDMUNDS

GODKIN, Edwin Lawrence (2 Oct. 1831–21 May 1902), magazine and newspaper writer and editor, was born in Moyne, near Dublin, Ireland, of English heritage, the son of James Godkin, a minister, and Sarah Lawrence. In 1851 Godkin took his degree from Queen's College, Belfast, where he had been introduced to the Utilitarianism of John Stuart Mill and Jeremy Bentham and, in general, acquired a liberal,

upper middle-class, socially conscious education. "John Stuart Mill was our prophet," Godkin recalled, "and [George] Grote and Bentham were our daily food" (*A Biography*, p. 9).

After a flirtation with the study of law in London at the Middle Temple, also in 1851, Godkin took a job as an editor on the *Workingmen's Friend*, a new magazine published by his father's radical friend John Cassell; early contributors included Jules Verne and Harriet Beecher Stowe. Among Godkin's contributions is his only known venture into fiction, "A Christmas in Rathnagru," a story about a college duel interlaced with the visit of a banshee to an English country home. This presented no threat to his sister, Georgina S. Godkin, who wrote several books of fiction from her home in Italy, where she had moved in the 1870s with an invalid sister and their widowed mother. The family seemed to dote on Edwin, the eldest, whom Georgina once described as a proud lad with a "fiery temper, but lovable and affectionate" (*A Biography*, p. 11).

Another of Godkin's contributions to the *Workingmen's Friend* was a series of historical sketches of Hungary that appeared between November 1851 and February 1852. Rewritten and expanded, they formed his first book, *The History of Hungary and the Magyars* (1853), prompted no doubt by his support of the Hungarian revolutionary Louis Kossuth. Godkin managed to temper such rhetorical stirrings in later writings, however, and even voiced some regret for his youthful "flush of enthusiasm" over the "Kossuth craze." Despite these musings, the book went through several printings, including an American edition, and earned Godkin accolades and a commemorative sword during a visit to Hungary in 1854 (*A Biography*, p. 16).

In late 1853 Godkin accepted an assignment from the London *Daily News* to be its correspondent at the Crimean War (1854–1856), which marked the first time that civilian journalists were organized to report on a war to a civilian population at home. (Previously, editors lifted news from foreign newspapers or hired junior officers to send letters from the battlefront.) Nearly fifty years after the war, Godkin wrote, "If I were asked now what I thought the most important result of the Crimean war, I should say the creation and development of the 'special correspondents' of newspapers." He added that the appearance of the special correspondent "led to a real awakening of the official mind. It brought home to the War Office the fact that the public has something to say about the conduct of wars, and that they are not the concern exclusively of sovereigns and statesmen" (*Life and Letters*, vol. 1, pp. 100–102).

Godkin's *Daily News* appointment probably had something to do with his book on Hungary and a letter he had written to the newspaper on the "Eastern Question" defending the claim of the Greeks to Constantinople. "I was only twenty-two," he recalled years later, "and knew nothing about either Greece, or the Greeks or Constantinople; but I was possessed of that common illusion of young men, that facility of composition indicates the existence of thought" (Pringle, "Godkin of the *Post*," p. 197).

Upon his return to Ireland, Godkin lectured on the war and became an editor on the *Northern Whig* of Belfast. On 19 October 1856, shortly after his twenty-fifth birthday, he resigned from the paper and set sail for the United States. He arrived on the eve of the presidential race between Republican John C. Frémont and Democrat James Buchanan, a spectacle he found more tolerable and more democratic than he had expected.

Among his special New York friends was Frederick Law Olmsted, the landscape architect whom he had met in London in 1851 and whose subsequent newspaper accounts in 1853 of his travels through the South had so impressed Godkin that he made a tour of the slave states himself. Between 1856 and 1857, he published in the London *Daily News* a series of letters based on his retracing of Olmsted's trip. Unlike Olmsted, Godkin could find no ethical justification for the institution of slavery.

Godkin returned to New York from New Orleans in January 1857 and resumed his legal studies, working in the office of David Dudley Field and passing the state bar the following year. In 1859 he married Frances Elizabeth Foote, whose cousins included Harriet Beecher Stowe and Henry Ward Beecher. They had three children. With his fledgling law practice foundering, the couple spent much of the next two years in England and on the continent. During his stay in Europe Godkin wrote nothing, aside from letters to the *Daily News*. They returned to New York in 1862 to find the country in the middle of the Civil War. Godkin's twice-weekly letters to the London newspaper indicated his sympathy for the North.

Meanwhile, Godkin was editing the *Sanitary Commission Bulletin* and writing regularly for the *New York Times* and the *North American Review*, whose editor, Charles Eliot Norton, had recently joined forces with two abolitionists, James M. McKim and George L. Stearns, to finance a new weekly newspaper. They called it the *Nation* and hired Godkin as editor in chief.

The *Nation*'s first issue appeared on 6 July 1865. Godkin and his colleagues promised a journal that would discuss the political and economic issues of the day "with greater accuracy and moderation than are now to be found in the daily press." He said it would advocate "whatever in legislation or in manners seems likely to promote a more equal distribution of the fruits of progress and civilization." It would seek to better the conditions of blacks. It would work at "fixing public attention upon the political importance of popular education, and the dangers which a system like ours runs from the neglect of it in any portion of our territory." It would also print sound and impartial criticisms of books and works of art (Ogden, *Life and Letters*, vol. 1, pp. 237–38). Within the first year, however, disharmony among stockholders enabled Godkin, McKim, and Olmsted (who had just returned from California and was brought in as a gesture toward

harmony) to take control of the *Nation* under the name of E. L. Godkin and Co.

In 1881, Godkin merged the *Nation* with the New York *Evening Post*, recently acquired by the journalist and financier Henry Villard. Godkin shared the editing with Carl Schurz, a former senator and presidential cabinet member, and Horace White, once editor of the *Chicago Tribune*. Friction soon developed among them, especially between Schurz, the editor in chief, and Godkin, who had expressed misgivings that "after sixteen years of absolute power I shall have to work with and defer to another man" (*A Biography*, p. 144). Schurz resigned in 1883 over Godkin's views on a labor strike, leaving Godkin in control of the newspaper.

As editor of the *Post*, Godkin was a leader of the 1884 Mugwump revolt among Republicans against James G. Blaine, the party's presidential candidate. Godkin endorsed Grover Cleveland and attacked Blaine in parallel columns that matched the candidate's statements and congressional record against his personal associations with railroad builders and financiers. Godkin believed that Cleveland's victory was proof that a group of well-organized, independent voters could put the public welfare ahead of party loyalty.

Generally, Godkin, among a growing number of editors who shunned political labels, championed property rights, a moderate tariff policy, and civil service reform. He opposed labor unions, assailed government interference in social issues, and deplored territorial expansion. He fought against government corruption and led the fight to defeat Tammany Hall. He insisted that socialism could not improve economic conditions and that the conservatism of Edmund Burke now made more sense than the liberal philosophy of Mill that he had once embraced. Yet he managed to stir sympathy for liberal causes among an intellectual elite that, like himself, was committed to public morality. Godkin observed the last half of the century, especially the period after the Civil War, when the United States became an industrial and imperial power. Mark Twain named it the Gilded Age for its bloated dreams, foolish optimism, and seedy rhetoric. Godkin called it the "chromo-civilization" when he wanted to express his disapproval of its most garish aspects ("Chromo-Civilization," *Nation*, 24 Sept. 1874, pp. 201–202).

Godkin's first wife died in 1875. He married Katharine B. Sands in 1884. He retired from the *Post* in 1900, and in 1901 the Godkins moved first to Ireland and then to England in early 1902 to Torquay near the sea. But Godkin's health declined rapidly and he died at Greenway House, Brixham, on the River Dart.

Godkin was one of the great editors of his day. Allan Nevins wrote of the *Evening Post* and its editor: "There was no other journal resembling it, and its dignity, integrity, thoughtfulness, scholarly accuracy, and pride of intellect were the reflection of Godkin's own traits" (Nevins, *The Evening Post*, p. 519). James Bryce, the British commentator, called the *Nation* the best weekly not only in America but in the world.

• Collections of Godkin's papers are at the Houghton Library, Harvard University, and in the Manuscript Division of the New York Public Library. Besides his many articles for newspapers and magazines, Godkin wrote books including *Reflections and Comments* (1895), *Problems of Modern Democracy* (1896), and *Unforeseen Tendencies of Democracy* (1898). William M. Armstrong, *E. L. Godkin: A Biography* (1978), is the most complete biography. Armstrong also edited *The Gilded Age Letters of E. L. Godkin* (1974) and wrote *E. L. Godkin and American Foreign Policy, 1865–1900* (1957), a study of Godkin's attitudes based on a selection of his *Nation* and *Evening Post* editorials. See also James Bryce, "Edwin Lawrence Godkin," in *Studies in Contemporary Biography*, (1903), a penetrating brief sketch of Godkin's career; Allan Nevins, *The Evening Post: A Century of Journalism* (1922); Henry F. Pringle, "Godkin of the *Post*," in *Highlights in the History of the American Press*, eds. Edwin Ford and Edwin Emery (1954); Edward Caudill, "E. L. Godkin and the Science of Society," *Journalism Quarterly* 66, no. 1 (Spring 1989): 57–64; and Michael Emery and Edwin Emery, *The Press and America: An Interpretive History of the Mass Media* (rev. 1992), the standard general history of American journalism. *Fifty Years of American Idealism: The New York Nation, 1865–1915* (1915), includes Wendell Phillips Garrison's obituary of Godkin. Rollo Ogden, ed., *Life and Letters of Edwin Lawrence Godkin (with Portraits)* (2 vols. 1907), is the "authorized" biography and contains Godkin's statement of purpose for the *Nation* and a list of his numerous publications.

RICHARD F. HIXSON

GODMAN, John Davidson (20 Dec. 1794–17 Apr. 1830), anatomist and naturalist, was born in Annapolis, Maryland, the son of Samuel Godman and Anna Henderson. His mother died when he was two years old, and he was sent to Wilmington, Delaware, to live with an aunt who in 1798 moved with him to Chestertown, Maryland. She died in 1800, the year after his father died, and he was sent to Baltimore, Maryland, to live with a sister. In 1811 he became a printer's apprentice, a position that was intellectually stifling and physically debilitating; within a year he contracted a tubercular infection that plagued him for the rest of his life. Perhaps as a result of this infection and the drudgery of his situation, he developed an interest in medicine and spent as much time as he could in the office of a local Baltimore physician. There he met William N. Luckey, a medical student at the University of Maryland, who inspired him to study chemistry in order to prepare for a medical career.

In 1814 Godman enlisted in the U.S. Navy and saw action against the British flotilla that bombarded Baltimore's Fort McHenry. Following his discharge the next year he returned briefly to his print shop before moving to Elizabethtown, Pennsylvania, to study medicine with Luckey, by now a practicing physician. In 1816 he returned to Baltimore to enter the University of Maryland. He proved to be a brilliant student of anatomy (he once lectured his fellow classmates on the subject over a period of several weeks while the regular professor recovered from an injury) and received an M.D. in 1818.

After graduation Godman opened a medical practice in New Holland, Pennsylvania, which he relocat-

ed the next year to Anne Arundel County on the outskirts of Baltimore. The life of a country doctor held little appeal for him, and he attempted to return to the University of Maryland as a professor of anatomy when that position became available in 1819. After being rejected because of his youth, he moved to Philadelphia, Pennsylvania, where he began lecturing on anatomy at the Philadelphia Anatomical Rooms, a private school associated unofficially with the University of Pennsylvania. Here he helped to pioneer a holistic method of teaching anatomy whereby the different parts of the body were considered in terms of their relationship to one another instead of as isolated segments. To this end he conducted his demonstrations on whole cadavers and allowed students to learn anatomy by performing their own dissections.

This new approach gained him national recognition, via word of mouth, among anatomists and surgeons, caught the attention of the medical profession, and in 1821 Godman was invited to become a professor of surgery and demonstrative obstetrics at the year-old Medical College of Ohio in Cincinnati, the second medical school founded in the West. That same year he married Angelica Kauffman Peale; they had three children. Disappointed by the Cincinnati school's small student body and disgusted by a rancorous power struggle between the school's founder and its faculty, he resigned after the first session and opened a surgical practice in Cincinnati. In 1822 he became cofounder and editor of the *Western Quarterly Reporter of Medical, Surgical and Natural Sciences*, the first medical journal published outside the original thirteen states, and wrote most of the articles that appeared in its first three issues.

Later that year Godman returned to the Philadelphia Anatomical Rooms, and in 1823 he became the school's director, a position he held for three years. He also embarked on a writing and editing career that quickly produced several important works on anatomy. *Anatomical Investigations, Comprising Descriptions of the Various Fasciae of the Human Body* (1824), provided a complete description of the fibrous membranes that cover, support, and separate muscles. This work dispelled much confusion concerning the variety and continuity of the fasciae and resulted in the naming in his honor of the fascia that extends from the base of the neck to the pericardium, the membranous sac that encloses the heart. From 1824 to 1826 he was a member of the editorial staff of the *Philadelphia Journal of the Medical and Physical Sciences*, the forerunner of the *American Journal of the Medical Sciences*. He also wrote *Contributions to Physiological and Pathological Anatomy* (1824), the first publication by an American devoted to these subjects; translated into English the French surgeon Jacques Coster's *Manual of Surgical Operations* (1825); and edited the English surgeon Astley P. Cooper's *Treatises on Dislocations and on Fractures of the Joints* (1825).

Throughout his life Godman also maintained an interest in natural history. In 1819 he became a member of Philadelphia's Academy of Natural Sciences, and in

1825, the year after he was elected to membership in the Franklin Institute, he was appointed the institute's first professor of natural history. During the latter year he began writing *American Natural History* (3 vols., 1826–1828), the first systematic treatment of the subject and one that also discusses the economic uses to which the various species were put.

In 1826, when dissident faculty members at Columbia University's College of Physicians and Surgeons opened a rival medical college in New York City affiliated with Rutgers University in New Jersey, Godman secured an appointment at the new school as a professor of anatomy and physiology. Forced to resign the following year when his health worsened, he went to Santa Cruz, Jamaica, to recuperate. He retired in 1828 to Germantown, Pennsylvania, and for the remainder of his life earned a living by writing. For *Encyclopaedia Americana* (1829–1833) he wrote all the articles on natural history beginning with the letters A through C. He also contributed a series of charming sketches concerning his observations of the Anne Arundel County and Germantown countryside to the Philadelphia weekly Quaker magazine, the *Friend*. After his death in Germantown these sketches were collected and published as *Rambles of a Naturalist* (1833), the work for which he is best remembered.

Godman contributed to American culture in two ways. His innovative teaching methods and textbooks advanced anatomical education in the United States, while his writings on American natural history provided a firm scientific base on which future naturalists could build.

• Godman's papers have not been located. Biographies are Stephanie Morris, "John Davidson Godman (1794–1830): Physician and Naturalist," *Transactions and Studies of the College of Physicians of Philadelphia*, 4th ser., 41 (Apr. 1974), pp. 295–303, and Eugene Fauntleroy Cordell, *The Medical Annals of Maryland* (1903), pp. 771–79. His medical contributions are discussed in Francis R. Packard, *History of Medicine in the United States* (repr. 1963). An obituary is in the *Western Journal of the Medical and Physical Sciences* (Jan.–Mar. 1831).
CHARLES W. CAREY, JR.

GODOWSKY, Leopold (13 Feb. 1870–21 Nov. 1938), pianist, teacher, and composer, was born in Soshly, a small town not far from Wilno (now Vilnius) in Lithuania, the son of Mathew Godowsky, a physician, and Anna Lewin, both Polish Jews. When his father died of cholera eighteen months after Godowsky was born, the boy and his mother moved to nearby Schirwinty. There Godowsky came under the influence of Louis and Minna Passinock, who were friends of his mother's. Neither of Godowsky's parents was musical; the childless Passinocks, however, were amateur musicians and enthusiastic music lovers, and they immediately recognized Godowsky's nascent musical ability. Louis Passinock, a violinist who ran a secondhand piano shop, began teaching Godowsky to play the violin when he was seven years old. Passinock discouraged him from learning to play the piano, on the theory that there were too many pianists, but his wife recognized

Godowsky's affinity for the instrument and encouraged his keyboard explorations. Godowsky basically taught himself to play the piano; by the age of five he was so advanced that he could play the transcription of Felix Mendelssohn's Violin Concerto in E Minor. He later vividly described his early attraction to the piano. "With me," he wrote in *Etude* in 1928, "music was as natural and necessary as breathing. . . . I started on [Passinock's] piano to penetrate the fascinating mystery of the ivory and ebony keys when I was three years old. It all seemed perfectly natural and obvious to me, as though I had always known how to play them. No one remembers how one learned to feed oneself. Playing the piano was like that to me."

Godowsky made his piano debut in Vilnius at the age of nine, and shortly thereafter Passinock arranged for Godowsky's first concert tour, through Poland and Germany. Godowsky subsequently was offered a full scholarship at the Imperial Conservatory of St. Petersburg, which he declined. In 1884 he was admitted to the Berlin Hochschule für Musik, but he studied there (with Ernst Rudorff) for only twelve weeks, before leaving for his first visit to the United States. His American debut took place in Boston on 7 December 1884; over the course of the next two years he performed with the American sopranos Clara Louise Kellogg and Emma Thursby at the New York Casino (where he alternated weekly with Teresa Carreño), and on tour with a concert company organized around the Belgian violinist Ovide Musin.

In 1886 Godowsky returned to Europe, with the intention of studying with Franz Liszt, but Liszt's death in July of that year prevented this. Instead, Godowsky settled temporarily in Paris, where he studied with Camille Saint-Saëns and earned a solid reputation as a performer. In October 1890 Godowsky returned to the United States; he made his Carnegie Hall debut on 24 April 1891, two weeks before the hall officially opened. Also in 1891 he married Frieda Saxe and became a U.S. citizen. The couple had four children. During the 1890s Godowsky performed and taught at the New York College of Music and the Broad Street Conservatory in Philadelphia; from 1895 to 1900 he served as head of the piano department of the Chicago Conservatory. It was during this period that he developed his pedagogical theory of "weight and relaxation," a concept asserting that pianistic power should come from the use of relaxed arm weight rather than from muscular force.

Godowsky's pedagogical ideas had remarkable effect on his own playing, and his 1900 concert tour of Europe (which commenced in July in France) was immensely successful. According to his biographer Jeremy Nicholas, Godowsky became an overnight European success as a result of his Berlin debut with the Berlin Philharmonic Orchestra on 6 December 1900. "With one recital," Nicholas writes, "Godowsky had conquered the musical capital of the world and assured himself of a place among the great keyboard players of history. Overnight he became one of the highest-priced of all instrumentalists." In the spring of

1901 Godowsky toured the United States and Canada with the Boston Symphony Orchestra, and after this tour he and his family returned to Berlin, where they lived until 1908. Godowsky taught privately and used the city as the base from which he launched concert tours; by 1910 he had performed in almost every country in Europe. During this period he performed almost the entire classical piano repertory, including chamber and orchestral works. In 1908 the Godowskys moved to Vienna, where Leopold served as director of the piano school at the Akademie der Tonkunst.

Godowsky was never as popular or charismatic a pianist as was his contemporary Ignacy Paderewski. Harold Schonberg suggests that perhaps Godowsky's tendency toward perfection inhibited the spontaneity of his public performances. To pianists and connoisseurs, however, Godowsky was the "ultimate phenomenon," "the superman of piano playing," and "one of the most remarkable pianists of all time"; Nicholas Slonimsky described him as "an outstanding technician of his instrument, extending the potentialities of piano technique to the utmost, with particular attention to the left hand." His playing was both powerful and intellectual; his technical prowess was prodigious and transcendental. The critic James Gibbons Huneker described Godowsky as "a pianist for pianists, as Shelley is a poet for poets," and Abram Chasins wrote that Godowsky's playing was "sheer enchantment . . . it had the cool, colorful clarity of a stained-glass window."

The Godowskys left Austria for the United States (via England) in 1914; thereafter, they made the United States their home. During World War I, Godowsky performed in the United States, despite the prevalent anti-German bias. In 1916 the family moved from New York to Los Angeles, where Godowsky concentrated on teaching, primarily in the master class format; in 1919 they moved to Seattle. After the war Godowsky resumed his hectic concertizing schedule, performing in solo recitals and with orchestras in Europe, Central and South America, and Asia.

Godowsky became increasingly despondent during the 1920s because of disillusionment, loneliness, and family disappointments. As an escape from depression he turned increasingly to composition—an activity he had first attempted at the age of seven and had pursued consistently throughout his life. Godowsky's compositions include works that run the gamut from simple pedagogy to extreme difficulty. He edited piano music of other composers, and some of these arrangements appeared in a series that he edited and that was published by the Art Publication Society of St. Louis from 1912 until the late 1920s. Godowsky also wrote theoretical works on piano pedagogy and made piano transcriptions of compositions by Brahms, Carl Maria von Weber, and Johann Strauss. His first arrangements of other composers' piano compositions date from the early 1890s; the most celebrated are his incredibly difficult arrangements of twenty-six of Frédéric Chopin's twenty-seven études, which form

the basis of Godowsky's reputation as a composer for piano.

In June 1930, while making a recording in London, Godowsky suffered a stroke that ended his performing career. When he returned to New York he continued to teach, compose, and make transcriptions of other composers' works. After his wife died in December 1933, he lived with one of his daughters in New York City but was increasingly lonely. Godowsky died in New York.

• The Leopold Godowsky Collection at the Library of Congress includes 52 holographs of his virtuoso piano music in addition to business papers, printed music, clippings, photographs, and other materials. There are also considerable Godowsky materials in the papers of John George Hinderer, a former student and intended biographer of Godowsky, at the Minnesota Historical Society. This collection includes Hinderer's research notes, his personal collection of Godowsky letters, musical scores, photographs, and other materials. Holograph letters from Godowsky are scattered in a variety of collections, including the Vladimir and Wanda Horowitz Collection and the Love Family Papers at Yale, the Harry Brunswick Leob Papers at Tulane, and the James G. Huneker Collection at Dartmouth. Several of Godowsky's own publications are useful for what they reveal concerning his thinking about music in general and piano playing in particular. These include "Self-Study in the Art of Music," *Etude* (Jan. 1928); "Piano Music for the Left Hand," *Musical Quarterly* (July 1935); and a pamphlet, *The Future of America* (1915).

The most comprehensive scholarly study of Godowsky's career is Jeremy Nicholas, *Godowsky, The Pianists' Pianist: A Biography of Nicholas Godowsky* (1989). Several books devoted to pianists include essays of significant length on his life and career, including Abram Chasins's *Speaking of Pianists* (1957; repr. 1981) and Harold C. Schonberg's breezy and somewhat anecdotal *The Great Pianists* (1963); shorter biographical essays include those by Robin H. Legge and Jerrold Northrup Moore in *The New Grove Dictionary of Music and Musicians* (1980) and (revised by Katherine Preston) in *The New Grove Dictionary of American Music* (1984). Other informative articles are by Arthur M. Abell in the *Musical Courier* (10 Oct. 1906), Harriette Brower in the *Musical Observer* (Dec. 1916), and Joseph Wechsberg in the *New Yorker* (10 Nov. 1956). Studies of Godowsky's music include Maurice Aronson, *Key to the Miniatures of Leopold Godowsky* (1935); David Cloutier, "A Comparison of the Transcription Techniques of Godowsky and Liszt as Exemplified in Their Transcriptions of Three Schubert Lieder" (Ph.D. diss., North Texas State Univ., 1987); Leonard S. Saxe, "The Published Music of Leopold Godowsky," Music Library Association, *Notes* (1956–1957), which includes a complete worklist; and K. S. Sarabji, "Leopold Godowsky as a Creative Transcriber," *Mi contra fa* (1947). Obituaries are in the *New York Herald Tribune* and the *New York Times*, both 22 Nov. 1938.

KATHERINE K. PRESTON

GODWIN, Frank (20 Oct. 1889–5 Aug. 1959), cartoonist and illustrator, was born Francis Godwin in Washington, D.C., the son of Harry R. Godwin, a newspaper editor, and Annie Stoppard. He began an apprenticeship with the *Washington Star*, where his father was city editor, around 1905, at the same time taking classes at the Corcoran School of Art. He later studied at the Art Students League in New York under illustrator James Montgomery Flagg, with whom he became friends and with whom at one time he shared a studio. Flagg's sponsorship allowed him to begin contributing to the major humor magazines of the day. His earliest recorded work appeared in *Judge* in 1908. He became a prolific cartoonist and illustrator, whose work appeared regularly in all the major magazines—*Cosmopolitan*, *Collier's*, and *Liberty* chief among them—and in a variety of lesser publications.

Now very much in demand, Godwin also did a great deal of advertising work and illustrated a number of children's classics, including Robert Louis Stevenson's *Treasure Island* and *Kidnapped* and Rudyard Kipling's *Kim*. In the 1930s he took up painting in oils, and among other commissions, he did murals for King's County Hospital in Brooklyn, New York, and the Riverside Yacht Club in Greenwich, Connecticut.

In the early 1920s, in addition to his freelance work, Godwin had become a staff artist for the Ledger Syndicate in Philadelphia. In 1924 *Vignettes of Life*, a weekly page of human interest panels, started appearing and eventually met with such success that he was asked a few years later to come up with a sophisticated "girl strip," which was a very popular genre in the 1920s. He started on this new assignment with his usual alacrity and in November 1927 the comic strip *Connie*, also a weekly, went into print. *Connie* began as a strip about a pretty young woman who lived with her well-to-do parents, went to costume parties and picnics with the upper crust, and did charity work among slum children.

Connie was a beautifully drawn feature, very much in the tradition of the best illustrators of the period, and by May 1929 had acquired a daily version. Unlike the Sunday page, which was mildly humorous, the daily strip firmly anchored the character Connie (whose full name was Constance Kurridge) to the field of high adventure. Among other exploits, she went searching for buried treasure in Mexico; became an investigative reporter for a daily newspaper; and was a field marshal in the republic of Anchovy. Soon adventure spilled over to the Sunday page, and the feature, daily and Sunday, became—in terms of imagery and invention—one of the best comic strips of the 1930s as well as one of the more intriguing, dominated as it was by its intelligent, self-assured heroine and her innocent beauty.

In addition to his work on *Connie*, Godwin took over *Roy Powers, Eagle Scout* (a daily credited to Paul Powell) a few months after its inception in 1937 and turned it into one of the most finely drawn of all newspaper strips before he abandoned it in 1942. (Other Ledger strips he may have worked on uncredited include *Babe Bunting* and *War on Crime*.)

In 1944 *Connie* came to an end, and for a while Godwin dabbled in comic books before returning to the newspaper field in January 1948 with his creation of *Rusty Riley* for King Features. A luminous strip of youth and the outdoors set in the Kentucky horse country, it was drawn with a vitality and verve that transcended the often trite story lines provided by Rod Reed and Godwin's brother Harold; it lasted until the summer of 1959, a few weeks before the artist's death.

Some time before the United States entered World War I, Godwin had married Grace Congleton, with whom he had four children before they divorced. He married Georgiana Brown Harbeson shortly after the end of World War II. The couple lived quietly in New Hope, Pennsylvania, until his death.

During his lifetime Godwin enjoyed greater fame as an illustrator than as a comic strip artist. He was an accomplished craftsman in the tradition of Charles Dana Gibson and James Montgomery Flagg. His style, consisting of a cursive but meticulous line and network of fine cross-hatchings, was highly regarded by his peers. He served as a vice president of the Society of Illustrators and was later inducted into its Hall of Fame.

Yet it is as an artist of the comics that he may ultimately be best remembered. He brought to the medium a sophisticated sense of style, an unerring eye for composition and design, and a graphic virtuosity that stamp him as one of the masters of the form. Recognition in this field came only posthumously to Godwin, first in Europe, then in his own country, and it is now firmly entrenched.

• For more on Frank Godwin's work in the comics, see Pierre Couperie and Maurice Horn, *A History of the Comic Strip* (1968); Maurice Horn, ed., *The World Encyclopedia of Comics* (1976); Maurice Horn, *Women in the Comics* (1977); and Ron Goulart, ed., *The Encyclopedia of American Comics* (1990). Examples and discussion of his illustration work can be found in Walt and Roger Reed, *The Illustrator in America 1880–1980*, 2d ed. (1984). An obituary is in the *New York Times*, 6 Aug. 1959.

MAURICE HORN

GODWIN, Parke (25 Feb. 1816–7 Jan. 1904), journalist and editor, was born in Paterson, New Jersey, the son of Abraham Godwin, a manufacturer and merchant, and Martha Parke. After graduating from Princeton in 1834, he returned to Paterson to study law. He lived briefly in Louisville, Kentucky, where he was admitted to the bar, but before establishing a practice, he moved to New York City. There he met William Cullen Bryant, editor of the New York *Evening Post*, in a rooming house where both were living. In October 1839 Bryant offered him a job on the newspaper, and by May 1841 Godwin had acquired a one-tenth share in the firm, which he retained until 1844. On 12 May 1842, he married Frances "Fanny" Bryant, the editor's daughter, without the approval of her parents. They had eight children, six of whom survived to adulthood. With $6,000 advanced by the *Evening Post*, Godwin tried unsuccessfully to establish his own newspaper. In 1842 he planned to publish a *Morning Post*, but instead bought the *New Era*. The following year he launched a weekly, the *Pathfinder*, which lasted only fifteen issues. He then rejoined the *Evening Post* as an editorial assistant.

Godwin was much interested at this time in the Associationist movement and found in the theories of Charles Fourier a corrective for what he perceived to be the growth of a moneyed aristocracy in the United States. He presented these ideas in two small books of 1844: *Democracy, Constructive and Pacific* and *A Popular View of the Doctrines of Charles Fourier*. He helped form a workingman's party, the National Reformers, and ran (unsuccessfully) for Congress on its ticket in 1844. He supported the Brook Farm experiment, wrote for *The Harbinger*, the colony's socialist organ, and became its editor (1847–1849) when it was moved to New York. He contributed articles on his social theories to William Henry Channing's short-lived journal, *The Present* (1843–1844), to the single issue of Elizabeth P. Peabody's *Aesthetic Papers* that appeared in May 1849, and to Channing's *The Spirit of the Age* (1849).

Godwin had also been a frequent contributor to *The United States Magazine and Democratic Review*, a journal that supported the liberal wing of the Democratic party. Godwin most often wrote social and economic articles, though he also completed a translation from the German of Heinrich Zschokke. Godwin edited a collection of Zschokke's *Tales* in 1845, including translations by himself, his wife, Christopher Pearse Cranch, and Gustav C. Hebbe. With a different group of collaborators—John H. Hopkins, Jr., Charles A. Dana, and John S. Dwight—he translated the first part and edited the whole of Goethe's *Autobiography* (1846–1847), which went through at least three editions. Over the next few years he wrote *Vala: A Mythological Tale* (1851), based on the career of Jenny Lind, and compiled a *Hand-Book of Universal Biography* (1852), which he later revised as *The Cyclopaedia of Biography* (1866, updated 1878).

Never on easy terms with his father-in-law, whom he once described as "cold, irritable and selfish," Godwin left the *Evening Post* a second time in 1846 and was appointed by President James K. Polk as deputy collector of customs at New York. After a trip to Europe in 1851, he joined the newly established *Putnam's Monthly Magazine* in 1853 as contributing editor in charge of political questions. Godwin launched a vigorous attack against slavery, sharply criticized the politicians of his time, and in 1856 supported the recently founded Republican party. He wrote its first (Free Soil) platform, based on an article he had published in the magazine. Politics, however, was not his only concern. In 1857 he sought appointment as professor of history at Columbia, but failed to secure it. His interest in history was sincere, for in 1860 he published the first volume (*Ancient Gaul*) of his *History of France*, a work he never completed.

After the demise of *Putnam's*, Godwin returned to the *Evening Post* in February 1859. Two years later he was encouraged to buy John Bigelow's one-third interest in the firm for over $111,000, the debt to be repaid from dividends. The *Evening Post* prospered, and Godwin was able to sell his share in 1868 for $200,000. He returned to a revived *Putnam's* as editor for eight months in 1870 and in the same year issued *Out of the Past*, a collection of nineteen previously published essays. During the early 1870s he was for various brief periods in charge of the *Post* and was named editor after Bryant's death in 1878; it was a position he held until the paper was sold in 1881. For a short time in the 1880s, he was editor of *The Commercial Advertiser*.

Godwin was selected to write the family-authorized biography of his father-in-law, and although he managed to keep his ill feelings toward the man out of its pages, he recovered so few of the poet's letters that he could not write a balanced account of his life. The book, in two volumes, appeared in 1883. Godwin also edited Bryant's *Poetical Works* and *Prose Writings* (2 vols. each, 1883–1884). In 1889 he issued a second collection of Zschokke's *Tales*, reprinting three of his earlier translations and including a new one by William P. Prentice. In 1895 he collected five speeches he had delivered on George William Curtis, Edwin Booth, Louis Kossuth, John James Audubon, and William Cullen Bryant in a book entitled *Commemorative Addresses*. In 1900 he published *A New Study of the Sonnets of Shakespeare*. He died in New York City.

Godwin was well thought of in his own day for his judicious mind and liberal principles. As an appreciative article in *Galaxy* put it in February 1869, he was "the foe of all forms of restriction, the advocate of the people, the lover of every beautiful act." His articles were "reasoned and persuasive, temperate without coldness, firm without prejudice."

• Major collections of manuscript materials are in the New York Public Library and the Princeton University libraries. There is no biography, but important information may be found in Frederick Marquand Godwin, *Genealogical Notes* (privately printed, 1958); Allan Nevins, *The Evening Post* (1922); Frank Luther Mott, *A History of American Magazines: 1850–1865* (1938); Clarence L. F. Gohdes, *The Periodicals of American Transcendentalism* (1931); John Preston Hoskins, "Parke Godwin and the Translation of Zschokke's Tales," *Publications of the Modern Language Association of America* 20, no. 2 (1905): 265–304; Charles H. Brown, *William Cullen Bryant: A Biography* (1971); and William Cullen Bryant II and Thomas G. Voss, eds., *The Letters of William Cullen Bryant* (6 vols., 1975–1992).

DONALD A. RINGE

GOEBEL, William (4 Jan. 1856–3 Feb. 1900), governor of Kentucky, was born in Carbondale, Pennsylvania, the son of Johann Christian Goebel, a cabinetmaker, and Augusta Greenclay. Both parents had recently immigrated from Germany. About 1863 the family moved to Covington, Kentucky. As a boy, William Goebel was influenced by a reform-minded, crippled cobbler, who lent him books. After finishing high school in Covington, William served as an apprentice in a Cincinnati store while attending business college. He graduated from Cincinnati Law School in 1877. One of his examiners, John White Stevenson, a former

U.S. senator and Kentucky governor, took Goebel into his firm to read law. Later Goebel practiced with U.S. congressman John G. Carlisle before rejoining Stevenson's firm. With these legal and political connections, Goebel prospered. Among the cases he won were a number directed against railroads.

In 1887 Goebel was elected as a Democrat to the state senate, representing Covington and surrounding Kenton County. Like his mentor Stevenson, he insisted on the right of the people to control chartered corporations. In the senate, therefore, he joined with Cassius M. Clay to fight the Louisville and Nashville (L&N) Railroad, whose economic importance and powerful lobby had won undue influence over the politics of Kentucky. Governor Simon B. Buckner in 1888 recommended that the powers of the Railroad Commission be increased. The railroad lobby then had a bill introduced in the state house to abolish the commission. A legislative committee, including Goebel representing the senate, then investigated the lobby.

Goebel led the investigation, drafted the report, and introduced it in the senate. The legislature accepted the highly critical report. Goebel pushed for an employers' liability law and full taxation of railroad property. In both the legislature and the constitutional convention of 1890–1891, he sought to preserve and strengthen the powers of the state's Railroad Commission. These actions did not endear him to L&N officials, nor did his bill to eliminate tolls endear him to turnpike owners. Nevertheless, by 1894 Goebel had been elected president pro tem of the Kentucky Senate.

Goebel erected a powerful political machine outside Louisville and the bluegrass region, where conservative planters and businesspeople held sway. Based in northern Kentucky and most popular among urban and labor constituencies, Goebel also gained a large following among agrarian voters in the western part of the state. The majority of the Goebel followers remained loyal to his program of ad valorum taxation of all railroad properties, a fellow-servant law, and control of corporations. These and other parts of his platform were implemented after his death. Goebel, nevertheless, did not style himself a "man of the people." Instead he modeled his speech on that of his former partners Carlisle and Stevenson, using few audience-pleasing phrases. In a state of heavy imbibers, he drank little, exercised religiously, and had regular habits. His often remarked-on pallor may have been occasioned by tuberculosis early in life, since both of his brothers had that disease. Described as aloof, Goebel had few close friends and never married.

In 1895 Confederate veteran John L. Sandford, a local political opponent, objected to a scurrilous personal attack made in a newspaper Goebel controlled. The two men, happening to meet in front of a Covington bank, exchanged words; then both drew pistols and fired. Sandford was killed. Since a credible witness stated that the dead man drew first, Goebel was not tried. However, the shooting made Goebel unpopular among Kentucky's Confederate veterans, who noted, too, his nonsouthern background and his father's service in the Union army.

In elections the same year and the next, the opposition Republican party won a series of victories. Goebel attributed these less to factionalism among Democrats than to corruption in the electoral process. In 1898, therefore, he drove an election bill through the legislature that virtually stripped the GOP of any role in selecting county election officials and centralized ultimate control of the process in the legislature, the upper house that Goebel led. Passed over the Republican governor's veto, this bill fed Goebel's rivals' suspicions of his ambition and fairness and provided a major issue for the upcoming 1899 gubernatorial election. Still, Goebel secured the Democratic nomination by sound strategy and clever maneuvering at the party's Louisville convention.

Goebel focused much of his campaign on the L&N, which backed his Republican opponent, W. S. Taylor. With a Populist and another, more conservative Democrat also in the field, the four-way race was fraught with tension, and Goebel declared, "I ask no quarter and I fear no foe." On election day both Goebel's and Taylor's partisans committed voting frauds. Taylor led the questionable count. Pressured by party leaders, Goebel agreed to contest the election before the legislature. On 30 January 1900, while walking to the capitol, Goebel was struck down by a shot fired from a state office building. Before he died, a majority of both houses declared him elected, and he was sworn in. Though Taylor and Republican secretary of state (and later congressman) Caleb Powers, among others, were indicted for complicity in the assassination, a series of highly partisan trials and overturned convictions left the true identify of the assassin unclear. Goebel's successor, J. C. W. Beckham, who had been placed on the ticket as a political maneuver, did not carry on the fight against the L&N, but much of Goebel's program was adopted.

• Some of Goebel's personal papers on microfilm are in the University of Kentucky Library; others are in the personal collection of the writer. Sources on Goebel are very biased. The only biography is James C. Klotter, *William Goebel: The Politics of Wrath* (1977), which accepts much of the view of his opponents, especially those who lived in central Kentucky. Urey Woodson, *The First New Dealer: William Goebel* (1939), deals primarily with his race for governor, is equally prejudiced, and is poorly organized. George R. Leighton, "Louisville: An American Museum Piece," an essay in his *Five Cities* (1939), presents a brief but fairer interpretation of Goebel and his principal opponent, Milton Hannibal Smith. R. E. Hughes et al., *That Kentucky Campaign* (1900), though distorted, provides much information on the Goebel-Taylor gubernatorial campaign that proved a major factor in his assassination. Thomas D. Clark, "The People, William Goebel, and the Kentucky Railroads," *Journal of Southern History* 5 (1939): 34–48, provides a fairer but limited portrait of Goebel. An obituary is in the *Cincinnati Enquirer*, 4 Feb. 1900.
BENNETT H. WALL

GOELL, Theresa Bathsheba (17 July 1901–18 Dec. 1985), archaeologist, was born in New York City, the daughter of Jacob Goell, a builder, and Mary Samowitz. The family soon moved from Manhattan to Brooklyn, spending summers at their house in Hunter, New York, in the Catskill Mountains. Theresa was a curious and active child, taking clocks and other mechanisms apart to see how they worked, ranging far afield in Hunter, always busy; she said later that the days were never long enough and implied that these early traits foreshadowed her "hands-on" approach to archaeology. Her family called her "the terrible Turk"—prophetically, as she is best known for her excavations at Nemrud Dagh in southeastern Turkey.

Goell studied at Syracuse University (1919–1921) and then transferred to Radcliffe College, majored in philosophy and social ethics, and graduated in February 1924. Professor James Ford encouraged Goell's interest in architecture. While at Radcliffe, she experienced a partial but permanent hearing loss, diagnosed as otosclerosis. After her junior year she married Cyrus Levinthal, a lawyer; they had one son.

Goell and Levinthal (she did not use her husband's name) spent the years 1926–1928 and 1930–1931 studying at Cambridge University, where she was affiliated with Newnham College and earned a B.A. in architecture. Her tutor, Theodore Fyfe, had been architect for the Knossos excavations; he divined her aptitude for archaeology and gave her assignments in architecture with "archaeological angles to them," as she put it. She came to realize that "I was going to be in transit for the rest of my life, and along the way my marriage came to an end." In the spring of 1933 Goell joined the American Schools of Oriental Research (ASOR) in Jerusalem and later the ASOR excavations at Gerasa, Transjordan. In Jerusalem, in the "flea-infested basement of the Schools," she learned to classify, draw, and reconstruct pottery, lamps, and figurines under the direction of William Foxwell Albright. At Gerasa she produced measured drawings of pottery from Tèl El Ful and cataloged photos of local churches; in the spring of 1934 she was architectural assistant there for the ASOR–Yale University Joint Expedition, drawing plans of architectural details and buildings and recording and reconstructing pottery and small finds. She then assisted E. L. Sukenik in compiling *Ancient Synagogues in Palestine and Greece* (1934) and *Ancient Synagogues of El Hameh* (1935). During this time she also designed some 200 buildings in Jerusalem, Haifa, and Tèl Aviv, a practical manifestation of her lifelong Zionism.

To get more training in classical archaeology, Goell returned to New York in 1935. She worked at Hearns department stores as "indoor architect," designing and decorating store interiors. Through a chance encounter she met Professor Karl Lehmann-Hartleben, director of the archaeology department of New York University's Graduate Institute of Fine Arts, who in 1939 suggested she study the "ugly monument" of Nimrud (now Nemrud) Dagh, a mountain in "Syria" (in modern Turkey). To write a term paper, she struggled through the scholarly German of *Reisen in Kleinasien und Nordsyrien* (1890), the report of an 1882–1883 expedition by Karl Humann and Otto Puchstein; she concluded that the monument was not ugly and that it deserved not a term paper but extensive investigation. Believing that it had been neglected because "it was too Oriental, barbaric and imperfect for the classical scholars, and too classical for the Orientalists," she was convinced that it showed influences of several distinct cultures, including Hittite. She continued to take courses at NYU and Columbia, to raise her son, and to work at Hearns. During World War II she worked as a draftsman for the navy, at first as the only woman among 1,200 men. Lehmann considered her "mercenary" to work rather than devote herself to scholarship, but she valued her independence. Like Albright before him, he emphasized that her sex and her deafness would rule out an academic career, thus making a Ph.D. unnecessary. This suited Goell, as she wanted to dig, not teach. As additional preparation for Nemrud Dagh, she did volunteer work in the laboratory of the Brooklyn Museum.

In 1945 Professor Hetty Goldman of the Institute for Advanced Study at Princeton University asked her to inspect the Tarsus excavations in Turkey, abandoned because of the war. Goell was architectural and archaeological assistant from 1946 to 1953; because of Goldman's illness, she was actually in charge of the dig and of writing up the results. During this time she made her first two trips to Nemrud Dagh, in 1947 and 1951. The journey was arduous, but she was more determined than ever to excavate there, undaunted by the dangers and discomforts. After the 1951 visit, Lehmann helped her get funds from the Bollingen Foundation and the American Philosophical Society; her older sister and brother-in-law, Eva and Philip Godfrey, also contributed, and in 1952 ASOR agreed to sponsor the dig. From 1953 to 1956 she worked with Friedrich Dörner, an epigraphist from Münster University (Germany) who had visited Nemrud in 1938; she then became director. In 1953 Goell and Dörner were assisted only by her brother Kermit and some forty workers; in 1954 there were about 160 workers, requiring more complicated and time-consuming administration.

Goell described herself as "a jack of all archaeological trades"; both at Tarsus and at Nemrud she participated in digging, surveying, photography, drawing the finds, reconstructing and cataloging pottery, and also in the management and lives of the crew. Water, food, and mail had to be brought long distances. Goell managed the supplies and cooking; shelter in a treeless terrain of extreme temperatures and furious winds; and medical care, which she generally provided herself, also treating local people unconnected with the dig. She learned Turkish and said she never felt afraid or unsafe, evidently earning the intense loyalty of her numerous local staff.

During her nine seasons at the site between 1953 and 1973, Goell uncovered the sanctuary of Antiochus I, the Hellenistic king who ruled c. 64 to 32 B.C., when the kingdom of Commagene was a buffer state between the Roman and Persian empires. Twenty centuries of weather and earthquakes had toppled or decapitated most of the statues; stones from the central tumulus had buried inscriptions, reliefs, and other elements; only human damage was minimal, because of the remoteness of the site. In several inscriptions in Greek, Antiochus claims descent from Alexander the Great through his mother and from Darius through his father; he declares the mountaintop his *Hierothesion* (place sacred to the gods). A central tumulus, some fifty meters high and 150 meters in diameter, is covered with stones produced in cutting three terraces built as sites for "everlasting" monthly rituals to observe Antiochus's birthday and his ascension to the throne. There are two sets of colossal seated figures, approximately twenty-four feet tall: Antiochus and four deities (the sun god, the local fertility goddess, the father of the gods, and the god of strength), flanked by lions and eagles. There are also reliefs portraying Antiochus's Greek and Persian ancestors and a sacrificial altar. A major effort to find Antiochus's tomb was unsuccessful.

Goell saw the sanctuary as evidence of a syncretic religion and art. She believed that it might illuminate the fate of the Hittites after they were conquered by the Assyrians in the eighth century B.C., for the shrine showed evidence of Hittite culture shaped by Hellenistic, Persian, and Mesopotamian influences. It was, she wrote, "one of the glories of the Hellenistic world," not, as some had thought, the crude work of a "semibarbarian monarch."

Although the Nemrud excavations were Goell's major contribution, she also worked at related sites. From 1953 to 1956, after work at the summit during the summers, she and Dörner excavated the shrine of Antiochus's father, Mithradates Kallinikos, at the foot of Mount Nemrud. This Hierothesion was in Arsameia (now Eski Kahta), a city on the Nymphaios (Nymph River) discovered by Dörner in 1951. In 1964, 1967, 1968, and 1970 Goell excavated Samosata, capital of Commagene (modern Samsat). Though she was able to excavate only part of the site, her finds illuminated Roman, Byzantine, Moslem Arab, and Turkish Seljuk occupation.

Goell was elected a corresponding member of the Deutsches Archäologisches Institut in Berlin (1962) and a life member of the Archaeological Institute of America. In 1973 she was the only American and the only female archaeologist invited to the fiftieth anniversary celebrations of the founding of the Republic of Turkey and was awarded a citation for her contributions to Anatolian history, culture, and art. In 1981 she learned that she had cancer, but she continued to work on the final report on Nemrud until she had a stroke in 1983. She died in New York City.

Goell's significance as an archaeologist lies in her imaginative grasp of the importance of a previously neglected site. Commagene, perhaps the richest of the small kingdoms conquered by the Romans, was a major crossroads of ancient Asia Minor. Goell's intelligence, determination, and energy enabled her to uncover its eclectic culture, adding significantly to our knowledge of the history of that busy, various, and contentious part of the ancient world.

Though there is little or no published record of her views on feminism, it is clear that Goell refused to accept the usual limitations her own culture imposed on women's independence and freedom. Her total involvement in each dig is also unusual: "Practically any job that anyone of my staff would have to do I'd do myself," she told an interviewer. Her independence was evident in her initial assessment of Nemrud Dagh, so different from Lehmann's; and even many a man would find life on a harsh, remote mountaintop, single-handedly managing scores of Turkish workers (as well as tourists, whom Goell found much more trying) an impossible physical and social challenge—while Goell said that each time she returned to Nemrud she felt as though she were coming home.

• The Schlesinger Library, Radcliffe College, and the Semitic Museum at Harvard University have divided Theresa Goell's papers between them, the former holding mainly personal and family papers and the latter the bulk of the archaeological records; at the time of writing, both collections were unprocessed but open to research. The Radcliffe College Archives has biographical data and some publications. The quotations above are from her personal papers, including an interview by Rebecca Latimer, and published articles. Most of Goell's publications report on the Nemrud Dagh or related excavations. With Friedrich K. Dörner she published *Arsameia am Nymphaios: Die Ausgrabungen im Hierothesion des Mithradates Kallinikos von 1953–1956* (1963); "The Last Resting-Place of Antiochus I, King of Commagene . . . ," *Illustrated London News*, 18 June 1955, pp. 1094–97; and "The Tomb Sanctuary of Mithradates of Commagene, and the Discovery of a Superb Relief . . . ," *Illustrated London News*, 2 July 1955, pp. 23–25. Under her sole name she published "The Excavation of the 'Hierothesion' of Antiochus I of Commagene on Nemrud Dagh (1953–1956)," *Bulletin of the American Schools of Oriental Research* 147 (Oct. 1957): 4–22, which describes the tasks and finds of the first four seasons. Three of her articles are in *National Geographic Society Research Reports*: "Geophysical Survey of the Hierothesion and Tomb of Antiochus I of Commagene, Turkey," *1963 Projects* (1968): 83–102; "The Nemrud Dagh (Turkey) Geophysical Surveys of 1964," *1964 Projects* (1969): 61–81; and "Samosata Archaeological Excavations, Turkey, 1967," *1967 Projects* (1974): 83–109. More popular and less technical are "Throne above the Euphrates," *National Geographic* 119 (1961): 390–405, and "Tarsus–'No Mean City'," *Radcliffe Quarterly* 35 (1951): 28–32. Because of illness, Goell was not able to finish writing up the Nemrud Dagh excavations. Donald Sanders has compiled her notes and photographs and published them as *Nemrud Dagi: The Hierothesion of Antiochus I of Commagene, Results of the American Excavations Directed by Theresa B. Goell* (2 vols., 1996). The National Geographic Society produced a motion picture about Nemrud Dagh.

Obituaries are in the *New York Times*, 21 Dec. 1985; by Mitchell Rothman in *ASOR Newsletter* 37 (Apr. 1986), and in *Biblical Archaeology Review* 12 (May–June 1986), and *Radcliffe Quarterly* 72 (June 1986). "A Jack-of-All-Trades," an interview in *Radcliffe Quarterly* 51 (May–June 1967): 5–9, by Paula Budlong Cronin, describes much of Goell's life and work.

EVA S. MOSELEY

GOESSMANN, Charles Anthony (13 June 1827–1 Sept. 1910), chemist, was born Karl Anton Goessmann in Naumburg, Germany, the son of Heinrich Goessmann, a medical doctor, and Helena Henslinger-Boetinger. Goessmann was one of four children; his mother died when he was fourteen. He was educated in the elementary schools in Naumburg but attended the gymnasium in Fritzlar, Germany, for his college preparatory work. On completing the gymnasium in 1842, he apprenticed himself to a pharmacist; four years later he had passed the examinations to qualify as a pharmacist. Over the next four years he worked as an assistant pharmacist in various communities, including as an assistant to the pharmacist at Göttingen University, while preparing to enter the university. He matriculated at Göttingen in 1850. In 1851 he was appointed a laboratory assistant in analytical chemistry and in 1852, a second assistant to Professor Friedrich Wöhler in the Göttingen Chemistry Laboratory. He was awarded a Ph.D. in December 1852.

Following receipt of his doctorate, Goessmann continued to work at Göttingen in the chemistry laboratory and to teach students as a privat-docent. His research at this time focused on the peanut, from which he isolated two hitherto unknown acids of the peanut, arachidic and hypogaeic acid. In 1854 he received a three-year leave of absence to study the chemical industries in France, Britain, and the United States. On 12 May 1857 he sailed from Southampton for the United States.

Although he had several academic offers in Germany, Goessmann chose to remain in the United States, becoming chemist and superintendent of the Eastwick Sugar Refinery in Philadelphia in 1857. He remained in this position for three years, except for a four-month leave in 1860 to study the sugar industry in Cuba. Goessmann's work at Eastwick focused on developing improved methods of sugar refining, as well as developing other sources of sugar cane, notably sorghum.

In 1861 Goessmann accepted an offer to become chemist and superintendent of the Onondaga Salt Works in Syracuse, New York. The application of chemical analysis to salt production was being more widely adopted at this time, in order to produce salt (sodium chloride) of uniform quality. Goessmann's encyclopedic interest led him to study salt in all its forms, but particularly the brines recovered from salt wells in the vicinity of Lake Onondaga. His objective was to develop methods of purifying the brines so that, following evaporation, the resulting salt would be quite pure. He developed a method of brine purification, called fractional crystallization, for use in the industrial production of salt. Much of the salt thus recovered was used to supplement the diets of farm animals, especially dairy cattle. While with the salt works, Goessmann traveled widely in both the United

States and Canada, looking at salt mines and salt wells. He visited Petite Anse, Louisiana, at the invitation of the U.S. Bureau of Mines, to look at the salt deposits there in 1866. Concurrently with his work at Onondaga, he taught chemistry and physics at Rensselaer Polytechnic Institute from 1862 to 1864.

In 1868, at the invitation of William S. Clark, the first president of the Massachusetts Agricultural College in Amherst, Goessmann became professor of chemistry at the new college. He and Clark had been fellow students at Göttingen in the early 1850s. Goessmann immediately set about organizing the instruction in chemistry (until 1884 he was the sole professor of chemistry), and establishing a chemistry laboratory. He continued experimental work in the college's laboratory and in his own private laboratory on the grounds of his house in Amherst. In 1878 he organized the first Massachusetts Agricultural Experiment Station with private support; in 1882 the station became a state-supported institution. Until it merged with the federally funded Hatch Experiment Station in 1895, by act of the state legislature, Goessmann headed the station.

Goessmann's experimental work centered on the chemistry of crops and agricultural soils. He did substantial work on sugar beets and sorghum as potential alternative sources of sugar from the sugar cane, and his fundamental work was the foundation of the sugar beet industry in the United States. He studied feed for farm animals, especially dairy cows and pigs, and did significant research on the use of corn ensilage as cattle feed. He conducted tests to determine the impact of legumes on the availability of nitrogen in the soil and studied the effects of phosphoric acid on the fertility of soils. He also investigated the growing conditions for fruits, especially peaches.

Goessmann was instrumental in getting the Massachusetts legislature to pass a law in 1873 requiring both the inspection and accurate labeling of fertilizers. In 1874 he was appointed the Massachusetts State inspector of fertilizers. Goessmann believed that if the chemical composition of fertilizers was clearly stated, farmers would be able to apply the exact amounts needed. This law was a model for other states. Chemists like Goessmann formed the leadership of the antiadulteration movement that led to the federal Pure Food and Drug Act and the Meat Inspection Act of 1906.

Generally regarded as the leading agricultural chemist of his day, Goessmann was active in the organization of professional societies, becoming president in 1880 of the newly created American Association of Agricultural Chemists. He participated in the formation of the American Chemical Society in 1876 and went on to serve as its vice president in 1882–1883 and its president in 1887. In 1865 he was elected a corresponding member of the New York Academy of Science and in 1875 was made a fellow. In 1889 he became a corresponding member of the Massachusetts Horticultural Society, and in 1893 he was a member of the Advisory Council on Chemistry of the World Congress Auxiliary of the Columbian Exposition. He retired from Massachusetts Agricultural College in 1907 and was made an emeritus professor in 1908.

In 1862 Goessmann married Mary Anna Clara Kinny, of Syracuse; they had six children. Her father, Edward Kinny, was instrumental in the foundation of the Roman Catholic Church of St. John the Evangelist in that city. A devout Catholic himself, Goessmann was an active participant in the group of Catholics in Amherst that arranged the construction of St. Brigid's Church. He died at his home in Amherst, Massachusetts.

• Goessmann's voluminous papers (he wrote 362 articles) are in the Archives of the University of Massachusetts at Amherst. These include several biographical descriptions and a book by Frederick Tuckerman, *Charles Anthony Goessmann* (1917). Goessmann also edited the second edition of George B. Emerson and Charles L. Flint, *Manual of Agriculture for the School, the Farm, and the Fireside* (1885).

NANCY M. GORDON

GOETHALS, George Washington (29 June 1858–21 Jan. 1928), engineer and military officer, was born in Brooklyn, New York, the son of John Louis Goethals, a carpenter, and Marie Le Barron. At the age of fourteen he entered the College of the City of New York. In April 1876, after three years of college, Goethals won a cadetship to the U.S. Military Academy at West Point. He graduated second in his class in 1880, a distinction that won for him a commission as second lieutenant in the Army Corps of Engineers.

Goethals remained at the military academy during the summer and fall of 1880 as an assistant instructor in practical astronomy. In 1881 he attended the Engineer School of Application at Willets Point, New York. His first field assignment came in the following year with his appointment as engineer officer of the Department of Columbia in Vancouver, Washington. His routine duties included reconnaissance, surveys, and astronomical work, while his most consequential project was the replacement of a 120-foot bridge across the Spokane River.

In September 1884 he transferred to Cincinnati, Ohio, as an assistant to Lieutenant Colonel William E. Merrill, who was in charge of the navigational improvements of the Ohio River. Goethals worked his way up from rodman on the hydrographic surveys to foreman of concrete work and, finally, to chief of construction. Also in 1884 he married Effie Rodman; they had two children. From 1885 to 1889 he taught civil and military engineering at West Point. He returned to the field in 1889 to assist Colonel John W. Barlow with navigational improvements on the Cumberland and Tennessee rivers.

In 1891 Goethals was promoted to captain and placed in charge of the completion of the Muscle Shoals Canal along the Tennessee River near Chattanooga. This was his first independent command, and his responsibilities included the design and construction of the Riverton Lock at Colbert Shoals. Goethals's recommendation of a single lock with an unprecedented lift of twenty-six feet was initially opposed by his superiors in Washington, and he was forced to persuade the conservative army engineers of the merits of his design. The success of the Riverton Lock inspired the eventual adoption of high-lift locks elsewhere, including those for the Panama Canal.

In October 1894 Goethals became the assistant to Brigadier General Thomas L. Casey, chief of engineers, in Washington, D.C. With the outbreak of the Spanish-American War in 1898, Goethals was made a lieutenant colonel of the Volunteer Service and assigned as chief engineer of the First Army Corps. In this capacity he designed and constructed the water and supply system for the army's camp at Chickamauga, Georgia, before directing the engineering operations of the First Army Corps in Puerto Rico. At the close of the war Goethals resumed his regular army status at the rank of captain.

In November 1898 Goethals returned to West Point to teach military engineering. Two years later he headed the coastal fortification and river and harbor work at the Corps of Engineers field office in Newport, Rhode Island. Following a general reorganization of the army in 1903, Goethals served on the newly created General Staff, where he remained until he became involved in the Panama Canal project.

The French had initiated construction of a canal across the Isthmus of Panama in 1880 but abandoned the project nine years later on account of a hostile environment, tropical disease, overextended supply lines, and mismanagement. After extensive investigation and debate, Congress decided in 1902 that the United States should undertake to build and operate the interoceanic canal. Under the direction of a seven-member Isthmian Canal Commission, construction by the American work force commenced in 1904. In March 1907 President Theodore Roosevelt (1858–1919) appointed Goethals to the commission.

By that time the commission had seen the resignation of two chief engineers: John F. Wallace and John F. Stevens. Convinced that continuity of leadership was essential to the success of the project, Roosevelt turned to the army for the next chief and on 1 April appointed Goethals. This solved the problem of resignations, but Roosevelt also wanted to centralize control in one person. Although he could not legally disband the commission, he effectively diluted its power by elevating the chief engineer to chairman of the commission and granting him supreme authority. Goethals was thus given complete control over all aspects of construction and made answerable solely to the president through the secretary of war. Administration of the Panama Canal Zone had effectively shifted from the commission form of government to a system of one-man control, which Goethals himself described as being "a sort of benevolent despotism."

Beyond the engineering challenges of the canal—which included excavating 262 million cubic yards of earth, building locks of unprecedented size, and damming the Chagres River to create the world's largest artificial lake—Goethals faced the equally difficult task of meeting the needs of a work force numbering more than 30,000. Housing, food, health care, schools, recreation centers, and a comprehensive judicial system had to be provided for the workers and their families. Moreover, Goethals had to deal with an atmosphere of skepticism about his appointment. Fearing the imposition of militarism, civilian workers expressed grave concern that Roosevelt had selected an army officer to head the canal project. Actually, the president did not turn the canal construction over to the Army Corps of Engineers; Goethals and the other engineer officers assigned to the Panama Canal did not report to the chief of engineers. Nevertheless, Goethals had to overcome this prejudice. This he did, aided in part by his policy of acting fairly on all grievances. He toured construction sites daily and prided himself on his thorough grasp of details. He was the ultimate authority, but he was known to be accessible, sympathetic, and fair. Goethals became a hero to the American work force in Panama, if not to the people of the United States and beyond.

Goethals's administration of the project was superb. The canal, which opened to traffic on 15 August 1914, was completed below budget and ahead of schedule. In the United States, Goethals's popularity soared. Congress thanked him, and there was even talk of his becoming a dark horse candidate in the 1916 presidential election.

All this fame failed to land him the assignment he wanted most, chief of the Army Corps of Engineers. Instead, President Woodrow Wilson appointed him governor of the Panama Canal Zone in April 1914. He retired from the army as a major general in 1916 and resigned as governor at the end of his term in 1917. He then accepted the position of state engineer for New Jersey, where he was responsible for developing a statewide highway system.

When the United States entered World War I, German submarine warfare was posing a deadly menace to Allied shipping. In an attempt to build up the nation's merchant fleet as rapidly as possible, President Wilson approved the U.S. Shipping Board's plan to construct an emergency fleet of wooden ships; he asked Goethals to help. Goethals agreed, and in April 1917 Wilson appointed him general manager of the board's Emergency Fleet Corporation.

From the beginning, however, Goethals doubted the wisdom of proceeding with the wooden ship plan, and the more he investigated the scheme the more profoundly opposed to it he became. Committed to technically superior steel ships, he devised a plan for their rapid construction and attempted to change the minds of the board members and the president but soon learned that technical matters made little difference to the turf-conscious Shipping Board members, who were firmly committed to the wooden ship program.

This situation infuriated Goethals, who had enjoyed great authority when building the Panama Canal. Although he prided himself on his persuasive abilities, his military and administrative experience had not focused on negotiation and compromise. Convinced of the validity of his position in light of the international crisis, Goethals sought to scotch the wooden shipbuilding program and turned to Wilson for support. The president, however, stood behind his previously endorsed policy, although he offered Goethals the option of simultaneously pursuing a steel shipbuilding program. Goethals was humiliated and felt forced to resign after only three months on the job. He viewed the shipbuilding experience as his first professional failure and was deeply bruised.

Goethals immediately asked the secretary of war to send him to France to head the army's engineering construction. As he wrote General John J. Pershing in August 1917: "My lack of training with troops could justly be taken by the Army at large as a bar to command in the field; but I do not see how any exception can be made to my assignment in charge of engineering construction, in which my experience has been rather extensive." Pershing, however, was unwilling to relieve the current engineer officers of their duties and declined Goethals's offer.

Goethals was nevertheless recalled to active duty in December 1917 and was appointed acting quartermaster general. He wrote his old patron Theodore Roosevelt about the job: "How long I am going to last here depends upon the support received and the lack of interference."

Frustrated again by his lack of complete authority, Goethals was relieved of the office in February 1918 and put in charge of the War Department's Division of Purchase, Storage and Traffic, another shift that left him angry and depressed. This time, however, the problems of the office led Wilson to give Goethals what he wanted: control over the department. He became, as one newspaper reporter described, "absolute dictator of purchase, traffic, and storage," a type of "supplies autocrat." Congress voted him the Distinguished Service Medal in 1918 "for especially meritorious and conspicuous service" in reorganizing the Quartermaster Department.

In March 1919 Goethals again retired and established a successful consulting engineering practice in New York City, where he remained active until his death. Among the important municipal, state, and private projects on which he consulted were the Inner Harbor Navigation Canal in New Orleans; the State of Washington's Columbia Basin Irrigation Project; the East Bay Municipal Utility District of Oakland, California; and the Lake Worth inlet in Florida. He worked as chief consulting engineer for the New York–New Jersey Port and Harbor Development Commission from 1917 to 1921 and remained in that position for the successor organization, the Port of New York Authority. As chief consulting engineer Goethals helped fashion a comprehensive plan for the coordination and modernization of all the rail facilities feeding into and out of the port; he was also one of the principal advisers for the construction of the Holland Vehicular Tunnel. His administrative skills were tapped during the 1923 anthracite coal strike when he served as fuel administrator of New York.

Goethals's work on the Panama Canal brought him a level of fame matched by few other engineers in American history. But success had its price. His accomplishments, along with his burning desire to be in complete control of all his subsequent assignments, contributed to a profound sense of frustration and lack of fulfillment that hounded him during the remaining years of his professional life. He died in New York City.

• The George Washington Goethals Papers are in the Manuscript Division, Library of Congress. The official documents associated with his service in various government agencies are in Record Groups 32, 77, 92, 165, and 185 at the National Archives. His publications include *The Isthmian Canal* (1909), *Government of the Canal Zone* (1915), *The Panama Canal: An Engineering Treatise*, (2 vols., 1916), *Slides at the Panama Canal* (1916), and *Columbia Basin Irrigation Project* (1922). His biography is Joseph Bucklin Bishop and Farnham Bishop, *Goethals: Genius of the Panama Canal* (1930). The best account of his work on the Panama Canal is David McCullough, *The Path between the Seas: The Creation of the Panama Canal, 1870–1914* (1977). His activities during World War I are analyzed in Phyllis A. Zimmerman, *The Neck of the Bottle: George W. Goethals and the Reorganization of the U.S. Army Supply System, 1917–1918* (1992).

JEFFREY K. STINE

GOETSCHIUS, John Henry (8 Mar. 1718–14 Nov. 1774), German Reformed clergyman, was born Johann Heinrich Götschi in Rheinegg, near Zürich, Switzerland, the son of Moritz Götschi, a minister, and Esther Werndli. The family name was often spelled Goetschy; John Henry preferred the Latinized version, Goetschius. After elementary schooling and tutoring in arts and ancient languages by his father (an excellent scholar), he entered the Latin school in Zürich at the age of sixteen, completing one-half year. His parents removed him from the school to emigrate to the New World. The father led a colony of some 250 emigrants who left Zürich in early October 1734. According to the account of a fellow passenger, Götschi's father was promised by a prominently placed Dutch official in The Hague an amply salaried position as a pastor if he would settle in Pennsylvania rather than in his intended destination, the Carolinas. More than half the band of emigrants accepted the change in destination along with the Götschi family. They arrived in Philadelphia on 29 May 1735, barely surviving a stormy passage, inadequate food and drink, and a tyrannical ship's master.

Unfortunately for the Götschi family, the father was mortally ill when he was taken from the ship and died the next day. This left Goetschius at the age of seventeen responsible for his mother and seven siblings in the strange setting. Despite his youth and inexperience, he was soon offered preaching posts in several German Reformed parishes, largely in the back country, which lacked well-trained and ordained pastors. In a letter of July 1735, sent back to Zürich, Goetschius reported that after landing and showing his credentials he was "almost compelled" to preach to adults and catechize children each Sunday on a schedule that

found him successively at Philadelphia, Skippack, Old Goshenhoppen, New Goshenhoppen, and Great Swamp. He hoped to be ordained so that he could administer communion, perform weddings, and baptize children.

Goetschius's first attempt in May 1737 to receive full ordination from the English-speaking Presbyterians failed when a committee of the presbytery found him lacking in collegiate and theological learning, though skilled in languages. They advised him to put himself under the care and direction of a competent minister, but in the meantime they gave him a temporary license to preach because of the shortage of qualified ministers. Goetschius continued his pastoral work, even performing duties reserved for those who had been ordained.

Goetschius began church record books in four colonial Reformed congregations. In one, that of New Goshenhoppen, he recorded that he preached at the places cited above and also at Saucon, Egypt, Maxatawny, Moselem, Oley, Berne, and Tulpehocken as well. A number of baptisms he performed are registered in these books. Because he was not fully ordained, some of his parishioners at Oley left the church.

Goetschius's active if informal pastoral ministry was hindered by the insistence of John Henry Boehm that all German Reformed preachers come under the control of a coetus responsible to the Classis of Holland at The Hague. Eventually, Goetschius bowed to this demand, suspended his preaching, and accepted instruction for one year under Rev. Mr. Peter Henry Dorsius in Bucks County. Subsequently, he was ordained in July 1741 by Dorsius, assisted by pastors Theodore J. Freylinghuysen (Dutch Reformed) and Gilbert Tennent (Presbyterian). All these men were in the Pietist camp and tended to be sharply critical of the lack of revivalist zeal among the orthodox clergy approved by the Pennsylvania coetus and the Classis of Holland. Dorsius was reprimanded by the Dutch officials responsible for Reformed congregations in America because of this ordination.

The action was taken to enable Goetschius to accept a call already extended to him to serve the combined Dutch-language parishes of Newtown, Jamaica, Hempstead, and Oyster Bay, all on Long Island, New York. He had become known to the Reformed there through his itinerant and irregular preaching in New Jersey and New York. After moving to the area to take up residence, he was installed in his office by Bernardus Freedman, an aged clergyman and fellow Pietist. Soon after his arrival, Goetschius preached a controversial sermon titled *The Unknown God*, based on a text in Acts 17, in which he admonished his hearers about their lack of demonstrated piety. Mere religious ritual, without heartfelt conversion, will result in damnation, not salvation, he contended. All Christians must be able to state and date the time of their personal regeneration. The sermon, with a praising foreword by Theodore J. Freylinghuysen, was printed in the Dutch language as *De Onbekende God* in 1743 by John Peter Zenger, who had become famous for his involvement in a trial that helped to establish the freedom of the press.

The belligerent stance of Goetschius provoked equally determined resistance by the orthodox. The Classis of Amsterdam mandated a commission of inquiry made up of other New York clergy to examine Goetschius. They censured his irregular ordination, his permitting unlicensed men to preach, and his barring from communion those parishioners whom he felt to be unregenerate; they also reported some personal indiscretions. Goetschius refused to answer the charges, maintaining that his critics were all "godless people." The panel ruled that Goetschius must refrain from administering the sacraments until the Classis in the Netherlands ruled on his ordination, but the unruly cleric went his own way, even when the verdict came back that his ordination was indeed invalid.

The result was a raging church fight that involved locked church doors and turbulent worship services, at times forcing Goetschius to preach outside the church building, or, if inside, to preach over the sound of congregational singing that attempted to drown out his voice. One biographer characterized him as "a stocky little man, ready of wit and not averse to a good fight" (Genzmer). His was one of a series of struggles between revival-minded pietists and tradition-minded confessionalists that wracked the Presbyterian/Reformed churches in the mid-eighteenth century.

Finally, to resolve the impasse, the Classis of Amsterdam suggested that Goetschius submit to an examination for a new ordination, with the understanding that, if approved, he seek ministry elsewhere than on Long Island. This took place in 1748, and Goetschius accepted a position as a senior colleague at Hackensack and Schraalenberg, New Jersey.

The shift moved the controversy from New York to New Jersey, because the traditionalist-minded senior pastor in these two parishes was soon accusing Goetschius of irregularities, such as visiting neighboring parishes to pursue his revivalist agenda without the permission of the regular dominie. In 1751 Goetschius conversed in New Jersey with the leading minister of the German Lutheran Church in Pennsylvania, Henry Melchior Mühlenberg, who was favorably impressed by Goetschius, probably because they shared a Pietist orientation.

Mühlenberg found Goetschius to have "an unusual zeal for furthering the power of godliness" and to be diligent in his ministry, if too vehement on the doctrine of predestination. When the senior colleague in the area complained that Goetschius was "too impetuous and hasty" and "too ready to begin all sorts of innovations," Mühlenberg counseled the colleague to overlook these weaknesses. The zeal of youth must be tempered by the wisdom of maturity. If they could unite in a good purpose their combined gifts could work to mutual advantage. One of the innovations was the founding of Queens College (now Rutgers University) in New Brunswick, New Jersey, with Goetschius a moving spirit as an early trustee. He also personally trained several young men for the ministry in the apprenticeship system then popular.

While in New Jersey in May 1750, he married Rachel Zabrowisky of Bergen County. After a long but turbulent pastoral career of thirty-four years with the Dutch Reformed Church in New Jersey, Goetschius died at Schraalenberg.

• An extended biographical sketch is in William J. Hinke, *Ministers of the German Reformed Congregations in Pennsylvania and Other Colonies* (1951), superseding the earlier chapter in James I. Good, *History of the Reformed Church in the United States, 1725–1792* (1899). The journey of the Götschi family from Switzerland to Pennsylvania is described in Hinke, *History of the Goshenhoppen Reformed Church, 1727–1799* (1920), based on Ludwig Weber, *Der hinckende Bott von Carolina* (1835), and its arrival in North America is documented in Hinke and Ralph B. Strassburger, *Pennsylvania German Pioneers . . .* , vol. 1 (1934), pp. 146–49. Hinke portrayed the struggles between Boehm and Geotschius in *Life and Letters of the Rev. John Philip Boehm* (1915), using the materials provided in the sourcebook edited by Hinke and Good, *Minutes and Letters of the Coetus of the German Reformed Congregations of Pennsylvania, 1727–1792* (1903). Reference to Goetschius's work in the Reformed parish at Oley is made in Philip E. Pendleton, *Oley Valley Heritage: The Colonial Years, 1700–1775* (1994). Randall H. Balmer included an extended discussion of Goetschius's character and theological orientation in *A Perfect Babel of Confusion: Dutch Religion and English Culture in the Middle Colonies* (1989), based in part on the sources published in the *Ecclesiastical Records of New York* (6 vols., 1901–1916). This material is repeated in Balmer, "John Henry Goetschius and the Unknown God: Eighteenth-Century Pietism in the Middle Colonies," *Pennsylvania Magazine of History and Biography* 113 (1989): 579–608, which provides the first full English translation of the Goetschius sermon. Mühlenberg's assessment is in Theodore G. Tappert and John W. Doberstein, *The Journals of Henry Melchior Muhlenberg*, vol. 1 (1942). There is brief mention of the New Jersey ministry in Theodore F. Chambers, *The Early Germans of New Jersey* (1895).

DONALD F. DURNBAUGH

GOETZE, Albrecht (11 July 1897–15 Aug. 1971), Assyriologist, was born in Leipzig, Germany, the son of Rudolf Goetze, a prominent psychiatrist, and Elsa Roemmler. He began his university education at Munich and Leipzig in 1915. The following year he fought in the German Imperial army on the western front. Thrice wounded, once critically, he was decorated for heroism and received a field commission. In 1918 Goetze began the study of Indo-European linguistics and Semitics at Berlin and Heidelberg, receiving his doctorate in linguistics at Heidelberg in 1922 on the subject of Italian phonology. His first monograph, *Die Schatzhöhle* (1922), was based on Christian oriental sources in Arabic, Ethiopic, and Syriac. In 1922 he married Frieda Schirbel. They had three children.

Goetze's expertise in Indo-European and cuneiform studies was ideal preparation for the study of the Hittites, an Indo-European people who settled in Anatolia in the second millennium B.C. and who left extensive records in Hittite (deciphered just as Goetze was a graduate student) as well as several other languages. Beginning in 1922, Goetze contributed fundamental publications to all aspects of Hittitology, including primary sources (*Keilschrifturkunden aus Boghazköi* [5 vols.] and *Verstreute Boghazköi Texte* [1930]), editions of texts with translation and commentary (*Hattušiliš* [1925], *Madduwattaš* [1928], *Die Annalen des Muršilis* [1933]), and numerous essays on philology, chronology, and geography. Goetze, gifted with a clear historical sense, published pioneering and authoritative studies of Hittite and Hurrian civilization, including *Die Hethiter-Reich* (1928) and *Kleinasien* (1933), the latter a masterpiece of fully documented synthesis. Goetze lectured at Heidelberg from 1922 to 1927, when he was called to Marburg as Ordentlicher Professor of Semitic Languages and Ancient Oriental History.

Believing that Hitler's rise to power spelled disaster for Germany, Goetze typed and distributed leaflets warning the Marburg community against nazism. This led to his dismissal in 1933. He escaped to Oslo and sustained himself by lecturing there and in Copenhagen for a year. Two substantial monographs emerged during this period, *Muršiliš Spachlähmung* (1934) and *Hethiter, Churriter und Assyrer* (1936).

In 1934 Goetze was invited to Yale University as a visiting professor. Goetze was thus at the forefront of German scholars of the ancient Near East whom nazism drove to the United States, where they revolutionized, vitalized, and enhanced Near Eastern studies. He became a U.S. citizen in 1940. Committed wholeheartedly to his country, Goetze published thereafter exclusively in English and often refused to speak German, even to former German colleagues. Not one to forget or forgive, he was proud to decline the Marburg professorship when it was offered to him once again, years after the war. He was appointed Laffan Professor of Assyriology at Yale in 1936 and Sterling Professor in 1956. During Goetze's years at Yale, he continued his leadership in Hittite studies, producing monographs on the *Hittite Ritual of Tunnawi* (1938) and *Kizzuwatna* (1940). His English translations of Hittite texts in *Ancient Near Eastern Texts Relating to the Old Testament* (ed. James B. Pritchard, 1956) were the first of their kind.

Goetze's interests in Assyriology spanned the entire discipline. His *Old Babylonian Omen Texts* (1947) was a major contribution to the arcane subject of Mesopotamian divination. In contrast to many of his contemporaries, he saw Sumerian administrative documents as a promising field of study and published numerous examples with analytic studies remarkable for their thoroughness and command of an enormous mass of material, including such subjects as reed mats (1948), leather objects (1955), foreign dignitaries (1953), Sumerian chronology (1960), and government (1963). He also contributed to Mesopotamian mathematics (1945, 1951) and chronology (1957, 1964, 1968).

Maintaining his interest in linguistics, Goetze published a series of grammatical studies on Akkadian verbs, number idioms, plural forms, passive constructions, dialects, phonology, and etymology. Like his other studies, these were characteristically incisive, succinct, original, and fully documented. Goetze quickly mastered new texts as they were discovered, including those in Ugaritic, a hitherto unknown Semitic language, written in alphabetic cuneiform script on clay tablets, discovered in Syria in 1929. He wrote more than 150 scholarly articles during this period.

Goetze had a taste for museum detective work and set about to catalog and make available for scholarship the thousands of Babylonian tablets scattered by the antiquities trade to museums and private collections throughout the United States. With Abraham Sachs and Thorkild Jacobsen in 1946 he founded the first U.S. periodical devoted exclusively to Assyriology, the *Journal of Cuneiform Studies*, and served as editor of the first twenty-three volumes (except for vol. 21, a festschrift). For the early volumes he wrote many of the articles himself and even typed the galleys on a rickety machine. Under Goetze, the journal developed into one of the world's premier periodicals in ancient Near Eastern studies.

Goetze throve on field work. In 1926 he explored much of Anatolia, mostly on horseback, and was keenly interested in all aspects of archaeology. In 1948 he became director of the Baghdad School of the American Schools of Oriental Research. Expelled from Iraq for political reasons, he eventually returned to participate in the school's Nippur expedition. The most noteworthy of his many publications of new discoveries in Iraq was the tablets of the earliest Babylonian law code, called the Laws of Eshnunna; published in 1956, this monograph initiated a new phase in the study of ancient legal codes.

Goetze spared no pains as a teacher, offering twelve or more class hours a week, writing out exercises himself in whatever languages he felt called on to teach, and serving virtually as a one-man department for decades of Yale graduate students in ancient Near Eastern studies. After his retirement in 1965, Goetze, who had few outside interests or leisure activities, felt deprived of the stimulus of students, colleagues, and administrative responsibilities and so labored on, his astonishing research capacities undiminished, but his mood was one of increasing personal loneliness and foreboding. He died while on a vacation trip in Garmisch, Germany.

• Goetze's extensive professional correspondence, including thousands of letters to and from the leading orientalists of his day, is in the Manuscripts and Archives Collection of the Sterling Memorial Library, Yale University. His scholarly manuscripts are in the Yale Babylonian Collection, Yale University. A bibliography of Goetze's scholarly publications was published by J. J. Finkelstein in *Journal of Cuneiform Studies* 26 (1974): 2–15. Obituaries include Finkelstein, *Journal of the American Oriental Society* 92 (1972): 197–203; H. G. Güterbock, *Archiv für Orientforschung* 24 (1973): 243–45; and T. Jacobsen, *Bulletin of the American Schools of Oriental Research* 206 (1972): 3–6.

BENJAMIN R. FOSTER

GOFF, Bruce Alonzo (8 June 1904–4 Aug. 1982), architect, was born in the remote village of Alton, Kansas, the son of Corliss Arthur Goff, a watch repairer, and Maude Rose Furbeck, an elementary-school teacher. The family moved frequently during Goff's childhood, residing for brief periods in other small towns in Kansas or Oklahoma. In 1915 they settled in Tulsa, Oklahoma.

Goff's parents thought he showed artistic talent, and in 1916 they arranged for him to begin working part time in the architectural office of Rush, Endacott & Rush, a well-established firm where Goff quickly advanced. His first design to be published appeared in 1918, when he was only fourteen, and his first design to be built, the B. L. Graves house in Los Angeles, was completed the next year. Following his graduation from Tulsa High School in 1922, he elected to continue working for the firm rather than attend college, and in 1929 he was named a full partner.

Goff was strongly influenced by Frank Lloyd Wright, whose work he discovered in an old issue of *Architectural Record*. His skillful adaptations of Wright's vocabulary were remarkable and prove his later claim that he was unusually precocious. His fascination with Wright soon led to an examination of all currents of modern architecture, which he explored through periodicals and books then readily available in Tulsa. He was particularly drawn to more individualistic currents, and beginning in 1920, reflections of Louis Sullivan, Antonio Gaudi, Eliel Saarinen, and Eric Mendelsohn can be detected in his early work. Among Goff's most important designs to be built during these years were the Boston Avenue Methodist-Episcopal Church, Tulsa, designed in 1926 under the close supervision of his former high school art teacher, Adah Robinson, and the Page Furniture Depository and Warehouse, Tulsa, designed in 1927 (demolished). Details of the former incorporate motifs of German expressionism, while the latter recalls work by Dutch expressionists. In other examples, such as the Riverside Studio, Tulsa (1928), a purer current of modernism is personalized with window patterns meant to suggest musical notation.

Architectural commissions declined during the Great Depression, and the firm (then Endacott & Goff) was dissolved in 1932. In 1934 Goff moved to Chicago to work for Alfonso Iannelli, who he had met in Tulsa and with whom he had become friends. Used to greater independence, Goff found the work frustrating. He began teaching part time in the Chicago Academy of Fine Arts in 1935 and tried freelance work, then in 1936 accepted an offer from the Libbey-Owens-Ford glass company to design architectural installations for their newly acquired glass facing material, Vitrolite. In 1937 he moved with the firm to Toledo, Ohio, but again found work unsatisfying and resigned later that same year, returning to Chicago. He resumed his teaching at the Chicago Academy and at last began to find clients of his own, mainly young families who wanted to build small houses for themselves in the Chicago suburbs. In these Goff adapted elements of work by George Fred Keck, as in the George Elin house, Northfield, Illinois (1938). He showed greater originality in a triangular weekend house for Irma Bartman, near Fern Creek, Kentucky (1941). Its taut linearity and crystalline forms presage mature work that was to follow.

During the Second World War Goff served with the U.S. Navy and was stationed in the Aleutian Islands in 1943, then in Camp Parks, California, in 1944 and 1945. He sketched "dream houses" for his military colleagues and designed recreational and ecclesiastical facilities for the naval bases where he was stationed, creatively reconfiguring standardized building systems such as Quonset huts. Following his release from service in December 1945, he chose to remain in California and opened a small office in Berkeley. In the work of this period, two designs (both unbuilt) in particular signal the end of his formative years: the Constance Gillis house, Bend, Oregon (1945) and the Don Leidig house, Hayward, California (1946). In the former, a curved stone wall was to enclose an open interior in which circular platforms, linked by a spiral ramp, overlooked a central volume. In the latter, open circular rooms were designed to appear as floating islands, informally joined by bridges over an extensive pool that was to cover the remaining areas of the floor. Various precedents can be cited, such as Wright's Jester house (1938) and Guggenheim Museum (1943), but these influences had been by now so completely absorbed and reworked that the product was uniquely Goff's.

In December 1946 Goff returned to Oklahoma to accept a teaching position at the University of Oklahoma in Norman, and in the spring of 1947 he was appointed chair of his department, officially known then as the School of Architecture. Under his direction, the school gained in reputation, and Goff's practice expanded. His work began to receive widespread attention in both the popular and the professional press, and major examples of his developing genius were built. Among these was the H. E. Ledbetter house, Norman (1947), an adaptation of the Leidig project with undulating stone walls and a suspended roof. For Ruth Ford, the owner of the Chicago Academy of Fine Arts, he designed a house of spherical elements, its structure adapted from Quonset hut components and its walls made of coal (Aurora, Ill. [1947]). Most impressive was the Eugene Bavinger house, designed for a university colleague (Norman, Okla. [1950]). Here Goff developed his Gillis house concept, enclosing an open volume within a logarithmic spiral of stone and glass cullet that rose to a high point at the center. There, from a steel mast, suspension cables supported both the curved roof and a series of circular platforms within. These were arranged at different levels like the treads of a spiral stair and, hovering over a pool below, took the place of conventional rooms. The remarkably complex interior that resulted stands as a high point of Goff's career. Other designs were geometrically simpler yet hardly less extraordinary, such as the James D. Wilson house, Pensacola, Florida (1950), designed for Goff's former commanding officer at Camp Parks, a series of cubes with angled corners that are linked to form a faceted volume. Many of his most remarkable designs remain unbuilt. These include the John Garvey house, Urbana, Illinois (1952), in which spheres were to be suspended within a translucent, trumpet-shaped volume, and the first design for the Joe Price studio, Bartlesville, Oklahoma (1953), in which irregular pentagons were joined together to outline a volume in which walls, ceilings, and portions of the floor were to slope; all references to conventional geometric enclosure would have been obscured.

Within the small, conservative town of Norman, Goff's homosexuality drew unwanted attention; in November 1955 he was arrested on a morals charge of dubious nature and forced to resign from the university. He moved to Bartlesville, Oklahoma, and opened an office in Wright's newly completed Price Tower. There he continued to design houses that captured popular attention, beginning with a second design for the Price studio (1956). Its more disciplined triangular forms still incorporate angled walls, and portions of the floor are shaped to form seating areas. Additions of a gallery in 1966 and a towered study in 1974 sustain the image of a crystal, as if the house were meant to symbolize the imagined space of a precious stone. In a proposal for the Vernon Rudd house (San Mateo County, Calif. [1959]; a simpler version was later built), Goff explored a linear theme in which sleeping areas and studies were to be housed in pentagonal units and linked to a central, undulating spine containing shared spaces. For the Albert Baxter house (Quincy, Ill. [1961]; unbuilt), he designed a tower containing one major room on each floor. In other proposals, Goff developed ideas that he had earlier initiated in Norman, depicting houses with various angular and circular shapes that sustained an image of wild modernity.

By 1964 work had slowed, and Goff accepted an invitation of work in Kansas City, Missouri, from a development company, Briar Associates. He moved there in April of that year and began designing prototypes for residential developments. These were not sufficiently convincing to gain needed financial support, and none were built. Other commissions led to happier results, as the Hugh Duncan house, near Cobden, Illinois (1965), a linear composition of cylindrical enclosures with circular doorways and windows. In 1970 he moved to Tyler, Texas, also in response to an offer of work: a series of houses and related buildings for a development known as Lake Village. A few of his housing prototypes were built, but again the results were disappointing; it seemed that Goff needed the stimulus of known clients to produce his best work. His designs in these years tended to be more subdued than in Norman or even in Bartlesville, and increasingly he focused on ornamental detail rather than exploring new spatial patterns.

Two late commissions elicited work of greater quality: the Mineola Community Center, Mineola, Texas, (1974; unbuilt), and the Shin'enKan museum, designed in 1978 for an unspecified site and realized after Goff's death as the Pavilion for Japanese Art at the Los Angeles County Museum of Art (1982–1988). Unlike most of Goff's later commissions, both were nonresidential. Both also proved Goff's undiminished skill at manipulating curvilinear geometries in unexpected ways. For the Mineola project, Goff planned an interior of curved and angled screens beneath a freely shaped canopy. To enhance openness, Goff proposed adapting radio transmission towers as spires from which the canopy would be suspended. This proved structurally unfeasible, and heavier towers were substituted, compromising its celebratory image. During the course of design, plan shapes, too, became more conventional configurations. Estimates still proved excessive, and ultimately the project was canceled.

For the Shin'enKan museum, Goff designed a light, translucent enclosure, also beneath a suspended roof. Inside, in a variation of the Guggenheim, a spiral ramp was to lead to curvilinear viewing platforms that overlooked niches made to resemble Japanese tokonomas. Goff died in Tyler, Texas, before the design progressed beyond preliminary design drawings, but his concept was faithfully developed by his trusted assistant, Bart Prince. Again it was necessary to modify the structure, and the result was visually heavier than Goff had envisioned, but in the essential continuity of its spaces and the beauty of its natural light, Goff's genius was honored.

Critics summarizing Goff's position in architecture accurately characterize him as an unpredictable, romantic loner who operated outside the bounds of conventional fashion. Although philosophically close to Frank Lloyd Wright, he never subscribed fully to Wright's concept of organic architecture, feeling its demands of cohesive unity and geometric coherence too restricting. Visually his work develops motifs of German and Dutch expressionism, and it has often been included with theirs in anthologies of fantastic architecture, yet his designs tended to be less theoretical and more pragmatic.

Affecting an unsophisticated manner, Goff worked best when designing specific solutions to specific problems for people to whom he could relate personally. His ability to envision new spatial configurations based on complicated combinations of untried geometries remains unsurpassed, but his tendency to articulate those geometries with materials, colors, and patterns judged by most critics as being in questionable taste obscured his accomplishments. His clients were primarily middle-class, self-made midwesterners whose own individuality was well served by his efforts. Not only the few artists among them, but also the automobile salesmen, real estate speculators, airline pilots, shoe manufacturers, doctors, and so on, were drawn to his daring challenges of architectural norms and tended to like things such as coal walls, feathered ceilings, and elaborately patterned mosaics of brilliantly colored tile or glass.

Goff described his work as expressive of what he called the "continuous present," naming the Bavinger house as one example: "earth-bound as it is, [it] is a primitive example of the continuity of space-for-living. . . . it is not a 'back-to-nature' concept of living space. It is a living *with* nature today and every day [in] space, again as part of our continuous present" (Goff, "Forty-four Architectural Realizations"). During his last years of practice he also strove (unsuccessfully) to create an example of what he called "absolute architecture," describing it as "something completely separate from utilitarian and symbolic functions. We might call it 'pure architecture' in the same sense that we now have 'pure music'" (Goff, "Notes on Architecture," unpaginated ms.). Neither concept seemed sufficient to provide convincing intellectual depth, however, and his work remains best appreciated as a manifestation of popular American culture.

• Goff's drawings and papers are maintained in the Art Institute of Chicago. His writings include "Design for a Limestone Residence," *Stone* 39 (Sept. 1918): 415; "Forty-four Architectural Realizations," an unpublished and unfinished manuscript begun in 1972, available at the Art Institute of Chicago; and "Notes on Architecture" (June 1957), published as "Notizen über das Bauen," *Bauwelt* 49, no. 4 (Jan. 1958): 78–88. For more information on Goff's life and work, see Jeffrey Cook, *The Architecture of Bruce Goff* (1978); David G. De Long, *The Architecture of Bruce Goff: Buildings and Projects, 1916–1974* (2 vols., 1977); De Long, *Bruce Goff: Toward Absolute Architecture* (1988); Takenobu Mohri, *Bruce Goff in Architecture* (1970); and Louis Muller and William Murphy, *A Portfolio of the Work of Bruce Goff* (1971).

DAVID G. DE LONG

GOFF, Frederick Richmond (23 Apr. 1916–26 Sept. 1982), rare-book librarian, was born in Newport, Rhode Island, the son of Francis Shubael Goff, an insurance executive, and Amelia Seabury. Goff attended Brown University, where he received an A.B. in 1937 and an M.A. in 1939. While still an undergraduate at Brown, Goff began work as the assistant to Margaret B. Stillwell of the Annmary Brown Memorial Library and editor of the Second Census of *Incunabula in American Libraries*. The study of incunabula, or books printed before 1501, would be central to Goff's entire career. The Second Census was published in 1940 and in July of that year Goff moved to Washington, D.C., to become assistant to Arthur A. Houghton, Jr., curator of the Rare Book Collection of the Library of Congress. Goff would spend the remainder of his professional career at the Library of Congress and his biography is largely the history of the development of the rare-book collections of the library.

Archibald Macleish, librarian of Congress, had only recently appointed Arthur Houghton curator of rare books. Houghton, president of the Corning Glass Company, assumed the position on the condition that he would devote only two days a week to the job. Many of the daily functions of administering the collection fell on Goff. Houghton, with business matters pressing heavily upon him, resigned the position in 1941. Goff became acting chief on 15 August 1941 and chief on 1 March 1945. It was in the previous year,

1944, that the rare-book collection became a full-fledged division in the Reference Department of the Library of Congress after being a unit of the Reading Rooms Division for some years.

Goff spent a total of thirty-two years in the Rare Book Division and during this period he gained a reputation as one of the most respected bookmen in the United States. In the 1940s Goff, along with consultant Lawrence Wroth from the John Carter Brown Library in Providence, Rhode Island, charted the future path of the national rare-book collection. The library hired Wroth, a veteran rare-book librarian and historian of printing and Americana, to aid the relatively new unit and its staff. He wrote a collecting policy in 1940 that Goff assiduously implemented and augmented. Wroth rightly believed that the Library of Congress should be the repository for the great works of Americana and have the strongest general collection of Americana in the country. Goff immediately began acquiring the monuments of American history and literature. Among his most notable acquisitions in his first decade or so at the library, either through purchase or gift, were the 1493 Rome edition in Latin of the *Letter* of Christopher Columbus that spread the news of his discovery to the world; the last known copy in private hands of the *Bay Psalm Book*, the first extant book printed in what is now the United States; the Alfred Whital Stern Collection of Lincolniana containing more than 6,000 pieces, including the printer's copy of the Lincoln-Douglas Debates with Lincoln's annotations, among other rarities; and the Carolyn Houghton Wells Collection of Walt Whitman. It was also under Goff that the final reconstruction of Thomas Jefferson's library took place. The third president's books, purchased from him after the British burned the Capitol and its library in 1814, form the cornerstone of the Library of Congress's collections. Over the years these books were pulled from the general stacks of the library and placed under the custody of the Rare Book Division. Under Goff's direction, Millicent Sowerby began the major bibliographical reconstruction of Jefferson's library in 1942; the work ended in 1952 with the publication of the five-volume catalog of the library. During these years the Library of Congress became the preeminent place in the world for the collecting and studying of Americana.

Goff's name is almost synonymous with the collecting and studying of incunabula in the United States. Beginning with his work on the Second Census of *Incunabula in American Libraries* until well into his retirement, he researched and collected these scarce and rare items. When Goff came to the Library of Congress, it had the tenth-largest collection of incunabula in the world, and in the United States it ranked behind the Henry Huntington Library. By the time of his retirement the library held more than 5,600 incunabula, holding first place in the Western Hemisphere and eighth in the world. This status came about primarily through Goff and the library's relationship with the great collector and businessman Lessing J. Rosenwald. Rosenwald, chairman of Sears, Roebuck & Co., was an avid collector of prints and illustrated books. The books Rosenwald bought were of the highest quality, and beginning in 1943 he began deeding them to the Library of Congress, a practice continuing until his death in 1979. Rosenwald's books, numbering some 2,600 titles, constitute the finest gathering of illustrated books in the United States. Included in this collection are more than 600 incunabula, a number that catapulted the library into its leading position in the United States.

Goff published the Third Census of *Incunabula in United States Libraries* in 1964, a work listing all known copies of incunabula in United States institutions. The book is so well known that one simply refers to it as "Goff." His supplement to the Third Census was published in 1973. Goff's name is still well known among scholars of early printed books because of the publication of these two censuses.

Goff not only focused on early Americana and incunabula but also collected for the library in a number of areas. Not least was his building on the strength of the library's contemporary fine printing collections. Goff added complete holdings of fine press books, a practice continued and expanded by his two successors as chief.

Goff wrote or oversaw the writing of a number of catalogs of the library's collections. He also wrote scores of articles on all facets of rare-book collecting and collections. He kept up his prolific publishing activity until his death. For instance, in the year before his death he had published an article on the library's purchase of the Gutenberg Bible, one of three known perfect copies on vellum. His interests in books were vast and encompassed all time periods and subjects. It is largely owing to his efforts that the Library of Congress became the leading repository of rare book in the United States.

Goff retired in 1972 and became honorary consultant in the Rare Book and Special Collections Division of the Library of Congress. He was a member of and held office in numerous professional associations, including the presidency of the Bibliographical Society of America in 1968–1970, and chair of the Rare Books and Manuscripts Section of the Association of College and Research Libraries in 1961. Throughout his career he was an articulate spokesman both for the Library of Congress and for the rare-book profession. He died in London, England.

• The papers of Frederick Goff are in the files and archives of the Rare Book and Special Collections Division of the Library of Congress. His collecting efforts are recalled in his *Delights of a Rare Book Librarian* (1975). The Third Census of *Incunabula in American Libraries* and its supplement are his most important and lasting works. He also compiled the catalog of the great Lessing J. Rosenwald Collection (1977). His guide, *The Rare Book Division: A Guide to Its Collections and Services* (1965), which details some of the collections that entered during his tenure as chief, is now supplanted by Larry E. Sullivan et al., *The Library of Congress: Rare Books and Special Collections* (1992). For a history of the Rare Book Division, including Goff's contributions, see Larry E. Sullivan, "The Rare Book and Special Collections Division," *Library of Congress Information Bulletin*, 12 Mar. 1991, pp. 83–87; and William Matheson, "Seeking the Rare, the Important, the Valuable: The Rare Book Division," *Quarterly Journal of the Library of Congress* (July 1973): 211–27.

LARRY E. SULLIVAN

GOFFMAN, Erving Manual (11 June 1922–20 Nov. 1982), sociologist, was born in Mannville, Alberta, Canada, the son of Jewish immigrants from the Ukraine (names and occupations unknown). He attended St. John's Technical High School in Winnipeg from 1936 until 1939, when he enrolled at the University of Manitoba. Goffman took a variety of classes at this university and was headed toward a career in chemistry, but in 1942 he interrupted his university education and began work at the National Film Board of Canada in Ottawa, where he worked until 1943. In 1944 he registered at the University of Toronto, where he began to take sociology classes, perhaps influenced by his earlier friendship with Dennis Wrong, whom he met while working at the Canadian Film Board. His two most influential teachers at Toronto were C. W. M. Hart and Ray Birdwhistell. In 1945 he graduated with a bachelor of arts degree from the University of Toronto.

Goffman enrolled as a graduate student in sociology at the University of Chicago in the autumn of 1945. He is remembered by fellow students for his quick wit and small size, as is indicated by his nickname at the time, "the little dagger." In his master's thesis of 1949 he used questionnaire data to study audience responses to a popular radio soap opera of the time called "Big Sister." The project was not very successful, and the thesis contains a detailed explanation of the difficulties inherent in quantitative studies of this kind. For his dissertation, "Communication Conduct in an Island Community," Goffman traveled to a small island off the coast of Scotland, where he spent an extended period of time as a participant observer of everyday life on an island he called "Dixon." During this time he pretended to be interested in crofting techniques used by the islanders. Although the dissertation is ethnographically oriented, it is not a typical case study. Instead, Goffman's field observations about the islanders' everyday behavior were recast as a general theory of face-to-face interaction. It is possible that the landscape of Dixon had an effect on his findings. The small island was very flat with little vegetation, and as a result the three hundred or so families lived in proximity to one another, with the ever-present possibility of being observed. Goffman's early theory of face-to-face interaction emphasized the extent to which individuals manipulate the way they appear to others. Goffman defended the dissertation toward the end of 1953. His defense was successful, although some felt that his abstract theorizing was detrimental to the ethnographic focus of his project.

In 1952 Goffman married Angelica Schuyler Choate, with whom he had one child. After finishing his graduate studies, Goffman worked as a research associate for Edward Shils of the University of Chicago on a project concerned with social stratification. Goffman also wrote a brilliant essay during this time about the problems facing individuals who endeavor to project positive self-images. He called this "face-work." The idea of saving face became a way of considering the deeply ritualistic elements of modern life.

This paved the way for what is perhaps Goffman's best-known book, *The Presentation of Self in Everyday Life*. First published in 1956 by the University of Edinburgh, the book analyzed the social world as a theatrical performance. Goffman demonstrated that this extended metaphor could be used to reinterpret a great variety of social interactions, perhaps any. His means made the everyday world appear strange. Goffman described a world in which individuals are performers striving to perfect their impression management. Performers manufacture images of themselves that are delivered in "front stage" settings and then "knowingly contradicted" backstage. The lasting message of this book, despite contradictory passages, is that the modern world is a profoundly cynical place. Although the first edition of his book was relatively obscure, the second edition, issued in 1959, established Goffman as one of the most prominent sociologists of the postwar period.

In his next major work, *Asylums* (1961), Goffman conducted ethnographic research at a mental hospital in Washington, D.C. As in his dissertation, the resulting analysis was abstract and comparative, and not strictly a case study. Goffman adopted Everett Hughes's term "total institution" to describe the general characteristics of organizations that control the time and space of the inmates who live and work in them. From Goffman's perspective, mental institutions had much in common with prisons, monasteries, military barracks, homes for the blind, etc. Perhaps more important, he suggested that the behavior of individuals in these organizations may be similar. *Asylums* describes everyday life in a total institution, from the initial moment of "civil death," when inmates are stripped of their personal identity, to their later efforts to protect themselves from the institution's attempt to engulf them. Goffman's book was a poignant reminder of the indignities of incarceration.

In 1957 Goffman accepted an appointment at the University of California at Berkeley. He thrived in the sociology department there, producing several important studies, *Behavior in Public Places* (1963), *Stigma* (1964), *Strategic Interaction* (1969), and *Relations in Public* (1971), each of which reexamined the everyday world, showing the extraordinary subtlety that accompanies apparently banal interaction. In the course of this work, Goffman developed a new vocabulary (for example, "impression management," "civil inattention," "spoiled identities") that has since permeated the entire sociological profession. In this period, in 1964, Goffman and his wife divorced.

By 1968, when he moved to the University of Pennsylvania, he had become one of the most significant sociologists in the United States. For the next four years he worked to complete the book he hoped would be his magnum opus, *Frame Analysis* (1974). This study analyzed the assumptions that make social interaction meaningful. The book was a long and engaged account of the processes by which we make sense of the social world. It was not, however, as well received as Goffman had hoped; critics complained of the book's length and of the difficulty of applying Goffman's analysis to empirical research.

In subsequent years Goffman turned his attention to the analysis of everyday talk. This was fitting because some of his students from his years at Berkeley, particularly Harvey Sacks, Emanuel Schegloff, and David Sudnow, had become influential in the developing fields of ethnomethodology and conversation analysis. This work resulted in his final book, *Forms of Talk* (1981), in which Goffman proposed a new framework for the understanding of replies and responses in conversations and offered empirical studies of the lecturing process, radio announcing, a person's "footing" in conversations, and even "spill-cries," such as "oops!" The overall effect is a dazzling redescription of apparently familiar aspects of everyday life.

In 1982 Goffman was elected president of the American Sociological Association, but he died of cancer before he was able to deliver his presidential address. He is remembered as an innovative sociologist who demonstrated both the complexity and charm of everyday life and as someone who appreciated the importance of ritual in the modern world. His moral outrage was genuine but understated. To a generation of sociologists concerned with either abstract theorizing or quantitative measurement, Goffman offered a sociological perspective that concentrated on the ability of individuals to create meanings in their often very different social worlds.

• Y. Winkin, *Erving Goffman: Les Moments et leurs hommes* (1988), is a biography. There are several book-length studies of Goffman's work. The most complete is Tom Burns, *Erving Goffman* (1992). A shorter study is by Philip Manning, *Erving Goffman and Modern Sociology* (1992).

PHILIP MANNING

GOFORTH, William (1766–12 May 1817), physician, was born in New York City, the son of Judge William Goforth and Catharine Meeks. Goforth began his medical studies in 1783 with Dr. Joseph Young, a New York physician, later studying with Dr. Charles McKnight, a distinguished surgeon and anatomist who was offering public lectures with the probable intent of forming a medical school. In 1788 "he and the other students of the forming school of that city, were dispersed by a mob, raised against the cultivation of anatomy" (Juettner, p. 16). Shortly thereafter, in the spring of 1788 he departed New York with a group of friends and relatives for Limestone (now Maysville), Kentucky, where Goforth set up practice in nearby Washington (now a part of Maysville), Kentucky. He practiced there for some eleven years. During this time he married Elizabeth Wood, the oldest daughter of the Reverend William Wood, a prominent Baptist minister and one of the founders of Washington, Kentucky.

In order to be closer to his father, Goforth migrated in 1799 to Columbia, Ohio, and a year later, because of a unique practice opportunity, he moved downriver to Cincinnati and took over the practice and home ("Peach Grove House") of Dr. Richard Allison, one of the city's busy practitioners who had announced his retirement. It was here on 18 December 1800 that fifteen-year-old Daniel Drake began his apprenticeship with Goforth. It continued until the summer of 1805 when young Drake was presented with a diploma attesting to his ability in medical practice. It was the first medical diploma issued west of the Alleghenies to any student of medicine. Goforth is also credited with the first use of small pox vaccination in the Northwest Territory (1801).

In an obituary published on 13 June 1817 in the newspaper the *Western Spy*, the writer (probably Daniel Drake) states,

Few things could have been more unfortunate for his [Goforth's] professional interests than his ardent devotion to the republican cause; and the reflection that he had been instrumental in facilitating the establishment of the new government, could have afforded but imperfect solace under the accumulated troubles, which a temporary neglect of his personal concerns and the loss of several wealthy patrons brought unexpectedly on him. His practice being, from this cause, somewhat reduced, the Doctor, in the spring of 1803, resolved on a summary mode of extricating himself from pecuniary difficulty.

The scheme involved an archaeological dig at Big Bone Lick in Kentucky where fossils had been found. According to Daniel Drake in his *Discourses Delivered by Appointment, before the Cincinnati Medical Library Association, January 9th and 10th*, Dr. Goforth was successful in uncovering "the largest, most diversified, and remarkable mass of huge fossil bones, that was ever disinterred at one time or place in the United States." Unfortunately, Goforth was swindled out of any possible reward for his efforts. In 1806 he entrusted the fossils for sale to a Thomas Ashe, alias Arville, who took them out of the country and sold them to various museums in Great Britain. Ashe embezzled all proceeds from the sale.

Goforth was described by Drake as a kindly and charming man. Drake wrote in his *Discourses*, "The pains taking and respectful courtesy with which he treated the poorest and humblest people of the village, seemed to secure their gratitude; and the more especially as he dressed with precision, and never left his house in the morning till his hair was powdered by our itinerant barber, John Arthurs, and his gold-headed cane was grasped by his gloved hand."

In 1807, contrary to the advice of friends, Goforth left Cincinnati for Louisiana, where he remained until 1816. During this time he served as parish judge in Bayou la Fourche and, in Attacapas, was elected by the Creoles to represent them at the Louisiana Constitutional Convention. During the British army attack on New Orleans he served as surgeon to one of the militia groups. After some nine years in Louisiana, Goforth determined to return to Cincinnati. The trip upriver took some seven months by barge. In February 1817, shortly after his arrival, he was struck with "inflammation of the liver," probably some form of hepatitis, incurred during his arduous voyage. He lingered only a few months more.

• The most complete body of bibliographical material regarding Goforth can be found in the writings of Daniel Drake at the Historical Medical Library of the College of Medicine of the University of Cincinnati. Drake's *Discourses Delivered by Appointment, before the Cincinnati Medical Library Association, January 9th and 10th* (1852) and *Natural and Statistical View; or, Picture of Cincinnati* (1815) are particularly detailed. A short biographical sketch is David A. Tucker, Jr., "Notes on the Early Medical History of Cincinnati," *Cincinnati Journal of Medicine* (Mar. 1936). Emmet Field Horine, *Daniel Drake (1785–1852) Pioneer Physician of the Midwest* (1961), and Otto Juettner, *Daniel Drake and His Followers: Historical and Biographical Sketches* (1909), are important sources.

STANLEY L. BLOCK

GOHEEN, Francis Xavier (9 Feb. 1894–13 Nov. 1979), hockey player, was born in St. Paul, Minnesota, the son of John William Goheen, an odd-job laborer, and Mabel Theresa Rotter. Popularly known as "Moose by his late teenage years," Goheen learned hockey on the outdoor rinks of White Bear Lake, Minnesota, where he grew up. He starred in hockey for the local town team while playing football and baseball for White Bear Lake High School, and at Valparaiso University in Indiana, he played football and baseball.

In the fall of 1915 Goheen joined the St. Paul Athletic Club, one of the strongest American amateur hockey teams of the time. Since professional hockey did not begin in the United States until 1924, St. Paul played in the U.S. Amateur Hockey Association (USAHA), the highest level of competition. Teaming with American stars Tony Conroy, Ed Fitzgerald, and Cy Weindenborner, he helped St. Paul capture the McNaughton Trophy in 1915–1916. The following year St. Paul retained that trophy and the next year also took the Art Ross Cup from the Lachine, Quebec, club. In April 1917, with U.S. entry into World War I, Goheen joined the army and served in France and Germany.

Returning to hockey in 1920, Goheen led St. Paul to successive second-place finishes in the USAHA in 1921–1922 and 1922–1923. The Boston Athletic Association (BAA) broke the string in 1923–1924. Goheen in 1958 recalled the final-game defeat: "It's hard to put a finger on any best night. One that gave me great satisfaction came in Boston against the BAA club. I scored the winning goal in the closing seconds. Trouble is, we came back to the Hippodrome [St. Paul] and lost the championship playoffs."

Goheen was selected as a member of the U.S. Olympic hockey team for the first Winter Games, held at

Antwerp in March 1920. Played under seven-man hockey team rules for the only time, the U.S. players finished second. The U.S. team won three games by wide margins, losing only to Canada 2–0 for the silver medal representing second place. Goheen was selected again for the 1924 Winter Games, but as he remembered: "I figured it would cost me too much in time to be away from my job, so Taffy Abel went in my place."

Goheen married Ruth Ann Goodrich in 1923; they had three children. In 1925–1926 the USAHA turned professional and became known as the Central Hockey Association. Reluctant to leave his position as a plant controller with the Northern States Power Company, Goheen refused offers from several National Hockey League teams. He continued to play with the now renamed St. Paul Saints until retiring in 1933. During this period he was chosen three times for the league all-star team. In addition to his playing career, Goheen coached the St. Paul entry in the Central League in 1932–1933; he officiated following his playing career.

Goheen performed primarily as a defenseman, but he frequently played forward. The era of seven-man hockey, which ended in 1920, also saw him play the rover position. Although not physically imposing at 5′9½″ and 170 pounds, he dominated play. Teammate Emmy Garrett recalled in a 1978 interview: "The team could be sluggish and then Moose would make one of those rink-long trips, split the defense, leave falling bodies and pour in the goal. From that point on, bedlam tore up the house and his team would become unbeatable." Oblivious to personal injury, Goheen had a strictly straightahead style. As a St. Paul sportswriter reported: "In the old days when Moose got the puck he took the shortest distance to the net. Fancy stickhandling and trying to dodge opponents was not for him. He just battered his way through the mob in a savage, relentless rush that caught the fancy of the scouts as well as the fans."

Throughout his career, Goheen was a great crowd favorite. A sportswriter recounted his appeal: "The crowds would sit and stand in bone-chilling temperatures in the old unheated State Fairgrounds Hippodrome. And then, suddenly, the sound would begin like the distant rumble of a locomotive. The building would tremble and shake, and the sound would become an explosion. 'Moose! Moose! Mosse!' they would cry. And the great shoulders and powerful thighs would be a blurred vision on the ice as the Mighty Moose Goheen wound up and began another of the shattering, game-breaking sorties which became his trademark."

Goheen was elected to the Hockey Hall of Fame in Toronto in 1952, only the second player who developed in the United States to be so honored. He was a charter member of the U.S. Hockey Hall of Fame, which opened in 1973. He died in St. Paul, Minnesota.

• Information on Goheen is located in the Hockey Hall of Fame, Toronto; the U.S. Hockey Hall of Fame, Eveleth, Minn.; and in scrapbooks maintained by his son John Goheen, in Louisville, Ky. For a good account of Goheen's playing style, see an undated game program from the 1949–1950 season of the former St. Paul Saints of the U.S. Hockey League. Goheen's popularity with fans is best described in a 1978 column (date unknown) by *St. Paul Pioneer Press* sportswriter Don Riley. (Both the program and column are owned by hockey historian Donald M. Clark in Cumberland, Wisc.) See also Clark, *USA Hockey Teams Results Book: Olympic and World Championship Competition 1920–1986* (1986), and Roger A. Godin, *United States Hockey Hall of Fame* (1984). An obituary appeared in the *Sporting News*, 1 Dec. 1979.

ROGER A. GODIN

GOING, Jonathan (7 Mar. 1786–9 Nov. 1844), Baptist minister and missionary administrator, was born in Reading, Vermont, the son of Jonathan Going and Sarah Kendall, farmers. The beneficiary of a gift from his uncle, Ezra Kendall of Kingston, Massachusetts, Going attended a preparatory academy in New Salem, Massachusetts, eventually graduating from Brown University in 1809. Upon graduation Going made plans to enter the Christian ministry and was licensed by his home congregation, First Baptist Church in Providence, Rhode Island, where the illustrious Stephen Gano was pastor. While there Going engaged in theological studies under Asa Messer, the Baptist president of Brown University who expressed an openness to Unitarian principles. Going was eventually ordained in 1811 and took a pastorate in Cavendish, Vermont; at the time he was the only Baptist minister in the entire state with a college education.

Beginning in 1800 mainstream Baptists in the United States began to form voluntary associations and societies for benevolent purposes such as mission and education. In 1815 the church at Worcester, Massachusetts, called Going as pastor, and he remained there until 1836, building the congregation into a substantial church that was mission-oriented. As a Baptist pastor he enthusiastically practiced the associational principle, holding that it was presumptuous of local churches to act alone in matters of ordination and church disputes. Consequently, in 1819 he helped to organize the Worcester Baptist Association.

Going organized one of the first sabbath schools in the Baptist denomination, also teaching in the Latin Grammar School in Worcester. Interested in public school education as well, Going assisted in the formation of one of the first teacher's conventions in Massachusetts. Guided by the principle that no one could teach without an education, he supported academic pursuits at every level. In 1819 he wrote a pamphlet outlining the establishment of a Baptist literary and theological institution in New England, recommending a system of manual labor to support the students. Going's plan eventually became the foundation for Newton Theological Institution, the first postundergraduate theological school for Baptists in the United States. Beyond the Baptist denomination, Going was also a founding trustee of Amherst College.

By the early 1830s Going had become preoccupied with domestic missions in the United States. After making a journey in 1831 to the West, principally through the Ohio Valley, he became convinced of the need to support Baptist missions in that region. During that trip he also met with prominent Baptist missionaries like Isaac McCoy and John Mason Peck who emphasized the importance of their work. Going secured a leave from his pastoral duties at First Baptist in Worcester in 1832, intent upon devoting his full support to missions organization. During a recess of the Baptist Triennial Convention in 1832 in New York City, Going spearheaded a drive to form the American Baptist Home Mission Society. Developed by Going and Peck, the society was based on the model of the American Home Mission Society and the practical experience of the Baptists in overseas missions. Going became the first corresponding secretary of the ABHMS, a position he held for five years, also editing its periodical, the *American Baptist and Home Mission Record*. Going's biographers later emphasized his pastoral concern for the missionaries and his vision for development of the Baptist cause in the West.

Characteristically, Going concerned himself with the development of religious education on the frontier in addition to his missionary pursuits. In 1831 during his trip to Ohio, he was one of the founders of the Ohio Baptist Education Society, and in 1837 he left the Home Mission Society to accept the presidency of the Granville Literary and Theological Institution (later Denison University). At Granville he again employed his plan for a denominational school which blended the arts and theological studies while simultaneously providing an income for students. Going also served as the first professor of theology and was instrumental in training numerous Baptist ministers and missionaries.

Going was a farsighted minister who brought the needs of the West to the attention of denominational interests in the Northeast. He died in Granville, Ohio, survived by his wife, Lucy Thorndike, who suffered from mental illness and was institutionalized throughout most of their marriage.

• Going's personal papers are in the archives at the American Baptist Historical Society, Rochester, N.Y., and at Denison University, Granville, Ohio. His published writings include sermons and addresses, notably *Outline of a Plan for Establishing a Baptist Literary and Theological Institution in a Central Situation in New England, By a Friend to an Able Ministry* (1819). Biographical details are in *Baptist Home Mission Monthly*, Nov. 1878, pp. 65–66; William B. Sprague, *Annals of the American Pulpit*, vol. 6, *Baptists* (1860); and Abial Fisher, "Discourse on the Life, Character, and Services of Rev. Jonathan Going, D.D." in *Annual of the Worcester Baptist Association* (1845). For a funeral sermon see Edmund Turney, *The Prospect of Death an Incentive to Christian Constancy and Faithfulness: A Discourse on the Death of Rev. Jonathan Going* (1845).

WILLIAM H. BRACKNEY

GOLD, Michael (12 Apr. 1893–14 May 1967), radical intellectual and writer, was born Itzok Isaac Granich on the Lower East Side of New York City, son of Cha-

im Granich and Gittel Schwartz, Jewish immigrants from Eastern Europe. His father was a storefront manufacturer of suspenders and a peddler but remained destitute all his life. Forced by economic stringency to leave school at age twelve, Mike Gold (at this point calling himself Irwin Granich) held a variety of jobs including night porter and clerk. He said he "had no politics . . . except hunger," until he was nineteen. But Gold was radicalized in 1914 when he witnessed and experienced police beatings at a demonstration by the unemployed at Union Square in New York City.

At the same time he bought a copy of *The Masses*, a cooperatively run magazine designed to unite literature and revolution, which helped shape Gold's fledgling radicalism and reinforced his desire to become a writer. Soon he had his first poem published in *The Masses*, and by 1917 he was a regular contributor. Gold consistently tried to combine literary and political pursuits. He joined the Industrial Workers of the World and the Socialist party, and he worked as a copyeditor for the Socialist paper the *New York Call*. During this time he also wrote three one-act plays for the Provincetown Players.

After a short, unhappy period as a special student at Harvard in 1916, Gold fled to Mexico in 1917 to avoid the draft. There he wrote for an English-language newspaper and worked on a ranch and in the oil fields before returning to New York in 1919. During the antiradical Palmer raids of 1919–1920 he chose, for the sake of anonymity, the name Michael Gold, and it stuck. In 1921 he became an editor of the *Liberator*, successor to *The Masses*, which had been closed down for its opposition to the war. The Russian Revolution had stimulated an extraordinary factionalism on the literary left, particularly between the old bohemianism and the new Communist influence. Gold, one of the very few intellectuals (of the many who were disgusted with bourgeois society) to actually join the Communist party, was in the thick of this fight. His increasing revolutionary convictions and Communist orthodoxy led to clashes with coeditors Claude McKay and Floyd Dell, but Gold emerged victorious. In 1922 the *Liberator* became an official arm of the Communist party.

After a sojourn in California as a journalist between 1923 and 1924, and after a visit to the Soviet Union in 1925, Gold moved to the *New Masses* as coeditor. In 1928 when Max Eastman resigned, Gold ran the magazine singlehandedly, and, reflecting his interest in a "proletarian" literature, he attempted to rely more upon the contributions of working men and women than on professional writers with radical sympathies. Gold at the helm also meant a steady drift into the orbit of the Communist party. For a time, however, he was far more tolerant of political deviation than was the official party press. For several years he accepted pieces from apostates such as Scott Nearing and V. F. Claverton, and even from "enemies" including anarchist Carlo Tresca and Socialist Upton Sinclair.

Returning from the Second World Plenum of the International Bureau of Revolutionary Literature in Russia in 1930, where he was an official delegate, Gold was increasingly enthusiastic about recruiting artists and writers for the revolutionary movement. He was soon subscribing to the theory that a writer's political affiliation, or more precisely, a writer's subservience to the Communist party, determined the value of his or her art. In this he did battle with more talented and less orthodox radicals including James T. Farrell and Philip Rahv.

Ironically and fortunately, Gold's most important work, his partly autobiographical novel *Jews without Money* (1930), did not reflect his Communist orthodoxy. It is straightforward and anecdotal and faithful to events of Gold's childhood. Except in the final tacked-on passages, including: "O workers' Revolution, you brought hope to me. . . . You are the true Messiah. You will destroy the East Side when you come, and build there a garden for the human spirit," the novel is not a vehicle for political propaganda. It neither glamorizes the proletariat nor romanticizes poverty. And if *Jews without Money* does not have more than modest aesthetic value, it is nonetheless an imaginative social document that puts us in touch with the challenges and confusions of urban America in the 1920s and the feel of immigrant poverty. Although his November 1930 article in the *New Republic*, eviscerating Thornton Wilder's writing as apolitical and decadent, and ridiculing the traditionalism of T. S. Eliot, attracted more attention at the time, the novel became a classic. That *Jews without Money* survives is testament to its authenticity.

Gold left a number of novels and plays unfinished. His inability to do sustained work, and the call of demonstrations, picket lines, and speaking engagements, prevented their completion. He produced nothing of literary value after 1930. He remained active, however, in party cultural affairs and wrote a column for the *Daily Worker* called "Change the World!"

Gold remained a Communist long after many other writers and artists had left the movement following the revelations of Stalin's murderous repressions in the 1930s. And between 1939 and 1941 he became increasingly strident in his criticism of those progressive intellectuals who, having been alienated by the Nazi-Soviet Pact of 1939, criticized or left the Communist party. He lashed out with ferocious personal slander at these "renegades" in his columns, some of which were published as *The Hollow Men* (1941). He was also vicious and uncompromising in his attack on those who dared to contend that a work of art could not be judged by its political correctness alone. In 1946, for example, Gold helped orchestrate the orthodox Communist condemnation of Hollywood writer Albert Maltz for having strayed from the party line.

In the late 1940s and early 1950s Gold made his home in France. Returning to the United States during the McCarthy period, he lived in abject poverty in the Bronx until a number of Communist newspapers made a collective decision to publish his column once again. During the last years of his life, from 1957 and into the 1960s, Gold lived in relative obscurity in California. There he wrote for the *Worker* and the *People's World*, a radical West Coast journal. He died in San Francisco.

Eugene O'Neill had admired Gold's early attempts at playwriting, and Edmund Wilson thought him the most "naturally gifted" of the American Communist writers. But Gold in his own time was more influential for his disastrous theories about art and politics than he was for his poetry and prose, never again producing anything comparable in value to *Jews without Money*.

• A representative sample of Gold's acerbic political articles can be found in *120 Million* (1929) and *Change the World!* (1937). For a sampling of the literature see Michael Folsom, ed., *Mike Gold: A Literary Anthology* (1972), which also contains important material on Gold's life and work. In addition, see Daniel Aaron, *Writers on the Left* (1961), and Harvey Klehr, *The Heyday of American Communism* (1984). An obituary is in the *New York Times*, 16 May 1967.

GERALD SORIN

GOLDBERG, Arthur Joseph (8 Aug. 1908–19 Jan. 1990), lawyer, jurist, and diplomat, was born in Chicago, Illinois, the son of Joseph Goldberg, a peddler, and Rebecca (maiden name unknown). Goldberg grew up in an immigrant slum on Chicago's West Side, where he led a life filled with hard work. Thanks to extraordinary intelligence and drive, he managed to graduate from Benjamin Harrison Public High School in 1924, the first member of his family ever to get that much schooling. He then attended Crane Junior College, from which he soon made his way into Northwestern Law School. During his three years there, Goldberg compiled the best academic record in the school's history up to that point and served as editor of the law review, while continuing to work part-time. He earned his bachelor of law degree in 1928, followed one year later by a doctor of science in law degree. He then joined the Chicago firm of Pritzger and Pritzger. In 1931 he married Dorothy Kurgans, an art student he had met at Northwestern; they had two children.

Unhappy with the bankruptcy work he was obliged to do and wanting to become his own boss, Goldberg established his own practice in 1933. His reputation as a skilled lawyer friendly to the left encouraged leaders of the Chicago branch of the Congress of Industrial Organizations (CIO) to approach him for help during a newspaper strike in 1938. Goldberg agreed to represent the strikers and to take other labor work that the CIO began steering his way. His acceptance of such cases stemmed from his own working-class origin and the sympathy it gave him for workers trying to unionize during the Great Depression. As Goldberg later explained this key change in his life and career, "I got attached to the CIO in Chicago because they were the down-and-outers at that time" (Stebenne, p. 15).

The United States' entry into World War II interrupted Goldberg's career as a labor lawyer. Eager to join the fight against fascism, he volunteered to serve in the Office of Strategic Services (OSS), the wartime intelligence agency. There he organized a labor branch, which gathered information from union members on the Continent for use in resisting the Axis advance and eventually aiding the Anglo-American invasion in Normandy. In the fall of 1944 Goldberg, convinced that the war was over and having exhausted his savings, returned to Chicago and resumed his law practice.

After the war ended, tensions within the CIO between its social democratic and more radical factions intensified, a division that led early in 1948 to the ouster of the CIO's top lawyer, the radical Lee Pressman. In Pressman's place, CIO president Philip Murray appointed Goldberg on 5 March 1948 as CIO and Steelworkers general counsel. For the next thirteen years Goldberg served as a leading Washington lobbyist for the American labor movement and the top contract negotiator for the Steelworkers, one of the country's largest and most influential unions. Among his most important achievements, in 1949 he helped to expel the CIO's radical-led affiliates; he negotiated that same year a pension plan for the Steelworkers that became a model for many other unions; he brokered the 1955 merger between the American Federation of Labor (AFL) and the CIO, which reunited the American labor movement for the first time since the mid-1930s; and he guided the Steelworkers union during its influential rounds of contract negotiations. Goldberg also played a major part in trying to rid the AFL-CIO of corruption, work that led him in the late 1950s to collaborate closely with Massachusetts senator John F. Kennedy. Serving in effect as Kennedy's tutor in the labor-management field, Goldberg became increasingly involved with Kennedy's successful bid for the presidency in 1960. Following the election, Kennedy named Goldberg secretary of labor. During his twenty months as labor secretary, Goldberg worked hard to settle strikes that imperiled American industries' long-term economic health and to provide federal support for the growth of public-employee unionism and for the growth of labor unions in Latin America.

Goldberg's tenure as labor secretary came to an early close in September 1962 when Kennedy appointed him to the Supreme Court, thereby producing a major change in its orientation. Like Chief Justice Earl Warren and Associate Justice William Brennan, whose views on the Court's role he essentially shared, Goldberg consistently supported efforts to expand legal protections for criminal defendants and suspects; to require state and local legislative bodies to reapportion themselves on the basis of one person, one vote; and to protect the civil rights of blacks menaced by segregationists.

Although he had intended to remain on the Supreme Court for the rest of his career, Goldberg reluctantly agreed to resign in July 1965 to become U.S. ambassador to the United Nations. Moved by President Lyndon Johnson's request that Goldberg go to the UN to help negotiate a Vietnam peace settlement, confident that he could persuade Johnson to seek such a peace, and unwilling to antagonize him by refusing, Goldberg took the new post. Johnson, however, ignored Goldberg's advice to halt escalation of the war effort until the unworkability of that policy became

clear in the spring of 1968. Goldberg left the administration shortly afterward. Two years later he ran unsuccessfully as the Democratic candidate for governor of New York. After his defeat, Goldberg returned to Washington, D.C., where he practiced law until his death there in 1990.

An organization man and aide to others for most of his life, Goldberg enjoyed an influence in the American labor movement and the postwar political and economic system greater than many of his contemporaries realized. As CIO and Steelworkers general counsel, he played a leading role in negotiating labor's post–World War II social contract or "New Deal" with management, and in sustaining it into the early 1960s. Goldberg is noteworthy, too, because he served in three high public offices, an unprecedented experience for an American trade unionist. A prototypical New Deal liberal, Goldberg's life and career reflected both the rise of American-style social democracy from the 1930s through the 1950s and its subsequent decline.

• Goldberg's papers are in the Library of Congress. His two major books are *AFL-CIO: Labor United* (1956) and *Equal Justice under Law: The Warren Era of the Supreme Court* (1971). For his career and life, see Dorothy Goldberg, *A Private View of a Public Life* (1975), and Daniel P. Moynihan, ed., *The Defenses of Freedom: The Public Papers of Arthur J. Goldberg* (1966). For a comprehensive list of Goldberg's writings, see Tim J. Watts, "A Bibliography of Arthur J. Goldberg," *Law Library Journal* 77, no. 2 (1984–1985): 307–38. The most complete scholarly assessment is David L. Stebenne, *Arthur J. Goldberg: New Deal Liberal* (1996). See also Robert Shaplen's two-part profile, "Peacemaker," *New Yorker*, 7 and 14 Apr. 1962; the reminiscences collected in *In Memoriam: Honorable Arthur J. Goldberg*, Proceedings before the Supreme Court of the United States, 15 Oct. 1990; "In Memoriam: Arthur J. Goldberg," *Northwestern Law Review* 84, no. 3–4 (1990): 807–31; and Emily Field Van Tassel, "Justice Arthur J. Goldberg," in *The Jewish Justices of the Supreme Court Revisited: Brandeis to Fortas*, ed. Jennifer M. Lowe (1994). An obituary is in the *New York Times*, 20 Jan. 1990.

DAVID L. STEBENNE

GOLDBERG, Leo (26 Jan. 1913–1 Nov. 1987), astronomer and astrophysicist, was born in Brooklyn, New York, the son of Polish immigrants Harry Goldberg and Ruth Ambush. When he was nine a fire destroyed the tenement where his family lived, taking the lives of his mother and younger brother. Three years later his father moved the remaining family to New Bedford, Massachusetts. Young Goldberg spent his summers on Nantucket Bay, where his frequent visits to the Maria Mitchell Observatory probably sparked his interest in astronomy. Financial support from a local businessman in 1930 allowed Goldberg to attend college. He completed both his undergraduate and graduate work at Harvard University under the supervision of Bart J. Bok. Bok introduced Goldberg to Donald H. Menzel, and the two worked together throughout college. Goldberg received a B.S. in 1936, an A.M. in 1937, and a Ph.D. in 1938. His dissertation applied theoretical calculations of atomic transition probabilities to the spectrum of the solar chromosphere and to the spectra of early type stars. After graduation he became an assistant at the University of Michigan, doing military research during the war years. In 1960 he returned to Harvard to perform space research and laboratory astrophysics. He became Higgins Professor of Astronomy at Harvard in the same year. Fifteen years later he was named Emeritus Higgins Professor, but he left to become director of the Kitt Peak Observatory in Tucson, Arizona, in 1977. Goldberg married twice: in 1943 to Charlotte B. Wyman with whom he had three children, and 1987 to Beverly T. Lynds, an astronomical colleague.

During his graduate years at Harvard, Goldberg was interested in spectroscopy and solar physics. He developed quantum mechanics into forms helpful for the interpretation of stellar spectra. His thesis concentrated on the intensity of lines in helium. He was known for his excellent writing throughout college, and part of his dissertation was awarded first prize in Harvard's Bowdoin Essay Competition. Because the Great Depression had left few openings for astronomers, he stayed at Harvard for three years as an assistant professor of astronomy. In 1938 he was awarded a special research fellowship. Three years later he became a research associate before moving to the University of Michigan.

At Michigan Goldberg worked his way up from associate professor to full professor in five years. He started as an assistant at the university's McMath-Hulbert Observatory, then responsible for private solar observation. At age thirty-three he became chairman of the astronomy department and director of the failing observatory. He recruited a strong new staff and established a graduate program in astrophysics. He then teamed with a fellow student of Menzel, Lawrence Aller, to write an introduction to astrophysics, *Atoms, Stars, and Nebulae* (1943), which became influential for both study and research. The McMath-Hulbert Observatory started to thrive; it constructed a 33-inch Schmidt telescope, which was placed off-campus to enjoy darker skies.

In 1951 Goldberg and his associates discovered the first carbon monoxide bands in the solar infrared spectrum. This significant discovery led to finding other gaseous mixtures in the solar atmosphere. Two years later, with funding from the National Science Foundation, Goldberg initiated a program in Ann Arbor, Michigan, that was similar to a summer program run at Harvard by Harlow Shapley. It allowed physicists and astronomers to share their ideas and work together. Walter Baade was the first speaker in the program, which became a great success.

Around this time, many scientists were arguing about the composition of the solar atmosphere. Goldberg joined with Aller and Edith Müller to resolve the debate. Their collaboration produced *The Abundances of the Elements in the Solar Atmosphere* (1960), which became the reference for standard abundances in the sun.

Goldberg, after teaching himself Russian, became chairman of the U.S. National Committee for the International Astronomical Union in 1956, but a struggle with the Chinese delegation and the U.S. visa office caused China to leave the union while the countries involved met in Berkeley, California. Despite his disappointment over this loss, Goldberg served as vice president of the union from 1958 to 1964 and as president from 1973 to 1976.

In 1958 Goldberg was asked to sit on the newly formed Space Science Board of the National Academy of Sciences and National Research Council, representing the field of astronomy. The board was created to advise the government on the proposed National Aeronautics and Space Agency (NASA). The next year he was approached to be responsible for the design and construction of a 700-pound experimental satellite package for solar physics. Goldberg gave up the directorship of the observatory in 1960 when Harvard offered him an experimental laboratory to expand his research. He saw the opportunity as a great leap for experimental physics and took the job.

Back at Harvard, Goldberg started the Harvard Solar Satellite Project, a program to observe from space the ultraviolet spectra of the sun. He used the Orbiting Solar Observatory series of rockets (OSO). At the same time, Donald Menzel became ill and had to leave the Harvard Observatory; Goldberg was chosen to become its director in 1966 and later was also named chairman of the astronomy department. In 1967 OSO 4 was launched; the program continued through OSO 6. With the help of his students and colleagues, Goldberg then began to explore auto-ionization and later, the problems of recombination lines of hydrogen in the radio spectrum. With William H. Parkinson and Edmond M. Reeves he established a technique to identify molecular and atomic lines in the sun's spectra. That year he also became chairman of NASA's Astronomy Missions Board, a position he held until 1970.

While Goldberg was director of the Harvard Observatory, the astronomy program grew tremendously. He led a drive to raise money for the new Perkin Laboratory for Astrophysics, which increased productivity at the university. In 1970, with colleagues from Britain and Canada, he worked on an experiment to photograph the ultraviolet rays of the sun during a total solar eclipse. The analysis led to the discovery of the Lyman-∞ solar corona and encouraged other astronomical programs to use the ultraviolet coronagraph to study the solar corona.

In 1971 Goldberg jumped at the chance to become director of the Kitt Peak Observatory in Tucson, Arizona. He installed first-class instruments and staff members in the decade-old observatory. Some critics argued that time allocated for staff observation on the equipment should have gone to visitors, and he resigned in protest in 1977. After his resignation he was appointed the first Martin-Marietta Chair of Space History at the National Air and Space Museum in Washington, D.C. He died in Tucson.

Goldberg won several honors for his research. He was elected to the American Academy of Arts and Sciences in 1956, and two years later to the American Philosophical Society and the National Academy of Sciences. From 1959 to 1969 he was a member of the board of directors for the Benjamin Apthorp Gould Fund. He was the founding editor of *Annual Reviews of Astronomy and Astrophysics* and continued in this capacity from 1961 to 1973. In 1973 NASA honored him with its Distinguished Public Service Medal. The same year the American Astronomical Society gave him its highest honor, the Henry Norris Russell Lectureship. Five years later, the Royal Astronomical Society gave him similar recognition with the George Darwin Lectureship, and he was named Distinguished Research Scientist at Kitt Peak. From 1976 to 1982 he was Harvard overseer and president of the American Astronomical Society; he prided himself on never missing a meeting.

As a graduate student Goldberg began applying quantum mechanics to the interpretation of stellar spectra. His pioneering research in this field profoundly influenced the development of stellar astrophysics. Despite his administrative responsibilities, he continued research, particularly in solar physics. He contributed extensively to both theoretical and observational astrophysics. He directed three important observatories—at Michigan, Harvard, and Kitt Peak. He built major graduate programs in astrophysical research, greatly encouraged international scientific cooperation, and was a strong proponent of national institutions for astrophysical research. In addition, he helped bring astronomy into the space era.

• Most of Goldberg's works are at the Smithsonian Institution. An early key paper by Goldberg is "Relative Multiple Strengths in LS Coupling," *Astrophysical Journal* 82 (1935): 1–25. He summarized research about the sun with A. Keith Pierce in "The Photosphere of the Sun," *Handbuch der Physik* 52 (1959). His pioneering papers about space astronomy include "Astronomy from Artificial Satellites," *Smithsonian Institution Annual Report, 1959* (1960), pp. 288–97; "Astronomy from Satellites and Space Vehicles," *Journal of Geophysical Research* 64, no. 11 (Nov. 1959): 1768–78; and "Project West Ford—Properties and Analyses," *Astronomical Journal* 66, no. 3 (Apr. 1961): 105–18. Late works include "Some Problems Connected with Mass Loss in Late-Type Stars," *Quarterly Journal of the Royal Astronomical Society* 20 (1979): 361–82. He edited, with Lois Edwards, *Astronomy in China: A Trip Report of the American Astronomy Delegation* (1979), and he contributed to Beverly T. Lynds, *Employment Problems in Astronomy: Report* (1975). Obituaries include those by Owen Gingerich, *American Philosophical Society Proceedings* (June 1992): 297–301, and by four former colleagues in *Physics Today* (Feb. 1990): 144–48.

RACHEL HERSHENSON
RICHARD BERENDZEN

GOLDBERG, Rube (4 July 1883–7 Dec. 1970), cartoonist, writer, and sculptor, was born Reuben Lucius Goldberg in San Francisco, the son of Hannah Cohn and Max Goldberg, a land speculator and campaigner for politicians. By the age of four, Goldberg was drawing pictures, and at eleven he began taking art classes from a sign painter. Evidently influenced by his father's attempts to discourage his artistic tendencies, Goldberg went to the University of California at Berkeley instead of enrolling in art school. As a college student, though, he drew cartoons for the yearbook and for humor magazines.

Upon earning his B.S. in mining engineering in 1904, Goldberg was hired to help design the San Francisco sewer system. While continuing to produce humorous sketches, he tried to publish some of them in the *San Francisco Chronicle*. After one of the sketches was finally accepted, the paper hired "Rube" Goldberg as a sports cartoonist (1905–1906). He then switched to the *San Francisco Bulletin* (1906–1907) before making the cross-country move that would truly establish his career. Goldberg's first employment on the East Coast was with the *New York Evening Mail* and the *New York Evening Journal* (1907–1925). In 1915 he started to draw cartoons for syndication, publishing with William Randolph Hearst's newspapers (1918–1934, 1950–1964), the McNaught Syndicate (1916–1930), the *New York Sun* (1938–1950), and the King Features Syndicate (from 1950 onward). In 1916 he married Irma Seeman, with whom he was to have two sons. By that year his cartoons were in three million homes every day, and in 1920 he was earning $185,000, which enabled the family to move into a five-story Manhattan townhouse.

Goldberg created at least sixty cartoon series and in the process a dozen or more indelible characters. His first long-running series was *Foolish Questions* (1909–1934). Example: "Is that a folding bed?" "No, this is a new box for my harmonica." *I'm the Guy* (1911–1934), *Life's Little Jokes* (1911–1935), *Father Was Right* (1912–1924), and other series followed. Goldberg based *Boobs Abroad* (1913–1914, 1918) on the first three of his twenty-five or more trips to Europe. Series characters include Book McNutt (hapless fall guy) and his luscious girlfriend Pearl, bunglers Mike and Ike (they look alike), pudgy social-climbing Countess Lala Palooza, and Professor Lucifer Gorgonzola Butts, the inventor of Goldberg's humorous machines.

The purpose of the professor's absurdly complicated devices, which Goldberg diagrammed for fifty-five years, was to accomplish essentially simple tasks; the artist's intent, however, was to satirize America's mania for gadgets. Take, for example, a cartoon captioned "Simple Alarm Clock." The artist includes directions labeled A, B, C, etc.: bird on an open bedroom windowsill catches worm; string attached to worm pulls pistol trigger; bullet pops balloon; balloon drops brick on atomizer; atomizer squirts sponge; weighted sponge pulls a string; string tilts board; cannon ball slides off, simultaneously falling on chest of sleeper and by attached string pulling cork off vacuum bottle filled with ice water; water falls on sleeper's face—"to assist the cannon ball in its good work." Only a dullard would wonder why the sound sleeper didn't buy an alarm clock—or a rooster. Other Butts inventions crack eggs, mash potatoes, hide gravy spots on vests, shine shoes, scratch backs, pull teeth, help wives pull up girdles, and so forth.

Goldberg, always versatile and plucky, was not inhibited about trying his hand at other forms of entertainment. From 1910 to 1915 he performed as a stand-up comedian in vaudeville, and in 1916 he designed several one-reel animated films that turned a profit. Short stories and articles of his appeared in the *American Magazine*, *Collier's*, *Cosmopolitan*, *Life*, *Redbook*, the *Saturday Evening Post*, and *Vanity Fair*, most of them from 1922 to 1930, and from 1927 to 1930 he wrote fifteen movie scripts.

The Great Depression did not diminish the audiences for Goldberg's cartoons until 1934. In 1938, after a year-long break from work, he started drawing political cartoons for the *New York Sun*, but in general they were much weaker than the sketches for which he remains best known. During World War II he traveled across the United States with some fellow cartoonists entertaining troops. Branching out again, he briefly tried his own radio show in 1944 and a television show four years later. He was a member of several convivial associations, including the Artists and Writers Golf Association, the Cartoonists Society, the Coffee House, the Dutch Treat Club, the Friars Club, the Lambs Club, and the Society of Illustrators. Among his numerous famous friends he could count Irving Berlin, George M. Cohan, F. Scott Fitzgerald, Ring Lardner, and Grantland Rice.

In 1946 Goldberg and a few other cartoonists formed a club and began giving annual prizes for artistic excellence. Each winner received a statue of an acrobatic team holding an ink bottle on high; designed by Goldberg, it was called the "Reuben." His 1947 cartoon "Peace Today," warning of the dangers of the atomic bomb, was awarded a Pulitzer Prize in 1948. In view of that award, it seems especially odd that he supported Joseph McCarthy from 1951 until 1953, when the senator's demagoguery became too obvious. After Goldberg retired from the *New York Journal-American* in 1964, he turned his talents to bronze sculpture. By 1970 he had created about three hundred pieces and sold six hundred copies—for up to $3,000 each—in four major exhibitions. Goldberg's bronzes are of animals as well as people. His purpose is to show their frailties, faults, and courage. Some are what Goldberg called three-dimensional cartoons. The surfaces of most are deliberately unfinished, lumpy, and what Goldberg's biographer Peter C. Marzio calls "temptingly tactile." In 1970 the Smithsonian Institution in Washington, D.C., held a retrospective Goldberg exhibition, which Goldberg gratefully attended on opening night just thirteen days before his death in his New York City home.

Goldberg's legacy can be found in standard dictionaries of American English. Starting in 1966, the term *Rube Goldberg* became a recognized colloquialism for preposterously complicated mechanisms used to accomplish simple tasks. In the 1980s engineering fraternities at Purdue University began holding annual Goldbergian contests featuring goofy, twenty-step devices—to toast a slice of bread, to break an egg for frying, to lick a postage stamp, etc. In the 1990s manufacturers of video game software packages presented Goldbergian challenges to computer addicts—perhaps to emulate Goldberg's cleverness, perhaps to satirize needless complexity of the sort Goldberg invited us to giggle at.

Unlike most American satirists, Goldberg was able to transcend his time by portraying the silliness of a basic human propensity. Not only do people slip into complicating something that ought to be simple, but they also are fascinated by intricacy as a form of sophistication and cleverness. Rube Goldberg's genius was to captivate his audience while at the same time gently mocking it.

• Some of Goldberg's correspondence and manuscripts are at the Bancroft Library, University of California, Berkeley. An excellent biography is Peter C. Marzio, *Rube Goldberg: His Life and Work* (1973), lavishly illustrated and with a list of Goldberg's cartoon series and a selective bibliography of his writings. For Goldberg in his own words, see *Rube Goldberg vs. the Machine* (1968). Selections of his invention cartoons are reprinted in *The Best of Rube Goldberg* (1944), comp. Charles Keller, and *Rube Goldberg: A Retrospective* (1983), with introductory material by Philip Garner. For studies of American humor that place Goldberg in context, see Jesse Bier, *The Rise and Fall of American Humor* (1968), and Walter Blair and Hamlin Hill, *America's Humor from Poor Richard to Doonesbury* (1978). The Purdue contests are described in "Rube Goldberg Award," *Popular Mechanics*, July 1988, p. 48. Obituaries are in the *New York Times*, 8 Dec. 1970 (on front page), and *Variety*, 9 Dec. 1970.

ROBERT L. GALE
PAUL BETZ

GOLDBERGER, Joseph (16 July 1874–17 Jan. 1929), medical research scientist, was born in Girált, Hungary, the son of Samuel Goldberger and Sarah Gutman, farmers. In 1881 he came to the United States with his parents, Jewish immigrants, who opened a small grocery on New York's East Side. The family lived above the store, which soon prospered. Joseph delivered groceries and ran errands.

Although he was a voracious reader, mathematics was his favorite subject at school, so he decided to become a civil engineer. Goldberger entered the College of the City of New York in 1890; within two years he stood fifth in a class of six hundred. When a friend invited him to attend a physiology lecture at Bellevue Hospital Medical College, he was inspired by the idea of the human body as a machine. He promptly decided to become a doctor. His parents reluctantly consented to this change of plans, and he enrolled at Bellevue in the fall of 1892. He received the doctor of medicine degree in 1895, graduating at the top of his class.

Goldberger interned at Bellevue (1895–1897) and practiced medicine in Wilkes-Barre, Pennsylvania (1897–1899), his first venture outside New York. He longed to see the world and in 1899, after being rejected by the Medical Corps of the U.S. Navy, took the competitive examinations of the Marine Hospital

Service (known after 1902 as the U.S. Public Health Service). He placed first and promptly enlisted.

His first assignment was at the Ellis Island immigration station, but his exceptional ability soon warranted a transfer to Reedy Island (Philadelphia), where he learned quarantine practice. In 1902 he requested a transfer to Tampico, Mexico, so that he could study yellow fever. He fell ill with the disease himself, but his subsequent immunity sped his research. He became an authority on yellow fever and its mosquito vector.

Goldberger joined the staff of the Hygienic Laboratory, the research arm of the Public Health Service (now known as the National Institutes of Health), in 1903 and remained there, when not on field assignments, until his death. From 1905 to 1909 his primary interest was helminthology (the study of parasitic worms), a field in which his mathematical and engineering skills proved useful: he developed a diagrammatic scheme showing the entire linear anatomy of trematodes (a class of parasitic flatworms). He also investigated typhoid fever along the Potomac River, dengue fever (which he contracted) in Texas, and straw itch in Philadelphia. In the case of the dermatological ailment, it took him only forty-eight hours to find the mite responsible.

Goldberger married Mary Humphries Farrar of New Orleans in 1906. They had four children.

In the fall of 1909 he investigated an epidemic of typhus in Mexico City and again fell victim to the disease he was researching. On his recovery, he successfully inoculated the typhus pathogen into monkeys and proved that the recently identified Rocky Mountain spotted fever is a separate disease from typhus, although they closely resemble each other. He also determined that the body louse is the vector of typhus (the tick is the vector of Rocky Mountain spotted fever), confirming an almost simultaneous finding of the French scientist Charles Nicolle. In 1910 he proved that the infectivity of measles is limited to the early stages of the disease.

Goldberger began the most dramatic work of his life in 1914—an investigation of endemic pellagra in the South. This mysterious, often fatal, disease was first diagnosed in the United States in 1906, and a frantic search for its cause and a cure ensued. After only a few weeks in the field, Goldberger linked pellagra to nutrition, specifically to a deficiency in the region's monotonous diet of cornbread, fatback, and syrup. He cured patients at hospitals for the insane and it orphanages, institutions where the disease was prevalent, by adding meat and milk to the diet. He successfully induced pellagra in prison inmates with a poor diet and, through a series of "filth parties" in which he, his colleagues, and even his wife injected or consumed blood, nasal secretions, scales from skin lesions, urine, and feces of pellagra patients, demonstrated that it could not be transmitted from one person to another by the usual methods. In a classic study of seven South Carolina mill villages (1917–1920), he linked pellagra to poverty: smaller incomes meant a poorer diet and a higher incidence of disease.

Many southern physicians resented the implications of the work done by the tall, gangling physician with the piercing eyes and rejected it. The normally soft-spoken Goldberger vigorously defended his findings, but his attempts at social engineering failed. There was little he could do to change the South's one-crop system of agriculture that fostered disease. In 1921 he returned to the laboratory to search for the pellagra-preventive (P-P) factor. He was able to induce black tongue in dogs, a disease analogous to pellagra, with a poor diet and then restore the animals to health through dietary therapy alone. He found the P-P factor in a variety of foods, especially in brewer's yeast. The discovery came in time to save hundreds of lives in the Mississippi River flood of 1927. The specific identity of P-P as niacin, a component of vitamin B, was made at the University of Wisconsin in 1937.

Goldberger died in Washington, D.C. His ashes were scattered on the Potomac River.

• The Joseph Goldberger Papers are in the Southern Historical Collection, University of North Carolina, Chapel Hill. Additional material is in the Goldberger-Sebrell Collection at the Vanderbilt Medical Center Library, Nashville, Tenn.; the manuscript collections of the National Library of Medicine, Bethesda, Md.; and the General Files of the United States Public Health Service (nos. 1648 and 0425–32) at the National Archives. Goldberger's scientific articles were published in *Public Health Reports* and the *Hygienic Laboratory Bulletin* (1907–1929). A convenient collection of his work on pellagra is *Goldberger on Pellagra*, ed. Milton Terris (1964). Elizabeth W. Etheridge, *The Butterfly Caste: A Social History of Pellagra in the South* (1972), places his work on the disease in a broader context. The most complete biography is Robert Percival Parsons, *Trail to Light: A Biography of Joseph Goldberger* (1943). An obituary is in the *New York Times*, 18 Jan. 1929.

ELIZABETH W. ETHERIDGE

GOLDBLATT, Harry (14 Mar. 1891–6 Jan. 1977), pathologist and medical researcher, was born in Muscatine, Iowa, the son of Lithuanian immigrants Philip Goldblatt, a merchant, and Jenny Spitz. When he was six, Goldblatt's family relocated to Montreal, Quebec, Canada, where his father developed a thriving business supplying coal, wood, and ice. In 1908 Goldblatt entered McGill University intending to pursue a career in mining engineering. Guided by Carrie Derrick, the first female professor at McGill University, Goldblatt developed an interest in biology and decided to study medicine. He received his medical degree in 1916 from McGill. After a year as a surgical resident at the Royal Victoria Hospital in Montreal, Goldblatt, who had retained his U.S. citizenship, enlisted in the U.S. Army Medical Reserve Corps, and served as head of orthopedics and fractures at American hospitals in France and Germany.

In 1919 Goldblatt took a position as pathologist at Lakeside Hospital in Cleveland, Ohio, where he also acted as a demonstrator in pathology for medical students at Western Reserve University. An unpaid position at the Lister Institute for Preventive Medicine in London, England (1921–1923), inspired him to study the dietary disease, rickets. He received a Belt Memorial Fellowship, sponsored by the Lister Institute, allowing him to pursue postgraduate training in experimental physiology at University College in London and in Vienna, Austria. In 1924 Goldblatt returned to Cleveland, where he was appointed assistant professor of pathology at Western Reserve University. His continuing investigations of rickets resulted in work demonstrating that sterol irradiated with ultraviolet light produced an antirachitic effect. In 1929 he married Jeanne Elizabeth Rea; they had two sons.

Promoted to professor of pathology in 1935, Goldblatt remained at Western Reserve until 1946, when he became director of the Institute of Medical Research at the Cedars of Lebanon Hospital in Los Angeles, California. In 1953 he returned to Cleveland as director of laboratories at Mount Sinai Hospital and professor of experimental pathology at Western Reserve. After his retirement from teaching, he directed the Louis D. Beaumont Memorial Research Laboratories at Mount Sinai Hospital in Cleveland until 1976.

In the 1930s Goldblatt joined the small number of researchers investigating renovascular physiology and made his classic contributions to hypertension research. As a pathologist at Lakeside Hospital, he performed autopsies on large numbers of patients with high blood pressure and observed extensive damage in the kidneys. His hypothesis about the relationship between impaired renal circulation, caused by disease or injury, and elevated blood pressure led him to develop an experimental animal model for studying benign essential human hypertension, defined as persistently elevated blood pressure of unknown origin. Goldblatt produced high blood pressure in experimental dogs by constricting the main artery of both kidneys using an adjustable silver clamp. In 1934 he published the first in a series of articles on the nature and production of hypertension (with J. Lynch, R. F. Hanzal, and W. W. Summerville, "Studies on Experimental Hypertension. 1. The Production of Persistent Elevation of Systolic Blood Pressure by Means of Renal Ischemia," *Journal of Experimental Medicine* 59 [1934]: 347–79), which did much to stimulate renovascular research.

From 1934 until his retirement Goldblatt conducted extensive studies of the role of renin, a pressor substance isolated from kidneys and part of the humoral mechanism responsible for the elevation of blood pressure. Together with his longtime associate biochemist Erwin Haas, he developed an effective method for large-scale isolation and purification of both human and animal renin. In 1943 Goldblatt introduced a unit of comparison for research involving renin. In 1974 the World Health Organization adopted the Goldblatt unit, the quantity needed to raise the blood pressure of a normal dog by thirty millimeters of mercury, as the international standard of measurement of human renin. In search of a means to reverse high blood pres-

sure, a major cardiovascular risk factor, Goldblatt and his associates performed extensive research on immunization using renin. Although he was able to reduce high blood pressure in dogs by immunizing them against dog renin, immunizing experiments on patients were not successful.

Seeking to develop an animal model in which to study elevated blood pressure, Goldblatt, like many investigators in the 1930s and 1940s, used the dog as his experimental animal. Since the 1930s the use of dogs in medical research had become a special focus for American antivivisectionists, who favored legislation to prevent medical researchers from obtaining dogs and cats from municipal pounds or animal shelters. In 1950 Goldblatt's active participation in the campaign against a proposed Los Angeles city ordinance barring release of impounded dogs to medical researchers made Goldblatt a target for extremists, who sent menacing letters, fired shots into the Goldblatt home, and telephoned a bomb threat to the Cedars of Lebanon Hospital, where he was director of the Institute for Medical Research. Noted for his gentle treatment of laboratory animals, Goldblatt continued to support the responsible use of animals in medical research. In 1955 one of the dogs in his laboratory colony received the Research Dog Hero Award from the National Society for Medical Research, a research advocacy group founded by physiologists Anton J. Carlson and Andrew Ivy in 1946.

For his research on hypertension, Goldblatt received many awards and prizes. Although he was never awarded the Nobel Prize for physiology or medicine, Goldblatt was nominated several times. He received the American Heart Association's Research Achievement Award in 1966, the American Medical Association's Scientific Achievement Award in 1976, and the Gold-Headed Cane Award from the American Association of Pathologists and Bacteriologists. He was inducted into the National Academy of Sciences in 1973. He died in Rochester, New York.

• The Dittrick Museum of Medical History of the Historical Division of the Cleveland Medical Library Association holds a substantial collection of Goldblatt's correspondence, including laboratory notebooks, autobiographical notes, equipment, research files, and reprints. Among his important publications not already mentioned are *The Renal Origin of Hypertension* (1948); with Y. J. Katz, H. A. Lewis, and E. Richardson, "The Bioassay of Renin," *Journal of Experimental Medicine* 77 (1943): 309–13; and "Hypertension Due to Renal Ischemia," *Bulletin of the New York Academy of Medicine* 40 (1964): 745–58. Sources for biographical information include John Laragh, "Harry Goldblatt 1891–1977," *Transactions of the Association of American Physicians* 91 (1978): 34–37; Erwin Haas, "Reminiscences and Reflections," *Journal of Hypertension* 4 (1986): S21–S25; and A. Clifford Barger, "The Goldblatt Memorial Lecture," *Hypertension* 1 (1979): 447–55. Also see A. McGehee Harvey, *Science at the Bedside: Clinical Research in American Medicine, 1905–1945* (1981). An obituary in the *New York Times*, 8 Jan. 1977, was followed by a correction, 11 Jan. 1977.

SUSAN E. LEDERER

GOLDEN, Harry (6 May 1902–2 Oct. 1981), journalist, was born Herschel Goldhirsch, in Mikulintsy, Galicia, the son of Leib Goldhirsch, a Hebrew teacher, and Anna Klein. Leib Goldhirsch and his eldest son, Jacob, came to the United States in 1904 and earned passage money for the rest of the family to emigrate the following year. (Immigration officials changed the family name to Goldhurst.) The family moved into a tenement on Manhattan's Lower East Side, and Leib taught at the Education Alliance and wrote for the *Jewish Daily Forward.*

Herschel Americanized his name to Harry upon graduating from Public School 20 in 1917. As a youth, he sold newspapers, hawked pretzels at ball games, and, at eleven, had a full-time job as a telegraph messenger. While attending East Side Evening High School, he blocked women's straw hats. He learned economic theory from his boss, Oscar Geiger, a furrier and advocate of Henry George's (1839–1897) single tax. Harry attended a weekly literary discussion group at Geiger's home. In 1923 he earned his B.A. degree from the City College of New York. When his sister Clara became a pioneering woman stockbroker, he wrote the house newsletter for the firm where she worked. Genevieve Gallagher, who worked as Clara's stenographer, became his wife in 1926. They had three sons but became legally separated in 1961.

In 1926 Goldhurst worked as an independent broker with Kable and Company, selling stock on the partial-payment plan. This short-lived career ended in his bankruptcy and conviction for mail fraud in 1929. Goldhurst was sentenced to a five-year prison term, of which he served three years, eight months, and twenty-two days. In prison he tutored inmates and catalogued the library. Upon his release, he managed a hotel in the New York theater district owned by his brother Jacob.

Between 1938 and 1941 he worked for the New York *Daily Mirror*, the New York *Post*, and the *Times-Advocate* of Norfolk, Virginia. Then, changing his name from Goldhurst to Golden, he went south, hoping to earn enough to send for his family. Later in 1941, the *Labor Journal*, a publication of the American Federation of Labor, in Charlotte, North Carolina, offered him the chance to write editorials. Instead, he decided to stay in Charlotte and start his own newspaper, the *Carolina Israelite*, a sixteen-page monthly of social commentary and nostalgic reminiscences. At the start he had two hundred subscribers. His was one of the few southern newspapers to back the 1954 *Brown v. Board of Education* decision. When Golden suspended publication in February 1968, the paper had a national circulation of forty thousand.

Golden often used humor in the name of reform. His Rent-a-Baby Plan was based on a stratagem devised by two black teachers who wished to see Laurence Olivier's *Hamlet* in a segregated cinema. They each borrowed a white child from friends and pretended to be nursemaids. This ruse gained them admission and gave Golden an anecdote to use in the service of integration. After the Supreme Court ended school segregation in 1954, Golden proposed his famous Vertical Negro Plan. Reasoning that no southerner objected to standing in line at shops or banks next to blacks, only to sitting beside them in buses or at lunch counters, he suggested replacing all seats in schools with stand-up bookkeeping desks so that students could learn vertically. Such a plan could also be extended to eating arrangements at lunch counters, he added.

Although Golden was frequently quoted in the *Congressional Record*, his newspaper suffered financially because of the hostility of white supremacists. To keep going, he had to borrow $20,000 from Jewish philanthropists between 1955 and 1958. His courageous stance won him the friendship of Eleanor Roosevelt; Adlai E. Stevenson II, for whom he campaigned in 1952 and 1956; and both John F. Kennedy and Robert F. Kennedy, who consulted him on civil rights matters. It also brought him an invitation to join a philosophy club at which Charlotte's intellectuals exchanged views at dinner once a month.

Golden's closest friend was Carl Sandburg, who had moved to North Carolina in 1945. Sandburg wrote the introduction to Golden's *Only in America*. Published in July 1958, the book sold 250,000 hardcover and more than 1.7 million paperback copies and remained at the top of the bestseller list for a year. Given this phenomenal success, Golden became a frequent guest on television talk shows, particularly Jack Paar's "Tonight." Jerry Lawrence and R. E. Lee turned *Only in America* into a Broadway play in 1959.

Golden was able to employ his son Richard as associate editor of the *Israelite* in 1958 and to make him his collaborator on four of his books: *Carl Sandburg* (1961), *Forgotten Pioneer* (1963), *Mr. Kennedy and the Negroes* (1964), and *A Little Girl Is Dead* (1965). Golden also produced with Richard a triweekly column for the Bell-McClure Syndicate that appeared in sixty-four newspapers from February 1960 on. Harry, Jr., who became a city editor at the Chicago *Sun-Times*, edited and arranged anthologies taken from Golden's *Israelite* columns: *For 2¢ Plain* (1959), *Enjoy, Enjoy* (1960), *So What Else Is New?* (1964), and *Ess, Ess, Mein Kindt* (1966).

Golden's report on the Eichmann trial was printed in the 21 April 1961 issue of *Life. The Israelis* (1971) is a compilation of sketches from the year he spent in Israel after the Six Day War. His autobiography, *The Right Time*, was published in 1969. Golden died in Charlotte after a long career as a journalist, crackerbarrel philosopher, raconteur, humorist, and racial reformer.

• Golden's manuscripts are preserved in a special "Golden Room" at the Charlotte Public Library. The most extensive source of information about Golden's life is his autobiography. See also Theodore Solotaroff, "Harry Golden and the American Audience," *Commentary* 31 (January 1961): 1–13. An obituary appears in the *New York Times*, 3 Oct. 1981.

RUTH ROSENBERG

GOLDEN, John (27 June 1874–17 June 1955), theatrical producer, songwriter, and playwright, was born in New York City, the son of Joel Golden, a teacher and proprietor of a summer hotel, and Amelia Tyreler. Raised in Wauseon, Ohio, he went to New York at age fourteen to pursue a career as an actor. For seven years he struggled, accepting odd jobs and selling comic verses, the latter written after the manner of W. S. Gilbert, to the weekly humor magazines *Puck*, *Judge*, and *Truth*. In 1895 Golden abandoned his acting career to sell industrial chemicals for the Oakes Manufacturing Company, where he rose quickly to an executive sales position. He continued meanwhile to write for the theater, composing a hit song, "I'm Willy Off the Boat," for the 1896 musical *A Good Thing*. Golden retired from chemical sales in 1908, and the following year he married actress Margaret Hesterich; they had no children.

During the next decade Golden wrote music and lyrics for six productions, most notably for musical revues and spectacles at the New York Hippodrome. His song "You Can't Play Every Instrument in the Band" (1913), after the style of Arthur Sullivan, was very popular, but his biggest hit was "Poor Butterfly," first heard in *The Big Show* (1916). Golden became a Broadway producer in 1916, underwriting a production of *Turn to the Right* with a royalty check of slightly more than $4,000 from his hit song "Goodbye Girls, I'm Through," written for the Hippodrome musical revue *Chin Chin* (1914). *Turn to the Right* (1916), which was dramatized by Winchell Smith from a story by John E. Hazzard, ran for 435 performances on Broadway and was repeatedly produced in stock and amateur theaters over the next fifteen years. Golden teamed up with Winchell Smith on two more successful productions. Smith doctored and then directed Frank Bacon's *Lightnin'* (1918), a sentimental comedy about an aging, rural reprobate who outmaneuvers a slick lawyer and an unscrupulous land developer to save his family home and reconcile with his estranged spouse. It ran for nearly 1,300 performances, a record at the time. Their third success was Austin Strong's *Three Wise Fools* (1918), again directed by Smith.

Early in his career as a producer, in 1918 Golden led his fellow producers in forming the Producing Managers' Association (PMA). He believed that managers should respond unilaterally to the demands of the actors' union, but after the PMA took an intransigent position that led to a devastating strike in 1919, Golden steered the two groups toward a mediated settlement.

Golden's reputation grew and his fortune as a producer increased until 1953, when he retired from theatrical production. He had produced about seventy-five plays on Broadway, nearly a third of which were hits that ran for at least 100 performances. In 1926 he built the Golden Theatre at 202 West Fifty-eighth Street, outside the theater district at that time. He sold the Golden Theatre to the Columbia Broadcasting System in 1932 and in 1937 purchased the Masque Theatre, which was in the theater district, and renamed it after himself.

Golden contributed on the home front during both world wars by producing special entertainments for soldiers and arranging for free theater tickets for those in uniform. His gifts to the City Center of Music and Drama in New York City in 1943 and to the Foundation Advisory Committee of the Theatre in 1944 are further evidence of his strong sense of social responsibility.

In addition to relying heavily on the skill and insight of playwright and director Winchell Smith, whom he had met in 1904 (while Smith was directing Arnold Daly in the plays of George Bernard Shaw), Golden formed close professional ties with actor-playwright Frank Craven, perhaps best known as the "Stage Manager" in Thornton Wilder's *Our Town* (1938). Craven appeared in, directed, or doctored several Golden productions because he was an adept of the folksy persona so vital to the Golden formula for success. As playwright George Ade observed, "John Golden has prospered as a producer because in each play he simply assembled some homely characters and steered them toward a happy ending" (quoted in John Golden's autobiography, *Stage Struck* [1930], p. xiv). Though the Golden formula also typically included the endorsement of traditional values stressing the primacy of home and family, Golden produced five plays by Rachel Crothers, then America's preeminent female playwright and director. Crothers, who also directed the plays, veered away from the Golden formula by representing the conflict experienced by women who were attracted both to traditional values and to the values identified with the "New Woman."

Golden characterized his career as "a fight for decency in the theatre" (*Stage Struck*, p. 196), and he was careful to choose "clean" plays, those without overt or covert sexual content. Placing audience satisfaction highest among his business priorities, Golden and his staff each year read hundreds of plays, mainly by established American writers. Either he or such associates as Smith and Craven would aggressively revise producible scripts to align them with the Golden formula. He then assessed the potential of each production by closely observing audience behavior at out-of-town tryouts.

An incident recorded in Rose Franken's autobiography illustrates Golden's working style. Franken had sent Golden a play based on her popular novel, *Claudia*, which concerned the maturation of a young bride who had a debilitating attachment to her mother. Franken had focused Claudia's transformation around hearing the news that she is pregnant. In discussing the script with Franken, Golden seemed upset by the play but clearly wanted to produce it. She could see that the copy on his desk had been heavily annotated, with lines and scenes cut or moved. "In my productions, nobody gets pregnant!" he insisted (*When All Is Said and Done*, p. 233). But Claudia was indeed pregnant in the play Golden produced in 1941 (which ran for 722 performances), for he recognized the dramatic necessity and the audience appeal of this crucial aspect of the title character. Franken emphasized Golden's irascibility, his contradictory manner, and "the sizzling tension of his presence" and concluded, "A strange man, John Golden. The most delightful, horrible, lovable rascal I've ever known" (p. 252).

Golden died at his home in Bayside, New York.

• The Theatre and Drama Collection of the New York Public Library has photographs, theater programs, clippings, souvenirs, advertising matter, press releases, minutes of American Theatre Wing (ATW) War Service, Inc., and other materials, some not relating to ATW, in its John Golden Collection. Correspondence from and to Golden is in the Kenyon Nicholson Papers and the Jean (Collins) Kerr and Walter Kerr Papers in the State Historical Society of Wisconsin; also in the Roy Wilson Howard Papers in the Manuscript Division of the Library of Congress. Golden's autobiography, *Stage Struck* (1930), written with Viola Brothers Shore, should be supplemented by accounts in the *National Cyclopedia of American Biography*, vol. 45, and *Current Biography 1944*. Rose Franken provides a personal view in *When All Is Said and Done: An Autobiography* (1963). An obituary is in the *New York Times*, 18 June 1955.

WELDON B. DURHAM

GOLDENWEISER, Alexander Alexandrovich (29 Jan. 1880–6 July 1940), anthropologist, was born in Kiev, Russia (now Ukraine), the son of Alexander Solomonovich Goldenweiser, a lawyer, and Sofia G. Munstein. His father was a major figure in the fields of criminal and civil law whose career was eventually chronicled by Goldenweiser himself for the *Encyclopaedia of the Social Sciences* (1931).

Goldenweiser grew up in a secular and cosmopolitan Jewish milieu in which the dominant languages were Russian and German. But he familiarized himself with other languages as well, steeped himself in their various literatures, maintained a profound interest in the visual arts, and studied piano. In short, he attained a high degree of cultivation at a relatively early age.

In 1900 Goldenweiser and his two brothers were taken to the United States by their father. He studied at Harvard for one year, then transferred to Columbia, where he was awarded an A.B. in 1902, an A.M. in 1904, and a Ph.D. in anthropology in 1910. He married Anna Hallow, a Russian, in 1906; they had one daughter. His teacher at Columbia, Franz Boas, advised him to spend several months in Germany, working at the Museum für Völkerkunde in Berlin. Writing to Alfred L. Kroeber on 24 May 1906, Boas said: "I sent him there because his mental make-up was such that he tended to develop very broad theories on slim material, and because he had difficulty in concentrating his attention upon special problems. I thought it best for him to take up detail work in a special region. . . . He is a very bright and promising man, and personally I should be quite willing to risk giving him work that requires some independence of mind."

Goldenweiser's Ph.D. dissertation was published as *Totemism: An Analytical Study* the same year he defended it (1910). In it he demonstrated that the presumed unity of totemic phenomena was an illusion. In fact, totemism itself, he argued, was a blanket term that concealed the actual heterogeneity of the factors involved, and the variety of their combinations. The idea prompted a lively debate among other anthropologists and provided the theoretical base for Claude Lévi-Strauss's *Le totémisme aujourd'hui* (1962). Goldenweiser continued to address this highly disputed problem in "Totemism: An Essay on Religion and Society" (1931), "A Final Note on Totemism" (1933), and an article on totemism written for the *Encyclopaedia of the Social Sciences* (1934).

Goldenweiser was recruited by Edward Sapir to carry out fieldwork among the Iroquois of Grand River Reserve, Ontario, in 1911, 1912, and 1913, but research of that kind did not suit him very well and he produced only a few brief reports. Throughout his career his paramount concern was social theory, and he once pointed out that he preferred theoretical works, even if their quality were not the highest, to almost anything else.

Goldenweiser's own theoretical gifts are perhaps most evident in his article "The Principle of Limited Possibilities in the Development of Culture" (1913), in which he argues that objects and institutions with a limited number of forms are almost certainly contrived independently by cultures located at a great distance from each other. Despite Sapir's airy dismissal ("I am sure," he wrote to Robert H. Lowie on 26 June 1917, "that you have something more fruitful to offer than the arid 'limited possibilities' and other futilities in which some intellectual gymnasts indulge"), the paper is an excellent contribution to the study of cultural dynamics, and illuminates those cases in which the idea of convergence provides a more satisfactory solution than the notion of diffusion.

Goldenweiser was an instructor in anthropology at Columbia beginning in 1910, and he also lectured at the Rand School of Social Science from 1915 until 1929. His classes attracted students because of his thorough knowledge of his subjects and his ability to instigate lively discussion. (As a student, Goldenweiser had organized a Karl Pearson Circle at Columbia, and several years later he began hosting a private discussion group called the "Unicorns," which provided his colleagues with a venue for debate on cultural and political topics.) After he was dismissed from Columbia in 1919 for allegedly disreputable behavior, he was appointed to the faculty of the New School for Social Research, which had been founded in New York City that same year. At the urging of his friend and publisher, Alfred A. Knopf, he published *Early Civilization: An Introduction to Anthropology* (1922), based on his lectures at the New School. Thus he became the first student of Boas (who did not himself attempt to write a textbook until the late 1930s) to provide a comprehensive summary of the field, predating Alfred L. Kroeber's *Anthropology* by a year.

Goldenweiser's unstable personal life and apparent womanizing adversely affected his scientific career and led to the deterioration of his marriage. Sapir commented on Goldenweiser's decline in a letter to Lowie (25 Mar. 1926): "I've not heard from Goldie in an age, but somebody told [Fay-Cooper] Cole and me recently that he was resigning from the New School—or had resigned—and was likely to get his divorce and go to Europe. It's going to be terribly difficult for Goldie to get a regular job in America. The ugly truth of it is he's become taboo in all academic circles. It's a hell of a shame but inevitable all the same."

In 1930 Goldenweiser left New York to become a professor of thought and culture at the University of Oregon Extension in Portland. That same year he married Ethel Cantor; they had no children. In 1933 he published *History, Psychology, and Culture*, a collection of previously published papers. While the book could be seen, in Goldenweiser's words, as little more than "a reheated meal," it provides an excellent overview of the full range of his interests. In addition to totemism, the various essays tackle such subjects as the complex relationship between psychology and cultural anthropology, the insights available to anthropology from the study of psychoanalysis, Durkheim's theories on the subject of religion, teaching as a means of influencing others and learning from their criticism, and the thorny issues of race and culture.

In 1937 Goldenweiser published *Anthropology: An Introduction to Primitive Culture*. Originally conceived as a revision of *Early Civilization*, the book eventually grew to become an independent work that mirrored the major concerns—greatly influenced by Boas's work at Columbia—of American anthropology at the time. Goldenweiser wrote on social organization and political institutions, symbolism in art, magic and religion, and the dynamics of culture from invention to migration and diffusion. While some of these topics are no longer fashionable, Goldenweiser's work remains of crucial importance.

Goldenweiser died in Portland. He remains the embodiment of a man with outstanding intellectual talents who was unable, because of other weaknesses, to make full use of them. Lowie characterized his career in a letter to Sapir written on 30 Aug. 1916: "In a purely cultural and scientific way he is a disappointment to me. He seems to me to be an essentially stationary individual. His point of view is always that of a highly sensitive and cultivated man, but his position never changes in essentials. . . . Still I must admit that in spite of all, though I do not seek his company, I cannot help enjoying it as a rule when circumstances bring us together."

This sense of a life of lost opportunities may be exemplified by Goldenweiser's projected book on Russia. Commissioned by the Carnegie Foundation and apparently completed in December 1918, it was never published, and the present whereabouts of the manuscript, if it still exists, is unknown. Whether the publication was halted by the Red Scare of 1919–1920 or for other reasons, a potentially significant work by Goldenweiser never saw the light of day.

• Goldenweiser's field research notes are in the Canadian Museum of Civilization (CMC) in Hull, Quebec, and the American Philosophical Society in Philadelphia. References to him also appear in Boas's letters at the University of California Archives in Berkeley; the Lowie papers at the Bancroft Library in Berkeley; and the Sapir papers at the CMC. He edited a symposium, *The Social Sciences and Their Interrelations* (1927), with W. F. Ogburn. Notable among his works is a literary venture, *Robots and Gods: An Essay on Craft and Mind* (1931). An informative and perceptive obituary is Wilson D. Wallis, "Alexander A. Goldenweiser," *American Anthropologist*, n.s. 43 (1941): 250–55.

PIERO MATTHEY

GOLDENWEISER, Emanuel Alexander (31 Jul. 1883–31 Mar. 1953), economist and author, was born in Kiev, Russia, the son of Alexander Solomonovich Goldenweiser, a lawyer, criminologist, and author of books on law and sociology, and Sofia Munstein. His father was also a friend and personal adviser to Count Leo Tolstoy. In 1902 Goldenweiser graduated from the First Kiev Gymnasium and then emigrated to the United States, where he was admitted to Columbia University. After receiving a B.A. from Columbia in 1903, he entered Cornell University, earning an M.A. in 1905 and a Ph.D. in 1907. In that latter year he also became a naturalized American citizen.

Goldenweiser had written his doctoral dissertation on the Russian immigration to the United States. That work led to a three-year appointment as a special investigator with the U.S. Immigration Commission, where in 1909 he published his study, *Immigrants in Cities*. After leaving that position, Goldenweiser served as a special agent for the U.S. Census Bureau from 1910 to 1914 and worked as a statistician for both the Department of Agriculture's Office of Farm Management from 1914 to 1919 and the Federal Trade Commission during World War I. In 1916 he married Anna Pearl Allen; the couple would have two children.

Goldenweiser spent the majority of the remainder of his life—a period that encompassed over thirty years—in the employ of the Federal Reserve Board, becoming a pioneer in the modern expansion of economic research in the federal government and contributing to the acknowledgment of the important role that economic analysis has in policymaking. His relationship with the Board began in 1919 when he took a job as an assistant statistician. That position lasted for six years until 1925, when he was appointed the assistant director of the Board's Division of Research and Statistics. By the following year Goldenweiser had been named director. Under his leadership, the Board introduced several innovative methods of economic intelligence; among these were the index of industrial production, which served during that era as the nation's leading indicator of economic health and trends as well as periodic surveys of consumer finances and statistical studies of money flow in major sectors of the economy.

While at this post Goldenweiser also wrote *Federal Reserve System in Operation* (1925), the general objective of which was to present in one single collection the workings of the Federal Reserve Board, which, until that time, had been scattered among several different publications. The book, according to its preface, was "intended to serve as an introduction to the study of the Federal reserve system [*sic*] by college classes in banking and by business and professional men who wish to have a general idea of the purposes, structure, and functions of the system." It seems that the business and professional men learned well, as many organizations in the private sector at that time began to make productive use of the economic information and analysis developed in the Federal Reserve System under Goldenweiser's guidance.

During Goldenweiser's tenure the Federal Reserve also became a working model emulated by central banks around the world. In fact, such imitation was actively encouraged, members of Goldenweiser's staff were directly responsible for organizing or reorganizing banks in such locales as Ceylon, Guatemala, Paraguay, and the Philippines. This spirit of internationalism was fitting in that Goldenweiser was the principal advocate for the creation of the National Advisory Council on International Monetary and Financial Problems, a body instrumental in coordinating international economic policy for the United States.

Goldenweiser did much of his work at a time when America was facing difficult economic conditions. It was during the depression of the late 1920s and the 1930s that he was asked to join the federal government's top technical committees on economics and finance. After those troubling times passed, Goldenweiser became involved in shaping the country's economic policy during World War II. From 1936 to 1945 he was the economist for the Federal Reserve Open Market Committee, where he played a major role in forming the financial policy of the New Deal. In 1943 he began to develop and negotiate the U.S. plan for the International Bank for Reconstruction and Development and the International Monetary Fund, which later became United Nations affiliates.

In addition to these duties, Goldenweiser was a fellow of the American Statistical Association and served as its president in 1943. In 1946, after retiring from the directorship of the Federal Reserve Board the previous year, he became president of the American Economic Association. During his retirement Goldenweiser dedicated himself to formulating a plan for postwar employment. He published a study, along with Everett E. Hagen and Frank R. Garfield, entitled *Jobs, Production, and Living Standards* (1945), in which he argued that employment should be guaranteed to anyone who is able and willing to work.

In 1946 Goldenweiser was asked to join the Institute for Advanced Study in Princeton, New Jersey. He remained there for four years, organizing seminars on monetary and financial policy and performing a series of investigations on behalf of the Committee for Economic Development. The principal aim of the investigations was to discover a method for avoiding inflation in war financing. While at the Institute he authored two books, *Monetary Management in the United States* (1949) and *American Monetary Policy* (1951).

Goldenweiser was a man who preferred his anonymity; thus, his many accomplishments were known only to those with whom he worked and others within the economic community. Elliott Thurston, a member of the Federal Reserve Board, said upon Goldenweiser's retirement that he "undoubtedly has contributed more, over a longer period of time, to important policy-making in the Federal Government than any other civil servant." Goldenweiser died in Princeton.

• Goldenweiser published the following works in addition to those previously mentioned: *Farm Tenancy in the United States*, with L. E. Truesdell (1924); and *Banking Studies* (1941). Obituaries are in the *New York Times*, 2 Apr. 1953, and in *American Economic Review* 43 (Sept. 1953): 632–33.

FRANCESCO L. NEPA

GOLDER, Frank Alfred (11 Aug. 1877–7 Jan. 1929), historian and library curator, was born near Odessa, Russia, the son of Minnie (maiden name not known) and Joseph Golder, a Talmudic scholar. To escape the virulent anti-Semitic pogroms of the early 1880s, the Golder family in about 1885 emigrated to the United States. They first settled in Bridgeton, New Jersey, where Joseph Golder took whatever odd jobs were available. A Baptist minister named Richard Minch found Frank Golder, whom he remembered as "a little Jew peddlar," on the streets and provided money for him to go to school. After a few years the Golders moved to Vineland, New Jersey, where they tried farming. In 1893 Golder enrolled in a preparatory school in Georgetown, Kentucky, perhaps aided financially by Reverend Minch. He graduated from it in 1896, then studied at Bucknell University on a two-year program, finally receiving a teacher's certificate in 1898. In 1899 he signed an American government contract, and from 1900 to 1902 he taught English to children on Unga Island, one of the Aleutian islands. At about this time Golder became a Unitarian.

In 1902 Golder entered Harvard, obtained his M.A. in history in 1903, and then continued toward his Ph.D. He studied in Paris and Berlin (1903–1904), returning competent in French and German, to teach history and economics at Arizona State Teachers College at Tempe (1906–1907). He studied again in Paris and Berlin (1907–1908) and taught at the University of Missouri from 1908 until 1909. He completed his dissertation, titled "Russian Voyages in the North Pacific Ocean to Determine the Relation between Asia and America," for his Ph.D. at Harvard in 1909. After teaching history at Boston University (1909–1910) and the University of Chicago (1910–1911), Golder taught at Washington State College at Pullman beginning in 1911, rising to the rank of professor and remaining there until 1920.

During the nine years he spent at Washington State, Golder took frequent leaves. He studied in St. Petersburg and Moscow on a Carnegie Institution grant from February to November 1914. His *Guide to Materials for American History in Russian Archives* (1917), which is still of value, was the result of his studies. Sponsored by the Carnegie Institution and the American Geographical Society, he revisited St. Petersburg from March to August 1917, observed the start of the Bolshevik revolution, and prepared the groundwork for his *Bering's Voyage: An Account of the Efforts of the Russians to Determine the Relation of Asia and America* (2 vols., 1922, 1925). From 1917 to 1919 he was a member of the Inquiry Commission, a group of experts appointed by President Woodrow Wilson and supervised by Colonel Edward Mandell House to formulate terms for a decent end to World War I. Some of Golder's recommendations now seem uncannily prescient; for example, the independence of Finland, Lithuania, and Poland, but not of the Ukraine. Well aware of his expertise and ambitious, Golder was disappointed when he was not invited to participate in the 1919 Paris Peace Conference.

In 1920 Golder accepted the position of curator at the Hoover War History Collection, founded the year before at Stanford University by Herbert Hoover, then secretary of commerce in President Warren G. Harding's cabinet and chairman of the American Relief Administration (ARA). Golder returned to Europe (Sept. 1920–Aug. 1921), traveled from Finland to Turkey and eastern Europe, and bought books for Stanford and the Hoover Library. He entered Soviet Russia (Aug. 1921) and traveled widely from headquarters in Moscow as an ARA representative to observe areas of famine. He was also active in Russia—and briefly in Europe (Apr.–June 1922)—as a collector of books, runs of periodicals, diaries, and other papers for his California affiliates and for Harvard and the Library of Congress when he could obtain duplicates. Golder met with communist officials but deplored their form of government and frequent acts of duplicity. However, his aims were always cultural, never political. Hoover described Golder's weekly reports in 1922 and 1923 as uniquely valuable, and his peers often expressed awe at his skills as a collector.

Golder began to teach at Stanford in September 1923. He also dug into the documents he had shipped to its library and to the Hoover Library, which together totaled about 25,000 volumes and 60,000 pamphlets and other small items. In September 1925 he again visited Soviet Russia, which was still not recognized by the American government, to attend meetings in Leningrad (formerly St. Petersburg, then Petrograd). After collecting more documents there and in Europe, he returned home in April 1926. A Rockefeller grant enabled him to assemble *Documents of Russian History, 1914–1917* (1927). At his urging, Stanford persuaded Lev Nikolaevich Litoshenko, an agricultural economist, to come from Moscow as visiting instructor for the 1926–1927 academic year. Golder went to Soviet Russia a final time in September–November 1927, ostensibly to help celebrate the tenth anniversary of the Russian Revolution. In reality, however, he had two other aims: to confer with Olga Kameneva, an official

trying to establish cultural relations between Soviet Russia and other countries, including the United States; and to persuade authorities to let Litoshenko return in 1928 to Stanford, where Golder was trying to establish a Russian Revolution Institute. Soviet authorities, however, not only blocked Kameneva's efforts but also refused Litoshenko travel permission. The communists did not want Kameneva to permit uncensored cultural publications or Litoshenko to continue to suggest privatization of Soviet agriculture. (Litoshenko was executed in 1938 by order of Joseph Stalin.)

Golder resumed teaching at Stanford in September 1928, but he was hospitalized with a worsening cold and was soon diagnosed as suffering from lung cancer. Golder held on to his dream of a Russian Institute at Stanford until his death in Palo Alto. He had never married.

Some of Golder's other publications are also significant: *On the Trail of the Russian Famine* (1927), coauthored with Lincoln Hutchinson, an economist and fellow ARA worker, detailed their observations, especially in the Volga region. *John Paul Jones in Russia* (1927) made use of Jones's letters Golder found in Russian archives and concerned Jones's association with Catherine II and her favorite, Grigori Aleksandrovich Potemkin. *The March of the Mormon Battalion from Council Bluffs to California: Taken from the Journal of Henry Standage* (1928), which Golder and two young colleagues prepared, narrates the story of recruits going west in 1846 to fight in the Mexican War. Topics of Golder's twenty or so articles include Alaska, Aleuts and Eskimos, Hawaii, Russian-American diplomacy during the War of 1812, the Crimean War, and the American Civil War. Golder impressed everyone with whom he came into contact as amiable, generous, and keenly intelligent. He untiringly sought international understanding, which the libraries his skills as a collector enriched have helped to promote.

• Most of Golder's papers are in the Golder Collection in the Hoover Institute on War, Revolution, and Peace, at Stanford University; and in the archives at Stanford. Other papers are in the library at Washington State University, Pullman. Alain Dubie, *Frank A. Golder: An Adventure of a Historian in Quest of Russian History* (1989), is an exhaustively documented biography and contains a full Golder bibliography. Terence Emmons and Bertrand M. Patenaude, eds., *War, Revolution, and Peace in Russia: The Passages of Frank Golder, 1914–1927* (1992), presents information in chronological order and annotates Golder's personal and official letters and reports. Wojciech Zalewski, *Collectors and Collections of Slavica at Stanford University* (1985), summarizes Golder's collecting successes. An obituary is in the *New York Times*, 8 Jan. 1929.

ROBERT L. GALE

GOLDFINE, Bernard (c. 1889–22 Sept. 1967), entrepreneur, came to the United States from his native Russian town of Avanta at the age of eight with his parents, Samuel Goldfine and Ida (maiden name unknown). He began working in his father's junk business as a high school dropout. With $1,200 of his savings, he and a friend began the Strathmore Woolen Company in Boston, which bought and sold textile remnants. His company prospered during World War I by supplying cloth for military uniforms. In 1917 he married Charlotte Goldblatt; they had four children. The Goldfine enterprises ultimately consisted of textile mills in four New England states, with the base in Lebanon, New Hampshire.

Political clout and self-promotion were essential to Goldfine's success. He cultivated most New England governors and was close to Boston's mayor James M. Curley. In 1951 he was host to an economic conference in Vermont, for which he chartered two planes to fly in three New England governors and newspapermen from Boston and New York. He also hired a public relations firm to boost his growing industrial activities. "You can't do business casually with Mr. B.," one of his legal acquaintances once said. "You must have lunch or dinner or drinks with him. There must be an exchange of glowing tributes: you're a great fellow, he's a great fellow, we're all great fellows."

Goldfine became best known for his legal difficulties and the downfall in 1958 of President Dwight D. Eisenhower's chief White House aide, former New Hampshire governor Sherman Adams, provoking an embarrassing political scandal for the president and the Republican party. In 1958 the House Interstate and Foreign Commerce Legislative Oversight Subcommittee revealed that Goldfine had tried to use his friendship with Adams to forestall punitive actions by federal agencies because of improper business conduct. When Goldfine was accused by the Federal Trade Commission in 1953 of mislabeling his textiles, he took his problem to Adams, who followed through by calling the chairman of the agency, Edward F. Howrey. The mislabeling continued, and so did the complaints. Adams, who then enabled Goldfine to meet with Howrey, explained that his actions were merely routine courtesies to help a friend in trouble with the federal bureaucracy. The charges were dropped. Adams intervened a second time in 1955 when the industrialist complained that the Securities and Exchange Commission was after him because the East Boston Company, another Goldfine holding, had failed to file annual financial reports over an eight-year period. Goldfine's flamboyant attempts to demonstrate his closeness to Adams helped to arouse suspicions.

Adams, known for his abrasive personality, had many political enemies and few defenders. The charges, as revealed by the House Interstate and Foreign Commerce Legislative Oversight Subcommittee in 1958, itemized gifts to Adams from Goldfine that included an expensive vicuna coat, a $2,400 oriental rug, and some $1,642.28 in hotel room accommodations billed to his industrialist friend. Adams denied that Goldfine had received favorable treatment. He also saw no reason to resign in disgrace. The president himself responded to the congressional disclosures by restating his faith in what had been Adams's legendary integrity, saying at a press conference, "I need him."

(It was later disclosed that Goldfine had also given President Eisenhower a gift of several yards of vicuna material.) The political pressures, however, were too great, the Goldfine intervention too brazen, and Adams's enemies too numerous. The president finally capitulated to realities and asked Adams to resign, a loss that then seemed crucial.

Goldfine received three prison sentences for contempt of Congress and for tax evasion; during the first sentence he was apparently transferred to a federal hospital in Washington, D.C., for psychiatric treatment. Goldfine, however, was never charged with additional findings that were later disclosed to the John F. Kennedy administration. Adams's former Washington landlady reported that he had paid his rent for years in cashier's checks. Internal Revenue Service investigators found that he had over $300,000 in unreported income. The new Democratic Justice Department was also confronted with the information that Adams had actually received "more than $150,000 in cash over a period of about five years" from Goldfine. Adams had "laundered" the payments at various banks and used the cashier's checks to pay his landlady.

The Kennedy administration weighed the wisdom of prosecuting Adams, but Goldfine's deteriorating mental and physical health made a court test somewhat risky. An additional consideration was former president Eisenhower, then in retirement at Gettysburg. Shown the allegations against his former aide by a Kennedy emissary, Eisenhower protested that Adams had been hurt enough. The ex-president left no doubt that he would be pleased to have the matter dropped. Eisenhower showed his consideration for the administration's handling of the Goldfine matter by agreeing with Senator Everett Dirksen to support the administration's Limited Nuclear Test Ban Treaty with the Soviet Union in 1963.

Goldfine had, by then, settled federal tax claims of $3.5 million from himself and $6.8 million from his wife, and he spent his final years in retirement at his home in Chestnut Hill, Massachusetts, outside Boston, where he died.

• Goldfine, his business activities, and the Adams affair are detailed in several memoirs and histories of the period. Among the memoirs are Sherman Adams, *Firsthand Report* (1961); Bobby Baker, *Wheeling and Dealing* (1978); and Dwight D. Eisenhower, *Waging Peace* (1965). For historical accounts see Stephen E. Ambrose, *Eisenhower the President* (1984); Michael R. Beschloss, *The Crisis Years* (1991); David A. Frier, *Conflict of Interest in the Eisenhower Administration* (1969); and two books by Herbert S. Parmet, *Eisenhower and the American Crusades* (1972) and *JFK: The Presidency of John F. Kennedy* (1983). An obituary is in the *New York Times*, 23 Sept. 1967.

HERBERT S. PARMET

GOLDIN, Horace (17 Dec. 1873–22 Aug. 1939), magician, was born Hirsh Goldstein in Vilna, Poland (at that time part of Russia), the son of a fruit grower and cantor; his parents' names are unknown. Goldin, who was eight years old when his father immigrated to the United States, remained for eight more years in Poland, where he studied music, hoping for a career as a concert violinist, and practiced magic tricks. When Goldin arrived in the United States, he joined his family in Nashville, Tennessee, where he worked in his father and uncle's general store and attracted customers with his magic tricks. These sleight-of-hand demonstrations had fascinated him ever since, at about twelve years of age, he had watched a gypsy magician at a country fair. Goldin depended even more on magic to draw customers when he became a traveling salesman, selling jewelry made by an uncle.

When Goldin happened to stay at the same boardinghouse as a traveling magician, magic became his life work. Only twenty years old at the time, Goldin went to see the magician's show. Impressed by the enthusiasm of the audience, he felt certain that he, too, could succeed as a magician. After serving as this magician's assistant for three months and saving $300, Goldin launched his career, incorporating into his show what he had learned from his own experience. From his work as a salesman he knew how to deal with people, and from his musical training he had a good sense of rhythm and timing. Because his English was still meager and his accent pronounced, his performances were almost silent demonstrations.

In the next few years, before he established himself in his new profession, Goldin had either to support his evenings of magic by daytime work or to perform as many as twenty-five times a day in "dime museums." But these hard years honed Goldin's acts, and he emerged from them an experienced magician determined on three things. He would pack more magic into his acts than any other performer; he would keep his show fast-paced by eliminating all talk; and he would strive to be topical in at least some of his acts. When put into practice, Goldin's formula proved successful. Audiences were enchanted with his huge, fast-paced show, staged with numerous assistants. Although he knew that his hard work and inventiveness had helped make him a great magician, Goldin, who had become a U.S. citizen (date unknown), gave his new country a large share of the credit for his success.

In 1902 Goldin performed in London, where he did four command performances in eight days and decided to call himself "the Royal Illusionist." After six months in England, during which his fame and income grew, he toured Europe, North and South Africa, and Australia. Each time he returned to the United States, eager audiences awaited him. Ever innovative, he constantly devised new tricks. The one for which he is especially remembered is his "Sawing a Woman in Half." A master in all feats of magic who was kind and helpful to other magicians, Goldin gave his profession a boost by making theater managers aware that magicians could attract large, lucrative audiences.

In 1919 when all of his show's equipment—costumes, scenery, and props—and much of his money were lost at sea, Goldin had to reshape his performances. Forced to speak more and to rely on smaller ob-

jects, Goldin—whose accent had diminished and whose vocabulary had increased—discovered that he could amuse audiences with his patter as well as his tricks. Even after he had built up his supply of equipment, talking remained an important part of his show.

During the later years of his life, Goldin found Europe more profitable than the United States and marriage more agreeable than bachelorhood. In 1927 he married Helen Leighton, whom he had courted for thirty years; the couple had no children. Openly acknowledged by his colleagues as the world's master magician, Goldin had a career in magic that spanned almost a half-century. Unlike his contemporary Harry Houdini, who specialized in feats of escape, Goldin preferred tricks in which he remained in the background while putting his assistants through weird perils. A life member of the Society of American Magicians—founded by Houdini—and the founder of the British publication *Magazine of Magic*, Goldin died in London.

• Goldin's career is amply documented in the clippings file of the New York Public Library for the Performing Arts, Lincoln Center. His autobiography, *It's Fun to Be Fooled* (1937), can also be found there. Milbourne Christopher, *The Illustrated History of Magic* (1973), has a detailed discussion of Goldin's career. Obituaries are in the *New York Times* and the *Herald Tribune*, both 23 Aug. 1939, and in *Variety*, 30 Aug. 1939.

PATRICIA FOX-SHEINWOLD

GOLDMAN, Edwin Franko (1 Jan. 1878–21 Feb. 1956), bandmaster and composer, was born in Louisville, Kentucky, the son of David Goldman, an attorney, and Selma Franko, a musician. He came from a long line of accomplished musicians—composers, conductors, pianists, violinists, and educators. After the death of Edwin's father, his mother moved the family to New York, where she placed two of the children, Edwin and his younger brother, Walter, in the Hebrew Orphans Asylum. There, Edwin studied both the cornet and the alto horn and played in his first band. He attended public schools but had religious and language studies at home. His mother gave him weekly piano lessons at the asylum. When his mother became financially able, she asked the brothers to return home, but Edwin chose to remain in the orphanage, where he enjoyed the many musical activities.

At the National Conservatory in New York, where Antonín Dvořák was the director, Goldman studied the cornet, first with Jules Levy and later with Carl Sohst. Dvořák was his composition teacher, and Goldman played in the school orchestra, which Dvořák conducted. One of the most memorable moments of Goldman's life was when Dvořák asked him to play the cornet parts of his "New World" Symphony before its Carnegie Hall premiere in 1893.

At the age of fifteen, Goldman was hired by his uncle Nahan Franko as music librarian and errand boy. This provided him with his first professional experience, performing with his uncle's orchestras and bands. In 1896, at the age of eighteen, Goldman turned down an offer to play first trumpet in the Boston Symphony Orchestra to remain in New York, where he joined the American Symphony as first cornetist under his uncle Sam Franko.

In 1901 Goldman joined the Metropolitan Opera Orchestra, where his uncle Nahan was concertmaster and conductor. He stayed with the orchestra for eight years. In 1906 he was on tour with the Metropolitan Opera during the disastrous earthquake in San Francisco. His uncle managed to save his Stradivarius violin, but Goldman lost a valued French Besson trumpet.

In 1908 Goldman married Adelaide Maibrunn; they had two children, one of whom, Richard Franko, later became a famous bandmaster. In 1909 Goldman left the Metropolitan Opera; in his unpublished autobiography he explained that he was "tired of playing in the orchestra" and did not want to be "part of a machine" for the rest of his life. He then went to work for the Carl Fischer Music Publishing House, where he wrote articles for *The Metronome*, revised wind instrument music, tested brass instruments, and composed. During that time he also wrote *The Foundations of Cornet Playing*, which became immensely successful.

Having conducted both the Nahan Franko Orchestra and Sam Franko's American Symphony, Goldman began to think about developing an ensemble of his own. "Slowly a dream was crystallizing of creating a band which would become a respected part of New York Musical Life—of showing the possibilities of wind instruments in tonal beauty and in their ability to produce serious music as satisfactorily as strings—above all, to bring good music not merely to the existing groups of music lovers but to everybody" (autobiography, p. 120). His New York Military Band gave a few concerts each summer from 1911 to 1917. In 1918 he gave the first regular series of free concerts, three concerts a week for ten weeks, at Columbia College. In 1928 the name was changed to "The Goldman Concert Band" and subsequently to "The Goldman Band." Money for these free concerts from 1918 to 1923 was raised through private donations. The most generous contributors were Murray and Daniel Guggenheim, who from 1924 on underwrote the entire season. The concerts were extremely popular from their inception and became one of the most important cultural events in New York. In 1923 the band changed its venue to Central Park, where at its opening concert it drew an audience of about thirty thousand people.

All through this period, while he was conducting, programming, and managing his band, Goldman continued to compose, writing over one hundred marches (including "On Guard," "On the Mall," "The Chimes of Liberty," and "The Pride of America") and also articles on band music and related topics for *Etude* and *Music Journal*. He wrote two books on bands: *Band Betterment* (1934) and *The Goldman Band System* (1936). Additionally, he guest conducted at many colleges and universities and taught part time at Columbia College.

Goldman was the founder of the American Bandmasters Association and served as its first president. Later, he was named Honorary Life President. He was the recipient of many other honors and awards, including John Philip Sousa's baton, the John Philip Sousa Centennial Medal, the Henry Hadley Medal, citations from New York, Los Angeles, and several European cities, and decorations from the governments of France, Italy, and Czechoslovakia. Goldman was also an avid collector of letters and other musical memorabilia, much of which he had inherited from Nahan Franko. According to Kirby Reid Jolly (pp. 120–21), Goldman bequeathed "several hundred items, dating from the time of Bach and representing nearly every noted composer, and many noted conductors and vocal artists" to the Metropolitan Opera and "a Mozart manuscript, a Schumann letter, a picture inscribed by Wagner, and a Sousa manuscript" to the University of Michigan.

Richard Franko Goldman considered his father's greatest achievements to have been in the area of programming and upgrading the image of the concert band. Henry Cowell stated, "That it is now possible to offer a program of fine art music of great variety and interest, all written expressly for the band by famous living composers, is very largely due to the efforts, influence and persuasiveness of Dr. Goldman" (*The Wind Band*, p. 86). In the early days of the band there was often only one original band work on the program; by 1953, some programs were made up entirely of original band music. Percy Grainger called Edwin "the patron saint of the modern concert band" (foreword to *The Band's Music* by R. F. Goldman). Goldman conducted his last concert on 15 August 1955. He died in New York City.

• Goldman's papers, including his unpublished autobiography, "Facing the Music," are in the Goldman Collection in the Music Division of the Library of Congress. A biography, "On the Mall," by his daughter, Louise Goldman Dooneief, is in the personal collection of his grandson, Daniel Franko Goldman. There are two dissertations: Kirby Reid Jolly, "Edwin Franko Goldman and the Goldman Band" (Ph.D. diss., New York Univ., 1971), and Noel K. Lester, "Richard Franko Goldman: His Life and Works" (Ph.D. diss., Peabody Conservatory of Music, 1984). Myron D. Welch, "The Goldman Band Library, Part 1," *Journal of Band Research* 19 (1984): 26–30, describes the Goldman library of band music housed at the School of Music, University of Iowa, donated by Richard Franko Goldman in 1967.

DOROTHY A. KLOTZMAN

GOLDMAN, Emma (27 June 1869–14 May 1940), anarchist and feminist activist, was born in Kovno, Lithuania, the daughter of Abraham Goldman and Taube Zodikoff, innkeepers and, later, small shopkeepers. Emma's lonely childhood was shaped by her parents' precarious social status and the contradictory influences of czarist anti-Semitism, the first stirrings of Russian feminism, and a growing revolutionary movement whose young members, especially the women, became Goldman's lifelong inspiration. After attending a *Realschule* in Königsberg, she entered a Russian high school in St. Petersburg, where her family moved in 1881, but straitened financial circumstances forced her to leave school after a year to work in a garment factory. In 1885 she emigrated with her sister Helena to Rochester, New York, where the rest of the family soon joined her.

In Rochester, Goldman met a fellow Russian immigrant, Jacob Kersner, to whom she was briefly married. Making shirtwaists in a sweatshop, she lived in an imaginary world of political intrigue, her mind filled with stories about the heroic Russian revolutionists who had been driven underground following the assassination of Czar Alexander II. She began following the trial and execution of the Chicago anarchists accused of setting off a bomb in Haymarket Square in the spring of 1886. A speech by Johanna Greie, a German anarchist, persuaded Goldman of the innocence of the accused men and perhaps also offered her a model of female activism that helped inspire her own flight from Rochester. Hungry for wider horizons and increasingly alienated from her husband, Goldman left for New York City, where she immediately became involved with the anarchist group around the flamboyant German agitator Johann Most. Within a few years Emma Goldman became one of the most controversial and charismatic figures in the international anarchist movement.

From the first, Goldman's life was entangled with that of Alexander Berkman, another Russian Jewish immigrant whose youthful belief in "propaganda by the deed" inspired his 1892 assassination attempt against Henry Clay Frick, manager of the Carnegie Steel Mills at Homestead, Pennsylvania. Goldman assisted in this attempt, though her complicity was never proven or acknowledged until the publication of her autobiography, *Living My Life*, in 1931. Berkman alone went to prison for fourteen years. However, the disastrous aftermath of his attempt, which neither killed Frick nor aroused the masses, convinced Goldman to relinquish her support for acts of violent individual protest, though not her admiration for those who were willing to sacrifice their lives for an ideal. She retained her belief in "direct action" as opposed to "political action" to effect revolutionary change but increasingly defined such action in terms of strikes, boycotts, acts of civil disobedience, and propaganda aimed at raising political consciousness.

At the time Goldman entered the anarchist movement, it was composed predominantly of small circles of German-, Russian-, Yiddish-, Italian-, and Spanish-speaking immigrants, most of them skilled workers and craftsmen. The Yiddish-speaking Jewish anarchists who increasingly made up the bulk of the movement after the turn of the century drew heavily on the ideas of Peter Kropotkin with his emphasis on ethics and his vision of a decentralized, stateless, communist society based on voluntary cooperation and mutual aid. Goldman tried to combine the anarchist communism of Kropotkin with the individualism of Max Stirner, Nietzsche, Ibsen, and the American individualist anarchists and midwestern free lovers, with whom she had considerable contact. As she explained in *Anarchism and Other Essays* (1911), anarchism meant "direct action, the open defiance of, and resistance to, all laws and restrictions, economic, social and moral." But it also meant a vision of society organized around "the freest possible expression of all the latent powers of the individual."

For Goldman, that individual was a woman as well as a man. The originality of her anarchist vision lay in her critique of gender inequality within anarchist theory and practice as well as within capitalist society, and her insistence on claiming for women the freedoms anarchists demanded for men. Though she remained aloof from the movement for woman suffrage, which she criticized as too puritanical and middle class, she spoke out strongly against the economic and social inequality of women, which made prostitution and marriage equivalent institutions. In Goldman's words, it was "merely a question of degree whether she sells herself to one man, in or out of marriage, or to many men." Criticizing the inadequacies of merely legal reform, Goldman emphasized that the emancipation of women required freedom from the "internal tyrants" of repressive social convention as well as from "external tyrannies" of political and economic inequality. Although Goldman extolled the glories of heterosexual love, she also urged tolerance for what she called "the intermediate sex," linking her very definition of anarchism to her defense of sexual minorities. "To me anarchism was not a theory for a distant future," she wrote in *Living My Life*. "It was a living influence to free us from inhibitions, internal no less than external, and from the destructive barriers that separate man from man."

By the turn of the century, Goldman had become a media star, a demonic figure to some, an inspiration to others. She had already served a year in Blackwell's Island Penitentiary in New York, for allegedly "inciting to riot" during a hunger demonstration in 1893. She was arrested on charges of inspiring the assassination of President William McKinley in 1901 but was released for lack of evidence. "Her name was enough in those days to produce a shudder," recalled her friend Margaret Anderson, editor of the avant-garde *Little Review*, in her autobiography, *My Thirty Years War* (1930). "She was considered a monster, an exponent of free love and bombs." An electrifying presence on the lecture platform, Goldman began making annual coast-to-coast tours, speaking out on a wide variety of subjects, from anarchism, anarchosyndicalism, and trade unionism to birth control and sex as an element of "creative work." She supported herself by working as a midwife, masseuse, and nurse—skills she had learned during a year of study at the Vienna General Hospital in 1895–1896. Her lectures in English attracted not only anarchists and other radicals but many liberals as well. She maintained ties with the radical wing of the labor movement, particularly the Industrial Workers of the World, whose strikes and free speech fights she often supported.

Upon Berkman's release from prison in 1906, the two comrades began publishing an anarchist monthly magazine, *Mother Earth*, combining cultural criticism and social analysis. With the emergence of bohemian communities in Greenwich Village and in cities around the country, Goldman began courting the intellectual avant-garde, who in turn embraced her as a heroine and inspiration. Emphasizing the need for a transformation of consciousness, she helped create libertarian schools through the "modern school" movement. She also lectured widely on literature, especially on the work of dramatists such as Ibsen, Hauptmann, Strindberg, Shaw, and others whose plays dramatized contemporary social evils. Her *Social Significance of the Modern Drama* (1914), offered one of the first political analyses of modern theater in English. Friendly with many actors and directors, she supported the "little theater" movement that created experimental regional theaters around the country.

Harassed by police and political officials, Goldman turned persecution into triumph as she organized free speech groups around the country to defend the rights of persecuted radicals and act as a support group for her own campaigns. Though she had long defended the right of women to control their own bodies, the arrest of Margaret Sanger in 1915 mobilized Goldman to more direct involvement in the campaign to legalize birth control. She spent two weeks in jail in 1916 for explaining birth control methods from the lecture platform and giving out free information.

World War I brought Progressivism to a halt in the United States, and Goldman and many of her comrades turned to antiwar activity. Arrested in 1917 for opposing the draft, Goldman and Berkman spent two years in prison. They were released at the height of the postwar Red Scare in 1919 and were promptly deported along with several hundred other immigrant radicals to the newly created Soviet Union. Although Goldman and Berkman had defended the Russian revolution and the fight against czarism, the Bolshevik vision of a highly centralized socialist state remained anathema to them and to most anarchists. Within a few months Goldman had grown alienated from the Bolshevik regime, particularly disgusted by the increasing persecution of anarchist and other left-wing dissidents from Bolshevism. In December 1921 Goldman, Berkman, and other anarchists left Soviet Russia for the West. In Stockholm, Berlin, Paris, London, St. Tropez, and Toronto, Goldman carried on an anti-Soviet campaign, condemning what she considered the Bolshevik betrayal of the masses and calling international attention to the plight of political prisoners in the jails and prison camps.

Finding herself increasingly isolated from all segments of the Left, not only the Communists but also the anti-Soviet socialists and even some anarchists, Goldman spent two years in a beautiful little house in St. Tropez where she wrote *Living My Life*. The autobiography used a conventional chronological narrative form to show how a lifelong commitment to anarchism opened new worlds of politics and love. Despite criticism from her comrades, she frankly described her tumultuous nine-year passion for a flamboyant Chicago physician, Ben L. Reitman, the only man who knew how "to love the woman in me and yet who would also be able to share my work."

Following publication of the autobiography, Goldman secured a ninety-day visa to lecture in the United States. But the Roosevelt administration feared alienating support for a more liberal immigration policy and denied her a permanent visa. In exile once again, she briefly realized her dreams in Barcelona in the fall of 1936, shortly after the start of the anarchist revolution and the civil war. The Spanish anarchosyndicalist organization the Confederacion Nacional del Trabajo-Federacion Anarquista Iberica (CNT-FAI) appointed her as its agent in London, where she campaigned for aid for her beleaguered comrades. With the small international anarchist movement badly split over the decision of Spanish comrades to enter the wartime government, Goldman attempted to reconcile factions while also criticizing CNT-FAI strategy. After the defeat of the anarchists by the Communists in 1937, and the fall of the republic in 1939, a grief-stricken Goldman traveled to Toronto to work on behalf of all refugees from European fascism. She died in Toronto and was buried in Chicago, in the country she always considered her home.

Emma Goldman's legacy within the anarchist movement remains controversial. Widely admired for her courage and tenacity in the face of persecution, she was also criticized as dominating and dictatorial. She remained like most immigrant radicals relatively blind to racism. For all her championing of the avant-garde, she preferred nineteenth-century realism and naturalism to twentieth-century modernism. She never succeeded in building an English-speaking movement, as she had hoped, though anarchist ideas had considerable influence within the Industrial Workers of the World and the Jewish trade union movement, as well as among middle-class intellectuals and artists. After 1921 Goldman's wholesale opposition to Marxism as well as her anti-Communism isolated her, not only from most of the western Left, including the anti-Soviet socialists, but also from much of the cultural avant-garde as well.

No other figure, however, so skillfully dramatized the rebellious social and cultural currents of Gilded Age and Progressive America. Certainly no other woman of her generation used her public persona so effectively to flout bourgeois conventions and taboos, using her own body on stage as a lightning rod for rebellion. Goldman brought keen theatrical gifts to the performance of protest, exploiting the controversy she created while lecturing in cities and towns across the country to educate and mobilize public opinion around a diverse array of progressive causes. Although more an activist than a theorist, she subjected anarchist ideas to a feminist critique, identifying the gender blindness in much anarchist theory and opening the way to the anarcho-feminism of the 1960s. She introduced a more sophisticated notion of psychology into anarchist thought, pointing out the subjective, often unconscious forces that helped maintain authoritarian or submissive attitudes even in those consciously opposed to all authority. *Living My Life* remains a compelling anarchist critique of America, as well as the record of a woman's lifelong resistance. Perhaps Emma Goldman's very originality conspired against the creation of a lasting anarchist movement, for to build such a movement she would have had to sacrifice the iconoclasm that remains her most enduring legacy.

• The Emma Goldman Papers are available on seventy reels of microfilm from Chadwyck-Healy, along with an extensive guide and index. All the Goldman biographies include useful bibliographies. Richard Drinnon's pioneering *Rebel in Paradise* (1961) stresses Goldman's identity as an American radical. Candace Falk's *Love, Anarchy and Emma Goldman* (1984) focuses more on her erotic life. Alice Wexler's two-volume biography, *Emma Goldman in America* (1984) and *Emma Goldman in Exile* (1989), emphasizes her feminism and offers a more critical perspective. Jose Peirats, *Emma Goldman: Anarquista de ambos mundos* (1978), stresses the Spanish Civil War years. There are two Twayne studies of Goldman, one by Martha Solomon (1987) and another by Marion Goldman (1992). Published collections of Goldman's writings include Alix Kates Shulman, ed., *Red Emma Speaks* (1972; rev. ed. 1983); Richard Drinnon and Anna Maria Drinnon, eds., *Nowhere at Home: Letters from Exile of Emma Goldman and Alexander Berkman* (1975); and David Porter, ed., *Vision on Fire: Emma Goldman and the Spanish Revolution* (1983). Goldman's *My Disillusionment in Russia* (1925) offers an anarchist critique of the civil war years. A provocative essay on *Living My Life* is Blanche H. Gelfant, "Speaking Her Own Piece: Emma Goldman and the Discursive Skeins of Autobiography," in *American Autobiography: Retrospect and Prospect*, ed. Paul John Eakin, (1991). Alice Wexler considers the process of writing about Goldman in "Emma Goldman and the Anxiety of Biography," in *The Challenge of Feminist Biography* ed. Sara Alpern et al. (1992).

ALICE WEXLER

GOLDMAN, Eric (17 June 1915–19 Feb. 1989), historian, author, educator, and presidential adviser, was born Eric Frederick Goldman in Washington, D.C., the son of Harry Goldman, a fruit and vegetable store owner and cab-driver, and Bessie Chapman. Goldman's parents divorced when he was very young, and he was raised mainly by his father. He attended public school in Baltimore but held out no hope of ever attending college because of his father's poor financial situation. On graduation from high school in 1931, however, he was awarded a scholarship and decided to enroll at Johns Hopkins University. Goldman moved on to graduate work at Johns Hopkins without ever completing the undergraduate program. He received an M.A. in American history in 1935 and a Ph.D. in the same subject in 1938, earning the latter degree at twenty-two years of age.

After receiving his doctorate, Goldman became a full-time instructor at Johns Hopkins. He left there in 1940 to join the staff of *Time* magazine, a position he held until 1942, at which time he returned to the academic world as an instructor in the history department at Princeton University. Goldman taught at Princeton

until 1985, moving through the ranks to become an assistant professor in 1943, an associate professor in 1947, and a full professor by 1955. In 1962 he became the first holder of the prestigious Rollins Professorship of History. Several times he was voted best lecturer by the Princeton senior class. Goldman noticed the irony of his becoming a successful college professor without ever having earned a bachelor's degree. He joked in an issue of *Current Biography* (July 1964) that "every year I introduce a motion that I be granted an honorary B.A., and every year I am defeated."

In 1941 Goldman served as the editor of *Historiography and Urbanization: Essays in American History in Honor of W. Stull Holt*, an essay compilation to which he also contributed a short piece. During the course of the 1940s Goldman would author three other books, in which could be seen hints of the themes of liberalism and reform that would dominate his later works. He also collaborated with Frederic Lane and others on a high school textbook, *The World's History* (1947), and made frequent contributions to the *New Republic*. He married Joanna Ruth Jackson in 1952; they had no children.

Goldman first rose to prominence on the national scene with the publication in 1952 of his book, *Rendezvous with Destiny: A History of Modern American Reform*, which focused on the liberal reform movement in the United States after 1865 and its two distinct and often competing traditions—the protection of the individual from big government and big business, and the use of centralized power on behalf of human welfare. Although written on such a scholarly subject, the book possessed an easy-to-read style that made it an instant success and garnered it Columbia University's Bancroft Prize for excellence in historical writing. Historian Arthur M. Schlesinger, Jr., applauded the book for giving its readers "a new sense of the variety and flexibility and strength, the vanity and gullibility, the shame and the glory of American liberalism" (*Current Biography* [July 1964], p. 156). In 1956 Goldman followed up his earlier success with the bestseller, *The Crucial Decade: America 1945–1955*, which presented an account of the United States's rise to the status of world power. The book's popularity spawned an updated version in 1961 in addition to a new preface chronicling Jimmy Carter's years as president that came out in a 1981 edition.

These two books helped to earn Goldman a reputation as an authority on public affairs. His writings on the subject appeared in *Harper's*, the *Saturday Review*, and the *New York Times*, among other publications. He became a current affairs lecturer as well, traveling on behalf of the State Department to Europe and India to give talks on the United States. In 1959 he was asked to serve as the moderator of the National Broadcasting Company's public affairs discussion program, "The Open Mind." As host of the television show, Goldman was, in the words of *Newsday* (5 Feb. 1964), "the picture of relaxation. . . . softspoken, erudite, and incisive, asking penetrating questions . . . [with] a knack for making his guests stick to the subject." The show ran until 1967 and won two Emmy awards.

Despite his success in these various mediums, Goldman is perhaps best known for his association with President Lyndon B. Johnson. The two men met at the recommendation of one of Goldman's former students, Richard H. Nelson, who worked in the White House as an assistant to presidential aide Walter Jenkins. Invited by Johnson to the White House for a discussion on 5 December 1963, Goldman spoke with the president for approximately forty-five minutes and, shortly thereafter, began working as an unpaid special consultant to the president. An official announcement of the appointment on 3 February 1964, stated that Goldman was to "serve as co-ordinator for the reception of the nation's scholars and specialists" and "would keep a continuous flow of specific proposals, general approaches, and opinions from a wide range of experts outside the government" (*Current Biography* [July 1964]).

Goldman's job was basically to function as a liaison between the administration and intellectuals and specialists outside of the White House. Some members of the press corps voiced their belief that Johnson had named Goldman to the post simply to serve as the token intellectual on the White House staff, but Goldman rejected such an idea. Near the beginning of his tenure, he informed *Current Biography* (July 1964) that the president was a "restless, adventurous kind of man [who] assumes that talent, energy and brains can solve problems."

Unfortunately, this union, which began with such promise, ultimately ended with bitterness on both sides. Johnson never felt completely comfortable around academics of Goldman's ilk, even though, by most accounts, he was an extremely intelligent man in his own right. In order to help dispel the pervasive notion that Johnson was an anti-intellectual, Goldman developed the idea of a White House Festival of the Arts, which was to be, according to Goldman, "an outgoing, warm, colorful White House salute" to artists, writers, and social critics. Despite those good intentions, the festival would contribute to the undoing of the relationship between Goldman and Johnson.

Johnson approved formal plans for the Festival of the Arts on 22 May 1965, with the gala to be held three weeks later on 14 June. This turned out to be bad timing for the president, who had recently ordered the systematic bombing of North Vietnam and U.S. military intervention in the Dominican Republic. The poet Robert Lowell sent an open letter to Johnson declining his invitation to the festival on account of the president's recent foreign policy decisions. The publication of the letter led to a debate among the invited artists over whether they should participate. The festival commenced as scheduled on 14 June, but the mood was one of considerable tension.

After the Festival of the Arts, Goldman's reputation was diminished within the White House. Johnson had been angered by Lowell's letter and the support it had received among many intellectuals. Their reaction caused Johnson to harden his stance against academics who opposed his war policies. However, these were the very intellectuals Goldman had hoped to recruit to share their ideas with the administration.

Goldman resigned from his position on 23 August 1966, although his decision was not made public right away. Johnson, who feared that Goldman would write a book detailing his experiences in the White House, wanted to downplay his departure. Goldman's resignation was finally revealed to members of the press on 7 September. White House press secretary Bill Moyers attempted to belittle Goldman's role in the administration, stating that "Goldman has spent most of his time working with Mrs. Johnson and Mrs. [Liz] Carpenter [Mrs. Johnson's press secretary] in the East Wing" (*Political Profiles, The Johnson Years* [1976], p. 221).

Johnson's fears were justified: Goldman did in fact write a book about his experiences in the White House, publishing in 1968 the bestseller, *The Tragedy of Lyndon Johnson: A Historian's Personal Memoir*, a critical assessment of Johnson's character and his limitations as president. In the book, Goldman wrote that Johnson was a man who "entered the White House unhailed, and functioned in it unloved. Only once did warmth and a degree of affection go out to him—when he told the country he was leaving the Presidency." Goldman's final assessment of Johnson was as "the wrong man from the wrong place at the wrong time under the wrong circumstances."

On leaving the administration, Goldman returned to full-time teaching at Princeton. He also continued his work in broadcasting, serving as a commentator for the *CBS Morning News* in 1975–1976. Goldman retired from his teaching duties in 1985. He died in Princeton, New Jersey.

• Among Goldman's publications not mentioned in the text are *Charles J. Bonaparte, Patrician Reformer: His Earlier Career* (1943); *John Bach McMaster, American Historian* (1943; repr. 1971); and *Two-Way Street* (1948). See also Donald R. Palm, "Intellectuals and the Presidency: Eric Goldman in the Lyndon B. Johnson White House," *Presidential Studies Quarterly* 26, no. 3 (Summer 1996): 708–25. An obituary is in the *New York Times*, 20 Feb. 1989.

FRANCESCO L. NEPA

GOLDMAN, Solomon (19 Aug. 1893–14 May 1953), Conservative rabbi, was born in Volhynia, Russia, the son of Abraham Abba and Jeanette Grossman. Brought to the United States as a child, he studied at New York University, Columbia University, the Rabbi Isaac Elchanan Yeshiva (now part of Yeshiva University), and the Jewish Theological Seminary, where he was ordained in 1918, having served the previous three years as rabbi of Congregation Petach Tikvah in Brooklyn. (He had received a most unusual recommendation from the chancellor of the seminary, Solomon Schechter, which allowed him to serve as rabbi before his ordination.) Also in 1918 he married Alice Lipkowitz; they had two daughters. Upon his ordination Goldman accepted the position of rabbi at B'nai

Jeshurun in Cleveland, Ohio. In 1922 he became rabbi of the Cleveland Jewish Center, which had formed out of a merger of two traditional, or Orthodox, synagogues, Anshe Emet and Beth Tephiloh.

A progressive voice within the nascent movement of Conservative Judaism in North America, Goldman instituted or oversaw many changes, including the instituting of bat mitzvah for girls, allowing women to read from the Torah and to be included in a minyan (the quorum of ten required for public prayers), the inclusion of musical instruments for worship services, amending prayers calling for the resurrection of the dead, and other liturgical changes. He sought to establish Conservative Judaism as a movement independent of Orthodoxy and as a corrective to the universalizing tendencies of Reform Judaism, which Goldman saw as weakening Jewish particularism through its posture away from Zionism, the use of Hebrew, and much traditional ritual. While serving as rabbi of the Cleveland Jewish Center, against strong opposition, he transformed the synagogue from Orthodox to Conservative. In the end the Orthodox opposition in 1926 took its complaint to the Court of Common Pleas of Cuyahoga County, Ohio, where his opponents charged Goldman with "violation of the Constitution and By-Laws which establishes the congregation as an orthodox or traditional congregation." The court held with Goldman in what became the first heresy trial of a rabbi conducted in an American court. In 1929 Goldman left Cleveland to assume the position of rabbi at the Anshe Emet Synagogue of Chicago, a position he held until his death.

Goldman became widely known as an orator, communal leader, scholar, and a strong advocate of Zionism in North America. Among his most notable achievements was the founding in 1946 of the Anshe Emet Day School, reportedly the first non-Orthodox Jewish day school in North America. Although Goldman appreciated the benefits of public education to American democracy, he was also convinced that only day schools, which combined secular and Jewish education, could effectively transmit a proper Jewish education. A Zionist activist throughout his career, Goldman sought to build popular support among American Jewry for the Creation of a Jewish state in Palestine. He served as president of the Zionist Organization of America from 1939 to 1942 and in that capacity was among those who chaired the convention of the World Zionist Congress held in Switzerland in August-September 1939, during the outbreak of World War II. Goldman's presidency of the Zionist Organization of America coincided with the years of the British White Paper on Palestine, which effectively put on hold Great Britain's previous commitment to the establishment of a Jewish homeland, restricting Jewish immigration to Palestine (eventually reducing it to zero in 1944) and restricting the purchase of land in Palestine by Jews. He also chaired the National United Jewish Appeal for Palestine (1937–1939).

In the area of Jewish scholarship, Goldman served as editor of a series of texts of Hebrew literature, including the works of Chaim Nachman Bialik, Ahad Ha'am, Moses Maimonides, and M. Z. Feierberg. In *The Jew and the Universe* (1936) Goldman offered his analysis of the medieval philosopher Maimonides. His books on the condition of American Jewry include *A Rabbi Takes Stock* (1931) and *Crisis and Decision* (1938). His numerous works on Zionism include *Undefeated* (1940) and *In the Words of Justice Brandeis* (1953). In his last years he began the publication of a study of the Bible and its influence on world literature; three volumes were completed: *The Book of Books* (1948), *In the Beginning* (1949), and *From Slavery to Freedom* (1958; also published as *The Ten Commandments*).

Goldman's lasting achievements are numerous. He was among those who created a strong Zionist movement in North America. He was a progressive voice for change within the world of Conservative Judaism. His vision in the creation of Jewish day schools has been imitated across the United States and Canada, and his works of scholarship in the Bible and Jewish philosophy remain valuable.

• Goldman's papers, including his manuscript sermons, correspondence, and other writings, are housed at the American Jewish Archives in Cincinnati, Ohio. His papers relating to his work on behalf of the Zionist Organization of America and other Zionist endeavors are housed with the Zionist Archives of the National Library of the Hebrew University in Jerusalem. Jacob Weinstein, *Solomon Goldman: A Rabbi's Rabbi* (1973), is an excellent biography. Alex Goldman, *The Greatest Rabbis Hall of Fame* (1987), is another useful source.

DANIEL ZEMEL

GOLDMAN, Sylvan Nathan (15 Nov. 1898–25 Nov. 1984), inventor of the folding shopping cart and businessman-philanthropist, was born in Ardmore, Indian Territory (later Oklahoma), the son of Michael Goldman and Hortense Dreyfus, owners of a general store. He received eight years of education in local public schools and in 1912 underwent his bar mitzvah in a Jewish Reform temple.

In 1913 the family moved to Tulsa, Oklahoma, and Goldman began working in nearby Sapulpa at his maternal uncles' wholesale grocery and produce business. He worked there until enlisting in the army in April 1917, overstating his age by eighteen months to meet the minimum-age requirement of twenty-one. Assigned to an engineers' battalion, Goldman trained at Camp Bowie, outside Fort Worth, Texas. He was named mess sergeant because of his grocery background and served in that capacity until mustered out in June 1919. His service included crossing the Atlantic by troopship and action in the Argonne campaign of 1918.

Upon his return to Oklahoma, Goldman returned to the wholesale grocery business, forming a partnership with his older brother, Alfred, and his uncle Henry Dreyfus. Their first warehouse in Cisco, Texas, was profitable, and they quickly expanded their enterprise to neighboring communities. This early success ended with a recession in 1921, causing the partners to return to Oklahoma. After a brief stint of retail working in California, Alfred and Sylvan were invited back to Oklahoma by their uncles to start a chain of grocery stores. The brothers opened their first store in 1926, and in two years they operated fifty Sun Stores in northeastern Oklahoma. They sold the chain to Skaggs-Safeway Stores in January 1929, taking stock as payment. By the end of the year their paper holdings of $300,000 had shrunk to $25,000 as a result of the stock market crash.

Despite this setback, Alfred and Sylvan Goldman rebounded quickly, purchasing five small grocery stores in Oklahoma City. They also married sisters, Sylvan marrying Margaret Katz in June 1931. The couple had two sons. The Goldmans' Standard Stores chain was run on a self-service concept, which they also incorporated in a second chain, Humpty Dumpty, added in 1934. Their combined operations grew more slowly in number than had the earlier Sun Stores because this time the brothers were developing larger units, which became known as supermarkets.

The enlargement of floor space and proliferation of items for sale enhanced profits, but Goldman was constantly searching for new ways to sell more groceries. In 1936, working late at his office, he had an inspiration. Shoppers, mostly women, could not buy more than they could carry, and the baskets they carried became heavy, thus abbreviating their visits. If they could push a cart with commodious baskets, women could buy more. Goldman got help from a store carpenter in tinkering with a frame similar to that of a folding chair, onto which two baskets could be affixed and pushed on casters. Goldman gave his helper, Fred Young, full credit for building the prototype according to his own inspiration.

Many inventors never get beyond having an intriguing idea. Goldman, in contrast, took additional steps in obtaining patents for his model that saved space by featuring baskets that could be stacked and carriers that folded and stacked vertically. He went on to manufacture his invention as the product of his Folding Basket Carrier Company, organized in 1937, and to overcome initial slow sales by a shrewd advertising campaign that included hiring actors to push his carts around a store, filming the activity, and having salesmen show the film to prospective customers. Later he developed the "nesting cart" that utilized a hinged rear slatted panel to allow the carts to "nest" in close storage. In the late 1930s Goldman manufactured over 70 percent of the shopping carts produced. Other companies developed similar products, however, and there were fierce competition and numerous patent infringement battles during the next few decades. Although Goldman's company continued to command a fair share of the market for carts, patents were impossible to maintain broadly enough to prevent competitors from gradually decreasing his market dominance.

Busy as he was with popularizing the shopping cart, Goldman did not neglect his grocery business. His brother and partner, Alfred, died in 1937, leaving him on his own to seek ways to expand his chain of stores both in Oklahoma City and in smaller Oklahoma communities. Goldman diversified his interests to include real estate. Seeking to ensure prime locations for his supermarkets, he began purchasing farmland around Oklahoma City in the 1940s, correctly anticipating the rapid expansion of the metropolitan area in the next three decades. He was able to use these purchases to launch shopping center developments, all anchored by Humpty Dumpty stores. In 1955 Goldman merged his chain of thirty-three stores with other chains located in different states, becoming president and a director of the new company, ACF-Wrigley. He became chairman of the board in 1958, then sold his interests in December 1959. In the 1960s Goldman organized a holding company, Goldman Enterprises, to handle his real estate, savings and loans, banking, hotel, and insurance businesses in Oklahoma, the Southwest, and Puerto Rico.

Although he kept an eye on Goldman Enterprises, Goldman went into semiretirement in his sixties, diverting much of his energy from making money to devising ways his Goldman Foundation could spend it. His philanthropies reflected a personalized approach that characterized his business acumen. In the 1950s he commissioned a number of sculptures, notably of Oklahoman Will Rogers, to adorn various public institutions in Oklahoma. One artist recalled Goldman's frequent visits to inspect progress on a life-size statue. On one occasion Goldman climbed a ladder to inspect the features already chiseled and pronounced them not entirely adequate. This personal attention to detail could be aggravating, particularly in the arts, but it served Goldman well in his business career and in philanthropy.

In 1972 the National Museum of History and Technology acquired Goldman's prototype, acknowledging the significance of his invention. Its widespread use in grocery and other retail establishments played an important role in modern merchandising and became a ubiquitous symbol of the nation's food industry and supermarket chains. Goldman died in Oklahoma City.

• Terry P. Wilson, *The Cart That Changed the World: The Career of Sylvan N. Goldman* (1978), is the only biography of Goldman. Works that deal with the retail industry he was associated with include Daniel Bloomfield, ed., *Chain Stores and Legislation* (1939); Frank J. Charvat, *Supermarketing* (1951); and M. M. Zimmerman, *The Super Market: A Revolution in Distribution* (1955).

TERRY P. WILSON

GOLDMARK, Henry (15 June 1857–15 Jan. 1941), civil engineer, was born in New York City, the son of Joseph Goldmark and Regina Wehle. His father, a physician who had served as a liberal member of the Austro-Hungarian Parliament, had emigrated from Europe following the revolution of 1848 and established an explosives factory in Brooklyn. Goldmark was educated in Brooklyn, attending the Collegiate and Polytechnic Institute. From 1874 to 1878 he attended Harvard, studying mathematics, sciences and literature. He then spent two years of postgraduate study at the Royal Polytechnic School in Hanover, Germany. He returned to the United States to pursue a career in civil engineering.

Goldmark was one of the first engineers to employ steel in the construction of railroad bridges. He first worked with the Erie Railroad, and then with the Texas and St. Louis Railroad, where he surveyed new routes. He also worked with the West Shore Railroad of New York. He then turned to metallurgy, visiting various metal factories to study their methods of production. He gained a thorough knowledge of the manufacturing process of metals and of the structural strengths of various beams and metal members used in bridge construction. During the late 1880s he was a consultant to a number of railroad companies on the safety of bridges and on their reinforcement.

In 1887 Goldmark completed a report on the Kansas City, Memphis and Gulf Railroad, suggesting that several bridges be condemned. He was then asked by the company to prepare plans for new bridges to replace those he identified as dangerous. These designs were his first independent ones. The bridges he built were heavier than the standard at the time and were still in service more than fifty years later.

In 1891 Goldmark was hired to help design several buildings for the World's Columbian Exposition in Chicago, including Machinery Hall. On 25 September 1892 he married Louise Condit Owens; they had no children, and she died in 1897. Goldmark took commissions to design a steel dam for a power company in Ogden, Utah, and the Connecticut Avenue bridge over Rock Creek Park in Washington, D.C., in 1897. From 1897 to 1899 he was design engineer with the U.S. Board of Engineers on Deep Waterways, which was studying the feasibility of a ship canal for the Great Lakes. While working on these studies, on 8 June 1899 he married Mary Carter Tomkins in Detroit, Michigan; they had two children. The work Goldmark completed on the beveled edges of canal locks while in Detroit became the basis for his later work on the Panama Canal.

Goldmark's early engineering work included a number of important projects in the United States and Canada. He received the Thomas Fitch Rowland prize in 1898 for a paper describing his engineering work on a hydroelectric plant in Ogden, Utah. In 1899, as resident engineer for the rebuilding of a railroad and highway bridge over the Missouri River at Atchison, Kansas, he gave a series of lectures on the history of locks and lock gates for ship canals; this series was published by Cornell University. He remained in Atchison from 1899 to 1902, working on improvements to protect the bridge during flood and ice conditions. He coupled his interest in waterways with his continued work on railroads. From 1902 to 1906 Goldmark worked in Canada on the design and construction of railroad shops for the Canadian Pacific Railway.

Goldmark's work with steel bridges, river dams, and canals, as well as his publications and recognition in these areas, made him a natural selection to work on the locks and auxiliary equipment for the Panama Ca-

nal. This was perhaps his most lasting contribution, and the main source of his national and international recognition. Many of the pieces of equipment Goldmark designed were still in fine working order a century later. Goldmark combined a knowledge of steel, years of experience in steel construction, and expert study of canal lock design, with dedicated on-site supervision both at the construction and prefabrication stage and at the installation stage.

Goldmark began his studies for the canal designs in 1906, spending two years working on preliminary plans. His responsibility was the design and installation of the lock gates, the water system for filling the locks, and the chain fenders which protected the gates from damage by ships. His contributions to the final canal design included electrical equipment, water intake and outlet valves, and movable emergency drains.

The valves were essential to the operation of the locks. The whole canal system relied on the power of water from Gatun Lake to lift and lower ships on their passage through the canal, and the system of locks, water tunnels, and water-valves was crucial to utilizing this force. The valves, which admitted water from immense tunnels or culverts into and out of the locks, were large sliding steel gates that moved on roller bearings in frames, like window sashes. Each valve consisted of two such gates, each weighing about ten tons. Opening of the intake valves or gates admitted water to the locks to raise the ship, and the opening of the outlet valve lowered it. At the bottom of each lock as many as fifteen well-holes served as drains for the outlet flow, designed to drain the lock rapidly and at the same time distribute the turbulence. A ship in a chamber could be lowered to the level of the outgoing basin in fifteen minutes.

The lock gates designed by Goldmark were the largest ever erected: each leaf of a gate weighed several hundred tons. The gates themselves were simply constructed, with a skin of steel plate riveted over a frame of steel girders and the interior left hollow. Although immensely heavy, as watertight chambers they floated slightly when the locks were filled with water, relieving pressure on the hinges. The heaviest of the gates were those on the locks at Miraflores, weighing 745 tons and able to withstand tidal forces at the Pacific side of the canal. Goldmark personally supervised the construction of the gates at shops in Pittsburgh, Pennsylvania, and their installation at the canal. His essays on this work were collected by George W. Goethals, along with those of other engineers, in *The Panama Canal: An Engineering Treatise* (1916).

When the canal was completed, Goldmark returned to New York, where in 1914 he opened an office as a consulting engineer. While there he worked with Goethals in designing the locks for the Inner Navigation Canal at New Orleans, which connected the Mississippi River with Lake Pontchartrain. He designed the lock gates, valves, electrical machinery, and an emergency movable dam for stopping floating logs. He also served on the board of engineers for the New York Barge Canal; and he designed the gates, valves, and electrical equipment for a new harbor at Chemulpko, Korea, under contract with the Japanese government. Other projects included a hydroelectric project in South Carolina and design work on a never-completed tidal-electric project for Passamaquoddy Bay in Maine. He was chairman of the inspection committee for the U.S. Navy airship *Shenandoah* and for an army airship.

Goldmark retired from full-time work but remained active. He served from 1923 to 1926 on the National Research Council as the representative of the American Society of Civil Engineers. He was also a member of the Engineering Institute of Canada, the Institution of Civil Engineers of Great Britain, and the Western Society of Engineers. In 1926 he prepared a report on plans for a proposed radio station near Shanghai, China, for communication with San Francisco. In 1927 he designed loading equipment for seagoing railroad-car ferries.

After retiring completely in 1928 Goldmark settled in Nyack, New York, where he remained active in professional organizations. He died after being struck by an automobile in Nyack.

• Goldmark's papers are at the City College Archives, City University of New York; other materials were microfilmed by the Yale University Library. Biographical sources include David McCullogh, *The Path between the Seas: The Creation of the Panama Canal, 1870–1914* (1977); "Memoir of Henry Goldmark," *Transactions of the American Society of Civil Engineers* (1941), pp. 1588–93; and George W. Goethals, *The Panama Canal: An Engineering Treatise* (1916). An obituary is in the *New York Times*, 16 Jan. 1941.

RODNEY P. CARLISLE

GOLDMARK, Josephine Clara (13 Oct. 1877–15 Dec. 1950), social reformer, was born in Brooklyn, New York, the youngest child of Joseph Goldmark and Regina Wehle. Her father, who had fled from Austria after the Revolution of 1848, was a physician and research chemist. His invention of a mercury compound that was used in making safety caps and cartridges during the Civil War enabled his family to live in comfort after he died when Goldmark was three years old. Goldmark went to Miss Brackett's School in New York City and then majored in English at Bryn Mawr College, graduating in 1898. She studied English at Barnard College for another year and tutored there from 1903 to 1905. While she was at Barnard, her sister Pauline introduced her to Florence Kelley, the dynamic general secretary of the National Consumers' League (NCL). Goldmark became a volunteer assistant to Kelley and quickly rose to the positions of publications secretary, chairman of NCL's committee on the legal defense of labor laws, and research director. The NCL's important *Child Labor Legislation Handbook* was published in 1907 under her supervision, as was its later *Handbook of Laws Regulating Women's Hours of Labor* (1912). These publications became blueprints for labor legislation throughout the country and earned Goldmark a reputation as a meticulous researcher and writer committed to social reform.

When an Oregon statute limiting women's working hours was challenged in court, Kelley and Goldmark asked attorney Louis Dembitz Brandeis, who had married Goldmark's sister Alice, to take on the case. Kelley and Goldmark did most of the research for what became the landmark Brandeis brief in *Muller v. Oregon* (1908). The brief gave only two pages to legal arguments but included more than one hundred pages of statistics successfully demonstrating the negative effect of overly long hours on women and their children. Goldmark performed the same research job when Brandeis submitted briefs defending other state laws limiting women's maximum hours and women's night work. Her organization of hundreds of national statistical reports enabled Brandeis to support his fact-driven sociological jurisprudence. In acknowledgement, Brandeis put her name on the title page of one brief, ignoring the fact that she was not a lawyer. He wrote that the material she amassed for their defense of an Illinois women's maximum hours' statute "makes available for the first time the world's knowledge of the results of the excessive hours of labor in industry" and "furnishes a broad foundation for legislative action." When Brandeis was appointed to the U.S. Supreme Court in 1914, his NCL cases were taken on by Felix Frankfurter, again assisted by Goldmark, who had the satisfaction of seeing the Court uphold Oregon's maximum hours law for men, just nine years after upholding the state's maximum hours for women.

In 1912 Goldmark was appointed to the committee investigating the Triangle Shirtwaist Company fire of 1911 and, along with Frances Perkins, Alfred E. Smith and Robert Wagner, participated in shaping the recommendations for state-enforced industrial safety and health standards made by the committee in 1914. She then undertook a survey of health conditions and hospitals in Cleveland, Ohio. After publication of her report in 1919, she was asked to serve as secretary of the Rockefeller Foundation's new Committee for the Study of Nursing Education. She turned the position into an investigative one, visiting more than seventy nursing schools and writing *Nursing and Nursing Education in the United States* (1923). The report profoundly affected the nursing profession, leading to the establishment of nursing schools at universities such as Yale, the affiliation of existing nursing schools with other universities, and the creation of national accreditation procedures.

In 1930 Goldmark published *Pilgrims of '48*, a study of the Goldmark, Brandeis, Wehle, and Dembitz families during the Austrian revolution and of their subsequent lives in the United States. It, and her later *Democracy in Denmark* (1936), expressed her beliefs in liberty, the importance of satisfying work that was neither overly demanding nor underpaid, and the ability of human beings to solve problems and create a just society. The beliefs were shared by many friends such as Brandeis, Frankfurter, Perkins, and Eleanor Roosevelt, and their influence with the New Deal administration enabled Goldmark quietly to help draft much of its labor legislation. Like her sister Pauline and many of their women friends, Goldmark remained unknown to the general public but played a major role in social reform.

Her final work, *Impatient Crusader*, a biography of Kelley, was written in Hartsdale, New York, where she and Pauline lived during her later years. Goldmark died in White Plains, New York.

• Many of Goldmark's letters, particularly those concerning industrial reform, are in the Schlesinger Library of Radcliffe College. Other letters and memoranda about child labor, wage-and-hour laws, migrant labor, and social security are in the National Consumers League Records in the Manuscript Division of the Library of Congress. Among her other publications are *Women in Industry* (1908), *Fatigue and Efficiency* (1912), *The Case for the Shorter Work Day* (1916), *The Case against Nightwork for Women* (1918), *Comparison of an Eight-Hour Plant and a Ten-Hour Plant* (1920), "50 Years: National Consumers' League," *Survey*, Dec. 1949, and many magazine articles. Although no biography has been published, some material about her life can be found in *Impatient Crusader* and *Pilgrims of '48*. See also Mary M. Roberts, *American Nursing* (1955). An obituary is in the *New York Times*, 16 Dec. 1950.

PHILIPPA STRUM

GOLDMARK, Peter Carl (2 Dec. 1906–7 Dec. 1977), inventor, was born in Budapest, Hungary, the son of Alexander Goldmark, a hatmaker, and Emmy (maiden name unknown). In 1919 Goldmark's family fled to Vienna, Austria, to escape the Communist revolution in Hungary. Goldmark studied for a year at the Berlin Technische Hochschule in Charlottenburg, Germany, and then transferred to the Physical Institute of Vienna, where he received his B.Sc. in 1930 and his Ph.D. in physics in 1931.

Goldmark's lifelong interest was telecommunications. In 1926 he built a miniature television receiver from a British-made kit and shortly thereafter earned an Austrian patent for a television picture–enlarging device. From 1931 to 1933 he worked for Pye Radio, Ltd., in Cambridge, England, as a television design engineer and then relocated to New York City to work as a television and radio consultant. In 1936 he joined the Columbia Broadcasting System (CBS) in its radio department but soon became its chief television engineer. Goldmark became a naturalized citizen in 1937. In 1939 he married Frances Trainer, with whom he had four children. After being promoted to director of engineering research and development in 1944, he became vice president of CBS Laboratories in 1951 and president in 1954, a position he held until 1971.

When Goldmark joined CBS, the fledgling television industry broadcast programs in black-and-white only, a situation that he resolved to change in 1940 after being enthralled by the vivid technicolor of the epic movie *Gone with the Wind*. He quickly invented the field-sequential system, which recorded images on a whirling disk of red, green, and blue and then transmitted the images to a similar, synchronized disk in the receiver. This system was used to make the first known color television broadcast in 1940. Although its development was delayed by World War II, the field-sequential system became the system of choice in closed-circuit applications such as medical education. However, despite being smaller, lighter, and simpler to operate and maintain than other methods of color broadcasting, Goldmark's system never gained widespread commercial acceptance because of the initial reluctance to retrofit millions of existing black-and-white sets with the whirling disk. However, in 1954 Goldmark invented a color television tube wherein the red, blue, and green phosphor dots were placed directly on the inside surface of the tube instead of on a phosphor screen attached to the tube in an unwieldy sandwich-type construction. This invention reduced the cost of manufacturing color tubes while also permitting the use of larger screens and was soon adopted as the industry's commercial standard.

During World War II Goldmark worked for the U.S. Office of Scientific Research and Development as a group leader for the Radio Research Laboratory. His group designed a jamming device that interfered with German radar and later created an "electronic spook navy" during the Normandy invasion by bombarding German radar with radio signals that imitated communications among naval vessels.

After the war Goldmark began developing the long-playing (LP) record. An accomplished cello and piano player, he loved listening to classical music on the phonograph but hated having to change the record every few minutes. By slowing a record's revolutions per minute from 78 to 33⅓, multiplying the number of grooves, and using vinyl instead of shellac as the pressing medium, he lengthened its playing time to about twenty minutes per side, long enough to hold an entire classical movement, while greatly improving the quality of the sound. Unveiled in 1948, the LP revolutionized the recorded-music industry and helped CBS to become a giant in the record business. He divorced his first wife in 1954 and that year married Diane Davis, with whom he had two children.

Under Goldmark's direction, CBS Laboratories invented more than 160 devices or processes in the field of acoustics, television, phonograph recording, and film reproduction. Two deserve special mention. The laboratory designed a lighter and smaller version of the field-sequential system for the National Aeronautics and Space Administration's Project Apollo, and in the late 1960s this system transmitted to Earth the high-resolution, close-up pictures of the Moon taken by both the Lunar Orbiter and the first people to walk on the Moon. More important, the laboratory created Electronic Video Recording (EVR), which permitted in-home viewing of a prerecorded film cassette via television and served as the forerunner of videocassette technology.

A resident of Stamford, Connecticut, Goldmark in 1968 joined its Urban Coalition to effect housing rehabilitation and job training for low-income residents. This involvement caused him to become increasingly concerned about the problems of America's cities, and he thought that one answer might be to get urbanites to move to the country to create what he called the

"New Rural Society." An integral part of this society would be a sophisticated telecommunications network built around EVR linking small towns with urban centers so that rural dwellers would not be deprived of educational and cultural events. In conjunction with Stamford's Fairfield University and the U.S. Department of Housing and Urban Development, he began studying ways in which to implement the New Rural Society in northeastern Connecticut's Windham County. In 1971 he retired from CBS to form Goldmark Communications, a subsidiary of Warner Communications, in order to "fulfill the promise of telecommunications as the instrument for social change," but his efforts in this regard were cut short by his untimely death.

Goldmark received a number of awards and honors recognizing his achievements, including the Institute of Radio Engineers' (IRE) Morris N. Liebman Memorial Prize (1945), the Television Broadcasters Association Medal (1954), the IRE's Vladimir K. Zworykin Television Prize (1961), the National Urban Service Award (1968), the Franklin Institute's Elliott Cresson Medal and the Institute of Electrical and Electronic Engineers' David Sarnoff Gold Medal (1969), the Carnegie-Mellon Institute Medal and the Industrial Research Institute Medal (1972), and the National Medal of Science (1977). He was elected to the National Academy of Engineering (1967), the American Academy of Arts and Sciences (1972), and the National Academy of Sciences (1972). He died near Rye, New York.

Although Goldmark's relationship with his employees was normally a cordial one, he often became quite demanding, if not unreasonable, when hot on the trail of an important innovation. He regarded himself as a gadfly because many of his inventions did not gain widespread acceptance. However, his contributions to the development of color television, the LP, and EVR mark him as one of the major shapers of twentieth-century culture.

• The whereabouts of Goldmark's papers is not known. His autobiography, written with Lee Edson, is *Maverick Inventor: My Turbulent Years at CBS* (1973). A good biography of Goldmark, which also includes a selected bibliography of his publications, can be found in Ernst Weber, "Peter Carl Goldmark," National Academy of Sciences, *Biographical Memoirs* 55 (1985): 293–303. His obituary is in the *New York Times*, 8 Dec. 1977.

CHARLES W. CAREY, JR.

GOLDMARK, Rubin (15 Aug. 1872–6 Mar. 1936), composer and teacher of musical composition, was born in New York City, the son of Hungarian Jewish immigrants. His father, Karl Goldmark, had been a well-known composer in Vienna. After attending City College of New York, Goldmark studied music in Vienna from 1889 to 1891. There he studied piano with Anton Door and composition with Robert Fuchs. In New York Goldmark did further study at the National Conservatory of Music, where he was a pupil of the Czech composer Antonín Dvořák.

Suffering from a chronic respiratory ailment, Goldmark went west in 1894 and he began his teaching career on the faculty of Colorado College in Colorado Springs; he remained there until 1901. Goldmark returned to New York, his health restored, and asserted his talent, establishing himself as a leading figure in the city's musical circles. He was one of the founders of the famous Bohemians Music Club, a leading supporter and promoter of music making in New York; at various times Goldmark served as the organization's president. Goldmark gained acclaim as one of the country's premier teachers of composition. He first taught privately, and then from 1925 to 1936 he taught at the Juilliard School, where he headed the school's department of composition. Among his pupils were Aaron Copland and George Gershwin. The world of composition was alive with many different, often warring, schools. As a teacher Goldmark never advocated any one school. While he advocated strong knowledge of classics, he was no mere pedant. His methods, particularly with talented students, always focused on helping them find their own true voice. Charming and friendly in manner, judicious in temperament, and intellectually acute, Goldmark was often asked to serve as a judge in composition competitions. During the depression he also headed an emergency relief commission to aid musicians.

Goldmark's own compositions are largely Romantic in harmonic language and style. There is a lilting quality to some of his melodies, and solid craftsmanship underlies his harmony and orchestration. Goldmark cared little for the innovations of such figures as Igor Stravinsky and Arnold Schoenberg, although he never discouraged talented students from following such pathways. Goldmark's leanings toward Romanticism meshed well with his desire to draw upon musical themes from American culture and history, and he was one of the first composers to employ identifiably American materials in formal compositions. *Hiawatha* (1900) was a tone poem drawing upon Native-American melodies. *Negro Rhapsody*, premiered in 1928, employed African-American spirituals and was the first such African-American concert piece performed at Carnegie Hall. Critics considered the works traditionally Romantic in harmony and construction. Modernists were critical of such traditionalism. Goldmark's *Requiem* (1919) musically eulogized the fallen of the Great War and based its thematic contours on Lincoln's Gettysburg Address. Some critics panned the work as old-fashioned, but audience appeal was widespread. The work gained popularity in Europe as well as in the United States; it later had the honor of being explicitly banned in Nazi Germany. Goldmark was among several notable composers of the early to mid twentieth century who demonstrated to audiences that American materials could provide a basis for concert compositions. Critics found the Romantic style of his work somewhat of a throwback to such nineteenth-century masters as Schumann and Brahms, but they recognized the music's appeal among general audiences. At the height of his popularity and regard as a teacher and composer, Goldmark's chronic respiratory problems reappeared, and he died suddenly in New York.

• There are no collected papers of Goldmark's, nor is there a biography. However, E. T. Rice, *Address Delivered in the Memory of Rubin Goldmark* (1936), summarizes key aspects of Goldmark's life and work. Goldmark is briefly discussed in Gilbert Chase, *America's Music* (1966); Ronald Davis, *A History of Music in American Life* (1980); and the *New Grove Dictionary of Music and Musicians* (1980). The major source materials are in the music reviews of the major New York newspapers that covered his music during his life.

ALAN LEVY

GOLDSBOROUGH, Louis Malesherbes (18 Feb. 1805–20 Feb. 1877), naval officer, was born in Washington, D.C., the son of Charles Washington Goldsborough, the chief clerk of the Navy Department, and Catherine Roberts. As a result of his father's political influence, Goldsborough was appointed midshipman in 1812, when he was only seven; however, he did not receive orders to sea until he was eleven. After being commissioned lieutenant in 1825, Goldsborough took a two-year leave of absence to travel and study in Europe.

Following his return to duty, Goldsborough completed a Mediterranean cruise and in 1830 became head of the newly created Depot of Charts and Instruments. In 1831 he married Elizabeth Gamble Wirt, daughter of William Wirt (1772–1834), Anti-Masonic candidate for president in 1832. They had three children.

Goldsborough then left the navy for several years, during which time he brought a group of German immigrants to his father-in-law's plantation in Florida and commanded a company of mounted volunteers in the Seminole War. He returned to the navy in 1841 and was promoted commander. Commanding the *Ohio* during the Mexican War, he served on blockade duty in the Gulf of Mexico and led an assault on the port of Tuxpan. Following the war, Goldsborough served on the commission that explored California and Oregon, 1849–1850, and headed the Naval Academy, 1853–1857. He was promoted to captain in 1855 and commanded the Brazil Squadron, 1859–1861.

On 23 September 1861 Goldsborough assumed command of the North Atlantic Blockading Squadron off Hampton Roads, Virginia. There he awaited the appearance of the formidable ironclad *Virginia*, which the Confederacy was building from the hull of the USS *Merrimack* at Norfolk. Early in 1862 Goldsborough's proposal to capture Roanoke Island, North Carolina, resulted in a combined army-navy expedition, the army commanded by General Ambrose Burnside and a fleet of some 100 vessels commanded by Goldsborough. Goldsborough's squadron destroyed the small defending Confederate naval force and provided protective fire for the 12,000-man unit that landed and secured the island. Despite his receiving the Thanks of Congress for the victory at Roanoke Island, Goldsborough was criticized by Navy Secretary Gideon Welles

for not being at Hampton Roads when the *Virginia* attacked vessels of the North Atlantic Squadron there, 8–9 March. Although he returned to Hampton Roads immediately upon learning of the danger, Goldsborough failed to lure the ironclad to deep water, where he believed he would have had a better chance of destroying it. His failure to act more aggressively resulted in severe criticisms from both the public and the press.

After the Confederates had themselves destroyed the *Virginia* when they evacuated Norfolk, Goldsborough sent vessels of his squadron to attack Drewry's Bluff on the James River. The vessels retreated, however, after encountering heavy enemy fire from the bluff. This naval operation was mounted in conjunction with the Peninsula campaign initiated by General George B. McClellan (1826–1885) in March 1862. As McClellan's reputation suffered from his failure to take Richmond, so did Goldsborough's. Despite this, in July 1862 he was promoted to rear admiral. That same month he lost more than a third of his squadron to a newly created James River Flotilla under the command of Commodore Charles Wilkes. Goldsborough's request to be relieved was granted on 4 September 1862.

Until late in the war Goldsborough performed administrative duties in Washington but without being allowed any role in major decision making. Welles had a poor opinion of Goldsborough, regarding him as "inefficient" with "no hard courage." Repeated requests for active command were denied Goldsborough on the basis that he could not be spared from his administrative duties. Finally, however, in February 1865, Goldsborough was placed in command of the European Squadron and ordered to locate and destroy any remaining Confederate raiders at sea or seize them if in port. The small squadron was not ready to sail until June, arriving in European waters long after the war had ended. The last Confederate raider at sea—CSS *Shenandoah*—managed to elude all pursuers and reached England in September. Thus Goldsborough was unable to redeem his reputation as he had hoped by performing a significant action. For the next two years he continued to command the European Squadron.

In 1867, with fifty-five years of service, Goldsborough was due to be retired. Despite the protest of Secretary Welles, Goldsborough's request to be continued in active service was approved by President Andrew Johnson. Goldsborough resumed administrative duties in Washington until finally retiring in 1873. He died at his home in Washington.

Although a competent officer, Goldsborough suffered from missed opportunities, a bad press, and a navy secretary who disliked him intensely. A fairer evaluation than Welles's is that of Admiral Samuel F. Du Pont, who although acknowledging Goldsborough's major personality fault, an "imperious nature," nonetheless recognized him as an able and conscientious officer with no interest in playing politics to advance his career.

• The Louis M. Goldsborough Papers are at the New York Public Library and the Library of Congress. See also *The Official Records of the Union and Confederate Navies in the War of the Rebellion* (30 vols., 1894–1922); U.S. Congress, House Ex. Doc. 27, 40th Cong., 1st sess. (1867), and House Ex. Doc. 66, 37th Cong., 2d sess. (1862); Thornton A. Jenkins, *Rear Ad. Goldsborough and the Retiring Laws of the Navy* (1868); A. B. R. Sprague, "The Burnside Expedition," in *Civil War Papers. Milt. Order of the Loyal Legion of the U.S.*, vol. 1, 427–46; and William Still, "Admiral Goldsborough's Feisty Career," *Civil War Times Illustrated* 17, no. 10 (Feb. 1979). An obituary is in the *Washington Evening Star*, 20 Feb. 1877.

NORMAN C. DELANEY

GOLDSBOROUGH, Robert (3 Dec. 1733–22 Dec. 1788), lawyer and planter, was born in Cambridge, Dorchester County, Maryland, the son of Charles Goldsborough, a lawyer, legislator, and large landowner, and his first wife Elizabeth Ennalls. When Robert was five and a half years old, his father married Elizabeth Dickinson, half sister of John Dickinson (1732–1808). Goldsborough was educated at home until 1752, when he went to London and entered the Middle Temple; he was called to the bar in February 1757. In 1755 he married Sarah Yerbury, daughter of Richard Yerbury, from whom he acquired title to property in London and an estate in Wiltshire. They had eleven children.

Upon his return to Maryland in July 1759, it appeared that Goldsborough would soon follow in the family tradition of service in the lower house of the Maryland General Assembly. In fact, Governor Horatio Sharpe wrote of the young Goldsborough in October 1760: "I doubt not but [Charles's] Son a Young Gentleman of good Abilities & Character who lately studied at the Temple will be elected by the People in his Father's Stead should the latter be made one of the Council." However, Charles Goldsborough was not admitted to the council until July 1762, by which time his son Robert was serving as sheriff of Dorchester County and was ineligible for election to the assembly. Robert Goldsborough was admitted to the bars of Queen Annes County and the provincial court in 1760 and to the bar of Dorchester County by 1772. He served in the general assembly of 1765–1766 and as attorney general of Maryland from June 1766 until his resignation in October 1768.

In addition to his profession as a lawyer and his political activities, Goldsborough directed the activities of his plantations in Dorchester County. He inherited over 4,500 acres in Dorchester County at his father's death in 1767 and by 1783 owned more than 8,600 acres and 123 slaves. Robert Goldsborough and his family lived at "The Point," the Goldsborough family plantation on the Choptank River in Dorchester County, in a style that was both gracious and lavish. He was connected by marriage or birth to many of the prominent families of Maryland.

When news of the Boston Port Bill reached Maryland, Goldsborough attended the first extralegal convention that met in June 1774 and was there elected to the First Continental Congress. For the next two years he alternated service between the increasingly powerful Maryland conventions and the Continental Congress. Politically aligned with men such as William Paca, Thomas Johnson, and Charles Carroll of Carrollton, Goldsborough worked at first for accommodation with England and, when it became apparent that that would not be possible, for the continuation of the conservative leadership that had controlled Maryland during the prerevolutionary period. Thus, Goldsborough favored property qualifications for voting and holding office, lengthy terms of office, and a benevolent power-from-above attitude toward the citizenry. One of the committee designated to prepare the first Maryland constitution in the fall of 1776, Goldsborough supported the final product—a conservative document that would preserve the status quo, with only the top layer of British and proprietary officials removed.

Following adoption of the new state constitution, Goldsborough served as one of the six Eastern Shore senators for the first term from 1776 to 1781 and during the second term from 1781 until his resignation in May 1783. Although elected again in 1783 and agreeing to serve "whenever his health would permit," Goldsborough did not again sit in the general assembly. He was elected as a Federalist to the Constitution ratification convention of 1788, but did not attend.

Robert Goldsborough died in Cambridge, Maryland. His obituary in the *Maryland Gazette* referred to him as "this distinguished Patriot" and remarked that at the time of the Revolution, Goldsborough, "embarking his extensive Fortune and Influence in the Cause of this Country, remained steadfast and inflexible in his opposition throughout the contest with Great Britain, nor did the Storms that often blackened over our Prospects at any Time shake his Courage." While Goldsborough does not stand out as an independent political leader or significant personage in the events of the day, it is clear from his continued reelection to office that his constituents saw in him the steady, competent, responsible leadership they wanted, and trusted his judgment in times of trouble.

• Basic information on Robert Goldsborough and his family is contained in Edward C. Papenfuse et al., eds., *A Biographical Dictionary of the Maryland Legislature, 1634–1789* (1979), and the files of the Legislative History Project at the Maryland State Archives. See also Henry F. Thompson and Anne S. Dandridge, "Hon. Robert Goldsborough," *Maryland Historical Magazine* 10 (1915): 100–9, and Dandridge (Roberta B. Henry, ed.), "Robert Goldsborough of Ashby and His Six Sons," *Maryland Historical Magazine* 34 (1941): 315–35. Goldsborough's legal career is outlined in Alan F. Day, *Social Study of Lawyers in Maryland, 1660–1775* (1989), and his politics are described in Ronald Hoffman, *A Spirit of Dissension* (1973). The quotation from the letters of Governor Horatio Sharpe can be found in William Hand Browne, ed., *Archives of Maryland*, vol. 9 (1890).

JANE WILSON MCWILLIAMS

GOLDSCHMIDT, Richard Benedict (12 Apr. 1878–24 Apr. 1958), geneticist, was born in Frankfurt am Main, Germany, the son of Solomon Goldschmidt, a coffee and confectionery shopkeeper and wine merchant, and Emma Flürscheim, who assisted with the family business. After attending the Gymnasium in Frankfurt, Goldschmidt studied medicine at Heidelberg University, where he was influenced by the noted zoologist Otto Bütschli, the comparative anatomist Carl Gegenbaur, and the biochemist Albrecht Kossel. In 1898 he transferred to the University of Munich, where he abandoned medicine for zoology, studying under Richard Hertwig. Returning to Heidelberg in 1899, Goldschmidt completed a dissertation describing egg maturation, fertilization, and early development of the trematode *Polystomum integerrimum*, obtaining his doctorate in 1902.

Appointed assistant to Hertwig at the Zoological Institute in Munich, Goldschmidt assumed the position in October 1903 after completing a year of compulsory military service. He remained in Munich for ten years, becoming privatdozent in 1904 and associate professor in 1909. In 1906 Goldschmidt married Elsa Kühnlein, the daughter of a professor of classical philology; the couple had two children.

Goldschmidt's teaching experience resulted in two books, a revised edition of Emil Seleka's widely used laboratory manual, *Zoologisches Taschenbuch für Studierende* (Zoological Pocketbook for Students; 1907), and the first German textbook on animal genetics, *Einführung in die Vererbungswissenschaft* (Introduction to Genetics; 1911), which was translated into Russian and went through five editions. In 1907 Goldschmidt founded the first specialist journal for cytological research, the *Archiv für Zellforschung*, which became after 1923 the *Zeitschrift für Zellforschung und mikroskopische Anatomie*.

Goldschmidt's earliest research carried on the tradition of classical German biology: microscopical studies involving cytology, histology, and embryology that focused on questions relating to morphology and evolution. A series of publications established Goldschmidt's reputation as a careful experimentalist. He also became known as a theoretician for his extension to metazoan cells of Hertwig's observations and interpretation of the presence of nuclear material in the cytoplasm of unicellular organisms. He developed his views into a general theory of cell functioning—the so-called chromidial theory, which envisioned two types of nuclear chromatin, one responsible for heredity and the other for metabolism—that roughly resembles later understanding of the functioning of nuclear DNA and cytoplasmic RNA.

Disenchanted with the prevailing descriptive, morphological approach to biological problems, Goldschmidt in 1909 turned to the new field of genetics. Beginning breeding experiments that spanned twenty-five years, he first used the nun moth, *Lymantria monaca*, and then the gypsy moth, *L. dispar*, to focus on two distinct problems: the evolution of geographical races and of melanic forms (in relation to speciation) and the determination of sex. From the beginning Goldschmidt conceived of genetics as involving both the inheritance of characters as well as their expression through development, an approach that became known as physiological genetics.

In January 1914 Goldschmidt became director of the division of animal genetics of the new Kaiser Wilhelm Institute for Biology in Berlin-Dahlem. While the institute was under construction, Goldschmidt traveled to Japan to collect different races of the moth *Lymantria*. Learning about the outbreak of World War I on his return voyage and prohibited by the British blockade from returning to Germany, he spent the remainder of the war in the United States, where he worked as a visiting professor in the Yale University laboratory of Ross Granville Harrison. Goldschmidt was joined by his family shortly before Christmas 1915.

During his stay in the United States, Goldschmidt learned firsthand about the work in *Drosophila* (fruitfly) genetics being conducted at Columbia University by Thomas Hunt Morgan and his students. Their classical book on transmission genetics, *The Mechanism of Mendelian Heredity* (1915), introduced the chromosome theory of heredity, which regarded the relation of genes to chromosomes as one of "beads on a string." This theory ran counter to Goldschmidt's functional understanding of genes as enzymes, and he became an early critic of the new static view of genes.

Goldschmidt became acquainted with many leading American zoologists by spending the spring and summer of 1915 breeding moths at the Bussey Institute of Harvard University and those of 1916 and 1917 at Woods Hole Biological Laboratory. With "war hysteria" sweeping America, Goldschmidt was arrested in May 1918 and interned with other enemy aliens in a detention camp at Fort Oglethorpe, Georgia, where he remained until the armistice was signed. He and his family finally returned to Germany in July 1919.

In Berlin Goldschmidt assumed his position at the Kaiser Wilhelm Institute for Biology (becoming second director under Carl Correns in 1919) and continued his research and writing. His 1921 paper on the nun moth was an early contribution to the study of the newly recognized phenomenon of industrial melanism (an increase in dark pigmented forms as a response to industrial pollution). But his most important and influential work in genetics came from his study of the genetics of sex determination in *Lymantria*, from which derived his physiological theory of heredity and the time-law of intersexuality. These were developed in a number of articles and several books, including *Die quantitative Grundlage von Vererbung und Artbildung* (The Quantitative Basis of Heredity and Speciation; 1920) and *Mechanismus und Physiologie der Geschlechtsbestimmung* (Mechanism and Physiology of Sex Determination; 1920). He also published a general work on genetics, *Der Mendelismus* (Mendelism; 1920).

Returning to Japan in 1924, Goldschmidt spent two years at the Imperial University in Tokyo teaching and continuing his breeding experiments. In 1927 he published *Physiologische Theorie der Vererbung* (Physiological Theory of Heredity), which presented his full view of the action of genes in development and was brought up to date in *Physiological Genetics* (1938). In 1929 he traveled for a third time to Japan. Between 1924 and 1933 he published a series of major papers presenting the results of his study of geographic races. Although in these works Goldschmidt accepted the neo-Darwinian conception of geographic races as incipient species, he later rejected this view, coming to believe that macroevolution resulted from major developmental alterations (saltations), not the gradual accumulation of variations. This idea was further developed in the Silliman lectures that Goldschmidt delivered at Yale in 1939, published as *The Material Basis of Evolution* (1940).

After the National Socialists came to power in Germany in 1933, Goldschmidt, who was a Jew, was able to retain his position at the Kaiser Wilhelm Institute until January 1936, when he was forced to retire. Accepting the offer of a professorship of genetics and cytology at the University of California in Berkeley, he left Germany with his wife for the United States that June. Although again declared an enemy alien in 1938, he became a naturalized U.S. citizen in 1942, taking as his middle name an old family name, Benedict.

Having turned to *Drosophila* genetics in 1929, Goldschmidt and a small group of Berkeley doctoral students became leaders in the investigation of what he named "phenocopies," abnormalities resembling those produced by mutant genes but obtained experimentally by altering the environmental conditions of developing pupae and larvae. This and further work on homoeotic mutants, including the podoptera effect, was taken up by later researchers and continues to interest developmental geneticists. These studies and Goldschmidt's mature views were presented in *Theoretical Genetics* (1955). Teaching until he reached the obligatory retirement age in 1948, Goldschmidt continued to pursue research as an emeritus professor until his death in Berkeley.

Goldschmidt's authorship of a number of popular scientific works reflected his conviction that it was the duty of scientists to make their "chosen field accessible to the general public . . . in a form which should combine pleasant reading with accurate information." In 1907 he described the world of microscopic organisms, *Die Tierwelt des Mikroskops (Die Urtiere)* (The Fauna of the Microscope). He explained the various processes of animal reproduction in *Die Fortpflanzung der Tiere* (Animal Reproduction; 1909). His engaging account of the biology of worms in *Ascaris, eine Einführung in die Wissenschaft vom Leben* (*Ascaris*: An Introduction to the Science of Life; 1922), illustrating basic biological processes, went through three editions and was translated into five languages. In 1927 he published an exceptionally popular exposition of genetics, *Die Lehre von der Vererbung* (The Theory of Heredity).

Goldschmidt was a controversial figure throughout his career. In addition to engaging in several heated scientific disputes, he consistently launched attacks on scientific orthodoxy, which served to marginalize him from the mainstream of classical genetics and later from the New Systematics, founded on the neo-Darwinian conception of gradualistic evolution and the new ideas of population genetics. Some of his views, such as his belief in the dynamic nature of hereditary material and his saltationist conception of macroevolutionary events, have enjoyed a revival among some scientists, although in a different formulation than that envisioned by Goldschmidt.

"Positive and negative attributes were curiously mixed in this great scientist," concluded Goldschmidt's biographer Curt Stern. "The sweep and penetration of his theoretical insights, the manifoldness of his objects of study, the courage to abandon seemingly established notions, including some of his own, stood side by side with the lack of rigor with which he could use imperfect observations when they fitted into his deductions, or sometimes disregard perfect ones when they failed to do so" (Stern [1967], p. 170). Goldschmidt credited his approach to three fundamental features of his mental makeup: an ability "to make quick factual discoveries based upon observation," "the absolute need of placing any new fact in its proper place within the whole realm of our science," and "an analytic tendency" that made him "skeptical of the scientific fashions of the day" (Goldschmidt [1960], pp. 312–13). These characteristics made him, if not a leader in genetics in the first half-century of its history, certainly a figure of considerable significance.

• Goldschmidt's papers are in the Bancroft Library of the University of California at Berkeley. Material relating to his career at the Kaiser Wilhelm Institute for Biology is in the archive of the Max-Planck-Gesellschaft zur Förderung der Wissenschaften in Berlin-Dahlem. Correspondence is in the genetics collections of the American Philosophical Society in Philadelphia; the Ross G. Harrison Papers at Yale; the Jacques Loeb Papers at the Library of Congress; the Frank Lillie Papers at Woods Hole Marine Biological Laboratory; the Ernst Ehlers Papers at Göttingen University Library; and in the manuscript collections of the Staatsbibliothek Preußischer Kulturbesitz in Berlin.

Goldschmidt was the author of more than 300 papers and eighteen scientific books, a listing of which is given in Curt Stern, "Richard Benedict Goldschmidt, 1878–1958," National Academy of Sciences, *Biographical Memoirs* 39 (1967): 141–92. He also left two autobiographical accounts: *Portraits from Memory: Recollections of a Zoologist* (1956), which was reprinted in the same year as *The Golden Age of Zoology: Portraits from Memory*, and *In and Out of the Ivory Tower: The Autobiography of Richard B. Goldschmidt* (1960). Goldschmidt's life and career were discussed in a special issue of *Experientia*, supp. 35 (1980), published separately as *Richard Goldschmidt: Controversial Geneticist and Creative Biologist. A Critical Review of His Contributions*, ed. Leonie K. Piternick (1980). Goldschmidt's scientific work has also been assessed by Garland E. Allen in "Opposition to the Mendelian-Chromosome Theory: The Physiological and Developmental Genetics of Richard Goldschmidt," *Journal of the History of Biology* 7 (1974): 49–92, and "The Historical Development of 'Time Law of Intersexuality' and Its Philosophical Implications," in his *Richard Goldschmidt: Controversial Geneticist and Creative Biologist*. See also Marsha L. Richmond, "Richard Goldschmidt and Sex Determination: The Growth of German Genetics, 1900–1935" (Ph.D. diss., Indiana Univ., 1986), and "Protozoa as Precursors of Metazoa: German Cell Theory and Its Critics at the Turn of the Century," *Journal of the History of Biology* 22 (1989): 243–76. An obituary is in the *New York Times*, 26 Apr. 1958.

MARSHA L. RICHMOND

GOLDSMITH, Grace Arabell (8 Apr. 1904–28 Apr. 1975), nutritionist and public health educator, was born in St. Paul, Minnesota, the daughter of Arthur William Goldsmith, an accountant, and Arabell L. Coleman. An only child, she attended the University of Minnesota before transferring to the University of Wisconsin, where she received a B.S. in 1925. Active in all sports and an accomplished dancer, she was physical director at the YWCA in New Orleans, Louisiana, before entering the Tulane University Medical School, where she received her M.D. in 1932. She gave dancing lessons to pay her bills and graduated first in a class of 108 that included only six women.

As a medical student she worked on the wards of Charity Hospital, where she saw many patients with pellagra, which was widespread in the South, and other dietary deficiency diseases. They sparked her interest in nutrition, a subject that medical schools neglected. She interned at the Touro Infirmary in New Orleans and in 1933 received a fellowship in medicine at the Mayo Clinic, where her interest in metabolic diseases was encouraged. While there she earned an M.S. in medicine at the University of Minnesota in 1936. That year she joined the Tulane University medical faculty as an instructor in internal medicine. She rose quickly through the ranks and became professor of medicine in 1949.

Goldsmith sensed the importance of training medical students in nutrition and, by introducing it as a separate course at Tulane, created the first program of its kind in the world. She also began postgraduate training in nutrition for physicians and biochemists. In 1946 she was named director of Tulane's newly established nutrition and metabolism unit, which became noted for the high quality of its graduates, who spread the gospel of nutrition in the United States and overseas.

Goldsmith was on the cutting edge of nutrition research. Focusing first on pellagra, she studied the role of vitamin C nutrition in the disease, determined the efficiency of the amino acid tryptophan as a precursor of the preventive agent niacin, and shed light on the relationship of pellagra to a corn diet. She researched the role of vitamin B_{12} in large cell anemias and was the first to report the response of anemia to folic acid. She determined the minimum daily requirements of various nutrients in the diet, especially niacin, thereby providing essential information to the national program of enrichment of bread and cereals. She also developed techniques to identify early signs of malnutrition. When deficiency diseases waned and threats to public health and cardiovascular diseases became the principal cause of death in the United States, Gold-

smith began clinical and laboratory studies on the role of dietary fat in arteriosclerosis. From 1940 to the 1970s she wrote almost 200 articles for scientific journals; her book, *Nutritional Diagnosis* (1959), became a standard work.

Recognizing that diet and the community are closely related, Goldsmith did nutritional surveys in Louisiana and Newfoundland. She became convinced of the value of school lunches and of such supplementary feeding programs as those for pregnant women. A social worker was an essential member of the staff in the nutrition clinic that she established at Tulane. As a representative of the World Health Organization, among other agencies, she traveled around the world studying nutritional problems. She saw the population explosion as a threat to health and became an advocate of both the green revolution and family planning.

These concerns found an institutional focus in 1967 when Tulane named her as the first dean of its newly created School of Public Health and Tropical Medicine. She held the position until 1972, when she returned to teaching. She was the first woman ever to head a school of public health in the United States.

Goldsmith's many honors for her work included honorary membership in the American Dietetic Association in 1963 and the American Medical Association's Goldberger Award in Clinical Nutrition in 1965. She was the first woman to become president of all three of the nation's leading nutrition organizations, the American Institute of Nutrition (1965), the American Board of Nutrition (1966–1967), and the American Society for Clinical Nutrition (1972–1973). Although she never considered her sex a significant handicap to her career, she welcomed the changed attitude toward women in medicine in the 1960s.

Goldsmith, who never married, loved music, gardening, and good food. She attended symphony concerts; grew roses, azaleas, and camellias in her yard; and entertained friends with gourmet meals she cooked herself. She was an enthusiastic swimmer and remained a popular dance partner all her life. Ironically, for one who knew so much about nutrition and health, she smoked, and she died in New Orleans of lung cancer.

• A file of articles and newspaper clippings about Goldsmith is in the archives of the Howard-Tilton Memorial Library, Tulane University. A bibliography of her published work, which includes chapters contributed to twenty-five edited books, also is there. "Efficiency of Tryptophan as a Niacin Precursor in Man," which was written with two colleagues, is reprinted in Kenneth Carpenter, ed., *Pellagra: Benchmark Papers in Biochemistry*, vol. 2 (1981). "Tulane Nutritionist Wins Many Distinctions: Sees Hope for Solution to World's Food Problems," *Tulane Report* No. 14 (Winter 1972), summarizes her life and work. Frances B. Simon, "From Pellagra Prevention to Public Health Dean," *Tulane Medicine* 23 (Autumn 1992): 28–29, concentrates on her work as an educator. The *Leaders of American Medicine* series of Alpha Omega Alpha includes a videotaped interview and is available through the National Library of Medicine. Obituaries are in the *Jour-*

nal of the American Dietetic Association 66 (June 1975): 618; and the New Orleans Times-Picayune, New Orleans States-Item, and the New York Times, 29 Apr. 1975.

ELIZABETH W. ETHERIDGE

GOLDSMITH, Joel Sol (10 Mar. 1892–17 June 1964), writer and lecturer on spirituality, was born in New York City, the son of Sol Joel Goldsmith, a prosperous lace importer, and his wife (name not available). Both parents were nonpracticing Jews. As a young man, Goldsmith became interested in Christian Science through his acquaintance with a woman whose father was a Christian Science practitioner. After himself being healed, he believed, of a serious illness through Christian Science, Goldsmith became a practitioner in 1928. About 1930 he married Rose Robb. Increasingly successful in Christian Science, in 1933 he set up an office in Boston across the street from the Mother Church. In 1943 he moved briefly to Florida. His wife died the same year.

By the end of World War II, Goldsmith had settled in Santa Monica, California. He married Nadea Allen in 1945, and in that year he reportedly underwent a series of mystical experiences that he saw as an initiation into deeper spiritual truth. The following year he withdrew from the Christian Science church and began his most famous book, *The Infinite Way* (1947), meditations on God as the sole power and reality. Though he had hoped to pursue a semiretired life in California, the recognition that this work brought him led to nearly twenty active years as an independent spiritual teacher, lecturer, and writer. He produced some twenty-two books, largely transcribed from lectures and classes by students, especially Lorraine Sinkler, and a number of audiotapes. These titles include *Living the Infinite Way* (1961), *A Parenthesis in Eternity* (1963), and *The Contemplative Life* (1963). After 1950 Goldsmith made his home in Honolulu. He was divorced in 1956 and married one of his students, Emma Lindsey, in 1957. He died in London while on a European lecture tour.

Goldsmith's teachings represent a radical monism in the Christian Science style. In the later independent phase of his life he placed less emphasis on healing than on the ramifications of Oneness for the inner spiritual life. He taught that God is the One Mind, the One Consciousness of which all beings are manifestations. The "many," which seem other than God, have only a superficial reality on the level of appearance. To establish awareness of the One by meditation is to tap into the source of healing. Besides the One, there is no other power or reality, and neither sickness nor death have real existence, for the One always is. Goldsmith believed in Christ and often used the words of the New Testament as bases for his instruction. But he saw Christ as an impersonal principle working for the healing of the world.

After leaving Christian Science, Goldsmith worked only with informal circles of pupils. He did not wish to establish a church or institution. Since his death, a modest organization has issued a newsletter and continued to make his audiotapes and books available.

• The only biography is Lorraine Sinkler, *The Spiritual Journey of Joel S. Goldsmith* (1973). A brief account may be found in J. Gordon Melton, *Biographical Dictionary of American Cult and Sect Leaders* (1986).

ROBERT S. ELLWOOD

GOLDSTEIN, David (27 July 1870–30 June 1958), Catholic lay evangelist, was born in Spitalfields, Middlesex, England, the son of Isaac Goldstein, a cigarmaker, and Anna (maiden name unknown). When he was a little over a year old, his family joined the exodus of working-class Jewish immigrants to New York City, where he was educated in the Henry Street and Fifth Street public schools and at the Hebrew Free School and Spanish Jewish Synagogue. At age eleven he left school to help support his family, which by then included three other siblings. After two short stints working as a cash boy, Goldstein became a tobacco stripper and an active member of the Cigarmaker's International Union. In his *Autobiography of a Campaigner for Christ* (1936), Goldstein reflects upon how his later career as a Catholic evangelist began at the factory bench and in the union hall, where he listened to fervent unionists and socialists endowed with a contagious "propaganda spirit." Two public figures especially impressed Goldstein in the mid-1880s, the union leader Samuel Gompers and the single-tax advocate Henry George (1839–1897), whom Goldstein ardently supported in his unsuccessful bid for mayor in 1886.

In 1888 Goldstein moved to Boston, where he joined the Cigarmakers' International No. 97 and became involved in the Socialist Labor party, running unsuccessfully for mayor of Boston on the party ticket in 1897. The most important legacy of Goldstein's socialist years, however, was his friendship with Martha Moore Avery, a Yankee woman nineteen years his senior. Goldstein and Avery became enmeshed in the factionalism within the socialist movement that spawned the Socialist party as well as in the heated disputes about the morality and political expediency of socialist clergyman George D. Herron's highly publicized divorce and remarriage in 1901. In the spring of 1903, Goldstein and Avery resigned from the Socialist party, convinced that it was a threat to the family and traditional morality, a position Goldstein articulated in his first book, *Socialism: The Nation of Fatherless Children* (1903). In 1905 Goldstein converted to Catholicism because he believed that the church, rather than the party, was the true safeguard of human dignity, justice, and the sanctity of the family. (Avery had been baptized in 1904.)

Goldstein was anxious to use the skills in oratory and persuasion that he had cultivated in the socialist movement in the service of the Catholic church. In 1910, after what seemed to Goldstein an interminable moratorium in his public life, Cardinal William Henry O'Connell of Boston asked him to join three other laymen and four priests to deliver lectures on Catholic social teachings to working-class Catholics in Boston. Goldstein's personal experience made him an extremely effective popularizer of the pro-union, anti-socialist position that American Catholic leaders had gleaned from Pope Leo XIII's watershed encyclical *Rerum Novarum* (1891), especially its premise that only by safeguarding the family and private property was true social justice to be achieved. This work in Boston led to national lecture tours sponsored by the Catholic Central Verein (1911) and the Knights of Columbus (1914–1924, 1928).

In 1917 Goldstein and Avery received permission from Cardinal O'Connell to launch their own organization, the Catholic Truth Guild, later renamed the Catholic Campaigners for Christ, which sponsored local and national lectures on Catholic beliefs, starting on Boston Common on 4 July 1917. The occasion gave Goldstein the opportunity to underscore a theme that became the centerpiece of his evangelistic work: the compatibility of American and Catholic values. His brand new, custom-built, yellow-and-white Model T lecture car, painted the colors of the papal flag, equipped with a portable podium and sounding board, and decorated with American flags and quotations from George Washington and Cardinal O'Connell, reinforced this message. This Ford automobile was the first in a series of spectacular cars and vans, all equipped with the latest sound systems, that became extensions of Goldstein's personality: his fearless and flamboyant oratorical style, his unshakable confidence, and his love of controversy. From 1917 until he retired in 1941, Goldstein lectured throughout the country, his presentations changing very little over the years, his purpose always to show that Catholic teachings on any topic, from sexuality to labor unions to doctrine, were the only tenable positions for intelligent, moral Americans. (Avery's poor health kept her in Boston.)

David Goldstein became a recognized public figure and an acknowledged spokesman for the Catholic church. After he retired from the lecture circuit he returned to Boston, exhausted from traveling and frustrated by his inability to persuade others to embrace his vision and his work. In 1942 he joined the Catholic opponents of the Massachusetts Birth Control Referendum and later explained his reasons in *Suicide Bent: Sangerizing Mankind* (1945). Until his death he wrote a regular column for *The Pilot*, the Boston archdiocesan newspaper, whose editors kindly kept him on even though his controversial tone sounded increasingly anachronistic in the postwar years, with the rise of a convert crusade that was very different from the one Goldstein had envisioned. A parish-based effort associated with Father John A. O'Brien of the University of Notre Dame, the postwar crusade stressed community-oriented evangelism rather than exhortations by flamboyant leaders like Goldstein. By the time of his death in Boston, there was a small army of Catholic lay people sharing their faith with their neighbors in inquiry classes or by distributing apologetical pamphlets; still others were involved in national evangelistic networks, such as the Convert Makers of America (1944). Goldstein, who remained aloof from the postwar crusade, remains an example of one kind of evangelistic career that an ambitious American layman could pursue within the pre–Vatican II church, but also a reminder of the limited appeal that such a ministry held for the Catholic laity at large.

• Goldstein's papers are in Boston College's Special Collections. Many contemporaneous accounts of Goldstein's work that appeared in Catholic periodicals and newspapers are available in the Goldstein papers. The *Autobiography of a Campaigner for Christ* remains the major source on Goldstein's life and work; however, the following works by Goldstein indicate the direction of his career after he retired from the lecture circuit: *Jewish Panorama* (1940), *Letters of a Hebrew-Catholic to Mr. Isaacs* (1943), *My Boston Pilot Column* (1956), and *What Say You?* (1945). In *From a Far Country: The Conversion Story of a Campaigner for Christ* (1939), Theodore H. Dorsey, who accompanied Goldstein on the road briefly during the 1930s, provides valuable details and one admirer's account of Goldstein's impact on his audiences. The only secondary works about Goldstein are by Debra Campbell: "David Goldstein and the Lay Catholic Street Apostolate, 1917–41" (Ph. D. diss., Boston Univ., 1982); "A Catholic Salvation Army: David Goldstein, Pioneer Lay Evangelist," *Church History* 52 (Sept. 1983): 322–32; and "David Goldstein and the Rise of the Catholic Campaigners for Christ," *Catholic Historical Review* 72 (Jan. 1986): 33–50. David Owen Carrigan, "Martha Moore Avery: The Career of a Crusader" (Ph.D. diss., Univ. of Maine, Orono, 1966), examines the single most important influence on David Goldstein.

DEBRA CAMPBELL

GOLDSTEIN, Fanny (1888–26 Dec. 1961), librarian and bibliographer, was born in Kamanetsk-Padolsk, Russia, the daughter of Philip Goldstein and Bella Spillberg. Soon after she was born, her family emigrated to the United States, settling in the North End in Boston, Massachusetts, by 1900. Because her father died at an early age, leaving her mother with five children, Goldstein's education was limited. There are no records of her attendance at school after the ninth grade. Later, as a young librarian, she took a few courses as a special student at Simmons College, Boston College, and Harvard University, but she never completed a degree.

In 1909 Goldstein obtained her first library position as assistant to Edith Guerrier at the North End Branch of the Boston Public Library. Guerrier was founder of the Saturday Evening Girls Club, which sponsored educational and cultural activities for immigrant girls. Goldstein edited its newsletter, the *S.E.G. News*, from 1912 to 1917. She remained active in the organization, acting as mentor to the younger girls, until it disbanded in 1917, and she maintained ties to some of the women as an adult. In 1917 she became a reference assistant at the central library. Two years later she transferred to the Tyler Street Branch, and in 1922 she became librarian at the West End Branch, where she remained for the rest of her career.

As the head of a branch library, Goldstein had some freedom to shape the collection and determine its direction. Influenced by her own experiences as an immigrant as well as her contacts with Guerrier, she tried to make the library more responsive to the immigrant communities of the West End by building up collections in Yiddish, Polish, and Italian. Soon, however, she began to focus her efforts on the American Jewish community. From 1931 to 1940 she published two bibliographies under the title "Judaica," with supplements called "Recent Judaica," as part of the Boston Public Library's Brief Reading List series. These bibliographies, listing books owned by the library, consituted one of the first attempts to publish an American Judaica bibliography for the general reader.

In 1925 Goldstein began a tradition that would become her legacy to Jewish library history. In December she put up a display of Jewish books, most in English, under a large menorah and posted a banner to encourage the giving of books as Hanukkah gifts. The exhibit was well received, and she repeated it the next year. In 1927 Rabbi S. Felix Mendelsohn of Chicago, Illinois, called for the observance of a Jewish book week, to be held during Lag b'Omer, the Scholars' Festival. Thus, Jewish Book Week, inspired by Goldstein's exhibit, became an annual celebration marked by exhibits, lectures, and readings in public libraries, synagogues, and Jewish community centers across the United States and Canada. Beginning in 1940, because of the strong association with gift giving, Jewish Book Week was celebrated during Hanukkah each year.

The observance of Jewish Book Week was coordinated in Boston by the Boston Jewish Book Week Committee, founded in 1930 and headed by Goldstein. The National Committee for Jewish Book Week was organized in 1940, with Goldstein serving as chair for the first year and after that as honorary chair along with Mendelssohn. The committee published the first *Jewish Book Annual* in 1942; offering articles and bibliographies in English, Hebrew, and Yiddish, it has remained an important guide to Jewish publishing in the United States. In 1943 the Jewish Book Council took over the duties of the national committee, and Jewish Book Week was extended to become Jewish Book Month. Goldstein was honorary president of the council from 1944 until her death.

In addition to her activities promoting Jewish books, Goldstein took a keen interest in interfaith efforts in Boston. She was a member of the National Conference of Christians and Jews, and with her encouragement the conference established a Religious Book Week and published a list of the fifty best books on Judaism, Catholicism, and Protestantism. Goldstein was well known in Boston for her Christmas-Hanukkah parties, invitation-only affairs intended to bring together influential members of the Jewish and Christian communities.

One of the roles Goldstein enjoyed most was mentor to aspiring American Jewish writers. She corresponded with writers such as Mary Antin, Charles Angoff, and Rachel Baker, inviting them to speak at Jewish Book Week events and arranging interviews to publicize their work. She often wrote enthusiastic reviews of their works for local newspapers and took personal pride in their success.

Until she retired in 1957, Goldstein remained active in Jewish Book Month. She also built up the collection of Judaica at the West End Branch. In 1954 this collection was moved to the central library and named the Fanny Goldstein Collection of Judaica; Goldstein was named curator. After she retired, she worked on the collection as curator emeritus.

Goldstein died in Boston. She had never married. Although she never attained a library degree, her activist vision of librarianship enabled her to make the West End Branch a vital neighborhood center. Her bibliographies and tireless promotion of Jewish Book Month helped to increase the audience for Jewish books.

• Goldstein's correspondence is in the American Jewish Archives in Cincinnati, Ohio. Other papers form an unprocessed collection at the Boston Public Library. The *S.E.G. News* is in the American Jewish Historical Society in Waltham, Mass. Goldstein's published writings include the "Judaica" bibliographies, Brief Reading List Nos. 44 (1931 and 1934). Supplements were published in 1936 and 1937. In addition, she published several bibliographies of Jewish children's books in the *Jewish Book Annual*, among them "The Jewish Child in Bookland," 5 (1946–1947): 84–100. "Jewish Fiction in English" was published in the *American Jewish Yearbook*, vol. 43 (1941–1942). *Suggestive Material for the Observance of Jewish Book Week* was published for 1938 and 1939. She also compiled "Bibliographic Material on the Jewish Woman," in *The Jewish Library*, ed. Leo Jung (1934). Goldstein wrote many articles, the most widely read of which was "Reading for Democracy," *Wilson Library Bulletin*, Feb. 1944, pp. 452–53. Another is "The Story of a Book Contest," *Wilson Bulletin for Librarians* 7, no. 2 (Oct. 1932): 118–20. Goldstein also wrote an autobiography and a history of the West End Branch. To her frustration, these were never published, and no copies of either survive.

JOY KINGSOLVER

GOLDSTEIN, Herbert S. (8 Feb. 1890–2 Jan. 1970), rabbi, was born Herbert Samuel Goldstein in New York City, the son of Morris Goldstein (born Jacob Joseph Schultz), a clothing manufacturer, and Sarah Miriam Mikler. After receiving his earliest formal educational training at Yeshiva Etz Chaim, an Orthodox Jewish elementary school on the Lower East Side, Goldstein enrolled in public school and continued his secular education at Columbia University, where he received his B.A. in 1911 and his M.A. in Judaica in 1912. Goldstein received ongoing training in traditional Bible and Talmud studies from private tutors before he enrolled in the Jewish Theological Seminary, from which he graduated as a rabbi in 1914. Concomitant with his seminary studies, which taught him the modern Jewish educational, homiletic, and pastoral skills to serve acculturating Jewish immigrants and their children, Goldstein received advanced Talmudic training from downtown immigrant rabbi Shalom E. Jaffe, who awarded him traditional ordination (*semicha*) in

1912. Uniquely credentialed as both a Conservative and Orthodox rabbi, Goldstein was able to speak to both first- and second-generation Jews of a variety of religious orientations, particularly those who had become disaffected from the religious civilization that had been transplanted from Europe.

Goldstein first displayed his skills as an English-speaking preacher who could project Orthodox teachings as compatible with the modern world in the months prior to his seminary graduation when he was appointed assistant rabbi of Congregation Kehilath Jeshurun in Manhattan's Yorkville section. In 1915 he began teaching homiletics at the Rabbi Isaac Elchanan Theological Seminary (RIETS), the Orthodox rabbinical school that was a forerunner of Yeshiva University. Goldstein would teach both homiletics and practical rabbinics at RIETS for the next fifty years, and he served as a role model for two generations of modern Orthodox rabbis. In 1915 Goldstein married Rebecca Fischel. They had four children.

In 1917 Goldstein made his most important contribution to the evolution of modern Orthodoxy when he founded the Institutional Synagogue. Situated in Harlem, then a community where acculturating, upwardly mobile Jews predominated, he established congregational programs that attracted assimilating Jews and their children. Religious, educational, and social activities were all consciously integrated into synagogue life. Goldstein believed that if he offered the right combination of classes, lectures, dances, sporting events, and other recreational activities to parents and children alike, families would together flock to his Jewish center and there reestablish their ties to their religion and ultimately to the observance of the faith's traditional commandments. Goldstein served in that uptown pulpit until 1937, when the synagogue moved to the West Side of Manhattan following the Jewish migration from a community that had become mostly African American. Goldstein remained rabbi of the West Side Institutional Synagogue until his death.

Goldstein also promoted the needs and concerns of Orthodox Jewry nationally through his presidency from 1924 to 1933 of the Union of Orthodox Jewish Congregations of America, an organization that monitored the preparation and distribution of kosher products and protected the rights of Orthodox Jews against onerous civil regulations, like "blue laws" that undermined religious commitments. Goldstein did comparable work in espousing American Orthodoxy's cause and creed as a founder in 1936 of the Rabbinical Council of America, a national organization composed primarily of RIETS graduates. He was its president from 1937 to 1939. As an advocate of Orthodoxy's status within the Zionist movement and the state of Israel, Goldstein affiliated both with the Mizrachi (Religious Zionist) and Agudath Israel movements. He raised monies in support of Israel-based institutions such as the Harry Fischel Institute for Research in Jewish Law, named after his father-in-law, and the Rabbi Herzog World Academy of Jewish Studies.

While president of the Orthodox Union, Goldstein became a founding member in 1925 of the Synagogue Council of America. From 1944 to 1946 he served as president of that national organization, which united all Jewish denominational leaders for nonreligious communal purposes, including defending Jews against anti-Semitism. However, in 1954 Goldstein resigned from that umbrella group, reflecting an American Orthodox withdrawal from implicit recognition of and cooperation with Reform and Conservative Jewish movements. At the same time, as an Orthodox rabbi who constantly sought to link his people with the larger American society and culture, Goldstein retained his membership in the National Conference of Christians and Jews and the World Fellowship of Faith, organizations that promoted interfaith ecumenical relationships. Goldstein's career projected and reflected changing American Orthodox attitudes toward the secular but generally tolerant American society in which twentieth-century American Jews lived. He died in New York City.

• The papers of the Institutional Synagogue, which document a major aspect of Goldstein's career, are in the Yeshiva University Archives in New York City. Most of Goldstein's writings were popular religious tracts designed to encourage greater commitment to traditional Judaism by American Jews. His biography of his father-in-law, *Forty Years of Study for a Principle: The Biography of Harry Fischel* (1928), chronicles the achievements of an Eastern European Jewish immigrant who rose socially and economically without surrendering his Orthodox identity. Aaron I. Reichel, *The Maverick Rabbi: Rabbi Herbert S. Goldstein and the Institutional Synagogue: A New Institutional Form* (1984), is a filiopietistic biography of Goldstein written by a grandson. Goldstein is put into a more objective historical context in Jeffrey S. Gurock, *When Harlem Was Jewish, 1870–1930* (1979). An obituary is in the *New York Times*, 4 Jan. 1970.

JEFFREY S. GUROCK

GOLDSTEIN, Israel (18 June 1896–11 Apr. 1986), rabbi and Jewish communal leader, was born in Philadelphia, Pennsylvania, the son of David Goldstein, a sexton (shammes), and Fannie Silver. When he was five Goldstein journeyed with his ailing mother to her home in Lithuania. He spent the next two and a half years there in traditional Jewish schools (cheder). He earned a B.A. at the University of Pennsylvania (1914) and an M.A. from Columbia University (1917); was ordained a rabbi at the Jewish Theological Seminary, Conservative Judaism's rabbinical school (1918); and earned a Doctor of Hebrew Letters (1927) for *A Century of Judaism in New York: B'nai Jeshurun 1825–1925* (1930).

Newly ordained, Goldstein became rabbi of B'nai Jeshurun, founded in 1825 in New York City and, in the years preceding Goldstein's lengthy tenure (1918–1960), plagued by frequent turnover in its rabbinate. Goldstein reshaped the synagogue to make it, as he claimed in dedicating its new community center (1928), into "a full-time spiritual power house radiating energy into the life of the entire community—men, women and children." The energy came from the variety of activities he introduced modeled on the emerging synagogue centers of the interwar years. These included, in addition to the community center, late Friday evening services, educational programs for every age, and a special focus on the youth, the future of the American Jewish community. Although his numerous Zionist activities and communal responsibilities often took him away from his pulpit and sometimes caused tension with his lay leaders, his synagogue supported his endeavors. Retiring in 1960 to fulfill his dream of settling in Israel, Goldstein returned annually to preach on the High Holidays.

Reflecting in his memoirs, *My World as a Jew* (2 vols., 1984), on the different career directions open to rabbis, Goldstein explained that he chose the rabbinate because it offered "a vehicle for public service." The plethora of his activities outside his congregation reveal that this was the main focus of his career.

First and foremost, Goldstein was an ardent Zionist, working to insure the establishment of Palestine as a Jewish state, raising funds to sustain it, and vociferously championing its cause among American Jews in an era long before they had overwhelmingly embraced Zionism. President of his first Zionist organization at the age of ten and of Young Judea (1928–1930), which took him for the first time to Palestine, he went on to become president of the Jewish National Fund (1933–1943) and vice president (1934–1943) of the Zionist Organization of America (ZOA). He was elected ZOA president (1943–1945) and simultaneously became president of the Synagogue Council of America and cochairman of the Interim Committee of the American Jewish Conference. These positions and his subsequent roles as founding president of the World Confederation of General Zionists (1946–1961), chairman of the United Jewish Appeal (1947–1948), cochairman of the United Palestine Appeal (1947–1948), and treasurer of the Jewish Agency (1948–1949) placed him within the vortex of the world Jewish crises of World War II and its aftermath—standing by impotently as European Jewry perished in the Holocaust, seeking havens for those who managed to escape, clamoring to open the doors of Palestine to Jewish immigration, and fighting to establish the Jewish state at the war's end. His Zionist work took him to wartime Britain, to displaced persons camps in Germany just weeks after the war ended in Europe, and to the midst of the War of Liberation in Palestine, where he strove to find funds to absorb the refugees streaming into the new nation. After he immigrated to Israel, he became world chairman of the Keren Hayesod–United Israel Appeal (1961–1971). Only in 1971 did he retire from Zionist public service.

Zionism was not the only area of Jewish public service to engage Goldstein. Virtually every area of Jewish life absorbed him, and he made substantive contributions to many Jewish organizations. He was president of Conservative Judaism's Young People's League (1921–1925). Committed to working across Jewish denominational lines, he became president of the New York Board of Jewish Ministers (1926–1928). Con-

cerned with interfaith work, he participated in the founding of the National Conference of Christians and Jews (1928). A champion of the rights of labor, he chaired the Social Justice Committee of Conservatism's Rabbinical Assembly of America (1931–1935). In the 1930s and again in the late 1960s he worked on behalf of the Falashas, the "Black Jews of Ethiopia." A particular interest was the presidency of the Jewish Conciliation Board (1930–1968), a voluntary Jewish court of arbitration that heard cases in Yiddish and whose history he detailed in *Jewish Justice and Conciliation* (1981). Recognizing that the Jews were the one major American religious group that had not sponsored a college, he helped launch Brandeis University by acquiring its campus in Waltham, Massachusetts (1946). As president of the American Jewish Congress (1952–1958), he worked to secure reparations for the survivors of the Holocaust.

In 1918 he married Bertha Markowitz, a teacher and lawyer, who joined him in his Jewish activism, frequently holding office in Jewish women's organizations. They had two children. Goldstein died in Tel Aviv, Israel, having devoted his entire life to the welfare of the Jewish people. He was one of a generation of American activist rabbis, among them Stephen Wise and Abba Hillel Silver, who believed that they could best serve Jews and Judaism by standing in the forefront of Jewish organizational life. In so doing they used their rabbinic knowledge and training as a springboard for a leadership that envisioned the synagogue, education, and Israel as the pillars of American Jewry.

• Goldstein's papers are in the Central Zionist Archives. Goldstein's writings detail the scope of his career and interests, especially his memoir and his published sermons and addresses, including *Toward a Solution* (1940), *American Jewry Comes of Age: Tercentenary Addresses* (1955), *Transition Years: New York–Jerusalem, 1960–62* (1962), *Israel at Home and Abroad (1962–72)* (1973), and *To Serve My People* (1983). *Shana b'Yisrael* (1950) covers the year he spent as treasurer of the Jewish Agency. He also wrote *Brandeis University: Chapter of its Founding* (1951). Some material is in the festschrift, Harry Schneiderman, ed., *Two Generations in Perspective: Notable Events and Trends, 1896–1956* (1957). Aharon Alperin's Yiddish biography, *A Lebn fun Shlikhes: Biografye fun Yisroel Goldshtayn* (1974), appeared in Hebrew as *Hayim shel Shelichut: Biografyah shel Doktor Yisrael Goldshtayn* (1977). In addition see Yehudah Bauer et al., eds., *Pirke Mehkar be-Toldot ha-Tsiyonut: Mugashim le-Yisrael Goldshtayn* (1976).

PAMELA S. NADELL

GOLDSTEIN, Kurt (6 Nov. 1878–19 Sept. 1965), neurologist and psychiatrist, was born in Katowice, Poland, then a part of Germany, the son of Abraham Goldstein, the prosperous owner of a lumberyard, and Rosalie Cassirer. Quiet, serious, and bookish as a boy, Goldstein earned the nickname "Professor" from his classmates at the local public school. Born Jewish, he strongly identified with the German poet Johann Wolfgang von Goethe and German Romanticism and regarded his Judaism more as a "destiny" than a "mission" (Robert Ulrich, in *The Reach of Mind: Essays in*

Memory of Kurt Goldstein, p. 13). After graduating from the Humanistische Gymnasium in Breslau, he studied philosophy and literature for a year at the University of Heidelberg before returning to the University of Breslau to take up medicine, with a focus on neurology and psychiatry. He explained his career choice as rising out of a desire to help the mentally ill, whom he perceived as the "unhappiest of all people." He received his medical degree in 1903 and then worked as an assistant to his former teacher, Ludwig Edinger. In 1906 Goldstein obtained a clinical position as privatdozent in the psychiatric clinic at the University of Königsberg.

His time at Königsberg began as a considerable disappointment. Goldstein was distressed by the therapeutically indifferent attitude many physicians there took toward patients. The emphasis in German psychiatry at this time on inherited factors had encouraged many psychiatrists to feel that if they made an accurate diagnosis and then arranged for their patient to receive proper custodial care, they had done all that could reasonably be expected of them. Goldstein's desire to create an alternative to this "therapeutic nihilism" was a powerful factor in his intellectual and professional development. During World War I he joined with psychologist Adhémar Gelb in founding a government-sponsored institute at Frankfurt dedicated to the study—and rehabilitation—of brain damaged and psychologically scarred soldiers. In 1919 Goldstein became professor of neurology at the University of Frankfurt.

At Frankfurt, Goldstein developed the key elements of his mature "holistic-organismic" approach to the problem of psychopathology and brain functioning. He argued, for example, that language was not an isolated skill with a localized "center" in the brain (as was then widely believed) but a mode of functioning that permeated the individual's total mental orientation. Above all, language allowed for the possibility of abstract thought, what Goldstein called "categorical behaviour." He contrasted this state with the more primitive "concrete" mental attitude associated with brain damage, in which an individual is at the mercy of immediate sense impressions. Brain damage to him was not just a question of a malfunctioning physiological system, it was also a human crisis. He called attention to the "catastrophic reaction" in brain damage: the existential anxiety of a patient forced to confront the fact that he is a diminished personality. Disclaiming therapeutic nihilism, Goldstein argued that even patients who could not be "cured," could be helped back to "health" if health was understood in a new way—as a state in which an individual life again could have personal meaning. Seen in this way, healing involved choice and courage in the service of "actualization." He was fond of quoting Kierkegaard: "To venture causes anxiety, but not to venture is to lose oneself."

In 1930 Goldstein left Frankfurt to become head of the Department of Neurology and Psychiatry at the progressive state hospital Moabit in Berlin. Because, however, this hospital had a reputation for being both "Jewish" and "red," it did not survive the rise of the Nazi regime in 1933. On 1 April 1933 a truckload of storm troopers raided the hospital and arrested the staff, including Goldstein. After a brief imprisonment (during which he was beaten with sand-filled hoses), Goldstein was permitted to leave the country and fled to Amsterdam. In 1935, supported by the Rockefeller Foundation, he emigrated to New York City. He secured a position at the New York State Psychiatric Institute and became clinical professor of neurology (without salary) at Columbia University. At the Montefiore Hospital in New York in 1936 he established a clinical laboratory, where he worked with Martin Scheerer on abstract versus concrete attitudes in brain-damaged patients.

In 1938–1939 Goldstein was William James Lecturer at Harvard; his lectures were published in 1940 as *Human Nature in the Light of Psychopathology*. His 1934 German magnum opus, *The Organism: A Holistic Approach to Biology Derived from Pathological Data in Man*, had appeared in English in 1938. From 1940 to 1945 the Rockefeller Foundation funded a clinical professorship for Goldstein at Tufts Medical School in Boston. He then returned to New York City, where he built up a private practice and taught at City College, Columbia University, and the New School for Social Research. Later, in 1957–1958, he served as a visiting professor at Brandeis University in Waltham, Massachusetts, but New York City remained his home until his death there.

The Goldstein archives at Columbia University paint a picture of rich collegial contacts and intellectual cross-fertilization, both with leading fellow exiles and with American friends who were intrigued and inspired by the holistic, humanistic alternatives Goldstein offered to classical Freudianism on the one hand and behaviorism on the other. Goldstein's views on the organismic urge to actualization played a central role in the rise of American humanistic or "third force" psychology and in humanistic revisions of classical psychoanalysis. His epistemological reflections influenced later developments in phenomenological philosophy.

Even though Goldstein's influence in exile was significant, he never achieved the professional stature he had enjoyed in Germany, and he never recovered from his disappointment with the native country that had betrayed him. In a reflection of his attitude toward Germany, he once reasoned that "those who hate so much that they cannot return, are the ones who really love [*Menschen, die aus Haß nicht zurückgehen, lieben*]" (Bach, p. 95). Although he became an American citizen in 1940, he never quite felt at home in his new country. English always remained an awkward language for him, and he suffered from a sense of disconnectedness from his cultural roots. Family tragedy also left its toll. In 1933 Goldstein had married psychiatrist Eva Rothmann, his second marriage. An earlier marriage, to Ida Zuckerman (date unknown), had produced three children. During World War II Eva

Rothmann-Goldstein began to show signs of severe depression; she committed suicide in 1960.

In his final years, Goldstein not only bore what colleague Hans Lukas-Teuber called an "amazing similarity in appearance" to Goethe but also increasingly identified with Goethe's concerns about the dangers of a mechanistic scientific world view decoupled from "human existence." His thoughts and writing now questioned the epistemological and moral requirements of science in the post-Hiroshima era. He had come full circle, turning from brain anatomy back to fundamental questions of philosophy and ethics. In a special issue of the *American Journal of Psychoanalysis* that honored Goldstein in 1959 (vol. 19), Frederick Weiss found a lyrical explanation for these "steadily widening horizons of [Goldstein's] life and work" in a Goethean quotation that had inspired Goldstein throughout his career: "If you want to stride into the Infinite, move but within the Finite in all directions."

• Most of Goldstein's unpublished papers and correspondence relevant to his American career are in the Rare Books Library of Columbia University. A selection of some of his most important published articles from both the German and American periods of his career were collected in *Selected Papers/Ausgewählte Schriften*, ed. A. Gurwitsch et al. (1971). A posthumous autobiographical essay is in E. G. Boring and G. Lindzey, eds., *A History of Psychology in Autobiography*, vol. 5 (1967). A range of biographical and interpretive essays on Goldstein's life and work were published in Marianne L. Simmel, ed., *The Reach of Mind: Essays in Memory of Kurt Goldstein* (1968). A 1958 interview with Goldstein, carried out by I. Bach, was published in German in L. Besch, ed., *Auszug des Geistes. Bericht über eine Sendereihe* (1962). K. A. Meyer, "The Path Not Taken: Kurt Goldstein's Theory of Self-Actualization in Theological Perspective" (Ph.D. diss., Divinity School, Univ. of Chicago, 1989), analyzes Goldstein's thought in the context of broader pastoral intellectual movements in the United States, with a particular focus on his relationship with the liberal Protestant theologian Paul Tillich. An extended discussion that focuses more on Goldstein in the context of the culture and politics of Weimar Germany can be found in A. Harrington, *Reenchanted Science: Holism in German Culture from Wilhelm II to Hitler* (1996).

ANNE HARRINGTON

GOLDTHWAITE, George (10 Dec. 1809–18 Mar. 1879), Alabama jurist and U.S. senator, was born in Boston, Massachusetts, the son of Thomas Goldthwaite and Anne Wilson. Anne, apparently deserted by Thomas, eked out support for her family by operating a boarding house. George attended the Boston Latin School and in 1824 received an appointment to the military academy at West Point. In his junior year he was expelled in connection with a hazing incident. He then moved to Alabama, read law in Montgomery under his brother Henry B. Goldthwaite, subsequently a justice of the Alabama Supreme Court, and was admitted to the bar in 1828. He formed a law partnership with his brother-in-law John A. Campbell, later a justice of the U.S. Supreme Court. In 1835 he married a fellow Bostonian, Olivia Price Wallach; they had six children.

In 1843 the legislature elected Goldthwaite over the incumbent to the office of circuit judge. During Goldthwaite's first term on the bench the state constitution was amended to give the election of circuit judges to the people, and in 1850 Goldthwaite was chosen by the voters to serve a second term. In 1851 the legislature appointed Goldthwaite to a three-man commission that was created to codify the state's laws. Initially allied with the Democratic party's Calhounite faction along with his brother Henry and his brother-in-law Campbell, Goldthwaite was convinced that a sectional conflict over abolition was inevitable. He was a delegate to the Nashville Convention of 1850 and on his return to Montgomery declared himself ready for disunion if the North refused to accept the South's just rights. During the 1850s, however, his views became increasingly unionist, and in 1860 he opposed immediate secession in response to the election of Abraham Lincoln. In December 1851 the legislature increased the size of the state supreme court from three to five justices, and in January 1852 it unanimously elected Goldthwaite to one of the new positions. He served until his resignation in January 1856.

Among his most controversial decisions were his opinions in 1854 that barred the state, on highly technical grounds, from recovering the defalcations of the state treasurer and the state comptroller. His most portentous decision for the future of Alabama, however, was his 1852 opinion that drew a sharp distinction between the property rights of tenant farmers and sharecroppers. Tenant farmers, he held, owned the crop that they raised and merely paid the landowner a portion of it as rent, whereas sharecroppers and landowners owned the crop jointly. Goldthwaite's opinions frequently contained learned discussions of the history of the common law and references to contemporary British precedents. For many years he subscribed to the most important English and Scottish reviews and had them bound for his personal library.

After his resignation from the supreme court, Goldthwaite formed a law partnership with Henry Churchill Semple, which was joined in 1859 by Samuel F. Rice. This partnership continued until Goldthwaite's election to the Senate. During the late 1850s Goldthwaite's wealth rapidly increased. The value of his real estate grew from $34,000 in 1850 to $101,500 in 1860, and his personal property in 1860 was placed at $310,000. The Civil War and emancipation, however, badly damaged his financial position. In 1870 his real estate was less than half, and his personal property barely a twentieth of its 1860 value.

Although Goldthwaite had opposed immediate secession, once the secession ordinance was adopted, he fully supported the southern cause. In January 1861 he was appointed to the position of adjutant and inspector general of Alabama troops, with the rank of brigadier general. He served until the fall of 1863. All four of his sons fought in the Confederate army.

In 1866 Goldthwaite was again elected a circuit judge, but the Reconstruction Acts deprived him of the position in 1867. In 1870 Democrats managed to capture control of the state house of representatives, though the state senate remained almost entirely Republican. In the election for U.S. senator, Republicans divided their votes between a carpetbagger and a scalawag. Democrats supported Goldthwaite, principally because both of Goldthwaite's law partners, Semple and Rice, had become Republicans, and Democrats hoped therefore to attract Republican defectors. This strategy worked, and Goldthwaite was elected by a margin of one vote. Republican state legislators filed a contest of this election, and Goldthwaite was not finally permitted to take his seat until 15 January 1872. His term in the Senate was undistinguished; he devoted his attention almost entirely to matters of local concern in Alabama. He did not seek reelection and was succeeded by John Tyler Morgan in March 1877. Thereafter his health failed rapidly, and he died in Tuscaloosa, Alabama.

• Goldthwaite's papers have not survived. He has not been the subject of any scholarly investigations, but there are brief sketches of his career in Thomas M. Owen, *History of Alabama and Dictionary of Alabama Biography*, vol. 3 (1921), p. 672, and in the *Dictionary of American Biography*, vol. 4, part 1, p. 368.

J. MILLS THORNTON III

GOLDWATER, Sigismund Schulz (7 Feb. 1873–22 Oct. 1942), hospital administrator and public health official, was born in New York City, the son of Henry Goldwater, a tobacconist and pharmacist, and Mary Tyroler. Goldwater attended public schools but left at age thirteen to go to work. By the age of seventeen he was writing for the *Cloak Journal*, a garment-industry publication. He became interested in labor problems and resigned his job to take courses in economics and sociology at the Institute of Social Economics. In 1894 Goldwater enrolled in a political science course at Columbia University; the following year he went to study sociology at the University of Leipzig. His interests became focused on problems of social reform, specifically in relation to public health. On his return to the United States, he applied for admission to New York University's Bellevue Hospital Medical College.

In 1901 Goldwater received his M.D. degree and did his internship at The Mount Sinai Hospital. Although considered a brilliant medical clinician, he decided to specialize in hospital administration and accepted an appointment as assistant superintendent at Mount Sinai. In 1903 he became the chief superintendent, one of the first hospital administrators in the country with a medical degree. The following year he married Clara Aub; they had three children, one of whom, Robert Goldwater, became a professor of art history at New York University's Institute of Fine Arts.

One of Goldwater's initial innovations at Mount Sinai was the establishment in 1906 of a department of social services (then found in only two other hospitals in the United States). He also set up a dentistry department and reorganized the hospital's medical education program. Always an advocate of voluntary (that is,

self-supporting, non-municipally funded) hospitals, he wrote a study on their funding, *The Appropriation of Public Funds for the Partial Support of Voluntary Hospitals in the United States and Canada* (c. 1908).

In 1914 Goldwater left Mount Sinai to serve for a year as New York City commissioner of health. He committed the city health department to the maintenance of minimum health and sanitary standards for all people, in accordance with his idea that the primary task of medicine was to prevent illness. He advised periodic physical examinations, established a Bureau of Health Education, and got a law passed requiring disclosure of the ingredients of patent medicines. His study *Dispensaries: A Growing Factor in Curative and Preventive Medicine* was published by the Board of Health in 1915. Goldwater returned to Mount Sinai in 1915 and two years later was appointed its director.

Goldwater often acted as a consultant in hospital planning and construction (in fact, he became a registered architect) in the New York area. In 1927 he went to England and helped plan the reorganization of the British voluntary hospital system. In later years he also served as a consultant to the U.S. Public Health Service and the Institute of Experimental Medicine in Leningrad.

Among Goldwater's guiding principles in the planning of hospitals was his preference for the general hospital in which all the branches of medicine were integrated to provide maximally efficient care. He recommended the pavilion layout rather than construction as a single unit, believing that the flexible pavilion plan would help a hospital adapt more readily to changing needs. As an advocate of preventive medicine, he encouraged the expansion of outpatient services. Above all, he held that the primary aim of any hospital is to prevent suffering, and that the most important person in the hospital was the patient.

In 1928 Goldwater resigned as Mount Sinai's director but remained active as a consultant. In 1934, at the height of the Great Depression—which had intensified the problems of the poor in paying for health care—he was appointed New York City's commissioner of hospitals. With the support of reform-minded Mayor Fiorello LaGuardia, he undertook the reorganization of the city hospitals, all suffering from years of neglect. Among his achievements were establishing the autonomy of medical staffs from city bureaucracy; bringing lay hospital staff into the civil service merit system; and setting up consulting boards in medicine, dentistry, nursing, and administration. Goldwater also obtained a $7 million municipal appropriation to build a new facility devoted to research on chronic diseases and the care of the chronically ill. Located on Welfare Island (now Roosevelt Island) in the East River, it was originally called Welfare Hospital but was renamed Goldwater Memorial Hospital in its founder's honor.

In 1940 Goldwater resigned as hospitals commissioner to become president of the Associated Hospital Insurance Service. Dedicated to the equitable distribution of medical care, Goldwater favored a system of nonprofit prepayment insurance (the so-called three-cents-a-day plan), which would be supported by government subsidies to general hospitals. He also set up Community Medical Care as a means of providing low-cost care in hospital wards; under the auspices of the Associated Hospital Insurance Service, it would coordinate the efforts of hospitals and physicians and labor and industrial groups.

Until his death Goldwater served as a construction adviser for institutions in the United States and Canada. He died of cancer at The Mount Sinai Hospital.

Goldwater was president of the American Hospital Association in 1908; vice president of the New York Academy of Medicine in 1913 and of the National Institute of Social Sciences, 1918–1921; and president of the American Conference on Hospitals, 1924–1926. He was an honorary member of the British Hospital Association and of the American Institute of Architects, which shortly before his death gave him an award.

• Some of Goldwater's articles were compiled and edited by Clara A. Goldwater and published posthumously as *On Hospitals* (1947); it includes a biographical note by Clara Goldwater and C.-E. A. Winslow), and a selected bibliography. An account of his work at Mount Sinai is in Joseph Hirsh and Beka Doherty, *The First Hundred Years of The Mount Sinai Hospital of New York* (1952), pp. 137–48. Obituaries are in the *New York Times*, 22 Oct. 1942 (with an editorial in the *Times*, 24 Oct. 1942) and in the *Journal of the American Medical Association*, 7 Nov. 1942.

ELEANOR F. WEDGE

GOLDWYN, Samuel (birth stated as 27 Aug. 1882, but more likely July 1879–31 Jan. 1974), motion picture pioneer, was born in Warsaw, Poland, the son of Aaron David Gelbfisz, a peddler, and Hannah Reban Jarecka. Goldwyn's early years are clouded. Although official records show his name at birth as Goldfish, he was in fact born Schmuel Gelbfisz. As the eldest child, he attended *cheder* and *payess* and received an Orthodox Jewish education. In 1895, on his father's death, Goldwyn made his way—alone—to Germany and then to Great Britain. In December 1898 he entered the United States and took the name Samuel Goldfish. Penniless, he found work as an apprentice glove maker in Gloversville, New York, for $3 a week. While he attended Gloversville Business College, studying English at night, Goldfish also became an expert glove cutter and in time began traveling as a glove salesman. On one of his trips, Goldfish met Blanche Lasky, the sister of vaudeville producer and performer Jesse L. Lasky, and they married in 1910.

In 1912 the American glove manufacturing industry suffered a downturn in sales, and Goldfish decided to enter show business with his brother-in-law. In 1913 he and Lasky formed the Jesse L. Lasky Feature Play Company and hired Cecil B. DeMille to direct motion pictures. Early hits, including DeMille's *Squaw Man* (1913), made the company a leader in early Hollywood. In 1916 the Jesse L. Lasky Company joined forces with Adolph Zukor and his enterprises and formed Famous Players–Lasky. Later renamed Paramount, this corporation became one of the largest and most influential motion picture producers, distributors, and exhibitors in the world. Famous Players–Lasky continuously pioneered business innovations. Recognizing that not all theaters were equal, the company's executives charged more for showings at new, larger movie palaces of the day. And if a theater owner wanted to show the films of major stars, such as Mary Pickford or Douglas Fairbanks, the owner also had to take the company's movies with less popular stars. Famous Players–Lasky was the first to tap Wall Street for the financing of feature films and later the construction of a its own chain of movie palaces. By 1920 Famous Players–Lasky had established the first national movie theater chain that in time, and for many years, would be the world's largest.

Through these innovations Goldfish played an inside role in creating the Hollywood studio system that came to dominate the movie business for half a century. But, although Goldfish liked this ever-growing power, he hated the associated infighting. He simply wanted to produce movies. So, late in 1916, he sold his shares and set up an independent motion picture production company with Broadway producers Arch and Edgar Selwyn. The enterprise was called Goldwyn—a combination of *Gold*fish and Sel*wyn*—and Samuel Goldfish liked the Goldwyn moniker so much that in his mid-thirties he officially became Samuel Goldwyn.

The Goldwyn Corporation recruited leading stars and writers and fashioned high-quality productions aimed at—in his publicists' words—audiences of "intelligence and refinement." Goldwyn followed this strategy throughout his career, in part because Paramount and the other major companies were willing to cede him this relatively small portion of the market for movies. But corporate infighting continued to trap him. In 1922 he was edged out of his own company. Two years later, the Goldwyn company became part of the grand merger that resulted in Metro-Goldwyn-Mayer, but Goldwyn had no affiliation with MGM.

Goldwyn sought a new alliance, and in August 1925 he joined United Artists. For the next sixteen years he distributed his meticulously crafted motion pictures through that studio. In time he was made a partner and produced such popular films as *Bulldog Drummond* (1929) and *Palmy Days* (1931). But Goldwyn grew unhappy with his partners, particularly Mary Pickford, Charles Chaplin, and David O. Selznick. He figured that he deserved the bulk of the company's profits since he supplied most of its highest-grossing films. His partners, however, voted him only a tiny cut. Goldwyn balked. The confrontation came to a head in 1939 when Goldwyn took his partners to court over terms of his distribution contract. Two years later, a deal was struck, and Goldwyn sold his stock back to United Artists.

In 1941 Goldwyn sought yet another company through which to distribute his films, signing and sticking with RKO until the end of his career. Indeed, only his final motion picture, *Guys and Dolls* (1955), was distributed through another company—Metro-Goldwyn-Mayer.

When not struggling over business matters, Goldwyn worked to make feature films with a "Goldwyn touch." He often took his inspiration from popular Broadway plays and acclaimed novels. Two of the most noted were *Dodsworth* (1936) and *The Little Foxes* (1941). But for every heralded serious drama, such as *Dead End* (1937) and *Wuthering Heights* (1939), Goldwyn mixed in emotional and simplistic melodrama starring Anna Sten and fluff musicals starring Eddie Cantor and the "Goldwyn Girls." Goldwyn took to the road to promote his latest film, bad or good, and initiated special handling of the press to assist favorable publicity.

Working with director William Wyler and cinematographer Gregg Toland, Goldwyn hit his acme with *The Best Years of Our Lives* (1946). Based on a MacKinlay Kantor novel and adapted for the screen by Robert Sherwood, this timely drama told the story of how three servicemen struggled to fit back into society after World War II. *The Best Years of Our Lives* dramatized real concerns of returning veterans to create an honest work of charm, richness, and beauty. Here Goldwyn was able to take full measure of the talents of his long-term alliance with director Wyler and cinematographer Toland. The film earned seven Academy Awards and Goldwyn praise from the filmmaking community around the world.

Goldwyn divorced his first wife in March 1916 and ceded custody of their four-year-old daughter Ruth to her. In 1925 he married former Broadway actress Frances Howard, who would survive him by two years. Frances Goldwyn managed the family's financial affairs, freeing him to labor obsessively on his films. At the end of his career Samuel Goldwyn took his son Samuel Goldwyn, Jr., as his business partner.

Goldwyn's final film was the Gershwin folk opera, *Porgy and Bess* (1959). During the later years of his career, he had specialized in musicals, with *Hans Christian Andersen* (1952) and *Guys and Dolls* (1955) being among the more successful.

Over his fifty-year movie career in Hollywood, Samuel Goldwyn discovered many noted stars, Vilma Banky, Eddie Cantor, Ronald Colman, Gary Cooper, Danny Kaye, Merle Oberon, and Teresa Wright, among others. He also brought more than his share of prestigious writers west, including Ben Hecht, Lillian Hellman, MacKinlay Kantor, Sinclair Lewis, and Robert Sherwood. Upon his death in Los Angeles, Goldwyn was already a legend as a shrewd, creative movie producer, able to hire the best talents to help him make films that in time would elevate the Samuel Goldwyn name to the very status of a true pioneer of moviemaking.

• The papers of Samuel Goldwyn are held in private by his son, Samuel Goldwyn, Jr. Only A. Scott Berg for his *Goldwyn: A Biography* (1989) has had the family's full cooperation and use of these papers. With help from his public relations staff, Goldwyn "wrote" a number of articles and one book,

Behind the Screen (1923). For representative articles from the popular press, see Goldwyn's "Do We Pay Our Picture Stars Too Much?," *Saturday Evening Post*, 17 Sept. 1934; "Hollywood Is Sick," *Saturday Evening Post*, 13 July 1940; "Our Movies Speak for Us," *Saturday Review of Literature*, 1 Apr. 1950; and "Is Hollywood Through?," *Collier's*, 29 Sept. 1951. Several thorough biographies of Goldwyn have appeared: Alva Johnson, *The Great Goldwyn* (1937); Carol Easton, *The Search for Sam Goldwyn* (1975); and Arthur Marx, *Goldwyn* (1976). Information about Goldwyn can also be found in autobiographies of his contemporaries; see Cecil B. DeMille's *Autobiography* (1959), Jesse L. Lasky's *I Blow My Own Horn* (1957), and Adolph Zukor's *The Public Is Never Wrong* (1953).

DOUGLAS GOMERY

GOLLNER, Nana (8 Jan. 1919–30 Aug. 1980), ballerina and teacher, was born Nana Ruth Gollner in El Paso, Texas. Little is known about her parents, whose names are unknown, except that her father was a native Texan and a construction engineer. Gollner was stricken with infantile paralysis at age two. One leg was severely affected, and an El Paso doctor suggested walking in sand; by age seven she had almost full mobility. The same doctor recommended dance classes, and Gollner began studying in her hometown. Shortly thereafter the family moved to Los Gatos, California, near San Francisco. Nana began taking classes with the Russian-trained choreographer and teacher Theodore Kosloff; from 1925 to 1927 he taught in both San Francisco and Los Angeles. When Kosloff decided to focus his energies in Los Angeles, Gollner's parents moved so their daughter could continue ballet classes with him.

At age fifteen, in 1934, Gollner made her first professional appearance as a dancer in Max Reinhardt's staging of *A Midsummer Night's Dream* at the Hollywood Bowl, a large outdoor amphitheater in the Hollywood Hills. That same year she worked briefly in New York with George Balanchine and Lincoln Kirstein's newly formed American Ballet. By 1936 she was a member of the Ballets Russes de Monte Carlo, managed by René Blum, brother of the French premier, Léon Blum. Gollner became principal dancer in 1937, the first American to achieve that distinction in a twentieth-century European company. She worked closely with the choreographer Michel Fokine in revivals of his old works and danced the lead in his three new ballets: *Don Juan* (25 June 1936), *L'Epreuve d'Amour* (4 Apr. 1936), and *Les Elements* (26 June 1937). An English review from 8 November 1937 noted, "Gollner's grace and certainty remind one strongly of the Pavlova of a quarter of a century ago." The English dance writer Arnold Haskell, in his book *Dancing around the World* (1938), reflected on the 1937 English season of the Ballets Russes de Monte Carlo. "To me the most interesting of the dancers was the young Californian Nana Gollner. She is proving herself to be one of those rare aristocrats of the dance" (p. 246).

René Blum sold his company at the end of 1937; ballet impresario Colonel W. de Basil became the manager and Léonide Massine the choreographer.

Among the many dancers who chose not to stay with the change of ownership was Gollner, who by December 1937 was back in California. She did a screen test, "My Heart is Dancing," and acquired Frank Tuttle as her agent. On 27 December 1937 Richard Pleasant, later a moving force in the development of Ballet Theatre, wrote to Gollner in California asking her to join the Mordkin Ballet for the 1938–1939 season. With no movie prospects in sight, she finally agreed in September 1939 to join Pleasant. He was ready to launch a new company called Ballet Theatre (later known as American Ballet Theatre), and Gollner danced in the January 1940 premiere performances.

Audiences and critics alike were astonished by Gollner's physical beauty, interpretive powers, and technical prowess. In the 1940 and 1941 seasons Gollner was applauded for her artistry in the classical ballets *Swan Lake* and *Giselle*. In those two years she also received acclaim for creating roles in new ballets: *Pas De Quatre*, by Anton Dolin, and Antony Tudor's *Gala Performance*. Writing in the *New York Herald Tribune* on 12 October 1941, the critic Walter Terry commented:

In Nana Gollner America finds its first top-notch ballerina. As last season's star of Ballet Theatre, Gollner proved that she is potentially the most vivid ballerina of our times. Beautiful and thoroughly glamorous, she boasts an amazing technical equipment which culminates in an arabesque that she seems to be able to sustain for indefinite periods. Some of her Texan background is discernible, for Gollner's movements are space-creating. Her leaps are broad and free, and even in static poses there is the impression of movement flowing out through her fingertips. As a classic ballerina she is showing the traditionalists that a Texas Swan Queen or an Aurora can hold her own with her Russian sisters in the balletic art.

In the summer of 1940 Gollner starred in Adolph Bolm's restaging of *The Firebird* at the Hollywood Bowl. She toured South America in 1942–1943 with Colonel de Basil's Original Ballet Russe. In Mexico City in 1942 Gollner married Paul Petroff, a Danish-born dancer who was also with de Basil's company. In 1943 Ballet Theatre arranged immigration papers for Petroff, and they both performed in New York for the 1944 and 1945 seasons. During the 1945 season, upon creating the role of Medusa in Tudor's *Undertow*, Gollner was praised as an outstanding dramatic performer. Gollner then returned to Los Angeles with Petroff and in 1946 gave birth to the first of her three children; in 1947 both husband and wife were guest artists for seven months with Mona Inglesby's International Ballet. Ballet Intime, the company Gollner and Petroff formed in 1948 with three supporting dancers, toured extensively to decidedly mixed reviews. According to a reviewer present at the New York performance in March, their reduced versions of classic ballets were unsuccessful.

Gollner returned to perform periodically with Ballet Theatre through 1955, and in 1951 she and Petroff formed another company that toured South America.

By 1952 the couple had moved permanently to Los Angeles, opening a school where they taught successfully for many years. Gollner was a guest teacher at the Banff Centre for the Fine Arts in Canada, and critic Terry, watching her teach in 1976, wrote: "She was as slender as she had been when I first saw her in *Giselle* in 1941, and what was even more remarkable was that her prowess appeared undiminished." In 1977 Gollner and Petroff left California, opening the Academy for Classical Russian Ballet in Antwerp, Belgium, where Gollner died. Petroff died in 1981.

Ballet was still in its infancy in America when Gollner decided to become a ballerina, and as Terry wrote, "Nana Gollner was not only a 'first' in the annals of American classical ballet accomplishment on the world stage but one of the best." During her many years as a teacher, she passed on to her students the knowledge, artistry, and high standards that characterized her performing career.

• Valuable primary material is in the Dance Collection of the New York Public Library for the Performing Arts, including correspondence and contracts related to performances, a scrapbook of Ballet Intime reviews, film segments of performances, photographs, and some clippings. Biographical information exists primarily in the obituaries: the *New York Times*, 12 May 1981; *Ballet News*, Mar. 1981; *Dancing Times*, Dec. 1980; *Dance Magazine*, Mar. 1981; and *Dance News*, Jan. 1981. Early life history is in Quentin Reynolds, "Ballerina without Accent," *Colliers*, 3 Feb. 1940, pp. 16 and 46. Two encyclopedias and one book also have information current through the late 1950s: Selma Jeanne Cohen, American ed., *Dictionary of Modern Ballet* (1959), Anatole Chujoy and P. W. Manchester, eds., *The Dance Encyclopedia* (1967), and Olga Maynard, *The American Ballet* (1959). It must be noted that there are many errors in all of the biographical information. Specific material relating to performances exists in Jack Anderson, *The One and Only: The Ballet Russe de Monte Carlo* (1981), Arnold L. Haskell, *Dancing around the World* (1938), Vicente Garcia Marquez, *The Ballets Russes: Colonel de Basil's Ballets Russes de Monte Carlo, 1932–1952* (1990), and Walter Terry, *I Was There: Selected Dance Reviews and Articles, 1936–1976* (1978).

NAIMA PREVOTS

GOMBERG, Moses (8 Feb. 1866–12 Feb. 1947), organic chemist, was born in Elisavetgrad, Russia (now Kirovograd, Ukraine), the son of George Gomberg and Marie Resnikoff. Little is known about his early life because he never wished to discuss it in his adult years. He attended the Nicolau Gymnasium in Elisavetgrad for six years, but in 1884 his father became involved in a political conspiracy and left Russia to emigrate to Chicago. Moses also came under suspicion and either fled with his father or left soon after. Biographers generally assume that his mother and sister also moved to Chicago, though they never mention the mother in America. Moses's sister, Sonja, found her way to Chicago and in later years joined her brother in Michigan and served as his housekeeper. Neither Moses nor his sister ever married. No other siblings were ever mentioned, and it is assumed there were none.

None of the Gombergs spoke English on arrival. For a time both Moses and his father worked at menial jobs in the rapidly developing stockyards of Chicago. In later years Moses insisted that Upton Sinclair's book *The Jungle* was an accurate story of what went on in the stockyards. He also attended public school and quickly mastered the English language. It is believed that he attended a local high school before entering the University of Michigan in 1886.

During the next four years Gomberg pursued the course in physical science in which he concentrated on chemistry, making up shortcomings in his background by intense self-study of subjects he had missed in earlier years in Chicago. He completed his bachelor of science degree in 1890 and was granted an assistantship by the chemistry department that enabled him to pursue his M.S., awarded in 1892, and his Ph.D., awarded in 1894. His work for both degrees was supervised by Albert B. Prescott and dealt with the chemistry of caffeine. Because Prescott's work involved not only chemistry but also pharmacy and medicine, Gomberg was able to earn extra funds by carrying out chemical analyses involving legal matters. He analyzed numerous samples assigned to him by Prescott and sometimes appeared in court when the samples involved patent matters. However, he soon dropped such work after completing the doctoral degree.

After completion of his Ph.D., Gomberg was given an instructor position in the chemistry department at Michigan and received regular promotions until he reached a full professorship in 1904. He became chair of the chemistry department in 1927, a position he held until retirement in 1936.

Gomberg took a leave of absence in 1896 and 1897 in order to pursue research work in Germany. He initially worked for two terms in the laboratory of Adolf von Baeyer in Munich, where he prepared two new compounds, isonitramino-butyric acid and nitroso-iso-butyric acid. He then moved to Heidelberg, where he worked in Victor Meyer's laboratory and prepared tetraphenylmethane but in poor yield. He left Heidelberg realizing, as did other chemists, that replacing four hydrogen atoms with four phenyl (C_6H_5) groups was creating a compound where one carbon was losing four hydrogen atoms, each weighing 1 unit, and adding four bulky phenyl groups, each weighing $6 \times 12 + 5 \times 1$ for $72 + 5$ or 77 units each. Thus 4 weight units of hydrogen were being replaced by four phenyl groups weighing 308 weight units, in each case surrounding a central carbon atom.

On returning to Ann Arbor, Gomberg improved the procedure for preparing tetraphenylmethane and obtained a significantly improved yield. He then sought to prepare the next hydrocarbon of the series, hexaphenylethane, $(C_6H_5)_3C-C(C_6H_5)_3$, a compound that many chemists believed would never be prepared. After a series of partial failures, he repeated his experiment in an oxygen-free atmosphere by shaking a solution of triphenylchloromethane in benzene containing fine particles of silver or zinc in an atmos-phere of carbon dioxide. A yellow solution resulted. After evaporating the benzene, still in the absence of air, colorless crystals were obtained. These showed properties expected of hexaphenylethane but also showed a chemical reactivity not characteristic of a hydrocarbon. The crystals reacted readily with chlorine, bromine, iodine, and oxygen, providing evidence that hexaphenylethane, when in solution, partially decomposes to a free radical, a reaction not expected in a hydrocarbon. Until that time, chemists had assumed that hydrocarbons were exceedingly stable because none that had ever been studied were prone to split into free radicals.

$$(C_6H_5)_3C-C(C_6H_5)_3 \rightleftharpoons 2(C_6H_5)_3C\cdot$$

| Hexaphenylethane (colorless) | | Triphenylmethyl (yellow) |

Determination of molecular weights established that the colorless solution of hexaphenylethane undergoes dissociation to yellow triphenylmethyl radicals to an equilibrium point. The free radicals combine with halogens (chlorine, bromine, iodine), producing triphenyl halides. With molecular oxygen two radicals form a colorless peroxide. Numerous other hexa-aryl-ethanes have been created and studied since then. Gomberg continued to study such substances for many years, and the studies have been continued by others. It is now accepted in most laboratories that formation of free radicals is not limited to triarylmethyls. There are numerous organic compounds that exist as free radicals.

Gomberg was a very active research chemist from the time he undertook graduate studies at the University of Michigan until the time of his retirement. His early publications to 1896 were mostly from his work on caffeine with Prescott. There were also a few papers that reflect his work on food and drug problems associated with his courtroom work. In his early years he published his research results in German in the *Berichte der Deutschen chemischen Gesellschaft* and in English in the *Journal of the American Chemical Society*. In later years he restricted his publications to the American journal.

After his return from Germany he guided a steady flow of graduate students working on the free radical problem. More than thirty-five students earned their Ph.D.s under his guidance from 1900 to his retirement. Particularly prominent students were John Bailar, Jr., who spent his career at the University of Illinois, and C. S. Schoepfle and Werner Bachmann, both of whom stayed at Michigan. Gomberg continued personal research in his private laboratory adjacent to the larger laboratory where his students worked. He visited their benches several times daily and reviewed their progress. Their evenings, and his, were devoted to study of the chemical literature.

During his years on the Michigan faculty Gomberg's sister kept up their modest home near the campus. When he retired, she was in poor health. Gomberg took care of her until his own health began to decline. He died in Ann Arbor.

Although the University of Michigan was already well recognized for its chemistry when he came to study with Prescott, Gomberg added a great deal to the reputation of its chemistry department by his early analytical work, his research on free radicals, his chairmanship of the department, and his influence on the education of numerous students of chemistry. He was highly respected by his graduate students for his firm but understanding guidance.

• Several reviews on free radicals were published by Gomberg in *Chemical Reviews* 1 (1924): 91–146, and 2 (1925): 301–14; *Journal of Industrial and Engineering Chemistry* 20 (1928): 159–64; *Science* 74 (1931): 553–57; and *Journal of Chemical Education* 9 (1932): 439–51. The best biography of Gomberg, with a portrait and bibliography, is that of John C. Bailar, Jr., in National Academy of Sciences, *Biographical Memoirs* 41 (1970): 141–73; Bailar reveals the personal characteristics of Gomberg very clearly. His doctoral students C. S. Schoepfle and W. E. Bachmann have published a biography in *Journal of the American Chemical Society* 69 (1947): 2924–25. *Free Radicals in Solution*, a symposium on free radicals held at the University of Michigan in 1966, the centennial date of Gomberg's birth, was published by the International Union of Pure and Applied Chemistry (1967) and contains a paper by A. J. Ihde titled "Gomberg's Role in the History of Free Radical Chemistry," pp. 1–13. An obituary is in the *New York Times*, 13 Feb. 1947.

AARON J. IHDE

GOMEZ, Lefty (26 Nov. 1908–17 Feb. 1989), baseball player, was born Vernon Louis Gomez in Rodeo, California, the son of Manuel Gomez, a dairy farmer, and Elizabeth (maiden name unknown). Tall, thin, and athletic, Gomez aspired to be a rodeo rider, but his greatest talent consisted in throwing a baseball left-handed with speed and movement. While still a teenager on San Francisco's sandlots, he attracted the attention of major league scouts. At age nineteen he was pitching for Salt Lake City in the Utah-Idaho League, and in 1929 he led the Pacific Coast League in earned run average with the San Francisco Seals. Nineteen-thirty saw him a member of the New York Yankees, although he was sent to St. Paul in the American Association "for more seasoning" as well as to have "his teeth fixed" and to be put "on a milk diet to fatten him up," wrote Yankees' general manager Ed Barrow in his memoirs.

Healthy and seasoned, Gomez was back with the Yankees to stay in 1931. That season he compiled an outstanding 21–9 won-lost record with a 2.67 ERA and became the left-handed mainstay of the New York pitching staff. In 1932 he improved his record to 24 wins and seven losses; in 1933, despite a victory total that dipped to 16, he led American League pitchers in total strikeouts for the first of three times. Also in 1933 Gomez married actress June O'Dea; the couple had four children.

Although the Yankees finished second behind the Detroit Tigers in 1934, Gomez had his finest season. He was first among the league's pitchers in better than a half-dozen categories: 26 wins, an .839 winning percentage, 25 complete games, 281 innings pitched, 158 strikeouts, a 2.33 earned run average, and he was so effective that opposing batters hit only .215 against him. After middling-good seasons in 1935 and 1936, he and the consistently reliable Red Ruffing paced the Yankees to a second straight pennant and a second straight "subway World Series" championship over the New York Giants in 1937. Gomez led the league that year in wins, shutouts, strikeouts, and ERA.

Gomez pitched well in three of the next four seasons (he was sidelined for much of 1940), but his most successful years were behind him. Even though he led the American League with a 15–5 record in 1941, the next season he pitched only 80 innings, and in 1943 he finished his career with a single appearance as a member of the Washington Senators.

Gomez's regular-season career totals were noteworthy. In 13 years with the Yankees he compiled a 189–102 record for a .649 winning percentage. He won 20 or more games four times, and by defeating the Philadelphia Athletics seven different times in 1932, he played a major role in the Yankees' toppling of the reigning world champions.

During postseason play, Gomez was undefeated in six World Series decisions, defeating the New York Giants twice in both 1936 and 1937. In 1933 he was the winning pitcher in the first major league All-Star game, and he had a 3–1 record in five All-Star appearances. He also drove in the first run in All-Star game history, an unlikely feat for a lifetime .147 hitter. "I had a good batting eye," he insisted, "but my right leg had a yellow streak."

According to baseball historian Lee Allen, Gomez combined "southpaw brilliance and ebullient wit." After losing a second consecutive opening day 1–0 shutout in 1936, he told reporters, "I wish history would take some bicarbonate of soda and stop repeating itself." Asked the best way to defend himself against a line drive hit back at the pitcher, he said: "Run in on it before it picks up speed." He described one home run hit off him in Yankee Stadium by Jimmie Foxx, a particular nemesis: "I don't know how far it went, but it takes 45 minutes to walk up there." Gomez's love of the spotlight took some of the pressure off the shy Joe DiMaggio, who often brought Gomez to speak for him at various engagements. On a typical occasion, the Yankees' star center fielder would begin: "Thank you for inviting me. Now you can hear Lefty tell some funny stories." It was said that Gomez was the only person who got away with kidding DiMaggio in public. "I actually made DiMaggio famous," Gomez said. "Until he played behind me, they didn't know how far he could go back for a ball."

Before retiring as a player, Gomez described his declining skills with characteristic wit. "I'm throwing twice as hard as I used to, but the ball is taking longer to get there." In 1946 and 1947 Gomez managed the Yankees' farm team at Binghamton, New York, to last-place finishes. After that he worked as a spokesman for a sporting goods corporation and was in demand as an after-dinner speaker. The Veterans Committee of the Baseball Hall of Fame selected him for a Cooperstown plaque in 1972.

Although Gomez did not reach the mark of 200 career victories that is arguably necessary for Hall of Fame status, he was an outstanding pitcher, especially respected for his ability in clutch situations. "Few people symbolized the sport more joyously or successfully," wrote *New York Times* sportswriter Joseph Durso. Gomez died in Larkspur, California.

• Bob Broeg's reminiscence of Gomez in the *St. Louis Post-Dispatch*, 23 Feb. 1989, is one of many useful clippings in the Gomez library file at the Baseball Hall of Fame in Cooperstown, N.Y. Other personal and statistical information on his career can be found in Lawrence Ritter and Donald Honig, *The Image of Their Greatness: An Illustrated History of Baseball from 1900 to the Present* (1979); Lee Allen, *Cooperstown Corner: Columns from the* Sporting News (n.d.); Maury Allen, *Where Have You Gone, Joe DiMaggio?* (1975); and Bill James, *The Bill James Historical Abstract* (1986). All figures from Gomez's major league career are taken from John Thorn and Pete Palmer, eds. *Total Baseball*, 3d ed. (1993).

LEE LOWENFISH

GOMPERS, Samuel (27 Jan. 1850–13 Dec. 1924), co-founder and first president of the American Federation of Labor, was born in the working-class East End of London, England, the son of Solomon Gompers, a cigar maker, and Sarah Rood, Dutch Jewish immigrants. At age six he attended the Jewish Free School, where he studied Hebrew and French, but four years later the family's economic needs required that he apprentice himself first to a shoemaker and then a cigar maker. Difficult economic times continued for the Gompers family, however, and with financial aid from his father's union, Samuel and his family immigrated to the United States, arriving in New York City on 29 July 1863.

At first Samuel, as the oldest son, worked side-by-side with his father rolling cigars in their tenement apartment on New York's Lower East Side. By 1865 Samuel entered the world of the cigar factory as a skilled worker, where he would remain in a succession of shops into the early 1880s. By Gompers's own admission, his youthful interests focused little on the labor movement. Rather, he joined with other immigrant working-class youth in a variety of social groups and fraternal orders and undoubtedly shared in that distinctly male world of popular entertainments and saloons. But when Gompers entered the cigar factory to work, he also entered a world of ideas and visions that would, in time, have a transforming influence on this young man. Cigar makers regularly "hired" one of their own to read aloud while the others worked; in return, the reader was paid in cigars at day's end so that no one lost wages. Through this form of working-class self-education (he "went to school at Hirsch's shop," he once remarked), Gompers was introduced to discussions of current political issues, the conditions of labor worldwide, and the work of such political economists as Karl Marx, Ferdinand Lassalle, Edward Kellogg, and Ira Steward. Within a few years

Gompers had joined a small group of skilled workers from different trades for regular intense discussions of the current standing and future prospects of labor. Nicknamed *Die Zehn Philosophen*, or "the ten philosophers," the group met regularly after work to continue these discussions, exploring the alternative paths of socialist politics and trade unionism. While specific ideas would change over time, Gompers and his comrades maintained a commitment to building the trade union movement for decades to come. In 1878, for example, the 28-year-old Gompers turned down a well-paid position at the Treasury Department in Washington to remain in the labor movement—a striking commitment to an ideal from a young, poorly paid, overworked man with family responsibilities.

Gompers had married Sophia Julian in 1867. They had ten, possibly twelve children (only five of whom lived to adulthood), and the family eked by on Gompers's salary of about $15 a week. Although Sophia exhibited a fierce loyalty to her husband and to his commitments, their marriage was not without its tensions. The very real poverty, the infant deaths of a number of the children, and her husband's frequent absences during these times of family crisis all had their effect. Further, it was during the first decade of his marriage that he became increasingly active in the affairs of the Cigarmakers International Union (CMIU).

As a skilled worker, Gompers entered the trade at a time when the process of making a cigar was undergoing a fundamental transformation. In 1868 a mold was perfected that performed mechanically the skilled tasks that had been the core of the cigar maker's craft. The effect of this transformation was to allow employers to hire unskilled workers, especially recent immigrants and female workers at lower wages, to replace the skilled men. Some in the CMIU urged that the union refuse to organize these workers, but Gompers and his friend, Adolph Strasser, president of Local 15 of the Cigarmakers Union, argued that technological innovation increased efficiency, was potentially beneficial for working people, and was in any case inevitable.

In 1877, when Strasser assumed the presidency of the national union, he and Gompers dramatically altered the internal structure of the CMIU and, in the process, established a model that would be largely followed by future unions of skilled, craft workers. To justify the new, higher dues, the new administration established a series of benefits—for travel in search of work, sick relief, and unemployment compensation—that deserving workers might receive from the union treasury. Second, borrowing from the British union experience, they inaugurated a system of equalization of funds, whereby the national officers could transfer money from financially stronger locals to weaker ones in crisis. Finally, they created a well-financed, centralized strike fund, under the control of the national officers who could and did withhold support in strikes they thought ill advised. Together, these and other new policies created a centralized union structure, with a firm oversight of the finances of the locals, one that acted as a brake on independent rank and file activity.

Contrary to the opinion of many later critics, in urging these changes Gompers was not looking to create a conservative, hierarchical union sympathetic to the business community's needs. Just the opposite was in fact the case. In the late 1870s, as Gompers looked back on more than a decade of his own trade union activism, what impressed him most was the fragility of America's union movement. Economic depressions such as had occurred in 1837–1842 and 1873–1879 devastated these unions, as many members of necessity placed basic survival for themselves and their families above union membership. Then, too, major strikes, such as the recent 1877 national railroad strike (toward which Gompers was sympathetic), frequently resulted in the further leveling of the trade union movement as employers, often working in consort with state and national elected officials, took the opportunity to eliminate the weakened unions. Gompers's emphasis on a strong centralized union was a response to such realities.

So too was his insistence that working people themselves achieve their own independence. Gompers, a profoundly political creature, nonetheless resisted the temptation to commit the unions officially in political campaigns for a given candidate or party. Influenced by the Marxist analysis of the International Workingmen's Association, Gompers held that until workers came to a consciousness of themselves as a class—a process that could occur only through the experience of work itself—political action would be premature. Individually, workers could and should be politically active, as Gompers himself had been in his public support for Henry George in New York City's 1886 mayoralty campaign. But, Gompers argued, a broader, work-derived group identity was a prerequisite to any effort to orchestrate working-class political behavior; otherwise, such political action would pit workers against each other, with disastrous implications for the union movement. This was true whether the politicians appealing for workers' votes were Democrats or Republicans, Socialists or independents associated with the Knights of Labor. Political action without a clear class perception would only reinforce the utopian hope that workers might escape their class standing without transforming the larger economic system.

To further these ideas Gompers, who now possessed a growing national reputation in labor circles, joined with others in 1881 in Pittsburgh to found the Federation of Organized Trades and Labor Unions. Elected president despite a series of disagreements with the majority Knights of Labor delegates concerning the composition of the organization, Gompers worked hard that first year to establish the organization and to diminish the influence of the Knights. At the Federation's second convention in Cleveland in 1882, it quickly became evident that he was more successful in achieving the latter aim than he was the former. The Knights were all but formally excluded from the Federation, but the organization itself remained underfunded, without a clear focus, and institutionally weak. It did engage in efforts to influence legislation of benefit to working people, especially in various state legislatures.

In 1886 Gompers and his allies among the organized skilled workers in the union movement transformed the rather ineffective Federation into a new institution they called the American Federation of Labor (AFL). Their intent was to distance themselves from the public image of unionists as wild-eyed anarchists that had become so prevalent in the aftermath of the recent Haymarket bombing in Chicago and to provide a sure institutional structure for the union movement that, in contrast with the Knights, would focus primarily on organizing skilled craft workers. Samuel Gompers was elected president of the AFL in 1886, as he would be every year after, save one, until his death.

The two guiding principles of the AFL reflected the intentions of Gompers and his supporters. Voluntarism, in regard to the institutional structure of the AFL, reaffirmed the right of the individual unions to join (and therefore to leave) at will this national umbrella organization of the trade unions. But there was another meaning as well to that term. Gompers and other AFL leaders formally rejected a role for the state in establishing either the general boundaries or the specific conditions of industrial relations. Employers and workers through their unions, Gompers held, were the only legitimate actors, and in 1883 he informed a Senate committee that the U.S. Constitution "does not give our National Government the right to adopt a law which would be applicable to private employments." The second principle, trade union autonomy, reasserted the independence of the national unions within their craft jurisdictions and affirmed their right to order their own internal affairs without interference from other national unions or from the AFL itself. These principles ensured a constitutionally weak office of the president for the new organization.

Gompers's enthusiastic support of these ideas was not capricious. In part, his objection to government regulation reflected his longheld belief that only workers themselves could effectively wage their struggles—an idea that owed much to Karl Marx. But there was another factor as well. As president of the Federation in 1884, Gompers had spent long hours in Albany, lobbying New York state legislators of both parties to pass a bill regulating the conditions of work in the tenement buildings in the state's major cities. His elation when a strong bill was enacted crumbled the next year when the state court (in *In re Jacobs*) declared the law unconstitutional. With the power of the judiciary in this and many other cases so consistently utilized on behalf of employers, Gompers and his associates turned even more emphatically to organizing workers, in the belief that the resulting collective power was the only reliable force when confronting employers.

Despite the obstacles presented by both government and employers, the AFL survived and grew modestly in its early years. Gompers was indefatigable, answering letters, traveling incessantly, and giving speeches to organize workers and to alter the public's impression of the labor movement. Despite his agreement with the AFL's emphasis on organizing skilled workers (it was thought that skilled workers, more difficult to replace, could more effectively strike to gain their ends), Gompers's letters and talks during that first decade reveal a persistent effort on his part to urge the affiliated unions to organize all workers regardless of skill. Most dramatically, Gompers used his limited constitutional power and his more considerable unofficial influence to deny for a number of years membership in the AFL to the International Association of Machinists on account of its white-only membership requirement. Although Gompers ultimately had to accept a compromise that allowed machinist locals to determine membership qualifications (in effect retaining a segregated union), in other areas his influence was more effective. Rejecting his earlier Marxism as unrealistic in an expanding, democratic American society, Gompers waged unrelenting war on socialists of every stripe who sought to influence AFL policy, and he sharply distanced the organization from the populist movement as well. In the early 1890s he courted the railroad brotherhoods and their charismatic leader, Eugene V. Debs, but then publicly dismissed Debs as a labor leader in the aftermath of the Pullman strike of 1894. Although he lost his bid for reelection as president of the AFL in large part as a result of these actions, in the long run the AFL remained inoculated against these tendencies that Gompers and others found so disturbing.

Despite the internal dissension, the adverse court decisions, continued political hostility on the part of many elected officials, and yet another major depression between 1893 and 1897, the AFL under Gompers achieved what no other national labor organization in America had ever done: it survived and continued to grow. From a largely paper organization in 1886, the AFL counted some 250,000 members in 1893; a little more than a decade later, in 1904, that figure reached 1.7 million. Not surprisingly, the organizing budget rose accordingly, from $450 to over $83,000 in 1904, and full-time organizers became a permanent feature of AFL strategy in 1899.

As important as these achievements were, Gompers recognized that serious obstacles yet confronted the AFL. Most employers remained implacably opposed to cooperating with unions, while a string of U.S. Supreme Court decisions in the first decade of the century (the most important of which were *Buck's Stove and Range Co. v. American Federation of Labor* and *Loewe v. Lawlor*, the famous Danbury Hatters case) severely restricted the labor movement. Then, too, the regulatory power of the state, dramatically evident after the Civil War in the enactment of the Interstate Commerce Act of 1888, continued to grow sharply in ways that affected organized workers. The manner in which Gompers and his closest advisers addressed these problems largely structured organized labor's responses during his lifetime and even decades after his death.

In an effort to offset the fierce employer resistance to unionization, particularly that organized by the local and regional businessmen in the National Association of Manufacturers, Gompers aligned with the National Civic Federation (NCF). A quondam reform group composed of the leaders of the nation's largest corporations, the NCF sought to win worker loyalty by providing a variety of benefits (stock sharing and pensions, for example), all the while firmly preserving the full range of management rights and prerogatives. Yet Gompers and others in the AFL, in the face of withering criticism from dissident labor activists, asserted a value to this association nonetheless. NCF meetings provided access to the nation's business leaders and encouraged nonbinding mediation efforts in times of crisis. Through these businessmen's contacts in government, Gompers hoped to at least soften potentially hostile legislative and regulatory action. The results were at best mixed, as most NCF executives rejected their own organization's involvement in disputes within their own corporations.

Gompers and his AFL advisers developed another approach in their effort to defend against the prevalent antiunion animus, and this strategy altered the very core of the AFL's position on political involvement. The AFL had long thought that lobbying for specific legislation could be consonant with its theory of voluntarism; thus, in 1906 Gompers presented labor's Bill of Grievances to President Theodore Roosevelt and the Congress. Following two years of inaction, Gompers addressed the platform committees of both major political parties for the first time and increased efforts to defeat labor's worst legislative opponents, regardless of their party affiliation. But political realities quickly eroded the AFL's voluntarist, nonpartisan stance. The Republicans were generally cool toward Gompers, while the Democrats responded generally more favorably. By 1912 this led Gompers and the AFL into new understandings concerning political life. Despite formal statements to the contrary, Gompers now acknowledged the legitimate right of the state to intervene in broad areas of labor's concern, although he always maintained an opposition to government setting the hours of work or to funding unemployment compensation or social security. Recognizing Republican party opposition, he dropped all pretense of nonpartisanship and actively supported the Democrat, Woodrow Wilson, in the 1912 campaign. In a few short years Gompers had led the AFL well along the path from partisanship toward an actual partnership with the Democratic party.

The actions of Wilson and of the Democrats in Congress suggested to Gompers and other AFL leaders the value of these efforts. The president appointed a former coal miner and union official, William B. Wilson, to head the Department of Labor, and in quick succession a host of bills were enacted that addressed some of labor's key concerns: the Clayton Anti-Trust Act (1914), which Gompers proudly proclaimed as "Labor's Magna Carta" for its presumed exemption of unions from antitrust prosecution; the Seamen's Act

(1915), establishing basic standards of work on American ships; and the Adamson Act (1916), which established the eight-hour day for railroad employees. Despite the fact that Gompers opposed the Adamson bill—to cede to government the power to set hours of work butted against even his expanded understanding of voluntarism—it was widely popular among railroad workers and their union officials. More to the point for Gompers, he had been able to express his opinion on a bill directly to the president, as he had done so many times since Wilson's inauguration.

With a federal policy more supportive of labor than ever before in American history, the membership of the AFL continued to grow, reaching approximately 2.4 million in 1917. The advent of American involvement in World War I spurred that growth even further and deepened organized labor's ties to both this Democratic administration and to the idea of an expanded government role in industrial relations. Gompers, for example, strongly supported the American war effort and dealt harshly with antiwar unionists and socialists within the AFL. When Wilson proposed the National War Labor Board in an effort to reduce strikes and industrial tension to assure continuous production of war material, Gompers was elated. Composed of representatives of labor, management, and the public, the Board formally acknowledged labor's right to organize—something no administration had ever done before—and threatened employers with penalties if they refused to comply. Under such a strong governmental aegis, the AFL's membership soared to more than 4 million by 1920. For Gompers, his involvement with the Board, coupled with his subsequent participation (as an adviser on the labor sections of the treaty) in the Versailles Peace Conference following World War I, represented the height of both his personal and organizational prominence and influence. In 1920, however, Sophia Gompers died. The following year he married Gertrude Annesley Gleaves Neuscheler.

The last years of this proud man's life dealt harshly with his expectations of continued prominence for the labor movement. During the last year of his administration, Wilson was quite sick and thus politically ineffective; and the 1921 inauguration of the new Republican president, Warren G. Harding, brought no friend of organized labor to the White House. Simultaneously, the nation was caught in a paroxysm of fear concerning the influence of the recent Bolshevik revolution on American institutions. The wave of postwar strikes in 1919 and the anti-immigrant feelings unleashed by wartime propaganda (ironically something Gompers and the AFL helped to foster in their own propaganda activities on behalf of the American effort) obliterated for many the distinctions between communists, socialists, trade unionists, and immigrant working people, with the result that labor found itself under sustained suspicion and attack. The nation's employers, including some of those formerly affiliated with the NCF, recognized the moment as opportune as well. Chafing from the forced recognition of labor during the war, they now took advantage of the new political conditions to break unions where possible and to reduce labor's political influence at every level. By 1924 AFL membership had fallen to 2.9 million, a decline that would continue throughout the decade.

Although Gompers never publicly acknowledged labor's dramatic decline in influence as well as its loss of members, one of his last efforts suggests how serious he thought the situation was. In 1924 Gompers openly supported the independent presidential candidacy of Wisconsin senator Robert La Follette in an effort to revive the progressive alliance that had proved so beneficial but a few short years before. The results, from Gompers's perspective, were dismal: not only did the Republican, Calvin Coolidge, win, but the majority of even working-class voters rejected La Follette. A month later, following a meeting of the Pan American Federation of Labor, Samuel Gompers died in San Antonio, leaving behind a legacy that, in both its victories and its failures, would profoundly influence the American labor movement for decades yet to come.

• The most important archival collections of Samuel Gompers's papers can be found in the Library of Congress; the President's Office File, AFL, at the State Historical Society, Madison, Wis.; and at the George Meany Memorial Archives, Silver Spring, Md. A microfilm collection, "The AFL Records in the Gompers Era," is also available. As his correspondents included a wide variety of individuals, there are numerous other collections in archives across the nation with Gompers material. A superb, multivolume letterpress edition of Gompers's papers, under the editorship of Stuart B. Kaufman, is *The Samuel Gompers Papers* (1986–). The key published text on Gompers is his own *Seventy Years of Life and Labor* (2 vols., 1925); an edited version of the autobiography, with an introduction by Nick Salvatore, was published in 1984. Earlier works still of interest include Louis S. Reed, *The Labor Philosophy of Samuel Gompers* (1930); Philip Taft, *The A. F. of L. in the Time of Gompers* (1957); Bernard Mandel, *Samuel Gompers, a Biography* (1963); and William M. Dick, *Labor and Socialism in America: The Gompers Era* (1972). Kaufman's insightful study, *Samuel Gompers and the Origins of the American Federation of Labor, 1848–1896* (1973), covers approximately half of Gompers's life. A useful introduction to the AFL and politics remains J. David Greenstone, *Labor in American Politics* (1969). An obituary is in the *New York Times*, 14 Dec. 1924.

NICK SALVATORE

GONSALVES, Paul (12 July 1920–15 May 1974), jazz tenor saxophonist, was born in Boston, Massachusetts. His parents came from Cape Verde; neither details about them, nor when and how he acquired his nickname "Mex," are known. At some point the family moved to Rhode Island. Gonsalves's father taught him to play guitar. At about age eleven he discovered jazz through recordings, and, after hearing Coleman Hawkins on record and later Jimmie Lunceford's big band at a local theater at about age sixteen, he was inspired to play tenor saxophone, which he studied diligently under Joseph Pietratelli in Providence.

After graduating from high school in 1938, Gonsalves began working as a saxophonist and guitarist in

Providence and then in New Bedford, Massachusetts. Drafted, he served in the army from 1942 until 1945. He may have made recordings with pianist Teddy Weatherford in Calcutta while stationed in India. There he received a job offer from Duke Ellington, who had heard him in Boston, but he could not accept. After his discharge he joined Sabby Lewis's big band in Atlantic City, New Jersey, in 1946. He replaced Illinois Jacquet in Count Basie's big band late in August 1946 and was featured on many recordings, including "Basie's Basement," "Sugar" (both made with a smaller group from the band), "South," and "Robbin's Nest," all from 1947. His importance in the band diminished somewhat from September 1948 until February 1949, when Basie employed Wardell Gray, but Gonsalves remained until midyear, when he briefly rejoined Lewis before working in Dizzy Gillespie's big band from about October 1949 until August 1950.

When Gillespie was forced to disband, Gonsalves came to New York and played in jam sessions. He realized a boyhood ambition in September when he contacted Ellington, who offered him an audition the next day and then a job on the strength of his being able to reproduce Ben Webster's solos note-for-note (although Gonsalves soon proved to be a highly original improviser in his own right). He remained with Ellington for the rest of his career, except for a brief period in Tommy Dorsey's big band in 1953 and absences caused by illness.

Like Webster, Gonsalves had a strong talent for interpreting ballads. His solo on "Solitude" (following the piano solo), recorded in December 1950, exemplifies his smooth, airy tone and warm, wide vibrato. In 1951 Ellington performed "Diminuendo in Blue" and "Crescendo in Blue" at Birdland in New York (preserved on a broadcast recording), and Gonsalves took a long solo linking the two. It finds him playing with somewhat of a Rhythm & Blues simplicity, but mainly it features a wild style in which Gonsalves does to swing what Eric Dolphy would do to bop a decade later: playing "outside," that is, stretching or contradicting the underlying chord progression. Five years later at the Newport Jazz Festival (July 1956), Ellington called for the linked pieces, and Gonsalves once again took a long solo, playing in a highly emotive R&B style that thrilled the audience; captured on record (*Ellington at Newport*), the performance is perhaps the single finest document of jazz's raw vitality, ritualistically linking musician and audience. The event, however, caused Gonsalves considerable frustration: the piece grew tiresome as Ellington was obliged to repeat it every night, owing to its (and Gonsalves's) newfound popularity, and Gonsalves's solo—renowned as much for length as for substance—was musically far less impressive than his playing "outside" or his finest improvisations on ballads, including "Laura," recorded in February 1956, in which beautiful melodic statements frame a swinging interlude, and "Chelsea Bridge," on the album *Concert in the Virgin Isles* (1965), in which he takes a much more florid approach to ballad playing.

Gonsalves may be seen in numerous film shorts and documentaries involving Ellington's band. He also recorded the sounds that Sidney Poitier acts out in the movie *Paris Blues* (1961). In 1968 his Portuguese heritage proved useful when Ellington's band toured Brazil and Gonsalves served as its interpreter at various festivities. Independent of the leader, he had a modest career in the recording studio, the majority of sessions involving Ellington's sidemen. He also recorded a number of albums as a leader of and soloist in small groups. The best are *Gettin' Together* (1960); with Sonny Stitt, *Salt and Pepper* (1963); and with Ray Nance, *Just a-Sittin' and a-Rockin'* (1970).

Having been ill for several years, Gonsalves died of natural causes at a friend's home in London while returning from Holland to New York. He had been married and had several children, but he and his family were estranged (details are unknown); his papers identified Ellington as next of kin.

"Gonsalves was a gentle, sensitive, and, I suspect, rather lonely man who dogged himself with living habits detrimental to his chances of a long and healthy life." His alcoholism repeatedly caused Ellington to tell him that he was fired, but the firing never actually happened. "Ellington has (had, I suppose) a tremendous affection and respect for Gonsalves, who was capable of creating beauty at will," Max Jones wrote. Although he had the capacity to play with beboppers Gillespie and Stitt, Gonsalves was one of the major improvising tenor saxophonists of his era to remain closely connected with the swing style, while maintaining an individuality within that realm.

• Early surveys are by H. P. [Hugues Panassié], "Un grand saxo ténor: Paul Gonsalves," *Bulletin du Hot Club de France*, no. 68 (1957): 3–7; and Barry McRae, "Paul Gonsalves," *Jazz Journal* 16, no. 7 (July 1963): 25–26. For additional information, see the unsigned interview, "Under the Influence of Ellington: Paul Gonsalves Tells His Own Story," *Crescendo*, Mar. 1964, pp. 22–23; and one by Stanley Dance, *The World of Duke Ellington* (1970), pp. 168–74, with additional personal stories of Gonsalves spread throughout the book. Chris Sheridan's *Count Basie: a Bio-Discography* (1986) details his years with the Basie band. Obituaries are in the *New York Times*, 17 May 1974; *Melody Maker*, 25 May 1974, p. 25, which also includes a tribute and interview (taken in 1963) by Max Jones, "Duke's Fiery Tenorist," pp. 54, 56; Graham Columbé, "Time and the Tenor Postscript: Paul Gonsalves, 1920–1974," *Into Jazz* 1, no. 5 (1974): 27; and Panassié, *Bulletin du Hot Club de France*, no. 288 (1974): 3–5.

BARRY KERNFELD

GONZALES, Ambrose Elliott (29 May 1857–11 July 1926), newspaper publisher and author, was born on a plantation in St. Paul's Parish (Colleton County), South Carolina, the son of Ambrosio José Gonzales, a Cuban educator in exile, and Harriet Rutledge Elliott, a member of a family long prominent in the region. During his early boyhood, Ambrose's nurses and playmates were slaves from the African West Coast. These associations would lead to an abiding interest in his later life in the Gullah blacks who had settled in the Low Country.

The devastation of the Civil War, during which William Tecumseh Sherman's army destroyed the ancestral home, left the Gonzales family destitute. In 1869 the family traveled to Matanzas, Cuba, where Ambrose's father had been appointed to a professorship. There Ambrose attended public school briefly. That winter, after his mother was fatally stricken with yellow fever, Ambrose's returned with his brothers and sisters to South Carolina to live with his mother's family. Their father rejoined them the following winter, and the reunited family struggled, with only limited success, to restore the family plantation. Ambrose's formal schooling in the United States consisted of a few months at an academy in nearby Beaufort and a short stay at a private school in Virginia. By the time he was sixteen, he had left home to work as a telegraph operator for the Charleston & Savannah Railway in Grahamville, South Carolina, and managed to send money home to help restore the family homestead. He and his younger brother, Narciso Gener, also produced a handwritten weekly newspaper, which they called *The Palmetto*. The two young men, who were very close, enjoyed the experiment enormously. They typically produced two copies of the paper each week, which, Gonzalez later recalled, circulated "from house to house through the village, [and] created much amusement."

Soon after his twentieth birthday, Gonzales landed a telegrapher's position with Western Union in New York City, where he worked until 1885. He then returned to the South to work as a traveling agent and correspondent for the *Charleston News and Courier*. He and his brother Narciso, who also worked for the paper, quickly became embroiled in the turbulent politics of the day. During the late 1880s, a powerful bloc of small farmers in the upstate region, led by Benjamin R. Tillman, wrested control of South Carolina politics from the Bourbon Democrats, a coalition of planters, lawyers, and businessmen whose base was in the Low Country, and rewrote the state constitution to drastically curtail the rights of black voters. Denounced as a demagogue by the Gonzales brothers in the *News and Courier*, Tillman nonetheless was elected governor in 1890.

The Gonzales brothers decided to carry on their fight by establishing their own newspaper. Backed by $20,000 contributed by business and professional leaders from throughout South Carolina, they launched *The State* at Columbia in 1891. Calling for a new, progressive leadership in the state, the newspaper crusaded against lynching, for improved schools and compulsory education, for more protective child-labor laws, and for honest government. Although the paper was well received, especially within liberal circles, it made determined enemies among the Tillmanites. In 1903 Narciso was shot and killed by James Hammond Tillman, a nephew of Ben Tillman and a candidate for governor. In the emotionally charged murder trial that followed, Tillman was acquitted, despite numerous eyewitness accounts that contradicted his plea of self-defense.

Joined by his brother William Elliott, Ambrose redoubled his efforts to improve *The State*, and soon it achieved a regional and national reputation for editorial courage and journalistic excellence. Long years of overwork sapped Gonzales's physical resources, however, and in 1922 he suffered a severe stroke that impaired his speech and left him in a greatly weakened condition.

It was at this point that a renewed interest in the African Americans of the Low Country who had impressed him so deeply as a child began to take up increasing amounts of his time. Writing in his spare time, Gonzales eventually produced four collections of stories in the unusual dialect of the Gullah blacks: *The Black Border* (1922); *With Aesop Along the Black Border* (1924); *The Captain* (1924); and *Laguerre, a Gascon of the Black Border* (1924). Critics applauded the books not only for the insights they provide into the lives of the Gullahs, but also for providing the first glossary of Gullah expressions and for Gonzales's highly original philological commentary. "This Gullah dialect is interesting, not merely for its richness, which falls upon the ear as opulently as the Irish brogue," Gonzales wrote in the introduction to *The Black Border*, "but also for the quaint and homely similes in which it abounds and for the native wit and philosophy of its users." Archibald Rutledge, among many other critics, was fulsome in his praise of Gonzales's scholarship and literary skill. "It is a triumph of truth," he wrote of *The Black Border*. "It has found its way into the hearts of the people—as indeed does every true work which comes from the heart of a true man." Another critic credited Gonzales with saving the Gullah dialect from oblivion.

Despite his physical infirmities, Gonzales worked at *The State* until the day before he died in Columbia.

• The bulk of Gonzales's papers is housed in the Southern Historical Collection at the University of North Carolina in Chapel Hill. A smaller collection is maintained at the South Caroliniana Library at the University of South Carolina, Columbia. S. L. Latimer, Jr., *The Story of "The State" and the Gonzales Brothers* (1970), the authorized history of the newspaper, is valuable for its compilation of many of Gonzales's editorials and other writings. Gonzales himself provides a useful account of his earlier years in his Foreword to N. G. Gonzales, *In Darkest Cuba* (1922). Gonzales is ably profiled in various histories of South Carolina, notably Yates Snowden and H. G. Cutler, eds., *History of South Carolina*, vol. 4 (1929). The twenty-fifth anniversary issue of *The State*, published on 18 Feb. 1916, contains many articles and recollections of Ambrose Gonzales. A lengthy obituary and numerous tributes are in *The State*, 12 July 1926.

RONALD TRUMAN FARRAR

GONZALES, Babs (27 Oct. 1916 or 1919–23 Jan. 1980), jazz singer and conversationalist, was born Lee Brown in Newark, New Jersey. His parents' names are unknown. Any sketch of his activities must be extremely shaky, owing to his fondness for hyperbole and disinformation. His birth year has always appeared as 1919 in reference works, but his *New York Times* obituary gave his age as sixty-three, hence the 1916 birth year.

In his first book Gonzales claimed to be four years younger than saxophonist Ike Quebec (who was born in 1918; hence c. 1922) and elsewhere in that book he made himself out to be still younger (for example, age eighteen in 1943; hence c. 1925), presumably none of which should be believed.

Gonzales reported that his brothers played basketball at a time when there was a star player called Big Babbiad, so they became Big Babs and Middle-sized Babs, and he, Little Babs. He also reported that his mother ran a whorehouse. Later she opened a restaurant where he met many well-known jazz musicians, and one summer, probably in the late 1930s, he toured as the band boy for Jimmie Lunceford's orchestra. At a fine arts school in Newark he studied piano and then played drums and sang. Around 1940 he toured regionally as a pianist in a Newark-based band.

In 1941 he toured with Charlie Barnet's big band for a few weeks, serving as a backup singer to Lena Horne. According to one of his accounts, he picked the surname Gonzales to pretend to be Hispanic and thereby avoid Jim Crow laws while on tour with Barnet, but elsewhere he claimed to have assumed the surname while working as a chauffeur for actor Errol Flynn in Los Angeles in 1943. During this year he sang with Benny Carter's band. In 1945 he joined Lionel Hampton's big band for about five months.

As Babs Brown he drummed while singing with his group Three Bips and a Bop, which included Tadd Dameron; he said that he grew tired of lugging around the drum set and focused on singing. The group formed at Minton's Playhouse in Harlem in 1946, transferred to Buffalo after a dispute over pay, and then returned to Minton's in 1947. In February of that year he recorded his compositions "Oop-Pop-a-Da" and "Low Pow," the latter arranged by Dameron. Later that year trumpeter Dizzy Gillespie made a version of "Oop-Pop-a-Da" that became a hit recording, and Gonzales subsequently toured with Gillespie's big band for about three months, until vocalist Joe Carroll took his place. Around 1947 or 1948 Gonzales published a now-obscure book, The Be-bop Dictionary and History of Its Famous Stars, which gives delightful definitions ("gestapo:" an out-of-town musicians union delegate) and brief colorful biographies.

In 1949 Gonzales made a few recordings, including "Capitolizing" and "Professor Bop," in New York City and Los Angeles with a crew of distinguished young jazz musicians among his sidemen. In 1951 he joined the Manhattan Singers to tour Scandanavia for four months with comedian Reverend Carl Davis. Gonzales remained in Scandinavia and then traveled to Paris, where he met saxophonist James Moody. Returning to the United States by December 1951, he recorded Moody's albums Cool Whalin' and The James Moody Story (both 1952–1953) and stayed with Moody as manager and singer until 1953, when they had a falling out and Eddie Jefferson took Gonzales's place. Later that year he toured Sweden leading a band that included trumpeter Buck Clayton and drummer Kansas Fields.

Gonzales worked as a disc jockey in Newark, and around 1955 he sang with tenor saxophonist Johnny Griffin's band at the Blue Note club in Chicago. At some point he wrote lyrics to instrumental jazz themes: Horace Silver's "The Preacher," Gillespie's "A Night in Tunisia," and Thelonious Monk's "'Round Midnight." He returned to Paris several times during the mid-1950s, and he also performed in Holland, Spain, Switzerland, and Egypt. Back in the United States, he worked as a singer and comedian in several major cities and on a southern tour. In 1958 he recorded the album Voilà, including "Lullaby of the Doomed," which he wrote for Billie Holiday, and the following year he made another album, Cool Philosophy.

Gonzales performed in nightclubs in southern California in 1962 or 1963, and in the latter year he recorded the album Sundays at Small's Paradise in New York. In July 1963 he held a two-week engagement at Ronnie Scott's nightclub in London, and he also worked in Amsterdam and Paris. He continued to make regular summer visits to Europe into the 1970s.

Sometime in the late 1960s Gonzales produced the album Tales of the Famous: Guess Who?, on which he tells outrageous stories about well-known musicians whose identities are only thinly disguised. In his final decade he was often seen at jazz concerts, selling his books. He died in Newark, New Jersey.

Writer Jack Cooke best captured Gonzales's art: "He has two methods of expression in his songs: one of them is a harsh, gravelly approach in which he spits out the words of things like Night in Tunisia and The Preacher before going into his scat singing, hand-clapping, shouting and foot-stamping routine; the other is a gentler approach he reserves for his ballad material." Though his voice had limited range, his ear for harmony and sense of timing were excellent. But, as Cooke writes, "More important than all his singing . . . was his talking. . . . He assumed the role of spokesman for the whole hipster world."

• Gonzales's autobiographies are I Paid My Dues: Good Times . . . No Bread (1967) and Moving on Down the Line (c. 1975). The Institute of Jazz Studies, Newark, N.J., holds a copy of his self-published bebop dictionary. Published surveys are by Valerie Wilmer, "Babs Gonzales," Jazz Monthly 9 (Aug. 1963): 6–10, repr. in Wilmer, Jazz People (1970); Jack Cooke, "Babs Gonzales," Jazz Monthly 9 (Sept. 1963): 15; and Bernard Niquet, "Babs Gonzales," Jazz Hot, no. 274 (July–Aug. 1971): 20–21, with a discography by Charles Delauney and Niquet. See also Leonard Feather and Ira Gitler, The Encyclopedia of Jazz in the Seventies (1976), and Buck Clayton and Nancy Miller Elliott, Buck Clayton's Jazz World (1986). Obituaries are in the New York Times, 24 Jan. 1980, Down Beat 47 (Apr. 1980): 12, and Jazz Journal International 33 (1980): 22.

BARRY KERNFELD

GONZALES, Narciso Gener (5 Aug. 1858–19 Jan. 1903), journalist, was born at Edingsville, on Edisto Island, South Carolina, the son of Ambrosio Jose Gonzales, a Cuban revolutionary, and Harriet Rutledge

Elliott, a scion of a prominent South Carolina family. In 1869 the family moved to Cuba, where the elder Gonzales secured a position as a professor at Matanzas. After Harriet Gonzales died of yellow fever in the fall of 1869, Ambrosio and most of the children returned to "Oak Lawn," a plantation near Charleston, South Carolina, owned by the Elliott family. Narciso and a younger brother remained in Cuba and returned to Oak Lawn in 1870. The children lived with their grandmother and aunts while their father pursued jobs in New York and elsewhere. The Civil War and the abolition of slavery cost the Elliotts much of their wealth, and the Gonzales children received little formal schooling. In 1873–1874 Narciso attended St. Timothy's Home School for Boys in Fairfax County, Virginia.

In late 1874 Narciso Gonzales moved to Grahamville, South Carolina, a small town where his elder brother Ambrose worked as a telegraph operator. Narciso learned telegraphy from his brother and in 1875 took a job as a telegraph operator. During the political excitement of the 1876 campaign (which brought the end of Reconstruction in South Carolina), the two brothers produced a handwritten newspaper, *The Palmetto*. Narciso also wrote short news items for the *Charleston Journal of Commerce* in 1876 and 1877. From 1877 to 1880 he worked as a telegraph operator in Savannah and Valdosta, Georgia, and also served as a reporter for the *Valdosta Times*. In June 1880 Gonzales was hired as a reporter for the *Greenville (S.C.) News*; two months later he became a correspondent for the *Charleston News and Courier*, the state's leading paper.

Gonzales spent the next ten years working for the *News and Courier*. From August 1880 to October 1881 he served as the paper's correspondent at Columbia, the state capital. From October 1881 to August 1882 he reported from Washington, D.C., and then returned to South Carolina, working briefly at Charleston before returning to Columbia in early 1883. In April 1885 the *News and Courier* established a formal bureau at Columbia, with Gonzales as its manager, to handle news, circulation, and business affairs in that city. His early reporting showed what would become trademarks of his style: an emphasis on crime and politics, with a heavy dose of sometimes venomous opinion. Gonzales did not shy from personal disputes. In an 1885 article he charged that John L. M. Irby, a prominent planter in Laurens County, had held a pistol on an enemy while a third man horsewhipped him. Irby threatened to shoot Gonzales on sight, but the journalist continued his attack in articles with titles such as "Irby Drunk Again."

The year 1890 marked a crucial turning point in South Carolina politics and in Gonzales's career. That year, Benjamin R. Tillman ran for governor, promising relief for the state's hard-pressed white farmers and attacking the "aristocrats" who he said controlled the Democratic party. In his reports to the *News and Courier*, Gonzales dismissed Tillman as the "Great Bamboozler" and warned that his Farmers' Movement would bring class warfare to the state. After Tillman won the Democratic nomination, Gonzales joined other disgruntled Democrats to back another candidate, whom Tillman handily defeated in the general election. Gonzales believed the *News and Courier* had been too timid in its opposition to Tillman, and in November 1890 he quit the paper to join his brother Ambrose and other anti-Tillmanites in founding a daily paper at Columbia. The first issue of *The State* appeared on 18 February 1891, with Narciso Gonzales as its editor and largest stockholder. Within three years the paper was the second largest in South Carolina, due largely to the efforts of the Gonzales brothers—Narciso as editor; Ambrose, first as general agent and, after 1893, as president; and William as telegraph and news editor.

Under Narciso Gonzales's leadership, *The State* defined for itself a position separate both from Tillman's pseudo-Populism and from the Conservatism of the old-line Democrats. The paper supported industrial development and compulsory education and opposed child labor and the convict lease system. These and other positions put Gonzales and *The State* within a nascent movement of southern progressivism. On racial questions as well, Gonzales's views were progressive for his day and region. He opposed the segregation of railroad cars and passionately denounced lynching, which, he argued, reflected an attitude "unworthy of a moral newspaper and a moral man." On the other hand, he supported limits on black education and wanted the federal government to finance black emigration from the South.

During the Spanish-American War, Gonzales served as an officer with Cuban émigré troops who opposed Spanish rule. On his return, *The State* published excerpts from his diary, which Ambrose later published under the title *In Darkest Cuba* (1922). In 1901 Gonzales married Lucie Barron, who before their marriage was state librarian in Columbia; they had no children.

In 1902 Gonzales found himself once again embroiled in a bitter political controversy, this time with James H. Tillman, lieutenant governor and nephew of Ben Tillman. After the younger Tillman announced his candidacy for governor, *The State* ceaselessly editorialized against him, calling him "a man without character" who was "both disgraceful and dangerous" in public office. Tillman placed fourth in the gubernatorial primary in August and in a public statement blamed his defeat on "the brutal, false and malicious newspaper attacks headed by N. G. Gonzales." On 15 January 1903 Tillman met the editor on a sidewalk in Columbia and shot him once; Gonzales died of the wound several days later. Gonzales was unarmed at the time of the shooting, but Tillman claimed self-defense and was acquitted in a highly publicized trial later that year.

Although his career was cut short, Narciso Gener Gonzales played an important role in a tumultuous period of South Carolina history. Descended from an aristocratic family with deep roots in the Old South, he helped define a brand of progressive journalism for the New South of the twentieth century.

• Letters from Gonzales to other family members are in the Elliott-Gonzales Papers at the Southern Historical Collection, University of North Carolina, Chapel Hill. The South Caroliniana Library, University of South Carolina, Columbia, also has a small collection of Gonzales family papers. Gonzales is profiled in Lewis Pinckney Jones, *Stormy Petrel: N. G. Gonzales and His State* (1973). See also S. L. Latimer, *The Story of "The State," 1891–1969, and the Gonzales Brothers* (1970). An autobiographical sketch appeared in *The State*, 15 Apr. 1892. The foreword to *In Darkest Cuba* (1922) was written by Ambrose Gonzales and contains much biographical information about Narciso. An obituary is in *The State*, 20 Jan. 1903.

STEPHEN A. WEST

GONZALEZ, Pancho (9 May 1928–3 July 1995), tennis player, was born Richard Alonzo Gonzalez in Los Angeles, California, the son of Manuel Gonzalez, a painter of houses and Hollywood movie sets, and Carmen Alire, a seamstress. Gonzalez's parents, who emigrated from Chihuahua, Mexico, and settled in a poor section of Los Angeles, were determined to give their seven children a decent childhood in the dangerous barrios of South Los Angeles. After a boyhood accident on a scooter that left Gonzalez with a scar on his cheek several inches long, his parents refused to give the twelve-year-old the bicycle that he wanted. Instead, his mother bought him a 51-cent tennis racket. The restless, energetic Gonzalez quickly discovered his natural athletic ability and became obsessed with the game of tennis, which he learned in the public courts of Exposition Park near the Los Angeles Coliseum.

Although he never took a formal lesson, Gonzalez soon became one of the best junior players in Southern California. Encouraged by his early successes, Gonzalez devoured the game of tennis and rebelled against the confinements of school. He spent much of his time in the tennis shop of the Exposition Park with teaching professional Frank Poulain, who often allowed the strong-willed Gonzalez to hide from the truant officer in the tennis shop.

During his early teenage years Gonzalez also formed a friendship with Chuck Pate, a fine player and a devoted student of the game. It was Pate who innocently pinned the nickname "Pancho" on Gonzalez. His family disliked the name, considering it an ethnic slur. Eventually, however, the Gonzalez family accepted the nickname with the graciousness with which Pate had intended it.

By age fifteen, Gonzalez had quit school entirely and devoted himself to tennis. When the Southern California Tennis Association learned that Gonzalez had left school, it barred him from all sanctioned tournaments. Dejected but even more determined, Gonzalez continued to improve as a player until early 1945, when he enlisted in the U.S. Navy. There he swabbed decks until he was discharged in 1947.

When Gonzalez was eighteen, his suspension was lifted, and he resumed his tennis career with a passion. He won the Southern California championships by beating Herbie Flam, who was the national junior champion in 1945 and 1946. At age twenty, ranked seventeenth and seeded eighth, Gonzalez won the 1948 U.S. championship at Forest Hills, New York, beating Eric Sturgess of South Africa in straight sets. He became what was at the time the second-youngest male singles champion ever. That same year Gonzalez married Henrietta Pedrin; they had three children before the marriage ended in divorce.

In the eyes of most tennis experts, Gonzalez's 1948 U.S. title was tainted because Ted Schroeder, considered the best amateur in the world, had not played in the tournament. When Schroeder entered in 1949, he and Gonzalez met in the finals. After falling behind two sets to none, Gonzalez shocked the experts by winning his second straight amateur U.S. championship, 16–18, 2–6, 6–1, 6–2, and 6–4.

In 1948 the Mexican government offered Gonzalez a free college education and a lifetime job at the Mexican consulate in Los Angeles if he would become a Mexican citizen and represent Mexico in international competition. Gonzalez was tempted but finally refused, saying, "I just decided that this country [America] was a pretty good place to live in." After his second U.S. championship in 1949, tennis promoter Bobby Riggs offered Gonzalez $72,000 to turn professional. This was more money than the Gonzalez family had ever seen, but for the inexperienced 21-year-old, accepting the offer was also competitive suicide. Riggs's contract called for Gonzalez to go on tour against the reigning professional champion, Jack Kramer. The overmatched Gonzalez lost ninety-six matches, won only twenty-seven, and became a has-been in professional tennis by age twenty-two.

No longer a drawing card, Gonzalez spent three years in relative obscurity, selling tennis equipment, stringing rackets, bowling, golfing, driving hot-rod cars, and gambling in high-stakes poker games. He never strayed far from tennis, however, and in 1954 he returned to the professional tour. At the peak of his physical and competitive skills, his style was the envy of his peers. His right-handed serve and overhead smash were the most powerful in the sport. His attacking serve and volley game off both first and second serve was devastating, yet he could also use a deft touch and precise angles to win crucial points. At six feet three inches, he was lithe and agile and possessed an intuitive all-court sense. His rich black hair, dark complexion, withering stare, and scar created a menacing presence that often intimated opponents even before the match began. He was moody, hot-tempered, contentious, and sometimes mean-spirited when he was extremely upset during a contest. On repeated occassions, Gonzalez verbally and even physically abused not only opponents but also line judges and sometimes hecklers in the crowd.

From 1954 to 1962 Gonzalez was clearly the best player in the world. He reigned as the king of the professional tour, now run by Kramer, whom Gonzalez once sued for a better percentage of the gate. A glowering lone wolf, Gonzalez won the U.S. professional title eight times during this period, dominating other tennis greats such as Frank Sedgman, Don Budge, Pancho Segura, Tony Trabert, Lew Hoad, Ken Rosewall, Rod Laver, Alex Olmedo, and Barry MacKay.

The great irony of Gonzalez's career is that, because he turned professional at such a young age, he was not eligible to play in the four Grand Slam tournaments during his prime, which was before the Open era. Kramer, in his comprehensive book on tennis, *The Game* (1979), estimated that Gonzalez would have won seven U.S. championships instead of two, and six Wimbledons, for a then-modern record of thirteen. Kramer, Budge, and other experts agree that Gonzalez was "the greatest player who never won Wimbledon."

Gonzalez finally got his chance to play the Grand Slams again in the twilight of his career, when the Open era began in 1968. Two months past his forty-first birthday, having already become a grandfather, he outlasted 25-year-old Charles Pasarell in what was then the longest match in Wimbledon history. The score of this epic match was 22–24, 1–6, 16–14, 6–3, and 11–9. It numbered 112 games, took five hours, twelve minutes to play, and spanned two days.

Gonzalez retired from competitive tennis several times in the 1960s, but he continued playing at a world-class level with remarkable success into the early 1970s. He won his last event in Des Moines, Iowa, when he was nearly forty-four years old. In later years he coached the United States in Davis Cup competition, worked at Paradise Island in the Bahamas, and for twenty years served as director of tennis at Caesars Palace in Las Vegas. Gonzalez married six times, the last to Rita Agassi, the sister of popular American tennis star Andre Agassi. He was the father of eight children, including one with Rita Agassi before their divorce.

Gonzalez's spectacular career in tennis spanned four decades. He was a great natural talent, a colorful showman, and the fiercest of competitors who felt he had to prove himself time and again to overcome the sting of prejudice he experienced in his youth. Gonzalez was a hero to tennis aficionados in general and to the Hispanic community in particular. For more than ten years he was the best tennis talent in the world but didn't get the chance to show it in the biggest events because they were closed to professionals. Gonzalez was elected to the International Tennis Hall of Fame in 1968. Upon his death from cancer in Las Vegas, Nevada, noted tennis writer Bud Collins said, "He was as good as there ever was."

• Gonzalez's autobiography, *Man with a Racket* (1959), was published at the peak of his career. He wrote three other instructional books on tennis: *Tennis* (1962), *Winning Tactics for Weekend Singles* (1974), and *Tennis Begins at Forty* (1976). A concise biography is Dave Anderson, *The Return of a Champion* (1973). Gonzalez is mentioned prominently in Jack Kramer, *The Game* (1979). There are also sections devoted to Gonzalez in Arthur Daley, *Sports of the Times* (1959); Ed Fitzgerald, *Heroes of Sport* (1960); B. McCormick, *Great American Athletes of the Twentieth Century* (1966); Trent Frayne, *Famous Tennis Players* (1977); *Bud Collins' Modern Encyclopedia of Tennis* (1980); Larry Lorimer, *Tennis Book* (1980); and Stan Hart, *Once a Champ* (1985). A juvenile source is Charles Morse and Ann Morse, *Pancho Gonzalez* (1993). An article worth noting is "The Power and the Fury," *World Tennis*, Sept. 1987, pp. 25–7, 75, 77. Obituaries are in the *Los Angeles Times* and the *New York Times*, 5 July 1995.

BRUCE L. JANOFF

GOOCH, Sir William (21 Oct. 1681–17 Dec. 1751), colonial governor of Virginia, was born in Yarmouth, England, the son of Thomas Gooch, a local official, and Frances Lone. Both parents died before William was sixteen, and he had a close relationship with his older brother Thomas, who became a bishop of the Church of England. William attended Queen's College, Oxford, and at nineteen entered the army. He served through the War of the Spanish Succession and against the Highlands uprising of 1715, attaining the rank of major. In 1714 he married Rebecca Staunton of Hampton, Middlesex; they would have one son. After opportunities for advancement slowed, Gooch left the army to live in Hampton and to seek a civil appointment.

Through the influence of the duke of Newcastle, the secretary of state, Gooch obtained a commission in 1727 as lieutenant governor of Virginia (the titular governor remaining, as was the custom, in England). A reputation for fairness and evenness of temper preceded him to Virginia, and on his arrival he was greeted warmly by the appointed Council and the elected House of Burgesses, who had not always had amicable relations with earlier governors such as Alexander Spotswood. For his part, Gooch invited the burgesses to take initiative in formulating legislation for the benefit of the colony. He also demonstrated a willingness to support the colony's interests, which during his administration came into conflict less with the government at Whitehall than with British merchants. Gooch could not wield immense political power in England, but because of good relations with Robert Walpole and others his voice had some influence.

Early in his administration Gooch forwarded a bill relating to tobacco, the colony's staple crop. The measure was similar to one that Spotswood had promoted without success. Planters would deposit barreled tobacco at official warehouses for inspection and sealing. As a benefit to the currency-poor economy, inspectors' certificates for deposited tobacco could be used as money. The bill also limited the inspectors' involvement in provincial politics by forbidding members of the assembly from serving as inspectors. Gooch prepared the way by writing to officials and merchants in England, then managed the bill through the House of Burgesses and the Council, who approved it in 1730. Despite objections from the commissioners of customs, he persuaded the Board of Trade that it would increase quality and prices (and therefore revenues). Some tobacco growers, distressed in particular by a requirement that tobacco rejected by inspectors must be burned, resisted implementation of the act. Gooch countered this opposition by writing, anonymously, *A Dialogue between Thomas Sweet-Scented, William Oronoco, Planters . . . and Justice Love-Country* (1732), a fictional exchange in which the sound reasoning of a local magistrate overcomes the doubts of two planters. The law provided means of assuring product quality and was given credit when prices rose. With periodic renewal and some modification, the 1730 act remained in effect through the colonial period.

Tobacco prices had been depressed since the mid-1720s but improved by the middle 1730s, and Virginia enjoyed a long period of what Gooch characterized as "peace and plenty" (Morton, *Colonial Virginia*, 531). It was his good fortune also that the prosperous planters who controlled the colony's politics generally resolved differences without overt conflict. On most issues Gooch found alliance with influential members of the provincial leadership. He determined that the best means of handling the aging James Blair—commissary of the bishop of London and a formidable political force in Virginia since the previous century—was to "kill him with kindness" (Morton, *Colonial Virginia*, 501). Through investments in land and in an iron mining venture, as well as by the eventual marriage of his son to a Maryland woman, Gooch also established personal ties to the society he oversaw on the Crown's behalf.

In 1740–1741 Gooch commanded colonial troops sent with a British expedition to take Cartagena, a fortified Spanish port on the coast of South America. The attack failed; Gooch contracted fever and a cannonball clipped his ankles, an injury that would trouble him long after. Within a few years, in fact, rheumatism and other complaints impaired his ability to keep up with his duties as governor. He was dispirited also by the deaths in close succession of his son, baby grandson, and brother-in-law. The Crown made him a baronet in 1746 and major general of the army the year after, but he quietly made plans to leave Virginia. In 1749 he returned to England, where he petitioned for repayment of personal funds advanced for the Cartagena expedition and sought a new post from the government. He died in Bath, England, where he had gone to succor his ailing health.

As governor, Gooch attempted to protect both the Crown's and the colony's interests. He promoted settlement of western lands, and in a single day in 1749 he and the Council granted to prominent Virginians over one million acres west of the Allegheny ridge. He allowed those grants, however, only after receiving approval from Whitehall. Near the end of his administration he said that it had been his policy to "act, according to the Dictates of my own Judgment and Conscience, determined, if possible, to avoid Displeasure" (*Journals, 1742–1749*, p. 241). The burgesses commended him as "a faithful Trustee" of his power and he in return pledged "to support them in their antient Rights and Privileges" (*Journals, 1727–1740*, p. 242). He was the beneficiary of a period of prosperity, but left his own mark by not allowing his office to become a source of political conflict.

• Modern historians have made use of a Colonial Williamsburg microfilm copy of informative letters that Gooch wrote to his brother in England. Official papers are in the Colonial Office series of the British Public Record Office documents. For Gooch's relations with the Assembly, see H. R. McIlwaine, ed., *Journals of the House of Burgesses of Virginia, 1727–1734, 1736–1740* (1910) and *1742–1747, 1748–1749* (1909). Andrew Karl Prinz, "Sir William Gooch in Virginia: The King's Good Servant" (Ph.D. diss., Northwestern Univ., 1963) contains biographical details. For Gooch within the larger context of colonial Virginia see also Richard L. Morton, *Colonial Virginia*, 2 vols. (1960); Warren M. Billings, John E. Selby, and Thad W. Tate, *Colonial Virginia: A History* (1986); Randall Shrock, "Maintaining the Prerogative: Three Royal Governors in Virginia as a Case Study, 1710–1758" (Ph.D. diss., Univ. of North Carolina, 1980); and Percy Scott Flippin, "William Gooch: Successful Royal Governor of Virginia," *William and Mary Quarterly*, 2d ser., 5 (Oct. 1925): 225–58, 6 (Jan. 1926): 1–38.

JAMES P. McCLURE

GOOD, James Isaac (31 Dec. 1850–22 Jan. 1924), clergyman and educator, was born in York, Pennsylvania, the son of William A. Good, a clergyman, and Susan B. Eckert. Early in his life Good evidenced potential for intellectual vigor and literary expression. When he graduated with honors from Lafayette College in 1872, his work on Alexander Pope was published as the college's Fowler Prize Essay of that year. After graduating in 1875 from Union Theological Seminary in New York City, he was ordained as a minister in the German Reformed church. He served three pastorates in Pennsylvania during the next three decades: the Heidelberg Reformed Church in York (1875–1877), the Heidelberg Reformed Church in Philadelphia (1877–1890), and the Calvary Reformed Church in Reading (1890–1905). While serving at Reading, Good also entered upon the second, and ultimately more significant, part of his career. In 1890 he began teaching in the theology department of Ursinus College in Collegeville, Pennsylvania.

The section of Ursinus College concerned with theological education soon became a School of Theology in its own right, and in 1893 Good became its dean. In that capacity he lectured on such topics as church history, dogmatics, and pastoral theology. In 1898 he was instrumental in physically separating the school from the college and in locating his divinity students amid Philadelphia's urban challenges. Educational work continued there for almost a decade, but in 1907 an institutional merger occasioned another change of scene. In that year Ursinus School of Theology joined with Heidelberg Theological Seminary to form Central Theological Seminary, located in Dayton, Ohio. Good was professor of church history and liturgics at the new institution, spending the fall semester of every year there from 1907 until his death. He spent the spring semester of each term back at Ursinus College, lecturing to undergraduates. Since he never married, such periodic shifts of residence were rather easily accomplished. When he died unexpectedly in Philadelphia, he was about to begin another round of undergraduate instruction.

The first time Good went to Europe, he was simply an unseasoned tourist in search of his German ancestral home. Over the next quarter-century he spent every summer as an increasingly experienced scholar who traced the roots of Calvinism among the Germans, Dutch, and Swiss. In the course of those travels he made extensive notes that served as foundations for several lengthy publications on the origin and history of Reformed ecclesiastical traditions. He also made arrangements for documents and archival deposits to be copied and transported to libraries in the United States, with the bulk of materials eventually accumulating at Central (now Eden) Theological Seminary in St. Louis, Missouri. Moreover, he amassed over the years a notable collection of books on Reformation topics. As voluntary purchasing agent, documents collector, and specialist in his own right, Good enhanced German Reformed historical scholarship in this country. His support of the field spanned thirty-four years of classroom activity; his material aids made it possible for later generations to continue those efforts and build on them.

Good served on many of the larger managerial structures in his denomination. He was, for instance, president of the board for foreign missions from 1893 to 1924. Beginning in 1903 he worked with a committee to revise the *Hymnal of the Reformed Church*, which eventually appeared in 1920. From 1911 to 1914 he occupied the prestigious office of president of the General Synod, and in 1914 he was also president of the American Society of Church History. Interested to some extent in ecumenical activities, he participated in the Reformed Alliance and the World Alliance of Reformed and Presbyterian Churches. Through these offices a lengthening list of addresses, sermons, and reports came from his productive pen. One specific theme worth noting was his defense of free worship. Some in his denomination wanted to provide written prayers for a uniform order of service that ended with the Lord's Supper as its high point. Good wanted by contrast to allow for extemporaneous prayers in church services and to have the sermon as their culmination.

In almost all questions Good was a thoroughgoing and undaunted conservative. He was content with the commonplace understanding of the Bible, creeds, and history held by most people in his denomination. He had no use for what he called the wild speculations of biblical criticism. Critical analysis was, in his view, a threat to faith and successful ministry; it tore the Bible apart and eroded the sure foundations on which Reformed theology rested. Good also denounced evolutionary theory or any other developmental explanation of the past. He rejected the liberal notion that dealing with social problems was part of a Christian's duty. He viewed such innovations as signs of deteriorating faith, symptoms of an age when proper theology was being put at serious hazard. His response was to accept the past as normative and to confront the present with uncompromising rigidity. As late as 1914 he was still defending the sixteenth-century Calvinist Heidelberg Catechism as a full and sufficient guideline for coping with all facets of twentieth-century American culture.

• Good produced a great many large volumes, the most important of which are *The Origin of the Reformed Church in Germany* (1887); *History of the Reformed Church of Germany, 1620–1890* (1894); *History of the Reformed Church in the United States, 1725–1792* (1899); *Women of the Reformed Church* (1901); *Famous Missionaries of the Reformed Church* (1903); *Famous Places of the Reformed Churches: A Religious Guidebook to Europe* (1910); and *History of the Reformed Church in the U.S. in the Nineteenth Century* (1911). Biographical material is in Carl H. Gramm, *The Life and Labors of the Reverend Prof. James I. Good, D.D., LL.D., 1850–1924* (1944), which includes a short autobiography. An obituary is in the *New York Times*, 23 Jan. 1924.

HENRY WARNER BOWDEN

GOODALE, George Lincoln (3 Aug. 1839–12 Apr. 1923), physician, botanist, and educator, was born in Saco, Maine, the son of Stephen Lincoln Goodale, a pharmacist and agricultural chemist, and Prudence Aiken Nourse. After serving an apprenticeship in his father's apothecary shop, he entered Amherst College in 1856; there he received instruction from Edward Tuckerman in botany, Edward Hitchcock in geology, and Charles Shepard in mineralogy. He received the A.B. in 1860 and remained at Amherst for a year as a chemistry assistant to William Clark, concurrently studying medicine with a local doctor. In 1861 he began more formal instruction in medicine at Portland, Maine, and in 1862 he matriculated at the Harvard Medical School, earning an M.D. with distinction in 1863, the same year Bowdoin College also conferred an M.D. on him.

Goodale then practiced medicine in Portland, Maine, for three years. He also served as city physician and instructor at the Portland Medical School. While a medical student he had been part of the scientific survey of Maine, and in 1862 and 1863 he published papers on the survey's botanical discoveries. In March 1866, troubled by poor health, he decided to go to California, traveling by boat and crossing the Isthmus of Panama by rail. His condition improved, and he visited areas of botanical interest in the West. This same year Amherst conferred the A.M. on him.

In December 1866 Goodale returned to Maine and married Henrietta J. Hobson of Saco, Maine; they had five children, but only two lived to maturity. Goodale toured a number of European countries in 1867 and became acquainted with their museums and botanic gardens. In 1868 he accepted a professorship at Bowdoin College, where he taught botany, zoology, and chemistry; he also taught materia medica at the Bowdoin Medical College.

In 1870 Goodale wrote to Asa Gray that he was having difficulty in continuing to study without guidance. He proposed to continue his work, especially on plant physiology, and to consult with Gray at his home periodically. During a winter vacation in 1870 he studied with Gray, who was impressed with his ability, and the next year he was appointed instructor in botany and university lecturer in vegetable physiology, assuming responsibility for some courses long taught by Gray. To the basic studies of plant morphology he began to add more material on plant anatomy and physiology. In 1873 he was named assistant professor of vegetable physiology and instructor in botany, and in 1878, full professor of botany.

Goodale was considered an excellent lecturer, not only knowledgeable in his field but also able to hold the interest of laymen as well as of students. He was a popular presenter to high school teachers at the Harvard Summer School, who often encouraged their colleagues to attend. He also lectured to the general public in Boston and other cities. Goodale was able to arouse enthusiasm in his audiences and enlist their support for his work, but his many activities did not permit him much time for independent research.

Goodale was also an excellent administrator and organizer, traits recognized by Gray, who convinced him to take over responsibility for the Harvard Botanic Garden. He was appointed director of the botanic garden in 1879, a position he held until his retirement in 1909. Because of his tact and sincerity he was able to appeal to the wealthy and influential to support the repair and replacement of structures, start an endowment fund, and hire trained personnel. Under his management, the garden regained its role as an educational asset.

Goodale authored two books. The first was *Wild Flowers of America* (1882), with colored plates prepared from watercolors by Isaac Sprague. Written to appeal to a general audience, this was one of the first nature guides prepared in the United States. The second, *Physiological Botany*, a treatise of 500 pages, was issued as volume 2 of Gray's *Botanical Textbook* in 1885. One of the earliest American books on plant physiology, this was lauded at the time, but rapid advances in the field reduced its long-term usefulness. Most of Goodale's publications consisted of short papers on botany, reviews, and administrative reports.

Louis Agassiz had planned a great natural museum complex to be built in Cambridge, and Goodale's untiring efforts made it possible for the botanical section of the museum to be completed in 1890. He saw it as a place for botanical instruction, offices, laboratories, a library, and a repository for the many botanical specimens accumulated by Harvard. Goodale needed a focal point around which he could effectively display materials already acquired. In the mid 1880s he became intrigued by the glass models of marine invertebrates made by Leopold and Rudolph Blaschka of Meissen, Germany. After some correspondence, he visited their home and presented his plan for glass models of plants. They were at first reluctant, since they had no experience with botanical objects, but, they agreed to prepare samples. Unfortunately, these arrived broken, but Goodale showed the fragments to prospective patrons. Elizabeth Ware and her daughter, Mary Lee Ware, agreed to finance the project in memory of their husband and father, Charles E. Ware, and thus the entire output of the Blaschkas was procured for the museum. Goodale himself arranged other displays around the glass flowers, still a popular attraction today.

During his tenure at Harvard Goodale traveled to many countries. He was an able linguist and had a broad range of interests. In 1890 and 1891 he traveled around the world, acquiring many objects for the museum and the garden. Over the years he became interested in economic botany, especially tropical agriculture; with funding from Edwin F. Atkins of Boston, he was able to establish a branch of the botanic garden in Cuba, where sugar cane and other tropical crops were studied.

Goodale belonged to many scientific and social societies and served as an officer in several. He was president of the American Association for the Advancement of Science in 1890–1891.

After Asa Gray's death in 1888, Goodale was appointed Fisher Professor of Natural History, a title he held until his resignation in 1909. The university then named him Fisher Professor, Emeritus, and honorary curator of the Botanical Museum. He maintained his interest in the museum and prepared the annual reports until shortly before his death in Cambridge.

• Goodale's administrative papers are in the Harvard University Archives; some letters and other papers are in the archives of the Gray Herbarium, Harvard University. B. L. Robinson, "Memoir of George Lincoln Goodale 1839–1923," National Academy of Sciences, *Biographical Memoirs* 21, no. 6 (1927): 1–19, contains a biography and a detailed bibliography of Goodale's publications, as well as a list of his obituaries. An obituary by R. T. Jackson is in the *Harvard Graduates Magazine* 32 (Sept. 1923): 54–59, and one by L. H. Bailey is in *Rhodora* 25 (1923): 117–20.

ANNA M. M. REID

GOODE, George Brown (13 Feb. 1851–6 Sept. 1896), zoologist, museum administrator, and historian of science, was born in New Albany, Indiana, the son of Francis Collier Goode, a merchant, and Sarah Woodruff Crane. Goode's mother died just eighteen months after his birth, and he was raised by his father and stepmother, Sally Ann Jackson. In 1857 his father retired to Amenia, about 100 miles north of New York City. Family study and private tutors prepared Goode for entrance into Wesleyan College in Middletown, Connecticut, from which he graduated with an A.B. in 1870. He attended the Lawrence Scientific School at Harvard University and apparently spent some time in Louis Agassiz's rapidly expanding Museum of Comparative Zoology before returning by late 1871 to Middletown, Connecticut. There he renewed his acquaintance with family neighbor Orange Judd, the prominent agricultural editor, and his daughter Sarah Ford Judd, whom Goode married in 1877; they had four children.

Appointed curator of the Orange Judd Hall of Natural Science at Wesleyan in 1871, Goode had the opportunity to continue his interest in natural history even as he established a collegiate museum for study and public display to the local community. Convinced that college students learned as much from helping to gather and identify the collections as from lectures and systematic instruction by the faculty, he wrote enthusiastically about his development of the collections in long annual reports to the trustees. At Eastport, Maine, in 1872 he met Spencer F. Baird, who was responsible for the collections of the Smithsonian Institution and had recently been appointed U.S. fish commissioner. Recognizing their mutual interests, Baird took the earnest curator into his circle of collectors and collaborators and soon established a close, mentoring relationship with Goode.

Over the next several summers Goode joined Fish Commission expeditions along the Atlantic coastline and became an expert in ichthyology. In the autumn and winter months, Goode spent periods of time in Washington, D.C., as an assistant curator at the Smithsonian, writing up research results and arranging for duplicate specimens to be shipped to Wesleyan. Much of the commission research involved the economic implications of the geographic distribution and migration of deep sea fish and reflected concern about the potential overfishing of some sites. A prolific writer, Goode contributed to the resulting literature and discussions about extending the habitats of useful fish. He was asked to conduct a survey of American fisheries for the Tenth U.S. Census (1880), and after Baird's death in 1887 Goode briefly held the position of fish commissioner. He resigned, preferring to devote himself to the National Museum. Goode also continued his scientific and taxonomic research and published significant studies of particular localities and species, including his early *Catalogue of the Fishes of the Bermudas* (1876). For years he worked with Tarleton Hoffman Bean, and together they produced an authoritative, two-volume study, *Oceanic Ichthyology* (1895), shortly before Goode's death. Goode's scientific productivity, while impressive, was overshadowed by his career as a museum theorist and administrator.

Work with Baird in preparing major displays on U.S. activities for a series of International Fish Commission exhibitions in the 1870s and 1880s revealed Goode's exceptional organizational and administrative talents. Contemporaries marveled as storage crates filled with fishes and charts were transformed into attractive and informative exhibits. As a result of his enthusiasm and innovation, the relatively young naturalist was chosen to plan and coordinate the Smithsonian's display of zoology for the Centennial Exposition in Philadelphia in 1876. This offered an unprecedented opportunity to draw national attention to the result of the Smithsonian's thirty years of acquiring specimens from government expeditions as well as other sources. Goode's 1876 exhibition catalog, *Classification of the Collection to Illustrate the Animal Resources of the United States*, reveals his idea that the human uses of the skins, skeletons, and other objects on display would be of predominant interest, even as the individual labels provided scientific nomenclature and descriptions to visitors. While in Philadelphia he also helped negotiate with representatives from other countries for an exchange of specimens.

Within two years, Congress had authorized a building for the new U.S. National Museum as part of the Smithsonian Institution, and Goode was offered a permanent position in Washington, D.C., as assistant to the director of the museum. Goode managed much of the day-to-day planning of the facility and the design of new display cases; perhaps equally important, he worked with Baird on plans to organize the specimens and artifacts for general public audiences. Goode, assisted by innovative staff members like anthropologist Otis T. Mason, systematically toured museums in the United States and abroad, reviewed in detail the exhibits at international expositions, and wrote about the past and the future of museum practice as part of the Smithsonian's planning process. *Circular Number 1* (1881) of the National Museum was a comprehensive plan for the museum that was so thorough that it was used as a guide for several decades and was widely cited by other museum administrators. In it Goode outlined his idea of the three basic functions for a major museum: to establish a record of scientific knowledge, to provide facilities for research on the collections, and to provide popular education through display of specimens and descriptive labels.

Goode began to speak and write about museum management. His articles made him widely known in this country and abroad as a thoughtful theorist who was simultaneously working to put his principles into practice at the U.S. National Museum. Under Goode, the museum continued to expand not only its zoological materials but also those in ethnology, anthropology, and history. Always insistent that the traditional and core responsibility of museums to foster research and preserve the "raw materials of science" for future reference be maintained, Goode concentrated much of his discussion on the aspect that he believed needed further attention, namely educational presentations in which the organization of materials and detailed labels explained current, expert interpretation of the specimens and artifacts. Contemporary scientific theories could best be demonstrated, he believed, by using descriptive labels and graphics accessible to a range of people with diverse educational backgrounds. A natural history museum should also be appropriate for its particular audience, and thus he offered no apology for a concentration on American materials even as the museum provided insights from other geographic and cultural areas. In 1895 he delivered the keynote address to the British Museums Association at its annual meeting in Newcastle on "The Principles of Museum Administration" and stressed the responsibility of curators to interpret their holdings for the culture and enlightenment of all people.

Although Goode was a firm administrator, Henry Fairfield Osborn noted that he was so successful in museum work because he "sought out the often-latent best qualities of the men around him and developed them." When Baird died in 1887, Goode was named director of the National Museum, whose range of holdings had vastly expanded in both scale and scope in the decade since the Philadelphia Exposition.

A sustained interest in history can be traced to Goode's early essays on American naturalists and his long-term and substantial genealogical study of the Goode family, *Virginia Cousins: A Study of the Ancestry and Prosperity of John Goode of Whitby, a Virginia Colonial of the Seventeenth Century* (1887). Increasingly interested in the pattern of scientific development in the United States, he gathered materials and wrote a pioneering series on "The Beginnings of Natural History in America" (Biological Society of Washington, *Proceedings* 3 [1884–1886]: 35–105), "The Origins of the National Scientific and Educational Institutions of the United States" (American Historical Association, *Papers* 4 [1890]: 53–161), and related topics covering the period from the nation's earliest exploration by Europeans to the late nineteenth century. His descriptions of prominent scientists and their work, particularly naturalists, were thorough, and he showed a remarkable capacity to discuss their activities in institutional and educational as well as conventional intellectual context. He also collected documents and wrote a massive history of *The Smithsonian Institution, 1846–1896* (1897). As an institution builder himself, he joined in the new American Historical Association, founded in 1884, and arranged to have its headquarters at the Smithsonian; the first reports of the AHA were published under government auspices. He collected history materials for the museum, caring for the memorabilia that accrued from political figures but also gathering the ordinary artifacts of life with the intention, he wrote, of having the children of the 1990s see the toys with which the children of the 1890s had played. He also sought to accommodate contemporary "arts and industries," and many of his collections of late nineteenth-century machinery, electricity, and manufacturing were the basis for the Smithsonian's Museum of Science and Technology (1964), which in 1980 became the Museum of American History.

Goode's vision was eclectic, and he struggled to find ways to manage the large collections that drew on science, technology, art, and history. From a relatively modest collection of about 200,000 items in 1872, the museum grew to more than 3 million items by the time of his death. Although the vision nearly outran the capacity of staff and space, Goode, who remained convinced that museums were an important measure of the civility of a people, believed that the Smithsonian represented the United States. Growth and reinterpretation were therefore essential, and Goode argued that "a finished museum is a dead museum."

By the 1880s Goode's leadership and wide-ranging interests made him a central figure in Washington's growing intellectual and cultural community. His list of affiliations and leadership roles grew longer as he became founding member of the Cosmos Club, served as president of the Biological Society of Washington, held various offices in the Sons of the American Revolution, and participated regularly in the Virginia Historical Society and the Columbian Historical Society of Washington, D.C. Interested in the environment along Rock Creek as it wound its way through the city, he built a home in Lanier Heights near the future site of the National Zoological Park, encouraged the development of roads through the area, and persuaded friends to purchase land and build near him. Brown (as he was known to his friends) enjoyed exploring this natural landscape within the District of Columbia with his family.

An intense, sometimes frenetic man, Goode suffered from many of the ailments common to the men of his generation, reporting bouts of neurasthenia and overwork throughout the course of his career. His death in Washington, D.C., of acute bronchitis, possibly emphysema, at the age of forty-five brought multiple eulogies and published obituaries for a man who Smithsonian secretary Samuel P. Langley remembered as having such remarkable integrity, judgment, and leadership that he could "maintain the discipline of a great establishment like the National Museum while still retaining the personal affection of every subordinate."

• Goode's extensive manuscript collections, which almost exclusively relate to his professional career, are at the Smithsonian Institution Archives. A small collection relating to his genealogical research is at the Virginia Historical Society, and others relating to the 1876 exhibition are in the Manuscript Division of the Library of Congress. His historical essays on museums and science are reprinted in Sally Gregory Kohlstedt, ed., *The Origins of Natural Science in America: The Essays of George Brown Goode* (1991). A complete bibliography of his nearly 400 publications (about a third jointly authored) as well as contemporary eulogies were published as "A Memorial of George Brown Goode" in the *Annual Report of the Board of Regents of the Smithsonian Institution: Report of the U.S. National Museum* for 1897, pt. 2 (1901). On his contributions to museum administration, see Edward P. Alexander, *Museum Masters: Their Museums and Their Influence* (1983), and to historical studies, see Kohlstedt, "History in a Natural History Museum: George Brown Goode and the Smithsonian Institution," *Public Historian* 10, no. 2 (1988): 7–26.

SALLY GREGORY KOHLSTEDT

GOODELL, William (14 Feb. 1792–18 Feb. 1867), missionary and linguist, was born in Templeton, Massachusetts, the son of William Goodell and Phebe Newton, farmers. Goodell's father was too poor to provide an education for his son but recognized that his mind was keen and that his physique was not suited for hard manual labor. Consequently he encouraged Goodell to seek aid from the charity fund at Phillips Academy in Andover. At the age of fifteen he packed all of his belongings and walked sixty miles to Andover, where he so impressed the preceptor John Adams with his first Latin recitation that his financial support was assured and a lifelong bond was created between them.

Learning that the first American foreign missionaries were to be ordained in Salem in February 1812,

Goodell walked in bitter cold from Andover to Salem to attend the service. He entered Dartmouth College, earned money by teaching school, and graduated with an A.M. in 1817. Three years later he graduated from Andover Theological Seminary. There he was active in the Society of Inquiry, a group of students interested in foreign missions. One of them, Asa Thurston, had been appointed to go to Hawaii in 1819 with the first company of missionaries, but he lacked the requisite wife. In his characteristically humorous style Goodell later recalled how he located a distant cousin, Lucy Goodale, introduced her to Thurston, and saw them married just in time for embarkation.

After receiving his license to preach in May 1820, Goodell was asked by the American Board of Commissioners for Foreign Missions to spend a year promoting the cause of missions in America before going overseas. For six months he studied medicine at Dartmouth (a standard preparation for missionary service). He then made a promotional journey to the Midwest, traveled on horseback through Kentucky, Tennessee, and Mississippi, and visited missions to the Choctaw and Cherokee Indians. Thirty-five years later in Turkey he received a letter and a donation from some of the Cherokees; expelled from their homelands by the U.S. government, they had traveled the "Trail of Tears" across the Mississippi and into Oklahoma where they had reestablished their churches.

In 1822 Goodell married Abigail Perkins Davis; they had nine children, one of whom died in childhood. He was ordained and sailed with his wife for Syria, with Jerusalem the intended destination. They arrived in Malta in January 1823 but were prevented by turmoil in Jerusalem from proceeding. For nine months Goodell preached in English and studied languages of the region. He and his wife, with colleagues Isaac and Ann Bird, then established the first Protestant mission in Beirut in November 1823. Mingling with the populace and preaching and distributing literature, Goodell also devoted major effort to the study of the languages used daily with visitors in his home: ancient and modern Greek, ancient and modern Armenian, Turkish Armenian (or Armeno-Turkish—Turkish written with Armenian letters), Arabic, and Italian. His house was plundered in 1828 when the city was attacked by a Greek fleet and Goodell was forced to return to Malta, where he supervised the mission press. In 1831, with assistance in translating from Bishop Dionysius, he published the first version of the Armeno-Turkish New Testament and began work on the Old Testament.

Goodell was then asked to establish a mission in Constantinople (now Istanbul, Turkey), with a special focus on work with the Armenian population. Arriving on 9 June 1831, his wife and two daughters found themselves the first American women in the capital of the empire. Their home and almost all of their possessions were destroyed two months later in one of the city's periodic fires; Goodell escaped narrowly, with his hat on fire. Amidst an alarm about cholera and plague in the village to which they moved, Goodell's wife gave birth to a son, the first American child born in Constantinople. Goodell entered vigorously into the cosmopolitan life of the city, conducting services and using several languages. Although Commodore David Porter, the American charge d'affaires, became a close friend, Goodell opposed the use of political leverage on behalf of the mission, preferring quiet genial diplomacy and friendship. One of his first projects was to plan and encourage the establishment of Lancastrian schools in which the older pupils monitored the younger; before the end of 1831 there were more than twenty, including one for girls in his own home. Because the people formed and supported their own schools, the charge of foreign control was avoided.

Goodell continued his vigorous work on Bible translation. In 1841 he produced an Armeno-Turkish version of the Old Testament directly from the Hebrew with the help of Greek scholar Panayotes Constantinides. Continually revising in an effort to achieve better accuracy and idiom, Goodell published his final version of the entire Bible in 1863.

Goodell believed that Christianity could be expressed through varying forms, with its essential center a personally realized faith in Christ and a devotion to Christ's moral teaching. He cultivated relationships with the ancient Greek and Armenian Orthodox churches and envisaged his mission as strengthening existing currents of reform rather than securing converts to Protestantism. But he was impatient with worships conducted largely in "dead" languages such as ecclesiastical Armenian and Greek unfamiliar to ordinary people, and he objected to emphasis on rituals not clearly derived from the Bible. When those whom the mission encouraged in a less liturgical and more Bible-centered faith were excommunicated by the Armenian patriarch, an Armenian Evangelical church was founded at Constantinople in 1846. A similar development occurred among the Greeks.

During his forty-five years of missionary service Goodell made only one visit to America (1851–1853). He traveled some 20,000 miles in eighteen states, preaching and promoting the cause of missions in more than 400 congregations as well as many educational institutions. Just before returning to Turkey his book *The Old and the New; or, The Changes of Thirty Years in the East* was published.

In 1865 the Goodells retired and returned to America, living in Philadelphia with one of their sons. Goodell died in Philadelphia.

• Correspondence between Goodell and the American Board of Commissioners for Foreign Missions is in the ABCFM papers at Houghton Library, Harvard University. E. D. G. Prime, ed., *Forty Years in the Turkish Empire; or, Memoirs of Rev. William Goodell, D.D.* (1876), is a major resource, consisting largely of extensive quotations from Goodell's journal and his letters, which display his wit and graceful style. Vivid personal reminiscences of Goodell are in *Services at the Seventy-Fifth Anniversary of the Establishment of the American Mission at Constantinople* (n.d.). An extended obituary is in the *Missionary Herald* 63, no. 5 (May 1867): 130–33.

DAVID M. STOWE

GOODELL, William (25 Oct. 1792–14 Feb. 1878), religious reformer, was born in Coventry, New York, the son of Frederick Goodell and Rhoda Guernsey. Goodell's parents were Connecticut natives who became pioneer settlers in upper New York State. During his childhood Goodell suffered a "crippling disease" that kept him bedridden for several years; this confinement resulted in his cultivating a lifelong interest in religious reading and writing. After the death of his parents, Goodell went to live in Pomfret, Connecticut, with his paternal grandmother, a convert of evangelist George Whitefield and an ardent defender of the democratic principles of the American Revolution. Goodell attended common school, but he did not have enough money to attend college. From 1811 to 1827 he held various business positions in Providence, Rhode Island; Wilmington, North Carolina; Alexandria, Virginia; and New York City. He was also a supercargo on a ship to Europe and east Asia. While in Providence, he met and, in 1823, married Clarissa C. Cady; they had two children.

Disillusioned with business, Goodell turned to his interest in writing and became a journalist. In 1827 he began to edit a "general reform" journal in Providence. Goodell crusaded in the paper against various social evils, especially the traffic in and consumption of alcoholic beverages. Goodell moved the paper to New York City in 1830. There, at the center of the "benevolent empire" of voluntaristic reform, he became a leader of the American Temperance Society.

In 1833, partly through the influence of William Lloyd Garrison, Goodell decided to focus his journalistic efforts on antislavery. He helped to organize both the New York City Anti-Slavery Society and the American Anti-Slavery Society (AASS). He was on the AASS Executive Committee and was named editor of the *Emancipator*, the official paper of the AASS. In this position, Goodell influenced public opinion by his forceful articulation of the principles of the abolition movement. He was one of the first reformers to link antislavery with the broader issue of civil rights for African Americans.

Goodell left the *Emancipator* in 1835. The next year he assumed the editorship of the *Friend of Man*, a paper affiliated with the New York State Anti-Slavery Society, based in Utica. There, among the revivalistic activists of the "burned-over district" of upstate New York, Goodell became a leading spokesperson for "political abolitionism," the movement to secure the elimination of slavery through independent political action. Goodell assisted in the 1840 formation of the Liberty party, an abolitionist political alternative to the Whigs and Democrats. He wrote the convention address, which was essentially a party platform, for the Liberty nominating convention in 1841. He also transformed the *Friend of Man* into a campaign sheet for abolitionist candidates; subsequently, upper New York became the strongest region of electoral support for the third party.

In 1842 Goodell resigned from the *Friend of Man* so that he could begin a new paper, the *Christian Investi-*

gator, which was dedicated to "ecclesiastical abolitionism," also known as "antislavery church reform"—the democratic restructuring of Christian congregations. Goodell believed that democracy and evangelical Christianity were natural allies but that denominational hierarchies, like slavery, were despotic and tyrannical. Thus, the reformulation of religious institutions was a necessary corollary to the reformulation of civil institutions. In the same manner that Christians were to withdraw from established political parties in order to organize a purified antislavery political party, so too, Christians were to withdraw from established denominations in order to organize purified antislavery congregations. These independent congregations, Goodell hoped, would unite together in their common commitment to radical social reform and create a "Christian union" among reformers. From 1843 to 1852 Goodell was the unordained pastor of one of these independent antislavery "Union" churches in Honeoye, New York.

In 1847–1848, when the majority of the Liberty party merged into the Free Soil coalition (and then, later, into the Republican party), Goodell became the leader of a minority faction of the Liberty party that fielded candidates until the Civil War. The faction was called by various names: the Liberty League, the Liberty party, and the Radical Abolitionist party. In the decade prior to the war, this rump party was the only political group that continued to advocate for the complete abolition of slavery and equal rights for African Americans. Goodell was the party's nominee for president in 1852 and, in 1860, its candidate for governor of New York. He also authored most of the party platforms. Some of his proposals included the direct election of federal officials, opposition to the Mexican War, civil rights for women and Native Americans, free distribution of public lands, abolition of economic monopolies, and the unconstitutionality of slavery. As early as 1847 Goodell began to see the interrelatedness of reforms due to the systemic connection between various social problems. He argued, for example, that the legal abolition of slavery should not be seen as a panacea, because continuing prejudice and economic deprivation could result in a virtual reenslavement of African Americans after emancipation.

During the 1850s Goodell edited another paper in New York City, the *American Jubilee*, later renamed the *Radical Abolitionist*. In the 1860s this paper became a weekly known as the *Principia*, a medium through which he hoped to press radical views on the Republican party. Specifically, Goodell urged Republicans to view the Civil War as a "Second American Revolution," an opportunity for them to realize long-delayed reform goals in order to create a more egalitarian society. He visited Abraham Lincoln twice in 1862, encouraging the president to make his comments on emancipation explicit regarding the establishment of civil rights for African Americans. "Justice and not merely military necessity," Goodell told Lincoln, should be the unambiguous message in all official pronouncements about the freeing of the slaves.

After the war, Goodell returned once more to the issue of temperance, and he helped to organize the Prohibition party. He and his wife moved to Goshen, Connecticut, in 1865, and later to Janesville, Wisconsin, where he died. Years later, Goodell's grandson William Goodell Frost, president of Berea College, had his remains brought to Berea, Kentucky.

• Goodell's papers, including manuscript sermons and correspondence, are located in the Oberlin College Archives and the library at Berea College. Further information about Goodell is available in the thirteen periodicals that he edited and the sixteen books or tracts that he wrote. Besides the newspapers mentioned above, his most significant writings include *Views of American Constitutional Law in Its Bearing upon American Slavery* (1844); *Come-Outerism, the Duty of Secession from a Corrupt Church* (1845); *The Democracy of Christianity* (1849); and, especially, *Slavery and Anti-Slavery* (1855), his interpretative narrative history of the abolitionist movement. Secondary sources are scarce, but helpful data can be found in M. Leon Perkal, "William Goodell: A Life of Reform" (Ph.D. diss., City Univ. of New York, 1972); Whitney R. Cross, *The Burned-Over District* (1950); James M. McPherson, *The Struggle for Equality* (1964); and Douglas M. Strong, "The Application of Perfectionism to Politics," *Wesleyan Theological Journal* 25 (1990): 21–41. Another good source on Goodell and his contacts in upstate New York is Lawrence J. Friedman, *Gregarious Saints: Self and Community in American Abolitionism, 1830–1870* (1982).

DOUGLAS M. STRONG

GOODENOUGH, Florence Laura (6 Aug. 1886–4 Apr. 1959), developmental psychologist, was born in Honesdale, Pennsylvania, the daughter of Linus North Goodenough and Alice Gertrude Day, farmers. Considered intellectually gifted early on, she attended a rural school in Rileyville, Pennsylvania. In 1908 she received a B.Pd. from Millersville (Pa.) Normal School.

Goodenough completed a bachelor of science degree in 1920 and a master's degree at Columbia University in 1921. While studying at Columbia, she served as director of research in the Rutherford and Perth Amboy (N.J.) Public Schools from 1919 to 1921. In 1924 she received a Ph.D. in psychology from Stanford University, where she assisted Lewis M. Terman, an authority on mental measurement, with his well-known studies of giftedness in children. She and Terman continued to collaborate throughout their careers, sharing views on intelligence and other seminal issues in psychology and education.

Goodenough relocated to Minnesota in 1925 to fill the position of chief psychologist of the Minneapolis Child Guidance Clinic. She joined the faculty of the University of Minnesota's newly established Institute of Child Welfare as an assistant professor in 1925 and was promoted to full professor in 1931. Throughout her career she was involved in developmental research as well as teaching and advising graduate students.

One of Goodenough's most enduring contributions to the field of developmental psychology is the Draw-a-Man Test (1926) developed from her doctoral dissertation, "Measurement of Intelligence by Drawings."

Standardized on hundreds of participants, the test purportedly assessed intellectual ability in children ages three to thirteen. The measure used children's drawings of a male figure and evaluated concept formation reflected in the presence and interrelationship of body parts in the drawings. The foundation of this work was Goodenough's interest in individual differences in intelligence and her own belief that the complexity of human figure drawings increases with development and in relation to intellectual ability. Her research with the measure suggested significant individual differences by age and ability, but more recent psychologists guard against its use as an index of intelligence. The Draw-a-Man Test, later revised by Goodenough's colleague Dale Harris, has been used worldwide and is now titled the Goodenough-Harris Drawing Test (1963).

Goodenough also maintained a particular interest in evaluating young children's intelligence. For this purpose, she designed the Minnesota Preschool Scale (1932, 1940, 1942), which assesses mental abilities. With Katherine Maurer, she contributed to *The Mental Growth of Children from Two to Fourteen Years* (1942) and to the notion that measured intelligence during early childhood may not be predictive of later assessments of mental abilities. This finding contradicted earlier widely held assumptions that intelligence remains stable across the life span.

Commentary on potential methodological innovations in empirical research was a common feature of Goodenough's work. Throughout her career, Goodenough was critical of the methodological designs of many of the studies conducted in the burgeoning field of developmental psychology. She contributed to numerous articles and a book, *Experimental Child Study* (1931) with John E. Anderson, to illustrate methodological problems and to suggest advancements within child psychology research. One such advancement suggested episode-sampling to acquire knowledge of children's behavioral characteristics. Goodenough's seminal study of emotional development, *Anger in Young Children*, exemplifies her pioneering methodology. Evaluating the systematic records maintained by mothers of preschool children, Goodenough devised a coding scheme to categorize young children's behavior and subjected her findings to rigorous statistical analysis.

Goodenough's *Developmental Psychology* (1934) was widely used and translated into several foreign languages. Through this work and "The Development of Human Behavior" (*Acta Psychologica*, 1935), she illustrated the importance of studying the chronology of developmental stages, the influences of individual differences, and the significance of examining development through adolescence and beyond.

During the 1930s and 1940s scholars engaged in passionate debates regarding intelligence tests, identifying both environmental and inherent factors that influence mental abilities. Goodenough led rigorous empirical evaluations to guard against the misuse of IQ measures and with Lewis Terman argued against claims that specific environments directly contribute to mental ability. This work drew her into a heated controversy with Beth Wellman, George Stoddard, and others at the University of Iowa concerning heredity and environmental influences on the development of intelligence. Goodenough argued against their claims that a child's environment, specifically nursery school attendance and an enriched home, substantially raises IQ, and she was highly critical of their statistical procedures and research methods.

Goodenough was invited to speak nationally on mental measurement and was regarded as an authority. She wrote numerous evaluative conference reports for the National Research Council and the White House Conferences on Children and Youth (1929–1946). She also contributed to the highly regarded *Handbook of Child Psychology* (1931, 1933, 1946). The controversy over the extent to which heredity and the environment influence intelligence, however, continues to be contested among scholars.

Goodenough won many honors and participated in numerous professional organizations. She was a noted scientist in *American Men of Science* (1936), indicative of her outstanding contributions when few women were bestowed this honor. She also served as president of the newly formed National Council of Women Psychologists in 1942. Elected president of the Society for Research in Child Development, she served from 1945 to 1947. She also held the position of secretary and president of the Division on Childhood and Adolescence of the American Psychological Association (1947–1948).

Goodenough's novel research in the areas of social and intellectual development and her pioneering observational studies of child behavior have greatly influenced experimental child study. Her work in the area of anger and aggression in young children is noted throughout the social behavior literature. Her methodological advancements continue to be recognized as influencing observational studies of children's social development. She has been described by Willard W. Hartup as an "innovator of the first magnitude in the observational study of child behavior. Her work on social development in addition to the work on intelligence has been of lasting value and remains cited as one of her most significant contributions."

Despite chronic diabetes, deafness, and near blindness, Goodenough remained as full professor at the University of Minnesota's Institute of Child Welfare until 1947. Upon retirement, she spent summers in Lisbon, New Hampshire, and winters in Lakeland, Florida, where she died. At her death, her vast library of scholarly works was left to the University of Minnesota. A reference room, established in her honor, provides students and faculty at the Institute of Child Development with exceptional resources.

Goodenough never married, devoting her life to her work. As her colleague Dale Harris recalled, "Florence Goodenough took the term 'child welfare' seriously. She felt strongly an obligation to return the results of science to the parents of children who had served as subjects" (Society for Research in Child Development, Fiftieth Anniversary Meeting, Mar. 1983). Her's insights into children's development and methodological advancements in the areas of observational and experimental child study continue to be cited throughout the child development literature.

• Personal papers and materials relating to Goodenough are in the University of Minnesota Archives. A complete collection of her works is available in the University of Minnesota Library. In addition to works noted above, she wrote *Your Child Year by Year*, with John E. Anderson (1930); *Developmental Psychology* (1934); "Measurement of Mental Growth in Childhood," in *Manual of Child Psychology*, ed. Leonard Carmichael (1946); *Mental Testing, Its History, Principles, and Applications* (1949); and *Exceptional Children* (1956). Her tests also include the Free Association Test (1940). Annotated bibliographies of her works from 1925 to 1947 are in *Publications of the Faculty of the University of Minnesota*. A tribute to Goodenough at the time of her death appeared in *Child Development* 30 (1959): 305–6.

CATHERINE LAWRENCE

GOODENOW, John Milton (1782–20? July 1838), Ohio jurist and congressman, was born in Westmoreland, Cheshire County, New Hampshire, the son of Nahum Goodenow. His mother's name is unknown. After a common-school education, he taught school and studied law in New Hampshire and, for a spell in 1803–1804, in New York and New Jersey. In 1805 or 1806 he moved to Wiscasset, Maine, where he failed in mercantile business about 1808 and then worked in various public offices. In September 1812 he moved to Steubenville, Ohio, where he studied law with John C. Wright, gained admission to the bar in August 1813, and began practice. In the same year he married Wright's sister, Sarah Lucy Wright Campbell. An opponent of the regular Jeffersonian Republicans, Goodenow was rejected as county prosecuting attorney through the influence of another relation by marriage, Benjamin Tappan, but was appointed collector of internal revenue in 1817.

Later that year Tappan, as president judge of the state district court, ruled that crimes under English common law could be punished in Ohio even in the absence of statutory legislation. Goodenow vehemently objected but found that few local lawyers agreed with him, and so he wrote, in eight weeks, a scholarly book of more than 430 pages, *Historical Sketches of the Principles and Maxims of American Jurisprudence, in Contrast with the Doctrine of English Common Law on the Subject of Crimes and Punishments*, and paid to have sixty copies printed in Steubenville in 1819. None were sold, and few copies reached law libraries, but the copies Goodenow distributed helped to persuade legal opinion in Ohio that only crimes defined by statute can be punished by the courts.

Fellow lawyer Charles Hammond had long considered Goodenow "a man of very infirm and peevish temper of mind, more tormenting to himself than to any body," and Goodenow now pursued Tappan with "a malignity of the most fiendlike character, . . . with a spirit of active, incessant, unrelenting bitterness." He tried unsuccessfully to have Tappan impeached by the legislature, then brought a case against him for slanderously claiming nearly seven years before that Goodenow had escaped from jail in New England and disguised himself in Ohio under a new name. Awarded $600 damages, Goodenow was elected to the general assembly in 1823, but the members held him "very cheap" for his vindictive behavior (Hammond to Wright, 15 Dec. 1822, 7 Jan. 1824, Hammond papers, Ohio Historical Society). He was defeated for reelection in 1824 despite advocating the political rights of unnaturalized aliens, who were numerous in his locality.

In the 1824 presidential election, Goodenow had initially favored a northern, non–slave-owning candidate like De Witt Clinton, but he soon recognized Andrew Jackson's popularity among local Scotch-Irish voters. Becoming "Jackson up to the hub," with "Jackson snuff, Jackson punch, Jackson whiskey" (Elisha Whittlesey to John McLean, 31 Aug. 1826, McLean papers, Library of Congress), Goodenow ran for Congress in 1826, assailing the incumbent, his brother-in-law Wright, for voting against Jackson in the 1825 House election. In a skillful anonymous pamphlet, *The Voice of the People*, he argued that "the *right of instruction*, and the *responsibility of public servants* have been disregarded, abandoned and set at nought by those who had the immediate agency in making Mr. Adams president." Goodenow narrowly lost in 1826 but won in the Andrew Jackson sweep of 1828.

Goodenow's real ambition, however, was for federal judicial preferment. "Being poor," he thought this proved him not such "an odd fellow" as his neighbors said (Goodenow to Robert Todd Lytle, 10 Sept. 1828, Lytle papers, Cincinnati Historical Society). He was appointed justice of the state supreme court in February 1830, which entailed his resignation from Congress during his first session there, but ill health forced him to give up the judgeship within a few weeks. He then purchased a farm in Bloomfield, Trumbull County, but "restless, peevish and dissatisfied," he moved to Cincinnati in the spring of 1832 to practice law (*Western Law Monthly* 5:176). In January 1833 he was appointed president judge of the local state judicial circuit, but almost immediately he fell into an undefying dispute over the appointment of the clerk of the court. Alienating the Cincinnati bar by his sensitivity to criticism, he resigned in November 1834 and set up practice in the spring of 1835 in St. Clairsville, where he spoke out against Ohio's highly popular efforts to acquire the Toledo area.

A devoted family man, Goodenow apparently married a second time; he had a daughter by each marriage. Disappointed at his failure to secure further preferment, Goodenow migrated to Texas in November 1837 but, "unsuccessful and unfortunate," decided to return to Ohio in the summer of 1838, leaving his wife behind. Taken sick en route, some later accounts claim that Goodenow died shortly after reaching Cincinnati. However, contemporary reports state that he died in New Orleans, and his remains were shipped to Cincinnati (*Western Law Monthly* 5:177; *Columbus Ohio Statesman*, 24 July 1838).

Generous and free in his habits, Goodenow was remembered as "a fine classical scholar, perhaps too much of a student for a politician, if not for a lawyer" (J. A. Caldwell, *History of Belmont and Jefferson Counties, Ohio* [1880], p. 439). Hammond thought Goodenow brought troubles on his own head by his "fretful and jaundiced temperament of mind" and his paranoid suspicion of persecution (*Daily Cincinnati Gazette*, 28 Apr. 1834). Ill health plainly contributed to his problems and ensured that this unhappy and somewhat strange man never fulfilled his promise in any field, despite his significant legal contribution.

• The main sources on Goodenow are his own publications relating to the various legal disputes in which he was involved. Details of his early life can be deduced from testimony in *Minutes of the Proceedings and Trial, in the Case of John Milton Goodenow vs. Benjamin Tappan, for Defamation* (1822). He is self-revealing in his introductions to his valuable pamphlets, *A Review of the Question whether the Common Law of England Is in Force in the State of Ohio* (1817) and the detailed *Historical Record of the Proceedings of the Court of Common Pleas and 'the Bar' of Hamilton County, Ohio, in Reference to the Appointment of Clerk of Said Court, 1833 and 1834* (1834). See also *Letter of the Hon. John M. Goodenow, on the Subject of the Northern Boundary of Ohio* (1835). His legal contribution is discussed in the anonymous "Sketch of John Milton Goodenow," *Western Law Monthly* 5 (1863): 169–79, and in William T. Utter, "Ohio and the English Common Law," *Mississippi Valley Historical Review* 16 (1929): 321–33. Goodenow's relationship with Tappan and his political outlook are insightfully discussed in Daniel Feller, "Benjamin Tappan: The Making of a Democrat," in *The Pursuit of Public Power: Political Culture in Ohio, 1787–1861*, ed. Jeffrey P. Brown and Andrew R. L. Cayton (1994), pp. 69–82.

DONALD J. RATCLIFFE

GOODHART, Arthur Lehman (1 Mar. 1891–10 Nov. 1978), lawyer and educator, was born in New York City, the son of Philip J. Goodhart and Hattie Lehman. He attended the Hotchkiss School in Connecticut and in 1912 earned his A.B. from Yale. The remainder of his formal education took place in the United Kingdom, beginning with his M.A. and LL.B. from Cambridge, both awarded in 1914. Goodhart was also awarded an LL.M. (1926), an LL.D. (1931), and eventually a D.Litt. (1969), all from Cambridge, as well as a D.C.L. from Oxford (1931).

Upon completion of his law degree at Cambridge, Goodhart returned to the United States and was admitted to the New York bar. His first position was that of assistant corporation counsel of New York City from 1915 to 1917. During U.S. participation in the First World War, Goodhart served as a captain in the Ordnance Department of the U.S. Army. Immediately following the war he was appointed by President Woodrow Wilson as counsel to the American fact-finding mission to Poland (1919).

Goodhart was made barrister at law of the Inner Temple, England, in 1919. The majority of his career thenceforth would be focused on the practice and teaching of law in the United Kingdom. His first post, which he assumed in 1919, was as fellow and lecturer in law at Corpus Christi College, Cambridge.

He edited the *Cambridge Law Journal* in 1921 and was named the editor of the *Law Quarterly Review* in 1926, a position he held until 1975. In 1929 he became a visiting professor at Yale and an associate fellow of Jonathan Edwards College at that institution.

In 1924 he married Cecily M. Carter. The couple had three sons: Philip Goodhart would serve as a member of Parliament, William Howard Goodhart would become a barrister associated with Lincoln's Inn, and Charles Albert Eric Goodhart would become an economist with the Bank of England.

After twelve years at Cambridge, in 1937 Goodhart was named a fellow and professor and awarded a chair of jurisprudence of University College, Oxford. He was decorated knight commander of the Order of the British Empire in 1948. In 1951 he became the first American named master of a college (University College) at Oxford.

During his teaching career Goodhart also held visiting professorships at Harvard Law School (1964), the University of Virginia Law School (1965), and McGill University Law School (1966). He was scholar in residence of the New York City Bar Association (1966–1967). In British academe he served as a delegate to Oxford University Press (1942), was appointed a fellow of Nuffield College, Oxford (1944), was admitted to the British Academy (1952), and was appointed curator at the Bodleian Library, Oxford (1947). Goodhart served in British government-related positions as chair of the Southern Region Price Regulation Committee (1940–1948) and as a member of the Lord Chancellor's Law Revision committee (1937), the Monopolies Commission (1954–1957), the Royal Commission to the Police (1960), and the Scottish Constitution committee (1969). For the police commission, Goodhart participated in composing the final report, which included his dissenting memorandum arguing for a national police force. Other offices held by Goodhart included chair of the International Law Association, vice president of the Société International de Philosophie du Droit, and president of the International Association of University Professors. He held additional memberships in the American Law Institute, Phi Beta Kappa, Alpha Delta Phi, and the Académie de France. Goodhart was also presented with numerous honorary degrees from both American and British universities.

His writings in the field of law and jurisprudence were numerous and wide ranging. The first publication that brought Goodhart to the attention of Anglo-American legal scholars was his landmark law review article, titled "Determining the Ratio Decidendi of a Case." This article is still cited widely in subject-related American law journals. Goodhart died in London.

• Goodhart's own works include *Poland and the Minority Races* (1920), *The General Strike* (1927), *Essays in Jurisprudence and the Common Law* (1931), *Precedent in English and Continental Law* (1934), *What Acts of War Are Justifiable* (1941), *English Contributions to the Philosophy of Law* (1949), *Five Jewish Lawyers of the Common Law* (1950), and *English Law and the Moral Law* (1953). He coedited, with H. G. Hanbury, Sir William Searle Holdsworth's *Essays in Law and History* (1946; repr. 1995) and *A History of English Law* (17 vols., editions vary, 1936 to 1972). Goodhart's memorial address for Holdsworth, titled *Sir William Searle Holdsworth, O. M., 1871–1944*, was also published (1954). He selected essays and provided an introduction for another book, Sir Frederic Pollock's *Jurisprudence and Legal Essays* (1961). Goodhart's more notable law review articles include "Determining the Ratio Decidendi of a Case," *Yale Law Journal* 40 (1930): 161; "The Brief Life Story of the Direct Consequences Rule in English Tort Law," *Virginia Law Review* 53 (1967): 857; "Blackmail and Consideration in Contracts," *Legal Quarterly Review* 44 (1928): 436; "Trespass and Negligence," *Legal Quarterly Review* 49 (1932): 359; "Lincoln and the Law," *American Bar Association Journal* 50 (1964): 433; "The Rule of Law and Absolute Sovereignty," *University of Pennsylvania Law Review* 106 (1958): 943; and "Costs," *Yale Law Journal* 38 (1929): 849. Goodhart had numerous letters printed in the *New York Times* concerning various political and legal issues of the day, among which are those of 8 Aug. 1974, 9 Apr. 1975, 16 Oct. 1976, and 8 Jan. 1977. An obituary is in the *New York Times*, 11 Nov. 1978.

BARRY RYAN

GOODHUE, Bertram Grosvenor (28 Apr. 1869–23 Apr. 1924), architect, was born in Pomfret, Connecticut, the son of Charles Wells Goodhue, a country gentleman, and Helen Grosvenor Eldredge. In 1884 he entered the New York architectural firm of Renwick, Aspinwall and Russell as an apprentice; he never attended college nor did he have formal architectural training. His first independent design was for the competition for the Cathedral of St. John the Divine, New York (1889). By 1891 he was working with Ralph Adams Cram, advocate of the Gothic revival style, and in the following year he formed the partnership Cram, Goodhue, and Ferguson. The firm, based in Boston, built churches, residences, and libraries in various revival styles—Gothic, Renaissance, Tudor, Greek, and Spanish. During this time Goodhue developed relationships with historians of medieval culture Charles Eliot Norton and Charles Herbert Moore at Harvard University; these men helped form Goodhue's notion of the Middle Ages.

Throughout his career, Goodhue was involved in publishing. In 1891 he did the drawings for Cram's *Church Building* and in 1901 the drawings for Silvester Baxter's *Spanish Colonial Architecture in Mexico*. He also designed title pages, decorations, and initials; invented the typeface known as Merrymount for *The Altar Book of the Episcopal Church* (1896); and designed the Cheltenham typeface (before 1904). Cram and Goodhue published a quarterly, the *Knight Errant*, linked to the English arts and crafts movement in the 1890s. Following his trip to Mexico in 1891, Goodhue published *Mexican Memories* (1892). Between 1896 and 1899 he prepared drawings and descriptions of fictive places —"Traumburg," "The Villa Fosca and Its Garden," and "Monteventosa"—which were published in 1914. In 1902 Goodhue visited Persia and was influenced by the exotic art he saw there; that same year he married Lydia Thompson Bryant, with whom he had two children. Goodhue's Boston experiences show his wide-ranging curiosity, eclectic talents, strong imagination, and love of the exotic, the romantic, and the beautiful.

The commission for the campus plan and additions for the United States Military Academy at West Point (1903–1910) marked a new stage in Goodhue's career. Goodhue opened a branch office in New York, where he became progressively independent of Cram until the dissolution of their partnership in 1913. His design for the Cadet Chapel at West Point, characterized by the use of a Gothic architectural vocabulary, is exemplary of the kind of work for which the New York office acquired a reputation in church building. Its two most successful projects were St. Thomas's Church, New York (1905–1913) and the Chapel of the Intercession in Trinity Cemetery, New York (1910–1914). In 1914 architectural critic C. Matlock Price described the latter as "a sort of Gothic at once rugged and refined; virile and massive without being heavy, and delicate without being trivial—and essentially scholarly without being archeological" (*Architectural Record*, June 1914). But Goodhue was outgrowing the Gothic style. In a letter of 1913 he wrote about St. Thomas's that "although I did the best that in me lay, it was always with the rather mournful conviction that to rival the past in this fashion could never result in anything but comparative failure" (29 Oct. 1913, Avery Library Archive).

Although Goodhue was deeply impressed by Giles Gilbert Scott's Gothic revival project for Liverpool Cathedral, which he saw on a trip to England in 1913, and although he continued to design in Gothic style (most notably, St. Vincent Ferrer, New York, 1914–1918) he was moving in new directions. He had already begun to experiment with Romanesque and Byzantine features in his 1909 project for the campus of Rice Institute in Houston, and his work for the Panama-California Exposition in San Diego (1911–1915) has been seen as launching the Spanish revival style in California. The influence of historian and architect W. R. Lethaby, with whom Goodhue claimed friendship in 1915 but whose books he probably knew much earlier, helps account for the increasing importance of Byzantine and Romanesque sources for his work. Yet Goodhue's design for St. Bartholomew's Church, New York (1914–1919) reveals that this expansion of historical referents was, more fundamentally, a search for an architecture of monumental spaces enclosed in stripped-down, geometric masses in which stylized ornament was closely integrated with tectonic forms. As head of one of the leading architectural firms in the country, his work between 1914 and 1919 (on the East and West coasts and in Hawaii) reveals his sensitivity to the regional vernacular in both style and material. But at the same time that his work showed greater variation from project to project, he also developed a personal vision of architectural form that would characterize his final period.

The works that best reflect his last style are the National Academy of Sciences Building, Washington, D.C. (1919–1924), the Nebraska State Capitol in Lincoln (1920–1932), and the proposal for the Liberty Memorial in Kansas City, Missouri (1921). Talbot Hamlin caught the essence of this style when, describing the project for the Liberty Memorial in 1925, he wrote: "It is the mass composition that dominates; a mass conceived with a tremendous sense of climax, so that the whole has an austere and tragic emotionalism characteristic only of very great art" (*Nation*, 10 June 1925, p. 661). Indeed, these last works embody an equilibrium between opposing qualities. The mass and space express purity, calm, reason, and objective order, while the optical impression of these works, richly textured and colored, suffused with symbolic imagery, and overtly dramatic, conveys Goodhue's personal image of sensuous beauty.

Despite the many tributes to him after his death from a heart attack in New York City, and although he was posthumously awarded the Gold Medal by the American Institute of Architects in 1925, by 1927 he was already seen as an old-fashioned architect whose works represented "not a transition but a tardy compromise" between traditional forms and modernism. As Fiske Kimball assessed him in the *Architectural Record* (1927): "In the final estimate of Goodhue's work there must be taken into account, beside the intrinsic quality of his works, the question of leadership. We must recognize that in the great movements on the stage of the world he made but a dilatory entrance, and that his steps were halting and uncertain. Essentially he was a belated romanticist and eclectic." Kimball is right: Goodhue was not a pioneer in modern architecture. Only in the postmodern period have scholars reevaluated his contribution in terms not only of their intrinsic quality, but also of their cultural significance. Goodhue's unusual facility as a draftsman made him an architects' architect, and the complexity of his creative process, in which historical references, personal vision, and objective principles of design vied among themselves, make him an interesting, if elusive, artistic personality.

• The main repository of documents regarding Goodhue (letters and drawings) is in the Avery Architectural and Fine Arts Library at Columbia University. The Department of Architecture at the University of Nebraska has a special collection devoted to Goodhue. A bibliography of works by and about Goodhue was published by Lamia Doumato, *Bertram Grosvenor Goodhue, 1869–1924* (1981). The classic study of his life and work is a volume of essays about and tributes to Goodhue edited by Charles Harris Whitaker in 1925, *Bertram Grosvenor Goodhue, Architect and Master of Many Arts*, 2d ed. (1976). A full-scale monograph on the architect by Richard Oliver, *Bertram Grosvenor Goodhue* (1983), includes a list of all of Goodhue's projects. The only book-length monograph on one of his buildings is Christine Smith, *St. Bartholomew's Church in the City of New York* (1988). An obituary is in the *New York Times*, 24 Apr. 1924.

CHRISTINE SMITH

GOODLOE, William Cassius (27 June 1841–10 Nov. 1889), lawyer and politician, was born in Madison County, Kentucky, the son of David Short Goodloe, a merchant, and Sallie Ann Lewis Clay Smith. He attended Transylvania College but withdrew in his senior year. When his great-uncle, Cassius Marcellus Clay, was appointed minister to Russia, Goodloe accompanied him as secretary of legation (Sept. 1861–May 1862). Upon returning to Kentucky, Goodloe joined the Union army with the rank of captain and was assigned to recruit volunteers. Injured by a fall from his horse, he resigned his commission in June 1864 and began the study of law. He was admitted to the Kentucky bar later that year and became a prominent defense lawyer. In 1865 Goodloe married Mary E. Mann of Mannville, Rhode Island. The marriage produced eight children.

Goodloe joined with Benjamin H. Bristow, James Speed, and Curtis F. Burnam to organize the Republican party in Kentucky. Aware of the paucity of Republican newspapers, he began publication of the *Kentucky Statesman* in Lexington in January 1867. In addition to reporting state and national news, the paper urged Kentuckians to forget the war and accept the Fourteenth and Fifteenth amendments to the Constitution.

Goodloe ran for the state house of representatives in 1867 but was defeated. The next year he was elected a delegate to the Republican National Convention, where he supported the nomination of Ulysses S. Grant. He was elected to the state house of representatives in 1871 and worked to promote better relations with the federal government. In 1872 he helped arrange the visit to Louisville of Russian grand duke Alexis. Although he had misgivings about the renomination of Grant in 1872, Goodloe campaigned for him. In 1873 he was elected to the state senate but lost his party's nomination for U.S. senator. As a state senator, Goodloe promoted the concept of the New South. After working unsuccessfully for the nomination of Bristow at the Republican National Convention of 1876, he actively supported the nomination and election of Rutherford B. Hayes. President Hayes appointed him minister to Belgium, and he served in this post from 1878 to 1880. As head of the Republican Oratorical Bureau after his return to Kentucky, Goodloe devoted himself to building up the Republican party in the state. In 1888 he helped establish in Lexington a new Republican newspaper, the *Kentucky Leader*. In return for his support of Benjamin Harrison (1833–1901) in the 1888 presidential election, Goodloe was appointed collector of internal revenue for the Lexington district in 1889.

In a strongly Democratic state, many of Goodloe's political positions were unpopular. Additionally, his arrogant and vitriolic manner of speaking antagonized many Republicans as well as Democrats. Among Republicans hostile to Goodloe was Armstead M. Swope, who had lost his position as collector of the Seventh Kentucky District through Goodloe's efforts. When the two men met at the Lexington post office they exchanged words, and Swope shot Goodloe in the abdomen. Pulling out a Bowie knife given him by his great-uncle, Goodloe then mortally wounded Swope. Goodloe died of his wounds, insisting that Swope had made the first move. The press eulogized Goodloe as a "man of high courage and spirit" with "irreproachable integrity." Goodloe was a man of principle who believed that the time had come for Kentucky to move forward by accepting the results of the Civil War; possessing a "logical, convincing, and brilliant mind," he courageously argued the cause of the New South in Kentucky.

• Isolated letters as well as two Civil War scrapbooks containing newspaper clippings and speeches of Goodloe are in Special Collections, Margaret I. King Library, University of Kentucky. The Benjamin H. Bristow Papers at the Library of Congress contain correspondence between Bristow and Goodloe. The best account of Goodloe's life is in Robert Peter, *History of Fayette County, Kentucky, with an Outline Sketch of the Blue Grass Region*, ed. William H. Perrin (1882), pp. 606–12. The Swope-Goodloe tragedy is discussed in L. F. Johnson, *Famous Kentucky Tragedies and Trials* (1916), pp. 282–91.

ROSS A. WEBB

GOODMAN, Benny (30 May 1909–13 June 1986), jazz musician and bandleader, was born Benjamin David Goodman in Chicago, the son of David Goodman, a garment worker, and Dora Rezinsky. His parents were Jewish immigrants from East Europe, and Goodman was raised in near poverty in Chicago's Jewish enclave.

In the years after 1907 the United States was swept by a fad for social dancing, which was creating a startling demand for musicians. Sensing an opportunity, Goodman's father encouraged his younger sons to take up instruments. At ten, Goodman began to study the clarinet, probably because it suited his size, at a local synagogue, and he went on to study at Hull-House, the famous settlement house. He proved to be gifted and came to the attention of Franz Schoepp, a renowned clarinet teacher, who gave him the basis of a sound technique, rare among jazz musicians at the time, most of whom were self-taught or had been instructed by relatively unskilled bandsmen.

Goodman was first influenced by clarinetist Ted Lewis, a commercial musician cashing in on the jazz craze, but he quickly began to model himself on the better early jazz musicians, such as Larry Shields of the very popular Original Dixieland Jazz Band. By the age of thirteen Goodman was beginning to get professional jobs, and at fourteen he dropped out of school to become a full-time musician. He quickly acquired a reputation among musicians as a player who could read, was technically adept, and could play good hot jazz. In 1925, at sixteen, he was asked to join the Ben Pollack orchestra, one of the new school of hot dance bands working from written arrangements. The group would include some to-be-famous jazz musicians, like Jack Teagarden and Bud Freeman, and soon became nationally popular as one of the hottest new dance bands.

Goodman began his recording career with Pollack in 1926, and through the next years he recorded frequently with Pollack, with other leaders as a sideman, and under his own name. These first recordings show that even as a teenager Goodman was a masterful improviser, always hot and swinging, and technically one of the most adroit instrumentalists in jazz. Typical solos from this period are "Waitin' for Katie," with Pollack, and "That's a Plenty," with his own trio, a pick-up group. Occasionally Goodman played solos on various of the saxophones, but although he was a competent section saxophonist, he was not an impressive soloist on the instrument.

In 1929 Goodman left Pollack after a personality clash and began to freelance full-time, making hundreds of radio broadcasts and scores of recordings. At first he was extremely successful, but, partly because of the depression, which badly hurt the recording industry, and partly because of his at times abrasive temperament, his earnings sagged.

For some while he had had it in mind to start his own band. The year 1934 was not auspicious for such a venture because hard times had closed many dance halls and cabarets. But some hot bands, like Casa Loma, were succeeding, and, given his freelance problems, it seemed a good course. Goodman put together a band to audition for a new club, Billy Rose's Music Hall in New York City. The band was chosen to open in the spring, and although the group was not properly rehearsed and lacked enough good arrangements, it hung on to the job.

In the fall the club closed. Fortunately, the National Biscuit Company was about to sponsor a three-hour national Saturday night radio show to be called "Let's Dance." By luck, the Goodman band was chosen for the show. It was, Goodman said later, "the biggest thing that ever happened to me." Not only was the band well paid, but there was a substantial allowance for arrangements, which permitted Goodman to build up the band's book. Furthermore, he now had a number of important musicians, including Gene Krupa and Bunny Berigan as well as lesser-known but excellent musicians like guitarist Allen Reuss and saxophonists Toots Mondello and Art Rollini. A valuable addition was vocalist Helen Ward, an alluring young woman with a lilting style.

Credit has often been given to Fletcher Henderson for creating the arrangements that made Goodman famous. Yet Goodman did not begin buying from Henderson immediately; the bulk of the band's early writing was done by Lyle "Spud" Murphy and others. However, very soon Henderson began contributing, and his pieces like "King Porter Stomp" and "Down South Camp Meeting" were among Goodman's early

hits. Other important arrangers were Horace Henderson, Jimmy Mundy, and Edgar Sampson, who wrote two of Goodman's most famous hits, "Don't Be That Way" and "Stompin' at the Savoy."

The "Let's Dance" program ended in May 1935, but it had brought Goodman to the attention of the music industry. He signed with MCA (Music Corporation of America), and, after a few unsuccessful bookings, in the summer of 1935 the band set out for a cross-country tour of one-nighters. When audience response was mixed, a discouraged Goodman was thinking of junking the group. But when it arrived at the Palomar Ballroom in Los Angeles, audience response, whetted by the "Let's Dance" show and the first records, was overwhelming. Goodman's orchestra was suddenly in demand. It is unclear why the band had its first great success at the Palomar engagement. Apparently some West Coast disc jockeys had been playing some of Goodman's early records; but it may simply have been that the few extra weeks the band had spent touring allowed a taste for his music to develop.

Not long before the cross-country tour, Goodman had jammed at a party with a drummer and with black pianist Teddy Wilson, already a consummate jazz musician. People at the party were enthusiastic, and shortly Goodman recorded some trio sides with Wilson and his regular drummer, Gene Krupa. The trio recordings proved to be popular, and in December 1935, as the band was playing in Chicago, the question of presenting the group live arose. Goodman was initially reluctant, for the United States was still largely racially segregated. However, he was persuaded by supporters to try the experiment at an informal concert. There were no objections, and soon Goodman expanded the trio to the Goodman Quartet, with the addition of another black musician, vibraphonist Lionel Hampton. Further expansion of the group to a quintet and then a sextet brought in more blacks, like Cootie Williams and Charlie Christian. Although the big dance band was the mainstay of the operation, the small groups played increasingly larger roles over time. All of these small group records are at a very high level; Goodman plays particularly fine solos in "Sweet Sue" and "Gone with What Draft." The Goodman small groups were exceedingly important to jazz, for not only did they produce superlative music, but they broke a major color barrier; and it is the opinion of some people, including Lionel Hampton, that these interracial groups paved the way for bringing down color bars in sports and other areas of American life.

Meanwhile, the success of the Palomar engagement produced an upswelling of interest in what was now being called "swing." Other leaders rushed in to emulate Goodman's success, and bands already in existence, like Casa Loma and Duke Ellington, were swept along in the wave. Jimmy Dorsey and Tommy Dorsey, Artie Shaw, Count Basie, Jimmie Lunceford, Glenn Miller, and many more became famous and wealthy. Not all swing music was good jazz; a great deal of it was built around the singing by good-looking young "boy" and "girl" singers of light, popular songs. But in the mix were a lot of driving hot numbers, with solos by the best jazz musicians of the time. Featuring trumpeter Harry James and Krupa, the Goodman band was one of the best and remained at or near the top in popularity through the swing period. It had big hits with "Bugle Call Rag," "One O'Clock Jump," and especially "Sing, Sing, Sing" featuring Krupa. It must be said, however, that not everybody enjoyed playing with the band. Goodman was a demanding leader and could be insensitive to the feelings of his musicians. Many of his sidemen grew to dislike him.

The band reached a peak of popularity during a 1937 engagement at the Paramount Theater in New York, when attendance records were broken and his fans jitterbugged in the aisles, to much publicity. Then, in 1938, the Goodman orchestra presented a concert of swing at Carnegie Hall. Jazz was still seen by most as a low form of music, and the juxtaposition of swing and the august concert hall caught the imagination of music fans. The recording of the concert remains one of the bestselling of all jazz albums.

In 1942 Goodman married Alice Hammond Duckworth, a woman from a wealthy and socially prominent family connected to the Vanderbilts. She was the sister of John Hammond (1910–1987), an important jazz critic and record producer, who had befriended Goodman early in his career. The Goodmans had two daughters.

In the early 1940s Goodman, growing bored with the style that had made him famous, worked with Eddie Sauter and other innovative arrangers, who created thick-textured pieces like "Superman" and "Clarinet à la King," which used unusual forms and advanced harmonies. (Goodman was exempt from the draft because of serious back problems that began in the late 1930s.) But the swing band period was nearly over. By 1946 most of the swing bands were giving up, Goodman's along with the others.

In 1947 Goodman tried again, in time hiring a number of young modernists involved with the new bebop movement, among them Red Rodney and Wardell Gray. The experiment was short-lived, and Goodman never had a permanent band again. He would, however, put together groups, both small and large, to play occasional concerts and tours. The best-remembered of these was a 1962 tour of the Soviet Union, which gained a great deal of publicity but was not entirely satisfying musically to serious jazz fans because of Goodman's insistence on playing the old 1930s numbers instead of more modern ones.

As time went on, Goodman concentrated more on his classical playing. In April 1938 he had performed the Mozart Quintet for Clarinet and Strings (K. 581) with the Budapest String Quartet. Over the years he concertized more frequently, playing works by Brahms, Weber, Mozart, and others he commissioned. Reviewers acknowledged the brilliance of his technique, but some questioned his interpretations,

which seemed not to extract full meaning from the music. He died in New York City.

Goodman's legacy, then, was as a jazz musician. Although the idea of the jazz-based swing band was not original with Goodman, he was the one who found the form that brought it to great popularity: relatively simple, straightforward arrangements played with swing and excellent musicianship. He was, additionally, one of the finest improvisers in jazz history, and his small group recordings are among the treasures of jazz. And finally, his willingness to break the color line in the band business had enormous consequences for American society.

• Goodman's papers are at the John Herrick Jackson Music Library at Yale University, but they are disappointingly thin. However, the library does have a great deal of unissued Goodman music and a fairly complete file of Goodman's arrangements. Goodman's autobiography, *The Kingdom of Swing* (1939), written with Irving Kolodin, is superficial and self-serving, but it is the main source for many details of his early life. The full-dress biographies are James Lincoln Collier, *Benny Goodman and the Swing Era* (1989), and Ross Firestone, *Swing, Swing, Swing: The Life and Times of Benny Goodman* (1993). D. Russell Connor, *Benny Goodman: Listen to His Legacy* (1988), a meticulously researched discobiography, containing the details of his engagements and recordings, is invaluable. Also useful are various oral histories of people associated with Goodman, lodged at the Institute for Jazz Studies, Rutgers University, Newark, N.J. An obituary appears in the *New York Times*, 14 June 1986.

JAMES LINCOLN COLLIER

GOODMAN, Joseph Thompson (18 Sept. 1838–1 Oct. 1917), writer, publisher, and archaeologist, was born in Masonville, Delaware County, New York, the son of Caleb Goodman. His mother's name is unknown. Little is known of his early life. Sometime during the 1850s, Goodman moved west with his brother and father and began to work as a typesetter for the *Golden Era*. In 1861, attracted by the favorable reports coming from the newly discovered Comstock Lode, he and Denis McCarthy purchased the *Territorial Enterprise*, a small, struggling weekly newspaper in Virginia City, and converted it to a daily.

Under their vigorous management, it immediately became profitable and soon became the main newspaper on the Comstock Lode and one of the great newspapers of the West. They quickly began to hire the best writers they could find, including Samuel L. Clemens in 1862 (who months later adopted the pen name Mark Twain and began his literary career) and other newspapermen who went on to achieve eminence either in journalism or in other fields, such as Dan De Quille, Rollin Mallory Daggett, Alfred Doten, James Townsend, and Stephen Edward "Steve" Gillis.

Goodman bought out McCarthy several years later and became the sole proprietor and editor. He expanded the paper and concentrated on establishing its reputation for having the most complete and reliable coverage of Comstock mining activity. This alone ensured that the *Enterprise* would be read all over the country and also in the world's main financial centers—New York, Boston, London, and Berlin—because investors everywhere closely followed developments on the Comstock.

Goodman was fiercely and fearlessly independent. He detested rumormongering and innuendo in journalism and adjured his reporters to first get all the facts from reliable sources and then write positively and forcefully. He gave his reporters free rein but expected them to be fully responsible for what they wrote. He was credited with having said that "you couldn't be a good Comstock newspaper man unless you could shoot straight, both with gun and pen," and he set an example to his staff on both counts by his personal conduct. In 1863 a dispute with a rival newspaper, the *Virginia Daily Union*, led to a duel with one of its editors, Thomas Fitch, who would later become a leading Nevada figure. Fitch fired first and missed. Goodman spared Fitch's life by shooting him in the knee.

In 1872 the *Enterprise* was among the first newspapers on the Pacific Coast to boldly describe as swindlers a company attempting to promote some Arizona property as diamond-bearing. Goodman wrote a fiery editorial denouncing by name General George McClellan and a number of leading San Francisco citizens for lending their influence to the hoax and denouncing another Virginia City newspaper for consenting to promote the scheme in return for a one-fifth interest. Also in 1872 one of Goodman's hard-hitting editorials destroyed the senatorial hopes of the wealthy but unscrupulous William Sharon in that election. Sharon retaliated by quietly buying up *Enterprise* stock until he held enough to present Goodman with the choice of either backing Sharon's policies or selling out and leaving town. Goodman sold his holdings in the paper in 1874 and left for San Francisco.

With enough money to be comfortable, Goodman tried his hand at several enterprises in California. First he worked on the editorial staffs of several San Francisco newspapers, among them the *Post*, but he did not stay with them for long. In 1877 he became a stockbroker but lost all his money by 1880. The "silver king" James Mackay had by then purchased half the shares of the *Enterprise* and offered to buy the other half and give it back to Goodman, but Goodman declined because he realized that the Comstock had passed its prime and was heading for oblivion. Instead, Goodman borrowed $4,000 from Mackay and started a raisin vineyard in the San Joaquin Valley near Fresno. He made a modest success of it but was restless as a farmer and in 1884 started a literary journal, the *San Franciscan*. Many of Goodman's literary friends, including Mark Twain, contributed to it, but Goodman sold the magazine after six months.

In 1870 Goodman visited the British Isles and Europe, vividly recounting his adventures and impressions in a series of letters reprinted in the *Enterprise*. He returned at least once more to Europe, but after he left the *San Franciscan* his attention turned to Central America. He became interested in the recently discovered Mayan ruins, undertook a study of the hieroglyphs, and succeeded in deciphering enough of them to be the first to recognize that they represented the Mayan calendar and that the calendar was a central cultural artifact. He published several books on the subject and laid the basis for this still valid theory, which later became known as the Goodman-Thompson-Martinez hypothesis.

Although not as proficient a writer as Twain or De Quille, Goodman nevertheless had some respectable literary ability of his own. While in Virginia City, he wrote drama reviews and poetry as well as editorials. Along with Rollin Mallory Daggett, he wrote *The Psychoscope*, a well-written play that was too far ahead of its time. It was short-lived because Virginia City audiences objected to its inclusion of some realistic scenes of prostitutes and work in the brothel, and the playwrights refused to delete or modify the scenes. Later in his life, he wrote some fiction, the burlesque "The Trumpet Comes to Pickeye" being the best known. In his later years, he published some of his reminiscences as newspaper articles.

Little is known of his married life. At his death in San Francisco, he left a widow, Mary, and four daughters. Mary was his second wife. His first wife, Ellen, died in 1894, leaving him the sole legatee of her estate.

Apart from his own achievements, Goodman also was an important influence on his circle of friends, especially Mark Twain. Though Twain was slightly older, he looked up to Goodman because of his courage, integrity, good judgment, and stability. Goodman supplied support and confidence at critical moments in Twain's career and remained a respected model and trusted adviser.

• For critical details of Goodman's life, see archival letters in the possession of the Mark Twain Project and the Bancroft Library of the University of California. See also microfilms of the *Territorial Enterprise* and other periodicals to which Goodman contributed. A collection of his memoirs, with an introduction, can be found in Phillip I. Earl, *Heroes, Badmen and Honest Miners: Joe Goodman's Tales of the Comstock Lode* (1977). One short story is available: "The Trumpet Comes to Pickeye" (1939). His best Mayan work is *The archaic Maya inscriptions* (1897). The only study of Goodman is Eva B. Adams, "Joseph T. Goodman: The Man Who Made Mark Twain" (M.A. thesis, Columbia Univ., 1936); as the title indicates, Goodman's relationship to Twain is the main focus of this work. Anecdotes about Goodman are common in such standard contemporary accounts of the Comstock as Myron Angel, *History of Nevada* (1881; repr. 1958); Ella Sterling Cummings, *Story of the Files* (1893); Samuel P. Davis, *History of Nevada* (2 vols., 1913); and Wells Drury, *An Editor on the Comstock Lode* (1936; repr. 1984). He figures prominently in Oscar Lewis, ed., *The Life and Times of the Virginia City Territorial Enterprise* (1971) and is mentioned frequently in Twain biographies and studies of Twain's early career. New information and more recent assessments of his career may be found in Lawrence I. Berkove, "Life after Twain: The Later Careers of the *Enterprise* Staff," *Mark Twain Journal* 29, no. 1

(1991): 22–28; and in *The Psychoscope*, ed. Lawrence I. Berkove (1994). An obituary is in the *San Francisco Examiner*, 3 Oct. 1917.

LAWRENCE I. BERKOVE

GOODMAN, Kenneth Sawyer (19 Sept. 1883–29 Nov. 1918), playwright, was born in Chicago, Illinois, the son of William Owen Goodman, the wealthy owner of a lumber business, and Erna Sawyer. Goodman, or "K," as those close to him called him, attended Chicago schools until he was fifteen, at which time he enrolled at the Hill School in Pennsylvania, where he boarded and where he began to write for the school paper. He continued writing while attending Princeton, where Dean Christian Gauss suggested that playwriting might best suit Goodman's talents. When he had completed his education, Goodman returned to Chicago and, as was expected, entered the family lumber business. Young men of high society were expected to take an interest in and support the arts, and Goodman thrust himself into the cultural life of Chicago with unusual vigor. He volunteered at the Art Institute of Chicago as director of its prints department, and in 1910 he joined the Cliff Dwellers Club, a meeting place for artists and their patrons.

At this time a grass-roots movement was growing across the United States, moving away from commercial theater and toward "art" theater, taking as its model the little theater movement in Europe. Goodman found himself at the forefront of this movement in Chicago, when in November 1910 he and another member of the Cliff Dwellers entertainment committee, Thomas Wood Stevens, began collaborating on a one-act play titled *Goya*, based on the painter's life. Within three weeks of its inception, the play was performed at the Art Institute, and a few days later Goodman and Stevens began working on their second piece, *The Masque of Quetzal's Bowl*. During the next few years, the fledgling duo collaborated on several other masques, which playwright and commentator Percy MacKaye describes as "actable poem(s) adapted to a special place and occasion for an audience directly cooperating" (Preface to *Masques of East and West*, p. 10). Goodman and Stevens's masque *Montezuma*, for example, was designed to be played on the central staircases of the Art Institute with the audience, in Aztec dress, seated in adjacent corridors.

To facilitate production of masques and other new plays as well as European classics, the Chicago Theatre Society was formed in 1911 by a group that included Goodman and Stevens, who also at this time began a publishing house for Chicago playwrights. Other local experimental ventures included Maurice Browne's Chicago Little Theatre, founded in 1912, and Mary Aldis's Players' Workshop, which, beginning in 1916, produced original plays and adaptations of short stories. Goodman was active primarily as a playwright but also as a director, actor, and financial supporter of the burst of theatrical activity.

In addition to his theatrical responsibilities, Goodman remained active in the family business and was married in 1912 to Marjorie Robbins. They had two children. That same year he began writing plays on his own, Stevens having left Chicago first for the University of Wisconsin and then in 1913 to form a theater program at Carnegie Institute of Technology in Pittsburgh. Two of Goodman's best solo efforts were written during this period. *Dust of the Road*, first produced in February or March 1913, is a sort of morality play, featuring a penitent Judas's confrontation with a couple attempting to steal a friend's inheritance. *The Game of Chess*, presented at the Fine Arts Theatre on 18 November 1913, deals with a revolutionary peasant's assassination attempt on a czarist governor.

By the end of 1913 Goodman had begun collaborating with the young journalist Ben Hecht, then establishing himself as a playwright and screenwriter. Together they wrote eight one-act plays, beginning with *The Wonder Hat* (1913), a harlequinade about love and magic and a hat that renders its wearer invisible, and ending with *The Hero of Santa Maria* (1918), an ironic story about a supposedly dead war hero who turns up for his memorial service alive and unheroic. Goodman and Hecht were associated with the Players' Workshop, but their collaborations were produced at small theaters throughout the country.

Meanwhile, Goodman became increasingly active with events surrounding the imminent world war, raising money for war relief, working with navy recruiting, and in May 1917 enlisting in the naval reserve. He was made a lieutenant fourth class and was assigned as an aide to the commander of the Great Lakes naval station. In the fall of 1918 he caught a cold while watching a football game between his unit and the naval academy in Annapolis; he subsequently contracted pneumonia and died at his parents' home in Chicago.

Goodman had planned to form a professional theater affiliated with a drama department, in which students would be taught by actors in the company. In 1922 his parents gave money to the trustees of the Art Institute to build a theater on its grounds dedicated to Goodman's vision and work. The Kenneth Sawyer Goodman Memorial Theatre opened its doors in 1925 with Goodman's former collaborator, Thomas W. Stevens, as artistic director. Goodman, in his unique capacity as both an artist and a patron of the arts, energized Chicago's little theater movement and encouraged theater as art. Although such important contributions tend to overshadow his work as a playwright, he contributed several fine examples to the genre of the one-act play. Goodman's philosophy is capsulized in his words, which are carved above the doorway of his theater: "To restore the old visions and to win the new."

• Material on Goodman, including manuscripts and personal papers, is located primarily in a collection at the Newberry Library in Chicago. A useful guide to this and other sources has been compiled and edited by Dennis Batory Kitsz in *Kenneth Sawyer Goodman: A Chronology & Annotated Bibliography* (1983). Included in Kitsz's work is a brief biographical sketch by Goodman's daughter Marjorie Sawyer Goodman Graff. Stuart J. Hecht, "Kenneth Sawyer Goodman: Bridging Chicago's Affluent and Artistic Networks," *Theatre History Studies* (1993): 135–47, offers a concise but comprehensive account of Goodman's life and work. Information on Goodman and the Goodman Theatre is available in clippings files and programs at the Theatre Collection of the New York Public Library, Lincoln Center. Some critical insight into his plays is offered by Percy MacKaye in his foreword to Thomas Wood Stevens and Goodman's *Masques of East and West* (1914), and by Stevens in his preface to Ben Hecht and Goodman's *The Wonder Hat and Other One Act Plays* (1925). Information on the little theater movement and Goodman's place in it can be found in Constance D'Arcy Mackay, *The Little Theatre in the United States* (1917), and Kenneth Macgowan, *Footlights Across America* (1929). An obituary is in the *Chicago Tribune*, 30 Nov. 1918.

JACK HRKACH

GOODMAN, Paul (9 Sept. 1911–2 Aug. 1972), libertarian social-cultural critic and man of letters, was born in New York City, the son of Augusta Goodman, of German-Jewish middle-class background and a traveling saleswoman of apparel. His father, Barnett Goodman, abandoned the family around the time of Paul's birth, and he was raised mostly by aunts and an older sister. Following a good record in humanities in New York City public schools, he majored in philosophy at the City College of New York (A.B., 1931). Then he worked as a counselor at a Zionist youth camp, was a sometime graduate student at Columbia University, and became a bohemian litterateur within a New York Jewish left-intellectual circle. His longest period outside the New York he fervently identified with was as a graduate student at the University of Chicago (1936–1940), studying literature and philosophy, finally receiving a Ph.D. in 1954.

Awkward, nearsighted, humorless, and defiantly sloppy in appearance, Goodman early developed a domineering, frequently belligerent yet earnest manner. With this went a pronounced role as a social dissident and public bisexual. He had two lengthy common-law marriages, from 1938 to 1943 to Virginia Miller, with whom he had one child; and from 1945 to 1972 to Sally Duchsten, with whom he had two children. He also was noted for numerous open homosexual relationships and for his insistence on polysexuality and pedophilia.

Goodman's teaching, reportedly of an "unsettling" didactic-therapeutic cast, was lifelong but intermittent. He was attached to Manumit School of Progressive Education (1942–1943), New York University (1948), Black Mountain College (1950), New York Institute for Gestalt Therapy (1951–1960), Sarah Lawrence College (1961), the University of Wisconsin (1964), San Francisco State College (1966), and the University of Hawaii (1969, 1971). He also gave lecture/therapy sessions at a wide range of institutions in the 1960s during which he was a figure of some celebrity as an antiwar and anticonvention social critic.

Goodman variously described himself as an "Enlightenment Man of Letters," a "utopian sociologist," and a "conservative anarchist." His early, and recurring, identification and work was as a literary avant-garde critic-writer. His literary studies went in several antithetical directions: from the minor neo-Aristotelianism of his published doctoral thesis, *The Structure of Literature* (1954), to such idiosyncratic left-psychoanalytic essays as *Kafka's Prayer* (1947) and many of the pieces later collected in *Creator Spirit Come! The Literary Essays of Paul Goodman* (1977), to loose but earnest defenses of literary humanism as against scientism, such as *Speaking and Language: Defense of Poetry* (1971). The most common responses to his writings: "arbitrary," "sloppy," and "eccentric."

Prolific, Goodman also wrote half-a-hundred stories and sketches, mostly during his early and middle periods. "The Facts of Life," an arch story about ambivalent Jewish identity, and "Our Visit to Niagara" and "A Statue of Goldsmith," implicitly self-satiric anecdotes about humorless pomposity, are probably the best of the "fractured and jargonish allegories." Goodman also wrote half a dozen novels. He later combined three of them (and added another) around autobiographical homosexual dilemmas and the failures of New York bohemian communalism in the allegorized-picaresque *The Empire City* (1959), whose quaint preachings a few have found "suggestive." *Parents' Day* (1951) and *Making Do* (1963) are semidramatized, didactic personal accounts of failures in early teaching and middle-aged protesting in marginal communities. Goodman also wrote a dozen or so plays in more or less experimentalist modes, some of which had brief performances by friends (as with the Beck-Malina Living Theatre in the 1960s). He also published many volumes of his verse jottings; see the posthumous *Collected Poems* (1974). In spite of the emphasized bathos of one who saw himself as "ugly" and "unappreciated," and a style uncertainly mixing archaicism and trite slang, the poetry has been cited for homoerotic candor and moral earnestness.

Far more significant were Goodman's essays in social criticism, which from his early thirties on took a libertarian perspective, perhaps especially from the influence of World War II anarchopacifists (see such journals as Dwight Macdonald's *Politics*, to which Goodman contributed, and the later *Liberation*, which he helped edit), as seems evident in his first essay collection, *Art and Social Nature* (1946). *Communitas: Means of Livelihood and Ways of Life* (1947; rev. ed., 1960) was done with his practicing architect brother Percival. It provides a sophisticated primer for thinking about city planning and the deeper issues of "human scale" and an aesthetic and just environment. With utopian imagination, it also juxtaposes three possible futures: the city as a Corbusier-style super department store for compulsive consumption; the city as a dual society in which a welfarist subsociety ameliorates the ruthlessly competitive mainstream; and the city as a "neofunctional" plan, aesthetically decentralized into rather medieval urban subcommunities, which the Goodmans obviously favor.

Continuing such imaginative sociology, Goodman applied, after a gap devoted to psychiatric therapy theory (1950s), anarchist perspectives (especially indebted to the Kropotkin tradition) to much of the American scene, as in his *People or Personnel: Decentralizing and the Mixed System* (1965), a fervent but often commonsensical critique of dehumanizing centralism and giganticism in organization. In *Utopian Essays and Practical Proposals* (1962), a variety of raggedly suggestive essays, he argued for abolition of censorship, banning automobiles from cities, debureaucratizing science, and eliminating war and other forms of authority. He propounded more direct forms of democracy, including deformalized work and learning, new rural communalism, participatory media, and other antihierarchical ways of doing and living.

A left-Freudian and early defender of sexual revolutionary Wilhelm Reich, Goodman wrote (with Frederick "Fritz" Perls) a rather abstractly tendentious biosocial psychological theory, *Gestalt Therapy* (1951), of which he was a practitioner—a forerunner of the "humanistic psychology" movement. He saw his quasi-religious psychology as part of a utopian therapeutics for transforming society. This was continuous with the earnest polemic that made him well-known, *Growing Up Absurd: Problems of Youth in the Organized System* (1960), an essay in pop-sociology in which he adapted a libertarian critique to reformist demands around the social discontents of young American males. (He oddly had little feminist or ethnic minority egalitarian sympathies.) Better polemics, such as *Like a Conquered Province: The Moral Ambiguity of America* (1967), an attack on American centralism, militarism, and repressive lifestyles, followed in his energetic and self-conscious role as prophet and scold of generational discontent. Such writings helped make Goodman a celebrity in the 1960s "protest movement," though he was later ideologically rejected by many "revolutionary" radicals.

Probably Goodman's most persuasive and influential radical stance was as libertarian critic of American education. Strikingly, he combined noncoercive "progressive" schooling for young children, as in *Compulsory Mis-education* (1964) with sweeping intellectualist, rather medieval, arguments for simplified autonomous universities, as in *The Community of Scholars* (1962). With acute insistence, he urged in *New Reformation: Notes of a Neolithic Conservative* (1970) the abolition of high schools and their replacement with youth corps, apprenticeships, and related "natural learning." He was an important voice, as Ivan Illich and others acknowledged, for the "de-schooling society" movement and similar libertarian responses.

Though not a rigorous libertarian theorist, and with both his writing and teaching heavily burdened with his personal messiness (which he insisted on as his identity), Goodman had for a time (1960–1972) a considerable public role. Perhaps most essentially, he applied the principle that "voluntary association has yielded most of the values of civilization" to a variety of mid-twentieth-century American institutions. An earnest provocateur, this anarchopacifist and bohemian dissenter to the warfare-welfare ordering posed the new abolitionism of radically de-schooling America, of enlarging sexual freedom, and of broadly seeking alternatives to power and domination in American technocracy. Up to near his death—at his farm in Vermont near North Stratford, New Hampshire—Goodman energetically helped enlarge libertarian advocacy of socioeconomic decentralization, democratic and aesthetic community, and utopian longings for "greater human autonomy" and enlarged direct responsiveness.

• In addition to the books mentioned above, Goodman published during his lifetime *The Society I Live in Is Mine* (1963) and *Tragedy and Comedy: Four Cubist Plays* (1970). Posthumous collections of his work include *The Collected Stories and Sketches of Paul Goodman*, ed. Taylor Stoehr (4 vols., 1970–1970); *Drawing the Line: The Political Essays of Paul Goodman*, ed. Stoehr (1977); and *Nature Heals: The Psychological Essays of Paul Goodman*, ed. Stoehr (1977). Stoehr also edited the posthumously published collection of Goodman's poems.

A partial bibliography is by Tom Nicely, *Adam and His Works: A Bibliography by and about Paul Goodman* (1979). Biographical information appears in the many introductions by Taylor Stoehr and in his lavishly devoted articles, such as "Paul Goodman and the New York Jews," *Salmagundi* 66 (1985): 50–103. Other devotee accounts may be found in a Goodman double-issue of *New Letters* 42, nos. 2–3 (1976), and in *Artist of the Actual: Essays on Paul Goodman*, ed. Peter Parisi (1986).

Critical discussions are included in Kingsley Widmer, *The Literary Rebel* (1965); Theodore Roszak, *The Making of a Counter Culture* (1969); Richard King, *Party of Eros: Radical Social Thought and the Realm of Freedom* (1972); Morris Dickstein, *Gates of Eden: American Culture in the Sixties* (1979); and a book-length study by Widmer, *Paul Goodman* (1980).

KINGSLEY WIDMER

GOODNIGHT, Charles (5 Mar. 1836–12 Dec. 1929), rancher, was born in Macoupin County, Illinois, the second son of Charles Goodnight and Charlotte Collier, farmers. After Charles Goodnight, Sr., died in 1841, Charlotte Goodnight married a neighbor, Hiram Daugherty, who moved the family to Texas in 1845, settling in Milam County. By then Charles Goodnight, Jr., had attended school for two years, which was all the education he ever received.

At age sixteen Goodnight found work in Waco as a teamster, employment he left about 1855 to join with an older stepbrother, J. W. Sheek, to travel to the gold fields of California. Before they could depart, Sheek's brother-in-law, Claiborn Varner, offered them 400 head of cattle to tend on the open range for ten years, their share being one-fourth of the increase in livestock. For the next decade Goodnight combined freighting and raising cattle in the Keechi Valley of Palo Pinto County with duty as Texas Ranger and scout, serving with Lieutenant Colonel James E. McCord's Frontier Regiment during the Civil War. In 1865, when the partnership was dissolved, Goodnight took his share, some 2,000 cattle, and sought a market.

Oliver Loving, a neighboring rancher, persuaded Goodnight to join him in quest of buyers in the Rocky

Mountains. Loving had driven cattle to Denver before the Civil War, disposing of animals profitably to miners, and he believed such connections could be reestablished. In early spring 1866 Goodnight and Loving combined some of their steers into a herd of about 2,000 animals and proceeded westward along the path of the Butterfield Overland Mail Route, through dangerous Apache, Comanche, and Kiowa Indian country, to the Pecos River, which they followed northward to Fort Sumner, New Mexico. There, government agents, who needed to supply garrisons and dependent reservation Indians, bought as many of the animals as they could handle, or most of the herd. With about 800 head remaining unsold, the cattlemen decided that Loving should proceed to Colorado in search of more buyers while Goodnight returned to Texas for additional cattle, which government agents promised to buy at eight cents a pound, on the hoof.

While Loving continued northward, ultimately selling the remaining animals to rancher John W. Iliff near Denver, Goodnight returned home, hired drovers, gathered a herd of 1,200 steers, and set out once more for New Mexico. At the Concho River, Goodnight encountered rancher John Simpson Chisum, who added animals to the drive over what ever since has been known as the Goodnight-Loving Trail. Their enterprise being most profitable, in 1867 Goodnight and Loving again gathered Texas cattle (including some of Chisum's) for delivery in New Mexico, but along the way they were repeatedly attacked by Indians, who drove off about 300 steers in one raid; in another, Loving was mortally wounded. Goodnight nevertheless continued on to Fort Sumner. Thereafter, for the next three years, Goodnight continued driving cattle to New Mexico, mostly in association with Chisum.

In 1871 Goodnight married Mary Ann Dyer of Belknap, Texas, and, with accumulated profits of about $50,000, abandoned the rigors of droving and resumed ranching. Developing separate spreads near Pueblo and Trinidad, Colorado, he emerged as one of the territory's most substantial cattle raisers. Goodnight also experimented with irrigated farming and founded the Stock Growers' Bank of Pueblo. The panic of 1873 virtually bankrupted him, leaving him landless and with only 1,800 head of cattle to his name, which he grazed on open range. In 1876, following the Red River War in which the U.S. Cavalry swept the Comanches and Kiowas from the Great Plains, he drove his livestock southward into the Texas Panhandle, wintering the animals in the relative shelter of Palo Duro Canyon.

When Goodnight returned to Colorado to arrange for his wife to join him, he met Englishman John G. Adair, who was eager to become a rancher. Adair and Goodnight struck a five-year partnership, whereby Adair would bankroll the establishment of the JA Ranch and Goodnight would run it, his share being a salary of $2,500 a year and one-third of the profits. Adair's money soon bought 25,000 acres of land, most of it strategically situated along the Prairie Dog Town Fork of the Red River, in Palo Duro Canyon. A half-mile-wide and 75-mile-long strip was purchased primarily from land speculators Jot Gunter and William B. Munson, and the rest of the acreage was judiciously scattered about the surrounding countryside in such a way as to discourage others from buying intervening tracts, which Goodnight and the JA treated like open range. Goodnight continued buying land and expanding the herd, and by 1882, when he and Adair renewed their agreement for another five years, the JA's assets—94,000 acres of land and 28,000 head of cattle—were valued at more than $700,000. Thereafter Goodnight bought additional land, some for as little as twenty cents an acre, leased more, and appropriated for JA's use much intervening public acreage. At the end of the second five-year period their operation spread over 1.3 million acres, on which they ran some 99,000 head of cattle.

As Adair had died three years before, in 1887 his widow divided the acreage and livestock with Goodnight, his share being the 140,000-acre Quitaque Division of the JA, or the F Ranch, and 20,000 head of cattle. In two transactions, in 1888 and 1890, Goodnight sold the F Ranch and semiretired to a small spread near the Texas Panhandle town of Goodnight. On that ranch Goodnight experimented with cattle breeding, including the crossing of Angus with bison to produce "cattalos." He also invested in a Mexican mining venture, which apparently was unprofitable.

During his declining years he divided his time between his ranch at Goodnight, during summers, and a home in Tucson, during winters. After the death of his first wife in 1926, on his ninety-first birthday he married 26-year-old Corrine Goodnight, to whom he was not related. By her he had one child, who failed to survive. Charles Goodnight died in Tucson and was buried in Goodnight.

• Goodnight's papers and collected recollections are scattered among the Goodnight Collection, Panhandle-Plains Historical Museum, Canyon, Tex.; the J. Frank Dobie Collection, Harry Ransom Humanities Research Center, University of Texas at Austin; the J. Evetts Haley Papers, Nita Stewart Haley Memorial Library, Midland, Tex.; and the Earl Vandale Collection, Barker Texas History Center, University of Texas at Austin. They concern trail driving, cattle ranching, and Indian depredation claims and include narratives by Goodnight and others regarding their frontier experiences. Published personal accounts penned by Goodnight appear in J. Marvin Hunter, comp. and ed., *The Trail Drivers of Texas* (1925). Although marred somewhat by the author's awe of his subject, J. Evetts Haley, *Charles Goodnight: Cowman & Plainsman* (1936), remains the classic biography, which should be supplemented with B. Byron Price, *Crafting a Southwestern Masterpiece: J. Evetts Haley and Charles Goodnight, Cowman & Plainsman* (1986). Laura Vernon Hamner, *The No-gun Man of Texas* (1935), is as laudatory as Haley's study but far less reliable. Useful are Harley True Burton, *A History of the JA Ranch* (1928), and biographical sketches of Goodnight in the following: James Cox, *Historical and Biographical Record of the Cattle Industry and Cattlemen of Texas and Adjacent Territory* (2 vols., 1894); J. Frank Dobie, "Charles Goodnight, Trail Blazer," *Country Gentleman*, Mar. 1927, pp. 26–27, 135–39; James W. Freeman, ed., *Prose and*

Poetry of the Live Stock Industry of the United States (1904); J. Evetts Haley, "Charles Goodnight, Pioneer," *Panhandle Plains Historical Review* 3 (1930): 7–17; George A. Wallis, *Cattle Kings of the Staked Plains* (1957); and Walter Prescott Webb and H. Bailey Carroll, eds., *The Handbook of Texas* (2 vols., 1952). The most detailed obituaries are in the Dallas *Morning-News*, 13 Dec. 1929; Fort Worth *Star-Telegram*, 12 Dec. 1929; and San Antonio *Express*, 13 Dec. 1929.

JIMMY M. SKAGGS

GOODNOW, Frank Johnson (18 Jan. 1859–15 Nov. 1939), professor of public administration, university president, and government adviser, was born in Brooklyn, New York, the son of Abel Franklin Goodnow, a cutlery manufacturer, and Jane Maria Root. In 1879 he graduated from Amherst College. Before enrolling at Columbia University Law School he worked briefly in a broker's office. While at law school he took courses in the School of Political Science, begun in 1880 by J. P. Burgess and including the departments of history, economics, public law, and social science. Goodnow earned an LL.B. degree in 1882 and entered a New York law office, where he practiced law for only a few months.

In 1882 a position opened in Columbia's School of Political Science. Goodnow was offered the post, provided that he study abroad for a year. He enrolled in and attended the École Libre des Sciences Politiques in Paris and the University of Berlin. Upon his return to Columbia in 1883 he was appointed instructor and began teaching courses in history and administrative law.

In 1886 Goodnow married Elizabeth Buchanan Lyall; they had three children. In 1887 Goodnow became adjunct professor of administrative law and in 1891 was promoted to professor. In 1903 he was named Eaton Professor of Administrative Law and Municipal Science. During the 1906–1907 academic year he served as acting dean of political science.

Goodnow was one of the nation's leading authorities on public administration. He has been called the "father of American administration," but it is important to note that he was also one of the first to recognize the importance of comparative public administration. His first book, *Comparative Administrative Law: An Analysis of the Administrative Systems, National and Local, of the United States, England, France and Germany* (2 vols., 1893), and the revised edition of *City Government in the United States* (1910), which incorporated considerable European material, influenced much of the work in the field prior to World War II.

Goodnow's book *Politics and Administration: A Study in Government* (1900) is a classic, establishing one of the most enduring debates in the field. "There are two distinct functions of government," Goodnow wrote, that "may for purposes of convenience be designated respectively as Politics and Administration." The politics-administration model as developed by Goodnow has been modified through the years, but it continues to influence thinking, if not practice, concerning the division of roles in government between

politics (as the sphere in which the will of the state is fashioned and expressed) and administration (as the sphere in which the policies expressing this will are executed).

Goodnow did much to reverse what James Bryce called "our most conspicuous failure": the government and administration of American cities. He authored a number of widely known works on municipal government and administration law, among them *City Government in the United States* (1904; rev. ed., 1910). This work was part of the American State series edited by his future colleague at Johns Hopkins, W. W. Willoughby. *City Government* discussed many aspects of municipal government from the point of view of organization and structure. Although his approach was legal in character, he was conscious of the interconnectedness of urban social and political problems. Goodnow believed that attempts to reform city government should not be confined to the mere structure of municipal institutions nor to the change of its relationship with the state. Because the problems experienced by city governments go beyond reform of the governmental machinery alone, efforts should also be made to improve the economic and social conditions of the urban population.

Goodnow was more interested in the application of public administration than in theory. As a result much of his scholarship has a practical or reform orientation. One reviewer remarked that Goodnow focused on "the physiology rather than on the anatomy of government. . . . His is a study of dynamics." In an address delivered at a luncheon in Goodnow's honor, Charles A. Beard observed that he "was the first scholar in the United States to recognize the immense importance of administration in modern society and to sketch the outlines of the field. This was in itself an achievement large enough to give his work a secure place in the rising structure of American political science."

Goodnow helped form the American Political Science Association and in 1904 was chosen to serve as its first president. He served one term but remained a member for life. He was also a member of the American Economic Association, the American Bar Association, and Phi Beta Kappa and a fellow of the American Academy of Arts and Sciences. For his scholarly publications and his contributions to the field of public administration, Goodnow received honorary degrees from Amherst, Brown, Columbia, Harvard, Johns Hopkins, Princeton, and the University of Louvain, Belgium.

James Bryce, the eminent British jurist, historian, and diplomat, asked Goodnow to write a chapter on New York's city government for his book *The American Commonwealth* (1888). Goodnow's chapter, titled "The Tweed Ring in New York City," became the subject of a libel suit against Bryce. A. Oakey Hall, who was mayor of New York between 1869 and 1871, brought suit in London alleging that the reference to him in connection with the "Tammany Ring" was defamatory. Bryce's defense was that the statements in the alleged libel were accurate, and much of his correspondence, preserved in the Frank J. Goodnow Papers, was devoted to this affair. Because the matter was still before the courts when the second edition of *The American Commonwealth* was scheduled to be released, the "Tweed Ring" chapter had to be omitted from the 1889 edition.

Goodnow brought his knowledge of public administration to bear on public affairs, serving as adviser to governments both foreign and domestic. In 1900 Governor Theodore Roosevelt appointed him to the commission charged with drafting a new charter for New York City. President William H. Taft in 1911 chose Goodnow to serve on his Commission on Economy and Efficiency, a panel of prominent citizens and scholars investigating the organization and work of the cabinet-level departments. In 1912 the new Chinese Republic asked that the Carnegie Endowment for International Peace nominate an American scholar to serve as technical adviser in constitutional and administrative law. In October 1912 Goodnow was named legal adviser to President Yüan Shih-K'ai, and the appointment took him to China in March 1913.

In 1914 Goodnow became the third president of the Johns Hopkins University. One of his first tasks was to complete the university's move to the Homewood site begun by his predecessor. After having completed the move, Goodnow led the efforts to devote the university's mission to graduate education. In 1925 a proposal was considered that would have abandoned the undergraduate program and reorganized the university into solely a graduate school. The "Goodnow Plan," as it was called, won approval by the trustees in 1926. Although the plan was eventually altered to allow the undergraduate program to continue, it had the effect of reinforcing the university's founding commitment to research patterned on the German model of graduate education.

Goodnow's work as an adviser in China may have been cut short by his being named president of the Johns Hopkins University the following year, but his interest and involvement in public affairs did not wane. In 1914 he led a governor-appointed panel that was to recommend how various Progressive Era ideas, such as civil service, labor, and tax and education reform, might be implemented in Maryland. Later he became regent of the University of Maryland, a member of the Baltimore Public School Board (1916–1931), and chairman of the State Budgetary Commission (1916), known as the "Goodnow Commission," which reformed Maryland's budget process, giving the governor the authority to prepare and propose the state's budget to the legislature. He also was named a member of the International Commission, established by President Calvin Coolidge in 1928 for the advancement of peace between the United States and China.

During Goodnow's administration at Johns Hopkins several programs were initiated, including the School of Engineering, the Institute of Law, the School of Hygiene and Public Health, the Walter Hines Page School of International Relations, and the Wilmer Institute of Ophthalmology. In 1929 he re-signed as president but continued to give lectures in the graduate program. Goodnow died in Baltimore, Maryland.

• The Frank J. Goodnow Papers are at the Johns Hopkins University Milton S. Eisenhower Library (Special Collections). His papers consist of over 12,000 items, spanning the years 1880 through 1940 and including correspondence, lectures, and other writings. Goodnow wrote several other books that pioneered the field of public administration. These books include *Municipal Home Rule: A Study in Administration* (1895), *Municipal Problems* (1897), *Municipal Government* (1909), and *Social Reform and the Constitution* (1911). He was the editor of *Selected Cases on the Law of Taxation* (2 vols., 1905), *Selected Cases on the Law of Officers* (2 vols., 1906), and *Selected Cases on Government and Administration* (1906). Despite the demands of being a university president at Johns Hopkins, he still managed to write three new books during his tenure: *The American Conception of Liberty and Government* (1916), *Principles of Constitutional Government* (1916), and *China: An Analysis* (1926). He also issued new editions of two earlier works, *Politics and Administration* (1914) and *Municipal Government* (1919). A festschrift for Goodnow, *Essays on the Law and Practice of Governmental Administration* (1935), was put together and edited by Charles G. Haines and Marshall E. Dimock, two of Goodnow's former students. This book features an introduction that assesses Goodnow's contributions to the field and nine original essays written by several members of the generation of public administration scholars inspired by his work. Goodnow is the subject of several articles, including Warren Wilmer Brown, "New President of John Hopkins and What He Thinks of His Job," *New York Press*, 18 Oct. 1914, and Munroe Smith, "The Professional Life of Frank Johnson Goodnow," *Johns Hopkins University Alumni Magazine* (1914), and a painting by Hannibal Knight, now hanging in the lobby of Garland Hall on the Johns Hopkins campus. Obituaries are in the *New York Times*, the *New York Herald-Tribune*, and the *Baltimore Sun*, all 16 Nov. 1939.

MICHAEL TOLLEY

GOODPASTURE, Ernest William (17 Oct. 1886–20 Sept. 1960), scientist and physician, was born near Clarksville, Tennessee, the son of Albert Virgil Goodpasture, Sr., a lawyer, farmer, publisher, and historian, and Jennie Willson Dawson. Goodpasture received a B.A. from Vanderbilt University in 1907. For a year he taught at Allegheny Collegiate Institute, Alderson, West Virginia, then entered Johns Hopkins University School of Medicine, where he earned an M.D. in 1912. He remained there in 1912–1913 as a Rockefeller fellow in pathology under William Henry Welch and George H. Whipple. From 1913 to 1915 Goodpasture was instructor in pathology at Hopkins and, for a time, acting resident pathologist at its hospital. In 1915 he was appointed resident pathologist at the Peter Bent Brigham Hospital and instructor at Harvard University Medical School. That same year he wed Sarah Marsh Catlett; the couple had one daughter.

On leave as a volunteer in the U.S. Navy Reserve Force, Goodpasture was posted to the pathology laboratory of Chelsea Naval Hospital near Boston in the fall of 1918, shortly after the influenza pandemic struck the nation. The worst in the nation's history, it resulted in as many as 550,000 deaths in ten months. Based on autopsies of victims, Goodpasture published papers on the pathology of influenzal phenomena in journals such as the *United States Navy Medical Bulletin* and the *American Journal of Medical Sciences*. His research undercut the dominant conviction that the causative agent was bacterial.

After a year on the faculty at the University of the Philippines, where he investigated the histopathology of cholera, leprosy, and yaws, Goodpasture was named director of the William H. Singer Memorial Research Laboratory, Allegheny General Hospital, Pittsburgh. There he and Oscar Teague studied the spread of herpetic viruses in the central nervous system, showing how they traveled along nerve paths to the brain.

In 1924 Goodpasture was named professor of pathology and head of the department in the new Vanderbilt University medical school. Vanderbilt had been selected by Abraham Flexner of the General Education Board, which administered portions of the Rockefeller fortune, to assist in establishing a leading institution for modern medical education in the South. While awaiting completion of the physical plant, Goodpasture spent a year as a Rockefeller scholar at the Institute for General and Experimental Pathology of the University of Vienna.

Whereas an earlier generation had focused on infectious diseases of bacterial origin, Goodpasture belonged to the generation that developed techniques for studying and controlling infectious diseases of a viral origin. Arriving at Vanderbilt in 1925, Goodpasture continued research on the fundamental nature of viruses and their propagation in the laboratory and in living tissue. Some of his most significant work, done with C. Eugene Woodruff and others, involved the tracking of the actual infectious agent within the virus of the fowl pox, first to inclusion bodies found in the nucleus or cytoplasm of diseased cells, then to extremely minute particles within the inclusion bodies, called Borrel bodies after their discoverer, French bacteriologist Amédée Borrel.

Needing to cultivate viruses for more study, Goodpasture and Alice Miles Woodruff found that the chorio-allantoic membrane of the chick embryo provided a sterile medium where they would flourish. Because they grow only on living tissue, viruses had until then been expensive to cultivate and difficult to keep free of bacterial contamination. A fertile hen's egg provided a cheap, virtually perfect environment. This technique enabled the large-scale, economical production of vaccines against yellow fever, influenza, smallpox, typhus fever, Rocky Mountain spotted fever, and equine encephalomyelitis (horse sleeping sickness). It also helped Goodpasture and his associates to develop new facts on cellular inclusions and on the physical conditions and chemical changes within the walls of cells invaded by bacteria as well as viruses. This research held important implications for understanding the complex relationship of susceptibility and resistance to disease.

Working with Claud D. Johnson, Goodpasture discovered the infectious agent causing mumps. Johnson and Goodpasture described their work in "An Investigation of the Etiology of Mumps" (*Journal of Experimental Medicine* 59, no. 1 [1934]: 1–19). The two scientists prepared bacteria-free filtrates of fresh saliva from humans in the first stages of the disease and inoculated monkeys with it, uniformly producing parotitis (swelling of the salivary glands) and fever. The isolation of the virus was confirmed when this serially passed material reproduced the disease in humans. While Goodpasture left the problem of poliomyelitis to others, his research demonstrated that the polio virus traveled along nerve fibers and ganglia and had an affinity for nerve tissue.

As a classroom teacher and lecturer, Goodpasture is remembered for his clarity of presentation. He favored teaching experimental pathology to undergraduate medical students as a way of demonstrating mechanisms underlying events in disease.

Goodpasture served as dean of Vanderbilt Medical School from 1945 to 1950. He was also an influential member of the panel headed by Walter W. Palmer that prepared the report on medical research policy for Vannevar Bush, wartime director of the Office of Scientific Research and Development. Palmer's panel recommended an independent medical research agency that would have given considerable autonomy to individual investigators. The proposal was never adopted. Instead, public support for scientific work began to emphasize grants-in-aid for focused projects, a trend that Goodpasture thought spelled danger for basic science, whose goal was understanding life processes.

Goodpasture helped promote research on the genetic effects of the atomic bombs dropped on Hiroshima and Nagasaki. He traveled to Japan in 1950 to outline this program for the Atomic Bomb Casualty Commission, which conducted a series of studies on radiation damage in cooperation with Japanese scientists.

In 1955 Goodpasture accepted the post of scientific director of pathology at the Armed Forces Institute of Pathology in Washington and oversaw its expansion and a huge production of research by its staff of army officers and visiting civilian pathologists. He found time to publish papers on neoplastic disease (including "The Pathology of Viral Neoplasia," *Texas Reports on Biology and Medicine* 15, no. 3 [1957]: 451–61), suggesting that viruses might provoke cancerous growth without being an essential component. Longing to pursue such studies, Goodpasture resigned in the winter of 1959–1960 and served a brief appointment in pathology at the University of Mississippi Medical Center before returning to Vanderbilt in the spring as emeritus professor.

After the death of his wife in 1940, Goodpasture wed collaborator Frances Katherine Anderson in 1945. Following their return to Nashville, the couple spent the last months of his life in the laboratory. He died at their Nashville home.

Goodpasture had advanced the scientific understanding of the pathogenesis of infectious diseases, parasitism, and a variety of rickettsial and virus infections. His technique for the laboratory cultivation of viruses brought him renown from both colleagues and laymen. Sir Macfarlane Burnet, Nobel laureate in medicine in 1960, said that Goodpasture should have had the award, and added, "He was one of the few dozen men from Pasteur and Koch to Florey and Enders who provided the basic discoveries that gave us, by 1955, control over disease that came from outside ourselves" (quoted in Shapiro).

John L. Shapiro, who succeeded Goodpasture as head of Vanderbilt's department of pathology, recalled his old teacher as "a quiet, soft-spoken, gentle man of good humor," yet one who could be "stern, critical, and uncompromising. His approach to questions was thoughtful and judicious. In mind, spirit, and behavior, he always was independent—sometimes fiercely so. He often walked alone."

• Goodpasture's papers, and copies of materials cited here, are in the Special Collections Department of the Eskind Biomedical Library, School of Medicine, Vanderbilt University. Goodpasture's most significant publications include "Transmission of the Virus of Herpes Febrilis along Nerves in Experimentally Infected Rabbits," with Oscar Teague, *Journal of Medical Research* 44, no. 2 (1923): 139–84; "The Infectivity of Isolated Inclusion Bodies of Fowl-pox," with C. Eugene Woodruff, *American Journal of Pathology* 5, no. 1 (1929): 1–9; "The Susceptibility of the Chorio-allantoic Membrane of Chick Embryos to Infection with the Fowl-pox Virus," with Alice M. Woodruff, *American Journal of Pathology* 7, no. 3 (1931): 209–22; "The Developing Egg as a Culture Medium," *Journal of Laboratory and Clinical Medicine* 26, no. 1 (1940): 242–49; and "Research and Medical Practice," *Science* 104 (1946): 473–76. A thorough assessment of his life and work is Esmond R. Long, "Ernest William Goodpasture; October 17, 1886–September 20, 1960," National Academy of Sciences, *Biographical Memoirs* 38 (1965): 111–44, which includes a bibliography. For a discussion of Goodpasture and the science/service dualism in medicine, see Timothy C. Jacobson, *Making Medical Doctors: Science and Medicine at Vanderbilt since Flexner* (1987). Robert D. Collins, a former student, describes the formative influences on and personal and scientific legacy of his mentor in "Dr. Ernest William Goodpasture: A Memoir," *Vanderbilt Medicine* 1 (1983): 20–25. A list of his pioneering contributions in pathology and a discussion of his personal relations and character can be found in John L. Shapiro (with Hugh J. Morgan), "Ernest William Goodpasture, 1886–1960," a memorial booklet printed by Vanderbilt University (n.d.). An obituary is in the *New York Times*, 22 Sept. 1960 (corrected 27 Sept.).

JAMES SUMMERVILLE

GOODRICH, Annie Warburton (6 Feb. 1866–31 Dec. 1954), nursing administrator and educator, was born in New Brunswick, New Jersey, the daughter of Samuel Griswold Goodrich, a life-insurance salesman, and Annie Williams Butler. As a young girl she moved to New York City and was tutored at home until 1877, when she entered a private school in Berlin, Connecti-

cut. Three years later she accompanied her family to her father's new assignment in London, England, and completed her secondary education at private schools in England and France. In 1885, when her father's health failed, she moved with her family to Hartford, Connecticut, but soon relocated to Boston, Massachusetts, where she supported herself as the companion of an unmarried socialite. In 1890 she returned to Hartford to help care for her mother's aged parents. Concerned by the lack of skill displayed by the nurse who served as their primary caregiver and needing a means of financial support, that same year she enrolled in the New York Hospital Training School for Nurses. She graduated two years later and immediately became a head nurse at the hospital.

In 1893 Goodrich became superintendent of nursing at New York Post-Graduate Medical School and Hospital. Four years later she also assumed the duties of directing the hospital's training school; she established a minimum entrance requirement of a high-school diploma and arranged for students to receive additional training at a nearby maternity hospital. In 1900 she became the superintendent of nurses at New York's St. Luke's Hospital, where she developed the concept of primary-care nursing. At the time the typical hospital patient was attended by a number of nurses, each of whom performed the same duty for every patient on a ward. Goodrich rejected this assembly-line approach and instead made one nurse responsible for the total care of a small group of patients. This innovation proved so successful in improving patient care and morale that it eventually became standard practice at virtually every hospital in the country.

In 1902 Goodrich returned to New York Hospital as superintendent of nursing; two years later she began teaching hospital economics part-time at Columbia University's Teachers College. In 1907, after the hospital's board of governors overturned many of her innovative practices, she left to become general superintendent of New York's Bellevue Hospital Training School, where she instituted a probationary period for new students as well as standardized instruction and testing. She was appointed inspector of training schools by the New York State Education Department in 1910 and began working to establish state registration and licensure of nurses, as well as higher entrance requirements and educational standards for New York's more than 130 training schools. In 1914 she became a full-time assistant professor of nursing-school administration at Columbia; in 1917 she assumed the additional duties of director of the Henry Street Visiting Nurses Service, a charitable organization that delivered health care and preventive medicine to some of the city's poorest residents.

Goodrich contributed to the American effort in World War I by serving as chief inspecting nurse of U.S. Army hospitals in the United States and France. In order to staff these hospitals with trained nurses, in 1918 she also organized the first U.S. Army School of Nursing in Washington, D.C. She served as its first dean until 1919, when she returned to Columbia and Henry Street.

In 1923 the Rockefeller Foundation's Committee for the Study of Nursing Education, of which Goodrich was a member, recommended the establishment of a nursing school affiliated primarily with a university rather than a hospital. When Yale University offered to create such a school that same year, Goodrich was appointed the school's first dean. Given the resources of the Connecticut Training School as a base on which to build, she immediately set about developing a 28-month curriculum that would train nurses how to prevent as well as cure illness and disease. In 1926 she established an entrance requirement of two years of college coursework and convinced Yale's administration to confer upon the school's graduates the bachelor of nursing degree—the first time that degree had ever been awarded in the United States and the first degree ever awarded by Yale to women. In 1932 she restricted admission to holders of baccalaureates, and two years later the school began conferring the master of nursing degree.

Two years after the publication of her book *The Social and Ethical Significance of Nursing* (1932), Goodrich retired from Yale. She spent the next four years lecturing at various schools in the United States, Europe, and China and touring European hospital systems on behalf of the Rockefeller Foundation. From 1938 to 1941 she served as a nurse-training consultant for Hartford's Institute of Living. As special nursing education consultant to the U.S. Public Health Service from 1942 to 1945, she helped to organize the Cadet Nurse Corps to replace public health nurses who were serving overseas during World War II. In 1946 she retired to Colchester, Connecticut. She died, having never married, in Cobalt, Connecticut.

Goodrich served as president of the American Federation of Nursing in 1909, the International Council of Nurses (ICN) from 1912 to 1915, the American Nurses' Association (ANA) from 1915 to 1918, and the Association of Collegiate Schools of Nursing in 1933. She was made ICN's lifetime honorary president in 1915. She was awarded the National Institute of Social Science's Medal (1920), the U.S. Distinguished Service Medal (1923), France's Médaille d'Honneur de l'Hygiène Publique (1928), the ANA's Walter Burns Saunders Medal (1932), the French Ministry of Social Welfare's Silver Medal and the Bronze Medal of Belgium (both 1933), the National League of Nursing Education's Mary Adelaide Nutting Award (1948), and the Yale Medal (1953). A Yale professorship was named in her honor, and she was elected to the ANA Hall of Fame in 1976.

Goodrich was a pioneer in the development of American nursing. Her efforts to establish high professional and educational standards for nurses—particularly her insistence that a college education provide the core of a nurse's training—contributed significantly to the improvement of patient care in the United States.

• Goodrich's papers are in the Department of Archives, Teachers College Library, Columbia University; the Nursing Archives, Mugar Library, Boston University; and the School of Nursing, Yale University. Biographies include Edna Yost, *American Women of Nursing* (1955); Harriet Berger Koch, *Militant Angel* (1951); and Esther A. Werminghaus, *Annie W. Goodrich: Her Journey to Yale* (1950). Obituaries are in the *New York Times*, 1 Jan. 1955, and the *American Journal of Nursing* 55 (Feb. 1955): 158–59.

CHARLES W. CAREY, JR.

GOODRICH, Benjamin Franklin (4 Nov. 1841–3 Aug. 1888), rubber goods manufacturer, was born in Ripley, New York, the son of Anson Goodrich and Susan Dinsmore, farmers. Goodrich's father died when he was about six and his mother two years later, whereupon he went to live with his mother's brother, John Dinsmore, not far from Ripley. Attracted to medicine, Goodrich studied in 1858 with his cousin Dr. John Spencer in Westfield, New York, and graduated from the Cleveland Medical College in 1860. The same year he opened a medical practice in Mayville, New York, only to find his life disrupted by the Civil War. Goodrich first served as a hospital steward in the Ninth New York Volunteer Cavalry. In early 1862 he was promoted to assistant surgeon and assigned to a battalion of engineers, serving in that capacity until November. He continued his medical studies at the University of Pennsylvania while on leave in late 1862 and early 1863. Goodrich assumed his old post with the engineers in the spring of 1863, taking charge of a small hospital for a short time. He served until September 1864.

After the war Goodrich tried his luck as a doctor but with little success. Moving first to Jamestown, New York, not far from Ripley, he soon went on to newly developing towns in the oil fields of Pennsylvania. By the fall of 1865 he was practicing in Pit Hole. Conditions there were primitive but expensive. Goodrich found it difficult to make ends meet because of the high cost of living in the boomtown. Lacking the patience and capital to persist as a doctor, Goodrich entered the employ of Brown Brothers Oil Company—a firm with which he had become acquainted in Pit Hole—as a member of its shipping department in New York City.

Goodrich's career change and move to New York City set the stage for his entrance into the rubber industry. He boarded in a private home and there became friends with a young attorney, John P. Morris. The men became involved in real estate enterprises together, several of which appear to have been quite profitable. At least one such venture was not, however. Ironically, it was this one that first involved Goodrich in the rubber industry. Goodrich had come to know Ezra Frost and others who owned the Hudson River Rubber Company, whose production works were at Hastings-on-the-Hudson, but whose head office was in New York City. Intrigued by what he saw in the company, Goodrich persuaded Morris to join him in offering to trade $10,000 worth of real estate in New York City for an equal value of stock in the company. Hudson River Rubber Company officers, facing intense competition and desperate for capital, eagerly accepted Goodrich's offer on 15 July 1869.

The Hudson River Rubber Company, burdened by rundown machinery and continued severe competition, was found by the new shareholders to be in poor shape. To protect their investment, Goodrich and Morris became still more deeply involved in the rubber business by buying out all of the other stockholders through a further exchange of $5,000 worth of New York City real estate and $5,000 in cash (from Morris) in late 1869. Goodrich then became president and manager of the company, while Morris served as its secretary and treasurer. Problems persisted. Seeking to salvage the operation and perceiving opportunities elsewhere, Goodrich closed the Hastings plant, leased a small rubber factory in Melrose, New York, and moved all of the Hastings equipment there. The relocation accomplished little, for Goodrich still encountered the problems of competition and inadequate financing there.

Far from discouraged, Goodrich sought rubber manufacturing opportunities farther west—away from the competition of large, well-established eastern firms. In fact, Goodrich was optimistic enough about his future to marry Mary M. Marvin of Jamestown, New York, the daughter of one of the state's leading jurists, in November 1869. The two had met in Jamestown during Goodrich's search for a place to practice medicine right after the Civil War. The couple had five children, two of whom, twins, died in infancy.

Goodrich spent much of 1870 seeking a new location for rubber manufacturing, eventually choosing Akron, Ohio, as the site for his future operations. Perhaps, as legend at the B. F. Goodrich Company suggests, Goodrich was traveling by train to Cleveland when by chance an Akron businessman entered into conversation with him and persuaded him to visit his city. More likely, however, Goodrich learned about Akron through a broadside that was widely distributed in the East in spring 1870 by the town's board of trade. Akron indeed had much to offer a budding industrialist like Goodrich: canal and railroad connections to raw materials, such as coal, and to regional and national markets for finished goods. Nearby rivers and a canal reservoir provided an ample supply of water.

Most appealing initially, Akron possessed a business elite eager to attract Goodrich's plant and willing to provide him with financial backing. When Goodrich visited Akron in fall 1870, he successfully presented his ideas to a meeting of Akron's businessmen. The response was favorable: altogether twenty-three business leaders pledged $15,000 to Goodrich (only $13,600 was actually paid). No doubt working in Goodrich's favor in their eyes was the fact that he was ready to uproot himself and his family, that he was willing to invest all of his own capital in the venture, and that he had pledges of additional financial support from friends and family in New York.

Assured of the needed financing, Goodrich dismantled the Melrose plant and moved to Akron to begin making rubber goods anew. On the last day of 1870, Goodrich and four others set up the partnership Goodrich, Tew & Co. under Ohio law, "for the purpose of carrying on the business of manufacturing India rubber goods of various kinds." The late nineteenth century was a period of tremendous expansion for American industry and cities; and Goodrich, Tew & Co.'s two leading products, fire hoses and rubber belting for machinery, both of which had been made in Goodrich's New York plants, benefited immensely from this growth. Nonetheless, Goodrich, Tew & Co. followed a policy of diversified production.

Initiating a strategy that would long distinguish his company from many later entrants into the rubber business, Goodrich was unwilling to have his company become excessively specialized. Goodrich, Tew & Co. made whatever rubber goods its owner-managers thought they could sell profitably. In addition to hoses and belting, Goodrich, Tew & Co. made wagon springs, steam packing, wringer rolls for washing machines, valves, billiard cushions, tubing, gas bags, and fruit jar rings. Footwear was one of the few rubber items the company did not initially make. Large eastern firms produced and sold boots and shoes at prices Goodrich, Tew & Co. had no hope of matching.

A major national depression in the mid-1870s severely injured Goodrich's fledgling firm. After being reorganized several times as a partnership, the company emerged as an Ohio corporation, the B. F. Goodrich Company, in 1880. B. F. Goodrich, headed by Goodrich, expanded during the 1880s to become a regional industrial firm of some repute. For the most part, B. F. Goodrich's strategy of diversified production worked. At the close of 1881, its first full year of operations, B. F. Goodrich possessed assets of $233,000, made sales of $319,000, and posted profits of $69,000. A month before Goodrich's death, the company had assets of $564,000, and in that year earned profits of $107,000 on sales of $696,000.

Goodrich lived to see his company benefit from several years of accelerating growth before his death, and as the major stockholder in the company he enjoyed the fruits of that growth. Some remembered Goodrich as a gentleman of quiet dignity, but there was more to him. Goodrich was also known as one of the best poker players in Akron. As his prosperity increased, Goodrich enjoyed driving fast horses and, his health permitting, trips to Europe, where he bet on horse races. In the end exhaustion and tuberculosis caught up with him, and he died in a sanitarium in Manitou Springs, Colorado. From these origins B. F. Goodrich would develop as one of the United States' leading rubber makers—always as a diversified corporation—in the early and mid-twentieth century. Moreover, B. F. Goodrich's success directly attracted other businessmen into the rubber industry in Akron, Ohio, making that city the rubber capital of the world by the early twentieth century.

• The papers of the B. F. Goodrich Company, deposited in the University of Akron Archives and open without restrictions, are the most valuable source of information about Goodrich and his firm. On Goodrich's personal life, see correspondence in the Dinsmore Family Papers located at the Arizona Historical Society Archives, Tuscon. No reliable full-scale accounts of Benjamin Goodrich's life or the early years of his company exist. Biographical sketches appear in two Summit County (Ohio) histories, Samuel Lane, *Fifty Years and Over of Akron and Summit County* (1887), and William Perrin, *History of Summit County with an Outline Sketch of Ohio* (1881). The most revealing obituary is in the *Akron Beacon Journal*, 4 Aug. 1888.

MANSEL BLACKFORD

GOODRICH, Carter (10 May 1897–7 Apr. 1971), college professor and government official, was born in Plainfield, New Jersey, the son of Rev. Charles Lyman Goodrich, a minister, and Jeanette Margaret Carter. As a student at Amherst College, Goodrich edited the *Amherst Monthly* literary magazine and formed a close friendship with faculty member Robert Frost. A poet was lost to the field of economics, however, when upon his graduation in 1918 the college awarded Goodrich a fellowship with which he financed a trip to Britain to study trade unionism.

After returning to America Goodrich completed a Ph.D. in economics at the University of Chicago (1921). His doctoral thesis was published as *The Frontier of Control: A Study in British Workshop Politics* (1921); it documented inroads made by workers into the decision-making prerogatives asserted by management in a wide range of British industries. Goodrich married Florence Perry Nielson in 1921; they had three children. Subsequently, he served as a fellow and instructor at Amherst (1921–1924) and taught at the University of Michigan from 1924 to 1931. His second book, *The Miner's Freedom: A Study of the Working Life in a Changing Industry* (1925), warned of the deterioration in the quality of the working life of coal miners as technological change brought decreased dignity and autonomy and increased supervision and productivity. Goodrich was a staunch advocate of strong unions and was closely involved with the Bureau of Industrial Research and the United Mine Workers.

In 1931 Goodrich became professor of economics at Columbia University, where he built a reputation as an extraordinary teacher. He served as the department's executive officer from 1946 to 1949 and remained at Columbia until 1963. While in this position he became very active as a governmental consultant and official and served on many international commissions.

From 1934 to 1936 Goodrich served as director of the Social Science Research Council's Study of Population Redistribution, and he was lead author of *Migration and Planes of Living, 1920–1934* (1935) and *Migration and Economic Opportunity* (1936), both quantitative studies of geographical mobility within the United States. Simultaneously he coauthored, with Sol Davidson, two important articles in the *Political Science Quarterly* that empirically tested Frederick Turner's "safety valve" thesis about the frontier's im-

pact on the labor movement. Goodrich was an active supporter of the New Deal and had deep faith in the possibility of solving problems through collective action. He was a member of the Department of Labor's committee that investigated labor conditions in the anthracite industry, the author of a study of earnings and standards of living among railway employees (1934), a consultant to the U.S. Resettlement Administration (1936), and a consultant to the U.S. Social Security Board (1937).

In 1936 Goodrich began representing the nation on the international stage, serving as U.S. Labor Commissioner in Geneva (1936–1937 and 1938–1940) and as the U.S. government's member of the Governing Body of the International Labor Office (1936–1946). Before the Second World War he pursued the goal of enacting international labor standards in areas such as child labor and the length of the workweek. Goodrich headed the ILO Board of Governors during the war years (1939–1945), a difficult period in which the ILO was forced to relocate from Geneva to Montreal and during which it was frustrated and marginalized with the ascension of new international agencies such as the United Nations, the International Monetary Fund, and the World Bank. During World War II he was also special assistant to the American ambassador to Great Britain (1941).

After the war Goodrich served as a consultant to the United Nations (1947–1951) and as chairman of the Preparatory Committee of the United Nations' Resources Conference (1948–1949). His most notable role was as UN special representative to Bolivia. Goodrich negotiated an arrangement by which a team of ten international experts were given high positions within the Bolivian civil service for a five-year period. Led by Goodrich, the team arrived in La Paz shortly before revolution erupted in April 1952. A well-organized campaign of vilification was mounted in the newspapers and on the streets, which charged the UN mission with infringing upon Bolivian sovereignty. Wall inscriptions warned "Goodrich Go Home" and "Death to the Gringos." However, Goodrich's leadership efforts kept the UN team together, and after the fighting subsided he built cordial ties to the new government, enabling the mission to continue. This was the first major technical assistance mission by the UN, and its success helped lay the foundation for the scores of UN Development Program offices that followed. For his efforts Goodrich was awarded the Order of the Condor of the Andes by the Bolivian government. His observations were published as *The Economic Transformation of Bolivia* (1955). Later (1955–1956) he was chief of the UN Economic Survey Mission to Vietnam.

Beginning around 1950 Goodrich made several important contributions to the field of economic history, serving as president of the Economic History Association from 1954 to 1956. The most influential of his scholarly works, *Government Promotion of American Canals and Railroads, 1800–1890* (1960), concluded that the efforts of government at all levels to build transportation infrastructure did much to promote

American economic growth during the nineteenth century. He also documented a "striking feature of the American experience," that "the public and private roles in promotion were almost always thought of as cooperative rather than competitive." Thus government aid generally diminished and died out when private enterprise no longer needed it. The importance of government in economic growth and the "state in, state out" pattern were further examined in several articles and two books edited by Goodrich, *Canals and American Economic Development* (1961) and *The Government and the Economy, 1783–1861* (1967).

Goodrich was known for his geniality, pragmatism, deep sympathy with his fellow man, omnivorous intellectual curiosity, and careful scholarship. As his colleague Mark Perlman put it, "What he wrote combined intellectual integrity with euphony." All these traits served him well in his diplomatic endeavors and his mastery of a succession of fields within economics. These traits give his published works enduring value and help them complement the more quantitative and theoretical cliometric research in economic history that has been published subsequently.

After his retirement from Columbia, Goodrich became Mellon Professor of History and professor of economics at the University of Pittsburgh. He died in a bus accident in Mexico City.

• Goodrich's papers (sixty-seven boxes of correspondence, notes, manuscripts, diaries, and interviews) are located in the Rare Book and Manuscript Library of Columbia University. The most informative biographical material on Goodrich is Mark Perlman, ed., *Carter Goodrich, 1897–1971* (1971), which consists of a brief biography and comments delivered at his memorial service.

ROBERT WHAPLES

GOODRICH, Charles Augustus (19 Aug. 1790–4 June 1862), clergyman and popular writer, was born in Ridgefield, Connecticut, the son of the Reverend Samuel Goodrich and Elizabeth Ely. He was the grandson of Elizur Goodrich, distinguished Yale College graduate, Congregational clergyman, and scholar; the older brother of Samuel Griswold Goodrich, author, publisher, and diplomat; the cousin of Chauncey Allen Goodrich, clergyman, educator, and lexicographer; and the uncle of Samuel's son, Frank Boott Goodrich, author and translator.

Early in life, Goodrich said he wanted to become a minister; so his father tutored him conscientiously at home and then sent him to Yale, at considerable financial sacrifice. After graduating in 1812, he read theology in East Hartford, Connecticut, and preached in Saratoga Springs, New York. In July 1816 he was invited by officials of the First Congregational Church of Worcester, Massachusetts, to settle there as the junior colleague of the Reverend Dr. Samuel Austin until the latter could be officially dismissed. Pastor there since 1790, Austin was a learned preacher and a vehement champion of orthodoxy against Unitarians and Baptists. He had offered a sermon critical of President Thomas Jefferson in 1811 and had vigorously opposed

the War of 1812. When Austin became president of the University of Vermont in 1815, his church authorities granted him a leave of absence, which some hoped would be made permanent. The vote inviting Goodrich to assist Austin was sixty-four in favor to two against. When Goodrich was installed in August 1818 at a salary of $900 a year, the vote was eighty-eight to two. He was ordained in October in an elaborate ceremony—including a sermon delivered by Goodrich's father, a consecrating prayer, a charge, an exhortation, an address and the right hand of fellowship, and a concluding prayer. In June of that same year Goodrich had married Sarah Upson, a minister's daughter. The couple had seven children.

All surely must have seemed well at the First Congregational Church, but Goodrich soon found that he had stepped into the middle of a controversy. Pro-Austin opposition quickly developed. With Austin's consent, twenty-eight church members protested before the ecclesiastical council convened to argue unsuccessfully against his dismissal. When Austin was released in December 1818, his followers continued to object to Goodrich as a person, as an administrator, and on doctrinal grounds as well. Some of the disaffected withdrew, while others were officially separated; many joined the Baptist Society or went into other religious organizations, and some formed their own Calvinist church. (Meanwhile, Austin continued as president at the University of Vermont until 1821, published extensively, became pastor of the Congregational church of Newport, Rhode Island, until 1826, but then sank into "religious melancholy" and died in 1830.)

Long before that time, however, Goodrich was in an untenable position. His work in Worcester was mainly notable for his helping establish the first Sunday school in that part of Massachusetts. But he was not a Calvinist of sufficiently extreme views; moreover, he felt that Jefferson had acceptable reasons for his political and diplomatic decisions. Goodrich's difficulties generated the publication of at least five pamphlets on the subject. Worn down and pleading poor health, he petitioned to be released and was officially dismissed in November 1820.

Goodrich then began a second career, one more congenial and successful. He returned home to Berlin, Connecticut, in 1820 and established himself as a popular, if pedestrian, writer of (often huge) informational books and texts on religion and travel for juvenile readers, lavishly illustrated with fine engravings and sometimes in question-and-answer form. His most significant titles are *A History of the United States of America* (1822), which went through more than 150 editions; *An Outline of Bible History* (1825); *A History of Connecticut* (1833); *The Ecclesiastical Class Book; or, History of the Church from the Birth of Christ to the Present Time* (1835); *Great Events in the History of North and South America* (1850); *A Geography of the Chief Places Mentioned in the Bible* (1856); and *The Land We Live in; or, Travels, Sketches and Adventures in North and South America* (1857). He worked some of the time with his brother Samuel, who, writing as "Peter Parley," combined energy, talent, and prissy piety. Goodrich also served one term in the state senate (beginning in 1838). From 1848 he and his family made their home in Hartford, where he held a pastorate for a time and where he died.

• Other important books by Goodrich are *Outlines of Modern Geography* (1826); *Lives of the Signers of the Declaration of Independence* (1829; trans. into German, 1842); *Outlines of Ecclesiastical History* (1829); *The Child's Book of the Creation* (1832); *The Child's Book on the Bible* (1832); *The Influence of Mothers* (1835); *Lectures to Children, on the Last Hours of Our Lord Jesus Christ* (1835); *The Universal Traveler* (1836); *The Family Tourist; or, A Visit to the Principal Cities of the Western Continent* (1839); *The Family Sabbath-day Miscellany* (1841); *The Bible History of Prayer* (1847); *A Pictorial and Descriptive View of All Religions* (1850); *The Family Encyclopedia* (1852); and *Greek Grammar* (1855). William Lincoln, *History of Worcester, Massachusetts, from the Earliest Settlement to September, 1836: With Various Notices Relating to the History of Worcester County*, vols. 1–2 (1862), gives details of Goodrich's ordination in Worcester, opposition to him, and his dismissal. Personal information on Goodrich is contained in Samuel Griswold Goodrich, *Recollections of a Lifetime; or, Men and Things I Have Seen* (2 vols., 1856), and Lafayette Wallace Case, *The Goodrich Family in America* (1889). Obituaries are in the *Hartford Courant* and the *Hartford Times*, both 7 June 1862.

ROBERT L. GALE

GOODRICH, Chauncey (20 Oct. 1759–18 Aug. 1815), lawyer, U.S. congressman, and U.S. senator, was born in Durham, Connecticut, the son of Elizur Goodrich, a cleric, and Catherine Chauncey. In 1776 he graduated from Yale College, which his father and four younger brothers also attended. He did not serve in the American Revolution. After receiving his baccalaureate, Goodrich remained to study at the college as a Berkeley scholar, then taught at the Hopkins Grammar School in New Haven in 1777 and 1778. Appointed a tutor at Yale in 1778, he pursued his teaching duties there from 1779 until 1781 while studying law. Admitted to the Connecticut bar in 1781, he commenced his legal practice shortly thereafter in Hartford, where he quickly distinguished himself.

A brief, childless marriage to Abigail Smith ended with his wife's death in 1788. In 1789 he married Mary Ann Wolcott, daughter of Governor Oliver Wolcott, thus cementing his membership in the state's "standing order" of political notables, most of them Congregationalists and members of the Federalist party, which effectively monopolized major Connecticut political offices until after 1815. The couple had no children.

In 1793 Goodrich entered elective politics, to which he thenceforth devoted most of his life, except for occasional service in organizations, such as the Connecticut Bible Society, associated with the state's political-religious oligarchy. As a member of the lower house of the Connecticut General Assembly in 1793 and 1794, he gained successively responsible positions. In 1794 he was elected to the first of three terms in the U.S.

House of Representatives, where his views were those of a conventional Federalist. He spoke and voted for such major party initiatives as the Jay Treaty of 1795 and the Alien and Sedition Acts of 1798. His intention to return to full-time legal practice upon his retirement from Congress in 1801 was frustrated by his election in 1802 to the governor's council, on which he served until 1807. In that year the state legislature elected him to succeed the deceased Uriah Tracy in the U.S. Senate, where, opposing the embargo of 1807 and voting against the declaration of war with Great Britain in 1812, he resumed his dependable advocacy of Federalist party policies. Because holding responsible office in more than one jurisdiction was not then illegal or considered injudicious, Goodrich in 1812 accepted the mayoralty of Hartford, a post he retained until his death. Upon his election as lieutenant governor of Connecticut in 1813 in a three-way race decided by the legislature, he resigned from the Senate but remained Hartford mayor and served on the state's wartime Committee of Safety.

In 1814 the legislature elected Goodrich, by then one of the leading public figures in the state, a member of the Connecticut delegation to the ill-fated Hartford Convention. While that gathering has often since been incorrectly accused of intending to foment rebellion against the policies of the James Madison administration and perhaps secession from the Union, in actuality it met to protest the conduct of the war with Britain, to propose alterations in the Constitution to improve the operation of the government, and to press for changes in the policies of the Madison administration. Goodrich did not play a major role at the convention. Yet because he was senior member of the convention's Connecticut delegation and thus in effect its leader, he was named at the close of the convention to a committee authorized to call a second meeting of delegates if its members judged conditions to warrant it. The conclusion of peace in 1815 obviated any further action.

As mayor of Hartford during the convention, Goodrich was also responsible for maintaining relations with federal troops stationed in the state capital to observe the convention and no doubt to remind its members of the authority of the national government. While conclusive evidence is lacking, indications are that Goodrich conveyed to other delegates the views of the troops' commanding officer, Thomas S. Jessup, especially Jessup's determination to maintain national authority. Goodrich may thus have helped hold the convention to legitimate protest rather than the more radical acts proposed by some, such as the withdrawal of New England from the Union. Goodrich died of heart disease in Hartford shortly after the gathering's end.

A conventional public figure in the early nation's most conventional and homogeneous state, Goodrich embodied both the strengths and limitations of his environment and professional circle. He was respected for his judiciousness and unwavering Federalist positions, but no distinctive policy or action was ever associated with him. He was repeatedly entrusted with senior public responsibilities because of his seriousness and dependability in promoting the policies of Connecticut's governing elite rather than for his imagination or inventiveness.

• No major collection of Goodrich papers has survived, but some papers are in the Connecticut Historical Society and at Yale University. A number of his letters concerning public affairs are printed in George Gibbs, *Memoirs of the Administrations of Washington and John Adams, Edited from the Papers of Oliver Wolcott, Secretary of the Treasury* (2 vols., 1846). The social and political setting of Goodrich's life is examined in Richard J. Purcell, *Connecticut in Transition, 1775–1818* (1918). A modern study of the Hartford Convention is James M. Banner, Jr., *To the Hartford Convention: The Federalists and the Origins of Party Politics in Massachusetts, 1789–1815* (1969). Goodrich's role as Hartford mayor while a convention delegate is discussed in J. C. A. Stagg, *Mr. Madison's War: Politics, Diplomacy, and Warfare in the Early American Republic, 1783–1830* (1983). Obituaries are in the *(Hartford) Connecticut Mirror*, 21 and 28 Aug., 1815.

JAMES M. BANNER, JR.

GOODRICH, Chauncey (4 June 1836–28 Sept. 1925), missionary to China, was born in Hinsdale, Massachusetts, the son of Elijah Hubbard Goodrich and Mary Northrup Washburn. After attending Hinsdale Academy and Union High School in Burlington, Vermont, he entered Williams College, where he excelled academically, graduating in 1861. At a young age, Goodrich decided he wanted to enter the ministry, and by his sophomore year in college he focused on becoming a foreign missionary. After college he attended Union Theological Seminary in New York for a year and then Andover Theological Seminary, graduating in 1864. He was ordained in the Congregational Church at Hinsdale on 21 September 1864. That same month, he married Abbie Ambler, who died ten years later in Tung Chou, China. Goodrich then married Justina Emily Wheeler in 1878; she died just three months later, also at Tung Chou. In 1880 Goodrich was married a third time, to Sarah Boardman Clapp. Two children survived him.

Goodrich and his first wife traveled to China under the auspices of the American Board of Commissioners for Foreign Missions, arriving in August 1865. Skilled at the study of Chinese, he was soon recognized as one of the most fluent and accurate speakers of Mandarin. He began preaching at Tung Chou shortly after his arrival but spent most of his years in China instructing and translating English works into Chinese. He taught astronomy and Christian evidences at North China College and at the mission's Gordon Memorial Theological Seminary, both located in Tung Chou. He was dean of the seminary for twenty-five years, teaching such subjects as Old Testament history, church history, homiletics, and pastoral theology.

Goodrich was working in China before the greatest influx of Protestant missionaries arrived. From 1890 to 1898 their numbers grew from 1,296 to 2,458, and by 1908 there were more than 4,000 of them. Many did not speak Chinese, and for this reason standard reference sources were needed. One such source was Goodrich's *A Pocket Dictionary (Chinese-English) and Pekingese Syllabary* (1891), which contains more than 10,000 characters. In 1898 he published *A Character Study of the Mandarin Colloquial*, another aid to the language containing 39,000 sentences. Both books were considered of great value to the Protestant missionaries working in northern China at the turn of the century.

Goodrich was resolved to translate the Bible into Mandarin. Elected to the Mandarin Translation Committee at the General Conference of 1890, he served as chairman of this organization for many years. He worked with Calvin Mateer and others on what would be Mateer's last big effort, the translation of the New Testament. Work was divided on this project between a number of participants, but "only Mateer and Goodrich served throughout, and the finished work was primarily theirs" (Hyatt, p. 198). Goodrich continued to work on translating the entire Bible and, with the help of a few others, completed this work in 1918; it was published the following year.

Goodrich's translations did not stop there. Interested in Chinese Christian music from his first days in the country, he edited with Dr. Henry Blodget a *Chinese Hymnal* (1877), translating many hymns from English and composing others in Chinese. The hymnal was extremely popular and went through several editions. In 1922 he issued another collection of forty-four hymns, thirty-four of which he had composed.

Goodrich dedicated his entire professional life to foreign mission work in China, distinguishing himself from many of his colleagues. He voiced his commitment to spreading Christian thought in that country when he said in 1894, "All China is to be changed. It is with this assuring hope in our hearts that we can work on with patience and enthusiasm. We believe our Bible and we trust our eyes" (Forsythe, p. 29). At the time of his death in Tsing Hua, Chihli, China, he was the longest-serving Protestant missionary in China.

• Information on Goodrich is located in Irwin T. Hyatt, Jr., *Our Ordered Lives Confess* (1976); Kenneth S. Latourette, *A History of Christian Missions in China* (1929); and Sidney A. Forsythe, *An American Missionary Community in China, 1895–1905* (1971). Other biographical information can be found in the records of Williams College, Williamstown, Mass., and in the *Chinese Reporter*, July, Oct., and Nov. 1925 issues.

THE EDITORS

GOODRICH, Chauncey Allen (23 Oct. 1790–25 Feb. 1860), educator, clergyman, and lexicographer, was born in New Haven, Connecticut, the son of Elizur Goodrich, a lawyer, judge, and mayor of New Haven, and Anne Willard Allen. He attended the Hopkins Grammar School in New Haven, passing from there in 1804 to "fitting" for college by Henry Davis. He entered Yale College in 1806 and joined the College Church by profession of faith in his sophomore year. At his graduation in 1810, he delivered an oration on "The Influence of Novelty."

It is difficult to determine when Goodrich decided to enter the Congregational ministry, and in fact for two years after graduating from Yale, he served as rector of the Hopkins Grammar School without following the customary pattern of being "fitted" for the ministry by a serving clergyman. But in 1812 he returned to Yale as a tutor and to study theology under Yale's president, Timothy Dwight, and on 27 September 1814 he was licensed to preach by the New Haven West Association. He also studied for a term at the new Andover Theological Seminary during the winter of 1815–1816, and in the spring of 1816 the Park Street Church in Boston called him as the successor to Edward Dorr Griffin. In the end, however, Goodrich answered a call nearer to home and was ordained and installed as pastor of the Congregational parish in Middletown, Connecticut, on 24 July 1816. Finally settled in a parish, Goodrich married Julia Frances Webster, the second daughter of lexicographer Noah Webster, that October. They had four children.

Goodrich was, however, "by nature shy and ill-fitted for the work of a pastor" (Wright), and his career in active ministry was cut short, first by illness and then by a call in September 1817 to take up the new professorship in rhetoric and oratory at Yale. He was dismissed by the Middletown church in December and began his work at the college in January 1818. Goodrich did not find the state of education in rhetoric at Yale very encouraging. English grammar was only being studied in the sophomore year and rhetoric only in the senior year, which Goodrich believed was inadequate for the training of public professionals who would rely on their rhetorical skills to communicate with and uplift a provincial American public. In describing the situation to President Jeremiah Day for Day's famous Yale Report of 1828, Goodrich recalled that even the senior training in rhetoric amounted to little more than a midweek tutorial while the texts used to provide examples were "chiefly unintelligible." Goodrich soon began campaigning for more time in the college curriculum for training in rhetoric and elocution and set about providing his own textbook, a fat compendium, *Select British Eloquence, Embracing the Best Speeches Entire of the Most Eminent Orators of Great Britain* (1852). Goodrich had, one student wrote, "some of the arts of the orator" himself but evidently not all of them, because his classroom manner was described as lacking in "tact and wisdom," particularly when it came to student discipline.

Goodrich was much happier when he could shift his attention away from student discipline to student religion. Despite his commitments to the college, he never lost a sense of his earlier calling as a minister, and he became "the great religious force in the student world" at Yale (Dwight, p. 87). He functioned informally as the college pastor, conducting a Sunday afternoon "prayer and conference meeting" in the Yale Athenaeum at which he usually "made an address on some topic relating to practical piety" and could relate to the students "simply as a pastor" and not a "strictly and minutely governmental" instructor. He was the moving force behind the Yale student revivals of 1825 and 1827, and in 1831 a collegewide Bible class led by Goodrich became the seedbed for a revival that "included nearly every man in the college" (including then-tutor Horace Bushnell). Throughout the 1850s Goodrich remained the chief representative of "the old-time revival spirit of the college" (Wright).

Goodrich was a particularly strong advocate for organizing a separate theological department for professionalized clergy training at Yale, especially after the disestablishment of Congregationalism in Connecticut in 1818 threatened to secularize education at Yale. Together with his classmate Eleazar Fitch, now Yale's professor of divinity, Goodrich helped raise the $20,000 necessary to open the department in 1822. He was especially interested in establishing a chair of homiletics and the pastoral charge in the theological department. In 1838 he helped to fund the chair with a contribution of $5,000 and eventually resigned from the college to fill it himself in 1839 when the first nominee declined. Goodrich was also closely tied theologically to the department's first professor of didactic theology, Nathaniel William Taylor. Both Goodrich and Fitch were supporters of Taylor's revisions and moderations of Edwardsean Calvinism that became known as the "New Haven Theology." When Taylor's views were publicly proclaimed in his celebrated *Concio ad Clerum* in 1828, Goodrich bought up the monthly newspaper *Christian Spectator* in 1829 and turned it into a theological quarterly for the defense of Taylor and the new theology. Goodrich remained the sole editor of what was retitled the *Quarterly Christian Spectator* until 1836 (it ceased publication in 1838).

Family connections rather than theological allegiances involved Goodrich in the massive project of revising and editing the famous *American Dictionary of the English Language*, produced in 1828 by his father-in-law. The strategy of the *American Dictionary* had been to reform and simplify American usage to liberate American spelling and grammar from the yoke of British custom on the basis of "rationality and analogy." Nonetheless, many of Webster's reforms were severely criticized by reviewers, and in an effort to boost sales Webster hired Goodrich and Joseph Emerson Worcester to produce a single-volume abridgment that could be marketed to schools. However, neither Goodrich (with his admiration for British elocutionary models) nor Worcester shared Webster's enthusiasm for radically Americanizing grammar and spelling, and when the Worcester-Goodrich abridgment appeared in 1841 most of the new Americanized spellings had been removed. Webster sharply disapproved of Goodrich's conservatism, but after Webster's death in 1843, the publishers of the *American Dictionary*, George and Charles Merriam, turned again to Goodrich as reviser and editor. Goodrich superintended a third revision of the dictionary, which appeared in 1847 together with a memoir of Webster, and a fourth edition, the "Pictorial," in 1859.

Despite his numerous educational and theological interests, Goodrich's contribution to the Webster dictionary remains his most significant achievement. As such Goodrich occupies very conservative ground, not only against Webster's attempted innovations, but also against philologists and lexicographers in the next decade who, unlike Goodrich, abandoned attempts to hold spelling and usage to models of English belles lettres and tried to mold American usage to popular and scientific usage. This conservatism of attitude also informed his support of Taylor and the New Haven Theology as the best ideological means for preserving the influence of Calvinism in the state once the Connecticut legislature had ended official state support for the Congregational churches in Connecticut. Goodrich planned a further unabridged version of the dictionary but suffered a stroke in February 1860 and died several days later in New Haven.

• Goodrich's family papers and letters are housed in the Goodrich Family Collection at the Sterling Memorial Library at Yale. He also produced two minor textbooks, *Lessons in Greek Parsing; or, Outlines of Greek Grammar* (1829) and *Lessons in Latin Parsing: Containing the Outline of Latin Grammar* (1832). He contributed a "Narrative of Revivals of Religion at Yale College" to the *American Quarterly Register* 10 (Feb. 1838): 289–310, and defended Nathaniel W. Taylor in "Review of Taylor and Harvey on Human Depravity," *Quarterly Christian Spectator* 1 (June 1829): 343–84, and "Brief Notice of Dr. Tyler's Vindication," *Quarterly Christian Spectator* 2 (Dec. 1830): 608–21. He also published an anonymous review of Horace Bushnell in *What Does Dr. Bushnell Mean?* (1849) and contributed a sketch of his grandfather, Elizur Goodrich, to W. B. Sprague's *Annals of the American Pulpit*, vol. 1 (1857). Goodrich's contributions to student life at Yale are discussed in Theodore Dwight Woolsey, *Discourse Commemorative of the Life and Services of the Rev. Chauncey Allen Goodrich* (1860); Timothy Dwight, *Memories of Yale Life and Men, 1845–1899* (1903); Franklin B. Dexter, *Sketch of the History of Yale University* (1887) and *Biographical Sketches of the Graduates of Yale College*, vol. 6 (1912); and H. B. Wright, "Professor Goodrich and the Growth and Outcome of the Revival Movement," in *Two Centuries of Christian Activity at Yale*, ed. James B. Reynolds et al. (1901). His work as the editor of Webster's dictionary is reviewed in Kenneth Cmiel, *Democratic Eloquence: The Fight over Popular Speech in Nineteenth-Century America* (1900). Two portraits of Goodrich (one from 1830, the other from the 1850s) survive at Yale, and Sterling Memorial Library owns a marble bust of Goodrich. An obituary is in the *New York Times*, 28 Feb. 1860.

ALLEN C. GUELZO

GOODRICH, Elizur (26 Oct. 1734–22 Nov. 1797), Congregational clergyman, was born in Wethersfield, Connecticut, the son of David Goodrich, a farmer and church deacon, and Hephzibah Boardman. Prepared for college by the Reverend James Lockwood of Wethersfield and supported financially by his father's elder brother, he entered Yale College at the age of fourteen and graduated in 1752. After studying divinity, Goodrich was licensed to preach in January 1755; in October he was back at Yale, employed as a tutor. A year later, in October 1756, he was invited to be the pastor of the Congregational church in Durham, Connecticut. Ordained on 24 November, Goodrich continued preaching from the Durham pulpit until his death more than four decades later.

In 1759 he married Catharine Chauncey of Durham; they had one daughter and six sons. The five boys who survived infancy were sent to Yale: the eldest, Chauncey Goodrich, would become a lieutenant governor of Connecticut and a U.S. senator; the second son, Elizur Goodrich, would serve in the House of Representatives; and the third, Samuel Goodrich, would become a minister.

In 1776, the year his first son graduated from Yale, Goodrich was named a member of the Yale Corporation; a year later, he was nearly elected as the college's president, and in 1781 he was seriously considered for professorships in both divinity and mathematics. Goodrich wrote manuscript treatises on difficult scriptural texts, a dissertation on a passage in the book of Genesis, discussions of the prophesies in Daniel and Revelation, essays on Hebrew terms, and an argument against the doctrine of universal salvation. Nevertheless, his reputation as a scholar, recognized by the College of New Jersey with a doctor of divinity degree in 1783, was based more on his abilities in mathematics and astronomy than in theology. These interests, first developed in his undergraduate years and reflected in his yearly computations of eclipses, are displayed in his 1783 "Observation of the Auroral Appearance," which his son later published in the *Memoirs* of the Connecticut Academy of the Arts and Sciences (vol. 1 [1810]: 137–39). Goodrich's command of modern science as well as ancient languages led Ezra Stiles, Yale's president from 1777 to 1795, to call him "an excellent & great Scholar, one of the greatest of the American Literati" (*Diary*, vol. 2, pp. 500–501). According to Stiles, Goodrich lacked the speaking abilities, but not the intellectual acumen, required of a college professor or president. A later Yale president, Timothy Dwight, who preached Goodrich's funeral sermon, noted his continuing service to the college as a member of the Yale Corporation. "No man living probably so well understood the interests of our University," Dwight declared, "or for more than twenty years took so active and important a part in its concerns" (*Discourse*, p. 33). While on a yearly inspection tour of college-owned farms, Goodrich died suddenly in Norfolk, Connecticut.

Goodrich published five sermons in his lifetime: four installation or ordination sermons for fellow ministers and a 1787 election sermon delivered before the Connecticut legislature. As a delegate to the annual convention of Connecticut Congregationalists and Presbyterians from the synod of New York and Philadelphia, he wrote a report assessing religious liberty in Connecticut. These yearly meetings, held from 1766 to 1775, were prompted by fears that the Church of England was preparing to gain power over dissenters by sending bishops to the colonies. In his report, submitted to the convention in 1774 and published twice in the nineteenth century (*Minutes of the Convention Delegates* [1843] and *Historical Magazine* [July 1868]:

34–43), Goodrich defended the colony's religious establishment. He admitted that his Puritan forebears had been too coercive on religious matters but argued that the present system (which would remain in effect until 1818) did not infringe on a Protestant's rights of conscience. Connecticut tolerated dissent from the tax-supported Congregational churches, he explained, by exempting Anglicans, Baptists, and Quakers from ecclesiastical taxes and, since 1770, exempting Separate Congregationalists from nonattendance penalties. Such a system was a step toward multiple establishment and not toward the "religious liberty" championed by most dissenters, who, like Thomas Jefferson and James Madison in the Virginia debates of 1784–1785, called for the complete separation of church and state.

In his 1787 election sermon, *The Principles of Civil Union and Happiness*, and in an unpublished 1795 Thanksgiving sermon, Goodrich declared his political sentiments. He argued that the early settlement of America, the patriot cause during the Revolution (which he had strongly supported), and the establishment of "a rational and free government" all testified that God had blessed the American commitment to the sacred cause of civil and religious liberty. "It was a great favour in divine providence that the American Revolution took at a time when the rights of mankind were better understood and more clearly defined than [at] any other period" ("Thanksgiving Sermon," 19 Feb. 1795). Preserving civil harmony and happiness, however, required more than a zeal for liberty; it required the close cooperation of government, churches, and schools to cultivate a moral citizenry. For Goodrich, the prospects of the new nation and the progress of Christianity remained rooted in the ideal of the New England covenant community.

• Goodrich's manuscript sermons and essays are included in the Goodrich Family Papers at Yale University. He also published the following sermons: *The Duty of Gospel Ministers* (1762); *A Sermon Preached at the Installation of the Rev. Mr. Benjamin Boardman* (1784); *A Sermon Preached July 6, 1786, at the Ordination of the Rev. Samuel Goodrich* (1787), for his son; and *A Sermon, Delivered at the Ordination . . . of . . . Matthew Noyes* (1790). His unpublished papers include "Extracts &c. laid before the General Convention at Stamford" (1773). Ezra Stiles discusses Goodrich's scholarship in his *Literary Diary*, vol. 2, (1901), entry for 24 Jan. 1781. Timothy Dwight, *Discourse Preached at the Funeral of the Reverend Elizur Goodrich* (1797), discusses its subject's character in the last few pages. For genealogical information, see Lafayette Wallace Case, *The Goodrich Family in America* (1889). On Goodrich's relationship to Yale, see Franklin Bowditch Dexter, *Biographical Sketches of the Graduates of Yale College*, vol. 6 (1912), pp. 282–85, and Edmund S. Morgan's biography of Stiles, *The Gentle Puritan* (1962), chaps. 19–21, *passim*.

CHRISTOPHER GRASSO

GOODRICH, Elizur (24 Mar. 1761–1 Nov. 1849), lawyer, politician, and law professor, was born in Durham, Connecticut, the son of the Reverend Elizur Goodrich, a Congregational clergyman, and Catharine Chauncey. Like his father, the younger Goodrich attended Yale College, and excelled academically. He was awarded a Berkeley scholarship upon graduation in 1779 and was chosen to give the Latin valedictory oration.

The most eventful episode of his college career had occurred earlier in 1779, however. When over two thousand British troops landed on the west side of New Haven harbor on the morning of 5 July 1779, Goodrich and other student volunteers, led by Yale Divinity professor Naphtali Daggett, joined a local militia of about three hundred men and marched out to meet them. The Americans could do no more than delay and harass the invasion force while New Haven citizens hid their valuables and ran for cover. Goodrich was one of nineteen Americans wounded in the engagement (twenty-seven were killed) before the British left the town two days later. He had suffered a knife or bayonet wound to the chest and was having the wound dressed in a nearby house when a British soldier entered. Goodrich supposedly leaped from the bed, threw the soldier against the wall, and chased him away, a deed that earned the patriot-student a special place in local lore and the college annals.

From 1781 to 1783 Goodrich served as a Yale College tutor and studied law with his uncle, Charles Chauncey; in 1783 he opened a law practice in New Haven. In 1785 he married Anne Williard Allen of Great Barrington, Massachusetts; they had three children, two sons and a daughter.

Goodrich's career in local, state, and national politics began in 1789 with the first of five terms on New Haven's common council. He would be a New Haven alderman until 1800, the city's mayor from 1803 to 1822, and then alderman again for two more terms. He first entered the Connecticut General Assembly as a representative in 1795, serving as clerk of the house for six sessions and Speaker for two. A staunch Federalist, in 1802 he gained a seat on the Governor's Council and kept it until a new state constitution was enacted in 1818. Along with his elevation to the council in 1802, he was named judge of probate for the district of New Haven, and in October 1805 Goodrich also became chief judge of the county court. However, he left these benches as political changes ushered in the new state constitution.

Compared to his long, uneventful service in local and state government, Goodrich's foray into national politics was brief and controversial. He was elected to Congress in 1799, serving in the last session to be held in Philadelphia and the first session in the new capital city of Washington, D.C. But he resigned his seat in early 1801 when a "midnight appointment" by President John Adams before leaving office made the Connecticut Federalist the collector of the Port of New Haven. President Thomas Jefferson quickly removed Goodrich from that office, having little sympathy for last-minute Federalist appointees in general and believing that Goodrich in particular had been involved with Federalist schemes to secure the presidency for a more cooperative Aaron Burr. New Haven merchants published a remonstrance against the removal of

Goodrich and his replacement by a 78-year-old Republican, Samuel Bishop. Jefferson's reply on 12 July 1801 defended the removal of Federalists on purely political grounds, which Federalists interpreted as a betrayal of his conciliatory inaugural address. The Goodrich removal ignited debates in the press about party politics and civil service; it was the first round of a long struggle between a Republican administration and the Federalist opposition over presidential patronage and partisan control of the judiciary.

While serving ably as a lawyer, judge, and officeholder, Goodrich continued to be involved in the affairs of Yale College. From 1801 to 1810 he was professor of law; among other topics he lectured on the law of nature and nations. From 1809 to 1818 he served as an ex officio member of the Yale Corporation, and then continued as secretary of the board from 1818 until 1846. He lived with various relatives after the death of his wife in 1818 and died in New Haven. Obituaries in the New Haven and Hartford newspapers, written by Professor James Luce Kingsley of Yale, recalled Goodrich's reputation as a judge who tried to mediate disputes without litigation, as a lawyer known for clarity and accuracy, and as a neighbor and church member noted for "kindness and affability." Kingsley also wrote that "his reading was extensive and minute, and what is not very common in public men, he kept up his acquaintance with the ancient classics to the last; being accustomed to read the writings of Cicero, Livy, Sallust, Virgil, and Horace down to the eighty-ninth year of his age, with all the ease and interest of his early days."

• Goodrich's papers, mostly correspondence relating to his law practice and lectures, are housed at Yale University. On efforts of Yale students and professors to repel the British invasion of New Haven, see Henry P. Johnston, *Yale and Her Honor Roll during the American Revolution* (1888); Franklin Bowditch Dexter, *Biographical Sketches of the Graduates of Yale College*, vol. 4 (1907); and Edmund S. Morgan, *The Gentle Puritan: A Life of Ezra Stiles* (1962), chap. 21, "Wartime President." For documents relating to Goodrich's removal as collector of the Port of New Haven, see Abraham Bishop, *New Haven Remonstrance* (1814); the broader significance of the issue is discussed in Richard E. Ellis, *The Jeffersonian Crisis: Courts and Politics in the Young Republic* (1971), chap. 3, "The Repeal of the Judiciary Act of 1801." For genealogical information see Lafayette Wallace Case, *The Goodrich Family in America* (1889). Obituaries are in the *New Haven Journal and Courier*, 2 Nov. 1849, and the *Hartford Courant*, 3 Nov. 1849.

CHRISTOPHER GRASSO

GOODRICH, Lloyd (10 July 1897–27 Mar. 1987), author, art historian, and museum officer, was born in Nutley, New Jersey, the son of Henry Wickes Goodrich, a lawyer and amateur artist, and Madeleine Lloyd. Interested in art from early boyhood and encouraged by his friend and neighbor Reginald Marsh, Goodrich's youthful ambition was to become a painter. After graduating from high school in 1913, he studied at the Art Students League and the National Academy of Design in New York from 1913 to 1918.

From the outset, Goodrich's outlook was progressive—his introduction to modern art was the momentous Armory Show of 1913, which he visited several times.

Goodrich discovered that he did not have the talent to succeed as an artist, but the friendships he made at the league and his firsthand experience with the aesthetic concerns and practical needs of creative artists influenced him profoundly. From 1918 to 1923 he worked first in the steel business and then as an editor in the religious books department of Macmillan Company, jobs he later characterized as "a real detour" in his career.

In 1924 Goodrich married Edith Havens; they had two children. She later helped Goodrich with much of his research. That same year he began writing for *The Arts*, one of the liveliest journals of the day. A year later he became associate editor of the magazine, contributing substantial essays on nineteenth- and twentieth-century American and European art as well as shorter reviews of New York exhibitions. Goodrich wrote pioneering reassessments of the Hudson River School and of the works of Winslow Homer. Another important essay treated Edward Hopper's paintings. This was the first critical article to appear about Hopper, and it marked the beginning of a long personal and professional relationship between the two men.

The Goodriches spent the 1927–1928 season in Europe, with Goodrich continuing as a European editor for *The Arts*. After they returned to the United States, Goodrich became keenly aware of the dearth of scholarship about American art, and he began devoting more time to researching and writing about the subject. Thomas Eakins was one of the American painters about whom little was known; in 1929, aided by a $500 loan from Marsh, Goodrich began writing a monograph about Eakins. During this period the Whitney Museum of American Art was in the process of formation, and in late 1929 Juliana Force, the institution's first director, asked Goodrich to join the staff as a writer, offering him a salary to complete his book. Goodrich readily accepted, and from then on he was intimately associated with the Whitney. After the publication of *Thomas Eakins: His Life and Work* (1933), the most ambitious study to date on an American artist of that generation, Goodrich worked closely with Force in administering the New York regional section of the Public Works of Art Project (1933–1934), the first New Deal art program.

At the Whitney, Goodrich, who became research curator in 1935, undertook a full program of exhibitions and publications. Among the many shows he organized were American Genre: The Social Scene in Paintings and Prints (1935), Winslow Homer (1936), A Century of American Landscape Painting (1938), The Hudson River School and the Early American Landscape Tradition (1945), Robert Feke (1946), Ralph Blakelock (1947), Albert Pinkham Ryder (1947), Yasuo Kuniyoshi (1948), Edward Hopper (1950), Arshile Gorky (1951), and John Sloan (1952). In the theme and survey shows, Goodrich played the present against the past whenever possible, including pertinent works by contemporary artists. In this way a pedigree was established for the living artists the Whitney was trying to promote.

By the 1940s Goodrich had emerged as the preeminent historian of American art. His familiarity with the field sensitized him to the problem of forgeries and the need for systematic authentication procedures. Accordingly, in 1942 he founded the American Art Research Council, a Whitney-sponsored consortium of museums and university art departments that assembled extensive written and visual documentation on American artists. The council was a casualty of a shrinking Whitney budget, but the information collected on the bodies of work of certain artists, such as Stuart Davis, Georgia O'Keeffe, and Maurice Prendergast, was at the time the most comprehensive data in existence.

In 1947 Goodrich was appointed associate curator of the Whitney, and a year later he became associate director. Upon this second promotion, Goodrich accepted increasing responsibility as a liberal activist in the art world. As a trustee of the American Federation of Arts, he protested McCarthyite attacks on artistic freedom and advocated that museums pay artists reproduction rights and a share of admission fees. From 1948 to 1954 Goodrich chaired the Committee on Government and Art, which represented twelve national art organizations. The committee's report, which was submitted to President Dwight Eisenhower in 1954, recommended and offered a plan for legislation on government support of the arts. It later led to the founding of the two national endowments.

Within the Whitney, Goodrich realized that the founder's descendants did not have the means to remain the sole source of the museum's financial support, and he guided its transition from a family institution into a public one. In 1956, to broaden support, he formed the Friends of the Whitney Museum, a group of collectors and art patrons devoted to furthering contemporary art. Under the aegis of the Friends, the museum made notable acquisitions by Davis, Willem de Kooning, Edwin Dickinson, Jasper Johns, Ellsworth Kelly, Franz Kline, Morris Louis, Louise Nevelson, Kenneth Noland, and Mark Rothko. In 1958 Goodrich was appointed director of the museum, and he further opened up the institution by soliciting trustees from outside the Whitney family. He also supervised the building of the museum's present quarters at 945 Madison Avenue, to which it moved in 1966. Often honored, Goodrich received four honorary doctorates as well as awards from *Art in America*, Brandeis University, the Art Dealers Association of America, the American Academy and Institute of Arts and Letters, and the Archives of American Art.

Goodrich retired from the museum to return to writing in 1968. He produced numerous articles and nearly two dozen books and catalogs, including *Edward Hopper* (1971), *Raphael Soyer* (1972), and *Reginald Marsh* (1972). Goodrich's finest and most magisterial book, a two-volume biography of Eakins that updated and expanded his previous work, was published in 1982 to universal acclaim. In the conclusion of *Thomas Eakins*, Goodrich articulated his preference for artists who expressed something elemental about the character of American life. Discussing why Eakins, Homer, and Ryder "were so little involved" with avant-garde movements, Goodrich observed, "The most enduring American art has not always been in accord with the changing currents of its time; more often it has come from the deeper springs of individual and national character" (vol. 2, p. 289). He died in New York City.

Lloyd Goodrich was a key figure in the protracted struggle of American art to gain acceptance and influence, of which the development of disciplined scholarship was a considerable part. When he noticed the lack of erudition in the study of American art, he moved to correct it. He was indispensable to the anointment of Eakins, Ryder, and Homer as the outstanding triumvirate of indigenous nineteenth-century painters; yet he was one of the first to write about these and other artists from a more sophisticated point of view and in a prose style that is admirable for its clarity of thought and expression. Goodrich effectively combined his labors on behalf of the past with an extraordinary sympathy for living artists. The latter was embodied not only in his books, essays, and purchases, but also in his vigorous public stance that called attention to vital issues in the visual arts. These activities helped to establish the Whitney Museum as a trusted institution. Goodrich's prodigious research and reporting on American art, especially his meticulous biographical spadework and gathering of corrective factual data on individual objects, are now the bedrock on which succeeding generations of art historians have constructed their own very different yet indebted scholarly edifices.

• With the exception of three important groupings, Goodrich's personal and professional papers are in the Whitney Museum of American Art and the Archives of American Art at the Smithsonian Institution. His archives on Eakins are at the Philadelphia Museum of Art; those on Homer are at the Graduate Center of the City University of New York; and those on Ryder are lodged at the University of Delaware. Goodrich is the subject of two lengthy and informative oral histories, one conducted by the Archives of American Art and the other by Columbia University. Both are available at the respective institutions, and an excerpt from the Archives interview, "Lloyd Goodrich Reminisces," was published in two parts in the *Archives of American Art Journal*: 20, no. 3 (1980): 3–18 and 23, no. 1 (1983): 8–21. Donna W. Gustafson and Christine W. Laidlaw, "Interview With Lloyd Goodrich," *Rutgers Art Review* 7 (1986): 105–19, contains several evaluations by Goodrich of his own achievement and the changing field of American art. Aspects of his life and career are also discussed in Raphael Soyer, *Diary of an Artist* (1977), and in Avis Berman, *Rebels on Eighth Street: Juliana Force and the Whitney Museum of American Art* (1990). An obituary is in the *New York Times*, 28 Mar. 1987, and the *American Art Journal* published a memorial issue (20, no. 2 [1988]) with reminiscences, articles, photographs, and a chronology.

AVIS BERMAN

GOODRICH, Samuel Griswold (19 Aug. 1793–9 May 1860), author, was born in Ridgefield, Connecticut, the son of Reverend Samuel Goodrich and Elizabeth Ely. The sixth of ten children, Goodrich received scant formal education, attending West Lane School House and Master Stebbins's Seminary.

Because the family's financial resources were limited and he had not demonstrated scholarly inclinations, he accepted work as a Danbury merchant clerk for his brother-in-law in 1808. Upon his first employer's death, Goodrich assumed a position as a dry-goods clerk in Hartford, then served reluctantly for six months in the War of 1812. With the aid of his older friend George Sheldon, a book-publisher's clerk, Goodrich began a system of home education to remedy his deficiencies. In 1816 Sheldon and Goodrich started a venture, publishing American authors, a financially risky activity. Sheldon died soon after, and Goodrich, less experienced than his partner, struggled with the business, often incurring losses. Goodrich married Adeline Gratia Bradley, a Vermont senator's daughter, in 1818. Four years after her death in 1822, he married Mary Boott, with whom he raised six children.

In 1823–1824 he traveled to Europe to meet leading literary figures, among them the English author Hannah More, a successful tract writer, from whom he conceived the plan of writing educational works for children. Goodrich believed that the materials available to children were dreadful. His disgust centered on the stories of Mother Goose, which had offended him even as a child. As an adult, he fulminated against these seemingly innocuous tales and rhymes, declaring in *Recollections of a Lifetime* (1856), "I am convinced that much of the vice and crime in the world are to be imputed to these atrocious books put into the hands of children, and bringing them down, with more or less efficiency, to their own debased moral standard." The other literary offerings available in the early nineteenth-century schoolroom consisted largely of priggishly moralistic texts. The few "readers" that did exist were scarce, and imported books generally had strong British biases, undesirable to a nation seeking its own distinctive vision.

To the rescue came Goodrich's fictional creation Peter Parley, a gouty old gentleman eager to instruct children in a variety of subjects. Goodrich felt that his genial persona, whose name was derived from the French *parler,* to speak, was exactly what American children needed—a friendly, knowledgeable companion who could regale them with intriguing, factually based stories of his adventures, imparting instruction without stuffiness or foolishness. The first Peter Parley book, *The Tales of Peter Parley about America* (1827), is an entertaining narrative of American history and geography, generously illustrated, the author sensing that young minds grasped information more quickly when it was accompanied by pictures. The work was successful enough to go through new editions in 1829, 1830, and 1831, a pace that continued until at least 1860. Parley's vocabulary was suited to the children's ages, and subsequent editions included questions about the contents of each page. Spurred by success, Goodrich wrote *Tales of Peter Parley about Europe* (1828), *Parley's Winter Evening Tales* (1829), *Parley's Juvenile Tales* (1830), *Tales about Africa, Tales about Asia,* and *Tales about the Sun, Moon, and Stars* (all 1830). The Parley books' ready reception is well documented: by the close of the century, some twelve million copies had been sold.

Also popular were the Peter Parley textbooks, including five readers. However, Goodrich did not write all of these books himself. The best known of his geographies, for instance, *Peter Parley's Universal History on the Basis of Geography* (1837), was written by Nathaniel Hawthorne, who noted in a letter to Elizabeth Peabody that Goodrich tended "to feed and fatten himself on better brains than his own."

Goodrich revolutionized children's schoolbooks, both by including illustrations to represent incidents and people discussed and by providing a beloved raconteur. He also stimulated other authors to create their own textbooks. Many of his "facts," however, could be considered offensive—as in the persistent anti-British slant that caused the *London and Westminster Review* to snap, "Peter Parley is a bad dealer in slip-slop on many subjects" (vol. 33, no. 1, p. 149). And Goodrich sometimes relied on fatuous generality, as in *Peter Parley's Method of Telling about Geography to Children* (1829), which proclaims:

The most wealthy and powerful country is Great Britain; the most polite nation is the French; the coldest and poorest place is Lapland; the pleasantest climate is that of Italy; the most cruel and despotic government is that of Turkey; the most mountainous country is Switzerland; the flattest is Holland.

Still, there is a certain charm to the Parley productions. Considering that people are still familiar with McGuffey's Eclectic Readers, which became prominent after Goodrich's texts had been established, it is odd that Goodrich is well known only to specialists.

Goodrich also created *Merry's Museum,* a children's magazine that he edited from 1841 to 1850. *Parley's Magazine,* another children's publication, was begun in 1833 and merged with the *Museum* in the 1840s. For adults, he wrote *The Outcast and Other Poems* (1836) and *The Token* (1827–1842), an annual gift book containing the works of the best contemporary authors, including Hawthorne. Of interest also is his rambling two-volume epistolary autobiography, *Recollections of a Lifetime,* which contains comments on such diverse topics as the social classes, the value of books, and natural history; the study affords a pleasant insight into nineteenth-century New England life. Goodrich also found time to involve himself in politics, serving in the Massachusetts legislature in 1837 and accepting the appointment of U.S. consul at Paris, a post he held from 1851 to 1853.

Goodrich spent his last years in Southbury, Connecticut, where he quickly became a local favorite. Affectionately referred to as "the old gentleman," he had grown very much into Peter Parley incarnate. During one of his periodic visits to New York City, Goodrich died. The greatest tribute to this prolific author was the wide imitation of the Parley books, both here and abroad.

• Goodrich claimed to have written some 170 works. The appendix to volume two of his *Recollections of a Lifetime* contains Goodrich's list of publications as well as commentary on the issue of the numerous spurious Parleys. Goodrich also published the children's series *Parley's Cabinet Library* (1843–1845), and a series of Christmas books, *Parley's Christmas Story Book* (c. 1835–1853), *Peter Parley's Christmas Tales for 1839* (1838), and *Peter Parley's Gift, for 1839* (1838). For adults he wrote *Fireside Education* (1838), a guide for parents; and *Sketches from a Student's Window* (1841), a collection of his contributions to *The Token*. For an understanding of Hannah More's influence on Goodrich, see *Cheap Repository Tracts: Entertaining, Moral, and Religious* (3 vols., 1903) and *The Works of Hannah More* (7 vols., 1835). Also useful is F. J. Harvey Darton, *Children's Books in England: Five Centuries of Social Life*, 2d ed. (1958). Daniel Roselle, *Samuel Griswold Goodrich, Creator of Peter Parley* (1968), provides an interesting biography and valuable bibliography. See also Rita Podell, "Samuel Griswold Goodrich or Peter Parley" (masters thesis, Columbia Univ., 1939). An obituary is in the *New York Evening Post*, 11 May 1860; repr. in *Littell's Living Age*, 9 June 1860, pp. 619–20.

KAREN N. SCHRAMM

GOODRIDGE, Sarah (5 Feb. 1788–28 Dec. 1853), painter of portrait miniatures, was born in Templeton, Massachusetts, the daughter of Ebenezer Goodridge, a farmer and mechanic, and Beulah Childs. Members of the large Goodridge family spelled the surname variously as Goodridge and Goodrich; documents signed by the artist herself show she used both spellings.

Goodridge's education in district schools was modest and her instruction in art informal. According to her sister Eliza, she showed a propensity for art as a young girl by drawing on bark she collected and in sand spread on the floor of her family's home when paper was not available. She studied drawing with an unnamed man who lived in the household of her eldest brother, William, in Milton, Massachusetts, and later in Boston with an unknown miniature painter who was said to have recently arrived from Hartford, Connecticut. Eliza also recollected that her sister read an art manual that described the technique of miniature painting.

American portrait miniature painting—the art of painting likenesses in watercolor on thin slices of ivory—found its immediate antecedents in England, where the art form first rose to prominence during the reign of Henry VIII. In the United States, miniature painting began to flourish in the years before the American Revolution; its popularity only subsided in the 1850s as photography supplanted the portrait miniature as an affordable medium by which accurate likenesses could be taken more quickly. Although Goodridge did take likenesses in chalk and watercolor on paper and in oil as early as 1812, by 1818 she is listed in the Boston city directories as a miniature painter.

Her talent in her chosen medium was soon recognized; her miniature of the Universalist minister Hosea Ballou was engraved by the noted Boston engraver Abel Bowen and published by his brother Henry that same year.

About 1820 Goodridge met Gilbert Stuart, who painted a miniature (Worcester Art Museum) after his portrait of General Henry Knox as a demonstration for her in how to paint a miniature. (Her own miniature of Knox after Stuart is now owned by the Bowdoin College Museum of Art, Brunswick, Maine.) Stuart also advised her to attend the drawing school of Englishman David L. Brown in Boston. Brown is listed in city directories as early as 1818 as a proprietor of a drawing academy. Indicative of their continuing friendship, Goodridge painted in 1825 a miniature of Stuart (of which there are three versions: Museum of Fine Arts, Boston; Metropolitan Museum of Art, New York; National Portrait Gallery, Washington, D.C.) that her mentor thought to be the most successful likeness ever painted of him. The miniature was engraved by Asher B. Durand in 1833 for *The National Portrait Gallery of Distinguished Americans* (4 vols., 1834). Goodridge also copied in miniature several of Stuart's portraits. For example, she painted a miniature of Russell Sturgis (Museum of Fine Arts, Boston) after one of Stuart's portraits of him (Worcester Art Museum).

About 1819 Goodridge became acquainted with the family of the statesman Daniel Webster, who lived in Boston and served as a U.S. senator from Massachusetts. Over the next two decades she painted several miniatures of Webster (Massachusetts Historical Society, Boston; Dartmouth College, Hanover, N.H.; and Amherst College, Amherst, Mass.). Correspondence between the two suggests they developed an intimate friendship and that she lent him a substantial amount of money that he never fully repaid. A highly unusual miniature depicting a woman's breasts (Manney Collection, New York), painted in Goodridge's style, is said to have been painted by her for Webster, according to his family. The senator undoubtedly encouraged her to visit Washington, D.C., in 1828–1829 and 1841–1842.

Goodridge showed exceptional talent in spite of little formal training. Her patrons were affluent merchants and professionals from notable Boston families and from across New England. She also painted family members (miniatures of her parents are in the Worcester Art Museum and of other family members in the Museum of Fine Arts, Boston). Her miniatures are distinctive for the careful delineation of facial features and details of costume and jewelry, especially in her likenesses of women. In her best portraits she achieved a decisive characterization of her sitters. She portrayed her subjects typically against a neutral background of blue-green and brown in a rectangular bust-length format in which the hands are omitted. One of her self-portraits, painted about 1845 (R. W. Norton Gallery of Art, Shreveport, La.), shows her intently engaged in painting a miniature set on a table-top easel with a glass of water for cleaning her brushes beside it. (Two other self-portraits are in the Museum of Fine Arts, Boston, and the National Museum of American Art, Washington, D.C.)

For more than forty years Boston remained Sarah Goodridge's home, and she lived briefly with a brother and then with her sister Beulah. Goodridge achieved a considerable measure of recognition in Boston during the 1820s, 1830s, and 1840s. She was prolific, painting two or three miniatures a week, according to her sister. Between 1827 and 1835 she exhibited her work at annual exhibitions at the Boston Atheneum. Devoted to her family, Goodridge, who never married, was able to support her aging mother after her father's death. She also cared for an ill brother and raised an orphaned niece. By the late 1840s her failing eyesight curtailed her painting. In 1850 she moved to Reading, Massachusetts. Three years later she died during a visit to Boston as the result of a stroke suffered on Christmas. Goodridge became known as one of New England's finest painters of portrait miniatures of the nineteenth century. She was one of the most accomplished women practitioners of that intimate art form, rivaled only by Anna Claypoole Peale of Philadelphia.

• Correspondence in manuscript between Goodridge and Daniel Webster can be found in the libraries of the Museum of Fine Arts, Boston, and the Massachusetts Historical Society, Boston. Sarah Goodridge rarely signed her miniatures, and consequently they are occasionally confused with those by her less well-known, but talented, youngest sister Eliza (also known as Elizabeth). Eliza provided the earliest and most detailed biography of Sarah to George C. Mason, who published it in *The Life and Works of Gilbert Stuart* (1879). Agnes M. Dods published a brief biographical note on Goodridge with a list of miniatures attributed to her at that time in "Sarah Goodridge," *Magazine Antiques* 51, no. 5 (May 1947): 328–29, though several of these attributions are now in question. John Hill Morgan devoted a chapter to Goodridge in *Gilbert Stuart and His Pupils* (1939). Recent catalogs that provide fuller biographies and good illustrations of her work are Dale T. Johnson, *American Portrait Miniatures in the Manney Collection* (Metropolitan Museum of Art, 1990), and Susan E. Strickler, *American Portrait Miniatures: The Worcester Art Museum Collection* (Worcester Art Museum, 1989).

SUSAN E. STRICKLER

GOODSPEED, Thomas Wakefield (4 Sept. 1842–16 Dec. 1927), clergyman and educational leader, was born in Glens Falls, New York, the son of Stephen Goodspeed, an unsuccessful small business entrepreneur, and Jane Johnson. An old stock Protestant, Goodspeed was set on a course for the Baptist ministry by his devout mother. He prepared for the ministry first in academies and preparatory schools in Glens Falls and Poughkeepsie, New York, and later in Galesburg, Illinois, after his family moved to the Midwest in 1855. In 1859 he entered the first University of Chicago, thereby beginning his involvement in a distinctive episode in the history of American higher education.

Following graduation in 1862, Goodspeed spent a year at the University of Rochester, where he received the A.B. degree (1863), before entering Rochester Theological Seminary. Ordained in 1865 and graduated in 1866, he served temporary ministerial charges in Avon and Chicago, Illinois, before accepting a permanent call to Vermont Street Baptist Church of Quincy, Illinois, where he served as pastor for five and a half years. In 1866 he married Mary Ellen Ten Broeke; they had two sons.

In 1872 he left Quincy to assist his ill brother, Edgar, in the demanding ministry at Chicago's Second Baptist Church. The next year he was elected to the Board of Trustees of the Baptist Union Theological Seminary, a financially troubled institution that he helped save through his fundraising efforts. He would later help transform it into the Divinity School of the (new) University of Chicago.

In 1876 he resigned his post at Second Baptist Church to raise funds for the seminary. As secretary of the seminary, he moved with the faculty to suburban Morgan Park where he also served as founding pastor (1876–1879) of Morgan Park Baptist Church. Goodspeed raised more than $250,000 to secure the seminary's financial future—an effort that took eight years to achieve. As a fundraiser, he became acquainted with the businessmen, including John D. Rockefeller (1839–1937), who would later help raise the money to build the University of Chicago. Goodspeed's enlistment of Rockefeller's initial gift of $30,000 for the seminary was the first step in a process of cultivation that resulted in a larger philanthropic effort years later.

On 5 April 1886, Rockefeller, vice president of the seminary board of trustees, wrote Goodspeed warning of Yale University's attempts to lure William Rainey Harper, a professor of Hebrew at the seminary, to New Haven. Goodspeed responded with a plan to relocate the old and failing University of Chicago to Morgan Park (near the seminary) and to make Harper its new president. Harper expressed interest in serving if funds to rebuild the university could be found, but Rockefeller offered no immediate help. In 1886 the old university closed its doors, and Harper went to Yale.

This seeming failure turned out to be the beginning of Goodspeed's most significant work. His proposal to Rockefeller initiated the conversation that resulted in Rockefeller's founding of the University of Chicago and Harper's return as its first president. Goodspeed functioned as advocate, fundraiser, and constituency builder. On 28 December 1886, he wrote Rockefeller asking permission to present ideas for a new university in Chicago. Two weeks later he asked Rockefeller for $100,000 to start the project. Rockefeller declined but then joined in conversations with Harper and Augustus H. Strong, president of Rochester Theological Seminary, about the need for a new university in the country. The next two years saw little progress as advocates lobbied for different sites and contended for various types of institutions, ranging from the small college Rockefeller initially seemed to favor to Strong's proposed $20 million graduate university.

During these years, Goodspeed worked with the Reverend Frederick T. Gates of Minneapolis to create the American Baptist Education Society, a denominational agency charged with studying the condition of education among Baptists. By 1888 the society concluded that a new institution of higher learning in Chicago was "an immediate and imperative denominational necessity." With his own denomination behind the Chicago proposal, Rockefeller finally committed $600,000 on 17 May 1889 to endowment for the new university, contingent upon the successful solicitation of $400,000 in additional pledges for land, building, and equipment.

Goodspeed later spoke of the campaign to secure the first million dollars for the University of Chicago as his greatest adventure. Less than a month after Rockefeller's historic decision, Goodspeed resigned his seminary position to devote full time to the campaign. Working first with Chicago Baptists, he soon branched out into the larger Chicago business community and into other religious groups. Occasionally landing a big contribution like Marshall Field's (1834–1906) gift of real estate on the city's South Side, he garnered most of the support in much smaller gifts from businesses, churches, and clubs of Chicago and other cities. On 23 May 1890, the Education Society reported to Rockefeller that they had raised more than the $400,000 he had mandated. By 9 September the new University of Chicago was incorporated and its new board elected. Goodspeed was its first secretary. For the rest of his life, he served the university as its de facto business manager, registrar, public relations officer, and fundraiser.

When Goodspeed announced in 1912 his plans to retire, President Harry Pratt Judson, Harper's successor, offered him the honorary position of corresponding secretary to the board. Judson's request opened a new vocational chapter for Goodspeed, who prepared at the president's urging a number of historical and biographical books that preserved the institutional memory of the University of Chicago's formative years. Goodspeed continued his literary projects up until the day of his death in Chicago when he was at work on the biography of President Harper.

As a founder of the University of Chicago, Goodspeed is an important figure in the development of the modern university in the United States. A progressive churchman and a lover of rustic outdoor life, he embodied an early form of the American ecumenism that sought to transcend denominational boundaries. Both in fundraising efforts that led him beyond his Baptist world and in his preparation of the materials used to help the university set aside the "forever unalterable" stipulation in its charter which required that two-thirds of its trustees and its president be Baptists, Goodspeed demonstrated the modern religiosity that suffused so much of the institutional creativity of the Gilded Age.

As James Weber Linn wrote in the *Herald-Examiner*:

More than any other man, with one possible exception, Dr. Goodspeed made the University of Chicago possible. The exception, of course, is the first president, William Rainey Harper, but it was Dr. Goodspeed who interested Harper in the plan, as he interested Mr. Rockefeller, and he interested the businessmen of Chicago . . . who were the local founders of the institution. Read their biographies as he has written them, or the history of the University as he has written that, and you would never guess that if they were the stars in the cast, he was the producer of the play.

• Goodspeed's papers are housed in the Department of Special Collections, Joseph L. Regenstein Library, University of Chicago. Important published works are *A History of the University of Chicago* (1916), *The University of Chicago Biographical Sketches* (2 vols., 1922–1925), *A History of the Hyde Park Baptist Church, 1874–1924* (1924), *The Story of the University of Chicago 1890–1925* (1925), and *Ernest De Witt Burton* (1926). His *William Rainey Harper* was published posthumously in 1928. The only full-length biography of him is Charles Ten Broeke Goodspeed, *Thomas Wakefield Goodspeed* (1932). An obituary appears in the *New York Times*, 17 Dec. 1927.

JAMES P. WIND

GOODWIN, Charles Carroll (4 Apr. 1832–25 Aug. 1917), editor and author, was born near Rochester, New York. (The identities of his parents are unknown.) Before finding his forte as a journalist, Goodwin tried a number of careers early in life: schoolteacher, lawyer, rancher, and miner. After going to California when he was twenty, Goodwin studied law and, until he discovered his aptitude at editing, taught school and practiced law. Like many other men of talent, Goodwin was attracted in the early 1860s to the newly discovered Comstock Lode in Nevada by the accounts of its great riches. He tried his hand at ranching and mining there without much success. While Nevada was still a territory, he served briefly as a probate judge. After Nevada became a state in 1864, he was elected district judge of Wahoe County, Nevada, and served for two years. This earned him the sobriquet of "Judge." By 1867 he had again tried his luck with mining, again without success. He then turned to politics and was an unsuccessful Republican candidate for Congress in 1872. In 1874 he became the private secretary of William Sharon, one of the Comstock's wealthiest, most powerful, and most ruthless entrepreneurs. In 1877 he married Alice Maynard of Carson City, Nevada; they had two children.

When Sharon acquired control of the Virginia City *Territorial Enterprise* in 1874, Goodwin was appointed associate editor under Rollin M. Daggett. This position turned out to be formative for the rest of his life. Under the editorship of Joseph T. Goodman, the *Enterprise* had become the leading newspaper on the Comstock and one of the great newspapers of the Old West. At one time or another, the editorial staff included such writers as Dan De Quille, Mark Twain,

Alfred Doten, Arthur McEwen, James Townsend, and Wells Drury. Goodwin knew these men and might have done some occasional work for the *Enterprise* during his earlier years in Virginia City, but once he began full-time work on the paper his talent for journalism became evident. Though his controversial editorials served Sharon's policies with force and conviction, he could also write with eloquence and grace, and he was widely respected. When Daggett was elected to Congress in 1879, Goodwin succeeded him as editor. In 1880, however, he moved to Salt Lake City as editor of the *Salt Lake Daily Tribune*, which he subsequently purchased.

Goodwin came into his own as owner and editor of the *Tribune* because he at last was in a position to establish his own policies. He did so quickly, and the *Tribune* soon became an impressive and influential newspaper in the West. From the beginning, Goodwin showed both a fearlessly independent spirit and also a tendency to extremely conservative positions. An early indication of the former was his attack on Mormonism in its very citadel. His editorials opposed the political power of the Mormon church and some of its religious practices, such as polygamy. He ran feature articles on some of the adverse and embarrassing episodes of Mormon history, such as the Mountain Meadows Massacre and Mormon attacks on Union army units during the Civil War. He also printed freelance articles that mocked Mormonism or challenged its leaders.

It was natural for him, as an editor in a western mining state, to favor the Free Silver movement and to object to the use of imported Chinese coolie labor, but Goodwin became a zealot on these issues. He engaged his former colleague, the Comstock journalist Dan De Quille, to write almost weekly diatribes for years against the gold standard, and he himself published a pamphlet in favor of free silver in 1891 and an attack on the gold standard in 1893. Although Goodwin had coexisted with Chinese laborers in the tolerant cultural and racial melting pot of Virginia City, he became increasingly convinced that the Chinese posed an insidious threat to democracy and white America. In his novel, *The Comstock Club* (1891), American miners who are being ably and loyally served by a Chinese cook and houseboy nevertheless conclude that the country would be better off without Chinese.

Goodwin was deeply sentimental about the "good old days" of the mining country of the 1860s and 1870s and was strongly loyal to his many friends from those times. This quality had both a good and a bad side. On the one hand, he could extend a saving hand to needy friends like Dan De Quille, whose alcoholism had caused him to be fired from his Virginia City jobs, and on the other he sincerely praised some of the most ruthless and dishonest men of the Comstock and other parts of the West, also his friends, for being captains of industry.

In 1913 Goodwin published his valuable memoir, *As I Remember Them*, vignettes of his friends and acquaintances of former times. This book captures the essence of both Goodwin and the Comstock spirit: their contradictory mixture of personal virtues and prejudices, of vision and short-sightedness, and of their unapologetic love of the romance of the pioneer era and the open land that made it possible. He died in Salt Lake City.

• An archive of Goodwin material exists in the Special Collections Department of the University of Nevada, Reno Library. Besides the novel and the book of memoirs cited above, Goodwin's publications include *Poems* (1857), *The Wedge of Gold* (1893), the pamphlet *The Omnipotence of Silver* (1891), the memoir *Steel Rails on the Old Trails in the Western Pacific Country* (1913), the magazine article "The Truth about the Mormons," *Munsey's Magazine*, June 1900, pp. 310–25, and a short-lived periodical, *Goodwin's Weekly* (1902). Little has been written on him directly, and not all accounts harmonize with each other, but some useful information on him can be found in various contemporary biographies and histories relating to the West: Ella Sterling Cummings, *The Story of the Files* (1893); James Dryden, "A Pioneer Bimetallist," *Overland Monthly*, June 1896, pp. 657–63; Samuel P. Davis, *History of Nevada* (2 vols., 1913); Myron Angel, *History of Nevada* (1881; repr. 1973); and Wells Drury, *An Editor on the Comstock Lode* (repr. 1984). More recent publications with information on him include Francis Phelps Weisenburger, *Idol of the West: The Fabulous Career of Rollin Mallory Daggett* (1965); O. N. Malmquist, *The First 100 Years: A History of "The Salt Lake Tribune" 1871–1971* (1971); and James W. Hulse, "C. C. Goodwin and the Taming of the *Tribune*," *Utah Historical Quarterly* 61, no. 2 (1993): 164–81. Goodwin's obituary is in the *Salt Lake City Tribune*, 26 Aug. 1917.

LAWRENCE I. BERKOVE

GOODWIN, Ichabod (8 Oct. 1794–4 July 1882), governor of New Hampshire and businessman, was born in North Berwick, York County, Maine, the son of Samuel Goodwin and Anna Thompson Gerrish, farmers. Raised in a Congregationalist family, Goodwin attended but did not graduate from the South Berwick Academy. (He later received, in 1857, an honorary M.A. from Darmouth College.) Shortly after leaving the academy, he moved to Portsmouth, New Hampshire, where in 1827 he married Sarah Parker Rice. They had seven children, including a daughter, Susan Boardman Goodwin, who married Admiral George Dewey.

Goodwin worked for twelve years for the counting house of Samuel Lord, first as a clerk, then as a supervisor of cargo, then as a ship master, spending a considerable amount of time at sea, before becoming master and partial owner of a fleet of sailing ships. By 1832 he had become a successful merchant and had invested in various business enterprises. He became the president of the Eastern and the Portland, Saco, and Portsmouth railroads; the First National Bank of Portsmouth; the Portsmouth Bridge Company; and the Portsmouth Steam factory, a leading textile company.

Goodwin won election as a Whig to the state house of representatives in 1838 and served as well in the years 1843, 1844, 1850, 1854, and 1856. Ideologically, Goodwin was a "Cotton Whig" par excellence: a conservative businessman who derided antislavery politicians, in and out of his party, as threats to both the Union and economic stability. He vehemently denounced abolitionists, opposed a joint congressional nomination Whigs made in 1847 with Free Soldiers in his district, and supported the Fugitive Slave Act. He served as a delegate in the party's national conventions in 1844, 1848, and 1852 and as a delegate in a convention in 1850 that revised the state constitution by eliminating the property qualification for holding state office. Goodwin unsuccessfully ran as a candidate in the congressional elections of 1845, which were still being conducted on an at-large basis.

Goodwin opposed the passage of the Kansas-Nebraska Act of 1854, which opened up the remainder of the Louisiana Territory to slavery on a popular sovereignty basis, but in 1855 he refused to join the anti-Catholic and antislavery American (or Know Nothing) party, which had suddenly risen to power in the state and which had supplanted both the Whig and Free Soil parties. Goodwin nonetheless permitted the American party to use his name for antislavery purposes. Fearful of defections in 1856, Know Nothings orchestrated a Whig convention that nominated Goodwin as its gubernatorial candidate, so as to allow antislavery Whigs who also opposed the American party's policies to participate without voting for the latter's principal opponents, the Democrats. The Whig platform of 1856 reflected Goodwin's moderate views: it demanded the mere restoration of the Missouri Compromise line rather than a congressional ban on slavery in all of the territories, and while it disdained the proscription of Catholics, it nonetheless blamed foreigners for altering the nation's "distinctive character." Goodwin won only 4.1 percent of the votes, but he may have helped prevent a Democratic victory, as the Know Nothing incumbent governor, Ralph Metcalf, won a plurality of the vote and gained another term.

In the 1856 presidential campaign, Goodwin joined the embryonic Republican party, but he announced that he had not surrendered his Whiggish principles. Such pronouncements, together with his lukewarm support of nativism, fatally undermined his attempts in 1857 to win either the party's gubernatorial nomination or election to the Senate by the legislature. In the first contest, he won roughly 40 percent of the votes on the first ballot; in the second, he won roughly 12 percent of the party's votes in caucus. In both cases former Democrats triumphed over Goodwin.

Goodwin almost unanimously won the party's nomination for governor in 1859, as more pragmatic, less ideological politicians gained preeminence in the party. Many now believed that a former Whig could safely head the state ticket without alienating former Democrats. Because the national Democratic party was badly divided between the prosouthern James Buchanan administration and Stephen A. Douglas's anti-Lecompton faction, many Republicans hoped that a moderate such as Goodwin could attract potential converts. (He had moved toward the moderate Republican position of opposing the extension of slavery, rather than the conservative position of reestablishing the Missouri Compromise line or the radical position of denying Congress's authority to establish slavery in the territories.) Although Goodwin won the election, such predictions proved unfounded. Democrats ran a strong campaign, attacking the state's prohibitory liquor law, its expensive judicial system, and a recently passed peddler act that discriminated against poor and alien merchants. Goodwin's 52.5 percent of the vote was slightly less than that achieved by Republicans the year before. The Republican-controlled legislature adopted several reforms Goodwin advocated. It weakened the liquor and peddler statutes, streamlined the judiciary, and reduced the state debt without raising taxes. Although the legislature passed resolutions critical of the *Dred Scott* decision and the Buchanan administration, at Goodwin's apparent urging it rejected a personal liberty bill that would have safeguarded the rights of accused runaway slaves.

By acclamation, Republicans renominated Goodwin in 1860. Republicans attacked Buchanan's prosouthern record while lauding their own modification of onerous legislation on the state level. Goodwin won 53.1 percent of the votes, defeating Democrat Asa P. Cate for a second time. In his second term, Goodwin signed legislation expanding the state reform school, stiffening voter registration requirements, and appropriating funds to combat a severe cattle disease that had affected much of New England. Although some Republicans favored his nomination to a third term, the principle of rotation in office worked against Goodwin.

During the secession crisis, Goodwin privately counseled Republicans to compromise with southerners on the slavery expansion issue, but after the Civil War broke out, he reacted positively to Abraham Lincoln's call for volunteers. As the lame-duck governor until June 1861, Goodwin used funds raised by individuals and banks to purchase munitions and outfit New Hampshire's First Regiment. Both of these executive decisions seemed unconstitutional, but when the legislature assembled, it validated Goodwin's actions and defeated a Democratic amendment to a war appropriation bill that denounced unlawful military requisitions.

After leaving office, Goodwin's role in politics diminished principally to that of an adviser. He presided over the state party convention of 1863, and he was a delegate in 1876 to a convention that revised the state constitution by abolishing the religious qualification for holding state office, thus allowing Roman Catholics to serve. Otherwise, he spent the last two decades of his life mainly involved in business affairs. Goodwin died in Portsmouth. His moderate views on the slavery issue and his stewardship in making less odious the peddler act and the judicial system helped secure a Republican majority in a politically competitive state.

• The Goodwin Family Papers are located at Strawbery Banke Museum and Library, located in Goodwin's house in

Portsmouth, and a smaller collection is held at the New Hampshire Historical Society. Goodwin's life is traced, albeit partisanly, in Frank Goodwin, "Hon. Ichabod Goodwin," *Granite Monthly* 3 (May 1880): 294–97; and his role during the secession crisis is discussed in William B. Hesseltine, *Lincoln and the War Governors* (1948). For Goodwin's role in state politics, see Lex Renda, "The Polity and the Party System: Connecticut and New Hampshire, 1840–1876" (Ph.D. diss., Univ. of Virginia, 1991). For genealogical information, see Samuel Goodwin, *The Goodwins of Kittery, York County, Maine* (1898). An obituary is contained in John M. Comstock, *Dartmouth Necrology: Obituary Record of the Graduates of Dartmouth College* (1883).

LEX RENDA

GOODWIN, John Noble (18 Oct. 1824–29 Apr. 1887), lawyer, congressman, and territorial governor of Arizona, was born in South Berwick, Maine, the son of John Goodwin, a lawyer, and Mary Noble. He was educated at Berwick Academy and Dartmouth College. After graduating from Dartmouth in 1844, he returned to his home town, read law in the office of John Hubbard, and was admitted to the bar in 1848. In 1854 he was elected to the state senate from York County and the following year was appointed to a special commission to revise the laws of Maine. In 1857 he married Susan Howard; they had one child who survived to adulthood. Goodwin supported the establishment of the Republican party and in 1860 was elected to Congress from the First District with a majority of 1,462 votes. He did not deliver a major speech during his term in Congress, but he was a member of the House Committee on Invalid Pensions. Although the rest of the state remained strongly Republican in the fall elections of 1862, Goodwin lost in his district to his Democratic opponent, Lorenzo Sweat, by the narrow margin of 247 votes.

In May 1862 Goodwin had voted in favor of a contested bill organizing Arizona as a territory separate from New Mexico. The bill eventually passed the Senate after the fall elections, owing largely to the influence of Ohio-based mining interests. Solely political considerations dictated the appointment of officials for the new territory. Goodwin was named chief justice along with a slate of other lame-duck congressmen, including John A. Gurley of Ohio, a chief supporter of the bill, as governor. Gurley became ill, however, delaying the departure of the appointees for Arizona. When Gurley died on 18 August, President Abraham Lincoln promoted Goodwin to the governorship.

The party of officials, traveling in a wagon train with a military escort, took three months to reach the Arizona border. On 29 December 1863 the party halted at a water hole called Navajo Springs, and there, on a snowy afternoon, the territory of Arizona was formally organized. In the new year Goodwin energetically set about establishing the government. He spent a month touring the mining districts and then went east as far as the Verde and Salinas rivers. In the spring he traveled to the southern part of the territory, visiting Tucson in early May. At his instruction, a census was conducted throughout the territory, and elections were held for a legislature. Goodwin was largely responsible for the establishment of a new town, named for the historian William H. Prescott, which became the first permanent territorial capital.

Although Arizona had been secured to the Union cause by July 1862, the southern origins of many settlers created the potential for instability. Goodwin dealt with this problem through a policy of conciliation. He appointed William S. Oury, a well-known Confederate sympathizer, the first mayor of Tucson and acknowledged the political importance of the southern part of the state by basing the First Judicial District there. Convinced of the enormous potential for economic development in Arizona, Goodwin encouraged the development of mineral wealth. He was preoccupied with improving postal and transportation links and was personally involved both in mining and in railroad speculation. In his message to the first territorial legislature, the governor provided an intelligent and optimistic assessment of the problems and opportunities ahead. Identifying the Apache Indians as the chief obstacle to progress, he recommended the formation of territorial ranger companies to assist federal troops and warned delegates that "a war must be prosecuted until they are compelled to submit and go upon a reservation." The governor urged the legislature to repeal the inherited New Mexico laws that permitted peonage and imprisonment for debt, which he regarded as "degrading to the dignity of labor." Following his lead, the first legislative session drafted a code of laws. Goodwin also tried to instigate a public school system and a university, arguing that "self-government and universal education are inseparable." But education seemed remote from the concerns of most early settlers, and in this area he accomplished little.

Although officially Goodwin remained governor until 10 April 1866, he left Arizona toward the end of 1865 after less than two years in the West. In September 1865 he defeated the incumbent Charles D. Poston for election as Arizona's delegate to Congress. Poston was incensed and produced a broadside alleging that Goodwin's election had been fraudulently secured with the assistance of the military authorities. Some confirmation of this charge was provided by General Irwin McDowell, who ordered all military personnel not to take part in Arizona elections in the future. Goodwin's profile was no higher in his second congressional term than in his first. His one speech was a futile attempt to prevent the transfer of Pah Ute County to Nevada.

Despite his principled commitment to the Republican party, Goodwin was not driven by ambition for political office. More comfortable in an administrative role, he decided not to seek reelection to Congress after the expiration of his term. He had been an able and constructive governor in difficult circumstances and in a short time had laid the foundations for stable civil government. However, Poston's insistence that Goodwin was uncommitted to the interests of the territory, although unfair, undoubtedly had some influence on the latter's reputation in Arizona. Goodwin's legacy was further harmed by the fact that he continued to draw his gubernatorial salary in addition to the one he received as delegate. He never repaid the difference in spite of repeated requests from the Treasury Department, and he never returned to Arizona. In 1867 he established a legal practice in New York City and three years later was appointed to a position in the Internal Revenue Department. Goodwin died in Paraiso Springs, California, where he had traveled in search of a climate that would suit his ailing health.

• Goodwin's papers are at the Arizona Pioneers' Historical Society in Tucson. Some of Goodwin's correspondence as governor is in the Interior Department, Territorial Papers: Arizona, in the National Archives, and his message to the legislature is in the *Journals of the First Legislative Assembly of the Territory of Arizona* (1864). Brief biographical information is in G. T. Chapman, *Sketches of the Alumni of Dartmouth College* (1867). A good, detailed discussion of his term as governor of Arizona is Jay J. Wagoner, *Arizona Territory 1863–1912: A Political History* (1970). Also useful are Odie B. Faulk, *Arizona: A Short History* (1970), and Thomas E. Farish, *History of Arizona* (8 vols., 1915–1918). The controversy over the election of the congressional delegate is highlighted by Lawrence Poston III, "Poston v. Goodwin: A Document on the Congressional Election of 1865," *Arizona and the West* (1963). An obituary is in the Portland, Maine, *Daily Eastern Argus*, 30 Apr. 1887.

ADAM I. P. SMITH

GOODWIN, Nathaniel C., Jr. (25 July 1857–31 Jan. 1919), comedian and actor, was born in Boston, Massachusetts, the son of Nathaniel C. Goodwin, Sr., a professional gambler, and Caroline Hinkel. Goodwin attended a private school in Maine. Then at an early age he became a dry goods clerk in Boston, only to be fired for showing up late and doing imitations of the customers. After two years of lessons with a retired actor, which started when he was thirteen, he began to give readings of Shakespeare but found more success in programs of impersonations of entertainers. In his stage debut as a performer, in *Law in New York* (1874) at the Howard Athenaeum, Boston, he played Ned the Newsboy and did impersonations.

Goodwin—a short, pudgy, red-haired, lantern-jawed youth—soon realized that comedy was his passport to success onstage. He made a hit with a comedy sketch at Tony Pastor's vaudeville house in New York in 1875 and in 1876 moved from a program of impersonations at the Lyceum Theatre to a role in a burlesque of *Black-Eyed Susan*. In 1877 he gained further attention as a rising comic in the comedy-farce *Evangeline*. The same year Goodwin married a member of the *Evangeline* company, Eliza Weatherby; she was nearly ten years his senior. With Weatherby, Goodwin had his only child, a son who died young.

Goodwin and his wife formed their own touring company, the "Froliques," and in the next few years performed together in a series of burlesques and farces. Goodwin's propensity for gambling complicated their lives. His comic skill and reputation kept growing through all his offstage ups and downs. A reviewer

for the *Spirit of the Times* exclaimed: "N. C. Goodwin is a born comedian, and season by season he increases his reputation" (11 Oct. 1879). By 1883 he was chosen as comedian for the Cincinnati Dramatic Festival, where he appeared with a number of dramatic stars and played the First Gravedigger in *Hamlet*.

In his twenties Goodwin seemed to take his work lightheartedly. An article in *Harper's Weekly* spoke of times when "it was his custom and his pleasure . . . to take the audience into his confidence across the footlights, to 'gag' his friends in the boxes, and to 'break up' [members of his company on stage with him]" (28 Oct. 1893). In his thirties, after his wife's death following a major operation in 1887, he began to reach for true stature in the theater. A major step toward this goal was the comedy-drama *A Gold Mine* (1889), where he played, for pathos as well as humor, the part of a shrewd if rough-hewn American up against the devious ways of an English aristocrat. Another success came in 1892 with *A Gilded Fool*. By now Goodwin's seemingly effortless comic technique on stage was a wonder to other theater professionals, including the young George M. Cohan.

Offstage, most of Goodwin's time was spent in bars, at poker tables, at the racetrack, or the boxing arena and with obliging women. He gambled on everything from cards to wildcat mining investments. His antics in private life, reported colorfully and repeatedly in newspapers, worked against the acceptance as a serious actor he wanted. Goodwin further undercut himself by the jokes he made in public about his private life and raffish background.

Goodwin's next role, in *In Mizzoura* (1893), did much to compel recognition that his gifts were not limited to broad comedy. A review of the play praised his performance for its "pathos and repressed force [as well as] dry humor" and said that with his acting in the play "Mr. Goodwin may well hope to attain that foremost position in his profession which his legitimate talents evidently entitle him to if he will but allow them fair play" (*Harper's Weekly*, 23 Sept. 1893). Yet, veering from the American homespun parts he played in his two greatest successes to date, Goodwin next tried playing the title role in a costume drama about a great actor, *David Garrick* (1895), with little success. He returned to an "American" part in *An American Citizen*, first tried out in 1896 during a tour of Australia.

With his entire company for the Australian tour engaged and within days of sailing himself, Goodwin met a statuesque brunette beauty, actress Maxine Elliott, in San Francisco. Badly smitten, Goodwin insisted that she become his leading lady on tour. Rumors that Goodwin and Elliott were having an affair while touring Australia soon emanated from members of the company. Neither was free: Elliott was getting a divorce and Goodwin was separated from Nellie Baker Pease, whom he had married in 1888. The supposed affair became a major scandal in the American press. To quell it, when Elliott and Goodwin returned to the

United States in 1897 to appear in *An American Citizen* and other Goodwin vehicles, they announced their engagement. In 1898, by now a successful team and both divorced, they married.

Maxine Elliott, though no great actress, made a good foil for the comic acting of Goodwin with her cool beauty. She also proved to be a shrewd judge of scripts that would show them both off to advantage. Meanwhile, she learned a lot from observing Goodwin's masterful skills on stage. Diana Forbes-Robertson, Maxine Elliott's niece, drew on family recollections to note especially Goodwin's attention to small movements of hands or "his inimitable feet, which could do such special, speaking things [with] a tiny twist of a toe or sag of an ankle" (p. 103). His supposed naturalness came from "hours of work in which gestures, facial expression and moves were mapped out . . . [and from] the most exact attention to timing—nothing too quick, nothing too slow—and a teamwork drilled into his actors that blended their timing exactly to his" (pp. 112–13).

The height of Goodwin's stardom came in plays Elliott urged on him during their marriage. One was the historical drama *Nathan Hale* (1898), in which he at last triumphed in a serious role. Next came *The Cowboy and the Lady* (1899), offering Goodwin another "American" part. In 1899 Goodwin brought this play and *An American Citizen* to London to a favorable reception. Success in London had long been one of Goodwin's ambitions. In 1900 came the pair's greatest success of all, the romantic comedy *When We Were Twenty-One*, in which they toured for two seasons.

Goodwin broke the chain of successes with his desire to appear in Shakespeare on Broadway. He played Shylock to Elliott's Portia in *The Merchant of Venice* (1901). Critical opinion was that both were out of their depth. The failure strained Goodwin's professional alliance with Elliott. She was already impatient of his bibulous set of pals and his offstage excesses, such as the double dose of morphine he took on tour that left him unconscious for two days and cost the cancellation of an engagement. The collapse of the marital partnership came in 1903, when Goodwin failed to please New York as Shakespeare's clown Bottom while Elliott made a hit starring alone in a modern play, and his production at the New Amsterdam Theatre was replaced by hers.

From that point on, Goodwin's career declined for some years. An interview in 1904 pictured him as a man overweight, showing the effects of late nights, "his reddish hair . . . slightly thin at the top," and with a "drooping mouth, that never takes an upward curve even when he laughs" (*Theatre Magazine*, Feb. 1904). His new plays did not equal his past successes, and he seemed to have misplaced his comic gift: on tour in *Cameo Kirby* in 1908, a review in the *Cincinnati Times-Star* spoke of him as "an actor who was once an artist." After a 1908 divorce from Elliott, he married a former Florodora Girl, Edna Goodrich, the same year. They were divorced in 1910. Goodwin was by now becoming notorious in the public eye for his string of marriages. A fifth marriage, to Margaret Moreland, came in 1913.

That year brought a professional ascent, with success on Broadway in a character role. He played Fagin in an all-star revival of *Oliver Twist*, to excellent reviews. Almost at the same time he played the same role in a film version of Dickens's book. A review in *Moving Picture World* exclaimed over his ability to adapt his stage technique to the new medium: "Deprived of the aid of speech and appearing for the first time as a photoplayer the result is remarkable" (1 June 1912). But he persisted in undermining his professional stature. In 1914 he published an autobiography, *Nat Goodwin's Book*. By ill-considered remarks about others there, including his wives, "he wrote himself down a bounder," said an old friend (*Chicago Herald-American*, 13 May 1945).

Goodwin made four more films in 1915 and 1916 and headlined in vaudeville in 1916. He also had more stage successes as a character actor, first in *A Celebrated Case* (1915) and then in *Why Marry?* (1917). The latter was a comedy hit in which he toured all through 1918, while he and his fifth wife divorced. On tour that year, by mistake he applied chloroform to an inflamed eye instead of eye lotion. He lost the sight of that eye, and in November 1918 it had to be surgically removed. He returned to touring before recovery was complete and declined badly in health. From playing in Baltimore, he returned in a state of illness to New York City and there—in the company of an actress who would have become his sixth wife—died of an apoplectic stroke.

In American theatrical history, Goodwin stands among the idols with feet of clay. His talents onstage won him fame. His notorious excesses offstage lost him the respect of the public. His obituary in the *New York Times* sums up the result: "Although long recognized as one of America's foremost actors, Nat Goodwin's personal eccentricities and the frequency with which his adventures figured in the newspapers in recent years have led the present public to regard him more as a unique personality than as a distinguished actor."

• Materials on the life and career of Nat Goodwin are in the Billy Rose Theatre Collection at the New York Public Library for the Performing Arts, Lincoln Center. A list of his stage appearances is in *Who Was Who in the Theatre: 1912–1976* (1978). Anecdotal information is in Allen Churchill, *The Great White Way* (1962), and in Diana Forbes-Robertson, *My Aunt Maxine: The Story of Maxine Elliott* (1964). Goodwin's appearances in vaudeville are covered in Anthony Slide, *The Encyclopedia of Vaudeville* (1994), which also lists his film appearances. Discussions of Goodwin early in his career are in two *Harper's Weekly* articles: "Music and Drama," 23 Sept. 1893, and "The New Mr. Goodwin," 28 Oct. 1893. A view of him in mid-career is in Ada Patterson, "Nathaniel C. Goodwin—An Interview," *Theatre Magazine*, Feb. 1904. A retrospective view is in Ashton Stevens, "Nat Goodwin Noted for Loves and Humor," *Chicago Herald-American*, 13

May 1945. Portraits and production photographs are in Daniel C. Blum's *Great Stars of the American Stage* (1952) and *A Pictorial History of the American Theatre* (1960). Obituaries are in the *New York Times* and the *New York Tribune*, both 1 Feb. 1919.

WILLIAM STEPHENSON

GOODWIN, Ruby Berkley (17 Oct. 1903–31 May 1961), actress and author, was born in Du Quoin, Illinois, the daughter of Braxton Berkley, a coal miner and union organizer, and Sophia Jane Holmes, who had nine other children. She graduated from high school there and, in 1920, moved with her parents to Imperial Valley in California. She attended San Diego State Teachers' College for one year and later taught in El Centro, where, in 1924, she married Lee Goodwin, an auto mechanic. They had five children and adopted another. In 1931 the Goodwin family moved to Fullerton, where she attended Fullerton Junior College, held various jobs, and was extensively involved in civic organizations. From 1936 to 1952 she worked as personal secretary to actress Hattie McDaniel and, more briefly, as secretary to actress Ethel Waters.

During the 1920s Goodwin had won a $100-prize in a short-story contest and was encouraged to pursue a writing career. However, she remained unpublished until 1937, when she wrote a series of "literary treatments" (sketches) of black life, to accompany *Twelve Negro Spirituals* (1937) by noted composer William Grant Still. Goodwin later wrote poems and articles for newspapers and magazines. The first collection of her poetry, *From My Kitchen Window*, appeared in 1942. "An Ode to Lincoln" is the best-known item in the collection, which also includes lyrics on a variety of social and religious themes. Another collection, *A Gold Star Mother Speaks*, followed two years later. Although Goodwin did not lose a son in World War II, she was inspired to write the war-related poems by the highly publicized deaths of the five Sullivan brothers.

Goodwin began her stage career in the 1940s, when she appeared in a Los Angeles production of *The Little Foxes*. She later appeared in *Nine Pine Street*, *Anna Lucasta*, *The Member of the Wedding*, and *The Male Animal*. During that decade she also wrote a musical, *American Rhapsody* (1942), a syndicated newspaper column called "Hollywood in Bronze," and a series of radio plays based on the lives of black leaders. She also continued her education, eventually receiving her A.B. degree from San Gabriel State College in 1949. And she began lecturing to organizations and at colleges and universities. Her topics were race relations, black music, and literature. In her most popular lecture, "Democracy Challenges America," Goodwin made a plea to end racial segregation, and in the process, she referred to her own mixed background of African-American, Native-American, and Scotch-Irish ethnic groups. She also wrote a novel about interracial marriage, entitled *Pure White*, which was accepted for publication but never appeared.

Goodwin's stage acting and her associations with Hattie McDaniel and Ethel Waters eventually led to a screen career. She appeared in *The View from Pompey's Head* (1955), *Strange Interlude* (1956), *The Alligator People* (1959), and *Wild in the Country* (1961), among other films. She also appeared in the television production of *The Life of Booker T. Washington* and in two noted TV dramatic programs, "The Loretta Young Show" and "Ford Theater."

Goodwin also continued to write. Her best-known book was her last, *It's Good to Be Black* (1953), a series of heartwarming autobiographical sketches that portray her early life in Du Quoin and stress the positive impact of family relationships. Much of the author's racial and family pride was derived from her father, a man of little education but much wisdom and energy, who had earned the respect of blacks and whites alike: "He was the eldest son of an ex-slave, but because mining was a hard and dangerous job, no one was too concerned about a miner's background. If he knew his business he was accepted as a fellow worker, and that was his admittance card into the great fraternity of free men." Although racism is not absent from the book, *It's Good to Be Black* explicitly rejects the notion that it was the central fact of black life in Du Quoin. As the author says, "We were colored, but what of it?" Widely praised, the book won the Commonwealth Award for the best nonfiction work by a California writer.

In 1955 the American Mothers Committee selected Goodwin as the California State Mother of the Year. By that time, she had moved to Los Angeles, where she died several years later.

• Goodwin has received very little attention, but she is included in *Black American Writers, Past and Present* (1975) by Theressa Gunnels Rush and others. In 1976 *It's Good to Be Black* was reprinted in a paperback edition by Southern Illinois University Press. Goodwin's obituary is in the *Los Angeles Examiner*, 2 June 1961.

JOHN E. HALLWAS

GOODWIN, William Watson (9 May 1831–15 June 1912), Eliot professor of Greek at Harvard, was born in Concord, Massachusetts, the son of Hersey Bradford Goodwin, a Unitarian minister, and Lucretia Ann Watson, both of old and prominent families. His parents died when he was an infant, and he was raised in Plymouth by his grandmother, Lucretia Burr Sturges Watson. He credited his uncle, Benjamin Marston Watson, with teaching him Greek. He graduated from Harvard in 1851, received his Ph.D. from Göttingen in 1855 (where three of the first five Eliot professors of Greek studied), returned to become tutor in Greek and Latin (1856–1857), tutor in Greek (1857–1860), Eliot professor until his retirement, and emeritus (1901–1912).

Goodwin was the first American classicist to be taken seriously in Europe, as witnessed by his honorary degrees from Cambridge (1883), Edinburgh (1890), and Oxford (1890), and he shaped the character of classical study in this country. Like his great contemporary Basil Lanneau Gildersleeve, he was a scientific grammarian who helped transplant German methods of scientific inquiry to the United States. He called his great work *Syntax of the Moods and Tenses of the Greek Verb* (1860), which he produced at the green age of twenty-nine, "an ephemeral production," but it has been a staple of the field since its publication. This precocious volume, along with the later work of Gildersleeve and Herbert Weir Smyth, established America's preeminence in the field.

When Goodwin studied under his German masters, Karl Friedrich Hermann, Friedrich Wilhelm Schneidewin, and August Böckh, grammatical study was caught between two quite different theoretical camps. One was the "metaphysical" grammar of Gottfried Hermann, who under the influence of Immanuel Kant tried to reduce the skein of grammatical rules to a fixed number that could be grasped by deduction. Instead, Hermann's work had the effect of muddying with philosophical abstractions the precise distinctions in the use of mood and tense, such as that between the time of an action and the nature of the action, or between expressions of absolute and relative time. The other school was the relatively new and uncertain field of comparative grammar, which tended to obscure problems unique to an individual language. Goodwin's great contribution was to remain independent of these two schools (as no German of the time could) and instead marshal examples and compose definitions as soberly and precisely as possible. The clarity of his organization, the depth of his learning, and the cogency of his argument produced a book so masterly that when expanded thirty years later, it needed almost no correction. Yet, like Gildersleeve, Goodwin taught his students that the study of grammar was not an end in itself, but the key to greater appreciation of literature. His greatest legacy was to bequeath his qualities of precision and independence to his many students, who themselves went on to solidify America's reputation in the field of grammatical studies.

He never produced anything else on the order of his *Syntax*. He adapted his principles for schools in his *Elementary Greek Grammar* (1870) and expanded these in his *Greek Grammar* (1879). He revised editions of his predecessor Cornelius C. Felton's translations of Aristophanes' *Clouds* (1858) and *Birds* (1861), as well as Isocrates' *Panegyricus* (1863). He produced minor editions of Xenophon and Herodotus (1877) and major ones of Demosthenes (*On the Crown* [1901]; *Against Midias* [1906]). The famous Harvard production of Aeschylus' *Agamemnon* in 1880 used Goodwin's graceful verse translation (published in 1906), which captured Aeschylean grandeur in a stately American idiom. In addition, he was a founder of the Archaeological Institute of America (1879) and the first director of the American School of Classical Studies at Athens (1882–1883).

He helped in Harvard's transformation from a small college into a university by promoting high standards in coursework and research. He supported President Charles W. Eliot's elective system but also championed a classical curriculum and deplored the lack of support for the ancient classics. He convinced other faculty to support collegiate courses for women and ul-

timately the establishment of Radcliffe College. He served with distinction on governing boards of Radcliffe and Harvard.

Distinctions came to Goodwin as have come to few men. He was twice elected president of the American Philological Association (1871–1872, 1884–1885) and was president of the American Academy of Arts and Sciences (1903–1908). In addition to those already mentioned, he received honorary degrees from Amherst, Chicago, Columbia, Harvard, and Yale, and his doctorate was renewed by Göttingen in 1905.

He married Emily Jenks sometime between 1860 and 1864, and with her he had two sons. Following her death, he married Ellen Chandler in 1882, without issue. He died in Cambridge, Massachusetts.

• There is a small collection of papers, mostly letters, in the Harvard University Archives, Pusey Library. In addition to the volumes named above, he published learned articles in the *American Journal of Philology, Transactions of the American Philological Association*, and *Harvard Studies in Classical Philology*. There is no biography; the chief sources for his life are the following memorial notices: Charles William Eliot, *Proceedings of the Massachusetts Historical Society* 46 (1912): 11–12; reprinted separately (1913); Herbert Weir Smyth, *Harvard Graduates' Magazine* 21 (Sept. 1912): 22–30; Smyth, *Proceedings of the American Academy of Arts and Sciences* 53 (1917–1918): 805–16; Smyth, *Proceedings of the American Philosophical Society* 52 (1913): iii–ix; and by various hands in *Proceedings of the Massachusetts Historical Society* 46 (1912–1913): 11–22.

WARD W. BRIGGS

GOODYEAR, Charles (29 Dec. 1800–1 July 1860), inventor, was born in New Haven, Connecticut, the son of Amasa Goodyear, an inventor and manufacturer of hardware and farm implements, and Cynthia Bateman. In four generations the Goodyear family produced seven inventors. Charles attended school at Naugatuck, Connecticut, until 1817, when he became apprenticed to a hardware manufacturer in Philadelphia. In 1821 he returned to New Haven to enter his father's business. He married Clarissa Beecher in 1824; they had nine children.

In 1826 Goodyear and his father established the first retail domestic hardware store in the United States at Philadelphia. They went bankrupt in 1830. Goodyear thereafter was mostly poor and often in debtors' prisons, where he carried out many of his rubber experiments. He frequently sold furniture and household items for food for his growing family. He began inventing and obtained six patents for mechanical inventions in the period 1830–1834. Early in his career he became intrigued with rubber, which he unsuccessfully tried to use in some of his inventions.

The modern rubber industry originated with the founding of the world's first rubber factory in 1820 by English coachmaker and inventor Thomas Hancock, who later pirated Goodyear's discovery of vulcanization because Goodyear was denied an English patent. In 1832 the India Rubber Company of Roxbury, Massachusetts, began manufacturing rubber bottles, mackintoshes, and overshoes, but they were hard in winter and soft in summer. During the summer of 1834 Goodyear visited the company's New York salesroom, where he became acquainted with the problems afflicting the new rubber industry. Recognizing rubber's valuable properties of elasticity, plasticity, strength, durability, nonconductance of electricity, and resistance to water, he developed a preoccupation with the material and devoted the remaining quarter-century of his life to experimenting with ways to improve, promote, and exhibit it, to the great detriment of his own and his family's finances and health.

Goodyear was neither a chemist nor scientist and used trial-and-error methods. His first successful improvement was to develop rubber sheeting, for which he received a silver medal from the Mechanics Institute of New York in 1835. Unfortunately, the sheeting did not age well and became soft and sticky in warm weather.

In 1838 Goodyear bought the Eagle India Rubber Company of Woburn, Massachusetts, from Nathaniel M. Hayward, whom he hired to work for him. Hayward added small amounts of sulfur to some of his rubber compounds, sometimes dusting sulfur over the surface of his rubber fabrics and exposing them to the sun ("solarization"). He patented this process and sold his rights to Goodyear. Hayward had all the essentials of vulcanization—rubber, sulfur, and heat—and if he had substituted a higher degree of heat for sunlight, he rather than Goodyear might have discovered the long sought "key to the riddle of rubber." However, like other rubber manufacturers, he avoided heat, which caused rubber to melt.

In January 1839, after more than five years of countless experiments, Goodyear accidentally placed a rubber sample that had been mixed with sulfur and litharge (lead oxide) on a hot stove. This chemical reaction of rubber with sulfur at a high temperature, still a poorly understood process, transformed it from a smelly, virtually useless substance into a stable, versatile commercial product with hundreds of uses. Hancock's friend William Brockedon proposed the name "vulcanization" for the process after Vulcan, the Roman god of fire and metalworking. The term became popular, and Goodyear reluctantly but repeatedly used the words "vulcanization" and "vulcanized" in his treatise of 1853.

Goodyear immediately applied the new process to the manufacture of various articles, despite periods of extreme poverty, ill health, and time spent in debtors' prison. He was manufacturing rubber sheet goods by 1841 and other items by 1843, the year in which he again went to debtors' prison and went bankrupt. U.S. patent number 3633 was granted to him on 15 June 1844, and profits from manufactured goods and license fees allowed him to pay his creditors.

Goodyear's discovery saved the ailing rubber industry and converted it into a multimillion-dollar enterprise. His vulcanization process was so simple that many persons used it without paying royalties, and he spent a great deal of time contesting infringements of his patent.

"The Great India Rubber Case," the most famous of these, was filed in Goodyear's name in 1852 by his licensee, the Shoe Associates, against Horace H. Day, probably the most flagrant of the infringers. The trial, considered the greatest American business lawsuit of the nineteenth century, received widespread press coverage because Goodyear's chief attorney was Daniel Webster, then U.S. secretary of state. On 28 September 1852 Goodyear's claim was upheld, but he spent time in debtors' prisons in the United States, England, and France because he used all his available funds on experiments, inventions, and exhibitions.

Goodyear considered himself a missionary for vulcanized rubber and went to Europe in 1851 for this purpose, not returning to the United States until 1858. On 16 April 1844, six weeks before Hancock's English patent of 30 May 1844, Goodyear had been granted a French patent for vulcanization, the first publication in any country to describe the process. However, he was deprived of all rights under this patent for a trivial cause: he had sent several American-made rubber shoes to France before taking out his French patent. For his large exhibit at the Exposition Universelle in Paris in 1855, Emperor Napoléon III awarded Goodyear the Grand Medal of Honor and the Cross of the Légion d'Honneur. Ironically, at the time of the second award Goodyear was in Clichy, the debtors' prison of Paris.

In March 1853 Goodyear's wife, who had shared his dreams, tribulations, and poverty for three decades, died. His single-minded preoccupation with rubber had prevented him from making many friends, and lonely and unaccustomed to caring for himself, he remarried on 30 May 1854 in London. His second wife was an Englishwoman, Fanny Wardell; they had three children. Goodyear returned to New Haven in 1858, reputedly pawning his wife's jewelry to pay for their passage. In 1859 he moved to Washington, D.C. He died in New York City, where illness had forced him to stop while en route to the funeral of Cynthia, his third daughter from his first marriage. The estimates of the debts that he left behind range from $200,000 to $600,000.

Since Goodyear's day, rubber technology has advanced in leaps and bounds and rubber companies are among the world's largest corporations. Goodyear's name lives on in Goodyear tires and the Goodyear blimp overhead. Paradoxically, neither Goodyear nor any of his family members or descendants were connected with the Goodyear Tire and Rubber Company, whose founder Frank A. Seiberling named it to honor one of the most famous U.S. inventors and the founder of an industry that is indispensable in modern life.

• Both volumes of Goodyear's book, *Gum-Elastic and Its Variety, with a Detailed Account of Its Applications and Uses, and of the Discovery of Vulcanization*, vol. 1 (1855) and *The Applications and Uses of Vulcanized Gum-Elastic; with Descriptions and Directions for Manufacturing Purposes*, vol. 2 (1853), together with Thomas Hancock's *Personal Narrative of the Origin and Progress of the Caoutchouc or India-Rubber Manufacture in England* (1857), were reprinted in facsimile as a single volume, *A Centennial Volume of the Writings of Charles Goodyear and Thomas Hancock . . .* (1939). Biographies include S. W. S. Dutton, *A Discourse, Commemorative of the Life of Charles Goodyear, the Inventor, Preached in the North Church, July 8, 1860* (1860); Ralph F. Wolf, *India Rubber Man: The Story of Charles Goodyear* (1939); and P. W. Barker, *Charles Goodyear* (1940). Biographical data are also found in J. D. McCabe, *Great Fortunes and How They Were Made* (1870); P. G. Hubert, Jr., *Inventors* (1893); G. Iles, *Leading American Inventors* (1912); Isaac Asimov, *Asimov's Biographical Encyclopedia of Science & Technology* (new rev. ed., 1978); Guido H. Stempel, in *American Chemists and Chemical Engineers*, ed. Wyndham D. Miles (1976); and George B. Kauffman, "Charles Goodyear—Inventor of Vulcanisation," *Education in Chemistry* 26 (1989): 167–70. Information on the family is found in G. G. Kirkman, *Genealogy of the Goodyear Family* (1899); and on the company in H. Allen, *The House of Goodyear: Fifty Years of Men and Industry* (1949), and Maurice O'Reilly, *The Goodyear Story* (1983).

GEORGE B. KAUFFMAN

GOOKIN, Daniel (1612–19 Mar. 1687), colonial magistrate and soldier, was the son of Daniel Gookin and Mary Byrd, the daughter of Richard Byrd, canon of Canterbury Cathedral in Kent, England. His father's family had been in Kent for many generations; Daniel may have been born in Kent or in Carrigaline, County Cork, Ireland, where his father held lands and was an important figure among the English Protestants who had settled in the southern part of Ireland early in the seventeenth century. The elder Gookin also invested in land in Virginia and went over himself in 1621 with fifty employees, passengers, and cattle. He returned to England but later sent Daniel and his younger brother John to manage his lands and to make their own way in the wilderness. Daniel first appears in the Virginia records in 1630 at age eighteen. In 1634–1635 he was granted land in his own right, 2,500 acres in the Nansemond area on the south side of the James River. By 1639 he was a widower; the year of his marriage and the name of his wife are not known. That year he returned to England, where he married Mary Dolling of London. They had nine children. Early in 1641 they returned to Virginia to settle on his property. He was made a burgess and a representative to the Virginia Assembly from Upper Norfolk County and was also appointed captain of train bands, the local militia.

Gookin was attracted to the Puritan lifestyle of religious self-searching, both privately and in churches with clergy chosen by the congregations, but Puritanism flourished only in the New England colonies. By 1641 when the civil war broke out in England, to choose this Puritan lifestyle was to mark one as a supporter of the parliamentary forces. Virginia's royal governor, William Berkeley, was determined to hold the colony for the king. Berkeley considered the parish system part of the governmental structure and was enraged to be informed that in the fall of 1642 one of the settlers from Upper Norfolk had traveled to Boston with the Nansemond Petition. Signed by Gookin and two others on behalf of seventy-one settlers, the petition requested that Puritan ministers be sent to the area to set up three new parishes. Three ministers were duly dispatched and quickly ejected by Governor Berkeley, who then had a law passed that all ministers were to be bound by the strict rules of the Church of England. The establishment of the Church of England caused endless trouble in Virginia in the next century.

According to Gookin's autobiographical account in his relation of conversion made to the church of Cambridge, Massachusetts, in 1648, Berkeley's actions prompted his move to New England. The death of his brother John in 1643 may have also cut his Virginia ties. He may have made a stop in Maryland; it is certain that he joined the First Church in Boston and was accepted as a freeman of Massachusetts Bay in May 1644. He lived in Roxbury while attending John Cotton's Boston church until, discouraged by the quarrels aroused by the antinomian controversy, he and his wife moved in 1648 to Cambridge. There they became members of Thomas Shepard's church, which was never rocked by heresy or scandal. Gookin enjoyed the affection and trust of Shepard, who on his deathbed chose Gookin to act as one of his executors. He also had a cordial relationship with Jonathan Mitchel, Shepard's successor. In 1665 a special committee was set up to oversee the output of Cambridge's two printing presses, and Mitchel honored Gookin by asking him to be one of two lay members of the committee.

The sources of Gookin's comfortable fortune are not entirely clear. He seems to have kept much of his land in Virginia and Maryland and to have owned trading vessels that sailed between the southern colonies and New England. The government periodically rewarded him with large grants of land in new townships, and Gookin kept one of the most elaborate houses in Cambridge. As he had in Virginia, he served the colony as soldier and as magistrate. He was first made captain of the military company in Cambridge in 1648 and kept the position until his death, meanwhile rising in the ranks of the colonywide military service until he was appointed major general in 1681. In 1649 and 1651 he was elected representative to the legislature from Cambridge; in 1651 he was chosen Speaker of the House. In 1652 he was elected assistant (member of the governor's council) and was reelected continuously until 1687, except in 1676, at the height of King Philip's War.

He moved easily between England and New England during the years of the ascendancy of the Puritans in England, 1650–1660, but never made any effort to move his family back to England. During the years of Oliver Cromwell's rule, he held positions of trust because he was well known as an expert on colonial affairs. The most important of his commissions from Cromwell's government was to try to persuade New England Puritans to settle on the recently captured island of Jamaica. Gookin had the Cambridge press print up a recruiting poster for this venture, but there were very few takers. On the restoration of King

Charles II in 1660 and the wholesale dismantling of the Puritan commonwealth in England, Gookin returned to America on the ship with the regicides Edward Whalley and William Goffe, who had signed Charles I's death warrant and were the subject of intensive search by the English government. He entertained them for months in his house in Cambridge before they were moved to safety in Connecticut. Gookin then turned his energies to dealing with problems of the Native Americans.

Gookin had been a devoted colleague of John Eliot, "the apostle to the Indians," since 1644, when he first settled in Roxbury, where Eliot was minister. He helped Eliot formulate the policy of setting up towns of "praying Indians," who had accepted the Puritan form of Christianity and were willing to conduct their lifestyles in the European manner. In return the Indians were protected from settlers encroaching on their land and abusing them. The most famous of these towns was Natick, about twenty miles southwest of Boston. Gookin accompanied Eliot on many of his missions to the Indians and in 1656 was designated "overseer" or "superintendent" of the Christian Indians. Because Gookin was busy on the island of Jamaica for most of 1656 and 1657, Humphrey Atherton took his place, and Gookin became permanent superintendent only in 1661. The Indians were largely self-governing under their own commissioners, but the superintendent had ultimate jurisdiction. Gookin was convinced that the only hope that these native people had of surviving in a society where they were at the mercy of the constant pressure of white settlement was to adopt European ways.

When the conflict known as King Philip's War broke out in 1675, Gookin was the only magistrate who stood with John Eliot in an effort to protect the praying Indians. He had most of them moved to the islands in Boston Harbor, where, although they were almost without food or shelter, they were safe from the unconverted Indians and from the wrath of the settlers, who made few distinctions between hostile and pacific Indians. Gookin was almost universally execrated by the general populace for his actions, and for the only time in his illustrious political career he was not elected to the Court of Assistants in 1676.

Gradually tempers cooled, and Gookin was able to resume his public career. In 1681 he was made major general of all the military forces of the colony. His son Nathaniel became minister of Cambridge. After Mary's death in 1683 he married a widow, Hannah (Savage) Tyng. They had no children. He died in Cambridge.

Gookin was genuinely fond of Native Americans and wrote two books about them: *Historical Collections of the Indians in New England* (finished by 1674) and *An Historical Account of the Doings and Sufferings of the Christian Indians of New England in 1675, 1676 and 1677* (finished in 1677). By 1674 he had finished half of "History of New England, Especially of the Colony of Massachusetts," but the manuscript did not survive. Unfortunately none of his works were published during the Puritan period. This is a great pity, for Gookin's attitude toward the Indians was much more enlightened than that of most of his contemporaries. He never let his rigid religious beliefs overpower his sympathetic understanding of humanity.

• Besides the original manuscript of the *Historical Collections*, the Massachusetts Historical Society possesses Gookin material that relates to his efforts to convert the Indians. The New England Historic Genealogical Society has some manuscripts relating to the church in Cambridge. The American Antiquarian Society owns the Shepard notebook. F. W. Gookin's life of his ancestor, *Daniel Gookin, 1612–1687: Assistant and Major General of the Massachusetts Bay Colony* (1912), reprints all the relevant documents, including much on Gookin's work with the Indians. The best genealogical account of the Gookin family is *Adventurers of Purse and Person: Virginia 1607–1624/5*, rev. and ed. Virginia M. Meyer and John F. Dorman (1987). For the Puritans in Virginia, see Babette M. Levy, "Early Puritanism in the Southern and Island Colonies," *Proceedings of the American Antiquarian Society* 70 (1960): 69–348. The Nansemond Petition episode is discussed in Jon Butler, "Two 1642 Letters from Virginia Puritans," *Proceedings of the Massachusetts Historical Society* 84 (1972): 99–109. The autobiographical relations of conversion by both Daniel and Mary Gookin were printed for the first time in Mary Rhinelander McCarl, ed., "Thomas Shepard's Record of Relations of Religious Experience, 1648–1649," *William and Mary Quarterly*, 3d ser., 48 (1991): 432–66. Gookin is only mentioned in passing in modern histories of King Philip's War, but a useful article on the Christian Indians is Neal Salisbury, "Red Puritans: The 'Praying Indians' of Massachusetts Bay and John Eliot," *William and Mary Quarterly*, 3d ser., 31 (1974): 27–54. Gookin's *Historical Collections of the Indians in New England* was first published in 1792 by the Massachusetts Historical Society in the first issue of their *Collections* and was reprinted in 1972. *An Historical Account of the Doings and Sufferings of the Christian Indians* was published by the American Antiquarian Society in *Transactions and Collections*, vol. 2 (1836).

MARY RHINELANDER MCCARL

GORDIN, Jacob (1 May 1853–11 June 1909), playwright and teacher, was born in Mirgorod, Ukraine, the son of Yekhiel Mikhel Ha-Levi Gordin, a prosperous merchant, and Ida (maiden name unknown). Gordin received both a secular education and a grounding in traditional Jewish studies. Most of his early jobs were as a Russian-language journalist, at which he made a name for himself for his vignettes of Jewish life. He may also have worked in the Russian theater. He married Anna Itskowitz in 1872; they had eleven children.

Gordin developed a political philosophy that aimed to transform Russian Jews into productive citizens of a revolutionary order. They were to become physical laborers on the land—he himself lived as a laborer for several years—and were to abandon all Jewish ritual and to see the Bible from a Tolstoyan perspective. In 1891 a project to found a Jewish socialist colony forced him to flee from czarist police to New York City's Lower East Side, one of many Russian-Jewish intellectuals who migrated within the same few years. There he began to write, primarily in Yiddish, still aiming to convert the Jewish community to his ideals of Tolstoyan spirituality and radical politics.

Although he was to make his greatest mark as a Yiddish dramatist, initially Gordin scorned Yiddish theater. Secular professional Yiddish theater had originated only fifteen years earlier, in Romania, and was flourishing, especially in America. Although its actors and music were often excellent, the plays were lowbrow, folksy, popular entertainments. In 1891, attracted by a vignette Gordin had published in a newspaper, a group of actor-managers approached him to write a new play. Gordin agreed, partly because he had a wife and children to support, but also because he felt he could improve the quality of Yiddish theater. Through his plays he hoped to uplift newly arrived, uneducated Yiddish audiences and secular Yiddish culture itself. "I wrote my first play," he recalled, "the way a pious man, a scribe, copies out a Torah scroll."

This first play, *Siberia*, a melodrama, opened at the Union Theater in New York in 1891. Rehearsals were stormy, for Gordin brought reforms to the production that reflected trends in contemporaneous avant-garde theater in Europe. He insisted on verisimilitude above all and on the primacy of the text. Both of these ideals required the actors to submerge their personalities in their roles; Gordin outlawed ad-libbing, clowning, and musical interpolations. A further ideal was the purification of Yiddish literary language, making it flexible and consistent. It had been less than a half-century since Yiddish had evolved into a medium for modern novelists and journalists. Common stage practice was to flip from vulgarisms, especially for comic dialogue, to grandly high-flown Germanicized forms for noble characters and sentiments. Gordin was the first champion of flowing colloquial Yiddish dialogue, tempered only by fidelity to the characters' "natural" ways of speaking.

All these austerities frustrated not only the actors, but the opening night audience as well, which found *Siberia* "dry" at first, despite the moving plot. But toward the final curtain, when the comic servant said a heartbroken farewell to his master, who had been exiled to Siberia, everyone in the theater wept. By general agreement, Yiddish theater was now considered a serious modern art form. Thus, the decade beginning with *Siberia* is generally called the Gordin Era, or sometimes the Golden Age, of Yiddish theater.

Gordin's plays were powerfully theatrical. Realism was his creed. However, like his hero Tolstoy, he did not jettison old-fashioned melodrama but heightened its emotional extremes, its shorthand symbolism, and the twists of suspense that intensify the logic of its developing plot. A trademark was the trenchant aphorism, especially used as an arresting curtain line. Gordin introduced minor characters for comic relief, often giving them a dark and grotesque quality reminiscent of Tolstoy's characters.

Gordin often wrote juicy roles for specific stars. Among the "Gordin actors" were most of the famous Yiddish players of his day. All seized the chance to identify themselves with a Gordin role and to revive it as frequently as possible. Jacob Adler played the title roles in *The Jewish King Lear* and *Shlomke the Charlatan*; David Kessler, Appolon and the Faust figure Hershele Dubrovner; Sara Adler, Bas-sheva, the immigrant woman who cannot adjust to a new life in *Without a Home*. Boris and Bessie Thomashefsky both enacted Gordin roles, and Sigmund Mogulesko, the inspired clown who once threw Gordin out of rehearsals because the author would not let him mug to the crowd, went on to create a number of characters both comic and heartrending. Keni Liptzin in the United States and Ester-Rokhl Kaminska in Poland both played Mirele Efros, the Jewish Queen Lear, a rivalry considered a public duel for supremacy. The beautiful Bertha Kalich is supposed to have coaxed Gordin to "write a play for my hair." Specifically for her he wrote the romantic dramas *Sappho* and *The Kreutzer Sonata*.

Gordin aimed to educate the Yiddish masses so they could participate in the culture of modern Western civilization. He based *God, Man, and Devil* on the Faust story; he founded *The Jewish King Lear* and *Mirele Efros; or, The Jewish Queen Lear* on Shakespeare's *King Lear*; he named the handsome musician in *Sappho* Apollon; in every case he made sure that the dialogue explained his sources, thus broadening the audience's education. He also used his plays as a forum for moral and specifically political issues. Among his deepest concerns were women's rights, international socialist brotherhood, and the distinction he perceived between religious orthodoxy and true goodness.

Outside the theater Gordin was a founder of the Educational League, dedicated to evening classes for workers. He lectured there and elsewhere. He constantly wrote in journals, exhorting Jews toward justice, enlightenment, self-respect, and socialist brotherhood. In 1897 he founded the Free Yiddish Folk Theater, a reading and discussion club dedicated to creating a better Yiddish theater. In 1901–1902 he put out a Yiddish newspaper, *Theater Journal and Family Paper*, which failed, and in 1904 he tried again with the *Drama World*, also in Yiddish and also short-lived. From podium or coffeehouse, through the force of his passions, as well as through the influence of his charismatic presence and good looks, he attracted many readers, hearers, and disciples.

Gordin wrote at least thirty-five plays. Possibly he wrote twenty or thirty more, under many pseudonyms, for to earn a living he turned out a constant stream of plays, and journalistic articles, and vignettes. By the turn of the century his position in the community diminished, and some of his political positions became controversial. Literary tastes among the intelligentsia shifted from melodrama to newer forms. Meanwhile, theatrical activity on the Lower East Side, which had been dominated by the radical intellectuals who arrived in the 1890s, now reflected a new wave of immigrants fleeing pogroms: uneducated Jewish workers, who were drawn to the Lower East Side's newest attractions, music halls and silent films.

Nevertheless, Gordin continued to write, and some of his plays remained popular for a long time on the Yiddish stage and in Yiddish films as well as in English, Russian, Polish, and Hebrew translation. *God, Man, and Devil* and *Mirele Efros* were still performed in the 1990s. Gordin's larger influence continued to be felt, as evidenced by the many amateur drama clubs named in his memory. He died in New York City.

Besides being an important community leader, Gordin was a major figure in the movement that created a modern secular intellectual life in the Yiddish-speaking communities of the United States and eastern Europe, establishing Yiddish culture as part of modern intellectual life. Through his influence, the higher aspirations of Yiddish culture became and have remained associated with Yiddish theater.

• Information about Gordin, including much archival material, is available in Yiddish at the YIVO Institute for Jewish Research in New York City. Volumes of many of Gordin's plays in the original language are available at YIVO and in the libraries of Brown University (the Harris Collection), Harvard University, the Jewish Theological Seminary of America in New York, the University of Tel Aviv, and the Hebrew University in Jerusalem. Several Yiddish film versions of his works are available through the Rutenberg and Everett Yiddish Film Library, YIVO, and a few commercial video outlets. An English version of Gordin's *The Kreutzer Sonata*, adapted by Langdon Mitchell, was published by H. G. Fiske in 1907; it can be found at the New York Public Library (Library and Museum of the Performing Arts). Another translation is the title work of Nahma Sandrow, ed., *"God, Man, and Devil": An Anthology of Yiddish Drama* (1997). Sandrow's *Vagabond Stars: A World History of Yiddish Theater* (1972; 2d rev. ed., 1996), pp. 132–63, is the fullest treatment of Gordin's life and career.

NAHMA SANDROW

GORDON, Andrew (17 Sept. 1828–13 Aug. 1887), Presbyterian missionary, was born in Putnam, New York, the son of Alexander Gordon, a Scottish missionary, and Margaret Martin. Gordon spent much of his childhood working to support his family and sporadically attending country schools and an academy. He graduated from Franklin College in Ohio in 1850 and then studied theology at the theological seminary in Canonsburg, Pennsylvania. In 1852 he married Rebecca Campbell Smith. They had five children, one of whom died in childhood. Licensed to preach on 2 November 1853, Gordon supplied pulpits for two years in the Delaware Presbytery of Delaware County, New York.

In 1853 a resolve by the Associate Presbyterian Synod of North America to send missionaries to India resulted in Gordon's ordination "to preach the Gospel in North India" in August 1854. The family embarked on their journey in September 1854, arriving in India in February 1855. Gordon's wife expressed reservations about their new life until a hunter's stray bullet narrowly missed their elder daughter's head and struck Rebecca's mother in the arm, an event the family interpreted as a message that their safety would be guarded in India. Upon their arrival, they immediately traveled 1,100 miles overland to Saharanpur to consider sites for the construction of a mission station. Because of the British annexation of Punjab in 1849, the area was relatively free of missionaries, and Gordon established the populous Sialkot as the center for his work. When the union of the Associated and Reformed Presbyterian churches created the United Presbyterian Church of North America in May 1858, the mission was given over to that body.

The establishment of the permanent mission in Sialkot coincided with the outbreak of the Sepoy mutiny of 1857. This uprising quickly engulfed northern India, and the rebels massacred many Europeans. In grave danger and far from government protection, the missionaries escaped to Fort Lahor. Upon their return, they found their neighboring Scottish missionaries, the Reverend and Mrs. Thomas Hunter, slaughtered in their home. Gordon's account cast an insightful look into these events. With the help of his sister Elizabeth, Gordon built several orphanages and schools during his ten-year tenure. He also succeeded in converting a small number of high-caste Hindus and a handful of Megs, a local weaver caste. At the end of his first tour in India, the mission counted thirty-four native communicants. The Gordons left India for health reasons on 28 November 1864.

Back in the United States, Gordon lectured for ten years on India and its need for missions. He supported his family by working in the lumber business in Cedar Rapids, Iowa, and peddling soap in Philadelphia, Pennsylvania. He returned with his family to India on 10 December 1875. Upon settling in Gurdaspur on 7 February 1876, he adopted a change in his missionary strategy. He devoted himself to preaching to the poor and outcast instead of the wealthy, educated audiences he unsuccessfully cultivated in Sialkot. This new approach represented his belief that the lower classes would adopt Christianity in greater numbers than the privileged peoples in India, who profited from the material and spiritual subjugation of others. He was extremely successful in converting the Chuhras, a scavenging cast of the Punjab. Gordon helped establish a hospital in Gurdaspur in September 1880. Upon Gordon's departure from India in April 1885, the North India Mission numbered over 2,000 communicants. At his death, the churches he founded claimed 4,019 practicing Christians. When he died he was working on a translation of the Psalms into Urdu, and many of these were accepted by the Sialkot Presbytery for use in Scripture and liturgy. Gordon died in Philadelphia.

By many accounts, Gordon was uniquely suited to the missionary calling. He was known to be kind, soft-spoken, and respectful of all Indians, an attitude that won him many hearers and perhaps saved his family's lives during the mutiny. One native testified that he had "never before met any one who presented the cause of Christ so well and did not get angry" (*Memorial to Dr. Andrew Gordon*, p. 29). The eventual success of the Punjab mission can no doubt be attributed to his character and reputation.

• Some of Gordon's papers are in the Department of History of the Presbyterian Church (U.S.A.) in Philadelphia. Gordon's only published work, *Our India Mission* (1886), details his own missionary labors and presents a history of the first thirty years of the North India Mission. Biographical information is in a collection of eulogies composed on his death, *Memorial to Dr. Andrew Gordon* (1887). An obituary is in the *Philadelphia Inquirer*, 15 Aug. 1887.

BRIAN K. PENNINGTON

GORDON, Anna Adams (21 July 1853–15 June 1931), temperance reformer, was born in Boston, Massachusetts, the fourth of seven children of James Monroe Gordon, a bank teller and treasurer of the American Board of Commissioners for Foreign Missions, and Mary Elizabeth Clarkson. She attended public schools and Mount Holyoke Seminary in 1871. After only one year she transferred to Lasell Seminary in Auburndale, Massachusetts, finishing her studies in 1875.

Upon graduation Gordon intended to spend one year abroad and then study music, specifically the organ. However, when she returned to the United States Gordon met Frances E. Willard at a revival meeting led by Rev. Dwight L. Moody. Immediately, the two became friends. Gordon became the older woman's secretary and soon began living with her in Evanston, Illinois. Although neither woman ever married or had a long-term relationship with a man, their relationship seems to have been more like that of a mother and daughter than that of lovers. Willard was elected president of the Woman's Christian Temperance Union (WCTU) in 1879; Gordon, still working as her secretary, was naturally drawn into the movement. Both separately and together, the two traveled across America, lecturing, holding rallies, and organizing chapters of the WCTU.

Gordon was especially involved with the children's branch of the WCTU, the Loyal Temperance Legion. In 1891 she was named superintendent of juvenile work for the World's Woman's Christian Temperance Union. Despite the prestige and demands of this post, Gordon still spent most of her time working for Willard, organizing her private affairs and WCTU involvements. Willard was a highly controversial figure in the union, arguing for, for example, an unpopular proposal to officially endorse the Prohibition party. By avoiding heavy involvement in the controversial issues dividing the WCTU, Gordon remained widely liked and friendly with all parties. However, she always firmly supported her friend and employer. Willard died in 1898. Devastated by her friend's death, Gordon wrote two tributes, the biographical *The Beautiful Life of Frances E. Willard* (1898) and *What Frances Willard Said* (1905). She also organized the construction of several memorials to her friend and successfully campaigned for Willard's birthday to become a school holiday in some areas. Willard's memorial statue in Statuary Hall in the Capitol in Washington, D.C., was unveiled in 1905, and in 1923 she was inaugurated into the National Hall of Fame of New York University.

Gordon continued work with the WCTU, serving as vice president under Lillian M. N. Stevens. Still heavily involved with the youth organizations of the temperance movement, she established the Young Campaigners for Prohibition in 1910. When Stevens died in 1914, Gordon became president of the WCTU. The organization was in the middle of an intensive campaign in cooperation with the Anti-Saloon League to pass a federal prohibition amendment. Gordon coined the slogan "Every White Ribboner a Prohibition Patriot," implying a link between temperance and patriotism. The campaign ended in success with the passage of the Eighteenth Amendment outlawing the manufacture, sale, or transport of alcohol in January 1919. The union continued education and public opinion work but also diversified into campaigns for social reforms, child welfare, and the integration of immigrants into American culture. Membership in the WCTU rose sharply in 1921, benefiting from the exposure afforded by its regional conferences. The "Jubilee Convention," two years later, also brought the organization publicity, most memorably through newspaper coverage of Gordon's pouring three hundred bottles of illegal whiskey down street sewers. The union's popularity resulted in an extremely successful fundraising campaign the following year and a membership drive that topped one million.

With the success of the prohibition campaign in the United States, Gordon's interests shifted to the international temperance movement. After a European lecture tour promoting temperance, she was elected president of the World's Woman's Christian Temperance Union in 1921. She resigned from the presidency of the national association in 1925 to devote herself fulltime to her office in the world organization. She died of myocarditis in a sanatorium in Castile, New York.

• For further information see Benjamin F. Austin, ed., *The Prohibition Leaders of America* (1885), and Helen E. Tyer, *Where Prayer and Purpose Meet: The W.C.T.U. Story* (1949). On Gordon's involvement with Willard see Mary Earhart, *Frances Willard: From Prayers to Politics* (1944), and Frances E. Willard, *Woman and Temperance* (1883). Obituaries are in the *New York Times* and the *Evanston (Ill.) News-Index*, 16 June 1931.

ELIZABETH ZOE VICARY

GORDON, Arthur Ernest (7 Oct. 1902–11 May 1989), Latin epigraphist, was born in Marlborough, Massachusetts, the son of Arthur Ernest Gordon, a storekeeper, and Susan Esther Porter. Growing up in modest circumstances, Gordon attended Dartmouth College (1919–1923) and, on the receipt of an A.B. in Latin, was sent on a Dartmouth fellowship to the American Academy in Rome (1923–1925). In 1924 he married Maddalena Belloni, with whom he had one child.

After two years as an instructor in Latin at Dartmouth (1925–1927), Gordon entered graduate studies at Johns Hopkins University as a student assistant in ancient history (1927–1928), further aided by a Dartmouth fellowship. In the following year he was a Johnston fellow at Johns Hopkins, earning a Ph.D. in 1929 in Latin with the dissertation "Local Cults of Latium" under the supervision of Tenney Frank. He then served a year as associate professor of Latin and ancient history at the University of Vermont. In 1930 he was appointed assistant professor of Latin at the University of California at Berkeley, in which department he rose to the rank of professor and was chair from 1953 to 1959, retiring as professor emeritus in 1970. His first marriage ended in divorce in 1936. In 1937 he married Joyce Anna Stiefbold, who was to become a fellow researcher and frequent collaborator in Latin epigraphical studies. They had no children.

Gordon continued a lifelong association with the American Academy in Rome, on whose advisory council to the School of Classical Studies he served from 1940 until his retirement, by returning as senior research fellow for 1948–1949, and again as Guggenheim fellow and Fulbright research scholar in 1955–1956, and finally as National Endowment for the Humanities senior fellow during 1972–1973, when he and his wife made an extensive tour of epigraphical collections.

From his dissertation and his student experience in Rome, Gordon produced "Cults of Aricia" and "Cults of Lanuvium" (*University of California Publications in Classical Archaeology* 2, nos. 1 and 2 [1934]: 1–20 and 21–58), early evidence of his ability to draw significant cultural evidence from epigraphical sources. His maturing as an epigraphist was demonstrated by articles on the first appearance of the cognomen in freedmen's inscriptions, on marble as a criterion for dating of inscriptions, and on supralineate abbreviations; these technical studies were harbingers of his powers of observation and mastery and reporting of epigraphical detail.

Each of the periods at the American Academy resulted in major publications. From 1948 the Gordons were studying inscriptions and collecting squeezes and evidence for the dating of Latin inscriptions. A number of incidental works emerged from this effort. In a visit to the storerooms of the Museo Nazionale delle Terme in Rome, Gordon noted a fragment that he identified and published as "A New Fragment of the *Laudatio Turiae*." The garden of the same museum yielded "Quintus Veranius Consul A.D. 49: A Study Based upon His Recently Identified Sepulchral Inscription" (*University of California Publications in Classical Archaeology* 2, no. 5 [1952]: viii, 231–352), which included a typical pair of invaluable appendices on *curatores* of temples and public works and of triumphal honors and statues set up in Rome during the empire. Work begun in 1948–1949 and continued in 1955–1957 produced the *Album of Dated Latin Inscriptions in Rome and the Neighborhood. Augustus to Nerva* (1958) and "Contributions to the Palaeography of Latin Inscriptions" (*University of California Publications in Classical Archaeology* 3, no. 3 [1957]: xii, 65–242), both in collaboration with Joyce Gordon. Giancarlo Susini wrote of these works, "A further, and in some respects definitive, step forward in the assessment of Roman inscriptions from the point of view of writing has been taken by Arthur and Joyce Gordon in their monumental re-

cent collection of dated Latin inscriptions and in their masterly contributions to the palaeography of Latin inscriptions" (*The Roman Stonecutter*, ed. E. Badian, trans. A. M. Dabrowski [1973], pp. 7–8). The 1973 visit and that to the Fondation Hardt in 1975 allowed the final site observations for the *Illustrated Introduction to Latin Epigraphy* (1983).

In 1952 Gordon was a member of the Second International Congress of Greek and Latin Epigraphy in Paris, and in 1953 he was a lecturer for the Archaeological Institute of America. In 1975 he held membership in the Fondation Hardt pour L'étude de l'antiquité classique. After his formal retirement from Berkeley he held two visiting professorships, at Ashland College (Ohio) for the autumn semester of 1970 and at the Ohio State University (Columbus) for the autumn quarter of 1971. Gordon died in Oakland, California.

As a classicist Gordon had an international reputation as a distinguished epigraphist, noted for his meticulous research, his carefully documented scholarship, his passion for accuracy, and his perseverance in major scholarly undertakings. The Gordons' magisterial *Album of Dated Latin Inscriptions* (7 vols., 1958–1965) is widely recognized as an enduring masterwork, and the concomitant "Contributions to the Palaeography of Latin Inscriptions" offers remarkable perceptions in an area too little treated. The *Illustrated Introduction to Latin Epigraphy* is far more than that; the detail of observations in the introduction and in the descriptive commentaries on the 100 inscriptions speaks to the expert as well as to the novice. The sum of his many articles, reviews, and monographs is characterized by his thoroughness and his strong sense that all the evidence should be made available to the reader and that precision in the knowledge of the ancient languages and of expression in the modern ones is a key to effective scholarship.

• A complete set of the writings of A. E. Gordon has been collected and is available for consultation at the Center for Epigraphical and Palaeographical Studies, Ohio State University, Columbus. Other important contributions to the field of Latin epigraphy include "On the First Appearance of the Cognomen in Latin Inscriptions of Freedmen," *University of California Publications in Classical Archaeology* 1, no. 4 (1935): 151–58; (with Joyce S. Gordon), "Roman Names and the Consuls of A.D. 13," *American Journal of Philology* 72, no. 3 (1951): 283–92; "Letter Names of the Latin Alphabet," *University of California Studies in Classical Antiquity* 9 (1973): i–ix, 1–70; "The inscribed *Fibula Praenestina*: Problems of Authenticity," *University of California Studies in Classical Antiquity* 16 (1975): 1–84; "Further Remarks on the Inscribed Gold *Fibula Praenestina*," *Epigraphica* 40 (1978): 32–39; and twenty-one articles on the Veranii in Pauly-Wissowa, ed., *Realencyclopädie der classischen Altertumwissenschaft* (1955).

CHARLES L. BABCOCK

GORDON, Caroline Ferguson (6 Oct. 1895–11 Apr. 1981), author and teacher, was born on Merimont farm, near Trenton, Kentucky, the daughter of James Maury Morris Gordon, a teacher and preacher, and Nancy Minor Meriwether, a teacher. Gordon's childhood at Merimont was both the inspiration for and the setting of her early fiction. From her mother's sometimes eccentric family of local gentry she heard stories of frontier, antebellum, and Civil War days, and she learned of strong southern women. Her father, a Virginian who was often exasperated by the clannish Meriwethers, contributed to Gordon's ability to appreciate the Meriwethers and the Southern past without lapsing into uncritical ancestor worship and nostalgia. She was for the most part educated privately by her parents, who stressed classical languages and literature. In 1912 she entered Bethany College in Wheeling, West Virginia, where she studied classics and graduated in 1916 with a bachelor's degree and an associate degree in pedagogy.

From 1916 until 1920 Gordon lived at Merimont or wherever her father was currently preaching, and she taught high school in nearby Clarksville, Tennessee. In 1920 she moved to her aunt's house in Chattanooga, Tennessee, and worked as a reporter and book reviewer for the *Chattanooga News*. In her spare time she wrote an autobiographical novel, "Darkling I Listen," which she later destroyed, believing it unfit for publication.

While on vacation at her parents' home in Guthrie, Kentucky, in the summer of 1924, Gordon met the youthful poet John Orley Allen Tate, known as Allen Tate, who was visiting the parental home of poet and novelist Robert Penn Warren, his former Vanderbilt University roommate. Before Tate's graduation in 1923, he and Warren had been major figures in the Fugitive literary movement, which embraced literary modernism and rejected the moonlight-and-magnolias approach to southern literature. Gordon had praised *The Fugitive*, the movement's publication, in a *Chattanooga News* article on 10 February 1923, so perhaps she was disposed to falling in love with Tate. After a series of misunderstandings caused by her pride and his wandering eye, they were married in New York City in 1925. They had one child. Tate introduced Gordon to many of the prominent concepts and writers of modernism and remained one of her best critics throughout and after their marriages.

For the next five years Gordon and Tate struggled to make a living by freelance writing, sometimes sharing a farmhouse near Pawling, New York, with poet Hart Crane. In Greenwich Village they associated with writers Malcolm Cowley, Katherine Anne Porter, and Josephine Herbst; and during Tate's 1928–1929 Guggenheim Foundation grant they moved in the Parisian expatriate circles of writers Ford Madox Ford, Ernest Hemingway, and F. Scott Fitzgerald. Gordon sometimes acted as secretary to Ford, who taught her the techniques of his "Master," novelist Henry James. Ford became Gordon's most influential mentor and encouraged her to finish and publish her first novel, a family saga titled *Penhally* (1931).

The 1930s was Gordon's most productive decade, despite her and Tate's frequent sojourns away from their home base, "Benfolly," in Clarksville, Tennessee, which they purchased in 1930. They returned to Paris for Gordon's Guggenheim in 1932; lived in Memphis, Tennessee, from 1934 to 1937; spent their last summer at Benfolly in 1937 before moving to a Chatauqua-type settlement in Monteagle, Tennessee, where for a year they shared a cabin with novelist and former Fugitive Andrew Lytle; and then headed east to Greensboro, North Carolina, where both Tate and Gordon taught at the Women's College at the University of North Carolina from 1938 to 1939. All these locales were grist to Gordon's artistic mill. She used her Meriwether background and a Clarksville setting for *Penhally* and for *None Shall Look Back* (1937), a Civil War novel. Earlier in the decade Gordon had attempted a novel about the contemporary South's class structure, later published as *The Garden of Adonis* (1937), but she was stymied in 1933 by the devastating discovery of Tate's affair with one of her cousins. For relief, she wrote, in her father's voice, a first-person account of a passion for hunting and fishing similar to that of an artist for his or her work. The novel was published in 1934 as *Aleck Maury, Sportsman* and became her most famous and loved work. From her time spent in the Greensboro area, Gordon gleaned the pioneer and Native American lore that she used in writing *Green Centuries* (1941).

Although Gordon enjoyed a distinguished career as a novelist, she remains best known as a writer of short fiction. Many of her most acclaimed stories were written in the 1930s and appeared in *The Forest of the South* (1945), a collection that Gordon assembled to show the deterioration of the South. She later published two other collections, *Old Red and Other Stories* (1963) and *Collected Stories* (1981).

During the 1940s and 1950s Gordon's career declined, Tate's reputation peaked, and their marriage deteriorated. Gordon and Tate moved to Princeton, New Jersey, in 1939, when Tate accepted a teaching job at Princeton University. Despite frequent travels and extended sojourns, Princeton remained Gordon's home base until 1973. She and Tate returned to Monteagle from 1942 to 1943 and shared a house with poet Robert Lowell and novelist Jean Stafford. She next accompanied Tate to Washington, D.C., where he served as poetry consultant to the Library of Congress from 1943 to 1944. In 1944 Gordon published her finest novel, *The Women on the Porch*, a bitter look at the South and men. In September 1945, while living in Sewanee, Tennessee, Gordon's anger stemming from her husband's philandering and prominence and her own relatively minor reputation caused her to leave him. She lived briefly in New York City, Princeton, and Maine. They were divorced in January 1946 but were remarried just three months later.

Although Gordon and Tate's second marriage lasted until 1959, when they were divorced again, they often lived apart while technically sharing homes in places dictated by Tate's employment: Princeton (sporadically until 1959); Chicago (1950); Minneapolis, Minnesota (1951–1954); and Rome, Italy (1954–1955). Gordon sardonically examined her marriage and the plight of the modern artist in two novels, *The Strange Children*

(1951) and *The Malefactors* (1956). With Tate she edited and wrote introductions for *The House of Fiction* (1950), a widely used anthology.

In response to her trials of the 1940s and 1950s, Gordon developed new sources of strength. In 1947 she became a Roman Catholic, believing that in addition to the consolations of faith, it would provide a historical tradition and system of beliefs to replace the vanished South of her childhood. Psychologist Carl Jung's views of myth and archetype also became part of her philosophy as a result of her Jungian analysis in Rome in 1955. Most important, though, she established a career as a teacher. Over the next three decades Gordon taught at many institutions, including New York University, Purdue University, the University of Washington at Seattle, and the University of Kansas, as well as at many writers' conferences. From 1973 to 1978 she helped establish a creative writing program at the University of Dallas in Irving, Texas. As a teacher, Gordon was known for her emphasis on the classics and for her high standards. She is particularly remembered for her great helpfulness to aspiring writers, including southern fiction writers Flannery O'Connor and Walker Percy, whom she taught informally via correspondence.

With the pressures of new interests, increasing age, and declining health, Gordon published relatively little in the last decades of her life. She revised her lectures on fiction and published them as *How to Read a Novel* (1957). Her lifelong interest in mythology culminated in a retelling of the story of Hercules called *The Glory of Hera* (1972). In 1978 she moved to the home of her son-in-law and daughter in Chiapas, Mexico, where she unsuccessfully attempted to complete two novels before her death there. For her tombstone she chose a line from theologian Jacques Maritain that she had also used as the epigraph for *The Malefactors*: "It is for Adam to interpret the voices that Eve hears." The statement is a sad but fitting conclusion to the career of a fine woman writer whose reputation remains overshadowed by that of her husband.

• Gordon's papers are in the Firestone Library of Princeton University. For further biographical information, see *The Southern Mandarins: Letters of Caroline Gordon to Sally Wood, 1924–1937*, ed. Sally Wood (1984); and Veronica A. Makowsky, *Caroline Gordon: A Biography* (1989), which also provides literary criticism of her works. Additional literary interpretations are in Thomas H. Landess, ed., *The Short Fiction of Caroline Gordon* (1977); Rose Ann C. Fraistat, *Caroline Gordon as Novelist and Woman of Letters* (1984); and Robert H. Brinkmeyer, Jr., *Three Catholic Writers of the Modern South: Allen Tate, Caroline Gordon, Walker Percy* (1985). In addition to that contained in the preceding works, bibliographical information is available in Robert E. Golden and Mary C. Sullivan, *Flannery O'Connor and Caroline Gordon: A Reference Guide* (1977).

VERONICA A. MAKOWSKY

GORDON, Dexter Keith (27 Feb. 1923–25 Apr. 1990), jazz tenor saxophonist, was born in Los Angeles, California, the son of Frank Alexander Gordon and Gwendolyn Baker. His father was a physician and surgeon who numbered among his patients the musicians Duke Ellington and Lionel Hampton. His father's personal interest in jazz encouraged Gordon at an early age, and he first studied clarinet and elementary music theory at age seven with the New Orleans-born clarinetist John Sturdevant, a disciple of Barney Bigard. Gordon's father died when Gordon was twelve, but he continued studying music, added the alto saxophone when he was fifteen, and played in the school dance band. Other contemporaries at Jefferson High School, where Sam Brown directed the bands, were Chico Hamilton, drums; Ernie Royal, trumpet; and Vi Redd, alto saxophone. Gordon studied saxophone with Lloyd Reese, lead trumpet in the Les Hite Orchestra, and Reese formed a rehearsal band of his students that included both Gordon and Buddy Collette on saxophone and Charles Mingus on bass.

At seventeen Gordon took up the tenor saxophone, played in local clubs, and quit school to play in a local professional band, the Harlem Collegians. In December 1940 he joined the Lionel Hampton Orchestra, recorded with Hampton in 1941, and remained with Hampton for three years. His tenor partner in the band was Illinois Jacquet. Returning from New York to Los Angeles in 1943, he worked briefly with the Lee Young Sextet, the Jesse Price band, and the Fletcher Henderson Orchestra. That same year, Gordon made his first recordings as leader of a quintet with Nat "King" Cole on piano and Harry Edison on trumpet.

Gordon played briefly, and recorded, with Louis Armstrong in 1944 and with the Billy Eckstine Orchestra during 1944 and 1945, the first big band to feature the new bebop style. Fellow musicians in the band included Sarah Vaughan, vocalist; Dizzy Gillespie, trumpet; Sonny Stitt, alto saxophone; Gene Ammons, tenor saxophone; John Malachi, piano; Tommy Potter, bass; and Art Blakey, drums. He left the band in St. Louis and returned to New York in 1945, had freelance associations with Charlie Parker at the Spotlite, led his own group at the Three Deuces, and began a regular series of recordings under his own name. These activities placed Gordon among the leaders of bebop.

For the next four years (1946–1949) Gordon traveled as a freelance artist to Los Angeles, Honolulu, and then alternately back and forth between the East and West coasts. Between 1947 and 1952 he gained increased musical celebrity for his "saxophone duels" with tenor saxophonist Wardell Gray, live and recorded performances in which the two soloists competed to outplay each other. Their 1947 recording for Dial Records, *The Chase*, became the model for many battles of the saxophones. Speaking of his association with Gray, Gordon said:

I came back to LA in '47. And the jam session thing was going on very heavily at that time, at several different clubs . . . various tenors, altos, trumpets and an occasional trombone. But it seemed that in the wee small hours of the morning—always—there would be only

Wardell and myself. It became kind of a traditional thing. (Quoted in Britt, p. 18.)

Gordon, like many jazz musicians of the 1940s and 1950s, suffered from heroin addiction and was incarcerated from 1952 to 1954 at Chino Penitentiary in California. Although his return from prison was followed by recordings and a successful comeback, his musical activities during the 1950s were seriously curtailed when he was jailed a second time for drug use from 1956 to 1960. After his second return, he made several recordings that were well received. In September 1960 he joined the West Coast company of Jack Gelber's play about drug addicts, *The Connection*, as composer, musician, and actor. The play received mixed reviews, and in 1962 Gordon returned briefly to New York, but his parole conditions and lack of a cabaret card prevented him from performing in New York City.

In September 1962 Gordon played engagements in Europe and Great Britain and settled in Valby, Denmark, a suburb of Copenhagen, for fourteen years, making brief returns to the United States in 1965, 1969, 1970, and 1972. While in Europe, he married a second time (details of his first marriage are not known), appeared at jazz festivals, toured Japan, recorded frequently with European musicians, and taught and played regularly in Denmark. His drug addiction persisted, and he was arrested and jailed once again in Paris in 1966. Overall, however, his years abroad were successful and artistically satisfying. Of his years abroad, Gordon commented:

Ira Gitler referred to me as an expatriate. That's true, you know, but at the time I hadn't really made up my mind to live there so I came back here in 1965 for about six months, mostly out on the coast. But with all the political and social strife during that time and the Beatles thing, I didn't really dig it. So I went back. . . . The fact that you're an artist in Europe means something. They treat you with a lot of respect. In America, you know, they say, "Do you make any money?" (Interview with Chuck Berg, *Down Beat*, Sept. 1989, p. 82)

A warm reception for his visit to the United States in 1976 led him to return permanently in 1977. He was selected Musician of the Year by *Down Beat* magazine in 1978 and 1980 and was elected to the Jazz Hall of Fame in 1980. He performed less frequently thereafter, but in 1986 he was acclaimed for his acting in the motion picture *Round Midnight*, for which he received an Academy Award nomination. The film, directed by Bertrand Tavernier, portrayed the trials of an expatriate jazz musician in France, and although the movie was based on the final years of Bud Powell's life, it was, in fact, hauntingly autobiographical for Gordon. Partially as a result of the publicity received from the film's success, he began playing again. He died on tour in Philadelphia. He was survived by his second wife, Maxine (maiden name unknown), and five children.

During his career, Dexter Gordon recorded prolifically, but a few of his more important and representative recordings are *Long Tall Dexter* (1946), *The Chase* (1947), *Doin' All Right* (1961), *Our Man In Paris* (1963), and *Homecoming* (1976). He did his most innovative work during the late 1940s and 1950s. When new styles developed in the late 1950s, he remained true to his ideals of bebop execution. Summarizing Gordon's career, Brian Priestley (*Jazz: The Essential Companion* [1987], p. 196) writes:

His combination of bop-inspired lines with an essentially pre-bop time feeling produced an inherent tension which was excruciatingly enjoyable. His tone quality, always vibrantly hot even when playing ballads, remained virtually unchanged for 40 years, despite adopting a few mannerisms from Coltrane in the 1960s and occasionally taking up the soprano. His authoritative delivery, however, only increased with the passing years.

Dexter Gordon was the first significant bebop tenor saxophonist, and he provided the key link between the music of Lester Young and John Coltrane. He combined a huge, hard tone with spare melodic lines and laid-back, behind-the-beat phrasing. An imposing figure, always elegantly attired and standing six feet five inches, he became, through his presence, manner, and expatriation, a representative African-American figure fighting racial and social injustice. In his portrayal of Dale Turner in *Round Midnight*, and in his music, Gordon achieves his own apotheosis as a black artist struggling against the terrors of drugs, alcohol, and racism.

• Oral history material and recordings are preserved at the Institute of Jazz Studies at Rutgers University in Newark, N.J., and the most complete listing of Gordon's published recordings with full discographical details is in R. Nieus, *A Discography of Dexter Gordon* (1986), and Thorsten Sjøgren, *Long Tall Dexter: A Discography of Dexter Gordon* (1986). Stan Britt, *Dexter Gordon: A Musical Biography* (1989), is a full study of the life and work, with an excellent discography by Don Tarrant. The critic most familiar with Gordon's music, Ira Gitler, focuses on Gordon in chap. 7 of his *Jazz Masters of the Forties* (1966; repr. 1983), and he gives an insightful account of Gordon's early career. Two substantive obituaries, one by Peter Watrous, the *New York Times*, 26 Apr. 1990, and another by Steve Voce, *The Independent*, 27 Apr. 1990, are both excellent. Also, an interesting report of memories of Dexter Gordon related to the author by musicians attending the memorial service in New York City on 6 May 1990 was written by Tim Gordon, the *New York Times*, 7 May 1990.

FRANK TIRRO

GORDON, George Angier (2 Jan. 1853–25 Oct. 1929), Congregationalist minister and theologian, was born George Gordon in Oyne, Scotland, the son of George Gordon, an estate overseer, and Catherine Hutcheon. As a boy he did farm work and attended schools in the nearby Aberdeenshire town of Insch. In 1871, at the age of eighteen, Gordon emigrated to the United States and for three years supported himself in trades and manual labor in Boston. In keeping with his earlier religious training, he joined the Presbyterian church. That congregation's minister, Luther H. Angier, recognized great potential in the young man and urged him to prepare for a ministerial career. For several years Angier provided Gordon with both encouragement and financial aid. The young man subsequently adopted Angier as his middle name in public acknowledgment of his patron's unflagging support.

Reversing the normal order of things, Gordon graduated in 1877 from a Congregationalist seminary in Bangor, Maine, and then enrolled as a freshman at Harvard College. He may have matriculated with a sense of remedial need, but by 1881 he had achieved an honors degree in philosophy. For a short while (1881–1884) he filled a Congregationalist pastorate in Greenwich, Connecticut, and was then called to historic Old South Church in Boston for a distinguished ministry that spanned forty-three active years. In 1890 he married Susan Huntington Manning, eldest daughter of the church's previous minister; the couple had at least one child.

Though he came from a Calvinist theological heritage, Gordon became an outspoken exponent of the liberal Protestantism that was developing in his day. As part of a vanguard of early liberals he popularized his ideas in a handsome urban church during a golden age of preaching. He was one of the clerical elite who broadcast new ideas before they became the mainstay of many seminaries and universities. Gordon conducted what he considered a teaching ministry to thoughtful people, and in it he did not hesitate to criticize traditional ideas when he found them out of keeping with current intellectual trends. For instance he strongly denounced the doctrine of arbitrary election because it contravened the optimism of his era regarding human capabilities. He also rejected belief in a fall from grace, original sin, and innate depravity in human nature. Instead of preaching limited atonement for a chosen few individuals, he insisted that the gospel was potentially available to everyone.

In some categories, however, Gordon sounded a less modernist note, and there he appeared as a forthright defender of orthodoxy expressed in contemporary idioms. He maintained, for example, that the free moral agency of people gave them the power actually to thwart God's divine love and offer of ultimate salvation. That position marked a crucial difference with local Universalists. More notably Gordon stood in strong contrast with Unitarians in his high Christology. While he tended in sermons to stress the similarity between divine and human nature, he also argued that one fundamental difference remained that presumption could not bridge. Jesus Christ had been a human person in historical fact, of course, but beyond the earthly figure stood an eternal, preexistent Son of God. With Unitarians Gordon agreed that Jesus was the model of human perfection and that his example inspired others to seek closer communion with God. But following a favorite theologian, Origen of Alexandria, he also held that the Trinity was an ineffable society within the godhead where the transcendental potence of Jesus's incarnation still retained powerful relevance. Christ was uniquely divine, the indispensa-

ble medium of human salvation. Lesser christological definitions robbed Christianity of its central focus.

While Gordon's apology for divinity warned against further drift into mere humanism, he still found room to celebrate the dignity and worth of human life. Many of his sermons touched on high qualities in patriotism, business sense, wisdom of the ages, and great men intent on doing good. He was invited to lecture at all the leading American universities, and there he offered considerations of a basis for idealistic principles, assurance for beliefs, and a defense of things that abide. He was also widely read, and his many books contained themes that enumerated the fatherly attributes of God, individual responsibility in religious affirmation, and the possibilities of moral progress. His mix of liberalism and orthodoxy helped him to serve as a mediating force between extremes. In another aspect of his many activities, Gordon remained strongly attached to Harvard and was immensely proud of his service on the college's board of preachers (1886–1890, 1906–1909) and its board of overseers (1897–1916, 1925–1929). Declining health forced him into semiretirement for two years before he died in Brookline.

• There is no known repository of Gordon's papers. His many writings include *The Witness to Immortality in Literature, Philosophy and Life* (1893), *The Christ of To-day* (1895), *Immortality and the New Theodicy* (1897), *The New Epoch for Faith* (1901), *Ultimate Conceptions of Faith* (1903), *Through Man to God* (1906), *Religion and Miracles* (1909), *Revelation and the Ideal* (1913), *Aspects of the Infinite Mystery* (1916), *Humanism in New England Theology* (1920), and *Unto Victory* (1927). Information about his life is contained in his *My Education and Religion: An Autobiography* (1925). See also William R. Hutchison, *The Modernist Impulse in American Protestantism* (1976). An obituary is in the *New York Times*, 26 Oct. 1929.

HENRY WARNER BOWDEN

GORDON, George Byron (4 Aug. 1870–30 Jan. 1927), archaeologist and museum director, was born in New Perth, Prince Edward Island, Canada, one of six children of James Gordon and Jane McLaren. Following a year at the University of South Carolina, he transferred to Harvard University. His archaeological career began in 1892 when he was appointed surveyor for the Harvard Peabody Museum's second expedition to the Mayan site of Copán, Honduras. Upon his return he changed the focus of his education from engineering to archaeology.

After graduating cum laude from Harvard's Scientific School in 1894, Gordon enrolled in its graduate program in archaeology. He then returned to Copán as the director of the Peabody Museum's Fourth Copán Expedition. When work there was suspended because of political unrest, he continued his explorations in other regions in Honduras. These expeditions were published in *Prehistoric Ruins of Copán, Honduras* (1896), *Researches in the Uloa Valley* (1898), *Caverns of Copán* (1898), and *The Hieroglyphic Stairway, Ruins of Copán* (1902).

Gordon received his doctorate in anthropology in 1903. His dissertation was later published as *The Serpent Motive and the Ancient Art of Central America and Mexico* (1905). In 1903 he became assistant curator of the Free Museum of Science and Art (as the University of Pennsylvania Museum was then known); the following year he was advanced to the position of curator of anthropology and became a lecturer in anthropology at the University of Pennsylvania. In 1907 he was promoted to assistant professor of anthropology, a position that he held until 1915. From the beginning, his energy, enthusiasm, and diligence in working with the collections drew attention and admiration, although his zeal and occasional blunt manner caused some to accuse him of overstepping bounds and exceeding his jurisdiction. A museum board member commented that his personality could be "as sharp as the needles of his waxed mustache." No doubt his long, waxed mustache stemmed from Gordon's lifelong love for all things British, which was the impetus behind his vaguely British accent, his dapper dress, and the British spellings he preferred for certain words.

As one of the country's first Ph.D.'s in the new discipline of anthropology, Gordon was instrumental in furthering the professionalization of what had been an avocational pursuit. During his first year at the museum, he urged the university to offer a program of instruction in anthropology that would include courses in somatology and linguistics as well as in archaeology and ethnology. He proposed a curriculum of ten courses, suggesting that he would teach all of them himself if necessary. When there were no funds for a course in American archaeology, he taught it voluntarily. His efforts were rewarded in 1907 when the university instituted a major in anthropology. He was active in the American Anthropological Association and the International Congress of Americanists and represented the museum in these forums. In 1906 he used the opportunity of his attendance at the International Congress of Prehistoric Archaeology in Monaco to visit his European colleagues, some archaeological sites, and several museums, establishing a professional network that would serve the museum in the decades ahead.

As curator, Gordon began a systematic collection of American ethnographic materials. He undertook two major expeditions to Alaska (1905 and 1907), establishing a network of suppliers and collectors and acquiring outstanding artifacts to fill gaps in the museum collections. His concern to acquire the best objects for the museum frequently led to financial disputes with the chronically under-funded institution. His supporters on the board, recognizing the excellence of his aesthetic vision and the way in which it advanced the museum's reputation, argued in favor of his unauthorized expenditures and frequently made up the unbudgeted costs through personal contributions. Gordon himself used his own money to purchase an important collection and gave it to the museum, asking only that his costs be repaid when possible.

In 1910 Gordon was appointed director of the museum, which until that time had operated with the loose structure of a Board of Managers and autonomous curators. Thus began the period of Gordon's most important work, as he reorganized the museum and shaped it into an institution renowned for research and education, with collections representing cultures from around the world. With his administrative skills and visionary goals, and his archaeological training and connoisseur's eye, Gordon was the perfect man for the job. He envisioned a museum of international rank, its walls encompassing nothing less than the entire history of human endeavor.

In the years following his appointment as director, Gordon's energies and acumen were instrumental in the realization of many of his goals. He launched major excavations, among them the joint expedition to Ur, which brought the museum the fabled gold and jewels from the royal tombs; he wooed benefactors to contribute important gifts and purchases for the museum collections; he directed the creation of new exhibitions; and he coaxed funds from reluctant board members to enlarge the building itself to house the major new collections. He also presided over the publication of excavation reports, initiated a quarterly journal, and built up an important research library. Gordon viewed the museum as a center for education as well as research, introducing a public lecture series and inviting Philadelphia schools to bring their students to the museum.

Gordon's actions were frequently controversial and his personal manner alienated some of the university faculty and staff. Although he could be charming and an engaging and loyal friend, he could also be imperious and patronizing. Some of the museum's curators left, and the anthropology department moved across campus, refusing to have anything to do with the museum. His prickly personality, however, could not detract from his contributions to the profession and the museum. Under his guidance the museum became known as one of the world's foremost scientific institutions, and Gordon himself was called one of the world's best-known archaeologists. He died in Philadelphia.

• Gordon's papers are in the University of Pennsylvania Museum Archives. Although most of his writing was directed to professional colleagues, he wrote *In the Alaskan Wilderness* (1917) and *Rambles in Old London* (1924) for a wider audience. A comprehensive discussion of his contributions is Eleanor M. King and Bryce P. Little, "George Byron Gordon and the Early Development of the University Museum," in Susan A. Kaptan's *Raven's Journey: The World of Alaska's Native People* (1986). Other publications in which his work is discussed are Percy C. Madeira, Jr., *Men in Search of Man* (1964), and Dilys Pegler Winegrad, *Through Time, Across Continents* (1993). Obituaries are in the *New York Times*, the *Philadelphia Evening Bulletin*, and the *Philadelphia Public Ledger*, all 31 Jan. 1927.

ELIN DANIEN

GORDON, Jean Margaret (1865–24 Feb. 1931), social reformer and suffragist, was born in New Orleans, Louisiana, the daughter of George Hume Gordon, an educator, and Margaret Galiece. Jean grew up in the Garden District of New Orleans; she attended public schools but graduated from Miss Shaw's School, a private finishing academy. Her parents had become converted to the cause of woman suffrage as early as the 1850s and raised their daughters to share their commitment. Jean and her family were members of the First Unitarian Church of New Orleans, where in 1896 Mary C. C. Bradford from Colorado delivered an address on woman suffrage. Inspired by the lecture, Jean and her sister Kate founded the Era Club (Equal Rights Association) on 9 May 1896. Affiliated with the National American Woman Suffrage Association (NAWSA), it eventually merged with the older Portia Club to form a statewide suffrage organization.

Gordon served the woman suffrage movement first as president of the Era Club from 1903 to 1904 and later as president of the Louisiana Woman Suffrage Association (LWSA) from 1913 to 1920. During these years, when the argument concerning states' rights reached a peak, she removed the LSWA from affiliation with the NAWSA, preferring a state provision for woman suffrage to a national amendment. Bitterly opposing the Susan B. Anthony Amendment to the U.S. Constitution because she feared it would enfranchise black women, she campaigned successfully against its ratification by the Louisiana legislature. When the Tennessee legislature ratified the Nineteenth Amendment, granting American women constitutionally protected voting rights, she lamented that "Tennessee has disgraced the South."

Although her sister Kate is well known for her association with the cause of woman suffrage, Jean Gordon is better remembered for her career in social service. She began by joining the Charity Organization Society of New Orleans in 1888. Through her contact with disadvantaged children she came to understand the need for a law restricting child labor. In 1896 she influenced the Era Club to form a committee to investigate conditions of child labor and presented a bill based on the results to the legislature. Her goal was a new law to regulate child labor and a constitutional provision to appoint women factory inspectors. The legislature balked until she launched a newspaper campaign to explain the problem and win support. In 1906 the Louisiana legislature passed the Child Labor Act and amended the constitution to grant women positions as factory inspectors. Gordon served as a factory inspector until 1911. In 1908 she was able to effect the passage of a bill prohibiting the hiring of children under the age of fourteen but was unable to reduce the workday for women and adolescents to nine hours. In 1909, therefore, with aid from Louisiana governor Jared Sanders and New Orleans mayor Martin Behrman, she persuaded a number of southern governors to hold a conference on child labor. The result was a series of annual conferences that by 1912 had led to the passage of child labor laws in most southern states. Gordon also served as president of the Southern Conference of Woman and Child Labor from 1910 to 1911 and helped to form a Louisiana branch of the National Consumers' League in 1913.

From 1909 until her death Gordon continued her active involvement in social work. When her work as inspector for factory labor brought her into contact with mothers who left their children at home alone because they had no day care, she established the New Orleans Day Nursery (1909) in Eleanor McMain's Kingsley Settlement House. Believing in the need for trained social workers, she helped to found the School of Applied Sociology in New Orleans (1914–1915). In response to the call for organized charity she aided in founding the Federation of Non-Sectarian Charity and Philanthropy (1914) and the New Orleans Central Council of Social Agencies (1921), predecessor to the Community Chest. She also helped to create the New Orleans Central Council of Social Engineers (1919) and served as director of the Louisiana State Society for the Prevention of Cruelty to Animals.

While working with child labor regulation and in her capacity as factory inspector, Gordon became convinced that some young women were unable to hold jobs because of mental deficiencies. At her behest, in 1919 the Alexander Milne Home for Girls became a training school and a home for mentally retarded girls. She gave her life to this work, eventually moving into the home and serving as president of its board until she died.

Because of her work with retarded girls, Gordon was appointed in 1922 to the board of the State Colony and Training School for the Feeble-minded. By 1926 she had become a follower of the eugenics movement. She and her sister Kate lobbied to disenfranchise the genetically unfit. She also campaigned for compulsory sterilization of the "feeble-minded." Because the Gordon sisters countenanced birth control, their efforts were opposed by the Catholic church and fundamentalist Protestant groups. Still, as director of the Milne Home for Girls, Gordon oversaw the sterilization of at least 125 girls.

Gordon died in New Orleans. As a tribute to her lasting achievements, Dorothea Dix wrote, "In her death New Orleans had not only lost one of its greatest daughters but perhaps its most useful citizen." Jean Gordon, a southern Progressive Era reformer who believed in the perfectibility of society, provides a striking example of the contrasts within progressive thought. She supported social work, child labor laws, woman suffrage, and birth control, but she couched these reforms within the proscriptive context of southern elitism, racial segregation, and social control through sterilization.

• There are no family papers for the Gordon sisters. Manuscript collections that have a few letters and material relating to Jean Gordon are the Jacob D. Dresner Collection, the Hutson Family Papers, and the First Unitarian Church Records, all in Manuscript Collections, Howard-Tilton Memorial Library, Tulane University, New Orleans. A vertical file on

Jean Gordon may be found in the Louisiana Collection, Howard-Tilton Memorial Library, Tulane University. The Alexander Milne Home for Girls Records, with reports written by Jean Gordon, are in the Historic New Orleans Collection, New Orleans. For the Gordon sisters' suffrage activism see Elizabeth Cady Stanton et al., eds., *History of Woman Suffrage*, vol. 4 (1902) and vol. 6 (1922); Eleanor Flexner, *Century of Struggle: The Woman's Rights Movement in the United States* (1959); Aileen S. Kraditor, *The Ideas of the Woman Suffrage Movement, 1890–1920* (1965); Kraditor, "Tactical Problems of the Woman-Suffrage Movement in the South," *Louisiana Studies* 5 (Winter 1966): 289–307; Anne Firor Scott, *The Southern Lady: From Pedestal to Politics, 1830–1930* (1970); Kenneth R. Johnson, "Kate Gordon and the Woman-Suffrage Movement in the South," *Journal of Southern History* 38 (Aug. 1972): 365–92; B. H. Gilley, "Kate Gordon and Louisiana Woman Suffrage," *Louisiana History* 24 (Summer 1983): 289–306; Elna C. Green, "The Rest of the Story: Kate Gordon and the Opposition to the Nineteenth Amendment in the South," *Louisiana History* 33 (Spring 1992): 171–89; and Marjorie Spruill Wheeler, *New Women of the New South: The Leaders of the Woman Suffrage Movement in the Southern States* (1993). For Jean Gordon's social work see Carmen Lindig, *The Path from the Parlor: Louisiana Women, 1879–1920* (1986), and Kathryn W. Kemp, "Jean and Kate Gordon: New Orleans Social Reformers, 1898–1933," *Louisiana History* 24 (Fall 1983): 389–401. Obituaries are in the *New Orleans Times-Picayune* and the *New Orleans Item*, 24 Feb. 1931.

ELIZABETH HAYES TURNER

GORDON, John Brown (6 Feb. 1832–9 Jan. 1904), soldier and politician, was born in Upson County, Georgia, the son of Zachariah Herndon Gordon, a minister, and Malinda Cox. After studies at a private school established by his father, John attended Pleasant Green Academy for a year before entering the University of Georgia in 1850. He did well at Georgia but did not graduate. In 1854 he moved to Atlanta to pursue a legal career. His practice, however, was not as successful as he had hoped, and he decided to explore other fields of employment. After a brief stint as a journalist covering the Georgia General Assembly, he joined his father in a coal-mining venture that quickly prospered. In 1854 he married Fanny Rebecca Haralson, with whom he had six children.

Gordon was an enthusiastic supporter of Georgia's secession from the Union. Although he lacked any prior military training, he was elected captain of the "Raccoon Roughs," a company he helped raise. On 14 May 1861 he became major of the Sixth Alabama Regiment. On 28 April 1862 he was promoted to colonel, and after the battle of Seven Pines he assumed command of a brigade. During the 1862 Maryland campaign, Gordon fought at both South Mountain and Antietam. In the latter contest, he was wounded five times. Knocked unconscious by the final bullet, which inflicted a terrible wound on his cheek and jaw, Gordon fell face forward into his cap. Only a bullet hole in the cap prevented his drowning in his own blood.

On 1 November 1862 Gordon was promoted to brigadier general, and with the help of his wife, he recovered rapidly from his wounds. On 30 March 1863 he returned to duty and on 11 April became a brigade commander in Jubal Early's division. That year Gordon and his brigade participated in the Chancellorsville, Gettysburg, and Mine Run campaigns. He further distinguished himself at the battles of the Wilderness and Spotsylvania in May 1864. At the Wilderness he conceived and led an attack that nearly rendered Federal communications useless. At Spotsylvania his leadership helped restore a badly broken Confederate line.

On 14 May 1864 Gordon was promoted to major general. He remained with the Army of Northern Virginia until June, when his unit was sent to the Shenandoah Valley to assist Early in retrieving southern military fortunes there. Despite initial successes that culminated in a raid bringing Early's army to the gates of Washington, Union forces under the leadership of Phillip Sheridan ultimately prevailed in the valley in 1864. In December Gordon's division returned to the Army of Northern Virginia, then besieged in front of Petersburg, Virginia. He eventually obtained command of the Second Corps but no promotion. On 25 March 1865 his troops made an unsuccessful attack against the Union position at Fort Stedman, setting the stage for the northern counteroffensive that caused the collapse of the entire Confederate line. Gordon commanded the army's rear guard during the retreat west and surrendered at Appomattox.

After the war, Gordon returned to Georgia, where he accepted positions with the Atlanta branch of the Southern Life Insurance Company and a New York–based publishing house. Eventually he entered politics and quickly assumed leadership in the effort to restore home rule. He also became a prominent member of the Ku Klux Klan. In 1868 he ran unsuccessfully for governor, but five years later he managed to win election to the U.S. Senate. During his first term, Gordon had the honor of being the first former Confederate to preside over that body. He led the fight to restore citizenship to former Confederates, opposed efforts to retire paper money, and made himself a rallying point for Georgia Democrats. He also established himself as a trustworthy ally for northern Democrats and promoted the image of a South that accepted defeat and simply sought to manage its own affairs.

Although reelected by the legislature in 1878 Gordon stunned onlookers by resigning his seat in May 1880 to accept a position with the Louisville & Nashville Railroad. Rumors immediately surfaced that Gordon, Governor Alfred H. Colquitt, and the man Colquitt had appointed as Gordon's replacement, former governor Joseph E. Brown, had struck a bargain by which Gordon had received inducements to allow the highly unpopular Brown to enter the Senate. Gordon firmly denied the charges. Apparently disillusionment with politics, anxiety over his health, and financial concerns were indeed the principal motives behind his resignation. After six years spent developing his business interests, which consisted of investments in stocks and bonds and involvement in numerous enterprises, the most significant of which was railroad development, Gordon won election to the governorship in 1886. In 1891 he returned to the Senate, where he served until 1897.

Brown, Colquitt, Gordon, and their associate Henry Grady, all shared a belief in the New South creed of promoting industry and railroad construction to move Georgia away from its overdependence on agriculture. For two decades Brown, Colquitt, and Gordon, the "Bourbon Triumvirate" as they came to be called, dominated Georgia politics. From 1873 to 1897 either Gordon or Brown held one of Georgia's U.S. Senate seats. For all but four of the years between 1876 and 1890, either Colquitt or Gordon was governor. The influence of the triumvirate extended beyond politics, as all three were powerful officials in a number of railroads and other major businesses.

When the United Confederate Veterans was organized in 1890 to aid surviving veterans and their dependents and ensure that the history of the Civil War would be presented in a way that dignified the southern cause, its leaders selected Gordon as commander in chief. He held this post the rest of his life and did much to make the UCV a vigorous institution. It became a particularly important tool in Gordon's efforts to promote sectional reconciliation, the great cause of his later years. In late 1903, searching for a climate that would help him recuperate from a speaking tour in the North, Gordon traveled to Biscayne Bay, Florida, where he died.

Few Georgians cast so long a shadow over nineteenth-century America as did Gordon. His valiant service during the Civil War has been most remembered, yet his service to the cause of sectional reconciliation afterward was equally honorable. His legacy to Georgia is more ambiguous. He succeeded in his efforts to restore home rule to the South but failed to see his dream of a New South, where industry as well as agriculture flourished, come to fruition.

• A fire at Gordon's home in 1899 destroyed many of his personal papers. However, many valuable materials related to his life and career are in the Gordon Family Collection at the University of Georgia. Official records for Gordon's tenure as governor are at the Georgia Department of Archives and History. Gordon's memoir, *Reminiscences of the Civil War* (1903), is valuable but must be read with care. The standard biography is Ralph Lowell Eckert, *John Brown Gordon: Soldier, Southerner, American* (1989). His wartime service can be traced in *The War of the Rebellion: A Compilation of the Official Records of the Union and Confederate Armies* (128 vols., 1880–1901). Douglas Southall Freeman, *Lee's Lieutenants* (3 vols., 1942–1944), remains the foremost study of the Confederate generals in Virginia, while C. Vann Woodward, *Origins of the New South, 1877–1913* (1951), fills the same function for its subject. See also Allen P. Tankersley, *John B. Gordon: A Study in Gallantry* (1955), and Grady Sylvester Culpepper, "The Political Career of John Brown Gordon, 1868 to 1897" (Ph.D. diss., Emory Univ., 1981). An obituary is in the *Atlanta Constitution*, 10–14 Jan. 1904.

ETHAN S. RAFUSE

GORDON, Kate M. (14 July 1861–24 Aug. 1932), suffragist and civic leader, was born in New Orleans, Louisiana, the daughter of George Hume Gordon, an educator, and Margaret Galiece. Both parents supported equal rights for women and instilled feminist principles in their children. Gordon enjoyed an affluent upbringing in New Orleans, where she received her early education and graduated from Miss Shaw's finishing school, a private institution for young women.

Upon completing her education, Gordon became involved in New Orleans civic work and Louisiana's campaign for woman suffrage, becoming the leader of the movement in that state. She joined the Portia Club, the first organization in New Orleans dedicated to the enfranchisement of women, shortly after it was formed in 1892 but found it too conservative and soon resigned her membership. With other suffragists, including her sister Jean, on 9 May 1896 she founded an "equal rights association," appropriately named the Era Club. This citywide organization and the Portia Club later united, forming the keystone of the statewide franchise movement, which Gordon headed from 1904 through 1913. In 1896 she also helped establish the Louisiana Woman Suffrage Association.

In 1899 Gordon sought to enlist New Orleans female voters (eligible since early 1898 because of their tax-paying status) to vote in the local water and drainage bond election. The Era Club sponsored a women's rally through which the Women's Sewerage and Drainage League was established, with Gordon as its leader. She compiled a list of more than 10,000 qualified female voters in the city and held parlor meetings to acquaint women with the relevant issues, with the goal of inducing them to cast their ballots in favor of an adequate water and sewer system. Although she was unable to persuade many traditional women to vote, she nonetheless obtained 300 proxies from them to vote in their stead. This experience proved significant to Gordon's development as an organizer and leader in the crusade to secure the vote for women. Through her civic work, she caught the attention of national suffrage leaders, including Carrie Chapman Catt, president of the National American Woman Suffrage Association (NAWSA).

In her early career Gordon participated in securing the vote on the national level through membership in NAWSA. Between 1902 and 1909 she served as the corresponding secretary for the organization. She was elected second vice president in 1911, then resigned her post after becoming disenchanted with NAWSA's goal of federal reform. That year she discontinued her advocacy of national suffrage and concentrated her efforts on reform at the state level, although she maintained close ties with NAWSA for several more years.

About this time a marked split in the woman suffrage movement arose between those who supported the Susan B. Anthony amendment, a constitutional suffrage amendment patterned after the Fifteenth Amendment, which protects the rights of African Americans to vote, and those who supported state-by-state ratification. Gordon, backed by a legion of southern suffragists, feared that a national amendment would threaten states' rights by interfering with the election process and determining who should vote. In this way, the federal amendment was a threat to white supremacy, and southern suffragists, certain that their state politicians would spurn the idea of enfranchising women if African-American women were also given a voice, created a southern splinter group. Gordon took the lead, calling a conference of southern suffrage leaders in November 1913, at which time a new organization was born, the Southern States Woman Suffrage Conference (SSWSC); a part of its political strategy was to convince the racist male legislators to grant white women the vote. Gordon was elected president and set the tone for the SSWSC's objectives, regarding her new group the equal of NAWSA.

In May 1914 the SSWSC established its headquarters in New Orleans and organized a press service. In October of that year the SSWSC began publication of a magazine, the *New Southern Citizen*, and in November held its first conference, at which it determined to urge the national Democratic party to adopt a woman suffrage provision in its platform. Gordon continued to push for this plank until it was finally approved in 1916.

In time the southern wing also split into two factions: states' rights advocates, like Gordon, and moderates who heeded the NAWSA leadership. Gordon began to lose support for her unyielding states' rights campaign as newly enfranchised women supported a federal amendment and as southern women gained renewed faith in both the Anthony amendment and NAWSA's strategies and abilities. In May 1917 the *New Southern Citizen* ceased publication, and by this time the SSWSC was essentially defunct, thus incapacitating the southern wing of the woman suffrage movement.

In July 1918, under pressure from Gordon and her cohorts, the Louisiana legislature passed a bill presenting a female franchise amendment to the state constitution for approval in the November general election. Though it was defeated, Gordon persisted. When the Anthony amendment ultimately passed Congress in June 1919, Gordon and other states' rightists allied themselves with opponents of woman suffrage to block ratification in her state. Although they succeeded, by August 1920 thirty-six states had ratified the amendment, thus enfranchising women in all states by federal action.

Gordon's other contributions throughout her varied career also came in the form of civic enterprise and equality. She led efforts to establish a New Orleans chapter of the Society for the Prevention of Cruelty to Animals in 1888, a city Anti-Tuberculosis League in 1906, and a permanent juvenile court in 1921. She also aided in the creation of the New Orleans Hospital and Dispensary for Women and Children and spent many years working to open a hospital for tuberculosis patients. The New Orleans Anti-Tuberculosis Hospital was founded in 1926, open to all patients regardless of race, social condition, or economic status. Gordon further battled to afford women access to Tulane Univer-

sity Medical School, eventually succeeding in her fight. She died in New Orleans, never having married.

Gordon dedicated her life to public service and reform. An obituary in the *New York Times* noted that "she took part in virtually every reform movement of importance in Louisiana in the last forty years." Her considerable contribution to Louisiana's suffrage campaign stands as a testament to her belief in progress and her willingness to fight for her principles. Through her leadership, tenacity, and allegiance to the movement, she advanced the cause of women's rights not only in her home state of Louisiana but in the entire southern region at a critical point in the development of U.S. history. Her belief in enfranchisement exclusively for white women represents an unfortunate element of the southern faction of the movement and stands as a historical document of the times.

• The Gordon family papers are unavailable to the public. For general information about Gordon's background, see the *New Orleans Directory 1870–75*; Amelia S. Pasteur, ed., *New Orleans' Society Reference* (1899–1909); *Men and Matters*, Dec. 1895; and the *New Orleans Times-Picayune*, 24 Feb. 1931 and 25 Aug. 1932. For data on her woman suffrage work, see Elizabeth Cady Stanton et al., eds., *History of Woman Suffrage*, vols. 4–6 (1902–1922); Ida C. Clarke, ed., *Suffrage in the Southern States* (1914); Kenneth R. Johnson, "Kate Gordon and the Woman Suffrage Movement in the South," *Journal of Southern History* 38 (Aug. 1972): 365–92; B. H. Gilley, "Kate Gordon and Louisiana Woman Suffrage," *Louisiana History* 24, no. 3 (1983): 289–306; the *New Southern Citizen* (New Orleans) for the years 1914 through 1917; and the index to the *New Orleans Daily Picayune*. Regarding her sewerage, drainage, and water campaign, see Mary R. Beard, *Woman's Work in Municipalities* (1915), and Daisy Breaux, *The Autobiography of a Chameleon* (1930). Caroline E. Merrick, *Old Times in Dixie Land* (1901), gives information about Gordon's fight to admit women to Tulane's Medical School, and the pamphlet *A True Picture of the Tuberculosis Situation in New Orleans* (1928) provides information on her antituberculosis activities. An obituary appears in the *New York Times*, 25 Aug. 1932.

ELIF Ö. ERGINER

GORDON, Laura de Force (17 Aug. 1838–5 Apr. 1907), suffragist, newspaper publisher, and attorney, was born in Erie County, Pennsylvania, the daughter of Abram de Force and Catherine Doolittle Allan. Her mother helped support the family through needlework because her father suffered from rheumatism and could not work. Gordon was educated in the public schools, and at age seventeen she changed her religious affiliation from Congregationalist to Christian Spiritualist. She soon began a career as a traveling trance speaker, touring New York and her native Pennsylvania. Her lectures were well received by audiences and the press, and she expanded her territory in the 1860s to include Maine, Massachusetts, and New Jersey.

In 1862 she married Dr. Charles H. Gordon, a native of Scotland and captain of the Third Rhode Island Cavalry. The couple moved to Virginia City, Nevada, where Gordon's husband practiced medicine and she continued to lecture. Lecturing on Spiritualism had become, for many women, a catalyst for early suffrage campaigns. Women Spiritualists like Gordon were accomplished speakers, and many expanded the scope of their lectures to include the topic of women's rights. Gordon was no exception; in 1868 she spoke on this issue in San Francisco, where her remarks were recorded and remarked upon for the first time by suffrage leaders Elizabeth Cady Stanton and Susan B. Anthony. Gordon followed up on her lecture with a speech on women's rights at a session of the California legislature. Her eloquence on the platform led to numerous invitations to speak, and she gave more than 100 lectures in California in 1870. That same year she and her husband settled in Lodi, California.

After the tour Gordon was in demand to speak to legislators on woman suffrage, and in 1872 she was part of a delegation that attended the national woman suffrage convention in Washington, D.C. Her fame had spread so far that the Independent party of San Joaquin County, California, nominated her for state senator, and she received an astonishing 200 votes.

In 1873 Gordon entered the newspaper business, beginning as an editor for the women's department of the *Narrow Gauge*, a Stockton, California, weekly. Later that year she became the editor and publisher of the *Stockton Weekly Leader*, the only paper then published by a woman. In 1876 she sold the paper; at the same time she abandoned the Spiritualist doctrine that had defined the early years of her life. She spent the years 1875–1878 editing the Oakland *Daily Democrat*, covering topics such as women's rights and Democratic politics.

In 1877 Gordon and her husband were divorced. Although the breakup of the marriage caused Gordon great pain for the rest of her life, the circumstances of her various careers had made it impossible for her to live as a traditional wife; however, the reason given for the divorce was her husband's adultery. In that same year Gordon began the next phase of her life: fighting to secure for women the right to practice law in California.

Gordon had read law in connection with her many lectures on women's rights. She was also acquainted with many attorneys who encouraged her to take up the profession of law, despite the fact that women were not admitted to the bar in California at that time. Her opportunity to change this occurred in 1877 when Clara Foltz, who had been studying law on her own, drew up a bill to remove the barriers against women becoming attorneys. The California Woman's Suffrage Society endorsed this bill and asked Gordon to lobby for its passage in Sacramento. She decided to join Foltz in enrolling at Hastings College of the Law, a division of the state university system. Although Foltz had passed qualifying examinations and Gordon had been studying assiduously, the women were denied admission. They took their case to the California Supreme Court, and in 1879 the court upheld a lower court's decision requiring Hastings to admit women. That year the two

women became the first to be admitted to the California bar. Gordon also drafted the text of Article 20 of the new state constitution, which stated, "No person shall, on account of sex, be disqualified from entering upon or pursuing any lawful business, vocation or profession."

In 1880 Gordon opened a law office in San Francisco, and in 1885 she made history again by becoming one of the first women admitted to practice before the U.S. Supreme Court. In the late 1880s she traveled around California mining towns, stumping for the Democratic party.

At the end of the nineteenth century Gordon cut back on her suffrage activities to concentrate on her law career. She gained unexpected fame for her 1880 defense of an Italian immigrant, which brought her honorary membership in the Royal Italian Literary Society of Rome.

In 1901 Gordon retired to a farm she had purchased in Lodi. Her original plan was to manage the twenty-acre spread with a syndicate of suffragists, but it apparently never materialized. In 1905 she identified herself as an agnostic "with leanings toward Theosophy," a notable change from the powerful Spiritualist beliefs of her early life.

Gordon's marriage had been childless, but around 1893 she adopted a boy, named Verne, from an impoverished home. Verne married his adoptive mother's niece, and the loss of their child in 1906 was a great shock to Gordon. Her last public appearance was at the state Democratic convention that same year. Gordon died in Lodi.

In an obituary published in the *Woman's Tribune*, 25 May 1907, Gordon's life was summarized as follows: "Hers was a genial, tender, loving soul, cast in heroic mold. She was so finely-endowed physically that she ought to have been a power in the world's work for years to come." The cause of women's rights—both suffrage and in the professions—owes much to Laura de Force Gordon's lifetime of work on behalf of American women.

• Gordon's correspondence at the Bancroft Library, University of California, Berkeley, is the most comprehensive collection of Gordon material. Secondary materials that are useful to a study of Gordon's life and work include Elizabeth Cady Stanton's *History of Suffrage* (1881). Newspapers are also useful, especially the *Woman's Tribune* and Nevada papers such as the *Territorial Enterprise*, 9, 14, 16, 20, 28, and 31 July 1870, 9 Feb. and 17 Dec. 1871, and 1 Feb. 1876, and the *Reno Crescent*, 12 Mar. and 9 and 23 July 1870.

LYNN DOWNEY

GORDON, Max (28 June 1892–2 Nov. 1978), theatrical producer, was born Mechel Salpeter in New York City, the son of Heschel Salpeter and Doba Friedman, Polish-Jewish immigrants who, like many of their countrymen and coreligionists, had settled on the city's Lower East Side. Heschel Salpeter found employment as a pants presser; on his meager salary of $11 a week he supported a family of ten. Neither parent ever assimilated to American culture; throughout their lives, Yiddish was the only language they spoke or read. Perhaps by way of reaction to his parents' lack of interest in anything other than work and the family itself, Max, as young Mechel was called, became an avid reader as a child. He developed an interest in the theater after his elder brother, choosing the name Cliff Gordon, became a star comedian in burlesque and vaudeville and, later, a producer of burlesque shows. At that time burlesque was family entertainment, not the vulgar enterprise of strip acts and off-color jokes it later became. Vaudeville was also family entertainment but a cut above burlesque in the quality of its acts. In his senior year at Townsend Harris High School, a prestigious public school for exceptionally promising students, Max dropped out a few months before graduation to take a job as advance man for the Behman Show, another burlesque company. With this career beckoning, he took his brother's adopted surname. In his employment, Max Gordon drummed up publicity for the Behman Show in cities where it was scheduled to play.

After spending a year at this work, Gordon was offered a similar position by his brother Cliff. He accepted but felt a growing need to be on his own. An opportunity came his way in 1911, when another young man, Albert Lewis, a vaudeville comedian, suggested that they team up as agents for and producers of vaudeville acts with the thought of one day producing plays on Broadway. After mulling it over for a few months, Gordon, with savings of $500 to invest, told Lewis that he was ready to form a partnership with him.

In their first year of booking acts, Lewis and Gordon made only enough money to meet their living expenses. This unsatisfactory experience convinced them that they should move on to the production of one-act plays for vaudeville. Unable, however, to convince any writer of merit to trust them with a play, they booked a British comedy act, the London Fire Brigade, into a theater in Trenton, New Jersey. It was a total failure. To make ends meet, Lewis had to go back to trouping in vaudeville, while Gordon continued to search for a play. Happily, Aaron Hoffman, a prolific author of one-acts, gave them a melodrama, *Straight*, which around 1911 or 1912 provided the success they were hoping for. With Hoffman as their silent partner, the pair continued to produce one-acts from 1913 to 1920, booking them into the national vaudeville circuits and frequently casting talented, well-known actors such as Judith Anderson and Roland Young.

Successful though they were, Gordon and Lewis were happy to end their career in short plays when the opportunity arose to join forces with the eminent Broadway producer Sam H. Harris. Their first production with Harris was Hoffman's hit *Welcome, Stranger* (1920), after which they broke with Hoffman over a financial dispute. Other successes that the partners presented with Harris were William Anthony McGuire's *Six Cylinder Love* (1921); John Colton and Clemence Randolph's *Rain* (1922), based on W. Som-

erset Maugham's story "Miss Thompson"; and Samson Raphaelson's *The Jazz Singer* (1925).

In 1921 Gordon married Mildred "Millie" Bartlett. At his insistence, but with no regrets, she abandoned a promising career as a stage and screen actress. The couple had no children.

Over the years, Gordon had begun to feel somewhat ill used in his working relationship with Lewis, who assumed the dominant role in their partnership. When the firm received a lucrative offer in 1926 from the vaudeville impresario Marcus Heiman, the head of the Orpheum circuit, to run Orpheum's production department and manage its bookings, Gordon was pleased to learn that Lewis, preferring to continue in the legitimate theater, was not interested. This left Gordon free to accept the offer on his own. But the advent of the sound film and the increasing popularity of radio had gradually diminished the audience for vaudeville. Although the creation in 1928 of a new corporation, Radio-Keith-Orpheum (RKO), an amalgam of radio interests and the Keith-Albee and Orpheum circuits, promised a revival of vaudeville, no such revival occurred, and RKO went on to concentrate on film production. Dismayed by these events, Gordon gave up his position after three years. At the onset of the Great Depression of the 1930s, with no job and very little money in the bank, he needed a new career; improbably, he found one as a Broadway producer.

In 1930, with a bank loan of $25,000 and $100,000 gathered from other sources, Gordon offered his first production, *Three's a Crowd*, an intimate revue starring Fred Allen, Libby Holman, and Clifton Webb, with songs mostly by Arthur Schwartz and Howard Dietz. The show was a hit, enabling Gordon to produce a second revue, *The Bandwagon* (1931), starring Fred and Adele Astaire, with songs by Dietz and Schwartz and sketches by George S. Kaufman. It too was a success.

With two highly praised productions running simultaneously, Gordon produced *The Cat and the Fiddle* (1931), a musical with a score by Jerome Kern and Otto Harbach. This was also a hit. But Gordon's fourth production, *Flying Colors* (1932), another revue with songs by Dietz and Schwartz, was, in his words, "a disaster." So severe was Gordon's reaction to the artistic and financial problems incurred by the production that he made two attempts at suicide and then entered a sanitarium to be treated for what was diagnosed as a nervous breakdown. Fortunately, this crisis did not cause his backers to lose confidence in him. His illness only briefly interrupted his career.

Among Gordon's foremost successes in the years that followed were Noël Coward's *Design for Living* (1933), Gordon's first nonmusical production, starring Alfred Lunt, Lynn Fontanne, and Coward himself; *Roberta* (1933), a musical with songs by Kern and Harbach; Clare Kummer's *Her Master's Voice* (1933); Sidney Howard's *Dodsworth* (1934), based on Sinclair Lewis's novel of the same name, starring Walter Huston; Clare Boothe's *The Women* (1936); Joseph Fields and Jerome Chodorov's *My Sister Eileen* (1940), based on stories by Ruth McKenney; Fields and Chodorov's *Junior Miss* (1941), based on stories by Sally Benson; Ruth Gordon's *Over Twenty-one* (1944); John P. Marquand and George S. Kaufman's *The Late George Apley* (1944), based on Marquand's novel of the same name; Garson Kanin's *Born Yesterday* (1946); and Howard Teichmann and Kaufman's *The Solid Gold Cadillac* (1954). Altogether he presented forty-five plays on Broadway.

On occasion, Gordon worked briefly—and with little enjoyment—in both film and television. In 1931 he went to Hollywood as an adviser on two Marx Brothers pictures, *Monkey Business* (1931) and *Horse Feathers* (1932), and in 1939 he produced the film version of Robert E. Sherwood's play *Abe Lincoln in Illinois*. Also in 1939, he contracted with NBC to secure rights for the production of plays on television, then still in an experimental stage. In 1951 he produced variety shows for CBS with Frank Sinatra as master of ceremonies. The sum of these experiences, none of which lived up to his expectations, convinced him that the theater was his true medium.

A gregarious man, Gordon had friends in all branches of show business. Among those he regarded with greatest affection were Coward, Kaufman, Harris, Oscar Hammerstein II, and Moss Hart. Kaufman and Hart invested in his plays, offered advice when he requested it (and sometimes when he did not), directed plays for him, and became his partners in the purchase of a Broadway theater, the Lyceum. In 1941, after the death of Harris, Gordon assumed Harris's role as the producer of the plays of Kaufman and his many collaborators. Kaufman was sometimes put off by a streak of brashness in Gordon's personality but admired him for his unfailing meticulousness in their business dealings.

Periods of depression marked Gordon's busy, seemingly contented life. He experienced a second severe breakdown in 1940. More often than not, however, he was in ebullient form, finding time, despite his hectic schedule, for golf, for attending horse races, and for singing old songs at The Players, the theatrical club of which he was a member. He died in New York City. A newspaper strike was under way at the time, preventing the publication of the lengthy notices that the death of so eminent a showman would ordinarily merit.

• Gordon's correspondence and business files are in the theater collection of the Princeton University Library. His scrapbooks are in the New York Public Library for the Performing Arts at Lincoln Center. The principal source of information on Gordon's life is his volume of memoirs, *Max Gordon Presents*, written with Lewis Funke (1963). An obituary is in *Variety*, 8 Nov. 1978.

MALCOLM GOLDSTEIN

GORDON, Ruth (30 Oct. 1896–29 Aug. 1985), actress and playwright, was born in Quincy, Massachusetts, the daughter of Clinton Jones, a factory foreman, and Annie Ziegler, a secretary.

Upon graduating from high school in 1914, Ruth Gordon Jones, an aspiring actress from the age of twelve, was accepted by the prestigious American Academy of Dramatic Arts in New York. Months later, after the academy's president concluded that she was unsuited to the stage and dismissed her from the program, she began her seventy-year career as a stage and screen actress, playwright, and screenwriter. Her first marriage, in 1918, to Gregory Kelly, a young actor with whom she briefly owned a minor stock company in Indianapolis, ended with his early death in 1927. Gordon's only child, Jones Harris, the son of the legendary producer Jed Harris, whom Gordon never married, was born secretly in Paris in 1929. Her forty-three-year marriage to Garson Kanin, with whom she collaborated on a number of screenplays, ended with her death at their home in Edgartown, Massachusetts, where she was at work on a new screenplay. She received an Academy Award for best supporting actress in *Rosemary's Baby* in 1968; a television Emmy for her appearance in Taxi in 1979; and the Holland Society's gold medal in 1980. In November 1984 Quincy, Massachusetts, dedicated an amphitheatre in her name.

Ruth Gordon's career is, in part, a history of the America theater and an account of its principal personalities from the era of the traveling repertory company to the postmodern world dominated by film and television. While her 1915 New York debut as Nibs, one of the Lost Boys in *Peter Pan*, drew the attention of the *New York Times* reviewer Alexander Woollcott, minor roles continued to characterize the first two decades of her career as a stock company player traveling to cities and towns, many of them far from the major theatrical centers of the country, to perform a new play nearly every week. As a touring company player, Gordon developed the flexibility and adaptability that made her equally successful, throughout her career, in both comic and tragic roles. The high-spiritedness, determination, and comic timing for which she is credited in countless reviews had its source in the grueling life of the traveling theater company, where she refined her talents as an actress and developed the resilience that sustained her career. She toured with road companies in *Little Minister* and *Fair and Warner* (1915–1917); toured in *Seventeen* (1919); and performed in *Clarence* in Chicago (1920). In 1925 she ran a stock company in Indianapolis with Kelly and performed in *The Fall of Eve*. Exposure to diverse audiences and critics tested her self-esteem. In the second of four animated memoirs, *My Side: The Autobiography of Ruth Gordon* (1976), she recalls her response to an attack by a Minnesota critic: "I *won't* give up. Why does everybody knock me even in damn places like Duluth where they should be glad any damn person comes?" Despite the arduous and uncertain life of the stock company player in the United States between the two world wars, Gordon honed her talent for creating unique and memorable characters out of the fabric of plays, though most of them were less than memorable. Her early career foreshadowed her screen career as a character actress famous for roles in such films as

Where's Poppa?, *Harold and Maude*, and *Brighton Beach*. The repertory years also included minor appearances in two early films, *Camille* (1915) and *The Wheel of Life* (1915).

Her first Broadway success in 1927 as the vacuous Bobby in Maxwell Anderson's *Saturday's Children* typecast her as the emptyheaded young bride, a role she temporarily exploited and then eventually rejected in favor of the more challenging, classical roles that are the measure of a career in the theater. Prior to her first international success, however, Gordon appeared in minor theatrical fare including *Serena Blandish* (1929); *Hotel Universe* (1930); *The Violet* (1930); *The Wiser They Are* (1931); *The Church Mouse* (1931); *Here Today* (1932); *Three Cornered Moon* (1933); *They Shall Not Die* (1934); and *A Sleeping Clergyman* (1934).

In her autobiography, Gordon recalls the telegram that altered the course of her acting career and elevated her status in the acting profession. At the request of Tyrone Guthrie, a director of international stature, she was offered the part of Mrs. Pinchwife in the London revival of William Wycherley's *The Country Wife*, in which she would appear, in 1936, with Edith Evans and Michael Redgrave. Gordon became the first American cast by London's Old Vic Company. She was a resounding success, according to the *New York Times* (7 Oct. 1936), which reported that "Ruth Gordon took London by storm." What followed were several London engagements that she repeated with great success upon her return to New York. Her most successful productions included *Ethan Frome*, in which she played Mattie Silver (1936); *A Doll's House*, as Nora (1937); *Here Today*, in Boston and Chicago (1941); *Portrait of a Lady* (1941); *The Strings My Lord Are False* (1941); and *The Three Sisters*, as Natasha (1942–1943). The role of Nora in *A Doll's House* was adapted for her by Thornton Wilder, a collaboration that later led Wilder to write the role of Dolly Levi in *The Matchmaker* for Gordon, who made the role internationally famous with productions in London and Berlin (1954) and in New York (1955).

In the 1940s Gordon entered a new creative period, stretching her talents to include both film acting and playwriting. Gordon's first major motion picture success was in the role of Mary Todd in *Abe Lincoln in Illinois* in 1939. Her marriage in 1942 to Garson Kanin, then a serviceman in the U.S. Army, inspired her early plays, including *Over 21*, in which she performed on Broadway from 1943 to 1945. She subsequently wrote *Years Ago* (1946) and *The Leading Lady* (1948). Testimonies to her versatility and durability are her additional ventures into film, including Mrs. Erich in *Dr Erich's Magic Bullet* (1939), *Two-Faced Woman* (1941), *Action in the North Atlantic* (1943), and *Edge of Darkness* (1943). *Two-Faced Woman*, Greta Garbo's last film, established Gordon's long-lasting working relationship with legendary film director George Cukor.

Screenplay collaboration with Kanin began in the late 1940s with several notable films written for George Cukor that helped establish the film careers of Katherine Hepburn and Spencer Tracy. They include *A Double Life* (1948), *Adam's Rib* (1949), *The Marrying Kind* (1952), *Pat and Mike* (1952), *The Actress* (1958), and *Rosie* (1958). In *The Actress*, Gordon retells the story of her earlier play, *Years Ago*, which, along with *The Leading Lady*, explore Gordon's own relationship with her father, who questioned her ambition to become an actress but proved supportive and proud of her early achievements.

Gordon's adaptability and durability allowed her to alternate between film and stage roles until 1976, appearing on stage in *The Good Soup* (1960); *A Time to Laugh*, London (1962); *My Mother, My Father, and Me* (1963); *The Loves of Cass McGuire* (1966); *Dreyfus in Rehearsal* (1974), as Zina; and *Mrs. Warren's Profession* (1976). Her film roles during the same period include *Inside Daisy Clover* (1965), *Lord Love a Duck* (1966), *Rosemary's Baby* (1968), *Whatever Happened to Aunt Alice?* (1969), *Where's Poppa?* (1970), *Harold and Maude* (1971), *The Big Bus* (1976), *Every Which Way but Loose* (1978), *Brighton Beach* (1979), *Any Which Way You Can* (1980), *My Bodyguard* (1980), and *Maxie* (1985). Gordon's television films include *Isn't It Shocking?* (1973), *Prince of Central Park* (1975), *Rosemary's Baby II* (1976), *The Great Houdini* (1976), *Perfect Gentlemen* (1978), *Scavenger Hunt* (1979), and *Don't Go to Sleep* (1983). Her televised plays include *The American Dream* (1963); *A Very Rich Woman* (1965); *Ho! Ho! Ho!* (1976); and *Blythe Spirit*, as Madame Arcati. In addition, she appeared on television episodes of "Kojak," "Rhoda," "Medical Story," and "Taxi." Unlike many actors whose skills are limited to one medium, Gordon carefully selected professional opportunities that consistently broadened and advanced her career.

Possessing a multifaceted talent, Gordon remains one of the most enduring theatrical figures of the twentieth century on screen. Her appeal as an actress and author transcends several generations. In *Harold and Maude*, Gordon's elderly character confronts a suicidal teenager and teaches him how to survive in a mad world. The role, in fact, typifies the wit, generosity of spirit, and candor that characterize Gordon's reminiscences and her anecdotal style. As she concludes in her autobiography, "[I]t's been a ball, it's been sad, it's been lonely, it's been hard work, it's come out right. I live in the past and the present and the future and haven't let them get me down and I wouldn't want to live anywhere else." The friend and confidante of many stage and film celebrities, Gordon's memoirs reflect the masterful discretion at the core of her ability to succeed in the complex worlds of theater and film. Her memoirs are a substantial contribution to the cultural history of the twentieth century.

• Despite some discrepancies in the reporting of dates and minor events, Gordon's four autobiographical memoirs—*Ruth Gordon: Myself among Others* (1971), *My Side: The Autobiography of Ruth Gordon* (1976), *Ruth Gordon: An Open Book* (1980), and *Shady Lady* (1981)—are primary sources for information about her career and about her personal life in the theater and film industries, including her marriages and romantic liaisons with two of the theater world's most influential producers. Gordon was profusely reviewed throughout her career, particularly in the *New York Times*. Obituaries are in *The Annual Obituary* (1985) and in the *New York Times*, 29 Aug. 1985.

PATRICIA FLANAGAN BEHRENDT

GORDON, Waxey (1888–24 June 1952), bootlegger, was born Irving Wexler on the Lower East Side of New York City, the son of poor Polish-Jewish parents. His formal education did not extend much beyond grammar school; he ceased attending in his early teens. He became one of the most successful bootleggers in New York during Prohibition, earning the sobriquet Public Enemy Number One from the state of New York in 1930 for his criminal exploits. He initially pursued a relatively normal criminal career among the tenements of his home neighborhood. His skill as a pickpocket earned him the nickname "Waxey" (for smooth fingered), while "Gordon" came from one of the numerous aliases he gave the police. In his late teens he served several short terms for grand and petty larceny in reformatories and other penal institutions. At this point in his career (c. 1912) he seemed destined for the obscurity of petty street crime.

Gordon's rise from obscurity to fame began with his membership in Dopey Benny Fein's street gang. Fein was a prominent pioneer in racketeering, a crime that extorted money from vulnerable small merchants in exchange for "protection" in urban ghettos in the early twentieth century. Alert to new opportunities to make money, Fein discovered that the fledgling garment workers' unions on the Lower East Side would pay for his services in protecting their members from physical abuse by employer goons. When Fein went to prison in 1914, Gordon continued working with the original gang under the leadership of "Little Augie" Organsky. This work was not only remunerative; it also gave Gordon contacts with several other major gangsters interested in racketeering, including Arnold Rothstein, New York's premier underworld figure at the time. In 1914 Gordon married Leah (maiden name unknown); they had three children.

Gordon's personal flair for illegal business seems to have evolved from his racketeering experiences. He began to invest in other criminal opportunities about this time. Cocaine had become a popular street drug on the Lower East Side during the first decade of the century. Public concern over drugs, expressed in the Harrison Act in 1914, contributed to a change in the marketing of cocaine. Since the drug was unavailable through legal sources, underworld entrepreneurs began developing ways to satisfy consumer demand for cocaine. Gordon was one of several criminals who developed this market. By 1917 he had become a partner in five cocaine syndicates that operated in Harlem, the Lower East Side, and Philadelphia. Gordon's participation in these syndicates, which engaged in smuggling as well as distribution of cocaine, probably made him a relatively rich man by 1920. The drug trade was

in fact so important to him that he continued it throughout the remainder of his criminal career.

Prohibition offered numerous opportunities for a successful criminal entrepreneur with cash and connections. Gordon's opportunity emerged in late 1920, when Max Greenberg, a St. Louis gangster who had moved to Detroit to smuggle liquor from Canada, approached Gordon about expanding his smuggling business. Greenberg's choice of Gordon was probably not purely coincidental, since Greenberg wanted an introduction to Arnold Rothstein, who he hoped would finance his scheme. Gordon knew Rothstein through their mutual interest in racketeering and arranged the introduction.

Although Rothstein rejected Greenberg's original idea, he offered to finance a smuggling operation between England and the United States. Gordon's experience with drug smuggling may have helped convince Rothstein of the efficacy of this idea (Gordon and Rothstein would in fact run a drug smuggling syndicate separate from, but associated with, the liquor smuggling).

As a junior partner in Rothstein's liquor syndicate, Gordon acquired his first investment opportunity in bootlegging, and he made the most of it. He and his partners developed a very large and very successful smuggling operation by 1925, using as a front a company that imported building materials from overseas. Gordon's own income was rumored to be $200,000 a month by this point. To celebrate his success, he bought a magnificent apartment on New York's Upper West Side and a mansion in New Jersey.

Gordon's good fortune encountered a temporary setback in September 1925 when federal agents raided his business headquarters. Although nothing came of the raid, Gordon decided to move his liquor investments onshore. Between 1925 and 1929 he systematically built a brewing empire that eventually owned thirteen breweries in three states. Gordon's expanding empire occasioned some opposition from equally ambitious bootleggers. (Two of his major rivals, Frankie Dunn and Bugs Donovan, died violently as Gordon expanded his interests.) To protect himself and his investments, Gordon arranged protection through New Jersey gangsters such as William Moretti (whose associates included Vito Genovese and Lucky Luciano).

By the late 1920s Gordon's syndicate had become one of the most powerful bootlegging groups on the East Coast. It belonged to the "Big Seven," a loose association of major bootleggers commonly thought to control most of the liquor business in the Northeast. He had become a millionaire bootlegger and narcotics dealer.

Gordon's prominence became a major weakness. The Internal Revenue Service legal team, which prosecuted Al Capone, transferred to New York and began a long investigation of Gordon's business and tax records. Led by U.S. state attorney Thomas Dewey, this team finally brought Gordon to trial in November 1933 and convicted him of tax evasion. Gordon spent the remainder of the decade in Leavenworth prison.

After his release in 1941, Gordon unsuccessfully attempted to reestablish himself as a major criminal entrepreneur. He tried his hand at black market operations, but that only resulted in another federal conviction in January 1943. Back on the streets a year later, he continued searching for ways to duplicate his earlier success. Heroin was emerging as a major street drug, and Gordon's familiarity with the world of drug smuggling seems to have given him a belated opportunity to recoup his fortunes. Disaster struck again, however, when federal agents arrested him in 1951 in possession of a large quantity of heroin. Since Gordon had three prior felony convictions on his record (the earliest for purse snatching as a teenager), the judge invoked the Baumes Law, which stipulated life imprisonment upon conviction for a fourth felony.

Gordon did not live long after his return to prison. Suffering from heroin addiction, he died in Alcatraz prison. His conviction for income tax evasion had essentially deprived him of the opportunity to emulate other major bootleggers who developed new and important careers in organized crime after the repeal of Prohibition.

• Among the works that provide various details of Gordon's life, the following are most useful: Alan Block, *East Side, West Side: Organizing Crime in New York, 1930–1950* (1980); Stephen Fox, *Blood and Power: Organized Crime in Twentieth-Century America* (1989); Albert Fried, *The Rise and Fall of the Jewish Gangster in America* (1980); Jenna W. Joselit, *Our Gang: Jewish Crime and the New York Jewish Community, 1900–1940* (1983); and Leo Katcher, *The Big Bankroll: The Life and Times of Arnold Rothstein* (1959). An obituary is in the *New York Times*, 25 June 1952.

DAVID R. JOHNSON

GORDY, John Pancoast (21 Dec. 1851–31 Dec. 1908), historian, philosopher, and teacher, was born in Salisbury, Maryland, the son of Elijah Melson Pancoast and Martha Ellen Shepard. Gordy began teaching in public schools in 1868 at the age of seventeen and was named principal of an academy in Farmington, Delaware, in 1871; later, between 1873 and 1875, he served as vice principal of another academy, this one located in Dover, Maryland. Following his graduation in 1878 from Wesleyan University of Pennsylvania, where he had studied logic, psychology, and ethics and specialized in English literature, Gordy began his graduate studies in Europe, receiving his Ph.D. from the University of Leipzig in 1884. After his return to the United States he served as professor of philosophy and pedagogy at Ohio University (1886–1896), professor of history and philosophy at Ohio State University (1896–1900), and professor of the history of education and American history at New York University (1901 until his death). In 1884 he married Eugenia Day, with whom he had one daughter.

Gordy's most-noted work was in education and philosophy. His *History of Political Parties in the United States*, originally published in two volumes in 1895 and revised and expanded into four volumes in 1900, was his most-popular work. Gordy's political texts were not intended to be specific treatments of selected political issues but rather general comprehensive works suitable for survey courses in university or college programs. The generally held expectation that he would extend his initial treatments on political parties was never realized. Gordy also authored several works that signaled his devotion to normal school/teacher education: *History of Modern Philosophy* (1887), *Lessons in Psychology* (1890), *Rise and Growth of the Normal School Idea in the United States* (1891), and his last published work, *A Broader Elementary Education* (1903).

What makes Gordy's work significant is that he was among the first scholars to prepare textbooks to be used exclusively by college and university students and, in particular, normal school or teacher education students. In appealing to those audiences, Gordy adopted a writing style that was more conversational and friendly than scientific and stuffy, and his writings are largely free of academic jargon. In addition, his pedagogical works contained the latest educational theories, fully discussed and debated, together with notations from important educational writers and professional academic and educational committees, such as the National Education Association's Committee of Ten. His developing educational philosophy, which centered on the social melioration of the masses, was thoroughly egalitarian. In *A Broader Elementary Education*, in the chapter titled "Democracy and Education," Gordy argued that: "the moment you begin to educate [a child of the masses], the moment you begin to increase his value . . . *that* moment you implant in his mind the germ of the belief that from his point of view [lessons] are supremely important matters, and the more you educate him the more quickly you will cause that germ to develop" (p. 52). Gordy also offered a challenge that was as timely at the beginning of the twentieth century as it was at the end:

. . . if our American political philosophy is true, if that form of society is best in which there is no discrimination between man and man, if men as such have an inherent right, if not to equality of opportunity, at least to freedom from artificial inequalities, then the thing to do is to work out an American theory of education based on the assumption that every member of society, without regard to birth, race, or sex, should receive that development of his or her powers which makes life most worth the living. (P. 51)

Gordy's views seem to have anticipated the later work of his up-town colleague, noted educational philosopher John Dewey, who in *Democracy and Education* (1916) presented what is arguably the first full-length American philosophical treatment on how individuals should be educated within a republican-democratic form of government. Gordy also anticipated, despite the aristocratic realities of his day and the influence of Marxist and other socialist theories, worldwide movement toward a form of democracy in which "unselfish rulers" would "make an effective alliance with the masses in bringing about progress toward democracy." Had Gordy lived, he might have cultivated a more-cogent educational philosophy than that of Dewey. His life, however, ended in tragedy. Gordy and his wife committed suicide on 31 December 1908, within a few hours of the untimely death of their only child, Gwendolyn.

• There are no known papers or collections of the works of Gordy, nor are there any biographies. His major works are noted in the text. An obituary is in the *New York Times*, 1 Jan. 1909.

DAVID WARREN SAXE

GORE, Christopher (21 Sept. 1758–1 Mar. 1827), Federalist statesman, diplomat, and lawyer, was born in Boston, Massachusetts, the son of John Gore, a paint and color dealer, and Frances Pinkney. Paternally, he was descended from a Puritan family that migrated from Hampshire in England to Roxbury, Massachusetts, in 1635. After attending the Boston Public Latin School, Gore entered Harvard College where he graduated in 1776. Although his Loyalist father fled Boston in 1776, Gore remained in Massachusetts and served the revolutionary cause as an officer in an artillery regiment. John Gore returned to America from England in 1785 and regained his citizenship. The taint of his father's Toryism persisted, however, and Gore's opponents used it against him when he was a candidate for the Massachusetts ratifying convention in 1787.

Admitted to the bar in 1778, Gore soon established a successful legal practice and numbered among his clients prominent individuals and commercial houses in the United States, Great Britain, and Nova Scotia. His marriage in 1785 to Rebecca Payne of Boston was childless, but his connection with the prominent Payne family furthered his professional career.

Through his legal practice, speculation in government securities, and ties with the Massachusetts Bank, Gore began to acquire a considerable fortune during the 1780s. Economic interest and a conservative viewpoint led Gore, amidst the rising radicalism of agrarian unrest in Massachusetts, to join the movement for a stronger federal union. As a member from Boston, Gore was a strong supporter of the 1787 Constitution in the Massachusetts ratifying convention. Elected from Boston to the state house of representatives in 1788 and 1789, he backed men favoring the new Constitution and worked for conservative measures such as indirect election of presidential electors and congressional districting that would strengthen friends of the federal government.

In 1789 President George Washington named Gore the first U.S. attorney for the Massachusetts district. He also became a director of the Boston branch of the Bank of the United States. Closely identified from the beginning with the Federalist party, Gore supported Alexander Hamilton's (1755–1804) financial policy as well as the administration's foreign policy. As district attorney he vigorously enforced the policy of neutrality when Britain and France went to war in 1793 by prosecuting privateers illegally fitted out in Massachusetts. He believed that John Jay's special mission to Britain was desirable, and he staunchly defended the treaty Jay negotiated in 1794.

Gore's ambition for a diplomatic appointment was realized in 1796 when Washington named him a commissioner to serve in London as a member of the joint Anglo-American commission on maritime spoliations provided by Article 7 of Jay's treaty to deal with American and British claims for the loss of ships and cargoes arising from violations of neutrality. As a member of the commission Gore effectively represented American interests, and he was well received by the English aristocracy and business community during his eight-year stay. Before the work of the commission was completed in 1804, Gore acted on two occasions as the American chargé d'affaires in the absence of the minister.

Returning to Boston in 1804, Gore resumed his legal career. An outstanding leader of the bar, his tutelage was sought by aspiring students like Daniel Webster, a grateful recipient of his kindness and advice. A shrewd investor, Gore continued to increase his fortune by strategic investments in transportation and manufacturing enterprises, such as canals, bridges, and textile mills. He also remained active in the cultural and social life of Boston as a vestryman of King's Chapel, a member of the American Academy of Arts and Sciences, and president of the Massachusetts Historical Society. Devoted to his alma mater, Gore served as an overseer and fellow of Harvard. An owner of farm land near Waltham, Gore for many years was interested in soil improvement, the introduction of new varieties of vegetables and fruits, and the breeding of improved livestock. Such interests made him one of the founders in 1792 of the Massachusetts Society for Promoting Agriculture. Desiring to lead the life of a country gentleman, Gore and his wife had begun planning a country mansion in Waltham while still in England. The completed house, "Gore Place," which reflected the elegant taste of the Gores, has remained a striking architectural monument of the Federalist era.

Despite his many interests, Gore did not abandon public life. In Federalist party politics he was a transitional figure between the old and young Federalists. Unlike many of his generation, he recognized the need for party organization, and he served faithfully as a member of the party's central committee in Massachusetts. At the national level he participated in the New York meeting in 1808 that promoted the candidacies of Charles C. Pinckney and Rufus King (1755–1827) for the presidency and vice presidency. Gore himself had been elected from Boston to the Massachusetts Senate in 1806 and to the state house of representatives in 1808. Defeated for governor in 1808, he was elected in 1809, but after an uneventful term was defeated by Republican Elbridge Gerry in 1810 and again in 1811. Gore's lavish display of pomp and ceremony in office alienated many and contributed to his defeat. Although sometimes branded by his political enemies as a member of the so-called Essex Junto, a small group of die-hard Massachusetts Federalists, Gore was never in the inner circle of that amorphous faction.

Strongly opposed to Republican foreign policy, Gore did not favor war with Great Britain in 1812 because he was convinced that Anglo-American friendship, despite its difficulties, was the wiser course. Appointed and subsequently elected to the U.S. Senate in 1813, he opposed the war measures of James Madison's (1751–1836) administration. Although Gore never joined the extremists who advocated secession of the New England states, he approved of the Hartford Convention, which he did not attend, as an expression of regional protest. Although a strong nationalist in his support of Alexander Hamilton's program during the 1790s, Gore as a senator defended predominant New England interests in his opposition to appropriations for internal improvements and the protective tariff of 1816. He was concerned that internal improvements would promote the growth of the West at the expense of his section and that higher import duties would adversely affect mercantile and shipping interests.

Resigning from the Senate in 1816 because of ill health, Gore retired from public life. Until his death in Boston he personified the spirit of Federalism in society and politics as well as the spirit of American enterprise in his capitalistic ventures. He left generous bequests to the American Academy of Arts and Sciences and the Massachusetts Historical Society. His bequest of $100,000 to Harvard was the largest ever made to the university up to that time. It was used to build Gore Hall, which housed the general library from 1841 until it was demolished in 1912. Gore's memory is preserved in Harvard Yard by the name of a residence hall of Winthrop House. Among his portraits preserved at Gore Place, the most impressive likeness was painted by John Trumbull (1756–1843).

• The only full-length biography is Helen R. Pinkney, *Christopher Gore, Federalist of Massachusetts, 1758–1827* (1969). Perceptive comments by David H. Fischer on Gore's political career are found in his "The Myth of the Essex Junto," *William and Mary Quarterly*, 3d ser., 21 (1964): 191–235, and *The Revolution of American Conservatism* (1965). There is no single collection of Gore's papers, but many of his letters are in the collections of friends and associates, most notably the Rufus King Papers in the New-York Historical Society library in New York City. Many Gore letters were printed in Charles R. King, ed., *The Life and Correspondence of Rufus King* (6 vols., 1894–1900). Documents concerning Gore's service as a member of the commission under Article 7 of Jay's treaty are in the National Archives; some of these documents were published in John Bassett Moore, ed., *International Adjudications, Ancient and Modern* (6 vols., 1929–1933).

MALCOLM LESTER

GORE, Thomas Pryor (10 Dec. 1870–16 Mar. 1949), U.S. senator, was born near the village of Embry in Webster County, Mississippi, the son of Thomas Madison Gore, a farmer and lawyer, and Caroline Elizabeth Wingo. Gore launched a political career by serving as a page in the Mississippi Senate in 1882. In Jackson he resided in the home of U.S. Senator James Z. George. As a result of two childhood accidents, the first sustained at the age of eight, Gore was totally blind at the age of twenty. Nevertheless he attended school in Walthall, Mississippi, excelled in debating, and gave the commencement address in 1888. After studying for two additional years Gore taught at the public school in Candaretta during the winter of 1890–1891. In the fall of 1891, after withdrawing as a Farmer's Alliance candidate for the state legislature because he was not yet twenty-one, Gore began to study law at Cumberland University in Lebanon, Tennessee. He received a Bachelor of Laws Degree in 1892 and started his practice in Walthall. By now a polished orator, Gore campaigned for the Populist ticket in 1892, following in the footsteps of his father and other relatives.

Seeking better opportunities, he moved to Corsicana, Texas, in 1894. However, he soon returned to Mississippi to actively engage in Populist party politics and was defeated in the 1895 election. He attended the Populist National Convention at St. Louis in 1896 as a delegate from Mississippi. After moving back to Texas, in 1898 Gore was nominated as a Populist candidate for Congress but was defeated. Thereafter he changed his party affiliation to Democrat. In December 1900 he married Nina Kay, daughter of a Texas cotton planter. In June of the next year Gore and his father moved to southern Comanche County in Oklahoma Territory. Unsuccessful in his bid for a land claim in the lottery, Gore bought a lot in Lawton and opened a law office. In 1902 he was elected to the territorial council for the 1903–1905 term. Thanks to his oratorical abilities, his driving ambition, and the support of the *Daily Oklahoman* in Oklahoma City, Gore became a prominent political figure. In 1907 upon the creation of the new state of Oklahoma, Gore was selected by the legislature as one of the first two U.S. Senators. He was the youngest member of the senate and the first blind person ever to serve in that chamber. Altogether an imposing figure, he was six feet tall, weighed two hundred pounds, and was prematurely gray. Seeking a second term, Gore became the first U.S. Senator directly elected by the people of Oklahoma.

In the Senate Gore allied himself with the progressive cause, opposing high tariffs and trusts, particularly the railroads. An early supporter of Woodrow Wilson, Gore endorsed his "New Freedom" legislative program. He served as chairman of the Committee on Agriculture and Forestry and played a prominent role in guiding agricultural bills and appropriations through the Senate. In addition, he devoted considerable attention to the oil industry and to Indian affairs, all three issues of vital concern to his Oklahoma constituency. In 1918 Gore offered an amendment to the Revenue Act granting exemptions to oil companies from taxation on a portion of their oil income. This depletion allowance in revised form subsequently was applied to other mineral industries as well.

However, in the neutrality controversy leading to American entry in the First World War, Gore followed a more pacifist-isolationist line. In 1916 he cosponsored a resolution informing American citizens that if they traveled on armed belligerent ships, they did so at their own peril. Though unable to vote against the war resolution owing to illness, Gore opposed the draft and most of Wilson's wartime policies. He further utilized his oratorical skills in opposition to the League of Nations. His stand against Wilsonian diplomacy was unpopular in Oklahoma, and in the 1920 Democratic primary he was defeated by Congressman Scott Ferris.

After his defeat Gore practiced law in Washington, specializing in tax matters while retaining an interest in Oklahoma politics. In 1924 he again sought a Senate seat but was defeated in the primary. In 1926 he filed for a seat in Congress but quickly withdrew. In 1930, as the depression deepened, he was elected again to the Senate. Though he endorsed Franklin Roosevelt in 1932, Gore had opposed the creation of the Reconstruction Finance Corporation during the Hoover Administration. He pursued this conservative stance during the New Deal, voting against most administration-endorsed measures because he believed they stifled private initiative and made balancing the budget almost impossible. Again out of step with his constituents, Gore was defeated in the 1936 Democratic primary by Congressman Josh Lee.

Gore remained in Washington, again resuming his law practice and retaining a lively interest in political affairs. He now added Indian affairs to taxation as his fields of special expertise. Gore died in his Washington apartment as a result of a cerebral hemorrhage. His chief significance as a senator lies in the example his career provides of superior achievement despite disability.

• Gore destroyed most of his papers after he left the Senate following his defeat in the 1920 primary. What papers remain from his earlier years are housed in the Carl Albert Center at the University of Oklahoma, which also contains his files from the 1930s and 1940s. The collection is divided into seven major sections, including correspondence, speeches, form letters, personal and family records, clippings, and so forth. Novelist Gore Vidal, the senator's grandson, possesses a small collection pertaining to his grandfather. See Martin J. Lahood, "Gore Vidal: A Grandfather's Legacy," *World Literature Today* 64, no. 3 (1990): 413–17.

Monroe Billington, *Thomas P. Gore*, is a comprehensive biography. Extended eulogies by members of Congress can be found in the *Congressional Record* on 16 March 1949, pp. 2616–18 and p. 2750. Editorials from various newspapers can be found in the *Appendix to the Congressional Record for the First Session of the Eighty-First Congress*, pp. A1065, A1817, A1911–12, and A2506.

RICHARD LOWITT

GORGAS, Josiah (1 July 1818–15 May 1883), soldier, was born at Running Pumps, Pennsylvania, the son of Joseph Gorgas and Sophia Atkinson, farmers and innkeepers. Apprenticed at seventeen to a newspaper printery in Lyons, New York, Josiah accepted appointment to the U.S. Military Academy in 1837 and was graduated sixth in his class in 1841. Brevet Second Lieutenant Gorgas selected the Ordnance Corps and drew assignment to Watervliet Arsenal, near Troy, New York. After a year's travel in Europe, 1845–1846, he joined General Winfield Scott's expeditionary force to Mexico.

A prominent role in placing guns for the Veracruz siege led to Gorgas's commanding the ordnance depot forming in the old fortress city. A bout with yellow fever plus the tedious routine of depot duty robbed the Mexican War of much drama for Gorgas. Still, service in that important assignment established his own faith in his abilities and called him to the favorable notice of his superiors. He also came to know several young officers who would work closely with him in the Confederate army in a few years.

A tendency toward independence involved Gorgas in an insubordinate correspondence with Secretary of State James Buchanan, hence also with Secretary of War William L. Marcy—a controversy that cost Gorgas a brevet promotion for Mexican services and that would hamper his career over the years.

Routine ordnance duties throughout the 1840s and 1850s took Gorgas to installations in the deep South and to scattered arsenals in the North. At Mount Vernon Arsenal in Alabama, he met Amelia Gayle, daughter of a former governor of Alabama. He and Amelia were married in 1853. She soothed the roughness of Gorgas's personality but could not heal the old Buchanan wound. They had six children; one, William Crawford Gorgas, would be a conqueror of yellow fever.

Promotions were slow for this dark-haired soldier with steady eyes, a large nose, and a straight mouth hidden by a full beard, and army service promised too little for his talents. When the Civil War came, Captain Gorgas commanded Frankford Arsenal in Philadelphia, Pennsylvania. Asked to join the Confederacy, Gorgas hesitated, but his wife's influence and his continuing troubles with superiors pushed him at last to accept a commission (effective 8 Apr. 1861) as major in the artillery of the Confederate states with assignment to the important duty of chief of ordnance. General P. G. T. Beauregard, who knew him slightly, had urged his appointment on President Jefferson Davis. The appointment would be one of Davis's best.

Gorgas's challenges were staggering. The South boasted scant manufacturing facilities, only one large foundry capable of casting heavy cannon (in Richmond, Va.), and although each state had an armory, arsenals capable of repairing or making arms were few. Across the Confederacy Gorgas counted only 159,010 small arms of all kinds, about 3.2 million cartridges of various calibers, powder enough for another 1.5 million bullets, and an indeterminate amount of cannon powder. Close to 3 million percussion caps were counted, along with saltpeter and sulphur enough to make an additional 200 tons of powder. Supplies were scattered across different states, and governors tended to guard their hoards with parochial jealousy.

Gorgas's first efforts were directed toward importation—from the North and from Europe. Next, he focused on expanding or creating existing industrial and mechanical capacity and on scavenging every battlefield. He developed mineral resources through a Nitre and Mining Corps. Various arsenals were overhauled and modernized; small ordnance shops were established in Tennessee, Mississippi, Virginia, and Texas. Gorgas realized that the rail system of the South inhibited a centralized procurement plan, which would have allowed the Ordnance Department to set up a few large works to distribute arms and munitions to railheads near the field armies. Without that luxury, he relied on decentralized distribution.

By 1862 Gorgas turned his attention increasingly to blockade running as a vital source of cannon, powder, lead, copper, arms, and other ordnance needs. He successfully urged creation of a Bureau of Foreign Supplies to organize overseas purchasing. His efforts led to the purchase of blockade runners for his and other supply departments and an efficient system of transshipment in Bermuda, Nassau, and Cuba. From 1861 to 1865 about 600,000 small arms reached the South. From December 1863 to December 1864, 1,933,000 pounds of saltpeter and 1,507,000 pounds of lead arrived.

Gorgas's programs succeeded. On 8 April 1864 he confided to his diary: "It is three years ago today since I took charge of the Ordnance Department. . . . I have succeeded beyond my utmost expectations. From being the worst supplied of the Bureaus of the War Department it is now the best. . . . Where . . . we were not making a gun, a pistol nor a sabre, no shot nor shell . . . —a pound of powder—we now make all these in quantities to meet the demands of our large armies." On 19 November 1864 Gorgas was promoted to brigadier general.

Gorgas performed logistical miracles to the end of the war. His wizardry lay in his judgment of subordinates. He picked able men to run his installations and to serve with the field armies, and he backed his men strongly. He and his department did more than most to sustain the Confederacy.

Gorgas's iron-making venture at Brierfield, Alabama, after the war ended in failure. On 1 July 1869 he became head of the Junior Department of the nascent University of the South at Sewanee, Tennessee, and on 10 July 1872 he was installed as head of that institution. A stormy tenure there ended with Gorgas's appointment (July 1878) as president of the University of Alabama. He enjoyed the town of Tuscaloosa and was a quick success with the faculty and student body. The Alabama move restored his self-confidence. Happiness was brief; illness forced Gorgas to resign the presidency in September 1879. Appointed librarian, he lived with his family on the university campus until his death there.

• The major collection of Josiah Gorgas Papers is in the Amelia Gayle Gorgas Library, University of Alabama. Included are Gorgas's manuscript diaries from the Mexican War through 1877, a travel diary for 1845–1846, and the records of his ill-fated postwar ironworks venture. Much genealogical material is to be found in this collection. See also Frank E. Vandiver, ed., *The Civil War Diary of General Josiah Gorgas* (1947), Vandiver, *Ploughshares into Swords: Josiah Gorgas and Confederate Ordnance* (1952), and Sarah Wiggins, ed., *The Diaries of Josiah Gorgas* (1995).

FRANK E. VANDIVER

GORGAS, William Crawford (3 Oct. 1854–3 July 1920), surgeon general of the U.S. Army and sanitarian, was born near Mobile, Alabama, the son of Josiah Gorgas, an army lieutenant, and Amelia Gayle, the daughter of Judge John Gayle, former governor of Alabama. Josiah Gorgas, though Pennsylvanian-born, gave up his U.S. Army commission to become Confederate Ordnance officer during the Civil War. Following the war he became president of the University of the South in Sewanee, Tennessee.

The eldest of six children, Gorgas was privately educated but was more interested in reading battle stories than studying in his early years. He adopted the manners and loyalties of his region during his boyhood in the Confederate South and lived in Richmond, Virginia, during the Civil War. Desiring a military career, he sought to enter West Point but was unable to secure an appointment. Notwithstanding, he decided to obtain entrance into the army by studying medicine. Gorgas spent six years at the University of the South, graduating in 1875 with a B.A., followed by three years of study at Bellevue Hospital Medical College in New York, from which he received an M.D. in 1879. After a yearlong internship at Bellevue, he received an appointment to the U.S. Army Medical Corps in 1880. For the next twenty years Gorgas served as an army doctor at posts in Texas, North Dakota, and Florida. In Texas he contracted yellow fever, then one of the leading scourges of the South. While he was convalescing, Gorgas met Marie Doughty, who was also recovering from a near-fatal case of the disease. They were married in 1884 and had one daughter. Because of his immunity to yellow fever, Gorgas was frequently sent to treat yellow fever epidemics. The majority of his career as an army doctor was spent at Fort Barrancas in Pensacola Bay, Florida, where yellow fever was endemic. Gorgas, along with most other physicians of the time, attributed yellow fever to lack of sanitation and thought that it was transmitted by contact with contaminated items such as bed sheets and clothing. Although a few physicians theorized that the disease was transmitted by mosquitoes, the lack of conclusive evidence caused their theories to be dismissed.

After U.S. troops occupied Havana, Cuba, in 1898 following the Spanish-American War, Gorgas was summoned to a yellow fever camp at Siboney, near Havana, where yellow fever had been endemic for 150 years. He served on a special commission with Dr. Carlos Finlay and Dr. Henry Rose Carter that diagnosed all suspected cases of yellow fever. Later that year he was appointed chief sanitary officer of Havana, and there promptly instituted strict sanitary codes, including the removal of garbage, human and animal corpses, and sewage from the streets; segregating the sick; and quarantining infected locations. His efforts resulted in a sharp reduction of smallpox, typhoid, and dysentery and a general improvement in health, but had no effect on yellow fever. Indeed, yellow fever cases rose in Havana, despite Gorgas's sanitation efforts, in part because of the influx of nonimmunes entering Cuba as immigrants during the U.S. occupation. In 1900 surgeon general George M. Sternberg sent a talented team of medical researchers headed by Major Walter Reed to assist Gorgas, Finlay, and Carter in their efforts to find the cause of yellow fever. They investigated the mosquito theory, which finally granted them the missing link to this elusive disease. The Reed Board proved conclusively in 1900 that yellow fever was not caused by contaminated articles but by the Stegomyia mosquito (since renamed the Aëdes Aëgypt), an insect that thrived in urban centers like Havana by laying her larvae in artificial containers of standing water near human habitation. The female Stegomyia, having bitten a yellow fever victim during the first three days of his illness, could then transmit the disease to other humans after incubating the disease in her own body from ten to fourteen days.

After this long-awaited medical breakthrough, Gorgas set out to eliminate mosquito-breeding areas. His campaign was thorough and effective. He divided Havana into twenty zones and sent health officials into each zone to carry out and enforce anti-mosquito measures. They covered rain barrels with mosquito netting and placed spigots on each one, sprayed kerosene on all pools of standing water, and restricted citizens' use of vases and other standing water that might prove friendly to Stegomyia larvae. He imposed fines for violation of his ordinances, but he seldom collected the fines once compliance had been achieved. By September 1901 Gorgas had caused the virtual extinction of Stegomyia mosquitoes in Havana and eliminated yellow fever in the region. He enjoyed widespread popularity among citizens of Havana, not only because of his sanitary genius, but also because of his kind temperament and his respect for others. His reputation grew as a sanitarian and as the conqueror of yellow fever in Havana.

When the United States began planning the construction of a canal on the disease-infested Panama Isthmus, Gorgas was selected to be the sanitary expert on the project. He was called to Washington in 1902 to prepare for his upcoming assignment. The French had attempted to build a canal in Panama a decade earlier (1881–1889) with disastrous results and an alarmingly high death rate from yellow fever and malaria (also transmitted by mosquitoes). Confident that the Americans would succeed only if they were able to conquer the diseases that had led to the defeat of the French venture, Gorgas familiarized himself with the French experience in Panama and visited both the Suez Canal in Egypt and Panama. The American Medical Association (AMA) had attempted but failed to obtain for Gorgas a seat on the seven-member commission heading the canal project. As a result, Gorgas was subordinated to a frugal commission that deemed preventive medical expenditures extravagant. Denied mosquito netting, trained personnel, and other supplies necessary for him to prevent a yellow fever outbreak by Chairman John Walker, an adamant opponent of the mosquito theory of yellow fever transmission, Gorgas sailed to Panama in 1904 empty-handed, with a foretaste of future administrative difficulties that would foil his efforts to conquer yellow fever efficiently there.

In Panama, Gorgas attempted the same measures of mosquito control that had been successful in Havana, but his limited resources were insufficient to prevent a yellow fever outbreak in 1905. He nevertheless carried on his work of mosquito-proofing buildings, sequestering yellow fever victims, draining swamp areas, and spraying kerosene in pools of standing water to kill mosquito larvae. The commission became annoyed that Gorgas persisted in fighting mosquitoes rather than devoting his time to improving sanitation in the Canal Zone and attempted to discredit him. They would have been successful had not Charles A. L. Reed of the AMA published a timely exposé in the *Journal of the American Medical Association* on 11 March 1905 that detailed the commission's medical ignorance and their obstruction of Gorgas's work, which had resulted in the deaths of many American workers by yellow fever. Shortly afterward, President Theodore Roosevelt dismissed the Walker Commission and established a new three-member commission headed by Theodore P. Shonts in April 1905. Although Gorgas initially faced resistance from the Shonts Commission, Roosevelt denied Shonts's request to have Gorgas removed and ordered Shonts to treat Gorgas fairly. As a result, Gorgas was given almost a free hand to carry out his disease control, which resulted in a notable decline in the cases of yellow fever. Roosevelt visited Panama in 1906 to inspect work on the canal and was impressed by the sanitary improvements Gorgas had effected. For a time Gorgas's obstacles were swept away. Although Colonel George W. Goethals, who was elected chairman of the commission and chief engineer in 1908, proved to be another unsympathetic superior, Gorgas had established respect in the medical field, resulting in his being elected president of the AMA in 1908. In spite of administrative difficulties, Gorgas's efforts were rewarded by a sharp decline in the cases of yellow fever in the Panama Canal Zone. The cities of Panama and Colon became models of sanitation. By 1910 the death rate on the isthmus was substantially lower than in some areas in the United States, causing Gorgas to be regarded as the foremost sanitary expert in the world.

Gorgas remained in Panama until 1913, when the Transvaal Chamber of Mines invited him to Rhodesia, South Africa, to study pneumonia among mine workers. In January of the following year he was appointed surgeon general of the U.S. Army with the rank of brigadier general. His first task as surgeon general was to improve sanitary conditions in Vera Cruz after American troops landed there in 1915. He traveled to South and Central America in 1916 with the International Health Board to fight outbreaks of yellow fever. The entry of the United States into World War I in 1917 interrupted Gorgas's fight against the disease. During the war, he enlisted, trained, and equipped medical staff and mobilized medical supplies. He expanded health care facilities and hospitals to care for Americans abroad who were sick or wounded. Additionally, he imposed strict standards of hygiene in areas where troops were concentrated to prevent disease and infection.

In 1918 Gorgas retired from the army and accepted a position with the International Health Board, which concentrated on eliminating the remaining pockets of yellow fever in South America. In 1920 he was awarded the Harbin Gold Medal in recognition of his "services to mankind." King Albert of Belgium presented Gorgas with the Star of Belgium in Brussels in May 1920. Gorgas had planned to sail to West Africa shortly afterward, but these plans were canceled with the collapse of his health in London in early June. Realizing that recovery was unlikely, King George of England visited Gorgas on his sickbed and knighted him for his service to humanity. A month later Gorgas died in London at the Queen Alexandria Military Hospital at Millbank. His funeral was held in St. Paul's Cathedral and his body sent to the United States to be buried at Arlington National Cemetery.

Gorgas's battle against yellow fever virtually eliminated the deadly disease in Cuba and Panama. His heroic sanitation improvements significantly reduced outbreaks of malaria and other tropical diseases. Without Gorgas's efforts to eradicate the mosquito that carried yellow fever, thousands of American lives would likely have been lost to tropical diseases during the building of the Panama Canal. After his death, countries in North and South America joined together to found the Gorgas Memorial Institute of Tropical and Preventive Medicine, which established health education in South America; and the Republic of Panama donated land for the Gorgas Memorial Laboratory in 1928 to carry out research on preventing and fighting tropical diseases and preventative sanitation measures.

• Gorgas's own writings include *Sanitation in Panama* (1915); "The Effect that Sanitary Work Accomplished in Cuba and Panama Has Had, and Will Have, upon the Sanitation of the Tropics," *Journal of the Southern Medicine Association* 9, no. 2 (Feb. 1916): 133ff.; "Tropical Sanitation in Its Relation to General Sanitation," *Journal of the American Medical Association* 65 (25 Dec. 1915): 2207ff.; and "Work of the Sanitary Department of Havana," *An Address Before the New York Postgraduate Clinical Society, May 22, 1903* (1911). Bibliographical accounts include John M. Gibson, *Physician to the World: The Life of General William C. Gorgas* (1950); Marie D. Gorgas (Gorgas's wife) and Burton J. Hendrick, *William Crawford Gorgas: His Life and Work* (1924), which includes a detailed personal description of Gorgas; F. H. Martin, *Major-General William Crawford Gorgas* (1924); and Thomas W. Martin, *Doctor William Crawford Gorgas of Alabama and the Panama Canal* (1947). Gorgas is also treated in Willard Hull Wright, *Forty Years of Tropical Medicine Research: A History of the Gorgas Memorial Institute of Tropical and Preventive Medicine* (1970); Ralph Emmett Avery, *The Greatest Engineering Feat in the World at Panama* (1915); Marshall Logan, *The Story of the Panama Canal* (1913); Hugh Gordon Miller, *The Isthmian Highway: A Review of the Problems of the Caribbean* (1929); and James S. Ward, *Yellow Fever in Latin America: A Geographical Study* (1972). Obituaries are by Robert E. Noble in *American Journal of Public Health* (Mar. 1929); and by J. F. Siles in *American Journal of Tropical Medicine* (Mar. 1922).

ANNE-MARIE E. NAKHLA

GORGES, Ferdinando (c. 1568–1647), author and sponsor of English exploration and settlement in New England, was born about 1565 in Ashton Phillips, Somerset, England, the son of Edward Gorges of Wraxall and Cicely Lygon, landholders. Knighted in 1591, Gorges became involved in the earl of Essex's 1601 conspiracy against Queen Elizabeth I. He was charged with treason but exonerated after testifying against Essex. These events marked Gorges as a royalist, a political position he held to strongly throughout his life, even during the Puritan Revolution. He had taken a commission with the navy during England's war with Spain (1588–1604) following the Spanish Armada, eventually becoming military governor of the port of Plymouth in 1604.

In 1605 George Weymouth presented Gorges with three of the Native Americans he had brought to Plymouth from the New England coast: Manida, Sketwarroes, and Tafquantum. After learning about the New World from them, Gorges became excited about the possibilities of establishing an English colony there, a hope that became a lifelong project and obsession. In 1606 he helped form the Plymouth Company, which with the London Company was given the rights to settle the lands along the eastern coast of North America. The Plymouth Company sent several unsuccessful expeditions to the northern reaches of this grant, and in 1614 Gorges hired Captain John Smith (1580–1631) to sail to New England for the company. Smith made three unsuccessful attempts to leave England, turning around each time because of troubles with his ships and the weather.

After Smith's failure the Plymouth Company sent two more expeditions to the northern parts of New England. In 1620 the Plymouth Company reorganized and was given all the grants for the lands between the fortieth and forty-eighth parallels from the Atlantic to the Pacific. Gorges personally took control of these grants along with John Mason, the founder of New Hampshire, and in 1623 a settlement was again attempted in the Atlantic coastal region Gorges called Laconia, bounded by the Merrimac, Kennebec, and St. Lawrence rivers. In 1635 Gorges resigned his charter but, in 1639, was given another grant for the Province of Maine. While he was arranging to visit New England, Gorges's company fell into debt and had to sell its ship. Thus, despite his long involvement with

New England settlement, Gorges never visited the New World. He probably died in Bristol.

Gorges wrote two works about New England. *A Briefe Relation of the Discovery and Plantation of New England* was published anonymously in 1622 but has generally been attributed to Gorges. It describes the attempts at exploration and settlement made by the Plymouth Company. A second work, *A Briefe Narration of the Original Undertakings of the Advancement of Plantations into the Parts of America*, was written by Gorges soon before his death and was included as part of a work by his grandson, also named Ferdinando Gorges, *America Painted to Life* (1658). *A Briefe Narration* is a much more personal view of the attempts made to settle New England than is *A Briefe Relation*. It pays particular attention to the political difficulties experienced in England that hampered American exploration and settlement. Though not considered major literary achievements, both works provide an important non-Puritan perspective on sixteenth-century English settlement in New England, stressing the interaction between European powers and North American settlements rather than the inner workings of a self-enclosed theocratic society.

• The only collection of Gorges's papers and works is James Phinney Baxter's three-volume *Sir Ferdinando Gorges and His Province of Maine* (1890), vols. 18–20 of the Publications of the Prince Society; a lengthy "Memoir" of Gorges's life appears in the first volume of Baxter's work. The only full-length biography is Richard Arthur Preston, *Gorges of Plymouth Port: A Life of Sir Ferdinando Gorges, Captain of Plymouth Port, Governor of New England, and Lord of the Province of Maine* (1953).

E. THOMSON SHIELDS, JR.

GORGES, Robert (1595–1624?), **William Gorges** (1606–1659), and **Thomas Gorges** (1618–1670), son, nephew, and cousin, respectively, of Sir Ferdinando Gorges, an English soldier, colonizer of New England, and proprietor of Maine, each served at different times as his deputy governor in the New World. They were the agents for his repeated attempts to settle territory for England, bring law and order to the area, and carve out a personal estate for himself in the 1620s, 1630s, and 1640s until civil war at home and his death in 1647 intervened.

Robert Gorges, soldier, was born in London, England, the son of Sir Ferdinando Gorges and Ann Bell. He served in the military in Europe and then with his father at Plymouth Fort in England, where he got into several scrapes as a young man, including a fight in which he killed another man. In 1622 he obtained a grant of land to "Massachusetts" from the Council of New England, of which his father was a member, and in 1623 a commission as governor for the entire region. His father wrote that he was "pitched upon" to bring an end to "the abuses committed by severall the Fishermen, and other Interlopers" who mixed "themselves with their women, and other beastly demeanors, tending to Drunkenesse" as well as "the overthrow of our Trade and dishonour of the Govern-

ment." Once in New England Robert Gorges was unable to get the cooperation of the settlers at Plymouth, who were justifiably wary of recognizing his authority, and he found the fishermen and "interlopers" exceedingly difficult to deal with. When he heard that support and funds for the venture were diminishing in England, he quickly returned home. William Bradford commented that Gorges had found New England unsuited to his "quality and condition" and departed having "scarcely saluted the country." His father excused him by saying that resources available to him were inadequate for the job. A modern evaluation sees him as "lacking in resolution" when dealing with settlers, concluding that overall his efforts were a "complete fiasco" (Preston, p. 228). Back in England Gorges may have tried for a naval position. If he obtained one it was briefly held, as he apparently died young and left no heirs.

William Gorges, soldier, was born in Wraxall, England, the son of Sir Edward Gorges, the older brother of Sir Ferdinando Gorges, and Dorothy Speke. He first served his uncle Sir Ferdinando as a lieutenant at Plymouth Fort and then as governor of the Province of New Somersetshire, a grant Sir Ferdinando obtained from the Council of New England when its territories were divided up in 1635. William Gorges went to New England in 1636 with other settlers, including "craftsmen for the building of houses and erecting of sawmills," as well as cattle for a private plantation to be established for his uncle.

As governor William Gorges became embroiled in a dispute with George Cleeve, a cantankerous early settler. Disturbed by the actions of the youthful governor, Cleeve departed for England, where he voiced his complaints to Sir Ferdinando, who then recalled his nephew in 1637. Sir Ferdinando later regretted this action, saying that Cleeve had deceived him. The result was that this effort to impose formal government and thereby further his private interests failed. Once back in England, William Gorges wrote that he had been "disappointed of my . . . voyage." What he did next is not clear.

Thomas Gorges, lawyer and English politician, was born at "Batcombe Farm," Somersetshire, England, the son of Henry Gorges, a lawyer, and Barbara Baynard. Along with two of his brothers, he studied at the Inns of Court, intending to practice law. He married twice, first to Mary Sanford and, after Mary's death, to Rose Alexander Mallack. He had at least six children.

The Council of New England ceased to exist in the mid-1630s. To implement his ongoing colonization schemes, Sir Ferdinando Gorges obtained a proprietary grant to the Province of Maine from the king in 1639. He then turned to his young cousin Thomas Gorges to pick up where his son and nephew had left off. He commissioned Thomas to organize government in the area on a firm footing while also overseeing his personal plantation started at Agamenticus (later renamed Gorgeana and now York).

As governor Thomas Gorges stayed the longest (1640–1643) and was the most successful of Sir Ferdinando's agents. Originally dismissed as "the boy, Gorges" by John Winter, a prominent and difficult settler, Gorges acted firmly and impartially to establish a government, administer justice, and improve his uncle's private estate. He traveled to the White Mountains in search of "precious metals" and with his Puritan sympathy even made a favorable impression on John Winthrop at Massachusetts Bay. When his actions in a case involving Winter and Cleeve were reversed in England, he stuck to his position backing the decisions of the local courts. Thomas Gorges had more determination than his predecessors, and he has been more positively evaluated by historians. Henry S. Burrage described him as "by far the one conspicuously attractive personality" in all of Maine's early history (*The Beginnings of Colonial Maine*, p. 312).

When Gorges arrived in Maine, Sir Ferdinando's manor house and estate were in great disrepair, with few household items or cattle remaining. He nevertheless wrote enthusiastic letters to his uncle, father, and other relatives, at first emphasizing the economic potential of Maine. He saw abundance everywhere, a great source of fish and lumber for future profits. He worked to increase the cattle on his uncle's land, fixed and operated a sawmill and a gristmill, "repaired the house & fenced the feild [*sic*], sowed & planted." He requested cooking pots and dishes. He worked on a code of laws and authorized additional local courts. But by the end of his stay his reports, reflecting the depression in the area that followed the Great Migration (the mass movement of Puritans from England to New England in the 1630s), noted empty houses and failing prices. His disillusionment probably also reflected resentment over Sir Ferdinando's meddling in Maine affairs, which Thomas thought under his authority.

By 1642 Gorges asked Sir Ferdinando to permit him to return to England, where the civil war had begun. While Sir Ferdinando was a Royalist, this cousin sided with Parliament. Returning in 1643, Thomas Gorges served as a commissioner of accounts for the Commonwealth and became a lieutenant colonel in the cavalry. He was elected to Parliament from Taunton in 1654, served again in 1659, and in 1660 was a member of the Parliament that reestablished the monarchy. He also practiced law, an occupation he had delayed assuming when he went to Maine. He died on the estate of his second wife at Heavitree, near Exeter.

For his service Gorges was given a grant of 5,000 acres on the Ogunquit River, at what is now Wells, Maine, by his uncle. Several of his children later turned to America and this grant, perhaps having imbibed an interest in the New World from their father. Henry Gorges, who inherited the Wells property, immigrated to Barbados. About 1674 Ferdinando Gorges went to Maine, where he occupied his brother's estate, then called "Batcombe" after the farm where their father had been born. He died there about 1688, the same year a stepbrother died in Virginia. Henry Gorges died in Barbados before 1740, leaving no children to inherit the Maine lands.

Sir Ferdinando Gorges persistently interested himself in the colonization of America, from the formation of the Virginia Company of Plymouth in 1606, through the Council of New England and a variety of its subgrants after 1622, to the proprietorship of Maine in 1639. Although stating that he intended to personally exercise powers of government in New England, he turned instead to his son Robert, nephew William, and cousin Thomas to act for him. Operating on the northern margins of British colonization, none of these youthful governors was truly successful in establishing a permanent government. But the Gorges family's involvement in Maine through them and their children continued for more than a hundred years. Although the colony of Massachusetts bought the proprietary title from the heir in 1677, the Gorges family remained in Maine.

• For genealogical information on the Gorges family see James P. Baxter, *Sir Ferdinando Gorges and His Province of Maine* (3 vols., 1890; repr. 1967), and Raymond Gorges, *The Story of a Family through Eleven Centuries . . . Being a History of the Family of Gorges* (1944). These two books also provide information on the three Gorges as governors. For specific material on William see Charles E. Banks, "The Administration of William Gorges, 1636 to 1637," *Maine Historical Society Collections*, 2d ser., 1 (1890): 125–31. For Thomas see Robert E. Moody, ed., *The Letters of Thomas Gorges, Deputy Governor of the Province of Maine, 1640–1643* (1978), and Moody, *A Proprietary Experiment in Early New England History: Thomas Gorges and the Province of Maine* (1963). References to Robert are scattered in these and the following sources. Still useful for general information on Maine are Henry S. Burrage, *The Beginnings of Colonial Maine, 1602–1658* (1914) and *Gorges and the Grant of the Province of Maine 1622* (1923). More modern evaluation is in Richard A. Preston, *Gorges of Plymouth Fort* (1953); John G. Reid, *Acadia, Maine, and New Scotland: Marginal Colonies in the Seventeenth Century* (1981); and Emerson Baker et al., eds., *American Beginnings: Exploration, Culture, and Cartography in the Land of Norumbega* (1994).

MAXINE N. LURIE

GORHAM, John (24 Feb. 1783–27 Mar. 1829), physician and teacher, was born in Boston, Massachusetts, the son of Stephen Gorham, a merchant, and Molly White. Graduating from the Boston Latin School and in 1801 from Harvard College, Gorham commenced a three-year apprenticeship under the eminent Boston physician John Warren and entered Harvard Medical School, from which he received a bachelor of medicine degree in 1804. He then spent two years visiting the principal medical schools and hospitals of London, Edinburgh, and Paris. In London, he studied experimental chemistry with Friedrich Accum, a world-renowned chemist.

Returning home in 1806, Gorham opened a practice in Boston. Business was extremely slow at first, and Gorham spent much of his time continuing the study of chemistry. Through the friendship and assistance of Aaron Dexter, professor of chemistry at Harvard,

Gorham was in 1809 appointed adjunct professor of chemistry. Dexter's recommendation also benefited Gorham by bringing him numerous private patients. In addition to his work as adjunct professor of chemistry, Gorham received an M.D. from Harvard in 1811 and began to teach a private course in chemistry, which he continued to offer until 1827. In 1816 Gorham succeeded Dexter as Erving Professor of Chemistry at Harvard. In his inaugural address as Erving Professor, Gorham promoted chemistry's value to society when he observed that the knowledge gained from this branch of science would improve "the arts which supply the wants, multiply the comforts," and "administer to the luxuries of social life." His address moved John Adams so much that the former president wrote Gorham commending him on his appointment and encouraging all chemists to pursue experiments that would benefit humanity.

Gorham was a popular teacher. When Harvard in 1824 instituted a policy requiring the Erving Professor of Chemistry to live in Cambridge, Gorham refused because it would interfere with his growing private practice. He continued to teach chemistry at Harvard until 1827, when the increasing demands of his extensive practice caused him to resign from the faculty.

As a teacher Gorham soon realized that his students lacked an adequate textbook on chemistry. Accordingly, he prepared a two-volume work, *Elements of Chemistry* (1819–1820), which was the first systematic treatise on chemistry written by an American. Dedicated to Dexter, Gorham's textbook became the standard American work on the subject. Besides his *Elements of Chemistry*, Gorham published several articles, most of which appeared in the *New-England Journal of Medicine and Surgery* and the *Boston Medical and Surgical Journal*. His journal publications on topics such as indogene, Indian corn, and calculi from the sublingual gland resulted from his chemical investigations. One of the founders in 1812 of the *New-England Journal of Medicine and Surgery*, Gorham was one of its editors for fifteen years.

A kind and friendly man who enjoyed music, art, and poetry, Gorham was active in the affairs of the Massachusetts Medical Society. He served the society as librarian (1814–1818), treasurer (1818–1823), recording secretary (1823–1826), and as a member of the publications committee. Gorham was also a fellow of the American Academy of Arts and Sciences.

In 1808 Gorham married Mary Warren, the daughter of his former preceptor John Warren. It is not known if they had children. After traveling through a snowstorm in an open sleigh to attend a patient, Gorham contracted pneumonia and died in Boston at the young age of forty-six.

• A small collection of Gorham's papers, covering the years 1824 to 1827, are in the Harvard University Archives. The archives of Harvard's School of Medicine document Gorham's association with that institution. Besides his textbook on chemistry, Gorham's other writings include four articles published in the *New-England Journal of Medicine and Surgery:* "Address Delivered on the Induction of John Gorham, M.D., as Erving Professor of Chemistry in Harvard University, December 1816" 6 (1817): 1–14; "Contributions to Chemistry, No. 1. Indogene" 6 (1817): 169–76; "Chemical Analysis of Indian Corn" 9 (1820): 320–28; and "Examination of Calculi from the Sub-Lingual Gland" 9 (1820): 329. James Jackson, "An Address Delivered at the Funeral of John Gorham, M.D." (1829), and Benjamin Silliman, "American Contributions to Chemistry: An Address Delivered on the Occasion of the Celebration of the Centennial of Chemistry . . . August 1, 1874," are useful, albeit brief, accounts of Gorham's life and career. See also Thomas Francis Harrington, *The Harvard Medical School: A History, Narrative and Documentary*, vol. 1 (1905); Walter L. Burrage, *History of the Massachusetts Medical Society* (1923); and "A Letter from John Adams to John Gorham, 28 January 1817," *Proceedings of the Massachusetts Historical Society* 10 (1867–1869): 90–92. Obituaries include "Death of John Gorham," *Boston Medical and Surgical Journal* 3 (1830): 107–9, and J. W. ["John Gorham"], *American Journal of the Medical Sciences* 4 (1829): 538–39.

THOMAS A. HORROCKS

GORHAM, Nathaniel (May 1738–11 June 1796), merchant and politician, was born in Charlestown, Massachusetts, the son of Nathaniel Gorham, a packet boat operator, and Mary Soley. The oldest of five children, Gorham was apprenticed at age fifteen to Nathaniel Coffin, a New London, Connecticut, merchant. He completed the terms of his apprenticeship in six years and returned to Charlestown in 1759. Gorham opened his own merchant house that same year and began to prosper during the later stages of the French and Indian War (1756–1763). He married Rebecca Call in 1763 and was the father of nine children.

Gorham sided early in the imperial crisis with the radical cause and opposed British measures to enforce custom duties more forcefully. His opposition to British imperial policies earned him election to the Massachusetts colonial assembly from 1771 to 1775, selection as a delegate to the extralegal Massachusetts Provincial Congress in 1774–1775, and service on the state's Board of War, 1778–1781. Gorham was active in privateering, a practice whereby private ships were commissioned by state governments to seize British ships and share the seized cargo with the government.

Gorham also enjoyed a successful career in state politics, serving as a delegate to the Massachusetts Constitutional Convention of 1779–1780, as Speaker of the Massachusetts House in 1781, 1782, and 1785, and as a state senator for a single term in 1780. He continued his plural officeholding for the state with his appointment as a judge for the Middlesex Court of Common Pleas in 1785. During the 1780s Gorham's political ascendancy took him into national politics. He was selected as a delegate to the Continental Congress in 1782, 1783, and 1785 through 1787. In 1786, while serving as the president of the Confederation government, Gorham, fearing the spread of Shays's Rebellion throughout the thirteen nascent states, sent a letter to Prince Henry of Prussia inquiring if the prince could be induced to serve as king of the Americas if the insurrection spread. Gorham had closely monitored the activities of Daniel Shays and his supporters in western Massachusetts as they grew from a protest movement against state taxes and debtor laws to an armed insurrection against the Massachusetts government. The uprising was quickly quelled by Massachusetts troops, and a Prussian monarch ruling the American states was never considered again.

Gorham's experience as president of the politically impotent Confederation made him an ardent nationalist in 1786. In 1787 he was selected as a Massachusetts delegate to the Constitutional Convention. In late May the convention's thirty delegates in attendance voted themselves a committee of the whole while waiting for the arrival of the remaining twenty-five delegates. Gorham was elected president of the committee and served until the middle of June. As a delegate, Gorham kept out of floor debates as he was not a gifted public speaker. At the convention he promoted a strong executive branch and was willing to compromise on slavery to gain southern support for the national government. He advocated a seven-year single-term presidency, ten-year terms for an appointed senate, and executive control of the judiciary through unqualified appointment powers of all federal judges. As a member of the Committee of Detail, he also supported Article I, Section 8, the "elastic" clause of the Constitution, which granted broad discretionary powers to Congress. Gorham is credited with delivering the decisive blow to the anti-Federalist forces at the convention by making a deal with Oliver Phelps of Berkshire in a land scheme that was based on speculation of continental securities. For his part, Phelps left the convention, weakening the anti-Federalist forces for a Federalist victory. After the convention Gorham was elected to the Massachusetts ratifying convention in 1788 and emerged as a leading Federalist in the state.

Gorham and Phelps entered a partnership to purchase 2.6 million acres of land in western New York for $1 million in Massachusetts currency. Gorham and Phelps assured their investors that depreciating values of the currency would require them to pay less than $200,000. By 1796, however, Secretary of the Treasury Alexander Hamilton's plans to assure all state debts actually drove the value of the currency upward. Unable to pay the full account, Gorham was bankrupted and died in Massachusetts from the strain. Gorham thus proved a victim of the strong national government he had helped to create.

• Gorham's papers are in the Massachusetts State Archives, the Massachusetts Historical Society, and the New York Public Library. Additional primary materials on Gorham are contained in Max Farrand, ed., *Records of the Federal Convention of 1787*, rev. ed. (1966); John C. Fitzpatrick, ed., *Journals of the Continental Congress* (1904–1937); Merrill Jensen, ed., *The Documentary History of the Ratification of the Constitution* (1976); and *Acts and Laws of the Commonwealth of Massachusetts* (1780, 1781, 1782, 1785). Most studies of Gorham's political career focus on his emergence as a Federalist and his role as a delegate to the Continental Convention. See Robert East, "Massachusetts Conservatives in the Critical Period," in *Era of the American Revolution*, ed. Richard Morris (1939), pp. 349–91, Forrest McDonald, *We the People* (1959), and Christopher Collier and James L. Collier, *Decision in Philadelphia* (1986).

RONALD J. LETTIERI

GORKY, Arshile (15 Apr. 1904–21 July 1948), painter, was born Vosdanik Adoian in Khorkom, Vari Hayotz Dzore, a village in Turkish-occupied Armenia, the son of Sedrag Adoian, a trader and carpenter, and Shushanik der Marderosian. In his native Armenia, Gorky attended local, American-run religious schools and had private tutors. From an early age he was fascinated by the iconography and art of Armenia, particularly that of its churches. His father emigrated to the United States in 1908 to avoid conscription in the Turkish army. In 1915 Gorky, his mother, and his sister Vartoosh fled from Turkish persecution. After four years of dislocation Gorky's mother died of malnutrition in Armenia. Gorky and his sister grew especially close during this time, and they maintained a regular and copious correspondence. This correspondence, primarily written in Armenian, is an important source for understanding his work, for in it Gorky expressed much of his aesthetic philosophy. Traveling with family friends, the siblings eventually reached Constantinople and from there emigrated to the United States via Ellis Island. In 1920 they were reunited with their father and older siblings in Providence, Rhode Island.

Gorky attended public school in Rhode Island and then moved to Boston in 1922. There he took courses at the New School of Design for two years and became an instructor. In 1924 he moved to New York City, where he began using the name Arshile Gorky. "Arshile" is the Armenian form of Achilles, and Gorky used several variant spellings (including Arshele and Archele) before settling on the final version. He took his new surname, "Gorky," from the Russian writer Maxim Gorky and fabricated a biography in which he claimed to be Maxim Gorky's cousin, to have been born in Russia, and to have studied art with Wassily Kandinsky and at the Rhode Island School of Design. In addition, "Gorky" means "the bitter one" in Russian—presumably Gorky knew this.

Gorky studied at the National Academy of Design and then at the Grand Central School of Art. He quickly advanced from student to instructor at the Grand Central School, and he was made a full faculty member in 1926, a position he retained until 1932. He remained associated with the school until the early 1940s, however, and was a popular and successful teacher. He also tutored students privately.

Gorky thought that drawing was "the basis of art. A bad painter cannot draw. But a good drawer can always paint." This dedication to technique, as well as his oft-stated debt to the Old Masters such as the early Florentine painter Paolo Ucello, allowed him to refine his dedication to abstraction by basing it on a solid foundation of draftsmanship and painterly skill.

In 1928–1929 Gorky met painters John Graham (a White Russian refugee, born Ivan Dambrowsky) and

Stuart Davis. The three painters were united in their devotion to abstraction and became close friends, referring to themselves as the "Three Musketeers." Through Graham, who made frequent trips to Paris, Gorky was kept abreast of developments in European art.

Gorky's early work was heavily based on the example and technique of Paul Cézanne. After encountering the work of the cubists, particularly Pablo Picasso and Georges Braque, Gorky began in the late 1920s and early 1930s to paint synthetic cubist still lifes. During this time he also worked on a number of portraits of his friends and family as well as self-portraits. These works, particularly the two versions of *The Artist and His Mother* (1926–1929, National Gallery of Art; c. 1926–1936, Whitney Museum of American Art), find Gorky mixing his experiments in modernism with his dedication to draftsmanship and an exploration of his Armenian heritage.

During this time Gorky's work began to be influenced by surrealism, particularly the work of André Masson. Soon he was combining his interest in surrealism with his earlier experiments. The paintings he executed in the early and mid-1930s are composed of abstract images that roughly recall living things such as birds and body parts. Works in this style include *Image in Khorkom* (c. 1938–1939, private collection) and *Khorkom* (c. 1938, private collection). These "biomorphic" elements remained a part of Gorky's work even as he developed a more abstract style.

Gorky's first museum exhibition was in the Museum of Modern Art's 46 Painters and Sculptors under 35 Years of Age exhibit in 1930, and it included works such as *Still Life* (c. 1929, private collection). Around this time he moved from Greenwich Village to Union Square, where he maintained a studio for the remainder of his life. In 1931 the Downtown Gallery included his work in two group exhibitions. However, the increasingly bleak economic situation in the United States soon caught up with Gorky, who had to work primarily at drawing because he was too poor to buy paints.

The Mellon Galleries in Philadelphia gave Gorky his first solo exhibition in 1934. That year he joined the Artists' Union, a leftist organization; however, he had no real interest in political activism and soon ended his association with the group. His friendship with Stuart Davis also ended at this time because of his lack of interest in political involvement.

Gorky had worked on the short-lived Public Works of Art Project in 1933–1934, and in 1935 he joined the Works Progress Administration's Federal Art Project. He was assigned to the mural division and began work on a mural titled *Aviation*, which was eventually placed in the Newark Airport Administration Building. This work, in which Gorky attempted through abstraction to portray the boundlessness of flight on a two-dimensional surface, was the subject of a laudatory article, "Murals without Walls" in *Art Front* (Dec. 1936). It was unveiled in 1937, but eight of the mural's ten panels were destroyed during renovations at the airport during World War II, and the other two were rediscovered under layers of paint only in the mid-1970s. Gorky was employed by the Federal Art Project off and on until 1941.

Gorky and Marny George, a midwesterner who had come to New York City to model and study fashion, had married in 1935. The independent George and Gorky soon clashed, however, and they were divorced a few months later. They had no children.

In 1939 Gorky completed the mural *Man's Conquest of the Air* (destroyed) for the Aviation Building of the New York World's Fair. That year he also became a naturalized citizen. In July 1941 Jeanne Reynal, a mosaicist and one of Gorky's early supporters, offered to arrange an exhibition of his work at the San Francisco Museum of Art, to open in August 1941. Gorky traveled cross-country with a group of friends that included sculptor Isamu Noguchi and Agnes Magruder, the daughter of a U.S. Navy admiral. Gorky had met Magruder earlier that year, and returning east in September, they were married in Virginia City, Nevada. The couple had two daughters.

Gorky emerged from his web of influences around 1940 with a series of works grouped around the theme of the *Garden in Sochi*. Though he named the paintings after a Russian Black Sea resort, Gorky created them by blending his memories of the Armenian gardens of his youth with the biomorphic forms he had introduced earlier into his work. *Garden in Sochi* (1941, Museum of Modern Art, New York City), is a good example of the works in this series. Associating with the surrealists in New York, including Matta Echaurren and André Breton, Gorky began titling his works with irrational and poetic titles, including *The Liver Is the Cock's Comb* (1944, Albright-Knox Gallery, Buffalo, N.Y.) and *Good Afternoon, Mrs. Lincoln* (1944, private collection). Echaurren encouraged Gorky to thin his oil paint with turpentine, allowing him to create ethereal, transparent splashes of color complemented by accidental stains and splotches.

Over the next two years Gorky spent time at the Connecticut farm of painter Saul Schary and at the home of his wife's parents, "Crooked Run Farm" in Hamilton, Virginia. Working from nature, Gorky introduced new forms into his paintings and drawings. He transmuted his many influences (Armenian iconography, Cézanne, cubism, surrealism, etc.) and created a style that has been termed by many critics as the bridge between surrealism and abstract expressionism. Partly at the instigation of Breton, art dealer Julien Levy presented a large exhibition of Gorky's work in 1945. A number of works sold, giving Gorky relief from financial worries. Levy became Gorky's dealer and showed his work regularly until Gorky's death.

The last two years of Gorky's life were fraught with a series of personal tragedies that were a counterpoint to the growing critical acclaim. In September 1945 Gorky and his wife had moved to Sherman, Connecticut, the home of architect Henry Hebbeln, who converted a barn into a studio for the artist. In January 1946 a fire in the studio destroyed many of Gorky's paintings and drawings from the previous year as well as his collection of books. The following month he underwent surgery to treat cancer. Recuperating at Crooked Run Farm, Gorky concentrated on drawing, completing nearly three hundred works over the course of the summer.

In contrast, at nearly the same time Gorky's exhibition, Paintings by Arshile Gorky, at the Julien Levy Gallery in New York City was hailed by critic Clement Greenberg in the 4 May 1946 issue of the *Nation* as "some of the best modern painting ever turned out by an American." During the next two years Gorky's work was shown in numerous exhibitions in both the United States and Europe.

The paintings Gorky created in the last years of his career were full of ambiguous imagery and were often composed with a darker, more somber palette. Works such as *Charred Beloved I* (1946, David Geffen Collection, Los Angeles) and *Charred Beloved II* (1946, National Gallery of Canada, Ottawa) are emblematic of his work at this time with their use of *grisaille* overlaid with hints of molten hues of red, reflecting a somber sense of mourning.

Gorky and his family returned to Sherman, Connecticut, in January 1947. There Hebbeln remodeled a farmhouse for their use. The house and Gorky's family were featured in the *Life* magazine article "Old House Made New" (16 Feb. 1948). During the next year Gorky was the subject of numerous exhibitions around the world. On 26 June 1948, while riding as a passenger in an automobile driven by Julien Levy, Gorky's neck was broken in a car crash, leaving his painting arm numbed and seemingly paralyzed. The next month mounting marital tension caused his wife to leave Connecticut with their two children. A few days later, Gorky hanged himself in the Sherman farmhouse, leaving the message "Goodbye My Loveds" in white chalk on a wooden picture crate.

Gorky presented a striking physical image, standing more than six feet tall with a thick shock of dark black hair, his face dominated by a long, drooping black mustache. Artist Jacob Kainen, a friend and neighbor of Gorky's from the 1930s, recalled in a memoir in the *Washington Post* (10 June 1979) that "in the company of a few like-minded friends, he could be tender and considerate, if always uncompromising in principle; but at larger assemblages, he was clearly reluctant to submerge his unique identity in the leveling mass." Intensely aware of his Armenian heritage, Gorky detailed his version of the Armenian people's history in his letters to his sister Vartoosh. Art historian Harry Rand has called Gorky "that rarest of creatures, a modern history painter; it was his own history that he painted."

Gorky has frequently been called "the last surrealist and the first abstract expressionist." In his later life, however, he distanced himself from surrealism, calling it (in a letter to Vartoosh) "academic art under disguise and anti-aesthetic and suspicious of excellence and largely in opposition to modern art." Early claims to Gorky's links to abstract expressionism were made by William Rubin in *Art International* (Mar.–Apr. 1958): "Arshile Gorky clearly emerges as the link between the Surrealist and the more liberated painting of the New Yorkers in the late forties."

• Examples of Gorky's work may be found in the Museum of Modern Art; the National Gallery of Art; the Whitney Museum of American Art; the Hirshhorn Museum and Sculpture Garden, Smithsonian Institution; the Philadelphia Museum of Art; and the Tate Gallery. Brief and very selected papers relating to Gorky are held by the archives of the Whitney Museum and the Museum of Modern Art. Harold Rosenberg, *Arshile Gorky: The Man, the Time, the Idea* (1962), offers an early critical appraisal of Gorky's contribution. For biographical information, see Ethel Schwabacher, *Arshile Gorky* (1957), and Diane Waldman's catalog for the exhibition organized by the Solomon R. Guggenheim Museum, *Arshile Gorky, 1904–1948: A Retrospective* (1981). Additional biographical material as well as translations of Gorky's Armenian correspondence can be found in the publications of Gorky's nephew Karlen Mooradian (son of Gorky's sister Vartoosh). These include *Arshile Gorky Adoian* (1978) and *The Many Worlds of Arshile Gorky* (1980). Harry Rand, *Arshile Gorky: The Implications of Symbols* (1980), is an important critical analysis. Dore Ashton's catalog for the exhibition organized by the Modern Art Museum of Fort Worth, *Arshile Gorky: The Breakthrough Years* (1995), concentrates on the last, most productive years of the artist's life. Jim M. Jordan and Robert Goldwater, *The Paintings of Arshile Gorky: A Critical Catalogue* (1982), lists all the artist's known oil paintings. Obituaries are in the *New York Times*, 22 July 1948, and *Art Digest*, 1 Aug. 1948.

MARTIN R. KALFATOVIC

GORMAN, Arthur Pue (11 Mar. 1839–4 June 1906), U.S. senator, was born in Woodstock, Maryland, the son of Peter Gorman, a contractor and farmer, and Elizabeth Brown. With no schools in his rural area, Gorman was quite literally schooled in politics when his father used his friendship with Maryland congressman William Hamilton to secure his son's appointment in 1850 as a page in the U.S. Senate. During the following decade and a half, Gorman was promoted to a succession of subordinate offices in the Senate, including messenger, assistant doorkeeper, and finally postmaster of the Senate. In these positions he learned what a later critic called all the "crafty, treacherous ways of smothering, of emasculating, of perverting legislation"; he also made important political friendships upon which he would later draw in his own career.

A conservative Democrat, Gorman became especially close to Andrew Johnson. This friendship caused Gorman to be dismissed from his Senate post in 1866. Johnson then appointed him collector of internal revenue for Maryland, a position Gorman retained until 1869. During these years Gorman successfully collected large accounts that were in arrears, and he cultivated important business and political contacts in Maryland. In 1867 he married his former Washington landlady, Hannah Donegan Schwartz, a widow of a Union army officer. The Gormans would have six children.

After Republicans removed him from the collectorship, Gorman turned his attention to Maryland politics in 1869. With the support of Hamilton, now a U.S. senator, Gorman was elected to the Maryland House of Delegates for six consecutive terms, serving as speaker during the last two. In 1875 he moved up to the state senate, to which he was re-elected in 1877 and 1879.

During this period Gorman helped build a political organization that would dominate state politics for much of the next three decades. Called the "Old Guard" by its friends and the "ring" by its opponents, this organization gave Gorman much of his power in Maryland as well as his unsavory reputation as a "boss" of the Democratic party. Gorman's rapid rise to prominence stemmed from his ability to exploit the conflicts between factional groups within the party; it did not reflect great personal popularity or any significant contribution to public policy. His political influence was further increased by his tenure (1872–1882) as president of the Chesapeake & Ohio Canal Company. A patronage position, it was not only financially lucrative, laying the basis for his substantial wealth, but it permitted him to build his political following by running the C&O as an adjunct of the Democratic party. Beginning in 1878 Gorman consolidated his power by becoming the Democratic state chair, a position he held until 1887. Although personally reserved and cautious, Gorman was often ruthless in maintaining his political power, especially by manipulating Maryland's electoral system and exploiting racial prejudice.

Gorman used his control over the state party machinery to eliminate his rivals and then to secure his own election as U.S. senator in 1880, 1886, and 1892. Gorman rarely introduced legislation as a senator but instead concentrated on learning the norms and practices of the Senate, understanding the desires and foibles of his colleagues, and promoting the interests of his party. A conservative, he took little interest in public policy questions except insofar as they had political implications. His open hostility to civil service reform reflected his attitudes.

In 1884 Gorman emerged as a national leader of the Democratic party when he was chosen to chair both the party's Congressional Campaign Committee and its National Executive Committee. A master of political strategy, Gorman managed successfully Grover Cleveland's presidential campaign, both providing organization and arranging finances. For this triumph Cleveland virtually handed control over federal patronage in Maryland to Gorman, who used it to secure further his command over the state and his party.

This victory also contributed to Gorman's growing power in the Senate, and in 1889 he was elected chair of the Democratic caucus, a key part of the machinery of the party and the Senate. His election indicated his influence among party colleagues; seniority did not control the decision. Well organized and methodical, Gorman chaired both the party's steering committee and its committee on committees. He attempted to maintain discipline among his fellow Democrats, but

the tumultuous issues of the day often eroded party unity. One Democratic senator described Gorman's techniques as "finding the common ground and leading his colleagues to enter upon it. He was indefatigable in his attention to all Democratic Senators," always using "the ingratiating influence of hospitality, favoring Senators in regard to Committees, helping them concerning pet measures."

Gorman's party leadership was vindicated in 1890 when he orchestrated the defeat of the proposing federal supervision of congressional elections in the South. This success finally brought him personal popularity and a presidential boom in 1892. Gorman did not actively seek the nomination but only reluctantly acquiesced in the renomination of Cleveland, whose uncompromising hostility to silver legislation threatened to split the party. Thereafter relations between the two Democratic leaders grew increasingly cool. Cleveland ignored Gorman in patronage matters in his second term, and the two engaged in bitter recriminations over the silver and tariff issues. Cleveland demanded unconditional repeal of the Sherman Silver Purchase Act in 1893; Gorman advocated compromise legislation in order to prevent the disruption of the party along sectional lines. Similarly, Cleveland's devious course in demanding tariff reform clashed with Gorman's attempt to maintain party unity and accommodate diverse Democratic interests by accepting protectionist amendments in the Wilson-Gorman Act of 1894.

Under increasing attack for both his stance against Cleveland and his "boss rule" in Maryland, Gorman was defeated for a fourth term in 1898 when Republicans and dissident Democrats combined to overthrow the Old Guard. But Gorman worked to rebuild the Maryland Democratic organization and was reelected to the Senate in 1902. He was again chosen chair of the Democratic caucus and minority leader in the hope that his organizational abilities could reunite his quarrelsome party. Tactical miscalculations and failing health, however, obstructed these efforts. He died in Washington.

• Gorman's correspondence, journals, and scrapbooks are in the Arthur P. Gorman Papers in the Maryland Historical Society, Baltimore. More scrapbooks and letterpress correspondence are in the Arthur P. Gorman Papers in the Southern Historical Collection at the University of North Carolina, Chapel Hill. A sympathetic and outdated biography is John R. Lambert, Jr., *Arthur Pue Gorman* (1953). Gorman's importance in the Senate is discussed in David J. Rothman, *Politics and Power: The United States Senate, 1869–1901* (1966). For aspects of his political career in Maryland, see Margaret Law Callcott, *The Negro in Maryland Politics, 1870–1912* (1969); James B. Crooks, *Politics and Progress: The Rise of Urban Progressivism in Baltimore* (1968); and Peter H. Argersinger, "From Party Tickets to Secret Ballots: The Evolution of the Electoral Process in Maryland during the Gilded Age," *Maryland Historical Magazine* 82 (Fall 1987): 214–39.

PETER H. ARGERSINGER

GORRELL, Edgar Staley (3 Feb. 1891–5 Mar. 1945), aviator and industrialist, was born in Baltimore, Maryland, the son of Charles Edgar Gorrell, a carpenter, and Pamelia Smith. He entered the U.S. Military Academy in 1908, graduating in 1912 with a commission as a second lieutenant of infantry. In 1915 he attended the army's Signal Corps Aviation School in Coronado, California, where he became a pilot. While serving with the First Aero Squadron during the Mexican Punitive Operation in 1916, he came to the attention of Brigadier General John J. Pershing, commander of the U.S. forces in Mexico. After leaving the expedition, Gorrell obtained an M.S. from the Massachusetts Institute of Technology and was then assigned to staff duty in Washington, D.C. He served on the staff of Colonel George O. Squier, chief signal officer of the U.S. Army. Squier, while himself not a pilot, was an early advocate of the development of air power, and he gathered around him a number of young officers who, like Gorrell, were committed to the creation of an American air service.

When the United States declared war on the German empire on 6 April 1917, Squier instructed Captains Gorrell and Benjamin D. Foulois to draw up a budget for the expansion of the U.S. Air Service. Gorrell and Foulois prepared a budget of $600 million, which Squier presented to Congress. In the fall of 1917 Gorrell accompanied Colonel Reynal C. Bolling on a mission to Europe to assess the needs of American air power for combat against Germany on the Western Front. General Pershing attached Gorrell to the Air Service staff of the General Headquarters, American Expeditionary Forces (AEF), and he became chief of the Technical Section of the Air Service. In November and December Gorrell became a disciple of British general Sir Hugh Trenchard, who advocated a strategic bombing campaign against German industrial and civilian targets. Gorrell believed, as did Trenchard, that an aerial bombing campaign into the heartland of imperial Germany would disrupt its war-making industrial complex and would seriously damage German civilian morale. Gorrell presented a plan, based on British concepts, to Pershing and the AEF, but because of the shortages of trained pilots and bombing aircraft and the emphasis of the army on observation and pursuit aircraft, his plan was not adopted. However, Gorrell's plan and his subsequent writing show him to be one of the first Americans to advocate a strategic air campaign like the one that would be waged against Nazi Germany from 1943 to 1945. After the end of World War I, however, it became painfully clear to Gorrell that air was considered to be a support weapon for infantry. He became a conservative as far as strategic airpower was concerned and concentrated on what was possible for American military air.

Promoted to colonel in early 1918, Gorrell remained on the AEF's air staff, serving under Major General Mason M. Patrick, chief of the Air Service. Gorrell's education made him a valuable member of Patrick's staff, and he made a serious contribution to the AEF's efforts by evaluating new aircraft technology. In No-

vember 1918 Patrick gave Gorrell the task of assembling all the reports, documents, and histories of the many units that made up the AEF's Air Service. Working from a large office in Tours, France, Gorrell received and cataloged thousands of documents. What he compiled was then sent back to the United States, forming the basis for what is known simply as "Gorrell's History" (unpublished), the main source of information on American air effort in the Great War.

In 1920 Gorrell resigned from the U.S. Army to pursue a career in industry. Disheartened at the lack of interest in building a strong air arm, he was equally distressed at the small appropriations for the armed services. As did almost every American officer who served in France during the war, Gorrell reverted to his former offering rank of captain. The army he saw offered little chance of advancement and seemed bound to a tradition that placed reliance on ground action as the decisive form of combat in war.

In 1921 he married Ruth Maurice; they had two children. Being an engineer with vast practical experience, Gorrell worked for several industrial firms. In 1925 he became the vice president of the Stutz Motor Company and in 1929 became its president. His main task was to guide Stutz through the grave economic difficulties caused by the depression. Despite his efforts the company ceased operations in 1935, whereupon Gorrell founded an investment firm and also became the director of Air Cargo, Inc. After his first marriage ended, in 1945 he married Mary Frances O'Dowd Weidman. They had no children.

Throughout his career Gorrell maintained his great interest in air power, and in 1934, at the request of President Franklin Roosevelt, he became a member of the Army Air Service Investigating Commission, or "Baker Board," which was formed to make recommendations about the future of the Army Air Corps. The board recommended an increase in the number of American military aircraft to 2,320 and also urged the creation of a general headquarters for the Army Air Corps, which was created in 1935. Gorrell, however, was not in favor of the creation of an independent air force.

In 1936 Gorrell became the president of the Transportation Association of America. Given his long advocacy of air transportation, he worked, with great success, to put the airlines of the United States on a paying basis. Two years later he led the effort to get the Civil Aeronautics Act passed. This act extended government control over civil aviation.

Before America's entry into World War II, Gorrell became a leading advocate of the buildup of the Army Air Corps. He wrote a number of articles and made speeches concerning the state of American preparedness. During the war Gorrell did little because of failing health; he died at his home in Washington, D.C. At his request his ashes were scattered over West Point by a military aircraft. Gorrell's main contributions to American history were his early advocacy of a strategic air campaign against an enemy's industrial might and civilian population centers, and also his compilation of the records of the Air Service of the AEF.

• Unedited memoranda from Gorrell are in RG 120, Records of the AEF, at the National Archives. An important source is Gorrell's *Measure of America's World War Aeronautical Effort* (1940). This book, based on his lectures at Norwich University in Vermont, gives key insights into Gorrell's work during World War I. Gorrell's memoranda from his war service are contained in Mauer Maurer, ed., *The U.S. Air Service in the Great War* (4 vols., 1978–1979). For a monograph on the air war, see also James J. Cooke, *The U.S. Air Service in the Great War, 1917–1919* (1996). See also Irving B. Holley, Jr., *Ideas and Weapons* (1953).

JAMES J. COOKE

GORRIE, John (3 Oct. 1802?–29 June 1855), physician and inventor, was born either in Charlestown on the island of Nevis, West Indies, or Charleston, South Carolina, of uncertain parentage. Because of his olive complexion and dark hair and eyes, some say his mother fled Spain for the West Indies where she bore John illegitimately. Mother and son accompanied Captain Gorrie, a Scots officer in the Spanish navy, to Charleston when John was twelve to eighteen months old in 1803. Gorrie left them in Charleston, and she received money from Spain until John graduated from college. Other accounts list Charleston as his birthplace in 1803 and his nationality as Scotch-Irish.

When Gorrie attended the College of Physicians and Surgeons of the Western District of the State of New York at Fairfield, Herkimer County, from October 1825 to 1827, he listed his hometown as Columbia, South Carolina. He earned his medical degree with honors in 1827 with a thesis on neuralgia. None of the three towns have records of Gorrie, his mother, or Captain Gorrie. He is reported to have worked as a Columbia apothecary's apprentice in 1824 before entering medical school. After graduation, Gorrie may have practiced medicine in Abbeville, South Carolina, c. 1828. From there he and his mother supposedly moved to Sneads, Florida, in 1831, and, after her death, Gorrie moved downriver to Apalachicola. Despite his murky beginnings, Gorrie distinguished himself upon arriving in the bustling Gulf Coast port in 1833.

Gorrie established his general medical practice and townspeople sought him for civic duties between 1834 and 1837. He served as assistant postmaster, then postmaster from 24 November 1834 to 18 July 1838 for $121.30 a year. Gorrie became the notary public for Franklin County in 1835. Apalachicolians elected Gorrie to the city council in 1835 and 1836 where he served as chairman and city treasurer; he was appointed vice intendant and then elected intendant (mayor) on 21 January 1837. In a letter to the city council Gorrie stated, "I am willing to serve the city . . . [and] expect to be endowed by you with the necessary powers and means of maintaining the peace, increasing the public health, and advancing the internal improvement of the city" (*Apalachicola Gazette*, 28 Jan. 1837).

He resigned on 22 November 1837. In 1841 he was elected justice of the peace for Franklin County.

Gorrie's business dealings included one-fifth ownership of the Mansion House Hotel, which he built in 1836. He was the incorporator of the Marine Insurance Bank in 1835, bank president of the Branch Bank of Pensacola in 1836, and director of the Apalachicola Mutual Insurance Company in 1840. He served on the committee to establish a local Masonic lodge, which appointed him secretary pro-tem on 28 December 1835 and later elected him treasurer. Although not an overtly religious man, Gorrie helped establish the local Episcopal church but did not have a pew. He married Caroline Myrick Beman, a widow with a young daughter, in May 1838. They had two children.

In 1838 Gorrie retired from active civic duties to concentrate on his medical practice; he subsequently decreased his patient load to discover a cure for malaria, prevalent in the subtropical climate. He spent four years in Apalachicola treating malaria patients as the attending physician at the Marine Hospital and his own hospital for the poor. He thought malaria was a volatile oil generated by decaying organic matter, moisture, and heat, and to eliminate the decay, he persuaded local citizens to fill in low waterfront areas and drain the higher wetlands. More important, Gorrie proposed controlling his patients' body temperatures by lowering the room temperature and removing atmospheric moisture. To accomplish this, he developed a method for cooling hospital rooms and making the artificial ice required for his cooling apparatus.

Gorrie developed his air-cooling system between 1838 and 1845. He published eleven articles in the *Apalachicola Commercial Advertiser* on malaria (6 Apr.–15 June 1844); an article in *American Journal of Science*, "On the Quantity of Heat Evolved from Atmospheric Air by Mechanical Compression" (1850); articles in the *New Orleans Medical and Surgical Journal* on blood (Mar.–May 1854) and malaria (Mar.–May 1855); a pamphlet, *Dr. John Gorrie's Apparatus for the Artificial Production of Ice, in Tropical Climates* (1854); and a series of articles for the *New York Lancet* in 1840 on "Equilibrium of Temperature as a Cure of Pulmonary Consumption." In 1845 he made artificial ice and had a working model built at the Cincinnati (Ohio) Iron Works in April 1848, demonstrating its ice-making ability. Locally, he announced his invention to French Consul Monsieur Rosan's guests at a Mansion House Hotel dinner on 14 July 1850. Gorrie filed a patent application on 16 March 1849, which the United States granted in May 1851 (No. 8080, "Improved process for the artificial production of ice"); the British granted him a patent in August 1850. His pump increased the air pressure in a chamber; after compression, the air was forced to expand rapidly to absorb heat from the water, thus producing artificial ice in a container in the chamber.

Gorrie needed financial backing to build a larger ice-making machine. Ridiculed by northern newspapers for preposterous claims to make artificial ice—a threat to the thriving natural-ice suppliers' monopoly—Gorrie lost his previous supporters. His financial condition precluded investing his own money. In 1847 a London debt collector sued Gorrie and his wife for payment on an 1842 mortgage of $6,548.64 for which Gorrie had not paid interest. Finally, in New Orleans he sold a half interest in the machine to an unnamed backer, who died suddenly before investing any money. Depressed by his failure to produce a commercial model of his ice-making machine, finances, and possibly ill health, Gorrie died at home in Apalachicola.

Gorrie's ideas for the prevention of fever place him at the forefront of sanitation experts in the South and make him a pioneer in malaria control. His innovative room air-conditioning and the invention of a practical ice-making machine have been overlooked outside Florida even after the state placed a statue—one of two allotted each state—of Gorrie in the U.S. Capitol's Statuary Hall in 1914. George Whiteside, a Florida iceman whose brother knew Gorrie, wrote about Gorrie's pioneering work in *Ice and Refrigeration* and lobbied Florida lawmakers to support the statue. A Frenchman, Edmond Carré used information from Rosan to base his 1860-patented ammonia-absorption refrigeration machine on Gorrie's work; not until 1903 would Willis H. Carrier install the first working air-conditioning system. Whiteside recognized Gorrie as "deserving of all the honor bestowed upon him as having obtained the first American patent on such a machine, as being the first to thus apply the compressed air principle to produce refrigeration and as the first, so far as is known, to advocate and apply the principle of mechanical refrigeration to relieve distress in the sick room, and in hospitals" (*Ice and Refrigeration*, June 1914, p. 316).

• Gorrie's personal papers were destroyed in the evacuation of Apalachicola during the Civil War. The Henry Alexander Ince Papers at Duke University include correspondence on Gorrie's property mortgage. In *The Fever Man: A Biography of Dr. John Gorrie* (1982), Vivian M. Sherlock published the most accurate full-length account of his life. Raymond B. Becker, *John Gorrie, M.D.: Father of Air Conditioning and Mechanical Refrigeration* (1972), provides detailed information on Gorrie's public service in Apalachicola. Gloria Jahoda, *The Other Florida* (1967), includes a substantial essay on the physician/inventor in chapter 5, "Dr. Gorrie's Wonderful Ice Machine." Earlier, Ruth E. Mier investigated and corrected the inconsistencies, contradictions, and misinformation about Gorrie published by George H. Whiteside, *Ice and Refrigeration* (May 1897 and June 1914), in "John Gorrie, Florida Medical Pioneer and Harbinger of Air Conditioning" (master's thesis, John B. Stetson Univ., 1938), and "More about Dr. John Gorrie and Refrigeration," *Florida Historical Quarterly*, Oct. 1947. An obituary is in the *New Orleans Medical and Surgical Journal* 12 (1855–1856): 288.

SUSAN HAMBURGER

GORTNER, Ross Aiken (20 Mar. 1885–30 Sept. 1942), biochemist, was born near O'Neill, Holt County, Nebraska, the son of the Reverend Joseph Ross Gortner, a Methodist minister, and Louisa Elizabeth Waters. His father had moved to Nebraska in 1882 to operate a homestead and preach on a local circuit. The family moved to Liberia in 1887 when Ross's father enlisted as a missionary but returned to Nebraska in 1888 when the reverend died, probably of malaria or yellow fever.

Gortner was educated at Nebraska Wesleyan University, receiving his B.S. in 1907. He was influenced by Frederick J. Alway to study chemistry and as an undergraduate published five papers with Alway. He then traveled to Canada, where he earned an M.A. in chemistry at the University of Toronto in 1908, studying under the physical chemist W. Lash Miller. He completed his education at Columbia University, where he worked under the organic chemist Marston T. Bogert. He received his Ph.D. there in 1909, while a Fellow in chemistry. That year, Gortner married Catherine Victoria Willis. Together they had four children, two girls and two boys. The sons followed their father's interests and became biochemists. In 1930 Catherine died, and in 1931 Gortner married Rachel Rude. The number of their children, if any, is unknown.

In addition to his studies, Gortner had begun to work as a chemist while still an undergraduate, having taken a post as a research assistant at Nebraska Wesleyan in 1906–1907. He was made an assistant chemist for the faculty of arts at the University of Toronto in 1907–1908, but his first employment as a professional researcher was as a resident investigator in biological chemistry at the Station for Experimental Evolution at Cold Spring Harbor, New York, part of the Carnegie Institution of Washington. He held the position from 1909 to 1914, and during this period his interest in biochemistry solidified. He was then hired by the University of Minnesota, where he held a series of posts dealing with biochemistry, starting as an associate professor of soil chemistry (1914–1916) at the College of Agriculture, becoming associate professor of agricultural biochemistry (1916–1917), and finally professor of agricultural biochemistry and chief of the Division of Agricultural Biochemistry at the Minnesota Agricultural Experiment Station (1917).

Gortner's studies covered a wide range of topics, from the formation of melanin to the chemistry of embryonic growth and the chemistry of soils. While at the Station for Experimental Evolution he joined forces with his friend and longtime associate, botanist James Arthur Harris, to study the chemical and physical behavior of plant saps. After 1926 he acted as a consultant to the Chemical Warfare Service and also served at various times as an associate editor of the *Journal of the American Chemical Society* and assistant editor of *Chemical Abstracts*. Gortner's most significant work, however, revolved around agricultural subjects, particularly his investigation of the protein complexes of cereal grains. Gortner recognized the importance of physical chemistry to biological systems and contributed original work on the application of colloid chemistry to biology. His pioneering work with cereal grains, which led to improvements in the quality of bread flour, was recognized when he was awarded the Osborne Medal in 1941 by the American Association of Cereal Chemists. Much of his research was based on a colloid theory of proteins, a position he shared with his friend and associate Wilder D. Bancroft, owner and operator of the *Journal of Physical Chemistry*, for which Gortner acted as an associate editor. When Jacques Loeb wrote *Proteins and the Theory of Colloidal Behavior* (1922), which questioned the colloid theory of proteins, Gortner and his student Walter F. Hoffman responded with "Physico-Chemical Studies on Proteins" in *Colloid Symposium Monographs* (1924), which defended the colloid theory. The colloid theory argued that proteins were made from indefinite aggregations of organic molecules. These smaller base units were held together by electrostatic forces or second valences and had their own rules of behavior. Loeb argued that proteins were definite chemical entities and followed the normal rules of chemical behavior established by physical chemistry. Gortner's textbook *Outlines of Biochemistry* (1929) was widely used and promoted the colloid theory of proteins.

Gortner was a good chemist and published more than three hundred papers and books, but his work as a teacher and scientific organizer is at least as important as his scientific work. While at the University of Minnesota, Gortner supervised more than eighty candidates for advanced degrees. He was frequently invited to speak and was the Wisconsin Alumni Foundation Lecturer (1930), the Priestley Lecturer at Penn State College (1934), and the George Fisher Baker Lecturer at Cornell University (1935–1936). He was a member of many scientific organizations and fraternal societies, including the American Society of Biological Chemists and Gamma Sigma Delta, and he was an honorary member of the Des Moines Academy of Medicine. He was on the executive board of the National Research Council and was serving at the time of his death as the chairman of the U.S. Committee of the International Committee on Biochemical Nomenclature for the Union of Pure and Applied Chemistry. He was an active member of the American Chemical Society, serving as chairman of the Biochemistry Division in 1919 and the Colloid Division in 1931, and in 1935 he was elected to the National Academy of Sciences. He also served as the president of the American Society of Naturalists in 1932 and of the honorary scientific society, Sigma Xi, in 1942. He died from heart failure at home in St. Paul, Minnesota, only a few days before a testimonial dinner was to be held in his honor.

• Some of Gortner's papers are held by the University of Minnesota Archive. A complete bibliography of his published works can be found in Samuel C. Lind's memorial in the National Academy of Sciences, *Biographical Memoirs* 23 (1945). A summary of his colloid work and theoretical position is in his *Selected Topics in Colloid Chemistry* (1937), which compiles his 1935–1936 George Fisher Baker Lectures at Cornell University. Also noteworthy is Frank D. Mann, "Ross Aiken Gortner and Bound Water, the Water of Life," *Perspectives in Biology and Medicine* 19 (1976): 142–44. Obituaries are in the *New York Times*, 1 Oct. 1942, and *Science* 96 (30 Oct. 1942): 395–97.

ANDREW EDE

GORTON, Samuel (c. 1592–1677), Puritan theologian and founder of Warwick, Rhode Island, was born in Gorton, England. Little is known of his background, but his father evidently had been a merchant and guild member in London. Instructed by competent tutors, Gorton became skilled in the classics and in English law but never attended university, engaging instead in the respectable middle-class trade of a clothier. He received his religious training in the English church but by the 1630s, under the influence of Puritan preachers, decided to leave London, where he had been in business, for New England. In 1636 he arrived in Boston with his wife, Mary Maplet, his eldest son, Samuel, and one or more other children. Gorton reached Boston at the height of the Antinomian controversy instigated by Anne Hutchinson, who offended the Puritan leaders by claiming that her words had come from God.

Though sympathetic to the plight and theology of the Hutchinsonians, Gorton remained apart from the immediate controversy and by 1638 moved within the Plymouth patent. There he ran afoul of the authorities and was tried on, among other charges, lay preaching that tended toward radical spiritism, the belief, which Puritans regarded as heresy, that the Holy Spirit dwelled within the true believer and dictated all of his actions. By 1639 Gorton relocated in the newly established settlement at Aquidneck where William Coddington, John Clarke, and others who had been forced from the Massachusetts Bay Colony after the Antinomian affair had joined the Hutchinsons. Soon enough, Gorton's penchant for controversy upset the delicate political alignment of this colony: he refused to acknowledge the authority of the local government in a trespassing complaint and for his seditious behavior was whipped and banished.

Matters went no better in Roger Williams's settlement of Providence, where, besides censuring the ministry, Gorton denied the efficacy of religious ordinances as means to attain salvation. Exasperating even the mild-mannered Williams, Gorton eventually moved on to what became Shawomet (later Warwick). By 1641 other settlers in the area became so annoyed at his obstreperous behavior that they decided to take the radical step of subjecting themselves to the Massachusetts Bay Colony's jurisdiction to rid themselves of this nuisance. By 1643 Gorton had been summoned to Boston on the complaint of Native Americans who charged that he occupied their lands illegally. When Governor John Winthrop's warning to Gorton drew the usual immoderate reply, the Bay magistrates moved against him. After a duplicitous attempt at negotiation, an expeditionary force led by Captain Edward Johnson captured Gorton and a small band of his supporters and brought them to Boston for trial as heretics and enemies to civil government. After hearing testimony and ordering Gorton to answer hermeneutical questions concerning his beliefs about the Holy Spirit, the court found the group guilty and sentenced them to hard labor. Within a few months, however, public pressure, influenced by the spread of toleration in England, forced the magistrates to overturn the sentences.

Gorton sailed for England to bring a formal, and eventually successful, complaint against Massachusetts for its harsh treatment of him. More important, he also became active in the burgeoning radical Puritan movement and published several important works that revealed his own theological bent. By the spring of 1646, for example, Gorton was preaching in Thomas Lamb's general baptist conventicle, in which one could hear Lamb or his fellow travelers, unordained "mechanick" preachers both male and female, emphasize Arminian theology, free grace, and universal salvation as well as the tenet of adult baptism that defined the baptist position. From contemporary accounts, Gorton was considered a valued participant in this and other radical Puritan activity in the 1640s.

Gorton could have returned to Rhode Island as early as 1646, after his favorable hearing before the parliamentary commission on foreign plantations. Instead, through the spring of 1648 he remained associated with the English radical underground, traveling as far afield as Lynn, in Norfolk, as an itinerant and publishing two lengthy works that define his radicalism. The first, *Simplicities Defence against Seven-Headed Policy* (1646), details his treatment at the hands of the New England authorities, criticizing them in particular for setting up a religious system as corrupt as that they sought to leave behind. The other, *An Incorruptible Key to the CX. Psalme* (1647), outlines Gorton's rejection of the civil magistrate's power to interfere in matters of conscience. The second work stands with Williams's own polemics in the New England radicals' espousal of total separation of civil and religious authority.

In 1648 Gorton returned to Warwick, Rhode Island, and settled into the process of colony building, holding many important civil offices in the new community. But he also continued to expound his own peculiar brand of radicalism to followers known as "Gortoneans" and reopened his dialogue with transatlantic Puritanism by publishing in London two more lengthy treatises, *Saltmarsh Returned from the Dead* (1655) and *An Antidote against the Common Plague of the World* (1657), both sharply anticlerical and antiauthoritarian works virtually unique in New England Puritan literature. Although attracted to the Quakerism that soon reached Rhode Island, he remained true to his own brand of radical Puritanism. Gorton died in Warwick, a well-respected citizen of what by then was a settled community in the colony of Rhode Island.

Through Gorton the ideology of such English radicals as John Saltmarsh, William Dell, and Thomas Lamb, among others, entered the religious discourse of Rhode Island and, eventually, all of New England. Gorton's case against the Massachusetts Bay Colony for paying little heed to English law in its suppression of religious opinions not consonant with its own found many sympathetic ears in England and cast doubt on the New England Puritans' claim to be the beacon for Protestantism. Gorton's significance thus resides not only in his religious mysticism but also in his threat to New England's self-image and the representation of that image in England. His writings and his personal example document a spectrum of radical Puritan beliefs on the American strand.

• The only extant Gorton manuscript, a lengthy (125 pages in minuscule hand) treatise on the Lord's Prayer, is at the Rhode Island Historical Society. Most biographical studies of Gorton are dated, but the following are still useful: Adelos Gorton, *The Life and Times of Samuel Gorton* (1907); John M. Mackie, "Life of Samuel Gorton," in *Library of American Biography*, ed. Jared Sparks, 2d ser., vol. 5 (1864), pp. 317–41; and Charles Deane, "Notice of Samuel Gorton," *New England Historical and Genealogical Register*, vol. 4 (1850), pp. 201–20. The outlines of his career are conveniently summarized in Kenneth W. Porter, "Samuel Gorton: New England Firebrand," *New England Quarterly* 7 (1934): 405–44, but the most detailed modern treatment is Philip F. Gura, "Samuel Gorton," in his *A Glimpse of Sion's Glory: Puritan Radicalism in New England, 1620–1660* (1984), pp. 276–303, which places Gorton in a transatlantic Puritan context.

PHILIP F. GURA

GOSLIN, Goose (16 Oct. 1900–15 May 1971), baseball player and manager, was born Leon Allen Goslin in Salem, New Jersey, the son of James Goslin, a farmer and trapper, and Rachel Baker. As a boy, he built his strength by performing hard farm chores. In 1917 the family moved to town, where Goslin attended high school (there is no record that he graduated), worked as a glassblower and elevator mechanic, and pitched for the semipro Salem All-Stars. Umpire Bill McGowan observed the awkward, friendly Goslin pitch for an industrial league in 1919 and encouraged him to enter professional baseball the next season as a pitcher for Columbia, South Carolina, of the South Atlantic League. The 5'11", 180-pound Goslin, who batted left-handed and threw right-handed, frequently appeared as an outfielder or pinchhitter. His manager at Columbia switched Goslin permanently to left field in 1921, and that season he led the South Atlantic League in batting (.390), runs scored, hits, and runs batted in. Nicknamed "Goose," Goslin lacked grace and speed on defense, resembling a bird flapping its wings as he ran after fly balls with his arms waving.

Clark Griffith, the owner of the Washington Senators, personally scouted Goslin at a 1921 game. Although one fly ball hit Goslin on the head and another barely missed him, Griffith signed him for $6,000 anyway because he belted three home runs. Goslin debuted in 1921 for Washington, hitting a bases-loaded triple off Red Faber to defeat the Chicago White Sox. Goslin, an excellent fastball hitter, played left field for the Senators, St. Louis Browns, and Detroit Tigers from 1921 through 1938 and ranked among baseball's best clutch hitters. Often crowding the plate, he possessed keen eyesight, quick reflexes, strong arms, and a natural swing. Goslin, who batted above .300 and knocked in more than 100 runs eleven times, led the American League in triples in 1923 (18) and 1925 (20). In 1924 he hit .344 and paced the American League with 129 RBIs, outdoing Babe Ruth (121 RBIs). Goslin's batting average rose to .354 in 1926 and peaked at .379 in 1928 as he edged St. Louis Browns outfielder Heinie Manush (.378) for the batting title. When the Senators played St. Louis in the season finale, Goslin did not want to bat in the ninth inning for fear of losing his precarious lead. Goslin's teammates, however, goaded him into doing so. After taking two quick called strikes, Goslin, hoping to get ejected from the game, argued vehemently with umpire Bill Guthrie. But Guthrie refused to take the bait. Goslin then singled to preserve the batting title. On three occasions (19 June 1926, 19 Aug. 1930, and 23 June 1932), he hit three home runs in a game.

Goslin starred for Washington in two consecutive World Series. In 1924 he batted .344 with 11 hits, 3 home runs, and 7 RBIs as the Senators defeated the New York Giants; he had 4 hits, including a three-run homer, in four at bats in game four, and he set a series record for most consecutive hits (6). Washington repeated as American League champions in 1925. Although Goslin hit well, batting .308, with 3 home runs, one double, 6 runs scored, and 6 runs batted in, the Senators lost the series to the Pittsburgh Pirates. Goslin possessed a strong throwing arm until he hurt it permanently at spring training in Tampa, Florida, in 1928. He wandered over to an adjacent field where high school shot putters were practicing and heaved the twelve-pound metal ball for half an hour as if it were a baseball.

In June 1930 the Senators traded Goslin to the St. Louis Browns for Manush and Alvin Crowder. Goslin established personal career bests with 37 home runs and 138 RBIs in 1930, and he batted in more than 100 runs the next two seasons. In December 1932 St. Louis traded him back to Washington, where the following season he helped the Senators win their last pennant. That autumn he hit one home run in a losing World Series effort against the New York Giants. The Detroit Tigers acquired him in a trade in December 1933. Goslin set a major league record by grounding into four double plays in one game that season, but he batted in 100 runs and hit safely in 30 consecutive games as Detroit captured the 1934 pennant. His single won the second World Series game, but the St. Louis Cardinals prevailed in seven games. In 1935 his 109 RBIs helped the Tigers to win the league title, and Goslin batted in three runs in the World Series against the Chicago Cubs. His ninth-inning single off Larry French in the sixth and deciding game scored Mickey Cochrane, giving Detroit a one-run victory and its first World Championship. Jubilant crowds danced in the Detroit streets that night, shouting "Yea, Goose!" In 32 career World Series games, Goslin batted .287 with 37 hits, 5 doubles, 7 home runs, 16 runs, and 19 runs batted in.

Goslin's last productive season came in 1936, when he hit .315 with 125 RBIs. After the Tigers released him in May 1938, Goslin ended his major league career with Washington. In 18 major league seasons he batted .316 with a .500 slugging percentage, 2,735 hits, 500 doubles, 173 triples, 248 home runs, and 1,609 RBIs in 2,287 games.

Goslin was player-manager of the Trenton, New Jersey, team in the Interstate League from 1939 to 1941. He married Marian Wallace in December 1940; they had no children. After he retired from baseball, he operated a boat and fishing tackle rental business in Salem. The Veterans Committee unanimously elected him to the National Baseball Hall of Fame in 1968. He died in Bridgeton, New Jersey.

• Goslin's reminiscences appear in Lawrence S. Ritter, *The Glory of Their Times* (1966). The National Baseball Library, Cooperstown, N.Y., has a file on Goslin. For biographical material, see Martin Appel and Burt Goldblatt, *Baseball's Best: The Hall of Fame Gallery* (1977); Lowell Reidenbaugh, *Cooperstown: Where Baseball's Legends Live Forever* (1983); Ritter and Donald Honig, *The 100 Greatest Baseball Players of All Time* (1981; rev. ed. 1986); Mike Shatzkin, ed., *The Ballplayers* (1990); and Robert Smith, *Baseball's Hall of Fame* (1973). Frederick G. Lieb, *The Detroit Tigers* (1946), and Shirley Povich, *The Washington Senators* (1954), also contain anecdotes about Goslin. Obituaries are in the *New York Times*, 16 May 1971, and the *Salem Sunbeam*, 17 May 1971.
DAVID L. PORTER

GOSNOLD, Bartholomew (1572?–22 Aug. 1607), sea captain and explorer, was the son of Anthony Gosnold, a Suffolk gentleman of Grundisburgh, Clopton, and Burgh, and Dorothy Bacon of Hessett, a kinswoman of Sir Nicholas Bacon, the lord keeper of the Great Seal of England. Bartholomew is first recorded on 20 October 1572, when his great-grandfather, Robert Gosnold of Otley, included him in his will. Bartholomew's education, at Cambridge University and the Inns of Court, was intended to fit him for life as a country gentleman: in 1587 he entered Jesus College; in 1589 he and his father together purchased land; and on 9 February 1593 he transferred from New Inn to the more prestigious Middle Temple.

How he came by his nautical knowledge and when he first went to sea are unknown. It has been suggested that his interest was stimulated by Richard Hakluyt, who from 1590 was the rector of nearby Wetheringsett. Though Gosnold was familiar with Hakluyt's *Principal Navigations* by 1602, and though the second edition of John Brereton's account of Gosnold's 1602 voyage included material clearly supplied by Hakluyt, there is no evidence that the two men were acquainted. Gosnold's interest more probably stemmed from his marriage in 1595 to Mary Golding. Among his wife's first cousins were Sir Thomas Smith, a leader in joint stock companies engaged in foreign trade, and the three sons, all sea captains, of Sir William Winter, the surveyor of the navy and master of the ordnance until his death in 1589. Perhaps by Hakluyt, but more probably by one of the Winter brothers or Smith, Gosnold was encouraged to go to sea.

In 1599, in the last years of the war against Spain, Gosnold commanded the *Diamond* of Southampton on a successful privateering cruise, which netted loot that September valued at 1625 17s 6d. In 1600 he planned another venture, in company with a Captain Streynsham. Nothing is known of this second voyage (it may never have taken place), but in 1602 Gosnold undertook the voyage of exploration on which his fame is based. His sponsor is unknown. It certainly was not Sir Walter Raleigh. According to William Strachey, it was the earl of Southampton, but in 1602 he was in the Tower of London and almost penniless. Captain Edward Hayes of Liverpool almost certainly helped to formulate Gosnold's plans, and Henry Brooke, Lord Cobham, was perhaps the expedition's prime mover. Its twin purposes were exploration and the establishment of a trading post, perhaps in Narragansett Bay, where Giovanni da Verrazzano had stayed in 1524.

On 26 March 1602 the bark *Concord* of Dartmouth sailed from Falmouth with thirty-two on board. Jointly captained by Gosnold and Bartholomew Gilbert, the latter "Lord Cobham's man," the *Concord* passed the Azores on 14 April and on 14 May made landfall on the Maine coast. Heading south, the vessel sailed first into Cape Cod Bay and then rounded the cape into Nantucket Sound. On 21 May an island to the south—probably Cape Poge (now part of Chappaquiddick)—was named Martha's Vineyard, from the grapes on the island and in honor of Gosnold's mother-in-law. This name the explorers later gave to the present Martha's Vineyard also.

Three days later, in "Gosnolls Hope" (Buzzards Bay), "Elizabeths Ile"—now the two islands of Cuttyhunk and Nashawena—was sighted and on 28 May adopted as the site for the trading post. While Gabriel Archer supervised the building of a fort on an islet in a pond there, and others felled cedars on Penikese and dug for sassafras roots, Gosnold explored the north shore of Buzzards Bay. Soon enough, however, the settlers decided that there were not sufficient victuals for the twenty under Gosnold who were to remain over the winter. The island and fort were abandoned on 17 June, and the next day the *Concord* left Martha's Vineyard, arriving off Exmouth exactly five weeks later, on 23 July 1602. The bark subsequently carried its cargo of furs, sassafras, and cedarwood to Dartmouth, Portsmouth (arriving on 27 July), and Southampton, whence part was shipped to London. Raleigh, who claimed the right to license all trade with his Virginia, was enraged by this interloping and enforced a settlement favorable to himself. He received the dedication of John Brereton's account of the voyage, published in 1602, and took the *Concord* into his service, contemplating a voyage in 1603 in his own name. Whether Gosnold was with the *Concord* during these events is unknown, but he was certainly not in Suffolk, for on 7 September, seemingly from London, he wrote to his father, excusing his delay and amplifying an earlier letter (which has not survived).

Between 1602 and 1606 Gosnold vanishes from the record. He must have been sometimes in Suffolk, for his three youngest children (Martha, his oldest, presumably had died in 1598) were christened in St. James's church, Bury St. Edmunds, on 16 December 1603, 11 December 1605, and 5 February 1607. By the last date, however, he was already on his way to Virginia. According to Captain John Smith, writing in 1612, Gosnold was "the first mover of this plantation, having many years solicited many of his friends, but found small assistants"; it was only after he had enlisted the help of Edward Maria Wingfield, John Smith himself, and others that a year later Gosnold made contact with "the Nobilitie, Gentrie, and Marchants" who secured the royal charter in April 1606. If Smith is correct, Gosnold had been planning the settlement of Virginia since 1604 at the latest. No other contemporary witness, however, gives Gosnold so important a role.

Christopher Newport, in command of the *Susan Constant*, was admiral of the fleet that set out in December 1606. Gosnold, in command of the *Godspeed*, was only vice admiral, but when the colonists reached the Chesapeake in late April 1607, Gosnold became one of the governing council of seven, who elected Wingfield their president. Antagonisms already existed among the councilors: Wingfield disagreed with Gosnold over the siting of Jamestown, thought John Smith no gentleman, and in mid-June apparently feared that Gosnold and his friend Gabriel Archer might unseat him. Wingfield was right to fear displacement—it occurred on 11 September—but by then Gosnold, after three weeks' illness, was dead, and it was clear that, far from being a threat to the president, Gosnold had been a peacemaker. Looking back, Wingfield termed him a "Worthy and Religious gent . . . upon whose lief stood a great part of the good success, and fortune of our government and Collony." George Percy recorded Gosnold's death on 22 August 1607, noting that "he was honourably buried, having all the Ordnance in the Fort shot off with many vollies of small shot."

• A handful of works have replaced older volumes and now permit a full survey of Gosnold's career. To Warner F. Gookin and Philip L. Barbour, *Bartholomew Gosnold, Discoverer and Planter* (1963), should be added Kenneth R. Andrews, *Trade, Plunder and Settlement: Maritime Enterprise and the Genesis of the British Empire, 1480–1630* (1984). The original documents are best consulted in David B. Quinn and Alison M. Quinn, *The English New England Voyages, 1602–1608*, Hakluyt Society ser. 2, 161 (1983); Philip L. Barbour, *The Jamestown Voyages under the First Charter 1606–1609*, Hakluyt Society ser. 2, 136 (1969); and David B. Quinn et al., *New American World: A Documentary History of North America to 1612* (1979).

DAVID R. RANSOME

GOSS, Albert Simon (14 Oct. 1882–25 Oct. 1950), agricultural leader, was born in Rochester, New York, the son of John Weaver Goss, a hardware merchant, and Flora M. Alling. When Goss was seven his family relocated to Spokane, Washington, and remained there for eight years before again relocating, this time to Portland, Oregon. With his father now established in the flour-milling business, Goss finished high school in Portland and completed his education at nearby Holmes Business College. He abandoned plans to become a bookkeeper and entered the milling business as a floor sweeper. In partnership with his brother he later bought and operated a mill in Walla Walla County, Washington, only to return home upon his father's death in order to run his father's business. While in Portland, Goss ran a country store in addition to his mill duties and in 1905 undertook his first effort at farming when he bought a small wheat farm. Shortly thereafter, he sold the farm and entered the telephone business, becoming the operator of the phone exchange in two small Oregon communities. He married Minnie E. Hand in December 1907; the couple had three children.

In 1914 Goss re-entered farming in Kennewick, Washington, where he operated a 100-acre dairy farm and soon became involved in the local branch of the Grange organization, the secret society established in 1872 that combined fraternal activities with rural political agitation. He became master of the local branch in 1916, the same year in which the Federal Farm Loan Act became law. Upon the passage of this important legislation, Goss convinced farmers in the Kennewick area to form a cooperative farm loan association, which could then make application for credit at the Federal Loan Bank in nearby Spokane. Serving the new association as president, Goss's astute management in guiding the organization through the post-1920 agricultural depression gained him notice among Grange officials. He moved to Seattle in 1920 and became manager of the organization's Cooperative Wholesale Society, and in that capacity he combined a number of Grange warehouses into a cooperative purchasing unit. Drawing on his knowledge of business operations, Goss also set up a centralized bookkeeping and auditing system and used his successes as a manager to advance the cause of cooperative organizations to anyone who would listen.

Meanwhile, incumbent Washington State Grand Master William Bouck had caused a major controversy when he urged members in 1921 to withhold support of the federal government until a variety of Grange demands were met. While a minority approved of Bouck's positions, many other members saw them as seditious in nature. The dispute erupted and soon escalated to the point where Grange halls were burned and members carried guns to meetings. Goss succeeded Bouck as Washington State Grand Master in 1922 and spent many of the next eleven years mending fences. He continued his efforts to boost cooperatives and also devoted considerable time and effort to such traditional Grange concerns as power development, improved rural roads and schools, and tax reform. The resentment many western Grange members felt toward that organization's alleged eastern bias found expression through Goss, and as a result he became a member of the Grange's national executive committee.

While busy in his efforts to heal the rift within the state Grange, Goss did not neglect the issue of farm credit. He became chairman of the Grange's executive committee and in his new position lobbied tirelessly for a broadening of Federal Land Bank lending policies. In 1927 he became a director of the Federal Land Bank in Spokane, which handled loans for farm and land purchases, and in 1931 he also helped set up for Washington State applegrowers a production credit corporation, which issued loans for annual expenses such as seed, feed, and fertilizer. With the advent of President Franklin D. Roosevelt's New Deal in 1933, Goss helped draft, as a consultant, the Emergency Farm Mortgage Act of 1933. When the Farm Credit Administration was established that same year, Goss became a land bank commissioner. Although he undoubtedly took pride at seeing his concept of cooperative credit installed at the national level, he eventually chafed at the Roosevelt administration's efforts to bring the Farm Credit Administration under the control of the federal Department of Agriculture and resigned his post in 1940.

In the following year the self-proclaimed "barnyard economist" became the master of the National Grange and entered into his most prominent role as agricultural spokesman. Long a critic of subsidies (claiming that "subsidies breed more subsidies"), Goss soon found himself a leading opponent of many New Deal agricultural policies. He appeared before the Senate Committee on Banking and Currency in both 1942 and 1943 to argue against subsidies, which he viewed as inflationary as well as wasteful. By March 1944, however, he was willing to compromise on the issue by selectively eliminating some subsidies while retaining others. His war years were also filled with service on the Land Management Commission of the War Powers Administration and the War Mobilization and Reconversion Advisory Board, and Goss led the Grange in conducting numerous blood donation drives, scrap metal salvage drives, and bond sales. By 1945 Grange membership stood at its highest level in years, in large part on account of Goss's support of local organizations. He also boosted Grange efforts at the national level by hiring a public relations man and obtained new headquarters for the organization in Washington, D.C.

With the end of the war in sight, Goss presided over the November 1944 Grange convention (he had been reelected in 1943) with a view toward the farmers' role in peacetime. Remembering all too well the ruinous effects of World War I's postwar agricultural depression, Goss offered three "Grange Guideposts" for determining effective foreign and domestic policy, namely, 1) that all prosperity arises from the production of wealth, 2) that individuals should receive financial compensation based on their own contribution to the general good, and 3) that government's main function is to protect citizens from outside aggression. In early 1945 Goss led the Grange into a new era of international cooperation when the organization endorsed the Dumbarton Oaks plan, the Bretton Woods conference (which produced the World Bank), and the International Food Conference. Goss also joined other agricultural leaders at the October 1945 meeting of the United Nations Food and Agricultural Organization in urging the creation of an international commodity control board. Such an organization, they believed, might serve the needs of both consumers and countries by transferring commodities from areas of surplus to areas of need without undue governmental interference or price swings in the marketplace.

In the years following the war Goss continued to lead the Grange (he was reelected Master in 1945, 1947, and 1949) and also served as a senior spokesman on agricultural policy. His most noted activity came in 1949, when he led the Grange in successful opposition to the so-called Brannan Plan, an ambitious proposal by President Truman's secretary of agriculture that featured lavish farmer subsidy payments (an "income support" formula) in an attempt to guarantee American farmers prosperity by shielding them from market price fluctuations. Again voicing some long-held convictions, Goss stated that "subsidies once accepted are very hard to abandon. They break down that commendable independence of spirit which is largely responsible for progress. . . . They tend to make beggars of us" (Benedict, p. 488–89).

Despite his outspoken opposition to key aspects of the New Deal, Goss had served Roosevelt in various capacities during World War II, and he likewise served Truman as a member of the Committee on Mobilization Policy during the early years of the Korean War. He died of a heart attack in New York City just minutes after giving a speech at the Waldorf-Astoria Hotel on farmer participation in the ongoing war effort.

Albert Simon Goss deserves to be remembered for his efforts within the Grange, his work in developing farm credit organizations, and his political advocacy. The Grange prospered under his leadership, and long after his death the agricultural credit infrastructure owed much to his pioneering efforts in the development of cooperative lending organizations.

• Numerous secondary sources contain information on Goss's life and career; among the best are Murray R. Benedict, *Farm Policies of the United States, 1790–1950: A Study of Their Origins and Development* (1953), Wesley McCune, *The Farm Bloc* (1943) and *Who's Behind Our Farm Policy* (1956), and Reo Millard Christenson, *The Brannan Plan: Farm Politics and Policy* (1959). An obituary is in the *New York Times*, 26 Oct. 1950.

EDWARD L. LACH, JR.

GOSTELOWE, Jonathan (1745?–3 Feb. 1795), joiner and cabinetmaker, was born in Passyunk, Philadelphia County, Pennsylvania, the son of George Gostelowe, a farmer who immigrated from Sweden, and Lydia (full name unknown), who was from England. Although some sources give his birth year as 1744, his obituary lists 1745. Gostelowe began to work in Philadelphia at a time when he had to compete against approximately thirty master joiners and cabinetmakers. He may have apprenticed with William Savery or, more likely, trained with George Claypoole. The 1754 Philadelphia tax lists include his name but not his holdings or occupation.

Gostelowe married Mary Duffield, niece of clockmaker Edward Duffield, on 16 June 1768. It is possible that this relationship developed through Gostelowe's production of tall-case clock cases for Duffield. Unfortunately, the marriage lasted two years; Mary died on 16 June 1770. They had no children. Gostelowe was left enough money to make him a rather wealthy man, and he became the owner of both land and houses. By 1770 a deed referred to him as a "master joiner," indicating he was already well respected in the city. Based on an attributed chest-on-chest (c. 1768), his shop was producing furniture still influenced by the simpler Queen Anne period.

Gostelowe's trade was expanding during the early 1770s. On 19 November 1772 he took on Jacob Crawford as an apprentice with a term of commitment of eleven years, eleven months, and eleven days. It is doubtful that Crawford fulfilled this contract, as it appears the Revolution may have made some agreements null and void. This may explain why Gostelowe signed Thomas Jones from London as a cabinetmaker journeyman to a four-year contract to work in the shop. Following the deaths of his wife and his mother, Gostelowe hired an indentured servant, Mary McQuaid, to run the household, so he could direct his efforts to business interests.

The Revolution found Gostelowe shifting his direction from a joiner and businessman to the war efforts, as Philadelphia was becoming the arsenal for the colonies. As specific needs for the war arose, Gostelowe became involved with Robert Towers, Sr., in an effort to improve the manufacture of saltpeter, used in making gunpowder. In addition, in June 1777, he was one of the first to sign an oath of allegiance to the new state.

A Corps of Artillery Artificers was mustered in the summer of 1777 under the command of Colonel Benjamin Flower. The first major to be commissioned in this unit, Gostelowe remained in Philadelphia throughout the war as commissary of military stores (CMS). His units stationed in Philadelphia and Carlisle were responsible for casting cannons, boring guns, and preparing munitions. There is evidence to indicate that Gostelowe was the CMS who, in September 1777, removed the Liberty Bell and the Christ Church chimes from their steeples to protect them from the British.

Gostelowe retired from the Continental army, and in May 1783 he joined the state militia as a captain in the Third Battalion, serving until 1789. In May 1789 he reopened his shop in Church Alley, where he remained for one year.

A year earlier, in 1788, both the Gentlemen Cabinet and Chair Makers and the Journeymen Cabinet and Chair Makers were formed, and Gostelowe became chairman of the first organization. This may be the reason Gostelowe was listed as a "joiner" before the Revolution but "cabinetmaker" after. On 4 July 1788 Gostelowe lead his "master" craftsmen, as he referred to them in a notice, in a procession to honor the Constitution, which actually may have been the first Independence Day celebration.

In 1789, nearly two decades after the death of his first wife, Gostelowe married Elizabeth Towers, the daughter of his friend Towers. There is no evidence of their having children. He was forty-five years of age, while she was thirty-one. This marriage, too, added to his wealth. They moved from the Church Alley shop in 1790 to his father-in-law's former shop at 66 Market Street.

In 1793 Gostelowe retired from business. He took out a large advertisement in the *Independent Gazetteer* on 11 May to sell his stock. Gostelowe moved to his property on Ridge Road, where he died.

Although Gostelowe must have turned out many excellent pieces during his career, he is probably best known for two pieces made for his wife Elizabeth as a wedding present, a walnut bureau and companion walnut dressing glass. The "Wedding Bureau," considered his masterpiece, has a serpentine front with canted corners having five flutes. To follow the canted corners, Gostelowe favored a three-piece molded bracket foot. Another Gostelowe technique was to pin the cockbead to the drawer rather than the case. He preferred to set off a piece with very ornate hardware but with simplified moldings. These characteristics and the skill with which they were executed made Gostelowe a rival of the best English cabinetmakers.

Gostelowe also made such items as card tables, chairs, and a baptismal font in St. Paul's Church in Philadelphia. Because Philadelphia had many cabinetmakers of that time, attribution to Gostelowe will always be difficult, especially since his label appears on only a few works. Gostelowe's statement to Philadelphia Chippendale was the boldness of English style in a society where Quaker restraint was so strong.

• For more information see Clarence Wilson Brazer, "Jonathan Gostelowe, Philadelphia Cabinet and Chairmaker," *Antiques*, June 1926, pp. 385–92, Aug. 1926, pp. 125–32; Joseph Downs, "Jonathan Gostelowe," *Pennsylvania Museum Bulletin* (Mar. 1926); Ethel Hall Bjerkow, *The Cabinetmakers of America* (1957); Helen Comstock, *American Furniture* (1962); Downs, *American Furniture: Queen Anne and Chippendale Periods in the Henry Francis du Pont Winterthur Museum* (1952); Deborah Anne Federhen, "The Serpentine-Front Chests of Drawers of Jonathan Gostelowe and Thomas Jones," *Antiques*, May 1988, pp. 1174–83; and William M. Horner, *Blue Book, Philadelphia Furniture* (1935).

RICHARD W. PENCEK

GOTCH, Frank Alvin (27 Apr. 1878–16 Dec. 1917), professional wrestler, was born south of Humboldt, Iowa, the son of Frederick Gotch and Amelia (maiden name unknown), farmers. Gotch's parents immigrated to the United States from Germany in 1863. Gotch, a fine all-around athlete, soon settled on wrestling as his primary sport. As a teenager, he excelled in informal matches around Iowa. In 1899 Martin "Farmer" Burns, one of the professional game's most scientific practitioners, discovered him. With Burns's help, young Gotch improved rapidly and made his pro debut at a local ballpark in Humboldt against highly regarded Dan McLeod. Gotch finally lost the long, exhausting match, fought on a bed of cinders from the nearby railroad roundhouse, but it was obvious that the youngster was going to be something special.

In 1901 Gotch journeyed to the Klondike and, under the name of Frank Kennedy, made a small fortune ($35,000) there by defeating the roughest miners in various camps in winner-take-all fracases. He also engaged boxer Frank Slavin in a boxing bout with less success, losing to his more experienced opponent on a foul in the fifth round. The following year he returned to Iowa, and with more polishing from Burns, he captured the American heavyweight wrestling title on 28 January 1904 from Tom Jenkins in a match held at Bellingham, Washington. Gotch then defended the title in a long series of contests, most of which he won handily. In 1906 he briefly lost his title to 169-pound Fred Beall, when the 202-pound Gotch struck his head against a ring post and was knocked unconscious. Sixteen days later he easily regained the crown in a rematch.

By 1908 Gotch felt that he was ready to tackle the famous "Russian Lion," George Hackenschmidt, for the latter's world title. On 3 April more than 10,000 spectators saw the two champions square off in Dexter Pavilion in Chicago. The contest lasted for two full hours and was fought almost entirely in the standing position. Eventually the faster, trickier American forced the heavily muscled Russian to default through exhaustion. Hackenschmidt continually complained to the referee that his opponent was greased to an extent that made it impossible to grip him and also that Gotch was continually allowed to rake the Russian's eyes with his fingers. More than three years later the two met again. On 4 September 1911 Gotch easily defended his world title before 30,000 fans, defeating Hackenschmidt in two straight falls in Chicago's Comiskey Park. For his short night's work Gotch earned $21,000. The Hackenschmidt camp claimed, with some justification, that the Russian had severely injured his leg in training but had been talked into performing by the promoters.

As a result of these triumphs, Gotch became a celebrity in the United States. He generally drew larger crowds to his matches than the heavyweight boxing champion, Jack Johnson, a black whom white boxing leaders and fans wanted to see dethroned. Gotch several times considered fighting for the boxing championship, despite his lack of experience in that sport. Gotch became known as the "Peerless Champion," and toys, buildings, farm equipment, and babies were named in his honor. He was invited to the White House on several occasions by President Theodore Roosevelt, a fitness fanatic. A natural businessman, the handsome champion was also very successful outside the ring in the Humboldt area, especially in real estate. He was a stockman, banker, and president of a street railway company and an electric light company. In January 1911 Gotch married Gladys Oesterich; the couple had no children. Following his retirement at the end of 1911, he wrote an autobiography, *Gotch: World Champion Wrestler.*

Gotch's overall wrestling record is usually placed at 394 wins in 400 matches. In addition, he was undefeated in hundreds of challenge matches at fairs and carnivals. Altogether he made nearly a half-million dollars, much of which he put into real estate. He has been widely regarded as the greatest professional wrestler of all time. After the second Hackenschmidt bout, he was never seriously challenged in any contest. Perfectly conditioned, Gotch combined strength and aggressiveness with great speed. At 5'11½" and 212 pounds, Gotch proved too fast and skillful for large opponents and too powerful for the rest. His use of the toe hold became the most effective move in the sport.

During the first two decades of the twentieth century, professional wrestling matches were usually "on the level." Spectators were willing to watch two large men maneuver slowly about the mat, sometimes for hours, before a decision was reached. In this static contest Gotch provided excitement with his speed and dominance. Even with Gotch, however, there were no flying tackles or dropkicks, none of the tumbling, pantomime, and buffoonery that came into the sport in the late 1920s.

Gotch was by no means a Boy Scout in the ring. He could be cruel, often preferring to force an opponent to surrender (usually with the toe hold) rather than to pin him. This behavior sometimes resulted in the maiming of less skilled adversaries. He also used questionable tactics when it served his purpose, as in the first Hackenschmidt match. In one 1909 bout he extended his hand for the customary prematch handshake with the ever dangerous Stanislaus Zbyszko, then suddenly flipped the surprised Pole over his shoulder with a flying mare for a 6.5-second pin. This sort of behavior may be mandatory today but was not typical of Gotch's era and belies his clean-cut reputation.

Shortly after his retirement and before he had really begun to enjoy the benefits of all his hard work and discipline, Gotch contracted uremic poisoning, which led to his premature death, probably in Humboldt. On his death the state of Iowa went into public mourning. He left behind an estate of $400,000.

• In addition to his autobiography, Gotch's book *How to Wrestle* (1913) is interesting historically as an accurate picture of the wrestling techniques of his day. George S. Robbins, *Gotch: World's Greatest Wrestler* (1913), is an old-fashioned biography but adequately detailed. Details of his most important matches may be found in Nat Fleischer, *From Milo to Londos* (1936), and in the *New York Times* sports pages for the days following the matches. See Mac Davis, *100 Great Sports Heroes* (1954), Graeme Kent, *A Pictorial History of Wrestling* (1968), George M. O'Brien, *Wrestling to Rasslin: Ancient Sport to American Spectacle* (1985), and Charles Morrow Wilson, *The Magnificent Scufflers* (1959). For more up-to-date insights see Mike Chapman, *A History of Wrestling in Iowa: From Gotch to Gable* (1981), and *Encyclopedia of American Wrestling* (1990). An obituary is in the *New York Times*, 17 Dec. 1917.

FRANK P. BOWLES

GOTTFREDSON, Floyd (5 May 1905–22 July 1986), cartoonist, was born Arthur Floyd Gottfredson in Kaysville, Utah. Little is known of his parentage except that his father was a farmer and salesman. Because of Walt Disney Studios' long-standing policy of secrecy about their employees and because of Gottfredson's reticence in talking about his private life, little is known of his family antecedents. He was brought up in a poverty-stricken home of strict Mormon orthodoxy where his love of drawing and his dreams of becoming a newspaper-strip cartoonist were discouraged. He left home as soon as possible, working as an advertising artist and movie projectionist for a small theater chain in Utah. After winning second place in a national drawing contest in 1928, he decided to move to Los Angeles in hopes of finding work with one of its seven newspapers. He settled for being a projectionist again until he found employment as an animation inbetweener with Walt Disney's fledgling studio at the end of 1929. When the following year Disney and his partner Ub Iwerks tired of turning out the daily "Mickey Mouse" strip they had created a few months earlier, Gottfredson took over the feature; when a Sunday page was added in 1932 it also was given to him.

Mickey's golden years were the 1930s, when Gottfredson was in closest control of his material. He made full use of the cast from the Mickey cartoon shorts, which included the irascible Horace Horsecollar, the hapless Clarabelle Cow, Uncle Mortimer, Mickey's dog Pluto, and his comic sidekick Goofy. Present almost from the first was Mickey's inamorata Minnie, for whose love Mickey was capable of summoning incredible amounts of energy, stamina, and sheer resilience.

Adventure was the keynote of the daily strips. There Mickey could fully reveal the extent of his prowess, whether fighting a ruthless gang of cattle rustlers out West, outwitting a phantom assassin, or vying for Minnie's favors against an oily city slicker. Mickey's adventures took him to the remotest corners of the earth, the lowest depths of the ocean, and the farthest reaches of space. His two most implacable enemies, Pegleg Pete and Sylvester Shyster, lay trap upon friendish trap for him, but Mickey always emerged triumphant from these encounters. In succession he beat out the unholy duo for the ownership of Uncle Mortimer's gold mine, left them stranded on an island of cannibals, thwarted their attempt to steal the sacred jewel of Zwoosh, and even foiled their mad plot to take over the world with their pirate dirigible. In addition to fending off Pete and Sylvester's schemes, Mickey found time at various odd moments to run a newspaper, enter a prizefighting contest, hunt for whales, and play monarch to the kingdom of Medioka.

The Sunday pages were more anecdotal. They were often given to sundry gags involving Mickey with his favorite foil, the slow-witted Goofy, or having him play host to his two mischief-making nephews, when he was not busy courting Minnie with clumsy attentions. Color greatly enhanced Gottfredson's exquisite artwork in the stories, and their irrepressible high spirits and inexhaustible gag-building rank them as classics of their kind.

In 1938 Gottfredson left the Sunday page in the hands of others, while he concentrated wholly on the daily strip. Its success in the 1940s necessitated his leaving more and more of the actual work to his assistants. But Gottfredson plotted out and penciled most of the strips, and he supervised the overall quality and consistency of the feature until his retirement in 1975. His forty-five years of continuous work on "Mickey Mouse" remained altogether anonymous, since the feature was simply signed "Walt Disney." Only in 1967, a year after Disney's death, was the veil of secrecy partially lifted and Gottfredson allowed to give his first interview, to a fan magazine.

In 1924 Gottfredson had married Mathilda (maiden name unknown), with whom he had three children. After relocating in the Los Angeles area he kept moving around southern California, whose scenery he liked to paint during his retirement years. He died in Los Angeles.

Since the 1930s Mickey Mouse has assumed the dimension of an international icon. The newspaper feature contributed to the permanence of Mickey's image worldwide more than any other medium, even ahead of the animated shorts, which were discontinued in 1953 while the newspaper strip endured. In this respect Gottfredson's classic work of the 1930s and 1940s is probably best known of all, through countless reprintings in the United States and abroad. This fact, coupled with the many innovations in story and drawing that he brought to the so-called "funny animal strip," secures his place among comic artists.

• For more on Gottfredson and his work, consult Don Thompson and Dick Lupoff, eds., *The Comic-Book Book* (1973); Maurice Horn, ed., *The World Encyclopedia of Comics* (1976); Bill Blackbeard and Martin Williams, eds., *The Smithsonian Collection of Newspaper Comics* (1977); and Ron Goulart, ed., *The Encyclopedia of American Comics* (1990). Examples of some of Gottfredson's best work, along with interesting biobibliographical material and a detailed breakdown of his contributions to Mickey Mouse during the forty-five years of his tenure on the strip, can be found in the mislabeled *Walt Disney's Mickey Mouse in Color* (1988): in actuality it is Gottfredson's Mickey Mouse.

MAURICE HORN

GOTTHEIL, Gustav (28 May 1827–15 Apr. 1903), rabbi, was born in Pinne, Prussia (now Pnierog, Poland), the son of Bernhard Gottheil and Bertha Adersbach, merchants. Gustav was given the customary education of a promising Jewish child and sent to a yeshivah in Posen (Poznan). In 1847 he was certified as a teacher and served first in Tierschtiegel, a small place near his home. Four years later he moved to Schneidemühl, and in 1854 to Goch, on the Dutch border. In these small towns, which did not have a rabbi to serve the community, it was customary for the Jewish teacher to fill a variety of functions. Thus, early in his career Gottheil assumed rabbinic duties and was often referred to as *Prediger* (preacher).

In 1855 Gottheil applied as a *Prediger* to the Reform congregation in Berlin and upon election became associated with the congregation's senior spiritual leader, Dr. Samuel Holdheim, perhaps the most radical of the rabbinical reformers, who probably ordained him as a rabbi. In Berlin, Gottheil had his first taste of the fledgling Reform movement and became an ardent, though not radical, disciple. He spent a good deal of his time broadening his Jewish and general education and acquired a doctorate in philosophy, most likely at the University of Jena. In 1856 he married Rosalie Wollman, with whom he had five children.

After serving in Berlin for five years, Gottheil was called to England to head the Manchester Congregation of British Jews (also known as the Park Place Synagogue). Because the congregation was composed primarily of German-born members, Gottheil preached at first in his native tongue (which he also taught at Owens College, later to become the University of Manchester). He soon acquired a good knowledge of English, and in time he spoke and wrote it eloquently. Slowly he introduced reforms into the synagogue ritual, such as a greater use of the vernacular in the service and confirmation for boys and girls. He showed his moderate leanings when he attended the 1869 Reform Jewish synod in Leipzig, where he advocated a return to the one-year cycle of Torah readings and the retention of traditional poetic selections (*piyyutim*). During these years his religious and intellectual mentor was Tobias Theodorus, a professor at the university.

In 1873 Gottheil was called to become the associate of, and eventual successor to, Rabbi Samuel Adler (1809–1891) at Temple Emanu-El in New York City, a congregation of national stature. Here he served for the rest of his life and left his most lasting imprint.

At Temple Emanu-El, Gottheil was asked at first to preach in German as well as in English, but in time the latter became the sole tongue of the pulpit. Gottheil soon was drawn into a much-publicized controversy with the senior rabbi's son, Felix Adler (1851–1933), who advocated a nontheistic Judaism and eventually left his faith altogether to form the Society for Ethical Culture. Gottheil's vigorous opposition was supported by his congregation.

As senior rabbi, Gottheil introduced various ritual changes and established the Emanu-El Sisterhood of Personal Service, which became a model for the National Federation of Temple Sisterhoods. He established close relations with Christian clergy and participated in numerous local and national activities. In 1893, the year his wife died, he was a prominent member of the Jewish delegation that represented Judaism at the World's Columbian Exposition's World Parliament of Religious.

Among those who Gottheil influenced was the poet Emma Lazarus, whose ringing sonnet "The New Colossus" (1883) is inscribed on the Statue of Liberty. Lazarus had been totally divorced from Jewish concerns but partly through Gottheil's influence returned to her roots. Similarly, the biblical scholar Arnold B. Ehrlich, who had converted to Christianity, came under Gottheil's sway and was led to regain his ancestral faith.

Gottheil, like many Reform Jews, had decried Jewish nationalism as an aberration and had eliminated all mention of Zion from the prayer service. But upon reading of the first Zionist Congress held in Basel in 1897, he became an ardent supporter and assumed a leading position in the Federation of American Zionists together with Rabbi Stephen S. Wise, who later became American Jewry's best-known advocate of Zionism. Gottheil's son Richard Gottheil, an eminent orientalist, was elected president.

Gottheil influenced Jewish cultural life significantly when he helped found the Jewish Publication Fund, a forerunner of the Jewish Publication Society. He also founded a rabbinical seminary, which, however, did not attract enough students and was closed after a few years. He became an influential member of the Central Conference of American Rabbis and contributed to its *Union Hymnal* and *Union Prayer Book*. On his seventy-fifth birthday he was honored by the establishment of a Gustav Gottheil Lectureship at Columbia University.

In 1899 Gottheil retired and became rabbi emeritus of Temple Emanu-El. Bertram W. Korn aptly characterized Gottheil as "a bridge between the German beginnings of Reform to its Eastern—as distinguished from Midwestern—American flowering" (*Encyclopaedia Judaica* [1971]). He died at his home in New York City.

• Among Gottheil's published works are *Moses and Slavery* (1860) and *Sun and Shield* (1896), "a book of devout thought for every-day use." His son, Richard J. H. Gottheil, published a large and lavishly documented biography of his father, *The Life of Gustav Gottheil, Memoir of a Priest in Israel* (1936). It differs in some respects from the articles by F. H. Vizetelli in the *Jewish Encyclopedia* (1904) and D. de Sola Pool in the *Dictionary of American Biography*, vol. 4 (1931–1932). See also I. S. Moses's eulogy in *Yearbook of the Central Conference of American Rabbis*, vol. 13 (1903). Obituaries are in the *New York Times*, 16 Apr. 1903; *American Hebrew*, 17, 24 Apr. 1903; and *Reform Advocate*, 25 Apr. 1903.

W. GUNTHER PLAUT

GOTTHEIL, Richard James Horatio (13 Oct. 1862–22 May 1936), professor and founder of the American Zionist movement, was born in Manchester, England, the son of Gustav Gottheil, a rabbi, and Rosalie Wollman. He was brought to the United States at the age of eleven upon his father's appointment as rabbi of Temple Emanu-El in New York City. He graduated in 1881 from Columbia College, where his classmates and associates included Nicholas Murray Butler, who later became the president of Columbia University.

Gottheil did his graduate work at the universities of Berlin, Tübingen, and Leipzig, where he received a Ph.D. summa cum laude in 1886. While in Berlin he also pursued traditional Jewish studies at an advanced talmudical academy and at the Hochschule für die Wissenschaft des Judenthums. His doctoral thesis, which was published in 1887, was on "The Syriac

Grammar of Mar Alia of Zobha." The extensive German antisemitism that he encountered, as well as his work in Berlin in 1882 with Russian Jewish refugees who had fled Tsarist pogroms, made a strong impression on him and helped influence him to embrace the cause of Zionism.

Rather than follow his father into the rabbinate, Gottheil decided upon an academic career in the nascent field of Orientalism, a forerunner to the modern study of Middle Eastern languages, literatures, and cultures. Returning to America in 1886, he was appointed lecturer in Syriac at Columbia College. The following year he became professor of Semitic languages and rabbinical literature through a chair that his father and Temple Emanu-El had been instrumental in endowing. He remained on the faculty until the end of his life. In 1891 he married Emma Léon, a young widow with two sons, whom he had met three years earlier on one of his frequent research trips to Paris. They had no children of their own.

Under Gottheil's guidance, a complete curriculum of Semitic courses was organized and the Semitics library of Columbia greatly expanded. His department attracted students from all parts of the United States and abroad, including Christian ministers, rabbis, and lay scholars, some of whom became the leading Orientalists, Arabists, and Jewish scholars of the twentieth century. Although Syriac, a form of Aramaic, was always Gottheil's first love, he was a published expert and teacher in numerous languages and cultures, including Hebrew, Turkish, Persian, and Arabic. His knowledge of the last made him almost unique among early American Zionists. In 1935–1936, during the Italian invasion of Abyssinia, he was the only teacher of Ethiopic languages in the United States. He published or edited numerous scientific articles and book reviews in his field as well as essays on international and historical subjects in various newspapers and periodicals.

Gottheil also served as trustee, officer, member, or founder of various societies, both Jewish and non-Jewish. These included the American Society of Biblical Literature (president, 1902–1903); the American Oriental Society (president, 1933–1934); the American School of Oriental Research in Jerusalem (director, 1909–1910); the Real Academia de la Historia, Madrid (corresponding member); the American Jewish Historical Society (founder and vice president, 1904–1936); the Educational Alliance of New York (member 1912–1919); the Jewish Chautauqua Society; the Jewish Institute of Religion in New York; and the Zeta Beta Tau Fraternity (founder in 1898 and supreme president, 1911–1920). As lifetime chief from 1896 of the Oriental Division of the New York Public Library, he built its collection of Orientalia and Judaica, which helped to transform it into a world-class institution.

Gottheil is perhaps best known as a founder and advocate of American Zionism. Shortly after his attendance at the Second Zionist Congress in 1898 in Basel, Switzerland, he was elected the first president of the Federation of American Zionists (1898–1904); his former pupil Rabbi Stephen S. Wise served as secretary. In 1899 he and Wise established the *Maccabean*, the first Zionist publication in English. Inspired by Theodor Herzl of Vienna, who sought to establish a Jewish homeland in Palestine, Gottheil became a member of the Central Committee of the Zionist Organization, corresponded extensively with Herzl and other European Zionist leaders, and traveled the United States on behalf of his cause. Unlike Herzl, he was in no way a charismatic leader, and the tiny American Zionist movement was particularly unpopular among Jews of Gottheil's background and class. On the other hand, his erudition, gentlemanly bearing, professorial prestige, and quiet persistence did much to win the adherence of both Jews and non-Jews who otherwise would not have considered Zionism, or indeed even Judaism as a whole, a subject worthy of their attention.

Although Gottheil ceased to be active in administrative affairs of the movement after Herzl's death in 1904, and became a virtual *persona non grata* among American Zionist officials during and after World War I, he remained an enthusiastic Zionist and prolific author on the subject until his death. His withdrawal from public Zionist affairs was due in part to his distaste and ill-suitedness for the practical details of national organizational life. In addition, the approach of World War I brought out in him a rabid anti-Germanism as he sought to expose those American Jews whom he suspected of undue sympathy with Imperial Germany. Although himself a product of the German-Jewish elite, he stressed his English birth and French-educated wife, repudiated any connection to Germany, and resigned his membership in all German learned societies. In tribute to his efforts for the Allied cause, he received the French Legion of Honor in 1919. Gottheil's experience was typical of the swift reorientation that took place among elite American Jews, who until World War I were still strongly influenced by German education and culture even if rarely by any actual political allegiance.

Never known for stirring oratory, passionate writing, or personal flamboyance, Gottheil is consistently described as the quintessential cloistered scholar and gentleman, who once admitted to a colleague that he never felt so happy as when he was copying and deciphering a difficult text. As an early Orientalist and teacher, however, he helped to transfer German university methods of critical scholarship to the United States and was an architect to an entire academic field. In teaching Hebrew and Semitic writings to pupils of all theological backgrounds, he successfully navigated a potentially explosive field with delicacy, tact, and a firm belief that a dedication to the principles of pure academic scholarship must ultimately overcome any conflict caused by individual religious differences. As a Zionist, he was one of the first to interpret the essentially European movement in terms that an American audience could understand, insisting that the doctrine did not require massive emigration of American Jews or leave them open to the charge of disloyalty to their country.

Finally, Gottheil played a quiet but significant role as a Jewish academic at a time when non-Christian students in American universities were few and Jewish professors virtually unknown. For almost fifty years he quietly served as the unofficial representative and advocate for Columbia University's Jewish community, helping to pave the way for future Jewish academics and giving Jewish topics a respected place in the university curriculum. Most important of all, his status and aristocratic bearing helped to inspire ethnic pride and identification in hundreds of young Jewish-American students at a time when Jewishness was still largely associated with immigrant status and negative, lower-class origins. He died in New York City.

• Gottheil's library was donated to Columbia University upon his death. The largest available collection of his letters and papers is at the American Jewish Archives in Cincinnati, Ohio, and the Central Zionist Archives in Jerusalem; a few can also be found at the American Jewish Historical Society in Waltham, Mass. A selective bibliography of his writings is Ida A. Pratt, "Selected Bibliography of R. J. H. Gottheil," *Journal of the American Oriental Society* 56, no. 4 (1936): 480–89. His academic writings include *Selections from the Syriac Romance of Julian the Apostate* (1906), *The Syriac-Arabic Glosses of Isha bar Ali* (1908–1928), *A Treatise on Syriac Grammar by Mar Elia of Sobha* (1887), and *Fragments from the Cairo Genizah in the Freer Collection*, with William H. Worrell (1927). Other works by Gottheil include *Zionism* (1914), the first full-length English history of the movement; and a biography of his father, *The Life of Gustav Gottheil: Memoir of a Priest in Israel* (1936), which includes some details of his own early life. For Gottheil's role in the early history of the Zionist movement, see Marnin Feinstein, *American Zionism, 1884–1904* (1965), and Evyatar Friesel, "The Knights of Zion of Chicago and Their Relations with the Federation of American Zionists, 1897–1916," *Zionism*, ed. Daniel Carpi and Gedalia Yogev (1975). Assessments of his life include George Alexander Kohut, "Prof. Gottheil—An Appraisal at Seventy," *Columbia University Quarterly* (June 1933), pp. 136–45; Joshua Bloch, "Richard James Horatio Gottheil," *Journal of the American Oriental Society* 56, no. 4 (1936): 472–79; and Louis I. Newman, "Richard J. H. Gottheil: A Biographical Sketch," *American Jewish Yearbook* 39 (1937–1938): 29–46. Tributes and eulogies from colleagues and students are in the *Zeta Beta Tau Quarterly* 18, no. 2 (Sept. 1936). See also the *New York Times*, 23, 25, and 26 May 1936. An obituary of Emma Gottheil appears in the *New York Times*, 13 June 1947.

MARIANNE SANUA

GOTTLIEB, Adolph (14 Mar. 1903–4 Mar. 1974), artist, was born in New York City, the son of Emil Gottlieb, the owner of a wholesale stationery business, and Elsie Berger. Gottlieb studied from 1920 to 1921 at the Art Students League in New York City with Robert Henri and John Sloan. The next year he traveled to Europe and studied at the Académie de la Grande Chauimère in Paris, later visiting Berlin and Munich. Gottlieb returned to New York City in 1923 and during the 1920s and 1930s painted representational still lifes, nudes, portraits, and figural groups, some of which were exhibited in his first show at the Dudensing Gallery in New York City in 1930.

In 1935 Gottlieb, along with Mark Rothko, was a founding member of The Ten, an independent group of painters favorably disposed to modern European art who worked in an expressionistic style. This group is not to be confused with another alliance of artists also called The Ten, who exhibited works together in 1898. Gottlieb was employed as an easel painter in 1936 on the Federal Arts Project (FAP); his paintings executed for the FAP include *Sun Deck* (1936). In the muted palette and sensitive application of paint, *Sun Deck* recalls the work of Milton Avery, an artist much admired in those years by Gottlieb and Rothko. Gottlieb left the FAP in 1937 and moved to Tucson, Arizona, with his wife of five years, Ester Dick. (The couple had no children.) While in Arizona Gottlieb responded to the local landscape, painting semiabstract still lifes and landscapes including images of bones, petrified wood, and cacti.

Returning to New York City in 1939, Gottlieb made summer excursions to Gloucester, Massachusetts, where from 1939 to 1941 he executed a series of surrealist-inspired still lifes, arranging seashells, coral, and starfish in compartmentalized boxes set against a deeply receding landscape, as in *Box and Sea Objects* (1941). He soon abandoned this motif, yet these still lifes anticipated certain formal qualities and the enigmatic content of his later "Pictographs," which he painted from 1941 to 1951. Pictographs is the word Gottlieb coined for paintings with two-dimensional symbolic motifs ranging from recognizable schematic forms to abstract signs positioned within rectilinear grids that flattened space and eliminated pronounced focal points. They were loosely painted predominantly in earth, clay, and mineral colors. Gottlieb's sources for the Pictographs were diverse. The grid format owed much to Paul Klee, Piet Mondrian, and Joaquín Torres-García, while the symbolic motifs—spirals, concentric circles, arrows, and anatomical fragments—were derived from Pablo Picasso and Joan Miró as well as classical myth, Native American, African, and oceanic art. His selection of symbolic motifs was subjective, inspired by the surrealist technique of automatism in which the artist suspends rational, judgment-based thought in order to draw or paint with spontaneity, expressing the unconscious mind. The Pictographs were, he said, "a form of picture writing or I thought of them . . . as using an automatic process that was akin to the automatic writing of the Surrealists" (Polcari, p. 165).

A letter written by Gottlieb, Rothko, and Barnett Newman and published in the *New York Times* on 7 June 1943 contains one of the fundamental statements about the content of abstract expressionism and reveals much about the meaning of Gottlieb's Pictographs. "Only that subject matter is valid which is tragic and timeless," they declared. "That is why we profess spiritual kinship with primitive and archaic art." Gottlieb's Pictographs also suggest archaic forms inspired by Carl Jung's theory of archetypes and the collective unconscious, recalled in ancient sign language, petroglyphs, and archaic motifs such as the spi-

ral and the arrow. Gottlieb's totemic themes, as in *Masquerade* (1945), were associated, he said, with journeys into "the catacombs of the unconscious" or "dim recollections of a prehistoric past" (Polcari, p. 165).

Gottlieb was president of the Federation of Modern Painters and Sculptors during 1944–1945. He was selected in 1951 to provide architectural decorations for Congregation B'nai Israel, a synagogue in Millburn, New Jersey. For this project, Gottlieb designed a large ark curtain incorporating stylized Jewish iconography. His most ambitious architectural commission was a 1,300-square-foot stained glass facade for the Milton Steinberg Memorial Center in New York City, which he erected during 1952–1954.

Meanwhile, also in 1951, Gottlieb began a series of imaginary landscapes composed of astral forms above broad, horizontal bands of color. In *Frozen Sounds I* (1951), the division of the canvas suggests a landscape, and celestial forms float above the dense mass of earth below. Gottlieb painted variations on this theme until 1957. That November through December a retrospective of his work dating from 1941 was held at the Jewish Museum in New York City.

By 1957 Gottlieb had simplified, condensed, and enlarged his pictorial forms to create the more immediate, universal, and monumental *Burst* series. *Blast I* (1957) is comprised of a sunlike disk above a more active, dynamic, or exploding form. According to art historian Martin Friedman, these works were "a statement of radical opposition, and these forms—one calm, defined and tightly contained, the other undisciplined, in flux—suggest interpretations ranging from the actual to the metaphysical: male and female, reason and emotion—positive negative entities essential to one another that interact across the charged field of the canvas" (Friedman, p. 7). In 1968 Gottlieb confirmed Friedman's interpretation, stating that the *Bursts* deal "primarily with polarities." He also noted, however, that "I try to resolve these conflicts and to . . . find some equilibrium for these opposing tendencies" (Polcari, pp. 180–82). During the 1960s Gottlieb continued with the *Burst* series, and they remain his most monumental and succinct artistic statement.

Gottlieb did not make preliminary drawings for his paintings but developed his visual ideas while working directly on the canvas. In paintings such as *Conflict* (1966), fragments, splatters, drips, scumbles, and pentimenti (faint, gestural markings that had been overpainted and that gradually reemerge on the surface of a painting) record Gottlieb's process. His painting style and the raw, unfinished quality of the paint itself characterize the dramatic immediacy evident in the mature works of other abstract expressionists such as Jackson Pollock and Willem de Kooning.

In November 1972 Gottlieb had a solo show at the Marlborough Gallery in New York City. Disabled by a stroke, he had completed the last painting for the show in a wheelchair. His mural-size painting *Flotsam* was finished in 1973, the year before he died in East Hampton, Long Island. Gottlieb played a leading role in abstract expressionism, a movement considered to be the first American art of international renown.

• Adolph Gottlieb's papers are in the Archives of American Art, Smithsonian Institution, and the Adolph and Ester Gottlieb Foundation, New York City. The most complete source of information on Gottlieb's life and art is Lawrence Alloway and Mary Davis MacNaughton, *Adolph Gottlieb: A Retrospective* (1981), an exhibition catalog that includes numerous color reproductions of the artist's works, two informative essays, and a comprehensive bibliography. One of the first comprehensive studies of Gottlieb is Robert Doty and Dianne Waldman, *Adolph Gottlieb* (1968). See also Stephen Polcari, *Abstract Expressionism and the Modern Experience* (1991), for a monographic chapter on Gottlieb that relates his art to the historical and cultural milieu. An exhibition catalog that focuses on Gottlieb's Pictographs is Alloway, *The Pictographs of Adolph Gottlieb* (1994). Additional one-man exhibition catalogs of significance are Martin Friedman, *Adolph Gottlieb* (1963), and *Adolph Gottlieb* (Marlborough-Gerson Gallery, 1964). Obituaries are in the *New York Times*, 5 Mar. 1974, and *Newsweek*, 18 Mar. 1974.

LEESA FANNING

GOTTLIEB, Eddie (15 Sept. 1898–7 Dec. 1979), professional basketball coach, promoter, and team owner, was born Edward Gottlieb in Kiev, Ukraine, the son of Morris Gottlieb and Leah (maiden name unknown). Gottlieb's family moved to the United States in 1907. While growing up in a Jewish section of Philadelphia, he learned basketball, and in 1918 he organized and promoted a team that represented the South Philadelphia Hebrew Association (Sphas). The Sphas soon ended their affiliation with the association but kept a six-pointed star and the Hebrew letters *samech, pey, hey,* and *aleph* on their jerseys. Other community professional teams that made up the Philadelphia League were dominated by Gottlieb's club. After the Sphas defeated the renowned Celtics in 1922, the New York Renaissance (Rens), and other American Basketball League (ABL) clubs during the 1920s, they became the toast of Philadelphia sports fans.

Gottlieb started in basketball at a time when the sport was trying to survive by serving as a prelude to community dances. Basketball was a local sport, operating on amateur and professional levels that provided inexpensive amusement integrated into local (in this case, Jewish) social life. Gottlieb remembered the days when the team's home court was the grand ballroom of the Broadwood Hotel, where men for 65 cents and women for 35 cents could watch a game and then enjoy a dance. "In those days," Gottlieb recalled, "many of the Jewish people wouldn't let their daughters go to an ordinary dance except when the Sphas were in action." Sometimes called "Gotty's Goal Gatherers," the Sphas, under Gottlieb's direction and led by Chick Passon, Babe Klotz, Davey Banks, and "Doc" Lou Sugarmen, dominated their opponents, winning three consecutive Philadelphia League titles in 1923, 1924, and 1925.

After the league's collapse in 1925, Gottlieb added two non-Jewish stars, "Stretch" Meehan and Tom Barlow. Gottlieb later renamed the Sphas the Philadelphia Warriors and entered them in the ABL. When that league collapsed after the 1931 season, Gottlieb revamped the team again, using solely Jewish players from Philadelphia and New York, including Cy Kaselman, Harry Litwack, and Moe Goldman. For sixteen seasons the Warriors dominated eastern professional basketball.

The Sphas' success and open identification as Jews served as an important vehicle for Jewish assimilation into American culture. Jewish fans relished the triumph of ethnic heroes who symbolized their own hopes for success.

Gottlieb was a driving force in the early days of the National Basketball Association (NBA). The NBA's forerunner, the Basketball Association of America, was formed in 1946 because arena managers (none of whom were professional basketball men) wanted to fill seats. All but one of the eleven charter member-founders of the BAA had hockey teams as their principal sport properties and tenants. As coach and part-owner of the Warriors, Gottlieb helped merge the BAA with regional leagues to form the NBA. Sparked by "Jumping Joe" Fulks, a Marine Corps star who perfected the jump shot (within a decade the primary offensive weapon in the NBA), Gottlieb's Warriors won the BAA title in 1947 and the NBA's first true league championship. Gottlieb's 263–318 professional coaching record included two more Eastern Division titles before his retirement in 1955.

Gottlieb built his Philadelphia basketball franchise around local collegiate stars, including Paul Arizin, Tom Gola, and Guy Rodgers. He was instrumental in securing Wilt Chamberlain, an all-time NBA star, out of Philadelphia's Overbrook High School. Playing in a summer league after graduating from high school, Chamberlain was coached by Red Auerbach, who tried to persuade him to attend a New England college so that the Boston Celtics could select him in the collegiate draft. But in 1955 Gottlieb convinced the other owners that he should be allowed to make Chamberlain an unprecedented "territorial pick" out of high school. Chamberlain began his illustrious professional career in Philadelphia after his college graduation. "We were fighting for survival in those days," Gottlieb recalled, and "hometown boys were big at the box office." In 1962 two credit card executives, Matty Simmons and Len Mogle, approached Gottlieb with an offer to buy the Warriors for an unheard-of $850,000—two or three times the selling price of most NBA franchises at the time. Gottlieb, who had purchased the franchise with $25,000 just fifteen years earlier, accepted the offer.

Besides his important coaching and promotional work, Gottlieb was an expert scheduler. He contended that he had been making schedules "since I was born." "Back in the old days," he said, "I was in charge of semipro baseball in Philly and I was scheduling two hundred baseball games a day. I made up schedules for the old Negro National League, I handled all baseball and basketball games around Philadelphia. At one time or another I guess I must have handled just about everything." Gottlieb promoted semipro black baseball teams during the major leagues' segregated era. "The Mogul," as he was called, promoted an all-black game in 1929 in Yankee Stadium, the first such contest in a major league park.

Gottlieb also organized overseas tours for the Harlem Globetrotters. He catered to the rapidly increasing fan interest in pro basketball by promoting doubleheaders and working to revise rules. As a powerful force on the NBA rules committee, he rarely resisted any idea that popularized and enlivened the game. He proposed the 24-second clock, supported the move to outlaw zone defenses, and backed the bonus penalty foul shot. Gottlieb was elected to the Basketball Hall of Fame as a contributor in 1971 for his twenty-five years on the rules committee. As a successful coach, owner of the Philadelphia Warriors, and long-time schedule-maker and administrator, he ultimately lived up to his nickname. He died in Philadelphia.

• The best scholarly treatment of the beginnings of professional basketball is Robert W. Peterson, *Cages to Jump Shots: Pro Basketball's Early Years* (1990). Stephen Fox, *Big Leagues: Professional Baseball, Football, and Basketball in National Memory* (1994), places the game's early history and evolving styles of play into the larger context of American sporting culture. Peter Levine has explored early Jewish participation in basketball in *Ellis Island to Ebbets Field: Sport and the American Jewish Experience* (1992). Other useful sources include Albert G. Applin, "From Muscular Christianity to the Marketplace: The History of Men's and Boy's Basketball in the United States, 1891–1957" (Ph.D. diss., Univ. of Massachusetts, 1982); Glenn Dickey, *The History of Professional Basketball since 1896* (1982); Neil D. Issacs, *All the Moves* (1975); Zander Hollander, *The Modern Encyclopedia of Basketball* (1973); Larry Fox, *Illustrated History of Basketball* (1974); and Robert Mendell, *Who's Who in Basketball* (1973). Gottlieb's obituary appears in the *New York Times*, 8 Dec. 1979.

STEVEN W. POPE

GOTTSCHALK, Louis Moreau (8 May 1829–18 Dec. 1869), the first internationally famous American pianist-composer, was born in New Orleans, Louisiana, the son of Edward Gottschalk, a London Jew who after his arrival in New Orleans around 1820 became a successful stockbroker, land speculator, and slave trader, and Marie Aimée de Bruslé, a fifteen-year-old Louisiana girl of Catholic faith and French ancestry, and niece of Moreau Lislet, distinguished Louisiana lawyer. Gottschalk began to play the piano when he was three. In 1841 he was sent to Paris for advanced study but was denied an audition at the Paris Conservatoire because "America was only a country of steam engines" (Gottschalk, p. 52); he studied piano with Camille Stamaty, a student of Felix Mendelssohn and teacher of Camille Saint-Saëns, and composition with Pierre Maleden. The audience of Gottschalk's 1845 Paris recital included Frédéric Chopin. His professional Paris debut in 1849 was well received, some critics comparing him with Chopin, Franz Liszt, and Sigismond Thalberg. Hector Berlioz wrote: "Mr. Gottschalk is one of the very small number of those

who possess all the different elements of the sovereign power of the pianist" (*Journal des débats*, 13 Apr. 1851). The New World ambiance of his first compositions, *Bamboula*, *La Savane*, and *Le Bananier*, had caught the attention of the public; publishers competed for his new pieces.

After touring France, Switzerland, and Spain, where he was knighted by Isabella II, Gottschalk returned to America in 1853. His New York debut, on 11 February 1853, was a critical success but lost money. That year his father died, bankrupt. Gottschalk assumed his father's debts and from then on supported his mother and six siblings. Because of poor health, Gottschalk spent 1854 in the warmer climate of Cuba. Returning to New York in 1855, his prospects improved: his publisher, William Hall, sponsored him in recitals featuring his compositions, the famous American piano manufacturing firm of Chickering engaged him to advertise its instruments, and the New York Philharmonic Society named him an honorary member. His popularity and reputation grew. Only Boston critic John Sullivan Dwight, who admitted to a bias for German music, attacked Gottschalk's compositions before hearing them; he remained hostile throughout the pianist's career, although he grudgingly acknowledged Gottschalk's virtuosity. Despite the death of his mother in 1856, Gottschalk finished the year in triumph, performing his *Grand Duo on Il Trovatore* (Verdi), the manuscript of which is lost, with the renowned Thalberg in New York on 26 December. A witness recalled Thalberg's remarkable trill "while Gottschalk was flying all over the keyboard in the 'Anvil Chorus,' producing the most prodigious volume of tone I ever heard from the piano" (Hoffman, p. 139).

Gottschalk performed with the New York Philharmonic in January 1857, then sailed with the young soprano Adelina Patti on a Caribbean tour. Drawn to the warmth of the tropics, he remained there for five years, performing throughout the Antilles. In 1860 he organized a festival of nine hundred musicians (the first of a series later called Monster Concerts) in Havana, premiering his symphony *La Nuit des tropiques*, the short opera *Fête champêtre cubaine*, and the finale of his incomplete opera *Carlos IX* (this manuscript is also lost).

In 1862, in the midst of the Civil War, Gottschalk returned to New York, declared his allegiance to the Union, and resumed his concert tours of the North and Canada. Everywhere he went he played *The Union*, a fantasy on "The Star-Spangled Banner," "Hail Columbia," and "Yankee Doodle" (dedicated to General George B. McClellan), never failing to arouse tremendous patriotic enthusiasm. President Abraham Lincoln and General Ulysses S. Grant attended his Washington concerts. In 1864 Gottschalk estimated that he had given more than four hundred concerts and traveled more than forty thousand miles by railroad since his return to the United States. To break the tedium of his incessant travels, he began writing letters and articles, in French, for the Paris journals *La France musicale* and *L'Art musical*, compiled posthumously by his sister Clara Gottschalk Peterson as his remarkable diary, *Notes of a Pianist*.

In May 1865 he sailed for California, intending to tour there and in the gold mining towns of Nevada. His visit ended disastrously when rumors spread concerning his relationship with a boarding-school girl; there was talk of tar and feathers. On 18 September he was spirited out of San Francisco by friends who feared for his safety. *The Golden Era* (1 Oct. 1865) blamed the press for exaggerating what was, "in reality, but an indiscretion." Gottschalk denied wrongdoing. From the start of his career, his romantic appeal, manners, dress, and French accent had made him a cult figure, and women threw themselves at him. The actress Ada Clare claimed that he had fathered her illegitimate son, and she pilloried him in her roman à clef *Only a Women's Heart*. Newspaper gossip frequently linked him with heiresses, but Gottschalk claimed that marriage was impossible for him because of his commitment to care for his siblings.

Humiliated, his plans disrupted, Gottschalk sailed to Panama. By November he was in Lima, Peru, where he resumed his recital career. For the next two years he traversed the Pacific coast of South America, organizing festivals in Valparaiso and Santiago, Chile. Sailing the Strait of Magellan, he reached Montevideo in May 1867. He premiered his *Grande Tarentelle* in Montevideo and made his Buenos Aires debut in November, shuttling back and forth between these cities until the spring of 1869.

Gottschalk arrived in Brazil in May 1869. His concerts in Rio de Janeiro were attended by the royal family, and Emperor Pedro II received him at the palace. For six months Gottschalk maintained a rigorous schedule that climaxed in a festival of 650 musicians on 24 November. The following evening Gottschalk performed for the Philharmonic Society his recently composed *Morte*; he then began his virtuosic etude *Tremolo* but was forced to stop, weakened by yellow fever and overwork from preparing for the festival. His health failing, he was taken to the salutary climate of suburban Tijuca, where he died of an intestinal disorder. His funeral in Rio de Janeiro occasioned an extraordinary expression of mourning. Everywhere in South America he had enjoyed enthusiastic receptions and attracted loyal friends and pupils; he had been honored and decorated. In 1870 his body was returned to America. After a requiem mass in St. Stephen's Church in New York City, he was buried in Greenwood Cemetery in Brooklyn, New York. The *New York Leader* remembered his generosity, charity, kindness to fellow artists, devotion to family, and love of country, though it noted humorously that he "never spoke nor wrote English (though he knew it well) unless obliged to."

Gottschalk composed a few orchestral pieces and songs and worked on several unfinished operas (many of his works were lost when his possessions were auctioned after his death). Using the pseudonym "Seven Octaves," he wrote many easier but not necessarily inferior pieces. The majority of his works are for piano: waltzes, polkas, mazurkas, galops, ballades, études, marches, nocturnes, opera transcriptions, and character pieces. Among the latter, *The Last Hope* and *The Dying Poet*, embodiments of Victorian sentiment, once could be found in every parlor. Especially appealing are the pieces inspired by folk music: *Bamboula*, *La Savane*, *Le Bananier*, and *Le Mancenillier*, based on Louisiana Creole and African-American songs; *Manchega*, *Souvenirs d'Andalousie*, and *La Jota aragonesa*, on Spanish airs; *Le Banjo*, *Columbia*, and *Pasquinade*, echoing spirituals, minstrel shows, and Stephen Foster's songs; *Ojos criollos (Creole Eyes)*, *La Gallina*, *Responds-moi*, *Suis-moi*, and *Souvenir de Porto Rico*, inspired by the Caribbean *danza*; and the remarkable symphony *La Nuit des tropiques* (not heard in the United States until 1955), in which he pioneered the use of Caribbean rhythms and percussion instruments in symphonic music. Gottschalk used American cakewalk and Cuban habañera rhythms as early as 1848, anticipating their appearance in ragtime around 1900 and in Latin-American dance music of the 1930s. Gottschalk's influence on these later styles cannot be established, but it seems unlikely that jazz musicians were unaware of his popular and widely disseminated compositions. In the last quarter of the nineteenth century, German classics dominated American programs, and Gottschalk's music was almost forgotten. But around 1930 a Gottschalk renaissance began, resulting in recordings, a collected edition, dissertations, novels, articles, a reprint of his memoirs, televised ballets of the *Grande Tarentelle* and *Cakewalk* (arr. Hershey Kay), and a reappraisal of Gottschalk as an important figure in American music. Richard Hoffman, who knew Gottschalk, considered him "the one American composer of genuine originality."

• The New York Public Library for the Performing Arts at Lincoln Center holds the largest Gottschalk collection in America. In 1984 the library acquired the historically invaluable collection assembled by Gottschalk's sister, Clara Gottschalk Peterson, including the French version of Gottschalk's *Notes of a Pianist* (English trans., 1881; ed. Jeanne Behrend, 1964; repr. 1979), the best account of his life. See John G. Doyle, *Louis Moreau Gottschalk 1829–1869: A Bibliographical Study and Catalog of Works* (1983), for this and other collections, literature, manuscripts, compositions, and recordings. F. C. Lange, *Vida y Muerte de Louis Moreau Gottschalk en Rio de Janeiro* (1951), gives a scholarly account of Gottschalk's final months. See Richard Hoffman, *Some Musical Recollections of Fifty Years* (1910), for a cameo of Gottschalk's personal magnetism. Gilbert Chase, *America's Music from the Pilgrims to the Present* (1955), and Wilfrid Mellers, *Music in a New Found Land: Themes and Developments in the History of American Music* (1965), reassess Gottschalk's historical significance. For a biography, see S. Frederick Starr, *Bamboula* (1994).

JOHN GODFREY DOYLE

GOUCHER, John Franklin (7 June 1845–19 July 1922), philanthropist and educator, was born in Waynesburg, Pennsylvania, the son of John Goucher, a doctor, and Eleanor Townsend. Goucher was raised in a devout Methodist household, the youngest of four children. Religion was a sustaining and motivating force throughout his life. Another important influence was a meeting with President-elect Abraham Lincoln, who remained one of Goucher's greatest heroes. After graduating from Dickinson College in 1868, he entered the Methodist Episcopal ministry in Baltimore. In 1869 he met Mary Cecilia Fisher, who was from an old Maryland family. They married on Christmas Eve, 1877. Of the five children born to the couple, three survived to adulthood. Her fortune, inherited from her father and bachelor uncle who were physicians, made it possible for the couple to exercise a shared philanthropic spirit throughout their married life. In Baltimore he was known as the "Builder of Churches," constructing fifteen churches during his twenty-one year pastorate.

The dominating purpose of Goucher's life, manifested in a variety of ways, was the spread of Christianity through schools and colleges for Christian education. Around 1880 the Gouchers volunteered for mission service with the Methodist Foreign Board. Special projects in their years of travel and work abroad included the establishment of a system of vernacular schools in India, which were attended by more than three thousand pupils at one time. He also built and generously supported schools in Germany, China, Korea, Mexico, and Japan. This work required many cross-country trips in the United States and dozens of ocean crossings. He relished the traveling and was noted for his courage and calm in dealing with the unexpected, such as the time he was a passenger on the SS *Republic* when it collided with the SS *Florida*. Since he always carried a pocket flashlight, he was able to lead others to the upper deck and rescue. He returned below to recover valuables and then, according to Bishop Earl Cranston, "he got tea and brewed it for the hysterical."

Perhaps Goucher's most lasting monument is the college in Baltimore that bears his name. A strong advocate of education for women, in 1883 he gave the land and early funding in the amount of $30,000 for the Woman's College of Baltimore. He was unanimously elected its second president in 1890, and after he retired in 1908 the college was renamed in his honor. His major failing as an administrator was an inability to put the college on a solid financial footing; it survived its first years in large part because financial deficits were met out of his pocket. They were, however, years of substantial growth; during his eighteen-year presidency, the college grew from forty students to 341, the plant greatly expanded, and strong academic standards were put into place. Because of inadequate preparatory education available to girls in the local schools at that time, the Girl's Latin School was established at the college to prepare students for its academic rigors.

Goucher was said to be a charming conversationalist, always ready to tell a story or a joke. Woman's College students of the time felt comfortable in his presence and enjoyed frequent hospitality in the Goucher home. Mary Goucher, too, was a favorite of the students, cultured, friendly, and generous with her attention.

Believing in opportunity for all, the Gouchers also were active in behalf of education for African Americans. They donated the land for Morgan College in Baltimore, and he served it for forty-three years as a trustee, thirty-nine years as president of its board of trustees. Goucher was also a chief benefactor of the Princess Anne Training School, later a junior college, in Princess Anne, Maryland.

Goucher received his master's degree in 1872, and he was awarded an honorary doctor of divinity in 1885 and an honorary doctor of laws in 1899, all from Dickinson College. In 1919 he was awarded the Order of the Rising Sun by the emperor of Japan and the Order of Chia Ho by China's president in 1921. He also served as president of the American Methodist Historical Society and the Maryland Bible Society. Some of his publications are *True Education* (1904), *Young People and World Evangelization* (1905), *Christianity and the United States* (1908), and *Growth of the Missionary Concept* (1911).

Goucher died at his Baltimore County home "AltoDale." On his death, the Baltimore *Evening Sun* quoted local ministers in describing Goucher as "the greatest figure in the Methodist Church . . . a towering figure. His mind was wonderful. He seemed to have studied every subject and to be at home discussing any of them."

• Materials related to both John Franklin and Mary Goucher are available in the Goucher College Archives and in the library of Lovely Lane Methodist Church in Baltimore. Goucher's life is outlined in Anna Heubeck Knipp and Thaddeus P. Thomas, *The History of Goucher College* (1938). The *Goucher Alumnae Quarterly* 2, no. 4 (1922) is devoted to him. Obituaries are in the *New York Times*, 20 July 1922, and the *Baltimore Evening Sun*, 19 July 1922.

NANCY L. MAGNUSON

GOUDSMIT, Samuel (11 July 1902–4 Dec. 1978), physicist, was born Samuel Abraham Goudsmit in The Hague, Netherlands, the son of Isaac Goudsmit, a wholesale dealer in bathroom fixtures, and Marianne Gompers, the proprietress of a millinery. Goudsmit's early interest in science was aroused at the age of eleven when he read a popular account of spectroscopy that related it to the structure of stars. Even earlier he had developed an uncanny skill of guessing the trends in Dutch women's hat designs, and would likely have joined his mother's business had she not closed her shop because of her health problems.

Graduating from high school one year early, Goudsmit enrolled at the University of Leiden in 1919. There he studied under the physicist Paul Ehrenfest, but he also spent two years studying egyptology. His talents for analyzing spectrographic data became quickly apparent, and while still an undergraduate he worked as the "house theoretician" in the laboratory of Pieter Zeeman at the University of Amsterdam. While in Amsterdam he also took an eight-month course in detective techniques, which would later prove invaluable to him. On 19 January 1927 he married Jaantje (Jeanne) Logher, an employee in his mother's hat shop; they had one daughter. Later that year he received his Ph.D., with a dissertation on the spectra of atoms, "Atoommodel en structuur der Spectra," directed by Ehrenfest.

Following the completion of his doctorate, Goudsmit immigrated to the United States and took a position at the University of Michigan; there he successively served as an instructor (1927–1928), an associate professor (1928–1932), and a professor (1932–1946). Together with his colleagues David M. Dennison, Otto Laporte, and George E. Uhlenbeck, he organized the Michigan symposia on modern physics from 1928 to 1940, which helped to bring new developments in physics to an American audience. Goudsmit became a naturalized U.S. citizen in 1937, and during the following year he was a Guggenheim Foundation Fellow in Paris and Rome. During World War II he was a staff member from 1941 to 1946 at the Radiation Laboratory of the Massachusetts Institute of Technology, where he worked on radar. From 1944 to 1946 he was the chief civilian scientific officer of the Alsos Mission. Goudsmit then returned to academic life as a professor at Northwestern University. However, he found that academia was no longer challenging, and so in 1948 he joined the Brookhaven National Laboratory on Long Island (then the nation's largest nuclear research center) as a senior scientist. He remained at Brookhaven until 1970, serving as head of the physics department from 1952 to 1960. Concurrently he was a visiting professor at the Rockefeller University (from 1957 to 1974), and the University of Nevada at Reno from 1975 until his death. His marriage ended in divorce in 1960; that same year he married Irene Bejach Rothschild.

Almost all of Goudsmit's scientific research was devoted to spectroscopy, for which his intuition and natural talent for bringing order to a jumbled collection of observations was ideally suited. He had published his first research paper at the age of nineteen when he employed relativity to explain the characteristic pairing in the spectra of alkali metals; this foreshadowed his later work on electron spin, although this was not recognized until years later. There followed six papers on spectroscopy; however, in May 1925, following Wolfgang Pauli's announcement of the need for a fourth quantum number in accord with his Exclusion Principle, Goudsmit suggested that—without physical interpretation—it be a half-integral number. Later that year Ehrenfest assigned him to tutor another graduate student, George E. Uhlenbeck, on recent developments in spectroscopy. This quickly developed into a fruitful collaboration, and in November Goudsmit and Uhlenbeck submitted their historic one-page letter on the spin of the electron to *Naturwissenschaften* (13 [Oct. 1925]: 953). This was followed by a more detailed letter, "Spinning Electrons and the Structure of Spectra" (*Nature*, 20 Feb. 1926, p. 264). Ironically, they feared that their initial results were wrong and asked Ehrenfest not to send the first letter for publica-

tion. However, Ehrenfest, who had already submitted the letter, cheerfully assured them that "You are both young enough to be able to afford a stupidity like that!"

The Uhlenbeck-Goudsmit proposal was off by a numerical factor of two; the correction was promptly supplied by Llewellyn H. Thomas, and it became known as the Thomas factor. By the middle of 1926 their idea had been accepted by quantum theorists; indeed, in 1928 the relativistic electron theory of Paul Dirac explicitly predicted their result. In a subsequent paper with Ernst Beck (1928), Goudsmit succeeded by an analysis of the hyperfine structure of bismuth-209 in ascribing a spin to the atomic nucleus. Goudsmit later admitted that he was more thrilled by this result than the discovery of electron spin, since it was the next step in establishing the notion of spin as a fundamental property of elementary particles. A flurry of papers on spectroscopy followed, along with books: the textbook *The Structure of Line Spectra*, co-authored with Linus Pauling (1930); and the research volume *Atomic Energy States as Derived from the Analysis of Optical Spectra*, with Robert F. Bacher (1932). Both books were very influential, and the latter led to important applications in nuclear physics.

The second stage of Goudsmit's career began with his selection as the chief civilian scientific officer for the Alsos Mission by General Leslie R. Groves. This was an inspired choice due not only to Goudsmit's scientific expertise, but also to his language skills and his extensive European scientific contacts. The Alsos Mission was a quasi-military group that accompanied frontline troops in capturing German nuclear scientists and seizing nuclear related facilities. Goudsmit had not been involved in the American bomb program; hence no secrets would be jeopardized in the event of his capture by the Germans. The name "Alsos" was taken from the classical Greek meaning "grove" or "sacred grove"—an apparent off-hand reference to Groves, who was reportedly not amused by the choice of project names. By November 1944 the mission had correctly ascertained that the German program would not be a serious threat.

In addition, largely because of Goudsmit's efforts, by the end of the war in Europe virtually all of the major German scientists had defected to the Anglo-American side. Goudsmit later wrote *Alsos: The Failure in German Science* (1947), which gave a popular account of his adventures and his analysis of the situation. The book proved controversial; although for a decade it was considered to be a definitive account, it eventually came to be considered too harsh and polemical. The book was re-issued in 1983 containing a useful foreword by Reginald V. Jones, a member of the British investigative team, which helped to place the book into a more proper balance.

Following the war Goudsmit made notable contributions to American physics by his leadership role at Brookhaven, and his editorial services for the American Institute of Physics. He served as managing editor of their flagship journal, *The Physical Review*, from

1951 to 1974, during the postwar boom in physics, and he was founder and editor of *Physical Review Letters* from 1958 to 1974. The latter was a new departure intended to facilitate the prompt publication of new results that were deemed exceptionally important to the physical community. Under his guidance both journals established high standards and assumed a position of international prominence that was maintained throughout the remainder of the twentieth century. Most of Goudsmit's own research publication gradually ceased as he became increasingly involved in the work at Brookhaven and his editorial duties.

Goudsmit was much honored during his lifetime. He was elected a member of the National Academy of Sciences in 1947; was a member of the Royal Netherlands Academy of Science, and an Officer of the Order of the British Empire (1948). In addition, he received the Medal of Freedom from the U.S. State Department in 1948; the Research Corporation Award in 1954; the Max Planck Medal of the German Physical Society in 1965; the Karl T. Compton Award for Distinguished Statesmanship in Science from the American Institute of Physics in 1974; and the Commander of the Order of Orange-Nassau of the Netherlands and the National Medal of Science, both in 1977.

One of the most colorful and fascinating figures of quantum theory, Goudsmit was unusually candid; regardless of whether or not one agrees with his views, his assessments of people and their work are engaging and enlightening. His collaboration with Uhlenbeck and their discovery of the spin of the electron was truly unique. Indeed, they made a formidable team: Goudsmit with his intuitive insight and relentless passion for following clues, and Uhlenbeck the more conceptually oriented theoretician. The Nobel Prize winner Isidor I. Rabi, a mutual friend, likened Goudsmit to a detective and commented that, "Physics must forever be in debt to those two men for discovering spin." He added on another occasion that why they never received a Nobel Prize "will always be a mystery to me." Notwithstanding his self-effacing manner, and often sardonic wit, Goudsmit was a complex character who always stood up for his convictions. Goudsmit died in Reno, Nevada.

• Goudsmit's papers are in the Niels Bohr Library, American Institute of Physics, College Park, Md. A transcript of a June 1976 interview with Goudsmit is in the Archive for the History of Quantum Theory at the American Philosophical Society. Goudsmit published an autobiographical sketch in *McGraw Hill Scientists and Engineers*, vol. 2, ed. Cybil P. Parker (1980). He provided his reflections on the discovery of the spin of the electron in "Pauli and Nuclear Spin," *Physics Today*, June 1951, pp. 18–21. Goudsmit offered a final assessment of the bomb program in the obituary notice "Werner Heisenberg (1901–1976)," *Yearbook of the American Philosophical Society 1976* (1976), pp. 74–80. Personal information about Goudsmit is in Daniel Lang, "A Farewell to String and Sealing Wax I and II," *New Yorker*, 7 Nov. 1953, pp. 47ff, and 14 Nov. 1953, pp. 46ff. A two-part article, "Fifty Years of Spin," *Physics Today*, June 1976, consists of Goudsmit's own "It Might as Well be Spin," and George Uhlenbeck's "Personal Reminiscences." A valuable historical survey, with complete references to the literature on the subject, is Bartel L. van der Waerden, "Exclusion Principle and Spin," in *Theoretical Physics in the Twentieth Century: A Memorial Volume of Wolfgang Pauli*, ed. Marcus Fierz and Victor F. Weisskopf (1960). Thomas Powers, *Heisenberg's War: The Secret History of the German Bomb* (1993), is a contemporary analysis that attempts to balance the American and German accounts of the program. Obituaries are in *Physics Today*, Apr. 1979, pp. 71–72; and the *New York Times*, 6 Dec. 1978.

JOSEPH D. ZUND

GOUDY, Frederic William (18 Mar. 1865–11 May 1947), typographer and printer, was born in Bloomington, Illinois, the son of John Fleming Goudy, a real estate broker, and Amanda Melvina Truesdell. The family moved to Shelbyville, Illinois, where, when he was sixteen, he received a commission to paste Bible verses to a classroom wall. He designed and cut some three thousand letters himself. In 1884 his family moved to Highmore, South Dakota (then part of the Dakota Territory), where his father was appointed federal probate judge. In 1888, after an attempt to establish a loan and mortgage company, Goudy moved to Minneapolis, Minnesota, to work as a bookkeeper for a department store. A year later he moved to Springfield, Illinois, but soon decided to return to South Dakota. As it happened he ventured no further than Chicago, Illinois.

In Chicago, Goudy held a number of positions, including bookstore clerk, which exposed him to book production and printing. Although the job did not last, he remained interested in books. Habitual bookstore visits exposed him to periodicals affiliated with England's Arts and Crafts movement and specifically to the work of William Morris's Kelmscott Press. In 1895 Goudy, with the assistance of C. Carron Hooper, founded the Booklet Press, soon renamed Camelot Press. Goudy's modest shop printed announcement cards, limited edition booklets, and a semimonthly magazine, *Chap Book*, an avant-garde publication established by two Harvard graduates, Herbert S. Stone and Ingalls Kimball that published H. G. Wells and Paul Verlaine as well as artwork by Aubrey Beardsley and Henri de Toulouse-Lautrec. In 1896 the Camelot Press fell into financial straits and closed. That same year Goudy designed his first typeface for commercial use, purchased for ten dollars by Dickerson Type Foundry in Boston, Massachusetts. It was christened "Camelot" and later appeared in the American Type Founders specimen book.

But Goudy found it difficult to make ends meet. In 1897 he married Bertha M. Spinks; they had one son. He then accepted a position as bookkeeper and cashier of the *Michigan Farmer*, located in Detroit, Michigan. In 1898 he was laid off and returned to Chicago. The loss of yet another job and the move brought Goudy to the realization that if work in general was unsteady he might as well commit himself to a career he loved. From that moment on he devoted himself to refining type and to raising the standards of printing. He pursued freelance work in advertising. In 1900 he was invited to teach at the Frank Holme School, where he met fellow typographers William Addison Dwiggins and Oswald Cooper. In July 1903 he, along with William Ransom, established the Village Press in Park Ridge, Illinois. The press's inaugural publication was William Morris's "Printing: An Essay." Goudy soon bought Ransom out and moved the press to Hingham, Massachusetts, and then in 1906 to New York City, where a fire destroyed the press in 1908.

In 1909 Goudy made several trips to Europe and a visit with Alfred W. Pollard, rare book curator of the British Museum, convinced him to resurrect the Village Press. Setting up shop in Forest Hills, New York, in 1914, the new Village Press produced an assortment of exceptional books, including H. G. Wells's *The Door in the Wall* (1911) and William Butler Yeats's *Nine Poems* (1914) as well as Goudy's *The Alphabet* (1918) and *Elements in Lettering* (1922), his pamphlet *Typographia* (1918–1934), and his periodical *Ars Typographica* (1911–1936).

A proliferation of type design ensued. In 1913 Goudy designed Goudy Old Style as a variation on fifteenth-century Roman letter forms. The name was changed, however, to Lanston, and the typeface was sold to the Caslon Foundry, London, England. By 1916 Goudy had developed and sold a total of eight typefaces to the Caslon Foundry as well as other faces to various companies in the United States. A new type face was christened Goudy Old Style in 1915 and was purchased by the American Type Founders for $1,500. This version of Goudy Old Style is available today, yet, Goudy never received royalties based on its sales. In 1915 he was appointed instructor of lettering at the Art Students' League in New York City, where he taught, until 1924 and in 1920 he became the art director of the Lanston Monotype Machine Company in Philadelphia, Pennsylvania.

The Village Press in Forest Hills did not have a printing press. All work was designed by Goudy, set by his wife, and printed, under Goudy's supervision, by another establishment. All type was designed for Goudy's Letter Foundry. Nevertheless, wanting to consolidate the foundry and the press, to make the Village Press, as Goudy said, "a working fact as well as a name," he purchased William Morris's Albion printing press, and moved the Village Press to an old farm in Marlboro, New York. The farmhouse, named "Deepdene," allowed Goudy the room to set up a printing press, design typefaces, cut matrices, and make fonts. At Marlboro the Goudys worked, as a family, much as one did in the sixteenth century.

On 26 January, 1939, the Village Press was once again destroyed by fire. All was lost, including the Morris press and some seventy-five typefaces. As was always his way, Goudy faced this obstacle with a determination that was the mark of his character. Between 1940 and 1944 he designed several more faces, including a distinguished Hebrew face for the Hebrew University in Palestine. In 1940 the University of California published Goudy's *Typologia: Studies in Type Design and Type Making.* Goudy died at Deepdene. His printing and typographic praxis echoed European tradition; his was an exquisite craft. He was of a kind, as Robert Hunter Middleton wrote of the late master, with Gutenberg, Jensen, Garamond, and Bodoni. Opting for integrity over financial reward, his genius was the introduction and incorporation of artistic perfection to American printing and typography.

• Material on Goudy is in the Robert Hunter Middleton Papers at the Newberry Library, Chicago, Ill. For information pertaining specifically to the Village Press, see Goudy's own *The Story of the Village Type* (1933) and Melbert B. Cary, Jr., *A Bibliography of the Village Press* (1938). Additional biographical material is in Peter Beilenson, *The Story of Frederic W. Goudy* (1939).

MICHAEL GOLEC

GOUGAR, Helen Mar Jackson (18 July 1843–6 June 1907), suffragist, temperance reformer, and lecturer, was born near Litchfield in Hillsdale County, Michigan, the daughter of William Jackson and Clarissa Dresser, farmers. After attending the preparatory department of Hillsdale College from 1855 to 1859, she moved to Lafayette, Indiana, to teach in the public schools in order to help support her family. There she joined the Second Presbyterian Church, where she met John D. Gougar, a promising young lawyer, whom she married in 1863. The couple, who had no children, made their home in Lafayette for the rest of their lives.

After her marriage Gougar became involved with local benevolent organizations, including the YMCA and community poor relief. By the early 1870s she began her lifelong work in temperance, joining the nascent Lafayette chapter of the Woman's Christian Temperance Union and establishing her reputation as a lecturer. She later recalled that in 1878 she felt compelled to enter public work as a result of the death of her washerwoman at the hands of the woman's drunken husband. Although at first Gougar "believed in praying away the evil," she soon "became convinced that the best way was to vote it away." In order to further her causes, from 1878 to 1880 she wrote a weekly column for the *Lafayette Daily Courier*, "Bric-A-Brac," which frequently addressed temperance and woman's rights issues. In the 1880s Gougar became active in the woman suffrage movement at both the state and national levels, subsequently serving as president of the Indiana Suffrage Association and as a representative from Indiana to the National Woman Suffrage Association.

A colorful character with a forceful platform presence, Gougar lectured frequently throughout the 1880s and 1890s to club meetings, temperance groups, and lyceum series and addressed state legislatures in New York, Illinois, Indiana, and Kansas as well as the U.S. Senate. By 1891 she estimated that she gave about 300 lectures each year. Never placing loyalty to any one organization above the need for public exposure of the causes she supported, she worked with both the National Woman Suffrage Association, headed by Susan B. Anthony and Elizabeth Cady Stanton, and its rival, the American Woman Suffrage Association, led by Lucy Stone, as well as with the local and state affiliates of these groups. She also tied her work to party politics, speaking on behalf of the Republican party, then the third-party efforts of Prohibitionists, and later the Democratic and Populist parties. In 1896 she campaigned for William Jennings Bryan in support of his position on bimetallism.

Although she had great appeal as a lecturer, Gougar brought to her work an apparently quarrelsome disposition and a penchant for controversy. In 1883 she brought a libel suit against Lafayette detractors who had accused her of adulterous behavior with her husband's law partner, DeWitt Wallace, during his 1882 campaign for a seat in the Indiana State Senate. Although she won a $5,000 judgment in her favor, claiming that saloon interests had fabricated the case, many Indiana suffragists felt the publicity was detrimental to their cause. In 1889 several colleagues in the Indiana Suffrage Association sought, unsuccessfully, to oust her from the organization's presidency to make room for May Wright Sewall. Gougar responded by accusing the newly merged National American Woman Suffrage Association with misappropriation of financial bequests. In 1892 she filed suit against the Attleboro (Mass.) *Sun* and Congressman Elijah Morse, who accused her of placing financial motives above reform principles. The same year she opposed Frances Willard's efforts to promote union between Prohibition and Populist interests, charging that Willard had compromised on the issues of temperance and woman suffrage. In 1893 May Wright Sewall blocked Gougar's effort to address the International Congress of Women at the World's Columbian Exposition in Chicago. Undaunted, if increasingly isolated from organized suffragist politics, in 1894 she attempted to cast a ballot in Lafayette for candidates in the state, county, and township elections. When refused, she filed suit against the local board of elections, claiming that the Indiana state constitution permitted women to vote. She secured admission to the state bar in order to argue her own case but ultimately lost her suit.

Gougar continued to write frequently throughout these years. From 1881 to 1885 she edited *Our Herald*, a weekly temperance and reform journal in Lafayette. After it merged with the *Inter-Ocean*, she continued to contribute to the journal. She also published in the reform monthly the *Arena* and in temperance papers, including the *Lever* and the *Voice*. Her arguments for her 1894 Indiana suffrage case appeared as *The Constitutional Rights of the Women of Indiana* in 1895, and *Matthew Peters: A Foreign Immigrant*, a didactic biography of achievement, assimilation, and moral rectitude chronicling the life of the husband of a co-worker, was published in 1898. In the late 1880s she began to travel frequently and added to her busy schedule paid lectures on her foreign excursions, often using these engagements to enunciate her antiimperialist sentiments. Her final volume, an account of her observations in Europe, Asia, and the Caribbean, *Forty Thousand Miles of World Wandering*, appeared in 1905. Gougar died in her Lafayette home of a heart attack.

During her lifetime, Helen Gougar gained prominence for herself and the temperance and woman suffrage reforms she espoused. An effective platform presence who spoke with a "magnetism to engage the closest attention of her hearers," she was less successful in the many organizational efforts in which she participated.

• The Tippecanoe County Historical Association contains a collection of materials by Gougar, primarily newspaper articles by her and copies of some issues of her weekly *Our Herald*, as well as clippings documenting her career and two useful unpublished sketches of her life by Mary Anthrop. Robert C. Kriebel, *Where the Saints Have Trod: The Life of Helen Gougar* (1985), recounts her colorful career in appropriately journalistic fashion; his research notes are included in the Tippecanoe County Historical Association file on Gougar. Additional manuscript materials by and about Gougar are available in Patricia G. Holland and Ann D. Gordon, eds., *The Papers of Elizabeth Cady Stanton and Susan B. Anthony*, microfilm ed. (1991), and in the Catharine Waugh McCulloch Papers, Schlesinger Library, Radcliffe College, Harvard University. Obituaries are in the *Lafayette Daily Courier*, 6 June 1907, the *Lafayette Morning Journal*, 7 June 1907, and the *Lafayette Leader*, 9 June 1907.

CAROL LASSER

GOUGH, John Bartholomew (22 Aug. 1817–18 Feb. 1886), temperance orator, was born in Sandgate, Kent, England, the son of John Gough, a pensioned British war veteran, and Jane (maiden name unknown), a schoolteacher. Although the family was poor, Gough attended an academy until 1829, when his parents, seeking better opportunities for their son, paid ten guineas to David Mannering, a neighbor planning to emigrate, to take Gough to the United States. The youth worked on Mannering's farm in Oneida County, New York, and joined the Methodist church during the revival then sweeping that region. Mannering, however, provided neither schooling nor a trade as had been promised, and in 1831 Gough left.

Going to New York City, Gough drew on his religious connection to become a bookbinder's apprentice for $2.25 a week (without board) at the Methodist Book Concern. He quickly mastered the trade and, finding other work at $3 a week, sent for his parents and sister. In 1833 his mother and sister arrived, but his father remained in England to keep his £20 annual pension. Soon after, Gough lost his job in a recession, and the family's situation became desperate during sporadic employment. In 1834 Gough's mother died and was buried in a pauper's grave, while his sister went to work as an ill-paid straw-bonnet maker. Gough then joined a convivial set of young men and began to drink heavily.

Possessing a fine singing voice and a talent for imitation, Gough performed in taverns in return for small amounts of money, which usually went for drink. He became an actor and in Boston took a role in a play satirizing the temperance movement. Like many men troubled with alcohol, he drifted in and out of jobs and towns and even went to sea. In 1839 he opened a book bindery in Newburyport, Massachusetts. That same year he married Lucretia Fowler. He continued frequent drinking bouts, during one of which, in 1841, he neglected his wife and infant child, both of whom died.

In 1842 Gough was drunk and homeless in Worcester, Massachusetts, when he was stopped on the street by Joel Stratton, a stranger, and urged to take the teetotal pledge not to use alcohol. The attempted reclamation of drunkards was a new trend in the temperance movement in the early 1840s. So was the organization of former drinkers into self-help groups called Washingtonian societies. Gough attended a temperance meeting and swore off liquor. Sober for five months, he relapsed but renewed his vow, and except for a widely publicized incident in 1845, which he believed had been deliberately plotted against him, he abstained for life. Gough repaid Stratton by providing for the latter's widow in her later years.

Drawing on personal experiences, Gough began to speak extensively against liquor. During 1843 he gave 383 temperance addresses, which were sufficiently lucrative that he had the means to marry Mary Whitcomb that same year. They honeymooned on the lecture circuit. In 1848, with money earned through speaking fees, Gough bought "Hillside," a fine country house near Worcester, that came to hold mementos of Gough's travels and an excellent library. Avoiding ostentation, the affluent, childless couple always received generously those seeking charity. They belonged to the Congregational church.

In 1844 Gough spoke to more than 20,000 Washingtonians encamped on Boston Common. This event, along with a brilliant speech in New York, led Gough to become one of the country's leading professional lecturers, receiving at the peak an average of $173 a talk. A natural orator, he followed this occupation with unusual popular and financial success until his death. In 1853 he took his lectures to Great Britain and attracted so much attention that he stayed until 1855. He returned to Britain to lecture in 1857–1860 and 1878–1879. After 1860 he lectured on topics other than temperance. In his entire career, Gough traveled almost a half-million miles to give nearly 10,000 lectures before more than 9 million people, and he personally collected 140,000 pledges. A celebrity, he sold one million copies of various lectures and 100,000 copies of his autobiography, which was first published in 1845 and frequently updated and reprinted.

Gough reached his audiences with emotion rather than reason and frequently reduced them to laughter or tears. Using a fine memory, a musical voice, and a talent for mimicry, he bounded across the platform with great energy, often telling stories through characters speaking Irish brogues or German immigrant dialects. His speech, rich with evangelical symbolism and flowery Victorian language, was filled with urgency. He once exhorted, "Snap your burning chains, ye denizens of the pit, and come up sheeted in the fire, dripping with the flames of hell, and with your trumpet tongues testify against the damnation of drink."

Gough never wrote a word of a lecture beforehand and always spoke without notes. This produced, he admitted, considerable anxiety, but his nervousness, unknown to the audience, was the wellspring from whence came his ability to bond with his audience's feelings. Once he had touched people in this fashion, he could lead them on a tour through all the emotions that he shared with them. His goal was to capture hearts, and the results could be startling. After attending a Gough lecture in Philadelphia, a wealthy merchant went home and emptied all the bottles in his wine cellar. In San Francisco an overwhelmed surveyor named a street in Gough's honor.

Gough's appeal to emotion was rooted in his belief, shared with other evangelicals, that temperance was primarily about individual conversion to a pledge of personal abstinence. After the Civil War he deserted the Republicans for the Prohibition party and reluctantly endorsed the idea of national Prohibition, which he warned could only succeed after public opinion had been properly prepared through individual pledges. He died in Frankford, Pennsylvania, a neighborhood outside of Philadelphia.

• John B. Gough, *An Autobiography* (1845) is the primary source. Anecdotes from his lectures are in *Sunlight and Shadow* (1880) and *Platform Echoes* (1885). Two good biographies are Carlos Martyn, *John B. Gough* (1893), and Honoré Morrow, *Tiger! Tiger!* (1930). For a critical account, see *Goffiana* (1846). Obituaries are in the *Boston Evening Transcript*, the *New York Times*, and the *New York Tribune*, all 19 Feb. 1886.

W. J. RORABAUGH

GOULD, Augustus Addison (23 Apr. 1805–15 Sept. 1866), physician and conchologist, was born in New Ipswich, New Hampshire, the son of Nathaniel Duren Gould, a music teacher and conductor, and Sally Andrews Prichard. Taking charge of the family farm at age fifteen, he prepared for college and entered Harvard University in 1821, receiving an A.B. degree in 1825. Thereafter, he served two years as tutor with the McBlair family in Baltimore County, Maryland. Deciding on a medical career, Gould studied with physicians James Jackson and Walter Channing in Boston and, having served an internship in the Massachusetts General Hospital, received an M.D. from Harvard Medical School in 1830. Immediately thereafter he began medical practice in Boston. He edited the *Medical Magazine* (Boston) with Abel L. Peirson, Joshua B. Flint, and Elisha Bartlett between 1832 and 1835 and was with the Boston Dispensary in 1834. From 1857 he was visiting physician at the Massachusetts General Hospital. Gould married Harriet Cushing Sheafe in 1833; they had ten children, seven of whom lived to maturity.

Gould's natural history interests began during his college years. As a member of the Boston Society of Natural History, he served as one of the general curators from 1831 to 1838, as curator of mollusks from 1841 to 1843 and from 1844 to 1845, and as corresponding secretary from 1843 to 1850, and in 1833 he gave a lecture course for the society. During the academic years 1834–1835 and 1835–1836, Gould lectured on botany and zoology in Harvard College. His publications in natural history began with a translation of *Lamarck's Genera of Shells* (1833), an entomological paper on Cicindelidae (tiger beetles) of Massachusetts (*Boston Journal of Natural History* 1 [1834]), and as editor of *System of Natural History* (1834). Thereafter, however, he concentrated his scientific studies on mollusks, work that was carried out during hours not devoted to his responsibilities as a physician.

In 1837 Gould was given charge of invertebrates (other than insects) for the Zoological and Botanical Survey of the State. A preliminary report, "Results of an Examination of the Shells of Massachusetts and Their Geographical Distribution" (*Boston Journal of Natural History* 3 [1841]), was followed in the same year by the final *Report on the Invertebrata of Massachusetts, Comprising the Mollusca, Crustacea, Annelida, and Radiata*. In these works, Gould gave early attention, among American naturalists, to geographical factors in the distribution of species, commenting especially on the influence of Cape Cod in limiting the territory occupied by some marine species. His state report delineated about 275 land, freshwater, and ocean mollusks and some 100 other invertebrates. With illustrations by the author, Gould's *Report* was the first to survey the molluscan species of a region of the United States and, while recognizing little of an economic or practical nature in the animals studied, was presented to be useful in the schools. During the same period, Gould published his work on a group of tiny land snails, "Monograph of the Species *Pupa* Found in the United States" (*Boston Journal of Natural History* 3 and 4 [1840–1843]), which demonstrated both his abilities with the microscope and his drawing talents.

In 1845 Gould was chosen to describe the new shells collected by Joseph Couthouy on the U.S. Exploring Expedition to the Pacific led by Lieutenant Charles Wilkes. Couthouy had left the expedition before its completion in 1842, and his specimens had been mishandled in Washington and his general notes lost before Gould took charge of the task. In order to expedite publication of his descriptions and establish priority, Gould published a series of papers in the *Proceedings of the Boston Society of Natural History* (2, 3 [1846–1850]). *Mollusca and Shells* (Exploring Expedition Reports, vol. 12) was released in 1852, and an accompanying atlas of illustrations (most of which were by persons other than Gould) was completed in 1856. Although the work was largely descriptive (encompassing nearly 450 species), Gould continued in it his geographical perspective, arguing that specimens from widely separated areas should be assumed, in the absence of confirming evidence, to be different species.

In 1848 Gould and Harvard zoologist Louis Agassiz coauthored *Principles of Zoology* for high school and college students. Gould also edited Amos Binney's posthumous *Terrestrial Air-Breathing Mollusks of the United States, and the Adjacent Territories of North America* (1851–1857). In the 1840s and 1850s he received the collections of various individuals, including some gathered by military personnel during the war with Mexico, and between 1859 and 1861 published on the mollusks that had been collected by William Stimpson on the 1853–1855 North Pacific Exploring Expedition (*Proceedings of the Boston Society of Natural History*, 6, 7, 8). In 1862 Gould issued a compilation of his work in *Otia Conchologica: Descriptions of Shells and Mollusks from 1839–1862*. The state of Massachusetts in 1865 appropriated $4,000 for republication of Gould's 1841 report on invertebrates; William G. Binney brought the work to completion, and the new edition was published in 1870.

Although Gould is remembered for his work as a conchologist, his interests and influence were shown in other areas. He was involved in the ether controversy that resulted from William T. G. Morton's 1846 demonstration at the Massachusetts General Hospital. During that year, Morton and his family resided with Gould, at which a tumor was surgically removed from the neck of a young patient, and on the evening before the MGH demonstration, Gould suggested an apparatus of valves to aid in controlling the ether that Morton used the next day. Gould was no partisan to the resulting controversy over credit for the discovery, however, and attempted reconciliation between Morton and his friend Charles T. Jackson, who claimed priority. Gould's medical service also included an extended term as treasurer of the Massachusetts Medical Society (1845–1847, 1848–1863). In 1863 and 1865 he presented papers to the Boston Society for Medical Improvement on "Climatology of Consumption," which drew on the census of 1860 and were published in the *Boston Medical and Surgical Journal* (69 [1863], 71 [1865]). Gould presented a paper on a similar topic to the National Academy of Sciences in 1864. He was joint author (with Frederic Kidder, and others) of *The History of New Ipswich* (1852).

Gould was made a member of the American Academy of Arts and Sciences in 1841 and was a charter member of the National Academy of Sciences. He was a constant laborer in his professional and scientific work but was friendly and a welcome companion in his circle. A careful and constructive reader, he was called on to review and critique work of others in various areas. He had a capacity for intense labor, shown not only in his scientific and professional work but in early projects such as the preparation of library catalogs (done for the Boston Athenaeum and for private collections). His real love of nature, in addition to his careful technical studies, was noted in contemporary memoirs. He died in Boston, Massachusetts.

During his career, Gould described nearly 1,100 molluscan species. His report on Massachusetts invertebrates was still considered a standard work on mollusks more than a hundred years later. But he was also broader in his zoological interests and abilities, as suggested by his friendship and collaboration with Louis Agassiz. He was one of a remarkable group of nineteenth-century American naturalists who were able, by great labor, to contribute substantially to a specialty while earning a livelihood by other means.

• After his death, Gould's extensive shell collection was sold to the New York State Museum (Albany); the types were transferred later to the Museum of Comparative Zoology (Harvard) and other specimens to the U.S. National Museum. Among the locations having Gould manuscript materials are the Boston Museum of Science and the Houghton Library and the Museum of Comparative Zoology at Harvard University, but no major collection of his papers is known. A brief autobiographical outline, to 1850, is in the records of the Harvard College Class of 1825, Harvard University Archives. A bibliography of his natural history and medical works is with the sketch of his life in National Academy of Sciences, *Biographical Memoirs* 5 (1905): 91–113; as first written by Jeffries Wyman, the memoir was published in the *Proceedings of Boston Society of Natural History* 11 (1867): 188–205 and was revised for the National Academy by William Healey Dall. Richard I. Johnson, *The Recent Mollusca of Augustus Addison Gould: Illustrations of the Types Described by Gould with a Bibliography and Catalog of His Species*, U.S. National Museum Bulletin 239 (1964), is the most important modern assessment and source for Gould's conchological work. Aspects of his medical career are in George E. Gifford, Jr., "The Forgotten Man of the Ether Controversy," *Harvard Medical Alumni Bulletin* 40, no. 2 (Christmas 1965): 14–19.

CLARK A. ELLIOTT

GOULD, Benjamin Apthorp (15 June 1787–24 Oct. 1859), educator and merchant, was born in Lancaster, Massachusetts, the son of Benjamin Gould and Griselda (or Grizzel) Apthorp Flagg. Gould's father was a veteran of the revolutionary war who was reduced to poverty in its aftermath. The family relocated in 1800 to Newburyport, Massachusetts, where Gould spent his youth. He attended Dummer Academy in Newbury, Massachusetts, and apparently also taught school in order to earn money for college. At last able to enter Harvard College at the age of twenty-three, he proved an excellent student, demonstrating particular proficiency in Latin and Greek. His progress was such that in April 1814, before his scheduled graduation, he was offered the position of principal of the Boston Public Latin School.

This school, founded in 1635 and noted for providing education to a long list of prominent men, including Cotton Mather and Benjamin Franklin, had fallen on hard times. Gould's predecessor, William Biglow, had run the school with an iron hand; his overemphasis on corporal punishment was draconian even by the standards of that era. Biglow's drinking problem had exacerbated matters, and the students were in open rebellion. The trustees of the school, who sought a new principal with the youth and vigor needed to overcome the problems facing the institution, eagerly seized upon Harvard president John Thornton Kirkland's proffered candidate. Despite leaving school early, Gould was awarded an A.B. with his class and an A.M.—as was customary in that era—three years later.

Gould's administration of Boston Public Latin spanned fourteen years and was marked by innovation and growth. He expanded the length of instruction from four to five years and introduced the use of detailed report cards, which included systems of "misdemeanor marks" and of measuring student performance during "declamations"—formal speeches that were another Gould innovation. Gould also raised the standards of instruction in both geography and mathematics for the two upper classes, bringing them in line with the entrance requirements of Harvard. Perhaps his most important accomplishment, given the circumstances of his arrival at the school, was the change in student discipline; under Gould the rules were strictly, and fairly, enforced. Enrollment increased from 180 in 1819 to a high of 237 in 1823. Of his students, who regarded Gould warmly, many attained future prominence; most notable were Ralph Waldo Emerson, Samuel Gridley Howe, Charles Francis Adams, Samuel Francis Smith (author of "My Country, 'tis of Thee"), Charles Sumner, Wendell Phillips, and the Reverend Henry Ward Beecher.

Gould took time from his administrative duties for his scholarship, which consisted of a revision of Alexander Adam's *Latin Grammar* (1825) and annotated editions of *Ovid* (1827), *Horace* (1828), and *Virgil* (1829), the first textbooks of their kind to be edited in the United States. Gould also edited *The Prize Book of the Publick Latin School in Boston* (1820–1824). He married Lucretia Dana Goddard in 1823. They had four children, one of whom (his namesake) became a noted astronomer.

In 1828, burdened by overwork and declining health, Gould resigned as principal. He maintained a number of connections with education, however, serving as the first president of the Latin School Association and as a trustee of his alma mater, Dummer Academy. A member of the American Academy of Arts and Sciences, he also served on the Boston School Committee and as a member of that city's Common Council from 1834 to 1837. In the year following his retirement from Boston Public Latin, Gould traveled throughout Europe and then returned to Boston, where he successfully became a merchant, acquired a number of ships, and participated in the highly lucrative trade with Calcutta, India. He died in Boston.

Gould rose from early poverty to make his mark as the head of the Boston Public Latin School. Fourteen innovative years at the head of that institution place him squarely within the ranks of the first generation of educational reformers who effectively reworked the American system of primary education in the first half of the nineteenth century.

• No organized collection of Gould papers appears to have survived; some scattered material is at the Massachusetts Historical Society in Boston. Additional manuscripts relating to his career at the Boston Public Latin School are held by the Boston School Committee. The best source of information on his life and career is Pauline Holmes, *A Tercentenary History of the Boston Public Latin School, 1635–1935* (1935). Obituaries are in the *Boston Transcript*, 25 Oct. 1859, and the *Boston Herald*, 25 and 26 Oct. 1859.

EDWARD L. LACH, JR.

GOULD, Benjamin Apthorp (27 Sept. 1824–26 Nov. 1896), astronomer, was born in Boston, Massachusetts, the son of Benjamin Apthorp Gould, a schoolmaster and merchant, and Lucretia Dana Goddard. He graduated in 1844 from Harvard, where he studied mathematics and the physical sciences under Benjamin Peirce. He then became master at the Roxbury Latin School. At the urging of Sears Cook Walker, one of the pioneers in the American appreciation of German astronomy, Gould began the study of foreign languages and eventually became fluent in German, French, and Spanish. In early 1845, eager to become grounded in the latest and best techniques in astronomical research, Gould began a three-year sojourn in Europe, visiting England, France, Russia, Switzerland, Italy, and Germany. He spent approximately two years in Germany, studying or working with some of the leading German astronomers, including Friedrich Wilhelm Argelander, Johann F. Encke, Karl Friedrich Gauss, and Heinrich Christian Schumacher. He received a Ph.D. in astronomy from Göttingen University in 1848.

Gould returned to the United States in November 1848. Having failed in an effort to be named director of the newly established Nautical Almanac, he spent the next three years as a private tutor teaching modern languages and mathematics in Cambridge, Massachusetts, and rejected a professorship from Göttingen in 1851. In December 1852 he was hired by the U.S. Coast Survey to succeed Walker in conducting longitudinal observations. He remained with the Coast Survey until 1867, often working on a part-time basis. While with the survey, Gould was director of the Dudley Observatory in Albany, New York, from 1855 through January 1859. On the death of his father in 1859, Gould took over the family mercantile business, which he gave up in 1864. In 1861 he married Mary Apthorp Quincy; they had five children. With his wife's financial help he was able to erect a private observatory in Cambridge, Massachusetts. During the Civil War he contracted to reduce the accumulated backlog of observations of the U.S. Naval Observatory. He also worked for the U.S. Sanitary Commission during the war as an actuary and conducted an extensive series of observations on the physical characteristics of members of the Union forces that were later published as *Investigations in the Military and Anthropological Statistics of American Soldiers* (1869). The data provided a unique opportunity to test theories correlating physical characteristics with nationality or ethnic group. In 1863 he was selected an original member of the National Academy of Sciences.

Gould was one of the leading American practitioners of astrometry—the determination of the positions of the stars and planets—of his day. Like his German mentors, he defined astronomy as "the investigation of those laws which govern the motions of the heavenly bodies" (*Reply to the "Statement of the Trustees" of the Dudley Observatory* [1859], p. 94). Like them, he emphasized mathematical rigor and sensitivity to sources of potential error. Also like them, he was uninterested

in the actual physical properties of celestial bodies, which was the realm of astrophysics or physical astronomy. Gould excelled in computation and organization rather than in personal observation, as he was extremely nearsighted. His first major publication (in *The U.S. Naval Astronomical Expedition to the Southern Hemisphere, during the Years 1849–'50–'51–'52*, vol. 3 [1856]), was a discussion of the solar parallax, in which he analyzed and criticized observations made by a number of other astronomers at four different observatories. In 1862 he published a catalog of the positions of forty-eight circumpolar and 128 time stars (*Standard Mean Right Ascensions of Circumpolar and Time Stars, Prepared for the Use of the U.S. Coast Survey*), which incorporated a century of observations and was adopted by the various American astronomical agencies. As a member of the U.S. Coast Survey, he conducted in 1866 the first telegraphic determination of the difference in longitude between Europe and North America, using the newly laid Atlantic cable. In that same year, working with Lewis M. Rutherfurd, a pioneer in astrophotography, Gould explored the application of photographic techniques to astrometry through photographs of the Pleiades and Praesepe clusters.

Gould's contributions to astronomical research during these years were only a part of his larger program to improve the state of American astronomy by disseminating German methodology and by establishing institutions modeled after their counterparts in Germany. His allies in this effort were the members of the Lazzaroni, an informal group of leading research scientists that was led by Alexander Dallas Bache, director of the Coast Survey. Other members included Peirce, Louis Agassiz, and Joseph Henry. Gould's one major success in this regard was his establishment in 1849 of the *Astronomical Journal*, modeled on the German *Astronomische Nachrichten*, which, edited by Schumacher, was the most prestigious astronomical journal in the world. Gould's publication became a major astronomical journal with an international readership. Although Gould discontinued publication of the *Astronomical Journal* in 1861 because of the Civil War, he resurrected it in 1886 after his return to the United States from Argentina.

Balancing this success was Gould's enormous failure as director of the Dudley Observatory. With the backing of the observatory's Scientific Council—Bache, Henry, and Peirce—Gould attempted to make Dudley the epitome of his vision of a research observatory. Instead, in what turned out to be his only opportunity to direct an observatory in the United States, his tenure was marked by a rapidly deteriorating relationship with the observatory's trustees over the question of its ultimate control and direction. Gould insisted that the power to make policy reside with him, not with the trustees. The disagreement quickly became widely publicized and disintegrated into a war of competing pamphlets and newspaper articles. Eventually, the trustees had Gould physically ejected from the observatory. (His residence was on the grounds.)

The events at Dudley polarized the American astronomical community. Although the Lazzaroni remained loyal to Gould, most American astronomers, either out of a dislike of Gould, distrust of the Lazzaroni, or on principle, supported the trustees. In an attempt to marginalize him, Gould's opponents made efforts to find an alternative publication to the *Astronomical Journal*. A national astronomical society was organized by C. H. F. Peters, Gould's former subordinate at Dudley, with the principal purpose of denouncing Gould as incompetent. Members of the Harvard College Observatory staff repeatedly questioned the accuracy of his 1862 circumpolar stellar catalog.

Ironically, in spite of his German education and ties to the German astronomical community, Gould was opposed to the hiring of foreign scholars for American professorships or for observatory directorships. Consequently, two German émigrés to the United States, both of whom directed observatories and held professorships, became Gould's critics.

By the mid-1860s, it appeared that Gould's career in astronomy was over. He had twice (1859, 1866) failed in his effort to become director of the Harvard College Observatory. A clash with his erstwhile mentor, Peirce, who had become director of the Coast Survey in 1867, had led to Gould's severing of his attachment to that organization. His negative reputation was secure. Unwilling to compromise or accept defeat gracefully, Gould inevitably antagonized his friends and foes. Henry noted in his letter to Bache of 18 September 1858, in the midst of the Dudley controversy, that "[Gould] has more personal enemies than any person with whom I am acquainted." More recent scholarship has suggested that Gould's mood swings, apparent paranoia, inability to compromise, and hostility to criticism, which was especially conspicuous during the Dudley episode, may have had its roots in mental illness (see James, p. 67).

In 1865 Gould began to explore the possibility of establishing a private observatory in South America. He gained the attention of Argentine Minister to the United States Domingo Faustino Sarmiento, who would become president of Argentina in 1868. The following year Sarmiento invited Gould to establish a national observatory for Argentina. Viewing this invitation as a godsend, Gould became director of the observatory at Córdoba in 1870. While waiting for the arrival of the principal instruments for the Córdoba Observatory, Gould's staff determined the magnitudes and positions of all stars in the southern sky that could be seen with the naked eye (Gould's nearsightedness precluded him from making these observations). Gould published the results as the "Uranometria Argentina" in volume one of *Resultados del Observatorio Nacional Argentino en Córdoba* (1879). These observations established the existence of "Gould's Belt" of bright stars, which intersected the plane of the Milky Way at an angle of twenty degrees. An additional fourteen volumes of *Resultados* appeared before Gould's death. Gould and his staff eventually provided the positions of 73,160 stars located between 23 and 80 degrees south declination in the zone-catalogs, and 32,448 in the more accurate general catalog.

Although professionally productive, the Argentine portion of Gould's life was marked by personal tragedy. In 1874 two of his children drowned in an Argentine stream. Nine years later his wife died during one of their visits to the United States. Gould died in Cambridge, Massachusetts, having held no positions after his return to the United States in 1885.

• There is no major collection of Gould manuscripts. The best bibliography was compiled by George C. Comstock in *Biographical Memoirs of the National Academy of Sciences* 17 (1924): 171–80. Gould's German experiences are discussed in D. B. Herrmann, "B. A. Gould and his *Astronomical Journal*," *Journal for the History of Astronomy* 2 (1971): 98–108. Two very different interpretations of the significance of the events in Albany are given in Richard G. Olson, "The Gould Controversy at Dudley Observatory: Public and Professional Values in Conflict," *Annals of Science* 27 (1971): 265–76, and Mary Ann James, *Elites in Conflict: The Antebellum Clash over the Dudley Observatory* (1987). Gould's Argentine experience is discussed in John E. Hodge, "Benjamin Apthorp Gould and the Founding of the Argentine Observatory," *Americas* 28 (1972): 152–75. For the Argentine perspective on Gould and his role in its national history, see Marcelo Montserrat, "La introdución de la ciencia moderna en Argentina: el caso Gould," *Criterio* 44 (25 Nov. 1971): 726–29, and Marcelo Montserrat, "Sarmiento y los fundamentos de su politica cientifica," *Sur: Revista semestral Sarmiento* 341 (July–Dec. 1977): 98–109.

MARC ROTHENBERG

GOULD, Chester (20 Nov. 1900–11 May 1985), cartoonist, was born in Pawnee, Oklahoma, the son of Gilbert R. Gould, a printer and publisher of a weekly newspaper, and Alice Miller. After two years at Oklahoma A&M, Gould transferred to Northwestern University in Evanston, Illinois, in 1921; he majored in marketing and commerce by day and attended the Art Institute of Chicago by night. Graduating in 1923, he worked at a variety of art jobs until landing in 1924 at William Randolph Hearst's *Chicago American*, where he did a couple of weekly comic features capitalizing on the emerging popularity of radio—*Radio Cats* and *Radio Lanes*—and then a daily syndicated strip called *Fillum Fables* in imitation of Ed Wheelan's burlesque of the movies, *Minute Movies*. With this modest success, Gould married Edna Gauger in November 1926; they had one child. But Gould was frustrated in his ambition to be syndicated by the Midwest's largest newspaper enterprise, the Chicago Tribune–New York Daily News Syndicate, headed by Joseph Medill Patterson. He had been submitting ideas for comic strips to Patterson since arriving in Chicago. After a decade of rejections, his persistence was rewarded: Patterson finally bought Gould's strip about a detective called *Plainclothes Tracy*.

The inspiration for the strip came from the front pages of the newspapers, which daily headlined bribery, extortion, graft, corruption, arson, and shootouts in the streets. Raised in the frontier traditions of swift justice that still prevailed in the Oklahoma Territory at the turn of the century, Gould was disgusted by the seeming triumph of gangsterism in Chicago during Prohibition. What was needed, he said, was the kind of incorruptible cop who would shoot known hoodlums on sight, a champion of law and order and "direct action, who could dish it out to the underworld exactly as they dished it out—only better. An individual who could toss the hot iron back at them along with a smack on the jaw thrown in for good measure" (Sheridan, pp. 121–22). Gould appropriated the persona of the hardboiled detective that had been flourishing in pulp magazines and, in visualizing his hero, gave him the chisel-jawed profile he associated with Sherlock Holmes. Al Capone had just been convicted of income-tax evasion and shipped off to Alcatraz when Gould's *Tracy* arrived on Patterson's desk in the summer of 1931. Wiring back that the idea had "possibilities," Patterson changed the name of the feature to *Dick Tracy* (observing that "they call plainclothes detectives 'dicks'") and outlined the opening sequence that established Tracy's character and the motive for his dogged crusade against crime.

Dick Tracy began as a Sunday feature in the *Detroit Mirror* on 4 October 1931; the daily series started on 12 October. Until *Tracy*'s debut, the newspaper continuity comic strip had focused on one of two extremes—exotic adventure or domestic intrigue. *Tracy* brought the excitement of adventure to its readers' front doors when Gould's cop began fighting contemporary crime in everybody's hometown. The strip was a success from the first, its popularity springing from its overt recognition and exploitation of the violence in American life. Tracy's first foe, Big Boy, was a scarcely veiled version of Capone; in the following spring, Gould capitalized on the sensation of the kidnapping of Charles Lindbergh's son, staging a blatantly similar crime in the strip. Raw violence on the comics page began with *Dick Tracy*; until then, gunplay and bloodshed had been nearly taboo. Gould changed that. His criminals were compunctionless brutes specializing in cruelty, and he delineated their crimes and foul deeds in unblinking detail—knifings, shootings, clubbings, throttlings, in short, death and maiming by every known means. Gould seemed to delight in submitting his hero (as well as countless innocent women and children) to physical torture at the hands of the crooks, and Tracy was plunged into and extricated from a morbidly fascinating series of outlandish death-trap situations. Retribution was dealt out to every miscreant in visual terms as graphically detailed as those that recorded their crimes: they died by drowning, freezing, impalement, crushing, mauling, hail of hot lead, and, Gould's specialty, a bullet between the eyes, depicted in dramatic close-up. But Gould's strip was more than a string of violent shoot-'em-ups. Tracy combined intelligence with action. And Gould was quick to adopt the realism of authentic police procedures and kept himself up to date on modern methods. He even anticipated some innovations: the use of closed-circuit television to monitor potential criminal activities in such places as banks and two-way wrist-radio communication.

Gould's achievement as a cartoonist arises from his pictures as much as from his stories. His drawing style is simple, almost geometrically so, liberally deploying solid flat blacks for characters' clothes and for modeling objects. The result is a stark rendition of reality—planes of black giving definition to planes of white (and vice versa) with uncompromising contrast. The strip is an exercise in black and white both graphically and philosophically: there are no grays in Gould's moral convictions either. Despite the precision of his technique, however, Gould's graphic treatment is not photographic in the illustrative manner; it is only semirealistic. It is a style that permitted Gould a dramatic deviation from naturalism. He created a gallery of ghoulish villains, caricatures of evil that underscored the moral of his strip: crime doesn't pay, and a life of crime will put one in daily communion with such creatures as *these*—Pruneface, Flattop, the Mole, Shoulders, B-B Eyes, the Brow, Shakey, Influence, Mumbles, none of them realistically rendered. All are grotesques, gargoyles of criminality. Hence the greatness of the strip: Gould's unique accomplishment was to combine realistic storytelling and graphic moralizing.

In the 1960s Gould took a long detour into science fantasy: inspired, no doubt, by his success at predicting technical advances, he invented the "space coupe," an interplanetary vehicle powered by magnetism, and he forthwith sent Tracy and his to the moon, where they discovered a race of horned humanoid beings. In his last years on the feature, Gould's championing of law and order became strident as he spoke out against the coddling of criminals that he saw in legal precedents that established rights for criminals. Gould retired from the strip with the installment for 27 December 1977, leaving the production of the strip to others. Gould died at his farm near Woodstock, Illinois, which he had purchased in 1936 with the first fruits of his success and where he worked on the strip daily except for the two days every week that he spent in his office at the Tribune Tower in downtown Chicago. One of the earliest straight adventure story comic strips and the first procedural detective feature, *Dick Tracy* set the pace for virtually every detective comic strip concocted thereafter. Gould created a host of memorable characters like B.O. Plenty, Gravel Gertie, and Vitamin Flintheart as well as his famed rogues' gallery, but Tracy was his most famous grotesque, a fiction as archetypal of his genre as Sherlock Holmes or Tarzan.

• Much of Gould's original art is in the possession of the International Museum of Cartoon Art in Boca Raton, Florida. Jay Maeder, *Dick Tracy: The Official Biography* (1990), has biographical material on Chester Gould as well as on his creation. And Bill Crouch, Jr., ed., *Dick Tracy: America's Most Famous Detective* (1987), includes autobiographical essays by Gould as well as reprints of the strip as produced first by Gould and then by his successors, novelist Max Allan Collins, initially with Rick Fletcher doing the drawing, then with

Dick Locher at the drawingboard. Also useful are John Culhane, "Dick Tracy: The First Law and Order Man," *Argosy*, June 1974, pp. 20–21, 44–47, and Herb Galewitz, ed., *The Celebrated Cases of Dick Tracy: 1931–1951* (1970), which includes biographical front matter and reprints several of the most famous of the strip's sequences. In Galewitz, ed., *Dick Tracy, the Thirties: Tommyguns and Hard Times* (1978), many of the strip's earliest stories are reprinted. Standard reference works on the comics also include biographical details: Martin Sheridan, *The Comics and Their Creators* (1944; repr. 1971); Coulton Waugh, *The Comics* (1947); and Stephen Becker, *Comic Art in America* (1959). An obituary appears in the *New York Times*, 12 May 1985.

ROBERT C. HARVEY

GOULD, George Jay (6 Feb. 1864–16 May 1923), businessman, was born in New York City, the son of Jay Gould and Helen Day Miller. As the eldest son of the era's most extraordinary financier, George Gould inherited the glory and the burden of an heir apparent who from the first was expected to follow in his father's formidable footsteps. At nineteen, after graduating from private school, he was made a partner in the brokerage house of Washington E. Connor after a brief apprenticeship with that veteran broker and Gould loyalist. On his twenty-first birthday he received a seat on the New York Stock Exchange and his father's power of attorney. As he took on more responsibilities in the family companies, he found himself dealing with the titans of Wall Street at the highest levels of business and finance.

Unlike his father, who was shy and abstemious in everything from personal habits to speech, George was affable and outgoing, fond of company and comfortable in society. He played the part of the dandy with his trim moustache and fashionable clothes. His tastes ran to sports, parties, clubs, and the theater. He became an excellent polo player and did much to establish the game in the United States. These qualities enabled George to escape the aura of distrust and notoriety that clung to Jay. Unfortunately, he also lacked his father's shrewd eye, penetrating intellect, ingenuity, and voracious appetite for work. George was somewhat slow of wit and mercurial of temperament, prone to ill-considered decisions. Where his father absorbed everything and revealed nothing, George absorbed little and concealed less.

In 1886 George provoked a strain in the Gould family circle by marrying Edith Kingdon, an actress renowned for her green eyes and hourglass figure. Although his father accepted the liaison gracefully, his mother, a rigidly proper Murray Hill matron, never reconciled herself to the match. The marriage produced seven children.

When his father died in 1892, George became fully responsible for the Gould business empire. That empire revolved around three great enterprises: a large system of railroads of which the Missouri Pacific was the centerpiece, Western Union Telegraph Company, and the Manhattan Elevated Railway. All three suffered from the depression of 1893–1897, competitive struggles, and public clamor for regulation or reform.

In his handling of these properties, and a host of other business interests, George proved utterly unequal to the legacy of his father. Fawned over by associates and rivals alike, hailed as the new Napoleon of business, he came to believe the flattery heaped on him. The Gould rail system, which Jay had left in decent shape, deteriorated steadily as George made little effort to master the details of its needs or character. As a result, when the depression lifted, he was in no position to profit from the massive increase in traffic.

Rather than devote close attention to managing his properties, George conceived a grand scheme to create the first true rail system running from coast to coast. This ambition locked him in mortal combat with Edward H. Harriman, the most talented railroad man in the nation, and the Pennsylvania Railroad, the most powerful system in the nation. Gould bought some roads, extended others, and undertook to build a new line from Oakland to Salt Lake City. The Western Pacific took seven years to construct and cost a staggering $80 million; other projects also soaked up alarming sums of money.

Such a bold campaign would have challenged the skills of Jay Gould; it utterly overwhelmed George, who spent much of his time hosting lavish entertainments at his huge mansion in Lakewood, New Jersey, or flitting off to Europe for prolonged vacations. These absences paralyzed his complex business ventures, for he insisted on making all key decisions himself. Many able officers left his employ, and Wall Street investors who had long followed the Gould properties abandoned them in exasperation.

The financial panic of 1907 dealt Gould's grand scheme a blow from which it never recovered. In 1911 he was forced to surrender control of the Gould railroads to the bankers. Weary of strife, he also sold out the family's interest in Western Union and Manhattan Elevated and invested the proceeds. Soon afterward he retired from active business and was content to manage his investments.

His private life was no less troubled. A bitter squabble among Jay Gould's six children over his estate led to a suit in 1916 charging George with mismanagement. For eleven years a series of suits, each more rancorous than the last, dragged the Gould name through the headlines and split the family forever. Dogged with woes, George entered into an affair with a showgirl named Guinevere Jeanne Sinclair, who bore him three children. He remained with Edith until her death in November 1921, then married Guinevere the following May and took her to Europe to live.

Long a sufferer from high blood pressure and heart trouble, George took ill after a visit to the newly opened tomb of King Tutankhamen in Egypt. After his death from pneumonia, the tabloids pronounced him another victim of King Tut's curse. But the true curse of George Gould's life was that of extravagant expectations. Ironically, he was the only one of Jay Gould's four sons who did not make a fortune on his own in addition to the spectacular inheritance shared by each.

• There is no collection of George Gould papers, nor is there a full biography. The most recent scholarly portraits are in Maury Klein, *The Life and Legend of Jay Gould* (1986), and the same author's "George J. Gould," in *Encyclopedia of American Business History and Biography: Railroads in the Age of Regulation, 1900–1980*, ed. Keith L. Bryant (1988). Edwin P. Hoyt, *The Goulds: A Social History* (1969), is a broader portrait but not always reliable. See also Ernest Howard, *Wall Street Fifty Years after Erie* (1923), and Burton J. Hendrick, "The Passing of a Great Railroad Dynasty," *McClure's Magazine* 38 (March 1912): 483–501.

MAURY KLEIN

GOULD, George Milbry (8 Nov. 1848–8 Aug. 1922), medical editor and writer, was born in Auburn, Maine, the son of George Thomas Gould and Eliza A. Lapham, professions unknown. His mother died when he was very young, and he moved with his father and stepmother to Salina, Ohio. He received his early education in the Salina public schools. In 1861, at the start of the Civil War, he enlisted in the Sixty-third Ohio Volunteers of the Union army as a drummer boy. He served for eighteen months before he was discharged because of illness. In 1864 he enlisted as a soldier in the 141st Ohio Volunteers and was discharged when the war ended. He attended Ohio Wesleyan University and graduated in 1873 with an A.B. To pay for his undergraduate education, Gould worked as a compositor in a printing shop. He left Ohio, entered the Harvard Divinity School, and graduated in 1874 with a bachelor of sacred theology degree, followed by postgraduate studies in Paris, Leipzig, and Berlin.

Gould returned to the United States and accepted a position as pastor of a Unitarian church in Chillicote, Ohio. He earned a small salary; to supplement his income he bought a partnership in a job printing shop and worked there during the week. After a year he resigned his position at the church but continued working in the printing shop; in 1876 he opened an art and book store in Chillicote. That same year he married Harriet Fletcher Cartwright; they had no children. In 1885 he gave up his business interests to enter the Jefferson Medical College in Philadelphia, Pennsylvania.

Gould graduated from Jefferson Medical College as president of his class in 1888 and immediately went into the practice of ophthalmology in Philadelphia. In 1889 he designed the cemented bifocal, which was an improvement on the bifocals developed by Benjamin Franklin. He developed a number of optical devices used in examining the eyes and improved the methods used to do refractions. He was a leader and originator in the area of visual corrections. From 1892 to 1894 he was an ophthalmic surgeon at the Philadelphia General Hopital, but he resigned in 1894 and acknowledged that he was not a surgeon. For his accomplishments in the medical specialty of ophthalmology, Gould was named the first recipient of the Doyne Medal awarded at the Ophthalmological Congress held at Oxford University in 1906. From 1908 to 1911 he lived and worked in Ithaca, New York. After that time he lived in Atlantic City, New Jersey.

Gould is known more for his contributions to medical literature than for his ophthalmology practice. In 1886, while still enrolled at Jefferson Medical College, in collaboration with Lawrence Webster Fox he published *A Compend of the Diseases of the Eye*. This publication was the first of many medical books and articles written by Gould and in collaboration with others. His interest in medical lexicography led to the publication of a number of dictionaries, the first of which was published in 1890; more than a half million copies of his dictionaries were sold.

In addition to his medical writings, Gould wrote poetry, essays, philosophy, biographies, history, psychological studies (of Thomas DeQuincey, Thomas Carlyle, and George Eliot in light of his eyestrain theory), and other diverse works. He wrote 416 titles in all.

Gould served as the editor of the *Medical News* from 1891 to 1895, of the *Philadelphia Medical Journal* from 1898 to 1900, and of *American Medicine* from 1901 to 1906. His work as an editor and writer put him on familiar terms with the medical publishing houses of Philadelphia and well-known medical teachers and scientists of Philadelphia. Gould was a social and political conservative particularly with regard to the conduct of the medical profession. Established precedents rather than experimental ideas were his criteria for accepting new concepts. He was a strong, aggressive, and enthusiastic individual, rarely discouraged, and hardly modest. As editor of various medical journals "his editorials were read and his criticisms feared."

Gould was an active member of professional and social organizations. He had a broad interest in all aspects of medical education, although he never taught at any of the Philadelphia medical schools. He was a member of the American Academy of Medicine, a national organization that advocated a four-year bachelor of arts degree as a prerequisite for admission into medical school. In 1895 he was elected president of the academy. He was a founder of the Association of Medical Libraries (now the Medical Library Association) and was elected its first president in May 1898. As an active participant in the association he was responsible for establishing a medical library duplicate exchange. In 1917 he married Laura Stedman; they had no children. Gould died at his home in Atlantic City.

• Major works by Gould include *New Medical Dictionary* (ten editions between 1891 and 1900), *An American Year Book of Medicine and Surgery* (1896–1905), *A Cyclopedia of Practical Medicine and Surgery* (1900), *Biographic Clinics* (6 vols., 1903–1909), and *The Jefferson Medical College of Philadelphia* (2 vols., 1904). Two retrospectives on Gould's life and career were published shortly after his death: *Medical Life*, Nov. 1922, and *American Journal of Ophthalmology*, Jan. 1923. A modern study is Marjorie B. Wanarka, "Dr. George Milbry Gould: Ophthalmologist and First President of the Medical Library Association," *Bulletin of the History of Medicine* 42 (1968): 265–71. Obituaries are in the *New York Times*, 9 and 10 Aug. 1922, and the *Journal of the American Medical Association* 79 (26 Aug. 1922): 756.

SAM ALEWITZ

GOULD, Hannah Flagg (3 Sept. 1789–5 Sept. 1865), poet, was born in Lancaster, Massachusetts, the daughter of Benjamin Gould and Griselda Apthorp Flagg. In a number of poems she commemorated the military career of her father, who led minutemen at the battle of Lexington, was the last to leave Charlestown neck when Continental forces retreated from Bunker Hill, and commanded the guard at West Point when Major John André was captured. In 1808 the family moved to Newburyport, where Gould remained, without marrying, for fifty-seven years. Known for her wit, moral sentiments, and loyalty to her father (to whom she was a constant companion for fifty years), she possessed a talent for light verse. In her mid-thirties she began writing poems for magazines and annuals. Her admirers brought these together with some unpublished works to make up her first volume, *Poems* (1832). Remarkably popular, the book was reprinted in 1833, 1835, and 1836. The second and third volumes of her *Poems* appeared in 1836 and 1841.

Gould remained popular throughout much of the nineteenth century, gaining favorable reviews and appearing in leading magazines and anthologies. Her work was compared to that of William Wordsworth in England and William Cullen Bryant, Fitz-Greene Halleck, and (most often) Lydia Sigourney in America. Edgar Allan Poe, somewhat skeptical of her talent, claimed that her reputation resulted from the "*frequency* of her appeals to the attention of the public." Her popularity had other explanations as well. She lent charm to the familiar and even homely aspects of daily existence. Moreover, as a woman writer, she managed her public role in a way likely to promote acceptance. "It was the habit of Miss Gould," one obituary noted, "to choose some simple theme pertaining to everyday life, and then, while engaged in her domestic avocations, or during her rambles on the banks of her beloved Merrimac[k], to weave it into rhyme." Her poems, short and unaffected, usually treat religious or patriotic themes. Her diction is rarely fresh, though her poetic subjects are often winning and occasionally arresting, sometimes because of her close observation of nature, and at other times because she treated topics commonly deemed not "poetic," as in her celebration of "The Steam-Boat." Some of her most interesting poems strive to reach beyond the domestic circle to engage political and moral issues of the public sphere.

Gould was particularly effective when she brought her simplicity, sincerity, and moral sensibility to bear on the issue of slavery in such poems as "The Black at Church" and "The Slave Mother's Prayer." Here she crosses racial lines and speaks from the perspective of the oppressed. She also gained many readers when her poems for children—"The Frost" and "The Pebble," for example—became standard fare in school readers. Her most significant publications, in addition to *Poems*, were a collection of articles entitled *Gathered Leaves* (1846), *The Mother's Dream, and Other Poems* (1853), *Hymns and Other Poems for Children* (1854), and *Poems for Little Ones* (1863). She also wrote occasional works, producing "an original hymn" for memorial services in Newburyport and a poem on the Bunker Hill monument, *The Rising Monument* (1840). She died in Newburyport.

Given that Gould's poetry is marked neither by stylistic innovations nor by depth of thought, she seems destined to retain only a small role in literary history. Nevertheless, her writing possesses a modest charm and serves to illustrate important tendencies in the popular poetry of the nineteenth century, especially through the portrayal of domesticity and the reliance on sentiment.

• Works by Hannah Flagg Gould not cited above include *The Mermaid's Cave* (1832), with music by C. E. Horn; *The Golden Vase: A Gift for the Young* (1843); *The Diosma: A Perennial* (1851); and *The Youth's Coronal* (1851). Few of her letters and manuscripts are still extant, and these are widely scattered. The best single collection of such material is in the Alderman Library, University of Virginia, which has eleven manuscripts and nine letters.

For biographical information, consult B. A. Gould, *The Family of Zaccheus Gould of Topsfield* (1895); J. J. Currier, *History of Newburyport, Massachusetts* (2 vols., 1906–1909); Sidney Perley, *The Poets of Essex County, Massachusetts* (1889); Boston *Transcript*, 6 Sept. 1865; *Daily Herald* (Newburyport), 7, 8 Sept. 1865.

For contemporary reviews and commentary, see "Poems. By Miss H. F. Gould," *The New England Magazine* 2 (May 1832), 435–37; "Literary Portraits: No. V. Miss H. F. Gould," *The New England Magazine* 4 (Apr. 1833), 309–13; "Miss Gould's *Poems*," *American Monthly Review* 2 (July–Dec. 1832), 75–78; "Mrs. Sigourney and Miss Gould," *North American Review* 89 (Oct. 1835), 430–53; Edgar Allan Poe, "Critical Notices," *Southern Literary Messenger* 2 (Jan. 1836), 112–17; "Our Female Poets," *Baltimore Literary Monument* (Nov. 1838), 72–83.

For brief mention in recent criticism, see Emily Stipes Watts, *The Poetry of American Women from 1632 to 1945* (1977), and Lawrence Buell, *New England Literary Culture* (1986).

KENNETH M. PRICE

GOULD, Jack (5 Feb. 1914–24 May 1993), journalist, was born John Ludlow Gould in New York City, the son of John W. Gould and Evelyn Fisk. His father was an engineer and automobile executive who died when his son was ten. Gould grew up in comfortable but not affluent circumstances. He attended two prep schools in Connecticut before receiving his high school diploma from the Brown School in New York City in 1932. Already an enthusiastic "ham" radio operator and a chain smoker, he lacked the money to attend college. He joined the staff of the *New York Herald Tribune* as a copy boy. The editor, Stanley Walker, spotted Gould's talents as a reporter, and he was soon covering general news. Within five years, Gould had begun to specialize in the entertainment industry. His repeated exclusives about the operations of the Federal Theater Project in New York City led the drama critic of the *New York Times*, Brooks Atkinson, to hire him away in October 1937 "in self-defense, for you were committing almost daily nuisance by scooping us in the *Tribune*" (Atkinson to Gould, 28 July 1954, Gould papers).

Over the next seven years Gould covered show business and night clubs for the *Times*. He developed especially close ties to the president of the American Federation of Musicians, James C. Petrillo. In 1938 he married Carmen Letitia Lewis, a Texas native and executive secretary to theatrical producers Harold Lindsay and Russel Crouse; they had three sons. Eye problems and chronic stomach ulcers kept him out of military service during World War II. In 1944, when the radio critic of the *Times* relinquished his post Gould succeeded him.

Following the war Gould moved his family to Connecticut where he wrote the reviews of television programs that he then phoned in to the *Times*. As the postwar boom in television commenced, his reporting and criticism in the nation's most influential newspaper made him an important force as the new medium evolved. The columns that appeared each Sunday provided him with the opportunity to comment on the major issues that television faced in areas of censorship, blacklisting of alleged Communists, live drama, and the social responsibilities of broadcasters.

The 1950s brought Gould to the peak of his impact as a journalist. He gave an important endorsement to the plays of Paddy Chayefsky and Rod Serling during what was called "the golden age of television." His favorable notices advanced the television careers of David Brinkley and Harry Reasoner, among others. Gould criticized the networks for their cowardice in the face of campaigns to blacklist performers with alleged subversive backgrounds. He urged executives to support live dramatic programming that challenged audiences, sought more women before and behind the cameras, and advocated the televising of congressional proceedings.

In 1954 Gould briefly left the *Times* to work in press relations at the Columbia Broadcasting System, but he returned to his post as critic after six uncomfortable weeks. Two years later, his observation that evangelist Oral Roberts provided "miracles on a weekly basis" (*Times*, 15 Feb. 1956) brought more than four thousand letters of protest. Later that year during the Suez Crisis, the networks failed to televise proceedings of the United Nations. Gould said that "the national electronic communication system made an absolute mockery of its obligation to serve the public interest" (*Times*, 31 Oct. 1956). His hard-hitting columns temporarily provoked the networks to devote more attention to the crisis. For his coverage of this episode, he won the George Foster Peabody Award in 1957. He had earlier received the George Polk and Page One awards for his reporting and criticism in 1953. At the height of the quiz show scandals in 1959 he criticized fellow reporters for accepting gratuities and gifts from corporate sponsors, a practice that he had earlier discontinued for himself.

During the late 1950s and into the 1960s Gould became progressively more disenchanted with the direction of television, as filmed dramas and game shows replaced the spontaneity of live programs. He believed that television had failed to realize its promise as a medium that could sustain democracy and educate the public while remaining a place for lively and interesting popular culture. He praised the work of Newton Minow at the Federal Communications Commission during President John F. Kennedy's administration to revitalize what Minow called "the vast wasteland" of television. At the *New York Times*, the retirement of Turner Catledge, the executive editor with whom he had worked harmoniously, brought in new editors who were less sympathetic to Gould's straightforward style of reporting and criticism. By this time he was telling family members that one dependable feature of television was that each year saw it grow worse than it had been a year earlier. In early 1971 he stated, "I'm really written out after looking at the screen after twenty years" (Gould to Lewis L. Gould, 30 Jan. 1971). Health problems stemming from his smoking intensified in the early 1970s, and he retired in February 1972. At the time, documentary producer and former CBS executive Fred Friendly said that Gould was the "conscience of an industry that too often could not find its own" (*New York Times*, 27 Feb. 1972). Gould regarded Friendly's phrase as pompous, but for many of his readers the judgment well summed up what Gould had meant to broadcasting during the first three decades of television. In 1974 he moved with his wife to Berkeley, California, where he died two decades later.

• Jack Gould's papers are in the possession of the author. There are materials about his career at the *New York Times* in the archives of the newspaper in New York City and in the Turner Catledge Papers, Mississippi State University. Other information is in the Newton Minow Papers and Lester Markel Papers at the Wisconsin State Historical Society, and in the Lyndon B. Johnson Presidential Library in Austin, Tex. Gould's own writings include a children's book, *All about Radio and Television* (1953); "Television Today—A Critic's Appraisal," *New York Times Magazine*, 8 Apr. 1956; "Quiz for TV—How Much Fakery?" *New York Times Magazine*, 25 Oct. 1959. For the best example of his daily criticism, see "Disgrace of the Networks," the *New York Times*, 31 Oct. 1956. Contemporary assessments of Gould's influence as a critic include Leon Morse, "Inside Jack Gould," *Television* 15 (Nov. 1958): 49–51, 94–95; "Cactus Jack," *Time*, 11 Oct. 1963, p. 58; and Fred Friendly, "Dear Jack Gould, They Say You've Retired," the *New York Times*, 27 Feb. 1972. A biographical study is Louis Carl Saalbach, "Jack Gould: Social Critic of the Television Medium, 1947–1972" (Ph.D. diss., Ohio State Univ., 1980). A skeptical view of Gould's impact on television is William Boddy, *Fifties Television: The Industry and Its Critics* (1990). Richard F. Shepard, *The Paper's Papers: A Reporter's Journey through the Archives of the New York Times* (1996), includes a brief chapter about Gould and his criticism. An obituary containing some factual errors is in the *New York Times*, 25 May 1993.

LEWIS L. GOULD

GOULD, James (5 Dec. 1770–11 May 1838), lawyer and judge, was born in Branford, Connecticut, the son of William Gould, a doctor, and Mary Foote. As a boy he suffered from gout, which affected his eyesight. He was educated at home and then in local schools. In 1787 he entered Yale College, where he had to have books read to him. Despite his poor eyesight, Gould graduated first in his class and delivered the salutatory oration "On the Origin and Progress of History, and the Utility of Historic Knowledge," for which he received the Noah Webster Prize. In college he was known as "a remarkably handsome young man of elegant figure and graceful manners" (Fisher, p. 17).

After teaching school in Connecticut and Maryland for two years, Gould read law in New Haven and then became a tutor at Yale in 1793. Two years later he enrolled as a student at the fledgling law school that Tapping Reeve had opened in Litchfield, Connecticut, in 1784. Gould completed the course in 1798 and was admitted to the bar. He settled in Litchfield and married Sally McCurdy Tracy, daughter of Uriah Tracy, a prominent Connecticut Federalist. They had eight sons and one daughter.

In 1798 Reeve became a judge on the Connecticut Superior Court. To continue the law school, which by that time had more than forty students, he needed an assistant to teach classes in his absence. Reeve asked Gould to join him, and the two men operated the school together for the next two decades.

Gould and Reeve made a good team. Reeve was more commanding and eloquent in court and classroom, while Gould emphasized logic and clarity. In fact, Gould spoke so slowly that his students could transcribe every word. One of them recalled that Gould "never aspired to high strains of impassioned eloquence, and rarely, if ever, addressed himself to the passions of the court and jury, but to their understanding only" (Baldwin, p. 473). Gould taught courses on pleading, real property, municipal law, and practicing law in Connecticut. He also published *A Treatise on the Principles of Pleading in Civil Actions* (1832), which was often reprinted during the nineteenth century.

During Gould's tenure at Litchfield, more than 800 students passed through the program. They included educator Horace Mann, three future Supreme Court justices (Ward Hunt, Henry Baldwin, and Levi Woodbury), and John C. Calhoun, who found Gould's style of argument persuasive and his Federalist politics unpalatable. The law school had a significant impact on the development of American legal education in the era before university-based law schools.

In 1816 Gould was appointed to the Connecticut Superior Court and Court of Errors, where he served for three years. His penchant for lengthy concurring opinions did not endear him to his colleagues on the court. After the Federalist party lost control of the Connecticut state government in 1818, Gould was not reappointed to his judicial position. Still, he remained a Federalist throughout his life. When an issue arose in the late 1820s about whether New England Federalists had contemplated a breakup of the union in 1804, Gould wrote a lengthy and vigorous defense of his father-in-law, Uriah Tracy, against the charges made by former president John Quincy Adams about secession sentiment in Connecticut and elsewhere. Historians have not found Gould's arguments compelling.

In the years that followed, Gould did not return to his legal practice. For the rest of his working life, he gave most of his attention to the operation of the law school. Judge Reeve retired from the school in 1820 with bad feelings toward Gould over the finances of the school. As part of an agreement made at Reeve's retirement, Gould provided his former mentor with a share of the tuition from the school. The awkward arrangement intensified the existing rancor between the families, with the Reeves spreading tales that Gould had a drinking problem. The quarrel persisted until Reeve's death in 1823. Gould then became the dominant figure in the school's affairs. He enlisted Jabez Huntington, a future U.S. senator, to assist him in teaching. The course of study took fourteen months to complete and featured moot courts over which Gould presided. In 1823 forty-four students enrolled in the program, the second largest class in the history of the school.

Changes in the way lawyers were trained, however, soon ended the active life of the Litchfield institution. Harvard had founded a law school in 1817, and Yale had followed in 1824. By 1833 the number of students at Litchfield had dwindled to six. Meanwhile, the aging Gould found his health failing. He closed the law school permanently in 1833 and died five years later in Litchfield. Gould was one of the important figures in the formative history of American legal education, and the school that he and Reeve operated provided in its time "the best professional instruction available in the United States" (Sutherland, p. 29).

• Gould's personal papers have not survived, but letters and documents relating to his life are in the manuscript collections of the Litchfield Historical Society, Litchfield, Conn., which also holds extensive records about the Litchfield Law School. Manuscript notebooks of law students from the school are at Yale Law School and Columbia Law School. Henry Adams, ed., *Documents Relating to New-England Federalism* (1877), reprints Gould's 1829 letter defending Uriah Tracy. For biographical information, see Samuel Church, "Address on the Occasion of the Centennial Celebration 1851," *Litchfield County Centennial Celebration, Held at Litchfield, Conn., 13th and 14th of August, 1851* (1851); Franklin Bowditch Dexter, *Biographical Sketches of the Graduates of Yale College*, vol. 4: *July, 1778–June, 1792* (1907); Simeon E. Baldwin, "James Gould, 1770–1838," in vol. 2 of *Great American Lawyers*, ed. William Draper Lewis (1907); Dwight C. Kilbourn, *The Bench and Bar of Litchfield County, Connecticut, 1709–1909* (1909); Samuel H. Fisher, *The Litchfield Law School, 1775–1833* (1933); and Fisher, *The Litchfield Law School, 1775–1833, Biographical Catalogue of Students* (1946). Arthur E. Sutherland, *The Law at Harvard* (1967), has a brief assessment of the law school, and Donald F. Melhorn, Jr., "A Moot Court Exercise: Debating Judicial Review Prior to *Marbury v. Madison*," *Constitutional Commentary* 12 (Winter 1995): 327–54, looks at the school in operation. An obituary is in the *Litchfield Enquirer*, 24 May 1838.

LEWIS L. GOULD

GOULD, Jay (27 May 1836–2 Dec. 1892), financier, was born Jason Gould in Roxbury, New York, the son of John Gould, a farmer and storekeeper, and Mary More. A frail, undersized child, Gould revealed early in life the characteristics that would make him formidable in business: a quick mind, perseverance, an indomitable will, far-ranging intellect, remarkable self-control, a fierce drive to succeed, and a bent for the practical. After attending a local school and nearby academy, Gould worked in his father's store and at night taught himself mathematics and surveying. At sixteen he operated his own survey business; at nineteen he completed an impressive history of his native Delaware County.

In 1856, with Zadock Pratt, a noted tanner, Gould built a tannery in the wilderness of eastern Pennsylvania; the village was named Gouldsboro in his honor. Three years later Pratt sold out to Gould and Charles M. Leupp. Disagreements between the new partners were compounded by Leupp's mental illness, which led to his suicide in October 1859. The episode forced Gould from the tanning field. Years later his critics twisted it into a grotesque myth that he had driven Leupp to shoot himself.

Gould turned his attention to Wall Street, where he again displayed a phenomenal capacity. Without money or connections during the turbulent Civil War years, he mastered the intricacies of finance with amazing speed. He also met Helen Day Miller, the daughter of a prominent merchant. Their marriage took place in 1863 and produced six children. For the rest of his life Gould devoted himself to business and family. No other figure who achieved such public notoriety ever lived a quieter or more proper domestic life.

In 1867 Gould thrust himself into the public eye when he and James Fisk (1834–1872) joined Daniel Drew in foiling the attempt of Cornelius Vanderbilt (1794–1877) to gain control of the Erie Railroad. The "Erie war" that followed became a Wall Street legend. Left with the bankrupt Erie after Drew defected to Vanderbilt, Gould and Fisk dazzled the business world with a series of audacious moves, including an alliance with William Marcy "Boss" Tweed, the Tammany Hall chieftain. For five years their blend of Appolonian and Dionysian energies outraged and bewildered the financial establishment.

Early in his career Gould revealed a gift for conceiving strikingly original plans and tactics. In 1869 he launched a campaign to expand the Erie into a major rail system. His brash maneuvers forced the nation's two strongest railroads—the Pennsylvania and the New York Central—to reverse policy and embark on expansion programs that inaugurated a new era of railroad competition.

That same year a complex chain of events linked to his rail campaign led Gould into a brazen effort to corner the nation's gold supply. The frenzy that followed on the gold exchange culminated in the infamous Black Friday that paralyzed New York's financial institutions for days. The fallout from this debacle dealt a fatal blow to Gould's ambitious plans for Erie and to his reputation. Together the Erie war and the gold corner fixed the image of Gould as financial predator for generations to come, thanks in large part to the caricature of him as the quintessential robber baron drawn by Charles Francis Adams (1835–1915) and Henry

Adams (1838–1918) in their scathing book *Chapters of Erie.*

In 1872 Gould's adversaries ousted him from the Erie and he resumed his career as a trader on Wall Street. The brokerage firm of Smith, Gould & Martin, which he had joined in 1867, had dissolved in 1870. He never again attached his name to a house but operated as a special partner in other firms; nor did he ever own a seat on the New York Stock Exchange. During the next two years he enhanced his reputation as a trader with a string of startling deals including a corner in Chicago & Northwestern stock.

Despite his genius at trading, Gould longed to be more than a speculator. He developed the art of buying weak properties (the only kind he could afford) and making them profitable through efficient, imaginative management. In 1874 he surprised the business world by capturing the Pacific Mail Steamship Company and the Union Pacific Railroad. Like the Erie, the Union Pacific was tainted by scandal, inefficiency, and an inept management that had gone through three presidents in four years. It also had a stormy relationship with the federal government that touched bottom with the Crédit Mobilier scandal of 1872–1873. The fit was perfect: Gould was seeking to escape his stereotype as a trader through some genuine achievement in business; the Union Pacific desperately needed someone to redeem its vast potential from a tarnished past.

To Wall Street's amazement, Gould turned the Union Pacific around, despite a major depression, by immersing himself in the road's affairs until his knowledge of them was encyclopedic. For six years he grappled with the road's problems. When his efforts to resolve its differences with the federal government failed, he concluded that his future lay elsewhere. A speculative miscalculation in 1878 that jeopardized his own solvency at a time when his chief asset was a large block of Union Pacific stock led Gould to play a daring gambit that transformed his role in the business world. He sold off his Union Pacific holdings and used the proceeds to put together a railroad system of his own.

Between 1879 and 1881 Gould forged an unprecedented business empire at a dizzying pace. In rapid succession he gained control of the Kansas Pacific, Wabash, Missouri Pacific, a half interest in the Denver & Rio Grande, and some lesser railroads. These holdings created a potential competing line with the Union Pacific. Using this threat, he sold the Kansas Pacific to his friends in the Union Pacific and used the profits to develop a system in the Southwest where he did not compete with them.

Defying the conventional wisdom that only a trunk line should serve as parent to a major system, Gould utilized the Missouri Pacific, a line between St. Louis and Kansas City, as the nucleus of his new system, adding to it the St. Louis, Iron Mountain & Southern; the Texas & Pacific; the Missouri, Kansas & Texas; and the International & Great Northern. On all these roads he launched ambitious expansion programs financed by some strikingly original methods. Furthermore, he did not confine himself to the Southwest.

Gould extended the Wabash into Detroit and Chicago, and in the East involved himself in the Lackawanna, the New York & New England, the Central of New Jersey, and the Philadelphia & Reading. By the winter of 1880 he controlled more miles of road (8,160) than any one person in the world.

This enormous rail dominion formed only one part of Gould's empire. He also executed brilliant coups in the telegraph and mass transit fields, making him the dominant player in the two most vital sectors of the industrial economy, transportation and communications. Early in 1881 Gould wrested control of Western Union from William H. Vanderbilt, obtaining command over most of the nation's telegraph system. That October he acquired the Manhattan Elevated system amid charges that he had used a major newspaper, the state attorney general, and a state supreme court judge as pawns in his campaign.

To Wall Street's surprise, Gould gave his three major properties sound, efficient management and left each stronger than he had found it. Possessing a fortune estimated at $75 million, he could have made several times that amount had he been content merely to pile up money. But Gould never considered diverting his money into safe investments to live off the proceeds. He was a driven man for whom business was a creative act. His obsession was to develop virgin country, lay rail, and forge rail systems where little settlement yet existed.

Gould's business tactics thrived on an expanding economy and a bullish market. A downturn that began in 1881 forced him to defend the empire he had erected with such swiftness. This struggle reached a crisis in May 1884, when a brief but severe panic rocked Wall Street. For months Gould fought to save his imperiled fortune and empire. Although he succeeded, the ordeal nearly broke his health. Once out of danger, he left Wall Street and devoted himself to his business interests. But he never escaped the reputation born of his early years on Wall Street. The gap between the legend and the reality of his business career widened steadily into a part of the national folklore.

After patching up his damaged rail empire, Gould launched an expansion program that more than doubled the Missouri Pacific system's mileage. As the catalyst for the expansion wars of the 1870s and 1880s, he did more than anyone else to reshape the railroad map of America in the late nineteenth century. During the last decade of his life Gould toiled at integrating his rail empire and making the Missouri Pacific a reasonably efficient system. The notoriety of Gould's roads for undermaintenance and poor service belonged more to the era after his death when his son George Jay Gould ruled the system.

Pulled in so many directions, Gould worked himself to death. Bouts of facial neuralgia tormented him with excruciating pain, and exhaustion forced him to take more frequent vacations to restore his strength. In 1888 Gould learned he had tuberculosis. He swore the doctor to secrecy and continued his work for four years without anyone—even his family—learning of his affliction. During these same years Gould became the target of constant, vicious criticism from the press, especially the New York dailies that feared his power over the telegraph and cable lines. He was caricatured as the "Wizard of Wall Street" or "Mephistopheles," and was labeled the most hated man in America.

So deeply did the worsening railroad rate wars concern Gould that, to the surprise of many people, he took the lead in seeking stability. The moving force behind meetings of railroad presidents at the home of J. Pierpont Morgan in 1888 and 1890, he advocated far more sweeping proposals than most of the others were willing to consider. To strengthen his position, Gould stunned Wall Street in the fall of 1890 with one last lightning stroke. He recaptured the Union Pacific, snatched Pacific Mail back from a group that had taken it from him, and bought large blocks of stock in two other major systems.

In peace as in war, Gould proved a man ahead of his time. Unlike most rail leaders, he understood that conditions were changing and was ready to move with them. Death claimed him before he could achieve his loftier goals, leaving much of the work he had started to be finished by the man who would dominate the next era of railroad history, Edward H. Harriman.

Apart from business, Gould's passions were books and flowers. He read voraciously, assembled a large library, and even devised his own catalog. Lyndhurst, his magnificent estate in Irvington-on-Hudson, boasted the largest private greenhouse in America. Orchids were his specialty, but Gould grew and studied a variety of plants to the point where his knowledge of horticulture may have rivaled his understanding of finance.

The death of his wife in January 1889 shattered Gould. In November 1892 his own disease entered its terminal phase. He died at his Fifth Avenue home in New York City, leaving a will as remarkable as its author. Not one cent went to anyone outside the family, and an intricate trust arrangement tried to compel the children to manage the fortune together for their common interest.

For ninety years Gould remained the archetypal villain of American history, the textbook stereotype of the robber baron. Only in recent years has modern scholarship restored the broader canvas of his achievements, which only a handful of entrepreneurs of that era can approach.

• Gould's papers are scattered in a variety of public and private collections. The only full scholarly biography, which sharply revises earlier interpretations of his character and reputation, is Maury Klein, *The Life and Legend of Jay Gould* (1986). More detail of Gould's Union Pacific activities can be found in the same author's *Union Pacific: The Birth of a Railroad, 1862–1893* (1987). Julius Grodinsky, *Jay Gould: His Business Career, 1867–1892* (1957) was the first scholarly study to challenge the negative view of Gould in popular accounts. The latter include Gustavus Myers, *History of the Great American Fortunes* (1910); Matthew Josephson, *The*

Robber Barons (1934); Robert I. Warshow, *Jay Gould: The Story of a Fortune* (1928); and Richard O'Connor, *Gould's Millions* (1962).

MAURY KLEIN

GOULD, Laurence McKinley (22 Aug. 1896–21 June 1995), educator, geologist, and explorer, was born in Lacota, Michigan, the son of Herbert Gould and Anna Updike, farmers. In 1914 he left the family farm and moved to Boca Raton, Florida, where he taught in a one-room schoolhouse. He also helped to found a Sunday school class and with his students published the *Boca Raton Semi-Occasional Newspaper*. Later he remembered the two years he taught in Boca Raton as "amongst the most productive of my whole educational career."

In the fall of 1916 Gould enrolled at the University of Michigan. He intended to study law but became interested in geology while rooming in the home of William H. Hobbs, the geology department's chair. World War I interrupted Gould's education. From 1917 to 1919 he served as a sergeant in the Army Ambulance Service in Italy and France and in Germany with the army of occupation.

After his military discharge, he resumed his studies at the University of Michigan, majoring in geology. He earned a B.S. in 1921, an M.A. in 1923, and a D.Sc. in 1925. He also started teaching geology at the university in 1921. He was promoted to assistant professor in 1926 and associate professor in 1930. Also in 1930 he married Margaret Rice. They had no children.

Gould commenced his career as a polar explorer in 1926 when he joined Hobbs on an expedition to Greenland. In 1927 he went with George P. Putnam's expedition to explore Baffin Island. (On both expeditions Gould was appointed second in command.) In 1928 Richard E. Byrd chose him to join him, again as second in command, on Byrd's first Antarctic expedition. During Gould's initial exploration, in March 1929, he got caught in a fierce blizzard and lost an airplane, and he and his party had to be rescued by Byrd. In November Gould led a party southward on an arduous and occasionally dangerous dog-sledge trek. Arriving at the Queen Maud Mountains, Gould and his companions mapped large areas and collected low-grade coal samples, indicating that Antarctica had once been considerably warm and forested. Then Gould traveled east and, as he described in *Cold: The Record of an Antarctic Sledge Journey* (1931), left a note on a cairn in a tightly covered tin can claiming the land as "a dependency, or possession of the United States of America" (although, in fact, the government never officially staked a claim in Antarctica). In January 1930, some eleven weeks after they had left, the party arrived back at their home base, having covered more than 1,500 miles.

In February 1930 Gould returned to the University of Michigan to teach. Two years later he accepted an appointment as professor of geology at Carleton College in Northfield, Minnesota. During World War II he took a leave of absence to head the Arctic section of the Air Force Arctic, Desert and Tropics Information Center. In 1945 he was named president of Carleton College. Over the next seventeen years he transformed the unremarkable Carleton into a leading small liberal arts college. He recruited top high school students, and, believing that scholarship required "constant renewal through some kind of research activity," he attracted a faculty dedicated to research as well as teaching, although his own original research was neglected while he was so busy as an administrator. He revised the curriculum to emphasize the humanities and introduced comprehensive examinations for seniors. Gould was also a successful fundraiser. During his presidency the school's endowment increased fourfold, and seven new buildings were constructed.

As occupied as Gould was at Carleton, he had not lost interest in Antarctica. In 1955 he led an American delegation at a multinational planning conference on antarctic research programs for the 1957–1958 International Geographical Year (IGY). At this Paris conference, sponsored by the International Council of Scientific Unions, an informal agreement was reached permitting scientists to travel in Antarctica without restrictions from territorial claims. The Paris agreement on the "coldest of all the continents," wrote Gould in the *Bulletin of the Atomic Scientists* (Dec. 1970), "witnessed the first thawing of the Cold War." As chair of the Committee on Polar Research of the National Academy of Sciences, Gould testified in June 1960 before the U.S. Senate Foreign Relations Committee on a multinational agreement to cooperate on scientific research in Antarctica. He urged approval of the treaty as the first step toward "some kind of permanent cooperation" among governments.

During the IGY, Gould, as director of the U.S. IGY Antarctic Program, supervised the scientific operations of American observation stations in Antarctica. He returned to Antarctica in 1969 with Grover Murray, whom he met when both served on the National Science Board, to visit a deposit near the Beardmore Glacier, where a vertebrate fossil of a partial skull closely resembling similar ones from South Africa had recently been found. Here was firm evidence that Africa and Antarctica had once been joined. Gould hailed the discovery as "not only the most important fossil ever found in Antarctica, but one of the truly great fossil finds of all time." It supported the then-suspect theory of continental drift.

Gould retired from Carleton in 1962 and accepted a teaching position at the University of Arizona in Tucson. Enjoying what he described as "a whole new wonderful career," Gould remained at Arizona until 1979, when he retired. Described by Charles Nader in the *New York Times Magazine* (31 Dec. 1995) as "charming, humorous, never stuffy," Gould spent his remaining years in Tucson. He died at a home for the elderly there.

During his long life, Gould won many honors. His standing as a polar explorer and scientist is made apparent by the bestowal of the David Livingston Medal of the American Geographical Society (1930), the Congressional Gold Medal (1931), the Explorers Club Medal (1957), the Navy Distinguished Public Service Award (1959), and the Cosmos Club Award (1981). He was also elected president of the American Association for the Advancement of Science (1965). His achievements as an educator are indicated by his selection as president of the United Chapters of Phi Beta Kappa (1958) and appointment as a trustee of the Ford Foundation and of the Carnegie Foundation for the Advancement of Teaching (1958–1962). Finally, he received twenty-six honorary degrees.

• Carleton College has a considerable collection of archival material, including full documentation of Gould's tenure as a professor and as president of the college. The collection also includes a wealth of photographic material. Diaries relating to the first Byrd antarctic expedition and material dealing with other polar matters are in the Dartmouth College Library. There is also a small collection of letters at the Boca Raton Historical Society. On Gould's years in Boca Raton and in the army, see Geoffrey Lynfield, "Laurence Gould, Explorer-Educator: From Boca to Antarctica," *Spanish River Papers* 11 (Spring 1983). Also helpful are obituaries in the *New York Times*, 22 June 1995, and the *Polar Times* (Fall–Winter 1995), pp. 3, 7.

RICHARD HARMOND

GOULD, Norma (1888–30 July 1980), modern dancer, teacher, and choreographer, was born in Los Angeles, California. Her father, Murray A. Gould, was a miller and her mother (name unknown) was a music teacher. Gould's parents encouraged her early interest in the arts, and she learned music from her mother, who combined formal instruction with the opportunity for creative expression. Gould entered Los Angeles Polytechnical High School in 1905, among the first group of students to enroll in what was then considered an experimental curriculum. Women were trained alongside men in business and college preparatory courses, and courses in music and art were exceptionally advanced. Gould was class historian and president of the Girls Club, a group that staged productions. Clippings in her scrapbook indicate that she studied dance in New York during summers while in high school.

After graduation from high school in 1908 Gould began teaching. She acquired a partner in 1911 when Ted Shawn came to Los Angeles from Denver, where he had studied ballet. Over the next three years Gould and Shawn performed in Los Angeles at the Angelus and Alexandria hotels in tango teas and for various clubs and groups. During a two-week engagement of five shows daily at the Majestic Theater in San Diego shared with other specialty acts, Gould and Shawn performed ballroom dances, Oriental interpretations, and Greek numbers. They made a short movie in 1913 for the Thomas Alva Edison Company, *The Dance of the Ages*.

In 1914 Gould and Shawn set out with a company of six on a trip to New York on the Santa Fe Railroad; they were hired as entertainers to play employee recreation centers along its line. Before arriving in New York they stopped in New Canaan, Connecticut, for one month to study at the Unitrinian School of Personal Harmonizing with the poet Bliss Carman and Mary Perry King; the course consisted of Delsarte exercises, free gymnastics, and movements based on expressive use of the voice and body. In New York Gould and Shawn appeared in recitals and then went their separate ways when Shawn met Ruth St. Denis, becoming her dancing partner, husband, and cofounder of the Denishawn School.

Gould went back to California and resumed her teaching and performing. After presenting her choreography at the Little Theater in Los Angeles in April 1915, she did a special presentation on 14 July for the Music Teachers Association of California in which she developed the idea of "music made visible" through dance, an idea that was later used by St. Denis and Shawn and called "music visualizations." Gould went on tour immediately afterward in Texas and Louisiana with the Don Philippini Symphony Band, and a newspaper review noted that "Miss Gould is very good. Her dancing is marked by strict observance of technique."

Gould was soon in great demand as a performer for the numerous women's volunteer clubs in and around Los Angeles; the lack of an established tradition in presenting the arts led the clubs to play an important role as performers showcased their talents in a serious environment for members and their guests. Among the clubs where Gould performed with her students were the Ebell, Gamut, Hollywood Women's, Wa-Wan, Matinee Music, Los Angeles and Pasadena Chapters of the Drama League, MacDowell, and Friday Morning Music. By 1915–1916 Gould had come under the management of an important Los Angeles impresario, L. E. Behymer; she was the only dancer in his stable of artists.

The years 1926 to 1929 signified widespread public acceptance of Gould as a major choreographer in Los Angeles. She appeared at Philharmonic Auditorium in *The Pearl of Kashmir* on 11 June 1926, accompanied by seventy-five dancers and Adolph Tandler's Little Symphony; on 30 August 1927 and 4 September 1928 she appeared on the Hollywood Bowl stage in two postseason evenings called "California Night of Music." In her 1928 Hollywood Bowl appearance she was again accompanied by Tandler's orchestra in the premiere of her new ballet, *The Shepherd of Shiraz*; and at the Windsor Theater on 15 June 1929 she presented a dance drama, *The Twilight of the Gods*. As the first native Californian asked to choreograph for the regular season of the Hollywood Bowl, Gould and her group appeared on 30 August 1929 in two pieces: one to Schubert's Symphony no. 8 and the other to Tchaikovsky's *Nutcracker Suite*.

Gould built up a large following in her studio and was one of the first professional dancers to become involved in higher education. In 1919 she began teaching at the University of California at Los Angeles and in 1920 at the University of Southern California. From 1919 to 1924 she functioned in a dual capacity at these two institutions: as a faculty member in the physical education department and as director of pageantry. Her legacy was carried on by her students who taught at the same two universities, at Stanford, and in public and private schools in Los Angeles. Another student, Dorothy Lyndall, opened her own studio and was the teacher of two well-known dancers, Myra Kinch and Yuriko.

In 1932 Gould created Dance Theater, an organization that had repercussions for Los Angeles dance and for those who went on to perform and work elsewhere. Based on her vision that all kinds of dance should be encouraged and seen, that audiences had to be developed, and that young dancers needed exposure to different kinds of techniques, she served as an impresario for a wide array of performances and classes. The Dance Theater was active through 1942, and the list of dancers and groups who performed and taught there is impressive and varied, including Carmelita Maracci, Tina Flade, Waldeen, Terui, Tom Youngplant and Hopi Indians, Angna Enters, Harold Kreutzberg, Lester Horton, Sumita Devi, and Lilivati Devi. There were special programs on Laban dance notation, dance and music, and Graham technique. Gould herself created *Lenox Avenue* in 1938 to the music of William Grant Still, and she mounted an exhibition of African-American cultural life with manuscripts, sculpture, photographs, and handicrafts.

Gould was less active in the late 1940s; by the 1960s she was already ill with Alzheimer's. She was placed in a nursing home in 1968 and remained institutionalized until her death in Santa Monica, California. She had never married.

Gould was an inventive, skilled, and theatrical choreographer, but her major contribution to dance was as a teacher and writer. Her Dance Theater brought artists together and influenced a whole generation of teachers and performers.

• The Archives at the University of California at Los Angeles and at the University of Southern California have records in the university catalogs of Gould's teaching. Information is also available from music scrapbooks in the main branch of the Los Angeles Public Library. For additional information on Gould see Naima Prevots, *Dancing in the Sun: Hollywood Choreographers, 1915–1937* (1987), and *American Pageantry: A Movement for Art and Democracy* (1990). There is discussion of Gould's work with Shawn in Ted Shawn, *One Thousand and One Night Stands* (1960); and there is some biographical material in Bruno David Ussher, *Who's Who in Music and Dance in Southern California* (1933).

NAIMA PREVOTS

GOULDING, Francis Robert (28 Sept. 1810–22 Aug. 1881), Presbyterian clergyman and author, was born in Midway, Georgia, the son of Thomas Goulding, a Presbyterian clergyman and a theologian, and Ann Holbrook, daughter of the revolutionary war hero Nathan Holbrook. When he was twelve, Francis moved

with his family from Midway to Lexington, Georgia. In 1830 he graduated from the University of Georgia and in 1832 from the Theological Seminary in Columbia, South Carolina. Goulding became a minister, and in 1833, at Savannah, he married Mary Wallace Howard, for whose use Lowell Mason composed the music for the hymn "From Greenland's Icy Mountains." Goulding held ministries in Sumter County, South Carolina, and in Greensboro and Washington, Georgia. He became an agent for the American Bible Society before he returned to preaching in Eatonton and Bath, Georgia, from 1843 to 1851. In 1842 he invented and built, but did not patent, a workable prototype of the sewing machine, the first of its kind in this country with pedal attachments.

In 1853 Goulding opened a school for boys in Kingston, Georgia, and began a work entitled *The Instincts of Birds and Beasts*. Two years later, after the death of his first wife, he married Matilda Rees and moved, with his six children, to her estate at Darien, near his birthplace. He was ministering there at the outbreak of the Civil War, during part of which he served as a chaplain. When his library was burned by Union troops in 1862, he moved to Macon, where he taught at a school for girls and continued to minister to and care for war casualties. It was here that he compiled a *Soldiers Hymn Book* for the Confederate army and wrote a series of articles for the *Army and Navy Journal* entitled "Self Helps and Practical Hints for the Camp, the Forest, and the Sea."

After the war Goulding was stricken with a throat infection that left him unable to preach. Desperate for money, he turned to writing. As early as 1844 he had published a story titled "Little Josephine." *Robert and Harold*, his most successful book, drawn largely from the life and personalities of his own family, was published in 1852. Renamed *Young Marooners on the Florida Coast, Robert and Harold*, a sort of *Robinson Crusoe* in America, went through several editions in England and France. By 1919 it had been through ten editions in the United States. This work was followed by a sequel, *Marooner's Island*, and *Frank Gordon*, both published in 1869. The Woodruff stories, named for Lorenzo Woodruff, a childhood friend, included *Sal-o-quah, or Boy Life among the Cherokees* (1870); *Sapelo, or Childlife on the Tide-Water* (1870); and *Nacooches, or Boy Life from Home* (1871). These works, while popular, never reached the audience of *Young Marooners*, on which his literary reputation rests. During this period Goulding also studied the subject of light, corresponding with English chemist and physicist Michael Faraday and other eminent scientists and ultimately publishing *What Is Light?* in 1858. Goulding died at Roswell, Georgia.

• Goulding's papers and letters are collected in the Emory University and the University of Georgia libraries. A master's thesis by Althea Jane Macon, "Francis Robert Goulding: Georgia Author" (1925), is at the University of Georgia. Goulding is mentioned prominently in E. A. Alderman and J. C. Harris, *The South in the Building of the Nation* (1909);

W. J. Northen, *Men of Mark in Georgia* (1907); and James Stacy, *History of the Midway Congregational Church* (1903). He is also discussed in M. L. Rutherford, *The South in History and Literature* (1907).

GERALD M. GARMON

GOULDING, Ray (20 Mar. 1922–24 Mar. 1990), radio performer and satirist, was born Raymond Walter Goulding in Lowell, Massachusetts, the son of Thomas M. Goulding and Mary Ann Philbin. After completing high school in 1939, he followed his older brother into work as an announcer at a Lowell radio station. In 1941 he moved on to a similar position at WEEI, a leading Boston station.

Goulding joined the U.S. Army in 1942. Despite his lack of formal education he became an officer and worked as an instructor in the officers' candidate school at Fort Knox, Kentucky. While in the army he met and married Mary Elizabeth Leader in 1945, with whom he had six children during a lifelong marriage.

Returning to civilian life in Boston in 1946, he joined radio station WHDH, where he met Robert B. "Bob" Elliot, the station's morning disc jockey. Goulding was originally assigned to read news summaries during Elliot's "wake-up" program, but the two would exchange bits of impromptu chatter as part of the show. These on-air segues gradually evolved into fully realized comic routines and became the comedy team known as Bob and Ray. Noting favorable audience response, WHDH gave them their own half-hour midday program, "Matinee with Bob and Ray." The popularity of the team grew, and they began doing a second, hour-long program, "Break Fast with Bob and Ray."

In 1951 Bob and Ray left local radio in Boston for New York to star in a Saturday night comedy hour heard coast-to-coast over the NBC radio network. Here the team developed some of its enduring sketches and characters. In "Mary Backstayge, Noble Wife," an ongoing parody of radio soap operas, Goulding played the title character; he would play all the female roles in the duo's routines. Send-ups of radio pitchmen and satires of commercials figured prominently in the pair's repertoire, and as a result Bob and Ray frequently alienated their own advertisers, forcing them to seek new sponsors.

Though American radio was rapidly shifting away from this type of comedy-variety programming toward strict musical genre or informational formats, "The Bob and Ray Show" stood against the trend and developed an enthusiastic national following. The comedians became the object of much critical acclaim, bringing desperately needed creativity to a medium that was otherwise being abandoned by comic performers. Syndicated columnist Harriet Van Horne characterized Bob and Ray as "the freshest thing on radio." John Crosby of the *New York Herald Tribune* commented, "They've a very adult, unusual and Charles Addams–like style about them."

NBC attempted to capitalize further on the success of its radio comedy stars, trying them on television several times, including efforts such as "Bob and Ray," a fifteen-minute daily variety program in 1951. ABC produced them in "The Name's the Same," a game show, in 1955. But the peculiar style of humor that Elliot and Goulding had developed proved unsuitable for visual exhibition, and the two focused their careers on radio. Over the years they would move their show to ABC, to Mutual, and back to NBC again, and, in the early 1980s, to a revival on National Public Radio. They are probably best remembered for their "Critics at Large" spots on NBC's "Monitor," a weekend news and information format that allowed them as many as fifteen appearances in five-minute routines over the course of a given weekend.

"Wally Ballou and Common Man's Views" was a typical Bob and Ray sketch. Elliot would play the part of Ballou, a radio reporter conducting a "man-on-the-street" interview putatively concerning some current issue or event. Goulding would play the anonymous interviewee:

Ballou: Did you hear the president's speech about the economy? Man: More or less. I was trimming the cat's toenails, but the TV was on in the other room. I could hear somebody talking and the voice sounded familiar. Ballou: Well, we're getting the reaction of people like yourself to his address. For instance, his point about declining productivity being a major cause of inflation . . . Man: Absolutely. You take that laundromat on the corner. Their dryers used to give you ten minutes for a dime. Now, it's up to fifteen cents they only run for eight minutes. Ballou: But when the president spoke of productivity . . . Man: I understood him perfectly—and I agree. Take the elastic in my shorts. It never gets dry in eight minutes. So, I'm stuck for an extra fifteen cents. Right?

In addition to their spoofs, Bob and Ray provided the voices for many legitimate commercials. They were, for example, Bert and Harry Piel in a long-running animated radio and TV campaign for Piels Brothers' Beer. Their stage show, *The Two and Only*, premiered on Broadway in 1970. Goulding made a rare solo appearance in a minor role in the film *Cold Turkey* (1971), and the team appeared together in *Author! Author!*, a 1982 comedy feature starring Al Pacino. Anthologized transcriptions of many of their best routines were published as books: *Write If You Get Work: The Best of Bob and Ray* (1975), *From Approximately Coast to Coast . . . It's the Bob and Ray Show* (1983), and *The New! Improved! Bob and Ray Book* (1985). As evidence of their popularity and the variety of their following, prefatory notes for the three books were written, respectively, by author Kurt Vonnegut, television commentator Andy Rooney, and radio personality Garrison Keillor.

Perhaps the closest approximation of their radio performances can be found on their recorded comedy albums. They produced several during the 1950s, including *Fun Time* and *Laugh of the Party*. Two of their later albums, *A Night of Two Stars Recorded Live at Carnegie Hall* (1987) and *The Best of Bob and Ray: Vol-*

ume One (1988), were nominated for Grammy Awards. *Vintage Bob and Ray* (1974) is considered the definitive collection of their radio work.

Bob and Ray won two George Foster Peabody Awards relatively early in their careers, receiving a 1951 Peabody as "the foremost satirists in radio" and a 1956 Peabody for "radio entertainment." They were honored by an exhibition of their work staged by the Museum of Radio and Television in 1989. Ray Goulding was a member of the American Federation of Television and Radio Artists, the Screen Actors' Guild, and the American Guild of Variety Artists. He died in his Long Island home.

• Frank Buxton and Bill Owen, *The Big Broadcast, 1920–1950* (1972), offers a fuller catalog of the Bob and Ray repertoire. Obituaries of Ray Goulding are in the *New York Times*, 26 Mar. 1990, and *Variety*, 28 Mar. 1990.

DAVID MARC

GOULDNER, Alvin Ward (29 July 1920–15 Dec. 1980), sociologist and educator, was born in Harlem, New York City, son of Louis Gouldner, a salesman, and Estelle Fetbrandt, a part-time department store clerk. Gouldner was, as he put it, "educated in the streets and schools of New York," which included De-Witt Clinton High School, Bernard Baruch College (now City College of New York), from which he received a B.A. in 1941, and Columbia University (M.A., 1945; Ph.D., 1953). In the latter two institutions, he joined a contingent of extraordinary students who would become national leaders in sociology and related fields during the three decades following World War II. In 1955 he married Helen Patricia Beem, who herself became a sociologist and academic administrator; they had one son. This marriage ended in divorce in 1965, and the following year he married Janet Lee Walker, their joint family eventually including their two sons and Janet's daughter by a previous marriage.

Gouldner's dissertation was published simultaneously in two volumes, *Wildcat Strike* (1954) and *Patterns of Industrial Bureaucracy* (1954), both of which enjoyed wide and continuous readership for more than twenty years as models of an unorthodox "functionalist" analysis. Also during graduate school, Gouldner worked temporarily on the famous "Studies in Prejudice" project brought to New York by the transplanted Frankfurt School, tenuously attached to Columbia University during World War II as a result of Paul Lazarsfeld's hospitality toward German Jews Max Horkheimer and Theodor Adorno. The project studied the connection between familial dynamics and the growth of fascism in Europe. This contact with the European critical tradition permanently influenced Gouldner. He left New York, his self-described spiritual home, to work from 1947 at the University of Buffalo, which itself had at that time a strong European component; from 1952 at Antioch College; and from 1954 at the University of Illinois, where he studied mathematics, factor analysis, and computers. In 1959 he became professor and chairman of sociology and anthropology at Washington University in St. Louis, where he built an illustrious academic unit that, for a time during the 1960s, rivaled much larger and older programs in the quality of its faculty, particularly in the areas of social theory and political analysis. He remained at Washington University, being named in 1967 the Max Weber Research Professor in Social Theory, until his premature death of a heart attack in Madrid, Spain.

Gouldner identified himself with the theoretical approach to sociology espoused by a line of distinguished Columbia professors who blended functionalism with the ideas of sociologists Émile Durkheim and Max Weber. In two early and important essays, "The Norm of Reciprocity" (1960) and "Anti-Minotaur: The Myth of Value-Free Sociology" (1961), Gouldner did battle with his intellectual patrimony, arguing over its strengths and weaknesses with unusual candor. In his best-known, though not necessarily most respected, book, *The Coming Crisis of Western Sociology* (1970), he singled out the Harvard tradition personified by Talcott Parsons for merciless critique and, in so doing, initiated a national debate about the value of sociology that continued to plague the discipline for the ensuing quarter century. Although he is remembered as a left-wing analyst of the social order, an inside critic of social science when practiced in ways he disapproved, and a virtuoso polemicist, his earliest works of empirical research, along with a remarkable monograph on Greek social philosophy and social life (*Enter Plato* [1965]) and several others from late in his life that exemplified Marxist social analysis, have endeared him to serious scholars, even those who discount his more virulent statements of opinion.

Gouldner also involved himself vigorously and outspokenly in the academic politics of this turbulent period. In 1962 he served as president of the Society for the Study of Social Problems, and in 1963 he founded and edited the popular and scholarly magazine *Transaction*. While teaching at the University of Amsterdam (1972–1976), he became reenamored of Marxism, a youthful enthusiasm, and founded an explicitly left-wing scholarly journal, *Theory and Society*, which has over its lifetime become one of the best English-language outlets for international work in social theory. In this journal, expanding on the ideas first offered in *The Coming Crisis*, Gouldner fashioned what came to be called "the sociology of sociology" and called for his more astute colleagues in social theory to begin practicing "reflexivity." By this he meant that sociologists must not consider their work only or principally at some remove from social life, under the illusion of "objectivity," but must instead admit to and work within the unavoidable condition of political and intellectual allegiances. The fact that Gouldner was much reviled for having initially stated this point of view, which has since become commonplace, indicates just how heterodox his position once was.

In the last decade of his scholarly life Gouldner produced a series of studies from within the Marxist tradition as it had been redefined in Europe during the

1970s. In several linked volumes, which he called *The Dark Side of the Dialectic*—including *The Dialectic of Ideology and Technology* (1976), *The Future of Intellectuals and the Rise of the New Class* (1979), *The Two Marxisms* (1980), and the opus posthumous, *Against Fragmentation: The Origins of Marxism and the Sociology of Intellectuals* (1985)—Gouldner brought his appreciative yet critical assessment of leftist analysis to its highest level. Even though the series could not accomplish everything it set out to do, the volumes nevertheless constitute a permanent part of the huge neo-Marxist wave that swept over intellectual life in Europe and the United States during the late 1960s and through the 1970s. When added to Gouldner's earlier works on industry and bureaucratization, ancient social thought, and sociology's foibles, the whole comprises an oeuvre that must be ranked high, even by the standards of that unusually gifted sociological generation of which Gouldner was one of the most outspoken members. If sociology endured a "crisis" after 1970, as he correctly predicted, this had less to do with Gouldner's presence in the discipline than with a dearth in the field of other scholars with his analytic ability and rhetorical power.

• Gouldner's professional papers have not yet been deposited in any academic library, nor do they yet appear in any of the standard bibliographical guides. In addition to the books mentioned above, he coauthored with Helen P. Gouldner and Joseph Gusfield, *Modern Sociology* (1963); and with Richard Peterson, *Notes on Technology and the Moral Order* (1962). Early in his career, he edited *Studies in Leadership: Leadership and Democratic Action* (1950) and later issued his collected essays in *For Sociology* (1973). He also wrote an introduction to the first English translation of Émile Durkheim's *Socialism and Saint-Simon* (1958). Useful sources on Gouldner include a detailed obituary by Charles Lemert and Robert K. Merton in the American Sociological Association's newsletter, *Footnotes* (Mar. 1981, p. 12); remarks delivered at a memorial service in St. Louis by Charles Lemert and Paul Piccone, published as "Alvin Ward Gouldner: 1920–1980," in *Theory and Society* 10 (1981): 163–67; and Walter R. Nord, "Alvin W. Gouldner as Intellectual Hero," *Journal of Management Inquiry* 1, no. 4 (Dec. 1992): 350–55. See also Anthony Giddens, "Alvin Gouldner and the Intellectuals," in *Social Theory and Modern Sociology* (1987), pp. 253–74; Ellsworth R. Fuhrman, "Alvin Gouldner and the Sociology of Knowledge: Three Significant Problem Shifts," *Sociological Quarterly* 25 (Summer 1984): 287–300; and John J. Stewart, "Is a Critical Sociology Possible?: Alvin Gouldner and the 'Dark Side of the Dialectic,'" *Sociological Inquiry* 54 (Summer 1984): 231–59.

ALAN SICA

GOVAN, Daniel Chevilette (4 July 1827–12 Mar. 1911), Confederate soldier, was born in Northampton County, North Carolina, the son of Andrew Robison Govan, a planter and politician, and Mary Pugh Jones. His parents moved to Somerville, Tennessee, in 1830 and to Marshall County, Mississippi, in 1832. After studying with a private tutor in his youth, Govan attended Columbia College (now the University of

South Carolina) but left school in 1848 before graduation. While at college, he drilled as part of a military company.

In 1849 Govan headed for the gold fields of California with his kinsman Ben McCulloch and nearly two dozen other Mississippians and Tennesseans. After experiencing only fair success panning along the San Joaquin and other rivers, Govan settled for steadier work as deputy sheriff of Sacramento when McCulloch was elected sheriff in 1850. Govan returned to Mississippi in 1852 to become a planter. He married Mary F. Otey, daughter of the first Episcopal bishop of Tennessee, in December 1853. They would have fourteen children. The Govans moved to Phillips County, Arkansas, a year later to engage in planting.

When Arkansas seceded from the Union in April 1861, Govan raised a company of Phillips County men, evenly divided between "plain country folk" and large farmers and planters. With Govan as captain, this band became Company F of the Second Arkansas Infantry in June 1861. The regiment, commanded by Colonel Thomas C. Hindman, served initially in southeastern Missouri but soon joined the Army of Tennessee at Memphis. The men elected Govan lieutenant colonel in October, and by mid-December the regiment had moved to Bowling Green, Kentucky. It first saw action at Rowlett's Stations (17 Dec.). Govan was promoted to colonel of the regiment in January 1862 and commanded it that year in the battles of Shiloh, Perryville, and Stones River.

In 1863, due to army reorganization and a shortage of general officers, Govan found himself commanding a brigade composed of mostly Arkansas troops, including the Second Arkansas. His men did not fare well at Chickamauga (19–20 Sept.) despite the Confederate victory. Three times in two days they broke in confusion, and had it not been for the quick thinking of one of Govan's regimental commanders, the men might have been caught between two Federal forces. Most of the brigade saw only limited action at Missionary Ridge, but at Ringgold Gap (27 Nov.) it held a critical passage through the mountains while the remainder of the army made good its escape from Tennessee.

In recognition of his service and the position he had been holding since taking over the brigade, Govan was promoted to brigadier general in February 1864 and given permanent command of his Arkansas brigade. He thus became one of five Confederate generals from Phillips County. Govan led his brigade through the Atlanta campaign (May-Sept. 1864) and turned in solid performances at Resaca, Pickett's Mill, and Kennesaw Mountain. His finest hour as a field commander came on 22 July in the battle of Atlanta when his men captured nearly seven hundred Federal troops, eight cannon, and the colors of the Sixteenth Iowa Infantry. Govan kept the captured flag until September 1883 when, being invited to a Federal soldier's reunion at Cedar Rapids, he returned it to survivors of the Sixteenth Iowa. The Hawkeyes displayed their gratitude by presenting Govan with a gold-headed cane.

In fighting near Jonesboro (1 Sept.), four Federal brigades overwhelmed Govan's brigade. Six hundred men, including Govan, surrendered after savage hand-to-hand combat. He was exchanged in time to join John Bell Hood's ill-fated Tennessee campaign (Nov.-Dec.). At Franklin, confronted by "heavy earthworks," "bristling bayonets," and the "glitter of Napoleon guns," Govan, like most of Hood's officers, advised against attack. After the battle, Govan informed his wife that he was lucky to have escaped "that bloody conflict," which claimed the lives of six Confederate generals. Govan did fall wounded a few days later in the battle of Nashville. His slow recuperation prohibited him from rejoining the army until April 1865 at Greensboro, North Carolina. In the final campaign through his native state, Govan led his old Arkansas brigade, now consolidated with Hiram Bronson Granbury's Texas brigade. He surrendered as part of the Army of Tennessee on 26 April.

Govan was a solid if unspectacular soldier. A sensitive and articulate man, he was praised by General William J. Hardee for being as "true and brave as he was courteous and gentle." He was a steady, patient commander, not charismatic but known for his common sense and coolness in battle. He seemed often to succeed because he surrounded himself with intelligent, active, and efficient officers who performed well under pressure. Yet, following the battle at Ringgold Gap, Major General Patrick R. Cleburne praised Govan and three other brigade commanders by saying, "Four better officers are not in the service of the Confederacy" (*War of the Rebellion*, vol. 31, pt. 2, p. 758).

After the war, Govan returned to his Arkansas plantation near Marianna, where he "lived a quiet and retired life," "very popular and much loved by all" (*Historical Memoirs*, p. 595). Still, one postwar resident of his neighborhood reported that Govan helped to lead the Helena chapter of the Ku Klux Klan during these years. In 1878 Govan wrote a brief history of Cleburne's division that was published shortly after his death in Fay Hempstead's *Historical Review of Arkansas* (1911). In 1894 Govan moved to Washington State to serve as American Indian agent for President Grover Cleveland. His wife died in 1896, and Govan moved back east to Tennessee in 1898. Thereafter he resided with one or the other of his children in Tennessee, Arkansas, and Mississippi. He died at the home of a daughter in Memphis and was buried at Holly Springs, Mississippi.

• The only collection of Govan papers is in the Southern Historical Collection at the University of North Carolina in Chapel Hill. His wartime battle reports are conveniently located in *The War of the Rebellion: A Compilation of the Official Records of the Union and Confederate Armies* (128 vols., 1880–1901). There is no biography of Govan. Among the best contemporary commentators are Irving Buck, *Cleburne and His Command* (1908); *Biographical and Historical Memoirs of Eastern Arkansas* (1890); Stan C. Harley, "Govan's Bridge at Pickett's Mill," *Confederate Veteran*, Feb. 1904, pp. 74–76; and Edward Bourne, "Govan's Bridge at New Hope Church," *Confederate Veteran*, Mar. 1923, pp. 89–90. Useful historical perspectives on Govan are provided by Albert Castel, *Decision in the West: The Atlanta Campaign of 1864* (1992); Peter Cozzens, *This Terrible Sound: The Battle of Chickamauga* (1992); Howell and Elizabeth Purdue, *Pat Cleburne, Confederate General* (1973); and Wiley Sword, *Embrace an Angry Wind: The Confederacy's Last Hurrah: Spring Hill, Franklin, and Nashville* (1992). Obituaries are in the Memphis *Commercial Appeal*, 13 Mar. 1911, and the *Confederate Veteran*, Sept. 1911), p. 444.

DANIEL E. SUTHERLAND

GOVE, Aaron Estellus (26 Sept. 1839–1 Aug. 1919), educator, was born in Hampton Falls, New Hampshire, the son of John Francis Gove, a blacksmith, and Sarah Jane Wadleigh. The family moved to Boston where eight-year-old Aaron attended the grammar schools and served as an apprentice to a nearby jewelry manufacturer. Tempted by western opportunities, the family later migrated to Illinois, and John Gove opened a blacksmith shop in the new village of Rutland. Aaron began his career as schoolmaster (his preferred title), attended Illinois State Normal University (later Illinois State University) between teaching terms, and graduated in 1861. When the Civil War began, he enlisted in the Thirty-third Illinois Infantry and was brevetted major for bravery at Vicksburg. When yellow fever sent him home on a cot in 1864, his father met the train with a coffin. But Gove recovered and traveled East to marry Carro Spofford of North Andover, Massachusetts, in 1865; they had four children.

Shortly after his marriage, Gove returned to Illinois and taught in the La Salle County and Normal Schools. In 1871 Gove and a colleague, E. C. Hewitt, acquired *The Chicago Schoolmaster*; and when *The Illinois Teacher* failed in 1873, they purchased that journal. That same year they merged these two publications to create *The Illinois Schoolmaster*, an educational journal that was popular statewide. In 1874 the Denver Board of Education elected him superintendent of District One. Upon his arrival in the frontier community that year, Gove found the educational system in chaos. A bitter quarrel engulfed the school board, and the district owed $75,000 in bonds. But Gove was an intrepid individual who believed that all children had the right to an education and that a common school could fulfill that right. He declared that good schools were essential for Denver's prosperity because they would attract settlers and spawn new businesses. He began to bring order out of chaos with his single-minded purpose to create a school system that would ensure a sense of democratic community and provide the highest quality of education affordable to Denver.

Three formidable issues confronted Gove during this critical era for Denver's educational system. First, new buildings were needed to address an escalating school population. Colorado experienced a persistent economic growth and thriving population until the panic of 1893. The census tallied 4,759 in 1870, but the city's population exploded to 106,713 by 1890. In one twelve-month period, student attendance climbed from 3,400 to 4,500—a 32 percent increase. Denver had two buildings, 1,012 students, and no high school in 1874. The conservative Gove adopted a pay-as-you-go philosophy, relying on tax levies rather than bonds. He thought that citizens deserved a dollar's worth of school for every tax dollar spent, and he delivered. The Board of Education permitted Gove considerable latitude in essential matters, and he benefitted from the ongoing harmony of their working relationship. At his insistence the buildings were designed to furnish a comfortable learning environment, and they were completed and paid for on time.

Gove then began the struggle to establish a high school. His opposition included religious groups who did not want the competition from public secondary education, and newcomers who thought a high school an unnecessary expense. But Gove discreetly won enough support to organize a high school in 1875. Its first class graduated in 1878 and later earned national recognition for its scholarship under principal James Hutchins Baker. In 1883 John D. Philbrick, Boston's noted superintendent of schools, visited Denver and praised the architecture as superior to other comparable eastern schools, expressed admiration for the quality of teaching, and extolled the board of education. When the 1885 school year opened, there were enough desks to accommodate all students in the district.

A second issue facing Gove concerned educational innovations that challenged him and other school administrators with questions of what to teach and how to teach it. Rapid industrial expansion induced reformers to promote manual training, to champion a child-centered curriculum that emphasized learning by doing according to ability, and to advocate uniformity in textbooks and instruction. These decisions were better left to local communities, not to legislators. Gove believed in limited government. Even compulsory education seemed to him an unnecessary intrusion upon family prerogatives, and free textbooks smacked of paternalism. Gove rejected these "experimentations" and called for teachers' colleges to test such methods thoroughly before allowing possible harm to the true function of the schools. For example, he asserted that individuals learn at different levels, a fact that absolute uniformity ignored. Gove did not oppose change, but he believed that time and experience would prove the value of reform measures. Keyed to a practical education, he proposed that schools teach what students could not learn outside. Many students left school after the fifth grade, and Gove strenuously argued that to compete in the real world, they must learn to read. Following noted educator William T. Harris, Gove favored a curriculum that stressed discipline through the classics, languages, and mathematics. Thus the school would teach Americans the meaning of responsible participation in a democracy. Gove finally yielded to change and accepted manual education, but in his view of education the teacher was the first priority and then the curriculum. He believed that both priorities required personnel with a proven character and steadfast dedication.

Acquiring and retaining competent teachers was Gove's third challenge. He was a hands-on superintendent who regularly visited his classrooms to encourage and counsel teachers. He saw the teacher as the school's "soul" who taught morality and responsibility more by example than by deliberation. Teachers had children daily for five hours and made an indelible impression upon their charges. To manage such responsibility, Gove demanded individuals with knowledge and character. During the panic of 1893 Gove confirmed their importance when he reduced his salary by $2,000 but left teachers' salaries alone. He developed written and oral exams to screen candidates, a practice that also eliminated favoritism. One candidate commented that one "knew" he or she had been thoroughly examined after meeting with Gove and his committee.

In his efforts to expand education, Gove established in 1885 the monthly *Colorado School Journal*, which became the official voice of Colorado's Department of Public Instruction, he helped organize the state historical and natural history society, and he proposed the State Teachers' Association. He was prominent in the National Education Association, serving as its president in 1887–1888 and sitting on its committee on the superintendency of the city school systems. Resigning from the Denver superintendency in 1904, he began a successful career as a lobbyist for the Great Western Sugar Company. Gove was credited with making a major contribution to the growth of the sugar beet industry in Colorado. He gained a reputation as one who wrote the best papers for legislative reference of any lobbyist in Washington, D.C.

Contemporaries credited Gove with the greatest influence on Denver's education during its most formative period. Perhaps a former Illinois student stated the most fitting epitaph when he recalled in 1895 that Mr. Gove's school "was the happiest place in which to be."

• Gove published one book, *Spelling Lessons: For Intermediate Grades* (1905), but the *Colorado School Journal* contains numerous articles and editorials by him that focus on the issues facing him from 1885 through 1905. The Denver Public Library Western History Department has four boxes of Gove's letters that date from his beginning in Denver and his work as a lobbyist for the Great Western Sugar Company. One can also find references to Gove throughout the National Education Association's reports. Dexter Takesue, "Aaron E. Gove: Denver School Superintendent, 1874–1890" (M.A. Thesis, Univ. of Denver, 1967) presents a fair evaluation of Gove's work through 1890. Two histories of Denver that offer interpretations of the city's early educational endeavors are Lyle W. Dorsett and Michael McCarthy, *The Queen City: A History of Denver* (1977; rev. ed., 1986); and Stephen J. Leonard and Thomas J. Noel, *Denver: Mining Camp to Metropolis* (1990). Leonard and Noel's endnotes are worth reading, particularly the references to the compilation by the Denver Public Schools, "Histories of Denver Public Schools," and Allen Zohn, "The Development of Public Education in Denver, 1859–1902" (M.A. thesis, Univ. of Denver, 1940).

JAMES A. DENTON

GOWEN, Franklin Benjamin (9 Feb. 1836–14 Dec. 1889), lawyer and railroad executive, was born in Mount Airy, Philadelphia County, Pennsylvania, the son of James Gowen, a wealthy merchant and farmer, and Mary Miller. Despite his father's wealth, Gowen never completed his formal education. He attended a Roman Catholic school in Maryland and a Moravian school in Pennsylvania, before his father apprenticed him to a storekeeper in Lancaster, Pennsylvania, at age thirteen.

Following his apprenticeship, Gowen moved in 1857 to Schuylkill County, Pennsylvania, a center of anthracite coal mining. In 1857 he managed a colliery that was owned by his father. The next year he formed a partnership with James G. Turner to mine anthracite. When coal prices fell the following year, the partnership collapsed. Although Gowen never again would directly operate a mine, he would spend the remainder of his life connected in some way with the anthracite industry. In 1858 Gowen married Esther Brisben of Sunbury, Pennsylvania. The couple had three children.

Following his failure as a mine owner, Gowen became a lawyer. He read the law under a Pottsville attorney and was admitted to the bar in 1860. In 1862 he was elected district attorney of Schuylkill County, but he resigned the position after only two years and returned to private practice. In 1865 the Philadelphia & Reading Railroad (the region's largest anthracite carrier) chose Gowen as its local counsel in Pottsville. Gowen quickly rose within the management of the railroad. In 1867 he became head of the legal department and moved to Philadelphia, the corporate headquarters. Two years later, when Reading president Charles E. Smith was ill, Gowen became the acting president of the company. Gowen was elected president of the railroad in 1870.

During Gowen's tenures as president of the Reading (he served on three separate occasions: 1870–1880, 1882–1884, and 1886), he attempted to expand the company from a small regional railroad to a major national corporation. He used his eloquence to win money from investors and concessions from legislators for the Reading's many battles with its crosstown rival, the Pennsylvania Railroad. The Philadelphia & Reading depended on anthracite coal for a vast majority of its traffic, and Gowen worked throughout his career to stabilize this volatile industry. An early example came in the 1870s when he used the power of Reading to help the mine owners crush a strong union. At the same time he tried to put together syndicates of mine owners to limit production and raise coal prices.

His first attempt in the 1870s to enlarge the Reading is an early example of vertical integration. Gowen wanted the railroad to own mines and retail distribution points. He thought this would ensure a stable traffic base for the company and help to end the chronic overproduction problems that plagued the anthracite industry because of its fragmented ownership. The Reading's charter, however, expressly prohibited the railroad from mining activities. It took Gowen two attempts at clandestine amendment before he was able to create a subsidiary that would become the Philadelphia & Reading Coal & Iron Company.

In 1872 Gowen was elected a Democratic delegate to the state constitutional convention. After he successfully represented the interests of the Reading on all matters related to railroad regulation, he resigned.

Gowen's purchase of coal lands pushed the Reading deeply into debt. In 1873 he went to London and convinced McCalmont Brothers (the British investment bankers who headed the syndicate that controlled the company) to loan the railroad more money using his eloquence and overly optimistic revenue projections.

In 1876 Gowen and Pennsylvania helped to blur the line between public and private interest when the commonwealth appointed him special prosecutor in the cases involving the Molly Maguires. The Molly Maguires were a secret Irish-American organization that allegedly had committed terrorism in the anthracite region against coal operators (including the Reading) during the 1870s. Gowen used railroad detectives and agents from the Pinkerton National Detective Agency to battle the Molly Maguires. One Pinkerton agent infiltrated the organization and testified at a series of politically charged trials. A number of reputed Molly Maguires were convicted, and many were executed.

During the 1880s, Gowen's attempts to expand the Reading met with repeated disaster. In 1880 the railroad went into bankruptcy. Gowen was replaced as president the next year when it became apparent that he had manipulated the annual reports of the railroad and its subsidiaries for years. He returned to office in 1882 after a proxy fight, with a new ally and a new plan. He and William H. Vanderbilt (of the New York Central) would build a railroad from Harrisburg to Pittsburgh to compete with the Pennsylvania. In 1884 Gowen resigned the presidency again and had George deB. Keim, a trusted aid, named his successor. Gowen became disenchanted with Keim when Keim refused Gowen's advice on the management of the company. Gowen watched helplessly as J. Pierpont Morgan killed his Pittsburgh line in a brokered deal between the Pennsylvania and the New York Central. In 1886 Gowen briefly regained the presidency of the Reading a final time, only to be forced out by Morgan following yet another bankruptcy. Gowen returned to the private practice of law after this final defeat. In 1889, while he was in Washington, D.C., preparing to present an antitrust case before the Interstate Commerce Commission, he purchased a revolver and killed himself.

Gowen was at the peak of his fame during the 1870s when he was the aggressive president of the Philadelphia & Reading Railroad. He added to his national reputation when he prosecuted the Molly Maguires in 1877. But with the failure of his expansion plans for the Reading in the mid-1880s, he slipped into obscurity. If Gowen is remembered at all it is because of his prosecution of the Molly Maguires and not because of his long association with the Reading. Overlooking his role as an unsuccessful railroad tycoon, however, misses the central part of his career. Gowen is a fascinating example of the executives who lost out in the great railroad consolidations of the late nineteenth century. For every Vanderbilt there were a dozen Gowens.

• The largest collection of Gowen's papers is in the Reading Company Collection of the Hagley Museum and Library, Wilmington, Del. Additional materials can be found in the Baltimore & Ohio Collection and Garrett Papers at the Maryland Historical Society. Although it is dated in places, Marvin W. Schlegal's *Ruler of the Reading: The Life of Franklin B. Gowen* (1947) remains the standard work on his life. All the major Philadelphia newspapers had articles and obituaries following his suicide, see, for example, the *Philadelphia Inquirer*, 15 Dec. 1889, and the *Philadelphia Public Ledger*, 16 Dec. 1889.

JOHN H. HEPP IV

GRABAU, Amadeus William (9 Jan. 1870–20 Mar. 1946), geologist and paleontologist, was born in in Cedarburgh, Wisconsin, the son of Rev. William Grabau, a Lutheran minister, and Marcia von Rohr. His mother died when he was six years old, and he was raised by his father and stepmother. His exceptional intelligence was recognized early by his family, who supported his youthful projects and interests. Grabau became interested in geology while taking a correspondence course in mineralogy from W. O. Crosby of the Massachusetts Institute of Technology. Crosby took a personal interest in young Grabau and encouraged him to enroll at MIT, from which he graduated in 1896. He then received an M.S. (1898) and a D.Sc. (1900) in geology from Harvard University. From 1899 to 1901 he was an instructor and then a professor of geology at Rensselaer Polytechnic Institute, while simultaneously lecturing in geology at Tufts College.

In 1901 Grabau married Mary Antin; they had one daughter. In the same year he took a position as lecturer in paleontology at Columbia University, advancing to a professorship three years later. During the next decade Grabau published pioneering reference works providing precise descriptions of sedimentary rock sequences and their contained fossils. He also carefully recorded, layer by layer, the stratigraphic range of fossils, using these data to infer the ages of rocks as well as their environments of deposition. He was an early leader in constructing paleogeographic maps and sequences of environmental change—eventually on a global scale. Grabau's collaborative effort with Hervey W. Shimer, *North American Index Fossils: Invertebrates* (1910), catalogs North American invertebrate fossils and their stratigraphic ranges. Through the 1960s, with revision, this book remained the standard reference for identifying North American fossil invertebrates and determining the age of the rocks enclosing them. Although gradually superseded for critical work by the multivolume *Treatise on Invertebrate Paleontology*, his "index fossils" has remained useful as a quick reference. Grabau's *Principles of Stratigraphy*—first published in 1913, with a second edition in 1924, and reprinted in 1960 with a prefatory note by Marshall Kay—continued to remain in print through the last half of the twentieth century. This book is a comprehensive account of the means by which earth history may be inferred from the rock record. It is notable for equally emphasizing rocks and fossils and for its innovative scheme of rock classification. Grabau recognized the importance of depositional environment as well as evolutionary change in determining the fossil content of rock units.

In 1919 Grabau was forced to leave Columbia University in the face of intense anti-German sentiment that had developed during the First World War. Although he was not considered disloyal to his country, he staunchly retained and articulated his respect for German science and culture in the face of popular denigration of all things German. These attitudes also created conflicts in his marriage. Mary Grabau was a Russian Jewish woman of great talent who published *The Promised Land* (1912) and lectured extensively for Allied causes during the war.

In 1920, having been estranged from his wife, Grabau moved to Beijing, China, to become China Foundation Research Professor at the National University and chief paleontologist of the Chinese Geological Survey. He was part of the American effort in China; there he became part of a community of American and European missionaries and professionals engaged in China's "modernization" (which began after the Sun Yat-sen revolution and continued until the Second World War).

Grabau's last major publications in the United States were *Geology of Non-Metallic Mineral Deposits other than Silicates*, vol. 1: *Principles of Salt Deposition* (1920) and *A Textbook of Geology* (1920–1921). Before leaving the United States, Grabau had completed many monographic studies of fossil gastropods, corals, and brachiopods, and important stratigraphic studies of North American Cambrian through Devonian rocks. He continued this research in China, extending his scope to Permian rocks and fossils, along with the history of early man. Grabau also organized China's first corps of professional geologists and paleontologists and founded the institutions and professional societies in which they served. His *Stratigraphy of China*, published in *Bulletin* 1 (1923) and *Bulletin* 2 (1928) of the Geological Society of China, provided the first comprehensive documentation of that country's geology.

All of Grabau's work in China was published in English. He was quite involved in efforts to send American and European geologists to work in China and in turn bring Chinese students and professionals into the United States for training. He also maintained his professional ties with American specialists in his fields of interest, many of whom financed his return to the United States to attend the Washington International Geographical Congress in 1933, his only visit to the United States after he moved to China.

During the last decade of his life Grabau developed two major theoretical concepts: the pulsation theory and the polar control theory. The pulsation theory explained the sedimentary rock record in terms of repeated expansion and contraction of the Earth. During times of expansion ("pulsations"), seas covered most of the continental area. Conversely, contractions ("interpulsations") deepened ocean basins into which the seas retreated. Rocks deposited during advances exhibited the effects of pulsation systems. These primarily marine sedimentary rocks constituted most of the sedimentary record. During interpulsations, erosion dominated, leaving widespread erosional surfaces (unconformities) and a scanty record of shoreline and nonmarine sediments. Grabau revised the geologic time scale into a series of pulsation and interpulsation systems, which he believed represented all of geologic time. His theories and data convinced many of his colleagues of the fundamental importance of eustatic changes in sea level, although few credited Grabau's proposed causal mechanism. However, the research thus stimulated ultimately led in the 1970s to P. K. Vail's theory of global rise and fall of sea level, thereby revolutionizing stratigraphic analysis.

Grabau's polar control theory, derived from his paleogeographic compilations, envisioned the outer crust shifting over the plastic interior of the Earth, bringing continental masses into polar position from time to time, thus causing episodic continental glaciation. A postulated continental glaciation in northern Africa during the Ordovician is an example. This particular glaciation was documented two decades later with the discovery of ancient glacial deposits in the Sahara. He also proposed that rearrangement of continental land masses would explain disjunct geologic patterns on continents now separated by oceans. (Plate tectonic theory, developed in the 1950s and 1960s, finally presented a different, generally accepted geophysical mechanism to explain crustal shifts proposed by Grabau.)

In Beijing, between 1934 and 1938, Grabau published four volumes of *Paleozoic Systems in the Light of the Pulsation Theory*. This was the first portion of a projected comprehensive work on the entire paleozoic system on a global basis. In 1940, stranded in the Chinese capital as a result of the Sino-Japanese war and facing advancing age and ill health, he published *The Rhythm of the Ages: Earth History in the Light of the Pulsation and Polar Control Theories*, outlining pulsation and interpulsation systems for the global sedimentary rock record, a project he realized he could not complete in detail. Unfortunately the book did not become readily available outside of China until the war ended.

In 1941 Grabau was interned by the Japanese in the British Embassy, where he remained until the Japanese surrender in September 1945. Although Grabau and his wife reconciled after wartime passions subsided, her illness and their daughter's illness, coupled with complications posed by the Sino-Japanese hostilities, prevented her from joining him in China. Grabau died on the premises of the Chinese Geological Survey in Beijing.

• George B. Barbour, *In the Field with Teilhard de Chardin* (1965), contains Barbour's memories of personal contacts with Grabau in Beijing. The Geological Society of China, *Bulletin* 27 (1947) contains a series of memorial articles on Grabau and includes a bibliography of 291 of Grabau's publications. Other sources include Hervey W. Shimer, "Memorial to Amadeus William Grabau," *Proceedings of the Geological Society of America: Annual Report for 1946* (1947): 155–56, which includes a portrait;; Edward C. Roy, "Grabau," in *Biographies of Geologists, Materials for the Study of the History of Geology 851, a Seminar in the History of Geology, 1953–1958, Second Supplement*, ed. Aurele La Rocque (1964), p. 27; Markes E. Johnson, "A. W. Grabau and the Fruition of a New Life in China," *Journal of Geological Education* 33 (1985): 106–11, an account of Grabau's interaction with the Chinese and European academic community in Beijing; Johnson, "A. W. Grabau's Embryonic Sequence Stratigraphy and Eustatic Curve," in *Eustasy: The Historical Ups and Downs of a Major Geological Concept*, ed. Robert H. Dott, Jr. (1992); H. Deighton Thomas, "Prof. Amadeus W. Grabau," *Nature* 146 (1946): 84–91; Shimer, "Dr. Grabau in China," *Science* 97 (1943): 555–56; and Shimer, "Amadeus William Grabau, An Appreciation," *Science* 244 (1946): 735–36. Two articles in *Interchange of Geoscience Ideas between the East and West, Proceedings of the XVth International Symposium of INHIGEO, 1990, Beijing*, eds. Hongzhen Wang et al. (1991), are also worth noting: Ursula B. Marvin, "Amadeus William Grabau's Global Theories in Light of Current Models," pp. 55–57; and Guang Yu, "Professor Amadeus William Grabau in Peking University," pp. 73–79. An obituary is in the *New York Times*, 27 Mar. 1946.

RALPH L. LANGENHEIM, JR.

GRABAU, Johannes Andreas August (18 Mar. 1804–2 June 1879), Lutheran pastor and church leader, was born in Olvenstadt, Germany, the son of Johannes Andreas Grabau and Anna Dorothea Jericho, farmers. He studied theology at the University of Halle for five years, graduating in 1829. He then taught school until 1834 when he was ordained in Erfurt and received a church position there.

In July 1834 Grabau married Christiane Sophie Burggraf; they had four children. In 1817 the Lutheran and Reformed Protestant churches of Prussia had, by royal command, united in a single Union church. Grabau, a strong partisan of the Lutheran confessions, was deeply troubled by the mixing of Lutheran and Reformed theology in the Union church. In 1836 he announced to his congregation that he would no longer use the official Union church liturgy but would instead substitute the old Lutheran order of worship. Removed from his position by authorities in 1836, Grabau continued to minister and attract allies, and in 1837 he was imprisoned by the Prussian government. He escaped in September, with the aid of one of his captors, Captain Heinrich von Rohr, and spent a year teaching and preaching throughout Central Germany, until he was recaptured in September 1838. In 1839, his health having deteriorated, the Prussian government allowed him to immigrate to the United States, and with a group of one thousand followers Grabau left Hamburg in the summer of 1839. He and a large group settled in Buffalo, New York, while a smaller group settled near Milwaukee, Wisconsin. In 1843 another 1,600 immigrants joined these two colonies.

In Buffalo, Grabau organized a congregation, which he served for forty years. He also started Martin Luther Seminary, one of whose first students was Rohr. On 15 July 1845 Grabau, Rohr, and other pastors met in Milwaukee and organized the Synod of the Lutheran Church Emigrated from Prussia, which later became known as the Buffalo Synod. Grabau was the leader and theologian of this synod, which he hoped would unite all the confessional Lutherans in the United States who accepted the authority of the sixteenth-century Lutheran confessions. By a number of accounts, however, he was authoritarian, and many resented his style. In 1842 he came into conflict with Carl F. W. Walther, the leader of another group of German Lutheran immigrants organized as the Missouri Synod, over the doctrines of ministry and ordination and the nature of the church. Grabau and the Buffalo Synod believed that the ministerial call and office were given by God to the pastor and ratified by the synod, which meant that the pastor had complete control over the congregation. The Missouri Synod, on the other hand, had a "lower" theory of ministry, which held that ordination was a power of the local congregation. This bitter controversy widened, with Missouri founding congregations in competition with those of the Buffalo Synod. The conflict, and Grabau's sometime arbitrary rule over the Buffalo Synod, resulted in a three-way split of the synod in 1866. The largest group, composed of twelve pastors, entered into the Missouri Synod; Rohr and others formed an independent synod; and Grabau was left with a small group of pastors and congregations that continued on as the Buffalo Synod.

After the split, the conflict with the Missouri Synod waned, and Grabau spent much of his time rebuilding his synod. He served the Buffalo Synod as senior minister, as teacher at Martin Luther Seminary, as editor of its paper, *Die Wachende Kirche*, and as leading theologian. The author of a number of theological works, mainly directed against the Missouri Synod, he also furnished the Buffalo Synod with a hymnal and a liturgical order of worship. In 1874 Rohr died. In 1877 the independent synod dissolved, and some of its pastors and congregations returned to the Buffalo Synod. Grabau died in Buffalo.

Grabau's influence on American Lutheranism was limited by the small size of the Buffalo Synod, yet his intellectual influence and challenge went beyond the borders of his denomination. His principled stance in Germany and his ideas about ministry and the church have continued to inform American Lutheranism.

• Grabau's papers are in the Archives of the Evangelical Lutheran Church of America, Chicago, Ill. A biography written by his son Johann A. Grabau, *Lebenslauf des Ehrwürdigen J. An. A. Grabau* (1879), is partly translated by E. M. Biegener in *Concordia Historical Institute Quarterly* 23 and 24 (1950–1951). Charles Lutz, ed., *Church Roots* (1985), tells the story of Grabau's life and imprisonment in Germany. William Cwirla, "Grabau and the Saxon Pioneers: The Doctrine of the Holy Ministry, 1840–1845," *Concordia Historical Institute Quarterly* 68 (1965), tells of his conflict with Missouri. See also P. H. Buehring, *The Spirit of the American Lutheran Church* (1940), for a history of the development of the Buffalo Synod.

MARK GRANQUIST

GRABLE, Betty (18 Dec. 1916–2 July 1973), film and stage actress, was born Ruth Elizabeth Grable in St. Louis, Missouri, the daughter of Conn Grable, a stockbroker, and Lillian Hofman. From Betty's infancy, Lillian Grable projected her own frustrated singing ambitions onto her daughter. A legendary stage mother, Lillian Grable suffered from an ambulatory problem, described as a "stiff hip," that was aggravated by her daughter's birth. Rigorously trained in tap, dance, voice, and saxophone, Betty began performing for private groups, in vaudeville, and in local public performances at the age of five. In 1929, to realize her daughter's career, Lillian Grable moved with her to Los Angeles, while her husband and other daughter remained in St. Louis. In Los Angeles Betty Grable was signed to a studio contract with 20th Century–Fox at thirteen. Her age was concealed, but she was dismissed when her youth was discovered after she had appeared illegally in the chorus line in several films.

Grable next signed a studio contract with Goldwyn–United Artists, and after several unnoticed appearances she moonlighted under the stage name Frances Dean in films by blacklisted director Roscoe "Fatty" Arbuckle. Her outside work resulted in a release from Goldwyn, and she performed as a vocalist for bands until she was signed to a contract by MGM at sixteen. Leased to RKO for *The Gay Divorcee* (1934), starring Ginger Rogers and Fred Astaire, Grable's performance in the dance number "Let's K-nock K-nees" attracted attention, and she was awarded the lead in *The Nitwits* (1935). Several similar "college capers" films followed.

The change in Grable's fortunes from small-time actress to major film star began with her romance with Jackie Coogan, the first American child superstar. Their engagement brought Grable a measure of fame, and she signed with Paramount. Following their 1937 marriage, Grable and Coogan made two films together for Paramount, capitalizing on the couple's fame. In *Campus Confessions* (1938) Grable was given her first top billing. Despite her blossoming career, the marriage quickly showed signs of strain as Coogan's business ventures failed. Grable supported Coogan until the conclusion of a suit he had brought against his relatives over his childhood earnings. When he was awarded a small settlement, she initiated divorce proceedings, citing irreconcilable differences; divorce was granted in 1939.

Following her divorce Grable returned to 20th Century–Fox, beginning a ten-year association with the studio that was characterized by her tumultuous relationship with the domineering studio chief Darryl F. Zanuck. At Fox, Grable was kept in the wings to control reigning studio star Alice Faye. Zanuck lent her to do stage work in *Dubarry Was a Lady* from 1939 to 1940, until Faye's sudden attack of appendicitis forced her replacement by Grable in the musical *Down Argentine Way* (1940), the film that brought Grable stardom.

Down Argentine Way was a tremendous financial success. 20th Century–Fox utilized the new color film process Technicolor, which complemented Grable's vibrant coloring, and her vivacious energy caught the audience's attention. The film featured several smart dance numbers in which Grable's legs, her most celebrated asset, were prominently featured. The film capitalized on her natural talents as a dancer and singer; she would spend the rest of her career in the musical genre.

As her career blossomed Grable was romantically linked with several leading men, including Artie Shaw and George Raft. Her mother continued to be a major influence in her life and always lived near her daughter, ready to offer advice. After living apart for more than a decade, her parents divorced in 1940. Grable kept a close relationship with both.

Following *Down Argentine Way*, Grable starred in *Tin Pan Alley* (1940), which was followed by a series of frothy musicals, all financial hits. In December 1941 World War II sobered the national mood, and Grable on screen provided relief. Not a femme fatale in the tradition of Bette Davis and Greta Garbo, she appealed to men and women alike. On screen and off she was characterized by personal warmth and a good-natured sense of humor. Grable saw herself as an inspiration for the soldiers and became personally involved in the war effort, as did many of Hollywood's leading ladies. Her movie *Song of the Islands* (1942) was a blockbuster and also introduced her to bandleader Harry James, her future husband. In 1943 she leaped from the eighth most popular Hollywood star to the first position; she also starred in the smash *Sweet Rosie O'Grady* (1943). Grable even appeared on the cover of *Time* magazine on 23 August 1948.

Grable's 1943 marriage to James only increased her popularity. James was a celebrity in his own right as a trumpeter and for occasional film appearances. Together, Grable and James presented a picture of a happy couple, and the birth of their two children confirmed this image.

In what would become her most famous deed, Grable posed for a still photo that later came to be known as the "pin-up shot." This photograph, snapped from behind, showed her in a white swimsuit and high heels, turning toward the camera with hands on hips, a smile on her lips, and a saucy wink. Three million copies were said to be in GI hands, decorating American military barracks worldwide. Grable's image in the pin-up pose was painted on warplanes, and a common wartime slogan for male soldiers was "I want a girl just like the girl who married Harry James."

Grable's physical beauty was at the center of her appeal. Her physical measurements were heavily publicized. Her famous legs were displayed in her movies and commented on by film critics. Graumann's Chinese Theater immortalized Grable's hands, feet, and right leg in cement for posterity. As a publicity stunt, 20th Century–Fox had her legs insured with Lloyd's of London for $1 million.

Fox capitalized on Grable's fame with *Pin-Up Girl* (1944), which despite poor critical reception was a box-office smash. In 1944 Grable averaged 10,000 fan letters a week, and her films over the next three years were the highest earners for 20th Century–Fox. Beginning in 1942 she stayed in the top ten of Hollywood's most popular stars for ten years. In 1946–1947 she was the highest-paid woman in the United States with a salary of $300,000, higher than Zanuck's.

A series of problems with 20th Century–Fox began in 1946. The conflicts between the studio, led by the authoritarian Zanuck, and Grable eventually led to her departure from films. Suspended for one year from Fox for refusing the role of Sophie in *The Razor's Edge* (1946), Grable devoted herself to her family. She had always viewed herself as a comic actress and had little confidence in her dramatic abilities. When she ventured outside the musical genre, she met severe criticism and was ignored by her public. She resisted acting in films other than musicals, a genre that has historically found little favor with critics. Her refusal to accept the dramatic role of Sophie was not surprising; her fears were confirmed when her dramatic attempt in *The Shocking Miss Pilgrim* (1947), a historical drama casting her as a suffragist, was a critical and financial failure. Grable quickly returned to her genre, and her public returned to her, with the first of four films with Dan Dailey, *Mother Wore Tights* (1947). She followed this with a series of generic musicals, true to form.

Grable's conflicts with the studio were not over. Despite the fact that her films had earned the studio more than $100 million over the years, she suffered repeated suspensions because of creative differences with Zanuck. Rising young star Marilyn Monroe was poised to replace the studio queen, and Grable's career was in its final stages. Grable starred with Monroe and Lauren Bacall in *How to Marry a Millionaire* (1953) before finally tearing up her contract with Fox in 1953.

At the height of Grable's popularity she and James invested heavily in horse racing, a costly mistake. After Grable left Fox, James's career declined, his gambling increased, and their marriage deteriorated. Their accountant mishandled funds, and James and Grable owed $500,000 in back taxes. The horse ranch was sold to pay bills, and Grable was reduced to supporting her family by appearing in a variety of second-rate entertainments, including television specials. Financial distress necessitated a return to 20th Century–Fox for *How to Be Very Very Popular* (1955). Her father's death in 1955 was deeply painful to her.

The James family's move to Las Vegas in the early 1960s exacerbated the problems. While Grable successfully established a career in theater, appearing in a Las Vegas show of various musical numbers from her films of the 1940s, gambling problems plagued her marriage. Despite the fact that Grable earned more than $3 million during her career, the couple had few assets and many debts. The death of her mother in 1964 caused her tremendous anguish. She finally divorced James in 1965.

After her divorce Grable continued her successful stage career, appearing in a popular touring company of *Hello, Dolly!* and in *Born Yesterday.* She also appeared in Geritol commercials. In 1971 she was honored by the film industry when she was asked to present the Academy Award for best musical score. She enjoyed a comfortable relationship with companion Robert Remick for nearly eight years. Grable had signed to star in an Australian production of *No, No Nanette* when she learned that she had inoperable lung cancer. She died in Santa Monica, California.

Icon of a generation, Grable was an integral part of the American collective consciousness of the war years. "As American as apple pie and Betty Grable" was a slogan of the time. Her warmth and dynamic verve captured the hearts of fans. Underappreciated and often vilified by critics during her lifetime, Grable's lasting appeal and status as a cultural icon were later reevaluated along with her significance to Hollywood and American culture.

• Several biographies appeared after Grable's death, notably Spero Pastos, *Pin-Up: The Tragedy of Betty Grable* (1986), and Doug Warren, *Betty Grable: The Reluctant Movie Queen* (1981). Later treatments include Larry Billman's exhaustive bio-bibliography of Grable's appearances (1993), and Tom McGee, *Betty Grable: The Girl with the Million Dollar Legs* (1995). The Arts and Entertainment cable network produced a video biography of Grable in 1995. See also Mel Gussow, *Darryl F. Zanuck: Don't Say Yes until I Finish Talking* (1971), and Zanuck, *Memo from Darryl F. Zanuck: The Golden Years at Twentieth Century–Fox,* ed. Rudy Behlmer (1993). An obituary is in the *New York Times,* 4 July 1973.

JENNIFER HUGHES DYER

GRACE, Charles Emmanuel (25 Jan. 1881–12 Jan. 1960), better known as Daddy Grace or Sweet Daddy Grace or by his self-proclaimed title, Boyfriend of the World, was one of the more flamboyant African-American religious personalities of the twentieth century. He was born, probably as Marceline Manoel da Graca, in Brava, Cape Verde Islands, of mixed Portuguese and African ancestry, the son of Manuel de Graca and Gertrude Lomba. In the charismatic church that he founded and headed, however, he managed to transcend race by declaring, "I am a colorless man. I am a colorless bishop. Sometimes I am black, sometimes white. I preach to all races." Like many other Cape Verdeans, Grace immigrated to New Bedford, Massachusetts, around the turn of the century and worked there and on Cape Cod as a short-order cook, a salesman of sewing machines and patent medicines and a cranberry picker.

Also known as Bishop Grace, he may have established his first church in West Wareham, Massachusetts, around 1919, but he achieved his early success in Charlotte, North Carolina, where he held evangelical tent meetings and attracted more than 10,000 followers in the 1920s. In 1927 in Washington, D.C., he in-

corporated the United House of Prayer for All People on the Rock of the Apostolic Faith. The phrase "All People" was said to indicate Grace's acceptance of the poor and disinherited who were unwelcome in more conventional churches. Grace established churches up and down the eastern seaboard, eventually numbering at least 500,000 people in some 100 congregations in nearly seventy cities. Most, but not all, members were African American.

In person, Daddy Grace presented a dramatic figure with his shoulder-length hair; six-inch-long fingernails painted red, white, and blue; and gold and purple cutaway coats and chartreuse vests. A master of public pageantry and showmanship, he sponsored bands and parades, outfitted his followers in uniforms, and staged colorful outdoor mass baptisms in swimming pools or with fire hoses. He promoted band music and once asked, "Why should the devil have all the good times?" He was generally surrounded by adoring followers who pinned dollar bills to his robe as he walked slowly down the aisle of one of his churches.

Many nonfollowers thought Daddy Grace an exploitative religious fraud and confidence man. The alleged escapism of his church was widely criticized, and E. Franklin Frazier, the Howard University sociologist, condemned the church for what he called its erotic dancing while disciples, mainly female, sang, "Daddy, you feel so good." Whatever spiritual or emotional satisfactions Daddy Grace provided his people, he also supplied apartment buildings, pension funds, retirement homes, burial plans, and church cafeterias that dispensed free food. He received a considerable income, invested heavily in real estate, and personally owned some forty residences. He bought the El Dorado on Central Park West in New York City, then the world's tallest apartment building. He purchased Prophet Jones's 54-room mansion in Detroit, which he had repainted red, white, and blue to the consternation of the neighborhood. In 1938 he acquired the kingdom of heaven property in Harlem of another charismatic leader, Father Divine.

The money came not only from the offerings of the faithful members of the United House of Prayer for All People but also from the numerous Grace-sponsored moneymaking enterprises that manufactured and sold such products as soap, hair pomade, vitamins, and ice cream. Followers reportedly believed these products had special powers bestowed by Daddy Grace. Healing was an important element in the movement, and Grace was widely believed by the faithful to have curative powers, particularly via buttered toast from which he had taken a bite. His *Grace Magazine,* which sold for ten cents, was also thought to be restorative when touched to the body.

Daddy Grace fused elements from the holiness and Pentecostal religious traditions, but his church (often referred to as a sect) depended largely on his charisma. He did not himself actually assert the divinity his followers attributed to him. "I never said I was God," he once stated, "but you cannot prove to me I'm not." He did say, however, "If you sin against God, Grace can save you, but if you sin against Grace, God cannot save you," as well as "Grace has given God a vacation, and since God is on His vacation, don't worry Him." He delighted in pointing out how many times the word grace appears in the Bible and was fond of repeating the classic Protestant formula that salvation is by grace alone.

Grace's considerable wealth attracted several lawsuits. In 1957 Louvenia Royster, a retired Georgia schoolteacher, claimed that Daddy Grace had married her in New York in 1923 under the name of John H. Royster but had deserted in 1928, leaving her with a daughter, now an adult. Grace responded that he was in the Holy Land at the time of the alleged marriage and had spent the night in question in the manger in which Jesus was born. The court dismissed her claim. Jennie Grace of New Bedford claimed that Daddy Grace had married her in 1909. She also was the mother of a grown daughter, whom she also said he had fathered. Whatever his relationships with these women, Daddy Grace apparently was the father of at least one child, a son, Marcellino V. Grace of Brentwood, Maryland.

The greatest legal difficulties came, however, after Grace's death, which occurred while he was visiting in Los Angeles. His finances were chaotic, and it was unclear what monies and property belonged to the church and what constituted his personal estate. There was some $25 million at issue, much of it in real estate but also including $3 million in cash in seventy-five banks in fifty cities and diamond-studded keys to numerous safe deposit boxes. Thirty-six lawyers became involved in the litigation. The Internal Revenue Service put a lien of $5.9 million against the estate at his death, claiming he owed that amount in back taxes, but settled in 1961 for $1.9 million. Grace was buried in New Bedford.

A fierce internal struggle for succession ensued. Bishop Walter McCollough took over the United House of Prayer after winning a lawsuit against rival contender James Walton. Much less flamboyant than Grace, McCollough concentrated on consolidating the denomination, making it more traditionally Pentecostal, and building a substantial low-income housing project. He moved the church, he said, "from the storefront to the forefront."

• General background information on Bishop Grace is in Marilyn Halter, *Between Race and Ethnicity: Cape Verdean American Immigrants, 1860–1965* (1993). Lenwood G. Davis compiled *Daddy Grace: An Annotated Bibliography* (1992). Two important articles are "America's Richest Negro Minister: Daddy Grace Heads Religious Empire Worth $10 Million, Claims He Is Neither Wealthy nor Negro," *Ebony*, Jan. 1952, pp. 17–23, and Robert Lovinger, "I Am the Boyfriend of the World," *New Bedford Standard Times*, 12 Jan. 1960. An obituary is in the *New York Times*, 13 Jan. 1960.

RICHARD NEWMAN

GRACE, Eugene Gifford (27 Aug. 1876–25 July 1960), industrialist, was born in Goshen, New Jersey, the son of John Wesley Grace, a ship's captain, and Rebecca G. Morris. In 1895 he matriculated at Lehigh University in Bethlehem, Pennsylvania, where he conducted experiments at the Bethlehem Iron Company while studying electrical engineering. In 1899 he received his E.E. degree and went to work for the renamed Bethlehem Steel Company, a major producer of heavy gun forgings and armor plate. After a six-month stint as an electric crane operator, he became a supervisor in the open hearth department. In 1902 he married Marion Brown, with whom he had three children. Also in 1902 he was promoted to superintendent of yards and transportation and over the next three years developed a system for handling incoming material and outgoing finished product that worked so efficiently that he came to the attention of Charles M. Schwab, president of Bethlehem Steel Corporation, the company's parent. Schwab was looking for someone to overhaul the Juragua Iron Company, Bethlehem's Cuban subsidiary and the producer of most of its iron ore, and in 1905 he made Grace the general superintendent of Juragua. After reorganizing that company's management and mechanizing its mining operations, Grace in 1906 returned to Pennsylvania, whereupon he was promoted to assistant general superintendent and put in charge of building a new mill in South Bethlehem.

That same year Schwab decided to decrease the company's dependence on military contracts by developing the Bethlehem Beam, a steel beam with a wide flange that was lighter, stronger, and less costly than conventional beams. Moreover, the Bethlehem Beam could be rolled in much longer sections than conventional beams, which had to be riveted together to make long sections, thereby facilitating the construction of taller buildings and contributing to the so-called skyscraper revolution. In order to produce this beam, Schwab promoted Grace to general superintendent and tasked him with the construction of a rolling mill dedicated to the beam's manufacture. This product was so well received by the commercial construction industry that within ten years Bethlehem Steel dominated the structural steel market in the eastern United States. The beam's success dictated a major reorganization of the company's entire operation, and in 1908 Grace was promoted to general manager with complete responsibility for integrating the company's buying, manufacturing, and marketing functions. He advanced to vice president in 1911 and president in 1913.

Despite the beam's success, Bethlehem Steel continued to manufacture military ordnance, and when World War I broke out Grace oversaw the production of huge amounts of war matériel for France, Great Britain, and Russia. In 1916 Schwab became chairman of the board of Bethlehem Steel Corporation, and Grace took on the additional duties of president of the corporation. When the United States entered the war in 1917, he upgraded and expanded the corporation's production of heavy guns, artillery shells, armor plate, and structural steel for the U.S. government. That same year he reorganized Bethlehem Steel's shipbuilding facilities into the Bethlehem Shipbuilding Corporation, and as president of this corporation he oversaw the construction of more than seventy destroyers and a number of submarines for the U.S. Navy as well as ten passenger liners and several hundred freighters for wartime service.

After the war Schwab embarked on a major acquisition campaign, and by 1929 Bethlehem Steel Corporation owned a railroad, substantial resources of iron ore and coal, and nine major mills that produced heavy steel products. As Schwab bought out various competitors, large and small, Grace integrated them into the operations of the corporation. When the Great Depression greatly decreased the demand for heavy steel, Grace converted several mills to the production of sheet and strip steel and several others to the production of tin plate, all for the automobile industry. When World War II broke out in 1939, he coordinated the corporation's conversion to wartime production. Under his direction, between 1939 and 1945 the corporation produced over 73 million tons of steel, most of which was used to fabricate approximately one-third of the naval guns and armor plate ordered by the U.S. Navy, while its shipbuilding facilities constructed more than 1,100 warships and freighters and converted or repaired almost 38,000 ships. During the war Grace also played a key role in developing, implementing, and administering a plan for allocating steel to the various military agencies and civilian contractors. So smoothly did Grace's plan function that it was used as a model for the development of similar plans for other scarce commodities that were essential to wartime production.

In 1945 Grace resigned as president of Bethlehem Steel Company and Corporation to become chairman of the board of both enterprises. For the next twelve years he directed a long-range modernization program that shifted production away from heavy steel products and into the manufacture of steel for consumer products.

Grace served as president of the American Iron and Steel Institute (AISI) in 1935–1936 and the Lehigh University board of trustees from 1924 to 1956. He was awarded AISI's Gary Medal in 1934, the Iron and Steel Institute of Great Britain's Bessemer Gold Medal in 1942, the American Institute of Mining and Metallurgical Engineers' Rand Medal in 1948, and the Boys Clubs of America's Silver Keystone with Silver Star in 1956. Lehigh's Grace Hall was named in his honor.

In addition to being a skilled executive, Grace was also a gifted athlete. He was the starting shortstop and captain of his college baseball team and was offered an opportunity immediately after graduation to play baseball professionally. He later became one of the finest amateur golfers in the United States; he won several cups and country club championships between 1917 and 1928, scored four holes-in-one in his lifetime, and helped to design two golf courses. In 1951 he helped organize the U.S. Golf Association's Amateur Golf Championship Tournament and received a special lifetime achievement commendation from the Metropolitan Golf Writers Association. In 1957 he retired to his home in Bethlehem, where he died.

Grace's managerial expertise combined with Schwab's financial acumen and vision to make Bethlehem Steel the largest shipbuilder and second-largest steel producer in the world.

• Grace's papers are in the Schwab Memorial Library, Bethlehem Steel Corporation, Bethlehem, Pa. His contributions are discussed in Robert Hessen, *Steel Titan* (1975); William T. Hogan, *An Economic History of the Iron and Steel Industry in the United States* (5 vols., 1971); and Edmund F. Martin, *Promise for the Future* (1967). An obituary is in the *New York Times*, 26 July 1960.

CHARLES W. CAREY, JR.

GRACE, William Russell (10 May 1832–21 Mar. 1904), founder of W. R. Grace & Co. and twice mayor of New York City, was born in Riverstown, Ireland, the son of James Grace, a landowner and farmer, and Eleanor Mary Russell. Grace, like so many Irishmen of his generation, left his famine-ravaged homeland in the mid-nineteenth century seeking a new life in the Americas. Well educated in Jesuit schools and coming from the minor gentry of Ireland, young William arrived in Peru in 1854.

Grace began his career as a purveyor of naval stores to the guano fleets gathered off the coast of Peru in the 1850s. Early on he showed an entrepreneurial gift that was to serve him well. The hundreds of ships that came to load guano off the Chincha Islands needed to revictual and refit for the return trip. To do so, they would go to Callao, the port serving the capital city of Lima almost a hundred miles to the north of the Chinchas. In 1854 Grace became a partner in the Callao firm of Bryce Brothers, purveyors of naval and ships stores to the guano fleets. He suggested that his firm anchor a supply ship in the midst of the fleets. It was a simple but immensely profitable idea. The Bryce-Grace storeship came to be known for providing goods and foods at a fair price. Grace learned to do business with the many American ship captains who came to load guano, the rich fertilizer that revitalized the depleted tobacco and cotton lands of the United States in the 1850s.

Among the travelers Grace met was Lillius Gilchrest, daughter of Mary Jane and George Gilchrest, captain of the ship *Rochambeau* out of Maine. Ship captains often traveled with their families on these long voyages, and Grace soon was enchanted with the seventeen-year-old daughter of the stern captain. William and Lillius were wed in 1859 in a small chapel in Tenants Harbor, Maine; they had six children.

In the 1860s Grace returned to Ireland via New York. He was fascinated by this thriving emporium and in 1866 moved his growing family to New York, bought a home in Brooklyn Heights, and opened W. R. Grace & Co. on Wall Street in the heart of the shipping district. From 1866 until 1880, when he was elected mayor of New York, Grace, his brothers, nephews, and other young business associates expanded their trade across the Americas, moving quickly to take advantage of new business opportunities as they arose. In the 1870s Grace, from New York, and his younger brother Michael, from Lima, invested and traded in a wide variety of businesses, none more profitable than in building the railroads of Peru.

The Graces made friends of Henry Meiggs, the flamboyant North American entrepreneur who built most of Peru's early railroads, and supplied Meiggs with everything from sewing needles to locomotives in the 1870s. Grace established a line of ships between New York and the west coast of South America—the Merchants Line—that was the predecessor of the Grace Line that dominated trade for the first half of the twentieth century between North America and South America. He imparted to his subordinates a warm feeling for Peru and its people.

"I like the Peruvians," Grace wrote to his brother John, who had come over from Ireland in 1872 to join his brothers in the Americas. "I always enjoyed their society and I never looked upon them as more deceitful than [other] people. . . . The English in foreign lands, I never liked; they are, in my experience, presumptuous and self-opinionated."

In a remarkable change of venue for Grace's energies and talents, in the 1870s he moved rapidly from political obscurity to political prominence, being elected mayor of New York in 1880—the first foreign-born Catholic to occupy that high office. Although earlier an admirer of Abraham Lincoln and the Republicans, by the mid-1870s Grace had gravitated to the Democrats as Ulysses S. Grant's Republican administration foundered in corruption.

Grace's true initiation in politics came in the summer of 1880 when he promoted his friend and old Brooklyn neighbor, Judge Calvin E. Pratt, for the Democratic presidential nomination. Although that darkhorse boomlet failed, Grace attracted the attention of Tammany Hall's boss, "Honest" John Kelly, who was searching for a progressive, honest candidate to put—and control—in office.

Grace agreed to accept the Democratic nomination, adding, "But, if elected, *I'll* be the mayor you know." As Marquis James reports in his brilliant biography of Grace: "What boss has not heard that talk? 'Sure,' said Honest John, 'Mr. Grace, *you'll* be the Mayor'" (James, p. 154). In fact, Grace successfully challenged Tammany's rule and became one of the first reform mayors of modern New York, even running with the support of a young maverick Republican, Theodore Roosevelt, when elected to his second term as mayor in 1884.

Grace brought probity and business experience to his two terms as mayor (1880–1882, 1884–1886) and achieved considerable reforms in education, public works, police administration, and sanitation, for example. In his first term, he reformed a corrupt street-cleaning department, then under police commissioners closely allied to Tammany, giving New Yorkers a new view—and cleaner streets—of what a reform-minded, honest mayor could accomplish. In education he appointed the first woman, Grace Dodge, to the board of education. She vindicated his confidence by successfully introducing industrial education into New York schools and helping found Teachers College of Columbia University. From the 1880s until his death, Grace remained a power in Democratic politics at both the state and national levels, especially sought after for his counsel on Latin American affairs.

Grace presided over an increasingly diverse business enterprise at the end of the century; it almost defies categorization. From the 1870s onward—even while he was mayor—the firm's range of interests and investments reflected Grace's immense versatility. His company helped build railroads in Costa Rica, participated in the rubber boom in Brazil, introduced the first steamers from New York to the West Coast, and at the end of the century Grace became one of the principal promoters for a transisthmian canal across Nicaragua. Even when his interests lost to the Panama lobby in 1902, Grace's enthusiasm for a canal helped internationalists such as Theodore Roosevelt realize his dream in the future Panama Canal.

Grace spent many of his last years at a home he had built in Great Neck, Long Island, although he always kept a residence in Manhattan, never too far from his interests not only in city politics but also in the ships that came and went with news and men and goods of his far-flung empire. Not simply a politician and businessman, Grace also gave generously to the Roman Catholic church. He founded and endowed the Grace Institute in New York for the ever-increasing number of young women then entering the industrial workforce. Not only were classes held in millinery, stenography, and bookkeeping, but also cooking, sewing, and laundry work were taught. It was Grace's way of giving girls and young women a better break as they sought to find work outside their homes in industrial America.

When he died in New York City, the *New York Daily News*, always with a penchant for the colorful phrase, perhaps produced the most apt epitaph: "Romantic life story of an Irish lad who ran away from home to be a Robinson Crusoe, who twice became Mayor of New York and died a multimillionaire." That was the embodiment of the American dream at the turn of the century, by which Grace's contemporaries remembered him best.

• The Grace papers in the Rare Book and Manuscript Collection of the Columbia University Library, New York, constitute the single most important source for the study of Grace and the company he founded. This is the most complete collection of papers relating to a U.S. company's early operations in Latin America as well as one of the finest sources of biographical information on William R. Grace. The collection was used extensively by Marquis James in his definitive biography of Grace, *Merchant Adventurer: The Story of W. R. Grace* (1993), which was written in the 1940s though published nearly half a century later. For more on Grace, but from the perspective of the affairs of the company, see Lawrence A. Clayton, *Grace: W. R. Grace & Co.: The Formative Years, 1850–1930* (1985). An obituary is in the *New York Times*, 22 Mar. 1904.

LAWRENCE A. CLAYTON

GRADLE, Henry (17 Aug. 1855–4 Apr. 1911), ophthalmologist and early proponent of bacteriology, was born in Friedburg, a suburb of Frankfurt-am-Main, Prussia, the son of Bernard Gradle and Rose Schottenfels Groedel. In 1859 Bernard Gradle emigrated to the United States and eventually established himself in the tobacco business in Chicago. Rose Gradle and her son moved to Darmstadt where Henry received his early education; she died in 1866 and two years later, when Henry had finished his elementary education, he joined his father in Chicago.

Completing his secondary education, Gradle entered the Chicago Medical College (now Northwestern University Medical School) and received his M.D. in 1874. After a year's internship at Mercy Hospital, Gradle spent the next three years in Europe (Vienna, Berlin, Leipzig, Heidelberg, Paris, and London). He worked especially with bacteriologist Robert Koch and physiologist Carl Ludwig. He also assisted in several ophthalmic clinics on the Continent and in London.

Returning to Chicago in 1879, Gradle began a general practice. By 1885 he was specializing in eye, ear, nose, and throat medicine and had left his earlier research interest in physiology. In 1881 he married Fanny Searls of Waukegan, Illinois. Searls had earned her M.D. from the University of Michigan but, unable to obtain an internship, took training and worked as a nurse before her marriage. The couple had two children, one of whom also became an ophthalmologist.

Gradle's academic positions reflected his interests. He served his medical alma mater as professor of physiology (1879–1884), lecturer in general etiology and hygiene (1892) and professor of those subjects in 1893, professor of general etiology and hygiene and of clinical ophthalmology and otology (1894–1896), and professor of ophthalmology and otology (1897–1906). From 1897 to 1906 Gradle was chairman of the Department of Ophthalmology. He served as attending eye and ear surgeon at Michael Reese and Wesley hospitals and as consulting surgeon in the same fields at Mercy Hospital.

After his studies with Koch, Gradle became an enthusiastic supporter of the new science of bacteriology. This was in spite of the opposition and ridicule of such important Chicago physicians as Nathan Smith Davis. In 1883 Gradle published a series of eight lectures under the title *Bacteria and the Germ Theory of Disease*. One of the first books in English on bacteriology, it stimulated wide interest; a Japanese naval surgeon translated it four years later. Gradle's writings ultimately included a substantial text, *Diseases of the Nose, Pharynx, and Ear* (1902), and nearly 100 journal articles.

Gradle's practical interest in bacteriology is shown by his skillful and widely recognized techniques. He suggested to Edward L. Holmes, founder of the Illinois Eye and Ear Infirmary in Chicago, that he use whiskey bottles lying on their sides as containers for experimental work with bacteria. In his 1883 book Gradle advised using gelatin in culturing the tuberculosis bacillus. A frequently told story has the famous surgeon and pathologist Christian Fenger ordering a young colleague who was having trouble with his bacteriological techniques to "go see Gradle." On Gradle's second trip to the Continent a European physician who had not understood his name when introduced told Gradle himself that the best place to start his bacteriological research was to study the valuable book by Henry Gradle of Chicago.

In 1883 Gradle lectured to the Chicago Philosophical Society on "The Germ Theory of Disease," published as a ten-page article that September in *Popular Science Monthly*. In it Gradle stated, "In the light of the germ-theory, disease is a *struggle for existence between the parts of the organism and some parasite invading it*" (p. 578). Gradle also reported on his bacteriological studies in several medical articles.

As an outgrowth of his interest in hygiene and public health Gradle recommended the boiling of water in Chicago to prevent the spread of disease and argued against the city pouring out its sewage into Lake Michigan, the source of its water supply. "No question of local sanitation," Gradle wrote in 1886, "has been more often and less intelligently discussed in Chicago, than the purity of our drinking water" (*Journal of the American Medical Association* 6, no. 20 [15 May 1886]: 544). D. J. Davis in *History of Medical Practice in Illinois* (1955) called Gradle's 3 June 1893 article, "What Benefits Can Ear Patients Derive from Nasal Treatment?" in the *Journal of the American Medical Association*, a "significant contribution."

In addition to belonging to specialty and regional medical societies, Gradle was a member of the Heidelberg Ophthalmological Society, and he served the Chicago Ophthalmological Society (of which he was a charter member) and the Chicago Laryngological and Otological Society as president in 1896 and 1909, respectively. The breadth of his scientific interests (and an indication of his intellectual curiosity) is shown by his memberships in the Illinois Microscopical Society and the Illuminating Engineering Society.

A fellow ophthalmologist described Gradle as "a man of unique personality" who was five-feet one-inch tall, stockily built with a large head and an untamed red moustache. One colleague referred to him as "The Little Giant" and another noted that "this was practically the only reference to his height that did not cause him mental discomfort" (*History of Medicine and Surgery* [1922], p. 161).

Gradle died of carcinoma of the bladder at his winter home in Santa Barbara, California. His widow and son donated his 4,000-volume collection and supporting funds to the John Crerar Library in Chicago.

A popular speaker, and an intellectually curious scientist, Henry Gradle contributed to the understanding and spreading of the new subject of bacteriology and to the teaching and clinical practice of ophthalmology and otology.

• There are no collections of Gradle's personal papers. Descriptions of Gradle and his work are in Thomas H. Shastid's entry on him in *The American Encyclopedia and Dictionary of Ophthalmology*, vol. 7 (1915), pp. 5619–21 (contains a portrait). Brief accounts, with some additional information, are in the obituary in the *Journal of the American Medical Association* (15 Apr. 1911): 1126, and in the Chicago Medical Society's *History of Medicine and Surgery and Physicians and Surgeons of Chicago* (1922), pp. 160–61 (portrait on p. 158).

WILLIAM K. BEATTY

GRADY, Henry Francis (12 Feb. 1882–14 Sept. 1957), diplomat, economist, and businessman, was born in San Francisco, California, the son of John Henry Grady and Ellen Genevieve Rourke. He earned his A.B. in 1907 from St. Mary's University in Baltimore, Maryland, and his doctorate in economics in 1927 from Columbia University. As a young man, Grady studied for the Roman Catholic priesthood, but his interest in economics and finance led him to overlapping careers in business, academia, and government. In 1917 he married Lucretia del Valle; they had four children.

Grady credited World War I for turning his attention to the problems of war and its prevention. His first service in government came in 1918–1919, when he worked as a member of the Bureau of Planning and Statistics for the U.S. Shipping Board. During 1919 and 1920 he worked as commercial attaché in London and traveled throughout Europe to report on postwar economic conditions.

After completing his doctorate in 1927, Grady took a position as professor of international trade at the University of California, Berkeley, and later served as dean of that university's College of Commerce. In 1937 he left academia and returned to government as a member of the U.S. Tariff Commission. A devout free trader, Grady joined Secretary of State Cordell Hull during the depression-plagued 1930s in working for lower trade barriers worldwide. Both men viewed international trade as an antidote to economic collapse and political instability. From 1939 to 1941 Grady served as assistant secretary of state for economic affairs.

From 1941 to 1947 Grady returned to the private sector to become president of the American President Lines, a shipping company. He nonetheless remained available throughout World War II for special government assignments. He led a mission in 1941 to southern Asia to survey the region's mineral wealth and study the feasibility of a raw materials stockpiling program. In 1942 he led the American Technical Mission to India to assess the subcontinent's potential to produce arms and other war supplies. Grady also served in late 1943 on the Allied Control Commission in Italy as a financial adviser.

The Second World War proved as important to the formation of Grady's views as had the Great War two decades earlier. He became convinced more than ever that the high tariffs of the 1930s had strangled economic recovery, encouraged political extremism, and ultimately produced war. A New Deal Democrat, he espoused the benefits of international capitalism, supplemented by modest but timely amounts of government-financed foreign aid. Viewing the Soviet Union as the one remaining threat to a liberal world order, Grady increasingly emphasized the importance of economic diplomacy in fighting the Cold War.

In March 1946 Grady joined an Allied mission to Greece to oversee that nation's elections. Civil war between leftist, Communist-led forces and the rightist supporters of the Greek monarchy made electioneering difficult. Staunchly opposed to a Communist victory, Grady and other mission members concluded that the elections had been generally fair, marred only by sporadic voting irregularities. Subsequent critics of U.S. policy contended that, since the left had abstained from participating, the newly elected government of Constantine Tsaldaris was hardly representative of the popular will. The messy outcome set the stage for the renewal of Greece's civil war and, in 1947, the pronouncement of the momentous Truman Doctrine, the anti-Communist declaration that accompanied President Harry Truman's decision to send U.S. economic and military aid to the Greek government.

Grady became a participant in another postwar controversy when President Truman appointed him to serve as the American representative on the Anglo-American Committee on Palestine and Related Problems (or the Morrison-Grady Committee). Grady met with British officials in London during July and August 1946 and gave support for a plan to place a unitary Palestine under United Nations trusteeship. The plan would have established a binational government, with provincial autonomy guaranteed to both Jewish and Arab populations.

The details of the Morrison-Grady plan remained vague, but the hope was to avoid the creation of a separate Jewish state and the Palestinian backlash that was sure to follow. The framers of the plan also hoped to facilitate the settlement in Palestine of hundreds of thousands of Jewish refugees, as had been called for by the Anglo-American Committee of Inquiry earlier that year. To bolster the new entity, the committee recommended the allocation of $200 million in loans from the Export-Import Bank. Despite its popularity with many British and U.S. officials, the plan faced strong opposition from both Zionist and Arab groups, and President Truman refused to endorse it.

In April 1947 Grady returned to full-time public service, when he became the first U.S. ambassador to India and Nepal. There he witnessed the end of British colonial rule and the bloody and chaotic partition of the subcontinent between Hindu and Muslim populations. Most important, Grady became one of the first American diplomats to advocate a special role for the

United States in the economic development of third world areas. He advised Washington that economic aid could help strengthen India's fledgling democracy and combat communism in Asia. However, Prime Minister Jawaharlal Nehru's policy of Cold War non-alignment, along with the outbreak of fighting between India and Pakistan over the northern border state of Kashmir, inhibited the unlocking of U.S. funds. At any rate, given the large expenditures associated with the Marshall Plan in Europe and the reconstruction of postwar Japan, the Truman administration could muster only meager funds for India and other developing nations.

Grady did oversee a massive economic and military assistance program when he returned to Greece in July 1948 as U.S. ambassador. The threat of a leftist victory in that nation's civil war and the declaration of the Truman Doctrine made Greece a testing ground for America's anti-Communist containment policy and the efficacy of foreign aid. During his critical two-year tenure, Grady supervised the distribution of $1.5 billion in assistance and pressured the corrupt, right-wing government of Premier Sophecles Venizelos to implement modest administrative and tax reforms. He also served as a member of the nation's war council, which directed the military effort. By early 1950, when Grady completed his assignment, the Greek leftists had been subdued, and Greece had aligned firmly with the Western camp.

Grady's last diplomatic assignment took him to Iran, where he served as ambassador from July 1950 through September 1951. He arrived just as Anglo-Iranian negotiations over the distribution of revenues generated by the Anglo-Iranian Oil Company (AIOC) reached an impasse. Sympathetic to Iranian nationalism, Grady traveled to London to urge British concessions, especially an increased allocation of company profits to the Iranian government to help finance the country's development plans. However, the British refused to bend. At the same time the State Department and White House, anxious not to disturb Anglo-American relations, rejected Grady's pleas for increased economic aid to help Iran through the prolonged negotiating period.

In March 1951 the Iranian Majlis passed legislation to nationalize the AIOC, and in October the new prime minister, Mohammad Mosaddeq, implemented the decree. U.S.–Iranian relations quickly deteriorated, and Grady's pro-Iranian views fell out of favor with Secretary of State Dean Acheson and other top State Department officials. In September 1951 Grady formally resigned from the Foreign Service. Two years later, after Mosaddeq had turned for support to the Communist Tudeh party and the American-backed Shah Mohammad Reza Pahlavi had fled Tehran, the Dwight Eisenhower administration directed the Central Intelligence Agency to support a coup that overthrew Mosaddeq and restored the shah to power. U.S. backing for the shah remained a constant element of U.S. foreign policy until Iran's 1979 Islamic revolution.

In retirement, Grady served as a foreign policy adviser to Adlai Stevenson II (1900–1965), worked in a group that advocated the recall of Senator Joseph McCarthy, and frequently spoke out in favor of trade liberalization. He died on a cruise to the Far East on board the *President Wilson*.

• Grady's papers, including his unpublished autobiography, are housed at the Harry S. Truman Library in Independence, Mo. Also see James A. Bill, *The Eagle and the Lion: The Tragedy of American-Iranian Relations* (1988); Dennis Merrill, *Bread and the Ballot: The United States and India's Economic Development* (1990); and Lawrence Wittner, *American Intervention in Greece, 1943–1949* (1982).

DENNIS MERRILL

GRADY, Henry Woodfin (24 May 1850–23 Dec. 1889), journalist and orator, was born in Athens, Georgia, the son of William Sammons Grady, a substantial merchant, and Ann Eliza Gartrell. He attended the local schools and the University of Georgia, from which he was graduated in 1868. He then spent a year as a postgraduate student at the University of Virginia. He excelled as a debater. The events of the Civil War and its tumultuous aftermath made a profound impression on Grady, whose father, an officer in the Confederate army, died of wounds suffered at Petersburg. In 1869 Grady entered the field of journalism, editing a succession of small newspapers in Rome, Georgia, before becoming part-owner and editor of the Atlanta *Daily Herald* in 1872. The *Herald* collapsed early in 1876. Meanwhile, in 1871, the young editor had married his childhood sweetheart, Julia King, and they became the parents of two children.

After the *Herald* failed, Grady became a special correspondent for the New York *Herald* and other out-of-town newspapers, and in the fall of 1876 he began to write for the Atlanta *Constitution*. He also became a successful freelance writer. In 1880, with a $20,000 loan from the businessman Cyrus W. Field, he bought a one-fourth interest in the *Constitution* and assumed the position of managing editor. Grady worked well with Evan P. Howell, the paper's principal owner and editor in chief, and he was responsible for the employment of Joel Chandler Harris. As editor he gave the *Constitution* a new format and directed its emergence as the most popular newspaper in the South. Grady was a first-rate journalist: a resourceful reporter, a clear and witty writer, an effective manager, and an editor with imagination and a flair for showmanship. Bright, charming, and ebullient, he was a captivating personage. "What a radiant and charming and accomplished man he was!" the North Carolina newspaperman Josephus Daniels recalled long afterward.

Grady exerted great influence in the public affairs of his city and state. An ardent booster of a greater Atlanta, he was closely identified with the International Cotton Exposition of 1881 and the Piedmont Exposition of 1887, with the visit of President Grover Cleveland to the city, and with many other civic enterprises. He played a major part in the election of every Georgia governor and U.S. senator in the 1880s. A skillful manipulator, he was a friend and collaborator of the Bourbon triumvirate of John B. Gordon, Joseph E. Brown, and Alfred H. Colquitt. In national politics Grady and his paper supported Democrat Grover Cleveland, although they were not enthusiastic about his tariff reform ideas, and after Cleveland's defeat in 1888 they looked for another candidate. The newly established Atlanta *Journal* became a strong advocate of Cleveland and tariff reduction and also clashed with the *Constitution* on local issues such as prohibition, which Grady upheld.

By the mid-1880s Grady was well known in his own section as a promoter of the economic and social rehabilitation of the South. He received mounting acclaim as a spokesman for southern regeneration, racial harmony, and sectional reconciliation—both in the columns of his newspaper and through his oratory. In December 1886 he addressed the New England Society of New York City on the topic of "The New South." That address, the most celebrated in the literature of the New South movement, gave the southern journalist a national audience and reputation.

To Grady the New South meant a South that utilized its dormant natural resources and diversified its agriculture. The South needed northern capital and technology in order to process its own raw materials, make full use of its own labor supply, and terminate its industrial and financial bondage to the North. "The old South," Grady explained, "rested everything on slavery and agriculture, unconscious that these could neither give nor maintain healthy growth." The New South, on the other hand, while "less splendid on the surface," was "stronger at the core—a hundred farms for every plantation, fifty homes for every palace—and a diversified industry that meets the complex need of this complex age." Coupled with the theme of economic change and renewal was a composite of related ideas emphasizing hard work and thrift, the dignity of labor, the image of the self-made man, and the ideal of success and material achievement.

Another component of the New South creed was an improvement in race relations. Grady assured northerners that racial problems were being solved in the South. "Nowhere on earth," the Georgian asserted, "is there kindlier feeling, closer sympathy, or less friction . . . than between the whites and the blacks of the South to-day." Racial peace and fair play were necessary, the editor acknowledged in pleading for northern forbearance and understanding, but "the supremacy of the white race of the South must be maintained forever."

A third element in the ideology of the New South was the theme of sectional reconciliation. Grady, a compelling orator, was, in the words of Harold D. Mixon, "an adept practitioner of the 'rhetoric of accommodation.'" Southerners, Grady and other apostles of the New South insisted, accepted the outcome of the war and were loyal to the Union: "The South found her jewel in the toad's head of defeat." The myth of the Old South, the valor of the Lost Cause,

and the imagery surrounding the New South elicited an increasingly sympathetic response from the North.

Grady died in Atlanta of pneumonia a few days after delivering a triumphant address in Boston. In his short career he rose to the top of his profession and achieved national recognition as a brilliant orator. His historical significance, however, stems from his role as a prophet of regional progress and as a propagandist for a New South. Although his ideas were quite conventional, he played the most important part in creating the image of a dynamic and successful South. He succeeded as a publicist in part perhaps because he was able to rationalize for his audiences beliefs that they wanted to hold. Inspired by a vision of economic regeneration, national reconciliation, and harmonious adjustment of the race question, he helped create a myth of his region's economic revitalization and social progress that remained a dream rather than a reality long after his death.

• Grady's surviving papers are located in the Emory University library. The Joel Chandler Harris Papers, another useful collection, are housed in the same repository. For other Grady documents, see Mills Lane, ed., *The New South: Writings and Speeches of Henry Grady* (1971). Raymond B. Nixon, *Henry W. Grady: Spokesman of the New South* (1943), is the standard biography. Gentry Dugat, *Life of Henry W. Grady* (1927), is an older, less scholarly work. Paul M. Gaston, *The New South Creed: A Study in Southern Mythmaking* (1970), is a revealing analysis of the New South movement that gives extensive attention to Grady's ideas. See also Timothy Curtis Jacobson, "Tradition and Change in the New South, 1865–1910" (Ph.D. diss., Vanderbilt Univ., 1974). Paul H. Buck, *The Road to Reunion, 1865–1900* (1937), throws light on the theme of intersectional reconciliation. For Grady's oratory, see Harold D. Mixon, "Henry Grady as a Persuasive Strategist," in *Oratory in the New South*, ed. Waldo W. Braden (1979), pp. 74–116, and Marvin G. Bauer, "Henry W. Grady: Spokesman of the New South" (Ph.D. diss., Univ. of Wisconsin, 1936). Obituaries are in the Atlanta *Constitution*, 23–24 Dec. 1889.

DEWEY W. GRANTHAM

GRAEBNER, Theodore Conrad (23 Nov. 1876–14 Nov. 1950), pastor, editor, and author, was born in Watertown, Wisconsin, the son of August L. Graebner, a professor at Northwestern College, and Anna Schaller. After prepatory training at Martin Luther College in New Ulm, Minnesota, he graduated from Concordia College in Ft. Wayne, Indiana, in 1894. He studied for the Lutheran ministry at Concordia Seminary in St. Louis, Missouri, graduating in 1897. After teaching German and history at Walther College in St. Louis from 1897 to 1900, he accepted a position as instructor of biology and English at the Lutheran Ladies' Seminary in Red Wing, Minnesota. He married Selma Brohm in 1900; they had five children. He taught at the seminary from 1900 to 1906 and was ordained there on 25 May 1902 in the Norwegian Lutheran church.

Graebner moved to Chicago in 1906, where he first served as a home missionary for the Norwegian church and then in 1907 for the Missouri Synod, helping the

Jehovah congregation grow from fifty to 950 members during his five-year ministry. In 1913 he returned to Concordia Seminary, where he remained the rest of his life, as editor and professor. Graebner provided important leadership for the Missouri Synod over the next four decades. He helped organize the Lutheran Laymen's League, the Lutheran Women's Missionary League, and the Walther League (a young people's organization). He also served on the board of the Concordia Historical Institute.

Graebner is remembered most for his prolific work as an editor and author. A key figure in helping the Missouri Synod make the transition from German to English, he provided many of the early works that enabled the Missouri Synod to express the theology of its German forebears in their children's language. He published several editorials in *Lessons for Sunday and Parochial School Teachers* in 1907 and was editor of the *Lutheran Herald* (1909–1913), *Homiletic Magazine* (1913–1918), and the *Lutheran Witness* (1913–1950). He ably spoke with authority to a church body feeling the pressures of acculturation. One of the great fears gripping the authorities in the Missouri Synod was that the shift to English would cause a compromise in the theological character of the immigrant church. Largely through Graebner's indefatigable efforts, the old Lutheran doctrine of the Synod's German founders was brought to a new English-speaking generation.

Graebner's books covered a wide variety of topics, but all had a practical and contemporary theological application. *Evolution* appeared in 1921, followed by *Essays on Evolution* (1925) and *God and the Cosmos* (1932). All three books were critical of Darwinian theory. Virulently opposed to Freemasonry, which he believed was a religion that compromised Christianity, he published *A Treatise on Freemasonry* (1914), *The Secret Empire* (1927), *Is Masonry a Religion?* (1946), and *Handbook of Organizations* (1948). His historical writings include *Lives of the Twelve Apostles* (1917), *The Dark Ages* (1916), *Here I Stand!* (1916), and *Church Bells in the Forest* (1944). All proposed to lead English readers into an appreciation of the Lutheran church and its theology. Finally, *Borderland of Right and Wrong* (1935) and *The Historic Lutheran Position on Non-Fundamentals* (1939) provided Lutheran pastors and laypeople a unique perspective on the relationship of form and substance.

Graebner was devoted totally to the advancement of the Lutheran church in America and dedicated himself to achieving this through expressing the old faith in a new language. He never swerved from the staunch conservatism of his church body, although he did criticize those whom he felt went too far in their zeal to defend orthodoxy. He died in St. Louis.

• Graebner's papers are collected at the Concordia Historical Institute in St. Louis, Mo. Besides those works noted above, Graebner wrote "For a Penitent Jubilee," *Concordia Historical Institute Quarterly* 45 (Feb. 1972): 3–28. The basic sources of information are William Arndt, "In Memoriam: Theodore Graebner, D.D., 1876–1950," *Lutheran Witness*, 12 Dec. 1950, pp. 396–97; Paul M. Bretscher, "Theodore Conrad Graebner, 1876–1950," *Concordia Theological Monthly* 2 (Jan. 1951): 1–8; John H. C. Fritz, "Zum Gedaechtnis," *Der Lutheraner*, 19 Dec. 1950, p. 412; Alex Graebner, "A Brief Commemorative Profile of Theodore Graebner, the Professional Churchman," *Concordia Historical Institute Quarterly* 44 (Feb. 1971): 13–16.

LAWRENCE R. RAST

GRAESSL, Dominic Laurence (18 Aug. 1753–c. 12 Oct. 1793), Roman Catholic missionary priest, was born at Ruhmannsfelden, Bavaria, the son of Lorenz Graessl (or Grässel), a tanner. (His mother's identity is unknown.) Graessl entered the Society of Jesus shortly before its suppression in 1773. In the novitiate he became a close friend of Johann Michael Sailer, later a noted theologian, educator, and bishop. Upon completion of his classical and theological studies he was ordained a secular priest in Augsburg in 1778. Although for a time he found no other employment than that of private tutor, he resigned a position with prospects of preferment in Munich to accept an invitation of Father Ferdinand Farmer of Philadelphia to come to that city. "God wants me to be in the New World," he explained to his parents, "where thousands and thousands of our brethren wander about without any spiritual shepherd."

Arriving in Philadelphia in late 1787, Graessl was named assistant at St. Joseph's and St. Mary's churches. He was obliged also, he told his parents, "to wander a great deal in the American forests to gather the scattered sheep" and to hear confessions in German, English, French, Dutch, and Spanish. He attended the dispersed Catholics not only of Pennsylvania but also of New Jersey and Delaware. He was, in fact, rejected by Philadelphia's German Catholics, who were drawn to another German priest, under whom they wished a parish of their own, a wish that Bishop John Carroll of Baltimore finally granted them with some reluctance. In 1788 Graessl became an incorporator of St. Mary's congregation. He also accepted an invitation to become a trustee of the College of Philadelphia. He urged noted publisher and economist, Matthew Carey to produce Catholic works and was among the first to subscribe to the Catholic Bible that Carey published in 1789.

The piety and learning of this "amiable ex-Jesuit" impressed Bishop Carroll—and even more the priests who attended the first diocesan synod in Baltimore in 1791. Soon thereafter Carroll petitioned the Holy See for a division of the diocese of Baltimore, which comprised the entire United States, or a coadjutor bishop with right of succession. Rome agreed to the latter proposal and instructed Carroll in 1793 to consult the older and wiser members of the clergy in his choice of a successor. The consultation took the form of an election by the clergy, a fact Carroll never revealed to the Roman authorities. "The election took place in the beginning of May," Graessl wrote, "and, dearest parents, the choice fell on your poor Laurence." Although

Carroll entertained doubts as to Graessl's future effectiveness as coadjutor because of his nationality, he supported the clergy's choice. He asked the Roman authorities to allow Graessl to omit from the oath of episcopal ordination the promise that he would "to the utmost of my power seek out and oppose schismatics, heretics, and the enemies of [the pope] and his successors." The Holy See permitted Graessl and all future bishops of the United States to take the oath allowed Irish bishops, which suppressed the objectionable promise, "so as to deprive sectarians of every chance of misrepresentation." The pope approved Graessl's appointment as coadjutor bishop of Baltimore in December 1793, and the briefs were immediately dispatched.

Less than two months after the election in May, however, Graessl knew that he would not live to be the second Catholic bishop of the United States. "Of this terrible burden I am set free by friendly death," he forewarned his parents, believing that he would soon die of consumption. As late as September, nevertheless, he was able to visit the Catholics of New Jersey. As it turned out, it was not consumption but yellow fever that felled, in addition to some 4,000 fellow citizens of Philadelphia, the first prospective German in the American Catholic hierarchy. The United States would not see a Catholic bishop of German extraction until 1833.

• For a series of letters from Graessl to his parents see *American Catholic Historical Researches* 21 (1904): 49–58. See also Henry F. Hebermann, "The Reverend Lawrence Graessel," *Historical Records and Studies* 8 (1915): 209–22; Peter Guilday, *The Life and Times of John Carroll: Archbishop of Baltimore (1735–1815)* (2 vols., 1922); Joseph L. J. Kirlin, *Catholicity in Philadelphia* (1909); and Graessl's obituary in the *Federal Gazette and Philadelphia Daily Advertiser*, 12 Oct. 1793.

THOMAS W. SPALDING

GRAFF, Everett Dwight (7 Aug. 1885–11 Mar. 1964), business executive and philanthropist, was born in the rural community of Clarinda, Iowa, the son of Valentine Graff, a merchant who had emigrated from Germany, and Nancy Elizabeth Fairley. Graff attended Lake Forest College in Illinois, graduating in 1906. His first job was with the company where he spent his entire working career, Joseph T. Ryerson & Sons, Inc., a Chicago firm that established a reputation as a distributor of steel products. He worked his way from the bottom of the organization to the top, beginning in the mail room in 1906 and ending as chairman of the executive committee in 1951. In the years in between, Graff held a number of positions, including posts in the store order and mill departments in Chicago before moving to Pittsburgh in 1909, where he was responsible for ordering steel from various mills. Graff also was involved in sales in Pittsburgh, and he continued this type of work after he returned to Chicago in 1915 as head of the country sales department. Later he became director of purchasing, but sales seems to have

been his strength, for his next assignments were to increase sales of cold-finished bars, special steels, and reinforcing rods.

During World War I, he worked with the War Industry Board's steel supply division in Washington, D.C. Graff married Verde Alice Clark of LaGrange, Illinois, in 1918, and the couple had three children. In the late 1920s, Graff began climbing the executive ladder in earnest, becoming vice president in 1928, director in 1929, and first vice president in 1932. Ryerson was purchased by Inland Steel in 1935 in an effort to expand outlets for Inland's steel products, but the merger agreement stipulated that the company would retain an independent identity as an Inland subsidiary. Moreover, Ryerson officials were integrated into Inland's board of directors. Graff was elected president of Ryerson in 1937, and in line with Inland's plans, oversaw expansion of Ryerson's operations across the country. Before Graff retired at the end of 1950, the company had become the largest steel service and supply company in the country. Graff also served on Inland's board of directors for several years during this period. In 1951 Graff completed his service with Ryerson as chair of the executive committee, although in retirement he remained on Inland's board until 1956 and on Ryerson's executive committee until 1959.

Graff's retirement from Ryerson permitted him the time to pursue his other main interest in life. Beginning in the early 1920s, he had begun to collect books, art, and other western Americana, and eventually he assembled one of the country's most comprehensive and important collections of materials on the Transmississippi West. Another leading collector and bookseller, Wright Howes, observed that Graff tried to cover all facets of western history, and the scope of the materials, donated to the Newberry Library in Chicago in the 1950s, indicates the success of his efforts. The Graff Collection, which contains about 5,000 items, includes, for example, the original account of the Lewis and Clark expedition presented to Thomas Jefferson. But western materials were not the only subject of Graff's interest, and he also had a fine collection of other art works.

His passion for collecting led Graff to a position as a cultural leader in Chicago. In 1944 he began twenty years as a trustee of the Art Institute of Chicago; he also served as vice president from 1949 to 1953, acting president during 1954 and 1955, and president from 1955 to 1958. Graff also was an important figure at the Newberry Library, joining the library board in 1948 and serving as president from 1952 until 1964. His role at both institutions was an active one. At the Art Institute, the addition of the Ferguson Memorial Building and a gallery rehabilitation project were launched during his tenure as president; he also made a number of substantial gifts to the Institute. Graff was honored for his work with an honorary doctorate of humane letters degree from Lake Forest College (1955) and an honorary doctor of laws degree from Northwestern University (1958). He was a member of several private clubs and professional associations, including the American Antiquarian Association and the American Steel Warehouse Association. Graff was in Rome, Italy, when he was stricken by a fatal heart attack.

Graff's combination of a successful career in sales and a passionate interest in the arts was not typical of most top executives in the American steel industry in the mid-twentieth century. The commitment of his wealth and time to important cultural institutions in Chicago was more in keeping with the patterns of business philanthropy and civic responsibility adopted by business leaders of the late nineteenth century. The results, however, provided an important legacy for both scholars and the city of Chicago.

• Information about Graff can be found in S. Pargelis, "Everett D. Graff: An Appreciation," *Newberry Library Bulletin* 5 (Dec. 1960): 187–89. A description of the Graff Collection at the Newberry Library is in Colton Storm, "The Everett D. Graff Collection in the Newberry Library," *Newberry Library Bulletin* 5 (Dec. 1960): 190–223, and in *A Catalogue of the Everett D. Graff Collection of Western Americana* (1968). Obituaries are in *American Antiquarian Society Proceedings* 74, no. 1 (1964): 7; *Art Institute of Chicago Quarterly* 58, no. 1 (1964): 3; and the *Chicago Tribune*, 12 Mar. 1964.

BRUCE E. SEELY

GRAFFENRIED, Christoph, Baron von (15 Nov. 1661–Nov.? 1743), promoter of Swiss and German settlement in early North Carolina and founder of New Bern, was born in the village of Worb near Bern, Switzerland, the son of Anton von Graffenried, lord of Worb, and Catherine Jenner. After studying at the Universities of Heidelberg and Leyden, he visited England about 1680, where he met the duke of Albemarle, Sir John Colleton, and other Lords Proprietors of Carolina. In 1683 he returned home and in 1684 married Regina Tscharner, with whom he had thirteen children.

Since rents from his estate and his income as a local government official failed to support his family and secure his fortune, Graffenried began discussing American enterprises with Franz Ludwig Michel about 1708. Michel's firm, Georg Ritter and Company, had already contemplated operating putative American silver mines and colonizing Swiss who were poor or religiously persecuted. Graffenried then renewed his English connections and in 1709 the Lords Proprietors of Carolina granted the Swiss firm 19,000 acres on the Neuse and Trent rivers, including 5,000 acres for Graffenried himself, whom they named "Landgrave of Carolina and Baron of Bernburg." Furthermore, Queen Anne offered to pay £4,000 in transportation costs for 100 families of German Palatines, 20,000 of whom had recently fled to Britain following the devastating War of the Spanish Succession. After very careful preparation and organization, Graffenried sent some 650 Palatine settlers to Carolina in 1710 under the leadership of John Lawson, the provincial surveyor general. Later that year, Graffenried followed with a contingent of about 150 Swiss and founded the town of New Bern.

Despite these auspicious beginnings, Graffenried's New World venture was destined to fail. The baron's social attitudes and expectations ill prepared him for life in one of America's most diverse and strife-ridden colonies. As a benevolent European landlord inspired by deep devotion to Reformed Christianity, he expected cooperation from his associates and respect from his social inferiors. Instead, he soon felt betrayed on all sides. Although the Tuscarora Indian uprising of 1711–1712 ultimately ended Graffenried's prospects of sustaining his colonial venture and of paying the large debts he had incurred in the process, he blamed disaffected, selfish whites, rather than Indians, for the enterprise's failure.

Both Graffenried's business associates and North Carolina officials seemed to let him down at every turn. After a disastrous voyage in which over half the initial immigrants died, Lawson sold the company's land to the settlers without authorization, leaving the settlers impoverished and vulnerable to the Indians. More than Lawson, however, Graffenried blamed "my ruin and that of the colony" on Thomas Cary, the deputy governor who refused to give up power to the new governor, Edward Hyde, in 1711. Unscrupulously, Cary led a combination of dissenters from the Albemarle Sound area and new settlers in the Cape Fear region against more established northern Anglicans. Cary refused to acknowledge Graffenried's status as a landgrave and his company's land claims, and Graffenried threw his support to the duly appointed governor and his chief northern ally, Thomas Pollock. In the midst of provincial civil war, the assembly claimed that they could not afford to supply Graffenried's settlers with food and cattle. As Graffenried explained in his narrative, he "was in great and pressing distress, since every one looked out for himself and kept what he had." Graffenried even blamed Cary in part for the Tuscarora uprising. Because Cary had destroyed the governor's reputation in the Indians' eyes, the baron asserted, the Tuscaroras almost killed Graffenried as well as Lawson in 1711, thinking for the moment that Graffenried was the governor.

Graffenried also blamed more humble settlers for the failure of his colonization scheme. Not only the "vile rabble" who supported Cary, but many of his own settlers turned against him. For example, a "disloyal Palatine" provoked devastating Indian attacks on the New Bern area by capturing and torturing a Tuscarora chief, contrary to Graffenried's orders, and by telling Indians that they should not trust Graffenried. It seemed that the baron's carefully selected colonists were no better than the treacherous, individualistic Anglo-Americans whose harsh treatment of the Indians and insubordination had helped produce the crisis.

After South Carolinians finally defeated the Tuscaroras, Graffenried urged settlers in the New Bern area to work for wealthier colonists and looked desperately to Virginia for a fresh start. Believing that silver mines existed near the falls of the Potomac River, he received a land grant from Governor Alexander Spotswood.

Nevertheless, his partner Michel failed to arrive with more Swiss settlers and the silver mines proved not to exist. In danger of being arrested for debt, Graffenried returned to England in 1713 in hopes of gaining political and financial assistance. His stay was cut short when a merchant who had received one of his notes threatened to prosecute him. In 1714 Graffenried returned to Switzerland permanently, although he long remained wistful about his American schemes, whose failure he blamed on "godless, rebellious people." He inherited the lordship of Worb on his father's death in 1730. He himself died in that village and was buried in the family church.

Graffenried never fully understood the sources of his failure in America because he viewed both colonial whites and Indians from an aristocratic perspective. His religious, social, and political outlook led him to expect that both groups would acquiesce peacefully in the rule of their enlightened "betters." However, the settlers' aspirations in a fluid, contentious society, and the Indians' sense that their land and lives were not safe in such circumstances, produced chaos and violence that destroyed even the best-laid schemes. Soon after Graffenried's departure from America, with the coastal tribes killed, subjugated, or driven away, and with the coming of Governor Charles Eden, North Carolina enjoyed unprecedented stability and growth. As Graffenried wrote his narrative from his home in Switzerland, he realized that others were reaping—though still rather selfishly and chaotically—where he had sown.

• Most of what we know about Graffenried comes from his own account of his American enterprises. An original manuscript is located in the public library at Yverdon, Switzerland. William L. Saunders, ed., *The Colonial Records of North Carolina*, vol. 1 (1886), includes an English translation of the French version of the original manuscript. Translations of both the French and German versions, edited by Vincent H. Todd and Julius Goebel, were published as *Christoph von Graffenried's Account of the Founding of New Bern* (1920) by the North Carolina Historical Commission. A source of useful details of family history, which also includes Julius Goebel's translation of the German version, is Thomas P. deGraffenried, *History of the deGraffenried Family from 1191 A.D. to 1925* (1925).

J. RUSSELL SNAPP

GRAFLY, Charles (3 Dec. 1862–6 May 1929), sculptor, was born in Philadelphia, Pennsylvania, the son of Charles Grafly and Elizabeth Simmons, farmers and shopkeepers. In 1879, when Grafly completed his public schooling in Philadelphia, he apprenticed at Struther's Stoneyard in Philadelphia. Two years later Grafly was placed in the public monument shop where he helped to carve Alexander Milne Calder's decorative sculpture for the new city hall. It may have been this experience that inspired him to study art, for in 1882 he attended drawing classes at the Spring Garden Institute and in 1884 entered the Pennsylvania Academy of Fine Arts in Philadelphia, where he studied with Thomas Eakins and Thomas Anshutz. In 1888,

accompanied by fellow student Robert Henri, he went to Paris to study at the Académie Julian where he worked under Henri-Michel Chapu.

Although he tried for admission to the more prestigious École des Beaux-Arts, Grafly's great disappointment of these years was that he never passed the entrance exams (although several accounts have mistakenly claimed that he studied at the École). In the spring of 1891, after receiving an honorable mention at the Paris Salon for his ideal piece *Mauvais Présage*, Grafly returned to Philadelphia to teach at the Drexel Institute. The following year he accepted a position at the Pennsylvania Academy, where he continued to teach until his death.

Grafly was active in the group that gathered around Robert Henri in the 1890s in Philadelphia, and it was he who introduced Henri to John Sloan. But while he was an enthusiastic participant in their iconoclastic discussions of contemporary art and shared in their good-natured camaraderie, Grafly never became part of their realist painting group. In 1895 he married Frances Sekeles and returned to Paris where, in 1895–1896, he studied privately with the academic sculptor Jean Dampt. During this time Grafly began work on a number of ideal pieces, including *Vulture of War* (Pennsylvania Academy), a larger-than-life, crouching male figure who steps on an orb (Earth) and drags a bag of pestilence behind him. In 1896, after the birth of the Graflys' only child, Dorothy, they returned to Philadelphia. It was their last trip abroad.

Grafly was part of the generation of artists who followed the lead of Augustus Saint-Gaudens and Daniel Chester French, producing portraits, public monuments, and symbolic allegories based on the invigorated style of naturalism taught in the French Academies. His early reputation was based on a series of allegorical works, including *Symbol of Life* (1897, Pennsylvania Academy), which depicts a young male nude, "Man," with a scythe and a larger female nude, "Nature," holding an ivory globe from which springs a shaft of wheat. This blend of symbolism in conception and realism in execution, typical of the Beaux-Arts style, was used to convey essential truths about the human condition. Other ideal works of the period include *From Generation to Generation* (1897–1898, Pennsylvania Academy), portraying an old man and a young boy in front of a winged zodiac clock, and *In Much Wisdom* (1902, Pennsylvania Academy), a nude woman holding a snake and a mirror. Works such as these earned Grafly a reputation for a "strong leaning to symbolism" that could, at times, be obscure. Like many artists of the period, he also did work for the world's fairs and expositions, and it was his *Fountain of Man* for the Buffalo exposition in 1901 that seemed so obscure that the critics, including Lorado Taft, called it "positively exasperating." The "Virtues and Vices" at the base of the fountain and the "Five Senses" on the second tier, all represented by nude figures, seemed clear enough, but the fountain was topped by a double-sided figure of "Man the Mysterious," and it was this shrouded figure, with its Egyptian reference in pose and costume, that bothered contemporary writers. It may be that Grafly took these criticisms to heart, for his subsequent exposition work was free of controversy. He did *Truth*, a nude woman on a pearl and oyster shell throne, for the Fine Arts Building in St. Louis in 1904 and the *Pioneer Mother Monument* for the Panama-Pacific Exposition in San Francisco in 1915.

Grafly received commissions for public monuments as well, including a figure and two busts for the *Smith Memorial* in Philadelphia (1898–1901), a *James Buchanan* (1925–1927) portrait figure for Lancaster, Pennsylvania, and his most important commission, the *Meade Memorial* (1915–1925), for the Mall in Washington, D.C. The latter, an eighteen-foot-high marble representation of Civil War general George Meade flanked by nude allegorical figures of Military Courage, Energy, Chivalry, Loyalty, Fame, Progress, and War, was considered his most outstanding public work.

However, Grafly is best known as a portrait sculptor and was frequently called "the Houdon of our time." Contemporary critics claimed "there is no sculptor in this country who can make a finer bust" and compared his male portrait heads favorably to those of Saint-Gaudens and French sculptor Auguste Rodin. Portrait busts constituted a large portion of his oeuvre and earned him a comfortable supplement to his income from teaching. His greatest pride was in the portrait busts he made of his artist friends, and he frequently exhibited these as a group. They include *Hugh Breckenridge* (1898, Pennsylvania Academy), *Walter E. Schofield* (1905, Pennsylvania Academy), *Edward W. Redfield* (1909, Philadelphia Museum of Fine Arts), *Thomas Anshutz* (1912, Pennsylvania Academy), *Frank Duveneck* (1915, Cincinnati Art Museum), *Paul W. Bartlett* (1916, Baltimore Museum of Art), and *Childe Hassam* (1918, Philadelphia Museum of Art). Today these are some of his best-known works. All of Grafly's portraits are noted for their truthfulness, energy, three-dimensionality, soundness of construction, and psychological insight.

Grafly won many honors, including gold medals at the Columbian Exposition in 1893, the Pennsylvania Academy of Fine Arts in 1899, the Paris International Exhibition in 1900, the Buffalo Pan-American Exposition in 1901, the Buenos Aires Exposition in 1910, and the National Academy of Design in 1918. He also received the Widener Medal at the Pennsylvania Academy in 1913 and the Potter Palmer Award at the Chicago Art Institute in 1921. He was a member of the Philadelphia Art Jury, a founding member of the National Sculpture Society, and an elected academician in the National Academy of Design. His long and successful career was marked by his thirty-seven years of teaching at the Pennsylvania Academy and twelve years as head of modeling at the School of the Boston Museum of Fine Arts, where he taught from 1917 until his death.

In 1905 he bought a farm in Lanesville, Massachusetts, built a studio, and spent most of his summers

there as an active member of the artist colony around Gloucester. He also took summer students there. His pupils, some of whom eventually became well known, included Albert Laessle, Paul Manship, Katharine Lane Weems, John Storrs, and Walker Hancock. All admired Grafly's demanding standards of craftsmanship and his ability to inspire them to hard work. When he died, the victim of a hit-and-run automobile accident in Philadelphia, he was one of the most respected sculptors of the old guard. While he was aware of the new modernist ideas represented by Constantin Brancusi and others, and tried to keep an open mind about them, his own work remained firmly entrenched in the naturalistic, academic tradition.

• Correspondence, documents, an unpublished biography written by his daughter, Dorothy Grafly, and a 200-piece collection of plaster casts are in the Grafly archives, Wichita State University, Wichita, Kans. Letters, files, and some of Grafly's most important works are in the Pennsylvania Academy of Fine Arts archives and collection. Grafly's one known piece of writing on sculpture is his article, coauthored with Dorothy Grafly, "Portrait Sculpture," in *Encyclopedia Britannica*, 14th ed., vol. 20 (1929). For a biography, bibliography, and *catalogue raisonné*, see Pamela H. Simpson, "The Sculpture of Charles Grafly" (Ph.D. diss., Univ. of Delaware, 1974). For discussion of Grafly by his contemporaries, see Vittoria Dallin, "Charles Grafly's Work," *New England Magazine* (Oct. 1901): 228–35; Dorothy Grafly, "Charles Grafly, Iconoclast and Trailblazer," *Philadelphia Record*, 29 Mar. 1936; Moissaye Marans, "Charles Grafly as Teacher," *National Sculpture Review* (Fall 1972): 20, 26; Lorado Taft, "Charles Grafly, Sculptor," *Brush and Pencil* (Mar. 1899): 343–53; John E. D. Trask, "Charles Grafly, Sculptor, An Appreciative Note," *Art and Progress* (Feb. 1910): 83–89; Uthai Vincent Wilcox, "A Tribute to Peace—The Meade Memorial," *American Magazine of Art* (Apr. 1927): 194–98. An obituary is in the *New York Times*, 6 May 1929.

PAMELA H. SIMPSON

GRAFTON, Charles Chapman (12 Apr. 1830–30 Aug. 1912), Episcopal bishop, was born in Boston, Massachusetts, the son of Joseph Grafton, a surveyor, and Ann Maria Gurley. Grafton grew up in prosperous circumstances and attended fine private schools until an eye problem forced him to study at home with a private tutor. He soon began to attend the Episcopal Church of the Advent and conceived the idea of becoming a priest. Despite this religious inclination, he studied law at Harvard, graduating with an LL.B. in 1853.

After graduation Grafton decided to pursue a career in the ministry and moved to Maryland, where he placed himself under the jurisdiction of Bishop William R. Whittingham, who shared Grafton's positive evaluation of ritual in religious services. Whittingham ordained Grafton as deacon in 1855 and as priest in 1858. After a brief period as chaplain to a house of deaconesses, Grafton served as the curate at Saint Paul's in Baltimore, remaining there until 1864. Throughout this period he felt a growing desire for monastic life, culminating in his decision to study the religious life in

England. At that time no religious orders for men existed in the Episcopal church.

Grafton spent his time in England studying monastic foundations and conferring with ecclesiastical leaders. On 27 December 1866 he joined with a small group of English and American priests to take religious vows, thus beginning the Society of Mission Priests of Saint John the Evangelist, also known as the Cowley Fathers. This small group lived as a community until Grafton left England in 1872, under the auspices of the society, to become rector of the Church of the Advent in Boston. Some of the Sisters of Saint Margaret, a related order for women, accompanied him and participated in his parochial work. Problems soon arose, however, due to the divided loyalties of the American members of the society. They owed loyalty to their diocesan bishops but had also sworn obedience to their superior, Father Richard Benson, in England. By 1882 such conflicts had led the American members of the society to withdraw and Benson to release them from their vows of obedience. For the next several years Grafton tried to begin a new religious community for men but failed. He was more successful at starting a new sisterhood, using the members of the Sisters of Saint Margaret who had stayed with him after the break as the nucleus of the Sisters of the Holy Nativity. Although he never lived in a religious community again, Grafton remained faithful to his vows of poverty and chastity and always considered himself to be a religious.

Grafton continued as rector at the Church of the Advent until 1888, when he moved to Providence to direct the Sisters of the Holy Nativity. Within the year he received word of his election as the second bishop of Fond du Lac, a small and poor diocese in Wisconsin. Although confirmation of his election took several months, he was finally confirmed in March of the following year and consecrated at the Cathedral of Fond du Lac on 25 April 1889.

Grafton had two primary tasks as bishop of Fond du Lac. First he needed to build up a weak diocese by recruiting more clergy, opening new churches, and putting the diocese on a sounder financial footing. Second he wanted to develop the Catholic principles of the Episcopal church by stressing various ritual elements of the worship service. He succeeded in the first task through his determined leadership and by making large financial contributions from his personal fortune as well as by soliciting funds from friends in the East. For the second task he stressed the following ritual practices: the use of clerical vestments, incense, and candles in the service; standing to the East of the altar to celebrate the Eucharist; reservation of the sacrament after celebrating the Eucharist for the purposes of further devotion to it as the true body and blood of Christ; and mixing water and wine in the eucharistic chalice. Grafton believed that incorporating these historical practices increased the beauty of the worship service and reinforced the devotional mood of the participants by emphasizing the presence of God, and he insisted that they be featured in worship services throughout the diocese of Fond du Lac.

Grafton's efforts to emphasize the Catholic nature of the Episcopal church through its liturgy aroused opposition on a variety of fronts and resulted in tension between him and some of the laypeople and clergy in his diocese. Most famous, however, was the national reaction to a picture of the bishops who participated in the consecration of Reginald Weller as coadjutor bishop of the diocese in 1900. Seventy by then, Grafton could no longer handle the full responsibility of the diocese, particularly the necessary task of visiting all the parishes, and Weller was consecrated to help him. Ten bishops participated in the consecration ceremony; among them were a Russian Orthodox bishop and a bishop from the Old Catholic church, a group who had broken from the Roman Catholic church in the nineteenth century. A picture of the bishops seated together in full ecclesiastical garb elicited widespread criticism of Grafton and his ritualism as tending to papistry and clerical arrogance. The reaction did not lead to a formal trial, but the opposition he aroused around the country probably set back the cause of the Catholic party within the Episcopal church.

Throughout this period, Grafton worked for the advancement of Catholic truth. Within the Episcopal church he criticized the Broad Church party, those who wanted to downplay historical doctrines and practices in order to accommodate modern ideas and to promote ecumenical unity, seeing them as Episcopalian Unitarians willing to sacrifice Christian truth. He criticized both the usurpations of Roman Catholicism and the schism of Protestantism. On the positive side, he strongly defended what he saw as Catholic truth, and he sought some form of reunion or at least recognition from the Eastern Orthodox churches and from the Old Catholics. He did so on the basis of the Catholic truth of the Episcopal church as revealed in its liturgy, in its maintenance of the apostolic succession, and in its ongoing life in the Holy Spirit. Until his death in Fond du Lac, Grafton remained one of the most controversial and outspoken leaders of the Catholic party in the Episcopal church.

• The diocese of Fond du Lac has the manuscripts of some of Grafton's writings, including his journals and correspondence for the period of his episcopate. The best source for his life is his autobiography, *A Journey Godward*; it is part of the eight-volume collection of his writings, *The Works of Charles Chapman Grafton*, ed. Talbot Rogers (1914). Scholars have written little on Grafton. John Mark Kinney, "C.C. Fond du Lac: The Life of Charles Chapman Grafton, Second Bishop of Fond du Lac" (master's thesis, Nashotah House, 1967), tells the story of Grafton's life and has a good bibliography of works, including contemporary newspaper articles, that make reference to him. For Grafton's family background see Henry Wyckoff Belknap, *The Grafton Family of Salem* (1928). Ernest C. Miller, "Bishop Grafton of Fond du Lac and the Orthodox Church," *Sobornost* 4 (1982): 38–48, treats his attitude toward the Orthodox church. E. Clowes Chorley, in *Men and Movements in the American Episcopal Church* (1961), and George E. Demille, in *The Catholic Movement in the American Episcopal Church* (1950), place Grafton's work in the context of the Episcopal church as a whole. An obituary is in *Churchman* 106 (Sept. 1912).

HARVEY HILL

GRAFULLA, Claudio S. (31 Oct. 1812–2 Dec. 1880), composer and band director, was born on the Spanish island of Minorca. Some accounts list him as Claudius Graffulla or Graffula, and one reference, unsubstantiated, gives the full name as Claude Serafu Grafulla. Nothing is known of his early years before he came to the United States in 1838. It has been suggested that he, like many others at the time, gained passage as a musician on a U.S. warship, and his absence from the index to passenger lists of vessels arriving in New York during that period makes the hypothesis credible. Later accounts state that soon after his arrival he assumed the leadership of the 27th Regiment Band of New York, while others mention a similar position with the New York Brass Band. Napier Lothian's New York Brass Band was considered the leading band of the city at the time and was regularly engaged by the 27th Regiment for its military functions. It is likely, therefore, that Grafulla served as the regimental bandmaster, directing Lothian's men for regimental functions. He also served as piccolo player in the New York Brass Band's nightly concerts at Castle Garden, where performances of many of his works established his reputation as a band composer and arranger.

His fame as an arranger having spread, Grafulla left the band in 1844 to devote himself to furnishing music to bands throughout the country. Bandsmen frequently exchanged arrangements, and the Hazens quote a letter from an Ohio musician offering another bandsman some Grafulla compositions in exchange for "four new pieces from Graffula" (p. 127). He was known for speed as well as accuracy in his arrangements. When one of the musicians for William Henry Fry's opera *Leonora* (presented in Philadelphia in 1845) performed in New York, he whistled some of the airs to Grafulla, who jotted them down. The musician was amazed to receive a completely arranged potpourri before returning to Philadelphia (White, p. 62).

The 27th Regiment, renamed the 7th Regiment in 1847, was having difficulty finding a suitable band for its functions. In late 1859 it engaged Grafulla as bandmaster and authorized him to develop a new band of thirty-eight musicians. Grafulla devoted the remainder of his life to serving the regiment and developed the band into one of the finest musical organizations in America. He accompanied the regiment when it was called to active duty in 1861 and provided music for the many social, civic, and military occasions it sponsored. These included parades, reviews, and inspections; formal concerts at New York's major festival hall, the Academy of Music; accompanying the regiment to Washington, D.C., for the dedication of a new statue of George Washington; annual summer encampments; sporting events; popular weekly armory concerts; fashionable society promenade concerts; and balls, weddings, and receptions.

From all accounts, Grafulla was a superb musician and had "a remarkable talent for organizing, governing, and disciplining" his musicians (Clark, p. 290). He was a quiet man, modest and unassuming, with a kind word and a genial smile for everyone. He never married and seemed to devote himself fully to music and to his regimental duties. He was a great favorite with the officers and men of the regiment, and when a mock army was organized in a club farce, Grafulla was named general. A testimonial reception and ball attended by the mayor, military officers, prominent members of society, and their wives was given for Grafulla by the regiment at the Academy of Music in 1876 in recognition of his long and faithful service. Age and ill health forced him to retire in September 1880, and he died soon thereafter in New York City. An indication of the esteem in which Grafulla was held may be seen from the fact that the music at his funeral was provided by the Dodworth Band, the only band in New York that rivaled Grafulla's in reputation and popularity.

The *Heritage Encyclopedia of Band Music* lists forty-seven known works for band by Grafulla and another twenty-seven quicksteps published for piano but most likely taken from band compositions. His compositions are included in the surviving Civil War band books of the 25th Massachusetts Regiment and the 3d New Hampshire Regiment (Port Royal Band Books) and in the earlier Manchester Cornet Band Books (1852). None of his many arrangements seem to have survived. His *Washington Greys*, dedicated to the 7th Regiment, "is regarded as one of the finest marches ever written and has become an international band standard" (Rehrig, p. 296). With a few exceptions, none of the others has remained in print. Twenty-eight of his works have been recorded in the Heritage of the March series (issued by Robert Hoe and given to many libraries).

• Colonel Emmons Clark includes some brief biographical details in his *History of the Seventh Regiment of New York 1806–1889* (1890). See also William Carter White, *A History of Military Music in America* (1944); Margaret Hindle Hazen and Robert M. Hazen, *The Music Men: An Illustrated History of Brass Bands in America, 1800 to 1920* (1987); and William H. Rehrig, *The Heritage Encyclopedia of Band Music* (1991). Obituaries are in the *New York Herald*, 3 Dec. 1880, and in the *New York Times* and the *New York Tribune*, 4 Dec. 1880.

RAOUL F. CAMUS

GRAHAM, Augustus (baptized 15 Apr. 1776–27 Nov. 1851), philanthropist, was born Richard King in Devonshire, England, the son of John King, a hatter or a clothier, and Mary Barrons. It is not known why he called himself Augustus Graham when he emigrated to the United States. In October 1806 in Frederick County, Maryland, he married Martha Cock, with whom he had two children. The following year he applied for U.S. citizenship and on 2 April 1808 was issued a certificate of naturalization. Graham, who worked in trade, and John Bell, a young Scotsman from Northern Ireland who worked for Graham in

Frederick, Maryland, started a successful stagecoach line from Frederick to Baltimore. Graham suggested to Bell that they "unite their capital, adopt a kindred name and relation, and proceed further north in quest of better fortunes" (Stiles, p. 838). Using a common name may have been a cover for a homosexual relationship. After leaving his wife in Maryland on her parents' farm, Graham settled in upstate New York with his new "brother." Together they ran a lumber business in Delhi, started a country store and a brewery and distillery in Norwich, and most likely helped to supply troops in the War of 1812. After that war's end in 1815 they moved to Brooklyn, New York. Some time after their arrival there they were joined by their "widowed sister," Maria Graham Taylor, who was born in Annandale, Scotland, and who lived with them until her death in 1829.

Augustus and John Bell Graham continued their brewery business in Brooklyn. When the building they rented near the navy yard to use as a distillery burned in 1816, its owner built them a new facility near the Fulton Street ferry. After retiring from their brewery business in 1822, the "brothers" divided their large fortune. That same year, to create jobs for the unemployed, Graham established a factory that helped to lay the foundation for the white-lead industry in the United States. To boost this endeavor John Bell Graham lent Graham two-thirds of his own estate, accepting stock in the Brooklyn White Lead Company as payment. The Grahams were well respected in the community and were recognized for their "probity and correct business habits" (Stiles, p. 838). Although John Bell Graham later moved to his own quarters and married his housekeeper, the two men continued to share the same horse for their separate carriages.

Within a few years after moving to Brooklyn Graham had become the spark that ignited progressive movements. Manifesting a "high and constant" concern "for the poor, the suffering, the young, and those" neglected "portions of the community," he made it his business to secure for them a larger "share of the great moral and intellectual privileges of the present state" (Trustee Minutes, p. 188). In November 1824 Graham and a group he had inspired started the Apprentices' Library to attract young workingmen away from grogshops and gambling resorts. To set a good example for these workingmen Graham, only two years after he had retired from the brewery business, became part of the first radical temperance movement in Brooklyn. With other library backers he made a pact not to offer liquor to visitors, even though the "ladies stigmatized the rules of the new society as *ungentlemanly*" (Stiles, p. 822).

First meeting in a room on Fulton Street, the Apprentices' Library became the center of community life after May 1825 when its building, whose cornerstone had been laid by the revolutionary war hero Lafayette, was opened for reading, lectures, and entertainment. Although the library's building was sold to the city in 1836 and its books stored, the library was revived by Graham in 1840, and the next year it rented the Lyceum Building (which Graham purchased for it in 1848). Rechartered and expanded in 1843 as the Brooklyn Institute, it offered the first ambitious program of evening classes in Brooklyn. In addition to ordinary subjects, such as grammar and bookkeeping, its classes included mechanical, architectural, landscape, and figure drawing. It also held a three-day horticultural show and a three-week painting and sculpture exhibit. In his will Graham endowed the Brooklyn Institute with $27,000 to establish a school of design and a gallery of fine arts. In the last decade of the nineteenth century that institution's name was expanded to the Brooklyn Institute of Arts and Sciences; during the second decade of the twentieth century it began to be called the Brooklyn Museum, and Graham was gratefully remembered as its founder. The museum annually awards a medal bearing Graham's name in recognition of community involvement, generous patronage of the arts, and outstanding contribution to the museum.

While in England in 1840 to attend the coronation of William IV, Graham did for his native Devonshire what he had done for Brooklyn. Using his given name, he established and endowed the Modbury Literary and Scientific Institution, which lasted until 1954, serving as both a social meeting place and an instrument of higher education.

In 1846 Graham donated $5,500 to establish the Brooklyn Hospital in a frame dwelling. Two years later he donated $25,000, followed by $2,000 more. In 1851 he laid the cornerstone for its new building, and he left the hospital $5,000 in his will. Over the years Graham financially assisted his abandoned relatives in both England and Maryland. These included his sister Ann Sherwell and her son Robert, the latter of whom came to Brooklyn to help manage Graham's white-lead business, and Graham's surviving child, Elizabeth Rebecca Graham Coleman, who with her husband and two children cared for Graham during the last months before his death in Brooklyn. She received $120,000 of his $300,000 estate, his English relatives received small bequests, and the other half of his fortune was divided among various institutions, including those connected with Unitarianism.

Graham had long supported the First Unitarian Church of Brooklyn and served as a model for its charitable endeavors. First meeting with the church's founders in 1833, he continued to do much to improve the image of the unpopular faith. In turn the church, despite rampant rumors about Graham's identity, buried him with respect and appreciation. On the Sunday following his funeral the church's minister, Frederick Farley, noted Graham's intelligence, "integrity and uniform and ready benevolence" as well as his "unostentatious bearing" (Trustee Minutes, p. 188).

After Graham's death it was said openly that he and John Bell Graham were not related. It was also claimed that Augustus Graham had verified that "fact" during a deathbed confession to his banker David Leavitt. It was further maintained that Graham had told

Leavitt that he had a "dark secret" and commented that John Bell Graham had been "a ministering angel to him" (*Brooklyn Eagle*, 4 Mar. 1906). Knowing that his deeds were more important than either of his names, Graham had requested a gravestone devoid of any inscription. His monument in Green-Wood Cemetery, sculpted by John Quincy Adams Ward, pictures, under an unidentified marble bust of Graham, in bas-relief on a box-shaped granite monument, the Brooklyn Institute and the Brooklyn City Hospital, two of Graham's gifts to the city he adopted, nurtured, and loved.

• For Graham's parents' names and the date of his baptism, see Modbury Parish Registers, and for information on his father's occupation, see Andrews Family Diaries, 1700–1870, Plymouth Record Office, England. For information on his gift to Devonshire, see "The Modbury Institute," in *A History of Modbury* (1971). Graham's will was contested, and a printed 1854 copy of it, as well as the court papers, are in the New York Public Library. The Brooklyn Historical Society has a folder containing Graham's passports and a few other papers, including Elizabeth Hayes Goddard et al., "Augustus Graham, Brooklyn, New York: Outline Chronology as of January 1965." For overviews of Graham's life, see First Unitarian Church Trustee Minutes 1:95, and Frederick Farley Sermon (30 Nov. 1851), First Unitarian Church Collection, Brooklyn Historical Society. See also Olive Hoogenboom, *The First Unitarian Church of Brooklyn: One Hundred Fifty Years* (1987); Henry R. Stiles, *History of Brooklyn . . .*, vol. 3 (1870); and Ralph Foster Weld, *Brooklyn Village, 1816–1834* (1938). For later newspaper accounts dealing with Graham, see "Three Tangled Lives," *New York Herald*, 24 Oct. 1886; "An Unsolved Brooklyn Mystery," *Brooklyn Eagle*, 4 Mar. 1906; and "Brooklyn Institute of Arts and Sciences," *Brooklyn Eagle*, 7 Oct. 1935. An obituary is in the *Christian Inquirer*, 6 Dec. 1851, and a death notice is in *Brooklyn Eagle*, 28 Nov. 1851.

OLIVE HOOGENBOOM

GRAHAM, Ernest Robert (22 Aug. 1866–22 Nov. 1936), architect, was born in Lowell, Michigan, the son of Robert W. Graham, a general contractor, and Emma Post. He attended public schools in Lowell during the day and at night worked for his father, performing a variety of general contracting duties. In 1885 he left home, solidly trained in construction and contracting, and settled in Grand Rapids, Michigan, where he joined the office of the architect William G. Robinson. Three years later he moved to Chicago, Illinois, and entered the architectural firm of William Holabird and Martin Roche, where he remained until 1891 as the chief of building operations.

Around 1890 a committee in Chicago began to plan the 1893 World's Columbian Exposition, appointing the firm of Daniel Burnham and John Wellborn Root as chief of construction. When Root died unexpectedly in January 1891, William Holabird, Chicago architect and friend of Burnham, recommended Graham to Burnham as a replacement for Root. Once hired, Graham was made assistant chief of construction for the exposition, a position that required supervision of more than 14,000 men. This appointment put the 25-year-old Graham in touch with the finest architects of the day, including Charles McKim, Richard Morris Hunt, and Louis Sullivan, all of whom were designing buildings for the fair grounds. In 1893 Graham married Carlotta V. Hall; they had no children. Upon the completion of the exposition, Burnham took Graham and two other assistants from the fair as partners in his firm, Daniel Burnham and Company, founded in March 1894.

Graham became Daniel Burnham's sole partner in 1899. While Burnham filled the role of designer for the firm, Graham became an exemplary office manager; he brought in clients, negotiated contracts, dealt with workmen, and maintained the general office routine. His firsthand knowledge of construction greatly assisted his dealings with contractors and his skill as a businessman won him the respect of many. Several important buildings were erected by the firm during his tenure including the Marshall Field Store, Chicago (1902 and 1914); Flatiron Building, New York (1903); Railway Exchange Building, Chicago (1904); Union Station, Washington, D.C. (1903–1908); U.S. Post Office, Washington, D.C. (1911–1919); Wanamaker Store, Philadelphia (1909); and the department store for Selfridges, London, England (1909–1928).

After Burnham's death in 1912, Graham became the senior member of the firm and joined Burnham's sons, Hubert and Daniel, Jr., and three other members of the office, Pierce Anderson, Edward Probst, and Howard J. White in forming Graham, Burnham and Company. This association lasted until 1917 when the Burnham brothers withdrew to form their own firm. Graham and the three remaining partners then officially joined together and created what would become one of the most prolific commercial architectural firms in the history of American architecture: Graham, Anderson, Probst, and White.

Each member of the firm carved out his own niche. Graham was again responsible for bringing in business, dealing with clients and contractors, and keeping the firm organized and running smoothly. He was in charge of an office of architects and engineers that at several times numbered into the hundreds. He understood the role of architect to be more than just a designer of beautiful buildings. He was only one member of a team whose mandate was to build not only an aesthetically pleasing structure but a financially sound one as well. In his introduction to the firm's privately published monograph, *Architectural Works of Graham, Anderson, Probst and White* (1933), Graham explained: "The architect must possess mastery over every aspect of the science of the building: he is expected to speak with authority on land values, on the appropriateness of site to purpose; on investment returns; and he must produce well-studied works, beautiful in form, complete in utility" (p. 5). As the firm's chief from 1912 until 1926, he applied these principles to the over two thousand commercial and civic commissions the firm received. His wife Carlotta died in 1923, and in 1925 he married Ruby Fitzhugh Leffingwell, a widow, and adopted her son William.

Like his predecessor Daniel Burnham, Graham contributed to the beautification of Chicago. He and his colleagues accomplished this through such buildings as the Field Museum of Natural History (1909–1920), Union Station (1913–1925), the Wrigley Building (1919–1924), the John G. Shedd Aquarium (1925–1930), the Civic Opera Building (1927–1929), and the Merchandise Mart (1928–1930). The firm was known throughout America by such other buildings as the Equitable Building (1913) and Chase National Bank (1926–1928) in New York; Mount Wilson Observatory, Pasadena, California (1914–1917); Union Station and Cleveland Terminal Group in Cleveland, Ohio (1917–1930); Pennsylvania Railroad's Broad Street (1924–1929) and Thirtieth Street (1927–1934) Stations in Philadelphia; Coe College master plan, Cedar Rapids, Iowa (1926); and the Alamo National Bank Building, San Antonio, Texas (1929).

Education was of great importance to Graham, and upon his death in Chicago, he willed the majority of his estate, valued at $1,570,000, to found an American school of the fine arts in Chicago that he hoped would rival the the École des Beaux-Arts in Paris. It was not until 1955, however, that his dream was fulfilled with the establishment of the Graham Foundation for Advanced Studies in the Fine Arts. The architect whose firm beautified American cities left in this legacy an opportunity for others to do the same.

• The business records, correspondence, diaries, photographs, drawings, commissions log, and other unpublished papers of Graham, Anderson, Probst, and White are located in the firm's private archives in Chicago. The Graham Foundation for Advanced Studies in the Fine Arts, holds other materials relating to him. His early work and affiliation with Daniel Burnham is discussed in Andrew N. Rebori, "The Work of Burnham and Root, D. H. Burnham, D. H. Burnham and Co., and Graham, Burnham and Co.," *Architectural Record*, July 1915; and in Thomas S. Hines, *Burnham of Chicago: Architect and Planner* (1974). A very informative work is Sally A. Kitt Chappell, *Architecture and Planning of Graham, Anderson, Probst, and White, 1912–1936: Transforming Tradition* (1992). Other references to Graham may be found in general discussions of Chicago architecture such as Carl Condit, *Chicago, 1910–1929: Building, Planning, and Urban Technology* (1973). John Zukowsky has also edited two general works on Chicago architecture: *Chicago Architecture, 1872–1922: Birth of a Metropolis* (1987) and *Chicago Architecture and Design, 1923–1993: Reconfiguration of an American Metropolis* (1993). An obituary is in the *Chicago Tribune*, 22 Nov. 1936.

VICTORIA M. YOUNG

GRAHAM, Frank Porter (14 Oct. 1886–16 Feb. 1972), university president and U.S. senator, was born in Fayetteville, North Carolina, the son of Alexander Graham, the superintendent of schools, and Katherine Sloan. Both parents were of Scotch Presbyterian ancestry.

At the University of North Carolina, which he entered in 1905, he was elected to Phi Beta Kappa in his junior year, and, as president of the YMCA, took part in evangelical Protestant programs to improve society. The college yearbook for 1909 called him "Frank, Laddie Buck. Everyman's friend, confidant and playfellow."

For some years after graduation Graham drifted. He completed two years of law school at the University of North Carolina and was admitted to the bar but never practiced. In 1916 he earned a master's degree in history at Columbia University. Despite frail health he sought in 1917 to enlist in the armed forces and persisted until the Marines commissioned him a second lieutenant. In 1919 he became the University of North Carolina's first dean of students, then assistant professor of history, but he left for three years of graduate studies at the University of Chicago, the Brookings Institution, and the London School of Economics.

In 1925, at the age of thirty-eight, Graham returned to Chapel Hill to resume his post as assistant professor of history with a renewed sense of mission. He sparked the Citizen's Library Movement, to foster the development of public libraries in the state, became president of the North Carolina Conference for Social Service (1928), and wrote and promoted an Industrial Bill of Rights.

His statewide renown and his popularity as a teacher led the trustees of the university to elect him president in 1930, though Graham, with characteristic modesty, sought to dissuade them. Two years later, after the Chapel Hill institution was merged with the North Carolina State College in Raleigh and the North Carolina College for Women in Greensboro, he was chosen president of the consolidated university. That same year he married Marian Drane, daughter of an Episcopalian rector; they had no children.

Graham quickly became a legendary university president. Neither an efficient administrator nor a profound thinker, he won respect and affection by his democratic style and his courageous stands on public issues, though his effort to reform intercollegiate athletics met defeat. "Dr. Frank" entertained students "at home" on Sunday evenings and knew thousands of them by name. The faculty cherished him, even when his attempts to pry funds from the legislature in the Great Depression fell short. "He is the only university president I know," one professor remarked, "who can announce a cut in salaries and receive a standing ovation from his faculty" (Ashby, pp. 129–30).

Graham's defense of academic freedom and his encouragement of scholars who dissected southern society attracted national attention to Chapel Hill. "In the university should be found the free voice not only for the unvoiced millions but also for the unpopular and even hated minorities," he declared in 1931. He stood up for the right to speak of controversial campus lecturers such as Bertrand Russell and Langston Hughes and insisted on bypassing a quota on admission of Jews to the medical school, even though the dean of the school resigned in protest. "In recent years the University of North Carolina has moved forward rapidly until it has become . . . the leading institution of higher learning in the South," reported the *New Republic* in 1936. "This development is largely the work of its president, Dr. Frank Graham" (Ashby, p. 138).

Graham's numerous public activities also put him in the national spotlight. In 1934 he chaired a government advisory council that gave birth to the Social Security Act, and in 1938 he accepted the chairmanship of the newly formed Southern Conference for Human Welfare, though the group was criticized for its advanced views on race and for admitting communists. For nearly three years during World War II, he shuttled between his university office in North Carolina and Washington, D.C., as a public member of the War Labor Board, where he wrote major statements on behalf of union security and equal pay for black workers.

Even after returning to the university in 1946, where the faculty had been chafing at his absence, he continued to take on time-consuming public assignments. In the fall of 1947 he became the most influential member of a mediation team for the United Nations that within four months achieved a truce between the Netherlands and Indonesian rebels, an important step toward creating the new state of Indonesia. He also aroused the ire of racists by serving on President Harry S. Truman's Committee on Civil Rights. He agreed with recommendations opposing discrimination, but he wrote a dissent disapproving of recommendations to achieve desegregation by coercion.

On 22 March 1949 the governor of North Carolina, W. Kerr Scott, named Graham to a vacant seat in the U.S. Senate, a move that delighted liberals but appalled conservatives who accused him of permitting Chapel Hill to become a haven for radicals. These charges arose again the following year when Graham ran for a full term in the Senate. In the Democratic primary, he received more votes than had ever been cast for a senatorial candidate in the state, but his total was not enough to avoid a runoff. In a second contest, marked by exceptional scurrilousness, supporters of his opponent raised the issue of race, and Graham went down to defeat by a slim margin, an outcome that drew a fault line through North Carolina politics still discernible a generation later.

In 1951, after a brief tenure as Defense Manpower Administrator during the Korean War, Graham accepted an appointment as United Nations representative for India and Pakistan to help resolve the Kashmir dispute, a vexing problem that consumed much of the next several years. He moved in 1952 to New York City, where he worked for the United Nations for the next nineteen years. He gave more than 2,000 talks about the United Nations while continuing to be active in social causes such as aid to sharecroppers. In 1967 the Grahams returned to Chapel Hill, where both died. They were interred under a dogwood in the ancient Chapel Hill cemetery beneath a headstone reading, "They had faith in youth and youth responded with their best."

Graham's contemporaries often found it hard to come to terms with a man who viewed the Sermon on the Mount as the most reliable guide to coping with modern-day problems. "That he is the best-loved man in the state admits of no more doubt than that he is the best-hated man there, too," wrote Gerald Johnson in 1941. Even some of his admirers believed that he sometimes used poor judgment in lending his name to causes and that he did not reckon the costs of always having to appear to be "on the side of the angels." A few wished that he had been more forthright in opposing segregation. Much more common, though, are the judgments of V. O. Key, Jr., who called Graham "by all odds the South's most prominent educator and versatile public servant," and of the historian Julian Pleasants, who concluded that "perhaps no other twentieth-century southerner better exemplified the South's attempt to adapt to the changing social and economic realities of the period from 1930 to 1950."

• The Frank Porter Graham Papers are at the Southern Historical Collection, University of North Carolina at Chapel Hill. Warren Ashby, *Frank Porter Graham* (1980), is the standard biography, but Julian M. Pleasants and Augustus M. Burns III, *Frank Porter Graham and the 1950 Senate Race in North Carolina* (1990), and William D. Snider, *Light on the Hill: A History of the University of North Carolina at Chapel Hill* (1992), are indispensable. Insightful shorter pieces include Pleasants, "Frank Graham and the Politics of the New South," in *The Adaptable South*, ed. Elizabeth Jacoway et al. (1991), and Edward C. Halperin, "Frank Porter Graham, Isaac Hall Manning, and the Jewish Quota at the University of North Carolina Medical School," *North Carolina Historical Review* 67 (1990): 385–410. An obituary is in the Raleigh (N.C.) *News and Observer*, 17 Feb. 1972.

WILLIAM E. LEUCHTENBURG

GRAHAM, Helen Tredway (21 July 1890–4 Apr. 1971), pharmacologist, was born in Dubuque, Iowa, the daughter of Harry Ennis Tredway, a merchant, and Marian McConnell. Graham attended local public schools and then traveled east to matriculate at Bryn Mawr. First in her class at this college, Graham received a B.S. in 1911 and an M.A. in chemistry in 1912. She then won a fellowship to pursue postgraduate study abroad. Her year at Georg August University in Göttingen, Germany, cemented her interest in organic chemistry. When Tredway returned to the United States in 1913, she entered the University of Chicago's graduate program in chemistry, from which she received a Ph.D. in 1915. While at Chicago, she met young physician Evarts Graham, and the two were married in 1916. Shortly thereafter they moved to Mason City, Iowa, where Evarts commenced practice; they had two children.

Marriage signaled the end of many women scientists' careers, but that was not to be the case for Graham—at least not in the long run. Little is known about what she did in the early years of her marriage. However, by the end of World War I, when Evarts was serving overseas in France, Graham had moved to Baltimore and was working as an assistant in pharmacology at Johns Hopkins University. When Evarts returned to the United States in 1919, he and Graham picked up stakes once more, this time moving to St. Louis, where Evarts had a job waiting for him at Washington University Medical School. For the next seven years, Graham concentrated on raising her two young sons.

But in 1926, when her children were in school, she returned to the laboratory bench as an instructor in the pharmacology department of the medical school. Conducting research with Nobel Prize winner Herbert Gasser, she spent the first half of her scientific career studying the physiology and pharmacology of peripheral nerve cells. She rose steadily through the academic ranks and was appointed an assistant professor in 1931 and associate professor in 1937. Graham enjoyed uncommon success for a woman in science, particularly in light of the fact that she managed to raise a family while she maintained her career.

Also rare for a married woman was the opportunity to proceed down the tenure track at the same institution as her husband. While other women in her position were consigned to research associate positions, less prestigious schools, or volunteer slots, Graham was treated as a valuable member of the Washington faculty. She realized how fortunate she was in this regard. In 1939 Johns Hopkins tried to lure Evarts away from Washington University but did not make any offers to hire Graham, viewing her as a "complicating factor" in the recruitment effort. Indeed she was. The couple opted to stay in St. Louis, and Graham continued to move up the Washington University hierarchy. In 1954 she was promoted to full professor of pharmacy.

By that point Graham had taken a step unusual for any scientist: at the age of sixty she decided to embark on an altogether new line of research, focusing on histamine, a compound released in response to an allergen. Graham was particularly interested in the role that histamine played during pregnancy and secured a grant from the National Institutes of Health to study this topic. She also devised a method to measure histamine levels in bodily fluids and discovered the histamine storage function of mast cells and blood basophils. Over the course of her career, she wrote or cowrote more than forty-five papers on both this subject and her earlier research areas. Her work appeared in a number of journals, including *The Pharmacologist*, the *American Journal of Physics*, and the *Proceedings of the Society of Experimental Biology and Medicine*. A respected member of her field, she belonged to the American Society for Pharmacology and Experimental Therapeutics as well as Sigma Xi.

Outside the laboratory, Graham worked hard at a number of causes. Along with her husband, she participated in the movement against air pollution in St. Louis. She also helped found the Junior College District of St. Louis and served as a trustee of both Bryn Mawr and the Community School in St. Louis. She was also active in a number of civic causes, serving as president of the St. Louis League of Women Voters and sitting on the city's board of freeholders. In her leisure time, she enjoyed hiking, gardening, and needlework.

In 1957 Evarts passed away, and the following year Graham was promoted to emeritus professor. Neither of these events shook her devotion to her work and her social causes. In the mid-1960s she was instrumental in the American Association of University Women's campaign against air pollution. In addition, she joined the movement against nuclear testing programs and became a founding member of the Committee for Nuclear Information. Eventually she served on the board of its offspring organization, the Committee for Environmental Information.

Throughout her life, Graham maintained a balance of these outside activities with those inside the lab. At the time of her death she was still active in both areas.

• Brief accounts of Graham's life can be found in the *National Cyclopedia of American Biography* and in Marian Hunt's article in the *Dictionary of American Medical Biography*, ed. Martin Kaufman et al. (1984). For more information on Evarts Graham and his relationship with his wife, see Lester Dragstedt's account in National Academy of Sciences, *Biographical Memoirs* 48 (1976). See Margaret Rossiter's *Women Scientists in America: Struggles and Strategies to 1940* (1982), for more information about the place of women in science in general. An obituary, in *Environment* 13 (June 1971): 23, also provides information on Graham's life and career.

SHARI RUDAVSKY

GRAHAM, Isabella (29 July 1742–27 July 1814), educator and philanthropist, was born Isabella Marshall in Lanarkshire, Scotland, the daughter of John Marshall and Janet Hamilton. She grew up in Elderslie, near Paisley, where she was educated in schools conducted by Rev. John Witherspoon (later the president of the College of New Jersey) and Betty Morehead. In 1765 she married Dr. John Graham, a physician in His Britannic Majesty's Royal American Regiment. The couple had four children.

Two years after the marriage Isabella Graham accompanied her husband and his regiment to Quebec, Canada. After brief stays in Quebec and then Montreal, the Grahams moved with the regiment to Fort Niagara (now Fort Niagara State Park in New York State), where they lived for four years. In 1772 the Grahams followed the regiment to the island of Antigua in the West Indies. In the autumn of 1774, while the couple was still in Antigua, John Graham died of an illness, leaving Isabella pregnant and with three infant children. She then moved back to Scotland, settling first in Cartside and later in Paisley.

Finding that her father had become impoverished while she was in North America and needing a means of support, Graham opened and operated a small school in Paisley. She explained her motivations in this and her later educational and charitable enterprises as flowing from her Christian belief in benevolence. At the urging of her friends, in 1779 she established a boarding school in Edinburgh that became quite successful. While in Edinburgh, Graham also was active in charitable activities. She founded the "Penny Society," a mutual-aid organization of poor people who donated a penny a week to a fund for the contributors when they fell ill. The organization later became the Society for the Relief of the Destitute Sick.

In 1789, with the encouragement of John Wither-spoon, Graham moved to New York City and opened a school for young women. In 1792 she opened an evening Sunday school for adults, notable because it enrolled both black and white students. In 1797 Graham, along with Elizabeth Seton and several others, established in her house the Society for the Relief of Poor Widows with Small Children. One of the first relief organizations for the poor in the United States, it was later renamed the Society for the Relief of Women and Children. In its first year the society provided aid to ninety-eight widows and 223 children. Following the prevalent notion that continued economic aid to the poor would foster dependence, the society employed widows in its own sewing and laundering businesses and as teachers in its own schools. The society also gave extensive moral and religious instructions to its charges.

In the first decade of the nineteenth century Graham continued to be prominent in the development of poor-relief organizations in New York City. In 1806 she presided at the founding meeting of the Orphan Asylum Society, established by her daughter Joanna Bethune, the first such organization in the United States. The Orphan Asylum Society took in six orphans after its opening, but soon grew rapidly, forcing the society to move from a small rented house on Raisin Street to a new building on Bank Street. Much later it moved to even larger quarters on Riverside Drive and 73d Street. In 1814 Graham founded the Society for the Promotion of Industry Among the Poor and opened a Sunday school in Greenwich Village for women and children of all races. Graham died in Manhattan later that year.

During the early industrial revolution, Graham was one of the leading figures in the movement to reform the poor that were rapidly filling the cities of the United States. Her work in founding and operating various self-help organizations and schools helped promote the idea that poverty was created by sloth and immorality and could be alleviated by teaching frugality, Christian principles, discipline, and genteel behavior.

• A great deal of illuminating correspondence and other writings by Graham was published by her daughter, Joanna Bethune, under the title *The Power of Faith: Exemplified in the Life and Writings of the Late Mrs. Isabella Graham, of New-York* (1816). It has been reissued several times. Joanna Bethune also edited *The Unpublished Letters and Correspondence of Mrs. Isabella Graham, from the Year 1767 to 1814, Exhibiting Her Religious Character in the Different Relations of Life* (1838). See also John M. Mason, *Christian Mourning: A Sermon Occasioned by the Death of Mrs. Isabella Graham* (1814).

THADDEUS RUSSELL

GRAHAM, James (c. 1658–1701), lawyer and politician, was born probably in Scotland, the son of John Graham and Isabella Auchinlick. Details of Graham's childhood and education are almost nonexistent, but he was probably descended from the Graham Clan infamous for its lawless depredations in the border region between Scotland and England. Graham seems to have received some form of education and an undetermined form of legal training, but almost nothing is known of his life before his arrival in New York in 1678.

Graham's career in New York was inextricably linked to his early association with Sir Edmund Andros, on whose ship he arrived in the New World. He was commissioned by Andros as one of the first six aldermen of New York City in October 1680 and quickly made a name for himself as a legal expert. Graham's acuity in drafting legislation and reports made him a valuable asset to Andros, and his activity as a trader in the Delaware Valley brought him to the attention of William Penn. In seeking to purchase the upper Susquehanna River Valley from the Iroquois Confederacy, Penn asked Graham to act as his commissioner along with William Haige. In that same year Graham became the first recorder of the City of New York under the new governor, Thomas Dongan, and simultaneously served as attorney general for the province.

Graham's legal skills and the precision with which he drafted state papers made him the logical choice to serve both as one of the first judges of the Court of General Sessions and clerk of the Court of Chancery, beginning in 1684. It may have been this last post that made him the equally obvious person to undertake, at the government's behest, an investigation into the collection of customs, a task he completed in 1687 to the satisfaction of his superiors.

Graham's longtime association with Andros and the many rewards he obtained from service to Andros, the king's choice to lead the Dominion of New England, explain his vehement opposition to Jacob Leisler's 1689 rebellion in New York. Jailed briefly by the Leislerians, Graham never wavered in his loyalty to Andros and the Stuarts. His Scots identity showed itself as well in his early interest in the rising fortunes of the young Robert Livingston. When Colonel Henry Sloughter arrived to reestablish royal authority under William and Mary, Graham, as speaker of the anti-Leislerian assembly signed that body's approval of Leisler's death sentence. He appears to have adopted a cautious role, however, in comparison with many anti-Leislerians who were as a whole vengeful against their political and social enemies.

His marriage to Elizabeth Windebank in 1685 produced six children and a further alliance to solid money. Graham carefully shepherded his fortune at "Morrisania Manor" in Ulster County as well as in smaller holdings elsewhere. His daughter Isabel married Lewis Morris (1671–1746), the nephew and heir to the elder Lewis Morris (1613–1691) with whom Graham may have bought lands in the Elizabethtown tract. Graham had no scruples about slavery; his manor boasted thirty-three slaves and an overseer in addition to his white servants. From his comfortable country seat, Graham continued to advance his political career, succeeding in 1691 to the post of Speaker of the House in the first General Assembly of New York. He retained this position over the next eight years, relinquishing it only on two brief occasions, each time quickly returned by the other members of the lower house who recognized his mastery of parliamentary procedure and the details of legislative business. His service in the 1690s extended to a seat on the governor's council during his absence from the House.

Graham's usefulness to Governor Benjamin Fletcher in dominating a pro-Leislerian assembly showed itself as he retained his role of Speaker until March 1699. But the arrival of Richard Coote, first earl of Bellomont, in April of the preceding year boded ill for Graham's political life. The elections of 1701 brought Abraham Governeur to the speakership of an even more partisan pro-Leislerian House. Graham had served both as clerk in the former chancery court, and on the Court of General Sessions. In 1701 a new court of chancery was created by order of the Lords of Trade. Later denounced in 1709 as an invasion of the assembly's privilege to create courts, the new chancery court nonetheless functioned without interruption. It subsequently became the focus of ferocious political intrigue since the governor held the office of chancellor. Graham, a steadfast defender of the governor's prerogative against the growing pretensions of the assembly, would have been the logical ally of the governor on this new bench. But Graham died in New York in the very year of the court's creation. As Speaker, he had managed to survive in the pro-Leislerian climate of the late 1690s and to defend the royal prerogative in an increasingly fractious political climate. Like other Scots arrivals in New York such as attorney David Jamison and merchants Samuel Vetch and James Emott, Graham represented a late manifestation of the duke of York's frustrated 1660s attempt to encourage immigration from Scotland to bolster loyalty in his proprietary colony. Graham managed to adjust his devotion to the House of Stuart sufficiently to support William and Mary, in part because of his detestation of the Leislerians' threat both to his personal life and to the social and political order he had devoted his life to creating.

• No known collection of Graham papers survives. His governmental work and a few letters are scattered in various New York colonial collections. Although he receives mention in more recent secondary historiography, there is no biography. See entries in Paul M. Hamlin and Charles E. Baker, *Supreme Court of Judicature of the Province of New York 1691–1704*, vol. 3 of *Collections of the New-York Historical Society* (3 vols., 1959); Richard S. Dunn and Mary Maples Dunn, eds., *The Papers of William Penn*, vol. 2 (1982), p. 342 n. 17; and Robert C. Ritchie, *The Duke's Province, A Study of New York Politics and Society, 1664–1691* (1977), pp. 126, 180–81, 198. Peter R. Christoph and Florence A. Christoph, eds., *The Andros Papers 1674–1680* (3 vols., 1991), is among several references found in the ongoing publication of the New York Historical Manuscripts Project.

A. G. ROEBER

GRAHAM, James Duncan (4 Apr. 1799–28 Dec. 1865), army officer, was born in Prince William County, Virginia, the son of William Graham, a revolutionary war veteran and physician, and Mary Campbell. Graham

enrolled in the U.S. Military Academy at West Point, New York, on 19 June 1813 and graduated on 17 July 1817. While at West Point, Graham studied mathematics under former U.S. astronomer Andrew Ellicott and natural and experimental philosophy under former surveyor general of the Northwest Territory Jared Mansfield. Despite administrative problems at West Point during this period, Graham was well prepared for his early career by these faculty.

Following graduation he was promoted from cadet status to third lieutenant in the First Artillery. Between 1819 and 1821 he served as topographical assistant to Major Stephen H. Long on Long's Yellowstone expedition to the Rocky Mountains, the first fully outfitted scientific expedition to explore the Great Plains. Initially dedicated to exploring the Missouri River and establishing an astronomically derived survey point through which to draw the U.S.–Canadian boundary, the expedition, because of fiscal shortfalls, was rerouted to the central Rocky Mountains. It ran into many difficulties that gave it a reputation as a failure. While under Long's command, Graham gained practical experience in topographical engineering, which he pursued for the rest of his life. In 1828 he married Charlotte Hustler Meade, General George G. Meade's sister. They had one child, William Montrose Graham, a distinguished Civil War general.

Upon leaving Long's service, Graham worked on various civil and military surveys in Vermont, Virginia, Alabama, Florida, Georgia, and Maine. He served as an inspector of harbor improvements on the Great Lakes. On 7 July 1838 Graham became one of the four majors in the newly formed Corps of Topographical Engineers. In 1839 he served as astronomer on the team that surveyed the border between the United States and the Republic of Texas. Returning from Texas, Graham was detailed as commissioner to survey the border between Maine and Canada (1840–1843). Between 1843 and 1847 he served as chief astronomer for the survey of the U.S.–Canadian border and was breveted lieutenant colonel as recognition for his service. Graham's position as astronomer was most important. Astronomy had gone from being a battleground for cosmological debate to becoming requisite to state diplomacy. Diplomats found it much easier to negotiate frontier boundaries by longitude and latitude rather than the older and less certain approach of river and watershed. The survey produced highly detailed maps of the border and the topography on both sides. Military planners valued Graham's maps, believing their precision and detail would be useful in the event of a confrontation with Canada. When the maps of that survey were consumed in a fire that destroyed the Topographical Bureau office, Graham's task became remaking them, which he did between 1848 and 1850 and between 1852 and 1853. Graham also resurveyed the Mason-Dixon Line in 1849–1850.

In 1850–1851, following the settlement of the Mexican War, Graham headed the U.S. detachment responsible for surveying the eastern portion of the U.S.–Mexican border. In the course of this duty, Arizona's Mount Graham was named for him. This assignment, however, sullied Graham's reputation, because he placed the Corps of Topographical Engineers into the political arena of expansionist politics. Dispute over the point at which the eastern New Mexico border would touch the Rio Grande had led to a series of concessions by the civilian U.S. commissioners in charge of the survey. Graham believed the concessions inconsistent with the intent of the Treaty of Guadalupe Hidalgo and the interests of the United States, because they jeopardized the only practicable southern route for a transcontinental railroad. Graham refused to allow his detachment of topographical engineers to survey the border until his interpretation of the border's beginning point was negotiated, he was recognized as second in command of the expedition, and he was included in all commission negotiations. For this, Graham was replaced as chief astronomer and head of the scientific corps. Ultimately, Graham's position was vindicated by the Gadsden Purchase in 1853. He returned to Washington to continue redrawing his U.S.–Canadian boundary maps.

By 1854 Graham had moved from leading topographical corpsmen on boundary surveys to serving as a supervising engineer for harbor works and lighthouse districts throughout the Great Lakes and Atlantic Coast. While serving as superintending engineer of the harbor improvements on the north and northwestern lakes (1856–1864), one of his many simultaneous duties between 1854 and 1864, he discovered a lunar tide on the Great Lakes (1858–1859). On 1 June 1863, after the Topographical Engineers and the Corps of Engineers merged, he was promoted to colonel. With that rank, he moved from the Great Lakes to the Atlantic Coast, where he took charge of maintaining harbor works along the entire East Coast of the United States, which, because of the Civil War, extended from Maine to the Chesapeake Bay. He also served as superintending engineer of sea walls in Boston harbor, in which capacity he planned and began construction to extend and repair sea walls there. Graham died at his Boston area home of complications from exposure to a winter storm, in which he was caught in the line of his duty. His first wife having died, Graham had married Frances Wickham (date unknown).

• Some of Graham's letters are in the LeConte Family Papers and the John Fries Frazier Papers held in the American Philosophical Society Library. Graham's personal papers do not appear to have been preserved in any publicly accessible archive. Their last known location was in the hands of his grandchildren. Graham's publications include *Report of Lieut. Col. J. D. Graham . . . on Mason and Dixon's Line*, 2d ed. (1862); Senate, *Report on the Mexican Boundary Commission*, 32d Cong., 1st sess., S. Exec. Doc. 121; and Senate, *Report on the Condition of Harbors . . .* , 34th Cong., 3d sess., S. Exec. Doc. 16. A detailed sketch of Graham's career is in George W. Cullum, *Biographical Register of the Officers and Graduates of the U.S. Military Academy . . .* (1891). The official chronicler of Long's Rocky Mountain expedition, Edwin James, recalls Graham's activities while on that expedition in his *Account of an Expedition from Pittsburgh to the Rocky Mountains* (1822–1823; repr. 1905). The most detailed account of any one portion of Graham's career, his participation in the U.S.–Mexican border survey, is found in William Goetzmann, *Army Exploration in the American West, 1803–1863* (1959; repr. 1991). His contributions to topographical and civil engineering are discussed in Aubrey Parkman, *Army Engineers in New England: The Military and Civil Work of the Corps of Engineers in New England, 1775–1975* (1978); as well as [anon.], *The Nation Builders: A Sesquicentennial History of the Topographical Engineers* (1988).

DENNIS C. WILLIAMS

GRAHAM, John (1774–6 Aug. 1820), diplomat and public official, was born in Dumfries, Virginia, the son of Richard Graham, a prosperous Scot merchant, and Jane Brent. He attended Columbia College, graduating in 1790. Graham subsequently moved to Mason County in northeastern Kentucky and in 1800 represented the area in the state legislature. He had earlier married Susan Hill; they had four children.

Graham traveled to Spain in 1801 to serve as secretary of legation at the American embassy in Madrid. He was later chargé d'affaires there, serving until 1803. The following year Thomas Jefferson named him secretary of Orleans Territory, which had been formed from a portion of the Louisiana Purchase. A valued aide to Governor W. C. C. Claiborne, Graham was at one point dispatched to negotiate trade issues with Spanish authorities in West Florida.

When Jefferson, in late 1806, finally roused his administration to determine precisely what his former vice president, Aaron Burr, intended to do on the southwestern frontier, he enlisted Graham's aid. Graham, then visiting Washington, D.C., was dispatched to trail Burr and directed to inquire after his intentions, to alert officials in the trans-Appalachian states to any possible conspiracy, to arrest Burr "if he made himself liable" (Abernethy, p. 86), and to take over the administration of Louisiana Territory from General James Wilkinson—himself a shadowy actor in Burr's shadowy designs (Graham declined appointment as governor of Louisiana Territory). Graham arrived in Marietta, Ohio, in November 1806 and questioned Burr's incautious confederate, Harman Blennerhassett. Blennerhassett, unaware that Graham was Jefferson's agent, told him that Burr's men intended to settle a tract of Louisiana land along the Ouachita River and, should war with Spain break out, proceed to invade Mexico. He denied, however, that Burr was actively intending to separate the western states from the Union as had been rumored. Graham suspected that the rumors were true, and his suspicions were strengthened by the reports of local people who had kept a watchful eye on Blennerhassett and Burr's activities. Graham reported to Ohio governor Edward Tiffin that a scheme was afoot to conquer New Orleans and revolutionize the West. Tiffin, in turn, had militia dispatched to seize ships and supplies that had been assembled by Burr's allies, an action that prompted the hasty flight of the latter from Blennerhassett's island in the Ohio River. Thus began the unraveling of Burr's southwestern ambitions, whatever they might have been. Thereafter Graham did not move quickly enough to catch up with Burr himself in Nashville, nor did he alert Kentucky authorities in time to prevent Burr from making his rendezvous with the Blennerhassett party on the lower Ohio. When Graham, in January 1807, finally confronted the harried Burr, who had surrendered to authorities in Mississippi Territory, Burr insisted that he had not been attempting to wrest the West from the Union.

Shortly after completing this mission, Graham was appointed chief clerk at the State Department, a post that he filled until 1817. At the beginning of the War of 1812, he reported on public opinion in Virginia, Ohio, and Kentucky to Secretary of State James Monroe and acted as an intermediary between agents of revolutionary Mexico and American officialdom. Like James and Dolley Madison, Graham had to flee Washington when the British fired it in 1814. In March 1817, during the first week of the Monroe administration, Graham served as interim secretary of state.

As Congress debated U.S. posture toward independence movements in Latin America, President Monroe, who wished to maintain a policy of strict neutrality, dispatched Graham, together with Caesar Augustus Rodney and Theodorick Bland, on a mission to South America in 1817. Although Graham was the only one of the three who understood Spanish (and he with a bit of difficulty), the commissioners were instructed to gather political, military, and commercial intelligence and determine the strength of both the revolutionary forces and their opponents, as well as their respective attitudes toward the U.S. government. Graham and Rodney traveled as far as Buenos Aires (Bland proceeded on to Chile), spending the early months of 1818 studying the situation in the United Provinces of South America (later the Argentine Confederation). The men, it seems, received distinctly different impressions, so much so that they found they could agree on little except that Spain's prospects of taking back the Río de la Plata region seemed dim. Rather than composing a single report, the commissioners submitted three, with Graham's lukewarm assessment falling midway between Rodney's embrace of the United Provinces government at Buenos Aires and Bland's disenchantment. Graham described contentions within the revolutionary ranks, separatist efforts in various provinces, the small popular base upon which the constitution of the United Provinces had been established, and what he regarded as the indolence of the people. Not surprisingly, with its principals in disagreement, the mission accomplished little, at least in official circles, toward resolving the question of whether the United States should recognize Latin American independence.

In 1819 the Monroe administration again sent Graham sailing south, this time as minister plenipotentiary to the Portuguese authorities in Brazil. The ill will conjured up by an obnoxious predecessor, as well as tensions left over from the War of 1812, assured that Graham could accomplish little toward improving U.S.–Portuguese relations in an abbreviated eight-month mission. He was sick by the time he returned from Rio de Janeiro and died not long afterward in Washington, D.C.

Three successive presidents—Jefferson, Madison, and Monroe—had entrusted Graham with important work. From the undermining of Burr to his assignments in South America, Graham had been their agent in grappling with assorted consequences of the United States's expanding role on the North American continent and in the Western Hemisphere.

• There is some Graham correspondence in the James Monroe Papers at the Library of Congress, Manuscripts Division, Washington, D.C. The reports of the South America commission were reprinted in William Manning, ed., *Diplomatic Correspondence of the United States Concerning the Independence of the Latin-American Nations*, vol. 1 (1925). On Graham's role in thwarting Burr, see Thomas P. Abernethy, *The Burr Conspiracy* (1954); Dumas Malone, *Jefferson the President: Second Term, 1805–1809* (1974); and Milton Lomask, *Aaron Burr: The Conspiracy and Years of Exile, 1805–1836* (1982). His Latin American diplomacy is discussed in Watt Stewart, "The South American Commission, 1817–1818," *Hispanic American Historical Review* 9 (1929): 31–59, and Arthur P. Whitaker, *The United States and the Independence of Latin America, 1800–1830* (1941).

PATRICK G. WILLIAMS

GRAHAM, Joseph (13 Oct. 1759–12 Nov. 1836), revolutionary soldier, political leader, and iron entrepreneur, was born in Chester County, Pennsylvania, the son of James Graham and Mary McConnell Barber, farmers. Graham's father rented the land he farmed. Upon his death in 1763, his mother joined the great Scotch-Irish migration to the South, moving her family to the Carolina back country via Charleston, South Carolina. Eventually the widow Graham and her five children—three sons and two daughters—settled in Mecklenburg County, North Carolina, where in 1771 she purchased a 200-acre farm near Charlotte.

Graham's mother placed great value on education and the Presbyterian faith. She was determined that her children would be appropriately educated. Graham attended Queen's Museum (later Liberty Hall Academy) in Charlotte. There he received a classical education under the direction of Presbyterian clergymen. Reputedly he "was distinguished among his fellow students for talents, industry, and the most manly and conciliatory deportments" (Morrison). As a youth he was present at the public meetings of 20 May and 31 May 1775, when the citizens of Mecklenburg County vented their anger against the tyranny of George III. Throughout his life, Graham believed that the Mecklenburgers had declared their independence on 20 May. He and his offspring were among the most vigorous proponents of the dubious Mecklenburg Declaration of Independence.

Whatever he observed, Graham was inspired to take up arms against the British. Between 1778 and 1781, serving as a volunteer, he fought in fifteen minor engagements. He rose from private to major while earning a reputation for reliability and valor. He commanded the rear-guard action that allowed William Richardson Davie's troops to escape Charles Cornwallis after the fall of Charlotte (26 Sept. 1780). He was wounded nine times and left on the field among the dead, but he survived to contest the British in the campaign for Wilmington the following year.

Given his ability and war record, Graham could anticipate a promising career in politics. By the age of thirty he had served as the Mecklenburg County sheriff (1784–1785), as a government commissioner of land transactions, and twice as a delegate to conventions considering the ratification of the U.S. Constitution of 1787. In the Hillsborough Convention (1788) he voted with the majority against ratification because the Constitution lacked an adequate bill of rights; however, this concern having been addressed, he voted to ratify in the convention of 1789. As a state senator from Mecklenburg County (1788–1793), he supported measures promoting public education and internal improvements. (He later imparted these lifelong interests to his son William Alexander Graham, the governor of North Carolina from 1845 to 1849.)

In 1787 Graham married Isabella Davidson; they had eleven children who survived infancy. Marriage diverted Graham's energies to another endeavor: the manufacture of iron. In the early 1790s he joined his father-in-law, John Davidson, and a brother-in-law, Alexander Brevard, in the nascent Lincoln County iron industry. Having bought an interest in a promising ore bank from Peter Forney, Graham, Davidson, and Brevard, with Forney, formed the Iron Company in 1791. The following year Graham built Vesuvius Furnace and settled his family in eastern Lincoln County. Over time the company underwent name and partnership changes, but Graham became a man of moderate wealth. He marketed his iron products in the western Carolinas. During the War of 1812 he sold the U.S. government 30,000 pounds of shot, shells, and cannonballs. He farmed and worked his furnace and forge principally with slave labor.

Graham, long a militia officer interested in military affairs, was called to active service late in the War of 1812. At British instigation the Creek Indians had risen, threatening the southern frontier. Graham was appointed as brigadier general to command a brigade of North and South Carolinians. The brigade, which was ordered to Alabama but arrived after Andrew Jackson's victory over the Creeks at Horseshoe Bend, performed only garrison duty. Subsequently, Graham served as major general of the Fifth Division, North Carolina Militia.

Until late in his life, Graham was active in the manufacture of iron and in public affairs, although he no longer held elective office. He was the councillor of state in 1814, a justice of the peace for some forty years, a trustee of Lincolnton's Pleasant Retreat Academy, a trustee of the University of North Carolina (1789–1790), and a ruling elder of the Unity Presbyterian Church. Long a student of history, Graham wrote a series of essays on revolutionary war events in the Carolinas. He wrote with few sources, largely from memory, but his accounts of battles were generally accurate. His vivid memories of the events of May 1775 became the principal authority for the disputed Mecklenburg Declaration of Independence. These essays and Graham's revolutionary papers, intended to assist Archibald D. Murphey in preparing a state history, eventually became a part of the archives of North Carolina.

Graham died of apoplexy at Earhart Plantation, his residence in Lincoln County. He was memorialized as an American patriot and devoted citizen. Of his devotion to country it was said: "To secure her liberties he spent many toilsome days and sleepless nights—for her he endured much fatigue, and sickness, and suffering without a murmur—for her his body was covered with wounds—to her welfare he consecrated his time, and treasure, and influence, during a long and unblemished life" (Morrison).

• Graham's papers are at the North Carolina State Archives in Raleigh and the North Carolina Collection at the University of North Carolina at Chapel Hill. Of particular interest are William A. Graham, *General Joseph Graham and His Revolutionary Papers* (1904), and the broadside by Robert Hall Morrison, *Obituary of Joseph Graham* (n.d.). See also Sarah Lemmon, *Frustrated Patriots* (1973); Lester J. Cappon, "Iron Making: A Forgotten Industry of North Carolina," *North Carolina Historical Review* 9, no. 4 (1932): 331–48; and William L. Sherrill, *Annals of Lincoln County, North Carolina* (1967). An obituary is in the *North Carolina Standard*, 7 Dec. 1836.

MAX R. WILLIAMS

GRAHAM, Martha (11 May 1894–1 Apr. 1991), dancer, choreographer, and teacher, was born in Allegheny, Pennsylvania, the daughter of George Greenfield Graham, a physician who specialized in mental disorders, and Jane (Jennie) Beers. Her father was of Irish descent and her mother proudly claimed to be a descendant of Miles Standish. In her memoirs, Graham vaunted her Puritan ancestry and made a disclaimer for her "Irish temper."

Graham divided her childhood into two distinct periods. The first years were spent in Allegheny, which she described as dark, grimy, and excessively puritanical in its attitudes—so much so that dancing was viewed as sinful and forbidden to her. Her loving Irish nursemaid introduced her to Catholic ritual and encouraged her sense of fantasy. Her father inspired both awe and fear. Graham, in interviews throughout her life, described how, when she was quite young, her father caught her up in a lie. She was intensely ashamed and tried to puzzle out how he knew. "Movement never lies," he replied, and implied that he could read her mind. Graham's later life as a choreographer utilized body language to convey interior emotional life; she used her powerful knowledge of nonverbal communication to portray her stage character's fictional experience. Allegheny was put behind her in early 1909 when the family moved to Santa Barbara, California. She was exhilarated by the change. She felt free for the first time, she confessed in her memoirs, and it is perhaps significant that her father retained his domicile in Pennsylvania for a full four years before he retired and joined the family in 1912. He died two years later and left the family impoverished.

Graham graduated from Santa Barbara High School in 1913, after staying for a fifth year to continue her studies. She enrolled in Cumnock College and studied liberal arts, with an emphasis on literature, art, and dramatics, and graduated three years later in 1916. That summer she fulfilled her dream and enrolled at the Denishawn School in Los Angeles. Some years earlier, when she was not quite seventeen, she had begged her father to take her to see a dance concert given by Ruth St. Denis and Ted Shawn. He gallantly did so, but he made it clear that the stage was not considered a suitable career for a young lady of her proper social standing. Nevertheless, she had been smitten by the performance and had determined to become a dancer.

The new college graduate was twenty-two years old and had never taken formal dance instruction. More than anything, she wanted to attach herself to "the goddess," as Graham referred to St. Denis, but the glamorous star was oblivious to this overage beginner who "worshipped" her. When her dancing partner Ted Shawn volunteered to work with Graham, St. Denis simply passed her along. Graham was crushed but stubbornly stayed with the program. Shortly after, she debuted with the Denishawn group as a priestess of Isis in a pageant staged in the amphitheater in Berkeley, California. Shawn groomed her to be his teaching replacement and years later to star opposite him. In 1917 she appeared in a Spanish solo that remained in her repertoire for many years, the *Serenata Morisca*. In 1920 she starred in New York in Shawn's *Xochitl*, a melodramatic ballet that capitalized on her exotic features and powerful stage presence. She toured with his company for four years until she was engaged as a solo dancer with the Greenwich Village Follies from 1923 to 1925.

When she was thirty-one, Graham realized that if she were ever going to accomplish anything she would have to delve deeply into her own creative imagination and become her own choreographer. It was a brave decision on her part, since she had no funds of her own or access to patrons. By 1922 Graham was teaching at the Eastman School of Music in Rochester, New York, and was experimenting with a movement style based on breathing techniques, later to be called "contraction and release." She was commissioned to choreograph an early film, *Flute of Krishna* (1926), which features Indian dancing maidens draped in silken saris. Her choreography, heavily reliant on pantomimed gestures lifted from Indian dance, was derivative of exotic Denishawn dancing. Graham was embarrassed when a copy of the "dreadful thing," which was intended to be "frankly decorative," resurfaced. The piece, with its disguised autobiographical material, anticipates her later work. In it, she reconstructs her family: a dominant Dancing Girl with two others (both her younger sisters danced), a fragile and passive

mother who swoons when confronted by her husband's infidelities, and a manipulative male who flirts constantly. The main female dancer occupies center stage, as Graham was to do throughout her performing career. The choreography is prescient in its glimpses of unusual emotional force. Three of its dancers joined Graham for her company's New York debut.

Graham opened a studio in Carnegie Hall, lived in the back room, and ate at the Automat. Her poverty did not prevent her from launching a career as a concert artist, without patronage of any kind, and she borrowed $1,000 to sponsor the New York debut of the Martha Graham and Concert Group. Her first concert in New York was given on 18 April 1926 at the 48th Street Theatre, with a total of eighteen pieces presented. Louis Horst accompanied her in solos danced to music of Schumann, Debussy, and Ravel, and the women's trio performed *Chorale* to the music of Debussy.

Graham gathered a band of devotees who performed without fee, and she attracted a cult of admirers who attended each performance. But the majority of observers remained skeptical about or even downright hostile to her work. *Dance Magazine* critic Stuart Palmer attacked her work as "macabre" and "unhealthy"; worse yet, she was smothered "in the trappings of death and decay." However, Graham became adamant in her opposition to that which was facile, decorative, and cloying. Her work became even more fierce, obscure, and tortuous. The contraction became central to her technique. Her choreography was marked by the use of torque in the central body and angular positions of the arms and legs—a far cry from the sensuous curves typical of St. Denis. Some of her most powerful pieces were assigned titles such as *Revolt* (1927), *Heretic* (1929), and *Lamentation* (1930). In *Heretic*, a diminutive figure dressed in white heroically confronts the bigotry of an implacable all-woman unit in black. Always experimenting, always changing, Graham shifted her emphasis from unison dance to separate groups in *Primitive Mysteries* (1931). The dance "was all planned architecturally," the critic Gertrude Schurr observed. Critics and audience alike were mesmerized by this Native American ritual dance associated with the essence of Christian rites that center about the Annunciation, Crucifixion, and Resurrection. Graham laughingly referred to this era of somber experimentation as her "long woolens" period, when dancers dressed in severe wool jersey outfits that she designed and cut on the bias to cling to the body.

If at first Graham's message seemed enigmatic or even inscrutable, gradually her work became more accessible to a wider public. As with many other early modern dancers at this time, she became intrigued with American subjects and themes. The text of her pieces became more human, outcomes less severe, attitudes less rigid or judgmental. Her next period, which could aptly be categorized as "American" to compare it with the "Greek period" that followed, culminated in the creation of her poetic masterpiece, *Ap-*

palachian *Spring* (1944). During the ten years from 1934 to 1944, eleven works out of twenty-five focused on American themes, and she created five of her most greatly admired works. *Letter to the World* (1940) was a lyric work based on Emily Dickinson's poetry, which was read aloud during the performance. *El Penitente* (1940) was based on Native American rites that Graham learned about during visits to the Southwest. *Frontier* (1935), with music by her mentor and lover Louis Horst, explored the perspective of the American frontier symbolized by a lone individual who delineated her space with marching steps, and then, with frisky skips, ventured away from the safety of a long fence. Particularly as patriotic fever rose before World War II, audiences were won over by her "devout patriotism."

American Document (1938) was a seminal dance-theater piece that foreshadowed a whole line of dramatically based productions. Graham took the structure of the minstrel show, a form historically associated with racial insult and stereotypes, and transformed it into a vehicle that portrayed injustice and suffering. This piece was Graham's first wide-scale success, and it played coast-to-coast to sold-out houses. No longer castigated for her "grim" and "sexless" dances, she was extolled for the boldness of her passionate love duet with Erick Hawkins, the first man to dance in her all-woman company. The piece, which stunned audiences, marked the beginning of her long association with Hawkins; they married in 1948.

But it was *Appalachian Spring* (1944) that became her signature piece and possibly one of the most beloved of all dance works of the twentieth century. Aaron Copland's score, commissioned by the Coolidge Foundation, has become a classic. Isamu Noguchi's spare set of a farmhouse wall is considered one of his finest designs. After the Library of Congress premiere, the *New York Times* critic John Martin enthused, "Nothing Martha Graham has done before has had such deep joy about it." Agnes de Mille called the piece "a love letter, a dance of hope, budding, fresh and beautiful." As the curtain rises, the wedding procession commences with a formal ritual walk: one by one enter four women who attend the wedding, the Pioneer Woman, the Preacher, the Husbandman, and finally the Bride. The Groom's eyes look far out toward the western frontier as he dances. The Bride, all agitated, reveals her apprehensions about the impending marriage with fluttering hands as she turns first one direction and then another and abruptly back again. The Preacher slips into a thundering sermon on the sins of the flesh, but his message, strangely inappropriate for a wedding day, is interrupted by the Pioneer Woman who blesses all participants and brings harmony to the celebration. The couple dance a duet that reveals their deep commitment. They bow formally to their guests, who depart, and take their places on the front porch of their new home. The Groom stands behind the Bride, places one hand protectively on her shoulder as she sits in the rocking chair, and together they gaze toward the horizon.

Graham's American period coincided with her becoming an American icon. In 1937 she was the first American dancer to perform at the White House, recognition that was much later confirmed by her award of the Presidential Medal of Freedom in 1976. Her name became a household word when she played "Miss Hush" on a radio mystery quiz show in 1947. College students and teachers came from all over the United States to study with her during summers at Bennington College. During this time she moved from being considered "a dangerous revolutionary" to a model for "orthodox ballerinas and choreographers in search of new ideas."

After *Appalachian Spring*, Graham produced no new works for almost two years. Plunged into dark depression and heavy drinking she reemerged and was seized with great creative energy as she entered her Greek period. The new works, based on Greek mythology, make up approximately one-third of her total output from 1946 to 1969. They have become so identified with her corpus that many do not realize how different they were from the highly abstract dances of her early days. Four of her great masterpieces of the Greek cycle followed hard on one another: *Dark Meadow* (1946), *Cave of the Heart* (1946), *Errand into the Maze* (1947), and *Night Journey* (1947). After a ten-year hiatus, she once again explored Greek mythology with a full-length work of great impact, *Clytemnestra* (1958). Some of her other great pieces from that period were drawn from Hebrew and Christian heroines or inspired by religious, celebratory themes, and they included *Diversion of Angels* (1948), *The Triumph of Saint Joan* (1951); *Seraphic Dialogue* (1955), *Embattled Garden* (1958), *Samson Agonistes* (1961; originally titled *Visionary Recital*), and *Legend of Judith* (1962).

The critic Margaret Lloyd termed these new works of the Greek period as the "Theatre of Martha Graham," and the label stuck. The pieces were highly dramatic and emotionally intense renderings of ancient classics. She took her plots and themes from the male-dominated Greek dramas but told them from the woman's point of view. In *Night Journey*, her version of the Oedipus cycle, she ignored the hero and concentrated on Jocasta the Queen; similarly, Clytemnestra's character is fully explored in the dance piece of that name whereas Agamemnon seems but a mere walk-on. Although she disdained the label "feminist," Graham refused to accept the supremacy of the conventional hero; if anything, men portrayed in her works tended to be figureheads or even caricatures of macho behavior.

During this period, three figures in Graham's life influenced her path. Her husband, Erick Hawkins, who had been a classics major at Harvard University, stimulated her interest in the Greek myths. Her analyst, Frances Wickes, favored the Jungian school of psychology, as did her friend the anthropologist Joseph Campbell. Intrigued by theories of how mythology relates to the subconscious, Graham explored ways dance could portray the complex emotions of mythic characters and so reveal archetypes or universals for our epoch.

The 1940s and 1950s were a time of great personal anguish for Graham, and many of her most powerful works reflected the turmoil of her private life and her increasingly unhappy marriage. Beginning with *Deaths and Entrances* (1943), Graham delved into antagonisms between herself and her sisters as mirrored in the prism of the Brontë sisters' lives. *Errand into the Maze* (1947) focused on a woman who confronts deep fear, and *Herodiade* (1944) portrays a woman who addresses the diminution of creative and physical powers. The tension between anticipation and anxiety concerning her impending marriage is depicted in *Appalachian Spring* (1944); she explores the dynamics of a wife's relationship to a considerably younger man who is her lover in *Night Journey* (1947). As Medea she portrayed the torments of jealousy in *Cave of the Heart* (1946), and as *Clytemnestra* (1958) she slayed her first husband for the sake of a selfish young lover. The autobiographical inspiration of these works could be disguised and refracted, but the emotional anguish was universal. As Graham wryly commented, "Greece is not so different from New England" (Stodelle, p. 180). Some of her greatest masterworks, then, derive from her own sufferings, but her genius lay in the ability to transcend them.

After her marriage broke up in 1954, Graham began to drink heavily, and insiders whispered that her work was affected. She continued to dance, but her waning physical powers caused critics to wonder aloud how much longer she could maintain her grasp on center stage. Her analyst lectured her, "Martha, you are not a goddess, you must admit your mortality." Despite pressure, she refused to hand over most of her signature roles. She could scarcely get up off her knees in *Cortège of Eagles* (1967), but it still took her two more years before she would agree to retire from the stage. For almost all of her life she had repeated as her personal mantra, "I am a dancer." When she could no longer perform, she confessed that she "wished to die."

A woman of indomitable strength and courage, Graham rose from the ashes of total despair and refashioned for herself a new career. "A phoenix," the choreographer Antony Tudor had called her once. She discovered to her astonishment that it was as a choreographer that she was to be remembered. With entirely new management and practically a whole new company, she opened the Martha Graham Dance Company in 1973 and began what was to be the final creative phase of her life. If her career had consisted only of the thirty-four new works from the last two decades of her life, she probably would still have been considered a major choreographer of the time.

Although she claimed she was not interested in nostalgia, Graham did revisit her roots. She revived anew or reconstructed early works and tinkered with themes from her early career. She devised her own choreography to Stravinsky's *Rite of Spring* (1984), in which she had originally danced the sacrificial maiden to Léonide

Massine's choreography in 1937. She created *Dances of the Golden Hall* (1982), with its parade of golden temple dancers, straight out of Denishawn. *Song* (1984) used the same text from "Song of Solomon" seen already in *American Document*. Her very last piece was *Maple Leaf Rag* (1990), reminiscent of the days when she would beg Louis Horst to play Scott Joplin's piano rags if ever she hit a creative hiatus.

Martha Graham became an institution in her final years. Even as she reviewed and reworked her artistic legacy, she became convinced that her technique, her works, and her company had to be preserved for future generations. She remade her personal image for public consumption, complete with Delphic interviews in the press and glamorous photographs in mink, gold designer gowns, and Cartier jewels of great value. Publicity agents repackaged her works as "radical Graham." The "Martha Graham Technique" was copyrighted and licensed for sale. She turned away from the discreet patronage of Baroness de Rothschild and others, who had supported her generously in the early days, and made use of jet-set celebrities to assist in fundraising on a mass basis. She borrowed Russian ballet dancers for "star" stints and presented her company on Broadway or on world tours. Some jokingly refer to this as her "Halston" period, a reference to the fashion designer's gold lamé loincloths that became standard uniform for her male dancers' costumes in contrast to the "long woolens" period.

Graham's lengthy list of honors reflects the extraordinary contributions of this great artist. She was awarded the Guggenheim Fellowship twice, the Aspen Award in the Humanities, the Henry Hadley Medal for Distinguished Service to American Music, the National Institute of Arts and Letters Distinguished Service to Arts Award, the first National Medal of Arts, the *Dance Magazine*, Samuel Scripps–American Dance Festival, and Capezio awards, and honorary degrees from nineteen colleges and universities. The queen of Denmark presented her with the *Ingenio et arti* medal, and the French minister of culture decorated her with the Légion d'honneur.

A revolutionary who shaped the world of modern dance, Graham has often been compared with such giants as Picasso and Stravinsky in terms of her far-reaching influence, her prolific artistry combined with longevity, and her ability to keep one step ahead of the avant-garde during the century. Her contributions to the theater arts in total are legion. With her collaborator Noguchi she changed the direction of theater design toward minimalist but evocative sets with symbolist overtones. She herself designed and sewed costumes of stunning visual impact that were widely imitated, and she helped change the look of lighting design. She commissioned scores from composers who were to become the great names of modern American music, including Aaron Copland, Gian-Carlo Menotti, Norman Dello Joio, and Paul Hindemith. Among the actors she trained in her movement style were Gregory Peck, Woody Allen, Bette Davis, Eli Wallach, and Joanne Woodward. Her dancers who went on to found their own companies included Anna Sokolow, Merce Cunningham, Erick Hawkins, Sophie Maslow, John Butler, Robert Cohan, Pearl Lang, Donald McKayle, Paul Taylor, and Glen Tetley. She guided the formation of spin-off companies in London and Israel. Through the invention and extension of her own personal idiom, the Martha Graham Technique, she irretrievably changed modern dance as well as ballet. She created the form of dance theater associated with some of her best-known works. Her body of work, some two hundred pieces in all, stands testament to the unique, courageous vision of this woman who plumbed the breadth and depth of human experience through dance.

• Graham's archives are at the Martha Graham School in New York City, but their use by outsiders is restricted. *The Notebooks of Martha Graham* (1973) offers great insight into her creative process. Her autobiography, *Blood Memory* (1991), appeared shortly after her death, as did Agnes de Mille's rather personal biography, *Martha: The Life and Works of Martha Graham* (1991). Ernestine Stodelle's *Deep Song: The Dance Story of Martha Graham* (1984) provides a sensitive interpretation of Graham's artistry. Merle Armitage, *Martha Graham* (1937; rpt. 1966), and Baroness Bethsabee de Rothschild, *La danse artistique aux U.S.A.: Tendances modernes* (1949), draw upon personal knowledge of her early years. Elizabeth Kendall sets Graham in the early modern dance context of Denishawn in *Where She Danced: The Birth of American Art-Dance* (1979). Her technique is discussed by Alice Helpern in "The Technique of Martha Graham," *Studies in Dance History* 11, no. 2 (1991), and Marian Horosko, comp., *Martha Graham: The Evolution of Her Dance Theory and Training, 1926–1992* (1991). Reviews of her work include Marian Horosko, "Frontier of the Mind: Martha Graham at 95," *Dance Magazine*, May 1989, and Margaret Lloyd, *The Borzoi Book of Modern Dance* (1949). Scholarly treatment of her work includes Maureen Needham Costonis, "Martha Graham's *American Document*: A Minstrel Show in Modern Dance Dress," *American Music* 9, no. 3 (Fall 1991): 297–310, and Arlene Croce, "Tell Me, Doctor," *Ballet Review* 2, no. 4 (1968): 12–18. LeRoy Leatherman published photographs of Graham and her company in *Martha Graham: Portrait of the Lady as an Artist* (1966), and Barbara Morgan captured almost her entire dancing career in her classic work, *Martha Graham: Sixteen Dances in Photographs* (1949; rev. ed. 1980). *Dance Magazine*, July 1991, and *Ballet Review* 19, no. 3 (Fall 1991), are special editions devoted to the memory of Graham. An obituary by Anna Kisselgoff is in the *New York Times*, 2 Apr. 1991.

MAUREEN NEEDHAM

GRAHAM, Philip Leslie (18 July 1915–3 Aug. 1963), publisher, was born in Terry, South Dakota, the son of Ernest R. Graham, a mining engineer and farmer, and Florence Morris, a schoolteacher. After several difficult years mining in the West, Ernest Graham moved his family to Dade County, Florida, where he managed an ill-fated experimental sugarcane plantation for the Pennsylvania Sugar Company. The plantation was unprofitable, but Ernest ended up with 7,000 acres of real estate near Miami just prior to the city's boom. Although Ernest Graham eventually became a wealthy man and an important figure in Florida Democratic politics, Philip came of age during the hard times. He grew into a high-strung, moody, and exceedingly bright young man, easily earning As at the University of Florida, where he received his B.A. in 1936. Graham then attended Harvard Law School, there becoming president of the law review and a protégé of Professor (later Supreme Court justice) Felix Frankfurter. He was among the elite for whom Frankfurter arranged Supreme Court clerkships. He received his law degree in 1939.

By 1940 Graham was deeply embedded in the New Deal power structure. As an attorney at the Office for Emergency Management and the Lend-Lease Administration, Graham became a member of the "goon squad," a group of young New Dealers who pushed President Franklin D. Roosevelt's military preparedness agenda through the bureaucracy. In 1940 Graham also married into money after falling in love with Katharine "Kay" Meyer, with whom he would have four children. Kay was the daughter of Eugene Meyer, a powerful and wealthy banker who also owned the fledgling *Washington Post*. Eugene Meyer was taken with the dashing and witty Graham, and after Graham's service in the intelligence wing of the Army Air Corps during World War II, Meyer prodded his son-in-law (who displayed some reticence) into succeeding him at the *Post*. Graham made the *Post* into one of the nation's dominant papers. With the newspaper as his base, Graham established himself as one of the key players in the Cold War liberal establishment.

Under Graham, the *Post* backed the foreign policy of President Harry S. Truman but was also an ardent defender of civil liberties and one of the foremost journalistic opponents of Senator Joseph R. McCarthy. Graham was a political pragmatist, tilting to the right in the 1950s, even endorsing Dwight D. Eisenhower for president in 1952. Yet the paper aggressively backed the cause of civil rights and demanded an end to segregation. (All the same, the *Post* published little about African Americans during this period and only gradually integrated its own office).

During his tenure at the *Post*, Graham revitalized the paper, reorganizing the business office, boosting salaries, and broadening the financial base. The *Post*'s successful purchase of the *Washington Times-Herald* in 1954 cemented its financial stability. A paper that had lost over $1 million annually during Meyer's first twenty years of ownership was soon making profits of $2 million a year. In 1961 the *Post* acquired *Newsweek*. Shortly after assuming control, Graham grandiosely declared that the journalist's responsibility is to write the "first rough draft of history."

Graham's power, both in politics and at the newspaper, grew from his charisma. He was dynamic and irreverent. He could charm the capital's elite at Georgetown cocktail parties and swap stories, profane or otherwise, with the newspaper's pressmen. Graham had sound editorial judgment and knew good writing; a steady stream of scribbled notes to reporters, alternately complimentary and cajoling, displayed his close attention to the content of the *Post*. When cartoonist

Herbert Block suffered a heart attack, Graham insisted on installing a large couch in his office to be used for siestas. The gesture aptly displayed Graham's style—both conscientious and intrusive, solicitous yet potentially overbearing.

Graham, his wife later observed, was fascinated with power. As a consummate insider, he cultivated close contacts with Lyndon Baines Johnson and John F. Kennedy. He was especially close to Johnson, serving as a key strategist and lobbyist for the 1957 civil rights act. Initially backing Johnson for the presidency in 1960, he later facilitated Kennedy's selection of Johnson as his running mate. Graham became one of a handful of people who could easily contact President Kennedy by phone.

Graham was also mentally ill, suffering from manic-depression. Consequently, between late 1957 and 1960, he only sporadically attended to his duties at the *Post*. His illness manifested itself in bouts of profanity and verbal abuse. Graham also turned against his father-in-law, seemingly resentful of the role the older man had played in his own ascent to power. He became virulently anti-Semitic. As his status increased and his media empire expanded, Graham became unhinged. He drank heavily, womanized openly, and harangued Kennedy and Johnson on the phone. ("Do you know who you are talking to?" he queried Kennedy at one point.) He also verbally and emotionally abused his wife Kay, ridiculing her weight, appearance, and intelligence. In early 1963 he moved in with a young Australian lover and announced his intention to marry her and will her the newspaper. As Graham gradually spun out of control, his behavior was the talk of Washington. Finally, at a conference of newspaper editors and publishers in Phoenix, Arizona, Graham delivered a blistering and profane attack on his counterparts. At the same time, he disclosed one of Kennedy's affairs. He was escorted from the stage after beginning to strip off his clothes, returned to Washington in a straitjacket, and committed to psychiatric care. On 3 August 1963, while convalescing at his estate in Virginia and seemingly recovering some sense of equilibrium, Graham shot himself to death.

Graham, David Halberstam observed, lit up a room when he entered—he was the "Sun King," exemplifying Kennedy-era liberal elitism. His talents as a fixer were great. ("If only *Phil* were still alive," Johnson reportedly lamented in the depths of Vietnam, "*Phil* could deal with this.") Yet, in some ways Graham's madness was merely the hypertrophy of the traits most essential to his power and success. Many of his most daring political gambits were the products of his manic stages. His talent was that of manipulation through sheer force of personality; his power was unratified by public vote and all too subject to the whims of personality and taste.

• Graham's papers are in the possession of Katharine Graham. Some relevant material can be found in the papers of Agnes and Eugene Meyer at the Library of Congress. The best information on Graham can be found in works on Katharine Graham and the *Washington Post*, particularly Carol Felsenthal, *Power, Privilege, and the Post: The Katharine Graham Story* (1993); Chalmers M. Roberts, *In the Shadow of Power: The Story of The Washington Post* (1989); and Katharine Graham's autobiography, *Personal History* (1997). The sections on Graham and the *Post* in David Halberstam, *The Powers That Be* (1979), are quite suggestive. See also Howard Bray, *The Pillars of the Post: The Making of a News Empire in Washington* (1980), and Tom Kelly, *The Imperial Post: The Meyers, the Grahams, and the Paper That Rules Washington* (1983). Deborah Davis, *Katharine the Great: Katharine Graham and the Washington Post* (1987), should be used cautiously with regard to both fact and interpretation. A memo by Graham describing his actions at the 1960 Democratic National Convention is reprinted in full in Theodore H. White, *The Making of the President: 1964* (1965), and nicely conveys a sense of the man.

PAUL V. MURPHY

GRAHAM, Sheilah (15 Dec. 1904?–17 Nov. 1988), author and columnist, was born Lily Shiel in London, England. Her parents' names are unknown. Her father, a tailor, died of tuberculosis while she was still a baby, and her mother, a cook in an institution, was forced to send Lily to the East London Home for Orphans when she was six. At the orphanage, she was constantly hungry and subject to humiliations such as having her hair shorn to protect against lice. Her mother, terminally ill, called her home to help care for her when Lily was fourteen years old and died of cancer three years later.

Graham's beauty got her a job selling toothbrushes at a department store in London. There she met Major John Graham Gillam, twenty-five years her senior, an agent for an iron and steel manufacturer. They married in 1926; they had no children. Graham kept her marriage secret and, with Gillam's encouragement, began a stage career. She formed her stage name at this point from a version of her own last name and her husband's middle name and invented a middle-class past for herself (even faking a baby picture). Though she enrolled in a drama school, her good looks led her to become a chorus girl. She also began writing sensational newspaper articles about the stage and selling them to the *Daily Express*, the *Daily Mail*, and the *Sunday Pictorial*. Her writing, she acknowledged, was mediocre, but it sold; she submitted her articles in person so that she could use her beauty to advantage.

Graham's husband was sexually impotent and tolerated and even encouraged her flirtations with titled upper-class men and allowed her to move to New York in 1933. That year her only novel, *Gentleman-Crook*, was published. In 1937 Graham divorced Gillam. Her career soared: she worked as a journalist for the *New York Mirror* and wrote a gossip column, "Sheilah Graham Says," for the *New York Evening Journal*. In 1935 publisher John Wheeler, who had helped her land the job at the *Mirror*, offered her the North American Newspaper Alliance's (NANA) syndicated Hollywood gossip column.

In Hollywood, Graham soon carved a niche for herself through her aggressive tactics and acerbic tongue.

In 1937 she was smitten by F. Scott Fitzgerald at a Hollywood party. Graham strove to conceal her origins, but Fitzgerald soon saw through her pretense, and on learning of her intellectual inadequacies determined to become her tutor in "the college of one," as she described it in her book of that title (1967). Fitzgerald relished the role of mentor but sometimes threw her origins in her face when they were fighting, to her utter humiliation. Graham perhaps saw him as a father figure, like Gillam, although when Fitzgerald was drinking, he was pathetically inept and dependent. Graham inspired the character of Kathleen in Fitzgerald's unfinished novel *The Last Tycoon*.

Fitzgerald credited Graham's physical resemblance to his institutionalized but once vivacious and beautiful wife Zelda for his initial attraction to Graham. Their affair lasted until his death in December 1940, although Graham broke off the relationship more than once after his alcoholic binges.

For the most part, though, their relationship was tranquil and their standard of living modest. Most of Fitzgerald's friends credited Graham with facilitating his ability to resume creative work. Graham used her relationship with Fitzgerald to fuel her writing career, starting with her first autobiography, *Beloved Infidel* (1958), her most significant work, written with Gerold Frank, and continued to recount details about the affair in about half her twelve books, as well as in numerous articles and interviews that related to Fitzgerald in part or entirely. After Fitzgerald's death, Graham asked, in order to get away from Hollywood and its associations with Fitzgerald, to be sent to England as a correspondent for NANA. There she met Trevor C. L. Westbrook, an aircraft manufacturer. While he was in Washington, D.C., on business, they married in Virginia in 1941. They had two children and divorced in 1946. Even before their divorce Graham returned to the United States with their children while he remained in England.

Again, her career flourished, and she met her goal of earning $5,000 a week, a salary commonly attainable only by the stars themselves. Eventually, in addition to her syndicated column, which reached American and English newspapers, she wrote a gossip column for the monthly *Photoplay* and had a radio segment. In 1947 Graham became a U.S. citizen. She married Stanley Wojtkiewicz in February 1953; they divorced two years later. In the 1950s she expanded her Hollywood gossip to television and wrote a column for *Daily Variety*.

Some critics condemned her for exploiting Fitzgerald's memory—a reviewer of the sequel to *Beloved Infidel*, *The Rest of the Story* (1964), remarked, "Miss Graham . . . is a self-satisfied egotist, dedicated to self-glorification and the perpetuation of what she considers her greatest claim to fame, her effort to rehabilitate F. Scott Fitzgerald" (*Best Sellers*, 1 June 1964). Another, Edmund Wilson, who knew Fitzgerald well, declared in the *New Yorker* that *Beloved Infidel* was "the very best portrait of Fitzgerald that has yet been put into print" (24 Jan. 1959).

Whatever the true measure of Graham's talent, her ambition was boundless. By the early 1960s she had eclipsed the Hollywood columnists who reigned when she was first given the column, Hedda Hopper and Louella Parsons. However, believing that Hollywood was no longer the center of the entertainment industry, Graham changed her column title from "Hollywood Today" to "Hollywood Everywhere" and finally called it "Speaking for Myself." She also moved to New York City.

Graham continued to write books involving her relationship with Fitzgerald, in addition to those stemming from her career as a gossip columnist. One reviewer of Graham's *The Real F. Scott Fitzgerald Thirty-five Years Later* (1976) was annoyed by her inability to surmount her popular style, concluding that

In tone the book is similar to Graham's earlier works: stylistically clumsy, self-justifying, highly subjective. An attempt to unite the conversational tone of a gossip columnist with the extensive quotation from primary sources that characterizes scholarly work renders the book awkward reading for both academic specialist and casual reader. (Oct. 1976)

Her books usually have a disordered chronology, and her procedure in them is largely anecdotal and fragmented.

Far more disturbing about Graham than her undisciplined writing style was her tendency to lie. Her credibility was not heightened by the fact that her primary vocation was as a gossip columnist. In order to substantiate her identity, she apparently forged a picture of her presentation at the British court with her husband John Gillam. She made much of the fact that she was virtually blackballed in the "red scare" during the McCarthy Era but never revealed publicly that she was Jewish, a reflection of both the external anti-Semitism of the times and her internalized shame. In *A State of Heat* (1972), she confesses many of the stratagems through which she snared men and landed writing jobs. By her own admission (she enjoyed comparing herself to the self-serving Becky Sharp of Thackeray's *Vanity Fair*), she was an opportunist.

Graham, like Zelda Fitzgerald, will probably always be better known for her connection with Fitzgerald than for her writings. Yet she made a name for herself through sheer determination and resolve. *The Rest of the Story* (1964) quotes her friend Buff Cobb Rogers as saying, "What a shame, what a waste, my dear, that we summed you up as merely a pretty girl with a gift for industry and a disagreeable ability to say a cutting thing." Rogers added further, "It took Scott the genius to make her known to herself and us." Graham died in Palm Beach, Florida.

• For autobiographical accounts of her life, besides the titles already mentioned, see her unproduced screenplay *Film-Struck* (1941) at the Library of Congress; *Books from the Library of Sheilah Graham* (1961); *The Garden of Allah* (1970); and *The Late Lily Shiel* (1978). Several books relied on her experience in Hollywood: *Confessions of a Hollywood Columnist* (1969); *Scratch an Actor* (1970); *How to Marry Super Rich*

(1974); *Hollywood Revisited* (1985); and *My Hollywood* (1984). The fullest and most accurate of accounts is by her son, Robert Westbrook, *Intimate Lies: F. Scott Fitzgerald and Sheilah Graham*, which sheds light on evasions in Graham's own works.

Other sources of biographical information on Graham are Jeffrey Meyers, *Scott Fitzgerald: A Biography* (1994), and Matthew J. Bruccoli, *Some Sort of Epic Grandeur: The Life of F. Scott Fitzgerald* (1981). *Annual Obituary 1988* (1990) contains a reliable entry on Graham, as does *Current Biography Yearbook* (1969, 1970).

JOSEPHINE McQUAIL

GRAHAM, Sylvester (5 July 1794–11 Sept. 1851), reformer and author, was born in West Suffield, Connecticut, the son of John Graham, a clergyman, and Ruth (maiden name unknown). After his father died when Sylvester was still very young, his mother, who apparently suffered from mental problems, had to let others raise her children. At age three he had to live with a neighbor; when he was five he lived with a local tavern keeper and at age six with a neighboring farmer.

Both Graham's father and grandfather had been Calvinist ministers who had taken part in the revivals of the Great Awakening when it swept through the Connecticut Valley, and this sparked Sylvester Graham's interest in the ministry. However, his family's poverty forced him to postpone those plans until he was twenty-nine. In 1823 Graham entered Amherst College. A mental collapse resulting from school and personal pressure forced him to drop out of school. While ill he prepared himself for joining the ministry. By 1826 he had recuperated, become a Presbyterian minister, and married a Miss Earl.

Between 1828 and 1831 his life arrived at a turning point. Apocalyptic visions filled his mind, propelling him from the pulpit onto the lecture circuit. On 13 December 1829 he delivered the sermon "Thy Kingdom Come" at Crown Street Church in Philadelphia. In the best temperance rhetoric he alarmed his audience with images of "millions of children" who, brought up without a proper religious education, would "soon unite in one dark and mighty confluence of ignorance and immorality and crime, which will overflow the wholesome restraints of society, and sweep away the barriers of civil law, and sap the foundations of our Republican institutions" (Abzug, p. 165). This fear of a social collapse prompted Graham to devote his efforts to issues of diet, nutrition, and human physiology.

From 1830 to 1831 he delivered addresses on human physiology, diet, and regimen for the Pennsylvania Society for Discouraging the Use of Ardent Spirits in Philadelphia. He argued that intemperance could be prevented by turning to a vegetable diet and avoiding all meats. Out of this idea he developed a theory that proper nutrition and a dietary regimen could cure virtually every disease.

As the country fearfully awaited the arrival of a cholera epidemic sweeping across Europe, Graham moved to New York City. From 1832 to 1833 he lectured to New Yorkers on the alleged dietary problems that supposedly caused the fatal disease. Many contemporaries believed that cholera had dietary causes because heavy vomiting in the early stages of the disease suggested the body's attempt to cleanse itself. While some asserted that hearty, heavy foods would help, Graham prescribed a bland, plain diet consisting of fruits, vegetables, and bread from unbolted flour or coarsely ground grain. Moreover, he urged his audiences to adopt a physiological and sanitary regimen of regular baths, exercise, and well-ventilated rooms. While it did not cure cholera, those who followed his advice certainly had healthier lives than most Americans at the time.

For Graham, salvation and the coming of the kingdom of God depended both on spiritual and on physiological compliance with the laws of God. He argued that "the millennium can never reasonably be expected to arrive until those laws which God has implanted in the physiological nature of man are, equally with the moral laws, universally known and obeyed" (Walters, p. 149). This connection between spirituality and human physiological nature led Graham to add sexuality to his lecture topics.

In his lectures on chastity, printed as *The Young Men's Guide to Chastity* in 1834, Graham preached sexual self-restraint not only outside but also within marriage. Sexual self-restraint was key for the reformers of the era, who believed that sexual excess depleted the life force of men and resulted in degeneracy and premature aging. Graham believed that a boy, if not properly socialized, would age prematurely and become

the wretched transgressor [who] . . . finally becomes a confirmed and degraded idiot, whose deeply sunken and vacant glossy eye, and livid, shrivelled countenance, and ulcerous, toothless gums, and fetid breath, and feeble, broken voice, and emaciated and dwarfish and crooked body, and almost hairless head—covered perhaps with suppurating blisters and running sores—denote a premature old age! (Kimmel, p. 47)

Only a complete physiological regimen, ranging from diet to exercise and sleeping habits could form a counterweight. In addition to his sanitary and dietary advice, Graham promoted sleeping on a hard wood bed, since the softness of a feather bed might have an unduly arousing effect. He published his lectures in two volumes as *Lectures on the Science of Human Life* (1839).

While he easily attracted audiences numbering as many as 2,000, Graham's appearances drew controversy as well. He was mobbed twice by Boston butchers for denouncing meat as sexually arousing. On one occasion a group of angry citizens kept him from delivering his lecture on chastity in front of a female audience because of the moral delicacy of the subject. In 1847 a mob of Boston bakers attacked Graham while he was extemporizing on the evils of consuming commercially produced bread and the dietary value of unbolted flour. The riotous bakers were subdued when

Graham's followers shoveled slaked lime from the windows of the lecture hall onto the crowd below.

At the time Graham's ideas enjoyed wide circulation and exerted considerable influence. Based on his ideas, the American Physiological Society was formed in 1837; its publication was the *Journal of Health and Longevity* (1837–1839). In 1838 Grahamites held their first national health convention. Two years later Oberlin College invited the editor of the *Journal* to take charge of the student commons.

As the movement that he had helped to originate broadened, Graham himself took a more narrow focus, which prevented him from assuming the position of leadership that he otherwise might have taken. Notwithstanding, Graham made lasting contributions to ideas about diet and nutrition. He popularized the use of unbolted flour, later named after him, like the cracker made of coarsely ground grain; and his lectures on diet and nutrition paved the way for the increased consumption of cereal and fruit. He died in Northampton, Massachusetts.

• For biographical information, see Jayme A. Sokolow, *Eros and Modernization: Sylvester Graham, Health Reform, and the Origins of Victorian Sexuality in America* (1983), and Stephen Nissenbaum, *Sex, Diet, and Debility in Jacksonian America: Sylvester Graham and Health Reform* (1980). Graham's life, significance, and contributions are also discussed in Ronald G. Walters, *American Reformers, 1815–1860* (1978); John S. Haller, Jr., and Robin M. Haller, *The Physician and Sexuality in Victorian America* (1974); Michael S. Kimmel, *Manhood in America: A Cultural History* (1996); Robert H. Abzug, *Cosmos Crumbling: American Reform and the Religious Imagination* (1994); and Charles G. Sellers, *The Market Revolution: Jacksonian America, 1815–1846* (1991).

THOMAS WINTER

GRAHAM, William Alexander (5 Sept. 1804–11 Aug. 1875), governor of North Carolina, secretary of the navy, and U.S. and Confederate senator, was born in Lincoln County, North Carolina, the son of Joseph Graham, a revolutionary war soldier, iron entrepreneur, and major general of a North and South Carolina brigade in the War of 1812, and Isabella Davidson. After attending preparatory academies in Lincolnton, Statesville, and Hillsborough, Graham graduated from the University of North Carolina in 1824, sharing first honors in a distinguished class. He read law with the eminent jurist Thomas Ruffin, later state chief justice, and in the late 1820s established a legal practice in Hillsborough, county seat of Orange County. He chose Hillsborough because it had an invigorating society; was located near Raleigh, the state capital, and promised an able young lawyer a lucrative practice in Hillsborough, Raleigh, and the surrounding counties. He became a successful lawyer, noted for his diligence, probity, and legal skill. In time Graham owned three plantations worked by slave labor. Two in the southwestern Piedmont were managed by overseers. With several hundred acres and nearly a hundred slaves, he was a substantial planter by North Carolina standards, but farming and the law were secondary to his interest in public affairs. In 1836 he married Susannah Sarah Washington. They had ten children, two of whom died in childhood.

Motivated by personal ambition and a sense of noblesse oblige, Graham entered politics and was a frequent officeholder from 1833 to 1865. He was a founder of the Whig party and was a delegate to the North Carolina House of Commons in 1833, 1834, 1835, 1836, 1838, and 1840, serving as Speaker in the 1838 and 1840 sessions. As a state legislator, Graham manifested an interest in public education, humanitarian reforms, and internal improvements. From 1840 to 1843 he served in the U.S. Senate, where he generally supported Henry Clay's opposition to "His Accidency," President John Tyler, and was a proponent of Clay's American System favoring a national bank, a protective tariff, and federally funded internal improvements. Elected governor for two terms, 1845–1849, Graham promoted humanitarian reforms, such as an asylum for the insane and a school for the deaf and dumb, and favored state-subsidized internal improvements, especially railroad construction. Much of his attention in his second term was absorbed by the Mexican War, of which he disapproved.

After declining European diplomatic appointments, Graham accepted Millard Fillmore's offer of the Navy Department, serving from 1850 to 1852. He was appointed secretary of the navy because he was a southern moderate from a consistently Whig state. He supported the passage and acceptance of the Compromise of 1850, advocating moderation to North and South alike. Beyond these political activities, he also proved to be an astute naval administrator. Secretary Graham was instrumental in a revision of the naval code, constructive personnel reforms, exploration of the Amazon basin, and planning the Matthew C. Perry expedition to Japan. Samuel Eliot Morison, the eminent naval historian, characterized Graham as one of the ablest nineteenth-century navy secretaries.

When the Whig party convention met in the summer of 1852, Graham was nominated to second place on a presidential ticket headed by General Winfield S. Scott. His role was to reassure the South that Scott was sound on the slavery issue. He failed, and Franklin Pierce was elected in a Democratic landslide that presaged the demise of the Whig party owing to the moral dilemma over slavery. A disappointed Graham returned to his Hillsborough home determined to leave politics to others while he provided for his numerous progeny. He served in the state senate in 1854 at the behest of his party but despaired when the Whig party disintegrated after the Kansas-Nebraska Act. Unlike many of his political friends who joined the American party, Graham still considered himself a Whig until the crisis of 1860 forced him to become a Constitutional Unionist. The efforts of conservative men to preserve the Union were frustrated by the election of Abraham Lincoln.

Vigorously opposed to disunion since the nullification crisis of the 1830s, Graham was a "reluctant secessionist" who advocated patience and conciliation between the November election and the firing on Fort Sumter. As a delegate to the secession convention of May 1861, he was nominated to serve as president in hopes of denying power to the original secessionists in the state, but to no avail. Next Graham and the conservatives he led proposed that North Carolina invoke the right of revolution as the appropriate remedy to tyranny. Eventually he voted for secession.

Graham and like-minded southerners found themselves allied with original secessionists in a war against the Union. Soon five of Graham's sons were Confederate officers. Two nieces were married to Confederate generals "Stonewall" Jackson and Daniel Harvey Hill. A third niece, then deceased, had been the wife of Brigadier General Rufus Barringer. Graham's only daughter married North Carolina chief justice Walter Clark. Graham had little choice but to support Confederate military efforts, but he was deeply troubled by the Jefferson Davis administration's policies. In particular he opposed the suspension of habeas corpus and Confederate conscription. By 1864, when he became a Confederate senator, Graham thought the fledgling southern nation "a lost cause." Serving until 1865, he joined the antiadministration forces in the Confederate Congress and supported peace negotiations on the basis of status quo antebellum. This unrealistic position was thwarted by the failure of the Hampton Roads conference. In February, Senator Graham opposed the arming of black troops despite the depletion of Confederate armies. He argued that the war would have been in vain if the institution of slavery were disturbed. In despair he bore a proposal from the peace faction in Congress to Governor Zebulon B. Vance that North Carolina seek a separate peace. This Vance declined to do. Graham's last wartime service was, with Vance's approval, to negotiate the surrender of Raleigh to William T. Sherman.

After the war Graham, though unpardoned, was elected to the U.S. Senate, but he and other southerners were denied their seats as Congress acted to frustrate presidential Reconstruction. Despite his antebellum Unionism, Graham's disabilities were not removed until 1873. He never filled another elective office but, as elder statesman, became an influential opponent of Reconstruction and a leading Democratic-Conservative. He became a white supremacist, contending that amalgamation of the races would destroy southern civilization. His sons, John Washington Graham and James Augustus Graham, reflected his views in the North Carolina General Assembly. An implacable opponent of the Republican governor, William Woods Holden, Graham was lead attorney in Holden's successful impeachment trial. During the 1870s, while seeking to repair his economic fortunes by practicing law, he called for a convention to revise the constitution of 1868. He hoped to reconcentrate political power in the state government in expectation that a Democratic party victory would "redeem" the state.

In 1867 Graham was appointed one of the original trustees of the Peabody Education Fund. He served in that capacity until his death, frequently traveling north for board meetings. He was also instrumental in reopening the University of North Carolina, an institution he served as trustee for some forty years. One of the three arbiters of the Virginia-Maryland boundary dispute, Graham died in Sarasota Springs, New York, while attending a meeting of that body.

Few men have enjoyed the public's confidence to the extent Graham did. He was arguably the preeminent North Carolinian of his age. At Graham's death, Samuel F. Phillips, an erstwhile Graham associate turned Republican, claimed: "He was altogether the wisest man of our time in North Carolina. He possessed in full measure that royal quality so rarely met—judgment" (Samuel F. Phillips to John W. Graham, 13 Aug. 1875).

• Most of Graham's manuscripts are in the Southern Historical Collection, University of North Carolina at Chapel Hill; the Duke Manuscript Collection, Duke University, Durham, N.C.; and the North Carolina Archives, Raleigh. For published documents see *The Papers of William A. Graham*, ed. Max R. Williams et al. (8 vols., 1957–1993), which includes memorial orations by Montford McGehee (1877) and Frank Nash (1910) in vol. 1. See also Williams, "William A. Graham, North Carolina Political Leader, 1804–1849" (Ph.D. diss., Univ. of North Carolina at Chapel Hill, 1965) and "Secretary William A. Graham, Naval Administrator, 1850–1852," *North Carolina Historical Review* 48 (Winter 1971): 53–72. Accounts of his death and burial proceedings can be found in the *Raleigh Daily Sentinel*, 11–16 Aug. 1875.

MAX R. WILLIAMS

GRAHAME, Gloria (28 Nov. 1923–5 Oct. 1981), actress, was born Gloria Hallward in Los Angeles, California, the daughter of Michael Hallward, an industrial designer, and Jean McDougall, an actress and teacher. She spent a comfortable early life in the suburbs of Pasadena, until the depression halted real estate development and her father lost his job. After the Hallwards divorced, Grahame's mother supported Gloria and her older sister Joy by teaching at private schools, directing plays, and giving acting lessons.

Grahame began performing at the Pasadena Playhouse at the age of nine. After appearing in a local production of *A Maid of the Ozarks*, as well as with the touring company of *Good Night Ladies* (for which she adopted the *A Star Is Born*–inspired stage name Vickie Lester), she was hired by Elia Kazan to understudy Miriam Hopkins in *The Skin of Our Teeth*. She never went on for the sturdy Hopkins, but the job led to roles in *Star Dust* (1943) and *The World's Full of Girls* (1943). The first died out of town; the second closed in a week. She had better luck with George Abbott's *A Highland Fling* (1944), a play that brought her good reviews and a seven-year, $250-a-week contract with Metro-Goldwyn-Mayer (MGM).

As Gloria Grahame (the last name belonged to her maternal grandmother), she had small parts in the comedies *Blonde Fever* (1944) and *Without Love* (1945). She spent most of her time in photo shoots and on United Services Organization tours, one of many bland starlets of the time. Director Frank Capra, who borrowed her from MGM to play the town flirt in *It's a Wonderful Life* (1946), was the first to spot Grahame's particular talent for portraying vulnerable bad girls. As Violet Bick, she used the incongruity of her tiny, childlike voice, inviting eyes, and bleached blonde looks to create the first of many complex fallen women. Cecil B. De Mille said she combined the manner of a schoolgirl with the eyes of a sorceress; film historian David Shipman called her the best of the 1940s floozies.

In 1947 Grahame played Frank Sinatra's girl in the musical *It Happened in Brooklyn*, a movie actress in the comedy *Merton of the Movies* with Red Skelton, a nightclub singer in the last of the Thin Man mystery series, *Song of the Thin Man*, and a trashy but sympathetic bar hostess in *Crossfire*. *Crossfire*, a study of anti-Semitism, marked her first foray into film noir. These particular types of dark, suspenseful thrillers used low lighting to point up the shadowy worlds of crime and deceit. Grahame found her niche in such films, playing all manner of morally ambiguous women—from prostitute to cheating wife—with sympathy and depth.

Crossfire brought Grahame an Oscar nomination for best supporting actress, though the film itself was buried by the similarly themed *Gentleman's Agreement*, released the same year, and by the blacklisting of director Edward Dmytryk and producer Adrian Scott. Grahame lost the Oscar but signed a new contract with RKO.

Grahame's director on her first RKO film, *A Woman's Secret* (1949), was Nicholas Ray. In 1948 Grahame divorced actor Stanley Clements, whom she had married in 1945, and married Ray. Late that year, their son was born.

Ray and Grahame teamed for *In a Lonely Place* (1950), a film noir love story with Humphrey Bogart that was said to parallel the disintegration of the Ray-Grahame marriage. Grahame was cast as a woman who falls in love with and then comes to fear and distrust suspected murderer Bogart. Jeff Stafford, writing in the *International Dictionary of Films and Filmmakers*, called it a "brilliant performance, alternating between passionate longing and paranoia." Grahame hoped to follow her success with the part of the doomed working-class girlfriend in *A Place in the Sun* (1951), one of the year's major films, but was bound by RKO to make Josef Von Sternberg's *Macao* (1952). Though *Macao* was a financial success, Grahame's small role as the mistress of a gambling den owner was no stretch. She ended her contract and began a lucrative career as a freelancer.

In 1952 Grahame appeared in De Mille's all-star circus film *The Greatest Show on Earth*, followed by the melodrama *Sudden Fear*, which found her terrorizing Joan Crawford with bad guy boyfriend Jack Palance. She then returned to MGM to play an unfaithful wife of a Hollywood screenwriter in *The Bad and the Beautiful*, a performance that won her the best supporting actress Academy Award.

After receiving the Oscar, Grahame landed starring roles in *The Glass Wall* and *Man on a Tightrope* (both 1953). After a short shoot on the ridiculous *Prisoners of the Casbah* (1953), she landed a fine and memorable film noir role in Fritz Lang's *The Big Heat* (1953), playing a streetwise prostitute who crosses over to the right side of the tracks, only to be disfigured when scalding coffee is flung in her face.

In 1954, after her 1952 divorce from Ray, Grahame married television writer Cy Howard and appeared in two melodramas: *The Naked Alibi*, with Sterling Hayden, and *Human Desire*, a disappointing reunion with *Big Heat* collaborators Lang and Glenn Ford. After a small but showy role in the English film *The Good Die Young* (1955), she was back on top in the hit musical *Oklahoma!* (1955). Though not a singer (she recorded her songs one note at a time), she was chosen by composer Richard Rodgers to play the girl who "Cain't Say No" over such musical performers as Debbie Reynolds and Celeste Holm. Her reviews were mostly good, though one reviewer dubbed her "the girl with the Novacaine lip," a tag that lent credence to stories of botched plastic surgeries on her mouth. Subsequent supporting performances in *Not as a Stranger* (1955) and *The Cobweb* (1955) were reviewed badly. Her last starring role was in *The Man Who Never Was* (1956), as a librarian involved with a fighter pilot during World War II.

In 1960, after a brief period of residence in France, the birth of a daughter, divorce from Howard, and minimal film work, Grahame married Tony Ray, Nick Ray's son by his first marriage. Public and family reactions were strong, sparking heavy coverage in the mainstream and gossip press. Despite the scandal, the couple remained married for fourteen years, often working together in stage productions, and they eventually had two sons.

As her film work diminished, Grahame returned to the stage, appearing in a Los Angeles staging of *The Three Sisters* (1960), regional productions of the *Marriage Go Round* (1961), *Laura* (1961), and *The Little Hut* (1963), and with Henry Fonda's touring company of *The Time of Your Life* (1972). Though she went into semiretirement to rear her children, she made guest appearances on television programs, including "GE Theater," "The Outer Limits," and "The Fugitive."

The bulk of Grahame's remaining work was in low-budget films. In *Blood and Lace* (1971) she was a murderer; in *The Todd Killings* (1971) she played the murderer's mother. *Tarot* (1973) was barely released in the United States. Most critics think that *Mama's Dirty Girls* (1974) was Grahame's worst movie, though *Mansion of the Doomed* (1976) was probably not much better.

In 1975 Grahame was diagnosed with breast cancer. For the balance of her life, she worked extensively on the English and American stage, in such diverse plays as *Rain* (1978), *A Tribute to Lily Lamont* (1978), *The Merry Wives of Windsor* (1979), *The Glass Menagerie* (1979), *Private Lives* (1980), and *Who's Afraid of Virginia Woolf* (1980). She also appeared in television movies and the first miniseries, *Rich Man, Poor Man* (1976), and on the big screen in supporting roles (usually as a mother) in *Chilly Scenes of Winter* (1979), *Melvin and Howard* (1980), and *A Nightingale Sang in Berkeley Square* (1979). *The Nesting* was released in 1982, after her death. She died in New York City.

• Sources that address Grahame's career include Nicholas Curcio, *Suicide Blonde* (1989); Peter Turner, *Film Stars Don't Die in Liverpool* (1984); Bruce Crowther, *Film Noir: Reflection in a Dark Mirror* (1988); Foster Hirsch, *The Dark Side of the Screen: Film Noir* (1981); *International Dictionary of Films and Filmmakers* (1986); James Robert Parish and Ronald L. Bowers, *The MGM Stock Company: The Golden Era* (1973); Nicholas Ray, *I Was Interrupted* (1993); and David Shipman, *The Great Movie Stars* (1980). An obituary is in the *New York Times*, 8 Oct. 1981.

DIANA MOORE

GRAINGER, Percy Aldridge (8 July 1882–20 Feb. 1961), composer, pianist, and musical experimenter, was born George Percy Grainger in Brighton, Australia, the son of John Harry Grainger, an English-born architect, engineer, and amateur painter and musician, and Rosa Annie Aldrich, an amateur musician. His father's philandering and alcohol abuse and his mother's harshly domineering manner probably contributed to the emergence of a number of unusual traits in their son as he grew into manhood. These included immature emotional ties to his mother that lasted until her suicide in 1922, masochism, rigid self-discipline that included strenuous exercise, pervasive freneticism, comically bizarre behavior, and virtually uninhibited flights of creative fantasy.

Grainger's first musical training was in piano, under his mother's tutelage. This instruction continued under Louis Pabst at the Melbourne Conservatory. Grainger began performing publicly in 1892. In 1895 Grainger and his mother moved to Germany, where he studied composition under Iwan Knorr at the Hoch Conservatory in Frankfurt-am-Main. This schooling, along with instruction in piano under James Kwast in Frankfurt and Ferruccio Busoni in Berlin, continued until 1901. During his years in Germany, Grainger associated with fellow students and budding twentieth-century composers such as Henry Balfour Gardiner, Norman O'Neill, Cyril Scott, and Roger Quilter. Also during this period, Grainger developed his concept of "free music" in a stream-of-consciousness style unencumbered by the traditional constraints of meter, bar line, and specifically defined pitch.

Grainger and his mother relocated to London in 1901. He soon became a leading concert pianist, but he found greater pleasure in composing. He suspected, however, that critical response to his often unconventional compositions would not be favorable. He therefore withheld most of his creative efforts until after the first successful public presentation of his works at the Balfour Gardiner choral and orchestral concerts in 1912.

Grainger's most significant experiment with avant-garde composition during his London years was "Ran-

dom Round" (1913), an early example of aleatoric, or "chance," music. Less adventurous but still forward-looking were two works titled "Hill Song" (1901–1902 and 1907). By 1914 his compositions were enjoying frequent performances in Britain despite conservative criticism. One of the critics' favorite targets was Grainger's use of coined English instructions such as "louden lots" instead of Italian cues like "molto crescendo." This mannerism reflected Grainger's attraction to Nordic languages and culture. He acquired much of this penchant from his early exposure to Anglo-Saxon literature and the writings of historians such as Edward Augustus Freeman.

From 1905 through 1907 Grainger collected numerous English folksong variants. This effort roughly coincided with those of Ralph Vaughan Williams, Gustav Holst, and Cecil Sharp, but it differed from theirs first in Grainger's utilization of Thomas Edison's cylinder phonograph and second in his meticulous notation of ornaments, metric shifts, and a variety of more subtle nuances. This care, which Grainger also exercised in collecting Scandinavian and Pacific island songs, often was deemed precious, but many scholars now consider it a paradigm of ethnomusicological discipline.

Grainger came to the United States in 1914 and became a citizen in 1918. His service to the war effort included active duty as an army musician. He also wrote "Country Gardens" in connection with the war-bond drive. While this piece represents neither his most advanced style at that time nor his mature artistry, it remains the work for which he is most widely known.

Grainger spent much of the decade following World War I performing, teaching at the Chicago Musical College, and composing. Many of his compositions from this period reflect both his fondness for woodwind timbres and his view of the folk idiom as an academically valid means of musical expression.

In August 1928 Grainger married Ella Viola Strom, a Swedish poet and artist, during a concert at the Hollywood Bowl. For the occasion, he composed an epithalamium, "To a Nordic Princess." They had no children.

In 1929 Grainger visited the English postromanticist Frederick Delius; their long friendship engendered Grainger's piano arrangements of several compositions by Delius and much mutual admiration and support.

From 1933 to 1955 Grainger assisted the musicologist Dom Anselm Hughes in transcribing medieval English music for the modern choir. He also transcribed about forty other works from the thirteenth through eighteenth centuries and was an active writer and lecturer. Grainger also founded the Grainger Museum, at the University of Melbourne, in 1935.

Many of Grainger's later works incorporated the idea of free music that grew more dominant as he matured. He ultimately pursued this concept through the use of tone-producing machines. In the 1930s Grainger composed for the Theremin, an electronic tone generator named after its Russian inventor. He also built several of his own machines that could read special notation that he invented. A particularly successful effort resulted from his collaboration in 1944 with Burnett Cross, a physicist. At the time of his death Grainger was using an updated version of the device, in which graphs drawn on sheets of plastic were scanned by photocells interfaced to transistor-controlled oscillator circuits. Unfortunately, their esoteric character and logistical problems with their performance have reduced most of Grainger's surviving free pieces to curiosities. He died in White Plains, New York.

The idiosyncrasies that placed Grainger ahead of his time psychologically, intellectually, and artistically also limited his success in achieving the recognition that his brilliance warranted, and posthumous appreciation of his significance has materialized slowly. Yet, to quote his observation about Delius, Grainger "set out to enjoy life, did so, and did not regret paying the price it cost."

• The Grainger Museum at the University of Melbourne is the principal repository of Grainger's surviving original documents, recordings, music machines, and various memorabilia. Manuscripts are also housed in the Sibley Music Library of the Eastman School of Music (Rochester, N.Y.), the New York Public Library, the National Library of Scotland (Edinburgh), the National Library of Ireland (Dublin), the British Library (London), and the Library of Upsala College (West Orange, N.J.). Records of Grainger's ethnomusicological studies can be found at the Royal Library of Copenhagen, the Vaughan Williams Memorial Library at the Cecil Sharp House (London), and in the Grainger collection of the Library of Congress. Important articles written by Grainger include "Collecting with the Phonograph," *Folk Song Society Journal* 3 (May 1908): 147–62; "Free Music," repr. in the *Grainger Society Journal* 8, no. 1 (1986): 57–63; "The Impress of Personality in Traditional Singing," *Folk Song Society Journal* 3 (May 1908): 163–66; "The Impress of Personality in Unwritten Music," *Musical Quarterly* 1 (July 1915): 416–35; "Melody versus Rhythm," repr. in the *Grainger Society Journal* 8, no. 1 (1986): 64–69; "The Orchestral Use of the Saxophone," repr. in the *Grainger Society Journal* 8, no. 2 (1986): 3–5; "The Saxophone's Business in the Band," *Instrumentalist* 4 (Sept.–Oct. 1949): 6–9; and "The Two-fold Vitality of Anglo-Saxon Music," *Etude* 37, no. 2 (1918): 81–82. Grainger's approximately 400 works are indexed in Teresa Balough, *A Complete Catalog of the Works of Percy Grainger* (1975). A short catalog appears in the *New Grove Dictionary of Music and Musicians* (1980). The definitive study of Grainger is John Bird, *Percy Grainger* (1976). Also important is Thomas Slattery, *Percy Grainger—the Inveterate Innovator* (1974). An important record of Grainger's London years is Kay Dreyfus, *The Farthest North of Humanness: Letters of Percy Grainger, 1901–1914* (1985).

J. MARSHALL BEVIL

GRAM, Hans Burch (13 July 1787–26 Feb. 1840), physician, was born Hans Benjamin Gramm in Boston, Massachusetts, the son of Hans Gram, secretary to the Danish governor of Santa Cruz, and Jane Burdick. After the death of his parents, he left Boston in 1806 or 1807 to claim his grandfather's estate in Copenhagen,

Denmark. Gram obtained a portion of the estate that allowed him to secure an education. Through the favor of his uncle, a Dr. Fenger, physician to the Danish king, he became a student at the Royal Medical and Surgical Institute. Fenger also provided him entrée to other schools and hospitals in northern Europe.

Gram was appointed in 1813 to the position of assistant surgeon at the National Military and Naval Hospital, with which he was officially connected during the last seven years of the Napoleonic Wars. He was at one point assistant surgeon to the king. By 1814 he had attained the rank of surgeon, and in 1816 he was awarded the degree C.M.L., or magister of surgery, the highest granted by the Royal Academy of Surgery. He then resigned his position and went into general practice in Copenhagen.

Through the influence of Hans Christian Lund, Gram became aware of the new system of homeopathic medicine, in which patients were treated with medicines which cause symptoms in the healthy similar to those of a given disease. Lund was Copenhagen's first and most prominent homeopath. He may have studied with Samuel Hahnemann, founder of the system, in Leipzig; although this is not documented, it is known that several Danes were students of Hahnemann at this time. Gram diligently studied the effects of homeopathic medicines in 1823 and 1824.

Gram wished to rejoin his family in the United States and to bring the doctrines of homeopathy there. He left his practice and sailed from Stockholm in 1824. In spring 1825 he arrived in Mount Desert, Maine, remaining there as the guest of Wendell Kittredge, the first physician on the island. Gram then sailed for New York City, where he resided with his brother, Neils B. Gram. He soon lost the bulk of his fortune by endorsing notes for his brother, and by necessity he resumed the practice of medicine.

Late in 1825 Gram published a 24-page pamphlet in the form of a letter to David Hosack, president of the New York College of Physicians and Surgeons. It was a translation of Hahnemann's *Spirit of the Homoeopathic Doctrine* (1813). Gram's imperfect translation, titled *The Character of Homoeopathy*, was distributed free to leading physicians and medical schools; it was not well received, and Hosack claimed never to have read it. Gram felt deeply the failure of his efforts. It was not until 1838 that Hahnemann's polemic was more perfectly translated into English.

In 1826 Gram became friends with Robert B. Folger, a fellow physician and Mason. After reading Gram's pamphlet and his unpublished manuscript on the "pharmacodynamic" properties of drugs, Folger initially ridiculed the small doses of homeopathy but later allowed Gram to treat several of his difficult cases. The patients' recoveries led Folger to learn German from Gram in order to study Hahnemann's works. Folger was Gram's assistant and student until he left New York in 1828. Gram intended to join Folger to go into practice in Charlotte, North Carolina, but he remained in New York when Folger gave up medicine for mining.

Folger had introduced Gram in 1826 to Ferdinand Wilsey, a merchant and prominent Mason who suffered from an ailment his physician, John Gray, was unable to relieve. Wilsey placed himself under Gram's care and was cured, boosting Gram's practice. Wilsey, the first American known to have been treated with homeopathic medicines, soon became a convert and Gram's student, later qualifying at the College of Physicians and Surgeons. Gray, who had reluctantly consented to allow Wilsey to be treated, believed the cure to be due to Wilsey's improved diet; finally, however impressed by Gram's cultivated air and broad learning, he submitted his difficult cases to homeopathic treatment and was converted by the results.

Gram was elected a member of the Medical and Philosophical Society of New York in February 1828; in July 1830 he became its president. From this office, and as a member of the New York County Medical Society, he was able to meet and eventually convert a number of prominent physicians. He also had two medical students.

Gram influenced the County Medical Society to adopt, about 1833, the rigorous German method of public examination to qualify for practice, but this practice was soon discontinued owing to the objections of medical schools.

Gram's converts treated cholera victims successfully during the epidemic of 1832, and New York became a center of homeopathic activity second only to Philadelphia. Physicians trained by Gram or his converts spread homeopathic doctrine through Connecticut, Massachusetts, New Jersey, and New York State. Gram continued as the group's guide, teacher, and counselor until May 1839, when he suffered a stroke in North Carolina that left him hemiplegic. He died in New York City after ten months of suffering, attended by Wilsey, Gray, and Curtis. He never married.

Gram was greatly admired for his culture, intellect, and independent views. He had been considered one of the most talented and learned men in the country by the leading physicians of the New York faculty until they learned he was a homeopath. Their subsequent enmity and persecution left him morose and taciturn in his last years. A Swedenborgian and a Christian, he strove be a good person. Wilsey said of him, "He was afraid of nothing earthly except doing wrong."

• The only work of Gram's ever published was *The Character of Homoeopathy* (1825). The most accurate accounts of his life are John Gray "The Early Annals of Homeopathy in New York," in *Transactions of the Homeopathic Medical Society of the State of New York* 1 (1863): 89–106; and John Smith's article in *The Homoeopathic Examiner* 1 (1840): 101. Henry M. Smith furnished further detail in *The New England Medical Gazette* 6 (1871): 91–95. Thomas Lindsley Bradford, *The Pioneers of Homeopathy* (1897), contains biographies of Gram and of his converts and students. Benjamin C. Woodbury, "These Many Years," in *Proceedings of the Forty-Seventh Annual Session of the International Hahnemannian Association* (1926), pp. 71–76, contains a biography with genealogical data. Gram's influence in the spread of the homeopathic doctrines from New York is presented in a documentary film by Julian Winston, *The Faces of Homeopathy* (1995).
CHRISTOPHER ELLITHORP

GRANGE, Red (13 June 1903–28 Jan. 1991), football player, coach, and broadcaster, was born Harold Edward Grange in Forksville, Pennsylvania, the son of Lyle Grange, a lumber camp foreman, and Sadie Sherman. When Grange's mother died in 1908, his father moved the family, which included Red's older sisters and his three-year-old brother, to Wheaton, Illinois, where the elder Grange had grown up. Years later, Red, as he was nicknamed because of his auburn hair, recalled that "at first I missed Forksville terribly," but as time passed he realized that Wheaton "offered a more civilized way of life."

Struggling to make a living and to provide care for his children, Lyle Grange sent his two daughters to live with his wife's relatives in Pennsylvania. The rest of family moved to a number of different residences in Wheaton, including a two-year period when they lived with one of Grange's uncles. After Lyle Grange joined the Wheaton police department in 1913 and became city marshal the following year, the family's financial situation improved. In 1917 Lyle Grange rented an apartment in the city's business district where he and Grange's brother lived until they were joined by Red, who had spent a year living on another uncle's farm on the outskirts of town.

Taking after his father, who had been renowned in the lumber camps for his strength and agility, Red Grange was a superb athlete from an early age. He once recalled, "I don't remember ever losing a footrace as a kid" and added that "the more important part of living came after school when I was able to play football, basketball, and baseball with my pals." Grange received ample encouragement from his father, who seldom missed one of Red's games or track meets despite often being the only policeman in Wheaton. At Wheaton High School Grange was a star athlete in four sports (track, baseball, basketball, and football) and earned 16 letters in four years. Although he always claimed his favorite sport was baseball, Red received his highest accolades playing football. While in high school Grange scored 75 touchdowns (only one of which came during his freshman year, when he played end instead of halfback) and kicked 82 conversions for a total of 532 points. During the summers he delivered ice to help support his family, which later earned him the nickname the "Wheaton Iceman."

Despite his prodigious athletic achievements, Grange was not heavily recruited. He decided to attend the University of Illinois because tuition there was inexpensive, his friends had decided to attend college there, and he was impressed by Illinois football coach Robert Zuppke, whom he had met at the Illinois state championship track meet. In 1922, as a freshman at Illinois, Grange nearly decided not to try out for football because about 120 other men were trying out for the freshman team, most of whom were bigger than he was. Grange recalled that, when he explained the situation to his fraternity brothers, they got hold of a paddle and had him bend over. At that point Grange immediately agreed that "football makes a lot of sense to me." The following day he returned to practice where he was issued his famous number 77 jersey. When later asked how he got such a high number, Grange simply replied, "the guy in front of me got 76; the guy in back got 78." Surrounded by other talented recruits (two of his teammates, Ralph "Moon" Baker and Frank Wickhorst, would be selected All-Americans at other schools), Grange was an immediate sensation on a freshman team that regularly beat the Illinois varsity squad in scrimmage games.

In 1923, his first varsity season, Grange led the Fighting Illini to an 8–0 record and a Big Ten Conference co-championship. His totals that season included 12 touchdowns and 1,260 yards rushing in just seven games. At the conclusion of the season Walter Camp selected him as halfback on his All-American team, a position he would retain in 1924 and 1925. The shy and modest Grange routinely depreciated his accomplishments. When later asked about his running ability, he replied that "it was God-given; I couldn't take any credit. Other guys could make 90s and 100s in chemistry. I could run fast. It's the way God distributes things."

In 1924 Grange became a national hero when he achieved one of the best individual performances in college football history against a powerful University of Michigan team. Playing before more than 67,000 spectators at the dedication of Illinois Memorial Stadium, Grange led the Illini to a 39–14 rout over the Wolverines. During the first quarter alone he ran for touchdowns of 95, 67, 56, and 45 yards, and he amassed 303 total yards. He added a 12-yard touchdown run in the third quarter and passed for a sixth touchdown in the final period. All told, Grange accounted for 480 yards by running and passing in just 41 minutes of play. Three weeks later Grange played another spectacular game against the University of Chicago in which he scored three touchdowns and accounted for 450 total yards to preserve a 21–21 tie against the eventual Big Ten champion Maroons. Although Illinois's record of 6–1–1 was good for only second place in the conference, Grange became a national celebrity. Chicago sportswriter Warren Brown nicknamed him the "Galloping Ghost," and nationally syndicated columnist Grantland Rice immortalized him in verse.

Illinois had a weaker team in 1925 and struggled in the early going with a 1–3 record, with Grange accounting for only three touchdowns. In the East, considered by many to be the cradle of football, some experts continued to question Grange's ability to measure up to their standards. Grange put that controversy to rest with another spectacular performance in a 24–2 rout of a highly rated Pennsylvania team on a rain-soaked field in Philadelphia. He scored three touchdowns and accounted for 376 total yards. After Illinois's last game against Ohio State, Grange shocked the nation by announcing that he was quitting college and turning professional. Grange had signed a contract with Wheaton theater owner and promoter Charles C. Pyle, who in turn contracted with George Halas of the Chicago Bears for Grange to play a series of games with the National Football League (NFL) team. Under the terms of the deal Grange and Pyle would split the gate receipts with the Bears and Grange would receive 60 percent of that sum. Because the NFL was in its infancy at the time and most college officials and some of the public frowned on the professional game, Grange received much criticism for his decision.

Grange made his professional debut on Thanksgiving Day 1925 before 36,000 fans at Cubs Park (later Wrigley Field) in Chicago. After playing another game in Chicago, the Bears began an eastern road trip in which they played eight games in 11 days. At the Polo Grounds, Grange and the Bears drew a then record 72,000 fans to a game against the New York Giants. After Grange was injured in Pittsburgh and could no longer play, the tour ended in Chicago two games later on 13 December. After a two-week rest Grange and the Bears embarked on a second tour of nine games that began in Coral Gables, Florida, and ended in Seattle. During this tour Grange drew 75,000 fans at the Los Angeles Coliseum in a game against the Los Angeles Tigers, a team made up of West Coast former college players. It is estimated that Grange made more than $100,000 on the tours. Grange's celebrity status and the two tours also gave the fledgling enterprise of professional football a much-needed boost; some believe that this was a turning point in the rise of the NFL.

After failing to gain an NFL franchise in New York (rivaling the Giants), Pyle, with financial support from Grange, established his own league, the American Football League (AFL), in 1926 with Grange playing for the the AFL's New York Yankees franchise. Grange and the Yankees drew large crowds, but both the AFL and the NFL struggled financially that year because of head-to-head competition in many cities. The following year Pyle made peace with the NFL. He agreed to disband the AFL, and the NFL allowed him to establish the Yankees as a second NFL team in New York. During the 1927 season, however, Grange sustained a serious knee injury that he aggravated by attempting to complete the season. As a result he was forced to sit out the 1928 season. Having dissolved his partnership with Pyle, Grange returned to the Chicago Bears in 1929 and continued to play until 1934. After his knee injury Grange was never again the breakaway runner he once was, but he was a steady straight ahead halfback and a superb defensive player. He was selected to the All-Pro team in 1930 and 1931. His professional totals include 56 touchdowns and four conversions for 340 points. Following his retirement as a player he became an assistant coach for the Bears and served in this capacity until 1937.

During the 1920s Grange made three motion pictures: *One Minute to Play* (1926), *Racing Romeo*

(1927), and a 12-episode serial, *The Galloping Ghost* (1929). In 1928 he briefly appeared in the top-billed vaudeville show *C'mon Red*. After he left coaching, Grange worked for a soft drink company before becoming an insurance broker in 1942. In October 1941 he married Margaret Hazelberg; they had no children. Grange became a part-time radio broadcaster in 1942 and by 1948 was working on radio and television broadcasts of the Chicago Bears and nationally broadcast college games. The first prominent athlete to become a sportscaster, Grange broadcast more than 480 games until his retirement in 1969. Grange was named to the College Football Hall of Fame in 1951 and the Professional Football Hall of Fame in 1963. In 1981 he received the prestigious Walter Camp Distinguished American Award. Grange died in Lake Wales, Florida.

• Materials relating to Grange's career are in the Professional Football Hall of Fame, Canton, Ohio. The University of Illinois Archives and the Wheaton College Archives also have collections on Grange. His autobiography, as told to Ira Morton, is *The Red Grange Story: An Autobiography* (1993). See also Robert S. Gallagher, "The Galloping Ghost: An Interview with Red Grange," *American Heritage* 26 (Dec. 1974): 21–24, 93–99; John Underwood, "Was He the Greatest of All Time?" *Sports Illustrated*, 4 Sept. 1985, pp. 114–35; and Richard Whittingham, *What a Game They Played: An Inside Look at the Golden Era of Pro Football* (1984). An obituary is in the *New York Times*, 29 Jan. 1991.

JOHN M. CARROLL

GRANGER, Francis (1 Dec. 1792–28 Aug. 1868), legislator and political leader, was born in Suffield, Connecticut, the son of Gideon Granger, the postmaster general under Thomas Jefferson and James Madison (1751–1836), and Mindwell Pease. His father's career as a lawyer, state legislator, and Democratic-Republican leader in Federalist Connecticut exposed Francis to politics and public service at an early age. He attended Yale College (graduating in 1811) and studied law before entering politics. By 1816 he had joined his father in Canandaigua, New York, where the elder Granger was practicing law associated with land sales. Francis married Cornelia Rutson Van Rensselaer in 1817; they had three children.

Granger's 1825 election to the state assembly as a supporter of Governor DeWitt Clinton and a National Republican inadvertently positioned him to play a major role in America's initial third-party movement. In September 1826 the bucolic peace of western New York was shattered by the kidnapping of William Morgan from Canandaigua, allegedly by Freemasons whose secrets Morgan planned to publish. When local investigations appeared thwarted by Masonic lawmakers and no trace was found of Morgan, public outrage escalated. Granger chaired a select committee of the assembly to which Anti-Masonic memorials were submitted, and while the committee's recommendations for an expanded investigation were defeated by the assembly in April 1827, Granger gained a reputation for fairness among Anti-Masons. Political organizer

Thurlow Weed saw the popular Granger, who was respected by National Republicans who were Masons as well as by Anti-Masons, as an ideal candidate for lieutenant governor on a fusion ticket against the Albany Regency in the 1828 gubernatorial contest. Granger thus received the National Republican nomination for lieutenant governor. Anti-Masons, however, refused to support the ticket and nominated their own with Granger at its head. Granger refused the nomination, apparently agreeing with Weed that fusion held the best chance for victory. Neither he nor Weed could dissuade the third-party effort that inevitably divided the anti-Regency vote and gave Martin Van Buren the governorship with a plurality and Democrats another decade at the helm of New York.

In 1830 a National Republican–Anti-Masonic alliance nominated Granger for governor, and he polled large majorities in western New York, losing the state by only some 8,500 votes. At that time William H. Seward, who was then an Anti-Masonic state senator, described his fellow legislator as "never great, but always successful." Persistent support of the Chenango Canal Bill brought Granger and the Anti-Masons votes from central New York, while social reform measures, such as the Mechanics' Lien Bill introduced by Granger in 1828, helped add some workingmen's ballots. Nonetheless, Granger's second run for the governorship in 1832 failed, a victim of continuing prosperity under the Regency and also, ironically, of Anti-Masonry's success in virtually shutting down Masonry across much of New York State. Weed, Seward, and Granger now turned to the organization of the new Whig party, which entered the lists against the New York Regency in 1834. This time Granger declined to run for governor.

From 1835 to 1837 Granger served in the House of Representatives and in 1836 launched another unsuccessful campaign, this time as the Whig/Anti-Masonic candidate for vice president. Granger's saddest political defeat, however, was to come at the hands of his own party in the New York State Whig convention of 1838. With the state now heavily indebted from a burst of canal building and the recent economic downturn, Whig victory appeared imminent, and Granger badly wanted the gubernatorial candidacy. Weed, however, engineered Seward's nomination on the fourth ballot. Granger responded like a true party man, calling for "every Whig . . . to take the place assigned to him without a murmur." Nonetheless, Granger's disappointment may have shaped his later party revolt.

Reelected to Congress, Granger served again from 1839 to 1841, when he resigned to assume the office of postmaster general in the cabinet of William Henry Harrison, allegedly at Weed's behest. The new president's death and the subsequent reorganization of the administration by John Tyler (1790–1862) sent Granger home to Canandaigua, but constituents quickly returned him to Congress to fill a vacancy (Nov. 1841 to Mar. 1843).

Declining to run again, Granger delighted in private life for the next several years until called to chair the 1850 New York State Whig convention. Although he had once supported John Quincy Adams (1767–1848) in his defense of the right of petition against the efforts of southern slaveholders, Granger was now known as a Fillmore conservative within the party, a proponent of the Compromise of 1850, and an opponent of Seward's antislavery stance. In the minority at the convention, Granger achieved perhaps his most lasting political fame by bolting with other conservative Whigs, subsequently known as the Silver Grays from Granger's flowing white hair, who were a distinct faction of the New York State Whig party until 1852. Generally considered synonymous with the Cotton Whigs of New York, they stood opposed to the Sewardites, or "Woolly Heads." Granger's last public role came as a delegate to the peace convention held in Washington in February 1861. He lived in Canandaigua, where he died.

Granger played a central role in the emergence of Anti-Masonry as a political force in its own right and in the broadening of the party's goals and appeal. A voice of reason and of pragmatic politics, he seemed an ideal public persona for backstage party-builder Weed, who remembered him succinctly as "a gentleman of accomplished manners, genial temperament, and fine presence, with fortune, leisure, and a taste for public life." While Granger helped smooth the transition to Whiggery in New York, ironically he also helped unravel that party and the second party system with the Silver Gray bolt at the beginning of the critical 1850s.

• The papers of Francis and Gideon Granger are in the Library of Congress, Manuscript Division. The New-York Historical Society has a small collection of Granger papers (Miscellaneous Manuscripts) and a number of Granger letters in several other collections. Granger letters can also be found in the George W. Paterson Papers, the William H. Seward Papers, and the Thurlow Weed Papers at the University of Rochester Library as well as in other collections of contemporaries. There is no biography of Granger, but insights are in Glyndon G. Van Deusen's biographies *Thurlow Weed: Wizard of the Lobby* (1947) and *William Henry Seward* (1967) and in John Niven, *Martin Van Buren* (1983). For incisive contemporary assessments see *Life of Thurlow Weed, Including His Autobiography and a Memoir*, ed. Harriet A. Weed (2 vols., 1884); *Autobiography of William H. Seward*, ed. Frederick W. Seward (3 vols., 1891); and Jabez D. Hammond, *The History of Political Parties in the State of New York* (2 vols., 1846). See also George S. Conover, ed., *History of Ontario County, New York*, comp. Lewis Cass Aldrich (1893); and DeAlva Stanwood Alexander, *A Political History of the State of New York* (3 vols., 1906–1909). Elizabeth Bruchholz Haigh, "New York Antimasons, 1826–1833" (Ph.D. diss., Univ. of Rochester, 1980), is useful on Granger's assembly career.

KATHLEEN SMITH KUTOLOWSKI

GRANGER, Gideon (19 July 1767–31 Dec. 1822), lawyer and politician, was born in Suffield, Connecticut, the son of Gideon Granger, a lawyer and politician, and Tryphosa Kent. Young Gideon's pastor prepared him for Yale, from which he graduated in 1787. About this time he met Oliver Phelps, a connection that was to influence his later life greatly. Admitted to the bar in 1789, Granger began practice in Suffield. The following year he married Mindwell Pease; they had three children. The most famous, Francis Granger, became an important politician in his own right.

Gideon Granger began his political career in 1792, serving in Connecticut's lower house seven times over the next nine years. Granger is usually credited with the authorship of Connecticut's important Common School Law of 1795. He was also a representative when Connecticut ceded its western land claims, forming a syndicate with Phelps to purchase large tracts. He also purchased Yazoo lands, contested Georgia property sold to unwitting Yankees, and in 1796 acquired a large portion of real estate in Ohio on the site of present-day Cleveland. The following year Granger delivered and published *An Oration Spoken on . . . the Fourth of July, 1797, at the East Meeting House in Suffield*, calling for westward expansion. Though he began his career as a Federalist, in 1798 Granger was an unsuccessful Republican candidate for Congress.

An ardent supporter of Thomas Jefferson in 1800, Granger accepted the new president's request to serve as postmaster general, because Connecticut continued to show its unwillingness to elect Granger or other Republicans to Congress. Though he advised Jefferson on patronage decisions in Connecticut, the postmaster general usually turned over patronage decisions for his own department to state political leaders like DeWitt Clinton of New York. Granger's political opponents ridiculed him for sending blank postmaster commissions to these Republican leaders, who almost always replaced popular Federalist or efficient politically neutral postmasters. Granger used his Connecticut connections to keep Jefferson informed of secessionist plots and other facets of New England politics. He used his postal connections to keep a close watch on Aaron Burr's devious machinations in the West. Actions like these earned Granger the derisive label "Jefferson's man" (*New York Evening Post*, 17 Apr. 1802). Other political enemies, like John Randolph, accused Granger of creating post roads more with an eye to increasing the value of his western lands than to the actual needs of the people. Enough evidence existed for Congress to begin an investigation of Granger, but nothing came of the inquiry. Through all of these political squabbles, Granger suffered from gout, gall stones, and other bodily infirmities.

Despite the accusations of Granger's detractors, historians usually describe him as an able administrator who successfully oversaw the tremendous expansion of the postal service that the new nation's rapid growth necessitated. During his tenure, Granger was a vociferous supporter of Jefferson's policies. In 1803 he penned *A Vindication of the Measures of the Present Administration*, a general defense of Jefferson's administration, especially its economic and fiscal reforms.

Granger defended the impost as the fairest type of taxation, because it was based on consumption. Under such a system, he pointed out, "the farmer pays least of all, because he lives most within himself." He also called for the economic integration of the West with the East. His 1808 *An Address to the People of New England* defended the embargo and railed against secessionist movements. The postmaster general sought a nomination to the U.S. Supreme Court in 1810, but President James Madison rejected him, claiming he was tainted by his Yazoo connections and remained too sickly. During the War of 1812 Granger was also involved with capitalist Joel Barlow in a "French business" venture that required "great delicacy, liberality, secrecy, talent." Granger remained postmaster general until the spring of 1814, when Madison forced his resignation, ostensibly because of a disagreement over the appointment of a Philadelphia postmaster but most likely because of revelations that Granger backed Clinton for president in 1812.

After his resignation Granger, worth almost $200,000 in real estate but chronically short of cash, moved to Whitestown, near Utica, New York, and resumed his law career. Granger, who had been involved in the litigation surrounding the Phelps and (Nathaniel) Gorham Purchase (a tract of land that included much of western New York) a full two years before Phelps's death in 1809, built a mansion in Canandaigua in 1815–1816 and soon moved his family to that burgeoning town.

In 1817 Granger was admitted to practice in New York's court of chancery. Long an admirer of Clinton, Granger backed his canal scheme in 1817 with a *Speech . . . Delivered before a Convention of the People of Ontario County*, arguing that from ancient times canals had aided the economic development of nations and locales. Contending that the proposed canal would help bind the Union together more firmly, he donated 1,000 acres in Steuben County to the state in 1819 in support of the cause. He became an ardent Clintonian essayist, defending Clinton's governorship in *Address of Epaminondas to the Citizens of the State of New York* (1819). Granger served as vice president of the Ontario County Agricultural Society for a time, and in 1820 he presided over the society's Cattle Show and Fair, where he presented a speech calling for the states to encourage manufactures if the general government failed to do so.

Granger served in the New York Senate in 1820–1821. In 1820 he backed Clinton for governor over Daniel D. Tompkins, using his seat in the senate to pester Tompkins about his botched War of 1812 accounts. Opponents charged Granger backed Clinton because Clinton promised all three of his sons patronage positions. Granger's proposal to have the state buy out the remaining holdings of the Holland Land Company, a Dutch land syndicate that had purchased much of western New York, and resell them on the open market caused an uproar in the state. He unsuccessfully tried to prevent the calling of a state constitutional convention, because the movement threatened

Clinton's governorship. Granger resigned his seat after the 1821 session, complaining of ill health, but he allowed the Federalists to put him up as a candidate to the constitutional convention. He lost, and the convention, controlled by Martin Van Buren, ousted Clinton from the governorship. Soon after his retirement, Granger presided over the retirement dinner of longtime state comptroller Archibald McIntyre, making several toasts in support of the canal and economic integration. In his last years Granger owned some two dozen lots in the burgeoning town of Rochester and was not above prosecuting trespassers or foreclosing on delinquent mortgages.

Granger died in his mansion in Canandaigua. Like William Few and Robert Wright, he represented the important commercial wing of the Republican party. Though a staunch partisan, he was also a vociferous patriot who sought to strengthen the nation and his personal wealth through a policy of economic growth not inimical to democratic republicanism.

• The most important primary sources are the Gideon Granger Papers at the Ontario Historical Society in Canandaigua, N.Y., and the papers of Gideon Granger and Francis Granger, 1800–1864, in the Library of Congress. Granger's Canandaigua mansion is now a museum owned by the Granger Homestead Society, which has photocopies of much of his correspondence in the Library of Congress and elsewhere. Though the most important secondary source, Arthur Hamlin, *Gideon Granger* (1982), was intended as a popular work and could use some scholarly elaboration, Hamlin was vice president of the Granger Homestead Society for a time. His book contains a good bibliography of primary and secondary sources as well as a short genealogy, but he missed Granger's letters in the Nathaniel Rochester Papers at the University of Rochester. The congressional investigation of Granger is in U.S. Congress, House, *Report of the Committee Appointed to Inquire into the Conduct of Gideon Granger, Postmaster General*, 9th Cong., 17 Apr. 1806, Shoemaker 2d ser., 11699. For his resignation and McIntyre's dinner, see the Ithaca *American Journal*, 7 Mar. 1821. For his legal actions in Rochester, see the Rochester *Telegraph*, 17 Nov. 1818 and 18 Mar. 1823. For his speech encouraging domestic manufactures before the Ontario County Agricultural Society, see the New York *Patron of Industry*, 30 Dec. 1820. The Albany *Argus*, 14 Apr. 1820 and 18 Apr. 1820, contains two detailed attacks on Granger's politics by "Brutus" and "Aristides."

ROBERT E. WRIGHT

GRANGER, Gordon (6 Nov. 1822–10 Jan. 1876), soldier, was born in Joy, Wayne County, New York, the son of Gaius Granger and Catherine Taylor. He received an English school education locally, then entered West Point in 1841. He graduated in 1845, thirty-fifth in his class of forty-one. Commissioned a brevet second lieutenant, he was first assigned to the Second Infantry Regiment at Detroit, Michigan, but was reassigned the next year to the Regiment of Mounted Riflemen at Jefferson Barracks, Missouri. This unit joined Winfield Scott's army in Mexico, and Granger participated with distinction in the siege of Veracruz and the battles of Cerro Gordo (18 Apr. 1847), Contreras (19–20 Aug. 1847), Churubusco (20 Aug. 1847), and Chapultepec (13 Sept. 1847) in the campaign to take Mexico City. During the Mexican-American War he was commissioned second lieutenant in May 1847 and was cited twice for gallantry. After the war he was assigned to duty in Oregon, visited Europe for a year while on leave, then joined the Mounted Rifles in Texas in 1852 for service against the American Indians. He was promoted to first lieutenant that year.

At home on sick leave at the outbreak of the Civil War, Granger was assigned temporarily to the staff of General George B. McClellan in Ohio, then returned to the Mounted Rifles and in May 1861 was promoted to captain. Assigned as adjutant general on the staff of General Samuel D. Sturgis in General Nathaniel Lyon's pursuit of Confederate forces into southwestern Missouri, Granger was in engagements at Dug Springs, 2 August 1861, and Wilson's Creek, 10 August 1861. He was cited for gallantry at the latter and was brevetted major in the U.S. Army. He then was appointed commander of the St. Louis Arsenal.

On 2 September 1861 Granger accepted an appointment as colonel of the Second Michigan Cavalry, assigned to the Army of the Mississippi, in order to get into the field. On 4 March 1862 he assumed command of the cavalry division of that army and was commissioned brigadier general of volunteers on 26 March 1862. Granger led the division in action at Island No. 10 and in the initial campaign against Corinth. He was promoted to major general on 17 September 1862 and assigned to command the District of Central Kentucky, Department of the Ohio, where he helped resist General Braxton Bragg's Kentucky invasion that autumn. In January 1863 he took over the Army of Kentucky, Department of Cumberland, which he commanded until the following June, when he was named commander of the Reserve Corps of the Army of the Cumberland.

Granger's command of the Reserve Corps was achieved despite opposition from some other commanders within the Army of the Cumberland. In Kentucky he had earned a reputation for being highly opinionated and for criticism of his superiors that verged on insubordination. General William Rosecrans, however, considered him a good fighter and named him commander anyway. This assignment provided the opportunity for Granger's most noteworthy accomplishment in the army, at the battle of Chickamauga on 20 September 1863, when he marched his corps to the relief of General George Thomas without orders and helped prevent the complete route of Union forces that day. For his performance, Granger was promoted brevet lieutenant colonel in the regular army, and when Thomas assumed command of the Army of the Cumberland, he rewarded Granger with command of the Fourth Army Corps.

Despite Granger's success at Chickamauga, his reputation continued to be a problem for him among his superiors. While his corps fought well at Chattanooga, Missionary Ridge, and in the relief of Knoxville, the decisive Granger seen at Chickamauga had disappeared. When Granger was sent to relieve Knoxville,

Ulysses S. Grant ordered William T. Sherman to join him and assume actual leadership, because Grant did not believe Granger had the energy or the capacity for such a large mission.

Thereafter, Granger was shuttled about and not reassigned to a full corps again until near the war's end. He spent much of this time in the Department of the Gulf under General E. R. S. Canby, campaigning against Mobile. In August 1864 he commanded a division that cooperated with naval forces under Admiral David Farragut in taking Forts Gaines and Morgan at the entry to the harbor. In December 1864 he was temporarily sent to Tennessee to help Thomas stop General John B. Hood's invasion. He then returned to the Mobile area, and on 18 February 1865 he was named to command Canby's Thirteenth Corps. He distinguished himself in the field when he personally led two divisions in fighting at Spanish Fort and Fort Blakely. For his personal heroism he was brevetted brigadier and major general in the regular army on the same day.

At the end of the war Granger and his Thirteenth Corps helped occupy Texas. He arrived at Galveston on 19 June 1865, assumed command of the District of Texas, and issued orders announcing the freedom of all slaves. While Granger efficiently dispersed his men throughout the state, his politics became an embarrassment to Republican officials. At Mobile he had written to President Andrew Johnson suggesting that Alabama be allowed to return immediately to the Union. Becoming friendly with former Confederates in Texas, he allowed local communities to organize citizen police forces despite General Philip Sheridan's orders to the contrary, assisted former slaveholders in enforcing labor contracts, and provided little assistance to the state's provisional government. Sheridan requested his removal, and Grant ordered Granger to report to the War Department for reassignment on 19 July 1865.

In 1866 Granger was mustered out of the volunteer service and that July was assigned to the Twenty-fifth Infantry as colonel. He subsequently had an uneventful career, assigned to command various districts in the Reconstruction South, trying to get President Johnson to send him to Europe to examine European militias, and recovering from ill health that had plagued him since before the war. In 1869 he married Maria Letcher. In 1871 he was sent to the District of New Mexico. After five years of service there, he suffered an apparent stroke, from which he died in Santa Fe, New Mexico.

• A short description of Granger's military career is in George W. Cullum, *Biographical Register of the Officers and Graduates of the U.S. Military Academy at West Point, N.Y.: From Its Establishment, in 1802, to 1890, with the Early History of the United States Military Academy*, 3d ed., vol. 2 (1891). His wartime activities are in Robert U. Johnson and Clarence C. Buel, eds., *Battles and Leaders of the Civil War*, vols. 1, 3, 4 (1887–1888). A full obituary is in the *New York Times*, 12 Jan. 1876.

CARL H. MONEYHON

GRANGER, Walter (7 Nov. 1872–2 Sept. 1941), vertebrate paleontologist, was born in Middletown Springs, Vermont, the son of Charles H. Granger, an insurance agent, and Ada Byron Haynes. He attended high school in Rutland, Vermont, for two years, after which he became employed at New York's American Museum of Natural History in 1890 through the influence of an acquaintance of his father. He acquired the remainder of his working knowledge while at the museum. In 1932, after he had become a recognized scientist, Middlebury College granted him an honorary D.Sc. Granger spent four years on the staff of the museum superintendent but worked mostly in the taxidermy shop, skinning and preserving animals that had died in the Central Park Zoo in New York City.

In 1894 Granger traveled to the Badlands region of South Dakota, where he collected mammals as part of an expedition led by Jacob L. Wortman, chief of the Department of Mammalian Palaeontology. His work in the fossil collectors' camps on the expedition led, in 1895, to his being transferred to the newly expanded Department of Vertebrate Paleontology. There he spent the remainder of his life as a collector, preparator, research investigator, editor, and administrator. Successively he held the position of assistant from 1896 to 1909, associate curator from 1911 to 1926, and curator of fossil mammals from 1927. From 1921 he was also curator of paleontology in the Department of Asiatic Exploration and Research. In April 1904 he married Anna Dean; they had no children.

From 1896 through 1918 Granger collected American Paleocene and Eocene faunas for the museum. From 1903 through 1906 he worked mostly in the Bridger Basin of Wyoming. In 1907 he collected vertebrate fossils in the Fayum beds of Egypt with Henry Fairfield Osborn. In 1909 he returned to Wyoming, working in the Wind River Basin and at Beaver Divide. From 1910 to 1918 he collected in the Lower Eocene of the Bighorn Basin of Wyoming. In 1912–1914 and 1916, he collected in the San Juan Basin of northwestern Colorado and southwestern Colorado and, in 1918, he worked in the Huerfano Basin of south central Colorado. Granger's collections and stratigraphic information were the basis of the Museum scientists' publications defining and describing the Early Tertiary paleontology of North America. The ultimate, tripartite subdivision of the Paleocene and Eocene of North America is based on this project. Granger also actively collaborated, mostly in association with William Diller Matthew, in preparing monographs that documented the Paleocene-Eocene projects.

Granger's international reputation was enhanced by his expeditions to eastern Szechwan, China, in 1921–1922 and during the winter seasons of 1922–1923 and 1925–1926 to collect Pleistocene vertebrate fossils. In April 1922 he traveled to Mongolia as a member of the museum's central Asian expedition. Almost immediately Granger found Mongolian fossil mammals in profusion. Although progressively hampered by the effects of the Chinese revolution and its aftermath, the expeditions returned a large number of fossil specimens. Among the items collected were the world's largest mammal, *Baluchitherium*, abundant skulls of early mammals, and a clutch of dinosaur eggs that attracted interest worldwide. More important, these expeditions filled in the largest remaining gap in international knowledge of vertebrate paleontology, which in turn led to an extensive revision of ideas about the origin and dispersal of vertebrate life.

After Matthew left the museum in 1927, and after Osborn died in 1935, Granger assumed greater curatorial, administrative, and editorial responsibilities. Eventually he took over the editorship of the entire series of publications of the central Asiatic expeditions, while at the same time retaining his two curatorial positions. Although he led no expeditions after 1931, he spent his summers in the field in the western United States collecting fossils.

During his career Granger was considered one of the most important collectors of fossil vertebrates. While he did not take the lead in writing reports of his investigations, he was listed as the second author of many reports by Matthew and by William K. Gregory. Matthew, according to George Gaylord Simpson (1942, p. 165), was

"worried . . . that readers unacquainted with the circumstances might think that Granger's name on the long, very important series of papers by Matthew and Granger had merely been a courtesy. In fact, as Matthew repeatedly emphasized . . . Granger contributed to this series of studies not only the indispensable materials and the field data . . . but also many of the ideas and observations and much of the knowledge and experience."

Granger was author or coauthor of more than 100 publications.

Granger was a fellow of the Geological Society of America, the Paleontological Society, and the Society of Vertebrate Paleontologists. He was president of the Explorers Club between 1935 and 1937 and was given an honorary membership, their highest honor at the time. He died in Lusk, Wyoming.

• A collection of Granger's correspondence is at the American Museum of Natural History. Granger wrote "Camp Life in the Gobi Desert, *Natural History* 31, no. 4 (1931): 359–73, a short account of life on the central Asian expedition. George Gaylord Simpson, "Memorial to Walter Granger," *Proceedings Volume of the Geological Society of America, Annual Report for 1941* (1941): 159–72, pl. 4, is an informed biographical appreciation of Granger's career. An obituary is in *Nature*, 29 Nov. 1941.

RALPH L. LANGENHEIM, JR.

GRANT, Cary (18 Jan. 1904–29 Nov. 1986), actor, was born Archibald Alexander Leach in Bristol, England, the son of Elias Leach, a presser, and Elsie Maria Kingdon (some claim that Kingdon was not his real mother). Grant's essentially local education soon took second place to his attendance at local theaters. By early 1918 he had already spent some time with Bob Pender's provincial variety troupe, where he learned to tumble, perform acrobatic dances, and share in performing music-hall songs. He rejoined Pender's troupe in 1919 after being expelled from school.

Grant was with Pender in 1920 when the troupe was booked into Charles Dillingham's immense Globe Theater in New York, where it shared billing with circus performers. After playing the Keith vaudeville circuit, Pender's troupe returned to Great Britain in 1921, but Grant remained in New York, living at the National Vaudeville Artists Club on West Forty-sixth Street and serving as a sometime sidewalk salesman and stilt-walker.

Still known as Archie Leach, in 1923 and 1924 Grant toured the western Pantages circuit with other former members of Pender's troupe, playing straight man in such sketches as "The Woman Pays." Minor theatrical roles preceded his musical debut in 1927 as Anzac in *Golden Dawn*, a highly serious Arthur Hammerstein production set in shadowy African jungles. It ran longer (184 performances) than any other Archie Leach stage production.

In 1928 Grant, who became his era's most popular romantic motion picture leading man, was replaced on the road as the lead in *Polly* and passed over for the lead in *Rosalie*. He appeared in the elephantine Jeanette MacDonald musical comedy *Boom Boom* (1929) and failed a screen test for Fox Pictures. The Shubert organization signed him for the operetta *A Wonderful Night* (1929) and for *The Street Singer* (1930), sending him to St. Louis in 1931 to appear in other musicals.

In his last performance as Archie Leach, Grant played Cary Lockwood in *Nikki* (1931), a semimusical based on screenwriter John Monk Saunders's Hemingwayesque tale of young World War I flyers unhappily clustered around Nikki (Fay Wray, Saunders's film-star wife). Although the show closed after thirty-nine performances, Grant went to Hollywood, tested for the screen again, was signed by Paramount-Publix Pictures to a five-year contract, and became Cary Grant—Cary for his *Nikki* character and Grant for its resemblance to the curt names of other current male stars.

Grant's film debut came as a raffish sailor in the 1931 short *Singapore Sue*. Patterning himself on performers he called "natural and well-dressed," such as Noël Coward, Jack Buchanan, and Douglas Fairbanks, Grant made twenty-one features for Paramount, usually as a glossy-haired sophisticate. However, in his first full-length film, *This Is the Night* (1932), he was an Olympic athlete, and in his eighth, *She Done Him Wrong* (1933), he proved an apt foil for Mae West's sexual humor.

In 1934 Grant, in England making *The Amazing Quest of Ernest Bliss* (1937), married actress Virginia Cherrill; they had no children and were divorced in 1935. On loan to Metro-Goldwyn-Mayer (MGM), Grant sang a duet with Jean Harlow in *Suzy* (1936), and for RKO, Grant was directed by George Cukor and costarred with Katharine Hepburn in the melodrama *Sylvia Scarlett* (1935). In the MGM comic fan-

tasy *Topper* (1937) his screen persona—jaunty, playful, romantic—blossomed. Likening the vagaries of stardom to an endless, crowded bus ride, Grant later commented, "Warner Baxter [the preceding decade's debonair romantic star] fell out the back and I got to sit down."

In the romantic comedies *The Awful Truth* (1937), *Holiday* (1938), and the Howard Hawks–directed screwball classic *Bringing up Baby* (1938), Grant's athleticism, timing, attention to detail, breezy, mid-Atlantic voice, and a sex appeal that spoke of savoir faire helped propel him to the top of box-office acclaim and earning power. His bouncy speeches ("Hello, Judy," "Come on, Judy") in the comedy-drama *Only Angels Have Wings* (1939) gave material to impersonators for the rest of his life. In the boisterous *Gunga Din* (1939), he was a Kiplingesque sergeant. F. Scott Fitzgerald wanted Grant as protagonist for a film of his short story "Babylon Revisited," but the film was never made. Raymond Chandler said he had visualized his private detective Philip Marlowe as Grant.

After the fast-talking newspaper comedy *His Girl Friday* (1940) and *The Philadelphia Story* (1940), a classic blend of the urbane and the screwball, Grant's image was fixed—"Cary Grant" was someone in control, someone who, if surprised, would land on his feet. A hint of vulnerability and imperfection—physically manifest in a tooth broken when he was thirteen—completed the attraction. The image made Grant greatly popular, but it was when he departed from it, in the sentimental *Penny Serenade* (1941) and the highly dramatic *None but the Lonely Heart* (1944), that he won Academy Award nominations. And under Alfred Hitchcock's direction in the suspenseful *Suspicion* (1941) Grant first drew upon his own inner insecurities to create an ambiguously menacing character.

Soon a very rich man, Grant donated large sums to the British World War II effort. He became an American citizen in June 1942, the year he married the wealthy Barbara Hutton. They had no children and were divorced in 1945. He received a low draft classification and made only one war film, *Destination Tokyo* (1944). It was later hypothesized that Grant, always secretive about his private life, spied for Great Britain on Nazi sympathizers in the film industry.

Although Grant remained popular after the war, his choice of films faltered ("I tried not to put myself into a movie that wouldn't be fun to make," he later said), although the romantic Hitchcock espionage yarn *Notorious* (1946) teamed him successfully with Ingrid Bergman. Grant redeemed the silly *The Bachelor and the Bobby-Soxer* (1947) with a routine recalled from his childhood ("You remind me of a man." "What man?" "A man with the power." What power?" "The power of hoodoo." "Hoodoo?" "You do." "You do what?" "You remind me of a man"). In 1949 Grant married actress Betsy Drake, who had appeared with him in *Every Girl Should Be Married* (1948). They had no children and were divorced in 1962.

In 1952 Grant announced his retirement from films to travel and study, experimenting with hypnotism. In 1954 he returned as a smooth cat-burglar in Hitchcock's *To Catch a Thief*. In 1956 Grant received the Producers Guild of America award for "historical contribution to the motion picture industry." Uncomfortable in the wide-screen adventure *The Pride and the Passion* (1957), he was more at home in romances such as *An Affair to Remember* (1957) and *Indiscreet* (1958). In 1958 and 1959 he experimented with LSD during psychotherapy. Perhaps the best of his later work was as another haunted hero in Hitchcock's *North by Northwest* (1959), its image of Grant fleeing a homicidal crop-dusting airplane one of the screen's most memorable. In the lightweight *Charade* (1963) and *Walk, Don't Run* (1966) he played amidst conscious echoes of his earlier roles. Ever protective of his reputation, he claimed to have appeared in only sixty-eight films, omitting four he found particularly awful. Athletic as ever, tanned, and with impeccable steely grey hair, he retired in 1966, saying it was no longer believable for him to be kissing young women on screen.

In 1965 Grant married actress Dyan Cannon; they had one child and divorced in 1968. In 1967 Grant made a commercial recording of a lullaby, dedicated to his daughter, whom he called "my best production." In 1970 he received a special Academy Award for contributions to the motion picture industry. He joined several corporate boards of directors. In 1981 Grant received the Kennedy Center Award for achievement in performing arts and also married Barbara Harris. In 1982 he began a nationwide series of thirty-six live "Conversations with Cary Grant," explaining the significance of each tiny detail in making a film. He told an interviewer, "If my films educated the public in any way, I would hope it was in the direction of politesse and grace. I would hope I added amusement to the public's life." He added, "I can make a detour around almost any question." Grant died in Davenport, Iowa, where he was giving a Conversation.

Maureen Donaldson, a companion of Grant's in the early 1970s, wrote of Grant's insecurity, "He felt his mother [confined in a British sanatorium between 1914 and 1934] deserted him. . . . He felt his wives had hated and abandoned him, though I suspect they all loved him but were forced to leave him in much the same way I was." Elizabeth Taylor, one of the few major women stars who never made a film with him, said, "He warmed you and made you feel super. He was what one would hope a movie star would be."

• Among many discussions and compilations on Grant, some that give particular insight are Lionel Godfrey, *Cary Grant: The Light Touch* (1981), Nancy Nelson, *Evenings with Cary Grant: Recollections in His Own Words and by Those Who Knew Him Best* (1991), and Graham McCann, *Cary Grant: A Class Apart* (1997). Among personal memoirs, Fay Wray, *On the Other Hand* (1989), and Maureen Donaldson and William Royce, *An Affair to Remember: My Life with Cary Grant* (1989), are persuasive. Grant's "Conversations" are covered largely in local newspapers such as the *Claremont (Calif.) Courier*, 16 Mar. and 17 Apr. 1985. A good obituary is in the *Los Angeles Times*, 30 Nov. 1986; for several days thereafter the newspaper continued to assess Grant's career.

JAMES ROSS MOORE

GRANT, Claudius Buchanan (25 Oct. 1835–28 Feb. 1921), lawyer, Michigan Supreme Court justice, and law and order advocate, was born in Lebanon, Maine, the son of Joseph Grant and Mary Ambrose Merrill. Claudius entered the University of Michigan at age twenty and received his B.A. (with highest honors) in 1859, his A.M. in 1862, and his law degree in 1866. He joined the Michigan bar the same year and earned an LL.D. in 1891. He married Caroline Lawrence Felch in Ann Arbor, Michigan, in 1863; they had five children.

Grant taught classics and served two years as principal in Ann Arbor schools before resigning in 1862 to raise a company for the Civil War. Entering the war as a captain of the Twentieth Michigan Volunteer Infantry, he eventually attained the rank of colonel and participated in numerous battles, including Fredricksburg, Vicksburg, Cold Harbor, the Wilderness, Spottsylvania Court House, and General Ulysses S. Grant's final campaign. In 1865 he returned to study law at the University of Michigan.

Following his admission to the bar, Grant formed a law partnership in Ann Arbor with his father-in-law, former governor, senator, and justice of the Supreme Court Alpheus Felch, and began his long legal and political career. He served as Ann Arbor postmaster and city recorder from 1866 to 1870 and in the Michigan legislature (1871–1874), where he was speaker pro tem (1873) and chaired the House Committee on Public Instruction and the Ways and Means Committee. His election and long arduous service as a regent of the University of Michigan (1872–1880) was highlighted by Grant's successful push for more independent control of university affairs by the Board of Regents. During this time President Grant appointed him state commissioner for the Centennial Commission (1872–1876).

Grant moved to Houghton, Michigan, in 1873 and formed a law partnership with former governor Joseph H. Chandler. He served as Houghton County prosecuting attorney (1876–1878) and, upon organization of the Twenty-fifth Judicial Circuit, became its first circuit judge in 1882. This began the judicial reform and law and order campaign that made him widely known throughout the state. In 1882 the new circuit suffered from consistent violations of liquor laws and from the presence of what one observer called the state's "vilest den of prostitution" (Reed, p. 385). To announce his reforms and his stand on law enforcement, Grant made public addresses in every city of the circuit, outlining the new policy and demanding that all local law enforcement officials adhere to the strictest enforcement of all laws. Circuit Judge Grant's reforming zeal was so successful that, upon his departure, the Twenty-fifth had the best reputation in the state for swift and strict law enforcement.

Grant was elected to the Michigan Supreme Court in 1889, where he served as chief justice in 1898, 1899, and 1908 before retiring in 1910. During his twenty-one years on the high court, Grant became known for his broad construction of the Michigan Constitution, his thorough investigations to ascertain proper statutory interpretations, and, of course, his law and order themes. His opinions appear in 81 volumes (79–159) of the Michigan Reports (Reed, p. 385).

Grant returned to private practice in 1910, serving as general counsel for the law firm of Warren, Cady, & Ladd in Detroit until his retirement in 1913. For the remaining years of his life Grant's chief activities were as head of the state's Law and Order League. As its spokesperson he traveled throughout the state and delivered nearly one hundred speeches and lectures on the subject. He died in St. Petersburg, Florida.

Grant's contributions in both law and education in Michigan spanned more than fifty years. He was a bold defender of local law enforcement powers and of judicial reform. A special resolution in the Michigan Reports (vol. 216) praised his long and distinguished service as a true pioneer in the state's development and history.

• The best available information on Grant exists in sketches of his legal and political life. Some information can be found in G. I. Reed, *Bench and Bar of Michigan* (1897), B. A. Hinsdale, *History of the University of Michigan* (1906), B. M. Cutcheon, *The Story of the Twentieth Michigan Infantry* (1904), *Michigan Biographies*, vol. 1 (1924), and the *Michigan Official Directory and Legislative Manual, 1909–1910.* An obituary is in the *New York Times*, 1 Mar. 1921.

JOHNIE D. SMITH

GRANT, Frederick Dent (30 May 1850–12 Apr. 1912), soldier and government official, was born in St. Louis, Missouri, the son of Ulysses S. Grant, a soldier and, later, U.S. president, and Julia Dent. Fred, as he was known, led a normal childhood until his father's rise during the Civil War afforded opportunities for extraordinary experiences. Ulysses S. Grant allowed Fred to accompany the armies during the Vicksburg campaign (Mar.-July 1863) and to escort him to Washington, D.C., when he went to be commissioned lieutenant general (Mar. 1864). Fred never served as a soldier, but he came under hostile fire while with his father, displaying coolness that General Grant acknowledged by an honorary staff appointment.

Although they were the stuff of grand reminiscence, Fred Grant's Civil War adventures precipitated severe illnesses and interrupted his schooling. By June 1864 Ulysses S. Grant had determined that his oldest son would attend West Point, and he enrolled him at an academy in Burlington, New Jersey. Placed under the tutelage of the West Point adjutant, Fred Grant passed the entrance examination and became a cadet on 1 July 1866. Not long before, his father had written, "I hope he will succeed though I have no expectation of him distinguishing himself in his studies."

Fred Grant barely fulfilled his father's low academic expectations and came perilously close to dismissal for excessive demerits. Also, in 1870 and 1871, after his father had become president, Fred became embroiled in a widely disparaged hazing incident and the alleged maltreatment of the first black cadet, James Webster Smith. Seemingly any irregularity at West Point involving Fred led to charges in newspapers or Congress that he used his relationship with his father to extort special consideration at the expense of regulations and less fortunate classmates. Fred survived an appearance before a congressional investigating committee in January 1871 and graduated on 12 June 1871, standing thirty-seventh in a class of forty-one.

Appointed second lieutenant, Fourth Cavalry, Fred Grant received leave to work as a civil engineer on the Union Pacific Railroad, a position his father secured through influential railroad manager Thomas A. Scott. He then accompanied General William T. Sherman on a European tour and was embarrassed when hosts assumed that the president's son was the principal member of the party. Following a scant three months at Fort Griffin, Texas, Fred Grant joined the staff of Lieutenant General Philip H. Sheridan early in 1873 as aide-de-camp with the rank of lieutenant colonel. This assignment stationed him in Chicago, where in 1874 he married Ida M. Honoré, the educated and elegant daughter of a wealthy businessman. The couple had two children.

The target of press barbs for his absences, Fred Grant did serve as a member of two exploring parties into contested Indian territory, the Yellowstone expedition (June–Aug. 1873) and the Black Hills expedition (June–Sept. 1874). After participating in the Bannock Indian war in 1878, Fred obtained leave to tour Asia with his parents. He departed with directions from General Sherman to observe the British army in India. Returning to duty in September 1879, Fred Grant resigned as of 1 October 1881 to pursue business opportunities.

Though he was not involved directly, the collapse of Grant & Ward, the financial firm of his brother, his father, and an unscrupulous partner, essentially bankrupted Fred Grant in May 1884. The discovery that his father suffered from throat cancer compounded the disaster. In January 1885 Fred Grant refused an offer from President Chester A. Arthur to rejoin the army as an assistant quartermaster and instead remained with his parents. He aided his father with his *Personal Memoirs* as a copyist and researcher and acted as the family's liaison to the many people wanting access to the dying hero. Fred Grant's conduct during this period earned plaudits.

After his father's death, Fred Grant plunged into New York politics, aligning himself with the Republican machine of Thomas C. Platt. He ran unsuccessfully for New York secretary of state in 1887, and on 20 March 1889, at Platt's urging, President Benjamin Harrison nominated Grant as minister to Austria-Hungary. He spent four congenial years in Vienna with his family and dealt satisfactorily with minor diplomatic matters involving trade, emigration, and citizenship. Unwilling to continue under a Democratic administration, he returned to New York City and accepted an appointment in 1895 as a police commissioner, joining Theodore Roosevelt (1858–1919) as one of two Republicans on the bipartisan commission. Believing that only paid "spies" were suited for the demeaning task of investigating brothels under cover, Grant condemned the practice of using regular police officers for this reprehensible duty. His resignation over this issue on 31 July 1897 caused an uproar and gave some credibility to Roosevelt's characterization of Grant as a "dolt" in private correspondence. Unquestionably scrupulous, Grant never fathomed the political and administrative possibilities of being police commissioner.

Though Grant had declined nomination as assistant secretary of war in April 1897, as hostilities neared between the United States and Spain he pressed President William McKinley for an army assignment. Taking the field as colonel of the Fourteenth New York Infantry, Grant received a commission as brigadier general of volunteers on 27 May 1898. He desired comparable appointment in the regular army and received a coveted commission as brigadier general in February 1901. His active service began as district commander in San Juan, Puerto Rico, responsible for improving sanitation in the cities and maintaining order in the country. Later he fought against insurgents on the Philippine island of Luzon.

Grant left the Philippines in 1902 to command the Department of Texas. In September 1904 he returned to New York City to command the Department of the East, a choice assignment. Promoted to major general as of 6 February 1906, he shouldered greater responsibility as commander of the Division of the East in 1910. Grant's peacetime duties followed standard executive routine, and he regularly attended veterans' reunions, civic gatherings, and social functions. He died from heart failure in New York City and was buried at West Point. Four years later, in 1916, his physician confirmed rumors that, like his father, Grant had suffered from throat cancer. A beneficiary of his father's name, Grant displayed sufficient competence as soldier, diplomat, and government official to command respect from most contemporaries.

• Documentary material related to Grant may be examined most conveniently in John Y. Simon, ed., *The Papers of Ulysses S. Grant* (1967–). Small numbers of revealing letters may be found in the papers of Russell A. Alger, William Clements Library, University of Michigan, Ann Arbor; and the papers of Sherman, Sheridan, Harrison, and McKinley, Library of Congress. Grant recalled aspects of his own life in occasional speeches and articles about his father. Most satisfying among a disappointing output are "My Father As I Knew Him," *New York World Sunday Magazine*, 25 Apr. 1897, and "With Grant at Vicksburg," *The Outlook*, 2 July 1898. His mother and brother supply impressions in Simon, ed., *The Personal Memoirs of Julia Dent Grant* (1975), and Jesse R. Grant, *In the Days of My Father General Grant* (1925). Frequently stinging views of Grant as a New York City police commissioner are in Henry Cabot Lodge, ed., *Selections from the Correspondence of Theodore Roosevelt and Henry Cabot Lodge, 1884–1918* (1925). George W. Cullum, *Biographical Register of the Officers and Graduates of the U.S. Military Academy*, 3d ed. (1891), and *Supplement*, vol. 5 (1910), summarize Grant's military career. Several works about his father, especially William S. McFeely, *Grant: A Biography* (1981), and Thomas M. Pitkin, *The Captain Departs: Ulysses S. Grant's Last Campaign* (1973), include valuable material on Fred Grant. For especially useful obituaries, see the *New York Times*, *New York Tribune*, and *Chicago Tribune*, 12 and 13 Apr. 1912.

WILLIAM M. FERRARO

GRANT, Heber Jeddy (22 Nov. 1856–14 May 1945), seventh president of the Church of Jesus Christ of Latter-day Saints (LDS), was born in Salt Lake City, Utah, the son of Jedediah Morgan Grant and Rachel Ridgeway Ivins. Grant's father, mayor of Salt Lake City and one of Brigham Young's two counselors, died when Heber was nine days old. A compensating bond developed between Heber and Rachel Grant, the seventh wife of the polygamous Jedediah. Rachel had high expectations for her only child, and she instilled these expectations in the boy, along with the Victorian attitudes that were so much a part of her personality. Grant's early life was difficult. While Rachel came from a family of prosperous New Jersey gentry, her religious conversion produced an unbridgeable gap between herself and her eastern relatives. As long as she maintained her Mormonism, the New Jersey Ridgeways and Ivins withheld their financial support, but she was equally determined. Taking in boarders and working as a seamstress, Rachel struggled to maintain herself and raise her boy.

Due to Rachel's sacrifice, young Grant received as good an education as pioneer Utah offered. He attended several "home schools" and later the private family school of President Brigham Young where teachers and the *Wilson* and *National* readers spoke of duty, success, and moral truth. He also attended the school of Mary and Ida Cobb, eastern-educated schoolmarms with an eye for up-to-date methods and curricula. Grant was good at math, memorization, and recitation and seemed to delight in attaining goals and overcoming obstacles. His school work (and his Utah family connections) were enough to secure an appointment to the U.S. Naval Academy at Annapolis, Maryland, which Grant refused. He feared that a prolonged absence from Utah would undermine his mother's emotional and financial well-being.

No doubt at his mother's insistence, Grant attended Salt Lake City's Thirteenth Ward congregation, one of Mormonism's most talented and prosperous flocks. Here he again found sturdy values and also several father figures, which partly compensated for the loss of his own father. Grant also became a member of the Wasatch Literary Association. The "Wasatchers," as the association's members were known, were a group of high-spirited young people who organized themselves for cultural exercises and social activity. Like the friendships gained at a British public school, the social ties of the Wasatch Literary Association continued through Grant's life and provided him with important, career-building connections.

Grant was a natural entrepreneur, and at the age of fifteen he left formal schooling for a series of office jobs including clerking for H. R. Mann and Company, Utah's leading insurance agency; at the age of nineteen Grant ambitiously bought out the business. During the next decades Grant branched from the selling of insurance to the partial ownership of a series of businesses: vinegar manufacturing, a wholesale wagon and agricultural implement company, the *Salt Lake Herald*, the Salt Lake Theater, a livery and cab business, the State Bank of Utah, and the Utah-Idaho Sugar Company.

Most of these businesses were inaugurated after Grant had become a church leader and were undertaken partly to counter the growing influence of non-Mormons and anti-Mormons in Salt Lake City. The merging of religion and business was a perfect match for Grant's interests and talents: he fully subscribed to the Gilded Age's (and Brigham Young's) idea of Christian stewardship. He hoped to serve society by creating jobs and wealth, and he believed himself on a Godly errand.

From early manhood Grant manifested a religious impulse. Like most LDS church leaders of the time, he entered into plural marriage by marrying Lucy Stringham, Huldah Augusta Winters, and Emily Wells (Stringham and Wells died before he became LDS president). At the unusually young age of twenty-three he accepted the nonpaid assignment to preside over the Tooele Stake in western Utah (roughly a diocese). Two years later, in 1882, he became a member of the Council of the Twelve Apostles, Mormonism's second-ranking leadership body. Occupying this position for thirty-six years, he spoke to local congregations; helped to direct the Church's youth organization, the Mutual Improvement Association; led the LDS effort to open Japan to LDS proselyting; and presided over the important European Mission, headquartered in Liverpool, England. During these years he also undertook several less formal assignments. In the aftermath of the panic of 1893, which brought hard times to Utah, Grant played a major role in preserving the Church's credit, and during the early twentieth-century Prohibition crusade, he became Mormonism's leading public activist in Utah's decade-long campaign to suppress the sale of alcohol.

Grant presided over Mormonism from 1918 to 1945. His presidency was characterized by a careful expenditure of funds during the economically difficult 1920s and 1930s. When the Great Depression deepened, he inaugurated a self-help welfare program that sought to preserve the self-sufficiency of Mormons. Grant also strongly advocated the LDS health code, "the Word of Wisdom," and made it a test of full membership. In addition, he worked tirelessly to reverse Mormonism's polygamy-tarnished image. Perhaps because he personified pioneer values so fully, many

leading American business and political leaders were drawn to him. Grant translated these friendships into favorable media coverage for his church.

During Grant's administration, church membership almost doubled, and Mormon congregations spread from the Intermountain West. Mormonism was becoming more than a regional American faith. According to one informal estimate, during his tenure as church president Grant traveled more than 400,000 miles and filled 1,500 appointments, including delivering 1,250 sermons and 28 addresses to state, national, civic, or professional groups. At his death he was eulogized not only for his business skill and dynamic church leadership but also for his personal kindness. Remembering the penury of his youth, he had throughout his long life consistently given his time and means to the unfortunate. Grant died in Salt Lake City.

• Heber J. Grant's papers are housed at the LDS Historical Department, Salt Lake City, Utah. This collection includes Grant's daily diary, which he kept from the time of his call to the Quorum of the Twelve Apostles, and copies of his extensive personal and official correspondence. For admiring surveys, see Bryant S. Hinckley, *Heber J. Grant: Highlights in the Life of a Great Leader* (1951); Francis M. Gibbons, *Heber J. Grant: Man of Steel, Prophet of God* (1979); and Ronald W. Walker, "Heber J. Grant," in *The Presidents of the Church*, ed. Leonard J. Arrington (1986). For accounts of various events of Grant's life, see Ronald W. Walker, "Crisis in Zion: Heber J. Grant and the Panic of 1893," *Arizona and the West* 21 (Autumn 1979): 257–78, repr. in *Sunstone* 5 (Jan.–Feb. 1980): 26–34; "Heber J. Grant and the Utah Loan and Trust Company," *Journal of Mormon History* 8 (1981): 21–36; "Young Heber J. Grant: Entrepreneur Extraordinary," *The Twentieth Century American West* (1983), pp. 85–119; and "Young Heber J. Grant's Years of Passage," *Brigham Young University Studies* 24 (Spring 1984): 131–49.

RONALD W. WALKER

GRANT, James Benton (2 Jan. 1848–1 Nov. 1911), metallurgist and governor of Colorado, was born in Russell County, Alabama, the son of Thomas McDonough Grant, a physician and owner of a plantation on the Chattahoochee River, and Mary Jane Benton. Both of his parents were natives of Halifax County, North Carolina. Grant's grandfather was a member of the Highland clan of Grants who, after having fought in the Battle of Culloden, were transported as rebellious subjects to North Carolina in 1746. Grant's father Thomas, after receiving an education in medicine in Philadelphia, Pennsylvania, and Charleston, South Carolina, migrated to Alabama to practice medicine and farm. Meanwhile, Grant's uncle, James Grant, who would play an important role in his life, migrated to frontier Chicago, Illinois, where he began practicing law in 1833.

After a rural education, Grant, at age seventeen, served in General Joseph E. Johnston's Confederate army from January through April 1865 and was involved in the last battle of the Civil War at Columbus, Georgia. Because his father lost his land during the war, however, Grant followed the lead of his brothers, sisters, and cousins and migrated in 1870 to Davenport, Iowa, to live with his wealthy and childless uncle James. James had moved from Chicago to Davenport, Iowa Territory, in 1838 and become a judge, a Democratic politician, a railroad director, and a prominent member of the local and state bar. As a railroad lawyer he had acquired a regional and even national reputation. With his uncle's financial backing, Grant attended Iowa State Agricultural College and Cornell University and from 1874 to 1876 studied at the mining school in Freiburg, Germany. Returning via a tour of the mining districts in Australia and New Zealand, Grant, with his uncle as a partner, set out for the mining frontier of Colorado in 1877.

Grant spent his first year assaying ore in Mill City and Central City, while scouting out other mining opportunities in Empire, Georgetown, and Fairplay before proceeding to Leadville in March 1878. A burgeoning local mining boom had started the year before when St. Louis capitalists had begun mining in the area. Grant, a trained assayer, recognized the wealth to be made in extracting silver, iron, and lead from the local carbonate ores. An essay he wrote in 1878 for a railroad reported on the incredible mineral wealth in the area and was instrumental in encouraging the Denver and Rio Grande to build a line to Leadville. With his uncle's financial support, Grant bought out mining and smelting concerns from St. Louis and Chicago that had established operations in the California gulch in Leadville, and he founded and operated the James B. Grant and Company smelting works, which were soon the largest silver mining and smelting operations in the region. Within three years Grant had joined the ranks of prominent men such as Horace Tabor, Jerome Chaffee, and Alva Adams, making a fortune and becoming very active in the boom town's booster ethos. In 1881 Grant married Mary Goodell; they had two children. (His wife was one of the five "Goodell Sisters of Leadville," daughters of the local postmaster, all of whom, in marrying prominent men in the regional elite, helped bring "gentility" to the urban West.)

When the Leadville plant burned down in 1882, Grant, who was already expanding his operations by buying other mines in Colorado, decided to relocate to a larger, more centralized establishment nearer to the railroad terminus at Denver, to which ore from around the region was shipped for smelting. Grant's decision the year before to move to Denver for political and social reasons also, no doubt, affected his business decision to relocate his company's operations there. He became known for his hard-nosed conservative methods and tough opposition to unions. He also became a prominent member of the Denver power elite that ruled the city for thirty years. As a member of the Denver Chamber of Commerce and, beginning in 1880, the Denver Club, Grant aggressively supported railroads, city improvements, and institutional development and helped organize the National Mining and Industrial Exposition in 1882. In addition to serving as the vice president of the Omaha and Grant Smelting

and Refining Company from 1882 until 1899, Grant was a member and director of the American Smelting and Refining Company from 1880 until his death in 1911. He also helped organize the Denver National Bank, serving as its first vice president from 1884 until 1911. Grant was also involved in the development of a water system in Denver.

Grant, perhaps more reluctantly than others, parlayed his economic and social power as a member of the "Capitol Hill" elite into political office. Taking advantage of factional and personal disputes among Republicans, Grant, a Democrat, was elected governor of Colorado in 1882 and served for two peaceful and prosperous years. As governor, Grant maintained independence from the Democratic party power structure by paying for his own campaign, refusing to participate in the patronage system, and, having broken the Republican monopoly of state government, declining to run again. Grant returned to business and philanthropy in 1885. For years Grant served on the Denver Board of Education and financially supported the fledgling University of Denver.

As a "captain of industry," Grant was representative of many native-born regional businessmen in the Midwest and West who after the Civil War rapidly expanded the scale of corporate capitalism and manufacturing and accelerated the pace of environmental resource extraction across the West. Like many of these capitalists, Grant acted within a power elite who ran the regional metropolis and sought, at the state, regional, or national level, to acquire influence in Gilded Age politics and society. He died in Excelsior Springs, Missouri.

• The James B. Grant Papers in the Colorado Historical Society are limited. Other Grant papers are at the Division of State Archives and Records in Denver. The James H. Grant Papers at the Putnam Museum in Davenport, Iowa, contain many letters between the young Grant and his uncle James during his school days and his first three years in Colorado. Useful biographical accounts of Grant can be found in the following: *History of the Arkansas Valley* (1881); James MacCarthy, *Political Portraits* (1888); *Portrait and Biographical Record of the State of Colorado* (1899); and *Sketches of Colorado*, vol. 1 (1911). Eugene Parson, "Colorado's First Governors," *Trail* 16, no. 12 (May 1924), is also useful. See also Grant, "Report on the Mines and Smelting Works near Leadville," in *The Pueblo and Oro Railroad* (1878), and *Inaugural Address of His Excellency James B. Grant, Governor of Colorado . . . January 9, 1883* (1883). For context regarding Leadville, see Don L. Griswold and Jean J. Griswold, *The Carbonate Camp Called Leadville* (1951), and Edward Blair, *Leadville: Colorado's Magic City* (1980). Lyle W. Dorsett and Michael McCarthy, *The Queen City: A History of Denver* (1986), is a standard work with some references to Grant. Obituaries are in the *Denver Post*, 2–4 Nov. 1911, and the *Denver Republican* and the *Rocky Mountain News*, both 2 Nov. 1911.

TIMOTHY R. MAHONEY

GRANT, Julia Dent (26 Jan. 1826–14 Dec. 1902), wife of President Ulysses S. Grant, was born at White Haven, near St. Louis, Missouri, the daughter of Frederick Dent, a planter, and Ellen Wrenshall. The fifth of eight children, she enjoyed a privileged childhood on her father's plantation and attended the Misses Mauros' boarding school in St. Louis. When she was seventeen, her brother Frederick introduced her to his former West Point roommate Ulysses S. Grant. After a two-year courtship and a four-year engagement, Julia Dent and Ulysses S. Grant were married in 1848 and began married life in the army posted to Sackets Harbor, New York. Over the next decade, they had four children.

For the next six years, at post after post, Julia Grant did her best to be a good army wife. Genial and sympathetic, she won the affection of her husband's subordinates, and she was properly respectful of his superiors. After Ulysses S. Grant resigned his commission in 1854, the family unsuccessfully cast about for a financial foothold. Julia Grant's prosperous family had always looked down on "dirt farmers," but, to their and her dismay, she found herself living a life of grinding poverty on a miserable, unproductive farm called "Hardscrabble" outside St. Louis. As she noted in her memoirs, the coming of the Civil War saved both her and her husband from desperate unhappiness.

No one understood Ulysses S. Grant better or knew how much he loved the army than his wife. She believed in him intensely and never wavered from her belief that he was destined for greatness. During the Civil War, Julia Grant spent more time in the field than any other general's wife. It was rumored that General Grant's aides summoned her to camp whenever he was drinking too much, but his letters tell a different story. Whenever he felt it safe enough, he would write anxious letters asking her to join him, which she eagerly did. An aide recalled evenings when she and the general would sit at headquarters in the field holding hands, looking shy and ruffled if anyone caught them. Julia Grant was nearly captured by the Confederates when they overran Holly Springs, Mississippi, in 1862, and she was with General Grant during the Vicksburg campaign in the spring of 1863.

After the war, with her husband a hero, Julia Grant shared in the glory and was delighted with its tangible manifestations. First, rich Philadelphians presented them with a splendid house with, she recalled, "closets . . . full of snowy fine linen, the larders and even the coal bins . . . full" (*Personal Memoirs*, p. 157). When the Grants moved to Washington, D.C., in 1866, the general's admirers had bought them another magnificent house in Georgetown. After her husband was elected president in 1868, Julia Grant looked forward to moving again, this time into the White House. Press interest in the Grants reached extraordinary heights, and the president's family was scrutinized as never before. Reporters applauded Julia Grant's replacement of Mary Todd Lincoln's extravagantly expensive carpets and draperies with simpler ones and her plans to convert the White House basement into a playroom for her two young boys. The press enjoyed greater rapport with the Grants than with any previous occupants of the White House. Julia Grant even gave occasional interviews, the first president's wife ever to do so.

With reporters looking on, Julia Grant held her first White House reception in the spring of 1869. "I felt a little shy," she recalled, but "I soon felt at home" (*Personal Memoirs*, pp. 174–75). A reporter watching Julia Grant that day described her as "fair, fat and forty" (Briggs, p. 169). She suffered from strabismus, a twitching eye, of which she was self-conscious, but she proved herself to be good-natured, well-meaning, and friendly. The same reporter noted approvingly, "She appears in grace and manner just as any other sensible woman would." Julia Grant wrote, "I am very fond of society and enjoyed to the fullest extent the opportunity afforded me at the White House" (*Personal Memoirs*, p. 177). Under her direction, the White House calendar blossomed with dozens of receptions, balls, dinners, and special parties. More than any previous presidential couple, the Grants dined out often, made social calls, and attended parties at private homes.

"My life at the White House was like a bright and beautiful dream and we were immeasurably happy," Julia Grant wrote in her memoirs of her eight years there, the longest period she and her husband lived together anywhere in their married life. It was not, however, without "some dark clouds in the bright sky." The darkest cloud for her personally intruded before she had lived in the White House a full year. "There was," she lamented, "that dreadful Black Friday." Black Friday, 24 September 1869, was the day the gold market collapsed, ruining scores of Wall Street investors. Among the revelations uncovered during the congressional investigation that followed was the fact that Julia Grant was probably among the speculators, a naive victim of flattery who succumbed to visions of the riches that had eluded her husband but which she believed they deserved.

Julia Grant left the White House at the end of two administrations with great reluctance. She reveled in the attention paid to her husband and to herself on the prolonged world tour on which they embarked to ease the transition to private life. The Grants retired to New York City, where Ulysses S. Grant, either gullible or greedy, lost all of their hard-saved money in a spectacular Wall Street smashup that left his family destitute and the object of national pity. Only his heroic efforts to complete his memoirs before he died left Julia and their children well provided for at his death in 1885.

Julia Grant lived for seventeen years after her husband. She returned to Washington, D.C., where some of her happiest years had been spent, and her daughter and grandchildren joined her. There she wrote her memoirs, the first president's wife ever to do so. She thought of publishing them immediately but was dissuaded, perhaps by potential publishers concerned by her sentimentality and her candor. Julia Grant died in Washington at the age of seventy-six. She was buried in New York City next to her husband in Grant's Tomb on Riverside Drive.

• Julia Grant's papers are dispersed among the repositories that hold her husband's papers. The largest collection of her letters are in the Ulysses S. Grant Papers at the Library of Congress, followed by a smaller collection in the Grant Family Papers at Southern Illinois University. While Ishbel Ross, *The General's Wife: The Life of Mrs. Ulysses S. Grant* (1959), is an adequate biography, heavy on the war years, a good full-length biography of Julia Grant has yet to be published. She tells her own story best in her memoirs, *The Personal Memoirs of Julia Dent Grant*, ed. John Y. Simon (1975). *The Papers of Ulysses S. Grant* (18 vols. to date, 1967–), also edited by John Y. Simon, reveal the closeness of the Grants' marriage, and Ulysses S. Grant's *Personal Memoirs of U.S. Grant* (2 vols., 1885–1886) calendar major events of their years together. Emily Briggs, who wrote *The Olivia Letters* (1906), was a Washington society reporter who covered the Grant White House and Julia Grant's every move. William McFeely's *Grant* (1981) is an outstanding biography of Ulysses S. Grant, which provides a sensitive evaluation of the Grants' marriage. William Seale, *The President's House: A History* (2 vols., 1986), offers an excellent description of Julia Grant as first lady. An obituary is in the *New York Times*, 15 Dec. 1902.

KATHRYN ALLAMONG JACOB

GRANT, Madison (19 Nov. 1865–30 May 1937), lawyer and naturalist, was born in New York, New York, the son of Gabriel Grant, a physician, and Caroline Amelia Manice. His parents were wealthy and supported his private education in New York, private tutoring in Germany, and extensive travel in Europe and the Middle East. He graduated from Yale University in 1887 and received his LL.B. from Columbia College (now Columbia University) in 1890. Grant practiced law after his graduation, but his primary interests were those of a naturalist. He also played an important role in restricting immigration in the United States in the 1920s.

Grant enjoyed experiencing nature through hunting and exploring. He became a member of the Boone and Crockett Club in 1893 and attempted to describe as a new species a type of caribou he observed in Alaska. Throughout his life Grant helped to make similar experiences available to the urban residents of New York City. In 1895 he helped to found the New York Zoological Society, along with other prominent men including Theodore Roosevelt, Henry Fairfield Osborn, and Elihu Root. He was the society's secretary from its founding until 1924, and president from 1925 until his death in 1937; he also chaired the executive committee from 1908 to 1936. Grant helped the society organize the New York Zoological Park. He also served on the planning commission for the Bronx River Parkway from 1907 to 1925; this was cited by the *New York Times* as his most important contribution to New York City. As both a naturalist and a lawyer, Grant also promoted wildlife protection and natural resource preservation. In 1905 he supported the founding of the American Bison Society, and in 1919 he formed the Save-the-Redwoods League, along with Osborn and John C. Merriam.

Equally important to Grant was his interest in the history of ethnic groups and its relevance to American immigration. An important figure in the nativist movements of the early twentieth century, Grant wrote several books in which he championed what he and many of his contemporaries referred to as the "Nordic races." In 1916 he published the first and best-known of these books, *The Passing of the Great Race*, which sold more than 16,000 copies. During the early twentieth century, Grant called for immigration restriction to keep out of the United States people he and many of his contemporaries considered inferior, especially immigrants from southern and eastern Europe and Asia. Grant advocated not only quotas on immigration but also efforts to purify the American population by means of selective breeding, or eugenics. He served as vice president of the Immigration Restriction League from 1922 to his death. He also used his legal skills to help write and pass the National Origins Act of 1924, also known as the Johnson-Reid Act, which eliminated immigration from eastern Asia and based quotas on the census of 1890. This act fell in line with the nativists' goals of Grant's Immigration Restriction League by allowing more immigrants to enter from northern and western European nations, and fewer from the southern and eastern nations that Grant and other nativists found unacceptable and even threatening. During this period Grant also served on the International Commission on Eugenics.

In *The Passing of the Great Race* Grant combined his racial views with his naturalist inclinations, claiming that climate and physical surroundings shaped the peoples of various regions. Grant claimed that what he called the Nordic race had been molded by the selective forces of weather, which eliminated the weak who could not withstand harsh winters, as well as those who could not plan for winter and work hard to prepare for it. In his last book, *The Conquest of a Continent* (1933), Grant made similar claims but used his theories to praise the American people in particular. He claimed, as had Frederick Jackson Turner in 1893, that the American frontier had formed the American character. Lauding the enterprise and initiative that must have driven the original immigrants, he described frontier America as a place that "took a heavy toll on weaklings" and led to "the survival of the able and the vigorous" (*Conquest of a Continent*, p. 92). Grant also believed that the small village provided the best environment for human beings to reach their fullest biological potential. At the same time, his naturalist proclivities made him ambivalent about this American and Nordic conquest. He explained, "Never since Caesar plundered Gaul has so large a territory been sacked in so short a time. Probably no more destructive human being has ever appeared on the world stage than the American pioneer with his axe and his rifle" (*Conquest of a Continent*, p. 221). Grant believed that the Nordic peoples had a special degree of strength, which had helped them conquer the Americas, but he also believed that that strength often was used in a manner destructive to nature.

Grant supported the formation and expansion of the New York Zoological Society and worked to save the threatened flora and fauna of the American West, making him an important figure in the American conservation movement of the early twentieth century. He was also an outspoken and openly racist activist who helped to develop the restrictive immigration policy of the 1920s, which persisted into the 1960s. Grant never married and had no children. He died in New York City.

• Grant's correspondence regarding the New York Zoological Society is held at the society in the Bronx. His eugenic views are reflected in the papers held in the Madison Grant file that is part of the Charles B. Davenport Papers at the American Philosophical Society Library in Philadelphia, Pa. The views of Grant and his colleagues are further discussed in Kenneth Ludmerer, *Genetics and American Society* (1971), and John Higham, *Strangers in the Land: Patterns of American Nativism* (1955). Grant wrote numerous articles on mammals in North America, including "The Vanishing Moose," *Century Magazine* (1894). He also edited two volumes with C. S. Davison: *The Founders of the Republic on Immigration, Naturalization, and Aliens* (1928) and *The Alien in Our Midst* (1930). An obituary is in the *New York Times*, 31 May 1937.

KATHY J. COOKE

GRANT, Percy Stickney (13 May 1860–13 Feb. 1927), Episcopal clergyman and poet, was born in Boston, Massachusetts, the son of Stephen Mason Grant and Annie Elizabeth Newhall Stickney. An 1883 graduate of Harvard University, he prepared for the ordained ministry at the Episcopal Theological School in Cambridge, Massachusetts, from which he received his B.D. in 1886. He earned an M.A. from Harvard in the same year. Ordained a deacon (1886) and priest (1887), he served three Massachusetts congregations (Church of the Ascension, Fall River, 1886; St. Mark's, Fall River, 1887–1893; Christ Church, Swansea, 1890–1893) before becoming rector of the Church of the Ascension in New York City (1893–1924).

At Ascension, Grant drew upon new styles of ministry advocated by other city clergy in order to develop a pattern that was uniquely his own. He combined the "institutional parish" model of William S. Rainsford (St. George's Episcopal Church) with the political preaching of Charles Henry Parkhurst (Madison Square Presbyterian Church). Following Rainsford, Grant eliminated pew rents and created fifty-one new parish activities and organizations. Like Parkhurst, he frequently spoke on political issues. Grant's approach resulted in increased attendance and an improved financial situation at Ascension.

The specific balance of activities at Ascension—a combination of cultural events and social gospel—reflected Grant's own personality. On one hand, he was a man of letters. He scheduled regular parish concerts, wrote poetry, produced essays on literary topics, toured the world (1899), and published a travelogue on Asia (1908). On the other hand, he saw himself as a spokesman for the working person.

An exposure to the woeful conditions of textile workers during the early years of his ministry in Fall River led Grant to become an advocate for working men and women. He spoke in support of unions and the right to strike, and he argued that the church had a responsibility to help the unemployed. Alexander Irvine, a Congregational minister who served as his assistant at Ascension (1907–1910), provided a public platform for Grant's views on the subject by converting Sunday evening revival services into the Ascension Forum (1907–1921), an arena for political and economic discussion. Grant also wrote occasional pieces for the *North American Review*, published two books on Christian social concerns, and played an important role in drafting the 1917 report of the Subcommittee on Industry and Employment of the Mayor's Committee on National Defense.

Grant's involvement led him to increasingly radical views. In his 1910 *Socialism and Christianity* he expressed sympathy for working people but doubts about socialism. By 1918, when he published *Fair Play for the Workers*, he had developed an admiration for the Industrial Workers of the World. The following year he called for the creation of a labor party in an address to the Episcopal Church Congress. In a 1920 sermon Grant compared exiled anarchists Emma Goldman and Alexander Berkman to passengers on the Mayflower.

Grant also became critical of the Episcopal church's policy on divorce, which until 1946 limited remarriage to the innocent party in a relationship ended by adultery. *Socialism and Christianity* attributed many divorces to economic hardship. A 1915 sermon called for a change in church practice. Seven years later, Grant announced his engagement to Rita d'Acosta Lydig, who had been divorced; the marriage was to be his first, but her third.

Grant's opinions did not always stand him in good stead with church authorities. In particular, he ran afoul of William Manning, bishop of New York from 1921 to 1946, a man whose election he had publicly opposed. Manning responded to the announcement of Grant's engagement to Mrs. Lydig with a threat to discipline any clergyman who presided at the wedding. The romance continued for some time, but marriage never took place.

The bishop also questioned the orthodoxy of a 1923 sermon in which Grant discounted most of the miraculous events in the life of Jesus and attributed others to "acts of autosuggestion." An intense debate followed, played out in the pages of the *New York Times* and reprinted in Grant's *Religion of Main Street* (1923). Manning, the author of an Episcopal house of bishops' statement on modernism of the same year, challenged Grant to either "accept the faith of the Church as set forth in the [Apostles' Creed] . . . or voluntarily resign." Grant responded by citing contemporary Anglican biblical scholars and arguing for understanding the creed "in the light of new knowledge." Jesus was, Grant said, the "portrait of the Invisible God, the perfect revelation of [the] Heavenly Father," but he lacked "the power of God." Though neither persuaded to resign his orders nor brought to a church trial,

Grant retired as rector of Ascension in the following year.

Grant died in Mount Kisco, New York. He had never married. His only child, adopted daughter Faith Willard Grant, had died in infancy.

Grant's early volumes of poetry, especially *Ad Matrem* (1905) and the *Search of Belisarius* (1907), attracted positive notice for his use of language and meter. In 1919 he was invited to read his work to the Phi Beta Kappa chapter at Harvard University. Reviewers were more critical of his final volume of poems, *Fifth Avenue Parade* (1922), in which he abandoned the classical and romantic themes of his early work in order to stir social consciences.

Grant's prose works fall into three categories: (1) advocacy of an increased Christian social conscience, (2) literary and cultural essays, and (3) a defense of theological modernism. In general these works are readable and clearly argued, but they did not break new ground.

• Grant's poetic works also include *A Song and Two Sonnets* (1896), *The Return of Odysseus* (1912), and *Welcome Home* (1919). His *Observations in Asia* (1908) and *Essays* (1922) treat cultural and literary topics. For an account of his conflict with Bishop Manning, see W. D. F. Hughes, *Prudently with Power* (1960), and the *New York Times*, 20 and 26 Jan. 1923, and 21 June 1924. An obituary is in the *New York Times*, 14 Feb. 1927.

ROBERT W. PRICHARD

GRANT, Robert (24 Jan. 1852–19 May 1940), novelist and jurist, was born in Boston, Massachusetts, the son of Patrick Grant, a patrician Boston commission merchant, and Charlotte Bordman Rice. Grant later sketched his early life on Beacon Hill in the first chapters of his juvenile novel *Jack Hall* (1887). He prepared for college at the prestigious Boston Latin School and, for one summer in the early 1860s, was tutored by Horatio Alger, Jr. Admitted to Harvard in 1869, he completed three degrees there: an A.B. from Harvard College in 1873, a Ph.D. in English philology (the first one so awarded) from the Graduate Department in 1876, and an LL.B. from Harvard Law School in 1879. "I passed ten years at Harvard—a record which I doubt has been surpassed or equalled by any other registered student," he later joked.

After his admission to the bar, Grant pursued a literary career in addition to practicing law. As he reminisced in his autobiography, "to read law in cold blood when I had a story fresh from the mint of imagination in embryo seemed like wasting opportunity." Grant's first novel, *The Confessions of a Frivolous Girl*, about a New York debutante influenced "by sense, noble purpose, and good breeding," appeared in 1880. During the next decade, Grant averaged a novel every other year, including *The Knave of Hearts* (1886), *Face to Face* (1886), and his "mugwump parable" *An Average Man* (1884); and he became a regular contributor to *Scribner's*. "Grant's fiction was often not merely autobiographical or politically allegorical," Christopher P. Wilson avers, "but more like inner-class parables,

fables coded with names or phrases his Boston cohorts were liable to identify." He was elected in the early 1880s to membership in the elite Papyrus Club of Boston artists, and on 28 June 1883 he delivered the Phi Beta Kappa poem at Harvard. Five days later he wed Amy Gordon Galt, daughter of the Canadian diplomat Sir Alexander Galt and granddaughter of the novelist John Galt. They had four children.

Meanwhile, the clubbable Grant was also embarking on a long career in public service. In 1882 he became private secretary to Samuel A. Green, the reform mayor of Boston; in 1886 he was selected secretary of the Bar Association of the City of Boston; in 1888 he was appointed a city water commissioner; and in 1893 he was appointed a judge of probate and insolvency for Suffolk County, a position he held until 1923. Elected an Overseer of Harvard in 1895, he served almost continuously on the board until 1921, the final four years as its president. Elected to the American Academy of Arts and Letters in 1915, Grant was chosen president of the National Institute of Arts and Letters in 1921. He was so well known for his judicial restraint that, in 1927, four years after retiring from the bench, he was appointed to a three-member advisory commission that reviewed the trial of Sacco and Vanzetti and censured the presiding judge but found no evidence to alter the verdict.

Grant minimized the importance of his early fiction because, as he explained, "my heart was set on writing a significant novel of American scope." *Unleavened Bread*, his most ambitious tale and his personal favorite among all his novels, appeared in 1900. In it, Grant satirized the pretensions of his middlebrow protagonist, Selma White, an uncouth Midwesterner who ascends the social scale through a series of well-calculated marriages. Grant both "detested" and "was fascinated" by his feminist heroine "for I knew her to be a true creation not hitherto portrayed in fiction." The novel became Grant's only bestseller, and a dramatic adaptation of it on which he collaborated was staged in New York, Philadelphia, and Boston in 1901.

In his next three novels Grant pondered the implications of marriage and divorce laws. *The Undercurrent* (1904) illustrated his conviction that religious opposition to "the remarriage of the innocent party" for any cause except infidelity was cruel and unjust; *The Orchid* (1905) was based on a rumored divorce settlement in which a woman had granted her husband custody of their child in exchange for $2 million; and *The Chippendales* (1909) described the legal consequences of a clandestine marriage between a Boston blueblood and his stenographer. In *The Bishop's Granddaughter* (1925) he again satirized "the fraudulence of American divorces." In his legal writings, too, Grant campaigned for a federal uniform marriage and divorce law to be enacted, if necessary, by constitutional amendment. Though he endorsed divorce on such grounds as adultery and desertion, he lamented the trend toward more liberal divorce on grounds of incompatibility, believing that such laws discriminated against poor women.

The author of more than thirty books, Grant was neither a writer nor a jurist of the first rank. Particularly "in writing short stories," he admitted, "I was always aware of my limitations." His novels comprise, in effect, the genteel or Brahmin response to such bourgeois realists as William Dean Howells. "I had long felt that the most salient novels on Boston had been written from the outside rather than the in," he wrote in his autobiography. Still, as his friend Edith Wharton remarked, Grant's satirical novels of manners plotted the very field "he was eventually to share" with such writers as Sinclair Lewis and Theodore Dreiser. Grant died in Boston.

• The largest collections of Grant's letters and other manuscripts are located in the Beinecke Library at Yale University, the Boston Public Library, the Princeton University Library, the Houghton and Baker Libraries at Harvard University, and at the American Academy of Arts and Letters. The most significant biographical sources are Grant's *Fourscore, an Autobiography* (1934) and his essay "Harvard College in the Seventies," *Scribner's*, May (1897), pp. 554–66. See also Wharton's *A Backward Glance* (1934); Frank Bergmann, *Robert Grant* (1982); and Christopher P. Wilson, "*Unleavened Bread*: The Representation of Robert Grant," *American Literary Realism* 22 (Spring 1990): 17–35. An obituary is in the *New York Times*, 20 May 1940.

GARY SCHARNHORST

GRANT, Ulysses Frank (1 Aug. 1865–27 May 1937), an early African-American professional baseball player, was born in Pittsfield, Massachusetts, the son of Franklin Grant and Frances Hoose, farm laborers. Grant's father died when the boy was only four months old, and in 1871 his mother relocated the family to Williamstown, Massachusetts, where Grant and his older brother played for the high school baseball team. Grant also played for the Greylocks, a South Williamstown sandlot team, in 1884. The following year he was living in Plattsburgh, New York, where he may have been working at a Lake Champlain resort. He also played for a local semipro club, the Nameless. In 1886 he signed with Meriden, Connecticut, in the Eastern League and established himself as a minor league player of considerable talent. He started at second base, sometimes pitched, and was leading the team in hitting when the club folded in midseason.

Grant had little difficulty finding a new team and enlisted with Buffalo, which had lost its National League franchise in 1885 and entered the International League. He played for Buffalo the remainder of 1886 and during the 1887 and 1888 seasons, compiling a cumulative batting average of .354. He hit for power and ran the bases well. Described as a flashy, yet consistent, fielder, he displayed wide range at second base. The 5'7½", 155-pound Grant was third in the league with a .340 batting average in 1886 and fifth at .346 in 1888. A *Sporting Life* story in 1888 called him the best all-around player to don a Buffalo uniform.

During a series of exhibition games against National League clubs in 1887, Grant had been regarded by the *Boston Post* as Buffalo's top player. A young and still improving athlete in one of baseball's toughest minor leagues, he was, according to baseball historian James E. Overmyer, "one of the few [blacks] who would have had the chance to make a long career in the majors or high minors." But the nation's shift toward greater segregation was about to drive the handful of black players in baseball's upper echelons out of integrated baseball.

In 1887 Grant was one of seven black players in the International League. That season witnessed several racially charged incidents in which whites refused to appear in team photographs with black teammates or to play with or against black players. In July the league's Newark team capitulated to Chicago White Sox manager Cap Anson, who refused to take the field for a well-attended exhibition game unless Newark played without its star black pitcher, George Stovey. That same month the league's directors voted not to approve any more contracts with black players. Although Grant played another season in the league, his future looked grim. So many rival players tried to spike or hurt him as they slid into second base that he left the infield for a safer spot in the outfield. He also encountered abusive tauntings from fans.

Grant barnstormed with the Cuban Giants after the 1888 season and did not go back to Buffalo the following spring. Only Moses Fleetwood Walker, of all the black players in the International League, returned for the 1890 season. Grant instead stayed with the Giants, a black club that played in the otherwise all-white Middle States League, a weaker minor league circuit. In 1890 he left the Cuban Giants for Harrisburg, an integrated team in the Eastern Interstate League. Harrisburg switched to the Atlantic Association in midseason, which meant that Grant was forced to travel farther south and face segregated dining and lodgings. Although he finished fifth in the league in batting with a .325 average, he signed with the Big Gorhams, a black team in New York City that barnstormed its way to a 100–4 record in 1891. Despite the players' ease of winning, the club lost money and disbanded. Grant returned to the Cuban Giants, with whom he played during the century's closing decade. He then played with the Philadelphia Giants, a top black club in 1902 and 1903, before drifting into athletic retirement at the age of thirty-eight.

He spent most of his later years in Manhattan, working as a waiter for a caterer. He died in New York City and was buried in a pauper's grave without a headstone.

Grant may have been the greatest black player of the nineteenth century. He sometimes was called the "Black Dunlap," a comparison to Fred Dunlap, considered at the time the best second baseman in the major leagues. Sol White, a black player of that era and the first chronicler of black baseball, wrote that Grant's "playing was a revelation to his fellow teammates, as well as the spectators. In hitting he ranked with the best and his fielding bordered on the impossible." Had he and other African Americans not been driven out of integrated baseball by the mounting racial enmity of the 1890s, Grant could have been the first black player in the "white" major leagues.

• The best source on Grant is "Frank Grant," by James E. Overmyer, *Baseball History 4* (1991). See also Robert Peterson, *Only the Ball Was White* (1970), and Jerry Malloy's article in *Nineteenth Century Stars* (1989).

ROB RUCK

GRANT, Ulysses S. (27 Apr. 1822–23 July 1885), Union army general and president of the United States, was born in Point Pleasant, Ohio, the son of Jesse Root Grant, a tanner and farmer, and Hannah Simpson. Baptized as Hiram Ulysses Grant, he was called Ulysses from infancy. When he was a year old, the family moved to Georgetown, Ohio, where Ulysses attended local schools and worked in his father's tannery, a job he hated, and on the farm. Shy and reticent with people, Ulysses loved horses and developed extraordinary skills of gentle discipline and command over them. At the age of seven he was driving a team; soon he took over much of the hauling for the tannery and plowing on the farm.

A hard-driving, self-made man who had risen from poverty, Jesse Grant expanded into the wholesale and retail leather trade and became a leading citizen and mayor of Georgetown. A Whig, Jesse opposed the annexation of Texas and the expansion of slavery, and Ulysses absorbed many of his father's opinions.

In 1839 Grant was appointed to West Point, where he registered as Ulysses Hiram Grant, transposing his given names because he did not want to be known by the initials H. U. G. In haste, the congressman who nominated him to the academy had misstated Grant's given names as Ulysses Simpson. An adjutant at the academy refused to correct the error; Ulysses Simpson was the name on the official appointment paper, and Ulysses Simpson it would remain. Grant's classmates inevitably turned his new initials into "Uncle Sam," and his nickname became Sam.

Grant's four years at West Point were distinguished mainly by his horsemanship. He could tame the most obstreperous beast; he set a jumping record that stood for decades. Yet when he graduated in June 1843 (ranking twenty-first in a class of thirty-nine) the army in its wisdom assigned him to the Fourth Infantry.

With little taste for a military career and hoping soon to secure appointment as instructor of mathematics (his best subject) at West Point, Grant joined his regiment at Jefferson Barracks in St. Louis on 20 September 1843. One day he rode five miles south to the home of his classmate Frederick Dent, Jr., to fulfill a promise to visit Fred's family. There Grant argued politics with Fred's father, Frederick Dent, a substantial slaveowner, planter, and Democrat. Grant's visits nevertheless grew more frequent because of Julia Dent, with whom he shared a love of horses. During their rides together this mutual passion ripened into

love. Before he could overcome Dent's opposition to his daughter's marriage to an impecunious second lieutenant, Grant's regiment was ordered in May 1844 to join the army being assembled by General Zachary Taylor near the Texas border to intimidate Mexico into acceptance of U.S. annexation of Texas.

When Congress approved annexation, Taylor in July 1845 moved his force to Corpus Christi at the mouth of the Nueces River. While Mexico and the United States bickered over the southern border of Texas (Mexico insisted on the Nueces and the United States claimed everything to the Rio Grande), tensions mounted. Grant's sympathies lay with Mexico, but President James K. Polk ordered the army to the north bank of the Rio Grande in March 1846. An attack by Mexican cavalry on U.S. dragoons north of the river on 25 April prompted a declaration of war by Congress on 13 May. By then Taylor had driven across the Rio Grande and won two victories, at Palo Alto on 8 May and Resaca de la Palma the following day. In command of his company part of the time, Grant exhibited the coolness under fire that became his hallmark at every subsequent level of command. He also demonstrated the same unpretentious control of men that he had previously shown with horses.

The Americans then pushed 150 miles deeper into enemy territory and attacked the Mexican stronghold at Monterrey. The exhausting march across barren wasteland at the height of summer demanded all the logistical prowess Taylor's small army could muster. Assuming that Grant's skill with horses would work equally well with mules and other apparatus of supply, his colonel appointed him regimental quartermaster despite Grant's protest that he wished to remain with his company and share its dangers.

Grant lived up to expectations as quartermaster. However, at the battle of Monterrey on 21–24 September 1846, he could not stand to remain behind in camp. He rode forward into the fighting and won temporary appointment as regimental adjutant when the regular adjutant was killed. During the next two days he distinguished himself as a combat officer, leading a successful charge and volunteering to ride back through sniper-infested streets to bring up ammunition. He accomplished this dangerous task without a scratch, galloping through intersections lying American Indian–fashion on the off side of his gray mare Nellie, which also came through safely.

When most of Taylor's regulars were transferred to General in Chief Winfield Scott for an invasion to capture Mexico City, Grant went with the Fourth Infantry to Veracruz, again as regimental quartermaster. Again he could not bring himself to remain in the rear when his regiment went into action. He was in the thick of the fighting at Molino del Rey outside Mexico City on 8 September 1847. Five days later, at the decisive battle of Chatultepec, he led volunteers in several dashes under fire and wrestled a cannon up a church tower to get an enfilading fire on Mexican defenders. For these feats he won promotion to first lieutenant and to a brevet captaincy. Yet his experiences confirmed Grant's abhorrence of the human wastage of war and regret for his part in aggression against Mexico.

Grant remained with his regiment until the Treaty of Guadalupe Hidalgo, yielding half of Mexico to the United States, was ratified in the spring of 1848. His four-year separation from Julia Dent had only made both hearts grow fonder. Grant's triumphant return to St. Louis overcame her father's opposition to the marriage, which took place on 22 August 1848. Captain James Longstreet was best man. The union produced four children.

Grant decided to remain in the army despite his distaste for military life. No civilian prospects offered equal security for the newly married couple. Stationed at army bases in Sackets Harbor, New York, and Detroit from 1848 to 1852, Grant took part in the convivial drinking of bored peacetime army officers, but in the spring of 1851 he took the cold-water pledge and joined the Sons of Temperance. In 1852 his regiment was transferred to the Pacific Coast, where explosive growth following the 1849 California gold rush required the enforcement of law and order.

Posted first to Fort Vancouver in Oregon Territory, Grant was promoted to captain and transferred to bleak Fort Humboldt in northern California in September 1853. Even a captain's pay did not enable him to bring Julia and their two sons. Grant tried several business and farming ventures on the side to supplement his salary. They produced only losses. Desperate with loneliness and frustration, he resumed drinking, more heavily this time. Rumors circulated of binges while on trips to San Francisco.

Truth is difficult to separate from legend in the matter of Grant's drinking. He apparently could not hold his liquor as well as many officers. He exhibited classic symptoms of alcoholism, which were then considered a moral defect. Grant himself so considered it and struggled to overcome a condition that shamed and humiliated him. With Julia at his side, he succeeded, but in the spring of 1854 Julia was not at his side. In April Grant resigned from the army. Whether he did so voluntarily or to avoid a court-martial for drunkenness has never been clear. In any case he returned to the family he had not seen for more than two years.

Grant turned his hand to farming the sixty acres south of St. Louis that his father-in-law had given Julia as a wedding present. The most valuable crop he produced on this land was firewood, which he sold in the city. To help him he hired free blacks whom, to the consternation of neighbors, he paid more than the prevailing wage. He stopped drinking, worked long hours, and named his farm "Hardscrabble." A hard scrabble it was, and by 1858 Grant recognized that he could not support his family by farming. He tried selling real estate and collecting rents in St. Louis, also without notable success. His downward mobility and sense of failure caused him to resume drinking, though without disastrous consequences.

Grant in March 1859 manumitted a slave he had acquired from Dent, though the money the man could have brought at auction would have solved Grant's financial problems. Nevertheless, he voted for James Buchanan in the presidential election of 1856 and considered himself a Douglas Democrat, because he feared that Republican victory would break up the Union.

In the spring of 1860 Grant moved to Galena, Illinois, where he went to work in his family's leather store, perhaps with the idea that he would take over its management when his brother Samuel, dying of consumption, had to step down. Tasting success in this work, he again stopped drinking, but as his prospects rose, those of the nation fell. When the Civil War erupted, Grant knew that he must again leave his family. To his father-in-law, who was leaning toward the Confederacy, Grant wrote on 19 April 1861 that "all party distinctions should be lost sight of, and every true patriot be for maintaining the integrity of the glorious old Stars and Stripes, the Constitution and the Union" (*Papers*, vol. 2, p. 3). Two days later he wrote to his father that, despite his preference for a domestic life, "having been educated for such an emergency, at the expense of the Government, I feel that it has upon me superior claims, such claims as no ordinary motives of self-interest can surmount" (*Papers*, vol. 2, p. 6).

Grant helped recruit a volunteer infantry company in Galena but declined election as captain because he believed his experience qualified him for command of a regiment. He went to Springfield to help organize the troops pouring into the capital. His remarkable knack for unostentatious leadership brought order out of chaos. Grant refused to pull political strings to obtain a colonelcy, so his Galena friends, including Congressman Elihu B. Washburne and the prominent lawyer John A. Rawlins, pulled them in his behalf. In June he was named colonel of the Twenty-first Illinois Volunteer Infantry.

Grant turned the unruly farm boys of the Twenty-first into a disciplined fighting force. He soon learned his first—and perhaps most valuable—lesson of combat command. Ordered to attack the camp of Confederate guerrillas in Missouri, Grant experienced great anxiety. He had seen plenty of action in Mexico, but now he was in command; he was responsible. As the Twenty-first approached the enemy camp, Grant wrote, "My heart kept getting higher and higher until it felt to me as though it was in my throat. I would have given anything to be back in Illinois." He kept on to discover that the enemy had fled. It dawned on Grant that his adversary "had been as much afraid of me as I had been of him. This was a view of the question I had never taken before" (*Personal Memoirs*, vol. 1, p. 250). It was one he never forgot.

In August Grant was promoted to brigadier general, an appointment obtained through the influence of Congressman Washburne. Assigned to command the troops assembling in Cairo, Illinois, he found himself at one of the most strategic points in the war, the confluence of four major rivers: the Cumberland, the Tennessee, the Ohio, and the Mississippi. When Confederate General Leonidas Polk occupied the heights above the Mississippi at Columbus, Kentucky, in early September, thereby violating that state's "neutrality," Grant immediately countered by dispatching troops to Paducah and Smithland, where the Tennessee and Cumberland rivers entered the Ohio.

In early November Grant received orders to create a diversion to draw off Confederate troops from another Union operation. He converted the demonstration into a full-scale attack on the Confederate outpost at Belmont, Missouri, across the Mississippi from Columbus, which the Confederates had fortified to block any Union traffic down the river. The whooping Illinois troops routed an enemy force of equal size on 7 November but were counterattacked by Confederate reinforcements ferried across from Columbus. Grant was in a tight spot, for the enemy threatened to cut him off from the steamboats that were his only means of retreat to his base at Cairo twenty-five miles upriver. Some of his officers panicked and advised surrender. With typical coolness, Grant responded, "We had cut our way in and could cut our way out" (*Personal Memoirs*, vol. 1, p. 276). So they did, with Grant the last man to embark.

Grant's close call at Belmont enabled Confederates to claim victory, but the battle fixed Confederate attention on defense of the Mississippi to the neglect of the Tennessee and Cumberland rivers. They turned Columbus into a bastion they proudly labeled "the Gibraltar of the South," while work languished on Forts Henry and Donelson on the two rivers just south of the Kentucky-Tennessee border. Grant recognized these forts as the key to the enemy heartland. Supported by Andrew H. Foote, commander of a fleet of new ironclad river gunboats, he sought permission from the Union commander of the Western Department, General Henry W. Halleck, to attack Fort Henry.

The cautious Halleck authorized the attack in February 1862. Grant and Foote moved quickly. On 6 February Foote's gunboats shelled Fort Henry into submission before Grant's infantrymen, who were slogging through the mud from their landing point downriver, could get there. Grant then marched his troops across the twelve miles that separated the Tennessee and Cumberland rivers to invest Fort Donelson by land, while Foote took his fleet down the Tennessee and up the Cumberland to shell the fort from the river. The Confederate gunners crippled the fleet on 14 February, and the southern infantry launched a breakout attack the next morning, while Grant was several miles downstream consulting with the wounded Foote. Returning, Grant found his right flank routed, but he calmly reorganized this sector and ordered his left to attack, penning the Confederates up again in their defenses. Cut off from reinforcements, Confederate General Simon B. Buckner, a friend of Grant from West Point days and the Mexican War who had lent Grant money on his return from California in 1854, requested terms of surrender. Grant bluntly replied, "No terms except an unconditional surrender can be accepted. I propose to move immediately upon your

works." These words made Grant famous; the phrase "unconditional surrender" gave new meaning to his initials U. S. He was promoted to major general, and Lincoln began to keep an eye on him; he had won the most significant Union victories of the war thus far.

The Confederate theater commander, Albert Sidney Johnston, then abandoned Kentucky and western and middle Tennessee and concentrated most of his forces at the rail junction of Corinth, Mississippi, just south of the Tennessee border. Grant commanded the forward movement of 40,000 Union troops to Pittsburg Landing on the Tennessee, where he was to be joined by another Union force under General Don Carlos Buell for a campaign against Corinth. Johnston did not propose to await Union attack. Backed by General Pierre G. T. Beauregard, who had come from Virginia to be his second in command, Johnston intended to attack Grant before Buell's troops arrived.

Having won decisive victories at Forts Henry and Donelson, Grant was overconfident. He did not entrench nor dispose his army for defense. When Johnston and Beauregard attacked on the morning of 6 April, he was caught by surprise. Nevertheless, he remained cool through the long, bloody day, as his troops were steadily driven back from the initial point of contact near Shiloh Church, which gave its name to the battle. Grant ranged all over the field, shoring up his breaking lines, encouraging division commanders, and forming a last-ditch line of artillery and infantry stragglers on the heights above the landing. A superb performance by one of his subordinates, General William T. Sherman, whose division bore the brunt of the initial attack, won Grant's admiration and cemented a partnership that would eventually win the war.

As dusk closed in on 6 April, Union forces held. General Johnston had been killed during the afternoon. The first reinforcements from Buell's army were arriving, but Grant's men had suffered such heavy casualties that some officers advised retreat. Grant replied, "Retreat? No. I propose to attack at daylight and whip them" (Catton, *Grant Moves South*, p. 241). So he did, decisively aided by three of Buell's divisions. Beauregard, in command since Johnston's death, broke off and retreated to Corinth.

However, victory at Shiloh won Grant few plaudits. The 13,000 Union casualties shocked the North. Grant incurred censure for having been caught by surprise, and baseless rumors of drunkenness rekindled. Lincoln parried pressures to remove Grant with the words, "I can't spare this man; he fights." Halleck had lost confidence in Grant. He came personally to Pittsburg Landing to take command of the combined and reinforced armies and gave Grant the meaningless designation as second in command. In a cautious campaign, Halleck captured Corinth on 30 May but allowed Beauregard's army to escape. Depressed by his empty role, Grant considered resigning but was talked out of it by Sherman.

When Halleck went to Washington, D.C., in July 1862 to become general in chief, Grant resumed command of the District of Western Tennessee and Northern Mississippi. The principal responsibility of his scattered forces was to administer and defend this area of 12,000 square miles against Confederate counterthrusts and guerrilla operations. One of his tasks was to devise a policy for the thousands of "contrabands" (former slaves) in this region. In November 1862 he appointed army chaplain John Eaton as superintendent of contrabands. Eaton worked to create as equitable a system of labor relations, education, and medical care for the freedpeople as was possible under wartime conditions, a system that established precedents for the Freedmen's Bureau after the war.

Union forces under Grant defeated Confederate efforts to regain territory in northern Mississippi at the battles of Iuka and Corinth on 19 September and 3–4 October. These victories prompted Grant to go on the offensive in a campaign to capture Vicksburg, the strongest remaining Confederate bastion linking the eastern and western halves of the Confederacy and blocking Union control of the Mississippi River. Grant's first Vicksburg campaign began in November 1862 with a march south from Memphis by 40,000 troops under his direct command and a river-borne move down the Mississippi by another 30,000 under Sherman. This campaign came to grief when cavalry raids in Grant's rear commanded by Nathan Bedford Forrest and Earl Van Dorn destroyed Union supply depots and communications, forcing Grant to retreat. Uninformed of these events because Forrest had cut the telegraph, Sherman attacked Chickasaw Bluffs above Vicksburg and was repulsed.

Grant brought his army downriver to regroup. Through early 1863, Union forces sought to penetrate the maze of bayous and swamps around Vicksburg to gain high ground east of the city. Nothing worked. Typhoid and dysentery claimed an alarming toll of Union soldiers, and clamors against Grant as an incompetent drunk rose in the North. Lincoln again refused to yield to such pressures. "What I want," said the president, "is generals who will fight battles and win victories. Grant has done this, and I propose to stand by him" (Foote, vol. 2, p. 217). With one or two possible exceptions (neither of them during active military operations), there is no reliable evidence of Grant drinking to excess during the war. His chief of staff John Rawlins and his wife, when she was with him, zealously guarded him from temptation.

In mid-April 1863 Grant set in motion a campaign that won acclaim as the most brilliant of the war. Because of its high risks, Sherman and other subordinates opposed his plan, but Grant, like Robert E. Lee, was a great commander because of his willingness to take risks. He sent Union cavalry under Colonel Benjamin Grierson on a raid through Mississippi as a diversion. He ordered Union gunboats and transports under Rear Admiral David Dixon Porter to sail directly past the Vicksburg batteries to a point thirty miles south, where they could ferry the troops, who had toiled through the swamps down the west bank, across the river. Most of the fleet got through, and once across the river, Grant's army cut loose from anything

resembling a base of supplies. They had to live off the country until they could fight their way back to contact with the river above Vicksburg.

Instead of driving straight north toward Vicksburg, Grant marched east toward the state capital of Jackson, where a Confederate army was being assembled by General Joseph E. Johnston. Grant then intended to turn west and invest Vicksburg, defended by another Confederate force under General John C. Pemberton. During the next three weeks Grant's men marched 130 miles, fought and won five battles against separate enemy forces that, if combined, would have nearly equaled Grant's 45,000, and penned the enemy behind the Vicksburg defenses.

These defenses were formidable, however, and enabled Pemberton to repel two Union assaults on 19 and 22 May. Grant reluctantly settled down for a siege, drawing the net ever tighter until Pemberton surrendered 30,000 half-starved men on 4 July. As a consequence, the 7,000 troops in the Confederacy's only remaining fort on the Mississippi, at Port Hudson, also surrendered four days later. Grant had cleaved the Confederacy in twain and opened the whole river to Union shipping. As Lincoln phrased it, "The Father of Waters again goes unvexed to the sea." Combined with other Union successes in that summer, especially the epochal victory at Gettysburg, the capture of Vicksburg was a crucial turning point in the war. "Grant is my man," said Lincoln, "and I am his the rest of the war" (T. Harry Williams, p. 272).

Much hard fighting lay ahead, and Grant would be in command of most of it. At the battle of Chickamauga on 19–20 September 1863, the Confederates dealt a sharp setback to the Union Army of the Cumberland's theretofore triumphant advance into northern Georgia. Driven back to Chattanooga, the besieged northerners seemed unable to break out. In this crisis, which threatened to undo the Union gains of the summer, the Lincoln administration sent reinforcements to Chattanooga. the most important reinforcement was Grant, whom Lincoln named commander of all Union forces in the theater.

Grant went personally to Chattanooga in late October. Within a month he had cleared the enemy away from his supply line and off Lookout Mountain. He then drove the Confederate Army of Tennessee twenty miles into Georgia with a spectacular victory at Missionary Ridge on 25 November.

Grant was the man of the hour. Congress revived the grade of lieutenant general, last held by George Washington. Lincoln promoted Grant to this three-star rank and appointed him general in chief of all Union armies. In the spring of 1864 Grant decided to make his headquarters with the Army of the Potomac, whose offensive against Lee's Army of Northern Virginia would decide the outcome of the war. Sherman remained in Georgia as commander of the other principal Union army. Believing that in the past three years Union armies in various theaters had "acted independently and without concert, like a balky team, no two ever pulling together," Grant devised a strategic plan for simultaneous and coordinated offensives on all fronts. Peripheral Union armies encountered frustration in Louisiana, southeast Virginia, and the Shenandoah Valley, but in a four-month campaign, Sherman captured Atlanta and prepared for his destructive marches through Georgia and South Carolina. Meanwhile in the bloodiest fighting of the war, Grant drove Lee seventy-five miles southward in a series of epic battles in May–June 1864 at the Wilderness, Spotsylvania, Cold Harbor, and Petersburg.

Heavy Union casualties sapped the morale of the northern people. Some in the North denounced Grant as a "butcher" because of his pounding tactics and severe losses, but the armies commanded by Lee suffered a higher percentage of combat casualties than those commanded by Grant. It was Lee, fighting skillfully on the entrenched defensive, who had turned the campaign into a war of attrition.

During the nine months of stalemate in the trenches fronting Petersburg and Richmond, Lincoln steadfastly supported Grant's strategy. "Hold on with a bulldog grip, and chew & choke, as much as possible," the president wrote him (Roy P. Basler, ed., *The Collected Works of Abraham Lincoln*, vol. 7 [1952–1955], p. 499).

While Grant held on like a bulldog, Sherman's thrust through the Lower South, General Philip H. Sheridan's victories in the Shenandoah Valley in the fall of 1864, and Lincoln's reelection in November weakened the Confederacy's capacity and will to resist. At the beginning of April 1865 the Confederate defenses at Petersburg cracked. Abandoning Petersburg and Richmond, Lee raced westward, but at Appomattox Court House the Army of the Potomac caught up and surrounded him. Lee had no choice; he was the third Confederate commander to surrender an army to Grant.

Instead of elation, Grant felt "sad and depressed . . . at the downfall of a foe who had fought so long and valiantly, and had suffered so much for a cause, though that cause was, I believe, one of the worst for which a people ever fought" (*Personal Memoirs*, vol. 2, p. 489).

After Lincoln's assassination, Grant was the most popular man in the North and an almost certain Republican candidate for president in 1868, but first he had to navigate the treacherous shoals of Reconstruction. After Grant's inspection tour of the South in November 1865, his report of southern acceptance of the war's results became fuel for President Andrew Johnson's lenient Reconstruction policy. Having promoted Grant to four-star rank in 1866, Johnson required him to accompany the presidential entourage on his "swing around the circle" in the congressional election campaign of that year.

Grant was disgusted by Johnson's performance and increasingly concerned about southern Democratic violence against freedpeople, Unionists, and federal troops. His concern moved him closer to the Republican program of Radical Reconstruction. When Johnson suspended Secretary of War Edwin M. Stanton in August 1867, Grant accepted the position of interim secretary to forestall the appointment of a more conservative man. When the Senate (under the Tenure of Office Act) refused in February 1868 to occur in Stanton's ouster, Grant incensed Johnson by readily yielding the office to Stanton. This action cemented Grant's rapport with Republicans and ensured his nomination for president. In the first national election in which a majority of black males had the right to vote (nearly all of them voting for Grant), the general carried his reputation as savior of the Union into the White House.

Polls of historians regularly rank Grant as one of the worst presidents. With no previous political experience, he relied on advisers who sometimes exploited his prestige for self-serving purposes. Honest himself, Grant was too trusting of subordinates. He appointed former members of his military staff as well as several members of his wife's family to offices for which they were unqualified. Some of them were later found guilty of corruption. His private secretary was involved in the infamous "Whiskey Ring," a network of collusion among distillers and revenue agents that deprived the government of millions of tax dollars. His secretary of war was impeached for selling appointments to army posts and American Indian reservations; Grant naively allowed him to resign to escape conviction. An attorney general and a secretary of the interior resigned under suspicion of malfeasance. Grant's inexperience permitted two notorious Wall Street buccaneers, Jim Fisk and Jay Gould, to manipulate him in an effort to corner the gold market, a misfortune narrowly averted when Grant and his secretary of the treasury recognized what was happening and flooded the market with government gold. In foreign policy Grant's unwise effort to acquire Santo Domingo (now Dominican Republic) collapsed into a fiasco that split the Republican party. Though Grant appointed a civil service commission to reform the spoils system, his supporters in Congress undermined the commission and sabotaged its recommendations.

Yet the Grant administrations scored solid achievements that should modify the generally negative appraisal of his presidency. Some government departments took the first steps toward genuine civil service reform during his years in office. Grant's ablest cabinet appointee, Secretary of State Hamilton Fish, negotiated the Treaty of Washington in 1871 to settle the vexing "*Alabama* claims" that had poisoned Anglo-American relations for nearly a decade. Under this treaty an international tribunal awarded American shipowners $15.5 million for damages caused by the CSS *Alabama* and other Confederate cruisers built in British shipyards. Grant's Treasury Department began the process of bringing the greenback dollar to a par with gold. In 1874 Grant vetoed a bill sponsored by antideflation congressmen to increase the amount of greenbacks in circulation. This veto set the stage for enactment in 1875 of the Specie Resumption Act, which by 1879 brought the U.S. dollar to a par with gold. Though controversial, especially in the South and West, where constraints on the money supply hurt farmers, these actions strengthened the dollar, placed government credit on a firm footing, and helped create a financial structure for the remarkable economic growth that tripled the gross national product during the last quarter of the nineteenth century.

The Fifteenth Amendment, banning racial discrimination in voting rights, was enacted and ratified during Grant's first year in office. Congress also passed and Grant signed a civil rights act and three laws to enforce the Fourteenth and Fifteenth amendments that were stronger than anything done by the federal government again in the field of civil rights until the 1960s. In 1871–1872 the Justice Department used this legislation to crack down on the Ku Klux Klan, employing federal marshals and troops to arrest several thousand Klansmen, convict hundreds of them (most received suspended sentences), and send sixty-five to federal prison. Consequently, the national election of 1872 was the fairest and freest in the South until 1968, with a solid black Republican vote helping Grant to win reelection.

The "southern problem" proved intractable during Grant's second administration. In accepting the presidential nomination in 1868, Grant had struck a responsive chord with his plea, "Let us have peace." During his entire adult life there had been no real peace between North and South on the issues of slavery and its aftermath. With ratification of the Fifteenth Amendment, millions of Americans, Grant among them, hoped that the strife was over. However, there was no peace. The level of counter-Reconstruction violence escalated again. Northern voters began to turn against Grant's use of troops to enforce black voting rights. In 1874 Democrats gained control of the House of Representatives. It was the handwriting on the wall, signifying the end of Reconstruction. The eruption of several scandals late in Grant's second administration accentuated the impression of presidential failure. The election of 1876 (Grant resisted pressure to run for a third term) resulted in disputed returns from three southern states that raised the specter of political instability. Grant kept the federal government on an even keel while Congress finally resolved the crisis in favor of the Republican nominee Rutherford B. Hayes.

Two months after leaving office, Grant embarked with his family on a trip to Europe that turned into a triumphal two-year circumnavigation of the globe. He returned home to a popular clamor, orchestrated by Republican "Stalwarts," that he run for a third term. Unwisely he succumbed to the blandishments, only to be defeated on the thirty-sixth ballot at the Republican National Convention.

Grant settled down as a private citizen in New York City. He invested his life's savings in a brokerage partnership with Frederick Ward, whose speculations crashed in a Wall Street panic in 1884. Grant was left $150,000 in debt. To keep bread on the table, in 1884 and 1885 he wrote three articles about his Civil War campaigns for *Century Magazine*'s "Battles and Leaders" series, revealing a previously unsuspected literary ability. In writing about the war, he employed the same straightforward, economical style that had made his written orders and dispatches models of clarity and conciseness twenty years earlier.

While writing the *Century* articles, Grant learned that he had incurable throat cancer. He accepted this verdict with the same outward calm and dignity that had marked his responses to earlier misfortunes and triumphs alike. To pay off his debts and support his family after he was gone, Grant almost accepted a contract with *Century* to write his memoirs for the standard 10 percent royalty. Mark Twain, who had formed his own publishing firm, persuaded Grant to sign up with him for 70 percent of the net proceeds of sales by subscription. It was one of the few good business decisions Grant ever made. In a race against death that won wide sympathy, Grant turned out chapter after chapter, despite intense pain. His death in Mount McGregor, New York, came just days after he had completed the final chapter. It was his last and greatest victory. The *Personal Memoirs* (1885–1886) were an extraordinary success, earning $450,000 for Grant's estate. Twain in 1885 and Edmund Wilson in 1962 judged them to be the best military memoirs since Julius Caesar's *Commentaries* in 51 B.C. To read *Personal Memoirs* today with knowledge of the circumstances in which Grant wrote them is to understand the indomitable will and moral courage that were keys to his military success.

In *Personal Memoirs* Grant described qualities that he admired in his first commanding officer, General Taylor. In doing so, he may have been subconsciously describing himself; the description can stand as the best summary of Grant's own character and qualities of generalship. "General Taylor never made any show or parade either of uniform or retinue." Neither did Grant. "But he was known to every soldier in his army, and was respected by all." So was Grant. "Taylor was not a conversationalist." Neither was Grant. "But on paper he could put his meaning so plainly that there could be no mistaking it." So could Grant. "General Taylor was not an officer to trouble the administration much with his demands, but was inclined to do the best he could with the means given him." The same was true of Grant, a trait that Lincoln greatly appreciated. "No soldier could face either danger or responsibility more calmly than [Taylor]. These are qualities more rarely found than genius or physical courage." So they are, and they explain why Grant has earned a reputation as one of the great captains of history.

• No single substantial collection of Grant's papers exists. Manuscript letters and other materials are located in various repositories, including the Henry E. Huntington Library, San Marino, Calif.; the Chicago Historical Society; the Illinois State Historical Library; the Library of Congress; the Missouri Historical Society; the Morris Library at Southern Illinois University; and the U.S. Military Academy Library. John Y. Simon, ed., *The Papers of Ulysses S. Grant* (18 vols., 1967–), has brought together personal and official letters and documents from these and other collections and publications through 30 June 1868. *The Personal Memoirs of U. S. Grant*

(2 vols., 1885–1886), are essential for any student of Grant's military career. Adam Badeau, Grant's aide, compiled a great deal of additional material in *Military History of Ulysses S. Grant* (3 vols., 1868–1881) and *Grant in Peace* (1887). Horace Porter, *Campaigning with Grant* (1897), is a valuable account of Grant in the last year of the war. The most recent and the best biography is William S. McFeely, *Grant: A Biography* (1981). For the years before the Civil War, the fullest account is Lloyd Lewis, *Captain Sam Grant* (1950), while the richest narratives of Grant's Civil War career are Bruce Catton, *Grant Moves South* (1960) and *Grant Takes Command* (1969). Important material on Grant's generalship can also be found in Shelby Foote, *The Civil War: A Narrative* (3 vols., 1958–1974); T. Harry Williams, *Lincoln and His Generals* (1952); Kenneth P. Williams, *Lincoln Finds a General* (5 vols., 1949–1959); and J. F. C. Fuller, *The Generalship of Ulysses S. Grant* (1929). For the political aspects of Grant's military career, see Brooks D. Simpson, *Let Us Have Peace: Ulysses S. Grant and the Politics of War and Reconstruction, 1861–1868* (1991). A useful collection of essays is David L. Wilson and John Y. Simon, eds., *Ulysses S. Grant: Essays and Documents* (1981). For Grant's presidency, two older studies are useful, William B. Hesseltine, *U. S. Grant, Politician* (1935), and Allan Nevins, *Hamilton Fish: The Inner History of the Grant Administration* (1936). They should be supplemented by William Gillette, *Retreat from Reconstruction 1868–1879* (1979). An obituary is in the *New York Times*, 24 July 1885.

JAMES M. MCPHERSON

GRANT, W. T. (27 June 1876–6 Aug. 1972), founder of the retail store chain named for him, was born William Thomas Grant in Stevensville, Pennsylvania, the son of William T. Grant and Amanda L. Bird. After failing as the owner of a small flour mill there, his father moved the family back to his native Massachusetts when Grant was about five years old. After the tea shop he owned in Fall River also failed, he supported his family with jobs as a salesman around the Boston area. Despite the family's meager income, Grant's thrifty mother managed to keep her three children in school.

Not much of a student, Grant worked as an errand boy while in high school and left after two years. Peddling in the streets and door to door and then working in stores around the Boston area and in Maine, he demonstrated a genuine flair for showmanship in sales promotion. That experience also taught him two other important lessons in merchandising: retailers could make good profits from the rapid turnover of low-priced items, but they needed to pay more attention to training their employees. At the age of thirty, when he was working as a buyer for a department store in Salem, Massachusetts, he decided to put those lessons into practice by starting a store of his own.

With three partners, whom he bought out nine years later, and his life savings, in 1906 he opened a department store in Lynn, Massachusetts. Selling household items, apparel, toiletries, and notions for no more than twenty-five cents, the store filled a niche above the successful Woolworth and Kresge dime stores across the street but below traditional department stores with more expensive merchandise. By strict economy of operations and volume buying, often

directly from manufacturers, the store was able to offer genuine bargains. As president of the company, Grant directed buying and merchandising and planned for expansion. When he added new stores, he chose the locations, usually other small industrial cities in New England, and the store managers, the marvels of mass marketing who were critical for profitable operations. In 1907 he married Lena Brownell; she had two children, whom Grant adopted.

Friendly and dynamic, he succeeded in building an efficient organization for mass retailing. A homespun motivator, he told his early associates, "Follow me and you'll wear diamonds." At the end of World War I, operating over thirty stores, with annual sales of $6 million, the W. T. Grant Company embarked on a more aggressive expansion program. To recruit, train, and retain good store managers, Grant relied on both his attention to human relations and a modern personnel department started in 1919. "Give the people in a business the opportunity for development," he later declared, "and the business will develop with them." To promote that development, the company trained prospective managers at a model store in New York City and then broadened their experience by frequent transfers. By 1928 the company operated over 200 stores, with annual sales over $50 million, and for the first time offered stock for public sale. Grant, who had become chairman in 1924, retained over 50 percent of the stock.

While his company flourished during the 1920s, Grant emerged as a prophet of American prosperity in which cooperation and coordination were replacing competition. His motto was "Nothing happens until somebody sells something." And, according to him, chain stores made good things happen for consumers and manufacturers of standardized products. By applying on a big scale both scientific management and market research, they modernized the distribution system, reducing waste and offering merchandise that customers wanted at prices they could afford. "The chain store has substantially contributed to raising the standard of living," he told a congressional committee in 1940, "and it should not be damned for doing an extra good job."

In 1930, shortly after his wife's death, Grant married Beth Bradshaw, who came to the marriage with a child, whom Grant adopted. The depression did not halt Grant's aggressive program for expansion. After acquiring several small chains, the company reincorporated in 1937 to raise capital to modernize its existing stores and to open new multifloor superstores, first in Buffalo in 1939 and later in Houston. In 1940 it abandoned its price-limit policy, expanded merchandise lines to include more costly items such as appliances and furniture, and introduced customer installment credit. Without entirely abandoning its origins as a limited-price variety store, W. T. Grant was coming to resemble the largest department store chains, Sears, Montgomery Ward, and J. C. Penney.

Despite his age and a serious illness in 1953, Grant expressed no interest in slowing down or pursuing a merger with other retail chains. During the 1950s he added over 550 new stores, concentrated in areas of rapid population growth, the West Coast and suburban markets. When he finally retired from the chairmanship in 1966 at the age of ninety, the company operated over 1,000 stores with about 60,000 employees, and almost 20,000 investors held its stock. Its return on equity reportedly was among the highest in the retail business.

But all was not well. The year that Grant retired, a national "credit crunch" revealed the company's vulnerability. By paying high dividends, opening many new stores, and expanding sales volume with low prices and generous customer credit, it had squandered its capital reserves. Meanwhile, its conservative merchandise line, which reflected its variety store origins, squeezed the company between the expanding Sears and Penney chains and the expanding discount chains, such as the K-Mart stores started by S. S. Kresge in 1962. Finally, overburdened with one of the highest debt to equity ratios and unable to pay suppliers, in 1975 the W. T. Grant Company became the biggest bankruptcy in retailing history.

Grant did not live to see that collapse. He had died in Greenwich, Connecticut, three years before. The William T. Grant Foundation, which he had established in 1936, survived him. It had once held about a quarter of the company's stock, but by diversifying its investments beginning around 1970, the foundation remained financially strong and was able to continue to provide assistance for the emotional development of children, youth, and family life.

• W. T. Grant did not deposit personal or corporate papers in any repository. The best sources for his ideas can be found in speeches printed and distributed as pamphlets by his company and in trade journals. G. Lynn Sumner, *The Story of W. T. Grant and the Early Days of the Business He Founded* (1954), is an authorized history. An obituary is in the *New York Times*, 7 Aug. 1972.

ALAN R. RAUCHER

GRANT, Zilpah Polly (30 May 1794–3 Dec. 1874), educator, was born in South Norfolk, Connecticut, the daughter of Joel Grant and Zilpah Cowles, farmers. The Grants were known for their "Scotch grit and toughness" and their "intellectual grace and strength." Although her father was killed in a farming accident when Grant was two years old, her mother maintained the family household and farm where Grant lived through her young twenties.

Grant attended the local district school until the age of fourteen, whereupon she began teaching in the district schools of Norfolk, Connecticut, and adjacent towns for twelve years. In 1813 she received baptism in the Congregational church. In 1816 she was diagnosed with pleurisy, and, although she recovered in two years, she would experience prolonged illnesses throughout her life. For one year, beginning in 1820, she attended Byfield Female Seminary directed by the Reverend Joseph Emerson, who would have a lasting impact upon her own teaching. Grant was strongly in-

fluenced by Emerson's recommendation of the Bible as an instructional tool and his vigorous advocation of education for women as "the foundation of society" and to whom "the education of both sexes is committed." While at Byfield, Grant taught various classes, aided in preparing Emerson's "Union Catechism" for press, and reading under his direction. At Byfield, Grant first met Mary Lyon, with whom she would have a deep personal and professional friendship until Lyon's death in 1849.

Although Emerson urged her to remain at Byfield, Grant left to lead a girls' school conducted in a private home in Winsted, Connecticut. In 1823 she returned briefly to Emerson's seminary, relocated to Saugus, Massachusetts. That same year she was urged to accept the offer of preceptress of the Adams Female Academy in Londonderry, New Hampshire, by its trustees and did so. In an article on the Adams Academy offerings, Grant described the three-year course of study as including reading, spelling, defining, arithmetic, chirography (penmanship), geography, English grammar, rhetoric, history, natural philosophy, chemistry, astronomy, drawing and painting, and scripture study. She was also successful in procuring the assistance of her friend, Mary Lyon, as a teacher at the academy. In this position, Grant has been called the first head of a college for women in the United States, because Adams, unlike the earlier Troy Seminary, issued diplomas. During the first few months of the new academy, Grant experienced personal tragedy through the news of the self-inflicted death of her mother. After four highly successful years as principal of the academy, Grant left in 1828 because of her objections to the teaching of dance and because of some trustees' concerns that the institution, established on liberal principles, had acquired under Grant's guidance a strictly Calvinistic character in its religious instruction.

From Londonderry, Grant accepted the principalship of the Ipswich Female Seminary in Ipswich, Massachusetts. As she had in Londonderry, Grant continued at Ipswich a systematic course of English study, the examination of prospective students for admission to its grades, and the issuance of a diploma at graduation. She added a formal insistence on the pupil's study of any area in which she was found deficient upon entrance and disciplinary self-reporting regarding the seminary's regulations. Grant announced as early as 1829 in the catalog that "for the benefit of those who are preparing to teach, and of teachers who have already had some experience" instruction would be given "on the manner of communicating knowledge to children and youth of different capacities, and in different stages of improvement, and also on the manner of correcting their faults, and improving their dispositions." This announcement of a course in teacher training was one of the first of its kind in America. This emphasis on pedagogy grew to the extent that the catalogs of 1837–1839, the last three years of Grant's principalship, referred to the school as "the Seminary for Female Teachers at Ipswich, Massachusetts." At the request of its editor, Grant wrote several accounts of Ipswich Academy and its pedagogy for *Annals of Education*. To provide education in the West, Grant established the Society for the Education of Females at Ipswich, a group that gave students loans to pay for their education as teachers and paid for their resettlement to the West when they began to teach. Mary Lyon served as Grant's assistant principal at Ipswich until autumn 1834, when she left to prepare for the founding of Mount Holyoke Seminary in South Hadley, Massachusetts. Grant provided both moral and material support for Lyon's seminary, although "she at first had little confidence in its 'domestic' work feature" (Guilford, p. 173). The first money given to Lyon's seminary came from the pupils of the Ipswich school. In the last months of Lyon's stay at Ipswich, Grant made her first trip west, a trip that prompted her founding of a society for sending teachers west. She also continued to appeal to subscribers for aid to the Holyoke Seminary in 1837. However, her health failed her again in 1837, rendering her unable to fulfill duties through most of 1838. Without the assistance of her lifelong friend Lyon, upon whom she had relied during prior illnesses, Grant was not able to recover. She rallied for the 1838 winter term but was forced to retire from Ipswich in April 1839 for reasons of health after thirty years of teaching.

During her recovery, she met William Bostwick Banister, an attorney, former Massachusetts state senator, and a Puritan who like her had "early set his feet in the straight and narrow way." They married in 1841, and, as his third wife, she presided over his large home and became a second mother to his two adult daughters. (They had no children together.) During the twelve years of their marriage, Grant remained productive, recruiting teachers for the West and writing in 1856 a pamphlet, *Hints on Education*, on her ideas on education. After Banister's death in 1853 and until her own in Newburyport, Massachusetts, Grant used the little money remaining to provide for herself, support charities, conduct her Bible class, and stay in close contact with former students, friends, and family. Grant's significance lay in her leadership in the promotion and development of college education for women, in her writings on pedagogy, and in her design of the first teacher-training course.

• The Zilpah P. Grant Banister Papers, 1803–1971, are in the Mount Holyoke College Archives and Special Collections. The collection includes 291 items and consists chiefly of letters by and to Grant, autobiographical sketches, writings, charts, a portrait, photographs, and biographical and secondary source documents. Source materials concerning Byfield Female Seminary, Adams Female Academy, and Ipswich Female Seminary are also housed at Mount Holyoke. The most extensive assessment of Grant's life is Lucinda T. Guilford, *The Use of a Life: Memorials of Mrs. Z. P. Grant Banister* (1885). See also Rev. John P. Cowles, "Miss Z. P. Grant—Mrs. William B. Banister: Memoir," *American Journal of Education* 30 (1880): 611–24, for a biographical sketch with an account of the schools at Londonderry and Ipswich; Leonard W. Labaree, "Zilpah Grant and the Art of Teaching: 1829,"

as recorded by Eliza Paul Capen, *New England Quarterly* 20 (1947): 347–64, on Grant's pedagogy; and Harriet Webster Marr, "Study of Zilpah Polly Grant Banister, Noted Educator of Ipswich Seminary," *Essex Institute Historical Collections* (Oct. 1952): 348–64. An obituary is in the *Boston Transcript*, 4 Dec. 1874.

CHERYL T. DESMOND

GRASS, John (1837/1844–10 May 1918), leader of the Sihasapa (Blackfoot) Sioux, was born at a camp along the Grand River in present-day South Dakota. His father and grandfather were important Sihasapa leaders; no information has been found on his mother. The Sihasapa were probably the last of the Teton Sioux to migrate from the woodlands into the Dakotas and were closely connected to the Hunkpapa and Sans Arc bands. Catholic mission records state that Grass, or Charging Bear, as he was known as a young adult, was baptized when he was three by the peripatetic Jesuit Father Pierre-Jean De Smet. Grass fought in battles against tribal enemies in the 1850s and 1860s. He married Cecelia Walking Shield in a traditional ceremony in 1867; they renewed their marriage in a Catholic ceremony in 1894. The Grasses had four children.

Grass appears regularly in the reports of the Standing Rock Indian Agency in North Dakota, to which the Sihasapa were assigned along with bands of Hunkpapa and Upper Yanktonais Sioux, as well as in the records of the commissions who worked to obtain land cessions from the Sioux in the 1880s. Grass counseled peace in the 1870s and gained influence after 1876 as he accepted government policies encouraging farming and education. Recognition of his willingness to cooperate marked him as "progressive," and he was named chief justice of the Court of Indian Offenses for the Standing Rock Agency, a position he held until his death. By the early 1880s Grass's influence increased as the Hunkpapa *bloutanka* (war leader) Gall came also to accept assimilationist policies. Gall and Grass became close friends and worked to protect the lands and interests of their people. Grass's willingness to cooperate with the government led Agent James McLaughlin to name him head chief of Standing Rock but also placed him and Gall at odds with other leaders, such as Sitting Bull, who remained more suspicious of government intentions.

Grass resisted government efforts to take more Sioux land in the 1880s. He claimed that the 1882 Edmunds Commission had lied to the Sioux about government intentions, and he led a united Standing Rock resistance to the 1888 Pratt Commission efforts to break up the Great Sioux Reservation, an effort that was assisted by McLaughlin. Initially, Grass opposed attempts by the Crook Commission (George Crook, Charles Foster, and William Warner) to receive Sioux approval for the sale of Sioux lands in 1889. Grass noted that the government had failed in the past to fulfill its promises regarding payments for land and the creation of reservation schools, and he felt that the offered payment of $1.25 per acre was too low. But he eventually succumbed, along with many others, to severe pressure and to arguments that if the tendered agreement for the cession of lands were not accepted, the government might simply take the land without compensation, an argument made privately to Grass and other Standing Rock leaders by McLaughlin. Government failure to live up to its treaty and statutory obligations after the Sioux approved the 1889 agreement led to the Ghost Dance Crisis, based on a spiritual movement whose practitioners believed that they, through the Ghost Dance, could make the whites vanish and could be rejoined with the spirits of their dead. Attempts by the army to suppress this movement led to the killing of Sitting Bull and the Wounded Knee massacre. Throughout this chaotic time, Grass counseled peace and worked to calm the situation. Subsequently in 1904 Grass led a Sioux delegation to Washington, D.C., to assert Sioux claims and grievances. Despite the government's inept handling of the Ghost Dance and the uneven implementation of Indian policy, Grass remained committed to peace and accommodation. As with many Indian leaders of that time, he saw no real alternative. He died at his home near Fort Yates on the Standing Rock Agency.

• The record of Grass's life is scattered through government records and recollection of individuals who knew him. Indian Agent James McLaughlin has high praise for Grass in *My Friend the Indian* (1910). Two recent biographies of Sitting Bull discuss Grass's role in the 1880s: Gary Anderson, *Sitting Bull and the Paradox of Lakota Nationhood* (1996), and Robert Utley, *The Lance and the Shield: The Life and Times of Sitting Bull* (1993). Brief mention of Grass's role during the Ghost Dance crisis can be found in James Mooney, *The Ghost Dance Religion and the Sioux Outbreak of 1890* (1896; repr. 1991); Utley, *The Last Days of the Sioux Nation* (1963); W. Fletcher Johnson, *The Red Record of the Sioux Life of Sitting Bull and History of the Indian War of 1890–'91* (1891); and Mildred Felder, *Sioux Indian Leaders* (1975). A brief obituary appears in the Catholic Bureau of Missions, *Indian Sentinel*, Apr. 1919, Washington, D.C.

DOUGLAS D. MARTIN

GRASSE, Comte de (12 Sept. 1722–14 Jan. 1788), French admiral, was born at Bar-sur-Loup (now in the department of the Alpes-Maritimes), France, the son of François, marquis de Grasse, an army officer, and Véronique de Villeneuve-Trans. His given name was François-Joseph-Paul. De Grasse was appointed to the Gardes de la Marine at Toulon in 1734 and received his naval training there and as a page in the Order of the Knight of Malta. During the War of Austrian Succession (1740–1748) he served in the Caribbean and the Mediterranean. In May 1747, while in a convoy bound for Canada, he was wounded and made prisoner by the English, but he was exchanged after giving his parole before the war ended. A lieutenant commander at the outbreak of the Seven Years' War in 1756, he took part in the defense of Louisbourg and was promoted to captain in 1762. Following the peace he served mostly in the Mediterranean. In 1764 he married Antoinette-Rosalie Accaron, who died in 1773; they had six children. While stationed at Saint Domingue (Haiti) in 1776 he married a wealthy widow, Catherine de Pien, who died only four years later.

In June 1778, shortly after France entered the War of American Independence, de Grasse was appointed commodore; he fought in the battle of Ushant the next month. In early 1779 he commanded a small squadron sent to reinforce Admiral d'Estaing in the West Indies. He participated in the capture of Grenada in July of that year and in the ill-fated expedition to Savannah shortly afterward. After further action the next year, he returned to France. In March 1781 he was named admiral and received command of a large convoy, including twenty ships of the line, some 150 vessels in all, that reached the Caribbean in late April. After a number of engagements in these waters, de Grasse put in at Saint Dominque in the beginning of July; there he found awaiting him a dispatch from the commander of the French army in the United States, the comte de Rochambeau, requesting naval and military assistance.

De Grasse's decision to comply with this request proved momentous. Taking immediate measures to implement his decision, he managed to arrange a loan from Spanish sources in Cuba and got the governor of Saint Dominque to furnish more than 3,000 troops under the command of the marquis de Saint-Simon. He wrote Rochambeau that in early August he was leaving for Chesapeake Bay where he would remain, with this army and his fleet, until mid-October. When this response reached the allied encampments outside New York on 14 August, George Washington and Rochambeau decided to march their armies southward to attack General Charles Cornwallis in Virginia, in order to take advantage of this unprecedented opportunity.

At the end of August de Grasse's fleet anchored at the southern end of Chesapeake Bay; a few days later Saint-Simon's troops began to disembark. On the morning of 5 September de Grasse was informed of the appearance of an English fleet commanded by Admiral Thomas Graves. The French quickly put to sea and engaged the enemy off the Virginia Capes that same afternoon. During the two hours of fighting that followed, both sides suffered severe damage and casualties, although the British losses were somewhat greater. For the next four days the two fleets stalked each other until both were dispersed by a storm on 9 September. De Grasse returned to Cape Henry where he met a French squadron, under Admiral Louis de Barras, that had recently arrived from Newport. French naval superiority in the Chesapeake was confirmed. On 13 September the English ships departed for New York. The trap around Cornwallis's army, holed up in Yorktown, closed.

Thereafter, de Grasse's primary contribution to the sieges of Yorktown and Gloucester (just across the York River) was to keep the British navy from reinforcing or evacuating Cornwallis's garrison, although he did provide some 800 marines from his fleet to the allied forces at Gloucester. He performed his mission well. The American and French armies gradually pressed the siege to a successful conclusion. The formal surrender on 19 October 1781 was as much the victory of de Grasse as of any of the allied commanders. The French admiral, however, was uneasy with having his warships at anchor. In fact, on 27 September when informed that an English squadron under Admiral Robert Digby was in American waters, de Grasse was ready to put to sea until dissuaded by the entreaties of Rochambeau and Washington. It was not long after the capitulation that he embarked Saint-Simon's army on his ships and set sail for the West Indies on 4 November.

Back in the Caribbean, de Grasse continued to enjoy victory, participating in the capture of St. Kitts, Nevis, and Montserrat in early 1782. On 12 April this success—and an entire career—came to a disastrous end. After four days of maneuvering, Admiral George Rodney's fleet of thirty-six ships of the line confronted de Grasse's fleet, reduced from thirty-three to thirty during the previous three days, off the Iles de Saintes. In the ensuing battle, five French ships of the line were captured (and two more a week later); French casualties exceeded 3,000, about triple the number of English losses; and de Grasse himself was taken prisoner. After his release and return to France, a "council of war," convened at Lorient in 1784, examined his conduct. Although he was exonerated in its final report, issued on 27 May, he was informed, "His Majesty, being displeased with your conduct . . . forbids you to present yourself before him." He then retired to his estate at Tilly (now in the department of the Seine-et-Oise), where he died survived by his third wife, Christine Marie Delphine Lazare de Cibon, whom he had married in 1786.

In France this brave, rather than brilliant, commander passed from disgrace to obscurity after his death. His contributions to the victory of Yorktown were better remembered in the United States: in 1784 the U.S. Congress voted to present him with four cannons, and a destroyer, the *Comte de Grasse*, was commissioned in 1978.

• There is no known repository of de Grasse's papers. Some information about the most important period of de Grasse's career can be found in *Correspondence of General Washington and Comte de Grasse, 1787, August 17–November 4*, 71st Cong., 2d sess., 1931, S. Doc. 211. Two conflicting evaluations of his conduct are presented in F. G. Shea, ed., *The Operations of the French Fleet under the Count de Grasse in 1781–1782, as Described in Two Contemporary Journals* (1864; repr. 1971). Most useful on the naval battle of 5 Sept. 1781 is Harold A. Larrabee, *Decision at the Chesapeake* (1964). Charles L. Lewis, *Admiral De Grasse and American Independence* (1945), reflects the concerns and interest of its author, who was a professor at the U.S. Naval Academy when he wrote it. Jean-Jacques Antier, *L'Amiral de Grasse: Héros de l'Indépendance Américaine* (1965), is somewhat more useful.

SAMUEL F. SCOTT

GRASSELLI, Caesar Augustin (7 Nov. 1850–28 July 1927), manufacturing chemist and business leader, was born in Cincinnati, Ohio, the son of Eugene Ramiro Grasselli, a manufacturing chemist, and Fredericka Eisenbarth. Grasselli was born into a family with a tradition in chemical manufacturing. His grandfather, Giovanni Angelo Grasselli, was one of the first manufacturing chemists in Europe, and his father was a pioneer in the American chemical industry. Eugene immigrated to the United States in 1836, settling in Philadelphia, Pennsylvania, where he worked for a chemical firm that manufactured pharmaceutical preparations. In 1839 Eugene migrated to Cincinnati, Ohio, then a major western meat packing and market center, where he established the Grasselli Chemical Company, the first sulfuric acid plant west of the Allegheny Mountains.

Grasselli developed an interest in chemistry and the family business at a young age. He received his formal education in the Cincinnati public schools and at St. Xavier's. In addition he received thorough scientific and business training under his father's direction while completing an extensive apprenticeship in the company's factories in Cincinnati and later Cleveland, Ohio, where the family moved in 1867 following his father's decision to build a new plant at the terminus of the Ohio Canal and the Cuyahoga River a year earlier. Grasselli assisted in its construction and operation, working as a stone mason, bricklayer, plumber, machinist, and boiler tender. Grasselli married Johanna Ireland on 1 August 1871. The couple had five children.

Grasselli's father made him a partner in the family business in 1873 under the name of Eugene Grasselli & Son. He became president of the company following the death of his father in 1882. In 1885 Grasselli consolidated with Marsh & Harwood Company, a rival Cleveland firm and incorporated with capital of $600,000 as the Grasselli Chemical Company, thus becoming the largest producer of acid in the country. Grasselli served as president until 1916, when he was succeeded by his son Thomas. By the time he retired, Grasselli Chemical had accumulated capital of more than $17 million, the value of its properties had increased to $30 million, and it was operating fourteen manufacturing plants throughout the eastern part of the United States. Grasselli served as chairman of the Board of Trustees from 1916 until his death.

Like his father, Grasselli was quick to utilize improved methods of manufacturing and introduce new chemical products for other industries. The years immediately following the Civil War were a period of rapid expansion for the petroleum industry, and since large quantities of sulfuric acid were essential for the distillation process, petroleum had a multiplier effect on the chemical industry. Cleveland's proximity to the Pennsylvania oil fields, as well as its combination of technology, transportation, and entrepreneurship, resulted in the city becoming the country's largest oil refiner by the late 1860s. The newly organized Standard Oil Company soon became Grasselli & Son's major customer for sulfuric acid, a business relationship that continued throughout Grasselli's career.

Around 1868 the family had become involved in the initial production of high explosives in the country. Grasselli convinced his father to manufacture the high-strength nitric acid needed to produce the nitroglycerin used in the construction of the Hoosac railway tunnel through the Green Mountains, the first practical demonstration to the technical world of the explosive's potential use. During the 1870s the Grassellis also supplied mixed acids to the Lake Shore Nitroglycerin Company in Fairport, Ohio; the Lake Superior Powder Company in Marquette, Michigan; and the California Powder Company in Newburgh, Ohio.

In the early 1870s the Grassellis, working without the aid of chemists, engineers, or technicians, developed their own process for manufacturing blue vitriol (sulfate of copper) for Western Union Telegraph Company electrical batteries. Around 1882 Grasselli produced a shipment of 97.75 percent sulfuric acid for the E. I. du Pont de Nemours Company, the first time sulfuric acid of greater strength than 66 percent on the Beaume scale was successfully made and sold in the United States.

In 1885 Grasselli pioneered in the production of domestic saltcake (sodium sulfate) for the glass industry. Up until then American glass manufacturers had relied almost entirely on saltcake imported from Great Britain. Confronted by an industrywide reluctance to the idea of using domestic saltcake, Grasselli decided to bypass management and personally cultivate the production workers in individual companies to demonstrate that he could provide a superior product at a lower cost. That same year, in response to pressure from Standard Oil for lower prices, Grasselli introduced a process allowing the use of sulfur-bearing iron pyrite ore in place of brimstone in the manufacture of sulfuric acid.

In 1893 Grasselli began manufacturing chloride of zinc as a wood preservative for the western railroads. Prior to the passage of protective tariffs in 1896, the American iron and steel, paint, rubber, leather, photograph, and plating industries had been dependent upon imported supplies of ammonium chloride, lithopone, and hyposulphite of soda. The new tariffs on these chemicals prompted Grasselli to enter the market, and his company was soon producing them at cost below their previous free market price.

Grasselli introduced the manufacture of acetic acid in 1900 and silicate of soda in 1902, as well as an improved process for producing ammonia in 1903. As a direct result of the increasing use of zinc sulfide in the production of sulfuric acid, Grasselli entered the zinc industry in 1904. Opening a plant near Clarksburg, West Virginia, his company became the country's second largest smelter of zinc. In 1905 Grasselli introduced the production of silicate soda for the manufacture of soap and as an adhesive for the manufacture of corrugated cardboard.

Grasselli's success in the chemical business brought him actively into other corporations. He was one of the founders of the Broadway Savings & Trust Company in 1885 and of the Woodland Avenue Savings & Trust Company in 1887, both of which he served as president until their merger into the Union Trust Company in 1921. He also served as a director of the Union National Bank and its successors, the Union Trust Company, the Broadway & Newburgh Street Railroad Company, and the Akron & Chicago Junction Railroad of the Baltimore & Ohio Railroad system.

Grasselli was a member of the American Chemical Society, the American Institute of Mining & Metallurgical Engineers, the American Institute of Banking, the American Academy of Political & Social Sciences, the Ohio Society of New York, the American Museum of Natural History, the Audubon Society, the Chemists' Club of New York, the National Civic Federation, the American Red Cross, the Cleveland Union Club, the Cleveland Museum of Natural History, and the Western Reserve Historical Society. He was also a founder of the Cleveland Museum of Art and helped reorganize the Cleveland Chamber of Commerce.

In 1910 King Victor Emanuel III of Italy decorated Grasselli Knight of the Order of the Golden Crown of Italy and in 1921 made him a commander of the order in recognition of Grasselli's relief efforts for victims of earthquakes and volcanic eruptions in Italy. In 1923 Pope Paul XI likewise conferred upon Grasselli the decoration of Commander of the Order of St. Gregory the Great.

Known to associates as "C.A.," Grasselli was a prominent figure in Cleveland's industrial, civic, and social life with a reputation for honesty and unfailing courtesy. Both a Republican and a Roman Catholic, Grasselli developed friendships with numerous prominent figures, including U.S. senator Marcus A. Hanna, President William McKinley, John D. Rockefeller and Samuel Andrews of Standard Oil, and Jephta Wade of Western Union.

As a memorial to his wife, who died in 1910, Grasselli gave the Cleveland Society for the Blind in 1918 a former family residence that became known as Grasselli House. In 1922 Grasselli gave the family summer residence in Euclid Village, Ohio, to the Cleveland Catholic diocese as a home for crippled children. Known as "Rose-Mary," the Johanna Grasselli Home for Crippled Children also served as a memorial to Mrs. Grasselli.

Grasselli's career spanned the period of greatest growth for the chemical manufacturing industry. A pioneer during the early industrial revolution when manufacturers faced both new opportunities and complex problems of production, transportation, selling, and finance, Grasselli proved to be a resourceful leader, building his family's business into one of the country's largest manufacturers of heavy chemicals. Grasselli died in Cleveland.

• The Grasselli Family Papers at the Western Reserve Historical Society in Cleveland, Ohio, include family and personnel papers and a manuscript of Grasselli's autobiography, *My Family and the Grasselli Chemical Company*, written for his family. The autobiography focuses more on scientific processes rather than business matters and is a good source for descriptions of how chemicals were processed at the time. The clipping files on Grasselli and the Grasselli Chemical Company in the Cleveland Press Collection at Cleveland State University are also useful. Elroy McKendree Avery, *A History of Cleveland and Its Environs* (1918), and Samuel P. Orth, *A History of Cleveland, Ohio* (1910), provide factual biographical sketches. Obituaries are in the *Cleveland Plain Dealer* and the *Cleveland Press*, both 29 July 1927, and the *New York Times*, 30 July 1927.

WILLIAM BECKER

GRASSO, Ella Tambussi (10 May 1919–5 Feb. 1981), state and federal legislator and governor of Connecticut, was born in Windsor Locks, Connecticut, near Hartford, the daughter of Giacomo Tambussi, a baker, and Maria Oliva. The daughter of Italian immigrant parents, she graduated magna cum laude from Mount Holyoke College in 1940 and then two years later earned an M.A. in sociology and economics from the same institution. She was fluent in Italian and proud of her working-class heritage. Also in 1942 she married Thomas Grasso, a schoolteacher, and they had two children.

Grasso devoted her entire adult life to governmental service. She worked for the Federal War Manpower Commission in Connecticut (1943–1946), did campaign work for the Democratic party after the war, won a seat in the state legislature in 1952, and then became Connecticut's secretary of state (1958–1970). She became active in Democratic politics on the national level, serving on the Platform Committee in 1960 and on the Resolutions Committee in 1964 and 1968. In 1970 she was elected to the U.S. House of Representatives and in 1974 won the governorship by almost a 200,000-vote margin. In 1978 she was reelected governor by a landslide, carrying three-quarters of the towns in the state. Esteemed by other governors, she was elected to chair the Democratic Governors Conference in 1979.

Throughout her political career, Grasso was known for her accessibility. As secretary of state, she turned her office in the state capitol building into a "people's lobby," where people could come to seek or give advice. As governor, she initiated a popular "open door" policy, called for creation of a consumer ombudsman, and instituted sunshine laws ensuring open meetings and full disclosure in government. She also avoided filling state jobs on a patronage basis, stating that the electorate expected her to hire on a strict evaluation of skills.

Grasso's concern for common people was also reflected in her liberal political record as a congresswoman. With defense cutbacks contributing to high unemployment in her congressional district, she helped lead a variety of congressional efforts to spur economic growth. She sponsored or promoted the Comprehensive Employment and Training Act (CETA) of 1971, an Emergency Education Act of 1971, an increase in the minimum wage, and laws providing additional money for transportation, medical

research, higher education, and benefits to veterans and the elderly. The liberal Americans for Democratic Action (ADA) gave her an 80 percent approval rating, and organized labor approved of her record except for her negative vote on a major military spending bill.

Despite Grasso's generally liberal record, she did not always score high marks from feminist groups. She faced criticism for her absence from Congress during a crucial vote on child care legislation and for her antiabortion stance. She respected the Supreme Court's decision to permit legal abortions as the law of the land, but as a Catholic, she quietly opposed abortion. As governor she refused to use state funds to finance abortions. Overall, however, advocates for women lauded her accomplishments. She was the first woman in the United States to be elected governor without the benefit of a husband's previous incumbency, and during the 1970s she was frequently mentioned as a possible vice presidential candidate.

Although Grasso acknowledged that she had benefited politically from the women's movement and often credited her membership in the League of Women Voters for her introduction to political issues, she consistently tried to downplay the significance of her gender. Critics tried to make her sex an issue in her gubernatorial campaign. Her opponent called her "Spenderella," and bumper stickers read "Connecticut can't afford a governess." Grasso asked voters to judge her on her own accomplishments, as an individual. Wanting no special treatment as a woman, either positive or negative, she said, "I expect to be treated as a person, and I usually am."

In her activity for the Democratic party in the late 1960s and early 1970s, Grasso spoke out against involvement in the Vietnam War. At the 1968 Democratic National Convention in Chicago, she collaborated on a minority report opposing the war. Along with others, she walked out of the convention in protest against the police brutality against antiwar demonstrators outside the convention hall.

As governor, Grasso sought to counter conservative charges that she was a liberal spender by turning back to the state a $7,000 increase in her own salary and administering state programs with frugality. While leading state efforts to help the elderly and the retarded, she also managed to uphold the Connecticut tradition of no income tax. To balance the budget, she reorganized and streamlined state operations, earning the enmity of state workers by cutting jobs, and limited welfare and aid to cities. She instituted more rigorous regulation of the profits of public utilities companies and gained special praise when she took personal charge of an emergency relief effort during a huge blizzard in 1978.

Grasso projected an image of compassion and care to constituents. "I'm just an old shoe," she explained. At the same time, she had a reputation among her staff for being demanding and tough. When she was diagnosed with cancer midway into her second term as governor, she conducted state business from her hospital room for several weeks before resigning. She died in Hartford.

• The Connecticut State Library at Hartford holds Grasso's official papers as governor. She is the subject of Susan Bysiewicz, *Ella: A Biography of Governor Ella Grasso* (1984). A biographical entry is in *American Catholic Who's Who*, vol. 23 (1979). Her career is discussed in a number of books on women in political life, including Herbert F. Janick, *A Diverse People: Connecticut to the Present* (1975); Hope Chamberlin, *A Minority of Members: Women in the U.S. Congress* (1973); Louise Greenbaum, *Contributions of Women: Politics and Government* (1977); Peggy Lamson, *Few Are Chosen: American Women in Political Life Today* (1968); Sharon Whitney, *Women in Politics* (1986); and Office of the Historian of the U.S. House of Representatives, *Women in Congress, 1917–1990* (1991). Ardyce Carlson Whalen, "Woman as Political Persuader" (M.A. thesis, Univ. of North Dakota), discusses Grasso's 1975 campaign for governor. A lengthy obituary is in the *New York Times*, 6 Feb. 1981.

EMILY S. ROSENBERG

GRATIOT, Charles (1752–20 Apr. 1817), frontier trader, was born in Lausanne, Switzerland, the son of David Gratiot and Marie Bernard, French Huguenot merchants. Educated in schools in Lausanne, Gratiot, at age seventeen, went to London to work with his mother's brother, a merchant, who then had him sent to Montreal, Canada. Arriving at Montreal in May 1769, Gratiot began working as a clerk in his uncle's office to learn the Indian trade in the Great Lakes region, which, though now under British sovereignty, continued to be controlled by French traders. In 1774 he went on a successful trading expedition for his uncle into the Illinois country but, on being less successful on a second venture of his own, established in 1777 a partnership with David McCrae, a Scottish trader in Montreal.

In December 1777 Gratiot opened a store in Cahokia, a French town settled in the early eighteenth century in the Illinois country. Gratiot's decision to locate in Cahokia reinvigorated its declining rural economy. His mercantile and agrarian knowledge, combined with his knowledge of the local Native Americans and his ability to speak English, enabled Gratiot to establish himself quickly as a member of the social elite and to assume the role of the local liaison between the French métis, French, and Indian residents of the region and their British rulers. When George Rogers Clark invaded the region the following year, Gratiot continued in the same role, this time supporting the Americans. However, Gratiot's support of the Americans combined with the disruptions of war and impending American takeover to cut off Gratiot's connections to Montreal. In 1781, therefore, he joined the migration of a number of merchants from nearby French towns to St. Louis, where, away from American control and under Spanish rule, he sought to reestablish himself as a trader via New Orleans. Gratiot quickly entered the social elite of St. Louis through his marriage in 1781 to Victoire Chouteau, the youngest daughter of Pierre de Laclède Liguest, the founder of St. Louis, and Marie Therese Bourgeois, the matri-

arch of St. Louis society. Gratiot and Victoire Chouteau had ten children.

Once in St. Louis, Gratiot formed a number of short-term relationships with prominent merchants of St. Louis, the Chouteaus and the Papins in particular, and then tried to establish himself as a forwarding and commission merchant between European merchants and the Indian trade. In pursuit of this grand design, most of which came to nothing, Gratiot went on several extended trips to the East Coast and Europe in the 1790s. Gradually, however, Gratiot realized that there were significant profits to be made in operating out of St. Louis as a regional wholesaling merchant. He acquired trade goods from New York through New Orleans and provided them to American newcomers and travelers, as well as to the Indians of the upper Mississippi and Missouri river valleys, in exchange for fur. John Jacob Astor supported this latter trade for many years. Gratiot's ability to speak English allowed him to acquire an especially lucrative trade with Americans settling in Spanish territory, as well as those who lived across the river in Illinois country and east up the Ohio River valley. During the same period he acquired an extensive land grant west of the village of St. Louis, on the eastern edge of which he established farms for himself and his sons. As was the practice among the elite French residents, Gratiot owned a number of slaves. Gratiot also went into land speculation, which made him a fortune, and established a salt works on the Merrimac, a distillery, and a tannery, making him one of the chief manufacturers in St. Louis.

Gratiot's continual support of and trade with the Americans made him a strong supporter of the transfer of power to the Americans in March 1804. Serving as interpreter, Gratiot, with other members of the elite, greeted American officials and helped raise the American flag over the frontier village. Serving as a trustee of the town for several years, he also became judge of the Court of the Quarter Sessions from 1807 to 1810, and afterward justice of the peace, while continuing his mercantile operations. Gratiot's social position was enhanced as several of his children married members of the Cabbanné, Chouteau, Labbadie, Demun, and Perdreauville families, all prominent in the intertwined social order of early St. Louis society. In his later years he remained active in local society, ruling as one of its patriarchs. In 1815 he was one of the first St. Louisans to welcome newcomer Thomas Hart Benton to the city. Gratiot's son Henry, a trader, explorer, and miner, helped open up the mines at the Fever River, near present-day Galena, Illinois, in 1825 and at Gratiot's Grove, Wisconsin, in 1827 and was an Indian agent for the Winnebago tribe during the Black Hawk War. Another son attended the U.S. Military Academy at West Point and became chief engineer for the U.S. Army. Gratiot died in St. Louis. As an early French trader in the Illinois country, Gratiot helped establish St. Louis as the center of the fur trade and as a regional entrepôt and played a considerable role in its early economic, social, and political development.

• The Charles Gratiot Papers are in the Missouri Historical Society. For genealogical records, see Paul Beckwith, *The Creoles of St. Louis* (1893), and Mary B. Cunningham and Jeanne C. Blythe, *The Founding Family of St. Louis* (1977). The best secondary source on his career remains Frederick L. Billon, *Annals of St. Louis* (1883), pp. 481–92. Also see James Neal Primm, *Lion of the Valley, St. Louis, Missouri* (1990), and J. Thomas Scharf, *A History of St. Louis City and County* (1883). Gratiot is also referred to in William Foley and C. David Rice, *The First Chouteaus, River Barons of Early St. Louis* (1983), and Winstanley Briggs, "The Pays des Illinois," *William and Mary Quarterly* 67, no. 1 (1990): 55. Also see Warren Lynn Barnhart, "The Letter Books of Charles Gratiot, Fur Trader: The Nomadic Years, 1769–1797" (Ph.D. diss., St. Louis Univ., 1971).

TIMOTHY R. MAHONEY

GRATTAN, Clinton Hartley (19 Oct. 1902–25 June 1980), writer and educator, was born in Wakefield, Massachusetts, the son of Leonard E. Grattan and Laura Campbell. Immediately after graduating from Clark College (now Clark University) with a B.A. in 1923, he served as head of the English Department at Urbana (Ohio) Junior College, until 1925. He then moved to Greenwich Village in New York City to become a freelance writer. His first publication, which appeared in editor H. L. Mencken's *American Mercury* in May 1924, was a thoroughly researched, sparkling essay downgrading poet and essayist James Russell Lowell by declaring his work passé. Beginning in the late 1920s, Grattan proved his competence and versatility as a freelance article writer. In 1925 he interviewed stage ingénue Beatrice Kay, and the two soon fell in love. They were married in 1926 and sailed the following year to Australia, where the talented actress went on tour with the musical *Sunny*. This trip was a turning point in Grattan's life. He became permanently captivated by Australia's geography, people, history, and culture. His several books on Australia, the result of later visits there—in 1936–1938, 1960, 1971, and 1975—represent his most significant work.

In 1934 Grattan and his wife, who had no children, were divorced. (Beatrice Kay later won considerable popularity as a featured singer in a radio series titled "Gay Nineties Review.") In 1936 the Carnegie Corporation of New York commissioned Grattan to study Australian economics, politics, and culture. He spent from December 1936 through September 1938 traveling in and around Australia on the project. In 1939 he married Marjorie Sinclair Campbell; the couple had four children.

Grattan produced a stream of books in addition to more than 200 articles for the *American Mercury*, *Harper's*, the *Nation*, the *New York Times Book Review*, the *New York World-Telegram*, the *North American Review*, *Scribner's*, and other periodicals, on subjects as diverse as economics, history, literature, politics, and sociology. His books ranged over several specific fields as well. In *Why We Fought* (1929) Grattan discussed the causes of World War I, analyzed wartime propaganda from the European belligerents, studied America's economic reasons for wanting an Allied victory, and surveyed American diplomacy. Generally well received, *Why We Fought* was criticized by a few specialists as somewhat derivative, hasty in spots, and inconclusive. Grattan's *Bitter Bierce: A Mystery of American Letters* (1929) presented known events in writer Ambrose Bierce's puzzling life and discussed his literary works and the salient ideas therein, somewhat improperly discounting Bierce's acrid philosophy and wit. In 1930 Grattan edited, and contributed an essay to, *Critique of Humanism: A Symposium*. This eclectic attack on the New Humanists of the 1920s, who loftily stressed the essential decency in people, the freedom of their will, and the supremacy of reason, augmented Grattan's reputation as a cultural critic. *The Three Jameses, a Family of Minds: Henry James, Sr., William James, Henry James* (1932) represents his finest work in literary criticism. A composite biography, it examined the physical, social, and intellectual ambiance of three remarkable members of a distinguished American family and their value in the evolution of the American mind.

Grattan's next significant work, *Introducing Australia* (1942), was a valuable, skillful, and concise survey, which had the advantage of timeliness. America had just entered World War II, and Australia was an ally about which too little was known. Grattan supplemented this discussion of Australian geography, history, economics, social conditions, policies, and culture with his *Lands Down Under* in 1943. In the midst of other work, he turned to the subject of adult education. His pioneering *In Quest of Knowledge: An Historical Perspective on Adult Education* (1955) surveyed the Western European history of the subject from preliterate times to the Industrial Revolution, then concentrated on specific British and American efforts in the field of adult education. The book was adversely criticized because it appeared to suffer from a paucity of material on which to base more objective research and conclusions. It was nevertheless soon translated into several foreign languages, including Hindi, Indonesian, Persian, and Urdu. He followed it with *American Ideas about Adult Education 1910–1951* (1959).

In the early 1960s Grattan produced his most significant works on Australia and its environs: *The United States and the Southwest Pacific* (1961), *The Southwest Pacific to 1900, a Modern History: Australia, New Zealand, the Islands, Antarctica* (1963), and companion volume *The Southwest Pacific since 1900, a Modern History: Australia, New Zealand, the Islands, Antarctica* (1963). Taken together, these books presented the political, economic, and cultural history of Australians and their neighbors, analyzed the actions and influence of European settlers, stressed American interests in Antarctica, and dealt with problems resulting from America's displacement of Great Britain as a military force in the Southwest Pacific. Grattan was widely praised both for his command of the material and for his crisp style.

Grattan also completed Paxton Hibben's harsh *Peerless Leader: William Jennings Bryan* (1929; rev. ed., 1973), and contributed essays to *Oceania and Be-*

yond: Essays on the Pacific since 1945, edited by F. P. King (1976), and other books. He edited Timothy Flint's 1826 classic, *Recollections of the Last Ten Years*, in 1932 and edited essays in a book titled *Australia* in 1947.

In 1964 Grattan accepted an appointment to lecture, with the rank of professor, on the history of the Southwest Pacific, at the University of Texas, in Austin. He was also appointed curator of the sizable Grattan Collection of Southwest Pacificana housed there. He continued in this dual capacity at the university until his retirement in 1974. In about 1960 and again in 1978, in response to questionnaires, Grattan wrote to the editors of *Contemporary Authors* (1962, 1981) that his expertise concerning the Southwest Pacific region had been superimposed on a preoccupation with America and, further, that his academic career was less important to him than his lifelong commitment to writing. He died in Austin.

• *The Oxford Companion to Australian Literature*, ed. William H. Wilde et al. (1985), has an informative, complimentary entry for Grattan. An obituary is in the *New York Times*, 30 June 1980.

ROBERT L. GALE

GRATZ, Barnard (1738?–20 Apr. 1801), and **Michael Gratz** (1740?–8 Sept. 1811), Jewish colonial and revolutionary merchants, were born in Langensdorf, Upper Silesia, the sons of Solomon Gratz, a moderately successful dry goods merchant. (Their mother's name has not been recorded.) Barnard attended school before his parents died in the late 1740s; he went in 1750 to London to work in the export and import business of his cousin Solomon Henry. While in London Barnard continued to study Hebrew, learned English, mathematics, and geography, and, of more importance, acquired business knowledge and skills. While working in Henry's business, he bought and sold sugar, tea, lumber, and textiles. The business opportunities in America and the close connections between Solomon Henry and David Franks suggest why Gratz decided in 1754 to go to Philadelphia to work in Franks's lucrative countinghouse. Barnard Gratz helped to keep the firm's books and thus developed a sense of prudence and discretion in business affairs. He was placed in charge of many accounts of Franks, working with clients in Newport, New York, Lancaster, and other colonial cities. Barnard purchased and sold furs, food, and apparel and helped to expand the firm's markets for these and other products. He left the employment of Franks in 1758 and that year became a business partner of Benjamin M. Clava. His business venture with Clava was not particularly successful, but the partnership Barnard formed with his brother Michael in 1759 proved to be a lucrative enterprise in colonial and revolutionary Philadelphia. In 1760 Barnard married Richea Myers; they had two children, only one of whom survived to adulthood.

Similar to that of Barnard, the early career of Michael Gratz revolved around merchant life. Michael's early education in Langensdorf consisted of courses in German, Hebrew, Yiddish, mathematics, and history. Michael followed his brother to London in 1756 to apprentice in the business of Solomon Henry. The adventuristic Michael in 1757 was given funds by Henry and was instructed to buy merchandise and to open new markets for his cousin's firm in India. He spent a little more than a year in India, developed some business contacts, returned to London in 1759, and sailed in April of that year for America. After his arrival in Philadelphia, Michael for a brief time also worked for Franks, learning to "keep shop" and selling hats, sheep shears, and knives and forks to importers in India. After the formation in 1759 of the partnership of B. and M. Gratz, Michael diligently worked from its headquarters on Fourth Street between Market and Chestnut to expand business operations in America, in the West Indies, and in Europe. In 1769 Michael married Miriam Simon of Lancaster; they had twelve children.

The Gratz brothers between 1769 and 1775 became involved in major business, political, and religious activities in colonial Philadelphia. Between 1760 and 1765 the brothers developed markets in many places. They imported sugar, chocolate, and rum from Curacao and St. Eustatius; sent shoes and leather goods to merchants in Quebec; and sold tobacco, coffee, kettles, and iron bars to those in London and Bristol. They also played an active role in the American coastal trade during the last years of the French and Indian War, selling grains, lumber products, hardware, clothes, and jewelry to merchants in Newport, New York, Charleston, and Savannah. To enhance their position in the coastal trade, the Gratzes purchased the ship *Rising Sun*. Problems, however, with England concerning the passage of the Stamp Act led the Gratzes on 2 October 1765, along with other Philadelphia merchants, to sign the first nonimportation resolutions, which greatly reduced trade with Britain. After 1765 the Gratzes became "western men" and attempted to open the West for settlement and commercial activities. Through their agent George Croghan, in 1766 and 1767 they sold food and clothes to settlers and American Indians in the vicinity of Fort Pitt and purchased furs and deerskins from them. The Gratz brothers in 1768 entered into an agreement with Joseph Simon and Levy Andrew Levy of Lancaster to promote the development of the Illinois colony. They provided funds that year for William Murray's expedition to Illinois and greatly profited from cargoes sent to settlements at Kaskaskia and Fort Chartres. Between 1770 and 1774 the Gratzes became involved in land companies to promote their western interests. As a result of their holdings in the Indiana Land Company, they operated a boat line from Fort Pitt and, without much success, tried to establish posts along the Ohio River in Kentucky and Indiana between 1770 and 1772. In 1773 they acquired shares in the Vandalia Company and unsuccessfully attempted to set up a settlement at Louisville. Having purchased the merchandise and land of the bankrupt firm of Baynton, Wharton, and Morgan in 1771, the Gratzes in 1773, along with Simon, Franks, and other investors, assumed an active leadership role in the newly created Illinois and Wabash Company and succeeded in developing new posts and markets in the Illinois country. In addition to their business ventures, the Gratzes were actively involved in the Mikveh Israel congregation. They purchased books and materials for this congregation, which first met in Cherry Alley. In February 1773, three years prior to the War of Independence, Barnard Gratz was elected as president, or *parnas*, of Mikveh Israel.

The Gratz brothers, in various ways, supported the cause of the American Revolution. They gave the patriots aid and were quite mobile during the War for Independence. In 1776 Barnard, from the firm's Pittsburgh store, sold needed clothes, shoes, blankets, and rifles to the Continental army; he returned to Philadelphia the next year to take the oath of allegiance to the Commonwealth of Pennsylvania and to the United States on 5 November. During the first four years of the war, Michael conducted business in Virginia; he sold American troops uniforms, food, and tobacco between 1776 and 1777, became involved in 1778 in the military supplies business with Carter Braxton, and the next year purchased shares in the ships *Neptune* and *General Mercer* in an effort to increase his shipping business. After the British left Philadelphia in 1778, Barnard Gratz returned to the city the next year, was named as secretary of the Illinois and Wabash Company, and with his brother continued during the war to support efforts to establish settlements in the Illinois colony. The Gratzes in 1781 formed a partnership with John Gibson to operate the firm's store in Pittsburgh and in July of that year provided military supplies to members of the George Rogers Clark expedition to Detroit.

Barnard Gratz continued to play an important role in Jewish activities in Philadelphia and also helped to promote efforts to end Jewish civil disabilities. With the Nathans of New York, the DaCostas of Charleston, the Sheftalls of Savannah, and members of other Jewish families who had come to Philadelphia to back the cause of the patriots after the British evacuated the capital, on 16 June 1782 he helped lay the cornerstone of the city's first synagogue, Mikveh Israel; on 13 September of that year he participated in its dedication ceremonies. In 1783 Barnard protested the clause of the Pennsylvania constitution that required Jews to recognize the "Scriptures of the Old and New Testaments" and, until its repeal in 1790, barred Jews from holding political office in that state. In 1797 Barnard Gratz and his son-in-law Solomon Etting spoke against a Maryland law that precluded Jews from holding political office in that state; this law was not repealed until 1824.

The closing decade of the eighteenth century witnessed the decline of the Gratz firm, a result of the advancing age of Barnard and Michael. Michael was actively involved in business until the decline of his health in 1798; he passed on the reins of the business to his sons Simon and Hyman. They decided to dissolve B. and M. Gratz in 1799 and to start their own firm. Barnard Gratz died during a visit to the Ettings in Baltimore. Michael Gratz died in Philadelphia and was buried in the Mikveh Israel cemetery. Of his children, the educator and philanthropist Rebecca Gratz was the best known.

Barnard and Michael Gratz were major contributors to colonial and revolutionary America. Their business and land ventures reveal much about the success of merchant capitalism and western expansionism in eighteenth-century America. They did much to develop the Philadelphia Jewish community and became strong advocates of the republican ideologies of the American Revolution. Similar to other members of minority groups who have come to American shores, the Gratzes believed in pluralism and consequently campaigned for the cause of political and civil emancipation of Jews in the early republic.

• There are many primary sources concerning the careers of Barnard and Michael Gratz. *The Gratz Papers, 1750–1830* (1915) were edited by William V. Byars and are on microfilm. Byars also edited *B. and M. Gratz: Merchants in Philadelphia, 1754–1798* (1916), which includes important letters and documents relating to their business careers. This work in many instances offers detailed explanations of their correspondence. The Historical Society of Pennsylvania, the Library Company of Philadelphia, the American Jewish Archives, and the American Jewish Historical Society house extensive collections of primary materials about the Gratzes. For a review of the primary and secondary sources relating to the Gratz brothers, see the bio-bibliographical essay by William Weisberger, "Barnard and Michael Gratz," in *Research Guide to American Historical Biography*, vol. 5 (1991), pp. 2537–42.

Although a comprehensive biography about the Gratzes has yet to be written, there are accounts concerning major facets of their lives. The best treatment of the business careers of the Gratzes is found in Jacob R. Marcus, *Early American Jewry*, vol. 2 (1955). Anita L. Lebeson, *Pilgrim People* (1975), and Jacob R. Marcus, *The Colonial American Jew* (3 vols., 1970), explain the involvement of the Gratzes in the western movement and their role as military contractors during the American Revolution. Edwin Wolf II and Maxwell Whiteman, *The History of the Jews of Philadelphia from Colonial Times to the Age of Jackson* (1956), and H. S. Morais, *The Jews of Philadelphia* (1894), examine the contributions of the Gratzes to eighteenth-century Philadelphia Jewry. Terse yet incisive accounts about the importance of the Gratzes in American history are found in Jacob R. Marcus, *United States Jewry, 1776–1985*, vol. 1 (1989), and in Howard M. Sachar, *A History of the Jews in America* (1992).

WILLIAM WEISBERGER

GRATZ, Rebecca (4 Mar. 1781–27 Aug. 1869), pioneer Jewish charitable worker and religious educator, was born in Philadelphia, Pennsylvania, the daughter of Michael Gratz, of Silesia, a merchant shipper, and Miriam Simon, of Lancaster, Pennsylvania. Gratz grew up in Philadelphia's wealthy society, and her brothers expanded the family financial interests to the West.

Gratz attended society balls and was part of a circle of young writers, including Washington Irving and James Kirke Paulding, who contributed to the Port Folio literary magazine, although she herself never published. After abandoning poetry, Gratz confined her literary talent to an extensive correspondence. Her correspondents included Maria Edgeworth, Catherine Sedgwick, and Fanny Kemble. The children of Alexander Hamilton (1755–1804), publisher John Fenno, and Rev. John Ewing, provost of the University of Pennsylvania, were among her closest friends. Irving asked Gratz to introduce Thomas Sully in Philadelphia when the artist moved there. The collected Gratz family portraits include many by Sully and by Edward Malbone and Gilbert Stuart.

Well educated for her day, Gratz attended women's academies and read the good literature, histories, and popular science in her father's extensive library. To it, Gratz herself added Judaica. Gratz remained unmarried and lived with her three bachelor brothers and an unmarried sister who died in 1817. In addition to synagogue activities and Gratz's own organizations, the Gratz siblings promoted the city's Athenaeum, the Deaf and Dumb Home, the Academy of Fine Arts, and various libraries.

At twenty, Gratz joined her mother, sister, and twenty other women, Jewish and Gentile, to found the nonsectarian Female Association for the Relief of Women and Children in Reduced Circumstances (c. 1801). Gratz was its first secretary and held that office for many years. In 1815 Gratz helped establish the Philadelphia Orphan Asylum and served as secretary for its first forty years. In the 1830s Gratz advised her sister-in-law on creating and running the first orphan asylum in Lexington, Kentucky.

Noting that Christian charitable women evangelized while aiding the poor, Gratz became convinced that Philadelphia's Jewish women and children needed their own charitable institution. In 1819 she gathered women of her congregation to found the Female Hebrew Benevolent Society, the country's first Jewish charity not directly connected to a synagogue. The FHBS provided food, fuel, shelter, and later an employment bureau and traveler's aid service. The FHBS served only Jewish women and their children but later coordinated its efforts with those of sewing and fuel societies serving needy local Jews. Gratz offered significant advice and aid to these societies as well. The FHBS remained an independent society.

Gratz's religious beliefs reflected her participation in Mikveh Israel, the oldest synagogue in Philadelphia. Although Gratz, like most Jewish women and some men, knew no Hebrew, her congregation's early use of prayer books imported from England, with English translations on facing pages, allowed her a satisfying and devoted synagogue experience throughout her life.

Around 1818 Gratz organized an informal Hebrew school in her home for the children of her extended family, instructed by a young rabbi hoping for employment at the synagogue to which she belonged.

Gratz thought that the freedom offered by the United States signaled the dawn of a new era free of religious persecution. She expected that under this freedom Jews would embrace their religion and bring their collective observance to new heights. Consequently, she was appalled by Judaism's nascent Reform movement, which renounced Zion and diminished ritual.

Gratz was the first to apply the Sunday school format to Jewish education. The FHBS women had hoped to provide religious education, but they were unable to do so until 1838 when Gratz established the Hebrew Sunday School (HSS), a coeducational institution, with herself as superintendent. She also served as secretary of the managing society and held both offices until she was in her eighties. Her sister congregants, Simha Peixotto and Rachel Peixotto Pyke, who ran a school in their home, joined her as teachers, and the Peixotto sisters wrote most of the textbooks initially used by the school. Students ranged in age from early childhood to early teens. The HSS soon attracted students and faculty throughout Philadelphia, and it continues to be an independent, citywide institution. The HSS offered Jewish women their first public role in teaching religion and determining curriculum in a Jewish school. Its teacher-training program offered them a religious education. Only female graduates were invited to join the faculty. Gratz advised Jewish women in Charleston, Savannah, and Baltimore on establishing similar schools. Gratz's efforts prompted the country's leading Jewish educators, especially Isaac Leeser, who wrote and translated Jewish catechisms for the school, to provide materials for their use. Leeser publicized the HSS and encouraged Jewish women around the country to take similar action.

By the 1840s Gratz happily noted that Jewish women were "becoming quite literary." She touted books by Grace Aguilar, a British writer who extolled Judaism and argued its importance to women, and she used Aguilar's books in the HSS. Gratz hoped the school would demonstrate that Jewish women equaled Christian women in religious piety, then considered a mark of civility. The school flourished, opened several branches, and served over 4,000 students by the end of the century.

The plight of an increasing number of Jewish immigrants in the 1850s convinced Gratz of the need for a Jewish foster home. Jewish orphan associations in New York and New Orleans, which relied on foster families, grew inadequate as immigration increased. The elderly Gratz became vice president of the Jewish Foster Home managing society, which later merged with several other institutions to form Philadelphia's Association for Jewish Children. Gratz died in Philadelphia.

By the end of her life, a legend about Gratz claimed her as the prototype for the character of Rebecca of York in Sir Walter Scott's novel *Ivanhoe*, the first favorable depiction of a Jew in English fiction. Jews pointed to Gratz, an Americanized Jewish woman who retained her Jewish loyalty, to argue the truth of the popular tale.

• Important collections of Gratz's letters are housed in the American Jewish Archives (Cincinnati), the American Jewish Historical Society (Boston), the American Philosophical Association (Philadelphia), and the Miriam Moses Cohen Papers in the Southern Historical Collection (University of North Carolina, Chapel Hill). David Philipson, *Letters of Rebecca Gratz* (1929), is an important source, although the letters are edited. See also Jacob Rader Marcus, *Memoirs of American Jews* (1955). Recent assessments of Gratz's life are in Ann Braude, "The Jewish Woman's Encounter with American Culture," in *Women and Religion in America*, ed. Rosemary Reuther and Rosemary Keller, vol. 1 (1981); Evelyn Bodek, "Making Do: Jewish Women and Philanthropy," in *Jewish Life in Philadelphia, 1830–1940*, ed. Murray Friedman (1983); and Dianne Ashton, "Souls Have No Sex": Philadelphia Jewish Women and the American Challenge," in *When Philadelphia Was the Capital of Jewish America*, ed. Murray Friedman (1993). See also Joseph Rosenbloom, "Rebecca Gratz and the Jewish Sunday School Movement in Philadelphia," *Publications of the American Jewish Historical Society* 47, no. 2 (1958): 71–75, and "Some Conclusions about Rebecca Gratz," in *Essays in American Jewish History* (1958). For an earlier assessment of Gratz's life, see Rollin G. Osterweis, *Rebecca Gratz: A Study in Charm* (1935). Other important sources are Joseph Rosenbloom, "And She Had Compassion: The Life and Times of Rebecca Gratz" (Ph.D. diss., Hebrew Union College, 1957); Leonard I. Beerman, "An Analysis of the Foremost Jewess of the Nineteenth Century as Reflected in Hitherto Unpublished Source Materials" (ordination thesis, Hebrew Union College, 1949); and Dianne Ashton, "Rebecca Gratz and the Domestication of American Judaism" (Ph.D. diss., Temple Univ., 1986). See also important material on the Gratz family in Edwin Wolf and Maxwell Whiteman, *The History of the Jews of Philadelphia from Colonial Times to the Age of Jackson* (1957). For older sources on Gratz see William V. Byars, ed., *B. and M. Gratz, Merchants in Philadelphia, 1754–1798* (1916); Sara H. Mordecai, *Recollections of My Aunt Rebecca Gratz* (1893); and Mary M. Cohen, *An Old Philadelphia Cemetery: The Resting Place of Rebecca Gratz* (1920). For the *Ivanhoe* legend see Gratz Van Rensselaer, "The Original of Rebecca in *Ivanhoe*," *Century Magazine*, Sept. 1882, which first popularized the legend; Joseph Jacobs, "The Original of Scott's Rebecca," *Publications of the American Jewish Historical Society* 22 (1914): 53–60; and W. S. Crockett, *The Scott Originals* (1912); but compare the dissenting views of Rosenbloom, Wolf and Whiteman, and Ashton.

DIANNE ASHTON

GRAU, Maurice (1849–14 Mar. 1907), music and theater impresario, was born in Brno, Moravia, the son of Emmanuel Grau and Rosalie (maiden name unknown). In about 1854 he immigrated with his parents to New York City, where they ran a boardinghouse. Grau began working in the theater for his uncle Jacob Grau while studying at the College of the City of New York. Upon graduating in 1867, he enrolled at Columbia Law School. But, preferring his uncle's profession, Grau left without graduating, instead holding "about every place that one can hold in the theater, except on the stage." Other members of Grau's family involved in theater management included a brother, two cousins, and a second uncle. Information regarding Grau's marital status is sketchy. Biographical sources indicate that he married Marie Durand in 1883, but obituaries list his widow as Jeannette.

Grau's first enterprises set the tone for his future as a manager. In 1872–1873 he ran the successful American tour of Aimée, a French opéra bouffe singer, and the joint tour of pianist Anton Rubinstein and violinist Henryk Wieniawski. From then on and with notable exceptions (e.g., Clara Louise Kellogg and Lillian Russell), Grau specialized in importing European musical and theatrical talent. His clients included the stars of the day. With Henry E. Abbey, Grau managed the English actors Ellen Terry and Henry Irving, the American tour of Jacques Offenbach, several French opéra bouffe companies, and tours of Sarah Bernhardt and Adelina Patti. In 1899 the French government made Grau a knight of the Legion of Honor for his services to French culture.

Grau's greatest success, however, came at the Metropolitan Opera. At its opening in 1883, he worked as acting manager for Abbey and John B. Schoeffel: the couple, however, was not asked to remain for the following season. In 1891 the three were invited back to perform under the corporate name of Abbey, Schoeffel, and Grau. Although the Metropolitan's seasons were successful, the firm lost money on other ventures, and in 1896 indebtedness forced a corporate restructuring. After Abbey's death in October of that year, Grau formed the Maurice Grau Opera Company, which performed at the Metropolitan from 1897 to 1903. He also managed London's Covent Garden from 1898 to 1900, bringing many of the operas produced in London during the spring and summer, along with their casts, to New York for the following winter season. In 1903 heart disease forced Grau to retire, and he joined his wife and daughter at Croissy-Chatou near Paris, where he died.

Grau's financial ups and downs exemplify the risks taken by many nineteenth-century impresarios and the potential for extremes of success and failure. But his eventual prosperity (he reportedly left an estate of over $600,000) convinced contemporaries that opera could be at once financially viable and artistically sound. Grau's key to success at the Metropolitan lay in the all-star casts that performed there. By expanding the size of the company, Grau ensured that several top-ranked singers, rather than the customary one or two, would appear in each performance. For the first time, the company included specialists in French, Italian, and German opera, enabling Grau to produce original-language performances that attracted large audiences and won critical acclaim. While generally favoring proven works, Grau took chances on new operas, staging such works as Ignacy Paderewski's *Manru* (1900), which he took on tour, and Ethel Smyth's *Der Wald* (1901), a production to which Grau invited the composer. He produced the American premiere of Puccini's *Tosca* in 1901 and the Metropolitan's first uncut production of Wagner's *Der Ring des Nibelungen* cycle in 1889. Ever looking out for new talent, Grau recruited Enrico Caruso, who first sang at the Metropolitan under Grau's successor, Heinrich Conried. Grau also expanded the company's touring schedule; in 1901–1902 the Metropolitan gave 145 performances

in twenty-seven cities, introducing the company to Atlanta, Birmingham, and Houston, among others.

Single-minded, tireless, self-effacing, and energetic, Grau was intrigued by the management problems
intrinsic to opera production yet remained indifferent
to its glamour. He also was regarded as an astute manager who helped to put the financially shaky Metropolitan on firm ground. He thus earned the confidence of
the patrons and the loyalty of most of his singers,
whom he paid well and who considered him kind,
courteous, and fair.

• Henry E. Krehbiel, *Chapters of Opera*, 2d ed. (1909), gives
an insightful firsthand account of Grau's Metropolitan career. Paul E. Eisler, *The Metropolitan Opera: The First Twenty-five Years, 1883–1908* (1984), documents and summarizes
Grau's achievement. Both writers offer year-to-year performance chronicles. Obituaries are in the *New York Times, New
York Daily Tribune,* and *New York Herald,* 15 Mar. 1907.

KAREN AHLQUIST

GRAUPNER, Gottlieb (6 Oct. 1767–16 Apr. 1836), musician and music publisher, was born Johann Christian Gottlieb Graupner in Verden, Germany, the son
of Johann Georg Graupner, an honored Hanover musician, and Anna Maria Agnesa Schoenhagen. He apparently bore no relation to famed composer Christoph Graupner of Darmstadt. At age fifteen Gottlieb
followed his father's profession and joined the nearby
Hanover regiment as an oboist. After his father's death
Gottlieb was discharged in 1788 and traveled to London where, in 1791–1792, he performed under Joseph
Haydn in the premieres of the first set of his "London"
symphonies. Graupner then immigrated to the United
States, probably through Prince Edward Island off the
coast of Canada. He gained employment as a musician
in a traveling Atlantic coast theater company on the
West and Rignall circuit. In April 1796 he married
Catherine Comerford Hillier, a widow with three children, a professional singer, and a member of the company. The Graupners settled in Boston in the winter of
1796–1797 and worked to improve the musical quality
of Boston's cultural life.

Once in Boston, Graupner organized subscription
concerts, accepted students on several musical instruments (oboe, flute, doublebass viol, guitar, and piano), and composed music. In 1801, with partners
Francis Mallet and Filippo Trajetta, Graupner established a music teaching studio (his "American Conser-
vatorio" or "Music Academy") at 6 Franklin Street, a
portion of which served as the Graupners' first Boston
home. With Mallet, Graupner started a rental library,
ostensibly for students, that they called the "Music
Repository"; but Graupner soon began to engrave,
publish, and retail music for the general public. Mallet
and Trajetta left the business in 1802, shortly after
Graupner began these activities. Graupner abandoned
the lending library but expanded both the academy
and his publishing business. From 1802 into the mid-
1920s he shipped printed music for resale to dealers in
Philadelphia, New York, Providence, Albany, Portland, and Newport. Graupner issued more than 200

imprints consisting principally of popular ballads;
short piano pieces; instruction books for clarinet,
flute, and piano; and collections of music from other
publishers in his *Musical Magazine* (1803–1805), *The
Monitor* (1806), and the *Anacreontic Vocalist* (1809).
Because of his success, Graupner is considered the
most important Boston music publisher of the first
quarter of the nineteenth century. Graupner also re-
tailed and wholesaled musical instruments and supplies, most of which he imported from Clementi in
London.

In addition to music publishing, retailing, teaching,
and developing subscription concerts in and around
Boston, Graupner and a violinist named Ostinelli created an orchestra of professional and amateur musicians called the Boston Phil-Harmonic Society.
Graupner played either oboe or doublebass, his favorites among the many instruments he played well, according to his stepdaughter Catherine Stone. The society, active from about 1810 until 1824, performed in
Graupner's concerts, hired out to other promoters,
and generally functioned as did city musicians in
Graupner's native Germany. Business records for
1816 indicate that Graupner netted almost $800 on a
series of summer concerts that included expenses for
fireworks and other entertainments.

In 1815 Graupner, A. Peabody, and Thomas Smith
Webb, a prominent Bostonian and high-order Freemason, invited Boston's singers to a March meeting in
Graupner's Music Hall to examine the need for a choral society. About fifty men, including Graupner, registered for membership that same evening in the soon-
to-be-influential Boston Handel and Haydn Society.
Webb was elected president, a post he held until his
death. The society enacted a bylaw prohibiting payment for services to any of its members. Shortly thereafter Graupner resigned his membership. He remained interested in the Handel and Haydn Society,
however; he sold or rented music and instruments to
the society at wholesale rates and performed as a freelance musician or with his Phil-Harmonic Society for
some of their concerts. His wife often sang the soprano
solos.

In 1818 Graupner hired Samuel Wetherbee to do
his music engraving, and he accepted some furniture
on consignment for sale in his store in the same year;
both of these represented departures from the successful ways he had been doing business. After his wife's
death in 1821, Graupner married Mary Hills. In 1825
Graupner's business activity began to decline. He died
in Boston.

Graupner was perhaps the first American entrepreneurial (as opposed to institutional) professional musician. "A tall, rather austere man, . . . of precise speech
and manner," according to Catherine Stone, Graupner
seemed determined to support his family by his musical skills. To accomplish this, he created a demand for
musical instruments, music publications, and musical
performers' services through his academy, his subscription concerts, and the music organizations he
helped to establish. The musical climate he, his associ-

ates, and his first wife created in Boston served as the foundation for the more publicized activities of leaders like Lowell Mason, George Webb, William C. Woodbridge, and others in the middle half of the century. To this second generation of Boston music activists we owe the American public school music program, a higher musical standard of hymnody, and the choral society movement of the later nineteenth century.

• Graupner's business records are in the John Hay Library at Brown University, Providence, R.I. A typescript of Catherine Stone's recollections and investigations into her stepfather's life is located in the Boston Public Library. The Newberry Library of Chicago and the John Hay Library hold most of his imprints. Most accounts of music in early Boston and most large music reference works contain biographical sketches of Graupner. Richard J. Wolfe's *Secular Music in America, 1801–1825* (1964) and *Early American Music Engraving and Printing* (1980), along with H. Earle Johnson's *Musical Interludes in Boston, 1795–1830* (1943) and the Sonneck-Upton Bibliography of Early Secular American Music (1945), contain more extensive information about Gottlieb Graupner.

J. TERRY GATES

GRAVES, Alvin Cushman (4 Nov. 1909–29 July 1965), physicist, was born in Washington, D.C., the son of Herbert C. Graves, a civil engineer and captain with the U.S. Coast and Geodetic Survey, and Clara Edith Walter, a teacher and census bureau clerk. He attended Eastern High School in Washington, excelling in oratory. He then entered the University of Virginia, from which he graduated at the head of his class in 1931 with a B.S. in electrical engineering.

Graves spent a postgraduate year at the Massachusetts Institute of Technology (MIT). While there, he developed an interest in nuclear physics after reading a book on the subject by the physicist Enrico Fermi. The Great Depression was under way and job opportunities were scarce, so Graves idealistically pursued his new interest rather than an engineering career. "I decided I didn't want to go by the book all my life," he later explained (Becker, p. 186). Around 1935 he won a graduate fellowship to study physics at the University of Chicago. While there he showed another physics doctoral student, Elizabeth Riddle, how to focus her microscope. They grew close and married in 1937; they had three children. In 1939 he received his doctorate upon completing his thesis, "The Packing Fraction Difference among Heavy Elements." Graves and his wife moved to Texas, where he taught physics at the University of Texas at Austin.

A few weeks after the Japanese attacked Pearl Harbor, the University of Chicago physicist Arthur H. Compton phoned Graves and asked him to join a secret military project. MIT had already offered Graves a job working on radar. "I asked Compton whether I could contribute more in his project than in radar, and he said yes," Graves later recalled (Becker, p. 33). Graves and his wife returned to the University of Chicago, where both worked in the Metallurgical Laboratory on an early phase of what would later be called the Manhattan Project. Its goal was to build the atomic bomb.

In 1942 Graves helped his idol Fermi develop a prototype nuclear reactor at the university squash court. Experimenters moved control rods in and out of the reactor to regulate the nuclear reaction. Graves and two associates—a so-called "suicide squad"—stood on a platform over the reactor and held buckets of a cadmium solution. In case the control rods failed, they were to dump the liquid onto the reactor to absorb neutrons and halt the reaction. But the experiment proceeded safely. On the afternoon of 2 December 1942, Fermi announced that a controlled nuclear chain reaction was under way—in his words: "The reaction is self-sustaining."

In 1943 Graves followed Fermi to Los Alamos, New Mexico, to continue their work on the Manhattan Project. The project climaxed in July 1945 with the successful test of a plutonium "implosion" bomb near Alamogordo, New Mexico. With a seismograph and other instruments, Graves and his wife monitored the effects of the first atomic explosion from a motel forty miles away. The blast was so strong that the motel shuddered. The next month, U.S. aircraft dropped atomic bombs on Hiroshima and Nagasaki, Japan. The Japanese government soon surrendered.

At Los Alamos on 21 May 1946, while Graves stood nearby, researcher Louis Slotin performed a "criticality" test on two hemispheres of plutonium for an atomic bomb. Slotin used a screwdriver to hold the hemispheres apart. Suddenly his screwdriver slipped. The hemispheres underwent a brief chain reaction and emitted a burst of intense gamma rays. Frantically, Slotin used his bare hands to separate the hemispheres. He, Graves, and the others suffered radiation injuries. "I'm sorry I got you into this," Slotin told Graves, referring to his own carelessness. "I am afraid that I have less than a fifty-fifty chance of living. I hope you do better than that." After ten days of severe pain, Slotin died.

Meanwhile, Graves spent three weeks in the hospital with radiation injuries that included nausea, exhaustion, and loss of hair on one side of his head. He was sterile for three years. He also suffered a cataract in his left eye that caused deteriorating vision in later years. Atomic Energy Commission (AEC) representatives told him he had received a radiation dose of almost 200 roentgens. In reality, he had received almost 400 roentgens; officials had told him the lower figure "for psychological reasons," as Los Alamos lab director Norris Bradbury later acknowledged (Fradkin, p. 90). Despite his suffering, Graves and the six others recovered. Their ordeal contributed much to knowledge of the biological impact of radioactivity.

In 1947–1948 Graves was the deputy science director of atomic tests in the Pacific Ocean. In 1948 he became the head of the Los Alamos weapons testing division, and in 1951 he was the deputy commander of blasts at Eniwetok Atoll in the Pacific, where concepts for a then-hypothetical new weapon, the hydrogen or fusion bomb, were tested. He served as the test director of U.S. nuclear explosions in Nevada from 1951 to 1954. "There are more than ten thousand steps involved in getting a test to the button-pushing stage," he said (Becker, p. 185). An especially nervous moment came when one bomb failed to detonate. Fearing a delayed blast, he crawled along the ground for 100 yards and examined circuits. The bomb was successfully detonated three days later. Despite a heart attack in January 1956, he continued to supervise tests until almost the end of his life.

Graves regarded himself as a stickler for safety. *Time* magazine (18 Apr. 1955) noted that he had postponed explosions at least fifty times over a fifty-day period. Before a test, Graves typically drove around the test site in a white, radio-equipped car, checking out equipment and talking to employees. He also consulted with weather experts to learn if winds might blow radioactive fallout over inhabited areas. Still, there were accidents: fallout sometimes fell on roads and inhabited areas. This would lead, decades later, to considerable litigation by area residents. As part of the AEC's effort to reassure the public, Graves gave speeches in local communities. Being a radiation survivor, he was an especially impressive witness.

Six feet tall and "outwardly easygoing" (Becker, p. 33), Graves told a writer for the *Saturday Evening Post*: "I am not in the atomic business because I like to manufacture things that kill people. I am thoroughly convinced that the reason we are not in a third World War now is because of the work the United States has done in atomic energy. Increasing our [nuclear] stockpile is our best safeguard for the future" (Becker, p. 33). Graves played the cello in the Los Alamos symphony, taught Sunday school in the local United Church, served on the school board, and cultivated zinnias.

Graves played a central role in testing and verifying the horrifying might of the U.S. atomic arsenal during its first two decades. He died of a heart attack while vacationing with his family in Del Norte, Colorado.

• On 27 May 1957 Graves testified to Congress's Joint Committee on Atomic Energy about the radiation accident; extracts of his remarks appear in "'I Took 200 Roentgens'—Testimony by Dr. Alvin C. Graves, AEC," *U.S. News and World Report*, 21 June 1957. Graves's view on the proposed nuclear test ban is cited in Glenn T. Seaborg and Benjamin S. Loeb, *Kennedy, Khrushchev, and the Test Ban* (1981). *Annals of Internal Medicine* (Feb. 1952) published a 231-page analysis of the radiation accident that befell Slotin, Graves, and the others in 1946. A lengthy profile of Graves is Bill Becker, "The Man Who Sets Off Atom Bombs," *Saturday Evening Post*, 19 Apr. 1952. For another profile see "He Gives the Word," *Time*, 18 Apr. 1955. A critical view of U.S. nuclear tests, including details on Graves's role, is Philip L. Fradkin, *Fallout: An American Nuclear Tragedy* (1989). Numerous references to Graves appear in Barton C. Hacker, *Elements of Controversy: The Atomic Energy Commission and Radiation Safety in Nuclear Weapons Testing, 1947–1974* (1994). An obituary is in the *New York Times*, 30 July 1965.

KEAY DAVIDSON

GRAVES, James Robinson (10 Apr. 1820–26 June 1893), Baptist preacher and editor, was born in Chester, Vermont, the son of Zuinglius Calvin Graves and Lois Schnell, farmers. His father died when Graves was an infant, and he received only rudimentary schooling. At the age of fifteen, he joined a Baptist church, although he had been reared in a Congregationalist family. He compensated for his lack of formal education through intensive private study, both before and after his family moved to Ohio when he was nineteen. He served as a schoolteacher, first at the Kingsville Academy in Kingsville, Ohio, and later at the Clear Creek Academy in Jessamine County, Kentucky. Meanwhile, he studied for the Baptist ministry and was ordained in 1842. He preached in Ohio for a short while before moving in the summer of 1845 to Nashville, Tennessee, where he opened an academy. That year he married Florence Spencer. After she died, he married Lou Snider. After her death, Graves married her sister, Georgie Snider. He had five children who survived him—three from his second marriage and two from his third marriage.

In Nashville, Robert Boyle Crawford Howell, the influential pastor of the First Baptist Church and editor of the *Baptist*, befriended Graves. Through Howell's influence, Graves became pastor of the Second Baptist Church by the fall of 1845, serving there for about a year. In 1846 he became an assistant editor for the *Baptist*. Two years later he succeeded Howell as editor of the renamed *Tennessee Baptist*, and soon after he became the leader of Tennessee Baptists. For the next forty years, Graves used the columns of the *Tennessee Baptist* (or the *Baptist*, as it once more became in 1867) to express his theological and ecclesiological ideas. The newspaper gained wide popularity during the 1850s; its 13,000 subscribers on the eve of the Civil War made it the largest denominational paper in the South and the largest of any sort in the Southwest. His audience extended far outside the boundaries of Tennessee, and the journal was especially popular along the lower Mississippi River. In 1847 Graves expanded his influence even further by organizing a publication society. By 1855 his South-Western Publishing House produced a variety of Baptist literature, which colporteurs sold and distributed across the South.

Graves rose to prominence among Southern Baptists as spokesman for the Landmark movement, which called for the restoration of distinctive, historic Baptist doctrines. Although he did not give the movement its name, he became the most articulate advocate of restoring the "old landmarks." Anxious to preserve a unique Baptist identity, he called for a meeting at Cotton Grove, Tennessee, in the summer of 1851. The "Cotton Grove Resolutions" adopted at this meeting warned churches against accepting members who had not been baptized by immersion in Baptist churches or opening their pulpits to preachers who came from other denominations or preached false ideas about baptism. Two tenets were central to Landmark theology. First, only Baptist churches were true churches, descended in unbroken succession from the first churches in apostolic times. Second, the local Baptist church was completely autonomous and had exclusive jurisdiction over preaching the gospel, conducting baptisms, and celebrating the Lord's Supper.

In 1855 Graves insisted that his newspaper was designed to be "the exponent of true Baptist faith and consistent Baptist practice" and would engage in "ceaseless war with error, whether advocated by Papists, Protestants, or Campbellites." Through his newspaper and his books, he upheld Landmark beliefs in controversies both against other denominations and within the Southern Baptist Convention. In 1858 James Madison Pendleton and Amos Cooper Dayton became assistant editors of the *Tennessee Baptist*, and together this "Great Triumvirate" expounded Landmark doctrines to a broad southern audience.

Landmark ideas divided Southern Baptists in many areas of the South; even in Nashville, Graves's ideas caused division. When Howell returned to Nashville in 1857, he and Graves quickly became embroiled in bitter controversy when Graves attempted to compete with the Southern Baptist Publication Society in supplying Southern Baptists with religious literature. The two men also clashed over control of the Bible Board and over Graves's establishment of a Southern Baptist Sunday School Union, which competed with the Southern Baptist Publication Society as well. The dispute spread into the Baptist press, and the First Baptist Church of Nashville, where Howell was pastor and Graves a member, eventually tried and excluded Graves. The dispute between Graves and Howell reached far beyond Nashville and threatened to divide the denomination. When the Southern Baptist Convention met in 1859, Graves unsuccessfully tried to defeat Howell's reelection as president and launched a broader attack on the convention itself.

The controversies waned during the Civil War. Graves fled Nashville when Union troops occupied the city in 1862. After the war, he moved his publishing activities to Memphis, and in 1867 he restarted the *Baptist*. In the postwar years, he continued to proclaim his Landmark doctrines through the press and from the pulpit with the same conviction, although with a more moderate tone. Through his writings, he also introduced Baptists to a form of dispensational theology, a view that God's interactions with the faithful varied in different periods of history. In August 1884 Graves suffered a stroke that permanently restricted his movements; but he was still able to deliver "chair talks"—sermons preached while sitting. In 1889 he turned his newspaper over to his son-in-law, who moved it back to Nashville and changed the name to the *Baptist and Reflector*. Graves died in Memphis, Tennessee.

Throughout his career as editor, author, and preacher, Graves used controversies to define who Southern Baptists were and who they were not. He wrote hundreds of editorials for the *Tennessee Baptist* between 1846 and 1889. He also authored nearly two dozen books. Graves began his book-length denunciations of other denominations with *Campbell and Camp-

bellism Exposed: A Series of Replies* (1854). In 1855 he published *The Great Iron Wheel; or, Republicanism Backwards and Christianity Reversed*, an assault on the doctrines of the Methodist Episcopal Church, South. During the next six years, the book went through thirty editions, sold nearly 50,000 copies, and provoked a response from Graves's Methodist counterpart, William G. Brownlow, in *The Great Iron Wheel Examined; or, Its False Spokes Extracted and an Exhibition of Elder Graves* (1856). In 1860 Graves attacked the Presbyterians in *The Trilemma; or, Death by Three Horns*. His influence in Southern Baptist life continued well into the twentieth century in the form of persistent localism in ecclesiology, dispensationalism in eschatology that requires a certain sequence of events before the ultimate return of Jesus Christ, and a penchant for literal interpretation of the Bible.

• Besides those works noted above, Graves wrote *The New Great Iron Wheel* (1884), in which he renewed his opposition to the Methodists; *Old Landmarkism: What Is It?* (1880), a classic presentation of Landmark beliefs; *Intercommunion Inconsistent, Unscriptural, and Productive of Evil* (1881); and *The Work of Christ in the Covenant of Redemption: Developed in Seven Dispensations* (1883), in which his mature theology is developed most fully. Despite his importance to the religious life of the Southwest in the nineteenth century, he has been the subject of only one published biography: Orren L. Hailey, *J. R. Graves: Life, Times, and Teachings* (1929), written by his son-in-law. For Graves's conflicts with Howell, see Homer L. Grice and R. Paul Caudill, "Graves-Howell Controversy" in *Encyclopedia of Southern Baptists*, ed. Clifton Judson Allen (1958); and Kenneth Vaughn Weatherford, "The Graves-Howell Controversy" (Ph.D. diss., Baylor Univ., 1991). James E. Tull, *Shapers of Baptist Thought* (1972), includes Graves. An examination of Landmark beliefs is provided in Tull, *A History of Southern Baptist Landmarkism in the Light of Historical Baptist Ecclesiology* (1980). Graves' theology is explored in Harold S. Smith, *Baptist Theologians*, ed. Timothy George and David S. Dockery (1990). Marty G. Bell, "J. R. Graves and the Rhetoric of Demagogy: Primitivism and Democracy in Old Landmarkism" (Ph.D. diss., Vanderbilt Univ., 1990), examines how Graves united political democracy and religious primitivism into a powerful populist ideology.

DANIEL W. STOWELL

GRAVES, William Sidney (27 Mar. 1865–27 Feb. 1940), army officer and author, was born in Mount Calm, Texas, the son of Andrew C. Graves, a Baptist minister and rancher who attended the 1875 Texas constitutional convention, and Evelyn Bennett. Graves taught school in Texas briefly before attending the U.S. Military Academy at West Point, from which he graduated in 1889. He was commissioned a second lieutenant on 12 June 1889 and ordered to Fort Logan, Colorado, where he served with the Seventh Infantry. He married Katherine Boyd in 1891; they had two children. During the 1890s Graves served at various posts, including instructor of small arms practice in the Department of Columbia in the Pacific Northwest from 1897 to 1899 and acting judge advocate from 1898 to 1899 in the Department of Columbia and the Department of Colorado.

In 1899 Graves was ordered to the Philippines with the Twentieth Infantry. He saw action in several campaigns during the Philippine insurrection, including the battle of Caloocan on 31 December 1901, for which he was cited for gallantry. He served again in the Philippines from 1904 to 1906. In April and May 1906 he was posted to San Francisco in the aftermath of the great earthquake.

In 1909 Graves joined the General Staff in Washington, D.C., serving as secretary to the General Staff Corps from January 1911 to July 1912 and again from September 1914 to February 1918. Promoted to the rank of major general in June 1918, Graves took command of the Eighth Infantry Division at Camp Frémont in California, where it was training for service on the western front.

Graves arrived in Palo Alto in July, but on 2 August 1918 he received secret orders to meet with Secretary of War Newton D. Baker in Kansas City, Missouri. There, Baker ordered Graves to Siberia to take immediate command of a small American Expeditionary Force, consisting of two infantry regiments and support units but no artillery. According to Graves's later published account, the secretary warned him of the volatility of the Russian situation, saying "you will be walking on eggs loaded with dynamite."

Baker gave Graves an aide-mémoire written by President Woodrow Wilson and shared with the Allied ambassadors on 17 July 1918. In the absence of a more specific statement of policy, Graves used that document to guide his actions in Russia. It categorically assured the Russian people that there would be no interference with their political sovereignty, intervention in their internal affairs, nor impingement on their territorial rights. The aide-mémoire directed American forces to guard military stores in Vladivostok and along the Trans-Siberian Railroad to prevent their falling into German hands, to aid the fifty to seventy thousand Czechs who had deserted the Austrians and were making their way through Siberia in an effort to join the Allied war effort, and to support efforts at self-government or self-defense by the Russian people if they were willing to accept assistance.

Most historians now believe that the underlying purpose of this American Expeditionary Force was to prevent the expansion of Japan's presence in the area, perhaps even its annexation of some portion of Siberia, an interpretation supported by Graves's reports from the scene. Allied forces included British, French, Japanese, and American troops, as well as smaller Polish, Czech, Chinese, Serbian, Canadian, and Italian contingents. The largest representations were the nearly ten thousand Americans and over seventy thousand Japanese.

During his year and a half in Russia, Graves interpreted his instructions strictly and resisted Allied encouragement to engage the Bolsheviks militarily. Those pressures accelerated after the armistice when the counterrevolutionary Whites, the Bolshevik Reds, and at least two sizable Cossack groups continued fighting one another in Siberia. Graves deplored the cruelty of the Cossacks, whom he believed were being financed and supplied by the Japanese, almost as much as Admiral Aleksandr Vasilevich Kolchak's ineffectual efforts to control them. Accused by the Japanese of sympathy for the Bolsheviks, Graves maintained impartiality toward all factions and abstained from any interference with internal politics. He wryly defined Bolsheviks as anyone in Siberia who did not favor restoration of autocracy.

Graves was also caught up in the conflicting intentions of his own State Department and War Department. His conscientious adherence to neutrality won him growing criticism from Consul General Ernest L. Harris at Irkutsk, Ambassador David R. Francis, and Acting Secretary of State Frank Polk. However, the chief of staff, General Peyton C. March, and Secretary Baker defended Graves and his applications of policy. When British prime minister David Lloyd George complained of Graves to President Wilson during the peace conference, Wilson asserted that any fault must lie elsewhere because Graves was "a man of most unprovocative character."

His World War I service brought Graves the Distinguished Service Medal; the Order of the Rising Sun, second class, from Japan; the Order of the Wen Hu (Striped Tiger) from China; and the War Cross from Czechoslovakia; and he was named a commander of the Order of the Crown of Italy.

In April 1920 Graves was given command of Fort William McKinley in the Philippines where he remained until October of that year. He subsequently commanded the First Brigade of the First Division in New Jersey and New York from December 1920 to April 1925; the First Division in New York from April to July 1925; the Sixth Corps Area, Chicago, from July 1925 to October 1926; and the Panama Canal Department from October 1926 to October 1927. His duties in the 1920s were primarily administrative. He requested retirement in 1928.

In 1931 Graves published *America's Siberian Adventure, 1918–1920*, an account of his assignment in Russia. It was sharply critical of Allied governments and military commanders as well as of the U.S. Department of State for trying to involve American forces in the Russian civil war but was complimentary to the War Department position of nonintervention. He lived in Shrewsbury, New Jersey, until his death there.

Graves had a reputation for loyalty, integrity, and high personal standards as well as kindliness and consideration for his officers and men. Strict attention to duty led him to become the primary custodian of American neutrality among the competing forces in Siberia from 1918 to 1920.

• Official documents of the Siberian expedition are included in *Papers Relating to the Foreign Relations of the United States, 1918, Russia* (3 vols., 1931–1932); *Foreign Relations of the United States, 1919, Russia* (1937); and *Foreign Relations of the United States, The Lansing Papers, 1914–1920* (2 vols., 1939–1940). Studies of the expedition Graves led and the geopolitical climate in which it occurred include John Albert White, *The Siberian Intervention* (1950); Betty Miller Unterberger's definitive study, *America's Siberian Expedition, 1918–1920: A Study of National Policy* (1956); George F. Kennan, *Soviet-American Relations, 1917–1920* (2 vols., 1956); Kennan, *The Decision to Intervene* (1958); Kennan, "Soviet Historiography and America's Role in the Intervention," *American Historical Review* 55 (1960): 302–22; and Robert J. Maddox, *The Unknown War with Russia: Wilson's Siberian Intervention* (1977). The context of American policy and presence in Russia at the end of World War I is discussed in Donald E. Davis and Eugene P. Trani, "The American YMCA and the Russian Revolution," *Slavic Review* 33 (1974): 469–91; Trani, "Woodrow Wilson and the Decision to Intervene in Russia: A Reconsideration," *Journal of Modern History* 48 (1976): 440–61; Trani and David L. Wilson, *The Presidency of Warren G. Harding* (1977); and Trani, "Herbert Hoover and the Russian Revolution, 1917–1920," in *Herbert Hoover: The Great War and Its Aftermath, 1914–1923*, ed. Lawrence E. Gelfand (1979). Obituaries are in the *New York Times* and the *New York Herald Tribune*, 28 Feb. 1940.

EUGENE P. TRANI
SUSAN ESTABROOK KENNEDY

GRAY, Asa (18 Nov. 1810–30 Jan. 1888), botanist, was born in Sauquoit, Oneida County, New York, the son of Moses Gray, a farmer and tanner, and Roxana Howard. He was educated in local schools, then the Fairfield (N.Y.) Academy, and, from 1829 to 1831, the Fairfield Medical School (also known as the College of Physicians and Surgeons of the Western District of New York). In 1831 Gray received his medical degree and for a brief period practiced medicine in western New York. However, his interest in botany, which had begun while he studied at Fairfield Academy, soon won out, and he abandoned his medical career. In 1834, after several years of piecing together a living through teaching, he moved to New York City to work on botanical research and writing with John Torrey. For the next eight years he studied, worked, and at times lived with Torrey. Torrey's status as the young nation's leading botanist provided the best botanical training and mentorship in the country. Torrey graciously shared his expertise and his contacts with Gray. The two evolved rapidly from teacher and student to colleagues, collaborating on a number of projects, most notably the revolutionary but unfinished *Flora of North America* (1838–1843). From 1836 to 1838, Gray served as the botanist of the U.S. Exploring Expedition (known also as the Wilkes Expedition), but repeated and prolonged delays caused him to resign before the expedition actually sailed. In 1842 he became the Fisher Professor of Natural History at Harvard University, a position he held until his death.

Gray's contributions were threefold: scientific, institutional, and pedagogical. With Torrey, Gray introduced the new, natural system of classification—based on biological similarity—then in use in Europe to America to replace the artificial, Linnaean system, which was based on convenient sorting markers. Both felt that adoption of the natural system and of type specimens for the classification of North American flo-

ra (which they also introduced) were crucial to bringing the United States into the world scientific community. The two volumes of the *Flora of North America* that they did complete were the first American attempt at a national flora that employed the natural system. Gray's synthetic works, most notably the *Manual of the Botany of the Northern United States* (1848, and five more editions in his lifetime), provided the United States with a single-volume, natural flora. The high standards of accuracy, scientific rigor, inclusiveness, and user-friendliness it modeled set new standards for regional flora as well.

Gray was one of British naturalist Charles Darwin's most trusted correspondents. Initially Darwin sought information from Gray about the North American flora, especially about issues of biogeography. This correspondence with Darwin led to an interest on Gray's part in the geographical distribution of species. His wide correspondence with amateur botanists throughout the United States allowed him to accurately set the ranges for many species, eventually enabling him to explain why the floras of eastern North America and Japan are more similar than those of eastern and western North America. This work, published in the *Memoirs of the American Academy of Arts and Sciences* (6 [1859]: 377–458), stands as Gray's most enduring piece of research. In it, Gray argued, originally and correctly, that species and genera common to both eastern North America and Japan were not the result of separate creations but rather were descendants of a common stock that moved south and separated during glaciation. Published just before Darwin's *Origin of Species*, this work provided a botanical example, using natural rather than supernatural influences, of the impact of the environment on species, an example that fit well into Darwin's scheme.

Through his Harvard professorship, Gray became the first American to make a living doing botany. His impact as a university teacher was arguably minimal as few of his students became professional botanists. In contrast he trained scores of collectors, raising the standards of how specimens were labeled and preserved and of the information recorded at the time of collection. Gray corresponded widely with both paid collectors and amateurs, who happily sent him specimens and observations in return for help with identifications. The work of both groups was elevated and transformed under his guidance. While Gray had little influence as a teacher himself, the impact of his texts—especially *How Plants Grow* and the *Manual*—on the teaching of botany was pivotal to the popularity of botany among the lay public. His influence made botany the science of choice in many American schools for much of the nineteenth century. His many textbooks for primary school to college level introduced thousands of Americans to botany and dominated the market for several generations.

Gray's impact on the profession of science is more difficult to assess. In exchange for the specimens that he received through his extensive correspondence with collectors throughout North America, Gray sent these amateurs and professionals specimens in trade, identification, information, collecting supplies, and sometimes cash. By greatly expanding the data base from which he was drawing conclusions, the specimens Gray received made his synthetic works possible. While Gray's reliance on specimens collected by others led some contemporaries to label him derisively as a "closet" or "armchair" botanist, history suggests that the enormous strides he made in viewing the North American flora as a whole were only possible because of the huge volume and variety of material he had at his disposal. By carefully instructing his collectors about what to gather, how to preserve it, and, especially, how to label it, Gray ensured the quality of his data base and thereby was able to model a style of botanical work that was new to America and to use it to advance the science.

It is arguable that Gray's greatest contribution to American science resulted from his relationship with Charles Darwin. Gray's work on the link between the floras of eastern North America and Japan arose from Darwin's request that Gray provide him with information about the geographic range of species. Long a trusted correspondent, Gray was one of the small handful of people with whom Darwin had shared his ideas on evolution as they developed. Gray was intrigued by Darwin's line of thought and supportive of Darwin both professionally and personally. One oft-quoted letter from Darwin to Gray begins, "I forget the exact words which I used in my former letter, but I daresay I said that I thought you would utterly despise me, when I told you what views I had arrived at." Clearly Gray's personal support was highly valued by Darwin, who even before the publication of the *Origin of Species* knew he was in for a battle not simply on scientific, but also theological, grounds. When the question of whether Darwin or Alfred Russell Wallace had first developed the idea of natural selection arose, Darwin's letters to Gray stood as evidence of Darwin's primacy. In 1859 Gray strove to ensure that Darwin's *Origin of Species* received a fair reception based on the scientific merits of the work. His review in the *American Journal of Science* (2d ser., 29 [1860]: 153–84), his debates with Louis Agassiz and others, and his later, more popular essays in the *Atlantic Monthly*, reprinted in his *Darwiniana* (1876), paved the way for the widespread acceptance of Darwin's work in the United States. Playing the role parallel to Thomas Huxley's role in Britain, Gray championed the American reception of Darwinian evolution. Philosophically, however, he took a very different tack from Huxley—who saw Darwinism as the triumph of science over religion—in his support of Darwin, arguing that natural selection and Protestant theology are compatible. He used the natural theology, especially the argument that if there is evidence of design then there must have been a designer, to assert that natural selection was simply more proof of God's work in the world. Although Darwin eventually rejected this line of reasoning, his respect and appreciation of Gray's work on behalf of his theory was profound: "No one person understands my views and has defended them so well as A. Gray, though he does not by any means go all the way with me" (Letter to James Dwight Dana, 30 July 1860). The success of Gray's endorsement of Darwin can be measured by the nearly universal acceptance of Darwinian evolution by working naturalists in America within a decade of the publication of the *Origin of Species*.

Gray married in 1848, choosing Jane Lathrop Loring over any of Torrey's daughters, whom many expected him to wed. His choice of a Loring brought him into Boston society, a role he never really enjoyed. Gray died childless in Cambridge. Well loved and respected by his peers who eulogized him as "our greatest botanist" and a "trump in all senses," Gray was a shy man who worked quietly and preferred scholarship to politics. Consequently, despite his scientific and pedagogical importance, he was relatively unknown to historians until the publication in 1959 of A. Hunter Dupree's major biography *Asa Gray: American Botanist, Friend of Darwin*. Today, however, his championing of Darwin and his influence on botanical pedagogy and practice are viewed as of sufficient importance to elevate him to the position of one of the most significant nineteenth-century American scientists.

• The largest collection of archival material on Gray is at the Gray Herbarium, Harvard University. Additional Gray material can be found in the letters of nearly every contemporary American biological scientist and many amateurs. Many of Gray's 780 articles and reviews appeared in the *American Journal of Science*. Collections of his writings include *Scientific Papers of Asa Gray*, ed. Charles S. Sargent (2 vols., 1889) and *Letters of Asa Gray*, ed. Jane Loring Gray (2 vols., 1893). A. Hunter Dupree, *Asa Gray: American Botanist, Friend of Darwin* (1959), is the major source for information on Gray. The most complete bibliography is Serano Watson and G. L. Goodale, "List of the Writings of Dr. Asa Gray, Chronologically Arranged, with an Index," *American Journal of Science* 36 (1888): 3–67 appendix. An obituary is in the *Boston Transcript*, 31 Jan. 1888.

LIZ KEENEY

GRAY, Clarence (14 Nov. 1901–5 Jan. 1957), cartoonist and illustrator, was born in Toledo, Ohio, the son of Val Gray, a store manager, and Laura Jane (maiden name unknown). After graduating from high school, he went to work for the *Toledo News-Bee* in the art department and was later promoted to be the paper's editorial cartoonist. In that capacity he became a respected, even feared, pen-and-ink editorialist, and his reputation was such that his drawings were rumored to have helped elect at least one mayor. At the same time he was contributing cartoons and illustrations to national magazines, and all this activity eventually brought him to the attention of the ever-vigilant William Randolph Hearst, who in 1930 had taken over the Central Press Association, a small syndicate located in neighboring Cleveland. In 1925 Gray had married Jessica Matthews and was now father to three children; when Central Press in the spring of 1933 approached him with a lucrative offer to draw an original newspaper strip they were planning to launch, he promptly accepted and relocated his whole family to Cleveland.

The new feature, called *Brick Bradford*, was the creation of veteran newsman William Ritt; the first daily installment appeared in August 1933, with illustrations by Gray. As originally conceived, Brick was a troubleshooter always ready to take part in any far-flung adventure, from discovering an underwater city deep in the Andes to thwarting a sect of assassins bent on the conquest of the world. Ritt's story lines were intricately plotted and suspense-filled, and Gray rendered them with an uncanny sense of mystery and an awesome power of evocation. Relying almost exclusively on black masses and white spaces, with very few half-tones, he delighted in depicting the action in cinematic terms, with frequent panoramics and lengthy sequences unbroken by any dialogue; his battle scenes and nocturnals were particularly effective.

In November 1934 a weekly page was added to the daily strip, and in this spacious format Gray could give free rein to his talent and flair for showmanship. Fired by Ritt's mythology laden tales, he enfolded his hero in spectacular settings of futuristic cities and primeval jungles, peopled by lost races and legendary monsters, bathing the whole proceedings in an atmosphere of eerie poetry and festive pageantry, to which the use of color added immeasurably. A companion strip, *The Time Top*, made a brief appearance for a few months in 1935, and its invention, the "chronosphere" (a device clearly derived from H. G. Wells's time machine) later found its way into the main feature, allowing Brick to span the eons, from earliest prehistory to the farthest reaches of the future. This plot development further enhanced the artist's opportunity for grandiose spectacle in his depictions of hypertechnological civilizations and primitive societies alike.

The 1940s saw the heyday of the strip. (Columbia Pictures, for instance, released a movie serial, *Brick Bradford, Amazing Soldier of Fortune*, in 1947.) Ritt, however, had become disenchanted with the strip and was leaving more and more of the writing to his collaborator, until Ritt was finally released of his duties. As a result, in 1950 Gray became the sole author of the feature; he intended to concentrate on more concise, more focused stories, but these ambitions were cut short when he was diagnosed with throat cancer later in the year. Inevitably his work began to suffer, and in 1952 he had to relinquish both the drawing and the writing of the daily strip to Paul Norris (who had earlier "ghosted" some sequences Gray had been too ill to draw). Retaining only the Sunday page, he turned it into a series of science-fantasy tales; there were still traces of brilliance in some of the pages, but the old dash was gone. Nevertheless he doggedly kept grinding out the *Brick Bradford* Sundays, now only pale reflections of their earlier incarnation, almost up to the day he finally succumbed to the illness in Rocky River, Ohio.

Clarence Gray was one of the inspired craftsmen of the comics, and *Brick Bradford* numbers among those creations that helped make the adventure strip in the 1930s and 1940s into one of the most exciting features of the daily newspaper as well as one of the most eagerly awaited by its readers (a fact borne out by all surveys of the time). While not on a par with such masters of the form as Hal Foster or Alex Raymond, he is remembered for work that was consistently attractive and involving, at least until illness and fatigue took their toll on him during the final years of his life.

• For more on Clarence Gray's work see Coulton Waugh, *The Comics* (1947); Pierre Couperie and Maurice Horn, *A History of the Comic Strip* (1968); Maurice Horn, ed., *The World Encyclopedia of Comics* (1976); and Ron Goulart, ed., *The Encyclopedia of American Comics* (1990). An obituary is in the *New York Times*, 7 Jan. 1957.

MAURICE HORN

GRAY, Elisha (2 Aug. 1835–21 Jan. 1901), inventor, was born in Barnesville, Ohio, the son of David Gray and Christiana Edgerton, farmers. By the time he was ten, Gray had heard about the first telegraph line, less than a year old, and had contrived his own working instrument. At twelve, after his father died, he quit school and went to work, becoming a carpenter and boat-builder. Meanwhile he read all he could about science, especially electricity, and tinkered with homemade batteries and electromagnets. Encouraged by an Oberlin College professor, he worked his way through preparatory school (1857–1860) and two years at Oberlin (1860–1862). In 1865 he married M. Delia Shepard of Oberlin, Ohio, who bore him one child.

Overwork had nearly wrecked Gray's health, and he was thirty-two by the time he fully established himself as a professional "electrician" (electrical expert) and inventor. In 1867 his first patent, for a telegraphic relay, won him the ongoing patronage of the Western Union Telegraph Company. The superintendent lent him the money to buy a half interest in a Cleveland shop that made telegraph instruments. He and his partner, Enos Barton, moved the shop to Chicago in 1869 and, with other investors representing Western Union, incorporated it in 1872 as the Western Electric Manufacturing Company. In three years Gray was able to sell his interest and to devote himself full time to invention.

In 1867 Gray had briefly experimented with the transmission of tones by sending a current interrupted at a set frequency through the coil of an electromagnet, the pulses of which would vibrate a steel reed tuned to that pitch. Early in 1874 Gray discovered that his young nephew had found a way of producing a sound with the current's frequency by inserting himself in the circuit in series with a zinc bathtub and rubbing the bathtub with his hand. Gray found that if the frequency of the current was varied, the pitch of the whining noise would follow suit. This stirred Gray to experiments with the electrical transmission of a varying frequency to a sounding device that would reproduce it. He evolved a metal diaphragm receiver identical to one devised—unknown to Gray—by Edward C. Pickering four years earlier. The tones Gray proposed to transmit were generated by current-interrupters, not by external sounds. But two months later, also unknown to Gray, Alexander Graham Bell conceived a transmitting device that would pick up sounds and transform them into equivalent electrical frequencies and amplitudes for transmission to a receiver of the Pickering type. In these experiments both Bell and Gray were primarily interested in generating and transmitting several fixed frequencies concurrently, so as to send several messages at once over a single telegraph wire, a goal Bell had already been pursuing for two years. It was this limited quest in which Gray and Bell became conscious rivals through 1875, having learned of each other's work through a mutual acquaintance late in 1874. In June 1875, however, Bell observed an effect that convinced him that his idea for speech transmission was indeed feasible, and in July he succeeded in transmitting vocal sounds, though not of intelligible quality. His backers' insistence that he concentrate on the financially more promising multiple telegraph delayed Bell's telephone patent application until 14 February 1876.

Gray later claimed to have independently conceived the telephone principle in November 1875, inspired by seeing a tin-can-and-string "telephone." However, he neither put his concept on paper nor mentioned it to anyone until he had spent nearly a month in Washington, D.C., making frequent visits to the Patent Office in connection with his multiple-telegraph patent applications, and until Bell's notarized specifications had for several days been the admiration of Patent Office personnel. It was on 14 February 1876, several hours after Bell's formal application was filed, that Gray entered a caveat, a mere notice of an untested idea existing only on paper.

Gray's patent lawyer informed him that by acting promptly Gray could delay the issuance of Bell's patent and file his own application. But Gray was engaged in other matters and saw little commercial value in the telephone, probably because of his long absorption with telegraphy. So he let the opportunity pass. Not until the immense importance of Bell's invention belatedly dawned on Western Union did the company acquire Gray's rights and present his claim to priority as a shield behind which the company could energetically infringe on Bell's patent. The ensuing legal battle inspired charges that Gray had been cheated by the corruption of Patent Office employees. Gray brooded for years, convincing himself that Bell had stolen his idea of a variable resistance transmitter, though Bell's priority in it was documented. If ideas had been stolen, the circumstances would have pointed to Gray as the thief, but a subtle difference between the variable resistance devices of the two men strongly indicates independence of conception. After court testimony and evidence, filling 600 printed pages and as many more pages of documentary exhibits, Western Union in 1879 gave up its case for Gray as hopeless. In hundreds of suits brought by the Bell interests against infringers on the Bell patent during the next decade, the various defendants tried to revive Gray's claim in or-

der to attack the validity of the patent. In every case, including one before the U.S. Supreme Court, Bell's patent was upheld.

Gray went on inventing, mostly in electrical communication, and made frequent contributions to technical journals. His "telautograph," transmitting facsimiles of handwriting, was in use until recent years. From it and about seventy other patented inventions, he made more money than Bell did from the telephone. He was further rewarded by honorary degrees, a French decoration, and other marks of professional esteem. Moreover, his remarkable near miss on 14 February 1876 had won him a secure though minor place in the history of technology. Nevertheless, he remained bitter until his dying day at having been denied the far greater glory that came to Bell. He had lived in Chicago since 1869, but died suddenly in Newton, Massachusetts, while visiting a friend.

• A small collection of Gray's letters is in the Division of Electricity, National Museum of History and Technology, Smithsonian Institution, Washington, D.C. Several of Gray's papers on electricity from 1874 to 1878 are printed in George B. Prescott, *The Speaking Telephone, Talking Phonograph, and Other Novelties* (1878). Further information and citations of other sources may be found in David A. Hounshell, "Elisha Gray and the Telephone," *Technology and Culture* 16 (Apr. 1975): 133–61, and Robert V. Bruce, *Bell: Alexander Graham Bell and the Conquest of Solitude*, 2d ed. (1990), which is also the best secondary source on the patent battle.

ROBERT V. BRUCE

GRAY, Gilda (24 Oct. 1899–22 Dec. 1959), silent film and stage dancer, was born Marianna Michalska in Cracow, Poland, the daughter of Maximilian Michalski and Wanda (maiden name unknown). The family emigrated to Bayonne, New Jersey, in 1907 and then moved to Cudahy, Wisconsin, where Marianna was educated at a parochial school. In 1912 she married bartender John Gorecki with whom she had one son, Martin.

Gray began her career in 1913, singing in seedy local saloons. Soon after, at around age fifteen or sixteen, she left her husband to pursue her career in Chicago. It was during this period that she created the risqué dance that would make her a ragtime legend. Dance historians have argued that the "shimmy" originated in India, the South Seas, Nigeria, or off the coast of California. However, other historians contend that Gray invented the dance and patrons named it when they misheard her explain, in a heavy Polish accent, the gestures by which she shook her chemise. Of her technique, which evolved naturally with the rhythms of the jazz age, Gray commented: "A ripple here, a quiver there, a shudder or two—and then I shake all the way up from my feet with everything" (*Newsweek*, Jan. 1960). Following her success in Chicago in 1918, she took her act to New York's Broadway as "Mary Gray." Sophie Tucker, the "Red Hot Mama," caught one of Gray's shows, befriended her and convinced her to adopt the stage name "Gilda Gray."

In 1921 Gray played in the Broadway comedy revue *Snapshots of 1921* at Gray's Theatre, which lasted only forty-four performances and sometime in the early 1920s danced a minor role in George White's long-running vaudeville revue *Scandals*. Gray, however, became a sensation in a principal role in the Ziegfeld *Follies* of 1922, earning the nickname "Golden Girl" from Florenz "Flo" Ziegfeld. During the revue's 541 performances at the New Amsterdam Theatre, Gray worked with vaudeville celebrities Will Rogers, Edward Gallapher, and Al Shean and regularly stopped the show during performances of the shimmy to the tunes *It's Getting Dark on Old Broadway*, and *'Neath the South Sea Moon*. Gray also played a lead dance role in the 1929 revue *Vaudeville*; reviewing her performance, a *New York Times* writer delared "Gilda Gray is as much as she ever was—possibly more" (Mar. 1929). Considered one of the top vaudeville performers of the 1920s, Gray earned $4 million in her ten years on stage and enjoyed an extravagant lifestyle during those years. In 1924 Gray divorced Gorecki to marry her manager, Gaillard Boag. Gray opened the popular club Rendezvous Room with Boag and continued to perform in other supper and vaudeville clubs that he managed.

Gray also performed in several films during this period. Most often she was cast as an exotic dancer, such as in the 1919 film *A Virtuous Vamp*, where she performed the shimmy. She also played minor characters in *Search of a Sinner* (1920) and the society melodrama *Lawful Larceny* (1923). Gray performed voluptuous dances in starring roles as Aloma in the melodrama *Aloma of the South Seas* (1926) and in the *Devil Dancer* (1927), as the Shite Muslim orphan Takla, whom an Englishman rescues and takes as his love. Her next two starring roles were in films that dealt with vaudeville; Gray played a poor girl who rises to stardom in *Cabaret* (1927) and received critical praise for her acting in the mystery-thriller, *Piccadilly* (1929), which was directed by E. A. Dupont. Gray's success came to a sudden halt in 1929, when the stock market crash devastated her savings. Shortly afterward, Gray divorced Boag.

In 1933 Gray married Venezuelan diplomat Hector Briceno de Saa, who was eight years younger than she. This marriage ended in divorce five years later. Gray's film career rekindled briefly; she was given a minor role of Belle in *Rose Marie* (1936) and played herself in *The Great Ziegfeld*, (1936), a lavish biography of Flo Ziegfeld, though she was cut from the final version. Gray's heyday ended in 1941, with a nostalgic review at Billy Rose's Diamond Horseshoe, where she shimmied to the "St. Louis Blues." In the same year, Gray filed for bankruptcy.

Her health failing, Gray retired to Colorado. In 1946 Gray sued Columbia Pictures for $1 million, claiming that the film *Gilda*, a romantic drama starring Rita Hayworth, was based in part on her career and thereby violated her privacy but then settled out of court. In 1952 Gray worked for a short time as a sex appeal consultant for young actresses. Gray died from heart failure in Hollywood, leaving behind an unfinished autobiography titled *Glamour Be Damned*. Gray's funeral expenses were paid with a donation from the Motion Picture Relief Fund. Characteristic of Gray is a late-life comment to a friend in which she lamented the passing of the Jazz Age, declaring: "They might roar more today, honey, but we had more fun" (*Time*, Jan. 1960).

• Details regarding Gray's film and dance career can be found at the New York Public Library for the Performing Arts Dance and Theater Collections, Lincoln Center. For biographical information, consult Joseph A. Wytrwal, *The Poles in America* (1969). The *New York Times* reviewed Gray's performance in *Vaudeville* on 26 Mar. 1929. Gray is cited in Ivan Butler's *Silent Magic: Rediscovering the Silent Film Era* (1987) and Sophie Tucker's *Some of These Days* (1945). For a reference to the shimmy, see William F. Pilch, *Social Dance* (1967), and Marshall Stearn and Jean Stearn's *Jazz Dance* (1968). An obituary is in the *New York Times*, 23 Dec. 1959; related tributes are in *Newsweek*, and *Time*, both 4 Jan. 1960.

PAULA M. GARDNER

GRAY, Glen (6 July 1906–23 Aug. 1963), saxophonist and band leader, also known as "Spike" Gray, was born Glen Gray Knoblaugh in Roanoke, Illinois, the son of Lurdie C. Knoblaugh, a clerk in the family store, and Agnes Cunningham.

Not an innovator nor performer of extraordinary gifts, Gray's significance was more historical than musical, residing in the transitional role he and his Casa Loma Orchestra played in the evolution of the large dance orchestra—the big band—between 1930 and the end of World War II. Together they helped to transform the "salon" commercial dance orchestra of the 1910s and 1920s into the swing-oriented bands that began to dominate the business during the mid-1930s.

Like most musicians who figured prominently in American dance music of that time, Gray's musical education began with hometown bands, especially his own Spike's Jazz Band, for which his sister was pianist. He also participated in musical activities at Roanoke High School, from which he graduated; at Illinois Wesleyan College, where he matriculated for part of an academic year; and during a brief residency at the American Conservatory of Music in Chicago. Following his brushes with higher education he took a job as a ticket cashier for the Santa Fe Railroad, still working local music dates at night.

From then on, his circle of activity gradually broadened to as far away from his north central Illinois home as Detroit, where he first played with the Orange Blossoms in 1924. This was a band he helped to organize, later to front, a collection of sidemen culled from what can best be called (and only partially in jest) the "Jean Goldkette Dance Orchestral Conglomerate." (It was not uncommon during the times for one ambitious impresario to keep several playing groups active, all under his singular imprimatur.) In 1929 the Orange Blossoms became a cooperative orchestra with its policies and empowerments determined by constituents' vote, known as the Casa Loma Orchestra, with Gray as its corporate president. The name "Casa Loma" was borrowed from a hapless nightclub in Toronto whose inaugural event the band was contracted to play. It lamely folded before the contract could be fulfilled, its name surviving only because members of the Orange Blossoms thought it a classy name. (And compared to "Orange Blossoms," who could disagree?) The band's first booking with its new name, following the Toronto debacle and, as it happens, the great Wall Street crash, was in the Roseland Ballroom, New York City.

Although he was its elected president, Gray did not front the Casa Loma group from the beginning. He took over, again by band vote, only after violinist Mel Jenssen had served briefly in that capacity. Late in the summer of 1931 the band went to Atlantic City, then toured the Midwest, returning by fall to a long stay at the Glen Island Casino in New Rochelle, New York. Gray and the band then moved to the celebrated Colonnades in New York's Essex Hotel in the fall of 1933, which unquestionably helped them secure a contract, during the same year, to be the resident band for the Camel Caravan radio show.

Sticking close to their radio show base, the Casa Lomans later began an extended engagement in the Rainbow Room atop Radio City, with occasional dates as well at the Terrace Room of the Hotel New Yorker and one brief runout to the Congress Hotel of Chicago. By the end of 1933 the new leader's national prominence had become so evident that the band's corporate name was legally changed to Glen Gray and the Casa Loma Orchestra.

An extended tenure at the Glen Island Casino provided additional radio time, which more than any other factor in the pop music mix of 1930–1945 paved the road to big-band success. An appearance at the Paramount Theater in Manhattan in 1935 marked the premiere of that theater's famous swing band series, one that in subsequent years became an institution, when "playing the Paramount" was tantamount to national canonization.

In 1937 the Casa Lomans began a transcontinental tour that ended at the famed Palomar in Los Angeles, the site of the Benny Goodman Band's passage into prominence just two years before. While there they were contracted to do George Burns and Gracie Allen's radio show, further proof of a soaring national identity. Indeed, by the spring of 1939 Gray and the Casa Loma Orchestra were virtual household items in the national popular music scene. They also enjoyed critical success, consistently receiving high votes in various industry polls, both in the "swing" and "sweet" categories. They won the *Down Beat* designation "Favored Dance Band" in 1938, having placed high in a similar *Metronome* poll the year before. The *Down Beat* poll of 1940 found them number two among the "sweet" bands and number six in the "swing" category. These dual placements suggest the principal basis for the Gray/Casa Loma success: it was a group of solid and tasteful entertainers who during an evening could switch continually (and with convic-

tion) from the romantic songs of vocalists Kenny Sargent and Connie Boswell to the jazz-inspired swing of original riff tunes.

The realization of Gray's musical values was made possible by several astute composer-arrangers who worked with him in forging the band's style. Larry Clinton was a crucial contributor beginning in 1935, as were Joe Bishop, Dick Jones, Frankie Carle, and even Glen Miller. But they were all preceded by a relatively unknown figure, Gene Gifford, whom Gray had known through his Goldkette association. Gifford's "Casa Loma Stomp" and "San Sue Strut" were musically adept, pure instrumentals cut from the same cloth he had heard in the work of John Nesbitt and Don Redman, both arrangers for the McKinney Cotton Pickers during the late 1920s. This new genre, the riff-motivated piece, would evolve in later years into the "jumps" that became surefire crowd pleasers; pieces like Count Basie's "One O'Clock" and Harry James's "Two O'Clock" were versions of the same basic format.

A fundamental ingredient of Gifford's style, and one that pointed toward the future, was the four-beat rhythm (or meter) he favored. First as a banjo player, and later as a guitarist, he laid down this progressive rhythmic base over the two-beat basis other members of the Casa Loma rhythm section provided. The four-beat pattern was a definitive departure from the old New Orleans tradition of rhythm backgrounds; it became emblematic of the more modern style that gradually emerged from the progressive big bands—Goodman's as well as Jimmie Lunceford's and Duke Ellington's—during the late 1930s. Thus Gray's Casa Loma, nudged along by Gifford, helped to replace two-beat jazz, which by the 1940s was known popularly as "rickety-tick."

The elegant show-business dress code imposed by Gray on his band (formal tails, white ties) and even his own handsome persona were not immaterial in the band's success. But there were more substantive reasons too. The precision of its sectional playing, a product of the unyielding concern of veteran trombonist Bill Rausch, made the band an enviable sonic unit. Such was not the rule in early traveling bands.

The band did not swing with the raw drive of Ellington's or Lunceford's or Basie's, but its "semi-swinging" groove was too well oiled not to produce conspicuous, and memorable, results. In this way it was influential in transplanting improvisational jazz in particular, and "hot music" in general, from the ethnic ghetto it had inhabited since early in the century. Gray ensured that a steady stream of great jazz artists was associated with the band, in short residencies as well as in recording dates. Over the years Mildred Bailey, Hoagy Carmichael, Lee Wiley, Louis Armstrong, Herb Ellis, Red Nichols, and Bobby Hackett joined the band for special occasions. Aside from its continuing output of recordings from 1929 (Okeh, Brunswick, Victor, Decca), the band's popular appeal was further confirmed when it appeared in two films, *Time Out for Rhythm* in 1941 and *Gals, Inc.* in 1943.

By then the Casa Loma Orchestra was the oldest continuing dance band in the country, and, with some sense of irony, its gradual decline can be traced to the year 1943 as meaningfully as to any other. Some of its key musicians, such as Sargent and clarinet soloist Clarence Hutchenrider, began to retire from the band in the early 1940s. The Casa Loma Corporation as such was dissolved in 1942, although Gray continued to lead the band in an active schedule of dance and recording dates until 1950, when he retired to Massachusetts. (Whether his retirement was cause or effect is moot.)

In 1956 he spent time in Hollywood, helping to preserve in new recordings many of the original arrangements of the most notable bands—his own as well as others—that were in danger of being lost forever. Produced with the assistance of superior studio musicians of the Los Angeles area, this journey into nostalgia was immensely successful. The project led to offers for Gray to once again organize a road band and tour, all of which he refused in order to spend more time with his wife, the former Marion Douglas, and their son. (The date of their marriage is unknown.) Gray died of cancer in his adoptive home of Peabody, Massachusetts.

• For quick access to a sonic essence of Gray's Orchestra, one should hear numbers such as "Casa Loma Stomp," "No Name Jive," and the ubiquitous—at least during the band's halcyon years—"Smoke Rings." (The first and last are Gifford compositions.) The "Casa Loma Stomp" is the band's only recording included in the Smithsonian *Big Band Jazz* collection. A larger and more detailed cross-section of the band's repertoire can be heard in *Glen Gray and the Original Casa Loma Orchestra's Greatest Hits* (MCA-122; 78 rpm); *Casa Loma and Hi Fi* (Capitol W-747); and *Sounds of the Great Casa Loma Band* (Capitol T-1588). Brief yet informative discussions of Gray and of the Casa Loma Orchestra are in Leo Walker, *The Big Band Almanac* (1978), Gunther Schuller, *The Swing Era* (1989), George T. Simon, *The Big Bands* (1967), and Albert McCarthy, *Big Band Jazz* (1974). Gray's obituary is in the *New York Times*, 25 Aug. 1963.

WILLIAM THOMSON

GRAY, Harold Lincoln (20 Jan. 1894–9 May 1968), cartoonist, was born in Kankakee, Illinois, the son of Ira Lincoln Gray and Estella M. Rosencrans, farmers. The family moved to Lafayette, Indiana, while Harold was young, and he worked his way through the local college, Purdue University, graduating in 1917 with a B.S. in engineering. Having sold cartoons to the *Lafayette Morning Journal* while in school, Gray decided to pursue an artistic career and immediately joined the art staff of the *Chicago Tribune*. He served in the U.S. Army (as an instructor in training camps) from May to December 1918, when he rejoined the *Tribune* staff, until 1920 when he left the *Tribune* to set up his own commercial art studio.

At about this time, Gray also became Sidney Smith's assistant on the comic strip "The Gumps" and began to submit ideas for a comic strip of his own to Joseph M. Patterson, chief of the Chicago Tribune–New York Daily News syndicate. In 1924 Gray suggested a strip about a curly-headed little orphan boy, which he called "Little Orphan Otto." Intrigued, Patterson accepted the idea but told Gray to change the sex of his protagonist and to call the strip "Little Orphan Annie."

The first major comic strip to venture into political commentary, Gray's creation seemed an unlikely candidate for that distinction when it debuted on 5 August 1924, but its heroine quickly demonstrated a spunky independence of spirit that was fundamental both to the success of the strip's stories and to its alleged politics. At the end of the strip's second month, Gray introduced the character who would shape the spirit of independence into a political stance. Annie is adopted by Oliver "Daddy" Warbucks, a millionaire industrialist, the epitome of Gray's idea of that culture hero: the self-made man who achieves success through hard work and canny capitalism. But a rich man's daughter leads a boring life, so Gray soon separated them; when Warbucks leaves on a business trip, Annie is driven from his home. Accompanied by a pet dog named Sandy that she acquired in January 1925, Annie takes refuge with a poor but kindly farmer and his wife. But she is no burden to them; through purposeful enterprise and her own ingenuity, the eleven-year-old waif is able to contribute to the couple's welfare and happiness. After a few months, "Daddy" Warbucks finally locates his missing adopted daughter and takes her and Sandy back to live in splendid comfort with him—until the girl is spirited away again. Thus did Gray inaugurate the cycle of separation and hardship, rescue and reunion that framed Annie's adventures as well as the quest motif that animated them throughout the strip's run.

Gray knew that the best way for a little orphan girl to make her way in the world without being simply a weepy milksop is for her to be self-reliant. Warbucks and the rest of Annie's ensemble were natural outgrowths of this pivotal notion. The strip reached the zenith of its popularity during the depression because it addressed and assuaged the greatest fear of the period. Annie's adventures proved again and again that the traditional American ethic of hard work was not bankrupt and that capitalism could still work. And as Gray's exemplar, Warbucks could scarcely espouse self-reliance and free enterprise during the Roosevelt years without, at the same time, attacking FDR's policies. The New Deal, after all, tended to encourage people to look to government for help rather than exhorting them to help themselves. "Little Orphan Annie" became unabashedly, unrelentingly "political" because the very essence of its story demanded it. Throughout the decade, Annie drifted from place to place, into "Daddy's" care and out of it, spending most of her time with the ordinary folk and reviving by precept and example their faith in the values of hard work and economy. But she also encountered a succession of greedy landlords and corrupt small-town politicians and outright evil megalomaniacs.

Gray's drawing ability seemed crude, but his artwork actually cast a spell that enhanced his story. Filling his drawings with solid blacks, heavy shadows, and darkly shaded nooks and crannies, Gray created a threatening and sinister world. In that world, Gray's characters seemed to stand around rigidly, posturing woodenly, as if they were paralyzed with fear and apprehension. The blank eyeballs for which Annie is celebrated were integral to this fearful mood: one walks through a threatening night gingerly, never looking behind or to the side for fear of seeing a dire presence there, eyes focused resolutely ahead in a kind of unseeing stare—precisely the effect that Annie's blank eyeballs have.

The ominous mysteriousness of Annie's world was amenable to the element of fantasy, and Gray sometimes subdued his villains with oriental magic. In February 1935 he introduced Punjab, a giant turbaned Indian, who, as Warbucks's assistant, banished evildoers from this world by spreading a blanket over them and muttering an incomprehensible incantation. Two years later, Warbucks gained another memorable henchman, a black-garbed, hooded-eyed agent of vengeance called the Asp. Later, Gray created Mr. Am, a white-bearded grandfatherly figure who seemed to have lived forever and whose powers exceeded even Punjab's.

Once the strip was established, Gray moved to the New York vicinity, initially to Croton-on-Hudson, then to Southport, Connecticut. He was married twice, first to Doris C. Platt (1921), who died in 1925; then to Winifred Frost (1929). He and his second wife took annual automobile trips around the country, stopping at roadside diners, farms, hardware stores, and the like, talking to people in small towns and big cities in order to understand what the reading public thought and felt and thereby to produce a better comic strip. In 1958 they bought a house in La Jolla, California, and thereafter their annual trips were coast-to-coast treks. The strip inspired a radio program, which ran from 1930 until 1943, several movies, and, in 1977, a Broadway musical.

For forty-four years, Gray wrote homey sermons on his favorite subjects for Annie to deliver while keeping her hands busy baking pies or sweeping out the store or doing the laundry, activities she habitually indulged in while she preached. Gray was as much against social pretension, religious intolerance, moral hypocrisy, abuse of power, and censorship of the press as he was for self-reliance and free enterprise. So personal a vision did the strip embody that it very nearly ended with his death. Unable at first to find a cartoonist capable of continuing the feature, the syndicate reprinted strips from the 1930s. But when *Annie* became a hit Broadway musical, Leonard Starr was persuaded to continue the feature, which he did ably but without hazarding Gray's conservative politics.

• Harold Gray's unpublished works and papers are at Boston University. His life story is very competently related in a book produced in support of the Broadway musical *Annie*, *The History of Little Orphan Annie*, by Bruce Smith (1982). The most insightful analyses of the strip's ethos can be found in Stephen Becker, *Comic Art in America* (1959), and Coulton Waugh, *The Comics* (1947). The strip has been reprinted variously. A volume was issued every year from 1926 through 1934; then, in 1970, *Arf! The Life and Hard Times of Little Orphan Annie* reprinted selected sequences from 1935 to 1945. A series, launched in 1987 by Fantagraphics Books, undertook to reprint the entire run of the strip from 1931 on. An obituary is in the *New York Times*, 10 May 1968.

ROBERT C. HARVEY

GRAY, Horace (24 Mar. 1828–15 Sept. 1902), jurist, was born in Boston, Massachusetts, the son of Horace Gray, a manufacturer, and Harriet Upham. He was a half brother of John Chipman Gray. Gray's mother died when he was still young. After preparation at private schools, he graduated from Harvard College in 1845 at seventeen, an early age even for the era. As was typical of a wealthy family, Gray had no urgent need to prepare for a profession. However, in 1847, while on a European tour, he received word that his father had suffered a severe financial setback. Gray turned to law and entered Harvard Law School in 1848, graduating the following year. As an undergraduate, he had developed a great interest in botany and ornithology, exhibiting the ability to memorize and to categorize specimens. That aptitude marked Gray's career in law.

After further preparation in the firm of Sohier and Welch and then with John Lowell, Gray was admitted to the bar in 1851. A short time later Luther S. Cushing, clerk of the supreme court of judicature, fell seriously ill, and Gray assumed his duties on a temporary basis. The office became Gray's permanently when Cushing died in 1854. The position was ranked only slightly below a judgeship, and its duties were well suited both to Gray's talents and proclivities. In particular, his extensive case notes reflected his search for historical truth as a basis for legal precedent. His notes on the writs of assistance question of 1761, in which James Otis had successfully argued against the royal government's use of general search warrants, and on slavery in the Commonwealth proved of value to his contemporaries and also to modern scholars, who have built on his thorough scholarship.

Besides his clerkship, Gray honed his skill as an advocate with the elite of the highly regarded Boston bar, which included Benjamin R. Curtis after Curtis's resignation from the U.S. Supreme Court in 1857. Gray's partners included Ebenezer Rockwood Hoar, future supreme judicial court justice and attorney general under President Ulysses S. Grant. Fully devoted to the law, Gray had little time for politics. Like his partner Hoar, however, he gravitated from "Conscience" Whig to Free Soiler to Republican. His opposition to slavery is further indicated in an attack, coauthored with John Lowell, Jr., on Chief Justice Roger B. Taney's *Dred Scott* opinion. Typically, the critique was solidly based on legal rather than political grounds. With the outbreak of the Civil War, Gray rendered significant legal advice to Republican governor John A. Andrew, although his support for the war was tempered by constitutional scruples over Abraham Lincoln's Emancipation Proclamation.

In 1864 Governor Andrew appointed Gray to the supreme judicial court, and in 1873, upon the death of Chief Justice Reuben Chapman, Gray succeeded to the chief justiceship. The court's heavy caseload involved its members as both trial and appellate judges. Opinions differed on Gray's courtroom demeanor and the extent to which his rigor was mitigated by kindness, but recognition of his capacity for work was unanimous. As chief justice he even proofread the court reports. In seventeen years on the Massachusetts court, Gray spoke for it 1,367 times. Moreover, the number of his opinions increased markedly once he became chief justice, as he seldom delivered less than a quarter of the seven-judge court's opinions each term. Remarkably, he dissented only once in seventeen years, an indication of his institutional commitment.

Gray's first opinion on the court was in a case involving ownership of a heifer. He expended five pages in notes, signaling that he was not changing his habits from his reporter days. Indeed, he contributed a number of essays on several points of law, ranging from ocean flats to the role of trustees in inheritance cases. He contributed to the court's assumption of more equity cases, as he was one of the few judges in the country with a mastery of the subject. Unnoticed at the time, Gray hired promising Harvard Law School graduates as clerks, a custom he continued on the U.S. Supreme Court. That practice became institutionalized on the Supreme Court when his successor, Oliver Wendell Holmes, Jr., maintained it. As one of Gray's early clerks, the brilliant Louis D. Brandeis demonstrated Gray's commitment to ability, and their working relationship served as a model for later clerks.

It was traditional in the nineteenth century for Supreme Court justices to be appointed from a particular circuit's most prominent state, which in the First Circuit was Massachusetts. In 1881, with the occupant of the First Circuit seat, Nathan Clifford of Maine, in his dotage and Republicans in control of the Senate and the presidency, Gray seemed certain to be appointed. The previous, image-conscious Rutherford B. Hayes administration had consulted Gray, though he was not a partisan, on Massachusetts patronage matters. To make the appointment unanimous, the Supreme Court justices informed President Chester Arthur, who made the appointment following James A. Garfield's assassination, that they favored Gray. He had come from being a lawyers' lawyer to being a judges' judge, and he took his seat on 9 January 1882.

Gray's twenty years on the Court are not easily categorized. Continuing a number of his career traits, his opinions often took the form of legal essays, he worked overtime to eliminate disharmony on the Court, and he maintained his penchant for precedent unabated. The image that emerges is the ultimate team player on the Morison R. Waite Court and the Melville Weston Fuller Court. Gray was the recognized historical scholar on the bench who could be counted on to do more than his share of the task. He worked closely with Fuller in securing passage of the Circuit Court of Appeals Act of 1891. The closeness of the brethren is indicated by Gray's marriage in 1889 to Jane Matthews, the daughter of his late colleague Stanley Matthews. The couple had no children. Gray had adhered to the doctrine of sovereign immunity, that government cannot be sued, as a Massachusetts judge, and he expounded it in his dissent in *Lee v. the United States* (1882), in which Robert E. Lee's heirs sued for the return of the family's estate confiscated during the Civil War. In general Gray supported the strengthened Union that had emerged from the Civil War. Thus in *Juilliard v. Greenman* (1884), his opinion for the Court sustained Congress's power to issue greenbacks (paper money), for which he was castigated by friends, even in their memorial tributes to him. Gray's commitment to precedent, or closely following prior decisions, explains his dissent along with Waite in the *Wabash* case (1886), in which the Court's decision overruled the *Granger* cases (1877) that had sustained state regulation of railroads. But Gray's adherence to governmental exercise of power and to following precedents was tempered by his conservatism. He frequently aligned with two of the most conservative members of the Fuller Court, and he joined the hysteria-driven 5 to 4 decision invalidating a congressional income tax in *Pollock v. United States* (1895). Perhaps Gray's best-known opinion was in *Won Kim Ark v. United States* (1898), in which he ruled that a person born to Chinese parents in the United States was a citizen who could not be excluded from returning to the country after a visit to China. Gray, however, had found grounds for not extending citizenship to a Native-American claimant in *Elk v. Wilkins* (1884) and joined his colleagues, with the exception of John Marshall Harlan, in what historian John Hope Franklin has called "the betrayal of the Negro" in the *Civil Rights* cases (1883), which invalidated the Civil Rights Act of 1875. In short, his record on equality for racial minorities under the Constitution was mixed.

A robust outdoorsman, Gray was six feet four inches tall and might be imagined in pursuit of an elusive hermit thrush. He enjoyed generally good health until his last years on the bench, which culminated in a stroke on 3 February 1902. To avoid burdening the Court, he resigned in July of that year, to take effect upon the appointment of a successor. He died in Nahant, Massachusetts.

George F. Hoar, one of Gray's classmates at Harvard Law School, had as a senator pushed for Gray's Supreme Court appointment. Hoar perhaps summed up Gray's career best: "In the first place, Judge Gray was a good lawyer. He did not make mistakes. In the second place, his devotion to his profession was like that of a holy priest to his religion." But Hoar also noted, "I think Judge Gray's fame . . . would have been greater . . . if he had resisted sometimes the temptation to marshal an array of cases, and had suffered his judgments to stand on his statement of legal principles without the authorities" (p. 165). It has been noted that Christopher Columbus Langdell, a law school classmate of Gray's, succeeded in formulating legal education the way that Gray applied law as a judge—laying out precedent in historical sequence within specific categories to demonstrate particular rules, or legal formalism.

• A useful capsule summary is Louis Filler, "Horace Gray," in *The Justices of the United States Supreme Court, 1789–1978,* ed. Leon Friedman and Fred L. Israel (1978). Also see Robert M. Spector, "Legal Historian on the United States Supreme Court: Justice Horace Gray, Jr., and the Historical Method," *American Journal of Legal History* 12 (July 1968): 181–210. A full-length work is Stephen R. Mitchell, "Mr. Justice Gray" (Ph.D. diss., Univ. of Wisconsin, 1961). The best of the contemporary evaluations is George F. Hoar, "Memoir of Horace Gray," *Proceedings of the Massachusetts Historical Society* 18 (1905). Gray is in Mark DeWolfe Howe, *Justice Holmes: The Proving Years 1870–1882,* chap. 4 (1963). Holmes followed Gray on both the Massachusetts Supreme Judicial Court and the Supreme Court.

DONALD M. ROPER

GRAY, James Harrison (17 May 1916–19 Sept. 1986), newspaper publisher, broadcast executive, and politician, was born in Westfield, Massachusetts, the son of Lyman Gray, an attorney, and Clara (maiden name unknown). James Gray spent his childhood in Springfield, Massachusetts, where his father served as district attorney. He received his A.B. in English from Dartmouth College in 1937, lettering in several sports and earning Phi Beta Kappa honors. After graduating Gray enrolled at the University of Heidelberg in Germany to study world history. While there in 1939 he contributed news articles about Nazi Germany to the *New York Herald Tribune.* Following his eight months in Germany, Gray worked as a political writer for three years, first for the *New York Herald Tribune* and then for the Hartford *Courant.*

In 1943 Gray married Dorothy Ellis of Springfield, Massachusetts. The couple had three children. He enlisted for army duty in World War II and was assigned to the 82d Airborne Division. After combat duty in Europe, Gray returned to Fort Benning in Columbus, Georgia, to become a paratroop trainer. While he was stationed at Fort Benning, Gray became familiar with rural southern Georgia. Through his wife's family he came to know the large farming and sporting "plantations" of celebrities such as golfer Bobby Jones. Gray predicted that the southern part of the state would be ripe for a postwar economic boom and settled in Albany, Georgia, where he established his own plantation.

A loan from his father-in-law, Dwight Ellis, allowed Gray to buy the local family-owned daily newspaper, the *Albany Herald,* in 1947. Gray had prearranged the deal with owner Henry McIntosh before moving south in 1946. Gray strengthened the paper's influence and streamlined its operations, quickly turning it into a profitable enterprise.

A gifted writer and orator as well as business manager, Gray made his first foray into politics with a 1946 speech before the Albany Rotary Club and the Chamber of Commerce titled "Why I Came South." The talk, published as a keepsake of the occasion, ably demonstrated Gray's historical knowledge and rhetorical skill. It also served as the northerner's political apologia. Praising Robert E. Lee's heritage and denouncing outside interference in southern politics, Gray professed his sympathy with conservative Democratic sentiment.

He concluded the speech with his views on racial integration: "As for the racial issue, we are capable of dealing with that in our own fashion. We know that a dual system is the only workable solution to the problem, that there has to be a line of demarcation between the two races, and no amount of legal justice dispensed by outside authorities can do anything but aggravate conditions." The event established important local business and political contacts for Gray, who continued to use his editorial position to influence public opinion.

Gray's dream was to build a successful media empire in southwestern Georgia. In 1954 he launched Albany's first television station, WALB. Gray continued to expand his business interests, incorporating in the 1970s as Gray Communications Systems and eventually owning several television stations throughout the South, an Albany radio station, a private aviation company, a rental car franchise, a communications consulting firm, and a restaurant.

Gray's record of civic involvement and his acquaintance with powerful Georgia leaders launched him into state politics in the late 1940s. He was instrumental in getting Herman Talmadge elected governor of Georgia in 1948, and he was elected in 1954 to the presidency of the Albany Chamber of Commerce, a post he held five times from the 1950s to the 1970s. A boyhood friend of the Kennedy family, Gray arranged for John F. Kennedy's speech to the Albany Chamber of Commerce in 1957. A year later Governor Ernest Vandiver appointed Gray chair of the Georgia Democratic party; Gray was the first non-native Georgian to hold the position.

Gray delivered the party's civil rights minority report at the 1960 Democratic National Convention that nominated Kennedy for president. In his markedly northern accent, Gray presented the Old South position, supporting discrimination in public schools and opposing the participation of uneducated blacks in government.

After black community leaders formed the Albany Movement in November 1961 to protest segregation, Gray maneuvered to maintain segregated facilities in the city. He bought the public swimming pool and for several years ran it as a private operation catering to whites only. Gray also claimed credit for preventing Martin Luther King, Jr., from provoking a confrontation and making an example of Albany, and after King was arrested for demonstrating in Albany in December 1961, Gray claimed that he used his Kennedy influence to arrange for King's release from jail in order to preempt a riot.

Gray remained active in state Democratic politics. He held the position of state Democratic party chair until Vandiver's loss to Carl Sanders in 1962. In 1964 he organized Georgia's Democrats for conservative Barry Goldwater. In 1966, when Vandiver suffered a heart attack while making a comeback bid, Gray took Vandiver's place in the gubernatorial race. Although Gray outspent his opponents, he came in fourth in the Democratic primary. He was reported to have offered Lester Maddox $100,000 to withdraw from the general election to avoid splitting the conservative vote. When Maddox eventually won, Gray was restored to the chairmanship of the state party and restored it to fiscal health.

In 1973 Gray succeeded Albany's mayor, who had died in office. After completing the unexpired term, Gray was elected mayor in 1975 and held the position until his own death. During his thirteen years in office Gray worked for downtown revitalization, though he did not live to see the fulfillment of most of his plans. He also eventually achieved a more amicable working relationship with black business and political leaders.

Gray's business ventures continued to succeed, though in 1975 the Federal Communications Commission directed him to break up his monopoly of the Albany media. All three of his children, James, Jr., Geoff, and Constance Greene, have been associated with the family business.

Having divorced in 1950, Gray married Cleair Ranger of Pelham, Georgia, in 1973; they had no children. While in Boston recovering from vascular bypass surgery, Gray died. The Albany Civic Center, which opened in 1983, was named for Gray over his objections. Although Gray thrived on power and was adept at manipulating both public opinion and private decisions, he remained an aloof figure, leaving a contradictory legacy of conservatism and progress.

• Some useful sources on Gray include Sharon Thomason, "James Gray, Albany's Mr. Power," *Brown's Guide to Georgia* 6 (Mar.–Apr. 1978): 75–86, and sections dealing with Gray in Numan V. Bartley, *From Thurmond to Wallace: Political Tendencies in Georgia 1948–1968* (1970); in Bruce Galphin, *The Riddle of Lester Maddox* (1968); and in Harold Paulk Henderson, *The Politics of Change in Georgia: A Political Biography of Ellis Arnall* (1991). Obituaries are in the *Boston Globe* and the *Albany Herald*, both 20 Sept. 1986, and the *New York Times*, 21 Sept. 1986.

BARBARA A. BRANNON

GRAY, John Chipman (14 July 1839–25 Feb. 1915), legal scholar, was born in Brighton, Massachusetts, the son of Horace Gray, a merchant, and Sarah Russell Gardner. The member of a distinguished Massachusetts family, Gray followed his elder half brother, later a U.S. Supreme Court justice, to Harvard, receiving an undergraduate degree in 1859 and a law degree in 1861. He studied for a third year at the law school and received his A.M. Gray was admitted to practice in 1862 but immediately volunteered for service in the Union army. He served in various staff positions, attaining the rank of major and judge advocate general of U.S. Volunteers in the Department of the South.

After the war Gray returned to Boston and began the practice of law in partnership with law school classmate John C. Ropes, founding the firm of Ropes & Gray. In addition to practicing law together, the two also assisted in founding the *American Law Review* in 1866. They edited the *Review* until 1870, when they yielded the duty to Oliver Wendell Holmes (1841–1935) and Arthur G. Sedgwick. In 1869, while continuing to practice law, Gray was appointed lecturer at the Harvard Law School. In 1873 he married Anna Lyman Mason; they had at least one child.

Gray's teaching career began the year before Dean Christopher Columbus Langdell revolutionized the teaching of law at Harvard (and elsewhere) by introducing the case method and Socratic dialogue. At first, Gray resisted the innovations, preferring, like many neophytes, the certainty of well-rehearsed lectures, but later he embraced Langdell's system with the enthusiasm of a convert. Although without a particular specialty when he was hired, Gray eventually settled in property law, when the retirement of Professor Emory Washburn in 1876 created a need in that area. In 1875 Gray was named to the newly created Story Professorship and in 1883 was transferred to the Royall Professorship, the school's oldest and most prestigious position. Although he refused several offers of appointment to the Massachusetts Supreme Judicial Court, Gray continued—with the permission of the Law School—to engage in the active practice of law with his firm, an exception to the full-time commitment Langdell's system normally required.

Gray's first book, *Restraints on the Alienation of Property* (1883), was prompted by his vehement disagreement with the Supreme Court decision in *Nichols v. Eaton* (1876), which upheld a "spendthrift trust," an arrangement by which property is placed in trust for a beneficiary but made immune from creditors. The device, which involves withholding from the beneficiary the power to alienate, encumber, or pledge the principal or income, was ideally suited to protect family fortunes from improvident heirs. The book failed to reverse judicial acceptance of this type of trust. By relentless argument, however, it powerfully reinforced the older ideal of unrestricted ownership, whereby wealth was available for productive investment but also exposed to the claims of creditors. In 1895 Gray produced a second edition; an unrepentant preface denounced "paternalism," which he described as "the fundamental essence alike of spendthrift trusts and of socialism." In fact, the two were at odds, trusts being used to safeguard the accumulated wealth of capitalists.

Gray's second book, *The Rule against Perpetuities* (1886), concerned limitations on the power of a disposer of property to guide its transmission from generation to generation. By postponing the vesting of unrestricted ownership, such power would also have helped to insulate the estate from the risk of loss due to spendthrift heirs. Despite ancient antecedents, the rule against perpetuities had not been formulated until the eighteenth century. Gray's self-assigned task was to produce a "model text-book" on the subject, one that would bring the rule's expression to "logical symmetry." The book succeeded, and courts in England as well as in the United States made it a standard reference. He produced two further editions in his own lifetime (1906, 1915), and his son Roland brought out a fourth edition in 1942. Also of great influence was Gray's *Select Cases and Other Authorities on the Law of Property* (6 vols., 1888–1892), a pioneering casebook that brought Langdell's method to the teaching of property law. Through a series of tightly linked successors, which were also produced by Harvard Law School professors, it shaped pedagogy in the field until the late twentieth century.

At age seventy Gray fulfilled a lifelong goal by publishing a book on jurisprudence, *The Nature and Sources of Law* (1909; 2d ed. by Roland Gray, 1921). Based on the Carpentier Lectures that he had delivered at Columbia Law School in 1908, the work remains of interest for the dogged honesty and simplicity with which it handles the enduring problems of legal analysis. While the book encouraged the kind of rigorous logicism later brought to near perfection by Wesley Hohfeld, one of Gray's student assistants, its constant concern with practical reality also suggested the development that Karl Llewellyn, Jerome Frank, and other scholars were later to call "legal realism." Gray died in Boston.

• Gray's correspondence during the Civil War, along with that of his law partner, has been edited by Worthington Chauncey Ford, *War Letters, 1862–65, of John Chipman Gray and John Codman Ropes* (1927). Gray's mature faith in the case method and Socratic dialogue is cogently set forth in "The Methods of Legal Education," *Yale Law Journal* 1 (1892): 159–61. A biographical sketch by his son and many reprinted tributes are in Roland Gray, *John Chipman Gray* (1917). A summary of his life and work by several of his colleagues at the Harvard Law School is in *Harvard Law Review* 28 (1915): 539–49.

JOHN V. ORTH

GRAY, John Purdue (6 Aug. 1825–29 Nov. 1886), physician, alienist, and asylum superintendent, was born in Half Moon, Pennsylvania, the son of Peter D. Gray, a Methodist minister and farmer, and Elizabeth Purdue. He received his early education at Bellefonte Academy and Dickinson College, from which he graduated with an A.M. in 1846. He studied medicine at the University of Pennsylvania, graduating in 1849 and immediately becoming resident physician at Blockley Hospital in Philadelphia.

At Blockley, Gray worked under Dr. Nathan Dow Benedict, who in 1851 became superintendent of the New York State Lunatic Asylum at Utica, where Gray joined him as third assistant physician. Gray became second assistant in 1852, and when Benedict was forced to resign for personal reasons in 1853, Gray became first assistant and acting medical superintendent at the age of twenty-eight. He served briefly as the medical superintendent at the Michigan State Lunatic Asylum in Kalamazoo, but in 1854 he was persuaded

to return to Utica to take over as full medical superintendent, a position he held until his death. He had become assistant editor of the *American Journal of Insanity* in 1852 and served as its full editor from 1854 until after he was shot in 1882. In 1854 he married Mary B. Wetmore; they had three children.

Gray's expertise in medical jurisprudence was evident in his testimony at several well-publicized court proceedings. He was consulted by President Abraham Lincoln several times for opinions on the sanity of criminals, and testified at several notable trials, such as that of Lewis Payne, who conspired with James Wilkes Booth to kill Lincoln. He also testified and was chief adviser to the government in the prosecution of Charles J. Guiteau, the assassin of President James Abram Garfield. In this role he suggested reliable prosecution witnesses, briefed attorneys on defense witnesses, and even drew up questions for cross-examination.

As an expert witness, Gray tended to opine that defendants were sane. While many of his colleagues believed that an inability to adhere to the moral dictates of society was the result of disease, not mere depravity, and that hence the accused were insane, Gray disagreed. He refused in court to acknowledge cases of moral insanity, insisting that individuals were entirely responsible for their actions as long as their reason remained intact. Many colleagues saw him as a conservative and challenged his approach to psychology, but Gray based his assessments on a belief in the freedom of the human will and the power of individuals to use reason to control their passions. Failure to exercise this control, Gray argued, was the result of depravity, not insanity. The debates Gray carried out with his colleagues, therefore, were over the relationship between the mind and the body.

In addition to his more notable activities in the realm of medical jurisprudence, Gray contributed immensely to the improvement of the treatment of the insane. Much of his work drew on his somatic belief that insanity was primarily a physical condition and not fundamentally hereditary, as many alienists believed. His rejection of hereditarian explanations of insanity led him to appoint a pathologist to the Utica Asylum staff in 1869 to undertake post-mortem examinations of patients to determine a pathology of insanity. He also worked to improve the conditions of asylums, giving his patients more fresh air and exercise and abolishing as much as possible the use of restraint and the practice of solitary feeding. With these innovations, Gray attracted the admiration of some asylum superintendents, and the hostility of many others. His empirical examinations of insanity, including microscopic study of the brain, made Utica one of the foremost asylums for the training of young alienists.

Actively involved in the medical community, Gray served as president of the Medical Society of New York in 1868; of the Psychological Section of the International Medical Congress in Philadelphia in 1870; of the Association of Medical Superintendents of American Institutions for the Insane in 1883–1884; and of the New York State Medical Association in 1885. In 1874 he became the chair of psychological medicine and medical jurisprudence at Bellevue Hospital Medical College, and in 1876 he occupied the same chair in the Albany Medical College. He was made an honorary member of the British, French, and Italian psychological societies and of the American Archaeological Association.

In 1882, while sitting in his office at Utica, Gray was shot in the face by a deranged man, Henry Remshaw, who was not a patient but had worked earlier as an attendant at Utica. While he lived for another four years, Gray never quite recovered from the attack, which seriously affected his breathing and general constitution. He took several years off to recuperate in Georgia and in Europe but, soon after returning to Utica in 1886, he died of kidney disease.

Gray's significance in American history lies in his championing of the rejection of hereditarian arguments of insanity and the empirical examination of the brain. His perspective caused tension in a number of the psychological associations to which he belonged in the United States, and much of the debate was carried out in the pages of the *American Journal of Insanity*, whose perspective, during Gray's editorship, was wedded to his. His insistence on close examination of the physiological conditions of insanity contributed a more detailed understanding of mental disease and an improvement to the conditions of asylums, testimony to which he witnessed when, during trips to Europe, he found in place several of his proposals for more sufficient heating of asylums.

• Few of Gray's personal papers seem to have survived. M. D. Raymond, *Gray Genealogy* (1887), is a source on Gray's family background. More detailed treatments of Gray's views are in Robert J. Waldinger, "Sleep of Reason: John P. Gray and the Challenge of Moral Insanity," *Journal of the History of Medicine and Allied Sciences* 34 (Apr. 1879): 163–79, and in Charles E. Rosenberg, *The Trial of the Assassin Guiteau: Psychiatry and Law in the Gilded Age* (1968). Much of the context of Gray's debates and activities is found in the essays in J. K. Hall et al., eds., *One Hundred Years of American Psychiatry* (1944). On Gray's tenure at Blockley Hospital, See John Welsh Croskey, *History of Blockley* (1929). Obituaries are in *American Journal of Insanity* 44, no. 1 (July 1887), *Medical Record* 30, no. 23 (Dec. 1886), and, by W. G. Tucker, "Memoir of John Purdue Gray, M.D. LL..D.," *Transactions of the Medical Society of New York* (1888): 541–44.

DANIEL J. MALLECK

GRAY, Wardell (13 Feb. 1921–25 May 1955), jazz tenor saxophonist, was born Carl Wardell Gray, in Oklahoma City, Oklahoma; his parents' names are unknown. During his childhood he moved with his family to Detroit. He attended Cass Tech High School there and began his musical life, first as a clarinetist, then as a saxophonist. While still a teenager he worked in local jazz bands, in the company of fellow jazz musicians Howard McGhee, Big Nick Nicholas, Sonny Stitt, and others. In 1943 he joined Earl Hines's big band, with whom he worked for two or three years as a tenor saxophonist, and with whom he made some early recordings. This engagement, playing with a fulltime road band, led him from Detroit to Los Angeles, where he played an important role in the development of the bebop jazz idiom.

While living in Los Angeles Gray made some early bebop records with alto saxophonist Charlie Parker, including "Relaxin' at Camarillo" (26 Feb. 1947, Dial 1012) and with tenor saxophonist Dexter Gordon, including a famous tenor saxophone musical battle, "The Chase" (12 June 1947, Dial 1017). A twenty-minute concert performance by the two tenor saxophonists, "The Hunt" (6 July 1947, Savoy 12012), was another well-known tenor battle, one that Jack Kerouac referred to in his novel *On the Road* ("They ate voraciously as Dean, sandwich in hand, stood bowed and jumping before the big phonograph, listening to a wild bop record I had just bought called 'The Hunt,' with Dexter Gordon and Wardell Gray blowing their tops before a screaming audience," p. 113, rev. 1957). Gray played in Billy Eckstine's big band in 1947, although he did not record with Eckstine.

In 1948 he joined clarinetist Benny Goodman's band, taking part in the famed swing-style clarinetist's brief attempt to move into the bebop idiom. He is heard on Goodman's "Stealin' Apples" (9 Sept. 1948, Capitol 10173) and "Bedlam" (14 Apr. 1949, Capitol 57-621). While playing in Goodman's band he traveled to New York City. Soon thereafter he left Goodman to work with pianist Count Basie's band and appeared on "Little Pony" (10 Apr. 1951, Columbia 39406). While in New York, he also worked with pianist Tadd Dameron and other bebop players, and in 1949 he recorded another famous piece, his blues tune "Twisted." (Singer Annie Ross subsequently wrote lyrics for Gray's theme and improvised solo and recorded her version in 1952.)

In 1951 Gray returned to the western United States, where he spent the rest of his life working as a freelance musician. His last recording date, with alto saxophonist Frank Morgan, was in early 1955. He died in or near Las Vegas, where he had gone to play an engagement with Benny Carter's band. His body was found on vacant land a few miles outside of town. His broken neck and head injuries suggested that he might have been murdered, though some of his colleagues said he was a heroin addict and might have died from a drug overdose. Las Vegas police arrested dancer Teddy Hale on suspicion of Gray's murder, but Hale claimed that Gray broke his neck when he fell out of bed after taking heroin. Hale also said that he panicked and dumped Gray's body in the open field, unintentionally inflicting head injuries in the process. He was found guilty of illegally moving Gray's body and sentenced to a brief jail term. No autopsy was performed, so the exact cause of Gray's death may never be ascertained.

Gray was one of the first tenor saxophonists to adopt the bebop idiom pioneered by Parker, trumpeter Dizzy Gillespie, and a few other players in the mid-1940s. His personal style was a blending of the smooth-toned, harmonically conservative approach of swing tenor saxophonist Lester Young and the newer melodic and rhythmic vocabulary of Parker. The gentler, Young-derived components of his style made it easy for him to fit in with the older style of playing favored by Goodman and Basie. At the same time, however, Parker's influence was so strong that Gray even borrowed entire phrases from some of Parker's improvised solos; these borrowings appear in "Twisted" and other recorded solos. Strangely, he favored a fast and prominent vibrato (especially in ballads such as "Easy Living"), while his role models Young and Parker favored slower and less pronounced vibratos. Despite his bows to his predecessors, his playing style was nonetheless distinctive and of musical importance. His colleagues ranked him as one of the best and had he lived longer he probably would have built a reputation equal to that of Gordon, Sonny Rollins, and other famous bebop tenor saxophonists. His music is heard to best advantage on two recording dates under his leadership, the quartet session that resulted in "Twisted" and "Easy Living" (11 Nov. 1949, Prestige 7008) and the sextet session that produced "Bright Boy," "Jackie," and "Farmer's Market" (21 Jan. 1952, Prestige 7009).

• Gray attracted little attention from the press during his brief career, however an article based on an interview appears in *Melody Maker* on 31 July 1954. A brief news item in the *Los Angeles Times*, 27 May 1955, states that the Las Vegas sheriff considered Gray's death a "probable murder," and subsequent details appear in *Melody Maker* on 4 June and 11 June 1954. Short biographies appear in Raymond Horricks, *Count Basie and His Orchestra* (1957), and the standard jazz biographical dictionaries. Robert Gordon in *Jazz West Coast* (1986) and Ted Gioia in *West Coast Jazz* (1992) paint vivid pictures of Gray in the context of the jazz world in the 1940s and 1950s.

THOMAS OWENS

GRAY, William (27 June 1750–3 Nov. 1825), merchant and public official, was born in Lynn, Massachusetts, the son of Abraham Gray, a shoe manufacturer, and Lydia Calley. His family moved to Salem sometime between the years 1760 and 1763. Gray served an apprenticeship under Samuel Gardner before he entered the counting house of Richard Derby, Salem's premier merchant. Gray learned the mercantile business well, and by the age of twenty-eight he had gone into business on his own. In this new capacity he signed his name as "William Gray, Tertius," to differentiate himself from others of the same name in Salem (including the privateer captain).

A member of the Salem militia, Gray responded to the call for action in 1775, but he did not see any direct fighting in the revolutionary war. Instead, he became the owner or the part owner of several ships that became privateer vessels and preyed upon British commerce during the Revolution. This activity moved Gray forward in his business designs, and in the years immediately following the Revolution, he became one of the merchant princes of Salem, sending ships to trade with Russia, India, and China. These were the heady days of early success in Salem, when the town sent ships to ports that previously had never received an American flag. In 1782 he married Elizabeth Chipman; they had ten children. Gray's merchant success was paralleled by his entry into politics. He served as a selectman of Salem (1783–1787) and was a delegate in January 1788, from Salem to the Massachusetts State Convention, where he voted in favor of ratifying the U.S. Constitution.

In 1798 Gray responded to the threat of war with France by subscribing $10,000 for the building of the frigate *Essex* in Salem. This was the start of a pattern for Gray; throughout the troubles engendered by America's neutral status in the Napoleonic wars, Gray would be a strong patriot. The height of Gray's mercantile success came in the period 1800–1807; he employed around 300 seamen annually, and his business profited greatly from the neutral status of the United States during these years. His prosperity, and that of his fellow merchants, was threatened, however, by the passage of the Embargo Act of December 1807, which prohibited American ships from leaving their ports with a cargo.

Surprisingly, Gray came out in favor of the embargo (*Salem Gazette*, 12 Aug. 1808). He soon found himself out of favor with the populace of Salem, which was suffering from the loss of trade. Gray served as the prefect for the port briefly in 1809, and his unpopularity grew apace. Therefore, in the summer of 1809, he and his family moved to Boston, where he continued his merchant business.

During the controversy surrounding the Embargo Act, Gray had switched from the Federalist party to the Republican party. He became a strong friend of John Quincy Adams, who had made the same switch of allegiance. When Adams went to Russia as the American minister in 1809, he shipped out on Gray's vessel, the *Horace*, and in Russia he advanced Gray's interests. Gray soon became the premier American merchant trading with Russia.

Gray served in the Massachusetts State Senate (1807–1809). Having made the switch from Federalist to Republican, he ran for and won the lieutenant governorship of Massachusetts and served under Governor Elbridge Gerry from 1810 to 1812. He also made unsuccessful runs for governor in 1814 and 1815 and lost three races for the Massachusetts Senate in 1818, 1819, and 1820. Both as lieutenant governor of Massachusetts and in his later capacity as president of the Boston branch of the Bank of the United States (1816–1822), Gray proved to be a strong supporter of President James Madison and the Madison administration's policies during the War of 1812. Gray's single most notable act of patriotism came in 1812. The USS *Constitution* was in Boston Harbor, preparing to sail, but it lacked men, money, and supplies. Gray came forward and gave money out of his own pocket to provision the ship and to pay the officers and men. Gray's service in this capacity was crucial; without his aid, the *Constitution* might not have sailed forth and won its victory over the British ship *Guerriere* (19 Aug. 1812).

Gray continued to be active as a merchant in his later years. At the time of his death in Boston, Gray had an estate that was valued at more than $1 million. At the height of his fortune, prior to the Embargo Act of 1807, his worth had been valued at $3 million.

Gray's life and career stand forth as an interesting testament to social mobility in maritime Massachusetts. Rising from middle-class circumstances to become a merchant prince of Salem and Boston, Gray demonstrated that vigor, intelligence, and luck could propel a man upward in a significant way. His career essentially belongs to the halcyon days of maritime Massachusetts, the period at the start of the nineteenth century when Yankee sea captains sailed the oceans from the Grand Banks to Canton, China. Although some controversy remains regarding Gray's motivations in supporting the Embargo Act of 1807, there seems little doubt that he was an active and sincere patriot of the United States as a whole. Gray's fortune was made by 1807, and he did not have to make a hard choice between patriotism and bankruptcy as did some of his fellows in Salem. Although he never recovered the goodwill of the people of Salem, Gray remained a memorable figure. At the time of his death in Boston, the Boston *Gazette* ran an obituary, which the *Salem Gazette* quoted, proclaiming his importance:

He has been an active merchant for more than half a century, and probably has been engaged in a more extensive commercial enterprise than any man who has lived on this continent in any period of its history; and it might be said without the slightest exxageration, that there was not a commercial place in the civilized world where his name was not familiar.

• Gray's papers were destroyed in the Boston fire of 1878. Some of the most valuable sources are Edward Gray, *William Gray of Salem, Merchant* (1914); Samuel Eliot Morison, *The Maritime History of Massachusetts, 1783–1860* (1921); and National Park Service, *Salem: Maritime Salem in the Age of Sail* (1987). Gray's relationship with John Quincy Adams and his involvement with the USS *Constitution* are related in Samuel Flagg Bemis, *John Quincy Adams and the Foundations of American Foreign Policy* (1949), and Bruce Grant, *Isaac Hull, Captain of Old Ironsides* (1947). Gray's taste in books is detailed in Harriet Silvester Tapley, *Salem Imprints, 1768–1825* (1927). One critical evaluation of Gray's support of the Embargo Act is in James Duncan Phillips, "Jefferson's 'Wicked Tyrannical Embargo,'" *New England Quarterly* 18 (Dec. 1945): 466–78.

SAMUEL WILLARD CROMPTON

GRAY, William Scott, Jr. (5 June 1885–8 Sept. 1960), reading expert, was born in Coatsburg, Illinois, the son of William Scott Gray, a schoolteacher and state senator from 1921 to 1923, and Annie Letitia Gilliland. After graduation from high school in 1904, Gray taught for a year in a one-room school in Adams County, Illinois, where he felt, in his own words, "distinctly unsuccessful" in teaching reading. From 1905 to 1908 he was principal and teacher in the village school in Fowler, Illinois. He entered Illinois State Normal University in 1908 and received his diploma in 1910.

At the university, he became immersed in Herbartianism, a humanistic philosophy of education focusing on children's interests and capacities. From 1910 to 1912 Gray served as principal and critic teacher supervising student teachers at the Normal University Training School. During this time he published his first professional writing, twelve articles in the *School Century* on the teaching of geography according to Herbartian principles.

In 1912 Gray went to the University of Chicago and received a B.S. in education in 1913. While at the university he met Charles Judd, head of the Department of Education and a proponent of the scientific study of education. Gray received an M.A. in 1914 from Teachers College, Columbia University, and worked there with Edward L. Thorndike, who, as the father of educational measurement, was another believer in scientific study. This approach involved experimentation in laboratories, quantified methods, and the use of statistics to study human learning and improve education. For his master's thesis Gray presented his "A Tentative Scale for Measuring Oral Reading." He further refined this test for his doctoral dissertation at the University of Chicago. Gray was appointed an instructor in education at the university in 1915; in 1916 he was awarded his Ph.D.; and was appointed dean of the College of Education in 1917. By 1921 he was a full professor. Also in 1921, Gray married Beatrice Warner Jardine; they had two children. He continued as dean until 1931, when the college was disbanded. Gray then served as executive secretary of the all-university Committee on the Preparation of Teachers until 1945 and, after his retirement in 1950, became director of research in reading. He was instrumental in founding the International Reading Association (IRA) and became its first president in 1955–1956.

In her book *Learning to Read: The Great Debate* (1967), Jeanne Chall calls Gray the "acknowledged leader of, and spokesman for, reading experts for four decades." Some of his success was undoubtedly due to his practical classroom experience as well as his ability to combine both humanistic and scientific approaches in his work. Gray's *Standardized Oral Reading Paragraphs* (1915) went through several major revisions and were widely used. The tests exhibited statistical measurements as well as concern for the comfort of both students and teachers. Because they were based on the analysis of reading errors, they led to diagnosis and remediation, gave insight into the nature of reading and the process of reading, and generated interest in the field. In 1922 Gray and his assistants published *Remedial Cases in Reading: Their Diagnosis and Treatment.* This landmark work, based on case histories and intended to pinpoint causes of reading disabilities and to plan individual instruction, utilized research in actual school settings and led to the development of remedial reading specialists.

One of Gray's special strengths was his talent for summarizing. His annual *Summary of Reading Investigations*, begun in 1925 and continuing until 1960, have since been published by the IRA. He summarized reading research for three editions of the *Encyclopedia of Educational Research* (1941, 1950, 1960), three important *Yearbooks of the National Society for the Study of Education* (1925, 1937, 1948), and the *Proceedings* of the University of Chicago Conferences on Reading. This work led to further research and presented a broadened view of the teaching of reading to include the development of readers' attitudes and problem-solving abilities in the elementary through adult years.

Gray's primary interest was the improvement of reading instruction. He was effective not because he was original but because he was knowledgeable, thorough, and practical. Although he never produced a reading methods text, he did publish *Improving Instruction in Reading: An Experimental Study* (1933), with Gertrude Whipple, and *The Development of Meaning Vocabularies in Reading: An Experimental Study* (1938), with Eleanor Holmes. These texts clearly and thoroughly disseminated the latest methods of teaching reading to educators throughout the country. They stressed the importance of systematic guidance and constructive leadership by administrators and led to an interest in content area reading (mathematics, science, social studies, etc.). Gray's work on adult reading increased interest in American illiteracy and readability formulas.

Gray became internationally involved as he analyzed the teaching of reading in Puerto Rico (1936) and Egypt (1950) and as he examined world literacy for the United Nations Educational, Scientific, and Cultural Organization (UNESCO) in *The Teaching of Reading and Writing: An International Survey* (1956). In this work he recommended a combination of teaching techniques, as a single method might not be effective for everyone. His influential model of reading, published posthumously, summed up his view of the reading process as an interrelated unit consisting of word perception, comprehension, reaction, and assimilation.

Gray's most famous work concerning the teaching of reading was his connection with the "Dick and Jane" readers, America's leading basal reader series, published by Scott, Foresman and Company. Coauthor of the *Elson Basic Readers* in 1930 and senior author of the revised *Basic Readers* of the 1930s, 1940s, and 1950s, Gray issued specific instructions to his authors. He wanted stories that were interesting and pertinent for children, that were full of action, suspense, and humor, and at the same time that presented a gradual increase in vocabulary, sentence structure, and plot complexity. He described his series in a 1932 letter to Nila Banton Smith: "an attractive, well-organized content of first-class authorship, amply provided with modern study-helps and well-illustrated by many well-known artists." One estimate in the 1950s found the readers successful in 86,000 schools. Their social values and teaching methods influenced generations of students and teachers.

Gray was a prodigious writer as well as a serious, modest, well-liked, and practical man. He died in Wolf, Wyoming. Evidences of his reputation include the William S. Gray Research Professorship in Reading, established by the University of Chicago; the title "Mr. Reading," bestowed on him by the IRA; and the IRA's William S. Gray Citation of Merit for outstanding contributions to reading.

• Papers concerning Gray are in the Special Collections of the University of Chicago under the following headings: William S. Gray, Charles H. Judd, College and Department of Education. Gray's own short autobiographical piece of 1931 is in the Gray Room, Judd Hall, University of Chicago. Together with his sister Lillian R. Gray, Gray privately printed *Record of the Family of Isaac and Sarah Hawkins Gray* in 1955, which contains photographs. The most comprehensive account of his life and work is Nancy A. Mavrogenes, "William Scott Gray: Leader of Teachers and Shaper of American Reading Instruction" (Ph.D. diss., Univ. of Chicago, 1985). See also the IRA booklet edited by Jennifer Stevenson entitled *William S. Gray: Teacher, Scholar, Leader* (1985); June R. Gilstad, "William S. Gray (1885–1960): First IRA President," *Reading Research Quarterly* 20 (1985): 509–11; and Allan Luke, "Making Dick and Jane: Historical Genesis of the Modern Basal Reader," *Teachers College Record* 89 (1987): 91–116. A shorter account of his career is W. J. Moore, "Pioneers in Reading I: William Scott Gray," *Elementary English* 34 (1957): 326–28, and Moore, "William S. Gray, 1885–1960, *Elementary English* 38 (1961): 187–89. Other brief biographical sketches are available from the University of Chicago Department of Education, President's Office, and Office of Public Information. Obituaries dated 9 Sept. 1960 are in the *New York Times*, the *Chicago Tribune*, and *Chicago's American*.

NANCY A. MAVROGENES

GRAYDON, Alexander (10 Apr. 1752–2 May 1818), author and public official, was born in Bristol, Pennsylvania, the son of Alexander Graydon, who had emigrated from Ireland in 1730 and become a Philadelphia merchant and lawyer, and his second wife, Rachel Marks. When her husband died in 1761, Rachel Graydon and her children moved from the family home in Bristol to Philadelphia, where to augment her slender means she took in boarders. Young Alexander dropped out of the College and Academy of Philadelphia at age fourteen to read law with an uncle but seems equally to have been studying his mother's boarders, among whom were sophisticated British officers and theater people. His somewhat reckless social life (recalled with evident pleasure in his *Memoirs*) was temporarily checked at sixteen, when his uncle placed him with a friend in York for six months of further study. He was not yet a lawyer at twenty-three when military matters took precedence.

Commissioned a captain by the Continental Congress in January 1776, he was entrusted with an important mission to General Philip Schuyler at Lake George in May. Returning to the troops that he had recruited and trained during the winter, he commanded his company in covering the retreat from Long Island and in the battle of Harlem Heights, where he was taken prisoner in September. Released months later on parole, he was formally exchanged in the spring of 1778. With no regiment to return to or suitable military opportunity in view, he resumed his legal studies, this time in Reading, Pennsylvania. He enlisted in the Berks County militia but saw no active service. Though he supported the Revolution, he was repelled by the harsh treatment of Loyalists and remained aloof from politics for a time. As a Federalist, he was a conspicuous early advocate of the Constitution and served as a delegate to the Pennsylvania state convention in 1790. Elected prothonotary of the newly formed Dauphin County, Pennsylvania, in 1785, he moved to Harrisburg. He continued in office until he was dismissed in 1799 by Thomas McKean, the new Jeffersonian governor. Graydon married his second wife, Theodosia Pettit of Philadelphia, the same year; his first wife, a Miss Wood of Berks County, whom he had married in 1778, had died in 1794. He had no children with either wife. Graydon lived the rest of his life on his small farm near Harrisburg, where he worked at various writing projects, including "Notes of a Desultory Reader," which appeared in seventeen issues (July 1812–Jan. 1815) of the *Port Folio*, the leading literary magazine, then being edited by young Nicholas Biddle.

The work for which Graydon is best remembered was first published anonymously in Harrisburg in 1811 as *Memoirs of a Life, Chiefly Passed in Pennsylvania, within the Last Sixty Years, with Occasional Remarks upon the General Occurrences, Character, and Spirit of That Eventful Period*. An Edinburgh edition appeared in 1822 with an appreciative introduction by Scottish novelist John Galt, which surfaced again in an edition of 1828 with a changed but hardly more informative title. Finally, in the Philadelphia edition of 1846, the contents were suitably indicated on the title page: *Memoirs of His Own Time, with Reminiscences of Men and Events of the Revolution, by Alexander Graydon*. Ten years later the editors of the *Cyclopedia of American Literature* characterized the book as "a choice volume . . . which has not been valued as it deserves to be" (vol. 1, p. 352). Never wholly lost sight of since then, the book (reprinted in 1969) has been cited chiefly for its historical information rather than its literary merit, though Graydon's intention was not only to write about the Revolution as he experienced it but also to reflect on its consequences. Both a chronicle of events and an introspective autobiography, the book is a personal narrative, conservative in outlook and Burkean in tone, by a man in his late maturity using his admirable literary skill to examine his life and instruct his fellow citizens.

• Unpublished letters and miscellaneous items relating to Graydon are in collections at the American Philosophical Society, Dickinson College, Haverford College, Lebanon Valley College, the Library of Congress, the New York Public Library, and the Pennsylvania Historical Society. The title of the second Edinburgh edition (1828) of Graydon's book reads *The Life of an Officer, Written by Himself during a Residence in Pennsylvania: With Anecdotes of the American War*. The Philadelphia edition of 1846, edited by John Stockton Littell, was reprinted in 1969. Robert Reed Sanderlin's unpublished "Alexander Graydon: The Life and Literary Career of an American Patriot" (Ph.D. diss., Univ. of North Carolina, Chapel Hill, 1968) presents in its first two chapters biographical material drawn from the *Memoirs* and adds information drawn from unpublished letters and public documents, some of them quoted in part in an appendix. An obituary is in *Poulson's American Daily Advertiser* (Philadelphia), 4 May 1818.

VINCENT FREIMARCK

GRAY LOCK (fl. 1723–1744), Abenaki war chief, was born probably along the Westfield River in Massachusetts, apparently the son of Woronoco (or Waranoke) parents. Gray Lock grew up in a time of catastrophic change and upheaval among the Indians of New England. In the great dispersal of Indian peoples produced by King Philip's War (1675–1676), Gray Lock's family retreated north away from the English frontier, and Gray Lock eventually settled at the Western Abenaki village of Missisquoi, near present-day Swanton, Vermont, on the northern end of Lake Champlain.

At a time when the Abenakis of northern New England were confronting growing pressure from the northern expansion of English colonies to the south, Gray Lock rose to prominence as a war leader. A refugee himself, he drew support from people displaced by conflict with the English. During Queen Anne's War (1702–1713) he was described as "a French Indian," since the Abenakis, along with many other Indians removed from New England, made common cause with the French in Canada in an effort to check English expansion. The Treaty of Utrecht, which ended Queen Anne's War, did not remove the root causes of Anglo-Abenaki tension or halt English encroachment on Abenaki land, and fighting broke out anew in 1722. By 1723 Gray Lock attracted a following of warriors from neighboring communities such as Caughnawaga, Schaghticoke, Bécancour, and St. Francis to his headquarters close to Missisquoi. French and English maps of the time noted the location of "Gray Lock's castle."

While the French, the colonists of New York, and the Iroquois watched from the wings, Abenakis from the coast of Maine to Lake Champlain battled against the Massachusetts colony. Known as Dummer's War, Lovewell's War, or Father Rasle's War in Maine, its western phase should more accurately be called "Gray Lock's War" since the Missisquoi chief dictated the course of the conflict in Vermont and western Massachusetts.

For several years Gray Lock and his warriors conducted guerrilla raids against the Massachusetts frontier, harrying the settlements, carrying off captives, and draining the colonies of their resources and morale. The government of Massachusetts built Fort Dummer, near present-day Brattleboro, Vermont, in an effort to check his raids, but to little avail. Gray Lock struck Northfield, Hatfield, Deerfield, Northampton, and other towns in the Connecticut Valley, but English counterstrikes failed to reach Missisquoi. Gray Lock consistently eluded his enemies and acquired the name Wawánolewát, meaning "he who fools the others or puts someone off the track."

By 1725 the war in Maine was winding down. Exhausted by years of fighting during which the English had burned some of their villages, the Penobscots and other Eastern Abenaki groups made peace with Massachusetts in 1725 and 1726. Abenakis from Canada agreed to peace terms in 1727. The English dispatched Indian emissaries to Gray Lock, inviting him to negotiate a settlement also, but Gray Lock refused to respond. The English attributed his intransigence to French influence and the fact that he had "done Much Mischief on ye fronteers & has doubtless a Guilty Conscience," but it is more likely that Gray Lock saw no reason to come to terms with enemies he had consistently beaten and eluded. He had fought the war for his own reasons and on his own terms, and it ended with him undefeated and defiant. Missisquoi remained a center of Abenaki resistance and independence throughout the French and Indian wars later in the century.

After the war Gray Lock all but disappeared from the records. French mission registers record that "La Tête Blanche" and his wife, Hélène, were baptized and that they had two children. The last mention of him seems to have been recorded when visiting Indians from Schaghticoke reported seeing "Gray Lock a Massesqueek Sachem" at Missisquoi in 1744.

Gray Lock died probably sometime before 1753. The exact date and circumstances of his death and his place of burial are unknown. His enemies' descendants paid Gray Lock belated tribute by giving his name to the highest peak in the Berkshire Mountains in Massachusetts.

• References to Gray Lock are scattered sparsely throughout colonial records and nineteenth-century histories. Colin G. Calloway, "Gray Lock's War," *Vermont History* 55 (1987): 212–27, and Gordon M. Day, "Gray Lock," *Dictionary of Canadian Biography*, vol. 3 (1974), pp. 265–66, draw together most of the available evidence. Calloway, *The Western Abenakis of Vermont: War, Migration, and the Survival of an Indian People* (1990), includes a chapter on "Gray Lock's War" and provides historical context on the Abenakis.

COLIN G. CALLOWAY

GRAYSON, William (1736–12 Mar. 1790), lawyer, soldier, and statesman, was born in Prince William County, Virginia, the son of Susanna Monroe and Benjamin Grayson, a merchant and factor. He attended the College of Philadelphia (now the University of Pennsylvania), graduating in 1760. Some controversy exists concerning whether he next proceeded to Oxford or to Edinburgh, but the absence of his name from the rolls at Oxford, coupled with his great devotion to the teachings of Adam Smith, seems to militate in favor of the Scottish university. According to tradition, he then received legal training at the Inns of Court. He married Eleanor Smallwood.

On returning to Virginia from Great Britain, in late 1765 or early 1766 Grayson took up law in Dumfries, where he lived within walking distance of his friend George Washington. He took the public stage in the Westmoreland County meeting that adopted the Asso-

ciation of 1766, the nation's first private association of men committed to foregoing purchase of British goods for political reasons.

In 1775 Grayson served in the Virginia Convention, which acted as the colony's legislature after Lord Dunmore prorogued the legal legislature. In 1776 Grayson was made a colonel of infantry in the fledgling Virginia army, but Washington soon drew Grayson into his military "family." Grayson was at Valley Forge and participated in the battles of Long Island and White Plains. Becoming a regimental commander, he fought in the battles of Brandywine and Germantown; his unit was first in the order of battle at Monmouth. When his brigade was absorbed by another, in 1779 he resigned his commission to serve as commissioner of the Board of War, where he stayed until 1781.

Grayson returned to law until he was elected to the general assembly in 1784. He was appointed to Congress from Virginia later that year. In Congress, as acting president, he offered energetic support to the Northwest Ordinance, which he privately hymned as beneficial to Virginians in excluding slavery, and thus potential competitors for the world tobacco market, from the Midwest. He returned to the general assembly in 1788.

Grayson's experience in the Continental Congress convinced him that the federal government should be yielded greater power. The proposal made by the Philadelphia convention of 1787 displeased him in its great nationalism, however, and he became an opponent of the proposed constitution in the ratifying convention held in Richmond. The friends of the states' predominance in American politics, whom their opponents mislabeled "Antifederalists," counted Grayson among their leading champions because he was, in the general opinion of his fellows, the single greatest debater in Virginia. As an orator he exhibited the breadth of his learning, his extensive relevant experience, a notable sense of humor, and a command of caustic sarcasm. He was tall, and his manners showed the polish of a man educated in Great Britain's finest schools. In addition, his family relations included fellow Antifederalist James Monroe, and "he was considered . . . the handsomest man in the Convention"—an appraisal borne out by the surviving portraits (Grigsby, p. 202).

Grayson's Antifederalism was founded on the premise that the other twelve states would never be able to sustain a union of which Virginia was not a member. The eastern states, he said, must have a union, for their fisheries were vulnerable to British depredations; New York and Pennsylvania could have no fur trade without union; the small states would never quarrel with the giants; and, in Britain, "Thank heaven, we have a Carthage of our own." The others would always need Virginia. If Virginia refused to ratify, the other states would alter the new charter to please Virginia, for citizens of all the states shared ties of law, religion, language, manners, and even marriage. If Virginia simply entered into the new arrangement, Grayson argued, the Old Dominion would soon find its interests subordinated to those of the carrying-state (northeastern) majority; representation offered no protection of a minority section's economic interests. The treaty power alone was sufficient, even without the commerce clause, to prompt him to oppose ratification. To support his position he pointed to the Jay-Gardoqui Treaty's provision for yielding the Mississippi River navigation to Spain, an action Grayson held to have been calculated to maintain New England's position in the Union by preventing population of the western lands. This point apparently cemented the Kentucky delegates' opposition to the proposed constitution.

Taxes laid on states as disparate as the parties to the proposed constitution could not be uniform, as the Philadelphia document required, without being oppressive to some and generous to others, Grayson contended. To Federalists' contention that the tariff would long be low, he responded that for an agrarian country with enormous expanses of unsettled lands, the day when manufactured items would not be imported was but a glint on the horizon. As a result of both of these taxation-related problems, the "producing," or non–New England, states would suffer. When an opponent stated that a future convention might undo an erroneous decision, Grayson retorted, "It is not so easy to dissolve a government like that upon the table" (Grigsby, p. 216).

Grayson had strong views about the necessity of reform. He would support "giv[ing] Congress the regulation of commerce" and laying the public debts on the western lands. The proposed government, though, was too strong for a federal and too weak for a national one. He would favor life senators, a triennial House of Representatives, and a life executive if there were to be a strong new government. However, following the baron de Montesquieu's teaching that a government should be designed to fit the genius of the people it is to govern and taking into account the rapid immigration and economic flux Americans were experiencing, he judged it too early a juncture for a thorough revision of the American polity. Though he trusted his friend Washington to act virtuously as president, saying, "We have no fear of tyranny *while he lives*," Grayson feared succeeding events. He insisted that amendments diluting the new government's national nature precede ratification.

The new charter was ratified by exactly the margin Grayson had privately predicted before the Richmond convention even met. Washington's support and the previous ratification of nine other states may have affected the outcome, but it seems unlikely. While the rhetoric of both sides was very learned, virtually all of the delegates had been elected on the basis of their announced intentions regarding the final vote on ratification, and almost no one's vote was changed by what he heard in Richmond. Virginia's leading Antifederalist, Patrick Henry, rewarded Grayson for his performance with election as the state's first U.S. senator. Grayson and Virginia's other senator, Richard Henry Lee, proposed constitutional amendments relating to the government's substantial new powers like the amend-

ments the Richmond convention had recommended, but they were rejected. The Senate also rejected the Virginia tandem's argument that Senate proceedings should be public. Additionally, Congress soon enacted what Grayson took to be a sectional tariff act. In sum, events seemed to bear out his dire expectations.

While vacationing between sessions of the First Congress, Grayson died of gout, from which he had suffered since 1786, at his brother's home in Dumfries, Virginia. By his will, he emancipated all of his slaves born after the Declaration of Independence.

• No collection of Grayson papers exists, but material on him is in the Virginia State Library, the Virginia Historical Society, and the major letterpress editions of those of such figures as James Madison and George Washington. See also the published primary collections relevant to the Continental Congress, including Paul H. Smith, ed., *Letters of Delegates to Congress, 1774–1789* (1985–1996). Biographical treatments of Grayson include James E. DuPriest, Jr., *William Grayson: A Political Biography of Virginia's First United States Senator* (1977), and Harry E. Baylor, Jr., "The Political Career of Colonel William Grayson, 1784–1789" (M.A. thesis, Univ. of Virginia, 1933). The most important source is Hugh Blair Grigsby, *The History of the Virginia Federal Convention of 1788* (1857; repr. 1969), by a longtime president of the Virginia Historical Society, member of the Va. convention of 1829–1830, and personal friend of the relatives of several participants in the events of the revolutionary period. Also very important for Grayson studies is John P. Kaminski et al., eds., *The Documentary History of the Ratification of the United States Constitution* (3 vols., 1988–1993).

K. R. CONSTANTINE GUTZMAN

GRAYSON, William John (12 Nov. 1788–4 Oct. 1863), politician and author, was born in Beaufort, South Carolina, the son of William John Grayson, a sheriff of the Beaufort District, and Susannah Greene. His father, who had been an officer during the American Revolution, died in 1797 at the age of thirty-seven; eleven months later Susannah Grayson married William Joyner, a widower and wealthy planter of the Beaufort District. Young Grayson early developed an insatiable desire for learning. From 1801 to 1803 he attended private academies in the North in preparation for admission to either Yale or Harvard. Accustomed to the gentility and hospitality of the South, he chose instead the new South Carolina College (now University of South Carolina).

Following graduation in 1809, he returned to the plantation of his mother and stepfather and led, as he recounted in his autobiography, a life of indolence until November 1813, when the voters of St. Helena's Parish elected him to the state legislature. There he poured his chief efforts into sponsoring a bill for statewide and state-supported education. On 6 January 1814 he married Sarah Matilda Somarsall, the daughter of a wealthy Charleston merchant and planter; they were to have seven children. He found himself faced with the everyday tasks of earning a livelihood, and thus he temporarily abandoned his dreams of a literary career. Except for the year 1816, when he was principal of Savannah Academy, Grayson held positions as teacher and assistant principal at Beaufort College from 1815 to 1819.

Grayson then studied law for fifteen months, passed the bar exam, and in 1822 began practicing law in the Beaufort District Court at Cossawhatchie. Believing himself unsuited and ill prepared for this profession, he turned to politics. He served as a state representative from 1822 to 1826 and then as a state senator until 1831, when he resigned to become commissioner in equity of the Beaufort District. During the nullification crisis in the 1830s he edited the *Beaufort Gazette*, organ of the Nullification and Free Trade party. He agreed with the states' rights beliefs of the Nullifiers but opposed the extreme measure of disunion, which some espoused. In 1833 Grayson was elected to the U.S. House of Representatives, was reelected in 1835, but was defeated for reelection in 1837.

In 1841 President John Tyler (1790–1862) appointed him collector of customs for the port of Charleston, a post he held for almost twelve years. When President Franklin Pierce was elected in 1852, Grayson was removed from office through the influence of the secessionists, whose views he publicly opposed. He had deserted the old Nullifiers when secessionism grew during the late 1840s and became a leader in his state in advocating preservation of the Union. In a pamphlet entitled *Letter to His Excellency, Whitemarsh B. Seabrook, Governor of the State of South Carolina, on the Dissolution of the Union* (1850), Grayson set forth the thesis that "disorder, violence, and civil war" would follow on the heels of disunion and would result only in disaster for the southern states. *Letters of Curtius* (1851), written in the caustic Swiftian style and published anonymously, further exposed the fallacies of the secessionists. Grayson advocated not political but social and economic separation—in essence, a boycott of northern manufactured goods, services, and institutions.

By April 1853 Grayson was able to purchase the magnificent "Fair Lawn" plantation near Charleston. With one dream fulfilled, he could reach toward another; in his sixties he seriously embarked upon a literary career. He helped his Charleston friends launch *Russell's Magazine* (1857–1860) by writing the leading article and became a frequent contributor of poems, essays, and essay reviews. The editor, Paul H. Hayne, in a post–Civil War reminiscence, "Ante-Bellum Charleston," fondly remembered Grayson as "tall, gray-headed, erect as a dart, the chief expression of whose face was a placid benevolence." At a time when the tenets of the British Romantics were making inroads, Grayson clung tenaciously to the neoclassical tradition, admitting that his taste was old fashioned, although he argued for the acceptance of various types of poetry and poets of varying degrees of talent. In "What Is Poetry?"—an essay published in *Russell's Magazine* (1857)—he argued that the chief difference between poetry and prose is not the choice of subject but its metrical form. Most of his poems have received little attention. He celebrated the charms of rural life in *The Country* (1858). "Chicora" is similar to Henry Wadsworth Longfellow's humane poetic treatment of the Indians. "Threescore Years and Seven," expressing genuine religious feeling, has been cited by Jay B. Hubbell as Grayson's best short lyric. Grayson's last sustained poem, "Marion," eulogized Francis Marion, the famous American revolutionary war general.

Grayson strongly resented the imputations heaped upon southern slave owners by British and Northern writers—especially Harriet Beecher Stowe in *Uncle Tom's Cabin* (1852). In his best-known didactic poem, *The Hireling and the Slave* (1854), Grayson chose his favorite form, the heroic couplet, to defend the institution of slavery. He painted an idyllic picture of contented slaves receiving full care and protection—a stark contrast to the squalid existence of northern and British day laborers. In a preface he proclaimed, "I do not say that slavery is the best system of labor, but only that it is the best for the Negro in this country." However, he did not advocate restoring the slave trade.

Grayson lived to witness the horrors of the Civil War, during which he penned a brief war diary, his autobiography, and a memoir of his lifelong friend James L. Petigru—all published posthumously. Fearing that Union troops would confiscate his valuable papers, he destroyed most of them himself. He died in Newberry, South Carolina.

Grayson's autobiography, considered by some critics his best prose, has received little attention until recently. Written in a lively style, it reflects his perceptive antisecessionist views—while, ironically, his best-known work is a poetic, tenacious justification of slavery. He is primarily remembered today as the author of *The Hireling and the Slave*, the most notable of the many replies to *Uncle Tom's Cabin*. Few can claim to have read its 1,500 lines, though segments from it appear in anthologies; its title is usually cited when Grayson's name is mentioned by historians.

• The extensive bibliography in Richard J. Calhoun, ed., *Witness to Sorrow: The Antebellum Autobiography of William J. Grayson* (1990), lists libraries where clippings and the like about Grayson may be found. The manuscript "Autobiography" in the University of South Carolina Library was edited, with an introduction, by Robert D. Bass, "The Autobiography of William J. Grayson" (Ph.D. diss., Univ. of South Carolina, 1933), and S. G. Stoney published it in part in the *South Carolina Historical and Genealogical Magazine* (1947–1950). *Selected Poems by William J. Grayson* (1907) was edited by Grayson's daughter, Mrs. William H. Armstrong. Grayson's other major publications include *The Union, Past and Future: How It Works and How to Save It* (1850); *The Hireling and the Slave, Chicora, and Other Poems* (1856); and *James Louis Petigru: A Biographical Sketch* (1866).

Also, see Thomas D. Jarrett, "The Literary Significance of William J. Grayson's *The Hireling and the Slave*," *Georgia Review* 5, no. 4 (1951): 487–94; Jay B. Hubbell, *The South in American Literature* (1954); Edd Winfield Parks, *Ante-Bellum Southern Literary Critics* (1962); and Edmund Wilson, *Patriotic Gore: Studies in the Literature of the American Civil War* (1962).

RAY M. ATCHISON

GRAYZEL, Solomon (1 Mar. 1896–12 Aug. 1980), historian and rabbi, was born in Minsk, Russia, the son of Dov-Behr Grayzel, a *melamed* (teacher) and former student at the renowned Slobodka Talmudic Academy, and Eta Kashdan. In 1908 Grayzel emigrated with his family to the United States, entering City College of New York in 1914 and graduating in 1917. In 1920 he earned an M.A. in sociology from Columbia and in 1927 a Ph.D. from the then Dropsie College. Shortly afterward, he married Sophie Solomon, the daughter of the well-known Conservative Rabbi Elias Solomon. The couple had no children.

Grayzel's professional activity commenced after his 1921 ordination from the Jewish Theological Seminary, when he became rabbi of Congregation Beth-El in Camden, New Jersey, where he remained until 1926, immediately preceding the completion of his doctoral studies. From either 1928 or 1929 to 1945 Grayzel served as registrar and professor of history at Gratz College in Philadelphia. The year 1927–1928 he spent in Europe, collecting materials for his *The Church and the Jews in the Thirteenth Century, 1198–1254* (vol. 1, 1933; 2d ed., 1966; vol. 2, posthumously ed. by K. R. Stow, 1989). This work, justly the source of Grayzel's scholarly repute, was the first critical and unbiased examination of papal attitudes toward the Jews; previous works by such scholars as L. Erler and Moritz Stern either contained anti-Jewish prejudice or lacked scholarly analysis. Grayzel may also have been the first Jew to have access to the papal archives at the Vatican for scholarly purposes.

In 1939 Grayzel added to his scholarly activity by becoming assistant editor of the Jewish Publication Society (then the major source of scholarly and semischolarly publications about Jews and Judaism in English) and within months was its editor, following the premature death of Isaac Husik. Grayzel remained in this post until 1966 (simultaneously serving, from 1956, as recording secretary of the American Jewish Historical Society). Between 1945 and 1950 he was also president of the Jewish Book Council, editing its publication, the *Jewish Book Annual*, from its inception in 1942 until 1945 and serving on its advisory board from 1962. Grayzel's stated goal in his work with the council and the annual was "to affect the intellectual interest of American Jewry."

As editor of the JPS, Grayzel oversaw the publication of Salo Baron's multivolume *A Social and Religious History of the Jews* (1952–) and chaired the JPS Bible project, leading to a new translation of the Hebrew Bible. Grayzel held this post until near his death. Under Grayzel's leadership, the JPS made available dozens of scholarly works of Judaica—long before Jewish Studies entered the curricula of public universities—to an audience that otherwise would have remained ignorant of their existence. All together, Grayzel edited 200 books, adopting an editorial stance that was at once thoughtful, but open to bold new conceptions, such as Will Herberg's *Judaism and Modern Man: An Interpretation of Jewish Religion* (1951). However, Grayzel rarely took sufficient credit for his

achievements and so received less acclaim than he deserved.

Based on his lectures at Gratz College, Grayzel wrote *A History of the Jews* (1947; rev. ed., 1968), a textbook aimed at increasing Jewish pride following the disasters of World War II. This book has been translated into numerous languages. Grayzel also wrote numerous pioneering articles. Indeed, nobody has analyzed the fourteenth-century papacy and the Jews as thoroughly as did Grayzel in "The Avignon Popes and the Jews" (*Historia Judaica* [1940]), "References to the Jews in the Correspondence of John XXII" (*Hebrew Union College Annual* [1950]), and, especially, "The Confessions of a Medieval Jewish Convert" (*Historia Judaica* [1955]), which has become a classic, portraying through translation the tension created by attacks, forced conversion, and the reactions of a "conscientious" Inquisitor, Jacques Fournier, the future Benedict XII. "The Jews and Roman Law" (*Jewish Quarterly Review* [1968]) was the first article ever to treat this subject directly. Perhaps Grayzel's best-known piece is "The Papal Bull 'Sicut Iudaeis'" (*Studies and Essays in Honor of A. A. Neuman* [1962]), a study of the fundamental document regulating medieval papal relations with the Jews. *Sicut Iudaeis*, Grayzel argued, established a permanent basis for Jewish legal stability. Yet, seventeen years later, and nearing his eightieth birthday, Grayzel produced the masterful "Popes, Jews, and Inquisition from 'Sicut' to 'Turbato'" (*Essays on the Occasion of the Seventieth Anniversary of Dropsie University* [1979]). Rejecting his earlier position, he said that *Sicut Iudaeis* theoretically made room for Jews in Christian medieval society but that the force of events eventually led the popes to opt for the spirit of *Turbato corde*, the bull authorizing the Inquisition to prosecute Jews who gave aid and comfort to heretics, especially apostate converts from Judaism to Christianity.

As a scholar, Grayzel was thus capable of rethinking positions even in his truly golden years. Herein lies his true legacy. Throughout his life, Grayzel committed himself to the dissemination of accurate knowledge about the Jewish past. This goal fueled his meticulousness (and even self-effacement) as an editor as much as it led him constantly to reassess what he himself had written and to embark with a sense of dispassionate scholarly drive on a hitherto essentially untraveled route, the history of the popes and the Jews. It is thanks especially to the probing questions Grayzel asked of his materials that the basic lines of the field were staked out. The history of the popes and the Jews became part of the history of the papacy as a whole, a topic subject to the normal canons of historical method and research, no longer just another chapter in a dismal, alternately moralizing or apologetic tale of medieval Jewish oppression.

Grayzel resided in Philadelphia until very shortly before his death. He died peacefully of cardiac arrest while resting after dinner at the home of his sister-in-law, Vivian Rous, in Englewood, New Jersey.

• Many of Grayzel's letters as JPS editor are housed in the Philadelphia Jewish Archives Center. Other important works by Grayzel include "Jewish References in a Thirteen-Century Formulary," *Jewish Quarterly Review* 46 (1955): 44–65; "The Talmud and the Medieval Papacy," in *Essays in Honor of Solomon B. Freehof*, ed. Walter Jacob et al. (1964), pp. 220–45; "Jews and the Ecumenical Councils," in *Seventy-fifth Anniversary Volume of the* Jewish Quarterly Review, ed. Abraham A. Neuman and Solomon Zeitlin (1967), pp. 287–311; and "Pope Alexander III and the Jews," in *Salo Wittmayer Baron Jubilee Volume on the Occasion of His Eightieth Birthday*, vol. 2 (1975), pp. 555–72. Biographies of Grayzel are by A. Alan Steinbach, "Solomon Grayzel: On the Occasion of His 75th Birthday," *Jewish Book Annual* 28 (1970): 110–15, and Kenneth R. Stow, "Solomon Grayzel, 1896–1980," *Jewish Book Annual* 39 (1981): 158–63. Jonathan D. Sarna, *JPS: The Americanization of Jewish Culture, 1888–1988* (1989), discusses Grayzel's tenure as JPS editor. No history which in any way touches that of the popes and the Jews fails to cite Grayzel's works, for example, Edward A. Synan, *The Popes and the Jews in the Middle Ages* (1965), and Shlomo Simonsohn, *The Apostolic See and the Jews* (1990).

KENNETH R. STOW

GRAZIANO, Rocky (1 Jan. 1919–22 May 1990), champion middleweight boxer and entertainer, was born Thomas Rocco Barbella in New York City, the son of Nicholas Barbella, a longshoreman and former boxer, and Ida Scinto. Graziano grew up impoverished on Manhattan's Lower East Side. He seldom attended school and dropped out before his teens. According to his own accounts, he and his friends were constantly stealing and getting into fights (he claimed to be "the best street fighter in history"). His heroes, he claimed, were Italian gangsters and tough-guy movie stars. Arrested at twelve for breaking into a subway gum machine, he was placed on probation. He was then caught stealing a bicycle and was sent to the Catholic Protectory in the Bronx, New York, a reform school, for the first of three terms he spent there. He prided himself on being tough, and he spent considerable time in solitary confinement. Each time he was released from incarceration, he returned to the streets and petty crimes. Rocky continued to be in and out of trouble in his late teen years. In 1938 he was sent to the State Vocational School in Coxackie and then to the New York City Reformatory in upstate Goshen, where he served three different stretches, interspersed with five months in the Tombs in New York City.

In 1939, at a friend's urging, Graziano visited Stillman's Gym near Madison Square Garden to test his street-fighting skills. After sparring unsuccessfully with a seasoned professional, he dropped the notion of becoming a prizefighter. However, he returned to Stillman's two months later and went on to a distinguished amateur career, capped off with the Metropolitan AAU welterweight award medal, which he said he pawned for $15.

During Graziano's third term at the reformatory in 1941, he got into so much trouble that he was sent to the city prison on Riker's Island, where he again spent an inordinate amount of time in solitary confinement. Released in October 1941, after serving five months,

he was drafted into the army three months later. He did not adjust to military discipline, and after arguing with a sergeant and beating up a captain, he went AWOL. To avoid arrest, he began fighting professionally under the name of his sister's boyfriend, Tommy Rocky Graziano. In less than two months he won seven of eight fights, including five knockouts. However, he was arrested and returned to the army in June 1942. He received a dishonorable discharge and was sentenced to a year at Fort Leavenworth, Kansas. There, he joined the boxing team, behaved according to the rules, and was released after nine months.

Graziano resumed his boxing career in early June 1943, training with the renowned Whitey Bimstein. Graziano became a great crowd pleaser because even at 5'7" he was a brawler with little concern for defense or finesse. That year he married Norma Unger; they had two children. By 1945 he had become a favorite of celebrities like Frank Sinatra and Al Capone. Usually fighting at 154 pounds, Graziano recorded thirty-two knockouts in his first fifty-four fights. In 1945 he twice knocked out welterweight champion Red Cochrane in nontitle matches, and in 1946 he scored a nontitle knockout of Cochrane's successor, Marty Servo.

Graziano became a leading middleweight and earned a match in New York with champion Tony Zale on 27 September 1946. Zale had won the championship in 1941, then joined the navy during the war. The fight at Yankee Stadium was attended by 39,827. Graziano had Zale in trouble in the early rounds, but the champion survived and knocked out Graziano in the sixth round. *Ring* magazine named Zale Fighter of the Year for his defense; boxing historians consider the match a classic.

Early in 1947 the New York State Athletic Commission suspended Graziano for failing to report a bribe offer in the Reuben Shank fight that was canceled when Graziano injured himself while training. One of his managers at the time, Eddie Coco, was considered a front man for Frankie Carbo, the alleged underworld czar of boxing. Despite the suspension, Graziano, a terrific box office draw, secured an Illinois license for a rematch against local hero Zale in Chicago. The July 1947 fight had a $422,918 gate, a record for an indoor arena. Graziano took a beating in the early rounds, but he persevered with a sixth-round knockout to gain the middleweight championship. After the fight, the Illinois legislature passed a law barring dishonorably discharged soldiers from boxing there. Graziano defended his crown in June 1948 against Zale in Jersey City, New Jersey. Zale regained the title with a third-round knockout. All three fights are considered to be among the most exciting in modern boxing history.

Graziano subsequently won twenty-one straight matches, which earned him a middleweight title shot on 16 April 1952 against Sugar Ray Robinson, who knocked him out in the third round. Graziano retired after losing his next match to former collegiate champion Chuck Davey. Overall, he compiled a record of 67 victories (52 knockouts), 10 losses, and 6 draws; he was named to *Ring* magazine's Boxing Hall of Fame in

1971. Experts consider him a good puncher and outstanding competitor, although not a great boxer. He was always a crowd favorite.

In 1952 Graziano's life story was told in *Somebody Up There Likes Me*, which was made into a motion picture (1956) starring Paul Newman. Graziano's fame and colorful personality led to a successful career in the entertainment field. He started out doing television commercials. A natural comedian, known for his fractured language and stereotypical New York accent, he became a regular on television's "The Martha Raye Show" from 1952 to 1955, earning up to $2,500 a week. He wrote a second autobiography and had several one-man shows of his paintings. A member of the President's Council on Physical Fitness, he coauthored *The Rocky Road to Physical Fitness* (1968). He died in New York City.

• Graziano's autobiography and a follow-up (with Ralph Corsel), *Somebody Down Here Likes Me Too* (1981), are colorful and anecdotal, but not entirely reliable. On his 1947 suspension, see "Nat Fleischer Says," *Ring* 27 (Feb. 1948): 10, and Barney Nagler, *James Norris and the Decline of Boxing* (1964). For views of Graziano's boxing career, see Dick Friendlich, "Blood over Newark," in *Best Sports Stories, 1949*, ed. Irving T. Marsh and Edward Ehre (1950), and W. C. Heinz, "Fighter's Wife," in *The Fireside Book of Boxing* (1961). For Graziano's record, see *Ring Record and Boxing Encyclopedia* (1984). An obituary is in the *New York Times*, 23 May 1990.

STEVEN A. RIESS

GREATHOUSE, Clarence Ridgley (17 Sept. 1843–21 Oct. 1899), lawyer and diplomat, was born in Shelbyville, Kentucky, the son of Ridgley Greathouse, a physician, and Mary Elizabeth Hancock. The family moved to California when Clarence was still young but returned to Kentucky in 1852 after his father's death from cholera. Little information is available about Greathouse's early life and education. He studied law and began his practice in Versailles, Kentucky. Returning to California in 1870, he became a resident of San Francisco, where he entered a law practice with Louis T. Haggin. Later he established a partnership with Gordon Blanding, and eventually that firm also included William T. Wallace. Greathouse invested in mining enterprises and helped organize the Bell Telephone Company in California. He purchased a part interest in the *San Francisco Examiner* and became general manager of that newspaper in 1883. A leading figure in state Democratic party circles, he was a close political associate of Governor George Stoneman. Although he enjoyed a reputation in San Francisco as a "lawyer of rare ability," he was also a notorious eccentric. He was absent-minded, never on time for appointments, and often stayed up all night walking the beat with the city's policemen. He never married, and his widowed mother resided with him until his death.

In 1886 President Grover Cleveland gave Greathouse a patronage appointment as consul general at Kanagawa (now Yokohama), Japan. Thereafter his contemporaries addressed him as "General" Great-

house. Although nothing remarkable characterized his service in Japan, the experience led to his appointment by the king of Korea as an adviser on foreign affairs on 12 September 1890. Why the king selected Greathouse in particular is not known, but the Korean government obviously sought his expert knowledge of the Western legal system. Known as the Hermit Kingdom, Korea had no diplomatic relations except with China through Beijing's ritualistic tribute system until Japan forced the country open with a treaty in 1876. In the two decades that followed, China and Japan competed for dominance in Korea, while Britain, Russia, and the United States maneuvered for commercial access. The Korean court considered the Americans less threatening than other outsiders and engaged several U.S. experts—military officers, lawyers, mining engineers, and others—to help Korea strengthen itself against foreign encroachment. In 1885 the government in Seoul named Owen N. Denny, an American attorney, as director of its foreign office and vice president of its home office. In these positions, Denny was a government official, not just a consultant, but he eventually resigned in frustration over Chinese intrigues in Korea. Following Denny's resignation, Korean leaders turned to Greathouse and another American, Charles W. LeGendre, to continue Denny's efforts to reform and manage the country's external and internal affairs.

Greathouse and LeGendre shared Denny's former title of vice president of the home office. In 1893 Greathouse also received the title of associate director of the new Korean Telegraph and Postal Service. Greathouse enjoyed the confidence of the king, and to some observers in the West, his role amounted to Korean attorney general or even prime minister. Despite his titles and closeness to the monarch, Greathouse's actual accomplishments were modest.

Greathouse had some definite impact on reform of the Korean legal system. He codified many Korean laws and brought Korea's statutes, especially commercial regulations, into closer conformity to international law. An American diplomat who knew Greathouse in Seoul recalled later that he "accomplished much in forming a legal procedure and establishing a principle in the nation's law and application" (Sands, p. 49). It was a "solid and permanent achievement," according to this observer, that equaled the more well-known Korean financial reforms of the Englishman John McLeavy Brown. Greathouse served as Korea's legal counsel in difficult negotiations with Japan over fishing rights and over Korean independence itself when Japan and China's struggle for superiority in the peninsula led to the Sino-Japanese War of 1894–1895. Despite the potential significance of Greathouse's reform efforts, neither he nor the other American advisers were able to transform Korea into a strong, progressive state. For example, the postal system remained inefficient even with Greathouse ostensibly in charge of it. Greathouse himself exhibited little personal ambition. His relaxed, indeed bohemian, manner and a faction-laden Korean political system prevented his work from making substantial transformations in Korea or attracting recognition for himself.

One notable event demonstrated Greathouse's salutary role but limited effectiveness as a legal reformer. In March 1896 thirteen Koreans were tried for their alleged participation in the brutal assassination of the Korean queen in October 1895. At the king's request, Greathouse supervised the trial and examined the witnesses. The *Korean Repository*, an English-language magazine in Seoul, reported that the proceedings were honest, open, free from torture, and "for general approximation to Western notions of justice and integrity . . . in every way remarkable." The testimony established that an incredible conspiracy involving Japanese diplomats and Korean reactionaries carried out the murder of the progressive and strong-willed queen, the real royal authority behind her weak husband. Greathouse's judicial findings on behalf of the effete king had little impact on Korea's destiny, however. Although Japanese involvement in the crime outraged American and European diplomats and missionaries, Western governments refused to get involved. With Japan having already defeated China in 1895, the future of Korea lay at the mercy of the Japanese and Russians, and Japan would eventually force its Russian rival from Korea in the Russo-Japanese War of 1904–1905. Greathouse did not live to see this denouement. He died in Seoul while still serving as the king's principal foreign adviser.

• No collection of Greathouse's papers is known to exist. Only a small number of items by or about him are in the Japanese consular records and Korean legation records in the General Records of the Department of State, National Archives, Washington, D.C. Brief sketches of his career are in William E. Railey, *History of Woodford County, Kentucky* (1975), and Oscar T. Shuck, *History of the Bench and Bar of California* (1901). The best scholarly analysis of Greathouse's service in Korea is Young I. Lew, "American Advisers in Korea, 1885–1894: Anatomy of Failure," in *The United States and Korea: American-Korean Relations, 1866–1976*, ed. Andrew C. Nahm (1979). Other useful sources are William Franklin Sands, *Undiplomatic Memories: The Far East, 1896–1904* (1930), and "The Queen's Death Again Investigated," *Korean Repository* 3 (Mar. 1896): 118–42. See also Spencer J. Palmer, ed., *Korean-American Relations: Documents Pertaining to the Far Eastern Diplomacy of the United States*, vol. 2, *The Period of Growing Influence, 1887–1895* (1963). An obituary is in the *San Francisco Examiner*, 18 Nov. 1899.

DAVID L. ANDERSON

GREATON, Joseph (12 Feb. 1679–19 Aug. 1753), Jesuit priest and missionary, was born in London, England. His parents' names are unknown. Nothing is known of his early years, but his family was probably middle class and Catholic. Coming of age as a Catholic in late Stuart England posed formidable challenges to even the most resolute members of the Catholic faith. He entered the Society of Jesus on 5 July 1708 and was professed and ordained on 4 August 1719. In the following year he was assigned to the Jesuit mission in Anne Arundel County, Maryland, at that time the only one of the twelve British North American mainland colonies that allowed Catholics to openly practice their faith.

Greaton resided at St. Inigo's in Maryland from 1721 to 1724. He then became an itinerant missionary, celebrating the mass in the homes of Catholics in Maryland, Delaware, and southern Pennsylvania. Penn's Colony, as it was originally called, was slightly more tolerant of Catholics than many other colonies. In 1729 Greaton went to Philadelphia and purchased a residence at the corner of Fourth and Walnut streets. In 1733 he purchased a lot on Fourth Street and established the small church of St. Joseph's, the first Catholic church in Pennsylvania and probably the first Catholic "town church" in any of the English colonies in North America. Starting with a congregation of perhaps a dozen people, Greaton expanded the size of his parish as the Catholic population of the city became more willing to expose itself in the open.

Serving in this ministry during the 1730s and 1740s was a trying affair, despite Greaton's dedication. A definite bigotry against Catholics remained, even in the City of Brotherly Love. In 1734 Patrick Gordon, the lieutenant governor of Pennsylvania, lodged a complaint against the very existence of the Catholic parish, but the city leaders were willing to permit the continuance of St. Joseph's. The advent of King George's War in 1744 increased the prejudice, as many Philadelphians suspected Greaton and his congregants of being in league or at least in sympathy with the French Catholic enemy during the war.

Greaton and his mission received a needed financial boost when a prominent English Catholic, Sir John James, set aside in his will £4,000 to be used for the support of the Jesuit mission in Pennsylvania. The following year Greaton's mission appeared in the official records of the Society of Jesus, under the title of St. Francis Borgia. Greaton received an assistant in 1741, the Reverend Henry Neale of the Society of Jesus. More importantly, the Society of Jesus sent two other priests to Pennsylvania to work among the German-speaking Catholics, who outnumbered their English-speaking counterparts. The 1757 census revealed 949 German-speaking Catholics and 416 English or Irish Catholics in the colony. For the German Catholics, Father Theodore Schneider and Father William Wapeler in 1741 founded in Goshen the mission of Goshenhoppen, some forty-five miles from Philadelphia. Greaton gave encouragement and support to his fellow Jesuits, and in 1748 he purchased approximately 473 acres of land for their rural mission.

Little is known of the rest of Greaton's career. He weathered the storms created by King George's War (1744–1748) and left his parish in the capable hands of Father Robert Harding in 1749. Greaton then retired to Maryland, where he spent the rest of his life.

Greaton was one of a handful of resolute and daring Catholics who founded small but significant institutions in the largely Protestant colonies. He was part of a much larger movement, the Catholic Counter Reformation, which intended to win all hearts back to what

Catholics believed was the true faith. Had Greaton adopted such a virgorous approach in the colonies, he would have been rooted out of existence by the animosity against Catholics. Cognizant of this, Greaton focused on establishing a foundation upon which later Catholic generations could expand. Greaton is revered in Catholic literature as one of the founders of Catholicism in Pennsylvania.

• Information on Greaton is in John Tracy Ellis, *Catholics in Colonial America* (1965); Henry de Courcy and John Gilmary Shea, *History of the Catholic Church in the United States* (1879); and Russell F. Weigley, ed., *Philadelphia: A 300-Year History* (1982). See also Eugene B. Gallagher, S.J., "Two Hundred and Fifty Years Ago: The Beginnings of St. Joseph's Church," *Records of the American Catholic Historical Society of Philadelphia* 93 (1982): 3–8; and Sister Blanche Marie, "The Catholic Church in Colonial Pennsylvania," *Pennsylvania History*, Oct. 1936, pp. 240–58.

SAMUEL WILLARD CROMPTON

GREATOREX, Eleanor Elizabeth (26 Mar. 1854–1897), artist, was born in New York City, the daughter of Eliza Pratt, an artist, and Henry Wellington Greatorex, a musician. After her father died, her mother supported her and her older sister Kathleen Honora by working as a professional artist. The family lived in Cornwall-on-Hudson with their mother's sister, Matilda Pratt Despard. In Cornwall-on-Hudson the young sisters accompanied their mother on her daily sketching excursions and received their first lessons in drawing from her.

Eleanor Greatorex began her formal art training at age seven. In addition to formal lessons from their mother at her studio in the New Dodsworth Building, the sisters enjoyed "the kind though not always flattering criticism of the colony of artists there established" (Wright, p. 69). Greatorex also studied at the National Academy of Design in 1869–1870 and later at the Art Students League.

In 1870 the sisters accompanied their mother on a trip to Europe. The Greatorexes spent the summer sketching the buildings and street scenes of Nuremberg. In Munich the following winter the girls studied German and music and worked with artist friends such as Toby Rosenthal and the American expatriate David Dalhoff Neal. In the gallery of the Pinakothek they copied old masters and made notes for original drawings. Later that year they traveled to Italy, visiting the galleries of Verona, Bologna, and Florence. They spent the next season in Oberammergau, where Eleanor Greatorex made a sketch for her painting *From Yuba's Kitchen, Ober Ammergau* (1876), which was the first picture she exhibited at the National Academy of Design in New York. Back in Munich that winter, the sisters began to work in color. They formed an atelier with a few other students and engaged Carl Otto as an instructor. A year later, after a summer spent sketching in Switzerland, the family returned to New York.

Eleanor Greatorex was brought up to be a professional artist. Her mother refused to let her exhibit until her works could "stand on their own merit, and not through the influence of her name" (Hanaford, p. 297). In New York the family of artists circulated in a world of literary, artistic, and business women brought together by Jane Cunningham Croly, the editor of *Demorest's Magazine* and founder of Sorosis, the first professional women's club. The Greatorexes were all savvy entrepreneurs who utilized the burgeoning popular art markets of the late nineteenth century. Panel painting, china decorating, illustration, and teaching were the most lucrative art fields open to women in the 1880s and 1890s. Greatorex worked in all of these. She also produced oil paintings, watercolors, etchings, and murals.

After returning from Germany Eleanor and her sister opened a studio in New York's Young Women's Christian Association building. There teaching provided their chief source of income, and they also painted panels and porcelain for sale. In 1873 Eleanor published, as illustrations for children's books, drawings taken on a sketching tour she made to Colorado with her family. Although she was not pleased with these reproductions, she continued to contribute to the illustration market until her death. In the 1890s she was a regular contributor to *Godey's Magazine*, for which she illustrated her own article "Christmas in Paris" in January 1893. In 1876 she began exhibiting and selling her work at the National Academy of Design in New York and the Brooklyn Art Association. Her pictures exhibited that year at the Philadelphia Centennial Exposition received honorable mention.

The Greatorexes returned to Paris in 1879, and there Eleanor and Kathleen worked under the instruction of the masters Carolus-Duran and Jean-Jacques Henner. During a trip to London in 1880 they met Scottish impressionist Arthur Melville, from whom the sisters learned to "flood" watercolors, instead of working in the more usual dry method. This technique became characteristic of Greatorex's style and can be seen in large paintings such as *Scottish Fisherwives* (1880) and *Roses* (1882), as well as in her magazine illustrations. She exhibited a large watercolor, *Mere Elizabeth a l'hotel Cluny*, in the Paris Salon that same year. The family spent the summers living in picturesque inns at Veules-en-Caux, Cheuvreuse, and the other French villages where artists congregated.

The Greatorexes demonstrated the seriousness of their search for the picturesque when they moved to Algiers in the autumn of 1880. The three women lived and worked on the Mustapha hills outside of the city and attracted attention whenever they ventured into town. Eleanor Greatorex concentrated on street and floral scenes in oils. But in Algiers she became gravely ill. In August 1881 she was brought back to New York an invalid and did not attempt to work until the next year. In February 1882 the family opened a studio in the Sherwood Building, where the sisters formed a class in flower and figure painting for professional artists. They spent the summers with their mother, sketching among the Shawangunk Mountains at Cragsmoor in Ulster County.

During the years at the Sherwood, Eleanor Greatorex gained recognition through her teaching and by producing a variety of art forms. She exhibited watercolors, oil paintings, and etchings at the New York Union League Club, the Brooklyn Art Association, the Philadelphia Society of Artists, and the New York Water Color Society. She was also one of twelve artists living at the Sherwood who collaborated on a decorative art project, each contributing a miniature oil painting on one blade of a lacquer fan (c. 1883, private collection). Roses, which exemplified the "glowing magnificence" of her color and the "broad, free sweep of her brush," were her most popular subject. Her work was collected by artists and the public alike. Some of her Algerian scenes appeared at the New York Water-Color Exhibition of 1882, the largest of which was bought by the noted artist Frederic Edwin Church.

Eleanor and Kathleen Greatorex also were cited by the *Art Amateur* as "the first women in this country who professionally mounted the painter's scaffolding." In 1884 the sisters were hired to decorate the ladies' reception room at the Dakota, a large apartment house near Central Park. Their brushwork covered the ceiling, walls, and curtains, the latter being done on huge stretchers in their studio.

The Greatorexes settled permanently in Paris in 1886. Eleanor Greatorex exhibited at the Paris Salon in 1888, 1889, and 1890, and her etchings appeared at the second Women Etchers of America exhibition, held at New York's Union League Club in 1888. Eleanor Elizabeth Greatorex died in Paris the same year as her mother.

Like most female artists of her era, Greatorex took advantage of opportunities offered by the decorative art market and publishing industry to establish her career. Fortunate in her early training and natural ability in fine art, Eleanor Greatorex secured her success by producing a diversified body of work—from floral paintings and panels to hotel murals and magazine illustrations. Critics praised her freely composed watercolor flowers and the "snappy manner" of her drawings as representative of her generation and her good luck in attaining "so young the artistic and material success that usually waits for much older heads and hands."

• The best contemporary biography of Eleanor Greatorex is Margaret Bertha Wright, "Eleanor and Kathleen Greatorex," *Art Amateur* 13, no. 1 (June 1885): 69–70. Eleanor Greatorex's work is discussed and reproduced in S. R. Koehler, "Second Annual Exhibition of the Philadelphia Society of Artists," *American Art Review* 2 (1881): 103–15; Union League Club, *Catalogue of the Work of Women Etchers of America* (1888); and "The Year's Art as Received in the Quarterly Illustrator," *Quarterly Illustrator* 1, no. 1 (Jan.–Mar. 1893), and 1, no. 2 (Apr.–June 1893).

APRIL F. MASTEN

GREATOREX, Eliza Pratt (25 Dec. 1819–9 Feb. 1897), landscape painter and etcher, was born in Manor Hamilton, Ireland, the daughter of the Reverend James Calcott Pratt, a follower of John Wesley. Her mother's name is unknown. As girls Eliza and her sister Matilda were allowed to study painting, literature, and music. For a time both girls sought literary careers. In 1840 the family moved to New York City, where Eliza Pratt began to concentrate on painting. In 1849 she married Henry Wellington Greatorex, an English emigrant and well-known organist; they had two children. The family traveled widely for Henry's frequent concert and teaching engagements, but they made their home in Hartford, Connecticut. On returning from a visit to England, Henry Greatorex died unexpectedly in Charleston, South Carolina, on 10 September 1858.

Until her husband's death Eliza Greatorex had practiced art as an amateur. She had joined a sketching club in New York City and in 1855 began exhibiting pen-and-ink drawings at the National Academy of Design. After Henry's death, Eliza Greatorex made art her profession, supporting her family by teaching and selling her art. Aided by friends in the sketching club, she opened a studio at the old Dodsworth Building on Broadway and continued to study under New York landscape artists William Wotherspoon, James Hart, and William Hart. During the 1860s and 1870s she taught drawing at Miss Haines's School for Girls, where, according to a contemporary biographer, she was given the "fullest liberty to work out her own peculiar ideas and methods of teaching" (Hanaford, p. 276). After 1858 she began to exhibit more extensively at the National Academy, the Salmagundi Club in New York, the Boston Athenaeum, the Philadelphia Academy of Fine Arts, and the Brooklyn and Washington Art Associations.

Eliza Greatorex belonged to several art associations and institutions. She was the only female member of the Artists' Fund Society of New York during the 1860s. Members had to be elected by ballot and contribute a picture worth $50 to $75 in lieu of annual dues. Greatorex's induction attests to her critical acclaim and financial success. In 1869 she was elected an associate member of the National Academy of Art in New York, one of the few women so honored.

In 1861 Greatorex traveled to Paris to work under the landscapist Emile Lambinet. Her first drawings of Chevreuse, a village near Paris, attracted immediate attention and brisk sales. She returned to Europe with her daughters in 1870. From their base in Munich, the Greatorexes traveled throughout Germany and Italy in search of picturesque scenes. They spent the summer in Nuremberg, where Greatorex prepared drawings (now in the Vatican collection) of Albrecht Dürer's home. In 1871 they traveled to Italy and Bavaria, where they attended the celebrated Bavarian passion play in Ober-Ammergau. Greatorex later published two books of etchings and diary text recording her travels in Germany: *Homes of Ober-Ammergau* (1872) and *Etchings in Nuremberg* (1875).

After the family returned to New York in 1872, Greatorex was sent by G. P. Putnam to procure sketches of Colorado Springs. One of the first artists to paint in Colorado, she spent the following summer in Manitou, a resort near Pikes Peak. There she prepared the drawings and wrote diary entries for her *Summer Etchings in Colorado* (1873). She also met the popular author Grace Greenwood (Sara Jane Clarke Lippincott), who wrote a preface for the volume.

Greatorex's success was due as much to her astute business sense as to her immense talent. She trained her daughters for artistic careers while they were small children and worked with them as a family firm until each daughter's work could stand on its own merits. By producing popular forms of art as well as expensive oil paintings, Eliza Greatorex was able to maintain critical recognition and support her family. Suspecting that there would be a strong market for centennial memorabilia, she had begun making pen-and-ink drawings of old colonial houses and other historical relics around New York in the early 1870s. She resumed this work upon returning from Colorado and in 1875 circulated a "prospectus" announcing the publication of "a series of fifty etchings of these relics, now almost daily disappearing." The series *Old New York, from the Battery to Bloomingdale* featured a commentary by her sister Matilda Pratt Despard. It became Greatorex's best-known work. She exhibited eighteen of the sketches at the Philadelphia Centennial Exposition.

While working on the sketches, Greatorex devised another centennial project. She collected panels and woodwork from historical homes and churches that were being demolished. In the center of the panels she painted or sketched historical scenes and events, while her daughters decorated the edges. They sold these works of "art history" at a gallery in their home. Eliza Greatorex culminated her centennial trade by having some of the drawings from *Old New York* lithographed in her *Souvenir of 1876*. This artistic entrepreneurial savvy was celebrated by Sorosis, New York's first professional women's club, which elected Eliza Greatorex an honorary member.

Inspired by modernist etching, Greatorex moved back to Paris in 1879 to study with Charles Henri Toussaint and to seek advice from Maxime Lalanne, a proponent of linear etching. At this time she moved away from documentary-style etching and adopted the "looser, painterly, light-imbued" style of the Barbizon school of landcape painting (Peet, p. 20). She practiced this style while living with her daughters in Algiers. During the 1880s she exhibited etchings of Cernay-la-ville and New York scenes at the Paris Salon and the first New York Etching Club exhibitions. Some of these were reproduced and reviewed by Sylvester Koehler in the *American Art Review*. Her work also appeared at the first *Women Etchers of America* exhibition held in 1887 at Boston's Museum of Fine Arts.

In 1886 Eliza Greatorex sold the contents of her gallery—the original pen-and-ink sketches for her etchings and the antique woodwork she had collected—and with her daughters moved permanently to France. From there she traveled to Italy, Norway, and Africa

and exhibited in Paris, Berlin, New York, and Boston. She died in Paris.

Critics praised the personal character of Greatorex's European landscapes and the "native style" of her etchings. Yet in documenting the vanishing landmarks of old New York she secured her reputation. Her success was exceptional at a time when the *New York World* called women's art "the most trivial and artistically worthless productions of the brush." The same article claimed that the "art of New York" owed a debt of gratitude to Greatorex and placed her among the "many women of great talent and of ability inferior to none of the other sex, who make art a source of income and at the same time do it honor."

• Greatorex's 1875 prospectus is available in the Gordon Lester Ford Collection of the Archives of American Art, Washington, D.C. The best secondary sources on Greatorex are Phyllis Peet, *American Women of the Etching Revival* (1988), and Charlotte Streifer Rubinstein, "Eliza Pratt Greatorex," *American Women Artists* (1982), pp. 71–72. Primary sources that give a good idea of Greatorex's contemporary reputation include S. R. Koehler, "Mrs. Eliza Greatorex," *American Art Review* 1, pt. 2 (1881); Phebe A. Hanaford, *Daughters of America; or, Women of the Century* (1883), pp. 276–78; and "Our Female Artists," *New York World*, 15 Mar. 1885.

APRIL F. MASTEN

GREB, Harry (6 June 1894–22 Oct. 1926), professional boxer, was born in Pittsburgh, Pennsylvania, the son of Pius Greb, a stonemason, and Annie O'Brien. After attending Immaculate Conception School in Pittsburgh (apparently, he never graduated), Greb held various jobs. In May 1913 he became a professional boxer. Lacking experience, he gradually improved until he was considered an outstanding main event fighter by 1917. Under the management of James "Red" Mason, he fought often and with great success.

From 1917 to 1921 Greb boxed many of the most highly ranked middleweights and light heavyweights in the world, usually winning the unofficial press decisions. In six fights with Battling Levinsky, the light heavyweight champion, Greb was proclaimed the unofficial winner, but he could not achieve the knockout considered necessary to take the title. He won "newspaper decisions" over several former world championship claimants, including Jack Dillon, Eddie McGoorty, George Chip, Jeff Smith, and Al McCoy. After losing to the great Mike Gibbons, he won the rematch. He was defeated twice by the great light heavyweight, Tommy Gibbons, but then defeated him twice. Among his other defeated opponents were Kid Norfolk, Buck Crouse, future light heavyweight champion Mike McTigue, Leo Houck, Tommy Robson, and Augie Ratner. Greb enjoyed success against highly ranked heavyweights, including Billy Miske, Bill Brennan, Charley Weinert, Bob Roper, Jack Renault, and Gunboat Smith.

Greb married Mildred Kathleen Reilly of Pittsburgh in 1919. Their only child was born ten months later. Soon afterward, his wife contracted tuberculosis and died in March 1923.

Greb won the American light heavyweight title in 1922 by defeating Gene Tunney. He successfully defended that title against Tommy Loughran in 1923, but he then lost it to Tunney. Finally, on 31 August 1923, he won the world middleweight title by defeating Johnny Wilson.

It was revealed by his physician after Greb's death that he had lost the vision in one eye even before becoming middleweight champion, but he concealed his impairment. Despite this condition, he attempted to regain the American light heavyweight title from Tunney but failed. However, he successfully defended his middleweight title against Bryan Downey, Johnny Wilson (in a rematch), Fay Keiser, Ted Moore, Mickey Walker, and Tony Marullo, before losing it to Tiger Flowers on 26 February 1926. Greb, in his last fight on 19 August 1926, attempted unsuccessfully to regain the middleweight title from Flowers.

Among Greb's most memorable fights were the first three of his five with Gene Tunney. In the first one, Tunney suffered a terrible beating. The second fight resulted in an unpopular decision being awarded to Tunney, who then won the third fight decisively. One of Greb's best matches came late in his career against Mickey Walker, who could not cope with his quickness, energy, and style.

Greb's fighting style was unorthodox and resulted in his nickname, "The Human Windmill." Standing 5'8" and strongly built, he had powers of endurance that his opponents could not match. Using his superior speed and quickness, he threw punches constantly and from nearly any stance or angle. Seldom setting himself sufficiently to deliver heavy blows, he knocked out few opponents, but he subjected them to heavy punishment while exhibiting such nimble footwork that he seldom was hit hard. His opportunistic methods almost always left his foes bewildered and harassed. Further, he often employed foul tactics, such as butting, elbowing, and "heeling." Because of his energetic style, he fought an unusual number of action-filled bouts.

In thirteen years as a professional, Greb had 299 fights. Most of his twenty or so losses came in the early years. His most active year was 1919, when he fought forty-five times.

Greb's personal qualities combined to make him one of the most controversial individuals in boxing history. Frequently abrasive and sarcastic, he was strongly disliked by some, but to others he displayed great kindness and generosity. New York City sportswriters were among his strongest critics, censuring him often for his roughness, yet revealing themselves as admirers by their praise after his death. He seemed to delight in mystifying and misleading the public about his personal affairs. For instance, he misled newspapermen into writing that he was actually Jewish and his name was Berg. Supposedly he did not train, but newspaper accounts reveal that he was actually among the best-conditioned fighters of his time, although his unorthodox methods were designed to promote endurance and quickness, with little or no

sparring. In the late stages of his career Greb's training did lapse somewhat, but, contrary to reports, he drank sparingly and did not smoke. After his wife's death, and perhaps because he liked nightlife and dancing, he acquired the reputation of a philanderer.

Following his second title fight with Flowers, Greb underwent an operation in Atlantic City, New Jersey, supposedly for a cataract but probably for removal of his blind eye and its replacement with a glass one. This operation was followed by another for facial repairs. He died, reportedly of heart failure, a few hours after the surgery.

Greb was one of the most colorful figures in sports during the 1920s. His unusual style of boxing, although immensely successful, was not successfully copied, perhaps because others lacked the endurance and quickness to emulate it. Harry Greb is best remembered as a unique phenomenon in boxing. He was elected to the International Boxing Hall of Fame in 1990.

• Greb's complete record is in *The Ring 1986–87 Record Book and Boxing Encyclopedia*, ed. Herbert G. Goldman. James R. Fair's *Give Him to the Angels: The Story of Harry Greb* (1946) is a badly flawed biography. The sports pages of the *Pittsburgh Post*, 1913–1926, give the details of most of his fights and provide information about his training methods, style, personality, and personal affairs. A series of biographical articles on Greb, by Robert G. Hoenig, appeared in the *Boxing Blade*, published weekly from 30 Oct. to 31 Dec. 1926. Another weekly series of biographical articles, by Charles Lesemann, appeared in *Boxing News* (England), 16 Apr.–21 May 1954. Other sources are Ed Van Every, "Harry Greb's Career," *Everlast Boxing Record* (1927), pp. 39–42; Edward Merrill, "The Human Windmill," *The Ring*, Nov. 1932, pp. 31, 37; Greb, "My Hardest Fight," *The Ring*, Feb. 1925, pp. 10–11; and Ken Merritt, "The Immortal Harry Greb," *The Ring*, Aug. 1992, pp. 47, 56–58. However, all of these articles and series contain errors. James E. Cashman of Lake Forest, Ill., who has had access to Greb family memorabilia and has interviewed many people who knew Greb, his family, and his daughter, contributed important information for this article. An obituary is in the *Pittsburgh Post*, 22–24 Oct. 1926.

LUCKETT V. DAVIS

GREELEY, Dana McLean (5 July 1908–13 June 1986), Unitarian Universalist minister, was born in Lexington, Massachusetts, the son of William Roger Greeley, an architect, and Marjory Ellen Houghton. He was educated at Harvard (B.S., 1931; S.T.B., 1933), and in 1931 he married a school friend, Deborah Allen Webster; they had four daughters.

After brief pastorates in Lincoln, Massachusetts, and Concord, New Hampshire, Greeley was called in 1935 to Arlington Street Church in Boston. This had been the pulpit of William Ellery Channing (1780–1842), the most distinguished Unitarian minister of the nineteenth century. The Arlington Street years were pleasing and useful ones for both minister and parish. The church's membership grew significantly, its resources were strengthened, and it became one of the leading Protestant churches in the city.

After the death in 1958 of the president of the American Unitarian Association, Greeley was selected as its new head. He worked for the merger in 1961 of the Unitarian Association with the Universalist Church of America and served for two terms (1961–1969) as president of the new Unitarian Universalist Association. With his quality of gentle persuasiveness, Greeley succeeded in creating an administrative model for the association that blended the Unitarian emphasis on a strong national organization with the Universalist emphasis on the authority and power of local churches and state conventions.

Greeley's concern for justice and human rights also enabled the association to establish a Department of Social Responsibility, which worked effectively for change with Martin Luther King's Southern Christian Leadership Conference, Clergy and Laymen Concerned for Vietnam, and other national groups during the civil rights struggle of the 1960s and during the debates and protests regarding the Vietnam War. The issues of black empowerment and reparations that were raised by many of his own church members in 1968 were not so easily adjudicated. Consequently, after he left office, Greeley wrote a spirited defense of his leadership titled *25 Beacon Street*.

Thereafter he was president of the International Association for Religious Freedom (1969–1972) and a visiting professor at Meadville/Lombard Theological School in Chicago (1969–1970). He was then called to the First Parish in Concord, Massachusetts, where he served sixteen years as senior minister. Greeley collaborated with numerous religious leaders such as Boston's Richard Cardinal Cushing and Rabbi Roland Gittelsohn to promote better interfaith relations between Christians and Jews. In 1962 he was one of the founders, and co-chair until his death, of the World Conference on Religion and Peace. The WCRP, headquartered at the United Nations, is a nongovernmental international organization that includes Buddhists, Christians, Confucianists, Hindus, Jains, Jews, Muslims, Sikhs, and others. Its goal is to foster interreligious dialogue and cooperation.

His last sermon, given just weeks before his death in Concord, reflected his view that "Life Is a Miracle." In recognition of this faith and as a way to continue his belief in world peace and human dignity, his congregation established the Dana McLean Greeley Foundation, a nondenominational organization that works throughout the world in behalf of peace and justice.

• Greeley's papers are held at the Andover-Harvard Theological Library of Harvard Divinity School, Cambridge, Massachusetts, where a computer-generated register (364 pages) is available. The Divinity School also holds the archives of the American Unitarian Association and the Unitarian Universalist Association. There is no biography, but some biographical details are given in his *25 Beacon Street* (1971). He published two short sermon collections, *Towards Larger Living* (1944) and *A Message to Atheists* (1948), and just before his death the Concord parish published *Forward through the Ages* (1986), a collection of his writings between 1970 and 1986. For a short assessment of his career, see Alan Seaburg, "Silence Is the Miracle," *Churchman*, Nov. 1987, pp. 8–9.

ALAN SEABURG

GREELEY, Horace (3 Feb. 1811–29 Nov. 1872), newspaper editor and political figure, was born in Amherst, New Hampshire, the son of Zaccheus Greeley and Mary Woodburn, poor New England farmers. Greeley's youth was marred by his father's struggle to improve his family's financial situation. During his first ten years, the family moved four times, from Amherst to Bedford, New Hampshire, back to Amherst, and in 1821 to Westhaven, Vermont. These years of economic uncertainty made a deep impression on young "Hod" Greeley. He was often absent from school because of the need to help his father; his formal education ended at the age of fourteen. Yet, both in school and on his own, he displayed a remarkable and lively intelligence. In later years Greeley paid tribute to the various influences of his Yankee childhood: the Scotch-Irish ancestry on his mother's side and his English forebears on his father's, the powerful hold of Calvinism, the promise of the Enlightenment from the revolutionary era.

In 1826 Greeley signed on as a printer's apprentice to Amos Bliss, editor of the *Northern Spectator* in East Poultney, Vermont. Here he mastered not only the skill of typesetting but also the art of concise writing. As he said, he learned how to "give in fewer words . . . the gist of information" (*Recollections*, p. 417). His family having moved to Erie, Pennsylvania, when the *Spectator* closed down in 1830, he joined them, and in 1831 he took employment on the *Erie Gazette*. Later that same year he went to New York City as an employee of the *Evening Post*. He subsequently worked as a printer for the *Spirit of the Times*, the *Morning Post*, and the *Commercial Advertiser*.

It was in the 1830s that he refined his talents as a journalist and editor, founding the literary weekly *The New-Yorker* with Jonas Winchester in 1834 and writing for other periodicals. Greeley's political commitment was confirmed when he joined forces with the leaders of New York's Whig party, Thurlow Weed and William Seward, who supported Greeley's new publication, the *Jeffersonian*, from 1838 to 1839. In 1840 Greeley launched the *Log Cabin*, which strongly endorsed the successful Whig presidential ticket of William Henry Harrison and John Tyler.

Greeley had courted and married Mary Youngs Cheney of Connecticut in 1836. While it was initially happy, the Greeleys' married life would repeatedly be struck by tragedy; of their seven children, only two lived to adulthood.

On 10 April 1841 Greeley published the first issue of the daily *New York Tribune*. This publication, the first daily Whig paper in New York City, brought him national fame and enormous journalistic power, despite such rivals as William Cullen Bryant's *Evening Post*, James Raymond's *New York Times*, and James Gordon Bennett's *Herald*. Later in 1841 Greeley took on Thomas McElrath as a business partner, and *The New-Yorker* and the *Log Cabin* were merged into the weekly *Tribune*. Over the years, in biting, witty editorials, Greeley crusaded against slavery, the conditions of penury, an unchecked aristocracy, suppression of women's rights, and capital punishment while supporting peace movements, vegetarianism, labor rights, Fourierist communities, and high tariffs. He also railed against tobacco, alcoholic beverages, and marital infidelity.

Under Greeley's guidance, the *Tribune* became one of the great American newspapers. By 1860 the *Tribune* in all its formats—daily, weekly, semiweekly—would reach a circulation of nearly 300,000. Renowned as a "political Bible" and distinguished for its excellent reporting of local, national, and global events, the *Tribune* in the 1840s, 1850s, and 1860s featured a galaxy of brilliant writers, among them, Solon Robinson on agriculture; Bayard Taylor on travel; Charles Dana, the managing editor; George Ripley and Margaret Fuller, the latter a close friend, on literary topics; and James Pike on Washington affairs. Perhaps the most intriguing Greeley reporter was Karl Marx, who wrote about European affairs in the 1850s. Greeley believed that while his editorials represented his personal perspective, a newspaper should be an open forum for the competing and colliding views of talented spirits. In this way, he sponsored an intellectual democracy. As well, Greeley remained committed to the principle of a free press as a check on the abuses of political and economic power. As he said, liberty "of the Press is the palladium of all true Liberty; with it despotism is impossible, without it inevitable" (Introduction, *Writings of Cassius Marcellus Clay* [1848], p. v).

In his editorials in the 1840s and 1850s, Greeley sharpened his political positions, informed primarily by his opposition to slavery. Like many other northerners, he opposed the Mexican War as a conflict prosecuted for the extension of slavery. Also, he objected to the Compromise of 1850 with its Fugitive Slave Act and condemned the Kansas-Nebraska Act because he believed its version of popular sovereignty would foster a new "slavocracy" in the West. In 1854 he resigned from his partnership with Weed and Seward and, with other northern Whigs, helped found the Republican party. He supported Republican John C. Frémont for president in 1856, condemned the Dred Scott decision, praised John Brown's goals while denouncing his advocacy of violence, and, after initial opposition, in 1860 supported the nomination of Abraham Lincoln for president.

During these years Greeley called attention not only to the condition of African Americans trapped in the institution of slavery but also to that of nominally free blacks in the North. He pointed to the hypocrisy of the legal and social postures of northern states that denied blacks the right to vote and even access to vehicles of public transportation. In a 4 July 1846 *Tribune* editorial, Greeley stated that "in the midst of our Democratic equity . . . we . . . sustain an Aristocracy of Color

more rigid and hateful than any Aristocracy known to the Old World. We . . . banish the children of Africa from our public conveyances, from our civic convocations, and even from practical equality as sinners in our assemblages to supplicate the mercy of God."

Greeley became famous for giving wide currency to the quotation "Go west, young man, go west," although the statement had originally been coined by John Soule, an Indiana editor, in 1851. Greeley in fact not only promoted the western movement but urged as well that Americans be continually willing to uproot themselves to seek a better life. Hence, he also urged his readers to consider underdeveloped regions in the East and in the South, especially after the Civil War.

Despite repeated tries for political office, Greeley was successful only in 1848, when he was elected to the House of Representatives. He served as a Whig only for a single session from December 1848 to March 1849. Among those serving with him was Abraham Lincoln. During his term Greeley introduced one of the first homestead bills. He upset many of his congressional associates with his attack on the abuses of the franking privilege and of the compensation received for mileage traveled by representatives between their districts and Washington, D.C. His call for reform made sense, but his invective approach made his efforts fruitless.

Greeley visited Europe for the first time in 1851, to serve as a jury chairman at the American exposition at the London World's Fair in the Crystal Palace. He reported on his adventures in his fine 1851 travelogue, *Glances at Europe*. In 1853 he purchased a farm in Chappaqua, New York, moved his family there, and experimented with farming techniques on his new land.

Greeley's busy life was punctuated by a number of infamous episodes of which his own accounts made much mockery. He contended with James Fenimore Cooper, who had brought a libel suit against the *Tribune* in 1842, an action dubbed by Greeley as the "Cooperage" of the *Tribune*. During a visit to the World's Exposition in Paris in 1855, he was incarcerated for two days because of a dispute with a sculptor. In January of 1856 he was caned by Arkansas congressman Albert Rust on the Capitol steps because of Greeley's adamant support of Republican Nathaniel Banks for the House Speakership. Fortunately, Greeley escaped mostly unhurt and "made merry" over the incident later.

In 1859 Greeley decided to follow the advice he had dispensed to a generation of young adult Americans and went west, to California. During his journey, which he made partially to advertise the necessity of a transcontinental railroad, Greeley wrote a series of remarkable dispatches, which were collected into a volume titled *An Overland Journey, from New York to San Francisco in the Summer of 1859*. Greeley commented on the sad plight of Native Americans, the rough conditions of Denver, the curious situation of the Mormons in Utah, the beauties of California. He also interviewed the powerful leader of the Mormons, Brigham

Young. Greeley complained of the discomforts of traveling by stagecoach, which consumed about half the trip, and ended the volume with a stirring call for a national railroad network.

On the eve of the Civil War, Greeley's perspective on secession seemed equivocal at best. In a controversial editorial published on 9 November 1860, Greeley, hoping for a peaceful resolution of the crisis caused by Lincoln's election, argued that it might be best for the Union to let the "erring sisters" go, but he also stressed here, as in later editorials, that he would acquiesce in withdrawal movements only if they were democratically supported. Hence Greeley condemned the ordinances of secession because they did not, in his estimation, represent the true voice of a majority of the citizens of the South. Once the guns at Fort Sumter were fired, Greeley pushed hard for Union victory, but his yearning for a peaceful resolution was not fully laid to rest. In 1864 Greeley participated in an abortive attempt to achieve peace in a meeting with southern "peace commissioners" in Niagara Falls, Canada. While permitting Greeley to go, Lincoln correctly predicted the futility of such a mission.

During the Civil War Greeley pressed the president to take steps to emancipate the slaves in rebellious states. In one of his most famous editorials, "The Prayer of Twenty Millions," appearing on 20 August 1862, Greeley called on Lincoln to enforce the provisions of the second Confiscation Act by authorizing military commanders to liberate the slaves of masters supporting the Confederate cause. The march of Union armies south would be a march for freedom. Lincoln, in a famous reply, stated that his paramount objective was to save the Union, with or without slavery. Unknown to Greeley, Lincoln had already drafted a version of the Preliminary Emancipation Proclamation, which he issued on 22 September 1862 after the Union "victory" at Antietam. Greeley immediately hailed this document and the final proclamation, issued on 1 January 1863. While it is doubtful that Greeley influenced Lincoln's decisions regarding emancipation policy, it is clear that his well-articulated concerns over the delay of liberation represented the views of many compassionate Union supporters, and the extent of his power as editor was demonstrated by Lincoln's felt need to reply.

Furthermore, Greeley exhibited enormous courage during the Civil War by refusing to vacate the *Tribune* offices during the New York City draft riots in early July 1863. He had supported conscription. Again, after initial opposition, he reluctantly endorsed Lincoln's renomination in 1864, and he saluted Union victory in 1865. As involved as he was during these critical years in the American experience, Greeley found time to write a major two-volume history of the Civil War, which he titled *The American Conflict* (1864 and 1866). Greeley's history, although biased, remains readable and is still important to Civil War scholars. Besides offering extensive accounts of battlefield events, Greeley traced compassionately the troubled story of African Americans.

During the Reconstruction years, Greeley advocated a policy of universal amnesty and universal suffrage. Adhering to his commitment to democratic processes, Greeley, like other moderates on this question, believed that true reconciliation would be achieved only with welcoming back to the Union fold all former Confederates and with incorporating African Americans into the national political fabric by granting them the power of the ballot box.

Greeley's *Recollections of a Busy Life*, published in 1868, is one of the great autobiographies of the nineteenth century and remains his most enduring book, instructive to this day and often compared, quite justifiably, to Benjamin Franklin's immortal work. Particularly fascinating is Greeley's narrative of his youthful adventures, including his entrance into the exciting metropolis of New York.

In 1871 Greeley published *What I Know of Farming*. In this volume Greeley summed up a lifelong devotion to agrarian economics by advocating a scientific approach to farming, or what was called "book" farming.

In 1872 Greeley was nominated for the presidency by both the Liberal Republican and Democratic parties in an effort to defeat Ulysses S. Grant. The Liberal Republican party began as an anti-Grant movement under the leadership of Senator Carl B. Schurz and Governor Benjamin Gratz Brown of Missouri; in 1870 it attracted Republican leaders such as Lyman Trumbull, Charles Francis Adams, George Julian, and Charles Sumner. It opposed Grant's supposedly vindictive southern policy, the corruption in his administration, his apparently dictatorial foreign policy, and his support of a high tariff. In some ways, Greeley, a compromise candidate, seemed suitable because of his flexible stance on Reconstruction. Greeley proved an embarrassing selection. He had not split with Grant until 1871, and he would not abandon his support of a high tariff policy.

Despite the many obstacles he confronted, Greeley launched a campaign marked by a succession of eloquent addresses. He articulated the theme of a benevolent American nationalism, based on an emerging American democratic community. He claimed that the Civil War was "fought in the interest of no section, of no party, but in the interest of universal humanity." He stressed that victory in the war was shared by all Americans, North and South: "Our triumph is the uplifting of every one to the common platform of American nationality" (speeches of 21 Sept. and 25 Sept. 1872).

Rarely has a presidential candidate met with such personal and public tragedy. On 30 October, Molly Greeley died. Six days later, Greeley suffered a crushing defeat at the polls, carrying only 44 percent of the popular vote and six states. Finding himself now insecure at the *Tribune* offices, Greeley died in Pleasantville, New York.

For all the ridicule Greeley received, particularly in the cruel caricatures of his disheveled appearance in Thomas Nast's cartoons during the campaign, he was also revered by millions, affectionately referred to as "Old White Hat," "Old Honesty," "Old White Coat," "Uncle Horace," and the "Farmer of Chappaqua."

Greeley represented the tensions and transformations of his era: raised in rural New England, he achieved success in the urban environment of New York City; a dedicated social reformer deeply sympathetic to the treatment of poor white males, slaves, free blacks, and white women, he still espoused the virtues of self-help and free enterprise; a Yankee nurtured in the Puritan tradition, he rejected Calvinism and embraced some of the currents of Transcendentalism; bred in the revolutionary heritage of the American Enlightenment, he abhorred violence and yearned for the peaceful resolution of conflicts.

Greeley was a great popular educator on the questions of his day, and he never lost faith in the promise of a buoyant American destiny. Much of his magical appeal lay in his championing of the dispossessed. As he said, "the Bread problem lies at the base of all the desirable forms which our age meditates. . . . Morality, Religion are but words to him who fishes in gutters for the means of sustaining life and crouches behind barrels in the street for shelter from the cutting blasts of a winter's night" (letter to Mrs. Pauline W. Davis, 1 Sept. 1852).

• Among other collections, there are the Greeley papers in the Library of Congress and in the New York Public Library. Materials are also at the Historical Society in Chappaqua, N.Y., in the New-York Historical Society, and in the Salmon P. Chase Papers in the Historical Society of Pennsylvania, among others. For an excellent biographical profile and annotated bibliography, see Suzanne Schulze, *Horace Greeley: A Bio-Bibliography* (1992). Glyndon Van Deusen, *Horace Greeley: Nineteenth-Century Crusader* (1953), remains the most definitive biography. James Parton, *The Life of Horace Greeley* (1855), is a charming, indispensable early biography. William Cornwell, *Life and Public Career of the Hon. Horace Greeley* (1874), Francis Zabriskie, *Horace Greeley, the Editor* (1890), Charles Sotheran, *Horace Greeley and Other Pioneers of American Socialism* (1892), William A. Linn, *Horace Greeley: Founder and Editor of the* New York Tribune (1903), Don C. Seitz, *Horace Greeley: Founder of the* New York Tribune (1926), Henry L. Stoddard, *Horace Greeley: Printer, Editor, Crusader* (1946), and William Harlan Hale, *Horace Greeley: Voice of the People* (1950), are all important biographies. Erik S. Lunde, *Horace Greeley* (1981), is one of the more recent treatments. See also Allan Nevins's excellent short biography in the *Dictionary of American Biography* (1934) and Karen Szymanski's essay (1979) and Daniel W. Pfaff's essay (1985), both in the *Dictionary of Literary Biography*. The chapters on Greeley in Vernon Louis Parrington, *Main Currents in American Thought* (1927), and in Constance Rourke, *Trumpets of Jubilee* (1927), are seminal. For a fine retrospective published some months after Greeley's death, see Junius Henri Browne, "Horace Greeley," *Harper's New Monthly Magazine* 46 (1873), pp. 734–41. For later nineteenth-century tributes, see John W. Forney, *Anecdotes of Public Men* (2 vols., 1874–1881); James G. Blaine, *Twenty Years of Congress* (2 vols., 1886); and Josiah Bushnell, *Men and Events of Forty Years* (1891).

ERIK S. LUNDE

GREELEY-SMITH, Nixola (5 Apr. 1880–9 Mar. 1919), journalist, was born in Chappaqua, New York, the daughter of Colonel Nicholas Smith, a lawyer in New York City, and Ida Lillian Greeley, who died when her daughter was two. Granddaughter of the well-known editor Horace Greeley, who founded the *New York Tribune*, she was born on the estate Greeley had left to her mother.

Greeley-Smith attended school at the Convent of the Sacred Heart in New York City until 1889 when her father was appointed American consul at Three Rivers, Quebec. She continued her education there and in Europe where he served as consul in Liège, Belgium, from 1893 to 1895. She became fluent in French in these early years, a skill that later resulted in an excellent interview with the actress Sarah Bernhardt, who appreciated Greeley-Smith's flawless French.

Greeley-Smith's writing began early, starting with a short play said to have been published in the *New York World* when she was twelve and a short story in *Harper's Magazine* when she was fifteen. Although these pieces apparently no longer exist, a November 1903 *Harper's Weekly* includes a romantic tale of a German princess by N. G. Smith.

After Greeley-Smith returned from Europe in 1895, she wrote to Joseph Pulitzer saying she wanted to work on a newspaper. Pulitzer, who had campaigned actively for Horace Greeley in his 1872 presidential nomination bid, hired her immediately. She started at the *St. Louis Post-Dispatch* and soon joined Pulitzer's *New York Evening World* in 1901. Although Pulitzer had reined in sensationalism at his papers after the distorted coverage of the Spanish-American War, newspaper stunts were in vogue when Greeley-Smith started her career in journalism. In this setting her vivid and scholarly writing style, combined with her interviewing skills and social finesse, distinguished her as a writer of quality. The Greeley name opened doors to New York's high-society matrons, and her disarming approach won her interviews with socially prominent women who would not otherwise have talked to a reporter. She interviewed celebrities as widely varied as President Woodrow Wilson's wife, Ellen, General Joseph Joffre, and Theda Bara. She popularized the serious personal interview and became particularly adept with topics appealing to women readers. During World War I she wrote many stories on the supporting role of women. Committed to woman suffrage, she not only participated in the movement but also supported that position in her writing.

Greeley-Smith's writing success attracted the attention of other publishers, including William Randolph Hearst and Lord Northcliffe, both of whom admired her work and tried to hire her away from the *World*. She declined these offers, but some time before World War I the News Enterprise Association lured her to its feature syndicate. Finding her assignments disappointing, she returned to the *World* where she remained for the rest of her career.

Greeley-Smith's writing style can be appreciated in her coverage of the sensational 1907 murder trial of

Harry K. Thaw, who was accused of murdering the fashionable New York architect Stanford White. Writing about Thaw's wife, Evelyn Nesbit, the beautiful heroine of the dramatic trial, she described her on the witness stand, noting that "the taking off of her white veil this morning revealed the fact that another white veil—the filmy fabric of lauded childhood, still wraps her, despite all the sins and shame she has been through."

Greeley-Smith was one of four women feature writers at the Thaw trial who were labeled "sob sisters" by Irvin Cobb, one of the other reporters covering it. Although the description did not fit her generally more intellectual style, in this case her assignment called for writing that was more emotional.

On 1 April 1910 Greeley-Smith married Andrew Watres Ford, who was then city editor at the *New York Evening Telegram*. The couple had no children. She died nine years later at a New York City hospital following an operation for acute appendicitis. She was buried in the Greeley family plot in Greenwood Cemetery, Brooklyn. Devoted to journalism, she earned a reputation as a sophisticated and skilled writer. Her work broadened the range of subjects covered by women reporters as well as increasing the dignity of the profession for women entering the field.

• See Ishbel Ross, *Ladies of the Press: The Story of Women in Journalism by an Insider* (1936), for a brief description of Greeley-Smith's career. Marion Marzolf, *Up from the Footnote: A History of Women Journalists* (1977), has a short entry on Greeley-Smith at the Thaw trial and the origin of the term "sob sisters." A short obituary notice, under "Death of Mrs. Ford," is in the *New York Times*, 10 Mar. 1919.

ALVI MCWILLIAMS

GREELY, Adolphus Washington (27 Mar. 1844–20 Oct. 1935), soldier and arctic explorer, was born in Newburyport, Massachusetts, the son of John Balch Greely, a shoemaker, and Frances D. Cobb, a cotton mill weaver. Greely graduated from Brown High School, Newburyport, in 1860, and in the following year, at the age of seventeen, he joined the Nineteenth Massachusetts Volunteer Infantry. He served as a private, corporal, and first sergeant and was hospitalized for wounds sustained at Antietam, including a facial injury, which he covered with a beard for the remainder of his life. On furlough in 1863 he accepted a commission as a second lieutenant in the Fourth U.S. Volunteers (later Eighty-first U.S. Colored Infantry), stationed in Louisiana.

After the war, Greely assisted in the organization of the Thirty-ninth Infantry and Ninth Cavalry, mustered out as captain and brevet major, and accepted a commission as second lieutenant, Thirty-sixth Regular Infantry, serving in Wyoming and Utah. In 1869 he joined the U.S. Signal Corps, in which service he served the bulk of his army career. For the next twelve years he inspected telegraph lines, surveyed flood lines, directed the construction of military telegraph lines in Montana, Dakota, Texas, and the Southwest, and engaged in weather prediction. He met Henrietta

H. C. Nesmith while on assignment in San Diego; they married in 1878 and eventually had six children.

In March 1881 Greely volunteered for the command of the International Polar expedition to Lady Franklin Bay, Greenland, one of thirteen sent out in a cooperative international effort to establish a ring of scientific stations at high latitudes. The 25-member expedition—including Greely, physician Octavus Pavy, two officers, eighteen enlisted men, and two sledge drivers—established Fort Conger at Discovery Harbor, Ellesmere Island. From this station they mapped the area, gathered scientific information, took regular weather readings, and sent out exploratory parties. In May 1882 one of these sledging parties led by Lieutenant Charles Lockwood successfully reached 83° 24′, the "farthest north" point yet achieved by explorers. Their expected resupply ship, blocked by ice in the Kane Sea, did not arrive during the summer of 1882. The next summer the relief ship, *Proteus*, also failed to arrive; it had capsized in the ice—its crew, rescued by a naval ship, left only a small cache of supplies for the Greely party.

Now out of contact for two years, Greely and his men, following prearranged instructions, abandoned Fort Conger in August 1883 and made their way by small boats and foot toward Cape Sabine more than 500 miles to the south, picking up some supply caches along the way. They expected to meet a party from the *Proteus* wintering at Littleton Bay but learned instead of the ship's demise. The men spent a hard winter and spring in a makeshift camp on Bedford Pym Island, north of Cape Sabine, subsisting first on limited rations and the meager results of hunting and fishing, then on small crustaceans, moss, lichens, and their leather equipment. Amid heightened public interest in the fate of the expedition and lobbying by Mrs. Greely and others, Congress authorized a naval rescue operation. By the time Commander Winfield S. Schley located the survivors in late June 1884, eighteen men had died—most of starvation, but one had been executed for stealing food, and one had drowned—and one died on the way home.

Greely and the remaining five enlisted men received national publicity and acclaim, but controversy soon surrounded the expedition. Schley reported that pieces of body tissue had been removed from six of the recovered bodies; Greely vehemently denied the newspaper charges of cannibalism. "I know of no law," he wrote in *Three Years of Arctic Service*, his 1886 two-volume account of the expedition, "human or divine, which was broken at Sabine." Greely's leadership and judgment also were questioned. As David Brainard, one of the survivors who remained in touch with Greely until his death, later recalled, Greely's "obstinate nature" and strict adherence to military conduct and orders shaped his command. Other arctic explorers, such as Robert E. Peary, debated whether those attributes also contributed to the expedition's disastrous outcome.

After two years spent recovering from the ordeal and preparing his official report, *Report on the Proceed-*

ings of the *United States Expedition to Lady Franklin Bay, Grinnell Land* (1888; also issued as U.S. 49th Cong., 1st sess., 1888, House Misc. Doc. 393), Greely received his overdue captain's promotion. He continued to be engaged by and to write extensively on arctic and polar exploration throughout his life, publishing books and articles in popular and scientific magazines. In 1887 Greely was appointed chief signal corps officer with the rank of brigadier general, a post he held until 1906, and through which he pursued his meteorological interests. His official congressional reports on western U.S. climatic conditions (U.S. 50th Cong., 2d sess., 1888, Sen. Exec. Doc. 91; U.S. 51st Cong., 2d sess., 1891, House Exec. Doc. 287) emphasized the diversity of arid regions and argued that no single irrigation plan would be applicable to the West. Under his command the Signal Corps expanded its weather forecasting service (until those responsibilities were transferred in 1891 to the Department of Agriculture), laid undersea cables and tactical wires during the Spanish-American War, and established the extensive Alaskan telegraph, cable, and wireless system.

At the end of his military career, Greely, promoted to major general, served as a replacement commander of western military divisions. As commander of the Pacific Division he directed the army relief for the San Francisco earthquake in April 1906. And in October 1906, as commander of the Northern Military Division, he sent a show of military force to persuade sojourning Utes to return to Utah from Wyoming. After retirement in 1908, Greely participated actively in numerous scientific organizations, clubs, and civic work, lectured and wrote extensively, and continued to be consulted, as he had been for many years, on all matters arctic. A founding member of the National Geographic Society, he published numerous articles in *National Geographic* magazine. He served as the first president of the Explorers' Club, New York, and represented the United States overseas at various international geographic and telegraph conferences. He received the Congressional Medal of Honor in 1935 and died later that year in Washington, D.C.

• The main collection of Greely's papers, which includes personal papers, military papers, and the most complete list of his published articles, is in the Library of Congress; smaller collections are located at Dartmouth College, Hanover, N.H., and the National Geographic Society Library, Washington, D.C. Additional materials from the Lady Franklin Bay expedition are located in the National Archives. Records, journals, and scientific materials left at Fort Conger and retrieved in 1899 by Robert E. Peary are located in the Explorers' Club, New York City. Greely's autobiographical writings include *Three Years of Arctic Service: An Account of the Lady Franklin Bay Expedition of 1881–84, and the Attainment of the Farthest North* (2 vols., 1886) and *Reminiscences of Adventure and Service: A Record of Sixty-five Years* (1927). His extensive published work includes popular books on arctic exploration, such as *Handbook of Arctic Discoveries* (1896) and *True Tales of Arctic Heroism* (1912); general surveys, such as *American Weather* (1888) and *Handbook of Alaska* (1909); and official reports, such as *Isothermal Lines of the United States, 1871–1880* (1881) and U.S. Army, Pacific Division,

Earthquake in California, April 18, 1906 (1906). William Mitchell, who served under Greely in the signal corps, wrote a laudatory biography, *General Greely: The Story of a Great American* (1936). The prominent published primary accounts of the Lady Bay Franklin expedition include an edited version of David L. Brainard's diary, *The Outpost of the Lost: An Arctic Adventure*, ed. Bessie Rowland James (1929); Charles Lanman, *Farthest North; or, The Life and Explorations of Lieutenant James Booth Lockwood, of the Greely Arctic Expedition* (1885), based on Lockwood's journal; and W. S. Schley and J. R. Soley, *The Rescue of Greely* (1885).

KATHERINE G. MORRISSEY

GREEN, Abel (3 June 1900–10 May 1973), entertainment journalist and editor, was born in New York City, the son of Seymour Green, a manufacturer, and Berta Raines. He was educated in public schools and attended New York University for one year. In 1919 Green left college to take a job writing obituaries and Tin Pan Alley squibs at *Variety*, where he would work for the rest of his life. The weekly, founded in 1905, was already a mainstay of the entertainment business. George Bernard Shaw read it with care, and Cardinal Francis Spellman is reported to have said on first meeting Green, "Mr. Green, I read your bible today." Green began as a "mug" covering films, radio, music, nightclubs, Tin Pan Alley, vaudeville, and Broadway. In 1921 he married Gracelyn Adele Fenn. The couple had no children.

His first major assignment at *Variety* came in 1929 when he was put in charge of organizing coverage of theatrical news of the capitals of Europe, North Africa, and Latin America. From 1930 to 1932 he directed the magazine's Hollywood office. He got the job of top editor in 1933 when Sime Silverman, the publication's founder, rose from his chair, said, "You sit here, Abel," and left.

Sit there Green did, invariably wearing a bow tie and sleeve garters, at a battered desk close to the window in a ground-floor office on West 46th Street. From there he directed *Variety*'s worldwide coverage, and he often traveled widely himself to maintain acquaintance with both luminaries and unknowns of the stage, sports, journalism, politics, radio, television, and movies. His obituary in the *New York Times* noted, "Walking down the street with him could be a nightmare. He would exchange greetings and perhaps engage in hasty conferences at the rate of a dozen or so to the block."

Green wrote for other publications as well, such as *Esquire*, *Collier's*, the *New York Times Book Review*, and *Cosmopolitan*. His book *Inside Stuff on How to Write Popular Songs* was published in 1927. A freelance songwriter, he wrote the lyrics to "Blue Baby," "Florida," "Variety Stomp," "Variety Is the Spice of Life," "Encore," and "Who's Who Are You?" He also wrote the 1933 Warner Brothers movie *Mr. Broadway*, about Silverman. He was coauthor and producer of the "Philco-Variety Radio Hall of Fame," a one-hour NBC program broadcast in 1941 and 1942. In 1951 he wrote an encyclopedic history, *Show Biz: From Vaude to Video*, with comedian Joe Laurie, Jr. In

1952 he edited both *Variety Music Cavalcade* and *The Spice of Variety*, the second book a collection of articles written for special editions of *Variety* by prominent entertainment figures.

Green's innovation, the Literati column in *Variety*, was widely read. But he is best remembered for his contribution to the slanguage and headlinese that became *Variety*'s hallmark. "All our staff are college men," he once said, "but we don't like square stories." Some "Varietyese," most notably "whodunit," "deejay," "hi-fi," and "sci-fi," became part of the King's English. Some of the headlines Green is credited with having written are still arresting: "STIX NIX HIX PIX" (country dwellers do not appreciate their portrayal in motion pictures) and "BLIZ BOFFS BIZ IN BUFF" (a Buffalo blizzard was disastrous for business there). *Variety* under Green made no apologies for its sense of priorities. Both Rita Hayworth's marriage to Aly Kahn and Grace Kelly's to Prince Rainier of Monaco were summed up: "Bride is film star; groom is non-pro."

Green's staccato style and his creative manhandling of English carried over into his personal communication. Asking friends to call he would say, "Gimme a quick Ameche one of these days," a reference to actor Don Ameche's portrayal of Alexander Graham Bell in the film biography of Bell. Canceling a meeting, he would tell an associate: "Can't meet you today—unforch."

He was a member of the Motion Picture Pioneers and of the American Society of Composers, Authors and Publishers. He received Italy's Commendatore di Merito in 1970.

At seventy-one Green responded to a request from *Who's Who in America* for thoughts on his life. "If you like what you're doing and so long as you can physically and mentally function," he wrote, "my credo long has been that I'd rather wear out than rust out." Green died in New York a few hours after completing another page one story for *Variety*.

• There are substantial Green entries in *Who Was Who in the Theatre* (1972), *Who's Who in the Theatre* (1972), *Biographical Encyclopedia and Who's Who of the American Theatre* (1966), and *Celebrity Register* (1959). Obituaries are in the *New York Times*, 11 May 1973, and *Time*, 21 May 1973.

BRUCE M. SWAIN

GREEN, Anna Katharine (11 Nov. 1846–11 Apr. 1935), mystery writer, was born in Brooklyn, New York, the daughter of James Wilson Green, a lawyer, and Catharine Ann Whitney. At age six she began writing and aspired to be a poet, an appropriately "feminine" mode of authorship of which her father approved. Unlike her sister Sarah, who cared for Green after their mother died and remained unmarried in the patriarchal household most of her life, Green planned a professional writing career. When she enrolled at Ripley Female College in Poultney, Vermont, in 1863, her teachers encouraged her interest in literature. After receiving her B.A. in 1867, she sought advice from

Ralph Waldo Emerson, who, while cautiously praising her poetry, discouraged her from making it her profession. Consequently she turned to fiction, secretly fearing her father's disapproval.

Nine years before Arthur Conan Doyle published "A Study in Scarlet," Green wrote the first popular American full-length mystery, *The Leavenworth Case: A Lawyer's Story* (1878). (Reading the manuscript to her father secured both his approval and support.) Contemporary research shows that she was not the first to write a full-length mystery story as earlier critics believed, but *The Leavenworth Case* nonetheless influenced succeeding generations of writers, including Agatha Christie and Mary Roberts Rinehart. Green had turned to fiction because she believed that becoming a published novelist would be a way to get her poetry published also. She was correct, for after the success of *The Leavenworth Case*, her publisher, George Putnam, printed *The Defense of the Bride and Other Poems* (1882) and a verse drama, *Risifi's Daughter* (1887).

The Leavenworth Case, which sold more than half a million copies and has been continuously reprinted, included a number of "firsts" that have since become part of detective fiction formula. Set in New York, the novel introduces Ebenezer Gryce, the first series detective, who appears in eleven other novels. A number of plot devices have become clichés. As Alma E. Murch points out, there is a body found in the library, a rich elderly man killed as he is about to change his will, a drawing of the scene of the crime, a butler and trained servants, a coroner's inquest, medical evidence indicating the time and cause of death, and a ballistics expert identifying the weapon (p. 162). Presumably drawing on Edgar Allan Poe, Green creates a "locked room" mystery in which Horatio Leavenworth is the victim, and the suspects include his nieces, Mary and Eleanore, a male secretary, and the servants. Much praised for its accuracy in depicting criminal procedure (Green acknowledged French writer Emile Gaboriau as a major influence), the novel was used by Yale College as a textbook demonstration of the deceptive potential of circumstantial evidence.

In 1884 the 38-year-old celebrity, then author of five mysteries, married 31-year-old actor Charles Rohlfs, the son of German immigrants. Rohlfs, who obtained approval from Green's father by promising to give up his acting career, settled on furniture design, which eventually earned him international recognition. After James Green's death he briefly returned to acting, taking a part in the dramatized version of *A Leavenworth Case* in 1891. Much of the couple's early married life was financed by Anna's literary earnings; the birth of two children as well as the financial dependency of Charles's mother and Anna's sister Sarah necessitated Green's continued literary output—three novels from 1886 to 1888. After Charles's mother died in 1888, the family moved from Brooklyn to Buffalo, New York. There another child was born, and Green continued to balance the dual roles of housewife and professional writer, claiming "'writing is only a part of my life'"

(*Literary Digest*, p. 48). Nevertheless, she produced nearly a volume a year until 1917. She published her last mystery novel, *The Step on the Stair*, in 1923 when she was seventy-seven.

Although modern critics fault Green's style as florid and melodramatic, they have universal praise for her plot construction (some based on the newspaper crime reports she collected) and sense of realism. She set her novels among the upper classes but maintained that "crime must touch our imagination by showing people, *like ourselves*, but incredibly transformed by some overwhelming motive" (*American Magazine*, p. 39). The central focus of what she called her "criminal romances" was always the mystery, not the romance.

Her detective Gryce is the antithesis of the romanticized predecessors created by Poe and Wilkie Collins. In fact, he is doggedly ordinary:

And here let me say that Mr. Gryce, the detective, was not the thin, wiry individual with the piercing eye you are doubtless expecting to see. On the contrary, Mr. Gryce was a portly, comfortable personage with an eye that never pierced, that did not even rest on *you*. If it rested anywhere, it was always on some insignificant object in the vicinity, some vase, inkstand, book, or button. These things he would seem to take into his confidence, make the repositories of his conclusions; but as for you—you might as well be the steeple on Trinity Church, for all connection you ever appeared to have with him or his thoughts. (*The Leavenworth Case*, p. 5)

Green's popularity with her American and British public continued with the novels that followed. Her works, in fact, were translated into five languages. Though none of these novels achieved the success of *The Leavenworth Case*, critics admired their plot construction and the characterizations of the detectives. By the end of the nineteenth century, however, Green's ornate style had gone out of fashion, and in the twentieth century her reputation declined until she was nearly forgotten.

In the 1970s and 1980s, feminist reevaluations of her work resulted in critical articles and a book as well as the republication of *The Leavenworth Case* in 1981. Much interest has been focused on Green's two female detectives, Amelia Butterworth, a wealthy middle-aged woman with curiosity and common sense (not always appreciated by Gryce) who first helps him in *That Affair Next Door* (1897) and appears in four additional novels; and Violet Strange, a society beauty secretly employed by a detective agency, in *The Golden Slipper and Other Problems for Violet Strange* (1915). Butterworth is the stronger, more independent character, although Strange herself, who keeps her profession secret from her father, reflects a frequent Green concern with dictatorial fathers (or father figures) who blight their daughters' lives. Violet, however, accepts the feminine facade of " 'silly little chit' " as she puts her clever mind to work solving a series of problems.

Some months after celebrating her golden wedding anniversary, Green died in Buffalo. Her admirers included Collins, President Woodrow Wilson, and future prime minister Stanley Baldwin. Variously known as the mother, godmother, or grandmother of the detective story, Green, who had a long, prolific, and internationally recognized writing career (thirty-five novels, four short-story collections, a play, and a volume of poetry over a span of forty-five years), is assured of a significant place in the history of mystery fiction.

• Scrapbooks of clippings and press photographs concerning Green may be found in the Rare Book Room of the Buffalo and Erie County Public Library. Barrie Hayne, "Anna Katharine Green," in *Ten Women of Mystery*, ed. Earl Bargainnier (1981), includes much of this material. Mary Alice Rohlfs, Green's daughter-in-law, has letters and other materials that flesh out the biographical information in the only book on Green to date, Patricia D. Maida, *Mother of Detective Fiction: The Life and Works of Anna Katharine Green* (1989). Maida's bibliography of Green's works is complete except for the omission of *Three Women and a Mystery* (1902). Important sources for Green's own comments include "Anna Katherine [*sic*] Green Tells How She Manufactures Her Plots," *Literary Digest*, 13 July 1918, p. 48; "Why Human Beings Are Interested in Crime," *American Magazine*, Feb. 1919, pp. 38–39, 82–86; and "Noted Buffalonians, Wed Half Century Ago, Happy," *Buffalo Courier Express*, 18 Nov. 1934, pp. 1–2. Her obituary in the *New York Times*, 12 Apr. 1935, extols Green's impact on mystery fiction and mentions her part in persuading British Prime Minister William E. Gladstone to support creation of an international copyright law. J. R. Broadus, *Critical Survey of Mystery and Detective Fiction*, ed. Frank Magill (1988), analyzes the main series characters and the works in which they appear. Michele Slung gives a brief historical introduction to *The Leavenworth Case* in the 1981 Dover edition. The examination of Green's detectives in Alma Murch, *The Development of the Detective Novel* (1958), is still worth reading. For a more recent argument that Green's characters are essentially feminist, see Kathleen L. Maio, "Anna Katharine Green," in *American Women Writers*, ed. Linda Mainiero, vol. 3 (1981), pp. 498–500.

MARIE T. FARR

GREEN, Anne Catharine (?–23 Mar. 1775), colonial printer, was born probably in Holland. Nothing is known of her family or of her life until her marriage on 25 April 1738 to Jonas Green, a journeyman printer, in Christ Church, Philadelphia. In 1738 Jonas received a position in Annapolis with the expectation of becoming the printer to the province of Maryland, and Anne Catharine accompanied him to the provincial capital to begin what would be a 101-year printing dynasty in Maryland.

For almost thirty years, Anne Catharine was known only as the wife of Jonas Green. She bore fourteen children, only six of whom lived past childhood. These were hard years financially. Jonas was confirmed as printer to the provincial government, but authorizations for payment came slowly and there were many debts. To obtain his press and supplies, Jonas had borrowed from his benefactors in Philadelphia, Benjamin Franklin and Andrew Bradford. The public printing included publication of the votes, proceedings, and acts of the General Assembly, government forms, and proclamations. For the first years, however, it was private printing that sustained the Green family. Notices of sales, handbills, and business forms were printed in the basement shop of their gambrel-roofed brick house on Charles Street.

In 1745 Jonas Green revived the *Maryland Gazette*, a newspaper that had been started in 1727 by William Parks, his predecessor as provincial printer. The *Maryland Gazette*, a four-page weekly usually published on Thursday, printed news from abroad and elsewhere in the colonies, a little local news, a few marriages and obituaries of well-known people, notes on shipping, extreme weather conditions, unusual events or natural phenomena, letters to the editor, poetry, and the advertisements that usually made up half of the paper and served as its major support.

To supplement the family income, Anne Catharine advertised coffee, raisins, and chocolate for sale at the printing office. There was always activity at the house on Charles Street. Customers stopped by to leave ads, pick up printing, pay for their papers, or to buy Anne Catharine's wares or the books, medicine, molasses, nails, and other goods that Jonas often advertised for sale at the office. From at least 1745 until 1764, Jonas Green served as postmaster, and the northern and southern post riders exchanged their packets at the printing office. In addition to running the household and feeding and caring for the family and the print shop apprentices, Anne Catharine probably assisted as a postal clerk and officiated behind the print shop counter.

Jonas Green died on 11 April 1767, leaving his wife with five unmarried children, the youngest just seven years old. In a notice beneath his obituary in the *Maryland Gazette* on 16 April 1767, Anne Catharine wrote, "I presume to address You for Your Countenance to Myself and numerous Family, left, without Your Favor, almost Destitute of Support, by the Decease of my Husband . . . and, I flatter myself that, with your kind indulgence and Encouragement, MYSELF, and Son, will be enabled to continue it on the same Footing." Her oldest son, William, was only twenty, however, so for the next nine months, Anne Catharine carried on the paper alone. She completed the votes, proceedings, and acts of the 1767 assembly, and in 1768 the legislature voted to pay her for the 1767 printing and named her public printer at the same salary that Jonas had received: 48,000 pounds of tobacco for a year with sessions of the assembly and 36,109 pounds of tobacco for those years in which there was no meeting of the legislature. In addition to the assembly printing and the government forms and proclamations, Anne Catharine also printed the government's bills of credit authorized in 1769. She continued as official public printer until her death, and the public contract was always in her name only, even during those years when her sons were listed with her as printers of the *Maryland Gazette*.

Anne Catharine Green continued the *Maryland Gazette* with no apparent loss of advertising and printed an annual almanac, begun by Jonas in 1750, as well as the usual handbills and notices of sales. In January 1768, a few weeks after his twenty-first birthday, William Green's name was added to the masthead—after his mother's. When William died in August 1770, Anne Catharine again published alone until her next son, Frederick, was almost twenty-two in January 1772. From that time until her death, the masthead read "Anne Catharine Green & Son."

As the dissention that resulted in the American Revolution grew in the early 1770s, the *Maryland Gazette*, under the editorship of Anne Catharine Green and her sons, served as a sounding board and open forum for all manner of political controversy. Complex, technical legal duels by such persons as William Paca, Charles Carroll of Carrollton, Samuel Chase, and the Reverend Jonathan Boucher were fought in the pages of the paper over issues such as the fees for government officials, the poll tax for support of the Anglican church, and, generally, the rights of citizens versus the established government. The *Maryland Gazette* printed news of the events leading up to the war: colonial reaction to the Townshend Acts, passage of the Boston Port Act and the resulting outcry throughout the colonies, and the *Peggy Stewart* affair in which a tea-carrying ship was burned in the Annapolis harbor. It balanced the votes, proceedings, and acts of the last proprietary assembly in 1774 with extracts from the Continental Congress of September 1774 and the proceedings of the extralegal Maryland conventions that began meeting in June 1774 in opposition to the proprietary government. Throughout this period Anne Catharine Green succeeded in keeping her paper reasonably unbiased and fair. Although the *Maryland Gazette* printed calls for meetings and letters on both sides of any question, the preponderance of news from antiestablishment groups weighted coverage on that side.

In addition to her regular printing jobs and the newspaper, Anne Catharine took on several special publications. Her publication of *The Charter and Bye-Laws of the City of Annapolis* (1769) is lauded by Lawrence C. Wroth as a "beautifully printed little volume of fifty-two pages, which for typographical nicety could hardly have been surpassed by the best of her contemporaries in the colonies." In 1774 she printed Elie Vallette's *Deputy Commissary's Guide*, with an engraved title page considered to be the best example of the work of Annapolis engraver Thomas Sparrow.

When Anne Catharine Green died in Annapolis, her newspaper carried her obituary, describing her as "of a mild and benevolent Disposition, and for conjugal Affection, and parental Tenderness, an Example to her sex." There was no mention of her business activity; yet, as the official Maryland printer and editor of a major colonial newspaper for eight years, Anne Catharine Green demonstrated an ability far beyond that considered natural for women of her time. Surely she had apprentices as well as sons to help her with the business; but while she may not have set every row of type, she supervised and directed those who did, and exerted a significant influence on prerevolutionary Maryland.

• For more information on Anne Catharine Green, see the *Maryland Gazette*, especially the issues of 16 Apr. 1767, 22 Sept. 1768, and 30 Mar. 1775. The original printers' copies of the *Maryland Gazette* are at the Maryland State Archives in Annapolis. The standard reference for the Greens and their imprints is Lawrence C. Wroth, *A History of Printing in Colonial Maryland, 1686–1776* (1922). Also helpful from a political standpoint are David C. Skaggs, "Editorial Policies of the Maryland Gazette, 1765–1783," *Maryland Historical Magazine* 59 (Dec. 1964): 341–49, and Josephine Fisher, "Bennet Allen, Fighting Parson," *Maryland Historical Magazine* 38 (Dec. 1943): 49–72, and 39 (Mar. 1944): 299–322.

JANE WILSON MCWILLIAMS

GREEN, Asa (11 Feb. 1789–c. 1837), physician and author, was born in Ashburnham, Massachusetts, the son of Oliver Green and Dorothy Hildreth. Green (sometimes spelled "Greene") entered Williams College at the sophomore level and there earned a "good reputation as a scholar." It is also at college where he is said to have been "distinguished for wit and vigor of thought," aspects of which are reflected in his later literary efforts. He received an A.B. from Williams in 1813 and an M.D. from Brown University in 1822 and from the Berkshire Medical Institution in 1827.

Green was thirty-eight when he began his medical practice in Lunenburg, Massachusetts, and it may not have been fulfilling to him. Within two years he had moved from Lunenburg to Townsend to Pittsfield and later to North Adams. In Pittsfield he established the *Berkshire American*. After moving to North Adams, he practiced medicine as well as continued publishing the newspaper. In a comment on his journalistic effort in the *History of Berkshire County*, Green is cited as "a ready writer, deservedly popular, well educated, and having both tact and talent."

Green's second journalistic effort, the *Socialist*, was founded in 1828. The *History of Berkshire County* called it an evocation of "good literary taste and a humorous style of composition." Both newspapers, however, failed sometime during 1828–1829. In 1829 Green moved to New York City. There he abandoned his medical career and became a bookseller in Beekman Street.

While selling books, Green also edited the *Evening Transcript*, a daily New York newspaper, and began to write novels. He wrote six in eight years. His first literary effort, *The Life and Adventures of Dr. Dodimus Duckworth, A.N.Q.* (1833), to which he added the extra title *The History of a Steam Doctor*, takes a satiric look at the medical profession. The perspective is initially that of a spoiled child who evolves into a reputable country practitioner. Its farcical and mock-heroic tone is found in his later literary works as well. Also in 1833 Green wrote *A Yankee among the Nullifiers*, based on a visit to North Carolina in 1832. The novel good-naturedly examines the South's feeling of opposition toward the North.

The Perils of Pearl Street, Including a Taste of the Dangers of Wall Street, by a Late Merchant followed in 1834. This story is notable among Green's oeuvre in that it is a quieter, more realistic volume, detailing the business failures of a country youth who comes to New York to make his fortune. The autobiographical overtones are stronger in this volume than in his previous works. *The Debtor's Prison* was also published in 1834. In 1835 Green returned to a more humorous bent in the novel *The Travels in America by George Fibbleton, Ex-Barber to His Majesty the King of Great Britain*. It is a satire on the Reverend Isaac Fidler's *Travels in America* and the writings of other English tourists.

A Glance at New York (1837); his final work, bears Green's name not only as author but as publisher. The novel, reflecting Green's usual humorous touch, deals with the harshness of life in a commercial city. The exact date of his death, in New York City, is unknown.

Green was one of America's earliest satirists. His works are noted for providing a humorous slant on American middle-class society. All his novels, except for *The Perils of Pearl Street*, are comical in tone. His contribution is not only that of satirist. His works, thought to be mainly autobiographical, provide a broad view of the business and the medical professions. As such, Green affords an invaluable glimpse into American professional life during the 1830s.

• A brief summary of Green's life is found in Ezra S. Stearns, *History of Ashburnham, Massachusetts, from the Grant of Dorchester, Canada, to the Present Time, 1734–1886* (1887). This volume also includes a genealogical register of Green's and other Ashburnham families. Other sources of information on Green's life include volumes associated with schools he attended, including the *General Catalogue of Officers and Graduates of Williams College* (1910) and the *Historical Catalogue of Brown University, 1764–1914* (1914). See also the Berkshire County records, Thomas Cushing, ed., *History of Berkshire County* (1885), and David Dudley Field, ed., *History of the County of Berkshire, Mass.* (1829).

LINDA K. WRIGHT

GREEN, Ashbel (6 July 1762–19 May 1848), Presbyterian pastor and educator, was born at Hanover, New Jersey, the son of Jacob Green (1722–1790), a Presbyterian pastor and physician, and Elizabeth Pierson, a daughter of the Reverend John Pierson, one of the College of New Jersey's founders. Raised in a family that maintained strict Sabbath observance, regular Bible study, and catechesis of children, Green began to question his faith at age seventeen while teaching English and later Latin at a local school.

Green served sporadically in the militia during the American Revolution and in 1782 entered the junior class at the College of New Jersey. The preaching of his brother-in-law, the Reverend Ebenezer Bradford, the same year generated a "rapture" in Green, and, at his father's urging, Green sought full church membership in Princeton. After giving the valedictory address at his graduation in 1783, Green tutored at the college for two more years. In 1785 Green married Elizabeth Stockton, the daughter of Robert Stockton of Princeton; they had three sons. Conversations with Samuel Stanhope Smith, a professor at the college, prompted Green to pursue the ministry rather than study under Richard Stockton, Jr., a relative of his father-in-law.

He continued to teach for a year and a half more as professor of mathematics and natural philosophy and was licensed to preach by the Presbytery of New Brunswick in February 1786.

The following spring the Second Presbyterian Church of Philadelphia asked Green to preach monthly in expectation of his becoming the assistant to the Reverend James Sproat. He experienced a physical and nervous collapse shortly thereafter that delayed his ordination until May 1787. Such ailments would continue to trouble Green during the numerous crises of his career.

While in Philadelphia, Green was elected to the American Philosophical Society. He also became a trustee of the College of New Jersey in 1790 and served with Bishop William White (1748–1836) as chaplain to the U.S. Congress from 1792 to 1800. At the turn of the century, he edited the *Works* (1800–1801) of his friend and college mentor, John Witherspoon.

After his first wife's death in 1807, Green became deeply involved in the establishment of Princeton Theological Seminary. Sharing the traditional Presbyterian insistence on an educated clergy, and discontent with the contemporary apprentice system under resident clergy, in 1809 he introduced the overture to the Presbyterian church in the United States of America (PCUSA) that led to the seminary's creation. He later helped formulate the plan for its structure, maneuvered its placement in Princeton, New Jersey, and in 1812 was elected chairman of its board of directors, a position he held until his death.

In 1809 Green married Christiana Anderson; they had one son. Three years later he succeeded Samuel Stanhope Smith as president of the College of New Jersey. Green did not believe that Smith had provided sufficient order to the school. He introduced the study of the Bible into the curriculum and founded a student Bible society. In 1813, Robert Stockton Green, Ashbel's favorite son, died, and one year later his second wife died of a miscarriage. To add to his difficulties, a student riot broke out in 1814. Student uprisings were relatively common on American college campuses at the time, and although Green was both mild and pliable in private, his public paternalistic style and inflexibility in discipline aggravated bad feelings with students and parents in this and later conflicts.

Green married Mary McCulloh in 1815, but she died two years later, again in a year of student unrest. Although the student population had grown during his presidency, Green's unpopularity generated conflict within the college's board of trustees. The board eventually maneuvered Green into resigning his position in 1822.

At the age of sixty-one, Green returned to Philadelphia and resurrected a dying religious periodical called the *Presbyterian*. As editor, Green renamed the monthly journal the *Christian Advocate* and for the next twelve years successfully managed its revival, writing many of its articles himself.

Green was a major presence in the Presbyterian church in the United States of America from 1790 until his death. He attended the PCUSA General Assembly as a member from 1790 to 1839 and occupied its chief elected executive office of stated clerk between 1790 and 1803. Green drafted the General Assembly's famous declaration against slavery in 1818 as well as numerous other statements for that body. In 1824 he was elected moderator of the General Assembly.

Green was a thorough-going Old School Presbyterian who believed in the predestination of God's elect and in the divine's absolute sovereignty over whether an individual receives faith. Although he had introduced an overture in 1790 for closer contact between the PCUSA and New England Congregationalist churches, he later came to distrust the results of institutional mingling with Congregationalists through the 1801 Plan of Union. This plan gave special permission for new congregations in New York and Ohio to seek ministers from and join either denomination. Inadvertently, it also fostered the growth of a New School Presbyterian party whose views on free will, election, and polity Green abhorred. Throughout the 1830s, Green, along with others, led efforts to bring New School Presbyterians like Albert Barnes (?–1870) to trial for heresy. Preferring division to doctrinal impurity, Green actively promoted the retrospective revocation of the Plan of Union that effectively expelled the majority of New School Presbyterians from the church in 1837. For these efforts, as well as for his influence and powerful speaking abilities, he became known to his opponents as the "old pope" of Presbyterianism and a "heresy hunter."

In his last years, Green expanded his *Lectures on the Shorter Catechism* (2 vols., 1841), a shorter version having been published in 1829, and he wrote a biography of John Witherspoon that was frequently used in manuscript form though not published until 1973. Green died in Philadelphia.

• The Green Family Papers are located in the archives of Firestone Library at Princeton University. Manuscript minutes of the College of New Jersey Board of Trustees and the Faculty are in the archives of Mudd Manuscript Library at Princeton University. Other papers relating to Green and his work are available at the New Jersey Historical Society at Newark and at the Archives of the Department of History of the Presbyterian Church (USA) and the Pennsylvania Historical Society, both in Philadelphia. Green produced several important volumes, including *Discourses Delivered in the College of New Jersey: . . . from Its Origin to the Accession of President Witherspoon* (1822); *Memoirs of the Reverend Joseph Eastburn, Stated Preacher in the Mariner's Church, Philadelphia* (1828); and *A Historical Sketch or Compendious View of Domestic and Foreign Missions in the Presbyterian Church of the United States of America* (1838). A largely autobiographical account of his life can be found in Joseph H. Jones, ed., *The Life of Ashbel Green, V.D.M. (1849).* See also PCUSA General Assembly, *Minutes*; Robert E. Lewis, "Ashbel Green, 1762–1848—Preacher, Educator, Editor," *Journal of the Presbyterian Historical Society* 35 (1957): 141–56; Mark A. Noll, "The Founding of Princeton Seminary," *The Westminster Theological Journal* 42 (Fall 1979): 72–110; Richard A.

Harrison, *Princetonians, 1776–1783: A Biographical Dictionary*, vol. 3 (1981); and William B. Sprague, *Annals of the American Pulpit*, vol. 3 (1856).

MILTON J COALTER, JR.

GREEN, Bartholomew (12 Oct. 1666–28 Dec. 1732), printer and journalist, was born in Cambridge, Massachusetts, the son of Samuel Green, a printer, and Sarah Clark, his father's second wife. As a youth, Green served his father as an apprentice. In 1687 he went to Boston to assist his half-brother Samuel, who managed Samuel Sewall's press in Boston after 1682. Both Greens continued to print after Sewall ceased his involvement. Bartholomew Green assumed control after Samuel Green died in July 1690. Soon after, a fire forced him to rejoin his father in Cambridge, where they produced jointly some dozen of his father's last imprints. In 1690 Green married Mary Short; the couple had four children who survived to adulthood. After his father's retirement in 1692, Green returned to Boston, doubtless taking with him much of the equipment and supplies assembled by his father, while also renting the press of Richard Pierce.

Green set up his shop on Newbury Street and was quickly licensed to print. For the next forty years, Green was the principal printer in New England, employing to productive effect his patronage by the colonial government and Harvard College. In addition to printing the acts and laws of Massachusetts, he printed the acts and laws of Connecticut to 1702 and those of New Hampshire to 1726. In the period from 1694 to 1704, Green often shared his imprint with John Allen, though there is no record of a formal partnership. After 1725 Green often collaborated with his son Bartholomew Green, Jr., Thomas Fleet, and Samuel Kneeland. He printed many of his books (epistles, sermons, and devotional tracts) in Algonquian, which he learned while working as an apprentice for his father.

Green produced a great many important titles, including sermons, histories, Indian captivity narratives, Harvard dissertations, and colonial documents, among a great variety of others. In 1690 he printed, along with his father, John Cotton's *Spiritual Milk for Boston Babes*, and in 1698, with John Allen, he printed Increase Mather's *Greatest Sinners Called*, the first book published in the Indian language in Boston. In 1709 the *Massachusetts Psalter* appeared, with parallel columns of English and Algonquian. (Green was assisted by James Printer, an Indian journeyman who had learned to print under Samuel Green in Cambridge and who worked on both volumes of the Indian Bible.) Green had much experience printing almanacs, beginning in 1691, and he produced the first book made with paper manufactured in North America.

Green produced other important titles. In 1696 he and Allen printed Joshua Scottow's *Massachusetts; or, The First Planters of New-England*, and in 1700 they printed Samuel Sewall's *The Selling of Joseph*, generally regarded as the first American antislavery pamphlet. In 1701 the two printers produced Michael

Wigglesworth's apocalyptic *The Day of Doom*, the first complete text of the poem, which finally appeared in its ninth edition. In 1707 Green published John Williams's *The Redeemed Captive, Returning to Zion . . .* , an important Indian captivity narrative. Green also produced a number of early schoolbooks: Nathaniel Strong's *England's Perfect Schoolmaster; or, Directions for Spelling, Reading . . .* (1710), Ezekiel Cheever's *Short Introduction to the Latin Tongue* (1724), and the anonymous *Epitome of English Orthography* (1697). Green also printed what may have been the first American autobiography, Roger Clap's *Memoirs of Capt. Roger Clap. Relating Some of God's Remarkable Providences to Him* (1731).

Green's work also produced several typographical innovations. The first portrait of an author in the British American colonies appeared in *Angelographia*, printed by Green and Allen in 1696; it is regarded as the first engraved portrait on metal in North America. The first music in a woodcut appeared in the ninth edition of the *Bay Psalm Book* (1698). In 1717 Green reproduced, in Hugh Peter's *A Dying Father's Last Legacy*, a woodcut frontispiece, a portrait copied from a line engraving that appeared in a London edition of the book. Green printed the first library catalog in America in 1723, the *Catalogus Librorum Bibliothecae Collegij Harvardini*, and he combined with Samuel Kneeland to produce the largest printing project of the first half of the eighteenth century, Samuel Willard's *A Compleat Body of Divinity*, a 927-page folio.

Starting with the first issue on 24 April 1704, Green printed, under the direction of Boston postmaster John Campbell, the *Boston News-Letter*, the first successful newspaper produced in the colonies. He continued printing it, except for the period 10 November 1707–1 October 1711, when it was printed by John Allen, until he succeeded Campbell as publisher on 7 January 1723. Green continued to publish the *News-Letter* until his death, when his son-in-law John Draper succeeded him. Initially, Green sought to evade controversy as he published "those Transactions only, that have no Relation to any of our Quarrels, and may be equally entertaining to the greatest Adversaries." But on 5 January 1727 Green renounced his practice of maintaining "a Thread of Occurrences of an Old Date," renaming his newspaper the *Weekly News-Letter* and renumbering it from number one. Green sought to select news, both domestic and foreign, that might be most acceptable to his readership. He took an important step by suspending recording the news and initiating reporting the news. His newspaper remained characterized by piety, containing much moral and religious reflection, but he recast its function in a manner that foreshadowed the evolution of journalistic practice. His obituary in the *Boston Weekly News-Letter* observed that "He began to be Pious, in the Days of his Youth; And he wou'd always speak of the wonderful spirit of Piety that then prevail'd in the Land, with a singular Pleasure" (4 Jan. 1733).

Green supported the Mathers, printing nearly two hundred of the titles written by Cotton Mather, including *The Short History of New England* (1694), the *Bostonian Ebenezer* (with John Allen in 1698), and *Decennium Luctuosum*, a history of King Philip's War, in 1688–1689 as well as, in 1710, *Bonifacius*, later retitled *Essays to Do Good*, and, in 1712, *Grace Defended*. Green had refused to print without imprimatur Benjamin Colman's *Gospel Order Revived*, a response to Increase Mather's similarly unlicensed pamphlet, *The Order of the Gospel*. Green then produced a handbill justifying his position.

Green was a deacon of the South Church. His first wife died in 1709, and in 1710 he married Jane Toppan, evidently a niece of Samuel Sewall, who performed the ceremony. They had one child, who died in infancy. After Green died, following "a long and painful Languishment of a Sore that broke inwards" (*Boston Weekly News-Letter*, 4 Jan. 1733), his will noted that his printing establishment was valued at £126. His son-in-law John Draper was one of a number of printers who had apprenticed with him, including Gamaliel Rogers, Thomas Short, Samuel Kneeland, Bartholomew Green, Jr., and Timothy Green.

Green was the most important printer in New England in the first quarter of the eighteenth century. Shortly after his death he was characterized as "esteemed among us . . . we may further remember his eminency for a strict observing the sabbath . . . his keeping close and diligent to the work of his calling; his meek and peaceable spirit; his caution of publishing anything offensive, light or hurtful . . . " (*Boston Weekly News-Letter*, 4 Jan. 1733).

• Among the most conveniently assembled compilations of information about Green is the article that appears in Benjamin Franklin V, ed., *Boston Printers, Publishers, and Booksellers, 1640–1800* (1980), while William C. Kiessel, "The Green Family: A Dynasty of Printers," *New England Historical and Genealogical Register* 104 (1950): 81–93, and George E. Littlefield, *Early Boston Booksellers: 1642–1711*, repr. ed. (1969), contain useful information, though much of it is derived from Isaiah Thomas, *The History of Printing in America*, repr. ed. (1970). A useful essay that contains a great deal of information about seventeenth-century printing in North America is William S. Reese, "The First Hundred Years of Printing in British North America: Printers and Collectors," American Antiquarian Society, *Proceedings* 99 (1989): 337–73.

WILLIAM L. JOYCE

GREEN, Benjamin Edwards (5 Feb. 1822–12 May 1907), lawyer, diplomat, and business promoter, was born in Elkton, Kentucky, the son of Duff Green and Lucretia Maria Edwards. He grew up in Washington, D.C., where his father, a determined supporter of Andrew Jackson, moved in 1825 to edit the *United States Telegraph*, used to attack President John Quincy Adams and laud Jacksonian reform. Green graduated from Georgetown College in 1838 and studied law at the University of Virginia. He began his law practice in New Orleans.

John C. Calhoun, whose son married Green's sister, used his influence to obtain for Green the post of secretary of the legation in Mexico on 24 May 1843. Green served as chargé d'affaires from 9 March until 1 September 1844. During the tense and increasingly hostile period prior to the Mexican War, he skillfully conducted negotiations on the disputed boundary of the Republic of Texas, an amended claims convention, and Mexican treatment of Texans captured during a disastrous engagement in late 1842 near Mier in the disputed area between Mexico and the Republic of Texas. He sought agreement on the Texas boundary and held out the promise of possible indemnification resulting from a boundary settlement. Mexican officials rejected the idea of an indemnification, because they did not intend to cede territory to the United States. Green retained a respectful and open relationship with Mexican officials, which allowed him to present the U.S. position and receive their replies. Because Mexican leaders refused to cede territory and U.S. leaders were determined to annex Texas with the largest possible borders, no meeting of minds was accomplished.

Green returned to Washington in 1845, where he practiced law and invested in railroads. Representing the Gosport (Va.) Iron Works, he, Simon Cameron, and another partner won a government contract to repair ships and to build the USS *Powhatan*. At this time and later, he wrote for newspapers on public issues related to political economy, including an 1846 article about the Oregon question for the Washington *Daily Union*, which he signed "Democrat." After the Mexican War, the Mexican government hired him to organize indemnity payments to U.S. citizens.

In 1849 President Zachary Taylor secretly dispatched Green to the West Indies with specific authority to negotiate with the Dominican Republic for the rights to a naval station. Green's chief success was to persuade Haiti to extend a one-sided recognition of U.S. consular officials. Secretary of State John M. Clayton described U.S. trade with Haiti as "extensive and profitable," making the ability to protect and extend commerce with agents who had access to the Haitian government a valuable concession. During Green's travels to Santo Domingo, he stopped for ten days in Havana, Cuba, from where he reported overwhelming popular sentiment for annexation to the United States despite the fact that he was held in quarantine the whole time of his visit.

Clayton instructed Green to ascertain the veracity of rumored British efforts to acquire a naval base at Samaná Bay and to observe French intrigues, which aimed to establish a protectorate over the Dominican Republic and Haiti. He was to determine "whether or not the Spanish race has the ascendency" in the government of the Dominican Republic. In the fall of 1849, he played on racism to appeal for aid to the white Dominicans against black Haitians. Green alleged that the French encouraged the Haitian invasions and conquest of the Dominican Republic so that Haiti could better service its French debt. A Haitian conquest of the Dominicans, he warned, would establish its vexatious commercial restrictions where U.S. merchants now experienced great freedom, and he proposed threatening Haiti with U.S. naval action unless it ceased its attacks on the Dominican Republic. When Green visited Haiti in April 1850, three U.S. war vessels accompanied him. The U.S. government wanted him to resolve the outstanding claims of U.S. citizens against Haiti without extending it recognition, but he was instructed to keep his official character secret from Haitian officials unless they clearly indicated willingness to negotiate a settlement of the claims, which totaled $300,000. In 1850 Green and his father became involved in a land and colonization scheme in the Dominican Republic, undermining his reputation and diplomatic efforts on the island because the project made the settlers (apparently U.S. whites) eligible for military service if the Dominican government went to war.

In 1850 Green founded the Dalton City Company to encourage industrial development in Georgia. His interests included the Dalton and Morgantown and the Dalton and Jacksonville railroads, the Central Transit Company, the Cherokee Iron Foundry, and the Texas Land Company. He later managed the Washington County (Tenn.) Iron Works for the Confederate government.

After the Civil War, the American Industrial Agency, a company organized to attract northern and European investments in southern agriculture, employed Green as solicitor and general manager. In 1866 he married Lizzie Waters; they had three children. He published *Letters and Remarks* (1866), which was addressed to the National Labor Congress that met in Baltimore on 20 August 1866. The pamphlet encouraged the establishment of savings banks for workmen under the American Industrial Agency, which would have raised capital for the enterprise's other objectives. However, the American Industrial Agency was an unsuccessful venture. Green then organized attempts to attract migrants to the South from the northwestern states and Germany and to generate interest in construction of a canal across northern Florida to connect the Atlantic Ocean and the Gulf of Mexico. As secretary of the Crédit Mobilier of America, he published its *Prospectus* (1873) as well as its history in the *New York Herald*, 6 February 1873.

Green translated (with a 59-page introduction and a 22-page postscript) Adolphe Granier de Cassagnac's *History of the Working and Burgher Classes* (1871). He also published several works related to economics and politics, such as *Opinions of John C. Calhoun and Thomas Jefferson on the Subject of Paper Currency* (n.d.); *The Irrepressible Conflict between Labor and Capital* (1872), which originally appeared as the introduction to Cassagnac's book; and *Shakespeare and Goethe on Gresham's Law and the Single Gold Standard* (1901). He left a number of unpublished manuscripts on the history of the 1840s, 1850s, and 1860s. Active in Georgia politics, he was instrumental in calling the Georgia Greenback party convention in 1880. He died in Dalton, Georgia.

Green participated in the search for a naval station on the island of Santo Domingo, relations with Mexico prior to the outbreak of war, and the economic and financial transformations of the United States during its Industrial Revolution.

• Green's numerous unpublished manuscripts are in private hands in Chapel Hill, N.C., and some of his writings, including a biographical sketch, are in the Duff Green Papers, Southern Historical Collection, University of North Carolina at Chapel Hill. The U.S. State Department's microfilmed records contain his official correspondence from Mexico (microfilm M97, reels 12 and 13) and from Santo Domingo (microfilm M37, reel 4). A biographical sketch is in John E. Findling, ed., *Dictionary of American Diplomatic History* (1989). His service in Mexico is described in James Morton Callahan, *American Foreign Policy in Mexican Relations* (1932), and Luis G. Zorrilla, *Historia de las Relaciones entre México y los Estados Unidos de América, 1800–1958* (2 vols., 1965). His service in Santo Domingo and Haiti is described in Henry Merritt Wriston, *Executive Agents in American Foreign Relations* (1929); Rayford Whittingham Logan, *The Diplomatic Relations of the United States and Haiti, 1776–1891* (1941); Charles Callan Tansill, *The United States and Santo Domingo, 1798–1873* (1938); and Sumner Welles, *Naboth's Vineyard: The Dominican Republic, 1844–1924* (2 vols., 1928). An obituary is in the *Atlanta Constitution*, 14 May 1907.

THOMAS SCHOONOVER

GREEN, Beriah (24 Mar. 1795–4 May 1874), abolitionist clergyman and educator, was born in Preston, Connecticut, the son of Beriah Green, a farmer and furniture maker, and Elizabeth Smith. He graduated from Middlebury College in 1819 and later attended Andover Seminary. In 1821 he married Marcia Deming; they had two children.

While waiting for an appointment from the American Board of Commissioners for Foreign Missions in 1821, Green accepted pastoral charges on Long Island and then in East Lyme, Connecticut. In 1822 he became pastor of the First Congregational Church in Brandon, Vermont, and was ordained one year later. His wife, Marcia, died in 1826. Six months later he married Daxara Foote; they had seven children.

Green then relocated to a "distinctly orthodox" Congregational church in Kennebunk, Maine, in 1829. A year later he accepted an appointment as professor of sacred literature at Western Reserve College in Hudson, Ohio. Promoted as the "Yale of the West" by its founders, who had migrated from New England, Western Reserve College became the center of controversy over the policies of the American Colonization Society. Organized in 1817, the ACS proposed to remove free blacks to the West African colony of Liberia and had the support of some slaveholders. The publication by William Lloyd Garrison of the *Liberator* in 1831 launched a direct attack upon the ACS, exposing its racist and proslavery policies. Garrison's paper and other abolitionist publications soon reached Western Reserve College, where his call for the immediate, unconditional, and uncompensated emancipation of the slaves sparked public debate among students and faculty.

Green angered the majority of the trustees and conservative clergy by using the chapel pulpit on four successive Sundays in November and December 1832 to attack slavery and supporters of the ACS. "It now is palpable as the sun in heaven, that the slaveholders and colonization party are united together to suppress the freedom of speech and of the press and even to exclude from the pulpits of our land those who plead for the immediate abolition of slavery," Green wrote Garrison in early March 1833. Because of his espousal of Garrisonian immediatism, Green expected to be purged by the conservative trustees. He submitted his resignation and left in 1833 to become president of Oneida Institute, a manual labor academy and college opened in May 1827 as Oneida Academy by George Washington Gale, a Presbyterian clergyman, in Whitesboro, New York.

The academy was chartered as the Oneida Institute of Science and Industry in 1829. Students participated in an obligatory manual labor program, working in fields and shops to offset their expenses and to demonstrate the benefits of combining physical labor with mental training. Most of the students were converts or supporters of the famous revivalist Charles G. Finney and were intent on a practical education for the ministry. Henry Highland Garnet and Alexander Crummell were two notable abolitionists who attended. Green radicalized the school by admitting more African-American students than any other college of the time, by making Oneida a center of abolitionist activity, and by making changes in the curriculum that included replacing the Greek and Latin classics with study of the original biblical languages.

In 1833 Green presided at the organizational meeting of the American Anti-Slavery Society. Known as an uncompromising opponent of slavery with expertise in moral theology and biblical interpretation, Green was encouraged by his abolitionist colleagues to answer the apologists of slavery who were using the Bible to defend "the peculiar institution." In the late 1830s, Green became preoccupied with refuting the claims of those he called the "grave and learned ecclesiastics" of the North, such as prominent theologians Moses Stuart and Charles Hodge. The fullest expression of Green's attack upon slavery, which was based on his blend of ethical principles derived from reason or natural theology and from revealed religion or the Bible, appeared in *The Chattel Principle* (1839).

Beginning with the financial panic of 1837, Oneida Institute entered a period of gradual decline. Compounding the school's economic problems was Green's loss of favor within conservative Presbyterian circles, which had provided some support. A schism rent Whitesboro's First Presbyterian Church in 1837, when Green led an exodus of abolition-minded members to form a "come-outer" congregation. Green asserted that the main issue was not church discipline but "whether the principle of human equality shall be carried out in the abolition of slavery—or whether, in opposition to this principle, the free shall be enslaved." As a result of the bitter battle within the church, Green felt more and more at odds with the religious establishment in the North and concluded that he had become a "troubler of Israel."

Unable to surmount its financial problems, Oneida Institute was sold to the Freewill Baptists in 1844. Green's experiment in radical humanitarianism had been an attempt to institutionalize abolitionism by making Oneida a model of the biracial society the United States would become if the abolitionist vision were to triumph. With the closing of his school, Green became more active in support of the Liberty party, a third party dedicated to the "One Idea" platform of abolitionism. In 1838 he had written prominent philanthropist and reformer Gerrit Smith, "I am well convinced that God, the God of the Oppressed, calls us into the field of Politics; and we must obey. I enter without any very great reluctance; as I am clear on the point of duty. And Politics is with us a Sacred Concern." The failure of the party to woo enough voters to have any significant impact on American politics, however, soured Green on the democratic process.

Green's personal political philosophy became increasingly idiosyncratic. He despaired of popular democracy and advocated rule by the wise, an oligarchy or modified theocracy, though he was never explicit about how to achieve righteous government. "The throne of God," Green wrote former Liberty party presidential candidate James G. Birney in 1847, "is the only Model on which a government can possibly be formed and maintained. . . . The wisest, strongest man in a community is its King, and Earth and Hell can by no means deprive him of the scepter."

Because of the closing of Oneida Institute and the refusal of colleagues in the abolitionist movement to embrace his notion of government by the wise, Green became increasingly bitter and disillusioned. He no longer ventured far from Whitesboro and tried to support his family by farming and preaching to a small congregation of abolitionists. His self-imposed isolation and quarrelsome personality were an enigma and irritation to his friends and colleagues, though they spoke highly of his intellect, integrity, and dedication to his principles.

Green published his collected writings in 1860 under the title *Sermons and Other Discourses with Brief Biographical Hints*. As the Civil War approached, he considered removing to Canada, for he had little sympathy for Lincoln and the Republicans, who he believed had betrayed the principles of pure abolitionism. As old age approached, Green engaged more zealously in the physical regimens he had followed for many years to maintain a healthy body and a healthy mind, especially cold-water baths and hard labor with his wood axe. Green died while delivering a temperance speech in Whitesboro. John Greenleaf Whittier, the Quaker poet and veteran abolitionist, wrote, "He has died as he would have wished to die, lifting his voice for God and humanity."

• No collection of Green's papers exists, but approximately 200 letters from Green to Gerrit Smith are in the Gerrit Smith

Papers, George Arents Research Library, Syracuse University. For a complete listing of Green's published essays, sermons, addresses, pamphlets, and books, as well as a fuller examination of his life and reform activities, see Milton C. Sernett, *Abolition's Axe: Beriah Green, Oneida Institute, and the Black Freedom Struggle* (1986). Additional information on Oneida Institute is in Sernett, "First Honor: Oneida Institute's Role in the Fight against Racism and Slavery," *New York History* 66 (Apr. 1985): 197–209. See Lawrence J. Friedman, "The Gerrit Smith Circle: Abolitionism in the Burned-Over District," *Civil War History* 26 (1980): 18–38, on Green's relationship with other abolitionists. The local context of Oneida Institute is sketched in D. Gordon Rohman, *Here's Whitesboro* (1949).

MILTON C. SERNETT

GREEN, Calvin (10 Oct. 1780–4 Oct. 1869), Shaker elder and writer, was born in Hancock, Massachusetts, the son of Joseph Green, a shoemaker, and Thankful Barce, a schoolteacher, both unmarried early followers of Mother Ann Lee. Barce was one of the earliest inquirers to visit Lee in Watervliet (formerly Niskeyuna), New York, near Albany. Lee, an illiterate mill-worker from Manchester, England, had led a small apocalyptic group of "Shaking Quakers" to America, arriving in New York Harbor in 1774. The group soon moved out into the New York wilderness. Green had the unusual distinction of being born among the Shakers, since his mother came to them when she was four-and-a-half-months pregnant, unmarried, and much concerned with her moral state. Unlike later biological families who joined the Shakers together but would then be sent to live in different Shaker families, Green continued to live with his mother through early childhood. He relates that her care was good, but she had to work hard to support him. They moved frequently, and he found it difficult living with a variety of scattered "out-families" of Shakers in New Lebanon and Hancock.

In 1788 Green joined his father, who soon united with the Church Family at New Lebanon. This did not cause a significant improvement in lifestyle for the child, however, for in the early days children shared fully in the work and difficulties of community building. Green was sent to work in the brickyard and, by his own accounts, was underfed, crowded in with many others, poorly clothed, and overworked; but all was endured with the zeal and enthusiasm of a growing and optimistic community. He was given special attention by Lucy Wright, the first female leader of the organized society and about twenty years older than Green. He noted in the biography he wrote of her, "She displayed that kind, heavenly love, & Motherly care toward me, as no other one ever did, nor was there another one that I loved with such filial love & grateful feelings. She has ever felt to me as my real Spiritual Mother."

Green felt from childhood that he would play an important role in Shakerism. At age ten he joined the church family, at nineteen he had a powerful "spiritual baptism," and at twenty-one he experienced a "conversion vision," all of which, he believed, fitted him to be a prophet and leader for Shakerism, and his early expectations were realized. Green served as a prominent elder for the society and was a key preacher at New Lebanon. As trusted theologian, he made two tours of the various societies (1807 and 1810) to explain developing theological positions to members. These included a gender-inclusive Christology that ranked Ann Lee alongside Jesus Christ as manifestations of the mother and father aspects of God. On his 1810 tour Green carried a draft of a work that was to become a key doctrinal treatise of the society, *A Summary View of the Millennial Church.*

Green also led the New Lebanon Gathering Order, the family in which newcomers resided, for some twenty-five years (1807 to 1832). This position involved considerable travel as a missionary "to the world." Between 1821 and 1831 he led extensive missions in the eastern states and was consulted in the formation of a new Sodus Bay community (later Groveland) in western New York State. In 1832 the ministry moved him from the Gathering Order back to the First Order. Green lamented this change, and it marked the end of his missionary period.

Green was one of the most trusted intellectual leaders of Shakerism and the key theologian for the eastern branch. His written contributions to Shakerism were considerable, including major theological works and tracts. Green also worked as an editor, scribe, and letter writer for the central ministry. With Seth Wells he wrote *A Summary View of the Millennial Church* (1823), the society's third doctrinal work. It was commissioned by the ministry as a summary statement of Shaker beliefs in response to severe attacks by former member Mary Dyer and others. Readable and extensively quoted by members, especially regarding celibacy, the work long held a prominent place within the society. It rejects the doctrine of the Trinity and develops a gender-inclusive doctrine of God. "The Almighty is manifested as proceeding from everlasting . . . and is the *Eternal Father*; and the Holy Spirit of Wisdom, who was *Co-worker* with him, from everlasting, is the *Eternal Mother*." Nevertheless, it also teaches the subordination of females to males, the theological basis being the Shaker belief that the masculine principle, or Father aspect of divinity, is primal, whereas the feminine principle, or Holy Mother Wisdom aspect, is derivative.

Although he wrote both *A Summary View* and the only biography of early leader Joseph Meacham in the 1820s, the bulk of Green's writing and editing was done between the 1830s and 1850s, after his missionary activity had ended. However, in spite of his accomplishments for the society and the trust they placed in him, Green came under severe criticism during this period, which coincided with the revival known as "Mother Ann's Work." Green expressed some reservations about the spiritualist manifestations that occurred during the revival, including questioning the efforts of noted Shaker medium Philemon Stewart. In the spring of 1838 he was reprimanded by Shaker visionaries and required to make multiple explanations and confessions about acting "against Order." Sometime after this event Green was asked, with Wells, to help edit a series of visions recorded by member Paulina Bates, one of the first women published by the Shakers. At first he balked but then had a vision that convinced him to go ahead. In 1849 the edited version of Bates's visions was published as *The Divine Book of Holy and Eternal Wisdom*.

Toward the end of his life Green served as elder of Groveland (1861–1863), and also produced some of his most significant writings. His manuscript biography of Lucy Wright (1861) shows his admiration for her and a sensitivity toward her struggles as the first regularly instituted woman leader of the organized society. He also wrote his autobiography between 1861 and 1866. His was an unusual account because Shakers who composed such narratives usually had joined the society in adulthood and wrote to detail their conversion to the faith. Green, however, considered himself to have been born and always lived as a fully committed Shaker and discussed instead his progress to the role of leader. This detailed account reveals many important facts about the progress of the society during its formative years and depicts its decline during the mid-1800s. Green was aware that his life spanned both the rise of Shakerism and the beginnings of its decline. In his autobiography he notes the drop in membership, his hopes for spiritual revival, and the increasing need for strong leadership. The place of his death cannot be ascertained.

As a born Shaker, Green was deeply committed to developing and preserving the best of the movement. His efforts in theology, biography, historical preservation, and oratory are impressive in Shaker society. Along with Wells and Benjamin S. Youngs, he was responsible for explicating the major tenets of Shaker theology. Unlike the others, he was also drawn to recording events that would otherwise have been lost to history, and he had a natural talent for making psychological and historical insights. He was an alert observer, devoted participant, and highly influential leader.

• The full title of the key doctrinal work by Green, written with Seth Wells, is *A Summary View of the Millennial Church, or United Society of Believers (Commonly Called Shakers) Comprising the Rise, Progress and Practical Order of the Society: Together with the General Principles of Their Faith and Testimony, Published by Order of the Ministry, in Union with the Church* (1823; repr. 1848). Green's biographical works that can be found in the Western Reserve Historical Society (Cleveland, Ohio) Shaker manuscript collection include "Biographic Memoir of the Life, Character, & Important Events, in the Ministration of Mother Lucy Wright" (New Lebanon, N.Y., 1861; VI:B-27); "Biographic—Memoir—of the Life and Experience—of Calvin Green" (Lebanon, N.Y., 1861–1869; VI:B-28); and "Biography of Elder Henry Clough" (Lebanon, N.Y., 1860; VI:B-24-26). Shaker journals can be found in this collection as well, such as the journal from 1811–1822 (V:B-80). Also see his "Biographical Account of the Life, Character & Ministry of Father Joseph Meacham, the Primary Leader in Establishing the United Order of the Millennial, Church. 1827," MS (copy dated 12 July 1859), Sabbathday Lake Society Library, also in Theodore E. Johnson, ed.,

Shaker Quarterly 10 (Spring 1970): 20–32, (Summer 1970): 51–68, and (Fall 1970): 92–102. Although no secondary source focuses solely on Green, books that elaborate on his life and/or work include Diane Sasson, *The Shaker Spiritual Narrative* (1983); Stephen J. Stein, *The Shaker Experience in America: A History of the United Society of Believers* (1992); Robley Edward Whitson, *The Shakers: Two Centuries of Spiritual Reflection* (1983); Linda A. Mercadante, *Gender, Doctrine, & God: The Shakers and Contemporary Theology* (1990); and Edward Deming Andrews, *The People Called Shakers* (1963).

LINDA A. MERCADANTE

GREEN, Constance McLaughlin (21 Aug. 1897–5 Dec. 1975), historian, was born Constance Winsor McLaughlin in Ann Arbor, Michigan, the daughter of Andrew McLaughlin, a professor of American history at the University of Michigan, and Lois Angell. Her father later joined the faculty of the University of Chicago, and the family moved to that city. Constance McLaughlin attended the University of Chicago High School, where she excelled in both academics and sports. After graduating in 1914, she spent a term as a student at a private secondary school in Munich.

Constance McLaughlin entered the University of Chicago as a history major in the fall of 1914; after two years there she transferred to Smith College, in Northampton, Massachusetts, and graduated with a bachelor's degree in history in 1919. She taught freshman English, first at the University of Chicago and then at Smith, until her marriage in 1921 to Donald Ross Green, a textile manufacturer. The couple settled in Holyoke, Massachusetts.

Constance McLaughlin Green had not planned on an academic career, but she found herself increasingly drawn to the study of New England history. In 1922 she enrolled as a graduate student at Mount Holyoke College, in nearby South Hadley, and received a master's degree in history three years later with a thesis on the New England Confederation of 1643. For some years afterward, she taught history part time at Mount Holyoke while bearing and raising three children. Also during this period, Green, a lifelong devotee of detective stories, tried unsuccessfully to write mysteries herself.

In 1933 Green enrolled as a doctoral student in American history at Yale, commuting between her home and the university campus in New Haven, Connecticut. Focusing on American industrial history, she received her Ph.D. in 1937—a year after her father had won a Pulitzer Prize for his book *The Constitutional History of the United States*. Green's dissertation, "Holyoke, Massachusetts: A Case History of the Industrial Revolution in America," won Yale's Edward Eggleston Prize and was published by Yale University Press in 1939.

In 1938 Green returned to Smith College as an instructor in the history department, specializing in the industrial history of the Connecticut Valley, and she directed graduate students in that field. She took a leave of absence from Smith in 1942, soon after the United States had entered World War II, to become historian of the U.S. Army Ordnance Department at the Springfield Armory in Springfield, Massachusetts, and remained in that post until the end of the war in 1945.

Following the death of her husband in November 1946, Green moved to Washington, D.C., to become consulting historian for the American Red Cross. Two years later she was named chief historian of the U.S. Army Ordnance Corps Historical Division. In that capacity she contributed to a series on the history of the U.S. Army during World War II. During her tenure there, her book *History of Naugatuck, Connecticut* (1949) was published by Yale University Press. Research for the book had been done during her years as an instructor in the history department at Smith.

In 1951 Green left the army to serve a one-year appointment as a Commonwealth Fund Lecturer at University College, London. She returned to Washington in 1952 and served for two years as a historian with the Department of Defense. In 1954 Green received a six-year grant from the Rockefeller Foundation, under the auspices of American University, to write a history of Washington, D.C. While she worked on this project, two studies by Green of industrialization and urbanization were published, *Eli Whitney and the Birth of American Technology* (1956) and *American Cities in the Growth of the Nation* (1957).

Following the expiration of the Rockefeller grant in 1960, Green obtained financial backing from the Chapelbrook Foundation of Boston to complete her Washington project, which she called an "interpretive rather than a comprehensive, foolproof history." The first volume, *Washington, Village and Capital, 1800–1878*, was published by Princeton University Press in 1962. The book was widely acclaimed by critics, including such leading American historians as Arthur M. Schlesinger, Jr., who called it "lucid" and "enthralling." In May 1963 it earned Green the Pulitzer Prize in history. Upon hearing the news of her award, Green celebrated—and paid homage to her father—by buying her grandson a pair of red suspenders. Nearly three decades earlier, when Andrew McLaughlin had received the Pulitzer Prize, his wife had urged him to buy "something fun" with the prize money. He had responded by buying red suspenders for himself.

The second volume of Green's history, *Washington: Capital City, 1879–1950*, was published by Princeton in 1963. During the 1960s Green wrote several more historical studies, including *The Rise of Urban America* (1965) and *Secret City: A History of Race Relations in the Nation's Capital* (1967). In 1971 she served as a visiting professor of history at Dartmouth College.

Green was an active member of several professional organizations, including the American Historical Association and the Economic History Association. In addition to her books, she wrote articles for the *Encyclopedia Britannica* and the *Encyclopedia Americana*, contributed chapters to several anthologies on American history, and published essays in both scholarly journals and popular periodicals, including the *Na-*

tion. Green was made an honorary member of Phi Beta Kappa at Smith College in 1943.

Green was a small, dynamic woman whom a journalist once described as having "a tartness in her talk." In addition to reading detective stories, she enjoyed walking, camping, and gardening as leisure activities. Her house in Washington, D.C., where she lived for many years, was directly behind the Supreme Court building.

After Green suffered a heart attack in 1972, she moved to the home of a daughter in Annapolis, Maryland. Although Green often said that she had no intention of retiring, frail health limited her activities in her last years. She died in Annapolis.

• Green's papers are at the Smith College Archives. Biographical information can be found in *Current Biography 1963*; the *New York Times*, 7 May 1963; and the *Washington Post*, 8 May 1963, and 7 Nov. 1972. An obituary is in the *New York Times*, 8 Dec. 1975.

ANN T. KEENE

GREEN, Duff (15 Aug. 1791–10 June 1875), journalist, political operator, and southern economic promoter, was born in Woodford County, Kentucky, the son of William Green, a revolutionary war veteran, and Lucy Ann Marshall. He was educated at home and briefly at Danville Academy in 1805. After studying medicine for a short time and teaching school, he enlisted as a private in the War of 1812, fighting in a number of battles under William Henry Harrison and emerging as a captain. In 1813 he married Lucretia M. Edwards, the sister of Governor Ninian Edwards of Illinois. They had nine children. Briefly a merchant in Kentucky after the war, he soon moved to Missouri, where he built up a large fortune as a land speculator, mail contractor, merchant, stagecoach operator, and lawyer. He was active in politics as well, serving in the Missouri constitutional convention in 1819 and as a member of the Missouri state legislature in the early 1820s.

In 1823 he began the career that brought him fame by purchasing a local newspaper, the *St. Louis Enquirer*, and running it as a committed political journal, first supporting John C. Calhoun and then Andrew Jackson for president in 1824. The next year Green moved to Washington and purchased the *United States Telegraph*, editing it as a militant, persistent assailer of the Adams administration and promoter of Jackson for the presidency. He was a strong states' rights and free trade advocate but became famous beyond his policy stances for his fiery attacks on John Quincy Adams and Henry Clay because of their policy and behavioral transgressions. His bitter, rousing editorials were widely copied by other Jacksonian newspapers, and he came to be seen as the main champion and interpreter of Jacksonianism for an emerging nationwide party press politically guided from Washington. After the election of Jackson in 1828, Green continued as the prime editorial spokesman and tone setter for the new administration. Congress elected him its official printer in 1829, and he served as an adviser to the president, although he later denied the contemporary assessment that he was a member of Jackson's Kitchen Cabinet.

Green was also close to John C. Calhoun, whose son had married one of Green's daughters. He supported Calhoun's presidential aspirations, which both expected to be fulfilled in 1832, when Jackson would presumably step down after one term. As Jackson came to think otherwise, and as Martin Van Buren emerged as a strong administration influence, Green, with Calhoun, grew increasingly critical of the president and his associates. Green's cranky independence led in 1830 to the establishment of a more dependable administration organ, the Washington *Globe*, edited by Francis P. Blair (1791–1876). Green finally broke with the administration in 1831 over a range of issues, some policy-oriented, others connected with the succession, as Van Buren won the battle with Calhoun to be Jackson's heir. Because of his support for Clay in the presidential election of 1832, Green lost the lucrative congressional printing post. Thereafter, he developed an increasingly militant, states' rights, prosouthern, antiabolitionist and antiparty perspective. As did Calhoun, Green became extremely sensitive to the sectional differences in the nation and the resulting tensions and what he saw as inevitable threats to southern security. He advocated complete resistance to the national party discipline promoted by the Van Burenites, which he considered dangerous to southern interests, and he called for the reorganization of parties along more ideological and sectional lines. In 1836 he supported the states' rights southerner Hugh L. White against Van Buren for the presidency.

Green gave up, on his doctor's advice, the editorship of the *Telegraph* in 1836. Although he edited a number of campaign newspapers for brief periods thereafter, he spent the rest of his life primarily as an active promoter and manager of transportation, mining, and industrial projects destined to make the South economically stronger and better able to sustain itself within the Union. He was a developer of canals and then of railroads, particularly of a route across the South from Washington, D.C., to the Mississippi River and beyond. He also invested in coal and iron mines in Virginia and Kentucky and in factories in Georgia.

Nevertheless, Green remained close to national political affairs in the late 1830s. His friendship with President John Tyler led the latter to send him to England in 1841 as an unofficial agent charged with promoting free trade, assessing British intentions in Texas, and encouraging acceptance of American predominance there. He continued to be active in Texas affairs after he returned home at the behest of Tyler and Secretary of State Calhoun, first promoting American emigration into the area and then going in 1844 to Galveston as American consul. From there he traveled into Mexico to work for annexation and further American expansion in the Southwest as well as to assess Mexico's possible reactions to American demands. He apparently tried to organize a revolution against the resisting Mexican government as part of his assignment.

After Tyler left the White House and war broke out under President James K. Polk, Green briefly tried to raise troops to fight against the Mexicans but soon returned to his interests in economic development. In the years that followed he was active as an investor in, and manager of, various economic enterprises. At the same time, he compiled informational volumes about the southern economy, such as the several volumes on finance and trade titled *Facts and Suggestions*, which were published in 1861 and 1864. He also wrote a great many pamphlets advocating the kind of mixed development that he hoped southerners would follow. During this period he was never far from the political world, usually in a behind-the-scenes role. He briefly edited another partisan newspaper, the weekly *American Statesman*, in 1857, and in 1860 President James Buchanan sent him as an unofficial agent to consult with President-elect Abraham Lincoln about the latter's attitudes toward secession and the use of force against the South. Although he himself was not a secessionist, Green went with the South during the Civil War, running iron mills in Alabama and Tennessee. In 1865 he briefly met with Lincoln again to pursue possible peace initiatives. After the war he retired to his estate in Dalton, Georgia, where he spent the rest of his life. His long and vigorous commitment to southern political power and economic independence in a hostile world marked a frame of mind and a program characteristic of many other opponents of what was perceived as the growth of national power dangerous to southern interests in antebellum America.

• The main body of Green's papers is in the Southern Historical Collection of the University of North Carolina at Chapel Hill. There is a smaller collection in the Library of Congress. No full-length biography of Green exists. Two articles by Fletcher Green are useful overviews: "Duff Green, Militant Journalist of the Old School," *American Historical Review* 2 (1947): 247–64, and "Duff Green: Industrial Promoter," *Journal of Southern History* 2 (1936): 29–42. There is a great deal about Green in Charles Wiltse, *John C. Calhoun* (3 vols., 1944–1951). See also David Wayne Moore, "Duff Green and the South, 1824–45" (Ph.D. diss., Miami Univ., 1983), and Kenneth Laurence Smith, "Duff Green and the United States' Telegraph, 1826–1837" (Ph.D. diss., College of William and Mary, 1981).

JOEL H. SILBEY

GREEN, Edith (17 Jan. 1910–21 Apr. 1987), teacher and congresswoman, was born in Trent, South Dakota, the daughter of James Vaughn and Julia Hunt Starrett, schoolteachers. When she was six her family moved to Oregon. She attended public schools and Willamette University in Salem, Oregon. After marrying businessman Arthur N. Green in 1933, she continued to teach and to further her own education. She graduated from the University of Oregon in 1939 and took graduate courses at Stanford. Edith and Arthur Green had two sons and were later divorced.

From 1930 to 1941 Green taught school in Salem, Oregon, and from 1943 to 1947 was an announcer at radio station KALE in Portland, Oregon. She became a leader in the Oregon Education Association, serving for a time as director of public relations. She entered politics in 1952, as the Democratic candidate for secretary of state of Oregon, but she lost the election. She was a delegate to the Democratic National Conventions in 1956, 1960, 1964, and 1968, chairing the Oregon delegation in 1960 and 1968. She was asked to second the nomination of Adlai E. Stevenson in 1956 and of John F. Kennedy in 1960. Oregon's Third Congressional District elected her to the U.S. House of Representatives in 1954 and reelected her for nine successive terms.

Over the course of two decades in Congress Green served on the following standing committees: Education and Labor (84th–92d Congresses), Interior and Insular Affairs (84th Congress), House Administration (85th–87th Congresses), Merchant Marine and Fisheries (88th–90th Congresses), District of Columbia (92d Congress), and Appropriations (93d Congress). She also was responsible for important legislation. For instance, she introduced legislation requiring equal pay for equal work. She also introduced the Library Services Act, signed into law by President Dwight D. Eisenhower in June 1956, which helped to extend public library services into rural areas at a time when more than twenty-seven million Americans had no access to public libraries. She had a direct role as well in writing numerous legislative measures that extended federal assistance to states for their educational programs and for handling juvenile delinquency problems. Also during her congressional career Green was a U.S. delegate to the Interparliamentary Conference in Switzerland (1958), a congressional delegate to the NATO Conference in London (1959), a delegate to the UNESCO General Conference (1964 and 1966), and a member of President Kennedy's Commission on the Status of Women.

Although Green's voting record indicates a liberal concern for educational, economic, and social issues, her support was not unqualified. She had always worked hard for improvements in education, but she opposed busing as a means to desegregation because, as she explained on the floor of the House, "We tonight cannot go back 100 years to correct the errors that may or may not have been made by our ancestors . . . I oppose busing because I do not think it is workable" (quoted in Wides, p. 15). Furthermore, it seemed to her to have been chosen as an easy way out of a complex situation and would therefore lead to the "deterioration of the public school system" (Miller, p. 18). She was concerned primarily for her middle- and lower-income constituents for whom there was not enough money for teachers and classrooms, let alone buses and drivers. Answering her critics, she reminded them that she had voted for every civil rights law but now felt obliged to "quarrel with the way the Civil Rights Act is being administered" (Miller, p. 18). Also, although Green voted for an increase in the minimum wage, she voted against increasing payments to welfare recipients. It was her view that Congress should show more concern for middle-income families who paid their taxes and then struggled to make ends meet.

Green was a vigorous supporter of President Lyndon B. Johnson's "Great Society" program, and as a member of the House Education and Labor Committee she played a crucial behind-the-scenes role in securing the enactment of related social-welfare programs. By drafting and pushing through amendments to the OEO Extension Act (1967), she effectively saved it from possible defeat. The amendments appeased the coalition of Republicans and Southern Democrats who wanted more state and local control over controversial social programs.

Just as vigorously, though, Green opposed President Johnson's Vietnam War policy. From 1965 on she spoke out forcefully and frequently against it and voted in opposition to all proposals to extend the war. She also was extremely concerned about the returning veterans and felt that the government should help them gain civilian employment. During the 1972 primary fight for the Democratic presidential nomination, however, she did not support antiwar candidate George McGovern but instead favored Washington senator Henry "Scoop" Jackson.

Because of her discriminating analyses of pending legislation and her independent voting habits, Green frustrated the Democratic party leadership and was criticized by others outside the party. In Ralph Nader's 1972 study of Congress, for example, she is characterized as a former "flaming liberal" who had become increasingly conservative (Wides, p. 28); she was also called "unpredictable" and a "political enigma" (Wides, p. 29). Her stand on busing, though carefully outlined, elicited the criticism that she showed a "scarcity of creativity" (Englebarts, p. 78). She incurred sharp opposition from the educational establishment as well; although her concern for the quality of education in the classroom was unwavering, she worried that the rising "educational-industrial complex" in America had more to do with lobbying than with improving education (Wides, p. 29). Not every evaluation was critical, however. Republican senator Mark Hatfield, a fellow Oregonian, called Green a powerful congresswoman who could "switch people's votes on the floor through the power of her intellect and her ability to persuade." People listened to her, he said, because "when Edith Green spoke, she spoke from the heart as well as the mind" (Hevesi, p. D31).

Green was an early advocate of women entering politics, pointing out, in 1955, that a government that does not involve a large segment of its population cannot be the best government. Her own involvement was effective; as a woman speaking on the House floor, she could issue "a rapid fire attack that was nevertheless delivered in a well-modulated, lady-like voice" (*Post and Times Herald*, quoted in *Current Biography 1966*, p. 227). Her son James S. Green described his mother as supporting women's rights but "without stridence." She realized, he said, that the key was to work with men, and that was something "she was very good at" (Hevesi, p. D31).

To preserve her voting independence, Green ran low-budget campaigns financed by small contributions. After serving in ten Congresses, however, she decided to retire, a highly unusual step for a successful, long-term member of Congress. In 1974 she moved from the House of Representatives to the college classroom as professor of government at Warner Pacific College. Her last political roles were as co-chairwoman of National Democrats for Gerald Ford (1976) and as a member of the Oregon Board of Higher Education (1979). Green died in Tualatin, Oregon.

• Edith Green's papers are at the University of Oregon Library. Her remarks in the House of Representatives are in the *Congressional Record* for the years 1955–1974, and major newspapers reported her speeches in and out of Congress. Edith Green, "The Federal Role in Education," in *Education and the Public Good* (1964), describes her legislative proposals to address education problems in the 1960s, whereas "Campus Issues in 1980," *PTA Magazine*, Apr. 1968, pp. 18–20, focuses on what she saw as potential educational problems of the future. Douglass Cater, "Aid to Higher Education: The One That Got Away," *Reporter*, 25 Oct. 1962, pp. 28–30, discusses why a particular education bill, the House version of which was chiefly Green's work, failed to pass. "Congress Urged to Equalize Pay for Equal Work by Both Sexes," *New York Times*, 27 May 1955, details the bill Green introduced in an attempt to improve the employment situation of women. Norman C. Miller, "Rep. Edith Green, a Bareknuckle Fighter," *Wall Street Journal*, 3 Dec. 1969, characterizes her style as a legislator. Rudolph Englebarts, *Women in the U.S. Congress 1917–1972* (1974), describes Green's district and constituents, analyzes her voting, and includes a bibliography. Louise Wides, *Edith Green: Democratic Representative from Oregon*, part of the Ralph Nader Congress Project: Citizens Look at Congress (1972), is indispensable for details on Green as a member of the Democratic party and as a representative of her constituents and on her campaigns, voting records, ratings by interest groups, and the policies she supported; its numerous footnotes provide references to many primary sources. *Current Biography 1956* is necessary for information on Green's life up to 1956. An informative and lengthy obituary by Denis Hevesi is in the *New York Times*, 23 Apr. 1987.

SYLVIA B. LARSON

GREEN, Ely (11 Sept. 1893–27 Apr. 1968), author, black activist, and clairvoyant, was born near Sewanee, Tennessee, the son of a college student, Edward H. Wicks, later a Texas attorney, and Lena Green, a fourteen-year-old kitchen servant and daughter of a privy cleaner who had been a slave. In Green's own words, he "was a half-white bastard." His mother died when he was eight. He was reared by Mattie Davis, a sympathetic neighbor who worked as a domestic. He did not finish the second grade but was largely self-taught. His phenomenal vocabulary came about because, so he said, "I studied from every man who would talk to me."

Green's youth, up to age eighteen, was spent in Sewanee, the site of the University of the South. He did odd jobs, such as shining shoes, carrying spring water to the third floor of dormitories, and selling peanuts at sports events. He had only indirect contact with his white family. When they came to Sewanee from Texas in the summer, he might play with the children, but the adults did not openly acknowledge a relationship. As a child Robin Hood, Green "borrowed" toys from white children and gave them to his black friends who had never seen such novelties.

In the nearby mountains and coves, Green hunted for small game—rabbit, squirrel, possum and quail—all edible when cooked by "Mother Mat." He became an excellent shot with rifle and pistol. He learned of a firm in St. Louis that would buy cured skunk skins. He prospered but spent earnings on friends, one of them needing expensive medicine for venereal disease. His superiority over the semiliterate "sagers" aroused their enmity, and Green was forced to leave in 1911 or be killed by the group of mountain whites he had offended. He escaped by night on a railroad handcar riding a perilous nine miles out of control down the steep tracks. He did not return to Sewanee until 1919.

At eighteen, Green found his way from Tennessee to Waxahatchie, Texas, where his mother had relatives. He was befriended by the most influential man in town, judge and banker Oscar E. Dunlap, and his family. Against the entreaties of his benefactors, Green volunteered for military service, thinking vainly it would make him a full-fledged citizen. He became an accomplished boxer, fighting to a draw the champion at Camp Travis, Texas. Overseas, he found that the American armed forces were among the most segregated parts of society, in contrast to the French, who treated their African colonials as equals. He marveled when he saw Marshal Ferdinand Foch kiss on both cheeks a black hero whom he was decorating for valor. Green was sergeant in an all-black stevedoring unit at St. Nazaire from 1918 to 1919.

Out of the army, Green never again held a steady job, but this was not because of any character defect. He was never charged with illegal use of alcohol or drugs, or of stealing. He lived at or near the poverty line, mostly in California after a stint in Texas, where he was "too black" to get a job in the lucrative new oil fields and "too white" to find security as a Pullman porter. He worked intermittently, in no particular chronological order, as handyman, body servant, butler, chauffeur, and as chef on a yacht that took him along the California coast and throughout the Caribbean. He worked for such elegant movie stars as John Barrymore, Lionel Barrymore, and Mary Pickford, usually as caterer for parties. He broke the color line at the Lockheed plant in California, where the company was willing to hire blue-collar blacks, but the unions would not give them cards. His standing up for principles cost him merciless beatings at the hands of police, who considered him obstinate and "uppity." On one occasion, he lost his front teeth and suffered a fractured cheekbone.

Throughout this period, Green wrote steadily but erratically in his "diaries." These were the notes and observations he used in composing his 1,200-page manuscript, which alone got into print. Green's frequent letters to his sweetheart were lost when she died while he was overseas. So also were those to and from the Dunlaps, who tried vainly to keep him out of trouble and who treated him like a son. The diary he kept in the oil fields was "borrowed" by an oil speculator who used its date as evidence in a claim to a half-million-dollar piece of property. The suit was won, the promise of a reward was not kept, and the diary was not returned. Green's sole legacy is the 1,200-page autobiography with its erratic punctuation, no paragraphing, hundreds of misspellings, and scattered dots where, he said, "I was resting my pen." This document, however, is the most compelling capsule of the subtle persecutions that erupted in the Civil Rights movement of the 1960s and 1970s. The autobiography was begun in the 1950s, two-thirds finished by 1963, and completed in the next two years. In his conversation and writing he would harangue listeners against the word *Negro*—a "slave word," he said. Ironically, *black* became acceptable usage about the time Green died.

Ely Green went to Sewanee in the summer of 1963 to visit his half-brother Edward Miller, custodian of the student union. He called on the employers of his youth and was referred to the university's historiographer. The following summer he returned with a small suitcase containing his "book" in six loose-leaf folders. More than a year was required to transcribe the difficult handwriting on unnumbered pages. It was edited into standard English and published as *Ely: An Autobiography* in 1966. The book covers his youth through age eighteen. The editor prevailed on the widely known author of *Strange Fruit*, Lillian Smith, to write the introduction, the last essay she did before dying in Atlanta of cancer. She called Green a "fabulous story-teller" who was "torn between love and hate" and was always in the limbo between the races of his father and mother.

At seventy, Green was unknown, unpublished, and broke. Sympathetic friends typed his manuscript. He lived to see the first edition enthusiastically reviewed by more than fifty magazines and newspapers, including the *New York Times*, which called him the "Grandma Moses of American literature." The book in its various (four) editions has been used as a text in religion and literature classes in college and high school. Prize-winning novelist Walker Percy wrote, "The love in it and the terrible reproach . . . wring the heart." *Christian Century* said, "Here is a microcosm of the tragedy and pathos of race relations."

The *Sewanee Review* in 1968 published a chapter, "The Aristocratic Mouse," and Green as well as the magazine received prizes of $1,000 each from the National Endowment for the Arts. Royalties at the time of his death had reached about $4,000, but his total estate came to less than $5,000 and thus was exempt from probate. After his death another $4,000 went to his widow, Beatrice McCarroll Green, whom he had married the year before. He knew before he died that the University of Massachusetts Press had accepted for publication his complete work as one volume. This became the second of the four editions.

Green died in Santa Monica, California, and was survived by two daughters whose mothers were sisters whom Green never married. He left only one book, but in it are the raw materials of sociology, ethics, and theology. It is an epic in black history, the story of a superior man, constricted by an imperfect society, bad laws, and illogical customs. As Rt. Rev. C. FitzSimons Allison, the thirteenth bishop of South Carolina, wrote in a review, "His is the story of injustice, grace, suffering, anger, pride, community, but above all a victory over the need to hate."

• Ely Green's original 1,200-page handwritten manuscript is in the Archives of the University of the South, Sewanee, Tenn. The diaries from which it was written are lost, as is his voluminous correspondence with his fiancée and the Dunlap family in 1918–1919. Fisk University in Nashville has an audiotape, hardly intelligible, on which Green, after the stroke that severely handicapped his speech in 1967, tried to expand on his autobiography. The first eighteen years of his life are described in *Ely: An Autobiography* (1966). The chapter "Aristocratic Mouse" appeared in *Sewanee Review* 76 (Winter 1968): 1–22. Green, *Ely: Too Black, Too White* (1970), is his life story through World War II; a condensed version appeared in paperback under the same title the same year. A new edition of *Ely: An Autobiography* was published in 1990 with the addition of a foreword by Bertram Wyatt-Brown, which deals with the cultural and historical context of the author's era. It repeats a literary evaluation by Lillian Smith and uses as afterword a biographical sketch by Arthur Ben Chitty. In the Sewanee Archives are letters to and from Green's agent and the four publishers, copies of dozens of newspaper and magazine reviews, and some correspondence from reviewers. An obituary is in the *New York Times*, 29 Apr. 1968.

ARTHUR BEN CHITTY

GREEN, Frances Harriet Whipple (Sept. 1805–10 June 1878), author, social reformer, and Spiritualist, was born in Smithfield, Rhode Island, the daughter of George Whipple. Her mother's name is unknown. She was married twice, first in 1842 to the artist Charles C. Green, whom she divorced in 1847, and later in 1861 to William C. McDougall (or McDougal) of California. She had no children. In between marriages, she lived in New York City with S. B. Brittan and contributed to his publications on Spiritualism. In all of these activities she maintained the strong individualist spirit that was so important in many of the antebellum reform movements.

During her years in Rhode Island, Green actively supported reform movements through her writings, which often stressed the dignity of manual labor and the importance of self-improvement as the best means to combat social injustice. These were the arguments implicit in her biography of Elleanor Eldridge, a free African-American woman whose life of hard work and thriftiness was portrayed as a model for other free blacks. Green wrote *Memoirs of Elleanor Eldridge* in 1838, as well as its sequel, *Elleanor's Second Book* in 1839, to raise money for Eldridge. Green explained that Eldridge had been cheated out of her property by a hypocritical Christian who had the support of racist public officials.

Green's concern for African Americans was also demonstrated in her antislavery writings. In 1840 she published *The Envoy: From Free Hearts to the Free*, an antislavery tract for children. *Shahmah in Pursuit of Freedom*, which Green published in 1858, was also an indictment of slavery. Shahmah was a naive, white Algerian, who had been briefly enslaved himself, traveling through the United States to study the freedom he idealized. His travels through the South gradually opened his eyes to both the horrors of slavery and the limits of freedom in the United States.

Green counseled self-respect and self-improvement to working people in her 1841 novel *The Mechanic*. She reinforced this message, particularly for women factory workers, during her short tenure as editor of the *Wampanoag and Operatives Journal*, published during 1842 in Fall River, Massachusetts. Her concern for the rights of working people surfaced again in her defense of Thomas Dorr's rebellion in Rhode Island, a conflict in which Dorr and his followers fought unsuccessfully to extend the right to vote to men who did not own property. Green defended Dorr and condemned his treatment by Rhode Island authorities in *Might and Right* (1844). Whether championing the rights of working people or African Americans, Green seems to have participated in reform movements primarily through her writings, concentrating on the economic and moral power derived from her pen.

Like many reformers of the period, Green moved on to Spiritualism as the moral reform impulse waned in the 1850s. Both in New York and in California, she wrote Spiritualist tracts from the 1850s onward, including the *Biography of Mrs. Semantha Mettler, the Clairvoyant* in 1853. In California, she delivered and published *The Baker Oration: Power and Permanence in American Institutions* in 1862. Claiming to have been visited many times by the recently deceased California senator Edward D. Baker, Green conveyed his message from the spirit world. The oration was a strong antislavery message that was more critical of slavery than anything the senator had said while alive. As a Spiritualist writer, Green maintained her belief in the importance of individual reform and, like many other Spiritualists, continued the anti-institutional impulse of the moral reform tradition by criticizing organized religions for their accumulation of wealth at a time when so much poverty existed and by attacking their emphasis on theology rather than social injustice. "The day of passive belief—the day of creeds, has gone by, and the time for ACTION—intelligent, direct, and concerted action, has arrived," she wrote (*Spirit Messenger and Harmonial Advocate*, 19 Mar. 1853, p. 356).

Green was a powerful writer who financially supported herself and others through her writings at the same time that she supported most of the important social and political causes of her time, including the antislavery movement, enfranchisement, and the elevation of workers. In addition to her books on social reform, she also wrote a textbook in 1855, *Analytical Class-Book of Botany, Designed for Academies and Private Students*. She died in Oakland, California.

• In addition to the books mentioned in this essay, Green also contributed to *Liberty Chimes*, printed in 1845 for the Ladies' Anti-Slavery Society of Providence, R.I., and she contributed on numerous occasions to the *Spirit Messenger and Harmonial Advocate*. The most extensive biography of Green is found in Sidney S. Rider, *Bibliographical Memoirs of Three Rhode Island Authors: Joseph K. Angell, Frances H. (Whipple) McDougall, Catherine Williams* (1880). An additional biography may be found in Alden Whitman, ed., *American Reformers: An H. W. Wilson Biographical Dictionary* (1985). An obituary is in the *San Francisco Chronicle*, 11 June 1878.

TERESA ANNE MURPHY

GREEN, George Hamilton (23 May 1893–11 Sept. 1970), keyboard percussionist, was born in Omaha, Nebraska, the son of George H. Green, a musician, and Minnie (maiden name unknown). He and his two brothers and younger sister were raised in a middle-class musical family. His father taught music harmony and composition at Nebraska University and held the position of bandmaster of the 7th Ward Band, then a well-known and important part of Omaha's cultural life. Green, who first studied piano and was considered a prodigy by age four, taught himself to play xylophone and at age twelve performed xylophone solos with his father's band. He subsequently enrolled in some music courses at Drake University, but he left college to pursue a career as a professional musician. Green married Georgia Ellen (maiden name unknown), a girl from the neighborhood, in 1913; they had a son and a daughter.

As a xylophonist, Green entered his professional career at exactly the right time. Aided by a fledgling recording industry, the popularity of the xylophone, a relatively new instrument to America, reached its peak between 1890 and 1925. Often paired with a piano or included in a small orchestra with two violins, flute, clarinet, two trumpets, and tuba, the xylophone appeared on numerous recordings of waltzes, polkas, marches, opera melodies, mazurkas, and galops that allowed much of the American audience to hear the instrument for the first time. In February 1917 Green made his first solo recordings with orchestral accompaniment for the Edison Company. These recordings were a series of twelve transcriptions of light classical pieces, including "Tannhauser March" and "Light Calvary Overture."

Around 1916 Green and his older brother Joe, a percussionist who had played with John Phillip Sousa, began touring the country. They performed in small clubs and hotels, including the Owashtanong Club in Grand Rapids, Michigan, and the Blackstone Hotel in Chicago. During the week they performed duets of standard xylophone repertory of the time—primarily transcriptions of light classical music. However, on the weekends Green and his brother played for afternoon dances with an orchestra, and Green had begun to gain the attention of other musicians for his improvisations over the waltzes he performed at these dances. In early 1917 the Green brothers left Chicago and moved to New York City at the invitation of bandleader and percussionist Earl Fuller.

Green and his brother began performing and recording in New York with society orchestras and dance bands. Fuller credits Green with first introducing the xylophone into dance-band music. Green improvised or played a written obligato virtuoso part in novelty ragtime style over the common dance-band repertory of marches such as one-steps, two-steps, and fox trots. The highly syncopated, technically demanding novelty rags not only prominently displayed Green's virtuosic technique but also satisfied the demand created by the dance craze of the 1910s and 1920s for music with a danceable beat. Green's unique style has been technically described as "based on the use of syncopated, accented double-stops in patterns combined with alternated single strokes" (Cahn, p. xii).

Between 1917 and 1940 Green made more than 1,000 recordings as a soloist, bandleader, and sideman, recording for virtually every major record label, including Edison, Victor, and Columbia. He recorded with his own groups under various names, including the All Star Trio, Blue and White Band, Castlewood Marimba Band, and the Green Brothers Novelty Band, in order to jump record contracts. Green would often record the same piece several times under different labels and with different solo lines. His recordings of "Frivolity" (Edison 50505, 1918), "Fluffy Ruffles" (Victor 18641, 1919), and "Yes, We Have No Bananas" (Edison 51177, 1923) are particularly noted for their intense rhythmic drive, even without the use of drums. Green also recorded with other top bands led by such noted musicians as Harry Yerkes, Earl Fuller, Fred Van Eps, and Harry Breuer. Green's recordings and compositions have influenced many jazz xylophonists and vibraphonists, including Red Norvo, who not only met Green but recalled listening extensively to Green's recordings as a teenager.

A particular highlight of Green's early career came during the last week of September 1928, when the Green Brothers—George, Joe, and Lew—recorded the effects for the sound track of the first Walt Disney cartoon, *Steamboat Willie*. The cartoon, which featured Mickey Mouse playing the "xylophone" on the teeth of a cow, was perhaps the beginning of the long association of xylophone music with cartoons.

From the time he learned to play the xylophone, Green was involved in inventing and making his own instruments. Throughout his career, he invented and developed instruments for the J. C. Deagen Company and is credited with having influenced the design of the modern xylophone. Green also composed. He published over 300 compositions, including character pieces arranged for wind band and xylophone, works for piano and xylophone, and about half a dozen Tin Pan Alley songs. One of these songs, "Alabama Moon," sung by Gladys Rice, became popular during the 1920s. He wrote several method books for his students, including his famous *50 Lessons for Xylophone* (c. 1924–1926) and *George Hamilton Green's Instruction Course for Xylophone* (1936), both of which remained in use well after his lifetime.

The advent of big band swing music in the 1930s had an adverse effect on Green's career. Since he continued to play novelty ragtime, which was no longer in vogue, he recorded and performed less often, but he did play a number of radio shows and worked from time to time as a sideman during the decade. However, shaken by the death of his brother Joe in 1939, Green reportedly walked out of a recording session with fellow xylophonist Harry Breuer sometime in 1940 and never played again.

After giving up music, Green made a living as a cartoonist. His watercolor cartoons appeared in *Collier's* and the *Saturday Evening Post*. Green and his family lived primarily in Yonkers, New York, but they also owned a house in Woodstock, New York. Sometime after his brother's death, Green moved permanently to Woodstock, where his wife owned and operated an antiques shop. Green died in Woodstock.

• Biographical information on Green can be found in Frank Powers, "George Hamilton Green," *Rag Times* 14 (July 1980): 2–3. Discographical information is in William Cahn, *The Xylophone in Acoustic Recordings (1877–1929)* (1979). See also Bruce Chaffin's record liner notes to *Masters of the Xylophone: George Hamilton Green and Joe Green* (1993).

KAREN HARROD REGE

GREEN, Grant (6 June 1935–31 Jan. 1979), jazz electric guitarist, was born in St. Louis, Missouri, the son of John Green, a security guard, and Martha Smith. His year of birth appears incorrectly as 1931 in standard reference sources, but his birth certificate confirms 1935, as Green himself asserted twice in interviews.

Green played guitar in grade school. His father, a blues and folk guitarist, gave his son some early instruction, and Green took lessons from Forrest Alcorn for one year. Otherwise he was self-taught. He explained to writer Laurie Henshaw, "I learned mostly from listening to records of [swing guitarist] Charlie Christian—and to [bop alto saxophonist] Charlie Parker."

As a teenager Green played gospel music in area churches. He then worked with accordionist Joe Murphy. Green mentioned that it was quite unusual to find an African American playing accordion, and his early experience in blending the guitar with this instrument may help explain why he was later so comfortable working with Hammond organists. Depending on how it is played, the accordion can sound like a cousin of the Hammond organ, particularly when it is amplified through a Leslie speaker.

Green married Annie Maude Moody in the mid-1950s. They had four children. Writer Dan Morgenstern reported a comment on Green's early years: "The first thing I played was boogie woogie. . . . Then I had to do a lot of rock and roll. It's all the blues, anyhow." By the latter part of the decade he was playing jazz with tenor saxophonist Jimmy Forrest, with whom he made an outstanding first album, *All the Gin Is Gone* (1959). He also worked with trumpeter Harry "Sweets" Edison; the date is unknown. He then performed with alto saxophonist Lou Donaldson, who encouraged Green to move from St. Louis to New York City in the late summer of 1960 and got him involved with Blue Note Records.

Green's recordings for this label extend into the early 1970s, but he was particularly active from 1961 to 1965, recording albums with saxophonists Donaldson, Stanley Turrentine, Hank Mobley, and Ike Quebec; trumpeter Lee Morgan; and organists Larry Young and Big John Patton. He also recorded numerous sessions under his own name, including *Grant's First Stand, Green Street* (both 1961), and *Talkin' About* (1964). During this period he performed in a number of trios consisting of organ, guitar, and drums.

From 1967 to 1969 Green was inactive because of problems with drug addiction. He participated in the Guitar Workshop at the Jazz Expo '69 show in London as a last-minute replacement for Tal Farlow, and in that year he resumed recording. He watered down his music on several of his late albums in a largely misguided attempt to reach a large popular audience. As with many musicians who took this path during the 1970s, Green's efforts to assimilate rock and pop into jazz frequently sounded halfhearted. Nonetheless he did have a modest hit with the title track of his album *Easy*, recorded in April 1978. In the fall of that year he was hospitalized for ten weeks for a blood clot near his heart. He refused to undergo open-heart surgery and resumed his career, performing in Los Angeles and then driving to New York City, where he died of a heart attack.

Few details of Green's life are documented, despite his stature as one of the greatest jazz guitarists. He holds a position in hard bop and soul jazz groups somewhat akin to that of cornetist Bobby Hackett in swing and Dixieland bands. He was not an innovator but, rather, a musician who perfected an existing approach, improvising immaculately clean, controlled, and tasteful melodies and accompaniments. From his early career he gained a deep feeling for idiomatic blues guitar playing, which made him—in his own restrained way—as soulful as any soul-jazz musician. Yet he was also able to combine this emotive approach with the fleet and comparatively abstract lines expected of a fluent hard bop player. Few other musicians have operated in both camps so well.

• Considerable information in this essay was provided by Green's daughter-in-law, Detroit-based newspaper reporter Sharony Andrews Green, who is preparing a biography of Green. Brief surveys and interviews include Dan Morgenstern, "Grant Green: New Guitar in Town," *Down Beat*, 19 July 1962, p. 23; Jack Cooke, "Halfway House," *Jazz Monthly*, Nov. 1963, pp. 10–12; Laurie Henshaw, "Three Guitar Greats," *Melody Maker*, 8 Nov. 1969, p. 26; "Grant Green Discusses His Approach to Modern Jazz Guitar," *Crescendo International*, Sept. 1971, p. 16; and Gary N. Bourland, "Grant Green," *Guitar Player*, Jan. 1975, pp. 10, 26, 29. See also Leonard Feather, *The Encyclopedia of Jazz in the Sixties* (1966), and Leonard Feather and Ira Gitler, *The Encyclopedia of Jazz in the Seventies* (1976). Obituaries are in the *Michigan Chronicle*, 10 Feb. 1979, and *Down Beat*, 22 Mar. 1979, p. 9.

BARRY KERNFELD

GREEN, Hetty (21 Nov. 1834–3 July 1916), private banker, money lender, and eccentric, also known as the Witch of Wall Street, was born Harriet Howland Robinson in New Bedford, Massachusetts, the daughter of Edward Mott Robinson, the owner of a prosperous whaling company, and Abby Slocum Howland, a member of one of the oldest and wealthiest families in New England. After the birth of her brother, who lived only a short time, Hetty's parents sent her to live in her grandfather Gideon Howland's household, where she was raised by her Aunt Sylvia. There she received her early education, reading the financial pages to her grandfather, whose sight was failing, and gaining a nascent understanding of financial markets. At age ten she attended a Quaker boarding school for three years, returning to New Bedford in 1847 after her grandfather's death.

After the death of her mother in 1860, Hetty Robinson received only $8,000 in real estate from her mother's estate, while her father took his wife's entire trust fund. Hetty's aunt Sylvia claimed that her sister had always intended for Hetty to inherit the trust fund. The resultant family quarrel caused Edward Robinson to break up the family firm and move to New York City. Hetty Robinson remained with her aunt. As Sylvia Howland's sole heir, she pestered her aunt with petty economies so as to preserve her inheritance. Howland finally banished her from the house, and Hetty moved to New York City. There she continued to badger her aunt by mail and tried as well to influence her father and his lawyer to construct his will in her favor.

On 14 June 1865 Edward Robinson died, followed closely by Sylvia Howland, who died on 2 July. From their two estates, Hetty Robinson expected to inherit $7 million. She was outraged to discover that her father had left her only $1 million outright, the remainder in trust; her aunt had bequeathed her the income from $1 million. Robinson challenged Sylvia Howland's will in a spectacular court trial that lasted for six years. She claimed that a later will existed. That will, when produced, proved to be a cooperative agreement between the two women that gave everything to the survivor. This document was without question a forgery, as a mathematician pointed out that the three signatures present on the second will, all determined by experts to be identical, had most likely been traced because the chances of any three signatures being coincidentally identical were approximately one in 2.6 sextillion. Robinson nevertheless convinced some leading public figures, notably naturalist Louis Agassiz and Dr. Oliver Wendell Holmes, to testify in her behalf. The lawsuit ended in 1868, dismissed over a technicality. It left Robinson with a lifelong disdain for lawyers and judges as well as a litigious approach to life.

In the meantime, she had married Edward Henry Green, a successful trader in international goods, in 1867. Edward Green had a net worth of $1 million at their marriage, but Robinson made him sign a prenuptial agreement to absolve her from any responsibilities for his debts as well as providing that he pay all household living expenses, an important protection for her wealth in the days before married women's property acts. After their marriage the Greens moved to London, where their two children, Edward Howland Robinson Green (called Ned) and Hetty Sylvia Ann Howland Green, were born.

In London, Hetty Green invested heavily and prospered mightily in the gold bond market and in railroads. While her husband lived in luxury, Hetty preferred to dress in shabby clothes and walk rather than pay for cabs or carriages. The panic of 1873 disrupted the Greens' business holdings and they returned to America, settling in Edward's hometown, Bellows Falls, Vermont. Green shifted her investments to real estate and ordered her bankers in New York, John J. Cisco & Son, to keep her account separate from her husband's.

From 1874 to 1885 the Greens lived in Bellows Falls, spending winters in New York and Chicago. When their son injured his knee in a sledding accident, Green, true to her miserly nature, refused him a doctor's care and treated the injury herself. When home remedies failed, she disguised herself and the boy and traveled to charity clinics to receive free medical care. When doctors learned her identity, they refused to help her unless she paid. Her actions led to tragedy; Ned's leg turned gangrenous and was amputated. His father paid the $5,000 bill. The son, surprisingly, did not seem to hold a grudge.

In 1885 the Greens separated after Edward lost his fortune and ran up a $700,000 debt, which the Cisco bank requested that Hetty Green pay. She refused and demanded that her money, some $550,000 on deposit as well as $25 million more in bonds, mortgages, and securities stored in the bank's vaults, be transferred to Chemical National Bank. The Cisco bank refused and, after two weeks of threats, tears, pleas, and public prayers in the bank's lobby, Hetty Green paid the debt, told Edward to move out, and loaded all of her remaining wealth into a hansom cab to transfer to Chemical National Bank. The removal of her accounts caused the Cisco bank to fail, and financier Jay Gould had to step in to prevent a financial panic.

The episode proved to be a turning point for Green, who thereafter referred to herself as Mrs. Hetty Green rather than use her husband's first name. She also began to take on a more public role in the financial markets. During the panic of 1893, she had plenty of cash on hand to provide loans to individuals, who usually provided real estate as collateral. She invested heavily in real estate, holding more than $17 million worth of property in California, Texas, New York, Denver, St. Louis, Cincinnati, and Chicago. She sent her son to Chicago and later to Texas to serve as her agent. His salary in Chicago for collecting $40,000 a month in rents for her was $3 per day; in Texas, she gave him a foreclosed Texas & Midland Railroad to turn around, which he did until stymied by competition from the Southern Pacific. Green survived a major crash in 1907, having converted all she had to cash or first mortgages. She became one of the few with money to lend—some to the New York Central Railroad, more than $1 million to New York City itself, and $6 million to the state of Texas.

Always eccentric in her personal habits and unpopular because of her success in bear markets, by the early 1900s Green began to exhibit increasingly bizarre behavior. She had for years worn the same black dress and bonnet, and she carried a black case and umbrella. Her habit, along with her piercing gray eyes and sharp tongue, earned her the sobriquet the Witch of Wall Street. She declared to the press that her father, aunt Sylvia, and husband, who died in 1902, had all been murdered. She carried a revolver for protection while asserting that the only things in life she truly feared were "lightning and a religious lawyer" (*New York Times*, 9 May 1902). Green moved frequently from cheap boardinghouses to cold-water walkups in Hoboken, New Jersey, with aliases on the mailboxes, hoping to throw off any assassins on her trail. Her peripatetic way of life also meant that she had no legal residency, thus avoiding taxes on her fortune. Newspapers interviewed her regularly, delineating her eccentricities as well as the secrets of her success. "I buy when things are low and no one wants them," she once said. "I keep them . . . until they go up and people are anxious to buy. That is the general secret of business success" (*New York Times*, 5 Nov. 1905). In fact, she was a brilliant investor, capable of manipulating the stock market by circulating rumors that she was buying or selling. She increased her wealth by making astute purchases in falling markets that accompanied financial panics. Few could match her resources.

In 1909 Green supervised the wedding of her 38-year-old daughter Sylvia to Matthew Astor Wilks, a 57-year-old millionaire. Momentarily, she reveled in her fortune, living at the Plaza Hotel, buying new clothes, visiting a beauty parlor, and hosting nuptial parties and a wedding feast. However, she reverted to her pecuniary habits shortly thereafter. In 1910 her son Ned arrived from Texas to help with his mother's affairs. He installed her in a flat in New York City, but she continued to change residences, alternating between that home and the home of Countess Anne Leary, a close friend, still trying to avoid establishing a city residence. She suffered a paralytic stroke in April 1916, following an exchange with the countess's cook over the cost of a meal, and died three months later at her son's house in New York City. At the time of her death Green was the richest woman in America. Her estate was valued at around $200 million but was taxed in Vermont (after considerable litigation) at an agreed-upon value of $50,000. It was divided equally between her children. Three hundred–pound Ned indulged his every whim, including marrying at age forty-eight a former prostitute and stripper named Mabel Harlowe.

He died in 1936. Sylvia, as eccentric as her mother, alternated her residence among three run-down estates in which she refused to have the hot water or heat turned on because of the expense. She died of cancer in 1951. The final distribution of Hetty Green's estate, some $150 million, was made in 1951 to innumerable charities, distant relatives, friends, and universities.

• No collection of Green's papers is known to exist. She gave numerous newspaper interviews that were printed in the Boston *Herald*; New York City's *Times, Tribune, Journal, Herald*, and *World*; and the New Bedford (Mass.) *Standard-Times*. Green also held forth in "Why Women Are Not Money Makers," *Harpers Bazaar*, 10 Mar. 1900, p. 201. Boyden Sparkes and Samuel Taylor Moore, *The Witch of Wall Street: Hetty Green* (1948), a reprint edition of their *Hetty Green: The Woman Who Loved Money* (1930), is not a scholarly monograph but is the most complete work on Green. Additional short works on Green are found in John T. Flynn, *Men of Wealth* (1941); Ishbel Ross, *Charmers and Cranks* (1965); Peter Wyckoff, "Queen Midas: Hetty Robinson Green," *New England Quarterly* 23 (June 1950): 147–71; and Janet Coryell, "Hetty Green," in *Encyclopedia of American Business History and Biography*, ed. Larry Schweikart (1990), pp. 233–39. Arthur H. Lewis, *The Day They Shook the Plum Tree* (1963), deals with the final distribution of Green's wealth and, although journalistic and sensationalistic, it is important for its discussion of her children's lives. Genealogical background can be found in William Morrell Emery, *The Howland Heirs* (1919), and *Gideon Howland's Kith and Kin* (1916). A colorful and highly inaccurate novel of Green's life during the Civil War era is William Kendall Clarke, *The Robber Baroness* (1979). An obituary is in the *New York Times*, 4 July 1916; an interview with her son is in the 9 July 1916 issue.
JANET L. CORYELL

GREEN, Horace (24 Dec. 1802–29 Nov. 1866), laryngologist, was born in Chittenden, Vermont, the son of Zeeb Green and Sarah Cowee, farmers. He received practically no formal education as a child. As a young man, he studied medicine with his brother Joel, a physician in Rutland, for several years before entering the Medical School at Middlebury (later known as Castleton Medical College). After receiving his M.D. in 1825, he returned to Rutland and joined his brother's practice; with the exception of a brief period in 1830–1831, when he attended lectures and dissertations at the University of Pennsylvania, he practiced with his brother for the next ten years. In 1829 he married Mary Sigourney Butler, with whom he had one child.

In 1835, two years after his wife died, Green moved to New York City, where he opened his own practice. In 1838 he took a five-month tour of hospitals and medical schools in London and Paris, and in 1840 he returned to Castleton Medical College as president and professor of medicine. In 1841 he married Harriet Sheldon Douglas, with whom he had ten children. He resigned from his positions at Castleton in 1843 to reopen his practice in New York City. In 1850 he co-founded the New York Medical College and became its first professor of the theory and practice of medicine. Over the next ten years he also served variously as president of the board of trustees and president of the faculty. In 1854 he co-founded and served as editor of the short-lived *American Medical Monthly*.

Green was the first physician in the United States to limit his practice to the treatment of throat diseases. He wrote *Treatises on the Diseases of the Air Passages* (1846; 4th ed., 1858), which investigated the history, pathology, and treatment of bronchitis, chronic laryngitis, and "clergyman's sore throat." In this work he advocated treating these conditions and a great many others by applying silver nitrate solution to the mucous membrane of the larynx or to the bronchial tubes, which he claimed to be able to reach by inserting a probang, a curved, ten-inch-long piece of whalebone with a tiny sponge on one end, through the vocal cords of the larynx. This assertion caused a general uproar in the medical community in the United States, France, and Great Britain. The laryngoscope had yet to be invented; therefore, because they could not actually see the larynx, many physicians refused to believe that it was anatomically possible to insert an instrument of any size through the vocal cords into the larynx, much less the bronchial passages. Moreover, Green's claims that he could cure pulmonary and laryngeal lesions in this manner struck physicians with a much better understanding of pathology than he possessed as simply absurd. He defended his claims for nine years against charges of fraud on the one hand and plagiarism on the other (he was accused of pirating his technique from an 1837 treatise on tuberculosis by Trousseau and Belloc, two French physicians). In 1855 Green arranged a demonstration before an investigative committee of the New York Academy of Medicine that was considering revoking his membership; the results did nothing to settle the controversy, although he was allowed to remain in the academy. Not until 1859, with the development of the first laryngeal mirror, was it shown conclusively that an instrument could indeed be inserted through the vocal cords into the larynx via a narrow slit known as the glottis, and on this count his critics in the medical community were forced to retract their accusations. However, his claims regarding his ability to insert the probang through the larynx in order to apply medication to bronchial tubes and tuberculous cavities were eventually proven to be totally without merit.

Despite this controversy, Green established and maintained a lucrative practice. He published a comprehensive study of the pathology of croup in 1849, and in 1852 he developed a surgical procedure for treating laryngeal polyps and edema of the glottis. In 1860, having contracted a case of tuberculosis so severe that it prevented him from performing surgery, he retired to Ossining, New York, although he spent two winters in Cuba trying to regain his health. He spent his remaining years writing *A Practical Treatise of Pulmonary Tuberculosis* (1864) and his autobiography, which was never published. He died in Ossining.

Green's understanding of laryngeal pathology was incomplete, thus he often espoused treatments that were ineffective; nevertheless, his innovative technique for medicating the larynx was an important contribution to the development of laryngology and establishes him as one of the pioneers in this field.

• The manuscript of Green's autobiography, as well as other archival material pertaining to his life, is in the New York Academy of Medicine Library. The significance of his work is discussed in William Snow Miller, "Horace Green and His Probang," *Johns Hopkins Hospital Bulletin* 30 (Aug. 1919): 246–52; Francis R. Packard, *History of Medicine in the United States* (2 vols., 1931; repr. 1963); Charles Snyder, "The Investigation of Horace Green," *Laryngoscope* 85 (1975): 2012–22; and Jonathan Wright, *History of Laryngology and Rhinology*, 2d ed. (1914). Obituaries are in the *New York Times*, 3 Dec. 1866, and the *New York Medical Journal* (Jan. 1867).

CHARLES W. CAREY, JR.

GREEN, James Stephens (28 Feb. 1817–19 Jan. 1870), politician, was born near Rectortown, Fauquier County, Virginia, the son of James S. Green and Frances Ann (maiden name unknown), farmers. He was educated in the common schools of Virginia, and in 1836 he moved with his family to Alabama before coming to Ralls County, Missouri, a year later. He purchased a gristmill and a sawmill with his brother, Martin E. Green, but was unable to make a success of it. He married Elizabeth Reese in 1838 or 1839. Green borrowed law books and studied while he worked at the gristmill. He was admitted to the bar in 1840 and established a practice with his brother-in-law in Monticello, Lewis County. He soon became active in Democratic politics as a protégé of Senator Thomas Hart Benton (1782–1858) and was chosen as one of the party's presidential electors in 1844. At the same time, he was elected a delegate to the constitutional convention of 1845. There he "first exhibited that talent for forensic debate which in after-life so distinguished him" (Bay, p. 521). Green was elected to Congress in 1846 from a northeast Missouri district that included many persons of southern origin. There he became a staunch defender of President James Polk's Mexican policy.

Following the death of his first wife, Green married Mary Evans in 1847. In the aftermath of the Mexican War, he adopted a strong states' rights stance, which opposed Free Soil doctrines, to represent the interests of his district. In this connection Green played a prominent role in the successful struggle to wrest control of the Missouri Democratic party from his former mentor Senator Benton because of the latter's failure to take a stronger stand in defense of the rights of slavery in the territories. Green did not stand for reelection in 1850, but when he attempted a comeback in 1852 he was defeated by his Whig opponent because of the split in the Democratic ranks over slavery extension.

President Franklin Pierce appointed Green chargé d'affaires to Colombia on 24 May 1853, but after a year there he declined appointment as minister resident because he found the climate unsuitable, and he was eager to return to the Missouri political fray. He was reelected to the House of Representatives in 1856, but before Congress convened, the Missouri legislature elected him to the Senate to replace David Rice Atch-

ison, whose seat had remained vacant for two years because of the disruption of Missouri Democratic politics. Green resumed his staunch support of the extension of slavery into the territories and defended the Lecompton constitution against Senator Stephen Douglas's attacks. When Douglas was deposed as chairman of the Senate Committee on Territories, the post went to Green, who later reported on the acts organizing Colorado, Dakota, and Nevada territories, with no mention of slavery, and secured their unanimous passage by the Senate. Although acknowledged by his legal and congressional peers as a master of debate and persuasion, it was also well known that Green had a drinking problem, which ultimately had a negative effect on his health as his difficulties over his prosouthern leanings mounted during the Civil War. In the midst of the secession crisis he declined reelection.

Green was arrested as a southern sympathizer by federal authorities in June 1861, when they moved into northeast Missouri, but he was paroled the following month. He later refused to go south with friends from his region who joined Confederate guerrillas. In 1864 he was reported to be actively involved in the Order of American Knights, a vague, secret, pro-Confederate organization that was rumored to be operating in the upper Mississippi valley. He openly admitted his support for Clement Vallandigham, one of the country's leading Copperheads. Green resumed his law practice in Lewis County after the war, but his health continued to decline until his death there.

• There is no known collection of Green's papers. Brief biographical sketches can be found in William V. N. Bay, *Reminiscences of the Bench and Bar of Missouri* (1878), and Walter B. Stevens, *Centennial History of Missouri*, vol. 2 (1921). His nephew James F. Green wrote a brief laudatory sketch, "James S. Green," *Missouri Historical Review* 21 (Oct. 1926): 41–44. An unsigned sketch entitled "A Forgotten Missourian—A Historical Sketch of the Life and Times of James S. Green, United States Senator, 1857–1861," appeared in *Reedy's Mirror*, 31 Dec. 1915. An evaluation of Green as senator is found in James G. Blaine, *Twenty Years of Congress: From Lincoln to Garfield*, vol. 1 (1884).

WILLIAM E. PARRISH

GREEN, John Cleve (4 Apr. 1800–29 Apr. 1875), philanthropist, railroad entrepreneur, and China trader, was born in Lawrenceville (formerly Maidenhead), New Jersey, the son of Caleb Smith and Elizabeth Green. His great-great-grandfather, Jonathan Dickinson, was first president of the College of New Jersey, which later became Princeton University; this family connection would later play a great part in Princeton's future.

Green's academic career began promisingly when he enrolled in the first class at what became the Lawrenceville School, but apart from some further schooling in Brooklyn, Green soon terminated further formal education. Instead, he joined the preeminent New York merchants, N. L. & G. Griswold, which specialized in overseas trade. Beginning in 1823 Green spent nearly a decade managing the sale of cargoes on the

Griswold ships dispensing trade in South America and China. By 1833 Green, then married to Sarah Griswold, the daughter of George Griswold, a junior partner in the Griswold firm, began his ascent into the loftier business cliques. His superior business skills and moral rectitude were acknowledged when he was offered a post with the dominant American house in the China trade, Russell & Company, a transplanted Boston enterprise, to bring the house's carefree business practices in line with an increasingly complex and competitive market and the firm's policy of fair dealing with its clients and the Chinese officials. Green became part of the secret trading world of Canton. His marriage and his new associates allowed him to enjoy the considerable and undeniable benefits of a rising star in the elegant world of merchant adventurers in their all male environment, absorbed in the single-minded promotion of trade. Like other Americans, Green was handicapped by a disinterested government in Washington, which left the twenty or so regular merchant adventurers at the mercy of Chinese officials. Green soon proved his worth to Russell's, and within a year he became head of its China operations, exporting tea and silks to a receptive American public. Opium became part of Russell's inventory following the end of the East India Company's entrenched monopoly in the China trade in 1833. Green benefited in two ways. First, his wealth increased along with that of his employers, whose sole objective was to amass as much wealth as possible within the shortest possible time. Second, he met John Murray Forbes and Robert B. Forbes, to their later mutual financial advantage. Green retired in 1839 at the beginning of the dominance of the clipper ships, and soon afterward, the Chinese high commissioner at Canton, Lin Tse Hsu, began the first of many attempts to undermine the foreign trade in opium. Despite Green's future intimacy with the Forbes family, Robert Forbes claimed Green surrendered too easily when he ceased his active ties with the Canton side of the business. Green ignored the accusations and returned to New York with his fortune intact.

Green then began to parlay his Chinese treasure chest into an even greater financial hoard. He retained his contacts in the China trade as consignee of tea cargoes and became a director of the Bank of Commerce and president of the Blocker Street Savings Bank. Green's greatest business coup was his investment in railroads. By 1846 Green was endorsing his old Canton trading associate, John Murray Forbes, the new president of the Michigan Central Railroad Company, who had bought both the "Democracy's Railroad"—that atrophying enterprise initiated by the Michigan Democratic regime to finance, build, and operate a state system of internal improvements based on a railroad snaking its way from Detroit in the general direction of Chicago—and the right to play with its trains as he saw fit. Green's trust, born from the China days, won him a fortune, because the railroad proved eminently profitable. So it was natural that Green became a "Forbes" man and gave him the loyalty demanded by

the leaders of these rigidly uncompromising corporate states, who believed in their right to reign over their territory and the captive freight traffic. In 1861 Green also championed Forbes when he headed a group that gained mastery over the great Chicago, Burlington & Quincy system, the most successful of the granger roads, which revolutionized the production of food and grains. For his support, Green was named a director of the CB&Q and the New Jersey Central until his death. Green's was not a token role. Forbes used him undercover to manipulate company business when the CB&Q was under threat during the River Roads scandal. Green's profit from these ventures, which received a heady boost during the Civil War, amounted to a 15 percent return; as a result he was worth $3 million by 1870.

Green, a devout Presbyterian, was now free to make his greatest contributions to American society. Even though he was a minor participant in the self-promotion frenzy beloved by many entrepreneurs, Green, with his capital resources, was encouraged by his belief that his business achievements demanded public respect; he sought to use his authority and influence to change American values before the nation would reject the destructive and destabilizing posturing of the railway men and their impact on its growth and commerce. Bereft of the love of his three children, all of whom died at an early age, Green sought solace in preparing others for life. He returned his wealth several-fold in good deeds to his community during his lifetime. Green donated significantly to the Deaf and Dumb Asylum. He also helped to found the Home for Ruptured and Crippled in New York City. He was a long-serving governor of the New York Hospital. However, his main interests lay with three institutions. Through his gifts and his estate his alma mater, the Lawrenceville Classical and Commercial High School, became one of the leading preparatory schools and a source of future Princeton undergraduates. He served Princeton Theological Seminary as a trustee for twenty-five years, and he endowed the seminary with a chair in church history and other gifts, including a professor's house. Princeton, however, received the lion's share of his largess. Green's philanthropy was an extension of his Presbyterian convictions, buoyed by an empathy for Princeton's evangelistic commitments. Green was one of the many self-made men who made large donations to higher education. He made his donations content in the knowledge that the university would be attended by like-minded students and teachers. His respect for academics extended beyond his family's connections with science and letters. Green thought beyond immediate railroad profits to a greater community good. He made the largest single donation up to that time and saved the university from a financial crisis. In 1866 he acquired a large tract of land in the northeast corner of the campus for the institution and paid for three critically acclaimed buildings, including the first library building, which was named after his brother, Henry Woodhull Green. He endowed three chairs in science. His major contribution to curriculum development came with his 1873 gift of the School of Science, named in his honor and supplemented with a benefaction from his will. The university continued to benefit from the estate into the 1890s with the construction of its first chemical laboratory. Green's presence still looms in Princeton, memorialized in Green Hall and his portrait in the Convocation Room in the Engineering Quadrangle.

Green participated in the creation of two great commercial adventures that profoundly affected American civilization. The China trade yielded the capital that generated a coterie of men who changed the American landscape and industrialized the nation through the railroads. Although Green's role in these fields was peripheral, he was center stage for the advance in education. He was an honest man with a well-earned reputation for fairness in commerce, a rare mix in his world. He died in New York City.

• Green's involvement in the China trade is addressed in Foster Rhea Dulles, *The Old China Trade* (1930), and in Ernest R. May and John K. Fairbank, eds., *America's China Trade in Historical Perspective; The Chinese and American Performance* (1986). His association with Forbes is described in R. B. Forbes, *Personal Reminiscences* (1878), and in Sarah Forbes Hughes, *Letters and Recollections of John Murray Forbes* (2 vols., 1899). Stewart H. Holbrook, *The Story of American Railroads* (1947), Caroline E. MacGill et al., *History of Transportation in the United States before 1860* (1917), John F. Stover, *The Life and Decline of the American Railroad* (1970), and James A. Ward, *Railroads and the Character of America, 1820–1887* (1986), discuss his role in railroads, as do John Lauritz Larson, *Bonds of Enterprise: John Murray Forbes and Western Development in America's Railway Age* (1984), and Albro Martin, *Railroads Triumphant: The Growth, Rejection, and Rebirth of a Vital American Force* (1992). V. Lansing Collins, *Princeton Past and Present* (1945), Alexander Leitch, *A Princeton Companion* (1978), and J. David Hoeveler, Jr., *James McCosh and the Scottish Intellectual Tradition: From Glasgow to Princeton* (1981), discuss Green's role in that institution. An obituary is in the *State Gazette* (Trenton, N.J.), 30 Apr. 1875.

RICHARD GROVES

GREEN, Johnny (10 Oct. 1908–15 May 1989), popular composer and film music director, was born John Waldo Green in New York City, the son of Vivian I. Green, a real estate agent and banker, and Irma Jellenik. Although his father planned a financial career for him, Johnny Green (he insisted on "John" late in life) said he was a musical pro from the beginning. At age twelve he performed for the composer George Gershwin. At fifteen he entered Harvard, where he started an orchestra. When André Charlot's London Revue came to New York in 1924, Green played piano at a party honoring its stars, Jack Buchanan, Beatrice Lillie, and Gertrude Lawrence. Lawrence later insisted that Green's "Body and Soul" emerged from her wailing attempts to play the saxophone under his tutelage.

In 1927, still at Harvard, Green collaborated with Gus Kahn and Carmen Lombardo on his first hit, "Coquette." In 1928 he received a bachelor's degree in ec-

onomics and briefly became a clerk in his uncle's brokerage office. When he quit, Lawrence hired him as accompanist. In 1929 his successful song "I'm Yours" was interpolated in the Broadway show *Simple Simon*. As a rehearsal pianist for New York's Paramount Studios he learned the basics of conducting from music head Frank Tours. He said he lost his "Coquette" royalties in the stock market.

"Body and Soul" was written for and first performed by Lawrence in 1929 as part of a four-song commission for $250. Green said, "I only knew I was writing for Gertie and for Wednesday. She wanted one comedy, one uptempo, one ballad, and one torch song. 'Body and Soul' was the bluesy one." After she sang it in London, the song was wanted for the 1930 Broadway revue *Three's a Crowd*. Lawrence gave the copyright (and a fortune in royalties) back to Green and his lyricist, Edward Heyman.

Musicologist-composer Alec Wilder called "Body and Soul" a "landmark," with "one of the widest ranges and one of the most complex releases and verses." "Its verse is as strange and unprecedented as its chorus." Because of its yearning melody and frank lyrics, "Body and Soul" was banned from American radio for a year. After tenor saxophonist Coleman Hawkins's recording in 1939, it became one of its era's most popular vehicles for improvisation. Green said in an interview, "I wrote what I felt, what that title required. People would like to force on me that I intended to use an inharmonious key relationship because it'd never been used in a popular song before. I didn't do that. . . . That was the middle strain that flowed out of the first strain and when I had conceived it, and locked it in, I thought it was good, I thought it belonged. . . . That 8 bars made a career."

In 1930 Green wrote "Out of Nowhere," another series of melodic surprises which became a jazz classic as well as Bing Crosby's solo recording debut. Songs from Green's first Broadway score, *Here Goes the Bride*, in 1931 outlasted the show; the most critically acclaimed song, despite its lyrics, was "Hello, My Lover, Goodbye." In 1932 his first "serious" work, *Six Improvisations for Three Pianos and Orchestra*, was performed by orchestras in New York, Boston, and London. Two more standards, "You're Mine You" and "I Cover the Waterfront," the latter illustrating the title of a film, were composed in 1933. Green and Heyman's songs were part of *Murder at the Vanities* (1933), an odd Earl Carroll stage show starring Bela Lugosi, which in 1934 became another film. Green went to London in late 1933 to write the score of the stage production *Mr. Whittington*, including "Oceans of Time," a trademark for Jack Buchanan. Green recorded much of the score in England.

In 1933, Green formed his own orchestra, which lasted for eight years. The big band historian and critic George T. Simon called it a "Good, hotel-room type band. . . . Replete with interesting sounds from a reed section that included flutes, oboes and English horns, it featured both the expert piano and the enthusiastic charm of Green himself." Fred Astaire's earliest recordings of songs from his films were with Green's orchestra. Green, who was also a musical director for radio, conducted an Irving Berlin testimonial in Los Angeles in 1936. His songs appeared in several more films. In 1939 his *Music for Elizabeth, Piano and Orchestra* was performed by the CBS and Eastman School symphonies.

In 1942 Green's life and career changed. After his Broadway show *Beat the Band*, he signed with Metro-Goldwyn-Mayer (MGM) as a composer, conductor, and arranger, and he settled in Hollywood. In 1943 he married Bonnie "Bunny" Waters, a swimming champion. His earlier marriages, to Carol Koshland and Betty Furness (with whom he had one child), ended in divorce. He and Waters had two children.

A nominal political liberal, he joined the Hollywood Independent Citizens Comittee of the Arts, Sciences, and Professions. After a dispute, Green left MGM briefly, returning as musical director for the 1948 film *Easter Parade*. He helped Berlin transcribe his songs for that picture. Green commented that it was no collaboration: Berlin might be musically illiterate, but he liked things the way he had written them in the first place. Green won an Academy Award for his scoring of the film. His next film, *The Inspector General*, won a Golden Globe Award. In 1949 he became MGM's general music director and executive in charge of music. He hired composers and performers such as André Previn, Miklos Rozsa, Bronislaw Kaper, and Adolph Deutsch.

After winning another Academy Award for the Gershwin musical *An American in Paris* in 1951, Green found himself threatened by the movie industry's political blacklist, but he was able to survive without repercussions.

Green remained at MGM through 1958, winning an Academy Award for the short musical film *The Merry Wives of Windsor Overture* (1958). He composed, arranged, and conducted for television productions. He won Oscars for his adaptations of the scores of *West Side Story* and *Oliver!*, and he was nominated for nine more. His score for the 1958 film *Raintree County* became *Three Themes for Symphony Orchestra*. Between 1959 and 1963 he was musical director and permanent conductor of the Los Angeles Philharmonic Orchestra's promenade concerts. He conducted Hollywood Bowl concerts and Academy Awards telecasts as well. Of the daily fresh carnation in his buttonhole, he said that it reminded him of the world's beauty and his obligation to protect and extend it.

Green served on the board of directors of the American Society of Composers, Authors and Publishers (ASCAP) between 1981 and 1989. In 1973 he was named to the Songwriters Hall of Fame and established musical awards at the University of Southern California. He became a governor of the Performing Arts Council of the Los Angeles Music Center and was the recipient of honorary academic degrees. In 1979 he was a visiting lecturer in music at Harvard. In 1978 his *Mine Eyes Have Seen* was performed by the Denver Symphony, and nine years later he conducted the London Symphony. He died in Beverly Hills.

• ASCAP holds much material on Green. One of the most interesting of the many interviews that Green gave during his lifetime is in the British Broadcasting Corporation (BBC) archives and was aired on the radio series "From Ragtime to Rock" in 1976. Another interview of interest is Elmer Bernstein, "A Conversation with John Green," *Film Music Notebook* (1976). Green's obituary in *Variety*, 19 May 1989, is highly detailed, as is Charles Champlin's in the *Los Angeles Times*, 16 May 1989.

JAMES ROSS MOORE

GREEN, John Patterson (2 Apr. 1845–30 Aug. 1940), lawyer and politician, was born in Newbern, North Carolina, the son of John R. Green, a tailor, and Temperance (maiden name unknown), free African Americans of mixed ancestry. He learned the rudiments of reading and writing at a private school for free blacks. His father died while John was a child, and in June 1857 his mother moved the family to Cleveland, Ohio.

After working as an apprentice to a harness maker in Oberlin, Ohio, Green returned to Cleveland and attended school briefly before being forced to withdraw because of the family's financial problems. Subsequently, he worked temporarily as a tailor, a waiter, and at other jobs. Green continued to study on his own, however, and at his own expense in 1866 published *Miscellaneous Subjects by a Self-Educated Colored Youth*. That same year, after returning from a lecture tour to promote his book, he entered Central High School in Cleveland, graduating in 1869. That same year he married Annie Walker; they had six children. Also in 1869 Green entered Cleveland's Union Law School, from which he graduated in 1870.

Green and his wife moved back to North Carolina in 1870. They remained there only a short while before settling in South Carolina, where Green was admitted to the bar and embarked on a lifelong political career in the Republican party. In 1872 he was elected a delegate to the state Republican convention and an alternate delegate to the national GOP convention. In the fall of 1872 Green returned to Cleveland and easily won election as a justice of the peace, a position which at that time had both judicial and some police powers. Green, one of the first black elected officials in the North, held this post for nine years while continuing to work as an attorney. In 1877 he apparently won election to the Ohio House of Representatives, but a recount gave the victory to the Democratic candidate; Green unsuccessfully claimed that the election had been stolen from him as a result of a fraudulent vote count.

In 1881 Green was renominated for a seat in the state assembly; this time he was elected. He was not reelected in 1883 but won handily when he ran again in 1889. In 1891 Green was elected to the Ohio Senate from a mostly white district—the only African American from the North to be elected to a state senate before World War I. His ability to win election to the state assembly and the state senate demonstrated both the power of the GOP and the racial liberalism of many white Clevelanders at the time. In the senate, he supported funding for Wilberforce University, an institution affiliated with the African Methodist Episcopal church, and in 1893 he helped defeat a bill designed to allow some local school districts to segregate students by race. Green became known best, however, as the sponsor of legislation establishing Labor Day in Ohio in 1893. The Ohio law served as a model for Congress when Labor Day was made a national holiday in 1894, and Green became known as "the father of Labor Day."

Throughout the 1890s, Green worked closely with the prominent black Clevelander George A. Myers, the owner of a barbershop that catered primarily to whites, in support of the Marcus A. Hanna faction of the Ohio Republican party. Green, who did not run for reelection to the state senate in 1893, became well known as a speaker on the Republican lecture circuit. He also wrote periodically for the Afro-American News Syndicate, which distributed his articles to numerous black newspapers. In 1896 he lectured throughout the state on behalf of William McKinley and was an alternate delegate-at-large at the Republican National Convention. Green's support for McKinley led to his appointment in 1897 as U.S. Postage Stamp Agent, a position that oversaw the printing and distribution of postage stamps. Green remained in this post until 1905, when he was named acting superintendent of finance for the Post Office Department. While holding these federal positions, he lived in Washington, D.C.

In 1906 Green left government service and returned to full-time law practice in Cleveland. Like most black lawyers in the North at the time, he drew his clientele mostly from the working class of both races. Following the death of his wife Annie in January 1912, he married a widow, Lottie Mitchell Richardson, in September 1912. In 1920 he published his autobiography, *Fact Stranger than Fiction*, a volume in the Horatio Alger mold that Green hoped would inspire young African Americans. After 1906 Green took little part in politics, except as an occasional speaker during election campaigns.

Green was typical of an elite group of light-skinned African-American professionals and businessmen who established themselves in Cleveland and other northern cities in the decades following the Civil War. Although by objective standards their income was at best middle class, they set themselves apart from the rest of the black community through their lifestyle, institutional affiliations, and frequent association with whites of similar or higher social status. Green was among the founders of St. Andrew's Episcopal Church, Cleveland's wealthiest African-American congregation, and was a member of the Social Circle, an exclusive African-American club that dated to 1869. He was also the first black member of the Logos Club, an elite group that met periodically to discuss important social issues of the day. He counted as his friends many prominent white Clevelanders and even had a passing acquaintanceship with John D. Rockefeller.

Green generally believed in the value of integrated institutions, but unlike some members of the city's African-American elite (such as Harry Clay Smith) he was not a leader in the fight against the rising tide of racism in the post-Reconstruction era. At a time when racial discrimination was becoming increasingly evident in Cleveland, Green described the city as an "asylum from prejudice and proscription" (*Fact Stranger than Fiction*, dedication page). As a politician, Green was cautious and conservative, and he never criticized Republican leaders on civil rights issues.

During a period when the northern black population was too small to provide an independent base of support for African-American politicians, Green was successful because he was a party loyalist who never rocked the boat. Even after retiring from political life, Green was unwavering in his allegiance to the GOP. In 1928 and 1932 Green spoke on behalf of Herbert Hoover. After most black voters switched to the Democratic party in 1936, he remained a committed Republican. Green was struck and killed by an automobile in Cleveland after disembarking from a streetcar. He was the oldest practicing attorney in Ohio at the time of his death.

• Green's papers, located in the Western Reserve Historical Society, and his substantial correspondence with George A. Myers in Myers's papers (Ohio Historical Society) are important sources. Green's upbringing, family life, and political career are discussed in his *Recollections of the Carolinas* (1881) and *Fact Stranger than Fiction: Seventy-Five Years of a Busy Life with Reminiscences of Many Great Men and Women* (1920). His career is assessed in Russell H. Davis, *Black Americans in Cleveland* (1972), and more extensively in Kenneth L. Kusmer, *A Ghetto Takes Shape: Black Cleveland, 1870–1930* (1976). An obituary is in the *Cleveland Gazette*, 7 Sept. 1940.

KENNETH L. KUSMER

GREEN, Jonas (28 Dec. 1712–11 April 1767), printer, was born in Boston, Massachusetts, the son of Timothy Green, a printer, and Mary Flint. His great grandfather Samuel Green had been the printer in Cambridge, Massachusetts, from 1649 to his death in 1702. The Greens were America's premier colonial printing family. Jonas Green grew up in New London, Connecticut, where he learned the printing business from his father, the colony's official printer. After Green finished his apprenticeship, he went to Boston as a journeyman printer, and then in 1736 moved to Philadelphia to work for Andrew Bradford. He married Anne Catherine Hoof in Philadelphia's Anglican Christ Church, in 1738; they had fourteen children, seven of whom survived to adulthood. Shortly thereafter he moved to Annapolis, having secured the position as Maryland's public printer.

For seven years, from 1738 to 1745, Green concentrated on job printing (forms and advertisements), government printing (the official materials the governor, council, and assembly paid him to print), and a few pamphlets that authors or others paid for. Green was probably in debt for his printing press and supplies and unable to venture his own publications. But in 1745 he took the gamble and started a newspaper. Green's *Maryland Gazette* followed Benjamin Franklin's *Pennsylvania Gazette* in trying to focus on local and American affairs, but Green printed more local compositions than Franklin. Though Philadelphia was larger than Annapolis, Green could draw upon an array of fine literary talent in Maryland, especially the prolific Dr. Alexander Hamilton (1712–1756) and the Reverend James Sterling. He also printed two of Franklin's best-known works, his free verse travesty of Sir William Gooch's confusing speech on the burning of the Virginia capitol and "The Speech of Miss Polly Baker" (*Maryland Gazette* 14 April and 11 August 1747), which Franklin never allowed to appear in his own paper.

Green became a member of Hamilton's Tuesday Club on 2 February 1748. In the *History of the Tuesday Club*, Hamilton said that Green's favorite subjects were "puns, conundrums, merrytales, and jests" and called him the ultimate club man: "for were there 50 clubs in the place, he'd be a member of every one." Green and Hamilton were the primary writers for the club—Green specializing in doggerel poetry and Hamilton in bombastic prose, both deliberate spoofs of the styles of British court writings. Green was appointed "P.P.P.P.P." ("purveyor, punster, punchmaker General, printer, and poet") of the club, but later requested to become merely "P.L.M.C." ("Poetica Laureatus, Magister Ceremoniam"). Some of his club poetry (particularly the anniversary odes) was set to music by Hamilton and by the Reverend Thomas Bacon. One rambunctious night (26 October 1752) the club met at Richard Dorsey's home, ate, sang, and danced, and then marched off, playing music, to Samuel Middleton's tavern, where they caroused until dawn. Near the conclusion of his mock heroic poem about the occasion, Green wrote:

Now Luscious toasts round the Room flew apace,
And the Claret flammd out on each nose & each face,
While with those that the bumpers of rack punch did
 swill,
The urine run off like the Sluice of a mill,
Full thirteen Quart bottles lay dead on the floor,
And nine Gallon bowls had been Emptied & more.

(Canto 3, ll. 119–24)

The Tuesday Club appointed Green and Hamilton its official punsters. From 30 January through 18 September 1750, each delivered two conundrums at every meeting. On 14 February 1750 Green asked, "Why is a wanton Lass in bed, like a book just printed?" The club failed to solve it, and Green replied, "Because she is in *Sheets* & wants *Stitching*." His second was, "Why is a dancing master Like a Shady tree?" Again the club failed, and Green answered: "Because he is full of *Bows/Boughs*." His puns occasionally even entered his newspaper obituaries: reporting the death of "Mr. Henry Crouch, Carver, who was deem'd by good

Judges to be as ingenious an Artist at his Business, as any in the King's Dominions," Green concluded, "altho' Mr. Crouch had very little Notice taken of him, and lived somewhat obscurely, yet it must be allowed, that he cut a good figure in life" (*Maryland Gazette*, 7 Jan. 1762).

On 29 July 1762 he printed the front page of his newspaper in three different types, "new English, new small pica, and new long pica." He had just bought the new types in order to print Thomas Bacon's *Laws of Maryland*, a hugh folio finally completed in 1766 that was Green's printing masterpiece. Lawrence C. Wroth said that it was not exceeded in beauty by any imprint of the colonial press. He was elected councilman of Annapolis on 28 October 1755 and an alderman of Annapolis on 11 April 1767.

Though a political moderate, Green, like almost all colonial printers, opposed the Stamp Act. He discontinued the *Maryland Gazette* during the period of the Stamp Act but occasionally issued an illegal "supplement" called *The Apparition of the Maryland Gazette Which Is Not Dead but Sleepeth*. Instead of the legal stamp, he substituted a death's head, surrounded by the words "The Times are Dismal, Doleful, Dolorous, Dollar-less." After he died in Annapolis, his wife became Maryland's official printer and continued the *Maryland Gazette* until her demise in 1775. Their descendants published it until 12 December 1839. Isaiah Thomas judged that Green's "printing was correct, and few, if any, in the colonies exceeded him in the neatness of his work." He made a major contribution to the intellectual and literary life of prerevolutionary Maryland, both by publishing other writers in his own urbane *Maryland Gazette* and by his poetic travesties and puns in Hamilton's facetious *History of the Tuesday Club*.

• Green's own file of *The Maryland Gazette* survives at the Maryland State Library, Annapolis. Lawrence C. Wroth lists and discusses Green's imprints in *A History of Printing in Colonial Maryland* (1922). Dr. Alexander Hamilton wrote an appreciative character sketch of Green, recorded his poems and sayings, and made a caricature wash drawing of him for *The History of the Tuesday Club*, ed. Robert Micklus (3 vols., 1990). Isaiah Thomas assessed his contributions in *The History of Printing in America*, ed. Marcus McCorison (1970). William C. Kiessel, "The Green Family: A Dynasty of Printers," *New England Historic and Genealogical Register* 104 (1950): 81–93, provides a brief account of the Green family. A biographical and critical sketch, together with a primary and secondary bibliography, is in J. A. Leo Lemay, *Men of Letters in Colonial Maryland* (1972).

J. A. LEO LEMAY

GREEN, Joseph (1706–11 Dec. 1780), poet and merchant, was born in Boston, Massachusetts, the son of Nathaniel Green and Elizabeth (maiden name unknown). Information about his parents' employment could not be obtained. He was educated at the South Grammar School and entered Harvard College in

1722, graduating in 1726. Few details of his life have been preserved, but it is known that he was part of the prosperous Boston merchant class and was said to own the largest private library in New England. He was also a pew-holder in the First Church of Boston, a man of Loyalist political sympathies, and a noted wit. He married Elizabeth (maiden name unknown) after 1742, but there is no evidence of their having any children.

Green is significant historically as one of the earliest American humorous poets, having earned the reputation as "the foremost wit of his day," according to Evert A. Duyckinck and George L. Duyckinck, the mid-nineteenth-century literary historians. The poems attributed to Green reveal him to be a keen social and political satirist. Samuel L. Knapp's 1821 sketch of Green notes that his business affairs afforded him "considerable leisure to attend his classical studies, of which he was a constant votary," and associates him with a "club of wits [who] watched every passing event . . . and turned every thing to merriment that was susceptible of it." Knapp also describes Green as "a retired, modest, unambitious, religious man, an enemy to parade and bustle, yet a bold opposer of arbitrary power, and a firm supporter of rational liberty."

A poet by avocation, Green left enough poems to suggest his tastes and talents. He initiated an exchange of satiric poems with Mather Byles, with "A Parody on a Hymn by Mather Byles" (1733), a burlesque of Byles's "A Psalm at Sea." Byles replied with a counter-parody, to which Green answered with "The Poet's Lamentation for the Loss of His Cat" (1733), mocking Byles's reference to his cat as his "muse." Green also wrote a lampoon of Boston's first Masonic procession of 27 December 1749, entitled *Entertainment for a Winter's Evening* (1750). The poem depicts the Masons as proceeding from church to their real destination, a tavern. Green also published a sequel to that satire, *The Grand Arcanum Detected* (1755). One of Green's more significant satirical poems, "The Disappointed Cooper," was called to the attention of scholars in 1974 by J. A. Leo Lemay, who recognized the poem as a satire of the Great Awakening.

Green remained a British Loyalist in the period preceding the American Revolution, joining other merchants in protests against the attempts to suspend commerce with England. As the revolutionary fervor increased in Boston, Green's position became increasingly precarious. In 1775 Green and his wife left Boston for England in apparent haste, leaving behind most of their possessions. He spent his last five years in England "in seclusion, but surrounded by every comfort that opulence could give" (Knapp). He was included in Massachusetts's 1778 Act of Banishment, and his abandoned possessions were auctioned. He died in London. Over thirty years before his death, an unnamed member of his "club of wits" had written a mock epitaph for him:

Siste Viator, here lies one,
Whose life was whim, whose soul was pun,
And if you go too near his hearse
He'll joke you, both in prose and verse.

Green remains of significance to American literary history as the author of several competent and amusing humorous and satirical poems, which illustrate one part of the poetic tastes of Boston's small literary class in the era before the American Revolution. His reputation as a "wit" suggests the value placed by that group on an attitude of critical and satirical detachment from important social and religious trends of the day.

• The best bibliographical and biographical guide to Green's scattered poems is the bibliography of Thomas V. Duggan, "Joseph Green—The Boston Butler" (master's thesis, Columbia Univ., 1941), which includes locations of both manuscripts and rare copies of printed sources. See also J. A. Leo Lemay, "Joseph Green's Satirical Poem on the Great Awakening," *Resources for American Literary Study* 4 (1974): 173–83. Poems that have been attributed to Green but deemed by Kenneth B. Murdock as "more or less dubiously ascribed to Green" (*DAB*, vol. 4, p. 553) are *A Mournful Lamentation for the Sad and Deplorable Death of Mr. Old Tenor* (1750) and *An Eclogue Sacred to the Memory of the Rev. Dr. Jonathan Mayhew* (1766). Samuel L. Knapp, *Biographical Sketches of Eminent Lawyers, Statesmen, and Men of Letters* (1821), provides a lively biographical portrait of Green. There is also information on him at various places in *The Memorial History of Boston*, ed. Justin Winsor (4 vols., 1882–1883). The most detailed biographical source is Duggan (cited above). Also useful is Kenneth B. Murdock's entry in the *Dictionary of American Biography*. On Green's literary place see Evert A. and George L. Duyckinck, *Cyclopedia of American Literature*, vol. 1 (1855), pp. 120–23; Moses Coit Tyler, *A History of American Literature, 1607–1765* (1878; repr. 1949), pp. 301–4; and the sketch by David Robinson in the *Dictionary of Literary Biography*, vol. 31: *American Colonial Writers, 1735–1781* (1984), pp. 99–100.

DAVID M. ROBINSON

GREEN, Leon (31 Mar. 1888–15 June 1979), legal theorist and educator, was born Abner Leon Green in Oakland, Louisiana, the son of William Morris Green, a businessman who made his living in agriculture-related pursuits, and Emily Frances McCormick. In 1908 he graduated from Ouachita College, a Baptist college in southern Arkansas. In December of the following year he married Notra Anderson; they had two children. He worked in various businesses in western Texas until he entered law school at the University of Texas at Austin in 1911. By the time he earned his LL.B. in 1915 he had been a practicing member of the Texas bar for three years. After graduation he started his career as a law school teacher at the University of Texas, staying until 1918, when he joined a Dallas law firm. The following year he became a named partner at a Fort Worth law firm, where, as an experienced trial lawyer, he specialized in the booming field of oil and gas litigation.

Overworked and ill, Green resigned in 1920 and was soon invited to rejoin the faculty at the University of Texas School of Law, where he remained until 1926. This period marks the true beginning of his scholarly career. One of its highlights came in 1922, when he took the lead in founding the *Texas Law Review*.

In 1926 Green accepted a visiting professorship at Yale Law School and the deanship at the University of North Carolina Law School. He spent his first year as dean away at Yale, where, it turned out, he remained until 1929, becoming a full professor in 1928. The collapse of North Carolina's state budget meant that he could not carry out his mandate, and so he was released from his contract. He left Yale to become dean at Northwestern University Law School, a position he held for eighteen years that would be the defining position of his academic career. In 1946 Attorney General Tom Clark offered him the job of solicitor general, but he turned it down. After stepping down as dean in 1947, Green spent the remainder of his career as distinguished professor of law at the University of Texas, teaching part-time until he retired in 1977.

Green made his academic mark in two areas, as a legal educator and as a tort law theorist. When he succeeded Dean John Wigmore, the renowned evidence scholar, at Northwestern, legal education in the United States was at a crossroads. Green spent his entire career as dean promoting higher standards and supporting the mission of law schools as a crucial part of the larger academy. At that time a formal legal education with uniform nationwide requirements, such as a three-year course of study preceded by a college degree, was not yet firmly established. Over the years he came up with multiple plans to improve the quality of legal education, plans that saw law school as a systematic and scientific process that would produce competent lawyers who understood the important role they had to play in the lives of the profession and the community. In enhancing Northwestern's considerable reputation, he hoped to mold a school that could compete with the elite eastern law schools and that would influence the direction of legal education in the United States.

Green's career centered on the theory, practice, and teaching of tort law, the area of law in which an action is brought to remedy a private or civil wrong or injury not covered by contract law. His first major contribution to tort theory, *Rationale of Proximate Cause*, appeared in 1927, and his second, *Judge and Jury*, in 1930. These two books, along with the casebooks on torts that he started publishing in 1931 and periodically updated and revised over the decades, established his reputation. They also resulted in his being linked to a collection of legal thinkers and reformers known as the "legal realists," who were prominent in the 1920s and 1930s, when the rise of the administrative state was becoming a legal and political reality.

In his first book, Green showed how the concept of legal or proximate cause had left legal liability in general and tort law in particular in disarray. Judges had fallen for the almost magical appeal of proximate cause, which assigns liability by identifying the act or event that produced the injury in question without which that injury would not have occurred. Green's goal was to strip the concept of extralegal meanings—metaphysical, theological, and moral—and to delimit its specific legal function. He hoped to clarify the process of adjudication for both judges and juries by using a functional analysis that described their respective responsibilities. In *Judge and Jury*, a collection of his most important articles that appeared after his first book was published, he expanded upon the argument of the earlier book by studying a greater variety of areas and concepts in tort law, shifting his emphasis from causal analysis to duty analysis.

Green wrote more than 120 articles for legal periodicals, a dozen book reviews, and a number of articles for Northwestern University information bulletins. He also compiled and edited numerous casebooks in tort law. The most influential of these was *The Judicial Process in Tort Cases* (1931), which went through three editions and provided the model for several other casebooks containing material relating to specialized aspects of tort law. Green brought his brand of legal analysis to the popular press in 1937, when he wrote two pieces for the *New Republic* that received much attention. The first was on President Franklin D. Roosevelt's controversial Court-packing plan, and the second was on the right of employees to use the weapon of the sit-down strike against their employers. In addition to his influential early books, he published *Traffic Victims: Tort Law and Insurance* (1958), which advocates replacing the failing system of liability insurance for traffic accidents with "compulsory comprehensive loss insurance," and *The Litigation Process in Tort Law* (1965; repr. 1977), which collects his most important articles that appeared after *Judge and Jury* and reprints "The Duty Problem in Negligence Cases" (1928; 1929), an important article that had appeared in the earlier volume.

Green was one of the leading tort theorists and legal educators during the 1920s and 1930s, and his contribution followed the path of the realists. Much of what they held, such as their attack on legal formalism or conceptualism, their commitment to social science research, and their recognition of the lawmaking function of the courts, became commonplace, even as their standing in the legal academy receded into the jurisprudential background. Green's powerful critique of the accepted understanding of legal cause earned him the respect of the academy but did not result in the disappearance of the concept. The functional approach to organizing casebooks in tort law that he developed produced champions and critics; subsequent generations of casebook editors would incorporate some of his ideas. He died in Austin, Texas.

• The Leon Green Papers are in the Tarlton Law Library, University of Texas School of Law, Austin. Northwestern University Archives, Evanston, Ill., has a biographical folder, and the Northwestern School of Law, Chicago, has materials relating to Green's tenure as dean. Green's life and thought have received significant scholarly attention. The *Il-*

linois Law Review 43 (1948): 1–22 was dedicated to Green, with articles by Charles McCormick, dean of the University of Texas School of Law and a longtime friend, on his theory of legal education (David W. Robertson and Robin Meyer edited and annotated a volume containing *The Correspondence between Leon Green and Charles McCormick, 1927–1962* [1988]); Charles O. Gregory on his contributions to tort law; and an appreciation by Thurman W. Arnold. A *festschrift* honoring Green on his ninetieth birthday was published by the *Texas Law Review* 56 (1978): 338–578. The issue includes his last published article, a bibliography of his writings, several personal appreciations by former students and colleagues, articles by leading tort scholars on topics indirectly relating to his work, and three articles on Green: James M. Treece, "Leon Green and the Judicial Process: Government of the People, by the People, and for the People"; Allen E. Smith, "Some Realism about a Grand Legal Realist: Leon Green"; and Robertson, "The Legal Philosophy of Leon Green." Robertson's article begins with a useful discussion of Green's background, career, and early intellectual development. For a fine account of the competing approaches to tort law and Green's role in those debates, see G. Edward White, *Tort Law in America: An Intellectual History* (1980). Brief obituaries of Green are in the *Texas Bar Journal* 42 (1979): 973 and the *New York Times*, 19 June 1979.

MARK MENDELL

GREEN, Nathan (c. 1784–1825), privateer captain, was a resident of Salem, Massachusetts. Almost nothing is known of his early years, and even his lineage has not been positively identified. It seems likely, though not certain, that his parents were John Green and Patty (full name unknown) of Salem and that he was baptized in Salem on 6 October 1797 at the age of thirteen. The obscurity of his upbringing does not disappear until his activities during the War of 1812, which was the only well-documented period of his life.

Green married Thankful Goodale in 1813. The couple had two daughters who died in infancy and a son who was born after Green's death. It seems very likely that Green was a merchant sailor or officer in Salem before his activities during the War of 1812. What is known for certain is that he received a commission as captain of the privateer *Grand Turk* (the third ship of that name) on 14 July 1814, and that on 6 August 1814 he led the ship out of Salem Harbor on its fourth privateer cruise during the War of 1812.

Green took the *Grand Turk* across the North Atlantic to a position about 100 miles west of the Scilly Isles, where he could intercept merchant ships bound for England. After being chased by a British sloop of war on 7 September 1814, Green headed his ship south to the Bay of Biscay and the coast of Portugal, where he encountered continued success in finding and capturing British merchant vessels. Ending a cruise that had lasted 103 days, Green brought the *Grand Turk* to Portsmouth, New Hampshire, on 17 November 1814. During the cruise, Green and his crew had captured eight ships, burned four others, and stopped twenty-three ships that turned out to be neutral vessels. Green had sailed with 150 men aboard his ship. At the time of his return he had only forty-four of his original crew on board; the rest had been assigned to prize vessels.

This fourth cruise of the *Grand Turk* was the most successful voyage made by any American privateer during the War of 1812. It was rivaled, in fact, only by the voyage of another ship from Salem, the *America*, captained by James W. Chever.

On 1 January 1815 Green took the *Grand Turk* out of Salem again. Unaware that the Treaty of Ghent had been signed on 24 December 1814, Green headed south to Brazil, where he soon took two prizes, one of which held about $17,500 in gold. On 10 March 1815 Green sighted a ship that turned out to be a British frigate. The *Grand Turk* fled from its foe, but the wind shifted, leaving both ships without headway. Between 10 and 12 March the *Grand Turk* used boats with sweeps to keep just out of range of two British frigates (a second had appeared soon after the first). By noon on 12 March the breeze had returned in enough strength that the *Grand Turk* could outdistance its pursuers. Green captured another merchant ship, the British *Acorn*, about a week later and learned of the signing of the Treaty of Ghent. Upon the receipt of this news, he turned for home and arrived in Salem on 28 April 1815, having captured three prizes during the fifth and last war cruise of the *Grand Turk*. In regard to Green's seamanship and skill, it can be said without exaggeration that his ship's escape from two British frigates over a period of two days was as remarkable as the escape of the USS *Constitution* from a British squadron in the summer of 1812.

Little is known of the rest of Green's life. The only documentary evidence indicates that he died from drowning in New York early in 1825 (*Salem Gazette*, 25 Feb. 1825).

Green's career as a privateer captain was notable for its conspicious success. Although he never became wealthy from his exploits (his share of the prizes from the fifth cruise came to about $4,000), Green exemplified the daring Yankee privateer skipper during the War of 1812, a conflict that did much to build a successful American naval tradition. It was fitting that men such as Green should have come from Salem and the other ports of maritime Massachusetts, the nursery ground for Yankee commercial enterprise and the American sailing tradition that came into full flower during the nineteenth century. Although British sources might still resent and resist the comparison, the activities of men such as Green and ships such as the *Grand Turk* resembled the stunning successes that the English sea dogs, such as John Hawkins, Francis Drake, and Martin Frobisher, had enjoyed against the Spanish galleons during the Elizabethan period. A little known and largely unsung hero of the heroic age of the Yankee privateers, Green deserves to be remembered and celebrated for his exploits.

• Amid a true paucity of sources regarding Green's life, Robert E. Peabody, *The Log of the "Grand Turk"* (1926), offers the only primary source, sections of Green's log. To ascertain his origins, the only source available is *Vital Statistics of Salem, Mass., to the Year 1850*, vol. 1 (1916), p. 388; vol. 3 (1924), p. 446; vol. 5 (1925), p. 299. Bits and pieces of information exist in Ralph D. Paine, *The Ships and Sailors of Old Salem* (1927), and Charles E. Trow, *The Old Shipmasters of Salem* (1905).

SAMUEL WILLARD CROMPTON

GREEN, Norvin (17 Apr. 1818–12 Feb. 1893), business leader, was born in New Albany, Indiana, the son of Joseph Green and Susan Ball, farmers. Green grew up in Breckenridge County, Kentucky, to which his parents moved soon after his birth. As a boy, he worked on his father's farm and attended the local schools. When his father's farm failed, he left home to make a living. At age sixteen, Green ran a grocery store from a flatboat that he floated down the Ohio and Mississippi Rivers, selling supplies to the lumbermen on the banks. Green also worked briefly as a lumberman himself.

Green's various business ventures provided him with enough money to pay his way through the Medical College of the University of Louisville, from which he graduated in 1840. In the same year, he married Martha English and began practicing medicine in Henry County, Kentucky. They had six children. Though Green would eventually give up medicine for telegraphy, he was known for the rest of his life as "Doctor" Green.

Green's involvement with telegraphy began in 1853, when he and several fellow Kentuckians established the New Orleans & Ohio Telegraph Lessees in order to help improve the financial standing of two telegraph firms—People's and the New Orleans & Ohio—that had fought a ferocious rate war that left both firms deeply in debt. Green had just completed two terms in the Kentucky legislature and may well have taken advantage of his political connections in arranging the deal.

Green quickly recognized the commercial potential of his investment and moved decisively to improve its equipment and expand the scale of its operations. The reorganized company soon began to turn a profit and to acquire a reputation as one of the best-run telegraph firms in the country. In 1860 it was formally incorporated as the Southwestern Telegraph Company, with Green as its first president. Green's experience with Southwestern helped to impress upon him the dangers of a rate war. Like most successful telegraph promoters, he had little faith in competition and recognized in consolidation a key to success. Toward this end, in 1857 he traveled to New York City with an early draft of an agreement, known as the "six-party contract" or the "Treaty of the Six Nations," that limited competition within the industry. This agreement led directly to the establishment of the "North American Telegraph Association," a cooperative agreement between the leading telegraph firms that laid the groundwork for the further consolidation of the industry following the Civil War.

During the Civil War, Green remained president of Southwestern. Though the firm survived the conflict, it was split into two operating units, one in the Union and one in the Confederacy; lost virtually all of its through traffic; and suffered a great deal of war-related damage. Following the war, Green once again turned his attention to the consolidation of the industry and in 1866 supported the merger of Southwestern into Western Union, which emerged as the first national corporate monopoly in the United States.

Green was offered the presidency of Western Union, but he refused it and accepted the vice presidency instead. Here he remained from 1866 until 1878, when he finally ascended to the presidency, a position he held from 1878 until his death. The most important challenge Green confronted during his presidency was the threatened takeover of the enterprise by Jay Gould in 1880. Green initially insisted on taking a hard line against Gould, but ultimately worked out a compromise that kept Green on as president while giving Gould a major voice in the decision-making process. Green also supported important improvements in telegraph technology, several reductions in telegraph rates, and the negotiation of noncompetitive agreements with various telephone promoters. In addition, he forcefully opposed the proposed nationalization of the industry. Why Green refrained from urging the takeover by Western Union of the nascent telephone industry is one question that historians have yet to satisfactorily resolve.

Green's opposition to the nationalization of the telegraph industry was consonant with his longstanding support for the Democratic party. "It is hoped," he wrote in 1883, "that the Government and people of this country have not entirely forgotten that sage maxim of President Jackson: 'That country is governed best which is governed least'" (Green, "The Government and the Telegraph," p. 434). To make his point, he wrote two influential essays for the *North American Review* that set out a rationale for keeping telegraphy under private control. In an age in which every other major telegraph industry in the world was a government monopoly, Green's defense of the industry as a private enterprise helped to give this controversial notion a measure of respectability. Green conceded that public control over the means of communication might be necessary in a monarchy but was dangerous in a republic, since it gave public figures too much control over public opinion. "The genius of our Government," Green wrote, "is that the people rule," making it "averse" to giving the administrative power "any such advantage in directing or controlling the popular will" (Green, "The Government and the Telegraph," p. 433). Green even defended the relatively high telegraph rates that prevailed in the United States, in comparison with those in Europe. These rates were necessary, Green declared, because the American telegraph industry, unlike its European counterparts, received no government subsidy. These low European rates, he speculated, had been instituted in order to "reconcile the people" to the "enormous engine of power and espionage" that the government possessed (Green, "Are Telegraph Rates Too High?" p. 574).

Green was for many years a prominent citizen of Louisville and represented the city in the Kentucky legislature between 1850 and 1853 and again in 1867. Shortly thereafter, he was seriously considered as a candidate for the U.S. Senate, losing out in a caucus on sectional grounds. He was also a member of the board of directors of several corporations, including Gold & Stock Telegraph, International Ocean and Telegraph, Southern Bell Telephone & Telegraph, and American Speaking Telephone. Between 1869 and 1873 he was president of the Louisville, Cincinnati, & Lexington Railway. Genial, gregarious, and well liked, Green was a capable business leader who helped to hasten the consolidation of the telegraph industry and to keep it under private control. He died in Louisville, though he spent much of the later years of his life in New York City.

• Green's business correspondence can be sampled at the Filson Club in Louisville, Kentucky, and the Western Union collection at the Smithsonian Institution, Washington, D.C. His personal papers are at the University of Kentucky (microform). Green testified before Congress on several occasions as Western Union's president; a number of his statements were issued as government documents. His two most important magazine articles are "The Government and the Telegraph," *North American Review* 137 (1883): 422–34, and "Are Telegraph Rates Too High?" *North American Review* 149 (1889): 569–79. On Green's role in the telegraph industry, see Robert Luther Thompson, *Wiring a Continent* (1947); James D. Reid, *The Telegraph in America* (1879); Lester G. Lindley, "Norvin Green and the Telegraph Consolidation Movement," *Filson Club History Quarterly* 48 (1974): 253–64; and Maury Klein, *The Life and Legend of Jay Gould* (1986). An obituary is in the *New York Times*, 13 Feb. 1893.

RICHARD R. JOHN

GREEN, Paul (17 Mar. 1894–4 May 1981), playwright and champion of human rights, was born Paul Eliot Green on his family's farm in Harnett County, North Carolina, the son of William A. Green and Bettie Lorine Byrd. The farm lay along the Cape Fear River, and cotton was the principal crop. The Greens also had tobacco acreage, raised hogs commercially, and grew corn for feed. Usually three or four black tenant families helped with the farm, and Paul's closest childhood friend was a tenant boy. When the boy died, Paul felt it like a death in the family but realized that his father looked on the death as merely the loss of useful farm labor. Awareness of this difference between himself and his father was an early step in the development of his identity.

Paul's mother taught music before her marriage and throughout life published poems in newspapers and church journals. When anyone of consequence visited the neighborhood, she invited the person for dinner and reminded her children that the visitor had started life with no more advantages than their own. To amount to anything, she told them, they must have ambition, education, and a large capacity for work.

Paul enrolled at the University of North Carolina in September 1916 but the next summer enlisted in the 105th Engineers. He took part in some of the ugliest trench fighting of the war and remained in Paris after the armistice as clerk in the U.S. Army Purchasing Office. He was discharged in June 1919. In Paris he studied French, explored museums, and kept up with the news as Allied leaders negotiated the Versailles treaty. The war had left him with a deep sense of waste and the conviction that Woodrow Wilson was right: a just and peaceful world order required a world government. Wilson remained a hero throughout Green's life. As he wrote during the months in Paris, Green felt "as if his ear were leaning to the heart of the world."

During his time in the army Green began writing poems. Back at the University of North Carolina in the fall of 1919, he majored in philosophy and turned to playwriting under the stimulation of Frederick Koch. Inspired by J. M. Synge, W. B. Yeats, and others of the Abbey Theatre group who were exploring the folklife of Ireland, Koch had founded the Carolina Playmakers to explore the folklife of North Carolina and the South. During Green's first year back at school, two of his plays were produced, and the experience of people in the subcultures of the region—tenant farmers and mill workers, Native Americans and blacks—remained at the heart of his concern throughout life.

Following graduation in the spring of 1921, Green stayed at the university for a year of playwriting and graduate work in philosophy. He married fellow student and playwright Elizabeth Lay in the summer of 1922, then went with her to Cornell for a second year of writing and study. The next summer the couple returned to Chapel Hill, where they lived the rest of their lives and raised four children. In the fall of 1923 Green joined the university's philosophy department. Although a conscientious teacher, he threw himself into his writing.

Green's play *In Abraham's Bosom* won the Pulitzer Prize in May 1927, which boosted his national reputation. He had already published two collections of plays, and the plays were being produced widely. In 1925 "The No 'Count Boy" had won the Belasco Prize in a national competition for the best one-act play of the year. Also in 1925 Green had become editor of *The Reviewer*, a lively literary magazine. His first number called for a new literature in the region, stressing the rich material for art in the South and the need for critical intelligence in dealing with it ("A Plain Statement about Southern Literature"). Through his plays and *The Reviewer* Green was already known to people interested in the arts, but *In Abraham's Bosom* brought his name to a larger public.

Green was an innovative playwright, and his earliest experiments had to do particularly with bringing authentic black experience into the drama. *Lonesome Road* (1926), one of his early collections of short plays, is subtitled *Six Plays for the Negro Theatre*. And *In Abraham's Bosom*, his first Broadway play, is the moving tragedy of a black man with Moses-like aspirations who fails to lead his people out of bondage because of their inertia, the racism of white society, and his personal flaws. The 1920s saw an awakening of the need to rid drama of stereotypical depictions of blacks. But among playwrights interested in black experience, Green was by far the best acquainted with the daily life of black people and thus best able to imagine the experience of a black person sympathetically.

In 1926, even before *In Abraham's Bosom* went into production, Green began work on a play that pioneered another kind of subject. *The House of Connelly* is among the early works of imaginative literature to forge that picture of the South later used in one version or another by William Faulkner, Lillian Hellman, Margaret Mitchell, and Tennessee Williams: a South whose aristocrats go back in memory to a time when social power and enlightened values coincide in their family but who in the present lack the will or character to act and therefore find themselves threatened with extinction. In 1931 *The House of Connelly* became the first production of the Group Theatre, which, until the advent of the Federal Theatre, was the most vital development in the American theater of the 1930s.

From the late 1930s on, much of Green's effort went into historical plays that he called symphonic dramas. Over the next forty-odd years, sixteen of these plays were produced, mainly in the South. For several summers, seven or eight of them ran simultaneously, and five were still running a decade after his death. The plays have affinities with early Greek drama and the mystery plays of medieval England. Like those works, they are designed for production outdoors before large audiences, and they dramatize themes central to their culture. *The Lost Colony* (1937), earliest of the outdoor plays, shows the origin of a democratic society founded on the principles of equality of condition and individual social responsibility.

The symphonic dramas were experimental in technique rather than subject matter. Always restive under the constraints of verisimilitude, Green in the early thirties began to explore ways of opening up the drama to all the presentational arts. *Roll, Sweet Chariot* (1935) has characters projecting thoughts over a speaker system and group movement choreographed with dancelike precision. *Johnny Johnson* (1936), a poignant antiwar musical written with Kurt Weill, has a full complement of songs, one of them performed by a battery of cannons. But it is the outdoor plays that gave his imagination full scope. He called them "symphonic" from the Greek root meaning "sound together," and it was the presentational arts he had in mind. The plays are filled with music, dance, special lighting—all "sounding together" with the action and dialogue of the plot.

The concerns of Green's plays were his social concerns as well. In the 1920s his racial views were, to say the least, uncommon. He was among the few white southerners who could envision integration. From the 1920s onward, he put time, energy, and money into the job of securing basic human rights for blacks and Native Americans, particularly fair treatment in courts of law and access to jobs and education. His efforts on behalf of the poor and uneducated in prison led him to advocate abolition of chain-gangs and capital punishment. At the university, where science and research attracted more and more attention, he was a force for the arts and humanities and for the importance of teaching. And he was a fierce opponent of the gag laws and loyalty oaths inflicted on the university in the aftermath of the McCarthy era. From the 1950s on, he became increasingly active in opposition to the cold war between the United States and the Soviet Union and the resultant arms race, and he was among the early opponents of American involvement in Vietnam.

Green dealt with problems at all levels. While he helped raise money to support a handful of Lumbee Indian children denied access to the high school in their county, he also served as a presidential appointee to the U.S. National Commission for UNESCO. Social issues inspired several of his imaginative works. *Cabin in the Cotton* (1932), his first motion picture, grew out of his concern for tenant farmers. "Hymn to the Rising Sun" (1936), a short but powerful play, came about as part of his campaign to abolish the chain-gang system. And *Wilderness Road* (1955), a symphonic drama, was in part an attempt to prepare the South to accept school integration. A need to deepen understanding between the races moved him to dramatize Richard Wright's *Native Son* (produced 1941) and to write the film script of John Howard Griffin's *Black Like Me* (1963).

Green died at his home near Chapel Hill. He had come into prominence in the 1920s just as the South was emerging from Reconstruction and North Carolina was acquiring a reputation as the most progressive of southern states. His life is a reason for the changes. A member of the generation that launched the Southern Literary Renaissance and the first playwright from the South to attract national and international attention, he also played a part in the broader social developments now associated with the emergence of the New South during the first half of the twentieth century.

• Green's work is unusually varied and includes two published volumes of poetry, five collections of essays, five collections of short stories, two novels, two books on folklore, twelve film scripts (sole or major responsibility), seventeen plays or collections of plays, sixteen symphonic dramas, and four songbooks from the symphonic dramas. In addition, many of his plays were published individually.

Letters from Green are in the collections of recipients in several libraries (for instance, the Barrett Clark and Richard Wright collections in the Beinecke Library at Yale), but the major repository of his papers is the Southern Historical Collection, University of North Carolina at Chapel Hill. That collection includes Green's personal papers (drafts and copies of his own letters plus letters to him from the 1920s on, and his diaries) along with drafts of many of his imaginative and expository works. Selections from his correspondence are published in *A Southern Life: Letters of Paul Green, 1916–1981*, edited by Laurence G. Avery (1994).

Biographical accounts include Barrett Clark, *Paul Green* (1928); Agatha Boyd Adams, *Paul Green of Chapel Hill* (1951); Elizabeth Lay Green, *The Paul Green I Know* (1978); and Frances W. Saunders, "A New Playwright of Tragic

Power and Poetic Impulse: Paul Eliot Green at UNC–Chapel Hill in the 1920s," *North Carolina Historical Review* 72, no. 3 (July 1995). Substantial discussions of his life and work are given in Myron Matlaw, *Modern World Drama: An Encyclopedia* (1972), and Joseph M. Flora and Robert Bain, eds., *Fifty Southern Writers after 1900* (1987).

LAURENCE G. AVERY

GREEN, Samuel (1615–1 Jan. 1702), printer, emigrated to Massachusetts from England in 1633 at the age of eighteen. His birthplace is not known, but his parents, Bartholomew Green and Elizabeth (maiden name unknown), were followers of the Reverend Thomas Hooker, who founded the first church in Cambridge, Massachusetts. Green's father died in Cambridge in 1635. Also in 1635, at the age of twenty, Green became a freeman of Massachusetts and was soon granted various official positions, from doorkeeper to the House of Deputies (the lower house of the legislature) to clerk of Harvard College.

Green became the manager of the first printing press in British North America as a result of the Harvard connection. The Reverend Jose Glover was bringing the press to Massachusetts in 1638 when he died on the voyage. His widow married Henry Dunster, the president of Harvard College, who put the press in the charge of Stephen Daye. Daye's son Matthew, who had some training in printing, actually operated the press. When Matthew Daye died in 1649, Dunster turned over the press to Green to run. When President Dunster resigned in 1654, he sold the press to the college. Green continued to run it for a total of fifty-four years.

Green never pretended to be a working printer—his main interests were serving in the militia and adding to his landholdings—but under his management the press issued just over 200 separate imprints. Green was the only printer of record in the British colonies until 1660, when Marmaduke Johnson, a skilled London printer, was brought in to print John Eliot's great *Indian Bible*. The press, which was subject to tight oversight by a committee nominated by the legislature, printed official documents only—ranging from summaries of the laws in operation, to almanacs based on the longitude of Boston, to the official psalm book, to Harvard College documents. The press would not have been kept in constant use had there not been a very specialized outside project funded directly from England that kept it busy for years. In 1649 Edward Winslow was sent to England by the colonists to ask for aid from the Puritan government then in power in the mother country. Winslow had considerable success raising money from pious English men and women who were interested in converting the Native Americans to Christianity. Being People of the Book themselves, the English Puritans were convinced that the American Indians would respond favorably to catechisms, primers, tracts, and above all, a Bible in their own language. Winslow could demonstrate that by this time John Eliot, minister of the church in Roxbury, had gained considerable mastery of the local language, Massachusett. On 27 July 1649 the Parliament voted an Act for the Promoting and Propagating the Gospel of Jesus Christ in New England, which set up a charitable corporation. Green was the designated printer for the Indian material.

In 1655 the commissioners of the United Colonies sent to England printed copies of the books of Genesis and Matthew as samples of what was intended for the Indian Bible, and a steady series of tracts on the subject of conversion followed. By 1659 the corporation in England had decided to finance the printing of the whole Bible. They agreed to pay not only for the services of a master printer for three years but for a whole new press and new specialized type. Johnson arrived in the summer of 1660.

Green and Johnson completed printing 1,500 copies of the whole Bible with the metrical psalms by late 1663. They kept on printing in an uneasy alliance in Cambridge until 1674. Because there was seldom enough local business to keep both printers busy, they cast around for English titles to reprint. In 1668 Green printed a devotional book, *A Drop of Honey*; two tracts, *Rule of the New Creature* and *The Way to a Blessed Estate in the Life*; the *Westminster Catechism*; a narration of the plague and fire in London; an anti-Catholic work, *Tidings from Rome*; and *The Young Man's Monitor*. He had a license to print for all of these from the president of Harvard College and Jonathan Mitchell, the pastor of Cambridge. Johnson was not happy with the restrictions put on his printing by the censors in Cambridge: beginning in 1668 he petitioned the authorities to let him move his press to Boston. The government finally granted his request in 1674. Ironically, Johnson suddenly died a few months later.

Green undoubtedly hoped that he might have his monopoly back, but instead Johnson's type and press went to John Foster, a young Harvard graduate without formal training in printing but with the support of John Eliot. When Foster died in 1681 Green's son, Samuel Green, Jr., who had set up a press in New London, Connecticut, was called to run the Boston press under the management of Samuel Sewall. Meanwhile Green, who had finally managed to secure the specialized type needed to print material in the Massachusett language, brought out a new edition of the *Indian Bible*. Green had the help of his second son, Bartholomew, who helped him print the few college items and almanacs that came his way. When Samuel Green, Jr., died unexpectedly in July 1690, Bartholomew Green went to Boston to work in the shop with the newer equipment. When the shop was destroyed by fire a few months later, he returned to Cambridge and set up the moribund press for its last few runs. The last item printed was Cotton Mather's *Ornaments for the Daughters of Zion* in 1692. Bartholomew then moved back to Boston, and the Cambridge press was abandoned.

Green was married twice. His first wife, Jane Bainbridge, whom he married sometime before 1640, died in 1657. They had seven children, including Samuel

Green, Jr. He then married Sarah Clark in 1663. They had at least eight children, including Bartholomew, who had a long and distinguished career as a printer in Boston after the Cambridge press was shut down. A third son, Timothy, was a printer in New London, Connecticut. Green's direct descendants can be traced as printers until 1845. He died in Cambridge.

Green was the only printer in the British colonies for much of the seventeenth century. He was content to practice his art under close government supervision. An honest workman, he made sure that New England's message was presented to the wider world in a clear and legible form.

• The fullest account of Green's career is George Parker Winship, *The Cambridge Press, 1638–1692* (1945). The Green family of printers is traced by William C. Kiessel in the *New England Historical and Genealogical Register* 104 (Apr. 1950): 81–93. All of Green's surviving impressions are available in microprint in *Early American Imprints: First Series (Evans), 1639–1800* (1955–1969), accessible through Clifford K. Shipton and James E. Mooney, eds., *National Index of American Imprints through 1800: The Short-Title Evans* (1969). See also Isaiah Thomas, *The History of Printing in America, with a Biography of Printers & an Account of Newspapers*, ed. Marcus A. McCorison from the 2d ed. (1970); and Hugh Amory, *First Impressions: Printing in Cambridge, 1639–1989* (1989), an exhibition at the Houghton Library and at the Harvard Law School Library, 6–27 Oct. 1989.

MARY RHINELANDER MCCARL

GREEN, Samuel Swett (20 Feb. 1837–8 Dec. 1918), librarian, was born in Worcester, Massachusetts, the son of James Green, a successful apothecary, and Elizabeth Swett. In delicate health for much of his early life, Green was reportedly quiet and rather shy, inclined more to studious concerns than to playing outdoors with neighborhood companions. He enrolled, nevertheless, in Mrs. Sarah B. Wood's private school and then attended public grammar school and graduated from the Worcester High School in 1854. Green excelled in mathematics and was fond of grammar. He attended, as did his older brothers, Harvard College, where his classmates included Winslow Warren, a lawyer and U.S. commissioner; Henry P. Walcott, a physician and public health administrator; and George A. Wentworth, a teacher of mathematics noted for his textbooks, which set a national standard for excellence. Despite his "bad general health and worse eyesight," Green graduated from Harvard in 1858 with a B.A. Although he did travel to Smyrna and Constantinople (now Istanbul), for the next three years Green stayed at home languishing as an invalid. Revived, he continued his studies in the Harvard Divinity School, starting in the autumn of 1860. He dropped out shortly thereafter as a result of poor health, but graduated in 1864. Ironically, Green was not rejected for the Civil War draft on the grounds of his ill health, but because of his short stature; he was only five feet, two inches tall.

Thinking his divinity work "unsalable," Green worked in banking, first as bookkeeper at Worcester's Mechanics National Bank and then as a teller. He resigned when he became afflicted with rheumatic fever and traveled in the West to recover. In 1870 Harvard awarded him an M.A. and later elected him an honorary Phi Beta Kappa member.

Beginning in January 1867, Green served as a director of the Worcester Free Public Library, which had been funded by his uncle, John Green, a Worcester physician. In January 1871 Green became the librarian of this institution. During his tenure, the library became noted for its pioneering public-service orientation toward its readers, especially its personal assistance to school children and factory workers. The library also was noted for its opening on Sundays starting in December 1872. Green established a lending collection of artwork (especially pictures and photographs); instituted interlibrary loans; and advocated use of the telephone in libraries as early as 1880. Today, though, Green is probably best known to librarians for the paper he delivered at the October 1876 Conference of Librarians in Philadelphia, "The Desirableness of Establishing Personal Intercourse and Relations between Librarians and Readers." His presentation forms the basis of modern library reference service and argues that librarians must acknowledge the presence of library users and interact with them by answering their questions. Green was a founder of the American Library Association in 1876 and served as its vice president twice and as its president in 1891; starting in 1892, he served on the original council of the association. Green wrote the well-received *Public Library Movement in the United States, 1853–1893* (1913) and taught at the School of Library Economy at Columbia University and the State Library of New York.

Considered a devoted son, Green never married, caring for his mother until her death at age ninety-three. After his death in Worcester, Green was remembered for his sympathy, geniality, versatility, patience, tact, energy, and wisdom in discharging his duties, for as he had said of himself, "There are few pleasures comparable to that of associating continually with curious and vigorous young minds, and of aiding them to realize their ideals." His service ideals continue to influence modern library service.

• Few of Green's papers are extant at the Worcester Free Public Library in Mass. The standard assessment of his life and contributions is Robert K. Shaw, *Samuel Swett Green*, American Library Pioneers, no. 2 (1926), which is now dated. See also Z. W. Coombs, *Samuel Swett Green, Worcester Free Public Library, Worcester, Mass.: Director, 1867–1971, Librarian, 1871–1909* (1909).

JOHN V. RICHARDSON JR.

GREEN, Theodore Francis (2 Oct. 1867–19 May 1966), governor and U.S. senator, was born in Providence, Rhode Island, the son of Arnold Green, a lawyer, and Cornelia Abby Burges. The eldest child in an aristocratic and wealthy family, he descended from colonists who arrived in Rhode Island with Roger Williams in 1636. Green graduated from Providence High

School in 1883 and Brown University in 1887, receiving an M.A. from Brown in 1888. He attended Harvard Law School from 1888 to 1890 and studied at the Universities of Bonn and Berlin from 1890 to 1892.

A lifelong bachelor, Green devoted himself to the law, politics, and civic, business, and cultural activities. Admitted to the Rhode Island bar in 1892, he long practiced law, taking time during the Spanish-American War to serve as a first lieutenant in the infantry. He served as president of J. P. Coats Company from 1912 to 1923 and Morris Plan Banker's Association from 1900 to 1929.

Green began his long career in public life in 1907 as a member of the Rhode Island House of Representatives, displaying early a zeal to reform state politics and government, which he considered ethnically divided and antiquated. Active in Democratic party politics as chairman of state committees and a delegate to the party's national conventions, he was an unsuccessful candidate for governor (1912, 1928, 1930) and a member of Congress (1920). Party loyalty, perseverance, and a depressed economy brought him the governorship in 1932.

As governor he directed his energies to welfare and unemployment relief, forging a relief bill three weeks before the New Deal began. During his two terms as governor (1933–1937), he made the Democratic party dominant in a traditionally Republican state, enlarged the importance of the governor's office, reorganized state government, won control of federal patronage, and cooperated with the New Deal to strive for economic recovery. He ended a violent textile strike by calling out the National Guard without losing organized labor's support.

In the Democratic party landslide of 1936, Green was elected U.S. senator, an office he held until 1960. Described as "the president's man," he was loyal to the Democratic presidents with whom he served and, to a larger extent than many other northern Democrats, to the Republican president Dwight D. Eisenhower. Green consistently displayed his faith in social measures, democracy, a strong national defense, and international cooperation.

Green vigorously supported domestic New Deal measures, including President Franklin D. Roosevelt's controversial Supreme Court retirement bill, braving the wrath of his constituents. He voted for the wages and hours and low-cost housing bills in 1937, and advocating farm and work relief, he sustained continuing appropriations for New Deal relief measures.

In view of the deteriorating international scene, Green advocated expansion of navy and army forces, revision of the neutrality laws despite isolationist opposition, and passage of the Lend-Lease Bill, which in one of his many radio talks he called "Aid to America." At times Green in his zeal outran both his constituents and the president, but vindicated by Pearl Harbor, he won reelection in 1942.

During World War II Green vigorously objected to a proposal to exempt farm workers from the draft as a means to increase agricultural production and secured passage of a law releasing government-owned silver for war purposes. He supported a law providing for absentee voting for servicepeople stationed in the United States and headed a Senate committee investigating violation of the Hatch Act that reported in favor of repealing the law.

Throughout his senatorial career Green supported civil rights legislation. He struggled to enact laws to ban the poll tax, to make lynching a federal crime, and to change Senate rules to make it easier to end filibusters. Consistently working closely with Majority Leader Lyndon B. Johnson, he helped secure eastern liberal support for the Civil Rights Law of 1957. As the nation moved to the right at midcentury, Green retained his liberal faith, voting to uphold President Harry Truman's vetoes of the restrictive McCarran-Walter Immigration Bill of 1952 and the McCarran Internal Security Act of 1950. During the McCarthy controversy, he voted for censure of his Republican colleague Senator Joseph R. McCarthy.

For twenty of his twenty-four years in the Senate, Green served on the Foreign Relations Committee, beginning in 1938 and interrupted from 1947 to 1949. An early and steadfast internationalist committed to the United Nations, he stoutly sustained President Truman's bold initiatives, including the Truman Doctrine, the Marshall Plan, the North Atlantic Treaty Organization, and intervention in Korea. At the 1952 meeting of the UN General Assembly, to which Truman appointed him as a delegate, Green expressed his faith in the world organization as the "last great hope of mankind." He stood with the minority of thirty-one senators who by one vote prevented the two-thirds majority necessary to pass an amendment initiated by Senator John W. Bricker to limit the president's powers in foreign policy.

Though wary of reductions in foreign aid programs with the coming of the Eisenhower administration, Green was one of the few northern Democrats to support administration measures in the Republican-dominated Senate of the Eighty-third Congress. At the age of eighty-nine he became chairman of the Foreign Relations Committee and, by his energy and meticulous attention to detail, quickly dispelled doubts about his capacity to discharge his duties. Over the years he had traveled widely, gaining an extensive knowledge of the world. As chairman he gave strong support to the Eisenhower Doctrine, authorizing the president to aid Middle Eastern nations resisting communism. When rebellion broke out in Lebanon in 1958, he supported Eisenhower's military intervention, because the president had first referred the matter to the United Nations.

Green differed with the president in 1958, when he thought Eisenhower intended to stretch a congressional authorization to defend Formosa to justify intervention two hundred miles away on the islands of Quemoy and Ma-tsu. When Communist China appeared to menace the islands, Eisenhower announced that he believed the Formosa resolution authorized him to act. Deeply concerned, Green wrote to Eisenhower that the executive should not take any military action unless it involved the security of Formosa. Eisenhower responded that he would not involve the United States "in military hostilities merely in defense of Quemoy and Matsu." Their correspondence was made public, and Green, without polling his committee, seemed to have restrained administration policy. From this time forward he was critical of Eisenhower's foreign policy.

In his ninety-second year, with his health failing, Green resigned his chairmanship. Three years before he retired from the Senate in 1960, he became the oldest man to that time to serve in Congress. He left behind a reputation as a stalwart party loyalist, an internationalist, a liberal in social and economic policy, a scholar, a dandy, and a favorite at Washington cocktail parties. He died in Providence.

• The Library of Congress holds Green's papers; principally on his Senate years, they number about 350,000. The John Hay Library at Brown University holds Green's miscellaneous writings. The *Congressional Record* contains his votes and speeches. Erwin L. Levine, *Theodore Francis Green* (2 vols., 1963; repr. 1971), is a fine study, essentially political and unrevealing of his personality. Obituaries are in the *New York Times*, 20 May 1966, and *Time*, 27 May 1966.

JAMES A. RAWLEY

GREEN, William (3 Mar. 1870–21 Nov. 1952), American Federation of Labor president, was born in Coshocton, Ohio, the son of Hugh Green, a coal miner, and Jane Oram. Green's father had come to the United States two years earlier, bringing with him a heritage of trade unionism and an unshakable Baptist faith, both of which he imparted to his son. Green was born in a miner's shack in the "Hardscrabble Hill" section of town. He was an energetic and precocious child, excelling at school and developing an appetite for reading. In a rare achievement for a miner's son at the time, he completed the eighth grade before his labor was needed to supplement the family income. An intensely religious youth, Green aspired to the Baptist ministry, but his family could not afford the training for such a career. Later, as a local union official, Green would conduct Sunday school classes, and as AFL president he welcomed opportunities to address church and religious organizations.

At fourteen, Green went to work as a water boy for railroad laborers. Two years later, he became his father's helper in the mines, and within a few years he was a skilled pick miner. Although he continued to entertain hopes of pursuing the ministry, he finally abandoned this dream in 1892 when he married Jennie Mobley, the daughter of a local miner. In time he fathered six children, and he remained in the mines for nineteen years.

Green followed his father into the local chapter of the Progressive Miners' Union in 1886. His education served him well, for he was one of the few men in his local who could read and write. In 1891, one year after the Progressive Miners' Union merged with the Knights of Labor District 35 to form the United Mine Workers of America, Green was elected secretary of his local. He threw himself wholeheartedly into union work and served his local as committee member, secretary, business agent, vice president, and ultimately as president. The union movement became the calling he had once sought in the ministry. Green's devotion to the union, along with his energy and administrative talent, led to steady advancement. He was elected subdistrict president in 1900 and president of the entire Ohio district in 1906. In 1909 he ran unsuccessfully for the UMWA presidency against the incumbent Tom Lewis, and a year later he failed to win the post of secretary-treasurer. Having lost two elections in two years, Green's future as a union official seemed unpromising. Counting on his popularity among local miners, however, he decided to seek a seat in Ohio's state senate as a Democrat in a largely Democratic district. He captured the nomination and easily won the election. In 1912 he was reelected and served as the Democratic floor leader. Green proved himself to be an adept Progressive politician, preparing and securing passage of the 1911 Workmen's Compensation Act, a law that established a maximum nine-hour workday for women, and a 1 percent income tax measure. Just when Green's political career seemed most promising, however, he returned to full-time work as a labor official.

In 1911 UMWA president John P. White, who considered Green "one of the finest young men in the Organization," appointed him union statistician. He served so dutifully between senate sessions that in August 1913 miners elected him UMWA secretary-treasurer, a post he would hold until 1924. Green was an unusually active secretary-treasurer, a champion of White's administration, and a frequent contributor to the union's journal. He remained secretary-treasurer during the presidency of the alcoholic Frank Hayes and the early years of John L. Lewis, who succeeded Hayes as president in 1919.

Meanwhile, in 1913, the death of an AFL vice president created a vacancy on the executive council, and AFL president Samuel Gompers offered the post to White because the powerful miners' union was unrepresented. When White scorned the position of seventh vice president as beneath his dignity, Gompers, still eager for a UMWA representative, offered the post to Green, who proudly accepted. As an executive council member, Green was a persistent critic of traditional AFL policy. As a first point of opposition, he was the highest-ranking advocate of industrial unionism in the craft-dominated AFL. In 1912 and again during World War I, he introduced resolutions to AFL conventions calling for the restructuring of the labor movement from its present craft orientation, in which unions organized only the skilled workers in a given trade, to an industrial orientation, in which unions offered membership to everyone within an industry. Green correctly perceived that industrial unionism was the only structure capable of organizing the millions of unskilled workers in mass-production industries. As a second point, Green rejected the AFL's opposition to labor legislation on behalf of working people, favoring national health insurance and an eight-hour-day law. The AFL's stance was based on the philosophy of voluntarism, which rejected any role for the state in establishing either the boundaries or the specific conditions of industrial relations. Unlike other AFL leaders, Green realized that political action was a viable means of advancing worker interests.

The death of AFL president Gompers in December 1924 was a severe blow to the organization. When none of the most powerful candidates to succeed Gompers could command a majority, John L. Lewis offered Green as the compromise candidate. This proved an easy task, for although Green had been a critic of AFL policy, he had always upheld majority rule, was well-liked by executive council members, and was not prone to aggrandize power. The new AFL president bore few signs of his struggles in the coal mines. Slight of stature and portly, wearing conservative suits and a gold watch chain, Green looked more like a minister or banker than a labor leader. In public he exuded sincerity and respectability. Labor reporters, accustomed to more charismatic union leaders, often ridiculed him as bland and boring.

The AFL presidency was a prestigious office but not a powerful one. Green's principal duties were presiding over executive council sessions and annual AFL conventions, lobbying on Capitol Hill, settling squabbles between affiliates, and publicizing the AFL's program. Throughout the twenty-eight years of his presidency, Green never questioned this role. On entering office, Green pledged to follow Gompers's precedent and leave the formation of strategy in the hands of the council. He did not consider it his duty or privilege to initiate policy, only to carry it out. In his first years in office he devoted most of his energies to publicizing the benefits of unionism. He directed the federation's massive but ineffective marketing campaign in the 1920s to "sell" unionism to industry and the public. Audiences responded favorably to Green's moralistic addresses in which he declared that the interests of labor and management were identical and that cooperation and morality had replaced conflict and self-interest in industrial relations, but the campaign netted few new union contracts.

The Great Depression clearly proved that AFL policies had failed. In response to poor economic conditions, extensive wage cuts and layoffs revealed that self-interest, not morality, determined corporate policy. As the economic crisis deepened, Green continued to preach cooperation. By 1932, his patience exhausted, he began predicting imminent class warfare and social revolution. He even made veiled threats about the need for a general strike and a labor party. The 1932 AFL convention witnessed perhaps the greatest fighting speech of his career. An exasperated Green declared that labor's patience with industrial management was at an end and that labor would not hesitate to use "forceful methods" to bring about full employment.

But militancy never suited him. As AFL membership rolls and wage rates plummeted, the rank and file grew increasingly discontented with federation inactivity, particularly its aversion to legislation. Discontent became powerful enough in 1932 to force the AFL to reverse its long-standing opposition to legislation and publicly endorse federal unemployment insurance and legislation for shorter hours. As the mouthpiece of the conservative executive council, Green had resisted this change in policy. But once the rank and file forced the issue, he happily assumed his chores as leading lobbyist for organized labor. His efforts had a part in shaping and passing many New Deal reforms, including the National Industrial Recovery Act (1933), the National Labor Relations Act (1935), the Social Security Act (1935), and the Fair Labor Standards Act (1938).

The promise of Section 7a of the National Industrial Recovery Act, which granted workers the right to organize, coupled with the despair born of years of depression, fostered a widespread and militant demand for unionism among unorganized workers across the country. But very few workers demanding unions joined and remained in the AFL. One reason for the ultimate failure of the AFL's organizing drives of 1933 through 1935 was Green's commitment to labor peace. Throughout his career, he was a conservative accommodationist; he sought the traditional goals of trade unions—higher wages, shorter hours, and better working conditions—not through strikes or work stoppages, but through appeals made to employers based on the economic benefits of unions, moral suasion, and negotiation. His opposition to strikes proved so discouraging to workers that most of those who joined the AFL in 1933 and 1934 departed by 1935.

The AFL's organizing failures encouraged a growing polarization of views within the federation between conservative craft union leaders, who dominated the executive council, and more militant industrial union advocates. The second group, led by John L. Lewis, pushed for aggressive campaigns to organize mass-production workers on an industrywide basis. Green personally continued to believe in industrial unionism, but he did not crusade for industrial unionism as AFL president, for he believed his principal duty was to maintain peace and unity within the labor movement. The defeat of Lewis's resolutions at the 1935 AFL convention and the subsequent rise of the Committee for Industrial Organization (in 1938 to become the Congress of Industrial Organizations) shaped the remainder of Green's career as a labor official. Green voted with the executive council majority in 1936 to suspend the CIO unions and in 1938 to expel them. For the rest of his life his energies would be consumed by a moralistic crusade against the rebel movement. The overriding factor behind his vindictive crusade against the CIO was his opposition to worker militancy. He considered the CIO's approach barbaric, futile, and immoral. He referred to the sit-down strike as "sabotage beyond the wildest dreams of the I.W.W.," and he remained unwilling to admit that such tactics could ever be successful. He even claimed the contracts that CIO unions signed with General Motors and U.S. Steel were failures for organized labor. Although he called for and attended numerous peace conferences with the CIO, the two labor federations remained divided until after his death.

The competition between the AFL and CIO coincided with the decline of Green's power and influence within the federation. In 1939 the executive council named George Meany secretary-treasurer of the AFL, and he immediately began to assume many of Green's administrative duties. In his declining years Green served largely as a figurehead, devoting much of his energy to publicizing the virtues of the AFL. In the 1940s he steadfastly held to the view that his office did not possess the authority to impose its will on affiliated unions. Thus, when criticism mounted over racketeering and corruption within unions, he claimed to be powerless to influence individual unions. He used the same argument when the federation was criticized for its failure to organize black workers and female workers.

After passage of the Taft-Hartley Act in 1947, Green began a campaign for its repeal. He branded those who voted for the act as immoral, but he failed to adequately mobilize the federation's political resources. Labor's League for Political Education, which Green established in 1947, adhered to Gompers's nonpartisan policy, and in 1948 Green and the AFL balked at an official endorsement of President Harry S. Truman. Only in 1952, when faced with the probable election of the Republican Dwight D. Eisenhower, did the federation endorse a candidate, Adlai Stevenson. This break with tradition reflected the growing influence of a new generation of AFL officials who sought greater political activism and unity with the CIO. Green died at Coshocton, Ohio.

Historians invariably depict Green as an impotent labor leader. His unwillingness to challenge conservatives on the executive council stymied the development of industrial unionism in the AFL and contributed to the split in organized labor in the 1930s. His inflexible opposition to labor militancy in the 1920s and 1930s contributed to the AFL's failure to meet the needs of millions of unskilled workers in mass-production industries. Under his leadership, the federation remained a weak and conservative organization of mostly skilled workers.

• Green's personal correspondence is on microfilm at the Ohio Historical Society, Columbus; most of his official correspondence as AFL president may be found at the George Meany Memorial Archives, Silver Spring, Md.; other important correspondence is located at the Wisconsin State Historical Society, Madison. Green's attitudes also are expressed in his editorials and articles in the *American Federationist*, his speeches and reports in the AFL's convention proceedings, and his book, *Labor and Democracy* (1939). Craig Phelan has written a full-length scholarly biography, *William Green: Biography of a Labor Leader* (1989). The same author has also written a critical essay, "William Green and the Limits of Christian Idealism," in Melvyn Dubofsky and Warren Van Tine, eds., *Labor Leaders in America* (1987). See also Charles A. Madison, "Coaldigger from Coshocton," in his *American*

Labor Leaders (1962), and Benjamin Stolberg, "Sitting Bill," *Saturday Evening Post*, 18 Oct. 1941. For the AFL drives in mass-production industries in the 1920s and 1930s and the rise of the CIO, see Irving Bernstein, *The Lean Years* (1960) and *The Turbulent Years* (1970). Philip Taft, *The A.F. of L. from the Death of Gompers to the Merger* (1959), is a valuable source on Green's role. A landmark study of the schism in the AFL is David Brody's "The Emergence of Mass Production Unionism," in John Braeman et al., eds., *Change and Continuity in Twentieth Century America* (1964). Melvyn Dubofsky and Warren Van Tine's *John L. Lewis: A Biography* (1977) provides the most exhaustive and sophisticated treatment of the emergence of the CIO.

CRAIG PHELAN

GREEN, William Thomas (May 1860?–3 Dec. 1911), attorney, was born in Canada, probably in St. Catharines, Ontario. His parentage is uncertain, but it appears that he was born into the family of Thomas and Mary Green, two African Americans who had migrated to Canada. His father was a laborer; neither parent was literate.

Green's early schooling is undocumented. He may have attended St. Catharines Collegiate Institute, but no records substantiate that. In 1884 he moved to the United States, probably to Chicago; no records support his claim that he became a naturalized citizen. Three years later he settled in Milwaukee, Wisconsin. Employed as a waiter in the prestigious Plankinton House, he was at home in the upper circles of Milwaukee's black society. While at Plankinton House Green probably benefited from the schooling that the African-American head of dining services, John J. Miles, established for members of his all-black crew.

Moving to Madison in 1890, Green received a patronage appointment as a janitor in the state capitol. He became known to politicians, one of whom, James H. McGillian, influenced him to apply to the University of Wisconsin Law School. Green received his law degree in 1892 and, returning to Milwaukee, joined James H. Stover, also a new attorney, for a year before establishing his own practice. Green was the first and, during his lifetime, the only black attorney in Wisconsin.

Green's rise to prominence was acknowledged by his leadership role in framing and lobbying for the state's first civil rights act. When a Milwaukee black, refused admission to the orchestra of a theater in 1889, took the theater owner to court, the suit galvanized the city's black community. Following a call signed by Green, among others, a meeting was held during which a substantial list of grievances was compiled and those in attendance asked the governor to recommend a civil rights law. The meeting also endorsed *New York Age* editor T. Thomas Fortune's idea of a national convention to support black commercial and political interests and urged that civil rights become the yardstick for race support of political parties.

Milwaukee's black leaders produced a civil rights bill a month later, but it was not introduced until 1891, at which time Green, the probable author of the bill, was the only African American to testify before the assembly judiciary committee. Although he made a favorable impression, it was not sufficient to overcome the opposition, and the bill died. Back in Milwaukee the next year, Green was elected to the state Republican convention, the first African American to be so recognized. His major contribution was a platform amendment denouncing the treatment of blacks by southern whites, a ploy for which the black press chided him but which was a strategically sound maneuver to get Republicans on record against discrimination for possible later use locally. When Republicans regained control of the legislature, Green's bill passed easily with a slight reduction of penalties and was signed into law in April 1895.

Twice thereafter Green was called on to lobby against bills that would ban intermarriage. One of these, known as the Cady bill, was defeated in the legislature in April 1901; two years later Green's testimony before the assembly committee was instrumental in having the similar Williams bill killed. He argued that the bill, based on "malice, prejudice and a desire to humiliate the Negro," was essentially a reintroduction of the Black Laws that had long since been repudiated by northern states. He maintained that a law grounded in "class hatred and or race or other prejudice was never beneficial to the state."

Associated with neither Booker T. Washington's network nor W. E. B. Du Bois's supporters, Green denounced prejudice and spoke out for positive action. The time had come, he urged a black audience in 1902, for the Negro to "carve out his own destiny." At other times he rejected color lines drawn by whites or blacks, endorsed the gospel of work, and believed that race amalgamation, that is, the interbreeding of blacks and whites over time to create a single race, "is the only salvation for the Negro." He urged blacks in 1906 to "keep up the fight, ever and always, for our constitutional rights."

Green's law practice flourished from the beginning. "We have the best Afro-American lawyer in the country," the black Milwaukee paper boasted in 1899, "and the best part of his clients are white people." He frequently traveled to other Wisconsin cities and to Chicago on legal business. As a defense attorney, his cases ranged from petty crime to corporate negligence, from debt recovery to divorce, from civil rights to murder. One of his most famous cases involved Nina Brown, who was accused of killing her paramour. Green offered an insanity defense; the prosecutor conceded, and the judge so instructed the jury. Both officials praised Green "for the manner in which he conducted this case." Four years later, when a well-established Milwaukee black was charged with murder, Green successfully entered a plea of self-defense to win the case. In each case he single-handedly defended his client. "If I engage counsel," he explained, noting his status as the only black attorney in Milwaukee, "and we won the case, some of my people would say, 'the white man did it.'"

Although a leader in black Republican circles and a faithful campaigner, Green was denied opportunities to run for city supervisor, assistant city attorney, and justice of the peace despite near-unanimous support from the black community and measurable endorsements from whites. "Our well-known attorney, Green, can tell you a thing or two, when it comes to Republican promises," the Milwaukee black weekly groused in 1906.

Active in the social life of the Milwaukee African-American community, Green also held leadership positions in the black Masonic order, where he often acted as orator, master of ceremonies, toastmaster, or introducer of prominent out-of-town speakers. An impressive speaker himself, he was well versed in local history, race matters, church affairs, and Wisconsin politics. A friend's description of his court appearances depicts him as "trembling with sincerity" and then using humor to "sweep the room with laughter."

There is no record of Green's marriage; he lived in single rooms and listed himself as a widower. At a probate inquiry, his only child, a son, testified that his mother was still alive. Green died in Milwaukee of kidney disease after a short illness. His funeral, the largest ever held in the city's St. Mark's A.M.E. Church, "was crowded to the doors," including "a large representation of lawyers and judges." He was, a white newspaper concluded, "one of the colored people's most ardent defenders, and always worked for the uplifting of his race."

• Because Green left no papers, information about him is scattered in a variety of sources. Two black Milwaukee weeklies, the *Wisconsin Afro-American* (1892–1893) and the *Wisconsin Weekly Advocate* (1898–1907), touch on his activities. See also Thomas A. Buchanan, "Black Milwaukee, 1890–1917" (master's thesis, Univ. of Wisconsin, Milwaukee, 1974). The 1861 Canadian census identifies his probable family, and the 1900 U.S. Census provides hard data. City directories, the 1910 U.S. census, and the 1895 and 1905 Wisconsin censuses are not helpful, however. Canadian sources such as St. Catharines Public Library Special Collections and Brock University Archives are accessible but not too useful. Green's probate record is filed with the Milwaukee County Register of Deeds. The Milwaukee County Historical Society file on African Americans is sketchy for Green, but they have published a useful pamphlet, *The Negro in Milwaukee* (1968), which includes "Negros in Milwaukee," Green's article from the *Milwaukee Sentinel*, 16 Oct. 1895, identified as "the earliest known historical treatment of Milwaukee's Negro population." The only two known published works about Green are Leslie H. Fishel, Jr., "The Genesis of the First Wisconsin Civil Rights Bill," *Wisconsin Magazine of History* 49 (1966): 324–33, and Frederick I. Olson, "Early Civil Rights Hero Honored in Sandburg," *UWM Report* 14 (1993): 15. The two best obituaries are in the *Milwaukee Free Press* and the *Evening Wisconsin* (Milwaukee), both 4 Dec. 1911.

LESLIE H. FISHEL, JR.

GREENACRE, Phyllis (3 May 1894–24 Oct. 1989), psychiatrist, psychoanalyst, and author, was born in Chicago, Illinois, the daughter of Isaiah Thomas Greenacre and Emma Leantha Russell. Although she planned to work in the field of psychiatry from an early age, she received her first special training in general pathology. She earned her S.B. from the University of Chicago in 1913 and her M.D. from Rush Medical College in 1916.

From 1916 to 1927 Greenacre worked as a resident and faculty member in the Department of Psychiatry of the Johns Hopkins Hospital and Medical School in Baltimore. As a member of the hospital's Henry Phipps Psychiatric Clinic, she performed early studies in neurosyphilis, schizophrenia, and obsessive-compulsive disorders. In 1919 she married Curt Richter, the director of the Psychobiological Laboratory of the Phipps Clinic; they had two children. The marriage ended in divorce in 1930.

Greenacre moved to New York in 1927, where she served until 1932 as a psychiatric consultant for the Westchester County Department of Public Welfare's child care division. She then went to work for the Department of Psychiatry of the New York Hospital and Cornell Medical College, first as an assistant professor and then as a professor of clinical psychiatry, a position she held until 1964. Until 1946 she was active in teaching and in the direction of the Psychiatric Outpatient Service, while in later years she served only as an occasional consultant.

In 1937 Greenacre graduated from the New York Psychoanalytic Institute, became a member of its faculty in 1942, and opened a private practice in psychiatry in Manhattan in the late 1940s. Greenacre became a prolific writer of journal articles on clinical psychoanalytic studies, especially developmental problems of early infancy. Particularly notable were those on the genetic and dynamic background of creativity, transference, and perversions such as fetishism. She published a total of ninety-one papers, the last in 1983 when she was eighty-nine years old. Most of her papers are compiled in her books, including *Trauma, Growth and Personality* (1952) and *Emotional Growth: Psychoanalytic Studies of the Gifted and a Great Variety of Other Individuals* (1971). Her work continues to be cited frequently in journals such as *The Psychoanalytic Study of the Child*, on whose editorial board she served from its inception in 1945 until her death. Greenacre also edited the book *Affective Disorders: Psychoanalytic Contribution to Their Study* (1953).

By 1950 Greenacre had won acclaim for her original investigations of infantile development in relation to the genesis of later neurotic disorders: "With her uncanny intuition and aptitude for painstaking and devoted attention to detail, she arrived at masterful reconstructions of actual infantile trauma as these contributed to pre-oedipal disturbances of ego development and orderly phase development" (Harley and Weil, p. 524). Her psychoanalytic studies were far ahead of her time, expanding the concept of pre-oedipal developmental processes and emphasizing autonomous ego growth and ego deficits years before anyone else.

Greenacre published two psychoanalytic biographies while in her sixties: *Swift and Carroll: A Psychoanalytic Study of Two Lives* (1955) and *The Quest for the Father: A Study of the Darwin-Butler Controversy, as a*

Contribution to the Understanding of the Creative Individual (1963). Greenacre believed that studying the lives of great historical persons in terms of their individual life settings and personal experiences and relationships could extend analytic knowledge in ways unattainable through traditional clinical settings. In her words, she used biographical studies "to contribute to our psychoanalytic understanding of clinical conditions in people who rarely come to an analyst" (*Emotional Growth*, vol. 1, p. xxvii). Although she wrote chiefly for students of psychoanalysis, her studies of famous individuals presaged much of the historical profession's later interest in psychobiography.

For over forty years Greenacre devoted herself to psychoanalytic practice, to which she made groundbreaking contributions. In recognition of her innovative work, she won the Elizabeth Blackwell Award in 1955 and the Menninger Award in 1959, and she delivered several prestigious lectures, including the 1953 Freud Anniversary Lecture, the 1956 Brill Memorial Lecture of the New York Academy of Medicine, and the 1959 Sophia Mirviss Memorial Lecture and Alexander Lecture of the Chicago Psychoanalytic Institute. She served as president of the New York Psychoanalytic Institute from 1948 to 1950 and as president of the New York Psychoanalytic Society from 1956 to 1957.

Greenacre was seen as personifying "the happy union of creative imagination and scientific detachment" (Harley and Weil, p. 525). She saw the practice of psychoanalysis "as containing aspects of the vision of both the hardcore scientist and the artist" (*Emotional Growth*, vol. 1, p. xii). Following her retirement in 1984, Greenacre moved to Garrison, New York. She died in Ossining, New York.

• The Abraham A. Brill Library of the New York Psychoanalytic Institute, New York City, contains papers related to Greenacre's presidential tenures at the New York Psychoanalytic Institute and the New York Psychoanalytic Society and materials related to her 1953 Freud Anniversary Lecture. For further information on Greenacre see the biographical sketches at the ends of her books. Gwendolyn Stevens and Sheldon Gardner, "The Women of Hopkins: Ten Women Who Helped Make American Psychiatry," at the Alan Mason Chesney Archives of the Johns Hopkins Medical Institutions, Baltimore, Md., also contains information on her role in the development of psychoanalytic theory. See also Heinz Kohut, "Phyllis Greenacre—A Tribute," *Journal of the American Psychoanalytic Association* 12 (1964): 3–5. Obituaries are in the *New York Times*, 25 Oct. 1989, and by Marjorie Harley and Annemarie Weil in the *International Journal of Psycho-Analysis* 71 (1990): 523–25.

CHRISTINE KEINER

GREENBERG, Clement (16 Jan. 1909–7 May 1994), art critic, was born in the Bronx, New York, to Russian parents who made a living as storekeepers. He attended the Art Students League in New York City from March to May 1925, then enrolled at Syracuse University, in Syracuse, New York, from 1926 to 1930. Greenberg studied literature and languages at Syracuse, where he earned a B.A. He married Edwina Ewing in 1934 in San Francisco; they had a son and were divorced in 1936. Greenberg's subsequent significant relationships included one with painter Helen Frankenthaler, whom he met in 1950 but never married, and with Janice Elaine Van Horne, whom he married in 1956. He had a daughter with Van Horne.

Although art criticism became Greenberg's main occupation, he held a variety of jobs, especially during the 1930s and 1940s. Greenberg worked for his family's dry goods business in St. Louis, Cleveland, San Francisco, and Los Angeles in the early 1930s. In 1936 he worked in New York as a clerk at the U.S. Civil Service Commission and then at the Veterans Administration. In 1937 Greenberg took a position with the U.S. Customs Service that he held until 1942. Also during the 1930s and into the late 1940s Greenberg translated books from the German. Greenberg's additional occupations included a year in the U.S. Army Air Force in 1943 (he was discharged for health reasons) and the position of adviser to the French and Company art gallery in New York from 1958 to 1960.

Greenberg first wrote art criticism for *Partisan Review*, a journal he edited from 1940 to 1942. His influential essay "Avant-Garde and Kitsch" appeared in this journal (Fall 1939), as did his article on abstract expressionism titled "'American Type' Painting" (Spring 1955). From 1942 to 1949 he wrote a regular column on art for the *Nation*, and in 1944 he became the managing editor of *Contemporary Jewish Record*. When this magazine was subsumed under *Commentary*, Greenberg held the position of associate editor from 1945 to 1957. He also freelanced for academic journals and for popular magazines such as the *Saturday Evening Post*. He published three artists' monographs during his lifetime: *Joan Miró* (1948), *Matisse* (1953), and *Hans Hofmann* (1961). He began but never finished a monograph on abstract expressionist Jackson Pollock. An anthology of his art criticism, *Art and Culture*, appeared in 1961.

Greenberg's most important contribution to criticism was his theory of modernism, which he developed in relation to European art movements and abstract expressionism, the movement he helped to define in the 1940s and 1950s. Sometimes called "Greenbergian formalism," a label the critic rejected as too reductive, his viewpoint held that the best contemporary art was that in which "formal" elements, such as shape, color, and line, played a greater role than representational subject matter. Arguing for the significance of contemporary abstract art, Greenberg wrote, "The presence or absence of a recognizable image has no more to do with value in painting or sculpture than the presence or absence of a libretto has to do with value in music. Taken by itself, no single one of its parts or aspects decides the quality of a work of art as a whole. In painting and sculpture this holds just as true for the aspect of representation as it does for those of scale, color, paint quality, design, etc., etc." (*Art and Culture*, pp. 133–34). By emphasizing form and downplaying recognizable content, Greenberg eventually arrived at a position wherein he considered avant-

garde art's admission of the picture plane, or the flat surface of two-dimensional art, to be its main contribution to art history. He viewed painting as evolving toward a conclusion of ridding itself of Renaissance pictorial illusion (that is, the convincing representation of objects in space). The ultimate end of this evolution was the "viable essence" of painting: abstraction. Thus he wrote in 1955, "Painting continues, then, to work out its modernism with unchecked momentum because it still has a relatively long ways to go before being reduced to its viable essence" ("'American Type' Painting," p. 209).

Greenberg viewed his formalist ideas as pertaining to the most ambitious and rigorous new art. When abstract expressionism first surfaced in the 1940s, the public failed to appreciate it and even viewed it, in Greenberg's words, as a "symptom of cultural and even moral decay" (*Art and Culture*, p. 133). Consistently comparing it to the work of the old masters, Greenberg presented the new American art as equal to the best European modern art.

Now-famous abstract expressionists whom Greenberg championed at an early date include William Baziotes, Willem de Kooning, Arshile Gorky, Robert Motherwell, Barnett Newman, and especially Jackson Pollock. Subsequently, he identified Morris Louis, Kenneth Noland, and Jules Olitiski as "Post Painterly Abstractionists." Greenberg's attention came with a price, however. Some accused him of causing artists to change their personal styles to suit his tastes, a well-founded accusation. Noland, for one, saw nothing wrong with Greenberg's interference. "I would take suggestions from Clem very seriously," he once stated, "More seriously than from anyone else. . . . I'm grateful for it. I'll take anything I can get that will help my art" (qtd. in Ziv, p. 58).

When Greenberg did not like an artist's work, he made his opinion known. Most often he denounced art that he perceived as having narrative content. Pop art in particular came under his fire. As Roy Lichtenstein said of Greenberg, "He didn't like my work. It was storytelling and it was vulgar and it was all the things the formalists didn't like" (qtd. in Ziv, p. 57). Greenberg himself put the matter in the most damning terms: "Roy Lichtenstein is a minor painter. The pictures look minor. When they're good they're minor, when they're bad they're bad" (qtd. in Ziv, p. 58).

Greenberg organized exhibitions for artists he championed. He curated nine exhibitions during his most active years, the 1950s and 1960s, and contributed to nearly twenty catalogs. Exhibits included Talent 1950 (1950, Kootz Gallery, New York), which showcased little-known artists Elaine de Kooning, Robert De Niro, Friedel Dzubas, Grace Hartigan, Franz Kline, Alfred Leslie, and Larry Rivers; Emerging Talent (1954, Kootz Gallery, New York), which presented Louis, Noland, and Philip Perlstein; Three New American Painters (1963, Norman MacKenzie Art Gallery, Regina, Saskatchewan), featuring Louis, Noland, and Olitiski; and Post Painterly Abstraction (1964, Los Angeles County Museum of Art), which showcased work by thirty-one artists from the United States and Canada. In addition, Greenberg curated exhibitions of Pollock, Adolph Gottlieb, Hans Hoffmann, and Barnett Newman (1952, 1954, 1955, 1958, Bennington College).

Throughout his career Greenberg conducted seminars on criticism and traveled internationally to jury shows. Of note are Greenberg's 1950 summer seminars at Black Mountain College, an experimental liberal arts institution in North Carolina known for its progressive faculty and visual arts programs. Here he taught "The Development of Modernist Painting and Sculpture from Their Origins to the Present Time" and an art criticism course based on Immanuel Kant's *Critique of Aesthetic Judgment* (Noland was a student). Greenberg gave the Ryerson lecture at Yale in 1954, "Abstract and Representational," published by *Art Digest* the same year, and held the Christian Gauss Seminar in Criticism at Princeton in 1958. In addition, he taught colloquia series at Bennington College in 1962 and 1971 and led workshops or lectured at Yale and Princeton. Exhibits that Greenberg juried included an international show in Buenas Aires (1964), the John Moores Biennial of Painting in Liverpool (1965), and a show called "Rose" in Dublin (1967).

During the late 1960s and early 1970s the tide turned against Greenberg. Tiring of his acerbic remarks and considering his evolutionary view of art to be reductive, many in the art world challenged his viewpoint. The demonization of Greenberg continued into the postmodernist period. He became an Oedipal figure who needed to be destroyed, so it seemed, in order to clear the way for a plurality of approaches to contemporary art. "Clembusting" was a term that referred to attempts to destroy his hegemony. Of this phenomenon Greenberg once said, "I was told by people at the Museum of Modern Art that my name was mud. Two people reported that I was the most hated person in the art world." Rationalizing his position, however, he wrote, "The first obligation of an art critic is to deliver value judgements" (qtd. in Ziv, p. 58). Such was Greenberg's fame and the rigor of his ideas, however, that he never fully lost the ability to sway the opinions of curators, art dealers, and other art patrons. He maintained this power to the end of his life. Greenberg died in Manhattan.

Late in the twentieth century a younger generation of scholar-critics such as Yve-Alain Bois, T. J. Clark, Michael Fried, Charles Harrison, and Rosalind Krauss were incorporating his thinking into their own work. This focus on Greenberg and his writings was prompted by John O'Brian's definitive four-volume edition on the critic's collected essays and by conferences in Vancouver (1986), Paris (1993), and New York (1995), in which Greenberg's important legacy was subjected to more balanced scrutiny. Editions of his writings then appeared in French, German, and Portuguese.

• Papers pertaining to Greenberg are at the Archives of American Art, Smithsonian Institution, Washington, D.C., and at the Getty Center for the History of Art and the Humanities, Santa Monica, Calif. Published sources on Greenberg include Thierry de Duve, *Clement Greenberg between the Lines* (1996); Gióra Gerreira and Cecilia Cotrim, *Clement Greenberg: e o Debate Crìtico* (1997); Donald B. Kuspit, *Clement Greenberg, Art Critic* (1979); Peter G. Ziv, "Clement Greenberg: A Critic's Forty-Year Challenge to the Art World," *Art and Antiques*, Sept. 1987; Caroline A. Jones, "La Politique de Greenberg et le discours postmodernistic," *Les Cahiers du Musée National d'Art Moderne*, Autumn/Winter 1993; and John O'Brian, *Clement Greenberg: The Collected Essays and Criticism* (4 vols., 1986–1993). An obituary, "Clement Greenberg, 1909–1994," is in *Art in America*, June 1994.

CATHERINE McNICKLE CHASTAIN
JOHN O'BRIAN

GREENBERG, Hank (1 Jan. 1911–4 Sept. 1986), major league baseball player and executive, was born Henry Benjamin Greenberg in New York City, the son of Romanian-Jewish immigrants, David Greenberg, owner of a cloth-shrinking business, and Sarah Schwartz. The upwardly mobile Greenberg family moved from Manhattan to the Bronx, where Greenberg developed into an outstanding athlete at James Monroe High School. After attending New York University for a semester on an athletic scholarship in 1929, he dropped out of college to pursue a professional baseball career, most of which was spent with the Detroit Tigers. Aside from one at bat for Detroit at the end of the American League's 1930 season, Greenberg toiled from 1930 through 1932 for minor league teams in Hartford, Raleigh, Evansville, and Beaumont. A first baseman/outfielder, he played for the Tigers from 1933 until 1941 and in 1945 and 1946.

Active army duty from 7 May to 5 December 1941, under the pre–World War II draft, followed by enlistment in the U.S. Army Air Corps immediately after Pearl Harbor, interrupted Greenberg's baseball career. His World War II service, during which he attained the rank of captain, included assignment to a B-29 bomber unit in the China-Burma-India theater.

On 1 July 1945, in his initial game back with the Tigers, Greenberg hit a home run. His comeback at the age of thirty-four was highlighted by a grand slam home run on the season's final day to clinch the pennant for Detroit. In 1946, his first complete season since 1940, he led the league in runs batted in (127) and home runs (44). Nevertheless, in the off-season, a salary dispute led Detroit to sell the aging slugger to the Pittsburgh Pirates of the National League. After spending the 1947 season there, he retired as an active player.

At 6'4", 215 pounds, Greenberg became among the most formidable power hitters in baseball history. Through determination and intelligence, he overcame a lack of speed and physical grace to achieve greatness on the field. Despite losing the equivalent of four and one-half seasons at the peak of his athletic prowess, he helped the Tigers win four pennants (1934, 1935, 1940, 1945), led or tied for league leadership in home runs four times (1935, 1938, 1940, 1946), had the highest RBI total in both major leagues in four seasons

(1935, 1937, 1940, 1946), was named to the American League All-Star team four times (1937, 1938, 1939, 1940), and received the American League's Most Valuable Player Award twice (1935, 1940). His career .605 slugging percentage is one of the highest in major league history. His 183 runs batted in during 1937 fell only one short of the American League record, and no right-handed batter surpassed his 1938 season total of 58 home runs. From 1941 until his retirement, Greenberg was the highest-paid player in baseball. His career totals, which included a .313 lifetime batting average, 1,276 runs batted in, and 331 home runs in only 5,193 at bats, earned him election to the National Baseball Hall of Fame in 1956.

Following his retirement as an active player, Greenberg remained in baseball as an executive for fourteen years. In 1948 Cleveland Indians owner Bill Veeck, Jr., with whom he shared a long association, hired him as an assistant. Subsequently, Greenberg served as farm director, treasurer, general manager, and part owner of the Cleveland franchise, but controversy over his personnel decisions prompted the board of directors to dismiss Greenberg in 1957. During his association with the Indians, the team set major league attendance records, won two pennants (1948, 1954) and the 1948 World Series, and promoted racial integration in the American League. In 1959, again allied with Veeck, Greenberg acquired stock in the Chicago White Sox and served as the organization's general manager and vice president. In 1959, the White Sox won their first pennant since the infamous 1919 Black Sox scandal. Partners Greenberg and Veeck, prompted by the latter's health problems, sold their interest in the team in 1961 and Greenberg went on to pursue different interests.

Greenberg married Caral Gimbel, the department store heiress, in 1946; they had three children before their 1959 divorce. Shrewd handling of his baseball earnings and subsequent success as an investment banker brought him substantial wealth. In 1966 he married the actress Mary Jo Tarola. They resided in Beverly Hills, California, where Greenberg died.

The social fabric of the United States in the 1930s gave Greenberg an enduring importance. During the Great Depression, economic distress intensified anti-Semitism. At the same time, many children of East European immigrants came of age. This second generation, sensitive to the often conflicting dictates of their ethnic heritage and the host society, found a symbolic standard bearer in Greenberg, the first great Jewish baseball player. His baseball exploits made him a highly visible figure and the media frequently noted his Jewish background. In September 1934 Greenberg's dilemma over whether to play baseball on the Jewish High Holidays, as Detroit competed for its first pennant in twenty-five years, or to attend synagogue, as did his religiously observant parents, dramatized pressures faced by many American Jews. Ultimately, Greenberg hit two home runs on Rosh Hashanah but he did not play on the more solemn Yom Kippur. Intelligent, circumspect, and ambitious, he offered Jews a prototype of an upwardly mobile lifestyle that attracted far more admiration than resentment from gentile America.

• Greenberg's file at the National Baseball Library, Cooperstown, N.Y., contains numerous newspaper articles. His posthumous autobiography, *Hank Greenberg: The Story of My Life* (1989), ed. Ira Berkow, remains the only book-length treatment. William M. Simons, "The Athlete as Jewish Standard Bearer: Media Images of Hank Greenberg," *Jewish Social Studies* 44 (Spring 1982): 95–112, examines his symbolic significance for Jewish and gentile Americans. See also Ira Berkow, "Greenberg: A Kind of Beacon," *New York Times*, 7 Sept. 1986, and Steve Jacobson, "A Hero We Can Call Our Own," *Newsday*, 28 Sept. 1986. An obituary is in the *New York Times*, 5 Sept. 1986.

WILLIAM M. SIMONS

GREENBERG, Hayim (1 Jan. 1889–14 Mar. 1953), Zionist leader and author, was born in the Bessarabian (Moldavian) village of Todoristi, then part of the Russian empire, the son of Itzhak Meir Greenberg, a grain merchant. The identity of his mother is unknown. Hayim grew up near the provincial city of Kishinev, where his father was known locally for his progressive views. In a fashion that was in keeping with such a family background, Hayim was schooled in basic Judaica by private tutors. He also read widely and taught himself to read and write Russian. Although he never received any further formal education, he became a young writer of some repute.

As a youth, he spoke and campaigned for the nascent Zionist movement, whose goals focused on rebuilding a Jewish homeland in Palestine. At the age of fourteen Greenberg was sent as a correspondent for the Odessa daily, *Odesskii novosti*, to cover the Sixth World Zionist Congress in Basel, Switzerland. Three years later he represented the socialist-leaning Ze'irei Zion (Young Zionist) party at a national conference of Russian Zionists held in Helsinki.

Greenberg lived for a while in Odessa (1910–1911), then a major focal point of Jewish literary, journalistic, and political activity in Russia, before moving to Moscow. There he was an editor and regular writer for the pro-Zionist Russian-language weekly, *Razsvet* (The dawn). During this period he continued to extend his reading and writing on classical religious and philosophical traditions, both Eastern and Western. When academic Jewish studies became permissible in Russia after the 1917 revolution, Greenberg served as an instructor in Hebrew literature at Kharkov University. During this period, Greenberg married his wife, Lea (the date of their marriage and Lea's maiden name are unknown); they had one child.

Growing political and police pressure against "bourgeois nationalism" (a label affixed to both Hebrew and the Zionist movement by the Communist regime) soon convinced Greenberg and other leading Zionist intellectuals to leave the Soviet Union. He was among several Zionist luminaries who took refuge in Romanian-held Kishinev in 1921. From there he and his family moved on to Berlin, where for three years he worked with other Russian Zionist émigrés to promote He-brew and Jewish cultural activities and coedited *Ha-'Olam* (The world), the Hebrew weekly of the World Zionist Organization.

Arriving with his family in New York City in No-vember 1924 on a fundraising mission on behalf of the World Zionist Organization, Greenberg eventually decided to settle permanently in the United States, given the alarming growth of anti-Semitism in Germa-ny. On New York City's Lower East Side, Greenberg joined the leading ranks of the Labor Zionist move-ment, a cluster of organizations with political ties to similar groups in Eastern Europe that were developing deeper links with American labor and were heavily in-volved in supporting the fledgling Jewish labor federa-tion and farming cooperatives in Palestine. Besides their efforts to win political and economic support for their confreres in Palestine, the Labor Zionists were also involved in resisting Communist inroads on the American Left. They also established an array of social and educational institutions in the United States, rang-ing from Yiddish and Hebrew schools and summer camps, to cooperative housing projects and medical insurance plans, to fraternal societies. These provided a framework for a significant sector of the Jewish im-migrant population, within which immigrants could maintain a Jewish group identity while integrating themselves into American society.

Greenberg served the Jewish community as one of its key inspirational figures. He edited the Yiddish weekly *Farn folk* (For the people)—later renamed *Yid-isher kemfer* (The Jewish warrior)—and in 1934 also undertook the editorship of the movement's English-language monthly, *Jewish Frontier*. As a leading figure among American Zionists, Greenberg was chosen to head the American Zionist Emergency Council during World War II, a coalition of Zionist organizations cre-ated in 1939 to mobilize American Jewish efforts and public opinion on behalf of European Jewry.

In 1946 Greenberg was appointed by the World Zi-onist Organization to head its Department of Educa-tion and Culture in the United States. As a lobbyist to the United Nations, he was instrumental in winning the support of key Latin American delegates for the November 1947 UN resolution in favor of the partition of Palestine, which paved the way for the creation of the State of Israel.

As a Zionist, Greenberg was an antidogmatist. He championed the use of the Yiddish language (a "folk" language unpopular among Israeli Zionists) alongside that of the preferred modern Hebrew. He was a spokesman for strengthening the Diaspora Jewish communities through educational and cultural efforts rather than insisting on an exclusively Israel-oriented Zionism. He stood for the primacy of Jewishness as an all-inclusive collective identity with ancient historical roots as opposed to a narrowly defined Zionist or Is-raeli nationalism.

As a prominent speaker and writer on the American Jewish scene, Greenberg was known for his intellectu-al depth and eclectic choice of subject matter. He wrote on British, Japanese, Russian, Indian, and clas-sical Greek philosophers as well as on Judaism, and his writing is imbued with a thoroughly humanistic spirit. As a liberal socialist, he championed the causes of human dignity, internationalism, and peace.

An educated, modern, secularized Jew, Greenberg rejected Orthodox traditionalism as being contrary to the modern temper while simultaneously affirming the positive social, cultural, and psychological value of spiritual search. Although clearly influenced by such seminal thinkers as William James and Mordecai Kaplan, he articulated his own brand of integral Jew-ishness that defied philosophical or denominational definition. Ben Halpern, another veteran American Zionist, remarked in his introduction to *'Ayin roi* (My mind's eye), a 1958 collection of Greenberg's essays that Greenberg was increasingly "inwardly drawn to the ethical and metaphysical content of the Judaic her-itage. Yet he never budged from his original path of free and critical inquiry. . . . His growing attachment to the heritage of his forefathers did not affect his openness to truth wherever he might find it" (my translation).

Greenberg died in New York City. His direct influ-ence is difficult to trace. After the 1950s, most of the Zionist organizations in the United States went into decline, their pro-Israel fundraising and political ac-tivities taken over by the Jewish communal apparatus at large and their educational functions becoming al-most exclusively the domain of individual synagogues. Labor Zionism, along with the American Jewish labor movement generally, decreased in significance, pres-tige, and membership as American-born Jews became overwhelmingly middle class. Also, a decline in quan-tity, quality, and diversity plagued the American Jew-ish press in the postwar period. Finally, the particular kind of integral Jewishness that Hayim Greenberg personified has rarely materialized in the denomina-tionally divided American Jewish community. Never-theless, the positions that he articulated on Israel-Di-aspora relations and on the link between ethnicity and religion have become commonplace among the Ameri-can Jewish intellectual and religious establishment.

• Greenberg's major essays are available in English, Hebrew, and Yiddish in several of his anthologies: *The Inner Eye* (2 vols., 1953, 1964), which includes English versions of the es-says that appear in his Hebrew collection, *'Ayin roi*; *The Hayim Greenberg Anthology*, intro. Marie Syrkin (1968); *Yid un velt* (The Jew and the world) (1953); *Bletlakh fun a tog-bukh* (Pages from a diary) (1954); and *Mentshn un vertn* (Peo-ple and values) (1954). To date, no biography exists, but Greenberg's contribution as a Jewish thinker is concisely as-sessed in Arnold Eisen, "Out of the Depths: On Hayim Greenberg and Religion," *Jewish Frontier* 51 (Nov./Dec. 1984): 48–50. The same issue of *Jewish Frontier* also contains reprints of two of Greenberg's important essays, "Jewish Cul-ture and Education in the Diaspora" (pp. 51–57) and "The Future of American Jewry" (pp. 57–63). A detailed review of Greenberg's life and work is given in the Yiddish literary lex-icon, *Leksikon fun der nayer yidisher literatur*, vol. 2 (1958), pp. 398–404. A more abridged account is offered in the *Encyclopedia Judaica*, ed. Geoffrey Wigoder, vol. 7 (1972). An obituary is in the *New York Times*, 15 Mar. 1953.

ELI LEDERHENDLER

GREENE, Belle da Costa (13 Dec. 1883–10 May 1950), library director, bibliographer, and art connoisseur, was the daughter of Richard Greene and Genevieve Van Vliet of Alexandria, Virginia. Her middle name came from her maternal grandmother, Genevieve da Costa Van Vliet. Specifics concerning Greene's childhood and education are scarce, because she preferred to keep them a mystery. When her parents separated her mother moved with her children to Princeton, New Jersey, where she gave piano lessons to support the family. Greene probably attended local schools, but in spite of early indications of her intellectual capabilities, lack of funds prevented her from attending college.

Greene's first position was librarian in training at the Princeton University Library, where she learned cataloging practices and reference services. While working there she met two men who greatly influenced her life. Her first mentor, a university librarian and bibliographer, Ernest C. Richardson, helped develop her interest in rare books; the second, Junius Spencer Morgan, an alumnus of Princeton and a collector of early manuscripts, was a nephew of the banker J. Pierpont Morgan. Knowing that his uncle was in need of someone to organize and catalog his sizable collection of manuscripts and rare books, Morgan recommended Greene. In 1905 Greene met and impressed the 68-year-old J. P. Morgan, who hired her as his private librarian. For Greene, he became a father figure who opened doors for her to the scholarly, the wealthy, and the collectors of museum-class art and books. Their instant rapport and continued mutual respect based on similar attitudes toward historical artifacts laid the groundwork for their interdependent, rewarding relationship. Morgan's increasing reliance on Greene's judgment in the acquisition and management of his growing collection made possible the assembling of a valuable, incomparable, private collection of medieval illuminated manuscripts, incunabula, early bindings, autographed manuscripts, rare books, paintings, and art objects.

The new Renaissance-style Morgan Library building at Thirty-sixth Street and Madison Avenue in New York City, designed by Charles F. McKim with an elegant and ornate interior planned by Morgan, became Belle Greene's work space for the next forty-three years. From 1905 to 1908 her main function was organizing Morgan's existing collection, but he also frequently sat with her for short chats and liked to have her read to him. From the onset she was loyal to her "boss," to the staff, and to her mission, willingly giving her very best in the smallest undertaking, gaining the respect of all who worked for her or needed her assistance. Humor, humility, and an energetic personality were essential ingredients of her quest for knowledge.

As Morgan came to depend on her judgment, Greene's duties expanded to include travel abroad to locate suitable additions for his collections. Her knowledge, coupled with Morgan's financial backing, had an effect on the book markets and auction houses of two continents. From the beginning of her employment, Greene was provided the means to live and work in the manner befitting an agent for a wealthy banker. In the early years at the library, she often wore Renaissance-style dresses or bustling brocades with appropriate jewelry. After 1908, when she traveled on buying trips for Morgan, she stayed at the best hotels, wore elegant clothing, including large, plumed hats, and sometimes brought her thoroughbred horse to London, England, to ride in Hyde Park.

Through Morgan Greene met in 1908 the noted art connoisseur Bernard Berenson, with whom she developed a lifelong attachment and a voluminous correspondence. Sydney Cockerell, the director of the Fitzwilliam Museum at Cambridge University, another of Morgan's acquaintances, taught her how to sharpen her critical evaluations and introduced her to European scholars from whom she could seek advice. She soon became well known and respected in museums, galleries, libraries, and upper-class homes throughout Europe. In spite of her growing expertise and acumen when evaluating rare objects she always consulted with experts before recommending a purchase to Morgan, who had the final say.

When Morgan died in 1913 Greene was devastated: "I feel as if life had stopped . . . it is all I can do to go on without him. He was much more than my 'boss.' He was almost a father to me" (Canfield, p. 152). She did remain in charge of the library when his son J. P. Morgan, Jr., inherited the collection, even though he was less involved than his father had been. She encouraged his interest in the library, and when some of the art collection had to be sold to settle the estate, Morgan relied on her to negotiate the best prices. It was at this time that she came to increasingly seek advice from Berenson, who continued to be an important influence on her intellectual pursuits as well as a friend.

With characteristic energy Greene approached war work when the United States entered World War I in 1917. In addition, her mother, who had been living with her since she first moved to New York in 1905, was joined by Greene's war-widowed, pregnant youngest sister who gave birth in her home. Several years later, when her sister remarried, she adopted her sister's child, Robert Mackenzie Leveridge, and took on the added responsibility of his education.

In 1920 Morgan decided to enlarge the collection, and Greene resumed her professional excursions to Europe. When Morgan incorporated the library in memory of his father in 1924, Belle Greene was named director, a position she held until she retired. As an endowed educational institution, the library took on a new orientation dedicated to scholarship. It was a challenge to turn a private collection into a semipublic one, and she and her staff took great interest in aiding scholars by increasing the availability and usefulness of the collection. When interviewed by Aline B. Louchheim, Greene recalled that even when it was a private collection, the elder Morgan said, "Of course, that man can come, someday they can all come." Expansion continued under Greene's direction, including an annex completed in 1928 that increased the research facilities and allowed for regular exhibitions and lectures. Large numbers of reference books were added, as well as files to accompany thousands of objects. On many of the fly leaves of books and in those files, annotations were added in her firm, clear writing as aids for researchers.

Over the decades Greene kept up a lively correspondence with scholars and friends and continued to travel to Europe for business and pleasure until 1936. By 1940 her life began to change radically. After an accident resulted in a broken arm she became fearful of falling and experienced other health problems. Within the next two years her mother and her older sister both died, her nephew was killed in action, and J. P. Morgan, Jr., died soon after.

By 30 November 1948, when she retired because of her failing health, Greene had spent twenty-five years as executive head and a total of forty-three years amassing a collection few librarians have had the opportunity or the ability to assemble. Her first devotion and responsibility was the Morgan Library, but she was often called on to make significant contributions to other institutions, for which she was honored during her lifetime. In recognition of her public service, the governments of Belgium, France, and Italy decorated her. After World War I she was made a member of the Committee for the Restoration of the Louvain Library and was one of the first women accepted as a fellow of the Mediaeval Academy of America. She was a fellow in perpetuity of the Metropolitan Museum of Art, a consultant to the Walters Art Gallery board of trustees, and a trustee of the Art Foundation, and she was elected to the board of the College Art Association, the Library Advisory Council of the Library of Congress, the Index Society, and the editorial boards of the *Gazette des Beaux-Arts* and *Art News*.

Among the many letters of praise she received on her retirement in 1948, the one from Eric Millar, former keeper of manuscripts at the British Museum, summarizes the distinction of her contribution to the shaping of a world-class institution: "It must mean something to you to know what a monument of your taste, enthusiasm, and wholehearted devotion to its interests you have built up to yourself in that wonderful institution, with which your name will always be associated." Greene died in New York City, where her legacy continues in the collection of the Morgan Library, which includes a 1913 portrait of her by Paul Helleu.

• Several publications contain valuable biographical information in relation to Greene's career, including *The First Quarter Century of the Pierpont Morgan Library: A Retrospective Exhibition in Honor of Belle da Costa Greene* (1949), contains a portrait. Dorothy Minor, ed., *Studies in Art and Literature for*

Belle da Costa Greene (1954), was conceived in 1949 and expanded after Greene's death by funds given in her honor. *The Pierpont Morgan Library: A Summary of the Annual Reports of the Director to the Board of Trustees, 1924–1929* (1930) and subsequent summaries covering 1930–1935 (pub 1937) and 1936–1940 (pub 1941), reflect her administrative strengths. Curt F. Buhler, "Belle da Costa Greene," *Speculum* (July 1957): 642–44, reprinted in his *Early Books and Manuscripts* (1973), is a modified version of a talk he gave at a celebration in her honor at the Morgan Library on 4 Apr. 1949. Cass Canfield, *The Incredible Pierpont Morgan: Financier and Art Collector* (1974), contains several references to Greene and a portrait. At the time of her retirement and the exhibition in her honor several articles and letters appeared in print: "Morgan Librarian," *Times Literary Supplement*, 13 Nov. 1948, p. 644; "Miss Greene Retires," *Art News* 47 (Nov. 1948): 13; "Belle of the Books," *Time*, 11 Apr. 1949, pp. 76–78; and Aline B. Louchheim, "The Morgan Library and Miss Greene," *New York Times*, 17 Apr. 1949. For information about Greene's relationship with Berenson see Ernest Samuels, *Bernard Berenson: The Making of a Legend* (1987). Obituaries are in *Publishers Weekly*, 10 June 1950, and the *New York Times*, 12 May 1950.

CONSTANCE KOPPELMAN

GREENE, Catharine Littlefield (17 Feb. 1755–2 Sept. 1814), wife of revolutionary war hero Nathanael Greene and principal financier of Eli Whitney's cotton gin, was born on Block Island, Rhode Island, the daughter of John Littlefield, a landowner and deputy to the General Assembly of Rhode Island, and Phebe Ray. Her early years among the nonconformists on Block Island, who shunned the rigid religious dogmas of the mainland, left an indelible mark on her personality; she remained forever an unconventional individualist.

At age ten, after her mother died, Catharine Littlefield lived in East Greenwich with her Aunt Catharine, wife of William Greene, Jr., a future governor of Rhode Island. She received some tutoring and was drilled by her aunt in social graces, especially the art of hostessing, a talent for which she would later be noted. She also came to know the men who gathered to discuss the growing split from England, among them the 32–year-old anchorsmith Nathanael Greene. They were married in 1774; five of their children lived to adulthood.

Less than a year after the marriage, Nathanael Greene rose from soldier in the ranks of a neighborhood militia to brigadier general. With the full advent of war, Catharine Greene joined him at his camps, a privilege his rank allowed. She endured the hardships of travel and camp life with courage and cheerfulness, bringing to the bitter headquarters her special high spirits and sharing the worst with fortitude; she won the abiding gratitude and devotion of George Washington during the harsh winter of Valley Forge. Uninhibited, witty, pretty, a stimulating conversationalist and raconteur, she made lifelong friends among such wartime acquaintances as Anthony Wayne, the marquis de Lafayette, Henry Knox, and Alexander Hamilton. Unfortunately, her openly flirtatious bonhomie aroused jealousy in some of the other officers' wives whose widespread gossip about her reached her Aunt Catharine, a probable cause of a rift between them. There were also domestic squabbles with her strict Quaker in-laws, who bore the brunt of managing the general's affairs and caring for whichever of the Greenes' children were not at headquarters with their mother.

At war's end, Nathanael Greene could not support his family in New England. Unsuccessful in his attempt to be reimbursed by a depressed government for personal notes he had signed to supply and clothe his southern command, he moved his family, including the children's tutor, Yale graduate Phineas Miller, to "Mulberry Grove," near Savannah, one of several confiscated tracts of land awarded him by impoverished southern states. The neighboring plantation owner was Anthony Wayne, and Catharine Greene's easy friendship with him caused gossip among the Savannah ladies. Georgia politician Isaac Briggs, an early visitor to Mulberry Grove, had heard those rumors and also that Nathanael Greene had made application for divorce from her in New England on grounds of adultery. Briggs had made inquiries while in New Port and "found 'twas all a lie." Charmed by "the Lady Greene," he defended her in a letter to a friend as a "lady who is superior to the little foibles of her sex, who disdains affectations, who thinks and acts as she pleases, within the limits of virtue and good sense.... In short, she is honest and unaffected enough to confess that she is a woman, & it seems to me the world dislikes her for nothing else."

Needing cash to put the long-neglected plantation into production, Nathanael Greene borrowed heavily from friends, pledging his lands as collateral. Mulberry Grove had just begun to prosper when, in 1786, Greene died suddenly of "sunstroke," leaving Catharine, five children, insurmountable debts, and no capital to put the other farms awarded him in operation.

Land-rich but money-poor, Catharine Greene was desperate. As far back as Valley Forge, General Greene, appointed by Washington to replace the quartermaster general who had abandoned his post, had used his own private funds and money from partnerships, signing personal notes for stores that the near-bankrupt government could not provide. Congress refused to reimburse him on grounds that his business enterprises had been secretly conceived without knowledge or permission of the governing body. With the advice and counsel of her now influential friends, Catharine Greene spent the next years traveling from Georgia to New England, gathering documents to prepare her indemnity petition to the government for reimbursement of her husband's wartime debts. Discouraged by those who deemed her cause hopeless, but privately encouraged by President Washington, she personally presented her case to the U.S. Treasury Department in December 1791. In April 1792 Congress approved an award of $47,000 to be paid in installments. Ecstatic, she wrote a friend, "I ... feel as saucy as you please.... I have gained comple[te] tr[i]umph over some ... who constantly tormented me to death to give up my *obstinancy.* ... O how sweet is revenge!"

In August 1791 Catharine Greene had quietly entered into a premarital agreement with Phineas Miller, the loyal tutor and friend she now depended on to manage Mulberry Grove. The legal document stipulated that Miller would disclaim any property that might be forthcoming from the disposition of the Greene estate. In order not to jeopardize her Congressional appeal as the destitute widow of General Greene, marriage was postponed. In the fall of 1792, as Catharine Greene's business manager, Miller sent a letter to Eli Whitney, a fellow Yale graduate from Connecticut, telling him of an opening as tutor at a neighboring South Carolina plantation. Whitney was invited to join Miller, Catharine Greene, and her children in New York for the journey south and to stop over at Mulberry Grove before going to South Carolina. Whitney, who hated teaching, remained at Mulberry Grove, claiming a misunderstanding about wages as the reason he abandoned the tutoring position. In truth, he enjoyed making and repairing items for his enchanting hostess and was becoming interested in the problem of ginning cotton. Inspired by talk of Savannah businessmen, he began work on a model for a cotton gin, confiding only in Greene and Miller. When the model proved promising, Greene authorized Miller to pledge her newly won money as capital in the cotton gin firm of Whitney and Miller. The enterprise was fraught with problems from the first, including patent infringements, lawsuits, monies pledged by enthusiastic Southern states and then rescinded, and a fire that left Whitney's New Haven manufactory in ruins. Hoping to get quick working capital, Greene and Miller made an ill-advised entry into what became known as the Great Yazoo Fraud. In 1795 four Yazoo companies, aided by liberal bribes and gifts of stock to corrupt Georgia legislators, succeeded in getting the assembly to pass a bill that sold them between 35 million and 50 million acres of Georgia's western territory for as little as one and one-half cents an acre. Following a public outcry the act was voided, rescinding the land sales. In 1802 Georgia ceded the land to the federal government and, after lengthy arguments of the land companies in Federal courts, Congress reimbursed investors in 1814, a resolution that came too late for Catharine Greene, who had lost ready cash tied up in estate property pledged as collateral.

Once again in financial distress, with the ginning company virtually bankrupt, Catharine and Miller, who had formally married in Philadelphia in 1796, saw Mulberry Grove go on the auction block for unpaid taxes. Moving with the children to Cumberland Island off the Georgia coast, where General Greene had laid the foundation for a future home, they oversaw the completion of "Dungeness" and developed a prosperous plantation. When Miller died tragically of blood poisoning from a thorn wound, 7 December 1803, Catharine again found herself widowed and encumbered by business complications and deals gone sour. Bedeviled by lawsuits stemming from the ginning firm and other ventures, emotionally involved with the friends she was financially indebted to, and constantly having to pledge the proceeds from the plantation to cover obligations, her last years were a continuing struggle.

She remained ever the cordial hostess, making Dungeness a refuge for relatives and friends, writing warm letters such as the one to Whitney telling him, "We have a party of Eighteen to eat Turtle with us tomorrow . . . I wish you were the nineteenth. Our fruit begins to flow in upon us—to partake of which I long for you." Struck down by a coastal fever of summertime Georgia, she died at Dungeness.

In an era when most women lived in semi-servitude with little hope of financial independence or personal freedom, Greene tested the boundaries of convention. She was a spirited, cheerful presence at army headquarters during the Revolution. She took measures, as a widow with children, to draw up a premarital agreement securing their future. She made a courageous public stand before the U.S. government to secure money owed her late husband and sought a place in the world of commerce by backing Whitney's cotton gin. Successfully managing two plantations, she jeopardized her own financial security by pledging crops and proceeds to cover debts, both personal and those incurred by the ginning venture. Stubborn, utterly charming, brave, and tenacious, she touched the lives of this country's notable men in a way that few have before or since.

• Greene's personal correspondence, found in collections at William L. Clements Library, University of Michigan; Yale University Library; South Caroliniana Library, University of South Carolina; University of Georgia Library; the American Philosophical Society; Historical Society of Pennsylvania; and Massachusetts Historical Society, reveals more about her than articles and books ever can. Notably lost are her letters to Nathanael Greene. A recent, full biography is John F. Stegeman and Janet A. Stegeman, *Caty: A Biography of Catharine Littlefield Greene* (1977; repr. 1985); this work contains an excellent bibliography, including manuscript collections. Richard K. Showman, ed., *The Papers of General Nathanael Greene*, vol. 1 (1976), is an excellent source for overview of areas of her life. Jeannette Mirsky and Allan Nevins, *The World of Eli Whitney* (1952), although uneven in its treatment of Catharine, is a good reference for her part in the development of the cotton gin.

JANET ALLAIS STEGEMAN

GREENE, Charles Sumner (12 Oct. 1868–11 June 1957), and **Henry Mather Greene** (23 Jan. 1870–2 Oct. 1954), architects, were born in Brighton, near Cincinnati, Ohio, the only sons of Thomas Sumner Greene, a bookkeeper, and Lelia Ariana Mather. Their father, who became a doctor in 1880, was interested in residential design and decided while they were still children that his sons would be architects. Early influences on the Greene brothers included four childhood years spent on a family farm, where the boys developed an interest in natural forms and materials, and their attendance at Calvin Woodward's Manual Training High School in St. Louis, Missouri (where the

family had moved in the early 1870s), which introduced them to the Arts and Crafts ideas of John Ruskin and William Morris.

In 1888 the brothers left St. Louis together to attend a two-year course in architecture at the Massachusetts Institute of Technology; Henry, who was interested in engineering, was more enthusiastic about this direction than Charles, who preferred painting, poetry, and photography. MIT's design curriculum was steeped in the Beaux-Arts tradition of classical styles, placing more emphasis on historicism than on design fundamentals, an approach that was in direct contradiction to the brothers' previous education and that they found frustrating and creatively stifling. After postponing the completion of their course of study while apprenticing with Boston-area architects, the young men received a partial certificate in 1891. They continued to work in the offices of various Boston architects until 1893.

Dr. Greene and his wife had meanwhile moved out to Pasadena, California, for health and financial reasons, and in 1893 they asked their sons to join them there. On the way out west, the brothers stopped in Chicago, Illinois, to visit the World's Columbian Exposition and were impressed by the half-scale replica of a Japanese temple they saw on display there; Japanese architecture later became an important influence in their work. In southern California they were intrigued by the mission buildings and the casual outdoor lifestyle. After a few months, the young men began planning a return to Chicago or Boston; however, when they received a commission for a small house from a family friend, they established their practice in Pasadena instead. During these years, both brothers began families. In August 1899 Henry married Emeline Augusta Dart: they had four children. Charles was married in February 1901 to Alice Gordon White, with whom he had five children.

The Greene brothers would eventually have a lasting impact on the development of American domestic architecture, introducing new formal expressions in their experimentation with wooden architecture and the California bungalow. But the first decade of their practice was marked by some stylistic confusion, as they searched for appropriate forms and materials to create an architecture for southern California's informality and mild climate. Torn between the popular styles of the day and the fundamentals of their earliest design training, their early work was marked by some of the eclecticism common in American architecture of the period, but the brothers gradually worked toward a simplification of forms and the reduction of applied ornament in their domestic designs (the firm designed only one commercial building, the Kinney-Kendall Building, in Pasadena in 1896).

Renewed exposure to Arts and Crafts ideas seems to have pushed the Greenes into the most productive period of their career. In 1901 Charles visited England on his honeymoon, where he saw many of the important buildings that that movement had produced; in the same year, Gustav Stickley began publishing his journal *The Craftsman*, in which the brothers found encouragement for their own efforts. Working primarily in wood, with exacting attention to craftsmanship, Greene and Greene developed a relaxed but vigorous architecture that related to the California landscape and reflected both functional and aesthetic concerns. Open sleeping porches, multigabled roofs with deep overhangs, an articulated timber structure, the design of furniture and interior fittings, and the integration of the house with surrounding walks, fencing, and gardens were hallmarks of the total architectural environments they created. Charles described their expansive design goals as being "1st, to understand as many phases of human life as possible; 2nd, to provide for its individual requirements in the most practical and useful way; 3rd, to make these necessary and useful things pleasurable."

From 1902 to 1907, the Greenes received many commissions, as their refined designs brought them to the attention of wealthy clients who wanted what one historian has called "ultimate bungalows," residences with the informality of that house type but with an attention to detail and material that raised the bungalow far above its humble beginnings. As in the Arts and Crafts movement generally, Greene and Greene put stylistic and symbolic evocations of vernacular and folk architecture to use for a largely genteel clientele. Charles's fertile artistic imagination, combined with Henry's sense of order and structure, allowed them to create a series of houses of unusual richness and simplicity.

The intense work of these years wore Charles down, and in 1909 he took his family to England for a year. Henry continued work on their existing commissions, but their busiest years were already behind them. The widespread and often shoddy use of bungalow designs by developers throughout California made them less appealing to wealthy clients, while only the well-to-do could possibly afford the kinds of materials and workmanship Greene and Greene insisted upon. With less work coming in, Charles turned more seriously to his writing and in 1917 moved his family to Carmel, California. The firm was reorganized under Henry's name in 1922, although the brothers continued to work together for the rest of their lives. However, none of their later work was to reach the level of their designs of 1902–1909, nor was it as influential. Henry died in Pasadena, and Charles died in Carmel.

Overlooked for several decades, the Greenes were honored with a citation from the American Institute of Architects in 1952. Their David Gamble house, built in 1908 for an heir to the Proctor and Gamble fortune and considered one of their best designs, was given to the city of Pasadena and the University of Southern California in 1966 and is jointly run as a museum. The Greene and Greene Library was added to the museum in 1968 on the centenary of Charles Greene's birth.

• Drawings, papers, and other memorabilia of the Greene brothers are in the Greene and Greene Library at the Gamble House in Pasadena and in the Rare Document Collection, Environmental Design Library, University of California at Berkeley. A large collection of Greene and Greene drawings is in the Avery Architectural Library, Columbia University. Writings by Charles Greene include "Bungalows," *Western Architect* (July 1908): 3–5, plates 1–9; "Impressions of Some Bungalows and Gardens," *Architect* (Dec. 1915): 251–52; and "Architecture as a Fine Art," *Architect* (Apr. 1917): 217–22. Randell L. Makinson's *Greene and Greene: Architecture as a Fine Art* (1977) treats the architects' careers chronologically, including their interior designs, and contains a complete bibliography. Books dealing significantly or entirely with Greene and Greene include Esther McCoy and Randell L. Makinson, *Five California Architects* (1960; rep. 1975); Clay Lancaster, *The Japanese Influence in America* (1963); William H. Jordy, *American Buildings and Their Architects*, vol. 3 (1972); William R. Current and Karen Current, *Greene and Greene—Architects in the Residential Style* (1974); Janann Strand, *A Greene and Greene Guide* (1974); Randell L. Makinson, *A Guide to the Work of Greene and Greene* (1974); and Timothy J. Andersen et al., *California Design 1910* (1980).

BETHANY NEUBAUER

GREENE, Cordelia Agnes (5 July 1831–28 Jan. 1905), physician and health reformer, was born in Lyons, New York, the eldest of five children of Jabez Greene and Phila Cooke. New England farmers and former Quakers turned Presbyterians, her parents settled in western New York along the banks of the Erie Canal shortly before her birth. Her father's piety was matched only by his interest in progressive education, and his active role as a trustee in the local public school no doubt sparked his daughter's lifelong concern with self-improvement. A serious student, she earned a teacher's certificate from the county while still in her early teens.

More than her intellectual achievement, however, Greene's interest in applied Christianity provides the best clue to understanding her subsequent career. Undergoing religious conversion during one of the waves of religious fervor that periodically swept the region, she transformed her religious impulses into social commitment and the pursuit of a professional career. In 1849, when her father gave up farming to found a water-cure establishment in Castile, New York, Greene became his nurse and assistant. Her later approach to medical therapeutics would always bear the influence of her early exposure to health reform and hydropathy, movements that emphasized a person's ability to manage health through proper diet, exercise, fresh air, and a variety of physical therapy techniques using water.

With money she earned from nursing, Greene, heartened by the recent graduation of Elizabeth Blackwell from Geneva Medical College in upstate New York, was the first student to receive a medical degree at the newly established Woman's Medical College of Pennsylvania in Philadelphia in 1853. She left Philadelphia in 1855 for Cleveland, where she assisted a friend of her father's in a recently established water cure in the city and attended the Cleveland Medical College (later Case Western Reserve). She graduated with honors in 1856 along with three other female pioneers of male-dominated professions, among them

Marie Zakrzewska, the future founder of the New England Hospital for Women and Children.

Returning to upstate New York, Greene spent the next six years gaining confidence and clinical experience as the assistant of Dr. Henry Foster, also a graduate of Cleveland Medical College, who owned the Clifton Springs Water Cure. Foster was a serious-minded and professionally oriented physician who kept abreast of new developments in medical practice and eventually turned his establishment into a fully equipped sanitarium and hospital. He shared his new recruit's religious orientation and, as one of his colleagues stated, believed with her that "a strong spiritual atmosphere has a mighty power as a curative agent" (Gordon, p. 12).

Greene's connection with sanitarium work was not merely fortuitous. Practicing at a water-cure establishment proved a particularly popular option for first generation women physicians. Female health was viewed as a woman's rights issue, and female invalidism and its treatment bound women together through companionship, mutual concern, and consolation. The water cure provided a locus where such bonds between women could be acted out.

Her father's death in 1864 gave Greene the opportunity to manage her own sanitarium. Urged by her brothers to take over the water cure in Castile, she consented after much soul searching. Thirty-four years old at the time, she would remain the medical director of Castile Sanitarium until shortly before her death. Her memoirs make it clear that she saw the proprietorship as a religious calling. "I have ever felt," she wrote, "that each patient was sent by a providential hand with the injunction Take this child and care for her for Me" (Gordon, pp. 16–17). A religious atmosphere pervaded the establishment; her first medical assistant was Dr. Clara Swain, a graduate of the Woman's Medical College of Pennsylvania and the first female medical missionary to India. Swain was only one of many successful women who worked with Greene in subsequent years. The medical work at Castile offered recent graduates important clinical experience and the sanitarium formed a link in a growing female professional network.

Greene supported women's rights activity and had strong ties to the Woman's Christian Temperance Union. Frances Willard and Mary A. Livermore of the WCTU were warm friends and supporters and came often to Castile to rest or visit. Susan B. Anthony was another frequent visitor. Like Anthony, Greene refused to pay her taxes one year because women were denied suffrage. She presided for several years over the local "Political Equality Club" and was active in the Wyoming County Suffrage Association. She donated large sums of money to support female social reform and was active in the home and foreign missionary boards of the Presbyterian church.

Greene believed that the study and proper application of hygienic principles to the life of the individual was a prerequisite for constructing a new role for women in the world. She often gave lectures on preventive medicine to mothers and young girls. Many of Greene's charges were middle and upper class women suffering from the vague symptoms of "nervous prostration." Greene took special interest in such cases. Known as an excellent diagnostician, she also must have been a woman of profound human insight.

Greene faithfully maintained her connections with the world of professional medicine, belonging to the American Medical Association and serving with Dr. Rosalie Slaughter Morton on its Committee for Preventive Medicine. She joined the New York State Medical Association and the local Wyoming County branch, where she served as president for a year, receiving warm support from male colleagues. She was active as well in women's medical organizations and for many years chaired the Educational Committee of the Woman's Medical Society of New York State.

Greene never married, though she liked to joke that she had looked in vain for Mr. Greene "for more than twenty years." She adopted six children, however, and lived an active family life. When Greene retired from the sanitarium, shortly before her death in New York City, she was succeeded by her niece, Dr. Mary T. Greene, who kept it a small but vital center for female professional medicine well into the first decades of the twentieth century.

• The best source for Greene's life is Elizabeth Putnam Gordon, *The Story of the Life and Work of Cordelia A. Greene, M.D.* (1925). Her own book, *The Art of Keeping Well; or, Common Sense Hygiene for Adults and Children* (1906), provides a key to her medical philosophy. For women physicians and water cure see Jane Donegan, *"Hydropathic Highway to Health": Women and Water-Cure in Antebellum America* (1986), and Susan Cayleff, *Wash and Be Healed: The Water-Cure Movement and Women's Health* (1987). See also "Dr. Mary T. Greene Sanitarium: 100 Year Celebration," *Medical Woman's Journal* 56 (June 1949): 21–25, and "Obituary—Cordelia Agnes Greene, M.D.," *Woman's Medical Journal* 15 (Apr. 1905): 80–81.

REGINA MORANTZ-SANCHEZ

GREENE, Edward Lee (20 Aug. 1843–10 Nov. 1915), botanist, was born in Hopkinton, Rhode Island, the son of William Maxon Greene and Abby Maria Crandall, probably farmers. The family moved to Illinois in 1855 and soon went on to southeastern Wisconsin, near Albion and Janesville. The boy was encouraged in natural history by his mother, who gave him *Botany for Beginners* (1833) by Almira H. Lincoln Phelps when he was six or seven. He also learned from Thure Ludwig Theodore Kumlien, a transplanted Swede who had studied natural history and knew the local plants well.

Greene attended Albion Academy for three years until 1862, when he enlisted as a private in the Thirteenth Wisconsin Infantry. His Civil War unit had light duties in Kentucky, Tennessee, and Alabama, so Greene observed plants; with him he carried Alphonso Wood's *Classbook of Botany* (1845). In 1865 he returned to the academy, receiving his Ph.B. the next year. On nearby field trips he and Kumlien noted problems in identifying Wisconsin plants in Asa Gray's *Manual of the Botany of the Northern United States* (1848). Reading botanical accounts in reports of Pacific Railway Surveys in Kumlien's library made Greene yearn to seek plants in unexplored regions.

From 1867 Greene's life was a compound of botany and religion. In Monticello, Illinois, from 1867 to 1870 he taught school while also preaching in a Methodist church. He corresponded with botanists Asa Gray, Alphonso Wood, John Torrey, and George Engelmann, and he wrote his first paper, "White Varieties of Flowers" (*American Naturalist* 2 [1869]: 656–57). In the spring of 1870 he went to Colorado to collect plants, carrying *Flora of North America* (1843) by John Torrey and Asa Gray, a cherished gift from the latter. Gray wrote, "I hope you may find some new things; but you will be sharp if you do" (6 Aug. 1870, quoted in Bartlett, p. 161). Gray had studied the plants obtained on the railway surveys and believed that all species in the region had already been collected. Greene found many new plants, but he delayed publishing in deference to Gray, who rejected one of his papers submitted to *American Naturalist*.

Greene enrolled in the Bishop's Collegiate and Divinity School in Golden City, Colorado, where he was ordained an Episcopal minister in 1873. While studying for the ministry, he taught botany at a high school for girls in Denver and served as minister for various Colorado churches. He asked the church for "a rural charge in order that the care of souls might be lightened by the pursuit of botanical studies," said historian Joseph Ewan (p. 62). Greene traveled in Colorado and Wyoming to collect plants, and he enjoyed finally meeting Gray at the dedication of Grays Peak in August 1872. In the intermontane region he traveled "on foot through dangerous and difficult country, often carrying only his plant press and a few changes of socks," wrote his biographer Harley Harris Bartlett (p. 163). He preached along the way. In 1876 he was sent by his church to Yreka, California, and the next year to Silver City, New Mexico, where he found many plants of interest.

In 1882 Greene was sent to Berkeley, California, as rector of St. Mark's. He resigned in 1885 and became a Catholic layman. That year he also became an instructor in botany at the University of California, Berkeley, rising to assistant professor in 1886 and professor in 1890, when botany became a separate department in the College of Natural Science. Students were attracted to Greene's courses by his knowledge, originality, and humor.

At the University of California Greene began publishing in earnest. He wrote six papers in a series, "Studies in the Botany of California and Parts Adjacent," published from 1885 to 1887 in the *Bulletin of the California Academy of Sciences*. Gray reviewed these sharply, saying Greene needed "less confidence as to specific distinctions, and a more restrained judgment about genera" (*American Journal of Science* 130 [3d ser., vol. 30], 1885, p. 320). Greene believed that species were immutable, so he defined plants in finer detail than did Gray, who was more inclined to regard regional variation broadly. Greene later said that his papers in 1885 broke down Gray's domination of American botany with his "rigidly conservative taxonomic principles" (quoted in Bartlett, p. 166). In 1887 Greene founded *Pittonia: A Series of Papers Relating to Botany and Botanists*; he paid for its printing until it ceased publication in 1905. He wrote the text of *West American Oaks* (1889–1890), *Manual of the Botany of the Region of San Francisco Bay* (1894), parts one to four of *Flora Franciscana* (1891–1897), and numerous papers.

In 1895 Greene became professor of botany at the Catholic University of America in Washington, D.C. There he had fewer students and limited facilities, but he continued writing and began a new intermittent publication, *Leaflets of Botanical Observation and Criticism* (1903–1912). He resigned in 1904 and stayed in Washington as an honorary associate in botany at the Smithsonian Institution, to which he transferred his library and herbarium. He wrote part one (to A.D. 1562) of *Landmarks of Botanical History* (1909), which he intended to expand to many more articles. In 1914 he transferred his library and herbarium to the University of Notre Dame, Indiana, and moved there as professor of botany. Greene never married. In 1915 he returned to Washington, D.C., to complete some writing and died in that city.

Before Greene displeased him, Gray named a genus in the composite family *Greenella* (now submerged in *Gutierrezia*) for him as "an enterprising botanist and most acute observer" (quoted in Ewan, p. 64). Greene's keen ability to distinguish small details led him to describe many species that have not been retained by later taxonomists, but some have lasted. His plant specimens from the western United States stand as long-term contributions to botany, and several species of the region bear the epithet *greenei*.

• Greene's correspondence is in the Archives of the University of Notre Dame. His herbarium specimens are in the Department of Biological Sciences at that university, and his collection of botanical books is in the University Libraries Department of Special Collections. Greene's publications are listed in Ellen D. Kistler, "Bibliography of the Botanical Writings of Edward Lee Greene," *Madroño* 3 (1936): 328–48. Biographical accounts include Angie Kumlien Main, "Life and Letters of Edward Lee Greene," *Transactions of the Wisconsin Academy of Sciences, Arts and Letters* 24 (1929): 147–85; and Harley Harris Bartlett, "The Botanical Work of Edward Lee Greene," *Torreya* 16 (1916): 151–75. Joseph Ewan in *Rocky Mountain Naturalist* (1950) discusses Greene's work in the Rocky Mountain area in detail. Memorials are in *American Midland Naturalist* 4 (1915): 228a–b, 335–38.

ELIZABETH NOBLE SHOR

GREENE, Francis Vinton (27 June 1850–15 May 1921), army officer and business executive, was born in Providence, Rhode Island, the son of General George Sears Greene (1801–1899) and Martha Dana. Entering the U.S. Military Academy in 1866, he graduated first in his class in 1870. He married Belle Eugénie Chevallié in 1879; they had six children.

Greene served in the regular army, becoming second lieutenant of artillery (1870), second lieutenant of engineers (1872), first lieutenant of engineers (1874), and captain of engineers (1883). From 1872 to 1876 he served as the assistant astronomer of the team that surveyed the forty-ninth parallel. Appointed military attaché at Moscow (1877), he accompanied the Russian army headquarters during the Russo-Turkish War, observing several engagements, including those at Shipka Pass, Plevna, and Philippopolis (now Plovdiv). He received two Russian decorations, the Order of St. Anne (Third Class) for bravery at Shipka Pass and the Order of St. Vladimir (Fourth Class) for bravery at Philippopolis. He then wrote *The Russian Army and Its Campaigns in Turkey in 1877–8* (2 vols., 1879) and *Sketches of Army Life in Russia* (1880). In 1882 he published *The Mississippi Campaigns of the Civil War*. From 1879 to 1885 he served as chief assistant to the engineer commissioner of the District of Columbia, in this capacity dealing with the public works of the federal district. His last service as a regular was as an instructor at the U.S. Military Academy (1885–1886).

Slow promotion proved discouraging. In 1886 Greene resigned his commission and became a businessman, seeking to capitalize on his fine appearance, his exceptional intelligence, and his literary achievements. Greene proved successful in an emerging industry, asphalt paving. First associated with the Asphalt Paving Company, he eventually became president of the Barber Asphalt Paving Company in New York. He continued to write, publishing a book on his distinguished ancestor, *The Life of Nathanael Greene, Major General in the Revolutionary Army* (1893).

Greene maintained his military associations, becoming a major in the New York National Guard in 1889. When his organization, the Seventy-first New York Infantry, volunteered for service in the war with Spain (1898), he became its colonel. On 27 May 1898 he was made a brigadier general of volunteers and ordered to the Eighth Corps being organized at San Francisco to campaign in the Philippines. Major General Wesley Merritt commanded this force, which was transported in three sections to Manila during June-August. Greene commanded the second section of 3,586 troops, which included two regiments of regulars and volunteers from several states. After reaching Manila Bay on 17 July, Greene assumed command of a brigade of the Eighth Corps, Brigadier General Arthur MacArthur commanding the other brigade. As Merritt prepared to attack Manila, Greene undertook delicate conversations with the commanders of Filipino insurgents who had invested the city. He managed to negotiate removal of Filipino troops between his position and the Spanish fortifications. While Greene and MacArthur prepared their assault, Admiral George Dewey reached a shadowy agreement with the Spanish commander, General Fermín Jáudenes, stipulating the capitulation of the city after a brief engagement designed to preserve the honor of the garrison. In return Merritt promised to keep the insurgents out of the walled city. He launched his attack on 12 August, intending to storm the city if necessary. Greene's brigade advanced on the left of the American line, which extended to the shore of Manila Bay. First he engaged Fort Antonio de Abad, which proved to be unoccupied. Scattered enemy fire caused a few casualties, but token resistance soon ceased. Greene's troops passed quickly through suburbs to the walled city. Meanwhile MacArthur's brigade moved on the right against limited resistance. Shortly after 11:00 A.M., a white flag appeared on the seawall of the city, and Dewey then completed arrangements for the capitulation of Manila. Greene sat on the commission that arranged the formal terms.

On 13 August Greene was made a major general of volunteers, but he did not remain long in the Philippines, returning to the United States in September. President William McKinley sought his views on the future of the Philippines. Greene's arguments in support of annexing the entire archipelago may have influenced the president's reluctant decision to do so. His final military service was to report on the condition of Havana, Cuba, an act that helped guide the refurbishment of the city.

Greene left the army in February 1899, soon returning to the asphalt business as president of the New Trinidad Lake Asphalt Company, but he undertook one more public service. Mayor Seth Low made him police commissioner of New York City in 1903–1904. His vigorous leadership directed a thorough reorganization of the police department and a marked improvement in discipline. Then he moved to Buffalo, New York, becoming the president of Niagara Construction Company and the Iroquois Construction Company. From 1910 to 1915 he served as president of both the Niagara, Lockport, & Ontario Power Company and the Salmon River Power Company.

After retiring in 1915, Greene became a civic leader in New York City and resumed his literary career. He was too old to serve in World War I, but he remained interested in contemporary affairs, writing *The Present Military Situation in the United States* (1915) and *Our First Year in the Great War* (1918). He was active in the New York Institution for the Instruction of the Deaf and Dumb, which he served as president (1918–1921). He died in New York City.

Greene's military service, while distinguished, was necessarily limited because he was active during an era of general peace. Like some other military professionals of the era, he turned to the business world and rose to positions of leadership in two industries, asphalt paving and electric power. Deprived of the opportunity to lead troops in the field except during the brief Manila campaign of 1898, he produced several works on military history and national defense, of which the most lasting is his book on the Russo-Turkish War.

• A collection of Greene's papers is deposited in the New York Public Library. A brief biography by General S. E. Tillman is in the *Fifty-third Annual Report of the Association of Graduates of the United States Military Academy* (1922).

Greene's military service during the war with Spain is discussed in Graham A. Cosmas, *An Army for Empire: The United States Army in the Spanish-American War* (1971), and David F. Trask, *The War with Spain in 1898* (1981). Obituaries are in the *New York Times*, 16 and 17 May 1921, and the *New York Tribune*, 16 May 1921.

DAVID F. TRASK

GREENE, George Sears (6 May 1801–28 Jan. 1899), civil engineer and soldier, was born in Apponaug, Rhode Island, the son of Caleb Greene, a shipowner, and Sarah Robinson. Greene attended the U.S. Military Academy at West Point from 1819 to 1823 and upon graduation became assistant professor of mathematics and engineering there. After four years of teaching, he served nine years in the artillery at posts in Maine, Massachusetts, and Rhode Island. In 1828 he married Elizabeth Vinton, who died four years later.

In 1836 Greene left the army, devoting most of the next twenty years to the construction of railroads in New England, Maryland, and North Carolina. In 1837 he married Martha Dana, the daughter of Congressman Samuel Dana. They had a daughter and five sons, two of whom became distinguished civil engineers; a third son was executive officer of the ironclad *Monitor* during the Civil War. In 1856 Greene accepted an engineering position with New York City's Croton Aqueduct Department. His most notable achievement during the next six years was the creation of a new Central Park reservoir that covered ninety-six acres and held 1.2 billion gallons of water. He also was responsible for the construction of a 1,400-foot wrought-iron pipe across the Harlem River High Bridge and the laying of a cast-iron pipe of unprecedented diameter (sixty inches) across Manhattan Valley.

With the outbreak of the Civil War, sixty-year-old Greene rejoined the army and served as a brigadier general of volunteers throughout most of the conflict. He fought in the battles of Cedar Mountain, Antietam, Second Manassas, and Chancellorsville, but he achieved his greatest distinction at the battle of Gettysburg, where his troops held off the Confederates at Culp's Hill and prevented them from turning the right flank of the Union forces. In October 1863 Greene received a severe bullet wound and did not return to his brigade until January 1865, serving the last months of the war with General William T. Sherman's army in North Carolina.

Returning to civilian life in 1866, Greene embarked on the most significant years of his long engineering career. From 1866 to 1871 he again applied himself to the expansion of New York City's water supply, becoming commissioner and chief engineer of the Croton Aqueduct Department. In that position he designed the Boyd's Corner reservoir, a basin covering 279 acres formed by a dam 670 feet long and 78 feet high. During the 1870s he took on a wide range of projects. He served for a short time as the chief engineer of the Board of Public Works of the District of Columbia, developing the city's sewage system. As a consultant,

he offered engineering advice on the water supplies of Detroit, Michigan, and Yonkers and Troy, New York, and on the sewage system of Providence, Rhode Island. He was instrumental in designing the streets and sewers of the present-day borough of the Bronx and was engineer to New York City's Rapid Transit Commission. Moreover, he was one of a team of engineers who reviewed the plans and estimated the cost of a ship canal linking Lake Champlain and the St. Lawrence River. From 1875 to 1877 he served as president of the American Society of Civil Engineers, an organization he had helped found in 1852. His consulting services remained in demand during the 1880s. In 1883 Greene was called on to consider the plans for the New Croton Aqueduct, and as late as 1886, at the age of eighty-five, he served on the Board of Examining Engineers investigating charges of malfeasance in the construction of the aqueduct. He died at Morristown, New Jersey, where he had lived since 1883. During the course of his life, Greene established himself as a pioneer in the civil engineering profession.

• Biographical sketches of Greene appear in *Transactions of the American Society of Civil Engineers* 49 (Dec. 1902): 335–40; Mark Mayo Boatner III, *The Civil War Dictionary* (1959); *A Biographical Dictionary of American Civil Engineers* (1972); and Stewart Sifakis, *Who Was Who in the Civil War* (1988). An obituary is in the *New York Times*, 28 Jan. 1899.

JON C. TEAFORD

GREENE, George Washington (8 Apr. 1811–2 Feb. 1883), author and educator, was born in East Greenwich, Rhode Island, the son of Nathanael Ray Greene and Anna Maria Clarke. Enrolled in Brown University before his fifteenth birthday, Greene left in his junior year for health reasons and journeyed to Europe to acquire a facility in the Italian and French languages and literature. In 1828 he met Henry Wadsworth Longfellow, who would become a lifelong friend, patron, and financial supporter in his later years. It is through the substantial correspondence between these two men, which continued until Longfellow's death in 1882, that we obtain a more complete view of Greene's activities.

Sometime between 1829 and 1831, Greene married Maria Carlotta, an Italian woman who accompanied him upon his return to the United States in 1831 or 1832. After an unsuccessful effort to secure a position as a professor of modern languages at Bowdoin College, Greene and his wife returned to Europe in August 1835. Two years later he was named as U.S. consul in Rome, a position held until 1845. During this time Greene launched his journalistic career with historical articles in the *North American Review* and with "Letters from Rome" in the *Knickerbocker*.

Throughout his consular life Greene felt that he was underpaid (compensation came in the form of fees from signing passports) and was not being fully appreciated. With both his diplomatic career and marriage ended, Greene journeyed alone to the United States in 1847.

Greene was the grandson of General Nathanael Greene of revolutionary war fame and sought to capitalize on that relationship by writing what he assumed was the definitive biography of his illustrious ancestor. His first work relating to his grandfather's career was *The Life of Nathanael Greene* (1846), which appeared as a volume in Jared Sparks's *Library of American Biography*, a work Longfellow had helped subsidize. In addition to preparing a multivolume biography of the general, Greene also began to write manuals on French and Italian, such as *Companion to Ollendorff's New Method of Learning to Read, Write, and Speak the French Language; or, Dialogues and a Vocabulary* (1850). Greene also found time to woo and win the hand of Catherine Van Buren Porter of Catskill, New York. They were married in February 1852 and had four children.

While Greene unsuccessfully pursued a teaching position among such institutions as New York University, Brown University, Columbia University, and Harvard College, he did serve as an instructor in modern languages at Brown University from 1848 to 1852. Through such friends as Longfellow and Charles Sumner, Greene also sought a directorship of the Astor Library, the Library of Congress, and the Smithsonian Institution. Greene met with continued frustration in such endeavors.

Meanwhile, after another unsuccessful effort to obtain congressional support for the publication of the collected papers of his grandfather, he turned in 1866 to pamphlet writing, attacking George Bancroft's presentation of Nathanael Greene in the ninth volume of Bancroft's major study of the American Revolution. Greene then followed this with the first of three filiopietistic volumes of the *Life of Nathanael Greene*, which appeared in 1867. This series (vols. 2 and 3 appeared in 1871) was subsidized to a great extent by Longfellow. Not only did Longfellow help with Greene's publications, in 1866 he purchased a house and furnishings for the Greenes in East Greenwich, Rhode Island, named "Windmill Cottage."

Greene dabbled in local politics and was elected as a Radical Republican to the Rhode Island House of Representatives in April 1866; he remained in that position until 1872. Greene also served as a lecturer at Cornell University before being named professor of history in 1873 after a protracted request for a change in title from that of nonresident professor. He continued to have complaints regarding his salary. Even before his termination from Cornell in 1875, Greene began to receive a monthly allowance of $50 from Longfellow, which largesse continued until the poet's death.

Through Longfellow's efforts, Greene was to publish additional historical studies such as *A Short History of Rhode Island* (1877) and numerous articles on revolutionary war themes in the *North American Review*, along with translations from Dante and other Italian poets. His lifelong desire to win recognition as a leading historian, lecturer, scholar, and linguist met with continued frustrations. He remained at Windmill Cottage until his death.

A man of many talents, Greene never achieved the eminence he sought. A language expert of Italian and French, he aided various authors with translations and with literary details. As a scholar he wrote a biographical study of his ancestor that relied on original source materials; and, as a traveler, Greene contributed countless travelogues to the leading journals of his day. Greene was highly regarded in his native state of Rhode Island, where he served in its legislature and where he was frequently called on to speak on historical occasions. Yet, with all these accomplishments, Greene was a financial failure who had to rely increasingly on his friendship with Longfellow for direct support.

• Greene's letters to Longfellow and Sumner are in collections at Houghton Library, Harvard University. Letters to Greene from Longfellow appear in Andrew Hilen, ed., *The Letters of Henry Wadsworth Longfellow* (5 vols., 1966–1982). A discussion of Greene's dispute with Bancroft over an interpretation of the career of General Nathanael Greene is summarized in Justin Winsor, *Narrative and Critical History of America*, vol. 8 (1889), p. 478. Genealogical information is contained in G. S. Greene and Louise B. Clarke, *The Greenes of Rhode Island* (1903). An obituary is in the *New York Times*, 3 Feb. 1882.

JACOB JUDD

GREENE, Henry Mather. *See* Greene, Charles Sumner, and Henry Mather Greene.

GREENE, Jerome Davis (12 Oct. 1874–29 Mar. 1959), educational administrator, was born in Yokohama, Japan, the son of Daniel Crosby Greene, a Congregational minister, and Mary Jane Forbes. His parents were the first missionaries to Japan of the American Board of Commissioners for Foreign Missions. Except for one year, Greene lived in Japan until 1887, when he entered Newton High School in Massachusetts. Graduating in 1892, he entered the Harvard College class of 1896 and supported himself with newspaper work and summer tutoring. He took a leave of absence his senior year to go to Europe as a tutor to an undergraduate and then to study law at the University of Geneva. From 1897 to 1899 he studied at the Harvard Law School but did not complete the LL.B. He received his Harvard A.B. in 1899. Greene was managing editor and president of the *Harvard Crimson* in 1895–1896 and edited the *Harvard Alumni Bulletin* in 1898–1899 and 1900–1901. From 1899 to 1901 he worked for the University Press of Cambridge as a salesman, plant superintendent, and assistant to its general manager. He married May Tevis in 1900; the couple had one son.

In 1901 Greene began his long career as a Harvard University administrator by becoming secretary to President Charles William Eliot. In 1905 Greene was elected secretary to the Harvard Corporation, serving under Eliot. A member of the faculty and of the undergraduate admissions committee, Greene helped to establish the first alumni directory and the weekly *Harvard University Gazette*. Popular with the alumni, he served three times on the Harvard Board of Overseers, 1911 to 1913, 1917 to 1923, and 1944 to 1950.

When Eliot left the presidency of Harvard in 1909, he favored Greene as his successor. The job instead went to A. Lawrence Lowell, and in 1910 Greene left Harvard to become general manager of the Rockefeller Institute for Medical Research in New York. In 1912 he began advising John D. Rockefeller, Jr., on business and philanthropic affairs. After obtaining in 1913 a charter from the New York legislature for the Rockefeller Foundation, Greene became its secretary and executive officer. During World War I he supervised relief supply shipments to Belgium for the Rockefeller Foundation. However, he resigned from the foundation on 1 March 1917, after its trustees appointed George E. Vincent to succeed Rockefeller as president. Greene remained a trustee of the Rockefeller Institute (subsequently Rockefeller University) until 1932. From 1928 to 1939 he also served as a trustee of the Rockefeller Foundation and of the General Education Board.

In 1916 Greene was a founder, trustee, and executive member of the Institute for Government Research, which became the Brookings Institution in 1928. In January 1918 he assumed his appointment as executive secretary of the American Section of the Allied Maritime Transport Council in London. At the postwar Versailles Conference, he was appointed executive secretary of the Reparations Section of the American Peace Mission. He was awarded three decorations, the French Legion of Honor, the Yugoslavian Grand Officer Order of St. Sava, and the Netherlands' Officer Order of Orange-Nassau.

From 1918 to 1932 Greene was a partner of the investment banking house of Lee, Higginson & Company, which he had joined in 1917. He chiefly managed overseas loan negotiations. Actively involved in public service organizations, he was treasurer of the American Social Hygiene Association from 1920 to 1932. He chaired the Institute of Pacific Relations' American Council from 1929 to 1932 and was international chairman from 1929 to 1933. When Greene was later called to testify before Senator Patrick A. McCarran's committee about the alleged communistic views of institute members, he defended its scholarly research (*Boston Sunday Herald*, 23 Mar. 1952).

After Lee, Higginson & Company voluntarily liquidated because of bankruptcy in 1932, Greene became Wilson Professor of International Politics at the University College of Wales in Aberystwyth. In 1934 he was appointed director of the 1936 Harvard Tercentenary Celebration and was given a free hand in arranging its events, which included conferences, symposia, the awarding of sixty honorary degrees, and addresses by Harvard president James Bryant Conant and alumnus President Franklin D. Roosevelt. These events Greene recorded in *The Tercentenary of Harvard College, Chronicle of the Tercentenary Year 1935–1936* (1937). From 1934 to 1943 he served as secretary to the Harvard Corporation under President Conant.

Throughout his long and varied career, Greene was a very competent and fair-minded administrator and trustee. "He was," observed President Conant, "a true gentleman, conservative in matters of taste yet a liberal on all academic questions" (James B. Conant, *My Several Lives* [1970], p. 148). Greene's deepest loyalty belonged to Harvard, which he demonstrated by opposing decisions that seemed to him to compromise its commitment to equality of opportunity and to religious toleration. During the 1920s he had opposed President Lowell's proposals to limit the number of Jewish students in Harvard College and to exclude black students from the Freshman Halls. Greene later took issue with the efforts of President Nathan Marsh Pusey and the chairman of the university's board of preachers to exclude non-Christian private religious services from the Harvard Memorial Church, built to honor the university's dead in twentieth-century wars. Greene decried "a tragic lack of Christian charity" in barring Jewish weddings and funerals, even though Jews had contributed generously to the church's construction and had died in war ("Right of Rite," *Harvard Crimson*, 12 Apr. 1958). His opposition and that of many faculty and alumni helped to open Memorial Church, by an action of the corporation, to all private religious services.

Greene's first wife died in 1941, and in 1942 he married Dorothea Rebecca Dusser de Barenne; they had one son. After retiring from Harvard, Greene remained active in Boston's civic and cultural organizations, serving as a trustee of the Boston Symphony Orchestra (later as president), of the New England Conservatory of Music, of Mount Auburn Hospital, and of the Isabella Stewart Gardner Museum (also as secretary and treasurer). He was president of the American Asiatic Association, the Japan Society, and the East Asiatic Society of Boston. Greene died in Cambridge, Massachusetts.

• Greene's papers in the Harvard University Archives contain correspondence, subject files, scrapbooks, and his writings, including a typed autobiography, "Recollections of a Varied Life." A substantial part of the latter was published as *Years with President Eliot* (1960) and as *Reminiscences* (1964). He occasionally commented or wrote on international issues, for example, *The League, Its Weaknesses and a Possible Remedy* (1935?). Other useful sources in the archives are Greene's biographical sketches in the *Harvard College Class of 1896* anniversary reports and his Quinquennial File, which contains a biographical sketch and clippings of his magazine and newspaper pieces. An obituary is in the *New York Times*, 30 Mar. 1959.

MARCIA G. SYNNOTT

GREENE, Nathanael (27 July 1742–19 June 1786), general in the American Revolution, was born in Potowomut (now Warwick), Rhode Island, the son of Nathanael Greene, an iron founder, and Mary Mott. Because his Quaker parents believed in manual labor and a minimum of education, he commenced working early in life at his father's forge without an opportunity for schooling. However, he was very bright and early acquired a love of books. A self-taught reader, he also became a fluent letter writer. During his lifetime he came to possess over 200 volumes on various subjects, especially military history and theory. In 1774 he married Catherine Littlefield; they had five children.

Greene began to show interest in public affairs when tensions between the colonies and Great Britain mounted in the mid-1770s. At that time he rejected the pacifism of his parents and organized the Kentish Guards in preparation for war. When he was rejected as an officer because of a limp caused by a childhood injury, he volunteered as a private in order to prove himself and spent his spare time studying military science. He also served on a committee empowered by the state legislature to prepare Rhode Island's defenses. Thus gaining the attention of the assembly, he received appointment in 1775 as general of the Rhode Island Army of Observation, being promoted over veteran officers of the Seven Years' War because of his likable personality, knowledge of military strategy, and political influence. In the next few weeks he organized three regiments and reported with them to General George Washington at the siege of Boston. The commander in chief was impressed by Greene's acumen and marked the young man for future responsibilities in the Continental army.

During his first year as a soldier Greene's performance was not particularly distinguished. He spent months in Boston and New York in a stalemate with the enemy, during which time he continued his studies of military matters and prepared Long Island's defenses. He was promoted to major general in August 1776, but he was too ill with a "raging Fever" to lead his troops when General William Howe attacked a month later. In November Greene was placed in command of Forts Washington and Lee, north of New York City. Partly because of his decision not to evacuate Fort Washington on Manhattan when it became endangered by the enemy, the British captured the fort, taking 2,800 prisoners. His confidence greatly shaken, Greene momentarily doubled his military acumen, as did others. However, he redeemed himself in December by helping Washington plan and execute the American retreat across New Jersey and the enormously successful attack on Trenton.

Over the next few months Greene made himself indispensable to Washington by taking on numerous tasks, not least of which was helping fend off Howe's attacks in New Jersey during the early summer of 1777. After the British landed at the head of Chesapeake Bay to drive toward Philadelphia from the south, he played a pivotal role in the battle of the Brandywine in September, marching his division four miles to thwart Howe's maneuver against Washington's right flank. A month later, at Germantown, he penetrated enemy lines before being compelled to carry out a masterful retreat, pressed hard by British general James Grant. In camp at Valley Forge during the following winter, he and Washington were accused of incompetence by several congressmen because of their defeats in Pennsylvania, but neither general was ever

in serious danger of losing command, and the grumbling soon faded.

In fact, Greene was in such high standing among Americans that he was soon urged by Congress and Washington to assume the vital post of quartermaster general. In deference to Washington's wishes, Greene accepted the post, but he disliked giving up battlefield command and later asserted that he considered the office "derogatory." In the next two years, despite enormous obstacles, he vastly improved the flow of matériel to the troops. Because inflation required them to pay huge prices for goods, he and his assistants were charged with profiteering, although the accusation was never proven. In August 1780 Greene resigned his post in disgust after a months-long battle with Congress. Throughout his tenure as quartermaster general, Greene had continued to serve Washington as an adviser and occasionally as a commander in the field. At the battle of Monmouth in June 1778 he took charge of Charles Lee's (1731–1782) troops after Washington relieved Lee for retreating without orders during the fight. He used his knowledge of his home state to assist John Sullivan in his Rhode Island campaign of 1778, and two years later he commanded at Springfield, New Jersey, when Baron Wilhelm von Knyphausen made a foray out of New York City to test American mettle.

In October 1780 Greene received the greatest opportunity of his military career: independent command in the Southern Department. During the previous summer British troops under Lord Cornwallis had gained control of Georgia and South Carolina and had defeated Horatio Gates at Camden. With North Carolina and Virginia seemingly in peril, Congress granted Washington the right to choose Gates's replacement. He immediately selected Greene, who at once commenced his journey southward. After pausing in Philadelphia to plead successfully for the addition of Henry "Light-Horse Harry" Lee's legion to his command, he proceeded to Virginia, where he appointed Baron Friedrich von Steuben to gather men and supplies. During his journey he studied maps of the South in preparation for his new duties. On 3 December 1780 in Charlotte, North Carolina, he took command from General Gates of his army of 2,200 troops, almost two-thirds of whom were militiamen.

Fully aware that Cornwallis was in Winnsboro, South Carolina, awaiting reinforcements from Virginia before attacking, Greene decided to make a bold stroke against his foe before the reinforcements arrived. Dividing his army, he sent Daniel Morgan westward with 600 men to shadow Cornwallis while he rebuilt his army at Cheraw, South Carolina. After Morgan's tactically brilliant victory over Banastre Tarleton's forces at Cowpens on 17 January 1781, Greene raced north ahead of an angry Cornwallis to rendezvous with Morgan and cross the Dan River to relative safety. Having successfully eluded his foe, he augmented his forces to a total of 4,200 men and recrossed the Dan, challenging Cornwallis to a battle at Guilford Courthouse, North Carolina. On 15 March he was attacked and after a furious fight was driven from the field. Cornwallis, having suffered 30 percent casualties, limped to the coast at Wilmington, where he refitted his army. Deciding to change his field of action to Virginia, he marched his troops northward to Yorktown.

Greene moved southward with 1,500 Continentals, his only remaining troops after militia departures, in an effort to overcome about 8,000 enemy soldiers garrisoned throughout South Carolina and Georgia. Although he was overpowered by the British in confrontations at Hobkirk's Hill and Fort Ninety-six, Greene, aided by partisans such as Francis Marion, Thomas Sumter, and Andrew Pickens, compelled his enemies to fall back from their interior posts. On 8 September he fought a drawn battle with Colonel Andrew Stewart at Eutaw Springs, after which Stewart withdrew to Charleston. A few weeks later Greene learned of Cornwallis's surrender to Washington at Yorktown. However, this American triumph did not bring an end to Greene's struggle in the South; the British still held Charleston and Savannah, and patriots and Loyalists still warred on each other throughout his command. Aided by General Anthony Wayne, he worked to restore peace in the South while continuing to apply pressure against the British in Charleston and Savannah until both cities were evacuated in 1782. His military labors ceased only when the final peace treaty was signed the following year.

After the war, both South Carolina and Georgia granted Greene large estates. Although he returned to the North in late 1783 as a conquering hero, two years later he and his wife settled in Georgia. His last years were plagued by accusations of profiteering in the closing months of the war and by a debt of thousands of dollars after a note that he had cosigned came due. Although he was vindicated of the profiteering charges, his debt woes continued, probably shortening his life. He died of an infection at "Mulberry Grove," his plantation near Savannah, leaving his family in financial straits until his debts were liquidated by Congress ten years later.

The first time Washington met Greene he declared that Greene could be relied upon to assume command of the Continental army should he become incapacitated. Thomas Jefferson asserted long after the war that Greene had no equal as a military thinker among his peers in the officer corps, and Francis Kinloch, a congressman who fought in the war, called him the "military genius" of the American Revolution. These assessments of Greene are borne out by his military record in both the North and the South, and historians today evaluate his military abilities as highly as did his contemporaries. Few would deny that he deserves to be remembered as the "strategist of the Revolution."

• Greene's papers are in the William L. Clements Library at the University of Michigan, the National Archives, the Library of Congress, and the American Philosophical Society Library. His correspondence is being published in *The Papers of General Nathanael Greene*, ed. Richard K. Showman et al. (1976–). The best biography is Theodore Thayer, *Nathanael Greene: Strategist of the American Revolution* (1960). In addition, Thayer has written a fine short sketch, "Nathanael Greene: Revolutionary War Strategist," *George Washington's Generals*, ed. George A. Billias (1964). See also G. W. Greene, *The Life of Nathanael Greene, Major-General in the Army of the Revolution* (3 vols., 1867–1871); William Johnson, *Sketches of the Life and Correspondence of Nathanael Greene, Major General of the Armies of the United States in the War of the Revolution* (2 vols., 1822); Douglas S. Freeman, *George Washington: A Biography* (7 vols., 1948–1957); M. F. Treacy, *Prelude to Yorktown: The Southern Campaign of Nathanael Greene, 1780–81* (1963); and John S. Pancake, *This Destructive War: The British Campaign in the Carolinas, 1780–1782* (1985).

PAUL DAVID NELSON

GREENE, Roger Sherman (29 May 1881–27 March 1947), diplomat, medical administrator, and lobbyist, was born in Westborough, Massachusetts, the son of Daniel Crosby Greene and Mary Jane Forbes, two of the earliest American missionaries to work in Japan. He received his early education in Japan, where he spent most of his life before college. At Harvard University he earned an A.B. in 1901 and an A.M. in 1902.

From 1902 to 1911 Greene filled several positions in the consular service in Brazil, Japan, Siberia, Manchuria, and China. As a diplomat he received much praise and several promotions, becoming consul general in Hankow in 1911. During the Chinese Revolution of 1911, Greene's work to ensure the safety of American citizens in China earned much official praise. At the same time, he argued against active American political involvement in Chinese domestic affairs, noting that such interference could prolong the conflict.

In 1914 the Rockefeller Foundation—of which Greene's brother Jerome was secretary—offered him a position on its commission to investigate the medical conditions of China. Having grown uncomfortable with his position in the foreign service, and despite being offered the position of assistant to the chief of the Division of Far Eastern Affairs, Greene resigned from government service to take a permanent position with the Foundation. The commission recommended the creation of the Chinese Medical Board (CMB), to help develop medical education in China by establishing hospitals and medical schools, fostering research, and creating a system of fellowships and grants to medical agencies and physicians. Upon the Board's creation in December 1914, Greene became its resident director in China.

During his years with the Rockefeller Foundation, Greene remained active and vocal in social and political matters within Asia. He was opposed to the proselytization practices of zealous evangelical missionaries in China, who treated the Chinese with contempt while pressing their strong religious views on them. He also became increasingly skeptical of the national commercial propaganda that seemed to drive much U.S. policy in the Far East. During the later 1910s, he began to criticize Japanese imperialist aggression against China, arguing against people like his brother Jerome, who felt the Japanese would exercise more restraint.

After the 1917 flood and famine in northern China, the Red Cross approached Greene to administer $200,000 worth of aid to the region. He set up a series of public works programs and returned a balance of $75,000 to the Red Cross. In 1919 he argued against allied intervention in the Russian Revolution, suggesting that the allies were siding with elites without considering the interests of the Russian people. He married Kate Brown in 1920; they had two children.

Greene was a major actor in the early years of the CMB. He became the board's director in 1921 and helped establish the Peking Union Medical College that same year. He became associate director of the college in 1927 and worked to "modernize" the values of both students and personnel, reasoning that this would facilitate the proper study and practice of modern western medicine. He also served as a vice president of the Rockefeller Foundation from 1927 to 1929.

In China Greene fostered strong ties with Chinese intellectuals and some key American diplomats. He used these connections to continue arguing against U.S. involvement in Chinese domestic affairs. After the beginning of the Nationalist Revolution in 1925, Greene successfully rallied opposition to the militant stance of J. V. A. MacMurray, U.S. minister to China. He argued that the Chinese should have the same freedom to fight their civil war as Americans had in the 1860s because only a decisive victor could end the persistent strife and pave the way to a unified nation. Greene further argued that the renunciation of American extraterritoriality in China would reduce the amount of interference by Americans in Chinese affairs. This change, however, was years away.

In the early 1930s, tensions developed within the Rockefeller Foundation that led to Greene's eventual resignation. The main source of conflict surrounded the existence of the religion department in the Peking Union Medical College. When the school was founded, John D. Rockefeller, Jr. had intended to maintain a strong religious aspect to the College's instruction, and his son sought to preserve this policy. But Greene questioned the advisability of such a practice. His concern was particularly relevant given the growth of Chinese nationalist sentiment and its hostility toward Western religious evangelism. In 1934, after a confrontation, Greene resigned from the board. Later that year he was also forced to resign from the college, which he left in July 1935.

For the rest of the 1930s, Greene maintained a strong interest in Asian affairs from inside the United States. He criticized the American government's trade with Japan during the Sino-Japanese War. In 1938 he joined the American Committee for Non-Participation in Japanese Aggression (or "Price Committee" after its founders Frank and Harry Price), becoming its chairman in December 1938. He argued that sanctions against Japan would help China in the war, thereby maintaining a balance of power in the Pacific. Despite popular support for its ideas, the Price Committee saw little legislative response to its assertions. In 1940 Greene joined the Committee to Defend America by Aiding the Allies (the "White Committee" after its founder William Allen White). He became its associate director and urged the committee, which was preoccupied with affairs in Europe, to consider China as an ally needing aid. The committee did not heed Greene's advice until after Japan signed the Tripartite Pact with Germany and Italy in September 1940.

During the Second World War, Greene served part-time with the Department of State's Cultural Affairs Division as a consultant on medical affairs in China. In 1942, after two decades of lobbying, he finally saw the renunciation of extraterritoriality rights. At the war's end, he watched with interest the power struggle between the Chinese Communist Party and the Kuomintang leadership. He saw positive merits in each but eventually favored the latter, although he did not live to see the eventual Communist victory. He died of cardiac failure and chronic nephritis in West Palm Beach, Florida.

While not a major public figure, Greene was influential in promoting constructive American contributions to the development of China. Through his affiliation with the Rockefeller Foundation, he oversaw great improvement in medical education and facilities. His access to Chinese intellectuals, American diplomats, and government figures provided him with a valuable perspective on U.S. involvement in China. While his lobbying activities did achieve major victories, like the opposition to MacMurray in 1925 and the renunciation of extraterritoriality in 1942, Greene's influence was not widely known.

• Greene's papers are located in the Houghton Library, Harvard University. The Price Committee Papers are also at Harvard; the White Committee papers are at Princeton University. The most thorough biography of Greene remains Warren I. Cohen, *The Chinese Connection: Roger S. Greene, Thomas W. Lamont, George E. Sokolsky and American-East Asian Relations* (1978). Greene's work on the China Medical Board is detailed in Mary E. Ferguson, *China Medical Board and Peking Union Medical College: A Chronicle of Fruitful Collaboration, 1914–1951* (1970). An analysis of the Rockefeller Foundation's work is provided in Frank Ninovich, "The Rockefeller Foundation, China, and Cultural Change," *Journal of American History* 70 (1984): 799–820, which includes a brief section on Greene's work with the foundation. An obituary is in the *New York Times*, 29 Mar. 1947.

DANIEL MALLECK

GREENE, Samuel Dana (11 Feb. 1840–11 Dec. 1884), naval officer, was born in Cumberland, Maryland, the son of George Sears Greene, a major general in the U.S. Army, and Martha Barrett Dana. Samuel Greene's brother, Francis Vinton Greene, became a general in the U.S. Army. Entering one of the first classes of the U.S. Naval Academy, Samuel graduated seventh in a class of twenty in 1859. One of his classmates was Alfred T. Mahan. Greene entered active service as a midshipman aboard the USS *Hartford*, a warship normally on station in the East Indies. He was promoted to lieutenant on 31 August 1861.

Greene returned to the United States and was reassigned to the iron-clad *Monitor* while it was still under construction in Brooklyn, New York. Although the famous warship would have five captains during its brief service of less than one year, Greene remained its only executive officer. He was at the launching in January 1862 and stayed with it until it sank in December of that year. Well beyond that time, the events surrounding the *Monitor*'s epic battle with a Confederate iron-clad had a profound effect on Greene's short life and his tragic death.

Greene's knowledge of the *Monitor*'s unique construction, particularly its distinctive revolving gun turret, made him indispensable to all of the ship's captains, particularly its first skipper, Lieutenant John L. Worden. The *Monitor* was formally turned over to the navy on 25 February and was dispatched to Hampton Roads, Virginia, nine days later.

The *Monitor*, its volunteer crew, and Lieutenant Greene were all but lost on the vessel's maiden voyage. Constructed in great haste, the low-riding warship leaked badly at the seam between the deck and the cylindrical turret. Additionally, when moderate seas were encountered, the *Monitor*'s exhaust and breather system flooded, hampering propulsion and urgently requiring bilge pumping. Under Greene's determined supervision, the crew made repairs. By 8 March, when the warship arrived off the Virginia coast twenty miles from Hampton Roads, the craft was combat worthy, albeit only in calm waters.

The *Monitor*'s arrival was none too soon. The crew could hear firing as they pulled toward Hampton Roads, and Worden correctly suspected the Confederate ironclad *Virginia* was engaging Union wooden-hulled craft near Fort Monroe. The captain ordered the *Monitor* cleared for action. Approaching the Union fleet, the *Monitor*'s crew saw a number of burning or grounded Federal ships. As darkness gathered, the *Monitor* was assigned to protect the grounded USS *Minnesota*, an easy prey for the *Virginia*, which the Federals believed would return the next day.

Soon after daylight on Sunday, 9 March, Lieutenant Greene began the most important and memorable day of his life. Several Confederate ships, including the *Virginia*, began making their way to the *Monitor* and the helpless *Minnesota*. To better protect the *Minnesota*, the *Monitor* moved toward the raiders, with Greene inside the turret ready to direct the ship's guns. Despite the *Monitor*'s 10 to 2 inferiority in guns, Worden ordered it to bear down on the *Virginia*. The wooden-hulled Confederate ships departed, and the two ironclads began a fierce battle. Greene conducted the firing in the turret of the *Monitor*. Captain Worden was wounded, and Greene took command after tending to Worden. At the helm Greene discovered that the *Virginia* was badly damaged and had turned away to safety. Firing a few parting shots, Greene returned his ship to protecting the *Minnesota*.

Although the *Virginia* had retreated and Greene's return to the *Minnesota* was judged correct by his superiors, the young lieutenant's brief conduct of command was criticized. Some believed he should have pursued the crippled *Virginia* and exacted revenge. Greene was the last officer to leave the *Monitor* when it went down in a gale off Cape Hatteras, North Carolina, on the night of 30–31 December 1862. His subsequent war service was as executive officer aboard the blockade ships *Florida* and *Iroquois*.

In 1863 Greene married Mary Willis Dearth. The couple had three children, the eldest of whom, Samuel Dana Greene, Jr., graduated first in his class at the U.S. Naval Academy in 1883. Mary Dearth Greene died in 1874, and in 1876 Greene married Mary Abby Babbitt. He was promoted to lieutenant commander on 11 August 1865 and to commander on 12 December 1872. He spent most of his postwar career as an instructor or member of the staff at the Naval Academy. He was also skipper of the USS *Juniata* (1875–1876), the USS *Monongahela* (1876–1877), and the USS *Despatch* (1882–1884).

The defense of his decision to abandon the fight with the *Virginia* and resume the defense of the *Minnesota* was an agonizing, lifelong task for Greene. While preparing a magazine article on the battle between the *Monitor* and the *Virginia*, he took his own life in Portsmouth, New Hampshire. His contemporaries concluded he could not bear to once again argue his role in history's first duel between two ironclads. Greene's decision to return to the original mission when the Confederate ironclad retired has been subsequently considered correct. Every facet of his career and the judgments of those officers who knew him best point to his competence as a naval officer. Greene was simply a delayed casualty of the intense passions surrounding the American Civil War.

• Greene's final account of the battle between the ironclads was published after his death and is available as "In the Monitor Turret," *Battles and Leaders of the Civil War*, vol. 1, ed. Robert U. Johnson and Clarence C. Buel (1887). A Greene family history is G. S. Greene and Louise B. Clarke, *The Greenes of Rhode Island* (1903). Obituaries are in *Proceedings of the U.S. Naval Institute* 11 (1885) and the *Concord Evening Monitor*, 12 Dec. 1884.

ROD PASCHALL

GREENE, Sarah Pratt McLean (3 July 1856–28 Dec. 1935), author, was born in Simsbury, Connecticut, the daughter of Dudley Bestor McLean and Mary Payne, farmers. The fourth child in a family of five children and granddaughter of the minister of the Congregational church in Simsbury, she was instilled with Puritan ideals and the value of learning. Her education included district and private schooling, but she was mainly taught by her mother. In 1872 she entered Mount Holyoke Seminary, where she demonstrated a capacity for warm friendship with teachers and students, an enjoyment of new adventures, and an early talent for writing, according to her biography in *Representative Women of New England* (1904).

After two years Sally McLean left school to accept a teaching position in Cedarville, Massachusetts, a small fishing village about thirteen miles from Plymouth. On returning to her family's home at the end of term, she recorded her fascination with the customs and speech of the inhabitants of the small Cape Cod village in the form of a novel. The narrator, an inexperienced schoolteacher and naive young woman, records her efforts to bring education and culture to the "rough" community of Wallencamp. Ultimately the narrator abandons her condescension toward the "Wallencampers" for an appreciation of the untutored dignity of their lives. Having intended to redeem these backward people, the schoolteacher discovers on leaving that, ironically, her own salvation has been wrought by their simple but genuine understanding of life and death. She muses, "Poor squalid, solitary, beautiful Wallencamp . . . thrilled me with a sense of some diviner, some half-comprehended glory" (p. 328).

Never intending to make her account public, McLean used the actual names of the villagers. Sometime later, her brother-in-law, who knew a junior member of the Boston publishing firm A. Williams & Co., encouraged his talented relative to submit something for publication. McLean apparently sent her unrevised novel. The manuscript was accepted immediately and published as *Cape Cod Folks* in 1881.

This first novel, which began McLean's career as an author, met with much popular and critical success. By the end of 1882 the novel had been reprinted eleven times. By 1883 nearly 20,000 copies had been sold. Critics emphasized McLean's memorable depictions of a singular and quaint way of life. The reviewer in *Harper's* (Nov. 1881) admired the "gift of humor" that enabled her to present "men and things with spirit and freshness" and to describe "the provincial traits of this most provincial of all the outlying New England settlements." The reviewer in the *Nation* (Sept. 1881) notes the "vivid force" of her portraits. McLean was quickly identified as a local color writer who had appreciatively presented the unique qualities of life in this Cape Cod fishing village.

Nevertheless, McLean's use of the actual names of the villagers resulted in lawsuits by several inhabitants of Cedarville. The court cases provoked a flurry of critical response and newspaper articles. Many of the reviewers argued that the sincerity and truthfulness of her portrayal of life in Cedarville mitigated the unfortunate use of real names. McLean, disturbed by the reaction of Cedarville, indicated in a letter to her publishers her lack of experience as a writer and her disbelief that a work "undertaken . . . so utterly without malicious motive . . . can prove so disastrous" (Hinckley, p. 462). As soon as the publishers were made aware of the problem, they agreed to change the names, although by this time the book was entering its third printing. Eventually one defendant was awarded $1,095 in an 1884 settlement. The novel was dramatized in 1906 by Earl W. Mayo and ran for twenty-four performances at the Academy of Music in New York City.

McLean's next two works evoked neither the critical acclaim nor the controversy of her first book. She published the novel *Towhead, Story of a Girl* in 1883 and a collection of short stories previously published in various magazines and titled *Some Other Folks* in 1884. In 1887 McLean married Franklin Lynde Greene in St. Louis, Missouri. Living near Chihuahua, Mexico, where her husband was involved in a silver-mining operation, and in Washington Territory and California, Sarah Greene evidently found the American West a suitable imaginative source for storytelling. *Lastchance Junction, Far Far West* (1889) and *Leon Pontifax* (1890) were both set in the West. In 1890 Greene returned to New England after the death of her twin sons and, later, her husband. Having traveled to Europe and Nova Scotia, she eventually settled in Lexington, Massachusetts, although she spent several summers touring various parts of Maine.

An isolated community set on the Maine coastline furnished the starting point for her second most popular novel, *Vesty of the Basins* (1892). The novel parallels *Cape Cod Folks* in its use of dialect, its careful representation of locale and local custom, and its exploration of the interaction between an outsider and the close-knit members of a small community living a simple life. Critical response to the novel has been uneven. The critic in the *Nation* (July 1892) asserted that Greene's unauthentic and exaggerated "caricature" of her "model" would at least save her publisher from further lawsuits. A later review, however, claimed the book "had phenomenal success" and believed the subjects of Greene's tale would "know their own manners and lives furnish the basis of the story" and continue to "read its pages with delight" (*Representative Women*, p. 263). Like *Cape Cod Folks*, *Vesty of the Basins* was popular enough to produce a dramatic adaptation.

Over the next twenty years Greene continued to write and publish fiction. Her later works include *Stuart and Bamboo* (1897), *The Moral Imbeciles* (1898), *Flood-Tide* (1901), *Winslow Plain* (1902), *Deacon Lysander* (1904), *Power Lot* (1906), *The Long Green Road* (1911), and *Everbreeze* (1913). One reader made special mention of *Winslow Plain*, set in a "quaint" New England village a half century earlier, noting it contains "rare poetic gems" (*Representative Women*, p. 264).

Greene's popular success in her own time is proven by a biographical account written in the midst of her long and productive writing career. Commenting on Greene's style and storytelling ability, the author mentions the "many, beautiful, helpful passages," the "enthralling interest of the story," and Greene's "voice so rich toned it might belong to a Southerner" (*Representative Women*, p. 264). By the end of her career Greene had acquired a measure of critical success and perceived acceptance into the literary establishment. She died in Lexington, Massachusetts. Her obituary in the *Boston Globe* notes a personal friendship with James Russell Lowell, Mark Twain, and Oliver Wendell Holmes and observes that John Greenleaf Whittier once said of her, "Young woman, thee hast a future."

Twain had praise for "her delightful unworldly people" in *Flood-Tide* (*Letters*, p. 769). Fifty years later another reader found *Cape Cod Folks* still deserving of high praise and argued that the work was "one of the most interesting books ever written" about the region (Hinckley, p. 454). He admired her "penetrating eye," willingness "to paint follies and foibles," and "sense of the pathetic and ridiculous and heroic elements in life" (Hinckley, p. 466).

Despite early critical praise and popular success, Greene's current reputation has fallen considerably. Her efforts to represent the life and speech of communities in the West and New England place her in the tradition of regional writing so popular at the turn of the century. Her interest in women's experiences link her to other, much better known, local color women writers of the time, such as Mary Wilkins Freeman and Sarah Orne Jewett. Her humor, witty commentary, and implicit social critique parallel another contemporary, Edith Wharton.

• A lengthy contemporary biographical entry is in Julia Ward Howe, ed., *Representative Women of New England* (1904). A lengthy review of the litigation over *Cape Cod Folks* is in Edward B. Hinckley, "Cape Cod Folks," *Harvard Graduates Magazine* 34 (June 1931): 452–67. For Mark Twain's comment on *Flood-Tide*, see H. N. Smith and W. Gibson, eds., *Mark Twain–Howells Letters* (1960), p. 769. For reviews, see the *Nation*, 22 Sept. 1881, p. 236, and *Harper's*, Nov. 1881, p. 954, on *Cape Cod Folks*, and the *Nation*, 14 July 1892, p. 34, on *Vesty of the Basins*. Obituaries are in the *Boston Globe*, 30 Dec. 1935, and the *New York Times*, 31 Dec. 1935.

DIANNE L. CHAMBERS

GREENE, William Cornell (26 Aug. 1853–5 Aug. 1911), rancher, mineowner, and investor, was born at Duck Creek, Wisconsin, the son of Townsend Greene and Eleanor Cornell, farmers. His father died when William was very young, leaving his mother apparently little choice but to split up the family of two sons and two daughters. As a result, Greene was brought up by his great aunt in Chappaqua, New York. He apparently obtained a decent education, given the standards of that day, then moved to New York at age seventeen to begin his business career as a clerk in a tea store. In 1872 Greene moved west, apparently working in the Dakotas, then in Texas, and finally drifting to Arizona, where he became a prospector in the Bradshaw Mining District in 1877. He was then twenty-four years old, brave to a fault, given to gambling, short in temper, and modest of means.

From 1880 to 1899, Greene lived in the Tucson/Bisbee region of southern Arizona, principally as a farmer and rancher but sometime prospector and miner both in Arizona and in Sonora across the Mexican border. Here he prospered, in part through his marriage in 1881 to Ella Roberts Moson, the sister of a business partner; they had two children. When his daughter Ella died in a drowning incident, Greene blamed the tragedy on a business foe and shot and killed the man in Tombstone. Greene claimed self-defense and was acquitted by a jury. In 1899 Greene's wife died of cancer. Two years later Greene married Mary Proctor, a woman half his age; they had six children.

By the mid-1890s, Greene had prospered as a farmer and rancher and had become a leading citizen of the Tucson/Bisbee region of southern Arizona. But it was the lure of copper mining that drove him and established his national reputation.

Fifty miles south of Bisbee, Arizona, lay the Cananea Mountains of Sonora, Mexico. Though long a lodestone to American investors, Cananea had produced little ore despite obvious mineralization. But Greene was not deterred. In 1896 he leased a number of mining claims from Elena Carraway, the widow and heir of General Ignacio Pesqueira, and so began his meteoric rise (and fall) in the copper industry. Greene quickly won the support of the Mexican president Porfirio Diaz and organized his first copper mining companies. He acquired more claims in the late 1890s, and then in 1899 he went to Wall Street to raise the capital to develop his two principal enterprises, the Greene Consolidated Copper Company and the Cananea Consolidated Copper Company. He now split his time between New York and Sonora before moving permanently to Cananea.

The first years of the twentieth century saw "Colonel" Greene's ascent as a copper tycoon. He raised huge sums on Wall Street and used the proceeds to develop his mines at Cananea, build reduction works, and acquire still more properties to form an integrated copper empire. As a result, Cananea became a large producer. But even as it did, Greene lived grandly and managed poorly. Although he hired some reputable engineers, most contemporary mining experts viewed his operations as wasteful and extravagant—ever in debt and always behind in payment. He also had dealings with the controversial stock manipulator Thomas W. Lawson, associated with the financial legerdemain of the era.

Greene's celebrated rise as a copper titan became a cropper almost as quickly. In June 1906 Mexican workers at Cananea struck for higher wages and shorter hours. They opposed company stores and supported the advance of qualified Mexicans into management—the opening blow (some say) in the revolution against Diaz and Mexico's domination by foreign capital. Greene reacted quickly. After a shooting in Cananea killed or wounded nearly fifty people, he got Arizona Rangers at Bisbee to cross the border to guard company property and break the strike under the guise that American lives were in danger. Mexican rurales arrived to finish the controversial work.

The great strike at Cananea marked the beginning of the end for Greene. Public embarrassment, fear of another strike, unpaid accounts, and falling copper prices overwhelmed his companies. Overextended, Greene and his associates had to sell out in 1906. He apparently made out well, but he was gone from the copper industry early the next year. The chief victims of his fall were unpaid Mexican workers.

Broken in health and spirit, if not in fortune, Greene spent the last few years of his life working his ranches in Sonora. On 31 July 1911 he was thrown from a runaway buggy; broken bones and a punctured lung brought on pneumonia, and he died in Sonora.

Although his careers in cattle and copper were long, Greene's reputation and notoriety, rest largely on his short career as a copper tycoon. As a promotor and speculator, Greene lived high and created his own legend—a legend celebrated by the sensationalist muckraking press of early twentieth-century America. While he was indeed the speculator, gambler, and shootist of his own legend, it was his energy that was responsible for opening and developing the Cananea copper mines.

• Greene's surviving papers rest in various scattered collections, public and private, and in the files of the Compania Minera de Cananea. The most complete modern treatment of Greene's spectacular career is C. L. Sonnichsen, *Colonel Greene and the Copper Skyrocket . . .* (1974). Sonnichsen's goal was to present the whole man and dispel the "infectious folklore"—pro and con—that has distorted Greene's reputation. For other information on Greene, see David M. Pletcher, *Rails, Mines, and Progress* (1958), and Marvin D. Bernstein, *The Mexican Mining Industry* (1964).

JAMES E. FELL, JR.

GREENER, Richard Theodore (30 Jan. 1844–2 May 1922), African-American educator, lawyer, and diplomat, was born in Philadelphia, Pennsylvania, the son of Richard Wesley Greener, a seaman who was wounded during the Mexican War while serving aboard the USS *Princeton*, and Mary Ann Le Brune. When he was nine, Greener and his parents moved to Boston but soon left for Cambridge, where he could attend "an unproscriptive school." Greener's father, as chief steward of the *George Raynes*, had taken his son on a voyage to Liverpool but then abandoned the sea in 1853 for the California gold fields. He "was taken sick, met with losses" and was never heard from again. When Greener was twelve years old he left school to help support his mother. Although he quit one of his positions after an employer "struck" him, those whom he met while "knocking around in . . . different occupations" often helped educate him, sharing their libraries and tutoring him in French and Latin.

When Greener wanted to attend college, his employer, Augustus E. Bachelder, offered financial help. Following Bachelder's suggestion, Greener enrolled in the two-year college preparatory program at Oberlin College in Ohio (1862–1864), where he received "considerable practice in speaking and debating," but because of "some colorphobia, shown by . . . classmates" he returned to New England. In 1865 he graduated from Phillips Academy in Andover, Massachusetts, and then attended Harvard, whose president, Thomas Hill, was eager to experiment in educating an African American. Although Greener received the second prize for reading aloud that year, he had been conditionally admitted to college because his background was uneven and he especially lacked mathematical training. Because Hill wanted the experiment "fairly tried," Greener repeated his first year. At the end of

his sophomore year he took the Boylston Prize for Oratory, and his senior dissertation, which defended the land rights of Irish peasants, won the first Bowdoin Prize for research and writing.

After becoming the first black to graduate from Harvard College (1870), Greener later could not recall "many pleasant incidents" there, but he had done well scholastically and made friends with whom he felt at ease. Hailed as a member of the Negro intelligentsia, he began the decade as principal of the male department of the Institute for Colored Youth in Philadelphia (1870–1872) and ended it in the Law Department of Howard University, where he began teaching in 1877 and was dean from 1879 to 1880. In between he was principal of the Sumner High School in Washington, D.C. (1872–1873); associate editor of *New National Era and Citizen*, a publication for blacks; and a law clerk in the office of the attorney for the District of Columbia. He also taught Latin, Greek, international law, and U.S. constitutional history at the University of South Carolina (1873–1877). As its acting librarian he rearranged and cataloged its books, completed a law degree there, and served on a commission to revise the state school system. In 1874 Greener married Genevieve Ida Fleet; five of their seven children reached adulthood. In 1876 Greener was admitted to the South Carolina bar and the next year to the bar of the District of Columbia, where he moved at the end of Reconstruction when doors in South Carolina were suddenly closed to blacks.

Having left the South rather than surrender to white supremacists, Greener heartily endorsed the Windom Resolution (introduced in the U.S. Senate on 16 Jan. 1879 by William Windom of Minnesota) encouraging black migration out of the South (primarily to Kansas). Fearing that the federal government would not give southern blacks the protection they needed, Greener was the spokesman for a delegation of "representative colored men" who saw Windom and called for a special but not legally exclusive black territory. Greener, who became secretary of the Exodus Committee, met in February with a group in Cincinnati and, along with Windom, took a central role in mid-April in organizing an Emigrant Aid Association in Washington. In December he went to Kansas to see firsthand the condition of new black settlers, who were called Exodusters. Disagreeing with Frederick Douglass, the distinguished black abolitionist who urged blacks to stay in the South where their freedom would depend on "right" rather than "flight," Greener brilliantly answered Douglass's objections, taking them up one by one at a congress of the American Social Science Association held in September 1877 at Saratoga Springs, New York.

Greener was without an academic appointment in July 1880 when the Howard University Board of Trustees temporarily disbanded its law department for lack of students. Having held two government clerkships before teaching at Howard and having in 1878 started a law firm, Cook & Greener, he continued his law practice, became a clerk in the office of the Treasury

Department's first comptroller, and remained in demand as a speaker and writer.

In 1880 Greener became involved in the case of Johnson C. Whittaker, which divided the nation and led to the dismissal of the commandant of the U.S. Military Academy at West Point. While teaching at the University of South Carolina, Greener had helped secure Whittaker's appointment to West Point, after choosing him from among 200 possibilities as the student most likely to succeed as the academy's only black cadet. Helping Whittaker secure an education, just as his own benefactors had aided him, Greener kept in touch with his former student, who on the morning of 6 April 1880 was found tied to his bed, bleeding and unconscious. Writing to Greener after he was accused of staging the attack and mutilating himself, Whittaker called it a "heinous plot engaged in by . . . cadets" and "sanctioned by the authorities."

Greener remained by Whittaker's side for most of the early inquiry and became a leading witness and assistant counsel in the court-martial that he called for and demanded to clear Whittaker's name (establishing the precedent that a West Point cadet is an officer of the U.S. Army). Because Greener had campaigned in six states for the Republican party and was one of the thirty members of James A. Garfield's Inaugural Executive Committee, he had access to important officials in both the departing Rutherford B. Hayes administration and the entering Garfield one. After army officers sitting on the court-martial found Whittaker guilty as charged, their decision was reviewed and overturned in March 1882 by Judge Advocate General David G. Swaim. Although, thanks to Greener, Whittaker was reinstated at West Point, Secretary of War Robert Todd Lincoln ordered him discharged for failing an examination he had taken immediately after his attack.

In 1884 Greener campaigned vigorously in eight states for the Republican party and in 1885 was made chief examiner of the New York City Civil Service Board, a position he held until 1889. Also in 1885 he became a trustee of the Grant Monument Association and was elected its secretary (1885–1892). A personal friend of Ulysses S. Grant, whom he had met in 1868 at Harvard and to whom between 1871 and 1876 he had led four delegations of black and white supporters, Greener was proud to be the chief administrative official of Grant's monument association and remained a trustee for the rest of his life. A lover of art who had enjoyed browsing through books on monumental art in the libraries at Harvard, Greener considered himself "better posted [on the subject] than any member of [the Grant Monument Association], and did not hesitate to attack . . . unworthy designs . . . foisted on the committee." After rejecting all proposals in the first competition, the association selected a design by John Hemenway Duncan from the second competition. "I was one of the first to point out the simplicity, dignity, and fitness of [Duncan's design]," Greener later noted, "as presenting the characteristics of the Conqueror of the Rebellion."

Greener was rewarded for campaigning for the Republican party with a political appointment abroad. In January 1898 he turned down an appointment as consul to Bombay because of a bubonic plague epidemic there, and in July he became the first U.S. consul to Vladivostok, Russia, where he served until 1905. His tour of duty began as his country emerged a world power from the Spanish-American War, and he witnessed both the completion of the Trans-Siberian railroad and the Russo-Japanese war. American newspapers often complimented Greener on his enthusiastic performance of his duties and his help to American businessmen. Few people objected to his Japanese mistress (his marriage having been dissolved years earlier). The Russians liked working with him, as did the British, who had him carry on their business when they were expelled from Vladivostok because of their pact with Japan, and the Chinese decorated him with the Order of the Double Dragon for aiding war victims during the Boxer Rebellion in 1900.

But Greener's decoration for services to Japan during the Russo-Japanese war went to his successor, Roger Greene, whose name the Japanese confused with his. The U.S. State Department, where blacks were sometimes referred to as "coons," refused to straighten out the mixup. Dismissed from the post in 1905 on charges of bad habits and dereliction of duty, Greener requested a special investigation, which was carried out by his successor. The charges were not confirmed; apparently he had been confused with another Greener living in Vladivostok. Back in the United States, he was denied a personal hearing over his dismissal.

In 1906 Greener moved to Chicago, where he worked as a special agent for an insurance company and championed black rights in numerous letters to newspapers and in lectures. In July of that year he joined with W. E. B. Du Bois and others in the second convention of the Niagara Movement at Harpers Ferry, West Virginia. Although Du Bois and his backers, who later founded the National Association for the Advancement of Colored People (NAACP), had formed the Niagara Movement to oppose the accommodationist philosophy of Booker T. Washington, Greener had hoped to make peace between the two black leaders. When his efforts failed he backed Du Bois, ending a 23-year friendship with Washington, and worked diligently for the NAACP.

Still brooding in 1912 over the Republican party's treatment of him and other African Americans, Greener backed Woodrow Wilson for president and lived to see him reintroduce segregation into the federal bureaucracy. Greener, who died in Chicago, was perhaps the most gifted of those whom Du Bois called the "talented tenth" of African Americans. But the end of Reconstruction cut short his promising career as an educator in the South, and the seven years he was away in Russia lessened his impact on fellow African Americans.

• Greener's papers, photographs (accompanied by a biographical leaflet), correspondence, and writings (including his Bowdoin Prize–winning dissertation, "The Tenures of Land in Ireland") are at the Schomburg Center for Research in Black Culture of the New York Public Library. His letters are also in the archives of Howard and Harvard Universities. Other material at Harvard includes Richard T. Greener, "Autobiographical Sketch," 19 May 1870, and the *25th Anniversary Report of the Class of 1870* (1895). See also Ruth Ann Stewart and David M. Kahn, *Richard T. Greener: His Life and Work* (1980); Allison Blakely, "Richard T. Greener and the 'Talented Tenth's' Dilemma," *Journal of Negro History* (Oct. 1974): 305–21; Emory J. West, "Harvard's First Black Graduates: 1865–1890," *Harvard Bulletin*, May 1972, pp. 24–28; Nell Irvin Painter, *Exodusters: Black Migration to Kansas after Reconstruction* (1977); Carter G. Woodson, *A Century of Negro Migration* (1918; repr. 1969); and John F. Marszalek, *Court-martial: A Black Man in America* (1972). An obituary is in the *Chicago Daily Tribune*, 4 May 1922.

OLIVE HOOGENBOOM

GREENHALGE, Frederic Thomas (19 July 1842–5 Mar. 1896), politician and lawyer, was born Frederic Thomas Greenhalgh in Clitheroe, Lancashire, England, the son of William Greenhalgh, a textile printer, and Jane Slater. In 1855 he immigrated to Lowell, Massachusetts, where his father was offered a supervisory position in the printing department of the Merrimack Manufacturing Company. Greenhalge, who changed the spelling of his family name, attended public schools in Lowell. He quickly demonstrated his literary and oratorical abilities and graduated from Lowell High School in three years.

In 1859 he entered Harvard College, where his debating skills proved impressive, but he was forced to withdraw after three years. Work stoppages in Lowell mills caused by the Civil War harmed the family finances, then Greenhalge's father became ill and died in October 1862. Greenhalge took a position as a schoolteacher in the town of Chelmsford. Later he studied law while employed at the law office of Brown and Alger in Lowell.

In 1863 Greenhalge attempted to enlist in the Union army but was denied because of ill health. While continuing to seek a commission, he obtained an appointment to the army's commissary department, arriving in New Bern, North Carolina, in November 1863. Although a civilian, he remained in New Bern when it came under southern attack and was given authority over the black soldiers of the Twenty-third Massachusetts Regiment. Later he contracted malaria and was ordered to return home in April 1864.

After recuperating Greenhalge resumed his law study and was admitted to the Massachusetts bar in 1865. His elective political career began in 1868 with his election to the Common Council of Lowell, to which he was reelected in 1869. In 1871 he was elected to Lowell's school committee, serving until 1873. In both bodies he demonstrated strong support for public education.

In his political career Greenhalge was a lifelong Republican with the exception of one year. In 1872, along with other "Liberal Republicans," who disapproved of the incompetence and corruption of the Ulysses S. Grant administration, he supported the Democratic presidential candidate, Horace Greeley. In 1872 Greenhalge ran as a Democrat for the state senate and lost.

In 1872 Greenhalge married Isabel Nesmith, with whom he had four children. His wife was the daughter of John Nesmith, a prosperous businessman who had served a term as lieutenant governor of Massachusetts during the Civil War. Through the 1870s Greenhalge pursued his legal career, developing a solid reputation as an able lawyer and courtroom advocate. He was appointed a justice of the police court in 1874, serving until 1884.

In 1879 Greenhalge was elected mayor of Lowell, to which office he was reelected for a second term without opposition. In 1885 he served for one year in the Massachusetts legislature, where he supported abolition of the poll tax and other reforms. He was defeated for reelection, partly because of his reluctance to campaign. He returned to his law practice until 1889, when he was elected to Congress.

In 1890 and 1891 Greenhalge represented the Eighth Congressional District in the rather tumultuous Fifty-first Congress. Owing to his membership on the Committee on Elections, which faced a large number of contested elections, many emanating from attempts to disfranchise southern blacks, his was an unusually visible freshman term. He made several impassioned speeches before the House on behalf of voting rights for blacks yet retained a degree of nonpartisanship in his votes on election disputes. In a similar vein Greenhalge supported a federal elections bill providing for federal supervision of elections, a measure defeated amid acrimonious debate. He actively supported civil service reform and the Sherman Antitrust Act. A protectionist, he voted for the McKinley Tariff of 1890. He was narrowly defeated in his run for reelection, in large part owing to negative reaction to the tariff bill, which contributed to a Republican loss of Congress and of many state offices, including governor.

In 1893 the onset of a depression assisted Greenhalge's successful bid for the governorship of Massachusetts. As governor he promised to continue reform policies already under way in the state, including civil service reform and regulation of quasi-public corporations, and he advocated woman suffrage. He also supported Republican national policies for gold-based currency and a high tariff.

A remarkable incident occurred in February 1894, Greenhalge's second month in office, when 5,000 unemployed people demonstrated in front of the state house for relief, including state-run farm and factory projects to provide jobs. Greenhalge addressed the crowd, expressing concern but also explaining the limitations of state government. His firm reaction to a socialist demonstrator's rhetoric headed off the possibility of violence. Months later, when the state created a commission to investigate the condition of the unemployed, Greenhalge nominated a socialist to be one of three commissioners.

Greenhalge adhered to his reform principles, most notably through vetoes. He vetoed a veterans' preference bill to exempt veterans from the civil service exam. That the bill passed over his veto attests to its popularity. He vetoed a bill to increase the capital stock of the American Bell Telephone Company, a measure with powerful supporters, on the grounds that it was not in the public interest. However, he demonstrated flexibility in vetoing a state takeover of the Holyoke police force, which he considered an unnecessary violation of home rule. He approved the 1894 Rapid Transit Bill, which authorized the nation's first subway in Boston, but only after successfully demanding the inclusion of provisions for public oversight.

Greenhalge was reelected twice by large majorities. In a speech during his second reelection campaign in 1895, he publicly denounced the rise of "religious bigotry." This statement for tolerance, in a period of rising anti-Catholic nativism, was widely hailed. An immigrant himself, he might have become a moderating voice in the Republican party on the issue of immigration restriction. However, early in his third term he became very ill, suffering from a kidney condition. He died at his home in Lowell. Always in demand as a speaker, his frenetic schedule of more than 300 appearances a year while in office was widely thought to have contributed to his early death.

• Apparently no manuscripts or personal papers of Greenhalge exist. A biography is James E. Nesmith, *The Life and Work of Frederic Thomas Greenhalge, Governor of Massachusetts* (1897). Written by his brother-in-law shortly after Greenhalge's death, it is understandably celebratory but does provide a comprehensive account of his life and career, including several of his speeches in full and excerpted, two of his published articles, and a selection of his poetry. For Massachusetts politics and society during Greenhalge's career, see Jack Tager, ed., *Massachusetts in the Gilded Age* (1985). The obituary in the *Boston Transcript*, 5 Mar. 1896, recounts his life in some detail.

JAMES F. BEAUCHESNE

GREENHOW, Robert (1800–27 Mar. 1854), government servant and historian, was born in Richmond, Virginia, the son of Robert Greenhow, a merchant, and Mary Ann Wills. Greenhow graduated from the College of William and Mary in 1816 and from the College of Physicians and Surgeons in New York City in 1821. After further medical study abroad, he practiced medicine in New York City from 1825 to 1828, when he took up a position as a translator and librarian at the Department of State in Washington. Among his responsibilities was preparation of historical works on diplomatic issues. He wrote *The History and Present Condition of Tripoli* in 1835. Also that year he married Rose O'Neal; they had four daughters. He prepared a report on the Pacific Northwest ("The Oregon Question") at the request of Senator Lewis F. Linn of Missouri in 1839, at a time of renewed interest in settling the question of sovereignty in the area. Congress published 1,500 copies of a revised version, entitled *History of Oregon and California*, in 1844.

An objective scholar whose work was based on original sources in several languages, such as Aaron Arrowsmith's *Map of All the New Discoveries in North America* (1795), Gabriel Franchere's *Relation d'un Voyage à la Côte Nord-Ouest* (1820), Ross Cox's *Adventures on the Columbia River* (1831), and the charter of the Russian-American Company, Greenhow is mainly significant as a historian and for the relationship of his historical works to important issues of the expansionist movement of the 1840s. In 1845 Greenhow's scholarly interests had caught the attention of the highest circles of American policy makers. During the period of increasing tension between the United States and Mexico, President James K. Polk and Secretary of State James Buchanan were asserting that the United States had the right to occupy Texas because it had become a part of the United States as a result of the Louisiana Purchase in 1803. Coincidentally, Greenhow had just completed a scholarly work—although it had not yet been published—entitled "History of Florida, Louisiana, Texas, and California, and of the Adjoining Countries, Including the Whole Valley of the Mississippi." In this manuscript, Greenhow clearly showed that Texas historically had never been part of Louisiana under either France or Spain and thus clearly was a Mexican possession. The work, with its damaging conclusions to the administration's position on the Texas boundary, was never published by the government, either because Greenhow, a loyal Democrat, did not wish to undercut Polk's claim; because Greenhow feared the loss of his job in the State Department if he did publish; or for some other reason. It was privately published posthumously in 1856.

In contrast to his work on Texas, which is principally of interest to historians, Greenhow's scholarship concerning Oregon affected contemporary foreign policy. During the debate in the U.S. Senate on the Oregon Treaty of 1846, expansionists demanding the line of 54°40′ as the northern boundary of the United States had to overcome the precedent that American diplomats had on several occasions, beginning in 1818, offered the line of the forty-ninth parallel, based on their belief that this line had been agreed to by the British and French commissioners at the Treaty of Utrecht in 1713 as the boundary between Canada and Louisiana west of the Lake of the Woods, perhaps as far as the Pacific Ocean. These expansionists found Greenhow's *History of Oregon and California* useful to their cause. In his work on the geography and history of the Pacific Northwest, Greenhow had shown through careful research that such a line had never been agreed to by the Anglo-French commissioners at Utrecht. Thus the earlier American proposals had no binding legal or moral force as precedents. Since the British claims to the Oregon Country also rested on the false Utrecht line, they too were removed as establishing any claim to Oregon. In spite of this attempt to apply Greenhow's work, the ultraexpansionists had finally to agree on the forty-ninth parallel boundary.

Greenhow's *History of Oregon and California* also contributed to the mass of literature published in the 1840s that helped persuade Americans to settle in the benign natural environment of the Oregon Country. Greenhow moved to California in 1850 to practice land law. In 1853 he became associate law agent of the U.S. Land Commission (established by congressional statute in 1851), investigating the claims of "each and every person claiming lands in California by virtue of any right or title derived from the Spanish or Mexican government." Greenhow died in San Francisco from injuries received in a fall. His wife later became a Confederate spy.

• Biographical information about Greenhow is in the biography of his wife, Ishbel Ross, *Rebel Rose* (1954). Works that deal with the significance of Greenhow's research in American diplomatic history are two studies by Frederick Merk, *The Monroe Doctrine and American Expansionism* (1966) and *The Oregon Question* (1967). Greenhow's obituary is in the (San Francisco) *Daily Alta California*, 28 Mar. 1854.

GORDON B. DODDS

GREENHOW, Rose O'Neal (1815?–1 Oct. 1864), Confederate spy, was born in Montgomery County, Maryland. Many O'Neals, their surnames variously spelled, inhabited the area. Speculation centers on a planter, John O'Neale, slain by a slave in 1817, and his wife, Eliza Henrietta (maiden name unknown), as her parents. In early adolescence she and a sister went to Washington, D.C., to live with an aunt, Mrs. H. V. Hill, who managed a popular boardinghouse on Capitol Hill. There she was tutored in the social graces as well as academic subjects and met many of the nation's powerful. Darkly beautiful, vivacious, and quick-witted, she was very popular and dubbed "Wild Rose." The boarder she admired most was John C. Calhoun of South Carolina, whose southern particularism and dedication to states' rights became her own political creed.

In 1833 Rose's sister Ellen married James Madison Cutts, a nephew of Dolley Madison, then Washington's premier hostess. Madison became a mentor, vigorously promoting both sisters' interests. Through the Cutts, Rose met Robert Greenhow, whom she married in 1835. Robert Greenhow, a cultivated Virginian who had studied medicine and law and was fluent in Spanish and French from study abroad, served in the State Department. At a time when rotation in office was becoming the political norm, he survived through numerous administrations with the help of his wife. Her lavish entertaining of present and future secretaries of state, foreign diplomats, and, indeed, anyone interested in affairs of state created webs of friendship, favors, and mutual obligations that increased the influence of both Greenhows. Besides caring for their four children, Rose Greenhow also assisted her husband's research on American land claims in the Pacific Northwest, learning skills of map interpretation and analysis of evidence that would prove useful later.

Rumors of political intrigue followed the couple. In her memoirs Jessie Benton Frémont reported that Rose was in the pay of the British during negotiations over Oregon during the James K. Polk administration and that sensitive state documents were withheld from Robert. At Calhoun's instigation, both Greenhows promoted expansion of slavery by supporting the efforts of Narciso López to liberate Cuba from Spanish rule (1849). Rose Greenhow also helped the dying Calhoun carry on his campaign against sectional compromise in 1850 by lobbying key editors and politicians.

After Robert Greenhow left the State Department in 1850, he traveled with Rose to Mexico City to study California land claims in the Mexican archives. Here he encountered José Limantour, who claimed a huge land grant in and around San Francisco. Recognizing the value of the claim and hoping to profit from establishing its validity, Robert moved to San Francisco, opened a law office, and with his wife's efforts tried to gain a position on the U.S. Land Commission, which could validate the claim. The best Rose could manage for her husband was assistant law agent for the commission, secured through her friend James Buchanan. In 1854, while Rose was in the East, Robert fell into a street excavation and died. Although the city awarded her $10,000 in compensation for his death, the Limantour claims proved fraudulent and a financial loss. In a trip to California in 1856 she promoted James Buchanan's presidential candidacy and advised him that a transcontinental railroad was the key issue in the state. On her return to Washington she moved to a smaller house, wrote comments on Washington society for the New York *Herald*, and capitalized on her association with Buchanan to secure favors for people. She also sought powerful new friends; her name was linked romantically to Senators Joseph Lane (Oreg.) and Henry Wilson (Mass.).

In May 1861, the Civil War having commenced, Captain Thomas Jordan of the U.S. Army, who intended to resign and join Confederate general P. G. T. Beauregard's staff in Virginia, recruited Greenhow to head an espionage ring in Washington. With southern sympathizers still in government jobs, many new officers and government workers eager to brag about their importance, and a general skepticism that women could be spies, information gathering proved all too easy. Greenhow claimed, with only slight exaggeration, to know almost immediately what transpired in cabinet and military staff meetings.

Greenhow's greatest service to the Confederacy came in three messages she sent prior to the Confederate victory at Manassas (Bull Run) in July 1861. These communications confirmed the orders to advance, described the route to be taken, and revealed how the Federals hoped to prevent the consolidation of Confederate forces in their front. Suspicion focused on Greenhow when she mentioned to the wife of a State Department official that she could communicate with Beauregard and openly brought food and clothing to captured Confederates, soliciting their names for forwarding to Richmond. Detective Allan Pinkerton was assigned to investigate her activities and associates, and on 23 August she was placed under house arrest. Although she was able to destroy some papers and smuggle others out, many incriminating items remained.

Greenhow still continued to transmit messages (although Confederate officials feared they were plants). Understanding the propaganda value in exposing the conditions of her confinement, she smuggled out copies of two scathing letters addressed to the secretary of state, which appeared in the newspapers. Following this embarrassment, the government transferred her to Old Capitol Prison in January 1862. With her youngest daughter by her side, she cultivated the image of the martyred "Rebel Rose." A hearing before a military commission in March resulted in a recommendation of exile to the Confederacy, but the release was delayed until June, possibly because negotiations regarding captured U.S. spies were under way. Wrapped in a Confederate flag and with a diary condemning her captors in hand, she departed for Richmond. Although many southerners were as shocked as northerners by female spying and publicity hunting, Jefferson Davis's public recognition of Greenhow (and award to her of $2,500), followed by similar congratulations from General Beauregard, confirmed her as a legitimate heroine.

In August 1863 Greenhow traveled to Europe. She met both Queen Victoria and Napoleon III, promoted Confederate bond issues, and published the popular and propagandistic *My Imprisonment and the First Year of Abolition Rule at Washington* (1863). Despite her popularity, European governments were reluctant to endorse her cause. She headed home on the British steamer *Condor* in August 1864. In a gale and pursued by Federal blockaders, the ship ran aground off Wilmington, North Carolina. Fearing capture, Greenhow insisted on being rowed ashore. The small boat overturned in high seas and, weighted down with gold, Greenhow drowned. Spared the trauma of outliving the Confederacy, she was buried with military honors in Wilmington.

• Items seized at Greenhow's arrest are in the National Archives. The North Carolina State Archives has a small collection of papers. Ishbel Ross, *Rebel Rose* (1954), is a biography. Louis A. Sigaud, "Mrs. Greenhow and the Rebel Spy Ring," *Maryland Historical Magazine* 41 (1946): 173–98, discusses her espionage, as do Harnett T. Kane, *Spies for the Blue and Gray* (1954), and John Bakeless, *Spies of the Confederacy* (1970).

PHYLLIS F. FIELD

GREENLAW, Edwin Almiron (6 Apr. 1874–10 Sept. 1931), Renaissance scholar and educator, was born in Flora, Illinois, the son of Thomas Brewer Greenlaw, educator and newspaper publisher, and Emma Julia Leverich. At age twelve he entered Chester High School and quickly became its top student, graduating two years later. He studied at Chester High School for an additional year after graduation, then taught classes in telegraphy, shorthand, literature, and business at Orchard City College. He entered Illinois College in 1893 but interrupted his education after a year to accept the presidency of Orchard City College. After serving two years at Orchard, he entered Northwestern University in February 1896, graduating with an A.B. in history in 1897 and an M.A. in history in 1898. In September 1898 he married Mary Elizabeth Durland; they had three children.

Greenlaw taught English and pedagogy at Northwestern and Northwestern Academy from 1897 to 1905, with one year's absence in 1901, when he began his doctorate at Harvard. Unsolicited, Harvard awarded him a master's in English in 1902. He became the head of the English department at Northwestern in 1903 and continued work on his Harvard doctorate at the University of Chicago. Harvard accepted this work, and Greenlaw received his Ph.D. in English in June 1904. The following year he became head of the English department at Adelphi College in Brooklyn, New York, and published his first book, *Selections from Chaucer* (1905). In 1913 he left Adelphi to accept a professorship at the University of North Carolina at Chapel Hill. Greenlaw's career at Chapel Hill would leave a permanent mark on many facets of the university.

In 1914 Greenlaw became chair of the English department. Under his leadership the department grew from eight professors in 1914 to thirty-seven in 1925. In 1915 he took on the editorship of *Studies in Philology*, a journal published by the university. He reorganized the journal, making it a quarterly and subscription-based, and accepting articles from outside the university. Within three years the magazine tripled in size and became one of the leading journals in the field.

In 1916 Greenlaw created an honors undergraduate program in language and literature, which included extensive independent readings, tutorials, a thesis, an oral examination, and an associated series of weeklong seminars given by visiting professors. He became head of the graduate school in 1918, and under his leadership, the school increased its enrollment from 125 in 1920 to 310 in 1925. In 1920 he supervised the creation of a department of comparative literature. His four-volume anthology, *Literature and Life* (1922–1924), intended for high school English, examines literature as an expression and exploration of the human condition, reflecting Greenlaw's conviction that "great literature is the biography of the human spirit."

In 1925 Greenlaw became the first Sir William Osler Professor of English at Johns Hopkins University. As a member of the academic council, he was also involved in directing the philosophy department. His primary professional specialization was in the work of the Renaissance poet Edmund Spenser. His publications on Spenser include an examination of "Mother Hubberd's Tale" and extensive work on a variorum edition, two volumes of which were almost ready for publication at the time of his death. While at Hopkins, he also published works on Shakespeare, Milton, and medieval romance. He founded the series Johns Hopkins Monographs in Literary History, personally contributing *The Province of Literary History* (1931) and *Studies in Spenser's Historical Allegory* (1932). He died in Chapel Hill.

Greenlaw was known as an expert on Edmund Spenser and a teacher who did much to develop the English and comparative literature departments as well as the graduate school at the University of North Carolina.

• Greenlaw published numerous scholarly articles. Besides those works cited above, he wrote *A Syllabus of English Literature* (1912), *Outline of the Literature of the English Renaissance* (1916), and *Builders of Democracy* (1918). He edited *Irving's Knickerbocker History of New York* (1909), *Familiar Letters* (1915), *National Ideas in English and American Literature* (1918), and *The Great Tradition*, with J. Holly Hanford (1918). An obituary is in the *New York Times*, 12 Sept. 1931.

ELIZABETH ZOE VICARY

GREENLEAF, Moses (17 Oct. 1777–20 Mar. 1834), mapmaker, writer, and promoter of the state of Maine, was born in Newburyport, Massachusetts, the son of Moses Greenleaf, a ship carpenter and a lieutenant in the American Revolution, and Lydia Parsons. In 1790 Greenleaf moved with his family to New Gloucester in the district of Maine, where his parents became farmers. From 1799 to 1806 he operated a general store, first in New Gloucester for three years, then in Poland, Kenduskeag, and Bangor. In 1805 he married Persis Poor; they had four children. One year after his marriage Greenleaf purchased from William Dodd of Boston a quarter interest in a township to be carved from Maine "wild lands" he had purchased from Massachusetts. Greenleaf agreed to manage the joint property (later incorporated as Williamsburg) and to settle forty families there by 1812. Greenleaf spent part of the winter of 1807 in Boston, where he promoted his new property and the separation of Maine from Massachusetts while the General Court was in session there. Although an ardent Federalist, he opposed the majority of his party on the issue of separation.

Greenleaf left Bangor in 1808 to live in East Andover and did not move to Williamsburg until 1810, when he brought seventy people with him including his own family. There he supervised surveying and explored the countryside to determine its accessibility and its agricultural and mineral worth. Beginning two years later and for many years following, he tried cases nearly every week as the chief acting magistrate of his area. In 1812 he became justice of the peace for Hancock County; in 1816, after the formation of Penobscot County, he became a justice of the Court of Common Pleas; and when that court became the Court of Sessions in 1819 he was appointed a justice on it.

Convinced that Maine land had never been estimated accurately, Greenleaf determined to find its worth. Beginning shortly after his arrival in Williamsburg, he collected statistics on which to base his estimates, and since there was no accurate map of the area, he began working on one. In 1815 he published his first map, showing nine Maine counties. It was "wonderfully accurate," a superb 40-by-26-inch example of mapmaking (Smith, p. 63). Early the next year to accompany his map Greenleaf published *A Statistical View of the District of Maine*. Based primarily on his own observation, it was the first book describing that area's undeveloped interior. By documenting its physical resources, the book brought Greenleaf recognition as the leading authority on the future state. These publications by a "far-seeing publicist" who had a greater understanding of the value of natural resources than did most of his contemporaries, informed prospective settlers of what to expect and promoted the separation of Maine from Massachusetts, while pressing the legislature of Massachusetts to build roads to open Maine's interior to settlers. Agreeing with Greenleaf's statement that "by neglect or mismanagement" Maine "may be depressed almost to a cypher," while "by directing the attention of settlers, it may be increased to a degree almost beyond calculation," Massachusetts legislators subscribed to a thousand copies of Greenleaf's *Statistical View* and its accompanying map (Smith, p. 42). The September issue of the *North American Review* used nineteen pages of a long article against the separation of Maine from Massachusetts to discuss this important book. Greenleaf's remarks, the reviewer stated, "shew a considerable knowledge of the science of political economy, and with every part of the country, . . . and his calculations and reasonings, respecting the settlement and future value of the interior, . . . discover a mind well accustomed to mathematical exactness, as well as to speculation, and reflection" (p. 371).

Also in 1816 Greenleaf spent twenty days helping to survey the interior near his settlement. While traveling and surveying the "wild lands" so that "a principal highway" could be built, Greenleaf noted the Indian names of lakes, rivers, and mountains and found that when translated these descriptive names helped him discover natural resources in the area. In 1824 he published these names and their meanings in a treatise on Native American languages in northern Maine.

Despite Greenleaf's map and published statistics, his town and other areas in Maine did not grow rapidly. When Maine became a state in 1820 and Greenleaf brought out a new edition of his map, Williamsburg's population had reached only 107. Even while discouraged over his town's slow growth—caused both by the severe depression after the War of 1812 and by the opening up to immigration of warmer western territories—Greenleaf worked tirelessly preparing his second great work, *A Survey of the State of Maine*. The result of even greater research and one of the most important works on Maine, it brought his former work up to date while increasing details and statistics and adding sections on the political economy and the state's educational interests. Published with this book in 1829 was a 50-by-42-inch map (for the first time accurately showing the complete boundary of the state and its interior lakes and streams), which George G. Smith, a distinguished contemporary Boston engraver, called the best "specimen of map engraving, of its class, . . . in this or any other country" (Smith, pp. 77–78). Also accompanying the new book was an atlas with six smaller maps and a meteorological diagram comparing the temperatures of various sections of the state. The first four maps were designed to help settle the dispute with Great Britain over the northern boundary of Maine with the fourth exhibiting great engineering skill in comparing the altitudes of the state's principal highlands and rivers. The fifth map outlines the state's chief grants and land sales and proved Greenleaf knowledgeable about Maine's history; the sixth map shows the progress of Maine settlement since 1778.

On one of his factfinding trips for his publications, Greenleaf and a helper penetrated so far into a forest that it was more than a week before medical help could reach him when he became seriously ill. Even though the typhoid fever, which he had contracted, left him weak for the remainder of his life, Greenleaf continued collecting material and improving his maps. As his biographer states, "only a man possessed of indomitable energy" and "unswerving purpose" could have achieved his accomplishments (Smith, p. 58).

Although famous in his lifetime, especially for his maps, Greenleaf failed to make money on any of his publications. The state legislature supported his 1829 publications with $8,540 in subscriptions and donations, but compiling and publishing these works came close to $10,000 (Smith, p. 20). When he died in Williamsburg of erysipelas, Greenleaf's estate was declared insolvent, but fortunately the year before he had been the chief promoter of a railroad that had received the first railroad charter granted by Maine. His shares in that railroad brought enough money to pay his estate's debts, leaving a small inheritance for his family. Realizing the importance of his father's work, his son and namesake completed, updated, and published in 1844 a new map for which Greenleaf in 1831 had started having plates engraved.

• There is a box of Greenleaf papers in the Massachusetts Historical Society; a few papers relating to his railroad grant are in the Greenleaf-Merrill Family Papers, 1819–1917, in the Maine Historical Society Library, Portland. For an idea of the breadth and depth of Greenleaf's work and for an understanding of what it did for Maine, see his three published works, which are mentioned in the text. Their full titles are *A Statistical View of the District of Maine; More Especially with Reference to the Value and Importance of Its Interior* (1816); *Indian Place-Names: Indian Names of Some of the Streams, Islands, &c., on the Penobscot and St. John Rivers in Maine, Taken from a Letter from Moses Greenleaf, esq., to Rev. Dr. Morse, Reprinted from the First Report of the American Society for Promoting Civilization and General Improvement of the Indian Tribes of the United States* (1814; repr. 1903); *A Survey of the State of Maine, in Reference to Its Geographical Features, Statistics and Political Economy* (1829). For a full biography of Greenleaf, summaries of his writings with contemporary comments on them and his maps, along with letters and other information, see Edgar Crosby Smith, ed., *Moses Greenleaf: Maine's First Map-Maker, a Biography: With Letters, Unpublished Manuscripts and a Reprint of Mr. Greenleaf's Rare Paper on Indian Place-Names, also a Bibliography of the Maps of*

Maine (1902). For a lengthy review of Greenleaf's first publication on Maine, see Benjamin Rand, "A Statistical View of the District of Maine . . . ," *North American Review* (Sept. 1816): 362–425.

OLIVE HOOGENBOOM

GREENLEAF, Simon (5 Dec. 1783–6 Oct. 1853), legal educator and scholar, was born in Newburyport, Massachusetts, the son of Moses Greenleaf and Lydia Parsons. Greenleaf was raised in Newburyport and in Maine. In 1801 he began the study of law with Ezekiel Whitman, later chief justice of the Maine Supreme Court. He entered into practice in 1806 in Maine, first in Standish, then in Gray, and from 1818 in Portland. He married Hannah Kingman in 1806. They had two daughters.

Politically a Federalist, Greenleaf was unsuccessful in capturing a seat in the Massachusetts Senate (1816), but as soon as Maine was admitted as a state, he served a term in the first Maine legislature; he then retired from political life. During his early years in practice the work did not consume his time, and he read extensively. In 1820 the governor of Maine appointed him as law reporter to the Maine Supreme Court, a position he kept for twelve years while still engaging in practice and in his private studies. In his capacity as reporter, Greenleaf compiled, edited, and annotated the decisions of the Maine Supreme Court. They were published as *Reports of Cases Argued and Determined by the Supreme Judicial Court of the State of Maine* in nine volumes from 1830 to 1832.

Harvard appointed Greenleaf as Royall Professor in its law school in 1833, and in 1846 he replaced Justice Joseph Story as Dane Professor. In 1848 he resigned from his teaching duties and became professor emeritus.

Before moving to Cambridge, Greenleaf was a Free Mason for a number of years and became Grand Master of the Grand Lodge of Maine. He had a devout and earnest personality, was a low-church Episcopalian, and belonged to numerous reforming societies devoted to Bible distribution, temperance, colonization, and other purposes. He was a trustee of the Maine Peace Society as early as 1818, served for many years as president of the Massachusetts Bible Society, and was vice president of the American Bible Society at the time of his death.

Greenleaf wrote on a variety of topics. Aside from his reports of the Maine cases, his first book was *A Brief Inquiry into the Origin and Principles of Free Masonry* (1820), and his first legal work was *A Collection of Cases, Overruled, Denied, Doubted or Limited in Their Application* (1821), both published while he was reporting and practicing law. He authored an American edition and adaptation of William Cruise's digest of English property law (3 vols., 1849) and a *Life of Joseph Story* (1845). He also wrote articles for legal periodicals. The work for which he became most noted was his three-volume *Treatise on the Law of Evidence* (1842–1853). This work became extremely popular with practitioners and appeared in numerous editions throughout the nineteenth century, long after Greenleaf's death. John Henry Wigmore, a prominent evidence specialist of the early twentieth century and himself the author of a multivolume examination of the subject, edited the final (sixteenth) edition of Greenleaf in the nineteenth century in 1899.

Early America enthusiastically embraced law as the basis of governance, but only English treatises were at first available. The great demand for American texts led to a massive outpouring of treatises by Joseph Story and James Kent, among others, in the first three decades of the nineteenth century; but these writers did not touch evidence, although there is considerable indication that the American law of evidence greatly changed during these years. These factors explain the popularity of Greenleaf's treatise, which is among the very earliest American work on evidence.

Greenleaf also wrote Christian apologetics; in 1846 he published *Examination of the Testimony of the Four Evangelists by the Rules of Evidence*. He was conservative in his views and reacted negatively to the 1837–1838 lectures and publications of the Grimkè sisters, early feminists. In the year following their Massachusetts tour, Greenleaf gave several lyceum lectures on the subject of women's rights; the tenor was that, although women were intellectually the equals of men, the common law already adequately protected women's rights during marriage. He published these views anonymously (as was the general practice) in the *Christian Review* (June 1840) as "On the Legal Rights of Women."

Greenleaf represented the victorious defendants in the final appellate stages before the U.S. Supreme court in the important *Charles River Bridge* case. Politically, this case was a victory for states' rights in the new Taney court; economically, it was a victory for dynamic new enterprise over initial start monopolies, monopolies given by government to enterprises that first undertake risky ventures; and doctrinally, it was a victory for a narrow interpretation of state grants of power to private corporations.

Greenleaf had retired from Harvard in 1848 due to ill health, but he appeared to recover thereafter. Nevertheless, he died suddenly in Cambridge. The huge success of his treatise on evidence, together with a high salary (for the time) of three thousand dollars annually from Harvard, brought Greenleaf considerable wealth, and his estate represented a large sum for the time.

• Harvard Law School Library holds Greenleaf's papers. An unpublished biography, Margaret H. Semple, *Simon Greenleaf, 1783–1853, A Maine Biography* (1981), is on file at the University of Maine School of Law Library. An obituary is in the *Boston Post*, 8 Oct. 1853. Biographical sketches include those in W. T. Davis, *Bench and Bar of the Commonwealth of Massachusetts* (1895), and William Willis, *A History of the Law, the Courts, and the Lawyers of Maine* (1863). References are in Charles Warren, *History of the Harvard Law School and of Early Legal Conditions in America* (2 vols., 1908). For modern published references, see Dianne Avery and Alfred S. Konefsky, "The Daughters of Job: Property Rights and Women's Lives in Mid-Nineteenth-Century Massachusetts," *Law and History Review* 10 (Fall 1992): 323–56, with information on Greenleaf's social and religious views; Stanley I. Kutler, *Privilege and Creative Destruction: The Charles River Bridge Case* (1971); and William L. Dawson, Jr., "Simon Greenleaf: Maine Lawyer and Legal Scholar," *Maine Bar Journal* 6 (Mar. 1991): 90–96.

DAVID J. LANGUM

GREENLEAF, Thomas (1755–14 Sept. 1798), printer and publisher, was born in Abington, Massachusetts, the son of Joseph Greenleaf, a justice of the peace and popular writer, and Abigail Payne. The family moved to Boston in 1771. One of Greenleaf's father's writings was published on 14 November 1771 in Isaiah Thomas's *Massachusetts Spy*; he used the pen name "Mucius Scaevola." This screed denounced colonial governor Thomas Hutchinson as "a usurper" whose signature on legislation was without legal force and added that "a ruler, independent of the people is a monster on government." Both Isaiah Thomas and Joseph Greenleaf were summoned before the Massachusetts Council. When neither appeared, the council declared Greenleaf's father in contempt and canceled his commission as a magistrate for Plymouth County.

Amid such challenges to royal authority, Thomas Greenleaf learned the printing trade under Isaiah Thomas. In 1773 his father purchased a printing house, which Greenleaf managed; it produced pamphlets and from July 1774 to March 1775 published a continuation of a Thomas venture, the *Royal American Magazine; or, Universal Repository of Instruction and Amusement*. The onset of the revolutionary war ended the Greenleafs' struggling Boston business.

Thomas moved his press from Boston to Worcester in 1775 and began to issue his *Massachusetts Spy* from Worcester in 1778; Greenleaf evidently remained in Boston. Some accounts have Greenleaf working as a "sub-editor" for the Boston *Independent Chronicle* published by the partnership of Edward Eveleth Powars and Nathaniel Willis, with Powars withdrawing from that paper from 1770 to 1786. From 1784 until September 1785 Greenleaf published the financially struggling *Boston Magazine* with Edmund Freeman, then left the partnership to move to New York City.

Once in New York, Greenleaf worked with Elizabeth Holt, the widow of John Holt, to publish the *New-York Journal; or, The Weekly Register*. Greenleaf's anti-Federalist connections were clear, for Holt was the mother-in-law of Philadelphia printer Eleazer Oswald. Greenleaf purchased the weekly newspaper from Oswald and Holt on 16 January 1787. In November 1787 Greenleaf changed to daily publication, altering the name to the *New-York Journal and Daily Patriotic Register*. It was published under that name until the end of 1793, when it became *Greenleaf's New-York Journal* and continued as a semiweekly. As Thomas observed, Greenleaf's newspapering strongly opposed the Federalists, "attacking the measures of the venerable Washington with a great degree of virulence."

Like his father, Greenleaf played with political fire. In association with Oswald's Philadelphia newspaper, the *Independent Gazetteer*, Greenleaf's *Journal* became a leading voice against the adoption of the Constitution, publishing the important "Centinel" essays in answer to the "Publius" essays of Alexander Hamilton, John Jay, and James Madison ("The Federalist Papers"). The writings of "Centinel" evidently were the work of Samuel Bryan, clerk of the Pennsylvania Assembly. Greenleaf's *Journal* also published Governor George Clinton's "Cato II" essays, which questioned the legality of the Constitution and asserted it had a southern, aristocratic origin. In July 1788 a mob broke into Greenleaf's printing house, scattering type and paper, breaking furniture and spilling ink. Greenleaf married Anna Quackenbos in 1791; they had three daughters and a son.

By 1795 Greenleaf's newspaper was called the *Argus; or, Greenleaf's New Daily Advertiser*, with type set for the daily reused in *Greenleaf's New York Journal & Patriotic Register*, published twice a week for circulation to outlying areas. As a visible critic of President George Washington and of the Federalists, Greenleaf—and other Jeffersonian Republican publishers— courted further trouble. Federalists used state seditious libel prosecutions and, after the Alien and Sedition Acts of 1798, had additional weapons to use to try to punish dissent. The threat of prosecution drove John Daly Burk of the *Time Piece* out of the country, leaving Greenleaf as the only anti-Federalist publisher among the nine newspapers then published in New York City. Historian James Morton Smith rated only the *Philadelphia Aurora* and the Boston *Independent Chronicle* as surpassing the *Argus* in political influence among the Jeffersonian newspapers of the late 1790s.

During the late summer of 1798 Greenleaf remained in New York City during a yellow fever epidemic, even though his apprentices and two-thirds of his customers had left the city. He contracted the disease and died. His newspaper eulogized him for his virtues as a good family man and neighbor. His obituary added, "If, at any time, he dipped his pen in gall," it was because he hated "political apostacy [*sic*]."

After his death Anna Greenleaf continued his business and like her late husband was buffeted by political turbulence. She was indicted under the Sedition Act for, among other things, calling the national government corrupt, and her paper was prosecuted for libel by Alexander Hamilton after it claimed Hamilton was behind an attempt to silence another Republican newspaper. These prosecutions led to the end of the *Argus* and the sale of the *New-York Journal*, leaving New York City with—as the Federalists had planned—no Republican newspapers.

In company with other newspapers opposing the Constitution and the presidencies of George Washington and John Adams, Greenleaf's journalism led to unofficial efforts at suppression via threats from mobs and official prosecutions under the Federalists' Sedition Act of 1798. Voices of protests such as Greenleaf's newspapers were not on history's winning side, unless one considers the adoption of the Bill of Rights. Those amendments to the Constitution, including the First Amendment rights of religion, speech, press, assembly, and petition, resulted from a political compromise reached to silence complaints about ratification of a Constitution lacking guarantees of civil liberties. The willingness of Thomas and Anna Greenleaf and their newspapers to oppose a Federalist majority helped to begin defining crucial freedoms in the United States.

• Greenleaf, along with many others who fought a losing battle against adoption of the Constitution and who attacked Federalist leaders, has not received his biographical due. Victor H. Palesits's sketch of Greenleaf's life in the *Dictionary of American Biography* is the starting point, with useful information to be found in Arthur M. Schlesinger, *Prelude to Independence: The Newspaper War on Britain, 1764–1776* (1958); Isaiah Thomas, *The History of Printing in America* (1814); and especially James Morton Smith, *Freedom's Fetters: The Alien and Sedition Laws and American Civil Liberties* (1956). Other information is in Herbert J. Storing, *The Complete Antifederalist* (7 vols., 1981); Robert Allen Rutland, *The Ordeal of the Constitution: The Antifederalists and the Ratification Struggle of 1787–1788* (1966); and John K. Alexander, *The Selling of the Constitutional Convention: A History of News Coverage* (1990).

DWIGHT L. TEETER, JR.

GREENLEE, William Augustus (1897–7 July 1952), National Negro League president and owner of the Pittsburgh Crawfords, was born in Marion, North Carolina, to a masonry contractor with the surname Greenlee (his mother's name is unknown). After dropping out of college, Greenlee hopped a freight train north to Pittsburgh in 1916 and settled in the Hill District, a gathering point for immigrants of many nationalities. He operated a steam drill, drove a taxi, shined shoes, and worked as a fireman at Jones and Laughlin's Southside Steel Works before serving overseas in the army's 367th Regiment during World War I. Returning to Pittsburgh in 1919, he bootlegged liquor and entered the nightclub business.

Greenlee ran a poolroom, then the Paramount Club, a restaurant and cabaret, then the Sunset Cafe before opening the Crawford Grill, the Hill's classiest nightspot. The club was the center for Greenlee's numbers game, a business that he and Woogie Harris popularized in Pittsburgh. The numbers were a lottery in which bettors wagered that a three-digit number would be the one to "hit" that day. The number was based on numbers drawn from transactions in the stock market, the commodity exchange, or a particular horse track. Greenlee and Harris turned the operation into the city's largest black-controlled enterprise during the 1930s. They made never-to-be-repaid loans to help families pay their bills, and Greenlee bankrolled many early black political efforts in Pittsburgh.

Greenlee also used the profits from numbers to become a sports patron. In 1926 he bought uniforms for the Crawfords, a popular sandlot club that took its name from the Crawford Bath House, a city facility for migrants. By 1930 the Crawfords were ready to take on the Homestead Grays, then among the nation's best black professional teams. The team asked Greenlee if he wanted to run the ballclub. Greenlee accepted the offer, but, according to captain Harold Tinker, "When he took the ballteam, he let us know that it was his intention not to leave it as a sandlot team. He was going to the top." Along with the Crawfords' cross-town rivals, Cumberland Posey and the Grays, Greenlee helped Pittsburgh become the center of black base-ball in those years.

Greenlee secured Negro League veteran Bobby Williams as his player-manager and soon began re-cruiting the best black players in the country. Over the next few seasons he added Negro League stars Oscar Charleston, Cool Papa Bell, Ted Page, Ted "Double Duty" Radcliffe, and Judy Johnson to the roster. Sev-eral of his recruits were lured from the Homestead Grays. The Crawfords could boast a battery of Satchel Paige and Josh Gibson, possibly the finest assembled, as well as three other future Hall of Famers, Charles-ton, Bell, and Johnson.

As the Crawfords overtook the Grays, Greenlee built the country's foremost black-controlled stadium. Costing more than $100,000, Greenlee Field opened on the Hill in 1932 and hosted Negro League baseball, black college football, soccer matches, and boxing.

Greenlee also began to piece together the Negro Na-tional League, one of the strongest national black insti-tutions of its time before its collapse in 1931 as the result of the depression and the death of its founder, Andrew "Rube" Foster. The NNL attained greater fi-nancial stability and public presence than any earlier black professional sport, and much of its success was due to Greenlee, the league's president. As the league's principal innovator during its first five years, he initiated an annual all-star game, the East-West Classic, first played in 1933 at Comiskey Park in Chi-cago. He also began four-team doubleheaders at Yan-kee Stadium in New York and Forbes Field in Pitts-burgh.

In 1937 the Negro American League was formed from the midwestern teams of the NNL. Greenlee re-tired as NNL president the same year, largely because of volatile Caribbean politics. Ciudad Trujillo, a team representing Dominican dictator Rafael Trujillo, per-suaded Paige, Gibson, Bell, and a half-dozen of their teammates to abandon the Crawfords for a summer season. Trujillo's team had lost the championship the previous summer, and his minions were determined not to repeat that humiliation. Ciudad Trujillo won the island championship, and Greenlee's Crawfords never recovered from the blow.

Greenlee gave up baseball before the 1939 season, and the Crawfords, who bore little resemblance to their former selves, played a few seasons in Toledo and Indianapolis before folding. Greenlee Field was torn down in 1938 and replaced by a public housing project.

Greenlee kept a hand in the sporting scene. In 1935 he purchased the contract of a 21-year-old boxer, John Henry Lewis, who, on 31 October, became the first African-American light heavyweight champion by winning a decision over Bob Olin. Greenlee thus be-

came the first black to manage a light heavyweight ti-tleholder. Lewis later was knocked out by Joe Louis in the first heavyweight championship bout between two black fighters. After Lewis quit the ring in 1939, Greenlee soon tired of boxing.

Greenlee later sought to reenter black baseball. De-nied a franchise in the Negro Leagues, he formed the United States League (USL) in 1945. The league last-ed two seasons, with franchises in Pittsburgh, Brook-lyn, Chicago, Detroit, Cleveland, Philadelphia, To-ledo, and Boston. Headquartered upstairs from the Crawford Grill, the USL had the endorsement of Brooklyn Dodgers' president Branch Rickey, who of-fered it the use of parks controlled by the Dodgers. During this period Rickey and Greenlee held discus-sions regarding the impact of integration on baseball. The USL detracted from the NNL and the NAL and left those leagues more vulnerable to Rickey's policy of signing players without compensating their Negro League teams.

After the USL's demise, Greenlee focused on the Crawford Grill, which he made into one of the city's foremost revenue-producing restaurants. In 1950, he became ill, and the following year the restaurant was destroyed by fire. By then, white numbers entrepre-neurs had taken over much of his territory, and the federal government was suing him for unpaid taxes. He died in Pittsburgh. The black-owned *Pittsburgh Courier*, which splashed news of his death across its front page, called Greenlee the city's "most fabulous sports figure."

• The most comprehensive treatment of Greenlee is Rob Ruck, *Sandlot Seasons: Sport in Black Pittsburgh* (1987). See also Donn Rogosin, *Invisible Men: Life in Baseball's Negro Leagues* (1983), and John Holway, *Blackball Stars: Negro League Pioneers* (1988). An obituary is in the *Pittsburgh Cou-rier*, 12 July 1952.

ROB RUCK

GREENOUGH, Horatio (6 Sept. 1805–18 Dec. 1852), sculptor, was born in Boston, Massachusetts, the son of David Greenough and Betsey Bender. A memorial to his father, a merchant, made note of the "careful manner" in which he raised his children and "the intel-lectual privileges afforded them." Raised in a cultured home, at school Horatio excelled in classical studies and English literature. It may have been the copy of an ancient statue of Phocion that stood in his father's gar-den that first inspired him to take up sculpture; in any case, while still a boy he carved wooden toys and mod-eled small figures in wax. These were displayed in a room of the Greenough house set aside for the pur-pose. There being no art schools then available to him, he learned about sculpture where he could, such as in the *Edinburgh Cyclopedia*. The local artisan-woodcarv-er Solomon Willard gave him some instruction, while a French sculptor named J. B. Binon taught him mod-eling and casting in plaster, and Alpheus Cary, a Bos-ton craftsman, taught him the rudimentary techniques of carving in stone. His father encouraged his artistic interests, but he also insisted that Horatio attend Harvard College.

At Harvard, beginning in 1821, Greenough blossomed intellectually through study of the classics, literature, and philosophy. At this time he met the painter Washington Allston, who had studied art in London, Paris, and Rome. "Allston was to me a father," wrote Greenough, "in what concerned my progress of every kind. He taught me first how to discriminate, how to think, how to feel." Allston also fired the youth with a desire to travel abroad, for by then Greenough had determined to become a sculptor, the first American to commit himself to the study of that art. In 1825, at the end of his senior year, he departed for Rome, where he would spend the next two years.

Rome exhilarated him, and its antiquity cast its spell upon him. He and his friends frequently roamed amid its ruins by moonlight, while in the many galleries he drew inspiration from the magnificent collections of ancient statues. The most famous neoclassical sculptor of that day, Bertel Thorwaldsen, gave him advice and criticism, and at the French Academy he drew from the nude figure—something not yet possible in Boston. In his own studio he attempted an ideal piece, a *Dead Abel*, which Allston later praised. But then suddenly he was struck down by "Roman fever" (possibly typhoid or malaria), and as soon as he could travel, he was forced to return home, in 1827.

His health restored, Greenough began working in Boston, Washington, and Baltimore, taking portrait busts. His own social graces and his family connections allowed him to move easily in the upper echelons of American society. In the national capital he modeled the likeness of a fellow New Englander, President John Quincy Adams (1828, Boston Athenaeum), confiding in a letter to his brother Henry: "I shall not (as Sully and others have done) make him look cheerful. . . . Gravity is natural to him and a smile is ill at home" (*Letters*, p. 26). He also met Robert Gilmor, Jr., of Baltimore, who became an important patron, giving him a commission for a bust of his wife, which was modeled in the library of the Gilmor home, and for an ideal figure that was to be executed once Greenough returned to Italy, which he did in 1828.

This time the young American chose to settle in Florence, where he lived for most of the rest of his life. He studied in the studio of Lorenzo Bartolini, who stressed the Renaissance tradition of naturalism over the neoclassicism that prevailed in Rome. In 1830 Greenough modeled portraits of his artist friends and fellow Americans Thomas Cole (Wadsworth Atheneum, Hartford) and Samuel F. B. Morse (Smithsonian Institution). He made the acquaintance of James Fenimore Cooper, who was then in Italy, and the author gave him a commission for a marble group titled *Chanting Cherubs* (unlocated). Cooper's intention was to send the group back to the United States on tour to establish the name of his young sculptor friend, but Americans were so unfamiliar with the art of sculpture that they criticized the cherubs' nudity and

so cloaked them with aprons; further, some felt cheated when they discovered that the group did not actually sing and demanded a refund of their admission fees. This only hinted at the problems Greenough would face when he tried to present his art in the United States. Most Americans of the period took little interest in such things and preferred, when they thought about art at all, something home grown that reflected contemporary American life as they knew it. Patrons like Cooper or Gilmor were the exception. For the latter Greenough began work on an ideal figure of Medora (Private Collection, Baltimore), inspired by Lord Byron's poem *The Corsair*. Meanwhile, to earn a living, he modeled portrait busts, one of the marquis de Lafayette (Pennsylvania Academy of the Fine Arts, Philadelphia) and another of Cooper (Boston Public Library).

Greenough was anxious to commence some grand piece that would challenge his abilities and establish his reputation. The opportunity came in 1832 when Congress appropriated funds for a heroic marble statue of George Washington that was to be placed in the rotunda of the recently completed Capitol. To execute sculptural decorations for the Capitol, the commission selected Greenough instead of one of the several Italian artists who had immigrated to America. This was the first major commission given by the federal government to an American sculptor. Greenough commenced modeling the figure in his Florentine studio, creating an image of Washington in a form that recalled the great ivory and gold statue that Phidias had made in the fifth century B.C. to adorn the Greek temple of Zeus at Olympia. He used the portrait bust taken from life by Jean Antoine Houdon as his model for the head, but the rest of the figure was an exercise in neoclassicism, showing Washington bare chested in a Roman cloak and wearing Roman sandals, surrendering a sword as emblem of military power in favor of constitutional authority. Greenough wished to imbue his image with the nobility of antiquity, casting his subject in the role of a revered statesman of republican Rome, with evocations of the greatest of all ancients, Zeus. The sculptor completed the clay model in 1835 and his studio workmen cast it in plaster; it was blocked out in marble at the quarry at Carrara and Italian stonecutters finished the carving in Florence. In September 1839 he wrote to his brother Henry that "the Washington is nearly done. I assure you [it] surpasses my expectations as a likeness, but what will be its reception as a work of art I know not" (*Letters*, p. 130). Greenough had reason to be concerned.

The statue, installed in the Capitol in 1842, at once became the subject of ridicule, for Americans could not see through the neoclassical presentation. One critic declared that the image looked more like a Hindu suttee than the nation's beloved Washington, while another referred to it as Georgy-Porgy. Even Philip Hone, former mayor of New York and friend to many artists, confided his disappointment to his diary when he saw it in April 1844: " . . . it looks like a great Herculean, warrior-like Venus of the Bath; a grand martial Magog, undressed, with a huge napkin lying across his lap . . . , and he preparing to perform his ablutions is in the act of consigning his sword to the care of an attendant until he shall come out of the bath." The statue soon suffered further indignities; once it was discovered that its weight was too great to be supported by the floor of the rotunda, it was moved outdoors, where it was subjected to inclement weather and generations of pigeons. Eventually it was sheltered in the Smithsonian Institution.

The next large commission Greenough received from Congress fared no better—*The Rescue*, erected on the eastern entrance to the Capitol in 1852. It represented a pioneer overpowering a hatchet-wielding Indian who is attacking his wife and child while a dog looks on passively. Later it was decided that the Capitol looked better without this sculpture than with it, and it was consigned to permanent storage.

Greenough was frustrated by the lack of appreciation his work received at home. In his later years he made numerous ideal pieces, such as the excellent oval relief, *Castor and Pollux* (1847–1851, Museum of Fine Arts, Boston). He also devoted much of his time to writing on theoretical matters, as in his *Travels, Observations and Experiences of a Yankee Stonecutter* (1852). In 1851, political unrest in Italy caused him to return to the United States with his wife, the former Louisa Gore of Boston, whom he had married in 1837, and their son. Late in the fall of 1852 he became ill with what was described as brain fever, and on 4 December he was hospitalized in Somerville, Massachusetts, where he died. Greenough was an urbane, cultivated man who loved his country yet enjoyed equally the life of the expatriate American. He holds a special place in the history of American sculpture as the founder of the American school of sculpture, as distinct from the efforts of artisan woodcarvers, and as the first American whose sculpture gained recognition in the European art world.

• A number of Greenough's letters are preserved at the Beinecke Library, Yale University; the Massachusetts Historical Society; and the Historical Society of Pennsylvania. Many have been published in Frances Greenough, ed., *Letters of Horatio Greenough to his Brother, Henry Greenough* (1887; repr. 1970) and in Nathalia Wright, ed., *Letters of Horatio Greenough, American Sculptor* (1972). Also by Wright are a biography, *Horatio Greenough: The First American Sculptor* (1963), and *The Miscellaneous Writings of Horatio Greenough* (1975). See also Horatio Greenough, *Form and Function: Remarks on Art*, ed. Harold A. Small (1947). Henry Tuckerman, mid-nineteenth-century art critic and friend of many artists, wrote a tribute to the artist in his *A Memorial to Horatio Greenough* (1853; repr. 1968). For brief reviews of Greenough's life and career, see Wayne Craven, *Sculpture in America* (1984), pp. 100–111, and Kathryn Greenthal, Paula Kozol, Jan Seidler Ramirez, and Jonathan Fairbanks, *American Figurative Sculpture in the Museum of Fine Arts, Boston* (1986), pp. 4–26.

WAYNE CRAVEN

GREENOUGH, Richard Saltonstall (27 Apr. 1819–23 Apr. 1904), sculptor, was born in Jamaica Plains, Massachusetts, the son of David Greenough, a wealthy Boston real-estate dealer and building contractor, and Elizabeth "Betsey" Bender. Early in life, Greenough demonstrated artistic talent. He also loved music and reportedly sang ballads before he could speak clearly. He attended a private school in Jamaica Plains and when the family moved to Boston entered the Boston Latin School, where he remained until 1836. But for temporary family financial reverses (his father died in 1836), he might have gone on to Harvard. Instead, he worked in the counting room of two of his brothers, who were commission merchants in Boston. He worked loyally but in his spare time devoted himself to drawing and modeling. In 1837 the same two brothers, observing his talent and discerning his desires, generously sent him to Florence, Italy, where their most brilliant brother, Horatio, had established a successful studio in 1828.

Greenough nominally studied under Horatio but seemed to need little guidance. He drew from antique statues and casts, visited established sculptors' studios (including that of Albert Bertel Thorwaldsen, the eminent Dane), sketched nudes in drawing classes, and modeled statues from them. After only about six months, however, he became ill and returned to Boston in 1838. He soon recovered his health, established a studio in 1839, worked uneventfully for a few years—and probably part-time as an accountant for his brothers again, as well—but then attracted notice with a fine plaster bust of the historian William Hickling Prescott, who purchased it and donated it to the Boston Athenaeum in 1844. More work followed. Greenough married Sarah Dana Loring in 1846; the couple had one son. Steady and considerable professional success, including a medallion head and portrait busts, enabled Greenough and his family to return to Florence in 1848, from where they soon moved to Rome. His 1849 marble bust of Cornelia Van Rensselaer, with its natural smile and attention to costume details, is proof of his success once he was back in Italy. American tourists commissioned him to do their portrait busts in marble. Neoclassical subjects, including Cupids and a Psyche, also ensued. Greenough modeled his *Shepherd Boy and Eagle*, returned to the United States with it in 1853, had it cast in bronze in Chicopee, Massachusetts, and sold it to the Boston Athenaeum in 1857 for $1,500. Meanwhile, he was commissioned to create statues of Benjamin Franklin and John Winthrop. The natural, dignified pose and homely details of his bronze *Franklin*, unveiled in Boston's city hall in 1856, won extravagant praise and seemed to the public to be worth the total price of $20,000. (His brother Henry Greenough designed its four-square pedestal, for which Greenough designed two of its pictorial bas-relief panels, while Thomas Ball designed the other two.) Greenough's seated *Winthrop*, modeled in clay in Paris in 1855–1856, put into marble for Mount Auburn Cemetery, Cambridge, and now at Harvard, is fussy and quaint as to costume and chair and expressionless as to face. Greenough accomplished more work in Paris, including a small equestrian statue of George Washington (now at the U.S. Military Academy, West Point), marble busts, and meticulously correct but rather vapid items. In the 1860s he established a studio in Newport, Rhode Island, but worked thereafter mostly in Paris and then Rome.

Although by this time Greenough had accomplished his best work, he continued to stay busy. He created an intricately costumed, striding figure of Winthrop (marble, 1876, U.S. Capitol, Washington, D.C.; bronze, 1880, First Church, Boston), an insipid *Circe* (1882, Metropolitan Museum of Art), and several more portrait busts—often somewhat vapid. His wife published novels and short stories, an 1872 collection of which was illustrated by their son, by then a competent artist. After his wife's death in Austria in 1885, Greenough placed a replica of his marble *Psyche* as a monument over her grave in the Protestant Cemetery in Rome. He died in Rome and is buried at Mount Auburn.

Greenough was part of the second wave of American sculptors to study, work, and live in Italy. The first wave had been dominated by Horatio Greenough, Thomas Crawford, and Hiram Powers. The second included a dozen or more, notably William Rogers, Randolph Rogers, and William Wetmore Story. In the small Florentine and Roman expatriate colonies, these artists and their families all knew each other, usually in a most amiable and mellow way. Greenough was a pioneer in the sense that he was the first expatriate American sculptor of note to work partly in Paris instead of exclusively in Italy. His work is now regarded as competent but seldom inspired and rarely innovative. The details of his ideal works usually stand out mainly to betray their meaninglessness in terms of the whole. The same may be said of many of his portraits, which, however, are often commendable for their naturalistic expressions.

• Nathaniel B. Shurtleff, *Memorial Inauguration of the Statue of Franklin* (1857), is a thoroughly documented history of Greenough's statue of Franklin. Henry T. Tuckerman, *Book of the Artists* (1867), Chandler R. Post, *A History of European and American Sculpture* (1921), Lorado Taft, *History of American Sculpture*, rev. ed. (1930), and Margaret Ferrand Thorp, *The Literary Sculptors* (1965), all discuss Greenough in context. The best succinct treatment of the whole Greenough family, including Richard Greenough, is Nathalia Wright, "Henry James and the Greenough Data," *American Quarterly* 10 (Fall 1959): 338–43. In her *Horatio Greenough: The First American Sculptor* (1963), Wright mentions Richard Greenough in passing. Thomas Brumbaugh, in "The Art of Richard Greenough," *Old-Time New England* 53 (Jan.–Mar. 1963): 61–78, provides a critical, often harsh, analysis, well documented and illustrated. A competent survey of Greenough's work is in Wayne Craven, *Sculpture in America*, rev. ed. (1984). An obituary is in the *New York Times*, 23 Apr. 1904.

ROBERT L. GALE

GREENSLET, Ferris (30 June 1875–19 Nov. 1959), publisher and author, was born in Glens Falls, New York, the son of George Bernard Greenslet, a merchant, and Josephine Ferris. Greenslet grew up in a genteel Victorian home filled with books and surrounded by natural beauty. After earning a B.A. at Wesleyan University in Middletown, Connecticut, in 1897, he enrolled in Columbia University, where he earned an M.A. in 1898 and a Ph.D. in 1900 in English literature. The university published his dissertation, *Joseph Glanvill—A Study in English Thought and Letters of the Seventeenth Century*, in 1900. In 1901 Greenslet moved to Boston, where he cataloged recently purchased Old French and Medieval Latin manuscripts in the city's public library. The following year he became associate editor of the *Atlantic Monthly* magazine, a position he retained until 1907. He married Ella S. Hulst of Cambridge, Massachusetts, in 1905; the couple had two children.

The professional turning point in Greenslet's life came in 1907 when he accepted a position as literary adviser of Houghton Mifflin, the distinguished Boston publishing house. Moving up the ranks in the firm, he became director and editor in chief of the trade department in 1910; a member of the executive committee in 1918; manager of the trade department in 1933; and vice president, general manager, and editorial director in 1936. From 1942 until his retirement five years later, he was literary adviser to the firm.

During his long and productive life, Greenslet combined three activities he equally revered. He was a magnificent editor-publisher, a scholarly author, and an avid fisherman. As publisher, he "discovered" several outstanding manuscripts, including *The Education of Henry Adams*, which it took a decade to procure from Adams. Greenslet's friendship with Willa Cather resulted in the publication by Houghton Mifflin of her first four novels. He enjoyed a long personal and professional friendship with John Buchan, the aristocratic Scottish author. After six publishers rejected the southern novelist Henry Sydnor Harrison's *Queed* (1911), Greenslet saw possibilities in the spicy work, which soon grossed $225,000. Among the minor writers he championed was the British ex-soldier Stuart Cloete, whose best fiction is set in Africa.

Greenslet's own books were attractively written. His highly competent dissertation places Joseph Glanvill among the other Cambridge Platonists, presents his subject's biography, and discusses Glanvill's philosophy, critical theories, and style. *The Quest of the Holy Grail: An Interpretation and a Paraphrase of the Holy Legends* (1902), a short book that stresses Celtic fancy, Christian symbolism, and chivalric ideals, is quaintly illustrated by reproductions of Edwin Austin Abbey's frieze decorations in the Boston Public Library. Abbey's Grail and Galahad episodes provide a framework for Greenslet's translations and redactions of the simpler accounts paralleling the pictures. Greenslet's *Walter Pater* (1903) has fared least well over the years. Ignored by some critics, it is depreciated by others for drawing exclusively on the reminiscences of Pater's friends, for wrongly reading his essays as autobiographical, and for showing no knowledge of his correspondence. Greenslet's *James Russell Lowell: His Life and Work* (1905), based largely on printed sources, provides a comprehensive evaluation of the writer's life and works and especially perceptive interpretations of Lowell's poetry.

Greenslet's *Life of Thomas Bailey Aldrich* (1908), which was immediately labeled Aldrich's authoritative biography by reviewers and critics, is a graceful discussion of his friend's career, temperament, and major works. Greenslet quotes extensively from Aldrich's letters and other writings and includes sympathetic reminiscences. In *Under the Bridge: An Autobiography* (1943), Greenslet takes pleasure in noting that he was personally acquainted with 192 of the 230 authors that cultural and literary historian Van Wyck Brooks mentions in his 1940 *New England: Indian Summer, 1865–1915*. Greenslet provides anecdotes about many of these writers and often adverts to his wide reading but is perhaps at his best when he recounts—with charm and easy shrewdness—the experiences in his own past. *The Practical Cogitator; or, The Thinker's Anthology* (1945), coedited with Charles P. Curtis, Jr., is an anthology crammed with excerpts, which have been documented, indexed, and often freshly translated, of writings from Confucius to James Joyce. Arranged by topic, such as man, the past, nature, on bettering oneself, peace, liberty, beauty, and love, the book has continued to delight readers through its reprinting in 1950, revision in 1953, and enlargement in 1962. *The Lowells and Their Seven Worlds* (1946) is a composite biography tracing the lives of eleven generations of Lowells, beginning in sixteenth-century England and continuing in seventeenth-century New England. Greenslet's presentation is learned and skillful, if sometimes too selective and sympathetic, and is often spiced with shy, sly wit. Especially well discussed are progenitor Percival Lowle [*sic*], born in England in 1571; John Amory Lowell, a mill owner and Harvard fellow; Augustus Lowell, a businessman; James Russell Lowell, the writer; dashing Civil War soldiers; Percival Lowell, the Orientalist turned astronomer; and Amy Lowell, the redoubtable poet. Greenslet also wrote innumerable articles about fishing, mainly for salmon and trout, for publication in anglers' journals worldwide.

Greenslet died in Cambridge, Massachusetts. A skillful handler of authors and their manuscripts and a shrewd businessman who understood all aspects of book publishing, Greenslet was also an adept biographer, autobiographer, and critic who wrote with a felicitous style.

• Greenslet's papers are widely scattered. Most, however, are deposited at Colby College, Columbia University, Harvard University, the University of Illinois, Indiana University, the Joint University Libraries at Nashville, the University of Oklahoma, and Yale University. A major source of information about Greenslet is his 1943 autobiography *Under the Bridge*. A fellow editor at Houghton Mifflin, Dale Warren, provides in "The Editor Who Outwhistled Shaw," *Saturday Review*, 9 Apr. 1960, pp. 21–23, 54–55, a detailed, affectionate memorial of his friend; the catchy title alludes to Greenslet's out-tooting the Irish-born English dramatist George Bernard Shaw in a friendly pennywhistle contest. James Woodress, *Willa Cather: Her Life and Art* (1970) and *Willa Cather: A Literary Life* (1987), and Edward Wagenknecht, *Willa Cather* (1994), discuss the profound influence Greenslet's friendship and professional judgment had on Cather. Obituaries are in the *New York Times*, 20 Nov. 1959, and *Publishers' Weekly*, 30 Nov. 1959.

ROBERT L. GALE

GREENSTREET, Sidney (27 Dec. 1879–18 Jan. 1954), actor, was born Sydney Greenstreet in Sandwich, England, the son of John Jack Greenstreet, a tanner and leather merchant, and Anne Baker. He attended the preparatory school Dane Hill in Margate, where he participated in sports as well as in school plays. In 1899 he traveled with a family friend to Ceylon to become a tea planter. While learning the tea business Greenstreet was the supervisor of a tea plantation, but because of the drought in that country his career plans changed.

Returning to England, Greenstreet "was manager of an agency in Harrow for Watneys, Coombes and Reed's Brewery, but he held that position for only a year" (Sennett, p. 8). Perhaps because of the long, lonely hours in Ceylon spent devouring Shakespeare, Greenstreet decided to attend Ben Greet's school of acting in London. His first public acting role was in 1902 at the Marina Theatre in Ramsgate, playing murderer Jim Craigen in *Sherlock Holmes* by Arthur Conan Doyle and William Gillette. From 1904 to 1909 he toured in Greet's Shakespearean Repertory Company in Great Britain and the United States. His Broadway debut was at the Garden Theatre as Good Fellowship in *Everyman* in 1905.

Known as an actor who could play a wide range of both comedy roles and major character parts, Greenstreet toured and acted with such stars and companies as Julia Marlowe, the Harry Davis stock company of Pittsburgh, Margaret Anglin, Maxine Elliott, and Sir Herbert Beerbohm Tree, who dubbed Greenstreet "the greatest unstarred star on the English stage." Greenstreet married Dorothy Marie Ogden in 1918; they had one son. Fortunately, he had a "long run" of two years as Martin Bennett in *The Rainbow Girl* at the New Amsterdam Theatre in New York City starting in April of that year, so touring did not disrupt his home life during that period. Greenstreet became an American citizen in 1925.

In the 1930s Greenstreet regularly acted in Theatre Guild productions on Broadway (the guild was the major producer of plays during the 1920s and 1930s). As usual, he received excellent (if brief) reviews for his supporting roles. Through the guild he began acting with Alfred Lunt and Lynn Fontanne, whose careers had also been greatly advanced by the guild. His final stage performance was with Lunt and Fontanne: he played the Finnish patriot Uncle Waldemar in Robert E. Sherwood's *There Shall Be No Night* in 1940. After the play closed on Broadway the company went on tour, ending up in California.

John Huston, at the time a scriptwriter, saw Greenstreet's performance at the Biltmore in Los Angeles and wanted Greenstreet to act in a motion picture. Lunt and Fontanne were taking a vacation, so Greenstreet was free to accept a role in a film. Although he was at first reluctant to take a screen role—partly because he was then in his sixties—Greenstreet accepted Huston's offer and was subsequently nominated for an Academy Award for his portrayal of the villain Casper Gutman in Huston's classic 1941 thriller, *The Maltese Falcon*. He was such a success that for the next nine years he acted in more than two dozen films—all except four of them for Warner Bros.

Through his work in *The Maltese Falcon*, Greenstreet was introduced to Peter Lorre, another actor who could play superb villains. Although the two became known as the "Laurel and Hardy of Crime," they actually worked together in only nine films—one of which was the renowned *Casablanca*, released in 1942. Greenstreet did not always play miscreants in his film roles; for instance, he was William Makepeace Thackeray in *Devotion* in 1946. His last film was the melodrama *Malaya*, released in 1950.

While he is chiefly remembered as being a film villain ("a florid, sybaritic monster"), actress Margaret Webster still remembered his 1938 portrayal of Uncle Peter Sorin in *The Seagull* in her 1972 book, *Don't Put Your Daughter on the Stage*. She praised him as a rare actor who "seemed able continuously to be what he was playing." It is true that despite his physical bulk he could portray a wide range of characters, from Shakespearean to musical comedy roles.

Greenstreet retired in 1950—earlier than Warner Bros. would have liked—because ill health plagued him. He admitted to weighing 285 pounds in his first film, and others have reported that his weight reached at least 325 pounds at one time.

• A major source of information on Greenstreet is Ted Sennett, *Masters of Menace: Greenstreet and Lorre* (1979). Other sources are *Current Biography: Who's News and Why, 1943* (1944); Roy S. Waldau, *Vintage Years of the Theatre Guild, 1928–1939* (1972); David Thomson, *A Biographical Dictionary of the Cinema* (1975); *Who Was Who in the Theatre* (1978); and David Quinlan, *The Illustrated Directory of Film Stars* (1986).

DONNA M. PAANANEN

GREENUP, Christopher (c. 1750–27 Apr. 1818), governor and congressman, was born in Loudoun County, Virginia, the son of John Greenup and Elizabeth Witten. He received his elementary education at home or perhaps in a local school; he learned surveying and studied law with Colonel Charles Binns of Charles City County, Virginia. Commissioned a first lieutenant on 2 February 1777, Greenup joined William Grayson's Additional Sixteenth Regiment in Charles Scott's brigade and probably saw action at the battles of Brandywine and Germantown. During the time of the Valley Forge encampment, Greenup, along with many other Virginia officers, resigned his commission (1 Apr. 1778). Subsequently he served as a colonel in the Virginia militia.

Greenup was one of the earliest settlers in Kentucky. In 1781 he moved to Frankfort, in Lincoln County, one of the three new Virginia trans-Allegheny counties. He was a land speculator and practiced surveying; he assisted John Filson in the making of the 1784 map of Kentucky. Greenup owned real estate and a store in Lexington. As an attorney he was admitted to practice law before the Fayette County court and also the district of Kentucky court at Harrodsburg and then Danville. He was justice of the peace for Mercer County in 1785, and from 1785 to 1792 he also held the post of clerk in the district court at Harrodsburg. Greenup served in the Virginia House of Delegates as a representative from Fayette County from 1785 to 1786. In 1787 he married Mary "Caty" Catherine Pope, of Hanover County, Virginia; they had six children who survived to adulthood. Greenup's wife died in 1807, and he did not remarry.

As a member of the Virginia General Assembly, Greenup served on committees for creating new counties in the Kentucky district and for amending a law regarding land entries and surveys. He became increasingly involved with politics. He helped found the Political Club, which lasted from 1786 to 1790 and was made up of prominent persons in or near Danville. The group's organization was similar to the Phi Beta Kappa Society of Williamsburg, Virginia. Benjamin Sebastian, a contemporary politician, said that the club "was the training school for the future statesmen of Kentucky." Greenup served as a quartermaster for Benjamin Logan's expedition of 1786 against the Shawnee Indians of the Ohio country and in 1791 was county lieutenant for Mercer County. He was clerk to a council of Kentucky leaders that met in April 1789 to supervise defense against the Indians.

Greenup enthusiastically supported the movement to separate Kentucky from Virginia. Contrary to accusations later leveled against him when he was governor, Greenup did not become involved with the so-called Spanish Conspiracy of 1788, when several Kentucky leaders flirted with the idea of separation from the United States and alliance with the Spaniards in America. Backing separation of Kentucky from Virginia, Greenup was a member of the Kentucky conventions held at Danville in December 1784–January 1785, May 1785, and July 1788, the latter of which made preparations for Kentucky to assume statehood.

When Kentucky became a state on 1 June 1792, Greenup was one of the electors who chose the first governor, senators, and judges. He briefly held an appointment as a judge of the new court of oyer and terminer from 28 June to 19 December 1792.

In 1792 Greenup was elected as one of the two Kentucky members of the U.S. House of Representatives, taking his seat on 9 November 1792. He was reelected twice, leaving Congress on 4 March 1797. A Jeffersonian-Republican, he voted against authorization to expand the army by 25,000 men in case of war emergency. He was one of twelve persons, including Andrew Jackson, who voted against House approval of the reply to President George Washington's last annual message of 17 December 1796 because the document was too unfavorable to France.

After leaving Congress, Greenup in 1798 was a member of the Kentucky legislature from Mercer County and from 1799 to 1802 was clerk of the state senate. On 24 December 1802 he was appointed a judge of the Franklin County Circuit Court. In the gubernatorial election of 1800, Greenup ran second of four candidates.

Greenup was elected governor of Kentucky as a Jeffersonian-Republican in 1804; unopposed he received 25,917 votes. Greenup's administration occurred during a time of prosperity and few domestic issues. He completely distanced himself from the Aaron Burr controversy of 1804–1807. Because of the Louisiana Purchase of 1803, the Mississippi River was open for transportation of Kentucky products. The state Bank of Kentucky was chartered. Greenup won a reputation for appointing capable and honest men to public office and the judiciary. He vetoed a bill for the repeal of the charter of the Kentucky Insurance Company on grounds that the legislature would be impairing the obligation of contracts, thus anticipating the later famous decision of John Marshall's U.S. Supreme Court. Greenup sought reform in the tax and criminal codes, and in his last annual address he recommended state aid to education.

After leaving office, Greenup resumed the practice of law. In 1809 he was a presidential elector for the Madison-Clinton ticket and three years later was appointed justice of the peace for Franklin County. Besides holding most of the elected and appointive offices of the state, Greenup participated in many community endeavors. He was an original trustee of Transylvania Seminary (now University) in 1784 and in 1787 one of the first trustees of Danville. He was a director of the Bank of Kentucky, a member of the Kentucky River Company (for the improvement of navigation of the state's rivers), and a founder of the Kentucky Society for Promoting Useful Knowledge (1787) and the Kentucky Society for Encouragement of Manufactures (1789). He held title to 4,055 acres of land.

In his later years Greenup suffered from crippling rheumatism and in walking had to use a crutch and a cane. He died while seeking relief at the Blue Licks Springs Resort. The town of Greenup and Greenup County, in northeastern Kentucky, are named for him. Greenup was the most "useful" of the early Kentucky leaders, so remarked a eulogist. A political moderate, he was admired for his statesmanlike qualities.

• The Kentucky Department for Libraries and Archives, Frankfort, has the Governor Greenup Papers: Executive Journals, Official Correspondence, and Enrolled Bills. Greenup correspondence is in the Harry Innes Papers and the Charles Simms Papers, Library of Congress. For Greenup's service as a member of the U.S. House of Representatives, see Joseph Gayles, comp., *Annals of the Congress of the United States, 1789–1824*, 2d, 3d, and 4th Congs. (1849). *The Papers of Henry Clay*, ed. James F. Hopkins, vol. 1 (1959), has documents pertaining to Greenup. Biographical sketches include Orlando Brown, "The Governors of Kentucky," Kentucky Historical Society, *Register* 49 (1951): 102–106, James F. Hopkins, "Christopher Greenup," in *Kentucky's Governors, 1792–1985*, ed. Lowell H. Harrison (1985), pp. 11–14, and "Governor Christopher Greenup," Kentucky State Historical Society, *Register* 1 (May 1903): 69–70. For Greenup and Kentucky government and politics, see Charles G. Talbert, *Benjamin Logan: Kentucky Frontiersman* (1962), Lowell H. Harrison, *Kentucky's Road to Statehood* (1992), Thomas Speed, *The Political Club, Danville, Kentucky*, Filson Club Publications, no. 9 (1894), William Littell, *Political Transactions in and Concerning Kentucky . . . to 1792* (1806; repr. 1926), William E. Connelley and E. M. Coulter, *History of Kentucky*, vols. 1–2 (1922), and Lewis Collins and Richard H. Collins, *History of Kentucky* (2 vols., 1874; repr. 1966). A death notice is in the *Kentucky Gazette*, 8 May 1818.

HARRY M. WARD

GREENWALL, Henry (1832?–27 Nov. 1913), theater manager, was born in Germany and brought to New Orleans by his parents (names and occupations unknown) in 1837 at the age of five. Details of his family background and his childhood are almost entirely lacking.

Sometime around 1865 Henry and an older brother, Morris, moved to Galveston, Texas, and opened a brokerage firm. In 1867 they rented a theater in the hope that they could enable a stranded actress to recover enough money to repay a debt to the firm. The venture proved profitable and launched Greenwall on a lifelong career as a theater manager in Texas and the South. He acquired a building that had been the first in Galveston designed specifically as a theater, formed Greenwall's Star Stock Company with actors and actresses he employed during a trip to New York, and opened the New Galveston Theatre on 21 November 1867. On 14 December 1868 he also leased the Perkins Theatre in Houston.

On 25 February 1871 the Tremont Opera House, financed by a group of influential Galveston businessmen supporting Greenwall, opened. It would serve as Greenwall's base of operations for at least twelve of the next seventeen years as he expanded his interests to include theaters in other Texas cities. In 1885 Greenwall's brother and partner, Morris, died, and his 26-year-old son, Edward, became his partner. They began the first of more than thirty years of management of the Dallas Opera House. By 1886 Greenwall's Texas Theatrical Circuit, as it was beginning to be called, included theaters in Galveston, Houston, and Dallas, which he managed personally, and theaters with local managers in the Texas cities of San Antonio, Austin, Waco, Fort Worth, and Texarkana and in the Arkansas cities of Little Rock, Hot Springs, and Pine Bluff.

In 1888 Greenwall moved to New Orleans, taking control of the Grand Opera House from David Bidwell and sparking a rivalry that eventually would lead, at least indirectly, to the development of the Theatrical

Syndicate. Bidwell, in retaliation, purchased a theatrical booking agency in New York and placed Charles B. Jefferson, Abe Erlanger, and Marc Klaw in charge. Direct competition was established, but it was several years before open rivalry began to heat up.

In April 1890 Greenwall's son, who had been managing the Texas Theatrical Circuit, committed suicide in New York. Greenwall changed the firm's name to H. Greenwall, Son and Bro. and called upon his brother Phil to act as his partner. Greenwall also purchased the Fort Worth Opera House, remodeled it, changed its name, and reopened it as the Greenwall Opera House.

In 1894, to combat the growth of Jefferson, Klaw, and Erlanger interests in the South, Greenwall formed a partnership with Albert Weis, a Galveston businessman, with the goal of protecting his own interests. Their American Theatrical Exchange established their own chain of nearly two hundred theaters in Texas and the South. On 10 March 1895 the *New Orleans Daily Picayune* reported that Greenwall controlled theaters in New Orleans, Galveston, Houston, Fort Worth, Dallas, Atlanta, Savannah, Charleston, Nashville, and Louisville.

In August 1896 the Theatrical Syndicate was officially formed. As a leader of the opposition to the syndicate in the South, Greenwall met with other independent theater managers in New York on 19 February 1897 to discuss ways to combat the syndicate. All but four of the independent managers joined the syndicate a short time later. Greenwall refused to give in. The season of 1897–1898 proved to be the turning point in Greenwall's career. That year he was able to bring an astonishing group of independent artists, including the Julius Grau Opera Company, Tim Murphy, Otis Skinner, and Nat C. Goodwin, to the Grand Opera House, apparently because of their loyalty to and respect for Greenwall. However, the following season, as the syndicate influence grew, he began having difficulty finding enough quality attractions and was forced to pull out of failing ventures in many southern cities.

Only through a return to the resident stock company was Greenwall able to remain active in theater in New Orleans when all other independent managers except one had been forced out by the syndicate. With the Baldwin-Melville Company, he remained at the Grand Opera House until 1904. He then built the Greenwall Theatre, which opened on 20 October 1904. After one year it became a burlesque house while Greenwall managed stock companies elsewhere—at the Lyric, then the Elysium, and then the Baldwin, which became the Dauphine Theatre.

By 1909 Greenwall's finances had become drained. He sold his share of interest in the American Theatrical Exchange and his theaters in Galveston and Houston to his partner, Albert Weis. His only remaining holdings in Texas, under the supervision of his brother Phil, were in Dallas, Fort Worth, and Waco. In 1910 he entered a three-year contract with the Shubert organization for first-class bookings at the Dauphine.

On 21 February 1913 the Shuberts and the syndicate agreed to avoid competition in the major cities. When the Shuberts agreed to book into the syndicate's Tulane Theatre in New Orleans, Greenwall was left without attractions for his Dauphine Theatre for the 1913–1914 season. The 81-year-old Greenwall traveled to New York once again to organize a stock company, which opened on 14 September 1913 in New Orleans at the Dauphine. Two months later Greenwall died in his apartment above the Greenwall Theatre in New Orleans.

Henry Greenwall's 46-year career as a theater manager and leader of the Deep South's opposition to the Theatrical Syndicate was one of significant achievement. It was the product of a man possessed of a remarkable business ability coupled with a great capacity for earning the loyalty and respect of his associates. His vast circuit of theaters in Texas and the South housed many famous actors and actresses of the day—Minnie Maddern Fiske, Lotta Crabtree, Clara Morris, J. K. Wallack, James O'Neill, Sarah Bernhardt, Richard Mansfield, Nat Goodwin, Otis Skinner, Sir Henry Irving, and Mme Helena Modjeska. Throughout his lifetime Greenwall displayed an unusual lack of self-interest and an undying dedication to the cause of artistic freedom in the American theater. Although his struggle against the syndicate was unsuccessful and reduced his holdings from a height of nearly 200 theaters in 1895 to merely five at the time of his death, he was one of only two theater managers who remained both independent and in business in the face of the monopoly.

• For Greenwall's career see Claudia A. Beach, "Henry Greenwall: Theatre Manager" (Ph.D. diss., Texas Tech Univ., 1986). Greenwall's years in Texas theater are best chronicled in Clyde Richard King, "A History of the Theatre in Texas, 1722–1900" (Ph.D. diss., Baylor Univ., 1963), and in Joseph Gallegly, *Footlights on the Border* (1962). The New Orleans years are best detailed in John S. Kendall, *The Golden Age of the New Orleans Theatre* (1952), and in Shirley Harrison, "A History of the Grand Opera House (Third Varieties Theatre) in New Orleans, 1871–1906: A History and Analysis" (Ph.D. diss., Louisiana State Univ., 1965). Obituaries are in the *New Orleans Daily Picayune* and the *New York Times*, both 28 Nov. 1913.

CLAUDIA A. BEACH

GREENWAY, Isabella (22 Mar. 1886–18 Dec. 1953), congresswoman, businesswoman, and community activist, was born Isabella Selmes in Boone County, Kentucky, the daughter of Martha Macomb Flandrau and Tilden Russell Selmes, a rancher and lawyer. After Isabella's birth, her mother took her to join Tilden Selmes in North Dakota, where Theodore Roosevelt was a neighbor. Her father and many others lost most of their livestock in the blizzards of 1886–1887, and he quit ranching and moved the family to St. Paul, Minnesota, where he practiced law. After her father's death in 1895, Isabella and her mother lived in New York City, where wealthy relatives sent her to a private girls' school. There she met Eleanor Roosevelt, and she was a bridesmaid at Eleanor's wedding to Franklin Roosevelt. At age nineteen, in 1905, Isabella married Robert H. Munro Ferguson, one of Theodore Roosevelt's Rough Riders. They had two children. After Ferguson developed tuberculosis, they homesteaded in New Mexico, where Isabella was active in community affairs. Ferguson died in 1922. The following year she married another Rough Rider, Brigadier General John Campbell Greenway. They had one child before John Greenway died in 1926.

Isabella Greenway had shared her second husband's interests in mining, ranching, and aviation as well as his concern for veterans of World War I. She organized a furniture cooperative in Tucson, Arizona, to provide work for wounded soldiers and their families, and she built a resort hotel, the Arizona Inn, furnished with their handiwork. Although the cooperative failed during the Great Depression, the inn was successful. She bought a ranch near the Grand Canyon and invested in a commuter airline.

"Jack" Greenway had also been active in politics, running unsuccessfully for the Democratic gubernatorial nomination in 1922 and serving as a delegate to the 1924 Democratic National Convention, where he was nominated for vice president. Isabella Greenway had made political contacts as his wife. After his death, she continued to be active in the Tucson community, and her work with the veterans received national attention. She was elected Democratic national committeewoman from Arizona in 1928 and waged a vigorous campaign for Al Smith.

Following the campaign, Greenway combined the men's and women's divisions of the Democratic party in Arizona and was reelected to her post in 1930. By 1932, when the depression had created political opportunity for the Democrats, she won the commitment of the Arizona delegation's votes for the nomination of her friend Franklin Roosevelt, and she seconded his nomination at the Democratic convention in Chicago. Roosevelt made a campaign stop at her mountain ranch in September.

Greenway, the only woman among Roosevelt's state leaders, organized Arizona Democrats to support his candidacy and campaigned for him throughout the state. After Roosevelt's inauguration in 1933, he appointed Arizona's only U.S. representative, Lewis W. Douglas, as director of the budget. Greenway ran for his vacant seat, using an airplane to reach scattered speaking engagements in a large state with poor roads. Her gender was not a real issue, although her opponents in the primary election referred to it indirectly. She downplayed her friendship with the Roosevelts, saying: "The Roosevelts have thousands of friends not qualified to be congressmen. I am not asking for votes on that basis, but on the basis that I feel qualified to do the work." She won both the nomination and the general election.

As a member of Congress, Greenway was active and independent. Within ten days of her election, she had secured promised funds from Secretary of the Interior Harold Ickes for irrigation and flood control projects in the state as well as a new post office in Phoenix to provide work for the unemployed. In her first speech in the U.S. House of Representatives, she confounded those who expected her to support the administration by criticizing Roosevelt's opposition to a veterans' benefits bill. The bill became law in 1934. That same year she was easily reelected to a second term. In 1935 she opposed Roosevelt over the Social Security Bill, urging passage of the popular old-age pension separately from more controversial aspects of the bill, such as state funding of old-age pensions and unemployment insurance. She also worked for legislation to help her state's hard-hit cotton and copper industries and for tax revisions to increase economic security. Her decision to retire in 1936 was attributed by some to her disagreements with Roosevelt, but those close to her believed it was more likely because of overwork as Arizona's sole representative in the House and her conscientious attention to constituent requests. In 1939 she married Harry Orland King, an industrialist from the New York City area. Greenway subsequently spent time both in the East and in Arizona, where she continued to operate the inn.

Greenway opposed Roosevelt's third-term candidacy in 1940, hoping to keep the United States out of the European war. Instead she worked for Democrats for Willkie, supporting Wendell Willkie, the Republican presidential nominee. After U.S. entry into the war, she was named chair of an organization to give civilian women defense training. She died in Tucson.

Greenway brought her considerable energy and originality to every aspect of a multifaceted life. The *New York Times*, in something of an understatement, observed in her obituary that she had been "one of the more colorful personalities who flashed to national prominence in the political upheaval that brought Franklin D. Roosevelt to the Presidency."

• Greenway's correspondence and papers are at the Arizona Historical Society in Tucson; papers and memorabilia are at the Dinsmore Foundation in Boone County, Ky., the site of her mother's family farm. Greenway's early life and congressional election are covered by Avan S. Probst, "Isabella Greenway: Arizona's 1933 Congresswoman" (master's thesis, Northern Arizona Univ., 1994). Her congressional career is summarized in Hope Chamberlin, *A Minority of Members: Women in the U.S. Congress* (1973). Her Tucson life is discussed in Blake Brophy, "Tucson's Arizona Inn: The Continuum of Style," *Journal of Arizona History* 24, no. 3 (Autumn 1983): 225–82. An obituary is in the *New York Times*, 19 Dec. 1953.

KRISTIE MILLER

GREENWOOD, Grace. *See* Lippincott, Sara Jane Clarke.

GREENWOOD, Isaac (11 May 1702–12 Oct. 1745), professor of mathematics and experimental philosophy, was born in Boston, Massachusetts, the son of Samuel Greenwood and Elizabeth Bronsdon (occupations unknown). Baptized and raised in Increase Mather and Cotton Mather's North Church, Greenwood followed the Mathers in their scientific interests. At Harvard College he became a favorite of tutor Thomas Robie, the successor of Thomas Brattle as New England's most knowledgeable mathematician and astronomer. Greenwood's obituary stated that Greenwood often reflected "with Gratitude upon the Assistances he received from [Robie], acknowledging that it was in a great Measure owing to his kind Directions and Encouragement that his love (tho' natural) to the Mathematicks was not quench'd or exchang'd for some earlier Employment."

The earlier employment he spoke of was the ministry. When Greenwood graduated in 1721, he turned his attention more fully to religion and was admitted into full communion in the Mathers' church in 1722. He decided on a career in the ministry but then considered a vocation in medicine. In 1721–1722 Greenwood supported Cotton Mather's and Thomas Robie's controversial advocacy of smallpox inoculation and was inoculated himself. Greenwood's *A Friendly Debate; or a Dialogue between Academicus and Sawny & Mundungus* (1722), ridiculed those who distrusted the dangerous practice. With letters of introduction to members of the Royal Society from Mather and Robie, Greenwood traveled in 1723 to England, where he found that many scientists, including Isaac Newton, were interested in hearing about the inoculations from an inoculant.

Greenwood socialized among fellows of the Royal Society and in late 1923 or early 1924 became the assistant to the popular lecturer and curator of the Royal Society's instruments Dr. Jean Théophile Desaguliers. In 1724 Greenwood sent a medical thesis to Robie in order to receive his master's degree from Harvard that year. While preaching among England's Dissenters, Greenwood met Thomas Hollis, who was prepared to endow a professorship in mathematics and experimental philosophy at Harvard College. Hollis's initial enthusiastic choice of Greenwood to be the recipient of his endowed chair waned when Hollis heard of Greenwood's financial misdealings. In 1726 Greenwood returned to Boston, running from substantial debts to friends in England. However, Cotton Mather and Benjamin Colman, a patron of Greenwood and agent between Hollis and Harvard, continued to ask Hollis to name Greenwood to the endowed chair. In the meantime Greenwood, "in Imitation of his Master Dr. Desaguliers," began giving popular scientific lectures in Boston.

Unlike Brattle and Robie, Greenwood did not have the desire and persistence required for ongoing precise scientific research and, instead, was best at popularizing science. "He had a happy Talent of adapting himself in such a Manner to the Capacity of his Hearers, of representing the most obscure and difficult Things in such plain and easy light, as could not fail to satisfy the most ignorant, at the same Time that it would please the most learned" (*Boston Gazette*, 26 Nov. 1745).

Appointed Hollis Professor of Mathematics and Experimental Philosophy in February 1728, Greenwood began teaching at Harvard while taking over from Ro-

bie as an American correspondent to members of the Royal Society. He married Sarah Clarke in 1729; they had five children. Between 1729 and 1731 Greenwood's observations on meteors, the aurora borealis, and the "vitiated air" in wells were published in the *Philosophical Transactions of the Royal Society*. His early lectures, *An Experimental Course of Mechanical Philosophy* (1726), were derived from Desaguliers's lectures and designed for general reading. He published later courses of lectures as *A Course of Mathematical Lectures and Experiments* (1738) and *A Course of Philosophical Lectures* (1739).

Greenwood's textbook for his algebra classes was never published, but his *Arithmetick Vulgar and Decimal with the Application Thereof to a Variety of Cases in Trade and Commerce* appeared in 1729. A simple overview for easy memorization and usefulness, *Arithmetick* devoted word problems and a special section to the use of math in business. Used at Harvard and Yale, it served as a precursor to textbooks in both math and business.

Greenwood's most important publication was *A Philosophical Discourse Concerning the Mutability and Changes of the Material World* (1731), which was published in honor of the death of Hollis. The *Discourse* did not report on any research but rather philosophically dilated on the mechanical laws that govern the mutability of nature. The essay fundamentally served to popularize Newtonianism.

Although active, Greenwood never lived up to his early promise. In 1738 he was dismissed from Harvard for intemperance with alcohol. His most significant publications, a beginning mathematics textbook and an essay on Newtonianism, exemplified his skills in simplification and popularization but did not meet the scientific standards of his Harvard predecessors, Brattle and Robie, nor of his successor John Winthrop. Although Greenwood had hoped to teach "Sir Isaac Newton's Incomparable Method of Fluxions, or the Differential Calculus," Harvard records do not indicate any greater understanding of calculus among students during Greenwood's professorship than during Robie's rudimentary tutoring.

After dismissal from Harvard, Greenwood continued to give popular lectures in Boston but was unable to make enough money. In the 1740s he created a traveling scientific show. Benjamin Franklin acted as Greenwood's Philadelphia promoter in 1740, arranging lecture rooms and apparatus from the Library Company. Greenwood's show may have been the spark that first set Franklin to try his hand at science.

Ultimately financially unsuccessful as an independent scientific showman, Greenwood joined the British Navy in 1742 as a chaplain. Discharged on 22 May 1744 in Charleston, South Carolina, he died there from excessive drinking five months later.

Greenwood is most well known for his public demonstrations, which helped popularize a Newtonian mentality in early eighteenth-century American society. A poem that appeared in the *Boston Gazette* (16 Dec. 1734) after one of his public lectures proclaimed that "No more we'll gaze with superstitious Fear" and asked him to continue to "Inform our Mind, and set our judgement right." His contributions as one of colonial America's first scientific showmen overshadow those as the nation's first professor of science. Greenwood's obituary speculated that he had left Harvard because "the Sphere of Action" was "too small and confin'd for the enterprizing Genius of Mr. Greenwood."

• A chronological list of Greenwood's writings is published at the end of David C. Leonard, "Harvard's First Science Professor: A Sketch of Isaac Greenwood's Life and Work," *Harvard Library Bulletin* 29 (1981): 135–68. Other life sketches are in Raymond Phineas Stearns, *Science in the British Colonies of America* (1970), pp. 446–55, and Clifford K. Shipton, *Sibley's Harvard Graduates*, vol. 4 (1942), pp. 471–82. See also Lao G. Simons' articles in *Scripta Mathematica*: "Isaac Greenwood's Arithmetic" 1 (1933): 262–64; "Isaac Greenwood, First Hollis Professor" 2 (1934): 117–24; and "The Adoption of the Method of Fluxions in American Schools" 4 (1936): 207–19. An obituary is in the *Boston Gazette*, 26 Nov. 1745.

RICK KENNEDY

GREENWOOD, John (17 May 1760–16 Nov. 1819), George Washington's dentist, was born in Boston, Massachusetts, the son of Isaac Greenwood, an ivory turner, mathematical instrument maker, and the first practical dentist in Boston, and Mary I'ans. Greenwood received the rudiments of an education at the North School in Boston. At age thirteen he was apprenticed for two years to his uncle, Thales Greenwood, a cabinetmaker in Portland, Maine.

When hostilities between England and the colonies broke out, Greenwood enlisted as a fife player in the military company in which his uncle was a lieutenant. Concerned for his parents' safety in Boston after the outbreak of war at Lexington and Concord in April 1775, he slipped out of Portland early one morning and walked back toward his parents' home. He was stopped at the British lines at Charlestown and prevented from crossing over to Boston. At Cambridge, in late May 1775, he enlisted in Captain Bliss's company as a fife major for eight months. When his parents learned that he was in the "rebel" army, they tried unsuccessfully to retrieve him by supplying the army with a substitute.

After the battle of Bunker Hill, Greenwood marched with his regiment to Montreal. When the Americans were defeated there, he retreated with the remnants of his company to Ticonderoga and Albany and returned to the main body of the army in time to engage in the battle of Trenton. Once his enlistment was up and Boston was free of the British, he returned to his parents' home. Three months later, in the spring of 1777, he shipped out as a steward's mate on a privateer, which was seized by the British. He was held prisoner for six months and released. He then returned home and signed on as a master-at-arms on another ship.

Sometime in late 1784 or early 1785 Greenwood settled in New York City, where he worked as a maker of mathematical and nautical instruments. Asked by a local physician to extract a tooth from one of his patients, Greenwood decided to study dentistry. Having already learned ivory turning and carving and practical dental skills from his father, he set out to learn as much as he could about the science of dentistry. He first advertised himself as a dentist on 28 February 1786; he was assisted in his dental practice by a younger brother, William Pitt Greenwood. In 1788, with improved finances, he married Elizabeth Weaver; they had at least two children.

A month after the newly named U.S. president George Washington arrived in New York—the nation's capital from 1789 to 1791—Washington saw a notice that Greenwood had placed in the *New York Packet* on 21 May 1789 advertising his services. Greenwood became Washington's favorite dentist, which was not a small matter, as the president had demanding dental needs and was an exacting patient. Washington's letters reveal that from 1791 to 1799 Greenwood was frequently called on to adjust or repair the president's false teeth or to send him materials for making the repairs himself. After Washington's death Greenwood advertised himself as "Dentist to the late President Washington." He continued "to make and fix Artificial Teeth" and to perform "every operation incident to the Teeth and Gums, from the fixing of a single tooth to a complete set" (*Dental Cosmos*, p. 991). He did not attend patients in their own houses "except it is to relieve pain in difficult cases . . . and that he will do gratis, if required."

Greenwood's special achievements as a dentist were a foot-powered drill that he made himself using one of his mother's old spinning wheels and the use of coiled gold springs to stabilize the patient's upper and lower dentures. As early as 1792 he utilized porcelain teeth in his denture construction. Like other dentists, he took impressions for dentures in beeswax. Initially, he carved the teeth from hippopotamus ivory; later, after a trip to France in 1806, he introduced the use of porcelain teeth with platinum pins. Like other dentists of his day, he implanted teeth, usually front teeth, in wealthier patients, after having extracted healthy teeth from poor patients, who were paid from one to four guineas per tooth. Greenwood died in his home in New York City. He was succeeded in his dental practice by his two sons.

• There is no known collection of Greenwood papers. For information on his life and work, see E. Bryan, "Mr. John Greenwood, Mechanical and Surgeon Dentist of the City of New-York," *American Journal of Dental Science* 1, no. 4 (1839): 73–77, no. 5 (1840): 97–105, no. 6 (1940): 113–19; *The Writings of George Washington*, ed. John C. Fitzpatrick (39 vols., 1931–1944): 31:216–17, 32:82, 35:120–21, 370–71, 374–75, 37:27–29, 82–83; Edward C. Kirk, "Pioneer Dentistry in New York: An Historical Study," *Dental Cosmos* 48 (1906): 981–97; and Charles R. E. Koch, ed., *History of Dental Surgery*, vol. 1 (1910), pp. 83–87.

DAVID KRASNER

GREER, David Hummel (20 Mar. 1844–19 May 1919), Episcopal bishop, was born in Wheeling, Virginia (later W.Va.), the son of Jacob Rickard Greer, a wholesale merchant, and Elizabeth Yellott Armstrong. In 1860 he entered the junior class of Washington College (now Washington and Jefferson College), Washington, Pennsylvania, and received the B.A. in 1862. After working in Wheeling, he studied at the Theological Seminary of the Protestant Episcopal church in the diocese of Ohio, Gambier (1863–1866). Bishop Coadjutor Gregory Thurston Bedell of Ohio ordained him deacon on 27 June 1866, and he began his ministry at Christ Church, Clarksburg, West Virginia. Bishop Francis M. Whittle of Virginia ordained him to the priesthood on 19 May 1868. From October 1868 until June 1871 he was rector of Trinity Church, Covington, Kentucky. While there he met and in 1869 married Caroline Augusta Keith; they had four children. In 1871–1872 he traveled in Europe, and on 15 September 1872 he began a sixteen-year rectorship at Grace Church, Providence, Rhode Island, where he became known as an outstanding preacher and helped to found St. Elizabeth's Home for Incurables. He represented the diocese of Rhode Island at the general conventions of 1877, 1880, 1883, and 1886.

In November 1888 he became rector of St. Bartholomew's Church, New York City, where he had a most effective ministry, especially among the poor and lower classes. St. Bartholomew's Parish House was the center of this religious and social work.

We have in St. Bartholomew's Parish a good many departments of parochial activity. We have not only our Sunday-schools, and missionary societies, and benevolent societies, but a Swedish mission, and a Chinese mission, and an Armenian mission, and a Syrian mission, and a lodging house and a loan bureau, and an employment bureau, and a coffee house, and a penny provident fund, and a girls' club, and a boys' club, and a men's club, and a gymnasium, and a parish press, and a kindergarten, and a surgical clinic, and a medical clinic, and an ear and eye clinic,—as well as all the ordinary activities which every thriving parish includes. (Slattery, p. 113)

In 1889 he delivered the Bedell Lectures at his seminary in Gambier. Published under the title *The Historical Christ, the Moral Power of History* (1890), these lectures displayed both his evangelical theology, with its commitment to the saving death of Jesus Christ, and his liberal views, with regard to modern science and biblical criticism. He was, in short, a liberal evangelical. When Phillips Brooks became bishop of Massachusetts, Greer was called to succeed him as rector of Trinity Church, Boston, but he declined. In 1895 he delivered the Lyman Beecher Lectures on Preaching at Yale University, then the most distinguished preaching lectureship in the United States. The lectures, published as *The Preacher and His Place* (1895), made the notable claim that "all truth is sacred, because all truth is God's." Greer represented the diocese of New York at the general conventions of 1895,

1898, and 1901. In 1897 he was elected bishop coadjutor of Rhode Island and, in 1901, bishop of western Massachusetts; he declined both.

Greer was elected bishop coadjutor of New York on 30 September 1903 and was consecrated at St. Bartholomew's Church, New York, on 26 January 1904 by Bishop Henry Codman Potter of New York. When Bishop Potter died on 21 July 1908, Greer succeeded him as the eighth bishop of New York, the position he held until his death at St. Luke's Hospital in New York City. While he was bishop of New York Greer supported the continuing construction of the Cathedral of St. John the Divine and opposed U.S. entrance into World War I. He also was committed to the ecumenical movement and the amelioration of social problems. A man of humility who eschewed the usual Episcopal clerical dress, he was also one of the great preachers of his age.

• Some of Greer's papers are in the archives of the diocese of New York, New York City, and the archives of the Episcopal church, Austin, Tex. His major publications include two volumes of sermons, *From Things to God* (1893) and *Visions, Sunday Morning Sermons at St. Bartholomew's, New York* (1898). The only major study of his life and work is Charles Lewis Slattery, *David Hummel Greer, Eighth Bishop of New York* (1921).

DONALD S. ARMENTROUT

GREER, Sonny (13 Dec. 1885–23 Mar. 1982), jazz drummer, was born William Alexander Greer, Jr., in Long Branch, New Jersey, the son of William Alexander Greer, an electrician for the Pennsylvania Railroad. His mother (name unknown) was a seamstress. Greer was first attracted to playing as the result of his contact with Eugene "Peggy" Holland, a drummer, singer, and dancer with J. Rosamond Johnson's touring vaudeville show. His few lessons with Holland (bartered for pool-shooting tips by Greer) provided him with the basic tools he needed to teach himself drums.

His first professional jobs began in the late 1910s with Wilber Gardner and Mabel Ross, and in society orchestras contracted by Harry Yerek and Will Marion Cook. At nineteen he worked with Fats Waller and violinist Shrimp Jones on the ocean boardwalk resort of Asbury Park. In 1919, while vacationing in Washington, D.C., Greer was asked to fill in as drummer with Marie Lucas at the Howard Theater, where he met Duke Ellington. While playing at the Howard, he also worked after hours at the Dreamland Café with pianist Claude Hopkins and trombonist Harry White. After spending several years in Washington, Greer returned to New York where, in 1923, he joined the Washingtonians, a five-piece band led by Elmer Snowden that included Snowden on banjo, Otto Hardwick on saxophone, Artie Whetsol on trumpet, and Ellington on piano. With the addition of Bubber Miley (replacing Whetsol) and Charlie Irvis, this group became the nucleus for the Duke Ellington Orchestra after Snowden departed. In 1928 he married Millicent C. (maiden name unknown), with whom he had two children.

From the early 1920s until 1951, Greer worked almost exclusively as Ellington's drummer. After leaving Ellington he freelanced in New York, playing with Johnny Hodges, Red Allen, Tyree Glenn, and Louis Metcalf. During the next decade, Greer played with two ex-Ellingtonians, saxophonist Eddie Barefield and trombonist J. C. Higginbotham, later fronting his own small group at the Garden Cafe in New York. He made an appearance (with Barefield and other band members) in the film *The Night They Raided Minsky's* (1968) and, in that same year, was featured in "Sonny," an eleven-minute film made by Midget Productions. During the 1970s Greer played with pianist and Ellington interpreter Brooks Kerr, recording an album of duos with him in 1975 (*Soda Fountain Rag,* Chiaroscuro CR 2001). He was active almost until his death in New York City.

Greer's career was remarkable not only for its longevity with one of the premier jazz bands of our century but for its complementary and unobtrusive playing style. Greer's best recordings were made in the late 1920s, when drummers, still influenced by earlier ragtime styles, were developing techniques that would later be used by drummers in the coming Swing Era. Perhaps most influential in forming Greer's playing style was the Ellington stint as house band at the Cotton Club in New York. Here, Greer was required to provide percussive effects for the many "Jungle" shows and productions performed nightly at the club. As a result, Greer collected perhaps the largest selection of percussion instruments of any drummer during the Swing Era, as numerous photographs of him taken at this time illustrate. At times some of these instruments found their way onto recordings made by Greer, including chimes ("Freeze and Melt," Columbia 1813D [1929]), temple blocks ("Arabian Lover," Victor V38079 [1929]), bells, and timpani.

At that time drum solos were de rigeur for any swing drummer, so it is surprising that extensive solos are rarely heard on recordings made by Greer. In fact, his infrequent and brief solos throughout his career are notable only for the fact that his playing can be heard clearly and plainly, since he most often remains in the background of many of the recordings he made with Ellington. Recordings representative of his best playing derive mainly from the 1920s, late 1930s, and early 1940s including, "East St. Louis Toodle-oo" (Columbia 953D [1927]), "Chasin' Chippies" (Vocalion [1938]), "Downtown Uproar" (Variety [1937]), "Cotton Tail," (RCA Victor [1940]) and "Jumpin' Punkins" (Victor, [1941]). These exhibit Greer's adherence to contemporary drum solo techniques, including those played by Gene Krupa, Chick Webb, and Cozy Cole.

• Information about Greer's career is mainly in sources about Duke Ellington, including Ellington, *Music Is My Mistress* (1973); Stanley Dance, *The World of Duke Ellington* (1980); and the *Duke Ellington Reader,* ed. Mark Tucker (1993). Some biographical information is included in Whitney Balliett, *Jelly Roll, Jabbo, and Fats* (1983), in a chapter titled

"New York Drummers"; and in Burt Korall, *Drummin' Men* (1990). Articles about his prolific career are few and, unfortunately, appear after he left the Ellington band in 1951. These include Jimmy Cooke, "Credit Where Due: A Short Study of Sonny Greer," *Jazz Monthly* 6, no. 6 (Aug. 1960): 7–8+; and Scott K. Fish, "Sonny Greer: The Elder Statesman of Jazz," *Modern Drummer* 5, no. 8 (Aug. 1981): 30. Also important are T. Dennis Brown, "A History and Analysis of Jazz Drumming to 1942" (Ph.D. diss., Univ. of Michigan, 1976); and Lee Jeske, "Sonny Greer, 83, Recalls the Time When the Aristocrats of Harlem Took London by Storm," *Jazz Journal International* 31, no. 11 (Nov. 1978): 22–23. Obituaries include Graham Colombé, "Sonny Greer," *Jazz Journal International* 35, no. 6 (June 1982): 6; Scott K. Fish, "In Memoriam: Sonny Greer," *Modern Drummer* 6, no. 4 (Mar. 1982): 72; and the *New York Times,* 25 Mar. 1982.

T. DENNIS BROWN

GREGG, Andrew (10 June 1755–20 May 1835), congressman, U.S. senator, and Pennsylvania political leader, was born in Carlisle, Pennsylvania, the son of Andrew Gregg and Jane Scott. His father, a native of Ireland, immigrated to Massachusetts, then moved to Pennsylvania in 1732 and took up farming. The younger Gregg was born on his father's farm and received a sound classical education, first at Reverend John Steel's Latin School in Carlisle and later at the Academy in Newark, Delaware. The Academy disbanded in 1777 when the British invaded Delaware, prompting Andrew, who had served in the Delaware militia, to return to Carlisle to help his father.

Thanks to his superb training, Andrew was hired in 1779 as a tutor at the College of Philadelphia (later University of Pennsylvania), where he spent four years. In 1783, using money he had saved from teaching, Gregg moved to Middletown in Dauphin County and set up business as a storekeeper. Four years later he married Martha Potter of Buffalo Valley, and in 1789 they moved to Penn's Valley in Center County, where Gregg took up farming. All of his children were born on this farm.

Well respected by his neighbors, Gregg was elected to the U.S. House of Representatives in October 1791. This election marked the beginning of a sixteen-year career in the House, as well as a long involvement in both state and national politics. Shortly after taking office, Gregg described himself as a "staunch Whig and a sincere Republican." Although political parties were still in their formative stages, Gregg's convictions placed him squarely on the side of the Jeffersonian Republicans in the struggle against the Federalists. Considering himself a "practical farmer" who perceived an "inseparable" connection between commerce and agriculture, Gregg supported the thrust of Jeffersonian political economy, with its emphasis on the development of an agrarian republic, and opposed Federalist plans for an industrial manufacturing economy.

In Congress, Gregg worked assiduously to guard the interests of his backcountry constituents, who were largely farmers themselves. On roll call votes Gregg generally voted with the bulk of other Republicans, often finding himself with a voting record nearly identical to Republican leader James Madison. But if Gregg followed his party on votes, he did not do so uniformly, even on the most important issues. Gregg showed enough independence to vote occasionally with Federalists on House measures. When the question of making appropriations for the Jay Treaty with England arose in 1796—perhaps the most decisive issue in the formation of political parties in America—Gregg broke with the Republicans, who bitterly opposed the treaty, to vote reluctantly in favor of funding. During the debate Gregg stated that while he did not like the treaty, he feared that rejection of a treaty already approved by the president and ratified by the Senate would do more harm to the country than its acceptance.

Back in Pennsylvania, Gregg found himself caught up in an internal Republican party struggle that had important ramifications for his later career. Pennsylvania Republicans were divided into a radical faction and a moderate or conservative band. Gregg followed the moderates, who included men like Thomas McKean, governor from 1799 to 1808, and Alexander J. Dallas. In local politics the moderates often found themselves allied with the Federalists to oppose the radical Republicans. The radicals saw themselves as the true descendents of Jeffersonianism, accusing the moderates of betraying party principles for the sake of a political allegiance with the Federalists; they also prided themselves on their common touch and often celebrated their lack of experience or education. On 13 January 1807, aided by Federalists, the moderate Republicans in the state legislature selected Gregg to a six-year term in the U.S. Senate. As he had been in the House, Gregg was a strong backer of the Jefferson and Madison administrations, supporting the Embargo Act and, later, the Non-Intercourse Act. Gregg also served as president pro tempore of the Senate from 26 June 1809 to 28 February 1810.

During Gregg's time in the Senate, however, the political climate in Pennsylvania shifted toward the radical Republicans, led by Governor Simon Snyder. Gregg was not reelected to a second term in the Senate and returned from Washington, settling in Bellefonte, Pennsylvania, in 1814. Gregg selected the town largely to be near good schools for his children and took a position as president of Centre bank. But Gregg's political career was far from over. Still actively engaged despite the triumph of the radical Republicans, Gregg was appointed secretary of the Commonwealth on 19 December 1820 by Governor John Hiester, an Independent Republican elected with some Federalist help.

In 1823 Gregg was nominated for governor by the Independent Republicans to run against the radical Republican John Schulze. Gregg, who was sixty-eight at the time, was attacked by the radicals who charged him with senility (some claimed he was as old as eighty-two) and ironically derided him as "The Farmer." After losing the governorship in 1820, the radical Republicans spared no efforts to win back the post in 1823. Since the Independent Republicans had often been allied with the Federalists, Gregg was tarred with the label of that discredited party. Gregg was further hurt by his initial skepticism, expressed in a letter to a friend in 1812, about the wisdom of declaring war against Great Britain—a further link to Federalism and a fact that his opponents used mercilessly against him. Despite an active campaign on his behalf, Gregg was defeated in a landslide. Shulze won by a majority of 25,000 votes (89,000 to 64,000) and swept forty-four counties. Following the 1823 election Gregg returned to his farm in Bellefonte, where he died.

Gregg was well liked and respected by his contemporaries, one of whom called him "a highly respectable inhabitant of this county, and for many years known as a public man in Pennsylvania and in the United States." Another praised him for his "sound and discriminating mind, agreeable and dignified manners, strict regard for truth, and unbending and unyielding honesty." Gregg was a well-educated, accomplished leader who succeeded in a variety of careers and was a participant in some of the most significant political events of his time.

• No substantial collection of Gregg's papers exists, although the Library of Congress has some papers, and the Historical Society of Pennsylvania has letters from Gregg in various collections. The best works on Pennsylvania politics and Gregg's role in them are Harry Tinkcom, *Republicans and Federalists in Pennsylvania* (1950); Sanford Higginbotham, *The Keystone in the Democratic Arch* (1952); and Philip S. Klein, *Pennsylvania Politics: A Game Without Rules* (1940). For an analysis of congressional voting activity in the 1790s, see John Hoadley, *Origins of American Political Parties, 1789–1803* (1986). For the ideological background and makeup of the Jeffersonian Republicans, see Lance Banning, *The Jeffersonian Persuasion* (1978), and Drew McCoy, *The Elusive Republic* (1980). For particulars on Gregg, see Sherman Day, ed., *Historical Collections of the State of Pennsylvania* (1843). A contemporary account (not always friendly to Gregg) of Pennsylvania and national politics in the early republic is Jonathan Roberts's *Memoirs* in the Historical Society of Pennsylvania. Gregg's own unfinished family history sketch is contained in W. H. Egle, *Pennsylvania Genealogies* (1886). An obituary is in *Poulson's American Daily Advertiser*, 28 May 1835.

TODD ESTES

GREGG, David McMurtrie (10 Apr. 1833–7 Aug. 1916), U.S. Army officer, diplomat, and Pennsylvania state official, was born in Huntingdon, Pennsylvania, the son of Matthew Duncan Gregg and Ellen McMurtrie (occupations unknown). He was the paternal grandson of U.S. senator Andrew Gregg and the first cousin of Andrew Gregg Curtin, Pennsylvania's Civil War governor. Graduating from the U.S. Military Academy at West Point in 1855, Gregg was commissioned in the dragoons in 1855 and served on the western frontier, occasionally protecting westward bound settlers. By the beginning of the Civil War in 1861, the young officer was stationed at Fort Tejon, California.

Declaring for the Union and returning to the East, Gregg accepted the rank of colonel of volunteers and the command of the Eighth Pennsylvania Cavalry. In this position, the colonel and his regiment participated in both the 1862 Peninsula and Maryland campaigns under the command of Union General George B. Mc-Clellan (1826–1885). During the former action, Gregg and his unit performed the task of preceding Union forces from Harrison's Landing to Yorktown, Virginia. Following the defeat of Union General John Pope (1822–1892) at the battle of Second Manassas (Second Bull Run) in late August 1862, Gregg's horsemen were relegated to rounding up northern stragglers and moving to protect Washington from the victorious Confederates. In October the colonel obtained a brief leave of absence to marry Ellen Frances Sheaff; the number of their children is unknown. On his return to duty, he was promoted to brigadier general of volunteers on 29 November. In the spring of 1863 Gregg, now a division commander, was involved in General George Stoneman's failed cavalry raid against Richmond.

Following the Union defeat at Chancellorsville, Virginia, in May 1863, Gregg participated in the reorganization of the Army of the Potomac's cavalry into a force more equal to the previously superior Confederate Army of Northern Virginia's mounted arm. At the battle of Brandy Station, only one month after the battle of Chancellorsville, the same Confederate cavalry that had been so capably handled by the flamboyant southerner, General J. E. B. Stuart, received a surprise and embarrassing check by northern troopers. Gregg and his men joined in that attack on Stuart's horsemen; however, Gregg's performance at Brandy Station was disappointing. Gaining Stuart's rear, the Pennsylvanian found his command in an excellent position to deliver a telling blow on the southerners. This advantage was surrendered when Gregg hesitated upon seeing the belatedly alerted Confederates wheel a single, six-pound howitzer into position and begin firing on the lead Union troopers. Wisely using the pause in the northern advance, Stuart's men fully recovered, and the ensuing engagement ended inconclusively. Given the previously acknowledged edge of Stuart's force over its Union counterparts, Gregg's mistake at Brandy Station, the loss of a golden opportunity, was overlooked. The northern officer, along with the rest of the Army of the Potomac's horsemen, gained respect and admiration from the unusual outcome of this cavalry action.

Later in June Gregg and his troopers had another opportunity to contest Stuart's men. When Lee moved the Confederate army northward for an invasion of Pennsylvania, he initially ordered his cavalry to establish a screen between the marching southerners and the trailing Army of the Potomac, under the command of Major General Joseph Hooker. The northern mounted arm was ordered to penetrate this Confederate cavalry screen, locate and report on Lee's main columns, impede Lee's northward progress, and harass the southerners. The instructions of the two leaders put the opposing cavalry units in a direct struggle. Gregg's horsemen fought several sharp battles in the region of Aldie, Upperville, and Middleburg, Virginia. The Pennsylvanian won the contest at Aldie but lost the better part of a regiment at Middleburg. In this initial phase of the Pennsylvania campaign, Stuart largely succeeded in keeping the Union cavalry from penetrating the southern horsemen's protective screen. However, by continually pressing the Confederate cavalry, Union troopers were able to identify Lee's general route of march, providing information to Hooker that confirmed other reports, such as sightings from Hooker's mountaintop signal posts. Additionally, the threat posed by Union cavalry caused some delay in Lee's march north. Gregg was praised for his role in these accomplishments by his immediate superior, the Army of the Potomac's cavalry chief, Major General Alfred Pleasonton.

At the battle of Gettysburg in early July, Union cavalry in general and Gregg's division in particular were initially dispersed on protection and reconnaissance missions. Gregg protected the northerners' right flank with a small contingent of 2,500 troopers. On the second day of the battle, Stuart arrived on the battlefield after his long-ranging raid, which had taken the exhausted Confederate horsemen far to the east and north of Gettysburg. Conferring with Lee, Stuart was directed to exploit the success the Confederate commander expected from the planned assault of George Pickett's division on the Union center the next day. Stuart would secretly position his troopers in such a way that they could attack the Union rear when Pickett broke through the northerners' lines. The stage was thus set for another cavalry encounter. The route for the Confederate mounted assault was near the Union right, that part of the Army of the Potomac's sector defended by Gregg's men, now reinforced by more Union horsemen.

On 3 July 1863 Gregg got the best of Stuart. As the latter moved into position, his column of horsemen was noticed and reported by Union signal officers. Gregg was notified, but he was then directed by Pleasonton to divide his command once more to assist the Union left. Realizing the potential danger to the Union rear, Gregg chose to disobey his superior's instructions. Fighting between the two cavalry forces broke out at 3:00 P.M., about the same time that Pickett's ill-fated assault on the Army of the Potomac's center was failing. Gregg and the Union cavalry held their ground.

Gregg's reputation for coolness under fire and competence continued to grow during 1864. On 1 August he was brevetted major general of volunteers. The Pennsylvanian played an important role at the battle of New Market Heights, where on 16 August Gregg led a determined assault, forcing the Confederates out of their defenses. The Union cavalryman and his men reached a point only seven miles from Richmond before Lee's forces rallied and drove them back. Six days later Gregg managed to cripple Confederate logistics by destroying three miles of the Weldon railroad, a vital artery for Lee's army.

On 3 February 1865 Gregg unexpectedly resigned his commission and forfeited his chances to see the Confederate surrender while still in uniform. The reason for his decision has never been satisfactorily explained. It is doubtful that the resignation was due to any dissatisfaction with his service on the part of his superiors. The senior Union cavalryman then, General Philip Sheridan, regretted Gregg's leaving, citing the Pennsylvanian for bravery, "firmness," and "unpretentious" professional ability.

Gregg became a farmer near Milford, Delaware, later moving to Reading, Pennsylvania. In 1874 he briefly served his country once more, this time as U.S. consul at Prague, an appointment made by his comrade in arms, President Ulysses S. Grant. After serving for a few months, Gregg returned to Reading and was elected state auditor general, a position he held for three years. In 1907 he published a pamphlet, *The Second Cavalry Division of the Army of the Potomac in the Gettysburg Campaign*. Information about where he died is unavailable.

If not a particularly brilliant officer, Gregg was certainly a respected and competent one, a leader who earned the admiration of his men. His wartime fate was to serve in an arm that was inevitably compared unfavorably with the corresponding arm of the opposing force. For much of the war, the Confederate cavalry in the eastern theater had no peer. However, from the summer of 1863 forward, the Union cavalry in the East garnered a growing reputation for skill and daring. Gregg contributed much to that development.

• Gregg's career is mentioned in Edwin B. Coddington, *The Gettysburg Campaign: A Study in Command* (1968); W. H. Egle, *Pennsylvania Generals: Scotch-Irish and German* (1886); *Military Order of the Loyal Legion of the U.S. Commandery of the State of Pennsylvania*, no. 6, ser. 1917; *The War of the Rebellion: A Compilation of the Official Records of the Union and Confederate Armies* (128 vols., 1880–1901); G. G. Meade, ed., *Life and Letters of George Gordon Meade* (1913); W. B. Rawle, *The Right Flank at Gettysburg* (1878); and Philip H. Sheridan, *Personal Memoirs*, vol. 1 (1904).

ROD PASCHALL

GREGG, John (28 Sept. 1828–7 Oct. 1864), lawyer and Confederate general, was born in Lawrence County, Alabama, the son of Nathan Gregg, one of the area's first white settlers, and Sarah Pearsall. Gregg moved with his family to La Grange, Alabama, when he was about eight years old. In 1847 he graduated from La Grange College, after which he taught school and studied law in Tuscumbia, Alabama. In 1852 he moved to Centerville, Texas, where he remained a short time before moving to Fairfield, Texas, where he practiced law. Gregg married Mollie Winston (date unknown). Following her death, he married Mary Frances Garth in 1855. Both marriages were childless. In 1856 he was appointed judge of the Thirteenth District and served in that position until 1860. Gregg enthusiastically supported secession and was appointed to the convention of January 1861 that took Texas out of the Union. He subsequently was a member of the Texas delegation to the Provisional Confederate Congress at Montgomery, Alabama.

Following the first battle of Manassas, Gregg resigned his seat in the Confederate Congress and returned to Texas to recruit the Seventh Texas Infantry, of which he was elected colonel. Posted to Fort Donelson, Tennessee, Gregg and his entire regiment surrendered when Ulysses S. Grant captured the fort in February 1862. He was imprisoned for nearly seven months at Fort Warren in Boston, Massachusetts, but his wife was apparently permitted to join him for part of his captivity. Following his exchange, Gregg was promoted to brigadier general to rank from 29 August 1862 and given command of a brigade of Tennessee and Texas troops stationed in Mississippi. After duty at Port Hudson, Louisiana, his brigade returned to Mississippi, where it served with distinction in spite of the Confederate defeat at Raymond, Mississippi, during the early stages of the Vicksburg campaign. Gregg and his command were then assigned to Joseph E. Johnston's Mississippi army and subsequently detached to reinforce Braxton Bragg's Army of Tennessee, with whom they participated in the battle of Chickamauga. On the second day of the battle, 19 September 1863, Gregg rode ahead of his brigade to reconnoiter. He rode on the skirmish line of the Sixty-fourth Ohio and was ordered to surrender. Gregg attempted to escape and was shot through the neck. The Union soldiers took Gregg's spurs and sword before they were driven off by members of John B. Hood's Texas brigade. Following his recovery, Gregg was assigned to command Hood's Texas brigade in the Army of Northern Virginia. On the second day of the battle of the Wilderness (May 1864), Gregg's brigade led James Longstreet's counterattack that repaired the break caused by the defeat of A. P. Hill's troops on the Plank Road. During their advance, General Robert E. Lee attempted to join Gregg's brigade in the charge. Fearing that Lee would be shot, Gregg's men refused to advance unless Lee went to safety in the rear. Lee relented, and Gregg directed a successful attack that blunted the Federal drive at a cost of nearly half of his eight hundred men. Gregg led his command through the subsequent battles of the Overland campaign with distinction. In the Union offensive of 29–30 September 1864 that overran Fort Harrison and threatened to penetrate Confederate defenses southeast of Richmond, Gregg was conspicuous for his inspired and successful defense of the Fort Johnson–Fort Gilmer line, which checked the Federal advance. Just over one week later Gregg was killed in action on the Charles City Road below Richmond. His wife desired that Gregg be buried in Aberdeen, Mississippi, where she planned to make her future residence. After a hazardous one-month journey across the wartorn South, Gregg's remains were laid to rest in Aberdeen in April 1865.

Gregg was a man who backed up his political conviction with personal action. Despite his lack of a military background, he developed into an accomplished soldier, inspiring in combat, who won the respect of his men and the accolades of his peers. The epitaph on his gravestone pays tribute to the man and the cause as he understood it: "To the memory of Gen. John Gregg, of Texas, a Christian soldier and a patriot. . . . fell before Richmond in behalf of Southern rights and constitutional liberty."

• For background on Gregg's life and military career, see Marcus J. Wright, *Texas in the War 1861–1865* (1965), and "John Gregg, Brigadier General C.S.A.," *Confederate Veteran* 22 (n.d.): 125. For Gregg's career as a Confederate army officer, see U.S. Department of War, *The War of the Rebellion: A Compilation of the Official Records of the Union and Confederate Armies* (128 vols., 1880–1901). A detailed account of Gregg's participation and wounding at the battle of Chickamauga is in Peter Cozzens, *This Terrible Sound: The Battle of Chickamauga* (1992). For Gregg's experience in the 1864 Overland campaign, see E. M. Law, "From the Wilderness to Cold Harbor," *Battles and Leaders of the Civil War*, vol. 4, ed. Robert U. Johnson and Clarence C. Buel (1884–1887). Also see Richard J. Sommers, *Richmond Redeemed: The Siege at Petersburg* (1981). The most accurate account of Gregg's death is found in *Confederate Veteran* 28 (n.d.): 12. Also see *Confederate Veteran* 29 (n.d.): 412. The remarkable journey to bury Gregg's remains is recounted in "Burial of Gen. John Gregg of Mississippi," *Confederate Veteran* 22 (n.d.): 463–64.

D. SCOTT HARTWIG

GREGG, John Andrew (18 Feb. 1877–17 Feb. 1953), African Methodist Episcopal (A.M.E.) bishop and educator, was born in Eureka, Kansas, the son of Alexander Gregg and Eliza Frances Allen. Early positive experiences in Sunday Schools and the Epworth League (a Methodist youth organization) encouraged him to develop good study habits and to expect successful results from his efforts. During the Spanish-American War, Gregg signed on for service in the Twenty-third Kansas Volunteers. Within a six-month period he rose from the rank of sergeant to that of lieutenant. This is all the more notable because very few African Americans were commissioned as officers in those days. His capacity for disciplined work blended with his proven ability to coordinate large-scale activities, and these qualities stood him in good stead through the following half century. In 1900 he married Celia Ann Nelson; they adopted one child. In 1945, four years after his first wife's death, he married Melberta McFarland.

In 1898 Gregg decided to enter the ministry and obtained a license to preach from the Kansas Annual Conference of the A.M.E. church. That same year he entered the University of Kansas, receiving his baccalaureate in 1902. While teaching school for a year at Oskaloosa, he was admitted to the Kansas Annual Conference. In 1903 he was ordained a deacon and appointed minister to Mount Olive Church in Emporia, Kansas. Shortly thereafter he volunteered to go overseas.

In 1903 Gregg became a teacher and administrator of the A.M.E. mission station in Cape Colony, South Africa, where he was a presiding elder. After returning to the United States in 1906 he was ordained an elder and appointed minister of Bethel Church in Leavenworth, Kansas. Two years later he became pastor of Ebenezer Church in Saint Joseph, Missouri, and served that congregation for half a decade. In 1913 he accepted the presidency of Edward Waters College in Jacksonville, Florida, showing once again how much he valued education alongside that of spiritual guidance as an element of human improvement. This strong commitment to intellectual training among African Americans was manifest in another instance when he filled the presidential chair at Wilberforce University in Ohio from 1920 to 1924, when he was elected a bishop of the A.M.E. church. That year he returned to South Africa to preside over his church's Seventeenth District. In 1928 he returned to America to assume responsibility for a succession of episcopal districts: the Fifth (Kansas, 1928–1936), the Fourth (Virginia, 1936–1948), (Florida, 1949–1958). Beginning in 1948 and serving until his death he also presided over the Bishops Council.

In the early 1940s the A.M.E. church joined the Colored M.E. church and the National Baptist Convention to form the Fraternal Council of Negro Churches, and in 1943 the council nominated Gregg to represent it in a visit to the White House. President Franklin D. Roosevelt gave him the task of touring U.S. troops in both the European and Pacific theaters. Gregg strove to boost morale among African-American soldiers and to encourage racial harmony. He wrote two pamphlets, titled "Superlative Righteousness" (1944) and "Of Men and Arms" (1945), based on his experiences. In 1947 he was presented the Award of Merit from the secretary of the army. He died in Jacksonville, Florida.

Throughout his career Gregg displayed no outstanding gifts as a scholar, writer, or public speaker. His intellectual grasp of doctrine and administrative procedures was firm, however, and his strength lay in helping people apply the basic principles of acquired skills and moral virtues in their lives.

• An obituary is in the *New York Times*, 19 Feb. 1953.

HENRY WARNER BOWDEN

GREGG, John Robert (17 June 1867–23 Feb. 1948), inventor of a type of shorthand, was born in Shantonagh, County Monaghan, Ireland, the son of George Gregg, a railroad stationmaster, and Margaret Courney Johnson. Gregg entered school in August 1872 and shortly thereafter received an ear injury. Because of the resulting hearing impairment he was considered slow both at home and at school, but this only inspired him to learn more on his own.

By the age of ten Gregg had developed a strong interest in shorthand. He studied many books and journals on different shorthand systems and read about the lives of their inventors. At fifteen he had mastered at least six shorthand systems; he then began developing his own method, which conformed to the natural flow of longhand writing.

After the family moved to Glasgow, Scotland, in 1878, young Gregg went to work as an office boy in a law office. In addition to working long hours, he broadened his education by reading in the free libraries and attending lectures, where he eventually became acquainted with the Pitman system of shorthand. Gregg was not pleased with this system or any of the others he knew. He resolved to construct a system that would be easier to learn and write.

Gregg entered a shorthand contest in 1885, winning a gold medal and a handwritten note from J. M. Sloan, the inventor of the shorthand system being used, testifying to Gregg's thorough knowledge of Sloan-Duployan Phonography. This was Gregg's certificate to start his career as a teacher of shorthand.

Gregg continued to develop his own system, choosing the best features he found in existing French, German, and American systems. His system was phonetic, with vowels joined in their natural order, and was based on a longhand slope using a horizontal flow. He completed his new system when he was nineteen.

In 1888 Gregg published his first shorthand manual, *Light-Line Phonography*, and opened his first school, the Light-Line Phonography Institute, in Liverpool, England. He continued to revise his shorthand in the following years. In 1893 he sailed to Boston, Massachusetts, where he published a revised form of the Light-Line system.

Gregg faced a great challenge in Boston, where many schools were teaching the styles of Graham, Beale, the Pitmans, and local inventors. He moved in 1895 to Chicago, where he became an American citizen the following year. There he established in 1895 the Gregg School, later Gregg College, which was sold to McGraw-Hill Publishing Company after Gregg's death. In 1952 the school was turned over to Northwestern University to operate under Gregg's name.

In 1894, however, Gregg had almost given up. He offered the copyright of his system to the publishing company of Charles Scribner. When he received no reply, he decided that the future of Gregg Shorthand was his responsibility and persevered in the efforts to sell it to the American people. By 1911, Gregg Publishing Company was selling more books than Scribner.

Gregg Publishing Company, founded in Chicago in 1896, flourished as the Gregg shorthand system was introduced to more and more schools throughout the United States and abroad. Gregg shorthand was markedly easier to learn and write than many other systems in use, so many public, private, and commercial schools switched to it. Gregg Publishing Company grew to include textbooks and magazines associated with all phases of commercial education. Their texts were translated into French, German, Spanish, Italian, Portuguese, Polish, and Esperanto.

Gregg wrote many shorthand texts, beginning in 1888 with 500 copies of *Light-Line Phonography*. This was followed by *Progressive Exercises in Gregg Shorthand* (1890), *Gregg Shorthand Dictionary* (1901), and *Gregg Phrase Book* (1901). *Gregg Speed Practice* (1907) was considered a great advance in the teaching of shorthand; it featured connected text, some in print with illustrated shorthand outlines, and some written

entirely in shorthand. The first text to present all practice material in its shorthand form, a new style of instruction, was introduced in *Gregg Speed Studies* (1917). Other notable texts were *Secretarial Studies* (1922), *Applied Secretarial Practice* (1941), and *The Private Secretary* (1943). Gregg also published seven magazines during his lifetime, most notably *The Gregg Writer* and *American Shorthand Teacher*, which became *Business Education World*.

Gregg married Maida Wasson in 1899; they had no children. After her death in 1928, Gregg married Janet Kinley in 1930 and had two children. Both his wives actively participated in Gregg's shorthand work.

Gregg was always interested in those who wanted to learn his method of shorthand. He took pleasure in helping those who did not have the resources to afford his courses or books. He took his theory to the students, offering courses in rural areas and even by mail and opening economic opportunities to many people. Many students of the Gregg system corresponded with him in shorthand.

Gregg also surrounded himself with those who excelled in and believed in his system. Many of his students were given jobs with his schools and publishing company. Gregg considered his shorthand acquaintances and his employees to be his family, and he helped many of them in times of personal and financial need.

Gregg was also an active supporter of many organizations. He was a charter member and honorary life member of both the National Commercial Teachers Federation (later the National Business Teachers Association) and the National Shorthand Reporters Association. He was also a member of the National Arts Club of New York City for more than forty years, serving on the board of governors and as president. He was a delegate to the International Shorthand Congress in Paris, France (1931), and to the International Congress on Commercial Education in Amsterdam (1929) and London (1932). Gregg received several honors, including a Distinguished Service to Education Award from the New York Academy for Public Education (1938), a gold medal for Notable Service to the Nation from the Ulster-Irish Society of New York (1936), and the King's Medal for Service in the Cause of Freedom from the British government. He died in New York City.

• Tributes to Gregg by Herbert A. Tonne appear in the *Journal of Business Education* 23, no. 6 (Mar. 1948): 6–7. See also F. Addington Symonds, *John Robert Gregg: The Man and His Work* (1963); Louis A. Leslie, *The Story of Gregg Shorthand* (1964); and Leslie Cowan, *John Robert Gregg: A Biography of the Shorthand Inventor, Educator, Publisher and Humanitarian, Whose Achievements Enriched the Lives of Millions* (1984). An obituary is in the *New York Times*, 24 Feb. 1948.

LARRY N. SYPOLT

GREGG, Maxcy (1 Aug. 1814–15 Dec. 1862), secessionist leader and Confederate general, was born in Columbia, South Carolina, the son of James Gregg, a lawyer, and Cornelia Maxcy. He graduated from

South Carolina College and practiced law in Columbia. Substantial inherited wealth enabled Gregg to devote himself to political pursuits, which displayed an ardently secessionist flavor, and to genteel artistic and scientific endeavors. He never married. Gregg proposed in 1850 "seizing California and closing the Mississippi." Furthermore, he argued that his native state should avoid attachment to a southern confederacy, consolidation with such friends being "only not quite so great an evil" as alignment with abolitionist states.

Gregg served in South Carolina's secession convention and then at once took the field as colonel commanding the state's first infantry regiment. Although he had served as a major of volunteers during the Mexican War, Gregg had heard no gunfire before 1861 other than that resulting from his involvement in duels. The colonel overcame this lack of experience by an earnest attention to duty. His zealous drilling of the eager but raw men who flocked to the colors brought them to a reasonable state of efficiency.

Gregg led his First South Carolina to Virginia after the fall of Fort Sumter and won a widely applauded, but now forgotten, skirmish near Vienna, on 17 June 1861. Soon thereafter the initial enlistments of his men expired, and most of the regiment returned home. After ardent exertion Gregg brought his regiment back to full strength by late July. On 14 December he received promotion to brigadier general, despite having clashed bitterly with Jefferson Davis over the president's treatment of one of Gregg's subordinates.

An observer who saw Gregg early in 1862 described him as "a very modest, quiet gentleman," with gray hair, "full whiskers . . . and a ruddy complexion," and a "jocular" manner. A colonel who knew him well wrote that the general possessed "an almost inflexible will," offset by "gentleness" and a smile that carried "almost the sweetness of a woman's."

Gregg commanded a detachment near Pocotaligo, South Carolina, during the war's first winter. He returned to Virginia the next spring to assume command of a sturdy five-regiment brigade in A. P. Hill's division of Robert E. Lee's army. At Gaines's Mill on 27 June 1862, Gregg led his men into the teeth of a mighty defensive position "with a zeal and energy, a power that commanded and inspired all men's hearts." At the end of August Gregg held his brigade sternly to a crucial position on the army's left at Second Manassas in what was clearly his greatest service to the Confederacy. The general again held the destiny of Lee's army in his grasp when he flung his command against an enemy advance during the final crisis of the battle of Antietam.

At the battle of Fredericksburg on 13 December 1862, Gregg and his brigade occupied a position well behind the front line, but Federals penetrated into the Confederate position and surged against the South Carolinians. As he rode in front of his men, Gregg fell mortally wounded by a ball that passed through his side to his spine. A. P. Hill and Stonewall Jackson paid emotional visits to Gregg as he lay dying at the Yerby house, "Belvoir." Early on 15 December Gregg

sent an entirely typical telegram to his governor: "If I am to die at this time, I yield my life cheerfully, fighting for the independence of South Carolina." Unlike many of his contemporaries who hotly sought secession, Maxcy Gregg converted his convictions into military service. His success in the field was at least as notable as that of any politician-turned-soldier in Lee's army.

• Maxcy Gregg's papers are at the University of South Carolina. The Joseph Jeptha Norton Collection at the same repository includes important material about Gregg's career and particularly about his mortal wounding and death; so do the David Gregg McIntosh Papers in the Southern Historical Collection, University of North Carolina at Chapel Hill. The only extended sketch of the general's life is Robert K. Krick, "Maxcy Gregg," *Civil War History* 19 (1973): 3–23. See also Louise Haskell Daly, ed., *Alexander Cheves Haskell* (1934); James F. J. Caldwell, *The History of a Brigade of South Carolinians, Known First as "Gregg's"* . . . (1866); and Benjamin M. Palmer, *Address Delivered at the Funeral of General Maxcy Gregg* (1863). Obituaries are in the *Charleston Daily Courier*, 16 Dec. 1862; *Richmond Dispatch*, 16 Dec. 1862; and *Yorkville* (S.C.) *Enquirer*, 24 Dec. 1862.

ROBERT K. KRICK

GREGG, Willis Ray (4 Jan. 1880–14 Sept. 1938), meteorologist, was born in Phoenix, New York, the son of Willis Perry Gregg and Jenny E. Ray, farmers. Gregg attended Cornell University, where he received an A.B. in 1903. The following year he began working for the U.S. Weather Bureau, where he remained the rest of his life.

Gregg spent the first three years of his career as an assistant weather observer at Grand Rapids, Michigan, and Cheyenne, Wyoming. In 1907 he came to the Mount Weather Observatory in Virginia, where under the supervision of physicist William R. Blair he conducted upper-air research using kites and balloons. In 1909 he became an observer and was involved in that capacity five years later with the Smithsonian Expedition to Mount Whitney, California. In 1914 he married Mary Chamberlayne Wall, and they later adopted one daughter.

That same year Gregg became assistant chief under Blair of the newly established aerology division in Washington, D.C. Three years later, Gregg became head of the division and remained there until 1933. Under his leadership, the division's work was expanded to assist the fast developing field of aeronautics. In 1914 meteorologists and pilots were all aware of the need for a weather service as a prerequisite to further progress in aviation, and Gregg's work at Mount Weather constituted the only continuous record of aerological data in the weather bureau, even though other meteorologists had previously conducted short surveys.

The U.S. entry into World War I provided an unexpected boost to the aerological division, as the army provided funding for the establishment of additional kite and balloon stations. During those years as chief of aerology, Gregg was stationed in various places and successfully advised pilots on several historical flights. These included in 1919 the navy's NC Transatlantic flight attempt (in which one of three dispatched machines reached Portugal) and the British dirigible R-34's crossing from England to Newfoundland. Such assistance was an early sign of Gregg's interest in developing military and civil aviation.

Expanding the aerological division was a slow process, however. Although Congress rejected requests for funding in the years from 1918 to 1920 to support the establishment of supplementary balloon and kite stations, Gregg was nevertheless able to expand his division's aviation services through the already existing weather stations and, within five years, to provide nightly forecasts for airmail flights. Finally in 1926, funds became available through the Air Commerce Act, making the U.S. Weather Bureau officially responsible for providing meteorological aid to aviation. With this stamp of approval, Gregg was further able to build his division, making it the largest in the U.S. Weather Bureau by 1934.

That year Gregg became chief of the U.S. Weather Bureau, replacing Charles Frederick Marvin. When he took over, Gregg faced serious budget cuts as a result of the depression. Nevertheless, he was able to implement many improvements in the activities of the bureau. Most of the appropriations made in the 1930s went to aviation services rather than to other divisions. Among the general services improvements that were implemented under Gregg's tenure was an expansion of the existing weather warning systems. A 1932–1934 review by the Presidential Science Advisory Board had revealed that the hurricane warning forecast was insufficient to track rapidly developing weather systems, since the stations were not operated twenty-four hours a day. Gregg deemed the situation "sadly sketchy" and plans were drawn up for the issuance of weather maps every six hours rather than every twelve. In addition, the flood service was expanded and given new means of measuring river levels, but limited funding prevented the installation of new, improved river gauges and the institution of hourly rainfall measurements that would allow effective estimates of flood risks. Progress was slow, and Gregg was well aware of the work that still needed to be done.

Unfortunately Gregg's work was cut short. While attending an aviation conference in Chicago, he was struck with coronary thrombosis and died a week later in Chicago. "America's No. 1 'weather man'," as the New York Times called him, left a remarkable professional legacy. A member of numerous aeronautical and meteorological organizations, including the American Meteorological Society (of which he was president in 1938), National Advisory Committee for Aeronautics, American Geophysical Union, and Royal Meteorological Society (England), Gregg fit well the description of the dedicated civil servant interested in furthering his organization's services. This was more than personal interest, though. Despite the progress meteorological sciences had made until then, much doubt remained as to the value of a methodical investigation of weather patterns to help farmers as well as aviators. Gregg's endeavor was thus essential to advancing the state of American meteorology and, in the wider context, that of safe aviation.

• The archives of the National Air and Space Museum of the Smithsonian Institution contain a biographical file on Gregg. A bibliography of his articles and addresses can be found in *Bulletin of the American Meteorological Society* (Feb. 1939): 54–59. Donald R. Whitnah, *A History of the United States Weather Bureau* (1961), and Roy Popkin, *The Environmental Science Services Administration* (1967), both contain material that helps place Gregg's legacy in context. J. McKeen Cattell and Jaques Cattell, *American Men of Science*, 5th ed. (1933), contains a useful summary of Gregg's work as he was about to head the U.S. Weather Service. An obituary is in the *New York Times*, 15 Sept. 1938.

GUILLAUME DE SYON

GREGORY, Charles Noble (27 Aug. 1851–10 July 1932), lawyer and educator, was born in Umadilla, New York, the son of Jared C. Gregory, a lawyer, and Charlotte Camp. Gregory received an A.B. in 1871 from the University of Wisconsin in Madison and an LL.B. a year later, immediately after which he was admitted to the Wisconsin bar. He began the practice of law in his father's firm, at that time organized as Gregory and Pinney, later as Gregory and Gregory, and finally as Gregory, Bird and Gregory. All three firms at various times represented the Chicago, Milwaukee and St. Paul Railroad. After more than twenty years at the bar, Gregory retired from practice at the age of forty-three. He had for some time been attracted more to the intellectual side of the law than to the hectic pace of the trial court, and in 1894 he took up an academic career at the University of Wisconsin in Madison.

Gregory entered the teaching profession in a decade during which new pedagogical practices in legal education were taking shape. Case study was then being promoted as a way to place legal study on a scientific basis. Teaching by the casebook method had grown steadily since its introduction at Harvard Law School in the 1870s by Christopher Columbus Langdell. The faculty at Columbia Law School, under Dean William Keener, and at Stanford, citing Keener as its role model, were already using the Harvard system. The leading state universities were also eager to import the Harvard model of legal instruction, and the 1890s saw the case method arrive at the University of Wisconsin College of Law when its president, Charles Kendall Adams, brought Gregory to Madison as associate dean of law to modernize the school along the lines of Harvard.

Gregory had only a vague notion of what the case study method was all about. A year after joining the law faculty, he was sent to Harvard to be coached by two of the men best equipped to instruct him: William Keener and James Barr Ames. Thereafter he became convinced of the possibilities of the new method. Gregory's dean at Madison, Edwin E. Bryant, was still wedded to running the law school more or less along the lines of "an ideal law office" and attacked the new case method as "narrow, slow and unprofessional." It was not until Harry Richards became dean in 1903 that the case method was finally adopted, and Bryant's views were repudiated.

Implementing the case study method was linked with other reforms in legal education, such as raising admission standards and professionalizing the faculty. Gregory was in advance of his times in accepting a full-time appointment to the College of Law, making a vocation of teaching law. Most law teachers continued to practice, at least part time. He helped to introduce these reforms in Wisconsin, and under his administration the course of study at the college was expanded from two to three years. One of his curriculum reforms was to place new emphasis on the study of international law. Gregory held the post at Madison until 1901, but when the deanship he expected did not come his way he accepted the deanship at the University of Iowa College of Law, where he spent the next ten years.

In his younger years Gregory had been regarded as one of the rising poets of his day. In reviews he was frequently styled "the Bryant of the West." While at Madison he had been an early promoter of the Literary Club.

The literary life held a certain attraction for him, and while at Iowa he wrote a biography of Justice Samuel Miller, a brief account of the man appointed by Abraham Lincoln in 1862 who became one of the towering figures on the Supreme Court. That Miller was elevated to the bench from his adopted state of Iowa in part explains Gregory's selection of him as a biographical subject.

In 1911 Gregory went to Washington, D.C., having been invited to become dean of the Department of Law at George Washington University. But in 1914 he retired from teaching and administration to devote all his time to professional and literary pursuits. He was much in demand as a public speaker, delivering many addresses to bar associations, educational institutions, and civic organizations all over the country. Most of his later career was devoted to writing articles for the leading English and American legal journals. He had two areas of interest: problems of legal education, particularly as they affected the practice of law, and international law.

Gregory was interested in politics at all levels. In Madison he had served as an alderman from 1880 to 1883 and was on the board of education in 1883. He furthered the enactment of progressive legislation, including Wisconsin's first corrupt practices act. He served as vice president of the American Bar Association, was on its executive committee from 1897 to 1900, and from 1908 to 1921 chaired its committee on international law. In 1888 he edited the *Tariff Reform Advocate*.

Gregory was one of the founding members and in 1909 the president of the Association of American Law Schools. He took part in founding the American Society of International Law, remaining active in its affairs until his death. In this connection he helped establish the *American Journal of International Law*, and he served on its board of editors from 1907 to 1923. At one time he was vice president of the American branch of the International Law Association based in London.

Gregory never married. He was an Episcopalian and made his home in Washington, D.C., where he died.

• A major work by Gregory is *Abstract of Cases Contained in Lloyd's Reports of Prize Cases*, published in four volumes in 1919. For information on Gregory's ancestry a good source is Grant Gregory, *The Ancestors and Descendants of Henry Gregory* (1938). A short memoir, *Charles Noble Gregory* (1911), written by Emlin McClain, is available on microform (#27718396) in Washington, D.C. On Gregory's years at the University of Wisconsin, see Charles F. Smith, *Charles Kendall Adams: A Life-Sketch* (1924), and William R. Johnson, *Schooled Lawyers: A Study in the Clash of Professional Cultures* (1978).

MARIAN C. McKENNA

GREGORY, Horace Victor (10 Apr. 1898–11 Mar. 1982), poet and critic, was born in Milwaukee, Wisconsin, the son of Henry Bolton Gregory, a self-taught chemist and businessman, and Anna Catherine Henkel, his former housekeeper. Of English and Irish descent on his father's side and German on his mother's, Gregory was born prematurely and burdened by tuberculosis of the bone, which paralyzed his left hand and foot and caused a slight tremor in his right hand. He walked with the aid of a cane all his adult life, and his frail condition kept him out of World War I.

In the summer of 1919 Gregory entered the University of Wisconsin, where he majored in English and studied Anglo-Saxon and Latin with William Ellery Leonard, the highly respected translator of Lucretius's *De Rerum Natura* (1915). After earning his B.A. and recovering from a nervous breakdown, he moved to New York in February 1923, determined to be a poet and to support himself by writing. He lived first in Chelsea and then in Greenwich Village, surviving at poverty's edge by doing reviews, scenario reports for Paramount Pictures, and advertising copy for a public relations firm. During this period his modest physical resources were further sapped by a bout of jaundice.

In the summer of 1925 he was introduced by Kenneth Fearing to Russian-born Marya Zaturenska, "a slight, dark-haired, beautiful girl," who had just completed two years at the University of Wisconsin's Library School on a Zona Gale scholarship. Sharing a passion for poetry, they were wed that same summer and rented a flat in Brooklyn the following year. In 1927, two months after the birth of a daughter, Gregory came down with scarlet fever, and they moved to a model housing project in Sunnyside, Queens, at the urging of Lewis Mumford. Like many literary contemporaries, he found himself drawn into the local Communist orbit, joining the John Reed Club in 1930–1931.

The impact of New York and the stock market crash of 1929 radicalized Gregory's poetics as well. In his memoir, *The House on Jefferson Street* (1971), he describes his first poetry collection, *Chelsea Rooming House* (1930)—a series of free-verse monologues set in an O. Henry milieu and obviously indebted to Robert Browning and Edwin Arlington Robinson—as "the beginning of my effort to combine the idiom of contemporary life with my early (and entirely literary) influences." A second collection, *No Retreat* (1933), was more traditional in its lyric mix of erudite elegies and nostalgic meditations, as was a heavily myth-oriented third, *Chorus for Survival* (1935). But he used the same street idiom of the Chelsea poems for his vigorous, slangy version of *The Poems of Catullus* (1931), his bid to restore "the vitality and freshness that Catullus must have had for *his* contemporaries."

Thanks to the generosity of English novelist Bryher (Winifred Ellerman), poet H.D.'s wealthy lover, the Gregorys and their two young children, a girl and boy, were able to go abroad for an extended visit in 1934. Upon their return, Gregory secured a post teaching classical literature in translation and modern poetry at Sarah Lawrence College, where he would remain until 1960, and the family moved permanently to Rockland County in upstate New York. Writing under her maiden name, Marya Zaturenska published a second volume of verse, *Cold Morning Sky* (1937), which won the Pulitzer Prize. She published six more collections over the next thirty-seven years. In 1946 she collaborated with her husband to produce the controversial *A History of American Poetry, 1900–1940*, which reflected their common engagé aesthetic.

Further enhancing his image as an old-fashioned man of letters who was open to experiment, Gregory also authored several bio-critical texts and edited, with Eleanor Clark, *New Letters in America* (1937) and *The Portable Sherwood Anderson* (1949). Among his critical studies are a profile of D. H. Lawrence's career, *Pilgrim of the Apocalypse* (1933), and *Amy Lowell: Portrait of the Poet in Her Time* (1958). In addition, he gathered his literary essays into two collections, *The Shield of Achilles* (1944) and *The Dying Gladiator and Other Essays* (1961), and in 1956 he published a new edition of his Catullus as *Poems, by Catullus*. His reputation as a creative translator of Latin poetry was augmented by his 1958 version of Ovid's *Metamorphoses*.

Gregory's own poetry, which included *Poems, 1930–1940* (1941) and *Selected Poems* (1951), helped land him a Guggenheim Fellowship in 1951 and an Academy of American Poets Fellowship ten years later. In his *Partisan Review* notice of the former collection, Allen Tate labeled Gregory "one of the best poets of his generation" (May–June 1941). Winning the Bollingin Prize in 1965 seemed to affirm his eminence in the field, but few critics and almost no literary historians have been as kind as Tate.

Though conversationally contemporary in tone and pace and at their best, as Tate noted, when dealing with elegies and nostalgia, deepened by classical allusions, Gregory's poems are more academic than passionate. Their strengths are theatrical and psychological, not lyrically intense. As he concedes in his memoir, "I feel that my poems are actually dramatic

poems overheard beyond the footlights of the scene." The most potent example of his mature technique and the poem most closely associated with his name is "Medusa in Gramercy Park," the title work of a 1961 collection. It intertwines Greek myth and urban sophistication in a deft first-person narrative that satisfies formal expectations without sacrificing poetic ambivalence.

Upon retiring from Sarah Lawrence in 1960, Gregory was awarded professor emeritus status. Confined to a wheelchair in his last decades but continuing to defy his wretched medical history, he died in a Shelburne, Massachusetts, nursing home less than two months after the death of his wife.

• Most of Gregory's papers are at the Syracuse University Library. The *Collected Poems* (1964) and a final collection, *Another Look* (1976), contain the bulk of Gregory's poetry. Both *The Shield of Achilles* and *The Dying Gladiators*, as well as three later essays, are in *Spirit of Time and Place: The Collected Essays of Horace Gregory* (1973). An obituary is in the *New York Times*, 13 Mar. 1982.

EDWARD BUTSCHER

GREGORY, John (17 May 1879–21 Feb. 1958), sculptor and educator, was born in London, England, the son of John Gregory, a shipmaster, and Amelia Elizabeth Read. Gregory's family moved to New Zealand around 1887, but domestic problems caused Gregory and his mother to return to England, where she supported them as a nurse. In 1893 they moved to Washington, D.C. For three years Gregory was a junior clerk in the U.S. Senate, and from 1897 to 1899 he worked for the Columbia Recording Corporation in Bridgeport, Connecticut.

Gregory began his artistic career around 1900, when he became the apprentice of the Scottish sculptor John Massey Rhind. He studied at night at the Art Students League of New York, working with sculptors George Grey Barnard and Hermon Atkins MacNeil. From 1903 until 1906 he continued his studies in Europe, spending a year in London attending Lambeth Art School and three in Paris at the École des Beaux-Arts. He returned to New York, where he worked in the studios of MacNeil, Gutzon Borglum, and Herbert Adams for the next six years.

In 1912 Gregory became a U.S. citizen. He also won a competition for a fellowship to the American Academy in Rome, where he studied from 1912 to 1915. These years defined the direction of Gregory's art. He said in an interview with *Arts and Decoration* in November 1919 that the academy "opened my eyes to what I wanted to see and I was absorbed into the modern classic school." This group of younger sculptors broke with the previous generation, who followed the French Beaux-Arts school in an attempt to recapture the original spirit of Roman and Greek sculpture.

After leaving the academy Gregory established his own studio in New York City and began a second career as an art educator. He accepted an appointment as associate in modeling at Columbia University from 1916 to 1925, and from 1921 until 1923 he was director of sculpture at the Beaux-Arts Institute of Design. He served the Navy Department during World War I as assistant inspector of naval construction in charge of camouflage.

Gregory's commissions during this time consisted of garden sculpture, including *Orpheus and Dancing Panther* (1916) for Charles M. Schwab of Loretto, Pennsylvania; *Wood Nymph* and *Bacchante* (1918–1920) for Mrs. Harry Payne Whitney of Long Island; and *Toy Venus* (1922) for Mrs. Egerton Winthrop of Syosset, Long Island. His reputation was assured when *Philomela* won the Architectural League of New York's medal of honor in 1921. That same year he received his first architectural sculpture commission for *The Voyage*, a bronze floor plate for the Cunard Building in New York City. In 1922 he married one of his students, Katharine Van Rensselaer; they had one child.

Although commissions for garden sculpture continued to occupy Gregory during the 1920s, he was soon designing larger public works, such as *The Forester* for Yale University (1923), the William Corcoran Eustis Memorial for the Corcoran Gallery of Art, Washington, D.C. (1924), a model of a pediment for the Philadelphia Museum of Art (1926–1927), panels depicting the four seasons and the four ages of man for the Henry E. Huntington Mausoleum in San Marino, California (1927–1929), and bas-reliefs for the Federal Reserve Bank of Washington, D.C. (1933). From 1929 until 1931 he carved nine reliefs depicting scenes from Shakespeare for the Folger Shakespeare Library in Washington, D.C. In 1933 he was awarded the George D. Widener Gold Medal by the Pennsylvania Academy of the Fine Arts for *Lyric Love*.

Gregory was at the height of his professional activities during the 1930s. He was president of the National Sculpture Society from 1934 to 1939. He not only provided a sculpture, *The Victories of Peace*, for the 1939 World's Fair in New York, but he also served on the selection committee for the fair exhibition *American Art Today*. He continued to win public and private commissions during the next decade. He executed a bronze equestrian statue of General Anthony Wayne for the city of Philadelphia (1940), a bronze *Orpheus* group for Brookgreen Gardens in South Carolina (1941), granite reliefs for the District of Columbia building in Washington, D.C. (1942), and a memorial to Albert J. Beveridge in Indianapolis (1946). In 1951 he contributed a seven-foot marble sculpture, *Memory*, to the World War I shrine at the American Military Cemetery in Suresnes, France.

The last decade of Gregory's life brought him the recognition due to one described by colleague Wheeler Williams in a letter to the *New York Times* (6 Mar. 1958) as "an ideal elder statesman of his profession." He was showered with honors by the National Sculpture Society, who elected him honorary president in 1953, gave him a medal of honor in 1956, and made him an honorary fellow in 1958. In 1954 he was honored by fellow members of the Architectural League of New York. By this time Gregory also held member-

ships in the National Institute of Arts and Letters and the Art Commission of New York City and honorary memberships in the Beaux-Arts Institute of Design and the American Institute of Architects, and he was an associate of the National Academy of Design. His last work was *Angel*, designed for the William Ziegler, Jr., Memorial in 1958. Gregory died in New York City.

Gregory and others of the modern classical school were an important force in American sculpture during the first half of the twentieth century. The Armory Show of 1913 had introduced Americans to abstraction and other modernist ideas from Europe, and these styles were accepted for small private works of sculpture. But in their parks and gardens and on their public buildings, Americans wanted to see the traditional classical forms of Gregory and his colleagues in the National Sculpture Society. It was not until after World War II that tastes changed enough to allow abstract sculptors to enjoy the same kind of success.

• Gregory's papers are in the Archives of American Art in Washington, D.C. General biographical information appears in Lorado Taft, *History of American Sculpture* (1930); Beatrice Gilman Proske, *Brookgreen Gardens Sculpture* (1968); Kineton Parkes, "A Classical Sculptor in America: John Gregory," *Apollo* 17 (Feb. 1933): 28–31; and "John Gregory, Sculptor," *Arts and Decoration* 12 (Nov. 1919): 8. For Gregory's role in the 1939 World's Fair, see the National Art Society's catalog *American Art Today* (1939). For the panels on the Folger Shakespeare Library, see Frederick Hard, *The Sculptured Scenes from Shakespeare* (1959). For Gregory's relationship to the Beaux-Arts tradition and his Philadelphia Museum of Art pediment, see Steven Eric Bronson, "John Gregory: The Philadelphia Museum of Art Pediment" (master's thesis, Univ. of Delaware, 1977). An obituary is in the *New York Times*, 22 Feb. 1958.

MELISSA L. BECHER

GREGORY, Samuel (19 Apr. 1813–23 Mar. 1872), founder of the first medical school for women, was born in Guilford, Vermont, the son of Stephen Gregory and Hannah Palmer, farmers. Little is known about his early life. He matriculated at Yale College, where he studied primarily English and history, but in his senior year he attended a lecture series in anatomy and physiology that changed the course of his life. After graduating from Yale with a B.A. in 1840, Gregory spent five years teaching English grammar in manufacturing towns in New England. During this time, Gregory also started lecturing on a variety of topics, including phrenology, public licentiousness, and the potential therapeutic effects of mesmerism. In 1844 he compiled some of his thoughts on young men and their sexual appetites into a published pamphlet, which sold more than 42,000 copies.

After earning a master's degree from Yale in 1845, Gregory focused his lectures on women's health care and obstetrics. In a pamphlet titled *Licentiousness: Its Causes and Effects*, published in 1846, Gregory argued that male doctors could not fail to compromise their female patient's modesty. The solution, Gregory realized, was to "enlighten [women] in relation to the principles of health and the means of preventing and relieving sickness." The only problem: no medical schools at the time admitted women. So Gregory, despite the fact that he himself had no official medical training, resolved to open a school exclusively for women.

Gathering together a faculty of four—including himself as chemistry professor—Gregory opened the doors to the Female Medical College in Boston in November 1848. The twelve women who comprised the school's first class, attracted by advertisements, came expecting to receive a medical education commensurate with their male counterparts. Gregory, however, was less concerned with the quality the education provided than with the gender of his pupils. At the close of the first term, Enoch Rolfe, one of the faculty members, protested the students did not have sufficient knowledge to become certified midwives and that their course of study amounted to nothing more than "Latin taught in twelve easy lessons." After Gregory argued that his students were owed certification, Rolfe consented to allow them to use his name as a reference.

Rolfe was not the only supporter of women's education to battle with Gregory. Throughout his days at the helm of the medical school, Gregory came into conflict with many of his colleagues over his lax attitude toward his students' preparation. Part of the problem may have been with the company he kept. While most supporters of women's medical education were feminist reformers, Gregory's chief goal in qualifying women to be physicians stemmed from his desire to offer women patients an alternative to male doctors. Soon after the school opened, Gregory organized the American Medical Education Society, which was incorporated in 1850 as the Female Medical Education Society, to help raise funds for the school. Within a year of its founding, the society had attracted about 1,500 members, including Horace Mann, Robert Francis Adams, Harriet Beecher Stowe, and other august lawyers, teachers, clergy, and businessmen.

The society's board members struggled to improve Gregory's operation. Although he envisioned the school's moving to a campus of its own, this was not financially feasible. Against his wishes, the board took preliminary steps to merging with Women's Medical College in Philadelphia in an effort to consolidate resources. In 1852 the two schools pooled faculty—offering classes in one city for a term and in the other the next. After a year it became clear that this arrangement was not workable. However, the flirtation with Women's Medical College had helped the school gain recognition. In 1852 it conferred its first medical degrees, and in 1856 the Massachusetts legislature reorganized it, renaming it the New England Female Medical College.

During the 1850s the school also took some crucial steps toward garnering respect from medical professions. In 1853 Gregory received an honorary degree from a medical college, albeit a marginalized one, the Eclectic Pennsylvania Medical College. More promisingly, in 1858 the school took over the management of Boston's Lying-In Hospital. At the urging of others, Gregory hired Marie Zakrzewska, a renowned female physician, as head of the department of obstetrics. It did not take long for the two to clash. From the moment "Zak," as she was known, arrived at the school, she balked at his seeming willingness to grant any student a diploma, regardless of her skill. Gregory, meanwhile, questioned Zak's demands for microscopes, test tubes, and thermometers, saying that they were "new-fangled European notions." Zakrzewska resigned in 1862, leaving to found her own haven for women physicians, the New England Hospital, that same year.

In some regards a pioneer of women's medical education, Gregory remains a troublesome figure in retrospect. Many critics charged that Gregory did not care about how competent the women doctors he produced were; he wanted only to ensure that there was, as he wrote early in life, "a class of female physicians, qualified at least to attend to the peculiar complaints of their own sex." Even Gregory's students recognized that he might not have their best interests at heart. In an attempt to emphasize their femininity, Gregory proposed that all graduates of the school should use the title "doctress" rather than doctor. The students refused, complaining that this term was demeaning. Yet, Gregory had offered these women an uncommon opportunity—a chance to become trained medical professionals. At the time of his death, nearly 100 women had received medical degrees from his school, including the first black female M.D. in North America.

The school faltered in the last ten years of Gregory's life despite his continued efforts to persuade society that only women doctors should attend women patients. The problems continued after Gregory died of consumption in Boston, and two years later the school merged with Boston University to become one of the first coeducational medical schools in the United States.

• Gregory's efforts to establish an institution to train women physicians have been chronicled in many histories of women in medicine. See, for instance, Regina Markell Morantz-Sanchez, *Sympathy and Science: Women Physicians in American Medicine* (1985); Ruth J. Abram, *"Send Us a Lady Physician": Women Doctors in America, 1835–1920* (1985); Mary Roth Walsh, *Doctors Wanted: No Women Need Apply* (1977); and Thomas Bonner, *To The Ends of the Earth: Women's Search for Education in Medicine* (1992). For a discussion of the move toward women's medical education in Boston, see Virginia Drachman, *Hospital with a Heart: Women Doctors and the Paradox of Separatism at the New England Hospital, 1862–1969* (1984).

SHARI RUDAVSKY

GREGORY, Thomas Watt (6 Nov. 1861–26 Feb. 1933), U.S. attorney general, was born in Crawfordsville, Mississippi, the son of Francis Robert Gregory, a physician who died in Confederate army service, and Mary Cornelia Watt. He grew up on his maternal grandfather's Mississippi plantation and graduated from Southwestern Presbyterian University in Clarksville, Tennessee, in 1883. After a year of studying law at the University of Virginia, he transferred to the University of Texas, graduating with an LL.B. in 1885. In 1893 he married Julia Nalle, with whom he had two daughters and two sons.

Gregory settled in Austin, where he practiced law from 1885 to 1913. In 1900 he formed a partnership with Robert L. Batts, and in 1908 a third partner, Victor Lee Brooks, joined the firm. In their most famous case, Gregory and Batts, representing the state of Texas, won an antitrust settlement of more than $1.5 million from Waters-Pierce Oil Company, a subsidiary of Standard Oil of New York.

Without ever holding elective office, Gregory became a leading Texas Democrat. He served as Austin assistant city attorney (1891–1894) and declined appointments as assistant state attorney general (1892) and state judge (1896). Ideologically, he was identified with southern progressivism. His moderate brand of reform looked to curb corporate power and eliminate business and government corruption. He favored Prohibition (until 1932), was lukewarm to woman suffrage, and opposed anti-Semitism and the resurgent Ku Klux Klan in the 1920s. Although he was no champion of racial equality, he supported education for African Americans and spoke against lynching.

Gregory served on the Credentials Committee at the Democratic National Convention in 1904 and was vice president of the 1912 Baltimore convention, where he led the Texas delegation in supporting Woodrow Wilson's candidacy. After Wilson won the presidency, Gregory's loyalty and his close friendship with Colonel Edward M. House, an influential Wilson adviser, led to a Washington appointment. In 1913 he became a special assistant to the attorney general concerned with antitrust enforcement. Soon after, he negotiated a settlement that forced the New York, New Haven, and Hartford Railroad to divest itself of its monopolistic transportation holdings.

In August 1914 Gregory succeeded his University of Virginia law school classmate James C. McReynolds as attorney general. In 1916 he passed up an opportunity to follow McReynolds to the U.S. Supreme Court, choosing instead to remain at the Justice Department.

During U.S. involvement in World War I (1917–1918), Gregory expanded and centralized the power and influence of his department and helped to create a national domestic security apparatus of unprecedented scope. Recalling the Alien and Sedition Acts of 1798, under Gregory the Justice Department drafted the Espionage Act (1917), amended as the Sedition Act (1918), which punished antigovernment and antiwar expression. Gregory led in rigorously enforcing these acts along with the Selective Service laws and the Alien Anarchist Act (1918). In a bureaucratic tug of war the Justice Department wrested primacy in pursuing German spies and domestic dissidents from Treasury secretary William G. McAdoo's Secret Service. In an atmosphere of national fear, suspicion, and intolerance of dissent the Justice Department's Bureau of Investigation (renamed the Federal Bureau of Investigation in 1935) cooperated with the Office of Naval Intelligence, Military Intelligence Division, Post Office Department, state and local police, private detectives, and 250,000 civilian volunteer auxiliaries organized as the American Protective League (APL). Collectively they investigated hundreds of thousands of persons and organizations. The result was the internment of 2,300 enemy aliens and the prosecution of more than 220,000 conscription and loyalty cases. By raiding its offices, confiscating its records and publications, and jailing more than 100 of its leaders, Gregory's men all but destroyed the radical Industrial Workers of the World. To enforce conscription laws, they mounted legally and ethically questionable dragnet "slacker raids," employing APL volunteers to round up thousands of men in New York and other cities who, if they lacked proper draft credentials, were then detained in overcrowded, makeshift lockups.

Despite such stringent measures, some conservative and patriotic legislators and journalists criticized Gregory and his special assistant John Lord O'Brian for not doing enough to control antiwar activity and disloyalty. But Gregory and O'Brian supported the rule of law insofar as they condemned vigilantism and rejected demands for military tribunals to control civilian opponents of the war.

In May 1919, after resigning his cabinet post on 4 March 1919, Gregory accompanied Wilson to the European peace conference as an adviser. From October 1919 to January 1920 Gregory was a member of Wilson's Second Industrial Conference, which convened representatives of employers, workers, and the public in an unsuccessful effort to improve labor-management relations. Then he returned to practicing law for a number of years in Washington, D.C., and afterward in Houston. In his later years Gregory was a major fundraiser for various projects, including the Stone Mountain Confederate Memorial, the Austin Presbyterian Theological Seminary, and, especially, the ex-students' association of the University of Texas.

In the 1920s Gregory, semiretired from politics, remained a loyal Democrat who idealized Wilson. Gregory never wavered in his defense of the Wilson administration and of his own stewardship of the Justice Department against a rising tide of revisionist history and journalism that condemned U.S. participation in World War I, including the government's treatment of aliens and dissenters. He continued to assert that the control of the alien population during the war was his greatest accomplishment as attorney general.

In declining health, Gregory nevertheless actively supported Franklin D. Roosevelt for president in 1932. It was shortly after a meeting with the president-elect that Gregory died in a New York hotel. As a political figure Gregory was always intensely loyal to the Democratic party and to his idol Wilson. Although on many issues he seemed inconsistent, Gregory should be understood as a moderate who always sought the "middle ground between competing extremes" (Anders, p. 24).

• Separate collections of Gregory's papers are at the Library of Congress and in the Southwest Collection at Texas Tech University. Some items relating to his attorney generalship are published in *The Papers of Woodrow Wilson*, ed. Arthur S. Link (1966–1994). Many more are in manuscript in Wilson's papers (and those of other Wilson cabinet members) at the Library of Congress. The General Records of the Department of Justice (RG 60) at the National Archives contain his official correspondence as attorney general. For overall interpretations of his public life see Evan Anders, "Thomas Watt Gregory and the Survival of His Progressive Faith," *Southwestern Historical Quarterly* 93 (July 1989): 1–24, and Homer S. Cummings and Carl McFarland, *Federal Justice* (1937). Examples of contrasting assessments of his wartime role are Paul L. Murphy, *World War I and the Origin of Civil Liberties in the United States* (1979), and Richard G. Powers, *Secrecy and Power: The Life of J. Edgar Hoover* (1987). A brief obituary is in the *New York Times*, 26 and 27 Feb. 1933. The *Houston Post*, 27 Feb. 1933, and the *Dallas Morning News*, 27 and 28 Feb. 1933, offer extended tributes.

CHARLES HOWARD MCCORMICK

GREGORY, William King (19 May 1876–29 Dec. 1970), paleontologist, was born in New York City, the son of George Gregory, a printer, and Jane King. In his youth Gregory had no interest in science or nature and intended to enter the Episcopalian ministry; however, he attended the Columbia University School of Mines, where a zoology course taught by Bashford Dean, curator of ichthyology at the American Museum of Natural History, caught his interest. He transferred to Columbia College to study zoology and vertebrate paleontology under Dean and Henry Fairfield Osborn, founder of the museum's Department of Vertebrate Paleontology and eventually its president. In 1899 Gregory became Osborn's research assistant, leading to his lifelong association with Columbia and the museum. He received his bachelor's degree in 1900, his master's in 1905, and his doctorate in 1910. While Osborn's assistant, Gregory also served as the first editor of the *American Museum Journal*, the predecessor of *Natural History*. He became a member of the museum's scientific staff in 1911 and a faculty member at Columbia in 1916. He married Laura Grace Foote in 1899. She died in 1937, and in 1938 he married Angela DuBois.

Working with Dean on fishes and with Osborn on the origin of mammals, as well as doing his own research, Gregory soon began publishing scientific articles. His monograph *The Orders of Mammals* (1910) is considered a classic in the field. Gregory applied changes of function, as well as morphology, as a way of understanding the adaptive purpose of characteristics to evolutionary and phylogenetic studies. An earlier work, *The Orders of Teleostomous Fishes* (1907), was a precursor to his lifelong interest in fishes. He rose through the museum's curatorial ranks, at one time holding a dual curatorship in the Departments of Ichthyology and Comparative Anatomy. At Columbia he was first appointed assistant professor of vertebrate paleontology, then promoted to full professor, and finally to Da Costa Professor of Zoology shortly before his retirement. Most of his graduate students took his courses on the evolution of vertebrates and on mammals at the museum, using its study collections. Gregory trained some of the most notable paleontologists and zoologists of America, including Alfred S. Romer, Charles L. Camp, G. Kingsley Noble, and James Chapin.

Gregory's most significant scientific contributions were in vertebrate morphology (the study of the form and structure of animals), which led him to innovative theories of evolution. He was especially interested in origins and the progression of evolutionary development. His research on marsupials led to his belief that evolutionary changes were adaptations responding to the environment. In "The Monotremes and the Palimpsest Theory" (*Bulletin of the American Museum of Natural History* 88 [1947]: 1–52), Gregory advanced the theory that every life form combines inherited and often primitive characteristics with advanced and evolved characteristics. He compared organisms to palimpsests, parchments that have been incompletely erased and reused.

Gregory's research on primate evolution dealt with the study of comparative muscle and skeletal structures and dentition, and also with habit or "habitus," function and heritage, and especially with motion. In several papers, including "Studies on the Evolution of Primates: Phylogeny of Recent and Extinct Anthropoids with Special Reference to the Origin of Man" (*Bulletin of the American Museum of Natural History* 35 [1916]: 258–355), Gregory presented his theory that "man and the anthropoids have been derived from a primitive anthropoid stock and that man's nearest existing relatives are the chimpanzees and gorillas."

Known as the museum's most sedentary scientist, Gregory still made a number of trips to the western states to dig for fossils, and he accompanied his colleague and friend Henry Raven to collect mammals in Australia for a museum hall that never materialized. In 1925 he sailed with William Beebe of the New York Zoological Society aboard the *Arcturus* to the Sargasso Sea, an expedition that resulted in the museum's Hall of Deep Sea Fishes; in 1929, with Raven, he went on the AMNH–Columbia University expedition to Central Africa to collect gorillas, resulting in a book, *In Quest of Gorillas* (1937), coauthored with Raven. In his later years he annually visited the Lerner Marine Laboratory in the Bahamas to continue his research on fish.

Gregory worked with some of the finest zoologists of his time and coauthored many important articles with Walter Granger, W. D. Matthew, George Gaylord Simpson, and Milo Hellman. He was remembered as a man of great charm, quiet, modest, enthusiastic, and absentminded. He was a member of numerous scientific organizations including the New York Academy of Sciences (president, 1932–1933), National Academy of Sciences, American Association of Anatomists, London Zoological Society, Linnean Society, Explorers Club, Paleontological Society of America, and Society of Ichthyologists and Herpetologists.

Gregory retired from the American Museum of Natural History in 1944 but continued his research as curator emeritus of fishes and comparative anatomy; in 1945 he retired from Columbia University. He died in Woodstock, New York, after surgery.

• Gregory's papers and publications are at the American Museum of Natural History. Among Gregory's extensive list of publications, *Evolution Emerging: A Survey of Changing Patterns from Primeval Life to Man* (1951) and *Our Face from Fish to Man* (1929, reprinted several times), best represent his interests in origins and evolutionary sequences. The best biography, including a comprehensive bibliography, is Edwin H. Colbert, National Academy of Sciences, *Biographical Memoirs* 46 (1975): 91–133. An obituary is in the *New York Times*, 30 Dec. 1970. A scholarly discussion of Gregory's scientific work is Ronald Rainger, "What's the Use: William King Gregory and the Functional Morphology of Fossil Vertebrates," *Journal of the History of Biology* 22 (1989): 103–39.

NINA J. ROOT

GRESHAM, Newt (20 Feb. 1858–10 Apr. 1906), labor organizer and editor, was born Isaac Newton Gresham in Lauderdale County, near Florence, Alabama, the son of Henry Gresham and Marcipia Narcissa Wilcoxon, tenant farmers. The family moved to Kaufman County, Texas, in 1859 (though some sources claim they moved after the Civil War). After his parents' deaths in 1868, Gresham lived with his older brother Ben.

Gresham went to Hood County, Texas, in 1877 and worked as a common laborer. He learned to read and write as an adult and attended Add-Ran College (now Texas Christian University) for one year. The school was sponsored by the Disciples of Christ, of which Gresham was a member. In 1881 Gresham married Ida May Cox (some sources give her maiden name as Peters); they had at least three children. He returned to tenant farming in Hood County after the marriage.

In this area of poor agricultural land and poor farmers, the agricultural community was eager to improve its lot through farming organizations. Gresham was a member of the Southern Farmers' Alliance and was elected an organizer in 1881. In that capacity he traveled through Texas, and in 1886 he began to organize farmers in Alabama as well. He and his family then spent four years organizing suballiances in Tennessee and Mississippi.

The alliance diminished, and in 1890 Gresham and his family returned to farming in Hood County. Gresham maintained an interest in farm rallies and turned to the Texas Populist movement. In 1897 he became the editor of a small country newspaper, the *Granbury Graphic Truth*, hoping to influence the organization of farmers through his work. He bought the paper the following year and was so eager to spread his views that he was willing to barter for subscription fees. The cavalier attitude toward financial matters that Gresham displayed in his consistently unsuccessful newspaper operations carried over into his personal finances and into his later positions in the farmers' union. He sold the paper in 1899 so that he could move to

Greenville, where he bought the (Greenville) *Hunt County Observer*. There he began to form his idea for a farmers' organization with the encouragement of O. P. Pyle, editor of the *Mineola Courier*, who became a close and influential friend.

Between 1900 and 1902 Gresham moved to Point, Rains County, Texas. There he published a small newspaper called the *Point Times*. He again encountered financial difficulties; consequently few people had faith in his plans, and he continued alone trying to organize farmers. In 1902 Gresham served on the platform committee of the Allied People's (Populist) party convention. The Populist agitation subsided, and Gresham again pushed forward with his plan for a new organization for farmers. Gresham and nine other men formed the charter membership of the Farmers' Educational and Cooperative Union of America, the purpose of which was to assist farmers in marketing and obtaining the best prices for their products. At the first meeting of the union, Gresham was named the general organizer, and he is credited with writing the constitution and bylaws of the organization.

Although Gresham had been politically active in both the Populist and Democratic parties, he insisted that the farmers' union should be nonpartisan. He did not want the union to have to fight against the charges of partisanship that had adversely affected earlier organizations such as the Grange and the Farmers' Alliance. The first local chapter of the farmers' union was organized in Smyrna, Texas; farmers were willing to join the new organization, particularly since the dues were low. Described as "a quiet, gentle man, slow and deliberate in his movements," Gresham had a great deal of success in his attempts to organize because his sincerity was apparent.

In 1903 Gresham moved to Emory, Texas, where he founded the *Password*, the official newspaper of the farmers' union. He relocated to Greenville, Texas, in 1904. The first state meeting of the union took place in February in Mineola, Texas. At this time Gresham became lecturer for the union's state organization, and in 1905 he became its secretary-treasurer.

Gresham inadvertently contributed to some of the early problems of the farmers' union. He was excellent at enrolling new members, but the growing membership was difficult to control, and when factions began to develop the union was in danger of becoming a partisan organization. In addition, Gresham failed to keep appropriate financial records. Many of the union's early records were destroyed in a fire in 1903, and he had no evidence to present in his defense when unsubstantiated rumors began to spread that year claiming that he had started the union for his own financial benefit. He did receive a salary from the union and built a small house with his income. In August 1905 Gresham's books were audited by an internal committee appointed by the union. The outcome of the audit, however, placed no blame for financial problems on Gresham. Still, this unprofessional approach to business matters was part of the reason the union changed its bylaws to restrict eligibility for officer positions to farmers only. This excluded Gresham, a newspaper-man, from his office.

In December 1905 the union began to nationalize, and without the restrictions of the state bylaws Gresham was elected its national organizer in 1906. As the national organizer he traveled throughout the South. Soon after presiding over the founding convention of the union in Tennessee, he suffered an attack of appendicitis and died at his home in Greenville.

Gresham's early death meant that he never saw the national prominence that his organization, today known as the National Farmers' Union, would gain. In honor of his contribution to rural life, the farmers' union raised a monument to Gresham in Point, Texas, on 9 October 1907.

• Robert Lee Hunt, *A History of Farmer Movements in the Southwest, 1873–1925* (1935), contains information about Gresham and the early years of the union in Texas and is based on early papers from the union's published proceedings. See also Gladys Talbott Edwards, *The Farmers' Union Triangle* (1941), which has additional data on the topic. One of the more current works about the farmers' union is C. E. Hunt and Eberhart Perry, *The Voice of the Family Farmer: A Short History of the Farmers' Educational and Cooperative Union of America* (1962). For information about Gresham and his friendship with O. P. Pyle, see Genevieve Pyle Demme (Pyle's granddaughter), *Owen Pinkney Pyle: Champion of the Farmer* (master's thesis, Rice Institute [now Rice Univ.], 1958). Contemporary works about the early days of the farmers' union movement include Charles Simon Barrett, *The Mission: History and Times of the Farmers' Union* (1909), which was written by an early president of the organization, and Commodore B. Fisher, *The Farmers' Union* (1920), which uses largely primary material about the subject.

CAROL A. LOCKWOOD

GRESHAM, Walter Quintin (17 Mar. 1832–28 May 1895), jurist and cabinet officer, was born in Harrison County, Indiana, the son of William Gresham, a farmer and cabinetmaker, and Sarah Davis. His father, serving as county sheriff, was killed by an outlaw when Walter was less than two years old, and Sarah Gresham later married Noah Rumley, a farmer. Gresham taught school and attended Indiana University's Preparatory Department, 1851–1852, before reading law with a prominent local Whig. He was admitted to the bar on 1 April 1854 and entered into practice at Corydon, Indiana.

After the Whigs collapsed, Gresham affiliated briefly with the Know Nothings and enlisted in the anti-Nebraska movement of 1854. That year he ran unsuccessfully for prosecuting attorney and the following year lost a bid for the county clerkship. By 1856 he had joined the Republican party, and his prominence grew with the new organization. In 1858 he married Matilda McGrain; they had two children.

In 1860 Gresham sought the nomination for state supreme court clerk at the Republican State Convention and lost. Later that year as Republican nominee for the lower house of the state legislature, he squeaked past his Democratic opponent by sixty votes. During the ensuing legislative session he

clashed with Republican governor Oliver P. Morton, and the two became bitter enemies. Initially a moderate on the slavery question, Gresham endorsed sectional compromise in the Indiana General Assembly debates during the secession winter of 1861. But he also pushed for military preparedness for the state, and with the fall of Fort Sumter he became an ardent foe of the southern rebellion. In the summer he joined the Union army, serving first as lieutenant colonel of the Thirty-eighth Indiana Infantry and later as colonel of the Fifty-third Regiment attached to the Army of Tennessee. After participating in the siege of Vicksburg he won promotion to brigadier general in August 1863, but the following July, during William T. Sherman's Atlanta campaign, a Confederate sharpshooter's bullet shattered his leg just below the knee. His fighting days ended, he left the army with the rank of brevet major general.

When his wound had sufficiently healed, Gresham resumed his legal practice at New Albany, Indiana. Returning to Republican politics, he ran for Congress in 1866 and 1868 and lost both times in a heavily Democratic district. Gresham soured on politics, and when his wartime friend, President Ulysses S. Grant, appointed him federal district judge for Indiana, he accepted in September 1869.

On the bench he handled cases on a variety of subjects, including patents, bankruptcy, railroads, the Whiskey Ring, and election fraud. During the 1877 railroad strike he issued injunctions against union interference with railroads in federal receivership, called upon President Rutherford B. Hayes to send troops to Indianapolis, and himself joined a local citizens militia to help preserve the peace.

The proprieties incumbent in the judgeship underscored Gresham's ambivalence about returning to politics. In 1876 he fought Morton's presidential candidacy and backed reformer Benjamin Bristow for the Republican nomination. After Morton's death in 1877 prospects brightened, and Gresham ran for the U.S. Senate in 1880. His clumsy campaign, however, had little chance of success against that of the adept Benjamin Harrison (1833–1901) who had replaced Morton as leader of the Indiana Republicans and as Gresham's political bête noire.

In April 1883 President Chester A. Arthur appointed Gresham postmaster general, a surprise move designed in part to thwart a prospective challenge from Harrison to Arthur's renomination. During the year and a half he occupied the office Gresham earned praise for implementing the new Pendleton Civil Service Act and for other reforms in the Post Office Department. He introduced competitive bidding for the purchase of supplies for local post offices, increased the standard weight for first-class mail, and negotiated revised railroad schedules to speed the mail between the East Coast and points west. He failed, however, in his moralistic attempt to ban the Louisiana Lottery Company from using the mails.

On the political front, Gresham used the patronage of his department in behalf of Arthur's bid for the

1884 presidential nomination, but he also cultivated a darkhorse candidacy of his own. Opposing a similar bid by Harrison, Gresham hoped that in a deadlocked convention Arthur's supporters would join with party reformers to nominate him. When the Republican convention chose James G. Blaine, whose probity Gresham and many others doubted, Gresham again soured on politics and longed to return to the bench. However, in September he acceded to Arthur's plea to accept an interim appointment as secretary of the treasury. While holding that office he made one brief campaign speech in New York, which generally departed from Blaine's advocacy of a high protective tariff. A week before the election Arthur appointed Gresham judge of the U.S. Seventh Circuit with jurisdiction over Illinois, Indiana, and Wisconsin. In this post Gresham encountered the same variety of cases he had seen as district judge. His views toward labor having mellowed, he won praise from workmen for his evenhanded treatment of strike cases. In the 1886 Wabash railroad receivership case he blocked a notorious example of "railroad wrecking" by Jay Gould and earned recognition as an enemy of monopoly.

Gresham's emerging reformist reputation formed the basis for his candidacy for the Republican presidential nomination in 1888. Although Indiana supported Harrison, Gresham entered the national convention with the second largest bloc of votes. In reality he had little chance for the nomination. As a moderate on the tariff issue, he was out of step with the party's movement to high protectionism. The opposition of Blaine's followers, who threw their support to Harrison, sealed the result.

Gresham gave only lukewarm support to Harrison in the national election, and during the ensuing four years he grew increasingly disenchanted with Republican policies, particularly as embodied in the highly protectionist McKinley Tariff. He spoke out against an emerging "plutocracy" and thereby attracted the attention of the new Populist party, many of whose members wanted to draft Gresham for president at its 1892 convention. He refused leadership of the Populist crusade, however, and instead threw his support to the low-tariff Democratic nominee, Grover Cleveland, who defeated Harrison.

Cleveland invited Gresham to be secretary of state in the new administration. Fearing the imputation of a pay-off for his election support, Gresham at first refused but later yielded to Cleveland's pleas. Aiming to further party realignment, Cleveland hoped the appointment would attract reformist Republicans, labor, and Populists to the Democrats. The idea miscarried, however, for the unpopularity of many of Gresham's policies as secretary of state proved an enormous political liability, with Republicans condemning nearly all his actions and few Democrats defending his controversial policies. Besides his anomalous political standing, Gresham suffered under other handicaps: a brusque indifference to diplomatic etiquette, insufficient personal wealth for official entertaining, and ill health. His lack of experience in foreign affairs forced him to spend large amounts of time studying the background of diplomatic issues.

As secretary of state Gresham followed patterns learned earlier in life. In domestic politics he had constantly warned of dangers posed to America's republican institutions by corruption and greed. In managing the nation's foreign relations he similarly saw a need to restore lost virtue. While others clamored for empire, either through territorial acquisition or enlarged economic penetration, Gresham tried to reverse what he considered the dangerous expansionism launched by the Harrison administration. With his limited background in foreign relations, he reverted to habits acquired on the bench, dealing with each problem as it arose and basing his opinions on international law, his understanding of traditional American interests, and his sense of justice and equity. Gresham defended traditional overseas interests, including economic interests, but he did so in a conservative, legalistic way that betrayed little desire to expand them.

Gresham's moralistic approach showed most clearly in his opposition to the annexation of Hawaii negotiated by Harrison after Americans had overthrown Queen Liliuokalani. Arguing that taking the islands would be tantamount to stealing territory, Gresham persuaded Cleveland to withdraw the annexation treaty from the Senate. At Gresham's prompting, the administration also attempted to restore the queen to power, but her enemies refused to relinquish control. In a similar vein, Gresham sought to terminate American participation with Germany and Britain in a condominium that controlled the Samoan islands, but Congress refused to act.

Toward Latin America Gresham offered a conservative but firm defense of the Monroe Doctrine. He pursued a legalistically neutral stance toward a revolt in the Brazilian navy in the harbor at Rio de Janeiro, while maintaining a watchful eye against undue European influence on the outcome. In Nicaragua he worked for an end to a British quasi protectorate over the Mosquito Indian reservation, even though American economic interests favored British over Nicaraguan rule. Believing the Monroe Doctrine inapplicable, he steadfastly refused to champion Venezuela in its dispute with Britain over the British Guiana (now Guyana) boundary. While this dispute was pending, Gresham died in Washington.

Ironically, the ultimate significance of Gresham's foreign policy was that it evoked a heated public controversy that spurred a growing expansionist feeling in the country. Republicans censured his often quixotic diplomacy in Hawaii, Samoa, and elsewhere, while many Democrats were embarrassed. Skepticism over his legalistic, "small" policy led many to question the nation's traditional role in international relations, and that questioning directly fed the imperialist urge that crested at the end of the 1890s. With the acquisition of a formal empire at the turn of the century, Gresham seemed in retrospect an anachronistic guardian of a bygone era.

• Gresham's papers are housed in the Manuscript Division of the Library of Congress. Gresham letters are also found in the papers of Thomas F. Bayard, Benjamin Bristow, Grover Cleveland, John W. Foster, John Bassett Moore, Carl Schurz (all in the Library of Congress), John Marshall Harlan (Library of Congress and University of Louisville Law School Library), Noble C. Butler (Indiana Historical Society), David Davis (Illinois State Historical Library), and Charles W. Fairbanks (Lilly Library, Indiana University). The National Archives holds Gresham correspondence from his service in the Union army and in the cabinet. His judicial opinions appear in the *Federal Reporter* and Bissell's *Reports*. A large portion of his diplomatic correspondence is published in *Papers Relating to the Foreign Relations of the United States*. The standard biography is Charles W. Calhoun, *Gilded Age Cato: The Life of Walter Q. Gresham* (1988). A family memoir, Matilda Gresham, *Life of Walter Quintin Gresham, 1832–1895*, was published in 1919.

CHARLES W. CALHOUN

GREW, Joseph Clark (27 May 1880–25 May 1965), diplomat, U.S. ambassador to Japan, and undersecretary of state, was born in Boston, Massachusetts, the son of Edward Sturgis Grew, a wool merchant, and Annie Crawford Clark. Grew's family was among the more well-off Bostonians, and he was a distant cousin of the financier J. P. Morgan (1837–1913).

Grew attended Groton School (1892–1898) and Harvard (1898–1902), where he received a B.A. degree. At these institutions the sense of noblesse oblige was instilled in him, and it played a role in his later choice of a career in government service. After college he took a world tour, which included a visit to the Far East, where, in Amoy, China, lying on his back in a cave, he shot a tiger as it leaped over him. This deed recommended Grew to Theodore Roosevelt (1858–1919) as a proper candidate for the foreign service.

Grew's father wanted him to secure a position in banking. After a failed attempt to gain employment in a publishing house, Grew thought the foreign service would sate his desire for travel to exotic places, and he announced that he wanted to go into government service, pleasing neither his father nor his mother. His first effort at appointment failed when a hearing loss caused by a childhood illness was mistaken for total deafness. He subsequently received an appointment to Cairo, Egypt, in 1904 and was among the last people to be transferred from the consular service to the foreign service before President Theodore Roosevelt instituted the system of competitive examinations for appointments in 1906.

In 1905 Grew married Alice de Vermandois Perry; they had four daughters, three of whom married foreign service officers. Grew's marriage proved of enormous benefit when he was later appointed ambassador to Japan. Alice Perry was the descendant of Commodore Matthew Perry, who opened Japan to the West in 1853, and she also had spent her youth in that island nation, developing many contacts there. Thus Grew had access to important people whom it took others years to cultivate, if ever.

After his marriage, Grew returned to Egypt briefly, was assigned to Mexico City as third secretary of the embassy in 1906, and was sent to Russia in 1907. He was promoted to second secretary at Berlin in 1908, first secretary at Vienna in 1911–1912, and was sent back to Berlin in the latter year. He returned to the United States in 1912. Because of his Republican family, Grew feared the new Democratic administration of Woodrow Wilson might replace him with a political appointee. He solicited the aid of Franklin Roosevelt and other Democratic friends and classmates from Groton and Harvard, probably saving his diplomatic career. It was only the first of several times that such contacts served him well. He spent 1913–1914 in Washington, and was in Berlin in 1915–1917, after which he returned again to Washington.

Grew gained a very prestigious post with the coveted equivalent rank of minister at the Paris Peace Conference in 1918, where he was put in charge of arrangements for the president's peace commission. Finding himself in the midst of the struggle for control of the mission, through tactful finesse he earned a reputation for evenhandedness and avoided antagonizing the various hostile elements. However, to ensure his position, Grew needed an appointment as chief of a legation, and he received this assignment as minister to Denmark in April 1920.

Representing U.S. interests at the Lausanne Conference on Near Eastern Affairs (1922–1923), Grew outmaneuvered British and French schemes to control oil concessions in Turkey. Although the separate treaty he negotiated with Turkey was rejected by the U.S. Senate, his negotiating skills and advice were warmly remembered by the Turks when he was appointed U.S. ambassador to Turkey in 1927. In the interim Grew returned to Washington to accept an assignment as undersecretary of state in Calvin Coolidge's administration.

These were not among Grew's happiest years. His diaries tell of conflicts with Secretary of State Frank Kellogg, who often called on him to give information to an inside group of advisers. They fired questions at him in a jumble of voices, which did not allow him to turn his good ear to each speaker, and the secretary became angry when Grew failed to give instant answers. The situation worsened when Grew became acting secretary of state in Kellogg's absence. Grew authorized the U.S. minister to China to join in a naval demonstration near Tientsin, and Kellogg accused him of nearly declaring war on China. Grew stayed on in this difficult arrangement in part because he wanted to see through the implementation of the Rogers Act of 1924, which authorized the reorganization and professionalization of the foreign service. By making it possible for career foreign service officers to be separated from consular appointments and not have to deal with such mundane items as issuing visas and reporting on business affairs of Americans in the various nations, the legislation distinctly separated the consular service from that category of foreign service officers who comprised the elite of the Department of State's overseas representatives. When this task was completed, he fled to the Turkish post with alacrity and relief.

In 1932 Grew was appointed and confirmed as the U.S. ambassador to Japan, the first career diplomat so honored, breaking the historic chain of political appointments to such posts. While Tokyo was a major capital, it was probably the least expensive place to be an ambassador, and thus Grew, whose fortune was adequate but not on a par with what would be required in London, Paris, or Berlin, could afford to accept the post.

Tokyo was the last overseas post for Grew and one where he intended to leave his mark in the annals of U.S. foreign policy. He spent the next ten years trying to explain the United States to the Japanese and vice versa in the hope that he could achieve success as a peacemaker between his suspicious employers and the aggressive leadership in that important island nation. That he failed in this ambition is partly attributable to conditions beyond his control, particularly the national ambitions and predilections of both governments. However, Grew bears some of the responsibility for the failure himself. With every new Japanese cabinet he advised the State Department to expect a better relationship because the premiers or foreign secretaries wanted to improve relations and the climate was better for a downgrading of the power of the military in Japan's government. As each Japanese cabinet fell, he retreated to gloomy predictions that relations could do nothing but get worse. These swings of mood and reporting caused reactions in Washington that were the opposite of what the ambassador sought, a greater appreciation for Japan's economic problems and greater leeway for the embassy to deal with policy decisions concerning Japan. He especially came into conflict with Stanley K. Hornbeck, who headed the Far East Division of the department until becoming special adviser to Secretary of State Cordell Hull on Far Eastern affairs in the late 1930s. Hornbeck accused Grew of being an appeaser.

Grew decided that the only way to avoid conflict was to illustrate to the Japanese that the result of failure to reach accommodation with the United States would be disaster. His famous "Straight from the Horse's Mouth" address to the America-Japan Society on 19 October 1939 warned that a change of course was requisite if the Japanese expected to avoid bringing the combination of U.S. economic and military power down on them. Despite attacks on him in the Japanese press, he thought that wiser heads in the government heeded his warning. He was, of course, mistaken.

Subsequently, Grew thought the only hope for peace was a direct meeting between President Franklin Roosevelt and Premier Prince Konoye Fumimaro. This failed to materialize, and Ambassador Grew contended thereafter that thus passed an excellent opportunity to save the peace. In fact there was little likelihood that such a meeting would have achieved anything save a stall for more time at best or a clearer case for rationalizing Japan's attack at Pearl Harbor on the basis of American intransigence at worst.

Grew returned to Washington in 1942 to become a special assistant to Secretary Hull and, in 1944, director of the Division of Far Eastern Affairs. From December 1944 to August 1945 he served once again as undersecretary of state. In this last post he opposed cooperation with the Soviets, based on long-held anticommunist views. He tried to prevent the use of the atomic bomb against Japan and played a role in preserving the emperor's position as titular head of the Japanese nation after the war. Grew retired from the State Department to serve on many private boards and commissions until his death at Manchester-by-the-Sea, Massachusetts.

• Grew's papers are in the Houghton Library at Harvard; the most important and informative information in this collection are the voluminous Grew diaries chronicling his long career and his views of U.S. policy. Much information about him is in the Department of State records in the National Archives, including all of his dispatches, and a large body of material, including correspondence, is in the Franklin Delano Roosevelt Library. Important material on Grew and his diplomacy is in the Columbia University Oral History Project. Grew's writings include *Sport and Travel in the Far East* (1910), *Ten Years in Japan* (1944), and *Turbulent Era*, ed. Walter Johnson assisted by Nancy Harvison Hooker (2 vols., 1952). Interested readers should also consult Waldo H. Heinrichs, Jr., *American Ambassador: Joseph C. Grew . . .* (1966), and Edward M. Bennett, "Joseph C. Grew: The Diplomacy of Pacification," in *Diplomats in Crisis*, ed. Richard Dean Burns and Edward M. Bennett (1974). Obituaries are in the *New York Times* and the *Washington Post*, both 27 May 1965.

EDWARD M. BENNETT

GREW, Mary (1 Sept. 1813–10 Oct. 1896), abolitionist and women's rights advocate, was born in Hartford, Connecticut, the daughter of Kate Merrow and the Reverend Henry Grew. Grew's father, an English-born Baptist minister, was well off, and Mary was always materially comfortable. She attended the Hartford Female Seminary, established and directed by Catharine Beecher. Grew shared her father's interest in social reform, and as a young girl in Hartford she had taught a Sunday school class for African-American children. After living in Boston during the early 1830s, the Grew family moved in 1834 to Philadelphia, where Mary joined the recently established Philadelphia Female Anti-Slavery Society (PFASS).

Mary Grew, who regarded abolition as "a noble mission for humanity," was engaged in many of the antislavery activities that proved so controversial during the 1830s and beyond. Besides running the PFASS's school for black children, she was active in a campaign to compile a petition urging Congress to abolish slavery in the District of Columbia. Despite her support for the abolitionist strategy of moral suasion, which eschewed direct involvement in the political process, Grew remained active in the petition campaigns during the 1840s and 1850s. In 1836 she was appointed corresponding secretary of the PFASS, and she also was selected to serve on the society's committee to arrange the first of many annual antislavery fairs that not only raised funds for the abolitionist movement but also gave women experience in public commerce. In addition to working in the Free Produce Association, which sought to attack slavery by promoting a boycott of slave-grown produce, Grew served as coeditor of the *Pennsylvania Freeman*, the organ of the Pennsylvania Anti-Slavery Society (PASS), from November 1845 until May 1850.

Grew was among the organizers of the antislavery conventions of American women held in New York City in 1837 and in Philadelphia in 1838 and 1839. The second of these gatherings, held in May 1838, provoked the ire of many Philadelphians. Offended by the spectacle of antislavery women addressing "promiscuous" audiences consisting of both men and women, an enraged group of Philadelphians burnt to the ground the newly built Pennsylvania Hall, which the antislavery women had used for some of their meetings.

Abolitionists were themselves divided over the question of women's appropriate "sphere." For many abolitionists, women's public participation in the antislavery movement was an unwelcome challenge to gender conventions, jeopardizing the success of the antislavery appeal. This issue was a major cause of the split in abolitionist ranks that occurred at the May 1840 meeting of the American Anti-Slavery Society. Like a majority of members of the PASS, Grew sided with William Lloyd Garrison—a public proponent of equal rights for women—in that rupture. The next month Grew attended the World's Anti-Slavery Convention in London, where the question of women's rights again proved contentious. After a debate in which her own father argued against the admission of the women delegates, Grew and the other women delegates sent by various antislavery societies in the United States were excluded from the proceedings. This experience served to galvanize Grew, Lucretia Mott, Elizabeth Cady Stanton, and several other abolitionist women to take a more active interest in the women's rights issue. Conscious of the legal as well as social bases of discrimination against women, Grew circulated petitions throughout eastern Pennsylvania supporting the passage of legislation that would protect the property rights of married women. In 1848 the Pennsylvania and New York legislatures passed laws providing such protection. The same year Grew was one of those who signed the call for the first women's rights convention, held in Seneca Falls, New York. Although her name is included in the convention's Committee on Social Relations, Grew is not listed among those who actually attended the gathering—ill health perhaps prevented her from traveling. Grew, however, was a key participant in the 1854 and 1860 women's rights conventions, working on their business committees and giving the closing address at the 1860 meeting.

During the Civil War, Grew worked tirelessly to promote emancipation and after the war to ensure that the freedom granted to African Americans was meaningful. At the war's end, Grew argued against the immediate disbanding of the antislavery societies, not only pointing out that several states of the former Confederacy sought to continue to discriminate against blacks but also noting that blacks in the northern states were also subjected to individual and institutionalized racism. Convinced that blacks would only achieve equality if they had the vote, she opposed the dissolution of the PFASS until it was clear that the Fifteenth Amendment would be ratified.

Having helped to secure the franchise for black Americans, Grew renewed her efforts to secure the vote for women, and in 1869 she was elected president of the newly established Pennsylvania Woman Suffrage Association, a position she held until 1892. After the split in the national women's movement in 1869, Grew had aligned herself with the American Woman Suffrage Association (AWSA), serving as its president in 1887. Whereas the rival National Woman Suffrage Association, led by Elizabeth Cady Stanton and Susan B. Anthony, regarded woman suffrage as one of a number of feminist objectives, Grew and her coadjutors in the AWSA were convinced that the woman suffrage issue was the most pressing problem. Only when women had secured the vote, they argued, could they achieve their other goals. Grew's interest in women's rights also impelled her to cofound and serve as the first vice president of Philadelphia's New Century Club. Like similar organizations elsewhere in the United States, the New Century Club addressed the particular difficulties facing American women, such as educational and vocational training. Grew's public lecturing career included addresses in Unitarian churches, the denomination to which she had converted from the Baptist faith.

Grew never married. She did have a wide circle of friends within the reform community. From the mid-1850s her closest companion was Margaret Burleigh, the widow of the abolitionist Cyrus Burleigh. Grew and Burleigh were housemates until Burleigh's death in 1892. Although Grew's contributions to public reform were interrupted on several occasions by serious illness, she nevertheless lived a long life and died in her Philadelphia home. Her reformist endeavors were well recognized by her coadjutors. Henry Blackwell, the husband of feminist-abolitionist Lucy Stone and himself an active participant in the antislavery and women's movements, praised Grew as "one of the most faithful and devoted" abolitionists and as "one of the most earnest and influential woman suffrage workers."

• Manuscript sources on Grew are included in the Anti-Slavery Collection in the Boston Public Library; the Sophia Smith Collection at Smith College; and the papers of the Philadelphia Female Anti-Slavery Society at the Historical Society of Pennsylvania, Philadelphia. Grew's abolitionist career is detailed in the *National Anti-Slavery Standard* and the *Pennsylvania Freeman*. Information on her postbellum involvement in the women's rights movement can be found in the *Woman's Journal*. The major biographical study of Grew is Ira V. Brown, *Mary Grew: Abolitionist and Feminist (1813–1896)* (1991). Information on Grew's life and contributions to abolitionism can also be found in Jean R. Soderlund, "Priorities and Power: The Philadelphia Female Anti-Slavery Society," in *The Abolitionist Sisterhood: Women's Political Culture in*

Antebellum America, ed. Jean Fagan Yellin and John C. Van Horne (1994), pp. 67–88; and Carolyn Luverne Williams, "Religion, Race, and Gender in Antebellum American Radicalism: The Philadelphia Female Anti-Slavery Society, 1833–1870" (Ph.D. diss., Univ. of California, Los Angeles, 1991).

CHRIS DIXON

GREW, Theophilus (?–1759), schoolteacher and mathematician, was of unknown parentage. There is no extant information on his early personal life or education. By the early 1730s he was skilled enough in astronomical computations to prepare almanacs, and presumably he resided in Maryland. His first known almanac, *The Maryland Almanack for the Year . . . 1733* was published in Annapolis, Maryland, in 1732. In it, he describes himself as a "Student in the Mathematics." Subsequently, he calculated almanacs that were published in Philadelphia, New York City, and Williamsburg.

When Grew took up schoolteaching is unknown, but the earliest extant newspaper advertisement for his Philadelphia school dates from 1734. In that school he taught a wide range of mathematical subjects, ranging from basic arithmetic to various academic and practical applications of mathematics, including surveying, navigation, astronomy, accounting, and the use of globes. From 1740 to 1742 he was headmaster of the Public School of Kent County, Maryland. In the latter year he returned to Philadelphia, where he reopened his school. He also served as a consultant on boundary issues, especially the boundary between Maryland and Pennsylvania. At the November 1750 meeting at New Castle, Delaware, he served as one of Pennsylvania's commissioners.

A friend of Benjamin Franklin's, in 1750 Grew was appointed the first professor of mathematics at the College and Academy of Philadelphia (now the University of Pennsylvania), the first nonsectarian colonial college. He held that position until his death in Philadelphia. From 1753, he was permitted by the trustees to simultaneously conduct a private evening school. The college granted him an honorary M.A. in 1757.

Grew was married three times: to Elizabeth Cosins in 1735, to Frances Bowen in 1739, and to Rebecca Richards in 1747. The first two marriages ended when his wives died.

His most important publication was a text for his students, *The Description and Use of the Globes, Celestial and Terrestrial; with Variety of Examples for the Learner's Exercise*. Appearing in 1753, this was the first student text on the use of globes to be published in the United States. He also contributed a number of mathematical puzzles and solutions to newspapers. In addition, he was among a number of Americans who observed Halley's Comet on its 1758–1759 return.

By most standards, Grew is not an important figure in the history of science. He made no original contributions. His focus was on the application of mathematics to everyday problems. What he does demonstrate is the knowledge level of mathematical practitioners in colonial America and the availability of basic knowledge in applied mathematics. Bedini describes Grew as "one of the most notable colonial schoolmasters" (p. 157), a fair judgment.

• What is known about Grew is derived almost entirely from his publications and newspapers. The most useful of the latter are the *American Weekly Mercury* and the *Pennsylvania Gazette*. For context, see Silvio A. Bedini, *Thinkers and Tinkers: Early American Men of Science* (1975).

MARC ROTHENBERG

GREY, Zane (31 Jan. 1872–23 Oct. 1939), author of romantic novels about the American West, was born in Zanesville, Ohio, the son of Lewis Gray, a dentist, and Alice Josephine Zane. His mother, aware that Queen Victoria's favorite color was pearl gray, named him Pearl Zane Gray. His middle name derived from his great-great-grandfather, Ebenezer Zane, whose service in the American Revolution had permitted him to settle land in south central Ohio. Growing up, Pearl had to fend off mischievous children teasing him about his name; even after he began his literary career he received letters addressed to "Miss Gray" or "Mrs. Gray." Eventually, he dropped Pearl from his name, kept Zane, and, showing that he, like his mother, could be influenced by the English, changed the "a" in his last name to "e," henceforth being known as Zane Grey.

He initially followed his father into dentistry, majoring in that subject while attending the University of Pennsylvania on a baseball scholarship. Not a serious student, he was more interested in developing his curve ball than in learning about teeth. After graduation, in 1896, he set up a practice in Manhattan but yearned for the out-of-doors he had known back in Zanesville. He played baseball for local leagues and fished at every opportunity. During one fishing trip, on the Delaware River near Lackawaxen, Pennsylvania, Grey met his future wife, Lina Roth, whom he called "Dolly." In 1902 his article "A Day on the Delaware" was published in *Recreation*, and in 1905 he was married to Dolly. They had three children.

His first novel, *Betty Zane* (1903), published at his own expense, was the beginning of what came to be known as the Ohio River trilogy. The other works comprising this collection were *Spirit of the Border* (1905) and *The Last Trail* (1906). In 1907 Grey met the renowned frontiersman Charles Jesse "Buffalo" Jones, who invited him to go west. This invitation changed Grey's life. For one thing, it induced him to give up dentistry and devote the rest of his life to writing. Also, the invitation determined the subject matter of his most popular books for the next several years and ultimately helped determine what millions of Americans over several generations would choose for their reading material. Grey wrote *The Last of the Plainsmen* (1908) about Jones.

His first popularly successful work, *Riders of the Purple Sage* (1912), is the book for which Grey is most remembered. Good reviews assured a wide readership (although Grey did not get on the bestseller list until

1915 with *The Lone Star Ranger*). The *Review of Reviews* liked *Riders* in part because it was "pure Americana." *Riders* dealt with the Mormons, whom Grey liked on an individual basis although he scorned the Mormon church as an institution. The sequel to *Riders, The Rainbow Trail*, continued his account of Mormonism in America.

Through his great-great-grandmother Elizabeth McCullough Zane, Grey claimed an Indian heritage. In his books he defended the Indians, saying they did not become brutal until they themselves were brutalized by the white man. His great Indian novel, *The Vanishing American*, was first published in 1925 and was reissued in an unexpurgated edition in 1982. In the latter edition, the main character, Nophaie, marries his white sweetheart, whereas he dies without marrying in the original edition because publishers in 1925 were unwilling to bring out a book in which a man and woman of different races became husband and wife.

Grey's novels refined the popular image of the cowboy. A typical Grey cowboy starts out in the East, where he is weak and sickly with a racking cough. He goes west—probably to Arizona—to see if his condition might improve. A few months later, this same person is strong and healthy; his cough is gone, he rides a horse and herds cattle, and he rescues fair damsels in distress. This formula of overdrawn characters and idealized descriptions caught on with the general reading public. In their day, Grey's books sold better than had any works in U.S. history, with the exception of the Bible and McGuffey's Readers.

Grey also authored about a dozen books on the subject of fishing. He held fishing records for a time, and it has been said (mostly in fanzines) that his experience in catching a big fish inspired his friend Ernest Hemingway's *The Old Man and the Sea*. Grey wrote about catching a big fish and having it ravaged by sharks in *Tales of Tahitian Waters* (1931). Over a hundred movies were made of his ninety-five western novels and fishing books.

Grey was often querulous, impatient with people in regard to royalty checks, appointments, and the like. Some reports claimed that for a time he was obsessed with the idea of fishing with the most famous angler of the early 1930s, President Herbert Hoover. His books, however, continued to belie any implication of social climbing with their sympathetic descriptions of the common man and scorn for the social elite.

For many years deemed "subliterary," Grey has come into his own as his works receive attention in high school and college classes. Ironically, as sales of his books decline, his popularity in classrooms increases. His works describe the Great West as it was before the era of fast highways and multitudes of tourists—in reality with reference to physical descriptions and in myth with reference to characters. They have remained important to much of the reading public (as evidenced by the stream of new paperbacks that come out each year) and because of their delineations, descriptions, and characterizations of another time are becoming academically significant.

Grey had homes all over the United States: in Lackawaxen, Pennsylvania; Key West, Florida; and Seabright, New Jersey, for example. His permanent residence, however, was in Altadena, California. In his Altadena home he installed a fishing rod attached to heavy weights that he used to practice for deep-sea fishing. While using this rod, he suffered a fatal heart attack.

• Grey letters and manuscripts may be found in the Daniel Beard Collection and Zane Grey Collection, Library of Congress, Washington, D.C.; the Robert Hobart Davis Collection, New York Public Library; the Edwin Markham Collection, Wagner College, Staten Island, N.Y.; and the Zane Grey Collection, University of Texas at Austin. Some of Grey's articles that provide insight into his life and philosophy are "Breaking Through: The Story of My Own Life," *American Magazine*, July 1924, pp. 11–13; "Down into the Desert," *Ladies' Home Journal*, Jan. 1924, pp. 8–9; "The Man Who Influenced Me Most," *American Magazine*, Aug. 1926, pp. 52–55, 130–36; and "What the Desert Means to Me," *American Magazine*, Nov. 1924, pp. 5–8. The best full biography is Frank Gruber, *Zane Grey* (1970), though it is loosely organized and does not discuss the motives behind Grey's work. Scholarly works dealing with aspects of Grey's life and writings include Carlton Jackson, *Zane Grey* (rev. ed., 1989); Candace Kant, *Zane Grey's Arizona* (1984); G. M. Farley, *Zane Grey: A Documented Portrait* (1986); Joseph Lawrence Wheeler, "Zane Grey's Impact on American Life and Letters: A Study in the Popular Novel" (Ph.D. diss., George Peabody College for Teachers, 1975); and Danny G. Goble, "Zane Grey's West: An Intellectual Reaction" (M.A. thesis, Univ. of Oklahoma, 1969).

CARLTON JACKSON

GRIDLEY, Charles Vernon (24 Nov. 1844–5 June 1898), naval officer, was born in Logansport, Indiana, the son of Franklin Gridley, a businessman, and Ann Eliza Sholes. Gridley's mother was more active than his father, who suffered poor health. Her work as a nurse during the Civil War was acknowledged by Generals Ulysses S. Grant, William T. Sherman, and Philip H. Sheridan. She would long be employed in the Patent Office and then the Land Office in Washington, D.C. She was a devout Episcopalian, as was her son.

Gridley entered Hillsdale College in Michigan as a preparatory student in 1857 and in 1860 received an appointment from Congressman Henry Waldron to the U.S. Naval Academy, Annapolis, while still short of his sixteenth birthday. Under the pressure of the Civil War, the USNA class of 1864 passed out early, the top half of the class in May 1863 and the lower half in September. Gridley was firmly located in the bottom half; of the twenty-one members of his class still on active duty in 1898, Gridley stood eighteenth.

Commissioned ensign on 1 October 1863, Gridley's first assignment was the USS *Oneida*, and on 5 August 1864 he saw action aboard the ship at the battle of Mobile Bay, where his conduct was commended. After the Civil War, Gridley experienced the typical life of an officer in the peacetime navy. He was promoted to master on 10 November 1866 and lieutenant on 21 February 1867, and he became a lieutenant commander on 12 March 1868, but it would be 10 March 1882 before he reached the rank of commander and 14 March 1897 before he received the rank of captain. The early promotions followed by the long wait to reach commander and captain were the result of the promotion hump the Civil War created in the officer corps.

Gridley's experience in the late nineteenth-century navy was considerable. He served in the *Brooklyn* on the South Atlantic Station from 4 October 1865 to 11 September 1868, after which he joined the *Kearsarge* on 24 January 1868 on the South Pacific Station, where he remained until October 1870. He was assigned to the *Michigan* on the Great Lakes in January 1871 when the ship was at Erie, Pennsylvania. In Erie, he married Harriet Frances Vincent, daughter of Judge John P. Vincent, in 1872; they had three children. Gridley was detached from the *Michigan* in July 1873 and joined the *Monongahela* on the South Atlantic Station in September of that year, where he remained until April 1875, when he joined the staff of the U.S. Naval Academy as instructor in seamanship. He was executive officer of the training ship *Constellation* for periods in 1877 and 1878.

Gridley joined the *Trenton*, flagship of the European Squadron, on 7 December 1879 as its executive officer. He served in this capacity until 9 November 1881. Shore assignments followed at the Newport Torpedo Station in 1882 and the Boston Navy Yard from 1882 to 1884. He commanded successively the training ships *Jamestown* and *Portsmouth* in the period 1884–1886. Gridley then became inspector of the Tenth Lighthouse District based in Buffalo, New York, from July 1887 to October 1891, convenient to the family home in Erie. He served briefly at the Washington Navy Yard before assignment to the Asiatic Station, where on 21 July 1892 he assumed command of the USS *Marion*. He decommissioned it in July 1894 at Mare Island, California, before taking up duty again as inspector of the Tenth Lighthouse District from August 1894 until April 1897.

Gridley returned to the Asiatic Station, where he assumed command of the USS *Olympia*, flagship of the Asiatic Squadron, on 28 July 1897. Commodore George Dewey became flag officer on the station at the beginning of 1898. With the outbreak of the Spanish-American War, Dewey's force sailed from Hong Kong for the Philippines, where the battle of Manila Bay was fought on 1 May 1898. As the *Olympia*, leading the American squadron, approached the Spanish fleet, Dewey waited until the range had fallen to about 5,000 yards when he told his flag captain: "You may fire when you are ready, Gridley" (Dewey, p. 214). Gridley fired several shots until satisfied he was in hitting range of the enemy. He then turned his ship parallel to the Spanish force to bring his port battery to bear and opened rapid fire, continuing at close range until the action ended.

Captain Gridley did not long outlive the victorious action at Manila Bay. His health failed rapidly, and he was found unfit for duty by a medical board of survey on 23 May. He was en route to the United States aboard the steamer *Coptic* when he died at Kobe, Japan.

Gridley's fame rests entirely on Dewey's instruction to him at the battle of Manila Bay. Otherwise, his career reveals nothing remarkable about the man. With a reputation as a good ship handler and popular with his crews, he typified the average rather than the extraordinary in the U.S. Navy of his era.

• Gridley's career can be followed in successive editions of Navy Department, Bureau of Naval Personnel, *Register of Commissioned and Warrant Officers of the United States Navy and Marine Corps*, and is summarized in Lewis R. Hamersly, *Records of Living Officers of the U.S. Navy and Marine Corps*, 6th ed. (1898). A full-length biography is Maxwell P. Schoenfeld, *Charles Vernon Gridley: A Naval Career* (1983), which contains source notes and a bibliography. Thomas Boslooper, *Capt. Charles Vernon Gridley* (1993), contains letters to, by, and about Gridley in 1898. There is a flattering account of Gridley in George Dewey, *Autobiography of George Dewey* (1913).

M. P. SCHOENFELD

GRIDLEY, Jeremiah (10 Mar. 1702–10 Sep. 1767), lawyer, was born in Boston, Massachusetts, the son of Captain Richard Gridley, a currier and minor public official, and Rebecca (maiden name unknown). Gridley received his A.B. (1725) and M.A. (1727) from Harvard and taught at Boston's South Grammar School from 1727 until 1733. About 1730 he married Abigail Lewis; they had three daughters. In 1731 he founded the *Weekly Rehearsal*, a literary journal that he edited until 1733. Though he had studied for the ministry, Gridley entered upon a career in the law. In 1734 his name begins to appear as attorney in the Superior Court records, and he was soon recognized as a leading lawyer. In 1742 the House of Representatives, wishing suit to be brought against delinquent Land Bank shareholders, elected him attorney general in defiance of Governor William Shirley's prerogative to fill that office. The House did not insist on Gridley's election, however, because the governor authorized the appointed incumbent to bring suit. In 1746, and again in 1761, Gridley was appointed a justice of the peace and of the quorum for Suffolk County.

One of the founders of Boston's West Church in 1737, Gridley was an "Old Light," a supporter of Puritan orthodoxy against the evangelistic "New Lights." He was active in manufacturing, real estate, and further literary ventures, and in 1742 he helped to establish the organization that he later incorporated as the Boston Marine Society. Joining St. John's Lodge of Masons in 1748, he rapidly became a leader in the order and served as grand master for North America from 1754 until his death. In 1755, after his wife died, Gridley moved to Brookline where he joined the First Parish Church, was perennially elected moderator, and held other local offices. From 1755 to 1757, he represented Brookline in the General Court. Support of the unpopular war measures of Britain's North American commander in chief, Lord Loudon, cost him his seat.

It was as a lawyer and teacher of lawyers that Gridley made his greatest contribution. In 1758, when John Adams sought and obtained his assistance in gaining admission to practice, Gridley was the acknowledged leader of the bar. He had trained many leading lawyers, including William Cushing, later a U.S. Supreme Court justice; patriot activist James Otis, Jr.; and Benjamin Prat, chief justice of New York from 1761 to 1763. Gridley's success as teacher was founded upon an encyclopedic and enthusiastic grasp of both the English common law and the Roman and civil law, the principal works of which were in his extensive library. For Adams, Gridley laid out a comprehensive course of study and offered timeless advice: "pursue the Study of the Law rather than the Gain of it. Pursue the Gain of it enough to keep out of the Briars, but give your main Attention to the study of it" (Adams, *Diary*, 25 Oct. 1758). Adams and other young lawyers continued to follow this advice, most notably in the "Sodality," a group organized by Gridley in 1765 that met weekly to read and discuss the classic works of the feudal law and inspired Adams's earliest serious writing on political theory.

In his most famous case, Gridley argued before the Massachusetts Superior Court in 1761 that the British Parliament could give, and had given, that court power to issue writs of assistance to royal customs officers even though they might invade the "Priviledge of House." Gridley prevailed, but for the youthful Adams, whose courtroom notes have preserved the scene, "the child Independance was born" in James Otis's eloquent and radical counterargument that the "Priviledge" was a fundamental principle that Parliament could not override. During the Stamp Act crisis of 1765, despite (or perhaps because of) this prior engagement for the Crown, Gridley was appointed, with Otis and Adams, to present to the governor and council Boston's arguments for reopening the courts.

In his last years, Gridley's life seems tinged with darkness. Adams described him as "in a very trifling Humour" and "not in Trim. . . . I never saw him more out of Spirits" (*Diary*, 13 Jan. and 28 July 1766). In the spring of 1767 Governor Francis Bernard appointed Gridley attorney general, as well as a colonel in the militia. He was also elected to represent Brookline in the General Court. These circumstances suggest a blatant use of patronage to secure his support in the House for the election of councilors favorable to the Crown. In any event, his legislative service was interrupted by illness in June 1767, and he did not appear as attorney general at the August term of the Superior Court.

Gridley died in Brookline of "a rising of the lights." Whether this statement in the First Parish Church records was a medical diagnosis or an allusion to Gridley's increasingly unorthodox theology is unclear. Despite rumors of unrepentance, his obituary, accompanied by a long poetic eulogy, stated that he died "with a Philosophical Calmness and Fortitude, that resulted from the steady Principles of his Religion." Whatever the theological context, his funeral was a spectacular parade of dignitaries, with Boston's arch political rivals, Lieutenant Governor Thomas Hutchinson and James Otis, among the pallbearers.

Gridley's example and teaching set new standards of learning and discipline for the generation of lawyers whose talents were essential to the American Revolution, the subsequent period of constitution making, and the early years of the new republic. He was well liked socially and active in public service, but his difficult public personality apparently barred him from a real leadership role. Rev. Charles Chauncy, a patriot unsympathetic to Gridley's moderate politics, said, "Haughtiness of spirit accompanied him wherever he went. . . . He had too high an opinion of himself, and was too unready to make those condescencions that are necessary to a Courtier. . . . The only way of access to him was by flattery" (Shipton, p. 529). Adams's observations strike a more sympathetic balance: "Gridleys Grandeur consists in his great Learning, his great Parts and his majestic Manner. But is diminished by stiffness and affectation" (*Diary*, Apr. 1759).

• The most authoritative biography of Gridley is in Clifford K. Shipton, *Sibley's Harvard Graduates*, vol. 7 (1945), pp. 518–30. John Adams's many contemporary observations and later recollections of Gridley are found in *Diary and Autobiography of John Adams*, ed. Lyman H. Butterfield et al., vols. 1–3 (1961). Gridley's service to Brookline is documented in *Muddy River and Brookline Records* (1875), pp. 180–217. His legal career is documented in the Massachusetts Superior Court records and files (1734–1767), Massachusetts State Archives. Numerous minutes and reports of his court cases, including detailed treatment of the writs of assistance argument, are in Samuel M. Quincy, ed., *Reports of Cases Argued and Adjudged in the Superior Court of Judicature . . . by Josiah Quincy, Jr.* (1865), and L. Kinvin Wroth and Hiller B. Zobel, eds., *Legal Papers of John Adams*, vols. 1–2 (1965). See also John A. Schutz, *William Shirley, King's Governor of Massachusetts* (1961), pp. 61–62, for his 1742 election as attorney general; M. H. Smith, *The Writs of Assistance Case* (1978), pp. 269–92, for his role in that case; and Daniel R. Coquillette, "Justinian in Braintree: John Adams, Civilian Learning, and Legal Elitism, 1758–1775," in *Law in Colonial Massachusetts* (1984), pp. 359–418, for his influence on the reception of the civil law. Obituaries are in the *Boston Gazette and Country Journal*, 14 Sept. 1767, and the *Massachusetts Gazette and Boston Newsletter*, 17 Sept. 1767.

L. KINVIN WROTH

GRIDLEY, Richard (3 Jan. 1711–21 June 1796), artilleryman, military engineer, and entrepreneur, was born in Boston, Massachusetts, the son of Captain Richard Gridley and his third wife, Rebecca, whose maiden name is uncertain. His father, a currier by trade and an active militia officer, died when young Richard was only three years old. In 1719 his widowed mother married Benjamin Landon, a Boston shopkeeper. After grammar school, Richard was apprenticed to a merchant. In 1731 he married Hannah Deming; they had nine children.

First a shopkeeper and then an innholder, Gridley somehow managed to acquire a technical knowledge of artillery and fortifications, with the help of instruction from the gunner at Castle William, the principal fort in Boston harbor, and from a British military engineer, Captain John Henry Bastide. War between France and England was declared in 1744. The following year, Gridley was appointed lieutenant colonel of the artillery train of the Massachusetts-led expedition against Fort Louisburg, a French bastion on Cape Breton that threatened New England fishing and navigation by sheltering privateers and naval vessels. After the death of the chief bombardier, Gridley took over that function as an added responsibility and won acclaim for his accuracy. While at Louisburg, he drew a plan of the town, harbor, and fort that was published in Boston in 1746. He was rewarded for his services with a commission as a regular British army captain, and he retired on half pay when his regiment was disbanded in 1749.

For several years, Massachusetts employed Gridley to build or upgrade fortifications in Boston harbor and in Maine, to ward off possible French attacks. Then, in 1755–1756, he served as a colonel of the provincial forces in expeditions against Crown Point. He was chief engineer and commanded both a regiment and the train. He also participated in the second capture of Fort Louisburg in 1758 and of Quebec the following year. Meanwhile, he was associated in a project to make potash in western Massachusetts.

With the coming of peace, Gridley and his sons established a fishery on the Magdalen Islands, in the Gulf of St. Lawrence, principally for taking walruses. He claimed to have received an exclusive license from Major General Jeffery Amherst, in recognition of his services in 1758–1759. This probably was true although confirmation is lacking. Petitions to the Crown for an outright grant of the islands were rebuffed. However, in 1773 Gridley did receive, under a Crown program, a grant of 3,000 acres of land in northern New Hampshire, which he sold a year later for £100.

In 1770 Gridley joined two others in purchasing Stoughtonham Furnace, located about eighteen miles south of Boston. The possibility of casting cannon in the event of hostilities was a motivating factor in the enterprise. With the onset of the revolutionary war, the owners, with the help of lessees, cast ordnance stores and some small cannon for Massachusetts and for privateers. An attempt to satisfy an order for forty howitzers from the Continental Congress in early 1777 seems to have been unsuccessful. At best, the furnace venture was only marginally profitable. From 1772 Gridley had made his home a few miles away in the present town of Canton.

Gridley was an ardent Freemason, a group strongly committed to the patriot cause, and he readily joined the Massachusetts troops gathering around Boston after the battle of Lexington on 19 April 1775. He was appointed chief engineer and commander of the artillery by the Massachusetts Provincial Congress. These responsibilities and his commission as colonel were continued in the Continental army, but the brevet rank of major general that had been granted by Massachusetts was dropped. Both Massachusetts and Congress promised to replace his British pension at the end of hostilities.

Gridley sited and built a number of fortifications designed to threaten the enemy in Boston and to protect against forays inland. On the night before the battle of Bunker Hill, he laid out the lines and helped supervise the troops engaged in digging the entrenchments. During the engagement the next morning, he was wounded in the leg and had to leave the field. He also planned the important fortifications on Dorchester Heights whose occupation was the immediate cause of the British withdrawal by sea in March 1776. When the American army moved south, the aging Gridley was left as chief engineer of the Eastern Department, responsible for erecting fortifications around the harbors of Boston and other New England ports to prevent the enemy's return.

After the Revolution, Gridley largely busied himself with his farm and grist mill and in settling the confused accounts of Stoughtonham Furnace, which he and his remaining partner had sold in 1777. He also developed a process for making steel, and he produced some swords that bore his name. A Universalist, Gridley is reported to have defended his unpopular belief with these words, "I love my God, my country, and my neighbor as myself. If they have any better religion, I should like to know what it is." The veteran soldier, and this country's first chief engineer, died at his home in Canton, Massachusetts.

• Original plans of six of the Boston forts, drawn by Gridley or under his supervision, are in the map collection of the Library of Congress. Sketches of the fortifications in New London Harbor, in his hand, are at the National Archives. For additional information on Gridley, see Daniel T. V. Huntoon, "Oration," in *Memorial Services of Commemoration Day Held in Canton, May 30, 1877, under the Auspices of Revere Encampment, Post 94, Grand Army of the Republic* (1877), pp. 5–29. This article was essentially reprinted (without citations) as a chapter in Huntoon's *History of Canton, Norfolk County, Massachusetts* (1893), pp. 360–79. It may also be found in the *Magazine of History* 7, no. 5 (1908): 278–83; 7, no. 6 (1908): 336–42; 8, no. 1 (1908): 29–38. Huntoon and the article on Gridley in the *Dictionary of American Biography* (1960) are wrong in stating that Gridley was actually granted the Magdalen Islands. The article by Stuart R. J. Sutherland in the *Dictionary of Canadian Biography* (1979) is reliable except for an assertion that the colonel had a second wife. For Gridley's contributions during the American Revolution, see Paul K. Walker, *Engineers of Independence* (c. 1976). For his Magdalen Island fishery, see PRO, CO 323, vol. 18, pp. 196–210; PRO, WO 34, vol. 86, f. 262, and vol. 91, f. 238 (copies are at the Canadian Public Archives); Paul Hubert, *Les Iles de la Madeleine et les Madelinots* (1926); and A. B. Warburton, *A History of Prince Edward Island* (1923), p. 154. Other sources that mention Gridley are *Massachusetts Soldiers and Sailors of the Revolutionary War*, vol. 6 (1889), and Samuel A. Drake, *Old Boston Taverns and Tavern Clubs* (1917), p. 82.

DAVID B. INGRAM

GRIDLEY, Selah (3 June 1770–17 Feb. 1826), physician and medical educator, was born in Farmington, Connecticut, the son of Timothy Gridley, a farmer and deacon of the West Hartford Congregational Church, and Rhoda Woodruff. Nothing is known of his schooling, but he seems to have been well educated: he had some French, Latin, and Greek, his penmanship was elegant, and he wrote many poems. As a young man Gridley taught school during two winters in the southern district of West Hartford. In 1791 he began the study of medicine with Lemuel Hopkins, a Hartford physician, and in 1794 the Connecticut State Medical Society accepted him as a qualified physician. The degree M.D. sometimes appears after his name, but it is doubtful that he attended any medical school.

Gridley practiced medicine briefly in Connecticut and in August 1794 moved to Vermont. In 1795 he married Beulah Langdon, with whom he had six children. In the same year he set up practice in Castleton, Vermont, where he became a well-respected, busy physician and a prominent member of the community. His home was a center of literary and musical events, and he was named a trustee of Rutland County Grammar School and later of Middlebury College. In addition to his professional activities, he found time to be the first postmaster of Castleton and proprietor of a general store.

Gridley is best known for his pioneering work in organized medicine in Vermont and as a founder of the first of its three medical schools. At the end of the eighteenth century there was no regulation of medical practice, and medicine was more a craft than a profession; anyone could offer his services to treat the sick, and many practitioners, even the best prepared, had learned by apprenticing themselves to established physicians. Gridley was one of a small group of Vermont doctors who, in an attempt to improve the status of medical practice, undertook to follow some other states in the formation of a society to examine applicants for membership and to certify those it considered adequately trained. He helped organize the Vermont State Medical Society in 1813 and served as its president in 1815 and 1816. Gridley proposed that each president present a scientific oration at the annual meeting. The minutes record that on 16 October 1816 he gave a dissertation on the functions of the human stomach in health and disease. At another meeting Gridley was appointed to serve on a committee to work with the New York society to establish a national pharmacopoeia.

In the first decades of the nineteenth century the population of Vermont was growing, and there was some movement toward the cities. More young people anticipated that it would be possible to earn a living as physicians, and there was growing interest in earning the M.D. as a supplement to the qualifications for medical practice. Until 1818 there were no medical colleges in Vermont, and few Vermonters could afford to go outside the state to attend the lectures on the theory of medicine that, in addition to practical training with a preceptor, were needed to earn the degree.

Gridley, again a leader, joined with two other physicians—neither of whom had themselves earned the M.D.—to start the first Vermont medical school. He and a younger colleague, Theodore Woodward, both popular preceptors, recruited John Le Conte Cazier to the effort. They applied to the legislature and received a charter for a medical school to be located in Castleton and named the Castleton Medical Academy. Gridley and Woodward contributed a building, some books, and apparatus. The contract, dated February 1818, provided that the three men were to be proprietors of the enterprise, collecting student fees and sharing in any profits. The term "proprietary," first used here, was later adopted to designate other privately owned schools. The original charter did not mention authority to grant the degree; the proprietors arranged to have nearby Middlebury College perform that necessary function, and the custom of delegating it persisted for several years until the charter was amended.

With Gridley as its first president, the school flourished during the years when a country medical college could provide lectures, personal contact with good teachers, and the opportunity to observe a few of the professors' patients—all that was needed to give the students a grounding in theory. Before it closed in 1862 Castleton graduated more than 1,400 doctors, more than any other New England institution including Harvard. Many of these people, following the shift of population westward, become pioneers in medical education in the early medical schools of the Midwest. In 1822 the school's name was changed to the Vermont Academy of Medicine, and in 1841 it became Castleton Medical College.

As he approached the age of fifty and the height of his career, Gridley's life began to fall apart. He gave up some of his duties at the medical school, and in 1822 his wife divorced him. The settlement awarded her most of his property and directed him to leave Rutland County. He moved to Exeter, New Hampshire, to live with his brother Timothy, made a short attempt at medical practice, and died there.

The cause of Gridley's decline is not known. In 1820 an old friend was killed in an accident for which Gridley felt partially responsible, and he was thought never to have recovered from feelings of guilt. It does not seem likely that a busy physician who must have encountered many misfortunes in his practice would have been devastated by this one event; it is more likely that he was suffering from a psychiatric illness. Unlike his early poems, those written toward the end of his life are almost uniformly sad. As a devout Christian, Gridley might not have tolerated the idea of suicide, but he welcomed death and wrote, "Rest I must find in the deep rolling waters." "Friends forsook and foes assailed to bruise my broken brain," another poem complained. In a letter to his daughter Mary he referred to himself as a "deserted and degraded father . . . deemed unworthy to enjoy my family or provide for their wants." He wrote that his exhaustion had been misrepresented as intemperance and his ill health as ill temper.

Gridley may not have had much influence nationally, but in Vermont he was recognized as one of the leading physicians of his time, a founder of the state's medical society and of its first and most prominent medical school, an innovative teacher, and an agent in helping to develop medicine from a craft to a profession.

• After Gridley's death his brother Timothy published a book of his poems, *The Mill of the Muses* (1828). A brief autobiography is included in J. Fellowes, *Reminiscences, Moral Poems and Translations* (1828). John McNab Currier, *Epitaphs of Castleton (VT) Churchyard* (1887), is a collection of tombstone inscriptions; many of those in rhyme were written by Gridley. Frederick Clayton Waite, *The First Medical College in Vermont* (1949), is the best source of information on Gridley's life and influence. See also Lester J. Wallman, "Early History," in *Vermont Medical Society Handbook 1963*, and M. Therese Southgate, "Castleton Medical College, 1919–1962," *Journal of the American Medical Association* 204, no. 8 (1968): 698–701.

LESTER WALLMAN

GRIER, Robert Cooper (5 Mar. 1794–25 Sept. 1870), associate justice of the U.S. Supreme Court, was born in Cumberland County, Pennsylvania, the son of Isaac Grier, a Presbyterian minister, and Elizabeth Cooper. After obtaining a solid classical education from his father, Grier enrolled as a junior in Dickinson College, graduating in 1812. He remained there as an instructor for one year before returning home to help his father run Northumberland Academy, a private school. When his father died in 1815, the academy appointed Grier principal. In addition to his teaching duties, Grier studied law, and in 1817 he was admitted to the bar. After practicing law for a year in Bloomsburg, Pennsylvania, he moved to nearby Danville, where he was an attorney for fifteen years. During this period Grier supported his mother and financed the education of his ten siblings. In 1829 he married Isabella Rose.

In 1833 Pennsylvania's governor appointed Grier judge of the District Court of Allegheny County, in the Pittsburgh area. Thirteen years later President James K. Polk nominated Grier, a Democrat, to the U.S. Supreme Court. That seat had been vacant for two years as Polk and his predecessor, John Tyler, struggled to obtain Senate confirmation for their nominees. The Senate unanimously and speedily confirmed Grier, however. Politicians in Pennsylvania and Maryland supported his nomination, in part for his "warm if not violent" opposition to abolition (Swisher, p. 231).

At that time each justice held court in circuits outside Washington, D.C., besides hearing cases together in the capital. Grier's circuit included Pennsylvania, a key state for slaves trying to escape the South. As a result, the new justice found himself in the midst of rising controversy, particularly after Congress in 1850 strengthened federal law to enforce the capture and return of fugitive slaves. Grier regarded fugitive slave rendition as a solemn constitutional obligation, and he railed against abolitionists who advocated violent resistance to the Fugitive Slave Act. Not long after its enactment, he requested that President Millard Fillmore make federal troops available in case of resistance.

While he was critical of abolitionists, Justice Grier denounced "fanatics and demagogues" on both sides (*Oliver v. Kauffman*, 1852), and he drew fire from Maryland's attorney general for his role in one of the most famous cases relating to fugitive slaves. In 1851 armed blacks skirmished with Marylanders searching for escaped slaves in Christiana, Pennsylvania. With the slaveowner killed and several others wounded, the press sensationalized the incident. In a clear case of overreaching, federal authorities secured indictments against Quakers and blacks for treason. Although Grier considered the killing "an outrage," the first trial ended in acquittal following his instruction to the jury that the defendant's actions did not rise to "the dignity of treason or a levying of war" (*United States v. Hanway*, 1851). This put an end to the treason trials, as federal prosecutors dropped the charges against the other defendants.

Grier played an unusual, albeit secondary, role in the *Dred Scott* case (1857). Two weeks before the decision was announced, Grier informed President-elect James Buchanan of the Court's internal deliberations. Grier, anxious that the justices might divide along sectional lines, worried about "some rather extreme views" of the southern justices (Grier to Buchanan, 23 Feb. 1857, Historical Society of Pennsylvania). In the end Grier was the only northern justice who voted to invalidate the Missouri Compromise (federal legislation prohibiting slavery in some western territories). The antislavery *New York Tribune* (17 Mar. 1857) attacked Grier for lacking "moral stamina."

Grier strongly supported the Union effort during the Civil War. His most important opinion came in the Prize Cases (1863), "one of the most momentous in the history of the Court's interpretation of presidential power" (Rossiter, p. 68). Writing for a 5–4 majority, Grier endorsed the Union blockade of southern ports, undertaken initially by presidential order without congressional authorization. In so doing, he articulated a broad view of the president's war powers and limited judicial scrutiny over executive decisions in war. That Grier acknowledged some limits to war powers is indicated by his joining the strong majority opinion in *Ex parte Milligan* (1866), which ruled military trials of civilians unconstitutional where civil courts are open.

At the height of the political struggles during Reconstruction, Grier sharply criticized the Supreme Court for shirking its duties. After the justices heard oral argument in *Ex parte McCardle* in 1868, Congress, fearing judicial invalidation of its Reconstruction policies, moved to deny the Court jurisdiction. When a majority of justices opted to put off decision, Grier objected. In his view, this case, involving the military trial of a southern newspaper editor, brought into question "the liberty and rights . . . of millions of our fellow citizens." "I am not willing to be a partaker of the eulogy or opprobrium that may follow" the

Court's action, he said. While some Republican papers condemned Grier for this, conservatives applauded his "nerve and honest independence" (Charles Warren, *The Supreme Court in United States History*, vol. 2 [1947], pp. 482–83).

Grier's health deteriorated during the 1860s. Although partly paralyzed, he remained on the bench until his colleagues persuaded him to resign. He left the Court in 1870 and died in Philadelphia a few months later.

Grier sat on the Supreme Court for nearly a quarter century in tumultuous years. He delivered major opinions in many areas, including bankruptcy law, commerce, patent law, and federal court procedure and jurisdiction. Several of these opinions were important in his day, but few had lasting doctrinal significance. In twentieth-century ratings of Supreme Court justices, Grier is ranked as average. His opinion in the Prize Cases, recognized by Ulysses S. Grant as a "great service" in the nation's "darkest hours," stands as his most important contribution to American constitutional law.

• Grier's papers are in the archives of the Historical Society of Pennsylvania and the Dickinson College Library. Carl B. Swisher, *The Taney Period, 1836–64* (1974), provides the most comprehensive review of Grier's work on the Supreme Court. For a useful discussion of Grier's opinion in the Prize Cases and its doctrinal context, see Clinton Rossiter, *The Supreme Court and the Commander in Chief* (1976). Some insight into Grier as a trial judge can be gleaned from Jonathan Katz, *Resistance at Christiana* (1974). An obituary is reprinted in the *Albany Law Journal* (15 Oct. 1870): 294–95.

STUART A. STREICHLER

GRIERSON, Benjamin Henry (8 July 1826–31 Aug. 1911), soldier, was born in Pittsburgh, Pennsylvania, the son of Robert Grierson and Mary Sheppard. In 1829 the family moved west to Youngstown, Ohio, where young Ben displayed a talent for music and by the age of thirteen was leading the Youngstown band. The Grierson family settled permanently in Jacksonville, Illinois, in 1849.

In 1854 Grierson married Alice Kirk, daughter of a wealthy entrepreneur. In an effort to increase his income, Grierson entered the mercantile business only to see it fail in the panic of 1857. The outbreak of the Civil War found him and his family in dire financial straits, living with his father in Jacksonville. Grierson enlisted as a private in an Illinois infantry regiment and experienced his first combat action against guerrillas in southeastern Missouri. He impressed his superior with his courage and quick grasp of military tactics and was promoted to lieutenant. Additional recognition came with appointment as aide-de-camp to General Benjamin Prentiss, commanding in the area. An ardent Republican and staunch supporter of Abraham Lincoln, Grierson had excellent political connections and used them in seeking a better assignment. On 24 October 1861 Governor Richard Yates appointed him as major in the Sixth Illinois Cavalry,

and less than a year later he was promoted to colonel and commander of the regiment.

During the latter part of 1862 and the spring of 1863, which he spent in a series of skirmishes and hot firefights along the Tennessee-Mississippi border, Grierson won the confidence of Generals William T. Sherman and Ulysses S. Grant. In April 1863 Grant chose Grierson to lead a brigade-strength raid into Mississippi to divert attention from Union efforts to capture the Confederate fortress at Vicksburg.

Grierson's sixteen-day (17 Apr.–2 May), 600-mile raid from La Grange, Tennessee, through the heart of Mississippi, and on to Baton Rouge, Louisiana, was a masterpiece of its kind. It aided significantly Grant's seizure of Vicksburg and brought Grierson national acclaim and promotion to brigadier general of volunteers. Grant remarked, "It was Grierson who first set the example of what might be done in the interior of the enemy's country without a base from which to draw supplies." Sherman declared the raid "the most brilliant expedition of the war."

Grierson's career suffered during most of 1864 while serving under timid commanders who were twice routed by Confederate forces led by General Nathan B. Forrest. Late in the year, however, he was once more given an independent command. He conducted another devastating raid into Mississippi in the winter of 1864–1865. By war's end he was a major general of volunteers, leading a division of cavalry in Alabama.

In July 1866 Grierson accepted appointment as colonel of the newly authorized Tenth U.S. Cavalry, an all-black unit commanded by white officers. Except for two years, 1873–1875, which he spent as superintendent of the Mounted Recruiting Service, Grierson served with his regiment on the western frontier until 1888. The Tenth's areas of operations for two decades were primarily in Indian Territory, West Texas, and New Mexico Territory. Despite constant prejudice and discrimination, the regiment fought with distinction in the Cheyenne War of 1867–1869, the far-flung Red River War of 1874–1875, and in the Apache Wars from 1879 to 1886. In the summer of 1880 Grierson personally conducted an impressive feat of guerrilla warfare against the elusive Apache chief, Victorio, and cleared West Texas of Apache raiders.

In June 1886 Grierson was appointed commander of the District of New Mexico, and in November 1888 he assumed command of the Department of Arizona. He was promoted to brigadier general in 1890 and retired from the service on 8 July of that year. His first wife died in 1888, and in 1897 he married Lillian Atwood King. He died at his summer home in Omena, Michigan, and was buried in Jacksonville, Illinois.

Grierson has never received the credit he deserved for his long service to his country. As much a builder and developer as soldier, Grierson devoted much of his time to surveying, mapping, and locating sources of water in the areas under his care, particularly in Indian Territory and West Texas. A prime example was Grierson's recommendation of the site for constructing Fort Sill, now one of the largest military installations in the country.

A big-hearted, humane, and fun-loving individual, Grierson was an outspoken champion of American Indian rights and was always quick to defend his black troopers, who carried out their duties under a near constant drumfire of criticism. His consistent intervention on behalf of minorities won him few friends in or out of the military. He paid the price by going twenty-four years without promotion.

• A large collection of Grierson papers is in the Illinois State Historical Library, Springfield. Other collections of papers are at Texas Technological University, Lubbock, and at the Fort Davis National Historic Site, Fort Davis, Tex. For a family biography of Grierson see William H. Leckie and Shirley A. Leckie, *Unlikely Warriors: General Benjamin H. Grierson and His Family* (1984). An excellent account of Grierson's 1863 raid can be found in D. Alexander Brown, *Grierson's Raid* (1962). Grierson's career in the West is detailed in William H. Leckie, *The Buffalo Soldiers* (1967). Shirley A. Leckie, ed., *The Colonel's Lady on the Western Frontier: The Correspondence of Alice Kirk Grierson* (1989), contains much useful information on the attitude of the Grierson family toward minorities. An obituary is in the Jacksonville (Ill.) *Daily Journal*, 2 Sept. 1911.

WILLIAM H. LECKIE

GRIERSON, Francis (18 Sept. 1848–29 May 1927), musician, writer, and mystic, was born Benjamin Henry Jesse Francis Shepard in Birkenhead, England, the son of Joseph Shepard and Emily Grierson. When Grierson was less than a year old, the Shepards migrated to central Illinois, where they took up frontier farming and became active in local abolitionist activities. The boy's parents taught him to read, using the Anglican catechism as a text. In 1858, when the family lived in Alton, Illinois, and during their first residence in St. Louis from 1859 to 1863, he may have had—the record is not clear—a little more than five years of formal schooling.

Grierson's musical life began when he was sixteen. He slipped into the house of an absent neighbor to try out the Steinway there and astonished himself by improvising genuine music. Although he later failed to deny reports that he never had taken piano lessons, he in fact studied with a professional teacher in 1865 after the family had moved to Chicago.

On the family's return to St. Louis in 1864, Grierson sought an audition from a professional vocal coach. His performance was so impressive that the coach immediately placed him in a major church choir. At twenty he gave recitals in several major U.S. cities, singing to his own accompaniment and improvising both music and words. When he went to Paris on his own at the age of twenty-one, the hypnotic power of his performances made him a favorite in recital halls and the salons of the social and cultural elite. Edwin Björkman, a contemporary critic, wrote of Grierson's music as "haunting" and as possessing "exquisite beauty, striking originality, a spiritual fullness that induces emotions of distinctly religious character."

These successes were duplicated in many other Continental cities and in London.

Becoming aware of the growing contention between a waning romanticism and a rudely vigorous realism in arts and letters, Grierson devoted himself to the cause of romance and philosophic idealism. Not until 1887, though, did he explicitly address the issues with a half-dozen retrospective essays published in the *Golden Era* of San Francisco. After 1871 he also became an avowed mystic. In 1874 he spent ten days at Chittenden, Vermont, with Helena Blavatsky and Henry Steel Olcott, the cofounders in 1875 of the Theosophical Society. Grierson held seances from time to time throughout his life.

From the mid-1870s through the mid-1880s he moved from city to city across Europe, the United States, and Australia. In Chicago, probably in 1886, he met Lawrence Waldemar Tonner, fourteen years his junior, with whom he formed an enduring relationship. They lived together until the end of Grierson's life.

Settling briefly in San Diego in 1887, Grierson became prominent among local Spiritualists, and he built the Villa Montezuma, a pretentious mansion financed by two San Diego admirers. For unexplained reasons he left the city abruptly in 1890 to spend five years in Europe giving recitals and renewing connections with old friends. During a residence in London from 1896 to 1913, he wrote eight of his nine books. Although they were frequently praised by competent critics, scattered evidence suggests that his writing produced only a modest income.

In 1899 he combined one of his given names with his mother's surname to produce the pseudonym by which he is known. He presumably took the new name to distinguish his reputation as a writer from the fame—or notoriety—he had earned as a musician and Spiritualist. He returned to the United States in 1913, partly because he foresaw the outbreak of World War I more clearly than had most of his contemporaries. He continued to support himself (and Tonner) by giving recitals and occasional lectures. His settling in Los Angeles in 1920 effectively marked his retirement. He lived there in poverty, but he continued to conduct recitals and seances until his death.

Grierson's piano improvisations evaporated as they were produced. He never wrote down a note, and his recitals, although not entirely impromptu on each occasion, were never twice the same. Partly for that reason, he is most likely to be remembered for his writing.

Although he was self-taught in writing, as in music, he somehow learned to produce a fluent and often sonorous prose. The essays give evidence of his wide and perceptive reading; their topics range through history, current affairs, and the arts. Although he usually worked from the premises of philosophic idealism, his reasoning was not always consistent or coherent.

Grierson's early essays (*Modern Mysticism* [1899]; *The Celtic Temperament* [1901]) are aphoristic—brief, sometimes charming, sometimes obscure, and always oracular in tone. The central technique is assertion; example and evidence are whimsical, partial, or absent. Broad generalization crowds out probing analysis.

Grierson's one durable work is *The Valley of Shadows: Recollections of the Lincoln Country, 1858–63* (1909). During his childhood he had absorbed vivid impressions of the prairie people and of the Sangamon region of Illinois. He witnessed the rising conflict of slavery and antislavery forces, and he came to regard Abraham Lincoln as a mythic hero. From this personal experience he shaped a book that is part historical fiction and part personal memoir. Although it lacks unity and focus, the work's undeniable power has been recognized by Roy P. Basler, Bernard De Voto, Carl Sandburg, and Edmund Wilson. Grierson's later collections of essays, notably *The Invincible Alliance* (1913) and *Illusions and Realities of the War* (1918), show his apocalyptic vision of an Anglo-American civilization threatened by Prussian militarism, hordes of Oriental immigrants, and the vulgarities of what he called a "ragtime" culture.

Writers such as Edwin Björkman and Claude Bragdon, who shared Grierson's mysticism, described him as a compelling and wise thinker, deserving of lasting fame. Arnold Bennett and Van Wyck Brooks, who viewed him primarily as a survival from the past, found him a comic figure and perhaps a charlatan, although they recognized some merit in his work. Those who have concentrated their attention on *The Valley of Shadows* find that book an enduring and in some ways original contribution to the annals of the nation. He died in Los Angeles.

• Grierson material is thinly scattered over fourteen locations. More than one or two letters are held by the Henry E. Huntington Library, San Marino, Calif.; the Newberry Library, Chicago; the Illinois State Historical Library, Springfield; Western Kentucky University Library, Bowling Green; the Horrmann Library, Wagner College, Staten Island, N.Y.; and the Charles Patterson Van Pelt Library, University of Pennsylvania, Philadelphia. Other material is held by the San Diego Historical Society. Works by Grierson not mentioned above include *Essays and Pen Pictures* (1889), *Pensées et Essais* (1889), *Parisian Portraits* (1910), *La Vie et les Hommes* (1911), *Some Thoughts* (1911), *The Humour of the Underman* (1911), *Abraham Lincoln, the Practical Mystic* (1918), and *Psycho-Phone Messages* (1921). Harold P. Simonson, *Francis Grierson* (1966), establishes Grierson's relationship to the intellectual currents of his time. Useful essays by Bernard De Voto and Theodore Spencer appear in *The Valley of Shadows*, 5th ed. (1948), and Edmund Wilson's generally favorable assessment of the work and its relationship to other Civil War books is in *Patriotic Gore* (1962). An editorial note and a brief obituary appear in the *New York Times*, 3 June 1927.

LYNN ALTENBERND

GRIFFES, Charles Tomlinson (17 Sept. 1884–8 Apr. 1920), composer, was born in Elmira, New York, the son of Wilbur Griffes, a manufacturer, and Clara Tomlinson. He was a precocious student, showing great flair and love for art and literature as well as for music. First bent upon a career as a pianist, Griffes, like most American music students of the day, studied in Europe (1903–1907). Among his teachers was the composer Engelbert Humperdinck. In Europe he perfected his pianistic technique and learned the crafts of harmony and composition. In course, Griffes discovered composition to be his true musical calling.

In 1907 Griffes returned to the United States and secured a position on the faculty at the Hackley School, a boys' preparatory academy in Tarrytown, New York. The post gave him a steady income and ready access to the publishers and general culture of New York City, but some critics have since felt that the drudgery of preparatory school life undermined his composing career, causing his genius to go underutilized and unappreciated. Most composers do spend much time teaching, however. Griffes's pupils were younger than those of many music teachers, but they ran the gamut of aptitudes that most composers face as teachers.

During school breaks and even while teaching, Griffes devoted his energies to composing. His early works exhibited a decided Germanic Romanticism, which appeared a bit old-fashioned. But by 1911 Griffes had turned away from this approach. At times he favored leaner musical textures and more dissonant harmonies, as exemplified by his Piano Sonata (1912). The sonata, which many critics regard as his greatest work, indicated the composer's potential for exploring the stark avant-garde aesthetics of the day.

A brilliant orchestrator, Griffes underscored the translucence of his music by the employment of exotic programmatic topics in many pieces. His orchestral transcription *The Pleasure Dome of Kubla Khan* (1912) musically depicted imagery both of medieval China and of the poetry of Samuel Taylor Coleridge. His *Sho-jo* (1917), an ensemble piece inspired by Japanese pantomime drama, and the five orchestral *Poems of Ancient China and Japan* (1917), in which he wove scales, harmonies, and instrumental colors of those Eastern cultures, were a thematic and harmonic revelation to his early twentieth-century American audiences.

It was in the impressionistic style of his French contemporaries Claude Debussy and Maurice Ravel that Griffes seemed to hit his stride and begin to gain professional recognition. Like other impressionists, Griffes possessed a keen sense of the lyrical qualities of each orchestral instrument and layered his music with rich and colorful orchestral textures. Griffes's harmonies and scales stretched listeners just beyond the bounds of traditional major/minor modality, as if to elevate them onto slightly unfamiliar pathways of emotions. The *Poem for Flute and Orchestra* (1918) holds the listener in a suspension of seamless melody, as the solo and orchestral accompaniment gently flow, with little perceptible cadence, in a kind of tense intoxication. Many critics applauded, and innovative conductors like Frederick Stock and Leopold Stokowski sought out Griffes and performed his works.

To what musical ends Griffes's considerable gifts would have led him is but sad conjecture. In December 1919 he came down with pleurisy complicated by pneumonia. As Griffes was convalescing at the Hackley School, some students and staff, fresh from the scares of the influenza epidemic, grew anxious to the point of hysteria. False rumors raged that Griffes was infectious with tuberculosis. Hackley's officials cowardly caved in, and Griffes had to be removed to a mountaintop sanitorium for consumptive patients. He did not belong there, and the banishment greatly depressed and weakened him. As he lay in his room he watched workmen digging about a water main and grew obsessed with the image that they were symbolically digging his grave. Surgeons drained a quantity of fluid from his lungs, but a second operation revealed that they had left a small metal piece in his chest, causing him even greater pain. Further emaciated and depressed, Griffes suffered a hemorrhage and died. He was only thirty-five and had written music for but thirteen years. The wealth of his short creative life and the portent of so much more led one critic to eulogize that his death "seems so unfair."

• There are several biographies of Griffes. For years the only work on the composer was John T. Howard, *Charles Tomlinson Griffes* (1923). Written shortly after Griffes's death, the work was very much a memorial and more a narrative of Griffes's life than an analytical study of his music. D. Boda, "The Music of Charles Griffes" (Ph.D. diss., Florida State Univ., 1962), capably analyzes many of the composer's works, as does an article by W. T. Upton, "The Songs of Charles T. Griffes," *Musical Quarterly* 9 (1923): 314. Two excellent books that thoroughly cover both Griffes's life and his music, as well as integrate the composer's career into the context of his era, are Donna K. Anderson, *Charles T. Griffes: A Life in Music* (1993), and Edward Maisel, *Charles T. Griffes: The Life of an American Composer* (1984).

ALAN LEVY

GRIFFIN, Appleton Prentiss Clark (24 July 1852–16 Apr. 1926), librarian and bibliographer, was born in Wilton, New Hampshire, the son of Moses Porter Griffin, a machinist, and Charlotte Helen Clark. The family moved to Medford, Massachusetts, in 1854 and after some public schooling there Griffin went to work at the Boston Public Library as a runner in 1865. He continued his education with private tutors and, rising steadily, he succeeded to more responsible positions: assistant (1869), assistant custodian (1872), custodian in the shelf department (1875), custodian of the building (1889), and finally keeper of books (1890), with extended duties in the acquisition of material. On 23 October 1878 he married Emily Call Osgood, with whom he had four children.

With the publication of his *Index of Articles upon American Local History in Historical Collections in the Boston Public Library* in 1889, Griffin was launched into bibliography, a course that would, by its conclusion, see him regarded as the field's foremost expert in any U.S. library. In 1894 his position was discontinued in a reorganization. A popular petition was offered for his reinstatement, citing his intimate acquaintance with the collection, his eminent standing in American bibliography, and his twenty-nine years' service, but to no avail. He then worked briefly for the Boston Athenaeum, which led to the publication of the *Catalogue of the Washington Collection in the Boston Athenaeum* in 1897. The *Washington Star* remarked of this work in 1903 that it was regarded "as the finest known example of logical and convenient arrangement."

He also worked for the Lennox Library in New York City and for the American Historical Association during this period. After the first building of the Library of Congress opened in 1897, John Russell Young, the librarian, brought Griffin to Washington, D.C., as an assistant librarian in the reading room. David C. Mearns, in his history of the library, described Griffin at that point in his career as "one of the most proficient technicians in the country." In 1900 Griffin was appointed the first chief of the library's bibliography division by Herbert Putnam. (They had just missed association at the Boston Public Library, Putnam having become director there in November 1895.) Griffin, himself a resource in American history, directed a staff of five working with a collection of nearly a million books and edited over fifty major bibliographies in the next eight years. The subjects of the bibliographies illustrate the attention of his unit to the political, economic, and social life of early twentieth-century America: Puerto Rico (1901); labor, government ownership of railroads, mercantile marine (1903); Chinese immigration, election of senators (1904); regulation of insurance (1906); railroads (1907); and workingman's insurance (1908). Many bibliographies began as answers to individual reference inquiries; many ended as publications of various government agencies or as congressional documents or were published by the library. Griffin's reference ability was quickly noted by both the Washington and the international press. The standard advice became: "When in doubt, ask Griffin." He was seen as "an explorer who doesn't travel" and pronounced "famous as a rediscoverer of facts."

With the death of Ainsworth R. Spofford in 1908, Griffin was appointed chief assistant librarian in his place. A tall, urbane man, Griffin was regarded by the staff as a wonder (Mearns, p. 145). Now second in command of the rapidly expanding national library, he became the library's highest authority for reference, research, and bibliography with responsibilities in the acquisition of material, his other long-term interest. The Brown University chapter of Phi Beta Kappa recognized him with an honorary membership in 1909. Although carrying much more administrative responsibility (he was acting librarian from December 1918 to September 1919), Griffin continued his genius with contributions to Appleton's *Cyclopaedia of American Biography* and Webster's *International Dictionary*, a bibliography on the ratification of treaties, an annotated catalog of the Finley collection at Knox College, and a work on the contributions of the Library of Congress to education. In keeping with the style set by the librarian and his other senior officers, he summered on the Maine coast, was a regular participant at Putnam's Round Table luncheons at the library, a gathering of which H. G. Wells had said, "I found at last a little group of men who could talk. It was like a small raft upon a limitless sea. I lunched with them at the round table" (*The Future in America*, 1906).

Griffin died in office after a brief illness. Putnam, who had been able to continue him in public service twice past the age of retirement, wrote two years later that he had "a remarkable flair for submerged material and a lifetime of experience in the disclosure of it."

Griffin had been a natural and forceful talent in handling bibliographic information at a time when the country's major scholarly libraries were in an early stage of development. He made his mark by establishing authority in citations, by acting as a resource in coping with a rapidly expanding field, and by setting a high standard of service.

• As no personal papers are known to exist and Griffin's only writings are bibliographies or short biographies of others, he is submerged and seen only in reflection in the organization of the archives in the libraries where he worked. Those of the Library of Congress are unusually rich. He does appear in David C. Mearns, *The Story Up to Now, the Library of Congress 1800–1946*, reprinted from the *Annual Report of the Librarian of Congress for the Fiscal Year Ending June 30, 1946*, and he is noted several places in the *Athenaeum Century, the Influence and History of the Boston Athenaeum from 1807 to 1907* (1907). His obituary is in the *Washington Evening Star*, 17 Apr. 1926.

JOHN D. KNOWLTON

GRIFFIN, Charles (18 Dec. 1825–15 Sept. 1867), soldier, was born in Granville, Ohio, the son of Apollos Griffin; his mother's name is unknown. He attended Kenyon College in Ohio but left in 1843 to accept an appointment to the U.S. Military Academy at West Point, from which he graduated twenty-third in his class in 1847. He was assigned to the Fourth U.S. Artillery as a brevet second lieutenant. On 12 October 1847 he was promoted to second lieutenant in the Second Artillery, with which he served in the war with Mexico, participating in General Robert Patterson's march from Veracruz to Puebla. Following the war he saw extensive service at various garrisons and on the frontier. His career with the Second Artillery took him to Florida, Virginia, New Mexico, Maryland, Pennsylvania, Massachusetts, Minnesota, and Kansas. He participated in an expedition against the Navajo in 1851, and in 1857 he conducted recruits from Carlisle, Pennsylvania, to Fort Leavenworth, Kansas. In September 1860 he was assigned as assistant instructor of artillery tactics at West Point.

On 25 April 1861, shortly after the firing on Fort Sumter, Griffin was promoted to captain in the Second Artillery and was ordered to form a battery of artillery from the regular army detachments stationed at West Point. Initially known as the "West Point Battery," it was subsequently designated Battery D, Fifth U.S. Artillery. At the first battle of Manassas on 21 July

1861, Griffin's battery was posted in a forward position on Henry House Hill, a key piece of topography on the battlefield. At a critical juncture in the battle, the Confederate Thirty-third Virginia Regiment was allowed to advance within musket range of Griffin's guns by the Union chief of artillery, because he thought they were Union troops. Griffin protested to no avail, and his battery was decimated by a volley delivered at point-blank range by the Confederate regiment. The great number of horses and men who were shot immobilized the battery, and Griffin was able to get only one gun off the field.

In 1861 Griffin married Sallie Carroll, a sister of General Samuel S. Carroll. They had at least one child. During the summer, fall, and winter of 1861, Griffin rebuilt and retrained his battery. His guns accompanied the Army of the Potomac on the Peninsula campaign, but on 9 June 1862 Griffin accepted a commission as brigadier general of volunteers and was assigned to command an infantry brigade in the Fifth Corps. On 27 June 1862 his brigade participated in bitter fighting at Gaines' Mill, where, after fighting stubbornly, they were swept from the field by an attack of Confederate general John B. Hood's division. On 1 July 1862, at Malvern Hill, Griffin commanded the batteries of General George Morell's division in addition to his own brigade. The guns and Griffin's infantry made a substantial contribution to repulsing the Confederate attacks in that battle. In the Seven Days' battles (26 June–1 July), Griffin's brigade lost 1,153 men.

Following the failure of the Peninsula campaign, Griffin's brigade was withdrawn and sent north to reinforce General John Pope's Army of Virginia. At Second Manassas on 29–30 August 1862, because of vague orders, Griffin's brigade took the wrong road and marched away from the battlefield. When the error was discovered, Griffin made no effort to find his way to the battlefield and was accused of making "ill-natured strictures" against army commander Pope. He was relieved of command until a court of inquiry could investigate charges of deliberate disobedience of orders levied against him by Pope. The invasion of Maryland by Robert E. Lee immediately after Second Manassas caused George B. McClellan, commanding the Army of the Potomac, to ask for Griffin's restoration to command until the campaign had been concluded. Lee's invasion may well have saved Griffin's career. His command served as a reserve at Antietam and was lightly engaged during the rearguard fighting at Shepherdstown, Virginia (now W.Va.), on 19–20 September 1862. No court of inquiry was ever convened against Griffin, and in fact, he was promoted to command a division in the Fifth Corps, which he led through the battles of Fredericksburg (13 Dec. 1862) and Chancellorsville (2–4 May 1863).

Following Chancellorsville, Griffin went on sick leave, but when he learned of the fighting at Gettysburg, he hastened to rejoin his division but did not arrive until the last day of the battle. He remained unwell and went on sick leave again on 24 October 1863.

When he returned in November he was assigned light duty, sitting on courts-martial until 3 April 1864, when he returned to command of his division in the Fifth Corps. His division participated in some of the bloodiest fighting of the battle of the Wilderness on 5–6 May 1864. On the afternoon of 5 May, after his division had not been supported as well as he thought it should have, Griffin rode to army headquarters and, in his characteristically blunt and bellicose way, complained to the army commander, General George G. Meade. Griffin's tirade was so virulent that Ulysses S. Grant's secretary, John A. Rawlins, thought it mutinous, and Grant suggested to Meade that Griffin should be arrested. Meade, who knew Griffin well, replied that it was merely "his way of talking" (Agassiz, p. 91).

This was not an isolated incident in Griffin's career. Colonel Charles Wainwright, chief of Fifth Corps artillery, described Griffin as "an inveterate hater, and so ugly in his persecutions" (Nevins, p. 348). On another occasion Wainwright described Griffin as "overbearing and supercilious as usual" (Nevins, p. 167). Griffin compensated for his unpleasant personality with a positive talent for leading men in combat. Richard Sommers wrote, "[Griffin] always fought his men and guns so well that he ranks as one of the most outstanding division commanders in Grant's entire army group" (Sommers, p. 231). Griffin was not always so careful of preserving his men's lives. During the fighting at Cold Harbor he asked Wainwright to place a battery in a highly exposed position, telling him, "You will lose lots of men, but then you will have a capital shot at the enemy." Nevertheless, it was officers of Griffin's tactical skill and pugnacious courage that maintained some level of effectiveness in the Army of the Potomac, despite the devastating losses they suffered during the spring and summer campaigns and the influx of unmotivated substitutes and draftees who replaced those lost troops.

Griffin commanded his division with distinction throughout the Richmond and Petersburg campaigns. At the battle of Five Forks on 1 April 1865, when the corps commander, General Gouverneur K. Warren, was relieved of command by General Philip Sheridan, Griffin assumed command of the Fifth Corps. He led the corps with characteristic aggressive energy during the pursuit of Lee's army to Appomattox and was appointed by Grant as one of the commissioners who carried out the terms of the Confederate army's surrender. One week before the surrender of Lee at Appomattox, Griffin received his promotion to major general of volunteers.

Following the war, Griffin was assigned to command of the District of Maine from August to December 1865 and then served as a member of the board that evaluated small arms for use by the army. On 28 July 1866 he was appointed colonel of the Thirty-fifth U.S. Infantry and was named commander of the District of Texas. On 5 September 1867 he took temporary command of the Fifth Military District, which included Texas and Louisiana. At the time he assumed command, Griffin's headquarters was located in Galveston, Texas, which was experiencing a yellow fever epidemic. His new temporary command authorized him to move his headquarters to New Orleans, and he was encouraged to do so for his own safety. Griffin wired a response to Washington, D.C., that to leave Galveston in the midst of the epidemic would seem like deserting his post. He remained, and within ten days he and his son were both dead from yellow fever.

General Joshua L. Chamberlain, who knew Griffin well, described him as "clear of vision, sharp of speech, true of heart, clean to the center." Despite the often unpleasant personality he displayed, Griffin developed into one of the outstanding soldiers of the Army of the Potomac. He has not received the attention that other more prominent officers did largely because he did not rise to corps command until late in the war.

• Griffin's official reports and some correspondence written during the Civil War are in *The War of the Rebellion: A Compilation of the Official Records of the Union and Confederate Armies* (128 vols., 1880–1901). Of particular interest is vol. 12, which covers the Manassas campaign and details the charges levied against Griffin by Pope. His military record is in G. W. Cullum, *Biographical Register of the Officers and Graduates of the United States Military Academy*, vol. 2, 3d ed. (1891). Many details about Griffin's Civil War career, particularly from 1863 to 1865, are in Allan Nevins, ed., *Diary of Battle: The Personal Journals of Colonel Charles Wainwright, 1861–1865* (1962), and in George Agassiz, ed., *Meade's Headquarters, 1863–1865: Letters of Colonel Theodore Lyman from the Wilderness to Appomattox* (1922). For operations of his division around Richmond see Richard Sommers, *Richmond Redeemed* (1981). Griffin's role in the final operations against Lee's army and the grand review of the Union army in Washington are described in Joshua Chamberlain, *The Passing of the Armies* (1915; repr. 1982). Obituaries are in the *New York Tribune*, 16 Sept. 1867, and the *New York Times*, 17 Sept. 1867.

D. SCOTT HARTWIG

GRIFFIN, Cyrus (16 July 1748–14 Dec. 1810), lawyer and judge, was born in Farnham Parish, Richmond County, Virginia, the son of LeRoy Griffin, a tobacco planter, and Mary Ann Bertrand. Upon receiving a share of his father's estate at age eighteen, Griffin went to study law at the University of Edinburgh. In 1770 Griffin, an Episcopalian, eloped with Lady Christina (Christiana) Stuart, a daughter of the Roman Catholic John Stuart, earl of Traquair. The next year Griffin enrolled in Middle Temple, one of London's four Inns of Court, remaining until 1774. He returned to Virginia that same year, but he went back to England in 1775 and tried unsuccessfully to obtain a share of the earl's estate for his wife. Money became a recurring problem for the Griffins, parents of two sons and two daughters. In 1776 Griffin was back in Virginia.

Griffin represented Lancaster County in the Virginia House of Delegates in 1777 and 1778 and served with Thomas Jefferson on judiciary committees. In 1778 and 1779 he was elected to the Continental Congress. Griffin attended Congress regularly from August 1778 to June 1780, allying himself with Middle States financial conservatives against radicals led by Virginian Richard Henry Lee. Consequently, the Lee party in Virginia criticized Griffin's congressional performance and ethics. Griffin served on the Board of Treasury, the Committee on Commerce, and the Committee of Appeals. He supported half-pay for life for army officers and protected the rights of Virginia.

In April 1780 Congress appointed Griffin to the new Court of Appeals in Cases of Capture, which heard all prize appeals from state courts. He was on the court longer than anyone else, serving until it was disbanded in 1787, when he was presiding judge. While on the court, Griffin moved his family to Philadelphia. He was appointed in 1782 one of the commissioners to meet at Trenton, New Jersey, to adjudicate a dispute between Pennsylvania and Connecticut over the jurisdiction of the Wyoming Valley. The commissioners decided for Pennsylvania.

Griffin's political fortunes in Virginia suffered some reverses, largely because he resided in Philadelphia. In 1783 he was defeated for election to the Confederation Congress, and in 1784 and 1786 he failed to be elected to the state's executive council. Lancaster County, however, sent him in 1786 to the Virginia House of Delegates, which he attended from October 1786 to January 1787. As a delegate, Griffin became friends with John Marshall, later chief justice of the United States.

In October 1787 and October 1788 Griffin was elected to Congress, attending and serving as president from January to November 1788. This appointment, he hoped, would help his children. He advocated the ratification of the U.S. Constitution, a document he called "beautiful in Theory . . . which will be found a Government of Safety and Energy." He kept fellow Virginian James Madison informed about the progress of ratification elsewhere. Observers praised Griffin's presidential performance, describing him as an intelligent, sensible, and affable man who did not permit his love of pleasure to affect his duties.

In December 1788 Griffin was elected to the Virginia Executive Council. Before taking his seat, he was appointed by President George Washington in August 1789 to a three-man commission to negotiate with the Creeks. Late in 1789 Griffin declined reappointment to the executive council because Washington named him federal judge for the district of Virginia. A sympathetic Washington realized that Griffin, a man of good character and a sound legal scholar, needed a well-paying office. Griffin had wanted to be ambassador to France and had enlisted the aid of outgoing ambassador Jefferson, but neither Washington nor Jefferson considered him fit.

As a circuit court judge, Griffin was involved in a case that became known as *Ware v. Hylton* (1796). In that decision, the U.S. Supreme Court upheld the circuit court's decision that treaty provisions compatible with the Constitution superseded state laws. In 1796 Griffin, expressing his loyalty to the Federalist party, wrote Washington asking that he be considered for the

Supreme Court. Two years later he asked Federalist president John Adams for a better-paying federal job because of his large family. Washington and Adams ignored his requests, although Adams appointed Griffin's eldest son a territorial judge after the son was recommended by Secretary of State Marshall.

In the 1800 sedition trial of Republican printer James Thomas Callender, Griffin shared the bench with Federalist Supreme Court justice Samuel Chase. Griffin made no effort to rein in the highhanded behavior of Chase, who refused to allow the constitutionality of the Sedition Act (1798) to be questioned. In 1802 Judge Griffin drifted into the Republican party and was welcomed by Republican president Jefferson, who congratulated him for no longer supporting the Sedition Act. Griffin's conversion saved him from being impeached along with Chase in 1804 by the Republican House of Representatives. In 1807 Griffin sat alongside Chief Justice Marshall in the Aaron Burr treason trial, where Griffin deferred completely to Marshall. He remained silent, and his existence is hardly noticed in the trial's three-volume record. Jefferson was appalled that Griffin did not intervene to restrain Marshall, a Federalist partisan. Three years later, as Griffin lay dying, Jefferson wrote President Madison that an independent man should be appointed district judge to replace Griffin, who had been "a cypher" and "wretched fool." Griffin died in Yorktown, Virginia.

• Griffin's papers are not extant. Some of his letters are in Paul H. Smith, ed., *Letters of Delegates to Congress, 1774–1789*, vols. 10–15 (1983–1988); Edmund C. Burnett, ed., *Letters of the Members of the Continental Congress*, vol. 8 (1936); and Robert A. Rutland and Charles F. Hobson, eds., *The Papers of James Madison*, vols. 10–11 (1977). The fullest biography is Henry S. Rorer, "Cyrus Griffin: Virginia's First Federal Judge," *Northern Neck of Virginia Historical Magazine* 15 (1965): 1346–57. For Griffin as an appellate prize court judge, see Henry J. Bourguignon, *The First Federal Court: the Federal Appellate Prize Court of the American Revolution, 1775–1787* (1977). For Griffin as a federal district judge, see Maeva Marcus, ed., *The Documentary History of the Supreme Court of the United States, 1789–1800*, vols. 2–3 (1988–1990); Albert J. Beveridge, *The Life of John Marshall* (4 vols., 1919); and Jane Shaffer Elsmere, *Justice Samuel Chase* (1980).

GASPARE J. SALADINO

GRIFFIN, John Howard (16 June 1920–9 Sept. 1980), author, was born in Dallas, Texas, the son of John "Jack" Walter Griffin, a wholesale grocery salesman, and Lena Mae Young. The family often moved to be with Jack Griffin, who traveled frequently. John Griffin was close to his mother, sharing her love of music. The second of four children, Griffin was described by his mother as a loner.

At age fifteen Griffin wrote to a French boarding school seeking admission. He was accepted and went abroad for the first time. In 1938 he graduated from the Lycée Descartes in Tours, France, and enrolled at the University of Poiters *Ecole de Medecine* to study psychiatry and work at an asylum. In September 1939, as war began, virtually all of the French medical staff of the asylum were conscripted. The nineteen-year-old American became head of the hospital's female sector. In his later writings Griffin noted how he utilized his position at the asylum to help smuggle German-Jewish families through France to England.

With France's surrender in 1940, Griffin returned to the United States. He joined the Army Air Corps and was soon on a three-year stint in the Pacific. Bored with his initial assignments, he volunteered for a post on the remote island of Nuni, where he was charged with gaining the islanders' trust. He married a native woman, but it was a tribal marriage, not legally sanctioned; within a year he was reassigned and never saw her again. At his next assignment, on the island of Mortai, he suffered severe head injuries while manning a radar tent during an artillery barrage.

In 1945 Griffin returned to the United States and received an honorable discharge. During his final physical exam he was shocked to learn he was legally blind. Subsequent visits to specialists revealed that he would lose his sight entirely. His medical career was cut short, but he was undaunted and returned to France to study musicology. There he became interested in the monastic life and Catholicism, and stayed for a period in a monastery. He returned to the United States a year later, engaged to a woman in France. Although they would never marry, he did find out that the informality of his first marriage would not prevent future marriages. Griffin and his French companion then lived on a farm in Mansfield, Texas. To earn a living Griffin became involved in animal husbandry and tutored local children in advanced piano. One of his pupils was a thirteen-year-old girl named Elizabeth Ann "Piedy" Holland.

In 1949, urged on by an encounter with New York drama critic John Mason Brown, Griffin began writing in a small space cleared out in the back of his barn. Griffin was able to dictate in French, then transcribe in English a first draft. It became his first novel, *The Devil Rides Outside* (1952). Dealing with the conflict of faith and temptation, it is based upon his stay in the monastery. The controversial book received an unusual amount of attention and was even banned in Detroit, Michigan. The ban was overturned by the U.S. Supreme Court in a landmark decision (*Butler v. Michigan*).

In 1953 Griffin married Piedy Holland, then seventeen years old. Griffin started work on a second novel. It was the tale of a professor's adventures on a small island. The book, *Nuni* (1956), closely follows Griffin's own experiences in the South Pacific. During this time Griffin was plagued by poor health. Already ailing with diabetes, Griffin also suffered from malaria. As part of a medical regimen, he took large doses of strychnine. In 1957 Griffin regained his sight and for the first time saw his wife and two small children. There was considerable controversy surrounding his blindness. Although his family was convinced of the medical basis for his disability, some of his friends were not. It was an event deemed worthy of national

attention: *Time* magazine reported that Griffin's blindness might have been "mainly, if not entirely, hysterical."

Nearly all of his writing up to this point had been fiction. With his sight back, Griffin turned his attention to journalism. In 1959, while conducting a study of suicide rates among southern black men, Griffin decided that "the only way I could ever hope to understand anything about the plight of black people would be to wake up some morning in a black man's skin." The idea for his third book, *Black Like Me* (1961), was born.

Griffin decided to dye his skin and travel the South without changing his name, background, or credentials. He was to be only a darker version of himself. It was a dangerous proposition because of the intense racial divisions of the time. Griffin declared that his motivation was his three children. He wanted a better world for them, free of the "dehumanizing poison of racism." *Black Like Me* describes in poignant detail the daily struggles caused by his skin color.

Immediately, the book was recognized for its innovative but controversial approach to an issue of national urgency. Griffin received death threats and was even hanged in effigy. A frenzy of media attention and social debate over the work ensued. He tabled his literary projects, including an autobiography, and devoted his literary energies to essays and articles on racism.

In 1968 Griffin was asked to write the biography of Thomas Merton, a close friend who shared Griffin's fascination with monastic life. From the onset of this project, however, Griffin was plagued by poor health; in 1973, with his condition worsening and the book still not complete, a crest-fallen Griffin was relieved of his authorship. From that time until the end of his life, he would occasionally find the strength to write in his daily journals, a lifetime undertaking.

Periodically isolated by his experiences as a young American in France, by his blindness, and by his interest in the monastic life, Griffin sought to illuminate for others what they could not see for themselves. A man simultaneously of the world and apart from it, Griffin's works concentrated on relieving the isolation of persecution and injustice.

• Griffin destroyed his personal journals written before 1950, but his journals from 1950 to 1980 and certain manuscripts are collected but unpublished, their location not determined. A collection of his letters is kept at the Harry Ransom Humanities Research Center at the University of Texas at Austin. Griffin wrote *The Church and the Black Man* (1969) and *A Time to Be Human* (1977), both studies of racial injustice. His personal writings while researching the book on Thomas Merton are found in *The Hermitage Journals: A Diary Kept While Working on the Biography of Thomas Merton* (1981). *The John Howard Griffin Reader* (1968) provides excellent selections of Griffin's novels as well as his magazine and newspaper writings. Beverly Stanford Frank, "John Howard Griffin: The Unshed Tear" (master's thesis, Univ. of Texas, 1989), gives a detailed account of Griffin from 1920 to 1956. Ernest

Sharpe, Jr., "The Man Who Changed His Skin," *American Heritage* (Feb. 1989), gives an account of Griffin's life, concentrating on his experiences while writing *Black Like Me*.

TODD C. FRANKEL

GRIFFIN, Marion Lucy Mahony (14 Feb. 1871–10 Aug. 1961), architect and artist, was born in Chicago, Illinois, the daughter of Jeremiah Mahony, a journalist from Cork, Ireland, and Clara Hamilton, a schoolteacher. Mahony grew up in Chicago in what is now part of suburban Winnetka, Illinois. She showed a facility for drawing and an interest in art that was fostered by her mother.

Following in the footsteps of her first cousin Dwight H. Perkins she studied architecture at the Massachusetts Institute of Technology, from which in 1894 she became the second woman to graduate. Her thesis project, "The House and Studio of a Painter," has been suggested as a prototype for the studio Frank Lloyd Wright built adjacent to his suburban home four years later. Returning to Chicago, Mahony drafted for Perkins for a year before beginning work in 1895 for Wright, then in his third year of independent practice. In 1898 she passed the new Illinois architects' licensing examination, the first such law in the nation, and became the first licensed woman architect in the country.

Beginning the same year Mahony commuted to Wright's new studio attached to his suburban Oak Park residence. She remained in his office on a regular basis until around 1904 and thereafter worked at irregular intervals until the studio closed in 1909. Mahony thus found herself at the heart of the progressive movement to create a modern American architecture. Centered in Chicago and inspired by the charismatic figure of Louis H. Sullivan, this group of architects, which included Wright, Perkins, Robert C. Spencer, Jr., and Walter Burley Griffin, has come to be called the Prairie School. In Wright's office Mahony designed furniture, glass, and decorative panels, including the fountain in his Susan L. Dana house (Springfield, Ill., 1904). She also made presentation drawings intended for publication and clients. By 1906 she had created a rendering style, partly based on Japanese prints, that became the hallmark of Wright's office for the next ten years.

Because Wright allowed his employees to accept outside commissions, Mahony occasionally prepared plans after regular business hours. In 1903 she designed for a family friend and mentor, the Reverend James Vilas Blake, All Souls Church, which was built in modified form in 1904 in Evanston, Illinois. Its crisp forms and geometric ornament betrayed the influence of Wright, coupled with Mahony's own decorative sense. In 1905 she painted an altar mural for the church, since destroyed.

By 1906 Mahony was living in Elkhart, Indiana, in the house she remodeled that year for her brother Gerald's family, and she was working part time as an independent architect. In 1908 she designed a house for William Burke in Three Rivers, Michigan, that, once again, was a variation of Wright's Prairie style.

In September 1909 Wright turned over his practice to Hermann Von Holst, a Chicago colleague, and left for a year-long European sojourn. Von Holst promptly hired Mahony to serve as chief designer, which involved completing buildings under construction, finishing the designs of other projects still on the drawing boards, and, in several cases, creating entire houses, including the Robert Mueller house in Decatur, Illinois, and the David Amberg house in Grand Rapids, Michigan, both in 1910. These are complex compositions derived from Wrightian forms, with characteristic ornamental designs that are Mahony's own.

For three large houses on the private street that included the Mueller house, Mahony convinced Von Holst to hire Chicago architect Walter Burley Griffin in 1910 to create a landscape plan. Griffin also lent a hand to the design of the Adolph Mueller house and helped Mahony with the major project remaining: a mansion for Henry Ford in Dearborn, Michigan, which Ford eventually chose not to build. Mahony had known Griffin in Wright's studio, where Griffin worked between 1901 and 1906; following their renewed acquaintance, in May 1911 Mahony and Griffin were married. They had no children.

Joining Griffin's office, Mahony created a new presentation format that consisted of interior and exterior perspective views combined with floor plans united into a single design. She also developed a technique of lithographing these ink-on-linen images to satin-finished silk, to which she applied watercolor washes. Otherwise, Mahony contributed to Griffin's work in much the same way that she had to Wright's: designing architectural ornament and decorative art objects.

In May 1912 Griffin won the international competition for the new capital city of Australia, Canberra, partly on the strength of Mahony's renderings. In July 1913 he traveled to Australia for five months to consult on construction of the city. Mahony was left in charge of the Chicago office. While in Australia, Griffin was offered a three-year contract to continue his work at Canberra. In the spring of 1914 the couple departed Chicago for Australia, making their home in Melbourne. Griffin's association with Canberra lasted until 1920, after which the couple decided to remain in Australia.

Mahony designed only one building in Australia under her own name, the Richard Reeves house, constructed in altered form in 1916 in East Malvern, near Melbourne. Her involvement in her husband's office varied through the years, but in general she devoted more and more time to artistic and social causes in Australia, to her deepening commitment to anthroposophy, and to the eccentric milieu of Griffin's planned suburb, Castlecrag, north of Sydney, where they moved in 1920. By the 1930s she had virtually abandoned architecture. However, she continued to work on spectacular drawings for a series of Australian trees, printed on silk and watercolored.

The Griffins returned to the United States in 1925 and in 1932, when Mahony designed a mural for Chicago's George Armstrong Public School. In 1935 Griffin designed the library for the University of Lucknow, India, and traveled in October to the site. Other commissions followed rapidly, and in June 1936 Mahony joined her husband. She managed the office, made working drawings, and drew watercolor perspectives of Griffin's final buildings. Once again, she created a rendering style that matched the magnificence of the architecture it portrayed.

In February 1937 Griffin died of peritonitis. Mahony closed the Indian office and returned to Australia, and by the following year she was back in Illinois. The outbreak of World War II prevented her return to Australia. She began writing an account of Griffin's Indian adventure that turned into a personal biography of herself and Griffin, eventually swelling into an unworkable manuscript of some 1,600 pages. Called "The Magic of America," it has never been published. She died in Chicago, Illinois.

If Marion Mahony Griffin was a capable architect and a pioneer among women architects, she was more important as one of the twentieth century's greatest architectural renderers, establishing the presentation style for which the Prairie School is known and giving visual expression to the revolutionary designs of Wright and Griffin.

• Many of Marion Mahony Griffin's renderings of Griffin's work as well as her own, are dispersed among Northwestern University, Evanston, Ill.; the Avery Library, Columbia University; and the Art Institute of Chicago, while her numerous drawings for Frank Lloyd Wright survive at that architect's archives in Scottsdale, Ariz. The two versions of her unpublished autobiography, "The Magic of America," are deposited at the Burnham Library at the Art Institute of Chicago and at the New-York Historical Society. General discussions of Marion Mahony Griffin's career include S. Berkon and J. Kay, "Marion Mahony Griffin, Architect," *Feminist Art Journal* 4, no. 1 (Spring 1975): 10–14; and A. Rubbo, "Marion Mahony Griffin: A Portrait," in *Walter Burley Griffin: A Re-View* (1988), which also includes J. Weirick's "*The Magic of America*: Vision and Text." Mahony's architectural projects are discussed in Weirick, "Marion Mahony at M.I.T.," *Transition*, no. 25 (Winter 1988): 48–54; and D. T. Van Zanten, "The Early Work of Marion Mahony Griffin," *Prairie School Review* 3, no. 2 (1966): 5–23. For analyses of her rendering style, see H. A. Brooks, "Frank Lloyd Wright and the Wasmuth Drawings," *Art Bulletin* 48 (June 1966): 193–202; and D. R. Munchick, "Marion Mahony's Architectural Drawings, 1900–1912," *Southeastern College Art Conference Review* 7 (Fall 1974): 5–14.

PAUL KRUTY

GRIFFIN, Walter Burley (24 Nov. 1876–11 Feb. 1937), architect and landscape architect, was born in the Chicago suburb of Maywood, Illinois, the son of George Walter Griffin, an insurance agent, and Estelle Melvina Burley. His family moved to nearby Oak Park and then to Elmhurst during his childhood; he attended Oak Park High School. In 1899 Griffin received a bachelor's degree from the University of Illinois in the architecture program instituted by Nathan Clifford Ricker. The program stressed a scientific and rational approach to the subject, with less emphasis on design and historic styles. Griffin returned to Chicago, and for the next two years he served as a draftsman in the offices of Dwight H. Perkins, Robert C. Spencer, Jr., and H. Webster Tomlinson, three among the handful of progressive Chicago architects who have come to be known as the Prairie School. Like Frank Lloyd Wright before him, Griffin came under the intoxicating spell of Louis H. Sullivan. Sullivan's call for a modern American architecture that was free from historic allusion was being answered by the architects for whom Griffin worked, and Sullivan's oration "The Young Man in Architecture" delivered in June 1900 completely changed the young architect's life.

In July 1901 Griffin passed the new Illinois licensing examination he was obliged to take before entering private practice, and he began working for Frank Lloyd Wright in Wright's famous Oak Park studio. Although not an actual partner, Griffin soon had a greater role in all phases of Wright's practice than his associates. He was also project supervisor for some of Wright's most important buildings, including the Ward Willits house (1902) and the Larkin Administration Building (1904). Wright permitted Griffin to maintain a small independent practice, which included designing the campus plan for the State Normal School at Charleston, Illinois (1901), and the William Emery house, built in Elmhurst, Illinois, in 1903. In 1904 Griffin began to supply landscape plans for Wright's buildings, and for three months in 1905 he took charge of the entire office while Wright was in Japan.

Early in 1906 Griffin established his own practice. During the next seven years he produced more than one hundred projects ranging from suburban estates to low-cost housing units. Beginning in 1909 these included an increasing number of landscape plans and schemes for subdivisions. His early buildings, including the houses for his brother Ralph (Edwardsville, Ill., 1909), for Harry Peters (Chicago, 1906), and for Frederick Carter (Evanston, Ill., 1910), are distinguished from Wright's Prairie houses by their heavier massing, their greater emphasis on symmetry and verticality, their interlocking, multi-level interior spaces, their termination in gabled rather than hipped roofs, and their use of diamond forms. Griffin's double house for Mary Bovee (Evanston, 1907), with its abstracted rectilinear massing, anticipated by two years Wright's famous house for Mrs. Walter Gale (Oak Park, 1909).

During 1910, when the *Architectural Record* still characterized Griffin's work as "strongly influenced by the success of Mr. Frank Lloyd Wright," his designs underwent a remarkable transformation. Bereft of overhanging eaves, buildings like the "Solid Rock" house for William Tempel (Winnetka, Ill., 1911) were massive, flat-roofed, and cubic, surmounted with roof gardens. Beginning in 1912 Griffin often added an expressive veneer of thick, rough-hewn coursed limestone in buildings such as the Joshua Melson house (Mason City, Iowa, 1912) and the Stinson Memorial Library (Anna, Ill., 1912), two of his masterpieces.

Because nothing survives of Griffin's reputed plan for an enlargement of Shanghai, China (c. 1905–1906), his earliest extant urban planning scheme dates to 1910. Griffin was mainly concerned with subdivision plans for suburban developments including the Trier Center Neighborhood (Winnetka, 1912), where he planned to live himself, but he also produced several campus plans, including the University of New Mexico (1915) and the Wisconsin State Normal School at Milwaukee (1914), and complete new towns such as Idalia, Florida (1911), and Mossmain, Montana (1915), none of which were carried out.

In 1911 Griffin married architect Marion L. Mahony, whom he had known for many years in Wright's office and who was then working for a Chicago architect, Hermann V. von Holst. Mahony, a fiery, theatrical figure, was the perfect match for the obsessive if serene and even-tempered Griffin. Mahony, who was one of the century's most talented renderers, became Griffin's de facto business partner as well.

Shortly before the Griffins' marriage the Australian government announced an international competition for the design of a capital city of 75,000 residents for the newly federated nation. Barely completed in time for the deadline in early 1912, Griffin's plan for Canberra was presented in stunning renderings by Mahony. On 23 May 1912 Griffin's design was selected as the winner from among 137 entries. The young architect was suddenly thrust into the limelight, both in the professional and popular press. After a period of negotiation the government offered to bring the winner to Australia for three months to inspect the Canberra site. An ecstatic Griffin embarked on 19 July 1913, leaving Mahony in charge of the Chicago practice. Griffin's letters home reveal how quickly he was enthralled by the Australian landscape.

Griffin's emerging prominence persuaded the University of Illinois to offer its famous alumnus the position of head of the department of architecture. After a period of discussion the actual offer was cabled to Melbourne in late September at the very moment that Griffin was negotiating with the Australian government for a three-year contract to oversee the construction of the new city. At the Canberra site Griffin had found that his plan was compromised by work that had already begun, and he was anxious to rectify the situation. Tempting as the Illinois offer was, Griffin rejected it to remain overseas. He soon embarked on a long, hard, and ultimately futile fight to save his capital plan. While in Australia Griffin also received commissions for town plans, subdivisions, and one of his masterpieces, Newman College (1915), the Catholic residential college of the University of Melbourne.

After years of professional abuse resulting from bureaucratic infighting, political squabbles, and changes of government, Griffin resigned his position as federal capital director in December 1920. For several reasons, including the closing of his Chicago office in 1917 after mismanagement by F. Barry Byrne, Griffin decided to remain in Australia, maintaining offices both in Melbourne, where the prospect of the commission for the Capitol Theater and office building loomed large, and in Sydney, where he had just acquired a substantial parcel of land that he intended to develop as Castlecrag, a planned community. His major works during years of financial hardship in the 1930s were an extraordinary group of garbage incinerators for local councils. He briefly returned to the United States in 1925 and again in 1932.

In September 1935 Griffin's design was accepted for a new library for Lucknow University in northern India. In October he agreed to travel to the site, and he was as exhilarated by the subcontinent as he had been twenty years earlier by Australia. He persuaded his wife to join him in May 1936. Commissions began to pour in, as the Griffins seemed to be reborn—he producing some of the most original designs of his career, and she providing yet another set of ravishing renderings.

In February 1937 Griffin suffered a ruptured gall bladder and died of peritonitis several days later in Lucknow. His wife closed the office in India, leaving the Australian practice in the hands of Griffin's partner, Eric Nicholls, and returned to Chicago to write her memoirs.

Griffin stands as the third great member, after Sullivan and Wright, of the Chicago movement to create a decorated modern architecture for the twentieth century. His buildings, landscapes, and town plans on three continents record a lifetime's dedication to this goal.

• The largest collection of source material on Griffin is at the Australian National Library in Canberra. The majority of the surviving drawings for Griffin's buildings, many of them executed by his wife, are in three American collections: the Avery Library at Columbia University, New York City; the Block Gallery at Northwestern University, Evanston, Ill.; and the Art Institute of Chicago. Part of the holdings of the Block Gallery are reproduced in David T. Van Zanten, *Walter Burley Griffin: Selected Designs* (1970). The standard biography of Griffin remains Donald Leslie Johnson, *The Architecture of Walter Burley Griffin* (1977), which is complemented by Peter Harrison, *Walter Burley Griffin: Landscape Architect* (1995). Griffin's surviving American buildings are fully documented in photographs in Mati Maldre and Paul Kruty, *Walter Burley Griffin in America* (1995). For Griffin's Australian work, see James Weirick et al., *Walter Burley Griffin: A Re-View* (1988), and Meredith Walker et al., *Building for Nature: Walter Burley Griffin and Castlecrag* (1994). For Griffin's work in India, see Kruty and Paul E. Sprague, *Two American Architects in India: Walter B. Griffin and Marion M. Griffin, 1935–1937* (1997). Two books that provide additional information on Griffin and his milieu are Mark L. Peisch, *The Chicago School of Architecture: Early Followers of Sullivan and Wright* (1964), and H. Allen Brooks, *The Prairie School: Frank Lloyd Wright and His Midwest Contemporaries* (1972).

PAUL KRUTY

GRIFFING, Josephine Sophia White (18 Dec. 1814–18 Feb. 1872), abolitionist, women's rights activist, and freedmen's aid reformer, was born in Hebron, Connecticut, the daughter of Joseph White and Sophia Waldo, farmers. Both parents were from prominent New England families. Though not much is known of Josephine's childhood and education, she embarked on a life of public activism after her marriage in 1835 to Charles Stockman Spooner Griffing.

Josephine Griffing left Connecticut for Litchfield, Ohio, in 1842 with her husband and became involved in the antislavery movement soon after. Their home was a stopping place on the Underground Railroad, and they were members of the Western Anti-Slavery Society. In 1850 Josephine Griffing was convinced by Abby Kelley Foster to become an antislavery lecturer, touring in Ohio, Michigan, and Indiana with Parker Pillsbury and Giles B. Stebbins. She wrote numerous articles for the *Anti-Slavery Bugle*, the organ of the Western Anti-Slavery Society. Griffing also began her active support for women's rights during this time.

Griffing's antislavery activism led her into the freedmen's aid movement during the Civil War. She joined the Loyal League, an organization of women who continued to petition Congress to free the slaves. Griffing then became interested in emancipation and petitioned the government to give women an official role in helping former slaves. "Your memorialists, women of the North and Northwest," she wrote, "pray that you will allow us to share more fully in the responsibility and labor, so remarkably laid upon the government and the men of the North, in the care and education of these Freedmen." Griffing's most important reform work was to be on behalf of the former slaves.

In 1863 Griffing and her three daughters moved to Washington, D.C., to work with the thousands of former slaves who had migrated there during the war while her husband Charles remained in Ohio. She joined the National Freedmen's Relief Association of the District of Columbia and urged the passage of the Freedmen's Bureau bill. In June 1865 Griffing was officially employed by the bureau as the assistant to the assistant commissioner for the District of Columbia. She emphasized her commitment to the bureau in a letter to General Oliver O. Howard, commissioner of the bureau, by stating, "No person has felt more interest in the creation and character of this Bureau than I have." Griffing's appointment was revoked in November 1865 after she gave speeches in the North to raise funds and to promote awareness of the impoverished situation of former slaves in Washington. The bureau leadership and some reformers disapproved of her methods and felt that the publicity would reflect badly on both the bureau and the freed people.

Undeterred, Griffing continued her efforts on behalf of the freedmen. In addition to distributing rations, fuel, and clothing, she also ran an industrial school for freedwomen and an employment agency. An important part of her mission in Washington was to transport former slaves to the North, where sympathetic whites, usually contacts of Griffing's from antislavery, freedmen's aid, and women's rights organizations, found them jobs and places to live. In this effort she was sometimes assisted by Sojourner Truth, who also worked with former slaves in Washington, D.C. Griffing was eventually rehired by the Freedmen's Bureau as an employment agent, but her relationship with them was never quite the same. While Griffing advocated a stronger bureau with an unlimited life span, Howard and other reformers turned to a laissez-faire approach to relief and the political solutions of radical reconstruction.

Griffing combined her interest in former slaves with women's rights. She was active in the woman suffrage movement in Washington and became the corresponding secretary for the National Woman Suffrage Association in 1869. In January 1870 she organized a large convention of the NWSA in Washington. However, Griffing's primary concern was for the freedmen. By 1870 northern interest had declined, and the Freedmen's Bureau and most northern aid societies had ended their operations, but she continued her efforts. When she died in Washington, D.C., in 1872, one of her obituaries stated, "she died of sheer overwork, faithful and earnest to the last" (*Woodhull and Claflin's Weekly*, 9 Mar. 1872).

During Reconstruction reformers and politicians debated the best means for integrating former slaves into American civic and economic life. Griffing was one of the few reformers who suggested that the government had a responsibility to all its citizens, including women and African Americans. She also belonged to a generation of women who saw their public status improved through voluntarism. Griffing proposed an alliance between women's voluntarism and the Freedmen's Bureau that would insure a place for women and blacks in American society. Most reformers disagreed with Griffing's position on the Freedmen's Bureau and argued that freed people should be independent of government support in order to prove their worthiness of freedom. As a result, Griffing and other female reformers had a less powerful voice in the federal government. The Freedmen's Bureau was a predecessor to the welfare state in America, but the American classical liberal traditions of self-reliance and private philanthropy undermined the impetus behind the bureau.

• A collection of Griffing's papers is at Columbia University, but many of her letters can be found in the Records of the Freedmen's Bureau in the National Archives, RG 105. The best source of information on Griffing is Keith Melder, "Angel of Mercy in Washington: Josephine Griffing and the Freedmen, 1864–1872," *Records of the Columbia Historical Society of Washington, D.C.* (1863–1865), pp. 243–72. For genealogical information see Waldo Lincoln, *Genealogy of the Waldo Family* (1902). The second volume of *The History of Woman Suffrage* (1970) also contains biographical information and an account of Griffing's activity in Washington. James McPherson, *Struggle for Equality* (1964), gives an excellent account of Griffing's freedmen's aid work in the context of other abolitionists' activities after the Civil War. George R. Bentley, *A History of the Freedmen's Bureau* (1955; repr. 1970), briefly describes Griffing's place in the internal politics of the Freedmen's Bureau.

CAROL FAULKNER

GRIFFIS, William Elliot (17 Sept. 1843–5 Feb. 1928), educator, clergyman, and author, was born in Philadelphia, Pennsylvania, the son of Captain John Limeburner Griffis, a coal dealer, and Anna Maria Hess, a pious young woman who for many years taught at an infant's nursery school and at a Bible school for young women at the First Independent Presbyterian Church of Philadelphia.

At the age of five Griffis entered a local dame school before attending one of Philadelphia's recently established public high schools, graduating from Central High School in 1859. Griffis served as a private in "H" Company of the Forty-fourth Pennsylvania Regiment, from June to August 1863. Promoted to color corporal, he missed seeing action at the battle of Gettysburg only because his unit arrived a few days too late to participate in the fighting.

After his discharge in the late summer of 1863, Griffis became editor of *Our Sunday School Messenger* (a publication of the Dutch Reformed church), engaged a tutor, and passed the entrance examination to Rutgers University in 1865. There he studied physics, chemistry, and mathematics. In 1869 he graduated fifth in his class and was inducted into Phi Beta Kappa. Following graduation from Rutgers and accompanied by his sister Maggie, Griffis embarked on a grand tour of Europe that enabled him to experience many of the cultural elements that were to shape his intellectual persona. He was especially influenced by his stay in the Netherlands, where his Dutch Reformed faith and his interest in Dutch history and culture were reinforced.

Upon returning to the United States in 1870, Griffis enrolled at the Rutgers Theological Seminary and taught at the Rutgers Grammar School (1867–1869), where the first Japanese students to study in the United States were his pupils.

Griffis's career was fundamentally shaped by the close ties between Rutgers and the Dutch Reformed church. In 1870 the Board of Foreign Missions of the Dutch Reformed church, responding to a request from missionaries in Japan, requested Rutgers to recommend a qualified person "to establish a scientific school on the American principle and teach the natural sciences." Griffis was ultimately offered the position, and he accepted it because, in addition to travel expenses, its terms included an annual salary of $2,400 (increased to $3,600 soon after his arrival), a western style house, and a horse. Sailing from San Francisco on 1 December 1870, Griffis arrived at the port of Yokohama on 29 December. After several weeks in Tokyo conferring with various officials and securing equipment, he arrived in the castle town of Fukui, in the interior of Japan, where he established the first chemical laboratory in Japan.

The Fukui in which Griffis lived for several months in early 1871 stood in sharp contrast to the relatively cosmopolitan Tokyo. Indeed, Fukui was still under the yoke of Japanese feudalism, which Griffis chronicled in great detail in his first book, *The Mikado's Empire*, which went through twelve editions between

1876 and 1912. Divided into two major sections, *The Mikado's Empire* provided English-language readers of his time with a rare reliable history of Japan, followed by a detailed recounting of Griffis's experiences in Japan and their relationship to Japan's modernization process. It was undoubtedly his most influential publication. One of the United States' most distinguished contemporary scholars of Japan, John W. Hall of Yale, wrote in 1966 that "in the United States, up to World War I, probably the most popularly read book on Japanese history was *The Mikado's Empire* (1876)"; and the distinguished historian of Japanese-American relations, Akira Iriye, has suggested that *The Mikado's Empire* "remained the best book on Japanese history for decades."

While gathering materials for his book, Griffis was able to make numerous contacts not only with many Japanese officials and dignitaries of the day but also with young students who in a few years would take important positions in the political, economic, and intellectual worlds of Japan. These men included a future prime minister, several ambassadors, prominent businessmen, and leading scholars, and they would serve as sources for a half-century of his subsequent writings on things Japanese. Returning to the United States in 1874, Griffis resumed his studies at the Union Theological Seminary, graduating in 1877 to pursue a dual career as a minister of the Dutch Reformed church and as a self-styled interpreter of Japan to the United States and the United States to Japan. In this role Griffis, through his teaching and his numerous contacts in Japan, sought to explain America and its institutions to the Japanese, while through his prolific writing and lecturing on Japanese society, politics, and history he served as an authority on Japan to his countrymen. His eighteen books and several hundred scholarly and journalistic articles on Japan and scores of public lectures established him as the leading Japan "expert" of his day. In addition, he also found time to write and lecture on topics dealing with the Netherlands and the United States.

Griffis married Katherine L. Stanton in 1879; they had three children. Following her untimely death in 1898, Griffis in 1900 married Sarah F. King. Griffis was twice awarded the Order of the Rising Sun, Fourth Class and Third Class, by the Japanese government in recognition of both his work in Fukui and Tokyo (1870–1874) and for his later extensive literary and journalistic efforts to explain Japan and the Japanese to his often skeptical countrymen.

The highlight of Griffis's later years was undoubtedly his sentimental return visit to Japan in 1926–1927 as a guest of the Japanese government. During this trip Griffis not only revisited the scenes of his youthful experiences, but also went to Manchuria and Korea, both occupied by the Japanese.

Griffis's reputation during his lifetime was as an earnest, sincere friend of the Japanese, but he was not a sycophant. Indeed, he was often a severe critic of the Japanese, notably Japan's actions in Korea. Shortly after returning from his 1926–1927 visit to Japan, Griffis traveled to his winter home in Winter Park, Florida, where he died after a brief illness. As a bridge between two cultures, Griffis was one of a small band of westerners who gradually made Japan known to the West.

• Griffis's extensive personal papers are housed in the Rutgers University Archives in New Brunswick, N.J. Containing approximately 15,000 items, this collection is a valuable source for the study of the role of foreigners in early Meiji Japan (1868–1880). Another somewhat different resource is the William Elliot Griffis Collection at Cornell University in Ithaca, N.Y. This collection consists almost exclusively of Japanese language works that were collected by or presented to Griffis, whereas the Rutgers Collection is overwhelmingly made up of Griffis's correspondence, his diary, and related materials—including English documents, clippings of newspapers, and manuscripts. In addition there is a small but useful Griffis Collection at the Fukui Municipal Historical Museum in Fukui.
There are a handful of biographical studies of Griffis and his career: Edward R. Beauchamp, *An American Teacher in Early Meiji Japan* (1976); Robert A. Rosenstone, *Mirror in the Shrine: American Encounters with Meiji Japan* (1988), a study of three Americans in Meiji Japan: Lafcadio Hearn, Edward S. Morse, and Griffis; and Frances Y. Helbig, "William Elliot Griffis: Entrepreneur of Ideas" (master's thesis, Rochester Univ., 1966), which contains useful material. Also see Ardath W. Burks, "William Elliot Griffis: Class of 1869," *Journal of the Rutgers University Library* (1966); Ardath W. Burks and Jerome Cooperman, "The William Elliot Griffis Collection," *Journal of Asian Studies* 20 (Nov. 1960): 61–69; Burks, ed., *The Modernizers: Overseas Students, Foreign Employees, and Meiji Japan* (1985); and Edward R. Beauchamp and Akira Iriye, eds., *Foreign Employees in Nineteenth-Century Japan* (1990). An obituary is in the *New York Times*, 6 Feb. 1928.

EDWARD R. BEAUCHAMP

GRIFFITH, Clark Calvin (20 Nov. 1869–27 Oct. 1955), baseball player, manager, and owner, was born in Clearcreek, Missouri, the son of Isaiah Griffith, a fur trapper, and Sarah Wright. His parents moved to Clearcreek just two years before Clark was born. His father died in an accidental shooting when Clark was only two, and by age ten he had become a professional trapper to help his mother. By age thirteen, however, Griffith contracted malaria, forcing his family to move to Bloomington, Illinois, where he recovered his health.
In 1887 Griffith began his baseball career pitching for the local Bloomington club, entered in the Central Interstate League. At the start of the 1888 season Griffith pitched for Milwaukee in the Western League. In his first recorded game, he beat Danville 3–1 with nine strikeouts. In 1890, his last season with Milwaukee, he compiled a 27–7 pitching record. Then he moved to St. Louis of the American Association (AA) in 1891 and finished the season with Boston of the AA, compiling a 14–9 record. The following year, after the AA merged with the National League (NL), Griffith joined the Tacoma, Washington, club in the Northern Pacific League; there he was 13–7 in 24 games. In 1893 Griffith pitched for the Oakland Oaks of the Pacific Coast League, where he compiled a 30–18 record.

By the close of the 1893 season Cap Anson had signed him to pitch for the Chicago Colts of the NL (later known as the Cubs).
Griffith stayed in Chicago until midway through the 1900 season. His first full season with Chicago Griffith put together a 21–14 record, the beginning of six straight years with 20 or more victories. The most amazing aspect of this feat was the fact that the Colts never finished higher than fourth during these years. In 1898 he also led the National League with a 1.88 ERA. All through his career Griffith earned his nickname, the "Old Fox," because of his cunning and guile. As a pitcher Griffith scuffed and doctored the baseball in order to improve his chances of winning. Ironically, later in his career Griffith became a strong advocate for banning the use of the spitball. As a manager and owner Griffith continued experimenting with all kinds of techniques to win, such as developing the regular use of relief pitchers and helping to develop the screwball pitch.
As a player, Griffith felt strongly that players' salaries were not sufficient; while in Oakland he had even led a strike when the owner would not meet the team's payroll. In his capacity as vice president of the Ball Players' Protective Association, he approached the NL about raising minimum salaries. When the league refused, Griffith in 1900 became a leading figure in the formation of the new American League (AL). He helped Ban Johnson, the first AL president, secure the services of over 35 stars for the new league's franchises, such as Jimmy Collins and Cy Young. Griffith himself became a player-manager of the Chicago White Sox, which he guided to the AL pennant in 1901, compiling a 24–8 record, the league's best winning percentage. Winning the AL flag gave Griffith a unique spot in baseball history because he was both player and manager when the White Sox won. He was the first to achieve that honor. He also became a relief pitcher, at the time a real innovation in the game.
Griffith went as player-manager to the New York Highlanders in 1903 to develop an AL team that would be a rival to the NL club already established in the city. By the 1906 season he had become predominantly a manager. In 1909 he became manager of the Cincinnati Reds of the NL; the team finished in fourth, fifth, and sixth place, respectively, during Griffith's three years at the helm. Then, in 1912, when he was convinced by Ban Johnson to join the Washington Senators to try to help revive the ailing franchise, Griffith embarked on a new phase of his career in baseball: he was to become a prominent, longtime owner.
Griffith had been a pitcher for 20 years, compiling a record of 240–144, with a career 3.31 ERA. He pitched 3,386 innings and completed 337 games; he gave up 774 walks while also registering 955 strikeouts. As a batter he hit .233 in 484 games and 1,380 at bats. In the coming years as manager of the Senators, he would compile a record of 1,491 victories and 1,367 losses, for a winning percentage of .522.
Griffith became not only manager of the Senators but also a member of the team's board of directors; in

doing so he mortgaged some property he owned to raise the money to buy 10 percent of the club's stock. He persuaded President William Howard Taft to throw out a ceremonial first pitch of the 1912 season, starting a tradition of presidents' appearing at the season opener for a major league team. By 1920 Griffith had increased his stock to a controlling share and became the team president; he remained with the Senators until his death. Though the club won the AL pennant in 1924 and 1925, the Senators never escaped financial difficulties. Griffith signed a number of genuine stars for the Senators, including first baseman Chick Gandil, who gave the team a big boost during Griffith's first years in Washington, and the pitching great Walter Johnson.

Griffith tried to improve the team's finances with a variety of publicity stunts, such as baseball clowns, a House of David pitcher, and the addition of lights to their stadium in 1941 to increase the attendance of working people. Griffith was also a pioneer in signing modern-era Cuban players Armando Marsans and Rafael Almeida for the Cincinnati club. For all his innovations in terms of publicity, Griffith made a crucial mistake by choosing not to develop a strong farm system, as other teams were doing in the 1930s. As a result Washington fell behind other clubs who relied on their own systems to breathe new life into their teams on a regular basis. Griffith did not want to spend any more money than necessary to keep Washington as a viable franchise.

By the 1940s Griffith showed a change in attitude from his early days in helping to form the new American League. He had not hesitated to use any encouragement necessary to draw players away from their NL contracts in the early 1900s. Then, when the Mexican raids took place in the 1940s, in which Mexican scouts offered big contracts to entice the best American players south of the border, Griffith led the cry against letting players sign contracts with anyone they wanted, claiming it would be detrimental to the future of baseball; in fact, Griffith worried about losing his players to teams that paid higher salaries.

Griffith worked with the government to raise money for the armed services during World Wars I and II. The Senators played benefit games to raise money for baseball equipment for servicemen overseas, and Griffith worked with the selective service to get special deferments for players until the baseball season ended. Believing baseball was important to the morale of the country, he also started playing baseball on Sundays so that those working in war industries could attend the games. During World War II he was part of a group that met with President Franklin D. Roosevelt to convince him that baseball should continue during the conflict.

Griffith had married Ann Robertson in 1900. They had no children, but they raised her brother's seven orphaned nieces and nephews. He adopted one of his nephews, Calvin Griffith, to groom as his successor. Starting as a mascot, a batboy, and a seller of concessions before moving up the chain of command, Calvin became president after Clark's death in Washington, D.C., and in 1960 he moved the team to Minnesota.

Griffith's many contributions to the game as a player, manager, and owner were recognized when he was elected to the National Baseball Hall of Fame in 1946. His many innovations, both in pitching and in publicity, have continued to influence the game.

• The National Baseball Library, Cooperstown, N.Y., has a large file on Griffith's career. Griffith's statistics can be found in John Thorn and Pete Palmer, eds., *Total Baseball*, 4th ed. (1995); and *The Baseball Encyclopedia*, 9th ed. (1993). Shirley Povich, *The Washington Senators* (1954), tells the story of Griffith's rise to the presidency and his work at the helm of the Washington franchise. Lee Allen, *The American League Story* (1962), discusses Griffith's and Johnson's roles in forming the new league and working to establish its credibility. The 21 Jan. 1937 issue of *Sporting News* contains a story about Griffith and his baseball career. In Lee Lowenfish and Tony Lupien, *The Imperfect Diamond* (1980), Griffith's various dealings with issues such as player salaries and the reserve clause are described. Henry Thomas, *Walter Johnson, Baseball's Big Train* (1995), is a wonderful source with lots of information about Griffith. Obituaries are in the *New York Times*, 28 Oct. 1955; the *Washington Post*, 29 Oct. 1955; and the *Sporting News*, 2 Nov. 1955.

LESLIE HEAPHY

GRIFFITH, Corinne (24 Nov. 1896–13 July 1979), actress, was born in Texarkana, Texas, the daughter of John Lewis Griffith, superintendent of the Texas and Pacific Railroad, and Ambolyn Ghio. As a small child, Griffith moved with her family to New Orleans where she attended the Convent of the Sacred Heart. Griffith's formal education ended at about age fourteen when her father, who had suffered serious financial reverses, died and her mother moved the family to the resort town of Mineral Wells, Texas. Accounts differ as to how Griffith entered the motion picture industry. According to some sources, the slender, dark-haired Griffith was offered a contract by Vitagraph Pictures after winning the "Queen of the Mardi Gras" title in New Orleans. Another version of the story has Griffith living with her mother in southern California and struggling to get into films. A beauty contest victory at the Santa Monica pier ballroom, along with the assistance of director King Vidor, whom she had known in Texas, resulted in her being signed to a contract by Vitagraph. In his autobiography Vidor says that he had met the ravishing young Griffith during a visit to Mineral Wells in the early 1910s. Some time later, after he had moved to California and established himself in motion pictures, he received a letter from Griffith asking for help in getting a job in films. Through an acquaintance of Vidor, Griffith was introduced to the director general of Vitagraph, who offered her a contract guaranteeing two days of work per week at a five dollars per day salary.

In 1916 Griffith began appearing as an extra in films produced at Vitagraph's West Coast studios in Santa Monica. She was promoted to supporting player roles in *Through the Wall* (1916), *The Cost of High Living* (1916), and other films. In 1917 Griffith transferred to

Vitagraph's more important East Coast facility in Brooklyn, New York, where she soon emerged as a major star. "Her particular type of incandescence charmed everyone on the sets—from prop boy to director. When she came on, the boys warmed up like arc lights," wrote Albert E. Smith, cofounder of Vitagraph, in his memoir *Two Reels and a Crank* (1952, p. 213). The studio dubbed Griffith "The Orchid Lady" or "The Orchid of the Screen" on account of her delicate features and coloring. She remained a popular box-office draw for the next decade. Among her films for Vitagraph are *Transgression* (1917), *The Menace* (1918), *The Love Doctor* (1918), *A Girl at Bay* (1919), *The Climbers* (1919), *The Garter Girl* (1920), *Moral Fibre* (1921), and *A Virgin's Sacrifice* (1922). From 1920 to 1923 Griffith was married to Webster Campbell, an actor-director also working for Vitagraph. The childless marriage ended in divorce.

In 1923 Griffith left Vitagraph to accept more lucrative offers from other companies. She freelanced for a short time, appearing in *The Common Law* (1923) for Lewis Selznick and *Six Days* (1923) for Samuel Goldwyn, then signed a contract with First National Pictures in Hollywood that set up a special Griffith production company. Her first three pictures for First National—*Single Wives* (1924), *Love's Wilderness* (1924), and *Lilies of the Field* (1924)—were all box-office hits. The success of these films earned Griffith the much-coveted lead role in First National's big-budget production of *Black Oxen* (1924), about a New York socialite who regains her youthful face and figure by undergoing rejuvenation treatments at a European clinic. Her effective portrayal of a middle-aged woman in the body of a young woman enhanced Griffith's reputation as an actress. Up to this point the striking brunette's career had been almost entirely dependent on her beauty. In 1924 Griffith married Walter Morosco, the son of theatrical producer Oliver Morosco. The couple had no children. Griffith made Morosco a producer with her film unit at First National.

Following her success in *Black Oxen*, Griffith appeared in screen versions of three prestigious stage plays—*Declassee* (1925), *The Marriage Whirl* (1925), and *Infatuation* (1925). Griffith turned to comedy with *Classified* (1925), in which she played a gum-chewing switchboard operator, and *Mademoiselle Modiste* (1926), a silent version of Victor Herbert's operetta. She also starred in the comedies *Syncopating Sue* (1926) and *The Lady in Ermine* (1927).

Griffith did not renew her contract with First National when it expired in 1928. Instead, she appeared in *The Garden of Eden* (1928), which she produced independently in conjunction with United Artists. The film was not a financial success but it did receive critical acclaim, and Griffith returned to First National under a new contract that made her the studio's highest paid star. She then made what is often considered her best-known film, *The Divine Lady* (1929), in which she played Lady Emma Hamilton to Victor Varconi's Lord Nelson. Produced as a silent, the film was released with a hastily added sound-effects score and one

song. Griffith spoke on screen for the first time in *Saturday's Children* (1929), a "part-talkie" based on Maxwell Anderson's play. Her first complete sound feature was *Lilies of the Field* (1930), a remake of her earlier film of the same name. Although Griffith had a pleasant voice and showed some talent with dialogue, she did not catch on as a sound-film performer. After making *Back Pay* (1930), costarring Grant Withers, for First National, she went to England to appear in *Lily Christine* (1932), for British Paramount. It was her final film, with the exception of a brief appearance as herself in *Stars in the Backyard*, a 1957 feature about Beverly Hills that never received general release.

Divorced from Walter Morosco in 1934, Griffith turned to the stage for a brief tour in Noël Coward's *Design for Living*. While appearing with the play in Washington, D.C., she met George Preston Marshall, a laundry-business millionaire and owner of the Boston (later Washington) Redskins professional football team. The couple wed in 1936. During her marriage to Marshall, Griffith was a busy member of Washington society and wrote the books *My Life with the Redskins* (1947), a memoir; *Papa's Delicate Condition* (1952), a semiautobiographical novel about a turn-of-the-century Texas family with an imbibing patriarch (made into a film with Jackie Gleason in 1963); and *Eggs I Have Known* (1955), a cookbook. She also wrote the words to the song "Hail to the Redskins," the team's victory chant, and involved herself in political causes, most notably a campaign to end the collection of income tax, which she considered unconstitutional.

Griffith was divorced from Marshall, with whom she had no children, in 1958. She returned to California where modest-priced land purchases she had made in the 1920s had turned into lucrative real-estate holdings, including valuable property in Beverly Hills. In addition to overseeing her real estate investments, she wrote books about cooking, collecting antiques, and other personal experiences.

In 1964 Griffith was briefly married to Daniel Scholl, an actor more than twenty years her junior. In divorce proceedings from Scholl, the seventyish Griffith testified that she was in her early fifties and was not the silent film star Corinne Griffith but a much younger look-alike who had assumed the name after the real Griffith had died in the 1930s. Griffith died at her home in Beverly Hills.

• The District of Columbia Public Library's Washingtoniana Collection has a clippings file on Griffith, mostly pertaining to the years of her marriage to George P. Marshall. Griffith's books not mentioned above include *Antiques I Have Known* (1961), *Hollywood Stories* (1962), *Taxation without Representation* (1962), *I Can't Boil Water, a Cookbook* (1963), *Truth Is Stranger* (1964), *Not for Men Only—but Almost* (1969), *This You Won't Believe* (1972), and *I'm Lucky—at Cards* (1974). Other sources of information on Griffith are DeWitt Bodeen, "Corinne Griffith: The Orchid Lady of the Screen," *Films in Review*, Nov. 1975, pp. 513–29, and Richard Lamparski, *Whatever Became of . . . ?* 2d ser. (1968). See also King Vidor,

A Tree Is a Tree (1953), and Albert E. Smith, *Two Reels and a Crank* (1952), a history of Vitagraph Pictures. An obituary is in the *New York Times*, 22 July 1979.

MARY C. KALFATOVIC

GRIFFITH, D. W. (22 Jan. 1875–23 July 1948), pioneer film director, was born David Lewelyn Wark Griffith in Oldham County, Kentucky, the son of Jacob Wark Griffith, a physician and Confederate veteran, and Mary Perkins Oglesby. The family plantation—Jacob Griffith had been a slaveholder—was no longer viable after the Civil War, and in 1889, four years after his death, Mary Griffith moved her large family (Griffith had six siblings) to Louisville, where she ran a boardinghouse. Griffith attended both country and city schools before going to work in a dry goods store and later in a bookstore. Although he originally intended to become a writer, Griffith was attracted by the theater, and in 1895 he joined an amateur acting company that toured Kentucky and Indiana. Within five years he was touring the country, playing bit parts under a variety of stage names. In 1906 he married Linda Arvidson Johnson, an actress whom he had met in San Francisco. They had no children.

In his spare time Griffith wrote fiction, poetry, and drama that he sold to magazines. His play *The Fool and the Girl* was produced briefly in Washington, D.C., and in Baltimore during the fall of 1907. Despite its lack of success, the play demonstrated that Griffith had a flair for inventing the dramatic, a talent he would later use in his film career. After the play's run, Griffith went to New York City and, while also working as an actor, began to submit story ideas to motion picture studios. The Biograph Company bought several of his synopses and in June 1908 offered him an opportunity to direct his first picture. *The Adventures of Dollie* and his other early films were successful enough that Griffith became the company's principal director.

Griffith made nearly 500 films for Biograph, mostly one- and two-reelers, and thereby established himself as a skilled and innovative director. These early films, many of which he wrote himself, with titles such as *The Tavern Keeper's Daughter* (1908), *Edgar Allan Poe* (1909), *Muggsy's First Sweetheart* (1910), and *A Pueblo Legend* (1912), covered a wide spectrum of subjects and genres. In presenting this diversity, Griffith developed a lyrical, compressed style and explored the systematic use of three cinematic techniques that were important in the evolution of the language of film: dynamic editing (joining separate shots for symbolic or metaphoric purposes), parallel editing (using alternate shots of separate actions to suggest that they are taking place simultaneously), and the last-minute rescue. Several of these films made use of on-location shooting. *The Musketeers of Pig Alley* (1912), one of the first films about urban crime, has an authentic look because it was shot on the streets of New York. Griffith also made a number of progressive movies, such as *A Corner in Wheat* (1909), adapted from the Frank Norris short story "A Deal in Wheat," which depicted the plight of poor Americans. These films reflect Griffith's naive view of poverty and his Victorian paternalism but nevertheless express his genuine concern about the plight of the poor.

Griffith also demonstrated a talent for handling actors, and at Biograph he developed a number of stars, including Mary Pickford, sisters Lillian and Dorothy Gish, Mae Marsh, and Henry B. Walthall. In the process he also pioneered a new acting style, one free of the theatrical excesses of the stage. Griffith recognized that the proximity of the motion picture camera necessitated the modification of grand gestures in favor of more subdued movements. He also recognized the revolutionary impact of the change, claiming rather grandiloquently in 1913, the year he left Biograph, to have founded the techniques of modern motion picture acting.

Griffith and his colleagues took credit for many cinematic innovations, some warranted, others not. With camera operators G. W. "Billy" Bitzer and Arthur Marvin, for example, he claimed to have invented the close-up, the long shot, and parallel montage. In truth, these techniques were already a part of the cinema repertoire before Griffith came on the scene, but he was the first director to put them to good use, and in the process he effectively explored the fluid, multidimensional qualities of film. By yoking these newly discovered dramatic qualities with the power of spectacle, Griffith fully realized the possibilities of the new medium and was the first to elevate it to an art form. His formidable presence also helped shift importance away from the cameraman as the major artistic figure in the creation of film and thereby established the aesthetic primacy of the director. Some critics believe that his early years at Biograph were Griffith's most significant as a director and that over the course of those five years he made his most-lasting and most important contributions to the art of the motion picture.

By 1912 Griffith had grown dissatisfied with Biograph's commitment to two-reelers. European film makers were already making longer films, and Griffith believed that was the coming trend. In his last years at Biograph Griffith had been going to California during the winter months to shoot, and in 1913, working under great secrecy because of spending considerations, he completed the first four-reel film made in America, *Judith of Bethulia*. The film overran its projected budget of $18,000, which increased tensions between Griffith and his studio bosses in New York. Even though the film was a great success after its release in 1914, Biograph was displeased by Griffith's increasingly independent behavior, and when he returned to New York he was informed that he would be allowed to produce, but not direct, a new series of films.

Griffith refused their terms, and after turning down a handsome salary offered by Adolph Zukor's Famous Players, he went to work for Reliance-Majestic, a production company of the Mutual Film Corporation that was owned by Harry and Roy Aitken, brothers who ran a number of film exchanges in the Midwest and two studios, the Reliance in New York and the Majestic in Los Angeles. Griffith's contract stipulated that he was to direct two films a year and supervise the production of others. The Aitkens negotiated an especially attractive deal because Griffith had persuaded several members of his technical crew from Biograph as well as many of the studio's best actors, including the Gish sisters, Mae Marsh, Blanche Sweet, Henry Walthall, Donald Crisp, and Bobby Harron, to move to Reliance-Majestic with him.

By the time he left for California during the winter of 1914, Griffith had already shot two films in New York, and he quickly completed two more after his arrival. These five- to seven-reel films *The Battle of the Sexes*, *The Escape*, *Home, Sweet Home*, and *The Avenging Conscience*, provided Griffith with much-needed experience shooting longer films, and they helped him hone his skills handling larger, more complex narratives. In addition, the profits they generated were used to help finance his next movie, an epic on the American Civil War. Griffith had wanted to do a film on that war for several years, and while he was at Biograph he had shot a number of short films with Civil War settings. Not surprisingly, many of these films, with titles such as *In Old Kentucky* (1908), *In the Border States; or, A Little Heroine of the Civil War* (1910), *Swords and Hearts* (1911), and *The Battle* (1911), contained material that eventually would appear in his larger-scale film.

In 1912 Frank Woods had written a treatment for a motion picture based on Thomas Dixon's popular novel and play *The Clansman* but the Kinemacolor company had abandoned the project. When Woods approached Griffith with a new treatment, he agreed to proceed with its production, which began on 4 July 1914. A complete script was never written for the movie, but with Woods's help, and with that of several assistants, Griffith researched the Civil War and Reconstruction periods in an attempt to make his new movie historically as well as socially accurate. At its release in 1915, the film, retitled *The Birth of a Nation*, was the longest (twelve reels) and most expensive ($110,000) motion picture shot in the United States to that time. The film was also to become one of the most controversial and most famous in motion picture history. Its portrayal of the struggle between North and South—and their ultimate reconciliation during Reconstruction through the rise of white supremacy as represented by the Ku Klux Klan—was set against large-scale historical events, but it also focused on the individual lives of those caught up in the events. Griffith thus achieved a film of epic sweep that also preserved an intimacy of feeling.

The Birth of a Nation and Griffith's other film epics depicted conventional and questionable views of history and reveled in pageantry and spectacle rather than on tightly drawn narratives. Nevertheless these films are extraordinarily individual and inventive. Billy Bitzer later explained how he and Griffith developed dozens of innovative ways to capture the huge battlefield scenes that the director envisioned for *The Birth of a Nation*. Director and cameraman used aerial shots, mobile camera takes, and various irising effects (which contract or expand the circular lens-masking device inside the camera to isolate or reveal an area of the frame for visual narrative or symbolic effect), all of which matched the epic with the personal. In dozens of ways Griffith and Bitzer, who shot the film almost entirely on his own with a single camera, created a sweeping and dramatically dynamic film that deserves the study it has received. The film's embarrassingly retrograde social attitudes and its racist conception of history, not its technical achievement, mar its viewing today.

The Birth of a Nation was hugely successful with white audiences; it made Griffith a fortune and did much to gain respectability for the motion picture as art. Because of its glorification of the Klan, the film produced widespread protest from progressives of both races and a number of African-American organizations, particularly the newly-formed National Association for the Advancement of Colored People (NAACP), which continued its campaign against the film until the late 1930s. Attempts to rally public opinion through leafleting and newspaper articles, legal action, and the creation of censorship boards had little effect on the film's distribution or exhibition. There were a few incidents of more aggressive protest, notably in Boston, which were also largely ineffectual. In response to *The Birth of a Nation*, members of the African-American community formed a film production company, which released *The Birth of a Race* (1915) to counterbalance the views depicted in Griffith's film. Public protests against *The Birth of a Nation* prompted Griffith to defend himself in a pamphlet on the right of self-expression, *The Rise and Fall of Free Speech in America* (1916).

Also as a result of public reaction to *The Birth of a Nation*, and in part because of his own directorial aspirations, Griffith's next motion picture, *Intolerance* (1916), was even longer and even more ambitious than his Civil War epic. The film interspersed stories from four different historical periods: ancient Babylon, Palestine in the time of Christ, sixteenth-century France, and the modern United States. The set for the Babylonian sequence was one of the largest and most magnificent ever constructed in Hollywood to that time. Although the movie apparently perplexed its audiences and lost Griffith a considerable amount of money, *Intolerance* had an enormous impact on future film makers, especially directors in the Soviet Union, who were interested in Griffith's style, especially his editing techniques.

Griffith's success in directing larger and longer, more intellectually and aesthetically complex movies did much to establish the need for an industrial base for movie making, and it earned him the popular title as "the man who invented Hollywood." In 1917 he signed with Adolph Zukor to make films for the Artcraft Corporation, and in 1919 he, Charlie Chaplin, Mary Pickford, and Douglas Fairbanks, Sr., formed the independent distribution company United Artists Corporation. Griffith's first film for United Artists was

Broken Blossoms (1919). In that year he also released, through other companies, seven more films and, in October, moved his production company to newly converted studios at Orienta Point on the Henry Flagler estate near Mamaroneck, New York.

Of the eighteen films Griffith directed between 1917 and 1924, among the most memorable were *Hearts of the World* (1918), *Broken Blossoms* (1919), *True Heart Susie* (1919), *Way Down East* (1920), *Orphans of the Storm* (1921), and *Isn't Life Wonderful* (1924). *Hearts of the World*, Griffith's propaganda epic about the recently ended First World War, became one of the most popular war films of its time with profits to match. The intimate, dreamlike qualities of *Broken Blossoms*, with its exquisite lighting, delighted both critics and audiences and provided a striking contrast to the epic qualities of his previous two movies. The most popular film of this period was undoubtedly Griffith's adaptation of the stage melodrama *Way Down East*. The harrowing rescue scenes shot on an ice flow during a winter storm are some of the most daring footage in motion picture history. Griffith's social drama about postwar Germany, *Isn't Life Wonderful*, filmed on location, proved that the old master could still create a film of exacting realism. Yet the success of these films was not enough to sustain Griffith's production studio, and by 1925 he was forced to direct films for others.

Even though Griffith continued to be a prolific film maker, his most prosperous days, between the release of *Intolerance* in 1916 and *Way Down East* in 1920, were over, and as the 1920s progressed, he experienced increasing financial and artistic setbacks. In 1921 the Wark Producing Corporation, which had been formed to distribute and produce *Intolerance*, declared bankruptcy. In 1922 Griffith renewed his contract with United Artists for three years, but there were increasing tensions within the company. The same year that his contract with United Artists ended he also sold his Mamaroneck studios.

In 1925 and 1926 Griffith worked for Paramount, and in 1927 he returned to Hollywood as a director for Joseph Schenck's Art Cinema Corporation. Griffith was unhappy directing other people's projects, however, and he became increasingly difficult to work with. In addition, his pictures were less and less successful, and this intensified his already strained and volatile relationship with the studios. Griffith shot his first sound film, *Abraham Lincoln*, with Walter Huston in the title role, in 1930. The slow, stagy film did little to rescue Griffith's sagging reputation. The following year he made *The Struggle* with his own independent company, but the film, about alcoholism and its effects, was very unpopular and ended Griffith's career. In 1932 he resigned the presidency of D. W. Griffith, Inc., the company he had founded in 1916, and in 1933 he finally sold his interests in United Artists. It is one of the ironies of Griffith's career—yet a commonality shared by many pioneers—that although he was acknowledged, even in his own lifetime, as one of the greatest and most prolific directors in the world, he

was unable to raise financial support for his later projects.

In 1936 Griffith and his wife were divorced after a 25-year separation, and he soon married 26-year-old Evelyn Marjorie Baldwin; they too divorced, in 1947. Also in 1936, the year the Motion Picture Academy honored Griffith with a special citation for his contribution to the industry, the Griffith Corporation went into receivership. Two years later Griffith gave his papers to the Museum of Modern Art in New York. In 1939 Hal Roach hired Griffith to work on the film *One Million Years, B.C.*, but he did little except collect his paychecks.

Despite his inability to work during his later years, Griffith began to receive increasing recognition for his place in the development of the motion picture. In 1940–1941 the Museum of Modern Art mounted the first retrospective of his films, and in 1945 the University of Louisville awarded him an honorary doctorate. Throughout the 1940s he continued to live in Hollywood and to attempt to secure backing for a number of movie projects. He died in Los Angeles. After a memorial service, his body was flown to Kentucky, where it was buried in the family plot at Mount Tabor Methodist Church in Centerfield, very near his birthplace.

Now known as "the father of the motion picture," D. W. Griffith was unquestionably one of the most important film directors of all time, and his creative influence has been felt worldwide. As many critics have acknowledged, he was the first important motion picture artist, and his pioneering efforts to extend the range and sensibilities of the new medium did much to legitimize the fledgling art form. Griffith popularized many new cinematic techniques, if he did not invent or discover them, and he helped to codify the grammar of film making. His early efforts to industrialize the film business were partly responsible for establishing, in a Los Angeles suburb, the corporate foundation that has come to be known as Hollywood.

• Griffith's papers are housed in the D. W. Griffith Archive of the Film Department of the Museum of Modern Art in New York City, which also has the most comprehensive collection of his films. The Motion Picture Section of the Library of Congress also has an extensive collection of Biograph films. The first scholarly biography of Griffith was Robert Henderson, *D. W. Griffith: His Life and Work* (1972). Richard Schickel's more recent study, *D. W. Griffith: An American Life* (1984), provides additional information on Griffith's life and career. Griffith's autobiography was published in *The Man Who Invented Hollywood* (1972), edited with notes and a memoir by Griffith's collaborator James Hart. Several personal reminiscences also make enjoyable reading: Linda Arvidson Johnson's memoir *When the Movies Were Young* (1925); Lillian Gish's charming *The Movies, Mr. Griffith, and Me* (1969); Karl Brown's *Adventures with D. W. Griffith* (1973), ed. Kevin Brownlow; and G. W. Bitzer's *Billy Bitzer: His Story* (1973). Iris Barry's monograph for the Museum of Modern Art, *D. W. Griffith: American Film Master* (1940), which was reprinted in 1965 with additional information by Eileen Bowser, constitutes one of the first full-length studies of Griffith's films, of which there is a growing number, especially for the films he made at Biograph. Thomas Cripps, *Slow Fade to Black: The Negro in American Film, 1900–1942* (1977), details the controversy over *The Birth of a Nation* and efforts by African-American organizations and publications to counter the film's racist depictions of blacks. Griffith's role in the early years of United Artists is outlined in Tino Balio, *United Artists: The Company Built by the Stars* (1976). An obituary is in the *New York Times*, 24 July 1948.

CHARLES L. P. SILET

GRIFFITH, Goldsborough Sappington (4 Nov. 1814–24 Feb. 1904), civic and religious leader, prison reformer, and philanthropist, was born in Harford County, Maryland, the son of James Griffith and Sarah Cox. His father died in the War of 1812, leaving Griffith, not one year old, the youngest of eight. His mother subsequently remarried and, when Griffith was twelve, moved to Baltimore with her husband and family of fourteen children. Griffith left school and obtained regular employment in a tobacco manufacturing house to help support the family. He continued his education in night school and devoted his leisure time to reading. Several years later he found a rewarding position as a paperhanger and, at the age of twenty-two, with $500 in savings and a knowledgeable partner, began a prosperous paperhanging and upholstery business. In 1854 he sold this thriving business to his half brothers and turned his attentions to his very successful wholesale and retail carpet business in which he was joined by his nephews.

Griffith married Elizabeth Durst, the daughter of a Swiss merchant who lived in Baltimore, in 1839; they had no children. They were deeply involved in the German Reformed church. Griffith represented the First Reformed Church of Baltimore in the state and the general synods of the Reformed Church of the United States. He was an American delegate to the Evangelical Alliance in Lübeck, Germany, in 1856, to the Alliance at Berlin in 1857, and in 1881 to the international Sunday-school convention in London. He was a popular Sunday school teacher and widely recognized as a leader in the development of Sunday schools. He was president of the Maryland Sunday School Union for twenty-eight years, during which more than twelve hundred Sunday schools were established to serve more than 137,000 children, a large proportion of whom were Americans of African descent. In 1859, after personally carrying religious teachings into prisons for more than sixteen years, Griffith organized the first prison Sunday schools in the United States, one for men and one for women, in the Maryland penitentiary.

Griffith was a tireless organizer of an extensive range of philanthropic projects and was devoted to spreading the gospel. In an article published in the 1850s in the *Reformed Messenger* he wrote, "It is the duty of every Christian to labor for the good of others." In 1860 with two associates he organized the Children's Aid Society, which endeavored to care for homeless children and protect delinquent children from exposure to confirmed criminals by keeping

them out of penal institutions. Griffith was a founder of the Asylum for Feebleminded Children and one of the incorporators of the News Boys' Home. He was a longtime supporter of the Young Men's Christian Association and a pioneer in temperance work. With colleagues Griffith established the Children's Aid Society, the Union Orphan Asylum, the Society for the Protection of Children from Cruelty and Immorality, the House of Reformation and Instruction for Colored Children, the Industrial Home for Colored Girls, and the Asylum and Training School for Feeble Minded Children. He was a trustee of the Union Protestant Infirmary and Franklin and Marshall College.

During the Civil War Griffith devoted considerable time, money, and effort to supplying food, clothing, medical supplies, and religious literature to wounded soldiers and prisoners of war in military camps and hospitals on both sides of the struggle. Toward these ends, on 4 May 1861 he founded and became president of the Baltimore Christian Association, the Civil War relief organization in the United States. When the United States Christian Commission was founded Griffith became chairman of its Maryland branch. His unquestioned loyalty to the North and sympathy with the South enabled him to ameliorate suffering during and after the war. At the conclusion of the fighting he formed the Maryland Union Commission, which worked to aid the thousands of war refugees in Maryland and speed the economic recovery of the struggling South.

Especially noteworthy was Griffith's lifelong commitment to the reformation of prisoners and the improvement of prisons. In 1869 he started and became president of the Maryland Prisoners' Aid Association, a society that worked for improvements in prison legislation, policies, and management and supported those recently discharged from institutions. Griffith was a member of the National Prison Association and a founder of the Maryland House of Corrections. He represented Maryland at national and international congresses on prison reform and was a member of the Howard Association of London and the Société Générale des Prisons of France. Griffith was able to make contributions to prison reform through his considerable organizational and management abilities and the promotion and enforcement of legislation limiting prison abuses. He regularly visited prisons and charitable institutions and used his pen and voice to raise and shape public awareness, to gather others to his cause, and to bring about immediate remediation. Griffith inspired the Probation of First Offenders' Act, passed in 1894, an accomplishment for which he worked with great determination and from which he derived great satisfaction.

Griffith frequently contributed articles on temperance, church matters, and penal reform to Baltimore newspapers and religious publications. In a pamphlet published in 1870, *An Argument on the Contract Labor System and the Reformation of Convicts*, Griffith argued that depriving prisoners of both liberty and employment increased the severity of their sentences. He wrote, "Steady employment, mental training, with religious instruction, all beautifully blended, are making impressions upon the prisoners which time will never erase." In another pamphlet Griffith wrote, "The man who curses another because he is black curses the God that made him so and challenges the infinitude of His wisdom."

Heartened by a continuing compassion for humankind, Griffith used his exceptional skills in organization and management to alleviate suffering in prisons, orphanages, and asylums, and on both sides during the Civil War. Known as the "John Howard of the South," he produced an admirable and enduring legacy as Maryland's first prison reformer. He worked all of his adult life to improve the physical, educational, moral, and religious welfare of the disadvantaged and to start them toward better lives. Through determination and frugality he was able to donate about $200,000 to the causes he supported. He died in Baltimore.

• Griffith's *Argument on the Contract Labor System . . .* , as well as two other published pamphlets, *Views on the Penal System of Delaware* (1892) and *The Prison System of the South* (1897), are at the Library of Congress. Other sources include the *Biographical Cyclopedia of Representative Men of Maryland and the District of Columbia, 1879*; George H. Nock, *The Story of a Great Life* (n.d.); and J. Thomas Scharf, *History of Baltimore City and County* (1881). Obituaries are in the *Baltimore Sun* and *Baltimore American*, 25 Feb. 1904.

KATHERINE M. KOCEL

GRIFFITH, Robert E. (1907–7 June 1961), theatrical producer and stage manager, was born in Methuen, Massachusetts, the son of Alfred Griffith (his mother's name is unknown). Griffith began in the theater as an actor, making his first Broadway appearance in a revival of Augustin Daly's melodrama *Under the Gaslight* in 1929. He had small roles in George S. Kaufman and Edna Ferber's *Dinner at Eight* in 1932 and in *Merrily We Roll Along*, by Kaufman and Moss Hart, in 1934. Hoping to move from acting to directing, Griffith became an assistant to director and producer George Abbott in the mid-1930s. Griffith never achieved his directing goal. Instead, he remained with Abbott for the next two decades, stage managing dozens of Abbott-connected productions, including the musicals *On Your Toes* (1936), *Pal Joey* (1940), *Best Foot Forward* (1941), *On the Town* (1944), *High Button Shoes* (1947), and *Call Me Madam* (1950). In 1937 Griffith married actress and former Ziegfeld *Follies* showgirl Otis Schaefer, with whom he had worked in *Merrily We Roll Along*. The couple had two children.

In 1949 21-year-old theater novice Harold Prince was hired to work under Griffith (known as Bobby to friends and colleagues) as assistant stage manager for the comedy revue *Touch and Go*. After serving a stint in the U.S. Army, Prince returned to work with Griffith in 1953 on the musical *Wonderful Town*, directed by Abbott. During the run of *Wonderful Town*, Griffith and Prince formed a producing organization (with Frederick Brisson, the husband of *Wonderful Town*

star Rosalind Russell, as a third partner). They chose as their first project *The Pajama Game*, a musical version of Richard Bissell's novel *7½ Cents*, a romance set amidst a labor-management dispute at a pajama factory. Mostly out of affection for Griffith, Abbott agreed to direct. Finding little enthusiasm for *The Pajama Game* among the usual Broadway show backers, the amiable, middle-aged Griffith and the young, energetic Prince pieced together funding from a variety of sources, including small amounts from *Wonderful Town* chorus members. *The Pajama Game*, with music and lyrics by newcomers Richard Adler and Jerry Ross, opened at New York's St. James Theatre on 13 May 1954. Only about a week's worth of advance ticket sales indicated minimal audience interest. Fortunately, rave reviews from nearly every New York newspaper drew hundreds of theatergoers to the box office the following morning. *The Pajama Game* won the Tony Award as best musical of the 1953–1954 season and ran for more than 1,000 performances.

Griffith, Prince, and Brisson followed up a year later with the equally successful *Damn Yankees*, based on the novel *The Year the Yankees Lost the Pennant*, by Douglas Wallop. An offbeat blending of baseball and the Faust legend, *Damn Yankees* did not seem promising material, but the great success of *The Pajama Game* made financial backing plentiful. Also directed by Abbott with a score by Adler and Ross, *Damn Yankees*, which opened on 5 May 1955 at the 46th Street Theatre, earned Griffith, Prince, and Brisson a second best musical Tony Award and enjoyed another thousand-plus performance run.

Griffith, Prince, and Brisson's third project was *New Girl in Town*, a musical adaptation of Eugene O'Neill's *Anna Christie*, featuring dancer Gwen Verdon, who had achieved star status via her femme fatale role in *Damn Yankees*. Opening in May 1957, *New Girl in Town*, directed by Abbott, with a score by Bob Merrill, was a modest success.

Frederick Brisson left the partnership after *New Girl in Town*. Griffith and Prince quickly moved on to *West Side Story*, the most influential of their collaborations. The landmark production introduced greater seriousness into the American musical without neglecting solid entertainment value. A bleak but ultimately hopeful tale of warfare between Manhattan youth gangs, *West Side Story* was another unlikely prospect for popular success. Directed and choreographed by Jerome Robbins, with music by Leonard Bernstein and lyrics by a young, untested Stephen Sondheim, *West Side Story* opened at the Winter Garden Theatre on 26 September 1957 and ran for 772 performances (after a national tour it reopened on Broadway in April 1960 and ran for another 253 performances).

Griffith and Prince's first attempt at producing a straight play proved a failure when the drama *A Swim in the Sea* closed during out-of-town tryouts in Philadelphia (the economical producers were still able to return more than half of their backers' investment). Griffith and Prince bounced back with *Fiorello!*, based on the life of New York mayor Fiorello LaGuardia. The musical reunited Griffith and Prince with Abbott. Jerry Bock and Sheldon Harnick provided music and lyrics. *Fiorello!*, which opened at the Broadhurst Theatre on 23 November 1959, won the Pulitzer Prize for drama (only the third musical to be so honored) and earned Griffith and Prince their third Tony Award for best musical. Although *Fiorello!* ran for an impressive 800 performances, Griffith and Prince believed it could have run for another six months if the Actor's Equity strike of 1960 had not caused the show to lose momentum by confusing the public in regard to performance schedules and ticket availability.

Griffith's background as a stage manager and actor, along with that of Prince, meant that his role as producer went far beyond raising financial backing. Concentrating their efforts on one project at a time, Griffith and Prince involved themselves in nearly every aspect of production. They employed no production assistants but instead dealt directly with creative personnel, offering suggestions and advice. Described in *Theatre Arts* in 1960 as seeming more like a "wise and kindly country lawyer" than a big-time Broadway producer, the bespectacled Griffith's calm personality and extensive practical knowledge of the theater complemented Prince's youthful dynamism. This combination of strengths helped Griffith and Prince productions to be of the highest professional standards yet refreshingly innovative. In his memoir *Contradictions*, Prince wrote of Griffith, "It is still difficult to analyze my relationship with Bobby. A brother, maybe, and certainly, in the area of stage managing, a teacher, a patient one. . . . A friend. We loved each other. Ironically, he helped me in very real ways to calm down, to enjoy my life, more in fact, than he was able to enjoy his own. He was generous, the delight of the panhandlers in front of the Lambs Club." Keeping in touch with his New England roots, Griffith maintained a home in Rowayton, Connecticut, in addition to a residence in Manhattan, and was a major investor in a boat-building company in Boothbay Harbor, Maine.

Discouraged by the failure of both the musical *Tenderloin* in 1960 and the straight play *A Call on Kuprin* in early 1961, Griffith decided to play a less active role in his partnership with Prince. Also, Prince wanted to become a director and had rejected as impractical Griffith's suggestion that they direct as a team, similar to the way they produced. Soon after Griffith decided to semiretire, he suffered a heart attack while playing golf with Abbott at the Westchester Country Club in Rye, New York, and died the following day at United Hospital in nearby Port Chester. Griffith's wife continued as a silent partner with Prince in two more productions, the comedy *Take Her, She's Mine* and Stephen Sondheim's musical *A Funny Thing Happened on the Way to the Forum*, before her own death in 1962.

• Little has been written about Griffith's career as a stage manager. Useful sources of information on his work as a producer are Carol Ilson, *Harold Prince: From "Pajama Game" to "Phantom of the Opera"* (1989), and Hal Prince, *Contradic-tions: Notes on Twenty-Six Years in the Theatre* (1974). See also Allene Talmey, "Biography of a Musical: *Damn Yankees*," *Vogue*, 1 Mar. 1956, pp. 152–53, 179–82; John S. Wilson, "Griffith and Prince," *Theatre Arts* (Oct. 1960): 20–21, 73–74. Richard Bissell, *Say, Darling* (1957), is a novel inspired by behind-the-scenes events in getting *The Pajama Game* produced. Bissell dedicated the novel to Griffith, who serves as a model for one of its characters. Obituaries are in the *New York Times* and *New York Herald Tribune*, both 8 June, 1961.

MARY C. KALFATOVIC

GRIFFITHS, John (fl. 1785–1797), was a dancing-master and choreographer. Nothing is known of his parentage or early life. He may have been related to one of the Griffiths families active on the English stage during the second half of the eighteenth century, but unlike many of his contemporaries, he made no claims of background or former teachers.

A teacher of social dancing who specialized in instructing young people in manners and deportment, Griffiths in 1788 published the earliest extant collection of country dances and cotillions to appear in the United States. In 1794 he published a revised and expanded collection and added instructions for polite deportment. The contents of this second book were reprinted by several rural New England and New York publishers over the next fifteen years. Through these publications and his itinerant teaching, Griffiths influenced the repertory of social dancing and behavior in rural New England ballrooms in the early Federal period.

For most of his known career, Griffiths based his activities in New York City (1785–1787, 1795–1797) or Boston (1788–1794) and divided his time between winter seasons in the city and summer classes in smaller towns in Connecticut, Massachusetts, and Rhode Island. The earliest record of his activity is from the spring of 1785, when, as assistant dancing master for the New York branch of Alexandre-Marie Quesnay's Academy of Polite Arts, he placed two advertisements for balls in New York at which his students performed for the public. He taught a course in New Haven that summer and in September gave at least two performances of the theatrical curiosity known as "Shades," stories acted out by puppets in silhouette. After another season in New York, Griffiths set out on an extended itinerant tour through Connecticut and Rhode Island to Boston, where for six years he held public classes, with additional sessions in Salem, Providence, and at private schools in Boston suburbs. In 1794 he made a brief tour to Northampton, Massachusetts, where he published his second volume of dances, and in the winter of 1795 he reopened his school in New York City. The last notice located for Griffiths is for a session he offered in Litchfield, Connecticut, in November 1797.

The ballroom in eighteenth-century America was a place where the demonstration of social skills was as important as the pleasure of the dance. The dancing-master taught not only dances but also how to behave in polite company, how to make bows and curtsies, and how to stand, sit, and walk with grace. In rural areas, basic manners were often lacking. The down-to-earth language in the section on "Instances of Ill Manners to Be Avoided by Youth of Both Sexes" in Griffiths's second book suggests that he was addressing a rural clientele and was sensitive to their needs and limited aspirations.

In the cities Griffiths taught complex dances of his own and others' composition: solo hornpipes, duos such as composed minuets, gavottes, allemandes, group dances such as English country dances and French cotillions, and ballets for larger groups of dancers to perform in the ballroom. When he held rural classes he focused on the plain minuet and simpler country dances and cotillions. For teaching purposes, he often adapted dances found in imported publications or created his own simple dances, publishing a number of them in his books. One of these was a country dance called "Fisher's Hornpipe," which appeared in both publications and became a favorite—200 years later it was still danced by traditional dancers in rural New England.

• The complete titles of Griffiths's two volumes are *A Collection of the Newest and Most Fashionable Country Dances and Cotillions. The Greater Part by Mr. John Griffith* [sic], *Dancing-Master, in Providence* and *A Collection of the Newest Cotillions, and Country Dances; Principally Composed by John Griffiths, Dancing Master. To Which Is Added, Instances of Ill Manners, to Be Carefully Avoided by Youth of Both Sexes.* Kate Van Winkle Keller, "John Griffiths, Eighteenth-Century Itinerant Dancing Master," in *Itinerancy in New England and New York*, ed. Peter Benes (1986), is the only study available and includes a facsimile of Griffiths's 1794 publication. Charles Cyril Hendrickson reconstructed the twenty-nine country dances in Griffiths's 1788 book in *John Griffiths, American Dancing Master: A Collection of 29 Longways Dances* (1989).

KATE VAN WINKLE KELLER

GRIFFITTS, Hannah (29 July 1727–24 Aug. 1817), writer, was born in Philadelphia, Pennsylvania, the daughter of Thomas Griffitts, mayor of Philadelphia and judge on the Supreme Court of Pennsylvania, and Mary Norris, a member of one of Pennsylvania's most established families. Despite the fact that Griffitts left a substantial collection of manuscript poems, letters, and essays, relatively little is known of her life. She was raised in a solidly Quaker household. Her penchant for writing suggests that she received at least a basic education. She never married, continuing to live with her parents until they died. In her later years she apparently struggled with financial difficulties, as she confided in a 1763 letter to a friend.

Perhaps poverty contributed to Griffitts's decision to remain in Philadelphia in 1777–1778 during the British occupation. She supported the patriots during the Revolutionary War, though not without reservation given their persecution of Quakers for pacifism. In a 1777 letter she unequivocally stated her position to General Anthony Wayne:

I am so good a whig that of Consequence I must be a little of a Politician. There was a time that I knew nor thought no more of Politics than I did of grasping a Sceptre but *now* the Scene is changed and I believe [*sic*] every Woman is desirous of being acquainted with what interests her Country.

Very little else is known of Griffitts's ninety-year life. Her correspondence, voluminous as it was, suggests that she saw herself as a retiring woman, careful not to step outside prescribed roles. The letter to General Wayne quoted above goes on to disparage women who write about politics because they move "entirely out of the sphere Nature designed her for and you know nothing can be lovely that is out of Nature." She apparently worried that even writing poetry might be inappropriate for women, and commented to Susanna Wright in a letter from 1763 that "though these little affairs [her poems] sometimes divert a dull hour, I hope I have . . . no[t] often visited the muses in a ragged petticoat binding, or been studying for verse when the stockin' ball was so much more necessary." Griffitts remained mentally alert and continued to write poetry, whatever her reservations about its propriety, until her death. Her handwriting indicates that she struggled in later years with gradually failing eyesight.

A Pennsylvania network of women poets apparently became one of Griffitts's most supportive audiences. She corresponded and exchanged verses with Wright, Elizabeth Graeme Fergusson, and Deborah Logan, but she charged her friends "to keep [the manuscripts] within the partial bounds of your family, where I am sure of that generous allowance I cannot expect out of it" (Griffitts to Wright, Nov. 1762). Despite encouragement, Griffitts resisted publication all her life. She signed her work with the pseudonym "Fidelia" at least in part to protect her anonymity. In a posthumous sketch, Deborah Logan, Griffitts's cousin and a poet herself, presented Griffitts as "averse to her pieces appearing in print, which they sometimes did, though without her knowledge." Late twentieth-century scholars interested in colonial women's history and in outlining the tradition of women's writing in the United States have included Griffitts's work in more recent narratives.

At her death, Griffitts left more than 200 manuscript poems. Her overwhelming concerns were religious. She frequently used her poetry-making as an act of devotion: "the Muse Long Banished and disused / I now will Consecrate to thee." But her interests were wide-ranging, nonetheless, and Griffitts wrote many secular occasional poems in addition to her religious verse. She wrote about political and social events, natural occurrences (earthquakes, storms, etc.), and friends. She wrote elegies, meditations, satires, and anniversary poems on the deaths of her parents as well.

Some of Griffitts's most memorable works recall events and figures of the American Revolution. "On the Death of John Roberts and Abraham Carlisle," for example, memorializes Roberts and Carlisle as Quaker martyrs to patriot nationalism. Charged with pacifism, they were convicted of treason and then hanged in 1778. Griffitts's strong conviction of the injustice of their deaths gives rise to one of her most moving poems:

And you, the guiltless victims of the day
(Who to a timid City's late reproach
And blush of its Inhabitants,) have fallen,
A Prey to Laws, disgraceful to the man,

. . . .

Long shall your Names survive the brutal deed,
And fair, transmitted down to better times
Stand the Reproach of ours.

Prominent patriots such as Thomas Paine were lucky that Griffitts chose not to publish her opinions of them: "Pane—Tho' thy tongue may now run glibber, / Warm'd with thy Independent glow, / Thou art indeed the Coldest fibber, / I ever knew, or wish to know" ("On Reading Some Paragraphs in 'The Crisis,' April, '77"). Of course, as a patriot sympathizer herself, not all her work is so critical. A 1775 poem that opens with the warning to Julius Caesar to "Beware the Ides of March" transforms itself into a warning to women to remember the boycott on British tea: "Then for the sake of Freedom's name, / (Since British wisdom scorns repealing) / Come Sacrifice to Patriot fame, / And give up Tea by way of healing."

Griffitts wrote poetry throughout her long life, much of it occasional work in the vein of the examples just cited. For that reason, her work opens a window to daily life in eighteenth-century Philadelphia. Some of the poems detail her attention to public events and figures, friendships, networks of correspondents, major natural events, and shifting political tides. Further, Griffitts's writing illustrates the popular neoclassical aesthetic of her times and suggests the continuing importance of manuscript culture to writers even as print culture and a burgeoning book and periodical trade are revolutionizing concepts of authorship. The full range of Griffitts's contribution remains to be studied, but the introductory material available to late twentieth-century readers indicates that such study will be worthwhile.

• Griffitts's manuscripts can be found in the Historical Society of Pennsylvania and in the Milcah Martha Moore Commonplace Book located in the Quaker Collection at Haverford College. A published edition of the commonplace book is *Milcah Martha Moore's Book: A Commonplace Book from Revolutionary America*, ed. Catherine La Courreye Blecki and Karin A. Wulf (1997). A small selection of her poems has been published in Pattie Cowell's *Women Poets in Pre-Revolutionary America, 1650–1775* (1981). Brief samples of the poetry are also available in Anne Wharton, *Through Colonial Doorways* (1893), Carl and Jessica Bridenbaugh, *Rebels and Gentlemen* (1962), and Linda DePauw and Conover Hunt, *Remember the Ladies: Women in America, 1750–1815* (1976). Because Griffitts's use of punctuation is erratic, I have regularized it for easier access to the quotations in this note.

Few published sources are available for reconstructing Griffitts's life, but handwritten notes by John F. Watson in F. W. Leach's typescript "Genealogies of Old Philadelphia Families," also located in the Historical Society of Pennsylvania, provide a sketchy (and occasionally contradictory) outline. Samuel Hazard, *Register of Pennsylvania* 8 (17 Sept. 1831): 178, prints Deborah Logan's account of Griffitts. Anecdotal references are available in several issues of the *Pennsylvania Magazine of History and Biography* 17 (1893): 28; 27 (1903): 109–11; 39 (1915): 286–87; and 75 (1951): 199; and in Linda K. Kerber, *Women of the Republic: Intellect and Ideology in Revolutionary America* (1980). John F. Watson, *Annals of Philadelphia and Pennsylvania in the Olden Times*, vol. 1 (1845), p. 559, provides a brief introduction to Griffitts, as does Katherine Jackson, *Outlines of the Literary History of Colonial Pennsylvania* (1906), and Karin A. Wulf, "A Marginal Independence: Unmarried Women in Colonial Philadelphia" (Ph.D. diss., Johns Hopkins Univ., 1993).

PATTIE COWELL

GRIGGS, David Tressel (6 Oct. 1911–31 Dec. 1974), geophysicist, was born in Columbus, Ohio, the son of Robert Fiske Griggs, a professor of botany, and Laura Amelia Tressel. He moved with his family to Washington, D.C., while he was still in high school when his father accepted a teaching position at George Washington University. In 1928 he matriculated at George Washington but left after one year to study physics at Ohio State University. As an undergraduate he accompanied the 1930 National Geographic Society Expedition to Alaska's Valley of Ten Thousand Smokes, which his father had discovered fourteen years earlier. Largely as a result of his experiences on this expedition, he developed an intense desire to apply the principles of physics to the study of geology.

After receiving his A.B. and A.M. in physics from Ohio State in 1932 and 1933, respectively, Griggs became an assistant in the Department of Geology at Harvard University, and in 1934 he was appointed a junior fellow. While at Harvard he experimented with the mechanical properties of rocks, particularly the deforming effects of heat, pressure, stress, and fluid on mineral crystals and rocks. In 1939, based on data derived from experiments with scale models that he had built, he advanced a controversial theory regarding thermal convection currents in the earth's mantle. Griggs postulated that the largest mountain ranges, such as the Rockies, Andes, and Himalayas, were driven upward from the mantle by currents of molten mantle rocks and minerals. As this material seeped upwards and then horizontally in an effort to rise to the surface, it dragged large sections of the earth's crust with it, so that both molten rock and the colliding edges of the sections piled up in the same location. The convection-current theory was rendered obsolete in the 1960s by the development of the plate tectonics theory; however, it contributed to the development of that theory and to a better understanding of the forces that mold and shape the earth's surface by focusing attention on the "softness" of the earth's crust and mantle.

Griggs contributed to the American effort in World War II by becoming a research associate at the Massachusetts Institute of Technology Radiation Laboratory in 1941. In this capacity he participated in the development of microwave radar as the program manager of an airborne radar system for tracking enemy aircraft. In 1942 he transferred to the Office of the Secretary of War in order to develop and implement radar for as many uses as possible against the Axis powers. In the course of developing the H2X, a radar system designed to increase the effectiveness of strategic bombing runs, he flew on a number of training and combat missions with the U.S. Strategic Air Forces in Europe. He was wounded during two of these missions and received the Purple Heart in 1944. After the surrender of Germany, he joined the Science Advisory Group of the Far East Air Forces and made many of the preparations for dropping the first atomic bomb on Hiroshima. In 1946, in recognition of his contributions to the war effort, he was presented with the Medal for Merit, the U.S. government's highest wartime civilian award.

In 1946 Griggs married Helen Avery; they had two children. The next year he helped found the RAND Corporation, a government-affiliated research institution, and served as the first head of its physics department. Although he continued to consult for the military until his death, in 1948 he resigned this position to return to the study of geophysics by accepting a professorship at the University of California at Los Angeles's Institute of Geophysics. In order to investigate rock deformation under pressures approaching 725,000 pounds per square inch and temperatures as high as 800 degrees(C), he designed and oversaw the construction of several instruments. Among these inventions were the "simple squeezer," the forerunner of the modern anvil device; the "cubic apparatus," a pressure vessel capable of plasticizing quartz crystals and other strong silicates; and the "DT apparatus" and "GB apparatus," cylindrical devices used to maintain rock and mineral samples in conditions of extreme pressure and temperature for up to nine months. These devices allowed Griggs and his colleagues to recreate the submicroscopic dislocation processes that transform rocks from the solid to molten state and to determine for the first time the physical laws governing the flow of molten minerals and rocks in the earth's mantle and crust.

Griggs's most important finding came in 1965, when he discovered that tiny amounts of water dissolved in quartz and other silicate crystals tremendously weaken the strength of their crystalline structure and promote their deformation. The data from these experiments were extrapolated and subjected to computer modeling to develop theories of fracture and seismicity, the flow of rocks in mountain building, and the global motions of the tectonic plates—all of which contributed to a more complete understanding of the natural forces that continue to shape the earth.

Although the bulk of his research after the end of World War II involved geophysics, Griggs continued to advise the U.S. military on matters of scientific importance. As the chief scientist of the Air Force in 1951–1952 and as a consultant for the Armed Forces Special Weapons Project from 1951 to 1956, he supported the decision to develop the hydrogen bomb; he also played an important role in the establishment of the Atomic Energy Commission's Lawrence Radiation Laboratory in California and in the implementation of underground nuclear testing. In 1954 he became embroiled in a controversy over the denial of a security clearance to J. Robert Oppenheimer, the moving force in the development of the atomic bomb but an opponent of the development of the hydrogen bomb. Griggs's testimony before the Personal Security Board in support of denial earned him the ire of many physicists who supported Oppenheimer's position. He also served on the Air Force Science Advisory Board from 1952 to 1974, the Defense Science Board from 1964 to 1974, and the Army Science Advisory Panel from 1965 to 1974.

In 1958 Griggs became involved in the Plowshares Program, an effort to use atomic energy for peaceful purposes, and suggested that nuclear weapons could be used to gain a further understanding of the ways in which earthquakes work. By detonating small thermonuclear devices in the earth's interior, he hoped to generate seismic waves that could be recorded and studied in an effort to predict future earthquakes. In the 1970s he played a significant role in the study of the "moon rocks" brought back to earth by the astronauts of various Apollo missions.

Griggs served as the president of the Tectonophysics Section of the American Geophysical Union from 1964 to 1968. He was awarded the Air Force Award for Exceptional Civilian Service in 1953, the American Geophysical Union's Bucher Medal and Ohio State's Centennial Achievement Award in 1970, and the Geological Society of America's Arthur L. Day Medal in 1974. He was elected to membership in the National Academy of Sciences. He died in Snowmass, California.

Griggs made two important contributions to the development of American science. His research into the ways in which rocks and minerals are weakened and deformed constituted a major step forward in the scientific understanding of the physical forces at work below the earth's surface. His work as an adviser to various branches and agencies of the U.S. military contributed materially to the development and application of technologically sophisticated weapons systems, such as airborne radar and the hydrogen bomb.

• A biography, including a bibliography, is Ivan A. Getting and John M. Christie, National Academy of Sciences, *Biographical Memoirs* 64 (1994): 113–33. An obituary is in the *New York Times*, 4 Jan. 1975.

CHARLES W. CAREY, JR.

GRIGGS, John William (10 July 1849–28 Nov. 1927), attorney general of the United States and governor of New Jersey, was born in Sussex County, New Jersey, the son of Daniel Griggs and Emeline Johnson, prosperous farmers. Griggs graduated from Lafayette College in 1868 after working as a railroad ticket agent to pay for his education. A later campaign slogan said he had moved "From Ticket Agent to Governor." He studied law for three years near Paterson, New Jersey, and formed a close friendship with Garret A. Hobart, who became vice president under William McKinley. Griggs was admitted to the bar in 1871. His first marriage was to Carolyn Webster Brandt in 1874; she died in 1891. He married Laura Elizabeth Price in 1893. He had seven children by these marriages.

Griggs made his first campaign for political office in 1875 when he won election on the Republican ticket to the General Assembly. He served two terms before being defeated and then became city counsel for Paterson, New Jersey, from 1879 to 1882. Griggs spent two terms in the state senate from 1882 to 1890 and was president of the senate in 1886. Associates said that "he was an intellect in a mold of ice," but his abilities as an orator and skill as a legislator made him a leader among New Jersey Republicans. He was a delegate to the Republican National Convention in 1888, and President Benjamin Harrison (1833–1901) considered him for appointment to the U.S. Supreme Court.

With the backing of Hobart, Griggs won the Republican nomination for governor in 1895 and defeated his Democratic opponent in the general election, the first gubernatorial victory for the party in nearly thirty years. President William McKinley asked Griggs to become U.S. attorney general early in 1898, and he became a close adviser to the president on legal and political issues. His views on the issue of corporate consolidation made Griggs reluctant to enforce the Sherman Antitrust Law (1890) with much vigor. The most important legal issues he faced were the Insular Cases concerning the jurisdiction of the laws of the United States over the overseas territories acquired in the war with Spain. Griggs's abilities as an advocate helped the government prevail in the Supreme Court.

Griggs retired from the cabinet in 1901 and sought without success the Republican nomination for the U.S. Senate from New Jersey in 1902. From 1901 to 1912 he served on the Permanent Court of Arbitration at The Hague, and he built a successful law practice in New York. Among his clients were the Marconi Wireless Telegraph Company and the Radio Corporation of America. Griggs remained a staunch Republican and criticized Woodrow Wilson during his rise to power in New Jersey politics.

Hunting, fishing, and shooting were his major diversions. He died in Paterson, New Jersey. Griggs was a competent and influential attorney general, but he left no permanent mark on the cabinet office itself.

• Griggs's personal papers do not appear to have survived. The New Jersey Historical Society, Newark, has some of his letters in their collections. His service as attorney general can be traced in the papers of William McKinley, Library of Congress, and in the records of the Department of Justice, National Archives. Some evidence about his legal career can be gleaned from the papers of Theodore Roosevelt, William Howard Taft, and Philander C. Knox in the Library of Congress. *Annual Reports of the Attorney General* (1898–1901) offer the official perspective. Among Griggs's own writings are *Addresses* (1930); "Have the United States Judges Adequate Salaries?" *Independent* 65 (19 Nov. 1908): 1155–58; and "The

World Status of the German-Russian Peace," *Forum* 59 (Apr. 1918): 393–402. For his policies toward the trusts, see "The Attorney General on Trusts and Combinations in Restraint of Trade," *American Law Review* 34 (Mar.-Apr. 1900): 253–55. Griggs's career in New Jersey is covered in William E. Sackett, *Modern Battles of Trenton: From Werts to Wilson*, vol. 2 (1914), and his tenure as attorney general is examined in Lewis L. Gould, *The Presidency of William McKinley* (1980). An obituary is in the *New York Times*, 29 Nov. 1927.

LEWIS L. GOULD

GRIGGS, Sutton E. (1872–1930), writer and Baptist minister, was born Sutton Elbert Griggs in Chatfield, Texas, the son of Allen R. Griggs, a prominent Baptist minister; his mother's name is not known. Sutton Griggs received his elementary education in the Dallas public schools and attended Bishop College in Marshall, Texas. After graduating in 1890, Griggs attended the Richmond Theological Seminary (later a part of Virginia Union University), graduating after three years. After his ordination as a Baptist minister, he was given his first pastorate at Berkley, Virginia, where he remained for two years. Griggs then moved to Tennessee where he spent thirty years, first at the First Baptist Church of East Nashville and later at the Tabernacle Baptist Church of Memphis, where he held ministerial office for nineteen years. Griggs married Emma J. Williams of Portsmouth, Virginia, in 1897; they had no children.

After reconstruction and the subsequent segregation and antiblack violence, Griggs, along with other African-American writers such as Charles Chesnutt, Paul Laurence Dunbar, W. E. B. Du Bois, and Booker T. Washington, responded by creating works that portrayed black Americans, often emphasizing their demands for civil rights. Griggs not only wrote five novels but also published a number of political and philosophical tracts. He published, promoted, and distributed these works himself, often by selling them door-to-door. One critic, Hugh Gloster, asserts that because of Griggs's strategy of taking his work directly to his audience, his books were more widely read and circulated than those of Chesnutt or Dunbar. In spite of Griggs's vigorous promotion of his own work, he maintained that all of his novels were financial failures.

The first, the most well known, and arguably the best of Griggs's five novels, *Imperium in Imperio*, appeared in 1899. It is, as are all of his novels, a political work. The story is centered around two individuals, Belton Piedmont and the mulatto Bernard Belgrave. Starting with their early childhood, Griggs traces the lives of these two characters through their contrasting social positions. Although Belton suffers intense discrimination (he is even hanged by a lynch mob but not killed), he adopts an accommodating and integrationist stance. Bernard, on the other hand, is well treated because of his white father. Nevertheless, Bernard becomes the more militant of the two. Perhaps most important, the story contains a description of a secret black government situated within the United States. The story's two protagonists wrestle with the problems of racism and segregation, as well as many of the political and philosophical ideas found in Griggs's other work.

Griggs's other four novels also deal with the themes he first examined in *Imperium in Imperio*. His second novel, *Overshadowed* (1901), deals with the harsh conditions imposed on blacks through segregation, painting a gloomy picture. *Unfettered* (1902), is the story of a young mulatto woman, Morlene, who falls in love with Dorlan Worthell, a courageous young black man. In this novel Griggs brings all of his characteristic melodramatic and sentimental tendencies to bear. In addition he tacks on an appendix, called "Dorlan's Plan." Foreshadowing his own more didactic work, the plan runs more than fifty pages, presenting a program to elevate the black race. In *The Hindered Hand* (1905), Griggs continued his probing inquiry of race relations through themes of lynching, miscegenation, and emigration to Africa. Griggs's final novel, *Pointing the Way* (1908), offers legal action as a possible recourse for blacks, a suggestion that also appears in his later writings.

After *Pointing the Way* Griggs abandoned the novel in favor of social and political tracts. He produced nearly three dozen such works. For the most part his themes remained the same, as he discussed problems such as lynching and mob violence, inadequate employment opportunities, miscegenation, and black suffrage. One of the longest of these works, *Wisdom's Call* (1911) is a reworking of two of his earliest tracts, *The Needs of the South* (1909) and *The Race Question in a New Light* (1909). In it Griggs directed his attention toward the intelligence and capability of blacks, concluding that their judgment is sound and reliable. *The Guide to Racial Greatness*, published in 1923 and one of his more well-known works, lays out a guide intended to solve many of the racial problems that Griggs detailed in his novels and tracts. As with his novels, Griggs published these tracts himself and sold them door-to-door.

Griggs's work was, for the most part, ignored until the 1940s. Since then there has been a reexamination of his writings, with critics labeling him everything from a radical-militant to an accommodationist.

Near the end of his life, Griggs returned to Texas. In Denison he served as pastor of Hopewell Baptist Church, a position his father had held. Griggs left Denison for Houston, intending to found a religious and civic institute. He died there, however, before the realization of his plan.

• Information on Griggs can be found in Hugh M. Gloster, "Sutton E. Griggs: Novelist of the New Negro," *Phylon* (Fourth Quarter 1943); Robert Bone, *The Negro Novel in America* (1958); C. W. E. Bigsby, ed., *The Black American Writer* (1969); Robert E. Fleming, "Sutton E. Griggs: Militant Black Novelist," *Phylon* (Mar. 1973); Arthur P. Davis, *From the Dark Tower; Afro-American Writers (1900–1960)* (1974); and Dickson D. Bruce Jr., *Black American Writing from the Nadir: The Evolution of a Literary Tradition, 1877–1915* (1989).

CHRIS RUIZ-VELASCO

GRIGSBY, Hugh Blair (22 Nov. 1806–28 Apr. 1881), historian, was born in Norfolk, Virginia, the son of Rev. Benjamin Porter Grigsby, a Presbyterian minister, and Elizabeth Blair McPherson. His father died in 1810 of yellow fever. Hugh's education and upbringing thus became the responsibility of his mother, a woman of intelligence whose substantial family means enabled her to give Hugh and his two siblings the advantages of a good education.

Grigsby attended several different Latin day schools in Norfolk before going off in 1815 to a boarding school in Prince Edward County. There he contracted typhoid fever and had to return home. His health returned slowly; for the rest of his life he suffered from a weak constitution and recurrent pulmonary problems. In 1824 he enrolled at Yale University with the intention of pursuing a career in medicine. Unhappy with this choice, he decided to study for a legal career. After sixteen months he withdrew from Yale and returned to Norfolk to study law on his own. After some years of desultory, independent study, he gained admission to the Virginia bar in 1828.

Grigsby never practiced law on a full-time basis but used it as a steppingstone to enter politics. In 1828 he was elected to the Virginia House of Delegates by the citizens of Norfolk. He served a single term, 1828–1830. A states' rights Republican, he supported Andrew Jackson for president but not the rising tide of democratic political reform associated with Jackson's presidency. For some years Virginia's small farmers living in the underrepresented western part of the state had been demanding a greater voice in the legislature and urging other democratic reforms. They succeeded finally in calling a convention in October 1829 to revise the state constitution. Grigsby attended the convention and stood solidly with the conservative Tidewater planter interests, which made only minor concessions to western demands. During the convention Grigsby decided to "delineate the personal appearance of the members." His character sketches of John Marshall, James Madison, James Monroe, John Randolph, and other Virginia luminaries were far more valuable than his contributions to the political debate. They became the basis for one of his later major historical volumes.

Grigsby's political ambitions were hampered by his continued poor health. He suffered from bouts of dizziness, a "weakness of the lungs," and tinnitus accompanied by progressive deafness. Immobilized at times by these infirmities, he doubted that he could continue in a career of public service. He stood for reelection to the assembly in 1830 but ran halfheartedly and was not greatly disappointed by his defeat. In the spring of 1830, hopeful that a change of climate would improve his health and outlook, Grigsby embarked upon a five-month walking tour of New England and upper Canada. He returned to Norfolk in October feeling much stronger.

Upon returning from his pedestrian tour, Grigsby became a partner in an apothecary, which he managed until 1834, when he acquired the *Norfolk American*

Beacon. For the next six years, as owner and editor of the daily newspaper, Grigsby worked exceedingly hard. The long hours and heavy workload weakened his health, forcing him to give up the business. The $60,000 that he received from the sale of the *Beacon* gave him the financial independence to pursue other interests.

In 1840 Grigsby married Mary Venable Carrington; they had two children. Mary's father, Colonel Clement Carrington, a revolutionary war hero and the master of the large estate of "Edgehill," died a few years after the marriage. Grigsby and his wife moved permanently to Edgehill, where Grigsby found the leisure time to pursue his scholarly interest while attending to the practical concerns of managing a large plantation.

Like so many enlightened farmers of his generation, Grigsby, a large slaveowner and tobacco planter, understood the need to improve agricultural practices in Virginia. He became active in the agricultural reform movement, joining agricultural societies, subscribing to scientific farm journals, and experimenting with deep plowing, hillside terracing, and other improved tillage methods designed to conserve and improve the soil. The encouraging results made the several-thousand-acre Edgehill estate a model farm whose success served as an example to neighboring farmers.

At Edgehill, surrounded by a superb library of more than six thousand volumes that he carefully selected, Grigsby finally found his life's true calling: the writing of history and biography. He had long been interested in history, having written at the age of eighteen a biographical volume on notable Virginians. Proud of Virginia's past and influenced by the great German historian Leopold von Ranke, he collected letters, papers, diaries, and other documents that would enable him to write historical accounts of the lives of prominent Virginians. The foremost Virginia historian of his day, Grigsby was a veritable storehouse of knowledge about the state's first families. This brought him into close association with Henry S. Randall, George Bancroft, Henry Adams, and other contemporary historians who corresponded with him seeking information about Jefferson, Patrick Henry, and other famous Virginians.

Grigsby's published work is almost exclusively biographical. Although uncritical and adulatory in tone, the volumes contain some useful descriptions of Virginia's public figures and preserve valuable anecdotes and personal material about them drawn from the oral tradition. The most important of his works include *The Virginia Convention of 1776* (1855), *The History of the Virginia Federal Conventions of 1788* (2 vols., 1890–1891), and *The Virginia Convention of 1829–30* (1854). He also published *Discourse on the Life and Character of the Honorable Littleton Waller Tazewell* (1860), *The Founders of Washington College* (1890), and *Discourse on the Lives and Characters of the Early Presidents and Trustees of Hampden-Sydney College* (1913). In addition Grigsby wrote many essays and genealogical studies for publication in the *Southern Literary Messenger* and especially the *Virginia Historical Register*, which was the organ of the Virginia Historical Society.

Despite his deafness, Grigsby did not withdraw from public life. He was very active socially and welcomed the opportunity to address any group, public or private, interested in his message. He spoke at Independence Day celebrations, to various college and university groups, to historical societies, and to state bar associations. He was active for many years in the Virginia Historical Society and led the successful effort to acquire a suitable facility for housing the society's valuable collections. He was elected president of that group in 1870. He was also a member of the American Philosophical Society and an honorary member of the Massachusetts Historical Society. From 1871 until his death he was chancellor of the College of William and Mary, which conferred on him an honorary LL.D. degree in 1885 for his efforts to promote learning. He died of pneumonia at Edgehill.

• The most important collection of Grigsby's letters and papers is the Hugh Blair Grigsby Papers at the Virginia Historical Society in Richmond, which contains over 4,000 items including most of his correspondence, diaries, commonplace books, account books, legal documents, drafts of his public speeches, and collected letters of Thomas Jefferson, John Tyler, Patrick Henry, Littleton Waller Tazewell, and John Randolph of Roanoke. Smaller collections are at the Norfolk Public Library, at the Alderman Library at the University of Virginia in Charlottesville, and in the William Cabell Rives Papers at the Library of Congress. Grigsby's important correspondence with Henry S. Randall is published in Frank J. Klingberg and Frank W. Klingberg, eds., *The Correspondence Between Henry Stephens Randall and Hugh Blair Grigsby, 1856–1861*, University of California Publications in History, vol. 43 (Berkeley, 1952). Alden Griswold Bigelow, "Hugh Blair Grigsby: Historian and Antiquarian" (Ph.D. diss., Univ. of Virginia, 1957), supplies biographical details and a useful interpretation of his life and work. In his introduction to Grigsby's *Virginia Convention of 1788* Robert Alonzo Brock penned a useful biographical sketch of Grigsby. An obituary is in the *Norfolk Landmark*, 3 May 1881.

CHARLES D. LOWERY

GRIGSBY, Snow Flake (13 Feb. 1899–22 Mar. 1981), civil rights advocate and trade unionist, was born in Newberry County near Chappells, South Carolina, the son of Fred Grigsby and Kitty (maiden name unknown), farmers. Named in the African manner for the unusual snowfall that fell on his birth date, he learned the lesson of fending for one's self in a family of twelve children raised by religious, education-minded, politically active parents. He embraced individualism but benefited from philanthropy and endorsed government activism. He left home to receive his high school diploma at Harbison Junior College (1923) in Irmo, courtesy of the Presbyterian Church. Heading north to look for what he called "rosy opportunities," he worked menial jobs by night and attended the Detroit Institute of Technology by day. He graduated in 1927 but failed to find employment as a pharmacist. Like his father, a one-time federal mail contractor, he became a postal employee. He married Eliza Red, and they raised a son and a daughter.

Confronting racism in the face of economic depression, he began a lifetime crusade of "militant insistence" upon equal opportunities for blacks, evolving from activist to unionist to political candidate. In each phase, he penned pamphlets in the revolutionary tradition: facts exposed lies and alibis to produce results, whereas confrontation without research wrought "blood on the conscience" but little change.

In 1933 Grigsby's research for "X-Ray Survey of Detroit" statistically demonstrated how disproportionately few municipal jobs were held by black citizens. Following a discussion of his finding at the Bethel African Methodist Episcopal Church, he and Reverend William Peck, formed the Civic Rights Committee and descended on the board of education. They presented data on the paltry number of black school employees and provided dossiers of numerous black college graduates, while also revealing that whites continued to be hired. They thereby undermined both the argument that no qualified black candidates were available and that budgetary limitations prevented additional hiring. Nineteen blacks were employed that day.

Thereafter, Grigsby headed the committee in what became known as formulistic protest. He sought to place blacks in the Recorder's Court and among firemen, and although he may have cost one judge re-election, he failed to succeed in either effort as he had with the school board. He proved more effective with the Detroit Edison Company, dramatically dragging thirty-two feet of black electricity payments before company representatives and, with other black leaders, negotiating jobs for black utility workers.

Essentially, Grigsby's effort was part of the "Jobs for Negroes" campaign occurring in several depression-racked cities, yet it lacked the chauvinistic tone and intimidating tactics of other more militant organizations in both New York and Chicago. He stressed community control over the influence of nationally established civil rights organizations and opposed pickets and marches. His criticism of apathetic black citizens and leaders of both races in "White Hypocrisy and Black Lethargy" (1937) resulted in his having few allies among them. He did not concentrate on the private sector or secure large numbers of jobs there; rather he broke barriers in municipal employment and laid the groundwork for future advances.

In 1939 Grigsby was forced to resign from the committee so he would not lose his government job for engaging in political activities. He may have done more than loudly protest the denial of a federal loan by the Home Owners Loan Corporation, for there were both blacks and whites in Detroit who considered him a rabble rouser. The Civic Rights Committee soon faded, partly because of his departure and partly because of the emergence of other more militant organizations (inspired by his example, the United Automobile Workers, and the Second World War).

Grigsby transferred his energies to the National Alliance of Postal and Federal Employees. In 1941 he won election as the editor of its *The Postal Alliance*. Over the next thirty-two years, he promoted union and racial concerns in his monthly magazine, which ultimately reached 40,000 members nationwide and every public official in Washington, D.C. During the war, he advanced the Double V campaign for victory over racism at home and fascism abroad, often through statements of others, for instance Detroiters involved in the Sojourner Truth Housing controversy of 1942; in that dispute he also mobilized Postal Alliance staff members to lobby congressmen and federal authorities for black occupancy of the defense units. Yet, he made the publication an integral part of the biracial union and served as one of its spokesmen.

Throughout the 1950s and 1960s, Grigsby expressed union concerns over automation and similar issues, while nudging postal workers toward the civil rights movement. He believed that both the causes of trade unionism and civil rights advanced equality of opportunity and human dignity; postal employees comprised "one big union," a microcosm of Reverend Martin Luther King's nonviolent efforts to integrate society. True to his beliefs, he rarely mentioned racial separatism and disorder.

Grigsby considered Detroit politics as important as "bread and butter" issues. In "Taps or Reveille?" (1956), he stressed the need for blacks to vote, yet failed nine years later in his bid for a common council seat, as did his petition for district rather than at-large elections (elections that would guarantee black representation). By the early 1970s, he circulated old and new material in publications, including "Are You Aware?" and "Think!" alerting voters to issues and "shafting" politicians. Nonetheless, he failed to obtain primary nominations as a county commissioner (1974) or community college trustee (1978).

From the Great Depression to his death from cancer in Detroit, Grigsby promoted achievement and pride. He wrote pamphlets for every black generation, including "Of This We Can Be Proud" (1961), and "Brainwashed—and Ignored" (1976). He also spoke widely during the racially aware 1960s, continuing in retirement to work as a researcher and consultant. A member of St. John's Presbyterian Church, the Republican Party, and the National Association for the Advancement of Colored People (despite having criticized it in the 1930s) combined a belief in individualism with collective action in an ongoing drive for self-improvement and racial justice. An "old Warrior" lifestyle reflected his propagandist creed: "A drop of ink may cause thousands to think!"

• Few sources exist on Grigsby's background although some information from newspaper clippings and other miscellany is available in the Snow F. Grigsby Reading Room file, Burton Historical Collection, Detroit Public Library. The collection also contains copies of many of his pamphlets, including "Ambitions That Could Not Be Fenced In" (c. 1945), which contains profiles of three siblings; and a sizeable, if incomplete set of *The Postal Alliance* for the years of his editorship.

His oral history is in the Blacks in the Labor Movement Collection of the Archives of Labor and Urban Affairs, Detroit, as are those of contemporaries such as Joseph Coles, Reverend Malcolm G. Dade, and Beulah T. Whitby, who evaluate him. Richard T. Thomas, *Life for Us Is What We Make It: Building black Community in Detroit, 1915–1945* (1992) covers his years as founder and chair of the Civic Rights Committee, 1933–1939. On this subject, see also Thomas S. Soloman, "Participation of Negroes in Detroit Elections" (Ph.D. diss., Univ. of Michigan, 1937). Newsworthy aspects of his later life, including his councilman candidacy, surfaced in the local black and white press; for examples see the *Michigan Chronicle*, 1 Sept. 1956, 19 June 1965, and 28 Mar. 1981, and *Detroit Free Press*, 24 Mar. 1981. Perhaps the best overall summary of his life is "Detroit Honors Its Volunteers," *Detroit News*, 11 Feb. 1981.

DOMINIC J. CAPECI, JR.

GRIM, David (28 Aug. 1737–26 Mar. 1826), tavern keeper, merchant, and antiquarian, was born in Stauderheim in the Palatinate, the son of Philip Grimm, a tanner and farmer, and Marguerite Dâher. He and his brothers Peter and Jacob dropped the second *m* from the family name. Grim immigrated to New York City with his parents and four older siblings in 1739. When Grim was about twelve, a painful lameness in his right leg, which he attributed to rheumatism, threw a hip out of joint and left him with one leg shorter than the other. He nevertheless served aboard two privateers during the French and Indian War. In the summer of 1757 he sailed under Captain Thomas Seymour on the *King of Prussia*, which during a voyage of ten months fought two successful engagements at sea and captured several French prizes in the West Indies. In December 1758 Grim sailed again under Captain Seymour aboard the *General Wolfe*, and the following March he returned to New York on a prize vessel carrying a valuable cargo of sugar and coffee. In 1759 he married Maria "Mary" Elizabeth Böcking. Of their seven children, three lived to adulthood.

Grim supported his family with a variety of commercial activities. In 1765 he was listed among the freemen of New York City as a cordwainer, and by 1767 he was operating a tavern at the Sign of the Three Tuns on Chapel Street. The German Protestants in the city celebrated the anniversary of the repeal of the Stamp Act at Grim's tavern on 18 March 1774. Also engaged in trade and speculation, he in April 1774 made a voyage to St. Thomas in the West Indies that, contrary to his expectations, yielded only a small profit. Grim's first wife died in 1779, and in 1781 he married Mary Alstyne Barwick, a widow, with whom he had no children.

During the American Revolution, when New York was occupied by the British army, Grim operated an establishment called the Hessian Coffee House, first on William Street and later on George Street. He evidently catered to German mercenaries, and in 1780 his daughter Mary Elizabeth married a lieutenant of the Anspach-Beyreuth troops. Nevertheless, Grim remained politically neutral during the war, unlike his brother Peter Grim, an avowed Loyalist who moved to St. John, New Brunswick, when the British evacuated New York City in 1783.

Between December 1782 and October 1784 Grim traveled with his son Philip to Wiesbaden, Germany, seeking relief at its famous spas for his recurring rheumatism. The warm baths, Grim believed, restored his health and lengthened his life, amply justifying the considerable expense of his long journey. The trip also enabled him to visit his birthplace and to tour Dublin, London, Frankfurt, and the major Dutch cities. On his return to New York, Grim was accused by a corrupt constable of having gone to Nova Scotia as a Loyalist refugee instead of to Europe, and he apparently was obliged to buy off this petty official to clear his name.

In the summer of 1785 Grim established a mercantile firm in New York to trade and speculate with Paul Beck, Jr., a prominent Philadelphia merchant, and he soon acquired several packet vessels to expand his operations. In 1794 Grim made his son Philip a partner in the firm, and in 1809 he retired from the business, leaving it in Philip's hands. Grim also was active in civic affairs before his retirement. He served as treasurer of the city's Lutheran church for a number of years, and he was president of the German Society of New York City from 1795 to 1802. In 1792 Grim collected subscriptions and received competitive designs for building the Tontine Coffee House on Wall Street, a cooperative project funded by the merchants of the city to provide a convenient business center for themselves.

In retirement Grim preserved his memories of eighteenth-century New York by making several detailed maps of the city as it appeared during his younger days and several pen and ink drawings of the city's early landmarks. These documents include *A Plan of the City and Environs of New York as They Were in the Years 1742–43 and 1744* (1813); *Plan and Elevation of the City Hall Formerly Standing in Wall Street* (1818); *Part of New York in 1742 Showing the Site of the Present [City Hall] Park; the Collect and Little Collect Ponds; and a Portion of the West Side of Broadway* (n.d.); a map of the parts of the city destroyed by the fires of 1776 and 1778; a watercolor of the banquet pavilion for the federal procession celebration in 1788; and two elevations of the Tontine Coffee House. Accompanying the maps and drawings are notes containing Grim's reminiscences of such diverse events as the "Negro plot" of 1741, the building of fortifications north of the city in 1745, an American Indian visit in 1753, and the fire of 1776.

A thoroughgoing antiquarian who valued the past for its own sake, Grim was more interested in changes in the surrounding cityscape than the great issues or personalities of his time. His maps and drawings were made largely for his own amusement, but he also intended to leave them for posterity. He consciously executed each document with painstaking attention to details and with the skill of an accomplished draftsman. In 1819 he presented two maps and the city hall sketch to the New-York Historical Society. A granddaughter gave his remaining works to the society in 1869. By recording what few others remembered much less bothered to preserve, Grim left an invaluable record of New York City during the years before it became a major commercial and cultural center of the new American nation. He died in New York City.

• The Grim manuscripts at the New-York Historical Society include, in addition to his maps, drawings, and notes on historical occurrences, two nearly identical copies of the account he wrote of his family and his life in 1816. Several of Grim's maps and drawings are reproduced in Isaac Newton Phelps Stokes, *The Iconography of Manhattan Island, 1498–1909* (6 vols., 1915–1928), and David Thomas Valentine, *Manual of the Corporation of the City of New York, for 1854, 1855, 1856, 1866*. For Grim's registration as a cordwainer, see "Roll of Freemen of New York City, 1675–1866," *New-York Historical Society Collections* 18 (1886): 206. For Grim's activities as a tavern keeper, see the *New-York Journal, or General Advertiser*, 29 Jan. 1767 and 24 Mar. 1774; the New York *Royal Gazette*, 28 Mar. 1778, 28 Oct. 1778, and 13 May 1780; the *New-York Mercury; or, General Advertiser*, 31 Jan. 1780; and William Harrison Bayles, *Old Taverns of New York* (1915). For Grim's involvement with the German Society, see Joseph A. Scoville, *The Old Merchants of New York City* (5 vols., 1863–1869). An obituary is in the *New-York Evening Post*, 27 Mar. 1826.

PHILANDER D. CHASE

GRIM, Ralph Early (25 Feb. 1902–19 Aug. 1989), mineralogist, was born in Reading, Pennsylvania, the son of Harry Grim, a cigar maker, and Annette Early. After attending public schools, he prepared for the College Board examinations with a two-month, intensive preparatory course at Roxbury School in Cheshire, Connecticut, and was accepted at Yale University in 1920, completing his bachelor's degree in 1924 and continuing there in graduate school. In 1924 he married Marie Claire "Peggy" O'Connor; they had no children. In the summer of 1925 he served as Harold Wanless's field assistant in mapping the Aledo Quadrangle for the Illinois State Geological Survey.

In 1926 Grim left Yale and accepted concurrent appointments as assistant professor of geology at the University of Mississippi and as assistant state geologist of Mississippi. In the summer of 1929 he began a study of the Eocene rocks of Mississippi. In the course of this work he made significant contributions to the knowledge of the Tertiary formations in the state. Also during this work he made the acquaintance of A. C. Trowbridge of the University of Iowa, who was carrying on similar investigations in Arkansas and Louisiana. When the governor of Mississippi, Theodore Bilbo, took control of the university's board of trustees and summarily discharged fifty faculty members, Grim was among those who lost their jobs. Inasmuch as he lacked resources to return to Yale for the additional year he would need to finish his doctorate, he accepted an instructorship offered by Trowbridge at Iowa and finished his doctorate there in 1931. In that year, on Trowbridge's recommendation, he joined the staff of the State Geological Survey of Illinois as a petrographer, serving until 1950. In 1936 he culminated

the study of Eocene rocks in Mississippi, publishing *The Eocene Sediments of Mississippi* as Bulletin 30 of the Mississippi Geological Survey. In 1940 he and his wife divorced. In 1945 he married Hazel Mae Tucker; they had no children. He was appointed research professor in the Department of Geology of the University of Illinois in 1948. He lectured on clay mineralogy in several countries and conducted an extensive international consultant practice in clay mineralogy, clay product manufacture, and mineral resource development, visiting every inhabited continent during the course of his work.

Grim was a petrologist and sedimentologist principally interested in the structure and composition of clays and the relation between their petrography and their properties. He wrote three textbooks in the field, *Clay Mineralogy* (1953; 2d ed., 1968), *Applied Clay Mineralogy* (1962), and, with Necip Guven, *Bentonite, Geology, Mineralogy, Properties and Uses* (1978). He also published a great many technical articles on this and other topics. His principal scientific contribution lies in defining the molecular structure and composition of clay minerals, in classifying clay minerals, and in determining their material properties. When he began his career, it had only recently been discovered that clay was actually composed of crystalline components susceptible to X-ray diffraction analysis. This sort of analysis made it possible to identify clay minerals and to determine the physical and chemical character of individual minerals in common clay mixtures. Grim was one of the first to enter this field and probably was the most productive and prolific student of clays during his lifetime. He was led into this field when he began working with Victor Allen of St. Louis University, who was engaged in a study of underclays, the clays found below coal beds, for the Illinois Geological Survey. Grim soon began collaborating also with George Clark and Roger Bray of the University of Illinois in, respectively, X-ray diffraction study and chemical study of Illinois clays. William F. Bradley, one of Clarke's graduate students in chemistry became Grim's collaborator for more than thirty years. In addition, Grim continually emphasized the practical applications of his research. His applied work began in 1950, when he served as consultant for the Illinois Clay Products Company, with whose president, Otis Jones, he maintained a long and productive association. He also worked extensively with Karl Terzaghi of Harvard and Ralph Peck of the University of Illinois, contributing clay mineral identification and analysis for applied studies on failure of earth materials affecting construction projects. From 1960 to 1973 he conducted an extensive mineral resources evaluation of the Republic of the Ivory Coast under the auspices of David Lilienthal and the Development and Resources Corporation. During the course of this work, in 1962, his second wife died, and in 1964 he married Frances Brown Reed; they had no children. He helped establish the Ivory Coast's government agencies for mineral research and in 1973 the republic named him a chevalier in its Ordre Nationale for his work. Grim asserted in his memoirs that this was "the greatest single event" in his scientific life.

In 1967 Grim retired from the University of Illinois as professor *emeritus* and in 1972 he accepted a position as adjunct professor of geology at Texas Technological University at Lubbock, Texas.

Very devoted to the advancement of his field, in 1948 he was the organizing chair of the National Research Council Committee on Clay Mineralogy, remaining as chair until the committee gave rise to the Clay Minerals Society of America in 1957. He instigated the location of the National Lime Association's research laboratory at the University of Illinois in 1959 and supervised its operations. He also chaired the National Research Council's Subcommittee on Digenesis and Committee on Sedimentation starting in 1953 and headed up the International Committee for the Study of Clays from 1952 to 1958. He was a fellow of the Geological Society of America, the Mineralogical Society of America (serving as vice president in 1958 and president in 1959), and the American Ceramic Society (serving as vice president from 1948 to 1960) and was the first Distinguished Member of the Clay Minerals Society. He was also a member of the Society of Economic Geologists, the American Association of Petroleum Geologists, the American Geophysical Union, the Society of Economic Paleontologists and Mineralogists, Sigma Xi, the British Ceramic Society, and the Association pour l'Étude des Argiles (serving as chair from 1948 to 1960). In 1983 he endowed a chair in geology at the University of Illinois, and in 1986 he donated funds to purchase a scanning electron microscope for the department.

Grim received many recognitions and awards. He was an honorary member of the British Clay Minerals Society and of the Society of Economic Paleontologists and Mineralogists and an honorary fellow of the Mineralogical Society of Great Britain; the National Academy of Sciences, Arts, and Letters of Modena, Italy; the Ceramic Society of Brazil; and the India Academy of Sciences, which awarded him a gold medal in 1957. The Clay Minerals Society of Spain awarded him a gold medal for outstanding contributions to clay mineralogy. The Mineralogical Society of America awarded him its prestigious Roebling Medal in 1974. He died in Urbana, Illinois.

• Bound copies of Grim's unedited memoirs, 689 typewritten pages, are in the library and in the archives of the University of Illinois–Urbana. Eleven boxes of his personal papers, including professional correspondence and manuscripts of some scientific papers and lecture notes, also are in the university archives. Grim recounts highlights of his career in "Acceptance of the Roebling Medal of the Mineralogical Society of America for 1974," *American Mineralogist* 60 (1975): 498–500. His comments are supplemented by Haydn H. Murray, "Presentation of the Roebling Medal of the Mineralogical Society of America for 1974 to Ralph E. Grim," *American Mineralogist* 60 (1975): 497–98. The *Annual Newsletter* of the Department of Geology of the University of Illinois–Urbana (1949–1989) makes frequent mention of Grim's work. Copies are available in the library and archives of the univer-

sity and in the department's files. Murray wrote two memorials of Grim, in the *Geological Society of America Memorials* 20 (1990): 85–87 and in the *American Mineralogist* 75 (1990): 1229–30; there is also a memorial by W. Arthur White in *Clay Minerals* 25 (1990): 1–2.

RALPH L. LANGENHEIM, JR.

GRIMES, Absalom Carlisle (22 Aug. 1834–27 Mar. 1911), Confederate mail runner and steamboat pilot, was born in Anchorage, Kentucky, the son of William Leander Grimes and Charlotte Platt Wright. He was born while his parents were visiting his father's hometown relatives. After he was one month old, his parents took him to their home at Saverton, Missouri (near Hannibal), where his father worked as a Mississippi River steamboat pilot. During his youth in St. Louis the rambunctious Grimes disliked school intensely and at the age of twelve stowed away on a steamboat to New Orleans, only to be retrieved by his anxious parents before he could carry out his plan to go to sea as a cabin boy. When he was sixteen, he worked briefly as a messenger boy for the Morse Telegraph Company when its service was first introduced to St. Louis, but later in the year he was introduced to steamboat piloting by his father. Ab, as Grimes was familiarly known, was so short at the start of his apprenticeship that he had to stand on a box to see over the boat's steering wheel. After obtaining his first annual license in 1852, he piloted various steamboats in the lively upper Mississippi trade between St. Louis and St. Paul until the start of the Civil War in 1861.

By the time Grimes applied for his license renewal in May 1861, the federal Steamboat Inspection Service required all applicants to take a Union loyalty oath. This demand, which seemed to be particularly offensive to Grimes since it was communicated to him through a naturalized German immigrant, prompted him to support the Confederacy. Along with fellow pilots Samuel L. Clemens and Sam Bowen, he refused the demand of federal military officials in St. Louis to pilot their steamboats. Seeking refuge in Hannibal, he joined Clemens and Bowen in a short-lived ragamuffin ranger unit. Their ill-equipped and untrained but fun-loving band straggled about nearby rural areas for several weeks to avoid federal apprehension.

When the unit disbanded, Grimes joined a militia force at Paris, Missouri. As part of that group, he participated in harassing the Hannibal & St. Joseph Railroad and joined the battle of Lexington before his unit was incorporated into the Confederate army. During subsequent campaigning in southwestern Missouri and participation in the battle of Pea Ridge in Arkansas, Grimes was captured twice by Union forces but with characteristic derring-do soon escaped both times.

Virtual Union control of Missouri by the spring of 1862 created the opportunity for Grimes's adventures as a Confederate mail runner. When Missourians serving in the Confederate army were forced south into Tennessee and Mississippi he proposed running mail through Union lines so that these troops could communicate with their Missouri brethren. In 1862 alone he made eight round trips from St. Louis carrying hundreds of letters both ways. His "grapevine circuit," as he styled it, was facilitated by a number of "distributors"—Missouri women who secretly collected mail and smuggled it to him and delivered letters from the troops. Their relatively broad network included gathering points and destinations in Kentucky and western Missouri. During his third trip, Grimes was commissioned by General Sterling Price as official mail carrier for the Confederate army with the rank of major. Despite his military rank, to the troops and other acquaintances he was always known by his steamboat designation, "Captain Grimes."

Grimes's escapades earned him instant notoriety. To Unionists he was a desperado and suspected spy. After being captured for the fifth time in the fall of 1862, he was sentenced to death by a court-martial for mail carrying and spying. After another daring escape he not only resumed mail running but in the early summer of 1863 became even more of a folk hero by smuggling mail through the federal blockade of Vicksburg, Mississippi. Pressed into active service, he piloted steamboats near Vicksburg before the besieged city fell to Union forces on 4 July 1863.

Grimes's mail-running days were ended by his sixth capture at Memphis in November 1863. Again sentenced to death, he was wounded while attempting to escape from the Myrtle Street prison in St. Louis. With the help of a sympathetic doctor he was granted a reprieve. Because of pleas by some of his Union steamboat friends and a prominent St. Louis clergyman, in July 1864 President Abraham Lincoln commuted his sentence to confinement in the state prison at Jefferson City. Lincoln's order specified that Grimes was to be released on 1 December provided he take a loyalty oath and post a $5,000 bond. Despite his pending release, he was mercilessly whipped on 27 November by order of the warden, for having violated a rule about passing notes to fellow prisoners. Two weeks after the savage beating, he was released.

On 7 March 1865, Grimes married Lucy Jones Glascock, to whom he had been engaged for seven years; they had seven children. After they took a steamboat honeymoon trip to New Orleans, he returned to piloting. Working mainly on the Missouri River, in both 1866 and 1867 he piloted boats to Fort Benton, Montana Territory, the head of navigation, which was then booming because of the Montana gold rush. He temporarily left steamboating in 1870 to operate a confectionery business in Hannibal, but two years later he returned to St. Louis, where he engaged in the steamboat excursion business until 1883, when he moved to Lincoln County. Until 1896 he managed the King's Lake Shooting Club, a favorite haunt of St. Louisans and for a decade following owned and operated the King Lake Club. His wife died in 1903, and in 1905 he married Nell Tauke, his twenty-year-old ward. They had no children. Soon after their marriage he shot a man for insulting her. After returning to St. Louis in 1907 he managed a movie theater, then a

shooting gallery, and last he worked for the General Compressed-Air Vacuum Cleaning Company. In 1910–1911, with the assistance of his daughter Charlotte Grimes Mitchell, he wrote a reminiscence from his wartime diary. M. M. Quaife later edited his work and published it as *Absalom Grimes, Confederate Mail Carrier* (1926). Grimes died in St. Louis.

• The Missouri Historical Society has a number of newspaper clippings about Grimes as well as a brief manuscript history of the Grimes family by Charlotte Grimes Mitchell. For an account of the activities of Grimes's initial participation in the Civil War with the ranger unit, see Mark Twain, "The Private History of a Campaign That Failed," *Century*, Dec. 1885, pp. 193–204. Obituaries are in the *St. Louis Globe Democrat*, 29 Mar. 1911, and the *St. Louis Republic*, 28 Mar. 1911.

WILLIAM E. LASS

GRIMES, Burleigh Arland (18 Aug. 1893–6 Dec. 1985), baseball player, manager, and scout, was born on the family's dairy farm near Emerald, St. Croix County, Wisconsin, the son of Nick Grimes and Ruth Tuttle. The family soon moved to Black Brook near Clear Lake in Polk County, and Burleigh began playing baseball, encouraged by his father and his uncle, Bird Grimes, who played for the Clear Lake town semiprofessional team. Always a pitcher, Grimes signed his first professional contract in 1912 for a Class D Eau Claire, Wisconsin, team that disbanded in midseason. Thereafter Grimes played first for a semiprofessional and then for progressively higher minor league teams, largely in quality southern leagues, and worked in the off-season driving a four-horse logging team in a Wisconsin lumber camp for a dollar a day. This changed when he was called up to the major leagues by the Pittsburgh Pirates in 1916.

From the beginning of his career Grimes was known as a fierce competitor who was never reluctant to throw at batters to unnerve them. He was reputed to have thrown at Frankie Frisch every time he faced him and, in 1934, to have thrown at Goose Goslin while the Detroit player was in the on-deck circle (for being too eager to get to bat). These accounts, like many baseball stories, may not be verifiable, but they testify to Grimes's belligerent attitude on the field. Grimes mastered a spitball pitch—for which he chewed slippery elm bark—and was one of seventeen pitchers allowed to continue throwing the pitch (as a concession to the fact that it provided their livelihood) after it was outlawed in 1920. He was also noted for not shaving before pitching appearances, causing the nickname "Old Stubblebeard": he claimed the bark he chewed would irritate freshly shaved skin, but it is just as likely it was another means of intimidation. These attributes helped make Grimes, after brief service as a machinist's mate in the navy during World War I, one of the dominant and most successful pitchers in baseball, particularly after he was traded to the Brooklyn Dodgers in a five-player deal that sent Casey Stengel to Pittsburgh in 1918. In 1921 he had an especially fine season, winning 22 games while losing 13, and leading the National League in victories, complete games, and strikeouts.

Pitching for Brooklyn until 1927, and then for New York, Pittsburgh again, Boston, St. Louis, Chicago, and St. Louis again in the National League, before ending his career with brief stints with the American League's New York Yankees and Pittsburgh for the third time, Grimes was one of the dominant players of his generation. An accomplished batter, base runner, and fielder, Grimes won 270 major league games while losing 212 (including his minor league service, his lifetime record was 356 wins and 269 losses) in a 19-year career, unusually long for a pitcher. A notable complete game Grimes pitched that resulted in no decision was a 20-inning 9–9 tie against Philadelphia on 30 April 1919. Appearing in four World Series (1920 with Brooklyn, 1930–1931 with the St. Louis Cardinals, and 1932 with the Chicago Cubs), he pitched in nine games and posted a won-lost record of 3–4. Grimes considered his career high point to be his performance in the 1931 World Series, when on 10 October he pitched the deciding seventh game, a 4–2 victory for St. Louis over the Philadelphia Athletics. Grimes claimed that the strain of this game, pitched when he was 38, ruined him as a pitcher.

Grimes left the majors after the 1934 season as the last legal spitball artist, and, after a season as player-manager with Bloomington, Indiana, of the Three-I League, he became a manager, both in the minors and in the majors with Brooklyn. After managing Louisville in 1936, he managed the 1937 and 1938 Dodgers. During the latter season Babe Ruth was added to the team as a coach, and Grimes was also assisted by infielder and team captain Leo Durocher. Grimes managed minor league teams with mixed success until 1953, with a year off in 1940–1941 after being suspended for "assault" (expectoration) on an umpire while managing a team in Grand Rapids, Michigan. His minor league managing career also included stops in Montreal, Toronto (on two occasions), Rochester, New York, and, briefly, Kansas City. He also saw service as a scout and coach for major league teams, ending his career in 1971 after nearly sixty years of service in professional baseball. He was elected to the National Baseball Hall of Fame in 1964, and in 1977 he joined the hall's veterans committee, which selects players for membership after their initial eligibility has expired. He was accused of settling old scores through decisions made by that group.

After making the major leagues, Grimes spent the off seasons raising prize hogs and breaking horses and mules on farms in Ohio and then Missouri, paid for with one of the highest salaries in baseball. Grimes made $2,600 annually as a rookie with the Pirates in 1916; by the time of his retirement, he was reported to be earning $25,000. It has been suggested, and Grimes himself agreed, that he may have been traded so frequently as a consequence of his salary demands. Grimes married five times: in 1913 in Memphis to Florence Ruth van Patten, from whom he was divorced in 1930; in 1931 to Laura Virginia (maiden name unknown), a marriage that also ended in divorce in 1939; in 1940 to Inez Margarete Martin, who died in 1964; to Zerita Brickell, widow of Fred Brickell, a Pirate teammate, in 1965; and after her death in 1974, to Lillian Gosselin in 1975. There were no children from any of these marriages. Late in life Grimes moved back to his boyhood home, Clear Lake, where he died.

Grimes's fierce, win-at-all-costs style of play represents the earlier era of baseball when professional players were usually drawn from rural and working-class backgrounds, and whose desire to win may have had roots in economic necessity. Grimes was a shrewd negotiator with his employers, ever conscious of his value to the team and determined to be paid what he was worth. Success on the ball field represented freedom from economic marginalization; for Grimes and players like him, professional sports were far removed from the official, public creeds of fair play and good sportsmanship, which represented the amateur ideals of the economically privileged. Grimes's reputation has consequently suffered because of his unconcealed desire to win in any way possible, epitomized by his reputation for success with a trick and later illegal pitch, the spitball.

• The National Baseball Library in Cooperstown, N.Y., has a large file of contemporary newspaper clippings on Grimes. A museum dedicated to Grimes and Senator Gaylord Nelson in Clear Lake and Davee Library of the University of Wisconsin–River Falls also have important holdings of Grimes materials. His career pitching statistics can be found in the various editions of *The Baseball Encyclopedia* and *Total Baseball*. Early editions of *The Baseball Encyclopedia* must be consulted for his batting record. An oral history of Grimes's service as a manager with the Brooklyn Dodgers can be found in Donald Honig, *The Man in the Dugout* (1977; rev. ed., 1995).

DANIEL J. J. ROSS

GRIMES, James Wilson (20 Oct. 1816–7 Feb. 1872), political leader, was born in Deering, New Hampshire, the son of John Grimes and Elizabeth Wilson, prosperous farmers. The boy attended Hampton Academy, preparatory to entering Dartmouth College in 1832. He left college midway through his junior year to read law in Peterborough. After one year of studying law, he left New Hampshire and headed west, arriving in Burlington, Iowa, in May 1836, a time when Iowa was still part of Wisconsin Territory. Grimes, not yet twenty, promptly opened a law office in partnership with William Chapman.

Within four months of his arrival in this frontier river town, the handsome young attorney won territorial-wide recognition by being appointed one of the commissioners to negotiate with the resident Mesquakie and Sauk tribes. Over the next several months two treaties were obtained by which the tribes were forced to cede the land, known as Chief Keokuk's Reserve, lying to the west of the area along the Mississippi River in Iowa that had been opened to white settlers in 1832 following the Black Hawk War.

In 1838 Iowa became a territory separate from Wisconsin, and Grimes was elected to its first territorial legislature. In 1841 he established a new law firm with Henry Starr, and the two were to remain partners for the remainder of Grimes's life. Grimes married Elizabeth Neally in 1846; their only child was adopted. In addition to being an officeholder and the town's most successful lawyer, Grimes became the region's leading horticulturist and served in 1853–1854 as an editor of the *Iowa Farmer and Horticulturist*, the state's major farm journal.

Although Iowa was predominantly Democratic, young Grimes, a staunch partisan Whig, had secured a majority of the votes in his district in his two campaigns for the territorial legislature. In 1852 he easily won election to the state legislature. In the general assembly, he successfully pushed through bills authorizing the building of plank roads, but he soon realized that railroads were preferable. He thus became an ally of those railroad interests that would dominate the state's politics for the next half-century. He was also insistent in his demand for a new Iowa constitution allowing the establishment of state banks, which the first state constitution of 1846 had prohibited. Twice he secured a majority in both houses calling for a constitutional convention only to have the bills vetoed by the Democratic governor. Frustrated as a legislator, Grimes in 1854 became the Whig candidate for governor. His narrow victory marked the beginning of the Democratic loss of power in Iowa.

During his term as governor (1854–1858), Grimes achieved a record of accomplishment few of his successors have approached. First on his agenda was a new constitution for Iowa. He also wanted to move the state capital from Iowa City to a more central location in Des Moines, but he assured Iowa City that the recently established state university would remain permanently in that city. Grimes's influence was reflected throughout the new constitution in such democratic provisions as an elective judiciary, two-year terms for all state officials, and the absence of restrictions on the legislature's freedom to regulate banks or railroads. The proposed constitution won the approval of the people by the narrowest of margins, but it has remained since 1857 the fundamental law of the state.

Major social legislation that Grimes shepherded through the legislature established Iowa's first asylums for the blind, the deaf, and the insane. A leading proponent for equality of opportunity for women, both in education and employment, Grimes insisted that the new state university be coeducational, the first in the nation. He also obtained a bill authorizing the first geological survey of the state. Although only thirty-eight when entering office, Grimes repeatedly demonstrated a sophistication far beyond his years in adept political management.

Grimes assumed leadership of the rapidly growing antislavery sentiment within the state. He warned that attempts to enforce the Fugitive Slave Act of 1850 in Iowa would be rigorously opposed by most citizens and that the state law officers would in no way assist federal marshals in capturing fugitive slaves. When it became clear that the national Whig party was not prepared to take a stand against the extension of slavery into the territories, Grimes led the Iowa Whigs and the Free Soil Democrats into the recently organized Republican party. He completed his term as a Republican. By 1858 Iowa's political turnabout was complete. The Democrats had lost control of all three branches of state government, and Grimes was generally credited by the people of his state for having "made Iowa Republican and allied it with the loyal states" (Salter, p. 115).

Grimes in 1857 announced he would not seek a second term in order to become a candidate for the U.S. Senate to replace the current prosouthern senator, George W. Jones. Grimes won an easy victory. In the Senate, he quickly caught the favorable attention of the antislavery bloc. Following the election of Abraham Lincoln in 1860, Grimes was chosen a member of the special Senatorial Committee of Thirteen to consider possible compromise measures that might prevent the secession of southern states. From the first, Grimes believed compromise was both impossible and dishonorable. He fiercely opposed the Crittenden Compromise, which would have forever protected slavery in all states and territories south of the 36° 30′ latitude, and he gloomily predicted that both secession and a devastating civil war were inevitable.

With the outbreak of the war, Grimes was placed on the important Committee on Naval Affairs, which he later chaired. He pushed for and succeeded in getting the pay for all naval personnel raised to that of the army, and he obtained rankings above commodore for the first time commensurate to the gradations in the army's rankings for generals. For these victories on its behalf, the navy was willing to forgive him for sponsoring the act that prohibited all spiritous liquors on naval vessels.

Although early labeled as belonging to the more radical wing of the Republican party in Congress, Grimes throughout his senatorial tenure remained a maverick who refused to follow blindly the party line. He never allied himself with his fellow Republican senator from Iowa, James Harlan. Although both were professed Radicals, they ignored each other in the Senate and headed opposing factions for patronage and power in Iowa.

Grimes had been an early supporter of Lincoln for the presidential nomination, but Lincoln as president was frequently subjected to Grimes's criticism, both for doing too little and for doing too much. Like the other Radicals in Congress, Grimes was impatient with the president's reluctance to move toward the abolition of slavery, but on the other hand, Grimes frequently excoriated Lincoln for assuming too much power at the expense of the legislature. Always a strict constitutionalist, Grimes regarded Lincoln's declaration of a blockade and his suspension of the writ of habeas corpus without the consent of Congress as acts of dictatorial power unprecedented in American history.

He had early in his public career been a leading advocate for a transcontinental railroad along a northern route, which would connect with the Burlington line then being built from Chicago across Iowa to a Council Bluffs–Omaha terminal. However, when with the departure of the southern obstructionists that dream became a reality, Grimes attempted to put a limit on the amount of stock any one individual could hold in the proposed transcontinental line. Grimes had led the fight to allow banking in his own state, but in the Senate he voted against the National Bank Act of 1863 because it did not provide for maintaining an adequate specie reserve within each member bank. He opposed one of his party's most sacred tenets, a high protective tariff. Even his beloved navy was to discover that there was a limit to Grimes's affection. Early in 1865, as the Union victory appeared inevitable, Grimes proposed a severe cut in the naval budget and the closing of several naval bases.

Along with his close Senate friends William Fessenden and Lyman Trumbull, Grimes turned against the increasingly radical proposals of such congressional leaders as Charles Sumner and Ben Wade in the Senate and Thaddeus Stevens in the House. From the moment he became active in Iowa politics, Grimes had courageously fought for the abolition of slavery and for racial equality, but he insisted that the freed slaves should not be favored by special class legislation. Consequently, he opposed Stevens's proposal to open exclusively to former slaves those lands in the South confiscated from southern white rebels. Moreover, he sought to amend the Homestead Act of 1862, which provided western lands only to married men and heads of families, so that any person, single or married, could be a homesteader. His amendment was defeated by one vote.

Following the death of Lincoln, Grimes, unlike many extreme Radicals, was under no illusion that the contest between the executive and the legislature for control of Reconstruction was now at an end. Grimes was certain that Andrew Johnson would attempt to pursue the same policies of easy reconciliation as his predecessor, the only difference being that Lincoln had been an effective statesman and Johnson, in Grimes's words, was "a man of low instincts, vindictive, violent and of bad habits" (Salter, p. 278).

As a member of the powerful Joint Committee of Fifteen, Grimes helped draft the report that in 1866 became the blueprint for Congressional Reconstruction, and he played a leading part in the passage of this plan over the president's repeated vetoes. In 1867, however, when he heard the first whispers within the Radical bloc promoting the impeachment of Johnson, Grimes privately made it clear that he would oppose such action unless it could be shown that Johnson was indeed guilty of "high crimes."

The impeachment of President Johnson in the spring of 1868 marked both the climax and conclusion of Grimes's senatorial career. The Wade-Stevens leadership was well aware that it could not rely on its former ally. After Johnson had been impeached by the House and his case came before the Senate for trial, however, Grimes refused to make any public statement until he had heard all of the evidence. Nor did the deluge of messages from Iowa urging conviction move him. He informed his constituents that, when sitting in the court of judgment, he was no longer their representative who must consider their partisan views but an independent judge who would cast his vote based on evidence presented and the dictates of his own conscience. Not until 11 May 1868, five days prior to the vote, did Grimes give a lengthy speech on the floor of the Senate, stating that the prosecution had failed to prove its case for conviction as defined by the Constitution and that he would give a "not guilty" verdict.

Two days after this speech, worn out by the stress of the trial, Grimes suffered a stroke, which left him paralyzed on one side. On 16 May, when the Senate gathered to give its verdict, a rumor spread that Grimes had died. Extreme partisans in the gallery were gleefully chanting, "Old Grimes is dead, that bad old man is gone," just as Grimes was carried into the Senate on an improvised stretcher. When his name was called, he was lifted to his feet and in a surprisingly strong voice announced, "Not guilty." A two-thirds vote of the Senate was necessary for conviction, and the president escaped by one vote.

Grimes never fully recovered his health. Keeping his Senate seat, he left for Europe in April 1869. While in Paris he suffered a second stroke, which convinced him that his senatorial career was over. From abroad he submitted his resignation. It was not until the summer of 1871 that he was able to return home. A series of heart attacks the following February brought death in Burlington.

Few politicians of his era had greater political influence on his state and nation than did Grimes. A progressive reformer in social legislation, he was at the same time a conservative in assiduously hewing to strict constitutionalism in an age of violent political upheaval.

• The official papers of Grimes as governor are in the archives of the State Historical Society of Iowa. Other archival collections of value, also in the Iowa Historical Society, are the papers of William Salter, William B. Allison, and a small collection of John Sherman papers. William Salter, *Life of James W. Grimes* (1876), is outdated and uncritical in interpretation but still valuable for the many personal letters and official correspondence and documents it contains. Other secondary sources are Dan Elbert Clark, *History of Senatorial Elections in Iowa* (1912); and an unpublished manuscript, Eli C. Christoferson, "The Life of James W. Grimes," in the State Historical Society of Iowa. Grimes's role in the impeachment and trial of Andrew Johnson is a much told story to be found in most histories of the Reconstruction Era. For a highly dramatic account of the incident, see John F. Kennedy, *Profiles in Courage* (1956). A brief, inaccurate obituary is in the *New York Times*, 9 Feb. 1872. A much fuller obituary is in the *Burlington* (Iowa) *Hawk-Eye* of the same date.

JOSEPH FRAZIER WALL

GRIMES, Tiny (7 July 1916?–4 Mar. 1989), jazz and rhythm-and-blues guitarist and bandleader, was born Lloyd Grimes in Newport News, Virginia. Grimes told interviewer Bob Kenselaar that he was unsure of his birth date, there being no certificate. He told writers Stanley Dance and Arnie Berle that he was born in 1917, but other published sources give 1916 or 1915. Details of his parents are unknown. Grimes took up drums in a Boy Scout marching band. He played regularly at a beach dancehall near Newport News until a storm and subsequent flood destroyed the hall and his drums. Around the seventh grade he dropped out of school to work typical boyhood jobs selling papers and shining shoes. He taught himself to play piano, and while living in Washington, D.C., he became a pianist and singer in a trio called Wynken, Blynken and Nod. The group performed regularly on radio on "Major Bowes's Original Amateur Hour" (c. 1936) and worked at a club in Alexandria, Virginia.

Grimes came to New York around 1937 or 1938 and taught himself to play tiple, a miniature guitar. He then bought an unusual acoustic guitar with four rather than six strings, because the thinner fretboard fit his small hands. For his entire career he would use such an instrument, tuned to the standard guitar's four highest pitched strings (in ascending pitch, the notes D, G, B, and E). After acquiring an electric banjo, with its four strings tuned the same way, he took up electric guitar and modified it accordingly. Much later in his career he played four-string electric guitars custom-made by the Guild company.

In 1940 Grimes joined a tiple and guitar group, Cats and the Fiddle, playing guitar, singing high tenor parts, and devising unnotated arrangements. After touring to California, he left Cats and the Fiddle to join bassist Slam Stewart in the duo Slim and Slam as a replacement for Slim Gaillard, who had been inducted into the army. Stewart and Grimes then joined pianist Art Tatum, forming a renowned trio from 1943 to 1944. Their recordings include "Cocktails for Two," "I Would Do Anything for You," "Body and Soul," "Topsy," and "Soft Winds." Accustomed to playing by ear, Grimes was as ready as anyone could be for Tatum's notoriously impetuous and difficult conception of harmony and rhythm: wherever Tatum's fingers went, the guitarist followed. "It was an honor, but certainly no pleasure," Grimes said. "It was a struggle trying to keep up with him." He testified that even the group's most intricate arrangements evolved on the bandstand, without rehearsal.

After Tatum broke up the trio to work again as a soloist, Grimes formed his own trio at Tondelayo's in New York, initially using pianist Clyde Hart and bassist Oscar Pettiford. Alto saxophonist Charlie Parker came regularly to sit in with Grimes's group. Grimes made a number of recordings in the summer of 1944, including "Blue Harlem," "Indiana," and "Hard Tack," all in tenor saxophonist Ike Quebec's band. A session with trumpeter Hot Lips Page featured Grimes playing tasteful obbligato lines in support of and in alternation with Page's singing on the ballad "I Got What It Takes" and on "Lip's Blues." Three days later, three takes of Grimes's own "Tiny's Tempo" offered fine examples of his melodic improvising, which followed swing guitarist Charlie Christian's manner of blending in catchy riffs while spinning out long lines; two other titles from this session, one being "I'll Always Love You Just the Same," offered rare examples of Grimes's bland singing (an experiment that he would not repeat until 1973), but the true importance of this date for the Savoy label was in providing a forum for the first substantial studio recordings of Parker's bop soloing. Later, in November 1944, Grimes twice recorded with drummer Cozy Cole, who featured him on a version of "Take It on Back."

During late 1944 or early 1945 Grimes moved from Tondelayo's to the Spotlite club, where he hired pianist Al Haig, and then to the Downbeat club, where he worked alongside tenor saxophonist Coleman Hawkins and singer Billie Holiday. Terry Gibbs, while working as a drummer rather than a vibraphonist, also played with Grimes's band at some point during this tenure in New York clubs. Grimes returned regularly to the Downbeat through 1946, and he accompanied Holiday in her first solo concert, at Town Hall in New York on 16 February 1946, and on several recordings, including "What Is This Thing Called Love" (1945) and "Good Morning Heartache" (1946). He also recorded with Quebec (1945), tenor saxophonist John Hardee, and his own swingtet (both 1946).

Around 1947 Grimes moved into the emerging rhythm-and-blues field. He had a hit that year with a version of "That Old Black Magic" with a group that included Hardee on saxophone and George Kelly on piano. Grimes's group became known as the Rockin' Highlanders when the members began wearing kilts and tam-o'-shanters as a gimmick. In 1948 they had begun a two-year stand at Gleason's in Cleveland. The Rockin' Highlanders made their first tour around 1949, returned to Gleason's until 1951, and then began extensive touring, spending summers entertaining in Atlantic City. Accounts of the band's personnel are confusing. Tenor saxophonist Red Prysock figured prominently. Pianist Sir Charle Thompson and bassist Ike Isaacs were members early on, and Kelly (as a tenor saxophonist, perhaps doubling on piano) joined or alternated with Prysock and other tenor players. Tenor saxophonist Benny Golson was a Rockin' Highlander around 1952. "Tiny's Boogie Woogie," recorded in 1951, exemplifies instrumental dance music well on its way to what would be known as rock 'n' roll; this title finds Grimes intentionally overdriving the amplifier to distort the speaker and thus achieve a harsher sound than in his days with swing groups. The Highlanders' recordings from the early 1950s include "Riverside Jump," "Call of the Wild," "Juicy Fruit," and "Second Floor Rear." The group disbanded in 1955 after a severe automobile accident. Grimes settled in Philadelphia, where he was inactive as a musician and separated from his wife. (Details of the marriage are unknown.)

From 1958 to 1961 Grimes occasionally organized and played on recordings for the Prestige company. The results included an album as coleader with tenor saxophonist Coleman Hawkins, *Blues Groove* (1958), and Grimes's own *Callin' the Blues* (1958) and *Tiny in Swingland* (1959). Pianist Erroll Garner then procured a recording session for Grimes on the United Artists label, resulting in what is regarded as his best album, *Big Time Guitar* (1962). Grimes performed at the Village Gate in New York in 1962. He stopped playing altogether in 1964, when he had the first of six operations on his leg.

Grimes resumed his career in New York late in 1966. In 1967 he was featured on "A Tiny Bit of Blues" on alto saxophonist Johnny Hodges's album *Triple Play*. The following year he toured Europe with tenor saxophonist Buddy Tate, organist Milt Buckner, and Cole, recording in Paris. He recorded with tenor saxophonist Illinois Jacquet in 1969. He returned to Europe in 1970 with Kelly and pianist Jay McShann and again recorded in France.

On 14 August 1971 he participated in a concert in the Great Guitarist series at New York's Town Hall, but the resulting recording is disappointing. For a few months in 1972 he joined pianist Earl Hines's touring band. In 1973 he gave his first performance at the Newport Jazz Festival (in New York), and he recorded the rather uneven album *Profoundly Blue*.

The year 1974 brought further performances and recordings in France, this time with tenor saxophonist Arnett Cobb and drummer Panama Francis. As coleader with trumpeter Roy Eldridge, Grimes recorded the album *One Is Never Too Old to Swing* (1977). Around 1979 he performed at the Nice Jazz Festival in France. The following year he had a hip replacement. After his recovery, he resumed a routine of festival appearances and performances in New York clubs. He died in New York City.

Not one of jazz's extraordinary talents, Grimes is remembered for his ability to deal with the complexities of Tatum's music and for his fostering of Parker's career. In rhythm and blues, he supplied, via his Rockin' Highlanders, a jazz-oriented approach to instrumental improvisation that was far meatier than the norm.

• A tape and transcript of Bob Kenselaar's Nov. 1983 interview with Grimes is at the Institute of Jazz Studies, Newark, N.J. Published surveys and interviews include Jacques Morgantini, "Tiny Grimes," *Bulletin du Hot Club de France* 181 (Oct. 1968): 3–6; 182 (Nov. 1968): 16–18; and 183 (Dec. 1968): 4–6; Hugues Panassié, "A Tribute to Tiny Grimes," *Down Beat*, 26 June 1969, p. 17; Dan Morgenstern, liner notes to Grimes's LP *Profoundly Blue* (1973); Stanley Dance, *The World of Swing* (1974), pp. 360–66, which includes a photo of the Rockin' Highlanders in Scottish dress; and Arnie Berle, "Tiny Grimes: The 4-String Jazz Guitarist of Swing Street," *Guitar Player* 15 (Jan. 1981): 58–60, 62, 64. See also John Chilton, *Billie's Blues: The Billie Holiday Story* (1975), and Arnold Shaw, *The Street That Never Slept* (1971; repr. in 1977 as *52nd Street: The Street of Jazz*). A catalog of recordings is by Marcel Chauvard and Kurt Mohr, "Discog-raphy of Tiny Grimes," *Jazz Statistics* 26–27 (June–Sept. 1962): 8–10. An obituary is in the *New York Times*, 7 Mar. 1989.

BARRY KERNFELD

GRIMKÉ, Angelina Emily (20 Feb. 1805–26 Oct. 1879), abolitionist and women's rights activist, was born in Charleston, South Carolina, the daughter of John Faucheraud Grimké, a planter and judge, and Mary Smith. A member of one of the wealthiest and most aristocratic families in Charleston, her father, who had been a captain in the American Revolution, traced his descent from the city's earliest Huguenot and German settlers and held the post of senior associate, equivalent to chief justice, of the South Carolina Supreme Court. Her mother's family had included two colonial governors. From an early age both Angelina and her older sister Sarah felt unusual sympathy for the slaves on their parents' plantation. At the age of five Angelina was so distressed at seeing a slave whipped that she begged a sea captain to help him escape to freedom, and at thirteen she objected so strongly to the Episcopal church's support of slavery that she refused to be confirmed. In 1829 she gave up a life of privilege and went to Philadelphia to join Sarah, who had become a member of the Society of Friends there.

The sisters were not very comfortable with the Quakers, however, and openly defied their rules of dress and speech. Above all, Angelina was dissatisfied with what she considered the Society's hypocrisy, feeling that their opposition to slavery was too moderate. Increasingly drawn to a more vigorous form of antislavery activism, she wrote a letter in 1835 to William Lloyd Garrison, editor of the radical abolitionist magazine *The Liberator*, encouraging him in his work. To her dismay, Garrison published the letter on 19 September. It caused a storm of protest, not only among the slaveholders of her own state but among the Philadelphia Friends, including her sister, who urged her to recant. But by now the demure southern belle was thoroughly committed, and instead of recanting she wrote a 36-page pamphlet, *Appeal to the Christian Women of the South* (1836), calling on her sex in the strongest terms to "overthrow this horrible system of oppression and cruelty, licentiousness and wrong." With this and a subsequent pamphlet, *An Appeal to the Women of the Nominally Free States* (1837), urging reform in the North, she became publicly linked with the abolition movement. As the first white southern woman to speak up forcefully against slavery, she was enthusiastically welcomed by Garrison and his followers. She was also bitterly reviled in South Carolina, where her pamphlets were publicly burned.

Sarah Grimké was soon persuaded to join her sister in antislavery activity, and in 1837 the two accepted an invitation from Elizur Wright, secretary of the American Antislavery Society, to speak to women's groups in New York. So moving were Angelina's accounts of the horrors of the slave system that her audiences soon came to include men as she and her sister went on the lecture circuit throughout New England. If their opposition to slavery had outraged the South, the idea of women speaking in public, and especially to "mixed" audiences, offended the North almost as much. They were attacked in the press and from the pulpit, by supporters of slavery and by conservative abolitionists; they were pelted with fruit, and the General Association of Congregational Ministers issued a "Pastoral Letter" forbidding any minister to open his church to women speakers. Undaunted, they both went on speaking. In some five months Sarah and Angelina separately toured sixty-seven New England towns, addressing more than 40,000 people in eighty-eight meetings. The climax of Angelina's tour was her three-day testimony on the evils of slavery before the Massachusetts legislature early in 1838. It was the first time the state house had ever been opened to a woman speaker, and her eloquence brought tears to the eyes of many.

Angelina, who in 1836 had written, "The investigation of the rights of slaves led me to a better understanding of my own," became a champion of women's rights, and in 1838 she wrote a scorching response to a pamphlet opposing engagement by her sex in political activism. Her *Letters to Catherine Beecher* was much ahead of its time. It argued that women should be allowed not only to help write the laws of the land but to sit in the seats of its government.

On 14 May 1838 Angelina married the abolitionist Theodore Dwight Weld, who had trained her for the lecture stage. The wedding in Philadelphia was a sensational event, including six former slaves of the Grimkés among the guests and employing Garrison to read the vows. Her marriage to a Presbyterian and Sarah's attendance at the unconventional ceremony resulted in the sisters' official expulsion by the Society of Friends, from which they had in any case long been estranged. The Welds had three children, and Angelina suffered one miscarriage. No longer physically able to bear the strain of public speaking, she and Weld retired to a New Jersey farm, accompanied by Sarah, who lived with them the rest of her life. Together they compiled *American Slavery As It Is* (1839), an influential exposé of the "peculiar institution" that provided Harriet Beecher Stowe with material for her 1852 novel *Uncle Tom's Cabin*.

In the 1840s the Welds gave up active involvement in abolitionism and began a school in which the sisters both taught. Pioneers in progressive education, they included young women among their students and gymnasium exercise, rowing, and diving in their curriculum. Ralph Waldo Emerson, Horace Greeley, and Henry David Thoreau were among the visitors who lectured there. Angelina and her husband moved to Hyde Park, Massachusetts, after the Civil War, and Angelina continued teaching until her retirement in 1867. Of her innovative educational practices, biographer and cultural historian Ernest Earnest has written, "It took American colleges seventy or eighty years to catch up with her ideas." She died in Hyde Park.

Angelina Grimké was among the first to synthesize abolitionism and feminism and to recognize the essential identity of the two causes. Viewed as a fanatic in her own time, she lived to see her beliefs vindicated and helped prepare the way for social reforms in both race relations and women's rights.

• The Angelina Grimké papers are in the Moorland-Spingarn Research Center at Howard University in Washington, D.C., and documents related to the Grimké sisters are in the Anti-Slavery Collection at the Boston Public Library and the Weld-Grimké Papers in the William Clements Library at the University of Michigan, Ann Arbor. Books dealing with Angelina Grimké include Theodore Dwight Weld, *In Memory: Angelina Grimké Weld* (1880); Catherine Birney, *The Grimké Sisters: Sarah and Angelina Grimké* (1835; repr. 1885, 1969); *Letters of Theodore Dwight Weld, Angela Grimké, and Sarah Grimké, 1822–1844*, ed. Gilbert H. Barnes and Dwight Dumond (1934); Gerda Lerner, *The Grimké Sisters from South Carolina* (1967); and Catherine Du Pre Lumpkin, *The Emancipation of Angelina Grimké* (1974). Objective examinations of the lives and careers of the Grimkés are in Benjamin P. Thomas, *Theodore Weld: Crusader for Freedom* (1950); Lawrence Lader, *The Bold Brahmins: New England's War against Slavery, 1831–1865* (1961); and Ernest Earnest, *The American Eve in Fact and Fiction, 1775–1914* (1974). See also Robert Abzug, *Passionate Liberator: Theodore Weld and the Dilemma of Reform* (1980), and Blanche Glassman Hersh, *The Slavery of Sex: Feminist Abolitionists in America* (1978).

DENNIS WEPMAN

GRIMKÉ, Angelina Weld (27 Feb. 1880–10 June 1958), poet and teacher, was born in Boston, Massachusetts, the daughter of Archibald Henry Grimké, an attorney and diplomat, and Sarah E. Stanley. Grimké's parents separated when she was very young, and she, an only child, was raised by her father. Her mother's absence undoubtedly contributed to Grimké's reverential treatment of maternal themes in her poetry, short stories, and especially her only published play, *Rachel* (1920). Her father dominated Grimké's life until his death in 1930; his continual insistence on her personal propriety and academic achievement seemed to inhibit his daughter's self-determination as much as it inspired her to make him proud of her.

Growing up in Boston, Grimké enjoyed a comfortable, middle-class life. Her distinguished family name gave her certain advantages, such as education at better schools and frequent exposure to prominent liberal activists. But as the daughter of a white woman and a man of mixed ancestry, she was no stranger to racial tension. Her sensitivity to racism was further enhanced by her family's history. Grimké was named for her father's aunt, the social reformer Angelina Emily Grimké Weld, who had campaigned for woman suffrage and for the abolition of slavery. Her father, the son of a slave, had dedicated his life to fighting prejudice. This heritage put enormous pressure on Grimké to carry on her family's tradition of embracing social causes. Timid and obedient as a child, she turned to writing as a release for her preoccupations: her need for a mother's attention, her diligence in living up to her father's expectations, and her inability to establish a lasting romantic partnership. Upon reaching adulthood, she remained introverted but began to use her writing as a public platform for denouncing racism.

In 1898 Grimké enrolled in the Boston Normal School of Gymnastics (which eventually became the Department of Hygiene at Wellesley College), graduating in 1902 with a degree in physical education. She then moved to Washington, D.C., where she taught physical education at the Armstrong Manual Training School, a vocational institution, until 1907. Apparently unhappy with both her duties and her work environment, Grimké left Armstrong in order to teach English at the M Street (later Dunbar) High School; she had prepared herself for this change by taking summer courses in English at Harvard University (1904–1910). She remained at M Street until she retired from teaching in 1926.

Although Grimké wrote most prolifically between 1900 and 1920, her first published piece, a poem titled "The Grave in the Corner," appeared in the *Norfolk (Mass.) County Gazette* when she was only thirteen (27 May 1893). During her postsecondary studies, Grimké published more of her verse in the *Boston Transcript*. However, not all of her work was well received. The editor of the *Transcript*, Charles S. Hunt, rejected Grimké's poem titled "Beware Lest He Awakes" on the grounds that its "implied threat of a bloody rising on the part of the negro" was anachronistic. The poem, eventually published in *The Pilot* (10 May 1902), reflects the crusade against racism that more typically characterizes Grimké's short fiction and *Rachel*. Another early poem, "El Beso," was published in the *Transcript* (27 Oct. 1909), accompanied by praise for Grimké's poetic talent.

Grimké's best-known poems include "To Keep the Memory of Charlotte Forten Grimké" (Grimké's aunt by marriage) (1915), "The Black Finger" (1923), "A Winter Twilight" (1923), "Tenebris" (1924), "For the Candlelight" (1925), "When the Green Lies over the Earth" (1927), and "Your Hands" (1927). These poems express her recurring themes of unfulfilled love and racial injustice or pay tribute to famous people. Other works feature tender depictions of children and mothers. A sense of despair pervades much of Grimké's verse, but only occasionally does her tone become strident or even moderately antagonistic. Her surviving manuscripts suggest that Grimké had, at one time, considered collecting her poetry into a volume tentatively titled *Dusk Dreams*. But the project never materialized, and the majority of Grimké's verse remains in holograph form among her personal papers. Much of this unpublished work consists of highly sentimental love poetry addressed to women by obviously female speakers. Some scholars have suggested that these lesbian overtones kept Grimké from publishing verse that might have brought scandal to her family name.

The dominant themes of Grimké's prose and drama are less varied than those of her poetry, focusing almost exclusively on lynching and the chagrin of African-American motherhood. Her short stories "The Closing Door" (1919) and "Goldie" (1920) combine these two topics in an effort to shock white readers into realizing how prejudice and racially motivated violence contribute to the disintegration of the black family. Both stories appeared in the *Birth Control Review* and were widely perceived as advocating childlessness among African Americans. The heroines of these stories fervently desire to bear children, but they sacrifice their maternal longings in order to avenge and prevent persecution of blacks by whites; the young women make this decision after they lose friends and family members to lynch mobs. Likewise, the title character of *Rachel* breaks off her engagement and forswears motherhood when her "adopted" children come home in tears from racist taunts hurled at them by white children.

Grimké is primarily regarded as a poet, yet her most celebrated work is her play, *Rachel*. Written in three acts, the play depicts the struggles of a young black woman and her family to deal with the racial prejudice that constricts their lives. Grimké unabashedly uses the story as a vehicle for antiracist propaganda, subtling it "A Play of Protest." Even critics who have faulted Grimké's dramatic technique have been unable to deny the impact of her message. When the Drama Committee of the National Association for the Advancement of Colored People fostered the original production of *Rachel* (3 Mar. 1916), Grimké became the first African-American woman to have written a publicly staged drama. The play underwent at least two other performances before its publication in 1920; it then disappeared for nearly seventy-five years, until its revival by the Spelman (College) Players (1991).

Critics and other readers have conjectured that parts of *Rachel* are autobiographical. The title character's physical description matches that of Grimké. More significantly, Rachel's decision to forgo marriage and motherhood parallels a conscious choice made by Grimké as a young woman. However, these similarities are largely superficial. Rachel abandons her dreams because of her heartbreak and anger over the racial injustice that she has seen affecting her loved ones; in contrast, Grimké's journals and poetry indicate that the writer's lesbian inclinations obliged her to spend her life in lonely, frustrated celibacy, her only socially acceptable option at that time.

A second play, *Mara*, was discovered among Grimké's personal papers. It was apparently written in the wake of *Rachel*'s popularity, but no record exists of its performance or of Grimké's attempt to have it published.

Throughout her life, Grimké never enjoyed good health, which may further explain why she eventually stopped teaching physical education in favor of English. A train accident led to a serious back injury in July 1911, and her retirement from teaching may have stemmed from physical incapacity. She nursed her father, who had retired to Washington, as he declined into death (1928 to 1930); then she moved to New York, where she spent the rest of her life in virtual seclusion. Her last significant publication consisted of a selection of poems featured in Countee Cullen's anthology *Caroling Dusk* (1927). After some thirty years of isolation, both artistic and social, Grimké died in New York.

For the most part, Grimké's published poems, stories, and play enjoyed moderate acclaim during her lifetime. Although she lived geographically remote from the hub of the Harlem Renaissance, she earned recognition from her more prominent contemporaries, notably Langston Hughes and Cullen. She also attended literary gatherings in the Washington, D.C., home of her close friend and fellow poet Georgia Douglas Johnson. Yet compared with her peers, Grimké published relatively few works. Her renown may have suffered further due to her failure to produce a collection of her poems or any other sizable volume. When she withdrew from the literary world, her works dwindled into obscurity, where they remained until they regained scholarly interest in the late twentieth century. Grimké's resurgent eminence as a poet stems not only from her skillful imagery and lyricism but also from her unusual perspective as a woman of color who felt compelled to suppress her sexuality.

• Grimké's papers, including unpublished works and private journals, are in the Angelina Weld Grimké Collection at the Moorland-Spingarn Research Center of Howard University (Washington, D.C.). A considerable cross section of Grimké's published and unpublished works appears in *Selected Works of Angelina Weld Grimké*, ed. Carolivia Herron (1991). Gloria T. Hull, *Color, Sex, and Poetry: Three Women Writers of the Harlem Renaissance* (1987), provides a thorough biographical and critical analysis of Grimké and her writing. See also David A. Hedrick Hirsch, "Speaking Silences in Angelina Weld Grimké's 'The Closing Door' and 'Blackness,'" *African-American Review* 26 (1992): 459–74.

LAINE A. SCOTT

GRIMKÉ, Archibald Henry (17 Aug. 1849–25 Feb. 1930), lawyer, diplomat, and protest leader, was born a slave on "Caneacres" plantation near Charleston, South Carolina, the son of Henry Grimké, a lawyer and planter, and Nancy Weston, the family's slave nurse. His parents probably never married, but his mother assumed the Grimké name. Grimké had an extremely difficult early life. After years of virtual freedom—he had attended Charleston schools for free African Americans though technically a slave—he and his brother Francis were returned to slavery in 1860 to serve his half-brother, E. Montague Grimké, as house servants. Archibald escaped in 1863 (Francis was sold to a Confederate officer) and spent the last two years of the Civil War in hiding, surfacing only after the fall of Charleston.

After the war Grimké briefly attended the Freedmen's Bureau's newly created Morris Street School before enrolling at Pennsylvania's Lincoln University in 1867. He earned his bachelor's and master's degrees in 1870 and 1872, respectively, and, with the aid of his newly discovered abolitionist aunts, Angelina and Sarah, he enrolled at Harvard Law School in 1872. He received his LL.B. in 1874, becoming the second African American to receive a university law degree.

At age twenty-four Grimké worked in the firm of prominent Boston lawyer William Bowditch, and in 1875 he gained admission to the Suffolk County bar. His Boston law practice and 1878 appointment as a justice of the peace had only a short-term influence on his ultimate career. In 1879 he married Sarah E. Stanley, a white minister's daughter; they had one child before separating in 1883.

For most of his life, Grimké played a leading role in the major organizations and events of the struggle for African-American rights. In 1883 he started the first African-American newspaper in New England—a weekly called the *Hub*—with the monetary backing of the Republican party and the personal backing of the future U.S. senator Henry Cabot Lodge. Through this paper and his positions as a leader of both the Massachusetts Suffrage League and the "Negro Independents" of the state, Grimké joined with the African-American newspaper editor T. Thomas Fortune and others who withdrew much of their support from the Republican party. In 1894 Democratic president Grover Cleveland appointed him to serve as counsel in Santo Domingo (Dominican Republic), a position he held until June 1898.

Grimké returned to the rights struggle in late 1898 during Booker T. Washington's ascendancy. A known and respected contemporary of Washington, Fortune, W. E. B. Du Bois, Calvin Chase, and Monroe M. Trotter, Grimké participated in and influenced all of the major African-American organizations of the times, especially the Afro-American League (later the Afro-American Council), the American Negro Academy (which he served as president from 1903 to 1919), the Niagara Movement, and the National Association for the Advancement of Colored People (NAACP).

In 1905 Grimké moved to Washington, D.C., where he placed himself at the center of the struggle for the rights of African Americans. He criticized President Theodore Roosevelt for his handling of the dishonorable discharge of 167 black soldiers of the Twenty-fifth Infantry in Brownsville (1906), which had resulted from charges in a murder investigation that later proved to be false. He attended the NAACP's founding conference in 1909, at which he was appointed to the committee of forty to create a permanent organization. Then, in 1911 he served on the committee of ten citizens who presented an antilynching petition to President William Howard Taft. As president of the Washington, D.C., branch of the NAACP (the nation's largest branch at the time) from 1913 to 1925, Grimké lobbied Congress and federal agencies and led the association's protests against the segregationist policies within the federal government that existed under Presidents Woodrow Wilson and Taft. During World War I he opposed—and then supported—the separate Officers Training Camp for African Americans at Fort Des Moines, Iowa. In 1916 he worked with the Amenia Conference, a conference held at the home of Joel Spingarn, an NAACP founder, to discuss the conditions of blacks in the United States. In 1919 the NAACP awarded him the Spingarn

Medal, its highest award, for service to the organization and in recognition of his role in the African-American struggle.

Grimké struggled with and against all of his more famous contemporaries. He opposed Du Bois's Pan-African Congresses (1919), his control of the *Crisis*, the official publication of the NAACP, and his "Close Ranks" approach to World War I; however, Grimké usually sided with Du Bois against Booker T. Washington's overt accommodationism in the Niagara Movement and during his stint on the *New York Age*. He wrote numerous editorials for this publication that clearly positioned him against accommodationism, even though *New York Age* was at the time controlled by Washington. In fact, he led factions in the Afro-American Council, the Niagara Movement, and the NAACP that severely criticized Washington, although he never openly abandoned Washington until the fallout over the Brownsville incident. Grimké differed with Boston's leading radical, Monroe Trotter, over the Niagara Movement, the NAACP, and the 1914 meeting with President Wilson, in which Trotter insulted the president while protesting segregation in Washington, D.C.

Grimké retired from active work with the NAACP in 1925 and lived in Washington, D.C., with his brother Francis and his daughter Angelina, a teacher at Dunbar High School. In his last years he supported A. Philip Randolph and Chandler Owen, the two leading young black radicals and socialists of the era. He died at home in Washington, D.C.

Though little noted, Archibald Grimké played a prominent role in the major struggles of African Americans in the late nineteenth and early twentieth centuries. His greatest assets were his extensive involvement, fierce independence within that struggle, and his ability to synthesize the best components of these diverse organizations and personalities. Even Du Bois came to recognize that Grimké's approaches to the issues raised during World War I were more practicable than his own initial pronouncements.

• The best sources of primary materials on Grimké are the Archibald Henry Grimké Papers, the Angelina Grimké Weld Papers, and the Francis J. Grimké Papers, all in the manuscript division of the Moorland-Spingarn Research Center at Howard University; see also the Weld-Grimké Papers, Clements Library, University of Michigan. Grimké's writings include "Why Disfranchisement Is Bad," *Atlantic Monthly*, July 1904, 72–81; and *The Shame of America; or, The Negro's Case against the Republic* (1924). Additional information may be gleaned from the E. Montague Grimké Papers at the University of South Carolina, the James Weldon Johnson Collection in the Beinecke Rare Book and Manuscript Library, Yale University, and the W. E. B. Du Bois Papers at the University of Massachusetts, Amherst. Other sources are *The Booker T. Washington Papers*, ed. Louis R. Harland and Raymond W. Smock (14 vols., 1972–1989); Minutes of Board of Directors, July 1918 and May 1920, NAACP Papers, Library of Congress; and issues of the Boston *Hub*. An excellent biography of Grimké is Dickson Bruce, *Archibald Grimké* (1993). Also see Angelina W. Grimké, "A Biographical Sketch of Archibald H. Grimké," *Opportunity* 3 (Feb. 1925): 45; Henry J. Ferry, "Francis James Grimké: Portrait of a Black Puritan" (Ph.D. diss., Yale Univ., 1970); Stephen R. Fox, *The Guardian of Boston: William Monroe Trotter* (1970); Alfred A. Moss, Jr., *The American Negro Academy: Voice of the Talented Tenth* (1981). Obituaries are in the *Washington Herald*, 27 and 28 Feb. 1930, and the *Washington Tribune*, 28 Feb. 1930.

JOHNIE D. SMITH

GRIMKÉ, Charlotte Forten (17 Aug. 1837–23 July 1914), educator, diarist, and essayist, was born in Philadelphia, Pennsylvania, the daughter of Mary Virginia Wood and Robert Bridges Forten, who were free blacks. Her father, a mathematician, orator, and reformer, was the son of wealthy sailmaker James Forten, a leading African-American activist in Philadelphia. Her mother, grandmother, and aunts had been among the founding members of the interracial Philadelphia Female Anti-Slavery Society (PFASS). Prominent figures such as abolitionist William Lloyd Garrison and Quaker poet and abolitionist John Greenleaf Whittier were friends of the Fortens. Whittier wrote a poem, "To The Daughters of James Forten."

Both privilege and misfortune marked the early life of Charlotte Forten. Although a very talented and well-educated man, Robert Forten never achieved financial stability. By the time he joined the family business, the sailmaking industry had been undermined by new steam-propelled vessels. Charlotte's mother died in 1840. Consequently, Charlotte spent most of her first years in the homes of her grandmother and of her aunt Harriet Forten Purvis, the wife of wealthy and mixed race Robert Purvis, who led the black reform community after James Forten died. Encountering a rapidly hardening racial climate, including mob violence and black disfranchisement in Pennsylvania, Purvis in 1842 moved his household from Philadelphia to the Quaker suburb of Byberry.

The inferior and segregated Pennsylvania schools prompted Robert Forten to send his daughter to Massachusetts to complete her education. In 1853 Charlotte was enrolled in the Higginson Grammar School in Salem. Following the examples of her aunts, particularly Margaretta Forten, a teacher, and Sarah Louise Forten, who composed poetry, Charlotte decided to teach and to devote her skills to "elevate the race." After graduating from the Higginson School in February of 1855 and the Salem Normal School in July of 1856, she began teaching at the previously all-white Epes Grammar School of Salem.

In Massachusetts Forten joined an expanding circle of abolitionists, including African Americans Charles Lenox Remond (in whose home she lived briefly) and his sister Sarah Remond, who were agents for the American Anti-Slavery Society, and white abolitionists Maria Weston Chapman and Lydia Maria Child, leading members of the Boston Female Anti-Slavery Society. This abolitionist community supported Forten's literary aspirations. In the *Liberator* Garrison published her "Poem for Normal School Graduates" in 1856. One of her last works, "Personal Recollections of Whittier," published in *New England Maga-*

zine in 1893, honored the poet who had immortalized her aunts more than a half century earlier. Although Forten possessed a facility for writing and would continue to publish her poems and essays in reform and literary magazines for decades to come, her ambitions as a writer were never fully realized.

Forten has become best known for the diary she began in 1854. Consisting of four volumes that record her thoughts and experiences between 1854 and 1864 and a fifth volume covering the years from 1885 to 1892, Forten's journal provides valuable insight into the experiences of the black elite. Early diary entries reveal the struggle of a young woman of African ancestry in an era when the assumption of Anglo-Saxon superiority went virtually unchallenged. Measuring herself against European standards of beauty and morality led to feelings of inadequacy and depression, which probably influenced her physical health. Severe headaches and ongoing respiratory illness interrupted her work as a teacher between 1857 and 1862, during which time she traveled back and forth between Philadelphia and Massachusetts.

When she recovered sufficiently, Forten joined the ranks of "Yankee School Marms" who traveled to the Union-controlled Sea Islands of South Carolina to educate erstwhile slaves left behind in large numbers by fleeing or absentee masters. Under the auspices of the Philadelphia Port Royal Relief Society, she became in 1862 the first African-American teacher on Saint Helena Island, working at a school conducted by the teacher and physician Laura Towne. Her writings from this period again reveal the tensions and contradictions in her life. She was, especially at first, enthusiastic about her mission, but her background—so very different from that of the population she served—sometimes limited her rapport with the Sea Islanders. Her relations with certain white colleagues, at the same time, were circumscribed by the racism that she suspected even some of the most well-disposed among them harbored. The death of her father, who had enlisted in the Union army and had been recruiting other African Americans, as well has her declining enthusiasm, ill health, homesickness, and poor living conditions, caused Forten to return north in May 1864. That same month and the next, *Atlantic Monthly* published her account of the Sea Islands.

From 1865 until 1870 Forten was secretary of the Teacher Committee of the New England Branch of the Freedmen's Union Commission in Boston, serving as a liaison between the teachers who labored among the newly freed people and their supporters in the North. In 1869 her translation of a French novel, Erckmann-Chatrian's *Thérèse; or, The Volunteers of '92*, was published. She spent the years 1870–1873 teaching, first at Robert L. Shaw Memorial School in Charleston and later at Summer High School, a black preparatory school in Washington, D.C. Turning to a profession newly opened to women during the Civil War era, she worked as a clerk in the Fourth Auditor's Office of the U.S. Treasury from 1873 until 1878, when she left to marry Francis Grimké, a divinity student twelve years her junior. A short time before their marriage Francis Grimké had been ordained and appointed pastor to the Fifteenth Street Presbyterian Church in Washington.

Forten's marriage to Francis Grimké completed a unique circle of black and white abolitionists. Grimké, the son of wealthy planter Henry Grimké of South Carolina and one of his slave women, Nancy Weston, was the nephew of two of the most famous white women abolitionists of the antebellum period, Angelina and Sarah Grimké, who briefly had been members of PFASS, which the Forten Purvis women had helped found. Francis Grimké conducted the marriage ceremony, an interracial union, of Frederick Douglass and his second wife, Helen Pitts.

The death a few months after the birth in 1880 of their only child, Theodora Cornelia, cast the only major shadow on the Forten-Grimké union. Illness plagued both at various times, and to improve his failing health, Francis Grimké was assigned to Jacksonville, Florida, where from 1885 to 1889 he was minister at the Laura Street Presbyterian Church. While in Jacksonville, Forten Grimké worked with the women of this church to provide social services for the local black community. She expanded these activities by becoming in 1896 a founding member of the National Association of Colored Women, which made major contributions to education, health, and other social services and to political activism, such as the antilynching campaign conducted by Ida B. Wells.

After returning to Washington, Forten Grimké assumed additional family responsibilities by helping raise her husband's niece, Angelina Weld Grimké, the daughter of Archibald Grimké and Sarah Stanley, a white woman, who had proved unable to shoulder the burdens of an interracial family. In the 1890s Archibald and Angelina Weld Grimké became permanent members of the household of Francis and Charlotte Grimké.

In Angelina, Forten Grimké found both a focus for her maternal care and affection and an opportunity to nurture a literary talent. Living up to the family tradition of social activism, Angelina Weld Grimké used her talent to promote racial justice. In 1916 she wrote the play *Rachel*, a denunciation of the widespread lynching of that period and the first play written by an African-American woman to be staged and performed, two years after the death of Forten Grimké.

After a long period of invalidism that left her bedridden for sixteen months, Forten Grimké died in Washington, D.C. Angelina Weld Grimké paid a final poetic tribute to her aunt in, "To Keep the Memory of Charlotte Forten Grimké," which eulogized the "gentle spirit" who was both substitute mother and bearer of the family standard of political activism and intellectual endeavor.

• The best source of information about Forten Grimké's life, character, and work are her diaries in the Moorland-Spingarn Research Center at Howard University, Washington, D.C. Ray Allen Billington edited the first four volumes of the diary, *The Journal of Charlotte L. Forten* (1953). A later edition of the full diaries, edited by Brenda Stevenson, *The Journals of Charlotte Forten Grimké* (1988), includes a very useful chronology of Forten Grimké's life. Among the writings Forten Grimké published during her lifetime are "Interesting Letter from Miss Charlotte L. Forten," *Liberator*, 19 Dec. 1862, p. 203; "Life on the Sea Islands," *Atlantic Monthly*, May 1864, pp. 587–96 (pt. 1) and June 1864, pp. 666–76 (pt. 2); and "Personal Recollections of Whittier," *New England Magazine*, June 1893, pp. 468–76. Also see the work of her longtime friend Anna J. Cooper, *The Life and Writings of the Grimké Family* (1951).

CAROLYN WILLIAMS

GRIMKÉ, Francis James (4 Nov. 1850–11 Oct. 1937), Presbyterian minister and civil rights activist, was born near Charleston, South Carolina, the son of Henry Grimké, a planter, and Nancy Weston, a mulatto slave. As the second son of an illegitimate dalliance that was familiar to plantations such as "Caneacres," young Grimké inherited his mother's status as servant. During the Civil War his white half brother sold him to a Confederate officer whom Grimké accompanied until the end of that conflict. The end of the war brought his manumission, and a benefactor from the Freedmen's Aid Society sent him to study at Lincoln University in Chester County, Pennsylvania.

Hard work and natural talent brought Grimké recognition on the campus. A newspaper account of the young scholar's outstanding record also attracted attention from his white aunts, Angelina and Sarah, who had been deeply involved in antislavery activities. After learning of the existence of a heretofore unknown nephew, the reformist sisters subsidized Grimké's education and remained in contact with him for the rest of their lives. After graduating from Lincoln in 1870, Grimké studied law for a time (1870–1871, 1872–1873 at Lincoln; 1874–1875 at Howard University) but at length decided to enter the Presbyterian ministry. In 1878 he completed training at Princeton Theological Seminary and was ordained.

In 1878 Grimké accepted an invitation to become pastor of the Fifteenth Street Presbyterian Church in Washington, D.C., inaugurating a ministerial career that spanned more than half a century. That same year he married Charlotte Forten, whom he had first met at a freedman school. The couple had one child who lived for a scant few months in 1880. The city of Washington grew rapidly in the last quarter of the nineteenth century, and Grimké made his church an eminent part of that rapid development. His fame as a pulpit orator spread, and members of all denominations as well as people with diverse ethnic identities attended his sermons.

Health problems due to overwork soon intervened, however, and Grimké viewed as providential an invitation to serve a church in Florida in 1885. He followed a more relaxed routine at the Laura Street Church in Jacksonville for four years, but he was ready to return to Washington when his old church pleaded for his help in 1889. Thereafter he became an even more important figure in esthetic and literary circles in the nation's capital. But more significant than recognition for erudition and genteel manners among the black elite, he developed a reputation for passionate advocacy in struggles for racial justice. As Jim Crow laws became more manifest and lynching increased, he moved from an accommodationist philosophy represented by Booker T. Washington to a more strident demand for government action in protecting the civil rights of black American citizens.

Grimké displayed powerful intellect and eloquence in his sermons. Using such standard components as biblical exposition and illustrative material from classical literature, he shaped most of his addresses into what he called "helpful" sermons. His preaching included ideas about salvation and proper doctrine, but it focused primarily on questions of social relevance. In Grimké's view the Christian ministry functioned essentially as a moral teacher, and he used contemporary issues to apply those lessons. In his day racial prejudice made itself known through lynchings, disfranchisement, and Jim Crow legislation, especially in the areas of education and public transportation. Grimké denounced those abuses and rallied African-American leaders to fight racist discrimination. He repeatedly stressed self-improvement as a means of achieving equal rights with other segments of American society. He urged character formation, moral integrity, and education as elements that commanded respect. Through industriousness black citizens could, he argued, insist on parity with whites because they deserved it.

In the years around 1895 Grimké moved from an accommodationist to a gadfly, impatient at slow progress and insistent on faster change. He criticized Booker T. Washington for being too meek, and his prophetic ardor did not diminish with age. In 1913, for instance, he wrote Woodrow Wilson that he had hoped Wilson's "accession to power would act as a check upon the brutal and insane spirit of race hatred that characterizes certain portions of the white people of the country." After faulting the president for lack of vigor, he reminded him that "all class distinctions among citizens are un-American, and the sooner every vestige of it is stamped out the better it will be for the Republic." He finally retired from the pulpit in 1928 and lived another nine years before dying in Washington.

• A collection of Grimké's personal papers, sermons, and addresses is housed in the library at Howard University in the District of Columbia. Scattered essays are brought together in *The Works of Francis James Grimké*, ed. Carter G. Woodson (4 vols., 1942). See also Henry J. Ferry, "Racism and Reunion: A Black Protest by Francis J. Grimké," *Journal of Presbyterian History* 50 (1972): 77–88, and "Patriotism and Prejudice: Francis James Grimké on World War I," *Journal of Religious Thought* 32 (1975): 86–94; and Louis B. Weeks, "Racism, World War I and the Christian Life: Francis J. Grimké in the Nation's Capital," *Journal of Presbyterian History* 51 (1973): 471–88.

HENRY WARNER BOWDEN

GRIMKÉ, Sarah Moore (26 Nov. 1792–23 Dec. 1873), abolitionist, writer-educator, and women's rights pioneer, was born in Charleston, South Carolina, the daughter of John Faucheraud Grimké, chief judge of the state supreme court, and Mary Smith. Sarah was educated by private tutors in subjects considered proper for well-bred southern girls—among them, French, watercolors, harpsichord, and embroidery. But from her older brother Thomas, a student at Yale, she learned Latin, Greek, mathematics, and geography. Raised in the upper classes of Charleston, Sarah gained firsthand experience with prosperity's underside, African slavery. Her father "owned" several hundred slaves, some of whom she taught to read before he (and the law of the state) forbade it.

A major turning point in Sarah's life came in 1819 when at the age of twenty-six she accompanied her dying father on a trip to Philadelphia. There she mingled with prominent Quakers and confronted their ideas about male-female equality. In 1821 she abandoned her ancestral Anglicanism, became a member of the Society of Friends, left her family, and moved to Philadelphia, where she worked and studied with Quakers. But the honeymoon was brief. Increasingly, Grimké chafed under mainstream Quaker attitudes toward blacks. When Grimké's youngest sister, Angelina, joined her in Philadelphia in 1829, they jointly began to protest the Friends' lukewarm position on slavery and the shabby treatment of blacks in Quaker meetings.

The physically fragile Angelina Grimké was a vital catalyst in Sarah's evolving religious perfectionism and activism. Twelve years younger than Sarah, Angelina had opposed slavery in Charleston; in 1835 she joined the Philadelphia Female Anti-Slavery Society and published an abolitionist letter in William Lloyd Garrison's radical abolitionist newspaper, the *Liberator*. A year later the American Anti-Slavery Society published a pamphlet written by Angelina—arguably, the most important tract published by a female abolitionist before the Civil War—entitled *An Appeal to the Christian Women of the South* and authorized her to hold women's abolitionist meetings in New York City. When Quaker leader Jonathan Evans publicly silenced Sarah at the Philadelphia Yearly Meeting of the Society of Friends, Sarah decided to join Angelina in New York City.

Once in New York, the two women zealously pumped energies into the abolitionist cause. In November 1836 they attended a course for abolitionist workers taught by lyceum speaker and reformer Theodore Dwight Weld. Inspired by the experience, Sarah in December of the same year wrote a pamphlet, *Epistle to the Clergy of the Southern States*. Swiftly published by the American Anti-Slavery Society, it refuted southern arguments of biblical justification for slavery. In early 1837 Sarah and Angelina addressed the Anti-Slavery Convention of American Women, the first major meeting of its kind in the nation, organized by the Grimkés and other women in response to male abolitionists' exclusion of women from reform society lecterns.

Controversy deepened when the sisters participated in an abolitionist speaking tour of New England; there they addressed "promiscuous" (mixed-sex) audiences of women and men and propelled dozens of listeners into both abolitionism and women's rights agitation;

they also inspired scholars and political oppositionists like Simon Greenleaf of Harvard to take to the road with anti-Grimké speeches. In July 1837 the Council of Congregational Ministers of Massachusetts issued a "pastoral letter" denouncing the sisters for addressing partly male audiences and for questioning male interpretations of the Bible. As they saw it, the sisters' speeches threatened "the female character with widespread and permanent injury" by leading women away from their "appropriate duties and influence." Women who abandoned dependency against the laws of nature and assumed "the place and tone of man as a public reformer" did not deserve the "care and protection" of men. In addition, the Grimkés disregarded taboos about public discussions of rape and women's bodies and so found themselves accused often of lewdness, mental imbalance, and ungodliness.

After publication of the clerical epistle in the *Liberator* (1838), and partly in response to repeated attempts to silence her, Sarah became an active speaker and writer for women's rights and what she termed "the ministry of women." Her 1838 *Letters on the Equality of the Sexes, and the Condition of Woman* (addressed to Mary Parker, president of the Boston Anti-Slavery Society) provided a book-length, penetrating examination of "the woman question." She mounted an argument for an original, divinely ordained equality between men and women; she also described the condition of women in the United States and abroad, examined American laws affecting women, enumerated the inequalities women faced in education, at work, and in parish halls, and explored the cultural roots of gender subjugation. She minced few words, on one occasion asking her "brethren" to "take their feet from off our necks, and permit us to stand upright on that ground which God designed us to occupy." Not least, she addressed the plight of female slaves, who epitomized patriarchal oppression, and deployed biblical texts in support of woman's spiritual, political, and economic equality. Referring to "the mistaken notion of the inequality of the sexes," Grimké called upon her readers "to rise to that degree of dignity, which God designed women to possess in common with men, and to maintain those rights and exercise those privileges which every woman's common sense . . . tells her are inalienable."

For the Grimké sisters, 1838 was a harrowing year. When Angelina married the Presbyterian Theodore Dwight Weld in May 1838, the Society of Friends expelled both sisters. Angelina and other women delivered an antislavery address to a mixed audience in a hall built by reformers in Philadelphia, ironically to encourage free speech; an angry mob threw brickbats through windows and, within a day, torched the hall. Shortly afterward, Angelina and Theodore Weld and Sarah Grimké withdrew from the lecture circuit and settled in Fort Lee, New Jersey. From that base, they circulated antislavery petitions and participated in associated reforms. In 1839 they published *American Slavery As It Is: Testimony of a Thousand Witnesses*, a compilation of articles on slavery clipped from southern newspapers that served, in turn, as a source for Harriet Beecher Stowe's explosive *Uncle Tom's Cabin* (1852).

In 1840 Grimké and the Welds moved to a farm near Belleville, New Jersey, retiring from antislavery agitation to care for the Welds' first child (born in 1839) and subsequent offspring. In 1848 the family began taking in boarding students to meet financial obligations; by 1851 they presided over a boarding school with twenty students. From time to time, the sisters contributed (often with letters of support) to the cause of women's rights, as with their widely quoted 1852 letter to the women's rights convention in Syracuse, New York.

In 1854 Grimké and the Welds moved to Perth Amboy, New Jersey, and opened a second school, Eagleswood, that operated successfully until 1862. When Theodore Weld decided not to resume a speaking career in 1863, the family relocated briefly to West Newton, Massachusetts, and, a year later, to Fairmount (near Boston), later called Hyde Park.

For Grimké the war years marked a sea-change, away from abolitionism and women's rights toward education reform and agitation for universal suffrage. Together the sisters taught in Dr. Dio Lewis's young ladies' boarding school in Lexington, Massachusetts, until it burned down in 1867. But the struggle to improve black-white relations also continued: in 1868, for instance, Sarah and Angelina welcomed into their homes two mulatto nephews, sons of their brother Henry and an emancipated black woman. The sisters helped Archibald Henry and Francis James Grimké attend and graduate from Harvard Law School and Princeton Theological Seminary, respectively. In 1868 the Grimké-Weld trio served as officers (with Sarah as a vice president) of the Massachusetts Woman Suffrage Association; two years later Sarah and Angelina led a group of Hyde Park women in unlawful attempts to cast ballots in a local election. On one occasion the 79-year-old Sarah tramped up and down the countryside distributing copies of John Stuart Mill's *Subjection of Women*. Her involvement with Massachusetts suffrage crusaders continued until her death in Hyde Park.

Grimké's contribution to antislavery agitation was pivotal, not only because of her considerable talent as a writer, speaker, teacher, and pamphleteer, but also because of her sex, southern nativity, and uncommon courage. As leaders of the female antislavery movement, Sarah and Angelina regularly risked physical harm and slander. They were the only women to brave social custom and charges of "heresy" in the 1837 speaking tour of New England; with Abigail Kelley, Frances Wright, Maria Stewart, and several others, Sarah made it possible for later generations of women to occupy public spaces without fear (as happened on one occasion) of having to run a gauntlet of jeering men and boys. Sarah's elegant mapping of similarities (and, occasionally, of differences) between white women in America and African-American slaves—and especially her insistence that white women learn to

empathize more completely with black women—elevated her to the first rank of social reformers and Christian-feminist theoreticians. As historian Larry Ceplair put it, Sarah Grimké and her devoted sister were genuine "revolutionaries" in a land not given to revolutionary change, "increasingly conscious that they were blazing a public path for women of courage who had seen a light or heard a voice of truth" (Ceplair, p. xi).

• Sarah Grimké's diary and papers have been preserved in the Weld-Grimké Collection at the Clements Library, University of Michigan, Ann Arbor. *The Public Years of Sarah and Angelina Grimké, Selected Writings 1835–1839*, ed. Larry Ceplair (1989), reprints many of Sarah's tracts and contains a chronology of the sisters' lives. Many of Sarah's essays have been published in small volumes or anthologized; see, for example, *Letters on the Equality of the Sexes and Other Essays*, ed. Elizabeth Ann Bartlett (1988), and material reprinted in general collections of documents about the history of women, such as Nancy Cott, ed., *Root of Bitterness* (1986), and Aileen Kraditor, ed., *Up from the Pedestal* (1968). Gerda Lerner, *The Grimké Sisters from South Carolina: Pioneers for Woman's Rights and Abolition* (1967), remains the best biography of the sisters. Other useful sources include *Letters of Theodore Dwight Weld, Angelina Grimké Weld, and Sarah Grimké, 1822–1844*, ed. Gilbert Barnes and Dwight Dumond (1934); Catherine Hoffman Birney, *The Grimké Sisters: Sarah and Angelina Grimké: The First American Woman Advocates of Abolition and Woman's Rights* (1885); and Theodore Dwight Weld, *In Memory: Angelina Grimké Weld* (1880), which includes a sketch of Sarah Moore Grimké. On Angelina especially, but also on Sarah Grimké and Theodore Dwight Weld, see Katharine DuPre Lumpkin, *The Emancipation of Angelina Grimké* (1974). See also the useful entry in Bartlett, *Liberty, Equality, Sorority* (1994), on Sarah Grimké's developing feminism.

SANDRA F. VANBURKLEO
MARY JO MILES

GRIMM, Charlie (28 Aug. 1898–15 Nov. 1983), major league baseball player and manager, was born Charles John Grimm in St. Louis, Missouri, the son of William Grimm, a house painter, and Emma Vierheller. Grimm completed only the first six years of school. Then, instead of joining his brothers in the family house painting trade, he hung around Robison Field, the home park of both the National League St. Louis Cardinals and the American League St. Louis Browns. While selling refreshments and doing favors for the players, he closely observed the skills of the outstanding ones. The famous but corrupt Hal Chase, then prince of first basemen, offered him a few tips on how to field the position. In his free time Grimm played baseball constantly, trying to improve his skills.

Grimm turned professional in 1916. At the time Connie Mack, manager of the Philadelphia Athletics, had his very worst team. He and his assistants signed allegedly promising players wholesale, trying to improve the ballclub. Ira Thomas, a one-time Mack player and active scout, observed Grimm and signed him. Despite having no minor league experience, Grimm played in a dozen games for the Athletics at the end of the 1916 season. Although not good enough to stay, his exposure to Mack's tutelage remained memorable. The years 1917, 1918, and 1919 found him playing mostly in the minors at Durham in the North Carolina League and then Little Rock in the Southern Association. Interspersed was another unsuccessful major league stint with the St. Louis Cardinals in 1918. By late 1919 his fielding skills brought him another try with the Pittsburgh Pirates, with whom he managed to stick.

From the end of 1919 until the mid-1930s, Grimm was a left-handed batting and fielding first baseman in the National League. He played with the Pirates through 1924 and from then on with the Chicago Cubs. Although he was too slow to reach stardom, he achieved distinction for his defensive dexterity, consistency, and durability. He led or tied National League first basemen in fielding percentage a record nine times. For his career he fielded a high .993. As a batter, he had 2,299 hits for a .290 career average, hitting as high as .345 in 1923. In two World Series he batted an impressive .364.

Grimm and his wife, the former Lillian Lyle, whom he had married in 1922, and their two children, found their home in Chicago with the Cubs. Grimm played for several years under Joe McCarthy, an excellent manager whom he greatly respected. Grimm was an important player on the strong 1929 team that won the pennant, only to lose the World Series to his old mentor, Connie Mack. In mid-season 1932 Grimm was promoted to player-manager. His immediate predecessor, the great player Rogers Hornsby, had managed like a Captain Bligh, thus practically necessitating a switch to a more easygoing leader. Under "Jolly Cholly," who had shown some skill in minor player-management relations, the team immediately surged to the pennant. However, in the World Series the Cubs were completely overwhelmed by the Babe Ruth–led and Joe McCarthy–managed New York Yankees.

As a manager—considering the extreme insecurity of the job—Grimm enjoyed remarkable success. A showman with a sense of humor, he used his attributes to coax and inspire capable players into performing successfully. His affable manner also made for excellent press and fan relations. He was able to rebuild or rally a fallen team fairly well. Grimm's leniency toward his players tended to lead to complacency, resulting in his replacement or voluntary withdrawal. He managed ten full and four partial seasons spread over three terms for the Chicago Cubs (1932–1938, 1944–1949, and 1960) and three full and two partial seasons for the Boston, then Milwaukee, Braves (1952–1956). His Cubs won 946 games and lost 784. Three times Chicago won pennants (1932, 1935, 1945). For Boston-Milwaukee he won 341 and lost 285. In his managerial career, Grimm won 1,287 games and lost 1,069 for a commendable .546 percentage. A World Championship escaped him, however, twice by narrow margins. Grimm also managed in the minor leagues, for the Milwaukee Brewers twice (1941–1943, 1951–1952) and the Dallas Eagles (1950).

For the Brewers, he won the prestigious Little World Series in 1951.

Between managerial stints Grimm served as a Cubs' coach (1941, 1961–1962) and radio announcer (1938–1940, 1960). From 1957 to 1959 he held the post of team vice president, and at intervals earlier and later he occupied the same office pro forma. In his later years he also filled the task of talent appraiser. Following the death of his first wife in 1961, Grimm married the former Marion Sayles. Grimm achieved financial well-being and a deserved remembrance as one of the leading figures on the Chicago sports scene. He died in Scottsdale, Arizona.

• No full-scale biography of Grimm has been published. Material on his career can be found in the Charles Grimm files, National Baseball Library, Cooperstown, N.Y.; Grimm, with Ed Prell, *Jolly Cholly's Story: Baseball, I Love You* (1968; repr. 1983); and the Sporting News, *Daguerrotypes of Great Baseball Stars* (1961). Statistical information is in Macmillan's *Baseball Encyclopedia*, 9th ed. (1993), and John Thorn and Pete Palmer, *Total Baseball*, 3d ed. (1993). For anecdotal material on Grimm's playing and managing careers with the Cubs and Braves, see Warren Brown, *The Chicago Cubs* (1946); Art Ahrens and Eddie Gold, *The Golden Era Chicago Cubs* (1985); and Bob Buege, *The Milwaukee Braves* (1988). Obituaries are in the *Chicago Tribune*, 16 Nov. 1983, and the *New York Times*, 17 Nov. 1983.

LOWELL L. BLAISDELL

GRINNELL, George Bird (20 Sept. 1849–11 Apr. 1938), conservationist and ethnographer, was born in Brooklyn, New York, the son of George Blake Grinnell, a businessman, and Helen Alvord Lansing. Grinnell grew up in an upper-class home and lived in several locations in his earliest years: Brooklyn, lower Manhattan, and Weehawken, New Jersey. In 1857 the family moved to "Audubon Park," the former estate of artist-naturalist John James Audubon on still-rural upper Manhattan. There, Grinnell's first teacher was Audubon's widow, Lucy Bakewell, who helped to develop his affinity for nature.

In 1866 Grinnell's father sent him, against his will, to Yale. A poor student, he barely graduated with an A.B. in 1870. In that same year, Yale paleontologist Othniel C. Marsh accepted him as a volunteer assistant on a "bone hunting" expedition that would travel west over the recently completed tracks of the transcontinental railroad, eventually reaching the Pacific coast. During the trip, he became acquainted with such figures as William F. "Buffalo Bill" Cody and the leader of the Pawnee Indian scouts, Frank J. North. His lifelong romance with the West had begun.

He returned to Yale in 1874 to assist Marsh at the Peabody Museum and to pursue graduate studies. Also in 1874, as a naturalist, he traveled with George Armstrong Custer's reconnaissance to the Black Hills of the Dakotas, and the following year he joined William Ludlow, an army engineer, on his survey of the Yellowstone region, preparing zoological reports for the expedition. In 1876 Grinnell became natural history editor of the hunting-and-fishing weekly *Forest and*

Stream. In 1880 he submitted a dissertation entitled "The Osteology of *Geococcyx californianus*" (roadrunner) at Yale and was awarded the Ph.D. Deciding not to pursue a scientific career, he acquired control of *Forest and Stream* and assumed the position of editor in chief.

Although Grinnell continued to live in the New York City area, he tried to spend a portion of each year in the West. Starting in 1885, he made regular trips to hunt and climb in the St. Mary Lakes region of northwestern Montana, where he discovered the ice mass later designated as Grinnell Glacier and named much of the prominent topography in what became the eastern portion of Glacier National Park. In 1899 he went with the Edward H. Harriman expedition to Alaska, compiling data on the salmon industry and on Alaskan natives.

Grinnell also edited (with Theodore Roosevelt and others) a series of books containing articles by members of the Boone and Crockett Club, an exclusive sportsmen's organization, on hunting, natural history, and conservation. His *American Duck Shooting* (1901) and *American Game-Bird Shooting* (1910), written for "the higher class of sportsman-naturalist," became classics. He also appealed to young readers, publishing seven novels in the so-called "Jack" series between 1899 and 1913—examples being *Jack the Young Ranchman* (1899) and *Jack among the Indians* (1900)—which were based on his own (or friends') experiences. In the same vein were his historical studies, *Trails of the Pathfinders* (1911) and *Beyond the Old Frontier* (1913).

Becoming increasingly interested in Plains Indians, he made summer trips to reservations and patiently recorded Native American history and culture. In 1895 President Grover Cleveland, aware of Grinnell's knowledge of Native American customs, had sent him as a special commissioner to help obtain a treaty with the Blackfoot and Fort Belknap Indians. Later, as President Roosevelt's personal emissary, he negotiated a land controversy on the Standing Rock Sioux Reservation in North Dakota. Over time, the number of his publications on Plains Indians steadily increased. In addition to articles in the *American Anthropologist* and the *Journal of American Folklore*, his collections of myths appeared in *Pawnee Hero Stories and Folk Tales* (1889), *Blackfoot Lodge Tales* (1892), *The Punishment of the Stingy and Other Indian Stories* (1901), and *By Cheyenne Campfires* (1926). *The Fighting Cheyennes* (1915) focuses on the clash between Native Americans and Euro-Americans, while *The Cheyenne Indians* (1923), his major monograph, is devoted primarily to cultural description. Scholars have criticized Grinnell for the "patronizing air" in his ethnographic writings, even in the 1923 work, but anthropologist Ruth L. Bunzel contended in 1960 that no book on any other tribe "comes closer to their everyday life than Grinnell's classic monograph on the Cheyenne" (Mead and Bunzel, p. 114).

Although best known for his publications on Plains Indians, Grinnell made his greatest impact on American history in the conservation of natural resources. As editor of *Forest and Stream*, he called attention to the rising dissatisfaction among sportsmen over the destruction of wildlife and channeled it into a crusade to husband both wildlife and habitat. He used his journal to launch successful campaigns to protect (and define) Yellowstone National Park, to end commercial hunting, to force the federal government to adopt European methods of scientific forestry, and to grant the president of the United States the right to set aside forest reserves. In an article in the September 1901 issue of *Century Magazine*, he initiated a campaign that ultimately resulted in the establishment by Congress of Glacier National Park in 1910. During these years, Theodore Roosevelt, a close friend, came to incorporate Grinnell's views into his own conservation philosophy. The *New York Times*, in listing Grinnell's accomplishments, later referred to him as the "father of American conservation."

Grinnell retired as editor of *Forest and Stream* in 1911 but otherwise remained active in environmental affairs. Earlier, he had founded the first Audubon Society group (1886) and cofounded the Boone and Crockett Club (1887); in 1911 he helped organize the American Game Association. He served as a director of the National Association of Audubon Societies; chaired the Council on National Parks, Forests, and Wildlife; and in 1925 succeeded Herbert Hoover as president of the National Parks Association.

By 1929, when he was struck down by the first of a series of heart attacks, Grinnell had played a significant role in most of the environmental campaigns of his day. He died of pneumonia at his New York City home. He was survived by his wife, the former Elizabeth Kirby Curtis Williams, whom he had married in 1902; they did not have children. Grinnell was representative of an elite group of educated easterners who went west when huge bison herds and native cultures remained intact on the plains. His writings as a naturalist and ethnographer are important legacies, for much of what he saw and heard soon vanished forever. Grinnell helped awaken the nation to the beauty and significance of the West, and he lived long enough to see his preservation efforts fulfilled.

• Grinnell's papers are in Yale University and the Southwest Museum Library, Los Angeles. His early life and western expeditions are covered in John F. Reiger, ed., *The Passing of the Great West: Selected Papers of George Bird Grinnell* (1972), supplemented by Reiger, ed., "With Grinnell and Custer in the Black Hills," *Discovery* 20 (1987): 16–21. The first book-length work that traces his entire life, and provides a good bibliography, is Cynthia Parsons, *George Bird Grinnell: A Biographical Sketch* (1992).

For Grinnell's conservation efforts to 1901, see Reiger, *American Sportsmen and the Origins of Conservation* (1975), and after 1901, James B. Trefethen, *Crusade for Wildlife: Highlights in Conservation Progress* (1961), and Stephen Fox, *John Muir and His Legacy: The American Conservation Movement* (1981). His campaign to preserve the St. Mary Lakes region of Montana is discussed in depth in Gerald A. Diettert, *Grinnell's Glacier: George Bird Grinnell and Glacier National Park* (1992).

Other major ethnographic works by Grinnell are *The Story of the Indian* (1895), *The Indians of Today* (1900), and *When Buffalo Ran* (1920). Historical studies include "Bent's Old Fort and Its Builders," Kansas State Historical Society, *Collections* 15 (1923): 128–91, and *Two Great Scouts and Their Pawnee Battalion: The Experiences of Frank J. North and Luther H. North . . .* (1928).

For analyses of Grinnell's ethnographic contributions, see Margaret Mead and Ruth L. Bunzel, eds., *The Golden Age of American Anthropology* (1960); Omer C. Stewart's foreword in the 1962 reprinting of Grinnell's *By Cheyenne Campfires* (1926); and Jarold Ramsey's introduction in the 1982 reprinting of Grinnell's *Punishment of the Stingy and Other Indian Stories* (1901). See also Andrew Giarelli, "An Indian Understanding of the Nature of Things: One Man's Education in the Field," *Yale Alumni Magazine* 45 (1982): 18–22, and Richard Levine, "Indians, Conservation, and George Bird Grinnell," *American Studies* 28 (1987): 41–55.

Detailed, unsigned obituaries of Grinnell can be found in the *New York Times* and *New York Herald Tribune*, both 12 Apr. 1938. Other useful obituaries are by John P. Holman in the *Journal of Mammalogy* 19 (1938): 397–99, and Albert K. Fisher in *The Auk* 56 (1939): 1–12.

JOHN F. REIGER

GRINNELL, Henry (13 Feb. 1799–30 June 1874), merchant and patron of exploration, was born in New Bedford, Massachusetts, the son of Cornelius Grinnell, a sea captain, and Sylvia Howland. The seaport of New Bedford was a center of the New England whaling industry, and young Henry took an early interest in the sea. After graduating from New Bedford Academy, Grinnell became a clerk at a shipping company, H. D. and E. B. Sewell, in New York City, and over the next seven years learned the shipping business. In 1814 his older brother, Joseph, had become a partner in another New York shipping firm, Fish & Grinnell. In 1825, after the retirement of Joseph Grinnell's partner, Preserved Fish, the three Grinnell brothers—Henry, Joseph, and Moses Hicks—joined together to continue the firm under the name Fish, Grinnell & Company.

In 1822 Grinnell had married Sarah Minturn, the sister of a merchant, Robert B. Minturn; they had one child. When illness forced Joseph Grinnell to leave Fish, Grinnell & Company in 1829, Robert Minturn replaced him; several years later the business was renamed Grinnell, Minturn & Company.

Initially, the company had been a shipper of whale oil; it later expanded its operations to include other commercial items as well as the ownership and management of more than fifty oceangoing vessels, including the famous *Flying Cloud* clipper. Through conservative and prudent administration by Grinnell and his partners, the company became one of the leading mercantile houses and earned a substantial profit. In 1850 Grinnell was able to retire as a wealthy man and turn his full attention to philanthropy.

For some years, Grinnell had been interested in Arctic exploration and the efforts by expeditions from several countries to find the Northwest Passage. The best known of these was the Franklin expedition, led by Sir John Franklin of Great Britain, which had disappeared in the Arctic in 1845. After several search parties had tried unsuccessfully to find him, Grinnell decided to sponsor another rescue mission. In 1850 he underwrote the cost of a U.S. government expedition to search for Franklin, paying to outfit two ships, the *Advance* and the *Rescue*, under the command of naval lieutenant Edwin J. De Haven.

Although the first Grinnell expedition was unable to find any traces of Franklin, new territory was discovered in the far north, between Davis Strait and Baffin Bay, and named Grinnell Land in honor of the expedition's patron. In 1853 Grinnell outfitted a second expedition, placing the *Advance* under the command of Elisha Kent Kane, a naval medical officer who had accompanied De Haven on the earlier mission. The second Grinnell expedition proved equally unsuccessful in locating Franklin's party and suffered great hardships and the loss of the *Advance*—but not before it had traveled to the highest latitude yet reached by a sailing vessel, discovering the Kennedy Channel and charting the coasts of Kane Basin.

The achievements of both expeditions encouraged Grinnell to continue supporting polar exploration. In 1860, as one of the founding members of the American Geographical and Statistical Society, he gave considerable financial support to the Arctic expedition of Isaac I. Hayes, which explored Ellesmere and Grinnell lands. In 1871 Grinnell contributed to the voyage of the *Polaris*, under the command of the eminent Arctic explorer Charles Francis Hall, which traveled even farther north than the *Advance* had nearly two decades earlier. In charting a pathway through the ice-filled channels of the Arctic, the expeditions of Kane, Hayes, and Hall helped later explorers, including the successful Robert Peary, in their quest for the North Pole.

In addition to his financial support of polar exploration, Grinnell was a major—but usually anonymous—contributor to many charitable causes in New York City. He was known as a modest and even shy man who avoided publicity. In 1859 he came out of retirement to enter the insurance business, serving for a decade as the U.S. manager of the Liverpool and London Insurance Company. In 1862–1863 Grinnell also served as president of the American Geographical and Statistical Society, an organization in which he remained active to the end of his life.

Henry Grinnell died in New York City. His son, Henry Walton Grinnell, who had served with distinction as a naval officer during the Civil War, later traveled in unexplored regions of the Far East and also became prominent in the American Geographical Society.

• Biographical information on Henry Grinnell and the Grinnell family is in Joseph Alfred Scoville, *The Old Merchants of New York City* (4 vols., 1863–1866), and Benjamin Rodman, *Memoir of Joseph Grinnell* (1863). For contemporary accounts of the Grinnell expeditions, see Elisha Kent Kane, *The U.S. Grinnell Expedition in Search of Sir John Franklin* (1854) and *Arctic Explorations: The Second Grinnell Expedition* (2 vols., 1856). For contemporary accounts of other expeditions funded by Grinnell, see Isaac I. Hayes, *The Open Polar Sea* (1867), and Joseph E. Nourse, *Narrative of the Second Polar Expedition Made by Charles Francis Hall* (1879). For a modern history of nineteenth-century polar exploration, including Grinnell's contributions, see Pierre Berton, *The Arctic Grail* (1988). Obituaries, which include biographical data on Grinnell, are in the *New York Tribune* and the *New York Times*, 2 July 1874.

ANN T. KEENE

GRINNELL, Joseph (27 Feb. 1877–29 May 1939), biologist, was born on an Indian agency at Fort Sill (now Oklahoma), the son of Fordyce Grinnell, the agency physician, and Sarah Elizabeth Pratt. Both parents were members of the Society of Friends. The family moved to Tennessee, then to the Pine Ridge Indian Agency in Dakota Territory. When he was four to eight years old, Grinnell's playmates were Sioux children, and he was a favorite of the leader Red Cloud. The family moved to Pasadena, California, to Carlisle, Pennsylvania, and back to Pasadena. Grinnell began collecting animals when he was quite young, with birds as his primary interest. He completed high school in Pasadena and entered Throop Polytechnic Institute there. On weekends and during summers he collected local birds and began publishing about them. As early as 1894 he declared his intent to compile a list of the birds of California.

With a friend of his father's, Grinnell visited Alaska in the summer of 1896 and wrote to his parents: "Think of it! In a new country, collecting new birds every day. It's my ideal of a good time." He received an A.B. from the institute in 1897. In the spring of the next year Grinnell joined a gold-seeking venture in Alaska for eighteen months. Although the venture was not a financial success, Grinnell collected about 700 birds and as many eggs and published "Birds of the Kotzebue Sound Region, Alaska" (*Pacific Coast Avifauna* 1 [Nov. 1900]: 1–80). His mother published his letters from the trip as *Gold Hunting in Alaska* (1901).

Grinnell entered Stanford University in 1901 for graduate studies in zoology. He received an M.A. that year, but before completing work for a Ph.D., he suffered a bout of typhoid fever in 1903. He went home to recover in Pasadena, where he accepted a position as instructor in biology at Throop Polytechnic Institute. He advanced to professor in 1905. He resumed collecting birds, often accompanied by students, and served as editor of *Condor*, the Cooper Ornithological Club's publication. In 1906 he married biology student Hilda Wood, who promptly became his field assistant on a study of the birds and mammals of the San Bernardino Mountains. The couple had four children.

Through one of his students, Grinnell met Annie Montague Alexander in 1907. She was heiress of a sugar-raising family of Hawaii and an enthusiastic hunter of game animals, and she had become concerned with conservation and wanted to found a museum at the University of California at Berkeley, where she had attended some classes. Her goals were to establish a collection of the terrestrial vertebrates, especially of Cal-

ifornia, and to gather "data that would have direct bearing upon important biological issues." She provided funds for Grinnell to tour a number of museums in the eastern United States, where he met many biologists with whom he had corresponded. She then arranged with the university for Grinnell to become the first director of Berkeley's Museum of Vertebrate Zoology in 1908, a position that he held until his death in 1939.

Not having completed his graduate studies, Grinnell queried his former professor at Stanford, Charles H. Gilbert, in 1912 about doing so. He was encouraged to submit a dissertation, for which he presented a summary of the mammals and birds of the Lower Colorado River valley. This submission was accepted, and he received a Ph.D. in zoology in 1913. He was then appointed assistant professor at the University of California and advanced to professor in 1920.

Grinnell donated his own collections to the new museum. He also began to lead summer trips to sample distinctive areas of the state, from the lowest deserts and the rocky coast to the highest mountains. A survey across the Sierra Nevada, including Yosemite Valley, was carried out by eight scientists intermittently between 1914 and 1920, and the results were published by Grinnell and Tracy I. Storer in *Animal Life in the Yosemite* (1924). Some museum expeditions were sent beyond the state for comparative material, but Grinnell himself participated in only one of these: into Baja California, Mexico, in 1925.

Graduate students were attracted to the growing collections and field trips of the museum, which in 1913 also instituted undergraduate courses in vertebrate zoology and later in economic zoology. Grinnell, once called "the field naturalist par excellence," encouraged his associates to study the animals in nature as well as to gather significant collections.

In 1934 the museum carried out a year's study of the pristine coastal region that became Point Lobos State Reserve, in a project to which the Carnegie Institution of Washington and the Save-the-Redwoods League contributed. Grinnell and Jean M. Linsdale summarized the study's results in *Vertebrate Animals of Point Lobos Reserve, 1934–35* (1936). This project interested Russell P. and Frances Simes Hastings of San Francisco, who, in conferring with Grinnell, donated their cattle ranch of 1,700 acres in Monterey County to the University of California in 1937 as a "biological reservation . . . where long-term studies of natural history processes could be carried on."

Grinnell was a pioneer in recognizing the significance of the ecology and the relationship of geographic zones and barriers to the evolution of the animals that he studied. His primary interest was birds, on which he published most of his 554 titles. The list of birds of California that he proposed in 1894 and repeated in *Condor* in 1901 became an extensive bibliography of references, published in three major papers (1915, 1924, 1939) that are still useful to researchers throughout and beyond California. Grinnell was senior author, with H. C. Bryant and T. I. Storer, of *The Game*

Birds of California (1918). With J. S. Dixon and J. M. Linsdale he published *The Fur-bearing Mammals of California* (1937), and he wrote several papers on the smaller rodents.

Grinnell continued editing *Condor* from 1906 until his death. In editorials he was an active proponent of conservation. He edited many papers for the *Pacific Coast Avifauna* series of the Cooper Ornithological Club and edited fourteen volumes of the University of California *Publications in Zoology*. When the American Ornithologists Union elected him as a Fellow in 1901, he was the youngest member to be so honored. He served as president of that organization from 1929 to 1932 and of the American Society of Mammalogists in 1937–1938. He died in Berkeley, California.

• Grinnell's papers are at the Museum of Vertebrate Zoology and Bancroft Library, University of California, Berkeley. His papers summarizing California birds were published in *Pacific Coast Avifauna*, "A Distributional List of the Birds of California," no. 11 (Oct. 1915): 1–217, "Bibliography of California Ornithology: Second Installment, to End of 1923," no. 16 (Sept. 1924), and "Bibliography of California Ornithology: Third Installment, to End of 1938," no. 26 (Dec. 1939). Biographies are by Hilda Wood Grinnell in *Condor* 42 (1940): 3–34, with bibliography; by Jean M. Linsdale in *Auk* 59 (1942): 269–85; and by Alden H. Miller in *Systematic Zoology* 13 (1964): 235–42.

ELIZABETH NOBLE SHOR

GRINNELL, Josiah Bushnell (22 Dec. 1821–31 Mar. 1891), preacher, reformer, and politician, was born in New Haven, Vermont, the son of Myron Grinnell, a farmer and schoolteacher, and Catherine Hastings. Grinnell's father died in 1831. Grinnell's guardian pressured him to take up farming, but instead he taught primary school to pay for his own additional education. In 1842 he enrolled at Oneida Institute, New York, where the instructors were radical abolitionists. It was, Grinnell believed, "the home of freedom" (Grinnell, p. 30). In the summer and fall of 1844 he distributed religious materials in Wisconsin for the American Tract Society and was a correspondent for Horace Greeley's *New York Tribune*. Returning to New York, he attended the Auburn Theological Seminary and upon graduation became a pastor of the Congregational church in present-day Greenwich, New York, in 1846.

Grinnell's abolitionist credentials and successful pastorship earned him in 1851 the opportunity to organize a Congregational church in Washington, D.C., where he openly attacked slavery from the pulpit. By early 1852 serious threats from the city's residents forced him to resign and assume charge of the Union Congregational Church in New York City, where he also established a school for poor boys. In 1852 he married Julia Ann Chapin; they had two daughters.

Ill health led to momentous changes for Grinnell. The legend he perpetuated is that Greeley spoke the famous words "Go West, young man, go West" to him. Greeley probably gave this advice to Grinnell, but he was not the first recipient, as Grinnell claimed.

While reporting on the Illinois State Fair for the *New York Tribune*, Grinnell investigated the possibility of founding a new settlement on the frontier. Fortuitously, he met Henry Farnam, president of the Rock Island Railroad, who intended to extend his railroad across Iowa. Fed inside information, Grinnell and several associates in March 1854 preempted over 5,000 acres along the proposed railroad route in central Iowa as the site for a Christian community, named Grinnell, where the residents would be dedicated to antislavery and temperance. Sales of the town lots would also fund a college. He urged settlers to consider agricultural diversification, and he introduced sheep ranching and fruit trees. The delayed arrival of the railroad in 1863 hindered the town's growth, but in 1859 Iowa College was relocated from Davenport to Grinnell (officially becoming Grinnell College in 1909).

In the meantime Grinnell entered politics. In 1856 he helped organize the Republican party in Iowa. At the convention in Iowa City, Grinnell was instrumental in "the delicate task" of bringing together abolitionists, temperance advocates, Know Nothings, and former Whigs. He won election to the state senate in 1856 and 1858 on the platform of temperance, free public education for all, and free soil. He tirelessly argued that not only were such positions morally correct, but they would bring prosperity by increasing the value of labor and the land. Despite securing a public school law, the creation of an agricultural college at Ames, and a temperance law, he was not renominated for a third term. His reputation might have been injured in February 1859, when he entertained and assisted John Brown and several fugitive slaves. Grinnell was a delegate to the 1860 Republican National Convention and became a devoted supporter of Abraham Lincoln. From 1861 to 1863 Grinnell was a special agent of the Post Office Department, giving him ample opportunity "to fan the fires of patriotism" and encourage army enlistments (Grinnell, p. 124).

With some difficulty, Grinnell was nominated for Congress from Iowa's Fifth District in 1862 and, thanks to a substantial soldiers' vote, won the election. He was reelected by a more comfortable margin in 1864. Grinnell could be counted among the Radical Republicans in favor of a vigorous prosecution of the war, the enlistment of blacks, and Radical Reconstruction measures. Years later he regretted not punishing the South further by insisting on "a territorial probation before admission" (Grinnell, p. 158). He did argue for black social and political rights in the South but opposed black suffrage in Iowa as too divisive politically. He also favored federal aid for railroad expansion, increased taxes, and higher tariffs. The latter position was not a common one in the agricultural West, and it may have contributed to Grinnell's failure to receive a third nomination. The nadir of his congressional career came on 14 June 1866, when Kentucky representative Lovell H. Rousseau, with whom he had quarreled over the Freedmen's Bureau Bill, caned him on the Capitol steps. Ridicule of his unwillingness to defend himself would plague the rest of his political career.

Grinnell's reputation was tarnished by vindictive enemies and through his own actions. In 1868 he served briefly as a special commissioner for the Treasury Department to classify wools at the New York Custom House. Always interested in railroad expansion, he helped negotiate the transfer of Cherokee lands in Kansas to a railroad company, and without evidence, political rivals charged that Grinnell and Secretary of the Interior James Harlan unscrupulously benefited from the transaction. The U.S. Supreme Court appointed Grinnell receiver of the bankrupt Central Railroad of Iowa in 1876, and enemies unjustly claimed he embezzled funds and ruined the railroad. His biographer admits, "When it came to business methods, Grinnell was dashing but careless" (Payne, p. 90). Overall, however, he served the railroad and the Court well.

Grinnell's political standing significantly declined after leaving Congress. At best his behavior was erratic. He failed to receive the Republican nominations for governor in 1867 and U.S. senator in 1869. He joined his old friend Greeley in the Liberal Republican movement in 1872, expressing disgust at Ulysses S. Grant's corrupt administration and the lack of reconciliation with southern whites. His new allies, however, would not nominate him for Congress. In 1873 Grinnell backed the Anti-Monopoly party but denied that the railroads were the villains, as portrayed in the party platform. In 1879 he failed in his campaign for the state legislature on the Greenback platform. By 1880 he was a supporter of James Garfield and back in the Republican fold.

Grinnell became mayor of the town he founded in 1880. When a tornado devastated the college and town in 1882, he quickly raised over $40,000. He was the founder and first president of both the State Horticultural Association and the Iowa Stock Breeders' Association. In 1885 he became president of the American Agricultural Association after service as vice president and director. He died at his home in Grinnell.

Grinnell's greatest successes came in his role as reformer and promoter for the young state of Iowa. Despite his political shortcomings and naïveté, contemporaries and historians recognized him for his unbounded moral energy in the promotion of his Christian community, his college and education in general, abolition, temperance, and the diversification of Iowa agriculture.

• Grinnell's papers are located at Grinnell College, Iowa. Shortly before his death, Grinnell completed his autobiography, *Men and Events of Forty Years* (1891). The only full-length biography is Charles E. Payne, *Josiah Bushnell Grinnell* (1938). A longtime friend published a useful and sympathetic assessment, Leonard Fletcher Parker, "Josiah Bushnell Grinnell," *Annals of Iowa* 2 (1896): 249–59. Specific aspects of Grinnell's diverse career are considered in John Scholte Nollen, *Grinnell College* (1953); Paul R. Abrams, "The Assault upon Josiah B. Grinnell by Lovell H. Rousseau," *Iowa Journal of History and Politics* 10 (1912): 383–

402; and Mildred Throne, "The Liberal Republican Party in Iowa, 1872," *Iowa Journal of History* 53 (1955): 121–52. Extensive obituaries are in the *Des Moines Iowa State Register*, 2 and 3 Apr. 1891.

M. PHILIP LUCAS

GRISCOM, John (27 Sept. 1774–26 Feb. 1852), teacher, chemist, and philanthropist, was born in Hancock's Bridge, New Jersey, the son of William Griscom, a farmer and saddle and harness maker, and Rachel Denn. Educated in country schools except for a few months in 1783 at Friends' Academy in Philadelphia, Pennsylvania, he was self-taught in chemistry and physics. Griscom began teaching at a log cabin school near Salem, New Jersey, when he was seventeen. In 1794 he took charge of the Friends' School in Burlington, New Jersey, where he taught chemistry to advanced pupils in a room in his house that he had converted into a laboratory.

In 1807 Griscom moved to New York City, where he taught for twenty-five years. There he presented courses of public lectures on chemistry and established a private school well equipped with imported laboratory apparatus. His institution was among the first in the city, along with Columbia College and the College of Physicians and Surgeons, to teach chemistry. In 1825 Griscom reorganized his school as the New York High School for boys and instituted the Lancasterian system of monitorial instruction in which teachers instructed older, advanced students, known as monitors, who in turn taught younger students. He continued to teach there until the school was sold in 1831. During these years, Griscom published two books on education, *Discourse on Character and Education* (1823) and *Monitorial Instruction* (1825). In extending a monitorial system of instruction from elementary education to high school, and in broadening it to cover every subject, Griscom sought to make education simultaneously cheap and thorough. In 1824 Griscom was awarded an honorary LL.D. from Union College. He also held professorships in chemistry and natural history at Queen's College, which became Rutgers Medical School (1812–1816, and again from 1826–1830), and at Columbia College (1812–1820). During his years in New York and throughout most of the rest of his life, he delivered public lecture courses in chemistry and other sciences, illustrated by demonstrations, to large audiences of subscribers. His colleague John W. Francis said of him, "For thirty years Dr. Griscom was the acknowledged head of all teachers of chemistry among us in New York" (*Memoir of John Griscom*, p. 424).

Griscom's chief contributions to chemistry were in teaching and disseminating European discoveries rather than producing original research. Well acquainted with foreign scientific literature, he prepared abstracts, selections, and translations for the *American Journal of Science* and *Journal of Franklin Institute*. He publicized the medicinal value of cod-liver oil as well as the utility of iodine in the treatment of goiter. In 1818–1819 he traveled to Europe to visit scientists and philanthropists, and to tour schools, factories, hospitals, charitable institutions, and prisons. He published detailed observations about life at these institutions in a popular book, *A Year in Europe* (2 vols., 1823), in which he also outlined the need for such institutions at home. During his years in New York, even before his European travels, Griscom acted on his philanthropic interests. At his home, he and a group of like-minded friends conceived the New York Society for the Prevention of Pauperism, which was publicly organized in December 1817. One of the society's many reports authored by Griscom studied juveniles in the penitentiary system and led to the establishment in 1825 of a House of Refuge for juvenile delinquents in New York as well as the founding of the Society for the Reform of Juvenile Delinquents.

Griscom married twice, first in 1800 to Abigail Hoskins, who died in 1816. They had two children who survived to adulthood. Griscom married Rachel Denn, a cousin, in 1843. His son, the physician John H. Griscom, followed in his father's footsteps by teaching chemistry before becoming a leader in public health.

In 1832 Griscom left New York to accept the post as principal of Friends' School in Provincetown, Rhode Island. Unhappy there because he found the Quaker sect at that school unwilling to accept science as an essential part of a serious education, he resigned in 1834 and moved to Haverford, Pennsylvania. There he lived with his daughters and arranged and supervised proof sheets for the *Journal of Franklin Institute*. In 1841 he returned to Burlington and served from 1842 as superintendent and trustee of New Jersey public schools almost until his death, in spite of near blindness during the last two years of his life. In this capacity he closely supervised schools by selecting teachers, interacting with both teachers and students, and examining all aspects of discipline and curriculum. He died in Burlington, New Jersey.

• The American Philosophical Society Library holds some correspondence by Griscom. Griscom's son compiled a memoir from an autobiography written by his father; see John H. Griscom, *Memoir of John Griscom, LL.D., Late Professor of Chemistry and Natural Philosophy* (1859). Secondary sources include Edgar F. Smith, *John Griscom, 1774–1852, Chemist* (1925), 27 pp.; F. B. Dains, "John Griscom and His Impression of Foreign Chemists in 1818–1819," *Journal of Chemical Education* 8 (1931): 1288–1310; and E. F. Smith, "John Griscom," *Journal of Chemical Education* 20 (1943): 211–18. Obituaries are in the *New York Times*, 28 Feb. 1852; *Friends' Review*, 6 Mar. 1852; *American Journal of Science* (Jan. 1860); Barnard's *American Journal of Education* 8 (1860): 325–47; and *American Chemist* (Aug.–Sept. 1874).

HELEN M. ROZWADOWSKI

GRISCOM, John Hoskins (14 Aug. 1809–28 Apr. 1874), physician and sanitarian, was born in New York, New York, the son of John Griscom, an educator and chemist, and Abigail Hoskins. He attended the Collegiate School of Friends and the New York High School, a school owned and run by his father, where he absorbed the elder Griscom's Quaker, philanthropic, and scientific outlook. After studying with anatomist John D. Godman and surgeon Valentine Mott and attending medical lectures at Rutgers Medical College, Griscom transferred to the University of Pennsylvania, where he received his M.D. in 1832. Appointed assistant physician to the New York Dispensary in 1833, he was promoted to physician a year later. He married Henrietta Peale, daughter of painter Rembrandt Peale, in 1835; they had eight children. He purchased the goodwill of a retiring New York City physician in 1837, acquiring a practice that he maintained until his death.

In addition to his private practice, Griscom held scientific and medical posts throughout his life, including professor of chemistry at the College of Pharmacy in New York from 1836 to 1838 and physician to the New York Hospital from 1843 to 1870. In 1840 he published *Animal Mechanism and Physiology*, which ran through several editions. His participation in the founding of the New York Academy of Medicine in 1846, his service as its vice president in 1854, and his work with the American Medical Association demonstrated his commitment to improving the status of the medical profession.

Griscom believed that, through the analysis of vital statistics, humankind could understand nature's laws and thereby design appropriate sanitary reforms to prevent illness and premature death. During his tenure as city inspector and as head of the New York City Health Department (1842), Griscom improved the reliability of the city's mortality statistics. He accomplished this by successfully promoting an ordinance requiring a city inspector's permit before the dead could be transported beyond the city limits. Although he was removed from these posts after a year because of his plans for reorganizing the structure of the city health department, he used the information gathered during these municipal appointments to form the basis of his most important work, *The Sanitary Condition of the Laboring Population of New York* (1845). Modeled on Edwin Chadwick's work on Great Britain, this report correlated the higher morbidity rate among the laboring class with their overcrowded, unventilated tenement living conditions. For Griscom, tenement reform required the provision of better ventilation so that the inhabitants might live in accordance with nature's laws. Cramped, unventilated spaces forced people to live in close quarters and breathe vitiated air, leading to a progression from declining morals to depression, illness, and unemployment.

Griscom's solution to this problem reveals his pietistic education and utilitarian outlook; for him, improving the physical health and moral sensibilities of the poor through education and legislation would benefit society as a whole. The poor, once freed from the ills of tenement living, would become useful and productive members of society. In *The Uses and Abuses of Air* (1850), he again stressed the importance of proper ventilation and offered concrete solutions for achieving it. Griscom's belief that immigrants and prisoners would benefit from these reforms is shown in the medical and sanitary rules he developed for the Emigrant Refuge and Hospital on Ward's Island while serving as Commissioner of Emigration (1848-1851) and in his well-known report *Prison Hygiene* (1868) for the New York Prison Association.

Griscom's influence extended beyond the confines of New York City. He corresponded with Massachusetts sanitarians Lemuel Shattuck and Edward Jarvis. In 1859 he presided over the Third National Quarantine Convention, confirming his national reputation. Griscom remained active in New York sanitary reform until his death. His tireless letter campaign contributed to the success of the Metropolitan Health Act of 1866, which established a Board of Health for New York City and served as a model for cities nationwide. Through his writings, lectures, and public service, John Hoskins Griscom helped lay the foundation for mid-nineteenth-century urban public health reform in the United States. His ideas came to fruition in the late nineteenth century with tenement reform laws and in the writings of later reformers including those of Jacob Riis. He died in New York City.

• Few manuscript letters of John Griscom survive; these are located in the New York Public Library, the New-York Historical Society (Gulian Verplanck Papers), the Henry E. Huntington Library of San Marino, Calif., and in the Francis A. Countway Library of Medicine, Harvard University, (Edward Jarvis Papers). The *Medical and Surgical Reporter* (Jan.–Apr. 1866) and the *New Jersey Medical and Surgical Reporter* (Feb. 1856–Mar. 1858) contain Griscom's printed letters. In the latter he published under the name of J. Gotham, Jr. His other published works include *First Lessons in Human Physiology* (1846), *Anniversary Discourse before the New York Academy of Medicine* (1855), *The Memoir of John Griscom, L.L.D.* (1859), and *Sanitary Legislation, Past and Future* (1861). Duncan Robert Jamieson, "Towards a Cleaner New York: John H. Griscom and New York's Public Health, 1830–1870" (Ph.D. diss., Mich. State Univ., 1972), provides a detailed chronology of Griscom's life as well as a primary bibliography and an annotated secondary bibliography. See also James H. Cassedy, "The Roots of American Sanitary Reform, 1843–1847: Seven Letters from John H. Griscom to Lemuel Shattuck," *Journal of the History of Medicine* 30 (Apr. 1975): 136–47; Charles E. Rosenberg and Carroll Smith Rosenberg, "Pietism and the Origins of the Public Health Movement: A Note on John H. Griscom and Robert M. Hartley," *Journal of the History of Medicine* 23 (Jan. 1968): 16–35; and Samuel W. Francis, "John H. Griscom," *Medical and Surgical Reporter* 15 (1866): 118–22.

CAROLYN G. SHAPIRO

GRISCOM, Lloyd Carpenter (4 Nov. 1872–8 Feb. 1959), diplomat, lawyer, and newspaper publisher, was born in Riverton, New Jersey, the son of Clement Acton Griscom, a shipping company executive, and Frances Canby Biddle. Shortly after his birth, Griscom moved with his family to Haverford, Pennsylvania. He enjoyed a privileged and cosmopolitan upbringing, attending private schools in Europe and mingling from childhood with America's political and business elite. He received his Ph.B. from the University of Pennsylvania in 1891 and then attended the university's law school.

Griscom's professional training and early career proceeded haltingly. In 1893, suffering from poor health, he left law school and took an unpaid position as private secretary to Thomas F. Bayard, U.S. ambassador to Great Britain. Back in the United States in 1894, he resumed his law studies at the New York Law School only to suspend them once more in early 1895, this time for a three-month journey to Latin America with author Richard Harding Davis. Admitted to the New York bar in 1896, he served in 1897 as deputy assistant district attorney of New York City until a recurrence of poor health prompted him to move to Arizona. During the Spanish-American War Griscom enlisted in the army, where he served as captain in the Quartermaster Corps and then as aide-de-camp to Major General James F. Wade in Georgia. In September 1898 he went to Cuba with Wade, who headed a commission to oversee the withdrawal of Spanish forces from the island. Griscom was discharged from the army in January 1899.

Ever since his tenure in London in 1893–1894, Griscom had longed for a return to diplomatic service, and in the summer of 1899 he parlayed his father's influence into an appointment as secretary of the U.S. legation at Constantinople. In December 1899 U.S. minister Oscar Straus went home on a leave of absence, from which he did not return. Griscom then became chargé d'affaires. In this capacity he took part in an elaborate campaign, directed from Washington, to extract a $90,000 indemnity from the Turkish government to compensate American citizens for property damaged during the Armenian massacres of 1894–1895. In June 1901, following a vaguely threatening visit by a U.S. warship to Turkish waters, the Turkish government finally paid the claims. Griscom's part in this affair, while less central than his memoirs later suggested, was sufficiently distinguished to merit the appreciation of Secretary of State John Hay, who appointed him minister to Persia. In 1901, just prior to assuming this post, Griscom married Elisabeth Duer Bronson, with whom he had two sons.

Griscom's mission to Persia ushered in a series of increasingly prestigious diplomatic appointments. In late 1902 he was named minister to Japan, where his diplomacy during the Russo-Japanese war of 1904–1905, though peripheral to the main channels of American mediation, earned him credit with President Theodore Roosevelt. In 1906 he was appointed ambassador to Brazil, where he helped arrange Secretary of State Elihu Root's visit to the Pan-American Conference in Rio de Janeiro. Griscom's final appointment, from 1907 to 1909, was as ambassador to Italy, where his principal contribution was organizing relief efforts after the devastating Messina earthquake of December 1908.

By then, the necessity of providing a more stable home life for his family, coupled with the expectation that incoming president William Howard Taft would look elsewhere to fill top ambassadorial posts, had convinced Griscom that he must leave the diplomatic service. In 1909 he returned to New York, where he practiced law and briefly involved himself in politics. In 1910–1911 he served as president of the New York County Republican Committee, attempting unsuccessfully to reconcile the Roosevelt and Taft wings of the party. After serving as a delegate to the 1912 Republican National Convention, he withdrew from active involvement in politics. In 1914 his wife died.

Following America's entry into World War I in 1917, Griscom enlisted in the army as a major in the Adjutant General's Corps. In 1918, after serving with the Seventy-seventh Division in France, he went to London as General John J. Pershing's personal liaison with the British War Office, using his diplomatic skills to help ease tensions among the Allies. During the war he achieved the rank of lieutenant colonel, and after the armistice he was awarded the Distinguished Service Medal. In 1919 King George V named him knight commander of St. Michael and St. George.

After the war Griscom became president of the Huntover Press, which published newspapers on Long Island, New York, and purchased the *Tallahassee Democrat*, a Florida daily. In 1929 he married Audrey Margaret Crosse; they had no children. Into old age he remained engaged in public affairs, corresponding with statesmen and writing articles on international events. He coauthored *Tenth Avenue*, a stage drama (1927) and motion picture (1928), and wrote *Diplomatically Speaking* (1940), a book of memoirs. He died in Thomasville, Georgia.

Griscom was an intelligent, hard-working, and vigorous man who spoke several languages, made friends easily, and relished humorous stories. He was a vivid and engaging writer, combining an aristocratic outlook with boyish irreverence. At home with nobility yet possessing the common touch, he ably represented his nation as it rose to a position of world power.

• A small collection of Griscom's papers is at the Library of Congress, Manuscripts Division. His typescript reminiscences, recorded in 1951, are in Columbia University's Oral History Collection. U.S. Department of State, *Foreign Relations of the United States* (1901–1908), contains the official records of Griscom's diplomatic career. Other references are in Elting E. Morison, ed., *The Letters of Theodore Roosevelt* (8 vols., 1951–1954). Salvatore Prisco, "Lloyd C. Griscom, New Jersey Patrician in Diplomatic Service, 1893–1909," *New Jersey History* 98, no. 1 (Spring–Summer 1980): 65–80, is a study of Griscom's diplomatic career. Richard Harding Davis, *Three Gringos in Venezuela and Central America* (1903), is an account of the 1895 journey to Latin America. An obituary is in the *New York Times*, 9 Feb. 1959.

SALIM YAQUB

GRISCOM, Ludlow (17 June 1890–28 May 1959), ornithologist, was born in New York City, the son of Clement Acton Griscom, a financier and corporate executive, and Genevieve Sprigg Ludlow. Both parents were from socially prominent and wealthy families. Griscom received his early education from private in-

structors until age eleven, when he enrolled in the Symes School for college preparation. At age fifteen, he passed the entrance examination for Harvard University; but, being too young to enroll, he remained at home for two years, concentrating on foreign languages and music. His parents strongly encouraged his keyboard training, and his skills were such that he briefly considered a career as a concert pianist. Having been on many trips to Europe with his family, Griscom developed an early aptitude for languages, which contributed to his parents' desire that he prepare for the foreign service. Although Griscom learned to speak five languages fluently and read another ten with ease, he found himself strongly attracted to natural history, particularly the study of birds. He enrolled at Columbia University in 1907 as a prelaw student and graduated in 1912 with an A.B. Griscom began graduate school in 1914 at Cornell University, where he was the first ornithology graduate student under Arthur A. Allen. Griscom taught ornithology at the University of Virginia summer school in 1915 and remained at Cornell as a biology instructor and graduate student in 1915–1916 after receiving an M.A. there in 1915.

Griscom decided not to pursue a doctoral degree and instead obtained an appointment at the American Museum of Natural History in New York City in late 1916. Initially assigned to the ichthyology department, he remained there until early 1917, when he accepted an opening in the ornithology department under Frank M. Chapman, the curator of birds. Although he went on his first Central American expedition soon thereafter, by midsummer 1917 he was on active duty in the U.S. Army, where he served until 1919 as a lieutenant in the intelligence branch. At the conclusion of his tour, he returned to the American Museum of Natural History, where he was appointed assistant curator of ornithology in 1921. It was during his years at the American Museum that he established his reputation as the leading promoter of field identification methods for bird study, a philosophy that challenged and replaced the long-prevailing "shotgun" school of ornithology, which required that a bird be collected to verify its occurrence. With the advent of prism binoculars, Griscom believed that birds could be identified by the use of field marks and song, a strategy that led to the pioneering work of Roger Tory Peterson in creating illustrated field guides. Part of Griscom's enthusiasm for this method stemmed from his extraordinary acoustic and visual acuity. Griscom's years at the American Museum were also marked by a growing output of scientific and popular literature, including his classic *Birds of the New York City Region* (1923). He organized or participated in a number of important expeditions while at the museum, including those to Nicaragua in 1917, to Panama in 1924 and 1927, to the Yucatan Peninsula in 1926, and to Pearl Cays in the Caribbean in 1927. A skilled botanist, Griscom also discovered and named many new plant species, and he worked as a volunteer on botanical collecting trips sponsored by Harvard's Gray Herbarium to the Gaspé Peninsula in 1923 and to Newfoundland in 1925. He acquired some 40,000 plant specimens, including many that he contributed to the Gray Herbarium. Much of the data on the flora of western Newfoundland in M. L. Fernald's edition of *Gray's Manual of Botany* was taken from Griscom's specimens and data.

Unfortunately, Griscom's personal relationship with Chapman became increasingly strained, and in 1927 Griscom resigned from the American Museum and accepted the position of research curator of zoology at Harvard's Museum of Comparative Zoology. He spent the rest of his professional career at the MCZ, becoming research ornithologist in 1948 and retiring in 1955. Griscom conducted many field trips during his decades at the MCZ, including a Harvard-sponsored exploration in Guatemala in 1930. In addition to his prolific output of taxonomic and distributional studies in scientific journals, Griscom produced a series of important book-length works, including *Distribution of Bird-Life in Guatemala* (1932), *Birds of Dutchess County, New York* (1933), *Ornithology of the Republic of Panama* (1935), *Monographic Study of the Red Crossbill* (1937), *Distribution of the Birds of Mexico* (1940), *Modern Bird Study* (1945), *Birds of Nantucket* (1948), *Birds of the Concord Region* (1949), *Birds of Massachusetts* (1955), *Distributional Check List of the Birds of Mexico* (1957), *The Warblers of America* (1957), and *Birds of Martha's Vineyard* (1959).

Griscom belonged to many scientific, educational, and conservation organizations. He served as a contributing editor to *Audubon Magazine* and associate editor of *Audubon Field Notes*. He was a trustee of the Boston Museum of Science, the Children's Museum, and the New England Museum of Natural History. An ardent conservationist, Griscom was actively involved in the National Audubon Society, which awarded him its Conservation Medal in 1956, and with the Massachusetts Audubon Society. He was a fellow of the American Ornithologists' Union, serving as its president in 1956, and a member of the Linnean Society of New York, which elected him to its presidency in 1927. He was also a member of the American Association for the Advancement of Science, the New York Academy of Sciences, the British Ornithologists Union, the Ecological Society of America, the Boston Society of Natural History, Sigma Xi, the Cosmos Club, the Nuttall Ornithological Club, and the Harvard Faculty Club.

Although Griscom could be warm and affectionate with close colleagues, he was considered brusque and discourteous in many of his relationships. Perhaps as a result of strict family life during his childhood, he tended to be strongly opinionated, rigid, and emotionally distant. Griscom married Edith Sumner Sloan in 1926; they had met in 1925, when Griscom was collecting plants in Newfoundland, where Edith was a nurse at one of the Grenfell missions. They had three children. A heavy smoker, Griscom eventually developed Buerger's disease, a dangerous vascular disorder, which probably contributed to the severe strokes

that he suffered in 1949 and 1956. He continued to travel internationally despite deteriorating health in later years. Griscom died at Cambridge, Massachusetts.

• Griscom manuscripts are at the American Museum of Natural History in New York; the Cornell University Library at Ithaca, N.Y.; the Peabody Museum of Salem Library, Salem, Mass.; and the Museum of Comparative Zoology at Cambridge. Many of his specimens are at Harvard University, with botanical materials at the Gray Herbarium and bird skins at the Museum of Comparative Zoology in Cambridge and at the American Museum of Natural History in New York. The major source on Griscom is William E. Davis, Jr., *Dean of the Birdwatchers: A Biography of Ludlow Griscom* (1994), which contains many photographs, a listing of manuscript resources, and an extensive bibliography. A useful sketch, based on years of close personal association, is Roger T. Peterson, "In Memoriam: Ludlow Griscom," *Auk* 82 (1965): 599–605.

MARCUS B. SIMPSON, JR.

GRISSOM, Gus. *See* Project Apollo Crew.

GRISWOLD, Alexander Viets (22 Apr. 1766–15 Feb. 1843), Episcopal bishop, was born in Simsbury, Connecticut, the son of Elisha Griswold and Eunice Viets, farmers. An uncle, Roger Viets, attended Yale College to study for the ministry of the Presbyterian church but was converted to the Church of England. In the year of Griswold's birth, Roger Viets, having been ordained a priest in England, returned to Connecticut to become the rector of the Simsbury church and the most important religious influence in the life of his nephew. Under Viets's influence, the Griswold family became Episcopalians. During the Revolution, Griswold's father and uncle were among those who "feared God, and honored the king." In 1785 Griswold married Elizabeth Mitchelson; they had fourteen children, only one of whom survived their father.

For about ten years after his marriage, Griswold farmed and studied law. He was active in the Protestant Episcopal church in Simsbury and became a communicant when he was twenty. In June 1794 he became a candidate for holy orders and was ordained a deacon on 3 June 1795. He began his ministry by officiating at five Connecticut towns: Plymouth, Harwinton, Litchfield, Waterbury, and Reading. He was ordained a priest on 1 October 1795, the last ordination performed by Bishop Samuel Seabury. While serving these small missions, Griswold supplemented his income by teaching and farming. In 1804 he was called to be the rector of St. Michael's Church, Bristol, Rhode Island.

In all of the New England states except Connecticut the Episcopal church was very weak. Furthermore, in those states, Congregationalism was very strong, and episcopacy faced great opposition. Under Griswold's leadership, a united convention was proposed to meet in Boston. On 29 May 1810 representatives from New Hampshire, Vermont, Rhode Island, and Massachusetts (then including Maine) met in Boston and organized the eastern diocese, the first diocese in the Episcopal church not to be coterminous with one state's boundaries. On 31 May 1810 Griswold was elected bishop, and he was consecrated on 29 May 1811 at Trinity Church, New York. The eastern diocese came to an end with the death of Bishop Griswold.

On 10 September 1817 Griswold's wife died. In 1828 he married Amelia Smith; they had no children. In 1830 he resigned as rector of St. Michael's and became the rector of St. Peter's Church, Salem, Massachusetts. He resigned from this position after five years and then gave himself full-time to the work of episcopacy. By seniority of consecration, Griswold served as the fourth presiding bishop of the Episcopal church from 17 July 1836 until his death.

Bishop Griswold delivered one of his major pastoral charges to the biennial convention of the eastern diocese on 28 September 1814. A copy was sent to England, where it was favorably noted in the *Missionary Register* of the Church Missionary Society. In this address Griswold pleaded with the people of the diocese for their wholehearted support of the missionary task. In the tradition of the Evangelical party of the Episcopal church, he urged that evangelism be their primary concern. "Let us do the work of evangelists. Let the work begin in our hearts, and in our families; let it extend to our friends and neighbors, and to the humblest cottage of our respective parishes; nor let it cease till it pervades our country, and all the ends of the world have seen the salvation of our God" (Stone, p. 612). Throughout his entire episcopate, Griswold was the chief evangelist in his diocese, preaching wherever he could, in schoolhouses, in wooded groves, and on hillsides. He formed mission societies and urged his clergy to begin new mission stations. He supported the Sunday School movement and stressed at every opportunity that the church's primary task is missionary work. Under his episcopal leadership the number of parishes in the eastern diocese increased from twenty-two to over one hundred. He confirmed over 11,000 persons.

Griswold was one of the leaders of the Evangelical party in the nineteenth century. In fact, many historians of the Episcopal church date the beginning of the Evangelical party with Griswold's consecration to the episcopate. "The year 1811 was memorable. It marked not only a revival of pure and undefiled religion, but also the emergence of two groups or parties in the Church—the Evangelicals and the High Churchmen" (Chorley, p. 33). ("Pure and undefiled religion" meant a Catholic Christianity free from the errors of Roman Catholicism.) As an Evangelical, Griswold considered preaching very important. He insisted that preaching should not be a defense of distinctive principles of the Protestant Episcopal church but should stress the essential doctrines of Christ and the necessary duties of Christians. A part of his Evangelicalism was concern about the Oxford movement and its ritualistic practices. In his address to the annual convention of 1841, Griswold expressed his concern about the Oxford movement's return to medieval practices: "I trust that

none in this Convention need to be reminded of the absurdity of going back to the dark ages of Christianity for the models of our Churches, or for the manner of worshipping in them; or of adopting any of the fooleries of ignorance and superstition. God requires us to act as rational beings, not idolatrous heathen." In the same address he insisted that the clergy face the people because "to turn from them to the communion table, implies the supposition that God is particularly present there, and sanctions the abominable doctrine of Transubstantiation. . . . We are sure, then, that Christ is, by his Spirit, among the people; but we have no assurance that he is on the table more than in any other part of the Church" (Stone, p. 425).

Griswold died in Boston. He was a leading Episcopal Evangelical bishop, a missionary bishop, and an opponent of the Oxford movement. A Congregationalist said of him, "He is the best representative of an Apostle that I have ever seen, particularly because he doesn't know it" (Chorley, p. 38). Griswold molded an Evangelical party that influenced the Episcopal church throughout most of the nineteenth century.

• Griswold's papers are in the Archives of the Episcopal Church, Austin, Tex. His major publications are *Christ's Warning to the Churches: A Sermon Delivered at the Opening of the General Convention of the Protestant Episcopal Church, Assembled in Trinity Church, in the City of New York* (1817); *Discourses on the Most Important Doctrines and Duties of the Christian Religion* (1830); *Prayers Adapted to Various Occasions of Social Worship* (1835); *The Reformation: A Brief Exposition of Some of the Errors and Corruptions of the Church of Rome* (1843); and *Remarks on Social Prayer-meetings* (1858). The major study of his life is John S. Stone, *Memoir of the Life of the Rt. Rev. Alexander Viets Griswold* (1844). Two brief studies are John N. Norton, *The Life of Bishop Griswold* (1857), and David W. Norton, Jr., *Alexander Viets Griswold of New England* (n.d.). W. W. Manross, "Alexander Viets Griswold and the Eastern Diocese," *Historical Magazine of the Protestant Episcopal Church* 4 (1935): 13–25, is helpful. Griswold's theological position is discussed in E. Clowes Chorley, *Men and Movements in the American Episcopal Church* (1946).

DONALD S. ARMENTROUT

GRISWOLD, Alfred Whitney (27 Oct. 1906–19 Apr. 1963), scholar, educator, and university president, was born in Morristown, New Jersey, the son of Harold Ely Griswold, an insurance broker, and Elsie Montgomery Whitney. He was a student at Peck School, Morristown, and at Hotchkiss School, Lakeville, Connecticut. He attended Yale beginning in 1925 and with the intention of becoming a journalist or a writer. He published columns and light poetry in the *Yale Daily News*, helped edit the *Yale Record*, and confounded the "Mountain," a literary society. Majoring in English, he obtained his B.A. in 1929. After clerking unhappily in a brokerage firm in New York City, he taught freshman English at Yale (1929–1930). He married Mary Morgan Brooks in 1930 (the couple had four children) and that summer went with her to Germany so that he could briefly study there. Starting in the fall of 1930 he pursued doctoral work in history at Yale and earned his Ph.D. in 1933.

That same year Griswold was hired as a history instructor at Yale. Two years later he became a research assistant in international relations. In 1938 he published *The Far Eastern Policy of the United States*, in which he analyzes American foreign policy beginning with the battle of Manila Bay in 1898 and the annexation of the Philippine Islands, examines subsequent policy phases, emphasizes changes motivating diplomatic papers, and concludes by considering the cautious U.S. response to Japan's aggression in China in the 1930s. Reviewers complimented Griswold for a coherent, absorbing, well-documented narrative. He was assistant professor of governmental and international relations from 1938 to 1942 and associate professor of history from 1942 to 1947. From 1942 to 1945 he also served as director of the U.S. Army Civil Affairs Training School and the Foreign Area and Language Studies of the U.S. Army Specialized Training Program. Both schools were located on the Yale campus. He was promoted to professor of history in 1947. *Farming and Democracy* (1948) was his second book. Written while he was on a Guggenheim fellowship, it evolved from his respect for Thomas Jefferson and develops the thesis that farming as a farm-family or an owner-operated enterprise is the backbone of democracy and the best defense of its values and institutions. In 1950, to his considerable surprise, the Yale Corporation appointed him the president of Yale.

Combining youthful energy and seasoned, liberal judgment, Griswold was a superb university president. He initiated fiscal, administrative, pedagogical, and hiring changes. In 1950 Yale owned $125 million in stocks and bonds but was running an annual deficit of $450,000. Griswold tripled the endowment, by inspiring a quadrupling of annual alumni donations and gifts from several foundations and millionaires. He restructured Yale's eleven schools, created a Drama School separated from the fine arts department, reorganized and strengthened the School of Engineering, and completed or began the construction of twenty-six new buildings. He encouraged high school programs to become more rigorous and liberal-arts oriented, suggested the development of advanced courses for qualified freshmen at Yale, and instituted a program for a master's degree in teaching. He defended academic freedom, criticized loyalty oaths and athletic scholarships, opposed the overuse of committees as problem solvers, more than doubled faculty salaries, brought internationally known scholars and scientists into the faculty, and obtained funding for fellowships to support the research of graduate students and instructors.

During his years as a creative administrator, Griswold did not neglect his lecturing, writing, and publishing. He assembled several of his addresses in defense of higher education in *Essays on Education* (1954). In this book he emphasizes the value of liberal education to counteract regimentation, specialization in technology, and vocationalism and calls on those who are well educated not only to support schools financially but also to do more creative thinking of their

own. Many reviewers praised the wit, charm, and persuasiveness of this book. *In the University Tradition* (1957) is more negative. While defending academic freedom in it, Griswold offers much barbed criticism. He called for emphasis in high schools on content and not methodology. And he discussed problems caused by collegiate athletics, going so far as to call scholarships for athletes of limited intellectual ability a national "swindle" to provide entertainment for alumni and others beyond college age. Several reviewers downgraded this book for being a disunified collection of reports, speeches, and articles. More effective is *Liberal Education and the Democratic Ideal and Other Essays* (1959), in which Griswold discusses the origins, history, and purposes of liberal education, defines the best environment in which it can perform its traditional and ongoing role, and calls for the energizing of America's spiritual powers. These essays originally appeared in such diverse publications as *Harper's Magazine*, the *Ladies' Home Journal*, the *New York Herald Tribune*, and the *Saturday Review*. An enlarged edition in 1962 added new material that had first appeared in the *Atlantic*, *Sports Illustrated*, and elsewhere, and prominently featured a candid interview of Griswold.

Two of Griswold's short essays, one early, one late, stand out. "New Thought: The Cult of Success" (*American Journal of Sociology*, Nov. 1934) came from his Yale dissertation and objectively traces the history of the new thought movement, the philosophy of which was that thoughts can become matter controllable by the opportunistic thinker to influence his fellows and achieve financial success. "The Fine Arts and the University" (*Atlantic*, June 1959; repr. as part of Griswold et al., *The Fine Arts and the University* [1965]) persuasively demands that the fine arts be recognized as a viable force in university and college curricula.

Griswold achieved the dual reputation of being not only a relentless pursuer of his well-specified liberal academic and social goals, often in the face of conservative political hostility, but also an amiable, humor-loving, self-deprecating, and versatile personality. He played the banjo, the flute, and the piano (once with President Harry S. Truman), enjoyed golf, and loved yachting around Martha's Vineyard. He was a voracious reader and a fine conversationalist. He received many awards and honorary degrees. He died of cancer in New Haven, Connecticut.

• The bulk of Griswold's papers are in the Yale administrative files. Some of his other correspondence is in the library at Radcliffe College. Obituaries are in the *New York Times*, 20 Apr. 1963, and *Life*, 3 May 1963.

ROBERT L. GALE

GRISWOLD, Matthew (25 Mar. 1714–28 Apr. 1799), jurist, deputy governor, and governor of Connecticut, was born in Lyme, Connecticut, the son of John Griswold and Hannah Lee, farmers. A fourth generation descendant of Lyme's founders, Griswold received his only formal education in one of the town's two district schools. In his late twenties he studied law and was admitted to the bar in New London County in 1742. In 1743 he married Ursula Wolcott, daughter of Governor Roger Wolcott. They had seven children, five of whom reached adulthood.

Griswold lived in Lyme and became a church member in 1741, during the peak of the Great Awakening. Affiliated with the New Light, he played a prominent role in the affairs of Lyme's First Society, whose minister, Jonathan Parsons, an ardent revivalist, was his brother-in-law. Griswold served as clerk of the society from 1742 to 1748, as a member of the society committee in 1760, and as a moderator of society meetings in 1760 and 1766. His commitment to the patriot cause by 1765 was typical of New Light eastern Connecticut.

Griswold's law practice was a successful one. Soon after his admittance to the bar, he represented Lyme before the county court in a case against New London. He was also agent for Lyme when it successfully opposed a group of petitioners who wanted to build a highway in the town. In November 1743 Griswold was appointed king's attorney for the county of New London, a position he held until 1776. He was made agent for New London County in 1754, 1757, and 1762. With William Samuel Johnson, he represented the town of Plainfield before the Connecticut General Assembly in 1757. Much of Griswold's practice dealt with collecting debts and settling estates. He was a popular and respected teacher of law.

In 1739 the Connecticut General Assembly appointed Griswold captain of the train band in Lyme. In October 1748 he was elected to serve in the general assembly as a deputy for Lyme, and he was reelected in May 1751 and every year from 1754 through 1759, in both regular and special sessions. While a member of the assembly, he was appointed an overseer of the Mohegan Indians "to lease out the lands, oversee, order and take care of the estate and affairs of the said Indians." In 1759 Griswold was elected to the prestigious Connecticut Council, the legislature's upper house and the inner circle of the political elite. He had been nominated several times during the 1750s, and after 1759 he was reelected with an ever-increasing popular vote for the next ten years.

Griswold's patriotic stance during the Stamp Act crisis and his support for the Susquehannah Company's claims in Pennsylvania led him to the deputy governorship of Connecticut. In spite of Connecticut's overt resistance to the Stamp Act, Governor Thomas Fitch agreed to take the required oath to carry out the provisions of the act. The council members, called assistants, were to administer the oath, but when they were informed of Fitch's decision, Griswold and other council assistants from eastern Connecticut withdrew from the chamber, leaving only four assistants to administer the oath. Governor Fitch and these four assistants lost reelection in 1766, and Griswold received his highest number of votes since his first nomination ten years earlier. When Governor William Pitkin, who succeeded Fitch, died in 1769, he was succeeded

by Deputy Governor Jonathan Trumbull. Griswold was elected deputy governor on the fourth ballot in the general assembly, and he held this position for the next fifteen years. As a New Light opponent of the Stamp Act and a supporter of the Susquehannah Company, Griswold aligned himself with the dominant political forces in prerevolutionary Connecticut.

In addition to replacing the governor during absences or incapacity and serving as an ex officio member of the council, the deputy governor was also chief justice of the superior court, a demanding position Griswold held from 1769 to 1783. As British-colonial relations worsened during the 1770s, Griswold's attention turned more often to imperial problems. While he consistently supported the patriot cause, the violence throughout Connecticut disturbed him, and he counseled restraint. Once the news of Lexington and Concord reached Lyme, he was among the first members appointed to the Council of Safety established to assist the governor with war matters when the assembly was not in session. Griswold was in regular attendance at the governor's "war office" in Lebanon throughout the war, absent only when superior court sessions demanded his presence. He was also in regular attendance at all sessions of the general assembly during these critical years.

When the ill Governor Trumbull decided not to seek reelection in 1784, Griswold was chosen governor by the assembly's vote, because he did not receive a popular majority. Both Griswold and Governor Trumbull were identified with the unpopular merchant interests in postwar Connecticut. Griswold was returned to office in May 1785. In April 1786 he again failed to receive a popular majority, and the assembly chose Deputy Governor Samuel Huntington as Griswold's successor.

The inadequacies of the Articles of Confederation were evident to Griswold as Congress attempted to execute the war. His own efforts to settle the 1782 Wyoming Valley land controversy deepened his doubts, and along with other Connecticut nationalists, he looked hopefully to the convention in Philadelphia. He was elected by Lyme residents to serve as a delegate to Connecticut's ratifying convention, of which he was chosen president. Griswold cast his vote with the majority of 128 to 40 in favor of the Constitution. He was asked by the assembly to help prepare an address to President George Washington and to be one of the dignitaries to greet him when Washington traveled to New Haven.

Griswold spent the last ten years of his life quietly at "Black Hall," the family estate in Lyme, where he died. While he is perhaps best known for his ardent patriotism during the revolutionary crisis, he was not a fiery leader. His life exemplifies the deeply conservative values that have earned Connecticut its reputation as a sober, steadfast state.

• Most of Griswold's papers are in the William Griswold Lane Collection at the Yale University Library. A secondary work that treats all of Griswold's life is an essay by John W.

Ifkovic, "Matthew Griswold: Lyme's Revolutionary Magistrate," in *A Lyme Miscellany, 1776–1976*, ed. George Willauer, Jr. (1977), which gives a complete picture of Lyme during the revolutionary era. See also Bruce P. Stark, *Lyme, Connecticut: From Founding to Independence* (1976). Julian P. Boyd, ed., *The Susquehannah Company Papers* (1930–1934; repr. 1962), documents Griswold's role in the company. Other works that treat Conn. during Griswold's life are Richard L. Bushman, *From Puritan to Yankee: Character and the Social Order in Connecticut, 1690–1763* (1967); Christopher Collier, *Roger Sherman's Connecticut: Yankee Politics and the American Revolution* (1971); and Oscar Zeichner, *Connecticut's Years of Controversy, 1750–1776* (1949; repr. 1970).

JOHN IFKOVIC

GRISWOLD, Roger (21 May 1762–25 Oct. 1812), lawyer and public official, was born in Lyme, Connecticut, the son of Matthew Griswold, a lawyer and Connecticut governor, and Ursula Wolcott, granddaughter of Governor Oliver Wolcott. After graduating from Yale in 1780, he studied law with his father and was admitted to the bar in 1783. He practiced law in Norwich until 1794, then moved his practice to Lyme. In 1788 he married Fanny Rogers. The couple had ten children.

In 1794 Griswold was elected to the lower house of the Connecticut General Assembly but soon surrendered his seat there to accept election to the U.S. House of Representatives, where he served until 1805. He quickly proved himself an engaging, skilled speaker and an energetic, partisan Federalist. The Federalist party was then in the majority in Congress and for another two decades was the effective monopoly party of Connecticut. His firm support of the policies of the George Washington and John Adams administrations and his opposition to those of Thomas Jefferson were the stands of an extreme Federalist. At the close of his administration in 1801, Adams offered him the secretaryship of war, but Griswold declined.

Griswold won enduring notoriety in 1798 for initiating the first recorded physical brawl on the floor of the House of Representatives. Vermont congressman Matthew Lyon, a radical Democratic Republican, spit in Griswold's face because of an alleged insult, and Griswold attacked Lyon with a hickory cane at the chamber's next meeting. After Lyon picked up a pair of fire tongs to strike back, other congressmen, with difficulty, pulled the combatants apart without injury. Neither representative was expelled.

After the Federalists became the minority party upon the election of Jefferson in 1800, Griswold became an increasingly bitter partisan and New England sectionalist. In 1804 he corresponded with other Federalists about the possibility of breaking up the Union by establishing a New England confederacy, and he kept the British ambassador in Washington apprised of these discussions. Concluding with others that New York's participation would be essential to these plans, he also worked with New York Federalists for the election of Vice President Aaron Burr to the governorship of that state. Because Burr was defeated, nothing came of these efforts. When Burr later set out on his ill-fated

adventure to create a separate confederacy out of some western states and territories, Griswold was not involved.

Following the election of James Madison to the presidency in 1808, Griswold was involved in 1809 in aborted plans for a convention of New England states to protest administration policies, especially the embargoes on foreign trade promoted by Jefferson and Madison, and to press for changes in them. Although nothing came of these convention plans, it can be said that they eventually bore fruit in the 1814 Hartford Convention, which Griswold did not live to attend.

Upon leaving the House in 1805, Griswold returned to the full-time practice of law and argued cases before the federal bench. In 1807 the legislature elected him to the Connecticut Superior Court, where he served until 1809, when he became lieutenant governor. Never an active churchgoer, he was in 1811 elected governor—the first chief executive in the state's history not closely associated with its powerful Congregational establishment. Reelected in 1812 to a second term, he served until his death.

While governor, Griswold refused to allow state's militia to serve under federal officers and inaugurated both a constitutional debate over dential power and three years of obstru among New England Federalist state gov obstructionism which frequently jeopardi ecution of the war with Great Britain. with others after the declaration of war terstate Peace party, composed largely and dissident Democratic Republican presidential candidate was DeWitt York. Clinton was not elected. Grisw disease in Norwich.

Skilled in avoiding compromise, extreme Federalist, willing to frust cies and even countenance disunio terests and old ways of Connecticu changing politics and culture. Ne the "standing order" of Connectic leading figure, long survived his

• Yale University possesses a small papers. An unpublished biography McBride, "Roger Griswold: Conn diss., Yale Univ., 1948). Conn.'s stances during Griswold's lifetime J. Purcell, *Connecticut in Transi*. obituary is in the *(Hartford)* 1812.

GRISWOLD, Rufus Wi 1857), editor and antholo Benson, Vermont, the so and farmer, and Debora reer consisted of a series for small-town papers When Horace Greeley cepted a temporary job to run the paper in hi

Griswold left the *New-Yorker* in November to compile an anthology of American poetry, which was published in 1842 under the title *The Poets and Poetry of America*. The book established Griswold's reputation as an expert on American poetry. In preparing the volume Griswold had consulted, by his own count, 500 volumes of poetry published in the United States. Griswold's early editorial work had already acquainted him with New York and New England poets, but the anthology revealed his sketchy knowledge of western and southern poets and included many poets unworthy of attention, weaknesses pointed out by reviewers in *Graham's* and the *Democratic Review*. Most reviewers, however, agreed with the *Knickerbocker* that the book was "by far the most satisfactory and in every way the best collection of American poetry that has ever been made."

Impressed with the anthology, George Graham hired Griswold in 1842 as associate editor of *Graham's Magazine*, replacing Edgar Allan Poe. During the next year and a half, under Griswold's direction, many popular writers contributed to *Graham's*, including William Cullen Bryant, James Fenimore Cooper, Elizabeth Barrett (not yet Browning), and Nathaniel Hawthorne. Griswold had married Caroline Searles in 1937. In 1842, just as Griswold was recovering from tuberculosis, Caroline died, leaving two daughters and setting Griswold, never very stable, emotionally adrift.

The 1840s were Griswold's period of greatest production. He edited a series of anthologies: *The Poets and Poetry of England in the Nineteenth Century* (1845), *The Prose Writers of America* (1847), and *The Female Poets of America* (1848). He edited collections of poet[ry]: *The Songs of Beranger in English* (1844), *The Poetic[al] Works of W. M. Praed* (1844), *Poems by Felicia [Hem]ans* (1845), and *The Poems of the Honorable Mrs. [Norton]* (1846). His name appears as editor on more [than] two dozen works of literature and history. He also [produ]ced a flood of gift books containing the senti[mental] poetry popular at the time.

[Grisw]old's *The Female Poets of America* helped to [recognize] women's writing before the Civil War and [was the s]tandard reference work on women's poetry [for severa]l decades. Other anthologies of women's [poetry ap]peared quickly thereafter. Griswold did not [believe, ho]wever, that women's poetry was equal in [quality to th]at of men, and his publication of *The Fe[male Poets of] America* did much to separate women's [from m]en's poetry in the nineteenth century.

[Griswold be]came a member of the New-York His[torical Society] in 1845 and wrote *Washington and the [Generals of the] American Revolution* (1847). He re[turned to the top]ic of Washington in the mid-1850s, [editing *Th]e Republican Court* (1855), a descrip[tion of the s]ociety during Washington's presi[dency.]

[Griswold i]s best known for his relationship [with Poe.] When Poe died, Horace Greeley [asked him to wr]ite an obituary for the *Tribune*. [He wrote] an uncomplimentary sketch

signed "Ludwig." Part of the sketch was borrowed from inaccurate material Poe had sent Griswold for *The Poets and Poetry of America*; part was based on an unsympathetic character in Bulwer Lytton's *The Caxtons*, whom Griswold felt resembled Poe. The "Ludwig" sketch alone might not have undone Griswold, had not Poe's mother-in-law, Mrs. Clemm, persuaded Griswold a few days after Poe's death to be his literary executor, claiming that Poe had asked for him. The news that Griswold would be the editor of Poe's collected works raised a clamor from Poe's supporters. Griswold was not willing to give up the executorship so long as he believed it was Poe's wish; Mrs. Clemm would not replace Griswold, who had promised her all the income from the project. Griswold used his editing of Poe's works to purge uncomplimentary references to his own work, and he inserted material into letters from Poe that made Poe seem dependent on him and treacherous to other editors such as George Graham, Louis Godey, and George W. Eveleth. His forgeries were not discovered at the time, and the edition sold well.

In 1845 Griswold had married Charlotte Myers of Charleston, but the marriage was never consummated, and they separated shortly thereafter. Griswold divorced Charlotte on 18 December 1852 in order to marry Harriet McCrillis, a wealthy spinster from Bangor, Maine. Despite Griswold's marriage, Charlotte filed an affidavit in September 1853 to have the decree set aside, barely two weeks before a son was born to Griswold and his new wife. Ultimately, a judge refused to vacate Griswold's divorce decree because the original decree had not been properly recorded even though numerous officials testified that the divorce had occurred. Technically, Griswold was guilty of bigamy. Harriet left for Bangor with the child. Alone in New York, Griswold's fragile health failed, and he died there of tuberculosis.

• The Griswold collection of correspondence and other manuscripts is located in the Boston Public Library. Other substantial collections are available in the Historical Society of Philadelphia and in the J. T. Fields Collection in the Huntington Library, San Marino, Calif. Griswold's son, William McCrillis Griswold, edited *Passage from the Correspondence and Other Papers of Rufus Wilmot Griswold* (1898), but the transcriptions are frequently inaccurate, and the work is sloppily produced. The only extant biography of Griswold is Joy Bayless, *Rufus Wilmot Griswold: Poe's Literary Executor* (1943), which is well written and accurate. Judy Myers Laue, "Rufus Wilmot Griswold's *The Female Poets of America*: The Politics of Anthologizing" (Ph.D. diss., USC, 1989), focuses on Griswold's impact on the American literary canon and his editing of women poets.

JUDY MYERS LAUE

GRISWOLD, William McCrillis (9 Oct. 1853–3 Aug. 1899), librarian, bibliographer, and indexer, was born in Bangor, Maine, the son of Rufus Wilmot Griswold, a minister, editor, and writer, and Harriet Stanley McCrillis. Griswold was raised in Bangor, graduated from Phillips Exeter Academy in 1871, and attended

Harvard University from 1871 to 1875. After graduating from Harvard he traveled in Europe for several years. In 1882 he married Anne Deering Merrill, with whom he had four children.

Griswold had an independent income and probably did not need to work for a living. However, his personal proclivities led him to pursue a career in librarianship. He joined the American Library Association in 1881 and the following year obtained a job at the Library of Congress, where he was employed until 1888 or 1889. He began work there as a clerk in the Copyright Office and does not appear to have advanced beyond that position. This job may have carried more responsibility than the title suggests, however; his obituary in *Library Journal* (Sept. 1899) indicates that for about four years Griswold was an assistant to Ainsworth Spofford, the Librarian of Congress. While working in the Copyright Office, he compiled and published *A Synopsis of Copyright Decisions*, which was used as a circular to respond to frequently asked questions.

During the 1880s Griswold produced and published a number of periodical indexes. The first of these publications, an index to *The Nation* covering the years 1865 to 1880, was published probably in 1881. This was followed by a series of cumulative indexes to individual periodicals such as the *International Review*, *Scribner's Monthly*, and *Lippincott's Magazine*; he also published cumulative indexes that covered several periodicals, such as *A General Index to the Contemporary Review, the Fortnightly Review, and the Nineteenth Century*. All of these were self-published under the pseudonym "Q. P. Index" between 1882 and 1887. The value of these indexes was significantly diminished by the publication of *Poole's Index to Periodical Literature*, which provided a combined index to a number of periodicals for the years 1802 to 1881. Poole did not utilize or acknowledge Griswold's indexes, though Griswold was a pioneer in the field of periodical indexing.

In 1882 Griswold began producing *Q. P. Index Annual*, an annual index to popular journals, the title of which changed to *Annual Index to Periodicals* in 1886, when Griswold began publishing it under his own name. Beginning as an annual index to nine popular American magazines, it evolved into an index covering several dozen English-, French-, and German-language periodicals printed in North America and Europe that was published until 1889. Although it was considered to be a more detailed index than *Poole's* for the journals it covered, the *Annual Index* was criticized for idiosyncrasies that made its use more difficult. An advocate of phonetic reform of the English language, Griswold incorporated phonetic spellings of certain words, such as "fotografy" and "paragraf" into his indexes, but did not use phonetic spelling consistently. His use of numerical codes to identify the periodicals and issues in his indexes, while ensuring the brevity of the publications, made them more difficult to use, especially since these codes changed from year to year. Although they were standard library reference books

at the time of publication, these indexes were eclipsed by the publication in 1888 and 1893 of supplements to the *Poole's Index*, which were more comprehensive in scope and easier to use. Another reference work produced by Griswold in the 1880s was the *Directory of Writers for the Literary Press*, which was issued in several editions between 1884 and 1890.

In 1890 Griswold moved to Cambridge, Massachusetts, where he devoted himself to a variety of literary endeavors. City directories from the 1890s list Griswold as a writer or journalist, which suggests that writing may have been his primary occupation. Assessing his significance as an author, however, is almost impossible. Although he is known to have written articles on travel and politics for popular periodicals, and to have been a frequent contributor to *The Nation*, his writings were almost always published anonymously or pseudonymously. His work as a bibliographer, compiler, and indexer is more easily documented. Between 1890 and 1897 Griswold published a series of annotated bibliographies of books, each of which focused on specific genres or subjects of literature, for example, *A Descriptiv List of Novels and Tales Dealing with the History of North America*. These bibliographies were judged to be extremely useful to librarians because of their "scientific classification and absolute accuracy" (*The Dial*, 16 Apr. 1898, p. 268). He also compiled articles describing travel in France, Italy, and Switzerland and published them with the indexes he produced. His final index, to the proceedings of the National Teachers Association and the National Education Association, was released in 1897. In 1898 Griswold published what is probably his best-known work, *Passages from the Correspondence and Other Papers of Rufus W. Griswold*, which documents the literary career of his father. Griswold died of unknown causes at his summer home in Seal Harbor, Maine.

Despite his numerous publications, Griswold is not a major figure in the history of the library profession. Although two of his bibliographies have been reprinted and one of his indexes has been published on microfilm, most of his publications are extremely rare and have been supplanted by more comprehensive reference books produced by the collective endeavors of librarians and indexers, such as *The A.L.A. Bibliography*, *The Poole's Index*, and *The Reader's Guide to Periodical Literature*.

• The papers of Rufus Wilmot Griswold, at the Boston Public Library, include some correspondence of William Griswold. A full-length biography of Griswold has yet to be published, but there are additional useful obituaries in *The Nation*, 31 Aug. 1899; *Harvard Graduate Magazine*, Dec. 1899; and *Publisher's Weekly*, 9 Sept. 1899. The genealogy of his family is outlined in Glenn E. Griswold, comp., *The Griswold Family England-America*, vol. 6 (1978), p. 105.

RICHARD HOLLINGER

GROESBECK, William Slocum (24 July 1815–7 July 1897), jurist, was born near Albany, New York, the son of John H. Groesbeck, a commission merchant and banker, and Mary Slocum. Taken by his parents to Cincinnati in 1816, Groesbeck was educated at Augusta College in Kentucky and at Miami University in Ohio, from which he graduated in 1835. After working in the law office of Vachel Worthington in Cincinnati, he was admitted to the bar in 1836 and was soon recognized as one of the foremost attorneys of the city, so successful that he was able to retire from full-time practice in 1857.

Groesbeck was always interested in politics. A lifelong Democrat, he was elected in 1851 to the state constitutional convention and in 1852 was a member of the commission to codify the Ohio code of civil procedure. Asked to become one of the judges of the new Superior Court of Cincinnati in 1854, he declined and ran unsuccessfully for Congress. In 1856 he was elected to the House of Representatives, where he served on the Committee on Foreign Relations and, in support of the Pierce administration, engaged in a debate with Alexander H. Stephens about the seizure of the filibuster William Walker. Three years after being defeated for reelection in 1858, Groesbeck, a strong Unionist, was a member of the Ohio delegation to the Virginia Peace Conference, and in 1862 he was elected to the state senate.

After the war Groesbeck opposed Congressional Reconstruction and in 1866 was a delegate to the Philadelphia National Union Convention. In 1868 he was one of President Andrew Johnson's counsel in the impeachment trial, a replacement for Jeremiah S. Black. He took little part in the early proceedings but delivered a forceful final speech in defense of the president. Pointing out the failure of the Tenure of Office Act to cover Edwin M. Stanton, who had been appointed by Lincoln, he demolished the case against Johnson as presented in the first eight articles. He also effectively ridiculed the attempt to impeach the president for believing an act of Congress to be unconstitutional, for speaking his mind freely, and for opposing the Reconstruction Acts. The fact that Groesbeck was not well while delivering his argument in the Senate made his appearance even more dramatic, and his speech was well received.

Groesbeck, a determined supporter of Civil Service reform, received two votes for president at the 1872 Democratic National Convention in Baltimore, which endorsed Horace Greeley. A firm believer in bimetalism, he was appointed a member of the 1876 monetary commission, which endorsed the coinage of both gold and silver in a ratio of 16 to 1. In 1878 he was one of three American commissioners to the International Monetary Conference in Paris, where he also favored bimetalism.

In 1837 Groesbeck married Elizabeth Burnet, the daughter of Judge Jacob Burnet; they had five children who survived infancy. A man of considerable wealth and an excellent speaker, he was one of Cincinnati's leading citizens, often called upon to welcome visiting dignitaries. His splendid mansion, "Elmhurst," faced the Ohio River and was an architectural marvel. He died in Cincinnati.

• There is no known collection of Groesbeck papers. Brief sketches of his life may be found in Charles Theodore Greve, *Centennial History of Cincinnati and Representative Citizens*, vol. 2 (1904); the *Biographical Cyclopaedia . . . of the State of Ohio*, vol. 6 (1885); and George Irving Reed, ed., *Bench and Bar of Ohio*, vol. 1 (1897). A description of the house is in Iphigene Bettman, "Elmhurst," *Bulletin of the Historical and Philosophical Society of Ohio* 18 (July 1960): 201–18. An obituary is in the *New York Times*, 9 July 1897.

HANS L. TREFOUSSE

GROFÉ, Ferde (27 Mar. 1892–3 Apr. 1972), composer and pianist, was born Ferdinand Rudolf von Grofé in New York City. Taken to California as an infant, Grofé grew up in a musical family. His father, Emil von Grofé, who was of French Huguenot extraction, was an actor and operetta performer, and his mother, Elsa Johanna Bierlich, was a cellist. Other family members, including his grandfather, Bernhardt Bierlich (cellist), and an uncle, Julius Bierlich (violin and concertmaster), were long-standing members of the Los Angeles Philharmonic Orchestra. From 1900 to 1906, shortly after his father's death, the family lived in Leipzig, where Grofé's mother studied at the Conservatory. On her return to the United States in 1907, she remarried and began teaching cello.

Grofé began to write popular songs at age thirteen. However, without the support of his stepfather, who insisted that the boy train for a more stable and traditional profession, Grofé ran away from home. He supported himself and his interest in the violin, piano, and drums by taking odd jobs and performing in the Los Angeles area. Grofé's first published piece comes from this period; he wrote "The Elks Reunion March" on commission for an Elks national convention in Los Angeles in 1909. In that year, at seventeen, he earned a position in the violin section of the Los Angeles Symphony Orchestra. He remained in the orchestra for ten years, but since orchestra positions were only part-time, Grofé also worked as a teacher, performer, and orchestrator. He played the violin and viola in local dance halls, including the Horseshoe Pier in Ocean Park. He also played in theater and film orchestras, vaudeville houses, and cabarets in San Francisco and formed his own popular jazz orchestra, for which he arranged the music. Grofé was thoroughly familiar with the traditional musical models provided by the symphony as well as the blues, jazz, and ragtime of popular music of the day. Throughout his career, his ability to synthesize concert and popular music styles was one of Grofé's most important characteristics.

In 1917 Grofé became an arranger and pianist for Paul Whiteman's orchestra, which came to be known for its "symphonic jazz," a style that brought together the instruments, techniques, and forms of popular music with those of more traditional concert music. Grofé's arrangements of "Whispering," "Avalon," and "Japanese Sandman" were very popular. He gained considerable fame with his arrangement of George Gershwin's *Rhapsody in Blue*, which was first performed with the Whiteman Orchestra at New York City's Aeolian Hall on 12 February 1924.

After the success of *Rhapsody in Blue*, Grofé devoted his full energies to arranging and composing. During his years with Whiteman and at a time when many American composers were exploring the history, culture, and physical landscape of their own country for inspiration, Grofé composed numerous pieces with descriptive titles that evoked American scenes. These included "Broadway at Night" (1924), "Three Shades of Blue" (1927), and "Metropolis" (1932), all for jazz band, and *Mississippi (A Tone Journey)* (1926). *Grand Canyon Suite* (1931), which was introduced by Whiteman on 22 November 1931, proved to be his most popular descriptive composition, in part because of the association of its "On the Trail" movement with a popular cigarette advertisement during the 1950s and 1960s.

In 1933–1934 Grofé conducted the orchestra for the Philip Morris radio program. He conducted a concert of his own works in Carnegie Hall in January 1937. That year, he became one of the first members of the American Composers' Alliance, a group organized by Marion Bauer, Aaron Copland, Elie Siegmeister, and others to secure rights to performance and recording fees for composers of symphonic music. Grofé taught arranging and composition at the Juilliard School from 1939 to 1942. He achieved considerable success with performances by his New World Ensemble on electric instruments at the 1939–1940 World's Fair in New York City. Grofé also brought his talent for integrating popular and symphonic sounds to Hollywood, composing scores for *The King of Jazz* (1930), *Yankee-Doodle Rhapsody* (1936), *Thousands Cheer* (1943), *Time Out of Mind* (1946), *Rocketship XM* (1950), and *The Return of Jesse James* (1950). He won an Academy Award for the score for *Minstrel Man* in 1944.

After his popular success in the 1930s and 1940s, Grofé continued to compose descriptive orchestral suites that emphasized regional American motifs. Some of his lesser-known later works in this genre include *Lincoln's Gettysburg Address* (1954), *Hudson River Suite* (1956), *Death Valley Suite* (1957), *Valley of Enchantment* (1959), *Niagara Falls Suite* (1960), and *World's Fair Suite* (1963). He occasionally experimented with nonmusical devices to contribute to an overall musical and pictorial effect, as in *Tabloid Suite* (1933), which uses typewriters, a police siren, a machine gun, whistle, and pneumatic drill; *Symphony in Steel*, commissioned in 1935 by the American Rolling Mill Corp., which uses drills, a locomotive bell, sirens, and two brooms; *Hollywood Suite* (1965), in which Grofé included the sounds of construction workers, a shouting film director, and tap dancers; and *San Francisco Suite* (1960), which features solos for foghorns and cable car bells. In these works, the nonmusical sounds were background to his melodic and rhythmic invention rather than avant garde or experimental compositional tools.

Grofé's work was notable for its melodic sophistication and evocation of American images. Nevertheless, his contribution to American music and to a national consciousness about creating a recognizably American idiom did not survive much past World War II, when a more international approach to musical modernism predominated.

Little information about Grofé's private life is available. He was married twice: in 1929 to Ruth Harriet MacGloan and in 1952 to Anna May Lempton. He died in Santa Monica, California, and was survived by his second wife and four children.

• There is no full-scale biography of Grofé, although he is mentioned briefly in a number of works on American music and in contemporary articles. See David Ewen, *American Composers: A Bibliographical Dictionary* (1982), *Popular American Composers* (1962), and "Paul Whiteman" and "Ferde Grofé" in *Men of Popular Music* (1944). See also H. Osgood, *So This Is Jazz* (1926; rev. ed., 1978); Ronald M. Radano, "Ferde Grofé" in *Who's Who in America*, ed. Stanley Sadie and H. Wiley Hitchcock (1970–1971), pp. 291–92. An obituary is in the *New York Times*, 4 Apr. 1972.

BARBARA L. TISCHLER

GRONLUND, Laurence (13 July 1846–15 Oct. 1899), socialist writer, was born and raised in Copenhagen, Denmark (names of parents unknown). After brief service in the Danish military, he completed his formal education at the University of Copenhagen, receiving his M.A. in 1865. He then studied law before emigrating to the United States in 1867. While teaching German in the public schools of Milwaukee, he finished his legal studies and joined the Chicago bar in 1869. Attracted to socialist gatherings among Chicago's German-Americans, he immersed himself in the literature of contemporary social philosophy and soon dropped the practice of law for a career in radical journalism and organizing.

Shortly after joining the new Socialist Labor party, Gronlund published *The Coming Revolution: Its Principles* (1878). A comprehensive elaboration of those principles appeared in 1884, titled *The Cooperative Commonwealth*. This was the first effort by an American socialist to present the general reading public with an accessible English-language exposition of Marxist revolutionary theory, or what Gronlund called German socialism as distinct from the communitarian or "utopian" tradition derived from the writings of French sociologist Charles Fourier.

In *The Cooperative Commonwealth*, Gronlund took pains to distance himself a bit from the harsher aspects of German socialism. He noted that his mind was "Anglo-Saxon in its dislike for all extravagances and in its freedom from any vindictive feeling against *persons*, who are from circumstances what they are." The revolution coming to change these circumstances, he stressed, was an evolutionary process, the climax of which lay decades in the future. Class struggle, the coiled spring of Marxist dynamics, remained mostly absent from his pages. References to English authorities David Ricardo, John Stuart Mill, and Herbert Spencer studded his text, while Karl Marx was mentioned only once in passing, as a "noble Jew" who opposed capitalistic speculation.

Nevertheless, Marxist economic determinism, grounded in the labor theory of value, governed Gronlund's analysis. He estimated that the capitalist profit system "fleeced" wage workers of roughly half their rightful earnings, which flattened their capacity to consume what they produced. To override this grim reality, capitalists resorted to techniques of monopoly concentration and control and a search for foreign markets. These tactics were immune to worker resistance or political reform. Trade unions were "absolutely impotent" to stop them; the drive for an eight-hour day was "futile"; ameliorative reforms did "immense mischief" by rendering "evils tolerable for the moment." Socialists, Gronlund asserted, cared "not a jot" about reform. Their aim was revolution.

Vagueness obscured Gronlund's explanation of the revolution's arrival. Socialists were not architects, he stated, and the details of social transformation, for all its inevitability, remained unclear. Whether violence would scar the process depended on the behavior of plutocrats, not revolutionaries. Somehow the whole mass of organized society, which Gronlund referred to as "the State," would replace the anarchic individualism of the plutocrats with the collective control of the emerging commonwealth. The corrupt apparatus of political parties, legislatures, state governors, and presidents would disappear, yielding to true "Democracy," defined as "Administration by the Competent." Competent administrators would be chosen from below, as workers, industry by industry, selected their supervisors. At the highest tier of supervision, industry chiefs would form a National Board of Administrators to govern the whole social organism of the nation, subject to the constraints of referenda. Politics, lawmaking, and litigation would diminish wonderfully, and lawyers would vanish.

The cooperative commonwealth promised to elevate the status of women. They would share economic and political equality with men but would not compete with men. Equal but different intellectually and physiologically from men, women would follow their own vocational pathways, while winning improved terms of education, marriage, and divorce. Meanwhile both sexes would enjoy the pleasures of more abundant leisure and consumer choice.

Gronlund anticipated that revolutionary socialism would spring up first in Europe. But the United States, free from foreign interference and open to popular agitation, provided the most likely arena for ultimate socialist success. Much would depend on arousing a purposeful minority, akin to the abolitionists of the 1850s, drawn from all classes to advance the cause. Gronlund hoped that his book might help mobilize this minority.

After 1884, despite his stated opposition to reform, Gronlund labored earnestly to gather a socialist elite beyond the narrow ranks of the Socialist Labor party. He supported Henry George's 1886 campaign for the New York City mayoralty despite his mistrust of George's single tax. When Edward Bellamy melded Gronlund's ideas with his own utopian vision in the novel *Looking Backward* (1888), Gronlund allied himself with the Nationalist movement inspired by the novel, although he still served on the Socialist Labor party's executive committee after 1888. In a new edition of *The Cooperative Commonwealth* (1890), he demurred from details of Bellamy's utopia, which he felt departed from authentic socialism. In *Our Destiny* (1891) he dwelt on the religious aspects of socialist thought and thereafter joined the Christian socialist William Dwight Porter Bliss in trying to launch a Fabian Socialist movement in America. In 1891, while employed in Washington, D.C., as a statistician at the Department of Labor, he proposed the creation of a secret society among academic scholars to promote the spread of socialism. The Populist movement momentarily inspired his hope for a farmer-labor alliance along lines urged by Henry Demarest Lloyd, but the agrarian obsession with currency inflation and the William Jennings Bryan campaign for free silver in 1896 confirmed his disillusionment with reform politics. Despite repeated disappointments, including a personal struggle with poverty that forced him to ask Lloyd for financial help in 1898, Gronlund never lost hope for the fulfillment of the socialist dream. His last book, *The New Economy: A Peaceable Solution of the Social Problem* (1898), again forecast state ownership of a trustified American economy.

Information about Gronlund's personal life has remained elusive. He dedicated the 1884 edition of *The Cooperative Commonwealth* "to my sympathetic wife." A biographical entry of 1909 reported a subsequent marriage in 1895. Throughout the last decade of his life, he traveled tirelessly, coast to coast, lecturing and proselytizing for his cause. One careful historian of the origins of American socialism described him in his final years as a "shabbily dressed Dane," often sleeping in parks or under steps with an empty wallet and an empty stomach (Quint, p. 276). Gronlund's writings soon fell into similar obscurity, but the impress of *The Cooperative Commonwealth* on contemporary critics of industrial capitalism, including among others Bellamy, Bliss, Daniel De Leon, and Eugene Debs, seems clearly established. Gronlund was employed as an editorial writer for the *New York Journal* at the time of his death in that city.

• Aside from Gronlund's published writings, which also include *Socialism vs. Tax-Reform: An Answer to Henry George* (1887) and *Socializing a State* (1898), primary sources are scant and scattered. The 1884 edition of *The Cooperative Commonwealth* was republished in 1965 with an admirable introduction by its editor, Stow Persons. Gronlund is prominent in the pages of Howard H. Quint, *The Forging of American Socialism: Origins of the Modern Movement* (1953). Solomon Gemorah, "Laurence Gronlund—Utopian or Reformer?" *Science and Society* 33 (1969): 446–58, concludes that Gronlund was a revisionist reformer. Obituaries are in the *New York Journal*, 16 Oct. 1899, and the *New York Times*, 17 Oct. 1899.

GEOFFREY BLODGETT

GROODY, Louise (26 Mar. 1897–16 Sept. 1961), musical comedy dancer and singer, was born in Waco, Texas, the daughter of Thomas J. Groody and Irene Ingraham. She spent her early years in Atlantic City, New Jersey, with dancing lessons as her principal education. While still a child Groody began winning contests at the carnivals on the city's Steel Pier and at the age of fourteen began dancing professionally in vaudeville. Later she joined the chorus of *The Spring Maid* on tour, after a vacancy occurred while the musical was playing in Atlantic City.

By 1914 Groody was in New York appearing in cabarets as a dancer. She went to Chicago for an acting role in a production of *Along Came Ruth* (1915). Back in New York the same year, she answered a casting call for a musical comedy, *Around the Map* and was given a small part as the Creole Girl. When the show closed, she returned to cabarets and vaudeville.

Her rise to fame began when producer Henry Savage saw her perform in a cabaret and featured her as a dancer in the musical *Toot! Toot!* (1918). She was diminutive, barely five feet tall, with "long and luxurious chestnut curls, which, worn down her back, swayed back and forth in perfect time with her twinkling feet when she danced" (*New York Herald Tribune*, 17 Sept. 1961). Besides a sparkling personality, Groody displayed boundless energy as a dancer. During the out-of-town tryout, the *Philadelphia Inquirer* said, "she is of the Whirlwind School of Dancing" (2 Feb. 1918). When the show came to New York, the *New York Times* noted that her "piquancy is one of the high spots of '*Toot-Toot*'" (31 Mar. 1918).

Later in 1918 she was featured as a dancer in *Fiddlers Three*. Though New York critics dismissed the production as a routine and even stale operetta, Groody made a personal success and stole the show. "It remained . . . for a virtual newcomer to score the hit of the evening. . . . Her voice is no better than it should be, but she has a trick of personality which stands out . . . like a rocket among the stars. And how she does dance! . . . she smiled and moved and rollicked her way into the very hearts of last night's audience, which for once burst into spontaneous applause. . . . it may safely be asserted that Miss Groody has arrived to stay" (*New York Times*, 4 Sept. 1918).

Groody continued her upward rise as a protégé of producer Charles Dillingham, who cast her in soubrette roles in two Jerome Kern musicals, *The Night Boat* (1920) and *Good Morning, Dearie* (1921). Both were successful, and so was she. In 1920 Groody married actor William Harrigan, but the marriage did not long survive her rapid elevation to high-salaried success and the luxurious life and public acclaim it brought. She was now able to spend summers in Paris, while Broadway theaters shut down during the hot months. There she met Wall Street broker William F. McGee, and the pair married early in 1922. Groody had no children in either marriage.

In 1923 Groody's summer in Paris was marred by court proceedings to determine whether McGee's dealings with a brokerage firm had caused its bankruptcy. McGee was accused of embezzling $4 million. The *New York Times* reported that "attorneys for the trustee and creditors of . . . E. M. Fuller & Co." were "awaiting with interest the return of Louise Groody [by ship from France]." They wanted to question her "concerning gifts of jewelry and money said to have been made to her by her husband shortly before the failure of [the firm] in June, 1922. . . . the value of these reported gifts was estimated at from $500,000 to $1,000,000" (29 July 1923). Groody denied any knowledge of the supposed gifts and went into rehearsal for *One Kiss* (1923). The marriage ended when her husband was convicted and sent to Sing Sing. "Her brother . . . told reporters that while it was not generally known, she 'sold everything she had for $1.5 million to cover the small investors when she found out [what McGee had done]'" (*New York Herald Tribune*, 17 Sept. 1961).

Groody went on to further success as the star of two Vincent Youmans musicals. In the first, *No, No, Nanette* (1925), she introduced "Tea for Two" and "I Want to Be Happy." In *Hit the Deck* (1927), she sang "Sometimes I'm Happy." In both she also danced with the whirlwind energy that was her style. Though she had long declared she would never cut her trademark hair, on opening night of *Nanette* "she electrified her audience by appearing with a most boyish bob" (*New York Herald Tribune*, 17 Sept. 1961). Describing Groody's years of stardom in these shows, the *New York Times* said "she earned a fortune, but spent money prodigiously" (17 Sept. 1961). In 1928 she was linked in gossip columns with Ogden Goelet, scion of a wealthy and socially prominent New York family, who was then an undergraduate at Harvard. Groody denied any serious involvement, calling Goelet "a perfectly charming boy. We were together a lot at Palm Beach, and, of course, these rumors are always cropping up. But there's no truth in this one" (*New York Times*, 4 June 1928). Rumor also had it that Goelet's father "threatened to disinherit his son . . . of $75 million dollars, if he married her. He did not marry her" (*New York Herald Tribune*, 17 Sept. 1961).

A 1928 summer in Paris brought a personal setback to Groody: she was injured in a diving accident at a resort swimming pool. A hospital stay resulted after "she struck against the rail in making a dive and fell flat on the water" (*New York Times*, 16 Aug. 1928). She never again danced in a Broadway musical. She continued to appear as a vaudeville headliner for several years, with reviews showing an increasing reliance on singing the hit songs she had introduced in earlier times. Also, she made singing appearances on radio shows. In the early 1930s she appeared as an actress in nonmusical plays on tour and in summer stock, where her name still had drawing power. By the end of the 1930s she had faded from public awareness.

During the World War II years, Groody joined the Red Cross and served as program director for officers' service clubs overseas, with postings from North Africa (1943) to Japan (1946–1947). In 1949 she married John Loofbourrow, an Associated Press editor; they had no children. Over the next years she appeared on television in small dramatic roles and as a panelist. A long struggle with cancer ended with her death at her summer home in Canadensis, Pennsylvania. Groody is remembered for heading the casts of some of the great musical comedy hits of the 1920s and for introducing several of the period's most memorable popular songs.

• Materials on the life and career of Louise Groody, including portraits, are in the Billy Rose Theatre Collection at the New York Public Library for the Performing Arts, Lincoln Center. A list of her stage appearances is in *Who Was Who in the Theatre: 1912–1976* (1978). For Victor Records she recorded, with Charles King, the song "Sometimes I'm Happy" (Vi20609) from *Hit the Deck*. Obituaries are in the *New York Times* and *New York Herald Tribune*, both 17 Sept. 1961.

WILLIAM STEPHENSON

GROPIUS, Walter (18 May 1883–5 July 1969), architect and educator, was born Walter Adolf Georg Gropius in Berlin, Germany, the son of Walter Gropius, an architect, and Manon Scharnweber. His family was long involved in architecture and government service. His father was an adviser for the construction of Berlin's police headquarters and his great uncle was Martin Gropius, a successful Berlin architect and student of the architectural giant Karl Friedrich Schinkel. Young Gropius apprenticed with Berlin architects Hermann Solf and Franz Wichards in 1903 while they were beginning the Imperial Patent Office Building; he then attended architectural classes in the Technical Universities of Munich and Berlin-Charlottenburg in 1903 and 1905–1907, respectively, with a stint between as a cadet in the Fifteenth Regiment of Hussars.

In 1906–1907 Gropius designed some small rural homes for an uncle and his associates in Pomerania (now in Poland), but his big break came in 1908 when he began a collaboration with Peter Behrens on the design of some buildings for the industrial conglomerate AEG. This work led him to open his own Berlin practice in partnership with industrial architect Adolf Meyer in 1910. Together, Gropius and Meyer created one of the legendary functionalist structures that greatly influenced the simplicity of structural skeletal facades in subsequent modern architecture: the Fagus Shoe Last Factory in Alfeld an der Leine, near Hanover, (1911–1925). The monumental power of the simple wall planes and structural forms in this factory was repeated in their Factory and Office Building at the Werkbund Exhibition in Cologne (1914, now demolished), giving the work of Gropius and Meyer widespread recognition and leading them to other industrial commissions. In 1915 Gropius married Alma-Maria Schindler Mahler, the widow of Gustav Mahler; they had one daughter before their divorce in 1923.

After service in World War I as a sergeant in his Hussars regiment, he reunited with Meyer in Berlin in 1919. Important projects from this era include the rustic-log house in Berlin-Steglitz for contractor Adolf Sommerfeld (1920–1921), the unornamented renovation of the City Theater in Jena (1921–1922) (both have been destroyed), and Gropius's famous minimalist entry to the *Chicago Tribune* competition of 1922. Those works have been said to contain ideas that Gropius was developing after his appointment in 1918 as director of the Saxon School of Arts and Crafts, which in 1919 became part of the world-famous school called the Staatliches Bauhaus in Weimar, or simply, the Bauhaus. Gropius's interest in the residential Prairie School architecture of Frank Lloyd Wright, which was published in Berlin in 1910 and 1911, was further developed in the Bauhaus years. Wright's architecture was clearly one of the influences on the construction, planning, and spaces of the Sommerfeld House and that client himself was a great patron of the Bauhaus in those formative years. In 1923 Gropius married Ilse Frank; they had one daughter.

Under Gropius's leadership, the Bauhaus became world-famous as the leading proponent of avant-garde education in art, architecture, and design, especially after its famed 1923 exhibition. This exhibition was meant to showcase the work of this new school and to counter charges that the school was unproductive. Although the exhibition publicized the Bauhaus and led to some industrial support, conservative politicians still criticized local government funding for the school. Because of growing local political opposition to this radical school, Gropius moved it north to industrial Dessau and reestablished the workshops there in a new building of his own design (1925–1926)—a building that was restored in the 1980s under the German Democratic Republic. By the time of this move, he was no longer in partnership with the more introverted Adolf Meyer, who continued to do mostly industrial buildings until his death in 1929. In addition to leading this important educational establishment (Gropius was head until 1928), he designed a number of significant projects and buildings that were characterized by the severe unornamented aesthetic of his early industrial works with Meyer. Famous examples that survive today include his housing settlement at Dessau-Törten (1926–1928), the Employment Office in Dessau (1927–1929), the Dammerstock Apartments in Karlsruhe (1928–1929), the Am Lindenbaum housing block in Frankfurt (1929–1930), and apartments within the Siemensstadt housing settlement in Berlin (1929–1930).

The worldwide depression of the early 1930s hit Gropius's practice as well, and his executed work from this era is slight. However, commissions ranged from designs for Adler automobiles and Oranier ovens to exhibition spaces such as a community room for an apartment building in the Berlin Building Exhibition of 1931 and, under the Nazis, the installation for nonferrous materials in the Deutsches Volk-Deutsches Arbeit (German People-German Work) Exhibition of 1934. After it became clear that the new regime under Adolf Hitler had little appreciation for radical modernist design outside an industrial or technical context—the Nazis closed the Bauhaus in 1933—Gropius decided to leave Germany for London, England, where he practiced with Maxwell Fry from 1934–1937. In 1937 he accepted an offer to teach architecture at Harvard University—a move that led him to change the course of America's architecture after World War II.

Gropius was chairman of the Department of Architecture at Harvard from 1938 to 1952, a position that gave him a secure base to reestablish himself and his design ideas over a long period of time (much as Ludwig Mies van der Rohe was able to do in Chicago's Illinois Institute of Technology) and thereby influence the course of American architectural education, and American architecture itself over those generations. He completely revamped the curriculum, which, until his arrival, had been locked in the educational traditions of turn-of-the-century Paris with a curriculum modeled on the École des Beaux Arts. During the late 1930s and early 1940s, he executed a number of modernist homes in the Northeast, including a house for himself and one, with and for his partner Marcel Breuer, both in Lincoln, Massachusetts. In 1944 he became a U.S. citizen.

Gropius used the security of his academic position to influence the development of postwar modern architecture throughout institutional and corporate America. Through his firm TAC (The Architects' Collaborative), and with other associate firms, he designed buildings such as the American embassy in Athens (1956–1961), an apartment block in the Hansaviertel housing exhibition in Berlin (1957), the Pan American Building in New York (1958–1963), and the Bauhaus Archive, originally designed for a site in Darmstadt but built in Berlin (1976–1979).

By the 1980s Gropius was criticized for the stark, sterile functionalism of his designs. But it cannot be denied that he had an incredible impact on the development of America's built environment after World War II. He received numerous awards, including the Gold Medal of the Royal Institute of British Architects (1956), the Gold Medal of the American Institute of Architects (1959), and the Gold Medal of the Royal Society of the Arts/London and the Goethe Prize/Frankfurt (both 1961). He died in Boston, Massachusetts.

• Gropius's archives are, principally, in the Busch-Reisinger Museum of Harvard University and, secondarily, in the Bauhaus Archive in Berlin. Other related drawings are in the Deutsches Architekturmuseum in Frankfurt. The following are useful sources: *MacMillan Encyclopedia of Architects*, ed. Adolf K. Placzek, vol. 2 (1982), pp. 251–63, Winfried Nerdinger, *Walter Gropius* (1986), and Nathan Silver, "Walter Gropius," *Contemporary Architects*, ed. Muriel Emanuel (3d ed., 1993), pp. 386–90. For the less well-known career of Meyer in relation to Gropius see Annemarie Jaeggi, *Adolf Meyer. Der zweite Mann. Ein Architekt im Schatten von Walter Gropius* (1994).

JOHN ZUKOWSKY

GROPPER, William (3 Dec. 1897–7 Jan. 1977), painter and caricaturist, was born in New York City, the son of Harry Gropper and Jenny Nidel, both workers in garment-trade sweatshops in New York's Lower East Side. When he completed grammar school, he won a scholarship to the National Academy of Design but stayed only a few months. Their requirement for drawing from casts disappointed Gropper, already experienced in drawing from life in classes at the Ferrer School with Robert Henri and George Bellows. This experimental school, established by a group of intellectual anarchists, was fortuitously located on 107th Street, where Gropper's family lived in 1911. He attended the New York School of Fine and Applied Arts part-time from 1915 to 1917 and on the strength of several prizewinning drawings was offered a position as a staff artist at the *New York Tribune*.

Gropper designed posters for the government in 1917 but also began to contribute drawings to the journals of the radical Left. He was sympathetic to the idea that art should advance social and political aims and produced caricatures for the *Rebel Worker*, published by the Industrial Workers of the World (IWW or Wobblies), and for *Revolutionary Age* and *Voice of Labor*, communist magazines. These activities cost him his position at the *Tribune* in 1919, when it began a campaign for the suppression of "unpatriotic papers."

In 1920 Gropper, already an imaginative, satirical draftsman for the daily and periodical press in New York, moved to Greenwich Village. He contributed to *Dial, Village Quill, Bookman, New Pearson's, Playboy, National Financial News, New York Evening Post, Literary Review, New York World, Liberator*, and others. He began to illustrate books with line drawings, among them a book of poems, *Chinese White* (1923), by Gladys Oaks, his wife from 1920 to 1924. He and Oaks had no children.

When Gropper married Sophie Frankle in 1924, her income as a hospital microbiologist permitted Gropper more freedom to draw and paint. She also organized the artist's archives, which were later maintained by the elder of the couple's two sons. Although Gropper received little or no remuneration from the radical papers, his mainstream drawings and yearly painting exhibitions at ACA Gallery in New York City, beginning in 1936, soon ensured a moderate income.

Gropper was always willing to draw for justified causes and for the unfortunate and disenfranchised of all races, countries, and creeds. Although he continually stated that he was neither a communist nor anti-American, he was accused of both. "I am accused of being a Red," he once said. "I don't belong to any political party. If a Jew is attacked, I am a Jew. If a Negro is attacked, then I am a Negro. Any minority—that's me." He left the *Tribune* in order to preserve his freedom of expression, and like Daumier, Goya, and Grosz, with whom he has been compared, he maintained an idealistic stance against injustice.

Early problems with authority set the pattern. Gropper's submission for the 1932 mural exhibition at the Museum of Modern Art, a portrayal of workers in combat against the upper classes, was not included in the traveling portion of the show. His 1943 attempt to become an army artist-correspondent was thwarted by Federal Bureau of Investigation reports of his support for Spanish civil war relief and other "tainted" memberships. He had been one of the founders of and early contributors to the *New Masses*, a contributing editor of the Yiddish-language communist daily *Morgen Freiheit* (1924–1948), and an unwitting contributor to the communist *Daily Worker*—associations cited as further evidence against his patriotism. During the 1940s and 1950s, when members of Congress sought out "subversives," Gropper appeared on every blacklist. Most damaging of all was his appearance on 6 May 1953 before Joseph McCarthy's Senate Sub-Committee on Government Operations, after which he was called a "Fifth-Amendment communist." His reputation destroyed, for many years he found few exhibiting opportunities. In the following three years he completed a portfolio, *Capriccios*, his personal indictment of "American inquisitions."

Gropper is relatively unknown today because formalist art criticism preferred apolitical, abstract art over social realism, and historical studies ignored popular media and politically engaged artists. In the 1930s and 1940s, however, he was a successful, well-respected person and artist. His August 1935 caricature for *Vanity Fair* of Japanese emperor Hirohito pulling a cart loaded with a diploma labeled "Nobel Peace Prize" caused an international furor. The public was pleased with this evidence of American daring. He was awarded a Guggenheim fellowship in 1937 to make studies of the dust bowl and the Boulder (now Hoover) and Grand Coulee dams. In 1939 his mural *The Construction of a Dam* was installed in the Department of the Interior, Washington, D.C. In 1938 he completed a mural for the Freeport, Long Island, post office and one on the automobile industry for the Northwestern Postal Station, Detroit (now in the student union building, Wayne State University). His submissions to juried shows received prizes and recognition.

Gropper was spoken of as a sensitive, intelligent, gentle, witty man and was honored at dinners in 1940 and 1944. He showed regularly at the ACA Gallery and exhibited widely in other one-person and group shows. He was included in several government-sponsored exhibitions, but *Advancing American Art* (1946) was the last. That exhibition was returned to the United States before its tour began when Congress withdrew funding because some of the works were by artists, like Gropper, with unacceptable political pasts.

In his later years Gropper won a 1965 commission for stained-glass windows at Temple Har Zion, River Forest, Illinois, and a 1967 fellowship to the Tamarind Lithography Workshop, Los Angeles. He continued to paint and to create etchings and lithographs until shortly before his death in Great Neck, New York. His legacy, a slashing, allusive, readable style, portrayed both society's defects and its ideals. He exemplifies a generation of artists who assumed that art has a direct role in creating a better world. He introduced censorship and freedom of expression as subjects into the language of fine art, subjects that once again seem new in the late twentieth century.

• Many of Gropper's papers are in the George Arents Research Library for Special Collections, Syracuse University, Syracuse, N.Y. In 1984 his family gave another group of papers to the Archives of American Art, Washington, D.C. His 1965 interview with Bruce Hooton is also at the AAA. Other papers, prints, and paintings are maintained by Gene Gropper, South San Gabriel, Calif. The catalog by August L. Freundlich, *William Gropper: Retrospective* (1968), includes a number of quotations from interviews with the artist, but Louis Lozowick, *William Gropper* (1983), is more accurate and inclusive. Dissertations include Norma S. Steinberg, "William Gropper: Art and Censorship from the 1930s through the Cold War Era" (Ph.D. diss., Boston Univ., 1994); Nancy Steele Hamme, "Images of Seamstresses in the Art of William Gropper" (Ph.D. diss., State Univ. of New York, Binghamton, 1989); and Joseph Anthony Gahn, "The America of William Gropper, Radical Cartoonist" (Ph.D. diss., Syracuse Univ., 1966). Steinberg investigates the political structures of the time and proposes an alteration of subjects, style, and media in Gropper's prints and drawings as the result of censorship. Hamme examines the issues of gender and stereotyping as portrayed in Gropper's images of seamstresses and tailors. Gahn outlines Gropper's involvement with artists' groups and Congress until the end of World War II and includes many quotations from interviews with the artist. All include substantial bibliographies.

NORMA S. STEINBERG

GROPPI, James Edward (16 Nov. 1930–4 Nov. 1985), Catholic priest and civil rights activist, was born in Milwaukee, Wisconsin, the son of Giocondo Groppi, a grocer, and Giorgina (maiden name unknown). James Groppi was the eleventh of twelve children. His father was a first-generation Italian immigrant who spoke broken English, a fact that Groppi said earned him "humorous contempt." This early introduction to prejudice had a lasting influence on Groppi, particularly since his father insisted that the Groppi children refrain from retaliating in kind when they were subject to ethnic slurs. A second influence on his attitudes about prejudice came indirectly from the church; the Irish Catholic parish the Groppis were expected to attend was less than friendly to Italian parishioners, many of whom responded by having their children baptised in a parish church in Milwaukee's Italian third ward.

Groppi attended Catholic schools and had his first personal encounter with a black man on the basketball court. Having thrown a body block that flipped his opponent and knocked him to the floor, Groppi held out his hand to help the young man up and was kicked in the stomach for his trouble. The two met and shared a sportsmanlike handshake when the game was over, and Groppi said in an essay for an English class that the incident had taught him something firsthand about brotherhood and racial justice.

A year after he graduated from high school Groppi entered Mount Calvary Seminary in Fond du Lac, Wisconsin. After his ordination in June 1959 he served as a parish priest for several years. In the early 1960s Father Groppi was assigned to a parish in a primarily black neighborhood in Milwaukee, the same time that he was becoming more actively involved in civil rights activities. He spent time in Mississippi assisting with voter registration programs and was working in Selma in the summer of 1965. During that trip he went to Montgomery, where he met the Reverend Martin Luther King, Jr., and participated in a march from the black ghetto to the capitol building as well as a march to the Dallas county courthouse. His work in Alabama catalyzed his civil rights concerns, prompting him to more active advocacy in his hometown of Milwaukee, where there was little activity. According to Frank A. Aukofer in *City with a Chance*, Groppi's method was to "create resistance and then agitate against it for all he was worth" (p. 95).

The first of his Milwaukee ventures involved serving as adviser to the Milwaukee NAACP Youth Council, and in 1966 the group campaigned to force the integration of the local chapter of the Fraternal Order of Eagles. The campaign was not a success, but it did represent the first time that Groppi received national attention. For the next ten years his name was prominent among civil rights activists and in national news coverage about civil rights activities. The most protracted battle he fought with the city of Milwaukee was on the issue of open housing. Beginning on 28 August 1967 Groppi and the Youth Council members held 200 consecutive marches demanding the passage of a Milwaukee open housing ordinance. Groppi was arrested eleven times during the marches. An ordinance was passed on 30 April 1968.

Groppi continued his civil rights activities, agitating for welfare reform and working for Native American rights. When armed Native American activists took over a vacant Alexian Brothers novitiate in January 1975, Groppi joined actor Marlon Brando as a peacemaker between the authorities and the activists. He also actively protested the Vietnam War. However, national interest in his public life virtually ended when he decided to marry Margaret Rozga in April 1976; they had three children. His action was against Catholic church precepts and led to his excommunication from the church.

After his excommunication, he attended Antioch Law School in Washington, D.C., where he drove a taxicab. Later, he studied for the Episcopal priesthood at Virginia Theological Seminary and was offered a job at an Episcopal church in Detroit. He refused the offer because he didn't want to leave Milwaukee. Eventually, he became a bus driver for the Milwaukee County Transit System and became president of its union in 1983.

Groppi's protest targets included the Catholic church, which he criticized for what he called its second-class treatment of women and of married clergy. He never submitted to the excommunication, and he freely admitted that he often said Mass with other married clergy in Milwaukee. Despite his differences with the church, after his death a Mass was said for him at St. Leo's Catholic Church in Milwaukee.

Groppi died in his home in Milwaukee, following surgery for a brain tumor that had left him partially paralyzed. While he is little known today, his persistence in pursuit of his convictions prompted national attention at a time when civil rights activities were often the purview of celebrities. His particular genius lay in his ability to empathize with the people he worked with and to get them to work together for a common goal.

• Groppi's personal papers are in the Milwaukee Manuscript Collection, University of Wisconsin, Madison. Most of his public life is recorded in newspaper articles, notably in the *Chicago Tribune*, the *New York Times*, and the *Milwaukee Journal*. Substantial information about his civil rights activities in Milwaukee is in Frank A. Aukofer's *City with a Chance* (1968). An interview by Albert Shannon is in the *Marquette University Education Review* 1, no. 1 (1970): 8–9, 15–22. Analysis of his rhetorical style is included in a presentation by Vonne Younger and Jan J. Meussling at the Annual Meeting of the Speech Communication Association held in San Francisco, Calif. in Nov. 1989. Obituaries are in the *New York Times* and the *Chicago Tribune*, both 5 Nov. 1985.

M. RINI HUGHES

GROS, John Daniel (1737–25 May 1812), clergyman, college professor, and philosopher, was born in the Bavarian Palatinate at Webenheim, near the city of Zweibrücken, Germany, the son of Lorenz Gros and Anna Magdalena. Little is known of Gros's upbringing and early education. His name is sometimes spelled Gross. Gros entered the University of Marburg in 1758 and then matriculated at the University of Heidelberg in 1761, partaking in theological studies. Having intentions of entering the pastoral ministry of the German Reformed church, Gros journeyed to America, landing in Philadelphia in 1764. As the North American population continued to increase, a growing need for pastors existed. Gros's esteemed German education and some influential connections led the German Reformed Coetus of Pennsylvania to ordain him in 1765. The coetus enacted the ordination without first receiving ratification from the Dutch Church Synod in Holland, which was the mandated procedure at that time. This was a precedent-setting act, as the German Reformed denomination in America began to break free from the church authorities in Europe.

Gros pastored German Reformed congregations in cities throughout Pennsylvania, including Allentown, Egypt, Jordan, Schlosser's, Saucon, and Springfield, from 1765 to 1772. While in Pennsylvania, Gros rose in prominence in the Reformed coetus, being elected clerk in 1768 and president the following year. Gros complained to the coetus in 1772 of being financially neglected and generally unsupported by his congregations, which led him to accept a call to pastor a church in Kingston, New York, from 1772 to 1783. In this frontier church, Gros encountered various dangers, particularly during the American Revolution. During the revolution he served as chaplain of regiments of the New York militia and was involved in the battles of Oriskany, Sharon, and Jamestown in 1781 and 1782. After the peace talks began, Gros moved to a congregation in the city of New York, which he pastored from 1783 to 1795. Gros became fairly wealthy through the purchase of soldiers' land warrants.

Gros was appointed professor of German and geography at the newly established Columbia College (earlier King's College) in 1784. In 1787 Gros became the professor of moral philosophy at Columbia. Gros was well known for both his geography and moral philosophy courses. His geography course was summarized as a "description of the globe in respect of all general matters . . . history with an ancient and geographical basis but with a modern political outlook" (Adams, p. 60). The course touched on world history, philosophy, and cultural developments from a broader orientation than the common British perspective. Herbert B. Adams remarked, "It was a highly creditable course, the best that the writer has found in the annals of any American College, at that early period. . . . [Gros] evidently represents a European current in American College instruction" (p. 60).

The text of Gros's moral philosophy course was published in 1795 as *Natural Principles of Rectitude for the Conduct of Man in All States and Situations of Life*. The course dealt with the nature of human persons in relation to God, whence were derived moral norms for all human conduct. The following excerpt from this text serves as an example of Gros's perspective on morality:

To endeavor to know and do all that is conducive to the well-being of soul and body, ought to be the most principal concern of every man who feels a desire to be happy. To assist our fellow men in this great work is the province of both the physician and the moralist. . . . It is therefore our first and indispensable obligation to endeavor to know what God in his infinite understanding has ordered for our happiness, and what his divine will commands us to do or to omit, that thereby we may be enabled to act in conformity to his laws and obtain their end, our own happiness. (pp. 2, 66)

Gros served as a regent of the University of the State of New York from 1784 to 1787 and as a trustee of Columbia College from 1787 to 1792. He received an honorary degree of doctor of divinity in 1789 from Columbia and was a well-admired teacher there. He resigned from Columbia in 1795 and went on to pastor a German Reformed church in Canajoharie, New York, from 1796 to 1800. Gros spent the last ten years of his life on a farm he purchased near Fort Plain, New York. He died in the neighboring town of Canajoharie.

As a philosopher Gros made steps to counter the Enlightenment movement, which sought to undermine the rationality of religious belief. Gros held that the Christian faith was rationally defensible and that the existence of God was evident to all persons. As a teacher he provided the newly freed American nation with an understanding of world history from a European perspective rather than from a solely British one, as well as a view of morality that would firmly ground the social and civic units of the developing society. Gros was also a significant influence in the German Reformed church as it matured in its identity apart from Dutch church authorities. While he did not rise to great prominence, Gros is one of many early Americans who played a small part in laying the theoretical and moral foundations of the United States.

• Gros's time at Columbia is chronicled in *A History of Columbia University: 1754–1904* (1904). For a description of Gros's courses, see Herbert B. Adams, *The Study of History in American Colleges and Universities* (1887). For a history of the philosophy department at Columbia, see Nicholas M. Butler, *A History of the Faculty of Philosophy: Columbia University* (1957). The most complete assessment of Gros is James I. Good, *History of the Reformed Church in the United States, 1725–92* (1899). Other biographical information can be found in Edward T. Corwin, *A Manual of the Reformed Church in America* (1902). For brief personal comments on Gros's time at Columbia, see John W. Francis, *A Discourse in Commemoration of the Fifty-third Anniversary of the New-York Historical Society* (1857). A complete obituary is in the *New York Columbian*, 5 June 1812.

STEVEN L. PORTER

GROSS, Milt (4 Mar. 1895–28 Nov. 1953), cartoonist and author, was born in New York City, the son of Samuel Gross and Rose Spivak. He grew up in the Bronx and had one and a half years of secondary schooling in Kearney, New Jersey, before leaving formal education at the age of sixteen to take a job as an office boy in the art department of William Randolph Hearst's *New York American*. The bull pen denizens for whom young Gross did chores included Harry Hershfeld, Gus Mager, Walter Hoban, Tom McNamara, Cliff Sterrett, Winsor McCay, and Thomas Aloysius Dorgan, who signed his cartoons "Tad" and who called Gross "Davenport" because the youth idolized the work of editorial cartoonist Homer Davenport. Gross, who at an early age had demonstrated an artistic bent, was in his element, and he was often able to put his pen to good use: "I used to ghost for artists who were late with their assignments," he told Martin Sheridan (p. 87).

In 1913 Gross became a staff artist for the American Press Association, a news service. Two years later he was back with Hearst, this time at the *Evening Journal*, for which he created his first comic strip, *Henry Peck, a Happy Married Man*. Like most newspaper staff cartoonists at the time, Gross devised a variety of cartoon features for his paper, some of which lasted only a few installments before yielding their place to his next creation. For the sports section, for instance, he did a strip called *Phool Phan Phables* and, later, *Sportograms*. In 1917 he left Hearst to join the Barre-Bowers Animation Studio, which produced Mutt and Jeff animated cartoons. His tenure there was interrupted by service in the U.S. Expeditionary Force with the Seventh Division in France during World War I. After the war, Gross went back to animation, working at the Bray Studios, and in 1920 he married Anna Abramson; they had three children.

By 1922 he had returned to newspaper cartooning—at the *New York World*, where he produced his most celebrated creations. Following the usual pattern, he drew an assortment of features and also began writing and illustrating with comic drawings a column called *Gross Exaggerations*. Many of the column's installments concerned the dilemmas of daily life in an imaginary Lower East Side apartment building where Mrs. Feitlebaum exchanges gossip with her neighbors. Written in a picturesque Yiddish dialect, the conversations of the residents wander from sympathetic analysis of the husband next door ("sotch a hanpacked poison") to discussions about the scion of another family who got caught in the "undertone" at "Coney Highland" or the unfortunate couple who bought a cottage with "sudden exposure." In a fourth-floor apartment is a "nize baby" who must be enticed into eating dinner by parents' telling "ferry tails," which Gross reported in detail, complete with blundering grammar and hilarious malapropisms. A collection of pieces from the column was published in 1926 as *Nize Baby*, and its enthusiastic reception was followed by the publication of *Hiawatta witt No Odder Poems* (1926), Gross's Yiddish dialect version of the Longfellow classic—a "parody which went beyond parody," according to Stephan Becker, who called it "a poetic triumph" to which "the author's inspired drawings added the final lunatic note" (pp. 370–71).

Nize Baby's success encouraged Gross to produce a Sunday comic strip with the same title. Starting in September 1926, it had run its course by February 1929, and Gross replaced it with his comic strip masterpiece, *Count Screwloose of Tooloose*, a weekly morality play about the prevailing insanity of the world at large. Every Sunday, Count Screwloose escapes from the Nuttycrest asylum, observes humanity in action, and returns to Nuttycrest, which he now perceives as a safe—and sane—haven.

Although the formula was trite, Gross endowed its weekly repetition with the comic genius of his graphic imagination and made it "more than just a variation on a theme." The count is dapper but diminutive, less than half the size of the other characters, and in drawing his pint-sized protagonist Gross crossed his goggle-eyed orbs, giving him the wildly comedic aspect that virtually defines "comic strip character." The rest of the cast partakes of the same conventions, resulting in a strip of almost manic ambience, which Gross enhanced with fast-paced action and a liberal dose of slapstick. Topping the *Count Screwloose* Sunday page was another Gross invention, *Banana Oil*, which took its title from the imprecation invariably shouted in the last panel as comic indictment of some minor fraud or misapprehension being perpetrated elsewhere in the strip; it became a popular expression, the equivalent of "baloney." Both features ceased on 28 September 1930, on the eve of the *World*'s collapse.

Gross continued to write books in the same vein as his 1926 volumes, and in 1930 he produced a pictorial novel entirely without words, *He Done Her Wrong*. Calling it Gross's "graphic masterpiece," Becker describes it as "a silent film transferred to paper" (p. 372). Inspired, doubtless, by Gross's experiences in the film colony where he had worked briefly with Charlie Chaplin on *The Circus* (1928), the novel mocks the grand passions and stock situations of Hollywood adventure films and the stage melodramas of the 1890s with its numerous homicides and chases, not to mention its dastardly villain, brave hero, and pure heroine.

After the *World* merged with the *New York Telegram* in February 1931, Gross created *Dave's Delicatessen* for Hearst's King Features Syndicate. A daily and Sunday strip of comedic continuity about the family and business of a delicatessen owner, the strip often ended with an extraneous panel in which a small boy observes his father at some nefarious activity and, heedless of the incompetence displayed, proclaims with joyful pride: "That's my Pop!" The panel became a stand-alone feature in about 1935. Titled *Grossly Xaggerated*, it was inevitably referred to by quoting the kid's proclamation. "That's my Pop!" became a catchword, and the feature inspired a radio program of the same name in the 1940s.

At various intervals, Gross lived in Hollywood, where he resumed writing scenarios for movies. He also wrote magazine articles and more humorous books in Yiddish dialect; he was a frequent guest on radio programs and often served as master of ceremonies at formal occasions. He died of a heart attack while returning to his California home from a Hawaiian vacation.

Drawing in a style that exemplified cartooning, Gross was nonetheless an original, a talent without predecessor or successful imitator. Becker reports that he was a man "who combined a brilliant career with absolute honesty and generosity to all men. No ego, no tantrums, no feuds. Just Milt Gross" (p. 374). When the National Cartoonists Society established a fund for the relief of indigent cartoonists, it was named the Milt Gross Fund as a mark of the profession's enduring regard.

• Gross's books not mentioned above include *De Night in de Front from Chreesmas* (1927), *Dunt Esk* (1927), *Famous Fimmales witt Odder Events from Heestory* (1928), *What's This?* (1936), *Dear Dollink* (1944), and *Shoulda Ate the Eclair* (1946); his illustrations appear in Margaret Linden's *Pasha the Persian* (1936). Gross's life and career receive fullest treatment in Stephan Becker, *Comic Art in America* (1959). Other books in which Gross receives more than token treatment are William C. Murrell, *A History of American Graphic Humor, 1865–1938*, vol. 2 (1967); Martin Sheridan, *Comics and Their Creators* (1944); and Ron Goulart, ed., *The Encyclopedia of American Comics* (1990). Obituaries are in the *New York Times*, 1 Dec. 1953; *New York Herald Tribune*, 30 Nov. 1953; and *Editor & Publisher*, 5 Dec. 1953.

ROBERT C. HARVEY

GROSS, Paul Magnus (15 Sept. 1895–4 May 1986), physical chemist and university administrator, was born in New York City, the son of Magnus Gross, an educator and city official, and Ellen Sullivan. He received a bachelor of science degree from City College of New York in 1916 and earned a master's degree and a doctorate from Columbia University in 1917 and

1919. Gladys Cobb Petersen, a Hunter College drama student, became his wife in 1918; they had two children.

Gross accepted an assistant professorship in chemistry at Trinity College in Durham, North Carolina, in 1919. Five years later, with the bequest of James Duke, the college became the nucleus of Duke University. He remained at Duke until his retirement, serving as William Howell Pegram Professor of Chemistry (1920–1965), chemistry department chairman (1921–1948), dean of the Graduate School of Arts and Sciences (1947–1952), and vice president for academic affairs (1949–1960). Gladys Gross directed plays at Trinity; her group became the Duke Players.

Gross was both a respected physical chemist and a key figure in the transformation of the then small college into a national university. As a chemist he published articles from 1921 to 1958 in three major areas, solution chemistry, molecular structure determination, and tobacco chemistry. He also wrote *Elements of Physical Chemistry* (1929). The greatest influence on his research career was the Nobel laureate Peter Debye, with whom Gross spent a 1929 sabbatical at the University of Leipzig. Debye had created the modern theory of the behavior of ions in solution and also pioneered the determination of molecular structure by means of dipole moments. Gross developed both areas by providing critical tests of the Debye theory and investigating the dipole moments of organic molecules and establishing their structures. His investigation of tobacco chemistry stemmed from his residency in North Carolina, where tobacco was the major industry. From 1927, with funding by tobacco companies, he examined the chemical composition of domestic and imported Turkish tobaccos, demonstrated the feasibility of growing imported types in southern soils, and showed how to best blend tobaccos to a constant composition for use in the most popular brands of cigarettes. In 1939 he developed a cigarette paper made from flax and hemp to replace expensive French cigarette paper.

As Duke administrator Gross believed that the quality of an educational institution depended on the quality of its faculty. He brought productive scholars to Duke, first as creator of an enlarged, greatly strengthened chemistry department and then as dean and vice president in all areas of undergraduate, graduate, and professional education. By the 1950s Duke had become a prominent university. He then initiated a second phase of expansion, becoming chairman in 1958 of the Long Range Planning Committee to place Duke in service to the South through research and development programs to aid southern education, research, and industry. His Duke administrative career, however, ended in controversy. He was forced to resign the vice presidency in 1960 with the revelation that he had secretly made administrative changes he thought were necessary.

During World War II Gross had contributed to the Army Air Force's training of aerial gunners. Between 1942 and 1945 he led a group of Duke, Princeton, and Bakelite Corporation researchers in developing a projectile to be fired from machine guns in bombers at target planes that would not damage the planes but only indicate hits. The outcome was the frangible bullet, a plastic bullet that enabled trainees to fire guns in air-to-air practice against fighter planes. He received from President Harry S. Truman in 1948 the Medal of Merit, the nation's highest civilian award, for this achievement.

Gross had a remarkably active career as a public servant in the postwar era. He believed that a major problem in the South was the loss of talented young people who went elsewhere for advanced training and never returned. He argued vociferously about the need to support and strengthen the South's educational institutions and to improve its business climate. To this end he founded in 1946 the Oak Ridge Associated Universities, a cooperative program among southern universities and medical schools for fundamental research in peaceful uses of atomic energy; from 1949 to 1969 he was its president. He also founded the Council of Southern Universities in 1952 and was its first president. From 1955 to 1958 he served on the committee that planned the North Carolina industrial area now known as the Research Triangle Park and as a member of the board of directors persuaded government and industry to locate research laboratories there. He also assisted in advancing the careers of young southerners. From 1953 to 1956 he was chairman of the Southern Regional Scholarship Committee, which selected Marshall Scholars for study in Great Britain. In 1958 Queen Elizabeth II appointed him honorary commander of the Order of the British Empire for his services on behalf of Anglo-American understanding.

With the increasing magnitude of the scientific effort in postwar America, the federal government selected Gross for a series of important positions. In 1950 Congress established the National Science Foundation, and President Truman appointed him to its executive governing board, a position he held to 1962. In that year he became president of the American Association for the Advancement of Science (AAAS), the world's largest scientific organization. In 1961 he was chairman of the Surgeon General's Committee on Environmental Health Problems. The committee issued a report that warned of the dangers of contamination of food, land, water, and air by chemical and other pollutants, that appraised needs in environmental health, and that suggested how these needs might be met. The report became the basis for federal environmental health policy and programs.

After Gross retired in 1965, Duke honored him by commemorating in 1968 the new Gross Chemical Laboratory and by awarding him in 1975 an honorary doctor of science degree during its fiftieth anniversary celebrations. Gross settled into a tranquil home life in Durham. He had a beach house on the North Carolina coast, where he engaged in his favorite recreations of sailing and deep sea and surf fishing. He died in Durham.

Gross combined administrative skills of a high order with a deep faith in the university as an instrument for making a better world. His achievement was to help build Duke into a prestigious university and to strengthen higher education, science, and research in the South.

• The Duke University Archives has a large collection of Gross material. Only brief treatments of Gross have been published to date. The most extensive is by Philip Handler in *Science* 133 (Feb. 1961): 463–65, written on the occasion of the selection of Gross as president of AAAS for 1962. *Chemical and Engineering News* 30 (26 May 1952): 2154 has a succinct account of his contributions to chemistry. An obituary is in the *New York Times*, 10 May 1986.

ALBERT B. COSTA

GROSS, Samuel David (8 July 1805–6 May 1884), surgeon and medical educator, was born near Easton, Pennsylvania, the son of Philip Gross and Johanna Juliana Brown, farmers. Samuel, one of six children, was raised in the Pennsylvania Dutch country speaking the Americanized German dialect. Gross first learned English at twelve and retained an accent throughout his life. His father died when Samuel was nine; his mother, a devout Lutheran, exercised a strong moral influence on her son.

Gross began the study of medicine at seventeen with a preceptor, Joseph K. Swift, as was customary. Aware of his educational deficiencies, Gross stopped his medical apprenticeship to continue his general education, first in Wilkes-Barre and later at the Academy of Lawrenceville, New Jersey. He resumed his medical studies with Swift in 1824. In 1826 Gross was headed for study at the University of Pennsylvania but instead, on the strength of his reputation, enrolled as a private pupil with Dr. George McClellan (father of the Civil War general). Gross matriculated at Jefferson Medical College in Philadelphia, which McClellan had founded in 1825. "McClellan was the master genius of the establishment, a fluent and popular lecturer, but utterly without system" (*Autobiography*, vol. 1, p. 33). Gross received his medical degree in 1828, with a thesis on "The Nature and Treatment of Cataract." That same year Gross married Louisa Ann Weissell, whom he had known since his student days at Jefferson; they had six children.

In his early months in Philadelphia (and with few patients), Gross busied himself translating important foreign medical works. These included Antoine Laurent Jesse Bayle, *A Manual of General Anatomy* (1828); Jules Hatin, *A Manual of Practical Obstetrics . . .* (1828); Alphonse Tavernier, *Elements of Operative Surgery* (1829), the first treatise on operative surgery published in America; and Valentin Johann von Hildenbrand, *A Treatise on Contagious Typhus* (1829). Gross, however, convinced that America should develop its own medical literature, never made any other translations. In 1830 he published *A Treatise on the Anatomy, Physiology and Diseases and Injuries of the Bones and Joints*.

By late 1830, in the absence of an adequate practice in Philadelphia, Gross was compelled to return to Easton, where he enjoyed some professional success. In 1832 he was sent by the Easton Town Council to visit New York City to investigate Asiatic cholera, which had appeared for the first time on the American continent.

In 1833, through the intervention of Dr. John Eberle, a former professor at Jefferson, Gross was appointed demonstrator of anatomy in the Medical College at Cincinnati, and in 1835 he was appointed to the chair of pathological anatomy at the newly organized Medical Department of Cincinnati College. There he organized and delivered the first systematic course of lectures on morbid anatomy ever given in the United States. In Cincinnati Gross also gathered the materials for his *Elements of Pathological Anatomy* (1839). The Cincinnati College closed in 1839, and the next year Gross accepted the chair of surgery at the Louisville Medical Institute, afterward renamed the University of Louisville. Gross spent sixteen years at Louisville, from October 1840 to September 1856. These were productive years that, beyond Gross's professional success at the university and in private practice, saw the publication of his *Wounds of the Intestines* (1843), one of the first exhaustive pieces of animal research for clinical purposes done in the United States. Gross also achieved eminence as a urologist by publishing *Practical Treatise on the Diseases, Injuries, and Malformations of the Urinary Bladder, the Prostate Gland, and the Urethra* (1851). A second edition appeared in 1855; a third, edited by his son, in 1876. It described his procedure for operation of lateral lithotomy (incision into the bladder to remove a calculus) for which he became famous. At Louisville he also completed his *Practical Treatise on Foreign Bodies in the Air Passages* (1854), a pioneer work. Some difficulties (not unusual in nineteenth-century medical colleges) at the University of Louisville caused Gross to accept the chair in surgery at the University of the City of New York for the winter of 1850–1851, but he rejoined the Louisville faculty in 1851.

In May 1856 Gross was elected professor of surgery by the faculty of Jefferson Medical College, his alma mater, where he remained in that position for twenty-eight years. During his long tenure at Jefferson his surgical clinics achieved both national and international fame. A steady procession of books and articles appeared, chief among them his *A System of Surgery: Pathological, Diagnostic, Therapeutic and Operative* (2 vols., 1859), which went through six editions, the last issued in 1882. Its first edition comprised two large octavo volumes of 2,360 pages with 936 wood engravings; the sixth edition included 2,300 pages with 1,600 illustrations. "The book comprised two thousand copies," Gross explained, "and cost a large sum of money, enough, as Blanchard & Lea assured me, to have enabled them to open a respectable mercantile house on Market Street" (*Autobiography*, vol. 1, p. 139). Other Gross works include *A Manual of Military Surgery* (1861), written for Civil War surgeons. (The so-called pirated edition for the use of Confederate surgeons was issued in Richmond in 1862.) In 1861 Gross also edited the voluminous *Lives of the Eminent American Physicians and Surgeons of the Nineteenth Century*. In 1868 he published his *Memoir of Valentine Mott*, and for the American centennial he issued *A History of American Medical Literature from 1776 to the Present Time* (1876) and *A History of American Surgery from 1776 to 1876* (1876), both invaluable bibliographical compendia.

In 1881 Gross published *John Hunter and His Pupils*. The *Autobiography of Samuel D. Gross, M.D., with Sketches of His Contemporaries* (1887), edited by his sons, is an important record of the medical history of most of the nineteenth century. Gross himself observed, "The devotion which I have shown to my profession may, perhaps, exert a salutary influence upon the conduct of young physicians, and thus serve to inspire them with a desire to excel in good deeds."

Gross was the founder of the Philadelphia Academy of Surgery (1879) and the American Surgical Association (1880). He served as president of the Philadelphia County Medical Society in 1863 and of the American Medical Association in 1867. Early in 1875 the Philadelphia artist Thomas Eakins began work on a portrait of Gross intending, in an elaborate setting with carefully selected details, to give dimensional meaning to Gross's work as a surgeon. The life-size portrait of Gross operating in his Jefferson clinic to remove a piece of dead bone from the thigh of a patient has become a classic in American art. Originally known as "The Portrait of Professor Gross," it is now universally known as "The Gross Clinic." It was first exhibited at the Philadelphia Centennial Exhibition of 1876 and purchased by the Jefferson Alumni Association in 1878.

Gross died in Philadelphia. In an obituary eulogy his colleague Dr. I. M. Hays noted: "It is safe to say that no previous medical teacher or author on this continent exercised such a widespread and commanding influence as did Professor Gross."

• The Gross Room and Endowed Library in the College of Physicians of Philadelphia contains Gross's 4,000-volume medical library left to the Philadelphia Academy of Surgery and permanently housed at the college, with some of his memorabilia in the Gross Room maintained by an endowment from his children. Also in the Gross Room is the manuscript of John Roberts, "Reports of the Surgical Clinics of Professor S. D. Gross in the Jefferson Medical College, for the Term Commencing October 6, and Ending December 30, 1874." The main source for Gross's life is the *Autobiography of Samuel D. Gross, M.D.* (1887), edited posthumously by his sons, Samuel W. Gross and A. Haller Gross. See also I. M. Hays, "A Memoir of Samuel D. Gross, M.D.," *American Journal of the Medical Sciences* (July 1884): 1–16; C. W. G. Rohrer, "America's Foremost Surgeon: Professor Samuel D. Gross," *Bulletin of the Johns Hopkins Hospital* 23 (1912): 83–94; A. L. Kotz, "Samuel D. Gross, M.D.," *Pennsylvania German Society* 30 (1930): 5–20; Frederick B. Wagner, "Revisit of Samuel D. Gross, M.D.," *Surgery, Gynecology, and Obstetrics* 152 (1981): 663–74; John Janvier Black, *Forty Years in the Medical Profession, 1858–1898* (1900); and Francesco Cordasco, *Medical Education in the United States* (1980). For "The Gross Clinic," see Elizabeth Johns, "The Gross Clinic, or Portrait of Professor Gross," in *Thomas Eakins: The Heroism of Modern Life* (1983), pp. 46–81.

FRANCESCO CORDASCO

GROSSINGER, Jennie (16 June 1892–20 Nov. 1972), businesswoman and philanthropist, was born in Baligrod, a village in Galicia, Austria, the daughter of Asher Selig Grossinger, an estate overseer, and Malke Grumet. Selig Grossinger sought a better life for his family in the United States. He traveled to New York City in 1897 and took a job as a coat presser. Jennie, her mother, and sister Lottie followed him to the Lower East Side three years later. Jennie had some Jewish elementary school education and four years of public school education at P.S. 174. She quit formal schooling to work as a buttonhole maker but continued to take some night school classes following her eleven-hour-day job.

Grossinger began to date her cousin Harry Grossinger from Chicago. He worked as a successful production man in the garment industry. The couple married in 1912 and eventually had three children, only two of whom survived infancy. They moved to an apartment next door to her parents, and she worked as a waitress in the new dairy restaurant business her father started. Her father became ill and could not keep up the eighteen-hour days necessary to meet expenses for his restaurant. Harry helped to relocate the entire family to a small farm in Ferndale, New York, in the Catskill Mountains.

In 1914 Grossinger's Kosher Farm was founded. The run-down seven-room house with an old barn, a chicken coop, and 100 acres of rocky land was a formidable agricultural challenge. According to different sources, it was either Grossinger's idea or her father's to take in boarders to help make ends meet. The boarding house, Grossinger's, appealed to fellow Jewish immigrants living in New York City who had moved into the middle class and wanted to vacation in the country. Word of good air and sun attracted them to Grossinger's. Prospective boarders also found the idea of Jewish resorts especially appealing since discrimination against "Hebrews" denied Jews entry into other establishments in the Catskills and Adirondacks. From 1900 to 1920 a ten-mile strip of farmhouses, converted into Jewish summer boarding houses created the "borscht belt." Grossinger's, or "G's" as it was often called, was one of these early Jewish resorts, and one of the largest ones.

Grossinger's extended family worked together as an economic network, pooling their collective resources. While her husband excelled at the business end of the venture, including marketing in New York City to attract guests, her mother, a renowned cook, presided over the kosher kitchen. Grossinger assumed whatever roles were needed from chambermaid to bookkeeper to hostess. Grossinger's charm was legendary as she conveyed a family atmosphere at the resort—a home away from home. She greeted guests by name and with genuine warmth. She was "the heart and soul" of Grossinger's.

The first year, 1914, Grossinger's hosted nine boarders a week at $9 each. The spring of 1915 six rooms were added to the house, making it suitable for twenty guests. That summer they also hired a chambermaid to help with the work. Grossinger took advantage of the popularity of the automobile and the thriving economy of the post–World War I era to expand Grossinger's. In 1919 she initiated the purchase of a neighboring hotel, a lake, and sixty-three wooded acres. In the 1920s she also introduced attractions such as tennis courts, a bridle path, a children's camp, a golf course, and resident professional entertainers. Many famous entertainers performed at Grossinger's, including Robert Merrill, Red Buttons, and Eddie Fisher, who started his career there. Over the years scores of famous people stayed there, including Jackie Robinson, Eleanor Roosevelt, Chaim Weizmann, and Governor Nelson Rockefeller.

Grossinger, aware of innovative business techniques, hired Milton Blackstone around 1927 to promote the resort. Blackstone, who had initially come to convalesce at Grossinger's, ended up advertising the hotel with slogans such as "Grossinger's has everything." Grossinger's published a house newspaper, the *Tattler*, to help with matchmaking among the guests. Blackstone created the public relations idea of giving any coupled who met at Grossinger's a free honeymoon at the resort. During the depression Grossinger's suffered along with the rest of the country. Despite hard times, Grossinger and her husband continued to improve the resort, and in 1934 they added a training facility for boxers and other athletes.

During World War II her mother worried about operating Grossinger's while American servicemen were at war. Grossinger went to Milton Blackstone to set up a canteen-by-mail program to send packages to U.S. servicemen. They also asked Eddie Cantor to broadcast a special radio program from Grossinger's. The price of admission to this program was a war bond. Grossinger's received a citation by the secretary of the treasury, Henry L. Morgenthau, Jr., for being the first hotel in the country to start a war bond drive. During the war, Grossinger's sold more than $10 million worth of war bonds and sent thousands of packages to American servicemen. After the war, despite the misgivings of Grossinger's mother, the resort broadened its appeal beyond Orthodox Jews. Thus, in 1948 Grossinger's offered entertainment on the Jewish sabbath.

Until the 1960s Grossinger's was a phenomenally successful hotel and resort. Grossinger's grew from a small farmhouse to a 1,200-acre estate, hosting as many as 150,000 guests a year, with a dining area seating 1,700 guests, two golf courses, a swimming pool, and its own post office. Even competitors liked Grossinger's since they were able to fill their resorts with the overflow from "G's." A general collapse of the Catskill economy occurred in the 1960s following a loss of clientele due to acculturation, rejection of the kind and

quantity of food, and the popularity of jet travel to alternative vacation spots.

Grossinger suffered from ill health throughout her long career. She endured chronic high blood pressure, severe headaches, back ailments, and bouts with depression. After her husband died in 1964, she gave responsibility for running her resort to her children, who had long been involved in its management. She died in her resort home in the Catskills.

Grossinger will be remembered as a famous hotelkeeper who was also a generous philanthropist, for which she received numerous awards. In particular she was a principal benefactor of medical centers in Tel Aviv, Israel, and Liberty, New York. She and Grossinger's touched the lives of many, Jews and non-Jews alike, and epitomized the culture of the Catskills for several decades of the twentieth century. Kanfer called her "the lodestar of the Catskills" (p. 7). A few years before her death Grossinger said, "You know, when I die, wherever I go, I hope there's a hotel there, and I hope they'll let me run it. I know I'll find a lot of my former guests and I'll remember what they liked to eat. And my mother will be there to do the cooking . . . and Papa . . . and Harry" (Kanfer, p. 263).

• Grossinger published recipes from her resort in *The Art of Jewish Cooking* (1958). Books about Grossinger include Joel Pomerantz's biography, *Jennie and the Story of Grossinger's* (1970); Harold Jaediker Taub, *Waldorf-in-the-Catskills: The Grossinger Legend* (1952); and the quite critical book about Grossinger by Tania Grossinger, *Growing Up at Grossinger's* (1975). Some information about her is found in Irene Neu, "The Jewish Businesswoman in America," *American Jewish Historical Quarterly* (Sept. 1976): 137–57. Articles about Grossinger include Morris Freedman, "The Green Pastures of Grossinger's," *Commentary* 18 (July 1954): 56–63 and 18 (Aug. 1954): 147–54; David Boroff, "The Saga of the 'G'," *Coronet*, July 1959, pp. 163–69; and Quentin Reynolds, "Jennie," *Look*, 13 July 1965, pp. 86–88. To place Grossinger in context, see Gerald Sorin, *The Jewish People in America: A Time for Building, the Third Migration, 1880–1920* (1992). Stefan Kanfer, *A Summer World: The Attempt to Build a Jewish Eden in the Catskills* (1989), discusses Grossinger and others in the borscht belt culture. A lengthy obituary is in the *New York Times*, 21 Nov. 1972.

SARA ALPERN

GROSSMAN, Albert Bernard (21 May 1926–25 Jan. 1986), musical promoter and manager, was born in Chicago, Illinois, the son of tailors. He graduated from Lake View High School in 1944 and briefly attended Chicago's Central YMCA College but walked out with others protesting quotas for blacks and Jews. He then studied briefly at DePaul University before entering the new Roosevelt College in 1946, from which he graduated in 1947 with a B.S. in commerce. He worked for the Chicago Housing Authority for a few years, then opened the Gate of Horn with Les Brown, a writer for *Variety*, in July 1956. It was the first folk music nightclub in Chicago and one of the first in the country. They booked Big Bill Broonzy, Bob Gibson, Odetta, Theo Bikel, Jo Mapes, and other folk performers, as well as comedians such as Shelly

Berman. In 1958 Brown sold his share in the club to Alan Ribback, who took over completely from Grossman by 1960. In 1962 Grossman married Betty Spencer but the marriage was shortlived and they divorced. In 1964 Grossman married Sally Buehler. He had no children from either marriage.

While still involved with the Gate of Horn, Grossman began to manage Bob Gibson and then Odetta, establishing Albert B. Grossman Concerts. Jazz impresario George Wein brought him into assisting with the first Newport Folk Festival in 1959. The next year he moved to New York City and joined Wein's Production and Management Associates. They produced the second Newport Folk Festival in 1960, with Grossman again selecting the musicians. As the folk music revival began to heat up in New York and throughout the country, he became manager for folk singer Peter Yarrow. By 1961, at Grossman's urging, Mary Travers and Noel Paul Stookey joined Yarrow in a potent trio, Peter, Paul & Mary, soon to become the preeminent folk group in the United States, with numerous hit records. His major artistic achievement, also beginning in 1961, was managing Bob Dylan, at first informally, then publicly in 1962. Peter, Paul & Mary, in turn, made hits of many of Dylan's songs, particularly "Blowin' in the Wind." By mid-decade, Grossman included Ian and Sylvia, Gordon Lightfoot, Richie Havens, John Lee Hooker, the Jim Kweskin Jug Band, and Hedy West among the artists he managed.

Not content with promoting only folk music, by decade's end Grossman had branched into rock 'n' roll, representing Janis Joplin, the Paul Butterfield Blues Band, Electric Flag, and the Band. His tussle with folklorist Alan Lomax at the 1965 Newport Folk Festival marked both a personality clash and the developing split between the seemingly traditional folk old guard and those who accepted rock 'n' roll. Grossman welcomed electric guitars and younger rock and blues performers, such as the Paul Butterfield Blues Band, and enthusiastically supported Dylan's musical transition toward rock 'n' roll. The Monterey Pop Festival in 1967 offered Grossman the chance to showcase Electric Flag as well as sign Joplin and arrange a Columbia Records contract for her. The Woodstock music festival in 1969 featured many of his artists.

Early on Grossman became aware of the economic potential of music publishing and formed publishing companies, first with Peter, Paul & Mary, and soon after with Dylan. Dylan separated from Grossman in 1969, however, and Peter, Paul & Mary broke up the next year. Grossman had been most closely identified with Dylan until their split, and, thereafter, their long-smoldering legal hassles proved nettlesome. The loss of Dylan as well as Peter, Paul & Mary, along with Joplin's death in 1970, led Grossman to withdraw from the active management of his artists. He had begun buying property in Bearsville near Woodstock, New York, in 1963, which soon became his home. He formed Bearsville Records there in 1971, to which he signed Todd Rundgren, Foghat, and Jesse Winchester, and built Bearsville Sound Studios, a state of the art recording facility. He also opened two restaurants at the Bearsville complex. He managed the record label, recording studio, a music publishing company, and extensive property until his unexpected death of a heart attack while flying to France in 1986.

Highly controversial, Grossman is credited with helping to revolutionize the music industry through his management prescience and skill, reputedly infallible taste, and combative style. His manner and approach drew praise but also engendered fear and dislike. Although not known for his involvement in contemporary political affairs, he encouraged Dylan as well as Peter, Paul & Mary to perform topical music, and he worked closely with filmmaker Howard Alk, who made *American Revolution II* and *The Murder of Fred Hampton*. Grossman can be seen in action in D. A. Pennebaker's film *Don't Look Back*, about Dylan's British tour in 1965. Yarrow has characterized Grossman as "brilliant, brutally honest, protective of his artists; he could be tough and combative as well as warm and loving." In its brief obituary, *Time* noted he was a "low-profile, high-intensity impressario of the 1960s" (10 Feb. 1986, p. 86). Steve Chapple and Reebee Garafolo, in *Rock 'n' Roll Is Here to Pay* (1972), believe Grossman was "the most important new style manager." Rock entrepreneur Bill Graham had met Grossman at the Monterey International Pop Festival in 1967, and with Grossman as a minor partner opened the Fillmore East in New York early the next year. Graham remembered him as a "tough cookie," but there "lurked a serene, sincere interior." One of the major players of the popular music industry in the 1960s and 1970s, Grossman left a personal legacy of admiration mixed with fractured relationships. He will be most remembered for his pathbreaking managerial style and representation of Bob Dylan, Peter, Paul & Mary, Janis Joplin, and the Band.

• A helpful source of information about Grossman is Rory O'Connor, "Albert Grossman's Ghost," *Musician*, June 1987, pp. 26–31. Scattered discussions of Grossman appear in Bob Spitz, *Dylan: A Biography* (1989), Anthony Scaduto, *Bob Dylan: An Intimate Biography* (1971), Robert Shelton, *No Direction Home: The Life and Music of Bob Dylan* (1986), Clinton Heylin, *Bob Dylan: Behind the Shades* (1991), Laura Joplin, *Love, Janis* (1992), Myra Friedman, *Buried Alive: The Biography of Janis Joplin* (1973), Marc Eliot, *Rockonomics: The Money behind The Music* (1989), and Fred Goodman, *The Mansion on the Hill: Dylan, Young, Geffen, Springsteen, and the Head-on Collision of Rock and Commerce* (1997). The obituaries are useful, but often misleading; see the *Woodstock Times*, 30 Jan. 1986, *Billboard*, 8 Feb. 1986, and the *New York Times*, 28 Jan. 1986.

RONALD D. COHEN

GROSSMAN, Mary Belle (10 June 1879–27 Jan. 1977), suffragist, attorney, and judge, was born in Cleveland, Ohio, the daughter of Louis Grossman, the proprietor of a meat and hardware business, and Fannie Engle. Grossman attended Cleveland public schools and graduated from the old Central High School and from the Euclid Avenue Business College. She worked in the law office of a cousin, Louis J. Grossman, from 1896 to 1912. She decided that a career as a lawyer was preferable to that of a stenographer and bookkeeper and enrolled in 1909 in the evening program of Cleveland Law School (now a part of Cleveland State University), the first law school in Ohio to accept women. She was awarded her LL.B. in 1912 and passed the Ohio bar examination that same year. After practicing law in her cousin's office for two years, she established her own law office and engaged in the solo practice of law through 1923. She never married.

As a candidate for judicial office in 1923, Grossman pointed with pride to her extensive experience in the law. She became in 1918 one of the first two women admitted to membership in the American Bar Association, and for a number of years she was the only female attorney admitted to practice in federal court in Cleveland. She described her own legal practice as two-thirds office work and one-third courtroom work. She defended individuals against criminal charges as serious as first-degree murder and had an extensive amount of work in the Cleveland Municipal Court.

Grossman was also active in civic affairs. She was chair of the League of Women's Suffrage and a charter member of the League of Women Voters and the Women's City Club. She was a member of the National Council of Jewish Women. She helped to incorporate the Women's Legal Service Bureau and represented their clients without compensation—an early example of what is now called pro bono work. As a judge, she worked to improve conditions at the Ohio Reformatory for Women.

Grossman's decision to seek election to municipal court was influenced by her own experience practicing law, by the passage of the Nineteenth Amendment granting women the vote, and by the ongoing study that resulted in the 1922 publication of *Criminal Justice in Cleveland*, directed and edited by Roscoe Pound and Felix Frankfurter. Commissioned by the Cleveland Foundation in 1920 as a result of a scandal involving the chief of police, that study called for the improvement of the judiciary.

The election of Florence Allen to the Ohio bench in 1920 made an impact on many women, including Grossman. Allen had wasted no time in testing the political waters; she ran for office the same year that the woman suffrage amendment became effective. Unlike her close friend Judge Allen, Grossman harbored no ambition for higher judicial office; she preferred the municipal court because it was closer to the people. She considered the court a social institution. She ran and lost in 1921 but was elected in 1923, winning the fifth-highest vote total in a 21-candidate race. She continued to win reelection, serving six consecutive six-year terms on the Cleveland Municipal Court until retiring in 1959. Her election campaigns were modern and insightful and sought broad-based community support, including that of many immigrant groups. Coverage of her 1941 effort, for instance, included stories in German-, Yiddish-, Italian-, and Polish-language newspapers, among others. Grossman earned the respect of both the general and legal communities, but the road she traveled was not always easy. She was not initially endorsed by the Cleveland Bar Association. However, two of its former presidents endorsed her and stated that the failure of the organized bar to endorse her was due to male bias.

In 1925 Grossman was the first woman to serve as a judge of an Ohio traffic court, a division of the Cleveland Municipal Court. She organized the morals court, another division, in 1926 and served there also. She emphasized the need to make health-care professionals a part of the criminal justice system. She was a firm judge with a reputation for being a tough sentencer. Grossman believed that drunk driving was the greatest menace to highway safety. When Cleveland traffic officers stopped drivers for speeding, they often quipped to male drivers, "Well, I guess you want to go before Judge Mary?" A Cleveland safety director stated that having her on the bench in morals court was equal to having added a hundred men to the police force.

Grossman's intellectual and moral qualities were joined to political skills. Before her 1929 election, she suggested that these were too many laws and that the legislature ought to meet next in a repealing session to repeal old laws rather than pass new ones. She also supported capital punishment and even, in extreme cases of cruelty, the public whipping of men who beat their wives or children.

Grossman had a reputation for being a fair, firm, courageous, and honest judge who thoroughly enjoyed serving the public by holding judicial office. She was an exemplar to young women considering careers in the law. She was honored in 1967 by the Women's City Club with the Margaret A. Ireland Award. Her legacy was improvement in society through fidelity to the law. She died in Cleveland.

• Grossman's papers, election campaign materials, and newspaper clippings are held by the Western Reserve Historical Society. Photographs and newspaper clippings are at the Cleveland State University Archives. She is portrayed in D. D. Van Tassel and J. J. Grabowski, eds., *The Encyclopedia of Cleveland History* (1987); Van Tassel and Grabowski, eds., *The Dictionary of Cleveland Biography* (1996); and Arthur Landever, "Hard-Boiled Mary," *Law Notes* (Cleveland-Marshall College of Law), Spring 1996. Obituaries are in the *Cleveland Press* and the *Cleveland Plain Dealer*, both 28 Jan. 1977.

PAUL BRICKNER

GROSVENOR, Charles Henry (20 Sept. 1833–30 Oct. 1971), congressman, was born in Pomfret, Windham County, Connecticut, the son of Peter Grosvenor, a farmer and veteran of the War of 1812, and Ann Chase. The family moved to Athens County, Ohio, in 1838. Grosvenor's formal education consisted of thirty weeks in a log schoolhouse; the rest of his education came from experience and self-instruction. He taught school, tended a store, and worked on a farm to earn a livelihood as a youth. After reading law under the supervision of Lot L. Smith, and Athens attorney, Grosvenor was admitted to the bar in 1857 and formed a partnership with S. S. Knowles. The next year Grosvenor married Samantha Stewart, who died in 1866, leaving one daughter. In 1867 he married Louise Currier, with whom he had two daughters.

During the Civil War, Grosvenor enlisted in the Eighteenth Ohio Volunteer Infantry as a private but quickly rose in rank and was commissioned a major in 1861. Promoted to lieutenant colonel in 1863, he was brevetted a brigadier general in 1865 for gallant services. He commanded a brigade at the battle of Nashville and was in command of a post at Chattanooga, Tennessee. Upon the conclusion of the conflict in 1865, Grosvenor resumed his law practice in Athens in a partnership with J. M. Dana that lasted fourteen years. He also held various township and village offices during this period.

Grosvenor entered state and national politics as a Republican in the 1870s. He was a presidential elector in 1872 and served in the Ohio House of Representatives from 1874 to 1878. He was Speaker of the house from 1876 to 1878, originating the practice of counting a quorum, the minimum number of members required to be present at an assembly before business can be transacted. He supported Representative James G. Blaine for the Republican presidential nomination in 1880 and later that year was a presidential elector for Representative James A. Garfield of Ohio, the Republican nominee for president. Four years later he again campaigned for Blaine, who obtained the party's nomination but lost the election to Democrat Grover Cleveland of New York.

In 1884 Grosvenor won his first election to the U.S. House of Representatives, where he served from 1885 to 1891 and again from 1893 to 1907, suffering defeat in the Democratic rout in 1890. He represented an agricultural and small-town region in southern Ohio that was generally regarded as Republican territory. A highly partisan individual and a skilled parliamentarian, he earned a reputation among colleagues for his debating skills, intellectual capabilities, political shrewdness, and devotion to Republican causes. Grosvenor was a member of the Committees on Ways and Means, Mines and Mining, Rivers and Harbors, War Claims, Rules, and Merchant Marine and Fisheries, serving as chairman of the latter in the Fifty-sixth, Fifty-seventh, and Fifty-eighth Congresses. As a member of a conference committee in 1897, he demanded protection for wool in the Dingley Tariff and threatened to vote against the entire bill unless legislators agreed to his stand, which they did. Some of Grosvenor's notable speeches in the House dealt with the benefits of tariff protectionism (1888 and 1895), his opposition to the creation of an Interstate Commerce Commission (1887), an endorsement of President William McKinley's prewar diplomacy (1898), and a rigorous defense of Theodore Roosevelt's record as president (1904).

Grosvenor was also a committed partisan outside the halls of Congress. In 1881, in a speech at Valley Ford, Meigs County, Ohio, he delivered a blistering attack on Democrats that was basically a compendium of what he perceived to be Democratic blunders on the state and national levels since the Civil War. In contrast to Democratic failures, Grosvenor pictured a glorious temple of liberty that had been built by Republicans. In 1888 he favored Senator John Sherman of Ohio for the presidential nomination and worked to line up delegates on his behalf. When Sherman lost the party prize to Benjamin Harrison, Grosvenor quickly transferred his loyalty to the Indiana Republican.

A delegate to the Republican National Conventions in 1896 and 1900, Grosvenor in 1896 joined Mark Hanna, a Cleveland industrialist, in promoting the presidential nomination of former Ohio governor McKinley. Grosvenor advised McKinley and Hanna during the campaign in 1896 against the Democratic challenger, William Jennings Bryan. Nicknamed "Old Figgers" because of his penchant for making arithmetical prognostications of election results, Grosvenor functioned as the official statistician of the party, issuing detailed statements of McKinley's strength in each state and forecasting results.

In 1906 Grosvenor was an unsuccessful candidate for renomination, ending his political career. He returned to Athens in 1907 to practice law with Evan J. Jones and Lawrence G. Worstell, with an office in the Athens National Bank Building. Grosvenor's interest in politics, however, did not cease with his retirement from Washington. In 1908, like Roosevelt, he endorsed Secretary of War William Howard Taft, a native Ohioan, over Ohio senator Joseph Benson Foraker for the Republican presidential nomination. He persuaded Taft to visit Athens in August and handled the local arrangements for the reception. "I should feel as if my country was on the road to ruin . . . if Bryan should be elected," he wrote to Taft.

Grosvenor was a well-known political figure during the late nineteenth and early twentieth centuries. He often appeared on the Chautauqua lecture circuit and on occasion debated the tariff and other national issues with Representative Champ Clark, a Missouri Democrat. Grosvenor labored endlessly for Republican success. He was also active in various community organizations and favored better regulation of hospitals for the insane. He served on the board of trustees of the Ohio Soldiers and Sailors Orphan Home in Xenia from 1880 to 1888. In addition he authored two books, *William McKinley, His Life and Work* (1901) and *The Book of the Presidents, with Biographical Sketches* (1902). Appointed chairman of the Chickamauga and Chattanooga National Park Commission, Grosvenor served in that capacity from 1910 until his death in Athens.

• A small collection of Grosvenor's letters, photographs, genealogies, and miscellaneous documents is in the Archives and Special Collections Department, Alden Library, Ohio University, Athens. Some letters are in the manuscript collections of his contemporaries, such as Joseph Benson Foraker (Historical and Philosophical Society of Ohio at Cincinnati); Charles Dick (Ohio Historical Society at Columbus); and John Sherman, James A. Garfield, Benjamin Harrison, William McKinley, Theodore Roosevelt, and William Howard Taft (Division of Manuscripts, Library of Congress). Grosvenor's speeches are in the *Congressional Record* from 1885 to 1891 and 1893 to 1907. Obituaries are in the *Athens Daily Messenger*, 30 Oct. 1917, and the *New York Times*, 31 Oct. 1917.

LEONARD SCHLUP

GROSVENOR, Gilbert Hovey (28 Oct. 1875–4 Feb. 1966), magazine editor, was born in Istanbul (then Constantinople), Turkey, one of a pair of identical twins born to Edwin Augustus Grosvenor, a clergyman and history professor at Robert College, and Lillian Hovey Waters. Grosvenor so appreciated being a twin that he later described it as "next to a wife . . . the greatest favor the Lord can give a man." Except for a short period during the Russo-Turkish War of 1878, the twins were raised by their parents in Turkey. When they were fifteen, Grosvenor and his brother arrived in the United States and attended preparatory school at Worcester Academy in Massachusetts. The brothers then entered Amherst College, where their father was then serving as a history professor, in the fall of 1893. Both were elected to Phi Beta Kappa and were honor graduates in 1897. The twins were the subject of an article in *Harper's Weekly*, which described their academic achievements and their performance as tennis players. Grosvenor's father was a friend of the inventor Alexander Graham Bell. Having read the *Harper's* piece, Bell's wife invited the Grosvenor twins to visit the Bell's summer home in Nova Scotia, Canada, in the summer of 1897.

When Bell, then serving as president of the National Geographic Society, sought a young editorial assistant for the struggling magazine in 1899, the position was offered on a trial basis to whichever Grosvenor twin might want to take it. Gilbert had for several years taught history, languages, algebra, and chemistry at Englewood Academy for Boys in New Jersey while working toward his M.A. at Amherst (he completed his degree in 1901). Edwin Grosvenor, then in law school, declined Bell's offer; Gilbert accepted the post at a substantial reduction in salary. Gilbert married Bell's daughter Elsie May in London in October 1900; they had seven children. Until her death in 1964, she was a staunch supporter of her husband and the National Geographic Society. She designed the society's flag and contributed three articles of her own to *National Geographic* in the 1950s.

Grosvenor's early efforts to stimulate interest in the society by gearing articles in the *National Geographic* to the public taste initially met with some opposition from the society's conservative trustees. Many of these men opposed the popularization of geography and considered Grosvenor's ideas about soliciting new memberships a form of unseemly hucksterism. With Bell's considerable help and that of several other prominent individuals—notably William Howard Taft, Grosvenor's second cousin and later president of the United States—the very capable Grosvenor, who became managing editor of the magazine in 1901, was soon able to stabilize his position. He was named editor in chief in 1903 and president of the society in 1920. Grosvenor's years abroad had given him a sense of the importance of geography. He was also able to take advantage of an enhanced public interest in world events, stimulated by the Spanish-American War and the acquisition of new American colonies in the Pacific and Caribbean.

While assisting his father, who was publishing a history of Constantinople in 1895, Grosvenor had learned something about the impact of photographic illustrations, then a rather new innovation. Grosvenor himself soon learned to take good pictures, some 400 of which appeared in the *National Geographic* over the years. He had the society set up a film laboratory and encouraged the development of color photographic techniques. The first *National Geographic* maps incorporating some color were published in 1906. One of the earliest books published by the society was *Scenes from Every Land* (1907), edited by Grosvenor and featuring an excellent range of photographs. Three other such compilations appeared in 1909, 1912, and 1918. Color photographs were first used in the magazine in 1910. Some color illustrations, he discovered, could be borrowed from government agencies. On one occasion, Grosvenor learned through his brother that the Department of Agriculture could not meet public demand for an illustrated pamphlet about common American birds. Making use of the department's color plates, he published them in the June 1913 issue of the *National Geographic*. Later, some $40,000 was invested in several well-illustrated issues concerning the larger (Nov. 1916) and smaller (Mar. 1918) American mammals. These were subsequently combined in a separate publication, among the first of many focusing on wildlife and conservation. Each of the wildlife books went through a number of editions.

Membership in the society, barely 900 when Grosvenor began work in 1899, had reached 11,479 by 1905, 285,000 in 1914, and 650,000 in 1918. The one million mark was passed in 1930, but the effects of the Great Depression reduced this by more than one-third. Recovery was swift, however, and membership rolls again reached one million in 1935; there were 2.1 million members by the time of Grosvenor's retirement in 1955. Hubbard Memorial Hall, the society's first permanent home, was built in Washington, D.C., in 1903. As the society's membership and staff grew, additional buildings constructed during Grosvenor's life were completed in 1914, 1925, 1932, 1947, and 1964. The society's sponsorship of exploring expeditions by land, sea, and air was vigorously expanded under Grosvenor's leadership. Accounts of these initiatives frequently graced the pages of the *National Geographic*. One particularly controversial issue centered on whether Dr. Frederick Cook or Admiral Robert Peary, who had received a $1,000 grant from the society, had first reached the North Pole in 1909. Grosvenor consistently backed Peary's claim, despite persistent questions then and later as to whether Peary ever actually reached his objective. Other grants from the society went to Hiram Bingham, dicoverer of Machu

Picchu in 1911; Admiral Richard Byrd, who flew over the North Pole in 1926; William Beebe, for his oceanographic researches in the 1930s; and many others.

Grosvenor, known as "the Chief" to his subordinates, was firmly in charge of editorial policy during his tenure. Although he stated in 1943 that "the members really own the society and, in addition to receiving the magazine, and the maps . . . share in the responsibility for the scientific expeditions which we sponsor," virtually all major decisions were made by Grosvenor and his trustees behind closed doors (Abramson, p. 153). Great emphasis was placed on accuracy, abundant illustrations, subject matter of permanent value, avoidance of trivia, kindly and nonpartisan coverage, avoidance of controversy and unpleasantness, and timeliness. This policy sometimes resulted in a failure to cover certain important issues, and often led to editorial blandness. The *New York Times* once took note of the *National Geographic's* "traditional tone of gentlemanly detachment from the ugliness, misery, and strife in the world" (quoted in Bryan, p. 349). A generally friendly and wide-ranging 1943 *New Yorker* profile characterized Grosvenor as a generally "kindly, mild-mannered, purposeful, pokerfaced, peripatetic man of sixty-seven, endowed with the sprightly air of an inquiring grasshopper." To the surprise of some on the *New Yorker* staff, Grosvenor was very appreciative of their coverage.

When World War II came, Grosvenor and his associates saw it, in the words of one observer, "as little more than an inconvenience," and "death was sanitized." The society's wartime map supplements, however, enabled the public, the president of the United States, and various military commanders to follow the course of events during the war. The society made a point of making complimentary sets available as well to Prime Minister Winston Churchill of Great Britain and other allied leaders. Many photographs and a good many maps, together with other information gathered by the society over the years, was provided to American military intelligence services during the war. On one occasion, the crew of a B-17 with the senior naval commander in the Pacific theater lost their way in a driving rainstorm but eventually found their destination using one of the society's maps. In the postwar world, Grosvenor directed the production of a new generation of maps, which reflected the widespread changes of national boundaries that had taken place.

Because of the magazine's widespread use in schools, Grosvenor refused to run any advertising matter deemed unsuitable for children, and advertisements that did appear either preceded or followed the substantive content of each issue. Grosvenor's editorial, hiring, and staff management policies were extremely conservative and did not undergo substantive change until after he stepped down from active direction of the society. Grosvenor and his wife traveled widely throughout his life. He played golf and tennis and enjoyed sailing large boats. When he retired in 1954, he was named chief of the society's Board of Trustees, a title he held for the remainder of his life. His son Melville Bell succeeded him as editor of the magazine. Grosvenor died at his summer home in Nova Scotia.

• Grosvenor's papers are in the Manuscript Division, Library of Congress. See two articles by Grosvenor, "The National Geographic Society and Its Magazine," *National Geographic*, Jan. 1936, a revised version of which appeared as the foreword to *National Geographic Magazine Cumulative Index, 1899-1946* (1948); and "The Romance of the Geographic: National Geographic Magazine Observes Its Diamond Anniversary," *National Geographic*, Oct. 1963. Information concerning Grosvenor and his work with the society and the magazine is in Geoffrey T. Hellman, "Geography Unshackled," *New Yorker*, 25 Sept., 2 Oct., and 9 Oct. 1943; Howard S. Abramson, *National Geographic: Behind America's Lens on the World* (1987); C. D. B. Bryan, *The National Geographic Society: 100 Years of Adventure and Discovery* (1987); and "Three Men Who Made the Magazine," *National Geographic*, Sept. 1988. See also a commemorative issue of *National Geographic* celebrating Grosvenor's half-century as editor, Albert W. Atwood, "Gilbert H. Grosvenor's Golden Jubilee," Aug. 1949, and a memorial by Frederick G. Vosburgh, with staff from the National Geographic Society, "To Gilbert Grosvenor: A Monthly Monument 25 Miles High," Oct. 1966. An obituary is in the *New York Times*, 5 Feb. 1966.

KEIR B. STERLING

GROSZ, George (26 July 1893–6 July 1959), artist and poet, was born Georg Ehrenfried Groß in Berlin, Germany, the son of Karl Groß and Maria Schultze. Grosz spent most of his childhood in Stolp, Pomerania, where his father, a failed restaurateur, became steward of a Freemasons' Lodge. After his father's death in 1900, his mother moved for two years to Berlin, where the family lived in meager circumstances; she then took a position as manager of an officers' club in Stolp. As a boy, Grosz became fascinated with America, especially through the stories of James Fenimore Cooper and Karl May. He showed early signs of artistic skill, copying cartoons from popular journals and composing his own drawings of battles, castles, and exotic characters. He also observed the arrogance and pettiness of the Prussian officers who frequented the club at which his mother worked.

Expelled from school at age fifteen for responding physically when a teacher struck him, Grosz was nevertheless able to study for two years (1909–1911) at the Royal Saxon Academy of Fine Arts in Dresden and for much of another two (1912–1913 and again in 1916–1917) at Prussia's Academy of Arts and Crafts (Kunstgewerbeschule) in Berlin, to which he won a scholarship. At Dresden he studied under conservative artists Richard Müller and Raphael Wehle, among others, and at Berlin notably with keen draftsman Emil Orlik, who was more sympathetic to modern trends (and in whose class Grosz met Eva Louise Peter, whom he married in 1920). Grosz also discovered much about newer artistic currents—the work of Eduard Munch and the futurists—outside the academy and explored the street and night life of the empire's capital. As early as 1910 he sold a cartoon done in the "line style" of art nouveau to *Ulk*, a supplement to the *Berliner Tageblatt*. On the side he also began to teach himself the fundamentals of painting in oil, which was not part of his course of study at either of the two academies. In 1913 he spent several months in Paris, formally at the Atelier Colarossi, where he claimed that he learned very little. But there and at Berlin's Autumn Salon later in 1913 he became better acquainted with cubism and futurism, both of which influenced his own work for several years.

World War I was a formative event in Grosz's life and work. He caricatured the exuberant response of many Germans to the coming of war but nevertheless enlisted for service late in 1914. Details of his brief experiences in the army remain obscure, but they were not happy ones despite his apparent escape from duty at the front. In 1915 he received a medical discharge and returned to Berlin, where he associated with literary young men with antiwar sentiments, among them Walter Mehring, Franz Jung, and the brothers Wieland Herzfelde and Helmut Herzfeld, who spelled their last names differently and the latter of whom anglicized his name to John Heartfield about the same time that Georg Groß changed his to George Grosz. In addition to his artistic work, Grosz, who liked to present himself in various social and sartorial disguises, staged a clowning cabaret act in which he read his poetry and danced. It was at this time that Grosz was "discovered" by Theodor Däubler, Count Harry Kessler, and others, who encouraged his artistic expression of rage at the hypocrisy and corruption, social and sexual, that he saw everywhere around him. He published several drawings in the short-lived *Neue Jugend* and a couple of portfolios (*Erste George Grosz Mappe* and *Kleine Grosz Mappe*) before being recalled in mid-1917 to military service, much of which he spent in various hospitals and psychiatric clinics, drawing and painting to keep himself sane, he claimed.

Upon his release from military service late in 1918, Grosz began the most frenzied and famous phase of his life. He embraced the revolution that accompanied the end of the war and took a leading role—as "Propagandada"—in Berlin's iconoclastic dada movement. In 1919 he joined Germany's nascent Communist party and contributed satirical drawings to short-lived dadaistic and revolutionary journals such as *Every Man His Own Football*, *Bankruptcy*, *Red Flag*, and the *Cudgel* (Der knüppel). One of his most famous oil paintings from these early postwar years, *Germany: A Winter's Tale* (1917–1919), its title appropriately borrowed from Heinrich Heine's poem satirizing Germany's "philistines," portrays a pastor, general, and schoolmaster supporting an anxious burgher as he defends his place in a chaotic scene of social disintegration. Grosz also ridiculed the moderate Majority Socialists, whom he and his colleagues accused of having betrayed the promise of revolution by selling out to the bourgeoisie and the officer caste.

Grosz's savage social and political satire from this period, much of it in published portfolios such as

"*God Is on Our Side*" (1920), *The Face of the Ruling Class* (1921), *The Day of Reckoning!* (Abrechnung folgt!) (1923), and *Ecce Homo* (1923), made his name. His mordant depiction, primarily in pen-and-ink drawings, of the sordid spectacle presented by a coarse, oppressive, and disrupted society—its bloated profiteers, exploited workers, reactionary officers, pandering churchmen, lascivious city slickers, leering and domineering patresfamilias, hardened prostitutes whose bodies showed through their clothing, and lust murderers—eventually became the stereotypical visual description of urban Germany during the Weimar era.

Such scathing social commentary also made Grosz's name infamous in many circles. He was prosecuted three times during the decade for what amounted to blasphemy against the established order, and Nazis—favorite targets of his—condemned him as the country's leading "cultural Bolshevist" and repeatedly threatened him (after January 1933 they dubbed his art "degenerate" and destroyed some of it).

However much Grosz attacked the few who in his view exploited the many, he was not kind to the masses, either, whether petit bourgeois or proletarian. The former he saw (early on) ready to embrace a Hitler; the latter he saw (perhaps more gradually) equally likely to succumb to freedom-destroying authoritarianism. His cynicism, much of it largely innate, became more marked after a disillusioning trip to Soviet Russia in 1922 and eventually led to tensions both within himself and between Grosz and his idealistic colleagues, who began to sense that he was not a true believer. He continued to publish satirical drawings in journals such as *Simplicissimus*, however, and in *Eclipse of the Sun* and *Pillars of Society*, large oils (both 1926), produced more fully developed caricatures of the greedy, debauched, and self-serving rulers of German society. Having lost faith in the building of a good society, he nevertheless thought that artists should shock viewers into awareness of underlying reality. In Grosz's case, the artist was also grappling with internal demons.

After mid-decade Grosz turned to "new objectivity" (Neue sachlichkeit). Through this style artists expressed social criticism with a greater degree of detachment and verisimilitude and with less emotional intensity than many exhibited just after World War I. Grosz's famous portfolios of drawings from this period, notably *Mirror of the Bourgeoisie* (Der spiesserspiegel) (1925), *The New Face of the Ruling Class* (1930), and *Love above Everything* (1930), lacked the polemical stridency of his earlier work while revealing "weariness with the injustice and suffering and boredom of the world" (Lewis, pp. 181–82). In these years Grosz produced well-known portraits of his mother-in-law, Anna Peter, of his poet friend Max Hermann-Neisse, and of himself as "warner." A portrait of boxer Max Schmeling won a gold medal at Amsterdam's Olympiade show of 1928, one of two awards he received that year. His works were featured in exhibitions throughout Germany and found buyers. He also continued to create stage designs, some of which evoked controversy, for Germany's leading avant-garde directors, as well as to take part in the public discussion about the purpose of art in a revolutionary era.

In 1931 Grosz had his first one-man show in the United States at New York's Weyhe Gallery. The following year brought an unexpected invitation to teach a summer course at the Art Students League. While in New York from June to October 1932 Grosz decided to move to the United States and returned to Germany to prepare for emigration. He and his wife left Germany on 12 January 1933, eighteen days before the Nazis came to power and went looking for him; they later stripped him of his citizenship. In the summer of 1933 Eva returned to Germany to bring their two children to the United States.

Late in 1932 Grosz explained himself in an autobiographical "comment" in *Americana* that one commentator has described as a mixture of "earnestness, cynicism, and enthusiasm." He wrote, "I have no programme. . . . Perhaps I am something of a muddlehead and certainly with one foot a petty-bourgeois. I still believe in certain forbidden metaphysical concepts like truth, justice and humanity. I am and wish to remain independent. . . . I do not really believe in progress, but agree that food and lodging might be better distributed. . . . I think America is a fine and astonishing land, and full of virile self-sufficiency. I hope to make my home here" (Flavell, pp. 81–82). Whatever hopes for success he harbored, Grosz recognized, as he wrote in 1933 to a friend contemplating a move, "This is not a land for dreamers—it's a land of hard work" (Flavell, p. 113).

The family settled on Long Island, first in Bayside (Queens), then in Douglaston, and finally, after 1952, in Huntington. Grosz threw himself into becoming American, which in many ways was the fulfillment of a lifelong dream. (He became a citizen in 1938.) He taught at the Art Students League (for minimal pay) and in 1933, with Maurice Sterne's help, opened a private school. He immediately set out to depict the various faces of New York in sketches and watercolors. Because he saw relationships there differently from how he had seen them in Berlin, this work lacked, however, the biting ferocity for which he had become famous. He experimented with different styles and motifs, especially from 1936 on, when the family began to spend summers on Cape Cod. For a while he drew and painted landscapes and studies of sand dunes, approaching storms, and sunsets—many of which, despite the serenity of his new environment, carried a hint of foreboding. He also continued to produce erotic art, from demure or Rubenesque nudes to exaggerated genitalia (the latter not made public until long after his death). Attacked by left-wing partisans for having abandoned the fight, he defiantly argued that he had left his rage behind and entered a new phase of his life, thereby contributing to the misconception that emigration had brought a complete break in his outlook and thus his art.

Grosz's work received considerable recognition in America, where it was accorded more than twenty individual exhibitions during his lifetime and occasionally found buyers. He received a Guggenheim fellowship for two years running (1937–1939), which provided him a break from teaching, after which, in 1941–1942, he taught at Columbia University's School of Fine Arts. He was nominated for membership in the American Academy and National Institute of Arts and Letters in 1954. He won several prizes, among them the Carol H. Beck Medal from the Pennsylvania Academy of Fine Arts in 1940 and the Gold Medal for Graphic Art from the American Academy and National Institute of Arts and Letters in 1959. He had friends and proponents—among them Edmund Wilson and John Dos Passos—and Richard O. Boyer profiled him sympathetically in three issues of the *New Yorker* late in 1943. Grosz also received occasional commissions for illustrations, notably for *Esquire* in the 1930s, O. Henry stories (1935), *The Divine Comedy* (1940), Sydney S. Baron's *One Whirl* (1944), Walter Mehring's *No Road Back: Poems* (1944), and *Life* magazine (1954). In 1952 he received a commission to portray "Dallas, its people, its industries, its character" in approximately twenty-five paintings and drawings.

But Grosz never felt himself to be a success in his adopted country, however much he tried to present himself differently. He generally had difficulty making ends meet; his works did not sell with adequate frequency; he was asked for illustrations far less often than he had hoped; and although he protested otherwise, he did not like having to teach for a living, either at the league, from which he took occasional breaks, or at his own school, which he conducted until 1937 and then off again and on again during the 1950s. Moreover, he felt out of step with the art world's preoccupation with abstract forms; an antimodernist as well as a modernist, he continued to champion art, however grotesque, that had some recognizable features even while expressing internal visions and torments. And despite the outward normality of his newfound life, he remained a man tormented by the fate of his homeland, by what he considered the collapse of a culture, and by internal demons (and a man given increasingly to drink).

Grosz poured his torments into some of the most compelling art he produced in the United States, albeit art that in the eyes of most critics failed to match the immediacy of that from his years in Germany. In 1936 he published *Interregnum*, a book of drawings that depicted conditions that had led to the terrors of Nazism but that also attacked leftist authoritarianism. The approach and then the destructiveness of another world war drove him to explore further the agonies of the human experience. His work increasingly evoked the tragic history painting of Goya and Bosch more than the caricature of Hogarth or Daumier, all of whom served as inspiration for Grosz at various times in his life. Notable in this regard are *The Survivor* (pen and ink, 1936; oil, 1945), *A Piece of My World II* (oil,

1938), *God of War* (oil, 1940), *Cain* (oil, 1945), *The Pit* (oil, 1946), and *The Painter of the Hole* (watercolor, 1947; oil, 1948), among others. He also borrowed explicitly from Dürer's apocalyptic horseman in a couple of works entitled *I Was Always Present*, one in pen and ink (1936), in which the deathly rider wears a gas mask, and one in oil (1942). Troubling and perplexing is the series of works known collectively as *The Stick Men* (begun in 1947), in which emaciated insectlike people with large heads struggle for existence (in the aftermath of atomic destruction?). Even more illustrative, perhaps, of Grosz's internal anguish are pencil drawings of dead mice, some caught in traps, that he executed early in the 1950s. Later in the decade he returned to dadaesque collages; one of them features his own clown face superimposed on the body of a female entertainer who holds a bottle of whiskey in one hand as the lights of New York shine in the background (1958).

Besides the poems and the essays that he wrote or cowrote in Berlin about the purposes of art, Grosz's major publication was his autobiography, *A Little Yes and a Big No*, first published in English translation (by Lola Sachs Dorin) in 1946, then, with some additions, in German in 1955. Although it provides more reflections about his life and times than concrete information, the book virtually radiates with ironic humor and insightful imagery. Grosz also carried on extensive correspondence with acquaintances old and new. The letters, too, reveal his many moods, his frequent efforts to convince others as well as himself that he had become fully American, his defense of nonabstract art, and his unwillingness to commit himself to partisan activities.

Ever the cynical ironist—he once proclaimed himself the "saddest man in Europe"—Grosz nonetheless retained a sense of humor and commitment to friends, especially those from his early days, even after their views about politics had diverged (e.g., Gottfried Benn to the right, Wieland Herzfelde to the left). He also held to the conviction that one must do Sisyphean battle against evil and social injustice in the ways that one could.

That conviction was one aspect of continuity in the life of this complex, not fully consistent, and at times dissembling artist. Some critics have discerned, especially in light of works made public in exhibitions in 1993 and in 1995, another form of continuity, one of ambivalence concerning sexuality. In Berlin, Grosz's preoccupation with "despised pleasures" had blended into his political and social satire; as one critic has noted, he "conferred on his loathsome bourgeois characters precisely those lusts that he himself shared" (Ziegler, p. 82). But in New York, where Grosz avoided political involvement, the sexual side of his art "became an autonomous component" (p. 82). It remained a private preoccupation, however, so much so that in 1950 Grosz stipulated to his agent in Berlin that the most daring of his erotic works should be displayed only at a time "when they will meet with greater understanding" (p. 81).

Although Grosz was welcome in Germany after 1945, he chose to live in the United States for another fourteen years. He visited France and Italy in 1951 and Germany in 1954 and 1958 but was always glad to get back to Long Island, however much he felt unappreciated by the artistic establishment. Becoming a member of the German Academy of Art late in 1958, with its official status and offer of a studio in Berlin, as well as receiving a large sum awarded by the German government as restitution for Nazi depredations, helped ease his decision to return for good, but it was largely in deference to his wife's wishes that they moved to Germany in June 1959. Even then Grosz intended to teach in New York for at least three months a year. He fell and died alone in a stairwell in West Berlin following a night of revelry with friends only weeks after his arrival there; heart failure was the official cause.

Grosz will long be the object of study. Not a modern or grand master, perhaps, he was nevertheless a master draftsman, an artist skilled in several mediums, and a powerfully penetrating and disturbing visual witness of his time.

• Holdings of Grosz materials, notably letters, diaries, and some photographs, can be found principally in the Grosz Archive in the Houghton Library at Harvard University and also in the Grosz Archives at the Akademie der Künste in Berlin and at the Estate of George Grosz in Princeton, N.J. Works by Grosz can be seen at the Museum of Modern Art, Metropolitan Museum of Art, and Whitney Museum of American Art, all in New York City; Chicago's Art Institute; the Wichita Art Museum; and the Los Angeles County Museum of Art. A selection of his letters is in *Briefe, 1913–1959*, ed. Herbert Knust (1979). Poems can be found in two works: *Gedichte und Gesänge* (1932) and *Ach knallige Welt, du Lunapark: Gesammelte Gedichte*, ed. Klaus Peter Dencker (1986). His autobiography and several famous books of drawings have been republished since his death. See also *George Grosz Drawings*, ed. H. Bittner, which contains Grosz's essay "On My Pictures" (1944); *George Grosz: 30 Drawings and Watercolours*, with an introduction by Walter Mehring (1944); *George Grosz: 85 Drawings and Watercolours*, ed. Imre Hofbauer, introduction by John Dos Passos (1948); and *Ade Withoi*, 51 plates, ed. Walter G. Oschilewsky, postscript by Otto Schmalhausen (1955). Much has been written about Grosz, both during his lifetime and afterward, and the literature contains bewildering factual and chronological discrepancies. See John I. H. Baur, *George Grosz* (1954); Beth Irwin Lewis, *George Grosz: Art and Politics in the Weimar Republic* (1971); Uwe M. Schneede et al., *George Grosz: His Life and Work*, trans. Susanne Flatauer (1979); Andrew DeShong, *The Theatrical Designs of George Grosz* (1982); Serge Sabarsky, *George Grosz: The Berlin Years* (1985); and M. Kay Flavell, *George Grosz: A Biography* (1988). Lewis and Flavell especially provide extensive bibliographies. Two articles that responded to the large retrospective of Grosz's work exhibited in both Germany and New York in 1995–1996 are Ian Buruma, "George Grosz's Amerika," *New York Review of Books*, 13 July 1995, pp. 24–28, and Ulf Erdmann Ziegler, "Despised Pleasures," *Art in America* 84 (Jan. 1996): 78–83; the brief one by Stephen Kinzer in the *New York Times* has a telling headline: *So*

Dazzled by New York, So Haunted by Berlin (19 Feb. 1995). Numerous obituaries include that in the *New York Times*, 7 July 1959.

C. EARL EDMONDSON

GROUARD, Frank (20 Sept. 1850–15 Aug. 1905), army scout, was born in the Paumotu Islands in the South Pacific, the son of Benjamin F. Grouard, a Mormon missionary, and a woman who was a native of the islands and reputed to be the daughter of the high chief, though her name remains unknown. When Grouard was two years old, his family moved to California, and his father turned him over to the Addison Pratt family of San Bernardino. Not long after, the Pratts moved to Beaver, Utah, where Grouard lived until he was fifteen. At that time he ran away from home, traveled to San Bernardino, and hired on as a teamster with a wagon train bound for the gold fields of Montana. He worked several different jobs during the next four years, and in January 1870 he was captured by the Sioux while carrying mail in Montana. Grouard's non-Caucasian features led the Indians to adopt him rather than kill him. He remained with them for six years, learning their language and gaining close acquaintanceships with Sitting Bull and Crazy Horse. He was accepted into the tribe, took a Sioux wife, and learned the tribe's ways and skills.

His sojourn with the Sioux ended in the fall of 1875, as he returned to the white world at Camp Robinson, Nebraska. The reason for his departure remains obscure, but he is reported to have had troubles with his Sioux in-laws (his wife did not accompany him when he left the tribe). He also had fallen out with Sitting Bull, though he remained on good terms with other factions in the tribe. In any case, war was brewing between the United States and the Sioux, and the army was looking for experienced scouts. In February 1876 Grouard hired on at Fort Laramie, Wyoming, to scout for the expedition of General George Crook. During the month of March, amid a late-season spell of brutal winter weather, Crook led a grueling campaign north from Fort Fetterman, Wyoming, in hopes of finding and defeating the Sioux. Grouard participated in an inconclusive skirmish on the Powder River (17 Mar.). The expedition proved a failure, but the officers of Crook's column were unanimous in praising Grouard as the most reliable of the scouts and a man of amazing skill in tracking.

In May Crook set out to try again, and Grouard was among the few scouts rehired for this expedition. Once again he performed excellently, undertaking a dangerous and important trek through enemy country to recruit allied Crow Indians to join the expedition. On 17 June he participated in the battle of the Rosebud. Foiled again despite Grouard's efforts, Crook withdrew. In July Grouard accompanied a small reconnaissance under Lieutenant Frederick W. Sibley, with twenty-five picked cavalrymen, seeking the whereabouts of a known Sioux war party. They found more Sioux than they had bargained for, and only Grouard's skill permitted their escape. He led the party by the

only possible escape route through the lines of the encircling Sioux, crawling through a dry wash on their hands and knees. Then on the long trek to safety, Grouard made skillful use of the terrain to foil Indian pursuit and utilized his knowledge of plants and animals to keep the men from starving.

Later that summer Grouard accompanied yet another of Crook's expeditions and again performed amazing feats of tracking, leading Captain Anson Mills and a picked force of 150 cavalrymen to a Sioux village at Slim Buttes, South Dakota. Their surprise attack gave the army its only victory of the summer's campaign.

The following year Grouard played a role in the capture and death of Crazy Horse, and this affair has become a matter of controversy. Grouard's own account of the Sioux leader's death varies with other witnesses' accounts enough to suggest to some modern historians a desire to conceal an aspect of his own involvement. Possibly Grouard mistranslated a statement by Crazy Horse to the commanding army officer to make the Sioux leader seem more defiant than he was. Historians speculate that Grouard may have done so to settle an old score with Crazy Horse from the days when Grouard lived among the Sioux. The full truth will probably never be known. Crook always had implicit faith in Grouard and accepted his report. Whatever may have been Crazy Horse's true state of mind, Crook, acting on Grouard's information, had the Sioux war leader arrested. While under arrest, Crazy Horse drew a knife and was fatally bayoneted by a soldier.

Grouard continued to work as a government scout in the years after the Sioux War. Most of this time he was stationed at Fort McKinney, Wyoming. In 1890 and 1891 the Sioux on the reservations in South Dakota and Nebraska became restless as a result of a religious movement known as the Ghost Dance Cult. During this time, Grouard was assigned to Pine Ridge Agency and proved extremely valuable in providing information about the activities and attitudes of the Indians. He returned to Fort McKinney in the spring of 1891. In 1894 he told a possibly embellished version of his life story to newspaper reporter Joe De Barthe, who subsequently published it. The following year Grouard retired and moved to St. Joseph, Missouri, where he died.

While some of his fellow scouts occasionally expressed doubts as to whether he had truly abandoned whatever allegiance to the Sioux he might have gained during his sojourn among them and some modern historians have questioned (probably to an unfair extent) the reliability of his memoirs, Grouard was nevertheless the most valuable and renowned scout in the service of the army on the frontier. His superiors had implicit confidence in him based on a solid record of performance, and, at least toward them and the success of their operations, he never betrayed that trust.

• The richest source of information, based as it is on the author's discussions with Grouard, is Joe De Barthe, *The Life and Adventures of Frank Grouard* (1894), though it must be carefully compared with other sources to guard against Grouard's problems of memory or veracity. The 1958 reprint edition edited by Edgar I. Stewart provides useful help on this score. Other firsthand or almost firsthand accounts of particular value are John F. Finerty, *Warpath and Bivouac; or, The Conquest of the Sioux* (1890), and George Crook, *General George Crook: His Autobiography* (1946). Among the work of modern historians, Evan S. Connell, *Son of the Morning Star: Custer and the Little Bighorn* (1984), and John S. Gray, *Centennial Campaign: The Sioux War of 1876* (1988), give brief but significant attention to Grouard's role in that campaign. Robert M. Utley, *Frontier Regulars: The United States Army and the Indian, 1866–1890* (1973), also touches briefly on Grouard.

STEVEN E. WOODWORTH

GROVE, Lefty (6 Mar. 1900–22 May 1975), baseball player, was born Robert Moses Grove in Lonaconing, Maryland, one of eight children of John Grove, a coal miner, and Emma Beeman. Grove left public school in the eighth grade to help support his large family. He first worked in a silk mill for 50 cents a day. In 1916 he loaded coal for a few weeks, filling in for an injured brother, but vowed never to go back after his brother returned. He worked for a time in a glass factory, and then in 1918 and 1919 he was an apprentice in the Baltimore and Ohio Railroad shops in Cumberland, Maryland, cleaning and repairing steam locomotives.

Lonaconing fielded no baseball team, but Midland, three miles away, had an amateur club; Grove, at age 17, began playing first base there. His manager shifted him to pitcher because he could throw harder than anyone else on the team. Grove's strong left arm attracted the attention of Bill Lowden, manager with the Martinsburg, West Virginia, team, which had joined the Class D Blue Ridge League in 1920. Lowden signed Grove for $125 a month.

Word about Grove's blazing fastball spread quickly. Jack Dunn, owner and manager of the Baltimore Orioles of the International League, scouted the young pitcher. Though he had only a 3–3 record, did not throw curves, and lacked experience on the mound, Grove was so impressive that Dunn purchased his contract for $3,000 plus a pitcher. Years later, Grove remarked that Martinsburg sold him because the team needed the money to expand the small grandstand and to build a fence around the ballpark.

The Baltimore Orioles, which Grove joined in June, ranked among the strongest minor league clubs. Grove contributed greatly to the Orioles' winning the International League pennant five consecutive years (1920–1924). During that time, he won 108 games and lost only 36. The 6′2½″, 175-pound, lefthander (later rosters list him at 6′3″, 190 pounds) relied on his fastball until 1923, when, as he commented in an interview after he had retired, "[I] tried to throw a curve ball as fast as the fastball, and it would only break a little ways. Maybe six inches. Just a wrinkle. Maybe they'd call it a slider today." To improve his control, Grove began to take more time between pitches; later in his career, he worked even more deliberately. In 1921, after his first season with Baltimore, he married

Ethel Gardner (his hometown sweetheart), with whom he had two children.

In the winter of 1924, Dunn sold Grove to Connie Mack's Philadelphia Athletics for $100,600—at that time unprecedented for a transaction involving only one player. The extra $600 was added to surpass the record $100,000 the New York Yankees had paid the Boston Red Sox for Babe Ruth in January 1920.

With the Athletics, Grove achieved his greatest fame. He led the American League seven consecutive seasons in strikeouts, five times in earned-run average, and four times each in wins and winning percentage. In 1931 he won 31 games and lost only 4. In nine years with the Athletics, he won 195 games and lost only 79. His combined won-lost record for the 1930 and 1931 seasons was a remarkable 59 victories and only 9 defeats. In three World Series, he won 4 games, lost 2, and saved 2 games in relief—one the crucial seventh game of the 1929 series against the Chicago Cubs. He was named to the *Sporting News* All-Star teams from 1928 through 1932 and won the American League Most Valuable Player Award in 1931. Grove considered one of his greatest accomplishments striking out Lou Gehrig, Babe Ruth, and Bob Meusel—known as the New York Yankees' Murderer's Row—on nine pitches, with the tying run on third base in the ninth inning.

The managerial skill of Connie Mack contributed greatly to Grove's success. Mack delicately handled his star lefthander, who exhibited a terrible temper, sulked, and possessed few friends. Although he never caused trouble by drinking or fighting, Grove berated his teammates if they made errors behind him, and at times he refused to pitch. He trained himself and would take no coaching. Mack patiently let Grove do as he liked. Grove regarded his manager as a father figure, though they frequently engaged in salary disputes, Mack also being part-owner of the Athletics.

Grove's temper reached its worst on 21 August 1931. He already had won 16 consecutive games to tie the American League record, but in trying for a seventeenth win that day, he lost 1–0 to the lowly St. Louis Browns. A rookie, substituted in left field for the absent Al Simmons, misjudged a line drive to let in the only run of the game. Angry not only at the rookie but also at Simmons, a great hitter who had been allowed to go home to Milwaukee to rest an infected toe, Grove smashed lockers, ripped his uniform to shreds, and threw benches, water buckets, and equipment around the locker room. His teammates avoided Grove for weeks afterward, but Mack treated his star player as if nothing had happened.

Grove's career in Philadelphia ended in December 1933. In the midst of the depression, the Shibe family and Mack, who owned the Athletics jointly, needed money to pay off obligations to a bank that had called in their loans. Philadelphia sent Grove, Rube Walberg, also an excellent pitcher, and Max Bishop, one of the better second basemen in the league, to the Boston Red Sox for $125,000 and two marginal players. According to rumors, the Red Sox actually paid

$250,000, with half the amount representing the price of Grove. Thus Grove may have been sold a second time for over $100,000.

Although sometimes displaying his former great fastball with the Red Sox, Grove frequently experienced arm problems. He suffered his first sore arm in spring training in 1934 and thereafter endured a variety of arm ailments. To compensate for his inability to throw hard, he improved his curve, developed a forkball, and gained remarkable control. During his final seasons with the Red Sox, Grove mellowed and became popular with his teammates and fans. His best friend, young Tom Yawkey, owned the team.

In his eight years with the Red Sox, Grove won 105 games, lost 62, and led the American League in winning percentage in 1938 and in earned-run average in 1935, 1936, 1938, and 1939. In 1940 and 1941, however, he struggled on the mound. Opposing batters hit him hard, and he often did not last beyond the sixth inning. With the goal of 300 career victories in sight, Grove at age 41 valiantly continued to pitch until on 25 July 1941 he reached his goal. He never won another game and was released unconditionally on 9 December.

Grove's impressive record, covering 17 major league seasons, gained him election to the National Baseball Hall of Fame in 1947. Authorities consider Grove one of the greatest lefthanded pitchers in baseball history, with 300 victories and only 141 losses for a .680 winning percentage. In 616 games, he pitched a total of 3,940⅔ innings, allowed 3,849 hits, struck out 2,266 batters, and walked 1,187. His earned-run average was 3.06. In 51⅓ innings during eight World Series, he struck out 36, walked only 6, had a 1.75 earned-run average, won 4 games, lost 2, and saved 2 others in relief. His lifetime regular-season earned-run average, normalized to the league average and adjusted for home park according to a formula developed by the editors of Total Baseball, was judged as of the early 1990s the best ever, even surpassing that of the great Walter Johnson.

After retiring from baseball, Grove moved back to Lonaconing, the small town in the Cumberland Mountains that he loved. Grove had invested his money carefully and had not suffered losses during the stock market crash. He had built homes in Lonaconing for himself and for his family and had helped one of his brothers begin operating bowling alleys, which Grove ran in his retirement. He rejected offers to coach and preferred to spend much of his time fishing. Formerly gruff, distrustful of strangers, and quick-tempered, Grove had become easily approachable, loaned money to former teammates, and managed Little League teams, which he supplied with baseball equipment.

Following the death of his wife in 1959, Grove lived with his son and daughter-in-law in Norwalk, Ohio, until his death there from a heart attack.

• There is a file on Grove in the library of the National Baseball Hall of Fame, Cooperstown, N.Y. The best articles on Grove can be found in Martin Appel and Burt Goldblatt, *Baseball's Best: The Hall of Fame Gallery*, 2d ed. (1980), and Bob Broeg, *Super Stars of Baseball* (1971). Grove's major league records are in Joseph Reichler, ed., *The Baseball Encyclopedia*, 9th ed. (1993), and John Thorn and Pete Palmer, eds., *Total Baseball*, 4th ed. (1995). Detailed accounts of Grove's years with the Philadelphia Athletics appear in Frederick G. Lieb, *Connie Mack, Grand Old Man of Baseball* (1945), and Connie Mack, *My 66 Years in the Big Leagues* (1950). For Grove's career with the Red Sox, see Al Hirshberg, *The Red Sox, the Bean, and the Cod* (1947), which also contains additional details about his life, and Ellery H. Clark, Jr., *Boston Red Sox: 75th Anniversary History* (1975). Red Smith's column in the *New York Times* of 26 May 1975 is an insightful character sketch occasioned by Grove's death. An obituary appears in the *New York Times*, 23 May 1975.

RALPH S. GRABER

GROVER, Cuvier (29 July 1828–6 June 1885), soldier, was born in Bethel, Maine, the son of John Grover, a physician, and Fanny Lary. Among Cuvier's younger siblings was La Fayette Grover, future governor of Oregon and U.S. senator. By 1843, at the age of fifteen, Grover had graduated from common school, and his father deemed his son ready to enter college. Grover refused, his heart set on either becoming a soldier or a merchant. Too young to be appointed to the U.S. Military Academy, he clerked for two years in Boston for Eben D. Jordan. On 1 July 1846 Grover entered West Point, being accredited to Massachusetts. Four years later he graduated fourth in his class, was commissioned brevet second lieutenant, and was assigned to the First U.S. Artillery.

On 16 September 1850 Grover was promoted to second lieutenant in the Fourth U.S. Artillery and joined his unit at Fort Columbus, in New York Harbor. Ordered to Fort Leavenworth, 27 October 1850, he served at that post as company officer until 17 April 1853. He was an engineer with the teams, headed by Governor Isaac Stevens of Washington Territory, given the mission of exploring a route for a Pacific railroad between the forty-seventh and forty-ninth parallels. In January and February, on snowshoes, with dog teams, and accompanied by four men, Grover crossed the northern Rocky and Bitterroot mountains. The going was rugged, the snow deep, and on one day the temperature fell to 38°F below zero.

On 3 March 1855 Grover was promoted to first lieutenant and assigned to the Tenth U.S. Infantry. By June 1857 he was en route to Fort Leavenworth, where he joined the Mormon expedition commanded by Colonel Albert Sidney Johnston. Upon the expedition's arrival in Salt Lake City, Grover was named provost marshal to oversee enforcement of martial law in Utah Territory.

August 1861 found Captain Grover stationed at Fort Union in New Mexico Territory. Ordered east in mid-November, Grover went on leave. He reported for duty on 14 April 1862 and was commissioned brigadier general of volunteers. Sent to the Virginia Peninsula, he joined the Army of the Potomac's Third Corps, assuming command of the First Brigade in

Brigadier General Joseph Hooker's division. A participant in the Yorktown siege, Grover first led troops into combat at Williamsburg (5 May 1862), where Hooker earned his nom de guerre of "Fighting Joe" and Grover was brevetted lieutenant colonel for gallantry and meritorious service. Although he and his troops were not engaged at Seven Pines (31 May–1 June), Grover was brevetted colonel. The Seven Days' battles found Grover and his people on the firing line at Oak Grove (25 June) and at Glendale (30 June). At the former, Hooker cited Grover for "the skillful disposition of his force and his gallant use of it in accomplishing our object," and at the latter he noted that when Grover and his troops counterattacked, "the enemy were rolled back through a part of [Brigadier General George] McCall's camp."

Back in northern Virginia, in the fourth week of August, Grover fought in the Second Manassas campaign. On the twenty-ninth Grover and his brigade advanced to attack troops of A. P. Hill's Light Division posted along the unfinished railroad grade. According to Major General Samuel P. Heintzelman, Grover's corps commander, they "made the most gallant and determined bayonet charge of the war. He broke two of the enemy's lines but was finally repulsed by the overwhelming numbers in the rebel third line." In twenty minutes Grover's brigade, which had numbered fewer than 2,000, lost 486 soldiers, nearly all killed or wounded.

On 10 November 1862 Grover was detached from the Army of the Potomac and ordered to report to Major General Nathaniel P. Banks, who had been named to replace Major General Benjamin Butler (1818–1893) as commander of the Department of the Gulf. Grover, upon reaching New Orleans, was placed in charge of the force that reoccupied Baton Rouge, and on 30 December he took command of the division General Banks had organized for the defense of the Baton Rouge enclave. In mid-March 1863 Grover and his division participated in the demonstration against Confederate-held Port Hudson in support of Rear Admiral David G. Farragut's 14–15 March passage of the rebel batteries with two ships. April found Grover campaigning on the Teche, where, on the fourteenth his troops beat the Confederates at Irish Bend.

Grover and his troops, on a march that took them across the Attakapas to Alexandria and back across the Mississippi, again approached the Port Hudson perimeter, this time from the north. On 27 May Grover's command was repulsed in their all-out assault on Fort Desperate. On 14 June, in an attack on Port Hudson that was no more successful than the first, Grover commanded the right wing of Bank's army. On 12–13 July, less than a week after the surrender of Port Hudson, Grover fought the Confederates at Donaldsonville. In mid-August he and his division were assigned to the newly formed Nineteenth Corps, led by Major General William B. Franklin. Returning to the Teche country, Grover campaigned with Franklin from 3 October to 30 November.

In mid-January 1864 Grover was ordered to duty in the defenses of New Orleans, and on 10 March he returned to the field, resuming command of the Nineteenth Corps's Second Division. He and his troops began the Red River campaign on 16 March, taking ten days to make the 140-mile march from Franklin to Alexandria. He and his division remained at Alexandria, and Grover commanded the post during Banks's army's four-week absence. Upon the completion of the Bailey Dam and the recoil from Alexandria, Grover and his troops were based in Morganza.

Early in July, Grover and his division, along with most of the Nineteenth Corps, were transferred by ship from Louisiana to the eastern theater of the war. Initially sent up the James River, Grover and his division were rushed to Washington, disembarking there on 1 August. Two weeks later, at Berryville, Virginia, he reported to Brigadier General William H. Emory, who had superseded General Franklin as leader of the Nineteenth Corps. Grover and his troops were center stage during Philip H. Sheridan's Shenandoah Valley campaign, as they were caught in the vortex of battle at Opequon (19 Sept.), Fisher's Hill (22 Sept.), and Cedar Creek (19 Oct.). At Cedar Creek Grover was wounded early in the day but remained with his troops. Seriously wounded in the arm late in the afternoon, he was compelled to leave the field. In recognition of his gallantry and meritorious service at Cedar Creek and in the Shenandoah Valley, Grover was brevetted brigadier and major general of volunteers, 19 Oct. 1864.

On 1 August 1865 Grover married Susan Flint. Mustered out of the volunteer service later that same month, on 24 August, he reported for duty as major of the Third U.S. Infantry on 18 November 1865, pulling duty at St. Louis and Fort Larned, Kansas. On 2 December 1866 he was promoted to lieutenant colonel and assigned to the Thirty-eighth U.S. Infantry, one of the four African-American infantry units authorized by Congress on 28 July 1866. His duty stations while assigned to the black unit were Jefferson Barracks, Missouri, and various posts in New Mexico. A reduction in the strength of the army from forty to twenty-five infantry regiments in the summer of 1869 left Grover without a line assignment, and he spent the next eighteen months as a staffer, on leave, and recruiting. During that time, in September 1869, his wife died.

On 20 Mar. 1871 Grover joined the Third U.S. Cavalry and served with it first in Arizona and then in Wyoming. He was acting assistant adjutant general for the Department of the Platte from 22 September 1874 to 6 March 1876. Promoted to colonel on 2 December 1876, he joined the First U.S. Cavalry, then stationed in Washington Territory. Grover, in addition to commanding the regiment, wore at various times a second hat as post commander of Fort Walla Walla (Dec. 1880-June 1884) and Fort Custer, Montana (June 1884-Mar. 1885). In 1875 he married again, to Ella Miller.

Suffering from "nervous prostration and a facial nervalgia" dating to his Civil War experience, Grover in the 1880s secured several lengthy sick leaves. He was on leave when he died suddenly from a hemorrhage of the lung at Atlantic City, where he had gone for treatment. He is buried at the U.S. Military Academy.

• For further information on Grover, see *Letters Received by the Commission Branch of the Adjutant General's Office*, National Archives, M-1064; U.S. Congress, Senate, *An Examination of the Reports and Explorations for Railroad Routes from the Mississippi to the Pacific*, 33d Cong., 2d sess., 1854–1855, S. Exec. Doc. 1, vol. 13; *The War of the Rebellion: A Compilation of the Official Records of the Union and Confederate Armies* (128 vols., 1880–1901); George W. Cullum, *Biographical Register of the Officers and Graduates of the U.S. Military Academy*, 3d ed., vol. 2 (1895); and Ezra J. Warner, *Generals in Blue: Lives of the Union Commanders* (1964). Obituaries are in the *Army and Navy Journal*, 13 June 1885, and the *New York Times*, 8 June 1885.

EDWIN C. BEARSS

GROVER, La Fayette (29 Nov. 1823–10 May 1911), lawyer, politician, and manufacturer, was born in Bethel, Maine, the son of John Grover, a surgeon, and Fanny Lary. He grew up among the Bethel elite; his father served in the Maine constitutional convention of 1819 and later in the state legislature. La Fayette received his early education in Bethel's common schools and the private Gould's Academy. After two years of study at Bowdoin College (1844–1846), he moved to Philadelphia, where he studied law in the office of Asa I. Fish and attended lectures at the Philadelphia Law Academy. He was admitted to the bar in 1850.

In the fall of that year Grover was persuaded to move to Oregon by congressional delegate Samuel Thurston, a fellow Maine native and Democratic boss of the new territory, who offered Grover a partnership in his law office. Grover accepted Thurston's proposal and made the six-month voyage from Philadelphia to Salem, Oregon. Thurston's unexpected death precluded the proposed law partnership, but in August 1851, a month after his arrival in Salem, Grover received his first political appointment as clerk of the U.S. district court and became prosecuting attorney a year later.

After recruiting and commanding companies of volunteers in the territorial militia campaigns against the Rogue River (1853) and Yakima (1855–1856) tribes, Grover was appointed federal claims auditor to investigate and repay the damages suffered by homesteaders in those conflicts. In 1853 and 1855 he served as a Democrat in the territorial legislature. In 1857 he was elected Marion County's delegate to the Oregon constitutional convention, where he drafted the state's bill of rights. After Oregon's admission to statehood in 1859, Grover was elected the state's first U.S. congressman, but he drew the short term and served only seventeen days. The takeover of the Oregon Democracy by a rival faction led by Joseph Lane prevented Grover's nomination for reelection.

Grover's political career was interrupted by the outbreak of the Civil War in 1861. During the Democrats'

wartime eclipse, Grover devoted himself to his private law practice and the Willamette Woolen Mills, the region's first major manufacturing enterprise, which he and several partners opened in 1857. In 1865 Grover married Elizabeth Carter; they had one child. Two years later Grover bought out his partners in the woolen mills and managed the business alone until he sold it in 1871.

In 1866 Grover became chairman of the state Democratic central committee. From 1866 to 1870 he oversaw the Democrats' return to power in Oregon, directing campaigns based on racist, anti-Chinese rhetoric. In 1870 he was elected Oregon's first Democratic governor since the Civil War. During his tenure as governor, from 1870 to 1877, he extended Democratic patronage and control over state politics by means of a series of public construction projects. He presided over the construction of the state house, agricultural college, and penitentiary. Grover funded institutional growth through sales of state lands. Careless surveys and fraudulent registration of those state lands during the 1870s and 1880s led to unprecedented cases of public malfeasance in the state, but those cases were not prosecuted or publicized until after the turn of the century.

Grover committed his most notorious act as governor by contributing to the dispute over the presidential election of 1876. In that election, Oregon was entitled to send three electors to the electoral college. The Republican ticket received a clear majority, but one of the three electors, John W. Watts, was a fourth-class deputy postmaster. Since the U.S. Constitution barred electors from holding other federal positions, Watts was ineligible to serve and resigned as postmaster. Following an Oregon state law that allowed electors to fill vacancies among their own number, Watts's two colleagues announced a vacancy and then promptly filled it with the newly eligible Watts.

Governor Grover refused to issue a certificate of election to the Republicans. Instead, Grover, acting on his authority to certify the election of all federal officials, issued a certificate of election to Democrat E. A. Cronin. According to Grover, a vacancy never existed among the Oregon electors since Watts had never been eligible. He therefore certified the three electors who had received the most votes, Watts's two Republican colleagues and the Democrat Cronin.

Accusations of bribery surfaced almost immediately but were never substantiated. The Senate Committee on Privileges and Elections discovered coded telegrams sent between Oregon Democrats and the national committee that alluded to the purchase of an elector, but apparently no money had actually changed hands. Had the Senate Elections Committee upheld Grover's certification of Cronin, Democratic candidate Samuel J. Tilden would have won the presidential election of 1876 by a margin of one vote in the electoral college. But the Committee rejected Grover's certification of Cronin and recognized Watts as the legitimate elector, as did the special Electoral Commission of 1877, and Republican Rutherford B. Hayes was elected president.

Despite the failure of Grover's attempt to influence the presidential election, his bid for a U.S. Senate seat in 1877 succeeded. He served one lackluster term that was marred by an investigation of his own election, to which Grover had to agree before he could be seated on 8 March 1877. After his Senate term expired in 1884, Grover retired from politics and focused on law and real estate development. He suffered severe business reversals late in life and died poor and obscure in Portland.

Grover's enemies called him corrupt or incompetent or both, and even his fellow Democrats sometimes found his actions hard to defend. But Grover was a hardline machine politician who valued loyalty above all. While many factors contributed to the compromise of 1877 and the end of Reconstruction, the disputed election of 1876 provided Democrats with the immediate political leverage they needed to force a Republican withdrawal from the South. Grover's small but crucial role in that election illustrated both the power of partisan solidarity and the importance of state-level officials in the federal polity of nineteenth-century America.

• Few of Grover's own writings survive; most of them are in the *Biennial Message[s] of Governor L. F. Grover* (1870, 1872, 1874, 1876). Grover published the legal reasoning behind his decision in the 1876 election dispute in *Executive Decision by the Governor of Oregon, in the Matter of Eligibility of Elector of President and Vice President of the United States, for 1876* (1876). His biography is in *History of the Pacific Northwest: Oregon and Washington* (1889) and H. K. Hines, *An Illustrated History of the State of Oregon* (1893). The latter reproduces almost verbatim a privately published biography, *Biographical Sketch of La Fayette Grover, of Oregon* (n.d.), which is also in the Oregon Collection at the University of Oregon's Knight Library. A brief biography is in William D. Fenton, "Political History of Oregon from 1865 to 1876," *Oregon Historical Quarterly* 2 (Dec. 1901): 343–44. For analyses of Grover's role in the disputed election of 1876, see Harold C. Dippre, "Corruption and the Disputed Election Vote of Oregon in the 1876 Election," *Oregon Historical Quarterly* 47 (Sept. 1966): 257–72; and Philip W. Kennedy, "Oregon and the Disputed Election of 1876," *Pacific Northwest Quarterly* 60 (July 1969): 135–44. Malcolm Clark, Jr., ed., *Pharisee among Philistines: The Diary of Judge Matthew P. Deady, 1871–1892* (1975), provides both a contemporary portrait of Grover from the perspective of fellow Democrat Deady and historian Clark's own assessment of controversies over Grover's election to the Senate and his participation in the election dispute of 1876. David Alan Johnson, *Founding the Far West: California, Oregon, and Nevada, 1840–1890* (1992), has insights into Grover's life, including his connection with Thurston and his significance as a Democratic machine politician in Oregon.

R. RUDY HIGGENS-EVENSON

GROVES, Leslie Richard, Jr. (17 Aug. 1896–13 July 1970), army officer and engineer, was born in Albany, New York, the son of Leslie R. Groves, Sr., a Presbyterian minister, and Gwen Griffith. When his father became an army chaplain, Groves accompanied him around various camps in the United States, Cuba, and the Philippines. In 1913 he enrolled for a year at the University of Washington and also completed two more years at the Massachusetts Institute of Technology before entering the U.S. Military Academy in 1916. Groves graduated fourth in his class in November 1918 and was commissioned a second lieutenant of engineers. He subsequently attended the Engineer School at Camp A. A. Humphreys (now Fort Belvoir, Va.) for an additional year of training before completing a three-month tour of occupation duty in France with the American Expeditionary Force immediately after World War I. By 1919 Groves was back at the Engineer School, where he completed several civil engineering courses and graduated in 1921. In 1922 he married Grace Wilson; they had two daughters.

For the next fifteen years Groves distinguished himself in a number of routine engineering assignments, including tours of duty in Hawaii (1921–1922), San Francisco (1922–1925), Texas (1925–1927), and Delaware (1927–1929). In October 1929 he was dispatched to Nicaragua to survey a proposed transoceanic canal, and his work garnered him the Medal of Merit from the Nicaraguan government. In 1931 he was assigned to the Office of Engineers in Washington, D.C., and rose to captain there in 1934. Ambitious for higher command, Groves graduated from the Command and General Staff College at Fort Leavenworth in 1936 and the Army War College in 1939. Between the two he also served as assistant to the divisional engineer in the Missouri River Engineering Division. By July 1940 Groves received promotion to temporary lieutenant colonel and was assigned to the War Department as chief of the Operations Branch, Corps of Engineers. In this capacity he directed construction of barracks, training camps, and munitions plants nationwide. By the onset of American entry into World War II, Groves was responsible for expending $6 million a month on military facilities of every description, including the newly designed Pentagon Building.

Groves accrued a reputation as a gruff and uncompromising problem solver who avoided army politics and focused on results. With the decline in domestic military construction in the spring of 1942, he sought and was tendered a combat assignment, but permission for him to transfer was inexplicably denied. Instead Lieutenant General Brehon Somervell informed Groves that he had been tapped by Secretary of War Henry L. Stimson and President Franklin D. Roosevelt to head up the top secret Manhattan Engineer District, the World War II atomic bomb project. Groves admitted to having little knowledge of nuclear physics, but his broad experience, no-nonsense managerial style, and ability to get results rendered him a natural choice. He assumed formal control on 7 September 1942 with the temporary rank of brigadier general.

Groves confronted the daunting task of unleashing the power of the atom with the primitive technology of the day. He was charged with making reality out of scientific theory, testing it, and fashioning a viable and potentially war-winning weapon. Underscoring this technological struggle was the moral imperative of acquiring nuclear weapons before Nazi Germany, which had its own atomic program. Fortunately, Groves could draw upon the scientific and intellectual largesse of the nation. At its height the Manhattan Project employed 600,000 workers and commanded a $2 billion budget. And while providing guidance, Groves was immeasurably assisted by a coterie of brilliant scientists, notably J. Robert Oppenheimer of the University of California, Berkeley. The two men, so different in training and temperament, forged a working relationship based on trust and mutual respect. Groves so thoroughly trusted Oppenheimer that he appointed him head of the Los Alamos, New Mexico, facility despite reports that focused on the scientist's youthful flirtation with left-wing politics. The lofty theorizing of one man and the hard-bitten practicality of the other facilitated America's nascent atomic bomb project.

Groves's immediate problem was to ensure that sufficient fissionable materials were available to build and test a bomb. Competing approaches devised at Columbia University, the University of Chicago, and the University of California consumed much time and money before being tested at nuclear facilities at Hanford, Washington, and Oak Ridge, Tennessee. Progress was sometimes deliberately hindered by Groves's insistence on total security. He restricted scientists to their bases, censored their mail, and forbade isolated project teams from communicating with each other. To minimize the potential for espionage Groves kept few written records and issued only oral reports to the chief of staff, secretary of war, and president. His steady progress culminated in promotion to temporary major general as of March 1944. By the spring of 1945, the project had amassed enough plutonium to create several weapons. When the first was detonated before an awed group of scientists at Alamogordo, New Mexico, on 16 July 1945, the atomic age had dawned.

In addition to promoting research and the design of nuclear weapons, Groves was closely involved with the high-level planning and policy making necessary for their deployment. Germany's surrender in May 1945 caused wavering in the scientific ranks, and many began questioning the bomb's continued relevance. Groves, however, pressed for a nuclear strike against Japan to end the war and save American lives. He proved instrumental in persuading President Harry S. Truman to proceed and also helped select the initial targets. On 6 August 1945 a 400-pound device nicknamed "Little Boy" demolished Hiroshima, a major military command center, killing 70,000 people. When Japan did not immediately surrender, a second weapon, "Fat Man," leveled Nagasaki four days later with an additional 45,000 casualties. On 14 August Japan unconditionally surrendered. What Groves had long considered a "2 billion dollar gamble" had paid decisive results.

After the war, Groves was retained as chief of the Armed Forces Special Weapons Project, a joint army-navy venture. Minor controversy ensued when, for security reasons, Groves opposed turning over nuclear research to the civilians in the Atomic Energy Commission in 1946. He also confidently predicted that the United States would sustain an atomic monopoly for fifteen to twenty years, a prognostication that was refuted when the Soviet Union successfully exploded an atomic device in 1949. Nevertheless, his work on the Mahattan Project earned him a Distinguished Service Medal and temporary promotion to lieutenant general in February 1948. Groves retired the following month, then served as vice president for research with the Remington Division of the Sperry Rand Corporation in Stamford, Connecticut. In 1961 he retired to Washington, D.C., where he died.

Groves's greatest contribution was in orchestrating, pacing, and facilitating one of the defining achievements of human science. By no means brilliant, his thirty years of military service revealed him to be a methodical, singularly determined individual with endless capacity for effective staff work. These qualities marked his tenure as head of the Manhattan Project. Brusque and demanding, Groves reveled in his unpopularity with the scientists but was a flexible problem solver willing to explore new avenues when deemed necessary. That such a complicated, far-reaching project came to fruition in only two and a half years is testimony to his management abilities. Unlike Oppenheimer and others who played key roles in the Manhattan Project, Groves never questioned the morality of his labors. He defended the project's value without remorse or reflection, fully convinced of the need to shorten the war and, in the long run, save lives.

• Groves's wartime diary is at the Modern Military Branch of the National Archives. Two related collections, "Manhattan Engineer District History" and "Manhattan Engineer District Records," are also deposited there. Other correspondence is at the Harry S. Truman Library, Independence, Mo., and the George C. Marshall Foundation Library, Lexington, Va. An account in his own words is Leslie R. Groves, *Now It Can Be Told* (1962). General overviews of the atomic project are Vincent C. Jones, *Manhattan: The Story of the Atomic Bomb* (1986); Richard Rhodes, *The Making of the Atomic Bomb* (1986); William Lawren, *The General and the Bomb* (1988); and Dan Kurzman, *Day of the Bomb* (1986). Firsthand accounts of the bomb drops are Charles W. Sweeney, *War's End: The Eyewitness Account of America's Last Atomic Mission* (1997), and Paul Tibbets, *The Tibbetts Story* (1978). For other various aspects of his work consult Roger M. Anders, "The President and the Atomic Bomb: Who Approved the Trinity Nuclear Test?" *Prologue*, no. 4 (1988): 268–82; Leslie R. Groves, "Some Recollections of July 16, 1945," *Bulletin of the Atomic Scientists* 26, no. 6 (1970): 21–27; Stanley Goldberg, "Racing to the Finish: The Decision to Bomb Hiroshima and Nagasaki," *Journal of American–East Asian Relations* 4, no. 2 (1995): 117–28; Allen C. Estes, "General Leslie Groves and the Atomic Bomb," *Military Review* 72, no. 8 (1991): 41–52; and Stanley Goldberg, "A Few Words about This Picture," *American Heritage of Invention and Technology* 7 (1991): 48–54. An obituary is in the *New York Times*, 15 July 1970.

JOHN C. FREDRIKSEN

GROW, Galusha Aaron (31 Aug. 1823–31 Mar. 1907), politician, was born in Ashford, Windham County, Connecticut, the son of Joseph Grow and Elizabeth Robbins, farmers. After Joseph Grow's death in 1827, the family temporarily scattered, and Grow went to live with his grandfather, Samuel Robbins, a hotel keeper. When he was nearly eleven, his mother purchased an old homestead of some 400 acres near Glenwood, Susquehanna County, Pennsylvania.

Elizabeth Grow was an overbearing, possessive mother who continued to make major decisions for the family long after her children had become adults. Her meddling may be the reason Grow never married; her standards for a suitable wife were just too high. Realizing that farming was insufficient to meet the family's needs, she opened a successful general store in her home and later added a lumber business. Grow and his brothers rafted boards to markets down the Susquehanna River and into Chesapeake Bay. During these early years, two things deeply impressed Grow and helped determine his political outlook: the inequitable land system, under which settlers grubbed out a living on marginal land while speculators prospered, and the evils of slavery that he witnessed on his trips to Maryland and Virginia.

When his mother insisted that he seriously pursue his studies, first at Franklin Academy (Susquehanna County) and then at Amherst, Grow obeyed. Although he had planned a career in law, he took his mother's advice and studied surveying as a practical alternative. As a college freshman he was ridiculed for his crude gestures and naiveté, indicative of the simple life in the Pennsylvania backcountry, but his remarkable skills as a debater soon won him respect and audiences. With increased self-confidence, he became an activist, with democracy, popular rights, and Jeffersonian idealism his favorite texts. Tired old systems, monopolies, and elitism were repugnant to him.

Upon his graduation from Amherst in 1844, Grow campaigned for the Democratic presidential candidate, James K. Polk. Afterward, he studied law with Chauncey Cleveland of Connecticut and later with R. B. Little and F. B. Streeter of Montrose, Pennsylvania. Neither his admission to the bar nor his partnership with David Wilmot, author of the famous proviso that would have excluded slavery from the territories acquired as a result of the Mexican War, kept him in law, however. Politics became his real passion. When opposition to Wilmot's bid for reelection to Congress in 1850 threatened to divide the Democrats, party leaders, at the insistence of Wilmot, selected Grow as a compromise candidate. Grow won the election on a free soil platform that promised to keep slavery out of the territories. He took his seat in the Thirty-second Congress as its youngest member.

In his first term, Grow pursued an independent course that met with the approval of a constituency that wanted to continue the radical tradition established by Wilmot. He ably supported Louis Kossuth, the Hungarian patriot who was attacked by opponents of intervention for asking for American aid to Hungary. Grow also defied the wishes of Democratic leaders by voting against the Compromise of 1850 as the "final" settlement, scolded his southern colleagues for accusing the North of deliberately violating the fugitive slave law, which he opposed, and defended the homestead bill by declaring man's natural right to the soil. Essentially the homestead bill offered free tracts of public land (160 acres) to bona fide settlers who would cultivate the land for a specific number of years.

Eventually Grow became the driving force in Congress behind the free-land measure. His own homestead bill remained before the House despite growing opposition from southerners, who believed that the bill was tainted by free soilism and abolitionism, and from nativists, who argued that the bill would open the door to increased immigration. Grow's bill was the most liberal. It extended benefits to any person twenty-one years or older, including foreigners who declared their intention to become citizens and to complete their naturalization during the required residence period of five years.

Once he was sure the Democratic party no longer spoke for free homesteads because it had fallen under the sway of southerners, Grow became a Republican. After passage of the Kansas-Nebraska Act in 1854, he helped organize the House Republicans. Newspaperman Horace Greeley called him a "young chevalier" who led the opposition for a free Kansas against the proslavery forces and the Democratic administration's policies in that territory. Grow's constant badgering of southerners triggered both a fistfight on the House floor with Lawrence Keitt of South Carolina and a challenge to a duel by Lawrence Branch of North Carolina.

His combativeness and leadership role among the radical Republicans enabled Grow to become Speaker of the House after the party's successes in 1860. His defiant attitude did not mellow. He warned that no foot of American soil would be sacrificed to the secessionists until it was first "baptized in fire and blood." The southern conspiracy against the Constitution had to be totally destroyed, he insisted. For many years afterward, he clung to the conspiracy theory and remained one of the last Republicans to abandon "bloody shirt" politics of recriminations against the Democrats and the South.

Political redistricting caused Grow's defeat for reelection in 1862. A heavily populated and Democratic county of Luzerne had been joined to Susquehanna to make up the new Twelfth Congressional District. Luzerne Democrats cried foul and charged Republicans with gerrymandering to consolidate their power and to "abolitionize" Luzerne. No doubt Grow's unyielding position on the South and his accommodating attitude toward emancipation helped upend him with moderate Republicans as well. Before he left office, he was pleased to see a version of his homestead bill become law.

For the next thirty years Grow fought machine politics in Pennsylvania as dictated by the powerful bosses Simon Cameron, Don Cameron, and Matthew Quay, none of whom liked Grow. He rejected their kind of party organization and discipline and believed in a more direct and honest approach to the voter. Because he disliked the Cameron dynasty, Grow supported the Liberal Republican bolt in 1872 and created his own in 1881, when he decided to run for the U.S. Senate.

His nonconformity thus denied him the opportunity to attain high office. The Camerons denied him the chance to become either senator or governor. He did participate as a delegate to several Republican National Conventions and in 1868 served as chairman of the state committee, but these assignments were simply small concessions to the pro-Grow forces. He refused a diplomatic appointment because it was nonelective.

Aside from politics, Grow invested in oil, coal, and railroad interests. In December 1865, for example, he helped organize the Reno Oil and Land Company and became its first president. This company purchased 1,200 acres on the Allegheny River above Oil City and proceeded to drill wells and lay out the town of Reno. It must have been strange for most people to see Grow in the unlikely role of speculator, but he only wanted a piece of America's economic dream. In the early 1870s he became president of the Houston and Great Northern Railway in Texas.

When he was no longer a threat to the party bosses, Grow was elected Pennsylvania's congressman-at-large in 1894 and was reelected four times. His unprecedented pluralities affirmed his popularity with the general voter. Now in his seventies, he became his party's grand old sage, a consistent defender of its policies and a leader who inspired younger men.

Upon his retirement in 1903, Grow fell on hard times. A scandal and subsequent blackmail tarnished his reputation and drained his life's savings. Many years earlier, Grow had befriended a woman and her adopted daughter. He lavishly gave the daughter money and jewelry and provided for some of her education. His generosity only led to swindle. Not knowing who her father was, the daughter later accused Grow of being her parent. She and her husband threatened to expose him and file charges unless paid. Distraught, ill, and confused, Grow wanted to avoid going to court and agreed to pay the extortionists a considerable sum of money. His friends later appealed to Andrew Carnegie for financial assistance, and the Pittsburgh industrialist agreed to contribute several thousand dollars in Grow's behalf.

Those who mourned Grow's tragedy remembered him for the Homestead Act, his stand against southern militancy, the struggle for a free Kansas, and his conscientious resistance to bossism. Grow died at his home in Glenwood.

• A few of Grow's remaining papers are in the Susquehanna County Historical Society, Montrose, Pa. Grow's addresses in Congress are in the *Congressional Globe*, 32d–37th Cong.,
and the *Congressional Record*, 53d–57th Cong. James T. DuBois and Gertrude S. Mathews, *Galusha A. Grow, Father of the Homestead Act* (1917), is a favorable treatment of his early life and career but ignores most of the post–Civil War period. The most complete political biography is Robert D. Ilisevich, *Galusha A. Grow, the People's Candidate* (1988). Also helpful are Edwin Maxey, "Galusha A. Grow, Father of the Homestead Bill," *Overland Monthly* 52 (1908): 75; Hubert B. Fuller, *The Speakers of the House* (1909); and Charles B. Going, *David Wilmot, Free-Soiler: A Biography of the Great Advocate of the Wilmot Proviso* (1924). Interesting autobiographical information is included in Rufus R. Wilson, "Personal Recollections of Honorable Galusha A. Grow," *Saturday Evening Post*, 19 Jan. 1901, pp. 2–3, and 2 Mar. 1901, pp. 4–5.

ROBERT D. ILISEVICH

GRUBE, Bernhard Adam (24 June 1715–20 Mar. 1808), Moravian missionary, was born in Walschleben near Erfurt, Thuringia, a German state. His parents' names are unknown. He studied at the University of Jena and became a minister in the Renewed Moravian church in 1740. Before immigrating to North America, he was pastor of Moravian congregations in the Netherlands and also taught at a seminary in Lindheim.

Arriving in the Moravian center at Bethlehem, Pennsylvania, in 1748, Grube served there as a teacher until 1752. In that year he began missionary work among the Indians in Monroe County; after studying the Delaware (Lenape) language for six months, he was transferred to Shamokin, visiting from that base Indian villages in the Susquehanna and Wyoming valleys.

In 1753 Grube led a group of twelve male Moravians to the Wachovia tract of North Carolina to establish the colony of Bethabara (a Hebrew word meaning house of passage), the first in an area that was to become the center of the southern Moravian region. Upon their arrival they sang a hymn of praise that he had composed. Grube was described in this context as "a German by birth, aged 37 years, *Ordinarius* [elder], *Pfleger* [pastor], and upon occasion, cook and gardener" (Fries, vol. 1, p. 73). In addition, he kept the detailed diary of the arduous daily tasks of founding a pioneer colony. Grube's name loomed large in the early annals of the North Carolina Moravian colony until he was recalled to Bethlehem, leaving in April 1754. He was not forgotten by the Carolinians in later years, as evidenced by repeated mention in the church diaries of the Moravians in Wachovia.

In 1754 Grube took up mission work at the Gnadenhütten station located at the confluence of the Mahoning and Lycoming rivers in Pennsylvania. When the Indian colony he led was attacked in November 1755 by other tribes, Grube and the other survivors retreated to Bethlehem where they remained for two years. Between 1758 and 1760 he led the Moravian mission in Litchfield County, Connecticut, then returned once more to mission work in Monroe County, Pennsylvania.

In the course of the Pontiac War in 1763 the mission outpost was again threatened, this time predominantly by belligerent white settlers, who chose in their fury to make no distinction between hostile Indians and peace-loving Moravian converts. Grube and the Indians abandoned their dwellings and retreated to Moravian centers at Nazareth and Bethlehem. They were soon ordered by the governor of Pennsylvania to move for their own safety to Philadelphia, where they were threatened by an angry band of Scotch-Irish militants known as the "Paxton Boys," who marched on the city vowing to kill all natives and anyone who would attempt to defend them.

From 1765 to 1785 Grube served as pastor of several Moravian congregations in New Jersey and Pennsylvania, including one in Lititz, Lancaster County, Pennsylvania. He attained an advanced age, spending the last years of his life in Bethlehem, where he died. When news of his death reached the Bethabara colony, their pastor announced "the calling home of our old Br. Bernhard Adam Grube, in Bethlehem, he being nearly ninety-three years old." Colonists in North Carolina took special interest in the news, "because he was one of the pioneers in the settlement of the Brethren in Wachovia, the first pastor, and he was always deeply interested in the welfare of the Wachovia congregation" (Fries, vol. 6, p. 2917).

Grube was a scholarly man who studied the Indian languages and manner of life. He mastered the Delaware (Lenape) language, in which he conducted all of his religious services for Indians after 1760. He compiled a hymnal, *Dellawaerisches Gesang-Büchlein: Wenn ich des Morgens früh aufsteh etc.* (1763), consisting of translations of Moravian German hymns into Delaware, preserving German captions. As a teacher of Indian boys, Grube emphasized music, teaching both German and Indian hymns. He also published a harmony of the Gospels, *Evangelien-Harmonie in die Delaware Sprache Uebersetzt* (1763). After the 1776 death of his first wife, Elizabeth Busse, whom he had married in 1755 and with whom he had a daughter, he married again in 1778, to Sarah Eberhardt. They had no children, and she died in 1793. Grube is considered one of the patriarchs of the Moravian church in North America.

• The standard Moravian history, J. Taylor Hamilton and Kenneth G. Hamilton, *History of the Moravian Church: The Renewed Unitas Fratrum, 1722–1957* (1967), provides both background and some detail for Grube's life and work in America; see also Allen W. Schattschneider, *Through Five Hundred Years: A Popular History of the Moravian Church* (1956). Helpful biographical information is found in John W. Jordan, "Biographical Sketch of Bernhard Adam Grube," *Pennsylvania Magazine of History and Biography* 25 (1901): 14–19. Grube's early pioneer efforts in Wachovia are also documented in Adelaide L. Fries, ed., *Records of the Moravians in North Carolina*, vols. 1–7 (repr. 1968–1970); see also John T. Spach, "The Long, Muddy Road to Middle Creek," in *The Three Forks of Muddy Creek*, ed. Frances Griffin, vol. 3 (1976), pp. 1–10, and Paul Larson, "Mahican and Lenape Moravians and Moravian Music," *Unitas Fratrum* 21/22 (1987): 173–87. For information about his books see K. J. R. Arndt and Reimer C. Eck, eds., *The First Century of German Language Printing in the United States of America . . .* , vol. 1:

1728–1807 (1989), and Charles R. Hildeburn, *A Century of Printing: The Issues of the Press in Pennsylvania, 1685–1784* (1885).

DONALD F. DURNBAUGH

GRUEBY, William Henry (10 Feb. 1867–23 Feb. 1925), ceramist, was born in Chelsea, Massachusetts, the son of Samuel A. Grueby, a spar maker, and Elizabeth W. Rich. Grueby attended public school until he was thirteen. In the Chelsea school system Grueby received practical training in drawing and design through the first state-mandated art curriculum introduced in the United States. After working for a Boston decorating firm and the J. and J. G. Low Art Tile Works in Chelsea, Grueby founded an architectural ceramics company in 1890. He and his partner, Eugene Atwood, produced faience—glazed terra cotta—for interior and exterior decoration at the South Boston plant of the Boston Terra Cotta Company. Atwood and Grueby dissolved their partnership around 1893, each man establishing his own faience company. Atwood Faience Company operated in Hartford, Connecticut, until 1899, when new owners changed the name to the Hartford Faience Company. Grueby Faience remained in South Boston.

By 1897, when Grueby Faience Company incorporated, the company was best known for architectural ceramics—altars, plaques, and wall treatments—based on historic models, especially Italian Renaissance masters. Grueby's partners were George Prentiss Kendrick, a designer of books and metalwork, and William Hagerman Graves, a wealthy, well-educated young man with connections to the Boston architectural community. With Graves as the business manager, Kendrick as designer, and Grueby providing glaze expertise, the company began to experiment with art pottery and developed a distinctive combination of hand-crafted vases with matte glazes, particularly matte greens.

In June 1899 Grueby married Lucy Frost Tent, also of Chelsea, and from 1900 to 1921 they lived in the fashionable Ashmont section of Dorchester, outside Boston. They had no children.

The Grueby Faience Company, and later its subsidiary, Grueby Pottery Company (inc. 1907), was soon recognized as a major force in the reform efforts of the American Arts and Crafts movement. Rejecting the glossy coldness of machine-made pottery, Grueby's workshop emphasized individualistic hand-thrown and hand-decorated ceramics. As early as 1898 one Boston critic noted, "The Grueby pottery has an individuality that gives it a distinctive position in this art, both in its glazes, which vary from the rich and brilliant in character to those with soft, dull blooms, and in its beauty of design, wherein every line is indicative of natural forms of floral life" (C. H. Blackall, *Brickbuilder*, Dec. 1898, p. 266). By 1902 Addison Le Boutillier, a multitalented architect, graphic artist, illustrator, and jewelry designer, replaced Kendrick as designer and created a successful line of Arts and

Crafts tiles, applying Grueby's classic matte glazes to animal, flower, and landscape designs.

The company was awarded medals for pottery at world's fairs in Paris (1900), Buffalo (1901), Turin (1902 and 1904), and St. Louis (1904). Grueby was particularly influenced by French potters who were also rejecting overdecorated, poorly designed ceramics in favor of simple forms and complex glazes. This impulse to reform, to return to nature, and to avoid excessive historical references is best typified by Siegfried Bing, who represented European and American artists, including Grueby, in his Parisian L'Art Nouveau gallery.

In the United States, Grueby and his partners were active in the Society of Arts and Crafts, Boston (SACB), founded in 1897 as the first American organization devoted to reviving handcraftsmanship and restrained design. The SACB sponsored juried exhibitions and traveling shows of members' work, opened retail showrooms, and facilitated working relationships among architects, designers, and craftsmen. Other art societies, museums, commercial galleries, and department stores displayed and sold Grueby's work across the country. Nationally prominent architects such as Greene and Greene; Andrews, Jacques and Rantoul; Heins and Lafarge; and Price and McLanahan specified Grueby tiles in domestic, commercial, and ecclesiastical commissions, including the New York City subway and the Cathedral of St. John the Divine.

Grueby's combination of rich color, matte texture, organic form, and hand-modeled leaves, buds, and flowers epitomized the Arts and Crafts ideals of decoration unified with form and harmony between form and function. To critics, the pottery was natural and honest in its design and manufacture. In 1901 exhibition reviewer Theodore Hanford Pond wrote:

There is a great deal of good pottery shown—pottery honestly made and useful as well as beautiful to the eye—and certainly the work of the Grueby Faience of Boston takes front rank in this department. Perhaps more than any other exhibit, this pottery expresses the spirit of the new idea in artistic handicraft. Aside from its simplicity of design, the beauty of its decorations, evidently inspired by direct contact with nature, and the richness of its coloring, it is essentially pottery, and could never be mistaken for anything else. ("The Arts and Crafts Exhibition at the Providence Art Club," *House Beautiful*, July 1901, p. 98)

Simplicity, handcraftsmanship, and rich glazes were extremely costly to produce. Grueby vases commonly sold for $10 to $50. Very fine examples were often priced at $100. Competitors took advantage of Grueby's popularity by imitating his matte green glaze on cheaper cast forms, sold at a fraction of Grueby's prices. Competition, combined with technical difficulties and financial instability brought on by high production costs, forced Grueby into receivership in 1909. Company assets were liquidated over the next four years to pay off creditors. Seven months after receivership proceedings began, however, Grueby Faience and Tile Company was incorporated to produce the architectural lines. Grueby never made art pottery again, unwilling to compromise his standards of craftsmanship to efficient production.

The company weathered a disastrous fire in 1913 and in 1919 was sold to a larger tile manufacturer, C. Pardee Company of Perth Amboy, New Jersey. In a lucrative deal, Grueby signed over his designs to Pardee, which kept them in production for several years. Grueby was made manager of Pardee's Faience Division and in 1921, when the South Boston plant closed, he moved to the Pardee offices in Manhattan. He worked for Pardee, in semiretirement, until his death in New York City.

Grueby's professional affiliations included Boston's prestigious St. Botolph Club from 1905 to at least 1919 and the Salmagundi Club in New York. He was an active member of the SACB from 1899 to 1924. In addition to being an exhibitor, he was a council member from 1904 to 1910 and in 1907 was awarded the society's highest honor for lifetime achievement, the Hors de Concours medal.

After a fifty-year hiatus, interest in Grueby's work was revived by the 1972 Princeton exhibition The Arts and Crafts Movement in America, 1876–1916. Editor Robert Judson Clark wrote in the accompanying catalog, "A major change in American pottery around the turn of the century was the introduction of mat [*sic*] glazes, and the person most responsible for this was William H. Grueby." Today Grueby pottery is still considered some of the finest work of its time and is highly sought after by museums and private collectors. Individual pieces have brought record high prices of nearly $50,000 at auction.

• The Addison B. Le Boutillier Archives at the Andover (Mass.) Historical Society contain original drawings, source material, and printed materials that relate to Grueby's role at the Grueby Faience Company. The records of the SACB at the Boston Public Library include exhibition catalogs and photographs that document Grueby's involvement with the society. Most of the finest examples of Grueby pottery and tiles have been acquired by private collectors. Public collections include the Newark Museum, the Metropolitan Museum of Art, the Everson Museum of Art in Syracuse, the National Museum of American History at the Smithsonian Institution, and the Museum of Fine Arts, Boston. Contemporary articles and exhibition reviews provide evaluations of Grueby's work by his peers but frequently contain factual errors. The most useful include C. H. Blackall, "The Grueby Faience," *Brickbuilder*, Aug. 1898; W. G. Bowdoin, "The Grueby Pottery," *Art Interchange*, Dec. 1900; Mary Chase Perry, "Grueby Potteries," *Keramic Studio*, Apr. 1901; "Boston's Art Product: Grueby Ware," *Crockery and Glass Journal*, 12 Dec. 1902; Annie M. Jones, ed., "The Grueby Pottery," *Scrip*, Mar. 1906; and Henry W. Belknap, "Another American Pottery," *Pottery and Glass*, Nov. 1908. A history of Grueby's pottery and tiles and his place in the international decorative arts reform movement is the subject of Susan J. Montgomery, *The Ceramics of William H. Grueby: The Spirit of the New Idea in Artistic Handicraft* (1993). In 1994 the

Hood Museum of Art mounted an important exhibition, Grueby Pottery: A New England Arts and Crafts Venture, with an accompanying catalog.

SUSAN J. MONTGOMERY

GRUEN, Victor David (18 July 1903–14 Feb. 1980), architect and planner, was born Viktor David Grünbaum in Vienna, Austria, the son of Adolph Grünbaum, an attorney, and Elizabeth Lea Levy. Reared in privileged surroundings, he assimilated at an early age the elegant and cosmopolitan cultural life of Vienna. He circulated among the actors, writers, and musicians of Vienna's flourishing theatrical world and with his family frequently traveled throughout central Europe.

Gruen's family lost its wealth after World War I, when Gruen's father died, and Gruen left school. With assistance from a court-appointed guardian, however, he enrolled in the State Vocational School for Building in 1918 and graduated in 1923. As a student he also worked for the architectural firm of Melcher & Steiner. He subsequently entered the Master School for Architecture at the Vienna Academy of Fine Arts and graduated in 1925. At the Master School, he studied under Peter Behrens, whose theories about town planning and housing inclined Gruen toward a lifelong fascination with urban environments.

In the late 1920s Gruen also met Adolph Loos, who had retired to Vienna. He admired Loos's "clear thinking and his attacking spirit." The example of an architect agitating public opinion through writing, speaking, and "fighting" excited him, and beginning in the 1920s he distinguished himself as a writer as well as an architect.

In 1926 Gruen was instrumental in creating a political cabaret in Vienna that promoted his socialist views. He wrote, directed, and acted in these iconoclastic theatrical productions until their suppression in 1934. In 1930 Gruen married Alice Kardos. Two years later, he opened his own architectural practice in Vienna. Although he received several commissions to design residential and commercial buildings, he concentrated on designing furniture, shopfronts, and interiors of apartments.

Following the 1938 *Anschluss*, he lost his architectural practice. In June 1938, under threat of arrest, he obtained a visa to the United States and fled to New York City. Despite his inability to speak English, he found work in the New York office of the stage and industrial designer Norman Bel Geddes. Energetic and enterprising, he was a principal organizer in New York of a theatrical company of exiled actors, writers, and musicians from Vienna. He rapidly broadened his contacts among exiled artists from Austria, Germany, and Hungary and relied on this core of emigrés to facilitate his entrance into architectural circles in New York.

Working on exhibitions for the 1939 World's Fair, he met Morris Ketchum, Jr., an architect, and Elsie Krummeck, a designer. Gruen subsequently collaborated with Ketchum on designs for two retail shops in Manhattan, Lederer de Paris (commissioned by a refuge from Hungary) and Ed Steckler. Widely publicized in architectural journals and praised for their "brilliantly imaginative" design, these shops conferred nationwide attention on both Gruen and Ketchum.

In 1939 Gruen also formed a partnership with Krummeck. Their firm, Grünbaum and Krummeck, specialized in merchandising and furniture design and introduced the flamboyancy and high-style modernism of Gruen's work in Vienna to chain stores across the country. A palette of warm colors, mirrored ceilings, multilevel window display cases, Carrara glass, undulating walls, corrugated surfaces, and neon signs typified their work.

In 1941, after Gruen divorced his first wife, he and Krummeck were married, and they opened an office in Hollywood. Gruen also renewed his career as an author and sought through his writing to promote his architectural practice. In 1943, when he was naturalized as a citizen and shortened his surname to Gruen, he published an innovative proposal to reconfigure downtown shopping districts by isolating pedestrians from traffic. In that year Gruen also recruited Rudolph Baumfeld, a classmate and fellow emigré from Vienna, to join his firm as the principal architectural designer, a position he held for four decades.

In his designs for the Milliron's Store (1949, Los Angeles; now Macy's), he realized his scheme for the "department store of tomorrow" by circulating shoppers through a series of ramps and escalators and directing traffic to rooftop parking. Widely publicized, the Milliron's project signified a new phase in his career and positioned him, along with Welton Becket, John Gardner, and Ketchum, Sharp & Ginà, as a leading designer of freestanding shopping complexes in suburban settings.

In 1949, a year after being honored as a fellow of the American Institute of Architects, Gruen boldly approached the owners of J. L. Hudson Company in Detroit with a proposal to develop a giant suburban shopping center. Intrigued, the company commissioned Gruen (with his associate Karl O. Van Leuven, Jr.) in 1952 to design a shopping center, the Northland Center (1954), outside Detroit. With eighty stores and 1.1 million square feet of colonnaded buildings, it was, when built, the largest and most successful shopping complex in the world. Surrounded by an enormous expanse of parking, the shopping center featured open-air pedestrian malls and courtyards enlivened with plantings, sculptures, fountains, and a public auditorium. Gruen pioneered the introduction of these amenities into suburban shopping complexes, which he envisioned as entertainment and cultural centers and twentieth-century adaptations of medieval European market towns.

In 1951, after divorcing Krummeck and marrying Lazette McCormick Van Houten, an interior design journalist (who died in 1962), he reorganized his practice as Victor Gruen Associates. By the mid-1950s, following enormous public and professional acclaim for

Northland and the multistoried Southdale Center (1954–1956) outside Minneapolis, the first fully enclosed, climate-controlled shopping complex, his firm became synonymous with regional shopping centers across the country. Beginning in 1954, with an essay in *Harvard Business Review*, Gruen applied his device of traffic-free suburban marketplaces to commercial districts of aging inner cities. To cities then embarking on urban renewal projects, he proposed "shock therapy" to "redeem" streets from automobiles and to restore human activity, which, he contended, had become servile to the "autoscape" and the "disease of urban sprawl."

In plans developed for Fort Worth (1956, unexecuted) and, subsequently, for Kalamazoo (1958), Rochester (1962, Midtown Plaza), Cincinnati (1962), and Fresno (1964), Gruen designed a network of "super blocks" where traffic was banished to perimeter highways and downtown streets, serviced by shuttle buses. These "superblocks" became landscaped, traffic-free corridors of meandering walkways, public art, fountains, and benches. His ambitious 300-acre "revitalization plan" for Fort Worth, lauded as the "most mature American response to date to the crisis of the central city" (James Marston Fitch, *Architecture and the Esthetics of Plenty* [1961], p. 225), and his equally far-reaching plan for Welfare Island (New York City, 1961) were his most influential contributions to theories about the spatial organization of cities.

Gruen's thoughts about urban "scatterization" and the tyranny of automobile preoccupied his work for the duration of his career. He tirelessly promoted his ideas in publications and in speeches and emerged by the mid-1950s in the forefront of international commentators on urban planning. His celebrity as a planner, architect, and author led to numerous commissions for large-scale developments, such as Palos Verdes Peninsula (Calif., 1956), Charles River Park (Boston, 1957), Government Center in Boston (1966), and the new city of Valencia, California (1965). In the 1960s Gruen Associates also became one of the largest and most influential architectural and planning firms in the United States.

In 1968 Gruen moved to Vienna, where in 1963 he had opened an international branch of his firm. His affection for Vienna, a place that had remained "magical" to him, guided his return to the city of his origins, despite the absence of 95 percent of its prewar Jewish population. In 1971 he began the two major projects of his retirement years in Austria: a new campus for the University of Louvain (Belgium) and a comprehensive plan, partially executed, for the historic center city of Vienna. In 1972 he received a Significant Artistic Achievement Award from the city of Vienna. Toward the end of his career Gruen acknowledged the incongruity between his advocacy of traffic-free cities and his contributions to the growth of suburban shopping centers across the country. He asserted, though, that concentrically organized cities, largely based on the historical plan of Vienna, could efficiently isolate pedestrians from traffic and serve as international models

for city planning in the future. Two children from his second wife and his fourth wife, Kemija Salihefendic, whom he married in 1963, survived him when he died in Vienna. He was remembered as a "busy and restless man," the "Father of the Downtown Pedestrian Mall," and, by his own description, an "environmental planner." Through his writings and his participation in the design of more than 1,000 projects, he was a major presence in American and international architecture for almost forty years.

• The leading archival sources for information on Gruen include the Victor Gruen Collection at the American Heritage Center of the University of Wyoming (Laramie) and additional collections at Pepperdine University and the Library of Congress (which published a register of its collection on Gruen in 1995). See also Gruen's article, "Dynamic Planning for Retail Areas," *Harvard Business Review* 32 (Nov.–Dec. 1954): 53–62, and his influential publication (coauthored with Larry Smith), *Shopping Towns U.S.A.* (1960). Biographical sources include Walter J. Guzzardi, Jr., "An Architect of Environments," *Fortune* 65 (1962): 77–80; and portions of Gruen's most widely read book, *The Heart of Our Cities: The Urban Crisis* (1964). Leading sources of information on his theories about architecture and planning include John Peter, *The Oral History of Modern Architecture* (1994), and the most scholarly study of Gruen, David R. Hill, "Sustainability, Victor Gruen, and the Cellular Metropolis," *Journal of the American Planning Association* 58 (Summer 1992): 312–26. A major listing of Gruen's extensive writings—and a partial listing of secondary sources on him—is Robert B. Harmon, *Victor Gruen, Architectural Pioneer of Shopping Centers: A Selected Bibliography* (1980); it, however, omits some of his works from the 1940s (e.g., "Shopping Center," *Architectural Forum* 78 [May 1943]: 101–3) and some of his writings published in Europe during the 1970s (a phase of his life that has been inadequately studied). A decisive event in his career, the commission to design his first suburban shopping center, is recounted in "Northland's Client," *Architectural Forum* 100 (June 1954): 117. An informative analysis of Gruen's career and his collaboration with Rudolph Baumfeld, with a detailed bibliography, is Otto Kapfinger, "Victor Gruen und Rudi Baumfeld, Traumkarriere einer Partnerschaft," in *Visionäre & Vertriebene, Österreichische Spuren in der modernen amerikanischen Architektur*, ed. Matthias Boeckl (1995). An obituary is in the *New York Times*, 16 Feb. 1980.

JEFFREY CRONIN

GRUENBERG, Louis (3 Aug. 1884–10 June 1964), composer, was born near Brest-Litovsk, Belorussia, the son of Abraham Gruenberg and Clara (maiden name unknown). His parents brought him to the United States when he was age two. Encouraged to take up music by his father, a violinist at the Yiddish theater in New York City, Gruenberg became a child prodigy on the piano. He left school at fifteen and worked as a peripatetic musician to help his mother pay for the upkeep of his six siblings, his father being frequently absent from home. At age nineteen Gruenberg traveled to Berlin to study piano and composition with Ferruccio Busoni. He made his professional debut as a pianist with the Berlin Philharmonic under Busoni's direction in 1912. In the same year he was appointed to teach at the Vienna Conservatory. His first two important works were an operetta, *The Witch of Brocken* (1912), and an opera, *The Bride of the Gods* (1913). Gruenberg developed a close pupil-teacher relationship with Busoni, performed with Arnold Schoenberg and Anton von Webern in Vienna, toured as an accompanist, and taught private students. But his finances were in dire straits, and at the outbreak of World War I he returned penniless to the United States.

Gruenberg was the accompanist for Caruso's final American concert tour. Thereafter he devoted himself entirely to composition. His first major success as a composer came with an orchestral symphonic poem, *The Hill of Dreams* (1920), which won the prestigious Flagler Prize. In the 1920s he drew much on sounds and techniques derived from jazz and popular music in his compositions, believing that jazz was "the musical expression of black, red and white people—'the American race.'" In 1926 he published a set of harmonized black spirituals. Among other pieces influenced by the jazz idiom were the *Jazz Suite* (1925), for orchestra; *Jazzettes* (1926), for violin and piano; and *The Daniel Jazz* (1924), a chamber vocal work based on a poem by Vachel Lindsay. These works are generally considered more distinctive and full of character than some of his larger works, such as the First Symphony (awarded the RCA Victor Prize in 1930). In 1930 he married Irma Pickova, a medical doctor from Prague; they had one daughter.

Gruenberg was a leading participant in the American Music Guild and the League of Composers. As president of the United States section of the International Society for Contemporary Music from 1928 to 1932, he advocated universality in music and internationalism in art. His greatest dramatic success came with the Metropolitan Opera production of his expressionist music drama *The Emperor Jones* (1933), with the baritone Lawrence Tibbett in the title role. This powerful work, based on Eugene O'Neill's play, had eleven performances in its first two seasons and was awarded the David Bispham medal. It was revived by the Chicago Opera Company in 1946, by the Rome Opera in 1950, and by the Michigan Opera Company in 1979. In 1937 Gruenberg's *Green Mansions*, a nonvisual radio opera, received its first performance on the CBS network.

From 1933 until 1936, Gruenberg was the head of the composition department at the Chicago Musical College. But teaching drained his creativity and energy, so he moved to Santa Monica, California, where he wrote several film scores. *The Fight for Life* (1940), a damning portrait of childbirth in the Chicago slums, won much attention and an Academy Award, as did *So Ends Our Night* (1941) and *Commandos Strike at Dawn* (1942). In 1944 Gruenberg wrote a Violin Concerto for Jascha Heifetz. This led to a celebrated recording of the work by Heifetz and the San Francisco Symphony Orchestra under Pierre Monteux.

Gruenberg was active in several societies promoting modern music and was elected to the National Institute of Arts and Letters in 1947. By that time he had stopped writing music for the movies and had settled into a solitary, withdrawn life of composition. In the 1950s he wrote the operas *Antony and Cleopatra* and *The Delicate King* (both in 1955) and the *Harlem Rhapsody* (1953) for orchestra. *Americana*, his symphonic pastiche of American tunes, received its first performance in Cleveland in 1956. One of his last major works was an oratorio, *A Song of Faith* (1959), dedicated to Mahatma Gandhi. He composed until his death in Beverly Hills, California.

Gruenberg wrote in many different musical genres—operas, operettas, chamber music, orchestral music, ballets, pantomimes, film scores, and incidental music. His music is an eclectic attempt to synthesize the styles and strains of Americana. His jazz-inspired pieces of the 1920s have elements of dissonance, atonality, and bitonality and also reflect his interest in spirituals. *The Emperor Jones* includes much declamation and plain speech and has a persistent percussive nature. The Violin Concerto has a romantic vein and includes country tunes and barn dances as well as strains from spirituals. As his career progressed, Gruenberg tried to find an ever larger audience for music. Unfortunately, he became increasingly isolated from the concert world in the last two decades of his life. These were years of significant creative achievement but also of frustration. Gruenberg was bitter about his failure to get many of his works performed and railed against the neglect of his own compositions and those written by other contemporary American composers. He became increasingly forgotten by performers and audiences, but some of his extensive range of compositions will no doubt be revived in the future.

• Gruenberg's manuscripts and papers are maintained at the New York Public Library. Manuscript scores, journals, speeches, and other materials by Gruenberg are at the George Arents Research Library for Special Collections, Syracuse University. His major works are listed in Carleton Sprague Smith, "Louis Gruenberg," in *The New Grove Dictionary of American Music*, vol. 2, ed. H. Wiley Hitchcock and Stanley Sadie (1986). Insight into Gruenberg's views on music can be found in his article "For an American Gesture," *League of Composers Journal* 1, no. 2 (1924): 27. An early appraisal of Gruenberg's music is Walter Kramer, "American Composers, III, Louis Gruenberg," *Modern Music* 8, no. 1 (Nov.–Dec. 1930): 3. Three modern studies by Robert F. Nisbett provide detailed analysis: "Louis Gruenberg: A Forgotten Figure of American Music," *Current Musicology*, no. 18 (1974): 90–95; "Louis Gruenberg: His Life and Work" (Ph.D. diss., Ohio State Univ., 1979); and "Louis Gruenberg's American Idiom," *American Music* 3, no. 1 (1985): 25–41. For a helpful overview of Gruenberg's career, see David Noble, "Louis Gruenberg," sleeve notes to *The Music of Louis Gruenberg* (GM Recordings, GM2015CD). Details about the premieres of several works by Gruenberg are given in Nicolas Slonimsky, *Music Since 1900*, 4th ed. (1971). An obituary and a tribute to his music are respectively in the *New York Times*, 11 June 1964 and 5 July 1964.

KENNETH MORGAN

GRUENBERG, Sidonie Matsner (10 June 1881–11 Mar. 1974), educator of parents, writer, and authority on children, was born near Vienna, Austria, the daughter of Idore Matzner, a failed merchant, and Augusta Olivia Besseches, who later was the U.S. partner in a rubber-importing company. In 1888 Sidonie and her family moved to Philadelphia but returned to Austria within a year, only to have her father leave again for the United States in 1893. Sidonie and her mother and siblings joined him in New York City in 1895 after spending a year and a half in Hamburg, Germany, where she attended the Höhere Töchterschule. After a few months of public school in Manhattan, Sidonie in early 1896 entered the Society for Ethical Culture's Workingman's School and gave the valedictory speech when she graduated from its eighth grade in 1897. Because a stroke had partially paralyzed her father, she took a secretarial job to help her family financially. In 1903 she married Benjamin Charles Gruenberg, a young chemist who the year before began teaching biology at DeWitt Clinton High School; they had four children. Their marriage was a true partnership, providing them both the stimulus for growth and the opportunity to collaborate as writers and experts in the field of child study.

In 1904 Gruenberg began a two-year normal course at the Society for Ethical Culture, and in 1906 she started advanced courses at Teachers College, Columbia University. During the first year of her marriage, she had become acquainted with the Society for the Study of Child Nature (a federation of semiautonomous parent groups, which was founded in 1888). One of the "new-style," less radical feminists of her generation, Gruenberg strongly believed that women needed outside stimulation to make them more effective at home. Looking for something that would help her and her family, she began attending federation meetings in 1908. Almost immediately she was asked to head a new committee to evaluate children's books, which reported on 200 titles that year. The next year the federation appointed her as the discussion leader of its second chapter, launching her on her life's work.

Winning a fifty-dollar prize in *Housekeeper* magazine's 1911 writing contest inspired Gruenberg to use anecdotes that parents told in her study group to illustrate points in articles on child development. The impact of these commonsense articles, making parents confident of their own intelligence as well as their ability to learn by observing their children, made the *Housekeeper* ask for more articles, which were collected and published in *Your Child Today and Tomorrow* (1913).

Gruenberg's writings made her an important spokesperson for the federation, which, because it was bent on understanding children, "accumulated expertise" and was in the forefront of the child-study movement. In 1914 she was asked by the *New York Tribune* to write a series of articles on older children and adolescents. These were collected and published in *Sons and Daughters* (1916), which parents found "sympathetic, respectful and instructive" (Wollons, p. 148).

Gruenberg and the federation were pioneers in the use of psychoanalysis to better understand children and their problems. Finding that using Freud's newfangled terminology made the formerly forbidden subject of masturbation easier to discuss, Gruenberg suggested sublimation when dealing with that problem and insisted that with the proper approach parents could teach their children "to feel there is something personal and private about their own bodies, yet nothing shameful" (*Encyclopedia of Child Care and Guidance*, p. 745). Feeling it unfair to children to let them be rude in the name of freedom, she advocated training them to be polite and teaching them to interact positively with other children and adults.

In 1917 Gruenberg set up a new federation chapter in Chicago and was designated the liaison with the many chapters outside of New York City. Continuing to rise steadily in the federation, Gruenberg in 1921 became its director. The next year the federation published *Outlines of Child Study*, covering fifty-one topics in a general survey of child development, which was edited by Gruenberg's husband.

Hoping to coordinate a national parent education program, the Laura Spelman Rockefeller Memorial fund underwrote the association's publications as well as its leadership training and membership development from 1923 to 1930. Its name was changed to the Child Study Association of America in 1924. With the new funds, Gruenberg published a regular newsletter—first called the *Bulletin* and later the *Child Study Magazine*—formulated a leadership training course through the Teachers College, and financed a "parent education marathon." Drawing more than 1,500 people to its first meeting this conference was widely acclaimed, and its published proceedings, *Concerning Parents: A Symposium on Present Day Parenthood* (1928), went through eight printings.

While continuing as the head of the Child Study Association, Gruenberg from 1928 to 1936 and in 1946–1947 was a regular consultant and lecturer at the Teachers College Institute of Child Welfare Research. She held a similar appointment at New York University in 1936–1937 and 1940, and at the University of Colorado in 1940 and 1942. Widely admired for her self-confident and commonsense style, she often lectured to organizations of parents, teachers, and social workers, and her audiences at times reached 9,000. She was also a member of the advisory council or board of some twenty organizations and participated in numerous national and international conferences, including White House conferences in 1930, 1931, and 1940.

In 1950 Gruenberg stepped down from her leadership position at the Child Study Association (remaining a special consultant there until 1974) and immediately became the Junior Literary Guild editor at Doubleday & Co., a position she also held until 1974. While there, Gruenberg wrote and edited more books, including *The Wonderful Story of How You Were Born* (1952; rev. ed., 1959 and 1970)—a classic that was translated into Japanese, Norwegian, and Swedish—

the well-received *Encyclopedia of Child Care and Guidance* (1954; rev. ed., 1968), and three more collections of children's stories (having already edited two). Besides the numerous articles that she wrote and the many books that she edited, Gruenberg published seven books and coauthored five more.

Shortly before her death in New York City, Gruenberg, who remained an optimist, spoke of her eighties as her best decade. A bridge between specialists and parents, she presented new concepts of child training in a tactful and nonthreatening way, helping parents to integrate these concepts with working ideas from the past.

• Gruenberg's papers are at the Library of Congress, Manuscript Division, and the papers of the Child Study Association of America are in the Social Welfare History Archive at the University of Minnesota, Minneapolis. Columbia University has a microfilm archive of part of the Child Study Association collection, and its Teachers College has the papers of that association's Book Committee, which Gruenberg headed, including its correspondence from 1920 to 1940 and fifty to sixty of its book lists and pamphlets. Other books by Gruenberg are *The Use of Radio in Parent Education* (1939); *We, the Parents* (1939; rev. ed., 1948); *Your Child and You* (1950), also published in Hebrew; *Our Children Today: A Guide to Their Needs from Infancy through Adolescence* (1952); and *The Parents' Guide to Everyday Problems of Boys and Girls: Helping Your Child from Five to Twelve* (1958). The books she coauthored are *Our Children: A Handbook for Parents* (1932), with Dorothy Canfield Fisher; *Parents, Children, and Money* (1933) and *Children for the Childless* (1954), both with her husband; and *The Many Lives of Modern Woman: A Guide to Happiness in Her Complex Role* (1952), with her daughter, Hilda Sidney Krech. For an excellent, well-balanced account of Gruenberg's early career, which includes material from eighteen interviews with her colleagues and children, see Roberta Lyn Wollons, "Educating Mothers: Sidonie Matsner Gruenberg and the Child Study Association of America, 1881–1929" (Ph.D. diss., Univ. of Chicago, 1983). An obituary is in the *New York Times*, 13 Mar. 1974.

OLIVE HOOGENBOOM

GRUENING, Ernest Henry (6 Feb. 1887–26 June 1974), journalist and U.S. senator from Alaska, was born in New York City, the son of Emil Gruening, a physician, and Phebe Fridenberg. Educated in private schools in New York, New England, and Europe, Gruening entered Harvard College at age sixteen; he received an A.B. in 1907 and an M.D. in 1912. In 1914 he married Dorothy E. Smith, with whom he would have three children.

Although Gruening earned a degree in medicine, he chose to pursue a career in journalism. In Boston he was a part-time reporter for the *American* (1911–1912), a reporter and editor with the *Herald* (1912–1914), and the managing editor of the *Traveler* (1914–1917) and the *Journal* (1917–1918). Gruening fought for editorial independence from advertisers and political bosses while advocating progressive causes: academic freedom, honest government, workers' rights, woman suffrage, and family planning through contraception. An early member of the National Association for the Advancement of Colored People, he also championed racial equality. In 1918 he moved to New York City to become managing editor of the *Tribune*. Although a supporter of American intervention in World War I, he soon left the paper in a dispute with the executive editor over wartime censorship of stories about lynching, discrimination against German-Americans, and U.S. government war propaganda. Between 1918 and 1920 he was business manager of the Spanish-language weekly *La Prensa*. He accepted an offer to become managing editor of the *Nation* in 1920. In this position, which he held until 1923, he collaborated with Oswald Garrison Villard, Irita and Carl Van Doren, Freda Kirchwey, and other dissenters on stories about political corruption, the mistreatment of minorities, and the political power of big business, and he played a major role in the magazine's crusade to end the American occupation of Haiti.

By the mid-1920s Gruening's interests turned increasingly to domestic politics and international relations. In 1924 he was director of publicity for the unsuccessful presidential campaign of Robert M. La Follette (1855–1925). After the election he traveled to Mexico for *Collier's Weekly* to report on postrevolutionary conditions. Inspired by his experience, he wrote *Mexico and Its Heritage* (1927), which was well received in both the United States and Mexico. He helped found the Portland, Maine, *Evening News* in 1927 and was its editor through 1932, during which time he exposed the monopolistic practices and weak corporate structure of the Insull holding company empire. His book *The Public Pays* (1932) summarized his critical findings about the state of the power-utility industry. In 1933 he returned to the *Nation* as its editor and used this forum to address the overriding problem of unemployment caused by the Great Depression as well as to support Fiorello H. La Guardia's successful campaign to be mayor of New York City. Meanwhile, as a member of the U.S. delegation to the Seventh Pan American Conference, he accompanied Secretary of State Cordell Hull to Montevideo, Uruguay, influencing both Hull and President Franklin D. Roosevelt to adopt the so-called Good Neighbor Policy toward Latin American states. In February 1934 he became the editor of the New York *Evening Post*, but he resigned in April in response to the owner's insistence on suppressing muckraking stories that involved large donors to the paper.

In the summer of 1934 Roosevelt appointed Gruening director of the Division of Territories and Island Possessions (1934–1939), a new agency in the Department of the Interior. Concurrently, he headed the Puerto Rican Reconstruction Administration (1935–1937). Believing, as he told FDR, that "a democracy shouldn't have any colonies," he tried to diminish the colonial status of Alaska, Hawaii, Puerto Rico, and U.S. Pacific island possessions, which were only represented in Congress by voteless delegates, by speaking vigorously on behalf of their interests. He also worked persistently to invigorate their economies, reduce their crippling dependency, and improve their quality of life through programs of social and economic investment. In Puerto Rico, for example, he acquired federal funds to subsidize local export industries, provide loans and relief aid to farmers, and construct medical facilities, power plants, schools, and university buildings. He encouraged reforestation, enlarged and improved the quality of the university faculty, and broke up large landholdings for redistribution to poor farmers.

In 1939 Roosevelt appointed him territorial governor of Alaska, a post he held for almost fourteen years. In this capacity he was a strong advocate of federal aid, economic development, highway construction, and statehood. Urging tax reform as well as jobs and benefits for labor, he sometimes clashed with the Alaskan legislature, which was heavily influenced by absentee owners in the canning, mining, and utilities industries. During and after World War II he disagreed with military authorities over their land-use and labor policies, concluding that "military encroachments upon the civil rights of any citizen must be implacably resisted." Favoring the conservation and wise use of natural resources, he was not, however, a champion of wilderness preservation.

Elected provisional U.S. senator in 1956 and then bona fide senator after the achievement of Alaska's statehood in 1958, Gruening continued to be a vigorous representative of Alaskan concerns as well as progressive national programs and international policies. He supported, for example, civil rights legislation and government funding for the distribution of birth control information; he opposed the granting of control over communications satellites to private, profit-making companies and the distribution of foreign aid to undemocratic countries. Deeply regretting President Dwight Eisenhower's retreat from New Deal and Fair Deal spending for domestic needs, he contrasted the Republican administration's frugality in regard to domestic spending with its largesse in the largely secret but well-funded American program of foreign aid. Initially hailing John F. Kennedy's election to the presidency in 1960, he soon became disappointed with what he saw as JFK's lack of commitment to domestic reform. On international issues, Gruening generally supported the economic aid provisions of Kennedy's Alliance for Progress but criticized the emphasis it placed on military aid to Latin American elites. He was also an early opponent of America's deepening involvement in Vietnam.

Despite his long, productive career in journalism and government, Gruening is most often remembered as one of only two senators who voted against President Lyndon B. Johnson's Gulf of Tonkin Resolution in August 1964. He opposed presidential escalation of the war and the deceptions it aggravated. As early as October 1963 he had spoken against Kennedy's interventions in Indochina, and in March 1964 he delivered a Senate speech calling on the United States to withdraw from Vietnam. Gruening subsequently welcomed the growth of the antiwar movement, opposed sending draftees to Vietnam, and defended conscientious objectors.

In 1968 the 81-year-old Gruening lost the Democratic senatorial primary election to 38-year-old Mike Gravel. But he continued to be active in national politics: he opposed the war, campaigned for George McGovern during the 1972 presidential election, testified on behalf of Daniel Ellsberg at his trial for leaking the Pentagon Papers, and criticized President Richard M. Nixon's expansion of the Indochina War, enlargement of the powers of the presidency at the expense of Congress, assault on the freedom of the press, and subversion of the electoral and judicial processes in the Watergate scandal. He died at his home in Washington, D.C. Those who knew him agreed that Gruening's own words characterized his public life: "I believed that the greatest battles are often fought by men who are defeated time and again, and keep on fighting."

• Gruening's papers are in the University of Alaska Archives, Fairbanks. His other books include *The State of Alaska* (1954) and *Many Battles: The Autobiography of Ernest Gruening* (1973). Claus-M Naske assesses Gruening's Alaskan record in "Governor Gruening and the Alaska War Council: The Battle for Civilian Control of Alaska during World War II," *Alaska Journal* 16 (1986): 48–54; "Ernest Gruening, the Federal Government, and the Economic Development of Territorial Alaska," *Pacific Historian* 28, no. 4 (1984): 4–16; "The Battle of Alaska Has Ended and . . . the Japs Won It," *Military Affairs* 49, no. 3 (1985): 144–51; and "Governor Ernest Gruening's Struggle for Territorial Status, Personal or Political?," *Journal of the West* 20, no. 1 (1981): 32–40. John A. Britton analyzes his writing on Mexico in "In Defense of Revolution: American Journalists in Mexico, 1920–1929," *Journalism History* 5 (1978–1979): 124–30, 136. Obituaries are in the *New York Times*, 7 June 1974, and in the *Nation*, 20 July 1974.

JEFFREY KIMBALL

GRUENTHER, Alfred Maximilian (3 Mar. 1899–30 May 1983), army officer, was born in Platte Center, Nebraska, the son of Christian Maximilian Gruenther, a newspaper editor, and Mary "Mayme" Shea, a schoolteacher. Alfred Gruenther entered West Point in June 1917, two months after the United States entered the Great War, and graduated fourth in his class on 1 November 1918, ten days before the armistice. Once the war had ended, his class was recalled to West Point as student officers in early December since their total cadet service had only been nineteen months. They graduated again in June 1919, in Gruenther's case into the field artillery.

In 1922 Gruenther married Grace Elizabeth Crum; they had two children. In the army of the interwar years promotion was very slow, and he was to serve as a lieutenant for more than sixteen years. His early assignments included eight years at West Point, ending in 1937, as instructor and assistant professor of chemistry and electricity. It was during those years that he became famous as an expert player and teacher of contract bridge as well as a favorite bridge tournament referee in New York City, in which capacity he refereed the celebrated Culbertson-Lenz matches of 1931–1932.

In 1937 Gruenther graduated from the Army Command and Staff College and, by then a captain, from the Army War College in 1939. Next followed his first and only field command—a field artillery battalion. His promotions beyond captain came very rapidly because of the World War II expansion of the army. He participated in the famous Louisiana maneuvers of September 1941 as deputy chief of staff to Brigadier General Dwight Eisenhower, Third Army chief of staff. These were the biggest peacetime war exercises in the country's history, and the future leaders and key staff officers, including Eisenhower and Gruenther, were those who made their mark there.

In mid-1942 General Eisenhower was sent to England to command all American forces there, and Gruenther, brigadier general, became his deputy chief of staff. On his first day of duty, Eisenhower assigned him the task of chief planning officer for Operation Torch, the invasion of North Africa, which began on 7 November 1942. After the North African campaign, Major General Gruenther became chief of staff to General Mark Clark, commander of the Fifth Army, which carried out the invasion of Italy.

When Clark subsequently became commander of the Fifteenth Army Group, Gruenther stayed on as his chief of staff for the remainder of the war. This command combined the forces of Americans, British, French, Poles, New Zealanders, Italians, and other nationalities. By now General Gruenther's reputation was as a staff officer with an unlimited capacity for detail but at the same time one who never lost his overall perspective. He was, in short, a well-known and highly respected military figure.

After the war Gruenther went to Austria for a year as deputy to Clark, who commanded the U.S. occupation forces there. After a brief tour as deputy commandant of the newly established National War College (1946–1947), General Gruenther served as director of the Joint Staff, Joint Chiefs of Staff (1947–1949), and the army's deputy chief for plans in the rank of lieutenant general (1949–1950).

When the Korean War began in June 1950, it was perceived by the West as part of a worldwide communist offensive, and it galvanized the North Atlantic Treaty Organization, which had been established in April 1949. President Harry Truman in that context appointed Eisenhower in late 1950 as the first supreme Allied commander, Europe (SACEUR). Eisenhower immediately tapped Gruenther as his chief of staff and recommended his promotion to four-star rank in 1951. Gruenther also, as he had in the past, became Eisenhower's bridge-playing colleague. Subsequently in the spring of 1952, when Eisenhower resigned to run for the presidency, Gruenther retained the same job under General Matthew Ridgway, Eisenhower's successor as SACEUR.

Shortly after Eisenhower became president in 1953, he changed his military chiefs of service, and Ridgway was brought home to be army chief of staff. About that time Gruenther was being recruited for a high position in industry. The president balked at Gruenther's proposed retirement, stating that he could not "possibly leave at this time without inflicting a sad blow amounting to near destruction of NATO." General Gruenther remained on active duty and was appointed supreme commander in the summer of 1953.

Gruenther's three and one-half years as supreme commander came at the high point of the Cold War, a period when NATO became committed to a nuclear strategy. One only need recall the Hungarian and Suez crises of November 1956, which came at the end of Gruenther's tour, to capture the tone. Asked at a press conference about the Soviet Union's threat to use missiles in Europe during these crises, Gruenther, invoking Eisenhower's massive retaliation doctrine, replied, "That would cause very serious damage to Russia, which would follow as definitely as day follows night."

Gruenther was one of the very best SACEURs, not only because of his competence but also for the very high regard the Europeans had for him. When Gruenther retired on 31 December 1956, Lord Hastings Lionel Ismay, NATO's secretary general, called him "a great soldier statesman," and Eisenhower declared him "one of the ablest all-around officers, civilian or military, I have encountered in my fifty years" (*Mandate for Change* [1953–1956]). Gruenther received, over time, decorations from some twenty nations, including the Soviet Union.

The day after his military retirement, Gruenther became president of the American Red Cross, serving until the end of March 1964. He was a most active president, traveling extensively and giving more than 800 talks during his tenure. He subsequently served as director of four corporate boards and on three presidential commissions. Thirty-eight universities, including Harvard and Yale, presented him with honorary degrees. He died at Walter Reed Army Hospital in Washington, D.C.

Gruenther was a major American military figure of the twentieth century. Competent, brilliant, self-assured, personable, and dedicated, he was an ideal service staff officer. In an Allied environment he was most effective as a soldier-statesman with whom representatives of other nations could identify. His most notable roles were as key staff officer in U.S. military operations in the Mediterranean area from 1942 to 1945 and as a brilliant supreme Allied commander, Europe, during the Cold War period from 1953 to 1956.

• Gruenther's papers are in the Eisenhower Library in Abilene, Kans. Curtis Mitchell, "Ike's Man—Gruenther," *American Weekly*, 11 May 1952, pp. 4, 5, 7, and 24, includes good family photos. Robert Kleinman, "Can Europe Be Defended?" *U.S. News and World Report*, 11 Sept. 1953, pp. 44–51, is a good cover story with interviews. Ernest O. Hauser, "The Army's Biggest Brain," *Saturday Evening Post*, 31 Oct. 1953, pp. 32, 33, and 165, is also an insightful article. Theodore H. White, "The Latest 'Gruenthergram,'" *New York Times Magazine*, 12 July 1956, pp. 12, 13, 41, and 44, is an excellent article on the SACEUR period. "NATO the Shield," *Time*, 6 Feb. 1956, pp. 24–28 and 31, is the cover story and presents an excellent development of Gruenther's relationship with the Europeans. Gertrude Samuels, "New

Command for Gruenther—The Red Cross," *New York Times Magazine*, 3 Mar. 1957, and Harvey W. Flannery, "Man with a Mission," *Ave Maria Magazine*, 13 July 1957, are both about Gruenther's method of operation as a civilian president of the Red Cross. Obituaries are in the *New York Times* and the *Washington Post*, both 31 May 1983.

DOUGLAS KINNARD

GRUMMAN, Leroy Randle (4 Jan. 1895–4 Oct. 1982), aircraft manufacturer, was born in Huntington, New York, the son of George T. Grumman, the owner of a carriage shop, and Grace E. Conklin. Grumman showed an early interest in aviation. Graduating second in his class from Huntington High School, he devoted his salutatorian address to a discussion of the infant aircraft industry. After receiving a degree in mechanical engineering from Cornell University in 1916, he joined the engineering department of the New York Telephone Company.

Grumman enlisted in the navy in June 1917, two months after the United States entered World War I. Accepted for aviation duty, he won his wings in September 1918. After a brief tour as a flight instructor, he was sent to the Massachusetts Institute of Technology for a navy-sponsored four-month course in aeronautical engineering. He worked as a test pilot and project engineer for the Naval Aircraft Factory in Philadelphia until he resigned his commission in October 1920.

Grumman joined the Loening Aeronautical Engineering Corporation of New York as a test pilot and engineer. Rising to the position of plant manager, then general manager, of the company, he was part of a team that produced the Loening Air Yacht. An amphibious biplane, the Air Yacht proved the most successful aircraft of its type in the United States during the 1920s.

Grumman married Rose Marion Werther in March 1921. The union produced four children.

When the Loening company became part of the North American Aviation complex in 1929 and relocated to Pennsylvania, Grumman and several Loening employees decided to strike off on their own. On 6 December 1929 they formed the Grumman Aircraft Engineering Company. Grumman, who invested $16,950 in the new company and acquired 46.7 percent of its voting stock, became president and chairman of the board.

The Grumman company opened for business with sixteen employees in a converted garage in Baldwin, New York, in the midst of a growing economic depression. At first, business centered on repairing damaged Loening amphibians. In 1930, however, the struggling concern received a $33,700 contract from the navy for two Grumman-designed floats for seaplanes that featured retractable landing gears. This marked the beginning of what was to become a long and mutually profitable association with the navy.

In 1932 Grumman obtained a production contract from the navy for twenty-seven FF-1 fighters. The first navy fighter with a fully retractable gear and the first to exceed 200 miles per hour, the two-seat FF-1 won high praise for its maneuverability and sturdiness, qualities that would become characteristic of Grumman aircraft over the years. In 1934 the navy ordered fifty-five F2Fs, a single-seat fighter; three years later, it ordered eighty-one of the improved F3F, the last of the biplane fighters.

The Grumman company prospered during the Great Depression. By 1937, when it moved to new plant facilities at Bethpage, New York, the company not only supplied fighters to the navy but also produced two amphibians for a limited civilian market. The firm employed more than 500 workers and had gross sales of $2.2 million. Back orders of aircraft, however, nearly led to bankruptcy from insufficient cash flow. A successful public stock offering solved the problem.

In 1940 Grumman received navy orders for the F4F, its first monoplane fighter. The Wildcat, which featured a folding wing that Grumman conceived personally and that increased by 150 percent the number of aircraft that could be embarked on a carrier, served as the navy's only operational fighter during the first thirty months of World War II. Grumman produced 1,971 F4Fs, while the Eastern Aircraft Division of General Motors Corporation built more than 6,000 more under license. In August 1943 the F6F Hellcat, the navy's premier wartime fighter, joined the fleet. Over the next two years, Grumman produced 12,275 F6Fs. The Hellcat destroyed 5,156 enemy aircraft—55 percent of all Japanese aircraft shot down by the navy and marine corps during the war—while losing only 270. Pilots came to prize this rugged product from what they called with admiration the "Grumman Iron Works" for its ability to absorb battle damage.

In addition to fighters, Grumman also produced the TBF Avenger. The company built 2,293 of this carrier-based torpedo-bomber, while General Motors turned out another 7,546 under the designation TBM. In all, Grumman manufactured 17,573 aircraft at its Bethpage plant during the war, while other companies produced 13,803 Grumman-designed aircraft.

Grumman took pride in the fact that his workers produced more airframe pounds per employee than any other aircraft manufacturer during the war. The company had one of the most generous noncontributory employee pension plans in the country. Although the firm had grown to more than 25,000 employees, Grumman maintained his paternalistic, easygoing, open-door management policy of the 1930s. He was a familiar figure on the production floor, usually in shirt sleeves, and always with a pipe in hand.

Shortly before the war ended, Grumman suffered a severe allergic reaction to a penicillin injection, leaving him with chronic eye irritation. Although he remained in active charge of the company as chairman of the board, he stepped down as president in 1946.

The company survived the lean postwar years, building everything from seaplanes to aluminum canoes. Prosperity returned with the Korean War, during which Grumman supplied the navy's main fighter, the F9F Panther, the company's first jet. Over the next decade, Grumman manufactured the successful swept-wing Cougar (3,370 built) and supersonic Tiger.

By the time Grumman retired from active management in 1966, his company was responsible for a wide range of products that included the sophisticated A-6A Intruder attack bomber, the most widely used crop duster, and the lunar module. One of the nation's largest defense contractors, the company employed more than 33,500 workers and had annual gross sales of over a billion dollars, with a net income of $27.6 million.

Grumman retired to homes on Long Island and in Florida. Honorary board chairman, he frequently visited the company's assembly line. He died at Manhasset, New York.

The premier manufacturer of aircraft for the U.S. Navy in the twentieth century, Grumman won the acclaim of several generations of naval airmen for his rugged and dependable airplanes. Grumman's aircraft made a pivotal contribution to victory over Japan in World War II and were the mainstay of naval aviation in Korea and Vietnam. A talented aeronautical engineer, he built a symbiotic relationship with naval aviators that brought great prosperity to his company while assuring the success of carrier-based air power.

• The best account of Grumman and his aircraft is Rene J. Francillion, *Grumman Aircraft since 1929* (1989). An obituary in the *New York Times*, 5 Oct. 1982, mistakenly reports that Grumman became blind as a result of his reaction to penicillin.

WILLIAM M. LEARY

GRUND, Francis Joseph (19 Sept. 1805–29 Sept. 1863), author and political journalist, was born in Reichenberg, Bohemia (then a part of Austria), the son of Wenzel Grund, a furrier, and Anna Weber. Details on his early life and education are sketchy, but he apparently studied in a technical school in Vienna; by 1821 he was in Brazil, where he studied mathematics at a military academy in Rio de Janeiro. He came to the United States and was in Boston in 1827. From 1828 to 1833 he taught in a private school, Chauncy-Hall, which was patronized by many of the Boston elite. He was skilled in both mathematics and languages and published several mathematics texts while at Chauncy-Hall. In 1829 he married Larissa Parke in Philadelphia; they had one son.

Grund's first known activity in American politics was in 1834, when he spoke to a Whig rally in New York City, apparently having been recruited to appeal to Germans there on behalf of the gubernatorial candidate William Henry Seward. The next year, he spoke in Boston on behalf of the Democrat Martin Van Buren, who contemplated succeeding Andrew Jackson in the presidency. In the election year of 1836 Grund campaigned actively for Van Buren in Pennsylvania, as part of a Democratic effort to win the important Pennsylvania German element.

In late 1836 and early 1837 Grund was in England and Germany, arranging for publication in both places

of the first of two books that would gain him a reputation as an author. *The Americans, in Their Moral, Social, and Political Relations* (1837) was aimed originally at a European audience and structured as a travel account, with running commentary on American life. This was followed in 1839 by *Aristocracy in America: From the Sketch-Book of a German Nobleman*. Both works were clearly influenced by Alexis de Tocqueville's *Democracy in America* (1835), to which Grund made reference in his texts. Both works were generally approving of the democratic and egalitarian spirit of America in the Jacksonian era. *Aristocracy in America* sounded a more specific theme: the ineffectiveness and futility of a self-made aristocracy in a country where democratic rule was well established. Grund's works differed from Tocqueville's in their greater wealth of concrete description, but his social analysis was considerably more superficial.

In 1840 Grund switched his political allegiance to the Whig party, editing a campaign newspaper directed at the Pennsylvania Germans and writing a campaign biography of presidential candidate William Henry Harrison. After the Whig victory he was the recipient of patronage rewards from the administration. Appointed in 1841 to a brief term in the consulate at Bremen by President John Tyler, he returned after the Senate failed to confirm the appointment. He served for a while in a post in the Philadelphia customs house, then in 1844 was named consul at Antwerp, where he remained until 1846.

Having returned to Philadelphia, Grund undertook the relatively new role of a Washington correspondent, remaining in the capital city while Congress was in session and reporting in detail on developments there. His dispatches appeared regularly in the *Philadelphia Public Ledger* (where he used the pseudonym "Observer") and in the *Baltimore Sun* (under the name "X"). Since these papers were nonpartisan, he could offer independent viewpoints, although generally his opinions showed a pro-Democratic bias. He supported President James K. Polk's conduct of the Mexican War and later was an advocate of the Compromise of 1850 and a supporter of Stephen A. Douglas's Kansas-Nebraska Act. He remained consistent throughout his career in his opposition to antislavery movements, arguing that slavery could not be ended without total disruption of southern society and that blacks as an inferior race could not survive in freedom. While his political allegiance in the 1850s remained Democratic, he pursued an erratic course through the factional divisions that plagued the party.

In 1855 he resigned his appointments as newspaper correspondent to support the political campaign of James Buchanan (despite difficult relations with Buchanan in previous years), spending much of his time speaking to German voters in the midwestern states. Following Buchanan's election, Grund remained loyal to the president, even after the administration split with Stephen A. Douglas, with whom he had also had a close relationship. In 1858 and 1859 Grund received the patronage plum of a special mission to Europe as a confidential reporter on matters of trade and diplomacy. In 1860 he was named consul at Le Havre, where he remained until the beginning of the Republican administration of Abraham Lincoln and the outbreak of the Civil War.

Returning to Philadelphia, Grund became the editor of the *Philadelphia Age*, supporting Democratic opposition to Lincoln's war policies. However, a final twist in Grund's political career became the occasion of his demise. On 28 September 1863 Grund appeared at the Union League Club, already a Republican stronghold, to announce his support of Lincoln's war policies. This aroused the immediate wrath of Philadelphia Democrats. The next evening a group of Democrats on their way to serenade General George McClellan, who was visiting his mother in her house nearby, paused in front of Grund's home. Hearing the noisy disturbance and fearing some violence, Grund escaped his house and fled to a nearby police station, where he collapsed and died. The coroner judged the cause of his death to be apoplexy.

Both political opponents in Grund's time and historians later have criticized him for his political inconstancy and opportunism. He was skillful at testing the political winds to determine which candidate would win and at seeking patronage when his candidate was successful. Except in the presidential elections of 1848 and 1860, he was on the winning side. His reports as a Washington correspondent were sometimes influenced by his desire to cultivate promising politicians; nevertheless, he set some of the standards for "inside" reporting that would later characterize political writing. Although Grund's skill as a writer and orator was widely acknowledged, politicians in his time probably overrated his influence on the German-American voters.

• The most thorough discussion of Grund's career is Holman Hamilton and James L. Crouthamel, "A Man for Both Parties: Francis J. Grund as Political Chameleon," *Pennsylvania Magazine of History and Biography* 97 (1973): 465–84, which cites a wide variety of sources. Maria Wagner, "Francis J. Grund neu betrachtet," *Yearbook of German-American Studies* 21 (1986): 115–26, draws on Grund's correspondence with his German publisher in the Cotta-Archiv in Marbach, Germany, and on Department of State records in the National Archives. An analysis of Grund's most famous book is Marc Harris, "A Would-be Whig Ascendancy of Fashion: Francis J. Grund's *Aristocracy in America* as a Satirical Account," *Yearbook of German-American Studies* 23 (1988): 73–90. The *Baltimore Sun* and the *Philadelphia Public Ledger* contain frequent political reports and opinions written by Grund from 1846 to 1855. An obituary is in the *Philadelphia Public Ledger*, 1 Oct. 1863.

JAMES M. BERGQUIST

GRUNDY, Felix (11 Sept. 1777–19 Dec. 1840), lawyer and politician, was born in Back Creek, Berkeley County, Virginia, the seventh son of George Grundy, a farmer and land speculator, and Elizabeth Beckham. The family moved to Pennsylvania in 1779 and then to Kentucky in 1780. At least three of Grundy's brothers were killed by Indians. Grundy's father died when Fe-

lix was very young. His mother, despite impoverished circumstances, managed to hold the family together and to provide her "youngest and favorite son" an education at the Bardstown Academy, run by James Priestly. After completing his studies, he read law under George Nicholas, one of the leading lawyers in the West. Grundy was admitted to the bar in Kentucky on 5 November 1795. He served as the commonwealth attorney from 1796 until 1806. During this period he married Ann Phillips Rodgers, a second cousin of John C. Calhoun; the couple had twelve children.

Despite his youth, Grundy rose to early prominence as a delegate at the Kentucky Constitutional Convention in 1799. He championed a plan for circuit courts, but it was not adopted. In 1800 he was elected to the Kentucky House of Representatives; he was twice reelected. He continued to push for his circuit court plan, and though he was twice defeated, he succeeded on his third effort.

In 1803 Grundy moved from Springfield (Washington County) to Bardstown and became a leader of the democratic forces against the entrenched bluegrass aristocracy. Henry Clay, as a representative of the latter, was a formidable foe, disagreeing with Grundy over the issues of franchise, banking, and court reorganization, among others. In December 1806 Grundy left the house and became a judge of the court of appeals, and in April 1807 he became the chief justice. Just as his career seemed established, Grundy resigned late in 1807 and moved to Nashville, Tennessee. Apparently he was dissatisfied with his prospects and the low salary.

Grundy quickly rose to prominence as a lawyer and politician in Tennessee. He was chosen as a representative of western Tennessee to the Twelfth Congress and soon joined with other young War Hawks calling for war with Great Britain. He served on the Foreign Relations Committee and proved to be a staunch supporter of the Madison administration. Reelected to the Thirteenth Congress, Grundy resigned in the summer of 1814, apparently because of the illness of his wife.

Returning to his law practice, Grundy soon gained a reputation as one of the outstanding criminal lawyers in the West. He was an exceptionally able speaker and debater. He was also a graceful, commanding, impressive figure, superb at cross-examination and a master at swaying a jury. He was called on to defend individuals in all of the states surrounding Tennessee. He lost only one criminal case in his career.

Grundy returned to politics when he was elected to the Tennessee legislature in 1819 as a champion of debtor relief. He sponsored several measures to establish a paper money system or loan office to increase the money in circulation and relieve the distress of farmers, particularly those of Middle Tennessee suffering from the effects of the panic of 1819. Grundy's "easy money" group achieved some success, but the creditor class fought back, and most of Grundy's measures were either declared unconstitutional or eventually repealed. His actions, however, did nothing to diminish his appeal to the mass of the people.

Grundy also served on a commission that resolved the disputed boundary line between Kentucky and Tennessee. Grundy was reelected in 1820 and served to the end of the legislature's session in 1823. Grundy ran for Congress in 1827, but in a hard-fought contest he was defeated by a rising young politician, John Bell.

Because of his loyalty to Andrew Jackson, the Tennessee legislature selected Grundy to succeed Senator John H. Eaton, who had been named Jackson's secretary of war. In the Senate, Grundy initially supported nullification, perhaps out of friendship for his wife's cousin, Calhoun, but when South Carolina nullified the Tariff of 1832, Grundy remained loyal to Jackson and led the administration's forces in the Senate against nullification. Reelected in 1833 after a long, difficult contest against Eaton, whom Jackson wished to see back in the Senate, Grundy nevertheless staunchly supported Jackson in his bitter contest with Nicholas Biddle and the Bank of the United States. Grundy then supported Martin Van Buren as Jackson's successor in the election of 1836 over fellow Tennessean Hugh L. White and others. After Van Buren's victory, White supporters and Whigs in the Tennessee legislature elected Grundy's successor in 1837, two years before his term of office ended. They also tried to get Grundy out of office by instructing him to vote against Van Buren's Sub-Treasury plan. Grundy complied with the instruction, but he used the occasion to publish a highly partisan, but well-received, condemnation of the Whig legislature.

On 1 September 1838 Van Buren appointed Grundy as attorney general of the United States. He served in this office only a little over a year, mostly working to reelect Van Buren, and resigned when he was reelected to the U.S. Senate in December 1839. He served in the Twenty-sixth Congress through the end of its first session. In the election of 1840 Grundy campaigned vigorously for Van Buren through the South. Exhausted and sick from a stomach disorder, he died in Nashville shortly after the election was over.

Grundy rose from humble origins to become one of the leading lawyers of the West and one of the leading members of the Jacksonian Democratic party. He never forgot his roots, and throughout his life he fought for the causes of the little man against the aristocracy. He was one of the staunchest advocates of democracy in his generation, consistently opposed to special privileges for certain groups and consistently supporting a broadened franchise and limited government.

• No major collection of Grundy papers exists, but some letters may be found in the Library of Congress, Manuscript Division, and in the papers of many of his contemporaries. The best source on Grundy's life and career is Joseph Howard Parks, *Felix Grundy* (1940). Parks also wrote an article, "Felix Grundy and the Depression of 1819 in Tennessee," East Tennessee Historical Society, *Publications* 10 (1938): 19–43. A valuable sketch of Grundy is in the *United States Magazine and Democratic Review* 3 (Oct. 1838): 161–70. Josephus C. Guild, *Old Times in Tennessee* (1878), was written by a close friend of Grundy. See also two works on Tennessee history and politics by Thomas P. Abernethy, *From Frontier to Plantation in Tennessee* (1932), and "Andrew Jackson and the Rise of Southwestern Democracy," *American Historical Review* 33 (1927): 64–77. An obituary is in the *Nashville Union*, 21 Dec. 1840.

C. EDWARD SKEEN

GRUNDY, Joseph Ridgway (13 Jan. 1863–3 Mar. 1961), business leader, lobbyist, and senator, was born in Camden, New Jersey, the son of William Hulme Grundy, a woolens manufacturer, and Mary Lamb Ridgway. Reared in an upper-class Quaker home in Bristol, Pennsylvania, he received a part of his early education at the Moravian School for Boys (Lititz, Pa.) and subsequently spent three years at Swarthmore College (two in its preparatory division). In 1880 he made a grand tour of Europe and after his return began work for his father's company. In 1885, after working in each of the mill's operations, he became a wool buyer. Following his father's death in 1893, he became the company's head and also the principal stockholder in the Farmers National Bank of Bucks County, originally founded by his great-great-grandfather. Under his leadership, Grundy and Company prospered, soon making him a multimillionaire. He never married.

Grundy entered politics through involvement in family lobbying activities and election to the Bristol borough council. In the course of his lobbying, he formed close connections with Pennsylvania's Republican senators and political bosses, Matthew Quay and Boies Penrose. In 1910 Grundy founded and became president of the Pennsylvania Manufacturers' Association (PMA), an organization that served both as the money-raising arm of the Penrose machine and as a powerful lobby for high tariffs, low taxes, and minimal legislative burdens on business. By 1919 he had gained recognition as a highly effective political fundraiser, an adroit defender of Pennsylvania's capital stock tax exemption and limited social legislation, and "high priest" of a protectionist creed that fostering manufacturing could allegedly serve labor and farm as well as business interests.

In 1920 Grundy was among the Republican leaders who helped swing the presidential nomination to Warren G. Harding. Following Penrose's death in 1921, Grundy became the dominant figure in Pennsylvania's Republican party and, through Secretary of the Treasury Andrew Mellon, an important influence on national economic policy. In 1924, by stressing the importance of political "investments," he raised the then astounding sum of $800,000 for President Calvin Coolidge's reelection campaign. In 1926, however, his dominance in Pennsylvania was challenged by William Vare of Philadelphia, who defeated Grundy's favorite, George Wharton Pepper, in the Republican senatorial primary and was subsequently elected. The election, Governor Gifford Pinchot claimed, was "partly bought and partly stolen." Pinchot refused to certify it to the Senate, and after protracted proceedings the Senate decided in 1929 to deny Vare his seat.

Governor John Fisher appointed Grundy, who at the time was in the spotlight because of his work in shaping the Smoot-Hawley Tariff Bill and because of a much-publicized appearance before the Senate Lobby Investigating Committee. There, in October 1929, Grundy created a sensation by holding his own against western progressives and southern Democrats. He declared a number of the western and southern states to be overrepresented "backward commonwealths" who by rights should be silent on the tariff issue. His performance made him a conservative hero, but in the West and South he became a symbol of the "haughty and rapacious East."

As Pennsylvania's junior senator (1929–1930), Grundy served on the Manufacturing, Banking, Naval, and Civil Affairs committees but spent most of his time working for higher rates on manufactured items in the Smoot-Hawley Tariff. When accepting his appointment, he had believed that he would have full party support in the special senatorial election of 1930. After Secretary of Labor James J. Davis entered the contest, this was not the case. The Vare machine supported Davis, as did a number of other Republican notables. In a contest widely interpreted as showing the limits of PMA power, Davis defeated Grundy in the primary and won his seat in the Senate.

Grundy's prominence as a national figure declined after 1930. He continued to be a power in state politics, a man with whom Republican governor Pinchot and Democratic governor George Earle tried to work. Grundy's lobbying organization led the fight against business taxes and Pennsylvania's "little New Deal." In 1938 he helped to elect Arthur James as governor. However, by that time he was sharing power in the party organization with oilman Joseph N. Pew, and in the late 1940s what was left of his power was largely destroyed by Republican governor James H. Duff. In 1947 Grundy also gave up his chairmanship of the PMA's executive committee, and after 1952 he withdrew from politics almost completely, refusing even to make political endorsements.

In the 1950s Grundy began spending his summers at his "Walnut Grove" estate near Bristol and his winters at "Jacaranda," a rented mansion in Nassau in the Bahamas. In addition to an amazingly active social life for a person of his age, he continued to maintain a business office in Philadelphia, devote considerable time to civic and philanthropic endeavors, and be especially generous to his hometown of Bristol. He died at his residence in the Bahamas.

In political parlance "Grundyism" became a synonym for extreme political conservatism, allegedly opposed to all change other than a return to the ways of the late nineteenth century. Yet Grundy had no use for the neoclassical tenets of what he called "swivel-chair economists." His greatest accomplishment was the creation of an organization that pioneered in the development of a new system of interest-group politics. For political reasons he became at times an ally of such reformers as Pinchot and a facilitator of such business-minded legislation as Pennsylvania's workmen's compensation law. He also played the role of "modernizer" in seeking cultural and recreational as well as economic development for his city, state, and nation. As an individual he remained remarkably untainted by the scandals arising out of Pennsylvania politics. He was noted for his cheerful amiability, social graces, code of honor, and candor as well as for his conservative creed, hard-hitting tactics, and exceptional skill in political backrooms. While often fighting change, he was also an influential figure in shaping the course that it took.

• A collection of Grundy papers is available at the Pennsylvania Historical and Museum Commission in Harrisburg. Relevant materials are also in the Pennsylvania Manufacturers' Association archives in Philadelphia and at the Grundy Memorial Museum in Bristol. The only biography is the overly laudatory Ann Hawkes Hutton, *The Pennsylvanian: Joseph R. Grundy* (1962). Aspects of Grundy's life are also covered in J. Roffe Wike, *The Pennsylvania Manufacturers' Association* (1960), and Herman A. Lowe, "Pennsylvania: Bossed Cornucopia," in *Our Sovereign State*, ed. R. S. Allen (1949). For a brief sketch with some insightful comments, see "Pennsylvania: From Joe to Jim," *Time*, 10 Mar. 1947, p. 20. An obituary is in the *New York Times*, 4 Mar. 1961.

ELLIS W. HAWLEY

GRYCE, Gigi (28 Nov. 1927–17 Mar. 1983), jazz saxophonist, flutist, and composer, was born in Pensacola, Florida, and grew up in Hartford, Connecticut. Gryce was the product of a highly musical family: his brother and four sisters all were classically trained on a variety of instruments. In his youth, Gryce attended music school in Hartford, developing his skills on flute, alto saxophone, clarinet, and piano. In 1946 he began performing in and around Hartford, both as a sideman and as the leader of his own 23-piece group. In 1948 Gryce moved to Boston to attend the Boston Conservatory, where he studied composition and instrumentation with Daniel Pinkham and Alan Hovaness. In 1952 he won a Fulbright scholarship to study music in Paris, where he continued his instruction in composition with the famed composer Arthur Honegger.

Gryce returned to the United States in 1953 and quickly established his reputation on alto saxophone as a dynamic and original soloist in a bebop style similar to that of Charlie Parker. In 1953 Gryce performed and recorded with Max Roach, Clifford Brown, and Howard McGhee in New York City; worked with the Tadd Dameron band in Atlantic City, New Jersey; and toured the United States and Europe with Lionel Hampton's group for six months. While in Europe, Gryce composed and recorded several original arrangements, including "Paris the Beautiful," "Capri," "Consultation," "Eleanor," "Simplicity," and "Brown Skins," which was performed by a twenty-piece orchestra featuring Clifford Brown on trumpet. In 1954 Gryce performed on recordings with Donald Byrd, Lee Morgan, and Thelonious Monk. In 1955 he led his own group, the Jazz Lab Quintet, which included Byrd on trumpet, Wade Legge on piano, Wendell Marshall on bass, and Arthur Taylor on drums. The group recorded one LP, *Gigi Gryce and the Jazz Lab Quintet* (1960), which ironically was one of Gryce's less experimental recordings but nonetheless received praise from reviewers. From 1955 through 1957 Gryce also wrote and performed with the Duke Jordan and Oscar Pettiford bands. From 1959 through 1961 Gryce led a new quintet, featuring Richard Williams on trumpet, Richard Wyands on piano, Julian Euell on bass, and Mickey Roker on drums. In 1960 this fivesome recorded *The Rat Race Blues*, considered by many jazz critics to be Gryce's finest and most original album.

Through the 1950s Gryce also produced several well-known compositions, most notably "Nica's Tempo," which he wrote for Art Farmer and the Jazz Messengers; "Capri," written for J. J. Johnson; and "Speculation" and "Minority," which were recorded by several bebop bands in the 1950s and 1960s.

In 1961 Gryce retired from performing and became a music teacher. He died in Pensacola, Florida.

Though never considered a virtuoso performer, Gryce was one of the most proficient alto saxophonists of the bebop era. His playing lent an unusual classical technique to the more "organic" structures of bop, yet he never sought to merge European music with jazz. He was better known for his writing, which included several compositions that became jazz standards, especially popular with bop and postbop groups of the 1950s and 1960s.

• An illuminating, biographical interview with Gryce is included in Raymond Horricks, *These Jazzmen of Our Time* (1959). See also Nat Hentoff, "A New Jazz Corporation: Gryce, Farmer," *Down Beat* 22, no. 21 (1955): 10.

THADDEUS RUSSELL

GUALDO, John (?–20 Dec. 1771), musician, composer, and wine merchant, was born Giovanni Gualdo. Details of his parents are unknown. He arrived in Philadelphia in the 1760s as a wine merchant. Little is known of Gualdo's youth and background before his arrival in Philadelphia. On 24 August 1767 it was announced in the *Pennsylvania Chronicle* that he was a wine merchant from Italy, but recently from London. While in London, Gualdo had had two sets of sonatas (op. 1 and 2) published under the name "Sig. Giovanni Gualdo da Vandero." His singing style, reminiscent of the music of Italian composers, suggests that he may have acquired his musical training in Italy.

Once in Philadelphia, Gualdo opened a wine store on Walnut Street, between Second and Front streets, and sold wine and spirits, as advertised in the *Chronicle*, "for ready money only." He revealed his musical interests in a 30 January 1769 advertisement in the *Chronicle*, in which he offered "for sale, A few violins, German flutes, guittars, mandolins, spinits, clavichords, together with a variety of music strings." Gualdo had also engaged people who could under his direction "improve and repair every kind of musical instrument." In his house resided a German gentleman who taught violin, violoncello, and french horn,

and a servant boy who could copy music. Gualdo was not affluent, and customers did not always repay their debts, but he continued to pursue his business activities.

On 21 November 1769 Gualdo wrote a flier to the Philharmonical Merchants and others stating that during the winter season he would direct nine concerts of vocal and instrumental music, one every other Thursday. He thought he could capably direct these concerts at Mr. Davenport's house on Third Street. The first concert occurred on 30 November 1769. The *Pennsylvania Gazette* announced the program to include vocal music by Handel, Arne, Giardini, Jackson, and Stanley and instrumental music by Geminiani, Barbelli, Capioni, Zanneti, Pellegrino, Abel, Bach, and the earl of Kelly in addition to Gualdo himself. A ticket for one evening was priced at five shillings.

The following year, on 8 November 1770, Gualdo advertised in the *Pennsylvania Journal* a public concert to be held on 27 December 1770 at the Assembly Room. The price of tickets was ten shillings, twice that of the previous year. The advertisement announced that new songs and selected pieces would be performed, with solos and concertos on various instruments including the mandolino. There exist, in addition to the twelve sonatas Gualdo wrote in London, six sonatas for two mandolins or two violins, and these were probably written in Philadelphia and performed in the 27 December concert.

The six sonatas of op. 2 and the six written in Philadelphia each consist of two short movements. The last movement of each of those scored for two mandolins or two violins is a minuet. The continuo part of all of his known sonatas consists of a thoroughbass, which gives the bass line and figures for the realization of the notes to be played above the bass line. The sonatas share the melodic style of other baroque Italian trio sonatas.

Records of the Pennsylvania Hospital in Philadelphia indicate that on 24 August 1771 Gualdo was admitted to the hospital for "Lunacy. Security of the poor." At that time, mental patients were kept in the unheated basement of the hospital because it was believed they did not feel cold. Gualdo died there about four months after he was admitted.

Gualdo is noteworthy as a musician and composer of quality. His music bears a resemblance to that of the European baroque composers, particularly in his use of thoroughbass notation. It is significant that during his lifetime Quaker Philadelphia had become cosmopolitan enough that residents could accept a man who promoted and enjoyed serious European music while the Quakers did not. Many immigrant musicians brought their own native contemporary music to the United States, but Gualdo was one of the first to do so.

• Music by Gualdo can be found at the Library of Congress in Washington, D.C.: the collection includes *Six Sonatas for two German Flutes or two Violins with a Thorough Bass for Harpsichord or Violoncello* (undated) and *Six Easy Evening Entertainments for two Mandolins or two Violins with a Thor-*

ough Bass for the Harpsichord or Violoncello (unpublished). A concert program of one of Gualdo's 1769 series, including mention of several pieces by Gualdo, is quoted in John Tasker Howard, *The Music of George Washington's Time* (1931), and in Edith Borroff, *Music in Europe and the United States* (1971).

MYRL D. HERMANN

GUARALDI, Vince (17 July 1928–6 Feb. 1976), pianist, bandleader, and composer, was born Vincent Anthony Guaraldi in San Francisco, California, of parents whose names are unknown. Guaraldi began his professional career in the newspaper business with the *San Francisco Daily News* in 1949, until he nearly lost a finger in an industrial accident. After this mishap, and helped by relatives Muzzy and Joseph Marcellino, who had strong ties in both music and television in San Francisco, he returned to his first (and apparently safer) love and talent, the piano. He played with local groups, most significantly with the Bill Harris-Chubby Jackson Sextette and later with the Georgie Auld Band (1953) and Sonny Criss (1955). He toured the continent with the Woody Herman Herd in 1956–1957 and later, in 1959, went on tours of Britain and Saudi Arabia. He was a member of Howard Rumsey's Lighthouse All Stars for a short period beginning in September 1959.

Guaraldi's most significant formative association came with the Cal Tjader Quintet. He joined the group in early 1957, after Tjader drastically reduced the Afro-Cuban repertoire through which he had gained public attention. With Tjader on vibes, Gene Wright on bass, Al Torres on drums, and Louis Kant on congas, Guaraldi contributed during his two-year tenure to Tjader's growing reputation, both as vibraphonist and bandleader, for "cool" jazz. Like Tjader, Guaraldi was eloquent in any idiom, from moving lyricism to hard-driving riff tunes.

As a pianist Guaraldi was respected as being adaptable, tasteful, and somewhat understated in his playing. He was prized as highly for the motivating backgrounds he could provide other artists as for his solo work, and he was coartist with some of the West Coast jazz greats of the 1950s and 1960s. In addition to Tjader, Harris, and Jackson, he played club dates with other sidemen from the Herman band, especially Conti Condoli and Frank Rosolino. He recorded on dates with Stan Getz, Eddie Durran, Billy Higgins, and Bola Sete. Indeed, Guaraldi helped to establish what became known as the "West Coast Sound," the kind of lean, cleanly articulated swing associated with Paul Desmond, Dave Brubeck, Chet Baker, Shorty Rogers, Gerry Mulligan, Jimmie Giuffre, Lennie Niehaus, Shelly Manne, Art Farmer, and Buddy Collette.

But Guaraldi seemed determined to exceed his success as a performer by leading groups, composing, and recording. The decided upswing of his career during the 1960s, when many jazz-based musicians suffered lean times, was probably due to this determination to use his breadth of talents to do well in the business.

As a composer he was best known for his jazz-driven scores for the "Charlie Brown" television specials. He won a Grammy in 1962 for his "Cast Your Fate to the Wind" (on *Black Orpheus*, Fantasy 8089), whose rapid sales of over 100,000 copies proved to be an early bonanza for the Fantasy label. His most ambitious work as a composer was his *Jazz Mass*, which premiered in San Francisco in 1965. It was recorded on an album titled *Vince Guaraldi of Grace Cathedral, San Francisco* (Fantasy 8367).

Other representative recordings of his own music, solo and with trio, are on the Fantasy label from the 1950s and 1960s; his composition "Blue Groove," with the Cal Tjader group, is on Fantasy; several pieces with the Herman band are on Capitol; and excerpts from *A Boy Named Charlie Brown* are on Fantasy. Some of his early unalloyed jazz playing can be heard in the 1956 *The Vince Guaraldi Trio* (Fantasy 3-225).

A resident of Mill Valley, Guaraldi suffered a sudden heart attack between sets during an engagement at Butterfield's Bar in San Francisco, death coming shortly thereafter in nearby Menlo Park, just south of the Bay City. Little can be ascertained about his personal life. He had married and divorced, and the obituary in the *Los Angeles Times* (8 Feb. 1976) mentions only that he was "survived by two children."

• A brief but informative article about Guaraldi as a pianist is "Vince Guaraldi," *Keyboard* 7, no. 7 (1981): 12. An extended discussion of his playing and career and of his association with Tjader can be found in Ted Gioia's *West Coast Jazz: Modern Jazz in California, 1945–1960* (1992).

WILLIAM THOMSON

GUARNIERI, Johnny (23 Mar. 1917–7 Jan. 1985), jazz pianist, was born John Albert Guarnieri in New York City. His parents' names are unknown. Through his father, a violinist and music teacher, Guarnieri represented the last remaining line descended from the world-famous Cremonese family of violin makers. Young Guarnieri's musical interest lay elsewhere, however, and at age ten he began classical piano studies. Two years later he was imitating the movement of the keys on his aunt's player piano, and by his late teens Guarnieri had become friends with the leading Harlem stride pianists—Fats Waller, James P. Johnson, Willie "the Lion" Smith, and Luckey Roberts—all of whom took his interest seriously and offered useful tips on playing.

After graduating from Roosevelt High School, Guarnieri joined the dance band of George Hall in 1937. He then toured with trombonist Mike Riley's comedy band and later rose to prominence by replacing Fletcher Henderson as Benny Goodman's pianist in December 1939. While performing in Goodman's big band and sextet, Guarnieri recorded "The Sheik" and "Poor Butterfly" with the smaller group in 1940. During this time he also participated in jam sessions with Kenny Clarke's group at Minton's Playhouse in Harlem.

Goodman, requiring an operation for sciatica, disbanded in July 1940, and Guarnieri was one of six sidemen who joined Artie Shaw's big band. Guarnieri achieved modest historical fame for the novelty of having played a harpsichord on recordings by Shaw's associated small group, the Gramercy Five, the most notable being "Special Delivery Stomp" and "Summit Ridge Drive." Still, these otherwise impressive sessions served only to confirm that the instrument is ill suited to jazz.

Guarnieri returned periodically to Goodman's ensembles from February to early June 1941, and in March he participated in a famous session by the sextet featuring guitarist Charlie Christian. The titles from this session, including "Good Enough to Keep" (also known as "Air Mail Special"), are among some of the greatest jazz recordings ever made, and even in a subsidiary role, Guarnieri is to be admired for his tastefulness as an accompanist. In May he also recorded with trumpeter Cootie Williams, who was then with Goodman.

Rejoining Shaw, Guarnieri also became a member of Jimmy Dorsey's big band from February 1942 to March 1943. In 1943, while working on CBS under the direction of Raymond Scott in the first racially integrated radio staff orchestra, Guarnieri spent his nights with clarinetist Hank D'Amico and drummer Cozy Cole at the Onyx Club on Fifty-second Street, performing as an instrumental trio and accompanying singer Billie Holiday. The following year he worked with bassist Slam Stewart and drummer Sammy Weiss at the Three Deuces on Fifty-second Street. Guarnieri also sat in with many other bands at clubs on Fifty-second Street. At one point during these inspired and energetic years of small combo swing, violinist Stuff Smith and Guarnieri took turns playing at each other's venue during their own intermissions.

At first, owing to a musicians' union recording ban that started in 1942, Guarnieri's small combo swing work went undocumented. But from late 1943, when the ban began to be resolved, through 1945, he made many important sessions, the most significant being with Lester Young in a quartet under the tenor saxophonist's leadership. With Young and the quartet, Guarnieri recorded versions of "Just You, Just Me," "I Never Knew," "Sometimes I'm Happy," and "Afternoon of a Basie-ite" in December 1943. Likewise, a septet led by Guarnieri recorded "These Foolish Things," "Exercise in Swing," "Salute to Fats," and "Basie English" in April 1944 (the last three titles composed by Guarnieri). Among the best of his many other recordings from this period are the 1944 sessions with trumpeter Roy Eldridge, tenor saxophonists Ben Webster and Coleman Hawkins, and trumpeters Hot Lips Page and Louis Armstrong. Also notable are 1945 recordings with clarinetist Barney Bigard, tenor saxophonist Don Byas, bassist Stewart, and tenor saxophonist Ike Quebec. Guarnieri recorded with Armstrong again in 1947.

Through the 1940s and 1950s Guarnieri was busy with studio work, including a long association with WMCA; in 1949 he was broadcasting twice nightly with his own jazz quintet on that station. Guarnieri recorded with trumpeter Ruby Braff in 1954, and in that year he joined the staff on NBC television, where he performed on "Broadway after Dark" and Dave Garroway's "Today Show." Guarnieri then recorded the quartet album *Songs of Hudson and De Lange* in 1956. In 1958 he participated in the television series "Art Ford's Jazz Party," and in 1961 he was featured alongside Hawkins and Eldridge in one of the finest jazz television shows, "After Hours."

Guarnieri moved to Hollywood in 1962, intending to break into the studio scene as a composer, but he found making the right contacts far more difficult than expected. To make ends meet, he resumed his performing career, playing at the Hollywood Plaza Hotel beginning in 1962, the Charter House Hotel in Anaheim beginning in 1966, and the Tail o'the Cock, a restaurant in Sherman Oaks, beginning in 1972. Guarnieri interrupted this last engagement for tours to Canada and Europe, and he resumed his recording career with an unaccompanied album, *Johnny Guarnieri Plays Harry Warren* in 1973.

Among the European visits was a French tour devoted to the music of Fats Waller in March 1975, during which Guarnieri recorded an album under his own name (*Walla Walla*, reissued in the United States as *Gliss Me Again*), as well as albums with bassist Stewart, guitarist Jimmy Stewart, and violinist Stephane Grappelli. Guarnieri later recalled the physical strain of that tour, as he was diabetic and no food was brought in during the lengthy program. In July 1975, however, he was back in France, where he recorded with trombonist Vic Dickenson.

Guarnieri held engagements at the Tail o'the Cock until 1982 and toured Europe again in 1983. Having come to New York to give a concert early in January 1985, he died in Livingston, New Jersey, two days later. He was survived by his wife Jeanne and their six children; her maiden name and the date of marriage are unknown.

Guarnieri once estimated that he had written about 5,000 compositions, but the vast majority are fragments, designed for radio and television cues and commercial breaks, and the exceptions—including classically oriented piano and violin concertos, as well as ragtime, stride, and swing pieces—had little impact outside his own sphere. He enjoyed designing virtuoso test pieces for pianists; "Walla Walla," for example, is a compendium of Waller's showiest and most exuberant stride piano techniques.

In the mid-1960s, as mainstream jazz was being submerged under the collective weight of rock music and free jazz, Guarnieri came up with the idea of reenergizing jazz interpretations of the classic American popular songs of Gershwin, Kern, Porter, Waller, and their colleagues, by performing these tunes in 5/4 meter. "I can forsee 5/4, within the next few years, sweeping the world completely," he told writer Leonard Feather in 1968 (Feather, p. 41). He pursued this concept to the end of his life, long after the craze for odd-metered jazz had faded away. His concertos are even in 5/4 time.

Guarnieri's significance was his ability to capture the essence of the pioneering piano styles developed by Waller, Tatum, Count Basie, and Teddy Wilson. Feather reported that on the 1945 recording of "Honeysuckle Rose" under Stewart, Guarnieri so closely imitated Waller's playing and singing that the disc was routinely mistaken for Waller's own. The previous year Guarnieri had recorded versions of this same tune in Webster's quartet using Basie's approach, his principal influence in the mid-1940s. "I've been accused all along of having no originality, no style of my own," he told writer Amy Lee. "I thought it was more important to play what sounded best for the occasion."

• Surveys and interviews with Guarnieri are in Amy Lee, "Guarnieri Plays Greatest," *Down Beat* 16 (1 July 1949): 2; Leonard Feather, "Johnny Guarnieri's New Bag," *Down Beat* 35 (2 May 1968): 24–25, 41–42; and Yvan Fournier, "Many Faces of Johnny Guarnieri," *Le point du jazz* no. 4 (Mar. 1971): 63–76. See also Arnold Shaw, *The Street That Never Slept* (1971; repr. as *52nd Street: The Street of Jazz* 1977); Herb Wong, liner notes to Guarnieri's album *Gliss Me Again* (1978); Bob Byler, "A Remembrance: Conversations with Johnny Guarnieri," *Mississippi Rag* 12 (Feb. 1985): 7–9; Chip Deffaa, "Johnny Guarnieri's Last Performance," *Mississippi Rag* 12 (Feb. 1985): 9; and Lowell D. Holmes and John W. Thomson, *Jazz Greats: Getting Better with Age* (1986). Further details of Guarnieri's affiliations with bands are in John Chilton, *Who's Who of Jazz: Storyville to Swing Street*, 4th ed. (1985), and D. Russell Connor, *Benny Goodman: Listen to His Legacy* (1988). A notated example of his playing in 5/4 meter appears in Feather, "Piano Giants of Jazz: Johnny Guarnieri," *Contemporary Keyboard* 4 (Dec. 1978): 58–59. For a critical assessment of his harpsichord work with Shaw, see Gunther Schuller, *The Swing Era: The Development of Jazz, 1930–1945* (1989). Obituaries are in *New York Times*, 9 Jan. 1985, and *Annual Obituary 1985.*

BARRY KERNFELD

GUÉRIN, Anne-Thérèse (2 Oct. 1798–14 May 1856), educator and religious leader, was born in Étables (Côtes-du-Nord), Brittany, France, the daughter of Laurent Guérin, a naval officer during the Napoleonic wars, and Isabelle Lefèvre. Anne-Thérèse received her basic education in reading, writing, and religion from her mother. At age nine she attended a small village school, which closed after one year. At about that time a young cousin of the Guérins, a seminarian studying for the priesthood, came to live with the family. He tutored Anne-Thérèse, and after his departure she continued her education by reading widely, in particular in literature and history.

Tragedy struck the family on 17 June 1814, when Laurent Guérin, while returning home from military service after an absence of three years, was killed by bandits. Isabelle Guérin, having already endured the loss of two children, became a semi-invalid and put the sixteen-year-old Anne-Thérèse in charge of the home and her younger sister, Jeanne-Marie.

Not until 1823 was Anne-Thérèse able to fulfill her desire to enter the Congregation of the Sisters of Providence, a group of women religious dedicated to education and the home care of sick poor people. After a

brief, six-month novitiate at Ruillé-sur-Loir, Anne-Thérèse, now known as Sister Theodore, spent the next seventeen years in education and administration. She became widely known as a leader in her chosen field and was awarded the medal of excellence by the French government in 1839. In addition to her work as teacher and administrator of schools, she put herself under the tutelage of a local doctor who taught her the elements of medicine and pharmacy.

In the summer of 1839 Célestine de la Hailandière, bishop of Vincennes, visited the motherhouse at Ruillé in search of missionary teachers for his sprawling American diocese, which included all of Indiana, one-third of Illinois, and part of southern Michigan. The superiors agreed to ask for volunteers from among the membership. Having suffered from poor health from the earliest days of her novitiate, Sister Theodore was afraid she would be a liability rather than an asset to the mission and so did not offer to go. Mother Marie Lecor, the superior general, selected five volunteers but was unwilling to send them without a strong leader. She made known her preference for Sister Theodore, who then acquiesced.

The journey from Ruillé began on 12 July 1840. After five months traveling by sailing vessel, canal boat, river steamer, and stage coach, on 22 October the six French-speaking sisters arrived at their destination, five miles west of Terre Haute in a deeply forested area that had been named Saint Mary-of-the-Woods by Simon Bruté, the first bishop of Vincennes.

The promised school and home were not yet finished. A local farmer, Isaac Thralls, welcomed the French sisters and let them use one of his two rooms and a loft. Four young women were waiting there to become the order's first American postulants. During the winter of 1840–1841 the ten women were crowded into one room in which Sister Theodore instructed the two French novices and the four American postulants in the rudiments of religious life. The Americans, in turn, taught the French sisters English. Before the first year ended, Sister Theodore, with the help of the bishop, was able to purchase the Thralls farmhouse for use as the first Providence convent.

When the building planned by the bishop was completed, Mother Theodore, as she was now known, found it "too grand" for a convent and decided to use it as the boarding school and academy, to be called Saint Mary's Female Institute. In July 1841 the school opened with five students, three of whom were non-Catholic. At that time, Indiana's educational system was in its infancy. Mother Theodore set about establishing free schools side by side with the order's popular female institutes or academies, both of which were open to Catholic and non-Catholic alike. By 1854 the congregation had grown to almost 100 sisters who were instructing more than 1,000 children in schools, academies, and orphanages in Jasper, Vincennes, Madison, Terre Haute, Fort Wayne, Columbus, and Evansville. Constantly concerned about the welfare of the sisters given the primitive living conditions of the frontier, Mother Theodore visited the schools regularly, traveling by the uncomfortable accommodations of the day. In order to give the missionaries some respite, she had them come each summer to Saint Mary-of-the-Woods for rest, relaxation, study, and spiritual retreat.

The harsh living conditions of the day were not Mother Theodore's most pressing trial, however. Local prejudice, fires, floods, cholera, and typhoid—all of these she took in her stride. More difficult to bear were seven years of conflict because of the French superiors' lack of understanding of the American situation compounded by Mother Theodore's problems with her bishop in the United States. Hailandière, like many of the early bishops, tried to control the religious women within his diocese. Provoked by her resistance to his interference in the internal government of the congregation, he expelled her from the diocese and forbade the sisters to have any contact with her—in effect removing her from office. Before the foundress could carry out Hailandière's unjust orders, however, his resignation from office was accepted by Rome. Under his successor, Bishop Jean Bazin, Mother Theodore was exonerated and restored to her congregation.

In 1854 Mother Theodore built a four-story brick convent to replace the old farmhouse the order had purchased from Thralls. There, debilitated by a life of physical hardship and painful trials, Mother Theodore died. Within a few years of her death, her sisters' influence had spread beyond Indiana to Michigan, Illinois, and Massachusetts. During the Civil War they served in military hospitals in Indianapolis and Vincennes. In 1920 they became the first American apostolic congregation to establish a mission for the education of women in China. In the last years of the century, the congregation numbered about 800 sisters who worked in a wide variety of ministries in twenty-seven states and Taiwan.

The legacy of dedication to education continues to be cherished by the Sisters of Providence. Saint Mary-of-the-Woods College, one of the oldest liberal arts colleges for women in the United States, stands on the site of that first academy. The Indiana Academy, which was inaugurated in 1971 by Associated Colleges of Indiana to honor Hoosiers "who have enriched the cultural and civic life of the state," in 1975 posthumously honored Mother Theodore for her contributions to Indiana.

The cause for Mother Theodore's beatification has been in process since 1908. On 11 July 1992 Pope John Paul II publicly recognized the heroic virtues of the servant of God and accorded her the title "Venerable," the first step in the Roman Catholic church's process of canonization.

• Correspondence and other papers of Mother Theodore Guérin are housed in the Sisters of Providence Archives at Saint Mary-of-the-Woods. Through her *Journals and Letters* (1937, 1978), she tells the story of the last sixteen years of her life. The first biography of Mother Theodore, written by Mary Theodosia Mug, *Life and Life-Works of Mother Theodore Guerin* (1904), relates the life of the foundress in the style and language of the day; although undocumented, it has the advantage of having been drawn from the testimony of living persons who had known Mother Theodore. Katherine Burton later wrote a popular life of Mother Theodore, *Faith Is the Substance* (1959). Among the theses and dissertations that include the story of Mother Theodore are Lawrence Gonner, "A History of the First Fifty Years of the Sisters of Providence in America" (master's thesis, Loyola Univ., Chicago, 1933), and Margaret Agnes O'Neill, "A History of St. Mary-of-the-Woods College" (master's thesis, Indiana State Teachers College, 1940). Also see H. Tracy Schier, "The History of Higher Education for Women at Saint Mary-of-the-Woods: 1840–1980" (Ph.D. diss., Boston College, 1987). In 1989 the Sisters of Providence published a pictorial history, *A Journey in Love, Mercy and Justice*, which tells, in both pictures and text, the story of Mother Theodore and the foundation at Saint Mary-of-the-Woods from 1840 to 1990. Mary Borromeo Brown, *History of the Sisters of Providence*, vol. 1 (1949), is a well-researched and fully documented history of the American order from 1840 to 1856. Anita Cotter Belsen, *Souvenir of the Fiftieth Anniversary or Golden Jubilee of St. Mary's Academic Institute* (1891), tells the story of the first fifty years of the academy from the point of view of a former student.

In 1987, in fulfillment of the requirements of the Congregation for the Causes of Saints in Rome, Sister Joseph Eleanor Ryan wrote a thoroughly documented life of Mother Theodore. Copies of this unpublished, two-volume work, "'Positio' on the Life and Virtues of the Servant of God, Mother Theodore Guérin," are in the Sisters of Providence Archives.

MARY ROGER MADDEN

GUÉRIN, Jules Vallée (18 Nov. 1866–14 June 1946), painter and illustrator, was born in St. Louis, Missouri, the son of Edwin Guérin (occupation unknown) and Louise Davis. His father's family was of Huguenot descent and had been in North America for at least a generation. In 1880 the family moved to Chicago, where Guérin probably received his first art instruction. In 1889 he is known to have lived in a Dearborn Street boarding house with Winsor McCay, creator of the comic strip "Little Nemo." The two became friends and influenced each other's styles of illustration.

Young Guérin gained some recognition in Chicago during the early 1890s, exhibiting at the Art Institute of Chicago and executing at least one painting of the buildings at the 1893 World's Columbian Exhibition. His biographers claim that he studied painting in Paris at the ateliers of Jean Joseph Benjamin-Constant and Jean-Paul Laurens, but this cannot be reconciled with what is known of his travels before 1900, when he established a studio in New York.

Guérin achieved his greatest fame as an architectural delineator, muralist, and magazine illustrator. His artistic influences derived from the flourishing school of magazine artists working with color lithography at the century's turn, from French impressionism, and from the classically trained painters and architects of the American Renaissance (1876–1917). Known for his bold perspective compositions and his flair as a colorist, he was acknowledged to be America's finest painter of architectural subjects during an era renowned for its illustrators.

Guérin's first national exposure came in 1901 when he was retained by Charles Follen McKim to prepare a few of the elaborate architectural renderings for the McMillan (Senate Parks Commission) plan for Washington, D.C., one of the cornerstones of the City Beautiful movement. His brilliant perspective drawings helped to sell the committee's visionary proposals for the Mall and led to commissions by other prominent architects, including Daniel Burnham, the father of City Beautiful planning principles. In 1907 Burnham and his partner, Edward Bennett, commissioned Guérin to prepare an extensive series of renderings for their monumental "Plan of Chicago." His dramatically lit and colored bird's-eye views became virtual icons of American city planning and remain his most famous works. He also collaborated with Bennett on plans for San Francisco and as "Director of Color" for the 1915 Panama Pacific Exposition held there; the fair was called the "Jewel City" for its brilliant Mediterranean palette.

In addition to his work with architects, Guérin achieved considerable fame for his magazine and book illustrations of travel scenes and architectural monuments. Working for *Century*, *Scribner's* and *Harper's*, he made hundreds of lithographs of buildings and cities in the United States and abroad. From 1909 to 1911 he toured the Middle East, Greece, and Turkey with the travel writer Robert Smythe Hitchens, producing his finest illustrations for such books as *Egypt and Its Monuments* (1908), *The Holy Land* (1910), and *The Near East* (1913). Because of their enormous popularity, many of his prints were marketed individually by such presses as University Prints and the DeVinne Press.

Prior to World War I Guérin had won recognition as a major illustrator, but his career as a serious painter had languished. During the final phase of his life he devoted himself increasingly to mural painting, decorating the buildings of such prominent architects as Cass Gilbert and the firms of McKim, Mead & White, and Graham, Anderson, Probst & White (the successor firm to Daniel H. Burnham & Company).

The commission for his best-known monumental paintings, the two sixty-foot-long murals in the cellar of Henry Bacon's Lincoln Memorial in Washington, D.C. (1911–1922), came as a result of his work as a delineator. Guérin's superb renderings of Bacon's designs for the memorial helped the architect win a limited competition against John Russell Pope's office in 1912. He was then invited to join Daniel Chester French and Bacon in preparing the decorative and sculptural program for the monument. The stiff, angular bodies in the "Emancipation" and "Reunion" murals (placed respectively above inscriptions of the Gettysburg and Second Inaugural addresses) are typical of Guérin's angular figure draftsmanship, always designed to support the lines of the architecture. Conceived by the artist to "typify in allegory the principles evident in the life of Abraham Lincoln," six groups of figures are depicted in a grove of cypress trees, symbolizing eternity. As a decorative painter he also distinguished himself in the large murals for McKim, Mead & White's Pennsylvania Station (1902–1911); decorations for the Chicago Civic Opera building and Merchandise Mart (1929); Cleveland's Union Trust and Terminal buildings (1924, 1926–1931); and the Liberty Memorial in Kansas City (1921–1935). Despite this, art historians have not viewed Guérin as a major painter of monumental subjects.

Jules Guérin was honored in his time by membership in the National Academy of Design (associate, 1916; member, 1931). He won medals for painting at the Paris Exposition Universelle in 1900, and at the Buffalo (1904) and San Francisco (1915) fairs. He was awarded the first Yerkes Medal in Chicago and was honored by the Philadelphia Water Color Club in 1913. He died in Avon, New Jersey, and was survived only by his wife, Mary Mulford Guérin.

• There is no known archive of Guérin papers, drawings, or personal memorabilia and no reliable biography. Brief biographical sketches exist in the following sources: Samuel Swift, "The Pictorial Representation of Architecture—The Work of Jules Guérin," *The Brickbuilder* 18, no. 9 (1909): 178–84; Mark A. Hewitt, *Jules Guérin: Master Delineator* (1983); Florence N. Levy, ed., *American Art Annual*, vol. 20 (1923), p. 540; and Robert Bruegmann, "Burnham, Guérin and the City as Image," in *The Plan of Chicago: 1909–1979*, ed. J. Zukowsky (1979), pp. 16–28. Guérin's best-known illustrated books not mentioned in the text are Daniel Burnham and Edward H. Bennett, *The Plan of Chicago* (1909); Jules Guérin, *Twelve Pictures in Color* (1925); Jules Guérin and Maxfield Parrish, *A Collection of Colour Prints by Jules Guérin and Maxfield Parrish* (1917); and Marie H. Lonsdale, *Chateaux of Touraine* (1905). Obituaries are in the *New York Times*, 15 June 1946, and *American Institute of Architects Journal*, Sept. 1946.

MARK ALAN HEWITT

GUERNSEY, Egbert (8 July 1823–19 Sept. 1903), homeopathic physician, was born in Litchfield, Connecticut, the son of John Guernsey and Amanda Crosby. His education at Phillips Andover Academy prepared him for a year's work teaching, after which he took a year's scientific course at Yale College. He began the study of medicine with Valentine Mott in 1845 and received his M.D. degree from the University of the City of New York in 1846. During the last year of his studies he acquired pharmacy experience and managed a large drug company, in addition to holding a staff position on a newspaper, the *Evening Mirror*. In 1847 he was a founder of the *Williamsburg* (Brooklyn) *Times*, which he edited for a year and a half. During this time he also established a medical practice. In 1848 he authored a widely used school text, *History of the United States of America*, a second edition of which appeared in 1867.

Guernsey had studied the work of Samuel Hahnemann, the founder of the homeopathic system of medicine, which treats disease by giving drugs that cause symptoms in the healthy similar to those of the disease. He consulted with a homeopath, George Cox, in a desperate case that was rapidly cured. He became more convinced of the efficacy of homeopathy by curing Sarah Lefferts Schenck of pleurisy. He married her in 1848; they had five children, only two of whom survived infancy.

Early in 1849 Guernsey was appointed city physician of Williamsburg. By December of that year he had suffered a breakdown from overwork and moved to Fishkill-on-the-Hudson. He soon became involved with the literary labors of Amos Gerald Hull, a pioneer of homeopathy in New York, who was editing the third American edition of George Jahr's *New Manual of Homeopathic Practice*. While at Fishkill, Guernsey treated many cases of cholera, testing to his satisfaction the alleged superiority of homeopathy. He claimed not to have lost a case, while multitudes had died under regular treatment.

After regaining his health, Guernsey, now an avowed homeopath, left for New York City in 1850 to establish a new practice. Although he did not entirely abandon orthodox methods, his belief in the superiority of homeopathic means led to his being dropped by old patients and to his expulsion from professional associations. Despite this, in 1851 he was appointed physician to a charitable institution, the House of Industry and Home for the Friendless, a position he held until 1865.

In 1851 Guernsey also became a member of the Hahnemann Academy, many members of which had been pioneers of homeopathy in the 1830s. The majority of these early converts, including Guernsey, continued to rely on orthodox medicine under some circumstances. Other members were unwilling to deviate from the strictures of Samuel Hahnemann, thus widening a split in the ranks of American homeopaths which had begun in 1832. Guernsey maintained his liberal viewpoint throughout his career.

Guernsey's first medical work, *Homeopathic Domestic Practice*, appeared in 1853 at a time when there were about fifteen other popular homeopathic manuals. Intended to accompany a family medicine chest, they were written to instruct and proselytize members of the public, especially those distant from professional homeopaths. Guernsey's was chosen by William Holcombe, an editor of the *North American Journal of Homeopathy*, as one of the best for its "superior literary finish." By 1890 the book had gone through eleven editions and had been translated into four languages. In 1855 Guernsey published a pocket manual, *A Gentleman's Guide To Homeopathy*; a second edition appeared in 1857.

In 1860 Guernsey was one of the founders of New York Homeopathic Medical College (now New York Medical College). He became professor of materia medica in 1862 and of practice of medicine in 1863, holding the latter position until 1865. He still upheld the superiority of drugs given on homeopathic principles, but he believed this was only one aspect of a trinity also including the chemical and mechanical use of drugs. In 1865 a reorganization of the faculty led Guernsey to resign. He continued his private practice and took on the duties of surgeon to the New York Sixth Regiment.

The Western Dispensary was founded in 1868 and brought Guernsey to prominence in public charity work in New York. After having been a director, he assumed the position of chief of the medical staff in 1875. By the end of 1877 the dispensary had served 99,780 patients. Guernsey commented, "While our transcendental friends are talking, we are quietly working," reflecting his growing antagonism to the purist wing of the homeopathic school. His success in fundraising among the wealthy made possible the establishment of Hahnemann Hospital and the opening of Ward's Island Homeopathic Charity Hospital in 1875. He served as chief of staff at Ward's Island until his death, dominating the board with the assistance of Alfred Hills.

In January 1873 Guernsey reentered the field of journalism as editor of the *Medical Union*, which in 1875 merged with the *New York Journal of Homeopathy* to form the *Homeopathic Times*, later the *New York Medical Times*, which he edited until his death. This journal, with Guernsey's editorials, was claimed by the editors of the *Medical Advance* to have done more harm to homeopathy than all the orthodox journals. Its divergent views, conflicts with the fundamental wing, and advocacy of deleting the homeopathic designation from journals and institutions led Guernsey into conflict with even the more moderate homeopaths. In consequence, the *Medical Times* was withdrawn from the American Institute of Homeopathy's list of recognized journals.

Because of Guernsey's deviations from homeopathy in the *Medical Times* and in the policy of the Ward's Island hospital board, the New York County Homeopathic Society formally requested that the hospital be reorganized. The board defied the society, drew up new resolutions, and presented them to the Charities Commissioners in January 1890. Guernsey's liberal views were evident in a resolution to allow hospital physicians to resort to means other than homeopathic. The *Homeopathic Physician* charged him with "delivering the hospital into the camp of the allopaths." In February 1890 the Homeopathic Society censured Guernsey and recommended that he resign from the society and have no further affiliation with homeopaths and their institutions. He would not recant, insisting that it was the duty of a physician to use whatever means would benefit the patient. He remained in the society despite the resolutions, which were expunged in 1899.

At Guernsey's instigation, the Ward's Island Hospital dropped the homeopathic designation in November 1893 and was renamed the Metropolitan Hospital. Subsequently he was removed from the board of the Middletown State Homeopathic Hospital and replaced by Timothy Field Allen, whose loyalty to homeopathy was known to be unwavering. The passing years, however, brought reconciliation, as evidenced by a standing ovation Guernsey received at a New York Homeopathic Medical College commencement. He continued to edit the *Medical Times* and headed the medical board of the Metropolitan Hospital until May 1903, when he resigned in ill health. He died at his home at Fishkill.

Little known today, and his minor contributions to the literature out of print, Guernsey is most significant as one whose attempts at the amalgamation of medical approaches actually hastened the demise of organized homeopathy in the United States. His liberal views were thought by the purist wing to be a confession of inability to apply the principles of homeopathy. His condemnation of sectarianism and exclusivism in medicine certainly contributed to the internal weakening of the homeopathic school. Guernsey's influence was largely felt in New York, where he was perhaps the city's most affluent and successful physician. His charity and institutional work provided medical care for many thousands. Perhaps his character is best portrayed in "The Man Whose Yoke Was Not Easy," written by his friend Bret Harte. There he is described as a man "who through long contact with suffering had acquired a universal tenderness and breadth of kindly philosophy . . . day and night at the beck and call of Anguish."

• A complete list of Guernsey's books and articles is in Thomas Lindsley Bradford, *Homeopathic Bibliography of the United States, 1825–1891* (1892). Egbert Cleave, *Biographical Cyclopedia of Homeopathic Physicians and Surgeons* (1873), contains the best account of the first several decades of his life. The *North American Journal of Homeopathy* 44 (1896): 398–99, describing a celebration of Guernsey's fifty years in medicine, offers details on his career and quotes by him. Frederick Dearborn, *The Metropolitan Hospital* (1937), provides an account of Guernsey's involvement with the hospitals of New York and touches on aspects of his career and character. Particulars of the censure by the New York County Homeopathic Society are in the *New York Times*, 22 and 23 Sept. 1890. The *Medical Advance* 10–17 (1880–1891), gives insight into the Hahnemannian homeopaths' contention with Guernsey and the *New York Medical Times*. The general doctrinal split in the homeopathic school is dealt with in Harris Coulter, *Divided Legacy*, vol. 3 (1973). Obituaries are in the *New York Times*, 20 Sept 1903; the *Brooklyn Times*, 19 Sept. 1903; the *New York Medical Times*, Oct. and Dec. 1903; *Transactions of the Homeopathic Medical Society of the State of New York* (1904); and *American Institute of Homeopathy Transactions* (1904).

CHRISTOPHER D. ELLITHORP

GUEST, Edgar Albert (20 Aug. 1881–5 Aug. 1959), journalist and poet, was born in Birmingham, England, the son of Edwin Guest, a copper broker, and Julia Wayne. When his copper brokerage failed, Guest's father moved to the United States, obtained a job as a brewery accountant in Detroit, Michigan, and sent for his family to join him in 1891. He lost his position in the panic of 1893, and young Guest worked at odd jobs after school to help out. In 1895 he began an association with the *Detroit Free Press* that was to last for the rest of his life. He started as a part-time office boy and soon moved into the accounting office. In 1898, after his father died, he quit school and became a full-time cub reporter and then exchange editor. In the latter capacity, he read other newspapers and clipped short items, including poems, to use as filler in *Free Press* pages. One day he wrote four lines of verse himself, offered them to his editor, and was asked to try some more. Soon his poems appeared in his own weekly column, titled "Chaff" and then "Blue Monday Chat," and later in a daily column called "Edgar A. Guest's Breakfast Table Chat."

Guest, who had been naturalized in 1902, married Nellie Crossman of Detroit in 1906. The couple had two children. In 1910 Guest collected a number of his poems and with his brother Harry set them in type by hand; Harry printed what became *Home Rhymes* on a press in the attic. The edition of 800 copies quickly sold out. In 1911 they published Guest's *Just Glad Things*, which sold 1,500 copies. In 1914, when word got out that a selection comprising Guest's *Breakfast Table Chat* was in production, the Detroit Rotary Club ordered 3,500 copies. Poems in his columns grew immensely popular; handled by the George Mathew Adams Syndicate, they were eventually distributed to 275 newspapers nationwide. In 1916 Guest's *A Heap o' Livin'*, his first bestseller, was published by Reilly & Britton, a commercial firm in Chicago. It was reprinted thirty-five times and sold more than a million copies. Remaining with that publisher, Guest eventually wrote a total of twenty-five books.

During his early years, Guest had had a great fear of poverty. He once told a friend that he went to an old journalist's funeral attended by only three people and determined to avoid such a fate. With the publication of *A Heap o' Livin'*, a comfortable future was assured. His first book titles, many of which hint at their contents, include *Just Folks* (1917), *Over Here* (1918), *When Day Is Done* (1921), *All That Matters* (1922), *The Passing Throng* (1923), *Rhymes of Childhood* (1924), *Mother* (1925), *The Light of Faith* (1926), and *Harbor Lights of Home* (1928). Traveling to Chicago, he read his verses on national radio on Tuesdays from 1932 to 1942, ultimately for $1,000 a week. He also made his verses the basis for numerous lecture appearances before various civic organizations. His weeping while reciting his verses evidently appealed to some women's clubs of his era. Many of his short poems appeared on greeting cards and calendars. During the period of his greatest popularity, his income exceeded $100,000 a year—the highest figure quoted being $128,000. Later titles include *Life's Highway* (1933), *All in a Lifetime* (1938), *Today and Tomorrow* (1942), and *Living the Years* (1949). He also published two optimistic, moralistic books in prose—*Between You and Me: My Philosophy of Life* and *Edgar A. Guest Says It Can Be Done* (both 1938). In March 1951 he starred in a short-lived NBC television program called "A Guest in Your Home."

Guest was always a good citizen of Detroit. He was chairman or otherwise served on numerous fundraising campaigns. He was an active member of the American Press Humorists, the Detroit Boys' Club, the Masons, and the Detroit Athletic Club. Beginning in 1942 and continuing to the end of his life, he was the Protestant co-chairman of the Round Table in Detroit of the

National Conference of Christians and Jews. He played golf at several clubs, one golf course being so close to his $50,000 home that he could tee off for the twelfth hole from his rear porch. More privately, he was a shrewd poker player, often winning because he appeared disarmingly harmless. He died in Detroit, leaving an estimated 12,000 poems.

Among authors of single books of poetry published between 1895 and 1975, only Robert Frost, Kahlil Gibran, Rod McKuen, and Ogden Nash outsold Guest. He is credited with having reached the widest popular audience since James Whitcomb Riley, whose style he admired. He was affectionately known as "the poet of the people." He was well aware, however, that he was too facile and called himself a newspaperman and not a poet. Although his favorite poets were Robert Browning and Walt Whitman, his own verse lacks their robustness and technical daring. His sense of humor is indicated by his confession that he read all the modern poets but was aware that they probably did not read him—unless to poke fun at him. Almost never acclaimed by reviewers or critics, his work was memorably skewered in a wicked couplet incorrectly attributed to Dorothy Parker: "I'd rather flunk my Wasserman test / Than read a poem by Edgar Guest." His efforts are now regularly described, when they are mentioned at all, as commonplace, didactic, homey, sentimental, and unvaried. They celebrate in singsong lines the proper role of parents; love of relatives, friends, and neighbors; the rewards of hard work and relaxing in natural settings; patriotism; and plain living. They frequently caution that since life is replete with sorrows as well as joys, a virtue of paramount importance is humility. Perhaps, however, Guest slips a touch of self-praise in these sly lines from "Success and Failure" (in *A Heap o' Livin'*): "I do not think all failure's undeserved, / And all success is merely someone's luck." "Home," his most famous poem (also in *A Heap o' Livin'*), is quite representative of his style and begins as follows:

It takes a heap o' livin' in a house to make it home,
A heap o' sun and shadder, an' ye sometimes
    have to roam
Afore ye really 'preciate the things ye lef' behind,
An' hunger for 'em somehow, with 'em allus
    on yer mind.

This quatrain may seem banality itself. All the same, Guest gave immeasurable pleasure to millions of ordinary readers, who were as sincere and unpretentious as himself.

• Guest's papers are in the Burton Historical Collection of the Detroit Public Library and in the Michigan Historical Collection at the University of Michigan. *Index to the Poems of Edgar A. Guest* (1935) is an early bibliography complete to its date. Biographical coverage is provided by Leonard Cline, "Eddie Guest: Just Glad," *American Mercury*, Nov. 1925, pp. 322–27; J. P. McEvoy, "Sunny Boy," *Saturday Evening Post*, 30 Apr. 1938, pp. 8–9, 42–44; Royce Howes, *Edgar A. Guest: A Biography* (1953); and Kit Lane, *Michigan's Victorian Poets* (1993). Alice Payne Hackett and James Henry Burke, *80 Years of Best Sellers, 1895–1975* (1977), mentions Guest's *A Heap o' Livin'* and *Over Here*. Obituaries are in the *Detroit Free Press* and the *New York Times*, both 6 Aug. 1959, and in *Time*, 17 Aug. 1959.

ROBERT L. GALE

GUFFEY, Joseph F. (29 Dec. 1870–6 Mar. 1959), U.S. senator and businessman, was born in Westmoreland County, Pennsylvania, the son of John Guffey and Barbaretta Hough, wealthy farmers. From an early age he was interested in politics, and he and his sister, Emma Guffey Miller, a Democratic national committeewoman in the 1920s and 1930s and Guffey's closest adviser, inherited their political orientations. The Guffeys had been Democrats since Andrew Jackson's days. Guffey's father was sheriff of Greensburg, Pennsylvania, and an uncle, James M. Guffey, moved to Pittsburgh, made a fortune speculating in oil, and became a state Democratic leader.

Educated at the Princeton Preparatory School, Guffey entered Princeton University in 1890. He joined the undergraduate Democratic Club and met Professor Woodrow Wilson, whom he greatly admired. Eager to get into business and politics, Guffey quit college after two years and, through his uncle's political influence, secured a supervisory position in the Pittsburgh post office. He left in 1899, when a family friend hired him to work for a public utilities holding company, of which he was soon general manager. Guffey also speculated in oil and coal, started the Guffey-Gillespie Oil and Atlantic Gulf Oil companies, and became a millionaire.

In 1912 Guffey was a delegate to the Democratic National Convention, where he worked with A. Mitchell Palmer and Vance McCormick to deliver Pennsylvania's support to Wilson. Upon becoming president, Wilson appointed Palmer and Mitchell to offices in Washington, and following their departure for the capital, Guffey assumed the chairmanship of the Pennsylvania Democratic State Committee.

During World War I, Guffey served as a dollar-a-year man in the Petroleum Division of the War Industries Board and as sales director for the Office of the Alien Property Custodian. When, because of a technicality in the law, the Treasury Department would not accept interest earned on seized enemy alien property, Guffey banked the funds and borrowed from them for his own business ventures. A postwar drop in oil prices bankrupted Guffey, and at the same time the Warren G. Harding administration indicted him for misappropriation of government money and tax avoidance. With loans from his sisters, Guffey managed to repay the government. Though he was never brought to trial and in 1930 the charges were dropped, his political opponents repeatedly brought up the episode. With his sisters' assistance, Guffey then speculated in East Texas oil fields and by the late 1920s had recouped his wealth.

Guffey's political fortunes also revived. Backing Alfred E. Smith's candidacy in 1928, he switched to Franklin D. Roosevelt and played a key role in swinging the Pennsylvania delegation to Roosevelt at the 1932 convention. During the campaign, Guffey became convinced that the Democrats could lure northern black voters away from their traditional Republicanism. After meeting with Robert L. Vann, publisher of the *Pittsburgh Courier*, the largest black newspaper in Pennsylvania, Guffey talked reluctant Roosevelt managers James A. Farley and Louis M. Howe into creating a black division of the National Democratic Committee and naming Vann to head it. While Roosevelt did not carry Pennsylvania in 1932, he did make inroads into the black community.

As president, Roosevelt largely turned Pennsylvania patronage over to Guffey, who urged further efforts to win over blacks. He persuaded Roosevelt to appoint Vann assistant to the U.S. attorney general and to place many other blacks in federal jobs. Guffey also convinced the Pennsylvania legislature to pass one of the first state laws against discrimination in public accommodations, and he saw to it that poor blacks were well represented on New Deal relief and work relief programs in Pennsylvania.

In Guffey's 1934 U.S. Senate race against the conservative Republican incumbent, David A. Reed, grateful blacks helped Guffey become the first Democratic senator from Pennsylvania since 1881. Realizing the electoral power of the renascent labor movement, Guffey championed unions and the closed shop, thereby earning the workers' votes as well.

Guffey did not forget who had put him on Capitol Hill. In 1935 he was cosponsor of the Guffey-Snyder Coal Act, which imposed federal regulation and price fixing in the bituminous coal industry along lines desired by both the United Mine Workers and many coal producers. When that act was held unconstitutional by the Supreme Court, he cosponsored the Guffey-Vinson Act of 1937, which reenacted the provisions in a form the Court upheld. Guffey also fought, unsuccessfully, for a federal antilynching measure and against the poll tax. He backed Roosevelt and the New Deal completely, even denouncing fellow Democrats who balked at the president's Court-packing plan.

While genuinely committed to New Deal liberalism, Guffey played the patronage politics of the old-time political boss. He interfered blatantly in the Pennsylvania Works Progress Administration, getting his man appointed state director, honeycombing its staff with Democratic party workers, and requiring that they, in turn, donate a portion of their wages to the party. Said Guffey, "It is better to raise funds from party workers than sell yourself to big business."

After the 1939 outbreak of war in Europe, Guffey, an interventionist, was one of the first Democrats openly to entreat the president to run for a third term. In 1940 he published *Roosevelt Again*, a campaign tract arguing the case for the president's reelection. Reciprocating, Roosevelt placed enough influence and patronage behind Guffey to enable him to vanquish a primary challenger and go on to win his race against Republican Jay Cooke.

During Guffey's second Senate term, his devotion to internationalism and liberalism continued. In 1943 he joined other Capitol Hill members in backing creation of the United Nations, and he called for a presidential commission to find ways to save Europe's Jews. He unsuccessfully battled the southern bloc on behalf of federal protection of servicemen's rights to vote and fruitlessly fought bills cracking down on unions and strikes. At the 1944 convention Guffey spearheaded the losing drive to keep left-wing vice president Henry A. Wallace on the ticket. Despite his disappointment, Guffey, always a loyal Democrat, campaigned hard for Roosevelt and Harry S. Truman.

President Truman, who disliked Guffey and his pro-Wallace, leftist liberalism, curtailed the White House patronage Guffey had enjoyed from Roosevelt. The national mood also grew more conservative, dooming Guffey's 1946 run for a third term. He lost to the former governor of Pennsylvania, Republican Edward Martin, by 600,000 votes. After retiring from the Senate, Guffey, who never married, continued to reside in Washington, D.C., where he died.

Guffey, a pedestrian orator, who was always more comfortable in political backrooms than in public debate, did not leave an impressive legislative record. The Guffey-Snyder and Guffey-Vinson Acts were the only important laws to bear his name. However, in the Roosevelt era he was a major player in the Democratic party. Journalists Joseph Alsop and Robert Kintner in 1938 dubbed him "one of the two or three most powerful men in American politics" and the "first of the liberal bosses" ("The Guffey: Biography of a Boss, New Style," pp. 5–7). His enduring accomplishment for the Democrats may well have come from his early recognition of the importance of the black vote and persuasion of the party to cultivate that constituency with favorable policies and patronage. While other elements of the New Deal coalition have long since fallen away, the devotion of African Americans to the Democratic party has continued.

• The Joseph F. Guffey Papers are in the Washington and Jefferson College Library in Washington, Pa., as is a copy of his privately printed autobiography, *Seventy Years on the Red-Fire Wagon* (1952). Biographical information is in Joseph Alsop and Robert Kintner, "The Guffey: Biography of a Boss, New Style," *Saturday Evening Post*, 26 Mar. 1938, pp. 5–7, 98–104; and Alsop and Kintner, "The Guffey: The Capture of Pennsylvania," *Saturday Evening Post*, 16 Apr. 1938, pp. 16–17, 98–103. For Guffey's indictment see Walter S. Sanderlin, "The Indictment of Joseph F. Guffey," *Pennsylvania History*, Oct. 1963, pp. 465–82. Guffey's role as a New Deal political boss is discussed in Arthur M. Schlesinger, Jr., *The Politics of Upheaval* (1960), Richard C. Keller, *Pennsylvania's Little New Deal* (1982), Andrew Buni, *Robert L. Vann of the Pittsburgh Courier* (1974), Bruce M. Stave, *The New Deal and the Last Hurrah: Pittsburgh Machine Politics* (1970), and J. David Stern, *Memoirs of a Maverick Publisher* (1962). For Guffey's career during World War II and his Senate race defeat see "Reminiscences of Henry A. Wallace," in the Columbia University Oral History Collection (COHO); John M. Blum, ed., *The Price of Vision: The Diary of Henry A.*

Wallace, 1942–1946 (1973); and Allen Drury, *A Senate Journal, 1943–1945* (1963). An obituary is in the *New York Times*, 7 Mar. 1959.

BARBARA BLUMBERG

GUGGENHEIM, Daniel (9 July 1856–28 Sept. 1930), industrialist and philanthropist, was born in Philadelphia, Pennsylvania, the son of Meyer Guggenheim, a merchant, and Barbara Meyer. At age seventeen Daniel Guggenheim ended his formal education and joined the family lace business. For the next eleven years he worked as a lace buyer in Switzerland, the nation from which his father and grandfather had emigrated a quarter-century earlier. By the time Guggenheim returned to the United States, his father had begun to invest in lead and silver mines in Leadville, Colorado. Although initially leery of shifting the focus of their business to mining, the younger Guggenheim soon committed himself fully to the new venture and eventually assumed a leadership role among his brothers. The family firm, M. Guggenheim's Sons, expanded its interests beyond mining, building the largest smelter in the world in Pueblo, Colorado. The shift in emphasis from extraction to the more technologically advanced smelting industry typified Daniel Guggenheim's increasing commitment to technological innovation as a fundamental corporate strategy. International diversification became a second part of that plan, as the family interests spread beyond the borders of the United States.

Attracted by low labor costs and apparent political stability, Guggenheim negotiated the first in a series of business concessions with Mexico's president, Porfirio Diaz, in 1890. Based on those concessions, the brothers opened their first Mexican smelter at Monterrey and soon emerged as the leading force in Mexican smelting. This low-cost Mexican lead and silver became significant in the family's rise to dominance in the American smelting industry.

Typifying the "merger mania" of the late 1890s, a number of smelting corporations formed the American Smelting and Refining Company (ASARCO) in 1899, in an effort to monopolize the industry in the United States. But in a style similar to that of Andrew Carnegie, Guggenheim relied on low-cost Mexican production and the efficiency of his domestic operations to defy the poorly managed trust. In 1901 ASARCO admitted defeat, buying out the Guggenheim smelters at a generous price, naming Daniel Guggenheim chairman of the board and installing four of his brothers as directors.

In the years that followed the ASARCO takeover, Guggenheim used ASARCO, M. Guggenheim's Sons, and the Guggenheim Exploration Company to build a vast empire that came to include mines, smelters, and refineries in the continental United States, Alaska, Mexico, Chile, and the Belgian Congo. Guggenheim drew on the resources of leading financial houses such as Kuhn, Loeb and J. P. Morgan to implement innovative technologies that made possible the exploitation of low-grade ores and reshaped mining and smelting into a single, continuous industrial process. For example, the Guggenheim-backed development of Bingham Canyon, Utah, demonstrated the feasibility of coupling mass extraction techniques with chemical concentration processes to treat low-grade copper ore. The subsequent application of these nonselective techniques to the Guggenheims' Chuquicamata mine in Chile transformed it into the largest open pit mine in the world.

The transformation of mining and smelting from high-skill, labor-intensive processes to capital-intensive, mechanized techniques prompted growing labor unrest. When workers struck against the resulting deskilling, displacement, and speedups, Guggenheim, like other industrialists, initially responded with private police forces and strike breakers. But in 1912 the Guggenheims reversed their view toward labor and instituted their "ethical policy," which included housing and medical benefits for their workers. Guggenheim became a leading advocate of corporate and federal industrial welfare policies to forestall attempts by workers to control the workplace. Guggenheim's innovative vision extended beyond the technology and management systems of mining to include labor relations and the sociology of the workplace.

While the business operations he shared with his brothers had made Guggenheim a pioneer in shaping modern American multinational enterprises, his immediate family prompted him to broaden his vision beyond business concerns. Over the years Guggenheim had donated generously to causes close to the heart of his wife, Florence Schloss, whom he had married in 1884. In 1924 they formed the Daniel and Florence Guggenheim Foundation, which contributed to such worthy causes as hospitals and educational institutions. It was also at this time that Harry Guggenheim, the second of Daniel's three children, drew his father's attention to the world of aeronautics.

Harry had served in the naval air corps during World War I and remained fascinated with flying after he returned to civilian life. His father agreed to support new advances in aeronautics, forming the Daniel Guggenheim Fund for the Promotion of Aeronautics. Before it was dissolved in 1930, the fund expended $2 million to support such pioneers of American aviation as Billy Mitchell and Charles A. Lindbergh (1902–1974) and to create the first American school of aeronautics at New York University. The fund also provided financial assistance to Dr. Robert Goddard for his research in rocketry. Yet as Daniel Guggenheim was launching these new ventures, his own pioneering spirit was leading the family enterprises into a disastrous undertaking.

By the end of World War I, Guggenheim had become convinced that a marvelous opportunity awaited in the Chilean nitrate industry. Developed by British and German capitalists during the last quarter of the nineteenth century, the industry had stagnated technologically and faced serious competition from synthetic producers in Europe. Guggenheim believed that by applying nonselective extraction and processing techniques to nitrates he could salvage the industry and create an international trust with synthetic producers. In 1923, despite protests by Harry and other young Guggenheim partners, Daniel sold a controlling interest in Chuquicamata to the Anaconda Copper Company in order to invest the proceeds in nitrates. He assured his brothers that "nitrates will make us rich beyond the dreams of avarice!" But the joint nitrate venture with the Chilean government collapsed in the face of the Great Depression, which sent nitrate prices plummeting and cut off essential financing from New York. Daniel Guggenheim was spared the failure of his last great venture in technological innovation. He died at "Hempstead House," his palatial estate on Long Island, more than two years before the Chilean government dissolved the joint venture early in 1933. The company never had to declare bankruptcy, and the family continued to maintain control over nitrate production facilities in Chile, securing profits from these operations during World War II. But the nitrate debacle had inflicted heavy losses on outside investors and toppled the Guggenheims from their dominant position in international mining.

Guggenheim, who by the early twentieth century headed the most important group of mining interests in the world, distinguished himself not only by the size and scope of his enterprises, but by his commitment to innovation. His significance transcends his mining and smelting empire, for he also pioneered new forms of labor relations, supported the development of American aviation and rocketry, and established a major philanthropy.

• Few of Daniel Guggenheim's business and personal papers are available to the public. The Daniel Guggenheim Papers in the Library of Congress focus on the activities of the Daniel Guggenheim Fund for the Promotion of Aeronautics. Although there is no full-length biography of Guggenheim, his life and work receive extensive treatment in several excellent family histories. Harvey O'Connor, *The Guggenheims: The Making of an American Dynasty* (1937), is highly critical but very informative. The best recent treatment of the family's business activities is Edwin P. Hoyt, Jr., *The Guggenheims and the American Dream* (1967). John Hagy Davis, a family acquaintance, had wide access to family records, and in *The Guggenheims: An American Epic* (1978) he provides considerable insight into the personal and social lives of the family. On the Guggenheim Fund and the development of aeronautics, see Richard Hallion, *Legacy of Flight: The Guggenheim Contribution to American Aviation* (1977). An obituary is in the *New York Times*, 29 Sept. 1930.

THOMAS F. O'BRIEN

GUGGENHEIM, Harry Frank (23 Aug. 1890–22 Jan. 1971), philanthropist, aviation pioneer, and newspaper executive, was born in West End, New Jersey, the son of Daniel Guggenheim and Florence Shloss. His family, refugees from the anti-Semitism of Switzerland, amassed a mining and smelting fortune and established a group of philanthropic foundations in which he played a major role.

Guggenheim was only ten years old when his father began nudging him toward the world of commerce by setting up a chicken business for him and a cousin at the family's summer home in Elberon, New Jersey. After graduation in 1907 from Columbia Grammar School in New York, he enrolled in the Sheffield Scientific School at Yale to study mining and metallurgy. When he quit school in order to marry Helen Rosenberg, his father put him to work at a smelter in Aguascalientes, Mexico. This was his initiation into the family firm, then called M. Guggenheim's Sons and later Guggenheim Brothers. In 1910 he married Rosenberg. That same year he resumed his education in England, at Pembroke College, Cambridge, where he studied economics, political philosophy, and government. He received a bachelor's degree in 1913 and a master's in 1918.

Upon graduation in 1913, Guggenheim became executive director of the family-owned Chile Copper. At the start of World War I he became a naval aviator. After the war, when the senior members of the firm proposed to sell the Chile Copper mine at Chuquicamata, he insisted it was still a valuable property. The family sold it anyway, and he resigned from the firm in 1923.

At about the same time, Guggenheim divorced his first wife, with whom he had had two children. In 1923 he married Caroline Morton Potter. Together they supervised the construction of a Norman mansion, "Falaise," completed in 1923 at Sands Point, on the north shore of Long Island, New York. With Caroline he had another child.

Despite the disagreement over the sale of Chuquicamata, Daniel Guggenheim relied on his son's judgment. The elder Guggenheim wanted to use some of his wealth to benefit his adopted country, and Harry Guggenheim advised him to invest it in the development of the fledgling aviation industry. To that end they created the Daniel Guggenheim Fund for the Promotion of Aeronautics in 1926, with Harry Guggenheim as president.

By the time it finished its work in 1930, the fund had built the scientific foundation of the industry by establishing six schools of aeronautical engineering at such prestigious institutions as the Massachusetts Institute of Technology and the California Institute of Technology. Monies from the fund were also used to demonstrate the feasibility of commercial passenger airlines, by setting up a model airline and aviation weather service, and to promote safety in a variety of ways, such as the development of instrumented flight.

Working for the fund, army aviator James Doolittle, later famous for leading a World War II raid on Tokyo, flew the world's first instruments-only flight at Mitchel Field, Long Island, in 1929. Guggenheim's work for the fund also brought him in contact with Charles A. Lindbergh. After Lindbergh's 1927 New York-to-Paris flight, the fund paid for his cross-country tour, and Guggenheim became a trusted friend. Lindbergh completed the manuscript of his book, "*We*" (1927), while a guest at Falaise.

It was during a Lindbergh visit to Falaise in 1929 that the two men read of the Massachusetts rocket experiments of Robert Goddard, and Lindbergh served as Guggenheim's emissary to Goddard. It was Guggenheim money, first from Daniel's personal funds and later from the Daniel and Florence Guggenheim Foundation, that helped Goddard operate his laboratory at Roswell, New Mexico. His experiments in the 1930s and early 1940s provided the basic technology that later led to the American space program.

Guggenheim, a fervid conservative, supported Herbert Hoover's 1928 presidential campaign, and Hoover made Guggenheim ambassador to Cuba in 1929. When Franklin Roosevelt succeeded Hoover in 1933, Guggenheim resigned. In the years after his return from Cuba, his second marriage deteriorated, and he had no full-time career. It was during this period that he purchased a racehorse—the first step toward owning his own stable, Cain Hoy.

Near the end of the 1930s, Guggenheim met Alicia Patterson, daughter of Joseph Medill Patterson, founder of the *New York Daily News*. She, too, was at the end of an unhappy second marriage. Though Patterson was far more liberal politically and sixteen years younger than Guggenheim, they divorced their spouses in 1939 and married.

To channel Alicia's energy, save her from an aimless life of wealth, and provide training for what he believed would eventually be a position of power at the *Daily News*, Guggenheim bought her a small newspaper plant in Hempstead, Long Island. In 1940 they established a new daily, *Newsday*. As president, he was the financier. As editor and publisher, she took care of the journalism. From the beginning they clashed over her lack of financial acumen and over politics. In the 1940 presidential campaign, for example, they wrote opposing columns—hers supporting Franklin Roosevelt, his backing Wendell Willkie.

When World War II began, Guggenheim rejoined the navy, took command of Mercer Field, a naval air facility in Trenton, New Jersey, and left the paper to his wife. He emerged with the rank of captain, and from then on, *Newsday* employees referred to him as "The Captain."

Alicia Patterson's support of FDR and her marriage to a Jew had caused a rift with her father, and upon his death in 1946 he did not leave her a major role at the *News*. He did leave her money, and she used it to seek part ownership of *Newsday*. Guggenheim would sell her only 49 percent, however, keeping 51 percent for himself. That two percent difference remained a major source of friction in their marriage. They were very different to begin with—temperamentally, emotionally, and culturally—and arguments over politics and business exacerbated those differences.

In the decade after the war, as *Newsday* grew rapidly, Patterson ran the paper, and Guggenheim busied himself, among other things, with his horses, one of which, Dark Star, won the Kentucky Derby in 1953. He also spent his time supervising the construction of the Guggenheim Museum, endowed by his late uncle, Solomon R. Guggenheim. It opened in 1959.

Guggenheim left editorial matters to Alicia Patterson, until she infuriated him in 1956 by giving the paper's endorsement to her close friend, Adlai E. Stevenson, despite Guggenheim's support of President Dwight Eisenhower. When he demanded more editorial control, she threatened to divorce him and resign. Eventually she decided to stay, allowing him to offer editorials on his views when they clashed with hers. In the 1960 campaign they wrote opposing pieces—hers for John F. Kennedy, his for Richard M. Nixon.

In 1963 Alicia died after ulcer surgery, and Guggenheim took control of the newspaper. He knew nothing about journalism, distrusted his own staff, and felt the need to hire a publisher with a big name. In 1967 he brought in Bill D. Moyers, the young press secretary to President Lyndon B. Johnson. Moyers and "The Captain" clashed when Moyers started publishing editorials critical of Nixon's conduct of the Vietnam War in 1969. Guggenheim had a series of strokes, became increasingly paranoid, and demanded that Moyers fire the "Communists" on the staff. Finally, Guggenheim sold the paper to the Times Mirror Company in 1970, without giving Moyers any role in the transaction; Moyers resigned.

A few months later Guggenheim became mortally ill. Confident of his own historical significance, he left his mansion to Nassau County for use as a museum—complete with instructions on how his naval uniforms were to be displayed in his closet. Visitors to Falaise can still see the mansion exactly as it was when Lindbergh and Guggenheim began their support of rocketry and when Guggenheim and Patterson started the most successful new newspaper of the postwar era. He died at Falaise.

Harry Guggenheim was a relentlessly serious, often stuffy man, whose driving philosophy was the belief that a rich man's duty was to use his wealth constructively. Though the strength of his personality and strongly held convictions could make him difficult to live with, those same traits enabled him to compile a list of accomplishments rare in their scope and variety.

• Harry Frank Guggenheim's complete papers are in the Library of Congress. His own books are *The Seven Skies* (1930) and *The United States and Cuba: A Study of International Relations* (1934). There is no biography devoted exclusively to Guggenheim, but he is discussed in John H. Davis, *The Guggenheims: An American Epic* (1978); Richard P. Hallion, *Legacy of Flight: The Guggenheim Contribution to American Aviation* (1977); Edwin P. Hoyt, Jr., *The Guggenheims and the American Dream* (1967); Robert F. Keeler, *Newsday: A Candid History of the Respectable Tabloid* (1990); Milton Lehman, *This High Man: The Life of Robert Goddard* (1963); Anne Morrow Lindbergh, *Bring Me a Unicorn* (1972), *Hour of Gold, Hour of Lead* (1973), *War Within and Without* (1980); Charles A. Lindbergh, *Autobiography of Values* (1978); Milton Lomask, *Seed Money* (1964); Harvey O'Connor, *The Guggenheims: The Making of An American Dynasty* (1937); and Woody Stephens, with James Brough, *Guess I'm Lucky* (1985).

ROBERT F. KEELER

GUGGENHEIM, Peggy (26 Aug. 1898–23 Dec. 1979), art patron, was born Marguerite Guggenheim in New York City, the daughter of Benjamin Guggenheim, who directed the mining and smelting interests of the Guggenheim clan, and Florette Seligman. She grew up in one of the most affluent and socially prominent Jewish families in New York, tutored at home except for a short stint at the Jacoby School. In addition to the loneliness imposed by her restrictive home life, her childhood was marked by her father's death in the 1912 *Titanic* disaster. After Peggy finished high school, her older sister persuaded her not to attend college; instead, she worked briefly for the Defense Department during the war and then at the Sunwise Turn, a radical bookshop and her first exposure to the cultural avant-garde.

In 1919, having come into her $450,000 inheritance, Guggenheim moved to Paris. There she fell in with the bohemian expatriate community. It was during this time that she began her career as an art patron, sending money to writer Djuna Barnes, who received a monthly check from her into the 1970s. In 1922 Guggenheim married Laurence Vail, an American writer whom she dubbed the "King of Bohemia." They had two children, but their stormy marriage did not last long; Guggenheim left him in 1928 for an English writer, John Holms. The pair never married, but Guggenheim described Holms as the great love of her life, and she was devastated when he died during minor surgery in 1934. She then lived briefly with Douglas Garman, an English publisher and writer.

After almost two decades of involvement with the world of letters, Guggenheim turned to visual arts with the 1938 opening of Guggenheim Jeune, her London gallery of modern art. The first show, works by Jean Cocteau, was curated by Marcel Duchamp, who continued to advise Guggenheim on her collection and galleries for many years. As Guggenheim knew little about art after the postimpressionists, Duchamp's guidance was important. At Guggenheim Jeune she showed Wassily Kandinsky, Alexander Calder, Henry Moore, Constantin Brancusi, Jean Arp, Max Ernst, Pablo Picasso, Joan Miró, and others. Guggenheim's own collection was begun during this period; she would buy "a painting or sculpture from each show, to console the artist," because the contemporary work she showed had not yet found many patrons.

Deciding that the gallery's sales were too modest to justify its upkeep, Guggenheim decided instead to found a museum of modern art in London and enlisted Herbert Read as director. She went to Paris to gather the first show in 1939, but the outbreak of war made the founding of a museum unthinkable. Instead, Guggenheim decided to purchase artwork for herself, attempting to buy "a painting a day" from artists such as Alberto Giacometti, René Magritte, and Georges Braque. In 1941, only days before the Germans arrived, she departed from France with hundreds of works of art and an entourage that included her ex-husband, his new wife Kay Boyle, the children from both his marriages, and Max Ernst. Guggenheim married Ernst shortly thereafter, divorcing him in 1946.

Many European artists gathered in New York during the war, establishing the city as the new international art capital. Guggenheim's new gallery, Art of This Century, where she showed her collection of surrealist and cubist art, was part of this development. The interior of the gallery was designed by architect Frederick Kiesler in a startling manner—concave walls, pictures mounted on protruding wooden arms—intended to reflect the nature of the work itself. When Art of This Century opened in October 1942, the staid New York art world did not know whether to take the gallery, its artists, or its proprietor seriously. It was the only Fifty-seventh Street gallery to show the work of European moderns as well as to introduce new American artists. By showing the founding fathers of modern art alongside new talents, Guggenheim stressed the continuities between them and gave legitimacy to the work of younger artists. Abstract expressionism was emerging in the early 1940s, and Guggenheim's gallery gave Jackson Pollock, Robert Motherwell, Hans Hoffmann, and Mark Rothko their first shows. While acquiring the work of her new stable of artists, especially Pollock, Guggenheim continued to collect early twentieth-century European art, including Piet Mondrian, Kasimir Malevitch, Arshile Gorky, Joseph Cornell, Marc Chagall, and Jacques Lipchitz. In 1946 she published the first volume of her memoirs, *Out of This Century*, describing her romantic life with a candor that shocked many.

Feeling that the energy of the early 1940s was fading, in 1947 Guggenheim decided to return to live in Europe and settled on Venice. She acquired a huge palazzo on the Grand Canal, installed her collection, and continued to attract a circle of artists and writers. At the 1948 Venice Biennale she was invited to show her collection at the Greek pavilion, which was empty because of Greece's civil war. This official recognition, after years of running commercial galleries, was very important to her. In 1960 she published a second volume of memoirs, less shocking than the first, entitled *Confessions of an Art Addict*.

After the 1950s Guggenheim withdrew from the forefront of modern art, devoting herself to her collection. She spent the rest of her life in Venice, opening her home as a museum in 1951 and establishing artists' studios in her cellar to encourage her protégés. She gave much of her collection away, often to small institutions to which she had little connection; she was strict about maintaining the coherence of her collection and frequently donated works that she loved but that were out of keeping with her emphasis on surrealist art. Her collection of later works, bought without the expert guidance of mentors like Duchamp, Ernst, and Breton, was not as strong as that she had acquired in the 1930s and 1940s. Although the overall quality of her collection and her importance in encouraging young artists are clear, many critics have attacked her for her abrasive character and miserly ways, as well as the lack of a unifying personal vision in the work she collected. But as curator Thomas Messer commented, "Peggy must be given credit for her advisors," since their taste dominated hers. Guggenheim's collection traveled to the Tate Museum in 1965 and to the Solomon R. Guggenheim Museum in New York (established by her uncle) in 1969. The New York museum acquired the collection and the palazzo in 1974 and continues to run the Venice institution. Guggenheim died in Padua, Italy.

• Guggenheim's papers are in the archives of the Solomon R. Guggenheim Museum in New York City. Her memoirs were reissued in a combined volume, with a foreword by Gore Vidal, as *Out of This Century: Confessions of an Art Addict* (1979). See also Angelica Zinder Rudenstine, *Peggy Guggenheim Collection, Venice: The Solomon R. Guggenheim Foundation* (1985); Jacqueline Bograd Weld, *Peggy: The Wayward Guggenheim* (1986); Solomon R. Guggenheim Museum, *Peggy Guggenheim's Other Legacy* (1987); Virginia M. Dortch, ed., *Peggy Guggenheim and Her Friends* (1994); and Laurence Tacou-Rumney, *Peggy Guggenheim: A Collector's Album* (1996). An obituary is in the *New York Times*, 24 Dec. 1979.

BETHANY NEUBAUER

GUGGENHEIM, Simon (30 Dec. 1867–2 Nov. 1941), business executive and philanthropist, was born in Philadelphia, Pennsylvania, the son of Meyer Guggenheim, an immigrant who founded one of the country's great fortunes by developing western mineral holdings, and Barbara Meyer. He was educated in Philadelphia public schools and at the Pierce School of Business.

The seven sons of Meyer Guggenheim formed the firm of Guggenheim Brothers, which for many years dominated the copper industry from Alaska to Chile. A Republican senator (1907–1913) from Colorado (a virtual Guggenheim fiefdom), where he settled as a young man and amassed immense wealth in mining and smelting, Simon Guggenheim, in the words of John Davis, was "one of the most farsighted benefactors of the arts and sciences in American history" (p. 226). During his years in Washington, the deeply conservative businessman who lobbied against creation of the Department of Labor was noted not for sponsoring legislation but for looking after his family's interests, seeking federal aid for his state, and entertaining in a manner considered lavish even in that sybaritic city. Aggressive in his business and political dealings but quiet and courteous in private relationships, he was fond of fine food, good wine, and strong cigars. His wife, Olga Hirsch, whom he married in 1898, was blessed with a wide understanding of the arts. Following his stint in public life the senator was named chairman of several of the family businesses: American Smelting and Refining, American Smelters Securities, and the Guggenheim Exploration Company. The family eventually made its home on Park Avenue in New York City. Guggenheim was to die in the city at Mount Sinai Hospital.

It was not his political or even his more noteworthy business career that causes Simon Guggenheim to be remembered today, however, but his enlightened response to a personal tragedy. In 1922 one of the couple's two sons, John Simon, died of mastoiditis just as he was to graduate from Phillips Exeter Academy and matriculate at Harvard. As a way of honoring the memory of their son, Simon and Olga, advised by Carroll Atwood Wilson (general counsel for Guggenheim Brothers), Frank Aydelotte (president of Swarthmore College), and Henry Allen Moe, created the John Simon Guggenheim Memorial Foundation, with Moe as its first general secretary. Both Aydelotte and Moe were Rhodes scholars, and the idea of "European scholarships" for younger men and women, encompassing the creative arts as well as the sciences and humanities, derived at least in part from the Rhodes model. John Simon's younger brother, George Denver, who suffered from a manic-depressive disorder, died some years later by his own hand; thus there was no heir to the family fortune.

Incorporated on 16 Mar. 1925, the Guggenheim Foundation from the beginning existed "to promote the advancement and diffusion of knowledge and understanding, and the appreciation of beauty, by aiding without distinction on account of race, color, or creed, scholars, scientists, and artists of either sex in the prosecution of their labors" (from the foundation's charter). As a result, thousands of creative individuals have enjoyed the financial reward and prestige of being named John Simon Guggenheim Memorial Fellows, free to use the funds in any way likely to enhance their scholarly and artistic efforts.

Being named a Guggenheim fellow has come to be regarded as one of this country's most cherished honors, and those so tapped constitute an extraordinary community, which encompasses more than sixty Nobel laureates, scores of Pulitzer Prize and National Book Award winners, hundreds of members of the National Academy of Arts and Sciences, and other major contributors to American cultural and academic life. The list includes Aaron Copland, Thomas Wolfe, Martha Graham, W. H. Auden, John Kenneth Galbraith, Linus Pauling, Langston Hughes, James D. Watson; Arthur Schlesinger, Jr., and Eudora Welty, to name just a few. The distinguished literary historian Alfred Kazin observed that the foundation "has by its support of the individual and by its concern with talent, done more for American thought, learning, and art than any other foundation in the United States" (Davis, p. 240).

Both the senator and his wife served on the foundation's board until their deaths. Among the senator's major contributions was the establishment in 1929 of a program for Latin American fellowships, which continues to flourish. In his will, the senator left $20 million to the foundation, and at Olga Guggenheim's death, at age ninety-three, the foundation received an additional $40 million. By 1992 the endowment, begun with a $3-million gift, stood at more than $135 million, and the number of those who had received awards exceeded twelve thousand. In the words of Brand Blanshard, Sterling Professor of Philosophy at Yale, "I cannot think how anyone could have made a more imaginative or decisive contribution to American scholarship than Senator Guggenheim did in his magnificent letter of gift. He was moved to make the gift because he had lost a son. He gained some thousands of sons and daughters who will always think of his name with thanks and honor" (Davis, p. 255).

• The following works contain useful information about Simon Guggenheim and the family fortune: Edwin P. Hoyt, Jr., *The Guggenheims and the American Dream* (1967); Milton Lomask, *Seed Money: The Guggenheim Story* (1964); and Harvey O'Connor, *The Guggenheims: The Making of an American Dynasty* (1937). Especially informative is John H. Davis, *The Guggenheims, 1948–1988: An American Epic* (1978; repr. 1988). An obituary is in the *New York Times*, 4 Nov. 1941.

JOEL CONARROE

GUGGENHEIM, Solomon Robert (2 Feb. 1861–3 Nov. 1949), industrialist, art collector, and museum founder, was born in Philadelphia, Pennsylvania, the son of Meyer Guggenheim, businessman, and Barbara Meyer, Swiss immigrants who had accompanied their parents to Philadelphia in 1847 to escape restrictions on Jews in their native land. By the time of Solomon's birth, the family had prospered, its good fortune hastened by Meyer's shrewdness in providing clothing and food supplies for the Union Army during the Civil War. After attending public school in Philadelphia, Solomon was sent to the Concordia Institute in Zurich, Switzerland, to polish his German and study business techniques. Together with his brothers Isaac, Daniel, and Murry, he became a partner in M. Guggenheim's Sons, the family lace and embroideries manufacturing and importing company (1877; incorp. 1882), and remained in Europe as manager of a branch of the family business in Saxony. The four brothers became the masterminds behind the Guggenheim empire.

The expansion of the Guggenheim fortune began in 1879, when Meyer Guggenheim bought a one-third interest in two lead and silver mines in Leadville, Colorado. With the development of these mines, Meyer propelled the family into worldwide economic power, based upon the extraction, smelting, refining, and marketing of mineral resources—copper, silver, gold, and lead. By retaining family control of numerous industrial enterprises in the American West, Alaska, Mexico, Chile, Africa, and South America, by forming syndicates with other empire builders such as J. P. Morgan and Jacob Schiff, by taking advantage of the cheap labor and raw materials of undeveloped countries, and by establishing vertical trusts, the Guggenheims by the First World War had created the greatest mining empire in the world, and in doing so had amassed multimillion-dollar fortunes.

With his brothers, Solomon helped to form in 1899 the Guggenheim Exploration Company or the Guggenex, an independent corporation whose purpose was to search throughout the world for potentially profitable mines, develop them, and invite public investment. His first great challenge as an industrial manager came early in 1891 when the family sent him

to Monterrey and Aguascalientes in Mexico to organize a new Guggenheim mining venture—the Compañia de la Gran Fundicion Nacional Mexicana. Although Solomon had assumed responsibilities in the family business earlier, especially in managing the sale of the family embroidery factories in Switzerland, as head of this new company he had to exert all his personal and business skills. He leased and purchased mines and plant sites, built new smelters, imported machinery, conducted searches for ore, obtained water rights, and entered into agreements with railroads. Possessing considerable personal charm as well as shrewd business sense, he succeeded in persuading Mexican politicians to grant concessions with respect to customs duties, land acquisition, and taxes; and he skillfully fended off the protests and obstructions of Mexican competitors. He also established labor policies for indigenous workers whose work ethic and culture were foreign to his own experience. For four years he traveled back and forth between New York and Mexico, building up the Mexican properties until they could run themselves. By 1895 the Guggenheim smelters at Pueblo, Monterrey, and Aguascalientes showed a net annual profit of over one million dollars, and the Guggenheim name became one of the most famous, as well as most feared, in Mexico. Solomon's activities in the Guggenheim partnership continued in Chile, where he served as president of the Braden Copper Company, and in Alaska, where he helped to found the Yukon Gold company (1906).

In 1895 Solomon married Irene Rothschild, the daughter of a New York merchant. Irene introduced him to art collecting. At first, Guggenheim's tastes ran to Old Masters, Early Renaissance Italian and Flemish art, and the paintings of the French Barbizons, but in 1926 a friendship with the Alsatian artist, the Baroness Hildegard (Hilla) Rebay von Ehrenwiesen, drew him into the orbit of European abstractionists. Convinced that their works constituted the art of the future and therefore merited his attention, with typical Guggenheim boldness and under the guidance and influence of Hilla Rebay, Solomon began to buy abstract, or Non-Objective, art. By 1939 he was ready to sell at auction most of his Old Master paintings and concentrate on avant-garde art.

Guggenheim was particularly drawn to the work of Vassily Kandinsky, by the 1920s an established artist with a widely held reputation as a member of the Weimar Bauhaus school and Blauer Vier (Blue Four) group. Known in the United States from his participation in the Société Anonyme exhibition in New York in 1920 and again in 1923, by the time the Guggenheims visited him at Weimar in 1929, Kandinsky had published many essays and books explaining his conception of the "spiritual in art," an aesthetic philosophy that sought to establish new artistic values by freeing images from recognizable objects. On that visit in July 1929, Guggenheim purchased *Composition 8* from Kandinsky, and he continued to acquire the artist's work at auctions, through agents such as the painter Rudolf Bauer of Berlin, a close friend of Hilla Rebay, or Otto Stangl of Munich, or Karl Nierendorff of New York, through direct purchase, and as gifts from the artist or the artist's wife. With Rebay's guidance, Guggenheim also purchased work by Laszlo Moholy-Nagy, Fernand Léger, Paul Klee, Marc Chagall, Robert Delaunay, Piet Mondrian, Albert Gleizes, Amedeo Modigliani, Georges Seurat, Edward Wadsworth, and Pablo Picasso.

As Guggenheim's collection grew in numbers and fame, concern for housing it in a building of its own resulted in various proposals, including an offer of ground space from the Rockefeller Foundation, which perhaps feared competition from the Museum of Modern Art. In 1936 the collection had its first public exhibition at the Gibbes Art Gallery in Charleston, South Carolina; the following year it traveled to Philadelphia to be exhibited at the Art Alliance. That year Guggenheim created The Solomon R. Guggenheim Foundation for the "promotion and encouragement of art and education in art and the enlightenment of the public" (Charter, 1937; Guggenheim Museum archives), named Hilla Rebay curator, and during the following two years doubled his collection. Throughout the decade of the thirties, Guggenheim entertained plans for a museum building, but it took the threat of war in Europe to impel him to act. With Rebay's assistance, on 31 May 1939 he rented space on East 54th Street in New York, which he and Rebay transformed into the Museum of Non-Objective Painting (renamed the Solomon R. Guggenheim Museum in 1952), designed to introduce the public to nonobjective art and to assist the artists themselves. Along with the permanent collection of works collected by Guggenheim, the museum exhibited paintings by American nonobjective artists; it also circulated traveling exhibitions in order to promote broader acceptance of this revolutionary kind of painting. Guggenheim's foundation also provided scholarships to deserving artists and financial assistance to needy artists during a time of economic depression; later, in the 1940s, as refugee artists from Europe began to arrive in the United States, the Foundation offered assistance to many of these, including Chagall, Léger, and the filmmaker Hans Richter.

In 1943 Rebay and Guggenheim began to make plans for a permanent building for the collection, which numbered more than three thousand modern paintings and works of sculpture. Rebay solicited the help and advice of Frank Lloyd Wright, and, with Guggenheim's approval, she and the architect determined the site of the building and worked toward its construction. Her definition of the philosophy behind nonobjective art influenced Wright's final design of the building, which, however, also was subject to Guggenheim's assent. Not until 1959 was the building completed, seven years after Rebay was dismissed as director, presumably for mismanagement of funds and the acquisition of works of art of poor quality. Guggenheim did not live to see the museum building completed, and Wright died a few months after its public opening.

In 1970 Guggenheim's niece, Peggy Guggenheim—who at the same time as her uncle had begun a collection of over three hundred objects, including examples of tribal art and decorative glass objects as well as Cubist and surreal paintings—decided to deed her collection and its building in Venice, Italy—the Palazzo dei Leoni—to The Solomon R. Guggenheim Foundation, thus amalgamating the two collections. Her collection, however, has remained in Venice and has retained its separate identity as a reflection of her personal taste.

The Solomon R. Guggenheim Memorial Museum and Foundation testified to Guggenheim's and especially his family's great economic achievement and to his personal tastes and philanthropy. A man with gourmet and artistic instincts, apparent in the eight homes he owned in Long Island, Elberon, New Jersey, Charleston, South Carolina, Idaho, and Scotland, Guggenheim was a well informed and committed art collector, who prized quality and personally participated in planning and developing his art foundation despite Rebay's influence and intervention. He was also an active sportsman, a generous philanthropist, a loyal patron, and a man admired for his "courage and assurance" (Davis, p. 470). He and Irene had three daughters: Eleanor May, who became Countess Castle Stewart, Gertrude, who established charities for children in Sussex, England, and Barbara, whose first husband, John Robert Lawson-Johnston, a member of the British diplomatic service, fathered the son who was to take over the direction of the Guggenheim Brothers's vast business enterprises. Solomon Guggenheim died at "Trillora Court," Sands Point, Long Island, New York.

• A collection of Guggenheim's personal papers, particularly his correspondence with Hilla von Rebay, is in the archives of the Solomon R. Guggenheim Museum in New York City, together with the scrapbooks and papers of Hilla Rebay and the Hilla Rebay Foundation. Manuscripts relating to the building of the museum are also in the Wright archives at Taliesen West in Scottsdale, Ariz. Other manuscripts are in the collections of the Archives of American Art: Dwinell Grant Papers, 1930–1988; Carl Zigrosser Papers, which include files relating to The Solomon R. Guggenheim Museum and Foundation, 1946–1971; Harry Callahan Correspondence and Papers, 1943–1975; and Rudolf Bauer Papers, 1918–1983. Biographies and studies of Guggenheim's contributions include Harvey O'Connor, *The Guggenheims: The Making of an American Dynasty* (1937); Philadelphia Art Alliance, *Second Enlarged Catalogue of the Solomon Guggenheim Collection of Non-Objective Paintings* (1937); Edwin P. Hoyt, Jr., *The Guggenheims and the American Dream* (1967); John H. Davis, *The Guggenheims: An American Epic* (1978); Angelica Zander Rudenstine, *The Guggenheim Museum Collection: Paintings, 1880–1945* (1976); Kendall Taylor and John C. Riordan, *The Benefactors: Solomon Guggenheim, Joseph H. Hirshorn, Roy R. Neuberger* (1980); Joan M. Lukach, *Hilla Rebay: In Search of the Spirit in Art* (1983); Vivian Endicott Barnett, *Kandinsky at the Guggenheim* (1983); and Frank Lloyd Wright, *The Guggenheim Correspondence*, selected and with commentary by Bruce Brooks Pfeiffer (1986). For Peggy Guggenheim's relationship with the Guggenheim Museum, see Rudenstine, *Peggy Guggenheim Collection, Venice* (1983), and the accompanying *Handbook: The Peggy Guggen-*

heim Collection, text by Lucy Flint, conception and selection by Thomas M. Messer (1983). An obituary is in the *New York Times*, 3 Nov. 1949.

LILLIAN B. MILLER

GUILD, Reuben Aldridge (4 May 1822–13 May 1899), librarian, was born in West Dedham (now Westwood), Massachusetts, the son of Reuben Aldridge Guild, a blacksmith, and Olive Morse. The younger Reuben received a sound elementary education in both public and private schools. During his early teens young Reuben worked in a variety goods store near his home, and at the age of sixteen he left home for employment in Boston with Charles Warren & Co., a wholesale and retail dry goods dealer. In later years Guild attributed his managerial skills to this early experience. After two years in this endeavor, he decided to dedicate himself to the Baptist ministry, which religion he had joined in 1840 and for which a collegiate education seemed necessary.

In preparation for college, Guild was undoubtedly influenced by the surprising number of Brown graduates who were his instructors at Worcester and Day's Academy (including Charles Coffin Jewett, who was to be Guild's predecessor as librarian at Brown), and because of the strong Baptist tradition at Brown, Guild entered Brown University in the fall of 1843. He proved to be a good student, graduating in 1847 sixth in his class of thirty-three and as a member of Phi Beta Kappa. In 1850 Brown awarded him a master's degree.

Upon graduation from Brown, Guild was invited to take a position as assistant to the university librarian, Charles Coffin Jewett. The invitation was undoubtedly prompted by the fact that Jewett had known Guild in pre-Brown days and also that Guild had been librarian of the United Brothers Society for two years while an undergraduate. Guild accepted, and it proved to be a fortunate career decision as, one year later, Jewett moved on to become the librarian of the Smithsonian Institution and Guild succeeded him as Brown University librarian. Guild married Jane Clifford Hunt on 17 December 1849. They had six children, two of whom died in childhood. The circumstances of Guild's home life have not been discovered, but the fact that one daughter wrote glowingly of him shortly after his death suggests that he was as appreciated at home as on campus.

Guild was only twenty-six when he became university librarian, but he was prepared to take on the responsibilities. As he later pointed out, he had had five years of experience in business, had managed the bookstore at Worcester Academy, had had two years of experience as librarian with the United Brothers Society while an undergraduate, and had been a year under the direction of Jewett. It is also true that at the time the library was not considered a major facility of the institution nor was the position of librarian considered a major office within the university. It was Guild's destiny to preside over the library of a major university during a period in which the library became a central instrument in the newly perceived mission of research within the university.

The struggle toward centrality to the mission of the university was not an easy one for Guild. When he took over the library in 1848, the collections consisted of about 20,000 volumes, only half of which had been cataloged. During his long tenure, he often was the sole practitioner in the library, and at best, he had a single assistant through some of the years. During this time he was responsible for ordering new materials, for auditing and paying all bills, for recording all accessions, for acknowledging all gifts, and for making monthly reports.

During the first thirty years of Guild's tenure the library was situated in the first floor of the chapel, Manning Hall. This is by no means a vast facility, and by 1870 it had become almost impossible for anyone other than the librarian to find anything. President Ezekiel Gilman Robinson, remarking in the early 1870s on the need for a new library, said, "the library was crowded into the dark room on the first floor of the chapel building, and was . . . crammed with books, two or three feet deep on the shelves." The opening of the new library in 1878 was probably the most important development in Guild's career as librarian at Brown.

It is not clear that Guild had any great influence on the plan of the building itself. He himself said that the architects repeatedly called upon him for his advice and that he passed on to them Jewett's views as modified and developed after years of observation and study. On the other hand, Guild was not on the building committee and his name was not mentioned in the official dedicatory remarks at the opening of the building. The facility itself was in line with other recent libraries, most notably the library at Princeton, in that it had a central rotunda with alcoves radiating from it. Guild had been among the pioneers in allowing students direct access to library materials (a policy he had instituted by 1858). To facilitate such use in the new library, Guild arranged the materials by subject within the various alcoves. In addition, there was an eighty-drawer card catalog of the holdings. This catalog was in the nature of a shelf-list, as no real cataloging, as the term is now understood, was undertaken until after Guild retired. The library was initially named after its principal benefactor, John Carter Brown, but was later renamed Robinson Hall after the president in whose regime the edifice was erected.

Guild's energies were not limited to the operation of the library. In 1853 he, along with Charles B. Norton, was instrumental in convening the first librarians' convention in September 1853. This venture in cooperation proved abortive, but Guild was again a central figure in the convention of librarians in 1876 at Philadelphia, during which the American Library Association was founded. He was elected a secretary of that convention and the following year traveled to London for the first International Conference of Librarians, serving on council.

Throughout his career at Brown Guild dedicated himself to various civic duties. Among those were member of the Common Council of Providence, seven years; member of the school committee, usually as secretary, fifteen years; secretary of the Brown University Alumni Association, fifteen years; president and essayist of the Rhode Island Baptist Sunday School Convention, seventeen years; and secretary of the Rhode Island Baptist Education Society, five years. In addition to these activities Guild edited several volumes of letters and sermons and wrote many biographical and historical sketches. His major works, *Life, Times, and Correspondence of James Manning* (1864), *History of Brown University* (1867), and *Early History of Brown University* (1897), remain important in the history of higher education in the United States and have served as the bases for subsequent histories of Brown University.

Although Guild was clearly a very busy man in his professional life, he apparently had a personal warmth and charm that helped to mold generations of Brown students. He kept up an extensive correspondence with graduates that supports an impression of genuine warmth and appreciation toward him. William Carey Poland was a Brown professor and former Brown student who remembered Guild as "cheery and helpful. He seemed to enter easily into our ways of looking at things. He gave us aid in our reading. He could understand us, and always treated our immaturity with consideration." Guild retired in 1893, having held the position of librarian at Brown University for forty-five years. He died where he had lived his adult life, in Providence, Rhode Island.

Although no one thing stands out, Guild's accomplishments are substantial. He contributed to the building of a library facility that was state-of-the-art in its time, oversaw the early stages of the founding of a great library collection by the acquisitions of such materials as the famous Harris Collection of American Poetry, was influential in the development of library cooperation, and wrote and edited a number of works very useful to the historian of American higher education.

• Guild's papers are in the John Hay Library, Brown University. No biography is devoted to him, but information on him can be gathered from American Historical Society, *Colonial Families* (1925); Walter C. Bronson, *The History of Brown University, 1764–1914* (1914); Henry M. King, *Memorial Discourse on Reuben Aldridge Guild* (1899?); and William C. Poland, *Reuben Aldridge Guild, LL.D., Librarian of Brown University* (1900). A death notice is in the *Providence Daily Journal*, 15 May 1899.

JONATHAN S. TRYON

GUILDAY, Peter Keenan (25 Mar. 1884–31 July 1947), historian and educator, was born in Chester, Pennsylvania, the son of Peter Wilfred Guilday, a textile plant foreman, and Ellen Keenan. After attending parochial schools in Chester and Philadelphia, Peter entered St. Charles Borromeo Seminary in Overbrook in 1902 to study for the Roman Catholic priesthood. There he re-

ceived a scholarship in 1907 to attend the American College in Louvain, Belgium, for his last two years of theological studies. He was ordained in 1909 and at the same time began graduate work in history at the University of Louvain. Having a facility for languages, he researched archives in France, Belgium, Spain, and Italy, and spent a full year in London. In 1914 he received a Doctorat en sciences morales et historiques for his dissertation on colleges and convents of the European continent that had supported Catholic refugees from Elizabethan England. The outbreak of World War I halted further research, and the young priest returned to his homeland.

With the cooperation of his sponsoring diocese, Guilday was invited in 1914 to become an instructor of history at the Catholic University in Washington, D.C. Serving there for the next thirty-three years, he became an associate professor in 1919 and a full professor in 1923, in the department of history. His first duties pertained to medieval and modern European church history, but as the years progressed, he turned increasingly to the almost pristine field of American Catholic history. With the exception of John G. Shea of the previous century, few historians had studied the field to any substantial degree, and Guilday responded with great zeal and acuity to the need for uncovering Catholic activities in past American culture. At his own institution, he inaugurated a seminar on the subject and nurtured both master's and doctoral graduate programs in American Catholic church history. This original series of courses and the students trained therein made Catholic University unique in the circles of higher education. Between 1922 and 1943 thirty-three monographs were produced under Guilday's professorial hand and were printed in the Studies in American Church History series. Dozens of master's theses simultaneously presented work of comparable quality.

In 1915, shortly after Guilday's arrival on campus, the *Catholic Historical Review* was first issued. Guilday served as one of its editors and soon assumed the bulk of editorial chores, which he retained until poor health forced him to relinquish those duties in 1941. Through the *Review*, he was able to strengthen and augment a serious appreciation of Catholic history in both hemispheres. The journal's pages offered guidance for beginning researchers and the finished work of accomplished scholars. Guilday provided lists of biographical sources for the American Catholic hierarchy, guides to American church materials in foreign libraries, and evaluative comments on archival sources. He also edited several book-length studies of church historians through two millennia and assessments of Catholic life in twentieth-century Europe. In recognition of his editorial contributions, the *Review* kept his name on its masthead until his death in Washington, D.C.

As another means of nurturing interest in his chosen field, Guilday founded the American Catholic Historical Association in 1919. Its subsequent annual meetings under his guidance and thereafter have continued to encourage scholarly research into all phases of the Catholic experience.

Guilday made his most lasting contribution through his books. Trained first as a Europeanist, he gave his career a new focus to meet a perceived need. From 1914 to 1932 he produced seminal studies of key American prelates, the conciliar hierarchy, crucial issues in American Catholic history such as trusteeism, and nativist hostility, the careful expansion of Catholic witness throughout the country, and compatibility of Catholic piety with American freedoms. His graceful, accurate prose remained informative and reliable even to later generations that asked different questions of the eras he covered. From his manual on method for beginners to his orations on George Washington's birthday, to learned sermons in churches near the campus, Guilday established American Catholic historical scholarship as a distinctive subcategory of the academic profession.

• Among Guilday's works that have not already been mentioned are *The English Colleges and Convents in the Catholic Low Countries, 1558–1795* (1914), which is part of a larger work, *The English Catholic Refugees on the Continent, 1558–1795* (1914); *The Life and Times of John Carroll, Archbishop of Baltimore, 1735–1815* (1922); *The National Pastorals of the American Hierarchy, 1792–1919* (1923); *An Introduction to Church History: A Book for Beginners* (1925); *John Gilmary Shea, Father of American Catholic History, 1824–1892* (1926); *The Life and Times of John England, First Bishop of Charleston, 1786–1842* (1927); and *A History of the Councils of Baltimore, 1791–1884* (1932; repr. 1969). For biographical information see John T. Ellis, "Peter Guilday: March 25, 1884–July 31, 1947," *The Catholic Historical Review* 33, no. 3 (Oct. 1947): 257–68. See also David O'Brien, "Peter Guilday: The Catholic Intellectual in the Post-Modernist Church," in *Studies in Catholic History in Honor of John Tracy Ellis*, ed. Nelson H. Minich et al. (1985). An obituary is in the *New York Times*, 1 Aug. 1947.

HENRY WARNER BOWDEN

GUILES, Austin Philip (23 June 1894–13 Nov. 1953), theological educator, was born in Lawrenceville, Pennsylvania, the son of Austin Greenclay Guiles (occupation unknown) and Hanna Davis. After serving with the U.S. Army Ambulance Corps in Italy (1917–1919), Guiles, called "Phil," earned degrees from Princeton University (A.B., 1921), Columbia University (M.A., 1923), New York's Union Theological Seminary (B.D., 1925), and the University of Edinburgh (Ph.D., 1934, with a dissertation entitled "Mental Therapy and the Forgiveness of Sins; A Clinical View of the Results of Sin, with Psychological Studies of Religious Leaders . . ."). He was ordained to the Presbyterian ministry in 1924 and became a Congregationalist in 1939. He served as pastor of Union Church, Palisade, New Jersey (1925–1927), and later as associate to pastors at the Old South Church in Boston (1931–1933). He married Louise Earhart in 1925; they had four children.

In the summer of 1928 Guiles was among the first ministers to undertake training for pastoral work with emotionally disturbed persons through a newly organized program at Worcester State Hospital in Worcester, Massachusetts, under the supervision of the Reverend Anton T. Boisen, staying on as Boisen's assistant through 1929. The Boisen program for the education of ministers within clinical settings was supported by the prominent Boston physician and educational innovator, Richard C. Cabot, and Cabot and Guiles soon formed an important professional relationship. When Boisen suffered a temporary psychosis in 1930, and Cabot promptly terminated his activities at Worcester, Guiles, faced with a conflict of loyalties, sided with Cabot.

In 1931, on the basis of this training and experience, and having served also for several years as a psychotherapist with the Neuro-Endocrine Foundation of Boston, Guiles secured a faculty appointment at Andover Newton Theological School, a newly merged Baptist and Congregational seminary. He thereby became the first clinically trained person ever appointed to a theological faculty. Promoted to Smith Professor of Pastoral Psychology in 1934, Guiles devoted the rest of his career to the vision of integrating clinical studies into the core of the theological curriculum and used his faculty position and his relationship with Cabot to develop clinical training programs for pastors throughout New England.

Guiles was the key figure in organizing the Council for the Clinical Training of Theological Studies in 1930, securing the necessary funding through his father-in-law's Earhart Foundation, and served as the council's first field secretary and interim director until his appointment of Helen Flanders Dunbar, M.D., as executive director in 1930. For reasons never entirely clear, conflict soon developed between Guiles and Dunbar; each was a promoter and entrepreneur, and a clash of personalities apparently occurred. In 1932 Guiles withdrew from the council and established his own organization, the New England Group, and its successor organizations, the New England Theological Schools Committee on Clinical Training (1938) and the Institute for Pastoral Care (1944). These organizations were the major vehicles for the clinical pastoral education movement in New England, and Guiles was the principal figure in creating and guiding them through their formative years. In addition, and not incidentally, Guiles (with Cabot) was also the principal figure in funding their numerous centers and programs through his father-in-law's financial resources.

Guiles was a charter member of the Joint Committee on Religion and Health in 1927 (a cooperative research venture of the New York Academy of Medicine and the Federal Council of Churches) and in 1937 its successor, the Federal Council's Commission on Religion and Health. In Boston he was a central figure in the Cabot Club, a group of clinical pastoral educators dedicated to developing pastoral theory and skill through clinical and empirical studies in the Cabot tradition. The most notable achievement of this group was its invention of the pastoral case conference, a teaching device that later became standard in all advanced training in pastoral care and counseling. Guiles also promoted advanced research and academic degrees in pastoral care and counseling, was instrumental in securing the significant appointment of the pastoral theologian Paul Johnson to the faculty of the Boston University School of Theology in 1944, and was the key figure in creating the *Journal of Pastoral Care* in 1947. He served on various boards and was a fellow of the American Psychological Association and the American Protestant Hospital Chaplains Association.

A zealous advocate of psychological methods in ministry (he was fired from a chaplaincy position at Massachusetts General Hospital in 1932 for appearing to practice psychiatry), Guiles was always very much a clinical supervisor and teacher as well as a builder of programs and organizations. Inspired by Cabot's ideal of learning ministry from clinical experience under supervision, Guiles developed clinically oriented courses at Andover Newton aimed at fostering pastoral competence and various courses in "clinical theology" on such topics as guilt and forgiveness. His teaching emphasized "being oneself" in ministry, feeling at home with other professionals, and attaining a knowledge of human nature as a means of promoting healthy religious and moral life. Though fascinated by the "rather daring" theories of depth psychology, his ultimate research interest was to develop a "clinical theology"—a theology derived empirically from clinical experience.

Edward Thornton writes, "A. Philip Guiles was a tall, handsome, vivacious, outgoing, and thoroughly disorganized man. He had a striking personality . . . [and] was seen by some of his early associates as an empire builder. His lack of organization limited him, however. He is said to have written three books, none of which were seen by publishers" (p. 76). Nonetheless, there is little doubt that Guiles was a giant in the early years of the clinical pastoral education movement, not only "a debonair educational entrepreneur" (Holifield, p. 242), but "the most creative spirit in the New England group, . . . one of the most influential lives in the history of clinical pastoral education" (Thornton, p. 110) and "the first to demonstrate that a clinically oriented man belongs on the Faculty of any Theological School" (Hiltner, *Andover Newton Theological School Bulletin* 46 [Feb. 1954]: 3).

Guiles's health failed in 1949, greatly reducing his role in the movement. He died in Boston five days before a celebration to announce the founding of an academic chair in his honor at Andover Newton.

• Guiles's papers are in the possession of the Department of Psychology and Clinical Studies of the Andover Newton Theological School. He published no books and only a few papers: "The 1935 Summer School in Clinical Experience," *Institution Bulletin: Andover Newton Theological School* 27 (Oct. 1935): 7–8; "For Clinical Training during the School Term in the Light of the Experience of the New England Group" and "Clinical Training and Classroom Pastoral Courses," in *Clinical Pastoral Training*, ed. Seward Hiltner (1945); "Andover Newton and Clinical Training," *Andover Newton Theological School Bulletin* 39 (Dec. 1947): 1–20; and "Our Objectives in Psychology and Clinical Training," *Andover Newton Theological School Bulletin* 46 (Feb. 1954): 5–17. Guiles's role in the history of clinical pastoral education is described by Edward E. Thornton, *Professional Education for Ministry: A History of Clinical Pastoral Education* (1970); see also Allison Stokes, *Ministry after Freud* (1985), and, for a broader cultural interpretation of the movement, E. Brooks Holifield, *A History of Pastoral Care in America: From Salvation to Self-Realization* (1983). Obituaries are in the *Journal of Pastoral Care* 8 (1953–1954): 30–35, and the *Andover Newton Theological School Bulletin* 46 (Feb. 1954): 3.

RODNEY J. HUNTER

GUILFORD, Joy Paul (7 Mar. 1897–26 Nov. 1987), psychologist and educator, was born in Hamilton County, Nebraska, the son of Edwin Augustus Guilford and Arvilla Monroe, farmers. He attended college at the University of Nebraska in Lincoln, where he earned both an A.B. (1922) and an M.A. (1924) in psychology. His undergraduate studies were briefly interrupted by service in the Army Signal Corps during World War I. Although Guilford was interested in a career as a chemist when he entered the University of Nebraska, his experience in psychology courses led him to choose a career in psychology.

Guilford was accepted as a doctoral student at Cornell University in 1924 and there completed a Ph.D. in psychology in 1927. While at Cornell, Guilford worked closely with one of the pioneers of psychology in the United States, Edward Bradford Titchener, who supervised Guilford's dissertation on "Fluctuations of Attention with Weak Visual Stimuli." His work with Cornell psychophysicist Karl Dallenbach taught him the value of precision in the collection and treatment of data, as well as the possibilities for mathematical treatment of psychological data. During his first year at Cornell, Guilford also benefited from a seminar led by the Gestalt psychologist Kurt Koffka.

Guilford served as an instructor in psychology at the University of Illinois in the academic year 1926–1927, during which time he also completed his doctoral dissertation. He spent 1927–1928 as an assistant professor of psychology at the University of Kansas. He then accepted a position at the University of Nebraska, where he served as an associate professor from 1928 to 1932 and professor from 1932 to 1940. During his tenure at Nebraska, Guilford spent one semester as a visiting professor at Northwestern University. From 1938 to 1940 Guilford also served as director of the Bureau of Institutional Research at Nebraska. In 1940 Guilford accepted a position at the University of Southern California, where he remained, except for military service from 1942 to 1946, until his retirement in 1962. After his retirement, Guilford continued his research, writing, and professional involvement until his death in Los Angeles. He married Ruth S. Burke, a psychologist, in 1927; they had one child.

Guilford had a long and productive career as a psychologist. He was a prolific researcher and producer of research reports, writing more than twenty-five books and more than 300 journal articles. Guilford also produced thirty tests for use in psychological evaluation.

His research and writing interests ranged from experimental studies of attention to statistical studies of personality and intellectual abilities. His early interests fit within traditional experimental topics: attention, psychophysics, and learning. In this early period, Guilford also contributed to the understanding of abnormal behavior. While he did not lose interest in these topics, his work in the 1930s shifted to statistical psychology. His first major book, and arguably his most influential, *Psychometric Methods* (1936), was widely used as a textbook and was issued in a second edition in 1954. Guilford's other major book on statistical methods in psychology, *Fundamental Statistics in Psychology and Education*, went through several editions (1942, 1950, 1956, 1965, 1973). Guilford's work in statistical psychology centered on test development and on factor analysis as a method of discovering intellectual abilities.

During World War II Guilford served as a colonel in the Army Air Corps, where he and his colleagues undertook a large-scale effort to develop appropriate measurement devices for the selection of air-combat personnel. Factor analysis was key to this effort and by war's end Guilford's team had developed screening tests that helped to significantly reduce the pilot training failure rate. Guilford received the Legion of Merit for his contributions to the war effort.

After the war, Guilford returned to the University of Southern California, where he continued his factor-analytic approach to elucidating the multiple abilities (e.g., creativity, the ability to grasp visual-spatial relations, visual memory, verbal comprehension, numerical facility, and mechanical knowledge) that he believed compromised intelligence. In his approach he diverged from the widely accepted view that there was one general factor that underlay all aspects of intelligence.

Guilford's empirical work led him to develop a model for the classification of mental abilities; the model became known as the Structure of Intellect (SOI). First presented at a conference in Paris in 1955, the SOI was presented in a fully developed form in Guilford's book, *Personality* (1959). The SOI came to be the central tool Guilford and his colleagues used to explore intellectual abilities. The SOI model was represented by a three-dimensional rectangular solid. According to Guilford, there are six kinds of operations (cognition, memory recording, memory retention, convergent production, divergent production, and evaluation), five kinds of contents (visual, auditory, symbolic, semantic, and behavioral), and six kinds of products (units, classes, relations, systems, transformations, and implications) that provide the underlying structure for the many abilities that facilitate information processing.

Guilford continued to refine the SOI and increasingly sought to apply it to the educational process. He believed that intelligence was not static and that people could be trained to be smarter. His ideas on education have been widely applied, especially in Japan.

Guilford's work had a significant impact on psychologists' understanding of intelligence and personality. His refinement of factor-analytic techniques made it possible to empirically test theoretical propositions about human abilities. Guilford's work continued to be influential in the field of psychological measurement at the end of the twentieth century.

Guilford's honors included membership in the National Academy of Sciences; presidencies of the Psychometric Society and the American Psychological Association; and receipt of the APA Distinguished Scientific Contribution Award, APA Richardson Creativity Award, and Gold Medal of the American Psychological Foundation.

• Guilford contributed an autobiographical sketch to *History of Psychology in Autobiography*, vol. 5, ed. E. G. Boring and G. Lindzey (1967). For biographical sketches of Guilford see A. L. Comrey et al., "J. P. Guilford (1897–1987)," *American Psychologist* 43 (1988): 1086–87; D. B. Lindsley et al., "American Psychological Association Distinguished Scientific Contribution Awards," *American Psychologist* 19 (1964): 941–54; and W. B. Michael et al., "J. P. Guilford: Psychologist and Teacher," *Psychological Bulletin* 60 (1963): 1–34.

WADE E. PICKREN

GUINAN, Texas (12 Jan. 1884–5 Nov. 1933), nightclub personality, was born Mary Louise Cecilia Guinan in Waco, Texas, the daughter of Michael Guinan, a grocery wholesaler, and Bessie Duffy, both of whom had emigrated to the United States from Quebec, Canada, although their forebears had emigrated to Canada from Dublin, Ireland. Guinan was first married to John J. Moynahan, a Denver newspaper cartoonist, in 1904. It was a brief union and Guinan was on her own again by 1907. She entered show business as a rodeo driver, appeared in an operetta, *The Snowman* (1907; later retitled *The Girls of Holland*), and had her own vaudeville act beginning in 1908. When she appeared at New York's Fifth Avenue Theatre, *Variety* noted on 29 May 1909 that "Miss Guinan has looks, and dresses well. Her well-trained soprano does the rest." In 1909 she also appeared in *The Gay Musician* and subsequently went into partnership with that show's producer, John Slocum. In 1910 she presumably married film critic Julian Johnson (there is some doubt that they were ever formally married). Guinan pursued a successful vaudeville and musical comedy career for several years, billing herself as "God's Masterpiece," and she appeared in the cast of *The Passing Show* (1912–1913). Teamed with musical comedy performer Billy Gibson in 1916, she performed the song, "Do What Your Mother Did, I'll Do the Same as Your Dad." In this era she began using a phrase that would be credited to her throughout her life: "Give the little girl a big hand." It was only one of several memorable catch phrases Guinan popularized throughout her extraordinary career.

In 1917 Guinan became a silent screen actress in westerns where she was featured as a female variation on silent western male favorite William S. Hart. It was a natural transition for Guinan who was quoted in her

New York Times obituary as saying, "I could twirl a lariat, rope a steer, ride and shoot to beat any tobacco-chewin' cowpoke." Her first film, a short subject made for Balboa Studios in 1917, was *The Wildcat*. Its popularity led to her appearances in a series of feature pictures for the Triangle Company, the Frohman Amusement Corporation, the Reelcraft Film Company, and Victor Kremer Productions, all early and now forgotten silent filmmakers. Guinan's first important performance was in *The Fuel of Life* (1917), in which she played a vamp. *Motion Picture News* wrote on 24 November 1917 that she "overacts considerably and can't quite shed her musical comedy mannerisms." However, when she switched to westerns, critics were more approving. Some of her notable appearances were in *The Gun Woman* (1918), *The Love Brokers* (1918), *The She Wolf* (1919), *I Am the Woman* (1921), and *The Stampede* (1921), as well as frequent two-reel shorts. In 1921 she formed Texas Guinan Productions and filmed *The Code of the West* and *Texas of the Mounted*, playing the leads herself. Guinan had divorced Julian Johnson in 1920. Of this marriage, she stated, "He was my idea of a good scout, a regular fellow. As husbands went he was all right—and he went!" She married her third husband, George E. Townley, soon after her divorce from Johnson, but this last attempt at marriage ended in divorce in 1925.

It was in New York nightclubs in the 1920s that Guinan became a legendary figure and the icon of the Prohibition era. She was first associated with the El Fay Club, which was backed by Larry Fay, a former cabbie. She moved on to the Club Moritz and the Three Hundred Club (151 West 54th Street), the last of which provided her permanent niche in New York night life. Guinan served as hostess and mistress of ceremonies, introducing acts, singing a little, joking with the customers, and introducing the dancers to wealthy patrons (although Guinan puritanically insisted that the girls always leave work alone, and she did not permit them to go to parties). In a famous wisecrack directed at the celebrated Broadway producer Florenz Ziegfeld, Jr., Guinan proclaimed that her dancers were "glorious girls who don't need glorifying." Among the dancers introduced by Guinan were Ruby Keeler, who later married entertainer Al Jolson and became a popular dancer in Hollywood films, and Peggy Shannon, who also became a well-known screen actress in the 1930s. Gregarious and high-spirited, Guinan was attuned to public tastes and her clientele's interest in the glamorous nightlife of the 1920s. She invented stories about herself and the denizens of her club that amused and fascinated the public throughout the heady days of the speakeasies and the flapper. Despite the various popular acts that played her club, Guinan herself was the main attraction and could be relied upon to pack the audience. Patrons delighted to hear her deliver her famous greeting, "Hello, suckers!"

In 1927 Guinan was arrested at the Three Hundred Club for violation of prohibition laws. She insisted in court that she was only the hostess of the club and that she herself never drank (which was apparently true). Guinan was acquitted after a sensational front-page trial. Shortly thereafter, capitalizing on her arrest, she appeared in a Shubert-produced Broadway revue, *Padlocks of 1927*. The Shuberts were known for popular risqué entertainments, but *Padlocks* was not well received by critics.

Guinan also made a few movie appearances in the early sound era. In these she either played herself, as in her brief cameo appearance in Paramount Pictures' *Glorifying the American Girl* (1929), or as imitations of herself in Warner Bros.' *Queen of the Nightclubs* (1929) and United Artists' *Broadway Through a Keyhole* (1933). Other actresses played "Texas Guinan types" throughout the years, such as Glenda Farrell's "Missouri Martin" in *Lady for a Day* (1933), Gladys George's "Panama Smith" in *The Roaring Twenties* (1939), and Diane Lane's "Vera Cicero" in *The Cotton Club* (1984). Guinan was also portrayed in a Paramount Pictures' film biography, *Incendiary Blonde* (1945), which starred Betty Hutton as Guinan, and she was also impersonated by Barbara Nichols in *The George Raft Story* (1961).

Guinan headlined at New York's Palace Theatre in March 1932, and in 1933 she toured with her own company in a revue called *Too Hot for Paris*. When the show played the Beacon Theatre in Vancouver, British Columbia, Canada, in November 1933, Guinan collapsed backstage during a performance and died the next day due to complications from an ulcerated colon. Her funeral, held at Frank Campbell's Funeral Home in New York, was attended by over 7,500 mourners, and the *New York Times* proclaimed her the "mistress of Broadway's high revel."

• For information on Guinan, see Louise Berliner, *Texas Guinan: Queen of the Nightclubs* (1993); William Bolitho, "Two Stars," *The Delineator*, Jan. 1931, p. 15; James Doherty, "Texas Guinan, Queen of Whoopee!" *Chicago Sunday Tribune*, 4 Mar. 1951, pp. 4–6; Abel Green, "Texas Guinan Helped Make B'way History During the Volstead Era," *Variety*, 4 Jan. 1956, p. 423; Texas Guinan, "How to Keep Your Husband Out of My Night Club," *Liberty*, 30 Apr. 1932, pp. 50–51; Will A. Page, *Behind the Curtains of Broadway's Beauty Trust* (1927); Glenn Shirley, *Hello Sucker!: The Story of "Texas" Guinan* (1989); and Anthony Slide, *The Encyclopedia of Vaudeville* (1994) and *The Vaudevillians: A Dictionary of Vaudeville Performers* (1981). Obituaries are in the *New York Times*, 6 Nov. 1933; the *Times* (London), 6 Nov. 1933; and *Variety*, 7 Nov. 1933.

JAMES FISHER

GUINEY, Louise Imogen (7 Jan. 1861–2 Nov. 1920), poet and scholar, was born in Boston, Massachusetts, the daughter of Patrick Robert Guiney, a lawyer and Union brigadier general in the Civil War, and Janet M. Doyle. She studied at the Jesuit Elmhurst Convent of the Sacred Heart in Providence, Rhode Island. In 1877, two years before she graduated, her father died from an old war wound; the martial and chivalric strains in her poetry have been attributed to his influence.

While still in adolescence Guiney settled on a literary career. Her early poems were published by John Boyle O'Reilly, editor of the Roman Catholic periodical the *Boston Pilot*, and many of these reappeared in her first volume of poetry, *Songs at the Start* (1884). She followed with a volume of essays, *Goose-quill Papers* (1885), and a second volume of poetry, *The White Sail and Other Poems* (1887). The fairy tales she wrote for *Wide Awake*, a children's magazine, were collected in *Brownies and Bogles* (1888).

By 1887 Guiney had won the friendship of Boston literary figures such as Annie Fields, wife of the publisher James T. Fields, the writer Sarah Orne Jewett, the patron Louise Chandler Moulton, and the genre writer Alice Brown. The essayist Oliver Wendell Holmes, Sr., punning on her name, called her his "little golden guinea." She also associated herself with Boston's artistic bohemia, a younger group of artists and writers who were aesthetically innovative and sexually ambivalent. Among this group were the architect Ralph Adams Cram and the photographer and publisher Fred Holland Day. Vigorous and athletic—she sometimes preferred men's clothing—Guiney was, according to Cram, "the most vital and creative influence in the lives of all of us" (*My Life in Architecture* [1936], p. 30).

In 1889 Guiney traveled to London with her mother and stayed two years. Her friend Day arrived and joined her in collecting Keats memorabilia. Alice Brown also visited and edited, with Guiney, a handbook for women, *A Summer in England* (1891). There has been speculation that Guiney was involved romantically with Brown or Day, or both.

After her return to America, Guiney completed work on her best collection of poetry, *A Roadside Harp* (1893). Small in scope, the volume comprised a variety of styles: chivalric or medieval-style poems; fifteen "Alexandriana" based on classical forms; and a dozen sonnets on contemporary London. Although the work displayed technical mastery, critics—whose acumen Guiney compared to that of pelicans—complained of the density and difficulty of her phrasing. Van Wyck Brooks found her poetry, with exceptions, to be "ventriloquistic and intensely bookish" (*New England: Indian Summer* [1940], p. 451) but admired her later essays.

Guiney's career as a poet slowed as her financial resources dwindled and she was forced to work. In 1894 she became postmaster at Auburndale, the small town outside Boston where she and her mother lived. Inhabitants she identified as "bigots of small intellectual calibre" boycotted the post office to protest being served by a Roman Catholic. Her friends came to her rescue by traveling to Auburndale to buy stamps. She found the postal work too distracting for producing poetry, but she continued to write prose and to edit or translate the work of other writers. She had already completed *Monsieur Henri* (1892), a romantic biography of a French counterrevolutionary, and in 1894 she brought out a book of deft character sketches, *A Little English Gallery*; among those portrayed was one of her

models, the essayist William Hazlitt. Guiney's only book of fiction, *Lovers' Saint Ruth's and Three Other Tales*, appeared in 1895. In 1897 she completed *Patrins* (a word meaning gypsy trails), a well-received book of essays that included a lighthearted defense of Charles II of England. She resigned from the post office after a serious illness in 1897. Later she accepted an appointment as a cataloger at the Boston Public Library and worked there for nearly two years.

In 1901 Guiney moved to England and made Oxford her home for the rest of her life. She never, however, gave up her American citizenship. In England, as one of her biographers Henry G. Fairbanks has observed, her work became religious and increasingly Catholic in focus (p. 199). She edited works by such largely forgotten seventeenth-century Catholic literary figures as Henry Vaughan, Katherine Philips, and Hurrell Froude. Eventually, she came to concentrate on the generation of English recusant Catholic poets—those who declined to attend the Church of England—and worked on a collection of their work until her death. Although she continued to write general-interest articles for English and American magazines, her concentration on the obscure inevitably subverted any hopes she had of widespread recognition. Not even the appearance of *Happy Ending: Collected Lyrics* (1908), reviewed enthusiastically in America, brought her celebrity in England.

Guiney visited the United States for the last time when she returned late in 1909 to nurse her dying mother. After returning to England her income dwindled to the point that she eventually had to give up her house in Oxford and move to progressively smaller quarters. In 1917 she suffered a stroke, which curtailed her work. She died at the Cotswolds village of Chipping Camden.

Some of Guiney's most substantial work appeared after her death. *Recusant Poets*, its editing completed by others, was published in New York and London in 1938 and 1939. An enlarged edition of *Happy Ending* was published in 1927. Her cousin, Grace Guiney, collected two substantial volumes of her letters (1926), which reveal, as much as does her poetry, the spirit and wit of the woman who has been called "the lost lady of American letters." Although she has not been considered a major poet, cultural historians have shown continuing interest in her role in Boston's literary-artistic ferment of the 1890s and as one of the first Catholic writers to gain recognition in Protestant New England.

• The Guiney Room in Dinand Library, Holy Cross College, Worcester, Mass., has substantial holdings of Guiney's letters, first editions, and memorabilia. The Library of Congress has approximately 1,000 letters centering on her correspondence with Fred Holland Day; the Huntington Library in San Marino, Calif., has a smaller collection. Guiney's other poetical works include *Nine Sonnets Written at Oxford* (1895), *England and Yesterday* (1898), and *The Martyr's Idyl and Shorter Poems* (1900). Her prose includes "Martha Hilton," in *Three Heroines of New England Romance* (1894), *Robert Emmet* (1904), and *Blessed Edmund Campion* (1914).

Letters of Louise Imogen Guiney, ed. Grace Guiney (2 vols., 1926), is the most substantial published autobiographical material. Biographies of Guiney include Alice Brown, *Louise Imogen Guiney* (1921); Eva Mabel Tenison, *Louise Imogen Guiney* (1923); Mary Adorita Hart, *Soul Ordained to Fail* (1962); and Henry G. Fairbanks, *Louise Imogen Guiney: Laureate of the Lost* (1972) and *Louise Imogen Guiney* (1973). Discussion of Guiney and her associates appears in Hyder Edward Rollins, *Keats and the Bostonians* (1951); T. J. Jackson Lears, *No Place of Grace* (1981); Stephen Maxfield Parrish, *Currents of the Nineties in Boston and London* (1987); and Douglas Shand-Tucci, *Ralph Adams Cram*, vol. 1: *Boston Bohemia, 1881–1900* (1995). A perceptive appreciation of her work is Daniel J. Berrigan, S.J., "Forgotten Splendor," *America*, 4 Mar. 1944, pp. 605–6. A brief notice of her death is in the *New York Times*, 4 Nov. 1920.

JAMES BOYLAN

GUITEAU, Charles Julius (8 Sept. 1841–30 June 1882), assassin, was born in Freeport, Illinois, the son of Luther Wilson Guiteau, a businessman, and Jane Howe. Left motherless at the age of seven, he grew up a hyperactive, lonely child, dominated by his strict father, whose only passion was for the Perfectionist doctrine of John Humphrey Noyes, which taught that sin and thereby death were illusions. When Charles failed his preparatory exams for the University of Michigan in 1860, he took up his father's religion and joined the Perfectionist community at Oneida, New York, drawn there more by the sexual communitarianism it practiced than by the theology it preached.

Life among the Perfectionist saints proved disappointing to Guiteau, whom Noyes regarded as "moody, self-conceited, unmanageable." Unpopular in the community, Guiteau left in 1867, determined to fulfill some great destiny, perhaps even the presidency. For a time he toyed with the idea of establishing a religious newspaper in New York, although he was virtually penniless. Then he studied law in Chicago, trying only one case, which he lost disastrously. After that he specialized in collecting bad debts, but he tended to pocket the proceeds rather than sharing them with his clients.

An accomplished deadbeat, Guiteau left behind a trail of unpaid loans and boardinghouse bills before returning to New York in 1871. He was accompanied by his wife of three years, Annie Bunn, a timid YMCA librarian who had been attracted by his outward show of piety. She was soon so disillusioned by his violent temper and frequent consorting with "lewd women" that she sued for divorce in 1873; they did not have children.

In 1872 Guiteau tried his hand at politics, delivering a disjointed speech for presidential candidate Horace Greeley that, he was convinced, entitled him to be minister to Chile in a Greeley administration. With Greeley's defeat, he turned again to theology, after a brief stint in jail for fraud and a narrow escape from commitment to a mental asylum for chasing his sister with an axe. For three years he was an itinerant evangelist, preaching a revelation brazenly lifted from the works of Noyes.

In 1880 Guiteau again took up politics, publishing a cliché-ridden speech for James A. Garfield, the Republican nominee for president, and hanging around Republican headquarters, stealing stationery and trying to look important. For these services he expected to be rewarded with a suitable diplomatic appointment, preferably consul general at Paris. For months he badgered Garfield and Secretary of State James G. Blaine, who finally threw him out of his office in exasperation.

Shortly thereafter, on the evening of 18 May 1881, an inspiration, which he presumed to be divine, began to possess Guiteau with the conviction that the faithless president had to be "removed" in order to save the Republican party and avert another civil war. Unable to resist the "pressure" of this call, Guiteau purchased a .44 caliber, ivory-handled pistol (with borrowed money) and began to stalk his prey. Presidents were not yet protected by either the Secret Service or by bodyguards. Most Americans would have agreed with Garfield that "Assassination can no more be guarded against than death by lightning; and it is not best to worry about either."

Guiteau caught up with the president on 2 July 1881 at the Baltimore & Potomac railroad station. Garfield was in a festive mood: his patronage troubles with Roscoe Conkling, leader of the pro-Grant "Stalwart" wing of the party, were behind him; a vacation lay ahead of him. Garfield was waiting for his train, deep in conversation with Blaine about a forthcoming speech on southern affairs, when Guiteau stepped behind him and pumped two bullets into the president's back. Leaving his wounded victim lying on the waiting-room floor, Guiteau coolly headed toward a cab he had prudently hired to take him to the safety of the District of Columbia jail. Before he could reach it he was arrested by police officer Patrick Kearny, to whom he explained, "I am a Stalwart."

Throughout the summer of 1881 the weakened president slowly slipped away despite, or perhaps because of, the constant attention of a small army of physicians. He died at Elberon, New Jersey, at 10:35 on the night of 19 September and was succeeded by Vice President Chester Alan Arthur.

After Garfield's funeral, which was conducted amid scenes of unmatched national mourning, Guiteau's trial began. The trial lasted from 13 November 1881 to 5 January 1882. It soon degenerated into a tasteless circus, largely because of the bizarre antics of the defendant who sang, raved, and interrupted the proceedings at will. If this behavior was intended to support the defense's contention that Guiteau was insane, it failed to impress the jury, which ruled him guilty after deliberating for only an hour and five minutes. Behind the clowning, the trial contained some serious aspects. It served as a showcase for the infant discipline of psychiatry, and it underlined the deficiencies of the prevailing M'Naghten rule, which held that defendants could be deemed legally insane only if they failed to understand the consequences of their actions. By that standard Guiteau was clearly sane, despite his apparent derangement. He was hanged in Washington, D.C., on 30 June 1882 while reciting a childish poem he composed for the occasion entitled "I Am Going to the Lordy."

Guiteau's sad career was eagerly seized upon by advocates of civil service reform. In their propaganda, Guiteau's tangled web of delusions was reduced to the single strand of "disappointed office seeker," and in that guise he was transformed into a symbol of the evils of the spoils system, a gross oversimplification that has been imposed upon history ever since.

• The indispensable source for Guiteau's life and crimes is the official three-volume transcript, *Report of the Proceedings in the Case of the United States vs. Charles J. Guiteau. . . .* (1882). This should be supplemented with a journalistic account by H. G. and C. J. Hayes, *A Complete History of the Trial of Guiteau* (1882), which includes Guiteau's "Autobiography" and a narrative of his married life by his onetime wife. Useful secondary works include Allan Peskin, *Garfield* (1978), and Charles Rosenberg, *The Trial of the Assassin Guiteau* (1968), which places Guiteau's trial in the context of Gilded Age psychiatry and law.

ALLAN PESKIN

GUITERAS, Juan (4 Jan. 1852–28 Oct. 1925), physician and public health official, was born in Matanzas, Cuba, the son of Eusebio Guiteras, an educator and author, and Josefa Gener. In 1867 he received an A.B. from Colegio La Empresa in Matanzas and began studying medicine at the University of Havana. Two years later he enrolled in the medical and graduate schools of the University of Pennsylvania, where he received an M.D. and a Ph.D. in 1873. After completing his internship at Philadelphia Hospital, he was there appointed resident physician in 1874 and visiting physician in 1876. Three years later he became a clinical lecturer at the hospital, an instructor in symptomatology at Pennsylvania, and a member of a U.S. National Board of Health commission investigating the causes of yellow fever in Havana.

Upon returning to the United States in 1880, Guiteras joined the U.S. Marine Hospital Service (later part of the Public Health Service), and for the next nine years he treated merchant sailors in various marine hospitals in the southern states and investigated yellow fever epidemics throughout the country. In 1883 he married Dolores Gener; they had one child. From 1885 to 1889, while assigned to the marine hospital in Charleston, South Carolina, he took on the additional duties of professor of clinical medicine at the Medical College of South Carolina. In 1886 he made the first positive identification in the United States of *filaria Bancrofti*, a worm-like, microscopic parasite injected into the lymph system by mosquito bite. After briefly studying pathology in Germany at the University of Frankfurt-on-Main with Carl Weigert, he returned in 1889 as a professor of general and anatomical pathology at the University of Pennsylvania, where he taught the first courses offered in the United States on the causes of tropical diseases. Two years later he was appointed pathologist at Philadelphia Hospital.

Like his father and father-in-law, Guiteras was an ardent supporter of Cuban independence from Spain. When the second Cuban revolution broke out in 1895, he became president of the executive committee of the Philadelphia-based Cuban Revolutionary party. Over the next three years he wrote one book and translated another, both of them intended to elicit U.S. support for Cuban independence. When the Spanish-American War broke out in 1898, he joined the American expeditionary force as a major in the medical corps and served in Cuba on General William R. Shafter's staff during the Santiago campaign.

After the war Guiteras joined the staff at Las Animas Hospital in Havana, where he resumed his earlier studies of the causes of yellow fever. Working closely with Walter Reed of the U.S. Army Yellow Fever Commission, who was investigating the transmission of the disease, he verified experimentally their hypothesis, first suggested in 1881 by the Cuban physician Carlos J. Finlay, that yellow fever is spread by the mosquito *Aedes aegypti*. He also attempted to develop a vaccine for yellow fever, but the death of three subjects convinced him that this feat was not possible. Although he later proved to be at least partially wrong on both counts—in the 1930s researchers discovered that a number of other mosquito species also carried yellow fever, and Max Theiler of the Rockefeller Foundation developed two vaccines—Guiteras's findings concerning the role played by mosquitoes in the spread of yellow fever directly contributed to the implementation of a mosquito-control program that eliminated yellow fever from Havana in 1901. This same program was employed in the Isthmus of Panama several years later and made possible the completion of the Panama Canal.

In 1899 Guiteras studied at the University of London's School of Tropical Medicine and returned the next year to the University of Havana as professor of pathology and tropical medicine, becoming the first holder of such a chair in the world. In 1900 he founded *La Revista de Medicina Tropical*, the first medical journal devoted to tropical medicine, and served as its editor for six years. When Cuba was granted its independence from the United States in 1902, he assumed the additional duties of president of the Havana commission for the diagnosis of infectious diseases and director of Las Animas. That same year he discovered ancylostomiasis, a form of hookworm disease that thrives in tropical climates amidst particularly unsanitary living conditions. In 1905 he was also made dean of the university's medical school. Although he continued to teach until 1921, in 1909 he resigned the rest of his positions to become director of Cuba's public health service. In this position he oversaw a nationwide campaign to rid the country of much of its debris and organic filth, thus reducing the population's susceptibility to ancylostomiasis.

In 1916 Guiteras joined the Rockefeller Foundation's Yellow Fever Commission and for the next four years investigated that disease throughout the Caribbean, northern South America, and west Africa. This commission identified Guayaquil, Ecuador, as the only endemic center for yellow fever in South America and oversaw the implementation of a mosquito-control program that led to the eradication of the disease from that city in 1919. In 1921 he was appointed secretary of public health and charities, and chief administrator and president of Cuba's national board of health. In 1922 he retired to his home in Matanzas, where he died.

Guiteras served as director of the *Boletin de Sanidad y Beneficiencia* from 1909 to 1917, president of the Second National Medical Congress of Cuba in 1914, member of the board of the Rockefeller Foundation from 1916 to 1925, and vice president of the Association of Health Officers of North America. He was also a founder and vice president of the American Public Health Association.

One of the foremost experts in tropical medicine of his day, Guiteras is remembered for his groundbreaking investigations into the pathology of yellow fever and other tropical diseases.

• Guiteras's papers have not been located. His contributions are discussed in George K. Strode, ed., *Yellow Fever* (1951). An obituary is in the *New York Times*, 29 Oct. 1925.

CHARLES W. CAREY, JR.

GULDAHL, Ralph (22 Nov. 1911–12 June 1987), professional golfer, was born in Dallas, Texas, the son of Olaf Guldahl and Anna Nordly, Norwegian immigrants. He became a caddy at the Lakewood Country Club at age eleven and then began playing regularly at the nine-hole Randall Park city course. In 1927 he captained the state champion Woodrow Wilson High School team and was also the individual interscholastic medalist with rounds of 65 and 71. He developed his game in the highly competitive atmosphere of the Tenison Park and Stevens Park public courses against Ray Mangrum, Gus Moreland, and other strong competition. He entered various Texas tournaments, whose fields included Jimmy Demaret, Ben Hogan, and Byron Nelson. In 1929 he won the Dallas city championship.

Guldahl turned professional in January 1930 at the Texas Open in San Antonio, which forced him to delay his final examinations for high school graduation. He was the youngest qualifier for the 1930 U.S. Open at Interlachen in Minneapolis, the site that year of Bobby Jones's third Grand Slam victory. Working as a Dallas club professional, he saved enough to attempt the California winter tournaments in 1931 and there earned his first money title, the Motion Picture Match Play Championship. He thus became, at nineteen, the youngest ever to win a Professional Golfers Association (PGA) event. During that year he married La Verne Fields of San Angelo, Texas; the couple had one child.

After finishing second by a single stroke to amateur Johnny Goodman at the 1933 U.S. Open, Guldahl entered a period of disillusionment, searching, and frustration. He recalled that both "my golf game and confidence went to pieces." Financially pinched, he tried unsuccessfully to sell automobiles in Hollywood before working as a carpenter on the Warner Bros. studio lot. There the likable, 6'3" Texan developed friendships with golfers such as Oscar-winning director William Wellman and western actor Rex Bell. From them and others he secured backing that allowed him to practice extensively and rejoin the PGA tour. With additional support, notably from Lawrence Icely, president of Wilson Sporting Goods, he reemerged brilliantly in 1936.

For the next four years Guldahl was the nation's dominant player in major tournaments, competing against Sam Snead, Craig Wood, Byron Nelson, and Denny Shute, among others. His record in the majors during this brief span matches those of Ben Hogan (early 1950s), Arnold Palmer (late 1950s–early 1960s), and Jack Nicklaus (early and mid-1960s). In 1936 he won the first of three consecutive Western Opens (then considered a major tournament), three regular tour events, and the Radix Trophy, forerunner of today's Vardon Trophy, for the lowest per-round average. His victory in the U.S. Open at Oakland Hills near Detroit highlighted a superb year in 1937, which included another Western title, a disappointing near-win at the exclusive Masters Tournament, six second-place finishes, and a sweep of all his matches for the American team against the British in his only appearance in the biennial Ryder Cup competition. He took a third Western in 1938, tied for second in the Masters, and won a second U.S. Open, in a magnificent come-from-behind effort at Cherry Hills in Denver, becoming only the fourth to claim consecutive U.S. Opens. His four titles in 1939 included the Masters, where his 279 total, while matched once, was not bested until 1953. For five straight years (1936–1940) he ranked among the top ten professionals in earnings.

This remarkable run placed Guldahl thirteenth among PGA tournament players for the period 1930–1945, a status that fellow players affirmed. His consistency in winning two U.S. Opens, declared Bobby Jones, proved that success in a major championship would demand not three but "four good rounds." Guldahl's deliberate style of play and extraordinary concentration did not endear him to sportswriters and some competitors. Tommy Armour in 1939 described him as the "most underrated golfer I ever knew" but the "best we have today." Snead, a close friend and competitor, considered Guldahl a "master" of sand play, while Walter Hagen judged him a "great" six-iron player.

In 1940, following a fifth-place finish in the U.S. Open and the last two of his sixteen PGA victories, Guldahl's winning percentage declined abruptly, and he ceased to be a tour regular. This turnabout generated ample speculation. Scrutiny centered on his swing, which he meticulously analyzed on film and in an astute, personally authored instructional book, *Groove Your Golf* (1939). Despite his close self-study and comeback in the mid-1930s, some critics insisted that he played by instinct and did not sufficiently grasp the game's technical aspects to recover the powerful on-line swing that had gone awry. Others blamed an inactive lower body, a style that placed excessive reliance on his hands and arms, perhaps the result of an earlier hip injury. Most plausible were Guldahl's later explanations that his competitiveness flagged; that he and his wife tired of the travel grind and incessant long-distance driving on hazardous two-lane highways; and that they desired a normal family routine for their young son.

Guldahl, rejected for active military duty because of a perforated ear drum, held positions at prestigious clubs in San Diego and the Midwest during World War II. He attempted the tour briefly in the late 1940s, failed to play up to his high standard, and then entered the insurance business in southern California. In 1961 he returned to golf as the first head professional at the new Braemar Country Club in Tarzana, California. A popular teacher and members' favorite, he remained at Braemar until his death. In the late 1970s and 1980s he was an original participant in the Legends of Golf tournament, which inspired the PGA Senior Tour. He was inducted into the PGA, the World Golf, and Texas Sports halls of fame. Guldahl died in Sherman Oaks, California.

• Published reminiscences are scant, but Guldahl's life from boyhood through his Masters' victory in 1939 is chronicled in "Highlights in the Golfing Life of Ralph Guldahl," a section of his now rare instructional book, *Groove Your Golf* (1939). The nature of his rise and triumphs in the mid- and late 1930s is best described in Robert Sommers, *The U.S. Open: Golf's Ultimate Challenge* (1987; repr. 1996), and Herbert Warren Wind, *The Story of American Golf: Its Champions and Its Championships*, 4th ed. (1986). Articles and entries of less scope include Nevin H. Gibson, *Great Moments in Golf* (1973), Michael Hobbs, *50 Masters of Golf* (1983), and Peter Alliss, *The Who's Who of Golf* (1983). Guldahl's departure from the tour is discussed in Wind and in Al Barkow, *Golf's Golden Grind: The History of the Tour* (1974). His post-tour years are encapsulated, largely through the recollections of his widow, in Curt Sampson, *Texas Golf Legends* (1993). The statistical story is detailed in Al Barkow, *The History of the PGA Tour* (1989), and John P. May, ed., *The Golf Digest Almanac, 1984* (1984). An obituary is in the *Los Angeles Times*, 14 June 1987.

JAMES A. WILSON

GULICK, John Thomas (13 Mar. 1832–14 Apr. 1923), missionary and naturalist, was born on Kauai Island, Hawaii, the son of Peter Johnson Gulick and Fanny Hinckley Thomas, Presbyterian missionaries. Primitive conditions made life difficult for the Gulick family. At the age of three Gulick contracted an inflammatory eye disease, and in an effort to protect his eyesight, he was often restricted to a darkened room until the age of five. For the rest of his life he suffered from impaired vision.

Gulick's weak constitution prevented him from studying the usual subjects, but his parents encouraged his interest in the Hawaiian environment. In 1853 this interest was cultivated through his meeting and association with the noted collector of Hawaiian land snails, Wesley Newcomb, who introduced Gulick to Charles Darwin's *Journal of Researches into the Geology and Natural History of the Various Countries Visited by H.M.S. 'Beagle'*.

Gulick was fascinated by the work of naturalists. After observing morphological differences from valley to valley of *Achatinellidae*, land snails of Oahu, Gulick collected these snail shells to compare his geographical distribution study to that of Darwin on various species of the Galapagos Islands. On 7 April 1853 Gulick presented "The Distribution of Plants and Animals," a lecture to the Púnahóu Debating Society near Honolulu. He noted three important principles found through the observations of naturalists: each species has its own geographical locality; each species has adapted to its surrounding environment; and a group of species in each area maintains its own harmony and correspondence. While expanding his studies on biological evolution, Gulick also enjoyed reading Hugh Miller's *Footprints of the Creator*, especially the last chapter, a critical introduction to Robert Chambers's theory of organic evolution.

In 1855 Gulick entered Williams College in Massachusetts and immediately joined the college's Lyceum of Natural History. In 1856 he was appointed member in charge of conchology, and for the half-year preceding his graduation he served as the society's president. After graduation Gulick attended Union Theological Seminary, where he continued his biological research and read Darwin's newly published *On the Origin of Species*.

In about 1861 Gulick's work on Hawaiian land snails attracted the attention of the naturalist Louis Agassiz, then a professor of zoology at Harvard University. Inspired by this recognition, Gulick interrupted his formal education for a shell-collecting tour to Aspinwall on the Isthmus of Panama. Then he extended his trip to Japan.

The Gulick family had produced a number of missionaries to the Pacific islands and Asia, and in childhood Gulick had resolved to follow in the footsteps of his father and brothers. As a result of Commodore Perry's expedition to Japan and the resultant treaty of 1854, Japan had recently opened to foreign visitation. In 1862 Gulick traveled to Yokohama and applied to the American Board of Commissioners for Foreign Missions (of the Congregational church) for assistance in working as a missionary in Japan. With the United States embroiled in civil war, however, the board rejected his application, indicating that it lacked the resources necessary to open work in a country that had maintained anti-Christian laws for more than 200 years and had not yet openly accepted Christian missionaries.

Gulick then resolved to carry out missionary work in China. In 1864, while visiting Hong Kong, he met and married Emily De La Cour, an educational missionary at an English school there. The couple proceeded to Peking and later Chang-kia K'ou, where they did missionary work; however, the climate in these places was so harsh that Gulick became seriously ill. In 1875, hoping to restore Gulick's deteriorating health, they traveled to the milder climate of Japan, but soon after their arrival Emily died suddenly. Their marriage was childless.

Gulick remained in Japan to serve as a missionary in Kobe until 1882, when he moved to Osaka to join his new bride, Frances A. Stevens, an educational missionary at Osaka's Baikawa Girl's School. During their stay in Osaka until 1899, they had two children. Gulick taught English grammar, conversation, and debate at two Christian schools, Taisei Boy's School in Osaka, and Hokuetsu Boy's School in Niigata. He also preached regularly in the Japanese language at Osaka's mission chapel centers.

Gulick was one of two American naturalists who introduced evolutionary theory to Japan. Unlike his counterpart, Edward S. Morse, Gulick consistently linked evolutionary theory to Christianity. He presented several lectures on evolution at a leading Christian school in Kyoto, Dôshisha University. At the Osaka Conference for Missionaries (1883 or 1884), he drew connections between his religious beliefs and biology in a lecture, "Evolution in the Organic World."

In 1899 Gulick and his family returned to the United States for a stay in Oberlin, Ohio. There Gulick finished the masterwork based on his life's research, *Evolution, Racial and Habitudinal*, which was published in 1905, the year he and his wife left Oberlin. Until Gulick's death they lived in Honolulu, Hawaii. Gulick had made significant contributions to the development of evolutionary biology, and his collection of Hawaiian land snail shells furnished important evidence on the geographical distribution of these species.

• Gulick's diary was published by his son, Addison Gulick, under the title *Evolutionist and Missionary: John Thomas Gulick* (1932). Most of his biological work and views on social evolution are described in his *Evolution, Racial and Habitudinal* (1905).

TOMOKO Y. STEEN

GULICK, Luther Halsey (10 June 1828–8 Apr. 1891), missionary physician and administrator, was born in Honolulu, Hawaii, the eldest son of Peter Johnson Gulick and Fanny Hinckley Thomas, missionaries of the American Board of Commissioners for Foreign Missions (ABCFM). After early years in Hawaii, Gulick was sent to the mainland for education. He graduated from Auburn Academy, New York, attended the New York College of Physicians and Surgeons, and on 9 March 1850 received the M.D. from New York University. While a medical student he engaged in city missionary work and began attending lectures at Union Theological Seminary. On 5 October 1851 he was ordained as a Congregational minister at Broadway Tabernacle, New York City. Two weeks later, on 29 October, he married Louisa Mitchell Lewis, who had been educated at Rutgers Seminary, New York City, had spent two winters in North Carolina teaching, and before her marriage was doing city missionary work in New York. They had seven children.

Intent on founding a mission to Micronesia, the Gulicks sailed from Boston on 18 November 1851 with Rev. and Mrs. B. G. Snow, under sponsorship of the American Board. Arriving in Honolulu on 28 March 1852, Gulick organized a Hawaiian Mission Children's Society for support of a Micronesia mission. Colloquially known as "the Cousins," the society became a major factor in Hawaii's development, as many of its members achieved prominence in business, professional, and political life. Its first project was to contribute $50 a year to the support of "Cousin Halsey" and his bride. On 15 July 1852 the Gulicks sailed on the brig *Caroline*, together with two other American and two Hawaiian missionary couples and three advisers, including Luther's brother John Gulick. A letter of commendation from the Hawaiian king Kamehameha III introduced them as "teachers of the Most High God, Jehovah."

After stops at Butaritari in the Gilbert Islands and at Kusaie, the missionary party made landfall at Ponape, a large, high island with a population of 10,000 divided among half a dozen rival tribes. The Gulicks settled among the Metalinim on the windward side, with one other American couple and a Hawaiian couple beginning work across the island. The Gulicks immediately began to learn the language and reduce it to writing. At the same time they built a house, a chapel for visiting seamen, a school, and a hospital. Local labor could only be secured by payment with tobacco, an addiction introduced by traders and whalers; no other currency was acceptable. Gulick made many translations into Ponapean and toured his area energetically on foot, combining medical practice with frequent preaching. When Louisa Gulick fell ill he had to undertake home duties; journal entries read, "Washed clothes, got breakfast, read some. . . . Got dinner. Read Gibbon, Meditated on sermon for tomorrow." Reading was always important; sending his gold watch home to the mission board in exchange for books, he wrote: "Books are Louisa's and my life. . . . We must have books if nothing else. To deprive us of them is cruelty." Eventually he had 600 of them in his wicker and palm-leaf house. Ponapeans loved the Gulicks' music, quickly became adept in it, and would travel miles to hear them play the melodeon. The first printing on the press that Gulick secured in 1856 included a hymn that he had composed.

In 1854 a passing whaler put two seamen sick with smallpox ashore to die. Natives took their clothing, thus engendering a raging epidemic. Gulick inoculated himself from an active case, cultured a vaccine, and then, with his fellow missionary on the other side of the island, inoculated thousands, helping to save half the population.

Gulick became exasperated by the wholesale prostitution of native women on board visiting New England whalers. In 1859 he wrote a public letter, widely distributed in New England, to "The Christian Owners of Whaleships." It stirred up a hornet's nest, and he was admonished by his supporters to write privately to pastors of offending captains rather than exposing their names publicly.

In 1859 the mission voted to send the Gulicks to Ebon Atoll in the Marshall Islands to provide medical service and otherwise strengthen a new mission there. A year later they were recalled to Hawaii for health reasons. Recovering, Gulick traveled on the mainland as a rousingly effective missionary speaker. In 1863 he became the first executive secretary of the Hawaiian Evangelical Association, newly organized to carry on the mission from which the American Board had withdrawn. It became the primary sponsor of the mission to Micronesia that Gulick had pioneered.

In 1871 Gulick was drafted by the American Board to establish new missions in "Papal Lands" of Europe. He settled in Barcelona, Spain, and inaugurated a mission in which his brothers William H. Gulick and Thomas L. Gulick also served. The venture proved enduring and helped to reinforce the small Protestant community in that country. Gulick was posted to Italy in 1873 to explore the desirability of a mission there in partnership with the indigenous Protestant churches. He concluded that an undesirable degree of dependence on American support and initiative would be inevitable, so he returned to the United States in May 1875.

In December of that year Gulick entered into the final phase of his career, serving as Far East agent for the American Bible Society. He was located first in Yokohama, where he established the Bible House, later moving to Shanghai. There he greatly increased the circulation of Bibles through a system of colporteurs working as itinerant salespeople. From 1885 to 1889 he also edited an important periodical, the *Chinese Recorder and Missionary Magazine*, interpreting developments in China for English readers in China and abroad. He died in Springfield, Massachusetts, after forty years of missionary service. His widow returned to Japan, and she died at Kōbe in 1894.

• Correspondence between Gulick and the American Board is in the papers of the ABCFM at the Houghton Library, Harvard University. Much of it is available in microfilm. For many materials, including *Reports of the Hawaiian Missionary Society* (1852–1862) and *Reports of the Hawaiian Evangelical Association* (1863–1891), the Hawaiian Mission Children's Society library in Honolulu is an important resource. Its *Missionary Album* (1869) has basic data on several members of the Gulick missionary dynasty. Except for one sermon of 1852, Gulick's only published writing in English is *Notes on the Grammar of the Ponape Dialect* (1858), reprinted in the *Journal of the American Oriental Society* 10 (1872). He made many translations from the Bible and religious writings into Ponapean. Issues of the *Missionary Herald*, 1851–1863 and 1871–1875, contain many references, as do the *Annual Reports of the American Board of Commissioners for Foreign Missions* for those years. A biography is Thomas Gulick Jewett, *Luther Halsey Gulick* (1891). Accounts of various aspects of Gulick's life and work are in David Crawford and Leona Crawford, *Missionary Adventures in the South Pacific* (1967); Albertine Loomis, *To All People* (1970); Fred Field Goodsell, *They Lived Their Faith* (1961); John Garrett, *To Live among the Stars* (1982); and David Hanlon, *Upon a Stone Altar* (1988).

Obituaries are in the *Bible Society Record*, 16 Apr. 1891; the *Friend* (Honolulu), May 1891, reprinted in the *Chinese Recorder*, July 1891; and the *Missionary Herald* 87 (1891): 237–39.

DAVID M. STOWE

GULICK, Luther Halsey (4 Dec. 1865–13 Aug. 1918), physical educator and sports administrator, was born in Honolulu, Hawaii, the son of Luther Halsey Gulick and Louisa Lewis, missionaries. His father's supervisory work for Presbyterian missions took Gulick as a child to Spain, Italy, Switzerland, and Japan as well as to Hawaii. In each place he stored up experiences that compensated for uneven schooling. His higher education, too, was irregular. From 1880 to 1885 he studied in a college preparatory program at Oberlin College, interrupted for a year by his parents' furlough; in 1886 he briefly attended the Sargent Normal School of Physical Training in Cambridge, Massachusetts, before enrolling as a part-time student in New York University's school of medicine. He paid his way at NYU by engaging in an unlikely array of activities: providing medical services to a YMCA branch, teaching in a Harlem school, serving as physical director of the YMCA in Jackson, Michigan, and organizing the physical education department at the new YMCA training school in Springfield, Massachusetts.

In 1887 Gulick married Charlotte Vetter; they had six children. Two years later he completed his medical degree at NYU. His lifelong concern for hygiene, human anatomy, and scientific physical measurement found expression in numerous articles and books, especially *Physical Measurements and How They Are Used* (1889), *Physical Education by Muscular Exercise* (1904), and a five-volume Gulick Hygiene Series of school textbooks (1906–1909). As a staff leader at the Springfield YMCA college from 1886 to 1900, he lectured and wrote widely, serving for sixteen years as secretary of the YMCA international committee's physical training department. During his college tenure he also edited *Physical Education* (1891–1896), *Association Outlook* (1897–1900), and the *American Physical Education Review* (1901–1903), and he created the YMCA triangular emblem representing the organization's physical, social, and spiritual ideals.

At the outset of Gulick's career the YMCA combined gymnastics and physical exercise with evangelical teachings and religious activities. He led the organization to embrace competitive sports as a means to cultivate and display Christian character. Although he had little experience as an athlete, he hammered out a biological, philosophical, and ethical rationale for competitive athletics. Appropriately, his guiding hand lay behind the creation of one of the world's major sports. In 1891 he required a Springfield college graduate class to imagine a new indoor game to supplement tedious gymnastics exercises, and from that assignment came James A. Naismith's invention of basketball. In 1894 Gulick and Naismith coauthored a handbook, *Basket Ball*, for the American Sports Publishing Company, and from 1894 to 1912 Gulick edited or contributed to almost all of the annual basketball guides in Spalding's Athletic Library. In 1909 *Proposed Changes in Basket Ball Rules* was published.

Gulick left Springfield in 1900 to become principal of Pratt High School in Brooklyn, New York. There he encouraged his teachers to conduct themselves according to the progressive standards of the day: teaching boys and girls rather than academic subjects, and applying evolutionary and psychological principles to pedagogy. Three years later, however, he returned to his primary interest, physical education, when he became president of the American Physical Education Association and in the same year director of physical training in New York City's public schools. From that office he encouraged brief daily exercise sessions and gymnastics classes, insisting that physical activity should be an integral part of the curriculum as an antidote to cramped muscles, sluggish circulation, and bad posture caused by prolonged desk sitting.

Working cooperatively with James E. Sullivan, the secretary of the Amateur Athletic Union, Gulick in 1903 initiated the nation's first Public Schools Athletic League. Financially supported by New York's wealthy citizens, not by the board of education, the PSAL first sponsored a large indoor track meet at Madison Square Garden, then extended the program to include basketball, baseball, and marksmanship competitions. To encourage average athletes as well as stellar ones, Gulick established age and weight divisions. At first, only boys in the New York City area were invited to compete, but in 1905 a girls' branch was added. To compete, students had to achieve satisfactory grades. The PSAL, widely publicized in the press, became a model for interscholastic sports throughout the United States.

Through Sullivan and the AAU, Gulick came into direct contact with the international Olympic movement. In 1904 he chaired the lecture committee and delivered several impressive talks at the first Olympics in the United States, held in conjunction with the St. Louis Exposition. From 1906 until 1908 he served on the American Olympics Committee for the Athens and London games.

More enduring was his biological theory of play that found expression in his activities on behalf of the public playgrounds movement. In 1906 he helped found the Playground Association of America, serving as its first president. The following year he accepted the chair of the Playground Extension Committee of the Russell Sage Foundation, which required him to relinquish his school administrative position. As a 1907 delegate to London for the Second International Congress on School Hygiene, from 1908 until 1913 he directed the division of children's hygiene under the Sage Foundation's auspices. In that capacity he traveled and lectured widely on the social benefits as well as the physical and psychological needs of children for public playgrounds, summer vacation schools, and indoor social centers. His efforts contributed to a vast growth in recreational facilities. Only ninety cities provided public playgrounds in 1907, but more than five hundred did so just three years later.

Between public speaking engagements, Gulick produced *The Efficient Life* (1907), *Mind and Work* (1908), *The Healthful Art of Dancing* (1910), and many pamphlets, handbooks, and magazine articles. Much of this material derived from lectures he delivered in the School of Pedagogy at New York University from 1905 until 1909, especially in summer school courses for public school teachers. As always, he emphasized good health and hygienic principles for "the efficient life." A great believer in preventive medicine, he urged an annual complete medical examination for everyone. In *Medical Inspection of Schools* (1908) he and a Sage Foundation colleague compiled examples of school boards taking the lead in conducting medical inspections for the early detection of physical defects in schoolchildren. As the title of one of his pamphlets suggests, Gulick considered himself a *Social Engineer in the Field of Public Health* (1911).

Gulick's love of the outdoors prompted him to assist in the founding of the Boy Scouts of America in 1910, and in 1912 he and his wife created the Camp Fire Girls as a means of educating young women for new roles in the community. On family property on a Maine lake they established a summer camp for girls in the new organization to swim, sail, canoe, study, and make pottery and metal craftwork at minimal expense. The camp's name, Wohelo, stood for work, health, and love.

His own health failing, Gulick rejected a doctor's advice in 1917 by volunteering his services to the YMCA on behalf of the war effort. He spent six weeks with U.S. troops in France, and he concluded that both the morale and morals of members of the American Expeditionary Forces could best be sustained by a more concentrated effort at providing athletic activities, wholesome literature, and dramatic presentations that characterized the YMCA's wartime work. Returning home, he engaged in an extensive YMCA lecture tour, recruiting young men to work with servicemen at home and abroad. Two books written during the war, *The Dynamic of Manhood* (1917) and *Morals and Morale* (1919), address the interaction of physical fitness and ethical behavior. Two other important summaries of his ethical perspective, *Food and Life* (1920) and *A Philosophy of Play* (1920), were published posthumously.

Fatigued by his wartime activities, Gulick died of an apparent heart attack in South Casco, Maine. Eulogies depicted him as one who combined visionary and pragmatic qualities. "He was a frontiersman," noted John Collier in the *Playground* (Oct. 1918). "What he wrote or uttered, he executed in life and in work. A horizon-builder, he was yet almost fiercely practical." Gulick himself provided the best clue to his significance when he urged readers of *The Dynamic of Manhood* to pursue life "as a splendid aggressive campaign." In the missionary spirit of his parents, Gulick energetically contributed to public discourse and institutions conducive to good health and physical fitness.

• Since no modern biography has been published, Ethel Josephine Dorgan's *Luther Halsey Gulick, 1865–1918* (1934) remains a solid, informative source that is best supplemented by the Luther Halsey Gulick File in the Naismith Memorial Basketball Hall of Fame in Springfield, Mass. Helpful, too, are items in the *Survey* 40 (24 Aug. 1918): 579–80; the *Playground* 12 (Oct. 1918): 251–55; and Ellen W. Gerber, *Innovators and Institutions in Physical Education* (1971), pp. 348–56. An obituary is in the *New York Times*, 14 Aug. 1918.

WILLIAM J. BAKER

GULICK, Sidney Lewis (10 Apr. 1860–24 Dec. 1945), missionary and author, was born on the island of Ebon in the Marshall Islands, the son of Luther Gulick and Louisa Lewis. His parents and various kin were active missionaries for the Congregational church, and although children usually did not follow the calling, Sidney did. He received a bachelor's degree in science at Dartmouth College in 1883 and attended Union Theological Seminary, where he was ordained to the ministry in 1886. He was sent to Kamakura, Japan, shortly after his marriage to Cara Fisher in 1887. They had five children. He studied Japanese diligently and taught English, but in 1890 a resurgence of conservatism and xenophobia in Japan thwarted missionary efforts. Gulick had become more and more an intellectual through intense study and writing about Japanese culture, and his theological interests turned to a lifelong task of interpreting Japan to the West. After a serious illness with cancer, he suspected a recurrence and resigned his position at Doshisha University, Kyōto, to return to the United States for treatment.

Gulick did not have cancer, but he soon decided that, although he had intended to return to Japan, he had received a new calling. The Federal Council of Churches in America (FCCA) offered him a position in 1914 as their expert on Japan. Gulick's long employment by the FCCA was as an advocate of a policy of understanding and reconciliation—work he considered an extension of his previous missionary career. He already loved the country and soon became such a sympathizer for its foreign policies that the Bureau of Investigation (predecessor to the Federal Bureau of Investigation) considered him a paid agent of the Japanese government and put him under surveillance (1921–1922). He was no agent, but he did interpret Japan's expansionist activities in China as the counterpart of America's own Monroe Doctrine and saw no harm in them. Gulick published five books on Japan, beginning with *Evolution of the Japanese* (1903). In this work he analyzed Japanese culture in light of the new social sciences, concluding that the people had modernized through a unique ability to adapt to new circumstances brought on by exposure to Western models of development. His extensive writing took two themes: first, the history and culture of Japan itself, and second, Japanese in the United States.

Gulick wrote his second book, *The American Japanese Problem*, in 1914, turning to the latter of these two interlinked concerns. He argued that Japanese were assimilable in American society and that agitation against them was based on fears of unlimited immigration swamping California. This, he said, was not their intention. He advocated immigration restriction and in 1922 began to champion the idea of a quota system. Gulick stressed the dangers of humiliating Japan and the benefits to be gained from promoting a policy of friendship with the emerging Orient. He condemned discriminatory legislation, such as California's Alien Land Laws (1911 and 1913), and urged tolerance. However, his preaching was in vain. Japanese immigration was banned by the National Origins Act of 1924, which he deplored as a needless humiliation of a proud people.

Gulick realized the two countries he loved were drifting closer toward war. He gave speeches nationwide, wrote countless articles, and made a final effort to head off the inevitable collision in another book, *Toward Understanding Japan* (1935). He was almost alone in his advocacy for Japan by this time, and his words reached a steadily diminishing audience, who judged the nation by its actions not rationalizations for them. He retired in 1934 and returned to Hawaii, where he was living when Japan attacked Pearl Harbor. He was not surprised, for he knew that the Japanese, if backed into a corner, would fight. He died in Boise, Idaho, at his eldest daughter's home.

• Gulick's papers are at the Houghton Library, Harvard University. The major biography of Gulick is Sandra C. Taylor, *Advocate of Understanding: Sidney Gulick and the Search for Peace with Japan* (1984). Roger Daniels, *The Politics of Prejudice* (1962; repr. 1973), sets his life in the larger context.

SANDRA C. TAYLOR

GULLIVER, Julia Henrietta (30 July 1856–26 July 1940), college president and philosopher, was born in Norwich, Connecticut, to the Reverend John Putnam Gulliver, college president and theological seminary professor, and Frances Woodbury Curtis. The family moved several times during her childhood because of changes in her father's employment. In 1865 he left his Norwich pastorate for another in Chicago; in 1868 he moved to Galesburg, Illinois, to serve as president of Knox College for four years and then to Binghamton, New York, where he held a Presbyterian pastorate.

Julia Gulliver entered the first class of Smith College and graduated with an A.B. in 1879. Thereafter she studied philosophy at home under the tutelage of her father, who had joined the faculty of Andover Theological Seminary in 1878. The second woman to receive a doctorate in philosophy and one of only two women to be granted doctoral degrees by Smith College, she received a Ph.D. in 1888. Two years later she was appointed head of the Department of Philosophy and Biblical Literature at Rockford Female Seminary (renamed Rockford College in 1892) in Rockford, Illinois. She remained at Rockford for the next twenty-nine years except for a brief interval of study (1892–1893) under the leading European psychologist, Wilhelm Wundt, at the University of Leipzig. In 1902 she became president of Rockford College, a position she held until 1919.

Although critics argued that women lacked the independence of mind to make significant contributions in scholarship, Gulliver showed considerable promise with the publication of her senior thesis, "The Psychology of Dreams," in the prestigious *Journal of Speculative Philosophy* (1880). Subsequently, she published six articles and two books, the first book in collaboration with Cornell psychologist E. B. Titchener on a translation of the first volume of Wundt's three-volume *Ethics* (1897), and later her own small book, *Studies in Democracy* (1917). Like most other nineteenth-century women Ph.D.'s, Gulliver had little opportunity to pursue scholarly research given the constraints of a heavy teaching load and administrative responsibilities.

Gulliver's philosophy included classical, realist, and pragmatist principles. From her classical education she drew such themes as order, harmony, the eternal; from the pragmatism of William James and John Dewey she drew notions of the useful, the workable, the changing. She believed that it was a mistake to separate the soul from the body, principle from fact, theory from practice. The most challenging intellectual task, she asserted, was to combine the universal with the particular, revealing how principles are applied in everyday life.

Gulliver's religious philosophy resembled that of many other Protestant liberals of her day. She espoused the social gospel and the creation of God's Kingdom on earth. She rejected the traditional view of God as static, incomprehensible, transcendent; for Gulliver, God was a "tremendous internal push of life and love and progress working in and through the organic whole of the universe and each of its organic parts."

Gulliver's philosophical contribution was minor, but her role as president of a leading midwestern women's college was major. The college included among its graduates Jane Addams (class of 1882), founder of Hull-House, and Catherine Waugh McCulloch (class of 1882), vice president and legal adviser of the National American Woman Suffrage Association. Women with advanced degrees were usually barred from professional and administrative positions except in women's institutions. One of the few women college presidents, Julia Gulliver served both as a role model and spokesperson for women. She proved an able college president. When she took office, Rockford College was struggling to survive. The freshman class of 1905 had only seven students, and the endowment was small. She raised the academic standing of the institution by hiring faculty with better credentials, abolishing the preparatory department, and winning national accreditation.

To attract more students and to prepare them for vocations, Gulliver added to the liberal arts curriculum classes in pedagogy (1906–1907) and library science (1914–1915), and she inaugurated four-year degree programs in home economics and secretarial work (1914–1915). She attacked the notion that vocational courses were demeaning. Rather, she equated

them with such male-dominated vocational disciplines as engineering and journalism that were gaining wide acceptance in the universities. She argued that a young woman with vocational training would be prepared to take an active role in the world rather than casting about for something to do with the general culture she had absorbed in college. She further predicted that all sciences taught at the college level would, in due course, become applied sciences because ignorance had resulted from the bifurcation of abstract principles and practical applications.

In 1918–1919 the enrollment of the college had increased to 216, a new hall had been constructed, and the endowment totaled $243,620. That year a rumor circulated that a male faculty member had solicited sexual favors from boys in the Rockford community. Gulliver's decision to quiet the rumors and help the man find another position caused a major rift with her 36-member predominantly female faculty, 22 of whom openly defied her. The leader of the dissidents was apparently Edith Bramhall, the head of the history department. "I am not in the business of ruining people," Gulliver wrote to her antagonist, whom she accused of "murdering" her career. The scandal forced Gulliver into retirement. Suggesting that only a male president could quiet the rebellious campus and elicit respect from the faculty, Gulliver urged the trustees to appoint a male to replace her. This they promptly did, and the next five presidents of the college were males. This gender arrangement, which was gaining acceptance in other women's colleges as well, further diminished the leadership opportunities of women academics, particularly those with Ph.D.'s. Gulliver retired with her sister to Eustis, Florida, where she discontinued her academic research and writing and where she died.

Gulliver's life story can be read as that of an extraordinary person. Fewer than two hundred women earned Ph.D.'s (or equivalent degrees) before 1900. Gulliver distinguished herself by being one of the only two of this group who served as presidents of colleges. Yet on other levels, her life reveals much about academic women's career constraints. Like a majority of the early female Ph.D.'s, she never married. She had limited access to graduate programs, and like nearly half of the female Ph.D.'s, she found employment in a segregated setting. She received low pay throughout her career and had limited options for advancement. Despite these constraints, Gulliver was deeply committed to improving society and devoted much time and energy to advancing women's education.

• Letters, clippings, presidential reports, grant proposals, and published articles can be found in the Julia Gulliver Papers and the William A. Maddox Papers in the Rockford College Archives. Other material is in the Smith College Archives. Her views about women's education are expressed in three brochures published by Rockford College, *Why Should a Girl Have a College Education and What Will It Do for Her?* (1913), *New Tendencies in Education* (n.d.), and *The New Renaissance and Woman's Place in It* (1914). Her philosophical ideas are in "The Substitutes for Christianity Proposed by

Comte and Spencer," *New Englander*, Mar. 1884, pp. 246–260. A good biographical article is Jodi Billstrom's "Julia Gulliver Faces Faculty Revolt," in *Rockford College: A Retrospective Look*, ed. C. Hal Nelson (1980). On her father see Hermann R. Muelder, *Missionaries and Muckrakers: The First Hundred Years of Knox College* (1984). Obituaries are in *Smith Alumnae Quarterly*, Nov. 1940, and the *New York Times*, 28 July 1940.

LUCY FORSYTH TOWNSEND

GUNN, James Newton (3 Sept. 1867–26 Nov. 1927), industrial engineer, was born in Springfield, Ohio, the son of James Winn Gunn, a minister, and Mary Catherine Johnson. He completed his secondary education in the Springfield public schools, but instead of attending college he received advanced training in engineering, mathematics, and languages from private tutors. Around 1890 he moved to Boston, Massachusetts, where he went to work for the Library Bureau, which had been established by Melvil Dewey, the inventor of the Dewey Decimal System, to help libraries develop cataloging and retrieval systems for their collections. While with the bureau, Gunn developed the concept of the vertical file system, whereby supplementary materials, such as leaflets, clippings, reprints, pictures, maps, and pamphlets, which are not suited for placement on the shelf with the regular collection because of their shape or ephemeral nature, are stored in folders in a filing cabinet. He also refined the card index system in a number of small but important ways; for example, he conceived of securing a tab to the top of the standard 3 × 5 index card, thereby providing an inexpensive but functional means for dividing catalog cards. Most of these improvements remained in use until the implementation of computerized cataloging in the late twentieth century.

Having become interested in business management, Gunn took several courses in that field before moving around 1898 to London, England, where he organized and managed a branch office of the Library Bureau. In 1901 he returned to the United States and founded Gunn, Richards, and Company, one of the first firms to specialize in industrial engineering. This discipline combines the principles of engineering and business management in order to develop production lines and sequences that eliminate all unnecessary steps and motions, thus making a company's manufacturing process as efficient as possible. One of his most important clients was the Pennsylvania Steel Corporation, which retained him to help reorganize its entire manufacturing operation. In 1902 he married Mabel Scott, with whom he had three children.

In 1911 Gunn moved to South Bend, Indiana, to become manager of the newly established automobile division of the Studebaker Corporation. Although the company was one of the seven major automobile manufacturers in the United States, its production facilities and processes were more suited to the manufacture of wagons and carriages, a business the company had been in since 1868. After two years Gunn, one of the first non-members of the Studebaker family to assume a management role in the company, completely reorganized its production processes so that it could remain competitive in a dynamic industry. In 1913 he became vice president of the United States Tire Company. His success in systemizing its operations led to his promotion two years later to president of U.S. Tire and vice president and director of its parent organization, the United States Rubber Company. During World War I he served on the War Industries Board as the Rubber Association's representative and in this capacity played a major role in allocating scarce supplies of rubber to the various manufacturers of military goods.

Gunn's interest in automobiles led him to play an active role in the affairs of the Lincoln Highway Association. Founded in 1913, this group sought to establish a coast-to-coast highway to honor the memory of President Abraham Lincoln and solicited construction money from state, county, and municipal governments as well as civic-minded businesses and individuals. Completed in 1928 with terminuses in New York City's Times Square and San Francisco's Lincoln Park, the Lincoln Highway (later known as U.S. Route 30 between New York and Salt Lake City) crossed twelve states and was billed as "America's Transcontinental Main Street." As one of the association's presidents, Gunn helped to develop what was in effect the first cross-country highway in the United States.

In 1923 Gunn's poor health forced him to retire from U.S. Rubber and U.S. Tire. That same year he became a consulting industrial engineer with Lockwood, Greene, and Company, and in 1924 he was appointed one of two receivers of the Hodgman Rubber Company. From 1925 until his death he lectured on industrial engineering at the Harvard Graduate School of Business Administration, Columbia and New York Universities, and the Massachusetts Institute of Technology.

Gunn served as chairman of the legislative committee of the National Automobile Chamber of Commerce and was a member of the executive committee of the Rubber Association of America. He died in New York City.

• Gunn's papers have not survived. His contributions to the automotive industry are discussed in *Automobile Topics*, 13 July 1918; 9 June 1923; 19 Jan. 1924; and 26 Jan. 1924. An obituary is in the *New York Times*, 28 Nov. 1927.

CHARLES W. CAREY, JR.

GUNN, John C. (22 June 1795?–22 Oct. 1863), physician and author of a popular domestic medical book, was born in Savannah, Georgia, the son of Christopher Gunn, a tavern operator and innkeeper, and Ann Marinow. Sources disagree about the date of his birth; his tombstone gives the year 1800. Beyond his basic education at the Mercantile and Mathematics Academy in Savannah, Gunn appears to have had no formal training other than an apprenticeship under an unidentified Virginia physician. Anecdotal material in his writings suggests that he left Savannah, probably after his father's death in December 1816, and traveled extensively, journeying from Cuba and France to New York before "reading medicine" (*Domestic Medicine* [1830], p. 431) and actively practicing for five years in Botetourt and Montgomery counties in southwestern Virginia and in Monroe County (now in West Virginia).

In 1827 Gunn settled in Knoxville, Tennessee, with his first wife (date of marriage and name unknown) and at least one child. Personable and outgoing to the point of flamboyance, he was well received as a professional and saw his practice grow until he expanded his interests into Tennessee politics. In 1829 he ran unsuccessfully for the post of state senator from Knox and Anderson counties, inveighing on behalf of the poor of the state against recent legislative funding for what is now the University of Tennessee. A supporter of Andrew Jackson, Gunn gave much lip service to the plight of the poor, but his more than comfortable lifestyle raised some question about his sincerity. Following his defeat at the polls, he moved his practice and his family, which by then included three children, approximately fifty miles south, to Madisonville, Tennessee.

Meanwhile, the book on which Gunn's significance in American social and cultural history would rest was being published in Knoxville. The first edition of *Gunn's Domestic Medicine, or Poor Man's Friend, in the Hours of Affliction, Pain and Sickness*, "printed under the immediate superintendance of the author," appeared in August 1830. For the remainder of his life, Gunn devoted most of his professional energy to promoting this work, arranging for a proliferation of local reprintings in Tennessee, Kentucky, Ohio, Pennsylvania, and New York. Enlarged under the author's supervision in 1857 and translated into German, the book remained Gunn's original basic text through the 1876 National Jubilee Edition, the 160th, down to the last recorded edition, the 234th, which was issued in New York in 1920. Over the years outdated practices were eliminated, but not much new material was added to the work.

Gunn's Domestic Medicine addressed serious health problems of frontier and rural families who lived great distances from even primitive medical care. Whether dealing with childbirth, broken bones, toothaches, cancer, epileptic fits, burns, or looseness of the bowels, Gunn wrote with clarity and assurance, carefully instructing and leading "home doctors" through what were often life-or-death crises. Though his methods did not differ from those of most of his contemporary physicians, his approach to health situations was apt to be more practical than theoretical. His emphasis on the value of locally available herbs and the adaptability of other natural things (the use of a goose quill as a catheter for a female patient, for example) reflected the sort of practicality made necessary by the isolation and restricted resources of most of his unsophisticated users. Intended as a guide for the layperson, the book covered virtually any possible miscarriage of health

and contained extensive references from the works of the major medical men of the time, which also made it a useful textbook for the largely self-taught doctors of the rural areas of the southern and western states.

In 1837 Gunn's private life became a matter of wide speculation when he "ran away" with Clarisa Montgomery Jarnagin, the wife of state senator Spence Jarnagin, who from 1833 to 1835 had held the position for which Gunn had been a candidate eight years earlier. Gunn and Mrs. Jarnagin settled in Louisville, Kentucky, where—after divorce proceedings initiated by the senator were finalized—presumably they were married. Although what happened to the first Mrs. Gunn is not known, the 1850 National Census indicates that Gunn's two sons from his first marriage, William and Hugh, were then living with him. Also listed in the census household was Anne, aged two years, apparently the offspring of Gunn's daughter Margaret, who had married Captain William C. Brown, a native of Louisville. Following Clarisa's death in 1851, the family members dispersed.

Gunn continued to live in Louisville, residing at the National Hotel and taking any opportunity—such as in city directory listings—to associate himself with his book. In 1857 he published a much enlarged revision with a fresh title, *Gunn's New Domestic Physician; or, Home Book of Health*. The 1860 edition contained a letter, dated 30 January, in which he stated that he was preparing for publication an autobiography entitled "The Poor Gentleman." There is no evidence, however, that this project was ever realized. He died in Louisville.

Gunn is remembered for the contribution made to American domestic medicine by the century-long lifetime of his principal work. The extent to which it was absorbed into the national psyche is suggested by its appearance in diverse literary works such as Mark Twain's *Huckleberry Finn* and John Steinbeck's *East of Eden*.

• No known Gunn manuscripts are extant. The text of his book is the only source on his early life and training. Isolated documents relating to him and his family are in courthouse records in Savannah, Ga.; Knoxville and Madisonville, Tenn.; and Louisville, Ky. The Allen papers in the Lawson-McGhee Library, Knoxville, contain information on Clarisa Montgomery Jarnagin. For *Gunn's Domestic Medicine*, see Ben Harris McClary, "Introducing a Classic," *Tennessee Historical Quarterly* 45 (Fall 1986): 210–16, and Charles E. Rosenberg, "Introduction to the New Edition," *Gunn's Domestic Medicine* (1986). Several efforts have been made at compiling a bibliography of the editions of this book, the most notable by William A. Harper, University of Colorado Libraries (1970), but none has reached print.

BEN HARRIS McCLARY

GUNN, Ross (12 May 1897–15 Oct. 1966), physicist, was born in Cleveland, Ohio, the son of Ross Delano Aldrich Gunn, a physician, and Lora A. Connor. As a high school sophomore in Oberlin, Ohio, Gunn developed a wireless radio, initiating a lifelong interest in electricity and high-frequency radiophysics. Before graduating from Oberlin High School in 1916, he earned a commercial wireless operator's license and worked as a ship radio operator on Lake Erie between Cleveland, Ohio, and Buffalo, New York. Gunn also developed one of the first long-range radio stations in Ohio before entering Oberlin College in 1916.

At Oberlin Gunn studied electrical engineering and worked as a research assistant for the Glenn L. Martin Company, a Cleveland aircraft manufacturer. He graduated from Oberlin in 1920 and entered the University of Michigan, where he earned an M.S. in physics in 1921 and served as a part-time instructor in engineering physics. After graduate school he became a radio research engineer with the U.S. Army Air Service at McCook Field near Dayton, Ohio. There he invented a frequency selective transformer that led to the development of pilotless aircraft during World War II. Gunn entered Yale University in 1923 to pursue a doctorate in physics. He taught engineering physics there from 1923 to 1927 and directed the Yale high-frequency laboratory from 1926 to 1927. At Yale he developed an aircraft altimeter, a vacuum-tube oscillator, and a vacuum-tube modulation system. He married Gladys Jeannette Rowley of Victoria, New York, on 8 September 1923; they had four sons.

Gunn received his doctorate from Yale and joined the Naval Research Laboratory in Washington, D.C., as a research physicist in the Radio Division in 1927. There he developed a theory that attributed diurnal variations of terrestrial magnetism to a high-level diamagnetic layer distributed over the earth's sunlit hemisphere; he invented an induction electrometer that produced an induced alternating voltage from an extremely small charge that could be amplified and recorded; and he proposed the fundamental principle behind the electric field meter, from which developed the vibrating reed electrometer used during World War II to measure atomic radiation.

In 1934 Gunn became the laboratory's technical adviser and, in 1938, superintendent of its Mechanics and Electricity Division. In the latter position he developed an amplification system for small direct-current voltages, used during World War II to detect enemy ships and aircraft by infrared radiation. His group revolutionized the testing of battleship armor by using 50-caliber bullets to predict the behavior of armor under attack by full-sized shells. Gunn also pioneered the use of light plastics for hardening aircraft protection and infantry body armor. He introduced the use of concentrated hydrogen peroxide as a source of oxygen for diesel powered submarines and long-range hydrogen-powered torpedoes. Gunn's work on closed-cycle diesel engines later contributed to the development of propulsion systems for nuclear-powered submarines. With Philip Abelson, he developed the thermal diffusion method for the separation and enrichment of uranium isotopes. This technique was one of several employed during the Manhattan Project at Oak Ridge, Tennessee, to separate uranium-235 from uranium-238 for use in the atomic bomb dropped on Hiroshima.

Gunn served as technical director of the Army-Navy Precipitation Static Project during World War II, investigating static interference on aircraft flying through ice-crystal clouds or snow. Gunn developed antenna treatments and materials that suppressed precipitation and eliminated the radio and navigational blackouts frequently encountered when aircraft flew through clouds composed of ice crystals. As superintendent of the Aircraft Electrical Research Division in 1944, he led an investigation of aeronautical electrical problems encountered during the war. In 1946 Gunn became superintendent of the Physics Division and technical director of the Army-Navy atmospheric electricity research project. From 1942 to 1954 he also worked as a consultant to the National Defense Research Committee, the National Advisory Committee for Aeronautics, the Research and Development Board of the Military Establishment, the Science Advisory Board of the U.S. Air Force, and the C. F. Kettering Foundation.

In 1947 Gunn became director of physical research at the U.S. Weather Bureau. In addition to research on rain produced by cloud seeding (which demonstrated that the technique was ineffective and of no economic value), he also made many contributions to the fundamental knowledge of cloud physics and the mechanics involved in the formation of natural precipitation. Gunn developed instruments to study precipitation, atmospheric electricity, thunderstorm electrification, the elastic and mechanical properties of the earth's crust, and fundamental mechanics of mountain building; he demonstrated the occasional interrelation of oceanic depths, mountain ranges, and volcanic chains. He also found that air pollution decreased the possibility of the formation of rain clouds, thus reducing the volume of rainfall. In 1958 he retired from the Weather Bureau and joined the American University in Washington, D.C., as a research professor in physics. He died in Washington.

• Gunn's papers and other materials on his career are in the archives of Oberlin College, Oberlin, Ohio, and the Historical Files of the Naval Research Laboratory, Department of the Navy, Washington, D.C. For Gunn's role in the development of underwater nuclear propulsion, see Norman Polmar and Thomas B. Allen, *Rickover* (1982), and Richard G. Hewlett and Francis Duncan, *Nuclear Navy, 1946–1962* (1974). For the history of the Naval Research Laboratory, consult Harvey M. Sapolsky, *Science and the Navy: The History of the Office of Naval Research* (1990). Obituaries are in the *New York Times*, 16 Oct. 1966; *Physics Today*, Mar. 1967; and the *Washington Post*, 16 Oct. 1966.

ADAM R. HORNBUCKLE

GUNN, Selskar Michael (25 May 1883–2 Aug. 1944), public health administrator, was born in London, England, the son of Michael Gunn, a theatrical manager, and Barbara Elizabeth Johnston. After attending Kensington Park College in London (1896–1900), Gunn went to the United States to enroll at the Massachusetts Institute of Technology. As a student of public health there, he had an opportunity to work at

MIT's pioneering Sanitary Research Laboratory and Sewage Experiment Station. He graduated with an S.B. degree in biology in 1905 and then started work as a bacteriologist, first at the Boston Chemical Laboratory (1905–1906) and next at the Iowa State Board of Health (1906–1908). He became a U.S. citizen in 1906. In 1908 Gunn was appointed health officer for Orange, New Jersey. Among other activities in that capacity, he organized an innovative program for the early identification of tuberculosis that drew on the collaborative efforts of the board of health, the local branch of the National Tuberculosis Association, and several private welfare agencies.

In 1910 Gunn returned to MIT as an instructor in sanitary biology; he later became associate professor. In 1911 he married Clara J. Coffin; they had one daughter. Besides teaching at MIT and at Simmons College (1912–1914), Gunn served on the Massachusetts State Board of Labor and Industries (1913–1914) and became the first director of the Division of Hygiene in the reorganized state Board of Health (1915–1916). He acted as sanitary consultant to the Milwaukee Bureau of Economy and Efficiency in 1911, was assistant secretary-general of the International Congress on Hygiene and Demography in 1912, and served as secretary of the American Public Health Association from 1912 to 1918. Gunn doubled the circulation of the APHA's *American Journal of Public Health* while serving as its manager (1912–1914) and editor (1914–1917).

In 1917 Gunn earned a certificate from the Harvard-Technology School for Health Officers. That same year, in the midst of World War I, he left MIT for France to become associate director of the Commission for the Prevention of Tuberculosis, a program sponsored by the Rockefeller Foundation and the French government. Gunn helped to organize several demonstration projects, a training program for French medical staff, and a survey of TB in northern France. Once the war ended, the French government assumed primary responsibility for the program, so in 1920 the Rockefeller Foundation's International Health Board sent Gunn to Prague, where he served as adviser to the Ministry of Health in the newly formed nation of Czechoslovakia. He returned to Paris in 1922 to assume overall direction of the Health Board's European program. In 1927 he became a vice president of the parent foundation, with new responsibilities encompassing all Rockefeller Foundation activities in Europe, and in 1930 he was also named associate director for the social sciences in Europe. He and his wife divorced that year, and he married Carroll McComas three years later; they had no children.

On a trip back from Paris in 1931, Gunn made a seven-week detour to China. That visit, which he called "unquestionably one of the most interesting experiences of my life," set a new course for the next eight years of his career. He returned to New York convinced that China offered a unique opportunity for the Rockefeller Foundation. Despite the instability of the government, the economic problems of the depression, and the rivalry among local institutions, Gunn concluded that "China has become plastic after centuries of rigid conventionalism." With the foundation president's blessing, Gunn went back for a second, much longer visit (1932–1933), and in January 1934 he submitted a 100-page report titled "China and the Rockefeller Foundation."

In this document Gunn stated that China's future depended on rural reconstruction, since 85 percent of the country's population resided in the countryside, most of them living in dire poverty. Local development officials were woefully ill trained, while few of the country's academic institutions showed much interest in the practical problems of their society. Gunn proposed that the foundation organize and underwrite a program that would focus the energies of the strongest academic institutions on training and research in rural redevelopment. He observed candidly that western-sponsored institutions like the Peking Medical College (a long-time beneficiary of the foundation) had neither the expertise nor the local standing to take a lead role; the Rockefeller Foundation must work primarily with Chinese institutions. Above all, it must promote the coordination of resources and talent to serve a common goal. Gunn's recommendations were endorsed by the foundation, and the "China Program" was formally launched in July 1935.

Gunn spent most of the next three years in China, during which he helped launch an ambitious program that included projects in agriculture, sanitation, preventive medicine, marketing, rural economy, and community works. Some progress was made in coordinating China's fragmented institutional resources, and several hundred young people were trained as rural administrators. However, the deteriorating military situation in the late 1930s brought the project to a virtual halt, and Gunn returned to the United States in 1937.

In 1938 Gunn took up his previous position heading the Rockefeller Foundation's Paris office. Fleeing the city just six days ahead of the Nazis' arrival in June 1940, he returned again to New York. A few months later the foundation loaned Gunn to the National Health Council to undertake a three-year study of America's voluntary health-care providers. After doing extensive interviews and research, Gunn left the project in 1943 to spend a year as health affairs adviser at the Office of Foreign Relief and Rehabilitation. He then returned to the survey project, but poor health prevented him from finishing the job; soon afterward, he died in Newtown, Connecticut. The project report, *Voluntary Health Agencies* (1945), was completed by his collaborator, Philip S. Platt.

Irish by ancestry, English by birth, and American by citizenship, Gunn spent much of his adult life in Europe and Asia. He was a talented administrator and planner, as well as a man of considerable sophistication and personal charm. Starting his career in the early days of America's urban public health movement, he lived to incorporate those principles into a broader vision of international community development. His most ambitious undertaking, the China Program, ended before its feasibility could be fully evaluated, but it remains a pioneering effort, remarkable both for the scale of its vision and the pragmatism of its approach.

• Gunn published a number of papers on sanitation, as well as *The Doings of Dinky* (1937), a children's story written for his daughter. The annual reports of the Rockefeller Foundation, 1917–1942, trace the path of his career and describe the various programs on which he worked, while additional relevant documents are in the Rockefeller Archives, Pocantico Hills, N.Y. The best account of the China Program appears in James C. Thomson, Jr., *While China Faced West: American Reformers in Nationalist China, 1928–1937* (1969). Raymond Fosdick, *The Story of the Rockefeller Foundation* (1952), provides a more general account of the foundation's activities during Gunn's career, though with few references to Gunn himself. Obituaries are in the *New York Times*, 3 Aug. 1944, and the *Rockefeller Annual Report* (1944), pp. x–xiii.

SANDRA OPDYCKE

GUNNISON, John Williams (11 Nov. 1812–26 Oct. 1853), topographical engineer, was born in Goshen, New Hampshire, the son of Samuel Gunnison and Elizabeth Williams, farmers. Gunnison's ancestors had first settled in New Hampshire in 1631. He grew up in a large family. In 1830 Gunnison attended Hopkinton Academy, thirty miles from his home, for one term. From 1831 to 1833 he taught in the Hopkinton village school and prepared for a career at the U.S. Military Academy at West Point. Letters of recommendation describe him as displaying "habits of temperance, industry and close application to study" and having "sound moral principles, perfect rectitude of conduct."

Gunnison stood 5'9" and had a light complexion. He was slim, active, and energetic, and as a youth he was well liked by his classmates and teachers. He was an Episcopalian and worked in the Young Men's Christian Association. He started at West Point in July 1833 and graduated second in his class of fifty students in June 1837. After graduation Gunnison was called into active duty as an ordnance officer in Florida, where the army was enforcing President Andrew Jackson's removal of the Seminoles. In 1838 Gunnison assisted in the removal of the Cherokees from Georgia. Also that year he transferred to the Corps of Topographical Engineers and became a topographical engineer. In 1840–1841 he served as engineer on the improvements of the Savannah and St. Mary's rivers. In April 1841 Gunnison married Martha A. Deloney of St. Mary's, Georgia; the couple had three children.

Between 1841 and 1849 Gunnison engaged in surveying the Great Lakes region, particularly the Wisconsin-Michigan boundaries, the coast of Lake Erie, and the marshy districts of northern Ohio. He was promoted to first lieutenant of the topographical engineers on 9 May 1846.

In 1849 Gunnison was appointed second in command under Captain Howard Stansbury to survey the Great Salt Lake and Utah Lakes—more than 2,000 miles. One of the islands of the Great Salt Lake was named Gunnison in his honor. He helped the Mormons with an Indian uprising on the Provo River in February 1850. He left Salt Lake at the end of August 1850 and returned to his family in Grand Rapids, Michigan. Stansbury wrote of Gunnison's "efficient and faithful services": "To high professional skill, he added energy, judgment and an untiring devotion." Gunnison went to Washington, D.C., in January 1851 to complete maps of the expedition.

As a consequence of his yearlong contact with the Mormons, Gunnison wrote *The Mormons or the Latter Day Saints* (1852), in which he argued that he believed internal dissent would splinter the Mormon movement and that, if left alone, Mormons would modify their practices to more traditional behavior. While in Washington, Gunnison met with President Franklin Pierce, who had sponsored Gunnison's nomination to West Point, and explained his beliefs that the Mormons should be given as much self-government as possible because continuing persecution would strengthen rather than weaken the church. Free interchange, he believed, would lead to exposure and correction of Mormon excesses such as polygamy. Mormons responded to the book by calling Gunnison "our much esteemed, though distant, learned very polite and unsolicited chronicler."

On 3 March 1853 Gunnison was promoted to captain. At the time he was engaged in harbor improvements on Lake Michigan. Two months later he was assigned to survey the Pacific Road for a central railroad route from the Mississippi River to the Pacific Ocean between the 38th and 39th parallels. The expedition set out in June to survey the Rocky Mountains by way of the Huerfano River in Colorado through Cochetopa Pass. Then they were to travel into the region of the Gunnison and Green rivers west to the Sevier River. The return would be north into the Utah Lake region, through the passes and various canyons of the Wasatch Range, and finally through South Pass to Fort Laramie. As well as exploring for the railroad, Gunnison wanted to prove the practicality of a wagon road across the mountains.

In addition to the survey party members, the expedition consisted of eighteen wagons and a military escort of thirty men. They traveled 1,050 miles from their base camp on the Kansas prairie, 500 of which were over unbroken ground. They crossed four major rivers and many difficult streams. They identified 128 new or rare botanical specimens, 27 varieties of mammals and birds, 26 reptiles and fish, and more than 50 varieties of insects.

Many of the geographic areas Gunnison explored were later named in his honor, including the Grand River, which became the Gunnison River; Poncha Pass, which was known as Gunnison Pass; Gunnison County, Colorado; two towns named Gunnison, one in Utah and one in Colorado; Gunnison National Forest; Mount Gunnison; the Gunnison Valley in Grand County, Utah; and Gunnison National Monument. The road he established served simultaneously as a road for the southern states to California, a road for immigrants who were late in starting across the plains, and a military road to Utah.

In the fall of 1853, when Gunnison arrived in Utah for the second time, he found the Mormons at war with the Indians. He stopped in Fillmore, a town in central Utah, which, like other Mormon settlements, had established rules of not venturing out of the fortified town without arms and a company of twelve or more men. Despite the tensions and perhaps because of impending winter, Gunnison split his party into one team to explore the canyon of the Sevier River and the other to survey the entrance of the river into its lakes. The parties would meet afterward and continue to Salt Lake.

On 26 October Pahvant Indians approached under cover of thick bushes within twenty-five yards of Gunnison's campfires. Gunnison rushed from his tent but was killed by fifteen arrows. His body was then mutilated. Of the twelve in his party, eight were killed and four escaped.

Gunnison's death aroused great controversy and animosity against the Mormons. The final entry in his service records reads "Massacred, 26 Oct. 1853, by Mormons and Indians in Utah." The massacre was never investigated by competent legal authority, and subsequent trials to prosecute supposed Indian participants were farcical. Most probably, Gunnison was murdered by Pahvants enraged by the killing of a chief and warriors by the Hildreth party of immigrants on their way to California. The massacre forms part of a larger struggle among the Mormons, Indians, and U.S. government for control over the Utah Territory and regulation of the people living there.

• A collection of Gunnison's letters is in the Henry E. Huntington Library in San Marino, Calif. His journal for the Stansbury Expedition of 1849–1850 is in the Marriott Library at the University of Utah. Accounts of Gunnison's life and massacre appear in Nolie Mumey, *John Williams Gunnison* (1955), and Robert Kent Fielding, *The Unsolicited Chronicler: An Account of the Gunnison Massacre, Its Causes and Consequences, Utah Territory, 1847–1859: A Narrative History* (1993).

ANN W. ENGAR

GUNSAULUS, Frank Wakeley (1 Jan. 1856–17 Mar. 1921), pastor, educator, and author, was born in Chesterville, Ohio, the son of Joseph Gunsaulus and Mary Hawley, occupations unknown. Gunsaulus attended the public schools in Chesterville and then graduated from Ohio Wesleyan University in 1875, was ordained to the Methodist ministry, and became the pastor of several small churches on a rural circuit near Harrisburg, Ohio. In 1876 he married Georgiana Long of Holly Meadows, West Virginia; they had no children. After serving Methodist congregations in Worthington, Ohio (1876–1878), and Chillicothe, Ohio (1879), Gunsaulus became a Congregationalist minister. Following two years as the pastor of the Eastwood Congregational Church of Columbus, Ohio, he accepted a call from the High Street Congregational Church in the same city. Health problems led him to resign this

position in 1881 and to move to Newtonville, Massachusetts, where he pastored a Congregational church and enjoyed a close relationship with Phillips Brooks, the renowned rector of Boston's Trinity Episcopal Church. After serving as the minister of the Brown Memorial Presbyterian Church of Baltimore from 1885 to 1887, he moved to Chicago, where he was to spend the remainder of his life, first as the pastor of the Plymouth Congregational Church (1887–1899) and then of the independent Central Church (1899–1919).

While ministering to these prominent Chicago congregations, Gunsaulus gained a reputation as the city's "premier pulpiteer," as one of the nation's "princes of the pulpit" during an age of outstanding orators. A powerfully built man, a gifted and dynamic speaker, and a man of broad interests, he attracted several thousand listeners every Sunday for three decades to hear his sermons. Visitors to Chicago flocked to hear him. One sermon he preached at Plymouth Congregational Church inspired his parishioner Philip D. Armour, who had made a fortune in the meat-packing industry, to pledge to provide up to $1 million to build a technical school in Chicago, especially to educate youth from working-class and poor families. Armour promised to give this money if Gunsaulus would devote five years of his life to establishing and administering the institute. Opened in 1893, the Armour Institute (later the Armour Institute of Technology) attracted thousands of students and during the early twentieth century ranked among the nation's leading technical schools. Armour eventually gave the institute almost $3 million, and Gunsaulus served as the school's president from its founding until his death. Despite his lack of background in engineering or higher education administration, Gunsaulus successfully directed the institute and sought to provide a scientific education complemented by training in the humanities.

In addition to pastoring Chicago's most renowned congregation and guiding the Armour Institute, Gunsaulus made major contributions to the city's cultural and civic life. A lover of art who collected paintings, prints, pottery, textiles, manuscripts, rare books, and music, he promoted painters Josef Israels and Anton Mauve. He raised large amounts of money to help cultural institutions such as the Field Museum and donated personal collections of Wedgwood and Near Eastern pottery to the Chicago Art Institute and a Mendelssohn manuscript of *Elijah* and many incunabula to the University of Chicago. While striving to improve Chicago's libraries, museums, and schools, Gunsaulus also worked to reform the city's political practices and remedy its social problems. He urged churches to establish kindergartens and founded Glenwood Farm, where each summer 300 boys from inner-city Chicago could experience fresh air, moral uplift, and new adventures. He served on the Chicago Vice Commission of 1910–1911 and was a long-standing member of the political action committee of the Chicago Union League Club. Believing that international relations should rest on the principles of honor, tolerance, equality, and humanitarianism, he resisted the imperialistic forces of the late nineteenth century and called for the freedom of Cuba in 1895 and just treatment of Puerto Rico and the Philippines in 1900. Convinced that the entry of the United States into World War I was justified, he sought to convince Americans to support the war effort.

By lecturing throughout the country and writing many books, Gunsaulus became well known beyond Chicago. In addition to teaching courses at the University of Chicago, McCormick Theological Seminary, and Chicago Theological Seminary, he lectured at Johns Hopkins University and Yale Divinity School and frequently spoke on the Chautauqua circuit. His favorite lecture topics included the great English poets, the influence of music in the church, Savonarola, Alfred Lord Tennyson, Matthew Arnold, William Gladstone, and Henry Ward Beecher. Gunsaulus donated most of the money derived from these addresses to the poor or used it to buy rare books or art objects to give to colleges or museums. He published two books of poetry, *Phidias and Other Poems* (1891) and *Songs of the Night and Day* (1896). His historical novel, *Monk and Knight* (2 vols., 1891), examined how the revival of learning during the Renaissance affected Erasmus, Thomas More, Francis I, Henry VIII, Charles V, Pope Leo X, and many other individuals. Especially significant were his theological studies. *The Metamorphoses of a Creed* (1879) explained the theological liberalism that undergirded his preaching and ministry. *The Transfiguration of Christ* (1886; 1907) analyzed the nature and significance of this event, emphasized the importance of Jesus to the Christian faith, and challenged the church to cultivate a deeper "consciousness of infinity" as a basis for its life and ministry. In his Yale lectures on preaching, titled *The Minister and the Spiritual Life* (1911), Gunsaulus sought to show how personal spirituality, which rested on friendship with and service of Jesus Christ, was related to orthodoxy, the preaching and power of ministers, and solving contemporary social problems. His numerous other books included *William Ewart Gladstone* (1898), *The Higher Ministries of Recent English Poetry* (1907), and *Prayers* (1922). His theological works sold well and were highly respected, especially by liberal evangelical Protestants. His historical novels and poetry received mixed reviews. One critic called his *Monk and Knight* "suggestive of the novels of Charles Kingsley" (*Dial* 12 [June 1891]: 48), while another declared that much of his poetry was "mere verbiage, with little display of rhythmical art" (*Dial* 20 [Feb. 1896]: 113).

Gunsaulus was a man of tremendous vision and immense energy who enjoyed many close friendships. His Puritan background, a contemporary argued, "made him practical, modest, firm, and conscientious" (Bancroft, p. 12). Writing in *Collier's* in 1912, Peter MacFarlane described him as a "man of many manifestations" who epitomized the "striving, conquering spirit of Chicago" (p. 16). A poet, popular lecturer, art connoisseur, educator, author, and, above all, an outstanding preacher, he had a significant influence on Chicago and on American Protestantism during the late nineteenth and early twentieth centuries. He died in Chicago.

• Some of Gunsaulus's personal correspondence is in the Newberry Library Modern Manuscript Collections and the Chicago Historical Society Archives and Manuscripts. In addition to the works cited in the text, Gunsaulus wrote *Loose Leaves of Song* (1888), *The Man of Galilee* (1899), *Paths to Power* (1905), *Paths to the City of God* (1906), and *Martin Luther and the Morning Hour in Europe* (1917). The best sources of information about his life are Peter Clark MacFarlane, "Frank Wakely [sic] Gunsaulus," *Collier's*, 3 Aug. 1912, pp. 16–17, 25; Edgar A. Bancroft, *Doctor Gunsaulus, the Citizen* (1921); and the unsigned *In Memoriam: Frank Wakeley Gunsaulus* (1921). For the work of the Chicago Vice Commission, see Graham Taylor, "The Story of the Chicago Vice Commission," *Survey* 26 (6 May 1911): 239–47. Obituaries are in the *Chicago Daily Tribune*, 18 Mar. 1921, the *New York Times*, 18 Mar. 1921, and the *Congregationalist*, 31 Mar. 1921.

GARY SCOTT SMITH

GUNTHER, John (30 Aug. 1901–29 May 1970), foreign correspondent and writer, was born in Chicago, the son of Eugene M. Gunther, a salesman, and Lisette Shoeninger, a schoolteacher. His mother stimulated Gunther's interest in literature and history; at eleven he already was compiling a personal encyclopedia of world affairs. The wide-ranging interests, energy, and enthusiasm displayed at this early age characterized his personal and professional life. At the University of Chicago, where he graduated in 1922, he became literary editor of the campus newspaper while building his personal library by reviewing books for other journals as well. Eager for a writer's career, he headed for Europe to soak up continental culture without waiting to receive his bachelor's degree.

He returned to Chicago as a reporter for the *Daily News*, while pressing for an overseas assignment. Failing to win one, he quit in 1924 and worked his way to London, supporting himself with part-time freelance jobs for several news agencies while producing some unsuccessful novels. He was rehired by the *Daily News* in Paris in 1927, with roving assignments to other European capitals. He continued to write novels, but it was as a journalist and writer on the international political and social scene that he made his mark.

As *Daily News* correspondent in Vienna from 1930 until 1934, with responsibility for the Balkan states as well, Gunther flourished in a circle of outstanding reporters that included such well-known figures as Marcel Fodor of the *Manchester Guardian* and Dorothy Thompson of the *Philadelphia Public Ledger*. Another correspondent described him at this time as "big and made bigger by baggy suits, jovial, friendly . . . good company." In a later novel Gunther depicted his Vienna colleagues as "a hard-working, respectable lot, with children growing up and never enough money to go around." With his wife, Frances Fineman, whom he married in 1927, he plunged into the social life of the Austrian capital, relishing the company of interesting, influential people as well as the pleasures of the table and the wine cellar. High living kept him constantly in debt; he once threatened his editor that he would close his office and work out of his apartment, with only his wife as secretary, to save on expenses.

Like other underpaid correspondents, Gunther sought to supplement his income by contributing articles on Europe's colorful but treacherous politics and society for journals such as *Harper's* and the *Nation*. He quickly showed a knack for such writing, enlivening it with memorable incidents and characters and a straightforward narrative style rather than an analytical approach. His success with this kind of reporting enabled him to break with journeyman correspondence altogether after the publication in 1936 of a highly popular book, *Inside Europe*. Written during his last days in Vienna and a few months as head of the *Daily News*'s bureau in London, where he hobnobbed with Britain's social and political elite, the book offered readers a spirited, comprehensive overview of Europe's approaching crisis.

Inside Europe combined data gleaned from Gunther's own observations with those provided by many colleagues and friends, both American and European. Organized on a country-by-country basis, it included gossip, intrigue, and psychological interpretations of national leaders—Hitler, Stalin, Mussolini—as well as lesser lights. Although criticized by some specialists as superficial, the book presented a wealth of solid, factual information in a popular, almost novelistic style. Appearing just as Americans were beginning to awaken to the ominous course of international politics, *Inside Europe* found an enthusiastic audience. It was named a Book-of-the-Month Club selection and eventually sold more than a million copies in successive, updated editions. Its reception made Gunther the best-known, most widely read correspondent of his generation.

With this success, Gunther was freed to range the globe as a freelance observer and writer. Other *Inside* books followed: Asia (1939), Latin America (1941), the United States (1947), Africa (1955), Russia (1958), and South America (1968), each preceded by extensive reading, research, interviews, and travel. Equally well received, they offered the general reader illuminating background on the trouble spots and issues that were capturing headlines.

During World War II Gunther served as overseas correspondent for NBC radio and as a consultant for the U.S. War Department. His personal life, meanwhile, had been darkened by the death of an infant daughter and by his divorce in 1944. In 1947 an adolescent son died of a brain tumor after a painful, gallant struggle memorialized by Gunther in *Death Be Not Proud* (1949), the most personal and moving of his books.

In 1948 Gunther married Jane Perry Vandercook, with whom he adopted another son. He continued to write, travel, and speak indefatigably—still savoring the good life and still driving himself to sustain it. By the time of his death, in New York City, world politics, economics, and technology had drastically changed the nature of foreign correspondence. Gunther's own work as a wide-ranging interpreter of international affairs had played a part in the changes. For his work in popularizing global consciousness, Gunther deserves to be remembered as a key contributor to the waning of American isolationism.

• Manuscripts of Gunther's works together with some correspondence are at the Regenstein Library, University of Chicago; the remainder are in Jane Gunther's possession. Biographical materials include Gunther's *A Fragment of Autobiography* (1962), and Richard Rovere, "Inside," *New Yorker*, 23 Aug. 1947. *An obituary is in the New York Times*, 30 May 1970.

MORRELL HEALD

GURLEY, Ralph Randolph (26 May 1797–30 July 1872), philanthropist, was born in Lebanon, Connecticut, the son of John Gurley, a Congregationalist minister, and Mary Porter. Gurley moved to Washington, D.C., following his graduation in 1818 from Yale. A charismatic orator, he gained popularity as a licentiate, preaching mainly in Presbyterian churches with a predominantly black membership. Later he served as the chaplain for the U.S. House of Representatives. In 1827 Gurley married his fourteen-year-old cousin Eliza McLellan; they had thirteen children. The couple made their home in Georgetown, District of Columbia.

In 1822 Gurley accepted a $600 annual salary to fill the clerical position of resident agent for the American Colonization Society. Gurley was a fervent believer in the society's promise to offer white American citizens atonement from God for the sin of slavery. The nature of this sin, however, was not primarily the inhumane treatment of fellow humans but the introduction of the inferior black race into white America. According to the society, God willed white Americans to return the "alien" black race to its native land. The founder of the society, Robert Finley, wrote in 1816: "Could [free blacks] be sent to Africa, a three fold benefit would arise. We should be cleared of them—we should send to Africa a population partly civilized and christianized for its benefit. And our blacks themselves, would be put in a better situation" (*African Repository and Colonial Journal* 1[Mar. 1825]: 2). To Finley, colonization meant both an American foothold on trade with Africa and an avoidance of contact between white Americans and an inferior race that threatened to contaminate their morals and industriousness.

Gurley zealously assumed the responsibilities of the society's secretary, Elias Caldwell, when Caldwell's health began to fail. Unlike Caldwell, Gurley not only retained and organized all of the society's papers but he filed them with an eye for preservation. Gurley bound in volumes all the correspondence of the society, started a library on topics related to African colonization, and took responsibility for compiling the society's annual reports. In addition to performing clerical tasks, Gurley from 1822 to 1824 preached the society's convictions as a traveling agent. His persuasiveness as a lecturer resulted in large contributions. In 1824 the society chose Gurley to act as an arbiter between the rebellious settlers of its African colony at Cape Mesurado in Liberia and the unofficial governing agent, Jehudi Ashmun. The settlers, threatened by starvation and fever, believed that Ashmun ruled with only one goal in mind: the eventual control of the colony's trade with American trading companies.

Gurley spent three weeks discussing the crisis with Ashmun on the Cape Verde Islands, to which Ashmun had fled. Gurley's advice was to avoid rule by force and to implement a new constitution. Gurley's "Plan for the Civil Government of Liberia" gave the settlers a voice in the government through appointed positions. Gurley then risked his standing with the society by reinstalling the out-of-favor Ashmun as the governing agent. Tensions in the colony soon diminished. Gurley recorded his experience and impressions in the biography *Life of Jehudi Ashmun, Late Colonial Agent in Liberia* (1835). He visited the colony twice more, in 1849 and 1867, to observe its progress.

Gurley's successful negotiations in Liberia earned him the society's respect as a policymaker. Upon his return to America, he was given the authority to formulate policies for the parent society in Washington, D.C. In June 1825 the society selected Gurley to replace Caldwell as secretary for $1,250 a year. In his new role, Gurley supervised agents, managed finances, and fueled a publicity campaign to develop a national movement. In his *Discourse Delivered on the Fourth of July, 1825, in the City of Washington*, Gurley emphasized that it was the moral obligation of every American citizen to take individual responsibility for social evils such as slavery. Since slavery was a national problem, Gurley argued, the American Colonization Society deserved a continuous flow of national funds until all slaves were emancipated. As evidence of the danger blacks posed to the morality of white citizens, Gurley described the poor living conditions of freed slaves in the North and presented surveys that showed the percentage of blacks in Northern prisons was much higher than in the general population. Gurley's effort to draw a connection between African colonization, patriotism, and missionary work inspired the American Board for Foreign Missions to arrange a mission to the Liberian Colony and clergymen to claim that support of colonization was a Christian duty.

Gurley encouraged the spread of the American Colonization Society's beliefs throughout America between 1822 and 1840, acting as the prime mediator among the society's branches in the North and South and between the branches and the society's parent organization. In 1826 Gurley embarked on a lecture tour, traveling from Philadelphia to Montpelier, Vermont, to gain support for the cause. His plea to Pennsylvania Quakers was answered by donations, including a pledge from abolitionist and women's rights advocate Sarah M. Grimké and the establishment of a state society in Pennsylvania. Gurley's campaign led to the establishment of twenty auxiliary societies within the year. In 1830 a state society in Massachusetts was founded in Boston. By 1832 Gurley had succeeded in making the American Colonization Society one of the nation's top "benevolent" societies.

The society began to falter in 1834 as a result of the accrual of heavy debts and the growing criticism that colonization was a ploy to perpetuate slavery. Gurley increasingly spent his time defending the society against criticisms made by William Lloyd Garrison, an antislavery advocate and proponent of immediate emancipation. Garrison's *Thoughts on African Colonization* accused the society of hypocrisy, injustice, and having un-Christian and anti-Republican sentiments. He labeled the society as an apologist of slavery, a servant to slaveholders, and an opponent of the education of blacks. He claimed the society referred to slaves as property in its literature, drove up the price of slaves by removing free blacks, and promoted racism in its every act. Before Garrison's haranguing, Gurley had been successful in gaining support and contributions from northerners and southerners alike. In the North, he had suggested that the society's goal was the eventual end of slavery; in the South, he had advocated the removal of free blacks as a threat to the slavery system. Garrison's attack on colonization split the society wide open, forcing Gurley to respond to Garrison's accusations directly. In the *African Repository and Colonial Journal* and a small pamphlet titled *Letter on the American Colonization Society* (1832), Gurley argued that his aim was national unity and that Garrison's invectives only alienated southerners, therefore demolishing any chance of attaining the consent of southerners for immediate emancipation. Furthermore, Gurley argued, Garrison unfairly used excerpts out of context from the society's journal to prove his points. In Gurley's effort to diffuse Garrison's argument, however, he confirmed Garrison's criticism that the society considered slaves property when he argued that immediate emancipation was an infringement on property rights.

Despite the damage done by the antislavery movement, Gurley did not falter. In an effort to spread the American Colonization Society's influence to the British Isles, Gurley contributed to a debate on colonization at Egyptian Hall in London and in 1841 recorded his experience in *Mission to England*. He continued as the editor of the journal and the secretary of the society through its decline in the 1860s. He died in Washington, D.C.

• For information on Gurley's contribution to the development of the African colonization movement, see copies of his correspondence in the massive archival collection for the American Colonization Society at the Library of Congress. An informative article written by Gurley is "Remarks on the Principles of the Colonization Society," *African Repository and Colonial Journal* 10 (May 1834): 65–72. For information on Gurley's character and family life, see Mason Noble, *A Discourse Commemorative of the Life and Character of the Rev. Ralph Randolph Gurley* (1872), and Albert E. Gurley, *The History and Genealogy of the Gurley Family* (1897). Gurley's contribution to the society and the African colonization movement is discussed in P. J. Staudenraus, *The African Colonization Movement, 1816–1865* (1961). Early Lee Fox, *The American Colonization Society, 1817–1840* (1919), interprets Gurley's position as a focus on national unity (in relation to Garrisonian radicalism) and an effort to liberate and save thousands of blacks from slavery. William Jay, *Inquiry into the Character and Tendency of the American Colonization, and American Anti-Slavery Societies* (1838), provides a description of the establishment of the American Colonization Society.

BARBARA L. CICCARELLI

GURNEY, Eliza Paul Kirkbride (6 Apr. 1801–8 Nov. 1881), Quaker minister, was born in Philadelphia, Pennsylvania, the daughter of Joseph Kirkbride and Mary Paul. Both parents came from Quaker families, and from childhood Kirkbride was acquainted with leading English and North American Friends. Three years in the Friends Boarding School at Westtown, Pennsylvania, reinforced such influences. Kirkbride's mother died in 1807 and her father in 1816. Thereafter she made her home with relatives who were equally active and prominent Friends. In 1827 she became engaged to John Howell, a Quaker from Woodbury, New Jersey, but he died the following year.

By 1827 Eliza Kirkbride had become active in the affairs of the Philadelphia Yearly Meeting of Friends. When the separation into Hicksite and Orthodox branches took place in 1827–1828, she identified herself with the Orthodox Friends, who emphasized the importance of acceptance of the authority of Scripture and the divinity of Christ. In this, and in other respects, the Orthodox were moving close to the dominant evangelical religious culture of the United States. In Philadelphia, Orthodox Friends were the majority, though Hicksites outnumbered them in the surrounding countryside.

During the 1820s and 1830s a number of English Quaker ministers, most with pronounced evangelical views, visited the United States to strengthen the Orthodox Quakers. One of the most important of them was Hannah Chapman Backhouse, who arrived in 1830. She and Eliza Kirkbride became fast friends, and in 1832 the Philadelphia Friends appointed Kirkbride a companion to travel with Backhouse and her husband, Jonathan, across the country. In the next three years they passed through seventeen states and Canada, visiting Orthodox Quaker communities to exhort them to hold firm against "Hicksism."

In 1836, at Backhouse's invitation, Kirkbride visited England and then accompanied her on a ministerial journey to Scotland and the north of England. Through Backhouse, she gained entry into the leading circles of English Quakerism. She became particularly close to the great English Quaker minister and prison reformer Elizabeth Fry and to Fry's brother, Joseph John Gurney, a Norwich banker and philanthropist who was probably the most influential Friend in Great Britain. In 1837 Gurney began a three-year journey through North America. Kirkbride returned to America on Gurney's ship, advising him on conditions in American Quakerism generally and among Philadelphia Orthodox Friends particularly, many of whom regarded Gurney's evangelical Quakerism with suspicion.

Gurney's three years in America were, for the most part, what the Quaker historian Rufus Jones called "a triumphant tour." He visited almost every Orthodox Quaker community in North America, urging Friends to greater scriptural knowledge and to join with non-Quaker evangelicals in good works. His attentions extended to non-Quakers—he disputed theology with Congregationalists at Yale and Andover, called on governors and legislators, and everywhere spoke in favor of abolition, prison reform, and education. He also remained in touch with Kirkbride, who watched his progress from Philadelphia.

In 1841 Kirkbride accepted Hannah Backhouse's entreaty to come to England and live with her. Soon after moving to England she was recorded a Quaker minister. Kirkbride's removal may have had another motivation as well, because on 21 Oct. 1841 she and the twice-widowed Joseph John Gurney were married. Thereafter she lived at "Earlham Hall," the Gurney estate near Norwich. No children were born to them. In 1843 the Gurneys, accompanied by Elizabeth Fry, visited France in the interest of prison reform and antislavery. The visit climaxed with a call on King Louis-Philippe and his family.

After the deaths of Joseph John Gurney in 1847 and Hannah Chapman Backhouse in 1850, Eliza Gurney returned to the United States, buying a small estate at West Hill near Burlington, New Jersey. She returned to find American Friends again badly divided. Most Orthodox Friends were in sympathy with her husband's interpretation of Quakerism, which moved them closer to evangelical Protestantism; they had become known as "Gurneyites." A minority, known as Wilburites (after their chief prophet, John Wilbur of Rhode Island), still viewed Gurney's teachings as dangerously innovative. At issue were sanctification, the resurrection, and links with other denominations. Gurneyites made sanctification, or the attainment of holiness, a second experience after conversion or justification, while Wilburites argued that the two were inseparable. Gurneyites emphasized the resurrection of the physical body, while Wilburites believed the resurrection to be spiritual. Gurneyites favored working with other evangelicals in reform causes, while Wilburites feared that links with non-Quakers, even for the best of reasons, endangered Quaker distinctiveness. Philadelphia Yearly Meeting was strongly Wilburite in sympathy, which put Eliza Gurney in an awkward position. Nevertheless she continued to travel widely among Quakers, upholding her husband's views. In 1854 she played a leading role in the bitter split among Ohio Orthodox Quakers, calling down divine judgments on the Wilburites. Her ministry was confined entirely to Quaker concerns.

Like all Quakers, Gurney was antislavery in her views, although there is no evidence of her involvement with the abolitionist movement. The outbreak of the Civil War confronted her with a cruel dilemma. As a staunch supporter of the Union and an enemy of slavery, she hoped for a Union victory, yet she could not break with Quaker pacifism. The conflict was the occasion for her most public ministry, however, when in October 1862 she, with three other Friends, visited Abraham Lincoln. Gurney felt moved both to comfort Lincoln and to exhort him to greater reliance on divine guidance. The visit evidently deeply impressed Lincoln because he later asked Gurney to write to him. "I have not forgotten, probably never shall forget, the very impressive occasion when yourself and friends visited me," he wrote to her in 1864.

After 1865, as her eyesight failed, Eliza Gurney became less active in Quaker affairs. She died at West Hill, New Jersey.

• Eliza Gurney's papers are not known to have survived, but some letters can be found in the Joseph John Gurney Papers in the Friends Library, London, and in the Haverford College Quaker Collection. The basic source for Eliza Gurney's life is Richard F. Mott, ed., *Memoir and Correspondence of Eliza P. Gurney* (1884). Good brief accounts are in William Robinson, ed., *Friends of Half a Century* (1891), pp. 166–72; Amelia Mott Gummere, *The Quaker in the Forum* (1910), pp. 309–17; and Gummere's biography in *Quaker Biographies*, ser. 2, vol. 2 (n.d.), pp. 99–130. For Eliza Gurney's role in the separation in the Ohio Yearly Meeting in 1854, which is ignored entirely by Mott, see William Hodgson, ed., *Selections from the Letters of Thomas B. Gould* (1860), pp. 353–74. See also David E. Swift, *Joseph John Gurney* (1962).

THOMAS D. HAMM

GUSTON, Philip (27 June 1913–7 June 1980), artist, was born Philip Goldstein in Montreal, Canada, the son of Lieb Goldstein, a machinist, and Rachel Ehrenlieb, Jewish immigrants from Russia. In 1919 Guston moved with his parents to Los Angeles, where his father, discouraged with his inability to support his family, committed suicide four years later. Guston began drawing seriously at age thirteen. After brief instruction in cartoon illustration, he enrolled in Los Angeles Manual Arts High School, where he befriended the young Jackson Pollock. Unimpressed by the institutional regimen, Guston left school and supported himself by working various odd jobs. After 1930 and another failed attempt in art school—this time at the Otis Art Institute (where he met Musa McKim, whom he married in 1937 and with whom he had one child)—Guston gained a mentor, artist Lorser Feitelson, who exposed him to Walter Arensberg's collection of works by Picasso, Leger, and De Chirico. Feitelson also nurtured in Guston a respect for the Italian masters, particularly Piero della Francesca. Exposure to modern and Italian Renaissance painting was key to Guston's development as an artist.

Guston first came to national prominence in the 1930s as a mural painter. He moved for the first time in 1936 to New York City, where he, like many artists from his generation, signed on with the Federal Art Project's mural division of the Works Progress Administration under Franklin D. Roosevelt's New Deal. Inspired by Picasso and De Chirico, Guston's widely acclaimed, large-scale murals, some of which included haunting images of the Ku Klux Klan, engaged issues of race, desperation, and discrimination so prevalent in American art and culture throughout the 1930s. One such mural, *Maintaining America's Skills*, completed for the 1937 New York World's Fair, received particular critical recognition.

After his stint with the WPA, Guston accepted a teaching position at the University of Iowa from 1941 to 1945. His tenure in Iowa as well as his stay at Washington University (St. Louis) as artist in residence from 1945 to 1947 allowed him to turn his attention exclusively toward easel painting for the first time in his career. Like his murals from the 1930s, Guston's easel paintings received wide critical approval. Stylistically, Guston's imagery from the early 1940s was a delicate synthesis of American social realism, European modernism, and Italian Renaissance that grew progressively more abstract and flat as the decade progressed. Public recognition reached an early peak for the artist when he was featured in a *Life* magazine article in 1946, three years before Pollock received the same honor.

In 1950 Guston relocated to New York City and became a leading practitioner of abstract expressionism, a loose artistic movement that included Pollock, Mark Rothko, Barnett Newman, Grace Hartigan, Franz Kline, and Willem de Kooning. By creating everchanging and evocative spaces using an anxious, linear application of pigment, Guston explored the aesthetic ground existing between the two branches of abstract expressionism perceived by some critics—action painting and color-field abstraction.

Throughout the late 1950s and mid-1960s, Guston became progressively dissatisfied with nonfigurative abstraction. He returned to depicting single objects in a large series of ink and charcoal drawings completed from 1966 to 1969. Many of the banal subjects painted by Guston in the 1930s—boots, light bulbs, and brick walls—reappeared in these drawings. Other more socially charged images, such as the Ku Klux Klan figures, were resurrected as well. The drawings constituted an evocative iconographic catalog that the painter used to create a new body of bizarre, large-scale figurative paintings.

Guston's critical departure from nonfigurative abstraction took place in relative seclusion. In 1967 he and his wife abandoned the New York art scene to set up permanent residence in Woodstock, New York. Away from New York City's plethora of competing dealers, critics, artists, and ideologues, Woodstock provided Guston with the necessary time and solitude to find and explore his personal vision. It would remain his home until his death.

Guston's new style was a tense synthesis of drawing and painting and a combative struggle between representation and abstraction. His lines, which in the 1950s were utilized to create quasigeometric abstractions, became attenuated in the later sixties and seventies, pushed, pulled, and bent by the artist to render flattened, cartoonish subjects on the canvas. The paintings also demonstrated the artist's renewed interest in narrative. Like his painting technique, however, Guston's storytelling from the late 1960s and thereafter is neither simple nor easily understood. Many paintings—particularly those from the mid-1970s containing a self-portrait as a lima bean cyclops head—suggest autobiographical narratives depicting Guston's struggles with alcohol and insomnia. Despite the self-reflexive nature of much of Guston's late imagery, it is difficult to assign definitive biographical interpretations to individual images.

The public's first exposure to Guston's new figurative paintings occurred in an exhibition in October 1970 at New York's Marlborough Gallery. His self-consciously crude painting technique and his use of narrative shocked his audience and enraged his critics.

The most negative criticism came from Hilton Kramer: "Mr. Guston is appealing to a taste for something funky, clumsy and demotic. We are asked to take seriously his new persona as an urban primitive, and this is asking too much. . . . Mr. Guston is clearly . . . turning to the popular visual slang of the old cartoonists as the basis of a new pictorial style. But it doesn't work. For one thing, there is no vitality here to rejuvenate" (*New York Times*, 25 Oct. 1970). Moreover, the cartoonish and banal subjects suggested to many concerned viewers that the artist had succumbed to the influence of pop art, the concurrent rival movement. To purist advocates of abstract expressionism, such as the formalist critic Clement Greenberg, Guston's new work seemed to mock the foundations of New York School abstraction.

Profoundly struck by the negative reception and the financial failure of the Marlborough exhibition, Guston left New York with his wife and accepted the position of artist in residence at the American Academy in Rome. Instead of elaborating on his new artistic discoveries in his studio at the American Academy, Guston wandered through Italian villages and visited the cultural landmarks in Florence, Venice, and Rome that he had admired as a student.

After he returned to the United States in 1972, Guston accepted a teaching position at Boston University, a post he would hold until the year of his death. Inspired by the monumentality of the Italian masterpieces he had just experienced, Guston returned to his controversial large-scale imagery, which became more disturbing and iconic as the decade progressed and as his health deteriorated. Living and working in Woodstock, where he maintained a residence during his tenure at Boston University, the artist exhibited his paintings widely and was awarded many honors, including a distinguished teaching award from the College Art Association of America in 1975 and a membership to the American Academy of Arts and Sciences in 1978.

While Guston's final years were marked by considerable professional success, they were also characterized by illness. With his health weakened by years of anxiety, exhaustion, and heavy drinking, Guston suffered a heart attack in 1979. He died in Woodstock from a second heart attack a year later.

Scholars of American art generally regard Philip Guston as an important transitional figure between abstract painting of the 1950s and the figurative art that reemerged in the 1970s and 1980s. However, viewers of his work should not understand Guston's seemingly radical break from abstract expressionism as his most

important artistic achievement. Rather, as the artist's oeuvre reveals and as Guston scholar Robert Storr aptly stated, "the value of Guston's example resides in . . . his concern for art's continuity" (Storr, p. 99).

• Most of the Guston papers are in the possession of Musa Mayer. Useful Guston materials on microfilm are at the Archives of American Art, Smithsonian Institution. The David McKee Gallery in New York City has been the primary dealer of Guston's paintings since 1974. Dore Ashton has written extensively on Guston; her *Philip Guston: A Critical Study* (1976) is one of the most important sources on the artist. Robert Storr, *Philip Guston* (1986), is a key monograph. Ashton's and Storr's texts contain excellent bibliographies. Guston's daughter, Musa Mayer, has written a more personalized account of the painter's life and career in *Night Studio* (1988). See also Ross Feld's exhibition catalog, *Philip Guston* (1980). Guston published numerous statements and essays in various art journals, including one of the most illuminating pieces, "Faith, Hope, and Impossibility," *Art News Annual* 31 (1966): 101–3, 152, 153. An obituary is in the *New York Times*, 10 June 1980.

RANDALL R. GRIFFEY

GUTENBERG, Beno (4 June 1889–25 Jan. 1960), seismologist, was born in Darmstadt, Germany, the son of Hermann Gutenberg, a soap manufacturer, and Pauline Hachenburger. Gutenberg entered the Realgymnasium in Darmstadt in 1898, where he showed an early interest in meteorology and an aptitude for mathematics and physics. He continued his studies at the Technische Hochschule in Darmstadt from 1907 to 1908. His original intention was to become a high school teacher, but his teachers were convinced that with his abilities he should continue his studies in mathematics and physics at the University of Göttingen, which he entered. in 1908. There he attended courses of such luminaries as Max Born, David Hilbert, Felix Klein, Edmund Landau, Hermann Minkowski, Woldemar Voigt, Hermann Weyl, and Emil Wiechert. His interests drifted into seismology, and he wrote his dissertation on microseisms, "Die Seismische Unruhe," under the direction of Wiechert. He received his Ph.D. in 1911.

Gutenberg continued his research at Göttingen after receiving his Ph.D. in collaboration with Wiechert's assistant, Ludwig Geiger. They began a study of an incomplete manuscript left by Karl Zöppritz at his death in 1908. Together they finished this work and perfected the Zöppritz method, which was a notable advance in computational methods.

Gutenberg next turned his attention to determining the depth of the earth's core. Wiechert had conjectured that the earth had a core in 1897, and Richard D. Oldham had proved the core's existence in 1906. Wiechert had guessed that the core lay at a depth of 1,500 kilometers, but until Gutenberg no one had launched a definitive investigation of the matter. In 1912 and 1913 he made a meticulous examination of seismic waves recorded at distant observation stations, and by intricate calculations (which he later modestly dismissed as being by "trial and error"), he determined the true depth to be 2,900 kilometers, a result that is essentially accepted today. This study is widely regarded as one of his greatest achievements, and in retrospect it was a *tour de force* of his analytical skills. The evidence also seemed to suggest that the core was liquid, but Gutenberg hesitated to draw that conclusion.

In 1913 Gutenberg became an assistant at the Central Office of the International Association of Seismology, which was then attached to the University of Strassburg. Then service in the German army during World War I interrupted his work, and from 1913 to 1914 he worked for the army's weather service as a meteorologist. In 1919 he married Hertha Dernberg; they had a son and a daughter. His principal occupation from the year of his marriage until 1929 was running his father's business. Nevertheless, in 1923 he became a Privatdozent at the University of Frankfurt-am-Main, and in 1926 he was appointed an associate professor of geophysics, positions that brought him little income. His father died in 1926, leaving him the business.

In the meantime Gutenberg produced a great many geophysical and seismological publications, which included his first two books, *Die Aufbau der Erde* (1925) and *Grundlage der Erdbebenwellen* (1927). He was also an editor of, and frequent contributor to, the *Lehrbuch der Geophysik* from 1927 to 1929 and wrote articles on earth science for the *Lehrbuch der Physik* (1928). He also returned to his early interest in meteorology with studies on the structure of the upper atmosphere, which included work on the relation between temperature and the speed of sound.

In 1929 Gutenberg attended a conference at the seismological laboratory of the Carnegie Institution in Pasadena, California. Already antisemitism was on the rise in Germany, and sensing that his academic prospects were limited, he accepted an offer to become professor of geophysics at the California Institute of Technology (Caltech) in 1930. He remained there for the rest of his life.

Gutenberg took up his position at Caltech at the height of his powers, and together with the staff already there—notably, Harry O. Woods, Hugo Benioff, and Charles F. Richter—set about making Caltech one of the world's major centers of seismological research. In particular, his collaboration with Richter was highly productive and lasted for almost thirty years. In 1933 he gave the first confirmation that mountains have "roots," that is, a thickening of the crustal layer beneath them. Perhaps the most fruitful result of the Gutenberg-Richter collaboration was their series of papers on seismic waves (1934–1939), which appeared in *Gerlands Beiträge zur Geophysik* and were noteworthy for their studies of the earth's core and travel times of waves. According to Richter it was Gutenberg who suggested the use of a logarithmic scale, and this has become known as the Richter magnitude scale. In 1936 Gutenberg became a naturalized citizen of the United States. During 1944 he worked as a civilian for the U.S. Navy, and from 1947 to 1958 he was director of the Seismological Laboratory in Pasadena (which had become part of Caltech in 1936).

Gutenberg continued to produce important reference and research volumes on seismology and geophysics as both an editor and contributor, including *Internal Constitution of the Earth* (1939; rev. ed., 1951); *Seismicity of the Earth* (1941; rev. ed., 1954), written collaboratively with Richter; and finally his last book, *The Physics of the Earth's Interior* (1959).

Although little known outside academic circles, Gutenberg received many honors from his profession. He was elected a member of the National Academy of Sciences in 1945. He was an honorary or foreign member of the Royal Astronomical Society, the Geological Society of London, the Accademia dei Lincei (Rome, Italy), and the royal societies of New Zealand and Sweden. He was president of the Seismological Society of America from 1945 to 1949 and the International Seismological Association from 1951 to 1954. His honors include the Prix de Physique du Globe of the Académie Royale de Belgique (1950); the William Bowie Medal, which is the highest honor of the American Geophysical Union (1953); and the Wiechert Medal of the Deutsche Geophysikalische Gesellschaft (1956).

In person, Gutenberg was a small, vivacious man who seemed to possess a limitless supply of energy. His vigorous productivity spanned the entire development of seismology from its beginning to its emergence as an organized discipline, and today the subject bears the indelible imprint of his genius and industry. All his work is characterized by a careful nondogmatic scholarship, which warns the reader against drawing overoptimistic conclusions. He died in Pasadena.

• The Gutenberg papers are held by the Institute Archives at the California Institute of Technology. Of special interest are Gutenberg's personal remarks in "Fifteenth Award of the Bowie Medal," *Transactions of the American Geophysical Union* 34 (June 1953): 353–55, and the biographical comments by Hertha Gutenberg in the Institute Archives at Caltech. Relatively few of Gutenberg's writings were intended for the general reader; however, his paper "Earth Physics," *Physics Today* 2 (Feb. 1949): 14–18, contains an overview of the problems that confront a working geophysicist. Also, section 1.1 of his final book, *Physics of the Earth's Interior* (1959), gives insight into his methodology and approach to science. A lucid account of the development of the seismological program at Caltech is in Judith R. Goodstein, *Millikan's School—A History of the California Institute of Technology* (1991), chap. 7. Obituary notices were written by Charles F. Richter, in *Proceedings of the Geological Society of American Annual Report for 1960* (Feb. 1962): 93–104, which contains a complete list of publications; and by Harold Jeffreys, in *Ouarterly Journal of the Royal Astronomical Society* 1 (1960): 239–42. An obituary also appears in the *New York Times*, 28 Jan. 1960.

JOSEPH D. ZUND

GUTHEIM, James Koppel (15 Nov. 1817–11 June 1886), rabbi, was born in Menne (in the district of Warburg), Westphalia, the son of Meyer Gutheim, a Hebrew scholar. (His mother's name is not known.) As a young boy, he received a traditional Jewish education at the Talmud Torah school of Warburg. He later obtained a teacher's education at the Lehrerseminar, and, simultaneously, he studied with the district's chief rabbi, Abraham Sutro, from whom he earned a diploma of Hebraic proficiency. He also studied classics with a Protestant minister in the city of Oberlistingen, where he taught Hebrew. From 1838 to 1842 Gutheim served as a preacher and a teacher in Sedenhorst, Westphalia.

Gutheim came to the United States in 1843 and worked in New York City as a bookkeeper in his brother's counting room. Shortly thereafter, he began contributing articles to the Anglo-Jewish press. By 1844, the editor of the *Occident, and American Jewish Advocate*, Isaac Leeser, noted Gutheim's potential and praised him for having "in so short a time acquired a great facility to express himself so generally correctly in the English language." Leeser's hope that Gutheim would soon be able to devote himself to "advancing the cause of Jewish faith" in the United States was fulfilled in 1846 when Gutheim accepted an offer to serve as the headmaster of a Talmud Torah school in Cincinnati.

Soon after his arrival in Cincinnati, Gutheim became rabbi of Congregation B'nai Yeshurun, thus launching his career as an American rabbi. At his suggestion, the congregation appointed a committee to revise the "order of worship" so as to improve service decorum. Gutheim's proficiency in English increased his appeal; he was one of only a handful of rabbis who could preach in the vernacular at the time. The oldest Jewish congregation in New Orleans, Shangaray Chessed, coaxed him away from Cincinnati in 1849 and elected him minister in 1850. Three years later, Nefutzot Yehudah, a New Orleans congregation receiving financial support from wealthy Jewish philanthropist Judah Touro, enticed Gutheim to accept the position of rabbi for a handsome annual salary of $2,000. In 1858 he married Emilie Jones of Mobile; they had one child.

After Union forces captured New Orleans in 1862, each citizen was required to either take an oath of allegiance to the United States or relocate to the Confederacy. Declining to pledge loyalty to the "Dictator of Washington," Gutheim fled to Mobile in 1863. For the remainder of the Civil War, he served two Confederate pulpits, the Hebrew Congregation of Montgomery and the B'nai Israel Congregation of Columbus, Georgia, visiting the latter every six weeks.

Although a passionate supporter of the Confederacy, Gutheim objected strenuously to a public proclamation issued by Alabama governor Thomas H. Watts in 1864 appealing to the "Christian people" of the state to pray for the welfare of the Confederacy. "It is the citizens . . . not a Christian people, nor a Jewish people," Gutheim wrote Watts, "that ought to be addressed by the constitutional functionaries." After the war, Gutheim agreed to resume his post at Nefutzot Yehudah, but soon after his return to New Orleans he accepted Shangaray Chessed's invitation to return to its pulpit.

In 1868 Congregation Emanu-El persuaded Gutheim to come to New York City to serve alongside its senior rabbi, Samuel Adler, as its English preacher. His years in New York City signaled his official association with Reform Judaism, and during this time he published numerous articles in the Anglo-Jewish press, a volume of his own sermons, metrical translations of many psalms, original hymns for Emanu-El's prayer service, and a translation of the fourth volume of Heinrich Graetz's *History of the Jews* for the short-lived American Jewish Publication Society. Nevertheless, Gutheim apparently found life in New York City less than satisfying. He longed to return to his beloved New Orleans, and the presence of a senior associate necessarily limited the scope of his ministry at Emanu-El. In 1870 his friends and admirers in New Orleans established a new Reform congregation named Temple Sinai, and as soon as its structure was completed in 1872, Gutheim accepted their invitation to become the temple's first rabbi—a post he held until his death.

Gutheim's name was allied with numerous Jewish and civic philanthropic organizations in New Orleans, including the Hebrew Benevolent Society, the Hebrew Education Society, the Hebrew Foreign Mission Society, and the Touro Infirmary. He was also founding president of the Conference of Rabbis of Southern Congregations. In addition, he served on the New Orleans School Board and the Conference of Charities and was a charter member of the city's Widows and Orphans Home.

Gutheim died in New Orleans. Often referred to as "the High Priest of Southern Judaism," he was the universally acknowledged leader of New Orleans Jewry's religious life for nearly forty years and a pioneering figure in the development of Reform Judaism in the United States.

• Many of Gutheim's papers, including his manuscript sermons, are in the American Jewish Archives, Cincinnati, Ohio, which also houses excellent indices of articles in the *American Hebrew, Die Deborah*, and the *Occident, and American Jewish Advocate*, all of which contain many references to Gutheim. Additional materials are in the Temple Sinai Collection at the Tulane University Archives. *Temple Pulpit* (1872) contains seventeen of his sermons and addresses given during the years 1854–1872. Other published addresses also survive, including sermons delivered at the consecration of B'nai Yeshurun in Cincinnati (1846), Adas Israel Synagogue in Louisville, Ky. (1849), and Shangaray Chessed in New Orleans (1851). For examples of Gutheim's hymns, liturgical compositions, and metrical psalms, see M. Thalmessinger, *Hymns for Divine Service in the Temple Emanu-El* (1871), and Isidor Wise, *The Sabbath Visitor* (1886–1887): 12, 74. The Conference of Rabbis of Southern Congregations published Gutheim's presidential address, *Cause, Development and Scope of Reform* (1886). Unfortunately, no critical studies assessing the significance of Gutheim's life and work exist. The most detailed biographical sketch is *The Record: Sketches of the Life of the Rev. James K. Gutheim, and the Solemn and Impressive Obsequies at his Death . . .* (1887). See also Leo Shpall, "Rabbi James Koppel Guttheim [*sic*]," *Louisiana Historical Quarterly* 22 (1939): 166–81. *The Jubilee Souvenir of Temple Sinai, 1872–1922*, written by Rabbi Max Heller, who succeeded Gutheim as rabbi of Temple Sinai in New Orleans, contains additional biographical data. Heller composed another concise assessment on Gutheim in *Central Conference of American Rabbis Yearbook* (1917). Other helpful sources include James G. Heller, *As Yesterday When It Is Past* (1942);

Bertram W. Korn, *American Jewry and the Civil War* (1970) and *Early Jews of New Orleans* (1969); and Jacob Rader Marcus, *United States Jewry, 1776–1985*, vol. 2 (1991). An obituary is in the *New Orleans Daily Picayune*, 12 June 1886.

GARY P. ZOLA

GUTHRIE, A. B., Jr. (13 Jan. 1901–26 Apr. 1991), journalist and author, was born Alfred Bertram Guthrie, Jr., in Bedford, Indiana, the son of Alfred Bertram Guthrie, an educator and newspaper publisher, and June Thomas. When Guthrie was six months old, the family moved to Choteau, Montana, on the eastern side of the Rocky Mountains and still very much a frontier town, where his father became the first principal of the new Teton County Free High School. Guthrie's father was interested in western history; this interest was passed on to his son. Growing up, Guthrie enjoyed hunting and fishing; he was later to give up both, hating to kill or see anything killed.

When he was fourteen, Guthrie went to work at the weekly newspaper the *Choteau Acantha*, formerly owned by his father. He was first a printer's devil and later a journeyman printer. He also "reported" for the paper on arrivals and departures at the Great Northern Railroad Station. After graduating from high school, he went to college to become a journalist. He entered the University of Washington at Seattle in the fall of 1919 but did not like the city or the climate and transferred for his sophomore year to the University of Montana at Missoula. He graduated in 1923 with honors and a degree in journalism.

For the next two years Guthrie worked at a series of jobs: at a ranch in Mexico, for Western Electric in Oakland, California, and as an agricultural census taker for the Forest Service in Choteau. His next job was in Attica, New York, working for an uncle and cousin at a feed company. When its mill burned down, another uncle found Guthrie a job in Kentucky as a cub reporter for the *Lexington Leader*. By 1927 he was writing editorials. He became city editor in 1929, then managing editor, and in 1945 executive editor. In 1931 Guthrie married his childhood sweetheart from Choteau, Harriet Helen Larson; they had two children. They would divorce by "common consent" in 1963. Guthrie married Carol Bischman Luthin in 1969.

Guthrie began his first book in 1936, *Murders at Moon Dance* (1943), a detective story with a western setting, but was not pleased with the result: "I can't say it is the worst book ever written, but I've long considered it a contender" (*The Blue Hen's Chick* [1965], p. 128). He was so ashamed of the book that he bought up all the hardcover copies in Lexington. In 1937 an anthology, *Headlining America*, included a story of his about the inauguration of A. B. "Happy" Chandler as governor of Kentucky. In 1938 Guthrie applied, unsuccessfully, for a Nieman Fellowship to study at Harvard.

After being stricken with encephalitis in 1943, Guthrie returned to Montana to recuperate. It was there that he decided to write a novel about the mountain men of the West. After three chapters, Guthrie

abandoned the project. He applied again for a Nieman Fellowship and this time was successful. At Harvard his adviser, Theodore Morrison, gave him the criticism and direction needed to progress on his book. In 1945 the family went home, and a publisher offered Guthrie $5,000 for the partially completed manuscript of *The Big Sky* (1947).

The Big Sky is about three fictional mountain men, composites of historical figures, who first live off the land and then see their way of life ending as settlers begin to move over the mountains to Oregon and California. Guthrie's love of the land is apparent with his often poetic descriptions of the mountains, rivers, and sky. In fact, Guthrie so captured the essence of Montana that the state adopted the nickname "Big Sky Country." The novel was made into a film in 1952.

Guthrie was able to quit his job at the *Lexington Leader* in 1947 and devote himself exclusively to writing. He planned to tell the story of the development of the West in a series of novels. *The Big Sky* takes place in the western wilderness and covers the years 1830–1843. His next novel, *The Way West* (1949), is the story of settlers moving over the Oregon Trail in 1845. By using one of the mountain men characters, Dick Summers, from *The Big Sky*, Guthrie tied the novels together. He showed how the wilderness life of the mountain men changed by having Summers become the guide of the new immigrants. Guthrie wrote this novel in six months. It was a Book-of-the-Month Club selection, won the Pulitzer Prize in fiction for 1950, and was made into a film in 1967.

In 1951 Howard Hawks, who directed the film version of *The Big Sky*, recommended Guthrie to write the screenplay for Jack Schaefer's novel *Shane*. Guthrie had never written a screenplay; in fact he "had never even seen one on paper." The film was nominated for an Academy Award for best picture, and Guthrie was also nominated for his screenplay. Guthrie wrote the screenplay to *The Kentuckian* for United Artists in 1955 and for his own novel *These Thousand Hills* in 1958.

After leaving the *Lexington Leader*, Guthrie taught creative writing at the University of Kentucky. In 1953 he moved back to Montana. In his autobiography, *The Blue Hen's Chick*, he wrote, "The Bluegrass landscape did not enchant me. . . . I liked my beauty grim. I liked it out of control, pristine, everlasting as man's work could never be"—the landscape of Montana.

The third novel of Guthrie's saga of the West, *These Thousand Hills* (1956), covers the years 1880–1887 and marks the end of the westward movement. The chief character, a descendant of the Oregon settlers of *The Way West*, moves east. Guthrie described this novel as "my most difficult and least successful book." Centered on cattle ranching in Montana, it, too, was made into a film. *Arfive* (1970) covers the time period 1910–1917, and *The Last Valley* (1975) brings Guthrie's saga of the "winning" of the West to the year 1946. In the novels the concept of winning and taming the West is also part of losing it. Progress brings the settlers and "civilization," but it also destroys the beaver trade, the buffalo, and the way of life of the Indians. A character in *The Last Valley* warns, "Watch out for progress because you can't backtrack."

Realizing he had left a forty-year gap between *The Way West* and *These Thousand Hills*, Guthrie wrote *Fair Land, Fair Land* (1982), the final novel in his series and a sequel to *The Big Sky* and *The Way West*. This novel continues the story of mountain man Boone Caudill, his Indian "wife" Teal Eye, and Dick Summers, all characters in *The Big Sky*. *Fair Land, Fair Land* has been described as a requiem for a way of life.

The land plays a major role throughout Guthrie's novels; he saw the western landscape as a "diminishing treasure." Toward the end of his life, Guthrie said, "if I had to do it over, I would have been a naturalist." Guthrie became an activist for preserving the wilderness in Montana and received an award for Conservationist of the Year, in 1988, from the Montana Environmental Information Center. He and his wife also worked for the protection of the grizzly bear, a position not highly regarded in their sheep and cattle ranching community. In 1988 a series of his environmental essays were collected in *Big Sky, Fair Land*.

Drawing on his experience as a newspaperman, Guthrie wrote an unsentimentalized series of novels about the West. As one critic said, "He put fact back into fiction." The novels are true historically and recreate the western experience, both moments of triumph and of despair as the movement of peoples stretches the nation westward.

Guthrie's final book, *A Field Guide to Writing Fiction* (1991), was published two weeks before he died at home in Choteau, Montana.

• Guthrie's manuscripts are at the University of Kentucky, Lexington. Guthrie also wrote short stories, which were collected in *The Big It and Other Stories* (1960); some poetry; *Once upon a Pond*, a collection of animal stories for children that were illustrated by his wife Carol; and a series of western "whodunits:" *Wild Pitch*, followed by sequels *The Genuine Article* (1977), *No Second Wind* (1980), and *Playing Catch-Up* (1985). A book-length study is Thomas W. Ford, *A. B. Guthrie, Jr.* (1981), part of the Twayne's authors series. A comprehensive annotated bibliography of both primary and secondary sources is in Martin Kich, *Western American Novelists*, vol. 1 (1995). A lengthy article with bibliography by Wayne Chatterton is in *A Literary History of the American West* (1987). Also see John Milton's chapter "The Historical Inheritance: Guthrie and Manfred," in *The Novel of the American West* (1980), and Sue Mathews, "Pioneer Women in the Works of Two Montana Authors: Interviews with Dorothy M. Johnson and A. B. Guthrie, Jr.," in *Women and Western American Literature* (1982). Articles in periodicals include Thomas Ford, "A. B. Guthrie's *Fair Land, Fair Land*: A Requiem," *Western American Literature* 23 (Spring 1988): 17–30; Michael Simmons, "Boone Caudill: The Failure of an American Primitive," *South Dakota Review* 22 (Autumn 1984): 39–43; Richard Astro, "*The Big Sky* and the Limits of Wilderness Fiction," *Western American Literature* 9 (Aug. 1974): 105–14; and Dayton Kohler, "A. B. Guthrie, Jr., and the West," *College English* 12 (Feb. 1951): 249–56. An obituary is in the *New York Times*, 27 Apr. 1991.

MARCIA B. DINNEEN

GUTHRIE, Edwin Ray (9 Jan. 1886–23 Apr. 1959), psychologist, was born in Lincoln, Nebraska, the son of Edwin Ray Guthrie, a piano-store owner, and Harriet Louise Pickett. Guthrie earned an undergraduate degree in mathematics in 1907 and a master's degree in philosophy in 1910 at the University of Nebraska at Lincoln. He then studied philosophy under Edgar A. Singer at the University of Pennsylvania, where he completed a dissertation on Bertrand Russell's logical paradoxes of self-reference and received his Ph.D. in 1912. After teaching mathematics at Boys Central High School in Philadelphia for two years, he accepted an instructorship in philosophy at the University of Washington in Seattle in 1914, and in professional philosophy journals he published articles on topics in logic. In 1919 he moved to the Department of Psychology and collaborated with Stevenson Smith on *General Psychology in Terms of Behavior* (1921), a classic of early behaviorism. He married Helen MacDonald in 1920; they had one child.

Guthrie is best known for his seminal contributions to "learning theory," an academic-research enterprise that developed theories of habit formation and rote learning from the results of the study of humans and animals in simple learning tasks in the psychology laboratory. Learning theory dominated American academic psychology from the 1930s to the 1950s. Guthrie's reputation as a learning theorist is based on publications that appeared in *Psychological Review* between 1930 and 1940; his *Psychology of Learning* (1935; rev. ed., 1952); and his *Cats in a Puzzle Box* (1946), coauthored with George P. Horton and based on research conducted between 1936 and 1939. Guthrie's achievements of the 1930–1940 period resulted in recognition and various honors, including the presidency of the American Psychological Association in 1945. In 1958 he became only the third psychologist to receive the Gold Medal Award of the American Psychological Foundation.

Guthrie's first important article on learning theory, "Conditioning as a Principle of Learning" (*Psychological Review* 37 [1930]: 412–28), was a daring interpretation of many of the findings reported by Russian physiologist Ivan Pavlov in his *Conditioned Reflexes* (1927). Guthrie treated Pavlov's findings as manifestations of the principle that the temporal proximity—"contiguity"—of stimulus and response is the primary determinant of the formation of associations. In his subsequent papers and books, Guthrie brilliantly extended the apparently simple principle of contiguity to account for a variety of complex learned behaviors, both in and beyond the psychology laboratory. His theory enjoyed an appealing parsimony and explanatory success, even though he did not carry out an extensive program of laboratory research to support it.

Guthrie's theory was "behavioristic" in emphasizing the importance of behavior in the organism's transactions with the environment; it was not "cognitivist," for the theory minimized the importance of higher mental processes, particularly in animals but also in much of the habitual conduct of humans. Finally, the theory was "peripheralist" in minimizing reference to hypothetical inner (cognitive, mental, or experiential) states. It claimed that stimulus-response (S-R) associations are the primary elements of learning and that the fundamental mechanism is S-R "contiguity"—rather than a principle of reinforcement such as was promoted by psychologists Edward L. Thorndike, B. F. Skinner, and Clark L. Hull, constituting a majority viewpoint at the time.

The fact that Guthrie had carefully read Sir Charles Sherrington's classic of reflex physiology, *The Integrative Action of the Nervous System* (1904), is apparent as early as 1921, in his text with Smith. Guthrie's vision as a theorist strongly reflected the Sherringtonian notion that an organism's overall behavior is a composite of elementary or "molecular" reflexes, a composite that is integrated by higher centers in the nervous system. Guthrie's emphasis on the molecular description of actions was largely bypassed by his contemporaries in the 1930s (Hull, Skinner, Edward C. Tolman, etc.), who regarded "molar" acts as sui generis, incapable of reduction to elementary constituent (i.e., molecular) movements. Consequently, by relying on explanatory models in physiology to develop his hard-headed scientific philosophy of psychology, Guthrie's theoretical style was reductionist, and it was peripheralist in minimizing reference to hypothesized inner ("central" or mental) states. Finally, his theory was quite distinctively "molecularist," rather than "molar."

Guthrie's intriguing *Cats in a Puzzle Box* made use of motion-picture analysis of the behavior that cats employed in escaping from a puzzle-box. The book's compelling demonstration of behavioral stereotypy in the cats' problem-solving acts corroborated Guthrie's "molecularism" and provided an enduring anomaly for other learning theories. The project was partially replicated and reinterpreted by B. Moore and S. Stuttard in "Dr. Guthrie and *Felis domesticus*; or, Tripping over the Cat" (*Science* 205 [1979]: 1031–33).

Guthrie's academic career was spent entirely at the University of Washington except for periods of military service during both world wars. Administrative responsibilities as dean of the Graduate College (1943–1951) occupied his later years. As dean, he carefully investigated teaching effectiveness and wrote on the topic (e.g., in *The Evaluation of Teaching: A Progress Report* [1954]); course evaluation surveys he devised for this task continued to be used decades later at Washington. Guthrie's military involvement in the early 1940s and his postwar administrative duties probably account for the fact—a fact treated as a shortcoming by most commentators—that he did not substantially modify or elaborate his theory after the fruitful decade of the 1930s. Portions of his theory were instead developed by other theorists in behavioral psychology, such as William K. Estes, Virginia Voeks, and Fred Sheffield.

Guthrie was not primarily an experimentalist: rather than cram his books with the findings of behavioral research, he described illuminating characteristics of human and animal conduct, often in natural settings,

to illustrate fundamental mechanisms of behavior. This approach was consistent with his self-description as one whose primary interests were in undergraduate teaching. Students have attested to personal qualities that made him an excellent teacher. These personal features and the fact that the University of Washington was largely an undergraduate teaching institution up until World War II surely diverted some of his energy from the learning-theory enterprise and probably hindered his influence. Guthrie retired in 1956 and died three years later in Seattle.

• Guthrie's papers and correspondence, spanning from 1921 to 1958, are in the archives of the University of Washington Library. Before he developed his learning theory, Helen and Edwin Guthrie collaborated in a French-to-English translation of Pierre Janet's *Principles of Psychotherapy* (1924). Guthrie's *Psychology of Learning* and a series of articles in *Psychological Review* are the primary statements of his theory; for its application to abnormal psychology, see his *Psychology of Human Conflict* (1938), and to educational psychology, see *Educational Psychology*, with F. F. Powers (1950). Guthrie's final exposition was "Association by Contiguity," in *Psychology: A Study of a Science*, ed. Sigmund Koch, vol. 2 (1959), pp. 158–95. An incisive critique of Guthrie's theory and scientific philosophy is in the chapter by C. Mueller and W. Schoenfeld in *Modern Learning Theory*, ed. W. K. Estes et al. (1954), pp. 345–79. G. H. Bower and E. R. Hilgard, *Theories of Learning*, 5th ed. (1980), and R. C. Bolles, *Learning Theory*, rev. ed. (1979), provide balanced appraisals of Guthrie's theory and influence in psychology. Obituaries are in the *Seattle Times*, 24 Apr. 1959, and, by former student Fred Sheffield, in *American Journal of Psychology* 72 (1959): 642–50, which includes an extensive bibliography.

STEPHEN COLEMAN

GUTHRIE, Jack (13 Nov. 1915–15 Jan. 1948), country music singer and composer, was born Leon Jerry Guthrie in Olive, Oklahoma, the son of John Camel Guthrie, a local blacksmith; his mother's name is unknown. He developed riding skills and musical abilities at an early age. His father was an old-time fiddler and a fan of the recordings of Jimmie Rodgers. As Jack was growing up, the family moved to different locations around the Southwest: to Amarillo in 1924, to Oklahoma City in 1929, back to Texas, to Sapulpa in about 1930, and then to Midlothian Oklahoma. During this time Guthrie absorbed the music he came in contact with; according to his sister Wava, he received instruction from a young Gene Autry.

During the depression and Dust Bowl, like so many "Oakies," the Guthrie family moved to California. Eventually they settled around Sacramento, where Jack Guthrie worked in forestry for the Works Progress Administration and utilized his trick-riding skills at local rodeos. In 1934 he married Ruth Henderson and created a novelty act whereby he snapped cigarettes out of her mouth with a bullwhip. In 1937 Guthrie's cousin Woody Guthrie joined him in California, and the pair worked up a radio act, "The Oklahoman and Woody Show," and appeared on radio station KFVD in Hollywood. During this time Woody wrote a new song that became "Oklahoma Hills," and Jack began singing it; when Woody left the coast to go to New York City in 1939, Jack continued to perform it and soon made it into a local favorite. When he was offered a contract with Capitol Records in October 1944 Jack had no trouble choosing what to record, his radio work and many shows having honed his repertoire.

The Capitol executives were delighted with the results, but before they could release the records Guthrie was drafted and sent to the Pacific, where he served on Iwo Jima. While he was there, the record was released and soon became the number-one seller in the country. All Guthrie could do was read his reviews and press clippings until January 1946, when he was able to return to the United States. For a time he played with Buck Ritchey out of Tacoma, Washington, but by 29 January he was back in the studio ready to resume his career. A major commercial success in country music during the 1940s, he eventually amassed a legacy of thirty-three recordings as well as a series of radio transcriptions. Among them were "This Troubled Mind of Mine" and "Oakie Boogie" (both 1947). His style combined the hard country vocals of Hank Williams with the smooth western swing that he had grown up with and fascinated younger musicians. Unfortunately, he began to have health problems and eventually was diagnosed with tuberculosis. He continued to try to record but by July 1947 was confined to a sanatorium near Livermore Hospital in Los Angeles, where he later died.

In later years both Woody Guthrie and Woody's son Arlo Guthrie kept Jack Guthrie's music alive, and many of the songs became country and folk standards.

• The best biographical account of Guthrie is the booklet written by Guy Logdson for the CD reissue of the singer's complete recordings, *Oklahoma Hills* (Bear Family BCD 15580, 1991).

CHARLES K. WOLFE

GUTHRIE, James (5 Dec. 1792–13 Mar. 1869), secretary of the treasury, U.S. senator, and businessman, was born in Bardstown, Kentucky, the son of Adam Guthrie, a planter and politician, and Hannah Polk. Educated at the McAllister Academy in Bardstown, he subsequently worked on Mississippi River flatboats. After reading law with John Rowan, who was later a U.S. senator, Guthrie was admitted to the bar in 1817 and established a practice in Bardstown. In 1820 he moved to Louisville to serve as commonwealth attorney. The following year Guthrie married Eliza Prather; the couple had three daughters before Eliza died in 1836. Guthrie's legal work was more than simply routine. At one point a rival attorney shot him, hobbling Guthrie for life.

In this period Guthrie entered upon a similarly contentious political career. After several failed campaigns, he was elected to the Kentucky House of Representatives in 1827. In 1831 he moved up to the state senate, serving there until 1840. A Democrat, he was his party's candidate for the U.S. Senate in 1835, but

he lost in legislative balloting to John J. Crittenden. A Jacksonian, Guthrie nevertheless enthusiastically supported state cultivation of economic development. He pressed the state government to undertake internal improvements, particularly to make rivers more navigable, and he secured charters for banks, railroads, and private road companies. His interest in such enterprises extended considerably beyond fostering them by beneficent state action, however, for his joining of active business and political involvements began relatively early in his career. He promoted the extension of a railroad from Louisville to Frankfort early in the 1830s, served as a bank director and as president of the Louisville and Portland Canal Company, and invested in paving roads. He prospered speculating in hometown real estate and became one of Louisville's civic leaders, sitting on the city council, promoting public education, and helping establish the University of Louisville.

Guthrie presided over Kentucky's constitutional convention in 1849, but two years later he again failed in a bid for a U.S. Senate seat. In 1853, however, president-elect Franklin Pierce appointed him secretary of the treasury. Seeking balance in his cabinet, Pierce chose Guthrie as a prominent southerner who was less identified with states' rights than Jefferson Davis, whom he appointed secretary of war. Serving until the end of Pierce's term in 1857, Guthrie employed funds accumulated in the Treasury to reduce the nation's debt by over half. He insisted that the independent treasury system be more rigorously enforced and directed that government funds parceled out to private agents be returned to federal depositories. He also sought to limit profiteering among customs officers and private contractors and required a more timely settlement of federal officials' accounts. For all this scrupulousness, Guthrie was not above political intrigue, removing factional enemies and Know Nothings from various Treasury offices. He continued to speak up for public support of economic development, becoming one of the chief advocates within the administration of federal aid for transcontinental railroad construction.

After leaving office, Guthrie was a prime organizer of what became one of America's most important north-south railways, the Louisville & Nashville. Serving initially as vice president, he proved a most successful salesman of company bonds, enabling it to complete construction between the two cities for which it was named. In 1860 Guthrie was elevated to the company's presidency, remaining in that post until 1868. He gave his official sanction to a program of continuing expansion, both through construction and acquisition of other lines.

Guthrie received some scattered support for the presidential nomination at the Democratic convention in Charleston in 1860, even as the party disintegrated into separate northern and southern organizations. Since his road extended from the northern reaches of a Border State into the southern heartland and he was a prominent figure, his attitude toward secession was of some consequence, but his stance was not immediately apparent. At the Washington Peace Conference of February 1861, he chaired the committee that crafted the convention's proposed compromise, a constitutional amendment that, in effect, would have required the unanimous consent of the states before slavery might be interfered with where it already existed. With the convention's proposal spurned by Congress, the Union dissolved, and Kentucky aspiring to neutral status, Guthrie kept his trains running both north and south. But as Confederate authorities interfered with northward traffic, seized rolling stock, and destroyed track to slow the advance of Yankee troops, Guthrie allowed his line to become an instrument of the Union war effort. The Louisville & Nashville (L&N) was an important means of supplying Federal armies as they penetrated the Confederacy's mid-section. Guthrie's relations with Federal authorities were far from pacific, however. Disagreements erupted over the rates the L&N charged the government, the respective claims of military and private shippers, and the expenses the company incurred because of wartime damage. All the same, the L&N prospered over the course of the war.

Even though his railroad was a tool of Union war making, Guthrie disapproved of other means the Abraham Lincoln administration employed. At the 1864 Democratic National Convention, Guthrie chaired the committee that crafted a party platform denouncing the administration's infringements on civil liberties and states' rights and seeming to make peace rather than union victory the priority. The following year, in an early sign of the Louisville & Nashville's influence in state politics, Kentucky legislators sent Guthrie to the U.S. Senate. An unwavering Democrat, he resisted the most important pieces of Reconstruction legislation in 1866, opposing the Freedmen's Bureau Bill and the Civil Rights Act and voting against the Fourteenth Amendment. "It is not necessary to secure the freedom of the African," he insisted. "Slavery does not exist. The ordinary process and proceeding of the law is ample for his protection" (*Congressional Globe*, 39th Cong., 1st sess. [1865–1866], p. 601). Increasingly Guthrie missed important votes, and citing ill health, he resigned from the Senate in February 1868. He died in Louisville.

• Collections of Guthrie's papers are at the Filson Club in Louisville and in the Southern Historical Collection, University of North Carolina, Chapel Hill. Official correspondence is in the General Records of the Office of the Secretary of the Treasury (RG 56) at the National Archives. For useful biographical sketches, see Robert Cotterill, "James Guthrie—Kentuckian, 1792–1869," *Register of the Kentucky Historical Society* 20 (1922): 290–96; and E. Polk Johnson, *A History of Kentucky and Kentuckians* (1912). Valuable discussions of various aspects of Guthrie's career are in Roy Nichols, *Franklin Pierce, Young Hickory of the Granite Hills* (1931); Robert G. Gunderson, *Old Gentleman's Convention: The Washington Peace Conference of 1861* (1961); and Maury Klein, *History of the Louisville & Nashville Railroad* (1972). See also Larry Gara, *The Presidency of Franklin Pierce* (1991).

PATRICK G. WILLIAMS

GUTHRIE, Joseph Hunter (8 Jan. 1901–11 Nov. 1974), Roman Catholic clergyman and philosopher, was born in New York City, the son of Jacob Francis Guthrie and Mary Ross. He excelled at Fordham Preparatory School and continued his classical studies after entering the Society of Jesus at St. Andrew-on-Hudson in Poughkeepsie, New York, on 30 July 1917. At Weston College (Mass), he pursued science and philosophy, and he earned his A.B. (1923) and M.A. (1924) in philosophy from Woodstock College in Maryland. He taught and coached drama at Vigan Seminary and then at the Ateneo de Manila in the Philippines. His *Ateneo Passion Play* was first performed at the Manila Opera House in 1927. Also in 1927 he returned to Woodstock by way of China, Japan, northern Africa, and India. His theological studies led to his becoming a Roman Catholic priest on 23 June 1930. He earned a doctorate in theology from the Gregorian University in Rome (1931), concentrated on ascetical theology at Tronchiennes and Louvain, Belgium (1932), and made his solemn profession of his Jesuit vows in Paris (14 Aug. 1934).

Guthrie's research was enriched by his studies at several universities, including Munich, Freiburg im Breisgau, Berlin, and Paris, under Martin Heidegger, Werner Jaeger, Emile Bréhier, and others. He was also familiar with Hans Hahn's Vienna Circle and was acquainted with religious and philosophical luminaries such as Edith Stein, Simone Weil, Jacques Maritain, and Etienne Gilson. After recuperating from tuberculosis in Asheville, North Carolina, he defended his dissertation before Professors André Lalande and Albert Rivaud of the Société française de philosophie and Jean Wahl, an early influence on Jean-Paul Sartre. For his phenomenological analysis, *Introduction au problème de l'histoire de la philosophie: La métaphysique de l'individualité a priori de la pensée* (Introduction to the problem of the history of philosophy: The metaphysics of individuality a priori to thought), the first study of parallels between scholastic existentialism and Heidegger's phenomenology, Guthrie became a docteur de l'université de Paris (Sorbonne) with highest honors in 1937.

Guthrie taught at Woodstock until 1940, chaired the philosophy department at Fordham University in New York until 1943, and was the dean of the graduate school, the chair of the board of regents and deans, and a member of the board of trustees at Georgetown University in Washington, D.C., until 1949. He brought Dietrich von Hildebrand to Fordham and Rudolf Allers to Georgetown. He championed international standards of scholarship and favored methodologies that stress questions over answers. An expert in scholasticism, he urged a curriculum that was grounded in Greek philosophy and concerned with contemporary thought. By admitting women to Georgetown's graduate courses in 1944 he broke a century-and-a-half tradition. He deplored the absence of a first-rate university in the nation's capital and, after becoming the forty-second president of Georgetown in 1949, made difficult decisions. He disbanded

Georgetown's football team, citing that intercollegiate football had become an unprofitable business, diverting funds from academics ("No More Football for Us!" *Saturday Evening Post*, 15 Oct. 1951). Guthrie brought Georgetown's Dental and Nursing schools under central administration, and his initiatives to do the same with the Foreign Service, Law, and Medical schools were completed by President Edward B. Bunn after Guthrie's departure in 1952. He recuperated from a recurrence of his lung ailment and in 1953 became a professor and sometime chair of philosophy at St. Joseph's University in Philadelphia, Pennsylvania.

An arresting speaker, fluent in four languages and able to read four others, Guthrie was an exchange specialist in education for the U.S. Department of State, traveling to every continent except Australia. His work in Central and South America in 1954 and 1958 allowed him to argue for the establishment of the Latin American Studies Program at St. Joseph's University in 1960. Professor emeritus in 1969, he died in St. Isaac Jogues' Infirmary in Wernersville, Pennsylvania.

Guthrie was a member of the U.S. Commission on Restructuring Education that met with British counterparts at Princeton to consider education based on democratic principles (1940) and a member of the Chartering Committee of UNESCO that met in Nice, France (1945). During Spain's bicentennial celebration of Francisco Suarez (1948), Guthrie received the Grand Cross of Alphonso X el Sabio for his publications on the philosopher and for his lectures at the Universities of Barcelona, Madrid, and Salamanca. He was presented with the Freedoms Foundation Award at Valley Forge for "bringing about a better understanding of the American way of life" (1950), was invested an officer in the Legion of Honor and Merit of Haiti for contributions to educational reform (1954), and received the Air University Award for his tie-breaking vote to establish the university at Maxwell Air Force Base (1958). In the 1950s film director Sam Bronston consulted with him for productions set in ancient Greece and Rome. A member of many societies, the Medieval Academy of America and the American Academy of Politics and Social Science among them, Guthrie was a cofounder in 1946 of the Catholic Commission for Intellectual and Cultural Affairs.

Familiar with German existentialism, logical positivism, and the beginnings of analytic philosophy a decade before most other American philosophers, Guthrie was able to evaluate the ferment that generated World War II. He saw nationalism, totalitarianism, and biological elitism as threats to freedom. Recognizing the links among philosophy, education, society, and politics, he stressed the predictable course that ideas may follow through education to disastrous sociopolitical consequences. He spent thirty-five years trying to improve colleges and universities at home and abroad. His foremost concern rested on the interrelation of internal and external freedoms of the individual in philosophy, school, and society.

• Most of Guthrie's papers were destroyed. What survives is in the archives of the Maryland Province of the Society of Jesus, Baltimore, Md., the collections of the universities he served, and the possession of Francis F. Burch. Guthrie's published works on St. Bonaventure, Suarez, Max Scheler, Henri Bergson, and other subjects appeared in journals such as *Thought* and the *Modern Schoolman* and in *Phases of American Culture* (1941); *A Philosophical Symposium on American Catholic Education* (1941); and D. D. Runes, *Dictionary of Philosophy* (1942). His translation of Yves Congar's *History of Theology* (1968) was a Catholic Book-of-the-Month selection. See Francis F. Burch, "J. Hunter Guthrie, S.J.," *National Jesuit News*, Mar. 1975, for a view of his life and career. His philosophy is discussed in Martin C. D'Arcy, *The Mind and Heart of Love* (1945), and Ralph Harper, *Existentialism: A Theory of Man* (1948). Obituaries are in the *New York Times*, 12 Nov. 1974, and the *Washington Post*, 13 Nov. 1974.

FRANCIS F. BURCH

GUTHRIE, Samuel (1782–19 Oct. 1848), chemist and physician, was born in Brimfield, Massachusetts, the son of Samuel Guthrie, a physician, and Sarah (maiden name unknown). Of his childhood it is known only that he had what his mother considered an "unwholesome" interest in anatomy and that he decided very young to become a physician. He studied medicine with his father, a typical method of training at that time.

In 1802 Guthrie set up his own medical practice in Smyrna, Chenango County, New York, probably because his grandfather had moved to nearby Sherbourne. Guthrie married Sybil Sexton in 1804; they had four children. During the winter of 1810–1811 he attended the College of Physicians and Surgeons in New York, and then the family moved to Sherbourne. During the War of 1812 Guthrie was an examining surgeon for the army; he participated in the second battle at Sackets Harbor, New York, on Lake Ontario. He returned to his medical practice in both Sherbourne and Smyrna. In 1815 he spent a month at the University of Pennsylvania for further medical study.

Impressed by Sackets Harbor during the War of 1812, Guthrie moved there with his family in 1817. They acquired a piece of wilderness land near the town alongside Mill Creek, which provided power for various kinds of mills. Guthrie practiced medicine but never joined the local medical society. He built a brick house and barns, and on his forty acres he grew produce, built a distillery for alcohol, and raised cattle, sheep, and hogs. His biographer Jesse Randolph Pawling says that Guthrie read the *Boston Cultivator* and experimented with crops not generally grown in the area, such as "Chinese tree corn," "Roan Potato," and sugar beets, which did not become very sweet.

Guthrie conducted chemical studies in a building near his house over a number of years before he wrote about them to Benjamin Silliman at Yale College, who summarized the researches as letters to the editor of the *American Journal of Science and Arts* in 1831 and 1832. Silliman commented, "I presume it was little suspected that such things were doing in a remote region on the shore of Lake Ontario" (21 [1831]: 92).

One item described Guthrie's efforts about 1830 to make sugar from potatoes. An acquaintance, Captain E. G. Potter, built machinery for processing about 4,000 bushels of potatoes into a rich sweet syrup, but it would not crystallize. Silliman noted that the sample he received was "nearly as rich as that from the sugar maple" (p. 93). Guthrie also reported on developing a process for removing resin from oil of turpentine by distillation; when mixed with alcohol, the oil burned in a lamp more clearly and without leaving resinous points on the wick.

Over many years Guthrie experimented with materials for priming gunpowder to speed up firing a rifle. The flintlock rifle of that day was slow to load, and in the early 1800s many inventors were trying to improve it. Guthrie at first created grains of gunpowder after heating black powder to fusion, although he said he "met with frequent and terrible disasters." He then used "chlorate of potassa" successfully, even though one time he "blew up fifty pounds of the composition in the grinding mill" while preparing an order for one ton of the powder (Pawling, p. 28). Guthrie's major contribution was forming the powder into pellets or "pills" about the size of mustard seed, but he was probably not the first to do so. From 1826 he was selling percussion priming pellets widely, some waterproofed. Separately, he created an effective punchlock or percussion cap to replace the slower flint mechanism of the rifle.

Guthrie was the first chemist to produce chloroform in the laboratory. Silliman described "chloric ether" in *Yale College Elements of Chemistry* (2 [Feb. 1831]: 20) as "one of the curiosities of the chemist's laboratory under the name of 'oil of the Dutch chemists'" and probably "from its constitution and properties . . . an active diffusive stimulant." Guthrie was interested. He mixed whiskey with chlorinated lime and reported to Silliman on about 1 July 1831 that he had supplied the liquid to "persons" in his laboratory, "to the point of intoxication," while seeking its usefulness as a medicine. Locally the liquid was called "Guthrie's sweet whiskey." He soon succeeded in distilling a pure form of the chemical; the French chemist Jean Baptiste André Dumas named it "chloroform" in 1834. By 1832 chloroform was used by some doctors as a treatment for asthma, scarlet fever, whooping cough, and similar ailments. Guthrie observed the salutary effect of a patient's inhaling the chemical while his broken arm was set (Pawling, p. 45), and, probably in 1848, he first used it himself as an anesthetic during the amputation of a leg. By 1847 the Scottish physician James Young Simpson was routinely using chloroform for women in childbirth. Chloroform replaced nitrous oxide as a general anesthetic and, except in obstetrics and some children's ailments, was itself generally replaced by ether in surgery in the later 1800s. Guthrie's production of chloroform in its pure state in July 1831 preceded that of German chemist Justus von Liebig (Nov. 1831) and of French chemist Eugène Soubeiran (Jan. 1832), who later argued over priority. By the 1880s Guthrie was universally credited with having discovered chloroform.

Guthrie operated various prosperous businesses from his farm and was locally noted for the high quality of his vinegar and alcohol. For such products as the percussion caps and "chloric ether" (chloroform) he dealt through agents in New York City. He served on school and library committees in his community. He died in Sackets Harbor.

• Guthrie is not known to have published any papers beyond those cited in the *American Journal of Science and Arts*. The primary biography is Jesse Randolph Pawling, *Dr. Samuel Guthrie: Discoverer of Chloroform* (1947).

ELIZABETH NOBLE SHOR

GUTHRIE, William Dameron (3 Feb. 1859–8 Dec. 1935), attorney and constitutional law expert, was born in San Francisco, California, the son of George Whitney Guthrie, the deputy surveyor of the Port of San Francisco and owner of several newspapers, and Emma Gosson. As a child, Guthrie lived with his parents in France for nine years and in England for three before settling with them in New York City at the age of fourteen. Two years later his father's financial reverses forced Guthrie to leave public school and become a stenographer at the Wall Street law firm of Seward, Blatchford, Griswold, and Da Costa, the predecessor of the present firm of Cravath, Swaine and Moore. Guthrie read law at the firm and attended Columbia Law School from 1879 to 1880. Following his admission to the New York bar in 1880, Guthrie returned to the Seward firm, where he became a partner after four years and remained until 1909. He subsequently established his own law practice. In 1891 he married Ella Elizabeth Fuller; they adopted one daughter.

Throughout his career, Guthrie represented major corporations in complicated and often politically controversial business transactions and litigation. More than just a hired advocate, he passionately believed in the causes of his clients, whose interests tended to coincide with Guthrie's virulent hostility toward governmental regulation of business enterprises and his ardent faith in the sanctity of private property. He argued many landmark cases, in which the U.S. Supreme Court delineated the scope of governmental power. At the age of thirty-six he successfully argued his most famous case, *Pollock v. Farmers' Loan & Trust Co.* (1895), in which the Court invalidated by a vote of five to four the first federal income tax enacted during peacetime. As the result of this decision, no federal income tax was possible until the Sixteenth Amendment in 1913 specifically authorized such a tax. This case established Guthrie as a leading champion of wealthy and conservative forces that fought the trend toward greater governmental intervention in economic affairs during the late nineteenth and early twentieth centuries. During 1895–1904 he successfully argued cases in which the Supreme Court invalidated a Minnesota statute prohibiting the sale of colored oleomargarine, a

New Hampshire statute that prohibited the sale of all oleomargarine that was not colored pink, and a Kansas statute regulating public stockyards.

Guthrie, however, unsuccessfully argued two major cases in which the Court upheld the power of Congress to enact regulatory legislation. In the first case, *Champion v. Ames* (1903), the Court sustained the power of Congress to prohibit the interstate transportation of lottery tickets. In the second case, *McCray v. United States* (1904), the Court upheld a federal statute that imposed a tax on manufacturers of oleomargarine. The Court's refusal to accept Guthrie's argument that the real purpose of the statute was to protect the butter industry represented another step toward judicial deference to federal regulatory legislation. By expanding the scope of Congress's ability to regulate business enterprises through its commerce and tax powers, the Court's decisions in these cases served as a precedent for other federal regulations of economic enterprise. Later in his career, Guthrie suffered another significant defeat when the Supreme Court in 1920 sustained the validity of the Eighteenth Amendment's prohibition on the "manufacture, sale, and transportation" of alcoholic beverages in the national Prohibition cases.

Five years later, however, Guthrie won a significant victory for the causes of both personal and economic freedom when he successfully argued *Pierce v. Society of Sisters* (1925), a landmark case in which the Supreme Court invalidated an Oregon law that required all elementary school-age children to attend public school. The Court's decision in *Pierce* ended a nationwide movement for compulsory public education that was motivated by nativistic hostility toward Roman Catholicism and aimed at destroying parochial education. The decision also signaled a greater willingness by the Court to scrutinize legislation that interfered with noneconomic liberties and has served as a foundation for the right to privacy.

Influential as a legal scholar as well as a practicing attorney, Guthrie in 1898 published a treatise on the Fourteenth Amendment that embodied many of his antistatist views and was long regarded as an authoritative work. From 1909 to 1922 he was a member of the political science and law faculties at Columbia University, serving as Ruggles Professor of Constitutional Law from 1913 to 1922. During 1907 to 1909 he was the Storrs lecturer at Yale University.

Guthrie was also active in professional societies and served as president of the New York Bar Association from 1921 to 1922 and as president of the Association of the Bar of the City of New York from 1925 to 1927. An ardent Francophile, he promoted Franco-American amity, served as an officer of Franco-American societies, and raised funds for French charities.

A devout Roman Catholic throughout his life, Guthrie provided significant legal services for the Roman Catholic church. In addition to his work in the *Pierce* case, he also successfully represented the church in *Gonzalez v. Roman Catholic Archbishop of Manila* (1929), in which the Court refused to permit a civil court to determine whether a Roman Catholic chaplain was qualified for his office. He was an expert in canonical law and served as counsel for the Roman Catholic church at the New York State constitutional convention in 1915.

Guthrie actively supported many Republican candidates for public office and was a vocal opponent of much social and economic reform legislation, particularly the unsuccessful federal amendment prohibiting child labor. Despite his keen interest in politics and his considerable political influence, he held only one public office, the mayorship of Lattington, Long Island (1931–1935), to which he was elected twice near the end of his life. Guthrie's irascible personality and his wholehearted identification with the forces of wealth and privilege may have foreclosed a political career and prevented his nomination to the U.S. Supreme Court. Widely admired for his brilliant mind, insatiable appetite for hard work, and steadfast dedication to the causes he served, he was also regarded as rigid, intolerant of views other than his own, and too much of a perfectionist. Guthrie remained active in legal affairs until his sudden death at his estate "Muedon," near Lattington, New York.

Guthrie's legacy is problematical. Even in his lifetime, the courts sustained the constitutionality of more economic legislation than they struck down, and the Supreme Court since 1937 has ceased to impose any significant restraints on statutes that regulate businesses. While courts continue to reject Guthrie's constitutional theories and his views remain in disfavor among most legal scholars, the trend toward rejection of governmental economic regulation may restore some of his views to fashion. Moreover, his theories in opposition to regulation of economic activity have in part provided the foundation for the Supreme Court's careful scrutiny of legislation that restricts personal liberties. In particular, the *Pierce* case provided a link between the old judicial scrutiny of economic legislation and the modern judicial scrutiny of laws that affect personal freedom. Guthrie remains a significant symbol of the constitutional theories that he so ably espoused.

• The largest single concentration of his letters is in the Charles Evans Hughes Collection at Columbia University. Some of his papers relating to the *Pierce* litigation are at the Oregon State Archives in Salem. His career with the Cravath firm is discussed in some detail in Robert T. Swaine, *The Cravath Firm and Its Predecessors 1819–1947*, vols. 1 and 2 (1946), which draws upon Guthrie's private correspondence. An obituary is in the *New York Times*, 9 Dec. 1935.

WILLIAM G. ROSS

GUTHRIE, Woody (14 July 1912–3 Oct. 1967), singer and songwriter, was born Woodrow Wilson Guthrie in Okemah, Oklahoma, the son of Charles Guthrie, a cattle rancher and real estate salesman, and Nora Belle Sherman, a schoolteacher. Guthrie's roots were in the soil of the American frontier. His maternal grandfather had been a dirt farmer in Kansas who settled in Oklahoma at the end of the nineteenth century, and his father's family had been cowboys in the territory.

Woody Guthrie's childhood was uneventful until he reached the age of seven, when he experienced a series of family tragedies that set the tone for his adult life as a loner, a wanderer, and, at the same time, a man who spoke for America's "little people." His sister was burned to death in a fire that his mother was suspected of setting, his father's business ventures failed, and the family lost a total of three homes. When his father was also injured in a suspected arson fire, his mother was institutionalized. She had begun to show signs of Huntington's chorea, the degenerative and hereditary disease of the central nervous system that would eventually kill her son.

Guthrie remained in Okemah when his family moved to Pampa, Texas, in 1927. He joined his family in Pampa later that year and developed his skills as a guitarist, performing locally in a trio with his aunt on accordion and his uncle on fiddle. He also played with local country and western bands. With the coming of the depression and the drought that caused his part of the country to be known as the Dust Bowl, Guthrie saw terrible economic conditions. His strong identification with the economic plight of farmers and workers can be seen in songs like "Dusty Old Dust," also known by the text of its chorus, "So Long, It's Been Good to Know Ya."

In 1937 Guthrie moved from the Dust Bowl region to California, eventually playing, talking, and singing on his own radio show on KFVD in Los Angeles. His show, "Here Come Woody and Lefty Lou," featured social commentary, homespun humor, and everyday wisdom, and it was an immediate success. During this period, he developed loose ties to several left-wing and progressive organizations that were striving to improve conditions for migrant workers in California. He summed up his political identification not in terms of party membership but in the context of the suffering of the common people when he said, "I ain't a communist necessarily, but I been in the red all my life."

In 1939 Guthrie moved to New York, where he met folk song historian Alan Lomax, who featured him on the CBS network show "Columbia School of the Air." Through Lomax, Guthrie also recorded songs and conversations for the Library of Congress Archive of American Folk Song and released his first commercial recordings of "Dust Bowl Ballads" for Victor. In 1941 he worked for the Department of the Interior, composing songs for and acting in a film about the Bonneville Power Administration.

Guthrie served in the merchant marine with his singing companion Cisco Houston. He wrote songs in favor of the war effort such as "When the Yanks Go Marching In," and he inscribed the words "This Machine Kills Fascists" on his guitar. Toward the end of the war, he was drafted and served a year in the U.S. Army. He published *Bound for Glory*, an autobiographical portrait of his early life, in 1943. Around this time, he joined the Almanac Singers, a group founded in New York by Pete Seeger, Lee Hays, and Millard Lampell to promote left-wing activism in trade unions and local communities. He wrote an occasional column for the Communist party's *People's Daily World* and continued to comment on the world and its injustice as he saw it. In "Union Maid" and "You've Got to Go Down and Join the Union," Guthrie argued that trade unions represented the democratic American response to the fascist threat in World War II. His views inspired the Almanac Singers in their albums, "Songs for John Doe" and "Talking Union." Many of Guthrie's songs, such as "Good Night, Irene," were popularized by the Weavers—Seeger, Hays, Fred Hellerman, and Ronnie Gilbert—who brought folk music to a wide audience. Guthrie also perfected the form of the "talking blues" as a way to tell a story. This form has been used effectively by such musical social commentators as Seeger, Bob Dylan, Tom Paxton, Phil Ochs, and Guthrie's son Arlo Guthrie.

After World War II, Guthrie traveled across the United States, documenting what he saw and felt in his music. Between 1932 and 1952, he composed more than 1,000 songs. He returned to New York and experienced the onset of Huntington's chorea. Hospitalized for most of the remainder of his life, he died at the Creedmore State Hospital in Queens, New York.

Guthrie was married three times, first to Mary Jennings on 28 October 1933. The couple had three children, and the marriage ended in divorce. Shortly after World War II he married Marjorie Greenblatt Mazia. They had four children, including Arlo, who established his own career as a singer and songwriter. After his divorce, Guthrie married Anneke Van Kirk, and they had one child.

Guthrie published *American Folksong* in 1947 and *Born to Win* in 1965. He also wrote an autobiographical novel, *Seeds of Man: An Experience Lived and Dreamed*, published in 1976 (posthumously) and based on earlier stories about his attempt to find a silver mine in Texas. His legacy is his songs about farmers, workers, unions, and everyday people. He inspired a generation of folksingers in the 1950s and 1960s who used music to comment on their society and culture with the idea of changing it. Today, Woody Guthrie's music, from his explicitly political and antifascist songs to his "Song to Grow On" for children, are sung everywhere, from elementary schools to television commercials. Guthrie's anger at the injustices of American society was combined with a strong and abiding patriotism that he expressed eloquently in "Pastures of Plenty"—if necessary he would defend this land "with my life" because "these pastures of plenty must always be free."

• Guthrie's manuscripts, memorabilia, correspondence, and sketches are housed in the Woody Guthrie Archive in New York. In 1990 Harper Collins released Guthrie's *Pastures of Plenty: A Self-Portrait*. Marjorie Guthrie edited *Woody Sez* (1975), with a foreword by Studs Terkel. The *Little Sandy Review* published a Woody Guthrie discography in 1960, and Richard Reuss published *A Woody Guthrie Bibliography, 1912–1967* in 1968. Henrietta Yurchenco, *A Mighty Hard Road: The Woody Guthrie Story* (1970), is a children's biography. See also Ed Robbin, *Woody Guthrie and Me: An Intimate Reminiscence* (1979); Joe Klein, *Woody Guthrie: A Life* (1980);

and Alan Lomax, *Hard-hitting Songs for Hard-hit People* (1967), which includes notes by the composer. In 1986 Wayne Hampton published *Guerrilla Minstrels: John Lennon, Joe Hill, Woody Guthrie, and Bob Dylan*. An obituary is in the *New York Times*, 4 Oct. 1967.

BARBARA L. TISCHLER

GUTMANN, Bernhard (24 Sept. 1869–23 Jan. 1936), painter, illustrator, and teacher, was born in Hamburg, Germany, the son of Zadig Gutmann and Elizabeth Biesenthal, merchants. After the death of his mother when he was two years old, Gutmann, the youngest of eight children, was reared by his father, then sent to boarding school. At age twenty Gutmann entered the internationally renowned art academy in Düsseldorf, transferring the following year to the academy in Karlsruhe. Unable to find employment in Germany after leaving school in 1892, he joined his brother Ludwig to work as an electrician at the Piedmont Electrical Illuminating Company in Lynchburg, Virginia. After only three years in Lynchburg, Gutmann began to make his mark on the creative life of the city. In 1895 he became the first supervisor and instructor of drawing in the Lynchburg Public Schools and concurrently taught drawing and painting at Randolph-Macon Woman's College. He also founded the Lynchburg Art League with students from his private art classes. An enthusiastic and creative teacher, he introduced courses on art history and modeling, organized an exhibition of his work for the college, had his students design illustrations for a college handbook, and painted a mural, *Wisdom Instructing Youth*, for the college library during the two years that he taught there.

In 1897 Gutmann's painting *Church Interior* was shown in the annual exhibition sponsored by the Art Institute of Chicago, providing Gutmann with his first national exposure in the year that he became a naturalized citizen of the United States. The following year he published his first book illustrations in Mary Tucker Magill's *Virginia History for the Young*. Gutmann also wrote a series of articles on methods of teaching art that were published in the *North Carolina Journal of Education* in 1898 and 1899.

Gutmann moved to New York City in 1899 in search of a more lively artistic milieu, believing that provincial life in Virginia had blunted his artistic skills. He attended classes in New York while he worked as a freelance illustrator. Frustrated by the inequities he encountered while doing freelance work, Bernhard founded the fine art printing firm of Gutmann & Gutmann with his brother Hellmuth in 1902, to which he contributed numerous designs for magazine and sheet music covers, book illustrations, and printed cards. In 1907 Gutmann married Bertha Goldman, the granddaughter of the founder of the investment banking firm Goldman-Sachs. Through the largess of Bertha's father, Julius Goldman, Bernhard and Bertha were provided with an annual annuity, enabling him to leave Gutmann & Gutmann to Hellmuth and his wife Bessie Pease Gutmann, whose popular

sentimental prints of babies kept the business flourishing.

Several months after their marriage, Gutmann and his young bride moved to Paris, then the international center of the art world. In Paris Gutmann's artistic horizons expanded when he encountered postimpressionism. Under the inspiration of Parisian influences, he loosened his brushwork and began to work with richer and lusher colors, creating dazzling landscapes, still lifes, and genre scenes. In 1911 the Gutmanns' first child was born in Paris, where they remained for several months after the eruption of the First World War. Gutmann participated in a group show in Paris in 1910, and his painting *Bébé* was shown in the internationally acclaimed Salon des Beaux-Arts of 1911.

Forced to return to the United States, the Gutmanns settled in bucolic Silvermine, Connecticut, in 1913, relatively isolated from the artistic ferment brewing in the New York art world. In Silvermine there was an active community of artists still linked to the traditions of American impressionism, and congenial Gutmann soon befriended the local coterie of artists and participated in their exhibitions.

Beginning with his inclusion in the 1912 annual exhibition at the Pennsylvania Academy of the Fine Arts, Gutmann actively pursued national recognition for his work. The following year he submitted *In the Garden* to the Armory Show, America's first major international exhibition of modern art. An article on Gutmann's painting appeared in the prestigious journal *International Studio* in 1914, the year he held his first solo exhibition in New York at the Arlington Art Gallery. That year he was included in group exhibitions at the National Academy of Design, the Corcoran Gallery of Art, and the Pennsylvania Academy of Fine Arts. His painting *A Nude* was featured in the 1915 Panama-Pacific Exposition in San Francisco.

Throughout the second decade of the twentieth century, Gutmann's paintings appeared in numerous annual national exhibitions and at the Macdowell and Salmagundi Club shows in New York. In 1917 he joined the Society of Independent Artists and exhibited two paintings in their first exhibition, which included Marcel Duchamp's scandalous urinal sculpture. Gutmann maintained his membership in the organization and participated in subsequent independent shows.

In 1918 Gutmann demonstrated his support for his adopted country in its war against the nation of his birth by donating a "typical work" to the Great Allied Bazaar in New York and by painting a billboard in New Canaan, Connecticut, to encourage contributions to the fourth Liberty Loan. In 1919 the Gutmanns' second child was born, and in 1920 Bernhard had his second major solo exhibition at the Folsom Gallery in New York. Although he participated as one of the founding members of the still-flourishing Silvermine Guild of Artists in 1922, Gutmann left the United States at the end of the year for an extended stay in Europe, going first to Spain and then to Paris in the spring of 1924. In Paris the following year Gutmann staged a solo exhibition at the prestigious Galérie Bernheim-Jeune and received a notice in the *Revue des Indépendants*.

Returning to Silvermine in 1925, Gutmann was immediately elected president of the guild, instituted the guild's ceramic program, and began making and exhibiting etchings. He had two subsequent solo shows in New York City at the Macbeth and Ferargil galleries and was chosen to direct the New Canaan regional Public Works of Art Project in 1934, shortly before his death of throat cancer in New York City.

Celebrated with a retrospective exhibition at the Grand Central Galleries in 1938, Bernhard Gutmann's career sank without a trace for over fifty years because of the absence of his work in any major public collections. Yet he produced a substantial body of luminous paintings that are hymns to the richness of life, that were well respected, and that earned him significant national and international acclaim during his life. The appearance of several of his paintings in the exhibition "Impressionism and Post-Impressionism: Transformations in the American Mode, 1885–1945" at the Grand Central Art Galleries in New York in 1988 revived interest in Gutmann's work. Daniel Terra purchased *Breton Lacemakers* (1912) from the show for the Terra Museum of American Art in Chicago, and in 1995 Abbevile Press published *Bernhard Gutmann, an American Impressionist*, by Percy North, the first major study of Gutmann's work.

• Gutmann's papers are in private collections and are held primarily by his grandsons Theodore Lehmann II and John Mollenhauer. They include letters to his wife and daughters, a memoir-journal in German, and reminiscences by his daughter Dorothea Gutmann Mollenhauer. During Gutmann's life the most significant assessment of his work appeared in W. H. de B. Nelson, "A Painter in Pure Colour: Bernhard Gutmann," *International Studio*, Feb. 1914, pp. 205–7. See also Evelyn Moore and Ruth Holmes Blunt, "Composition, Color, and Sometimes Humor: Artist Bernhard Gutmann of Lynchburg," *Virginia Cavalcade* 31, no. 4 (Spring 1982): 206–15; Robert Preato, Sandra L. Langer, and James D. Cox, *Impressionism and Post-Impressionism: Transformations in the American Mode, 1885–1945* (1988); and Ashton Sanborn, *The Works of Bernhard Gutmann: Memorial Exhibition* (1938).

PERCY NORTH

GUTTERSON, Albert Lovejoy (23 Aug. 1887–7 Apr. 1965), track and field athlete, was born in Andover, Vermont, the son of Charles Milton Gutterson, a farmer, and Elizabeth Lovejoy. Gutterson received his primary education in Simonsville, Vermont, and Peaseville, Vermont. In 1903 Gutterson's father sold his farm and moved his family to Springfield, Vermont, in order for Albert to continue his secondary education. While attending Springfield High School, Gutterson participated in track and field and began to display his ability as a sprinter, hurdler, long jumper, high jumper, and discus thrower.

Following his graduation from high school, Gutterson enrolled at the University of Vermont in 1907. There he joined the track and field team and enjoyed continued success. The high point in Gutterson's collegiate career came in a dual meet against the University of Maine in 1911, when he won the 100- and 220-yard dashes, the 220-yard low hurdles, the high jump, the long jump, and the discus throw events. He also was the runner-up in the 120-yard high hurdles. His long jump performance of 23′ 5½″ during the meet was the best in the nation that year. In 1912, after winning the long jump in the Penn Relays, Gutterson finished second in this event at the U.S. Olympic trials to Harry Worthington of Dartmouth College. Gutterson overcame this setback and won the long jump in the 1912 Olympic Games in Stockholm, Sweden. The winning jump of 24′ 11¼″ established American and Olympic records and missed the world record (established in 1901) by one-fourth of an inch. Gutterson's American record in the long jump lasted until 1921, when Ned Gourdin bounded 25′ 3″, and his Olympic record lasted until 1928, when Edward Hamm reached 25′ 4½″.

Gutterson received his bachelor's degree in mechanical engineering from the University of Vermont in 1912. Four years later he married Florence Greer; they had no children. After retiring from competition Gutterson worked as an engineer in Springfield, Vermont. In 1950 he was named president of Lovejoy Tool Company; he also served his community through leadership roles in the Manufacturer's Association, the Springfield Savings and Loan Association, and the New England Chapter of the U.S. Olympians Society. Gutterson also continued to serve his alma mater, and from 1954 to 1960 he was a University of Vermont trustee. Shortly before his death, a newly constructed athletic-physical education complex at the university was named after him, in recognition of both his athletic achievements and his generosity to the university. Gutterson died in Burlington, Vermont. While he by no means ranks as America's greatest long jumper, his Olympic performance reflects the dominance of U.S. athletes in this event throughout the twentieth century.

• The sports information department of the University of Vermont contains biographical information on Gutterson. Statistical information on Gutterson's Olympic performance is found in David Wallechinsky, *The Complete Book of the Olympic Games*, rev. ed. (1988). For Gutterson's place in the history of athletics, see Roberto L. Quercetani, *A World History of Track and Field Athletics* (1964). An obituary is in the *New York Times*, 7 Apr. 1965.

ADAM R. HORNBUCKLE

GUTTMACHER, Alan (19 May 1898–18 Mar. 1974), physician and birth-control advocate, was born in Baltimore, Maryland, the son of Adolf Guttmacher, a leading Reform rabbi, and Laura Oppenheimer, a social worker. Alan had an identical twin, Manfred, with whom he was very close throughout his life, and a sister. His early years were happy ones in a household where Judaism set the guiding tone. Alan's paternal great-grandfather had been the chief rabbi of Gratz, and when the family immigrated to the United States they maintained their faith. But Guttmacher renounced his faith after his father died suddenly when Alan was sixteen. Two years later, in 1915, the twins entered Johns Hopkins University. Alan originally planned to pursue a career in English or history, but a brief stint as a private in the army in 1918 changed his direction.

After Alan and Manfred received their bachelor's degrees in 1919, both young men decided to continue at Johns Hopkins in its medical school. During medical school, Alan developed a strong interest in anatomy and in research. In 1921 he and Manfred published their first scientific paper together. They tossed a coin to see which twin's name would go first; Alan lost. In 1923 both twins graduated from Johns Hopkins Medical School. Reports conflict about where Guttmacher went next. Some suggest that he taught anatomy for two years, first at Johns Hopkins University and then at the University of Rochester; other accounts place him in an obstetrics internship at Hopkins immediately after his medical school graduation. During this period he studied with both Johns Hopkins's J. Whitridge Williams, a leader in obstetrics, and in New York with Mount Sinai Hospital's Robert Frank, the founder of gynecologic endocrinology. In 1927 he was named an instructor in obstetrics at Johns Hopkins.

Guttmacher's early years in medicine were relatively quiet ones, during which he concentrated on setting up his practice in Baltimore and on his young family. In 1925 he had married Leonore Gidding, with whom he had three daughters. His brother also remained in the area, and the two men delighted in pretending to be one another when patients went to the wrong office. His brother would enjoy a distinguished medical career himself, eventually becoming medical adviser to the supreme court bench in Maryland.

From the start of his career, Guttmacher had ties to the birth control movement. During his internship, he was inspired to join the nascent movement after he saw a woman who had died from a botched abortion. He was also known for his practice of giving patients a "straight-forward account" of what they should expect in their pregnancies. Most other doctors did not discuss this topic, considered a delicate one. In 1933 he wrote a frank guide for expectant mothers and fathers, titled *Life in the Making*. In 1943 he was named chief of obstetrics at Sinai Hospital in Baltimore. Four years later he won the prestigious Mary Lasker Award for his work with Planned Parenthood, and in 1952 he was promoted to associate professor at Johns Hopkins.

That same year, New York's Mount Sinai Hospital recruited him to become the first director of their newly combined obstetrics/gynecology department. At the same time, Guttmacher was named a clinical professor of obstetrics and gynecology at Columbia University. His years of practice had already persuaded him that every child born should be a wanted one, and in his position of chief of obstetrics he started programs on abortion, sterilization, and contraception—three areas that physicians had hitherto found too controversial to

address. He rapidly became known for his liberal views concerning abortions. The procedure was then illegal throughout the United States, unless a woman could get a medical dispensation on the grounds of her own health. The hospital finally asked Guttmacher to cease performing so many abortions, to avoid gaining a reputation as an abortion mill.

But Guttmacher continued to campaign for birth control. When he got to New York, he immediately joined the national Planned Parenthood organization and served on their National Medical Committee. Shocked to learn that doctors could not prescribe contraceptives—particularly for the poor—he set about trying to reverse the ban. In 1958 he was finally successful. He was also an early advocate for artificial insemination, which struck some as a form of adultery but which he referred to as "decent and humane." In 1959 he published *Babies by Choice or Chance*. The following year, he sought a publisher for a book he wanted to write, a compendium on birth control. Two publishers turned down his proposal, wary of the subject, before Ballantine accepted it. In 1961 two books by Guttmacher appeared, *The Complete Book of Birth Control* and *Planning Your Family*. He spent that year at Boston's Harvard Medical School as a visiting professor of maternal and child health.

In 1962 Guttmacher returned to New York to assume the presidency of the Planned Parenthood Federation. Although he was chosen for his medical expertise and liberal outlooks, as one colleague, Frederick Jaffe, wrote of him after his death, "He looked like an old-fashioned man and had a penchant for old-fashioned virtues."

Guttmacher was also a consummate and caring clinician. By the end of his career, he estimated that he had personally delivered about 7,000 babies and had borne clinical responsibility for the delivery of more than 100,000. Though some considered him egotistical, he had a very human side. He was an avid tennis player and had a warm sense of humor. In his office he displayed a figurine of an Indonesian fertility goddess who had nine children attached to her.

Guttmacher nevertheless was remembered more for his efforts to prevent children from being brought into the world. On Guttmacher's death, Alden Whitman, in a *New York Times* obituary, observed that "what Dr. Guttmacher sought was to assure women the right to plan their whole lives, including when and if to have children." This was a right that Guttmacher wanted to assure not just for American women but for women around the world. Soon after becoming president of the federation, he traveled throughout Asia, Africa, and Latin America, spreading the gospel of birth control to these countries. He was known for saying that the world's two major problems were atomic energy and the population explosion.

As president of Planned Parenthood during the early years of the Sexual Revolution, Guttmacher witnessed one of the major changes in birth control in this century—the advent of the birth control pill. Although some doctors urged caution, Guttmacher came out wholeheartedly in favor of hormonally regulating the ability to conceive. Throughout the 1960s, as sexual mores started to loosen, Guttmacher was called upon to comment. In 1966 he testified before Congress, saying, "We really have the opportunity now to extend free choice in family planning to all Americans, regardless of social status and to demonstrate to the rest of the world how it can be done. It's time we get on with the job."

A popular speaker on college campuses, Guttmacher took the following position: "When you give the kids the keys to your car, be sure to give them contraceptives too." Often students were too embarrassed to ask him questions in front of their peers so they would submit them in writing. In response to the question of "What advice would you give a woman who never intended to marry?" Guttmacher responded, "Don't die a virgin." In 1970 he collected the wisdom he had shared in person into a book, *Understanding Sex: A Young Person's Guide*. Numerous colleges recognized him for his work, bestowing on him the Margaret Sanger Award in 1972.

Known as the elder statesman of the birth-control movement, Guttmacher died in New York City of chronic myelogenous leukemia, the same disease that had taken his brother seven years before him. One of the final triumphs of his life was seeing the repeal of the ban on abortion in 1972.

• Guttmacher's papers are at Harvard University's Countway Library. An interview with him is in the Family Planning Oral History Project at the Schlesinger Library at Radcliffe College. For more information on Guttmacher's life, see Joseph J. Rovinsky, "In Memoriam," *Mount Sinai Journal of Medicine* 41 (1974): 503–4. For accounts of Guttmacher's fight to legalize abortion, see Michael S. Burnhill, "Humane Abortion Services: A Revolution in Human Rights and the Delivery of a Medical Service," *Mount Sinai Journal of Medicine* 42 (1972): 431–38. See also, Malcolm Potts, "Natural Law and Planned Parenthood," *Mount Sinai Journal of Medicine* 42 (1975): 326–33, and George J. Langmyhr and Harold I. Lief, "Alan Guttmacher, M.D.: His Role in Teaching Human Sexuality," in the same volume, pp. 445–51. Obituaries are by Frederick Jaffe in *Family Planning Perspectives* 6 (1974): 1–2, and by Alden Whitman in the *New York Times*, 19 Mar. 1974.

SHARI RUDAVSKY

GUYASUTA (c. 1725–c. 1794), Seneca chief and diplomat, was probably born on the Genesee River in New York into the Wolf clan of the Senecas. As Guyasuta grew to adulthood, the western Seneca (those of the Genesee Valley westward into the Ohio country) generally pursued a pro-French policy. Nevertheless, Guyasuta is said to have guided the young George Washington in 1753 when Washington delivered an ultimatum demanding that the French, who were building Fort Duquesne, withdraw from the forks of the Ohio (at present-day Pittsburgh). Two years later, on the other hand, he served as part of the French-Indian force that routed Major General Edward Braddock's force attacking Fort Duquesne. Both his pro-French attitude and his rising political influence are

evidenced by the fact that he led a delegation of twenty Senecas to meet with Governor Pierre de Rigand de Vaudreuil in Montreal in the autumn of 1755. The purpose of the delegation was to cement symbolically the Seneca-French alliance through performance of the condolence ritual and to request that French trader and agent Philippe-Thomas Chabert de Joncaire return to reside among them. The governor promised to send Joncaire to the Seneca country in the spring.

With the British victory on the Plains of Abraham near Quebec in 1759 and the consequent extinction of French power in North America, former French allies were faced with the problems of dealing with the new all-powerful British regime. Guyasuta appears to have been among those who advocated continued hostility toward the British. In 1761 he and fellow Seneca Tahahaiadoris passed among western Indian nations a large red-painted wampum belt, known as the war hatchet, as a call to attack the British. Sir William Johnson, Britain's superintendent for Indian affairs in the northern colonies, managed quickly but temporarily to place a lid on the simmering kettle when he met privately with Guyasuta in a Detroit conference that same year.

By 1763, however, even the considerable skills and connections of Johnson could not prevent a widespread revolt. During the decades of French-British conflict in North America, the Indian nations had become accustomed to, even dependent upon, goods given them by colonial powers courting their favor. With the French threat extinguished, some in the British service argued as an economy measure that such payments should cease. Defying the advice of his own Indian Department, commander in chief of British forces in North America, Jeffrey Amherst, denied essential supplies to the Indian nations in the West, and the frontier erupted in a general war in June. The Ottawa chief, Pontiac, has received credit, or blame, for carrying on this war, but others have suggested that Guyasuta was equally influential. While both leaders probably fostered rather than retarded the development of hostilities, the widespread outbreak reflected a more general dissatisfaction with the severe economic constraints recently imposed by the British.

Guyasuta did fight in the West, at the unsuccessful siege of Fort Pitt (formerly Fort Duquesne). However, oral tradition suggests that he did not participate with other Senecas at the major victory at Devil's Hole (on the Niagara Gorge, N.Y.) in 1763. Despite initial successes, the uprising of the followers of Pontiac and Guyasuta and their allies was doomed to certain defeat because in the absence of a rival European power they lacked a source of arms and ammunition to support a war against the British.

Following the failure of the Pontiac-Guyasuta war of 1763, Guyasuta shifted his loyalties to Sir William Johnson, who had strong ties to the Iroquois confederacy, particularly its easternmost members, the Mohawk (his Mohawk "housekeeper" or wife was the influential and powerful Mohawk Mary Brant). Guyasuta assumed the dangerous and difficult role of intermediary between the ethnically mixed native population of the Ohio country and the firm alliance (the "covenant chain") uniting the Iroquois confederacy of New York and the British Indian Department, which was controlled by Johnson, his kinsmen, and his followers.

The modern term "shuttle diplomacy" could describe Guyasuta's activities during the decade preceding the outbreak of the American Revolution. He traveled back and forth constantly from the British and their Iroquois allies to the potentially hostile towns in the Ohio country, carrying wampum belts of peace from the former and complaints from the latter of depredations on native communities by frontiersmen. In this role, he served British interests, which coincided with the interests of the Iroquois confederacy (including the Seneca) in New York. At one point his ties to the British became so notorious that during his travels among the Indians of the Ohio country he needed the protection of an escort of fifty Seneca fighting men. The relative infrequency of hostile outbreaks during this decade is partly a tribute to the sagacity of Johnson and the skills of Guyasuta as his deputy in the Ohio country.

After Johnson's death in 1774 and the beginning of the American Revolution, the rebels courted Guyasuta's favor, the Continental Congress voting him a colonel's commission and a silver gorget. It was inevitable, however, that most native peoples would take the side of the Crown, since the British Indian Department seemed willing to prevent or at least regulate large-scale land losses. In contrast, those rebelling against the Crown seemed to represent the portion of the colonial population coveting Indian lands. Of the Iroquois confederacy, after a period of neutrality, the vast majority of the Senecas, Cayugas, and Mohawks opted to support the royal cause in 1777, and Guyasuta concurred.

In 1777 Lieutenant Colonel Barry St. Leger commanded a British-Indian-Loyalist force that besieged Fort Stanwix (Rome, N.Y.), and Guyasuta was with the large Indian contingent that ambushed and repulsed with heavy casualties a relieving force of Mohawk Valley militia at Oriskany. Lack of artillery, however, caused St. Leger to abandon the siege. Although there is evidence that Guyasuta participated in other actions during the American Revolution, he was probably more important to the British-Loyalist cause in his familiar role as diplomat to the Ohio country. In 1780 Guy Johnson, Sir William Johnson's son-in-law, dispatched him to attempt to hold Indians of the region, which had been invaded by rebel forces under George Rogers Clark, firm in their alliance with the British.

After the British were defeated, the new American republic attempted to use Seneca influence, including that of Guyasuta, to establish peace with the Indians of the Ohio country. Although Guyasuta's younger kinsman Cornplanter was more active than the aging diplomat in this endeavor, Anthony Wayne, the American military commander, did meet with Guyasuta in 1792 and 1793. Cornplanter's efforts to establish peace between the Seneca and the states of the new American republic led Pennsylvania to grant him a personal tract of land on the Allegheny River. It was there that Guyasuta died and was buried.

Guyasuta was the product of a society that valued the skills of the diplomat. He clearly honed such skills and played an important role in the complex network of fragile alliances and latent or open hostilities that both united and divided Indian nations and colonial powers in northeastern North America in the late eighteenth century. He was a major player in the events of both war and peace on that frontier.

• The longest biographical treatment of Guyasuta is found in C. Hale Sipe, *The Indian Chiefs of Pennsylvania* (1927). The Bouquet papers and Haldimand papers in the British Library (London), the Gage papers in the Clements Library (Ann Arbor), and the Draper manuscripts in the State Historical Society of Wisconsin (Madison) contain information relative to Guyasuta's career. His activities and the significant events of his time and place are documented in published collections such as James Sullivan et al., eds., *Papers of Sir William Johnson* (1921–1965); E. B. O'Callaghan and B. Fernow, eds., *Documents Relative to the Colonial History of the State of New York* (1853–1887); L. P. Kellogg, ed., *Frontier Retreat on the Upper Ohio, 1779–1781* (1917); and R. C. Knopf, ed., *Anthony Wayne, a Name in Arms: . . . The Wayne-Knox-Pickering-McHenry Correspondence* (1960). The best monograph treatment of Guyasuta's era is still Randolph C. Downes, *Council Fires on the Upper Ohio: A Narrative of Indian Affairs in the Upper Ohio until 1795* (1940).

THOMAS S. ABLER

GUYON, Joseph Napoleon (26 Aug. 1892–27 Nov. 1971), professional football and baseball player, was born in Mahnomen, Minnesota, the son of Charles M. Guyon and Mary (maiden name unknown). A full-blooded Chippewa Indian, Guyon was born O-Gee-Chidea, which means "brave man" in the Chippewa language. He grew up on the White Earth Reservation in Minnesota, where he received an elementary education. He entered Carlisle Indian School in Pennsylvania in 1912 on an athletic scholarship.

Guyon, known as "Indian Joe," starred as a football tackle and halfback for two years (1912–1913) at Carlisle. Coached by the legendary Glenn "Pop" Warner, the Carlisle team won the national championship in 1912, finishing the season with a 12–1–1 record and defeating Army 27–6 to clinch the title. At 5'11" and weighing 190 pounds, Guyon opened holes as a tackle for Carlisle's premier halfback, Jim Thorpe, in the 1912 season. The team averaged 36 points per game. The following year Guyon replaced Thorpe in the backfield, and Walter Camp named him second-team All-American. The 1913 Carlisle team finished with a 10–1–1 record.

In the summer of 1914 Guyon entered Keewatin Academy in St. Augustine, Florida. Though Keewatin did not field a football team, Guyon remained there three years. In 1917 he enrolled at Georgia Tech, where he played football for two seasons (1917–1918) under coach John W. Heisman. He never graduated.

The 1917 Georgia Tech team became the first southern school to win the national championship by going undefeated at 9–0–0 and averaging 54.6 points per game, outscoring its opponents 491–17. As a half-back Guyon rushed for 344 yards on only 12 carries. The next season Georgia Tech finished at 6–1–0, losing to the eventual national champion, the University of Pittsburgh, 32–0, to end a 33-game winning streak. Guyon was named consensus All-American at tackle for the 1918 season.

Guyon had grown to 6'1", 180 pounds when he began his professional football career in 1919. He played eight years in the American Professional Football Association (APFA) and the National Football League (NFL). For the first six years Guyon was teamed in backfields with Thorpe, which hampered Guyon gaining renown. Guyon and Thorpe played together in the 1919 and 1920 seasons with the Canton Bulldogs of the APFA, which became the NFL in 1921, the same year the two men joined the Cleveland Indians. In 1922 and 1923 they both played in the backfield with the Oorang Indians of Marion, Ohio, one of the more colorful early professional teams.

The Oorang team fielded only Native-American players, with Guyon and Thorpe the featured players. Playing most of their games on the road, Oorang was a weak team that finished 3–6 in 1922 and 1–10 in 1923. But the Oorang team could entertain crowds wherever they played by entering the stadium in full Indian dress and offering up a number of war whoops. In 1924 Guyon and Thorpe played their last season together with the Rock Island (Ill.) Independents.

Guyon played for the Kansas City Cowboys in the 1925 season and then took a one-year hiatus. In 1927 he returned to the NFL with the New York Giants and led the team to an 11–1–1 record and the league championship. Out from under the shadow of Thorpe, in the 1927 season Guyon made a name for himself. On both offense and defense he proved to be a stellar passer, runner, kicker, and tackler. In the decisive game of the season Guyon paced the Giants to a 13–7 victory over the Chicago Bears.

While earning a reputation as a professional football star, Guyon also played professional baseball. In 1925 he signed to play with the Louisville Colonels of the minor league American Association. Playing in the outfield, Guyon led the league in hitting in 1925 with a .363 average, while the Colonels won the first of two consecutive league pennants. In 1927 Guyon's baseball career ended when he crashed into the outfield wall in Indianapolis.

Guyon garnered several honors for his professional football career. In 1920 he returned a punt 95 yards, which remained an NFL record for fifty years. In 1966 he was inducted into the Professional Football Hall of Fame and in 1971 into the National Football Foundation's College Hall of Fame.

Eventually settling in Louisville, Kentucky, Guyon lived for a time in Harrah, Oklahoma, and Flint, Michigan. After coaching high school football in Louisville in the 1930s, he worked as a bank guard in Flint. After he retired he returned to Louisville, where he died from injuries sustained in an automobile accident. He and his wife, Christine Denney, had two children.

• A file on Guyon, Student File 4213, Carlisle Indian School, Records of the Bureau of Indian Affairs, RG 75, is in the National Archives, Washington, D.C. The Professional Football Hall of Fame Research Library, Canton, Ohio, also holds Guyon material. An obituary is in the *New York Times*, 29 Nov. 1971.

BRIAN S. BUTLER

GUYOT, Arnold Henry (28 Sept. 1807–8 Feb. 1884), geographer and educator, was born in Boudevilliers, Switzerland, the son of David Pierre Guyot and Constance Favarger. Born into a family that had converted to Protestantism in the mid-sixteenth century, Guyot initially planned to become a minister. After graduating from the College of Neuchâtel in Switzerland in 1825, he studied German and classics in Stuttgart and Karlsruhe and then completed a two-year course in theology at Neuchâtel in 1829. Returning to Germany, he continued his study of theology in the classes of Frederick Schleiermacher and Johann Neander at the University of Berlin in 1829. Fellow students and professors at institutions where he studied (especially naturalist Louis Agassiz of Karlsruhe), however, stimulated his interest in the natural sciences, and in 1830 Guyot decided to pursue a doctoral degree in this field. Following five years of study of physics, chemistry, and geology with many renowned scientists, most notably geographer Carl Ritter, and the completion of his thesis, "The Natural Classification of Lakes," Guyot was awarded a Ph.D. by the University of Berlin in 1835.

Guyot spent the next five years as a private tutor for the sons of count de Pourtales-Gorgier in Paris. During the summers he made excursions into the Alps to study glaciers, especially to test Agassiz's theory that a significant portion of Europe had experienced an "ice age." In 1838 Guyot reported his discoveries about glacial formation, structure, and movement in a paper he presented to the Geological Society of France. His own modesty as well as an agreement with Agassiz to later collaborate on a major book on the glacial age led Guyot not to publish his research. As a result, credit for his findings about glaciers was given to others, especially Agassiz, who in many cases merely confirmed Guyot's discoveries. His scientific studies did, however, lead to an offer to teach at the Academy of Neuchâtel in 1839. Joining Agassiz on the faculty, Guyot served as a professor of history and physical geology at Neuchâtel until the Grand Revolutionary Council of Geneva closed the institution in 1848. While teaching at Neuchâtel, he continued to investigate glaciers in the Alps, collected thousands of rock specimens, and began to publish some of his findings.

At the urging of Agassiz, who had settled in the United States in 1846, Guyot left the political turmoil of Switzerland and immigrated to America in the summer of 1848. In 1849 he gave the prestigious Lowell

Institute Lectures in Boston. Their publication that same year as *The Earth and Man* quickly made him one of America's most respected geographers. This volume sought to explain the relationship between people's physical environment and their social, political, and moral development. From 1849 until 1854 Guyot lectured to more than 1,500 teachers each year on instructional methods in geography under the auspices of the Massachusetts Board of Education. This experience led him to publish a series of geography textbooks between 1866 and 1879, which strongly influenced how the subject was taught in American schools for many years.

In 1854 Guyot moved to Princeton University to accept a chair in physical geography and geology, which he occupied for the next thirty years. While at Princeton he was active as a teacher, lecturer, researcher, technical adviser to many scientific enterprises, and author. He taught courses to many different groups including schoolteachers, students at Princeton and Union theological seminaries, and the staff of the Smithsonian Institution. During the 1870s he founded the Elizabeth Marsh Museum (now the Guyot Hall Natural History Museum) at Princeton and filled it with geological specimens he had collected and classified. Under Smithsonian direction he worked to establish and equip stations, especially in New York and Massachusetts, to observe weather conditions. He measured the heights of peaks from Maine to South Carolina and devised topographic maps of the Appalachian and Catskill mountains. In 1858 Guyot published the results of these investigations as *Tables, Meteorological and Physical, Prepared for the Smithsonian Institution*. During the late nineteenth century many countries used his meteorological tables, and his textbooks and wall maps enjoyed a wide circulation in the United States. His atlases and textbooks in geography were awarded the Medal of Progress at the Vienna Exposition of 1873 and a gold medal at the Paris Exposition of 1878. In 1867 he married Sarah Doremus Haines, daughter of a former New Jersey governor; they had no children.

Guyot's humility, demanding teaching responsibilities, extensive geological investigations, desire to have more facts, and discomfort with English sometimes led him to postpone publication of his discoveries; as a result he did not always receive the recognition he deserved. During the last thirty years of his life, however, Guyot presented numerous papers to scientific organizations and published many articles on his geographical findings and conclusions in both European and American scientific journals. Perhaps his most notable paper was his "Memoir on Louis Agassiz," which he read in two parts to the National Academy of the Sciences in October 1877 and April 1878.

A deeply committed Christian, Guyot joined philosopher James McCosh, Princeton's president from 1868 to 1888; botanist George Macloskie; and other Princeton colleagues in an effort to reconcile nineteenth-century scientific discoveries and theories with biblical teaching. Guyot argued in a paper that he presented to the Evangelical Alliance in 1873 that the "sublime grandeur," "symmetrical plan," and "positive historical character" of the biblical narrative contrasted sharply with "the fanciful, allegorical cosmogonies of all heathen religion," whether ancient or modern, displayed God's superintendence of the Bible, and argued for its truthfulness ("Cosmogony and the Bible; The Biblical Account of Creation in the Light of Modern Science," *History, Essays, Orations, and Other Documents of the Sixth General Council of the Evangelical Alliance* [1874], p. 276). In 1884 he published *Creation, or the Biblical Cosmogony in the Light of Modern Science* to provide scientists as well as ordinary Christians with "new reasons for accepting" the Bible as "the revelation of a God of love to man" (p. xii). Guyot insisted that both biblical and scientific records came from the same author and therefore complemented each other and together constituted God's revelation. *Creation* explicated the plan of the biblical book Genesis's narrative of creation—what God intended this narrative to teach—and demonstrated how the findings of modern science could help Christians understand this account. Guyot devised charts to show how the seven "cosmogonic days" described in Genesis were consistent with many specific discoveries and hypotheses of modern science. He also attempted to explain apparent inconsistencies between the biblical account of creation and modern scientific conclusions. Although creationists in the last quarter of the nineteenth century frequently hailed him as a champion of their position, in *Creation* Guyot expressed his belief that limited evolution had occurred through natural causes (without accepting the idea of Darwinian natural selection).

Guyot's investigations, maps, tables, textbooks, and articles significantly influenced the development of both American and international geography during the second half of the nineteenth century. His research and publications provided important data about many geological formations and stimulated other geographers to do their own fieldwork. His extensive meteorological observations contributed to the establishment in 1870 of the U.S. Weather Bureau (now the National Weather Bureau). A generous, energetic, devoutly religious man who enjoyed many close friendships, Guyot hiked and climbed mountains to obtain scientific information well beyond his seventieth birthday. He died in Princeton.

• Guyot's personal papers are in the Manuscripts Division, Department of Rare Books and Special Collections, Princeton University Libraries. For biographical sketches, see James D. Dana, "Memoir of Arnold Guyot, 1807–1884," National Academy of Sciences, *Biographical Memoirs*, 2 (1886): 309–47, and Leonard Chester Jones, "Arnold Henry Guyot," *Faculty Papers of Union College*, vol. 1 (1930), pp. 31–65, both of which discuss Guyot's chief scientific works in considerable detail and provide an extensive list of his publications and papers. David Livingstone, *Darwin's Forgotten Defenders* (1987), and Gary Scott Smith, *The Seeds of Secularization: Calvinism, Culture, and Pluralism in America, 1870–1915* (1985), analyze his efforts to reconcile scientific discoveries with biblical teachings about creation. Obituaries are in the *New York Tribune*, 9 Feb. 1884, and *Science*, 22 Feb. 1884.

GARY SCOTT SMITH

GUZIK, Jack (between 1886 and 1888–21 Feb. 1956), bootlegger and gambling entrepreneur, was born probably in Russia, the son of Max Guzik and his wife (name unknown). Guzik was brought to Chicago in 1891–1892 and became a U.S. citizen through the naturalization of his father in November 1898.

By 1910 Guzik, like his brother Harry, was hustling a living in Chicago's Southside redlight district. In 1914, for instance, he arranged protection for his woman, Elsie Cusick (an early spelling of his last name), at 2222 Wabash Avenue, where she oversaw two prostitutes. After a 1914 campaign to close the redlight district, both Guzik and his brother moved their vice activities to blue-collar suburbs. As a vice entrepreneur, Guzik made contacts with underworld figures like John Torrio and Al Capone and with politicians, including Michael Kenna and John Coughlin, who, between them, represented the downtown First Ward in the city council until the 1940s. Such contacts were central to his meteoric rise in the 1920s.

With the onset of Prohibition in 1920, Guzik and Capone joined Torrio as he organized a coalition of bootleggers to distribute illegal alcohol in Chicago and its suburbs. On election day in April 1924, Capone-led gunmen seized the polls in Cicero, Illinois, and assured the victory of friendly politicians. Afterward, Guzik and Capone spent much time there overseeing gambling houses and bootlegging activities. Concurrently, an uneasy truce among Chicago bootleggers collapsed, and bootleg wars broke out that earned Chicago and Capone worldwide fame. In 1925 Torrio was convicted of bootlegging and was shot by rivals. As a result, he returned to New York and left the Chicago operations to his associates.

Thereafter the varied illegal operations associated with Capone's name were in fact coordinated by four equal partners: Al Capone, his older brother Ralph, their cousin Frank Nitti, and Jack Guzik. These four, in turn, entered into partnerships with various persons to operate individual enterprises. For instance, they entered into partnership with Sam Guzik, Jack's younger brother, to operate slot machines in the western suburbs and with Louis Lipschultz, Jack's brother-in-law, to deliver beer in Cicero and nearby suburbs. This structure allowed oversight by the four partners within a basically decentralized system in which various individuals assumed responsibility for daily management of separate enterprises. After the notorious St. Valentine's Day Massacre on 14 February 1929 completed the decimation of the Northside gang, the partners not only expanded bootlegging into the northern part of the city but also became involved in the lively nightclub area on the near Northside. In 1927, too, they joined with Edward J. O'Hare to establish in Cicero the Hawthorne Kennel Club for dog racing, a popular activity that made money from illegal betting.

The murderous bootleg wars and Capone's notoriety focused government investigative efforts on the four partners, and all went to prison for income tax evasion. Jack Guzik was convicted in November 1930 and went to prison in April 1932 after the U.S. Supreme Court refused to hear his appeal. In December 1935 he emerged from prison into a new world. Prohibition was over, and Al Capone, still in prison, would never resume an underworld role. Guzik immediately returned to a central place within the Chicago underworld, first as a partner with Frank Nitti and, after Nitti's suicide in 1943, as a partner with Tony Accardo.

Guzik's chief focus was gambling. Working closely with Hymie Levin, he became and remained until his death the central figure whose permission was needed to operate bookmaking and other gambling enterprises in downtown Chicago. His relations with Alderman Kenna in the late 1930s were so close that Guzik received his mail at Kenna's city hall office. After World War II Guzik and Accardo also used strong-arm tactics to become partners in policy gambling syndicates operated by blacks and whites out of the Southside black ghetto.

About 1940 Guzik and Levine began distributing sports information to betting parlors in and around Chicago. Later they joined with others in demanding a share in the national race wire operated by James Ragen. When Ragen refused, they established a rival company called Trans-America Publishing and News Service and recruited underworld associates in other cities to establish local outlets for their company. In 1946 Ragen was assassinated, apparently by gunmen associated with Guzik; thereafter Guzik and his partners merged their news service with the rival company.

In other ways, too, Guzik and his associates extended their business interests and influence beyond Chicago. In 1926 Guzik purchased land in Florida and began to spend time there. By the 1930s, with his Chicago associates, he had invested in Florida dog and horse tracks. In 1949 Guzik and Accardo muscled in on the S&G Syndicate, which dominated bookmaking in the Miami area. Guzik and Accardo also invested money in the Riviera, one of the casino hotels that transformed Las Vegas into America's fastest-growing city after World War II. During the famous Senate investigations into organized crime under the leadership of Estes Kefauver, Guzik was subpoenaed as a witness and at his appearance in March 1951 refused to testify on Fifth Amendment grounds.

Guzik and his wife, Rose (maiden name unconfirmed but probably Lipschultz), whom he reportedly married in the early 1920s, raised three children (one of them adopted) in their modest Chicago home. Barely five feet tall, Guzik looked like a squat penguin, and he generally avoided the notoriety of his more flamboyant partners. He may nevertheless have been the most significant criminal leader in Chicago during the twentieth century. The lack of careful attention to him is reflected by the fact that, although his friends called him Jack and he used either Jack or John as his legal name, newspaper stories and most crime histories refer to him as Jake. From the time that he and Capone became partners in 1926 until his death in Chicago—a full thirty years—Guzik remained at the center of those criminal entrepreneurs who exercised extensive influence on Chicago politics, steadily expanded their hold on the underworld of the city, and extended their interests into Florida, Las Vegas, and other locations.

The best primary sources on Guzik are the files of the Chicago Crime Commission, including files no. 65 and 65-100. The intelligence files of the Internal Revenue Service are invaluable but not currently open. Because Guzik was Capone's partner, the extensive IRS file on Capone (SI 7085-F) contains much information on Guzik, including his financial records in envelope 80 and an interview in envelope 25. Later the intelligence division opened an investigation on Guzik and Accardo (file no. 42739-FR). Valuable information is also available in file no. 5-23-283, Central Files of the Department of Justice, in the National Archives in Washington, D.C., which has records on the prosecution and appeal of the income tax case in the 1930s. Arthur W. Mitchell was the attorney who later negotiated the settlement of Guzik's civil tax liabilities; his correspondence with his client and with the government is in the Mitchell papers, Chicago Historical Society.

• Guzik has not been the subject of a biography but appears in the major secondary works on Capone or the twentieth-century Chicago underworld. Generally Guzik is not treated as an active partner but instead is inaccurately referred to as Capone's accountant or as a money handler for the mob. Discussion of Guzik can be found in John Kobler, *Capone: The Life and World of Al Capone* (1971); Jack McPhaul, *Johnny Torrio: First of the Gang Lords* (1970); Ovid Demaris, *Captive City* (1968); Estes Kefauver, *Crime in America* (1951), chaps. 3, 4, and 7; and Virgil W. Peterson, *Barbarians in Our Midst* (1952). For a brief analysis of the structure of the so-called Capone bootlegging operations, explaining Guzik's partnership interests, see Mark H. Haller, "Illegal Enterprise: A Theoretical and Historical Interpretation," *Criminology* 28 (May 1990): 215–23. An obituary is in the *New York Times*, 22 Feb. 1956.

MARK H. HALLER

GWIN, William McKendree (9 Oct. 1805–3 Sept. 1885), politician and entrepreneur, was born in Sumner County, Tennessee, the son of James Gwin, a Methodist minister, and Mary (maiden name probably Adair). He pursued legal studies in Gallatin, Tennessee, and gained admittance to the state bar. Gwin matriculated at Transylvania University in Kentucky in 1825 for the purpose of studying medicine. He received his medical degree on 5 March 1828 and practiced medicine for several years.

In 1830 Gwin moved to Mississippi. He lived in Vicksburg, Clinton, and Natchez at various times. Gwin married Caroline M. J. Sampson; they had two children before she died in 1833. In 1837 he married

Mary Elizabeth Hampton Bell. His second marriage produced four children.

A Jacksonian Democrat, Gwin became one of Mississippi's most powerful politicians. In 1833 President Andrew Jackson selected him as U.S. marshal for the District of Mississippi. He assumed office on 12 October. On 18 June 1838 his position became U.S. marshal for the Southern District of Mississippi. He resigned this office in the winter of 1840–1841. During the mid-1830s, Gwin and his older brother Samuel, who was the register at a federal land office in the state, became embroiled in a bitter dispute with U.S. Senator George Poindexter. The dispute derived from Poindexter's opposition to the appointments of the Gwin brothers, the senator's charge that Samuel Gwin had joined interests with land speculators to defraud the federal government and exploit actual settlers, and Poindexter's support of South Carolina's nullification of the tariff. William Gwin played a key role in Poindexter's losing his Senate seat to Robert J. Walker by vote of the Mississippi legislature in January 1836.

Meanwhile, Gwin amassed considerable wealth from his fees as marshal and his land dealings. He joined prominent Mississippians such as Walker and John A. Quitman in a maze of speculations. A member of two consortia, Gwin acquired plantations, Vicksburg lots, and undeveloped tracts in Mississippi, holdings in Texas and Arkansas, and almost two hundred slaves. He also was a partner in two commission firms that marketed cotton.

Elected to Congress in 1840, Gwin served as U.S. representative from 1841 to 1843. During his House term, Gwin primarily fought for legislation designed to benefit his state, such as a law creating a marine hospital at Natchez. However, he also strongly opposed protective tariffs and came under the influence of John C. Calhoun. Though Gwin declined his party's nomination for a second term, he remained politically active. In 1844 he championed the annexation of Texas, served as a delegate to the Democratic National Convention, and campaigned in Mississippi and Tennessee for James K. Polk. In the winter of 1844–1845, Gwin returned to Washington, D.C., where he represented the Chickasaw Indians in claims against the U.S. government. Gwin secured a settlement on behalf of the Chickasaws for $112,042.99 but charged the tribe half of the award for his services. (Gwin's fee became the subject of an inconclusive congressional investigation in 1850.) Gwin served as one of Vicksburg's delegates to the Southern and Western [Commercial] Convention in Memphis, Tennessee, in 1845. He made an unsuccessful bid for a U.S. Senate seat in 1845–1846. In 1846, after receiving an appointment from the Department of the Treasury to oversee the construction of a customhouse in New Orleans, Gwin moved to that city. He held this position until 31 March 1849.

Gwin moved to California in 1849. Before he left New Orleans, he wrote to an acquaintance that his decision was prompted by his ambition for a U.S. Senate seat. Apparently with that end in mind, he entered

California politics soon after his arrival at San Francisco on 4 June. He participated in the ongoing agitation for statehood and was elected to represent San Francisco at the California constitutional convention (3 Sept.–13 Oct. 1849). That December California's legislature selected Gwin as one of the state's first U.S. senators. Gwin took his seat in September 1850. He served in the Senate until 3 March 1855 and from 13 January 1857 to 3 March 1861. He chaired the Committee on Naval Affairs from 1851 to 1855.

As senator, Gwin upheld the interests of California's Anglo settlers against Spanish and Mexican claimants to the state's domain. According to the Treaty of Guadalupe Hidalgo, which ended the Mexican War, the United States would respect legitimate Mexican titles to land in California secured prior to 13 May 1846. However, many Mexican grantees had failed to satisfy stipulations of Mexican law necessary to formalize their titles, and American settlers tried to preempt their tracts. When Gwin's California colleague John C. Frémont introduced a bill creating a board of commissioners to resolve disputed claims, Gwin proposed a substitute measure, which carried, giving the U.S. government the right to appeal to federal courts decisions hostile to the claims of American settlers. Similarly, Gwin championed Anglo settlers regarding U.S. Indian policy in California. He attacked and helped defeat the ratification of eighteen treaties signed by federal commissioners that would have provided more than 7 percent of California as reservations for the state's tribes. He was unsuccessful, however, in his efforts to get the federal government to fund California and Oregon volunteers to subdue the Indians. He was also unable to defeat a measure that provided for small military reservations in the state where the natives could live but not receive fee simple title to the land.

One of the country's most energetic commercial and territorial expansionists during the 1850s, Gwin helped push a bill through Congress creating a navy yard in San Francisco Bay and advocated legislation to establish transcontinental railroad, telegraph, and regular overland mail delivery service to California. He also supported William Walker's (1824–1860) filibuster to Lower California, promoted Henry Crabb's filibuster to Sonora, cosponsored a Senate measure to help American whalers and increase U.S. trade in the Far East, urged trade reciprocity with the Hawaiian kingdom to facilitate its eventual absorption into the United States, conducted negotiations (on behalf of the Buchanan administration) in 1859 regarding the American purchase of Alaska from Russia, and supported U.S. annexation of Cuba.

Gwin retained landholdings and slaves in the South and advocated many of the causes of his native region during the events preceding the Civil War. He supported the Kansas-Nebraska Act, the *Dred Scott* decision, the Lecompton Constitution, and John C. Breckinridge's presidential candidacy. Gwin played an instrumental role in the Senate Democratic caucus's decision in 1858 to replace Stephen A. Douglas as chairman of the Committee on Territories. Desirous of preserving the Union during the secession winter, he supported the Crittenden Compromise. In early March he took on the role of intermediary between Secretary of State William Seward and Confederate leaders in Seward's negotiations to postpone hostilities over Fort Sumter in the hope of leaving the door open to peaceful reunion.

After the Civil War erupted, Gwin returned to California, where he discovered that his political support had eroded and that he was under suspicion both as a Confederate sympathizer and for harboring plans to create a new Pacific republic—an idea that he had alluded to in an 1860 speech in Congress. Gwin left San Francisco on 21 October 1861, intending to make his way to New York. However, he was arrested before his vessel reached Panama by Union general Edwin V. Sumner, who happened to be aboard the same steamer and suspected Gwin of collaboration with the Confederacy. Sumner paroled Gwin days later on condition that Gwin remain in New York after his arrival pending a ruling on his status by Secretary of State Seward. On 16 November 1861 Gwin was arrested according to Seward's instructions. On 18 November Union authorities confined him at Fort Lafayette in New York City. Formal charges were never filed in his case, and he was released unconditionally on 2 December. Gwin subsequently returned to his Mississippi plantation.

After his plantation was destroyed by Union military forces in 1863, Gwin traveled to Paris, France. There he interested Emperor Napoleon III in a project by which Gwin would colonize Mexico's northern frontier with western miners, pacify Indian tribes, and develop the region's silver resources. In 1864 and 1865 Gwin traveled back and forth between France and Mexico to promote his plan. However, he never gained the cooperation of France's puppet ruler in Mexico, the Archduke Maximilian, and his project ran counter to the mood of resurgent nationalism sweeping Mexico in 1865. That summer Gwin abandoned the scheme and returned to American soil. He intended to make his way to France, where his family was staying, but he was intercepted by Union military authorities and sent to report to General Philip Sheridan, commanding at New Orleans. Sheridan immediately telegraphed the Department of War for instructions. Apparently under the influence of rumors that Gwin intended his colony as a base for attacks by Confederate exiles against the recently reunited Union, President Andrew Johnson, on 29 September 1865, had orders telegraphed to Sheridan for Gwin's arrest and imprisonment. Sheridan confined Gwin at Fort Jackson. Once again, federal authorities never filed charges explaining the cause for Gwin's arrest. He was not released until May 1866. He returned to Paris and then, in 1868, to San Francisco. His last years were devoted to an array of business projects, including a Panama railroad enterprise. He was a delegate to the 1876 and 1880 Democratic National Conventions. He died in New York City.

• The best collection of Gwin manuscripts is the William Mc-Kendree Gwin Papers, Bancroft Library, University of California, Berkeley. There is also a William McKendree Gwin Collection at the California Historical Society Library, San Francisco. Gwin's correspondence can be found in the J. F. H. Claiborne Papers at three repositories: the Library of Congress; the Southern Historical Collection, University of North Carolina; and the Mississippi Department of Archives and History. Small numbers of Gwin letters can be found in such collections as the Charles D. Fontaine Papers, Mississippi Department of Archives and History; the James K. Polk Papers, Library of Congress; the Powhatan Ellis Papers, the Center for American History, University of Texas; and the Archibald Hamilton Gillespie Papers, University of California at Los Angeles Library. Gwin's memoirs, edited by William Henry Ellison, were published in the *California Historical Society Quarterly* 19 (1940): 1–26, 157–84, 256–77, 344–67. Lately Thomas [pseud.], *Between Two Empires: The Life Story of California's First Senator, William McKendree Gwin* (1969), though often imprecise, provides a biography about Gwin's life. Secondary works, including Edwin A. Miles, *Jacksonian Democracy in Mississippi* (1960); Joseph Ellison, *California and the Nation, 1850–1869,* repr. ed. (1969); and Joseph Allen Stout, Jr., *The Liberators: Filibustering Expeditions into Mexico, 1848–1862, and the Last Thrust of Manifest Destiny* (1973), help clarify several phases of Gwin's public career. Gwin's role at the California constitutional convention can be traced in J. Ross Browne, comp., *Report of the Debates in the Convention of California, on the Formation of the State Constitution, in September and October, 1849,* repr. ed. (1973). An obituary is in the *New York Times,* 4 Sept. 1885.

ROBERT E. MAY

GWINNETT, Button (bap. 10 Apr. 1735–19 May 1777), merchant and political leader, was born in Gloucester, England, the son of the Reverend Samuel Gwinnett and Anne Emes. Gwinnett left England as a young man and for a number of years after arriving in America was a merchant in the colonial trade. In April 1757 he married Ann Bourne, with whom he had three children. His business activities took him from Newfoundland to Jamaica, and at times brought him into conflict with other merchants and with legal authorities. Never very successful, he moved to Savannah in 1765 and opened a store. When that venture failed, he bought (on credit) St. Catherines Island, off the coast of Georgia to the south of Savannah, and attempted to become a planter. Though his planting activities were also unsuccessful, he did make a name for himself in local politics.

In 1769 he was elected to the Commons House of Assembly, where he helped prepare a "Humble Address" protesting the taxing of parishes not represented in the assembly. Largely as a result of financial problems, he served only one term in the legislature; in 1773 he put his property up for sale and withdrew from public life. He seems to have played no role in the 1774 protests of the Intolerable Acts, and he did not attend the meetings at which men from his parish (St. John's) tried to take control of the Whig movement from men of Savannah and surrounding Christ Church Parish. At this time he was organizing a "nocturnal Cabal" among Whigs in rural parishes, working to persuade them that it would be in their own best interest to join St. John's against the conservative Christ Church–led coalition. He organized an alliance of coastal and backcountry Whigs (variously termed the country party, the popular party, or the radicals) determined to create a more democratic government of which they would be the leaders. The first indication of the strength of his creation came in early 1776, when Georgia's provincial congress elected Gwinnett as commander of the state's Continental battalion. Leaders of the Christ Church coalition threatened to withdraw from the congress as a result, so, in a compromise, Gwinnett accepted election to the Continental Congress instead, and the military post went to Lachlan McIntosh, a wealthy planter from southern Georgia with strong ties to the Savannah faction.

Gwinnett arrived in Philadelphia on 20 May 1776. In Congress he was appointed to a number of committees, including one to study the feasibility of forming a confederation of the states. Although there is no record of his having made any speeches on separation from England prior to 2 July, on that date he voted to accept the resolution calling for independence. He voted to approve the Declaration of Independence on 4 July, and he signed the document on 2 August. Not long afterward, he returned to Georgia, hoping to receive command of the newly authorized Georgia brigade. Frustrated when that post went to his old rival McIntosh, he turned his energy and influence to the task of helping his party to gain control of the provincial congress then being elected. Successful, he became Speaker and headed the committee that drew up the state's first real constitution. This democratic document put power in the hands of Gwinnett's backcountry allies and signaled a shift that would bring an end to Christ Church's political domination. Meanwhile Gwinnett began to purge the army of officers not loyal to his faction, many of whom were friends and relatives of Lachlan McIntosh.

After the legislature adjourned in mid-February 1777, the president of the council of safety, Archibald Bulloch, died, and Gwinnett was chosen to replace him. Now in command of the state militia, "president" Gwinnett determined to undertake an expedition to Florida in order to capture St. Augustine. General McIntosh, believing the invasion was designed to enhance Gwinnett's political career, withheld Continental troops. In the midst of preparations for the expedition, Gwinnett arrested McIntosh's brother for treason, and tension between the general and the president escalated. The invasion was finally launched, but it quickly bogged down. Gwinnett had to ask McIntosh for help, which was reluctantly given. But genuine cooperation between the two men was impossible, and the expedition ultimately failed. In early May 1777 the first assembly under the new constitution met, and Gwinnett was defeated in his bid to be chosen governor. However, when the legislature investigated the Florida invasion, it found that Gwinnett had acted properly. McIntosh, taking this finding as a charge against his own conduct, publicly denounced

Gwinnett as "a Scoundrell & lying Rascal." Gwinnett immediately challenged McIntosh to a duel, and his challenge was accepted. On the morning of 16 May 1777 the two met just outside the city of Savannah. Both were wounded; but while McIntosh's injury was not serious, in Gwinnett's case "a Mortification came on" and he died three days later.

Gwinnett's friend Lyman Hall eulogized him as "a Whig to excess," a description on which both friend and foe would have agreed. His ambition had fanned the flames of partisanship and in many ways retarded the revolution in Georgia. But he had also brought the backcountry into the conflict on the Whig side, and that may have turned the tide toward independence.

• Little has been written about Gwinnett, but the best sources on his life and political activities are Harvey H. Jackson, "Button Gwinnett and the Rise of the 'Western Members': A Reappraisal of Georgia's 'Whig to Excess,'" *Atlanta Historical Journal* 24 (1980): 17–30, and *Lachlan McIntosh and the Politics of Revolutionary Georgia* (1979); and Charles F. Jenkins, *Button Gwinnett: Signer of the Declaration of Independence* (1926).

HARVEY H. JACKSON

H

HAAGEN-SMIT, Arie Jan (22 Dec. 1900–17 Mar. 1977), biochemist, was born in Utrecht, Netherlands, the son of Jan Willem Adrianus Haagen-Smit, the chief chemist of the Royal Mint of the Netherlands, and Maria Geertruida van Maanen. He began studying chemistry at the University of Utrecht in 1918 and received his A.B. in 1922. He continued his work as a graduate student at the University of Utrecht, receiving his A.M. for work in organic chemistry in 1926, and his Ph.D. in 1929. He worked with P. Van Romburgh on natural products chemistry and with Leopold Ruzicka on isoprenoids. Haagen-Smit's Ph.D. research dealt with the chemistry of sesquiterpenes; in particular, he uncovered the structure of terpenes, the hydrocarbon compounds in essential oils and flavors. In 1930 he married Petronella Francina Pennings; they had one child before she died in 1933.

The University of Utrecht appointed Haagen-Smit chief assistant in organic chemistry in 1929 and lecturer in chemistry and natural products in 1933. He assisted Fritz Kogl in studies of plant hormones, then known as "the plant growth substance," and isolated auxin in 1934. In the summer of 1935 he worked with Frits Went of the California Institute of Technology (Caltech) to isolate substances that mimicked the action of other plant hormones; this work contributed to the development of chemical controls to plant growth, including chemical weed killers and selective herbicides. That same summer Haagen-Smit married Maria Wilhelmina Bloemers of Zutphen; they had three children.

In 1936 Kenneth Thimann, who had just started a plant hormone laboratory at Harvard University, invited Haagen-Smit to Harvard as lecturer in chemistry and natural products. The next year Went and Thomas Hunt Morgan persuaded Haagen-Smit to accept a position at the California Institute of Technology in Pasadena, California, as an associate professor of bioorganic chemistry. He was appointed full professor in 1940. His early work there continued to focus on plant hormones. Together with James Bonner, he worked to understand and isolate the structure of "traumatic acid," or "the plant wound hormone." During the 1940s he successfully synthesized hormones that could aid in the healing of wounds in both animals and plants. He also pursued his interest in flavors and essential oils, studying the oils in pines and desert plants, and the flavorings in other natural materials, winning the Fritzche Award of the American Chemical Society in 1949 for his work in this area.

In the mid-1940s Haagen-Smit began to study the smog that had been increasing in Southern California, especially since the end of World War II. His early experiments used simple tools to measure oxidant levels in the air. In one set of experiments from 1946, he and his colleague C. Bradley pulled air through rubber tubing and measured the amount of time it took the tubing to crack in order to ascertain the level of oxidants in the air. He also created smog in his laboratory, providing incontrovertible proof of its causes. These tests and others that he developed throughout his career provided the groundwork for understanding and decreasing air pollution in Southern California and elsewhere. In 1948 he began acting as a consultant for the Los Angeles County Air Pollution Control District, and in 1950 he took a leave of absence from Caltech in order to direct research at the laboratories of the district. During that year he discovered the photochemical oxidation that is an important aspect of modern pollution. In 1956 he took a second leave of absence to direct research for the Southern California Edison Company; in those experiments he was able to learn about the way in which stacks from central power stations contributed to smog.

Haagen-Smit's expertise made him party to many efforts to curb smog, and by 1958 he was becoming a vocal critic of pollution. He advocated greater attention to conservation and ecology, and in 1959 he appeared on the television program "The Next Hundred Years" to advocate greater urban planning to prevent problems with pollution. As Bonner remembered, Haagen-Smit was "one man against an establishment that at first insisted that petroleum and automobiles could not possibly be the source of smog." His smog studies made Haagen-Smit unpopular with oil and automotive companies, but they also brought him widespread acclaim. According to one report, he realized the power his research had over the automotive companies, exclaiming after one smog victory over Volkswagen, which had failed to file a compliance certificate with California regulations about clean air: "I shut down all their sales in California until they complied. That's real power."

Haagen-Smit's work was crucial in understanding the causes of smog and air pollution and in fostering early efforts to overcome this important problem. He was widely recognized for these efforts. In 1957 he received the Los Angeles County Clean Air Award, and in 1958, the Frank A. Chambers Award from the Air Pollution Control Association. He received the American Chemical Society's Award for Pollution Control in 1973. He was a member until 1973 of the Motor Vehicles Pollution Control Board, which became the California Air Resources Board in 1968. He was chairman of the National Air Quality Criteria Advisory Committee for the Environmental Protection Agency and a member of the Committee on Motor Vehicle Emission for the National Academy of Sciences. He served on committees for the Atomic Energy Commission and the National Institutes of Health and was also a member of President Richard Nixon's Task Force on Air Pollution in 1970. Haagen-Smit received the Hodgkins Medal of the Smithsonian Institution, the Cottrell Award of the National Academy of Science (1972), the $50,000 Alice Tyler Ecology Prize (1973), and the National Medal of Science (1973). He was also a trustee of the American Chemical Society. He retired to become professor emeritus of biochemistry at Caltech in 1971. He died of lung cancer in Pasadena.

• The California Institute of Technology maintains a historical file on Haagen-Smit, but the location of his papers is unknown. Important articles by Haagen-Smit include "Smell and Taste," *Scientific American* 186, no. 3 (Mar. 1952): 28–32; "Essential Oils," *Scientific American* 189, no. 2 (Aug. 1952): 70–74; "Progress in Smog Control," *Engineering and Science* 21, no. 9 (June 1958): 5–11; "Air Conservation," *Science* 128 (17 Oct. 1958): 869–78; "The Control of Air Pollution," *Scientific American* 210, no. 1 (Jan. 1964): 25–31; and "Man and His Home," *Vital Speeches of the Day*, 28 Apr. 1970. James Bonner wrote an interesting tribute to his colleague, "Arie Jan Haagen-Smit, 1900–1977," *Engineering and Science* 40, no. 4 (May–June 1977): 28–29. Obituaries are in the *New York Times*, 17 Mar. 1977, and the *Washington Post*, 20 Mar. 1977.

KATHY J. COOKE

HAAN, William George (4 Oct. 1863–26 Oct. 1924), army officer, was born in Crown Point, Indiana, the son of Nicholas Haan and Anna Marie Weins, farmers who had emigrated from Germany in 1850. Nicknamed "Bunker" early in his youth because of his large physique, Haan entered the U.S. Military Academy in West Point, New York, in 1885. He graduated in 1889, ranking twelfth in a class of forty-nine, and was commissioned a second lieutenant in the artillery.

Over the next several years Haan served with artillery regiments in California and New York and taught military science and tactics at the Northern Illinois Normal School. From 1898 to 1901 he was stationed in the Philippine Islands, where he was cited on two occasions for "conspicuous gallantry" in actions with his artillery battery against the Spanish in the final days of the Spanish-American War and against insurgents in the early days of the Philippine Insurrection. After successively holding the posts of depot, brigade, and district quartermaster, Haan became assistant secretary to the military governor of the Philippine Islands. Following two years of troop duty after his return to the United States in the summer of 1901 Haan, then a captain in the coast artillery, was named one of the original members of the newly created War Department General Staff, 13 August 1903 to 13 August 1906. While with the General Staff he went to Panama on a confidential mission to report on conditions there after its revolt from Colombia in November 1903, and from 1 May 1904 to 1 August 1905 he attended the Army War College. Also in 1905 he married Margaret Hawes, the daughter of an army officer. Haan was acting chief of staff, Pacific Division, from 18 April 1906

to 15 July 1906 and chief of staff, Maneuver Camp at American Lake, Washington, from 15 July 1906 to 30 September 1906.

From 1906 to 1917 Haan rose to the rank of colonel while holding a variety of field, staff, and special assignments. As acting chief of staff of the Pacific Division in 1906, he helped to direct relief work following the San Francisco earthquake and fire. Other posts indicate Haan's increasing importance: military secretary of the Army of Cuban Pacification from 1906 to 1907; chief of staff of the Eastern Department from 1913 to 1914, the most important staff position in the army at that time; and two stints with the Land Defense Board in the Office of the Chief of Artillery. After the United States entered World War I in April 1917 Haan was promoted to the temporary rank of brigadier general and given command of the Fifty-seventh Field Artillery Brigade. At the end of the year he was promoted to the temporary rank of major general and appointed commander of the Thirty-second Division, then training at Camp MacArthur, Texas, and made up of units that were originally part of the Michigan and Wisconsin National Guards. In early 1918 Haan took his division to France, where it initially served as a depot division, providing replacements for combat divisions and labor troops for the Services of Supply. Then the Thirty-second Division was designated a combat division and prepared for combat in Alsace before being sent to the Marne sector.

In late July 1918 Haan's division was sent to the Marne sector to participate in the Marne-Aisne offensive. From 29 July to 7 August the soldiers in the division were in almost constant action with the Germans in the Allied drive down the spine of the Marne Salient, pushing the Germans off the banks of the heavily defended Ourcq River and seizing the town of Fismes in heavy fighting. When the combat-weary Thirty-second Division was unable to gain control of a bridgehead across the Vesle River, some staff officers in the French Sixth Army and the American III Corps suggested that the division suffered from a lack of drive and recommended that Haan be relieved. But Haan's superiors believed that the fault lay with the inadequate artillery and engineer assistance he had received and that Haan had demonstrated a determined ardor in leading his men in the face of stiff German resistance. Several weeks later Haan successfully fought a tough five-day battle to capture and secure the town of Juvigny and surrounding points on the western side of the salient during the Oise-Aisne offensive.

After a month's rest to absorb 5,000 soldiers, mostly recent draftees who were virtually untrained, to replace the 6,800 casualties suffered in the summer's fighting, Haan's division took part in the American First Army's Meuse-Argonne offensive. Entering the battle on 4 October, nine days after the offensive had started, Haan's division and those flanking it reached the formidable heights northwest of Romagne by 10 October, after enduring unrelenting German artillery and machine-gun fire. Four days later, in a brilliant feat, the Thirty-second Division captured the vital

Côté Dame Marie, helping to crack the *Kriemhilde Stellung* (Hindenburg Line) and to pave the way for the American advance to the Meuse River.

Shortly after the war's end in November 1918 Haan became commander of the VII Corps, part of the American occupation army in Germany. Returning to the United States with the Thirty-second Division in the spring of 1919, he was appointed director of the War Plans Division of the General Staff. For the next two years he worked on the postwar demobilization and reorganization of the army. Haan retired from the army in 1922 with the permanent rank of major general.

Haan was a soldier who, despite his hard-driving style, earned the affection of his troops and was highly respected by his wartime superiors for his tactical skills and dependability in carrying out difficult assignments. Having begun his career when the army was little more than a frontier constabulary, he epitomizes the officers of his generation who successfully met the challenge of command in modern war as the American army emerged as a major fighting force in the international arena. Haan died in Washington, D.C.

• Haan's papers, which cover his career unevenly, are in the State Historical Society of Wisconsin in Madison. The best source for Haan's service during World War I is *The 32nd Division in the World War: 1917–1919* (1920), a concise history prepared by the division's historians that includes excerpts from Haan's letters to his wife. Assessments of Haan's generalship can be found in Robert L. Bullard, *Fighting Generals* (1944); Edward M. Coffman, *The War to End All Wars: The American Military Experience in World War I* (1968); and Allan R. Millett, *The General: Robert L. Bullard and Officership in the United States Army, 1881–1925* (1975). The most important sources for biographical information about Haan are *General Cullum's Biographical Register of the Officers and Graduates of the U.S. Military Academy*, vols. 4, 5, and 6 (1901, 1910, and 1921); and *Fifty-seventh Annual Report of the Association of Graduates of the United States Military Academy* (1926).

JOHN KENNEDY OHL

HAAS, Francis Joseph (18 Mar. 1889–29 Aug. 1953), priest and government official, was born in Racine, Wisconsin, the son of Peter Haas, a grocer, and Mary O'Day. He studied at St. Francis Seminary in Milwaukee, was ordained a priest in 1913, and received a Ph.D. in sociology from the Catholic University of America in 1922.

Haas served on the faculty of St. Francis Seminary for nine years and then in 1931 was appointed director of the National Catholic School of Social Service in Washington, D.C., an institution established during World War I to train young women for careers in social work. With the inauguration of President Franklin Roosevelt in 1933, Haas was recruited into government service. He served on the National Recovery Administration's Labor Advisory Board and its General Code Authority, and also on the National Labor Board, a bipartisan panel appointed in 1933 to mediate threatened work stoppages. He was a member of the

Committee to Report on Changes in Business and Labor Standards after the demise of the NRA and, in 1934, was coauthor of the Haas-Dunnigan Plan, which brought an end to the violent truckers' strike in Minneapolis.

In 1935 Haas was recalled to Milwaukee as rector of St. Francis Seminary, but he returned to Washington two years later, this time as dean of the School of Social Science at Catholic University. His government work resumed immediately. He served as special commissioner of conciliation for the Department of Labor, as a member of both the Wisconsin Labor Relations Board and the Labor Policies Board of the Works Progress Administration, and as White House emissary in efforts to heal the split between the American Federation of Labor and the Congress of Industrial Organizations.

In May 1943 President Roosevelt appointed Haas to chair the reconstituted Fair Employment Practices Committee. That summer he presided over hearings into alleged discrimination in hiring practices in the railroad and in other defense industries and spent three days in Detroit investigating the causes of a violent racial disturbance.

After four months with the FEPC, Haas was transferred to Michigan as bishop of Grand Rapids. As the number of Catholics in his diocese increased during the postwar years, he erected new parishes, enlarged the school system, and expanded services to the poor and elderly. He also continued his government service, arbitrating several strikes for the Department of Labor and serving on President Harry Truman's Committee on Civil Rights in 1946–1947.

Haas wrote numerous articles and pamphlets supporting collective bargaining, higher wages, and better working conditions. They include *Man and Society* (1930), *Catholics, Race and Law* (1947), and *Seven Pillars of Industrial Order* (1952). He also was a frequent speaker at local and national labor conventions. He was a big man physically, six feet tall and 200 pounds, with a head of sandy hair that earned him the nickname "Red" long before conservative business leaders adopted it to suggest what they considered his leftist labor views. At his death, in Grand Rapids, Michigan, he was remembered as "the big friend of the little guy."

• The major collection of Haas's papers is in the Department of Archives and Manuscripts of the Catholic University of America. Additional materials can be found in the Archives of the Archdiocese of Milwaukee and of the Diocese of Grand Rapids, the State Historical Society of Wisconsin, the Franklin D. Roosevelt and Harry S. Truman libraries, and the pertinent government collections in the National Archives. A full-length biography of Haas is Thomas E. Blantz, C.S.C., *A Priest in Public Service: Francis J. Haas and the New Deal* (1982). Shorter studies are Blantz, "Francis J. Haas: Priest and Government Servant," *Catholic Historical Review* 57 (Jan. 1972): 571–92; Franklyn Kennedy, "Bishop Haas," *The Salesianum* 39 (Jan. 1944): 7–14; Philip Land, S.J., "Bishop Haas and Monsignor Ryan," *America*, 12 Sept. 1953, pp.

573–74; and Constance Randall, "A Bio-Bibliography of Bishop Francis J. Haas" (M.A. thesis, Catholic Univ. of America, 1955).

THOMAS E. BLANTZ

HABERLE, John (1856–3 Feb. 1933), painter, was born in New Haven, Connecticut, the son of George Frederick Haberle, a tailor, and Katherine Meyer, German immigrants. At the age of fourteen he was apprenticed to Punderson and Crisand, New Haven printers, working there for four years as a lithographer and engraver. He continued in this trade in Montreal, Providence, and New York City until returning to New Haven in 1880. Yale University's Peabody Museum of Natural History then employed him as a designer and preparator.

Haberle's only formal art training was at the New York Academy of Design in 1884–1885. Back in New Haven, he resumed work at the Peabody Museum and established a home studio, becoming the local specialist in small trompe l'oeil paintings. One of his currency paintings, *Imitation* (Berry-Hill Galleries, New York City), was purchased in 1887 by the prominent collector Thomas B. Clarke for $5,000. The work was described as "an assortment of familiar objects painted with microscopic detail and descriptive imitativeness of observation and skill." Clarke wrote, "W. M. Harnett . . . studied the picture . . . and said that he had never seen such deception anywhere." Haberle's career was launched.

From 1887 to 1897 Haberle produced at least a hundred trompe l'oeil works, many still unlocated. These illusionistic deceptions, painted to exact scale in an impeccable oil technique, were the wittiest and most original of the period. These paintings were primarily composed of small, flat, ordinary objects—often including paper currency—that were casually arranged against a flat background, defying gravity, and were frequently signed with a simulated tintype self-portrait. Haberle's currency paintings were so accurate that the U.S. Secret Service threatened to arrest him for forgery.

While Haberle did exhibit at various art academies, his main venues were hotel and theater lobbies, stationery stores, bookstores, and even saloons, as well as large expositions in the Midwest. The official art world dismissed trompe l'oeil painting as deceptive visual trickery. His clients were primarily businessmen.

In 1889 Haberle's painting *USA*, a conglomeration of currency, laudatory newspaper clippings, and postage stamps, was exhibited at the Art Institute of Chicago. The *Chicago Interocean*'s art critic accused Haberle of fraud, asserting that the objects were just pasted onto the canvas. Furious, Haberle confronted the critic, who had to retract his statement. The newspaper reported that "Eastman Johnson, dean of American painters . . . had a very serious time proving to himself that Mr. Haberle's painting was not what it appeared to be [i.e., painted not pasted]." This publicity brought Haberle commissions and more sales. His compositions grew larger and more complex, often including ambiguities and ironic personal references.

Time and Eternity (1888, New Britain [Conn.] Museum of American Art) is Haberle's version of the *vanitas* theme. A man's pocket watch hangs above a newspaper clipping entitled "Time and Eternity, Bob Ingersoll." At right, rosary beads are suspended over playing cards, theater stubs, a woman's photograph, and pawnbroker and lottery receipts. The whole ensemble suggests that the noted agnostic lecturer's celebrated preaching had been rejected in favor of Christianity.

Bachelor's Drawer (1890–1894, Metropolitan Museum of Art, New York City) is Haberle's most famous, most complex, and most autobiographical painting. An assortment of about fifty objects, mostly flat and with witty personal references, is casually arranged against the exterior of a bureau drawer, which is nailed shut. Laudatory news clippings, currency, and playing cards, along with theater, lottery, and steamship ticket stubs, among other items, create a complex arrangement at right. A used cigar box top nailed to the wooden surface and holding a comb, corncob pipe, shoelace, and other personal objects is the centerpiece. A tintype of the artist is wedged above a nude "girlie" photograph. *Bachelor's Drawer* represents the end of the carefree life of the bachelor. (Haberle married Sarah Emack of New Haven about this time.) In 1894 the *New Haven Evening Leader* stated, "The artist's eyes were nearly ruined in painting it . . . it is the last of its kind Mr. Haberle is to make."

In 1890 Haberle completed his two largest works, *Grandma's Hearthstone* (Detroit Institute of Art) and *Japanese Corner* (Museum of Fine Arts, Springfield, Mass.). *Grandma's Hearthstone*, a depiction of an American colonial fireplace and overmantle cluttered with antique bric-a-brac, with a fire crackling on the hearth, was commissioned by James T. Abbe, a rich businessman who longed for the "good old simple days" in preindustrial New England. *Japanese Corner* strikes an exotic note, showing an elaborate grouping of Japanese objects enclosed by a black lacquer screen. It represents the late Victorian taste for newly discovered Japanese art and culture. Both works were painted in Haberle's studio in Morris Cove outside New Haven, where the artist moved in about 1886 with his wife and two daughters.

With his eyesight failing, around 1895 Haberle shifted to a loose, impressionist style, painting still-life and animal compositions. His fame and prosperity faded. He died in Morris Cove poor and forgotten until a chance rediscovery in 1949 by art scholar Alfred Frankenstein restored him to American art history.

Haberle's trompe l'oeil paintings remain significant because of their affinity with twentieth-century surrealism and pop art. Ordinary, incongruous objects, even discards, casually arranged, are the subject in many Haberle paintings, as they are in the works by surrealists such as Duchamps and Dali. Their compositions ironically debunk conventional art subject matter and elevate ordinary objects to the category of art.

Pop artists such as Andy Warhol used dollar bills, soup cans, and photographs of movie stars in their paintings as Haberle used similar commercial objects in his. Haberle's unique achievement reflects the timeless American taste for the tangible and the real in a materialist society, as well as the fondness for a good practical joke.

• The Alfred Frankenstein Papers in the Archives of American Art, Smithsonian Institution, Washington, D.C., contain Haberle's notes and related material. Haberle is included in Frankenstein, *After the Hunt: William Harnett and Other American Still Life Painters 1870–1900* (1960), pp. 115–22. Gertrude Grace Sill, *John Haberle, Master of Illusion* (1985), an exhibition catalog, is an important source. See also Sill, "John Haberle: Master of Illusion," *Magazine Antiques* 126 (Nov. 1984): 1227–33, and "Two Rediscovered Paintings by John Haberle," *Magazine Antiques* 132 (Nov. 1987): 1118–21. See the discussion of *Bachelor's Drawer* by Doreen Bolger Burke in *American Paintings in the Metropolitan Museum of Art*, vol. 3 (1980), pp. 277–81. Haberle is discussed in Russel Burke and William Gerdts, *American Still-Life Painters 1690–1960* (1971), pp. 157–58. An obituary is in the *New Haven Register*, 5 Feb. 1933.

GERTRUDE GRACE SILL

HABERSHAM, James (June 1715?–28 Aug. 1775), planter-merchant in colonial Georgia, royal councilor, and acting governor, was born in Beverly, Yorkshire, England, the son of James Habersham, a dyer and innkeeper, and Elizabeth Sission. His mother died when he was seven; subsequently his father apprenticed him to his uncle, Joseph Habersham, a London merchant. From him he mastered the import trade in hides, indigo, and sugar. By the age of twenty-one he had assumed charge of two sugar-refining houses connected with his uncle's interests. In 1736 Habersham came under the religious influence of George Whitefield and his evangelical ministry. Within a few months of first hearing the young deacon, Habersham had become both zealous convert and close, devoted friend. As such, he determined to accompany Whitefield on a mission to Georgia despite objections from his uncle.

In May 1738 the two men arrived in Georgia and took responsibility for religious and orphan affairs in Savannah. Upon Whitefield's return to England for ordination a few months later, Habersham found himself supervising both matters alone. Personality and religious conflicts soon developed between Habersham and William Stephens, Savannah-based secretary and authority figure for the Georgia Trustees, the philanthropic group in England that had full responsibility for governing and developing the colony in its first twenty years. To curtail the conflict, Habersham removed the orphans to Bethesda, a self-sustaining school and religious community being developed by Whitefield ten miles from Savannah. Although religious matters in Savannah continued to attract Habersham's interest, Bethesda became both his home and primary workplace until 1744. While superintendent at Bethesda in 1740, he met and married Mary Bolton, a sixteen-year-old student at the orphanage whose fa-

ther, a Philadelphia merchant, had been converted by Whitefield. Ten children were born during their 23-year marriage, but only three survived infancy and childhood.

In 1743 Habersham formed a partnership with Francis Harris, former clerk in the Trustees' store in Savannah, for transporting supplies directly to Bethesda from Charleston. The partnership flourished even as the Trustees' monopoly over trade and supplies for Georgia loosened with colonial growth. Seizing an obvious trade opportunity, the partners began merchandising provisions for the fledgling colony. By 1744 they were keeping a store in Savannah, and in 1745 Habersham resigned his post at Bethesda to enter full-time trade in town. He and Harris thereafter made arrangements with a London factor to initiate direct Savannah-London trade in 1748. Their company became colonial Georgia's first truly successful transatlantic merchant house during the Trustee era.

Habersham's efforts so impressed the Georgia Trustees that they named him in 1749 to the board of assistants supervising their affairs in Georgia. When the Trustees surrendered their charter in 1752, the Crown continued Habersham's political position by naming him to the colonial royal council. During his term as a councilor, Habersham's relationships with Georgia's royal governors varied from power-control conflicts with John Reynolds to close friendship and collaboration with Sir James Wright (1716–1785) the third and last royal governor.

The 1750s royalization of Georgia also prompted changes in Habersham's economic position. By finalizing the Trustees' termination of restrictions on land ownership and slavery, which had occurred at the urging of Habersham and other Georgia landowners, the British Crown advanced the ambitions of an emerging Georgia upper class eager to emulate South Carolina's rice-planter elite. Armed with financial resources and government connections, Habersham acquired nearly 6,000 acres along Georgia's coastal rivers and just under 200 slaves before the end of the colonial era. His wise retention of merchant connections, while engaging in rice planting, gave him an estimated annual income of £2,000 and premier status among the planter-merchant oligarchy that controlled Georgia on the eve of the Revolution.

The first echoes of rebellion that reached Georgia with the Stamp Act crisis of 1765 dismayed Habersham. Wealthy and comfortable, he had no quarrel with Britain, and he supported Governor Wright throughout the crisis. Thereafter he assisted Crown efforts to keep the Georgia "liberty faction" subdued in controversies between Britain and America. In 1771 Governor Wright, describing Habersham as a "firm friend of Government," designated him acting governor while Wright visited England. In this capacity, Habersham dissolved the Georgia Assembly of 1772, with the prior approval of the Crown, rather than accept rebellion-prone Noble Wymberley Jones as Speaker. Yet, limited by poor health as he aged, Habersham had no real desire to be London's political voice in Georgia in uncertain times. He welcomed with relief Governor Wright's return in 1773.

Although Habersham remained supportive of royal government throughout the next year, one of his own sons had joined the revolutionary faction in the colony before the end of 1774. Poor health, the mental agony of father against son, and finally the news of Lexington and Concord overwhelmed Habersham's last feeble efforts to help Wright maintain royal government in 1775 by supporting resolutions and proclamations denouncing rebellion. He took passage in July with his youngest son on a northbound ship, ostensibly to recover his health. With the resignation of someone who knows his time and cause are passed, he died a month later at Brunswick, New Jersey.

In his lifetime Habersham helped transform colonial Georgia from a philanthropic experiment into a merchant-planter-slave culture linked to the transatlantic commercial world of Great Britain. As part of the governing elite of that culture, he despaired when revolution threatened its destruction even as age and gout threatened his own. With his death, Providence granted his expressed preference to live in America no longer than it was subordinate to, and protected by, Great Britain.

• Habersham letters are widely scattered. Significant manuscript locales include the Habersham papers in the Georgia Historical Society Library, Savannah; Habersham Family Papers in the Perkins Library of Duke University; and the Manuscript Colonial Records of Georgia at the University of Georgia Library and the Georgia Department of Archives. Published letters can be found throughout Allen Candler, ed., *The Colonial Records of the State of Georgia* (1904–1916; continuation edited by Kenneth Coleman and Milton Ready, 1976–), and in *Collections of the Georgia Historical Society*, vol. 6 (1904). A brief published survey of Habersham's life is William B. Stevens, "A Sketch of the Life of James Habersham," *Georgia Historical Quarterly* 3 (1919): 151–68. Larger accounts include Erwin Surrency, "The Life and Public Career of James Habersham, Sr." (master's thesis, Univ. of Georgia, 1949), and W. Calvin Smith, "Georgia Gentlemen: The Habershams of Eighteenth-Century Savannah" (Ph.D. diss., Univ. of North Carolina, 1971). See also W. W. Abbot, *The Royal Governors of Georgia, 1754–1775* (1959), and Kenneth Coleman, *Colonial Georgia: A History* (1976).

W. CALVIN SMITH

HABERSHAM, Joseph (28 July 1751–18 Nov. 1815), revolutionary leader, merchant, and politician, was born in Savannah, Georgia, the son of James Habersham and Mary Bolton. His father had followed George Whitefield to Georgia and eventually became the young colony's leading merchant. He was acting governor in the early 1770s and a Loyalist until his death in 1775. Out of concern for Joseph's health, his father sent him to Princeton, New Jersey, at age eight. Joseph attended the College of New Jersey (now Princeton University) from 1763 to 1767. The elder Habersham was disappointed in the results of this education and sent his son to England to be a merchant apprentice under Graham, Clark, and Company in 1768. James Habersham's friends enrolled the boy in

Woolwich Academy for several months to improve his handwriting and mathematics before putting him to work. Although Joseph's English career was reasonably successful, he was unhappy and disliked the English. He returned to Savannah in 1771.

At home Habersham joined first his brother James Habersham, Jr., and later his cousin Joseph Clay in trade partnerships. By 1774 he and Clay had emerged to the forefront of Savannah's revolutionaries. Habersham was a ringleader in the "Liberty Boys," who in 1775 raided Savannah's royal powder magazine. In meetings at Tondee's Tavern, he sat on a committee that drew up resolutions condemning the Intolerable Acts, and he served as a Georgia "Minute Man." He also outfitted a schooner, which he used to intercept the British munitions ship *Philippa*. As a member of Georgia's Council of Safety trade committee, he enforced trade regulations and participated in the appointment of militia officers and the ordering of arms and ammunition for the war effort.

In 1775 Habersham became a planter with approximately 4,300 acres and sixty-six slaves inherited from his father. The next year he married Isabella Rae; the couple had ten children. Nevertheless, revolutionary activities continued to preoccupy him. In 1776 he arrested his father's old friend, Georgia's royal governor James Wright. As a major and later colonel in Georgia's battalion in the Continental line, Habersham participated in early military engagements in the South. A fracas led to the accidental death of a fellow officer, and Habersham served as McIntosh's second in the controversial Gwinnett-McIntosh duel, angering the radical St. John's Parish faction. He resigned his commission in 1779 and spent the rest of the war in political posts, partly in exile in South Carolina and Virginia after the fall of Savannah.

Habersham, his brothers, and his cousin Clay actively worked to rebuild Georgia after the British evacuation in 1782. They were part of a clique numbering about twenty men who dominated Georgia politics and had leading places in the state's economy. The three Habersham brothers and Clay frequently served in the legislature. Joseph Habersham was Speaker of the house in 1785 and later served on the committee that drew up a revised constitution for the state. He also served in Georgia's convention that unanimously ratified the 1787 U.S. Constitution. His opposition to the notorious Yazoo land deal, which sharply divided Georgia politics, placed him in James Jackson's victorious faction. Habersham allied himself with Jackson to oppose a large land grant to an out-of-state company that the Jackson group believed was less favorable to the state than a local offer. The Jackson group pointed to gifts of stock to members of the legislature as evidence of corruption. The issue became central to the Jackson group's control of Georgia politics for the next decade.

During the 1780s and 1790s Habersham was increasingly prominent in Savannah affairs. He served on Savannah's new city council and became mayor in

1792–1793. At the same time, he rebuilt his plantation and reentered trade.

President George Washington appointed Habersham postmaster general in 1795. During his tenure, the number of miles of post roads increased from 1,875 to 20,817, and the number of post offices went from 75 to 903. He also experimented with government mail stagecoaches. Rapid growth helped promote rapid expansion of settlements. Under pressure from Thomas Jefferson, he resigned in 1801. The new president and Habersham differed over appointment policies: should civil servants be permanent or rotate in office? Habersham opposed wholesale replacements of postal officials for political reasons. Jefferson offered him a judgeship or the position of treasurer, but Habersham refused, preferring to return home to aid his brothers' widows and attend to family fortunes.

From 1802 to 1815 Habersham served as head of the Savannah branch of the Bank of the United States, which involved him in a court struggle over state taxation of the bank. Managing his dead brothers' estates and financial difficulties caused by a lawsuit brought by a British merchant against his father's heirs meant that Habersham needed to devote much of his attention to family affairs. He ran one of Georgia's early cotton commission and factorage businesses, laying the foundations for a prosperous enterprise that his sons continued. He was active in the affairs of Christ Church Parish, serving both as vestryman and warden, and he continued an interest in Bethesda, an orphanage school founded by Whitefield that was revived after the Revolution.

Habersham's name occasionally cropped up in a political context. In 1807 he chaired a meeting protesting the attack of the British *Leopard* on a U.S. naval vessel, the *Chesapeake*. In 1809 he presided over a meeting planning Savannah's Independence Day celebration, during which he presided over a banquet of the "Federal Republicans." Habersham apparently leaned toward the old Whig idea of nonpartisan government. He thought that the president should be chief executive of the country, not a party.

Habersham died in Savannah, having served his country, his state, his community, and his family. Although he was a hotheaded youth, he learned to direct his energy into patriotic service and economic advancement. History remembers him as a fiery revolutionary Liberty Boy, a conscientious public servant, and a successful merchant, planter, and banker who did much to aid Georgia in its transition from colony to state.

• Most of Habersham's surviving personal papers are at the Georgia Historical Society in Savannah. The society also holds the papers of his father, James Habersham, partially published in the *Collections of the Georgia Historical Society*, vol. 6 (1904), and his cousin Joseph Clay, partially published in the same series, vol. 8 (1913). The society's George Noble Jones Collection is also helpful. The Habersham family papers at Duke University, the papers of the Bank of the United States (microfilm copy at the American Philosophical Society in Philadelphia), and the Postmaster General Letterbooks at

the National Archives are other valuable sources. Additional important printed sources include Alfred Candler, ed., *Revolutionary Records of the State of Georgia*, vols. 1–3 (1908), especially vol. 2, pp. 84–87; and early Ga. newspapers. Indexes to the newspapers are at the Georgia Historical Society. W. Calvin Smith, "Georgia Gentlemen: The Habershams of Eighteenth-Century Georgia" (Ph.D. diss., Univ. of North Carolina, 1971), is by far the most complete and accurate account of Habersham's life. Kenneth Coleman, *The American Revolution in Georgia* (1958), gives background for the period 1763–1789. Genealogical information in Joseph G. B. Bulloch, *A History and Genealogy of the Habersham Family* (1901). Leonard White treats Habersham's administration of the post office in *The Federalists: A Study in Administrative History* (1948). George Lamplugh, *Politics on the Periphery: Factions and Parties in Georgia, 1783–1806* (1986), fills in Habersham's place in Ga. postrevolutionary politics.

FRANCES HARROLD

HACKETT, Bobby (31 Jan. 1915–7 June 1976), cornetist, trumpeter, and bandleader, was born Robert Leo Hackett in Providence, Rhode Island. His father was a blacksmith; his parents' names are unknown. Hackett played ukelele at age eight and studied violin for a year at age ten. He had added banjo by age twelve, when he acquired his first cornet. At fourteen he quit school to play guitar in what he described as a lousy band at a Chinese restaurant; he endured the job by courting Edna (maiden name unknown), his childhood sweetheart and future wife. He played banjo and guitar in little-known bands in Providence and Syracuse, where he began performing on cornet as well. From 1933 to 1934 he worked alongside Pee Wee Russell on Cape Cod and in Boston, and during this time he began drinking heavily. After performing from late 1934 in Providence while his father was suffering from terminal cancer, he returned to Boston early in 1936.

Moving to New York in 1937, he joined clarinetist Joe Marsala's band. Hackett married Edna in the summer of 1937; they had two children. He began many years of freelance recording in bands accompanying singers, his restrained, tuneful approach being well suited to that role, and many years playing a hybrid of Dixieland and swing in Eddie Condon's bands at Nick's club. He impersonated the sound of the legendary Bix Beiderbecke at Benny Goodman's celebrated Carnegie Hall concert on 16 January 1938. He regretted this performance in later years because his main inspiration was Louis Armstrong (though his miniaturized and polished adaptation of Armstrong's trumpeting recalled Beiderbecke's gentle manner) and because, with his own subtle originality, he hated to be called a copycat. Nonetheless it brought him to prominence.

The next day he began a long-standing affiliation with Condon on record, which later included a beautiful solo on "When Your Lover Has Gone," 1944. Apart from Nick's they also performed at concerts, with Hackett as a featured soloist at the Carnival of Swing on Randall's Island in the summer of 1938; in Hackett's own short-lived big band, which recorded "Embraceable You" in 1939; and on television, beginning with the first televised jazz show in 1942. After the failure of his big band put Hackett $2,300 in debt, he joined Horace Heidt's dance orchestra from September 1939 to June 1940 and again in November. When dental surgery temporarily prevented Hackett from playing cornet, Glenn Miller generously hired him as a guitarist, a job that lasted from 10 July 1941 until 24 September 1942. Soon Hackett was playing cornet again; he was the soloist on Miller's "String of Pearls" (1941).

He worked as a staff musician at NBC until November 1943, rejoined Marsala in August 1944, and toured with Glen Gray's Casa Loma Band from October 1944 to September 1946, during which time he stopped drinking. After leaving Gray he began fifteen years of work for ABC. For several years he and trumpeter Billy Butterfield were paired as the studio's "hot" soloists, and they developed an agreement whereby either was free to work independently as long as the other remained available. In 1947 Hackett participated in Armstrong's concert at Town Hall; that same year he also recorded "Body and Soul" with Frank Sinatra. Among many other recordings were a series of six romantic albums issued under Jackie Gleason's name, including *Music for Lovers Only*, and two albums as a co-leader with Jack Teagarden, *Coast Concert* (1955) and *Jazz Ultimate* (1957). By the time of this last album he had switched from cornet to its more brilliant cousin, the trumpet, at the urging of Armstrong, but he soon resumed playing both and continued to prefer cornet.

Sometime during the 1950s he became diabetic, though he said it was not a serious impediment. From late in 1956 to March 1958 he led a band at the Henry Hudson Hotel in New York. His saxophonist, Bob Wilber, described him thus (p. 71):

Bobby was a lovely man, a very gentle soul who had nothing bad to say about anybody. Even when a friend, exasperated by his perpetual good nature, asked him what he thought about Adolf Hitler, Bobby paused for a moment and replied in his deep voice, "Well, you gotta admit he was the best in his line." (!) He had a zany sense of humor, a funny way of looking at life, but also a definite paranoid streak. The two great dangers as far as he was concerned were the mafia and Communism. He always used to refer to the *New York Times* as the "Uptown Daily Worker."

Hackett played in Goodman's small group from October 1962 to July 1963, temporarily replaced an ailing Ray McKinley as the head of the New Glenn Miller Orchestra in summer 1964, and he toured Europe with Tony Bennett in 1965 and 1966. From 1967 he led groups at the Riverboat club in New York; singer Maxine Sullivan joined him there in 1969. The album *Live at the Roosevelt Grill*, recorded in April and May 1970, captures the sound and joy of Hackett's music at a time when he was leading a quintet that included Vic Dickenson. He moved from New York to Chatham, Massachusetts, on Cape Cod in 1971. That same year he performed in Japan with pianist and jazz entrepre-

neur George Wein. In 1972 he temporarily replaced Butterfield in the World's Greatest Jazz Band, with which he recorded three albums. He resumed his association with Goodman from 1973 to 1974, and again later in 1974, after a battle with pneumonia, and in 1976. He died of a heart attack at his home in Chatham. As a cornetist in jazz and popular music, Hackett was widely admired for his imaginative and tasteful lyricism and for the perfection of his playing.

• Interviews with Hackett are by Pat Harris, "'Bouquets to the Living': All Schools Dig Bobby Hackett," *Down Beat*, 9 Feb. 1951, pp. 1–2, 18–19, which includes recollections from fellow musicians; Richard Sudhalter, writing under the pseudonym Art Napolean, "A Conversation with Bobby Hackett," *Jazz Journal* 26, no. 1 (Jan. 1973): 2–6; Whitney Balliett, "Profile: More Ingredients," *New Yorker*, 12 Aug. 1972 (repr. in *Alec Wilder and His Friends* [1974]); George Simon, *Glenn Miller and His Orchestra* (1974), pp. 267–71; Ron D. Johnson, "Talking to Hackett," *Mississippi Rag*, June 1976, pp. 6–7; Warren W. Vache, Sr., "The Jazz Philosophy of Bobby Hackett," *Mississippi Rag*, June 1985, p. 1; and Max Jones, *Talking Jazz* (1987), pp. 113–25. Condon remembers Hackett in Eddie Condon, *We Called It Music* (1947); numerous photos from this affiliation appear in Condon and Hank O'Neal, *The Eddie Condon Scrapbook* (1973). Notes on Hackett's years in New York appear in Arnold Shaw, *The Street That Never Slept* (1971; repr. as *52nd Street: The Street of Jazz* [1977]), and in Robert Hilbert, *Pee Wee Russell: The Life of a Jazzman* (1993). Bob Wilbur describes the engagement at the Henry Hudson Hotel in his autobiography, written with Derek Webster, *Music Was Not Enough* (1987), pp. 71–73. For a chronology of Hackett's years with Goodman, see D. Russell Connor, *Benny Goodman: Listen to His Legacy* (1988). Max Jones surveys his career in an obituary, "Hackett: Beauty in Brass," *Melody Maker*, 19 June 1976, pp. 33, 36. Colorful descriptions of his playing style are Balliett, "Maestro," in *Ecstasy at the Onion* (1971), pp. 104–6, and Digby Fairweather, in *The Blackwell Guide to Recorded Jazz*, ed. Barry Kernfeld (1991), pp. 195–97. A listing of his recordings with other leaders is by Steve Holzer in *Record Research* 159–60 (Dec. 1978): 14; 161–62 (Feb.–Mar. 1979): 10; and 165–66 (Aug. 1979): 15.

BARRY KERNFELD

HACKETT, Francis (21 Jan. 1883–25 Apr. 1962), editor and writer, was born in City Kilkenny, Ireland, the son of John Byrne Hackett, a physician, and Bridget Doheny. Francis Hackett's youth was shaped in part by sociocultural conflicts within the family (between the Hacketts' education and social identity and those of the more provincial and less educated Dohenys), conflicts between Dr. Hackett's fervent Parnellism and the anti-Parnellites (those in Kilkenny, Clongowes Wood, and other Irish settings who opposed the nationalism of Charles Steward Parnell on pro-British or other political grounds and those who joined some Roman Catholic clergy in morally condemning Parnell's connection to Kitty O'Shea and thus Parnell), and Francis's rejection of Roman Catholicism and British imperialism. Frustrated because his family could not afford to pay for a postsecondary education, daunted by the prospect of becoming a clerk in the local bank for the rest of his life, hostile to both British and Roman Catholic influence in Ireland, Hackett decided, as had his brother Eddie Byrne Hackett and other relatives before him, to find a career in America. Hackett arrived in New York on 6 October 1901, well prepared for professional success in urban America. Educated by the Jesuits at the secondary level at Clongowes Wood College from 1897 to 1900, he was also widely read in British and American literature and qualified to write literary essays.

Hackett worked as a clerk in the Philbin, Beekman and Menken law firm and in *Cosmopolitan*'s advertising department, sold bookcloth at Holliston Mills, hired on as assistant paymaster on the SS *Pennsylvania* (a prep school/sea-voyage venture that instantly failed), and in December 1904 became a clerk in Chicago on the Chicago and Alton Railroad. In his first years in the United States, he read European, American, and Russian literature, wrote poetry and essays published in Irish and Irish-American periodicals, served as an Irish cultural propagandist (assisting John Quinn in founding an Irish literary society), and joined the Gaelic League in Chicago. (His brother Dominick and his sister Florence, in Kilkenny, also joined the Gaelic League.) Hackett coordinated Dr. and Mrs. Douglas Hyde's fundraising visit to Chicago. (Hyde, later the first president of Ireland, had translated Irish tales from Gaelic and had founded the Gaelic League in the 1890s.) Irish connections (Young Mary Prindiville linked him to Clara Laughlin among others) introduced Hackett to the Little Room, the headquarters of Chicago's genteel culture.

Little Room connections (Laughlin) brought Hackett work as a freelance writer, including a short muckraking series for Bobbs-Merrill's the *Reader* magazine on the life of the clerk and cub reporter. He worked briefly in Marshall Field's wholesale house basement and for William Randolph Hearst's *Chicago American* and by 1906 was writing reviews, features, and editorials for the *Chicago Evening Post*. *Evening Post* and Little Room connections (Laughlin had introduced him to Franklin Head, Lorado Taft, Hamlin Garland, Harriet Monroe, Robert Herrick, Edith Wyatt, and Henry Blake Fuller, who, in turn, connected Hackett to his cousin Tiffany Blake, literary editor of the *Post*) led him also to a year of residency and teaching in Hull-House and to a new social life with the affluent and culturally hungry young professionals of Chicago's suburbs in the early years of the emerging reform period known in its political aspects as the Progressive Era.

As literary editor of the *Post* in 1908 and as founding editor of the paper's influential literary supplement, the *Friday Literary Review*, in March 1909, Hackett (with Floyd Dell, his associate editor and successor) supported literary realism, cultural radicalism (an attitude toward culture in an anthropological sense, partly drawn by Hackett from the writings of Thorstein Veblen, William James, George Bernard Shaw, H. G. Wells, and Russian and European writers, challenging conventional American and British assumptions about moral, intellectual, and economic behavior as well as

literary expressions of behavior), and socialized democratic reform. He excited influential readers with the quality of his literary criticism and the audacity of his comments on racial, sexual, gender, and cultural liberation (advocating, for instance, sexual love outside marriage, the liberation of women from gender-stereotyped roles, miscegenation as the way to turn Americans from their assumptions regarding "Negro" inferiority, and a literature capable of expressing all experience). Leigh Reilly, the *Post*'s editor, had helped Hackett create the influential supplement and had protected him as much as possible from the business office and the publisher's disturbed responses to reader reactions. But Hackett's capacity for irritated reaction and stubborn resistance emerged when the *Post* sought to curtail his personal references to a journalist he held in particular disdain. This and frustration brought on by the failure of the second of two disastrous love affairs led him to resign and spend the winter of 1911 on a farm near Madison writing portions of a novel. Hackett also resented being treated as a lackey in his role as Quinn's secretary at the Democratic National Convention in Baltimore in 1912. Defeated in love and friendship, his promising literary career stalled or worse, his father dying in Kilkenny, a broken Hackett returned to Ireland in 1912. There he read, wrote, nursed his father, considered job offers from the United States, and did some freelance work in Dublin and London.

Hackett returned to America in October 1913 and, at Herbert Croly's invitation, joined Croly, Walter Lippmann, Walter Weyl, and Philip Littell as founding editors of the *New Republic*, a magazine that quickly became politically, intellectually, and culturally influential. From the first issue in November 1914 until 1922, Hackett continued in this larger arena to support radical progressivism (supporting labor, women's rights, civil rights, and socialist movements and the extension of reform beyond politics and economics), cultural pluralism, and the widest range of expression in literature. His influence is clear in the enthusiastic response he received in 1918 and 1921 for collections of his *Friday Literary Review* and *New Republic* essays. In time his fierce independence, as it had with the *Evening Post* and John Quinn, led Hackett to break first with Lippmann and eventually with Croly over *New Republic* editorial positions, especially concerning Irish independence and agreements made in Europe at the end of World War I, the League of Nations, and radicalism in the early 1920s. His opposition to what he considered a *New Republic* desertion of Irish independence (eased he believed for some by British support for a Jewish homeland), Croly's religious preoccupation and disinterest in aggressive reform in the early 1920s, differences over the merits of the Soviet revolution in Russia, and the failure of others at the magazine sufficiently to share his disaffection and criticism led him to an increased sense of frustration. Having married Signe Toksvig in 1918, and having presumably secured (through his *New Republic* writings, his books, and his speeches on Ireland) short- to mid-term economic security, he resigned. In 1922 he and Toksvig began long freelance writing careers in Europe and America.

Although the couple would achieve a number of literary and financial successes, they often had very little income. Hackett's earlier income sources quickly vanished as Americans lost interest in Ireland and in the league. Hackett and Toksvig lived in England and France and (from 1927) in Ireland on loans from friends in New York and Chicago and on income from pieces published in American magazines. Hackett wrote a first novel (*That Nice Young Couple* [American ed., 1925]) praised by many significant critics in England and America, a financially and critically successful psychological history of Henry VIII (*Henry the Eighth* [1929]), a biography of Francis I (*Francis the First* [1935]), a novel that successfully examined the Ireland of his youth (*The Green Lion* [1936]), and a novel based on the life of Anne Boleyn (*Queen Anne Boleyn: A Novel* [1939]). His last novel (*The Senator's Last Night*), written and set in the United States, appeared in 1943.

The Irish censored novels by both Hackett and Toksvig. As a result, and now economically unable to continue to live as they had since 1929, they moved first to Denmark in 1937 but soon fled Nazi expansion and returned to America. There Hackett supplemented their shrinking income with pay as a critic at the *New York Times* (1944–1945) and as a literary editor at the *American Mercury*. His critically praised last collection of cultural essays (*On Judging Books*) appeared in 1947. He attacked especially Nazi totalitarianism and imperialism in an autobiographical volume (*I Chose Denmark* [1940]) and again in a 1941 book (*What "Mein Kampf" Means to America*). In 1935 and 1949 he and Toksvig brought lawsuits in defense of their literary property rights. Hackett sued Maxwell Anderson, asserting that his "Anne of a Thousand Days" had taken material from Hackett's earlier works on Anne Boleyn and Henry VIII. Toksvig sued a writer for having used without permission material from her published biography of Hans Christian Andersen. They bought a house near Bethel, Connecticut, and Hackett became a naturalized citizen of the United States in 1948. Financial difficulties, however, led them to sell their home, and from the early 1950s they lived in Denmark on very little money. Friends, especially Felix Frankfurter (one of the founding supporters, writers, and advisers for the *New Republic* and a Harvard law professor and U.S. Supreme Court justice; he had renewed his broken friendship with Hackett in 1929), helped connect them with literary work and foundations. Despite contracts and grants, Hackett turned from an unenthusiastic study of Charles V to write a play based on his Anne Boleyn novel and a book of reminiscences based on his first years in the United States (*American Rainbow: Early Reminiscences*, published posthumously in 1971). Despite initial support from businessman Huntington Hartford (heir to a retail fortune) and the interest of various actresses, the play was not performed. Hackett died in Virum, Denmark.

• The main collection of Hackett's correspondence is in the Royal Library, Copenhagen, but large holdings also exist in the Felix Frankfurter and Benjamin W. Huebsch papers in the Library of Congress. Hackett's published periodical works are in the files and indexes of American and European periodicals, in the columns of the Chicago *Evening Post* and its *Friday Literary Review*, in the *New Republic*, and in the *New York Times*. Hackett's reviews have also appeared in anthologies, but the three major collections of his literary essays are *Horizons* (1918), *The Invisible Censor* (1921), and *On Judging Books*. Hackett's historical writings include his 1936 and 1939 novels, his Irish volumes, and his biographies of Henry VIII and Francis I. Hackett's Irish studies are *Ireland: A Study in Nationalism* (1918) and *The Story of the Irish Nation* (1922). Hackett's autobiographical accounts are in many of his essays but are especially evident in *The Green Lion, I Chose Denmark*, and *American Rainbow*. Hackett's attacks on fascism and other expansionist and antidemocratic tendencies and his praise especially of small, socialized democracies appear in essays scattered through much of his career as a journalist but especially in his essays for *Survey* in the 1920s, *I Chose Denmark*, and *What "Mein Kampf" Means to America*. Unpublished secondary studies of Hackett include Hyland Packard, "Critic as Witness: Francis Hackett and His America, 1883–1914" (Ph.D. diss., Louisiana State Univ., 1970). Published essays on Hackett include Philip Littell, "F.H.," *New Republic*, 12 Oct. 1918, pp. 308–10; James Delehanty, "The Green Lion: In Memoriam Francis Hackett (1883–1962)," *Kilkenny Magazine*, Summer 1962, pp. 49–53; George A. Test, "Francis Hackett: Literary Radical without Portfolio," *Midcontinent American Studies Journal* 5 (Fall 1964): 24–37; Charles Angoff, "Francis Hackett," in *The Tone of the Twenties* (1966), pp. 209–16; and Hyland Packard, "From Kilkenny: The Background of an Intellectual Immigrant," *Eire-Ireland* 10 (Autumn 1975): 106–25. Obituaries are in the *New York Times* and the *London Times*, both 26 Apr. 1962.

HYLAND PACKARD

HACKETT, James Henry (15 Mar. 1800–28 Dec. 1871), actor, was born in New York City, the son of Thomas C. Hackett, a lieutenant in the Life Guards of the Prince of Orange when he migrated to New York in 1799. The name of his mother, the daughter of the Reverend Abraham Keteltas of Jamaica, Long Island, is unknown. Hackett was three when his father died, and he was brought up by his mother. Her close touch with wealthy Knickerbocker families, both in New York City and upstate, gave him a solid start in life. He attended school first at Union Hall Academy in New York City and then, at age fifteen, for one year at Columbia College. He dropped out after a serious illness and began reading law with General Robert Bogardus. But Hackett was soon enticed into the profitable grocery business, an activity that took him in 1820 to the thriving upstate town of Utica, New York, to run a business on his own. Along with him came Catharine Lee Sugg, an actress at the Park Theatre, whom he had married the previous year; the couple had one child. Though his enterprise failed, Hackett learned a good deal about the townspeople and particularly about the New England Yankees trading in the area. This background led him into a career of developing and acting native folk characters when he went on the stage in 1826.

After returning to New York City in the early 1820s, Hackett entertained his friends with Yankee folk stories and mimicries of English actors such as Edmund Kean. But when he saw English comedian Charles Mathews at the Park Theatre play his English, Irish, Scottish, and Welsh characters, all lightly satirized, he apparently saw how he could put his skill at mimicry and storytelling to work on the stage in satirizing Americans. After Mathews had returned to London, he had collected his American experiences into a full entertainment titled *Trip to America*, featuring Yankee Jonathan Doubikins, and its fame had spread to America. Mathews had pointed the way, and now it moved Hackett toward a stage career with materials Americans could make their own. Within a few years Hackett had not only introduced his version of the Yankee character but also other American folk types such as Kentucky backwoodsman Nimrod Wildfire and Dutchman Rip Van Winkle, the latter adapted to the stage from Washington Irving's folktale. Hackett had discovered a line of native comedy American actors could fully exploit.

A variety of "Yankees" had been seen on the American stage since Royall Tyler first gave him life in *The Contrast* in 1787. David Humphrey had further developed the folk character in *Yankey in England* (1815) and in the printed edition of that play appended a lexicon of Yankee speech, and in 1822 Samuel Woodworth had given his notion of the Yankee primary focus in *The Forest Rose*. But Hackett's approach, now influenced by Mathews, was not just that of making a prototype American as the others had, but of showing a realistic New Englander in all of his eccentricities. What Hackett first put together, probably working alone on his own material, set a line of comedy that was taken up by a string of native-born actors; when playwrights were available, a line of plays featured a smart, sly country bumpkin who could outsmart and outrun his city cousin. Hackett's penchant for telling Yankee stories—long, complex, and mostly without point—was worked into the format. Though he came from New York City, many thought he had caught the essence of the New Englander close to real life and turned the character into a primary stage entertainment.

Only a few months after he first took up acting in New York in 1826 Hackett went to London, undoubtedly to enhance his reputation, and the critics there give us a very good idea of his early work. His impersonations of Edmund Kean and Charles Macready were well received, even lauded, by both critics and audiences, but his "Yankees" were shouted off the stage. "Imagine an unknown actor," wrote one critic, "in an uncouth disguise, without ceremony or explanation, advancing to the front of the stage, and entertaining an audience with a cock-and-bull story in relation to persons and peculiarities of which nine out of ten of the spectators had not a single previous conception." He wore a black hat, a blue coat, a flowered waistcoat, blue-striped trousers, and a pigtail tied with a green eelskin. So eccentric and startling was Hackett's characterization that the critics, along with the audience, argued over whether Hackett was revealing an "authentic" Yankee or just doing a bad piece of acting. When Hackett returned to London again in 1832, his Yankee characters were much better received. But this time critics castigated him for converting Solomon Gundy, the principal character in George Colman's *Who Wants A Guinea?* into an American Yankee, especially when Colman himself, then the lord chamberlain, had to license the playing of this corrupted work. But the lord chamberlain gave reluctant permission, and Hackett not only played Solomon Swap, as he called his new character, in London but made it a permanent part of his repertoire in America, convulsing audiences wherever he played it.

On his return from London, to obtain playable pieces Hackett set up a play contest, offering $300 to the winner. James Kirke Paulding, then a budding writer, won with *Lion of the West; or, A Trip to Washington* (1831), whose main character, a "raw Kentuckian" and a genuine backwoods "screamer," was obviously a thinly disguised Davy Crockett figure. So successful was Colonel Wildfire that Hackett solicited two more versions, one by American John Augustus Stone, and the other, placing the colonel in New York, by English playwright Bayle Bernard.

By 1835 Hackett's repertoire included *The Kentuckian; Jonathan in England* (Solomon Swap); *Job Fox: The Yankee Valet; Major Jack Downing; Jonathan Doubikins; Rip Van Winkle; The Militia Muster*; and *Mons. Morbleu*, a satire on a French émigré. In addition, he did imitations of Edmund Kean and Charles Macready. Hackett stayed with this collection of pieces as he traveled America through the 1830s, gradually giving them up only when younger comedians such as George Hill (the "authentic Yankee") and Dan Marble ("the Yankee Jumper") came into competition with strong support from play reviewers. He first played his version of Rip Van Winkle at the Park Theatre in New York on 22 April 1830. Later Charles Burke and Joseph Jefferson both played Rip, with the latter becoming the Rip of renown, but Hackett had led the way and had made places in American comedy for the others.

Hackett's career, however, was far from over. Earlier he had taken up the playing of Shakespeare—*The Comedy of Errors, Richard III*, and even *Othello* (Iago). When he saw he had none of the gifts for tragedy, he gave that up and played Falstaff for most of his acting career in both parts of *Henry IV* and *The Merry Wives of Windsor*. In this role he was highly praised by both American and London critics.

When Hackett published his *Notes, Criticism, and Correspondence upon Shakespeare's Plays and Actors* in 1863, he brought to his subject his longtime experience. Essays on *Hamlet* and *King Lear* stand side by side with his comments on such Shakespearean actors as Edmund Kean, William Charles Macready, Charles Kemble, George Vandenhoff, Edwin Booth, Charles Kean, and Edwin Forrest. The most valuable parts of the book today are Hackett's detailed and specific comments on how they played their roles.

Over many years Hackett had managed a number of theaters: Howard Athenaeum in Boston, and in New York the Chatham Garden, the Bowery, the National (opera), and the Astor Place Theatre (during the 1849 Forrest-Macready riot). Hackett the businessman thus linked his early years in Utica with his later ones as theater manager. Out of this work, along with his acting career, he amassed a comfortable fortune.

In 1845 Catharine Lee Sugg died. In 1864 Hackett married Clara Cynthia Morgan, and out of this union, in 1869, James Keteltas Hackett was born. When the elder Hackett died in Jamaica, Long Island, New York, he was praised as one of America's finest actors and a comedian-innovator of the first rank.

• The Enthoven Collection at the Victoria and Albert Museum, London, has many of the pieces Hackett played in London in 1827–1828 and in 1832. See also the Lord Chamberlain's Collection at the British Museum, London. James Hackett, *Notes, Criticism, and Correspondence upon Shakespeare's Plays and Actors* (1863), is also useful as a measure of his whole career. The *New York Mirror* followed Hackett's career from the beginning and published a lithograph. See also the *Spirit of the Times* for his early years. The London newspapers for 6 Apr. 1827 and 18 Nov. 1832 are rich in critical detail. For Mathews's influence, see the *Memoirs of Charles Mathews*, ed. Anne Jackson Mathews (1839), and drawings of *Trip to America* (1824). Noah Ludlow, *Dramatic Life as I Found It* (1880), records much detail about Hackett's playing in the West, and George Odell and Joseph Ireland cover the New York scene. Montrose Moses, *Famous Actor-Families in America* (1906), provides an overview of the Hacketts, father and son. Francis Hodge, *Yankee Theatre* (1964), places James Hackett against the other actor-comedians in this genre and includes Humphrey's lexicon, an annotated listing of Yankee Theatre plays, and a useful bibliography. For a useful obituary see John Durand, "Souvenir of Hackett the Actor," *Galaxy* 14 (Oct. 1872): 550–56.

FRANCIS HODGE

HACKETT, James Keteltas (6 Sept. 1869–8 Nov. 1926), actor and theater manager, was born in Wolfe, Ontario, Canada, the son of James Henry Hackett, an actor best known for his portrayal of Falstaff, and Clara Cynthia Morgan. His father died two years after Hackett's birth. Hackett displayed his propensity for the theater early; at the age of eighteen he won much admiration as Touchstone in *As You Like It* and two years later as Othello. He also successfully acted as an amateur in the role of Carraway Bones, the undertaker in *Turned Up*. By the time he left the College of the City of New York in 1891 (with no degree), Hackett had committed himself to the theater. At his mother's insistence he briefly studied law at Columbia University but soon abandoned his studies and left for Philadelphia. In March 1892 he made his professional debut there in a three-line role as François in *The Broken Seal*, despite veteran manager Albert M. Palmer's criticism that he was too tall and too plain for the stage. For a short time Hackett toured as leading man to Lotta Crabtree, a popular entertainer-actress of the time,

until illness forced her off the stage. Hackett then joined Augustin Daly's renowned stock company for the 1892–1893 season. Several undistinguished temporary engagements ensued.

Late in 1895 Hackett joined Daniel Frohman's company at the Lyceum Theater in New York, leaving after one season to become the leading man for Daly's company. In 1897 he married Mary Mannering, an English actress who had come to the United States in 1896. The couple had one child before they divorced in 1910. In 1911 Hackett married Beatrice H. Beckley, a London actress with whom he had appeared earlier; the number of their children, if any, is unknown.

Early in Hackett's career audiences identified him with romantic roles of the "cloak and sword" school, such as the protagonists in *The Prisoner of Zenda, Don Caesar de Bazan*, and *Rupert of Hentzau*. He strove to rid himself of this reputation by appearing in Shakespearean productions. His first major Shakespearean role was Mercutio in *Romeo and Juliet* (Maude Adams and William Faversham appeared in the title roles) in 1899. He further attempted to broaden his scope with his appearance in 1902 in *The Crisis*, a dramatization of a bestseller by the American novelist Winston Churchill. Hackett played Captain Stephen Brice, displaying what critics called "becoming modesty," "quiet manliness," and "chivalrous warmth." Nevertheless, Hackett reverted to earlier form in a 1904 production of *The Fortunes of the King*, a melodramatic treatment of Charles II. In 1902, with Harrison Grey Fiske, Mrs. Fiske, and Henrietta Crosman, Hackett organized and presided over the Independent Booking Agency in an attempt to control his own bookings. The Theatre Syndicate, which held a monopoly on the American theater, allowed the Independent Booking Agency to function for two years, then destroyed it by disallowing its use of theaters adequate for their productions. Hackett had no choice but to rejoin the syndicate.

After the success of his 1905 production of Alfred Sutro's *The Walls of Jericho* Hackett rented a theater in New York and renamed it the Hackett Theater. His fortunes varied in the new facility; by 1908 he had appeared in *The Prisoner of Zenda*, a successful romantic potboiler produced with the hope of boosting ticket sales. In 1912 Hackett filmed the production for the Famous Players in Famous Plays Company, founded by Adolph Zukor to film the theater's greatest dramas.

In 1914 Hackett came into a fortune of more than $1 million, willed to him by his niece Millicent Hackett Trowbridge. The two were never on good terms, but Trowbridge died intestate and incapable of rewriting her will, so the courts awarded Hackett the money as her next of kin. Freed from financial worries, Hackett immediately plunged into Shakespeare, producing and starring in *Othello* in 1914 and *Macbeth* in 1916. During World War I Hackett appeared in *Out There* with an all-star cast, netting the Red Cross $700,000 in three weeks. In 1919 he performed with the Theater Guild in New York, creating the title role in *The Rise of Silas Lapham*.

In 1920 Hackett's company produced *Macbeth* in London. The success of the production led to an invitation to play in Paris; there Hackett received the Legion of Honor in 1921 for his acting. Hackett also played Othello in Paris, London, and Stratford-upon-Avon; subsequently he was twice the guest of the king and queen of England at Buckingham Palace. Hackett returned to the United States in 1924 but did not act there again. While seeking medical treatment for an ongoing liver problem, he died in Paris.

Although Hackett won stardom and money playing dashing romantic heroes, his Shakespearean endeavors proved substantial achievements. For his role as Macbeth, for example, he studied with Louis Calvert, considered the ablest Shakespearean director of his time. The *New York Times* applauded Hackett's modesty and intelligence, calling his Macbeth "the most nearly adequate since Henry Irving." Critic John Corbin, also reviewing *Macbeth* for the *New York Times*, praised Hackett's voice, which he considered "always an organ of great range and power." Corbin also noted that Hackett showed Macbeth's "underlying goodness which turns to weakness, the morbid mysticism which has more than a touch of psychic degeneracy." London critics agreed, claiming that "he played with dignity and natural command with which no English performance within memory can compare to complete advantage." Other critics gave Hackett mixed reviews. Of his Mercutio, William Winter in *Shakespeare on the Stage* said, "Mr. Hackett embodied Mercutio as a jolly good fellow, a roisterer, shallow in feeling and metallic in style, but his delivery of the text was, in general, refreshing, by reason of his clear articulation: the Dream Speech, however, was for some inscrutable reason, spoken mostly in a whisper."

Hackett's employment of Joseph Urban as scenic designer helped advance the New Stagecraft movement in the United States. Urban, an Austrian, introduced many techniques into the United States that were later adopted by American-born designers, including the simplified and cleaner designs typical of the New Stagecraft. Theater historians have summed up Hackett's career by suggesting his romantic style limited his accomplishments in the great Shakespearean roles, however valiant his efforts along those lines.

• The New York Public Library Theatre Collection at Lincoln Center holds a substantial scrapbook of Hackett materials. Hackett's published articles include "Macbeth," *Green Book Magazine*, June 1916, pp. 1107–9; "My Beginnings," *Theatre*, Oct. 1906, pp. 275–76; "Some Accidents and Others," *Green Book Album*, Aug. 1909, pp. 368–73; "The Stage Villain," *Green Book Album*, Jan. 1909, pp. 201–2; and "A University for the Drama," *Independent*, 23 Apr. 1903. See also Margherita Hamm, *Eminent Actors in Their Homes* (1902); Montrose Moses, *Famous Actor-Families in America* (1906); Daniel Frohman, *Memories of a Manager* (1911); and Lewis C. Strang, *Famous Actors of the Day in America* (1900). A detailed obituary is in the *New York Times*, 9 Nov. 1926.

STEPHEN M. ARCHER

HADAS, Moses (25 June 1900–17 Aug. 1966), scholar and educator, was born in Atlanta, Georgia, the son of David Hadas and Gertrude Draizen, Russian-Jewish immigrants. His father was a shopkeeper, a scholar, and a writer in Hebrew and Latin on the rabbinical exegesis of the Pentateuch. After studying Greek and Latin at Boys High School in Atlanta, Hadas earned his B.A. at Emory University in 1922 and his M.A. in classics at Columbia University in 1925. For scholarly, not theological, reasons, he began study in 1922 at the Jewish Theological Seminary in New York and received a rabbinical degree in 1926. He taught for two years at the University of Cincinnati (1926–1928), after which he returned to Columbia and earned his Ph.D. in 1930. His dissertation, *Sextus Pompey*, was published in 1930 and is still considered the definitive treatment of the subject.

He married Ethel J. Elkus in 1926 and had two children with her; they divorced in 1945. That same year, he married Elizabeth M. Chamberlayne, a former student of his, with whom he had two children. Meanwhile, he had begun a long, solid, distinguished academic and publishing career. His residence was on fashionable Riverside Drive, in upper Manhattan. At Columbia nearby, he rose steadily in academic rank: instructor (1925–1926), assistant professor (1930), associate professor (1946), and professor (1953). He was appointed Jay Professor of Greek, a signal recognition, three years later. Together with colleagues such as Gilbert Highet, Hadas made his classics department one of the best anywhere. His phenomenal accomplishments were unusual: he was an early example of a successful American Jew in what was then a pervasively anti-Semitic profession. However, his rise in the ranks may be explained to a degree by his formal, ferocious rejection of both traditional Judaism and official Christianity. He preferred Plutarch, one of his most beloved authors, and Voltaire, an iconoclastic intellectual exemplar. During World War II Hadas was a civilian employee of the Office of Strategic Services, assigned to North Africa and also to Greek resistance movements in the eastern Mediterranean area (1943–1946). He occupied the Jay chair until his death in Aspen, Colorado.

In addition to being a demanding professor much sought after by the best students, Hadas was a productive scholar and a skillful translator of works in Greek, Latin, Hebrew, and German. In just under forty years, he published upward of forty books, which may be divided into specialized studies, general histories, editions, and translations. His most original books include *Hellenistic Culture: Fusion and Diffusion* (1959); *Humanism: The Greek Ideal and Its Survival* (1960); *Old Wine, New Bottles: A Humanist Teacher at Work* (1962); and *Heroes and Gods: Spiritual Biographies in Antiquity* (1965; coauthored with Morton Smith). More general works include *A History of Greek Literature* (1950); *A History of Latin Literature* (1952); *Ancilla to Classical Reading* (1954); *Imperial Rome* (1965; coauthored with the editors of Time-Life Books); and *The Living Tradition* (1967).

He translated and edited Euripides, *Electra* (1950); *Aristeas to Philocrates: Letter of Aristeas* (1951); *The Third and Fourth Books of Maccabees* (1953); *Three Greek Romances* (1953); *Heinrich Heine*, Heine's autobiography (1956); *A History of Rome from Its Origins to 529 A.D., as Told by the Roman Historians* (1956); Julius Caesar, *The Gallic War, and Other Writings* (1957); Heliodorus, *Ethiopian Romance* (1957); Plutarch, *On Love, the Family, and the Good Life* (1957); *The Stoic Philosophy of Seneca: Essays and Letters of Seneca* (1958); *Latin Selections: Florilegium Latinum* (1961; coauthored with Thomas Suits); *The Plays of Seneca* (1965), having earlier published separate translations of *Oedipus* (1955), *Medea* (1956), and *Thyestes* (1957); and Berechiah ha-Nakdan, *Fables of a Jewish Aesop* (1967). He also translated three plays by Seneca in *Roman Drama . . .* (1965).

He was a cotranslator of Alfred Körte, *Hellenistic Poetry* (1929), and translated Joseph ben Meir Zabara, *The Book of Delight* (1932); Hermann Vogelstein, *Rome* (1940); Tacitus, *Complete Works* (1942); Elias Bickerman, *The Maccabees: An Account of Their History from Their Beginnings to the Fall of the House of the Hasmoneans* (1947); Ferdinand Gregorovius, *The Ghetto and the Jews of Rome* (1948); Jakob Burckhardt, *Age of Constantine the Great* (1949); Karl Viëtor, *Goethe, the Poet* (1949); Walter F. Otto, *The Homeric Gods* (1954); and Livy, *A History of Rome* (1962).

He edited *The Complete Works of Tacitus . . .* (1942); *Solomon Maimon: An Autobiography* (1947); Plato, *Euthyphro, Apology, Crito, and Symposium* (1953); *The Greek Poets* (1953); Cicero, *Basic Works* (1961); *Essential Works of Stoicism* (1961); Aristophanes, *Complete Plays* (1962); Suetonius, *The Lives of the Twelve Caesars* (1963); *Greek Drama* (1965); and *The Complete Plays of Sophocles* (1967). He also prepared an abridgment of Edward Gibbon's *The Decline and Fall of the Roman Empire* in 1962 and over the years published fifty or more articles in *Classical Weekly* and *Classical World* and essays in other journals as well.

Four books may be cited as representative of the work of the formidably erudite Hadas. *A History of Greek Literature* has great range, makes use of the best scholarship, employs modern techniques of literary analysis, and is inspirited by a style combining precision and liveliness. *A History of Latin Literature* traces and appreciatively analyzes Roman writing from its beginnings through the Dark Ages, including Saint Augustine and other Christian authors. *Heroes and Gods* studies the mythmaking and divinization processes of early biographers, who conflated facts and fables to create awe-inspiring personalities. *The Living Tradition* probes the origins of the humanistic vision and reveals the slowly evolving concept of the primacy of humankind. Hadas also wields a style that is pithy, witty, sensitive, flexible, and erudite. All his professional life, Hadas argued for a classically grounded education in what he regarded as a world grown dangerously materialistic, scientific, and technological.

• Much of Hadas's correspondence, many of his manuscripts, and some memorabilia are in libraries at Columbia University. There are autobiographical touches in his *Old Wine, New Bottles* (1962) and "The Religion of Plutarch," *South Atlantic Quarterly* 46 (Jan. 1947): 84–92. An informative, laudatory sketch is Gilbert Highet, "Moses Hadas, 1900–1966," *Classical World* 60 (Nov. 1966): 92–93. A long obituary, with photograph, is in the *New York Times*, 18 Aug. 1966.

ROBERT L. GALE

HADDEN, Briton (18 Feb. 1898–27 Feb. 1929), magazine founder and editor, was born in Brooklyn, New York, the son of Crowell Hadden, Jr., and Elizabeth Busch. Crowell Hadden, a stockbroker, died in 1905; Elizabeth Hadden married William Pool in 1911. Briton Hadden's mother strongly encouraged his childhood fascination with satirical writing and word games. At both the Hotchkiss School and Yale, Hadden edited the student papers and displayed a remarkable willingness to experiment with the presentation of news. He also became a friend of a rival student journalist, Henry R. Luce. During World War I, the two were officers in the U.S. Army Artillery; at Camp Jackson, South Carolina, they began discussing founding a newspaper or magazine. Contacts with soldiers, most of whom appeared ignorant of current events, convinced them that the American news media did a poor job informing readers. Hadden returned to Yale and graduated in 1920; his classmates voted him the most likely to succeed. He briefly worked as a reporter at the *New York World* and then, with Luce in tow, went to the *Baltimore News* in November 1921. The two quit in February 1922 to plan their own publication.

After considering starting a newspaper, Hadden and Luce settled on a magazine that they dubbed *Time*. It would present the week's most important news in a concise (no entry was to run more than 400 words) and knowing manner. "Each page," Hadden and Luce declared in their prospectus, "brings to the reader a FINAL REPORT on a whole world of news." Although *Time* would carry no editorial page, it would not, like the comparable and well-entrenched *Literary Digest*, lack a point of view. To secure money for *Time*, the two used their Yale connections, driving to different parts of the country to seek investors among classmates and their parents. They eventually raised $86,000.

With a modest staff, consisting mainly of other recent male graduates of Ivy League colleges, *Time* first appeared on 27 February 1923. For most of the next six years, Hadden edited the magazine; Luce was publisher. Although he and Luce would occasionally change positions, Hadden crafted the periodical's distinctive and all-important style. *Time* in its first ten years relied almost exclusively on clever summaries of newspapers stories. A 1938 company memoir admitted that "*Time*'s news source was a big bundle of newspapers dropped at the office door morning and evening." Disingenuously, *Time* offered descriptive inclusions, referring, for example, to the "buzzard-bald" mayor of New Orleans, that gave the magazine an "in-the-know" quality. This attribute was reenforced by the magazine's often startling willingness to sneer at newsmakers. A 27 February 1927 entry began, "General Carlos Ibanez, peppery and choleric, is not so much the Dictator as the Playboy of Chile." Under Hadden, the magazine invented words (e.g., "socialite" and "cinemactor") or cleverly used words (e.g., "pundit" and "tycoon") as descriptive titles. Hadden encouraged a Homeric compounding of words and inversion of sentences. "As it does to many men," *Time* reported 10 August 1925, "a 43d birthday came to Benito Mussolini." Although faulted by language mandarins, *Time* quickly became a model for many younger journalists. Still, it took nearly ten years for *Time* to achieve an editorial consistency and truly distinctive language. By then, Hadden's cousin, John S. Martin, had become managing editor; Martin more effectively and fiercely imposed Hadden's ideas on the magazine.

Politically and culturally, *Time* reflected the self-conscious cosmopolitanism of the post-World War I upper middle class. Hadden greatly admired Sinclair Lewis and H. L. Mencken, who regularly mocked the country's provincials. All in all, *Time*'s politics were irreverent, mirroring Hadden's smart-alecky personality. Nevertheless, *Time* never challenged political or economic convention; both Hadden and Luce were progressive Republicans, anxious to become millionaires.

Time's parent company, Time Incorporated, began publishing the *Saturday Review of Literature* in 1924, only to sell the periodical two years later. In 1928 Hadden started *Tide*, an advertising trade journal, and experimented with radio programs to promote *Time*. Yet, Hadden lacked Luce's ambitions for Time Inc. He opposed founding the business periodical *Fortune*, which Luce started early in 1930. Nor did Hadden wish to see *Time*'s circulation (243,400 in 1929) increase greatly. He imagined a readership like himself, better educated and well-to-do.

Hadden fell ill with blood poisoning late in 1928 and died in Brooklyn, New York. He had never married. Luce secured enough of Hadden's shares of Time Inc. stock to assure control of the company.

• Noel F. Busch, *Briton Hadden* (1949), is the only biography; the author was Hadden's cousin. Hadden is discussed in Robert T. Elson's house history, *Time Inc.: The Intimate History of a Publishing Enterprise, 1923–1941* (1968); "Fifteen Years," *Time*, 28 Feb. 1938, pp. 37–40; Joseph J. Firebaugh, "The Vocabulary of 'Time' Magazine," *American Speech* 15 (Oct. 1940): 232–43; and James L. Baughman, *Henry R. Luce and the Rise of the American News Media* (1987). Obituaries are in the *New York Times* and the *New York World*, both 28 Feb. 1929.

JAMES L. BAUGHMAN

HADDOCK, Charles Brickett (20 June 1796–15 Jan. 1861), educator and legislator, was born in Salisbury (later Franklin), New Hampshire, the son of William Haddock, a tanner, currier, and shoemaker, and Abigail Eastman Webster, Daniel Webster's older sister. He graduated first in his class from Dartmouth College in 1816. After spending two years at Andover Theological Seminary, Haddock returned to Dartmouth in 1819 as professor of rhetoric and oratory until 1838, when, declining the presidency of Bowdoin College, he became professor of intellectual philosophy and English literature. He married Susan Saunders Lang in 1819; they had nine children. Starting in 1844, he served as professor of intellectual philosophy and political economy at Dartmouth until his retirement in 1854. A successful and well-liked, if not inspiring, teacher, Haddock was an impressive figure who possessed elegant manners and a striking resemblance to his famous uncle.

Haddock simultaneously held his professorship and public office. He served from 1845 to 1848 as a Whig in the New Hampshire house of representatives, where he achieved regional distinction for successfully advocating the extension of a rail line across New Hampshire from Concord to Lebanon on the Connecticut River. He overcame the western New Hampshire farming Democrats' fears of losing teamster jobs and becoming indebted to urban centers by emphasizing the savings that rail transportation to the Boston market would produce. Aided by Haddock's sponsorship of a bill that enabled the railroad company to acquire its right of way, the Northern Railroad was completed to Lebanon in November 1847.

Haddock raised an even stronger legislative voice for the reform of common schools. "The improvement or neglect of our own children" was to him an issue more pressing than southern slavery, which he opposed. He stumped his state calling for educational change: the schoolhouses or "knowledge boxes" were in disrepair and insufficient; the low pay of schoolteachers was scandalous; the creation of high schools was an imperative. Proclaiming that a prudent, moral, and intelligent citizenry guarantees a prosperous commonwealth, he steered the legislature toward establishing a state commissioner of common schools. Whig governor Anthony Colby appointed Haddock as the first incumbent of this post in 1846. Journeying 300 miles in his own carriage to New Hampshire school districts, he solicited statistics on schooling and teaching conditions and on the tax support given each county. He called for teacher training institutes. His work culminated in *Report of the Commissioner of Common Schools to the Legislature of New Hampshire* (1847), which was modeled after the reports submitted in Massachusetts by Horace Mann, the preeminent public school reformer of Jacksonian America. Haddock's report marked the beginning of New Hampshire's system of public schools.

Devoted to his college and state and admired as an orator in an age of great oratory, Haddock was guided by Christian republicanism. His speeches owed much to the Puritan heritage, reflected the academic moral philosophy that he taught, and carried over elements of old New England federalism into the practice of Whig politics. According to Haddock, tradition would be salvaged if economic and educational life were ordered and consolidated to avert the chaos and contempt for the past that he saw in the Jacksonian era. Effective schooling for all would restore civic self-discipline. Echoing John Adams (1735–1826) and Benjamin Rush, he declared, "The only way of securing a Republican equality and, of course, an equal legislation, equal rights and common privileges is by general education. . . . There must first be an aristocracy of intellect before there can be an aristocracy of power. . . . Public intelligence and public virtue are the best securities of liberty and equal laws." These words succeeded in winning localist, but egalitarian, New Hampshire citizens to Haddock's common school crusade and established him as the Horace Mann of New Hampshire.

Though ordained as a Congregational minister in 1824, and a frequent preacher in Hanover and the vicinity, Haddock never held a pastorate but always insisted upon clerical control of Dartmouth's affairs. After the death of his first wife in 1840, he married Caroline Kimball Young in 1841. On leave from 1850 to 1854, he served as U.S. chargé d'affaires to Portugal. Upon his return from Europe in 1856 he lectured on "Life in Lisbon" throughout the northern states, while he made his home in West Lebanon, New Hampshire, where he died.

• Haddock's papers in the Baker Library at Dartmouth College include chiefly his addresses and lectures in manuscript. Those delivered before he left the legislature were published as *Addresses and Miscellaneous Writings* (1846). The fullest biographical sketch is Samuel Gilman Brown, *A Discourse Commemorative of Charles Brickett Haddock, D.D.* (1861). A modern assessment that stresses his moral philosophy is Wilson Smith, *Professors & Public Ethics: Studies of Northern Moral Philosophers Before the Civil War* (1956). Haddock's career at Dartmouth is treated in Leon Burr Richardson, *History of Dartmouth College* (1932). His part in establishing the Northern Railroad is described in James Duane Squires, *Headlights and Highlights: The Northern Railroad of New Hampshire, 1844–1848* (1948), and his efforts for statewide education are related in Everett S. Stackpole, *History of New Hampshire*, vol. 3 (1916). Haddock's close relationship to Webster is apparent in C. M. Wiltse, ed., *The Papers of Daniel Webster*, vol. 1, *Correspondence* (1974), and his Websterian conservatism is analyzed in Daniel Walker Howe, *The Political Culture of the American Whigs* (1979). As late as 1842 Haddock spelled his family name Hadduck.

WILSON SMITH

HADFIELD, George (15 Sept. 1763–5 Feb. 1826), architect, was born in Florence, Italy, the third of five gifted children of Charles Hadfield and Isabella Pocock. The scion of a well-known Manchester (England) family of textile manufacturers, Charles Hadfield, an art collector and dealer, owned and managed three hotels in Tuscany, where his children were brought up in the Roman Catholic faith, with Italian their first language, but after his death they moved to London. Maria Hadfield, the eldest, married the artist Richard Cosway in 1781, the same year that George Hadfield was admitted as an architectural student to

the Royal Academy, where he had an outstanding career; only weeks later he won the silver medal. For several years Hadfield exhibited at the Academy, and in 1784 he also won the gold medal.

Hadfield worked for James Wyatt as an architectural assistant from 1784 to 1790, while also executing a number of engravings. During a visit to Paris in 1789, Hadfield was introduced to his elder sister's friend Thomas Jefferson. In 1790 he won the Royal Academy's three-year traveling scholarship and went to Rome. During 1792 Sir James Wright, a well-known patron of the arts, commissioned Hadfield to make measured drawings and reconstructions of the temple at Palestrina, near Rome; these were exhibited in 1795 at the Royal Academy. Hadfield stayed on in Rome for a year and worked as an architect, including designing chimneypieces for the Prince of Wales and others. After his return in 1794, he designed a house in Ireland. In September 1794 Hadfield was asked by the American painter John Trumbull if he would consider superintending work at the Capitol in Washington, D.C., and in March 1795 Hadfield formally agreed to a trial year. The war with France and resultant difficult economic situation, family difficulties, and what was perhaps an unhappy love affair were all good reasons for his departure.

Arguably the first professionally trained architect to come to America apart from Hallet, Hadfield arrived with enthusiastic letters of introduction, his portfolio of drawings, his books, and the latest architectural and technological information. After three troubled years, in May 1798 he finally left his Capitol post, because the city commissioners had used his designs for the four executive office buildings without paying him. The executive buildings had fifteen bays, two stories with basement, and giant porticos with Ionic columns—the earliest use of a Greek order in America. Several of Hadfield's designs for the Capitol were later adopted by other architects.

In 1800 Hadfield patented the first brick and tile making machine in the United States and established a manufacturing company. In 1801 he advertised for students at his Architectural Academy; his one known pupil was William P. Elliot, best remembered for designing the U.S. Patent Office, who trained for five years with him. In 1802 Hadfield was the first person to become a naturalized citizen in Washington, D.C., and the following year he was elected a city councillor as a Jeffersonian Republican.

Over the next few years, recommended by Jefferson and by the city commissioners, Hadfield successfully designed a number of public buildings, including the arsenal in 1803; the marine barracks and commandant's house, which survives albeit somewhat altered, in 1801–1803; and the city jail, completed in 1801 (it was later converted into a hospital and burned to the ground in 1861). He corresponded with Jefferson about dry docks and worked on several other projects as well. Hadfield was long a prominent member of the Columbian Institute for the Promotion of Arts and Sciences (subsequently absorbed by the Smithsonian

Institution), whose objectives included the establishment of a museum and the U.S. Botanic Garden.

Also at this time Hadfield worked on several private commissions, including the Washington Theatre, opened in 1804; Commodore David Porter's splendid house on Meridian Hill, designed in 1798 but not finished until 1819, which had a wonderful geometrical staircase; the Tayloe row houses (later transmogrified into the Willard Hotel); the Way brothers' row houses; and Weightman's Row (1816). In 1802 Hadfield designed Arlington House for G. W. P. Custis as a residential reliquary commemorating President George Washington; the dramatic and austere façade of the first temple-form and "most conspicuous residence in America" (now in Arlington National Cemetery) can be seen from much of the city. After the Washington Theatre burned in 1820, Hadfield was asked by the Carusi brothers to design its replacement; a number of inauguration balls were held in this famous building, which contained the theater, assembly rooms, and convention hall.

Hadfield also designed, in 1822, the Assembly Rooms on Louisiana Avenue. In later years he designed his own house in Washington; several other houses; alterations, including the second roof of the Octagon; and, in 1824, the Washington Branch Bank of the second Bank of the United States. At the end of his life, in 1825–1826, he designed the Van Ness mausoleum, a beautiful, small tempietto now in Washington's Oak Hill Cemetery. Hadfield, who died in Washington, is buried in the Congressional Cemetery. William Elliot entered his designs for the Washington National Monument competition posthumously.

Washington City Hall, Hadfield's most important public commission, was not completed until 1849, although the cornerstone was laid in August 1820. The intended rotunda was never built. The central section is set on a stepped terrace; the beautifully proportioned Ionic hexastyle portico was derived from the Erechtheum in Athens; the hyphens on either side have recessed round-headed windows, and the two wings end with distyle in antis porticos. The originality of the exterior is matched by the interior use of space.

Several architects were strongly influenced by Hadfield's architecture, particularly Andrew Jackson Davis, who drew and engraved Hadfield's buildings in considerable detail, and Davis's partner Ithiel Town. Disseminated through the designs of these architects and those of the next generation, the influence of Hadfield's work was considerable and is reflected throughout the Midwest and the Northwest, in both private and public buildings. Hadfield was a modest, reserved, and sensitive man, but according to Jefferson and others he did not push himself forward sufficiently, and some of his achievements have gone almost unrecognized. Hadfield's elegant, intellectual, and original architecture introduced the Greek Revival to America, as exemplified by Washington City Hall, which is "a noble and durable monument of his correct conceptions in the art to which his life was devoted

[and] will hand down to posterity the name, the genius, and the talents of George Hadfield" (Records of the Columbian Institute, minutes, 11 Feb. 1826).

• Until 1900 Hadfield's papers were at the Smithsonian, but their whereabouts are now unknown. Little has been written about him, and the main articles are G. S. Hunsberger, "The Architectural Career of George Hadfield," Records of the Columbia Historical Society 51–52 (1955): 46–55, and John Walker, "The High Art of George Hadfield," American Heritage, 37, no. 5 (1986): 74–81. Obituaries are in the Daily National Intelligencer, 13 Feb. 1826, and the Washington National Journal, 7 Feb. 1826.

JULIA KING

HADLEY, Arthur Twining (23 Apr. 1856–6 Mar. 1930), economist and university president, was born in New Haven, Connecticut, the son of James Hadley and Anne Twining. From his earliest years, Hadley's education was shaped by his father, a professor of Greek at Yale University. Early academic pursuits included mathematics, science, and literature, and Hadley had learned German by the age of twelve. Hadley enrolled at Yale in 1872 at the age of sixteen, the same year his father died. He began postgraduate work in 1877 at Yale, which was followed by two years in Europe. Hadley studied for a year and a half at the University of Berlin, where he focused on political economy under the guidance of Adolf Wagner.

Hadley's first professional position, tutor of freshman Greek at Yale, began in 1879. Between 1879 and 1883 he also taught Latin, Roman law, logic, and German. A teaching position in political economy remained elusive, however, and Hadley left Yale for a career as a freelance writer in the summer of 1883. That same summer Yale offered Hadley the opportunity to teach political economy. Hadley was appointed as an instructor in political science, teaching a new course in the fall of 1883 titled "Railroads and Their Industrial Effects." Simultaneously he became editor of the Railroad Gazette. In 1891 he became a full-time professor at Yale. That year he married Helen Harrison Morris; they had three children. In 1892 Hadley became dean of the courses of graduate instruction, a post he held for three years, and became a founding editor of the Yale Review that same year. Hadley actively taught for fifteen years at Yale, offering courses that ranged from general economics to industrial growth and its associated legislative problems.

A participant in several professional societies, Hadley was a charter member of the International Institute of Statistics, which was founded in 1886, and contributed to the publications of the American Statistical Association. He also published a number of articles in the Railroad Gazette, the Yale Review, the Quarterly Journal of Economics, and the Economic Journal. In 1885 he incorporated both lectures and articles into his first book, Railroad Transportation, Its History and Its Laws. In this widely cited work, Hadley skillfully applied economic analysis to problems of the railroad industry. Specifically, Hadley addressed the setting of rates as well as the financing of railroads. Further, he developed theories of monopoly and price discrimination, of cartels, of short-run loss minimization for firms, and of the characterization of railroad regulation as stemming from private interests. These private interests—which included some railroads that sought legalized cartelization—consisted of all those who were in a position to gain from regulation of the railroads. His book remains one of two or three classic references on the preregulatory period in the railway industry.

Hadley's most comprehensive work was an introductory economics text, *Economics: An Account of the Relations between Private Property and Public Welfare* (1896), which was used widely in American universities for roughly twenty-five years. Hadley wrote this work in reaction to Marshall's *Principles,* a leading introductory economics text first published in 1890, which, according to Hadley, was "incomplete" because it omitted political economy. The organization of Hadley's text departed from the work of classical predecessors such as Adam Smith, James Mill, and David Ricardo, which typically were developed around the traditional theories of production, distribution, exchange, and consumption. While Hadley's "principles" developed these theories, he also addressed at length such topics as speculation, investment, property rights, public goods, and the interface between law and economics. Hadley emphasized the importance of encouraging individuals to engage in entrepreneurial activity, recognizing the importance of a profit incentive to compensate for the undertaking of risk. He argued that the potential to earn profit provides an incentive to acquire property, while supernormal returns, which are abnormally high profits, are usually avoided by competition.

Advances toward modern day contestability theory and dynamic limit pricing were also made by Hadley in his discussion of the combination of capital. Hadley recognized that potential entry into an industry disciplines a monopolist and promotes near competitive conditions. These conditions occur when price is high enough for an incumbent firm to earn super-normal returns, which induces entry into the industry by firms willing to offer a product at lower prices to attract customers and profits and then exit the industry. The concept of limit pricing, or of maintaining rates at nearly equal to cost, was seen as a means of increasing the volume of business in the long run. Hadley noted that monopolized industries that may be exposed to competition imminently will be forced to maintain low rates and a higher volume of business or face new entrants who will erode monopoly profits through the competitive process. The practice of limit pricing maximized long-run returns to firms while promoting consumer welfare. His *Economics* displayed an early understanding of economic theories that were developed in the next century. His notions of contestability theory and limit pricing were clearly prophetic of the progress of American contributions to the discipline of economics in the twentieth century.

Hadley was elected president of the American Economic Association in 1899. Later that year he became president of Yale at the age of forty-three. He was the first layman to hold the office, a position he filled successfully for twenty-two years. Some of Hadley's achievements as president included the construction of laboratories, dormitories, and other buildings on campus, eliminating the separation between the Sheffield Scientific School (a school within Yale) and Yale College, reorganizing the medical school, and increasing Yale's endowments throughout his tenure. In 1901 he began conducting roughly every other year an "outside" lecture series at major universities across the United States. He also became an original trustee of the Carnegie Foundation in 1905 and served as chairman from 1917 to 1920. His reputation as a railway economist led President William Howard Taft to appoint him chairman of the Railroad Securities Commission in 1910, and in 1913 Hadley accepted a position on the board of directors of the New York, New Haven, and Hartford Railroad.

Hadley retired as president of Yale in 1921. He remained active as a trustee of the Institute for Government Research, the Institute of Economics, and the Brookings Institution of Washington. He also served as a special editor in charge of definitions in economics for *Webster's New International Dictionary.* He died in Japan during a world cruise.

• Most of Hadley's work, both published and unpublished (including personal papers), can be located in the Yale University Library. A biography by his son Morris Hadley, *Arthur Twining Hadley* (1948), contains an excellent bibliography of Hadley's work. For more of his work on railroads, see Hadley, "The Prohibition of Railroad Pools," *Quarterly Journal of Economics* 4 (Jan. 1890): 158–71. See also two articles by M. L. Cross and R. B. Ekelund, Jr., "A. T. Hadley on Monopoly Theory and Railway Regulation: An American Contribution to Economic Analysis and Policy," *History of Political Economy* 12, no. 2 (Summer 1980): 214–33, and "A. T. Hadley: The American Invention of the Economics of Property Rights and Public Goods," *Review of Social Economy* 39, no. 1 (Apr. 1981): 37–50; and D. P. Locklin, "The Literature on Railway Rate Theory," *Quarterly Journal of Economics* 47 (Feb. 1933): 167–230. Obituaries are in the *Economic Journal* (Sept. 1930): 526–33, and the *American Economic Review* (June 1930): 364–68.

AUDREY B. DAVIDSON
ROBERT B. EKELUND, JR.

HADLEY, Henry Kimball (20 Dec. 1871–6 Sept. 1937), composer and conductor, was born in Somerville, Massachusetts, the son of Samuel Henry Hadley, a public school music instructor, and Martha Conant, a concert pianist and singer of local prominence. Prodigiously talented, Hadley received his earliest musical training in piano, violin, and conducting from his father. Later, from 1885 to 1894, he studied with outstanding teachers in Boston: violin with Henry Heindl, Charles N. Allen, and Jacques Hoffmann; harmony with Stephen A. Emery; and counterpoint and composition with his friend and mentor George

W. Chadwick, head of the New England Conservatory of Music. He continued his counterpoint studies with Eusebius Mandyczewski in Vienna in 1894–1895.

When he returned from Europe, Hadley succeeded Horatio Parker as director of music at the prestigious St. Paul's School on Long Island; he held the position until 1902. During these years, Hadley composed many of his most important early works, including his Symphony no. 1, entitled *Youth and Life*, which was premiered by Anton Seidl in 1897 and performed by Victor Herbert and the Pittsburgh Symphony a year later. In 1899 Hadley won his first prize for composition, a $250 award given by the *Musical Record* for his cantata *In Music's Praise*, which was premiered by Frank Damrosch at Carnegie Hall in 1901. Later that year his Symphony no. 2, *The Four Seasons*, premiered by the New York Philharmonic on Hadley's thirtieth birthday, won both the $500 Paderewski Prize and the $400 New England Conservatory Prize. Hadley's late Romantic, programmatic style of composition clearly reflected European influences, especially those of Richard Strauss: characteristics include a highly descriptive manner of suggesting scenes, movements, and sounds of life and nature in his works, brilliant orchestration, and an interest in composing operas and songs as well as instrumental works.

Determined to gain further training and experience, Hadley returned to Europe in 1904, his sojourn partially financed by the success of several of his light operas and operettas, such as *Nancy Brown*, which was produced on Broadway in 1903. His experiences over the next five years proved invaluable, as he increasingly won critical acclaim as both a composer and conductor. Praised by Richard Strauss, whom he met in London in 1905, as the only American "who knows the orchestra!" and encouraged by his study in composition with Ludwig Thuille in Munich from 1905 to 1907, Hadley completed both his symphonic poem *Salome* and his Symphony no. 3 in 1906. These works, premiered in 1907 by the Boston Symphony Orchestra and the Berlin Philharmonic Orchestra respectively, were heralded throughout Europe and the United States, receiving numerous performances by many major orchestras, often under Hadley's direction. Hadley merited further recognition when he became a conductor at the Mainz Stadttheater from 1907 to 1909, a unique position for an American. There, in 1909, he conducted the highly successful premiere of his first serious opera, the one-act *Safié*, based on the Persian legend of the love of Princess Safié for an envoy, Ahmad.

Hadley's success in Europe generated increased appreciation in the United States of his compositions and conducting abilities. In 1908 he was elected to the National Institute of Arts and Letters, and when he returned to the United States a year later, he launched the most successful career of any contemporary American composer-conductor. Hadley became the first native-born American conductor of a major orchestra and the highest-paid conductor in the United States. He served as conductor of the Seattle Symphony Orchestra (1909–1911) and of the San Francisco Symphony Orchestra (1911–1915), associate conductor of the New York Philharmonic Orchestra (1920–1927), and the founder and conductor of the Manhattan Symphony Orchestra in New York City (1929–1932), which performed thirty-six works by American composers during his three-year tenure. In addition to numerous guest-conducting opportunities with major orchestras in the United States and Europe, Hadley became the first North American to appear as a guest conductor of a South American orchestra, when he conducted the Asociacion del Profesorado Orquestral in Buenos Aires in 1927. According to the *Buenos Aires Herald*, Hadley, conducting entirely from memory, "showed himself a conductor of great merit, his principal qualities being a sympathetic understanding of the works given, respect for the composer's intentions, and a sobriety of gesture which enables him to get the greatest effect from the orchestra" (12 June 1927). In 1930 he became the first American to conduct in Japan, when he was invited by the Japanese government to conduct the New Symphony Orchestra of Tokyo.

Composing with consummate ease, Hadley had the distinction of contributing "not only more extensively but more successfully to all the accepted sorts of serious composition than any of his colleagues" (*Detroit News*, Feb. 1920). In 1917, his opera *Azora, the Daughter of Montezuma* (1914), performed by the Chicago Opera with Hadley conducting, was hailed by critics as the "first genuinely all-American operatic production" (*Current Opinion*, 1 Feb. 1918). The subject—the love between Azora and Xalca, a captive warrior from an opposing tribe, set in 1519 during the reign of Montezuma when Cortez brought Christianity to the Aztecs—was American; the libretto and music were written, conducted, and performed entirely by Americans; and the scenery was designed by an American. *Azora* won the Bispham Medal in 1925. His third opera, *Bianca* (1917), which won the $1,000 Walter Wade Hinshaw prize, was performed in New York in 1918; the opera is based on Carlo Goldoni's story of Bianca, the mistress of an inn, who is wooed by several suitors before she finally accepts Fabricio, her humble servant. In 1920 Hadley became the first American to conduct one of his own compositions at the Metropolitan Opera House, when he conducted his opera *Cleopatra's Night* (1918). Based on Théophile Gautier's "Une Nuit de Cléopatra," the opera centers around Cleopatra's pact with the hunter Meiamoun: if she gives him one night of love, he must meet death at sunrise. The work became the first American opera to be performed more than one season at the Metropolitan.

Hadley's orchestral works include five symphonies (no. 4, *North, East, South, and West*, 1911; no. 5, *Connecticut*, 1935), several symphonic poems, three overtures, and a rhapsody entitled *The Culprit Fay* (1908), which won a $1,000 award presented by the National Federation of Music Clubs in 1920. Hadley also composed chamber music, suites, cantatas, operettas, piano pieces, and music for twenty-five films. His film scores included one for *When a Man Loves* (1926), which was, according to Canfield, "the first musical score to be recorded and played in synchronism with an entire motion picture" (p. 239). Many of Hadley's approximately 200 songs were dedicated to and performed by his wife, Inez Barbour, the internationally renowned American soprano whom he had married in 1918; they had no children.

To honor his accomplishments as a composer and conductor, Hadley was elected to the American Academy of Arts and Letters in 1924 and was made an Officier d'Académie by the French government in 1924. In addition, as one of the foremost proponents of American music and musicians, Hadley founded the National Association for American Composers and Conductors in 1933 which had as its sole purpose "the banishing of old illusions with regards to American 'inferiority' and European 'superiority' in music" (*New York Herald Tribune*, 7 Sept. 1937). Later, this association endowed the Henry Hadley Memorial Library, one of America's preeminent collections of American music, now housed at the New York Public Library. He also founded the Berkshire Music Festival in 1934 and conducted the New York Philharmonic Orchestra there for the first two seasons.

Hadley died in New York, after a five-year battle with cancer. He was eulogized by Gene Buck, president of the American Society of Composers, Authors, and Publishers, for "more than any figure in America, carrying American music to the four corners of the earth. Also, I know of no figure in American music who has contributed more to the musical scene of America than he. He has carried the torch higher than anyone I know in the field of musical culture" (Hadley Scrapbook, vol. 19, p. 3).

After Hadley's death, he was honored in memorial programs by more than a hundred of the major symphonic and concert units of the Works Progress Administration's Federal Music Project in recognition of the significant place he held in America's musical life. In January 1938 the Henry Hadley Foundation was established to promote and encourage American musicians and composers by providing financial assistance and performance opportunities.

Even though Hadley's compositions are seldom performed, his contributions to America's music and musicians are inestimable. He served as an ambassador at large by becoming the first American to achieve international acclaim as a composer-conductor, and he influenced and stimulated the development of an American school of composition by championing the cause of American composers. According to the *Holyoke Daily Transcript and Telegram*, "Henry Kimball Hadley . . . will go down in history as the American musician who did the most to make the world understand that America could produce music" (8 Sept. 1937).

• The Henry Hadley Papers were bequeathed to the New York Public Library by Mrs. Henry Hadley. Many of Hadley's published compositions are available from his principal publishers, Ditson, G. Schirmer, and Schmidt; some manuscripts may be rented from the National Association for American Composers and Conductors. The most complete modern assessment is John Clair Canfield, Jr., "Henry Kimball Hadley: His Life and Works (1871–1937)" (Ed.D. diss., Florida State Univ., 1960), which includes a complete list of Hadley's compositions, an extensive bibliography, and a note on sources. Other significant sources include a full-length biography by Herbert Boardman, *Henry Hadley, Ambassador of Harmony* (1932); and a complete list of works published by Paul P. Berthoud, *The Musical Works of Dr. Henry Hadley* (1942). See also his obituary in the *New York Times*, 7 Sept. 1937.

SHERRILL V. MARTIN

HADLEY, Herbert Spencer (20 Feb. 1872–1 Dec. 1927), politician, lawyer, and educator, was born in Olathe, Kansas, the son of John Milton Hadley and Harriett Beach, farmers. He earned an A.B. in 1892 from the University of Kansas and an LL.B. in 1894 from Northwestern University. In 1901 he married Agnes Lee; they had three children.

In 1894 Hadley began the practice of law in Kansas City, Missouri, and soon entered public life as a Republican. In 1898 he became assistant city counselor of Kansas City and in 1901 became prosecuting attorney of Jackson County, Missouri. In his first year in office he won 206 of 208 criminal cases. He was elected in 1904 to the post of attorney general of Missouri. During his four years in office, he gained much favorable publicity for successfully prosecuting the Standard Oil Company and certain other companies and railroads for violations of Missouri antitrust statutes. The convictions, which involved technical rate practices, had little practical effect. However, through the reluctant testimony of management officials, Hadley called attention to the utter contempt their firms had for the public welfare.

In 1908, as a Liberal Republican, Hadley won a four-year term as governor by a 15,879-vote margin over Democratic candidate William S. Cowherd. Hadley became the first Republican governor in forty years in a campaign marked by no great issues. He won because a bitter Democratic primary battle carried over into the general election. His legislative program, which called for higher taxes and home rule for major cities, bogged down in partisan politics and generally failed to pass. He only prevented a deficit by using an executive order to raise the saloon tax. In Kansas City, he tried unsuccessfully to check the rise of the corrupt Pendergast organization by trying to stop illegal voting practices and appointing reformers to the city's state-controlled police board.

Ineligible under the state constitution to seek another term as governor, Hadley left elected politics to practice and study law. Citing frail health, he left Missouri and moved to Colorado. In 1917, after a short semiretirement, he accepted a position as a law professor at the University of Colorado. For two years he was also a counsel for the Colorado State Railroad Commission. In his law classes, he tried to make his students see that the achievements of classical civilization had application to modern life. He elaborated on this theme in a popular book, *Rome and the World Today*

(1922). He contended that the United States, just as Rome in its greatest days, had the necessary social, economic, and moral foundations to enter upon a mission with the potential of creating two hundred years of peace and prosperity in the Western world. "I have a deep conviction," he said, "that the life and experiences of the people of one time are of value and important to all who come after them."

In 1923 Hadley accepted a position as chancellor of Washington University in St. Louis. An advocate of necessary changes in criminal procedures, he served on the National Crime Commission and the Council of the American Law Institute. He participated in producing the comprehensive *Missouri Crime Survey* of 1926, a massive sociological study of the criminal justice system. Shortly before his death from heart disease and arteriosclerosis in St. Louis, he became a trustee of the Rockefeller Foundation.

• The Herbert Spencer Hadley Papers are in the Joint Western Historical Manuscript Collection of the University of Missouri and the State Historical Society of Missouri. Among Hadley's writings is "Criminal Justice in America," *American Bar Association Journal* 11 (Oct. 1925): 674–79. For more information see Edwin C. McReynolds, *Missouri: A History of the Crossroads State* (1962). Obituaries are in the *St. Louis Post-Dispatch* and the *Kansas City Times*, 2 Dec. 1927. Also see W. H. H. Piatt et al., *In Memoriam: Herbert Spencer Hadley* (1928), and T. M. Marshall, "Herbert Spencer Hadley," *Washingtonian* 5 (Dec. 1927): 1–5.

LAWRENCE H. LARSEN

HAESSLER, Carl (5 Aug. 1888–1 Dec. 1972), journalist and socialist trade unionist, was born in Milwaukee, Wisconsin, the son of Herman F. Haessler and Elizabeth Wagner. The political life of that city was dominated at that time by immigrant German social democrats. Haessler earned a B.A. at the University of Milwaukee, was elected to Phi Beta Kappa, and won a Rhodes scholarship to Oxford University, where he studied for two years. He completed his formal education with a Ph.D. degree from the University of Illinois, where he also taught. In 1917 he married Mildred Barnes; they had two children.

In the years directly preceding American entry into World War I, Haessler was on the staff of the *Milwaukee Leader*, a daily newspaper closely allied with the city's militant trade union movement then dominated by German immigrants. Like most socialists of his day, Haessler opposed American entry into World War I, believing it involved workers fighting other workers in the interest of their capitalist employers. When drafted in 1918, he refused to serve and was sentenced to twelve years at the military prison in Leavenworth, Kansas. After leading a strike of prisoners there, he was sent to the prison at Alcatraz Island, only to be given amnesty in 1920 as American war fever abated.

Upon his release, Haessler joined the Federated Press (FP) to begin the work with which he would be associated for decades. The FP sought to be a national wire service specializing in the issues of greatest importance to labor and reform publications in the manner in which commercial services like Reuthers served the conventional press. Beginning with thirty-two subscribers in 1919, the FP would reach a high of 250 in 1946 before falling victim to McCarthyism after World War II. Although the FP was not directly targeted, it suffered from its ideological openness. The unions that were purging themselves of Communist party influence withdrew from using the FP due to its refusal to take a similar course of action while retaining its longstanding policy of giving voice to the most radical wing of the trade union movement. Haessler headed the group for most of this 35-year-period.

Haessler excluded no one because of party affiliation or ideology. Communists, anarcho-syndicalists, socialists, liberals, and trade union conservatives were all included on his editorial board and as reporters. Well-known journalists who reported for the FP were Robert Dunn, Fred Hewitt, Len De Caux, and Harvey O'Connor. The service never attracted many commercial newspapers and thus its fortunes waxed and waned with those of the trade union newspapers and journals. As head of the FP, Haessler played a role in the founding of the American Newspaper Guild in 1933.

In 1936 Haessler was asked by John L. Lewis to serve as an organizer for the fledgling United Auto Workers Union (UAW) during its historic sit-down strike against General Motors in Flint, Michigan. He founded and edited the UAW's newspaper. Haessler made no secret of his belief that Walter Reuther had improperly built his fame on the basis of that strike when, in fact, other leaders had urged the tactics that won the strike over Reuther's objections. (Reuther belonged to the Socialist party, and other members of his party had gone over his head to the leader of the party, Norman Thomas, to gain approval for the actions that proved successful in the strike.) Through the years Haessler usually opposed Reuther in various disputes within the UAW, considering Reuther insufficiently militant and bent on building a monolithic union with himself as undisputed leader. Haessler sided with the broad left-wing coalition in the UAW, which had strong Communist party elements. When Reuther was elected president of the UAW after World War II in a bitter election, most of the left-wingers were purged or resigned. In the final struggle for control of the union with the Reuther faction, Haessler edited a particularly irreverent opposition newsletter whose acronyms were popularly interpreted as obscene personal references to Walter Reuther.

During the turbulent 1930s, activists such as Haessler frequently took part in various unions simultaneously, going back and forth to strikes and rallies. In addition to his work with the UAW, Haessler played a role in the massive United Rubber Workers' 1937 sit-down strike in Akron, Ohio, another key moment in the building of the Congress of Industrial Organizations (CIO). This was the most radical period of the CIO. In the summer of 1936 CIO president John L. Lewis had created an organizing committee whose staff included sixty known Communist party members. For the balance of the decade numerous radicals of various ideological backgrounds were in the forefront of organizing drives that brought millions of workers to the new CIO unions.

In addition to his work at the FP during this time, Haessler lectured at Commonwealth College at Mena, Arkansas. This involvement is indicative of Haessler's commitment to worker education with a socialist orientation. Commonwealth had been founded in 1923 by socialists led by Kate Richards O'Hare, one of the few women organizers in the American Federation of Labor. Commonwealth classes dealt with immediate organizing strategies as well as labor history. In 1940, his first marriage having ended, Haessler wed Lucy Whitaker; this marriage produced no children.

Although Haessler remained organizationally unaffiliated, his form of freewheeling radicalism was out of step with the rightward thrust of organized labor after the Taft-Hartley Act of 1947. Nor did it help that Haessler was a longtime foe of Reuther. Mainline unions withdrew their newspapers from the FP while the more radical unions fought for their very existence. The FP influence plummeted and the service closed in 1956.

Haessler continued to write articles and pamphlets on labor topics and to speak at labor events, still expounding the militant but democratic Debsian radicalism of his native Milwaukee and the direct-action populism characteristic of the Industrial Workers of the World and the fledgling CIO. At the time of his death he was living in Detroit, where younger radicals often regarded him as an elder statesman of labor. In a gesture much in keeping with his life's work, he bequeathed his body to the Medical School of Wayne State University. Haessler was eulogized as a major figure in leftist trade-union journalism.

• Haessler's personal papers are at the Reuther Library, Wayne State University; Federated Press materials may be examined in the Taminent Library, New York University. Haessler's career with the Federated Press is exhaustively covered in Stephen J. Haessler, "Carl Haessler and the Federated Press: Essays on the History of the American Labor Journalism" (master's thesis, Univ. of Wisconsin, 1977). Material on working for Haessler is found in Jessie Lloyd O'Connor et al., *Harvey and Jessie: A Couple of Radicals* (1988). An obituary is in the *New York Times*, 3 Dec. 1972.

DAN GEORGAKAS

HAGAR, Jonathan (1714–6 Nov. 1775), land speculator, assemblyman, and town developer, was born in the duchy of Westphalia, Germany; the names of his parents are unknown. Hagar (also spelled Hager) arrived as a freeman in Philadelphia from Rotterdam on the ship *Harle* on 1 September 1736, at the age of twenty-two. He was one of the many German-speaking settlers who began to migrate to the western areas of Maryland in the 1730s and 1740s. While most of these settlers first spent a few years in eastern Pennsylvania (sometimes as indentured servants to pay for

their passage), high land prices in that settled land forced new arrivals to establish their own homes farther west and south.

The exact date of Hagar's arrival in the backcountry is unknown, but in 1739 he made his first purchase of land, 200 acres, in what is today Washington County (then Prince George's County). There were very few people living in the region at that time, despite the fact that in 1732 the fifth lord Baltimore had declared the region open to settlement and had tried to encourage settlement by offering 100 acres (families 200 acres) free, with exemption from paying a quitrent for three years. Settlement westward had been impeded in part by boundary disputes between the Penns and the Calverts, which often led to violence in the contested areas. Furthermore, although western Maryland had some of the finest farmland in the country, in an era of water transportation the area's location behind the fall line was an inhibiting factor. It took land speculators, often colonial officials like Daniel Dulany, but also ambitious men like Hagar, to encourage movement westward. By 1775 the western areas of Maryland had a population of about 30,000.

In 1740 Hagar married Elizabeth Kerschner. Hagar was naturalized 20 October 1747, most likely to protect his property rights. Steadily he began to acquire land throughout the region. He sold lots at higher prices than he had paid and with his profits acquired yet more land. As a result of his timely arrival and efforts he was able to obtain both wealth and power. The Hagars had at least three children, two of whom survived to adulthood.

In the earliest records, Hagar is listed as a blacksmith. Perhaps this trade made him aware of the need for a provisioning town on the western side of the Blue Ridge similar to the flourishing town of Frederick on the eastern side. Settlers were coming south from Pennsylvania to the rich lands of Maryland, Virginia, and North Carolina. Hagar laid out a town in September 1762. He called it Elizabethtown in honor of his wife, but in a short time people called it Hagerstown. The name became Hagerstown officially in 1814, when the town was incorporated.

Hagar's original plan called for 520 lots, each 82 feet by 240 feet, approximately one-half acre. By 7 September 1772, the perceptive English traveler William Eddis reported of Hagar's town, in *Letters from America* (ed. Aubrey C. Land [1969], p. 68):

About thirty miles west of Frederick Town I passed through a settlement which is making quick advances to perfection. A German adventurer, whose name is Hagar, purchased a considerable tract of land in this neighborhood, and with much discernment and foresight determined to give encouragement to traders and to erect proper habitations for the stowage of goods for the supply of the adjacent country. His plan succeeded; he has lived to behold a multitude of inhabitants on lands which he remembered unoccupied; and he has seen erected in places, appropriated by him for that purpose, more than an hundred comfortable edifices, to which the name of Hagerstown is given in honor of the intelligent founder.

By the time of his death in 1775, Hagar had leased 160 of his lots. Thirty-five years later, the census of 1810 recorded 2,342 people living in Hagerstown. Hagar had also acquired more than 10,000 acres of land in Washington County. His personal property indicated a man of comfortable wealth. He had leased much of his farm and equipment shortly before death, however, so the extent of Hagar's farming cannot be easily determined.

Hagar, like a number of other German settlers, acted as a mediator between English officialdom and the settlers. He became a leader in both the English and the German communities. He served in the militia, where he attained the rank of captain. In 1771 he was elected to the lower house of the Maryland assembly. English law prevented naturalized citizens from serving, but the assembly changed the law to allow naturalized delegates. Hagar's seat was declared vacant and a new election was held, which Hagar won. A new complication arose when he was reelected in 1773. Although the governor had signed the naturalization bill into law, the assembly had unknowingly passed the law after the sixth lord Baltimore had died. The lower house, for political reasons unrelated to Hagar's case, ruled that the naturalization law was therefore invalid and that Hagar could not serve. The seat was again declared vacant.

Perhaps this experience helped lead Hagar to support the patriots, expecting that a new system would allow him to hold political office. On 2 July 1774 he was chosen to serve on a committee to aid the people of Boston. On 12 September 1775 he was named to the committee of observation. Further service to the patriot cause was prevented by his accidental death when he was crushed by a log at his sawmill. His son Jonathan would go on to serve in the Revolution. The younger Hagar was captured at the battle of Long Island in 1776 and held by the British in Halifax. Both his son and daughter married prominent members of the community. People in the region who are of German descent felt looked down on by neighbors of English descent, but Hagar was able to achieve such a high level of wealth and status that his children were considered part of the elite, bearing no stigma of being children of a German immigrant.

Hagar embodies the great American success story—he rose from poor young immigrant to rich and powerful settler. His grave is located in the churchyard of Zion Reformed Church in Hagerstown.

• There are limited Hagar papers housed at the Maryland Historical Society. More useful but harder to retrieve are the bits and pieces from the extensive Frederick County records, which are deposited in the Maryland State Archives. Because heirs contested the distribution of property after Hagar's death, there are also relevant Chancery records in the Maryland State Archives in Annapolis. Information on Hagar's election can be found in the printed archives, William H. Browne et al., eds., *Archives of Maryland* (1883–), vol. 63, pp. 92–93, 100, 107, 174–175, 238, 309 and vol. 64, pp. 22–23, 436. David C. Skaggs, *Roots of Maryland Democracy, 1753–1776* (1973), untangles the complexities of the election controversy and, in general, describes Md. colonial politics in the mid-eighteenth century. A concise summary of information on Hagar can be found in Edward C. Papenfuse et al., *A Biographical Dictionary of the Maryland Legislature, 1635–1789*, vol. 1 (1979), pp. 379–80. Old-fashioned compilations of information on the county with some reference to Hagar can be found in John Thomas Scharf, *A History of Western Maryland* (2 vols., 1882), and Thomas J. C. Williams, *A History of Washington County, Maryland* (1906; repr. 1968). Helpful, but to be used with caution, is Basil Sollers, "Jonathan Hagar, the Founder of Hagerstown," *Society for the History of Germans in Maryland*, Report 2 (1888), pp. 17–30.

ELIZABETH A. KESSEL

HAGEDORN, Hermann Ludwig Gebhard (18 July 1882–27 July 1964), author, was born on Staten Island, New York, the son of Hermann Hagedorn, a financier, and Anna Schwedler. His German-born father, a member of the New York Cotton Exchange, permitted only German to be spoken at home, and young Hermann learned English only after being enrolled in a private school, the first in a series that ended at the Hill School in Pottstown, Pennsylvania, where he endured such ridicule for his two middle names that he dropped them. But winning a mile race in a critical track meet made him a school hero, and at his graduation in 1901 he had the welcome sense of beginning to merge into American society.

Hope of further education collided with his father's insistence that Hagedorn train for a career in business. But office boy duties so bored him that he sought more congenial work and found it, in 1903, as contributor to a literary magazine, *The Reader*. That fall he entered Harvard, where he did well enough in course work to earn election to Phi Beta Kappa but was more interested in contributing to both the *Harvard Advocate* and the *Harvard Monthly*. At the 1907 commencement, as the elected class poet he read "A Troop of the Guard," replete with patriotic idealism. Within days it was reprinted nationwide in newspapers.

Hagedorn's marriage in 1908 to Dorothy Oakley, of a long-established family, further strengthened his sense of belonging in America. The honeymoon year was spent in New York, where he took advanced courses at Columbia and published his first book, *The Woman of Corinth, a Tale in Verse*. The next year he returned to Harvard as an instructor in English, but resigned two years later to devote full time to writing, completing in 1914 both a novel, *Faces in the Dawn*, and a play, *Makers of Magic*. The outbreak of war in Europe that year turned his attention to more serious matters, and by 1916 he and like-minded friends, Julian Street among them, were busy as Vigilantes, instructing young Americans in responsible citizenship. After American entry into the war, he published *Where Do You Stand?* (1918), a carefully worded appeal to his fellow citizens of German extraction. It was praised generally, but numerous well-established German Americans chided him for betraying his heritage, while overzealous patriots charged him with disloyalty bordering on treason. What made writing such a book an agonizing experience was the fact that his father, after retiring from the Cotton Exchange, had returned to Germany with most of the family, and that two of his sisters had married officers in the Kaiser's army, while a brother had become a prominent government official—as Hagedorn reported in detail in his last major book, *The Hyphenated Family* (1960).

The year 1916 brought another important change in Hagedorn's life, when a casual acquaintance with Theodore Roosevelt turned into enduring friendship. At lunch one day Roosevelt asked Hagedorn to write a book about him and would not take "no" for an answer. Issued in 1918 as *The Boys' Life of Theodore Roosevelt*, it was popular enough to require several editions and to prompt Hagedorn to produce seven more Roosevelt books, the best-loved being *The Roosevelt Family of Sagamore Hill*, a 1954 Book-of-the-Month Club selection and a runaway bestseller. Shortly after TR's death in 1919 Hagedorn joined others of his admirers in organizing the Theodore Roosevelt Memorial Association. As its first secretary and eventual executive director he assembled the nation's oldest presidential library, housed first in Roosevelt's birthplace on East 20th Street in Manhattan but later transferred to Harvard. He also led the drive to restore Sagamore Hill at Oyster Bay and was gratified when both it and the birthplace became national historic sites in 1962. His most ambitious proposal, for a memorial in Washington complementing those of Lincoln and Jefferson, never won congressional support. But the association bought an 88-acre island in the Potomac, known thereafter as Roosevelt Island, and deeded it to the government. His final contribution to the cause was serving as national director of TR's centennial in 1958, for which he lectured in cities across the nation and added three more titles to his already extensive Roosevelt canon.

Having discovered his talent for biography, he applied it to men with Roosevelt connections—General Leonard Wood, who helped organize the Rough Riders in the war with Spain, in *Leonard Wood* (1931), and William Boyce Thompson, a mining tycoon who served as first president of the Theodore Roosevelt Memorial Association, in *The Magnate* (1941). He also wrote biographies of his long-time friend and fellow poet Edwin Arlington Robinson in 1938 and Albert Schweitzer in *Prophet in the Wilderness* (1946). Each was carefully organized, and all were about men he admired. He also wrote occasional poems, including "The Bomb That Fell on America" (1946), prompted by the dropping of atomic bombs on Japanese cities in 1945, which drew at least as much popular attention as his Harvard graduation poem had almost forty years earlier.

Tall, dark-complected, and handsome, this poet, biographer, and champion of Theodore Roosevelt, busy though he commonly was in multiple activities, found time to enjoy social contacts in his clubs—Century, Harvard, Authors in New York and Cosmos in

Washington—albeit with a dignity and reserve that strangers often took for snobbishness. He spent his final years in Santa Barbara, California, where his two daughters had settled earlier; his only son had died in early middle age. Hagedorn died of a heart attack while in his car in Santa Barbara. Never one to stop work, he left unfinished a memoir of an Indian chieftain.

• Collections of Hagedorn manuscripts, correspondence, and memorabilia range widely in size and location—from Colby College in Maine to the Beinecke and Sterling libraries at Yale, the Butler Library at Columbia, the Houghton Library and Theodore Roosevelt Collection at Harvard, the Manuscript Division of the Library of Congress, the American Academy and Institute of Arts and Letters in New York, and libraries at the universities of Pennsylvania, Syracuse, and Southern California. Hagedorn's daughter, Dorothea Parfit of Santa Barbara, holds relevant family correspondence and other materials.

Self-estimates by Hagedorn can be found in the twenty-fifth and fiftieth anniversary class books of 1907 Harvard graduates, but his book *The Hyphenated Family* (1960) comes closer to substantive autobiography. A short biographical sketch by John Allen Gable, " 'He Loved the Soaring Spirit of Man': The Life and Work of Hermann Hagedorn," *Theodore Roosevelt Association Journal* 3 (Fall 1977): 9–13, includes a brief account of his long service to the association, paragraph summaries of several of his books, and a report of his activity in the Moral Rearmament Movement as one phase of his ecumenical liberalism. Scholarly evaluation is provided by Alan R. Havig, "Presidential Images, History, and Homage: Memorializing Theodore Roosevelt, 1919–1967," *American Quarterly* 30 (Fall 1978): 514–32, and Phyllis Keller, *States of Belonging: German-American Intellectuals and the First World War* (1979).

WILLIAM PEIRCE RANDEL

HAGEN, Hermann August (30 May 1817–9 Nov. 1893), entomologist and physician, was born in Königsberg, East Prussia (later the Russian enclave of Kaliningrad), the son of Carl Heinrich Hagen, a professor at the Albert University and counselor to the King of Prussia, and Anna Dorothea Linck. As a youth, Hagen was strongly influenced by his grandfather, who had been a professor of natural history at the university. Hagen graduated from the local gymnasium in 1836 and earned an M.D. from the University of Königsberg in 1840. Early on he became interested in dragonflies, and his medical thesis constituted a study of the European species of this insect. His first entomological paper, a study of the dragonflies of East Prussia, appeared in 1839, when he was twenty-two.

In company with his zoology professor, M. H. Rathke, Hagen visited and studied the major entomological collections in Norway, Sweden, Denmark, and Germany before completing his medical degree. He also undertook additional medical studies in Berlin, Vienna, and Paris between 1840 and 1843. He then practiced as a surgeon in Königsberg while continuing to study dragonflies and other insects between 1843 and 1866. During his last four years in Königsberg, he served as vice president of the city council and as a member of the city's school board. In 1851 he married Johanna Maria Elise Gerhards.

Between 1855 and 1860, Hagen published several volumes of his monograph on termites, *Monographie der Termiten*. At the suggestion of Baron Carl R. R. von Osten-Sacken, the noted contemporary Russian entomologist, whom he had met in 1856, Hagen turned his attention to a broader study of neuropteroid insects in the Americas. His *Synopsis of the Neuroptera of North America*, which included a list of the South American species, was published by the Smithsonian Institution in 1861. Though Hagen had not yet visited the United States or any American museum collections, he made extensive use of materials sent to him by Osten-Sacken. Originally drafted in Latin by Hagen, the text was translated into English by Phillip R. Uhler, who was then on the staff of the Museum of Comparative Zoology at Harvard University. Hagen's *Bibliotheca Entomologica* (2 vols.; 1862, 1863) was his magnum opus. A comprehensive account of entomological works published to that time, it was based on extensive research Hagen had completed in a number of European libraries and was described by some entomologists as "the entomologists' bible." Hagen also published a number of shorter papers concerning the Neuroptera, including both recent and fossil forms. These publications embraced not only dragonflies and termites, but also lace wings, ant lions, and other species, and included specimens found in amber.

Baron von Osten-Sacken again took a hand in his younger colleague's career by encouraging Louis Agassiz to invite Hagen to join the staff of the Museum of Comparative Zoology at Harvard University and establish a department of entomology there. Hagen accepted and began working as an assistant in entomology at the museum in 1867. He replaced his translator Philip Uhler, who had taken an appointment as a librarian at the Peabody Institute in Baltimore. Hagen rose quickly at Harvard, becoming an assistant professor in 1868 and a full professor in 1870. His was the first appointment of a professor of entomology in any American institution. In spite of the fact that Hagen never fully mastered the English language and could be impatient and temperamental, he was regarded as a sympathetic and generous professor and colleague. Sometimes difficult to understand in lecture halls, Hagen carried on much of his instruction with individual students in classrooms and laboratories, some of whom later became noted entomologists in their own right.

From 1868 to 1890, Hagen expended much effort systematically arranging and cataloging Harvard's insect collections, to which he contributed his own private collection in 1875. Hagen had some skill as an artist, and some of his sketches appeared in his published papers. He occasionally made errors, as when he suggested to a colleague in 1890 that the gypsy moth could not be dangerous because it attacked too many different tree species. Hagen made one major trip to the western United States in 1882, traveling by way of the Northern Pacific Railroad, and collecting many injurious insects in Montana and in the Pacific coast states.

Hagen, who enjoyed high standing among American scientists, was regarded as one of the premier world entomologists. After suffering a paralytic stroke in the fall of 1890, he was devotedly nursed by his wife until his death, in Cambridge, Massachusetts.

• Hagen's papers are at the Museum of Comparative Zoology at Harvard University. Biographical sketches are in Arnold Mallis, *American Entomologists* (1971) and in E. O. Essig, *A History of Entomology* (1931). An obituary sketch by Samuel Henshaw, Hagen's assistant and then his successor at Harvard, is in *Proceedings of the American Academy of Arts and Sciences*, n.s., 21 (1894). See also *Entomologists' Monthly Magazine* (Jan. 1894); a sketch by P. P. Calvert in *Entomologists' News* (Dec. 1893); and Henry Osborn, *Fragments of Entomological History* (1937).

KEIR B. STERLING

HAGEN, Walter Charles (21 Dec. 1892–5 Oct. 1969), professional golfer, was born in Rochester, New York, the son of William Hagen, a blacksmith, and Louise Balko. Hagen grew up less than a mile from the Country Club of Rochester, in the Corbett's Glen neighborhood of suburban Brighton. The proximity to a golf course was instrumental to Hagen's early development. He began playing golf at age five; by the age of seven he was caddying for 10 cents an hour. Hagan quit attending school regularly at the age of 12, as he jumped out of a schoolroom window, headed for the golf course.

Though Hagen aspired to be a professional baseball player, he became an assistant golf professional at the Country Club of Rochester in 1907 and thus began a pathbreaking career in professional golf. Hagen entered his first professional tournament in 1912, finishing 11th. His first, and perhaps most important, career breakthrough came in 1914 at America's premier professional golf event, the U.S. Open at Chicago's Midlothian Country Club. Despite suffering from a virulent case of food poisoning on the eve of the tournament, Hagen shot an opening-round 68—the lowest 18-hole score then recorded at a U.S. Open. His winning four-round total of 290 tied the Open record for the lowest score. Following his Open victory, Hagen capitalized on his newfound fame by playing exhibition matches around the country with fellow professionals. Hagen's showmanship and regal air on the course made him a crowd favorite wherever he played, thus attracting large audiences and high exhibition fees.

Hagen's penchant for expensive cars, the finest clothes, the most beautiful women, and all-night parties contributed to his increasing fame and popularity. On 29 January 1917 Hagen married Margaret Johnson of Rochester. The couple had one child before the marriage was dissolved in the spring of 1921, in part because of Hagen's frenetic travel schedule and his fondness for other women.

Shortly after the birth of his only child, Hagen accepted a position as head professional at the elite Oakland Hills Golf Club in Detroit, Michigan. But in 1919, during an age when golf professionals worked strictly at a course for financial survival, Hagen made the precedent-breaking decision to play exhibitions and tournaments full time. Thus Hagen paved the way for young men "to make their living not as golf professionals but as professional golfers" (Wind, p. 90).

Hagen won several more professional tournaments as the decade closed, including the first $1,000 purse at the Panama Exposition and the 1919 U.S. Open. But Hagen's career and reputation reached their peak in the 1920s. Hagen, along with famed amateur Bobby Jones, dominated the major championships. Hagen won his first of four British Open titles in 1922, thus becoming the first American-born professional to win the coveted claret jug (his other titles came in 1924, 1928, and 1929). Hagen also won five Professional Golfers Association (PGA) championships (1921, 1924, 1925, 1926, and 1927).

Hagen's dominance of the PGA championship, then played as matches in which contestants competed head-to-head rather than attempt to compile the lowest 72-hole total, crystallized his reputation as a master of golfing psychology. Hagen would often employ theatrics and gamesmanship to get the better of an opponent. One of his favorite methods was to arrive just minutes before his scheduled start, jogging to the first tee dressed in a wrinkled tuxedo and dancing pumps—evidence of an all-night party for which Hagen was notorious. Unbeknownst to his opponent, whose guard was now down, Hagen had staged the entire event.

Hagen's fondness for match play competition also contributed to formalizing matches between leading European and American golf professionals. Hagen captained the first seven American teams in the biennial matches, which became known commonly as the Ryder Cup (1927, 1929, 1931, 1933, 1935, 1937, and 1939). Perhaps not surprisingly, Hagen's "greatest thrill in golf" occurred in match play competition, a 72-hole contest against the legendary Jones played in 1926. Hagen pocketed $7,600 for his 12 and 11 trouncing (leading by 12 holes with only 11 holes remaining) of the Georgian amateur.

Hagen wed again in the spring of 1924, but the marriage to Edna Strauss did not last, as domestic life simply did not agree with his lifestyle; they divorced after 10 years. He did, however, experience much more success in making an important business decision. Specifically, in 1927, Hagen invested in manufacturing golf clubs bearing his name and design, a move that augmented his wealth and fame long after his playing career ended.

Hagen continued to play competitively well into the 1930s, but with the onset of the Great Depression, and with fees for exhibitions in the United States dwindling, Hagen took his game and appeal abroad. In so doing he became the first prominent American golf ambassador, as he played throughout the South Pacific, the Far East, Africa, and Europe.

Hagen retired from competitive golf in 1940, having won 75 tournaments and having played in more than 2,500 exhibitions. He was also the first golfer to win more than $1 million in prize money. Despite his retirement, Hagen's presence and popularity within golfing circles did not diminish. Professional golfers in particular realized that the game's popularity and the large tournament purses were attributable partly to Hagen's showmanship, his flair for competition, and his visibility around the world. According to his fellow competitor Gene Sarazen, "I think Walter Hagen contributed more to golf than any player today or ever" (quoted in Fimrite, p. 76). For his many contributions to the game, Hagen was inducted as a charter member of the PGA Hall of Fame in 1940, and he was elected to golf's most elite body, the Royal & Ancient Golf Club of St. Andrews, Scotland, in 1968. The following year Hagen died at his estate in Traverse City, Michigan.

• Though Hagen left no known unpublished personal papers, the Rochester Historical Society, Rochester, N.Y., houses an extensive collection of newspaper and magazine articles about him. The best, and most complete, single-volume account of Hagen's career is his autobiography, *The Walter Hagen Story* (1956). Other sources chronicling aspects of Hagen's career and personal life include Ron Fimrite, "Sir Walter," *Sports Illustrated*, 19 June 1989, pp. 74–86; Geoff Russell, "Walter Hagen: The Rochester Years," *Golf Digest*, June 1989, pp. 129–34; Charles Price, "Sir Walter and the Emperor Jones," *Golf Digest*, April 1992, pp. 58–63; and Herbert Warren Wind, "The Sporting Scene: The Haig and Some Recent Masters," *New Yorker*, 18 May 1987, pp. 89–106. An obituary is in the *New York Times*, 7 Oct. 1969.

DAVIS W. HOUCK

HAGERTY, James Campbell (9 May 1909–11 Apr. 1981), presidential press secretary, was born in Plattsburgh, New York, the son of James A. Hagerty, a journalist, and Katherine Kearney, a schoolteacher. In 1912 the family moved to New York City. Hagerty grew up with an understanding of the media; his father was a political reporter for the *New York Times*. Hagerty himself served as a campus reporter for the *Times* while a student at Columbia University. Upon his graduation in 1934, he worked four years on the paper's city desk in New York. In 1937 he married Marjorie Lucas, with whom he had two children. He moved to the Albany bureau to cover the statehouse in 1938, and in 1943 he joined the administration of Governor Thomas E. Dewey as its spokesman.

Through his experience with Dewey both in Albany (until 1952) and during the governor's presidential campaigns (1944 and 1948), Hagerty came to understand the requirements of an executive and of national political reporters and editors. For example, he understood the benefits of coordinating executive branch information at a time when others did not. While press secretary to Dewey, Hagerty established a Public Information Council composed of the people in each department working on public relations issues. The individuals coordinated the release of information in an effort to evenly distribute material throughout the week and avoid a situation in which too many items were released simultaneously. That way each item would get the attention the administration desired. His successful communications policies earned him the attention of Dwight Eisenhower and appointment in 1952 as presidential press secretary.

Hagerty's success was attributable to his training and talent but also to the relationship he developed with President Eisenhower. He was a good judge of people and knew how to get the best from them. Eisenhower described him as "possessed of an agile mind, a canny capacity for judging people, political shrewdness, and a healthy Irish temper" (Eisenhower, *Mandate for Change*, p. 117). Together Hagerty and the future president fashioned a modus operandi during a game of golf following the 1952 Republican National Convention. "You'll know everything I'm doing," Eisenhower told Hagerty. "If you have anything you don't know the answer to, come to me and I'll tell you." Hagerty reported that Eisenhower was true to his word. "It was as simple as that," said Hagerty. "If I wasn't in his office when he made a decision, [he'd tell the person present,] even including the Secretary of State, . . . 'Stop in at Jim's office as you go out and tell him what we decided'" (Hagerty oral history interview transcript, p. 56).

Hagerty was at the center of all publicity operations during Eisenhower's administration. At the time of the president's heart attack in 1955, Hagerty's smooth handling of a potentially difficult situation eased anxieties in Washington, D.C., and around the nation. Eisenhower also called on his press secretary for political advice, such as whether he should run for a second term. The close personal relationship the two men shared made it easier for Hagerty to know the mind of the president and not only to speak for him but also to anticipate his needs.

The nature of news organizations and the changes unfolding in the electronic media also were important to Hagerty's success. His White House tenure occurred at a time when television was coming into its own, and Hagerty understood its importance in allowing the president to present his own case to the public. For example, when Eisenhower was criticized by newspaper columnists for not responding more vigorously to Senator Joseph P. McCarthy (R.-Wis.), Hagerty arranged for Eisenhower's press conferences to be on television. "We'll go directly to the people who can hear exactly what Pres[ident Eisenhower] said without reading warped and slanted stories," Hagerty noted in his diary (4 Mar. 1954). Equally important, Hagerty worked with news organizations on technology, such as lighting. He wanted broadcasts that could be televised without glaring lights distracting the president. He also retained control over the film editing. Broadcasts were aired the same day they were filmed but only after Hagerty checked them for problems.

An incident related by Eisenhower in *Mandate for Change* highlights the confidence both he and the press had in Hagerty's media management. During the 1952 campaign, a photographer traveling with the candidate got up early to take pictures at 5:30 A.M. of General and Mrs. Eisenhower greeting local residents from the back of their railroad car. When his sleep-in colleagues heard of the coverage, they prevailed on Hagerty to restage the event for them. At Hagerty's request, the Eisenhowers reenacted the whole scene later in the day, bathrobes and all.

Hagerty's career reflects the transition from reporter to press secretary to professional government spokesperson. It also reflects the transition of communications from print to electronic media. In 1960 Leonard Goldenson, the president of the American Broadcasting Company, asked Eisenhower if he might talk with Hagerty about coming to ABC once he left the White House. Goldenson was interested in the press secretary because of Hagerty's contact with reporters during his sixteen years of association with political office. "He had a good perspective on who was good," Goldenson observed (interview with Goldenson). Hagerty's career ended at ABC, where he initially worked as the vice president of the news division (1961–1963), building the reportorial staff of the news department. Among the persons brought to ABC by his efforts were William Lawrence, a political reporter formerly of the *New York Times*; John Scali, the Associated Press diplomatic correspondent; and Howard K. Smith, who became an anchor on the evening news. Hagerty became vice president of corporate relations in 1964 and retained this position and title, despite suffering a stroke in 1975, until his death in Bronxville, New York.

In serving President Eisenhower, Hagerty set a performance standard for all press secretaries who followed. His strength was his ability to win the support of both government officials and reporters with an innate instinct for meeting their mutual news needs. In a position that has since become known for antagonism, Hagerty was respected for his talent to satisfy both reporters and the White House officials they covered on their beat. His concept of the organization of information was a major contribution to the role of the modern press secretary. He understood in a way his predecessors had not that how information was organized and released to news organizations was critical to promoting a president's image and best interests.

• The most important materials dealing with Hagerty are in the Dwight D. Eisenhower Library, Abilene, Kans. The most illuminating item is the diary Hagerty kept during 1954 and 1955, which reveals his relationships with reporters and with White House people, especially Eisenhower. The diary material is collected in Robert H. Ferrell, ed., *The Diary of James C. Hagerty: Eisenhower in Mid-Course, 1954–1955* (1983). Hagerty's files contain materials relating to press conferences, particularly the preparations for them, and information relating to the foreign travel of the president and his retinue of reporters. The oral history interviews, especially the one with Hagerty, also give valuable information on his relationships with the president, White House staff members, and the reporters covering the White House. Most of the oral histories are at Columbia University as well as at the

Eisenhower Library. Eisenhower's accounts of his years in the White House, *Mandate for Change, 1953–1956* (1963) and *Waging Peace, 1956–1961* (1965), are useful resources. See also Stephen E. Ambrose, *Eisenhower: The President* (1984). An excellent account of Hagerty's press operation appears in Patrick Anderson, *The President's Men* (1968). Additional information is in Elmer Cornwell, *Presidential Leadership of Public Opinion* (1965). The interview with Goldenson was conducted by Martha Joynt Kumar on 16 Dec. 1991 in New York. An obituary is in the *New York Times*, 12 Apr. 1981.

MARTHA JOYNT KUMAR

HAGGERTY, Melvin Everett (17 Jan. 1875–6 Oct. 1937), educational psychologist, was born in Bunker Hill, Indiana, the son of John Wright Haggerty and Phoeba Ellen Hann, farmers. His early education was in the rural schools of Indiana. After earning his A.B. in 1902 at Indiana University, he taught English in local high schools. That same year he married Laura Caroline Garretson, of Pendleton, Indiana, with whom he had three children.

Haggerty taught high school in both Indiana and Massachusetts as he pursued graduate work, studying during 1904 at the University of Chicago but returning to the University of Indiana for his A.M. in 1907. He continued graduate work in animal behavior and intelligence at Harvard University, where he earned a second A.M. in 1909 and the Ph.D. in psychology in 1910. Haggerty studied both psychology and philosophy (psychology was still in the Department of Philosophy at Harvard) and benefited from the help and influence of such important early psychologists as Hugo Muensterberg, Robert Yerkes, and William James (after whom he named his son). The influence of Yerkes seems to have been decisive, turning Haggerty toward the study of animal psychology and intelligence testing. During the summer of 1908 Haggerty studied the intelligence of monkeys at the Bronx Zoo under Yerkes's direction. This early interest in animal intelligence became the foundation for Haggerty's scholarly career, leading to publications in that field and then on the measurement of intelligence and of educational achievement.

After rising rapidly on the faculty of Indiana University, where he taught from 1910 to 1915, Haggerty was recruited by the University of Minnesota in 1915. He would continue at the University of Minnesota for the rest of his life, as chair of the Department of Educational Psychology and as dean of the College of Education. Haggerty interrupted his academic career during World War I, serving from January 1918 to March 1919 as a major and lieutenant colonel in the Surgeon General's Office of the U.S. Army, where he had responsibility for the reeducation of disabled soldiers.

Both before and after his war service, Haggerty was able to put into practice on a large scale his interest in educational measurements and to promote the value of educational psychology in reforming and modernizing school curricula. He directed a study of reading in twenty Indiana cities in 1915. Beginning in 1919 he directed surveys of educational achievement in the schools of Virginia (1919), North Carolina (1920), and

New York (1921). Haggerty's large-scale surveys of educational achievement helped establish testing as a basic instrument of education. The surveys also promoted the need for professional psychologists to direct the testing programs; by the early twentieth century, psychologists based their claims for professional status on the value of standardized tests for the measurement of intelligence and educational achievement. The role of testing in education remained a fundamental concern for Haggerty and became the area where he made his most important contributions to psychology as a discipline and a profession. At the University of Minnesota he chaired the University Committee on Educational Research (1924–1937), which studied a variety of educational problems, including testing and achievement. Haggerty continued work on instruments to measure various achievements and other behaviors. The "Delta II" was an important addition to intelligence testing for children in grades three to nine. The Haggerty-Olson-Wickman Behavior Rating schedules for kindergarten through twelfth grade, first published in 1930, remained in print until the 1960s. The Minnesota Reading Examination for College Students (published 1930 to 1935) by Haggerty and Alvin C. Eurich, remained in print until at least 1983.

As a member of the second generation of academic psychologists in the United States, and as an academic administrator, Haggerty showed a special concern for scholarly work. He directed a study on the quality of faculty at institutions of higher education that demonstrated that faculty scholarship correlated more highly than any other factor in the quality of an institution. As dean of the College of Education at the University of Minnesota from 1920 to 1937, Haggerty also worked to foster scholarship among the faculty members of the College of Education. He managed to find both free time and grants for younger scholars. His success led to the recruitment of many of these successful young scholars by other institutions. Haggerty also became an educational statesman. He was active in the Department of Superintendence of the National Education Association and in the National Society for the Study of Education. He helped direct a study for the North Central Association of Colleges and Secondary Schools to determine objective criteria for judging institutions of higher education.

Haggerty's broadness of vision allowed him to see not only beyond his institution but also beyond academia. He believed that the vital link between the individual and his or her surroundings had declined with the spread of industry and standardized commodities. This industrial trend has "too often destroyed the sincerity of our lives." With help from the Carnegie Foundation, he was able to launch the Owatonna Art Project in Owatonna, Minnesota. The grant provided an art teacher for the schools who also became a consultant to the community. Adult art classes followed, then invitations from families to discuss furnishings, decorations, and other art problems in the home. As the community became more aware of art, more and more decisions included some art element, from discussing how to improve the appearance of the school to inviting the art instructor to help decide what color to paint the boiler room in the power plant. Haggerty believed that the need for art arose from the most primitive sources of human life. "Life becomes rich," he wrote in *Enrichment of the Common Life* (1938), "as the desires of men are favored by an atmosphere in which they can thrive" (p. 9).

Haggerty established his importance as a psychologist through his work in standardized testing. His influence, however, reached much farther than the tests he wrote. The preparation of students for careers as teachers and scholars under his leadership at the University of Minnesota was the best contribution Haggerty could give to his profession and his country. He died unexpectedly of coronary thrombosis in Minneapolis, Minnesota.

• Haggerty's publications on standardized testing and educational achievement are extensive and include *The Ability to Read* (1917), *Rural School Survey of New York* (1922), and "Studies in Examinations," in *Studies in College Examinations* (1934). He authored or coauthored three of the volumes in the series *The Evaluation of Higher Education*, including *The Faculty* (1937) and (with George Frederick Zook) *Principles of Accrediting Higher Institutions* (1936). His account of the Owatonna Art Project appears in *Enrichment of the Common Life* (1938). Haggerty's early work with monkeys was followed with interested amusement by the *New York Times* in the summer of 1908. An article titled "Animal Intelligence" appeared in the *Atlantic Monthly*, May 1911, pp. 599–607. An obituary is in the *New York Times*, 7 Oct. 1937. A longer obituary was written by A. C. Krey for *School and Society*, Feb. 1938, pp. 273–75.

JOHN C. SPURLOCK

HAGGIN, B. H. (29 Dec. 1900–29 May 1987), music critic, was born Bernard H. Haggin in New York City, the son of Byron Haggin and Dorothea (maiden name unknown). Educated in Manhattan schools, Haggin studied music from a historical rather than a performance perspective but showed a particular ability as a writer during his student days. Too young for military service during World War I, he completed his high school education near the war's end in 1918 and went on to receive a bachelor's degree from the City College of New York in 1922. The next year he published his first music review, thereby launching a commercial writing career that would span more than fifty years.

Haggin contributed freelance reviews on music and dance until 1934, when he was named music critic of the *Brooklyn Daily Eagle*, where he remained on the staff until 1937. In 1936 he was appointed music critic of the *Nation*, an influential position he held until 1957. It was there that his reputation was made. As critic and poet Randall Jarrell wrote of Haggin's dramatic sense and incisive prose, "Mr. Haggin is, as anybody can see, a born critic—a man who is doing exactly what he was put in the world to do" (*Saturday Review*, Nov. 1949). Not given to self-doubt, Haggin attributed the reputation he earned in the *Nation* to "a musician's ear, and an ability to assemble words in or-derly, clear statements" (*S.H. Weekly News*, 21 Dec. 1980).

Although Haggin's native abilities were more than sufficient to warrant such self-confidence, the fact that his career unfolded during what may be termed a "parenthetical period" in American music criticism gave his reputation an added boost. When he began writing for the *Nation*, an era dominated by the renowned critics of the 1910s and 1920s was drawing to a close. Three of the most influential music critics of that period, James G. Huneker, Deems Taylor, and William J. Henderson, had either retired or died, and with them had passed an era in which the length of newspaper reviews allowed a level of technical analysis that was no longer possible in the late 1930s. By then, a combination of depression-era printing costs and declining sales of newspapers in the wake of radio's growing popularity, coupled with the expanded headline coverage prompted by Adolf Hitler's rise in Europe, relegated opera, symphonic, and dance reviews to increasingly smaller columns. This parenthetical period was tailor-made for the precise, well-crafted prose with which Haggin graced the *Brooklyn Daily Eagle*, the *Nation*, and somewhat later the *New York Herald Tribune*. Over the years he also contributed articles, commentaries, and reviews to the *Hudson Review*, the *Yale Review*, the *New Republic*, and *Musical America*, among others.

Although Haggin's prose was admired and often praised by many of his contemporaries, others observed an increasing rigidity of viewpoint in his work, especially as the years passed. "Many found his opinions narrow," said critic Tim Page in an obituary tribute in the *New York Times*, citing as evidence Haggin's well-publicized contempt for most twentieth-century music, especially that of Béla Bartók, Arnold Schoenberg, and Charles Ives. "In his later work," Page added, "he also developed the habit of attacking other critics, sometimes vitriolically." One such critic was Samuel Chotzinoff, whose much-publicized 1956 book, *Toscanini: An Intimate Portrait*, contained revelations about the often boorish behavior of legendary conductor Arturo Toscanini, whom Haggin revered. These revelations impelled Haggin to condemn Chotzinoff's book in *Conversations with Toscanini* (1959; rev. ed., 1979), a calculated rebuttal to what Haggin regarded as Chotzinoff's unforgivable breach of Toscanini's privacy.

The writing career that Haggin began in 1923 continued uninterrupted until he was well past eighty. By the time of his death, in Manhattan, he had published more than a dozen books that, taken together, chronicled the musical life of New York City for nearly half a century.

• The published writings of Haggin include *A Book of the Symphony* (1937), *Music on Records* (1938; rev. eds., 1943, 1945), *Music for the Man Who Enjoys "Hamlet"* (1944), *The Listener's Musical Companion* (1956; rev. eds., 1967, 1971), *The Toscanini the Musicians Knew* (1967), *The Ballet Chronicle* (1970), *Music Observed* (1964), *A Decade of Music* (1973), *Dis-*

covering Balanchine (1981), and *Music and Ballet, 1973–1983* (1984). His reviews for the *Nation* were published in edited form under the title *Music in the Nation* (1949). An extensive assessment of Haggin as a critic is in *Ballet Review* 20, no. 2 (Summer 1992): 49–56. An obituary is in the *New York Times*, 30 May 1987.

JAMES A. DRAKE

HAGGIN, James Ben Ali (9 Dec. 1822–12 Sept. 1914), mine owner, land developer, and horseman, was born in Harrodsburg, Kentucky, the son of Terah Temple Haggin, a lawyer and farmer, and Adeline Ben Ali, a schoolteacher. Haggin's mother was said to have been the daughter of Ibrahim Ben Ali, an exiled Turkish army officer who settled in England and then moved to Philadelphia in the mid-1790s. Ben Ali's residence in England is well attested, but there is no record that he ever lived in Philadelphia, where he supposedly settled and practiced medicine. Haggin may not have descended from a Turk, but he gloried in the name Ben Ali.

Haggin's education is uncertain, but he was admitted to the bar in 1845 and opened a legal practice in Shelbyville, Kentucky. The following year he moved briefly to Natchez, Mississippi, where he married Eliza Sanders; they had five children. Then they moved to New Orleans, where he again practiced law. Haggin followed the gold seekers to California, but instead of digging for gold he opened a law office in San Francisco early in 1850. The following year in Sacramento he went into partnership with Lloyd Tevis, a Kentucky friend who soon became his brother-in-law.

Haggin and Tevis flourished as lawyers and then as investors in real estate, mining properties, and other California corporations, most notably Wells, Fargo & Company. Haggin's first great landholding was the Rancho del Paso, 44,000 acres just east of Sacramento, which he acquired with Tevis in 1862 in settlement of a legal fee. Haggin developed the ranch for sheep and cattle on higher elevations and grain and hay on the American River bottomlands. Haggin began raising blooded horses around 1870, trotters at first and then thoroughbreds, but did not race under his own colors until 1882. The ranch's private railroad shipping point was called Ben Ali, as was his colt that won the Kentucky Derby in 1886. Haggin withdrew from racing in 1891, after the death of his son, Ben Ali Haggin, who managed his eastern racing interests and pursued a long financial dispute with other horsemen. Haggin continued as a horse breeder in California until 1905, when he gave up the business as no longer profitable.

From 1872 onward Haggin gradually acquired several hundred thousand acres in the southern end of the San Joaquin valley, eventually incorporating his holdings as Kern County Land Company (1890). After prolonged litigation and legislative lobbying over water rights, Haggin negotiated a fruitful compromise in 1888 that enabled the large-scale and very profitable development of his Kern County holdings.

Haggin knew nothing about mining, but he developed a remarkable talent for identifying those who

did. He owned interests in at least sixty gold, silver, and copper mines scattered from Alaska to Peru, often in partnership with George Hearst and Marcus Daly, as well as Tevis until his death in 1899. Haggin was a founder and for many years a director of the Anaconda Copper Mining Company in Montana, as well as a major shareholder of the Homestake mine in South Dakota and Cerro del Pasco in Peru.

In 1897 Haggin purchased Elmendorf near Lexington, Kentucky, and gradually enlarged the property to 10,000 acres, the largest Bluegrass horse farm. In addition to breeding thoroughbred racehorses, Haggin raised beef cattle, sheep, and hogs and built a large dairy operation. For some years prior to 1905 he owned more thoroughbreds than any other American horseman.

Haggin's wife died in 1894, and three years later he married her 28-year-old niece, Margaret Voorhies, known to friends as Pearl. He erected a lavish mansion at Elmendorf for his bride and named the house Green Hills. Their principal residence was in New York City, for he sold his Nob Hill mansion in San Francisco before 1900. Haggin remained vigorous in business and society until a few months before his death, acquiring a rich copper mine in Peru, buying land for a new Fifth Avenue mansion in New York, and building the Ben Ali Theatre in Lexington.

Haggin died at his summer home in Newport, Rhode Island, and was buried at Woodlawn Cemetery in New York City. His estate, variously estimated between $15 million and $100 million, was left almost entirely to his family. On his death many newspapers remarked that little was known of his private life, although he was called the "greatest mine owner of earth" by the *New York Times*, which noted that tales of his Turkish ancestry only made his life more glamorous. To the *Lexington Herald* he "was always a man of mystery." Many recalled his dark complexion and Turkish appearance, but he would never confirm or deny stories of his ancestry. Haggin was an astute man of business, never the speculator, regarded by many business associates as aloof and silent but always loyal to his friends and true to his word.

• There are a number of James Ben Ali Haggin items in the Haggin Family Collection at the University of Kentucky Library, and a few letters and more extensive business papers at the Bancroft Library of the University of California, Berkeley. There is an extensive clipping file on his racing interests at the Keeneland Library in Lexington, Ky. A biographical source is Lois E. Mahoney, "California's Forgotten Triumvirate: James Ben Ali Haggin, Lloyd Tevis, and George Hearst" (M.A. thesis, San Francisco State Univ., 1977). All accounts of Haggin's youth must be treated with suspicion. Ibrahim Ben Ali is described in William Jones, *Memoirs of the Life, Ministry, and Writings of the Rev. Adam Clarke* (1838), and also the anonymous *Life of the Rev. Adam Clarke, L.L.D.* (1841). For the water rights dispute, see *Lux v. Haggin*, 10 Pacific 674 (1886). Haggin was known beyond California chiefly as a horseman, and brief wire service obituaries appeared throughout the nation. There are detailed accounts in the *New York Herald*, the *New York Sun*, the *New York*

Times, the San Francisco Chronicle, the San Francisco Examiner, and the Lexington Herald, all 13 Sept. 1914, as well as the Thoroughbred Record, 19 Sept. 1914.

PATRICK J. FURLONG

HAGLER (?–30 Aug. 1763), chief of the Catawba Indian Nation, who was also known as Nopkehe and Haigler, was probably born during the first decade of the eighteenth century along the Catawba River on the border of North and South Carolina. Nothing is known about his life before 1750, when, as a prominent warrior and kinsman of the previous ruler, Yanabe Yatengway ("Young Warrior"), he became chief, or in Catawba, *eractasswa*. It was a time of crisis for the Catawbas. Yanabe Yatengway and fifteen headmen had died during the previous year while on a trip to Charleston, European diseases and raids by native enemies had decimated the population, and colonial farmers were encroaching on Catawba territory. Hagler played a vital role in preserving the Catawba Nation. In the summer of 1751 he led a Catawba delegation to Albany to make peace with the Iroquois, the Catawbas' principal foes. To cement his people's ties to the British, he led Catawba war parties against the French and their Indian allies during the Seven Years' War. He then played upon Anglo-American gratitude for this aid to lobby for a reservation that would help protect part of the Catawba homeland from further encroachment. In July 1760 Crown officials agreed to establish a Catawba reservation of 144,000 acres.

Hagler's accomplishments rested on his ability to balance adherence to traditional Catawba ways with a shrewd understanding of colonial society. He spoke some English and was friendly to colonists but insisted on negotiating exclusively in Catawba and rejected missionaries' attempts to convert him to European ways. Similarly, despite Anglo-American efforts to encourage him to take on the role of king, Hagler, like every *eractasswa* before him, worked closely with the Catawba council. Throughout his career he used his colonial connections to further the interests of his people. Knowing British America's need for Indian allies, Hagler drove a hard bargain, insisting that colonial authorities ship food, clothing, and weapons to the Catawbas in exchange for their service. To increase the supply of these and other precious commodities to his people, he played one province against another, simultaneously arranging deals with Virginia, North Carolina, and South Carolina.

Hagler's skills as a diplomat are best illustrated by an incident in the spring of 1759. The governor of North Carolina had promised the Catawbas beef, but the colony's agent had sent the Indians meat of poor quality, pocketing the savings himself. Hagler traveled to Salisbury, North Carolina, walked into its next court session, and informed the assembled officials that the agent was cheating the colony's taxpayers. The fact that he knew where to make his complaint, when to arrive, whom to approach, and how best to frame his argument suggests his considerable abilities and helps to explain the occasional references to him as "the Haggler." By the time a Shawnee war party killed Hagler near Catawba lands, his reputation was assured. Catawbas still regard him as one of their greatest chiefs. Americans were so grateful for his cooperation that Camden, South Carolina, later adopted him as its patron saint and commissioned the construction of a weathervane in his image that, since 1826, has overlooked the town.

• The official records of Virginia, North Carolina, and especially South Carolina are the best sources on Hagler's career. They contain speeches that he gave in meetings with colonists and letters written on behalf of the Catawba council by colonial scribes. See especially William L. McDowell, Jr., ed., *Documents Relating to Indian Affairs, May 21, 1750–August 7, 1754* (1958), and *Documents Relating to Indian Affairs, 1754–1765* (1970); South Carolina Council Journals, in William Sumner Jenkins, comp., Records of the States of the United States of America (microfilm, 1949); and William Henry Lyttelton papers, William L. Clements Library, Ann Arbor, Mich. Scholarly works include Douglas Summers Brown, *The Catawba Indians: The People of the River* (1966), and James H. Merrell, " 'Minding the Business of the Nation': Hagler as Catawba Leader," *Ethnohistory* 33 (1986): 55–70, and *The Indians' New World: Catawbas and Their Neighbors from European Contact through the Era of Removal* (1989).

JAMES H. MERRELL

HAGOOD, Johnson (21 Feb. 1829–4 Jan. 1898), Confederate soldier and politician, was born in Barnwell County, South Carolina, the son of James O'Hear Hagood, a physician and planter, and Indina Allen. After graduating from the Citadel, the military college of South Carolina, in 1847, he read law with a Charleston judge and was admitted to the bar in 1850. Hagood returned to Barnwell County where, like his father, he combined planting with his profession. In 1851 he was appointed deputy adjutant general of the South Carolina militia and elected county commissioner in equity. In 1856 he married Eloise Brevard Butler, daughter of Andrew Pickens Butler, one of South Carolina's U.S. senators. The Hagoods had one child.

When South Carolina seceded, Hagood was elected colonel of the First South Carolina Regiment and participated in the attack on Fort Sumter. Shortly thereafter, the regiment was ordered to Virginia where it saw action in the first battle of Manassas. Returning to South Carolina, Hagood became very much involved in the defense of Charleston. His valor at the battle of Secessionville (June 1862) led to his promotion to brigadier general. In May 1864 his brigade (Twenty-first South Carolina) was ordered to Virginia, where they participated in battles around Petersburg, including Drewry's Bluff, Bermuda Hundred, and Cold Harbor. In August 1864, after fierce hand-to-hand combat, he successfully led a detachment of 200 men back to Confederate lines when it appeared they would be surrounded. During the siege of Petersburg, he commanded a section of the trenches and, according to his own account, only 700 of the 2,100 men assigned to him survived. In December 1864 Hagood's troops reinforced the remaining Confederate forces in eastern

North Carolina. On 26 April 1865 he surrendered his unit with Joseph E. Johnston's army near Durham.

After the war, Hagood returned home and resumed his local political career. In the 1865 elections authorized under Presidential Reconstruction, he was elected to represent Barnwell County in the South Carolina House of Representatives. When Congressional Reconstruction was implemented in 1867, Hagood, like many of his class, found himself outside the political mainstream. Defeated in an 1868 congressional contest, he turned his energies to reopening his alma mater, the Citadel, and to improving the state's agriculture. In 1865 he was named to the Citadel's board of visitors and in 1878 became chairman of the board. The first president of the South Carolina Agricultural and Mechanical Association (1869), he led by example, engaging in a variety of agricultural experiments in an attempt to find crops suitable for diversified farming. He also spearheaded the successful effort to build a cotton oil plant in Columbia.

Although out of public office, Hagood did not abandon politics. He was chairman of the executive committee of the Barnwell County Democratic party and attended the 1871 and 1874 taxpayers' conventions. The conventions provided the only means for many South Carolinians to register their protest against what they considered the excesses of the Reconstruction regime. Hagood created a strong Democratic organization in his home county and was prepared for the 1876 elections prior to the state Democratic party convention. He served as vice president of that convention, received the party's nomination for comptroller general, and became a key adviser to Wade Hampton (1818–1902) in his gubernatorial campaign.

Elected comptroller general in 1876 and reelected in 1878, Hagood typified the conservative Hampton wing of the South Carolina Democratic party; he was a Confederate hero, a fiscal conservative, and thought that government should do as little as possible, no matter how great the need. In 1880 he was selected by the conservatives as their gubernatorial candidate against the rabble-rousing Martin W. Gary. With Hampton's personal support, Hagood received the unanimous nomination of the state convention and easily triumphed over his Republican opponent in the general election.

As governor, Hagood was instrumental in convincing the general assembly to pass legislation authorizing the reopening of the Citadel. He supported the passage of the Election Act of 1882, the so-called "Eight Box Law," and the redrawing of South Carolina's congressional districts to create a "black district." Both measures were designed to improve the Democrats' political position and to reduce the influence of black voters. Although he was South Carolina's "most agriculturally-minded governor" (Cooper, p. 138), Hagood failed to understand the difficulties facing the state's farmers. He considered the crop-lien law harmful to individual farmers and to the state's economy but did nothing to support repeal efforts. He did, however, support the creation of a stronger railroad commission in 1882. After one term in office, he decided not to stand for reelection and retired to Barnwell.

As Benjamin Ryan Tillman's populistic movement began to gather steam, Hagood was drawn back into politics in support of his old friends in the Hampton wing of the party. In 1890 he was mentioned as a possible gubernatorial candidate in an attempt to block Tillman, just as he had been used in 1880 to block Gary, Tillman's spiritual mentor. He demurred, in part because of his age and in part because he could see that opposition would be futile—Tillman's forces had taken control of the Barnwell Democratic party, which the former governor had dominated since the war. Tillman's triumph made hollow Hagood's comments following his defeat of Gary in 1880: "I think everything will go smoothly now" (Cooper, p. 64). After the elections, Hagood once again retired from politics, and in 1892 he stepped down as chairman of the Citadel's board of visitors. He died in Barnwell.

Hagood was not as well known at the end of the twentieth century as he was at its beginning. While there is little doubt that white Carolinians would have overthrown the Reconstruction regime in 1876, they opted not to resort to overt violence as had Mississippi and other states of the Lower South. Some contemporary observers credit Hagood with developing the successful plans for the 1876 election campaign. As governor, he helped implement the conservatives' plans for gradually reducing the influence of black voters. However, like his fellow conservatives, he was blind to the economic distress that afflicted the great majority of the state's white farmers and did nothing to alleviate their difficulties. His inaction, and that of his like-minded successors, led to the triumph of Tillmanism in 1890.

• There is a collection of Johnson Hagood Papers in the South Caroliniana Library (Columbia), but it contains little correspondence of any note. There are scattered Hagood letters in various other manuscript collections in that library and in the South Carolina Historical Society (Charleston). Hagood's *Memoirs of the War of Secession, from the Original Manuscripts of Johnson Hagood, Brigadier-General, C.S.A.* (1910) is in the tradition of most turn-of-the-century Civil War writings. Other accounts of his wartime experiences are in *Confederate Military History* (1899; repr. 1987) and E. Milby Burton, *The Siege of Charleston, 1861–1865* (1970). Hagood's devotion to the Citadel is discussed in John Peyre Thomas, *The History of the South Carolina Military Academy* (1893), which also includes a lengthy biographical sketch. For information regarding his place in post–Civil War South Carolina politics, there are a number of secondary sources. Francis Butler Simkins and Robert Hilliard Woody, *South Carolina during Reconstruction* (1932), discuss fully the political situation and the taxpayers' conventions. Discussions of his role in the 1876 campaign can be found in John S. Reynolds, *Reconstruction in South Carolina* (1905), and Alfred B. Williams, *Hampton and His Redshirts: South Carolina's Deliverance in 1876* (1935). Both of these books are typical of the "unreconstructed" South Carolina point of view; however, the prominence they give to Hagood explains his political power base. The best analysis of Hagood as governor and a conservative Democrat is found in William J. Cooper, Jr., *The Conservative Regime: South Carolina 1877–1890* (1968).

WALTER B. EDGAR

HAGOOD, Margaret Loyd Jarman (26 Oct. 1907–13 Aug. 1963), sociologist and demographer, was born in Newton County, Georgia, the daughter of Lewis Jarman, who became president of Queens College in Charlotte, North Carolina, and Laura Harris. Hagood was the second of four daughters and two sons, and she was one of two daughters to earn a doctorate. In 1926 she stopped attending Scott College in Atlanta, Georgia, to marry her childhood sweetheart Middleton Howard Hagood. One year later she had her only child, a daughter also named Margaret. In 1929, at the age of twenty-two, Hagood earned an A.B. at Queens College. One year later she earned an M.A. in mathematics at Emory University in Atlanta. In 1936 she was divorced from her husband, and the following year she completed her Ph.D. in sociology at the University of North Carolina at Chapel Hill.

Both before earning her doctorate and after, Hagood worked at various institutions. In 1930–1931 she was an instructor at Druid Hills High School in Atlanta. From 1931 to 1935 she taught at National Park Seminary College in Forest Glenn, Maryland. Two years later, in 1937–1938, Hagood became a fellow at the Julius Rosenwald Fund. From 1938 to 1942 she returned to the University of North Carolina at Chapel Hill as a research associate at the Institute for Research in Social Science.

Hagood's first book, *Mothers of the South* (1939), was published just two years after she received her doctorate. This important piece of qualitative research analyzed the life of poor white farm families in the southern United States during the Great Depression and is "considered one of the best records available of the daily experience of white Southern farmers in the midst of the Depression" (Deegan, p. 158). While qualitative research constituted her first book, it would be her contributions in quantitative methods for which Hagood would receive international recognition. *Statistics for Sociologists*, first published in 1941, "was to influence the quantitative methods of a generation of social scientists" (Willits et al., p. 128). In 1952 the text was revised and published again.

In 1942 Hagood moved to Washington, D.C., to join the professional staff of the Division of Farm Population and Rural Life, which was housed in the U.S. Department of Agriculture (USDA) within the Bureau of Agricultural Economics (BAE) from 1919 to 1953. The first unit in the federal government solely devoted to sociological research, the division and its staff played a leading role in developing the discipline of rural sociology. The division was a pioneer in applying sociology to the federal public agenda and became the authoritative source for current information on farm population situations and trends.

While at the division, Hagood researched farm population and rural levels of living using sophisticated statistical methods and contributing to the advances in sampling techniques in the larger BAE. Hagood's "most popularly known and widely used contribution" was her County Level of Living Index, published in book form in 1952 entitled *Farm Operator Family Level-of-Living for Counties in the United States; 1930, 1940, 1945, and 1950* (Taylor, p. 97). This index provided a quantitative method for measuring rural living at the county level. Developed during a time when the discipline of rural sociology was itself increasingly quantitative, this index provided a way to compare rural living, county by county, across the United States. Data on rural areas had only begun to be systematically collected twenty years earlier, and this index provided an invaluable tool for rural sociologists and nonsociologists alike. For example, by employing Hagood's index, it became possible to identify and delineate the rural cultural regions and subregions of the United States. Moreover, maps constructed from the indexes were also widely used. In 1948 findings from the division's levels of living indexes were used in a BAE report on agricultural policy requested by the House Committee on Agriculture.

In 1941 Hagood joined the Rural Sociological Society. Formed just four years earlier, this professional organization brought together rural sociologists from across the country. In these early years of the society, Hagood was one of only three women to publish more than a single article in the society's professional journal, *Rural Sociology*. Indeed Hagood's six articles were the most published by any of the journal's women contributors in 1949. Most of Hagood's articles focused on her measures of rural living.

Hagood's participation in professional societies quickly grew. In 1943 she was honored with a membership in the Sociological Research Association. Four years later she became president of the District of Columbia Sociological Society and honorary member of the International Population Union. In 1949 she was made a fellow of the American Statistical Association. The next year Hagood became vice president of the American Sociological Society (later the American Sociological Association), the national professional organization for sociologists in the United States. She also served as president in 1954 of the Population Association of America, the national professional organization for demographers. From 1958 to 1961 Hagood served as the District of Columbia representative on the Council of the American Sociological Society and as a member of the Board of Directors of the American Statistical Association from 1953 to 1955.

In 1950 Hagood began taking on leadership roles in the Rural Sociological Society. That year she was elected to the Committee on Research, where she served for several years. In 1954 she was elected vice president of the society and became a member of the Executive Committee. In 1956 Hagood became president of the Rural Sociological Society, "the only woman in the first 50 years of the organization to hold that office" (Willits et al., p. 128).

In addition to her numerous professional publications and technical reports, Hagood wrote four of the chapters in *Rural Life in the United States* (1949). This text was a key introductory text for sociologists and rural sociologists. Hagood's work also extended beyond professional publications. For example, in 1947 she participated in the World Statistical Conference. That same year Hagood was made an honorary member of the International Population Union. From 1948 to 1953 she served as a consultant on the Manpower Panel of the Research and Development Board of the National Military Establishment. The following year Hagood participated in the World Population Conference, and in 1949 she participated in the World Statistical Conference. In 1955–1956 she worked as a population expert and consultant with the United Nations Technical Assistance Mission to Barbados, West Indies. She also served on the Technical Advisory Committee on Population for both the 1950 and 1960 censuses. In 1951 Hagood was a visiting professor at the University of Wisconsin, and in 1955 her alma mater Queens College conferred to Hagood an honorary degree of doctor of science.

In 1952 Hagood became head of the Division of Farm Population and Rural Life. Following in the auspicious shoes of Charles J. Galpin and Carl C. Taylor, she headed the division for its final year in existence. After the division was abolished in 1953 as part of Secretary of Agriculture Ezra Benson's reorganization of the Department of Agriculture, Hagood became chief of the resulting Population and Rural Life Branch. She remained with the USDA until 1962, when she left due to health considerations. She died one year later of a heart attack in San Diego, California.

Hagood was internationally recognized in both demography and statistics. Her contributions were numerous as she established a "notable career as a sociologist and a demographer" (Taylor, p. 97). She was also a trailblazer, maintaining a strong career at a time when women in the professional ranks of social science were few and far between. In this way and through her many professional contributions, Hagood left an indelible mark on the development of the discipline of rural sociology. Carl C. Taylor summarized Hagood's work this way: "Her contributions are so solidly written into the framework of research methods that they will continue to fructify social research for many years in the future" (p. 97).

• For information on Hagood, see "In Memoriam: Margaret Jarman Hagood, 1907–1963," in *Social Forces* 41 (1963); Olaf F. Larson et al., eds., *Sociology in Government: A Bibliography of the Work of the Division of Farm Population and Rural Life, U.S. Department of Agriculture, 1919–1953* (1992); Olaf F. Larson et al., *Sociology in Government: The Galpin-Taylor Years in the U.S. Department of Agriculture, 1919–1953* (1998); Mary Jo Deegan, ed., *Women in Sociology: A Bio-Bibliographical Sourcebook* (1991); and Fern K. Willits et al., "Women in the Rural Sociological Society: A History," *The Rural Sociologist* 8 (1988): 126–141. An obituary is Carl C. Taylor, "Margaret J. Hagood (1907–1963)," *Rural Sociology* 29 (1964): 97–98.

JULIE N. ZIMMERMAN

HAGUE, Arnold (3 Dec. 1840–14 May 1917), geologist, was born in Boston, Massachusetts, the son of William Hague, D.D., a Baptist minister, and Mary Bowditch Moriarty, a relative of astronomer-mathematician Nathaniel Bowditch. In Arnold's twelfth year, the family moved to Albany, New York, where he graduated from the Boys' Academy in 1854. They then moved to New York City. In 1861, after being rejected on physical grounds as a Union army volunteer, Hague entered Yale's Sheffield Scientific School, where he was educated by professors George Brush, James Dana, and Samuel Johnson, and befriended by senior Clarence King. Hague received a Ph.B. in chemistry from Sheffield in 1863. Failing again to be accepted by the army, he spent the next three years in chemical and mineralogical studies at the university in Göttingen, in Wilhelm Bunsen's laboratory at Heidelberg, and with Bernard von Cotta at the Bergakademie at Freiberg in Saxony. White at Freiberg in 1865, Hague met Samuel Franklin Emmons, a Harvard graduate trained by Bunsen and at Paris's École des Mines, who had entered the Bergakademie the previous summer. Emmons became Hague's informal adviser.

Hague returned to the United States late in 1866, as King sought sponsorship by the U.S. Army Corps of Engineers for a survey of the economic resources of a wide strip across the West, from the eastern base of the Sierra Nevada to the eastern front of the Rocky Mountains, that included the lines of the Central and Union Pacific railroads. When Congress and President Andrew Johnson authorized the U.S. Geological Exploration of the Fortieth Parallel on 2 March 1867, King appointed Hague's older brother James, a graduate of Harvard's Lawrence Scientific School who also had studied at Göttingen and Freiberg, as the civilian-staffed survey's principal assistant in geology. King made Arnold Hague his second assistant and "Frank" Emmons (whom Arnold introduced to King) joined the organization as its unsalaried third assistant. Between 1867 and 1872, King's field parties systematically and comprehensively mapped (for publication at 1:253,440) and assessed the topography, geology, and natural resources of 87,000 square miles of western lands flanking the transcontinental railroad. James Hague left the survey in 1870 for consulting as a mining engineer, but Arnold remained with King. James Hague's *Mining Industry* (1870), the initial volume of the survey's final reports, set standards for the contemporary federal surveys of the West. The text and its atlas contained Arnold Hague's analyses and maps (with topographer Frederick Clark) of Nevada's Comstock and White Pine mining districts; Arnold's improvements of Washoe chemical smelting saved "millions in formerly lost silver and gold" (Thurman Wilkins, *Clarence King* [1988], p. 139). Also in 1870, King, Hague, and Emmons studied the dormant volcanoes of the Cascade Range; their discovery of active glaciers on Mounts Hood, Rainier, and Shasta, and on Lassen Peak, refuted the popular belief that no true glaciers existed in the United States outside Alaska. King's team completed field work in 1872 and began, using the latest laboratory methods and instruments, to prepare their folio atlas and the remaining quarto final reports as parts of *Engineer Department Professional Paper 18*. These volumes included Arnold Hague and Emmons's *Descriptive Geology* (1877) of the entire region surveyed, in which they introduced the term "Laramie Formation" to encompass the age-troublesome stratigraphic units that straddled the Cretaceous-Tertiary boundary associated with the demise of the dinosaurs. King merged his field data with those of Hague and Emmons as the basis for King's own volume *Systematic Geology* (1878), his geologic-orogenic synthesis of the results of the reconnaissance.

On 3 March 1879 the Forty-fifth Congress and President Rutherford Hayes established the U.S. Geological Survey (USGS), adopting in part recommendations the legislators had requested of the National Academy of Sciences (NAS). King, who had advised the NAS's committee and helped to write the plan and the statute, became the new agency's director. King appointed Arnold Hague and Emmons two of the USGS's five principal geologists. Since 1877, Hague had served as a contract mining geologist to national governments, first in Guatemala (where he also studied volcanoes) and then in China. Early in 1880 Hague returned from China and, with assistants Joseph Iddings and Charles Walcott and topographer Clark, began an examination of Nevada's Eureka mining district as one of the primary investigations by the agency's Mining Geology Division. The results of this study appeared as the atlas (1883) and the text volume (1892) of the "Geology of the Eureka District, Nevada" that form *USGS Monograph 20*. In this volume, Hague and Iddings introduced the descriptive term *phenocryst* for the larger crystals found in generally fine-grained porphyritic rocks. They also published innovative microscopical analyses of the Fortieth Parallel survey's rocks and those in new collections from the Comstock and Central America.

In 1883 Hague, Iddings, and a new team, including geologist Walter Weed, physicist William Hallock, and chemist Frank Gooch, began to map and study the geology of more than 3,000 square miles in the decade-old Yellowstone National Park and adjacent areas of Wyoming and Montana. Hague focused his own investigations on the nature and origin of the park's geysers and hot springs, spending nine years in continuing and expanding work begun during the 1870s by federal geologist Albert Peale to include the forest-reserve areas west of the park. Hague also studied the Tertiary volcanic rocks at the north end of the Absaroka Range. He recognized that protecting the park's resources depended on the conservation of adjacent forests, watersheds, and wildlife. He recommended successfully in 1891 the establishment of the Yellowstone Forest reserve east and south of the park. Most

of the results of the Yellowstone project appeared as the text (part 2, 1899) and 1:125,000-scale atlas (1904) of "Geology of the Yellowstone National Park" as *USGS Monograph 32*. Earlier versions of the topographic and areal geologic maps of the six quadrangles in the 1904 atlas comprise folios 30 (1896) and 52 (1899) of the *Geologic Atlas of the United States*.

Beginning in the 1880s, Hague's work won him many academic and professional honors, including election to the NAS (1885; home secretary, 1901–1913) and the American Philosophical Society (1903), and the presidency of the Geological Society of America (1910). In 1893 Hague married Mary Anne Bruce (Robins) Howe, of New York City, the widow of attorney-legislator Walter Howe; the Hagues had no children. Hague's stepson Ernest, who served as a USGS geologist during 1900–1910, accompanied Hague to two of the three International Geological Congresses—at Paris in 1900 and at Toronto in 1913—where Hague served as a vice president. Hague also joined several prominent social organizations, including the Cosmos Club in the Capital and the Century Club in New York City. Hague died in Washington, D.C. Ernest Howe, a consulting geologist since 1910, acted as Hague's executor.

In addition to Hague's studies of the areal geology and mining districts of Nevada, Utah, Wyoming, and Montana, his work with Gifford Pinchot in 1896 on the NAS's Committee on the Inauguration of a Rational Forest Policy for the Forested Lands of the United States led directly in the next year to the establishment of thirteen new reserves. Hague's influence on geology continued to be felt through the work of his collaborators Iddings, Weed, volcanologist Thomas Jaggar, and others who served with him in the West. The work Hague directed in the Yellowstone National Park, or undertook there himself, has recently been described by an earth scientist with extensive experience in the area as "the largest and most in-depth study of Yellowstone that has ever been done, or probably ever will be done," and the "foundation for future research" (USGS geologist-emeritus J. David Love, quoted in Mary Fritz, *American Association of Petroleum Geologists Explorer* 16, no. 12 [Dec. 1995], p. 23.

• The Geologic Division's portion of Record Group 57 (Geological Survey) at the National Archives and Records Administration's Archives II facility in College Park, Md., contains the records of the Fortieth Parallel Exploration, "Arnold Hague Papers, 1880–1916" and other documents, including his field notebooks, that Hague generated during his federal service. Other manuscript materials are in the James Hague Papers at the Huntington Library, San Marino, Calif. *U.S. Geological Survey Bulletin* 746 (1923): 437 lists Hague's principal publications; most of these data also are available on CD-ROM as part of the American Geological Institute's "GeoRef" online bibliographical database. Three articles by two of Hague's contemporaries in the USGS provide personal and career data and perspective, and bibliographies: Joseph S. Diller, "Arnold Hague," *American Journal of Science*, 4th ser., 44 (1917): 73–75; Joseph P. Iddings, "Memorial of Arnold Hague," *Geological Society of America Bulletin* 29 (1918): 35–48; and Iddings, "Biographical Memoir of Arnold

Hague," *National Academy of Sciences Biographical Memoirs* 9 (1920): 21–38. Hatten S. Yoder, Jr., reevaluates the Hague-Iddings collaboration in "Joseph Paxson Iddings, 1857–1920: A Biographical Memoir," National Academy of Sciences *Biographical Memoirs* 69 (1996): 3–34. Mary C. Rabbitt, *Minerals, Lands, and Geology for the Common Defence and General Welfare*, vol. 1: *Before 1879* (1979), vol. 2: *1879–1904* (1980), and vol. 3: *1904–1939* (1986), place Hague's work in the context of federally sponsored geology.

CAROL A. EDWARDS
CLIFFORD M. NELSON

HAGUE, Frank (17 Jan. 1876–1 Jan. 1956), mayor of Jersey City, New Jersey, was born in Jersey City, the son of John Hague, a blacksmith and railroad worker, and Margaret Fagen. Both parents were Irish immigrants. Hague's career followed a classic trajectory in urban politics. He grew up in the Irish-American tenement neighborhood of Jersey City called the Horseshoe District, which remained his power base for the rest of his life. Jersey City was then a rapidly expanding industrial center: a major rail hub for the shipment of goods across the Hudson River to New York City, a thriving manufacturing locale, and an important immigrant destination.

After leaving school at age fourteen, Hague drifted from job to job, but he found his true vocation in ward politics and was elected constable of the Second Ward in 1899. Over the next two decades he gradually mastered the arts of patronage, alliances, and betrayals, even portraying himself as a "reformer" to attract votes. Elected city commissioner in 1913, he headed the patronage-rich police and fire departments, and in 1917 he attained his goal: mayor of Jersey City and unchallenged boss of local politics.

Hague introduced no innovations into the art of urban politics, but he practiced the mechanics of machine organization with unrivaled rigor. The heart of the machine was its control of city jobs. From anyone seeking to gain or to hold a city job, the machine demanded unconditional loyalty, votes and labor at election time, and, not least, a 3 percent annual salary kickback. Suppliers and especially contractors who dealt with the city were assessed at 10 percent of their contracts. Finally, the machine took its cut from the rackets it protected. For example, Jersey City had so many bookmakers that it was known in the 1920s as the "Horse Bourse."

For those citizens not directly beholden to the machine, Hague promised reliable city services, especially police and fire protection. As he asserted with characteristic bluntness: "Nobody can beat me as long as I give the people service. And I give them service." He was particularly proud of his twenty-year campaign to construct the Jersey City Medical Center, which eventually comprised seven grand towers with more than 2,000 beds, at the time the third-largest municipal and county hospital system in the world. The first of the seven towers was the Margaret Hague Maternity Hospital, completed in 1922 and named after his mother, perhaps the only recorded example of sentimentality in Hague's political career.

Hague protected his base in Jersey City through the power he also exercised at the county and state levels. His control of Jersey City meant control of Hudson County, New Jersey's second-largest with 700,000 people, which gave Hague de facto appointive powers over the county sheriff, the county tax board, and the board of elections. In 1919 Hague's choice for governor, Edward I. Edwards, was elected, a victory that sealed Hague's leadership of the statewide Democratic party. For the governorship Hague favored respectable progressive Democrats who understood the need to appoint Hague's choices to the Hudson County prosecutorship and judiciary.

Protected from investigation, Hague never scrupled to hide a lifestyle that bore no relationship to his mayor's salary, which never exceeded $7,500: a fourteen-room duplex in Jersey City's most fashionable apartment house; a grand summer house at the Jersey Shore; and rented villas every winter in Miami or Palm Beach. Tall, well dressed, imperious, he lived like a millionaire but never lost the swagger and grammar of the slums. In 1903 he married Jennie W. Warner; they had three children.

At his peak in the 1930s, Hague was a virtual dictator in Jersey City, the most important Democratic leader in New Jersey, and a significant figure in national politics. A strong backer of Alfred E. Smith through the 1932 Democratic convention, he switched his loyalties so decisively to Franklin Roosevelt that Roosevelt channeled his New Deal recovery programs for Hudson County through Hague's machine. This enabled Hague to construct the capstone to his Jersey City Medical Center, the 23-story, 1,000-bed Surgical Tower.

The 1930s also saw Hague enveloped in national controversy stemming from his dictatorial control of the police and the judiciary. His famous statement, "I am the law," made in 1937 when he ignored state regulations in order to obtain working papers for two underage teenagers, accurately reflected his basic viewpoint, especially regarding civil liberties.

Despite his political ties to the New Deal, Hague's attitude toward the social movements of the 1930s was closer to the reactionary wing of the Catholic church. In particular, he hated the newly formed Committee on Industrial Organization (CIO), partly because he viewed it as comprised of dangerous "reds," but also because he wanted to enhance Jersey City's reputation for "a good business climate." One of his favorite slogans was "Jersey City Has Everything for Business."

In 1937 Hague decided to bar CIO labor organizers from the city, and CIO activists were beaten and jailed by Hague's police, then "deported" across the Hudson River to New York City. No hall would rent its space to CIO or civil liberties organizations, and they were refused all permits for outdoor rallies. When in 1938 the *New York Post* and *Life* magazine reported on these facts, the police ordered the offending publications removed from Jersey City newsstands. In that same year, when socialist leader Norman Thomas attempted to speak at a public rally, he was seized by the Jersey City police and put on the ferry to Manhattan.

The CIO and the American Civil Liberties Union (ACLU) responded with a lawsuit against Hague, and a landmark ruling from the U.S. Supreme Court was required to extend the First Amendment to Jersey City. The case, *Frank Hague et al. v. the Committee on Industrial Organization et al.* (1939), was an important precedent for civil liberties in the United States, for it established the citizen's right to use public space for the expression of opinion.

Hague's problems in the 1940s, however, did not come from the ACLU nor the CIO but from the ward politicians and ordinary voters, whose interests Hague had long been neglecting. Hague's penchant for the good life in Florida and the Jersey Shore had made him a virtually absentee mayor. Moreover, the Hague machine's appetite for patronage jobs had burdened Jersey City with the highest tax rate of any city its size in the United States. Although Hague's beloved police were the best paid in the nation, the public schools were especially neglected.

Most seriously, Hague's refusal to extend the circle of high-level patronage positions beyond the Irish-American community gave rival politicians their chance. In 1947 Hague, planning to retain power behind the scenes, resigned as mayor in favor of his nephew Frank Hague Eggers. This attempt to establish a "Hague dynasty" ran into the opposition of John V. Kenney, an Irish-American ward politician who put together a multiethnic coalition, including Italian, Polish, and Jewish voters, that reflected the changing demographics of Jersey City.

In the March 1949 Democratic primary, the Kenney forces decisively defeated Hague's machine, and Kenney was chosen mayor. At the state level, Hague's power had also been waning since the election of a reform Democrat, Charles Edison, in 1940 and two subsequent Republican gubernatorial victories. In the November 1949 elections, Hague's handpicked Democratic nominee for governor was beaten by the Republicans, a defeat that virtually ended Hague's power at the county and state levels. In April 1952 he was stripped of the last vestige of his power, Democratic national committeeman from New Jersey, an office he had held since 1922. He died in New York City.

Dour, ruthless, and dictatorial, Hague lacked the warmth and wit that have endeared other urban bosses to posterity. Formed by the narrow world of his youth, he never grasped the wider forces of social and economic change that were engulfing his city. While the Hague machine dominated local patronage politics, the Port Authority of New York and New Jersey and other agencies were reshaping the whole region, promoting middle-class suburbanization and the highway-based decentralization of industry. Both industry and the white, ethnic middle class fled the high taxes, pervasive corruption, and decaying infrastructure that they saw as the Hague machine's legacy to Jersey City. The city that had "everything for industry" lost its industrial base. Hague's monument, the towers of the Jersey City Medical Center, now stand largely abandoned in the midst of a surreal landscape of urban decay.

• None of Hague's personal papers survives. Richard J. Connors, *A Cycle of Power: The Career of Jersey City Mayor Frank Hague* (1971), is a competent academic work; but David Dayton McKean, *The Boss: The Hague Machine in Action* (1940; repr. 1967), is a classic account in the Lincoln Steffans tradition of investigative journalism. See also Mark S. Foster, "Frank Hague of Jersey City: 'The Boss' as Reformer," *New Jersey History* 86, no. 2 (Summer 1968): 106–17; and Thomas J. Fleming, "I Am the Law," *American Heritage* 20, no. 4 (June 1969): 32–48.

ROBERT FISHMAN

HAHN, Archie (13 Sept. 1880–21 Jan. 1955), Olympic sprinter, was born Charles Archibald Hahn in Dodgeville, Wisconsin, the son of Charles Hahn, who was in the tobacco business, and Mary Howell. Portage High School, from which Hahn graduated, had no track team, but the muscular 5′5-¾″ teenager was an outstanding running back, reputedly the best football player in Wisconsin. He attended the University of Michigan as a prelaw student. Coach Fielding Yost considered him too small for football, so Hahn turned out for the track team, coached by the future American Olympic Games leader Keene Fitzpatrick. Hahn's first sprint victory was at the 1900 Wisconsin State Fair, 10.1 seconds for 100 yards, but injuries restricted him to a single victory in the Western Intercollegiate Conference (precursor to the Big Ten). In 1903 he won both American and Canadian national championships at 100 and 220 yards. He never was beaten at the start of a race, a *St. Louis Globe-Democrat* reporter calling him "a wonder in breaking away."

In 1904 Hahn joined the Milwaukee Athletic Club, qualified to compete in the Olympic Games in St. Louis that year, and won the 60-, 100-, and 200-meter dashes, becoming the fastest human in the world. He had gained instant athletic fame as "the Michigan Midget" or the "Milwaukee Meteor." His times (7.0, 11.0, and 21.5) were world records. A contemporary, Charles J. P. Lucas, wrote in *The Olympic Games, 1904*: "At the crack of the gun, Hahn was off his mark like a 12-inch shell out of a coast gun, leaving his competitors as if they were anchored on their marks. Hahn's 200-meter time was a record as he beat the University of Pennsylvania's Nathaniel 'Nate' Cartmell by inches. After the race, Nate gasped: 'Archie's little, but he certainly can run.' The mark of 21.6 remained an Olympic record until 1932."

The International Olympic Committee did not sanction the 1906 Athens Olympic Games, but most of the world's great amateur athletes participated. These well-organized events contrasted with the chaotic festivals in 1896, 1900, and 1904. In 1906 Hahn won the only sprint race—the 100-meter dash. Lawson Robertson competed in that race and recalled: "We all knew the starter would fire his ancient muzzle-loading horse pistol immediately after shouting 'Etami' (get set!), and we decided to start at that moment. But

Hahn was smarter than the rest of us and fled off the mark as the Greek spoke his first syllable. No one ever beat Archie away from the start, no matter who officiated. Archie won with ease." Hahn was acknowledged the first great Olympic Games sprinter. In the same year (1906) that he won his fourth gold medal, he graduated from the University of Michigan. Rather than pursue a law degree, he became a professional footracer, competing at innumerable state fairs in the United States, Europe, New Zealand, and Australia. In 1908 he married Sarah Fidelia Abernethy; they had three children.

After a precarious and itinerant career as a pro, he began a successful thirty years as track coach, first at his alma mater, then as assistant at Princeton University, and finally an illustrious two decades at the University of Virginia. His 1923 book, *How to Sprint*, was considered the best text of its kind, and nearly seventy years after its publication was still acknowledged as being scientific, practical, and useful to athletes and coaches. He died in Charlottesville, Virginia.

• For additional information about Hahn, see John Kieran et al., *The Story of the Olympic Games* (1977), pp. 42–43, 54; David Wallechinsky, *The Complete Book of the Olympics* (1992), pp. 3, 14; Roberto L. Quercetani, *A History of Modern Track and Field Athletics, 1860–1990* (1990), p. 17; F. A. M. Webster, *Olympic Cavalcade* (1948), p. 36; Bill Mallon, *Quest for Gold* (1984), p. 302; June W. Becht, "America's Premier Olympics," *Olympian* 10 (Mar. 1984): 12, 19; John Lucas, "American Involvement in the Athens Olympian Games of 1906—Bridge between Failure and Success," *Stadion* 6 (1980): 217–28; James E. Sullivan, "American Athletes in Ancient Athens," *American Review of Reviews* 34 (July 1906): 43–48; and Charles J. P. Lucas, *The Olympic Games, 1904* (1905), p. 76. Obituaries appear in the *New York Times* and the *New York Herald Tribune*, both 23 Jan. 1955.

JOHN A. LUCAS

HAHN, Michael Decker (24 Nov. 1830–15 Mar. 1886), governor of Louisiana, was born Georg Michael Decker Hahn in Klingenmünster, Bavaria. Hahn's mother, Margaretha Decker, relocated the family to the United States after the death of his father, whose name remains unknown. The family eventually settled around 1840 in New Orleans, Louisiana, where Michael attended the public schools and subsequently studied law with Christian Roselius and at the University of Louisiana (now Tulane University). After earning a law degree from that school in 1851, he began a successful law practice and in 1852 won election to the New Orleans school board.

An advocate of trade, industry, and free labor, Hahn gained prominence during the 1850s as an opponent of the agrarian elite who controlled Louisiana politics. A Democrat, he supported Stephen A. Douglas in 1860 and, during the winter of 1860–1861, served on a committee that campaigned against the election of secessionists to the state convention convened in the aftermath of Abraham Lincoln's election. Unlike many Unionists, Hahn remained in New Orleans after Louisiana seceded. He refused to take the oath of loyalty to the Confederacy in renewing his commission as a notary public but otherwise avoided taking actions that would antagonize Confederate authorities.

When Union forces occupied the Crescent City in early 1862, Hahn swore his allegiance to the United States and worked to organize Union Associations in the city. To facilitate the process of reconstructing Louisiana, the Lincoln administration ordered congressional elections to be held in the two districts then under Union control. On 3 December 1862 Hahn won election from the Second District, but controversy over the legitimacy of the elections in Louisiana prevented him from taking his seat until 3 February 1863, less than a month before his term expired. He introduced a bill providing for further congressional elections in Louisiana that passed the House but was filibustered to death in the Senate. After his term expired, Hahn returned to New Orleans as prize commissioner and throughout 1863 advised Lincoln, with whom he had established an amiable personal and professional relationship, on affairs in Louisiana.

By the end of 1863 Hahn had emerged as the leader of the Free State party, around which Lincoln hoped to build a loyal government in Louisiana. In January 1864 Hahn purchased the *Daily True Delta* and turned the formerly conservative paper into a leading moderate voice in New Orleans. When the Free State party held a convention in February 1864 to nominate candidates for state elections, the radical faction, dissatisfied with the Lincoln administration's reluctance to support full civil and social equality for African Americans, walked out, and Hahn was unanimously nominated for governor. In the campaign Hahn looked to build a broad Unionist coalition by appealing to urban laborers and rural yeomanry. Thus, he presented himself as the candidate of moderation: in favor of emancipation but opposed to measures that would elevate African Americans politically, socially, or economically. General Nathaniel Banks, commander of Union forces in the state, threw his full support behind Hahn's candidacy, and on 4 March 1864 Hahn was inaugurated as the first Republican governor of Louisiana.

Later that month Banks, who remained the true source of authority in the Union-occupied portions of Louisiana, ordered the election of delegates for a constitutional convention. Moderates, thanks to Banks's and Hahn's patronage, dominated the convention that met in the spring and summer of 1864. The constitution it produced abolished slavery in Louisiana, established a state school system for both races, included political reforms to diminish the power of the planter elite, and instituted a minimum daily wage and a nine-hour day for workers. However, despite Lincoln's 13 March letter to Hahn suggesting the extension of suffrage to "very intelligent" blacks and those who had served in the Union army, it did not authorize the enfranchisement of African Americans. Hahn expressed approval of the new constitution, as did Lincoln, who was anxious to see his mild Reconstruction policy implemented. On 5 September 1864 the new constitution was ratified by Louisiana voters. During its first session under the new constitution, the legislature ratified the Thirteenth Amendment at Hahn's urging.

On 3 March 1865 Hahn resigned the governorship to accept election to the U.S. Senate. By this time Hahn, concerned about efforts to consolidate Unionist authority in the aftermath of Banks's removal from command, had moved toward advocacy of immediate black suffrage. Upon reaching Washington, D.C., Hahn found that the new president, Andrew Johnson, had sided with the conservatives against Lincoln's moderate policies, and in protest Hahn chose not to take his seat in the Senate.

After returning to Louisiana, Hahn suffered a gunshot wound in the leg during the July 1866 anti-black riots in New Orleans after giving a speech advocating African-American suffrage. Although he never fully recovered from the wound, Hahn was able by 1867 to start a new paper, the New Orleans *Republican*. Yet by this time his ability to influence the course of Reconstruction was in irreversible decline. After the legislature's rejection of his candidacy for the U.S. Senate in 1871, he folded the *Republican* and decided to focus his energy on his sugar plantation in St. Charles Parish and a new paper, the *St. Charles Herald*. He nonetheless remained active in state politics and went on to serve in the state legislature from 1872 to 1876. As Speaker of the house in 1875 he played a key role in exposing efforts to fraudulently alter that year's appropriations act, and his service as state registrar of voters during the election of 1876 won him praise for his personal impartiality. In 1879 he was appointed a federal district judge, a post he held until 1885, when he entered the U.S. Congress as a Republican. He had been in office a little more than a year when he died in Washington, D.C.

Hahn's control over events in Louisiana was severely circumscribed by the tumultuous environment in which he was forced to work. Although Hahn was a man of ability and personal integrity, as Lincoln's effort to develop and implement a mild Reconstruction policy crumbled, so did Hahn's power and importance. For two years, however, his role as a political leader and adviser to Lincoln made him one of the most important actors in the debate over how to reestablish loyal governments in the South during the Civil War.

• No collection of Hahn's personal papers is known to exist. A work that focuses on Hahn specifically is Amos Simpson and Vaughn Baker, "Michael Hahn: Steady Patriot," *Louisiana History* 13 (1972): 229–52. See also U.S. Congress, *Memorial Addresses on the Life and Character of Michael Hahn (a Representative of Louisiana), Delivered in the House of Representatives and in the Senate, Forty-ninth Congress, First Session* (1886). As a central figure during Reconstruction, Hahn figures prominently in Willie M. Caskey, *Secession and Restoration in Louisiana* (1938); Joe Gray Taylor, *Louisiana Reconstructed* (1974); and Peyton McCrary, *Abraham Lincoln and Reconstruction: The Louisiana Experiment* (1978). Obituaries are in the Washington, D.C., *Evening Star*, 15 Mar. 1886, and the New Orleans *Times-Democrat*, 16 Mar. 1886.

ETHAN S. RAFUSE

HAID, Leo Michael (15 July 1849–24 July 1924), abbot-bishop and educator, was born Michael Hite in Westmoreland County, Pennsylvania, the son of John Hite, a cooper and nurseryman, and Mary A. Stader (sometimes given as Stetter), later a domestic. The Hites named the fourth of ten children and their third son Michael at birth, but upon entering monastic life (1868) he acquired the religious name Leo; by 1872 the spelling of his surname had been altered to Haid, apparently to appease American pronunciation. He was raised in modest circumstances by his immigrant parents. Devout Catholics, the Hites had settled in Westmoreland County to be near the Benedictine monastery of Saint Vincent. In 1861, after his father's death and mother's remarriage, Haid assumed residence at Saint Vincent as a pupil in the monks' school. He won respect there as a boy of intelligence and character.

At age nineteen Haid began his preparations for the life of a Benedictine monk-priest. Following the ordinary sequence, he entered novitiate at Saint Vincent (12 Sept. 1868), professed temporary vows (17 Sept. 1869), then began his seminary studies. Three years later, on 5 October 1872, Leo Haid pronounced his solemn vows, promising to live as a monk in perpetuity. On 21 December 1872 he was ordained a Catholic priest. In September 1872 Haid was appointed to the faculty of his monastery's schools. He found teaching congenial and displayed a particular talent for inspiring the young and imparting high ideals. This success led Haid to begin his enduring effort to articulate a comprehensive philosophy of education, a project that was crucial to the character of the several schools he conducted in succeeding years. He also wrote plays during this period and saw them published.

On 14 July 1885 Haid was elected the first abbot of the new Benedictine abbey in Gaston County, North Carolina, called Maryhelp (later known popularly as "Belmont Abbey"). Since its foundation in 1876, Maryhelp had amassed a dismal record: every monk but one who had ever served there sought assignment elsewhere; school enrollment after nine years numbered only twenty-seven; even the monastic farm had failed. The Carolina abbey was thought to hold so little promise that the first man elected abbot there, Dom Oswald Moosmueller, had refused the office. Nevertheless, Haid, who had never seen North Carolina, accepted the abbacy and was later confirmed (30 Aug. 1885) and blessed (26 Nov. 1885) in office. As abbot he also became president of the monks' college in North Carolina, Saint Mary's (later "Belmont Abbey College").

Under Abbot Leo, Maryhelp's prospects were gradually but unquestionably reversed. To a significant degree, the improvement followed upon a widely accepted, highly romanticized public perception of Haid—promoted by press and clergy—as a sedulous monk/scholar/missionary/farmer/educator, struggling against imposing odds in the most Protestant state in the Union. The Haid image attracted national attention and won warm popular regard and response, especially from Catholics in the Northeast. With this attention came new prosperity for Maryhelp: enrollment increased in both monastery and college, imposing permanent buildings were constructed, and the Benedictines' presence in the South began to stabilize. This progress was also noted by the American hierarchy, who induced Catholic officials in Rome to expand Haid's venue. On 7 December 1887 Pope Leo XIII named him the new vicar apostolic of North Carolina, making him the Roman Catholic bishop of the entire state. Haid was also invested with the title of titular bishop of Messene (Greece). Ordinarily an abbot leaves his monastery if appointed bishop, but Haid protested and was allowed to reign concurrently over his abbey and vicariate. His ordination as bishop was performed in Baltimore by James Cardinal Gibbons on 1 July 1888.

Despite Haid's zeal, Catholic progress in North Carolina was slow and labored. His most vexing problem was the state's rancorous clergy. From the beginning of Haid's episcopal tenure, the monastery's priests and the clergy of the vicariate mistakenly perceived themselves as rivals for the abbot-bishop's time and attention. The internecine struggle that resulted effectively fettered Haid's episcopacy, hampering Catholic melioration in the state and impeding enduring stability.

Beyond the borders of North Carolina, Haid's labors focused on the cloisters and educational work of the Order of Saint Benedict. He created monasteries out of Benedictine parish commitments in Richmond, Virginia (1887), Savannah, Georgia (1887), and Pasco County, Florida (1889), endowing each with a school (1887/1911, 1902, 1889, respectively). In 1894 he founded another monastery and school, this time in Bristow, Virginia. Haid provided staffing for each of these ventures, while acting as president of each school and major-superior of each monastery. From 1890 to 1896 he also served as *praeses* (abbot-president) of the American Cassinese Congregation of Benedictine monks, overseeing a period of expansive growth for the order and the acquisition of various promotions and honors; among these was archiabbatial rank for the monastery of Saint Vincent (1892). As *praeses*, Abbot Leo journeyed in 1893 to Rome, where he successfully argued against imparting substantial powers to the Benedictines' abbot-primate. In 1914 Pope Pius X named Haid a count of the apostolic palace and assistant at the pontifical throne.

In 1908 Haid began seeking means to exempt his monks from their continuing conflicts with the vicariate's priests. That effort culminated in 1910, when he persuaded Pope Pius X to make Maryhelp an *abbatia nullius dioceosis* (an "abbey of no diocese"). As a *nullius*, Maryhelp enjoyed a quasi-diocesan character. That status invested Haid with a third prelacy ("abbot-*nullius*"); it gave the monks an exclusive pastoral territory; and it imparted cathedral rank to the abbey church at Maryhelp. The abbot-bishop considered the *nullius* to be the principal constituent in the patrimony he left to his monks. It was also unique, the only *nullius* jurisdiction ever created in the United States. Unfortunately, the Catholic clergy of North Carolina did not welcome the *nullius*. They saw the Benedictine "diocese" as evidence of the monks' avidity and ambition. Moreover, it seemed to substantiate the priests' suspicion that Haid favored his monastery over his vicariate.

Bishop Haid's missionary zeal was crushed by the clergy's condemnation of the *nullius*, and during the remaining fourteen years of his life he gradually retreated from the broad travels and incessant activity of his episcopacy. Haid's appearances in the vicariate came to be reserved for official and ceremonial occasions, as he returned to his full monastic routine and occupations of the classroom. With this reorientation of his activities, Haid strove to bring fresh integrity to the observance of his several monasteries. Also in this period he effected the maturation of his educational philosophy, revising curricula and rules of conduct in each of his schools, most notably at Belmont Abbey College in 1922.

Although the person and character of Leo Haid eventually regained the general affection and esteem of Catholics in North Carolina, his professional reputation never recovered. Haid's dual reign over the vicariate and monastery created a tension that sullied, perhaps excessively, much of the eminence and achievement of a 39-year abbacy and a 36-year reign as bishop. He died at Maryhelp.

• The official repository of the papers of Leo Haid and the records of his monasteries and schools is the archives of Belmont Abbey (Belmont, N.C.). Published works by and about Haid are collected at the Abbot Vincent Taylor Library on the campus of Belmont Abbey College (N.C.). Smaller but significant holdings of the abbot's letters are found in the archives of Saint Vincent Archabbey and the American Cassinese Congregation of the Order of Saint Benedict (both in Latrobe, Pa.), Saint John Abbey (Collegeville, Minn.), and the Collegio Sant' Anselmo (Rome). The best contemporary studies of Haid's work are two essays by Felix Hintemeyer (published anonymously) in *The Catholic Church in the United States of America* (3 vols., 1912–1914); vol. 1 has an account of Haid's monastery (pp. 50–54), and vol. 3 documents his dioceses (pp. 260–74). The only full biography of Haid is Paschal M. Baumstein, *My Lord of Belmont: A Biography of Leo Haid* (1985). Baumstein has also written a history of the *abbatia nullius*: "An Abbatial Diocese in the United States," *Catholic Historical Review* 79 (1993): 217–45. The only concise treatment of Abbot Leo's educational philosophy is Baumstein's "Benedictine Education at Belmont Abbey," *Crescat* 9 (Lent–Summer 1986): 1–8. For a generally reliable obituary see the *Saint Vincent Journal*, Oct. 1924.

DOM PASCHAL BAUMSTEIN

HAIG, Al (19 July 1922?–16 Nov. 1982), jazz pianist, was born Alan Warren Haig in Newark, New Jersey, the son of Arthur Alexander Haig, an engineer; his mother's name is unknown. His birth year is widely given as 1924, even in his own publicity material, but it seems unlikely that he entered college just after turning sixteen; the Oberlin College biographical form gives 1922, placing him there at the normal age of eighteen. The same Oberlin form lists his birthday as

19 July, rather than the commonly cited date of 22 July. Raised in Nutley, New Jersey, Haig began classical piano studies at age nine. While in high school he studied clarinet and saxophone, and he played piano in a dance band.

After graduating from high school in 1940, Haig entered Oberlin College in Ohio to major in piano. He enlisted in a Coast Guard band in 1942 and found himself stationed on Ellis Island, New York, where he played clarinet in a marching band and piano in a dance band. The proximity to Manhattan afforded opportunities to play informally and attend jam sessions in the city. He was discharged from the service in the spring of 1944. In June he married Grange Margaret Rutan, known as Bonnie; they had two sons.

Haig found his first professional work with saxophonist Rudy Williams in Boston, Massachusetts. That same year he also worked in Boston in Jerry Wald's orchestra. While performing in Michigan, he heard a broadcast of trumpeter Dizzy Gillespie playing "A Night in Tunisia" at the Onyx Club in New York City. He returned to the city and played various jobs while waiting the standard six-month period for his local union card to come through. (Perhaps the work in Boston came during this wait; the chronology is unclear.) He subsequently worked with Williams's quartet, with saxophonist Tab Smith, and with guitarist Tiny Grimes's quartet at the Spotlite. Gillespie and alto saxophonist Charlie Parker sat in with Grimes's quartet, auditioning Haig on the bandstand. Gillespie asked Haig to attend rehearsals with bassist Curley Russell and drummer Stan Levey. While working with Grimes and with Les Elgart's big band in Westchester County, Haig learned pieces that would become anthems of the emerging bop style, including "Groovin' High," "Shaw Nuff," "Ko-Ko," "Salt Peanuts," and "Hot House." In April 1945 the well-prepared Parker-Gillespie quintet opened at the Three Deuces on Fifty-second Street and caused a sensation. In May Haig figured prominently in Gillespie's seminal recordings of "Salt Peanuts," "Shaw 'Nuff," and "Hot House."

Membership in this quintet at the Three Deuces was the highlight of Haig's career, and rightfully so, as it was the first full flowering of the bop style. In later years he lamented that the group was so short-lived. When Gillespie took his first and unsuccessful big band, the Hepsations of 1945, on tour of the South, Parker and Haig stayed in New York City. They soon returned to the Three Deuces with tenor saxophonist Don Byas in Gillespie's place. Parker then left, and the group continued with tenor saxophonists Byas and Allen Eager, bassist Al McKibbon, and drummer Levey.

In October 1945 Haig recorded with tenor saxophonist Charlie Barnet's big band, replacing pianist Marty Napoleon. He toured with Barnet in California and again recorded with the band in December, playing solo on "E-Bob-O-Lee-Bob." In Los Angeles Haig rejoined Gillespie and his Rebop Six, which, during Parker's frequent absences, included vibraphonist Milt Jackson and tenor saxophonist Lucky Thomp-

son; the job was largely unsuccessful. While in Hollywood, Gillespie's sextet recorded five titles, including "Diggin' for Diz" (a bop version of "Lover") and "'Round about Midnight" (Feb. 1946). In New York two weeks later Haig recorded "Anthropology" and other titles with Gillespie's reconstituted septet and sextet, including Byas and Jackson. While Gillespie founded a second big band, Haig remained with the trumpeter's small group into the spring, working at the Spotlite and recording four titles on 15 May 1946 with a further revised sextet that included Jackson, alto saxophonist Sonny Stitt, and drummer Kenny Clarke. That day he also recorded four titles, including "Tilford Blues," with tenor saxophonist Ben Webster's quintet. He worked in Webster's quartet at the Three Deuces.

In an abrupt stylistic change, Haig joined Jimmy Dorsey's big band for about eight months during 1946 and 1947. In November 1946 he made his first recordings with singers Dave Lambert and Buddy Stewart, who initiated a fad for bop scat singing. He also recorded with instrumental bop bands, including a group with trumpeter Fats Navarro under the leadership of tenor saxophonist Eddie "Lockjaw" Davis (Dec. 1946).

In the summer of 1948 Haig returned to the center of bop upon joining Parker's quintet at the Three Deuces with trumpeter Miles Davis, bassist Tommy Potter, and drummer Max Roach. He remained with Parker when Kenny Dorham replaced Davis in December 1948. He also participated in Parker's residencies at Basin Street West, Birdland, and Café Society and traveled to France to perform with Parker at the first Paris Jazz Fair in May 1949. During layoffs from Parker, Haig worked with tenor saxophonists Stan Getz and Coleman Hawkins, and he took a four-week American tour with Jazz at the Philharmonic (Sept. 1950). Among his many recordings from these years were several sessions with Getz; with tenor saxophonist Wardell Gray in "Stoned" and "Matter and Mind" (both Apr. 1948) and "Easy Living" (Nov. 1949); and with Miles Davis on the first and finest "Birth of the Cool" session (Jan. 1949). His work was heard in a technologically low fidelity but musically high quality "live" performance in Paris released under Roach's name (May 1949). He was also recorded in Navarro's last studio sessions, including "Go," "Infatuation," and "Stop," made under the leadership of tenor saxophonist Don Lanphere (Sept. 1949), and with his own small groups, including a trio that made versions of "Liza," "Stars Fell on Alabama," and "Stairway to the Stars" (Feb. 1950).

By 1951 Haig had left Parker and was performing with Getz's group, whose work was captured in a renowned recording made at the Storyville Club in Boston in October. He recorded "Now's the Time" with Parker's quartet in August 1953, by which time he was no longer working regularly in jazz. In 1954 French pianist Henri Renaud sought out Haig in New York. In an unsuccessful attempt to revive Haig's career, Renaud recorded the first of Haig's three sessions from that year, including a trio album on the Esoteric label. Haig replaced pianist Russ Freeman in Chet Baker's quartet in California in December 1954, but Baker and Haig did not get along. Already separated from his wife, he returned to the New York City area to attempt a reconciliation. After subsequently playing with a rhumba band in Puerto Rico and at a striptease club in Miami, he recorded the album *The Young Bloods* with trumpeter Donald Byrd and alto saxophonist Phil Woods (Nov. 1956). He also joined Gillespie's big band for a State Department tour, but he lost his place in the band, reportedly owing to some problem with his union card.

During the next decade and a half Haig worked in trios, duos, and as a soloist in the New York City area. He accompanied Miriam Makeba at the Village Vanguard around 1960 but mainly worked outside the city in lesser-known restaurants and supper clubs. In October 1968 his wife was found dead in their home. Haig was tried for murder and acquitted in June 1969. Published accounts are irreconcilably contradictory regarding the circumstances of her death.

During the 1970s it became known that a giant of the bop era was playing as well as ever: Haig worked steadily in New York at small bars, clubs, and restaurants. In 1974 he made the first of several visits to England, where in January he recorded the superlative trio album *Invitation*. In his final years Haig recorded more than a dozen albums, including *Special Brew* (1974), *Chelsea Bridge* (1975), the unaccompanied *Solitaire* (1976), and as coleader with bassist Jamil Nasser, *Expressly Ellington* (1978). He also participated in "Dizzy Gillespie's Bebop Reunion" concert for an episode of the PBS television show "Soundstage" that aired in January 1977. He married Joanne Dioszegi in 1978. The following year Haig performed with a trio at a festival in Buffalo and as a soloist at the Newport–New York Jazz Festival. He died at his home in New York City.

It is not surprising that Haig expressed an admiration for pianist Teddy Wilson; Haig's style, founded in elegance, clarity, and restraint, may be understood as a bop analogue to Wilson's swing style. As one of the most important bop pianists, Haig was known early in his career for the tasteful and appropriate sparseness of his accompanying chords and for the crispness of his solo melodies. A definitive example of the latter is "Salt Peanuts," in which his improvisation lacks the outlandishness of Parker and Gillespie's inventions but matches them in the ability to toss off a relaxed, varied, well-shaped, and swinging melodic line at an extremely fast tempo. His instrument's function in the bop style at first afforded few opportunities to demonstrate his ability to play equally well in a more richly ornamented and pianistic manner, with the exception of performances on such ballads as "Tomorrow" (actually, Jerome Kern's "Yesterdays") from the 1949 Paris session and "Stars Fell on Alabama" from 1950. This side of his musical personality came out more strongly in the albums from 1974 onward. The greatest bop pi-

anist, Bud Powell, called Haig "my idea of a perfect pianist."

• Miscellaneous documents concerning Haig are in the Oberlin College Archives in Oberlin, Ohio. For interviews with Haig, see Mark Gardner, "Al Haig," *Jazz Monthly*, no. 186 (Aug. 1970): 4–7, and John Shaw, "The Reminiscences of Al Haig," *Jazz Journal International* 32 (Mar. 1979): 4–5, 9. Alun Morgan surveys Haig's career and catalogs his recordings in "Al Haig: An Introduction and Discography," *Jazz Monthly* 2 (Oct. 1956): 26–28; (Nov. 1956): 27–28. Further surveys are in Max Harrison, "Al Haig Quartet," *Jazz Review* 3 (June 1960): 22–24; George Hoefer, "Al Haig," *Down Beat* 32 (21 Oct. 1965): 17, 38; Henri Renaud, "Bebop Highlights," *Jazz hot*, no. 305 (May 1974): 18–23; and Raymond Horricks, "Another Case of Haig," *Jazz Journal International* 34 (May 1981): 16–17, (June 1981): 18–19. Another survey, Leonard Feather, "Al Haig," *Contemporary Keyboard* 6 (Oct. 1980): 58–59, includes a notated example of a 1977 improvisation on "Salt Peanuts." Further catalogs of recordings are in Brian Davis, "Discography [*sic*] of Issued Recordings by Al Haig, 1974–1978," *Jazz Journal International* 32 (Apr. 1979): 17–19, and in "Al Haig," *Swing Journal* 37 (Jan. 1983): 200–205. Powell's quote is from an interview made in Paris and dated 15 Jan. 1963 (but probably made in mid-1963 or 1964) available on the *Inner Fires* LP (Elektra Musician, El-60030). See also "Pianist Haig Charged with Murder of Wife," *Down Beat* 35 (28 Nov. 1968): 12; "Defense Fund Formed for Pianist Al Haig," *Down Beat* 36 (9 Jan. 1969): 10; "Al Haig Appears at Own Benefit," *New York Times*, 31 Mar. 1969; and "Al Haig Acquitted of Wife-Murder Charge," *Down Beat* 36 (7 Aug. 1969): 10. Obituaries are in the *New York Times*, 17 Nov. 1982; *Chicago Tribune*, 18 Nov. 1982; *Down Beat* 50 (Feb. 1983): 13; and *Jazz Journal International* 36 (Feb. 1983): 20.

BARRY KERNFELD

HAIGHT, Henry Huntley (20 May 1825–2 Sept. 1878), attorney and governor of California, was born in Rochester, New York, the son of Fletcher Mathews Haight, a lawyer and New York legislator, and Elizabeth Stewart MacLachlan. In 1844 Henry, the eldest son among twelve children, graduated from Yale, determined to follow the family profession. In 1846 he joined his father in St. Louis, Missouri, and became his law partner in 1847. The next year Henry published the *Barnburner*, declaring that the territories should remain free of slavery. A consistent, lifelong political ideology led him to champion a classical republicanism that emphasized "the virtue and the intelligence of the people," whom he defined as "the free white laboring and industrial classes." Just as firmly, Haight supported "southern rights" and slavery in the states where it existed.

In January 1850 Haight followed several family members to California, where he practiced law, first with James A. McDougall, later a U.S. senator, and then in 1854 again with his father. On a trip to St. Louis in 1855 he married Anna E. Bissell, daughter of a slave owner, which may serve as an indication of his racial views. Three of their five children survived to adulthood.

With its many-faceted immigration, gold rush California politically resembled the border state Haight had left. In 1852 he acted with David Broderick's Free Soil Democrats, but in 1856, with the Democratic party tangled in gridlock, Haight and his father opportunistically switched to the newly formed Republican party. In 1857 and 1859 Republicans failed to nominate Fletcher Haight as a state supreme court justice, but in the latter year they chose Henry Haight as chairman of the Republican State Central Committee.

In 1859 Haight began a twenty-year trusteeship for elite Calvary Presbyterian Church and came under the influence of his good friend, the Reverend Dr. William Anderson Scott, who fervently believed in the southern cause. The next year Haight supported Republican party regularity and angled for a nomination for district (superior) court judge but remained unenthusiastic. He voted for Abraham Lincoln since the lack of a clear victor would "break up the country," but he "regret[ted] exceedingly" his choice.

After southern secession, the San Francisco *Bulletin*, on 28 February 1861, carried Haight's conciliatory advice, "The Duties of Citizens in Reference to Our National Crisis." On 3 May 1861 Haight revealed that his Republican party ideology had vanished. Not only was the high protective tariff the "climax of folly," but with the news of Fort Sumter at hand, Haight incredibly argued that President Lincoln should accept the "stupendous reality" of a disrupted nation. Lincoln's policy to use coercion to preserve unity was "wholly impracticable." Haight acknowledged "no allegiance to any party." He emerged from his father's shadow after Lincoln appointed Fletcher Haight to a federal judgeship in southern California. Becoming a loner, he did not mingle socially, kept out of politics, and chose young, unknown lawyers as partners.

Quietly, Haight became attractive to Democrats because of his conservatism and racial views. In July 1863 299 party delegates nominated him for the state supreme court, but he quickly declined. In late September the municipal People's party asked him to be a district court judge, and Haight replied with a political manifesto. He would "sustain the Government to the fullest extent in its efforts to suppress the rebellion," he said, but he refused to accept any constitutional alterations. That document "confers all necessary power for war as well as peace." Haight's 101-page brief in the summer of 1864 challenged the Legal Tender Act, which allowed the issuance of paper money, and the "war power" school of thought, which "threaten[ed] to sweep away all the landmarks of constitutional government." Openly campaigning for the Democratic presidential candidate in late October 1864, he declared, "Under the policy of emancipation and confiscation, the rebellion never could be suppressed."

Haight's chance for office came in 1867. Democrats, with their loyalty during the Civil War severely questioned, were politically revived by the issue of race. The "suffrage of negroes, Chinese and Indians," their platform declared, would "end in the degradation of the white race and the speedy destruction of the Government." Concurrently, a growing workingman's movement feared competition from lower-paid, able Chinese laborers. While 1,000 black voters posed no threat, the addition of 50,000 Chinese to an active voting population of 110,000 could be terrifying. Haight, with no antiwar record to deny, became the perfect candidate for governor and was nominated by acclamation at the Democratic party convention on 20 June 1867. Stressing the race issue, he warned that a diverse electorate "would introduce the antipathy of race into our political contests and lead to strife and bloodshed."

Victory came after the Union party split, but even Haight's foes acknowledged his upright character, incorruptible honesty, and manifest abilities. Though Haight had no experience in government and much preferred the "congenial profession" of the law, he became an effective governor. Democratic control of the assembly in 1867 and both houses in 1869 allowed him to block acceptance of the Fourteenth and Fifteenth amendments to the U.S. Constitution. His desire to foster education blossomed with the creation of the University of California in 1868 and the opening of the State Normal School to train teachers in 1871. Another educational interest led to a commission to codify the laws, making California the first state to do so.

Energized workingmen contributed to Haight's victory, and they received a law establishing an eight-hour day. A principle from Haight's Republican past led him to call for legal equality for every resident and "the removal of all barriers to the testimony of any class or race." His party refused to let Chinese and American Indians appear in court against whites, but codification of the laws vindicated the governor. Haight's firm racial ideology reappeared on 8 May 1869, when he celebrated the transcontinental railroad as the "crowning work of Saxon civilization." The fiscally conservative governor reduced the state debt by one-third and cut the tax rate by one-fifth.

Governor Haight ran for a second term in 1871 to prevent the Central Pacific Railroad, as he said, from gaining "control" of California. He had vetoed bills binding counties to give "forced" financial aid to railroads, but then he lost credibility after signing a law that allowed county voters to grant railroads subsidies up to 5 percent of their taxable base. Anti-railroad sentiment led to defeat at the polls, and in 1872 Haight returned to the practice of law and helped organize the San Francisco Bar Association. As befitted Haight's educational record, he served from 1872 to 1874 as a regent of the University of California. His sudden death, apparently from a heart attack, in San Francisco precluded his participation in the 1878 constitutional convention.

Haight was by nature neither a public speaker nor an active politician, much preferring the solitary and reflective practice of law. Yet a desire to see a limited constitutional government preserve the liberties of free white citizens overrode all other considerations. His old-fashioned views fit the mood of a state tired from the stress of war. Commanding his attention were an invigorated labor movement fearful of an influx of alien Chinese, an economic depression precipitated by a flood of cheap eastern goods carried over iron rails, and monopolistic corporate power. The honest and incorruptible Haight worked hard to provide answers.

• Haight's manuscripts are at the Henry E. Huntington Library, San Marino, Calif. A. Russell Buchanan published the most significant letter as "H. H. Haight on National Politics, [3] May 1861," *California Historical Society Quarterly* 31 (Sept. 1952): 193–204. It places Haight's "political conversion" much earlier than historians have reported. Apart from newspaper and legislative journal articles, Haight's writings include *The Currency Question: In the Supreme Court of the State of California, "James Lick v. William Faulkner"* (1864); *Speech of H. H. Haight, Democratic Candidate for Governor, Delivered at the Great Democratic Mass Meeting at Union Hall, Tuesday Evening, July 9th 1867* (1867); *Letters of Gov. Haight on the Constitutional Power of the Legislature to Authorize Cities and Counties to Donate Bonds to Railroad Corporations* (1870); *First Biennial Message of Governor H. H. Haight* (1869); and *Second Biennial Message of Governor H. H. Haight* (1872). Haight hid his personality, but the Bancroft Library at the University of California, Berkeley, has two oral histories, "Dictation of Anna Bissell Haight, 1890" and "Interview with Un-Named Person re Haight, 1878," probably his private secretary Edward R. Taylor. Oscar T. Shuck, *Representative and Leading Men of the Pacific* (1870), gives bland remarks but presents Haight's 1869 railroad address. The long sketch in Alonzo Phelps, *Contemporary Biography of California's Representative Men* (1881), is laudatory, while Republican Theodore H. Hittell, in *History of California* (1897), was the first to detail Haight's career as governor. H. Brett Melendy and Benjamin F. Gilbert, *The Governors of California: Peter H. Burnett to Edmund G. Brown* (1965), provides the most extensive and balanced view, and Philip J. Ethington, *The Public City: The Political Construction of Urban Life in San Francisco, 1850–1900* (1994), emphasizes Haight's pivotal political role through his classical republican ideology.

ROBERT J. CHANDLER

HAISH, Jacob (9 Mar. 1826–19 Feb. 1916), inventor and businessman, was born in Consul Baden, Bavaria, Germany, the son of Christian Haish and Christina Layman, farmers. In 1836 the Haish family immigrated to the United States and took up farming, first in Pennsylvania and then in Crawford County, Ohio. In 1846 the young Jacob Haish moved to Kane County, Illinois, where he worked as an agricultural laborer. In 1847 he married Sophia Ann Brown, the daughter of the farmer for whom he worked. In 1848 Haish bought a farm in DeKalb County, Illinois, and tried farming on his own. In 1851 he sold the farm and worked as a carpenter. In 1853 Haish moved to DeKalb, Illinois, where he lived the rest of his life. Four years later, in 1857, Haish opened a successful building contractor and lumber business.

As a former farmer and as a lumber merchant, Haish was well aware of the fencing problems that farmers faced on the treeless prairies and plains of the western United States. Wood was scarce and expensive; hedges of thorny brush like osage orange took time, effort, and skill to grow. Haish later wrote that this problem "led me to think out and provide a substitute therefor." According to Haish, barbed wire was the result of this search. Introduced in the 1870s,

barbed wire revolutionized prairie agriculture by providing a cheap and effective fencing material. Entire farms and ranches, regardless of size, could be fenced with barbed wire. The era of the "open range" ended.

Haish was a central figure in the confusing question of who, exactly, invented barbed wire. Although Haish always maintained that he was the sole inventor of barbed wire, two other residents of DeKalb, Joseph F. Glidden and Isaac L. Ellwood, also claimed the credit. While this controversy remains unresolved, it is safe to consider Haish as at least the co-inventor of barbed wire. In December 1873 Haish applied for a patent, which was granted on 20 January 1874. However, Glidden had received a patent for a very similar barbed wire two months earlier. A long, complicated, and bitter personal and legal battle ensued over the patent rights to barbed wire.

In 1876 Glidden and Ellwood sold their patents to Washburn & Moen Manufacturing Company of Worcester, Massachusetts, the largest manufacturer of plain wire in the country (and later part of what would become the U.S. Steel Corporation). Washburn & Moen, with Glidden and Ellwood as partners, attempted to monopolize the booming production of barbed wire by forcing "moonshine" barbed wire manufacturers either to quit or to become licensees. Haish, who was manufacturing his own so-called "S" barbed wire in a large, 100-employee factory in DeKalb, defied the nascent monopoly. Washburn & Moen threatened not only manufacturers who violated their patents, but also the merchants who sold the "illegal" wire and even the farmers who purchased it. In this struggle, Haish posed as the champion of farmers across the West who wanted the lower prices of patent-less competition. Haish allied himself with the Farmers' Protective Association and stoked the flames of agrarian discontent with the publication of his annual antimonopoly circular, the *Haish Barb Wire Regulator*, of which hundreds of thousands were distributed throughout the West. Haish claimed that this mass-distribution publication was the first of its kind and represented a "new era in advertising."

The legal struggle over the patent rights to barbed wire lasted from 1876 to 1892. In a landmark ruling, the U.S. Supreme Court decided the issue on 29 February 1892; lower court rulings that had sided with Haish and the farmers were overturned, and the Glidden patent ruled preeminent. Haish later wrote that the legal battle over barbed wire "disclosed to me the greed and avarice that often impelled officers and stockholders of great corporations to pounce upon the weaker members of enterprises working along the same lines."

While Haish was finally forced to settle with the holders of the Glidden patent, he continued to amass a fortune based on his manufacturing operations and on royalties from patents he had received for various barbed wire manufacturing machines. As Haish later noted, "It was these devices that made barbed wire a merchantable product." Ironically, Haish's opponents in the long patent struggle came to use his machines.

In all, Haish received twenty patents, nine for barbed wire machinery. His companies, in addition to manufacturing barbed wire and its numerous accessories, made agricultural implements and gasoline engines.

Haish was a great benefactor to the town of DeKalb. Perhaps most importantly, in the early 1890s he joined with his old foes Glidden and Ellwood to help attract to DeKalb the new State Normal School for the training of teachers (now Northern Illinois University). Haish built rent-free apartments and houses for his employees and provided the funding for the local public library. In 1888 he ran for Congress as a Democrat and was only narrowly defeated in the overwhelmingly Republican district.

In 1910 Haish wrote a memoir entitled *A Reminiscent Chapter from the Unwritten History of Barb Wire, Prior to and Immediately Following the Celebrated Decision of Judge Blodgett December 15, 1880*. Haish, of course, argued that he had been the most important man in the founding of the barbed wire industry. By this time, Glidden and Ellwood were dead.

In 1916 Haish retired from the barbed wire and other manufacturing concerns, but he retained his bank, the Jacob Haish State Bank. Even though he was in his nineties, he went to the bank every day, sat in a rocking chair in the lobby, greeted customers, and conducted business. Haish died in DeKalb, Illinois.

• There is no official collection of Haish's papers. However, the Regional History Center of Northern Illinois University in DeKalb maintains files on Haish, along with a copy of the only biography, a short, unpublished piece by Steve Bigolin, "This Was Jacob Haish" (1977). A very good introduction to the importance of the invention of barbed wire, the legal battle that was waged over the patent rights, and Haish's role in these matters is Earl W. Hayter, "An Iowa Farmers' Protective Association: A Barbed Wire Patent Protest Movement," *Iowa Journal of History and Politics* 37 (Oct. 1939): 331–62. The founding and early growth of the barbed wire industry is covered in Joseph M. McFadden, "From Invention to Monopoly: The History of the Consolidation of the Barbed Wire Industry, 1873–1899" (Ph.D. diss., Northern Illinois Univ., 1968). Correspondence and records pertaining to the long patent fight are at the Industrial Museum, American Steel and Wire Company, Worcester, Mass. A front-page obituary is in the *DeKalb Daily Chronicle*, 19 Feb. 1926. A shorter obituary is in the *Chicago Tribune*, 20 Feb. 1926.

JAMES D. NORRIS

HAKLUYT, Richard (c. 1552–23 Nov. 1616), British geographer and anthologist of travel literature, was born in London, the son of a merchant father, orphaned at five, and reared by his uncle (the names of his parents and uncle are not known). He was descended from the Welsh Hakluyts of Herefordshire, whose family seat was Eaton, near Leominster. Richard was a queen's scholar at Westminster school; during that period he visited his namesake, a cousin twenty years his elder, at Middle Temple, where he was introduced to "certeine bookes of Cosmographie, with an universall Mappe" and the Bible, and felt an immediate passion for "that knowledge and kinde of literature." He entered Christ Church, Oxford, in 1570 and

after earning his M.A. in 1577 began to give there the first public lectures in England on geography, lectures that "shewed both the old imperfectly composed, and the new lately reformed Mappes, Globes, Spheares and other instruments of this Art." He also began a lifetime of voracious reading of "whatsoever printed or written discoveries and voyages I found extant either in the Greeke, Latine, Italian, Spanish, Portugall, French, or English languages."

His first book, *Divers Voyages Touching the Discoverie of America and the Islands Adjacent unto the Same* . . . , which appeared in 1582, is an early work that is now regarded as already urging the settling of America. During this period he made several visits to Bristol, hoping to join Sir Humphrey Gilbert on his voyage to discover the Northwest Passage. But Hakluyt was instead sent by the government as the chaplain to Sir Edward Stafford, named English ambassador to Paris in 1583. Once there, Hakluyt also followed the instructions of treasury secretary Sir Francis Walsingham, collecting information on French and Spanish travel and "making diligent inquirie of such things as might yield any light unto our westerne discoverie in America." At Sir Walter Ralegh's request, Hakluyt began writing *A Discourse of Western Planting* (published 1584), putting forth reasons to persuade Elizabeth I to plant the English in unsettled parts of North America. His intentions were to promote national pride and confidence as well as thoughts of commerce and empire. He gave the queen a copy of his work and won from her the next vacant prebend at Bristol, to which he was admitted in 1586, although he did not return to England until 1588. In time he held other benefices as well—a canonry at Westminster, livings at Wetheringsett and Gedney, and a chaplaincy at the Savoy. But his desire to collect records of travel remained foremost, and, combining the instincts and talents of the antiquarian, the historian, and the archivist, he became England's foremost accountant of the country's growing imperialism. His ever-expanding compendium of firsthand reports of voyaging—ships' logs, salesmen's records, secret economic intelligence, captured enemy papers, and, above all, sailors' narratives—took its place as the nation's most significant promotion of an English presence in the New World and in the settlement of America.

The Principall Navigations, Voyages, and Discoveries of the English Nation (1589) is one large volume divided into three parts focusing on Asia, on the Northeast Passage and profitable trade routes to Russia, and, largest of all, "navigations" and "travels" into the New World. In a new three-volume edition of 1598–1600, his 700,000-word anthology more than doubled to 1.7 million words, and the word *Traffiques* (trade) was added to its title. The work was now more than geography; it was also economic history and brief, arguing that the real wealth in the New World was not in imaginary gold mines, but in the potential fur trade. In addition, this massive account of voyaging, beginning in the first volume with an account of the Spanish Armada against England in 1588, caused his compendium to become as well the first sustained history of the British navy. This larger edition moved backward in time, to before 1500, then forward to 1600, extending considerably the range of the 1589 text. But the general approach and substance are similar: Hakluyt always prefers firsthand accounts and first-person narratives, giving public voice to such persons as Edward Hayes and Arthur Barlowe, who might otherwise never have been recorded in history. Hakluyt's books are characterized by energy, scope, and directness, although their immediacy could sometimes mislead the naive reader or the ambitious traveler. Yet, whenever he could, Hakluyt carefully checked each episode for accuracy—it is recorded that he once rode 200 miles to check certain facts about the relatively insignificant expedition of Master Hore to America in 1536. And his influence was immeasurable: virtually every ship in the seventeenth century that came to the American colonies had on board a copy of Hakluyt's second edition. The accounts in this text of earlier expeditions, describing flora, fauna, climate, and native customs, also revealed Virginia before Jamestown was founded and New England before it was "discovered" by Pilgrims and Puritans. Hakluyt translated French Huguenots' early reports on South Carolina and their descriptions of experiences in Florida and the West Indies. He also circulated the reports of Spanish explorers on the North American interior. His pioneering efforts, lasting his entire lifetime, also profoundly influenced initial American histories, *Of Plimmouth Plantation* by William Bradford (1590–1657) and the *General History of Virginia* by John Smith (1580–1631), both of whom acknowledge their indebtedness. Hakluyt died without survivors and was buried in Westminster Abbey on 26 November 1616, although an erroneous entry in the Abbey register records the burial as occurring in 1626.

More even than the explorers Ralegh and Sir Francis Drake, Hakluyt is responsible for the English settlement in America. Besides pursuing his own work, Hakluyt encouraged Robert Parke to translate Mendoza's *History of China* (1588–1589) and John Pory to translate *Leo Africanus* (as *A Geographical History of Africa*) in 1600. A number of manuscripts that Hakluyt assembled for still another edition were published in part after his death by Samuel Purchas; still more notes that he collected, written by contemporary authors, are preserved at the Bodleian Library in Oxford.

• The standard modern edition (of the 1598–1600 text) is that of the Hakluyt Society (12 vols., 1903–1905), although there is a good edition in the Everyman's Library, ed. John Masefield (8 vols., 1907). Volume 2 of *The Hakluyt Handbook* (Hakluyt Society, 2d ser., no. 145), ed. David B. Quinn (1974), provides a thorough concordance, list of sources, and primary and secondary bibliography for the 1598–1600 text.

ARTHUR F. KINNEY

HALAS, George Stanley (2 Feb. 1895–31 Oct. 1983), professional football player, coach, and owner, was born in Chicago, Illinois, the son of Frank J. Halas, a businessman, and Barbara Poledna. Halas acquired a lifelong commitment to the values of hard work, frugality, and personal loyalty from the example of his parents, first-generation immigrants from Bohemia, whose personal fortunes expanded from a modest tailor shop to a grocery store and saloon to extensive real estate holdings, and by growing up in an ethnic, working-class neighborhood in southwest Chicago dominated by St. Vitus Roman Catholic Church and the Pilsen Sokol (community center).

A three-sport letterman in high school, Halas worked for a year after graduation in the payroll department of the Western Electric Company in Cicero, Illinois, before entering the University of Illinois in 1914. While majoring in civil engineering, he played defensive end for legendary football coach Bob Zuppke, led the basketball team to a Big Ten championship and captained the squad as a senior, and starred on the conference championship baseball team. On completing requirements for the bachelor's degree in January 1918, he joined the U.S. Navy and was assigned to the sports program at the Great Lakes Naval Training Center, where he received an ensign's commission and played basketball, baseball, and football. On the gridiron he earned second-team All-America honors, and, thanks to the opportunity presented when the Tournament of Roses hosted service teams during World War I, he was named most valuable player of the 1919 Rose Bowl in leading Great Lakes to a 17–0 victory over the Mare Island Marines.

Halas signed with the New York Yankees after being discharged from the navy in March 1919. The swift, switch-hitting outfielder unexpectedly made the major league roster, but a hip injury suffered while sliding into third base during spring training and a .091 batting average after twelve games led to his demotion to St. Paul of the American Association. Halas quit professional baseball after the season and accepted a position as a bridge designer for the Chicago, Burlington, and Quincy Railroad. Despite his nagging hip, he agreed to play semipro football on Sundays with the Hammond, Indiana, Tigers. In March 1920 he accepted an offer from the A. E. Staley Company of Decatur, Illinois, to learn the starch products business but primarily to play on the company's semipro baseball team and serve as player-coach of its football team. On 17 September he represented the Decatur Staleys at a meeting of twelve midwestern football clubs in Canton, Ohio, which resulted in the formation of the game's first professional circuit, the American Professional Football Association. Under player-coach Halas, the Staleys won the APFA title in 1920 with a 10–1–2 record. In 1921 Staley, weary of the financial cost of underwriting a sports program, literally gave the football team to Halas, who moved it to Chicago. Lacking sufficient money to operate the club, Halas took in fellow teammate Edward "Dutch" Sternaman as an equal partner. But it was Halas who assumed primary responsibility for coaching and administrative duties in leading the club to a second championship with a 10–1–1 mark. The next year was a banner year for Halas. He not only married Wilhelmina "Min" Bushing, he also convinced fellow owners to change the name of the circuit to the National Football League (effective the 1923 season) and renamed his team the Bears because they shared Wrigley Field with baseball's Chicago Cubs.

As the team's founding father, Halas was popularly known as "Papa Bear," and through his roles as owner, coach, and player he personified the franchise for sixty-four years—the longest continuous association with a single team in sports history. The association was deeply personal as the Bears and pro football gave shape and meaning to his life. He immediately drew on his alma mater for many of the team's players and coaches and for the uniform colors—blue and orange—worn by the Staleys and Bears. With Sternaman unable to contribute much to the club's finances, Halas drew extensively on family investments to underwrite operations. After Sternaman in 1926 violated Halas's strict code of loyalty by considering overtures from a syndicate hoping to establish a second pro football team in Chicago, the partnership existed in name only; determined to obtain full control, Halas in 1931 finally bought out Sternaman for $38,000. Distrustful of "outsiders" who did not share his personal stake in the team, Halas thereafter kept the Bears a family affair.

Initially, Halas led by example. His aggressive, hard-hitting style of play at end from 1920 to 1929 earned him designation as a member of the All-NFL team of the 1920s. His greatest thrill as a player came in 1923 when he recovered a fumble by the great Jim Thorpe and ran ninety-eight yards for a touchdown—a record that would stand until 1972. A perfectionist who was unable psychologically to entrust the on-field fortunes of what he always called "my Bears" to another person, Halas simultaneously performed the duties of owner and coach for four separate ten-year periods—1920–1929, 1933–1942, 1946–1955, and 1958–1967. The lone hiatus occurred when he volunteered for naval service during World War II. From 1942 until 1945 he served as a lieutenant commander with the Seventh Fleet, receiving the Bronze Star for his role in organizing recreations in the South Pacific and Austria.

Dubbed the "Monsters of the Midway" by the press for their especially rough and physical style of play, the Bears reflected the personality of their coach. Under Halas the team won eight NFL championships (1921, 1932, 1933, 1940, 1941, 1943, 1946, 1963) and eleven divisional titles. Perennially successful, they finished second fifteen times and fell below the .500 mark only six times. The highlight of his career came in 1940 when the Bears played a nearly flawless game to defeat the favored Washington Redskins 73–0 for the NFL championship. At age seventy-three, Halas retired after forty seasons as by far the winningest coach in pro football history with 326 wins, 150 losses, and 31 ties for a career-winning percentage of .673. Under his tutelage such gridiron greats as Red Grange, Bronko Nagurski, Sid Luckman, Bill George, George Blanda, Mike Ditka, and Dick Butkus—nineteen Hall of Famers in all—developed their skills. The old hip injury finally drove Halas from the sidelines. "I knew it was time to quit," he snapped, "when I was chewing out the referee and he walked off the penalty faster than I could keep up with him."

Halas's reputation as the "Father of the NFL" is only slightly exaggerated. The only person associated with the league throughout its first half-century, he exerted predominant influence on the development of professional football as a game and as a business. As one of the league's charter owners, he brought much-needed publicity to the fledgling pro game by signing college star Grange and sponsoring a three-month barnstorming tour in 1925. He astutely used mass communications to promote the Bears (and pro football) by cultivating newspaper reporters in the 1920s, taking the lead in authorizing radio broadcasts of home games in the 1930s, and televising games as early as 1947. He also joined sportswriter Arch Ward in founding in 1934 the annual College All-Star Game, which, by pitting the current NFL champions (the Bears in 1934) against the best college seniors, brought great attention to the pro game as well as money to *Chicago Tribune* charities. As coach, Halas was the first to employ full-time assistant coaches, deploy coaches as "spotters" in the press box to suggest plays and formations, use classroom lectures and game film as instructional devices, and hold summer camps, preseason two-a-day drills, and daily practice during the season. While other teams used the fashionable single-wing formation, Halas and Ralph Jones, who coached the Bears from 1930 to 1932, devised the revolutionary man-in-motion T formation that became the basic offensive alignment in pro football. The chair and most influential member of the league's rules committee, Halas was primarily responsible for three fundamental rule changes that distinguished the professional from the college game by emphasizing the offense: in 1933 establishing hash marks to allow the offense to put the ball in play at an advantageous point away from the sidelines and moving the goal posts from the back line of the end zone to the goal line in order to facilitate kicking field goals, and in 1934 permitting a forward pass from anywhere behind the line of scrimmage to create a "wide open" game and more scoring. He also was responsible for the 1938 rule imposing a penalty for "roughing" the passer in order to protect the quarterback from injury. And as the de facto head of the league by virtue of being its senior owner and coach, Halas worked closely with NFL commissioners to move the circuit toward fiscal stability by insisting that home teams share gate receipts and pool television revenue, supported league parity despite the Bears' dominant position by providing the critical support necessary to create the draft of college players in 1936, and advocated the 1966 merger of the NFL and the American Football League. On the other hand, it is widely believed that Halas was primarily responsible for the unofficial ban on blacks in the NFL during the 1930s and 1940s.

A self-made man for whom football symbolized life itself, Halas has been called accurately "the first buccaneer and the last puritan" of pro football. To persons inside the Bears organization, he was a parsimonious, paternalistic autocrat who relished playing the role of father figure for his players and regarded personal loyalty and self-sacrifice as cardinal virtues. He took assistant coach George H. Allen to court in 1965 to prevent him from breaking his contract with the Bears to join the Los Angeles Rams. When Mike Ditka during a salary dispute in 1966 said the penurious owner "tosses nickels around like manhole covers," Halas promptly traded his all-pro tight end. Still, if he underpaid his players and publicly drove them relentlessly toward excellence, he also privately assisted many of them generously with their personal financial affairs. To the rest of the NFL, Halas was a crusty, combative, conniving curmudgeon. His motto, "Always go to bed a winner," found expression not only in berating and cursing officials, but in such unsporting actions as tripping opposing players, using binoculars to spy on opponents' practices, and withholding soap and towels from the visitors' locker room. He candidly admitted: "I like to win, and I fought for everything in the book. Nothing else mattered."

When the Bears' success declined after World War II, Halas increasingly was criticized for clinging proprietarily to the positions of coach and owner and for stubbornness and inflexibility that put him and the team increasingly out of touch with the rapid changes in the game. While the Bears maintained their reputation as a strong defensive team, thanks to assistant coaches Clark Shaughnessy and George Allen, the offense, closely controlled by Halas, failed to keep pace with new running and passing strategies, most notably shunning the use of a "flanker," or third pass receiver. And if charges of racism directed toward Halas remained unsubstantiated, the Bears in the 1950s and 1960s were one of the last clubs to use African-American players and in the 1970s and 1980s lagged behind other clubs in employing black coaches and administrative personnel. In some respects the game Halas did so much to create passed him by, but he remained ever the shrewd businessman. His fiscal management policies made the Bears one of the most profitable NFL franchises, while extensive investments in oil, real estate, and sporting goods made him the wealthiest coach in pro football history and earned him posthumous election in 1987 to the U.S. Business Hall of Fame.

Although his personality and demeanor brought infrequent public praise and considerable private derision from contemporaries, Halas was universally respected for his coaching and entrepreneurial acumen as well as for providing the crucial leadership that transformed professional football from a largely regional Sunday diversion to a national sports industry. He was a visionary on and off the field, doggedly pursuing his dream of making pro football a major attraction at a time when the college game dominated public attention. Personal animosities and jealousies preclud-

ed his election to the NFL presidency, but he served from 1970 until his death as the first president of the National Football Conference in recognition of his role in merging the NFL and AFL. Halas was among the charter members elected in 1963 to the Pro Football Hall of Fame. At the time of his death in Chicago, he was actively performing the duties—owner, chairman of the board, and chief executive officer—that he had begun sixty-four years earlier. "He was to us," declared NFL Commissioner Pete Rozelle, "what Dr. James Naismith was to basketball when he put up peach baskets and invented a winter sport. George Halas *was* the National Football League."

• Valuable clippings are in the George Halas File, Pro Football Hall of Fame, Canton, Ohio. Important if biased autobiographical accounts are George Halas with Gwen Morgan and Arthur Veysey, *Halas by Halas: The Autobiography of George Halas* (1979), and George S. Halas, "My Forty Years in Pro Football," *Saturday Evening Post*, 23 Nov. 1957, pp. 34–35ff.; 30 Nov. 1957, pp. 30ff.; and 7 Dec. 1957, pp. 36ff. The best biography is George Vass, *George Halas and the Chicago Bears* (1971). See also Myron Cope, ed., *The Game That Was; The Early Days of Pro Football* (1970); Frank Deford, "I Don't Date Any Woman under 48," *Sports Illustrated*, 5 Dec. 1977, pp. 36–38ff.; Ray Didinger, "George Halas: He Invented Pro Football," *Football Digest*, Feb. 1984, pp. 32–35; and Sid Luckman, "Football's Unforgettable George Halas," *Reader's Digest*, Nov. 1985, pp. 110–15. Analytical obituaries include articles by Dave Anderson and Joseph Durso, *New York Times*, 1 Nov. 1983; Jerry Kirshenbaum, "Papa Bear," *Sports Illustrated*, 14 Nov. 1983; and Cooper Rollow, "Papa Bear," *Sporting News*, 14 Nov. 1983.

LARRY R. GERLACH

HALDEMAN, H. R. (27 Oct. 1926–12 Nov. 1993), President Richard Nixon's chief of staff, was born Harry Robbins Haldeman in Los Angeles, California, the son of Harry Francis Haldeman, a plumbing, heating, and air conditioning supplier, and Katherine Robbins. His father's business ventures enabled Haldeman to have a comfortable, upper middle-class upbringing. An Eagle Scout, Haldeman completed high school in 1944 and joined the U.S. Navy Reserve's V-12 program at Redlands University and the University of Southern California, narrowly missing wartime service. He graduated from the University of California at Los Angeles (UCLA) in 1948 with a degree in business administration.

Haldeman was a strong supporter of the anti-Communist movement sweeping southern California during the postwar years. As a member of UCLA's Interfraternity Council, Haldeman had fought to keep student organizations free from Communist influence. Congressman Richard Nixon's activities on the House Un-American Activities Committee, especially his attempt to push an antisubversion bill through Congress, inspired Haldeman. In 1949 Haldeman married Joanne Horton; their marriage produced four children. That same year he became an account executive with the J. Walter Thompson advertising agency in New York City, returning to Los Angeles in 1952 to manage the firm's branch office. Haldeman exhibited strong organizational ability but, as the office's stagnating profits showed, lacked the vision to move the office forward.

In 1951 a college classmate introduced Haldeman to then senator Nixon. The meeting was unremarkable, but his interest in Nixon's political career deepened. In 1952 he volunteered to work on Nixon's vice presidential campaign and later served as an advance man for the vice president in the 1956 effort. Haldeman's organizational skills and attention to detail earned him the vice president's attention. Haldeman also worked on Nixon's unsuccessful presidential campaign of 1960 and his disastrous 1962 California gubernatorial race and gradually moved into Nixon's inner circle of advisers.

Unlike those motivated by party loyalty or personal ambition, Haldeman demonstrated a strong personal loyalty to Nixon. Following Nixon's 1960 defeat, Haldeman helped Nixon prepare his memoir, *Six Crises*, a defense of his political career. One of the few advisers able to relate to Nixon on a personal level, Haldeman listened to his thoughts and often provided reassurance during the low points of his career.

Resigning from J. Walter Thompson, Haldeman served as campaign chief of staff for Nixon's 1968 presidential campaign. He realized that earlier campaigns, which had relied heavily on numerous personal appearances at campaign rallies, had wasted Nixon's physical energy and destroyed his judgment. Drawing on his experience in advertising and marketing, Haldeman formulated a campaign strategy that maximized media exposure while carefully limiting the candidate's personal appearances. Although sharing Nixon's disdain of the media, Haldeman nonetheless believed that it could be manipulated. Haldeman zealously took on the task of limiting access to the candidate. He determined who could see Nixon and what business required his personal attention. Nixon, naturally reclusive, welcomed Haldeman's effort.

When Nixon took office as president in 1969, Haldeman became White House chief of staff, continuing his role as Nixon's "gatekeeper." His control over the president's schedule and the information directed to the president gave him unprecedented power. Haldeman was also instrumental in Nixon's effort to bypass the permanent bureaucracy, which was often slow to respond to presidential demands. Employing Haldeman as a shield and a demanding taskmaster, Nixon created a highly centralized administration, which placed much of the responsibility for policy implementation in the hands of the White House staff. Under constant pressure from the crew-cut Haldeman, who described himself as Nixon's "son of a bitch," the White House staff sought to respond promptly and without question to any presidential request, often without weighing the political consequences should their actions become known. Beyond official duties, Haldeman continued to serve as a close personal adviser, making himself available day and night to attend to pressing business. As confirmed by his diary, published in 1994, his constant access to the president assured that he was familiar with all issues facing the administration.

The intensely private Haldeman, who preferred working behind the scenes, first gained notoriety for his role in the Watergate scandal when it became a highly publicized political crisis with widely televised Senate hearings during the summer of 1973. Spurning the national media, Haldeman continued to restrict the flow of information from the White House, drawing the wrath of reporters who referred to him as a "Prussian guard." Eventually Haldeman's central role in the Watergate cover-up was revealed in Nixon's secret Oval Office tapes, which, when publicly released, showed that during the critical summer of 1973 and continuing until 1974 he had failed to dissuade Nixon from obstructing the Federal Bureau of Investigation probe of the break-in. Increasing pressure led Nixon to accept Haldeman's forced resignation as chief of staff on 30 April 1973. Indicted for his role in the Watergate cover-up, Haldeman was convicted of perjury, obstruction of justice, and conspiracy to obstruct justice in 1975.

After his release from prison in 1978, Haldeman returned to Los Angeles, serving as a business consultant, president of Murdock Hotels, and senior vice president of the Murdock Development Company before retiring in 1987. Remaining an intensely private person in his later years, he died in his home in Santa Barbara, California.

Haldeman's drive for control of Nixon's staff and loyalty to the president were crucial in the engineering of the Watergate cover-up. In his memoir, *The Ends of Power* (1978), Haldeman admitted that the atmosphere of secrecy and loyalty he created within the Nixon White House was largely responsible for this enveloping crisis. However, he denied that he was guilty of any specific crime. Haldeman's conduct as chief of staff underscores the perils of equating an administration's survival with the public good. Although conceding that Nixon's presidency comprised numerous mistakes, he continued to take pride in its positive accomplishments.

• *The Haldeman Diaries: Inside the Nixon White House* (1994) reveals Haldeman's extensive role within the administration. The most complete descriptions of Haldeman appear in Theodore H. White, *Breach of Faith* (1975) and *The Making of the President* (1972). See also Dan Rather and Gary Paul Gates, *The Palace Guard* (1974). For Haldeman's role in Watergate see Carl Bernstein and Bob Woodward, *All the President's Men* (1974), and Stanley Kutler, *The Wars of Watergate: The Last Crisis of Richard Nixon* (1990).

VINCENT W. GASSER

HALDEMAN, Samuel Stehman (12 Aug. 1812–10 Sept. 1880), naturalist and philologist, was born at Locust Grove, Lancaster County, Pennsylvania, the son of Henry Haldeman, a businessman, and Frances Stehman (her name and Samuel's middle name are sometimes spelled Steman or Stedman). Haldeman's Swiss ancestors had acquired considerable property in the Susquehanna Valley and had occupied positions of prestige in Pennsylvania. His grandfather John B. Haldeman had been elected to the general assembly of Pennsylvania, and his great-great-grandfather Jacob Haldeman had been a member of the colony's Committee of Safety during the Revolution. His great-grand-uncle Sir Frederick Haldimand had served as commander in chief of the British forces in Canada.

Haldeman's mother, an accomplished musician, died when he was ten years old, but she had imparted to him an acute sense of hearing that later facilitated his philological and natural history investigations. On his parents' estate south of Harrisburg, Pennsylvania, the boy collected shells, insects, birds, minerals, learned Pennsylvania Dutch from his German neighbors, and read extensively in his father's library. From 1826 to 1828 he attended John Miller Keagy's school for classics in Harrisburg, and from 1828 to 1830 he studied under the geologist Henry D. Rogers at Dickinson College in Carlisle, Pennsylvania. Tiring of the school regimen, he left college without earning a degree. Thereafter he studied independently, while attending medical lectures at the University of Pennsylvania and scientific discussions at the Academy of Natural Sciences of Philadelphia and the American Philosophical Society in Philadelphia. Even while managing the family sawmill from 1830 to 1835, Haldeman found time for extensive field trips and reading. In 1835 he married Mary A. Hough, with whom he had four children, and the couple moved to a new house at Chickies, overlooking the Susquehanna. There he joined two brothers in the manufacture of pig iron. Haldeman left the management of the commercial side to his brothers and applied his chemical knowledge to the scientific and technological aspects of iron smelting. In two articles in the *American Journal of Science*, "On the Construction of Furnaces to Smelt Iron with Anthracite" (1848) and "The Results of Smelting Iron with Anthracite" (1848), he demonstrated the advantages of anthracite coal furnaces over the traditional charcoal furnaces, an innovation that soon transformed the American iron smelting industry.

In 1836 Haldeman's mentor Rogers appointed him to the New Jersey Geological Survey. A year later Haldeman assumed charge of field work for the south-central portion of the Pennsylvania Geological Survey. In the field as survey naturalist and independent scholar, Haldeman gathered materials for his *Monograph of the Freshwater Univalve Mollusca of the United States* (8 pts., 1840–1866), which was the first comprehensive treatment of American mollusks.

In 1842 Haldeman led the drive to organize the Entomological Society of Pennsylvania, the first such society in America. During its brief existence, the society facilitated contact among American entomologists and between them and their European colleagues. Its members published hundreds of descriptions of American insects and assembled the first permanent American insect collections. Haldeman's monographs on the long-horned beetles, "Materials toward a History of the Coleoptera Longicornia of the United States"

(1847) and additions and corrections to the preceding (1847), constituted the first comprehensive treatment of these insects. With John L. LeConte, he edited Friedrich Ernst Melsheimer's *Catalogue of the Described Coleoptera of the United States* for publication by the Smithsonian Institution (1853), initiating a monograph series on various insect orders that helped advance American entomology to equal standing with the field in Europe.

Prompted by his desire to move on to new fields and also by problems with his eyesight, Haldeman turned to the study of human and animal sounds. His acute sense of hearing enabled him to "observe," record, and duplicate with his own voice fine distinctions in sounds. In 1848 he published his discovery of sound organs in certain moths. Being particularly interested in the languages of American Indians, he traveled widely to hear the speech of tribes in the East and Midwest. He often met visiting Indian delegations in Washington, D.C., and he solicited Indian vocabularies from naturalists in the West. His paper "On Some Points in Linguistic Ethnology, with Illustrations chiefly from Aboriginal Languages of America," delivered at the 1849 meetings of the American Association for the Advancement of Science and American Academy of Arts and Sciences and published in the proceedings of the latter (1849), immediately established his reputation as a first-rate philologist.

In place of the normal approach to the study of language from literature and the written word, Haldeman listened to sounds and studied their meanings. Over the course of six trips abroad between 1847 and 1875 he extended his investigations to the polyglot cities and provinces of Europe, where he became adept at languages from all corners of the globe. The result was a widening stream of publications on such topics as Latin pronunciation for naturalists, the adoption of the Latin alphabet to Indian languages, the relationship between Chinese and Indo-European languages, the origin and use of affixes, Pennsylvania Dutch, and a general outline of etymology. His *Analytic Orthography: An Investigation of the Sounds of the Voice, and Their Alphabetic Notation* (1860) won the international competition for the Trevelyan Prize for reform in English spelling. Though philologists objected to Haldeman's proposal to add letters to the alphabet in cases where sounds were not based on ancient Latin, they applauded his proposal to eliminate silent letters in words ("labor" in place of "labour").

Haldeman helped found the American Philological Association, serving as first vice president (1874–1876) and president (1876–1877), and he presided at the International Convention in Behalf of the Amendment of English Orthografy [sic], a group that organized in Philadelphia in 1876 to advocate spelling reform. He was professor of zoology at the Franklin Institute in 1842–1843; professor of natural history at the University of Pennsylvania from 1850 to 1853; chemist and geologist to the Pennsylvania State Agricultural Society in 1852; and professor of geology and chemistry at Delaware College (now University of

Delaware) from 1855 to 1858. In 1869 he became the first professor of comparative philology at the University of Pennsylvania, a position he retained until his death at Chickies.

Haldeman was a prolific writer. Louis Agassiz's *Bibliographia Zoologicae et Geologicae* (1852) lists seventy-three publications by Haldeman in natural history up to 1852, and an incomplete bibliography prepared by Haldeman's daughter Eliza Figyelmesy after his death lists a total of 122 publications in the fields of conchology, entomology, arachnology, crustacea, annelids and worms, geology and chemistry, philology, and archaeology, among others. His publications range over many subjects and explore many styles, including his first publication, a "Refutation of Locke's Moon Hoax" (1835), which exposed a widespread hoax of purported sightings of animals on the moon; his monograph on Pennsylvania's oldest fossil plant, *Scolithus linearis* (1840); technical reference works, such as his edition of *Taylor's Statistics of Coal* (1855); his ingenious *Tours of a Chess Knight* (1864), which demonstrated how the knight can pass over the whole chessboard, touching each square but once; and his humorous *Rhymes of the Poets*, under the pseudonym Felix Ago (1868), an anthology of false rhymes of prominent writers. He was also editor of the *Pennsylvania Farmer's Journal* (1851–1852) and associate editor for the department of comparative philology and linguistics of *Johnson's New Universal Cyclopaedia*, and he edited the *Narrative of the United States Expedition to the River Jordan and the Dead Sea* by William Francis Lynch (1849).

Late in life Haldeman turned his attention to archaeology. His report of a prehistoric cave shelter on his property, "On the Contents of a Rock Retreat in South-eastern Pennsylvania" (1878), along with other publications extended his scientific versatility to this field.

Haldeman epitomized the post-1812 generation of scholars who, prompted by patriotic and intellectual motives, advanced American science and letters to a position of true cultural independence from Europe. Living at a time when specialists were replacing generalists, Haldeman excelled in many areas. He set new standards in conchology, entomology, and linguistics, and he wrote knowledgeably on a wide variety of other topics as well.

• Haldeman's correspondence and papers on entomology and other natural history topics are in the library of the Academy of Natural Sciences of Philadelphia. No collection of his correspondence and writings on philology appears to exist. Some Haldeman letters are in the Smithsonian Institution Archives, Washington, D.C., and others whose present location is unknown are described in H. B. Weiss, "Some Historical Material Relating to Professor S. S. Haldeman," *Journal of the New York Entomological Society* 46 (Mar. 1938): 45–48. His specimens, artifacts, and books are widely scattered. His mollusks are at the Academy of Natural Sciences and at the Delessert-Lamarck collection in Paris; his archaeological collections are at the Academy of Natural Sciences, the American Philosophical Society, the Smithsonian Institution, the American Museum of Natural History in New York, and the Linnaean Society of Lancaster County, Penn.; and his annotated dictionaries are at the Library Company of Philadelphia. On the dispersal of his books see the *Catalogue of the Library of Prof. S. S. Haldeman* (1881).

The most extensive accounts of his life are J. P. Lesley, "Memoir of Samuel Stedman Haldeman 1812–1880," National Academy of Sciences, *Biographical Memoirs* 2 (1886): 139–72, and Charles Henry Hart, *Memoir of Samuel Stehman Haldeman LL.D.* (1881), reprinted from the *Penn Monthly*, Aug. 1881, which includes an assessment of his philological work and Figyelmesy's bibliography. Haldeman's career in entomology is placed in the context of his times in W. Conner Sorensen, *Brethren of the Net: American Entomology 1840–1880* (1995).

W. CONNER SORENSEN

HALDEMAN-JULIUS, Emanuel (30 July 1889–31 July 1951), author and publisher, was born in Philadelphia, Pennsylvania, the son of David Julius, a bookbinder, and Elizabeth Zamost. Both of his parents were Jewish immigrants from Odessa (Ukraine) who came to America in 1887; their original name was Zolajefsky. Emanuel grew up surrounded by books, and, although he dropped out of school in the seventh grade, he never ended his education. As a teenager he worked as a theater usher and bellhop before he found his place as an intellectual. After meeting several radicals in Philadelphia, he joined the Socialist party and turned to journalism. His first article, based on an interview with the author, was "Mark Twain: Radical" for the *International Socialist Review*. In his early twenties, he worked as a reporter for *The Call* in New York, *The Leader* in Milwaukee, and *Chicago World*, all socialist newspapers.

In 1915 Julius moved to Girard, Kansas, with Louis Kopelin in an attempt to salvage the *Appeal to Reason*, which had previously been the most popular socialist newspaper in the nation with a circulation of 500,000 and which boasted Eugene V. Debs as its most frequent contributor. After the death of its founder, J. A. Wayland, in 1912, however, the newspaper had foundered.

In Girard, Julius met Anna Marcet Haldeman, the niece of Jane Addams, a well-to-do Republican Presbyterian, and a feminist. They married in 1916, changing both surnames to Haldeman-Julius. The couple had two children. With a loan from his wife, Haldeman-Julius bought the presses of the *Appeal*, hired Kopelin to oversee them, and launched his own career as a publisher. He had been enchanted by the *Rubáiyat of Omar Khayyam* as a teenager and had dreamed of producing an edition cheap enough to get into the hands of everyone. The *Rubáiyat* was the first book produced by the Haldeman-Julius Publishing Company, and it sold for twenty-five cents. Next came Oscar Wilde's *The Ballad of Reading Gaol*.

Haldeman-Julius had found his niche, and he became phenomenally successful almost at once. He believed that there were millions of readers who could not afford handsome, hardcover books—gift books that go unread, as he described them—and he began mass producing paper books, all with the same blue, nondescript cover, all the same 3½″ × 5″ size, all printed in eight-point type on cheap paper, few with as many as eighty pages. For the first few years Haldeman-Julius merely reprinted classics—Plato, Shakespeare, Ibsen, Hugo—and sold them through ads in newspapers and magazines. By increasing his print runs in response to the great numbers of orders he received, he was able to offer each book for five cents and still make a profit. (He estimated his printing costs at one cent per book.) Within ten years Haldeman-Julius had sold 150 million copies of 1,500 different titles; at his death in 1951, he had sold 500 million copies.

In *The First Hundred Million* (1928), Haldeman-Julius explains that he merely tapped into the bottomless American desire for self-improvement. When he recognized that hunger, he began producing practical "how-to" books—knot-tying, masonry, dessert cookery, furniture refinishing—and books about health care, particularly birth control and sexual hygiene. He then moved into basic education: *Chemistry Self-Taught*, *Italian Self-Taught*, *Sociology Self-Taught*, and so forth. He found another huge market in ethnic jokes, proverbs, and anecdotes. But ideas, especially philosophical and religious ideas, were his favorite topics, and he invited such thinkers as Will Durant, Clarence Darrow, Margaret Sanger, and Joseph McCabe to write for the Little Blue Books. An agnostic anticleric, Haldeman-Julius once wrote, "I have been accused of saturating the series with skeptical books because I wish to print propaganda . . . and thus convert everyone to my own way of thinking." He then agreed with his accusers.

If a title sold less than 10,000 copies per year, Haldeman-Julius took it to the "hospital," where it was "rejuvenated." Often that meant simply retitling the text, as in the case of Francis Bacon's *Apothegms*, which became *Terse Truths about the Riddle of Life*. Sometimes, however, it meant editing, as when "the duller portions" were taken out of Tennyson's *Lady of the Lake*.

Haldeman-Julius wrote two novels with his wife, Marcet Haldeman-Julius, a playwright and a loan officer at the Girard State Bank. Their 1921 bestseller, *Dust*, told of the drudgery of farm life on the Kansas plains. Reviewers compared it favorably with the work of Willa Cather, Sinclair Lewis, and Ruth Suckow. Their second book, *Violence!* (1929), was also successful. A separation in 1934 ended their collaboration. Marcet Haldeman-Julius died in 1941, and shortly afterward Haldeman-Julius married an employee, Susan Haney; the marriage produced no children. He drowned in his swimming pool in Girard, Kansas, ten years later. Just before his death he was convicted of income tax evasion.

Haldeman-Julius was frequently criticized for his sensational methods of promoting books, his frequent lapses from good taste (alone he wrote "Everybody: A Fable for Voyeurs," which described every known sexual practice and was rejected by his publisher), and his tendency toward self-aggrandizement. He contin-

ued to write and publish *Appeal to Reason*, retitling it first *Haldeman-Julius Weekly* in 1923 and then *American Freeman* in 1929, and it became an outlet for his own idiosyncratic opinions, rather than mirroring an ideology. His standard for excellence was, "Do I like it myself?"

Haldeman-Julius is best remembered for revolutionizing America's reading habits. The Little Blue Books were found in prisons, on subways, on farms, and in ghettos, and their presence led to the ubiquitous cheap paperbacks of later years.

• The papers of E. Haldeman-Julius are divided among Pittsburg State University, Kans.; the University of Illinois, Circle Campus; and the Lilly Library at Indiana University. Haldeman-Julius's autobiographical works are *The First Hundred Million* (1928), *Why I Believe in Freedom of Thought* (1930), and *My First and Second Twenty-five Years* (2 vols., 1949). Some of his essays and articles were compiled in Albert Mordell, ed., *The World of Haldeman-Julius* 1960. A good contemporary criticism of his work is Louis Adamic, "Voltaire from Kansas," *Outlook and Independent*, 25 June 1930, p. 282. Biographical material can be found in Alden Whitman, ed., *American Reformers* (1985), and the introduction by Gene DeGruson to the reprint of *Dust* (1992). An obituary is in the *New York Times*, 1 Aug. 1951.

BETTY BURNETT

HALDERMAN, John Adams (15 Apr. 1833–21 Sept. 1908), soldier, politician, and diplomat, was born in Fayette County, Kentucky, the son of Susan Henderson Rogers and John A. Halderman, a physician. Subsequent to the death of Halderman's mother in 1843, Halderman's father remarried and moved to Illinois, but the younger Halderman remained in Kentucky in the care of his maternal grandparents. Little else is known of his early years except that he aspired to a military career and thus sought appointment to the U.S. Military Academy at West Point. When these efforts were frustrated, Halderman attended McKendree College in Lebanon, Illinois, Xavier College in Cincinnati, Ohio, and the University of Louisville. His most important educational experience, however, came in the Lexington law office of his uncle, Colonel C. C. Rogers, where he read law. In the spring of 1854 Halderman was admitted to the bar.

At this time Halderman also became intrigued by the prospects for a young man in the newly created territory of Kansas, and he was soon on his way west. Slavery was the defining issue in the territory and the nation during this tumultuous decade, giving rise to a new political party that objected to the Kansas-Nebraska Act of 1854. The "popular sovereignty" provision of this controversial measure reopened the issue of slavery's extension into the territories by repealing the Missouri Compromise of 1820. According to at least one source, Halderman's father opposed slavery and supported John C. Frémont's Republican candidacy in 1856. But Halderman identified himself with Stephen A. Douglas's wing of the Democratic party, and although he later insisted that he too opposed the institution of slavery, he supported the principle of popular sovereignty and was identified with Kansas's "proslave" party. Halderman probably arrived in the Kansas Territory in October 1854. In November he became private secretary to the territory's first governor, Andrew Reeder. Subsequently, as secretary of the first territorial council in 1855, Leavenworth County's first probate judge in 1855–1856, a member of the territorial council of 1857, and a Douglas delegate to the 1860 national convention, he worked to make Kansas a Democratic state. But, like his Illinois mentor Douglas, in 1857–1858 he opposed the infamous Lecompton constitution, which sought to force slavery on an unwilling Kansas populace. He even purchased a partnership in the *Leavenworth Journal* as an oracle for that opposition. "While I controlled or owned it [the *Journal*]," wrote Halderman in 1881, "it favored a free state in Kansas, fought Lecompton, and supported Douglas." The split among "proslave" partisans over the ill-advised Lecompton effort further weakened the fledgling Kansas Democracy, and Halderman's party-building efforts were to no avail. The Free State (Republican) party won the day in Kansas, and at some point during the Civil War (probably in 1861), Halderman switched his party allegiance.

During the war's second month, May 1861, President Abraham Lincoln called for troops, including one regiment from the infant state of Kansas. In the late spring recruits for eleven companies made up the First Kansas Volunteer Infantry and were placed under the command of Colonel George W. Deitzler of Lawrence. Halderman, who helped recruit the regiment, was Colonel Deitzler's second in command with the rank of major. Within two months these raw Kansas troops experienced their first engagement of consequence at Wilson's Creek (10 Aug. 1861), near Springfield, Missouri. There, Federal forces under Brigadier General Nathaniel Lyon met General Sterling Price's Confederates in the first major battle west of the Mississippi River. The First Kansas experienced heavy fighting and proved to be a surprisingly effective force. The regiment went into the battle with 644 soldiers, and 77 of them were killed and 255 wounded—a 51 percent casualty rate. General Deitzler, who, according to Colonel Samuel D. Sturgis, "led his regiment into a galling fire as coolly and as handsomely as if on drill," was badly wounded, and early in the six-hour battle Major Halderman led the charge of four companies, crying, "Forward, men, for Kansas and the old flag." In July 1861 Halderman served General Lyon as provost marshal general of the Army of the West, and in the spring of 1862 he resigned his commission with the First Kansas in order to accept appointment as major general of the Kansas State Militia with responsibility for organizing the northern division. He left the service for good in late 1864.

Halderman married Anna B. Dorrien during the latter part of 1861. Before divorcing, they had seven children, four of whom died as infants. To support his growing family during the postwar period, Halderman expanded his business interests and pursued his law

practice in Leavenworth. He served as mayor of that city for two terms (1867 and 1870) as a regent of the state university at Lawrence (1870–1873), and as a member of the state house of representatives (1870) and state senate (1875–1876). Although his record as a state and local leader was commendable, Halderman's interests went beyond the borders of his adopted state, and he traveled extensively during the early 1870s to Europe, Egypt, Syria, Turkey, and Palestine. When he aspired to diplomatic service in the late 1870s, support came from an unlikely corner—the pugnacious Leavenworth editor Daniel R. Anthony, his local rival and sometime political adversary. Anthony, an uncompromising abolitionist during territorial days and one-time commander of the Seventh Kansas Cavalry (Jennison's Jayhawkers), praised Halderman's mayoral service and pledged "carte blanche for anything . . . that I can give" with regard to Halderman's pursuit of a federal appointment.

Initial efforts were unsuccessful, but in 1880 Halderman was appointed the first U.S. consul to Bangkok, Siam (now Thailand). He arrived in September of that year and was well received by the nation's monarch. Effective in his efforts to promote U.S. interests, he was advanced to consul general in 1881. Although he failed to land a desired position in Moscow in 1882, Halderman was rewarded in 1883, when he was named first U.S. minister to Siam. Halderman "was apparently able to establish close and cordial relationships with the royal family. Commentators have said that his contribution to good American-Siamese relationships was substantial. He laid a foundation for friendship that has continued to this time. Indeed, Siam, later Thailand, may have been the most consistent friend the United States has had in Southeast Asia during the past century" (Wilson, p. 92).

While in this far-off post, Halderman focused on two main problems and made positive contributions. The first issue pertained to American liquor importers, who by treaty had been given some significant legal advantages over Siam's domestic distillers. Halderman worked to eliminate some of the worst abuses that arose under this system, which was driving local vendors out of business and denying the Siamese government much-needed revenue. Under the minister's leadership, new treaties were finally negotiated that gave the local government the sole right to license retail liquor dealers and to increase duties on such imports. His second accomplishment related to communication. With Minister Halderman's support and assistance, telegraph lines linked Bangkok to the outside world, and Siam joined the International Postal Union.

Halderman resigned his diplomatic post in July 1885, rightly confident that he had made a difference. The king of Siam honored him with the title knight commander of the Most Exalted Order of the White Elephant, and King Norodom and the French government made him a commander of the Royal Order of Cambodia. Former president Grant called his career in southern Asia "one of the highest successes in American diplomacy."

Halderman seemed to prefer his military salutation to the others he could claim and offered his services in the 1898 war against Spain. His offer was respectfully declined. He spent the last two decades of his life in Washington, D.C. Sources vary as to Halderman's place of death; he was buried in Arlington National Cemetery.

• Halderman's papers are scattered among several depositories and contain relatively little of his own writings, but useful collections are at the Kansas State Historical Society, Topeka, Kans.; the University of Kansas, Lawrence, Kans.; the Virginia State Historical Society, Richmond, Va.; and the Smithsonian Institution, Washington, D.C. Paul E. Wilson, "John Adams Halderman: Our Eldest Brother," *Journal of the Kansas Bar Association* 54 (Summer 1985): 84–95, is a fine article-length biography based on extensive research in the available primary and secondary sources. Obituaries are in the *New York Times*, 23 Sept. 1908, and the *Leavenworth Times*, 24 Sept. 1908.

VIRGIL W. DEAN

HALE, Arthur William (16 Mar. 1896–17 Oct. 1971), radio news broadcaster, was born Arthur William Glunt in Altoona, Pennsylvania, the son of George Alexander Glunt, a general store and property owner, and Ida J. Nail. In 1912 Glunt helped organize Altoona's Musicians' Union local, graduating from Altoona High School the following year. Glunt also clerked in his father's store and played the piano in a local movie house. Entering Gettysburg College in 1914, he led the Sophomore and College Orchestra and was Glee Club pianist. When the United States entered World War I in April 1917, he left college to join the U.S. Army. Ten months later he was shipped to France and was discharged honorably on 21 August 1919 as a second lieutenant, having served as battalion gas officer in the 312th Field Artillery, 79th Division.

Before returning to the United States, he spent a semester at the University of Grenoble in 1919 and then graduated from Gettysburg College that year. College aspirations for a law career were put aside, and he worked as a claim correspondent with the B. F. Goodrich Rubber Company in Philadelphia during 1920–1922, followed by two years with the Edson Insurance Company developing an automobile insurance plan that was later adopted by Ford Motors. In 1924 he returned to Altoona to manage the family interests, while working as a graph specialist (preparing graphs relative to economic performance, numbers of passengers and passenger miles, and similar data) with the Pennsylvania Railroad and directing a local theater orchestra.

In 1929 he returned to Paris in hopes of studying with the famous pianist Nadia Boulanger, who recommended against a concert career. Moving to New York the next year, Glunt joined the staff of radio station WOR as an "announcer, pianist, writer, producer, sound-effects etc." He wrote and announced program notes for live musical performances from venues such as Carnegie Hall. During one of those broadcasts the failure of the landline (telephone-cable connection of performance hall, studio, and transmitter) led Glunt to fill in the time with an impromptu radio premiere of the piano score of George Gershwin's *Rhapsody in Blue*.

Glunt, although not a journalist, possessed a natural "radio" voice that was his entry into the rapidly emerging radio news business. In 1935 Transradio Press Service chose Glunt, renamed Arthur Hale, to be the newscaster for its 11:00 P.M. news spot on WOR. He was credited with being the first to popularize sponsored news broadcasts at a late hour, as well as originating the sign-off "And that's the news." In July 1939, as the European crisis gathered momentum, Transradio started the fifteen-minute "Confidentially Yours—Arthur Hale" on WOR three nights a week, soon going to five nights a week. In December one of the sponsors, Richfield Hi-Octane, "Champion of Gasolines," offered a free European news map, and, to Richfield's astonishment, in two months 99,850 maps were given out. Richfield reported that over a three-month period, "Sales increased at almost THREE TIMES the rate of increase of the whole industry!"

In 1940 *Time* (15 Jan. 1940, p. 48) reviewed Hale's first weekly Saturday broadcast of "Confidentially Yours." Behind Hale's "glib, confidential voice," *Time* pointed out, was Transradio Press Service, Inc., directed by ex–United Press man Herbert Samuel Moore. Transradio (which served 250 radio stations and some forty newspapers worldwide) was "acclaimed in the radio business for accuracy, wariness and brevity. . . . [It] got wide kudos during the war-bulletin period for keeping its editorial head screwed on tight, broadcasting no scare heads." "Confidentially Yours" was carried nationally three nights per week (Tuesday, Thursday, and Saturday) from 7:30 to 7:45 Eastern Standard Time, alternating on the Mutual Network with Raymond Gram Swing (Monday, Wednesday, and Friday). In early 1940 Hale reportedly had a 9.2 Hooper rating with 30 percent of the New York metropolitan audience, matching the popularity of Paul Sullivan and topping Mutual's other news broadcasters, Swing and Gabriel Heatter. Hale also narrated movie shorts. He later recalled that during 1943–1944 a series of "Confidentially Yours" newsreel shorts for the Embassy Newsreel Theatre group led to his "face" becoming "known to headwaiters and [his] tables were further from the kitchen door." Although initially a supporter of the New Deal, by 1940 he had become a personally outspoken opponent of President Franklin D. Roosevelt and was set for his lifelong support of the Republican party.

Transradio wrote the scripts, and Hale had no authority to change them; each broadcast ended with the statement, "The material for 'Confidentially Yours' is gathered and prepared by Trans-Radio." Ironically, Hale reported a story on 15 August 1944 for which he was held responsible. That program contained a three-minute item on atomic energy that led the Federal Bureau of Investigation to descend immediately on

Transradio Press and Mutual Broadcasting in New York and WKBO in Harrisburg, Pennsylvania, impounding scripts, destroying program recordings, and questioning everyone connected with the program. Eric Barnouw said that the "leak" infuriated the military censors, who demanded a censor posted at every radio station. Despite the furor, Hale went back to his broadcasting, but he was not allowed to break the secrecy surrounding the affair even after the dropping of the atomic bomb on Japan a year later. Stories of the incident written by Hearst newsman Bob Considine in December 1951 left Hale convinced that his patriotism had been unjustly impugned by Manhattan Project chief General Leslie Groves.

Despite an estimated 5 million listeners, Richfield canceled "Confidentially Yours" in 1947, apparently because the company, like other gasoline companies, did not see a need to advertise a product in short supply, and Arthur Hale left the air, claiming that he needed a long-overdue vacation, along with time to travel, write, and work on a musical comedy composition. Financially comfortable, he never worked in the media again, although he had been a pioneering figure among early news broadcasters who kept America informed during the critical years of World War II. Hale, who never married, died in Harrisburg, Pennsylvania.

• Hale's diaries from the 1950s, a plaster bust, phonograph records relative to his career, and some of his papers are on deposit at the Pennsylvania State Historical Society Library, Harrisburg. Musical scores and papers relating to Hale's radio career remain in the hands of the family. The "Scoop of the War," as Hale termed it, is the subject of an article, including a copy of the offending script, by K. R. M. Short, "Radio's Scoop of the War: The Atomic Bomb, 1944!" *Historical Journal of Film, Radio and Television* 5, no. 1 (1985): 101–8. See also Eric Barnouw, *A History of Broadcasting in the United States*, vol. 2: *The Golden Web, 1933–1953* (1968).

KENNETH R. MacDONALD SHORT

HALE, Charles Reuben (14 Mar. 1837–25 Dec. 1900), Episcopal bishop, was born in Lewistown, Pennsylvania, the son of Reuben C. Hale and Sarah I. Mills. He received his early education in Lewistown and Philadelphia, and then graduated from the University of Pennsylvania with an A.B. in 1858. While a student at the University of Pennsylvania, he and two other students wrote and published a paper on the Rosetta Stone, giving original translations of the hieroglyphic, demotic (a simplified form of the ancient Egyptian hieratic writing), and Greek inscriptions. This 1859 publication attracted the attention of scholars of his day and began Hale's career as a student of Eastern Orthodox Christianity and Mozarabic liturgies.

Hale studied for the ministry of the Episcopal church on his own and was ordained a deacon on 8 January 1860 and a priest on 17 October 1861. For the first two years of his ministry, he was curate at Christ Church in Germantown and at All Saints' Church in Lower Dublin, Pennsylvania. In 1863 he was appointed a chaplain in the U.S. Navy and remained in that position until 1870. From 1863 until 1865 he was associate professor of mathematics at the Naval Academy, then at Newport, Rhode Island. In 1871 he was named the rector of St. John's Church in Auburn, New York, and worked there until 1873. While in Auburn he married Anna McKnight in 1871. They had no children. In 1873 he moved to New York City, where he assisted in founding Episcopal missions for immigrants, especially Italians. In 1875–1876 he served as rector of St. Mary the Virgin Church in Baltimore, Maryland, and from 1877 until 1885, he was assistant minister at St. Paul's Church in Baltimore. His last parochial responsibility was as dean of Trinity Cathedral in Davenport, Iowa (1886–1892).

On 17 May 1892, the diocese of Springfield, Illinois, elected Hale assistant bishop (bishop coadjutor); he was consecrated on 26 July 1892. Sometimes mistakenly referred to as the "bishop of Cairo," Hale was assistant bishop of Springfield until his death.

Hale's major contributions were as a scholar and ecumenist. In 1869 he became secretary of the Italian Church Reformation Commission, and in 1871 he was secretary of the Joint Committee of the General Convention of the Russo-Greek Church, which corresponded with the authorities of the Russian and other branches of the Oriental church for the acquisition of authentic information. In 1874 he was named by the General Convention to three additional ecumenical or intercommunion agencies: he was clerk to the Commission of the House of Bishops on Correspondence with the Hierarchs of the Eastern Churches; clerk to the Commission of the House of Bishops on Correspondence with the Hierarchs of the Old Catholics; and American secretary of the Anglo-Continental Society of England. In 1877 he was named secretary of the Commission on Ecumenical Relations of the General Convention.

It was as a scholar that Hale made his most lasting contributions. Several of his books were efforts to understand the confusion and multiplicity of Episcopal sees throughout the world. He published *A List of the Sees and Bishops of the Holy Eastern Church* (1870) and *A List of All the Sees and Bishops of the Holy Orthodox Church of the East, Translated and Compiled From Russian Official Documents* (1872). His major work in this area was *The Universal Episcopate: A List of the Sees and Bishops in the Holy Church Throughout All the World, Compiled From Official Documents, and From Other Trustworthy Information* (1882). This volume was originally prepared for and published in the *Living Church Annual* (1883). It began with a list of the Anglican churches, since "to say the least, none come nearer, in all essential respects, to the Primitive Church." Then come the "Old Catholic" churches, which "hold fast all Catholic doctrine, while . . . rejecting the innovations of later days." Next are listed the Eastern Orthodox churches, which "have, in good degree, preserved the Christian traditions of the first ages." The fourth major listing is the Latin churches.

Hale was also a liturgist who published four major studies: *The Mozarabic Liturgy, and the Mexican*

Branch of the Catholic Church of Our Lord Jesus Christ Militant Upon Earth (1876); *An Order for the Holy Communion, Arranged from the Mozarabic Liturgy* (1879); *An Office for Holy Baptism, Arranged From the Mozarabic and Cognate Sources* (1879); and *Mozarabic Collects, Translated and Arranged From the Ancient Liturgy of the Spanish Church* (1881). These studies made the Mozarabic (Spanish) liturgies and rites available to English liturgical scholars.

In his lecture, "The Greek Church," delivered before the Church Club of Connecticut at Christ Church in Hartford and published in *Five Lectures Upon the Church* (1896), Hale stated his ecumenical vision: "When each church fairly and fully realizes what the other intends, in word and deed, the time of reconciliation will doubtless be close at hand. God will surely then give each church grace to do away with whatever may hinder godly union and concord" (p. 72).

Hale was a leading Episcopalian of the nineteenth century and an early advocate of the ecumenical movement, especially in regard to the Eastern-rite churches. He died in Cairo, Illinois.

• Hale's papers are in the Archives of the Episcopal Church, Austin, Tex. Among his other publications are: *The Attitude of the Church towards Movements in Foreign Churches* (1874); *Innocent of Moscow, the Apostle of Kamchatka and Alaska* (1877); *The Orthodox Missionary Society of Russia* (1878); *Russian Missions in China and Japan* (1878); *The Russian Church* (1880); *The Eucharistic Office of the Christian Catholic Church of Switzerland, Translated and Compared with that in the Missale Romanum* (1882); *England's Duty Toward Egypt* (1884); *A Visit to the Eastern Churches in the Interest of Church Unity* (1886); and *Missionary Relations Between the Anglican and the Eastern Churches* (1894). His parish work is noted in Francis F. Beirne, *St. Paul's Parish, Baltimore: A Chronicle of the Mother Church* (1967), and Frederick Ward Kates, *Bridges Across Four Centuries: The Clergy of St. Paul's Parish, Baltimore, Maryland, 1692–1957* (1957). An obituary is in the *Living Church* 24 (5 Feb. 1901): 389.

DONALD S. ARMENTROUT

HALE, Clara McBride (1 Apr. 1905–18 Dec. 1992), humanitarian and founder of Hale House, was born in Philadelphia, Pennsylvania, where she grew up. Her father was murdered when she was a child, and her mother died when Clara was sixteen. She left high school without graduating, although she eventually earned her high school equivalency diploma at the age of eighty-seven. After high school, she married Thomas Hale and moved with him to New York City. There she did cleaning, worked as a domestic, and studied business administration by taking night classes at City College. When she was twenty-seven, her husband died, leaving her with three children.

The conflicts of financially supporting and physically caring for three young children spurred Hale to begin caring for children in her home. She became a licensed foster parent, taking in seven or eight children at a time. Between 1941 and 1968, she reared more than forty foster children.

Hale's work with addicted babies began in 1969, after her retirement as a domestic, when she took in the

baby of a heroin addict; within months she was caring for twenty-two infants in her Harlem apartment. Her home was licensed as a child care facility and in 1970 was incorporated as the residential center called Hale House. She later moved to a five-story brownstone. Hale's prescription for caring for infants was simple: hold them, rock them, love them, and tell them how great they are.

Hale's work with and for children extended well beyond the care of infants. With her daughter, Dr. Lorraine Hale, she created numerous other programs for children and families including Community-Based Family, a program for troubled youngsters; Children Helping Children, an apprenticeship program for juveniles; and Time Out for Moms, a haven to which children may be brought when their parents need relief. In addition, Hale House launched research programs on the problems of drug- or alcohol-addicted mothers and their infants, founded a home for mothers and infants infected with HIV, and established programs for housing, educating, and supporting mothers after detoxification.

In 1986 Hale was honored by President Ronald Reagan as "an American hero" in his State of the Union address and was appointed with her daughter, Lorraine E. Hale, to Reagan's National Drug Free America Task Force. Also in 1986 the Women's International Center presented Hale with their Living Legacy Award "to honor women for their great contributions to humanity."

Mother Hale, as she was known, traced her philosophy and values to her Baptist upbringing and to the difficulties she experienced in her youth. Until shortly before her death in New York City, she kept at least one infant in her own room.

• Hale's papers are privately held. See Darlene Clark Hine, ed., *Black Women in America* (1993); Jessie Carney Smith, ed., *Notable Black American Women* (1992); and Herschel Johnson, "Healing Baby 'Junkies' with Love," *Ebony*, May 1986. An obituary is in the *New York Times*, 20 Dec. 1992.

CHERYL LAZ

HALE, David (25 Apr. 1791–20 Jan. 1849), journalist, was born in Lisbon, Connecticut, the son of David Hale, a clergyman, teacher, and farmer, and Lydia Austin. He attended his father's family school, leaving at the age of sixteen to embark on a business career as a clerk for a store in Coventry, Connecticut. He became a clerk in a Boston commission house in 1809 and returned to Coventry in 1812 to teach in a district school. He earned a reputation for being a strict schoolmaster; the parent of a student he had "whipped severely for misdemeanor" unsuccessfully sued him (Thompson, p. 19). Hale married his first cousin, Laura Hale, in 1815. They had four children before her death in 1824. A serious illness ended another stint in business in 1817. Hale married Lucy S. Turner of Boston in 1825.

Hale contributed to his cousin's newspaper, the *Boston Daily Advertiser*, and later wrote for the *Boston*

Recorder, a Presbyterian newspaper established in 1816 with Gerard Hallock as part owner. Between 1817 and 1827, Hale engaged in several unsuccessful business ventures. He was a partner in a powder mill that exploded in 1821. He also was associated with a woolen factory that ultimately went bankrupt sometime around 1824. Hale became business manager of the newly established *New York Journal of Commerce*, founded in September 1827 by philanthropic businessman Arthur Tappan for the dual purpose of being a commercial newspaper "conducted upon principles of sound morality" and "scrupulous regard for the Sabbath" (Thompson, p. 47). Tappan invested $30,000 in the newspaper during its first sixteen months, then turned it over to his brother Lewis Tappan, who agreed in 1829 to relinquish control of the newspaper two years later to Hale and Hallock, making them sole proprietors. Hale continued as business manager and contributed editorial commentary; Hallock, formerly part owner and editor of the *New York Observer*, became editor.

Hale and Hallock continued with the newspaper's original policies, rejecting advertisements for theaters, lotteries, and businesses that operated on Sundays. In an editorial published on 28 June 1844, "Closing Stores on the Sabbath," Hale wrote: "The laws requiring a proper observance of the Christian Sabbath are good and wholesome laws. . . . All experience proves that there can be no well regulated liberty where the public morals are generally depraved, and that about in proportion as the Sabbath is disregarded in any community, is the depravation of its morals."

Hale once editorially complained about the "immorality" of newsboys hawking newspapers on Sundays, calling the practice a "public nuisance" that corrupted the Sabbath's religious purpose. Newspaper proprietors "ought at least to be restrained, both by their own sense of propriety and by the arm of the law if needful, from encroaching upon the peace of their fellow citizens by sending a thousand boys to fill the streets with confusion," he wrote. "The evil complained of is of recent origin, and it is high time it was abated" (*Journal of Commerce*, 10 July 1839). The *Journal of Commerce* permitted no editorial and production work between midnight Saturday and midnight Sunday, even though the Monday morning edition was published an hour later than its rivals'.

To gain advantage in New York's competitive newspaper market, especially against its archrival, James Watson Webb's *New York Courier and Enquirer*, the *Journal of Commerce* developed innovative newsgathering practices. The newspaper began using pilot boats in 1829–1830 to meet incoming transatlantic ships with foreign intelligence that provided an important source of news. A 24-horse pony express–style relay between Washington, D.C., and New York City was established to expedite congressional proceedings and other government information. Under Hale's leadership the *Journal of Commerce* joined other newspapers to initiate the cooperative news gathering system that became the Associated Press; Hallock was the New York Associated Press's first president.

Hale and the *Journal of Commerce* supported free trade policies, strenuously objecting to any government regulation of commerce. "Let us have 'Free Trade and No Combinations,'" he wrote in denouncing "the degrading tyranny" of trade unions that "subdue the moral sense, the self respect, the happiness, the interests of all who will submit to them" (*Journal of Commerce*, 10 Apr. 1835). Hale editorialized against imprisonment for debt and was an advocate for bankruptcy legislation (Havas, p. 86).

The *Journal of Commerce* took an ardently antiabolitionist editorial stance, advocating instead a "colonization" policy to resettle freed slaves in Africa. In a 28 July 1835 editorial Hale called abolition an "impracticable bundle of absurdities." He wrote, "The spirit of radicalism and insubordination which is inherent in the system of Abolition as now preached would overturn the institutions of society everywhere and bring in an age of anarchy over which angels might weep." He believed that abolitionist agitation for the immediate cessation of slavery had thwarted colonization efforts. Hale wrote, "The chief thing to be regretted among the effects of the Abolition fanaticism, is, that it has prevented so many intelligent and property-owning blacks from emigrating. Liberia wants them, and to supply their place by liberated slaves requires years of training" (*Journal of Commerce*, 14 May 1847). The South had "reason to complain loudly" about the "inflammatory conduct of the furious Abolitionists," Hale editorialized on 7 August 1835, "and if their course should ever come to be pursued by the great mass of northern men, the South would have reason to look about for remedies, perhaps even for those which are violent."

When an antiabolitionist mob murdered publisher Elijah Lovejoy and destroyed his Alton, Illinois, newspaper office in November 1837, Hale wrote: "Men must be gentle in their feelings and conduct, if they would get along without trouble. . . . We do not ask them to compromise principle, though we beg them to distinguish between a steadfast adherence to principle, and a stubborn self-will" (*Journal of Commerce*, 24 Nov. 1837). The Alton riot prompted Hale to criticize abolitionists' complaints about the press. "If anything is said against them, it is a dreadful thing—a deliberate attempt to get up a mob," he wrote. "Yet a course of conduct pursued by themselves, which they know will result in a mob, is perfectly harmless—nay, highly meritorious. Their right to the licentious use of the tongue and the press is sacred; another man's right to the same things is the hight [*sic*] of presumption" (*Journal of Commerce*, 7 Dec. 1837). Hale died of influenza in Fredericksburg, Virginia, and is buried in Greenwood Cemetery in New York City.

David Hale and the *New York Journal of Commerce* often were criticized for their high-toned puritanical editorial policies that were once described as "exclusive morality, patent religion, and extreme decency" (Havas, p. 86). Frederic Hudson, an early historian of the press, described Hale as a "brusque, vigorous man" who was "not afraid of anyone." Hale had "two religions, in both of which he was orthodox. One religion was as a member of the Old Tabernacle Church. . . . Hale's other religion was opposition . . . to the *Courier and Enquirer*" (Hudson, p. 364).

Under Hale's leadership, the *Journal of Commerce* became an aggressive innovator in gathering news that appealed to its mercantile audience. Hale emerged as an influential and outspoken antiabolitionist voice, prophetically warning his New England readers that the South's reaction to "abolition fanaticism" might result in the divisive violence of civil war.

• Joseph P. Thompson, *Memoir of David Hale, Late Editor of the "Journal of Commerce," with Selections from His Miscellaneous Writings* (1850), is an important source. John M. Havas, "Commerce and Calvinism: The *Journal of Commerce*, 1827–1865," *Journalism Quarterly* 38 (1961): 84–86, offers a concise overview of the newspaper's major editorial positions. For a general overview of David Hale's role with the *Journal of Commerce* and his cooperative news gathering efforts, see Frederic Hudson, *Journalism in the United States from 1690 to 1872* (1873); Victor Rosewater, *History of Cooperative News-Gathering in the United States* (1930); and Richard Schwarzlose, *The Nation's Newsbrokers* (1989). See also William H. Hallock, *Life of Gerard Hallock* (1869).

A. J. KAUL

HALE, Edward Everett (3 Apr. 1822–10 June 1909), author, reformer, and Unitarian minister, was born in Boston, Massachusetts, the son of Nathan Hale, a journalist, and Sarah Preston Everett. His father was a nephew of revolutionary war hero Captain Nathan Hale, and his maternal uncle and namesake was the orator and statesman Edward Everett. Hale's formal education began at age two and continued at the Boston Latin School and Harvard College, which he entered at thirteen. He was elected to Phi Beta Kappa, was named class poet, and, though often bored with his studies, graduated second in the class of 1839.

After teaching Latin at the Boston Latin School for two years, Hale gained invaluable journalistic experience working as a legislative reporter on Boston's first daily paper, the *Daily Advertiser*, which his father owned and edited from 1814 to 1854.

Meanwhile, through private study, Hale also prepared for the ministry and was licensed to preach in 1842. He spent the next four years as a substitute preacher until he felt he was ready to be ordained. In 1846 he became a minister to the Congregationalist Church of the Unity in Worcester, Massachusetts.

During those years as a substitute preacher Hale embarked on a career as a writer of stories and, later, novels and essays, which he pursued throughout his long life, and which brought him to national prominence. Unable to sell his first stories, Hale contributed them to the *Boston Miscellany*, which his brother Nathan edited. His first printed story, the somewhat allegorical "A Tale of a Salamander," was published in January 1842 and was the first of some 100 stories Hale published during the next fifty-five years.

But Hale's interests extended beyond mere storytelling, for he felt his writings should have some didactic purpose. Further, since he was raised in the privileged Brahmin world of antebellum Boston and was personally acquainted with eminent figures such as Henry Clay and Daniel Webster as well as Ralph Waldo Emerson, James Russell Lowell, Oliver Wendell Holmes, and Julia Ward Howe, Hale developed an active social conscience. He thus used his journalistic skills to publicly oppose slavery as early as 1845 in his pamphlet *A Tract for the Day: How to Conquer Texas before Texas Conquers Us*, in which he advocated Texas's admission to the Union as a free state. He later expanded the theme in 1854 in his book *Kanzas* [*sic*] *and Nebraska* (incidentally, the earliest book written on Kansas), in which he proposed mass emigration from the northern states into Kansas as a means of ensuring its becoming a free state.

In 1852 Hale, the outspoken abolitionist, married Emily Baldwin Perkins of Hartford, Connecticut, the niece of Harriet Beecher Stowe and Henry Ward Beecher and the granddaughter of Lyman Beecher. They had eight children.

After serving ten years in the ministry in Worcester, in 1856 Hale left to accept the post of pastor of the South Congregational Church in Boston, a position he held until his resignation in 1899. During this long tenure Hale's reputation as a writer grew, and he became what William Dean Howells described as "an artist in his ethics and a moralist in his art."

With the September 1859 *Atlantic Monthly* publication of his first successful and important story, "My Double and How He Undid Me," Hale received national acclaim. This humorous tale of an overworked clergyman who hires a slow-witted lookalike to fill in for him at tedious meetings was widely anthologized. The minister's plan of having the double make only one of four all-purpose clichéd responses when spoken to, such as "I agree, in general, with my friend on the other side of the room," eventually backfires on the cleric. Among Hale's stories, this work represents one of his dominant types of tales, the humorous anecdote; the other type is the serious fable, although as his biographer John R. Adams pointedly observed, "This distinction is only moderately helpful since most of his humorous tales develop a serious purpose." Straddling this line is a class of his sociological fables that take the form of utopian fantasies, such as his novella *Sybaris* (1869) and "The Brick Moon" (1869), a proto-science fiction story that presents the earliest fictive account of an artificial earth satellite.

Perhaps the most serious of Hale's purposeful stories is "The Man without a Country" (1863). Although written during the Civil War to rally support for the Union generally, and specifically to influence the Ohio electorate to vote against the Peace Democratic candidate for governor, Clement L. Vallandigham, "The Man without a Country" was not published in the *Atlantic Monthly* until December 1863, too late to influence the Ohio election (in which Vallandigham was, at any rate, defeated). Yet this story made a far greater impact than its author could have imagined, for it became a minor American classic and is the story for which Hale is best known. "The Man without a Country" is the tale of the traitor Philip Nolan, who upon conviction said in court that he wished, "I may never hear of the United States again!" His punishment was lifelong banishment from the United States in the form of confinement at sea on a series of some twenty naval vessels over the course of fifty-six years.

This work created so strong a sentiment that even twenty-two years later it was hailed in *Century* magazine as "the best sermon on patriotism ever written" and as having done "much, and will do more, to foster the idea of national unity." Furthermore, at Hale's death the story was described in the *Nation* as "probably the most popular short story written in America." Still, there was also a minority view by the turn of the century that the story was "the primer of jingoism."

In the years following the Civil War Hale's national prominence and liberal theological views led him to help establish the Unitarian Church of America. An indication of the inclusiveness of Hale's Christian belief and his distance from the more fundamentalist views of the day is evident in an essay Hale wrote in 1886: "For myself, I can attend the service of the Roman Church with pleasure and profit. If I find myself in a Catholic town in Europe, where there is no Protestant Church, I always go to worship with the Catholics."

Another aspect of Hale's increasingly popular public career is best encapsulated in remarks he made in 1871 in his Alpha Delta Phi address: "*Noblesse oblige*, our privilege compels us; we professional men must serve the world . . . as those who deal with infinite values, and confer benefits as freely and nobly as nature." This theme of promoting good works through social action is embodied in many of his books, especially *Ten Times One Is Ten* (1871), and several of his eighteen novels, as well as in a number of his stories published in the magazine he founded in 1869, *Old and New*. The premise of *Ten Times One Is Ten* is that doing good for others can create a positive chain reaction: if the one helped goes on to help ten others, and then those ten each help yet another ten, the expansion of goodness would be geometrical, resulting in what Hale called a "Happy World!"

Hale's "athletic morality" was not lost on one Harvard junior who first met with Hale in the 1870s. In fact Theodore Roosevelt became one of Hale's enthusiastic supporters and, as president, described Hale as "one of the most revered men in or out of the ministry in all the United States." Hale's association with Roosevelt and his successor, William Howard Taft (whose inauguration Hale attended), spanned a century of the American presidency, for as a young man Hale had been the guest of Dolley Madison and also John Quincy Adams in their homes.

With advanced age many accolades came to Hale. So highly esteemed had he become that for a civic ceremony to welcome the new century, before a crowd gathered on the Boston Common, he was asked to read the Nineteenth Psalm at midnight on 31 December 1900 from the balcony of the Massachusetts State House. After retiring from his chuch post in 1899, Hale was nationally honored in 1903 by being unanimously elected chaplain of the U.S. Senate, a position he held into the last year of his life. In 1904 he was among the first ten writers elected to membership in the newly established Academy of Arts and Letters. At his death in Boston Hale was effusively eulogized. The *Review of Reviews*, for example, described him as "a more truly national personage, in his knowledge and sympathies, than were any of the other New England thinkers and leaders" (July 1909, p. 79).

Although Hale's popularity as a writer has long faded, his work provides, as John R. Adams observed, "a mirror of his period. . . . He is more significant as an educator and as a journalist than as a creative writer." Indeed, while best remembered as the author of "The Man without a Country," his reform-minded advocacy of a variety of issues, from the abolition of slavery and improved race relations to religious tolerance, public education reform (to include half-year schooling and the abolition of grades and examinations), and even government regulation of monopolies and expanded public ownership, is most notable. Edward Everett Hale may well be viewed, to use Theodore Roosevelt's words, as "an American of whose life all good Americans are proud."

• The principal collection of Hale's papers is in the New York State Library in Albany. Other major collections of his papers and letters are at the Huntington Library, San Marino, Calif.; the Massachusetts Historical Society; the Library of Congress; the Houghton Library at Harvard; the American Antiquarian Society; the John Hay Library at Brown University; the Princeton University Library; the University of Rochester; and the Beinecke Library at Yale. In addition to Hale's own autobiography, *Memories of a Hundred Years* (1902; rev. and enl., 1904), two reliable biographies exist: *The Life and Letters of Edward Everett Hale* (1917), by his son Edward Everett Hale, Jr., and Jean Holloway, *Edward Everett Hale: A Biography* (1956). Holloway also compiled the definitive checklist of Hale's writings in three installments in the *Bulletin of Bibliography* 21 (May–Aug. 1954, Sept.–Dec. 1954, and Jan.–Apr. 1955). John R. Adams's critical assessment of Hale's life and career, *Edward Everett Hale* (1977), is highly estimable. Other useful accounts include William Sloane Kennedy, "Edward Everett Hale," *Century*, Jan. 1885, pp. 338–43. Obituaries are in the *New York Times*, 11 June 1909; *Nation*, 17 June 1909; and Massachusetts Historical Society, *Proceedings* 43 (1910): 4–16.

FRANCIS J. BOSHA

HALE, Edwin Moses (2 Feb. 1829–15 Jan. 1899), homeopathic physician, was born in Newport, New Hampshire, the son of Syene Hale, a physician, and Betsy Dow. In 1836 the family moved to Fredonia, Ohio, where Hale attended public school until the age of fifteen, when he removed to Newark, Ohio, to learn printing. He became associate editor of the local newspaper and, briefly, deputy postmaster. He then gave up journalism for the study of law.

A severe attack of pneumonia, successfully treated by Alonzo Blair, directed Hale to the study of homeopathic medicine, a system in which disease is treated by administering a substance that produces symptoms similar to the symptoms of the disease. It was the most popular of the theories of treatment rivaling orthodox medicine in the mid-nineteenth century, with most of its practitioners being graduates of the leading universities and medical colleges.

Blair served as Hale's preceptor, preparing him for entry into the Western College of Homeopathic Medicine at Cleveland in 1850. Scant evidence suggests, however, that young Hale did not obtain a diploma.

Hale began practice in Jonesville, Michigan, in 1852. His first publication, in 1858, was a pamphlet, *Homeopathy and Its Principles Explained and Defended.* He also began to contribute articles on materia medica to the *North American Homeopathic Journal;* one of these introduced *Caulophyllum,* an indigenous medicinal plant, to homeopaths. Hale was responsible for bringing many other American medicinal plants to the attention of homeopaths. In 1855 he married Abba Ann George; they had two children.

Early in his career he became concerned about abortion and published *The Homeopathic Treatment of Abortion* in 1860, expanding it into *A Systematic Treatise on Abortion* in 1866. Hale asserted, "I hold in no instance should the health of the mother be sacrificed to save that of an impregnated ovum" (1866, p. 319). This was interpreted by some as a view favoring abortion for reasons other than saving the life of the mother. This brought almost immediate censure against Hale. The subject of criminal abortion was very controversial at this time, and some state homeopathic medical societies passed resolutions condemning it. At least one society branded Hale an abortionist. Hale then published a disavowal of induced abortion (except to save the life of the mother), and the remaining copies of his book had a revision of the equivocal statement pasted over it. Hale also authored papers on the jurisprudence of criminal abortion in 1867 and 1869.

By 1860 Hale was an associate editor of the *North American Journal of Homeopathy* and the *Medical Investigator,* writing book reviews and papers on materia medica and diseases of women. He gained the first serious attention of the profession in 1862 with *A Monograph on Gelsemium,* a compilation of existing knowledge on that plant, coupled with his own experiments with the drug on animals. In May 1862 Hale delivered expert testimony in a case of manslaughter brought against Edwin Lodge, a noted editor, pharmacist, and homeopathic physician who had been accused by orthodox physicians of poisoning a woman during a "drug proving," or test, with tincture of Gelsemium. Hale's testimony aided in winning acquittal and upholding the legality of drug provings.

In 1864 Hale published a work on domestic practice, *The Soldier's and Traveller's Manual,* and read a paper on Uterine Therapeutics before the Illinois State Homeopathic Medical Society. He also continued edi-

torial work for the *North America Journal,* having left the *Medical Investigator* in 1863.

The most important of Hale's works, *The New Remedies,* appeared in 1864. It was intended to be a compilation of all that was known about various American medicinal plants. Hale stated that he would be satisfied if the profession were to find the work "eminently suggestive." However, many homeopathic physicians, such as Adolph Lippe, a leading professor of homeopathic materia medica, warned that Hale's work tended toward generalization, rather than the strict individualization of the case and patient required of the homeopathic method. The book combined information from orthodox botanic sources and those of the eclectic physicians, who drew from all methods of treatment, along with crude homeopathic drug provings and empirical observations, with the result that it appealed to the more eclectic sector of the homeopathic school. It went through five editions, introducing some drugs that came to be used in all schools of medicine.

In 1864 Hale moved to Chicago and formed a partnership with Alvan E. Small. He began teaching adjuvent materia medica at Hahnemann Medical College the same year. In June 1865 he was elected to membership in the American Institute of Homeopathy; he became a member of its board of materia medica the following year. Hale remained at Hahnemann, in 1870 assuming the chair of medical botany and therapeutics, in 1871 that of diseases of the heart, and in 1872 therapeutics of new remedies. In 1869 he formed a partnership with his brother, P. H. Hale, which ended at the time of the great Chicago fire of 1871.

In 1876 Hale resigned from Hahnemann Medical College. He had been attacked by a fellow professor, Gaylord Beebe, and had responded with a pamphlet, *An Open Letter to the Medical Profession,* in which he defended his 1860 work on abortion.

Hale then accepted the chair of materia medica at Chicago Homeopathic Medical College, a position he held from 1877 until his retirement from active practice in 1891. He continued to write articles, publishing his last major work, *A Practice of Medicine,* in 1894. After his move to Orange Grove, Florida, in 1895, his last monograph, *Saw Palmetto,* appeared. It was a concise little work on the indigenous palms of Florida and their therapeutic uses, coupled with all that was known of chemistry, botany, pharmacology, and drug tests on the healthy.

Hale died in Chicago. Shortly before his death he had completed the manuscript of *Presenility and the Diseases of Old Age,* but it was never published.

Until late in life Hale defended his theory of a law of dose. Samuel Hahnemann, founder of the homeopathic school, had noted in 1796 the opposing "primary" and "secondary" effects of drugs when tested on the healthy. He had not directed this phenomenon to be used to determine the dose. Hale loosely interpreted this observation to mean that small doses should be administered for similar primary symptoms in the sick and larger "stimulating" doses given when the secondary symptoms were manifested in patients. Hale's theory was discredited by the most able of materia medica teachers and branded a crude folly. Hale was characterized shortly after his death as "in fact an Eclectic with homeopathic proclivities." This deviation from proven principles, coupled with his practice of polypharmacy, the endorsement and development of patent medicines, and his eclectic teaching, has led Hale's influence to diminish greatly, though he is acknowledged as having introduced, however imperfectly, important medicines into daily practice.

• Hale's *Lectures on the Diseases of the Heart* (1871, 2d ed., 1877) was reprinted in 1983. He coauthored, with Charles A. Williams, *The Compendium of Health* (1884), a domestic and veterinary treatise, part of which was reprinted as *The Cat and Its Diseases* the same year. The majority of Hale's works are listed in Thomas Lindsley Bradford, *Homeopathic Bibliography of the United States, 1825–1891* (1892). The remaining titles are found in Francesco Cordasco, *Homeopathy in the United States* (1991). Hale's biography appears in Egbert Cleave, *Biographical Cyclopedia of Homeopathic Physicians and Surgeons* (1873). Obituaries are in the *Medical Advance* 36 (1899): 488; *Hahnemannian Monthly* 34 (1899); *Eclectic Medical Journal*, May 1899; *American Institute of Homeopathy Transactions* 55 (1899): 927–28; the *Homeopathic News* 28 (1899): 93; and the *Chicago Tribune*, 16 Jan. 1899. The scrapbooks of Thomas L. Bradford in the archives of Hahnemann University, Philadelphia, provide more information, as does a short sketch of Hale's life in William Harvey King, *History of Homeopathy and Its Institutions in America* (1905).

CHRISTOPHER D. ELLITHORP

HALE, Ellen Day (11 Feb. 1855–11 Feb. 1940), oil and mural painter and etcher, was born in Worcester, Massachusetts, the daughter of Edward Everett Hale, an author, orator, and Unitarian clergyman, and Emily Baldwin Perkins. Hale was the eldest child and only daughter in her family of seven brothers, of whom only five lived to adulthood. She assumed the surrogate mother duties of an eldest daughter, extending her caretaking to serving as her father's hostess in Washington, D.C., from 1904, when he was appointed chaplain to the U.S. Senate, to his death in 1909. From an early age she determinedly pursued a career in art, working and traveling as much as her commitment to family responsibilities would allow. Hale's mother encouraged Ellen and her brothers, who included the artist Philip Leslie Hale, to draw while they were growing up. Philip acquired much of his early art training from Ellen, who was ten years older than he. Her father taught her photography, which she practiced most of her life, and her aunt, the artist and writer Susan Hale, gave Ellen art lessons.

From her socially and intellectually prominent Boston family came several strong female role models, three of whom set a precedent for Hale as single, professional women. In addition to writing many books, her aunt Susan was a world traveler who taught art and conducted classes for women in literature during the 1870s. Another aunt was the author Lucretia Peabody Hale, popularly known for her Peterkin stories for children. Ellen Day Hale's great-aunts were Harriet Beecher Stowe, the author of *Uncle Tom's Cabin*, and Catherine Beecher, an author and advocate of women's scientific education to professionalize homemaking. The latter's *Treatise on Domestic Economy for the Use of Young Ladies at Home and at School* instilled in many women a sense of authority, dignity, and self-esteem through a feeling of pride in their domestic work.

Ellen Day Hale was a member of the first generation of American women who were determined to acquire professional art training equivalent to that available to men. In Boston she studied art in 1873 with William Rimmer, who emphasized tight, academic drawing. The next year Hale entered the art school for women run by the painters William Morris Hunt and Helen Knowlton, also Hunt's student. From Hunt and Knowlton, Hale learned how to use her brush expressively in the style of the French painter Thomas Couture and how to paint from nature in the more radical style of Jean-François Millet, with whom Hunt had studied in Barbizon, France. Hunt's method, which used charcoal to portray nature spontaneously, producing broad areas of light and shade, became the foundation for Hale's work. While still attending Knowlton's Boston class once a week, Hale opened her own studio in 1877. She painted portraits on commission, took private students, and taught at Marlborough School. On trips to Philadelphia to visit her cousin, the artist Margaret Lesley (later, Margaret Lesley Bush-Brown), in 1878 and 1879, she attended the Ladies' Life Class at the Pennsylvania Academy of the Fine Arts.

Anxious to begin her European training, Hale accompanied Knowlton to Europe in 1881. She took Emmanuel Frémiet's drawing class at the Jardin des Plantes, studied briefly in the class for women at the Académie Colarossi with Louis-Joseph-Raphael Collin and Gustave-Claude-Étienne Courtois, and then entered the women's class taught by Émile-Auguste Carolus-Duran and Jean-Jacques Henner. In 1882 Hale toured Spain with her father and her aunt Susan. She visited the painter Anna Lea Merritt in London and exhibited at the Royal Academy. In the fall she began several months' study at the Académie Julian and exhibited a portrait in the 1883 Paris Salon before returning to Boston.

On a visit to Philadelphia in 1883 Hale met Gabrielle Clements, a Philadelphia painter who became her closest friend and lifelong companion. Hale traveled with Clements and Clements's mother in France in 1885. The two artists studied at Julian's with William Adolphe Bouguereau and Tony Robert-Fleury. Clements taught Hale to etch while they were on a sketching tour. By the late 1880s the two women, influenced by French etching in color, were pioneering color etching in America. While still abroad, Hale exhibited her self-portrait in the 1885 Paris Salon.

Identifying herself as an "American Impressionist" after her trip to France in 1885, Hale painted landscapes and portraiture with broad brush strokes to emphasize tonal masses and heighten the contrasts of light and shade. While she did not use line work in her paintings, her early etchings demonstrate her ability to create a sparkling sense of light with the delicate line of an etching needle. By the early 1890s her prints had become more bold and broad, like her paintings, as she experimented with painterly printmaking techniques such as soft-ground etching, aquatint, and adding color *à la poupée* (dabbing colored ink onto the plate with a small rag bag for each run through the press). The exceptions to these progressive prints were her etchings of California and its missions, which she sold to tourists when she made lengthy visits to the state twice between 1891 and 1893.

Hale had begun to build her extensive exhibition record in the 1870s as she carried out her ambitious plan to establish herself as a professional artist. In 1876 she entered a painting of a boy reading in the U.S. Centennial Exposition and sent a charcoal sketch to the exhibition of the American Society of Painters in Watercolors in New York. She joined the Boston Art Club, which held an exhibition of "Paintings in Oil and Water Colors by Miss Susan Hale, Miss H. M. Knowlton, and Miss E. D. Hale" in 1878. The next year a landscape was exhibited at the Boston Museum of Fine Arts in a show of contemporary painting that included the French Barbizon artists. The Boston Museum also included Hale in its 1880 and 1883 exhibitions of contemporary American artists. She was represented in an 1881 auction by Boston's Lewis J. Bird & Company of "the first sale ever in the United States exclusively of lady artists." Hale exhibited her French etchings in the first museum exhibition of women's work, "Women Etchers of America," which was held at the Boston Museum of Fine Arts in 1887. Her exhibition venues included other Boston art organizations, the Pennsylvania Academy of the Fine Arts, the Art Institute of Chicago, the New York Etching Club, the Salmagundi Club, and the Massachusetts Charitable Mechanic Association, as well as several of the large world expositions.

Hale enjoyed painting from nature along the coasts of New England and on her frequent travels. Her family had spent summers on the coast at their home in Matunuck, Rhode Island, where in the 1870s she began to paint. In 1877 she stayed with Knowlton in her summer home at Magnolia, Massachusetts, to join the artists' colony around Hunt. By the summer of 1887 she worked at Rockport, on Cape Ann near Gloucester, eventually acquiring her own home and studio where she and Clements spent summers. Hale's brother Philip described how they held forth at their dinner table, Clements at one end with a "loud, confident voice" and Hale "silent" at the other.

Each year the two artists traveled abroad, usually in Europe, in search of subject matter. Hale traveled to Algiers in 1895, and in 1929 she and Clements traveled to Palestine, Egypt, and Syria to gather ideas for church murals. During World War I they spent winters in Charleston, South Carolina, where they taught and established an etching club.

During the 1920s and 1930s Hale returned to the experiments with soft-ground etching and aquatints *à la poupée* that she had begun in the late 1880s. She and Clements taught color etching to other Cape Ann artists. Notes that Clements made of their process are in the National Museum of American History, Smithsonian Institution.

In the twentieth century the Smithsonian exhibited her color etchings. Hale also exhibited at the Corcoran Gallery in Washington, D.C., the J. B. Speed Art Museum in Louisville, Kentucky, and the Worcester Art Museum. Her extremely active exhibition record, evidence of her lifelong drive for professional recognition, includes many shows with galleries and artist associations in the Rockport-Gloucester area, Washington, D.C., Baltimore, Chicago, and Boston.

Hale's intellectual pursuits included fluency in six languages. She wrote art reviews from Europe during the 1880s for the *Boston Traveler*. Her expertise in art history led her to produce a small and seldom-read book, *History of Art: A Study of the Lives of Leonardo, Michelangelo, Raphael, Titan, and Albert Dürer*, which was published in Boston and Chicago in 1888.

Disabled by arthritis and a broken hip when she was seventy years old, Hale persevered with her work until she was forced into a nursing home in Brookline, Massachusetts, where she died. She had worked to establish a place for herself in the professional art world, which thousands of women had entered, yet few had succeeded in gaining lasting acknowledgment. Although she was far more active than most women artists, Hale remained at the margin of national recognition. Hale expressed her self-consciousness about violating traditional mores for women by being ambitious in a letter to Margaret Lesley in the mid-1880s: "Hear me boasting and baperring and being worldly and ambitious! No matter my Margaret. I don't mind giving myself away to you, et ce n'est pas pour la première fois either." With lifelong determination she built an autonomous role for herself outside the traditional family structure, yet her proper New England upbringing kept her modest and limited her associations to her own class and to circles considered appropriate for women.

• The Archives of American Art, Smithsonian Institution, contain Hale's papers. Her brother Philip Leslie Hale's papers in the archives are also useful. The Hale Family Papers in the Sophia Smith Collection, Smith College, Northampton, Mass., contain Hale's diaries for 1901 and 1904. Her letters to Margaret Lesley (Bush-Brown), 1877–1886, are in the Bush-Brown papers at Smith. See also Caroline Penniman Atkinson, ed., *Letters of Susan Hale* (1919), and Nancy Hale, *A New England Girlhood* (1936) and *The Life in the Studio* (1969). The Boston Museum of Fine Arts holds her 1885 self-portrait. The National Museum of Women in the Arts, the National Museum of American History (Smithsonian Institution), the Pennsylvania Academy of the Fine Arts, and the Philadelphia Museum of Art own works by Hale. Exhibition catalogs issued during her lifetime include the Boston Art Club, *Paintings in Oil and Watercolors by Miss Susan Hale, Miss H. M. Knowlton, and Miss Ellen Day Hale* (1878); Goodspeed's *Exhibition and Sale of Etchings and Soft-ground*

Aquatints in Color of French, Italian and American Subjects by Ellen Day Hale and Gabrielle DeV. Clements (1924); and J. B. Speed Memorial Museum, *Exhibition of Etchings in Color by Ellen Day Hale, Gabrielle DeVeaux Clements, Lesley Jackson, Margaret Yeaton Hoyt, Theresa F. Bernstein, and William Meyerowitz* (1935). Biographical information appears in Alanna Chesebro, *Ellen Day Hale, 1855–1940* (1981), and the National Museum of Women in the Arts, *American Women Artists* (1987). Phyllis Peet, "The Emergence of American Women Printmakers in the Late Nineteenth Century" (Ph.D. diss., UCLA, 1987) and *American Women of the Etching Revival* (1988), are the most thorough sources.

PHYLLIS PEET

HALE, Eugene (9 June 1836–27 Oct. 1918), U.S. senator, was born in Turner, Maine, the son of James Sullivan Hale and Betsy Staples, farmers. Hale was educated in local schools and attended Hebron Academy. After studying law in the office of Howard & Stout in Portland, Maine, he gained admission to the bar in January 1857. Settling in Ellsworth, Maine, he practiced law and served as Hancock County attorney. He won election to the Maine House of Representatives as a Republican in 1867 and 1868. In 1871 he married Mary Douglass Chandler, daughter of Senator Zachariah Chandler. They had three sons.

Hale ran successfully for the U.S. House of Representatives in 1868 and was reelected four times. He declined President Ulysses S. Grant's offer to become postmaster general in 1874 and also turned down President Rutherford B. Hayes's request that he serve as secretary of the navy. Hale lost his House seat in 1878, when the Greenback party protest was strong in Maine. A year later he was elected to the Maine House once again. In 1881 the state legislature elected him to the U.S. Senate, where he served for the next thirty years.

Hale emerged as one of the important figures in the Republican leadership associated with Nelson Aldrich of Rhode Island and his senior GOP colleagues. In his early senatorial years, Hale defended the practice of assessing candidates for campaign contributions. He chaired the Appropriations Committee and the Naval Affairs Committee, and in the latter post he promoted the growth of the U.S. Navy during the 1880s and 1890s. While Hale was a strong protectionist, in 1890 he endorsed the idea of his fellow Maine politician, James G. Blaine, that trade reciprocity would open wide markets for American products. He introduced a key amendment to that effect for the McKinley Tariff of 1890. By the end of the 1890s, however, Hale had cooled on reciprocal tariffs. Of a possible trade agreement with Canada in 1898, he said, "Better no treaty" than one that would hurt Maine's timber interests.

Hale was skeptical about imperialism and opposed both the Spanish-American War and the Treaty of Paris in 1898. The stance cost him some support among his Maine constituents, but he won a fourth term in 1899 nonetheless. As Hale's power in the Senate grew, he became more conservative in his opposition to the expansion of national power that Theodore Roosevelt represented. Hale urged Charles W. Fair-

banks to accept the Republican vice presidential nomination in 1908 and opposed Roosevelt's intentions to "dictate his successor."

Hale's main confrontation with Roosevelt came over the nation's naval policy. By the early 1900s Chairman Hale had become convinced that the military had received too much in the way of appropriations. He questioned whether the navy, for example, needed to spend as much as Roosevelt and naval reformers wished to on modern battleships. In the process, Hale became identified with the existing naval establishment that resisted Roosevelt's desire to change the structure of the navy and to give more attention to readiness for potential war with Japan or European powers. Hale opposed Roosevelt's intention to send the "Great White Fleet" around the world in 1907–1909, and the senator managed hearings on the issue of battleships and their defects in 1908 in a way that pleased the navy brass and angered Roosevelt. The president numbered Hale among those who were "malevolent enemies of the navy." During the spring of 1908 Hale led the senatorial struggle against Roosevelt's request to build four modern battleships. The chairman reduced the figure to two battleships and did not provide funding for them. Hale then resisted the attempt of Senator Albert J. Beveridge of Indiana to add language restoring funding for four battleships. In the end, the Senate agreed to build two battleships a year and appropriated the money for their construction. The outcome was viewed as a rebuke to Hale and the senatorial leadership.

The political climate in Maine began to turn against Hale by 1910, and he announced his retirement that spring. His last battle was against President William Howard Taft's campaign for tariff reciprocity with Canada. He lived in Washington until his death there. His son Frederick Hale was elected to his Senate seat in 1916.

A cold and aloof man of small stature, Hale was "one of the most scrupulously correct dressers in the Senate" ("A Statesman from Maine," p. 529). He did not speak often on the Senate floor but could be sarcastic and cutting in debate. Despite his closeness to Aldrich and his conservative views, Hale did not command the respect accorded to other leaders of his time, such as William Boyd Allison and John Coit Spooner.

Hale's career illustrates the complexity of Republican conservatism in the era of Theodore Roosevelt. He was conventional in his advocacy of the protective tariff and opposition to increased government regulation. His stance against imperialism, campaign against a bigger navy, and suspicion of Roosevelt's ambitious foreign policy goals anticipated some aspects of later isolationist thinking.

• A small collection of Hale's papers is at the Maine Historical Society. Information about his political career is in the Nelson Aldrich, Theodore Roosevelt, and William Howard Taft papers, Library of Congress; the Charles W. Fairbanks Papers, Indiana University; and the George H. Moses Papers, New Hampshire Historical Society. Hale's infrequent speeches are in the *Congressional Record* for his House (1869–1879) and Senate (1882–1911) service. Martin Meadows, "Eugene Hale and the Navy," *American Neptune* 22 (July 1962): 187–93, examines a key area of Hale's Senate influence. "A Statesman from Maine," *Munsey's Magazine* 30 (Jan. 1904): 528–29; and "Men We Are Watching: Eugene Hale of Maine," *Independent* 66 (4 Feb. 1909): 258–59, offer contemporary assessments. A biographical essay is in Louis C. Hatch, ed., *Maine: A History, Biographical* (1919). Ari Hoogenboom, *Outlawing the Spoils: A History of the Civil Service Reform Movement* (1961), discusses Hale and campaign reform. Richard Cleveland Baker, *The Tariff under Roosevelt and Taft* (1941), deals with Hale and trade policy. See Elting E. Morison et al., eds., *The Letters of Theodore Roosevelt*, vol. 6 (1952), for Roosevelt's negative opinion of Hale. An obituary is in the *New York Times*, 28 Oct. 1918.

LEWIS L. GOULD

HALE, George Ellery (29 June 1868–21 Feb. 1938), astrophysicist, was born in Chicago, Illinois, the son of William Ellery Hale, a paper salesman, and Mary Scranton Browne. As a young boy, Hale was fascinated by tools and optics. By the time he was fourteen, he had built a workshop/laboratory that included a steam-driven lathe, a microscope with a camera for photographing slide specimens, and a telescope; the steam engine and telescope he made by himself. Having developed a great interest in astronomy while still in high school, he mounted a refracting telescope on the roof of his house to observe and take photographs of solar phenomena such as partial eclipses and sunspots.

In 1886 Hale matriculated at the Massachusetts Institute of Technology (MIT), where he studied physics, chemistry, and mathematics; he received his B.A. in 1890. Also in 1890 he married Evelina Conklin; they had two children. While at MIT, he served as a volunteer assistant at the Harvard College Observatory. Aided financially by his father, who had become wealthy manufacturing and installing hydraulic elevators, during summer breaks he designed and built a spectroscopic laboratory on a vacant lot next to his house in Chicago in order to photograph the sun. He particularly wanted to take pictures of prominences, the clouds of gas that rise high above the sun's surface, in full daylight in order to record and study them more completely. With this purpose in mind, in 1889 he designed and built the world's first spectroheliograph, an instrument that photographs the sun by using monochromatic light, or the light of a single wavelength or color. Although the prototype performed poorly, Hale was able to remedy the problems and attached the improved version to a twelve-inch telescope. In 1891 he mounted the new equipment in a building and dome attached to the spectroscopic laboratory, which became known as the Kenwood Observatory, and took the first photographs ever taken of prominences in full daylight. By focusing the spectroheliograph on the H and K Fraunhofer lines (narrow wavelengths in the solar spectrum that are very bright), in 1892 he discovered "flocculi," gaseous clouds that develop and change rapidly over the sun's surface. He postulated that the occurrence of flocculi near sunspots was some-

how related to the occurrence of magnetic storms on Earth, an observation that would lead to a monumental discovery several years later.

Between 1889 and 1891 Hale published nine articles on the results of his work with the spectroheliograph. Consequently, when he went to Europe in 1892 to meet the eminent astronomers of the day, his reputation preceded him. Hale intended to publish a new journal devoted to bringing physicists and astronomers together, and with the endorsement of those whom he met he started and coedited *Astronomy and Astrophysics* that same year. Renamed the *Astrophysical Journal* in 1895, it quickly became an important forum for the publication of astrophysical breakthroughs, especially Hale's.

In 1892 Hale joined the faculty at the University of Chicago as associate professor of astrophysics. He soon learned of two forty-inch disks of optical glass that were available at cost and seized upon the idea of procuring them for the university and using them to build a telescope. Accordingly, he proselytized a number of wealthy businessmen before convincing Charles T. Yerkes, the Chicago streetcar magnate, to donate the money to buy the disks, turn them into lenses, mount them in a telescope, and construct an observatory. Hale himself donated the dome, telescope, and equipment from Kenwood and raised enough money from other sources to pay for operating expenses and maintenance. In 1897 the Yerkes Observatory was completed in Williams Bay, Wisconsin. Hale served as director of the observatory until 1904 and made many important observations of sunspots, prominences, and the chromosphere (a gaseous envelope surrounding the sun) from there.

However, Hale dreamed of studying the spectra of the brighter stars on the same scale as he studied the solar one, and to accomplish this task he needed an even bigger telescope. In 1902 Hale learned that the Carnegie Institution of Washington, D.C., was interested in supporting a long-term effort devoted to pure research. As secretary of its Advisory Committee on Astronomy, in 1904 he managed to convince the institution's executive committee to fund the establishment of an observatory on Mount Wilson near Pasadena, California, equipped with a sixty-inch telescope, the largest in the world, and with himself as director. Mount Wilson Observatory began operating that same year with a 24-inch telescope from Yerkes; not until 1908 did the sixty-inch telescope become fully operational. The new observatory included a tower, designed by Hale, for housing the new instrument that greatly reduced the blurring effect of heat waves at ground level. As a result, he was able to make two remarkable discoveries about sunspots.

The first discovery, made in 1905, was that sunspots are not hotter than the surrounding surface but cooler. This discovery, augmented by experiments in a physical laboratory that correlated the spectral line strength of a number of elements with the temperature of those elements, enabled Hale and his associates to calculate the temperatures of the various lines on the sunspot spectra. In time, the results of this line of investigation enabled other astrophysicists to quantify the relationship linking temperature, brightness, and distance, thereby using spectroscopy to determine the distances between Earth and the larger stars.

The second discovery was that the sun is a gigantic whirling magnet. In 1907 Hale began observing a Fraunhofer line with a longer wavelength, and almost immediately he detected that sunspots lay at the centers of attraction for swirling hydrogen flocculi known as solar vortices. He also noticed that the arrangement of these flocculi around the sunspots bore a striking resemblance to the arrangement of iron filings around a magnet, an observation that reinforced the suspicion he had had in 1891 that a relationship existed between flocculi and terrestrial magnetic storms. Consequently, he spent the rest of his life amassing data that supported his belief in a general solar magnetic field. His investigations were aided greatly by the construction of a taller tower in 1910, the installation of a 100-inch telescope in 1917, the frequent upgrading of spectro-heliographs, and the help of many associates whose experiments in the physical laboratory provided data to which Hale could compare his observations. In 1913 he discovered that sunspot polarity reverses itself in the two solar hemispheres at the beginning of each 11½-year sunspot cycle. When this discovery was confirmed in 1922, Hale postulated the law of sunspot polarity, a major step toward proving the existence of a general solar magnetic field.

In addition to these discoveries, Hale made other contributions to the development of science. Not long after he became director of Mount Wilson, he was asked to assist with the development of Throop Polytechnic Institute, a small technical school founded in Pasadena in 1891. Hale became a trustee in 1906 and helped pilot the school on a course that emphasized pure and applied research in the sciences without overlooking the importance of instruction in the humanities. In 1920, as a member of the executive council, he persuaded Robert A. Millikan, the eminent physicist, to join the faculty and chair the executive council, which was tantamount to acting as school president. Under Millikan's leadership, Throop, known today as the California Institute of Technology (Cal Tech), came to be recognized as one of the foremost centers for scientific research in the United States. During this same time, Hale had become friendly with Henry E. Huntington, a wealthy collector of rare books, manuscripts, and paintings. When Huntington asked Hale for advice on how he should dispose of his collections, Hale outlined a plan that in time led to the creation of the Henry E. Huntington Library and Art Gallery in San Marino, California, one of the most important facilities for literary and historical research in the country.

A member of the National Academy of Sciences since 1902, Hale felt strongly that the academy should contribute its expertise to the U.S. military effort during World War I. After raising this proposal before the academy in 1916, he was made chairman of the organizing committee of what came to be known as the National Research Council. As first chairman of the council, he secured a grant from the Carnegie Foundation to build a headquarters and fund the council's administration. The organization proved to be so valuable that President Woodrow Wilson issued an executive order continuing the council during peacetime so that it might serve as a forum for promoting scientific research. Hale also played an instrumental role in the creation in 1905 of the International Union for Cooperation in Solar Research and in 1919 of what became known as the International Council of Scientific Unions.

Hale played a major role in the transformation of research in the physical sciences that took place in the United States in the early twentieth century. Prior to World War I scientists were isolated from the larger American community and conducted their research in accordance with the dictates of local benefactors and their own personal fortunes and whims. Moreover, the results of their efforts were poorly understood outside the scientific community and rarely applied by industry or government. The onset of the war convinced many American scientists that a greater degree of government involvement in guiding and funding research projects such as prevailed in Europe and especially in Germany was essential to the future well-being of the United States. To this end Hale worked assiduously and vociferously to achieve a coalition among scientists, federal officials, and philanthropic organizations that would establish goals for and fund major research projects in the physical sciences. This campaign aroused a good deal of ill feeling from scientists and was not immediately successful, although in time Hale's vision prevailed.

All this activity eventually took its toll on Hale's health. Due largely to the strain of overwork, he suffered nervous breakdowns in 1910, 1913, and 1921. When he failed to recover fully from the last breakdown, he resigned as director of the Mount Wilson Observatory and began work on the small Hale Solar Laboratory in Pasadena. But while building this new observatory, Hale conceived of a plan to construct a 200-inch telescope, and in 1928, despite his deteriorating health, he began lobbying the General Education Board, the Carnegie Institution, the National Academy of Sciences, the Rockefeller and Carnegie foundations, and Cal Tech for the money to build such an instrument. Although Hale did not live to see it, this telescope was installed at the Hale Observatory in 1948 and named the Hale Telescope in his honor. He died in Pasadena.

During his lifetime, Hale received many awards and honors for his discoveries and contributions to science. A partial list includes the Janssen Medal of the Paris Academy of Sciences (1894 and 1917), the Rumford Medal of the American Academy of Arts and Sciences (1902), the Draper Medal of the National Academy of Sciences (1904), the Gold Medal of the Royal Astronomical Society (1904), the Silva Medal of the Sociedad Astronómica de México (1908), the

Bruce Medal of the Astronomical Society of the Pacific (1916), the Galileo Medal of the University of Florence, Italy (1920), the Actonian Prize of the Royal Institution of Great Britain (1921), the Elliott Cresson Medal (1926) and the Franklin Medal (1927) of the Franklin Institute, the City of Pasadena's Arthur Noble Medal for Civic Service (1927), the Gold Medal of the Holland Society of New York (1931), and the Sir Godfrey Copley Medal of the Royal Society (1932). In 1920 he was made a commander of the Order of Leopold II of Belgium and a commander of the Order of the Crown of Italy. He received a dozen honorary doctorates and was awarded membership in the National Academy of Sciences, the Franklin Institute, the academies of sciences of Amsterdam, Athens, Belgium, France, Holland, Italy, Norway, Russia, Sweden, and Vienna, and the royal societies of London, Edinburgh, Dublin, and Uppsala. From 1948 to 1980 the observatories at Pasadena and Mount Wilson were operated jointly by the Carnegie Institution and Cal Tech as the Hale Observatories.

Hale was one of the giants of modern science. The citation accompanying the Royal Society's Copley Medal described his discovery of sunspot magnetism as "the most vital thing accomplished in solar astronomy in 300 years." By marrying the observational skills of the astronomer to the experimental skills of the physicist, Hale, more than any other single individual, fathered the discipline of astrophysics. His infectious energy and boundless enthusiasm for solar research enabled him to raise enough money to construct in the United States four telescopes, each of them the largest in the world at the time of its completion, and three fine observatories in which to house them. He disseminated the findings that these instruments allowed him to make to a curious world in six books and more than 550 scholarly articles in fifty-five publications in the United States and Europe. The research facilities that he helped to establish at Yerkes, Mount Wilson, Pasadena, Cal Tech, and the Huntington Library continue to this day to further the work of research in the sciences and humanities.

• Hale's papers are located in the George Ellery Hale Papers at Cal Tech as well as the George Ellery Hale Collection and the Mount Wilson Observatory Archives at the Huntington Library. Biographies are Walter S. Adams, "George Ellery Hale," National Academy of Sciences, *Biographical Memoirs* 21 (1941): 181–241; Helen Wright, *Explorer of the Universe: A Biography of George Ellery Hale* (1966); and Donald E. Osterbrock, *Pauper and Prince: Ritchey, Hale & Big American Telescopes* (1993). Adams includes a complete bibliography of Hale's publications, and Wright includes a list of other biographical works concerning Hale. Wright et al., eds., *The Legacy of George Ellery Hale* (1972), discusses the importance of Hale's work on the evolution of astronomy and scientific institutions in the United States. It also contains reprints of several of Hale's most important papers, such as "A Plea for the Imaginative Element in Technical Education," *Technology Review* 9, no. 4 (Oct. 1907): 467–81; "Solar Vortices and Magnetic Fields," *Proceedings of the Royal Institution of Great Britain* 19 (1909): 615–30; "National Academies and the Progress of Research" (paper presented at the Nov. 1913 meeting of the National Academy of Sciences); and "The Possibilities of Large Telescopes," *Harper's*, Apr. 1928, pp. 639–46. Daniel J. Kevles, *The Physicists* (1978), discusses Hale's role in the transformation of American science. An obituary is in the *New York Times*, 22 Feb. 1938.

CHARLES W. CAREY, JR.

HALE, Horatio Emmons (3 May 1817–28 Dec. 1896), ethnologist, was born in Newport, New Hampshire, the son of David Hale, a lawyer, and Sarah Josepha Buell, a writer and journalist. After his father's death when Hale was five years old, he and his four siblings were raised in a literary household headed by his mother, who had active intellectual interests. As a student at Harvard, inspired by the then romantic appeal of the vanishing Indians of the Northeast, Hale took the opportunity presented by a chance encampment of Indians on the campus to collect a small vocabulary; from his analysis of it, Hale determined that the group was a branch of the Algonkian-speaking Micmac. The resulting publication he set in type and printed privately in 1834 for a few of his friends. It was a period when the study of languages and the comparisons of their vocabularies and grammars promised to reveal the particular histories of linguistic communities as well as the historical relations between the culturally and racially distinct constituents of the human species. In 1836 Congress authorized its first overseas exploring expedition, to be led by Captain Charles Wilkes, both to collect scientific and navigational information and to explore commercial possibilities in the South Pacific. Hale, after his graduation in 1837, joined the scientific corps as ethnologist and philologist. The Wilkes Expedition did not return to its home base until 1842, after one of its two vessels was destroyed while visiting the Northwest Coast, but Hale left the expedition to pursue a several-month-long intensive study of the varied languages of the Oregon Territory and then to return overland to Philadelphia. The result of his intensive efforts was the 700-page *Ethnography and Philology* (1846), the first of the expedition's several scientific memoirs to be published. Restricted to a small edition because of budgetary reductions and therefore little known and generally neglected, the memoir was the first extensive publication of its kind in the United States. Reviewed very favorably, it was described by a contemporary English ethnologist, R. G. Latham, as "the greatest mass of philological data ever accumulated by a single inquirer" (*Natural History of the Variety of Man* [1850]). Hale's effective comparison of carefully collected vocabularies and grammars, which he used as the basis for determining the migrational history of the widespread Polynesian groups, was a forerunner of more highly professionalized work in comparative linguistics that would be conducted a generation later.

Despite the intensity of his apprenticeship as a member of the Wilkes Expedition and the professional success of his memoir, Hale, still a young man, seems almost purposefully to have given up his scientific interests. After writing his memoir, which he left for his mother to see through to publication, he spent some time in Europe. Upon his return he studied law, married Margaret Pugh in Jersey City, New Jersey, in 1854, and moved to Chicago, where he was admitted to the Illinois bar in 1855. A year later he moved to a large tract of land belonging to his wife's family near Clinton, Ontario, Canada, which he developed along with other business activities. He participated actively and successfully in Clinton's social and commercial development. Although Hale thought that the separation from his Philadelphia library and his disengagement from ethnology would be only temporary, he remained in Clinton, where he was an active citizen until his death there.

The ethnographic interests of Hale's youth, which had been pushed to the background by the more immediate concerns of family and business, finally reemerged in 1869 through the beginnings of a correspondence with Lewis Henry Morgan, then the most distinguished of a developing community of American ethnologists. As in his earliest fieldwork, Hale took advantage of the nearby Indian settlements at the Six Nations Reserve, whose residents, though primarily Iroquoian, still kept alive remnants of both the Algonkian and, through a single surviving Tupelo speaker, Siouan languages. Stimulated by Morgan's recent attempts to work out the migrational history of the American Indians through a comparison of basic elements in kinship systems, Hale returned again to language as the most valid criterion for the establishment of historical ethnic relationships. From his first visit to the Six Nations Reserve in 1870 to his death in 1896, he was again the ethnologist, Morgan's successor as a student of Iroquois language, culture, and history. He made important contributions to ethnology as it developed into anthropology. His single most important contribution was his edition of *The Iroquois Book of Rites*, first published in 1883, in which he best exhibits his holistic view of ethnology as an investigative discipline.

At least as important as his particular contributions to linguistics, ethnology, and the preservation of Iroquois culture was his contribution to the development of American anthropology through his influence on the early work and thought of Franz Boas, the most distinguished and influential American anthropologist for half a century. As a result of the first overseas meeting of the British Association for the Advancement of Science in 1884 in Montreal, a committee was established to make a survey of and to publish reports on the varied peoples and cultures clustered along the northwest coast of North America. Hale was appointed as a member with the expectation that he would resume the fieldwork he had initiated forty years earlier. By the time the survey was begun in 1887, however, Hale, recognizing that at the age of seventy he was no longer able to return to the field, became its active director. Boas, then a young man only recently arrived from Germany, had already done extensive fieldwork among the Eskimo and on the Northwest Coast and was appointed to do the field surveys. Although he

was eager to do the work and was excited by the opportunities afforded him, Boas had his own ideas about method and substance and often felt frustrated by the rigidity of Hale's plan and the continuing flow of his precise instructions communicated in a stream of letters from Clinton. As difficult as it was, and lasting only two years, the tutorial relationship was very important to Boaz's development. From it he derived several ideas about the nature of anthropology, such as the importance of language as a cultural indicator, the value of native texts collected in the original languages, the close comparisons of languages and the importance of their differences, a distrust of progressionist evaluations of cultures and the importance of a relativistic outlook, a distrust of the use of biological criteria as significant factors in ethnic differentiation: these were important elements in Hale's concept of ethnology and became important elements in the anthropology that Boas was constructing at the turn of the century. Despite his complaints about Hale's direction while in the field, Boas wrote at Hale's death, with something more than eulogistic need, that "ethnology has lost a man who contributed more to the knowledge of the human race than perhaps any other single student."

• Very little primary material with reference to Hale's life and work appears to be extant. Much of that dealing with his years on the Wilkes Expedition was probably destroyed when his ship, the *Peacock*, went down in a storm at the mouth of the Columbia River; even more was lost in a fire that destroyed his home in Clinton sometime after his death. Although occasional letters are scattered through the collections of his various correspondents, the largest series is that to Franz Boas, now in the Boas collection in the American Philosophical Library in Philadelphia; a relatively unimportant series of fourteen letters from Hale to Morgan is in the Morgan Collection of the Rush Rhees Library in the University of Rochester Library. For biographical material, see William N. Fenton's introduction to his edition of Hale's *The Iroquois Book of Rites* and Jacob W. Gruber, "Horatio Hale and the Development of American Anthropology," *Proceedings of the American Philosophical Library* 111 (1967): 5–37. Obituaries are in *American Anthropologist*, Jan. 1897; *Science* 5 (1897): 216–17; *Popular Science Monthly*, July 1897, pp. 401–2; and *The Critic* 27 (1897): 40–41.

JACOB W. GRUBER

HALE, James Webster (21 Nov. 1801–17 Aug. 1892), entrepreneur, was born in Boston, Massachusetts, the son of Benjamin Hale, a sail maker, and Marianna Foxwell Lowell. Hale was a restless youth who, after attending public school in Boston, went to sea at age fifteen. He sailed to Europe, Asia, Africa, and the West Indies, eventually becoming a sea captain. It was probably Hale's maritime exploits that brought him into contact with Eng and Chang, the well-known Siamese twins with whom he toured for a time and about whom he wrote a popular pamphlet in 1829.

In 1826 Hale retired from the sea and settled in Boston. The next year he married Almira Howe Davenport, with whom he would have seven children. Nine years later he moved to New York City, where he worked for many years as a news vendor on Wall Street in the commercial heart of the city. For a time he was employed by Robert E. Hudson in Hudson's News Room. By 1839 Hale had purchased Hudson's establishment and renamed it the Tontine Reading Room. The Tontine Reading Room was a popular meeting place for sea captains, merchants, and professional men. There Hale posted the latest news, sold newspapers and magazines, coordinated the delivery of overseas letters, a service the postal system did not yet provide, and acted as agent for the *John W. Richmond*, a steamship that ran between New York City and Providence, Rhode Island.

Hale used his connection with the *John W. Richmond* to help merchants circumvent the high cost of letter postage. Initially he confined himself to introducing trustworthy steamboat travelers to merchants with Boston-bound packages. In 1839 he persuaded railroad agent William Harnden to carry these packages on a regular basis for a set fee. To help Harnden get started, Hale secured for him a favorable contract with the *John W. Richmond* and brought his new service to the attention of Jacob Little and other leading brokers.

Harnden took up Hale's suggestion and began carrying packages between New York and Boston in a satchel, partly by steamboat and partly by railroad. When Harnden grew discouraged with his small earnings, Hale reminded him that the imminent establishment by the Cunard Company of a fast steamship line between Liverpool and Boston would greatly increase popular demand for his services. Hale's prediction proved correct, and Harnden's venture soon grew into the express industry, a major nineteenth-century enterprise.

Harnden loathed conflict and took special pains to avoid running afoul of the various laws that restricted competition with the postal system. Hale was more combative. Frustrated by the failure of publicists such as Barnabas Bates to persuade Congress to lower the basic letter rate, Hale undertook to demonstrate the practicality of the proposed reform. The linchpin of his strategy was Hale & Co., an independent letter delivery firm he established in late 1843 that competed directly with the government. Hale convinced himself—but not, he freely conceded, many others—that his venture was legal. His views were unusual but hardly unique. Other entrepreneurs with similar ideas included Lysander Spooner and Henry Wells, the founder of a letter delivery firm with which Hale was allied.

Hale's venture was an immediate success. At its peak in the summer of 1844, Hale & Co. employed 1,100 agents and carriers and served 110 offices, mostly in major commercial centers along the Atlantic seaboard and in the Midwest. Some of these offices were supervised directly by Hale and others by business allies such as Wells.

Hale's success owed a good deal to public dissatisfaction with the high rates of letter postage. While the government charged 18¾ cents to send a letter from New York to Boston, Hale charged as little as 5 cents, a decrease of more than 300 percent. In addition, he charged by weight rather than number of sheets, another cost savings for letters containing banknotes and other enclosures. To facilitate prepayment, Hale printed up labels, or stamps, an innovation that had recently been introduced in Great Britain but had not yet been widely adopted in the United States.

Hale's success quickly drew the ire of postal officers, who saddled him with several hundred lawsuits, making him, he later quipped, the "*most arrested* man in the world" (Hale, "History of Cheap Postage," p. 183). His legal expenses totaled $10,000, a large sum for the day and a striking indication of the seriousness with which the government took the threat that he posed. The most celebrated of these lawsuits was *Hale v. United States*, which was argued in Philadelphia in September 1844. Speaking for the prosecution was George M. Dallas, then the Democratic vice presidential nominee. Dallas charged Hale with violating the various federal laws that protected the postal monopoly. Hale lost the case. Yet Dallas freely conceded—or so Hale later recollected—that, by demonstrating the practicality of low postal rates, Hale had done more for the country than every postmaster general since the adoption of the Constitution (Hale, "History of Cheap Postage," p. 183).

Hale's venture lasted until July 1845, when Congress reduced the letter rate to a level competitive with Hale's and closed the various loopholes that Hale had exploited. Little is known about the remaining forty years of his life. His wife died in 1880. He died probably in New York City. Hale deserves to be remembered as a catalyst in the campaign for cheap postage, an innovation that a contemporary aptly hailed as "one of the most important reforms that the mercantile world has ever experienced" (Stimson, p. 63). His initiative forced Congress to significantly lower the basic letter rate, a major innovation that spurred commerce and helped make letter writing accessible to the public at large.

• Hale described his brief foray into mail delivery in "History of Cheap Postage," *American Odd Fellow* 10 (1871): 182–84. Late in life he published a series of letters describing his youth and early adulthood that are collected in *Old Boston Town, Early in this Century, by an 1801-er* (1883?). Hale's *Historical Account of the Siamese Twin Brothers, from Actual Observations* (1829) went through many editions. See also the unsigned "Father of Cheap Postage," *United States Mail and Post Office Assistant* 11 (Jan. 1871); A. L. Stimson, *History of the Express Business* (1881); and "The Early Days," *Express Gazette* 18 (10 Feb. 1893): 33.

RICHARD R. JOHN

HALE, John Parker (31 Mar. 1806–19 Nov. 1873), senator and diplomat, was born in Rochester, New Hampshire, the son of John Parker Hale, a lawyer, and Lydia C. O'Brien. On the death of her husband in 1819, Hale's mother took her thirteen children to Eastport, Maine, to live near her relatives and supported her family by taking in boarders. Despite the expense, she sent fourteen-year-old John to Phillips Exeter Academy in 1820 and to Bowdoin College in 1823. Although Hale was not an outstanding student, his cleverness carried him through scholastically, while his heartiness and resonant speaking voice made him a strong debater. After graduating in 1827, he trained for several years in law offices in Rochester and Dover, New Hampshire, before embarking on a successful law career in Dover in 1830. In 1834 he married Lucy Lambert; they had two children.

Politically Hale had several choices. He had grown up in a Federalist family and had trained under Federalist and National Republican lawyers. At Bowdoin, however, he had come under the influence of Franklin Pierce and other Jacksonians, and by 1830 the Jacksonians were in firm control of New Hampshire. Hale first favored the National Republicans, then briefly joined the Workingmen's party in 1832 in order to be elected to the state house of representatives, and finally committed himself to the Jacksonian Democrats. After making a name for himself as a temperance reformer during his one term in the house, he was in 1834 appointed U.S. district attorney for New Hampshire.

Removed from office by the Whigs in 1841, Hale was elected to the U.S. House of Representatives in 1843 and was soon involved in the slavery question. In his early career he had followed the Democratic party line of opposing abolition and in 1835 had spoken out harshly against the main speaker at an abolitionist meeting. However, gradually he had been drawn to the political antislavery movement. A strong believer in civil liberties, he was particularly distressed by the suppression of the abolitionists' freedom of speech. When parishioners at his Unitarian church in Dover criticized their pastor in 1842 for opposing slavery, Hale successfully defended the clergyman's right to preach on the subject. Although not an abolitionist, Hale was sufficiently antislavery by 1843 to vote against the gag rule in the House. When the annexation of Texas was proposed in December 1844, the state legislature passed resolutions instructing its representatives to support annexation, but Hale refused, saying that it would add slave territory. On 11 January 1845 he appealed to his constituents by sending them a letter defending his position.

Led by Pierce, their party chairman, the state Democrats held a convention on 12 February and removed Hale from their congressional slate. Almost immediately a group of antislavery Democrats held their own meeting and nominated him for Congress. After winning enough votes in the March election to force a runoff, Hale engaged in a yearlong battle with his opponents. The high point came in Concord in June 1845, when Hale and Pierce engaged in a heated debate. Calling himself a "doomed man," Hale shouted at the end that he would never "bow down and worship slavery." Hale did not win his seat in the House, but in June 1846 a combination of Whigs, Independent Democrats, and Liberty party men in the legislature elected him to the U.S. Senate.

Hale's brave fight for freedom of speech and his refusal to back down made him a popular figure. The abolitionist John Greenleaf Whittier wrote his poem "God Bless New Hampshire!" and in the fall of 1847 the antislavery Liberty party nominated Hale for president. When he arrived in Washington in December, the first senator to be elected because of his antislavery views, he was greeted as the antislavery leader of the Senate. Responding quickly, he attacked the Mexican War, blaming it on the expansion of slavery. He opposed a bill calling for more troops, refused to back a resolution applauding the valor of the American soldiers, and voted to reduce the amount of land to be acquired in the peace treaty. In the spring he spoke out against a proslavery mob that had forcibly removed seventy-seven fugitive slaves from the schooner *Pearl* on the Potomac River. He aroused the anger of southern senators by proposing a riot bill and by offering a resolution to bring in a bill ending slavery in the District of Columbia. Although both proposals failed, his sharp exchanges with Senators Henry S. Foote and John C. Calhoun made him the hero of the antislavery movement. During the presidential election in the fall he continued in that role, even though he dropped his bid for the presidency and backed the Free Soil candidate, Martin Van Buren.

In the debates over the Compromise of 1850, Hale delivered a long address on 19–20 March, in which he spent most of his time countering the speeches of Calhoun and Daniel Webster given earlier. The impact of his address was weakened by his failure to attack slavery directly. He was more successful in his persistent effort to abolish the daily ration of grog and the practice of flogging in the U.S. Navy. Largely because of Hale, Congress outlawed flogging in September 1850 and finally, in 1862, did away with the grog ration. In 1851 Hale also successfully defended in court the antislavery leaders who had rescued the runaway slave Shadrach in Boston.

Hale's political career was temporarily interrupted by the spirit of compromise in the early 1850s. When he ran for president as a Free Soiler in 1852, he received only half the vote that Van Buren had won four years earlier. In December the Democrats in New Hampshire were able to block his reelection to the Senate. For the next two years Hale was forced to turn to private pursuits as a lawyer in New York City and as a speaker on the lyceum lecture circuit. By 1855, however, the resumption of sectional conflict brought him back into prominence. In April of that year he won another runaway slave case in Boston, representing abolitionists accused of obstructing the return of Anthony Burns. When the New Hampshire legislature met in June, Hale's antislavery supporters made an arrangement with members of the nativist Know Nothing party, now a force in the state, and sent him back to Washington to serve out an unexpired term in the Senate.

Returning to the Senate, Hale was no longer the center of attention. Now only one of some half-dozen antislavery senators, his speeches seemed moderate compared to those of men such as Charles Sumner and Benjamin Wade. His speech "The Wrongs of Kansas" in 1856 was far more temperate than Sumner's "The Crime against Kansas." In a speech in January 1858 opposing the Dred Scott decision, Hale dealt more with property rights than with morality. He continued to speak out against slavery, but he never regained his position as the antislavery spokesman of the Senate. Now a Republican but something of a maverick, he never became a strong figure in the Republican party, even though his "wit," "earnestness," and "masterly eloquence" made him a much sought-after orator and political campaigner (Julian, p. 871). In 1858 he over-came the New Hampshire tradition of rotation in of-fice and won a third term as senator. His sixteen years in the Senate set a state record that lasted into the twentieth century.

During the Civil War Hale followed the radicals in supporting antislavery measures. Most of his energy, however, was spent on a feud with Secretary of the Navy Gideon Welles. As chairman of the Senate Naval Affairs Committee, Hale attacked Welles for suppos-edly condoning corruption and for giving the secre-tary's brother-in-law, George D. Morgan, control of the purchase of naval vessels. Hale, however, was also vulnerable, for he had tried to influence Welles to give naval contracts to New Hampshire firms and later re-ceived a large fee for securing the release of Major James M. Hunt from jail, where he was being held on charges of fraud while selling steamboats to the gov-ernment. Hale was not found guilty of misconduct, but his behavior contributed to his failure to be re-elected.

The final chapter in Hale's career began when he was named minister to Spain in 1865. He was unsuited for the position since he lacked any training in diplo-macy and spoke no Spanish. Facing few issues of im-portance, he was unable to leave a record of any great accomplishments. What record he did leave was marred by another controversy over his use of influ-ence, when he reportedly took advantage of his posi-tion to import goods duty free and then sold them at a profit. Although the charges were never proven, he was replaced as minister in 1869. A broken man, he suffered a stroke soon after returning to Dover in 1870 and died there.

Hale's own assessment of his career can be seen in the words on his headstone, taken from his Concord debate with Pierce: "He who lies beneath surrendered office, place and power rather than bow down and worship slavery." Although somewhat misleading since Hale's career ultimately benefited from his at-tacks on slavery, the statement does properly reflect the combativeness and independence that for a few years after 1845 made him a leader of the antislavery movement.

• A large collection of Hale papers is at the New Hampshire Historical Society, with smaller collections at Dartmouth College, the Minnesota Historical Society, and Phillips Exeter Academy. Richard H. Sewell has written an excellent biography, *John P. Hale and the Politics of Abolition* (1965). Hale's role in the Democratic party is explored in Donald B. Cole, *Jacksonian Democracy in New Hampshire, 1800–1851* (1970). For Hale's revolt in 1845 see Lucy Lowden, " 'Black as Ink—Bitter as Hell': John P. Hale's Mutiny in New Hampshire," *Historical New Hampshire* 27 (Spring 1972): 27–50, and John L. Hayes, *A Reminiscence of the Free-Soil Movement in New Hampshire, 1845* (1885). Gideon Welles gives a hostile opinion of Hale in *Diary of Gideon Welles, Sec-retary of the Navy under Lincoln and Johnson*, ed. Howard K. Beale (3 vols., 1960). See also George W. Julian, "A Presi-dential Candidate of 1852," *Century Magazine*, Oct. 1896, pp. 870–73; New Hampshire General Court Committee on Hale Statue, *The Statue of John P. Hale* (1892); Ezra S. Stearns, ed., *Genealogical and Family History of the State of New Hampshire*, vol. 3 (1908), pp. 1042–49; and Charles H. Bell, *The Bench and Bar of New Hampshire* (1894), pp. 415–20. Obituaries are in the *Boston Evening Transcript* and the *New York Tribune*, both 20 Nov. 1873; and the Concord, N.H., *Independent Statesman*, 27 Nov. 1873.

DONALD B. COLE

HALE, Lilian Clarke Westcott (7 Dec. 1880–7 Dec. 1963), artist, was born in Hartford, Connecticut, the daughter of Edward Gardner Westcott, a businessman employed by the Lee Arms Company, and Harriet Clarke, a piano instructor. She began to draw as a child and received her first commission at age fifteen. In 1897 she enrolled at the Hartford Art School, an institution that particularly fostered the artistic aspira-tions of young women. Lilian studied there for three years, primarily with Elizabeth Stevens; she also at-tended classes given by William Merritt Chase and then worked with Chase at his summer art school in Shinnecock, New York, in 1899. In 1900, with a scholarship from the Hartford Art Society, she entered the School of the Museum of Fine Arts in Boston, skipping the preliminary drawing classes (taught by her future husband) and directly entering the ad-vanced painting classes of Edmund Tarbell. She fin-ished the formal program at the school in 1904 but continued to take occasional classes there until 1906.

Lilian Westcott was introduced to painter Philip Hale in Hartford, Connecticut, during the summer of 1901 at the home of Hale's maternal uncle Charles Perkins. Their friendship turned quickly to romance, and despite her reservations about the effects that mar-riage would have on her career, the couple wed in 1902. Lilian Hale found her husband to be enthusias-tic and supportive of her profession; her self-confi-dence was bolstered by his advice and seniority. In 1904, after her matriculation from the museum school, the couple traveled abroad, and Hale spent her time studying Old Master paintings in London and in Par-is. She had been introduced to the impressionist style by her husband, and in August 1904 the Hales visited Monet in Giverny and painted landscapes there in the company of Philip Hale's friend Theodore Butler.

Soon after her return to Boston, Hale and her hus-band took separate, adjoining studios in the newly constructed Fenway Studio Building, which became the center of Boston's art community and the head-quarters of the Boston school. Hale began to exhibit her work in Boston and at the important art annuals in Philadelphia, Washington, and New York. In 1906 she painted *The Convalescent* (now titled *Zeffy in Bed*, Sheldon Memorial Art Gallery, Univ. of Nebraska), the first of many figure studies Hale made of Rose Zeffler, a model whom she dressed in elaborate gowns and posed in elegant interiors, often with flowers. Hale's first solo show, held in 1908 at the Rowlands Galleries in Boston, contained eighteen such studies, mostly of Zeffler. This exhibition consisted entirely of charcoal drawings, carefully crafted with thin vertical strokes. Hale considered this medium to be as well-suited for finished works of art as oil paints were; she frequently made images in charcoal and in oil that differ only slightly in detail, continuing this practice throughout her career. Soon after her successful 1908 exhibition, Hale gave up her studio in Boston and established one in her new home in Dedham, Massachusetts. In May 1908 she gave birth to her first and only child, Anna Westcott Hale, called Nancy. Nancy became the model for many of Hale's finest drawings, including *Flower* and *The Cherry Hat* (both Museum of Fine Arts, Boston).

Hale's style became more complex after about 1910; her compositions now included more of the room surrounding her model, and her technique, particularly in charcoal, became even more subtle and refined. The interior and exterior of their house appears frequently in her work after 1912, when the family moved to "Sandy Down," a quintessential New England farmhouse in Dedham. In addition to her periodic solo shows, Hale continued to display her work nationally, and she won a gold medal in 1915 at the Panama-Pacific International Exhibition for her painting *Lavender and Old Ivory* (private collection) and the more prestigious medal of honor for her charcoal drawings.

By the early 1920s Hale's style shifted once again. She began to paint and draw her rural surroundings, winning acclaim for her snow-filled winter scenes, often viewed through the windowpanes of her Dedham house. Her figural compositions were simpler and emphasized the individual features of her sitters. She soon won many portrait commissions, most often for likenesses of children. Some of her paintings, particularly *Home Lessons* of 1919 (Phillips Collection), reflect Philip Hale's influence on his wife's work; this carefully constructed interior recalls his passion for the seventeenth-century Dutch master Jan Vermeer.

Lilian Hale enjoyed both popular and critical success throughout the 1920s. She was elected an associate member of the National Academy of Design in 1927 (and an academician in 1931), received many portrait commissions, and began to show her work in New York more frequently, particularly at the Grand Central Art Galleries. She won the Altman Prize in 1927 at the National Academy for her portrait of her new son-in-law, Taylor Hardin (private collection), and her work was featured in an article in the *American Magazine of Art*. This period of accomplishment ended abruptly with the death of Philip Hale in February 1931; it took several years for Lilian Hale to regain her equilibrium and to paint again. In 1936 she had a solo exhibition of drawings at the Guild of Boston Artists that featured some of her finest winter scenes and still lifes, but despite the favorable acclaim she received, Hale began to feel that her representational work, dedicated to ideals of beauty and craftsmanship, was out of step with her times. She continued to make portraits, landscapes, and still lifes for the rest of her life, working during the summer in Rockport, Massachusetts, and in the winter in Dedham (and after 1953 in Charlottesville, Virginia, where she moved to be closer to her daughter). At the age of eighty-three, she won her last prize, at the Rockport Art Association, and she traveled to Italy for the first time. She died shortly thereafter in St. Paul, Minnesota, while visiting her sister in Minneapolis.

• Hale's papers are divided between the Archives of American Art, Smithsonian Institution, and the Sophia Smith Collection, Smith College, Northampton, Mass. During her lifetime Hale was featured in Rose V. S. Berry, "Lilian Westcott Hale—Her Art," *American Magazine of Art* 18 (Feb. 1927): 59–70; her daughter, writer Nancy Hale, recalled her parents' artistic careers in *The Life in the Studio* (1969). The most complete study of Hale's career is Erica E. Hirshler, "Lilian Westcott Hale (1880–1963): A Woman Painter of the Boston School," (Ph.D. diss., Boston Univ., 1992), which contains a complete bibliography and a checklist of Hale's work.

ERICA E. HIRSHLER

HALE, Lucretia Peabody (2 Sept. 1820–12 June 1900), children's writer and humorist, was born in Boston, Massachusetts, the daughter of Nathan H. Hale, a newspaper owner and advocate of the "editorial," and Sarah Preston Everett. During her youth, Hale attended several schools, including Susan Whitney's, Elizabeth Peabody's, and, ultimately, George B. Emerson's School for Young Ladies, where she earned the equivalent of a bachelor's degree. Following her matriculation, Hale held various occupations such as private tutor and instructor for a correspondence school. In addition, she also founded several culinary arts institutes, in 1874 became the first woman to serve on the Boston School Board, and helped her brothers Charles and Edward edit and proofread *Today* and *Old and New*, their respective literary magazines.

Hale—a devout Unitarian who neither married nor had any children—wrote with her brother Edward a religious novel, *Margaret Percival in America* (1850). In 1858 she created a book of light religious narratives titled *Seven Stormy Sundays*. Shortly thereafter, Hale produced a number of domestic tracts, four of which centered on the virtues and techniques of needlework. These essays, along with an abundance of short fictional sketches and humorous anecdotes, were her main source of income following her father's demise in 1863. Indeed, Hale's best-known work—that which showcased the unconventional Peterkins—appeared during the two decades after her parent's death.

In April 1868 one of Hale's whimsical children's stories, "The Lady Who Put Salt in Her Coffee," was printed in the juvenile magazine *Our Young Folks*. This successful nonsensical tale was rapidly followed by five other light sketches about the peculiar Peterkin family and their exaggerated domestic dilemmas. Mr. and Mrs. Peterkin and their six silly children—Agamemnon, Solomon John, Elizabeth Eliza, and the three nameless little boys best remembered for their odd habit of constantly donning and shedding their beloved india rubber boots—appeared regularly in both *Our Young Folks* and its successor, Scribner's *St. Nicholas*.

Indeed, Hale's 1880 release of *The Peterkin Papers*, a collection of twenty-two such nonsensical yet realistic tales, achieved much popularity, perhaps in part because the Peterkins poked fun at both unrealistic Victorian family ideals and constraining codes of conduct for children. The format for these sketches is simple; each story begins with the introduction of a seemingly perplexing problem. As the tale continues, the tension—which appears unnecessarily created and distorted—is humorously augmented by the lack of common sense found in the Peterkin household. Ultimately, panic erupts, and every member of the Peterkin family—from Father down to the three little boys with their india rubber boots—is consulted about the unmanageable imagined dilemma; yet, all advice proves comically useless. In each case, the pattern of the Peterkins' peculiar obsession with futile solutions is broken by the introduction of logical, clearheaded advice from their dear family friend Mrs. Leslie, otherwise known as "the lady from Philadelphia." This fictional savior-in-petticoats—who is thought to be modeled after Hale's devoted lifelong friend and schoolmate, Susan Inches Lyman—fixes everything from the fate of a cup of coffee that has inadvertently been seasoned with salt instead of sugar, to the dilemma of an awkwardly placed piano that can only be played by standing on the porch and reaching into the house through the parlor window.

Ultimately, Hale authored or co-wrote twenty book-length works, including a second volume about the silly Peterkin clan, *The Last of the Peterkins, with Others of Their Kin* (1886). Other titles by Hale include *Wolf at the Door* (1878); *An Uncloseted Skeleton* (1888), with Edwin Lassetter Bynner; *Stories for Children: Containing Simple Lessons in Morals: A Supplementary Reader for Schools, or for Use at Home* (1892); *The New Harry and Lucy: A Story of Boston in the Summer in 1891* (1892), with Edward Everett Hale; and *Six of One by Half a Dozen of the Other: An Everyday Novel* (1872), a collaboration with her brother Edward, Harriet Beecher Stowe, and three other writers. Many of Hale's titles are no longer in print; however, the impact of her innovative writing style—one in which the young reader's enjoyment, rather than his or her moral training, is the goal—transformed the nature of children's literature. By allowing her young characters to speak their minds and interact with adults, Hale simultaneously satirized society's peculiarities and altered the nature of juvenile fiction. Indeed, as both author and

social reformer, Hale is best remembered for her ability to temper the didactic with humor.

Hale died in Belmont, Massachusetts.

• Hale's papers are with the family records and papers in the Sophia Smith Collection, Smith College Library, Northampton, Mass. Biographical information concerning Hale, including a detailed list of her works, can be found in Diane Telgen's article "Lucretia Peabody Hale," *Contemporary Authors*, vol. 136 (1992), pp. 175–77. For an indepth discussion of *The Peterkin Papers*, see R. Gordon Kelly's "Lucretia P. Hale," in *Twentieth-Century Children's Writers*, 3d ed., ed. Tracy Chevalier (1989), pp. 1097–98. Also helpful are Madelyn C. Wankmiller, "Lucretia Peabody Hale and *The Peterkin Papers*," *Hornbook Magazine* 34 (Apr. 1958): 95–103, 137–47, and Eliza Orne White, "Lucretia P. Hale," *Hornbook Magazine* 16 (Sept.–Oct. 1940): 317–22. See also Amy Schwartz's "Author's Note" in the 1989 book-length republication of Hale's *The Lady Who Put Salt in Her Coffee*. Other modern citations appear in Virginia Blain et al., *The Feminist Companion to Literature in English* (1990), Claire Buck, ed., *The Bloomsbury Guide to Women's Literature* (1992), and Nancy Hale's introduction to *The Complete Peterkin Papers* (1960). An obituary is in the *Boston Transcript*, 12 June 1900.

SUSAN M. STONE

HALE, Nancy (6 May 1908–24 Sept. 1988), writer, was born Anna Westcott Hale in Boston, Massachusetts, the daughter of Philip Leslie Hale and Lilian Clark Westcott, painters. Descended from a distinguished New England family, her grandfather was the orator, author, and Unitarian clergyman Edward Everett Hale, and two of her great-aunts were the writers Harriet Beecher Stowe and Lucretia Peabody Hale. Philip L. Hale achieved some success as a neo-impressionist painter of the Boston School but probably had a greater influence as an instructor at the Boston Museum School and as an art critic for Boston newspapers. Lilian W. Hale, the more talented artist of the pair, was well known for her portraits and landscapes in oil, pastel, and charcoal. Nancy began writing at an early age, producing a family newspaper, the *Society Cat*, at age eight and publishing her first story, in the *Boston Herald*, at age eleven. She also devoted considerable energy to the study of art under her parents' tutelage. After graduating from the Winsor School in 1926, she studied at the Boston Museum School from 1926 to 1928.

In 1928 Hale married aspiring writer Taylor Scott Hardin and moved with him to New York City. The couple later had one son. Hale was hired to work in the art department at *Vogue*; however, almost immediately she was put to work as an assistant editor and writer. Under the pen name Anne Leslie, she wrote "chatty news" items, fashion news, and editorials. Hale's true ambition was to write fiction. Jobs at *Vogue* and later *Vanity Fair* provided financial support while she built her reputation as a writer by producing pieces on commission for a variety of magazines, as well as freelance fiction. Hale's first novel, *The Young Die Good* (1932), was a chronicle of the shallow lives of the post-flapper "smart set" in New York. In 1933 one of her stories, "To the Invader," won the O. Henry Memorial Award

Prize. A second novel, *Never Any More*, was published in 1934.

Hale was hired by the *New York Times* as its first female news reporter in the spring of 1934, a job she left after an exhausting six months. By then, she and her husband had been living apart for some time. They were divorced late in 1934. A year later Hale married author and journalist Charles Christian Wertenbaker. They settled in Charlottesville, Virginia, and had one son. Her next book, *The Earliest Dreams* (1936), was a selection of short stories already published by Hale in such magazines as the *New Yorker*, *Harper's*, *Redbook*, and *Ladies' Home Journal*. Fiction writing was now her primary means of financial support.

After several separations, Hale and Wertenbaker divorced in 1941. In 1942 she married Fredson Thayer Bowers, professor of English at the University of Virginia. Hale's third and best-known novel, *The Prodigal Women*, was published later that year. It is an immense book—over 700 pages—that, in the words of Anne Hobson Freeman, "dramatized, with unflinching candor, the psychological cost of being a woman at that time" (Freeman [1980], p. 214). It is the story of three women, each taking advantage of the freedoms offered by the post–World War I rejection of Victorian social mores.

The troubled nature of her second marriage combined with intense self-criticism about her work led to physical ailments and bouts of anxiety throughout this period. In 1938 and again in 1943 the anxiety was severe enough to result in hospitalization. In 1943 she was fortunate to find a psychoanalyst, Beatrice Hinkle, who helped her begin to solve what Hale called "this problem of who to be."

During the 1950s Hale published a collection of stories; the first of two much-loved volumes of "autobiographical fiction," *A New England Girlhood* (1958); and three novels. Included among these was Hale's favorite long work, *Heaven and Hardpan Farm* (1957), a humorous and humane novel about a group of "neurotic" women and their Jungian doctor in a small country sanitarium.

In 1961 Hale sold twelve stories to the *New Yorker*, more than any other writer in the magazine's history. In that same year, she put together *The Realities of Fiction*, a volume of lectures on writing, which were given primarily at the Bread Loaf Writers Conference in 1959 and 1960. Another novel, a collection of stories, and an anthology of writings by New England authors followed. One of Hale's most popular books, *The Life in the Studio*, was published in 1969. "My mother died and I felt more than I could stand without expressing it," Hale told a *Charlottesville Daily Progress* reporter (c. 1980). Advertised as "an affectionate recollection of some singular parents," *The Life in the Studio* is as much about coming to terms with their memory and their loss. Hale blurred the boundaries of fiction and fact to discover for herself "the meaning of the past," but also "to awaken an echo in other lives; to arouse a

consciousness where perhaps formerly there was none" (*Realities of Fiction*, pp. 4, 196).

It is clear that Hale shared her parents' artistic philosophy as described in *The Life in the Studio*. The artist's role is to create a subtle marriage of objectivity and subjectivity, to use "the interplay of the painter's subjective view with the way the light actually falls upon the object" to "render" its essence and its meaning (*Life in the Studio*, p. 20). In *Mary Cassatt* (1975), a biography commissioned after the success of *The Life in the Studio*, Hale was clearly aiming for "the special marriage of subject and object." Written with an authority quite different from that conferred by scholarly credentials, the text combined personal knowledge of Mary Cassatt's social and artistic milieu with the style that Hale developed in her "autobiographical fiction."

Hale then turned her attention to stories for children, publishing *The Night of the Hurricane* in 1978 and, in the mid-1980s, writing a collection of stories for young dyslexic readers. She died in Charlottesville, Virginia.

It is difficult to neatly characterize Hale's large and varied output. She is probably best known for her short stories. Her protagonists are most often women, usually rather well-to-do. As they go about their daily lives, skillfully drawn through careful attention to the minutest of details, these women come to an epiphany. They are, in the words of Anne Hobson Freeman, "penetrating portraits of women who may seem calm, and even satisfied, but beneath the surface are struggling to retain their self-esteem and individuality" (Freeman [1980], p. 218). Their moments of illumination bring better understanding of the patterns of their lives, but Hale's epiphanies confer what William Maxwell called "a sad wisdom."

In interviews throughout her life, Hale expressed amazement that the writing she felt was most private and personal evoked the strongest response in others. "I seem to do better by the world when I am acting for what is most inwardly myself" (Nancy Hale Papers, Sophia Smith Collection). She was described as elegant, regal, distinguished, and formidable, but with a disarming frankness and deep understanding, what Mary Gray Hughes called "a sense of risk along with the beautiful manners." Her writing reflects this complexity. Often described as "poetic," with what one writer called a "delicate balance of understatement and passion" (*New York Herald Tribune*, 12 Apr. 1936), Hale's "subtle and unsparing" work (*New York Times*, 15 Sept. 1960) "depicts the quiet horror of life with a directness that is positively unnerving" (*Saturday Review*, 17 Sept. 1960). Whether writing fiction, autobiography, or biography, Hale strove not so much for the literal, factual truth as for the emotional truth that lies beneath the surface. In a 1958 interview, she described most of her work as psychological. "I'm never writing about what I appear to be writing about. Anything that is worth conveying cannot be said directly."

• The largest collection of Hale's personal and family papers, including correspondence and manuscripts of published and unpublished works, is in the Sophia Smith Collection at Smith College. A smaller collection of papers is in the Alderman Library at the University of Virginia. Additional published works by Hale include the novels *The Sign of Jonah* (1950), *Dear Beast* (1959), and *Black Summer* (1963); collections of stories, *Between the Darkness and the Daylight* (1943), *The Empress's Ring* (1955), *The Pattern of Perfection* (1960), and *Secrets* (1971); and the anthology *New England Discovery: A Personal View* (1963). Other useful articles include "Nancy Hale of New England," *Boston Transcript*, 2 Apr. 1932; "Nancy Hale—An Analyzer of the Feminine," *New York Times Book Review*, 8 Nov. 1942; "Nancy Hale Writes to Please Herself," *Richmond Times-Dispatch*, 13 June 1958; and "Nancy Hale: A New England Person," *Boston Globe*, 2 Dec. 1973. Important published sources are a profile and obituary by Anne Hobson Freeman in the 1980 and 1988 *Dictionary of Literary Biography* yearbooks, the latter with tributes by colleagues and friends. Other obituaries are in the *New York Times*, 26 Sept. 1988; the *Washington Post* and the *Boston Globe*, 27 Sept. 1988; and *The Times* (London), 8 Oct. 1988.

MAIDA GOODWIN

HALE, Nathan (6 June 1755–22 Sept. 1776), martyr of the American Revolution, was born in Coventry, Connecticut, the son of Richard Hale and Elizabeth Strong, successful farmers. A sickly infant, he barely survived his first year, but as he grew he became an outdoorsman and a powerful athlete. He enjoyed reading, and his father decided to prepare him for the ministry, first by hiring Rev. Joseph Huntington to tutor him and then by sending him in 1769 to Yale College. At Yale he was widely admired by his teachers and fellow students. Dr. Eneas Munson, a resident of New Haven, described him as "almost six feet in height, perfectly proportioned, and in figure and deportment . . . the most manly man I have ever met. . . . His personal beauty and grace of manner were most charming. . . . [He] was overflowing with good humor, and was the idol of all his acquaintances." After graduation in 1773, instead of becoming a minister, Hale taught school in East Haddam and New London, Connecticut.

When the American Revolution commenced in April 1775 with the fighting at Lexington and Concord, Hale took the floor at a New London town meeting and made a resounding speech in favor of rebellion against Great Britain. Matching his words with actions, he joined the Continental army at Boston as a lieutenant in Colonel Charles Webb's regiment. On 1 January 1776 he was promoted to captain and in September, while on duty in New York, helped seize a supply vessel on the East River from under the guns of the British warship *Asia*. Impressed with Hale's exploits, Lieutenant Colonel Thomas Knowlton chose Hale to command a company in Knowlton's Rangers.

At about the same time, General George Washington, desperate for intelligence about British plans and strength, called upon Knowlton to supply him with a volunteer for a spy mission behind enemy lines. After Knowlton made two unsuccessful calls for a volunteer, Hale stepped forward to undertake the task. He disguised himself as a Loyalist schoolmaster, departed his

own lines at the northern end of Manhattan on 12 September and shortly thereafter entered British territory on Long Island. For the next few days he gathered information about enemy positions, making drawings of fortifications and writing descriptions of everything he saw. As he was returning to Washington's headquarters on 21 September, he was apprehended by the British and taken before General William Howe, who ordered him to be hanged the following day as a spy. He spent his last night writing letters to his brother Enoch and to Colonel Knowlton. The next morning he calmly mounted the scaffold, from which he addressed his foes in firm tones: "You are shedding the blood of the innocent; if I had ten thousand lives, I would lay them down in defence of my injured bleeding country." Then he uttered his final words, "I only regret that I have but one life to lose for my country." He died as he had lived, with nobility and dignity.

Almost immediately after his death, Hale became a hero of the American revolutionary cause and a symbol of the struggle for freedom. His tutor at Yale, President Timothy Dwight (1752–1817), composed a poem on the young man's life, and in 1812 a fort at the entrance to the New Haven harbor was named for him. In 1846 a granite memorial in his honor was dedicated at Coventry, and forty years later the state of Connecticut commissioned Karl Gerhardt to create a bronze statue of him for the capitol at Hartford.

• Hale's papers are at the Connecticut Historical Society in Hartford. Other sources on Hale's life are in the Connecticut State Library in Hartford and the Yale University Library. The best biography is H. P. Johnston, *Nathan Hale, 1776: Biography and Memorials* (1914). See also E. E. Hale, *Nathan Hale* (1881); Isaac W. Stuart, *Life of Captain Nathan Hale: The Martyr Spy of the American Revolution* (1856); Benson J. Lossing, *The Two Spies: Nathan Hale and John André* (1886); and *Diary of Frederick Mackenzie . . .* , ed. Allen French (2 vols., 1930).

PAUL DAVID NELSON

HALE, Philip Leslie (21 May 1865–2 Feb. 1931), painter, teacher, and writer, was born in Boston, Massachusetts, the son of Edward Everett Hale, a clergyman and author, and Emily Baldwin Perkins. Philip Hale grew up in a close-knit family of extraordinary accomplishment. Like his eldest sister Ellen Day Hale, a painter, and his younger brother Herbert Dudley Hale, an architect, Philip Hale had cultivated an interest in the arts since childhood. He finished his primary education at the Boston Latin School and his secondary schooling at Roxbury Latin School. At his father's insistence he successfully completed the entrance exams for Harvard College, an achievement that won him his father's permission to attend art school instead; Hale enrolled at the School of the Museum of Fine Arts in Boston in the fall of 1883. He studied there with Edmund Tarbell for one year, then moved to New York City to continue his training at the Art Students League under the direction of Kenyon Cox and J. Alden Weir.

In January 1887 Hale left for Paris, seeking to complete his artistic education. He enrolled at the Académie Julian, where he worked with French academicians Jules-Joseph Lefebvre and Gustave Boulanger. Hale cultivated and enjoyed a bohemian lifestyle in Paris, formed a society of compatriots called the "Anti-Pretty Club," and became one of the earliest Americans to paint at Giverny, home of impressionist master Claude Monet. However, in contrast to these avantgarde inclinations, he also submitted his paintings to the more conservative Salon exhibitions. His work was displayed at the Salon in 1888, 1889, 1890, 1893, and 1897. During the spring of 1890 Hale traveled to Spain to study the work of seventeenth-century master Diego Velasquez.

Hale returned to Boston in June 1890 but went back to Paris later that same year to join his love interest, Katharine Kinsella. Hale spent that winter in Paris, the summer of 1891 in Giverny, and the next winter in London, where he visited John Singer Sargent and studied the collections of London museums. He continued his itinerant lifestyle for the next several years, dividing his time among Paris, Giverny, Boston, and the Hale family's summer home in Matunuck, Rhode Island. He took a position as instructor of drawing after the antique at the School of the Museum of Fine Arts in Boston in 1893; his affair with Kinsella ended at about the same time. In 1895–1896 Hale was briefly engaged to Boston graphic artist Ethel Reed.

Throughout the 1890s Hale experimented with a bold, postimpressionist style. In paintings such as *Girls in Sunlight* (1895, Museum of Fine Arts, Boston), he used the fields at Matunuck as his setting and painted women outdoors in full sun, silhouetted against brilliant light. To capture the haloed effects, he used a high-keyed palette often dominated by chrome yellow and pulled thin strokes of paint over his figures. For a few years beginning in 1898 Hale offered summer art classes in Matunuck; several of his models were his students. The ambitious and daring compositions Hale crafted in Matunuck, both in oil on canvas and in pastel, were exhibited in New York in late 1899 at the Durand-Ruel Galleries, the dealers for the French impressionists. The paintings met with mixed reviews. Critics found Hale's dissolution of the human figure too extreme, so he reacted by shifting to a more conventional style. In the following decade he won acclaim for paintings such as *The Crimson Rambler* (c. 1908, Pennsylvania Academy of the Fine Arts, Philadelphia), in which he united an impressionist palette and concern for light effects with solid draftsmanship and form. He exhibited frequently at the National Academy of Design (he was elected an associate in 1907), the Pennsylvania Academy, the Corcoran, and at major annual shows, often winning prizes. He also had several solo exhibitions in Boston at the St. Botolph Club and the Guild of Boston Artists.

During the winter months Hale taught. In addition to his work at the Museum School in Boston, where he became the chief instructor of drawing, teaching artistic anatomy and life drawing, Hale offered classes at the Worcester Art Museum (1898–1910), the Pennsylvania Academy of the Fine Arts (1913–1928), and Boston University (1926–1928). These positions provided Hale with a steady source of income to supplement the money he made from portrait commissions. Even after his marriage to painter Lilian Westcott in 1902, Hale was determined to be his family's sole source of support, despite Lilian W. Hale's considerable financial success. The couple had one daughter.

Hale took a studio at the newly constructed Fenway Studio Building on Ipswich Street in Boston in 1905 and kept it for the rest of his life. While his wife created most of her paintings at their Dedham home, Hale seldom worked there, preferring to work at his city studio. His paintings became increasingly academic as he sought to imbue modern subjects with the attributes of the greatest art of the past. His nudes, while set in modern rooms and surrounded by contemporary accessories, are posed after the paintings of Jean Auguste Dominique Ingres and Jean Léon Gérôme, while his sporting figures, particularly a large design for a mural of football players, *Around the End* (c. 1905, Harvard University), take on the attributes of a classical frieze. In 1919 Hale won the prize for the most popular picture at the Pennsylvania Academy exhibition for his poetic composition *Flowers in Moonlight* (c. 1918, now titled *Moonlit Pool*, private collection), depicting a nude woman floating in a moonlit lake surrounded by flowers.

A keen intellectual, Hale wrote frequently about art. He began with modest contributions about art life in Paris for the magazine *Arcadia* (1892) and about Boston's artistic circles for the *Springfield* (Ill.) *Republican* (1896). From 1905 to 1909 he wrote a regular column of critical reviews for the *Boston Herald*, and he offered occasional features thereafter for both the *Herald* and the *Boston Evening Transcript*. His most important literary contribution was the monograph *Jan Vermeer of Delft* (1913; rev. and repr. 1938), the first American book dedicated to the seventeenth-century Dutch master. Vermeer was highly admired by painters of the Boston School, and Hale's book offered both a history of his work and a lesson on the relevance of Vermeer's paintings to contemporary art. Conservative in his taste and eloquent in promoting his ideas among his students and in the popular press, Hale used his admiration for Vermeer and other old master painters as an argument against recent developments in modern art, particularly abstraction.

Hale continued to paint throughout the 1920s, although he exhibited his work less frequently. He turned his greatest attention toward his students and offered private lessons in his studio in addition to the formal classes he taught in Boston and Philadelphia. He died suddenly of a ruptured appendix. His wife, Lilian Westcott Hale, organized a memorial exhibition of his paintings at the Museum of Fine Arts, Boston, in 1931.

Hale played a key role in establishing the intellectual foundation for the traditional artistic style characteristic of the Boston School. He expressed his philosophy both in his paintings and in his written work, and while he was always an active painter, Hale was aware that his greatest artistic legacy was in the lessons he taught his students.

• Hale's papers are divided between the Archives of American Art, Smithsonian Institution, and the Sophia Smith Collection at Smith College, Northampton, Mass. Hale's daughter, Nancy Hale, recalled her father's career in *The Life in the Studio* (1969). Other sources include Frederick W. Coburn, "Philip L. Hale: Artist and Critic," *World To-Day* 14 (Oct. 1907): 59–67, and Carol Lowrey, "The Art of Philip Leslie Hale," *Philip Leslie Hale, A.N.A.* (1988), a Vose Galleries catalog. Obituaries are in the *New York Times* and the *Boston Herald*, both 3 Feb. 1931.

ERICA E. HIRSHLER

HALE, Robert (29 Nov. 1889–30 Nov. 1976), lawyer and politician, was born in Portland, Maine, the son of Clarence Hale, a judge, and Margaret Rollins. Hale came from a prominent Maine Republican family, his father having been active in Maine politics leading to his appointment as a U.S. district judge, and his uncle Eugene Hale and cousin Frederick Hale both having served in the U.S. Congress.

Hale graduated from Bowdoin College summa cum laude in 1910 then attended Oxford University as a Rhodes scholar, receiving his B.A. in 1913. He attended Harvard Law School in 1913–1914 and returned to Oxford for an M.A. in 1921. Throughout his life, Hale was very active in Bowdoin alumni affairs.

Admitted to the Massachusetts bar in 1914, Hale began practicing law with Choate, Hall & Stewart in Boston in 1914. After two years, he returned to Maine, passed the bar there, and began practice with the firm of Verrill, Hale, Booth & Ives in Portland in 1917.

Hale's legal career was interrupted by two years of military service during World War I. He enlisted in the army on 27 November 1917 and fought as a second lieutenant in the American Expeditionary Force in France. From March to July 1919, before returning home, Hale served as a legal adviser to a field mission sent to Finland, Estonia, Latvia, and Lithuania by the American Commission to Negotiate Peace.

Hale resumed his law practice in 1920 (the firm had now become Verrill, Hale, Dana & Walker). He married Agnes Burke, a writer, in 1922; they had one daughter. He continued practicing law until 1942, when he won election to the U.S. House of Representatives.

Hale's election to Congress was the end result of a long and successful career in Maine state politics. First elected as a Republican member of the Maine House of Representatives in 1922, he served from 1923 to 1930 and won election to the posts of majority floor leader in 1927–1928 and Speaker in 1929–1930.

Following his election to the U.S. House of Representatives from Maine's First District in 1942, Hale served for eight terms (3 Jan. 1943–3 Jan. 1959), at that time the longest tenure of any Maine representative in this century. During his congressional career, Hale served as a member of the Interstate and Foreign Commerce Committee and the Merchant Marine Committee.

In 1956, Hale barely won reelection. After the state impounded the ballots for a recount, Hale was declared the winner by a mere twenty-nine votes. His Democratic opponent, James C. Oliver, had formerly served as Republican congressman from Hale's district from 1937 to 1943 but had been defeated by Hale in the 1942 Republican primary. There is a final footnote to this remarkable political rivalry: after failing in 1954 and 1956, Oliver succeeded in his third bid as a Democrat to oust Hale, ending Hale's congressional career in 1958.

Following his defeat, Hale chose to stay in Washington. President Dwight D. Eisenhower appointed him to the United States–Switzerland Permanent Commission on Conciliation in 1959. Admitted to the bar in Washington that year, Hale began practicing with the firm of Davies, Richberg, Tydings, Landa & Duff. He continued there until his death; indeed, he died on the way to work, having just turned eighty-seven the day before. For burial, his body was returned home, to Evergreen Cemetery in Portland.

Hale, a Republican from a traditionally Republican state, once described himself thus in *Harper's* magazine (May 1934): "I am by temperament and education a Tory. . . . My native bent is for agreeable food and attractive beverages in the homes of the affluent and the well-connected." In another *Harper's* article (June 1934) he wrote: "I believe in individuals and their exertions and their souls. I regard the acceptance of a government job or a government dole as a surrender. . . . I still believe in minimal governments kept simple and comprehensible and inexpensive."

It was also in *Harper's* that Hale published a highly controversial article in 1936. "Definitively, articulately, vociferously, I hate Roosevelt," Hale wrote. He condemned Franklin D. Roosevelt for his "shallow falseness," insisted he was "the chief enemy of our Republic," and explained his hatred in economic terms: the "consciousness that as a social and economic class we, who have lived or tried to live in any part on money saved, are being liquidated is the tie that binds Roosevelt haters whether they have a million a year or twenty dollars a week and fifty dollars in the savings bank." When he was first elected to Congress in 1942, *Time* reported that although Hale "had to defend himself" against that article, the voters of Maine apparently liked his defense: "I am probably the most outspoken advocate in Maine of President Roosevelt's foreign policies. Also, I guess I am the most outspoken critic of his domestic policies" (16 Nov. 1942). Perhaps so, but there is more evidence of the domestic policy criticism than the foreign policy praise, and the pattern continued beyond Roosevelt. When Hale died, the *New York Times* said accurately that he had been "a caustic and witty opponent of Democratic administrations." He not only opposed Truman's Asian policies but also became a part of an aborted impeachment effort over Truman's seizure of the steel industry.

When Hale received his honorary degree from Bowdoin in 1947, the citation read in part, "representative in Congress now for three terms of the First Maine District made famous by Thomas Brackett Reed and carrying on his tradition of ability, integrity, and courage; public servant who can state clearly and urgently the issues before his constituents and who can alternate the boredom of long, tedious House sessions by writing verses for the *New Yorker*." Hale did indeed publish poetry in a variety of magazines, including the *New Yorker, Catholic World*, and *Christian Century*. His other writings included *Early Days of Church and State in Maine* (1910) and a memoir of his beloved Cushing's Island on the Maine coast in *Down East* magazine (Sept. 1972).

• Hale's personal and congressional papers, correspondence, diaries, photographs, and sound recordings are in the Bowdoin College Library, Portland, Maine. There apparently is no biography of Hale. A brief sketch appears in the *General Catalog of Bowdoin College* (1978). Hale's *Harper's* articles appeared in May 1934, p. 752; June 1934, p. 122; and Aug. 1936, pp. 268–73. Helpful obituaries are in the *New York Times*, 2 Dec. 1976; and *Bowdoin Alumnus* 51, no. 2 (1977).

DAVIS D. JOYCE

HALE, Robert Safford (24 Sept. 1822–14 Dec. 1881), lawyer, judge, and congressman, was born in Chelsea, Vermont, the son of Harry Hale, a merchant, farmer, and miller, and Lucinda Eddy. He attended the South Royalton (Vt.) Academy and graduated from the University of Vermont in 1842. Hale taught at the academy in Montpelier before going back to Chelsea to study law. In January 1844 he moved to the village of Elizabethtown in northern New York and continued his legal studies at the office of Augustus C. Hand. Hale married Lovinia Sibley Stone, but the date of their marriage is unknown. They had a son and four daughters.

Hale was admitted to the bar in January 1847, and he then began a law partnership with Orlando Kellogg in Elizabethtown. The partnership continued until the fall of 1856, when Hale was elected county judge of Essex County. The "persuasive advocate" became "one of the most upright magistrates" (Hale, p. ix) and served on the bench for the next eight years before returning to private practice. During this time, Hale was recognized for his alert and accurate mind, impeccable scholarship, and authoritative knowledge of English literature and the classics. He was appointed a regent of the University of the State of New York and was active with that board from 1859 until his death. He was also an 1860 presidential elector for Abraham Lincoln.

In 1865 Hale was elected as a Republican to the Thirty-ninth Congress to fill the vacancy caused by the death of his former partner Kellogg. He served on the Committees on Militia, Manufactures, and Retrenchment. In 1866 he was a delegate to the National Union Convention in Philadelphia, where men of both parties hoped to elect a Congress that would unite moderate Democrats and moderate Republicans to stem the tide of radicalism. They were not successful. Hale left Congress at the end of his term and was then retained by Edwin M. Stanton, Lincoln's secretary of war, as counsel in Stanton's case against his removal by President Andrew Johnson.

During the years 1868–1870, Hale was a special counsel for the Treasury Department before the U.S. Court of Claims, charged with the defense of claims for abandoned and captured cotton. In 1870 he was nominated for judge of the New York Court of Appeals but was defeated in the election that went against the Republicans. In 1871 he was asked to return to Washington for the most important of the services he rendered his country.

President Ulysses S. Grant named Hale as agent of the United States before the Mixed Commission of American and British Claims, established under the Treaty of Washington. This treaty, negotiated between the United States and Great Britain in 1871, addressed complicated and controversial issues resulting from the Civil War and created the Mixed Commission to deal with the claims upon each government by the other. The commission met from May 1871 through September 1873, described by Hale in his report to Secretary of State Hamilton Fish as two years and more of "severe and unremitting labor." The commission was presented with and passed on nearly 500 claims, many dealing with international and legal fine points resulting from the recent war and transactions between the neutral nations of Europe and the former Confederacy.

It was Hale's job to present and support claims on behalf of his government and to answer claims against it, to represent the country in all investigations and decisions, and to act also as counsel for the United States. He was solely responsible for answering the claims of British subjects against the United States, about 90 percent of all the claims before the commission. The small number of American claims against Great Britain were handled by private counsels of the claimants with general supervision from Hale.

Hale's "Report," submitted to Fish on 30 November 1873, details the 478 British claims presented to the commission. Hale noted that the time allowed by the treaty for examination of the claims was short. Nevertheless, the tremendous volume of work was accomplished, and the outcome of the commission's investigations was most favorable. "The entire amount of the awards against the United States, including interest, allowed by the commission was . . . a trifle over two percent," or $1,929,819, although British claims against the United States totaled about $96 million.

Hale's last national public service was in Congress as a Republican representative from New York State. He was elected to the Forty-third Congress (4 Mar. 1873–3 Mar. 1875) and was chairman of the Committee on the District of Columbia. He did not seek reelection and returned to his mountain home, of which he spoke "with enthusiasm and with reverence" (Hale, p. xii). He was chosen the first president of the village of Elizabethtown in 1875 and 1876. In April 1876 he was appointed a commissioner of the state topographical survey and was still serving in this job when he died in Elizabethtown. Hale's pride in his Puritan heritage resulted in a detailed family genealogy, in which he traced his ancestry back to Thomas Hale of Watton, England, in the 1500s. The genealogy manuscript was edited and posthumously published, because, as the editor states, it contains "a vast amount of information outside of mere genealogical record" (Hale, p. v).

Hale was admired for his cultivated and alert mind, his courage, and his independence. As a legislator he was conscientious and well informed, and he practiced the same discretion that ruled his professional and private life. His friends felt the warmth of his companionship, and the board of regents appreciated his wise influence. A colleague on the board lamented, "His pleasant way of amending a written report by suggestive interlineations, . . . can never be forgotten" (Hale, p. x).

• Robert Safford Hale, *Genealogy of Descendants of Thomas Hale of Watton, England, and of Newbury, Mass.* (1889), is essential. It contains tributes to his memory presented at the annual meeting of the board of regents following Hale's death, which, while laudatory, include details from various perspectives on his intellect, character, and public service. The *Genealogy* also provides biographical information on Hale. For an understanding of Hale's most important service, see *Papers Relating to the Treaty of Washington*, vol. 6, *Washington Arbitration and General Appendix* (1874). An obituary is in the *New York Times*, 15 Dec. 1881.

SYLVIA LARSON

HALE, Sarah Josepha Buell (24 Oct. 1788–30 Apr. 1879), magazine editor, was born in Newport, New Hampshire, the daughter of Gordon Buell and Martha Whittlesey, farmers. She was educated at home, first by her mother and then by her brother, Horatio, who during his years at Dartmouth College outlined a course of study for his sister that paralleled his own. She taught school from 1806 until 1813. In 1813 she married David Hale, a lawyer, who continued her education. He died of pneumonia in 1822, leaving her with little money and the fear that their five children would be "deprived of the advantages of education." She subsequently began writing, she later said, "in the hope of gaining the means for [their] support and education." Friends of her husband helped establish her and her sister-in-law in a millinery business, but Hale did not succeed in the venture. In 1823 the same friends backed the publication of a book of her poetry, *The Genius of Oblivion*, by "A Lady of New Hampshire." At about this time, Hale also began publishing poems and short stories in literary journals. In 1827 she published a successful novel, *Northwood*, notable for its lucid prose style as well as for its portrayal of the domestic habits of the postcolonial period. It is also one of the first American novels to deal with the question of slavery, which Hale called a "stain on our national character . . . [which] crushes the talents and dwarfs the soul of both master and servant."

Hale's growing literary reputation led a Boston publishing firm to ask her to become the editor of the first American periodical planned exclusively for women. She accepted, and in the first issue of the *Ladies' Magazine* (Jan. 1828) she established her editorial policy: she would print only original material, rather than clipping articles from British periodicals as did other American journals; she would include women among her contributors; and she would print material of substance that would aid "female improvement." After arranging for four of her children, the eldest of whom was thirteen, to go to school or to live with relatives, she moved to Boston with her youngest son, then five. Hale's innovative editorship made the *Ladies' Magazine* very successful, and after a few years she became part owner. Then in 1837 Hale accepted the position of literary editor of *Godey's Lady's Book*, a women's periodical started by the enterprising Louis Godey in Philadelphia in 1830. Incorporating the *Ladies' Magazine* into *Godey's*, she remained in Boston until her sons graduated from Harvard, editing the Philadelphia-based magazine from a distance. Her purpose was still to improve the "moral and intellectual excellence" of women. In 1841 she moved to Philadelphia, where she lived for the rest of her life. She retired as editor of *Godey's* in 1877.

During her years as an editor, Hale led numerous causes. She spearheaded the fundraising effort necessary to complete the Bunker Hill Monument, and she worked to preserve the then-deteriorating Mount Vernon as a national shrine. In the 1860s she led the campaign to make Thanksgiving a national holiday. She also founded the Seaman's Aid Society, which set up employment and housing cooperatives for women as well as free libraries and job-training centers. She sponsored the Fatherless and Widow's Society to help alleviate the financial problems of poor women. At the *Ladies' Magazine* Hale was able to be more outspoken than she was at *Godey's*; Louis Godey would not allow political and religious issues to be discussed in his magazine. At both magazines, however, she focused on her principal themes: education for women and the advancement of women. She advocated the employing of female teachers and urged the establishment of state normal schools for women; she encouraged the growth of female seminaries; she worked closely with the founders of Vassar College and was responsible for the decision to appoint women to its faculty. Hale helped found schools for girls and was a close friend of educator Emma Willard. Although Hale was not a suffragist, she advocated women's entrance into many traditionally male areas of employment. She believed that all women should have the training and ability to support themselves "should the necessity occur." She was also an early advocate of married women's property rights.

Godey's Lady's Book is well known for its fashion plates (which Hale unsuccessfully opposed), but even more important were Hale's hard-hitting editorials, which expressed strong positions on issues of particular importance for women. In an age when women were regarded as natural invalids confined to the home, she urged the necessity for women doctors, women nurses, and women teachers and helped found schools for their training; she advocated physical exercise and fresh air for women, sensible dress, and an end to tight lacing. In addition, she supported the use of any labor-saving devices that would make domestic work easier, such as the sewing machine and the washing machine, and, in spite of religious opposition, she fought for the use of anesthesia for surgery and in childbirth. The influence of Hale's magazines derived from the unusual combination of the popular and the progressive. The fashion plates and Hale's conventionally feminine approach (she did not support woman suffrage, and from the first she appealed to men, pointing out that her magazine would not offend but would make women better wives and mothers because they would be better informed) captured the popular mind. They made her editorial positions on progressive issues all the more persuasive because they emanated from such an apparently inoffensive source.

In addition to her duties as editor, Hale wrote many books. She published a revised version of *Northwood* in 1852, with a preface making a plea for the Union, and the next year the novel *Liberia*, which outlined her plan to put an end to slavery and stressed the need for the education of blacks. Concluding that blacks would never receive fair treatment in a white society, Hale advocated colonization. Also in 1853 she published her most ambitious work, *Woman's Record; or, Sketches of Distinguished Women*, containing short biographies of over 2,000 women. This book was revised and reprinted several times. Hale's other books include *Flora's Interpreter* (1832), *Traits of American Life* (1835), *The Ladies' Wreath* (1837), *Ladies' New Book of Cookery* (1852), and *Manners* (1867). She also wrote books for children, the most significant of which was *Poems for Our Children* (1830), which contained her famous poem "Mary Had a Little Lamb." This and other poems were reprinted, often without credit, in the *McGuffey's Readers* and other collections for young people.

• Letters from Hale can be found at numerous repositories, including the Houghton Library at Harvard University, the Schlesinger Library at Radcliffe College, the Pierpont Morgan Library in New York City, Vassar College Library, the Historical Society of Pennsylvania, and the Huntington Library in San Marino, Calif. Hale published brief biographical sketches of herself in *Godey's Lady's Book*, Dec. 1850, Dec. 1877; *The Ladies' Wreath* (1837); and *Woman's Record* (1853). Biographies include Ruth E. Finley, *The Lady of Godey's: Sarah Josepha Hale* (1931), and Sherbrooke Rogers, *Sarah Josepha Hale: A New England Pioneer* (1985).
JOYCE W. WARREN

HALE, Susan (5 Dec. 1833–17 Sept. 1910), writer and painter, was born in Boston, Massachusetts, the daughter of Nathan Hale, owner and editor of the *Boston Daily Advertiser*, and Sarah Preston Everett, a linguist, writer, and the sister of statesman Edward Everett. Susan Hale grew up in a literary and intellectual environment that served as the major educational force of her early years. She studied with private tutors until she was sixteen and then attended George B. Emerson's private school in Boston. Hale began her career as a teacher, offering classes for young boys in her parents' Boston home and continuing to teach after the family moved to Brookline in 1860.

In 1867, after both of her parents had died, Hale accompanied her sister Lucretia to Egypt to visit their brother Charles, who served as the U.S. consul general there. Upon her return to Boston in 1868, Hale took rooms at 91 Boylston Street and resumed teaching. She also contributed articles in support of various local benefits, including the Sanitary Commission Fairs, and acted as editor for their publications. Her interest in painting, evident since she was a young girl, continued to develop, and in 1872 she traveled to Europe, where she spent a year studying art in Paris and Germany. Hale settled in Boston once again in 1873 and offered classes in watercolor painting at the Boston Art Club; she also offered her services as a reader to several upper-class, elderly Bostonians, and she contributed articles on travel, literature, and Boston's colonial past to several local newspapers. She was an active preservationist and edited the journal *Dial of the Old South Clock*, which was published in connection with the effort to restore Boston's Old South Meeting House in the late 1870s. During the summer Hale traveled along the coast of New England, frequently to Maine, where she made series of watercolor sketches that she exhibited at the Boston Art Club in the fall.

In 1881 Hale collaborated with her brother, Reverend Edward Everett Hale, to write the first of a series of illustrated books, *A Family Flight through France, Germany, Norway, and Switzerland*. This volume was followed by five other travel books covering Egypt and Syria (1882), New England (1884), Mexico (1886), Spain (1886), and young Americans abroad (1898). Hale also provided many of the illustrations for these volumes; on her own, she wrote six other books: *A Family Flight through Spain* (1883), *Self-Instructive Lessons in Painting with Oil and Water-Colors* (1885), *Life and Letters of Thomas Gold Appleton* (1885), *The Story of Mexico* (1889), *Men and Manners of the Eighteenth Century* (1898), and *Young Americans in Spain* (1899).

The close relationship Hale shared with her brother Edward and his children was strengthened by the summers they all spent together at Edward's country house in Matunuck, Rhode Island. Susan Hale first stayed there in 1883 to help care for her young nephews; two years later she adopted it as her own home, spending every summer there and traveling—to Europe, California, Mexico (with the painter Frederic Church), Algeria, Egypt, and Jamaica—during the winter. She is often counted as the first art teacher of her talented niece and nephew, Ellen Day Hale and Philip Leslie Hale. She and Ellen exhibited their work together, along with that of their friend Helen Knowlton, at the Boston Art Club in 1878. Hale's watercolors, predominantly landscapes made during her travels, are characterized by their free handling and broad strokes of wash.

An insatiable reader both in private and for genteel public entertainments, Susan Hale was also a prolific and descriptive letter writer, most frequently to her sister Lucretia, to whom she vividly described her many journeys. Together with her watercolor sketches, Hale left a legacy of enthusiasm and intellectual accomplishment that had a lasting effect on her family and associates. Hale never married; she died in Matunuck.

• Hale's papers and some of her sketchbooks are included in the Sophia Smith Collection, Smith College, Northampton, Mass. Selections from her letters were edited and published by her friend Caroline P. Atkinson as *Letters of Susan Hale* (1919); this volume, with its biographical introduction by her nephew Edward Hale, is the main source of information on Hale's life. Hale is mentioned in Clara Erskine Clement and Laurence Hutton, *Artists of the Nineteenth Century* (1879). Obituaries are in the *New York Times*, 18 Sept. 1910, and *Boston Evening Transcript*, 17 Sept. 1910.

ERICA E. HIRSHLER

HALEY, Alex (11 Aug. 1921–10 Feb. 1992), writer, was born Alexander Palmer Haley in Ithaca, New York, the son of Simon Alexander Haley, a graduate student in agriculture at Cornell University, and Bertha George Palmer, a music student at the Ithaca Conservatory of Music. Young Alex Haley grew up in the family home in Henning, Tennessee, where his grandfather Will Palmer owned a lumber business. When the business was sold in 1929, Simon Haley moved his family to southern black college communities, including Alabama Agricultural and Mechanical College in Normal (near Huntsville), Alabama, where he had his longest tenure teaching agriculture. The three sons of Bertha and Simon Haley, Alex, George, and Julius, spent their summers in Henning, where, in the mid-1930s, grandmother Cynthia Murray Palmer recounted for her grandsons the family stories of its history.

After graduating from high school in Normal, Alex Haley studied to become a teacher at Elizabeth City State Teachers College in North Carolina from 1937 to 1939. In 1939 he enlisted in the U.S. Coast Guard. Two years later Haley married Nannie Branch. They had two children. Haley spent twenty years in the coast guard, advancing from mess boy to ship's cook on a munitions ship, the USS *Murzin*, in the South Pacific during World War II. To relieve his boredom, he began writing, love letters for fellow shipmates at first, then romance fiction, which brought many rejection letters from periodicals such as *True Confessions* and *Modern Romances*. Finally, Haley sold three stories on the history of the coast guard to *Coronet*. In 1949 the coast guard created the position of chief journalist for him. Haley did public relations, wrote speeches, and worked with the press on rescue stories for the coast guard until he retired in 1959.

Failing to find other work and sustained by his military pension, Haley moved to Greenwich Village to work as a freelance writer in 1959. Casting about for

his subject and voice, his early articles included a feature on Phyllis Diller for the *Saturday Evening Post*. Two articles for *Reader's Digest* were better indicators of Haley's future work. One was a feature on black Muslim leader Elijah Muhammad; the other was an article about his brother George, who was the first African-American student at the University of Arkansas law school in 1949 and would be elected to the Kansas state legislature in the 1960s. In 1962 *Playboy* hired Haley to produce a series of interviews with prominent African Americans: Miles Davis, Cassius Clay (Muhammad Ali), Jim Brown, Sammy Davis, Jr., Quincy Jones, Leontyne Price, and Malcolm X. The last interview was the genesis of Haley's first important book, *The Autobiography of Malcolm X* (1965). Based on extensive interviews with the religious leader, the book was Haley's artistic creation and has won an important place in American biography. His marriage to his first wife ended in 1964; that same year Haley married Juliette Collins. They had one child before their divorce in 1972.

Haley's second important book was even more his own story than *The Autobiography*. Recalling stories recounted to him by his grandmother twenty-five years earlier, he had begun research on his family's history as early as 1961. Backed by a contract from Doubleday, Haley began serious work on a book that was initially to be called *Before This Anger*. His research trips across the South took him to Gambia, West Africa, where a griot identified an ancestor as Kunte Kinte. In 1972 Haley founded and became the president of the Kinte Foundation of Washington, D.C., which sought to encourage research in African-American history and genealogy. *Roots: The Saga of an American Family* (1976) finally appeared in the bicentennial year to great fanfare. A historical novel that invited acceptance as a work of history, it told the story of the family's origins in West Africa, its experience in slavery, and its subsequent history. A bestselling book that won a Pulitzer Prize, *Roots* had even greater impact when it was made into a gripping television miniseries. Broadcast by ABC in January and February 1977, it was seen, in whole or in part, by 130 million people. It stimulated interest and pride in the African-American experience and had a much greater immediate impact than did *The Autobiography*.

In 1977, however, Margaret Walker brought suit against Haley for plagiarism from her novel *Jubilee*. Her case was dismissed. Subsequently, however, Haley reached an out-of-court settlement for $650,000 with novelist Harold Courlander, who alleged that passages in *Roots* were taken from his *The Slave*. Haley acknowledged that *Roots* was a combination of fact and fiction. By 1981 professional historians were challenging the genealogical and historical reliability of the book. A third lawsuit for plagiarism was filed in 1989 by Emma Lee Davis Paul. The symbolic significance of the linkage in *Roots* of the African-American experience to its African origins for a mass audience continues to be important. Yet, by the time of Haley's death, renewed interest in Malcolm X and questions about the originality and reliability of *Roots* seemed to have reversed early judgments about the relative importance of the two books.

In 1988 Haley published *A Different Kind of Christmas*, a historical novella about the Underground Railroad. When he died in Seattle, Washington, Haley was separated from his third wife, Myra Lewis, and there were legal claims of more than $1.5 million against his estate. The primary claimants were First Tennessee Bank, his first and third wives, and many creditors, including a longtime researcher, George Sims. The bank held a mortgage of almost $1 million on Haley's 127-acre farm near Norris, Tennessee. His first wife claimed that their 1964 divorce was not valid, and his third wife claimed entitlement to one-third of the estate. The executor of Haley's estate was his brother George, who had been chief counsel to the U.S. Information Agency and chaired the U.S. Postal Rate Commission. George Haley concluded that the estate must be sold. In a dramatic sale on 1–3 October 1992, Alex Haley's estate, including his manuscripts, was auctioned to the highest bidder. His novel *Queen: The Story of an American Family*, based on the life of his paternal grandmother, was published posthumously in 1993 and was the basis of a television miniseries that aired in February 1994. A second novel, *Henning*, which was named for the small community in West Tennessee where Haley lived as a child and is buried, remains unpublished.

• Alex Haley's literary estate is dispersed. Two manuscripts of his early interviews for *Playboy*, including the one with Malcolm X, are in private hands, but the rest of them, research files on Malcolm X, and forty-nine volumes of *Roots* in various languages are at New York City's Schomberg Center for Research in Black Culture. Haley's manuscript of *The Autobiography of Malcolm X* is in private hands, but the publisher's copy is in the Grove Press Archive at Syracuse University. The manuscript and research material for *Roots* are at the University of Tennessee, Knoxville. On Haley's development as a writer, see Haskel Frankel, "Interviewing the Interviewer," *Saturday Review*, 5 Feb. 1966, pp. 37–38; Robert Bain et al., eds., *Southern Writers: A Biographical Dictionary* (1979); and Mary Siebert McCauley, "Alex Haley, a Southern Griot: A Literary Biography" (Ph.D. diss., George Peabody College for Teachers of Vanderbilt Univ., 1983). On *Roots*, see Alex Haley, "Roots: A Black American's Search for His Ancestral African," *Ebony*, Aug. 1976, pp. 100–102, 104, 106–7; David Gerber, "Haley's *Roots* and Our Own: An Inquiry into the Nature of a Popular Phenomenon," *Journal of Ethnic Studies* 3 (1977): 87–111; David L. Wolper, *The Inside Story of TV's "Roots"* (1978); Gary B. and Elizabeth B. Shown Mills, "Roots and the New Faction: A Legitimate Tool for Clio?" *Virginia Magazine of History and Biography* 89 (Jan. 1981): 3–26; Philip Nobile, "Uncovering *Roots*," *Village Voice*, 23 Feb. 1993; pp. 31–38; Jesse T. Moore, Jr., "Alex Haley's *Roots*: Ten Years Later," *Western Journal of Black Studies* 18 (Summer 1994): 70–76; and Helen Taylor, " 'The Griot from Tennessee': The Saga of Alex Haley's *Roots*," *Critical Quarterly* 37 (Summer 1995): 46–62. An obituary is in the *New York Times*, 11 Feb. 1992.

RALPH E. LUKER

HALEY, Bill (6 July 1925–9 Feb. 1981), singer and bandleader, was born William John Clifton Haley, Jr., in Highland Park, Michigan, the son of William Haley and Manda Green. He grew up during the depression in the area of Chester, Pennsylvania, where his father had found work in a shipyard. The Haley household enjoyed music; Bill's father played the mandolin, and his mother played and taught piano. Bill received his first guitar at age seven and soon began to play and sing cowboy and hillbilly songs. His musical tastes came partly from his father, a Kentuckian, and his models were radio singers and cowboy film stars of the period—performers such as Hank Williams, Gene Autry, and Bob Wills. Loss of sight in his left eye (from a childhood operation) kept him out of military service, and so at a time when young men expected to be drafted at age eighteen, Haley could hawk his musical wares at fairs, auction barns, and amusement parks in eastern Pennsylvania and adjacent states. With guitar, cowboy boots, and hat, advertising himself as "Yodeling Bill Haley," he was determined to leave his mark on the world of country music.

There followed several years of obscurity, experimentation, and travel. Starting as a guitarist and yodeler on a radio show in Wilmington, Delaware, in the early 1940s, he played with the Downhomers in Fort Wayne, Indiana, and with the Range Rovers. He performed on the National Barn Dance radio show and other local programs. He married Dorothy Crowe in 1946, and the first of their two children was born in 1947. He returned to Chester at the end of the 1940s, tired and somewhat discouraged. There he worked at the local radio station and formed his first band, the Four Aces of Western Swing, renamed the Saddlemen in 1949. Finding country music limiting for the local (Philadelphia area) market, he began to branch out, seeking to "crossover" to broader popular music, to rhythm and blues, or both—the sort of musical intermixing being practiced by artists such as Red Foley ("Chattanooga Shoe Shine Boy"), Bob Wills and his western swing, Tony Bennett ("Cold, Cold Heart"), and Patti Page ("Tennessee Waltz"). Fats Domino and other singers had begun to make black, "race" music popular with white people.

Anxious to find his niche, Haley exploited all these trends. The Saddlemen began to pick up the beat, feature different instruments, and show more life on stage. In 1951 Haley agreed to record "Rocket 88," a hot rhythm and blues song about a car (the Oldsmobile 88). Then came "Rock the Joint," a loud and lively piece often used in public appearances. Haley considered "Rock the Joint," which caught on with young people, the first rock and roll record. The transformation became complete in 1953 when the band exchanged boots and hats for tuxedoes, and the Saddlemen became Bill Haley and his Comets. The Comets' first recording, Haley's own composition, "Crazy, Man, Crazy," became the first rock and roll record to reach the top-twenty list. It also led to a contract with Decca, a first-rate recording company.

The first session with Decca in 1954 produced "Rock around the Clock," a rock piece already recorded by another band. Sales were disappointing, not as large as for another record released later that year, "Shake, Rattle and Roll," which eventually reached sales of 1 million. Then in 1955 "Rock around the Clock" was adopted as the theme for *Blackboard Jungle*, a grade-A movie about juvenile rebellion. The record then took off, standing as the national bestselling single for seven consecutive weeks. Featured later in another film, the song became Haley's trademark and stood for many years as an anthem of a new wave of popular music, if not of an emerging subculture of youth. Worldwide sales by the 1980s had passed 30 million.

Haley's years of glory came in the last half of the 1950s, especially in 1955–1956. The Comets turned out many records, of which "See You Later, Alligator" became a third multimillion seller. Haley was in constant demand for interviews and personal appearances in all aspects of the entertainment media. Popularity in the United States was duplicated in travel abroad, in Mexico, in Europe, and especially in Britain, where in 1957 he received an exceptionally friendly and noisy welcome.

The Comets as a rule comprised six or seven men playing mostly stringed instruments, drums, and a saxophone. Personnel frequently changed; perhaps the steadiest and most talented performer was saxophonist Rudy Pompilli. Haley played guitar and was lead singer. The music was loud, driving, and highly danceable. The musicians performed various antics onstage: the bass fiddle player twirled the instrument, and Pompilli played lying on his back. A Comets performance produced an atmosphere of excitement and spontaneity, a message that it was acceptable, and a great deal of fun, to let oneself go—a precursor to rock performances of years to come.

The star, however, did not shine long. Haley's popularity lasted longer in foreign countries, but it dropped with remarkable speed in the United States. There always had been detractors, of course, people who saw only immoral and dangerous elements in this new music. *Blackboard Jungle* had identified rock music with alienation and rebellion, and the Comets' concerts at times did produce rowdyism if not destructive behavior from young people in the audience. But Haley's popularity waned not because rock music lost its appeal but because its form shifted and he could not compete with younger, more creative and timely performers. Elvis Presley, with a new style and enormous sex appeal, surfaced only a year or so after Haley. This chubby-faced married man with short hair and wayward left eye, now approaching middle age, seemed out of touch with the cultural themes that emerged in the 1960s and early 1970s.

Haley's personal life contributed to his decline. After his first marriage ended in divorce, in 1952 he married Barbara Joan Cupchack, with whom he had two children, only one of whom survived infancy. They also were divorced. He began to drink heavily. A terri-

ble manager of money, in 1962 he fled to Mexico to escape debts and taxes. That same year he married Martha Velasco, a Mexican dancer. The band folded and reformed with different people. Pompilli died in 1976. In some years the band produced no records, and those that did appear were mostly recycled old music, country songs, and even some records in Spanish. Haley lived his last years mostly in Texas or Mexico. Little was heard from or about him except during periods of nostalgia about the 1950s. Quests for the origins of rock invariably led to brief bursts of recognition and acclaim, as occurred in New York in 1969 and London in 1964, 1968, and 1979. But they changed nothing. At the end Haley was a broken man, an alcoholic given to bizarre and irrational behavior. He died in Harlingen, Texas, of a heart attack.

Haley arrived on the stage of American entertainment at a time of transition. The swing music that had dominated for some two decades had run its course. That there was a restlessness, especially among youth, and that the time had come for something different could be detected in the popularity of the "rebels," notably Marlon Brando and James Dean, in the movies. In popular music, as perhaps in society in general, the mood called for more spirit and freedom and less structure and inhibition, in tune with rhythm and blues, or what for years had been identified as black music. Haley entered this void, and the appearance of *Blackboard Jungle*, which provided astonishing international exposure, was an enormous stroke of luck. His songs of the mid-1950s became the first nationally and internationally popular rock and roll records. The Comets soon fell victim to new moods and new rock stars, but Bill Haley's name still stood as one of the first of a small group of people who started American popular music and, indirectly, social behavior on a new, far-reaching course. Haley was inducted into the rock music hall of fame in 1986, one of its first members.

• John Swenson, *Bill Haley: The Daddy of Rock and Roll* (1982), is a useful and sympathetic but candid account that relies heavily on interviews. Shorter discussions of Haley's career appear in Arnold Shaw, *The Rockin' 50s: The Decade That Transformed the Pop Music Scene* (1974), which includes an interview with Haley; Anthony De Curtis and James Henke, *The Rolling Stone Illustrated History of Rock and Roll* (1980); and Lee Cotten, *Shake, Rattle and Roll: The Golden Age of American Rock, 1952–1955* (1989). William Clark, "'The Kids Really Fit': Rock Text and Rock Practices in Bill Haley's 'Rock around the Clock,'" *Popular Music and Society* 18, no. 4 (1994), analyzes Haley's best-known song. An obituary is in the *New York Times*, 10. Feb. 1981.

ROSS GREGORY

HALEY, Jack (10 Aug. 1899–6 June 1979), comedian, singer, and dancer, was born John Haley in Boston, Massachusetts, the son of John Haley, a ship's navigator, and Ellen Curley. Haley's desire to be in show business began in childhood, when he appeared in a church entertainment at the age of six. After completing his schooling at Boston English High School, he became an apprentice electrician at his mother's urging. As soon as he had saved up some of his apprentice earnings, however, he left to make his way on the stage.

According to his account in *The Vaudevillians*, Haley joined a friend in Philadelphia and took tap dancing lessons there while working as a song plugger for a music publishing company. His teacher placed him as a juvenile with a musical comedy sketch playing small-time vaudeville. Later he joined another troupe, the Lightner Girls and Alexander, as a comic. He then teamed up with another Bostonian, Charley Crafts, to form the song, dance, and comedy duo of Haley and Crafts. So successful was the new act that in six months, in 1920, they played vaudeville's great showplace, the Palace in New York City.

The song-and-dance team continued to tour the vaudeville circuits for the next three years. Haley remembered his vaudeville days with appreciation. "One of the great things about vaudeville," he said later in a press release, "was that you learned to play before so many different kinds of audiences . . . you learned to think fast and to act fast and to adapt your act to the crowd." Nevertheless, he said in *The Vaudevillians*, "we all dreamed of getting into a musical comedy . . . because then we could have an apartment. Wouldn't have to live out of a trunk, as we usually did" (p. 133). Haley's chance came when he was cast in the revue *Around the Town* (1924). Another revue, *Gay Paree* (1925), followed. Between a matinee and evening performance during the show's run, Haley married Florence McFadden, a dancer whom he had met while both were with the Lightner troupe.

Haley now formed a vaudeville act with his wife, and the pair toured for the next two seasons. In 1927 he went to Los Angeles to appear as an entertainer in a short talking film for Vitaphone. More shorts for Warners in New York followed. His comedy persona was by now established: he played a wide-eyed, somewhat shy and ingenuous fellow, what he called a "Milquetoast" character. He also made use of a pleasing tenor singing voice. Offstage, he was a steady family man with a good head for business. Liking the settled life that the movie colony offered, Haley in 1927 took a job as master of ceremonies for the stage productions at a silent-film theater, Loew's State, in Los Angeles.

In 1928 Haley was offered a place in the Chicago company of the hit musical comedy *Good News*. It proved to be the break he had been looking for. So successful was he in the show that its producers gave him one of the comedy leads in another musical, *Follow Thru*, that opened on Broadway in 1929. In it he introduced the hit song "Button up Your Overcoat." The show was a spoof of country club life, and Haley's "burlesque of golfing" with another of the show's comics was rated "bully nonsense" (*New York Herald Tribune*, 10 Jan. 1929). He returned to Hollywood to play in the film version of *Follow Thru* (1930). The film reviewer for the *New York Times* declared him "by far the most amusing character in this cinema offering" (13 Sept. 1930).

Haley's next success in Broadway musical comedy was with Ethel Merman in *Take a Chance* (1932). They sang together another song hit of the period, "You're an Old Smoothie." The *New York Times* reviewer found him "the least studied of our mountebanks. Droll and joyous and slightly demented, he is as irresponsible as a college buffoon. . . . When he sang 'Smoothie' with Miss Merman at the opening performance the audience roared with [show-stopping] pleasure" (28 Nov. 1932). Reportedly, the first night crowd demanded thirteen encores before the show could continue.

Now in demand for screen musicals, Haley and his wife and two children spent the next years in Hollywood. He appeared with Ginger Rogers in *Sitting Pretty* (1933), in which he introduced another hit, "Did You Ever See a Dream Walking?" He made three musicals with Alice Faye: *Poor Little Rich Girl* (1936), *Wake Up and Live* (1937), and *Alexander's Ragtime Band* (1938). The star of *Poor Little Rich Girl* was Shirley Temple, with whom Haley appeared again in *Rebecca of Sunnybrook Farm* (1938). During the 1930s Haley began investing his movie earnings in California real estate. He deemed it an obvious business move: a biographical sketch in the *Dictionary of American Biography* by Michael Goldberg quotes him as saying, "A man had to be an idiot not to succeed in buying, selling and developing land in Southern California over the years."

In 1939 Haley was cast as the Tin Woodman in *The Wizard of Oz*. He was brought in as a replacement for dancer Buddy Ebsen, who proved to be allergic to the metallic make-up required for the part. At the time it was just one more movie role for Haley, and an especially arduous one because of the discomfort of his costume and make-up. His son, the television director and producer Jack Haley, Jr., recalled that when some of the make-up got into his father's eye, the result was a week in a totally darkened room so that the eye could recover. He had a dance number in the movie, to "If I Only Had a Heart," that Naomi Cohen-Stratyner notes as showing his "specialties" as a dancer: "his ability to handle complicated rhythms, his isolated movements, and his exceptional balance as seen in the exaggerated leanings and sways."

Haley did not think much of the movie's script. "There was no acting," he was quoted in *The Making of the Wizard of Oz*. "It was all movement. We were running all the time. We were always afraid. We had three lines and then we were off to see the Wizard" (p. 158). Only gradually, according to his son, did he "realize that this movie would represent the pinnacle of his long and successful career. I suspect he thought there were other efforts more worthy of recognition—but the enduring popularity of *Oz* eventually got to him. He finally joined the other millions who gathered each year to watch the television broadcast of this wonderfully endearing film" (p. ix).

In the 1940s Haley enlarged his field of activities to include radio shows and Broadway entertainments—*Higher and Higher* (1940), *Show Time* (1942), and *In-*

side U.S.A. (1948)—as well as more motion pictures. His Los Angeles real estate holdings also enlarged greatly until, as Jack Benny quipped, "Every time you drive down Wilshire Boulevard, you're trespassing on Jack Haley's property." In 1949 he willingly retired from show business to manage the properties that had made him a millionaire. Vernon Scott, interviewing him years later, wrote that "he flashed his Irish grin and said 'There's a time to take the center of the stage, and a time to walk into the wings. A smart performer knows when to get off.'"

He appeared occasionally on television talk shows during the 1960s, sharing his show business memories. He also made a cameo appearance in his son's movie *Norwood* (1970). His last appearance was with Ray Bolger, fellow performer in *The Wizard of Oz*, in the 1979 Academy Awards ceremony produced by his son. He died in Beverly Hills, California.

• Materials on the life and career of Haley are in the Billy Rose Theatre Collection at the New York Public Library for the Performing Arts, Lincoln Center; two press releases from the 1940s in the collection give extensive information on Haley. His reminiscences are quoted in Bill Smith, *The Vaudevillians* (1976). Other Haley comments and biographical details are in Vernon Scott, "Haley Smiles in the Wings," *Jersey Record*, 8 Sept. 1974. His role as the Tin Woodman is discussed in Naomi Cohen-Stratyner, "Jack Haley," *Biographical Dictionary of Dance* (1982); Aljean Harmetz, *The Making of the Wizard of Oz* (1984); and Jack Haley, Jr.'s introduction to *The Wizard of Oz: The Official 50th Anniversary Pictorial History* (1989). Obituaries are in the *New York Times* and the *Los Angeles Times*, both 7 June 1979.

WILLIAM STEPHENSON

HALEY, Margaret Angela (15 Nov. 1861–5 Jan. 1939), leader of the Chicago Teachers Federation, was born in Joliet, Illinois, the daughter of Michael Haley and Elizabeth Tiernan. Haley's mother was born in Dublin; her father was born in Canada of Irish immigrants and learned his trade in construction on the Illinois and Michigan canals. During Haley's early youth, her father was a farmer, and Haley attended a rural one-room schoolhouse. When she was ten, her father lost his farm and moved the family to a number of towns in northern Illinois, where he operated a stone quarry and later a construction firm. Haley attended grade school in Channahon, Illinois, and St. Angela's Convent in Morris. At age sixteen she was, as she recalled, "catapulted" into teaching by her father's financial troubles, and she taught at country schools in Dresden Heights, Illinois, and a grade school near Joliet. After a semester of teacher training at the State Normal School at Bloomington, she moved to Chicago in 1880, having resigned from her teaching job after she was refused an increase of five dollars a month.

Haley began teaching in Chicago area schools in 1882, taking a semester's leave in 1884 to study at the Cook County Normal School under its new principal, Colonel Francis W. Parker, already renowned for his promotion of classroom instruction based on children's self-discovery. From 1884 to 1900 Haley taught

in the Hendricks Elementary School in the town of Lake, a sprawling stockyard district in an area south and west of Chicago that was annexed to the city in 1889. Following her continuing interest in progressive pedagogy, Haley maintained her connections with the Cook County Normal School and attended summer school at the Buffalo School of Pedagogy.

Haley joined the Chicago Teachers Federation (CTF), organized in 1897 under the leadership of teacher Catherine Goggin to represent elementary school teachers in response to an attack on the newly instituted teachers' pension law. Haley's activism with the CTF accelerated with the 1898 Harper Commission's proposal to reform Chicago schools, a plan that included the creation of a smaller and more powerful school administration, the adoption of business principles in school management, and a freeze on teacher salary increases previously promised by the Chicago Board of Education. Haley, now district vice president of the CTF, took on the investigation of the shortage of school funds that the board claimed necessitated the freeze. She found that a number of Chicago's largest corporations, including the Pullman Company, were being underassessed for taxes by the Chicago Board of Equalizers. In 1902 the CTF secured a writ of mandamus forcing that board to assess the corporations their full value. The companies appealed the case to the Illinois Supreme Court, which in 1907 upheld the lower court ruling. The CTF was eventually successful: the corporations paid nearly $600,000 in back taxes to Cook County, $250,000 of which went to the board of education. When the board voted to use the funds for school maintenance rather than teacher salaries, the CTF again resorted to court action to win the promised salary increases. Haley's leadership of the fight for tax equity gained national attention, drawing the support of former state governor Judge John Altgeld, Jane Addams, and William Randolph Hearst's muckraking *Chicago American*. The fight also spurred teacher membership and loyalty to Haley and the CTF: by 1900 over half of all Chicago elementary school teachers were members of the Chicago Teachers Federation.

As the emerging leader of the CTF, Haley molded the group into a powerful political force in Chicago politics. She consistently advocated improved teachers' working conditions, a secure pension plan, increased salaries, and tenure laws. To strengthen the authority of the CTF, she negotiated an unprecedented affiliation with organized labor by joining with the Chicago Federation of Labor in 1902. In 1916 the CTF became Local 1 of the newly formed American Federation of Teachers.

Haley's vision of the CTF as a professionalizing force for teachers led her to advocate a broad platform of educational and administrative reforms, including representative teacher councils in schools, improved teacher education, and the promotion of democratic, child-centered pedagogy. Under Haley, the CTF sponsored Saturday and after-school classes and lectures for teachers, provided curriculum resources, and reported on new and progressive ideas in education in the monthly *Chicago Teachers' Federation Bulletin* and the *Margaret Haley Bulletin*. The CTF also conducted investigations and surveys of Chicago and other city schools and inquiries of teachers' needs. Under Haley, the CTF developed great political clout in Chicago, and through the 1920s, it took stands opposing corporate contributions to schools, vocational education, and the cost-efficient rationale of the double session class schedule known as the platoon system. It supported child labor laws, direct primaries, woman suffrage, and local Democratic candidates who supported labor and teachers.

Haley's activism drew her outside of Chicago politics to the national education stage. In 1901 she became the first woman and first elementary school teacher to speak from the floor of the National Education Association. She mobilized her forces to pressure the NEA to liberalize its voting procedures to include classroom teachers. In 1910 she organized a successful campaign to elect Chicago superintendent and CTF friend Ella Flagg Young to be the first woman president of the NEA. In her notorious 1904 speech before the NEA, "Why Teachers Should Organize," Haley laid out her reform proposals not only for the organization of protective unions for teachers, but also for an expanded notion of teacher professionalism that included the opportunity to develop progressive pedagogy, improve educational practice, and promote the democratic participation of teachers in school administration.

The breadth of Haley's political objectives often worked against her, and she was forced to balance her broader social goals with achieving the material goals in salary, benefits, and working conditions that her membership demanded of her. To accomplish such goals, Haley often practiced particularly undemocratic policies. In 1900 Haley left the classroom to become the paid business representative of the CTF, a position she held until her death. She never returned to the classroom, although she always considered herself a teacher who worked for teachers' interests. As a leader she was both dynamic and controlling, dominating CTF meetings with expansive monologues about injustice and lecturing directives to her membership. She increasingly expressed frustration with the shortsighted, self-interested views of teachers and railed against their political conservatism.

Haley's CTF was at its peak influence between 1909 and 1915 when Young was superintendent of the Chicago schools. In 1915, however, the board of education adopted the Loeb rule—what Young called the "Dred Scott decision of American education"—which forbade teachers from membership in labor unions or any organization affiliated with trade unions or in any organization that had officers who were not teachers. Haley sought protection from the courts and a newly passed state tenure law, but in 1917 she was pressured to withdraw the CTF from the AFL. Through the antilabor 1920s the CTF declined in power when a new superintendent abolished the teacher councils that had

been introduced by Young and instituted the notorious platoon system of school scheduling that Haley argued was the ultimate in the "factoryization" of education. Haley spent her last years in semiretirement and died in Chicago.

Haley's individual politics took her across a wide spectrum of the American Left. She supported woman suffrage, was a member of the Women's Trade Union League, and served on the executive committee of a newly formed Labor party that ran John Fitzpatrick, president of the Chicago Federation of Labor, for mayor of the city in 1919. She lived and worked in a wide circle of women friends, colleagues, and political leaders, including Jane Addams, Ella Flagg Young, and Goggin, with whom Haley lived for fifteen years until Goggin's death in 1916. Although Haley was a swaggering giant in Chicago and educational politics, in physical appearance she was petite and always neatly dressed. Tiny even as a child, Haley could disarm her opponents by her femininity and maneuver loyalties among city, labor, and education officials. She was notorious in local Chicago politics for being a constant irritant to her opponents and for being almost untouchable herself. Carl Sandburg wrote in the Chicago daily *Day Book*: "For fifteen years this one little woman has flung her clenched fist into the faces of contractors, school land lease holders, tax dodgers and their politicians, fixers, go-betweens and stool pigeons," and never have her enemies "been able to smutch her once in the eyes of decent men and women of this town who do their own thinking" (24 Sept. 1915).

• The papers of the Chicago Teachers Federation, at the Chicago Historical Society, contain a wealth of original material on Haley, including the complete run of the *Chicago Teachers' Federation Bulletin* (1901–1908) and *Margaret Haley's Bulletin* (1915–1916 and 1925–1931), some correspondence, and transcripts of federation meetings led by Haley. See also *Battleground: The Autobiography of Margaret A. Haley*, ed. Robert L. Reid (1982). Contemporary articles of interest include William Hard, "Chicago's Five Maiden Aunts," *American Magazine*, Sept. 1906, pp. 481–89; David S. Ricker, "The School Teacher Unionized," *Educational Review* 30 (Nov. 1905): 344–46; George Creel, "Why Chicago Teachers Unionized," *Harper's Weekly*, 19 June 1915, pp. 598–600; and Carl Sandburg, "Margaret Haley," *Reedy's Mirror*, Dec. 1915, p. 445. Several monographs study Haley's role in Chicago's educational politics at the turn of the century, including Mary J. Herrick, *The Chicago Schools: A Social and Political History* (1971); Julia Wrigley, *Class, Politics and Public Schools: Chicago 1900–1950* (1982); and David Hogan, *Class and Reform: School and Society in Chicago 1880–1930* (1985). Studies of American teacher unions that analyze Haley's role as a union leader are Wayne J. Urban, *Why Teachers Organized* (1982); Marjorie Murphy, *Blackboard Unions: The AFT and the NEA 1900–1980* (1990); Cherry Collins, "Regaining the Past for the Present: The Legacy of the Chicago Teachers' Federation," *History of Education Review* 13 (1984): 43–55; and Maureen McCormack, "Margaret A. Haley, 1861–1939: A Timeless Mentor for Teachers as Leaders," in *Inside Out: Contemporary Critical Perspectives in Education*, ed. Rebecca A. Martusewicz and William M. Reynolds (1994). See also

Marjorie Murphy, "From Artisan to Semi-Professional: White Collar Unionism among Chicago Public School Teachers, 1870–1930" (Ph.D. diss., Univ. of California, 1981).

KATE ROUSMANIERE

HALL, Abraham Oakey (26 July 1826–7 Oct. 1898), politician and journalist, was born in Albany, New York, the son of Morgan James Hall, a wholesale merchant whose business was in New Orleans, and Elsie Lansing Oakey. In 1830 his father died of yellow fever and his mother moved to New York City, where she ran a boardinghouse. Relatives helped his mother finance his education, and Oakey (as he preferred to be called) graduated from New York University in 1844. He attended Harvard Law School for one term but decided that study in a law office would allow him to practice law sooner. Living with an uncle in New Orleans, he studied under noted states' rights Democrats John Slidell and Thomas Slidell and won admission to the Louisiana bar in 1846. In New Orleans the clever and witty Hall also continued the practice, begun in college, of writing for newspapers and magazines. Although a lawyer by profession, he loved the arts. Throughout his life, writers, actors, producers, poets, and fellow devotees of the arts would be his closest friends, and he himself would write not only pieces for the news journals but plays, stories, children's books, and thousands of verses, none of them, however, regarded seriously either then or now.

Since New Orleans offered economic opportunities but few cultural amenities, Hall returned to New York City in 1848 and was admitted to the New York bar in 1849. He married Katherine Louise Barnes in 1849, with whom he had seven children. Noted lawyer Nathaniel Bowditch Blunt became Hall's benefactor, helping him to arrange a law partnership with Aaron Vanderpoel and Augustus Brown and hiring him as his assistant in the New York district attorney's office. After Blunt's death, Hall ran for district attorney as a Whig in 1853 and was elected every three years thereafter until 1869 with the exception of 1859–1861.

Hall loved the drama of the courtroom and the public attention it brought. He took his job seriously, prosecuting 10,000 cases, including several sensational murders. He collected a large crime library, proposed a metropolitan police force in 1857 under state control, and gave popular lectures on crime and criminals. He was also politically savvy, failing, for example, to prosecute those who violated the unpopular liquor laws. His police reforms kept police patronage out of the hands of his political opponents. As the Republican party, which had succeeded the Whigs, proved unpopular in the city, he drifted toward the Democrats. Support from a dissident faction of Democrats enabled his election in 1861, and by early 1864 he had abandoned the Republicans entirely and enrolled himself as a member of the Democratic organization, Tammany Hall. As editor of Tammany's newspaper, the *Leader*, until 1871, he articulated Tammany's positions to the public. Hall's political prominence brought many clients to his law firm. Wealthy, culti-

vated, and highly regarded, he was asked to join the exclusive Union Club in 1861.

Following the Civil War, William Marcy Tweed gained control of Tammany. Seeking a genteel and respectable but politically pragmatic candidate to replace Mayor John T. Hoffman, who had been elected governor in 1868, Tweed's associates approached Hall. Hall was elected overwhelmingly to a post that at the time was largely ceremonial. Tweed, however, as state senator, pushed through the legislature a reformed city charter, which strengthened the mayor's power and made him, along with Tweed and two other city officials who were Tammany members, a board of audit to approve city expenditures. The plan was to undertake new building projects badly needed by the city and to create dedicated supporters through overpayments to contractors and kickbacks to politicians. Those who protested the corruption were paid off. The Republican *New York Times* and *Harper's Weekly*, however, carried on a protracted campaign against the Tweed "ring" on behalf of taxpayers concerned about economy and efficiency. The pun-loving mayor, at first a background court jester in Thomas Nast's famous cartoons in *Harper's*, soon became a sinister "Mayor Haul."

During his four years in office, Hall looked to the urban masses for support. The political machine offered jobs and other favors. Symbolically appealing to the Irish, Hall was the first mayor to dress head to toe in green to review the St. Patrick's Day parade. Such open acknowledgement of Irish Catholics created problems among Protestant Democrats, especially in 1871, when Hall tried to prevent a parade by Irish Protestants. State intervention allowed the parade to go on, but a riot costing more than thirty lives ensued. Assessing blame for the disaster split the Democratic party; reform Democrats joined the hue and cry against the Tweed ring.

Hall faced trial three times from 1871 to 1873 on charges that he had approved fraudulent overpayments as mayor. His unconvincing defense was that the volume of warrants he had to review (39,257) was too great for him to detect problems. No one testified to an intent to defraud, nor could anyone point to any great increase in Hall's property holdings or bank account. The first trial ended in mistrial, the second in a hung jury, and the third (on Christmas Eve) with a not guilty verdict.

Despite acquittal, Hall's reputation was shattered. He was "cut" socially and had to resign from the Union Club and his law firm. His marriage soured. When he wrote and acted in a play, *The Crucible* (1878), about a falsely accused man, it closed after twenty-two performances. A lecture tour in 1877–1878 was canceled because audiences only wanted to hear about the Tweed ring, a topic he would not discuss. In 1878 he became city editor of the *World* but was fired in 1882 when it lost money. In 1883 he started his own penny paper, *Truth*, but it too failed.

James Gordon Bennett (1841–1918) the younger, also a social pariah, assisted Hall by hiring him in 1883 to write from London for the *Herald*, and he served as Hall's chief client when the latter began practicing law in England. Moving in London's artistic circles, Hall met a widow, Mrs. John Clifton (given name unknown), whom he married after his first wife's death in 1897. He sued British scholar James Bryce over his description of Hall's role as a participant in the corrupt Tweed ring in the *American Commonwealth* (1888), and although the case was dropped, Bryce revised the chapter. Returning to New York in 1892, Hall remained there, occasionally writing for the papers, until his death in that city. His controversial mayorship dominated all assessments of his life.

• Hall manuscripts are in the New York Public Library. Croswell Bowen, *The Elegant Oakey* (1956), is a biography. See also Leo Hershkowitz, *Tweed's New York: Another Look* (1977), and Alexander B. Callow, Jr., *The Tweed Ring* (1966). An obituary is in the *New York Times*, 8 Oct. 1898.

PHYLLIS F. FIELD

HALL, Adelaide (20 Oct. 1901?–7 Nov. 1993), vaudeville, musical theater, and jazz singer and actress, was born in New York City, the daughter of William Hall, a Pennsylvania German music teacher at the Pratt Institute, and Elizabeth Gerrard, an African American. She made many jokes about her birth year; on her birthday in 1991 she declared that she was ninety years old, hence the conjectural 1901.

Hall and her sister sang at school concerts. After her father's death she began her stage career. From its debut in 1921 and into 1922 she appeared in the pioneering African-American musical revue *Shuffle Along* as one of the Jazz Jasmines chorus girls; she also sang a duet with Arthur Porter, "Bandana Days." In the revue *Runnin' Wild* (1923) she introduced the song "old Fashioned Love." At some point in 1925 she performed at the Club Alabam in New York City. In May of that year she traveled to Europe with the *Chocolate Kiddies* revue. By one account she married her manager Bert Hicks, a Trinidadian merchant navy officer, in 1924, and he would not allow her to tour with *Chocolate Kiddies* to the Soviet Union; elsewhere the marriage is dated 1936. They had no children.

Back in New York, Hall was featured in *Tan Town Topics* (1926), and she starred in *Desires of 1927*, which toured from October 1926 to early 1927. In October 1927 she recorded two titles, including "Creole Love Call," as a guest member of Duke Ellington's orchestra. Following the death of actress Florence Mills, Hall was chosen to star on Broadway with dancer Bill Robinson ("Mr. Bojangles") in *Blackbirds of 1928*, in which she introduced the songs "I Can't Give You Anything but Love" and "Diga Diga Do." The show opened in May 1928 and then traveled the following year to Paris, where Hall remained, starring at the Moulin Rouge and the Lido. Dazzlingly beautiful, a formidable dancer (partnering her tutor Robinson), and equally comfortable singing jazz melodies or risqué cabaret songs, Hall in these days rivaled Josephine Baker as the leading African-American female entertainer.

In 1930 Hall starred in *Brown Buddies on Broadway*. She toured widely in the early 1930s as a soloist accompanied by pianist Joe Turner (not the singer of that same name), Benny Payne, or Art Tatum, or guitarist Bernard Addison. In Europe she performed in the *Cotton Club Revue* of 1931, and she recorded with Turner and Carter in London that year. In 1933 she recorded two titles as a leader accompanied by Ellington's orchestra.

Hall was featured in the film short *All Colored Vaudeville Show* (1935). From 1936 she lived in Europe, and through her marriage to Hicks she became a British citizen (perhaps in 1938), but accounts of these few years are somewhat confused. In Paris she recorded "I'm Shooting High" and "Say You're Mine" with Willie Lewis's orchestra in the spring of 1936, and Hall and Hicks opened their own club, La Grosse Promme (The Big Apple). She also worked with Ray Ventura's orchestra in France. After touring Europe, she settled in London in 1938, when she starred in *The Sun Never Sets* and recorded with Fats Waller. Hall and Hicks opened the Florida Club, but it was destroyed by a German bomb in the Blitz. She then toured, entertaining troops in battle zones.

After the war, Hall had her own radio series. She performed in London in *Kiss Me Kate* (1951), *Love from Judy* (1952), and *Someone to Talk to* (1956). She came to New York to work in the show *Jamaica* (1957), and then returned to London, where she and her husband opened the Calypso Club. Hicks died in 1963. Hall's activities lessened considerably after his death, but she performed in the show *Janie Jackson* (1968), recorded her first album, *That Wonderful Adelaide Hall* (1970), and sang at St. Paul's Cathedral in a memorial service following Ellington's death in 1974.

In 1977 Hall created a one-woman show with which she toured widely for the remainder of her life, giving concerts in New York in 1988 and 1992. She was the subject of the documentary made for BBC television, "Sophisticated Lady" (1989). Pneumonia and an infection resulting from a fall led to her death in London.

In jazz circles Hall is remembered specifically for her first session with Ellington, on which she set aside her mainstream, smooth-toned, quavering, vaudeville-style singing voice and instead delivered a wordless vocalization imitating the sound of Bubber Miley's growling, plunger-muted trumpet-playing. More broadly, Hall was a leading actress and singer in African-American musical theater who helped to introduce the genre in the 1920s and to assure that it would be remembered at the century's end.

• An interview of Hall is held in the Oral History: American Music Collection at Yale University. Other sources include Chris Ellis, "Adelaide Hall: The Singing Blackbird," *Storyville*, no. 31 (1 Oct. 1970): 8–11; Derrick Stewart-Baxter, "Blues and Views," *Jazz Journal* 24 (Feb. 1971): 12–13; Henry T. Sampson, *Blacks in Blackface: A Source Book on Early Black Musical Shows* (1980); Howard Rye, "Visiting Firemen, 10(a): Adelaide Hall, Joe Turner, and Francis J. Carter," *Storyville*, no. 114 (Aug.–Sept. 1984): 211–12; John Chilton, *Who's Who of Jazz: Storyville to Swing Street*, 4th ed.

1985; and Barry Singer, *Black and Blue: The Life and Lyrics of Andy Razaf* (1992). Obituaries are in *The Times* (London), 8 Nov. 1993, and the *New York Times*, 10 Nov. 1993.
                                          BARRY KERNFELD

HALL, Al (8 Mar. 1915–18 Jan. 1988), jazz string bass player, was born Alfred Wesley Hall in Jacksonville, Florida, the son of Henry Hall, a cement finisher, and Alene K. (maiden name unknown), a dietician. (His birth date is often given as 18 Mar., but 8 Mar. appeared on his driver's license, in the *New York Times* obituary, and in one interview.) Hall was raised in Wilmington, Delaware, from age two and Philadelphia from about age five. His aunt Marie Gilchrist gave him his first lessons on piano, which he studied until he was fourteen. At age eight he concurrently took up violin, which he subsequently played in school orchestras before switching to string bass in 1932. He hoped to work in a symphonic orchestra but found that path closed to African Americans. After graduating from high school, and while performing in jazz and dance bands in Philadelphia and Atlantic City from 1933 until 1935, he continued his music education at the Mastbaum Music School, where he concentrated on string bass but took up cello and tuba as well.

Hall moved to New York City in August 1936 and joined the swing band Billy Hicks and his Sizzling Six, with which he made his first recordings in 1937 under Hicks's name and accompanying singer Midge Williams. He married shortly after his arrival in New York; details are unknown. He worked for reed player Campbell "Skeets" Tolbert and in 1938 began recording with Teddy Wilson. He was a guest member of Benny Goodman's sextet on the CBS Camel Caravan radio show on 10 January 1939 and a founding member of Wilson's big band from April 1939 into 1940. The group was pared down to a sextet, and he remained with Wilson until May 1941, also recording in Wilson's trio, including "Rosetta" (Apr. 1941).

Hall's second marriage dated from about 1940; again details are unknown, except that the couple had three children and were divorced in 1950. Their first daughter was born while Hall was working in violinist Stuff Smith's combo in Chicago around 1941. Returning home, he joined pianist Ellis Larkins's trio (1942–1943) and Kenny Clarke's group (early 1943). In 1943–1944 he was a staff musician at CBS radio and played on Mildred Bailey's show. Continuing to work in piano trios, he accompanied Mary Lou Williams, with whom he recorded in 1944–1945, and Erroll Garner, intermittently from 1945 until 1963. Also in 1944–1945 he regularly recorded in swing groups for the armed forces V-Disc label. His steady timekeeping was equally useful as a house bassist at Decca for the newly emerged rhythm-and-blues style and also for the newly emerged bop style, the latter including recording sessions with Dizzy Gillespie and Charlie Parker in Clyde Hart's group (Jan. 1945), the Be Bop Boys under Kenny Dorham and Sonny Stitt, Fats Navarro and Gil Fuller's Modernists, and Clarke (all 1946).

Hall contributed to the integration of black and white hiring and working practices in Broadway theater orchestras, initially in George Abbott's production of *Barefoot Boy with Cheek* (1946), in which he was the only African-American musician. Concurrently he played in jazz clubs, including a period at Eddie Condon's club early in 1947 and a recording session uniting Louis Armstrong and Jack Teagarden (10 June 1947). He also ran his own record company, Wax, from 1946 until 1948; it was then acquired by Atlantic. The small Wax catalog revolved around Ben Webster, pianist Jimmy Jones, drummer Denzil Best, and Hall.

In 1950 he attended television school to learn to be a producer and director and then spent five years unsuccessfully trying to get a job, because of racism in the industry. From the 1950s through the 1970s he continued playing in Broadway shows, including *The Music Man* (1957), *Gypsy* (1959), *Fiddler on the Roof* (1964), and *Ain't Misbehavin'* (1978). He joined Count Basie's big band for a few weeks in 1952 and rejoined Erroll Garner around 1953. Among his many recordings as a freelancer was a jam session under Condon's leadership (24 June 1954) including "Blues My Naughty Sweetie Gives to Me," on which Hall plays a walking bass solo (following Edmond Hall's clarinet solo). During another of his stays with Garner, he recorded "Misty" (1956). He accompanied Memphis Slim and Muddy Waters in concert at Carnegie Hall on 3 April 1959, French singer Yves Montand on an American tour, and Eubie Blake at the Newport Jazz Festival (both 1960) while recording within Duke Ellington's circle in sessions with Ellington and Johnny Hodges, Billy Strayhorn, Shorty Baker, Harold Ashby, and Paul Gonsalves.

Hall appeared in WABC television's "Salute to Eddie Condon" on 27 March 1965, and that same year he worked with pianist Phil Moore. As a member of Benny Goodman's small group from May into November 1966, he participated in the Comblain-La-Tour Jazz Festival in Belgium in August; the group's performances were telecast the following year. He played in the film *The Night They Raided Minsky's* (1968). Late in 1969 he worked with pianist Hazel Scott's trio. At Carnegie Hall in May 1970 he accompanied Big Joe Turner, Eddie "Cleanhead" Vinson, and T-Bone Walker, and later that year he recorded the album *Just a-Sittin' and a-Rockin'* with Gonsalves and Ray Nance. He played in Tiny Grimes's trio in 1971.

Around 1974 Hall married Elizabeth Hoeffner Turner, an art professor. He toured France in 1976 with the Harlem Song and Dance group. In 1978 he joined Alberta Hunter at the Cookery in Greenwich Village, and with her he recorded the soundtrack to the movie *Remember My Name*. He also worked at the Village Vanguard, at Gregory's, and in his final years with Doc Cheatham at Sweet Basil, all in New York City, where he died.

Hall was among the pool of string bassists who were regularly called on as accompanists in swing, bop, and rhythm-and-blues groups. "The Man I Love," recorded with Garner at a prolific recording session on 7

June 1956, summarizes his art: in the first minutes (taken at a ballad tempo), he plays with a beautiful tone, rock-steady rhythm, and a tasteful selection of notes; for the remainder of the piece (as the tempo quadruples in speed), he reliably underpins Garner's bouncy swing rhythms.

• The definitive source is Hall's own oral history, taken by Ira Gitler for the Smithsonian Institution on 11–22 Nov. 1978 and held on disc and in transcript at the Institute of Jazz Studies, Newark, N.J. John Chilton, *Who's Who of Jazz: Storyville to Swing Street* (1985), supplies the most complete single chronology of Hall's life. Additionally, bits of his career may be pieced together in greater detail from Albert McCarthy, *Big Band Jazz* (1974), pp. 302–3; David Meeker, *Jazz in the Movies* (1981); James M. Doran, *The Most Happy Piano* (1985), which includes a brief interview, pp. 79–80; and D. Russell Connor, *Benny Goodman: Listen to His Legacy* (1988). An obituary is in the *New York Times*, 21 Jan. 1988.

BARRY KERNFELD

HALL, Asaph (15 Oct. 1829–22 Nov. 1907), astronomer and discoverer of the moons of Mars, was born in Goshen, Connecticut, the son of Asaph Hall, a clock factory owner, and Hannah C. Palmer. Because Hall's father and grandfather had the same name, in the twentieth century he is sometimes referred to as Asaph Hall III; the eldest of his four sons, Asaph Hall IV, also was an astronomer. Although Hall's father had inherited a large estate, an unsuccessful business venture led to financial disaster. The clock business was not lucrative, and his father's death when Hall was only thirteen left the family in difficult circumstances. At age sixteen Hall was apprenticed to a carpenter for three years and as a journeyman established a reputation as a skillful house builder.

Influenced by books from his father's library, including the histories of Gibbon and Hume, Hall sought a formal education and by 1854 had saved enough money from his meager carpenter's salary to enter Central College at McGrawville, New York. Here he met Chloe Angeline Stickney, a strong-willed and intelligent woman who taught him mathematics. The two married in 1856 and eventually had four children. Chloe was destined to have a considerable effect on his professional life. For reasons that remain unknown, by this time Hall had decided to become an astronomer. Immediately after their marriage the Halls went to the University of Michigan at Ann Arbor, where Hall studied observational astronomy under Franz Brünnow. Perhaps because of lack of money, they remained only three months, but Brünnow's instruction laid a solid foundation for Hall's further study. On their return east Hall and his wife taught at Shalersville Institute in Ohio and arrived in Cambridge, Massachusetts, by mid-1857. Here Hall took several steps crucial to his career: he entered Harvard's Lawrence Scientific School, attended the lectures of Benjamin Peirce, and undertook observations for William C. Bond at the Harvard College Observatory. The latter work, which consisted chiefly in observing star positions with the transit circle, was com-

pensated at the rate of three dollars per week, a salary Hall supplemented by observing transits of the moon for longitude determinations of the army engineers' survey of the western United States, at one dollar per observation. He also observed comets and determined the elements of their orbits, setting a pattern of activity in both observational and mathematical astronomy that would mark his career.

Handicapped by his meager salary, Hall applied for the position of aide at the U.S. Naval Observatory in Washington, D.C., the national observatory for the United States comparable to Greenwich Observatory in England. On 25 July 1862 Superintendent James Melville Gilliss made the appointment, to take effect on 1 August. By May of the following year, after pleas from his wife on the basis of merit, Hall was elevated to the position of professor of mathematics in the U.S. Navy. Thus, in the tumultuous surroundings of Civil War Washington, Hall began a career at the U.S. Naval Observatory that extended until 1891.

Hall's career at the naval observatory was devoted to the routine work of positional astronomy, which in the latter half of the nineteenth century reached a golden age before the science of astrophysics began to predominate. While carrying out this routine work, Hall focused on specific problems of considerable importance. From 1862 to 1866, as assistant astronomer on the observatory's 9.6-inch equatorial telescope, he worked with astronomer James Ferguson to determine positions and orbits for asteroids and comets. After Ferguson's death in 1867, Hall took charge of the instrument and continued this work, in addition to positional observations made with the standard meridian instruments of the time: the transit circle, mural circle, and prime vertical. Both the meridian and equatorial observations (the latter made in conjunction with his colleagues such as Simon Newcomb and William Harkness) were published in the "Washington Observations," as well as in the scientific journals of Europe and the United States.

In 1875 Hall was placed in charge of the 26-inch equatorial, which had arrived at the observatory in October 1873 and was then the largest in the world. With this instrument Hall made a new determination of the rotation rate of Saturn, correcting the old value by almost a quarter of an hour. This episode made Hall doubt the conventional wisdom in astronomical observations, and it was in this context that in 1877 he undertook the work for which he is most remembered, the discovery of the two moons of Mars. Although many had previously searched for Martian moons, Hall used a technique to search very close to the planet. On 11 August he briefly spotted the first moon, confirming the observation on 16 August. On 17 August, while watching for the first moon, he discovered another one; he chose to name them Phobos and Deimos, respectively. Hall later wrote that he might have given up the search had it not been for the encouragement of his wife, who insisted that he discover the moons. Even with a large telescope, the small size of the moons (both now known to be potato-shaped and less than 12 miles on the longest axis) made this a discovery of the first order, and the reversal of conventional wisdom gave Hall an international reputation.

Throughout his career, Hall observed not only the satellites of Mars, but also the satellites of Saturn, Uranus, and Neptune, with the end in view of a more accurate determination of the masses of those planets and thus an improved knowledge of their mutual gravitational perturbations. Of particular importance was his work on Saturn's satellites Hyperion and Iapetus; his colleague G. W. Hill called Hall's 1885 memoir on the latter "among the most admirable pieces of astronomical literature." Hall also made significant contributions to double star work, publishing his observations made from 1875 to 1879 in 1881 and those from 1880 to 1891 in 1892. In the midst of his major programs of planetary satellites and double stars, Hall did not neglect the special astronomical events of his time. In particular, he was active in the solar eclipse expeditions to Siberia in 1869 and to Sicily in 1870, the transit of Venus expeditions to Vladivostok (1874) and San Antonio (1882) for determining the scale of the solar system, and the transit of Mercury observations.

An active participant in the administrative duties of his institution, Hall served on the site selection board for the new naval observatory and was the senior member of the board determining specifications for repairing and remounting the instruments at the new site. Although Hall retired more than a year before the formal removal of the observatory to the new site in 1893, his legacy to astronomy lived on both in his scientific and institutional contributions and in his son Asaph IV, who held his father's position as head of the observatory's Equatorial Division (including the 26-inch telescope used to discover the moons of Mars) from 1908 to 1929.

After his retirement and the death of his wife in 1892, Hall remained two more years in Washington before moving in 1894 to his native town of Goshen. In 1896 Hall's career came full circle when he began to teach celestial mechanics at Harvard University, remaining a faculty member there for five years but residing in Cambridge only while classes were in session. In the fall of 1901 he married Mary B. Gauthier. He died in Annapolis, Maryland.

Hall was the recipient of many awards, including the Gold Medal of the Royal Astronomical Society and the Lalande and Arago prizes of the French Academy of Sciences. He was elected to the U.S. National Academy of Sciences in 1875, even before his discovery of the moons of Mars, and served as its vice president for six years. In 1902 he served as president of the American Association for the Advancement of Science. Hall made contributions to both observational and mathematical astronomy and often sought the broader implications of his work. Not satisfied simply to determine cometary orbits, he showed that there was no apparent retardation due to a resisting medium in space. Despite his observations of double stars, Hall believed those observations did not yet warrant the extension of the law of gravity to stellar systems, an example of his

caution in drawing scientific conclusions. By all accounts he was a simple, generous, and sincere man who rose from poverty to the heights of scientific achievement through sheer perseverance. H. S. Pritchett, a one-time colleague at the naval observatory and later MIT president, ranked him in 1908 among the most important half-dozen mathematical astronomers.

• The Asaph Hall Papers are located at the Library of Congress, Washington, D.C. Other relevant material can be found in the records of the U.S. Naval Observatory, Record Group 78, National Archives, Washington, D.C. Hall's principal works were published in the naval observatory volumes entitled *Astronomical and Meteorological Observations Made during the Years . . . at the United States Naval Observatory*, including "Observations and Orbits of the Satellites of Mars" (1878), "Observations of Double Stars" (1881 and 1892), and "The Orbit of Iapetus" (1885). The best source for Hall's life is George W. Hill, "Biographical Memoir of Asaph Hall," National Academy of Sciences, *Biographical Memoirs* 6 (1908): 240–309, which includes an extensive list of "Published Writings of Asaph Hall," comp. William D. Horigan. Also useful is H. S. Pritchett, "Asaph Hall," *Popular Astronomy*, Feb. 1908, pp. 66–70. For Hall's personal life, see the memoirs by Hall's sons, Angelo Hall, *An Astronomer's Wife* (1908), and Percival Hall, *Asaph Hall: Astronomer* (privately printed, n.d.); the latter reprints a considerable amount of correspondence related to the discovery of the moons of Mars.

STEVEN J. DICK

HALL, Basil (31 Dec. 1788–11 Sept. 1844), captain in the British navy and author of scientific works and books of travel, was born in Edinburgh, Scotland, the son of Sir James Hall, a geologist of repute who published on a variety of other subjects as well, including architecture, and Helen Douglas. After a basic education in Edinburgh, Basil at age fourteen joined the Royal Navy and set out on the first of many voyages. By age twenty he was made lieutenant and at twenty-nine was a captain.

Hall constantly wrote of his experiences, on ship as well as on land, including a two-year journey on the continent of Europe (1818–1819). On one long voyage, begun in 1816, he commanded the ten-gun *Lyra*, escort to the *Alceste*, which was carrying William Pitt as ambassador to China. His account of this voyage, subsequently revised and lengthened, had some ten editions by 1865, the last version being called *Narratives of a Voyage to Java, China, and the Great Loo-Choo Island*. His final command, as captain of the *Conway*, was to South America and resulted in *Extracts from a Journal, Written on the Coasts of Chili, Peru, and Mexico, in the Years 1820, 1821, 1822*, which by 1826 had appeared in five editions in English and one each in German and French. Not only did Hall report his own activities and those of his fellow seamen, but he also interviewed Napoleon on St. Helena and wrote of scientific matters well enough to be elected to a number of learned bodies, including the Royal Society, the Royal Astronomical Society, the Royal Geographical Society, and the Geological Society. His interests, like those of his father, were wide-ranging, and his publications were popular. The best known, designed especially for younger readers, was the nine-volume *Fragments of Voyages and Travels*, first published in 1831.

In 1823 Hall resigned from the Royal Navy. In 1825 he married Margaret Hunter, daughter of Sir John Hunter, the consul-general to Spain. With his wife, small daughter, and the daughter's nurse, Hall spent fourteen months of 1827–1828 touring the United States and, for nine weeks, Canada. Aided by his literary reputation and more than 100 letters of recommendation, he dined with famous people such as President John Quincy Adams, the governors of several states, and artists and academics, among them Washington Allston, Gilbert Stuart, and Jared Sparks, the president of Harvard. With his wife he attended lavish balls. He sat in on federal and state legislative functions, and he inspected hospitals, prisons, and manufacturing plants. His party of four toured all the chief eastern rivers, including the Alabama between Montgomery and Mobile, as well as the Great Lakes, the chief canals, and the Gulf of Mexico between Mobile and New Orleans. Hall's most significant land journey was by carriage across Georgia, an adventure far different from any in the more advanced eastern states, and one that included his being feted by the Creek Indians. Altogether he claimed to have traveled 8,800 miles in the United States and Canada.

Hall's three-volume *Travels in North America in the Years 1827 and 1828*, published in 1829 in Edinburgh and London, was one of the most widely read of over 200 such books written by British travelers to North America before the Civil War. Like all of these books, however, it was in general condemned by American readers inordinately sensitive to and defensive about any European's judgments concerning the new nation's political experiments, its classless society, and its system of slavery which, especially to Britons at the time, was becoming more and more abhorrent. Nevertheless, perhaps in part because of Hall's intent to help his countrymen "think the Americans more worthy of regard and confidence," perhaps in part because he was determined to learn about America only from Americans, Hall's *Travels* was more nearly acceptable in the United States than contemporaneous accounts by Trollope, Dickens, and, especially, the outspoken Marryat, another retired naval captain who visited the United States in 1837–1838. Readers today, especially Americans, will in fact find Hall's keen, detailed, and well-written observations to be both just and significant. One highly original side feature of this American journey was the collection of forty drawings Hall made with the help of the camera lucida, and which he published simultaneously with the *Travels* in a small volume that underwent several editions. The *Travels* itself had two more editions in its first year.

After his return to Britain in July of 1828, Hall restricted his travels to the continent of Europe and his writings to revisions of earlier works, to books about Austria, and to a volume, *Patchwork* (1841), that consisted of "Sketches of Travel in Italy, France, and Switzerland." He and his wife had two more children. He became mentally ill in 1842 and entered the naval hospital near Portsmouth, where he died.

• Indiana University at Bloomington has 169 of the sketches Hall made during his North American travels. A number of Hall's works are autobiographical, and some are partly fictional. Nearly all are to be called travel literature and most are partly scientific. Biographical material can be found in *Voyages and Travels of Captain Basil Hall* (1894); *Travels in India, Ceylon, and Borneo*, selected and edited with a biographical introduction by H. G. Rawlinson (1931; repr. 1972); and especially the three reprints of *Travels in North America* (1965, 1973, 1974). An important volume to go with Hall's works is *The Aristocratic Journey, Being the Outspoken Letters of Mrs. Basil Hall Written during a Fourteen Months' Sojourn in America 1827–1828*, ed. Una Pope-Hennessey (1931).

PERCY ADAMS

HALL, Calvin Springer (18 Jan. 1909–4 Apr. 1985), psychologist, was born in Seattle, Washington, the son of Calvin S. Hall, a justice of the state supreme court, and Dovre Johnson. Like most of his generation, Hall's education in psychology reflected his teachers' behaviorist views. He first studied psychology as an undergraduate at the University of Washington, where he worked with behavioral learning theorist Edwin R. Guthrie. For his senior year, he transferred to the University of California at Berkeley because he opposed the ROTC course required by the University of Washington. At Berkeley he studied with Edward C. Tolman, whose concern for "purpose" began tempering Hall's commitment to purely behavioristic explanations of psychological phenomena. He earned his B.A. in 1930 and then continued there as a graduate student with Tolman and Robert C. Tryon, earning his Ph.D. in 1933. The year before he had married Irene Hannah Sanborn; they had one child.

Hall's most influential work at Berkeley was an extension of Tryon's early experimental studies on the inheritance of ability in rats. Tryon interpreted his results to prove that he could breed rats to do well or poorly in learning mazes. In his own experiments, Hall bred rats to exhibit behaviors that he construed as either unusual fearfulness or unusual fearlessness; he thus claimed to have demonstrated the inheritance of emotionality, at least in rats.

Upon receiving his Ph.D., Hall taught for three years as an assistant professor at the University of Oregon. In 1937 his growing research reputation led to his appointment as a professor and the department chair in psychology at Western Reserve University in Cleveland, positions that he held for the next twenty years. During the 1940s he began his systematic research into dreams, developing methods, producing findings, and formulating theories that would put him at the center of dream studies. In the following decade, he gained further professional influence and even popular success with several publications. His chapter in *The Handbook of Experimental Psychology* (1951) became one of the founding statements of behavior genetics as the field was conceived in the latter half of the twentieth century. *The Meaning of Dreams* (1953), Hall's first book intended for a nonprofessional audience, sold well and interested many people in keeping diaries of their dreams. He then published two more bestselling volumes, *A Primer of Freudian Psychology* (1954) and *Theories of Personality* (1957, written with Gardner Lindzey), which were clearly written expository works that helped create an emphasis on personality within psychology over the next two decades.

Hall's studies of dream content, however, became his foremost accomplishment. His early work on dreams was based on reports written anonymously by college students, whose interest in subjective experience and willingness to answer questions made them, from Hall's perspective, ideal subjects. He soon began to collect dream reports from children, older adults, people in other parts of the world, and those who kept dream diaries. (By the time he died he had collected more than 50,000 dream reports.) The research started with thematic analyses of fifteen to twenty-five dreams reported by each student, with the aim of looking for obvious patterns. Hall soon developed a quantitative coding system that divided dream content into settings, objects, characters, interactions, emotions, misfortunes, and several other categories. On the basis of his empirical studies, Hall developed a cognitive theory of dreams that states that dreams express an individual's "conceptions" of self, family members, friends, and social environment and reveal such conceptions to be "weak," "assertive," "unloved," "domineering," and "hostile." Hall also developed a metaphoric theory of dream symbolism that was supported, so he argued, by similar metaphoric expressions in slang and poetry. This work represents one of the earliest examples of the "cognitive turn" in psychology that through the 1960s and 1970s gradually superseded behaviorism's dominance of the field.

Hall contended that his empirical work showed that dreams of groups of people from all over the world are more similar than they are different, and he explained the variations that he found by reference to other cultural differences. At the same time, he found large individual differences in the frequency of dream elements; these, he believed, corresponded with waking concerns, emotional preoccupations, and interests, suggesting what Hall called a "continuity" between dream content and waking thought. His work with dream diaries recorded over several years, or even over decades by a few people, showed a high degree of consistency in dream content, although Hall at times found changes that he interpreted as consistent with changes in the dreamers' waking lives.

After twenty years at Western Reserve, Hall taught briefly at Syracuse University (1957–1959), the University of Miami (1959–1960), and, as a Fulbright scholar, at the Catholic University of Nijmegen, the Netherlands (1960–1961). It was during this time that he and his wife separated.

From 1961 through 1965, Hall studied dreams collected in the sleep laboratory he established at his Institute of Dream Research in Miami, Florida, concluding that the content of an individual's dreams does not vary during a single night. At Miami he and Robert L. Van de Castle, then affiliated with the University of Denver, developed their influential comprehensive coding system, which was set forth, along with Hall's normative findings, in a jointly authored work, *The Content Analysis of Dreams* (1966). Hall went into semiretirement in Santa Cruz, California, in 1966, continuing his research and occasionally lecturing at the local campus of the University of California. During these years he coauthored a book with Richard Lind on Franz Kafka, *Dreams, Life, and Literature* (1970), and one with Alan Bell, *Personality of a Child Molester* (1971). He published another popular exposition of his primary research, *The Individual and His Dreams* (1972), which sold widely, and he wrote *A Primer of Jungian Psychology* (1973) to complement his earlier book on Freud. Hall died in Santa Cruz, California.

Hall's early work in behavioral genetics is regularly cited in histories of the field. His open-field apparatus for studying emotionality, a brightly lit white arena that is a potentially frightening environment for rodents, is still frequently used in the many ongoing studies of emotionality in mice and rats. The system of content analysis he finalized with the help of Van de Castle in 1966 was used by researchers in Canada, Switzerland, India, and Japan as well as the United States, and became one of the standard aspects of most quantitative studies of dream content. Hall had a great impact on psychology during his lifetime through his widely read books, but his greatest legacies to the field are his careful new methods and sound empirical findings in both behavioral genetics and dream research.

• Hall's early work on animal temperament is best summarized in his "The Inheritance of Emotionality," *Sigma Xi Quarterly* 26 (1938): 17–27. His work on the genetic basis of audiogenetic seizures in mice appears in "Genetic Differences in Fatal Audiogenetic Seizures between Two Inbred Strains of House Mice," *Journal of Heredity* 38 (1947): 2–6; and "The Genetics of Audiogenetic Seizures in the House Mouse," *Journal of Comparative and Physiological Psychology* 42 (1949): 58–63, coauthored with a student, Governor Witt. All of Hall's work on temperament and genetics is summarized in his "The Genetics of Behavior," in *The Handbook of Experimental Psychology*, ed. S. S. Stevens (1951). Hall's first important article on dreams is "Diagnosing Personality by the Analysis of Dreams," *Journal of Abnormal and Social Psychology* 42 (1947): 68–79; his first report of quantitative findings, "What People Dream About," *Scientific American* 184 (1951): 60–63, anticipates many later results. His highly original theoretical article on dreams is "A Cognitive Theory of Dreams," *Journal of General Psychology* 49 (1953): 273–82; his metaphoric theory of dream symbols can be found in "A Cognitive Theory of Dream Symbols," *Journal of General Psychology* 48 (1953): 169–86. An excellent overview of Hall's work can be found in Robert Van de Castle, *Our Dreaming Mind* (1994). For a comprehensive presentation of all reliable findings related to the Hall/Van de Castle coding system, as well as new developments and theories based on it, see G. William Domhoff, *Finding Meaning in Dreams: A Quantitative Approach* (1996). A fine appreciation of Hall and his work appears in the obituary by his longtime friend Gardner Lindzey, "Calvin Springer Hall (1909–1985)," *American Psychologist* 42 (1987): 185.

G. WILLIAM DOMHOFF

HALL, Charles Cuthbert (3 Sept. 1852–25 Mar. 1908), Presbyterian minister and educator, was born in New York City, the son of William Cooper Hall, a successful businessman, and Jane Agnes Boyd. The sickly boy, often called by his middle name, was educated largely by tutors until he entered Williams College on his sixteenth birthday. Here he improved his musical gifts, found his religious faith deepened in part through the influence of president Mark Hopkins, and won academic honors. Graduating in 1872, he entered Union Theological Seminary in New York City the same year. After two years of study there, he completed his final year at theological colleges in London and Edinburgh.

In 1875 he became pastor of a Presbyterian church in Newburgh, New York, where he was ordained. Hall's thoughtful preaching power, magnetic personality, industrious leadership, and warm friendliness quickly attracted attention. Before two years had passed he was called to the First Presbyterian Church of Brooklyn, located on Columbia Heights, then a choice residential location for business leaders. Here he remained for twenty years, contributing significantly to tripling the membership and becoming widely known as an eloquent preacher for special occasions and for college sermons. In August 1877 he married Jeanie Stewart Boyd; four children were born of the union.

Theologically, Hall was a liberal evangelical, clinging to many orthodox convictions but finding biblical criticism a helpful way to deeper understanding of Christian truth. He respected persons of various opinions and proved to be a good reconciler. Long a member of the Union Theological Seminary Board of Directors, he consistently supported the controversial Charles A. Briggs during and after the trials that led to Briggs's suspension from the Presbyterian ministry. In 1897 Hall was called to the presidency of Union, serving also as professor of pastoral theology, missions, and homiletics. With characteristic energy, he threw himself into his new tasks, making himself readily available to students. He began to set the patterns Union was to follow deep into the twentieth century in his inaugural address on "The Expansion of the Seminary," insisting on the importance of high academic standards, of involving the laity, of social service to working people, and of deepening the spiritual and ecumenical life of the institution. Many impressive faculty appointments were made during his administration—for example, George William Knox in the philosophy of religion, Thomas C. Hall in ethics, Julius A. Bewer in Old Testament, and Hugh Black in practical theology—and plans for the Morningside Heights buildings (dedicated in 1910) were prepared under his watchful eye.

Invited to deliver the Barrows series of six lectures at five university cities in India and four in Japan in 1902–1903, he was granted a long leave. Though stating his own Christian position clearly in the lectures and in many other addresses, he took other world religions seriously and made a great impression—so much so that he was invited to give a second set of Barrows lectures in 1906–1907. Faced with vast crowds and many demands, he apparently contracted an infection never fully identified. Unable to complete the series in Japan, he returned home in the spring of 1907, revived briefly, but died in his native city.

• The archives of Union Theological Seminary in New York contain seven boxes of Hall's papers, including addresses, clippings, classroom and special lectureship notes, extensive correspondence, notebooks, manuscripts, sermons, and miscellaneous items. Among Hall's many books, often collections of sermons and addresses, are *Into His Marvellous Light* (1892), *Does God Send Trouble?* (1894), *The Gospel of the Divine Sacrifice* (1897), *Bible Truth in Hymns* (1899), *Christ and the Human Race* (1906), and *The Silver Cup* (1909). The two series of the Barrows lectures were published as *Christian Belief Interpreted by Christian Experience* (1902; repr. 1903, 1905) and *Christ and the Eastern Soul* (1909). His biography was written by Basil Douglas Hall, *The Life of Charles Cuthbert Hall: "One Among a Thousand"* (1965); it is an informative tribute that contains many illuminating passages from his father's papers and correspondence. For the Union years, see also chapter 5 in Robert T. Handy, *A History of Union Theological Seminary in New York* (1987). An obituary is in the *New York Times*, 26 Mar. 1908.

ROBERT T. HANDY

HALL, Charles Francis (1821–8 Nov. 1871), Arctic explorer, was born in Rochester, New Hampshire. The names of his parents and the circumstances of his early years are unknown. It seems likely, though not certain, that he did not finish high school. In fact, the verified historical record of his life did not really commence until 1849, when he appeared in Cincinnati, Ohio, with a handful of possessions and a wife named Mary. Nothing is known of his wife's parentage either; what is certain is that the couple had two children.

Hall thrived on the mercantile impulse present in the Midwest during the 1850s. He became in succession a seal-die molder, an engraver, and the proprietor of a small newspaper, the *Cincinnati Occasional* (1858–1860). In the capacity of printer and publisher, he noted the major news events of the day, and he appears to have become thoroughly entranced with the stories of Arctic travel spurred on by the failed English expedition of Sir John Franklin and the American explorer Elisha Kent Kane. By 1860 Hall had decided that he too would go to the Arctic, where he intended to search for the men who he believed had survived the Franklin expedition.

Hall left his wife and children and went to New York City and New London, Connecticut. There he familiarized himself with the details of finding a way to the Arctic. He won the tentative support of Henry Grinnell (who had financed Elisha Kent Kane's expedition), and on 29 May 1860 he sailed from New London aboard the commercial whaler *George Henry*.

Hall was put ashore by the whaler on Baffin Island on 30 July 1860. He spent much of the next two years there. In the process of exploration, he ascertained that what had been thought to be Frobisher Strait was actually a bay. He found sea coal from Martin Frobisher's expedition of 1577 and made a firm and lasting friendship with two Eskimos, Ebierbing and Tookoolito, whom he called Joe and Hannah. Hall and the Eskimos sailed for home aboard the *George Henry* on 9 August 1862 and arrived at New London on 7 September. He had learned of the advent of the Civil War during his stay in the Arctic, and although he was devoted to the northern cause, he now wished only to find a way to return to the Arctic.

During his two-year stay in the United States, Hall visited only twice with his family in Cincinnati. He sought funding for his future explorations, met with sponsors in New York City, and gave speeches on the need for exploration. During this time, the son born to Joe and Hannah died. Needing to escape from all this, Hall, Joe, and Hannah sailed from New London on 1 July 1864 for the Arctic.

Hall spent the next five years in the Arctic. He lived on Depot Island in Roes Welcome Sound (1864–1865); at Repulse Bay at the base of the Melville Peninsula (1865–1866); on King William Island (1866), where the second son born to Joe and Hannah died; and at Repulse Bay again (1866–1867). He went up the Melville Peninsula (1868) and returned to the United States in 1869, again in the company of Joe and Hannah. In the summer of 1869 he quarreled with and shot a sailor, Patrick Coleman. Coleman died on 13 August 1869. Hall was never charged with any crime; neither the United States nor Great Britain sought or claimed jurisdiction in the matter.

Upon his return to the United States in 1869, Hall was hailed as a hero. Momentum had gathered for government support for an expedition to the North Pole. President Ulysses S. Grant signed (12 July 1870) an act that appropriated $50,000 for that purpose. The United States steamer *Periwinkle* was refitted and renamed *Polaris*. Launched from the Washington navy yard, the *Polaris* left New London on 3 July 1871 with Hall, fourteen men, and two interpreters (Joe and Hannah).

Hall led the *Polaris* north, into the Kane Sea and the Kennedy and Robeson channels. On 30 August 1871 he reached the furthest northern point yet attained by any Arctic explorer (82° 11′N, 61°W), 250 miles north of the point reached by Elisha Kent Kane aboard the *Advance* in 1853. Confronted by the Arctic ice pack, Hall turned the ship back and found refuge on the northwest coast of Greenland in what he named Thank-God Harbor at 81°38′N, 61°44′W).

On 10 October 1871 Hall led a party of men by sledge to explore their surroundings. He returned to the *Polaris* on 24 October and asked for a cup of coffee immediately upon boarding the ship. Soon after drinking the coffee, he was taken ill. He felt bilious, a condition that progressed into seizures and extreme paranoia. He accused virtually every member of the ship's crew with attempting to kill him before he died. He was wrapped in an American flag and buried near Thank-God Harbor. The crew of the *Polaris* sailed for home on 12 August 1872, but the ship was lost on 13 October. A number of the survivors floated on ice packs for six months before they were rescued by a Newfoundland whaler on 30 April 1873. The remainder of the crew was rescued on land in July 1873, ending the saga, but not the mystery, of the *Polaris* expedition.

A naval board of inquiry looked into the matter and determined that Hall had died from an attack of apoplexy, as had been stated by the expedition's doctor. Considerable suspicion over this decision lingered, however, and in 1968 author and historian Chauncey C. Loomis led a group to Hall's grave, where the body was exhumed and an autopsy was performed. The autopsy revealed that Hall had ingested a large quantity of arsenic before his death. Although no final determination can be made, it seems likely that Hall was poisoned, and it seems plausible, but not certain, that the German doctor aboard the ship, Emil Bessels, was responsible for Hall's death.

Hall was one of a handful of daring individualists who brought the American flag to the Arctic during the mid- to late nineteenth century. Irascible and domineering, he may well have planted the seeds of his own death. His only truly enduring relationships seem to have been with the two Eskimos, Joe and Hannah, both of whom mourned his passing. High-strung and contentious, he possessed to a rare degree those qualities of determination and recklessness that impelled him and a small number of others (Elisha Kent Kane among them) to leave the comforts of civilization for the Arctic.

• Many of Hall's notebooks are in the division of naval history at the Smithsonian Institution. Other primary sources are Rear Admiral C. H. Davis, U.S.N., *Narrative of the North Polar Expedition* (1876). Some of the best secondary sources are Chauncey C. Loomis, *Weird and Tragic Shores: The Story of Charles Francis Hall, Explorer* (1971), and Leslie H. Neatby, *Conquest of the Last Frontier* (1966). Articles include Chauncey C. Loomis, Jr., and M. A. Wilson, "The 'Polaris' Expedition, 1871–1873: A Newly Found Graphic Record," *Prologue: Journal of the National Archives* 2 (1970): 1–9, and Liz Cruwys, "Henry Grinnell and the American Franklin Searches," *Polar Record* 26 (1990): 211–16.

SAMUEL WILLARD CROMPTON

HALL, Charles Martin (6 Dec. 1863–27 Dec. 1914), inventor and industrialist, was born in Thompson, Ohio, the son of Heman Bassett Hall, Congregational minister and Caribbean missionary, and Sophronia Brooks. His educated, pious parents of modest means moved the family to Oberlin, Ohio, when Hall was ten so that the seven children might attend the college of their parents. As a youth, Hall read widely in the libraries of his father and of the college. He also became an accomplished pianist. A true son of the age of invention, for which the *Scientific American* was the weekly bible, he became interested in chemistry and decided to seek his fortune in developing a practical process for extracting aluminum from its abundant ore. At the time, aluminum was a semiprecious metal because extraction was difficult. On his own in precollege years, Hall developed a fascination with experimentation that was to last a lifetime.

When Hall entered Oberlin College in the fall of 1880, he met Frank Jewett, professor of chemistry and world traveler. Educated in chemistry at Yale, at Göttingen, Germany, and through an assistantship at Harvard, Jewett had just completed four years of teaching chemistry at the Imperial University in Tokyo. Jewett was also interested in aluminum and possessed a sample of it. Although Hall did not take a formal course in chemistry until his junior year, the common practice in those days, he soon began experimental work with Jewett's help on a deliberate research program in aluminum metallurgy and on improved filaments for electric lights. Upon graduation with a B.A. in 1885, Hall intensified his experiments on aluminum production. On 23 February 1886 in the woodshed attached to his family's home, he obtained his first globules of aluminum metal. The process was the electrolysis of aluminum oxide dissolved in a mixture of molten cryolite and aluminum fluoride in a graphite crucible. Hall had fabricated the furnace, the batteries, and the crucible, and he had synthesized most of the chemicals. His older sister Julia, who had studied chemistry in college and had taken the reins of the family following their mother's fatal sickness, encouraged Hall in his experiments and served as an informed witness of the discovery.

After Hall applied for a U.S. patent for his invention in July 1886, he learned that the young Frenchman Paul Héroult had applied for a U.S. patent for a similar process in May. The February discovery date gave Hall precedence, however, under U.S. law, and a U.S. patent was finally issued in 1889. In November 1889, with the financing of Alfred E. Hunt and others at the fledgling Pittsburgh Reduction Company (ultimately Alcoa), Hall produced his first aluminum metal on a commercial scale. The price of aluminum soon fell from twelve dollars to fifty cents per pound as he improved the process. Many regard Hall's tenacity and success in converting the process from the laboratory scale to an industrial scale as a greater achievement than the discovery itself. Twenty-two U.S. patents bear Hall's name. He was the principal technical person at Alcoa until shortly before his death.

Aluminum, which previously had been used only in jewelry and dinnerware and for special purposes such as the lightning-rod cap of the Washington Monument, soon became an important industrial metal. The modest early uses of inexpensive aluminum for utensils and the like were outstripped by its crucial roles in cables for long-distance electric power transmission, in the emerging aircraft industry, and in other structural applications. As an inexpensive, lightweight, permanently lustrous metal, aluminum revolutionized

thinking about the uses of metals. In its first year Pittsburgh Reduction produced 10,000 pounds of aluminum metal; in 1914, the last year of Hall's life, Alcoa produced nearly 100 million pounds.

When aluminum production facilities were built at Niagara Falls in the mid-1890s in order to gain access to this source of abundant and inexpensive electric power, Hall established his home and his laboratory there. As one of the founders of a rapidly growing industry and as a financially astute person, Hall began to accumulate a personal fortune. At last, he had the resources to free himself and his whole family from their modest way of life. Although Hall never relinquished the puritanical attitudes of his upbringing, he adopted some of the practices of the wealthy in his later years. He was able to travel, to attend performances of opera and other serious music, and to pursue growing interests in oriental rugs and Chinese porcelains. He also supported the emerging conservation movement as an extension of his own strong interest in nature. Throughout his adult life, Hall renewed his spirits by playing the piano. He was skilled enough to play informal concerts for his friends and associates.

After Hall's fiancée from college years grew tired of waiting for him to make a fortune and ended their engagement, he turned his attentions to his large family and to his college, which he served as a trustee and as a financial angel. Hall's career, however, was interrupted by serious illness when he was in his mid-forties. A diagnosis by Sir William Osler in England and surgeries at the Mayo Clinic and in New York did not extend his life for long. What was almost certainly leukemia caused his death in Daytona Beach, Florida, at age fifty-one. The leukemia was probably caused by experimentation with radioactive materials, not by work with aluminum chemistry.

Hall gained wide recognition. He was elected to membership in the American Institute of Mining Engineers in 1890 and held memberships in the American Philosophical Society and the Franklin Institute. He was chosen vice president of the American Electrochemical Society upon its founding in 1902. In 1911 Hall became the fifth recipient of the Perkin Medal, which was awarded for "valuable work in applied chemistry" by the combined action of the Electrochemical Society, the American Chemical Society, and the Society of Chemical Industry (Great Britain). At the award ceremony, Paul Héroult gave a graceful speech acknowledging Hall's contributions and recalling his own. It is fitting that the aluminum refining process is now known as the Hall-Héroult process.

At the time of Hall's death in 1914 his estate was worth about $15 million, most of which was designated for higher education. By the time of its full distribution in 1928, the estate had increased in value to about $45 million. One-third went to Oberlin College, one-sixth to Berea College, and one-sixth to the American Missionary Association, then engaged in developing higher education for black Americans. The remaining third, under the administration of the trustees of the estate, provided endowments for twenty-two colleges in Greece, the Middle East, India, China, and Japan and for education about Asia in the United States, including the founding of the Harvard Yenching Institute.

• Letters from Hall to his sister Julia, notebooks, annotated documents, legal testimony, copies of patents, and records of his estate are in the Oberlin College Archives, Oberlin, Ohio. The principal biography of Hall is Junius Edwards, *The Immortal Woodshed* (1955). For a full account of Hall's experimental work en route to discovering the electrolytic process, see Norman C. Craig, "Charles Martin Hall—The Young Man, His Mentor, and His Metal," *Journal of Chemical Education* 63 (1986): 557–59. George David Smith, *From Monopoly to Competition* (1988), gives the business history of Alcoa and describes Hall's crucial technical role in the early years.

NORMAN C. CRAIG

HALL, Edmond Blainey (15 May 1901–11 Feb. 1967), clarinetist, was born in New Orleans, Louisiana, son of Edward Blainey Hall, a plantation and railroad worker, and Caroline Duhé. His father had earlier played clarinet with a brass band in Reserve, Louisiana. Edmond's four brothers all became professional musicians. His brother Herb Hall had a distinguished career in jazz.

Edmond taught himself to play guitar and then one of his father's clarinets. He worked occasionally with such New Orleans trumpeters and cornetists as Kid Thomas Valentine, Lee Collins, and Chris Kelly around 1919–1920. From 1921 to 1923, while with Buddy Petit's band in New Orleans and around the Gulf Coast, he began playing alto saxophone as well. He traveled to Pensacola, Florida, with trumpeter Mack Thomas, then joined pianist Eagle Eye Shields in Jacksonville in 1924 and brought trumpeter Cootie Williams into the band. In 1926 Hall and Williams joined Alonzo Ross's big band, in which Hall reluctantly played soprano saxophone rather than clarinet. Ross's De Luxe Syncopaters spent nine months in Miami and the remainder of the year touring regionally and, on the strength of recordings made while in Savannah in August 1927, were invited to the Rosemont Ballroom in Brooklyn in March 1928. The Ross band lost the job after two weeks and disbanded, with Hall and Williams joining drummer Arthur "Happy" Ford at Happyland, a dime-a-dance hall. They parted company when Williams joined Chick Webb's orchestra, with Hall staying at Happyland until July 1929, when he began working in Billy Fowler's band at a dance hall in Atlantic City. Two months later he joined pianist Charlie Skeets in a band that played another dime-a-dance hall in New York. By year's end Claude Hopkins had replaced Skeets and assumed the leader's position. Hopkins's group played at the Savoy Ballroom for seven months in 1931. From 1931 to 1934 it was the house band at Roseland Ballroom, from which it broadcast nationally. During this period Hall, featured on clarinet and baritone saxophone, also toured extensively and recorded regularly with Hopkins. With Hopkins's orchestra, Hall left Roseland to perform steadily at the Cotton Club, again with national broadcasts several times per week, from March 1935 until around December, when Hall quit the band.

In 1936 Hall joined trumpeter Billy Hicks and his Sizzling Six at the Savoy. He recorded with Frankie Newton and then, after John Hammond heard Hicks's band at the Savoy Ballroom in June 1937, with Mildred Bailey and Billie Holiday, whose session included "Me, Myself, and I"; Hall's solos on two versions of this delightful song are characteristically joyful and bouncy but somewhat stiff, especially in contrast to those of fellow sideman Lester Young. His last job in big bands was as a saxophonist with Lucky Millinder late in 1937. In 1938 he married Winifred "Winnie" Henry; they had no children. After rejoining Hicks, Hall joined Zutty Singleton's trio at Nick's club early in 1939 and Joe Sullivan's band at the downtown location of Barney Josephson's Café Society in October. Josephson took a great liking to Hall's clarinet playing, and no matter what the band, Hall would work at either the downtown or the uptown location for the next seven years: with Henry "Red" Allen from late in 1940; with Teddy Wilson from late 1941 to 1944; and with his own groups from September 1944 through the fall of 1946. From 1942 he also performed regularly in Eddie Condon's concerts at Town Hall. Recordings from this period include Singleton's "Shimme-sha-wabble" and "King Porter Stomp," Allen's "Down in the Jungle Town" (all from 1940), and his own "Jammin' in Four" and "Profoundly Blue" (from 1941). This last session may have been modeled after the sound of Benny Goodman's quartet (with Meade Lux Lewis's celeste serving as a parallel to Lionel Hampton's vibraphone) and thus underscored the conventional wisdom that Hall's personal style on clarinet was modeled after Goodman's, although modified by Hall's persistent use of a husky tone, achieved by humming while blowing.

Hall led bands in Boston until 1950, including one with Ruby Braff and Vic Dickenson at the Savoy. After a three-week engagement in San Francisco, he began playing at Eddie Condon's club in New York in July 1950, and recording with Condon and his colleagues. He also recorded two sessions with Vic Dickenson's septet, including "I Cover the Waterfront," "Russian Lullaby" (both from 1953), "Nice Work If You Can Get It," and "Everybody Loves My Baby" (both from 1954). After recording Condon's album *Bixieland* in 1955, he toured internationally from 12 September 1955 with Louis Armstrong's All Stars, performing in the movie *High Society* and the film documentary *Satchmo the Great*, both from 1956. That year writer Max Jones described Hall as a quiet, modest man whose energies were channeled in two directions: his exuberant clarinet playing and his love for fast European cars.

Pianist Joe Battaglia observed, "Edmond got so tired and bored playing the same twenty tunes at every concert that he just had to resign" (Selchow, p. 425), and Hall quit the Armstrong band in July 1958. Having toured Africa with Armstrong in the course of filming the documentary, he moved to Ghana in the fall of 1959, with the intent of settling there to play and teach. But he found local musicians to be uninterested and unreliable, and after three months he returned to New York. He toured Czechoslovakia as a featured soloist with local musicians in 1960 and then made wide-ranging tours of Europe, as a member of English trombonist Chris Barber's band in 1962 and again as a soloist. He also rejoined Condon and in the summer of 1964 played with cornetist Jimmy McPartland. Soon after performing in January 1967 at a concert at Carnegie Hall and at the Boston Globe Jazz Festival, he died at his home in Boston.

Hall sometimes played with bands associated with the revival of New Orleans jazz (for example, on recording with Mutt Carey in 1947), and he often played blues, but neither situation showed him to advantage. Rather, his considerable stature as a jazz clarinetist derives from his interpretations of popular songs in a swing style, lightly touched by Dixieland jazz, as best represented on record by his work in Vic Dickenson's septet.

• The definitive source is Manfred Selchow, *Profoundly Blue: A Bio-Discographical Scrapbook on Edmond Hall* (1988), incorporating a discography by Selchow and Karsten Lohman. A comprehensive interview tracing Edmond's career to 1956, originally published in Melody Maker, is reprinted in Max Jones, *Talking Jazz* (1987), pp. 13–20. There are interviews from 11 April 1957 and 18 July 1958 in the archives of Tulane University. John Postgate surveys his recorded legacy in "The Happy Jazz of Edmond Hall," *Jazz Monthly*, July 1964, pp. 11–16. Barry McRae presents a brief overview for newcomers in "A.B. Basics No. 48: Edmond Hall," *Jazz Journal* 23, no. 12 (Dec. 1970): 24. Gilbert M. Erskine offers a critical assessment of Hall's work with Condon in "Four New Orleans Clarinetists: Sidney Arodin, Irving Fazola, Edmond Hall, Raymond Burke," *Second Line* 27 (Fall 1975): 14–18. Hall's tenure with Hopkins is detailed in Warren Vache, Sr., "'I Would Do Anything for You': The Story of Claude Hopkins," *Mississippi Rag* 13, no. 5 (Mar. 1986): 8–11 and no. 6 (Apr. 1986): 10–13. Further information on the family is in Clive Wilson, "Herb Hall," *Footnote* 12, no. 3 (Feb.–Mar. 1981): 4–8; and Lawrence Brown, "Herb Hall," *Storyville*, no. 113 (June–July 1984): 172–90. Obituaries are in *Down Beat*, 23 Mar. 1967, pp. 13–14, and the *New York Times*, 13 Feb. 1967.

BARRY KERNFELD

HALL, Eugene Raymond (11 May 1902–2 Apr. 1986), zoologist, was born in Imes, Kansas, the son of Wilbur Downs Hall and Susan Effie Donovan, farmers. He was raised on the family farm in nearby Le Loup, Kansas, a short distance south of Lawrence, and began trapping animals at an early age. He evidently gave some thought to possibly pursuing this activity in Canada when his schooling was completed. Hall later recalled having had to give away his dog and sell his horse when the family moved to Yakima, Washington, after his sophomore year in high school. His father made an abortive effort to become an orchardist, but poor financial conditions there obliged the family to return to Kansas. Hall completed his senior year at

Lawrence High School, entered the University of Kansas, and majored in zoology. His first published paper, an account of a warbler he had shot—the first of this species collected from Kansas—appeared in the *Auk* (1921).

At the suggestion of Remington Kellogg, another Kansan and a zoologist who was a staff member with the U.S. Biological Survey in Washington, Hall entered the University of California as a graduate student in 1924. At Berkeley, Hall became a student of Joseph Grinnell, who had established one of the nation's leading academic programs in zoology there. Hall received his M.A. in 1925 and his doctorate in 1928 with a dissertation consisting of a taxonomic revision of American weasels. This study, later published in 1951, has continued to be an influential work. In it Hall concluded that the thirty species of weasels hitherto recognized by mammalogists should be reduced to three.

From 1927 until 1944 Hall was Curator of Mammals at the Museum of Vertebrate Zoology at Berkeley. While there he completed work on *The Mammals of Nevada* (1946), which has since set the standard for state faunal accounts. He was also acting director of the Museum of Vertebrate Zoology in succession to Grinnell from 1938 to 1944. In 1944 he was appointed professor and chair of the Department of Zoology at the University of Kansas and director of the Museum of Natural History there. Hall played an important role in persuading Ralph Ellis, a wealthy book collector, to donate his large collection of zoological works to the University of Kansas Libraries early in his tenure.

Under Hall's aegis, the zoology program at Kansas became a regional and national leader. Its continuing influence was due in large measure to Hall's strong leadership and sometimes controversial personality, his own published contributions to zoology, the vigorous support given to the university museum's important publishing program, and to the record made by Hall's graduate students. Hall saw to it that many of them were provided with needed financial assistance at a time when organized programs of support for graduate study in zoology had yet to become widespread. A number of them contributed research for his major work, *The Mammals of North America*, which was funded in part by a grant from the Office of Naval Research. Hall was an extremely hard-working and somewhat formal individual who maintained extremely high standards in his own work and was an exacting taskmaster to his students. Their caliber is reflected in the fact that many of them became leaders in zoology education in their own right, and four of them subsequently became presidents of the American Society of Mammalogists. Hall himself held this post in 1940 and 1941 and was later (1964) elected an honorary member of the society. In 1958 Hall was named Summerfield Distinguished Professor at Kansas. He was granted emeritus status in 1967 but continued with his research and writing until his death.

Hall completed the two-volume *Mammals of North America* in 1959 with the assistance of Keith R. Kelson. It was revised two decades later (1981) by Hall alone. This massive study has constituted the foundation for most subsequent research efforts in North American mammalian systematics and biogeography and has been recognized as one of the leading works of its kind in the world. In it Hall did much to reduce the taxonomic confusion left behind by earlier mammalogists.

Toward the end of his life, Hall was engaged in a taxonomic study of North American brown and grizzly bears. He did not live to complete the major work he had projected on this subject, but some outline of his thinking appeared in "Geographic Variation among Brown and Grizzly Bears (Ursus arctos) in North America" (*Special Publication, Museum of Natural History, University of Kansas* [1984]). One conclusion he reached was that the many species previously recognized worldwide should be reduced to fewer than half a dozen, though he recognized certain races and subspecies.

Hall authored nearly 350 books, monographs, and articles during his career. In addition to his work as a zoologist, Hall became increasingly dedicated to conservation. During his early years in California, he became a vocal critic of the federal government's program of poisoning predators and noxious rodents in the West, pointing out the very real dangers it posed to humans and to domestic livestock. For many years he continued with his efforts to have this program brought under better control. In Kansas he was instrumental in the creation of the Tallgrass Prairie National Park. The Kansas Wildlife Federation (1968), the governor of his state (1972), and the U.S. Environmental Protection Agency (1980) all recognized Hall's contributions to conservation. Hall married Mary Frances Harkey in 1924. They had three sons, each of whom became practicing scientists in their own right. Hall died in Lawrence, Kansas.

• Biographical sources include James S. Findley, "Eugene Raymond Hall," *Journal of Mammalogy* 70 (1989); Stephen D. Durrant, "Eugene Raymond Hall—Biography and Bibliography," *Miscellaneous Publications, Museum of Natural History, University of Kansas* (1969); Frank Graham, Jr., "Hall's Mark of Excellence," *Audubon* 86 (1984); and C. Jones, "Additions to the Obituary of E. Raymond Hall," *Journal of Mammalogy* 71 (1990). A brief biographical summary is in Elmer C. Birney and Jerry R. Choate, eds., *Seventy-five Years of Mammalogy (1919–1994)* (1994). An obituary is in the *Lawrence (Kans.) Journal World*, 3 Apr. 1986.

KEIR B. STERLING

HALL, Frederick Garrison (22 Apr. 1878–16 Oct. 1946), artist, was born in Baltimore, Maryland, the son of Joseph Thomas Hall, a clerk, and Myra Isabelle Garrison. Although he was descended from many generations of Marylanders, Hall did not remain there long. His parents separated in 1887 and his mother took him and his younger brother to live with her sister in Brookline, Massachusetts, where he spent his childhood. He entered Harvard College in 1899.

During his undergraduate years, Hall developed an interest in the visual and performing arts. It is clear from his work both as an undergraduate and in his later career that he had received a thorough background in art history and was particularly interested in the old masters of northern Europe and in the arts and crafts movement popular at that time. His distinctive talent for design found a place on the pages of the Harvard *Lampoon*, for which he drew cartoons, designed covers, and served as president. In 1901 Hall collaborated with two fellow students, Edward Revere Little and Henry Ware Eliot, Jr., in the production of a book, *Harvard Celebrities*, that contained caricatures and poems about fourteen prominent members of the Harvard community. Hall's contribution to the book was its design, which included elaborate decorations framing each caricature and ornamental initials for each poem.

At the end of the nineteenth century, the art of the bookplate (a small pictorial or typographic label pasted to the inside front cover of a book to identify its owner and often his or her interests) developed extensively in the United States. As an undergraduate and in the years after his graduation, Hall received a number of commissions for bookplates. In 1905 a small volume was published that contained twenty-three plates designed by Hall. In an introductory essay, Richard Clipston Sturgis, Jr., a Boston architect and author, remarked that the plates "have a place of their own among the foremost productions of the day." Hall continued to design bookplates for another decade, producing at least fifty-two in all.

After leaving Harvard in 1903, Hall continued his studies, taking a course in architecture at the Massachusetts Institute of Technology and then going to Paris, where he studied with Henri-Paul Royer, French landscape and portrait painter, at the Julien Academy. Although Hall's activities during this time are somewhat unclear, a diary/sketchbook indicates that he left Paris on 31 August 1907, feeling pleased with his accomplishments. Hall then went to Italy, where he remained for at least two months, studying and drawing. He was in Paris again in 1909 and subsequently studied in Boston with William McGregor Paxton, a leading Boston painter.

As an artist, Hall was best known for his etchings, which he began in about 1917. His earliest efforts consisted of landscapes around the Gloucester and Salem, Massachusetts, areas, but he soon devoted his efforts to architectural subjects. The degree to which Hall mastered the medium of etching and earned an international reputation through the production of only thirty-five plates is a tribute to his taste, talent, and painstaking, thoughtful workmanship. Arthur W. Heintzelman, keeper of prints at the Boston Public Library and himself an etcher, wrote in the April 1948 issue *More Books, The Bulletin of the Boston Public Library* that Hall, "through a few well-chosen subjects mastered etching to degree of international prominence, becoming one of the most talented architectural etchers." In addition to the Bibliothèque Nationale in Paris and the Uffizi in Florence, Hall's prints are in the collections of many of the major art museums in the United States, to a large extent as a result of his winning prizes in juried exhibitions. Among the prizes Hall won were the Bijur Prize, Brooklyn (1920); the Silver Medal, Sesquicentennial Exposition, Philadelphia (1926); the Logan Prize, Chicago (1926); the Brinton Gold Medal, Philadelphia (1927); the Eyre Gold Medal, Philadelphia (1927); and the Sesnan Gold Medal, Philadelphia (1928).

As a painter, Hall liked to portray still-life subjects, particularly arrangements of Chinese porcelain figures and elegant brocades, both of which he painted with meticulous care. He devoted equal attention to figure painting, both portraits and "subject pieces," showing beautiful young women engaged in genteel activities. His choice of subjects was very much in keeping with the "Boston School" of which he was a part. Since he had received most of his honors for his etching, Hall was particularly pleased to be elected an associate of the National Academy for his work as a painter in 1938.

In 1909 Hall married Evelyn Ames, daughter of Massachusetts governor Oliver Ames; they had no children. The couple shared an interest in music and the theater and were active participants in the social life of Boston, entertaining during the summers at a large stone house overlooking Gloucester Harbor. She was an accomplished pianist, and he studied the harp with Mildred Dilling and Bernhard Zighera. It was perhaps this musical interest that led to his friendship with Harpo Marx, who owned two of Hall's paintings. After Evelyn's death in 1940, Hall married Ariel Wellington Perry, a professional harpist, in 1943.

At the height of his career Hall maintained studios at Carnegie Hall in New York and at the Fenway Studios in Boston. A convivial, outgoing person with a well-developed sense of humor, he belonged to many clubs, including the Players and Coffee House clubs in New York and the St. Botolph and Tavern clubs in Boston, as well as numerous professional organizations. He died in Boston, struck down by an automobile.

While Hall's paintings were often accorded special praise in reviews of exhibitions, it is as an etcher that he made his most significant contribution to American art. Although few in number, their distinctive character and superior quality add to the dimension of etching in America.

• Summaries of Hall's life may be found in the Annual Reports of the Harvard Class of 1903, and a modest collection of papers and printed ephemera is in the Archives of American Art, Smithsonian Institution. The Boston Public Library has the most complete collection of his etchings, augmented by drawings and bookplates. Elton W. Hall, *Frederick Garrison Hall: Etchings, Bookplates, and Designs* (1972), illustrates all of Hall's known etchings and bookplates and contains a memoir by Hall's widow, along with reprints of three contemporary articles about his work. An obituary is in the *Boston Globe*, 18 Oct. 1946.

ELTON W. HALL

HALL, Granville Stanley (1 Feb. 1844–24 Apr. 1924), psychologist and educator, was born in Ashfield, Massachusetts, the son of Granville Bascom Hall, a farmer and local leader, and Abigail Beals. Raised in a family of Congregational piety and intellectual and social ambition, Hall graduated from Williams College with a B.A. degree in 1867 and attended Union Theological Seminary from 1867 to 1869. Interested in a philosophical career, he then spent fifteen months of study in Berlin, where he was drawn to Hegelian philosophy and evolutionary naturalism. Although he returned to Union and earned a divinity degree in 1870, he did not want to preach. After teaching philosophy and literature at Antioch College from 1872 to 1876, he decided to focus on physiological psychology. At Harvard University he studied under William James and received a Ph.D. in psychology in 1878, the first doctorate to be awarded in the new field of psychology in the United States.

Hall emerged quickly as a champion of scientific psychology. In "Philosophy in the United States," an article that has since become a standard source, he declared philosophical instruction in American colleges and universities to be "rudimentary and medieval" (*Mind*, Jan. 1879). Unable himself to get a professorship, he returned in 1878 to Germany, where he studied physiological psychology in the laboratories of Emil du Bois-Reymond, Carl Ludwig, and Wilhelm Wundt. While in Berlin he married American art student Cornelia Fisher; they had two children. In 1880 the couple returned to the United States, where Hall lectured, wrote, and sought an academic appointment. After successful public lectures at Harvard University on pedagogy, he briefly launched an effort to reform education on the basis of scientific psychology and undertook a pioneering study, "The Contents of Children's Minds" (*Princeton Review* [1883]).

In 1882 Hall was appointed lecturer, and in 1884, professor of psychology and pedagogy, at Johns Hopkins University, the first chair devoted to the new psychology in the United States. Hall turned his attention first to making psychology scientific and oriented his program to both the rising scientific interests of his educated generation and their still powerful religious heritage. Establishing a psychological laboratory, he avoided controversial metaphysical discussion and urged the investigation of specific problems by laboratory methods. At the same time he added a poetic gloss to mechanistic psychological theory that would reconcile modern culture and religious sentiments: he wanted to flood "the new and vaster conceptions of the universe and of man's place in it . . . with the old Scriptural sense of unity, rationality, and love beneath and above all" ("The New Psychology," *Andover Review* 3 [1885]: 134, 247–48). Hall's own work in the laboratory was meager, but he played a major role in organizing the new science. In 1887 he founded the *American Journal of Psychology*, a platform from which he attacked psychical research and introspective, or theoretical, studies, and in 1892 he called together the

American Psychological Association and served as its first president.

In 1888 Hall moved to Worcester, Massachusetts, to become the first president of Clark University. While its founder, Jonas Clark, a retired local businessman, had preferred to create an undergraduate college, Hall convinced him to establish a graduate university. Gathering a talented faculty, which included anthropologist Franz Boas, chemist John Ulric Nef, biologist C. O. Whitman, and physicist Albert A. Michelson, Hall made Clark the model of advanced university education, an education whose primary method and goal were scientific research. Clark, however, who kept daily control of the purse strings, soon balked at the costs and the lack of local support for Hall's project. Deceiving Clark about the university's expenses and the faculty about Clark's reluctance, Hall alienated both. In 1892 most of the faculty was hired away to the new University of Chicago.

The demise of Hall's hopes for Clark University and his embattled position as scientific advocate were compounded by personal tragedy: the accidental death in 1890 of his wife and daughter left him alone with a young son. By the end of the decade, Hall managed to recover and in 1899 married Florence Smith, a teacher; they had no children. In 1900 Clark's will established an undergraduate college with which Hall was forbidden contact, but the will also supplemented the endowment of the university and allowed Hall to maintain it as a small graduate center. In the mid-1890s Hall also reoriented his psychological program around evolutionary theory. Genetic psychology expressed his faith in nature, the "all mother" ("Address at the Bryant Centennial," *Bryant Centennial* [1894], p. 67), and focused his study on psychopathology and critical stages in the individual life cycle, topics that were marginal to laboratory-oriented academic psychology but of personal urgency to himself and to the wider audience that he increasingly addressed.

Hall had early recognized the potential uses of psychology in education and had founded the *Pedagogical Seminary* in 1891 to draw teachers into alliance with psychology. In 1893 he launched a child study movement among teachers in kindergartens, schools, and normal schools and became the first president of the child study department of the National Education Association in 1894. Believing that the development of the individual recapitulates the evolutionary development of the species and that instincts rule development, Hall looked for specific "nascent periods" of interests and aptitudes that would provide a blueprint for education and child-rearing. The heterogeneous materials that teachers collected never provided that blueprint, but Hall nonetheless popularized a program of biological and romantic naturalism, interlaced with the disciplinary concerns and idealistic inhibitions of Victorian culture. He stressed children's physical health needs, the imaginative character of childhood, the postponement of adult requirements, the crucial role of adolescence as a period of deep feeling and struggle, and the importance of sublimating sexu-

ality. Hall was also a major propagandist for the importance of sex differences in mental ability and education, although his stress on imagination and feelings had the effect of incorporating these "feminine" characteristics into the male life cycle and the school curriculum. Hall's message had wide influence on school reform and, through such students as H. H. Goddard, Lewis M. Terman, and Arnold Gesell, on the fields of clinical psychology, mental testing, and child development.

Hall's interest in psychopathology led him to collaborate with Adolf Meyer and others at nearby mental hospitals. In 1909 Hall brought Sigmund Freud and Carl G. Jung to the second decennial conference that celebrated the founding of Clark University. Although he interpreted Freud in the light of his own genetic psychology, Hall's writings and the conference helped to spread the influence of psychoanalysis in the United States. He retired from Clark in 1920 and died in Worcester, leaving his estate to the university for research in genetic psychology.

Expressed in a biological idiom that included racial inheritance and sexual differences, Hall's ideas and reputation were eclipsed by the 1920s. His importance was primarily as a promoter of academic scientific psychology in the 1880s and early 1890s, and of developmental psychology, school reform, and popular psychological interest in the Progressive Era.

• Hall's papers, as well as newspaper clippings of his career and copies of many of his articles and speeches, are in the Clark University Archives. His major works include *Adolescence: Its Psychology and Relations to Physiology, Anthropology, Sociology, Sex, Crime, Religion, and Education* (2 vols., 1904), *Educational Problems* (2 vols., 1911), *Founders of Modern Psychology* (1912), *Morale: The Supreme Standard of Life and Conduct* (1920), *Senescence: The Last Half of Life* (1922), and *Life and Confessions of a Psychologist* (1923), a revealing autobiography. The most complete modern study is Dorothy Ross, *G. Stanley Hall: The Psychologist as Prophet* (1972), which also contains an extensive bibliography of works by and about Hall. See also Stewart H. Hulse and Bert F. Green, Jr., eds., *One Hundred Years of Psychological Research in America: G. Stanley Hall and the Johns Hopkins Tradition* (1986); Joseph F. Kett, *Rites of Passage: Adolescence in America, 1790 to the Present* (1977); T. J. Jackson Lears, *No Place of Grace: Antimodernism and the Transformation of American Culture, 1880–1920* (1981); John Neubauer, *The Fin-de-Siecle Culture of Adolescence* (1992); and Rosalind Rosenberg, *Beyond Separate Spheres: Intellectual Roots of Modern Feminism* (1982).

DOROTHY ROSS

HALL, Grover Cleveland (11 Jan. 1888–9 Jan. 1941), journalist, was born in Haleburg, Alabama, the sixth and youngest son of William Rabun Hall, a farmer, and Permelia Ann Davis. Grover Hall's grandfather, Reuben H. Hall, moved to Henry County, Alabama, from Washington County, Georgia, in the 1840s; he owned over three-thousand acres of land and twenty-six slaves at the outbreak of the Civil War. As a member of the Sixth Alabama Infantry Regiment in the Civil War, William Rabun Hall was wounded at Gettysburg and forced to return home in 1863.

Grover Hall attended the Haleburg school, an ungraded, one-room structure typical of rural communities in the late nineteenth century. His teacher, William E. Glover, encouraged Grover to rise above the limits of his formal education and may have first suggested journalism as a career choice. Grover's older brother, William Theodore (W. T.) Hall, the first journalist in the family, was employed by the weekly *Wire-Grass Siftings* in nearby Dothan in 1898. W. T. became editor of the paper in 1903 when it was converted to a daily and renamed the *Dothan Daily Siftings*. Grover's first newspaper job was as a printer's devil for the *Siftings* in 1905. In 1908, after W. T. left the *Siftings* to launch the *Dothan Eagle*, Grover was made editor of the *Siftings*. When he raised the ire of the local Methodist minister by editorially defending a traveling vaudeville troupe, Grover was forced to resign a few months after becoming editor.

Grover Hall left Dothan in 1908 to work brief stints for newspapers in Jackson, Mississippi; Bessemer and Selma, Alabama; and Pensacola, Florida. In 1910 he accepted an editorial writer's post in Alabama, at the *Montgomery Advertiser*, and found his permanent niche in the profession. He married Claudia McCurdy English of Lowndesboro on 14 May 1912, and the couple had one son.

As a young editorial writer for the *Advertiser*, Hall was attracted to eccentric characters such as Alice Roosevelt Longworth and controversial political issues such as progressivism and prohibition. He also developed physical trademarks that featured a bow tie, a rosebud in his lapel, and an onyx-handled cane. Having gained the confidence and respect of the new publisher, Victor H. Hanson, Hall was named editor of the *Advertiser* in July 1926, upon the retirement of Will Sheehan. Hall immediately convinced Hanson to support an anti–Ku Klux Klan campaign in the 1926 statewide election. Hall editorially attacked the Klan and its political allies, such as gubernatorial candidate Bibb Graves and senatorial candidate Hugo Black. Even so, the plurality ballot system used by the Democratic party allowed most Klan candidates to win with less than a majority of the total vote.

Because of a more pronounced Klan influence after the 1926 elections, Hall continued to focus upon their activities. When a particularly brutal Klan flogging in Blount County was publicized in 1927, Hall used the incident as a vehicle to call down the public wrath upon the Klan and its cronies. He not only assailed the violent tactics and obscurantism of the Klan, but also urged political and law enforcement authorities to reign in the culprits. His editorials, not without considerable financial risk to the *Advertiser*, were the basis for Hall's nomination and award of the 1928 Pulitzer Prize for editorial writing in the 1927 Klan series.

By the time of his Pulitzer Prize, Hall's reputation had expanded his professional friendships. He became a correspondent with leading journalists, including

H. L. Mencken in Baltimore, Louis Jaffe in Norfolk, Virginius Dabney in Richmond, Julian L. Harris in Columbus, Georgia, and William Allen White and E. W. Howe in Kansas. Buoyed by national recognition and support from his publisher, Hall continued his offensive against the Klan's political allies such as Senator J. Thomas Heflin, who refused to support Democrat Al Smith in the 1928 Presidential campaign. The *Advertiser*'s influence was instrumental in the party's decision to bar Heflin from seeking future office as a Democrat, a maneuver which ended Heflin's political career in 1930.

During the depression of the 1930s, Hall staunchly supported Franklin D. Roosevelt's New Deal on the national level and promoted pragmatic reform government at the state level. Hall and the *Advertiser* were leading backers of the successful gubernatorial reform candidacies of Benjamin Meek Miller in 1930 and Frank Dixon in 1938. Because he simply liked people of all kinds, Hall often wrote editorials which defended minorities. His lengthy 1938 editorial, "The Egregious Gentile Called to Account," was a stirring defense of the Jewish people at a time when they faced mounting persecution in the United States as well as Europe. Hall defended blacks against discrimination and abuse, although he stopped short of calling for an end to the Jim Crow system of segregation. He maintained significant friendships among black leaders, including Dr. George Washington Carver at Tuskegee.

Perhaps the epitome of Hall's personal struggle with the race issue was his involvement in the infamous Scottsboro trial in the 1930s. Nine black youths were convicted in 1931 of raping two white women on a freight train in north Alabama. Questions about the evidence and credibility of the victims caused nationwide negative publicity for Alabama. Hall did not debate the guilt or innocence of the defendants, but for the sake of relieving further public stigma upon Alabama he urged the governor to pardon them. He offered his services to the Scottsboro Defense Committee, headed by Allen Knight Chalmers of Boston, as an intermediary with Governor Bibb Graves to obtain a pardon. The governor's refusal to make a tough political choice and grant the pardons was perhaps the emotional nadir of Hall's career.

Hall grew to love the *Advertiser* as well as Montgomery and found it difficult to leave. On different occasions during the 1930s, Hall was offered the editor's chair of both the *Atlanta Constitution* and *Atlanta Journal* but reluctantly refused the opportunities. The long illness of Hall's wife and his grief over the Second World War, which interrupted the writing of his memoirs for publisher Alfred Knopf, were factors which led to a bleeding ulcer and his death in a Montgomery hospital, two days short of his fifty-third birthday.

Hall's gregarious personality, wit, and lively writing style made him popular, if often controversial, among his readers. While he was not a radical, his editorial challenges to various southern traditions and institutions gained him respect among his peers as one of the South's foremost editors.

• Hall's papers are located in the Alabama Department of Archives and History in Montgomery. Also, a number of his letters are included among the papers of H. L. Mencken, Franklin D. Roosevelt, William Allen White, Allen Knight Chalmers, Louis I. Jaffe, Virginius Dabney, Julian L. Harris, and George Washington Carver. These and other references are cited in the bibliography of Daniel Webster Hollis III, *An Alabama Newspaper Tradition: Grover C. Hall and the Hall Family* (1983), which comprises a full account of Hall's life, career, and family connections. Among Hall's writings published outside the editorial pages of the *Montgomery Advertiser*, see "Alabama and the New Armageddon," Baltimore *Evening Sun*, 7 Aug. 1925; "Alabama Didn't," Baltimore *Evening Sun*, 1 Feb. 1927; "E. W. Howe and H. L. Mencken," *Haldeman-Julius Monthly* 2 (22 July 1925): 163–67; "Man's New Curiosities Most Helpful Sign of Modern Times," New York *World*, 28 Dec. 1930; and "We Southerners," *Scribner's Magazine* 83 (Jan. 1928): 82–88. Although initially printed in the *Advertiser*, 4 Dec. 1938, "The Egregious Gentile Called to Account" appeared in numerous other publications, including the *Congressional Quarterly* and foreign language translations. See also, Daniel W. Hollis III, "Grover Cleveland Hall: The Anatomization of a Southern Journalist's Philosophy," *Alabama Historical Quarterly* 42 (1980): 87–101. Among the many obituaries, not only the 10 Jan. 1941 *Montgomery Advertiser*, but also the *Atlanta Constitution* gave front page coverage to Hall's death. A full obituary with a photograph of Hall appears in the *New York Times*, 10 Jan. 1941.

DANIEL WEBSTER HOLLIS III

HALL, James (29 July 1793–5 July 1868), writer and editor, was born in Philadelphia, Pennsylvania, the son of John Hall, the secretary of the Pennsylvania land office and a U.S. marshal, and Sarah Ewing. He was educated at home until entering an academy in Lamberton, New Jersey, in 1805. He studied law with his uncle Samuel Ewing. In March 1813 Hall volunteered for the Washington Guard, was transferred to the Ordnance Department, was promoted to first lieutenant, and chose his duty to be at the Pittsburgh arsenal, where he could also continue his law study with James Ross, his father's friend. On 11 September 1817 Hall was court-martialed and his rank taken away. The official charges were disobedience of orders and neglect of duty as well as conduct unbecoming an officer. Hall was ordered to arrest a deserter and sent soldiers to make the arrest, but he did not accompany them. A soldier was killed as the deserter's friends tried to prevent the arrest. Hall was blamed by his superior officer, who also claimed that Hall had submitted a false report. Hall was found not guilty of the main charges, but he was cashiered. Though he resigned on 30 June 1818, he was vindicated, however, in that he eventually received a presidential pardon and was restored to rank. He was admitted to the bar in April 1818 and found another career at hand.

While in the army, Hall wrote some pieces, titled "The Wanderer, by Edward Ennui," emulating Joseph Addison for the *Pittsburgh Gazette*. Of the fourteen essays produced between 22 May and 1 Decem-

ber 1818, the most telling for his future interests is number twelve (3 Nov.), in which he advocates the establishment of a journal concentrating on the West. He felt the public would be naturally attracted to articles by and about the people of the frontier. Acting on his own advice, Hall moved to Shawneetown, Illinois, in May 1820 and bought a half-interest in the *Illinois Emigrant*. Hall's reputation as a "western writer" began with his character sketches he included in his newspaper and with their republication in the *Port Folio*. In "Christmas Gambols" (29 Dec. 1821) and "Fiddlers' Green" (5 Jan. 1822), Hall creates a stereotypical western character—the buckskin-clad hunter with moccasins, rifle, and powderhorn—anticipating James Fenimore Cooper's more developed descriptions of similar character types.

In December 1820 Hall was appointed attorney to the Fourth Judicial Circuit, and he was known as "Judge" Hall for the rest of his life. In 1823 Hall married Mary Harrison Posey, granddaughter of General Thomas Posey, governor of Indiana Territory. In 1827 Hall was elected state treasurer and moved his family to Vandalia, where he bought a half-interest in the *Illinois Intelligencer* (17 Jan. 1829) and organized the state's first historical society on 8 December 1827. Hall's first major literary work was *The Western Souvenir: A Christmas and New Year's Gift for 1829* (1828), containing sketches by Nathan Guilford, Morgan Neville ("The Last of the Boatmen" contains the first appearance of Mike Fink), and Hall himself. In "Pete Featherton" Hall created the first stock "backwoods marksman" character that led Fred Lewis Pattee to label Hall "the real pioneer of western fiction" (Pattee, *The Development of the American Short Story: An Historical Survey* [1923], p. 55). Hall then began the *Illinois Monthly Magazine*, again a periodical focusing on the resources, literary and literal, of Illinois. Hall wrote many realistic descriptive sketches of Illinois as well as fictional tales.

When the political winds changed in the early 1830s, Hall, a Jacksonian, lost his job in the state government and was soon in debt. The elections were fought mostly at the level of personal attacks rather than issues. Hall supported William Kinney for governor in the 1830 election; when Kinney lost to John Reynolds, Hall was accused of mishandling the books. In August 1832 his wife died of complications from the birth of their fourth child, who lived only until October of the same year. Hall left his children with his wife's parents in Kentucky, moved to Cincinnati in 1833, and edited his magazine under the new title, *Western Monthly*. Hall's new journal was successful (having 3,000 subscribers), wide ranging (covering science and history as well as poetry and short stories), and not prejudiced against women writers (Harriet E. Beecher won the fiction prize for "A New England Sketch" [Apr. 1834]). Also in 1833 Hall edited perhaps his most successful literary production, *The Western Reader: A Series of Useful Lessons*, a compendium of American writers (including Benjamin Franklin, Thomas Jefferson, Cooper, and Henry Clay) designed to make schoolchildren more aware of their American heritage. The volume was adopted by the Cincinnati schools and sold more than 200,000 copies. In this same period, Hall also published his only novel, *The Harpe's Head* (1833), which, though weakly plotted, contains some memorable "rascals" and accurate descriptions of western landscapes and manners; it was republished in London as *Kentucky* (1834). Though Hall's next effort, *Tales of the Border* (1835), contained only three previously unpublished stories out of seven, they are noteworthy because of their sympathetic portraits of Indians. They depict native Indian culture as enlightened and as legitimate as white culture. Hall resigned as editor of the *Western Monthly* in June 1836. In his essay "The Catholic Question" (June 1835), Hall reviewed Lyman Beecher's anti-Catholic polemic, *A Plea for the West*, by reminding readers that Catholics were democratic and loyal citizens and urged the debates to be conducted about theology rather than patriotism or citizenship. Hall probably did not resign his editorship as a direct result of the public turmoil about the Catholic question but more as a result of his taking on of new duties on the Board of Directors of the Commercial Bank of Cincinnati.

Hall thereafter devoted himself primarily to financial affairs. He was elected in 1836 to the Board of Directors of the Commercial Bank of Cincinnati, was made president of the bank in 1853, and retired in 1865. Yet he was still known for his literary productions, which were still in print. Hall moved his children to Cincinnati around 1838, married Mary Louisa Anderson Alexander in 1839, and was the father of five more children.

Hall continued to produce many volumes, but most were simply reworkings or reorderings of materials published earlier. For example, his last volume of short stories, *The Wilderness and the War Path* (1846), contained only two new stories, while *The Romance of Western History; or, Sketches of History, Life, and Manners in the West* (1857) reordered chapters written twenty-two years before. Hall's last important work, written with Colonel Thomas Loraine McKenney, was *History of the Indian Tribes of North America*. Over several years Hall transcribed and edited oral sources and collected paintings of Indian culture. The *History* was originally published in twenty parts (1836–1844) and is important as well because some of the original paintings by Charles King and George Catlin were lost in an 1865 fire in the Smithsonian. Hall died in Cincinnati.

• The largest collection of Hall's papers is at the Historical and Philosophical Society of Ohio. Additional writings by Hall include *Letters from the West; Containing Sketches of Scenery, Manners, and Customs; and Anecdotes Connected with the First Settlements of the Western Sections of the United States* (1828), *Legends of the West* (1832), *The Soldier's Bride and Other Tales* (1833), and *The Harp's Head: A Legend of Kentucky* (1833). The best secondary source is Randolph C. Randall, *James Hall: Spokesman of the New West* (1964).

DEAN G. HALL

HALL, James (12 Sept. 1811–7 Aug. 1898), geologist and paleontologist, was born in Hingham, Massachusetts, the son of James Hall, a textile mill superintendent, and Susanna Dourdain. Hall was drawn to science by Martin Gay, a founding member of the Boston Society of Natural History, whom he often assisted during Gay's public lectures on chemistry. In 1830 Hall walked over 200 miles from Hingham to Troy, New York, to enroll in the Rensselaer School (now Rensselaer Polytechnic Institute).

Directed by Amos Eaton, Rensselaer developed a model science curriculum with many innovations, including student teaching and summer field courses in geology and botany taught from boats along the Erie Canal. Hall graduated in 1832 with a bachelor of natural science degree, and he received a master's degree in 1833. Retained by Eaton as school librarian and an assistant in chemistry, he soon advanced to the rank of chemistry professor (1835–1841). In 1838 Hall married Sarah Aikin, the daughter of a Troy lawyer; they had four children.

Hall's classroom teaching was increasingly limited by his subsequent geological career, starting in 1836 with the New York State Survey. Under the organization of the survey, the state was divided into four districts, each with its own geologist. In charge of the Second District covering the Adirondack region was Ebenezer Emmons, who had taught chemistry at Rensselaer before Hall. Emmons hired Hall as an assistant geologist. So many unidentified fossils were collected after the survey's first year of operation that Timothy Conrad, in charge of another district, was reassigned as staff paleontologist. In 1837 Hall was promoted to geologist in charge of the Fourth or Western District, where he gained experience with fossil-rich strata of Silurian and Devonian age.

With the survey's termination in 1842, Hall was awarded the office of state paleontologist, a position created to complete the description and illustration of fossils collected throughout the state during the survey years. The stratigraphic systems then being described in the British Isles and Europe were well defined by fossils. Hall examined the British fossils brought to the United States by Charles Lyell in 1841–1842, and he accompanied Lyell on an extensive tour of New York State. It was clear that the labor of the New York geologists in establishing their own stratigraphic nomenclature depended on an equally precise use of fossils. The *Paleontology of New York* was intended to fill this need as a single quarto volume comparable to other volumes on the state's botany, animal life, and agriculture.

Hall fought yearly for additional appropriations that enabled him to expand the project until it reached the monumental size of thirteen quarto volumes with 4,320 pages of descriptions and 980 illustrated plates. During its long period of serial publication (1847–1894), the *Paleontology of New York* expressed techniques of scientific illustration changing from steel engravings to a lithographic process that permitted superior representation of continuous tones. Many of the early drawings were executed by Hall's wife, but eventually a staff of professional artists and lithographers was employed. The end result was a taxonomic compilation that attracted international attention to the rich Paleozoic record of fossils in New York State.

Hall kept his Albany workshop active through years of lean or nonexistent appropriations, often paying his staff privately from his own funds. While maintaining headquarters in Albany, he even assumed survey duties in Michigan (1850–1851), Iowa (1855–1858), and Wisconsin (1857–1862). The threat of Hall's permanent departure for Montreal to assume the job of chief paleontologist for the Canadian Geological Survey in 1854 was instrumental in reinstating salaries by the New York legislature.

Hall's name is linked with strident opposition to a major concept resulting from eastward extension of the New York Survey's work. His early benefactor, Emmons, was the author of the Taconic System, first promulgated in part three of Geology of New York (1842). Emmons insisted that his system embraced strata older than any previously defined, and he traced them into adjacent New England. Dated on the basis of a "primordial" trilobite fauna from eastern New York State in 1844, Emmons's interpretation was bitterly contested by Hall, who asserted that the trilobites belonged instead to "Lower Silurian" (now understood as Ordovician) strata.

Emmons persisted and saw the name Taconic System adopted on a geological chart published in 1849 by James Foster for use in secondary schools. Hall wrote angry denunciations of the chart in the Albany newspapers, enlisting support of other prominent geologists. A resulting libel case brought by Foster summoned Emmons to the defense of his system in a bizarre 1851 Albany court case. Foster lost his case, and the Taconic System never emerged from the dark cloud of disrepute that Hall had generated. Emmons's trilobites are now recognized as older than Hall realized, but the strata containing them were improperly correlated by Emmons with many younger New England strata.

The important geosyncline concept took root, however, as a direct outcome of Hall's experience beyond the western borders of New York State. Comparing the tremendous thicknesses of Appalachian strata with their thin equivalents in the mid-continent, Hall suggested that thick sequences subsided under their own weight to acquire features of surface folding and the injection of igneous rocks at great depth. Originally delivered as a presidential address to the Association for the Advancement of Science in 1857, Hall's novel concept of mountain building was expanded in volume six of the Paleontology of New York (1859). In 1873 James D. Dana applied the name geosyncline to this concept. The term still survives, although thick sedimentary wedges are no longer believed to generate their own mountains but result as the erosional product of mountain belts formed by plate tectonics.

Through his long career, Hall attracted many young apprentice paleontologists to Albany. Some who succeeded to their own careers were Charles E. Beecher, John M. Clarke, Fielding B. Meek, Charles D. Walcott, Robert P. Whitfield, and Charles Schuchert. Hall was among the first fifty members elected to the U.S. National Academy of Sciences in 1863, and several of his former apprentices followed their mentor as members. Hall also was elected the first president of the Geological Society of America in 1889 and was succeeded in that office by three of his former apprentices. He died at Echo Hill, New Hampshire.

• The major collection of James Hall Papers in the New York State Library is maintained by the New York State Archives in Albany. A complete list of Hall's geological publications is given in *U.S. Geological Survey Bulletin* 746 (1922). A full biography, *James Hall of Albany* (1923), was written by John M. Clarke. A shorter biography is summarized by Donald W. Fisher in the *Conservationist* 31 (1976): 12–16. Hall's contribution to the geosyncline concept is analyzed by Robert H. Dott, Jr., in *Centennial Special Volume 1* (1985), pp. 157–67, a publication of the Geological Society of America. A special James Hall issue of *Earth Sciences History* (vol. 6, no. 1) was issued in 1987 in commemoration of the sequicentennial of the New York State Geological Survey. An obituary is in the *New York Times*, 9 Aug. 1898.

MARKES E. JOHNSON

HALL, J. C. (29 Aug. 1891–29 Oct. 1982), greeting card manufacturer, was born Joyce Hall in David City, Nebraska, the son of George Nelson Hall, a nondenominational lay preacher, and Nancy Dudley Houston. The grandson of men who had fought on both sides at the Battle of Shiloh in the Civil War, he lost his father at an early age and went to work in 1900 as a door-to-door salesman for the California Perfume Company, later renamed Avon Products. Two years later his family moved to Norfolk, Nebraska, where his older brothers, Rollie and William, bought a book and stationery store. Joyce worked there after school and on weekends to help support his semi-invalid mother and his sister Marie. In 1903 he traveled with Rollie on sales trips through Nebraska, Wyoming, and South Dakota, selling candy and postcards, along with a sawdust sweeping compound. Two years later the three Hall brothers each invested $158 to form the Norfolk Postcard Brokerage Company, with Joyce, who had taken the middle name Clyde, listed as "J. C. Hall, Manager." They had moderate success selling picture postcards, imported from England and Germany, to Norfolk shopkeepers. In 1910 the young entrepreneur finished school and moved to Kansas City, Missouri, where he attended business college at night and, with savings of $3,500, established his own business as a postcard jobber in his room at the Young Men's Christian Association. Within a few months the volume of his sales compelled him to open a separate office.

In 1911 Hall was joined in Kansas City by his mother, sister, and brother Rollie. Noting a decline in the postcard market, he added greeting cards to his stock the next year. He and Rollie opened a retail card and stationery store, Hall Brothers, in the Corn Belt Bank Building in 1914 and printed a few of their own Christmas cards. The next year their office, plant, and full inventory were destroyed by fire, leaving them $17,000 in debt. They borrowed enough to reopen the business and purchase a local engraving firm. As Hall Brothers Paper Craft they introduced an informal style of "everyday" greeting card, already enclosed in an envelope, to a market previously limited to expensive engraved Christmas cards and valentines. Tastefully decorated with what Hall called "the art of the masses," their messages of congratulation for birthdays, weddings, and anniversaries and their expressions of sympathy for illness and death caught on quickly. They added nonoccasion "friendship" cards and, when the United States entered World War I, a popular line of cards saying "I miss you." In 1920 their brother William joined the company as office manager, and the next year J. C. married Elizabeth Ann Dilday; the couple had three children.

Hall Brothers Company was incorporated in 1923, with J. C., Rollie, and William Hall as equal shareholders. That year they began using the name "Hallmark" to identify their line, and by 1928 the name was printed on the back of every card. The name was registered as a trademark in 1954. During the 1920s they greatly increased their range of designs and messages. After beginning with 600 images, the firm grew to offer over 14,000 new designs annually by 1979. It produced as many as 500 different valentines in a year and established some 3,000 "sending situations," offering such personalized messages as congratulations on finding a new apartment, sympathy for a friend who has been hit by a car, and one reading "Sorry you're sick on St. Patrick's Day." For a time the firm carried six different cards specifically for tonsillectomy patients. Hall originated the use of humorous greeting cards and was the first to introduce pleated cards that unfold to tell a continuous story.

The company's first departure from greeting cards was decorative gift wrap, introduced in 1926. Another of its important innovations was the development in 1936 of display racks that made it easier for customers to select cards and for dealers to monitor their inventory. In 1944 Hall coined the memorable slogan, "When You Care Enough to Send the Very Best." A pioneer in advertising, he was among the first to sponsor radio and television shows, beginning with "Tony Wons' Radio Scrapbook" in 1938. The prestigious television series "Hallmark Hall of Fame," which premiered in 1951, was critically acclaimed, in 1961 winning Hall the National Academy of Television Arts and Sciences' first Emmy awarded to a sponsor. Although the show cost the company more than it generated in sales, Hall sustained it on the premise that "Good taste is good business." His determination to associate his product with quality was also evidenced in his selection of art for his cards; he was one of the first to use the work of such modern masters as Andrew Wyeth, Georgia O'Keeffe, Pablo Picasso, and Salvador Dali, as well as images by such popular artists as Norman Rockwell and "Grandma" Moses. In 1950 he secured the rights to use Winston Churchill's paintings for

Christmas cards. Hall's instinct for what the public wanted was confirmed by the company's continuing success. During his presidency, his taste for frank sentimentality expressed in easy-to-digest doggerel made Hallmark the largest greeting card company in the world, with 20,000 employees and annual sales of over $2.5 billion in 100 countries.

A Mason and a regular churchgoer, the stately and solemn "Mr. J. C.," as his employees called him, was known as a benevolent autocrat who personally supervised every element of his business. He was also noted for the generous benefits he provided his workers. In 1927 Hall Brothers was one of the first major companies in America to offer employee bonuses, and in 1936 it established a retirement plan, medical aid, life insurance, and vacation pay. In 1956 *Fortune* magazine credited Hallmark with "the country's most liberal employee-benefit and profit-sharing plan." Hall retired as president and chief executive officer of Hallmark in 1966, turning the post over to his son Donald but retaining the title of chairman of the board until his death in Kansas City. The bulk of his personal estate, estimated at more than $100 million, was left to charity.

• Hall's autobiography, *When You Care Enough* (1979), gives a full account of his life. See also Don Eddy, "A Million Greetings a Day," *Coronet*, Aug. 1949, pp. 143–46; "Card Shark," *Time*, 13 Feb. 1950, p. 78; the *New York Times*, 13 Aug. 1950 and 30 Nov. 1952; and Joseph J. and Suzy Fucini, *Entrepreneurs* (1985). For a detailed description of Hallmark Cards, see Milton Moskowitz et al., *Everybody's Business* (1990). An obituary is in the *New York Times*, 30 Aug. 1982.

DENNIS WEPMAN

HALL, John Elihu (27 Dec. 1783–12 June 1829), lawyer and editor, was born in Philadelphia, Pennsylvania, the son of John Hall, a member of a prominent Maryland landholding family, and Sarah Ewing, an author. The eldest of ten children, Hall grew up in a literary household with strong ties to Philadelphia's cultural elite. His maternal grandfather, John Ewing, was provost of the University of Pennsylvania. After studying for a time at Princeton without taking a degree, he returned to Philadelphia in 1804 and entered the law office of Joseph Hopkinson, a leading practitioner. Hall married Fanny M. Chew of Philadelphia, whose family included many notable community leaders and lawyers. In 1805 he was admitted to the Pennsylvania bar but soon moved to Baltimore, Maryland, to pursue his profession.

Hall combined his legal and literary interests by editing the first American legal periodical, the *American Law Journal*, which he published in six volumes from 1808 to 1817. Designed to inform attorneys and merchants of major differences in state laws affecting interstate commercial transactions, the *Journal* printed important new decisions and statutes that were not otherwise available. In addition, Hall translated portions of civil law codes and texts that dealt with maritime and commercial matters for his readers. Unlike the English law magazines of the time, the *American*

Law Journal was not narrowly professional but treated many subjects of general interest to the educated community. Hall hoped that his venture would encourage uniformity in state laws and contribute to the creation of a more systematic national jurisprudence. Although bar leaders praised the *Journal* and cited it in arguments before state supreme courts and the U.S. Supreme Court, financial difficulties forced Hall to suspend its publication after 1817. When he attempted to revive the magazine in 1821 as the *Journal of Jurisprudence*, it failed after only one issue.

Despite the demands of an active practice, Hall also engaged in some purely literary work. Under the pseudonym of "Sedley," he began in 1804 to contribute occasional essays to Joseph Dennie's *Port Folio*, the leading Federalist magazine of the early nineteenth century. In keeping with the *Port Folio*'s conservative temper, the "Sedley" pieces generally offered well-written reflections on the low state of American society and manners. Hall's most ambitious effort was the "Memoirs of Anacreon," a fictional account of the Greek poet, whose *Odes* had recently been translated by the Irish poet Tom Moore. On a visit to Philadelphia in 1804, Moore met Hall and encouraged the project. The first installment appeared in the March 1806 issue of the *Port Folio*, but Hall did not complete the work until 1820. When he serialized the enlarged version from April to September 1820, it attracted much favorable criticism from the *Port Folio*'s readers. Hall further enhanced his literary reputation by editing *Poems by the Late Dr. Shaw* (1810), to which he contributed a useful memoir of the Baltimore poet that drew upon material from his diaries. In 1813 Hall's attainments won him a prestigious appointment as professor of rhetoric and belles-lettres in the recently created University of Maryland. The post proved to be purely honorific, however, because the School of Arts and Sciences was not in fact organized until the 1830s. Of more immediate consequence was Hall's election to membership in the American Philosophical Society in 1814.

A staunch Federalist in politics, he opposed the War of 1812 and almost died at the hands of a Baltimore mob. On 27 July 1812 he joined a small group of fellow dissidents in defending the office of Alexander C. Hanson's (1786–1819) *Federal Republican* against the attacks of anti-British rioters. The next day municipal authorities persuaded the defenders to accept safe conduct to the local jail, but that evening a mob stormed the facility and severely beat the prisoners, leaving Hall and several others for dead. Shortly thereafter Hall published in Philadelphia an anonymous pamphlet, *To the People of the United States* (n.d.), which provided a valuable firsthand account of the incident and condemned the violence.

In 1816 he abandoned his Baltimore practice and returned to Philadelphia to edit the *Port Folio*, which his brother Harrison had purchased. Under Hall's direction the magazine survived until 1827 but never regained the popularity it had enjoyed during Dennie's editorship. Hall promised his readers that the *Port Folio* would defend American literature and manners against foreign criticism and partially redeemed this nationalistic pledge by publishing many pieces on life in the West. His mother and brothers James and Thomas Mifflin regularly contributed to the magazine until ill health and mounting debts forced Hall to discontinue its publication. During his years as editor he published three literary works: *The Lay Preacher by Joseph Dennie, Collected and Arranged by John E. Hall* (1817); *The Philadelphia Souvenir: A Collection of Fugitive Pieces from the Philadelphia Press* (1826), which contained a valuable sketch of Dennie, whose biography Hall intended to write; and *Memoirs of Eminent Persons, with Portraits and Facsimiles* (1827). He died in Philadelphia.

Hall's enduring importance derives primarily from his legal publications, which included *The Practice and Jurisdiction of the Court of Admiralty* (1809), *An Essay on Maritime Loans, from the French of Balthazard Marie Émérigon with Notes, to Which Is Added an Appendix* (1811), *Tracts on Constitutional Law, Containing Mr. Livingston's Answer to Mr. Jefferson* (1813), and *Office and Authority of a Justice of the Peace in the State of Maryland; to Which Is Added a Variety of Precedents in Conveyancing* (1815). Together with the *American Law Journal*, these works did much to shape early nineteenth-century American legal culture by bringing major Continental legal thinkers to the attention of American lawyers and judges.

• There is no biography of Hall, or any major collection of unpublished papers. Useful biographical sketches of his career, with special reference to his association with the *Port Folio*, appear in Frank Luther Mott, *A History of American Magazines, 1741–1850* (1930), and Harold Milton Ellis, *Joseph Dennie and His Circle* (1915). On the nature of American legal periodicals in the early nineteenth century, see Roscoe Pound, "Types of Legal Periodical," *Iowa Law Review* 14 (Apr. 1929): 257–65, and Maxwell Bloomfield, *American Lawyers in a Changing Society, 1776–1876* (1976). For a good discussion of the establishment of the University of Maryland and its schools, see George H. Callcott, *A History of the University of Maryland* (1966). Hall's obituary is in the *National Gazette* (Philadelphia), 13 June 1829.

MAXWELL BLOOMFIELD

HALL, Juanita (6 Nov. 1901–28 Feb. 1968), performer in Broadway musicals, was born in Keyport, New Jersey, the daughter of Abram Long, a farm laborer, and Mary Richardson. Of mixed African-American and Irish parentage, she was raised by maternal grandparents and received a training in classical music at New York's Juilliard School of Music. Although one source mentions an earlier marriage to Clayton King, most sources state that, while still in her teens, she married actor Clement Hall, who died in the 1920s. There were no children from the union, and Hall never remarried. Despite severely limited opportunities for African Americans on Broadway in the 1920s, Hall managed to break into the chorus of *Show Boat* in 1928 and joined the Hall Johnson Choir in the chorus of *The Green Pastures* in 1930. She remained with the Hall Johnson Choir as soloist and assistant director from 1931 to 1936.

In 1936 Hall served as musical arranger and director for *Sweet River*, a George Abbott adaptation of *Uncle Tom's Cabin* at the Fifty-first Street Theater. She conducted a Works Progress Administration chorus in New York City from 1936 to 1941 and meanwhile also organized the Juanita Hall Choir. She directed the latter group in a Brattleboro Theater production of *Conjur* in Brooklyn in 1938 and also appeared in radio broadcasts with Kate Smith, Rudy Vallee, and the Theatre Guild of the Air.

Hall began to reestablish her presence on Broadway with a bit part in S. N. Behrman's *The Pirate* (1942). This was followed by appearances in the musicals *Sing Out, Sweet Land* (1943), *St. Louis Woman* (1946), and *Street Scene* (1947). In 1948 she made her debut as a nightclub singer at New York's Old Knickerbocker Music Hall, singing, among others, songs written for her by Langston Hughes and Herbert Kingsley.

The break in her career came when Hall appeared in "Talent '48," an annual talent showcase sponsored by the Stage Managers Club. There she was seen by the songwriting team of Richard Rodgers and Oscar Hammerstein II, who were then in the process of writing *South Pacific*. As recalled later by Rodgers in the *New York Times*, "As soon as we heard her, Oscar and I knew that at least one part in 'South Pacific' had been filled. There was our Bloody Mary—high spirited, graceful, mischievous, proud, a gloriously gifted voice projected with all the skills of one who knew exactly how to take over a song and make it hers." When she opened in the original cast of *South Pacific* in the Majestic Theater on 7 April 1949, Brooks Atkinson commented, "Juanita Hall's bustling, sharp-witted performance is a masterpiece" (*New York Times*, 5 June 1949).

Bloody Mary became Hall's signature role for the remainder of her career. Her rendition of her big number, "Bali Ha'i," in the words of *Variety* (6 Mar. 1968), "virtually stole the show from its principals Ezio Pinza and Mary Martin and gave her name status." The short, stocky actress walked away with both the Donaldson and Antoinette Perry (Tony) awards for best supporting actress in a musical that season. She left the show after 900 performances for a year of nightclub singing and then returned at the request of Rodgers. She later recreated the role in summer stock and notably for a revival at the City Center (1957); she finally committed it to film for the movie version of *South Pacific* (1958). Her other song from the show, "Happy Talk," eventually became her favorite for its positive outlook; according to Mary Martin, Hall had worked out the number's singular hand movements herself.

Thanks to her multiracial heritage, Hall found herself in demand for a variety of character roles. After the Tonkinese Bloody Mary, she played a West Indian brothel keeper in Harold Arlen's *House of Flowers* (1954), appearing opposite Pearl Bailey and Diahann Carroll. In 1958 Rodgers and Hammerstein cast her as

a Chinese-American marriage broker in their *Flower Drum Song*. (Joshua Logan, *South Pacific*'s director, had originally thought Hall was Chinese.) She also appeared in the movie version of *Flower Drum Song* (1961).

Hall made numerous television appearances with "The Ed Sullivan Show," "The Coca-Cola Hour," "The Perry Como Show" and "The Dave Garroway Show." She also sang with her Juanita Hall Choir in the movie *Miracle in Harlem* (1949). Among her other stage appearances were *Sailor, Beware* with the Lafayette Players (1935), *The Secret Room* (1945), and *The Ponder Heart* (1956). She was also the recipient of a citation from Israel in 1952 for her efforts in the Bonds for Israel drive.

Suffering from failing health and eyesight because of diabetes, Hall scored her last triumph in a one-woman show, "A Woman and the Blues," at the East 74th Street Theater in 1966. Her program combined the blues and jazz of her nightclub acts with the show stoppers of her Broadway career. A benefit on her behalf was staged the year before her death by the Actors Fund of America. She died in Bay Shore, Long Island, and was buried in her hometown of Keyport.

Hall's interpretation of Bloody Mary set the standard for the perennially popular *South Pacific* for half a century. Hall expanded opportunities for African Americans during the American musical theater's golden age. Her versatility in roles other than as African-American characters, while not exactly nontraditional casting, may have helped point the way to that later practice.

• There is no collection of papers, though a vertical file on Hall is at the Schomburg Center for Research in Black Culture, New York City. Biographical entries appear in Rayford W. Logan and Michael R. Winston, eds., *Dictionary of American Negro Biography* (1982), and Darlene Clark Hine, ed., *Black Women in America: An Historical Encyclopedia* (1993). Articles on Hall are "After 21 Years," *Time*, 6 June 1949, pp. 74–76; and Doug Anderson, "The Show Stopper," *Theatre Arts* 36, no. 10 (1952): 26. The principal obituary is in the *New York Times*, 1 Mar. 1968, and Richard Rodgers wrote an appreciation for the *New York Times*, 10 Mar. 1968.

J. E. VACHA

HALL, Lyman (12 Apr. 1724–19 Oct. 1790), member of the Continental Congress and governor of Georgia, was born in Wallingford, Connecticut, the son of John Hall, a Congregational minister, and Mary Street. After graduating from Yale in 1747, Lyman served briefly as a minister in Fairfield and then became a physician by apprenticeship, practicing in Wallingford. In 1752 he married Abigail Burr, who died a year later. He then married Mary Osborne (date unknown), the mother of his son John, born in 1765.

In 1756 or 1757 Lyman and Mary Hall moved to Charleston, South Carolina, where he practiced medicine. Within several years they joined earlier New England Congregational immigrants in a move to the Midway settlement south of Savannah, Georgia. In 1760 Hall was granted land on which he established a rice plantation, "Hall's Knoll," and later he built a townhouse in Sunbury. He also continued his medical practice. By mid-1762 he had returned to South Carolina, advertising himself as "practitioner in physic and surgery" and a vendor of family medicines.

By 1774, however, Hall had moved back to Georgia and had become deeply involved in the politics of revolution. Georgia's reluctance to break with Britain disturbed him and his allies in St. John's Parish. When chosen by neighbors to attend the Continental Congress, Hall at first refused, probably because other parishes did not concur. Elected again in his own parish in March 1775, Hall went to Philadelphia and was unanimously voted a member by the Second Continental Congress. Hall and the Georgia delegates who joined him, Button Gwinnett and George Walton, signed the Declaration of Independence. They demurred from only that part of Thomas Jefferson's draft condemning King George for continuing the foreign slave trade and were partly responsible for the deletion of the clause.

Hall took little part in floor debate in Congress but was active in committees. He worked on ways to increase funds and the supply of lead and salt, evaluated the health of the army and the state of its medicines, conferred with General George Washington and his aides on future military plans, and inquired into "the causes of the miscarriage in Canada," the disastrous defeat of revolutionary forces that had invaded Quebec. Hall was reelected through 1780 but remained in Philadelphia only until February 1777, when he returned to Georgia, believing that state affairs should take precedence.

Hall had an ex officio seat in the new Georgia assembly, which was riven by controversy. He favored the faction that was rural, liberal, and wary of military dominance over civil affairs. In 1778 Savannah again fell under British control. Hall's Knoll and the Sunbury home were burned, and Hall stood accused of treason by the British, who confiscated his property. He escaped with his family to Charleston and, later, to relatives in Connecticut, where he remained until the British evacuated Savannah in 1782. In 1783 he was elected to the Georgia House of Assembly, which appointed him to a one-year term as governor. In that office Hall exiled adamant Tories and rewarded patriot soldiers with frontier land. He sought to restore the state's depleted finances by selling confiscated estates, reopening an office for sale of public land, and urging taxation upon the assembly. He advocated state support of education, an initiative responsible for the eventual chartering of the University of Georgia. In 1790 Hall moved to a new plantation in Burke County, where he died a few months later.

Hall was six feet one inch tall, courteous and dignified, generally mild in manner but fervent in his patriotism. No authentic portrait seems to have survived.

• No collection of Lyman Hall's papers exists, fires having destroyed his important records. The following publications are useful: Worthington C. Ford, ed., *Journals of the Conti-*nental Congress* (1904–1937); Edmund C. Burnett, ed., *Letters of Members of the Continental Congress* (1921–1936); and Allen D. Candler, comp., *The Revolutionary Records of the State of Georgia* (1908). Biographies include James W. Hall, *Lyman Hall, Georgia Patriot* (1959), and sketches by Charles C. Jones, Jr., in his *Biographical Sketches of the Delegates from Georgia to the Continental Congress* (1891); Franklin B. Dexter in his *Biographical Sketches of the Graduates of Yale College* (1896); J. H. Young in *Physician Signers of the Declaration of Independence*, ed. George E. Gifford, Jr. (1976), and in *Georgia's Signers and the Declaration of Independence*, ed. Edwin C. Bridges (1981), which contains genealogical information on Hall by Kenneth H. Thomas, Jr.

JAMES HARVEY YOUNG

HALL, Pauline (26 Feb. 1860–29 Dec. 1919), singer and actress, was born Pauline Fredericka Schmidgall (or Schmitgall) in Cincinnati, Ohio. Little is known of her parents other than that her father was an apothecary and her mother was a keeper of an actors' boardinghouse. Pauline's humble background was significant to her career primarily because the actors living in her childhood home caused her to be stagestruck at an early age. She was young when she committed herself to the "profession," as she called it, performing at age fifteen in a ballet presented by R. E. J. Miles at Robinson's Opera House in Cincinnati, "where she stepped out of the chorus to sing a small part" and "then chose the stage name of Hall" (Clippings File). She then went to the Grand Opera House until Miles, still her manager, put his "America Racing Association and Hippodrome" on the road, and Hall was featured in the street tableaus and drove a chariot in races at the indoor entertainments.

In 1878 Hall joined the chorus of Alice Oates's company and later appeared in minor roles with Samuel Colville's Folly company. For a brief period she acted in subordinate parts in legitimate drama, including Lady Capulet in *Romeo and Juliet* and Widow Melnotte in *The Lady of Lyons*. But tiring of these roles she returned to comic opera and burlesque, signing with J. H. Haverly for the role of Elsa in his *Merry War* in 1883. After this engagement she opened with Ned Rice's company at the Bijou Opera House in New York, where she created the role of Venus in *Orpheus and Eurydice*, a major success for her, and continued in the role until the show closed. The following season Hall duplicated her success in the role of Hasson in a revival of *Bluebeard*, touring with the company until July 1884.

In August 1884 Hall began an engagement at Niblo's Gardens as Loresoul in Poole and Gilmore's *The Seven Ravens*, a singing role that increased her popularity with young, "about town" men. In February 1885 she worked with the Percy Ixion company at the Comedy Theatre, thereafter debuting, in German, in *Die Fledermaus* at the Thalia Theatre.

For the 1885–1886 season Hall was engaged by Rudolf Aronson at the Casino Theatre as Ninon de l'Enclos in the first English presentation of *Nanon*. The part was a prelude to the most important role of her career, her interpretation of Erminie in the work by the same name, in which she played eight hundred performances touring across the country. She attributed her success at the Casino to Aronson, who possessed "the rare facility of determining the adaptability of a singer or performer to certain roles" and in whom she had such confidence that she would "cheerfully accept whatever he may assign me" (Pauline Hall, File of Clippings, 1880).

After leaving the Casino, Hall practiced her art peripatetically, touring for a time with her own companies (1892–1896) and later entering vaudeville. In 1894 she was at Harrigan's Theatre as Prince Raphael in *The Princess of Trebizonde*, as pretty as ever and singing "very sweetly," but "her shapely woman-figure destroyed all illusion as to the sex of the prince" (*Annals of the New York Stage*, vol. 15, p. 618). In 1912 and 1913 she was in the revivals of *Robin Hood* and *The Geisha*. In 1919, Hall was stricken with first a cold and then pneumonia while playing in David Belasco's comedy, *The Gold Diggers*, and she died a week later at her home in Yonkers, New York.

Hall was on the American stage continuously for forty-four years. Although when she began her career the bit parts she played paid for her shelter and heat but not for her supper, she was remarkably consistent in maintaining herself as an actress. She was equally consistent in sustaining her dark beauty, her curvaceous form, and a dazzling effect on the young men in her audiences. To one interviewer she was as magnificent as the Andalouse, whom Alfred de Musset immortalized, "her well-shaped head, encircled by black hair, illumined by her dark eyes of extreme limpidity" (*Theatre*, p. 60). She also developed a performance style that was so mellow she was reputed to have cured insomniacs, having the same effect on them as a lullaby. At one rehearsal of *Erminie*, she sang a ballad without moving a muscle of her face above the lips. "'Why not add a little life to it, Miss Hall?' asked the stage manager. Turning on him reproachfully with her limpid black eyes, she replied, 'Am I not supposed to be in a dream? Should a dreamer gesticulate?' The manager wilted, and Pauline went on blooming" (*Illustrated American*, p. 264).

As an actress reputed for face and figure, it is not surprising that her career declined in her later years. Shortly before her death she wrote, "I am glad to have even a small part in a successful play. . . . But . . . [n]o one who has played the leading part enjoys the transition to a lesser one. That is what time does" (File of Clippings, 1919). Her final role in *The Gold Diggers* seemed to personify her career—a distinguished stage beauty reduced to selling soap to younger and more beautiful women of the stage.

Offstage, Hall was married and divorced twice. She married Edmund White in 1881 and divorced him in 1889 because he was a "man about town." Remarried in 1891 to George B. McLellan, with whom she had one child, she divorced him in 1904.

Hall was a tolerably good singer and actress, but "her figure, after all, was the secret of her popularity" (*New York Herald*, 18 Nov. 1881). One of the most statuesque women on the American stage, her dignity and grace drew audiences for nearly half a century. During Hall's lifetime her name was a household word.

• Material on Pauline Hall is scant. The primary source for clippings and photographs from newspapers and journals published during her lifetime is the Billy Rose Theatre Collection at the New York Public Library for the Performing Arts, Lincoln Center. Specific articles contained within that file include "The Queens of Burlesque," *Theatre*, p. 60; *New York Herald*, 18 Nov. 1881; and "Our Gallery of Players," *Illustrated American*, 27 June 1891, p. 264. References to her performance history appear in George C. D. Odell, *Annals of the New York Stage*, vols. 10–15 (1938–1949). Also see Lewis Strang, *Prima Donnas and Soubrettes of Light Opera and Musical Comedy in America* (1900).

LYNNE GREELEY

HALL, Prince (1735–4 Dec. 1807), Masonic organizer and abolitionist, was born in Bridgetown, Barbados, the son of a "white English leather worker" and a "free woman of African and French descent"; his birth date is variously given as 12 Sept. 1748 (Horton). He was the slave of William Hall, a leather dresser. At age seventeen, Hall found passage to Boston, Massachusetts, by working on a ship and became employed there as a leather worker. In 1762 he joined the Congregational Church on School Street. He received his manumission in 1770. Official records indicate that Hall was married three times. In 1763 he married Sarah Ritchie, a slave. In 1770, after her death, he married Flora Gibbs of Gloucester, Massachusetts; they had one son, Prince Africanus. In 1798 Hall married Sylvia Ward. The reason for the dissolution of the second marriage is unclear.

In March 1775 Hall was one of fifteen African Americans initiated into a British army lodge of Freemasons stationed in Boston. After the evacuation of the British, the black Masons were allowed to meet as a lodge and to participate fully in Masonic ceremonies, but full recognition was withheld. After a series of appeals, African Lodge No. 459 was granted full recognition in 1784 by the London Grand Lodge. Hall became the lodge's "worshipful master," charged with ensuring that it followed all the rules of the "Book of Constitution." He served in that position until his death.

During the revolutionary war, Hall worked as a skilled craftsman and sold leather drumheads to the Continental army. Military records indicate that he likely fought in the war. During the war, Hall also agitated on behalf of abolition. In 1777 he and seven other African Americans, including three black Masons, petitioned the General Court to abolish slavery in Massachusetts so that "the Inhabitanc of these Stats" could no longer be "chargeable with the inconsistency of acting themselves the part which thay condem and oppose in others." The petition was referred to the Congress of Confederation, but slavery was not abolished in Massachusetts until 1783.

Throughout the 1780s, Hall served as the grand-master of the Masonic Lodge and owned and operated a leather workshop called the Golden Fleece. During that period he also emerged as a leading spokesman for black Bostonians. When Shays's Rebellion broke out in western Massachusetts in 1786, Hall and the African lodge offered to raise a militia of 700 black soldiers to assist the government in putting down the rebellion. "We, by the Providence of God, are members of a fraternity that not only enjoins upon us to be peaceable subjects to the civil powers where we reside," Hall wrote, "but it also forbids our having concern in any plot of conspiracies against the state where we dwell." The offer was turned down by the governor.

In 1787 Hall and seventy-two other African Americans, perhaps resentful of the state government's dismissive attitude toward them, signed a petition asking the state legislature to finance black emigration to Africa. "We, or our ancestors have been taken from all our dear connections, and brought from Africa and put into a state of slavery in this country," the petition stated, in marked contrast to the patriotic language of the petition on Shays's Rebellion. "We find ourselves, in many respects, in very disagreeable and disadvantageous circumstances; most of which must attend us, so long as we and our children live in America." This was the first public statement in favor of African colonization made in the United States. The legislature accepted the petition but never acted on it.

Shortly after the emigration petition, Hall drafted another petition to the Massachusetts legislature, this one protesting the denial of free schools for African Americans who paid taxes and therefore had "the right to enjoy the privileges of free men." In 1788 Hall drafted a petition, signed by twenty-two members of his lodge, expressing outrage at the abduction by slave traders of three free blacks in Boston. After a group of Quakers and other Boston clergy joined the call, in March 1788 the General Court passed an act that banned the slave trade and granted "relief of the families of such unhappy persons as may be kidnapped or decoyed away from this Commonwealth." Diplomatic actions obtained the release of the three captured freemen from the French island of St. Bartholomew. Hall and the African lodge organized a celebration for their return to Boston.

In 1792 Hall delivered a lecture on the injustice of black taxpayers' being denied free schools for their children. The lecture was published as *A Charge Delivered to the Brethren of the African Lodge on the 25th of June, 1792* (1792). After failing to convince the state government to provide education for black children, Hall in 1796 established a school for black children in his own house. He recruited two students from Harvard College to serve as teachers. In 1806 the school's increased enrollment prompted Hall to move it to a larger space at the African Society House on Belknap Street.

Hall died in Boston. The Prince Hall Masons, still the largest and most prestigious fraternal order of African Americans, was established one year after his death.

Hall was one of the most prominent and influential African Americans in the era of the American Revolution. As a leading spokesperson, organizer, and educator, Hall served as a principal agitator for abolition and for civil rights for black Americans in the period. He was also a pioneer in the establishment of fraternal organizations of African Americans at a time when such activities were deemed solely the province of whites.

• The most complete account of Hall's life is Charles H. Wesley, *Prince Hall, Life and Legacy* (1977). An excellent but condensed biography is in Sidney Kaplan, *The Black Presence in the Era of the American Revolution, 1770–1800* (1973). See also William C. Nell, *The Colored Patriots of the American Revolution* (1855); William H. Grimshaw, *Official History of Freemasonry among the Colored People in North America* (1903); and James Oliver Horton, "Generations of Protest: Black Families and Social Reform in Ante-Bellum Boston," *New England Quarterly* 49, no. 2 (June 1976).

THADDEUS RUSSELL

HALL, Samuel (2 Nov. 1740–30 Oct. 1807), publisher, bookseller, and printer, was born in Medford, Massachusetts, the son of Jonathan Hall and Anna Fowle. As a youth, he served an apprenticeship to his uncle, Daniel Fowle, publisher of the *New Hampshire Gazette*. Hall then moved to Rhode Island where in August 1762 he became the partner of Anne Franklin (the mother of James Franklin) in publishing the *Newport Mercury*. Although the patriot printer and historian Isaiah Thomas stated that Hall married Franklin's daughter, no record of the marriage has been found. After Anne Franklin died the following spring, Hall became sole proprietor, published the *Mercury*, and did substantial government printing. In March 1768 he sold the newspaper to Solomon Southwick. A month later Hall set up the first printing press in Salem, Massachusetts. On 2 August he started the *Essex Gazette*, to advance "a due sense of the Rights and Liberties of Our Country." His brother Ebenezer joined him there in 1772.

Hall proved to be a partisan of the patriot cause, as the *Essex Gazette*, in the phrase of Isaiah Thomas, was "well conducted, and ably supported the cause of the country." Hall also produced several almanacs and political pamphlets in Salem, including Stephen Sayre's *The Englishman Deceived: A Political Piece* (1768) and Timothy Pickering's *Easy Plan of Discipline for a Militia* (1775). Isaiah Thomas had to move his Boston press to Worcester in the spring of 1775. At the urging of the Provincial Congress, Hall and his brother moved their press to Cambridge, where they might be conveniently located to advance the patriot interest. In May 1775 Hall and his brother initiated the *New England Chronicle; or, The Essex Gazette* at Stoughton Hall, Harvard College. After his brother died, Hall moved to Boston in April 1776, changing the name of his paper to the *New England Chronicle*. Soon thereafter, in June, he sold the paper to Edward E. Powars and Nathaniel Willis, who renamed it the *Independent*

Chronicle. During the Revolution, Hall printed but few titles, probably owing to a shortage of paper, producing four in 1776, one in 1777, none from 1778 to 1780, two in 1781 (including a broadside announcing Cornwallis's surrender), and four in 1782.

On 18 October 1781 Hall returned to Salem and assumed publication of Mary Crouch's *Salem Gazette.* At that time, he also expanded his efforts as a publisher, producing around ten books per year, including the *New-England Primer Improved* (1784) and two Latin grammars. The tax on newspapers of 1785, however, obliged him to suspend publication with the 22 November issue. He returned again to Boston and on 28 November 1785 began to publish the *Massachusetts Gazette.* In June 1787 J. W. Allen became his partner; Hall relinquished his interest to Allen that September. For a brief period, in 1787 and 1788, Hall published Noah Webster's *American Magazine* and in 1789 the *Courier de Boston* in French for Joseph Nancrede. Hall was increasingly focused, however, on publishing sermons, children's books, and school texts. In the 1790s he became a prolific publisher, publishing more than sixty titles in 1795 alone. Of these, approximately one-third were children's books, one-third were sermons, and the balance were almanacs and books on science and literature.

As a publisher of juvenilia, Hall produced catechisms, including Rebecca Wilkinson's *Sermons to Children* (1797) and those of Joseph Priestley, Isaac Watt, and Cotton Mather; chapbooks such as *The Death of Cock Robin* (1791), *The Entertaining History of Honest Peter* (1794), and *The History of Little Goody Two Shoes* (1797), which was ornamented with cuts; and didactic works such as *Virtue and Vice; or, The History of Charles Careful and Harry Heedless* (1792) and *Food for the Mind* (1798?) by "John-the-Giant-Killer, Esq." He also published foreign-language books such as Arnaud Berquin's *Looking-Glass for the Mind* (1795), which was translated from the French by Samuel Cooper, and the *Golden Treasury for the Children of God* by Karl von Bogatzky and translated from the German (1796).

Hall published many primers and alphabet books, such as *Tom Thumb's Folio* (1791), *The Royal Primer* (1796), and, for older children, titles like Eleazar Moody's *The School of Good Manners* (1790) and James Dana's *A New American Selection of Lessons in Reading and Speaking . . .* (1792). As a publisher of textbooks, Hall produced *A Short and Easy Guide to Arithmetick* (1794), two editions of Samuel Temple's *Concise Introduction to Practical Arithmetic* (1796 and 1798), English grammars by Caleb Alexander (1792) and Benjamin Dearborn (1795), the first two editions of Caleb Bingham's spelling book, *The Child's Companion* (1792), and William Perry's spelling book and his *Royal Standard Dictionary* (1796).

As a publisher in the 1790s, Hall produced many sermons, including those of John Allyn, William Symmes, Isaac Backus, Abiel Holmes, Jeremy Belknap, Jedidiah Morse, and Peter Thacher. As publisher of some of the founding members of the Massachusetts Historical Society, Hall had contacts that led to his publishing several volumes of the society's *Collections* (1795, 1798, and 1800) and its *Catalogue of Books* (1796). Hall also published the first edition of Morse's *Geography Made Easy* (1791).

Hall published several medical books, including William Cheselden's *Anatomy of the Human Body* (1795), John Holliday's tract on the yellow fever (1796), and James Sims's *Observations on the Scarlatina Anginosa* (1796). Hall also published numerous editions of British fiction, including works by Daniel Defoe, Henry Fielding, and Samuel Richardson, including the first Boston editions of *Pamela* (1793), *The History of Sir Charles Grandison* (1794), and *Clarissa* (1795). He published a little poetry, captivity narratives such as John Williams's *The Redeemed Captive,* and execution literature such as Ezra Ripley's *Love to Our Neighbor* (1800), on the occasion of the execution of one Samuel Smith for burglary. Hall sold his business to Thomas Edmands and Ensign Lincoln in 1805 and retired. He died two years later, presumably in Salem.

Hall's publishing efforts were aimed principally at producing juvenilia, which were important not only for the variety of titles but also for their attractiveness, as well as many sermons and numerous literary, historical, and scientific works. He played a modest role in the events of the Revolution, producing a few important imprints and providing useful information through publication of his newspapers, but his principal contribution was as a regional publisher of many works (religious, devotional, literary, and educational) that reflected the expansion of American culture in the post-Revolution period.

• The article on Hall in Benjamin Franklin V., ed., *Boston Printers, Publishers, and Booksellers, 1640–1800* (1980), is a useful summary of Hall's career. Additional information may be found in Isaiah Thomas, *The History of Printing in America,* repr. ed. (1970); in Joseph T. Buckingham, *Specimens of Newspaper Literature,* vol. 1 (1850); and in Rosalie V. Halsey, *Forgotten Books of the American Nursery,* repr. ed. (1969).

WILLIAM L. JOYCE

HALL, Samuel (23 Apr. 1800–13 Nov. 1870), shipbuilder, was born in Marshfield, Massachusetts, the son of Luke Hall, a shipmaster, and Anna Tuels. Hall had little formal education. Since the North River at Marshfield was then a shipbuilding center, it was natural for him to be apprenticed as a shipwright. Hall served his apprenticeship in the shipyard of Deacon Elijah Barstow in Hanover and with his brothers, Luke and William, built several vessels in the Hanover-Marshfield area in the years 1825–1827. The *Waverly,* a 230-ton brig, was the last ship Hall built in Marshfield. When he achieved his majority, Hall left Barstow's yard with "twenty-five cents in his pocket and a broadaxe on his shoulders."

Hall first settled in Medford, Massachusetts, to work in the shipyards on the Mystic River, then a center for the construction of wooden ships. From there he went up to the Penobscot River, near Camden,

Maine, where he worked as a shipwright and ship's carpenter. Hall had a habit of getting the wood for a ship himself and was known to lead gangs of men into the woods of eastern Maine to search for ship frames. In 1837 Hall moved to Duxbury, Massachusetts. He worked as a shipwright in the yards of Ezra Weston, the premier shipbuilder on Cape Cod. Hall then built for a time on his own in Duxbury. In 1839 he moved to East Boston, then an island in Boston harbor, where William H. Sumner and the East Boston Company were attempting to establish shipbuilding as a commercial enterprise. Hall, the first shipbuilder to move to the island, set up his shipyard at the foot of Maverick Street.

Hall's first East Boston ship, the *Akbar*, was built for Boston merchant R. B. Forbes and was used in the China trade. The 650-ton *Akbar* was an unusually fast ship; Hall is believed to have modeled it after a schooner of the Baltimore clipper type. In 1842 Hall launched the schooner *Zephyr* and in 1843 the brig *Antelope*, both for Forbes. Hall built twenty-eight small ships at his Maverick Street yard between 1840 and 1850. In 1850 he launched the *Surprise*, the first clipper ship to be built in Massachusetts and the vessel that made his name. The *Surprise* had a long, sharp bow, considered best for speed, with a full, powerful afterbody. Before the clipper ship, designers had to choose between carrying capacity and speed. With the launch of the *Surprise*, Hall was one of the first designers to show that this choice was not an absolute. When the vessel stopped in New York to take on cargo for San Francisco, the *New York Herald* said that it was the handsomest ship ever seen in that port. A fast and profitable ship, the *Surprise* sailed for twenty-five years, until destroyed by a drunken pilot off the coast of Japan. For a time Hall was the most eminent shipbuilder in Massachusetts.

Over the next five years, Hall constructed a number of clipper ships, whose excellence was surpassed only—and not always—by those ships built at the nearby East Boston yard of his friend Donald McKay. The *Game Cock* (1850), the *Race Horse* (1850), the *R. B. Forbes* (1851), the *John Gilpin*, *Flying Childers*, *Hoogly*, and *Polynesia* (all 1852), the *Amphitrite*, *Mystery*, *Wizard*, and *Oriental* (all 1853) were remarkable, elegant, fast vessels. In 1852 the *John Gilpin* raced McKay's *Flying Fish* from New York to San Francisco, losing by a day in what Howe and Matthews in *American Clipper Ships* (1926) call the "most celebrated and famous ship-race that has ever been run." Hall built most of his ships for the large merchant fleets owned by wealthy Boston families, such as the Bacons and the Forbeses, and occasionally for the concern of Pierce & Hunnewell. He built the *Wizard* on his own account, however, and sold it in New York for $95,000.

Hall was a master shipbuilder, a visionary in some respects, but he was not a naval architect. Unlike McKay, who designed all his own ships, Hall had the plans of several of his large ships, including the *Game Cock* and the *Surprise*, drawn up by Samuel Hartt Pook, the first independent naval architect in New England. Even so, Hall, who had a national reputation, was the equal of the greatest shipbuilders of his time. In all, 110 ships were launched from Hall's East Boston shipyard.

Hall was one of few artisans active in East Boston politics. He represented the East Boston ward on the board of aldermen in 1850 and was instrumental in having water piped from Lake Cochituate to the island, which was in desperate need of a freshwater source. Grateful citizens rewarded him with a $1,000 silver service for his accomplishment. Hall did well in real estate speculation and was quite successful in business. He was president of the East Boston Dry Dock Company from 1847 until 1858, president of the East Boston Ferry Company from 1852 until it was bought out by the city of Boston, and president of the Maverick Savings Bank from its inception, in 1854, until his death. Early in 1870 Hall testified before the Lynch Committee, a select committee of the U.S. Congress, in his capacity as a prominent shipbuilder. Hall argued for the elimination or reduction of duties imposed on imported materials used in the construction of wooden ships. Continued imposition of such duties, Hall claimed, would put an end to an already depressed wooden shipbuilding industry.

Hall married twice. His marriage to Christina Kent was childless. Hall had eight children with his second wife, Huldah B. Sherman. He died at his home in East Boston.

• There are Hall papers in the East Boston Dry Dock collection at the Baker Library in the Harvard Business School. The Hall family is mentioned in L. V. Briggs, *History of Shipbuilding on the North River, Plymouth County, Mass.* (1889), and also in M. A. Thomas, *Memorials of Marshfield* (1854). W. H. Sumner gives a fair amount of detail on Hall as shipbuilder and public citizen in *A History of East Boston* (1858), a work that also contains a complete list of Hall's ships. Other works that discuss Hall are A. V. Clark, *The Clipper Ship Era* (1910); S. E. Morison, *The Maritime History of Massachusetts 1783–1860* (1921); O. T. Howe and F. C. Matthews, *American Clipper Ships* (2 vols., 1926–1927); and John G. B. Hutchins, *The American Maritime Industries and Public Policy, 1789–1914* (1941). Hall's complete testimony before the Lynch Committee is available in U.S. House of Representatives, *Causes of the Reduction of American Tonnage and the Decline of Navigation Interests* (17 Feb. 1870). Obituaries are in the *Boston Transcript*, 14 Nov. 1870, and the *East Boston Argus-Advocate*, 19 Nov. 1870.

GEORGE M. O'HAR

HALL, Sarah Ewing (30 Oct. 1761–8 Apr. 1830), essayist, was born in Philadelphia, Pennsylvania, the daughter of the Reverend John Ewing, pastor of the First Presbyterian Church, and Hannah Sergeant. She was educated at home by her father and by the instructive conversation of his learned guests. In 1782 she married John Hall and for the next eight years lived in relative seclusion on his Maryland farm. The couple returned to Philadelphia in 1790 when John Hall became secretary of the Pennsylvania land office. By the time of his death in 1826 they had ten children, two of whom died in infancy.

Sarah Hall retained a love of both contemporary and classical literature all her life, and during her late twenties she took up a regimen of remaining awake for hours each night, reading and writing. This continued for the rest of her life. She published some of her essays under the pen names "Constantia" and "Florepha," though others were written anonymously. Her writings cover a wide range of subjects, like the work of her contemporary Charles Lamb, the English essayist and critic, to whom she may be compared. In her "Reminiscences of Philadelphia" she contrasts the frugalities and war-time constraints of life during the American Revolution with later luxuries. Several of her essays deal with the place of women in the world of her time. "On Female Education" maintains that a father's money should no longer be spent exclusively on sons. Daughters should also be sent to school at the age of eight to learn grammar, geography, history, and modern languages. She did not advocate the study of Latin and Greek by most women, though they were every bit as qualified as men to master such learning, since this knowledge would soon fade away, just as it does with many men; she doubted whether a typical "merchant could still construe Greek." "Defence of American Women" laments that girls are kept so busy helping their mothers with domestic tasks, such as sewing for their brothers, that they have little time for sustained reading. In two essays on the subject of dueling, Hall advocated a community-wide coalition of wives and mothers to put an end to this practice, since they did not desire to see their husbands and sons slaughtered in single combat.

Hall was a contributor to the initial volume of Joseph Dennie's *Port Folio* in 1801, one of only two women so honored. At that time, to write for the *Port Folio* was considered no small honor. After Dennie's death, the publication of this periodical became an enterprise of the Hall family. Her son Harrison Hall published it, while another son, John Elihu Hall, edited it from 1816 to 1827. Their brothers James Hall (1793–1868) and Thomas Hall, as well as their mother, wrote for it. It was said that Sarah Hall's "sprightly essays and pointed criticisms" were written with "wit and felicity of language."

A lifelong student of the Bible, Hall learned Hebrew in 1811, at the age of fifty, in order to better interpret the Scriptures. She published her commentary, *Conversations on the Bible*, in 1818. In this 365-page book she adopted the guise of "Mother" responding to questions from "Catherine" and "Fanny." Four American editions of the book appeared, as well as one in England. For the second edition of the book in 1821, the author added a second volume, extending the commentary "to the end of the Acts of the Apostles." The format of the book included an introduction by "Mother" of each book of the Old Testament and the Gospels, followed by questions from the children. The phenomenal success of the book surprised the author because, as she said, "I had never written a single hour without interruption."

Sarah Hall died in Philadelphia. Three years later Harrison Hall published several of her essays, along with extracts from her letters, in a volume entitled *Selections from the Writings of Mrs. Sarah Hall, Author of Conversations on the Bible, with a Memoir of Her Life.*

• Harrison Hall, ed., *Selections from the Writings of Mrs. Sarah Hall, Author of Conversations on the Bible, with a Memoir of Her Life* (1833), is in the research collection in the catalogue room of the New York Public Library. Articles about Sarah Hall can be found in S. Austin Allibone, *Critical Dictionary of English Literature: American Authors and Books, 1640 to the Present Day*, 3d rev. ed. (1965), and P. A. Hanaford, *Daughters of America* (1882).

RUTH ROSENBERG

HALL, Thomas Seavey (1 Apr. 1827–1 Dec. 1880), inventor and manufacturer, was born in Upper Bartlett, New Hampshire, the son of Elias Hall, a clergyman, and Hannah Seavey. Hall attended Middlebury College in Middlebury, Vermont. He then established a textile company in Stamford, Connecticut, specializing in woolen products. Being very successful in this enterprise, Hall retired in 1866. That year Hall was traveling on a train that wrecked because a switch was misplaced. Although he was not injured, the event impelled him to find a better method for warning trains of other trains on the same track. His interest expanded from signaling devices to prevent accidents caused by misplaced switches and came to include prevention of mishaps at open drawbridges and highway crossings.

As a result of this interest, Hall developed an electrical automatic signal (railroad switch alarm) that would sound an alarm to indicate oncoming traffic and to give trains sufficient time to stop. In February 1867 he acquired a patent for this device, and later that year he founded the Hall Drawbridge and Signal Company, based in Stamford. In 1868 Hall's signal was used for the first time, on a track in Stamford. When Hall discovered that inclement winter weather such as snow and ice hindered the operation of his signal device, he invented the "banjo" signal, his most famous invention, for which he received a patent in April 1869.

In the banjo signaling system, the signal was controlled by a wire circuit through track treadles. A red silk disk was held in an "all-clear" position by an electromagnet powered by a local battery, which supplied a permanent current. When a train passed over the treadles, breaking the circuit, the red disk dropped and became visible through glass windows on each side of the signal. The watertight signal assembly was mounted on a pole positioned alongside the track. In daytime the disk was visible by daylight. At night a kerosene lantern situated behind the glass illuminated the signal.

Later the signal was made in the form of a blade, with the colorless glass behind it replaced by a pane of ground glass. The addition of internal lights gave the signal the same appearance by day and night. Hall's signal was used exclusively in the United States. Many electrically operated signals used open circuits and alternating induction currents to rotate signals on an axis close to the center of gravity.

Hall's invention led to the "automatic block" system of train control. The automatic block system ensured that only one train was on a section of track at one time. The block signal, operated by two electromagnets, each in series with its own switch and with a battery delivering a continuous current, stood at the entrance to a block section of track. The default position of the switch at the entrance to the block section was a closed circuit, delivering power to the electromagnet that held the signal in the white "all-clear" position. When the train passing over the switch broke the circuit, gravity pulled the signal into the red "danger" position. The default position of the second switch, positioned 1,500 to 2,000 feet beyond the block section, was an open circuit. A train passing over this switch closed the circuit and operated the second electromagnet, which held the signal in the danger position until the last car of the train had cleared it, after which the switch reopened and the first electromagnet could return the signal to the all-clear position. This configuration added a measure of safety by providing a delay in delivering the all-clear signal behind the passing train that accommodated the longest of trains at the slowest of speeds. Hall received many patents for different aspects of his signaling system.

The automatic block system was first installed in 1871 on a sixteen-mile section of the Eastern Railroad of Massachusetts. It was later used extensively on the New York, New Haven and Hartford, the Boston and Albany, and many other railroads.

Hall also invented and designed signals for drawbridges. These signals generally operated through a circuit controlling device, which was activated by the draw itself; this alerted water traffic coming from both directions. A patent was also issued to Hall in 1879 for a device to protect highway crossings. Many of the principles incorporated in Hall's inventions have remained in use on American railroads, providing safe travel for people and cargo. Thus did a train accident motivate a retired, successful textile manufacturer to embark on another career as an inventor of rail safety devices.

Hall was married to Sarah C. Phillips (date unknown); they had one son. He died in Meriden, Connecticut.

• Hall patented many railroad safety devices, which can be researched at the U.S. Patent Depository, Crystal City, Va., or through the *U.S. Patent Office Index of Patents*, which is available in hard copy and on microfilm, for the years 1867–1879.
C. Herschel Koyl, "The Evolution of Railroad Signaling," *Journal of the Franklin Institute* 99 (Jan. 1890): 36–59, provides a brief history of railroad safety signals. G. Kecker, "Railway Signaling," *American Society of Civil Engineers, Transactions* 29 (Aug. 1893): 495, is a paper prepared for the World's Columbian Exposition that compares railroad signaling devices up to that time. John P. O'Donnell, "Railroad Signaling—The Block System," *American Society of Civil Engineers, Transactions* 32 (Nov. 1894): 421–53, provides a good

history and description of the block system and Hall's contributions to it.

For more information on the Hall family, D. B. Hall, *The Halls of New England* (1883), is a valuable resource.

LARRY N. SYPOLT

HALLAM, Lewis (1714–1756), and **Mrs. Lewis Hallam Douglass** (?–1773), actors, led the first significant acting group to perform in the North American colonies. Lewis Hallam was born in London, England, the son of Adam Hallam and Anne (maiden name unknown). His mother was an important actress in Covent Garden in London, and four of the five sons in the family turned to the theater for their careers. Lewis Hallam appears to have first taken the stage in his older brother William Hallam's theater in Goodman's Fields, London. It is not known when he met and married his wife (whose full maiden name, date and place of birth, and parentage remain unknown), but Mrs. Hallam appears to have been a more talented actress than her husband; she often played leading roles while he took on subordinate ones.

In 1752 the Hallams and their children, including Lewis Hallam, Jr., formed the London Company of Comedians and planned to go to North America. There were few precedents for any type of theater in the British colonies, so the Hallams sent Robert Upton as their advance agent to Virginia, where he determined that there were good prospects for developing a successful operation. The Hallams sailed on the sloop *Charming Sally* in May 1752 and arrived at Yorktown, Virginia, in June of the same year. They soon acquired what was called "Finnie's Theater," a property built by Williamsburg innkeeper Alexander Finnie and intended as a theater for an earlier touring group. The Hallams gave their first performance on 15 September 1752, a rendition of *The Merchant of Venice*, in which Lewis Hallam played Lancelot Gobbo and Tubal, while Mrs. Hallam played Portia. The play was well received, and the family continued to perform throughout the autumn of 1752. A notable social success occurred on 9 November when the Hallams performed *Othello* for Governor Robert Dinwiddie and a number of prominent members of the Cherokee Indian nation who were visiting Williamsburg. Despite their popular success, however, the Hallams lost money on the enterprise, and on 10 October 1753 they lost possession of the playhouse.

The Hallams went on to perform in New York City (July 1753–Feb. 1754), Philadelphia (Apr.–June 1754), and Charles Town (now Charleston), South Carolina (Oct.–Dec. 1754). The Hallams then sailed to Jamaica, seeking to recruit new actors. Lewis Hallam soon contracted yellow fever and died. After a period of mourning, Mrs. Hallam married David Douglass, who assumed leadership of the former Hallam company. The Douglass-Hallam troupe performed in Jamaica and the Danish West Indies for several years before it returned to the North American coast in 1758.

The American Company troupe (as it was by then named) toured in New York, Philadelphia, Annapolis, Upper Marlborough, and Williamsburg, Virginia, from 1758 to 1761. During this period Mrs. Hallam Douglass continued to play the important, leading roles that might ordinarily have been assigned to a younger woman. The troupe went on to perform in Rhode Island, New York, Virginia, and Charles Town from 1761 to 1766. Mrs. Hallam Douglass gradually released her leading roles to her talented niece Nancy Hallam, while her son, Lewis Hallam, Jr., became the leading male player for the company. Mrs. Hallam Douglass retired from the stage and died in Philadelphia.

Although the Hallams' troupe and its successor, the American Company, never gained a strong audience in New England, their successful performances in the middle and southern colonies indicated a new interest on the part of colonial British Americans in the culture of the British Isles. Coming as it did at the time of the last of the French and Indian wars (1754–1763), the tour of the Hallam and Douglass companies battled economic vicissitudes, but a new pattern had been set, one that would encourage the spread of Shakespearean drama in the North American colonies.

• There are very few sources available for study of the Hallams. Most significant is Hugh F. Rankin, *The Theater In Colonial America* (1965). Other sources include William Dunlap, *A History of the American Theatre* (1832), and George W. Geib, "Playhouses and Politics: Lewis Hallam and the Confederation Theater," *Journal of Popular Culture* 5, no. 2 (1971): 324–39.

SAMUEL WILLARD CROMPTON

HALLECK, Charles Abraham (22 Aug. 1900–3 Mar. 1986), politician, was born in Demotte, Indiana, the son of Abraham Lincoln Halleck, an attorney and politician, and Lura I. Luce, an attorney. Halleck grew up in a conservative Republican family. His father served in the Indiana state legislature for a brief time and then returned to his law practice. Coming from a family of professionals who respected education, Halleck excelled academically.

In 1918 Halleck graduated from high school and entered the army. He remained in the continental United States during World War I, reaching the rank of second lieutenant. Immediately following his honorable discharge after the armistice in November 1918, Halleck entered Indiana University, where he received his B.A. in the spring of 1922. He thereupon entered Indiana law school and graduated at the top of his class in 1924. In 1927 he married Blanche White; they had two children.

Like his father, Halleck used his law degree to enter politics. In his first year as a lawyer, he won election as prosecuting attorney of the Thirtieth Judicial Circuit of Indiana as a Republican. He held that position from 1925 to 1935. During the 1920s his rural midwestern constituency tended to reject the characteristics of modern urban America, such as drinking, liberalized roles for women, and ethnic diversity. Halleck shared his constituency's values, and his early political career set the precedent for his future role as a hard-driving, conservative spokesman. The most controversial issue of the 1920s was Prohibition. While some politicians gave only perfunctory attention to antiliquor laws, Halleck strictly enforced the statutes during his tenure as prosecuting attorney.

By the mid-1930s many of Halleck's constituents had grown wary of President Franklin Roosevelt's New Deal. Halleck shared their concerns and used his public record to win the Republican nomination for the Second Congressional District in a special election held on 29 January 1935. His campaign slogans criticized the changing role of the federal government instituted by the Roosevelt New Deal. While he favored "humanitarian legislation," Halleck argued that federal spending had become lavish and wasteful. He mocked the notion of federal welfare, stating that Americans wanted jobs, not the dole. Central to his popular appeal was an underlying fear of federal power. "The people of the local units know more about their problems than any bureaucracy situated in Washington," Halleck maintained, "and I intend to fight for the return of home rule to our people." His district's voters agreed and elected him over his Democratic opponent George Durgan.

Entering a Congress dominated by Democrats, Halleck became a staunch partisan who consistently supported the Republican House leadership. His dependability won the confidence of the powerful Republican minority leader, Joe Martin, and led to his appointment to the House Rules Committee. Halleck's clout increased further in 1940, when his support helped fellow Hoosier Wendell Willkie win the Republican presidential nomination to run against Roosevelt's bid for a third term. A short time later, however, he broke with Willkie over U.S. foreign policy during World War II. Again reflecting the conservatism of his district, Halleck endorsed isolationism, voting against the Lend-Lease Act to aid Great Britain's war effort in the spring of 1941. "Enemy ships," he said, "would have to come up the Potomac River before Congress would declare another war." It took the Japanese attack on Pearl Harbor in December 1941 to change the congressman's mind.

Following the end of World War II, Halleck played an important part in the Republican gains in the 1946 congressional elections. As the chairman of the Republican Congressional Campaign Committee, he helped organize and raise money for Republican candidates nationwide. His conservative credentials endeared him to wealthy businesspeople, who gave him generous campaign contributions. In addition to his fundraising successes, he traveled by train through the country, publicly endorsing Republican candidates. When the GOP won both houses of Congress in 1946, his election efforts provided him with enough influence to capture the position of majority leader. For the first time in his career, he had the opportunity to execute his conservative philosophy in Washington and roll back New Deal policies. His most significant contribution was his floor leadership of the Taft-Hartley Act, a law curbing federal protection of labor unions. When Robert Taft encountered delays in the Senate, Halleck helped write an acceptable House version, steered it out of committee, and won a floor vote. Thereafter Halleck remained a powerful Republican leader of the House.

In 1954, following Republican losses in that year's midterm elections, Halleck sought President Dwight D. Eisenhower's support to replace the aging House leader Martin. The president rebuffed Halleck, preferring to preserve party unity. Halleck deferred to Eisenhower's judgment, biding his time for another opportunity. Halleck's next chance came in the wake of the stunning Republican defeat in the 1958 congressional elections. Using his popularity among his peers, he maneuvered a narrow victory over Martin to become Republican House minority leader.

In this leadership position, Halleck used his partisanship to successfully hold Republican representatives together against the Democratic House majority. In addition, he worked closely with President Eisenhower and Republican Senate minority leader Everett Dirksen (R.-Ill.) to decrease federal spending. The president used his veto power, and Halleck pressured Republican representatives to sustain Eisenhower's actions. During one debate to sustain Eisenhower's 1959 budget veto, he successfully appealed to his GOP colleagues, saying: "This is a straight political issue. Are you going to let the Democrats get away with it?"

When the Democrats regained both the White House and Congress in 1960, Halleck found himself in the familiar role of an outspoken opponent. He and Senate minority leader Dirksen held frequent press conferences, dubbed the "Ev and Charlie Show," to maintain the GOP stance against President John F. Kennedy's New Frontier legislative proposals. In the three years of Kennedy's presidency, Halleck helped uphold the Republican and southern Democratic alliance against liberal measures to expand government aid in areas such as health care and education.

By 1963, however, the congressman found common ground with the president on civil rights. Halleck visited the White House several times to confer with Kennedy about this issue and eventually supported the Democratic proposal. After Kennedy's assassination in November 1963, Halleck endorsed the civil rights bill subsequently introduced during the Lyndon B. Johnson administration in 1964.

The Democratic landslide of 1964 undermined Halleck's hold on the minority leader spot. As in Halleck's tactics against Martin in 1959, Gerald Ford used Republican disenchantment following this devastating defeat to unseat Halleck the next year. Three years later Halleck announced his decision to retire. After his retirement, he returned to Indiana. He died in Lafayette, Indiana.

Halleck's career personifies the American reaction against the unprecedented growth of the federal government in the twentieth century. His success as a politician was owed to the fact that a large minority of Americans shared his viewpoint. His highly vocal and visible opposition earned him standing as an important national champion of conservative sentiments. His long professional life also embodied the best principles of the American two-party system. Despite the repeated Republican setbacks during his nearly forty years in public office, Halleck's dogged commitment to conservative ideals won him a major leadership post, which he used to contain and at times to defeat Democratic legislative initiatives.

• The most valuable primary sources on Halleck are the oral histories in the presidential libraries of Harry C. Truman (Independence, Mo.), Dwight D. Eisenhower (Abilene, Kans.), John F. Kennedy (Boston, Mass.), and Lyndon B. Johnson (Austin, Tex.). The Office of the Staff Secretary in the Eisenhower Library houses the minutes of the president's legislative meeting in which Halleck played a significant role. The Kennedy Library's Congressional Liaison Office Files contain information on Halleck's actions from 1961 to 1963. The Office Files of Lawrence F. O'Brien in the Johnson Library have similar data on Halleck. Henry Z. Scheele's biography, *Charlie Halleck: A Political Biography* (1966), surveys Halleck's life up to 1965. An obituary is in the *New York Times*, 4 Mar. 1986.

R. SCOTT HARRIS

HALLECK, Fitz-Greene (8 July 1790–19 Nov. 1867), poet, was born in Guilford, Connecticut, the son of Israel Hallock (the son preferred the alternate spelling), a merchant and an Episcopalian who had been a Tory during the American Revolution, and Mary Eliot, a descendant of John Eliot, the "Apostle to the Indians." Halleck was educated in the Guilford schools until the age of fourteen, when he became a clerk in the store of a relative, Andrew Eliot, and embarked on a business career that was to be his main support in life. During these years he also wrote poems, two of which were printed in the *New York Columbian* in 1810. In May 1811 he moved to New York and by July had found employment in the bank of Jacob Barker, where he worked until the business collapsed, leaving most probably late in 1828. Halleck joined "The Iron Grays," a state militia company formed to defend New York in 1814.

In 1813 Halleck became the close friend of Joseph Rodman Drake, and this association led to Halleck's first real success as a poet. The two collaborated on "The Croakers," a series of light verses that satirized prominent New Yorkers. The poems appeared in the *New York Evening Post* and the *National Advocate* from March to July 1819. Drake, who began the series as "Croaker," was joined by Halleck as "Croaker, Junior," and the two composed some poems jointly as "Croaker & Co." The success of the series undoubtedly encouraged Halleck to write *Fanny*, a satiric poem reminiscent of Byron's *Beppo*. Published in 1819 and expanded for a second edition in 1821, *Fanny* portrays the rise of a merchant and his daughter to wealth and social position, satirizes the *nouveaux riches* and the society into which they move, and ends when the merchant overreaches himself and the pair sink once again into their original obscurity. Before the second edition appeared, the death of Drake from tuberculosis in September 1820 moved Halleck to write an elegy in his memory.

During the 1820s Halleck wrote the few remaining poems on which his reputation rests. A visit to the ancestral home of the Percys during his visit to Europe in 1822 yielded "Alnwick Castle" (1823). The first half of the poem invokes a romantic image of the storied past, contrasted ironically in the second half with the mercantile present in which "Lord Stafford mines for coal and salt, / The Duke of Norfolk deals in malt, / The Douglass in red herrings," and a descendant of the Percys conducts visitors through the castle "From donjon-keep to turret wall, / For ten-and-sixpence sterling." Though the contrast is very effective, contemporary critics, including Edgar Allan Poe, preferred the first half and objected to the satire in the second.

More widely admired was "Marco Bozzaris" (1825), a poem strongly influenced by Byron, which celebrates a hero who died storming a Turkish camp during the Greek War for Independence. Much of its popularity derived from American enthusiasm for the Greek cause at that time, and the poem was often used for public recitation. Poe believed that its "prevailing feature" was the force of its expression, derived from the "well-ordered metre, vigorous rhythm, and a judicious disposal of the circumstances of the poem," but he thought it lacked "*ideal* beauty." "Marco Bozzaris" was reprinted in Great Britain and was translated into French and Modern Greek.

Other poems of the decade include "Connecticut" (1826), intended as part of a longer poem that was never completed, and "Burns" (1827), a tribute to the Scottish poet. A small collection, *Alnwick Castle, with Other Poems*, appeared in 1827. By this time Halleck had become friends with other important New Yorkers, including William Cullen Bryant, Gulian Crommelin Verplanck, Robert Sedgwick and Henry Sedgwick, and James Fenimore Cooper, to whose Bread and Cheese Club Halleck belonged. Other noteworthy poems, all published in 1828, are "The Field of Grounded Arms," unrhymed verses on the battlefield at Saratoga; "Red Jacket," a portrait of the Seneca chief that treats both his noble and savage qualities; and "The Recorder," a satire on Richard Riker, the recorder of New York City.

From 1832 to 1848 Halleck was employed as confidential secretary by John Jacob Astor (1763–1848), during which time he wrote little. He published an edition of Byron's works in 1833 and an anthology of British poetry in 1840. Collected editions of Halleck's poems began to appear in 1847 and continued to be issued through the 1860s. In 1849 Halleck retired to Guilford, where, with a small legacy bequeathed him by Astor, he lived in straitened circumstances with his sister Maria. He published an addition to "Connecticut" in 1852, and *Young America*, a satire on American materialism, in 1865. Although he planned to issue a new edition of his poems, he died in Guilford before it

could be published. In his memorial address (3 Feb. 1869), Bryant praised Halleck's serious poems for "the rich imagery, the airy melody of verse, [and] the grace of language" they contain; he described the humorous poems as "marked by an uncommon ease of versification, a natural flow and sweetness of language, and a careless, Horatian playfulness and felicity of jest." Halleck's statue was erected in New York City's Central Park in 1877.

In his personal life, Halleck was, like his father, a conservative in religion and politics. He never married. A convivial man, he enjoyed an extensive social life in New York and continued to visit his friends there after his retirement to Guilford. Halleck was a talented member of the Knickerbocker group of writers whose forte was light verse satire. Highly regarded as a poet in his own time, his reputation has long since faded.

• *The Poetical Writings of Fitz-Greene Halleck*, ed. James Grant Wilson (1869), also contains "The Croakers," including the poems by Joseph Rodman Drake. The major source for Halleck's letters and uncollected poems—mostly juvenilia—is Wilson, *The Life and Letters of Fitz-Greene Halleck* (1869), based on primary materials that have since been lost. The standard biography is Nelson Frederick Adkins, *Fitz-Greene Halleck: An Early Knickerbocker Wit and Poet* (1930). It contains additional uncollected letters and poems.

DONALD A. RINGE

HALLECK, Henry Wager (16 Jan. 1815–9 Jan. 1872), soldier, author, and businessman, was born at Westernville, Oneida County, New York, the son of Joseph Halleck and Catherine Wager, farmers. Raised on the family farm but unwilling to accept agriculture as his life's work, he ran away from home in 1831 to seek a formal education. He was adopted by his maternal grandfather and attended Union College, where he earned an A.B. degree in 1837. Halleck then entered the U.S. Military Academy, graduated third in the class of 1839, and received appointment in the highly regarded Corps of Engineers.

Halleck remained at the Military Academy for one year as a French language instructor. In 1840 he was sent to New York City to work on fortifications. There he wrote "Report on the Means of National Defense," a study of coastal fortifications that was published by the Senate. During this time he also wrote a treatise on the uses of asphalt. In 1843 Halleck received an honorary A.M. degree from Union College; he soon after declined an engineering professorship at Harvard.

In recognition of Halleck's achievements, the army sent him on a six-month inspection trip of the harbor defenses of France in 1844–1845. On his return he delivered a series of lectures on military theory at the Lowell Institute of Boston. These were published in 1846 as *Elements of Military Art and Science*. In them, Halleck expounded the importance of concentration, interior lines of communication, and maneuver and argued that the occupation of key places was more advantageous to victory than the destruction of the enemy's army. An updated edition, published in 1861, became a standard reference manual for volunteer officers in the Civil War.

At the outset of the Mexican War in 1846, Halleck was sent to California. During the seven-month voyage he translated for publication Baron Antoine Henri Jomini's biography of Napoléon Bonaparte. As an army engineer on the Pacific Coast, he planned defensive works at Monterey, California, and accompanied several military expeditions into the interior. He received a brevet promotion to captain on 1 May 1847 for gallant conduct and meritorious service. Halleck also served as secretary of state in the military government of California. He was aide-de-camp to Commodore William B. Shubrick during the capture of Mazatlán on Mexico's west coast, 11 November 1847, and performed the functions of lieutenant governor of the city.

Returning to California, Halleck was at the forefront in efforts to gain admission to the Union. He played a major role in framing the state constitution. A man of great mental ability, he studied law while serving as lighthouse inspector and engineer of Pacific Coast fortifications. He was also chief director of a quicksilver mining concern. In 1849 he formed the law partnership of Halleck, Peachy, and Billings. Although promoted to the permanent rank of captain of engineers on 1 July 1853, Halleck was influenced by more fruitful civilian pursuits. He resigned from the army on 1 August 1854. The next year he married Elizabeth Hamilton, a granddaughter of Alexander Hamilton. They had one son.

Halleck expanded his professional and business interests in the years prior to the Civil War. In 1855 he was president of a California railroad. He published books on mining law, followed by a volume on the laws of international commerce. In 1860–1861 he was major general of the California militia.

Responding to the national emergency, Halleck reentered the regular army on 19 August 1861 with an appointment as major general. After reporting, he was assigned to St. Louis on 18 November 1861 to replace Major General John C. Frémont as commander of the Department of the Missouri. The department included several trans-Mississippi states plus Illinois and western Kentucky. He found the department in a state of "complete chaos." The troops were ill equipped and unpaid, and secession forces controlled large portions of Missouri. Halleck increased the number of inspectors and put an end to wasteful and fraudulent contracts. He established garrisons throughout Missouri to counter a growing guerrilla menace. By year's end his troops were adequately trained and supplied and ready to assume the offensive.

The enemy's strongest presence was along a line that extended from Bowling Green to Columbus, Kentucky. The line included Confederate Forts Donelson and Henry on the Cumberland and Tennessee Rivers. Halleck reasoned that the "true line of operations" against the enemy front would be at the center, along the route of the Tennessee River. To break the line and to drive the enemy from Missouri, Halleck devised simultaneous advances along the Tennessee and Mississippi Rivers and in southwestern Missouri. Responsibility for carrying out the offensive fell to Brigadier General Ulysses S. Grant, while Halleck managed the campaign from headquarters in St. Louis. By mid-March 1862 all three advances had gained their major objectives, and Halleck was acclaimed throughout the North as the "directing genius" of the campaign.

Victories at Forts Henry and Donelson seemingly reinforced Halleck's emphasis on the capture of the strategic places as a means to defeat the enemy, for the Confederates had responded by abandoning their line. Halleck next concentrated on the capture of Corinth, Mississippi, an important railroad junction and the key to further occupation of enemy territory. By this time he had grown fretful over certain irregularities in Grant's field reports and rumored personal habits. The near defeat of Grant's forces at Shiloh, Tennessee, 6–7 April 1862, convinced Halleck to take personal command of the forces in the field. He professed to find the army disorganized and wanting in discipline. Hampered by bad weather and illness among his troops, Halleck launched his drive against Corinth on 4 May. In two days he closed to within six miles of the enemy works. Halleck then reverted to siege tactics, having decided to maneuver the enemy out of Corinth. Union troops entered Corinth on 29 May without bringing on a general engagement. Halleck had taken another strategic point, but he was criticized in the press for allowing the enemy to withdraw intact.

Meanwhile, President Abraham Lincoln, worried by the lack of coordination between various Union armies, had settled on the need for a competent military adviser. Halleck's theories and successes had impressed the president, and upon the endorsement of retired major general Winfield Scott, Lincoln appointed Halleck general-in-chief of all Union land forces on 11 July 1862.

Initially, Halleck embraced the position with vigor and assertiveness, although he privately told his wife that the administration seemed "willing to give me more power than I desire on some points." However, he eventually formulated a precise, if narrow, definition of the role of general-in-chief. In a 16 February 1864 letter to Major General William T. Sherman, Halleck wrote that he was "simply a military advisor to the Secretary of War and the President and must obey and carry out what they decide upon, whether I concur with their decisions or not. If I disagree with them in opinion, I say so, but when they decide it is my duty faithfully to carry out their decision. . . . It is my duty to strengthen the hands of the President as Commander-in-Chief " (*The War of the Rebellion*, vol. 22, pt. 2, pp. 407–8).

By September Halleck had grown weary from the responsibility of the job, especially in his dealings with the recalcitrant major general George B. McClellan. The Union defeat at Second Manassas, brought about in part by McClellan's hesitancy to abandon the Peninsula Campaign, transformed and diminished Halleck. Lincoln observed that Halleck "broke down—

nerve and pluck all gone—and has ever since evaded all possible responsibility—little more than a first rate clerk."

On 1 January 1863 the president ordered Halleck to visit Major General Ambrose E. Burnside in the field, study his next proposed movement, and approve or disapprove the plan. "Your military skill," wrote the president, "is useless to me if you will not do this." Halleck responded by submitting his resignation, stating, "I am led to believe that there is a very important difference of opinion in regard to my relations toward generals commanding armies in the field." The president, on further consideration, rescinded his order, and Halleck withdrew the resignation.

During much of 1863, acting usually on instructions from Lincoln, Halleck directed his efforts toward the support of Grant's campaign against Vicksburg, Mississippi. Wherever possible he transferred regiments to Grant from other armies and ordered other commanders in the theater to make demonstrations that would draw off enemy reinforcements.

In the East, Halleck had slowly come to the conclusion that the capture of Richmond was not as important as the defeat of General Robert E. Lee's army. When Lee moved into Pennsylvania in June 1863, Halleck rejected the proposal of Major General Joseph Hooker to capture the Confederate capital. Hooker was directed to follow Lee; at the same time Halleck countermanded Hooker's orders to attach the garrison at Harpers Ferry to his army. When Hooker used Halleck's perceived interference as an excuse to resign as commander of the Army of the Potomac, Halleck recommended Major General George C. Meade to replace him.

Halleck's relations with Meade were at times strained by the general-in-chief's tendency to preach doctrine. Halleck failed to persuade Meade to pursue Lee's retreating army out of Pennsylvania after the Union victory at Gettysburg.

On 9 March 1864, when the president appointed Grant to the newly revived rank of lieutenant general, Halleck gladly surrendered the post of general-in-chief. He then assumed the offices of chief of staff, with most of the same duties as before. "With Grant as general-in-chief," observed Halleck's biographer, Stephen Ambrose, "the North possessed a commander willing to make decisions and execute them; with Halleck as chief of staff the Union had found a brilliant administrator" (Ambrose, p. 195). During the July 1864 raid of Confederate major general Jubal A. Early, Halleck rallied heterogeneous forces in defense of Washington until the Army of the Potomac could send relief.

After Lincoln's assassination, Secretary of War Edwin M. Stanton assigned Halleck to command the Military Division of the James, with headquarters at Richmond. Over the next two weeks, while trying to carry out War Department directives regarding the surrender of Confederate forces in North Carolina, Halleck issued orders that embarrassed and countermanded the efforts of his close friend Sherman. Although the

offense was unintentional and deeply regretted, Halleck lost the friendship of one of the few men who had staunchly supported him throughout the war.

While in command at Richmond, Halleck was responsible for saving the larger portion of the Confederate archives, which was later published in the massive reference work, *The War of the Rebellion* (1880–1901). Halleck's conservative tendencies in reestablishing order and normality in Richmond alarmed Radicals in Washington. He was transferred, on 30 August 1865, to San Francisco, where he filled the perfunctory role of commander of the Military Division of the Pacific. On 16 March 1869 he left California for Louisville, Kentucky, to command the Division of the South. He ultimately died there of an unspecified illness.

Though much maligned by his contemporaries, who thought him a "cold calculating owl," incapable of cultivating cordial relations, Halleck was nonetheless recognized as a man of great intellect. Nicknamed "Old Brains," he brought professionalism and organization to an army saddled with political appointments and militia mentality. He correctly placed priority on the war in the West, and made every effort to initiate and sustain simultaneous advances across a broad front. His dispatches to the field characteristically were petulant and argumentative, a trait that drew the ire of commanders who faced unforeseen difficulties. Consequently, he was the target of vitriolic outbursts in many postwar memoirs. His abilities are best appreciated when divorced from the personal animosities that clouded his every effort.

• Halleck's personal correspondence in the form of a letter book, is housed in the Library of Congress. The orders and official correspondence of Halleck are in the collection he fostered and helped preserve: U.S. War Department, *The War of the Rebellion: The Official Records of the Union and Confederate Armies* (128 vols., 1880–1901). His principal biography is Stephen E. Ambrose, *Halleck: Lincoln's Chief of Staff* (1962). Ambrose portrays Halleck as an able administrator hampered by political interference and frustrated by unresponsive generals. Glimpses of Halleck's opinions and work are in Frank Freidel, *Francis Lieber: Nineteenth-Century Liberal* (1947); Ulysses S. Grant, *Personal Memoirs of U. S. Grant* (1885–1886); and William T. Sherman, *Memoirs of General William T. Sherman* (1875). The overseeing hand of the general-in-chief in the prosecution of the war is evident in Warren W. Hassler, Jr., *Commanders of the Army of the Potomac* (1962), and T. Harry Williams, *Lincoln and His Generals* (1952). An obituary is in the *New York Times*, 10 Jan. 1872.

HERMAN HATTAWAY
MICHAEL D. SMITH

HALLET, Etienne Sulpice (18 Mar. 1755–Feb. 1825), architect, was born in the small village of St. Soupplets, diocese of Meaux, northeast of Paris, the only son and eldest child of Claude Jacques Hallet, schoolmaster and clerk of that parish, and Gabrielle Robin. Nothing is known of Hallet's early studies, architectural training, or projects; his name has not been found in the surviving lists of students who attended the leading schools of art and architecture. His later drawings clearly reveal a natural talent for the design arts, but he needed much more than that to establish himself as an architect in Paris. He was there as early as 13 January 1780, when he married Marie Françoise Gosalle. After her death he married, on 10 May 178[9?], Marie Françoise Gomain, the youngest daughter of Claude Gomain, clerk of the Parlement de Paris and, by her later account, a close associate of its last president, Barthélemi-Gabriel Rolland d'Erceville. Such a connection would have been a useful one for an aspiring architect from the provinces, at least until the French Revolution began to accelerate.

Hallet had the means to purchase the office, or *charge*, of *architect expert-bourgeois* on 5 October 1784 and thus appeared in the list of *experts jurés du roi* published in the *Almanach Royal* for 1786 (pp. 544–46). His success as an architect can be deduced from the fact that he was made secretary of the Masonic lodge of *Les Frères unis de St.-Henri* in Paris almost immediately upon joining it in 1787 (Francmaçonnerie archives, Bibliothèque Nationale). However, his position and livelihood now depended on the uninterrupted operations of the ancien régime. When the Assemblée Nationale abolished income-yielding offices such as his, Hallet found himself "sans état," as he later described his situation to Thomas Jefferson, leading him to seek a new life in America. Family tradition holds that the Hallets fled France as a consequence of the French Revolution, in 1789.

Yet Hallet was likely still in Paris when the *Almanach des Bâtiments* for 1790 was printed. At some time during that year, it seems, he became associated with the Scioto Company and sailed with his family for America, apparently expecting to be employed in the planning and construction of the company's projected settlement on the Ohio River at Gallipolis. Marie Gomain Hallet later wrote, in a remarkable letter to Jefferson, that she and her husband had endured hardship and distress in the "lands of the savages," implying that they were among the prospective French settlers who made the trek to Gallipolis; however, their family names have not been found in the surviving records of the Scioto Company (held in the New-York Historical Society and the Cincinnati Historical Society).

Whatever his personal disappointment in the Scioto affair, Hallet was living in Philadelphia, then the temporary national capital, on 1 November 1791, when Tench Coxe, assistant secretary of the treasury, informed Secretary of State Jefferson that he had "just discovered a Monsr. Hallet who is said to be a very excellent Draughtsman." Hallet was then in the employ of Narcisse Pigalle, a French engraver in Philadelphia, and engaged in making a reduced copy (for the purposes of preparing an engraver's plate) of Pierre L'Enfant's large manuscript plan of the new "Federal City." Jefferson also commissioned Hallet to make "two drafts" of the same work (these were displayed in Congress in Dec. 1791). Owing to the fact that L'Enfant had retrieved his manuscript plan soon after depositing it with Pigalle and thereafter had refused to make it available, Hallet proved indispensable in the preparation of the first engraved plans of the new national capital. But the Washington administration's decision to hold architectural competitions to secure designs for the principal public buildings presented him with a much greater opportunity, and he confidently drew plans for both the President's House and the U.S. Capitol. The drawings he submitted for the former have been lost; those he produced for the Capitol render him a noteworthy figure in the history of the early republic.

In late 1791, it seems, Hallet had presented Jefferson with his own, first ideas (later referred to as his "fancy [i.e., fanciful or imaginative] piece," seemingly a sketch) for a building to house the Congress. The design he actually submitted in the U.S. Capitol competition, a peripteral rectangular temple, resembled Jefferson's Virginia State Capitol in Richmond; it was either suggested by Jefferson or prepared in hope of winning the premium by flattering him. Hallet's entry, as well as all others received prior to the competition deadline (15 July 1792), failed to gain President George Washington's full approval, but the French architect was so skilled a draftsman that the administration could not afford to lose his talents. The following month Hallet and another competitor, George Turner, were invited to visit the Capitol Hill site and to submit additional drawings. After these were still judged lacking, Hallet was hired (13 Oct. 1792), under the authority of the Board of Commissioners of the Federal District, to fashion an acceptable design for the building. Then in late January 1793 Dr. William Thornton was permitted to submit what proved to be the winning post-competition entry. Hallet, bitterly disappointed, was awarded the second-place prize; his predicament was summed up in Washington's observation to the commissioners of 31 January 1793: "Some difficulty arises with respect to Mr. Hallet, who, you know, was in some degree led into his plans by ideas we all expressed to him."

After the president had approved Thornton's design for the Capitol, the commissioners instructed Hallet, still in their employ, to make estimates; his report, which included a new set of drawings, raised alarming questions about design and structural inadequacies as well as costs. Following a conference held at the president's residence in Philadelphia on 15 July 1793, chaired by Jefferson, Hallet's "simplified and abridged" version of Thornton's design (which also incorporated more elaborate, curvilinear legislative chambers) was designated the working plan of the Capitol, although its central feature, a recess that was to replace Thornton's dramatic east portico and rotunda (modeled after the Pantheon of Rome), was not approved. The president deferred a final decision, pending review of additional sketches and explanations. Nevertheless, once assigned to superintend construction, Hallet proceeded to lay foundations according to still another revised plan, now without basement story, in which he revived the east portico but left an open square court behind it in the center of the building, making no provisions for the rotunda.

When Washington visited Capitol Hill in late June 1794 to inspect construction, he angrily ordered Hallet to leave the site, then apparently instructed the commissioners to gain custody of the architect's working drawings. Hallet, confused and no doubt overwrought, refused to produce these papers and as a consequence was fired by the board on 28 June 1794; he would work at the site in an unofficial capacity, however, for several months longer under terms of an agreement he reached (and the commissioners appear to have sanctioned) with a major local landholder, James Greenleaf. Upon his appointment to the board of commissioners in September 1794, Thornton was instructed to restore the central part of his premiated design; however, he did this by making use of Hallet's revised ground plan, which, in general, continued to govern the building.

The events surrounding Hallet's dismissal from the U.S. Capitol can only be understood in the context of the political struggle that raged within President Washington's cabinet in the early 1790s. There is no evidence of any insubordination on the architect's part prior to the events surrounding his dismissal—he had a family to support and relied on Jefferson (with whom he communicated in French), as well as on the commissioners, for directions. It is inconceivable that he would have taken it upon himself to defy George Washington. If he became convinced that his revisions to the premiated design enjoyed official sanction, as indeed he did, such an impression was certainly conveyed to him by his superiors. The most likely explanation for the confusion is either that Jefferson had not fully understood Washington's thinking, or, more probably, that Jefferson had chosen, owing to the political implications in certain features of Thornton's design (notably the "great repository" beneath the rotunda intended for Washington's tomb, which each of Hallet's revisions eliminated), to give a different interpretation to the findings of the Philadelphia conference.

Hallet was never given a full explanation for his downfall. He eventually relinquished his drawings, received back and additional payments for his competition prize and work at the Capitol, then returned to Philadelphia, where he set up an evening school of architecture. Little is known of his life thereafter. He resided between 1809 and 1821 in New York City (Marie Gomain died there in 1812). In 1809 he (with Joseph Cerneau) received a patent for an improvement to Joseph Michel Montgolfier's hydraulic ram, a device for raising water, which, with the assistance of Thornton, then superintendent of patents, he promoted for use in the capital (Hallet to James Madison, 9 Sept. 1809, *The Papers of James Madison: Presidential Series*, ed. Robert A. Rutland, vol. 1 [1984], pp. 368–89). Hallet lived for a time in Havana (one of his daughters was born there in 1800) and, according to passport documents, returned to Havana with three of his eight children in May 1821. Family records place his death in New Rochelle, New York.

• Biographical sources are found in the parish records of St. Soupplets, Meaux (Seine-et-Marne) and in a manuscript index to marriages in Paris parish registers, 1700–1792 (Seine), France (films of which are in the Family History Library, Salt Lake City, Utah); in letters the Hallets wrote to Thomas Jefferson, particularly his of 21 Sept. 1792 and 13 Mar. 1793 and hers of c. 6 Oct. 1792 (Jefferson papers, Library of Congress); and in Marie Gomain Hallet's letter to George Washington of 5 May 1795 (Washington papers, Library of Congress). The biographical account published in I. T. Frary, *They Built the Capitol* (1940), was based on information provided by Hallet's great-granddaughter; her typescript summary deviates in some details from documentary records (e.g., she has Hallet born 17 Mar. 1755; see Elima A. Foster to Frary, 4 Dec. 1938, Ihna Thayer Frary Papers, Ohio Historical Society). The notarized document of Hallet's purchase of his *charge*, dated 5 Oct. 1784 but not registered until 17 Aug. 1785, is in the Archives Nationales, Paris (Series V 1, art. 521, no. 232).

Hallet's role in preparing the L'Enfant-Ellicott map of Washington, D.C., and his work on the U.S. Capitol are documented in the Records of the Board of Commissioners for the District of Columbia, RG 42 (and Microcopy 371), National Archives, and in the Thomas Jefferson Papers, Pierre L'Enfant Papers (two collections), William Thornton Papers, and George Washington Papers, Library of Congress; most of the pertinent texts are in *The Papers of Thomas Jefferson*, ed. Julian Boyd et al. (1950–); *Papers of William Thornton*, ed. C. M. Harris (1995–); and *The Papers of George Washington*, ed. Donald Jackson et al. (1983–).

Some twenty of Hallet's drawings for the U.S. Capitol survive in the Prints and Photographs Collection of the Library of Congress. The dating, proper sequences, and in some cases the identifications of these drawings remain in dispute, yielding quite different interpretations. Several have been reproduced: see Glenn Brown, *History of the United States Capitol* (2 vols., 1900–1903; repr. 1970); Wells Bennett, "Stephen Hallet and His Designs for the National Capitol, 1791–94," *Journal of the American Institute of Architects* 4 (July–Oct. 1916): 290–95, 324–30, 376–83, 411–18; and Pamela Scott, "Stephen Hallet's Designs for the United States Capitol," *Winterthur Portfolio* (1992): 145–70. A few additional drawings and related documents concerning Hallet are held by the Office of the Architect of the Capitol, U.S. Capitol. Notices of Hallet's school were published in the (Philadelphia) *Pennsylvania Packet*, 21 Dec. 1796, and *Federal Gazette*, 25 Nov. 1797; his passport records are in the New-York Historical Society.

C. M. HARRIS
MARILYN MARRS GILLET

HALLIBURTON, Richard (9 Jan. 1900–?24 Mar. 1939), travel writer and adventurer, was born in Brownsville, Tennessee, the son of Nelle Nance, a music teacher, and Wesley Halliburton, a civil engineer and land developer. He was brought up in an affluent household in Memphis, Tennessee. Although his father wanted him to stay in Memphis, his mother wanted him to go away to school. Halliburton attended the Lawrenceville prep school, a stepping stone to nearby Princeton, which he entered in 1917. Novelist F. Scott Fitzgerald described the period at Princeton in *This Side of Paradise* as "lazy and good-looking and aristocratic." Halliburton, who had been an introspective boy, relished the camaraderie and festivities. He flouted university rules even as a freshman, refusing to don the beanie cap traditionally worn by first-year students. When he completed his schooling he was voted "Most Original Member of the Class."

In addition to his propensity for writing (he was editor of the Princeton *Pictorial*), Halliburton also showed enthusiasm for travel. Without informing his parents, he took a train to New Orleans during a summer break and became a seaman on a freighter bound for Europe. The next summer he and three classmates took a pack trip in the Rocky Mountains. He sold his first travel article about this trip to *Field & Stream* (May 1921, pp. 18–20).

Immediately on graduating in 1921 Halliburton set off with a classmate for Europe. They established a pattern of feats and pranks he attempted to top throughout his career: he climbed the Matterhorn, was arrested for taking pictures of a militarily secure area of Gibraltar, and went bust at Monte Carlo gaming tables. Halliburton and his friend separated while they were still in Europe, and Halliburton subsequently traveled through India, China, and Japan, before returning home in the spring of 1923. The trip was the subject of his first book, *The Royal Road to Romance* (1925), which became a bestseller.

Halliburton's next book was *The Glorious Adventure* (1927), in which he tried to recreate (with various side trips) the path of Ulysses in the *Odyssey*. Lord Byron was one of Halliburton's heroes, and, like Byron, Halliburton swam the Hellespont (the Dardanelles). For *New Worlds to Conquer* (1929), he traveled throughout Latin America and became the only person ever to swim the full distance of the Panama Canal, including the locks. Both *The Glorious Adventure* and *New Worlds to Conquer* were bestsellers.

During the 1920s Americans were politically isolationist but fascinated by Halliburton's carefree style travels, even if they only enjoyed it secondhand in the *Ladies' Home Journal*. In addition to communicating through his writings, Halliburton commanded large audiences on speaking tours. With a bent for the theatrical, he appeared on stage carrying a derby hat and black silver-tipped cane and wearing spats, a double-breasted Chesterfield overcoat, pearl-grey suede gloves, and a flamboyant necktie. Despite his showmanship and popularity, he failed to interest Hollywood in making movies of his books but did appear in *India Speaks* (1933), a feature film that flopped.

By age twenty-six Halliburton was making $70,000 a year. As fast as he made money, however, he spent it, enjoying fine clothes and good living. During the depression he bought a Packard touring sedan and built "Hangover House" overlooking Laguna Beach, California. The house cost three times more than projected. Halliburton could be flamboyant and generous but also temperamental and self-centered. He wrote sentimentally about the women he met on his travels, but his longest relationship apparently was with Paul Mooney, who helped him write and lived with him at Hangover House.

Halliburton avoided writing about the unpleasantness of poverty, illness, deprivation, and strife. Reviewers described his books as sentimental and juvenile, but he responded in a Chicago news conference that "the American public is starved for romance." He wove his travel books into two volumes intended for a juvenile audience, *Richard Halliburton's Book of Marvels: The Occident* (1937) and *Richard Halliburton's Second Book of Marvels: The Orient* (1938).

In spite of his success, Halliburton was always concerned that he had not done more serious work. He was particularly interested in writing a biography of the British poet Rupert Brooke, who died during World War I. He tried to get Brooke's mother to assist him, but she did not take Halliburton's work seriously and refused. His notes and research on Brooke later were used by Arthur Springer, who wrote a comprehensive Brooke biography.

In every adventure Halliburton felt pressured to outdo previous stunts. With pilot Moye W. Stephens, he flew a Stearman two-place open cockpit biplane around the world, landing in Timbuktu and other remote places where planes had not been seen before. The resulting book was called *The Flying Carpet* (1932). A public relations man convinced him to be the first person to walk across the Golden Gate Bridge, which Halliburton did, holding on to cables and girders, while the bridge was still under construction.

Halliburton's final adventure came in 1939. He left Hong Kong in a junk he planned to sail to the Golden Gate International Exposition in San Francisco. The vessel was unseaworthy and manned by a ragtag crew. Halliburton was plagued with money worries, but he set sail anyway. A little more than two weeks after leaving Hong Kong, the junk was caught in a typhoon, and radio contact was lost. Neither Halliburton nor his crew was seen again.

• Halliburton's first-person travelogues are not a completely accurate guide to his life. Although he seems to have undertaken all the adventures he ascribed to himself, he embellished them to heighten the drama and color. His papers are at the Firestone Library at Princeton University. Letters to his mother and father, which are part of that collection, appear in *Richard Halliburton: His Story of His Life's Adventure* (1940). His parents edited sections they thought were unpleasant or unflattering. Biographies of Halliburton are Jonathan Root, *The Magnificent Myth* (1965), and James Cortese, *Richard Halliburton's Royal Road* (1989). An informative profile is found in David M. Schwartz, "On the Royal Road to Adventures with 'Daring Dick,'" *Smithsonian*, Mar. 1989, pp. 159–78.

JOHN MAXWELL HAMILTON
CAROLYN PIONE

HALLIDAY, John (14 Sept. 1880–17 Oct. 1947), actor, was born in Brooklyn, New York. His parents' names are not given in biographical sources. The father is identified only as a London artist who took Halliday to Britain in infancy. Halliday was educated there, studied at Cambridge, and earned a degree as a mining engineer in Scotland. He served in the British Army in the Boer War from 1901 to 1902.

Halliday came to Canada around the turn of the century, eventually making his way south to take part in the Nevada gold rush. He was successful: his Jumbo Mine in Goldfield, Nevada, earned him $180,000. Halliday then staged an amateur production of *H.M.S. Pinafore* there on 4 July 1905, casting himself as the hero, Ralph Rackstraw. According to the *New York Times*, "During the first act the miners began celebrating the holiday by shooting up the scenery. Swept by this tide of feeling, Mr. Halliday stepped to the footlights, which his fellow miners were endeavoring to shoot out, and sang in British accents 'My Own United States.' The miners were so delighted that they shot out the remainder of the lights" (18 Oct. 1947).

The comedy star Nat Goodwin, then in the vicinity for a Nevada divorce, was in the audience that night and offered Halliday a job touring the West Coast with his company. At the time Halliday did not accept. Six months later, however, having lost his entire fortune through bad investments, he took the job. After touring with Goodwin, he obtained work with a Sioux City stock company and played many roles, including Hamlet. By one account, the troupe's property manager was a former cowboy and tried to use a buffalo skull as the remains of Yorick. Halliday then returned to the West Coast to act with the stock company of Fred Belasco in San Francisco and Los Angeles, California. Following a tour of Australia and the Orient with T. Daniel Frawley's company, he then joined an Albany stock company.

Halliday's coolness in covering up for another actor who forgot his lines and fled the stage impressed New York producer William A. Brady, who was in the audience that night. Halliday's aristocratic looks and British accent were what Brady needed for a New York production of an English melodrama, *The Whip* (1912), and Halliday made his first Broadway appearance in the play as the Earl of Brancaster. Soon afterward he made his first film, *New Beginnings* (1912). *The Whip* succeeded as a thriller, but Halliday remained unnoticed as an actor. Nevertheless, he returned to acting, spending the next three years in a Cleveland stock company, where he was known as Jack Halliday. He appeared on Broadway again in *Stolen Orders* and *The Ware Case*, both in 1915, and made another film, *The Devil's Toy*, a year later.

Halliday married actress Camille Personi during this period, although the precise date is unknown. In 1916 he returned to acting with a stock company, this time in San Francisco, California. Soon afterward an article in *Variety* (1 Sept. 1916) reported his ambiguous involvement with an actress implicated in the suicide of an actor's wife. In this article Camille Personi was said to be "separated" from her husband but "friendly" to him.

For the 1917–1918 season, Halliday performed with a Denver stock company. Then he returned to Broadway in an English drama, *A Place in the Sun* (1918). The *New York Times* reviewer (29 Nov. 1918) wrote that "the son is very ably played by John Halliday—a performance which deploys, fold by fold, the rather intricate and surprisingly rational psychology of the young man." Halliday gained further recognition with his performance in *Three For Diana* (1919), when a *New York Times* reviewer called him "handsome and sympathetic . . . in a very Anglo-Saxon manner" (22 Apr. 1919). Likewise, Halliday received warm reviews as the young lover from the Malay States in *The Circle* (1921). He also appeared in three other films in 1920.

Now established as a New York actor, Halliday became known in the following decade as a reliable performer in roles calling for a distinguished appearance and "articulate and lucid" diction. Other appearances in the 1920s included *East of Suez* (1922), *Dancing Mothers* (1924), *The Spider* (1927), *Jealousy* (1928), and *The Humbug* (1929). Halliday's roles in these called for him to range from a cad of a lover to a polished charlatan to a medical quack. Although newspaper accounts show that he was unable to act because of illness at various times in 1927 and 1928, he nevertheless scored a personal success in the leading role of *Damn Your Honor* (1929), playing a dashing pirate. Halliday was noted for his "very elegant romanticism" in the production, but the play itself failed. During this period, at dates not given in biographical sources, he also married and divorced actress Eva Lang. In 1929 he married for a third time, wedding actress Eleanor Griffith.

Halliday entered Hollywood's talking pictures in 1929, remaining a competent character actor until 1941. According to *Variety*, he gave a "suave and engaging" performance as a district attorney in *Scarlet Pages* (1930), proving "suave again as a titled Englishman" in *Smart Woman* the following year. He returned to the New York stage for *Rain from Heaven* (1934), with one *New York Times* critic writing, "He returns to Broadway to play the exiled music critic like an actor and a gentleman" (25 Dec. 1934). Back in the movies after that, Halliday played a duke in *Peter Ibbetson* (1935) and the rascally partner of a jewel thief (played by Marlene Dietrich) in *Desire* (1936).

Halliday's last Broadway appearance was as the Russian exile Prince Mikail in *Tovarich* (1936), a comedy success that began in New York and toured until 1938. More films followed with Halliday starring as Deanna Durbin's father in *That Certain Age* (1938) and Katharine Hepburn's father in *The Philadelphia Story* (1940), among other roles. His last film appearance was in *Lydia* (1941). For the final years of his life, Halliday lived in Honolulu, Hawaii, where he was active in the Honolulu Community Theatre. He died in Honolulu. From theatrical records he appears to have been a competent, versatile actor whose career was based on his look of distinction and his upper-class voice. Unfortunately, Halliday never found the great success in a particular role that might have raised him to Broadway stardom, but he was nevertheless a star of numerous local companies from the beginning to the end of his career, successfully making the transition from the stage to character roles in films with equal competence and versatility.

• Materials on John Halliday are in the Billy Rose Theatre Collection at the New York Public Library for the Performing Arts, Lincoln Center. Accounts of his career are in "Visits in the Wings," *New York Times*, 11 May 1919; "Who's Who in Pictures," *New York Times*, 26 Feb. 1933; and Edward J. Eustace, "An All-American Halliday," *New York Times*, 5 Oct. 1938. The most nearly complete listing of his films is in the *American Film Institute Catalog*, vols. 1911–1920, 1921–1930, 1931–1940. A brief assessment of his film career, including a portrait, is in James Robert Parish, *Hollywood Character Actors* (1978). Portraits and production photographs are in Daniel C. Blum, *A Pictorial History of the American Theatre* (1960), and Blum, *A New Pictorial History of the Talkies* (1968). Obituaries are in the *New York Times*, 18 Oct. 1947, and *Variety*, 22 Oct. 1947.

WILLIAM STEPHENSON

HALLINAN, Paul John (8 Apr. 1911–27 Mar. 1968), Roman Catholic archbishop, was born in Painesville, Ohio, a small city on Lake Erie, thirty miles east of Cleveland, the son of Clarence Hallinan, a florist and nurseryman, and Rose Laracy. He received all of his education in Catholic schools: St. Mary's parochial school in Painesville, Cathedral Latin School in Cleveland, and the University of Notre Dame. After graduating from college in 1932, Hallinan entered Our Lady of the Lake Seminary in Cleveland and was ordained a priest of that diocese by Archbishop Joseph Schrembs on 20 February 1937. Each summer from 1927 to 1936 Hallinan also worked as a newspaper reporter and developed a lifelong flair for journalism.

After ordination, Father Hallinan spent the next five years as a curate in the Cleveland parish of St. Aloysius, where he excelled in youth work. In 1942 he joined the army as a chaplain and served for almost three years in the South Pacific, where he received the Purple Heart. On his return to Cleveland after the war, he involved himself in the Newman Movement, an effort to provide for the spiritual care of Catholic students in secular colleges and universities. From 1946 until 1958 Hallinan was active in this work in Cleveland, serving from 1947 to 1958 as director of Newman Hall at Western Reserve University. His success in Cleveland led to his election in 1952–1954 as president of the National Association of Newman Club Chaplains and national chaplain of the National Newman Club Federation.

On 9 September 1958 Hallinan was appointed bishop of Charleston, South Carolina, a diocese in which Catholics constituted only 1.5 percent of the total population. His appointment coincided with the beginnings of the civil rights movement in the South. Hallinan ordered the integration of all five Catholic hospitals in his diocese, but he proceeded cautiously with the more volatile issue of school integration. Together with the bishops of Savannah and Atlanta, on 15 February 1961 he issued a joint pastoral letter promising that the Catholic schools would be integrated "no later than the public schools," a decision that won approval from several moderate civil rights advocates, such as Atlanta editor Ralph McGill.

On 21 February 1962 the Diocese of Atlanta was elevated to the status of an archdiocese, and on that same day, Hallinan was named its first archbishop. As in Charleston, Roman Catholics constituted a small fraction of the population, and most of them were concentrated in Atlanta and its suburbs. Hallinan integrated both the Catholic hospitals and the Catholic schools, took an active interest in community affairs, supported moderate civil rights leaders, such as Martin Luther King, Jr., and established excellent relations with Protestant and Jewish leaders.

Hallinan's appointment to Atlanta occurred in the same year as the opening of Vatican Council II (1962–1965). Hallinan attended three of the four sessions; a severe attack of hepatitis in 1964 prevented him from attending the third. At the council Hallinan aligned himself with the progressive wing, supporting the Vatican Council's Declaration on Religious Freedom, welcoming greater contact between Catholics and non-Catholics, supporting a vernacular liturgy that stressed popular participation, and encouraging a greater role for women in the church. His most important contribution at the council was as the only American member of the conciliar liturgical commission; in that role he was instrumental in winning approval for the Constitution on the Sacred Liturgy, which was promulgated by Pope Paul VI on 4 December 1963. At the council Hallinan also was a founding member of the group that evolved into the International Committee on English in the Liturgy, which produced a uniform translation of the liturgical texts for all English-speaking countries.

After the council, as chairman of the Bishops' Committee on the Liturgical Apostolate (later renamed the Bishops' Committee on the Liturgy), Hallinan was important in the process of implementing the mandated liturgical changes to the vernacular in the United States. His generally centrist positions displeased extremists on both the right and left. The same was true of the reaction to the joint pastoral letter on the Vietnam War that Hallinan and his auxiliary bishop, Joseph Bernardin, issued in October 1966. The letter's carefully hedged criticism of the war drew fire from both antiwar activists and militant supporters of the war.

In the early 1960s Hallinan served as episcopal moderator of the Newman Clubs and during that time was instrumental in organizing the loosely affiliated clubs into a centralized body known as the Newman Apostolate. Hallinan also found time to complete the graduate studies he had commenced in Cleveland and to earn a Ph.D. in history from Western Reserve University in 1963 with a dissertation on the second bishop of Atlanta, Richard Gilmore. He never really recovered from his severe attack of hepatitis in 1964, and at his request, on 9 March 1966, Joseph Bernardin was appointed as his auxiliary bishop. Hallinan's death in Atlanta at the relatively early age of fifty-seven deprived the American hierarchy of one of its most progressive young members. His critics faulted him for fatuous optimism, especially in the areas of ecumenism and liturgical reform; they doubted that the progressive changes would bring about a spiritual renewal in the church. However, had he lived longer (at least during the pontificate of Paul VI), he might reasonably have expected advancement to one of the most important sees in the United States. At his death, Ralph McGill commented: "He was a frail, small man, who was ill for a long time, [but he was] a giant who made many of his clerical contemporaries appear as pygmies."

• Hallinan's papers are in the archives of the Archdiocese of Atlanta and the Diocese of Charleston. The Archives of the Catholic University of America contain material pertaining to Hallinan's role in the Newman Movement and at Vatican Council II. A selection of Hallinan's sermons and writings has been published as *Days of Hope and Promise*, ed. Vincent Yzermans (1973). For a perceptive memoir, see John Tracy Ellis, "Archbishop Hallinan: In Memoriam," *Thought* 43 (1968): 539–72; for a full-length biography, see Thomas J. Shelley, *Paul J. Hallinan, First Archbishop of Atlanta* (1989).
THOMAS J. SHELLEY

HALLOWELL, A. Irving (28 Dec. 1892–10 Oct. 1974), anthropologist, was born Alfred Irving Hallowell in Philadelphia, Pennsylvania, the son of Edgar Lloyd Hallowell and Dorothy Edsall, occupations unknown. After graduating from a three-year manual training high school he matriculated at the University of Pennsylvania's Wharton School of Finance and Commerce to prepare for a career in business but decided instead to become a sociologist after taking an elective course in that discipline. He received his B.S. in 1914 and financed his graduate studies in sociology at the university by working for Philadelphia's Family Society as a social worker. Because this position involved working with a wide variety of ethnic groups, he became interested in the factors that determine cultural diversity and began to study anthropology. He received his M.A. in 1920, gained an appointment as an instructor in anthropology at the university in 1923, and received his Ph.D. in anthropology in 1924.

Hallowell's dissertation brought to light the existence among many of the aboriginal peoples of northern Eurasia and North America of an extensive system of rituals and attitudes concerning the bear. Although these ceremonies and beliefs varied from one people to another they were quite similar in a number of important respects, particularly concerning the bear's quasi-divine origins, its kinship to humans, and the proper conditions under which it could be killed and eaten. Hallowell also demonstrated that archaeological finds and cave pictures dating back to the early Upper Paleolithic period indicate that these rituals and attitudes had persisted for perhaps as long as 50,000 years. These revelations, published as "Bear Ceremonialism in the Northern Hemisphere" (*American Anthropologist* 27 [1926]: 1–175), marked a major contribution to the development of comparative ethnology.

In 1928 Hallowell was promoted to assistant professor. Having begun a long-term general study of acculturated Algonkian-speaking Indians in eastern sub-

arctic Canada while still in graduate school, he now focused on the relationship between their kinship terms and cross-cousin marriage practices. In 1930 he added to his study the Saulteaux tribe, a branch of the Ojibwa Indians who lived in the Lake Winnipeg region of central Manitoba. Much to the surprise of most anthropologists, he revealed that the preferred spouse for a member of this tribe was a first cousin. He continued to study the Saulteaux for the next forty years and in the process documented the gradual transformation of their society as it became increasingly acculturated to Western modes of behavior and thought.

Hallowell's early studies of the Saulteaux, who still clung to their traditional beliefs and worldview despite having adopted to varying degrees modern tools, clothing, and diet, involved conventional ethnographic topics of a mostly descriptive nature. In 1936, the same year he was promoted to associate professor, he documented the gradual withdrawal of the tribe's members from the Grand Medicine Society, an ancient Ojibwa conclave dominated by shamans, prophets, and seers that conferred social status and mystical knowledge upon its initiates. In 1938, the year before he was promoted to full professor, he reported on certain aspects of Saulteaux material culture and the decline of their practice of polygamy. Although Hallowell continued to address such topics he gradually became more interested in larger questions of a psychoanalytical nature, such as the importance of primitive culture as a variable in the development of aboriginal personality. He began to study phenomena such as the role played by fear and anxiety in the cultural and individual development of the Saulteaux as well as the Freudian symbolism of some of their dreams.

In the course of his work Hallowell became attuned to the theories of Kurt Lewin, the German-American social psychologist, concerning the development of personality. Like Lewin, he rejected the traditional atomistic approach to personality development, which held that an observer registers physical perceptions in a piecemeal fashion. Instead he preferred the new albeit controversial theories of Gestalt psychology, which held that such perceptions are instead registered in light of the observer's past perceptual experience. Accordingly he made extensive use of the various techniques of projective testing, and in 1941 he began publishing the findings he obtained by using the Rorschach test. This technique involves asking the subject to identify a series of accidental inkblots that actually represent nothing. In theory the subject's responses are supposed to enable the tester to identify the subject's deeper personality traits and impulses; in fact no standard interpretation of responses exists, and the usefulness of the test depends in large part on the intuition of the tester. Hallowell's use of these techniques in an anthropological setting drew fire from almost as many critics as did the techniques themselves, although Hallowell also relied on a number of other methods and was quick to acknowledge the Rorschach's limitations. The most controversial of his findings concerned the existence of the aboriginal personality type, an individual whose isolation from the mainstream of world civilization and whose cultural beliefs made him a part of nature rather than a manipulator of nature. Hallowell believed that it was the aboriginal's immanence that made him extremely well suited for the life of a hunter-gatherer while also making it tremendously difficult to cope with acculturation to a "modern" way of life.

Hallowell married Maude Frame in 1942; the couple had no children. In 1944 he left the University of Pennsylvania to become professor of anthropology at Northwestern University. Three years later he returned to his former position at Penn; he also became a professor of anthropology in psychiatry in the university medical school and curator of social anthropology in the university museum. By the early 1950s he had become convinced that human evolution involved psychological structuralization and cultural development as well as biological change. Consequently he devoted a great deal of his later efforts to outlining the steps in hominid behavioral evolution that led to the development of an ego structure, thus permitting humans to perceive themselves objectively and participate appropriately within the framework of a moral social order. Although much of his work involved the pathological effect of Western culture on Native Americans, in 1957 he contributed to the growing field of ethnology by publishing the first of several papers regarding the impact of Native Americans on Euro-American culture.

Hallowell retired from Penn in 1963 but maintained an office at the university where he continued to advise students while involving himself with various projects for the National Academy of Sciences. During his retirement he also taught occasionally at the University of Wisconsin as well as at several colleges in the vicinity of Philadelphia.

Hallowell served as president of the American Anthropological Association in 1949, the American Folklore Society, the Society for Personality Assessment, and the Society for Projective Techniques. He also served as chair of the National Research Council's Division of Anthropology and Psychology from 1946 to 1949 and as editor of the Wenner-Gren Foundation's Viking Fund Publications in Anthropology from 1950 to 1956. He was awarded the Viking Medal for outstanding achievement in anthropology in 1956 and was elected to membership in the National Academy of Sciences in 1961. He died in Wayne, Pennsylvania.

Hallowell was a pioneer in the development of modern cultural anthropology. By introducing the ideas and techniques of modern psychology to the study of primitive societies he enabled anthropologists to analyze a society's observable behaviors and thereby gain a more profound insight into the commonly held, deep-seated thoughts and feelings of that society. In so doing he contributed significantly to a better understanding of the evolution of human personality and self-awareness.

• Two important collections of Hallowell's articles are *Culture and Experience* (1955) and *Contributions to Anthropology: Selected Papers of A. Irving Hallowell* (1976); the latter work includes a brief autobiography. A biography that includes a bibliography is Anthony F. C. Wallace, "Alfred Irving Hallowell," National Academy of Sciences, *Biographical Memoirs* 51 (1978): 195–213. A festschrift that includes some biographical data is Melford E. Spiro, ed., *Context and Meaning in Cultural Anthropology* (1965). An obituary is in the *New York Times*, 15 Oct. 1974.

CHARLES W. CAREY, JR.

HALLOWELL, Anna (1 Nov. 1831–6 Apr. 1905), civic leader and education reformer, was born in Philadelphia, Pennsylvania, the daughter of Morris Longstreth Hallowell, a prominent Quaker merchant, and Hannah Smith Penrose. She was reared in a family that grappled with religious and social concerns. In 1827 Anna's parents had allied themselves with the liberal Hicksite ("heterodox") branch of the Society of Friends. Within their social circle were Hicksite activists like abolitionist Lucretia Mott, whose granddaughter married Anna's brother. The Hallowell home served as a station on the underground railroad, and visitors included radicals like William Lloyd Garrison and Charles Sumner, who recuperated in the Hallowell summer house after being beaten with a cane in the Senate in 1856. Anna's brother Richard Hallowell, a member of the group that escorted the body of John Brown (1800–1859) to New York State in 1859, was instrumental in recruiting African Americans for the famous Fifty-fourth and Fifty-fifth Massachusetts Volunteers during the Civil War.

Within this sometimes unsettled, always stimulating milieu, young Anna Hallowell internalized moral earnestness to such an extent that her teacher at Miss Longstreth's School advised less ostentatious punctiliousness. Even her mother noted her tendency to suffer "unnecessary stings of conscience." By the age of fifteen Anna had become a social activist who organized reading, writing, and arithmetic lessons in the Hallowell laundry for neighborhood African-American children each Sunday. Thereafter, she taught one evening a week at Clarkson Hall, a school for "colored youth." Meanwhile, as was the custom with wealthy nineteenth-century young women, formal education ended. Informal education continued, however, under the tutelage of her father, with whom she read, studied, and in 1850 toured Europe.

Of Hallowell's personal life we have only fragmentary information. She never married. Indeed, she never left the home of her adored father. In the years after the European tour, as the oldest daughter of a mother in delicate health, she assumed responsibility for bringing up the other children. But even during these years she balanced domesticity with social concerns. In 1855 she helped to organize the Home for Destitute Colored Children and for six years served as secretary to its board. In 1859, in the company of Lucretia Mott, she attended the trial of the fugitive slave Daniel Dangerfield, later helping him to hide in the Hallowell home. In 1861, as friend and champion of Ann Preston, the first woman physician in Philadelphia, she accepted appointment to the board of Woman's Hospital and Woman's Medical College, even enrolling in some medical classes.

With the Civil War came trying times. Quaker pacifism notwithstanding, all four of Hallowell's brothers enlisted in the Union army. When two were wounded, she turned the Hallowell home into a hospital for Union soldiers, a group that included Oliver Wendell Holmes, Jr. (1841–1935), who referred to this sanctuary as the "House Beautiful." Here and in other improvised hospitals, Hallowell worked as a nurse, a role that would be cited in her obituary many years later as evidence of the wartime emergence of American women in the "outer world of effort and labor for nation, State, and city" (*Philadelphia Press*, 9 Apr. 1905). Meanwhile, her father's firm failed when he refused to placate southern clients by trimming his antislavery sentiments. Hallowell helped to support the family as a teacher of Latin and French at the Longstreth School and later as a private tutor when the family moved briefly to New York.

What was later referred to as "Miss Hallowell's work" took place after these difficult years, most of it after her father's death in 1880. The primary focus was philanthropic: attempts to alleviate the poverty and suffering of freedmen and freedwomen after the Civil War and attempts to improve the condition of women and children in institutions. Hallowell was a manager of the House of Industry, a philanthropic organization run by female Hicksite Quakers. She was also the first woman member of the board of visitors for the Seventh Ward, the first woman member of the Central Board of Charity, and in 1882 chair of the Philadelphia County Visitors for the State Board of Charities—in which role she was instrumental in modifying punishment for children and in improving institutional diet and medical services. In 1883 she founded the Children's Aid Society of Pennsylvania, serving as its first president. Meanwhile, she had also sponsored the Harvard Examinations for Women in Philadelphia, an effort at "coordinated" education that lasted from 1877 to 1881, during a time when few eastern colleges were open to women. The examinations sought to certify women's accomplishments without providing classroom instruction.

In 1879 Hallowell was instrumental in opening the first kindergarten in Philadelphia, a private institution for poor children at first viewed by her as an extension of her philanthropic activities. Gradually, however, influenced perhaps by the writings of reformers like Elizabeth Peabody, Hallowell came to view universal access to kindergartens as a way to reform all of society. In 1887, when the Philadelphia Board of Public Education assumed financial responsibility for what was by then a network of private kindergartens, Hallowell, the chief instigator of this reform, was appointed to the Philadelphia Board of Education, the first woman so named. She served on the school board until forced to retire for health reasons in 1898, a respected, indomitable figure conspicuous for her work in pro-

moting industrial arts at the James Forten School for the children of immigrants, tireless in her efforts to improve the training of women as teachers. She died in Philadelphia.

The death of Hallowell occasioned an outpouring of editorials and commemorative services that testify to the high esteem in which she was held by her contemporaries. To dismiss her activities as mere volunteerism is to misunderstand the courage of one who became a public persona in an era when outlets for women were limited at best. A reformer who, following the tenets of the Society of Friends, sought "to change from within by convincing, rather than by bringing pressure from without" ("Autobiographic Notes," p. 12), Hallowell's public actions were far more lasting in their impact than were those of many politicians of her time.

• Nine cases of books and papers, including Hallowell's records of the Civil War and of the "House Beautiful," were destroyed in a Boston fire. Hallowell's "Autobiographic Notes" (1900), a typescript of twenty-seven pages, is in the Friends Historical Library, Swarthmore College, as is a copy of William Penrose Hallowell's *Record of a Branch of the Hallowell Family Including the Longstreth, Penrose, and Norwood Branches* (1893). A tribute to Hallowell appears in the *Friends' Intelligencer* (June 1905), also in the Friends Historical Library. *Addresses Made at the Meeting Held in Memory of Anna Hallowell at the Philadelphia Normal School, May 11, 1905, Together with Letters and Resolutions Then Received* (1905), a useful compilation of reminiscences and testimonies, including one by Carey Thomas, president of Bryn Mawr College, is in the Historical Society of Pennsylvania. The library of the School District of Philadelphia holds Annual Reports of the Board of Public Education during Hallowell's tenure there. The "House Beautiful" is mentioned by Oliver Wendell Holmes, Sr., in "My Hunt after 'The Captain,'" *Atlantic Monthly*, Dec. 1962, pp. 738–64. References to the Hallowells also appear in *Touched with Fire: Civil War Letters and Diary of Oliver Wendell Holmes, Jr. 1861–1864*, ed. Mark De Wolfe Howe (1946). See also John Trevor Custis, *The Public Schools of Philadelphia: Historical, Biographical, Statistical* (1897), and Lewis R. Harley, *A History of the Public Education Association of Philadelphia* (1896). Thomas Woody, *A History of Women's Education in the United States*, vol. 2 (1929), traces the history of Harvard Examinations for Women. Obituaries appear in the *Philadelphia Evening Bulletin*, 8 Apr. 1905, the *North American*, 8 Apr. 1905, and the *Philadelphia Press*, 8 Apr. 1905, which also published an editorial the following day on Hallowell's achievements.

ELIZABETH SHERMAN SWING

HALPERT, Edith Gregor (25 Apr. 1900–6 Oct. 1970), art dealer, was born Edith Gregoryevna Fivoosiovich in Odessa, Russia, the daughter of Gregor Fivoosiovich and Frances Lucom. Her father, who died in 1905, was a grain broker but also conducted a wine-and-spirits business with his wife. In 1906 Edith, her mother, and her sister left Russia for New York. There her mother shortened the family name to Fivisovitch. In 1914 Edith began to attend painting classes at the National Academy of Design in New York. Accounts of her next few years are murky and contradictory. It appears, however, that in 1916 she changed her name to Fein and, while continuing to study painting, took a job as a comptometer operator at Bloomingdale's department store. By 1917 she had shown sufficient talent to become an assistant to the advertising manager of the Stern Brothers department store. In that position she not only created sketches for advertisements but also wrote copy.

While at the National Academy of Design, she frequented art galleries and was particularly impressed by the gallery of Newman E. Montross, who specialized in contemporary art. She also became active in the People's Art Guild, which staged exhibitions for the underprivileged in settlement houses and churches. At the age of eighteen, she married the artist Samuel Halpert, whom she had met at the Guild. They had no children. From Stern's she moved on to other managerial positions in New York. From 1921 to 1925 she served as personnel manager and head of correspondence for S. W. Straus & Co., an investment banking house. While in France with her husband in the summer of 1925, she accepted an offer to reorganize the Galeries Lilloise, a department store in Lille.

On her return to New York, she realized that her true interest lay in fine art, not the world of big business. In 1926, with her husband and a partner, Berthe Kroll Goldsmith, she opened a gallery in Greenwich Village. The original name chosen for it was Our Gallery, but after the first year she changed it to the Downtown Gallery because of its out-of-the-way location. Although she moved the gallery in 1940 to the first of three uptown sites, it remained the Downtown Gallery.

The sculptor William Zorach, a sometime member of Edith Halpert's "stable" of artists, maintained in his memoirs that behind her decision to operate a gallery was her belief that she could do a better job of selling her husband's work than could Charles Daniel, then his dealer. In 1929, however, only three years after the opening, she initiated divorce proceedings against Halpert. He died in 1930, with Edith at his side. Edith and Goldsmith continued to own the Downtown Gallery jointly until 1935, when Halpert bought her partner out. Halpert's second marriage, to Raymond Davis in 1939, was dissolved the following year.

As a new entrant to the trade, Halpert decided to specialize in contemporary American art. Her first artists included Peggy Bacon, Stuart Davis, Yasuo Kuniyoshi, Reuben Nakian, and Charles Sheeler. All were members of the Whitney Studio Club, a group founded in 1918 by Gertrude Vanderbilt Whitney and Juliana Force for the fostering and promotion of American talent. In 1931 Halpert expanded her inventory to include American folk art, which she gathered with the assistance of Holger Cahill, an authority in the field who in the previous year had organized a folk-art exhibition for the Newark Museum. Foremost among Halpert's clients in this division of her business was Abby Aldrich Rockefeller. With Halpert's aid, Cahill staged a major exhibition of folk art at the Museum of Modern Art in 1932; most of the works on view were from the Rockefeller holdings. They are now housed in the Abby Aldrich Rockefeller Folk Art Center in Williamsburg, Virginia.

Representation was the mode of all of Halpert's first artists, painters and sculptors alike. During the depression, when "American scene" painting achieved its apogee of popularity, Halpert truly came into her own. She developed "a 1930s eye," as Charles Alan, her associate from 1945 to 1953, put it. When the Federal Art Project of the Works Progress Administration was founded in 1935 to provide work and a weekly wage for needy artists, Halpert invited several of its painters to join the Downtown Gallery. At the same time she cleverly cultivated an acquaintance with the reclusive Alfred Stieglitz, a pioneer dealer in avant-garde art. From his gallery, An American Place, she was able to secure paintings by Georgia O'Keeffe, John Marin, Charles Demuth, and Marsden Hartley. She took no interest at all in abstract expressionism when it came into spectacular being in the 1940s. Modernist though she may have been at the beginning, her taste changed very little in her later years.

In the gallery and out of it, Halpert was a mixture of moods. She would breathe fire if a speculator in art asked how much the value of a work on view might be expected to rise in a year's time but would often complain about having to increase her artists' prices or lose them to other dealers. Among her most agreeable qualities were her readiness to encourage young painters and her patience with casual visitors to the gallery, even when it was evident that they had very little money to spend on art. Collectors with shallow pockets were perennially grateful to her for the pre-Christmas sales in which small but characteristic works by gallery artists were offered at very low prices.

As the years passed, however, much that had endeared Halpert to her acquaintances and the public gradually slipped away. She began to lose her talent for friendship. One unprejudiced and shrewdly insightful witness to her life from the early 1930s to the end was Dorothy C. Miller, the chief associate of Alfred H. Barr, the director of the Museum of Modern Art. Some four years after Halpert's death, Miller remarked, "She was such a good person at the beginning, and in the end she didn't have a friend or a person who could work with her, and it was some sort of self-destructive element in her personality as I analyze it."

What started Halpert on her downward spiral was a flaming controversy over the works of William M. Harnett, the nineteenth-century "magic realist" painter whose talent she first recognized in 1935. She bought one of Harnett's paintings and, much impressed, searched for more and had no difficulty finding buyers for them. Trouble began just after World War II, when Alfred Frankenstein, the art critic for the *San Francisco Chronicle*, made the discovery that many of the paintings signed with Harnett's name and sold as his works were in fact not his but were painted by John Frederick Peto, his contemporary. Halpert could not accept Frankenstein's findings, even though they were backed by solid evidence, including Peto's genuine signatures hidden under the forged signatures of Harnett. According to Dorothy Miller, Halpert believed that the critic's intention was to attack her personally, and in the wake of this sorry affair she gradually became "a little bit crazy."

Nevertheless, Halpert was entirely committed to her profession. She had a vacation house in Connecticut, but she made her home in an apartment above the Downtown Gallery, much like the immigrants of the turn of the century who lived "over the store." Her vocation was her life; when she was not at the gallery, she associated exclusively with artists and collectors. Unwell in her last years, she died in New York. Three years after her death, her personal collection was sold at auction in four installments. The first and most important of the sales brought in $3.6 million.

• The business records, correspondence, and scrapbooks of the Downtown Gallery are in the Archives of American Art, Washington, D.C. See also the transcribed interviews with Charles Alan, Alfred Frankenstein, Sidney Janis, and Dorothy Miller in the Archives of American Art Oral History, and William Zorach, *Art Is My Life* (1967). Halpert's Greenwich Village years are covered in Diane Tepfer, *Edith Gregor Halpert and the Downtown Gallery Downtown, 1926–1940: A Study in American Art Patronage* (1989). For a full account of the Harnett-Peto controversy, see Frankenstein, *After the Hunt: William Harnett and Other American Still Life Painters, 1870–1900* (1953). An obituary is in the *New York Times*, 7 Oct. 1970.

MALCOLM GOLDSTEIN

HALPINE, Charles Graham (20 Nov. 1829–3 Aug. 1868), journalist and soldier, was born near Oldcastle, County Meath, Ireland, the son of Nicholas John Halpin, a clergyman ordained in the Church of Ireland (Episcopal), and Ann Grehan. The scholarly Halpin devoted considerable time to the education of his son, who early demonstrated gifts as a writer of both prose and poetry. By the age of ten, Charles was accomplished in French and Latin, and shortly before his fifteenth birthday he enrolled in his father's alma mater, Trinity College, Dublin. He left Dublin before graduation and read law at Lincoln's Inn, London; held a minor political office at Somerset House; and wrote articles and poems for a variety of English newspapers and magazines. In 1849 he married a childhood sweetheart, Margaret G. Milligan. They had seven children. In February 1850, soon after the birth of their first child, he left his wife with her parents and, in search of fame and fortune, joined the exodus of the Irish to the United States. The family was reunited in 1853.

Charles began his new life in the United States by adding an "e" to his surname and by changing his middle name from Grehan to Graham, after a deceased brother. These changes reflected the tensions between Halpine and his parents, who were ardently pro-English and anti-Catholic, while he just as ardently hated the English and allowed Irish-Americans to assume he was a Catholic. This uneasy family relationship may have contributed to the stammer that plagued Halpine

all his life and caused him to assume the not-always-congenial role of the comic.

In 1851 Halpine began to write in Boston for Benjamin Shillaber's sparkling weekly newspaper, the *Carpet-Bag*. In Shillaber's temporary absence, many readers became offended by the extreme ridicule in Halpine's satires of the public's taste for trashy novels and excessive displays of patriotism, and as a result the paper stopped publication in 1853.

After he moved to New York City the next year, Halpine's journalistic career was launched by one of his poems published anonymously in Horace Greeley's *Tribune*. "Hail to the Stars and Stripes" (better known as the "Flaunting Lie") protested the use of U.S. troops to return a fugitive slave (Anthony Burns) to his master:

> Tear down the flaunting lie!
> Half-mast the starry flag!
> Insult no sunny sky
> With this polluted rag!
> Destroy it, ye who can!
> Deep sink it in the waves!
> It bears a fellow-man
> To groan with fellow-slaves.

It is possible that Halpine, like other aspiring writers, wrote the poem to please his editor, for as an Irishman and a Democrat his views on slavery and other issues were not compatible with those of an abolitionist who became a Republican. Later the two men disagreed openly over public policy. It is a tribute to Halpine's engaging personality that Greeley nevertheless remained the younger man's friend and patron. By the time of the Civil War, Halpine was writing for all the major New York dailies, especially the *Herald*, and had published at least six novels serially in the *Irish-American* dealing with his homeland. He also had become editor and part owner of the *New York Leader*, a pro-Stephen A. Douglas and anti-Tammany Hall weekly newspaper.

Among the first to respond to Abraham Lincoln's 15 April 1861 call to arms, Halpine served for three months with New York's Sixty-ninth Regiment of Irish volunteers. Late in the summer he became an officer on the staff of General David Hunter. As such, he helped compile the bill of particulars against John C. Frémont that resulted in that officer's removal from command in Missouri in 1861; he accepted the surrender of Fort Pulaski, Georgia, in 1862; he witnessed and later defended publicly the futile attack of the monitors on Fort Sumter in 1863; and he was at Hunter's side during the 1864 expedition up the Shenandoah Valley to Lynchburg, Virginia, and during the disastrous retreat through the mountains of West Virginia.

Following the antidraft riots in New York in July 1863, Halpine was assigned to the staff of General John A. Dix, commander of the Department of the East, and given the responsibility of building support for the war among the Irish in New York and elsewhere who opposed it. He accomplished this objective by describing the brash exploits of a mythical "Private Miles O'Reilly," who practiced the democratic egalitarianism he heard so much about in the United States by telling his superior officers, including his commander in chief, how to win the war. Broad burlesques, but published in the *Herald* as straight news (and at first often mistaken for it), "Miles O'Reilly" stories and poems became popular throughout the North. One poem, "Sambo's Right to Be Kilt," helped lessen the widespread opposition to the army's recruitment of African-American men by arguing that every time a black soldier was killed or wounded a white one was spared.

In widely reprinted comic poems and stories, "Private Miles O'Reilly" evolved into an early representation of the Lovable Irishman, luckless but happy, unlettered but wise, boastful but innocent and affectionate. As a vigorously outspoken Union soldier, he helped change the image of the Irish in the North and gave the Irish themselves a sense that they had a future in the United States, that the country was worth fighting for.

After the war Halpine published the *New York Citizen*, a literary weekly that took a forceful stand against Tammany Hall, the Democratic machine that for years looted the city by manipulating ignorant Irish voters. "Miles O'Reilly" appeared frequently in the *Citizen* but was less effective in the cause of good government than he had been in the cause of the war. Halpine also continued to write on a broad range of subjects for the big dailies. His largely fictional book *Prison Life of Jefferson Davis* (1866), ascribed to John J. Craven, M.D., aroused sympathy in the North for the ex-Confederate president and helped enable President Andrew Johnson to release him from prison in 1867. As a Democrat, Halpine supported the president's reconstruction policies. He opposed the enfranchisement of southern blacks (except those who had served in the army) on the grounds, he argued in a much-publicized poem, "Black Loyalty," that they had given more support to the South than to the North.

As the creator of the famous "Miles O'Reilly" and a journalist with many important connections, Halpine was able to pursue a political career independent of Tammany Hall. At the time of his sudden death, he was Register of the County of New York, the highest-paid elective office in the country, and was contemplating running for a safe seat in Congress.

Halpine's exuberant personality, quick intelligence, and gifts as a writer and observer endeared him to many powerful friends, who warned him frequently about his alcoholism. He made strenuous, if short-lived, efforts to control his drinking. In June 1868 he made a solemn pledge of total abstinence that caused him great suffering and sleeplessness, from which he sought escape by breathing chloroform. In August, in a room in the Astor House near the *Herald* office, he breathed too much of it (whether deliberately or accidentally is not known) and died.

• The largest collection of Halpine's papers, together with copies of his letters found in the collections of prominent friends, is in the Huntington Library, San Marino, Calif. The Library of Congress has scrapbooks kept by Margaret M. Halpine. Edward K. Eckert, "*Fiction Distorting Fact*" (1987), is a detailed analysis of *Prison Life* based upon Jefferson Davis's own annotations. Halpine's other books are *Lyrics by the Letter H.* (1854), *The Life and Adventures . . . of Private Miles O'Reilly* (1864), and *Baked Meats of the Funeral* (1866). His friend Robert B. Roosevelt edited a volume of Halpine, *Poetical Works* (1869), and included a sympathetic biographical essay. In "Charles Graham Halpine: Life and Adventures of Miles O'Reilly," *New-York Historical Society Quarterly* 51, no. 4 (1967), John D. Hayes and Doris D. Maguire introduced Halpine to twentieth-century writers. William Hanchett, *Irish: Charles G. Halpine in Civil War America* (1970), is the only book-length biography and contains an extensive bibliography.

WILLIAM HANCHETT

HALSEY, Frederick Arthur (12 July 1856–20 Oct. 1935), mechanical engineer, journalist, and prominent opponent of the metric system, was born in Unadilla, New York, the son of Dr. Gaius Leonard Halsey, a physician, and Juliet Carrington. He attended Unadilla Academy and went on to study engineering at Cornell under the noted professor John E. Sweet, with whom he maintained close contact throughout his career.

Halsey graduated from Cornell in 1878 and returned to Unadilla to work as a machinist. In the fall of 1879 he secured his first professional position as manager of the testing room of the Telegraph Supply Company (later the Brush Electric Company). Halsey left in the spring of 1880 to work as a draftsman for the Delamater Iron Works in New York City. Later in 1880 he joined the Rand Drill Company of New York as an engineer. Halsey married Stella D. Spencer of Unadilla in 1885. They had two children, Marion and Olga.

At the age of twenty-two Halsey settled down to a career in mechanical engineering. Over the next few years he invented the "Slugger" rock drill and described it in his first article in the American Society of Mechanical Engineers (ASME) publication *Transactions*. In 1890 he published his first book, *Slide Valve Gears*. He also developed a uniquely effective response to the labor disturbances of the 1880s, the Halsey Premium Plan. All efforts to talk Rand's New York management into adopting it proved futile, but in 1890, when Rand placed Halsey in command of its new Canadian operation, he was able to test it himself. In 1891 he described his efforts in a second *Transactions* article, "The Premium Plan of Paying for Labor." Halsey's plan, which was to have more influence on manufacturing over at least the next fifteen years than any variant of Frederick Taylor's more widely discussed system, advocated the addition of a premium to piece rates when workers exceeded normal output. By thus rewarding productivity, Halsey hoped to counter organized labor's resistance to piece-work wages and to foster a sense of worker participation in the employer's success. In a 1903 discussion, he pointed out that his plan paid a premium "as a reward for the workman's use of his wits and his intelligence," while Taylor rewarded them for doing nothing more than "following orders and producing expected results."

In 1894 Halsey left Rand to join the *American Machinist* as associate editor. During his seventeen-year tenure with the magazine he elevated it to first rank among engineering journals. He increased its emphasis on machine design and construction, management, and economics. In 1896 the American Economic Association published his paper on the Premium Plan in *The Adjustment of Wages to Efficiency*. In the late 1890s Halsey founded the "junior movement" within ASME, an effort to encourage publication by the younger members of the society. In 1902 he became embroiled, along with others who were identified with "scientific management," in efforts to democratize the society.

In that same year, in a paper titled "The Metric System," he alerted ASME to the fact that the House Committee on Coinage, Weights, and Measures had favorably reported a bill to convert federal government operations to metric measurement. In view of its support by scientific societies, the new discipline of electrical engineering, and the recently established National Bureau of Standards, it was likely that the bill would become law unless immediate opposition was organized. Halsey thought that conversion of the nation's industrial measuring equipment to a foreign system was both unwarranted and uneconomical; he was firmly opposed to government interference in manufacturing. The mechanical engineering community had registered its opposition to metric conversion twenty-two years earlier, when 80 percent of ASME's membership voted against it. Nevertheless, many of the society's most prominent members had close ties to academic and scientific groups who favored the idea. Halsey urged the membership to speak up, and in a repeat survey they did: again, 80 percent registered opposition to compulsory metric adoption. The society itself declined to take a public position, but Halsey had succeeded in setting the antimetric forces in motion. In 1904 he published *The Metric Fallacy* and testified at length before the House committee. In his testimony, he took direct aim at metric advocates: "It is simply monstrous and unthinkable that these enthusiasts . . . should force this thing on the manufacturers, who are opposed to it and who have the problems to face and the bills to pay." In recognition of his successful efforts, the National Association of Manufacturers presented him with an award and a finely crafted clock.

In 1907 the *American Machinist* made Halsey its editor in chief. He retired in 1911. During the early years of his retirement he published a number of significant engineering works, including *Methods of Machine Shop Work for Apprentices and Students in Technical and Trade Schools* (1914) and *Handbook for Machine Designers, Shop Men and Draftsmen* (1913). Both his interest in scientific management and his opposition to

metric adoption continued unabated. In 1917 he founded the American Institute of Weights and Measures, the organization that successfully led the fight against metric adoption for the next twenty years. In 1923 ASME awarded Halsey a medal in recognition of his efforts to rationalize wage structures in manufacturing.

During the last years of his life he traveled widely and actively promoted Anglo-American relations. He was an avid collector of rare technical books and an accomplished ballroom dancer. Halsey died in New York City.

Throughout his career Frederick Halsey exemplified and promoted a practical, businesslike approach to mechanical engineering. Although academically trained, he retained a strong belief in the apprenticeship system and in the machine shop as the heart of the engineering discipline. Unlike the founders of the profession, he had little reverence for age and social position and no desire to join forces with either the government or the scientific and academic communities. In many ways he was a prototype of the twentieth-century American engineer.

• A collection of Halsey family papers is in folder 2966, Department of Manuscripts and University Archives, Cornell University Libraries. Halsey wrote a number of books on engineering subjects, including those cited above. He published numerous articles in *Transactions*, the publication of the American Society of Mechanical Engineers (ASME), the *American Machinist*, and the *Bulletin* of the American Institute of Weights and Measures. A summary of his life is in "Cornell Engineers: Frederick A. Halsey, BME '78," *Sibley Journal of Engineering* (Dec. 1935): 149. His impact on ASME is discussed in Bruce Sinclair's *A Centennial History of the American Society of Mechanical Engineers* (1980). His Premium Plan of Paying for Labor is discussed in ASME, *Transactions* 24 (1902–1903): 1465–67; "The Premium System in Great Britain," *American Machinist*, 22 June 1905, pp. 828–32; and almost any work on scientific management. Halsey's antimetric views are thoroughly presented and explored in ASME *Transactions* 23 (1902–1903): 397–466; *The Metric Fallacy* (1904); and in his congressional testimony: U.S. House Committee on Coinage, Weights, and Measures, *Hearings on H. Rept. 8988*, 59th Cong., 1907. His career is outlined in obituaries in *Transactions* 58, no. 2 (Feb. 1936): RI-54, RI-55; the *American Machinist* 6 Nov. 1935; and the *New York Times*, 21 Oct. 1935.

ROBERT R. JENKS

HALSEY, John (1 Mar. 1670–1716), privateer and pirate, was born in Boston, Massachusetts, the son of James Halsey (occupation unknown) and Dinah (maiden name unknown). Born in North America's principal seaport in a time of naval rivalry and consequent naval warfare, John Halsey is reported to have first gone to sea as a sailor in HMS *Nonsuch* at the beginning of King William's eight-year war with France, the War of the League of Augsburg (1689–1697). In his early twenties he became a captain of one of the many small vessels coasting from Boston south to the lower colonies and the West Indies, part of a significant trade in New England livestock and building materials for the Caribbean and rum and molasses for Massachusetts Bay. In 1693 he is reported as master of a Boston sloop called *Adventure* making voyages to Virginia, and by the early 1700s he appears as a privateer in southern waters. *The Calendar of State Papers: America and West Indies, 1704–05* records that he brought three prize barks to Barbados in 1703 and refused to pay the customary one-tenth of their value to the lord admiral.

John Halsey seems to have been a merchant captain alert to privateering opportunities. In 1704 he brought a ship and cargo into Newport and shortly received a privateering commission from Rhode Island governor Samuel Cranston "to fight and destroy any privateers and others, subjects and vassalls of France and Spaine, for 12 months if the War continue so long." Halsey's vessel was the Boston brigantine *Charles*, variously described as from 80 to 100 tons in measurement and mounting eight guns, a ship fitted out as a privateer by Boston merchants the previous summer, stolen and used for piracy in 1703 by John Quelch and his crew, and returned to Boston in June 1704. The war cited by Governor Cranston was the War of the Spanish Succession (1701–1713).

Privateering, a patriotic piracy legalized by governments at war, was dangerous for a ship's crew and risky for a ship's owners, although the profits could be large. John Halsey was a successful privateer who brought a Spanish prize valued between £4,000 and £5,000 to Rhode Island on 30 May 1705, causing Governor Joseph Dudley of Massachusetts to declare that his neighbor Cranston had no authority to create Rhode Island privateers. A judge of the vice admiralty court briefly agreed with Dudley, but by the end of June the prize was condemned in favor of Halsey, his crew, and his vessel's owners. Halsey was given a new privateering commission by Governor Cranston and sailed first to the Grand Banks, then to the Azores, the Canaries, and finally to the Cape Verde Islands, capturing several Spanish vessels and losing another in a fierce engagement in which Halsey's *Charles* and a 40-gun would-be prize were deck to deck, with their men fighting hand to hand.

After taking on wood and water at Brava in the Cape Verdes, Halsey turned pirate. His latest privateering papers were shortly to be invalid, and it has been speculated that the previous year's dispute over his commission and prize vessel in Rhode Island had made him weary of dealing with politicians. An equally likely reason is the fortune a ship and crew could acquire in as little as a year of Red Sea and Indian Ocean piracy. Robbing the Mogul trading vessels of India, the India-to-Arabia pilgrim ships on their way to Mecca, and the rich, slow cargo carriers of Europe's India companies was extraordinarily profitable. By 1706 it had been known for twenty years on the waterfronts of Europe and America that "robbing the Moors" was the way to wealth. Red Sea piracy was an obvious opportunity for a man like Halsey, experienced in sea fights and willing to take risks for financial gain.

The last of Captain John Halsey's history is given to us by Captain Charles Johnson in his *General History of the Robberies and Murders of the Most Notorious Pirates*, published in 1724 and still the world's principal pirate reference. Halsey, says Johnson, "intended to rob only the Moor ships," and this caused a mutiny aboard his *Charles*. Captain William Kidd had a similar experience in the same waters ten years before. This mutiny was quelled, but a later dispute over a prize saw some of Halsey's crew desert in the captured vessel while Halsey and the remainder sailed for the Straits of Malacca.

In Malayan waters they encountered only ships too strong for them. In need of water, wood, and more manpower they headed west again to one of the pirate ports of Madagascar. Refreshed, repaired, and with augmented crew, they sailed for the Red Sea, where they encountered "the Moor's fleet from Mocha and Jeddah" in the Strait of Bab-el-Mandeb. The Moor's fleet, galleys, rowed away in a calm and escaped. But soon Halsey and his crew found four English merchant ships, chased them, and captured two, along with £50,000 in coin. A merchant seaman's wage in the first decade of the eighteenth century would have been from £1 to £4 per month, so the value of £50,000 can be appreciated.

They returned to Madagascar with the spoils and were joined there by merchants from one of the two English ships they had taken, the merchants hoping to buy back the stolen cargo at what Captain Johnson called "an easy rate." While this transaction was in progress, a 26-gun Scottish ship came into the anchorage to trade with the pirates for stolen goods. Soon enough, Halsey's pirates, their own three vessels wrecked by a storm, saw the wisdom of stealing the vessels and the money of both the English merchants and the Scottish traders.

Captain John Halsey died while this was taking place, and it is best to give Captain Johnson's account:

As to Captain Halsey, while the Scotch ship was fitting, he fell ill of a fever, died and was buried with great solemnity and ceremony. The prayers of the Church of England were read over him, colours were flying, and his sword and pistol laid on his coffin, which was covered with a ship's jack; as many minute guns fired as he was years old, *viz*: 46, and three English volley, and one French volley of small arms. He was brave in his person, courteous to all his prisoners, lived beloved and died regretted by his own people. His grave was made in a garden of water melons, and fenced in with pallisades to prevent his being rooted up by wild hogs, of which there are plenty in those parts. (P. 422)

• The most complete account of John Halsey's career is in Captain Charles Johnson, *A General History of the Robberies and Murders of the Most Notorious Pirates*, ed. Arthur L. Hayward (1926). A new edition of this standard pirate reference, edited by Manuel Schonhorn and published by the University of South Carolina Press, is Daniel Defoe, *A General History of the Pyrates* (1972). Many people believe that Captain Charles Johnson was Daniel Defoe writing under a pseudonym, but this has not been conclusively established. Captain

Halsey's privateering career is treated in Howard M. Chapin, *Privateer Ships and Sailors* (1926), and background on Captain Halsey, his profession, and his era can be found in George F. Dow and John H. Edmonds, *The Pirates of the New England Coast* (1923).

JOSEPH GRIBBINS

HALSEY, William Frederick, Jr. (30 Oct. 1882–16 Aug. 1959), naval officer, was born in Elizabeth, New Jersey, the son of William Frederick Halsey, an officer in the U.S. Navy, and Anne Masters Brewster. Always intending to follow in his father's footsteps, Halsey, after a year at the University of Virginia, secured a place at the U.S. Naval Academy. He ranked forty-third of sixty-two graduates in 1904.

Midshipman Halsey served aboard the battleship *Missouri* in 1904–1905 and was commissioned as an ensign in 1906 while assigned to a captured gunboat, *Don Juan de Austria*. When Theodore Roosevelt chose to wave his big stick by dispatching the "Great White Fleet," Halsey went along, circumnavigating the globe aboard the battleship *Kansas*. In 1909 he was promoted to lieutenant and given command of the torpedo boat *Dupont*. The same year Halsey married Frances "Fanny" Cooke Grandy; they had two children.

Through the following two decades, Halsey spent his service at sea almost entirely aboard small, quick destroyers. He served briefly aboard the *Lamson* in 1910 and later commanded the *Flusser* (1912–1913) and the *Jarvis* (1913–1915). The latter was dispatched to Tampico and Veracruz when the United States briefly intervened in revolutionary Mexico. Prior to American entry into the First World War, Halsey's shore duty included command of a training camp at the Norfolk Navy Yard (1910–1912) and assignment to the Discipline Department at the Naval Academy (1915–1917). Halsey, who enjoyed liquor and cigarettes and distrusted fighting men who did not, particularly disliked enforcing the academy's tobacco ban.

Promoted to lieutenant commander in 1916, Halsey returned to destroyers after the United States entered World War I. Based in Ireland, he served aboard the *Duncan*, then commanded the *Benham* and the *Shaw*, escorting convoys and patrolling for German submarines. His ships never saw combat. After the armistice Halsey skippered the destroyers *Yarnall* (1918–1920), *Chauncey* (1920), *John Francis Burns* (1920), and *Wickes* (1920–1921) before serving at the Office of Naval Intelligence in Washington and as naval attaché in Germany and Scandinavia (1922–1924). After commanding the destroyers *Dale* and *Osborne*, he served aboard the battleship *Wyoming* as executive officer. Promoted to captain in 1927, he returned to the Naval Academy to supervise its prison ship and other boats. There he became intrigued by naval aviation, but in 1930 he again assumed a destroyer command, this time leading a squadron of nineteen ships in the Atlantic Fleet. Between 1932 and 1934 Halsey studied at the Naval War College, then at the Army War College.

At this point Halsey's career took a decisive turn. He had cut his teeth on destroyers, but it was his late-blooming interest in aviation that fitted him to play an outsized role in a changing navy. When offered command of the aircraft carrier *Saratoga* in 1934 upon condition that he complete an aviation observer's course in Pensacola, he leaped at the opportunity. Indeed, Halsey somewhat mysteriously secured formal training as a pilot, even though he had earlier failed the requisite eyesight examination. After commanding the *Saratoga*, he returned to the Pensacola Naval Air Station in 1937 to serve as commandant. Promoted to rear admiral the following year, Halsey took charge of Carrier Division Two, which included the *Yorktown* and the *Enterprise*. In 1939 he moved to Carrier Division One, again aboard the *Saratoga*. In June 1940 Halsey was promoted to vice admiral and appointed to lead the Aircraft Battle Force as well as Carrier Division Two. He thus commanded the Pacific Fleet's carriers and their air groups as U.S. relations with Japan deteriorated.

Aircraft carriers were the linchpins of the naval war that followed. Fortunately, Halsey's ships were not at Pearl Harbor on 7 December 1941, the day of the Japanese bombing. Halsey himself was returning from Wake Island aboard the *Enterprise*. He was therefore able, in February and March 1942, to lead carrier task forces in what he called "morale raids" against Japanese positions in the Marshall and Gilbert islands and on Wake and Marcus islands. Though modest sorties, these represented the United States' first offensive actions in the Pacific. He participated in another such operation in April, commanding the carrier force from which James Doolittle launched his bombing raid on Tokyo. Ironically, Halsey missed Midway, the naval battle that in June began actually to turn the tide in the Pacific. Forced into a mainland hospital by a severe skin inflammation, he had relinquished command to Raymond Spruance. Halsey termed his absence from Midway "the most grievous disappointment of my career."

Halsey returned to the Pacific in September 1942. He had begun by this time to draw the American public's attention, both as an aggressive commander and as a rough-hewn but affable character (he claimed to dislike the nickname "Bull" with which he was tagged). He evinced the most visceral hatred of his foe, declaring that his strategy was to "kill Japs and keep on killing Japs." Halsey was given the opportunity to apply this principle after being named commander, South Pacific Force and South Pacific Area, in October 1942. Put in charge of naval and air forces and also ground troops operating in the island groups northeast of Australia, his most immediate task was to relieve hard-pressed American forces on Guadalcanal in the Solomons. Halsey, who was appointed a full admiral that November, proved more willing than some other commanders to make the requisite sacrifices in American ships, planes, and lives. His naval and air forces drove off Japanese reinforcements but sustained considerable losses. The Japanese finally evacuated Guadalcanal in February 1943. This victory allowed Allied forces more decisively to assume the offensive in the

South Pacific, not only in the Solomons but also in New Guinea, where Douglas MacArthur was in charge. Through the balance of 1943 Halsey's forces hopped up the Solomons through the Russells, New Georgia, Vella Lavella, and Bougainville and headed toward Rabaul, Japan's chief stronghold in the theater. By early 1944 Halsey and MacArthur had effectively quarantined Rabaul.

As Allied forces closed in on the Philippines and the Central Pacific islands nearer Japan, Halsey entered upon a "double-echelon" arrangement with Admiral Spruance, in which the pair alternated command of the same force of ships, designated the Third Fleet when led by Halsey and the Fifth Fleet under Spruance. As one led an operation, the other would prepare for subsequent actions. Halsey took charge of the "Big Blue Fleet" in August 1944, flying his flag on the battleship *New Jersey*, and supported operations in the Western Caroline and Palau islands. Third Fleet raids on the central Philippines suggested that Japanese occupiers were ill prepared, and Halsey successfully urged that American landings there be moved ahead to October. To pave the way, Halsey's fleet struck hard at Luzon, Japan's Ryukyu Islands, and Taiwan.

MacArthur's landings in the Philippines set the stage for what, in terms of tonnage engaged and territory covered, was the greatest naval battle to that time, the battle for Leyte Gulf (23–26 Oct. 1944). Knowing their foe well, the Japanese sent a stripped-down force of carriers toward the Philippines from the north in hopes that, in pouncing upon it, Halsey might leave the Leyte beachhead vulnerable to battleship groups approaching from the south and west. After his planes had shot up one of these forces, Halsey, understanding that his orders were to strike at the heart of the enemy fleet rather than to linger around Leyte, did indeed steam north, intending "to put those carriers out for keeps" (Potter, p. 296). This left the Seventh Fleet to fight off the Japanese force moving upon Leyte through Surigao Strait and the one, earlier hit by Halsey, approaching through San Bernardino Strait. To the surprise of other commanders, Halsey had left the San Bernardino Strait unguarded. Poor communications between the two U.S. fleets facilitated the deft Japanese manipulation of Halsey's combativeness, which, like his improvisatory operational style, had previously served him well. Planes from Halsey's task force sunk the carriers of the decoy "Northern Force," but before the fleets could become fully engaged, a terse message from Admiral Chester Nimitz forced Halsey to turn back to attempt to finish off the Japanese ships withdrawing through San Bernardino. Halsey, however, did not return in time for anything but the denouement. The destruction of a straggling ship was the only surface action this carrier admiral ever actually witnessed. Though its losses ensured that the Japanese navy could never again fight as a fleet, Americans could not avoid second guesses. Halsey claimed to regret only that he had to turn back rather than running down the "Northern Force." Others insisted that Bull had recklessly left American forces exposed.

Halsey hardly seemed chastened by the events at Leyte Gulf and, in the following months, continued an aggressive support of American operations, raiding Luzon, Taiwan, Okinawa, and in the South China Sea. His determination to carry out his missions may well have contributed to his fleet's stumbling into deadly typhoons in December 1944 and June 1945. Halsey could plead insufficient meteorological information, but courts of inquiry suggested that he had not taken necessary precautions. Given his record and his popularity with both sailors and the public, Halsey kept his command nevertheless.

After several months off, Halsey had returned to his fleet in May 1945, and his new flagship was the battleship *Missouri*, though not the same *Missouri* he had served aboard forty years before. His forces supported the offensive on Okinawa and through July and early August struck at targets on the Japanese mainland. Halsey witnessed the signing of the formal surrender documents by Japanese officials aboard the *Missouri* that September.

Halsey stepped down as Third Fleet commander in November 1945 and the following month was elevated to the navy's highest rank, Fleet Admiral. Essentially retired by the end of 1946, though still on the payroll into 1947, he settled in Charlottesville, Virginia. He moved to New York City a few years later and sat on the boards of several corporations, including International Telephone & Telegraph. Halsey died at Fishers Island, New York.

• A collection of Halsey's papers is at the Library of Congress, Manuscripts Division. He wrote a memoir with J. Bryan III, *Admiral Halsey's Story* (1947). E. B. Potter, *Bull Halsey* (1985; 2d corr. printing, 1988), is a comprehensive biography. Several of America's most distinguished historians have studied aspects of Halsey's service in depth, especially C. Vann Woodward, *The Battle for Leyte Gulf* (1947), and Samuel Eliot Morison, *History of United States Naval Operations in World War II*, vol. 5 (1949), vol. 12 (1958), vol. 14 (1960). Halsey is, of course, prominently featured in many other histories of the war in the Pacific such as Clark Reynolds, *The Fast Carriers: The Forging of an Air Navy* (1968). An obituary is in the *New York Times*, 17 Aug. 1959.

PATRICK G. WILLIAMS

HALSTEAD, Murat (2 Sept. 1829–2 July 1908), journalist, was born in Paddy's Run, near Cincinnati, Ohio, the son of Griffin Halstead and Clarissa Willets, farmers. His mother used the local *Hamilton Telegraph* as a primer to teach Halstead to read before he was four. He attended Paddy's Run Academy until he was nineteen, then entered Farmers' College in Pleasant Hill, Ohio, to study for a legal career. After several interruptions, during which he taught school, Halstead graduated in 1851 and embarked on a career in journalism.

While in college Halstead contributed articles to the *Hamilton Intelligencer* and the *Rossville Democrat*. In 1851 he worked briefly for two Cincinnati newspapers, the *Atlas* and the *Enquirer*, before making an abortive attempt to publish a Sunday newspaper called the *Leader*. For the next two years he wrote about literary topics for two popular weeklies, the *Columbian* and the *Great West*. In March 1853 he joined the *Cincinnati Commercial*, the newspaper he would lead to prominence over the next four decades. Halstead became editor in chief in 1859. In 1854 Halstead purchased a one-sixteenth interest in the newspaper and gradually increased his share until he acquired a controlling interest in 1866. He married Mary Banks of Cincinnati in March 1857. The marriage produced twelve children, including four sons who entered journalism.

As a political reporter for the *Commercial*, Halstead became nationally recognized for his coverage of the Democratic and Republican conventions of 1856 and 1860. His dispatches about the 1860 conventions were published as a book, *The Caucuses of 1860* (1860), which has become a valuable historical resource. He also was recognized for his reporting during the Civil War and the Franco-Prussian War. Halstead was a staunch supporter of Abraham Lincoln during the Civil War, but he could be bitterly critical of the first family. In 1864, when a friend failed to receive a postmastership, Halstead wrote that Lincoln was "a miserably weak man" and called the president's wife "a fool."

Halstead's career as a political reporter and editor was marked by a gradual turn from reformist idealism to conservative, partisan pragmatism. He emerged from the Civil War as a dynamic newspaper proprietor who invested in the newest printing presses and equipment and made the *Commercial* a leader in innovation west of the Alleghenies. Under his guidance the *Commercial* rivaled the *Chicago Tribune*, the *Chicago Daily News*, and the *St. Louis Post-Dispatch* among newspapers in the Midwest. In 1866 he was a leader in the emergence of the Western Associated Press. Through most of the 1870s Halstead championed independent journalism that was free of party control, but by 1880 he had yielded to partisanship.

Halstead was one of the first Republican editors to break publicly with the Ulysses S. Grant Administration over political corruption and to oppose the president's renomination in 1872. He was a leader in the Liberal Republican movement of 1872 as a member of a group of editors who called themselves the "Quadrilateral." The group opposed the nomination of David Davis at the party's convention in Cincinnati and used their newspapers to engineer his defeat. However, when the nomination went to Horace Greeley, Halstead at first gave his fellow editor only mild support in the *Commercial*. Eventually, the paper began to emphasize Greeley's strong points, but this support lost the newspaper circulation and advertising revenue. It was Halstead's last experiment in independent journalism. By 1876 the *Commercial* was a mainstream Republican newspaper.

Halstead supported Rutherford B. Hayes in 1876 and grew close to the Ohioan after his election. Halstead helped to guide the party's strategy in the dispute over electoral votes. He advised Hayes on the selection of his cabinet and served as a middleman, on at least one occasion, between Hayes and Republican editors. In the election of 1884 Halstead was chosen to edit a Republican campaign newspaper in New York City, the *Extra*. Halstead's support of Benjamin Harrison in 1888 earned him a nomination as minister to Germany. However, the Senate rejected him, apparently in retaliation for articles Halstead had written about the purchase of senatorial seats.

Halstead's political prominence masked the growing financial difficulties of the *Commercial*. By 1880 the newspaper was in a financial decline that had been brought about, at least in part, by poor fiscal management, union walkouts, and the challenge of the sensational and populist *Cincinnati Enquirer*. Negotiations that began in the fall of 1883 led to the merger of the *Commercial* with its Republican rival, the *Gazette*, by January 1884, with Halstead as editor in chief.

Halstead's financial control of the *Commercial Gazette* gradually slipped away until it was gone by 1890, and he left to become editor of the *Brooklyn Standard-Union* in New York. He also contributed articles to the leading magazines of the day and became well known on the lecture circuit as a champion of American imperialism at the time of the Spanish-American War. Halstead wrote nearly twenty books on contemporary history and politics. Most were compiled with scissors and paste pot and sold by subscription. None was memorable, but a biography of President William McKinley that Halstead churned out after the president's assassination sold nearly 700,000 copies. In 1899 he had returned to Cincinnati, where he lived until his death.

• Halstead's papers are held by the Historical and Philosophical Society of Ohio at the University of Cincinnati Library. An authoritative biography is Donald W. Curl, *Murat Halstead and the Cincinnati Commercial* (1980). Halstead's role in the Liberal Republican movement of 1872 is detailed in Earle Dudley Ross, *The Liberal Republican Movement* (1919; repr. 1970), and Joseph Logsdon, *Horace White, Nineteenth Century Liberal* (1971).

JOSEPH P. McKERNS

HALSTED, George Bruce (23 Nov. 1853–16 Mar. 1922), professor of mathematics, was born in Newark, New Jersey, the son of Oliver Spencer Halsted, Jr., a lawyer, and Adela Meeker. He attended Princeton University, as had his father, grandfather, great-grandfather, and other members of the family. After obtaining his bachelor's degree there in 1875, he briefly attended the Columbia School of Mines before becoming a student of James J. Sylvester at Johns Hopkins University, where he received a doctor of philosophy in 1879. Sylvester, one of England's most renowned mathematicians, helped establish mathematics as a field of research in the United States during his tenure at Johns Hopkins.

In 1884 Halsted became the professor of mathematics at the newly established University of Texas in Austin. During the next eighteen years he had a number of students who were to become distinguished mathematicians, including Robert L. Moore and

Leonard E. Dickson. In Austin in 1886 he married Margaret Swearingen, and they raised three children. Student reminiscences picture Halsted as one of the more colorful professors in the university's early history and a popular speaker on and off campus whether talking about his travels to Germany, Mexico, Japan, and Hungary or about religion and science or about geometry. In a classroom of freshmen one of his main purposes was to challenge what he regarded as the ill-founded notions that pervaded the teaching of geometry. He could, for example, always count on a student in such a class giving him the common but not mathematically satisfying definition of a straight line as the shortest distance between two points. His criticism of such a definition could be the starting point for a discussion of the fundamentals of geometry. His teaching method may have been one of the inspirations for the Moore Method of teaching mathematics that his student R. L. Moore later developed with great success. In this method, students learn by conducting their own, independent mathematical research under the general guidance of the teacher, who provides the foundation and sets the ground rules. Students present their work to the rest of the class and the teacher for criticism.

Halsted was outspoken in his opinions not only of students and colleagues, but also of administrators and members of the governing board of regents. This quality was evidently prized in Austin only up to a certain point, for his criticism of the regents as political appointees appears to have been the immediate cause of his dismissal in 1902. Thereafter he taught at a succession of institutions: St. Johns in Annapolis in 1903; Kenyon College in Gambier, Ohio, 1903–1906, where he carried on an unpopular battle against student hazing practices; and finally at Colorado State Teachers College in Greeley, Colorado (now the University of Northern Colorado at Greeley), 1906–1912, where he was dismissed after charging that the college was being mismanaged. This last controversy led to the college administration being investigated by a grand jury and by two committees appointed by the state governor. Halsted spent most of the last years of his life continuing with his mathematical writing while working as an electrician in the family-run electrical supply store that he had established in Greeley.

Halsted published textbooks in elementary geometry in 1885 and 1893, but his principal work in this area was *Rational Geometry* (1904), which was translated into French in 1911 and contains original work in the foundations of double elliptic geometry. His greatest influence in mathematics, however, has probably been in his furtherance of non-Euclidean geometry. His articles in professional and popular scientific journals publicized for the first time in English the new geometries, which, though they had been discovered decades earlier in Germany, Hungary, and Russia, were only beginning to be generally understood and accepted by mathematicians in those countries in the 1870s. In addition to appearing in his many brief journal articles, this new information was presented in his

"Bibliography of Hyper-space and non-Euclidean Geometry" (*American Journal of Mathematics* 1 [1878]: 261–76, 384–5; 2 [1879]: 65–70), and in his translations of J. Bolyai, *The Science Absolute of Space* (1891); N. I. Lobachevsky, *Geometrical Researches on the Theory of Parallels* (1891); and G. Saccheri, *Euclides Vindicatus* (1920). Halsted was one of the early supporters of the *American Mathematical Monthly*, and he contributed over ninety articles to it, including many biographies of mathematicians.

Halsted died in New York City.

• The G. B. Halsted Collection in the Archives of American Mathematics at the University of Texas at Austin, University Archives, includes letters and manuscripts. His letters to Paul Carus, editor of the *Monist*, are in the Special Collections, Morris Library, Southern Illinois University. Two manuscripts of his writings are at the archives of the University of Northern Colorado. He wrote well-received translations of H. Poincaré's *Science and Hypothesis, The Value of Science*, and *Science and Method*, which were published together under the title *The Foundations of Science* (1913). Further details of his career at Texas can be found in Albert C. Lewis, "The Building of the University of Texas Mathematics Faculty, 1883–1938," in *A Century of Mathematics in America: Part III*, ed. Peter Duren (1989), and more on his years in Greeley can be found in Robert W. Larson, *Shaping Educational Change: The First Century of the University of Northern Colorado at Greeley* (1989).

ALBERT C. LEWIS

HALSTED, William Stewart (23 Sept. 1852–7 Sept. 1922), surgeon, was born in New York City, the son of William Mills Halsted, the president of Halsted, Haines and Co., a textile-importing firm, and Mary Louisa Haines. Privately educated as a child, he graduated from Andover in 1869 and after a further year of preparation entered Yale University in 1870. There he had an undistinguished academic career and was known for his sporting prowess; he served as captain of the football team. He attributed his interest in medicine to the purchase of *Gray's Anatomy* and John C. Dalton's *Physiology* textbooks in his senior year at Yale. After his graduation from Yale (A.B., 1874), Halsted began medical studies at the College of Physicians and Surgeons in New York City. There he became the assistant of the professor of physiology, John C. Dalton—the author of the textbook that had led him to a medical career. An outstanding medical student, Halsted won a place for himself as an interne at Bellevue Hospital, where he met William H. Welch, who was to become a founding member of the Johns Hopkins Medical School.

Halsted received an M.D. in 1877 with honors. He then took a position as house physician to the New York Hospital. During the visit of English surgeon Joseph Lister that same year to New York, Halsted became convinced of the utility of antiseptic surgical techniques. In 1878 Halsted went for two years to Europe, where he studied embryology, histology, and surgery, mainly in German-speaking medical centers, spending the largest amount of time in Vienna. On his return to New York in 1880 Halsted took charge of the

Roosevelt Hospital outpatient surgical department. In addition he taught medical students, was an anatomy demonstrator at the College of Physicians and Surgeons, and during these years in New York became associated with five other New York hospitals (the Charity, Emigrant, Bellevue, Presbyterian, and Chambers Street hospitals). It was a period of intense work: he spent his mornings at the Roosevelt, his afternoons and evenings at the other hospitals as he was needed, and he was also teaching.

Interested in transfusions, Halsted intervened in 1881 when his sister almost died from a postpartum hemorrhage. By his own account, according to Samuel James Crowe, "After checking the hemorrhage, I transfused my sister with blood drawn into a syringe from one of my veins and injected immediately into hers" (p. 21). His sister survived. A year later Halsted saved his mother by operating on her to remove gall stones.

Around 1884, Halsted was at the height of his career as a New York surgeon. In September of that year Carl Koller announced at the Ophthalmological Congress in Heidelberg his discovery that injections of cocaine could be used to anesthetize the conjunctiva and cornea of the eye. Hearing of this Halsted (along with some colleagues) began experimenting on the anesthetic properties of cocaine. He used himself as an experimental subject and became addicted first to cocaine and then to morphine. He was apparently unable to shake the morphine addiction for the rest of his life. Through these experiments Halsted found that if cocaine was injected into the trunk of a sensory nerve, all of its branches were numbed to pain. So by using a small amount of cocaine carefully injected, a large area of the body (or jaw) could be anesthetized. Halsted had discovered neuro-regional anesthesia, or nerve-blocking, which was particularly important for the development of oral and dental surgery. This research gained Halsted in 1922, shortly before his death, the gold medal of the American Dental Association. At the time of his experiments, however, his addictions resulted in a noticeable deterioration in Halsted's performance, and by 1886 he was forced to leave New York, his once promising career in ruins.

In early 1886 Halsted appealed to his old friend Welch for assistance. Welch tried to cure him—and it is believed that he was cured of his cocaine addiction—and got Halsted a position in his own laboratory at Johns Hopkins. It was generally believed that Halsted had been entirely cured, although his once outgoing personality had been permanently altered, and he remained a rather withdrawn personage for the rest of his life.

In 1889, the opening year of the Johns Hopkins Hospital, Halsted was appointed acting surgeon to the hospital and head of the dispensary (Outpatient Department) and associate professor of surgery. Halsted had been the second choice of the committee (which included Welch and the famous clinician William Osler) and was appointed for only a year at first because of worries about his performance. Halsted's appoint-

ment became permanent: in 1890 he became surgeon-in-chief to the hospital, and in 1892, professor of surgery. Thus he was the founding professor of surgery at the Johns Hopkins Medical School, which opened in 1893.

During his time at Johns Hopkins, Halsted made the contributions to surgery for which he is famous. He was noted first for the development of an organized system of training surgeons, in replacement of the former apprenticeship method; one of his most famous articles is "The Training of the Surgeon," reprinted in the *Johns Hopkins Hospital Bulletin* ([1904]: 267–75). Second, he was credited with changing the surgical philosophy in America from an aggressive and somewhat unsafe approach to a more conservative one that depended heavily on a knowledge of anatomy and physiology. Halsted became a pioneer of the post-anaesthesia, postantisepsis era. Where previously speed had been the essence of good surgery, Halsted was known for operating slowly and deliberately, controlling blood loss and minimizing the damage to tissues. In so doing, Halsted was an originator of modern surgical practice. Halsted had many prominent students, including John M. T. Finney, Hugh Young, and the pioneering neurosurgeons Harvey Cushing and Walter Dandy.

Halsted also discovered numerous new surgical techniques. He was known for his surgery of the blood vessels, particularly related to aneurysms and was the first to routinely produce successful results when operating on hernia of the groin. He also introduced methods for treating goiters and for operating on the gall bladder and its ducts. He is famous, or perhaps infamous, as the man who developed techniques of radical mastectomy for breast cancer. Although his method was largely superseded in the 1960s in favor of the modified mastectomy, at the time Halsted's procedure, although mutilating, was viewed as an advance that provided hope for otherwise terminal breast cancer patients.

In late 1889 or early 1890 Halsted played a role in the introduction of surgical gloves, an important step in the move away from antiseptic surgery toward aseptic surgery. His head nurse at Johns Hopkins had complained about the dermatitis from which she suffered as a result of the use of antiseptic mercuric bichloride during surgery. Halsted asked the Goodyear Rubber Company to make thin rubber gloves for use by the surgical staff and in June 1890 married the nurse in question, Caroline Hampton; they had no children.

Halsted died in Baltimore, his reputation restored, and his addiction still a secret. One of the first surgeons to grasp the implications of anesthesia and antisepsis (later asepsis) for surgery, he made clean, slow, careful, and controlled techniques his trademark and passed these along to a new generation of surgeons.

• Halsted's surgical papers are collected in *Surgical Papers in Two Volumes* (1924; repr. 1961). Information relevant to Halsted's life can be found in an unpublished book by William

Osler, "The Inner History of the Johns Hopkins Hospital" at the Osler Library, McGill University, Montreal, Quebec, Canada, and in the papers of Harvey Cushing at Yale University. Halsted's original biographer, William George MacCallum, published *William Stewart Halsted: Surgeon* (1930) and "William Stewart Halsted," National Academy of Sciences, *Biographical Memoirs* 17 (1936). Another biography is Samuel James Crowe, *Halsted of Johns Hopkins: The Man and His Men* (1957). Short biographical notices include Irving B. Rosen and Mark Korman, "Halsted: His Success and His Secret," *Annals of the Royal College of Physicians and Surgeons of Canada* 29, no. 6 (1996): 348–51; and Wilder Penfield, "Halsted of Johns Hopkins," *Journal of the American Medical Association* 210 (1969): 2214–18. Penfield was the first to publicly reveal Halsted's long-term addiction to drugs. A particularly engaging account of Halsted's life is Sherwin B. Nuland, *Doctors: The Biography of Medicine* (1989), chap. 13. For an overview of his contributions to surgery, see Owen H. Wangensteen and Sarah D. Wangensteen, *The Rise of Surgery: From Empiric Craft to Scientific Discipline* (1978).

TERRIE M. ROMANO

HALSTON (23 Apr. 1932–26 Mar. 1990), milliner and fashion designer, was born Roy Halston Frowick in Des Moines, Iowa, the son of an accountant and a homemaker (names unknown). (The name Halston came from his maternal grandfather, Halston Holmes.) Halston spent his boyhood in Iowa. His first design was a red hat and veil he created for his mother to wear on Easter Sunday 1945 to the Central Presbyterian Church in Des Moines. After World War II the family moved to Evansville, Indiana, where as a teenager, Halston was known as the best dresser at Bosse High School. Following high school Halston attended Indiana University but left two years later for the Art Institute of Chicago. Halston attended the Art Institute for only two semesters and did not graduate.

After college Halston began his career as a window designer for Carson Pirie Scott, a Chicago department store. He convinced a friend, a hairdresser at Chicago's Ambassador Hotel, to display some of his hats, and the resulting display brought him his first client, Fran Allison of the television show "Kukla, Fran and Ollie." Halston moved to New York in the late 1950s and began to produce hats for Lily Daché. In 1959 he started working for Bergdorf Goodman department store. As a milliner his most famous hat was the beige pillbox worn by Jacqueline Kennedy at the 1961 presidential inauguration. In 1966 Halston opened a boutique in Bergdorf Goodman's and created dresses that were somewhere between made-to-order (couture) and ready-to-wear. Couture designs represent the latest creation of a designer and are made specifically for one person and employ the highest level of workmanship. Ready-to-wear designs are bought directly off the rack. Halston credited his earlier work with hats as having been instrumental to his later success as a dress designer. He said, "You learn to think in three dimensions, so your dresses have a sculptured quality. Also, you think in terms of small details" (quoted in Gaines, p. 99).

Halston left Bergdorf Goodman in 1968 and opened Halston Limited. His first customer was Babe Paley,

the wife of television executive William S. Paley, who ordered an argyle pantsuit. Halston Limited became the place for New York socialites to get made-to-order clothes. Halston's customers included Jacqueline Kennedy Onassis, Baronne Guy de Rothschild, Lauren Bacall, Liza Minnelli, Doris Duke, and Catherine Deneuve. In 1973 Halston sold his company to Norton Simon, Inc., the consumer goods conglomerate, for approximately $12 million. The relationship with Norton Simon would contribute to Halston's ready-to-wear business, which by then had begun to diversify into luggage, rainwear, and furs. The diversification would continue until Halston had four lines of clothing, ranging from couture to ready-to-wear, distributed through J. C. Penney department store. He also designed cosmetics, fragrances, loungewear, handbags, leather goods, gloves, swimsuits, airline uniforms, and uniforms for adult Girl Scouts. The alliance with Norton Simon freed Halston from the strain of running a business and set him up as the creative genius for a variety of products. Halston's merchandise for Norton Simon catered to the very wealthy with his couture collections and to the middle class with ready-to-wear clothes and other products bearing his name. In 1977 these products were valued at more than $100 million.

Norton Simon was bought out by Esmark, owners of Playtex, in 1983. Esmark was bought out shortly thereafter in a hostile takeover by Beatrice Companies. Halston's new business managers were far more interested in profits than in creativity, and the new owners and he were in continual conflict, as management required him to lower the quality of his merchandise in order to suit market demands for inexpensive clothing. In July 1984 Beatrice suggested to Halston that he take a vacation. In his absence, his company was dismantled. That October Halston was asked to stop producing for the company though his contract remained in force. Halston attempted to buy back his business but to no avail. The man who had designed fourteen collections a year was now only doing small projects, among them a line of dance costumes for choreographer Martha Graham. In January 1990 he sold his New York townhouse and moved to California to be near his two brothers and one sister. Halston died of AIDS at Pacific Presbyterian Hospital in San Francisco at the age of fifty-seven.

Halston's designs were marked by a number of innovations. In his 1972 fall collection he launched polyurethane into couture with his ultra-suede shirt dress. In the late 1960s, when paisley prints and fringe were everywhere, Halston revived jersey, cashmere, and silks, creating clothes in traditional styles that women could wear both to the office and out for the evening. His critics panned his style as being too plain, referred to him as a stylist but not a couturier. In the fashion industry, the Coty Award, begun by Coty cosmetics in 1942, is comparable to the Academy Award in Hollywood. Although Halston won four Coty Awards (1962, 1969, 1971, and 1972), his primary achievement was bridging the gap between couture and ready-to-wear. In the late 1960s and early 1970s a significant percentage of American Women entered the workforce. They needed clothes that were practical rather than the trendy and unrealistic outfits then being created by other designers. Clothes for a new class of professional women were needed, and Halston's styles were a perfect fit.

• A biography of Halston is Steven S. Gaines, *Simply Halston: The Untold Story* (1991). For more information on Halston and his designs see "Throwaway Chic for Fall," *Newsweek*, 21 Aug. 1972, pp. 48–56; "From Rags to Riches," *Newsweek*, 15 Oct. 1973, p. 86; "Couturier's Coup," *Time*, 22 Oct. 1973, p. 82; Jerry Bowles, "Will Halston Take Over the World?" *Esquire*, Aug. 1975, pp. 69–73; Nicholas Lemann, "The Halstonization of America," *Washington Monthly*, July 1978, pp. 8–15; Edith Loew Gross, "Halston: Style . . . and Something More," *Vogue*, June 1980, pp. 154–60; "Roy Frowick Fights for Freedom from the Company That Bought His Middle Name: Halston," *People Weekly*, 6 Jan. 1986, pp. 82–83; and Nina Darnton, "The Inimitable Halston," *Newsweek*, 7 Aug. 1989, pp. 64–66. An obituary is in the *New York Times*, 28 Mar. 1990. A reminiscence by Liza Minnelli and Polly Mellen is in *Vogue*, July 1990, pp. 62–68.
CAROLYN HAMBY

HAMBIDGE, Jay (13 Jan. 1867–20 Jan. 1924), artist and theorist, was born Edward John Hambidge in Simcoe, Ontario, Canada, the son of George Fowler Hambidge, occupation unknown, and Christina Shields. At the age of fifteen he ran away to the United States. He took a job as a surveyor's assistant in Council Bluffs, Iowa, and lived there for several years. He left for Kansas City in 1885, taking a job as a printer's apprentice at the *Kansas City Star*. He subsequently became a reporter, and after refining his journalistic skills he joined the staff of the *New York Herald* in 1895.

Not long after arriving in New York, Hambidge enrolled in night classes at the Art Students League, where he studied under William Merritt Chase. There he met the illustrator Walter Appleton Clark, who seems to have gotten Hambidge interested in professional illustration. Pursuing this occupation, the young illustrator accepted assignments from *McClure's* and *Century* magazine. In 1900 the editor of the *Century*, Richard Watson Gilder, sent Hambidge to Girgenti, Greece, to draw classical ruins and artifacts. On his return to the United States, Hambidge presented a paper based on his studies, "The Natural Basis of Form in Greek Art," wherein he proposed that the Greeks had used a mathematical constant in the measurements and ratios of their designs. He contended that this mathematical constant existed within the symmetrical forms and patterns of nature, such as the structure of the human skeleton or the spiraling seed distribution of the sunflower.

Hambidge received professional encouragement from Sir Francis Cranmer Penrose, the head of the Department of Greek Antiquities at the British Museum and one of the leading scholars on the Parthenon. For the next ten years, Hambidge lived mostly abroad, sketching Greek architecture and accepting illustra-

tion assignments in his spare time. With the conclusion of his research, Hambidge received an opportunity to present his theories to the Society for the Promotion of Hellenic Studies in London, although the outbreak of World War I prevented him from staying in Great Britain.

On returning to the United States, Hambidge initially found few opportunities in which to advance his theory of Greek design, which he now called dynamic symmetry. In 1916, however, he began a series of lectures at the residence of his friend George Whittle, the former assistant art director at the *Century*. The lectures gradually attracted well-known artists such as Robert Henri, George Bellows, and Leon Kroll, who were interested in the practical applications of dynamic symmetry. Hambidge continued to promote his theory and in 1917 published *Dynamic Symmetry*, which restated his earlier findings and provided the mathematical basis of his theory.

According to the tenets set forth in his publications, Hambidge's theory of dynamic symmetry rests primarily on the geometric manipulation of rectangles and the illusionistic tension of diagonal lines. According to Hambidge, the Egyptians developed the system and then passed it to the Greeks, who seemingly abandoned the system in the fourth century in favor of another measurement system. He proposed that the fifth-century Greeks had used a measurement system based on the diagonals and square roots of rectangles rather than the standard measurements of length used thereafter. Fixed units such as the foot and meter or the square and triangle create static symmetry in that these units may be divided into regular areas.

In contrast, Hambidge found the perfect sense of proportion and balance to be in the root five rectangle, which may be diagrammed as any rectangle in which a square constructed on the longer side occupies five times the area of a square constructed on the shorter side or a value of 1,618. Dynamic symmetry deals first and foremost with area and with a property Hambidge called the "rectangle of whirling squares," in which the artist constructs a logarithmic spiral of increasingly smaller squares within the rectangular frame of design. Although the areas constructed through dynamic symmetry provide a basis for composition, Hambidge insisted that dynamic symmetry was a tool for the artist rather than a steadfast rule and was not meant to hamper creative intuition.

Having published the basics of his theory, Hambidge then published a periodical called *The Diagonal* in 1919, which consisted of twelve issues. By this time Hambidge had found support among a number of leading American scholars and institutions, including Gisela M. A. Richter of the Metropolitan Museum of Art, L. D. Caskey of the Museum of Fine Arts, Boston, Denman W. Ross of Harvard University, and William Sergeant Kendall of Yale University. Through Kendall's influence, Hambidge received an honorarium from the Trowbridge fund (which was established at Yale for archaeological research), allowing him to return to Greece to make further measurements of the Parthenon and other monuments of Greek architecture. During his stay in Greece, his monograph *Dynamic Symmetry: The Greek Vase* was released in 1920.

While there was much scholarly support for dynamic symmetry, there was also opposition. Both Rhys Carpenter and Edwin M. Blake wrote criticisms of Hambidge's theory in 1921, stating that dynamic symmetry not only was arbitrary in application but also lacked any historical justification to prove its existence. Caskey attempted to publish a rebuttal to Carpenter in the *American Journal of Archaeology*, which had published the latter's criticism, but was turned down. Caskey subsequently published his own *Geometry of Greek Vases* in 1922.

During this time, Hambidge returned to the United States to publish a series of books based on his research in Greece: *Dynamic Symmetry in Composition, as Used by the Artists* (1923) and *The Parthenon and Other Greek Temples: Their Dynamic Symmetry* (1924). A lengthy lecture tour coupled with the trips to and from Europe eventually affected his health. During one of his lectures, Hambidge suffered a stroke. He died several hours later at Roosevelt Hospital in New York City.

Hambidge had married Cordelia Selina de Lorme in January 1889; they had no children, and their marriage ended in divorce. In 1917 he had married Mary C. (maiden name unknown); they had no children. After Hambidge's death, Mary published a collection of his lectures and notes under the title *Practical Applications of Dynamic Symmetry* (1932). She later established the Jay Hambidge Art Foundation, eventually renamed the Hambidge Center for Arts and Sciences, in Rabun Gap, Georgia, which provided seminars for artists and designers that actively used dynamic symmetry. The center still exists.

Even though critics in the decades following Hambidge's death generally dismissed his theory of Greek design and his books went out of print, artists continued to use dynamic symmetry as a technique of design. Many artists in the 1910s and 1920s in particular found dynamic symmetry to be a rational alternative to the seemingly eclectic nature of modernism. Since modernism, which generally depended on the emotions and thoughts of the artist rather than a formula or fixed technique, was often regarded as highly subjective and chaotic, artists like Bellows gravitated toward dynamic symmetry and its rules for composition. At the same time, the mathematical and scientific basis for dynamic symmetry gave it a modern feel.

• Aside from Hambidge's own works on dynamic symmetry, there are several publications on the theory, including Harold J. McWhinnie, "A Review of the Use of Symmetry, the Golden Section, and Dynamic Symmetry in Contemporary Art," *Leonardo* 19 (1986): 241–45; L. Lutz, "Dynamic Symmetry as an Archetype: A Reunification of Mathematics and Art" (Ph.D. diss., Univ. of Illinois, 1973); and E. Walter, "Jay Hambidge and the Development of the Theory of Dynamic Symmetry" (Ph.D. diss., Univ. of Georgia, 1976).

The Rhode Island School of Design held a retrospective exhibition of dynamic symmetry in 1961 entitled *Dynamic Symmetry*. An obituary is in the *New York Times*, 21 Jan. 1924.

MARK ANDREW WHITE

HAMBLETON, Thomas Edward (17 May 1829–21 Sept. 1906), blockade runner and financier, was born in New Windsor, Maryland, the son of Thomas Edward Hambleton, a dry-goods merchant and entrepreneur, and Sarah Slingluff. His parents moved in 1831 to Baltimore, where Hambleton received his early education before enrolling in St. Mary's College, from which he graduated in 1849. He then entered into a partnership in Baltimore that manufactured agricultural implements. In 1852 he married Arabella Stansbury, with whom he had three children.

In 1855 Hambleton entered his father's dry-goods business as a junior partner; in the next year he assumed greater responsibilities after his father retired. The business, then known as Hambleton Brothers & Company, underwent steady growth in Baltimore before the Civil War. With the coming of war, Hambleton, who had a great deal of his business based in the South and who was thoroughly southern in his sympathies (like many Baltimoreans), removed to Richmond, Virginia. While based in the capital of the Confederacy, Hambleton served briefly as a private in the First Maryland Cavalry but soon embarked on an even more adventurous path. He became affiliated with the Richmond Importing & Exporting Company, a firm that was heavily involved in the dangerous but potentially lucrative business of running the Federal blockade that surrounded the Confederacy on the high seas. This hazardous trade usually involved running cotton to Bermuda from the port cities of Wilmington, North Carolina, and Charleston, South Carolina, and returning with badly needed supplies and weaponry for the Confederacy.

Hambleton traveled to England, where he purchased a ship (the *Coquette*); he later built another ship, the steamer *Dare*. The hazards of his new profession were never more clearly evident than on 8 January 1862 when, hotly pursued by five Union ships, Hambleton was forced to beach and then destroy one of his ships on the South Carolina coast near Georgetown. He gained in the process a measure of revenge not only by evading capture but also by capturing the boarding party sent out to apprehend him. Before his first voyages Hambleton engaged in the even riskier business of carrying secret messages from President Jefferson Davis across the Potomac, an activity that would have been punishable by death had he been captured.

After the end of the war Hambleton returned to Baltimore and entered the realty business before joining his brother John in 1868 in the stock brokerage business. John A. Hambleton & Company, which also served as a private bank, expanded rapidly in the booming postwar economy. The firm handled security transactions for the People's Gas Company and the Consumer Gas Company (both of which were later amalgamated into the Consolidated Gas Company), the Norfolk Water Company, the Indianapolis Water Company, the West Virginia and Central and Pittsburgh Railway Company, and the Piedmont and Cumberland Railroad Company. Hambleton also served on the reorganization committee of the Cincinnati, Washington & Baltimore Railroad.

Interested in the potential profit of mass transit systems, Hambleton formed the People's Passenger Railway in 1878. The early transit lines were horse-drawn, run inefficiently, and likely to operate in the red. A new innovation, streetcars that were propelled by steam-driven underground cables, made its appearance about this time, and it was in this area that Hambleton made his greatest contribution. In search of additional capital he journeyed to Philadelphia, where he successfully interested men such as Peter A. B. Widener, W. L. Elkins, and Thomas Dolan in his plans.

Returning to Baltimore, Hambleton bought the North Baltimore Railway Company and then organized the Baltimore Traction Company. The so-called traction line began operations in July 1892, with Hambleton serving as president. He soon brought the competing lines of the Citizens', Pimlico & Pikesville, Powhatan, and Curtis Bay & Baltimore under the control of Baltimore Traction. The propulsion system proved impractical, however, and after the acquisition of the City & Suburban Railway Company the line was converted to electric power. Although Hambleton had retired by the time of the ultimate consolidation in 1899, which resulted (from the joining of Baltimore Traction with the City Passenger, Baltimore & Northern, and Central systems) to form the United Railways Electric Company, he maintained an interest in railroads, serving as president of the Albany & Northern Railroad.

Following the death of his first wife in 1893, Hambleton married the widow Theodosia L. Talcott in 1899. He retired from his firm, Hambleton & Company, on 31 January 1905 and died at his home, "Hambledune," near Lutherville, Maryland.

Hambleton was one of many enterprising men who survived the cataclysm of the Civil War and achieved notable success in the growing economic conditions that followed the war. While changes in both technology and society completely ended the run of the Baltimore streetcars in 1963, his efforts on behalf of mass transit development stand as an example of the possibilities open to capitalists during his career.

• No collection of Hambleton's papers is known to exist. Information on his life and career can be gleaned from several sources, including J. Thomas Scharf, *Baltimore: Its History and Its People*, vol. 2 (1912), pp. 158–61; Sherry H. Olson, *Baltimore: The Building of an American City* (1980); and Herbert H. Harwood, Jr., *Baltimore and Its Streetcars* (1984). An extensive obituary is in the *Baltimore Sun*, 22 Sept. 1906.

EDWARD L. LACH, JR.

HAMBLIN, Thomas Sowerby (14 May 1800–8 Jan. 1853), actor and theater manager, was born in London, England. After a schoolboy performance of the role of Hamlet enticed him away from a business career, Hamblin's first professional theatrical engagement was at the Adelphi Theatre in London as a ballet dancer before 1815. Between 1815 and 1823 Hamblin gained prominence playing a variety of roles at numerous theaters, including Sadler's Wells and Drury Lane, as well as theaters in Bath, Brighton, Dublin, and Sheffield. During this period he married Elizabeth Blanchard, a well-known actress and the daughter of eminent London actor and playwright E. L. Blanchard.

Hamblin and his wife immigrated to the United States in 1825. His first engagement was at the Park Theatre in New York during the first week of November, and he played Hamlet, the Stranger, William Tell, Virginius, Rolla, Petruchio, Pierre, Macbeth, and Othello. His performances received an unusually warm response, and the *Albion* declared him "a very excellent actor." Hamblin followed with a second engagement in Albany later in the month, playing the same repertoire opposite the young Edwin Forrest's Jaffeir, Macduff, and Iago.

A large part of Hamblin's appeal was his physical appearance. T. Allston Brown, in his *History of the New York Stage*, wrote, "He was tall and commanding, but so admirably proportioned as . . . to conceal his almost towering height. Deep set eyes black as jet were surmounted by a lofty brow, crowned by clusters of curling dark hair in . . . rich profusion" (vol. 1, p. 129). These qualities, however, were "more than balanced by the husky, disagreeable tones of his voice, which always gave the appearance of hard labour to everything he undertook" (Wemyss, p. 106).

After five years of touring, Hamblin began his career as an actor-manager in August 1830, when he and James H. Hackett took over operations of the Bowery Theatre in New York. Hamblin assumed full control a month later, and the years 1830 to 1836 were the most profitable and prolific period of Hamblin's lifelong tenure at the Bowery. Hamblin understood the importance of pleasing his audience, and although critics denigrated him for not using his talents to elevate the drama and the tastes of his audience they could not deny that Hamblin's efforts brought both him and his theater notable success. The Bowery under Hamblin could be counted on to deliver new and ever more spectacular melodramas as well as novelty programs. He innovated longer runs of up to a month and continued the innovations of a previous Bowery manager, Charles A. Gilfert, in his effective use of publicity and advertising.

His most important contribution, however, was best relayed by the words of his contemporary, Francis Wemyss: "The American stage is more indebted to Mr. Hamblin for discovering and fostering native dramatic talent, than to all his contemporaries" (p. 107). Among the playwrights "fostered" at the Bowery were Charles W. Taylor, James B. Phillips, and Louisa Medina. The role of Arbraces in the latter's *The Last Days of Pompeii* became one of Hamblin's most popular vehicles later in his life. The emphasis on lively spectacle and melodramas earned the Bowery the nickname "The Slaughterhouse." Indeed, Hamblin's particular and successful mix of repertoire was immortalized by contemporary terms like "Bowery actors" and "Bowery melodrama."

Hamblin's success in this period, as throughout his life, can be attributed to his business acumen. While all sources report him as strictly honorable in his dealings, an anecdote by Joe Cowell sheds light on his hardball attitude, which was undoubtedly part of the reason for his success. Cowell, who had known Hamblin in England and who esteemed him "as a brother," was engaged at the Bowery in 1830 when Hamblin took control. The new manager believed that "friendship [had] nothing to do with business" and Cowell, who "was unreasonable enough to believe that it should," found it necessary to terminate their theatrical connections after only three nights (Cowell, p. 96).

Hamblin's rise was marked by his ability to begin purchasing shares in the Bowery from its original builders, the New York Association, in the spring of 1834; within eighteen months he owned a controlling majority of shares. Bad luck and personal difficulties were, however, also close at his heels. After his wife returned from a European tour in 1831, she began divorce proceedings, which concluded in 1834. One of the stipulations of the verdict was that Hamblin could not remarry while his first wife lived. This, of course, did not prevent Hamblin from his infamous philandering; however, his relationship with the young and promising actress, Naomi Vincent, known euphemistically as "Mrs. Hamblin," soon ended tragically in July 1835 when she died in childbirth. Hamblin then began a long relationship with one of his star playwrights, Louisa Medina.

In September 1836 Hamblin showed once again his desire to promote interesting new talent when he introduced the young Charlotte Cushman to the New York stage for the first time. He had enough confidence in what he saw to engage her in a three-year contract; however, only a week after her debut, the Bowery Theatre burned to the ground, putting an end to the first phase of Hamblin's management career.

Despite the heavy financial loss, Hamblin completed his purchase of the theater property. Over the next three years, the site was rented to W. E. Dinneford and Thomas Flynn, who raised a new theater while Hamblin acted as adviser and spent his time touring and liquidating his debts. In February 1838 the Dinneford-Flynn Bowery Theatre burned, and Hamblin returned to build yet another new and more splendid structure that opened, under Hamblin's management this time, in May 1839.

The 1840s were more difficult than Hamblin's first decade in America. There was more diverse and intense competition in New York, and it was becoming harder to build a profitable audience. Hamblin's reaction was to add even more "blood and thunder" spectacles to his repertoire, including new pieces by J. S. Jones and C. H. Saunders, but this proved insufficient, and Hamblin found the need to bill more circus shows, exotic acts, and other variety entertainments.

In April 1845 the Bowery burned for the third time, and Hamblin's acute business sense led him to see the potential of building a theater on Broadway; however, his attempts to be the first to establish such a theater on this thoroughfare failed because of resistance from the community. He was forced to rebuild on the Bowery site for the third time in his career and to turn over the management to A. W. Jackson. During this period Hamblin appeared less and less frequently on playbills and suffered increasing physical and financial difficulties.

His style of acting was falling out of favor, as described by the *Albion* critic on 9 September 1848: "The dignity, the finished and elaborated elocution, and the high artistical execution of that school [formed on the model of the Kembles and the Siddons] were occasionally brought most vividly to our remembrance in Mr HAMBLIN's delineation of Hamlet, weakened however at times . . . by a dash of the melo-dramatic style and the laboured pompousness he has acquired by long practice of his art at the Bowery."

In the summer of 1848 Hamblin began his last period at the Bowery, also taking control of the Park Theatre following the collapse of Edmund Simpson's long reign. After major renovations, he reopened the Park to mixed reviews in September; while the critic of the *Albion* liked the new theater, he doubted its potential for success with the competition of Forrest on Broadway. In December 1848 Hamblin's fiery nemesis struck yet again when the new Park Theatre burned to the ground. Hamblin continued to struggle at the Bowery until the end of his life. In 1849, shortly after the death of his ex-wife, Hamblin married the respected English actress Elizabeth Mary Ann Trewar Shaw. They had four children.

Hamblin died of brain fever (either cerebral syphilis or cerebral meningitis) at his home on Broome Street in New York City. Even after his death, Hamblin's influence could be felt on the New York stage as his second wife and his two children from his first marriage, William and Elizabeth, continued to act regularly. The Bowery Theatre also remained in control of the Hamblin family until 1867.

• Hamblin's personal papers and journals from his Bowery years are held in the Harvard Theatre Collection; the Folger Library, Washington, D.C.; and in the New York Public Library Theatre Collection. Weldon B. Durham, ed., *American Theatre Companies, 1749–1887* (1986), contains a very detailed account of the Bowery Theatre as well as a lengthy bibliography. Francis Wemyss, *Twenty-six Years of the Life of an Actor and Manager* (1847), and Joe Cowell, *Thirty Years Passed among the Players of England and America* (1844), provide personal contemporary insights. Joseph Ireland, *Records of the New York Stage from 1750 to 1860* (1866–1867); George Odell's multivolume *Annals of the New York Stage* (1927–1949); and T. Allston Brown, *A History of the New York Stage from the First Performance in 1732 to 1901* (1903), all provide surveys of productions and personnel covering the years of

Hamblin's career. See also Lillian Hall, comp., *Catalogue of Dramatic Portraits in the Theatre Collection of the Harvard College Library* (1930), pp. 181–82; and Jürgen Wolter, ed., *The Dawning of American Drama* (1993). An obituary is in the *New York Tribune*, 10 Jan. 1853.

GLEN NICHOLS

HAMER, Fannie Lou Townsend (6 Oct. 1917–14 Mar. 1977), civil rights activist, was born in Montgomery County, Mississippi, the twentieth child of Jim Townsend and Lou Ella (maiden name unknown), sharecroppers. When Fannie Lou was two the family moved to Sunflower County, where they lived in abject poverty. Even when they were able to rent land and buy stock, a jealous white neighbor poisoned the animals, forcing the family back into sharecropping. Fannie Lou began picking cotton when she was six; she eventually was able to pick 300 to 400 pounds a day, earning a penny a pound. Because of poverty she was forced to leave school at age twelve, barely able to read and write. She married Perry ("Pap") Hamer in 1944. The couple adopted two daughters. For the next eighteen years Fannie Lou Hamer worked first as a sharecropper and then as a timekeeper on the plantation of B. D. Marlowe.

Hamer appeared destined for a routine life of poverty, but two events in the early 1960s led her to become a political activist. When she was hospitalized for the removal of a uterine tumor in 1961, the surgeons performed a hysterectomy without her consent. In August 1962, still angry and bitter over the surgery, she went to a meeting in her hometown of Ruleville to hear James Forman of the Student Nonviolent Coordinating Committee (SNCC) and James Bevel of the Southern Christian Leadership Conference (SCLC). After hearing their speeches on the importance of voting, she and seventeen others went to the courthouse in Indianola to try to register. They were told they could only enter the courthouse two at a time to be given the literacy test, which they all failed. On the trip back to Ruleville the group was stopped by the police and fined $100 for driving a bus that was the wrong color. Hamer subsequently became the group's leader. Marlowe called on her that evening and told her she had to withdraw her name. Hamer refused and was ordered to leave the plantation. Pap had to stay until work on the plantation was finished. For a time, she stayed with various friends and relatives, and segregationist night riders shot into some of the homes where she was staying. Nevertheless, she remained active in the civil rights movement, serving as a field secretary for SNCC, working for voter registration, advocating welfare programs, and teaching citizenship classes.

Hamer gained national attention when she appeared before the credentials committee of the 1964 Democratic National Convention in Atlantic City, New Jersey, on behalf of the Mississippi Freedom Democratic Party (MFDP), an organization attempting to unseat the regular, all-white delegation. Speaking as a delegate and cochairman of the MFDP, she described atrocities inflicted on blacks seeking the right to vote and other civil rights, including the abuse she had suffered at the Montgomery County Jail, where white Mississippi law enforcement officers forced black inmates to beat her so badly that she had no feeling in her arms. (Hamer and several others had been arrested for attempting to integrate the "white only" section of the bus station in Winona, Mississippi, during the return trip from a voter registration training session in Southern Carolina.) After giving her dramatic testimony, she wept before the committee. Although her emotional appeal generated sympathy for the plight of blacks in Mississippi among the millions watching on television, the committee rejected the MFDP's challenge.

That same year Hamer traveled to Ghana, Guinea, Nigeria, and several other African nations at the request and expense of those governments. Still, her primary interest was in helping the people of the Mississippi Delta. She lectured across the country, raising money and organizing. In 1965 she ran as an MFDP candidate for Congress, saying she was "sick and tired of being sick and tired." While many civil rights leaders abandoned grassroots efforts, she remained committed to organizing what she called "everyday" people in her community, frequently saying she preferred to face problems at home rather than run from them. In 1969 she launched the Freedom Farm Cooperative to provide homes and food for deprived families, white as well as black, in Sunflower County. The cooperative eventually acquired 680 acres. Still, she remained active at the national level. In 1971 she was elected to the steering committee of the National Women's political caucus, and the following year she supported the nomination of Sissy Farenthold as vice president in an address to the Democratic National Convention.

After a long battle with breast cancer, Hamer died at the all-black Mound Bayou Hospital, thirty miles from Ruleville. Civil rights leaders Andrew Young, Julian Bond, and Eleanor Holmes Norton attended her funeral.

• Hamer's papers are in the Amistad Research Center at Tulane University, the Mississippi Department of Archives and History, and the Wisconsin State Historical Society. Other papers and speeches are in the Moses Moon Collection at the National Museum of American History of the Smithsonian Institution and the Civil Rights Documentation Project at the Moorland-Spingarn Research Center at Howard University. A full-length biography is Kay Mills, *This Little Light of Mine: The Life of Fannie Lou Hamer* (1993). Hamer is the subject of a chapter in George Sewell, *Mississippi Black History Makers* (1977); three articles in Vicki L. Crawford, ed., *Women in the Civil Rights Movement* (1990); and a short sketch in Juan Williams, *Eyes on the Prize: America's Civil Rights Years, 1954–1965* (1987). See also Jerry DeMuth, "Tired of Being Sick and Tired," *Nation*, 1 June 1964, pp. 548–51; J. H. O'Dell "Life in Mississippi: An Interview with Fannie Lou Hamer," *Freedomways*, Spring 1965, pp. 231–42; Susan Johnson, "Fannie Lou Hamer: Mississippi Grassroots Organizer," *Black Law Journal* 2 (Summer 1972): 155–

62; and Art Peters, "Marked for Murder," *Sepia*, Apr. 1965, pp. 29–33. An obituary and a follow-up article are in the *Washington Post*, 17 Mar. 1977 and 19 Mar. 1977.

MAMIE E. LOCKE

HAMER, Thomas Lyon (July 1800–2 Dec. 1846), lawyer and congressman, was born in Northumberland County, Pennsylvania, the son of a farmer of moderate means. Almost nothing is known of his parents. The family moved to upper New York near Lake Champlain in 1812 and then to a farm in southwestern Ohio in 1817. Determined to stand on his own feet, Hamer took up schoolteaching in Clermont County. "Friendless, without means, and with only a common education," the seventeen-year-old Hamer borrowed law books from local professional men, and for some time he lived at Bethel with the family of Thomas Morris, who supervised his legal studies (Morris, pp. 398–99). In the spring of 1821 he was admitted to the bar and in August opened practice at Georgetown, the new seat of justice of neighboring Brown County, where he resided for the rest of his life. He soon married Lydia Bruce Higgins, the daughter of Colonel Robert Higgins, a prominent local citizen. They had seven children.

Hamer rapidly won a local reputation as a jury lawyer and an eloquent public speaker. For two years, commencing in January 1824, he edited the county's first newspaper, the *Benefactor and Georgetown Advocate*, supporting Andrew Jackson's bid for the presidency. In 1825 he was elected state representative and was rewarded for strenuous party efforts by nomination in 1828 as a presidential elector on the successful Jackson ticket. In 1828 and 1829 he was again elected to the general assembly, despite opposition charges that he thought "more than one half of the people were damned fools anyhow" (Brickman, p. 13). Unanimously chosen Speaker of the Ohio House in December 1829, he gave his own party command of only eight out of fifteen standing committees and voted against caucus nominees he thought unqualified. Stirring public controversy in Columbus by this opposition to "whole-hog" partyism, he chose not to run for reelection in 1830 (*Ohio State Bulletin*, Jan.–Feb. 1830).

Disapproving of President Jackson's vetoes, Hamer ran for Congress in 1832 as an independent Jacksonian, defeating the regular nominee, his former mentor Thomas Morris, by a narrow plurality. Unhappy with the party's antibank tendencies, he flirted with the movement to create a third force under John McLean in 1833–1834 but quickly recognized that his constituents were committed to the Democratic party. In 1834 and 1836 he secured reelection as a loyal party man, stumping the region in 1836 for Martin Van Buren. According to Charles Hammond, Hamer possessed a "clear, strong, vigorous, discriminating mind," but "for the sake of gratifying personal ambition, lends himself to base party purposes, whenever, by so doing, he can secure consideration for himself, with his party" (*Cincinnati Gazette*, 16 Nov. 1836).

Hamer's speeches in Congress showed a powerful, precise mind and a commitment to positive government unusual in a Jacksonian Democrat. By 1838 Daniel Webster thought him "the man of most talent of the [Democratic] party" (C. M. Wiltse, ed., *Papers of Daniel Webster: Correspondence*, vol. 4 [1974–1985], p. 295). In 1835 Hamer spiritedly advocated Ohio's claims in the dispute over the boundary with Michigan. In 1836, as a member of the select committee on petitions concerning slavery, he supported the gag rule and spoke eloquently in favor of Arkansas's admission as a slave state. Convinced—in contrast to Morris—of the need to conciliate slaveholders, he refused in 1838 to defend a local clergyman, John B. Mahan, who stood accused of assisting runaway slaves; instead, Hamer acted for the prosecution in the Kentucky courts. Advocating aid for banks that resumed specie payments after the panic of 1837, Hamer became the state's leading conservative Democrat and was seriously considered in 1838 for nomination as governor and for the U.S. Senate.

After declining reelection, partly through disillusionment with the national administration, Hamer retired from Congress in 1839 and concentrated on building up his professional reputation and a lucrative law practice. His political activity did not, however, cease. In 1840 he served as president of the state convention and, during the campaign, toured with the Democrats' gubernatorial candidate, Wilson Shannon, in order to buttress him against the superior eloquence of the Whig candidate, Thomas Corwin. In the banking crisis of the early 1840s, the pragmatic Hamer publicly insisted that Ohio's banks must be rechartered; he claimed that his "hard-money" opponents had "raked up . . . the crude generalities" of John Taylor of Caroline "from the rubbish of a past generation and made them the standard for the Ohio Democracy" (*Columbus Daily Ohio State Journal*, 2 June 1842). Facing down radical demands that he be read out of the party, Hamer opposed the renomination of Van Buren in 1844 and toured the state campaigning for James K. Polk. As reward, President Polk offered him the office of commissioner of Indian Affairs in October 1845, which he declined, and his name was again pressed for the governorship. That same year, following the death of his first wife in January, Hamer married Catharine Johnston, the daughter of Dr. William Johnston of Mason County, Kentucky.

In 1846 Hamer enthusiastically stumped for the Mexican War and volunteered for service as a private. As "the most conspicuous man in Ohio," he was elected major of the First Regiment of Ohio Volunteers in June and within a week was promoted by the president to brigadier general in the army. In September he distinguished himself in the attack on Monterrey, taking command when General William O. Butler was wounded. In October, while absent in Mexico, the new military hero was elected to Congress without opposition. In December he suddenly died of a fever outside Monterrey at the age of forty-six.

Zachary Taylor declared that Hamer's "loss to the army, at this time, cannot be supplied," while fulsome eulogies were pronounced in Congress and at Columbus as well as in Georgetown, where he was buried with Masonic honors at the state's expense. His former neighbor Ulysses S. Grant later claimed that Hamer, had he lived, would have been elected president in 1852 (Spalding, p. 10; Grant, p. 103). Unprepossessing in appearance, with an unwieldy mop of red hair, Hamer was infectiously vivacious, cheerful, generous, and hospitable. He had many friends, including opponents like Corwin; as a congressman, he unhesitatingly nominated Grant to a cadetship at West Point, despite his political enmity with Grant's father. He remained as interested in law as in politics, advocating reform of the cumbersome Ohio court system in 1841 and encouraging Timothy Walker to start the *Western Law Journal* in Cincinnati in 1843. Reflective and philosophical, he read widely on religion, corresponded with Alexander Campbell, and in 1837 underwent conversion in a Methodist revival.

• For a politician highly regarded in his own time, the materials on Hamer are surprisingly scanty. No collection of papers survives, but material may be found scattered in the collections of his contemporaries, including Herbert Weaver et al., eds., *The Papers of James K. Polk* (1969–). His *Review of the Opinion of the Attorney-General* on the Michigan boundary question may be found in the *Columbus Western Hemisphere*, 20 May and 3 June 1835; his congressional speeches were reprinted as pamphlets, and copious extracts from his speech on the admission of Arkansas are reprinted in Thomas Hart Benton, *Thirty Years' View*, vol. 1 (1854), pp. 634–35. The most intimate biographical treatment is *The History of Brown County, Ohio* (1883), pp. 343–52, with a portrait on p. 115. Hamer also comes to life in Lloyd Lewis, *Captain Sam Grant* (1950). The fullest treatment of his political career is Franz J. Brickman, "The Public Life of Thomas L. Hamer" (M.A. thesis, Ohio State Univ., 1940), though greater insight is provided by James Roger Sharp, *The Jacksonians versus the Banks* (1970), pp. 127–37. The local memory informs Benjamin F. Morris, *The Life of Thomas Morris* (1856), pp. 398–99; Ulysses S. Grant, *Personal Memoirs of U. S. Grant*, vol. 1 (1885), pp. 33–34, 103; and Byron Williams, *History of Brown and Clermont Counties, Ohio* (1913), pp. 416–17. The most informative obituary is Rufus P. Spalding, *Eulogy upon Gen. Thomas Hamer Pronounced before the General Assembly of Ohio, at Columbus, Jan. 18, 1847* (1847).

DONALD J. RATCLIFFE

HAMID, Sufi Abdul (6 Jan. 1903–30 July 1938), religious and labor leader, was born, according to his own statement, in Lowell, Massachusetts. According to Harlem historian Roi Ottley, however, he was born in Philadelphia, Pennsylvania. At various times Hamid also claimed to have been born in different places in the South. Little is known about Hamid's early life, including his parents' identities. According to Ottley, his original name was Eugene Brown. In an interview with writers from the Works Progress Administration, Hamid claimed to have been taken to Egypt at the age of nine, then to Athens, Greece, where he received his schooling through the university level. According to

the interview, he returned to the United States in 1923 and began to work for the William J. Burns Detective Agency in St. Louis, Missouri, and Memphis, Tennessee. Hamid soon left that job and moved to Chicago, where he joined the Ahamidab movement, an Islamic organization based in India. During this time he changed his name to Bishop Conshankin. In 1928 he left that organization and formed the Illinois Civic Association, which led several boycotts of white-owned businesses in black areas of Chicago that refused to hire African Americans. Sponsored by the Chicago *Whip*, a black newspaper, and J. C. Austin, a minister of a black Baptist church, the association successfully waged boycotts with the slogan DON'T BUY WHERE YOU CAN'T WORK. The group claimed credit for the hiring of eighteen hundred African Americans in Chicago from 1928 to 1930.

In 1930 Hamid moved to New York City, changed his name to Sufi Abdul Hamid, and began to call for boycotts of white-owned businesses in Harlem that did not employ African Americans. He founded the International Islamic Industrial Alliance, a boycott organization that later changed its name to the Negro Industrial and Clerical Alliance. Through 1932, however, most of Hamid's political work took place atop stepladders on the streets of Harlem, where he became famous for his orations demanding jobs for African Americans in the stores along the neighborhood's main commercial thoroughfares. Dressed in a turban, cape, and riding boots, Hamid was one of Harlem's most-colorful characters. Although his soapbox oratory was laced with references to the Qu'rān and various Asian religions, his message was economic organization, and it gained him a significant following in a section of New York that suffered from an unemployment rate that was higher than 50 percent throughout the depression.

During the summer of 1933 Hamid organized the picketing of small stores in the area of 135th Street. Several of the store owners capitulated and hired African Americans as clerks. Emboldened by this success, Hamid in the spring of 1934 moved his campaign to the large chain and department stores on 125th Street, Harlem's commercial and cultural axis. In May he organized a picket line around Woolworth's after the manager refused to hire members of the Negro Industrial and Clerical Alliance as sales clerks. Hamid's successes spurred other black leaders in Harlem, among them, ministers, various black nationalists, and Communists, to mount their own boycott campaigns. Hamid was invited to join a coalition of groups in leading a boycott of Blumstein's department store, but he was soon expelled after insisting that any newly hired black sales clerks should be made members of his organization. After his expulsion, he began to appeal to African Americans to "drive Jewish businessmen out of Harlem." Hamid was accused by the Communist party of being a "Black Hitler" and of taking money from merchants who agreed to hire black workers. Similarly, mainstream black ministers and newspapers denounced Hamid for his anti-Semitism, and he was often accused of embezzling dues money from the Negro Industrial and Clerical Alliance

In the fall of 1934 a group of Jewish businessmen met with Mayor Fiorello LaGuardia to complain that Hamid was conducting a race war against Jews in Harlem. In October Hamid was arrested on charges of "spreading anti-Semitism in Harlem." Following four days of conflicting testimony he was acquitted. A few weeks after his acquittal Hamid changed the name of his organization to the Afro-American Federation of Labor.

In January 1935 Hamid was arrested for publishing and selling a pamphlet without a license and was sentenced to ten days in jail. By this time the Harlem boycott movement had ebbed, and after his release Hamid declared that he would return to studying and teaching black magic and mysticism. He continued to speak atop his stepladder on Harlem streets and to operate a headquarters that housed a grocery store and the remnants of the Afro-American Federation of Labor, and his organization continued to picket stores in an attempt to force them to hire African Americans, but Hamid's rhetoric often veered into a mystical racialism, and his group became increasingly isolated. In July 1935 one of Hamid's targets, the Lerner Company, won a court injunction against the activities of the Afro-American Federation of Labor, effectively disbanding the organization. The company had argued that Hamid's aim was to drive white people and Jews in particular out of Harlem. Hamid then dropped out of public view for more than two years, during which time he reputedly studied Asian religions.

In 1938 Hamid formed the Temple of Tranquility, a quasireligious organization and economic cooperative in Harlem. The organization established a cooperative wholesale fruit and vegetable market as well as a parking garage and an automobile service station. Hamid died that same year in an airplane crash.

Hamid was the catalyst behind the Harlem boycott movement of the early and mid-1930s, one of the defining events in New York's black community during the Great Depression. He was also one of the first African-American leaders to publicly espouse anti-Semitism, an issue that vexed relations between African Americans and Jews for the rest of the twentieth century.

• An interview with Hamid and various conflicting biographical accounts are included in the "biographical sketches" section of the Negroes of New York, 1936–41, project of the Writers' Program of the Works Progress Administration, on microfilm at the Schomburg Center for Research in Black Culture, New York City. The most useful biographical studies of Hamid are in Roi Ottley, *New World A-Coming* (1943), and in Claude McKay, *Harlem: Negro Metropolis* (1940). There is a well-developed literature on the Harlem boycotts. See especially William Muraskin, "The Harlem Boycott of 1934: Black Nationalism and the Rise of Labor-Union Consciousness," *Labor History* 13 (Summer 1972): 361–73, and Mark Naison, *Communists in Harlem during the Depression* (1983).

THADDEUS RUSSELL

HAMILTON, Alexander (26 Sept. 1712–11 May 1756), physician and writer, was born in Edinburgh, Scotland, the son of Mary Robertson and William Hamilton, professor of divinity and principal at the University of Edinburgh, where Hamilton received his medical degree in 1737. Following the example of his oldest brother, John, Hamilton emigrated to Maryland in 1738 to establish a medical practice. By the time he died eighteen years later, he was regarded as "the most eminent Physician in Annapolis" (Upton Scott, Howard Family Papers, Maryland His. Soc.). In 1739 Hamilton joined the Ugly Club of Annapolis (the immediate precursor of the Tuesday Club), and in 1743 he was elected common councilman of Annapolis, an office he held until his death. By that time he was suffering from signs of consumption. To improve his health, he spent the summer of 1744 away from the muggy Maryland climate touring the northern colonies. Along the way, he kept a diary of his observations, the *Itinerarium* (first published in 1907), which has been called "the best single portrait of men and manners, of rural and urban life, of the wide range of society and scenery in colonial America" (Lemay, p. 229). The *Itinerarium* provides a running comic commentary on the aspects of colonial life a gentleman such as Hamilton found irritating, particularly the many breaches in privilege and decorum he witnessed during his travels. Hamilton viewed the average colonial as uncouth, impertinent, easily prone to lie, and although naive in other areas, a conniver in money matters. "As to politeness and humanity," he concluded, life throughout the colonies was "much alike"— meaning crude—"except in the great towns where the inhabitants are more civilized, especially att [*sic*] Boston."

Following his return to Maryland, Hamilton helped to form the Tuesday Club of Annapolis, which was the center of social and intellectual life in colonial Annapolis from 14 May 1745 to 10 February 1756, when it met for the last time, shortly before Hamilton's death. Almost everyone of some importance in the northern Chesapeake Bay area—including the Reverends Thomas Bacon, Thomas Cradock, Alexander Malcolm, and James Sterling; Jonas Green; Stephen and John Beale Bordley; the sons of Daniel Dulany (1685–1753); and Benjamin Franklin (1706–1790)—either joined or visited the Tuesday Club. As its secretary, Hamilton recorded the club's minutes shortly after each meeting; he then compiled the "Record of the Tuesday Club," a careful revision of the minutes; and from 1752 until his death he worked on the draft and on the final version of *The History of the Ancient and Honorable Tuesday Club* (first published in 1990), a fictionalized account of the club's proceedings in three volumes and nearly 1,900 manuscript pages. *The History* satirizes the proprietary struggles in colonial Maryland and what was perhaps the greatest social issues of the 1750s, the outcry against luxury. In Hamilton's day many feared that the domestic vices associated with luxury—drunkenness, gluttony, lust, avarice, ceremony, vanity, effeminacy, and affection—inevitably led to the political vices of ambition, pride, enervation, bribery, corruption, and subjection. That is precisely what happens in *The History*, where Hamilton mocks the Jeremiahs of his age by posing as one himself and by comically depicting the rise and fall of the Tuesday Club as a result of the harmful effects of luxury. *The History* is a splendid gauge of eighteenth-century wit, loaded with pseudo-learned essays and digressions, surprising metaphors and allusions, raillery and repartee, bombastic letters and speeches, doggerel verses and mock trials, brain-teasing riddles and conundrums, delicate and often indelicate puns, even nonsensical hieroglyphics and missing passages—and, of course, a generous dose of scatological humor and what Hamilton referred to as "polite smutt [sic]." Hamilton's wit runs the gamut of eighteenth-century comedy in *The History*, creating a comedic extravaganza matched, perhaps, but unsurpassed in eighteenth-century literature.

Most of Hamilton's time was taken up by his medical practice and by the hours he spent serving and writing about the Tuesday Club. But he found time to pursue other interests as well. From 1746 to 1750 he contributed numerous pieces to the *Maryland Gazette*, including an essay on the impertinent question, "What News?" (7 Jan. 1746); a cure for distempered authors and a mock advertisement to catch a runaway wit (4 Feb., 18 Mar. 1746); a dream vision on the fate of the contributors to the *Gazette* (29 June 1748); a tale for melancholic scribblers (31 Aug. 1748); and a parody of Masonic ceremonies (24 Jan. 1750). In 1747 Hamilton married Margaret Dulany, the daughter of Daniel Dulany the Elder; they had no children. In 1749 he and several other Tuesday Club members founded a Freemasons' lodge in Annapolis. In his "Discourse Delivered . . . by the Right Worshipful the Master, to the Brethren of the Ancient and Honourable Society of Free and Accepted Masons" (1750), Hamilton elaborated upon the principles by which he and his companions sought to regulate their lives, concluding his speech by reminding them that the "upright man," in control of his passions and guided by the "Lights of Reason" in his pursuit of liberty, was obliged to perform works of "*Charity, Benevolence,* and *Brotherly Love.*" In 1751 Hamilton participated in one of the leading medical debates of his day, publishing *A Defence of Dr. Thomson's Discourse on the Preparation of the Body for the Small Pox*, which defended Dr. Adam Thomson's method of inoculation and attacked what Hamilton considered the rash of "Quacks, Imposters, and Empirics" who knew nothing about medical theory. With the aid of the Dulanys, in 1753 he represented the Court party and was elected a member of the Lower House; he resigned from that office in 1754, probably because of poor health.

Hamilton died of consumption in Annapolis. In the *Maryland Gazette* for 13 May 1756, his good friend Jonas Green lamented the passing of the man he and other Tuesday Club members had come to love:

The Death of this valuable and worthy Gentleman is universally and justly lamented: His medical Abilities, various Knowledge, strictness of Integrity, simplicity of Manners, and extensive Benevolence, having deservedly gained him the Respect and Esteem of all Ranks of Men.—No man, in his Sphere, has left fewer Enemies, or more Friends.

• Archival materials concerning Hamilton can be found in the Huntington Library, San Marino, Calif.; the John Work Garrett Collections, Eisenhower Library, Johns Hopkins University; the Peter Force Collection, Library of Congress; and the Maryland Historical Society, Annapolis. Published editions of Hamilton's works are Carl Bridenbaugh, *Gentleman's Progress: The Itinerarium of Dr. Alexander Hamilton, 1744* (1948; repr. 1992); Elaine G. Breslaw, *Records of the Tuesday Club of Annapolis, 1745–56* (1988); and Robert Micklus, *The History of the Ancient and Honorable Tuesday Club* (1990). For commentaries, see Micklus, *The Comic Genius of Dr. Alexander Hamilton* (1990), and J. A. Leo Lemay, *Men of Letters in Colonial Maryland* (1972).

ROBERT MICKLUS

HAMILTON, Alexander (11 Jan. 1757?–12 July 1804), statesman and first secretary of the treasury, was born in Nevis, British West Indies, the second of two illegitimate sons of James Hamilton and Rachel Faucett Lavien. (The year of birth is often given as 1755, but the evidence more strongly supports 1757.) The father deserted the family when Hamilton was eight; the mother died three years later. Hamilton was apprenticed to a firm of international merchants and proved to be so gifted in commerce that he was soon left in full charge of the business. At fifteen he was "discovered" by a Presbyterian minister, who arranged financial support to send him to the College of New Jersey at Princeton. After a year at a preparatory school he passed the stiff entrance exams at Princeton, but when the president refused to allow him to advance at his own pace rather than with the regular classes, he went to King's College (now Columbia) in New York instead.

That was a fateful decision, for it placed Hamilton in a center of radical patriot activity just as the long struggle between the American colonies and the mother country was coming to a climax. Hamilton did not neglect his studies, but he was increasingly drawn into the public arena. He spoke at rallies and during the winter of 1774–1775 published two major political tracts that, though not up to his mature standards, elicited considerable praise. He also prepared himself to fight; by the following winter he had learned the rudiments of soldiery, studied artillery, organized an artillery company, and been commissioned a captain in the Continental army. Driven by a hunger for glory, throughout 1776 he repeatedly saw action in the field: if he had a flaw it was that of being excessively bold.

His prowess as a warrior was overshadowed by his skills as an organizer and administrator, and he received offers from several generals to serve as aide-de-camp, which he turned down until an invitation came from George Washington. He became almost indispensable to Washington and served with him (as a lieutenant colonel) until February 1781. Then he sought a field command, which he obtained in July. In October he was ordered to storm one of two crucial redoubts in the battle of Yorktown, and he and his men carried out the assignment heroically.

During his military service several things happened that influenced his future. One was that he made his first explorations into the subject of public finance. Another was that his nationalism grew more intense even as he was growing disgusted with the indecision, weakness, and corruption of Congress. Related to his attitude toward Congress was his disillusionment with American society, which he saw as plagued by "voluptuous indolence," provincialism, and oligarchy. And in December 1780 he married Elizabeth Schuyler, daughter of a wealthy New York aristocrat; the couple eventually had seven children who survived infancy. He married for love, but the political connections would prove invaluable.

Resigning his commission to take up his responsibilities as a husband and father, Hamilton devoted the first ten months of 1782 to training himself to practice law, and he passed the rigorous New York bar examination in October. To accomplish this feat, he wrote a book—a compilation of entries from a large number of legal tracts—and committed it to memory. The book was subsequently published and became a standard manual for New York lawyers.

On 22 July 1782 the New York legislature appointed Hamilton to represent the state in the Continental Congress. There he became involved with Robert Morris, Gouverneur Morris, James Wilson, and others in a scheme to combine the lobbying power of public creditors with "the terror of a mutinying army" to induce Congress to pass and the states to ratify amendments to the Articles of Confederation vesting Congress with independent sources of revenue. The army, encamped at Newburgh, New York, was discontented over arrears of pay, and the situation got out of hand. Only a dramatic confrontation between Washington and the officers prevented a mutiny. That killed the scheme: Hamilton's maiden effort to harness private self-interest to further the public interest came a cropper.

As a practicing lawyer, Hamilton quickly rose to the top rank among the lawyers in New York City. His most important early case, *Rutgers v. Waddington* (1784), is often but inaccurately cited as a precedent for the doctrine of judicial review. Hamilton did argue that the statute applicable to the case violated the state constitution and was therefore void, but the judge expressly disavowed any power to overturn a statute ("for that were to set the *judicial* above the legislative"), though his ruling favored Hamilton's client on other grounds.

Lucrative and busy as his law practice was, Hamilton had his eye on a public career and was preparing himself for one. His boyhood craving for military glory had been slaked at Yorktown; after the war his "ruling passion" became hunger for fame—immortality in the form of the grateful remembrance of posterity,

earned by noble services to one's country. By 1786 he knew the capacity in which he wanted to win his fame, namely as minister of the nation's finances. He derived the idea from Jacques Necker, the erstwhile French finance minister, whose memoirs Hamilton read early in 1786. His thinking on the subject was also powerfully influenced by Sir James Steuart, Adam Smith, and David Hume.

He began a two-front campaign toward his goal. One was in state politics. All the state legislatures except New York's had ratified an amendment to the Articles of Confederation granting Congress power to collect import duties; in April 1786 Hamilton ran for and won a seat in the state legislature, hoping to persuade it to ratify. It did not meet until the following January, at which time he argued brilliantly but futilely for the measure. In the meantime, he had acted on another front. Through the influence of friends he was appointed as one of New York's delegates to an interstate commercial convention that met in Annapolis in September 1786. There he joined forces with James Madison and John Dickinson and pushed through a resolution calling for a general convention to meet in Philadelphia the following May "to render the constitution of the Federal Government adequate to the exigencies of the Union."

When that call was issued it seemed unlikely to evoke a positive response, and at first it did not. Congress in effect tabled the proposal, and only five states voted to send delegates. But then, early in 1787, two dramatic events took place: Shays's Rebellion exploded in Massachusetts, and New York definitively rejected the revenue amendment. In desperation, Congress endorsed the convention call, and seven more states voted to send delegates. Somewhat incongruously, since the legislature was dominated by Governor George Clinton's antinationalist friends, New York was one of them; even more incongruously, Hamilton was chosen as one of the state's three delegates.

Hamilton attended the convention intermittently and was of minor influence in it. His one major speech, which consumed the whole day on 18 June was a profound analysis of the nature of man, society, and government, but except for raising the general philosophical level of the proceedings, it accomplished little. A delegate from Connecticut observed that Hamilton had "been praised by every body" but "supported by none." Hamilton had, at the end of his speech, proposed a strong central government, consisting of a president and senate chosen by electors for life, a lower house elected by universal manhood suffrage for three-year terms, and an appointive supreme court also serving for life. He did not, as was later charged, propose a monarchy; he declared that "we ought to go as far [toward monarchy] in order to attain stability and permanency, as republican principles will admit."

In truth, though he would have preferred a more "high toned" (the phrase is his) government than the one crafted by the convention, he cared little for forms and was determined to sign and champion the ratification of whatever the convention produced. His best-known effort in behalf of ratification was his coauthorship of the eighty-five essays signed "Publius," collectively termed *The Federalist* and generally regarded as the greatest commentary on the Constitution and federalism ever written. John Jay wrote five of the essays; James Madison is credited with twenty-four and Hamilton with fifty-six.

Though the contributions of the two principal authors were complementary and formed a well-rounded whole, there were differences between them. Hamilton, the epitome of self-confidence, emphasized the need for "energy," particularly in the executive; Madison, not fully trusting himself, was less prone to entrust power anywhere and emphasized the checks and restraints provided by the Constitution. Madison praised the system as "partly national, partly federal"; Hamilton disliked the federal features and tended to downplay them. His own concept was that each level of government was sovereign as to matters entrusted to it. Madison had no firm conception of judicial review, whereas Hamilton offered a full-fledged defense of it. These differences would rise to the surface three years later.

The Federalist was written primarily to influence the election of delegates to New York's ratifying convention, and in that cause it failed. Opponents of the Constitution (Antifederalists) dominated the convention; Jay and Hamilton were among the minority. The convention did, however, ratify the Constitution but not because of the Federalists' rhetorical skills. Some antis crossed over on learning that the requisite number of states had ratified, meaning that the new government would go into effect no matter what New York did. Enough others changed their votes in response to a rumor, spread by Hamilton and Jay, that if the state did not ratify, New York City would secede and apply for admission to the union on its own.

Once New York ratified, Hamilton became eligible to serve in the new government. The call came in the fall of 1789. Months earlier, Washington had asked Hamilton to be his finance minister, but Congress did not create the Treasury Department until September. On 21 September, two days before adjourning until January, the House of Representatives directed Hamilton to prepare a plan for support of the public credit and "to report the same to this House at its next meeting." The phraseology was significant. It meant that the Treasury, unlike the other executive departments, was responsible to the House as well as to the president.

That suited Hamilton entirely, for it facilitated the implementation of grand designs he had for the government and for American society. Establishing public credit was important to him for its own sake, but he saw it also as a means to broader ends. The Constitution did not preclude the development of something approximating the British ministerial system, in which the chancellor of the exchequer was the "prime" minister; Hamilton's having one foot in the House and another in the executive branch might make that development possible. As Madison later observed, Hamilton sought "to administer the Government . . . into what it ought to be," instead of what its authors had intended. This did not mean that Hamilton was lukewarm in regard to freedom. In the Constitutional Convention he had "professed himself to be as zealous an advocate for liberty as any man whatever, and trusted he should be as willing a martyr to it," but he differed from Madison in what he regarded as the most "eligible" means of securing it.

The other part of Hamilton's design was to reshape American society to make it fluid, energetic, and market driven. He believed that Americans "labour less now than any civilized nation in Europe" and that habits of industry were "essential to the health and vigor" of the nation. Americans had little incentive to work hard, for earning a subsistence was easy whereas improving one's lot was difficult. Wealth and status came not from labor or talent but from the possession of (usually inherited) landed estates. And Hamilton abhorred inherited status. (Indeed he was an active participant in New York's antislavery movement.) To transform the established order, Hamilton proposed to "monetize" society: to erect fiscal machinery that would become so convenient and necessary to the transaction of ordinary economic activity that money would become the measure of all things. Bourgeois values would then be embraced, oligarchies would come tumbling down, and men of merit would rise to the top.

The opening steps in the unfolding of Hamilton's fiscal plans were contained in his First Report on the Public Credit, presented to Congress on 14 January 1790. The public debts, as Hamilton described them, were of three broad descriptions. The foreign debt, owed to the government of France and to bankers in Holland, amounted to about $11 million and fell due in installments over several years. The domestic debts were in great confusion but came to roughly $40 million owed by the nation and about $25 million owed by the several states. Hamilton believed that if France proved willing to defer receipt of scheduled principal payments, he could refinance the entire foreign debt in Holland at reduced interest rates, and that was more or less the way it worked out.

His approach to the domestic debts was more complex. Unlike many members of Congress, who wanted to pay off the debts as rapidly as possible, Hamilton chose to "fund" them. That is, he asked Congress to provide semipermanent appropriations for interest payments on the debts, federal and state. Redemption of the principal would be at the discretion of the government but could be no more than 2 percent of the total annually. To stabilize the new government securities that were issued to retire the old certificates and to maintain them at or near their face value, a "sinking fund" would be created, financed by the profits from the post office.

Congress received the funding and sinking fund proposals favorably, but the proposal to assume responsibility for the state debts faced strong opposition. Several states had retired most of their debts, and their representatives were averse to paying taxes for the benefit of states that had not. Among the states without large debts was Virginia, and Madison—who had become a leader in the House—headed the opposition to assumption. The result was that it was defeated in the House by two votes. At that point a famous political deal was struck. The Virginians were anxious that the permanent national capital be located on the Potomac. Secretary of State Thomas Jefferson and his friend Madison held a dinner party for Hamilton at which it was agreed that Hamilton would find northern votes for the Potomac capital site, and they would find votes for assumption of the state debts. And thus the funding and assumption plan became law on 4 August 1790.

When Congress reconvened in December 1790 Hamilton greeted it with a Second Report on the Public Credit, this one proposing to create a national bank. The Treasury needed a reliable source of short-term credit to compensate for the seasonal flow of revenues from imports, and experience had taught Hamilton that the three existing banks in America were not entirely trustworthy. Moreover, Hamilton wanted to use the bank notes as a form of currency. He therefore asked Congress to grant a twenty-year charter to a private corporation, the Bank of the United States. It would be capitalized at $10 million, of which one-fifth would be subscribed by the federal government, the government's share to be paid with funds borrowed from the bank itself. The crucial feature was that private purchases of the bank's stock were payable one-fourth in gold or silver and three-fourths in government securities. Because everyone expected the bank to earn tremendous profits, the price of the stock would soar, which would also raise the price of government securities since they were interchangeable. And public credit would be soundly established.

Congressional response was strongly favorable, but a formidable obstacle arose: Madison objected during the debates in the House that chartering a corporation was beyond the scope of the powers of Congress as itemized in Article 1, Section 8, of the Constitution. The bill was passed anyway, but Madison's objections so disturbed Washington that he asked Jefferson and Attorney General Edmund Randolph for advisory opinions. Both held that the bill was unconstitutional.

Washington then asked Hamilton whether he could justify the creation of the bank constitutionally. Hamilton responded with the classic formulation of the doctrines of implied powers and "loose construction." The basis of his argument was the clause at the end of Article 1, Section 8, empowering Congress "To make all Laws which shall be necessary and proper for carrying into Execution" the enumerated powers. Randolph and Jefferson, Hamilton pointed out, had interpreted the word "necessary" so narrowly that, if their view prevailed, government would be paralyzed; they read the Constitution as if the words "absolutely" or "indispensably" preceded "necessary." Besides, he

went on, Jefferson had confused means with ends. The ends to be served by chartering the bank were clearly constitutional; the bank was merely a means of carrying out those legitimate functions. And, "If the end be clearly comprehended within any of the specified powers," he said, and "if the measure have an obvious relation to that end, and is not forbidden by any particular provision of the constitution—it may safely be deemed to come within the compass of the national authority." (Chief Justice John Marshall used Hamilton's reasoning and much of his language in the decision in *McCulloch v. Maryland* [1819].) Washington signed the bill into law on 25 February 1791.

Despite their policy differences, Hamilton and Jefferson were at that point on cordial terms, but a break was less than two months away. One evening in April Vice President John Adams, Jefferson, and Hamilton chanced to dine together. The conversation turned to political philosophy, whereupon Adams declared that if the British constitution were purged of its corruption and if representation in the House of Commons were equalized, "it would be the most perfect constitution ever devised by the wit of man." Jefferson was upset by his old friend's remark, but he was astonished to hear Hamilton's response. "Purge it of its corruption," Hamilton said, paraphrasing an essay by David Hume, "and give to its popular branch equality of representation, and it would become an *impracticable* government: as it stands at present, with all its supposed defects, it is the most perfect government which ever existed." Brooding on Hamilton's comment and reviewing his policies, Jefferson became convinced that Hamilton was scheming to erect an American version of the British system.

Jefferson saw every subsequent Hamiltonian action as an attempt to subvert the Constitution—including Hamilton's abortive Report on Manufactures, presented to Congress the following December. He shared his "discovery" with Washington, who refused to believe it; indeed, remembering what he and his armies had suffered because of a lack of public credit and a weak government, the president regarded Hamilton as something of a miracle worker. Jefferson then turned to Madison, who did believe him, and the two began laying the foundation for an opposition political party, which they styled Republican, in a pointed suggestion that Hamilton was a monarchist. Jefferson induced friends in Congress to begin a succession of harassing investigations of the way Hamilton ran the Treasury Department. They uncovered no wrongdoing, but that did not deter them from continuing the attacks.

Hamilton never understood the source of Jefferson's enmity, and he was bewildered and pained by the estrangement from Madison. Nor did he become a "party man" just yet. He still held the belief that parties were inimical if not fatal to republics, and not until Adams was president, and the party system had grown so entrenched and rancorous that every public man had to take a stand one way or the other, did Hamilton refer to himself as a "Federalist."

Soon genuine and deeply felt substantive concerns arising from the French Revolution exacerbated the rift between the department heads and the nascent political parties. When the revolution began in 1789 Hamilton was thrilled, for in common with most Americans he believed that Louis XVI was a friend of liberty who would give France a limited, constitutional monarchy. By the winter of 1792–1793 France had proclaimed itself a republic, executed the king, and announced its intention to "liberate" all Europe. These developments, in Hamilton's view, portended serious trouble for the United States. The country was bound to France by perpetual treaties of commerce and alliance signed when France agreed to help the United States in 1778. The United States was not obliged to join the war on France's side, for the alliance pertained only to defensive wars. Nonetheless, Hamilton believed that if America did not maintain the strictest neutrality it could be dragged into the conflict. The young nation could not afford a war, and particularly a war with Britain (a partner in the coalition against France), which would cut off most of the import revenues that supported Hamilton's financial system and the government itself. The problem became urgent in April 1793 upon the arrival of a minister from France, Citizen Edmond Genêt. In response to his doings, Hamilton and Secretary of War Henry Knox urged Washington to issue a neutrality proclamation and suspend the 1778 treaties; Jefferson insisted that as only Congress could declare war, only it could declare neutrality. Washington split the difference, issuing the proclamation but taking no action concerning the treaties. The cabinet remained bitterly divided until Jefferson resigned at year's end.

By that time new perils had arisen—from the British side. British naval commanders began seizing American vessels under secret orders. Cries for war swept America, cries that were intensified by news that the British were inciting Indians to attack in the Northwest Territory and were arming slave insurrectionists in Hispaniola. Hamilton recommended preparation for war to strengthen the American position to negotiate a peace. A provisional army was authorized, and Chief Justice John Jay was sent to England to negotiate.

As the negotiations proceeded, Hamilton was involved in a domestic episode that was only tangentially related to the international imbroglio. Since the passage in 1791 of an excise on whiskey, the inhabitants of western Pennsylvania had resisted the collection of the tax. Genêt had added to their spirit of resistance by promoting "democratic-republican" societies—pro-French political clubs—the most militant of which were near Pittsburgh. When further violence erupted in 1794, Hamilton believed that the rule of law and ordered liberty were gravely threatened. He also believed that only a prompt and massive display of counterforce by the government could restore law. Accordingly, he urged Washington to call out 12,950 militia troops from four states to crush the "Whiskey Rebellion." Hamilton accompanied the troops for the entire march. The display of force was effective; the rebellion evanesced, and the democratic-republican societies were discredited.

The domestic scene seeming well in hand and the prospects for continued neutrality appearing favorable, Hamilton felt that he could safely resign and attend to his long-neglected private financial affairs. As of 31 January 1795 he returned to his law practice. He became one of a handful of attorneys who were transforming the law by developing the law of contracts based on market determinations and pioneering (through cases, not statutes) a market-driven law of commercial paper, corporate privileges and obligations, and marine insurance. One suit in an unrelated area, *Hylton v. U.S.* (1796), involved the first ruling by the Supreme Court on the constitutionality of an act of Congress.

His retirement from public life, however, was not complete. The president and several department heads repeatedly asked him for advice. In many ways he seemed to be a prime minister in absentia. He wrote Washington's seventh annual message to Congress for him, and in 1796 he composed much of Washington's Farewell Address. And he was still forced to defend what he had done as secretary of the Treasury. He was publicly charged with having paid blackmail to a petty swindler named James Reynolds to cover department irregularities. Hamilton feared that if the charges were believed the integrity of his financial system and of public credit would be undermined. Accordingly, he rebutted the charges in a lengthy pamphlet that detailed an amorous affair he had had with Maria Reynolds that underlay James's blackmail demands. Thus he chose to give great pain to his wife, whom he loved, in order to protect his public reputation.

Soon a new call to service arose. Relations with France had again deteriorated, and in response to public clamor for war President Adams asked Washington to come out of retirement and serve as commander in chief. Washington agreed, but on condition that he would go on active duty only in case of invasion and that Hamilton be appointed his second in command. Adams had no option but to accept the conditions, but he mistrusted and envied Hamilton and thenceforth moved from being an avid hawk to being an ardent dove. The two years (1798–1800) of the Quasi-War with France were a time of great frustration for Hamilton. His efforts to organize the army were stymied by incompetence in the War Department and foot-dragging by the president.

In 1800 Hamilton determined to try to defeat Adams's bid for reelection—not by supporting Jefferson but by urging Federalists to vote for Charles Cotesworth Pinckney of South Carolina. When Jefferson and Aaron Burr tied for the lead, each having a majority, the election went into the House of Representatives. Hamilton regarded Burr as an extremely dangerous man, a "Caesar in embryo," and so threw his support behind Jefferson. Jefferson's election, for practical purposes, ended Hamilton's public career. He established a newspaper, not to oppose but to act as a responsible critic of the Jefferson administration, but in the main he stuck to his law practice.

One of his last cases was of enduring importance. The printer of an upstate newspaper, Harry Croswell, had been charged with libel for writing that Jefferson had paid a pamphleteer to defame Washington and Adams. The charge was true, but under the common law truth was not a defense, and Croswell was convicted. On appeal, Croswell engaged Hamilton as counsel. Hamilton delivered one of his most brilliant arguments, contending that truth, if not used "wantonly," must be reckoned by all reasonable men as a defense. Otherwise, "you must for ever remain ignorant of what your rulers do. . . . I never did think the truth was a crime . . . for my soul has ever abhorred the thought, that a free man dared not speak the truth." The court was divided, and the conviction stood. But members of the state legislature had come to hear Hamilton's argument and were so persuaded by it that the following year they enacted into law the principle of truth as a defense. By that time Hamilton was dead.

The New York gubernatorial election of 1804 had been a heated contest in which Hamilton had fiercely opposed Burr's candidacy. Burr lost and a few weeks later sent a representative to Hamilton to demand an explanation for remarks Hamilton had allegedly made. The matter could not be satisfactorily resolved, and Hamilton and Burr met on the dueling ground in Weehawken, New Jersey, where three years earlier Hamilton's eldest son, Philip, had been killed in a duel. By accident or design, Burr shot Hamilton in his right side, and the ball passed through his liver. He died in New York thirty-six hours later.

For a century and a half after his death, Hamilton's place in the pantheon of American demigods seemed secure. More than any other man save possibly Washington, he was regarded as the person who breathed life into the Constitution, and without exception he was viewed as the father of capitalism in America. Then, during the Great Depression of the 1930s, the latter appellation took on sinister tones, and Hamilton came to be seen as the founder not of a benign economic system but of a malevolent plutocracy. Despite his fall from grace among historians in general and in popular culture, however, his biographers continued to sing his praises. For, as the Virginian William Heth put it after a congressional investigation in 1794, "The more you *probe*, examine, & investigate Hamilton's conduct; rely upon it, the *greater* he will appear."

• See *The Papers of Alexander Hamilton*, ed. Harold C. Syrett et al. (27 vols., 1961–1987). *The Law Practice of Alexander Hamilton*, ed. Julius Goebel, Jr. (2 vols., 1964, 1969), makes available the remainder of Hamilton's extant writings. One of the best and most scholarly biographies is Broadus Mitchell, *Alexander Hamilton* (2 vols., 1957, 1962). Also useful are John C. Miller, *Alexander Hamilton: Portrait in Paradox* (1959), and Jacob E. Cooke, *Alexander Hamilton: A Biography* (1982).

For a fuller study of the man with particular emphasis on his economic ideas and policies, see Forrest McDonald, *Alexander Hamilton: A Biography* (1979). For greater focus on Hamilton's political ideas, see the more specialized studies by Clinton L. Rossiter, *Alexander Hamilton and the Constitution* (1964); Gerald Stourzh, *Alexander Hamilton and the Idea of Republican Government* (1970); Alpheus Thomas Mason, "The Federalist—A Split Personality," *American Historical Review* 57 (1952): 625–43; and Gottfried Dietze, "Hamilton's Federalist—Treatise for Free Government," *Cornell Law Quarterly* 42 (1957): 307–28, 501–18. Gilbert L. Lycan, *Alexander Hamilton and American Foreign Policy: A Design for Greatness* (1970), provides a balanced account of Hamilton's role in international affairs. Hamilton's public career in the context of the Washington administration is drawn concisely but fully in McDonald, *The Presidency of George Washington* (1974). A study that places Hamilton in the emerging political context in a different way is Joseph Charles, "Hamilton and Washington: The Origins of the American Party System," *William and Mary Quarterly* 12 (1955): 217–67.

FORREST MCDONALD

HAMILTON, Alice (27 Feb. 1869–22 Sept. 1970), physician, was born in New York City, the daughter of Montgomery Hamilton and Gertrude Pond. Her family resided in Fort Wayne, Indiana, dependent on an inherited fortune. Because her parents did not believe in conventional education, Alice and her siblings did not attend school. They were taught by both parents. She had two years of formal education before entering the University of Michigan Medical School. After that, a long period of professional training and deep feelings of social commitment prepared her for work in occupational health. The professional training was an accomplishment for a woman of her generation. She received the M.D. from the University of Michigan in 1893, then spent two months as an intern in the Hospital for Women and Children in Minneapolis, Minnesota, and nine months at the New England Hospital for Women and Children near Boston. She was then advised that if she wished to pursue a career in bacteriology and pathology, study in Germany was necessary to make her an expert. She went to Germany to study at Leipzig and Munich for one year. The following year she studied at the Johns Hopkins University, Baltimore.

In 1897 Hamilton accepted her first job, teaching pathology at the Women's Medical School of Northwestern University. During the years she taught at Northwestern, she lived at Hull House in Chicago, where she started a well baby clinic. Her concern with social and humanitarian issues matured, due in part to experiences while she resided at Hull House. Jane Addams, Florence Kelly, and Julia Lathrop influenced Hamilton, and the experience of living close to working people who suffered from injustice, poverty, and disease affected her social conscience. These experiences aroused interest in a cause in which she could utilize her capabilities and expertise to effectuate change. Her autobiography, *Exploring The Dangerous Trades* (1943), described this desire to help the unprotected worker: "It was my experience at Hull House that aroused my interest in industrial diseases. Living in a working-class quarter, coming into contact with laborers and their wives, I could not fail to hear tales of the dangers that working men faced, of cases of carbon monoxide gassing in the great steel mills, of painters disabled by lead palsy, of pneumonia and rheumatism among men in the stockyards."

From 1897 to 1910, while Hamilton taught at Northwestern and lived at Hull House, she educated herself about industrial diseases. She saw what harsh, unhealthy working conditions did to the working men and women with whom she had daily contact. She saw unorganized workers contend with the pressing problems of low wages, long hours, poverty, and exposure to industrial diseases. She learned about the labor movement and the needs of working men and women, and at the same time she studied all available information on industrial diseases.

In 1910 Governor Deneen of Illinois appointed an occupational disease commission to inquire into the extent of industrial disease in that state—the first such survey undertaken in the United States. The commission had one year to study six industrial poisons—lead, arsenic, brass, carbon monoxide, cyanides, and turpentine. As a member of this commission, Hamilton's long professional and social experience came to fruition. From that time (1910) her interests and energies focused on industrial health. At the age of forty-one she began her pioneering efforts in the unexplored field of occupational medicine. She remained actively involved in this field until after World War II. Her last major project was the revision of her textbook *Industrial Toxicology* (with Harriet Hardy, 1934), published in 1949 when Hamilton was eighty.

In 1910 Hamilton's investigations for the Illinois commission focused on the lead hazard. In 1912 she undertook a similar survey for the U.S. government. At this time a major need in the new field of industrial health was to survey existing occupational hazards. Thus Hamilton's surveys made a major contribution to the study of occupational disease. Her most important contributions were descriptions of the extent of industrial disease in the United States. From 1911 to 1920 she was special investigator for the Federal (Bureau) Department of Labor (1913) Bureau of Labor Statistics. Industries she studied included lead (pottery, tile, porcelain enamel sanitary ware, the painters' trade, and the making of storage batteries); rubber; munitions, including poisons utilized in the manufacture of explosives; and viscose rayon. She coauthored *Industrial Toxicology*, the first book of its kind, served on numerous committees, chaired the industrial hygiene section of the American Public Health Association, and received many honors and accolades for her work.

In 1919 recognition as an authority in the field of industrial medicine brought Hamilton an appointment as assistant professor at the Harvard Medical School. She became the first woman on that faculty at a time when the Harvard Medical School still refused admission to women students. The appointment caused much comment and occasioned a number of newspaper articles. Hamilton's sharp comment about the appointment, which was an honor, reveals much about her: "Yes, I am the first woman on the Harvard faculty—but not the first one who should have been appointed!" When Hamilton retired from the Harvard faculty in 1935, however, she was still an assistant professor.

To Hamilton, occupational health was a part of the larger field of medicine, especially public health. She understood the public-health problems of poverty, slum housing, inadequate nutrition, inequality, and inadequate medical care. Her contributions to the field of occupational health had so great an impact that they submerged her involvements in social reform. It is generally acknowledged, on the basis of her contributions to occupational medicine alone, that Hamilton was an outstanding woman of her generation. However, if one also considers her involvements with social issues, her status increases to an even greater degree. During her professorship at Harvard Hamilton worked for many liberal causes. She was appointed in 1924 as the only woman member of the health committee of the League of Nations; she participated for many years in international public-health programs, including control of epidemic and endemic diseases (malaria, smallpox, sleeping sickness, tuberculosis, and leprosy), reduction of infant mortality, and control of the opium trade. Always committed to social reform, she never feared endorsing controversial causes. She advocated family planning (birth control) at a time when such a position was unpopular. Her interest derived from firsthand knowledge of the lives of women who suffered from lack of information and social constraints. She had also seen the debilitating effects of unlimited childbearing.

In the second decade of the twentieth century, Hamilton also took a stand for protective labor legislation for women and against an equal rights amendment which she believed would negate any modest gains made by women to protect themselves at work. She spoke for unorganized, easily exploited, largely unskilled and inarticulate women who worked in textile mills; laundries; canneries; biscuit, box, and candy factories; and telephone exchanges, or as hotel chambermaids and office scrubwomen; she committed herself to a policy that sought to keep and extend protective legislation for women in industry, a commitment she would not renege on in order to see an equal rights amendment passed. In 1952, when Hamilton no longer feared that women workers would lose gains in the area of protective health legislation, she supported an equal rights amendment to the U.S. Constitution.

Hamilton used her scientific findings to show the need for protective legislation. She studied the employment of women in the poisonous trades and published some of her findings in a U.S. Department of Labor bulletin, *Women Workers and Industrial Poisons*. Most of her data on the part played by sex susceptibility to industrial poisons derived from the lead industries. She said women were more susceptible to lead poisoning, discussed effects of lead poisoning on offspring, and cited evidence that women who worked in lead trades were likely to be sterile, or incapable of carrying a child to term or of bearing a healthy child.

In 1935, when Hamilton became professor emeritus, she moved to Hadlyme, Connecticut. During her retirement from Harvard, she remained in touch with the field of occupational health. She was medical consultant to future U.S. Secretary of Labor Frances Perkins, who was then industrial commissioner in New York State. She studied carbon disulphide poisoning in the rayon industry, continued to present papers, and revised *Industrial Toxicology*. Hamilton died in Hadlyme in the same year the Occupational Safety and Health Administration came into existence.

The career of this remarkable woman spanned almost fifty years. Her professional and social reform work began in the Progressive Era and continued through World War I, the New Deal, World War II, and the Fair Deal. As the field of occupational health expanded and became more complex, she changed from a pioneer investigator to a consultant, teacher, troubleshooter, and codifier. In the absence of any governmental regulatory authority, she took upon herself the responsibility to make industry safer.

Hamilton described herself as a pioneer in the unexplored field of occupational medicine. In that field she did much to bring about change and alert others to the poor and deteriorating occupational health status of American workers. She made valuable contributions as a teacher and investigator into the extent of industrial disease in the United States. Very much a part of the humanitarian sector of the progressive movement, Hamilton implemented change in the health status of American workers.

• Hamilton's papers, including letters, are at the Arthur and Elizabeth Schlesinger Library on the History of Women in America, Radcliffe College, Cambridge, Mass. Her scientific publications include *Industrial Poisons in the United States* (1925) and *Industrial Toxicology*, with Harriet Hardy (2d ed., 1949). Hamilton wrote a number of bulletins for the U.S. Bureau of Labor (after 1913, U.S. Department of Labor, Bureau of Labor Statistics), notably *Lead Poisoning In the Smelting and Refining of Lead* (1914), *Lead Poisoning In Potteries, Tile Workers and Porcelain Enameled Sanitary Ware Factories* (1912), *Industrial Poisons Used or Produced In The Manufacture of Explosives* (1917), *Hygiene of the Painters' Trade* (1913), *Hygiene of the Printing Trade* (1917), *Effect of the Air Hammer on the Hands of Stonecutters* (1918), *Women In the Lead Industries* (1919), *Industrial Poisoning in Making Coal-Tar Dyes and Dye Intermediates* (1921), and *Carbon Monoxide Poisoning* (1922). Hamilton also published in bulletins of the Women's Bureau, U.S. Department of Labor, and in the U.S. Department of Labor, Division of Labor Standards in the 1930s and 1940s. She published articles in the *Journal of Industrial Hygiene* in 1924, 1927, 1928, and 1929.

The best biography is Barbara Sicherman, *Alice Hamilton: A Life In Letters* (1984). There are a number of published articles about Hamilton in a variety of journals including: *The New England Journal of Medicine* (1976), *Professional Safety* (1990), and *Job Safety and Health* (1977). Two doctoral dissertations about Hamilton are Angela Nugent Young, "Interpreting the Dangerous Trades: Workers' Health in America and the Career of Alice Hamilton 1910–1935" (Ph.D. diss., Brown Univ., 1982); and Wilma Ruth Slaight, "Alice Hamilton: First Lady of Industrial Medicine" (Ph.D. diss., Case Western Reserve Univ., 1974). An obituary is in the *New York Times*, 23 Sept. 1970.

JACQUELINE KARNELL CORN

HAMILTON, Andrew (?–26 Apr. 1703), merchant, proprietary governor, and organizer of the first intercolonial postal service in English North America, was born in Scotland. Nothing is known of his parents or early life. Hamilton first appears on the pages of history in 1683 as an Edinburgh merchant involved in the recruitment of settlers for the English and Scottish investors who had recently acquired the proprietorship of East Jersey. Hamilton strongly supported the proprietary effort to create an enclave of Scottish settlement in East Jersey that would be made up of large estates controlled by wealthy landholders and worked by indentured servants and tenant farmers. In 1683 Hamilton acquired a one-twentieth proprietary share of East Jersey and dispatched ten indentured servants to work what was to become his 6,000-acre estate in the colony. Hamilton's services in Scotland to the proprietors led a number of them in 1686 to appoint him as an agent to investigate the conduct of their business affairs in America.

The appointment launched Hamilton's career as the foremost defender of proprietary authority in the Jerseys during the twilight years of the proprietary regime. Arriving in America with his family in 1686, Hamilton quickly rose to a position of commanding influence in East Jersey affairs. He became a member of the East Jersey Council and the East Jersey Board of Proprietors, and in March 1687 he succeeded Lord Neil Campbell as deputy governor of East Jersey, thus beginning the first of three terms of proprietary gubernatorial service in America during the next fifteen years. Hamilton proved to be an adroit defender of the political authority and landed prerogatives of the East Jersey proprietors. But his first administration was overshadowed by James II's challenge to chartered and proprietary colonies, which led to the incorporation of East Jersey and West Jersey into the Dominion of New England in August 1688, terminating Hamilton's first gubernatorial term.

The collapse of the Dominion of New England and the resumption of governing rights by the East Jersey and West Jersey proprietors in the wake of the Glorious Revolution led to the second phase of Hamilton's American career. In April 1692, having returned to England two years before, he became proprietary governor of East Jersey and West Jersey as well as deputy to Master of the Mint Thomas Neale, who had recently received a patent from William and Mary authorizing him to establish a postal system in the mainland colonies from Virginia northward. Hamilton confronted the challenge of reestablishing proprietary government in the face of opposition from imperial administrators still anxious to royalize all chartered and proprietary colonies, New York officials eager to reacquire jurisdiction over the Jerseys, and local settlers hostile to proprietary rule.

Hamilton enjoyed mixed success during his second term of gubernatorial service in America. He led the way in reestablishing the basic institutions of proprietary government in East Jersey and West Jersey, but he failed to overcome the underlying sources of popular discontent with the proprietary regime, especially in the former colony. Hamilton summoned all of his political skills to persuade the East Jersey Assembly to contribute men and money to the defense of strategically vital New York during King William's War. But he failed to convince it to approve his proposals for obtaining long-term financial support for the proprietary government or for settling a long-standing dispute between the proprietors and settlers over the payment of quitrents. Moreover, as chief judge of the Court of Common Right and Chancery, he took part in highly unpopular judicial decisions affirming strongly contested proprietary land and quitrent claims. In contrast, by aligning himself with the dominant Quaker faction in West Jersey and allowing it to contribute indirectly to the defense of New York, Hamilton there enjoyed a highly effective administration.

In the midst of governing the Jerseys Hamilton helped to strengthen the bonds of empire by organizing the first intercolonial postal system in English North America. In his capacity as Thomas Neale's deputy, Hamilton prevailed on New Hampshire, Massachusetts, Connecticut, New York, Pennsylvania, and Virginia to pass legislation fixing uniform rates for intercolonial service and establishing post officers and riders for the regular delivery of mail. Though the rates proved to be too low, producing a deficit of £2,360 in 1697, for example, the system Hamilton established generally served the colonies well until it was incorporated into the British postal service in 1707.

The second phase of Hamilton's gubernatorial career came to an unexpected end in April 1698 owing to a misinterpretation of the Act of Trade passed by Parliament in 1696. Erroneously assuming that this measure forbade Scots to hold public office in the colonies, the East Jersey and West Jersey proprietors replaced Hamilton as governor with Jeremiah Basse. But because he lacked the royal approval required of colonial governors under the 1696 act, Basse immediately encountered widespread opposition to his authority in both parts of the Jerseys, and the imperial administration decided to challenge the proprietors' right to govern these colonies.

The proprietors appointed Hamilton to succeed Basse in the hope that he would restore order in East Jersey and West Jersey while they arranged a surrender of their governing rights to the Crown in return for confirmation of their landed prerogatives. Arriving back in America in December 1699 without the requisite royal approval, Hamilton spent the next two and one-half years fending off sometimes violent challenges to his authority from opponents of proprietary rule in East Jersey and West Jersey. While the proprietors in London negotiated with the imperial administration

in London about relinquishing their rights to govern these colonies, popular violence in East Jersey rose to such heights that in March 1701 Hamilton was attacked by a mob and temporarily incarcerated while presiding over the trial of a suspected pirate. Although the majority of proprietors sought to make Hamilton's appointment as royal governor a condition of surrender, a minority opposed him. After New Jersey was finally royalized in April 1702 the office went instead to Edward Hyde, Lord Cornbury, the royal governor of New York as well. From then until his death Hamilton served solely as deputy proprietary governor of Pennsylvania, an office to which William Penn had appointed him in November 1701. He enjoyed a largely uneventful administration.

A capable administrator and an upright man, Hamilton ably defended proprietary authority in the Jerseys until it was undermined by the combined forces of imperial centralization and popular discontent. Little is known of his private life other than that he was married three times—the second time to the daughter of Governor Thomas Rudyard of East Jersey—and that he had a son by his first marriage, John Hamilton, who enjoyed a distinguished career in his own right as royal postmaster general in America and as a New Jersey councillor. At the time of his death Hamilton appears to have been an Anglican.

• The only substantial corpus of Hamilton letters is in the William Penn Papers in the Historical Society of Pennsylvania. His career in New Jersey is amply covered in William A. Whitehead et al., eds., *Archives of the State of New Jersey* (43 vols., 1880–1949), vols. 1–2, 14. See also John E. Pomfret, *The Province of West New Jersey, 1609–1702* (1956); Pomfret, *The Province of East New Jersey, 1609–1702* (1962); Frederick R. Black, "The Last Lords Proprietors of West Jersey: The West Jersey Society, 1692–1702" (Ph.D. diss., Rutgers Univ., 1964); and Wesley E. Rich, *History of the U.S. Post Office to the Year 1829* (1924).

EUGENE R. SHERIDAN

HAMILTON, Andrew (c. 1676–4 Aug. 1741), colonial lawyer and political figure, was probably born in Scotland and educated at St. Andrews University. But nothing has been documented conclusively about his origins and early life before coming to the colonies. He arrived in Virginia about 1697, settling in Accomac County, where for a time he kept a classical school while preparing himself for the practice of law. Since he did not begin to practice until three years after his arrival, it seems unlikely that he arrived as a trained lawyer. In any case, his practice flourished from the beginning, and he was soon one of the most active attorneys in the county. In 1706 he married Anne Brown Preeson; they had three children. Two years later they moved to Kent County, Maryland, where Hamilton's growing practice brought him as far north as Philadelphia. On one of his visits to Philadelphia he met James Logan, William Penn's proprietary agent, and he thereafter began handling legal affairs for the Penn family. In 1713 the Penn connection took Hamilton to England, where he enhanced his professional standing by gaining admission to Gray's Inn and becoming a member of the English bar. After his return from England he served briefly in the Maryland Assembly before moving permanently to Philadelphia sometime in late 1715 or early 1716.

The move to Philadelphia marks the beginning of Hamilton's rise to professional and political prominence. In 1717 he was appointed attorney general of Pennsylvania, and in 1720 he became a member of the provincial council, a position he accepted only on condition that it should not interfere with his law practice. Hamilton spent 1724 and 1725 in England on business for the proprietors, and he played an important role in the litigation and negotiations that led eventually to the settlement of the boundary dispute with Maryland. After returning to Philadelphia in 1726, he became increasingly active in public affairs. In June 1727 he was appointed master of the rolls, recorder of Philadelphia, and prothonotary of the supreme court. In October of the same year he was elected to represent Bucks County in the assembly. Two years later he was elected Speaker of the assembly, an office he held until his retirement in 1739 except for the year 1733, when he was not a member.

Hamilton's independence and integrity won him the confidence of all factions in the assembly. On one occasion at least he was elected to the Speakership unanimously. Most of the measures passed during his Speakership dealt with fiscal and administrative matters, with one notable exception. In 1730 the assembly passed a law for the relief of insolvent debtors, a sensible and progressive measure that became a model for similar legislation in other colonies. Prior to 1729 the assembly had no regular meeting place, and Hamilton played a leading role in providing it with its own building. He not only purchased the land but designed and personally supervised the construction of the building later known as Independence Hall.

Hamilton's greatest professional achievement was his brilliant defense in 1735 of John Peter Zenger, publisher of the *New York Weekly Journal*, against charges of seditious libel brought by the administration of New York governor William Cosby. When Zenger's attorneys, James Alexander and William Smith, were disbarred for challenging the authority of Chief Justice James De Lancey to preside at the trial, secret arrangements were made to bring Hamilton into the case. He was by then the most famous attorney in the colonies, and his unexpected appearance on behalf of Zenger stunned the prosecution. Hamilton immediately took the offensive and turned the tables on Zenger's accusers. He admitted that Zenger had published the articles in question but contended that they were true and therefore not libelous. This, as Hamilton surely knew, was not the law, because in cases of seditious libel the issue was not truth or falsity but whether the articles undermined respect for government. He also urged the jury to bring in a general verdict of acquittal that left nothing for the judges to decide. This was also contrary to law, because the only function of the jury in such cases was to determine who had published the articles; the judges would then decide, as a matter of law, whether the articles were libelous. Since the judges were controlled by Governor Cosby, at whose pleasure they served, leaving the legal issue to them would have meant certain conviction for Zenger. Finding the law and the court stacked against him, Hamilton boldly argued for jury nullification of the law. No one should be punished for publishing the truth, he declared, and keeping the press free to publish the truth was an essential safeguard of free government. Although instructed by Chief Justice De Lancey to ignore such arguments as improper and contrary to law, the jury ignored De Lancey instead and brought in a verdict of not guilty. The verdict was widely hailed in New York and other colonies as a victory for free speech and political liberty. An English commentator on the case noted approvingly that, while Hamilton's position might not be the law, "It is better than law, it ought to be law, and will always be law whenever justice prevails."

Hamilton returned to Philadelphia in triumph after Zenger's acquittal. In 1737 he was appointed judge of the vice admiralty court, the last of his many public offices. Hamilton's wife had died the year before, and his own failing health forced his resignation from the assembly in 1739. He died two years later in Philadelphia. One of his sons, James Hamilton, became deputy governor and twice acting governor of Pennsylvania.

The loss of court records makes an objective analysis of Hamilton's legal career impossible, but to his contemporaries he was a towering eminence, the most formidable trial attorney of his time. His defense of Zenger did not change the law of seditious libel or free the colonial press from the threat of prosecution, but it did have a powerful effect on the political consciousness of Americans. Years later, Gouverneur Morris hailed the outcome as "the germ of American freedom, the morning star of that liberty which subsequently revolutionized America."

• The most complete accounts of Hamilton's life are Burton A. Konkle, *The Life of Andrew Hamilton, 1676–1741* (1941; repr. 1972), a useful but flawed biography; William H. Loyd, Jr., "Andrew Hamilton," in *Great American Lawyers*, ed. William D. Lewis (8 vols., 1907–1909); and Joshua F. Fisher, "Andrew Hamilton, Esq. of Pennsylvania," *Pennsylvania Magazine of History and Biography* 16 (1892): 1–27. The best source for information on Hamilton's early career is Foster C. Nix, "Andrew Hamilton's Early Years in the American Colonies," *William and Mary Quarterly*, 3d ser., 21 (1964): 390–407. For Hamilton's role in the Zenger case, see Peleg W. Chandler, *American Criminal Trials* (2 vols., 1841–1844); William Smith, *History of the Late Province of New York* (2 vols., 1830); and Richard B. Morris, *Fair Trial* (1952). Zenger's own account of the trial is reproduced in Livingston Rutherfurd, *John Peter Zenger: His Press, His Trial and a Bibliography of Zenger Imprints* (1904). The relation of the case to freedom of speech in America is treated in Livingston R. Schuyler, *The Liberty of the Press in the American Colonies before the Revolutionary War* (1905); Leonard W. Levy, *Emer-*

gence of a Free Press (1985); and Julius J. Marke, "Peter Zenger's Trial and Freedom of the Press," *New York University Law Center Bulletin* 10 (Summer 1961): 4–8.

EDGAR J. McMANUS

HAMILTON, Andrew Jackson (28 Jan. 1815–11 Apr. 1875), politician and provisional governor of Texas, was born in Madison County, Alabama, the son of James Hamilton, a planter, and Abagail Bayless. He was educated in the local public schools, studied law, and was admitted to the bar in 1841. He married Mary Jane Bowen in 1843. The couple had seven children, one of whom was adopted.

In 1846 the Hamiltons moved to a farm at La Grange, Texas. Hamilton practiced law in the area and was active in the Democratic party. Recognized widely as an excellent stump speaker, in 1850 Hamilton was appointed acting attorney general of the state and moved to Austin. He was elected without opposition as state representative from Travis County in 1851.

Hamilton proved to be a political maverick. In 1855 he broke with his party to join the Know Nothings, then later rejoined the Democrats to help defeat them. He split with the Democrats again in 1858 over local issues and in 1859 ran for Congress and won as an Independent Democrat opposed to the prosecession stance of party regulars. In 1860 and 1861 he continued to oppose secession and ran for the state senate on that platform in March 1861; he was elected despite his Unionist position.

Fearing for his life because of his unpopular political stance, he fled from Texas in 1862. In the North he became a popular speaker, recognized for his support of the policies of the Lincoln administration and his criticism of secession, calling it a conspiracy of the slave-owning oligarchy. He urged an invasion of Texas, and in the autumn of 1862 he received a commission as brigadier general of volunteers in the Union army. President Lincoln also appointed him military governor of Texas, with authorization to reestablish loyal government in the state. In December 1863, following the occupation of parts of southern Texas by Union forces under General Nathaniel P. Banks, Hamilton carried out the president's design but had to withdraw from the area when Banks pulled out most of his troops in May 1864. Hamilton remained in New Orleans until the end of the war.

In June 1865 President Andrew Johnson appointed Hamilton provisional governor of Texas. Hamilton believed that the new government should be made up of prewar Unionists, but in the state constitutional convention of 1866 he discovered that the war had created divisions among Unionists that could not be reconciled. He left the state for Washington, D.C., following the convention's adjournment, convinced that secessionists had returned to power. There he lobbied against readmission of the state under its new government. During this period he was active in the Southern Loyalists Association, which opposed the Reconstruction policies of President Johnson, and he aligned himself with the national Republican party.

Hamilton returned to Texas in the autumn of 1867, following the inauguration of Congressional Reconstruction and the appointment of Elisha M. Pease as governor. He was appointed associate justice of the state supreme court by General Joseph J. Reynolds, and in 1868 he was elected to the state constitutional convention as a Republican. At the convention he led what became known as the Conservative Republican faction against the Radical Republicans. He blocked efforts by the Radicals to divide Texas into three states, disfranchise former Confederates, and expand black rights. In 1869 he ran for governor as a Conservative Republican against Edmund J. Davis, the Radical candidate. After being narrowly defeated by Davis, Hamilton promoted and lobbied for railroad interests. In 1873 he engaged in his last major public role as an attorney in the case of *Ex parte Rodriguez*, arguing that the state election of 1873 was unconstitutional. Despite a favorable decision in the Texas Supreme Court, this legal action failed to prevent the Democratic party from taking control of the state government.

Following the Democratic resurgence, Hamilton retired to "Fair Oaks," his farm near Austin, where he died.

• A few of Hamilton's letters are in the Andrew J. Hamilton Papers at the Barker Texas History Center, University of Texas at Austin, and in the Governors' Papers, Texas State Archives. John L. Waller, *Colossal Hamilton of Texas: A Biography of Andrew Jackson Hamilton, Militant Unionist and Reconstruction Governor* (1968), is a full-length study of Hamilton's life. For his Reconstruction political career, see Carl H. Moneyhon, *Republicanism in Reconstruction Texas* (1980).

CARL H. MONEYHON

HAMILTON, Billy (16 Feb. 1866–15 Dec. 1940), baseball player and manager, was born William Robert Hamilton in Newark, New Jersey, the son of Samuel Hamilton, a cotton mill worker, and Mary McCutchin. He grew up in Clinton, Massachusetts, where he worked with his father in the mill. Though it is reputed that he signed his first contract with Waterbury, Connecticut, of the Eastern League in 1886, his name never appeared in a box score. Hamilton played his first three seasons in the New England League, batting .380 for Lawrence, Massachusetts, in 1886 and for Salem, Massachusetts, the following season. The 5'6½", 165-pound outfielder was hitting .352 in 61 games for Worcester, Massachusetts, in 1888 when he was sold to Kansas City of the American Association. Hamilton finished the 1888 season with Kansas City, playing in 35 games and compiling a .264 batting mark, his only sub .300 season until his final season in the major leagues.

Hamilton, who both batted and threw left-handed, jumped to the National League in 1890, signing with Harry Wright's Philadelphia club. From 1890 through 1895 he starred in one of the most outstanding outfields in baseball history, being teamed with Ed Delahanty and Sam Thompson. Hamilton, who was moved to center field in 1893, had an acrobatic instinct for catching flies off-balance, matching his uncanny ability to anticipate where the ball would be hit.

In an era when stolen bases occurred more frequently than home runs, no player stole more than "Sliding Billy" Hamilton, who perfected the head-first slide. Hamilton, who had been a 10.75 sprinter in high school, stole his first base in 1888 at the expense of Baltimore catcher Chris Fulmer. The next season he swiped 117 bases while batting .301. Among his teammates on the Phillies in 1890 was future evangelist Billy Sunday, who led the league in stolen bases with Pittsburgh before being traded to Philadelphia. By August Hamilton had overtaken Sunday, posting 102 steals for the year. By 1896 he had stolen 100 bases in a season three times and 90 bases two more times.

Hamilton led the league in hitting in 1891 with a .340 average. Following a season shortened in 1893 because of typhoid fever, he won his second batting title with a .380 mark. His best season was 1894, when his .399 average ranked fifth best in the league behind Hugh Duffy's record .438 and three of his Philadelphia teammates. Hamilton played in 131 of the team's 132 games, scoring a record 196 times on 223 hits, including a 36-game hitting streak. He amassed 126 walks for an on-base average of .523 and stole 99 bases, including seven in one game, tying Chicago's George Gore's 1881 record.

In an unpopular trade, after the 1895 season the Phillies sent Hamilton to Boston for third baseman Billy Nash, who subsequently played poorly in Philadelphia. Hamilton played with the Boston Beaneaters for the rest of his big league career. In 1896 he joined Duffy and Jimmy Bannon in the Boston outfield. Hamilton was an instant success, stealing a club-record 83 bases and batting a team-leading .365. In 1897 he scored 152 runs to lead the league for his fourth and last time, batting .343. The Beaneaters won the 1897 pennant by two games in a fierce struggle with Ned Hanlon's Baltimore Orioles, who defeated the Beaneaters in the postseason Temple Cup Series. Hamilton had been benched for the fifth and final game because of an error he had made in the previous game.

Knee injuries limited Hamilton's effectiveness the next two seasons. His stolen bases dropped to just 19 in 84 games in 1899. After scoring more than 100 runs for the eleventh time in his career in 1900, Hamilton rejected an offer in 1901 to play for the Boston Pilgrims, a charter member of the upstart American League, preferring to finish his major league career with the Beaneaters.

After his release from the major leagues, Hamilton returned to the New England League, where he played the outfield and managed the Haverhill, Massachusetts, team from 1902 through 1904. He moved to Harrisburg, Pennsylvania, in the outlaw Tri-State League in 1905 and 1906, returned to Haverhill from 1906 to 1908, and played for Lynn, Massachusetts, in 1909 and 1910. His .412 average for Haverhill led all of organized baseball in 1904. Hamilton scouted for Boston in the National League from 1911 to 1912 and

managed Fall River in the New England League in 1913. He managed with Springfield, Massachusetts, of the Eastern League in 1914, and in 1916 he served as manager and part owner in Worcester, his last affiliation with baseball.

Hamilton had married Rebecca Jane Carr in 1888, and they had four daughters. Unlike many players of his era, Hamilton invested his earnings wisely and owned a considerable amount of property, which allowed him to live comfortably in Clinton, Massachusetts, until his death in Worcester.

Hamilton's outstanding 14-season major league statistics include 2,163 hits in 1,593 games, 1,692 runs, 915 stolen bases with 779 in the National League (a record not surpassed until the St. Louis Cardinals' Lou Brock in 1979), and 1,187 walks. Hamilton proved himself the bane of league outfielders, being especially adept at taking the extra base on a hit to the outfield gaps. He was the league's batting leader twice, led in runs scored four times, led five times in walks, and led seven times in stolen bases. His on-base average of .455 ranks second only to John McGraw among nineteenth-century players.

Along with New York outfielder George Gore and Philadelphia first baseman and outfielder Harry Stovey, Hamilton was one of just three nineteenth-century major league players who amassed more runs scored than games played. He compiled a .344 career batting average, one of the best in baseball history. The game's first outstanding lead-off hitter, "Good Eye Billy" combined raw speed and daring base running. Many historians rank him as the best player of the 1890s.

Hamilton was inducted into the Baseball Hall of Fame at Cooperstown, New York, in 1961. Many of his contemporaries thought he should have made it much sooner. Jesse Burkett, another nineteenth-century great, who was inducted into the Hall of Fame before his own death, said of Hamilton in 1946, "Why didn't they pick Hamilton, too?"

• Archival information can be found in the William Hamilton File, National Baseball Hall of Fame Library, Cooperstown, N.Y. Other information on Hamilton is found in Martin Appel and Burt Goldblatt, *Baseball's Best: The Hall of Fame Gallery* (1977); Gene Karst and Martin Jones, Jr., *Who's Who in Professional Baseball* (1973); Paul McFarlane, ed., *TSN Daguerreotypes of Great Stars of Baseball* (1981); Lowell Reidenbaugh, *Cooperstown: Where Baseball's Legends Live Forever* (1983); John Thorn and Pete Palmer, *The Hidden Game of Baseball* (1984); and Mike Shatzkin, ed., *The Ball Players* (1990). Newspaper articles include Roy Mumpton, "Sports Lens," *Worcester Telegram*, 21 Dec. 1960; and *Sporting News*, 25 Jan. 1961. Obituaries are in the *Worcester Telegram*, 16 Dec. 1940, and *Sporting News*, 26 Dec. 1940.

WILLIAM A. BORST

HAMILTON, Clayton (14 Nov. 1881–17 Sept. 1946), educator and drama critic, was born in Brooklyn, New York, the son of George Alexander Hamilton, a merchant, and Susan Amelia Corey. Christened Clayton Meeker Hamilton, he deleted his middle name before he reached age twenty-one. His interest in a life of letters began during his youth. He received a B.A. from the Polytechnic Institute of Brooklyn in 1900 and an M.A. from Columbia University in 1901. Hamilton married Gladys Coates in 1913; they had two children.

Hamilton began a teaching career immediately after his graduate schooling. Between 1901 and 1904 he tutored English at Barnard and Columbia, and in 1903 he began teaching a course in current theater at Columbia's extension school, one of the first such courses in the United States. He taught at Columbia until 1923. He also held appointments at a number of other schools, including the Brooklyn Institute of Arts and Sciences (1913–1919), Dartmouth College (1916–1917 summers), Classical School for Girls (1900–1920), Gardner School (1904–1920), Finch School (1906–1908), Miss Spence's School (1908–1920), and the Jacobi School (1918–1919). He embarked on lengthy lecture tours of the United States in 1924–1926 and 1932–1933. In 1932 Hamilton received the Columbia Medal for Service, and in 1936 he was appointed honorary fellow in drama at Union College in Schenectady, New York.

Hamilton was also active as a drama critic. He held appointments at the *Forum* (dramatic critic, 1907), the *Bookman* (dramatic editor, 1910–1918), *Everybody's Magazine* (dramatic editor, 1911–1913), and *Vogue* (dramatic editor, 1912–1920). His views are best captured in his three-book series on the theory and writing of plays: *The Theory of the Theatre* (1910), *Studies in Stagecraft* (1914), and *Problems of the Playwright* (1917). Other critics at the time tended to dwell on the spectacle of individual performances, costumes, and other theatrical effects. Hamilton, by contrast, engaged in criticism at a more abstract level, examining the psychology of audiences and especially technical problems about play structure. In particular, he urged playwrights to devote more attention to the "strategy" of drama and to the "grandeur of the general conception" of their work; too many, he complained, displayed great cleverness in the minor "tactics" of the stage but "could not draw a leading character consistently throughout a logical success of four acts."

Hamilton also published critical commentaries in book form that provide fascinating accounts of important American dramatists and theatrical events of the day. *Seen on the Stage* (1920) and *Conversations on Contemporary Drama* (1924) both include sections on Hamilton's contact with and influence on Eugene O'Neill. If his account in *Seen on the Stage* is to be believed, it was Hamilton who counseled a young O'Neill in his early playwriting attempts and advised him to write about the sea, something done successfully in novels and short stories but not drama. Of course, the sea plays were O'Neill's entrée into drama. Hamilton also served as editor for collections of plays, including *The Social Plays of Arthur Wing Pinero* (1919) and *Plays by Richard Brinsley Sheridan* (1926).

Like many critics before and during his time, Hamilton was a playwright himself. His works include *A Night at the Inn* (1906); *The Love That Blinds*, with Grace Isabel Colborn (1906); *Heart of Punchinello* (1906); *It'll All Come Out in the Wash*, with Gilbert Emery (1906); *The Stranger at the Inn* (1913); *The Big Idea*, with A. E. Thomas (1914); *The Morning Star*, with Bernard Voight (1915); *Thirty Days*, with A. E. Thomas (1916); *The Better Understanding*, with A. E. Thomas (1917); and *Friend Indeed*, with Bernard Voight (1926). Hamilton enjoyed mixed success with his plays. Brooks Atkinson was intrigued with the *The Big Idea*, a play he found charming and novel, but rated *Friend Indeed* amateurish and slight.

Hamilton's accomplishments led to his membership in the National Institute of Arts and Letters in 1912. The same year, he was appointed to the three-member Pulitzer Prize Committee on drama. He served in that capacity a total of sixteen times between 1912 and 1934; as chairman in the latter year, he became embroiled in his only public controversy. Along with playwright Austin Strong and Walter Prichard Eaton, a drama professor at Yale, Hamilton selected Maxwell Anderson's *Mary of Scotland* as the recipient for 1934. The advisory board of the Columbia University School of Journalism, however, overruled the jury and awarded the prize to Sidney Kingsley's *Men in White*. The controversy over the award became public, and all three jurors refused to serve the following year. Hamilton died in New York.

Hamilton's contribution was not as a creative artist but as a theorist and critic, especially in drama. He broadened access to theater classes and championed drama as a legitimate field of study at a time when serious attempts to teach playwriting were being advanced by respected institutions such as Harvard (with George Pierce Baker's celebrated course) and Columbia (where Brander Matthews taught and was a mentor to Hamilton). Without these early attempts, drama might not have become a valid part of higher education until after World War II, when the discipline enjoyed further expansion.

• A collection of Hamilton's papers is at the New York Public Library. In addition to the works cited in the text, he was also author of *On the Trail of Stevenson* (1915), *Wanderings* (1925), and *So You're Writing a Play* (1935). His book *Materials and Methods of Fiction* (1908) appeared in revised form as *A Manual of the Art of Fiction* (1918) and *The Art of Fiction* (1939). *The Theory of the Theatre and Other Principles of Dramatic Criticism* (1939) reprints, with revisions, much of his three-volume series on drama, plus *Seen on the Stage*. A useful source on Hamilton's drama criticism is Frederick J. Hunter, "The Technical Criticism of Clayton Hamilton," *Educational Theatre Journal* 7 (1955): 285–93. An obituary is in the *New York Times*, 18 Sept. 1946.

KENT NEELY

HAMILTON, Earl Jefferson (17 May 1899–7 May 1989), economic historian, editor, and educator, was born in Houlka, Mississippi, the son of Joseph William Hamilton and Frances Regina Anne Williams. After graduating from Mississippi State University in 1920 with honors, Hamilton studied at the University of Texas, where he received an M.A. in 1924. He then went to Harvard University, where he completed both an A.M. (1926) and a Ph.D. (1929) in economics. In 1923 he married Gladys Olive Dallas; they had one child.

Hamilton became an assistant professor at Duke University in the fall of 1927. He spent the next twenty years studying the impact of treasure from the Americas on prices, wages, and money in Spain, publishing *American Treasure and the Price Revolution in Spain, 1501–1650* (1934), *Money, Prices and Wages in Valencia, Aragon and Navarre, 1351–1500* (1936), and *War and Prices in Spain, 1651–1800* (1947). A one-volume Spanish version of these studies, titled *El Florecimiento del Capitalismo y Otros Ensayos*, appeared in 1948.

One of the earliest quantitative studies in economic history, Hamilton's work showed economists how price data could be assembled from archival records; it also showed historians how the tools of economic analysis could be used to reconstruct that data in order to highlight certain key relationships. His conclusion was that the price level in Spain in the sixteenth century rose more than fourfold because of the importation of precious metals from the Americas (previous studies had estimated price increases of anywhere from twofold to tenfold). His study also showed that the importation of more silver than gold changed the bimetallic ratio of gold and silver, thereby making silver the monetary standard in most of western Europe.

In 1944 Hamilton accepted an appointment at Northwestern University, where he taught for three years. Then in 1947 he went to the University of Chicago, remaining there until 1967. He edited Chicago's *Journal of Political Economy* from 1948 to 1954 and contributed to its publication, *Landmarks in Political Economy* (1962). He served as president of the Economic History Association for the year 1951–1952. In anticipation of his retirement from the University of Chicago, he was appointed distinguished professor of economic history at the State University of New York at Binghamton in 1966, a position he held until 1969.

While the importance of Hamilton's quantitative work is widely acknowledged, the theoretical argument he developed both in the three-volume series and elsewhere regarding the relationship of prices and wages has been criticized. The wage-lag hypothesis he used to explain the relationship between price inflation and wage changes specified that changes in wages lagged behind changes in price levels because the Spanish labor markets exhibited inertia. For him, the wage lag accentuated disruptions to the economy's equilibrium process, thereby explaining the extraordinary profits of the commercial elite during the inflationary period of the price revolution and the business losses suffered during periods when price levels fell faster than wages. Hamilton's wage-lag hypothesis was criticized by Reuben A. Kessel and Armen A. Alchian, who argued in 1960 that Hamilton did not pay proper attention to the role of real forces in the price-wage relationship. Once the role of real forces is acknowledged, Hamilton's own time series show that

wages did not lag behind inflation and there was no significant change in real wages during the inflationary period. Kessell and Alchian's critique also gained prominence because it was indirectly a criticism of Keynesian economics. In volume two of *A Treatise on Money* (1930) John Maynard Keynes used Hamilton's price-wage lag as a historical example of his monetary theory.

Although the Kessel-Alchian critique of his analysis of prices and wages sidetracked Hamilton's research program, he was able to return to the quantitative analysis of prices and wages in Europe later in his career. This time his focus was the economic impact of the French introduction of paper money backed only by stock in John Law's Compagnie des Indes between 1716 and 1720. When expectations of profits from the Americas decreased in 1720 and the stock price fell, the resulting economic collaspe (the "Mississippi Bubble") caused a rapid escalation of prices in France. Hamilton was able to provide several measures of the price inflation and to show that wage increases lagged behind prices, creating a decrease in real wages of as much as 25 percent. He also contributed an essay on the impact of the Americas on Europe to *First Images of America: The Impact of the New World on the Old*, edited by Fredi Chiappelli (1976). In his last years he began research related to the inflationary impact of war. Hamilton died in Oak Ridge, Tennessee.

• Hamilton's papers and a significant portion of his personal correspondence are in the Special Collections Library of Duke University. His library of books on economic history is in Rare Books, Special Collections, University of Chicago Library. Alongside his three-volume series, Hamilton's "Profit Inflation and the Industrial Revolution, 1751–1800," *Quarterly Journal of Economics* 56 (Feb. 1942): 256–73, and "Prices as a Factor in Business Growth," *Journal of Economic History* 12 (Fall 1952): 325–49, discuss his wage-lag hypothesis. The most important criticism of that hypothesis is found in R A. Kessel and A. A. Alchian, "The Meaning and Validity of the Inflation-Induced Lag of Wages Behind Prices," *American Economic Review* 50 (Mar. 1960): 43–66. Hamilton's essays on John Law's banking system are "Prices and Wages at Paris under John Law's System," and "The Political Economy of France at the Time of John Law," *History of Political Economy* 1 (Spring 1969): 123–49. The early results of his study of the inflationary impact of war were published in "The Role of War in Modern Inflation," *Journal of Economic History* 37 (Mar. 1977): 13–19.

ROSS B. EMMETT

HAMILTON, Edith (12 Aug. 1867–31 May 1963), author, educator, and classicist, was born in Dresden, Germany, the daughter of Montgomery Hamilton and Gertrude Pond. Her father's wealthy and cultured family, prominent citizens of Fort Wayne, Indiana, had sent him to study in Europe in 1863 after he left Princeton University and served briefly in the Union army. There Montgomery Hamilton met and married Gertrude Pond, daughter of a New York sugar importer and Confederate sympathizer who had relocated his family abroad during the Civil War.

Edith Hamilton grew up on the Hamilton family's downtown Fort Wayne estate. She was educated at home, receiving formal instruction from her parents and tutors in Latin, Greek, French, and German and undertaking independent reading and research projects assigned by her father. Worship at the First Presbyterian Church and biblical and theological study loomed large in her girlhood. From 1884 to 1886 she attended Miss Porter's School for Young Ladies in Farmington, Connecticut, as had three Hamilton aunts and as would her younger sisters. After his wholesale grocery partnership failed during Edith's years at Farmington, Montgomery Hamilton withdrew to his library, drinking heavily and estranging himself from his wife and children. Gertrude Hamilton nurtured her daughters' ambitions and independence: all four eschewed marriage and pursued careers.

In 1891 Edith Hamilton entered Bryn Mawr College, majoring in Greek and Latin. After earning A.B. and A.M. degrees in 1894, and spending a further year at Bryn Mawr as a fellow in Latin, she was awarded the college's prestigious Mary E. Garrett European fellowship. The fellowship allowed her and her sister Alice Hamilton, the renowned industrial toxicologist and social reformer, to travel to Germany for a year of graduate study, first in Leipzig and then in Munich.

Her family's financial reverses forced Hamilton to abandon plans for a doctorate in classics. In 1896 she accepted the offer of M. Carey Thomas, president of Bryn Mawr College, to head the Bryn Mawr School, which Thomas had founded in her native Baltimore as the first all-female private secondary institution in America with an exclusively college preparatory curriculum. During Hamilton's twenty-six years as Bryn Mawr headmistress, she cultivated the social elite of Baltimore, seeking support for her efforts to establish rigorous academic standards and fund the tuition of girls from less advantaged families. The students were awed by the power of her personality and an intellectual philosophy summed up in Plato's phrase "Hard is the good." Yet she endeared herself by her sense of humor and her inspired teaching of the senior Latin class. Her differences with Thomas over conditions of employment for faculty and staff caused her to resign her post in 1922.

In 1923 she purchased and moved to a house at Sea Wall, Mt. Desert Island, Maine, with Doris Fielding Reid. A former Bryn Mawr School student twenty-eight years Edith's junior, Reid was the daughter of old Baltimore friends. The two women made a home together for the rest of Hamilton's life. Maintaining Sea Wall as a summer residence, in 1924 they took an apartment at 24 Gramercy Park in New York City, where Reid eventually joined a Wall Street investment firm. From 1923, when he was five years old, the son of Reid's brother lived with the two women and was legally adopted by Hamilton. His younger siblings came to live with the couple for extended periods.

Rosamond Gilder and Dorothea McCollester, Gramercy Park neighbors and literary staffers at the *Theatre Arts Monthly*, persuaded Hamilton to write about ancient drama and culture for their readers. Between 1927 and 1929 she published six articles and a translation of Aeschylus's *Prometheus*. The next year she published her widely acclaimed first book, *The Greek Way* (revised, expanded, and reissued in 1942 as *The Great Age of Greek Literature*). Other volumes on Greek, Roman, and biblical antiquity followed: *The Roman Way* (1932), *Prophets of Israel* (1936), *Three Greek Plays* (1937), *Mythology* (1942), *Witness to the Truth* (1948, rev. ed. 1957), *Spokesmen for God* (1949), *The Echo of Greece* (1957), and *The Ever-Present Past* (1964). With Huntington Cairns, she coedited *The Collected Dialogues of Plato* (1961).

After Hamilton moved with Reid to Washington, D.C., in 1943, her activities expanded to include radio and television broadcasts and lectures for scholarly and religious organizations. Recipient of several honorary degrees, she was elected to the National Institute of Arts and Letters in 1955 and the American Academy of Arts and Letters in 1957. That same year, at a public ceremony in the ancient theater of Herodes Atticus, preceding a performance of her translation of *Prometheus*, she was presented with the Gold Cross of the Order of Benefaction and proclaimed an honorary citizen of Athens. She was cited for distinguished service at the seventy-fifth anniversary of Bryn Mawr College in 1960 and sought out by the new Kennedy administration the next year. When she died at age ninety-five in Washington, D.C., she was hailed as "an ambassador of an ancient civilization," illumining "all that she touched upon."

The immense popularity of Hamilton's books with educated readers facilitated the development of classics courses in translation on U.S. college campuses, a phenomenon that revived the study of Greco-Roman antiquity in this country. Leading American intellectual and political figures admired her writings: Robert F. Kennedy drew lasting solace from her books after his brother's death, incorporating her translations of phrases from Greek literature into memorable speeches ("to tame the savageness of man and make gentle the life of the world," resounded in his eulogy for Martin Luther King, Jr.). But her works, although elegantly written, interpret ancient texts idiosyncratically, at times mistranslating passages or taking them out of context. In emphasizing "truths of the spirit" and the contributions of the Greeks as "the first Westerners" and lovers of freedom, she idealized the achievements of Greek culture but undervalued those of the Romans, whom she viewed as the Greeks' "spiritual inferiors" and "insensitive to human suffering." To Hamilton, the Greeks achieved a "balance in every field," between "particular and general, mind and spirit," which has not been repeated.

• Some of Edith Hamilton's papers have been deposited with the Hamilton Family Papers in the Schlesinger Library, Radcliffe College. Both the M. Carey Thomas Papers, Bryn Mawr College Archives, and the archives of the Bryn Mawr School in Baltimore contain some material on Hamilton and the Bryn Mawr School. Material on Hamilton may also be found in the W. W. Norton and Co. Papers in the Special Collections, Columbia University; the Houghton Library, Harvard University; the John Mason Brown Papers, Princeton University; and the Huntington Cairns Papers in the Library of Congress Manuscript Division. Although written with affection by Hamilton's long-time companion, the biography by Doris Fielding Reid, *Edith Hamilton: An Intimate Portrait* (1967), is selective and not always accurate. For the Hamilton family, the best sources are Alice Hamilton's autobiography, *Exploring the Dangerous Trades* (1943), and Barbara Sicherman, *Alice Hamilton: A Life in Letters* (1984). Rosamond Randall Beirne, *Let's Pick the Daisies* (1970), provides extensive information about Hamilton's years at the Bryn Mawr School. See also John Mason Brown, "Heritage of Edith Hamilton: 1867–1963," *Saturday Review*, 22 June 1963, pp. 16–17, and John White, "The Hamilton Way," *Georgia Review* 24, no. 2 (1970): 132–57, for appreciations by close friends. On Edith Hamilton's appeal to Robert F. Kennedy, see Arthur Schlesinger, Jr., *Robert Kennedy and His Times* (1978), and Harris Wofford, *Of Kennedys and Kings: Making Sense of the Sixties* (1980).

JUDITH P. HALLETT

HAMILTON, Elizabeth Schuyler (9 Aug. 1757–9 Nov. 1854), statesman's wife and charity worker, was born in Albany, New York, the second daughter of Philip Schuyler, a revolutionary war general, and Catherine van Rensselaer. Schooled at home, her early years were typical of most young women of colonial, aristocratic families. At the age of twenty-two, she met Alexander Hamilton, a dashing aide-de-camp of General George Washington, at the home of Mrs. John Cochran, her aunt. For Elizabeth it was love at first sight, a love that remained strong through the many scandals ahead. Accepted into the Schuyler family despite his illegitimate birth and lack of wealth or social standing, Alexander Hamilton held political beliefs similar to those of his future father-in-law. Both supported a strong centralized government and General Washington. Both had been soldiers as well as members of his military staff. The entire Schuyler family revered Alexander as a young political genius. As for Alexander, it is possible that he considered marrying Elizabeth for her family's money and status, for the Schuylers were one of the most influential families in the state of New York. Yet, his true love seemed evident in their courtship correspondence, which was intimate and childlike. Believing his sincerity, Elizabeth, with no formal education, became interested in military and political affairs, and Alexander even discussed Benedict Arnold's treason with her. In many of his letters Alexander also expressed his worry about his poverty and ability to provide for his future wife. The pair were finally married on 14 December, 1780; he was just shy of the age of twenty-four, and she was twenty-three.

The Hamiltons' marriage was both blessed with many children and fraught with scandal and credit problems. Elizabeth bore eight children between the years 1782 and 1802, miscarrying at least once. Ironically, her eldest son Philip, aged nineteen, was killed in a duel by an associate of Aaron Burr. After Philip's untimely death, her eldest daughter, Angelica, named after Elizabeth's sister, went insane. Six months later, Elizabeth bore her last child, also naming him Philip. Alexander adored children, both his own and Fanny Antil, a daughter of a fellow revolutionary war veteran, whom Alexander adopted. Elizabeth's frequent pregnancies often prevented her attendance at social functions at which Alexander was accompanied often by Elizabeth's eldest sister, Angelica. Both of the Hamiltons adored Angelica, but Alexander's affection appeared to exceed mere brotherly sentiment. It is unclear if this attraction actually turned into an affair. Alexander believed that his marriage vows to Elizabeth were unbreakable promises, but between 1791 and 1792 Alexander did have an affair with Maria Reynolds. Elizabeth and the children spent summers in Albany, New York, away from the disease-ridden summers of urban Philadelphia, leaving Hamilton alone. Maria claimed to be an abandoned relative of several prominent New York families, and Hamilton's pity for her plight resulted in a liaison. Probably entrapped by Reynolds's husband, James, Alexander publicly confessed the affair by publishing his personal account. Elizabeth forgave him; if she had not, his career and reputation would have been irrevocably ruined.

Despite Alexander's actual and rumored affairs, the Hamiltons' personal relationship was one of mutual respect. Elizabeth accepted his flirtatiousness. Alexander continued to solicit her advice on political and family matters, as he had early in their courtship. Before their marriage, he had trusted his wife to negotiate the purchase of a house. Throughout their married life, he often read selections of his writings to her, seeking her opinion and approval. She listened to his early drafts of Washington's "Farewell Address" and excerpts from the *Federalist Papers*. She probably copied some of the *Federalist Papers* for Alexander to distribute.

Never idyllic, the Hamiltons' marriage was hampered by incessant credit problems. Alexander resigned from military service and qualified for the bar in 1782. From 1789 to 1795, he worked for the fledgling American government as the first secretary of the treasury and as a member of President Washington's cabinet. He resigned in 1795 and returned to his New York City law practice. The Hamiltons struggled financially, never accepting assistance from General Schuyler, with the exception of food and goods from Schuyler's estate. With credit already stretched, Alexander bought fifteen acres in Harlem Heights, New York, to build his own estate, "The Grange," named after his ancestral home in Scotland.

Tragically, Elizabeth's life changed dramatically in 1804 with the deaths of both her husband and father. Aaron Burr and Alexander Hamilton had quarreled over Hamilton's alleged personal slurs against Burr's reputation and political aspirations, and Burr challenged Hamilton to a duel, which took place on 11 July 1804. Told he was just having spasms to prevent her hysterics, Elizabeth rushed to the mortally wounded Alexander. He left Elizabeth and his family virtually destitute.

Left to pay her husband's debts and raise their children (the youngest was two), Elizabeth relied on the help of friends and family. The death of her father four months after her husband's provided her with some financial relief through her inheritance of property and money. She was able to repurchase The Grange, which had been sold at public auction. She also petitioned the government for her husband's army pension that he had waived. Not granted until 1837 through a special act of Congress, her petition provided her with $30,000 and included land.

Even though Elizabeth spent her widowhood in poverty, she was active in charitable organizations. She held positions in the New York Orphan Asylum Society and founded orphanages in New York City and Washington, D.C. She was known to take homeless children into her own home. To establish her husband's political legacy and repair his reputation, she spent nearly fifty years after his death collecting and preserving his papers and letters. She corresponded with and visited the leading Federalists to collect papers and other information concerning her husband. Ironically, none of her correspondence to Alexander survived, although she did save his letters to her.

Throughout her life Elizabeth Hamilton staunchly defended her husband against his critics, maintaining his authorship of Washington's "Farewell Address" and refusing to acknowledge his responsibility in the duel and sexual scandals of his life. James Monroe had accused Alexander of financial irregularities during the Reynolds affair. Steadfast until the end, Elizabeth demanded a complete apology, which Monroe would not give, but before her death he visited Elizabeth to reconcile their differences concerning her husband's reputation. Alexander Hamilton's papers were not published until 1850–1851 by his son, John Church Hamilton, and after the U.S. government had purchased them in 1849. Elizabeth lived her final years in Washington, D.C., with her daughter Eliza Hamilton Holly. She was buried with her husband in the graveyard of Trinity Church in New York City.

• Most of the information on Elizabeth Hamilton must be gleaned from biographies written about her husband. Broadus Mitchell has written widely on Hamilton, including *Alexander Hamilton* (2 vols., 1957–1962). Allan McLane Hamilton, the grandson of Alexander and the son of Philip, the youngest child, has selected and compiled many letters and other documents written by Hamilton in *The Intimate Life of Alexander Hamilton* (1910). His narrative is one of the more comprehensive for information on Elizabeth. Other useful biographies include *Forrest McDonald, Alexander Hamilton: A Biography* (1979); Robert A. Hendrickson, *The Rise and Fall of Alexander Hamilton* (1981); Noemie Emery, *Alexander Hamilton: An Intimate Portrait* (1982); and Jacob Ernest Cooke, *Alexander Hamilton* (1982). For the later years of her life and charity work, see George W. Bethune, *Memoirs of Mrs. Joanna Bethune* (1863).

JENNY L. PRESNELL

HAMILTON, Gail. *See* Dodge, Mary Abigail.

HAMILTON, James, Jr. (8 May 1786–15 Nov. 1857), congressman and governor of South Carolina, was born near Charleston, South Carolina, the son of James Hamilton, a rice planter and formerly an aide to George Washington, and Elizabeth Lynch, whose brother Thomas Lynch had signed the Declaration of Independence. He was educated in Newport, Rhode Island, and Dedham, Massachusetts, and then read law in Charleston. Admitted to the bar in 1810, he established a practice with William Drayton. About a year later he became secretary to Governor Henry Middleton and subsequently enlisted in the infantry during the War of 1812. Promoted eventually to major, Hamilton served under General George Izard in northern and western New York. In 1813 he married Elizabeth Heyward, whose dowry included three plantations and two hundred slaves; the couple would have eleven children. After being discharged from the army in 1815, Hamilton established himself on a cotton plantation in Beaufort District, South Carolina. Always restless, he soon returned to law in partnership with James Louis Petigru. In 1819 Hamilton moved to Charleston. He continued to acquire land in South Carolina, Georgia, Alabama, and Mississippi, however, eventually owning fourteen plantations and more than four hundred slaves.

This Carolina grandee seemed so heartily to embody the mores of southern chivalry that he moved contemporaries (and some historians) to superlatives. British writer Harriet Martineau termed him "the perfect representative of the Southern gentleman" (Sibley, p. 168). Hamilton's standards of honor were so extravagant that he fought fourteen duels; it was considered to his credit that his opponents invariably ended up wounded but never dead.

Hamilton was an exemplar of another sort: his political career reflected the progress in the 1820s of many of South Carolina's leaders from nationalism to states' rights truculence. He served in the state house of representatives from 1819 to 1822 and in that period seemed to hold a fairly expansive view of federal powers and responsibilities. But as Charleston's intendant (mayor) the following year, Hamilton played an important role in scotching Denmark Vesey's slave conspiracy—a plot in part inspired by congressional debates over slavery. As slavery intruded into national politics and as protective tariffs taxed Carolina planters' dwindling profits for the benefit of building up northern manufacture, Carolinians rethought their posture toward the national government. Hamilton made explicit the connection that many of his peers were implicitly drawing between slavery and the tariff, arguing that if Congress's mandate to promote the general welfare could be interpreted to allow protection of specific industries, it might also be interpreted to allow the national government to finance the emancipation of slaves. Elected to Congress in 1822, Hamilton served until 1829, chairing the Committee on Military Affairs and supporting General Andrew Jackson's claims to the presidency. By the time Old Hickory was inaugurated in 1829, however, Hamilton had already taken his stand for nullification, the doctrine that states might abrogate federal laws they deemed unconstitutional. This stand put South Carolina on a collision course with Jackson.

Hamilton did as much as any Carolinian to turn the idea of nullification into reality. A unionist opponent concluded, "But for him it would have fallen stillborn" (Sibley, p. 167). The nullifiers were already well enough organized to have Hamilton elected governor by the legislature in 1830. Sensing that their momentum might be flagging, however, he undertook the next year to build up an infrastructure for agitation. The governor made sure that local branches of a new States Rights and Free Trade Association were formed to involve the populace in the issue, and he organized a statewide meeting that arranged for the regular production and distribution of nullification propaganda. He also mobilized support through ceremonial inspections of local militias. After Congress failed to lower the offending duties sufficiently in 1832, nullifiers won majorities in the state legislature. Hamilton had it call a state convention, over which he was elected to preside. This body passed an ordinance voiding the enforcement of the tariff within the state's boundaries and threatening secession should the federal government attempt coercion.

Hamilton's stint as governor ended as the convention closed late in 1832, but he remained in the thick of things. He became brigadier general of a state militia force of more than 25,000 men, raised to meet federal attempts forcibly to suppress nullification; he also allowed a shipment of his sugar to be seized, apparently to test the will of both parties to the dispute. The confrontation with the federal government eased early the following year with the passage of a compromise tariff that gradually reduced rates, and the consequent repeal of the nullification ordinance. Hamilton, however, remained militant, wishing to purge the state militia of unionists and to enforce an oath on state officers affirming their primary allegiance to the state. Yet when the state in 1834 seemed about to explode over the issue of a test oath, Hamilton turned conciliatory. He arranged a compromise with James L. Petigru, his former law partner and a leader of the unionist opposition, that effectively rendered the oath unobjectionable, and he worked for its acceptance among his own faction.

Hamilton served in the state senate between 1834 and 1838, but his political involvements were increasingly eclipsed by his status as one of Charleston's grandest entrepreneurs. He helped to found and directed the Bank of Charleston, established a mercantile firm, promoted several local insurance companies and southern railroads, and speculated in land. The effects of the panic of 1837 and his own recklessness, however, crushed some of his ventures, cost him the leadership of the bank, and left him deeply in debt.

Even before the panic, however, Hamilton seems to have sensed that the grass might grow greener (and the cotton thicker) west of the Sabine. He lent money to the infant Republic of Texas, interested himself in

land and banking there, and late in 1836 was offered command of its army. In 1839 Texan president Mirabeau Lamar appointed Hamilton loan commissioner. He soon sailed to Europe to secure $5 million for Texas. Over the next several years, Hamilton won Dutch recognition of Texas, negotiated several commercial treaties with Britain, and meddled in other diplomatic matters, but he could not arrange the loan. In 1842 he was dismissed by Texas's new president, Sam Houston, a Jackson protégé who had little use for nullifiers—or for men whose ambition and flamboyance rivaled his own.

For the next fifteen years Hamilton bustled among his Texas landholdings, an Alabama plantation, South Carolina, and Washington. One of his chief preoccupations was trying to secure payment of his $210,000 claim against the impecunious Texas government. In fact, the positions the earnest nullifier took on such issues as Texas annexation and the Compromise of 1850 seem largely to have been dictated by his estimation of how best to advance the prospects of repayment.

Hamilton made an attempt to claim John C. Calhoun's Senate seat on the latter's death in 1850, but questions arose over whether he could still legally be considered a South Carolinian. He settled in central Texas in the mid-1850s. He died when a ship upon which he was returning from Washington sank in the Gulf of Mexico: Hamilton, ever the gallant, had given up his life preserver to a woman and her child.

A central figure in South Carolina's experimenting with means by which the rights of a slaveholding minority could be defended *within* the Union, Hamilton drowned before the same interest took his state, and the rest of the South, *out* of the Union.

• The chief collection of Hamilton papers is at the Southern Historical Collection, University of North Carolina, Chapel Hill; the South Caroliniana Library, University of South Carolina, Columbia, has some correspondence. Documents related to Hamilton's diplomatic activities on behalf of Texas are at the Center for American History, University of Texas at Austin. See Virginia L. Glenn, "James Hamilton, Jr., of South Carolina: A Biography" (Ph.D. diss., Univ. of North Carolina at Chapel Hill, 1964). Also helpful is N. Louise Bailey et al., *Biographical Directory of the South Carolina Senate, 1776–1985* (1986). William W. Freehling has written engagingly on Hamilton; for his role in nullification, see Freehling, *Prelude to Civil War: The Nullification Controversy in South Carolina, 1816–1836* (1966). Hamilton's Texas years are well covered in Marilyn McAdams Sibley, "James Hamilton, Jr., vs. Sam Houston: Repercussions of the Nullification Controversy," *Southwestern Historical Quarterly* 89 (1985–1986): 165–80.

PATRICK G. WILLIAMS

HAMILTON, John (c. 1740–12 Dec. 1816), colonial merchant, Loyalist, and British consul, was born in Scotland. Nothing is known of his education. In 1756 he joined his brother Archibald in Nansemond County, Virginia, as a partner in a mercantile company, which included an uncle in Glasgow as a third partner. The Hamiltons extended their operations into North Carolina, where they established an extensive trading center at Hamilton Hill near Halifax; they had stores and warehouses for retail and wholesale trade in imported and colonial goods, a tavern, and shops for a blacksmith, a cooper, a hatter, and a tailor. By 1776 the Hamiltons, who operated under the name of John Hamilton and Company, had become the largest commercial house in the colony. Throughout its existence, the company maintained an excellent reputation with North Carolina farmers and merchants, who benefited from its ample provision of purchasing credit.

Despite their good relations with North Carolinians, John Hamilton and his family remained loyal to the British Crown at the outbreak of the Revolution. He and his brother, along with many others, refused to take the required oath of allegiance to North Carolina in 1777 and were banished from the state. Hamilton and his company left behind an investment of approximately £200,000 in land, goods, and accounts. After leaving North Carolina, Hamilton entered the British military service at New York. Authorized to recruit Loyalist troops for a southern campaign that began with the occupation of Savannah in December 1778, Hamilton eventually raised nearly 750 men, mainly from North Carolina. This command, of which he became lieutenant colonel, was the Royal North Carolina Regiment and fought with the British forces in Georgia and the Carolinas.

Hamilton and part of his regiment accompanied Cornwallis on the march into Virginia and surrendered at Yorktown. During his military service Hamilton was wounded three times. Cornwallis testified that Hamilton's conduct "as a citizen and soldier" was "highly meritorious" and deserved "the gratitude of his country." A fellow Loyalist, Charles Stedman, wrote in his account of the Revolution that "the British nation owed more [to Hamilton] than to any other individual loyalist in the British service."

In 1782 Hamilton went to St. Augustine and rejoined his regiment, which was sent to Nova Scotia in 1783 and there disbanded. From 1784 to 1790 Hamilton resided in London, where he sought compensation from the British government for losses suffered by Loyalist merchants. The Hamiltons recovered less than £14,000 of the £200,000 they had lost. Hamilton himself received an officer's half pay for life and land grants in the Bahamas, but he failed to obtain the governorship of the islands. He was, however, named British consul in 1789 at Norfolk, Virginia, where he remained until the outbreak of the War of 1812.

From 1790 until he returned to Britain in 1812, Hamilton performed his consular duties to the great satisfaction of British officials and subjects and those American citizens with whom he dealt. During the French revolutionary and Napoleonic wars, he rendered valuable service to the British navy as an agent for intelligence and supplies for warships frequenting the Chesapeake. In Anglo-American crises, such as that arising from the *Chesapeake-Leopard* encounter off the Virginia Capes, Hamilton exercised a moderating influence. Jovial and hospitable, Hamilton, "a short, stout, red-faced man; well bred and well fed," was liked and respected by Americans for his integrity and kindness.

Hamilton spent his last years in London. His wife, Claudia, whom he had married while prosecuting Loyalist claims in England during the 1780s, survived him, but there were no surviving children. On leaving Norfolk in 1812 and at the time of his death in 1816, John Hamilton's official conduct and personal character were highly praised, even by the anti-British local press.

• Letters by Hamilton and documents concerning him are found principally in the Public Record Office, London. There is no full-length biography of John Hamilton, though biographical sketches are in Lorenzo Sabine, *Biographical Sketches of Loyalists of the American Revolution with an Historical Essay* (2 vols., 1864) and in Wilbur Henry Siebert, *Loyalists in East Florida, 1774 to 1785* (2 vols., 1929). A brief sketch by Marshall De Lancey Haywood appears in Samuel A. Ashe, ed., *Biographical History of North Carolina* (8 vols., 1905–1917), and another by Arthur C. Menius and Carole Watterson Troxler in William S. Powell, ed., *Dictionary of North Carolina* (1979–). Sources pertaining to Hamilton's career during and immediately after the Revolution are in the Muster Rolls of the North Carolina Volunteers and the Royal North Carolina Regiment in the Public Archives of Canada, Ottawa; the Treasurer's and Comptroller's Papers in the North Carolina State Archives, Raleigh; and Land Grant Records in the Bahamas Registrar General's Office, Nassau. Contemporary appraisals of Hamilton as a person and public figure may be found in Charles Stedman, *The History of the Origin, Progress, and Termination of the American War* (1794); Wilfred S. Dowden, ed., *The Letters of Thomas Moore* (2 vols., 1964); *Norfolk and Portsmouth Herald*, 29 July 1812; and *American Beacon and Norfolk and Portsmouth Daily Advertiser*, 5 March 1817. Charles Christopher Crittenden, *The Commerce of North Carolina, 1763–1789* (1936), and Robert O. DeMond, *The Loyalists in North Carolina during the Revolution* (1940), are important background studies for Hamilton's North Carolina years.

MALCOLM LESTER

HAMILTON, John Brown (1 Dec. 1847–24 Dec. 1898), surgeon general of the United States, was born in Jersey County, Illinois, the son of Benjamin Brown, a clergyman, and Martha Hamilton. Of Scottish descent, the family founded and ran a country academy that offered students a classical education. Hamilton attended this school in his early years, helping out with the family farm in his free time. When he turned sixteen, he arranged to be apprenticed to Joseph Hamilton, a local physician, apprenticeship being a common path in those days to a career as a doctor. After a year of apprenticeship, Hamilton joined the G Company of the sixty-first Illinois Regiment and served throughout the rest of the Civil War.

When the war ended, Hamilton entered Rush Medical College in Chicago, from which he graduated three years later in 1869 with high honors. He returned to southern Illinois, where he was born, to practice medicine from 1869 to 1874 in Kane. During this period he married Mary L. Frost, with whom he would later have two children. Three years after the two married, they had tired of the rural life, and Hamilton decided he wanted a more public career. He returned to the army, serving as a surgeon at Jefferson Barracks in Missouri and Fort Colville in Washington. In 1876 he accepted an appointment to the Marine Hospital Service as an assistant surgeon and a year later was put in charge of the oldest and most esteemed hospital in that wing of the service, the Marine Hospital in the port of Boston, Massachusetts.

Despite the hospital's reputation, when Hamilton arrived there he instantly faced a problem. The hospital's primitive sewer system emptied into a salt marsh and produced a stench that angered many of its neighbors in Chelsea. In addition, the poor sewage system was thought to be responsible for a rash of postoperation illnesses and even death. Assessing the situation, Hamilton ordered that all patients be moved to the third floor and set about remodeling the hospital, primarily the water closets and ventilation system.

In this position, Hamilton reported to John Maynard Woodworth, who had become the nation's first surgeon general in 1871. When Woodworth died in 1879, Hamilton was one of fifteen physicians who took the civil service examination. The fact that he topped the list on performance on the exam coupled with his record in Boston helped him gain the surgeon general post, although the 31-year-old Illinois doctor had no prior experience in national politics. Such experience might have stood him in good stead, for in taking the surgeon general post, he was stepping into a political battle that was almost a decade old.

From the day that Woodworth was appointed, John Shaw Billings, an army physician, coveted his post and powers. However, the legislative act that created the post of surgeon general mandated that it be filled by a civilian, disqualifying Billings for the post. Undaunted, Billings proceeded in his quest to head a national agency in charge of the public's health. In 1878 Congress passed the Quarantine Act, ceding authority over quarantines to the Marine Hospital Service. Shortly thereafter, Billings covened his own agency, the National Board of Health. Composed of representatives from all branches of the military and the Department of Justice, the board volunteered its services to oversee public health matters. Adding to its strength was the organizational backing it carried; many of its supporters were staunch members of the American Medical Association or the American Public Health Association (APHA).

Hamilton, on the other hand, was not well situated to fight this battle; he did not even belong to the APHA, the leading public health organization in the United States. In the early years of his tenure as surgeon general, Hamilton lost a few minor skirmishes to Billings and his board. By the end of 1879, Billings had managed to secure control over quarantines for the board, start a yellow fever commission in Havana, Cuba, and acquire the editorial reins of the *Bulletin of the Marine Hospital Service*, whose name he changed to the *National Board of Health Bulletin*. Hamilton, however, did not surrender to Billings's blustery style.

In fact, Hamilton returned with some salvos of his own. In the summer of 1882 he persuaded Congress to take away the $100,000 that the National Board of Health had been granted to prevent the spread of contagious diseases, arguing that the board was too reliant on a patronage system. In addition, he said, the Marine Hospital Service could do the same job for less. Friends of the board stepped in, and that organization was given the green light to continue its quarantine activities with the caveat that it restrict its efforts to yellow fever, cholera, and smallpox. Hamilton continued to whittle away at the powers of the National Board of Health.

Hamilton marshaled support to his side, lobbying states' rightists against the actions of the board, which was frequently perceived as meddling in local affairs in the interest of preventing the spread of disease. Even more crucial to Hamilton's cause was his foresight when the board had managed to capture federal powers related to quarantines. Although Hamilton could not stop the board at this point, he did maneuver the bill so that the board's mandate would expire in four years. By 1883, when the board's powers came up for renewal, Hamilton commanded enough support to enable him to wrest the authority away from it. Thus on 2 March 1883 the law according this authority to the board expired, stripping the board of the mainstay of its existence. Although the board continued to exist for another decade, as of that point the Marine Hospital Service received control over all quarantine and public health matters.

Throughout this period, Hamilton had taken other steps to strengthen the Marine Hospital Service. Despite Billings's protests that the service should remain a four-institution system, Hamilton had secured funding from Congress in 1882 to give him money to open four new hospitals, in Cincinnati, Ohio; Baltimore, Maryland; New Orleans, Louisiana; and Cairo, Illinois. In addition, Hamilton began a crusade to increase professional standards of the service. Because medical credentials at that time could be achieved through a variety of paths—not all of them through an elite school—Hamilton wanted to ensure quality among his officers. (He himself remained an active participant in the medical community, serving on the surgery faculties of Georgetown and Providence Hospital from 1883 to 1891.) In 1889, at Hamilton's urging, U.S. president Grover Cleveland signed a bill saying that all the officers of the service would be appointed by the president after they passed a standardized examination.

Perhaps Hamilton saw that Billings was not through with his attempts to head his own federal public health agency. In the late 1880s, Billings petitioned the Congressional Committee on Commerce to host a favorable hearing on establishing a national board of health under the aegis of the Interior Department. Not surprisingly, many of the former members of the National Board were vocal supporters of this agency, which would take over all the activities of the Marine Hospital Service except quarantine. Hamilton saw through this ploy of Billings and appeared in front of the committee himself, arguing that the whole idea for this new agency grew out of efforts of the service. Indeed, a few years before, the service had started the National Laboratory of Hygiene on its Staten Island campus, a precursor to the National Institutes of Health.

Soon thereafter, Hamilton began his own campaign to change the name of the Hospital Service to the Public Health Service in recognition of its broader mission. Although the service's name did not change officially until 1912, Hamilton's work helped ensure that the service became the major federal public health agency. By the end of the 1880s, Nathan Davis, a former editor of the *Journal of the American Medical Association*, said that the service "has now become a health department in all but name."

Despite all these successes, Hamilton resigned abruptly on 1 June 1891 from the position of surgeon general, offering no explanation for his action. The resignation appears to have been voluntary; after Hamilton left, President Benjamin Harrison appointed Hamilton's protégé Walter Wyman as his successor and named Hamilton a surgeon in the Marine Hospital Service. After resigning, Hamilton returned to Illinois, accepting a post on the surgery faculty of Rush Medical College and serving as editor of the *Journal of the American Medical Association*.

In 1892, at Wyman's request, Hamilton returned east briefly to help the service deal with the cholera epidemic in New York. Hamilton was instrumental in the establishment of a camp on Sandy Hook, New Jersey, that could hold more than 1,000 people. Perhaps in recognition of his fine work on this project, the service offered Hamilton a promotion that would entail a transfer to San Francisco, California. Rather than move further west, Hamilton resigned from the service altogether. In 1896 he accepted a position as superintendent of the Northern Illinois Hospital for the Insane in Elgin, Illinois. He died there two years later.

• Collections of Hamilton papers are at the Library of Congress and the Armed Forces Institute of Pathology in Washington, D.C. The details of Hamilton's life are best pieced together by reading through a variety of histories of the Public Health Service. Bess Furman, *A Profile of the United States Public Health Service, 1798–1948* (1973), contains a detailed account of his years in office, as does Fitzhugh Mullan, *Plagues and Politics* (1989). Briefer descriptions of his years in office can be found in John Duffy, *The Sanitarians* (1992), pp. 171–72.

SHARI RUDAVSKY

HAMILTON, John William (18 Mar. 1845–24 July 1934), bishop of the Methodist Episcopal church, was born in Weston, Virginia (later W.Va.), the son of William Cooper Patrick Hamilton, a Methodist Episcopal clergyman, and Henrietta Maria Dean. Hamilton's father was a respected clergy member of the Pittsburgh Conference who served churches in western Pennsylvania, western Virginia, and eastern Ohio.

Another of his sons, Franklin E. E. Hamilton, also was elected a bishop of the Methodist Episcopal church.

After attending Summerfield Academy, John Hamilton taught school at the age of fifteen (the locations of the academy and the school are unknown). In April 1861 he attempted to enlist in the Union army but was rejected because he was too young. Later he served with General Don Carlos Buell's troops in Kentucky (dates unknown). He received his A.B. from Mount Union College, Ohio, in 1865. In 1871 he was graduated from Boston University School of Theology with an S.T.B.

Hamilton was licensed to preach in 1865 and joined the Pittsburgh Conference on trial in 1866. From 1866 until 1868 he was appointed to the Newport Circuit, Ohio. He was ordained deacon in 1868 by Bishop Calvin Kingsley and transferred his ministerial membership to the New England Conference, where he was ordained elder in 1870 by Bishop Levi Scott. He was pastor of several congregations in Massachusetts, including Maplewood (1868–1870), Somerville (1870–1872; 1884–1888), First Church, Boston (1872–1875), People's Church, Boston (1875–1884), and East Boston (1888–1892). Hamilton's pastorate at People's Church was especially noteworthy because he was responsible not only for its founding but also for its development into the largest Methodist congregation in Boston. It was Hamilton's intent from the outset that this congregation be open to everyone, regardless of social standing, race, or national origin.

From 1892 until 1900 Hamilton was corresponding secretary of the Freedmen's Aid and Southern Education Society, an agency of the Methodist Episcopal church created after the Civil War to establish and maintain educational institutions in the southern states for the benefit of freed slaves and other underprivileged youth. Held in high esteem by his colleagues, Hamilton was elected as a delegate to the denomination's General Conferences in 1884, 1888, 1892, 1896, and 1900. He was an eloquent advocate of temperance and the rights of African Americans and women, and as a delegate in 1892 he proposed a constitutional change that ultimately made it possible for women to serve as delegates to the General Conference, the chief legislative body of the denomination.

Hamilton was elected to the episcopacy in 1900, and from then until 1908 he resided in San Francisco. After the devastating earthquake of 1906, he organized the reconstruction of Methodist work in the city. He was also a pioneer in the establishment of Methodism in Alaska and Hawaii. From 1908 until 1916 Hamilton resided in Boston, where he was responsible for the denomination's ministry in New England. In 1916, when he reached the mandatory age of retirement, Hamilton succeeded his brother Franklin as chancellor of the American University in Washington, D.C. During his six-year administration the university's academic program improved and its financial position became more sound. In 1922 he was appointed chancellor emeritus. Also in these years he was a leader in raising funds for the restoration of John Wesley's living quarters at Lincoln College, Oxford University.

During the course of his various ministries Hamilton was both an editor and writer. Among the volumes he edited or wrote are *Memorial of Jesse Lee and the Old Elm* (1875), *The People's Church* (1877), *Lives of Methodist Bishops* (1882), *The People's Church Pulpit* (1884, 1885), *American Fraternal Greetings to the Wesleyan Conferences in Ireland and England* (1898), and *Gordon Battelle, Preacher, Statesman, Soldier* (1916).

During his lifetime Bishop Hamilton, known for his effective preaching, wise administration, and ecumenical leadership, was one of the most influential figures in the Methodist Episcopal church. He was recognized as a progressive regarding the social issues that confronted his nation and as a leader in the world Methodist community. He addressed the important world Methodist Ecumenical Conferences in London (1901) and Toronto (1911). Hamilton was winsome, energetic, and intelligent. His "striking face, flowing hair, booming voice, and erect, soldierly bearing" made him an impressive figure (Earl and Godbold, p. 1063).

Hamilton was married twice. In 1873 he married Julia Elizabeth Battelle of Covington, Kentucky; she died in 1883. He married her sister, Emma Lydia Battelle, in 1888; she died in 1915. Hamilton was the father of two children, one from each marriage. He died in Boston.

• There is no known repository of Hamilton's papers. References to Hamilton and his ministry appear in the various standard histories of Methodism, including Emory Stevens Bucke, ed., *The History of American Methodism*, vol. 3 (1964). The chief sources of biographical information are Jesse A. Earl and Albea Godbold, *Encyclopedia of World Methodism*, vol. 1 (1974), pp. 1062–63, and *Journal of the Thirty-second Delegated General Conference of the Methodist Episcopal Church, 1936*, pp. 685–88. Obituaries are in the *Minutes of the Annual Conferences of the Methodist Episcopal Church*, Spring 1934, and *Zion's Herald*, 1 Aug. 1934.

CHARLES YRIGOYEN, JR.

HAMILTON, Margaret (12 Sept. 1902–16 May 1985), actress, was born Margaret Brainerd Hamilton in Cleveland, Ohio, the daughter of Walter J. Hamilton and Jennie Adams. Her father was a prominent lawyer in Cleveland and frowned on his daughter's intentions to become an actress. Faced with her parents' insistence that she prepare herself for a reliable career, Hamilton attended Hathaway Brown School before studying voice with Grace Probert from 1917 to 1921. Her parents pushed her toward teaching, and she attended Boston's Wheelock Kindergarten Training School from 1921 to 1923, while also studying acting with Maria Ouspenskaya. She worked as an assistant kindergarten teacher while continuing her acting studies and made her debut in 1923 at the Cleveland Playhouse, where she took occasional roles while teaching. She ran her own nursery school from 1924 to 1927 before teaching kindergarten at the Rye Country Day School in 1927. When a friend encouraged her to audi-

tion for a part in the 1932 Broadway play *Another Language*, Hamilton got the part and scored a personal success in the role of a waspish wife, Helen Hallam.

Hollywood made a screen version of *Another Language* in 1933, and Hamilton was hired to recreate her role. Her solid performance led to a fifty-year career as one of Hollywood's most popular and enduring character actresses. She had married Paul Meserve in 1931, shortly before she made her transition to acting, and they had one son. She and Meserve were divorced in 1933, and Hamilton, left with her young child to support, worked as many acting jobs as she could. Her sharp features and withering scowl meant that most of her roles were as flinty, reproving spinsters and starchy New Englanders. Within these limits, however, Hamilton wrought many unique variations. She was also fortunate to work with some of the outstanding screen talents of the golden age of Hollywood. She appeared as a small-town frump with Mickey Rooney and Judy Garland in the screen version of the Richard Rodgers and Lorenz Hart musical, *Babes in Arms* (1939), as a frontier-town busybody with Mae West and W. C. Fields in *My Little Chickadee* (1940), as Spencer Tracy's acerbic maid in Frank Capra's *State of the Union* (1948), and as a disapproving matron opposite Bing Crosby in *Riding High* (1950). She also appeared in such notable screen efforts as *The Farmer Takes a Wife* (1935), *The Ox-Bow Incident* (1943), *Johnny Come Lately* (1943), *The Sin of Harold Diddlebock* (1947), *The Red Pony* (1949), and *Wabash Avenue* (1950).

However, Hamilton's greatest role, and undoubtedly her most challenging, was as the Wicked Witch of the West in Metro-Goldwyn-Mayer's classic 1939 technicolor screen version of L. Frank Baum's children's book, *The Wizard of Oz*. Under the direction of Victor Fleming (after some false starts with other directors), and costarring with Judy Garland (in the role that made her a star), Bert Lahr, Ray Bolger, and Jack Haley, Hamilton won the role after actress Gale Sondergaard was rejected as "too glamorous." Hamilton, as the *New York Times* wrote at the time of her death, "unnerved generations of children" as the hideous green-faced harridan who stalked Garland's Dorothy seeking the magical ruby slippers placed on Dorothy's feet by Glinda, the Good Witch of the North. Although Hamilton was already a familiar face to moviegoers, *The Wizard of Oz*, both in its original theatrical run and as a television holiday perennial, provided her with screen immortality as it emerged as one of Hollywood's most enduring classics. In 1974 she was again associated with it when she provided the voice for Auntie Em in the animated sequel, *Journey Back to Oz*. She occasionally played the Wicked Witch of the West in stage productions of *The Wizard of Oz*, and this role would continue to be associated with her for the remainder of her career. In subsequent years, Hamilton recalled the film's unique qualities and the experience of making it:

I don't think any of us knew how lovely it was at first. But, after a while, we all began to feel it coming together and we knew we had something. I can watch it again and again and remember wonderful Judy [Garland], Bert [Lahr], Ray [Bolger], Jack [Haley], Billie [Burke], Frank [Morgan] and how wonderful they all were. The scene that always gets me, though, and I think it's one of the most appealing scenes I've ever seen, is the one where the Wizard gives the gifts to them at the end. Frank was just like that as a person. And every time I see him do it, the tears come in my eyes. I listen to the words. I think of Frank, and I know how much he meant what he said, and how much the words themselves mean. (*New York Times*, 17 May 1985)

Although Hamilton's screen appearances became less frequent after the early 1950s, she occasionally returned for a memorable performance, including her turn as Daphne Heap, an irascible dowager, in *Brewster McCloud* (1970).

As film roles became less frequent, Hamilton returned to the stage, appearing in the celebrated Lincoln Center Music Theatre revivals of *Oklahoma!* as Aunt Eller and in *Show Boat* as Parthy Hawks during the 1960s. In the mid-1970s she toured the country as Madame Armfeldt in the national touring company of Stephen Sondheim's musical, *A Little Night Music*.

Hamilton also appeared frequently in character roles on radio and television, including such television series as *The Egg and I*, *Ethel and Albert*, and *That Was the Week That Was*, as well as two long runs in soap operas. She also acted in the 1972 television film *The Night Strangler*. It was in television that Hamilton found another role that brought her considerable recognition. As Maxwell House Coffee's friendly Cora, proprietor of a New England general store, she became recognizable through a series of homey commercials to yet another generation.

Despite the busy career she maintained as an actress, Hamilton also found time to maintain a connection to her original profession in education. She founded a kindergarten in a Beverly Hills church and was also president of the Beverly Hills Board of Education for many years. Hamilton retired from acting completely by the end of the 1970s and died of a heart attack in a Salisbury, Connecticut, nursing home.

• For information on Hamilton, see Buddy Ebsen, *The Other Side of Oz* (1993); Aljean Harmetz, *The Making of the Wizard of Oz* (1977); Ephraim Katz, ed., *The Film Encyclopedia* (1994); Doug McClelland, *Down the Yellow Brick Road: The Making of the Wizard of Oz* (1989); Salman Rushdie, *The Wizard of Oz* (1992); John Russell Taylor, ed., *The Wizard of Oz. 50th Anniversary Edition with Original Script and Songs* (1989); and Rhys Thomas, *The Ruby Slippers of Oz* (1989). An obituary is in the *New York Times*, 17 May 1985.

JAMES FISHER

HAMILTON, Maxwell McGaughey (20 Dec. 1896–12 Nov. 1957), diplomat, was born in Tahlequah, Oklahoma, the son of Wallace Maxwell Hamilton, a clergyman, and May Calvin Dobson. After graduating from Sioux City (Iowa) High School in 1914, he attended Washington and Jefferson College in Washington, Pennsylvania, for one year; he then enrolled at Princeton University, where he earned a B.Litt. degree. Following graduation in 1918, he entered the U.S. Army. With the end of World War I in November of that year, he was discharged, and in 1919–1920 he taught at the Jacob Tome Institute, a preparatory school in Port Deposit, Maryland.

Hamilton's 32-year career as a diplomat began in 1920, the year he entered the United States Foreign Service. He requested and was assigned to duty in East Asia and after training as a Chinese-language officer at the legation in Beijing was transferred in 1922 to the consulate in Canton. He began his consulate work with the rank of vice consul and junior interpreter but was soon promoted to senior interpreter (1923) and to consul (1924). While serving in Canton, in December 1924, he married Julia Fisher, with whom he would have one child. In 1925 Hamilton was assigned to Shanghai, where he held the post of assessor in the Mixed Court until 1927.

During his seven years in China Hamilton earned a reputation as an astute reporter on the momentous political changes then taking place in that country, and thus he was summoned by his superiors in Washington to the U.S. State Department's Division of Far Eastern Affairs, where from 1927 until 1943 he was at the center of shaping U.S. policy in East Asia. Staff members of the Division of Far Eastern Affairs were sharply divided over the appropriate U.S. response to the various political crises in Asia that were seriously straining diplomatic relations between the United States and Japan. Hamilton became a protégé of Stanley Hornbeck, the highly opinionated chief of the division, who, in 1931, established especially for Hamilton the position of assistant chief, which he held until 1937. Hamilton frequently disagreed with Hornbeck, however, urging restraint in dealing with Japan because he recognized the limited power of the United States in the Pacific. In 1934, for example, Hamilton counseled the United States not to take action against Japan after it issued the Amō statement—declaring, in essence, a Japanese Monroe Doctrine for Asia—because he believed that the earlier Manchurian Crisis (1931–1932) had shown that the United States lacked the political will to counter Japanese aggression. At the same time, Hamilton was skeptical about the prospects for meaningful agreement between the two governments. Dismissive of what he viewed as naively optimistic reports from Tokyo by U.S. ambassador Joseph Grew, Hamilton was critical of President Franklin D. Roosevelt's plan to implement a policy of neutrality among the Pacific nations as a means of alleviating growing tensions. The Division of Far Eastern Affairs' response, which Hamilton drafted, argued against the proposal, asserting the instability of the region in general and Japan's unpredictability in particular. The memorandum annoyed the president, who viewed it as defeatist thinking.

In August 1937—one month after the outbreak of the Sino-Japanese War—Hamilton was promoted to chief of the division, and Hornbeck was simultaneously appointed to the position of political adviser to Secretary of State Cordell Hull. Hamilton soon discovered that he would not be given the kind of authority that Hornbeck had wielded as chief, and in many ways Hornbeck continued to have more influence in shaping American foreign policy. Yet as relations between the United States and Japan worsened, long-held differences between Hornbeck and Hamilton could no longer be suppressed, and sometimes Hamilton's views prevailed. In 1938, for example, during the State Department's consideration of a loan to China, Hamilton argued that because the United States was not prepared to provide substantial assistance over an extended period, the aid would be insufficient to help China and would serve only to antagonize Japan. Although his political adviser took the opposite position, Secretary Hull ultimately favored Hamilton's cautious approach. That same moderation was reflected in a speech that Hamilton gave to the Army War College the following January in which he stressed that neither treaty obligations nor national security was threatened by Japanese aggression in China; further, he alleged, Japan was becoming so bogged down in China that it would not be able to expand farther.

Even after German victories in the spring of 1940 left European colonies in Southeast Asia vulnerable to Japanese expansionism and further elevated Japanese-American tensions, Hamilton remained an advocate of caution. In the debate over whether or not to impose economic sanctions in an attempt to restrain Japan, Hamilton argued vehemently against a proposed oil embargo, asserting that a desperate Japan would likely attack the Netherlands East Indies. Secretary of the Treasury Henry Morgenthau, who along with Hornbeck led the hawkish element in the Roosevelt administration, blamed Hamilton for being the primary obstacle to a tougher—and in the secretary's view, successful—policy toward Japan. Hamilton's fears proved to be well founded, however, and as the crisis in the Pacific intensified in the fall of 1941, he continued to press for a diplomatic solution.

In January 1942 as Japan was completing its conquest of Southeast Asia in the wake of its devastating attack on Pearl Harbor, Hamilton was already formulating postwar policy in Asia, noting in his writings that the Pacific war would have unusual political and psychological consequences because it involved so many colonial peoples. Hamilton helped to establish the division's postwar objectives of encouraging the emergence of China as a major power and liberalizing colonial policy in Asia. He believed it was in the interest of the United States to provide strong military assistance to the Kuomintang government, to support China's membership on wartime boards and commissions, and to encourage cooperation between the Kuomintang government and the Communist movement.

Just as postwar planning entered its most important stage, however, Hamilton was transferred to Moscow, where he served as minister-counselor of the U.S. Embassy from June 1943 to September 1944. The Moscow assignment marked the end of Hamilton's career as a significant policymaker, as he moved from brief assignment to brief assignment, his views no longer carrying much weight. Two months after Hamilton returned to the State Department as a special assistant to Hull, the ailing secretary of state resigned, and a month later Hamilton was sent to Helsinki as the U.S. representative. In September 1945 Hamilton was named minister to Finland, a position he held until January 1948, when he was returned to Washington in order to work on the Japanese peace treaty. Following that assignment, in November 1949 he was appointed to the eleven-member Far Eastern Commission as the U.S. representative, later serving as chairman. Although in name the commission was charged with establishing postwar occupation policy in Japan, in practice U.S. military and diplomatic personnel in Tokyo and Washington made all the important decisions.

After his retirement in 1952, Hamilton spent his remaining years in Palo Alto, California, where he died.

• The Hamilton papers are at the Hoover Institution at Stanford University. Materials on Hamilton can also be found in the papers of Stanley Hornbeck (Hoover Institution), Nelson Johnson (Library of Congress), and John V. A. MacMurray (Princeton University). Volumes covering Hamilton's years as chief of the Division of Far Eastern Affairs, in U.S. Department of State, *Foreign Relations of the United States*, are excellent for tracing his foreign policy views. For more on his relationship with Hornbeck see Edward M. Bennett, "Joseph C. Grew: The Diplomacy of Pacification," and Richard Dean Burns, "Stanley K. Hornbeck: The Diplomacy of the Open Door," both in *Diplomats in Crisis*, ed. Richard Dean Burns and Edward M. Bennett (1974). For a discussion of American foreign policy formulation in the Hamilton years see Dorothy Borg, *The United States and the Far Eastern Crisis, 1933–1938* (1964). Relations between the State Department and the White House, and Hamilton's role in formulating East Asian policy, are discussed, respectively, in Norman Graebner, "Hoover, Roosevelt, and the Japanese," and James C. Thomson, Jr., "The Role of the Department of State," both in *Pearl Harbor as History*, ed. Dorothy Borg and Shumpei Okamoto (1973); Hamilton's role in the crisis is examined also in Jonathan Utley, *Going to War with Japan, 1937–1941* (1985), and Waldo Heinrichs, *Threshold of War: Franklin D. Roosevelt and American Entry into World War II* (1988); for a retrospective account see Akira Iriye, *Power and Culture: The American-Japanese War, 1941–1945* (1981). An obituary is in the *New York Times*, 13 Nov. 1957.

GARY R. HESS

HAMILTON, Paul (16 Oct. 1762–30 June 1816), statesman, was born in St. Paul's Parish, South Carolina, the son of Archibald Hamilton and Rebecca Branford, planters. He attended common school in Charleston until June 1776, when a British fleet appeared off the coast and threatened the harbor. At that time he retreated to Dorchester, South Carolina, at the head of the Ashley River, where he later studied with the celebrated tutor James Hamden Thomson. The sudden death of his father and two brothers created financial difficulties for the family and forced Hamilton to withdraw from Thomson's school in December 1778.

Hamilton joined the Willtown Hunters militia company during the spring of 1779 in response to General Augustine Prevost's advance against Charleston. During the British retreat, he participated in an artillery engagement, winning honor as one of the last to be driven from the battlefield. That September he again distinguished himself with Continental forces in the ill-fated attempt to retake Savannah. In March 1780 Hamilton narrowly escaped capture when his militia company was routed by General Henry Clinton's advance scouts as they cut off Charleston's westward routes of retreat. After the British captured the city, he retired northward, joined Continental forces at Hillsborough, North Carolina, and on 16 August 1780 served with General Horatio Gates during the humiliating American defeat at Camden. For the remainder of the war Hamilton fought with several partisan leaders, including Francis Marion and William Harden, and saw action at little-known engagements such as Pee Dee River, Saltketcher Bridge, and the American capture of Fort Balfour. In 1782 Hamilton married Mary Wilkinson; the couple had six children.

In March 1783 Hamilton acquired twenty-three slaves from his father-in-law's estate. The following October he received from his father's estate Continental bonds that provided the opportunity to purchase land in Willtown, where in 1784, after an unsuccessful season growing indigo on Edisto Island, he began cultivating rice. His public service began the following year, when he was appointed a tax collector for St. Paul's Parish, and in 1786 he was named justice of the peace for the county. In 1787 Hamilton was elected as a Republican to the first of two consecutive terms to the state house of representatives, and in 1789 he served as a member of the state convention that ratified the federal Constitution. Elected to the state senate in 1794 and reelected in 1798, he remained in that office until 1799, playing an instrumental role in reforming the state's judicial system.

In 1799 Hamilton became the first comptroller for the state of South Carolina, a post he held without opposition until 1804. During his tenure he reversed the state's dismal financial situation. His frugal management allowed the state to purchase $300,000 of stock in the South Carolina State Bank and provided funds to charter and establish South Carolina College. Although he wanted to retire to private life, he allowed himself in December 1804 to be elected to a two-year term as governor. While holding that office, he worked to reform the state's system of apportionment and its penal code, to bolster the state's defenses, and to prohibit the African slave trade.

President James Madison, who owed his election to Republicans in Congress, offered Hamilton the position of secretary of the navy in 1809 to satisfy political debts. Although Hamilton had no experience with naval affairs, he supposedly understood financial responsibility—something needed in the nascent department—and he had military experience during the Revolution. The first two years of his secretaryship ran smoothly as he enhanced the program for educating midshipmen, enforced high personal and professional standards for officers, reformed the system for procuring supplies, ordered his officers to vigorously enforce the slave trade laws, and helped win congressional passage for the establishment of the Naval Hospital Fund. He also reformed and reorganized the Washington Navy Yard, argued for increasing the size of the seagoing navy, and promoted technological innovations, such as torpedoes and blockships.

At the beginning of the War of 1812 Hamilton supported President Madison's decision to use the nation's small fleet to fight a *war against commerce*. After early successes, Hamilton in September 1812 divided the fleet into three small squadrons designed to threaten British commerce and force the Royal Navy to reconsider its naval operations. These squadrons accounted for most of the U.S. Navy's victories during the war and prompted the British to vigorously blockade American ports.

With the beginning of the war Hamilton's administration appeared suddenly to deteriorate. Contemporary critics charged that the secretary's problems resulted from excessive drinking. Hamilton's drinking may have contributed to the department's disorganization, but other problems were more pressing. Lax record keeping prevented the department from accounting for most of its funds. Moreover, the secretary had appointed more officers than allowed by law, had given jobs to unqualified candidates, and had approved overpriced equipment contracts from friends and associates. The bitter criticism from congressmen, cabinet members, and naval officers hastened Hamilton's desire to retire. Madison was reelected in the fall of 1812, and the president tactfully persuaded Hamilton to tender his resignation. On 31 December 1812 the secretary resigned. Hamilton returned to South Carolina to face creditors who were forcing him to sell slaves to recover their debts. He spent the remainder of his life trying to recover his lost fortune. He died at Beaufort, South Carolina.

As South Carolina's first comptroller and later as governor, Hamilton gained regional recognition. His national notoriety, however, is based largely on his lackluster performance as secretary of the navy at the beginning of the War of 1812.

• The Paul Hamilton Papers are in the South Caroliniana Library, University of South Carolina. Hamilton's autobiographical "Extracts from a Private Manuscript, Written by Governor Paul Hamilton, Sr., during the Period of the Revolutionary War, from 1776–1800," *Year Book—1898: City of Charleston, So. Ca.* (1898), pp. 299–327, provides details of his early life and activities during the Revolution. Mabel L. Webber, "Grimball of Edisto Island," *South Carolina Historical and Genealogical Magazine* 22 (Jan. 1922): 1–7, offers materials concerning the family but only briefly mentions Hamilton. Edward McCrady, *The History of South Carolina in the Revolution, 1780–1783* (1902), and Henry Lee, *Memoirs of the War in the Southern Department of the United States* (1876), offer insight into his service during the Revolution. David Duncan Wallace, *The History of South Carolina* (1934), and Harriette Kershaw Leiding, *Historic Houses of South Carolina*

(1921), furnish material on his tenure as comptroller. His duties as secretary of the navy have been chronicled in several sources, including Charles Oscar Paullin, "Naval Administrations under Secretaries of the Navy Smith, Hamilton, and Jones, 1801–1814," *Proceedings of the U.S. Naval Institute* 32 (1906): 1289–1328; Frank L. Owsley, Jr., "Paul Hamilton," *American Secretaries of the Navy*, ed. Paulo Coletta (1980); Christopher McKee, *A Gentlemanly and Honorable Profession: The Creation of the U.S. Naval Officer Corps, 1794–1815* (1991); and William S. Dudley, ed., *The Naval War of 1812: A Documentary History*, vol. 2 (1992). An obituary is in the *City Gazette of Charleston*, 4 July 1816.

GENE A. SMITH

HAMILTON, Thomas (26 Apr. 1823–29 May 1865), journalist and antislavery activist, was born in New York City, the son of William Hamilton, a carpenter and community leader who participated in the rising abolitionist and black convention movements of the early 1830s. His mother's name and occupation are not known. Although young Thomas gained a rudimentary education in the city's African Free Schools and African Methodist Episcopal Zion Church, the primary influence on his career choice seems to have been growing up in the Hamilton household, where he was introduced to abolitionism and the reform press at an early age. A few months after his father's death in 1836, he went to work as a carrier for the *Colored American*, a local African-American weekly read in black communities throughout the North. Before long, he became a bookkeeper and mailing clerk for the *New York Evangelist*, a leading religious journal, and the *National Anti-Slavery Standard*, the official organ of the American Anti-Slavery Society.

In October 1841, after carefully observing the operation of the religious and reform journals for which he worked, the precocious Hamilton established a newspaper of his own called the *People's Press*. Although the weekly reached a limited readership, he continued to edit it for nearly two years, drawing on the assistance of his brother Robert Hamilton and several youthful acquaintances. The paper's militant tone prompted the *Colored American* to label it "a spicey little sheet." While devoted to the economic egalitarianism and antimonopoly principles of the Loco-Foco (or Equal Rights) political party in New York State, most news and editorials discussed issues of particular concern to the northern free black community, such as the appropriate strategies for attacking racial prejudice and winning civil rights. When diplomatic entanglements between the United States and Britain over the latter's capture of a slave ship brought the two nations to the brink of war in 1842, Hamilton instructed his black readers to maintain a studied neutrality, as their previous services in America's armed forces had been rewarded with continuing slavery and racial discrimination.

After the demise of the *People's Press* in 1843, Hamilton, a naturally quiet and modest person, preferred to work for a time behind the scenes. He returned to his positions with the *New York Evangelist* and the *National Anti-Slavery Standard*. In addition, he found

work with the New York *Independent*, a leading Congregationalist weekly. To supplement his income and assist various reform causes, he operated as a bookseller, distributing books and tracts on African-American, antislavery, and temperance themes from 48 Beekman Street in New York, the offices of the American Anti-Slavery Society. In 1844 he married Catherine Anne Leonard of New York. She apparently died some time later. In 1852 he married Matilda Ann Africanus of Brooklyn; this union produced at least one child, a daughter.

In 1859 Hamilton began publishing two periodicals—the *Anglo-African Magazine* and the *Weekly Anglo-African*—that made him a preeminent African-American journalist of the Civil War era. In initiating these ventures, he was motivated by the biased coverage that blacks often received in the white press. Believing that white journalists were partly to blame for the plight of African Americans, Hamilton pledged that his new publications would give a "thorough and impartial review" of the condition of blacks in the United States.

The *Anglo-African Magazine* was inaugurated in January 1859 and appeared monthly through March 1860. Hamilton served as editor during its entire run. Its aims were to publish accurate information about the African-American population, to present biographies of prominent blacks throughout the world, to review publications by black authors, and to serve as a forum for black intellect and talent. Hamilton envisioned that the magazine would function as an African-American *Atlantic Monthly*. These lofty goals were largely achieved. In its brief run of fifteen issues, the *Anglo-African* published hundreds of articles, essays, poems, and short stories by prominent and rising African-American writers and activists, including Frederick Douglass, James McCune Smith, and Alexander Crummell. Among the most significant and original literary pieces published in the magazine were Francis Ellen Watkins Harper's short story "The Two Offers" and the serialization of Martin R. Delany's novel *Blake*.

Hamilton initiated the *Weekly Anglo-African* on 23 July 1859 and forged it into the most influential black journal of the period. Under his guidance, the newspaper aggressively championed African-American concerns, and his vigorous editorials explored a variety of major issues, ranging from slavery and secession to the racial implications of Darwinian thought. Hamilton organized a corps of dozens of unpaid correspondents from San Francisco to Boston who regularly reported on life and culture in their communities, giving the journal a national appeal. But faced with persistent financial problems, he sold the paper in March 1861 to the Haytian Emigration Bureau, an agency that advocated and coordinated African-American settlement in Haiti, and relinquished the editorship. It was soon renamed the *Pine and Palm*. Five months later the Hamilton brothers—disturbed by reports from Haiti and enthused by the new prospects presented by the coming of the Civil War—established a second *Weekly An-*

glo-African. Although Robert edited the paper, Thomas worked behind the scenes to shape its direction and content over the next four years.

The Civil War raised Hamilton's hopes that America would finally realize its egalitarian ideals. He helped forge the *Anglo-African* into a pro-Union forum. Frequent editorials analyzed the meaning of the conflict. Correspondents reported regularly from the battlefield. After the War Department permitted African Americans to join the Union army in early 1863, he encouraged black enlistment and made sure that copies of the *Anglo-African* were distributed to black soldiers at the front. Hamilton also began a new venture, publishing books and pamphlets by and about African Americans. He hoped this would hasten the coming of equality and emancipation by increasing black pride and giving white Americans a more positive image of his race. Among the works published were Robert Campbell's *Pilgrimage to My Motherland* (1861) and William Wells Brown's *The Black Man: His Antecedents, His Genius, and His Achievements* (1863), important early pieces of African-American nonfiction.

Hamilton died of typhoid fever at his residence on Long Island. Messages of condolence poured in from African-American communities throughout the nation. New York blacks eulogized him as "one of those untiring heroes, who, however quietly they labor, lift the people as they lift themselves" (quoted in Bullock, p. 59).

• Only a few letters or other papers by Hamilton exist in archives. But dozens of editorials and other relevant documents can be found in the 1859 to 1865 issues of the *Weekly Anglo-African*. Two key editorials from the *People's Press* are reprinted in the 1 Apr. and 13 May 1842 issues of the *Liberator* (Boston). A brief biography of Hamilton appears in C. Peter Ripley et al., eds., *The Black Abolitionist Papers*, vol. 5 (1992). Overviews of his career as a journalist can be found in I. Garland Penn, *The Afro-American Press and Its Editors* (1891), and Penelope L. Bullock, *The Afro-American Periodical Press, 1838–1909* (1981). Other key sources include an obituary in the 14 July 1865 issue and a retrospective piece in the 8 June 1872 issue of the *Elevator* (San Francisco).

ROY E. FINKENBINE

HAMILTON, William John, Jr. (11 Dec. 1902–17 July 1990), mammalogist, naturalist, and educator, was born in Corona, Queens, New York, the son of William John Hamilton and Charlotte Richardson. His interest in nature was kindled in boyhood by a Sunday school teacher who gave him a plant to care for when Hamilton was seven. He was soon involved in gardening (which would remain a major avocation all his life), bird watching, muskrat trapping, and kindred activities. In his teens, he raised needed income by supplying timber rattlesnakes to the New York Zoological Society's Bronx Zoo and moth cocoons to a shop on lower Fifth Avenue in New York City.

Hamilton graduated from Flushing High School and had been accepted at Harvard; however, he was diverted by catalog descriptions of the zoology courses

offered at Cornell. Originally a premedicine student, he soon focused his attention on the vertebrate zoology courses offered through Cornell's Department of Entomology. He completed his undergraduate studies in 1926, his M.S. in 1928, and his Ph.D. in vertebrate zoology in 1930. He was a graduate assistant in zoology throughout the four years he pursued his doctorate. Hamilton's doctoral mentor was Albert Hazen Wright, but perhaps his closest colleague during his graduate student years was Francis Harper, another Flushing High School product and a 1925 Cornell Ph.D., who was Hamilton's laboratory instructor in vertebrate zoology. They later were Cornell faculty colleagues for a number of years. As a graduate student, Hamilton did some collecting of mammal and bird specimens in Cuba and of mammals in Central America. In the early 1930s he completed a survey of the mammals of Southampton Island, at the northern end of Hudson Bay, with George M. Sutton. These studies comprised the only field research done by Hamilton outside of the United States. In 1928 Hamilton married Nellie R. Rightmyer, a malacologist who had been a student in one of his laboratory sections. They had one son, who became a well-known environmentalist in his own right, and two daughters.

Hamilton joined the faculty as an instructor in vertebrate zoology in the New York State College of Agriculture at Cornell in 1930, but within several years he moved into the recently created Department of Vertebrate Zoology. He became assistant professor in 1937 and associate professor in 1942. In 1948, the year after his promotion to full professor, Hamilton helped to establish a Department of Conservation (later the Department of Natural Resources), where he made his academic home until his retirement in 1963, when he became professor emeritus. He was also a research associate in the Department of Mammalogy at the American Museum of Natural History, New York City, from 1958 until 1971.

Primarily a mammalogist, Hamilton specialized in the life history and ecology of the smaller common species in the vicinity of Ithaca and western New York. His doctoral dissertation dealt with the biology of the star-nosed mole, and some of his early papers concerned New York weasels (1933), the life history of the rufescent woodchuck (1934), and field mouse and rabbit control in orchards (1935). Hamilton was responsible for developing the Cornell collections of mammal specimens, particularly the skins, skulls, and skeletons of rodents, insectivores, and small carnivores. These were utilized both for research and as teaching aids. He was probably the leading authority of his time on the food habits of North American vertebrates, notably amphibians, reptiles, and birds, and was also particularly well versed on their economic importance and interrelationships. He spent some years researching the life cycles and population dynamics of the common field mouse and gave some attention to methods of controlling the damage this species did to agriculture. Many of his published papers had to do with the mammals and other vertebrates of western

New York and Long Island. A projected volume on the mammals of New York State was never completed, although he did publish several dozen definitive papers on a wide range of small mammals found there, most of them rodents, shrews, moles, and small fur-bearers.

Hamilton's *American Mammals: Their Lives, Habits and Economic Relations* (1939) was one of the earliest text books in the field dedicated to North American species and was a standard for some years. His *Mammals of Eastern United States* (1943; rev. ed., with J. O. Whitaker, 1979) was based on fieldwork in twenty-one of the twenty-seven states east of the Mississippi River and became something of a classic in the field. Hamilton was a pioneering figure in the area of conservation, and his *Conservation in the United States* (1939; rev. ed., 1949), with A. F. Gustafson, H. Ries and C. F. Guise, was another major work. Hamilton was an effective and popular researcher, teacher, and mentor for more than three decades. Through his spring vertebrate zoology course, where he focused on mammals, birds, and reptiles, he influenced a number of students to enter the field of vertebrate zoology. He was famous for his sense of humor, and his penchant for practical jokes was such that he became known as "Wild Bill" to both colleagues and students.

During World War II Hamilton was a captain in the U.S. Army Medical Corps, principally concerned with rodent and typhus control. He was stationed in the United States and Europe and underwent some training at a military government school at Boston University. His interest in Florida mammals began when he was stationed in the state for a period of time during the war, and he frequently revisited Florida in later years. A number of his published papers centered on the small mammals of the state, principally in Lee County. For some months in 1945 he served as a military governor of Mannheim, Germany. Later that year he was discharged as a major and returned to Cornell.

Hamilton was active in a number of professional organizations, including the American Society of Mammalogists (president, 1951–1952) and the Ecological Society of America (president, 1955). He was zoological editor of *Ecological Monographs* from 1951 to 1955. Seven organisms were named in his honor, including a subspecies of black bear. Hamilton died at his home in Ithaca.

• The best concise survey of Hamilton's life and career is an obituary by two former students, James N. Layne and John O. Whitaker, Jr., in the *Journal of Mammalogy* 73, no. 3 (1992): 693–706, which also contains a bibliography of Hamilton's 233 articles, reviews, and books. See also the sketch by Joseph Bongiorno in *Biographical Dictionary of American and Canadian Naturalists and Environmentalists*, ed. Keir B. Sterling et al. (1997). His career is discussed briefly in Elmer C. Birney and Jerry R. Choate, eds., *Seventy-five Years of Mammalogy (1919–1994)* (1994), and Richard H. Stroud, ed., *National Leaders of American Conservation* (1985). The high points of his career are summarized in *American Men and Women of Science* (1992).

KEIR B. STERLING

HAMILTON, William Thomas (8 Sept. 1820–26 Oct. 1888), congressman, senator, and governor, was born in Hagerstown, Maryland, the son of Henry Hamilton and Anna Mary Hess. Some accounts incorrectly give his middle name as Tiffany. His parents died when Hamilton was still a boy, and he was raised by an uncle in Boonsboro. Hamilton attended Jefferson College in Canonsburg, Pennsylvania, until 1840. He returned to Maryland to read law under John Thomson Mason of Hagerstown and was admitted to the bar in 1843.

Three years later Hamilton ran successfully for the Maryland House of Delegates. Although he was elected as a Democrat, he strongly supported Whig governor Thomas George Pratt's financial policies, including repayment of interest on the state debt. Hamilton was renominated in 1847, but the growing strength of the Whig party in Washington County defeated his reelection bid in 1848. That year he served as a Democratic presidential elector for Lewis Cass.

In 1849 Hamilton was elected to the U.S. House of Representatives, where he served until 1855. In 1850 he married Clara Holmes Jenness; they had six children. During his congressional career, he ardently opposed protective tariffs. The slogan "tariff for revenue only" formed the basis of his platform in all of his campaigns. True to his Jacksonian roots, Hamilton mistrusted the concentration of economic power in the federal government's hands and opposed banks as well. He once commented that he was "not too favorably disposed to banks, or a banking system." During his last term as congressman (1853–1855), he was chairman of the Committee on the District of Columbia and supervised the construction of the aqueduct that brought water to Washington from the Great Falls of the Potomac. Hamilton was outspoken in his southern sympathies. He was convinced that northern abolitionist agitation and later the Republican party were responsible for sectional strife. He strongly supported conciliatory measures and voted for Henry Clay's Compromise of 1850.

Hamilton was defeated for reelection in 1855 amid the rise of the Know Nothing party in Maryland. After this defeat, he returned to private law practice in Hagerstown and became active in local affairs. He was a prominent advocate of improved agricultural methods.

With the advent of the secession crisis of 1860–1861, Hamilton modified some of his attitudes toward the South. Although he felt that southern states had a legal right to secede, he nevertheless disapproved of secession itself. With his law partner, Richard H. Alvey, he became a leading member of the Peace party, which attempted to elect General George B. McClellan to the presidency in 1864.

During the war years, Hamilton remained in private practice but returned to political office in 1868, when he was elected to the Senate, serving from 1869 until 1875. Still favoring southern interests, he voted for the rapid readmission of southern states to the Union, the reestablishment of "home rule" (that is, the rule of native white Democrats) within each readmitted state, and for the rapid resumption of specie payments. He voted against the Fifteenth Amendment. When Congress enacted a 40 percent retroactive pay raise in 1873, Hamilton vigorously opposed what would become known as the "salary grab" and refused to accept the salary increase. His firm stand eventually forced Congress to repeal this unpopular legislation.

When his term as senator expired in 1875, Hamilton ran unsuccessfully for the governorship of Maryland. He won election in 1879. Hamilton's administration was known for his attempts to streamline state offices and reduce the budget and for his untiring battle against the powerful but corrupt elements within the state's Democratic party. He was sometimes described as rather brusque and lacking in tact, and he was outspoken in his criticisms of men whose ethics fell short of his own high standards. His personal manner and his commitment to reducing the state government's expenditures caused frequent clashes with local politicians.

Hamilton's opposition to a Chesapeake canal, which Democratic leaders strongly supported, also brought him into constant conflict with the state legislature. The state senate was at that time powerfully influenced by the canal supporters and thus rejected many of Hamilton's reform proposals. For example, his attempt to establish a sinking fund for the repayment of state debts was defeated, as were his efforts to abolish redundant or ineffective state offices, such as the tax commissioner, the insurance commissioner, and the Land Office.

For the rest of Hamilton's life, however, his administration was respected for an untiring commitment to political reform and careful attention to the state's finances. His clashes with the state legislature and the ensuing enmity of the Democratic party did not diminish the affection and loyalty of the people. Known as the "farmer governor," he continued to take a strong interest in the work of the Maryland Agricultural College. His term ended in 1884, and Hamilton returned to private life in Hagerstown, where he died.

By the end of his life, Hamilton was one of the wealthiest and most influential members of his community. He served as the president of the Hagerstown Bank, the Washington County Water Company, and many other boards and commissions. He was responsible for many improvements in Hagerstown, including electric lights, a waterworks, a hotel, and better streets.

As governor, Hamilton was outspoken in favor of "rigid economy in all branches of the public service." Although many of his reform efforts failed, he maintained a reputation for his commitment to lower taxes, ethical government, and reduced government spending. His last speech to the state legislature summed up his legacy as a public servant: "In returning to the private walks of life I shall bear with me the consciousness of having fairly, honestly and faithfully endeavored to discharge the important and imposing obligations then assumed, and of having faithfully endeavored to meet the just expectations of the people."

• Hamilton left no important body of papers. For brief biographical sketches, see H. E. Buchholz, *Governors of Maryland* (1908); T. J. C. William, *A History of Washington County, Maryland* (1906; repr. 1968); and Frank R. Kent, *The Story of Maryland Politics* (1911; repr. 1968). Although he made few speeches, the *Congressional Record* contains an account of his activities in Congress. Obituaries are in the *Baltimore Sun* and the *New York Times*, 27 Oct. 1888.

SILVANA SIDDALI

HAMLIN, Albert Comstock (10 Feb. 1881–29 Aug. 1912), politician, was born in Topeka, Kansas, the son of Andrew Jackson Hamlin and Fanny (maiden name unknown), former slaves who had migrated from Tennessee. Like many of the so-called "exodusters," the Hamlins moved on to Oklahoma Territory in 1890 and began to farm in Logan County. Educated in Topeka and in Logan County, Albert Hamlin continued to work the family's farm after his father's death in 1891. In 1899 he married Katie Weaver; the couple had five children.

Logan County's population was nearly one-quarter black in 1900. African Americans were especially numerous in such settlements as Langston, an all-black town, and Guthrie, the territorial capital. Hamlin took advantage of such opportunities as their numbers still afforded black Oklahomans, serving on the school board and as a trustee of Springvale Township, where his farm was located. In 1907 Oklahoma became a state, and the next year Hamlin ran for a seat in the legislature. The local black leadership was hardly united in support of his candidacy, however. Convinced that African Americans should be politically independent, the two prominent editors of black newspapers in the county rarely deigned even to mention Hamlin in their columns, no doubt put off by his loyalty to the Republican party. Nevertheless, he won his race by a better than 2 to 1 margin, becoming the only African American to sit in the second legislature.

Hamlin's election as the new state's first black legislator was the most conspicuous manifestation of the black electoral power that increasingly turned white Democrats' thoughts to disfranchisement. With little choice but to accept the more formalized segregation likewise being fastened upon the state, Hamlin evidently sought as a legislator to ensure that if "separate but equal" was to prevail, the latter condition truly be enforced. He helped carry through the legislature a $35,000 appropriation to establish a state school for blind, deaf, and orphaned black children and secured passage of a resolution calling on Oklahoma's Jim Crow railroads to provide genuinely equal accommodations for black patrons. A member of the African Methodist Episcopal church, he also pressed Sabbatarian legislation, and a bill he sponsored banning theatrical performances and baseball games on Sunday passed the legislature in amended form.

Hamlin's efforts to be reelected to the legislature in 1910 came to naught. Supporters claimed he won a majority of several hundred votes but was "counted out" by local officials. Less than two years later Hamlin died of unknown causes on his Logan County farm. He lived long enough to see a literacy restriction on the franchise, together with a "grandfather clause" grafted onto the Oklahoma Constitution. More than half a century passed before another African American sat in the state's legislature.

• Remarkably little about Hamlin's legislative career is in the surviving files of two Logan County African-American papers, the *Western Age* (Langston) and the *Oklahoma Guide* (Guthrie). Kaye M. Teall, ed., *Black History in Oklahoma: A Resource Book* (1971), contains some information from several other contemporary sources. A photograph of Hamlin is in Gene Aldrich, *Black Heritage of Oklahoma* (1973).
PATRICK G. WILLIAMS

HAMLIN, Alfred Dwight Foster (18 Sept.? 1855–21 Mar. 1926), architectural educator, was born near Constantinople, Turkey, the son of Cyrus Hamlin, a Protestant missionary, educator, and founder of Robert College, and Harriet Martha Lovell. After a preparatory education in his father's American school in Turkey, Hamlin embarked for the United States to attend Amherst College in 1871. A brilliant student in the classical Congregationalist education offered there, he was elected to Phi Beta Kappa, won several academic prizes, and graduated with honors in 1875.

Drawn immediately to teaching, Hamlin spent the next two years as an instructor in New England private schools before turning his attention to architecture. In 1876 a critical year as a special student in the architectural program at the Massachusetts Institute of Technology (MIT) brought him into contact with his mentor, William Robert Ware. Ware founded the first school of architecture in the United States at MIT in 1869. At Ware's urging, Hamlin chose to go to Paris to complete his architectural studies. His cosmopolitan education and knowledge of French made him an ideal candidate for the École des Beaux-Arts, where the better part of his professional training was acquired.

In Paris from 1878 to 1881, Hamlin enrolled in the atelier of the influential professor of theory, Julien Guadét. Guadét's 1904 opus, *Eléments et Théorie de l'Architecture*, is considered the last and most modern of the many treatises on composition and design published by École professors. Because of his direct tutelage by Guadét, Hamlin became one of the most persuasive Beaux-Arts pedagogues in the United States in the years to come. Although he received a number of mentions in monthly competitions, he did not stay long enough to receive a *diplôme*, leaving the academy in 1881. Like most American students in Europe, he spent several months traveling throughout the Continent, sketching and visiting the great monuments of Western architecture. Returning to New York in 1882, he immediately went to work for the newly formed firm of McKim, Mead and White.

With a French education and the mentorship of New York's leading architects, Hamlin might have prospered in architectural practice. But he cut short his apprenticeship after a year, choosing instead to follow his father's path to a career in education. In 1883

he accepted an invitation from his MIT professor, Ware, to teach at the new School of Architecture at Columbia University. Thus at age twenty-eight Hamlin entered the nascent field of organized architectural education, where he would make his largest mark. Columbia's program, then in the School of Mines, was the fourth of its kind in the United States and would be one of the most influential. Hamlin's initial responsibilities at the school included teaching courses in architectural history, conducting travel tours, and serving as a studio critic. Ware's program at this time only marginally influenced by École pedagogy, without organized outside ateliers or distinguished practicing architects on the faculty. Hamlin helped to change the course of the program while continuing in the spirit of his mentor.

Ware's failing health caused him to be removed as head of the department in 1903, precipitating something of a crisis at the school. As senior critic, Hamlin was appointed interim director of the program. In order to strengthen ties with the profession, Columbia president Nicholas Murray Butler courted Charles Follen McKim to become the new director of the school, but the busy architect demurred. By 1905 a suitable practitioner had not been found to fill the post. Though Butler initially intended Hamlin's role to be that of a mere caretaker, Hamlin remained in the directorship until 1912, presiding over the formative years of the School of Architecture, now independent of the School of Mines.

Hamlin faced a daunting task, caught between the German-influenced structure of the typical American university curriculum and the demands of an emerging profession. He brought in a number of distinguished practicing architects to teach design, instituting an experimental system of ateliers outside the school. He strengthened courses in architectural history, nurtured the development of the Avery Library collection, and maintained close ties with the Beaux-Arts Institute of Design, an independent educational organization founded by graduates from Paris. Like Ware, Hamlin well understood both the problems and advantages of translating the Beaux-Arts system into an American university curriculum. Pushing for ties with the arts community, Hamlin's most controversial initiative was to merge the architectural program with a new School of Fine Arts. This semiautonomous art, music, and architectural school was to be cosponsored by Columbia, the National Academy of Design, and the Metropolitan Museum of Art, thereby creating a comprehensive academy similar to the École in France. While the idea had its backers, it fizzled, and President Butler was compelled to reconstitute the original School of Architecture program in a new Avery Hall building under new leadership.

After the appointment of Austin Lord as director in 1912, Hamlin returned to teaching and writing, entering his most fertile creative period. From his two popular history courses he developed comprehensive books, *A Textbook of the History of Architecture* (1896, with later editions), and *A History of Ornament* (2 vols., 1916–1923). The former joined Sir Bannister Fletcher's monumental *A History of Architecture on the Comparative Method* (1896) as one of the pioneering attempts to organize and interpret Western building for the English-speaking student. The latter, despite its limited scholarly reach, is still one of the only thorough documentary sources on architectural ornament in English. Both texts give evidence of Hamlin's orderly and measured point of view, a synthesis of the French rational tradition and American pragmatism.

As a critic, Hamlin had a limited but significant influence through sporadic writings in leading architectural journals such as the *Architectural Record*. His articles on the impact of the École des Beaux-Arts on American architecture, on the American country house, and on problems of style and technology in modern architecture are still cited as definitive for their time. Writing during a period when architectural criticism was dominated by journalists and social critics such as Herbert Croly, Montgomery Schuyler, Royal Cortissoz, and Marianna Van Rensselaer, Hamlin brought the disciplined voice of an academic to bear on fin-de-siècle discourse.

To the very end of his life, Hamlin maintained active ties to organized religion, following in his father's Congregationalist footsteps. He rose to become a senior deacon of the Broadway Tabernacle Church in 1925. A civic-minded New Yorker, he also contributed strongly to many city beautification efforts, especially to the construction of the cathedral of St. John the Divine in Morningside Heights.

Hamlin had married Minnie Florence Marston of Hartford, Connecticut, in 1885; they had four children, and he was a devoted father, molding the education of his son Talbot Faulkner, who became a distinguished architect, critic, and historian in his own right. Hamlin died when he was struck and killed by an automobile on his way to church in New York City.

Hamlin played a major role in the development of the system of architectural education now followed in collegiate degree programs throughout the United States. During his more than forty-year career as a professor of architecture at Columbia University, he helped to define a standard curriculum in architectural history and design. As a critic and historian, he served as a persuasive voice for Beaux-Arts–inspired principles of academic eclecticism in the United States.

Hamlin's papers, drawings, and memorabilia are in the Avery Architectural and Fine Arts Library and in the Columbiana Room at Low Library, Columbia University. In addition to the two books mentioned in the text, his major writings include "The Problems of Modern Architecture," in *Congress of Arts and Science: Selected Papers*, from the Universal Exposition, St. Louis, vol. 3 (1904); "The influence of the École des Beaux-Arts on Our Architectural Education," *Architectural Record* 23, no. 4 (Apr. 1908): 241–47; "Architectural Education in America," *RIBA Journal*, ser. 3, vol. 17 (18 Dec. 1909): 141–62; "Twenty-five Years of American Architecture," *Architectural Record* 40 (July 1916): 1–14; "The American Country House," *Archi-tectural Record* 42 (Oct. 1917): 291–391; and "The Architectural Problems of Concrete," *American Architect and Building News* 91 (4 May 1907): 163.

• The best scholarly source is Peter S. Kaufman, *American Architectural Writing, Beaux-Arts Style: The Lives and Works of Alfred Dwight Foster Hamlin and Talbot Faulkner Hamlin* (1991), microfilm. On Hamlin at Columbia see Richard Oliver, ed., *The Making of an Architect 1881–1981* (1981), and Theodor K. Rohdenburg, *A History of the School of Architecture, Columbia University* (1954). On the Hamlin genealogy, see Henry Franklin Andrews, *History of the Hamlin Family with Genealogies of Early Settlers of the Name in America, 1639–1894* (1894), and Simon Moulton Hamlin, *The Hamlins of New England, Descendants of James and Anna Hamlin, Barnstable County, Massachusetts, 1639–1936* (1936). An obituary is in the *New York Times*, 22 Mar. 1926.

MARK A. HEWITT

HAMLIN, Charles (13 Sept. 1837–15 May 1911), Civil War officer and lawyer, was born in Hampden, Maine, the son of Hannibal Hamlin, a lawyer, politician, and vice president of the United States, and Sarah Jane Emery. After graduation from Bowdoin College in 1857, Hamlin studied law in his father's office, was admitted to the bar in October 1858, and began a law practice at Orland, Maine. He was a political confidant of his father and accompanied the new vice president at Abraham Lincoln's inauguration in March 1861.

In August 1862, after serving as a recruiting officer in eastern Maine, Hamlin received a commission as major in the Eighteenth Maine Infantry, reorganized as the First Maine Heavy Artillery. Later serving in the III Corps, Army of the Potomac, he was officially commended for his conduct at Little Round Top during the battle of Gettysburg (2 July 1863) and saw action in a number of other engagements. He was subsequently stationed in Washington, D.C., as assistant to the inspector of artillery and in March 1865 was brevetted brigadier general in the U.S. Volunteers.

Hamlin was present at the assassination of President Lincoln (14 Apr. 1865) and called out the troops of his command to secure the streets of Washington against anticipated civil unrest. Hamlin resigned his commission in September 1865 but remained active throughout his life in veterans' activities. He commanded the Maine chapter of the Military Order of the Loyal Legion and edited and contributed to *Maine at Gettysburg* (1898), the report of the Maine Gettysburg Commission, of which he was executive committee chairman. Known for the rest of his life as "General" Hamlin, he died in Bangor and was buried in his uniform.

On his return to Maine in 1865, Hamlin established a law practice in Bangor, where he lived and worked until his death. As a private practitioner, he concentrated on bankruptcy and insolvency law. He was actively involved in business and had a major role in the development of banking institutions as drafter of a law regulating building and loan associations (1887), organizer of the Bangor Building and Loan Association (1885) and similar associations elsewhere in the state, and a founding and continuing trustee of the Penobscot Savings Bank (1869–1911). Hamlin was the driving force in the establishment and success of Bangor's Eastern Maine Hospital, which he served as president from 1892 until 1911.

Hamlin was Bangor city solicitor in 1867–1868. He served as register in bankruptcy for the U.S. District Court at Bangor from 1867, when that quasi-judicial position was created by the new federal Bankruptcy Act, until 1878, when the 1867 act was repealed. In 1867 Hamlin was also appointed as one of the additional U.S. commissioners authorized for each district court under the federal Civil Rights Act of 1866; he exercised the minor judicial powers of that office until his death. He represented Bangor for two terms in the Maine House of Representatives, 1883–1886, serving as Speaker of the house in his second term. In 1888 he was appointed reporter of decisions by the Maine Supreme Judicial Court and served in that capacity until 1904, producing volumes 81–98 and a portion of volume 99 of the *Maine Reports*.

When Maine enacted its own insolvency law after repeal of the federal Bankruptcy Act in 1878, Hamlin drew on his experience as register to write a short treatise, *Insolvent Laws of Maine* (1878), relating the new Maine legislation to its federal predecessor and similar laws of other states. Hamlin also published a series of six articles on the history of the supreme judicial court in the professional journal the *Green Bag* (1895–1896), and a biography of Maine's most noteworthy nineteenth-century chief justice, John Appleton, in volume five of *Great American Lawyers* (1908), edited by William Draper Lewis. In 1898 Hamlin was one of the founders of the original University of Maine College of Law, located in Bangor, and was a lecturer on bankruptcy and federal procedure there from the opening of the school until his death. In 1909 the honorary degree of Doctor of Laws was conferred on him by the University of Maine.

In 1860 Hamlin had married Sarah Purinton Thompson of Topsham, Maine; she predeceased him in 1905. They had four children. Charles Eugene Hamlin, the eldest, was the author of *The Life and Times of Hannibal Hamlin* (1899), a work that drew heavily on Charles Hamlin's notes and recollections of his father and material gathered by him for a biography.

Charles Hamlin was typical of a generation that used leadership skills, courage, idealism, and sense of civic responsibility acquired in the Civil War to make the communities to which they returned more ordered and humane places. In his private practice and business activities, he was an important builder of civic and economic institutions. He also made significant contributions to the stability and growth of Maine through his legislative and judicial service and his role in the development of banking and other institutions. With his legal writing and teaching, he helped to reestablish an intellectual framework for the law in a state that for a time before the Civil War had abandoned requirements of education and examination for admission to the bar.

Hamlin was greatly respected and admired by his contemporaries not only for these achievements but as a man of great culture and humanity. In resolutions passed upon his death, the Penobscot County bar mourned him as "almost the last link . . . between the lawyers of today and those of a former generation," whose "high ideals . . . found in him their full expression." The resolutions also recognized his war service and subsequent professional and public activities and noted that "[h]is manners were gentle, cordial and democratic, . . . his integrity unquestioned, his personality rich and winsome" and that "[h]e was devoted to his family, and kind and loyal to his neighbors and friends."

• Hamlin's extensive correspondence with his father, c. 1855–1891, and other papers are in the Hannibal Hamlin Papers, Fogler Library, University of Maine, Orono. His account of events in Washington at the time of Lincoln's assassination appears in his essay, "Darkest Hour," in the Maine Commandery of the Military Order of the Loyal Legion, *War Papers*, vol. 1 (1898): pp. 254–59. Hamlin's legal writings include *Catalogue of Bankrupts of the District of Maine* (1873); "The Growth of the Constitution," *Maine Law Review* 1 (1908): 51–54; and Preface, *The Peters Banquet Tendered the Honorable John A. Peters by the Penobscot Bar* (1900). His relationship with his father is documented and discussed in Charles E. Hamlin's work cited in the text and in H. Draper Hunt, *Hannibal Hamlin of Maine: Lincoln's First Vice-President* (1969), the authoritative biography of the elder Hamlin. See also H. Franklin Andrews, *The Hamlin Family* (1902); Horace H. Shaw and Charles J. House, *The First Maine Heavy Artillery* (1903); Merritt C. Fernald, *History of the Maine State College and the University of Maine* (1916), pp. 307–19, 406–7; and William E. Walz, "General Charles Hamlin: In Memoriam," *Maine Law Review* 5 (1912): 251–53. A memorial resolution and several tributes appear in Penobscot County Bar, "Services in Memory of Franklin A. Wright and Charles Hamlin" (1911). Charles Hamlin's obituary, an editorial eulogy, and an account of his funeral are in the *Bangor Daily News*, 16, 18, and 19 May 1911.

L. KINVIN WROTH

HAMLIN, Hannibal (27 Aug. 1809–4 July 1891), fifteenth vice president of the United States, was born in Paris, Maine, the son of Cyrus Hamlin (1769–1829), a physician, sheriff of Oxford County, and farmer, and Anna Livermore. Hannibal was schooled locally and attended Hebron Academy for a year (1826–1827), worked as a clerk, learned surveying, and taught school briefly before returning home to run the family farm after his father died unexpectedly in 1829. Drawn into politics, he became co-owner of the local Democratic newspaper but soon left the concern.

Deciding to become a lawyer, Hamlin studied law on his own and served a stint in the Portland law office of Samuel Fessenden. Fessenden, Maine's premier abolitionist, failed to convert Hamlin to his cause. Hamlin believed, then as later, that while slavery was morally wrong and should be confined to the southern states where it existed by law, abolitionism was too radical a remedy on constitutional grounds.

Hamlin passed the Maine bar in 1833 and in that year married Sarah Jane Emery; they had four children. The couple eventually settled in Hampden, a village near Bangor, where he hung out his shingle. Handily elected as a Jacksonian Democrat in 1835, Hamlin served six one-year terms in the Maine House of Representatives (1836–1841, 1847), three of them as Speaker. He fought unsuccessfully to abolish capital punishment and championed the right of antislavery petitions to be fully aired, condemning slavery as a plague.

In 1843 Hamlin was elected to Congress, serving two terms in the House. Hamlin fought at John Quincy Adams's side to rescind the "gag rule," which barred abolitionist petitions from consideration by the House. He opposed Texas annexation on antislavery grounds and saw the Mexican War as a southern plot to expand the "peculiar institution." Hamlin helped formulate the Wilmot Proviso, which proposed to ban slavery from any territory acquired from Mexico.

Losing his bid for a seat in the U.S. Senate in 1846, Hamlin then served a term in the Maine House, where he authored antislavery resolutions, condemning the "peculiar institution" as evil and supporting the Wilmot Proviso exclusionary principle. In 1848 he entered the senatorial race to fill the seat vacated by the death of U.S. senator John Fairfield and this time succeeded.

As senator Hamlin opposed the prosouthern elements of the Compromise of 1850 while championing admission of free California. He fought a desperate fight for reelection against so-called proslavery Maine Democrats, who believed Hamlin's views endangered national unity and, by irritating the South, threatened to interfere with the lucrative New England carrying trade in cotton. The senator won a paper-thin victory in the Maine legislature.

Opposed to the expansion of slavery, Hamlin broke with his party to oppose the Kansas-Nebraska Bill (1854), and in 1856 he abandoned the Democratic party altogether. Converting at once to the new Republican party, he won the Maine governorship by a huge margin in a rousing contest. He served only a few weeks as governor, however, before the legislature returned him to the U.S. Senate early in 1857. In 1856, his first wife having died the previous year, Hamlin married her half-sister, Ellen Vesta Emery; they had two sons.

During his second year in the Senate, Hamlin had become chairman of the Committee on Commerce and in due course a renowned authority on U.S. commercial matters. Shipping, customs and revenue, river and harbor improvements, and other commercial matters were grist for his mill. He also championed the rights of American fishermen throughout the 1850s. Giving up his chairmanship upon conversion to the Republican party was one of the great disappointments of his public career. Hamlin also supported the transcontinental railroad. He bitterly attacked southern dominance in national affairs, as exemplified by the Buchanan administration's endorsement of the

Dred Scott decision and the Lecompton Constitution. Hamlin prided himself on being a "working" rather than a "talking" senator and proved especially adept at rounding up jobs and other patronage favors for Maine supporters, at least until he broke with the Democrats.

In 1860 the Republican National Convention nominated Senator Hamlin for vice president. The former Democrat from Maine balanced nicely the former Whig from Illinois, and Hamlin was perceived as a supporter of William H. Seward (incorrectly, since he feared the N.Y. senator would lose the election), with many delegates eager to offer a consolation prize to the disappointed Sewardites. Hamlin indicated that, had he been at Chicago, he would have declined the nomination, but he was a "good soldier" and accepted. The "powerless second office in the land" had no appeal to a powerful senator skilled in garnering and distributing patronage, but he made the most of it. During the campaign, southern demagogues rumored that Hamlin, a man of exceptionally swarthy skin, was a mulatto. Like Abraham Lincoln, Hamlin did not campaign, write, or speak for attribution, but he corresponded widely.

Hamlin found the vice presidency as frustrating and hollow a job as he had feared. True, the president-elect summoned him to Chicago to consult on cabinet appointments and let him choose the New England member, Gideon Welles of Connecticut, who became secretary of the navy, but once in office, Hamlin was rarely consulted by Lincoln. The vice president lamented that the federal government moved both slowly and unsatisfactorily regarding military and emancipation policy and that nobody paid any attention to his advice. Hamlin took a more radical position than Lincoln on slavery issues during the war, urging emancipation and the use of black troops long before Lincoln felt ready to take those steps.

Lack of influence over patronage particularly frustrated Hamlin. He groused in 1864, concerning his efforts to have a Maine general promoted, that the president and secretary of war paid no attention to his recommendation. Hamlin came to think of the vice president as standby equipment who could do little to help his friends. Yet he clearly wanted and expected renomination at the 1864 National Union party convention. His replacement on the ticket by Andrew Johnson of Tennessee stunned the sturdy Maine Republican. President Lincoln's role in the substitution of Johnson for Hamlin has been the source of considerable historical controversy, since Lincoln ostensibly left the choice of his running mate entirely to the convention. However, evidence suggests that the president worked behind the scenes to endorse Johnson's nomination, since as a War Democrat from a southern state, he would bring far more strength to the ticket than Hamlin. Unaware at the time of Lincoln's decisive role in his removal, Hamlin put on a brave face and loyally campaigned for the Lincoln-Johnson ticket. He spent much of that summer playing soldier as color corporal and company cook in a militia unit in Kittery, Maine.

After the war, Hamlin served briefly as collector of the Port of Boston and from 1869 to 1881 as U.S. senator. He chaired the Senate Foreign Relations Committee beginning in 1877 and, to his credit, strongly opposed the Chinese Exclusion Bill. He gave his support to federal efforts to protect carpetbag regimes in the reconstructed states. Senator Hamlin's loyalty to President Ulysses S. Grant was amply rewarded by jobs for the senator's friends. He found President Rutherford B. Hayes far less responsive and came to regard him as a political enemy because of clashes over patronage and the president's decision to end Reconstruction.

In 1881 Hamlin went to Spain as U.S. minister. He seems to have been essentially a tourist and sightseer, his post a reward for faithful party service. He returned to the United States in 1882 and died while playing cards at his Bangor club.

Although not a statesman of the first rank, Hamlin was a premier antislavery leader in Maine, and his career as vice president illustrates well the nineteenth-century limitations of that office.

• The Hannibal Hamlin Papers are located in the Raymond S. Fogler Library, University of Maine. Charles Eugene Hamlin, *The Life and Times of Hannibal Hamlin* (1899), is a laudatory but still useful biography by the statesman's grandson. H. Draper Hunt, *Hannibal Hamlin of Maine: Lincoln's First Vice-President* (1969), is the only modern biography. The best source for Maine politics in this period is Louis Hatch, ed., *Maine: A History* (3 vols., 1919).

H. DRAPER HUNT

HAMLIN, Talbot Faulkner (16 June 1889–7 Oct. 1956), architect, professor, and librarian, was born in New York City, the son of Alfred Dwight Foster Hamlin, a professor of architecture at Columbia University, and Minnie Florence Marston. He began his writing career at the age of twelve with a translation from the Latin of Pliny's letter describing his Laurentine villa. He received a B.A. in classics and English at Amherst College (1910), where he was elected to Phi Beta Kappa. From there he proceeded to Columbia School of Architecture, where he received a B.Arch. in 1914. That same year he began to work as a draughtsman in the New York architectural firm of Murphy and Dana. In 1916 he married Hilda B. Edwards; they had three sons. That year he published his first book, *The Enjoyment of Architecture*, illustrated by many sketches in his own hand and became an instructor of architectural history and theory at Columbia University's extension school.

Hamlin became a partner of Murphy and Dana in 1920, and the firm was renamed Murphy, McGill, & Hamlin. In 1926, a few years after his first marriage ended in divorce, he married Sarah H. J. Simpson, a historian, who died in 1930. The following year he married Jessica V. Walters. He formed his own practice in 1930. As a practicing architect he worked on housing projects and educational institutions both in America and in Asia, the most significant of which

were Ginling College (1920) in China and the College of New Rochelle (1925) in New York.

Hamlin was appointed director of the Avery Architectural Library at Columbia University in 1934, at which time he gave up his architectural practice, although he continued to write and to teach. As librarian he made many contributions to the field of architectural librarianship, and it can be said that it was he who brought Avery to the international distinction that it has enjoyed until the present time. With the aid of a grant from the Rockefeller Foundation he made a study tour of European libraries and published the results as *Some European Architectural Libraries: Their Methods, Equipment, and Administration* (1939). In this he outlines the problems created by the special nature of architectural materials straddling three types of institutions: libraries, archives, and museums. He also reports the lessons gleaned from European libraries at a time when American libraries were in turn studied by Europeans for their modern equipment and methods.

Although the first Avery librarian, Edward R. Smith, had already explored the idea of a periodical index, it was Hamlin who devoted time and resources to the creation and development of as complete a record as possible of the periodical literature on architecture, architects, and building. The *Avery Index to Architectural Periodicals* is consulted in paper or electronic form all over the world. Hamlin also developed an obituary index of architects through newspaper clippings, and increased the collection of drawings and archives through a systematic pursuit of significant donations.

Hamlin gave up the Avery librarianship when he became a full professor at Columbia's School of Architecture in 1946; he continued to teach until his retirement in 1954. Kenneth Frampton, in his essay on Hamlin in *The Making of an Architect* (1981), calls him one of the most prolific writers of his generation and highlights his role as a kind of "public conscience" or "intellectual guardian of the public weal" during the New Deal, not only through his almost daily critical writing but through his thirteen-year-long association with the U.S. Housing Authority Architectural Advisory Committee, of which he was a member from 1941 through 1954.

Of his books, the most significant are *Greek Revival Architecture in America* (1944), which is both an authoritative historical study and a benchmark of Hamlin's search for an adequate architectural expression for the democratic ideals of American life and government; *Forms and Functions of Twentieth-Century Architecture* (1952); and the biography of *Benjamin Henry Latrobe* (1955), for which he won the Pulitzer Prize in 1956.

Forms and Functions of Twentieth Century Architecture was a multivolume compilation for which Hamlin was both the general editor and a major contributor. Published under the auspices of Columbia's School of Architecture, it was an attempt to revise and recast Julien Guadet's *Elements et Théories de l'Architecture*

(1902), which summed up the precepts and practices of the French École des Beaux-Arts at the turn of the century, and thus to provide a theoretical framework for the study and teaching of architecture in America in the second half of the twentieth century.

Hamlin's other writings span a broad range of subjects that portray his eclectic interests and well-rounded erudition, from essays on the burlesque, through the various associations reflected in the ownership plates of books in Avery's rare book collections, to sailing. With his wife, Jessica, he coauthored a delightful book, *We Took to Cruising* (1951), documenting their travels and life on a yacht, the *Aquarelle*. He died in Beaufort, South Carolina.

• Hamlin's drawings, manuscripts, and correspondence are in the Avery Architectural and Fine Arts Library at Columbia University, where there are more than 150 articles by and about him. For additional information, see the chapter on Hamlin by Kenneth Frampton in *The Making of an Architect, 1881–1981*, ed. Richard Oliver (1981), issued on the centenary of the founding of the Graduate School of Architecture at Columbia University.

ANGELA GIRAL

HAMLIN, William (15 Oct. 1772–22 Nov. 1869), engraver and maker of scientific instruments, was born in Providence, Rhode Island, the son of Samuel Hamlin, a pewterer, and Thankful Ely. When he was four years old, he was taken to Middletown, Connecticut, remaining there until he was twenty-one. At the age of fifteen he was apprenticed to Samuel Canfield, a goldsmith and silversmith. Hamlin had wanted to be a painter, but his father made him follow a trade. He also took lessons in engraving from Richard Brunton. After completing his apprenticeship, he went to New York City and worked for Dudley Mann in Maiden Lane and for Peter Allison on Broadway, both silversmiths. After a few months, however, he returned to Providence to care for his ailing parents.

Hamlin started a silversmith business in Providence, but he soon began to engrave and print bank notes for most of the banks in the state. In 1797, when he was proposed for membership in the Providence Association of Mechanics and Manufacturers, he was called an "engraver and goldsmith." In 1804 he became a member of Mount Vernon Lodge No. 4, a Masonic lodge. He also joined the Cadet and Providence Artillery companies, two military organizations.

In 1798 Hamlin engraved a certificate for the Providence Marine Society, across the bottom of which is the earliest printed view of Providence, and in 1803 he made the first engraved map of Providence. He also engraved portraits, views of churches, and trade cards. He made his own engraving tools and probably made his copperplate printing presses. (Two small presses of his, both mounted on one stand, are now owned by the Rhode Island Historical Society.) His engravings were mostly mezzotints or a combination of mezzotint and stipple engraving, and his style has been called naive.

On 18 October 1806 the *Providence Gazette* advertised that Hamlin sold fancy goods—"Gold, Silver, plated and Britannia Ware, with numerous other Articles in the Fancy Line." By December of the following year he was also selling musical instruments, books of instruction, sheet music, and violin and bass-viol strings. Hamlin played the flute, fife, and drums. On 15 July 1809 he announced that he had formed a partnership with his brother John H. Hamlin to sell jewelry, fancy goods, and military goods, and he engraved a trade card for the new firm. In April 1810 Hamlin married Eliza Bowen, daughter of Isaac and Sarah Whittaker Bowen; they had four children.

Hamlin later began to make and repair nautical and scientific instruments, and he also sold nautical books and charts. He was listed in city directories beginning in 1824, the date of the first Providence directory, through 1855–1856 as an engraver and mathematical instrument maker. From 1857 on he was listed as a maker of mathematical instruments only, except between 1867 and 1869, when he was called a nautical instrument maker. In Benjamin F. Moore's *The Providence Almanac and Business Directory for the Year 1843*, he is not listed under "engravers" but under "Miscellaneous. Compass Maker." In subsequent volumes he is listed as a mathematical instrument maker.

In 1840 Hamlin moved his shop to 69 South Water Street on the Providence waterfront, and by 1847 it was at 131 South Water Street. Two different trade cards with the latter address are known, one of which shows the corner of the building containing his shop, at the "Sign of the Quadrant." It indicates that he made and repaired compasses, quadrants, sextants, spyglasses, reflecting telescopes, and microscopes. An oil portrait of him now owned by a descendant shows him holding a spyglass. The other card adds that he also did engraving and copperplate printing.

In July 1826 Hamlin completed a reflecting telescope, the earliest telescope known to have been made in America. In August he set it up near the First Congregational Church (at which he was a pew holder) and sold tickets, letting people view the planets Jupiter and Venus, which were then in conjunction. The engraved tickets show a telescope and a woman leaning on an anchor. A short biography of Hamlin published in the *Providence Journal* on 9 March 1867, a few months before his death, described his workplace: "He is generally to be found in his work-shop, busy in grinding a large lens for a telescope. . . . In one corner stands a well-used printing-press, and the walls are hung with old-fashioned quadrants, and different parts of nautical and astronomical inventions, and models of hydrostatic machines. Everything around gives the room the appearance of a curiosity-shop." The article also said Hamlin was very interested in astronomy and conversed on the subject with great enthusiasm.

Hamlin made numerous other things, including fraternal badges, a brass belt buckle, a commemorative plaque, various pieces of silverware, and an embossed leather cockade, for which he also cut the steel dies that stamped it. Hamlin died in Providence, having been active until a week before his death. He is buried in Swan Point Cemetery in Providence. He was one of the first engravers in America, the first American to build a telescope, and a craftsman of considerable versatility.

• Two general biographical articles about Hamlin are Gladys R. Lane, "Rhode Island's Earliest Engraver," *Antiques* 7, no. 3 (Mar. 1925): 133–37; and Eugene Van Wye, "William Hamlin, Providence Engraver," *Rhode Island History* 20, no. 2 (Apr. 1961): 33–44. A few additional details about his life can be found in Philip J. Weimerskirch, ed., "An Unpublished Obituary of William Hamlin, Rhode Island's First Engraver," *American Historical Print Collectors Society News Letter* 17, no. 2 (Fall 1992): 5–6; and James E. Mauran, "William Hamlin," *Providence Journal*, 9 May 1869. Hamlin's work as a maker of scientific instruments is discussed in Anne MacDougall Preuss, "William Hamlin: An Elusive Providence Instrument Maker," *Rittenhouse, Journal of the American Scientific Instrument Enterprise* 3, no. 4 (1989): 135–40. His telescope making is described in Silvio A. Bedini, "William Hamlin and His Telescopes," *Rittenhouse, Journal of the American Scientific Instrument Enterprise* 4, no. 3 (1990): 87–95. A cockade made by Hamlin is described in Robert P. Emlen, "From the Collections: An Embossed Leather Cockade by Providence Engraver William Hamlin," *Rhode Island History* 44, no. 2 (May 1985): 58–59. His certificate for the Providence Marine Society is described in L. Earle Rowe, "An Interesting Certificate," *Antiques* 19, no. 1 (Jan. 1931).

PHILIP J. WEIMERSKIRCH

HAMLINE, Leonidas Lent (10 May 1797–23 Mar. 1865), bishop of the Methodist Episcopal church, was born in Burlington, Connecticut, the son of Mark Hamline, a farmer and schoolmaster, and Roxanna Moses. His father added an *e* to Hamlin. Inspired by his son's intellectual precosity and religious disposition, Mark Hamline, a member of the Congregationalist church, prepared him educationally for the ministry. Extremely conscientious, Leonidas Hamline suffered a nervous and mental breakdown in 1815, after which he spent time recovering in South Carolina. Although he enjoyed success briefly as a Presbyterian minister in Pittsburgh, Pennsylvania, he felt his religious experience was lacking and decided to leave clerical office and enter the bar. He moved to Ohio. In 1824 he married Eliza Price; they had one child who survived infancy. Although records indicate that he joined the Zanesville bar in 1825, he is quoted as stating that he was admitted to the Lancaster, Ohio, bar in 1827. After the death of his infant daughter in 1828, Hamline converted to the Methodist church on 5 October 1828 while on a trip to New York State and returned to the ministry. He was licensed to the itinerant ministry in Ohio in November 1829, became a probationary member of the Ohio Conference in 1832, and was ordained deacon in 1834. That year he was stationed as junior pastor at Wesley Chapel, Cincinnati, until his ordination as elder in 1836. His wife died on 27 March 1835, and in 1836 he married Melinda Truesdell. They had no children.

To the dismay of Hamline's congregation, only three months after his appointment as minister in Co-

lumbus, Ohio, the General Conference elected him assistant editor of the *Western Christian Advocate* in Cincinnati. He began in September 1836 and was reelected in 1840. During his term in office he gave his support to the German mission in Cincinnati, whose existence was under threat, and at his instigation a German newspaper was founded, *Der Christliche Apologete*, which was popular from the first issue, 4 January 1839. His promotion of missions was constant throughout in his career. For example, in 1847, a year before gold was discovered in the Sacramento Valley, Hamline requested the establishment of a Californian mission. During these years Hamline and his wife also supported the holiness revival led by Phoebe Palmer, regularly attending her Tuesday Meeting for the Promotion of Holiness in New York City.

As a delegate to the General Conference of 1840, Hamline took the chair of the Committee on the Memorial to Establish a Periodical for Females. He accepted the editorship of the proposed *Ladies Repository and Gatherings of the West*, which at his instigation began experimentally in 1841 as a Christian counterpart to popular women's magazines. The journal, to which Hamline contributed many articles, rapidly gained prestige, and its continuance was firmly approved by the General Conference of 1844, held in New York City. At this conference, Hamline took a leading role in the central debate over the slaveholding bishop, James O. Andrew, and was rewarded with election to the episcopacy.

The debate focused on the right of the General Conference to suspend a bishop. Hamline was placed on the Committee of Six formed to conciliate between the northern and southern delegates over the resolution that Bishop Andrew desist from his office until he no longer held slaves. In Hamline's memorable speech, which was described by a contemporary as "authority in all the future history of the Methodist Episcopal Church," his oratorical skills and training at the bar came to the fore. Upholding the resolution, he argued the legal principle that, constitutionally, the General Conference was authorized to suspend a bishop's office. Eleven days afterward, on 7 June, he was elected bishop by the Ohio Conference. That same year he had begun to suffer from heart disease (angina pectoris). While Hamline had determined that his condition should not affect his agenda, the schedule of constant travel along with the ecclesiastical politics engendered by the division of the church brought him to a state of nervous exhaustion, and in 1852 he tendered his resignation, seeking to return his ordination papers to the General Conference.

This unprecedented move further challenged the General Conference over the question of the episcopacy. Hamline's offer of resignation demonstrated his belief in the principle that the bishop was solely an officer of the General Conference and that the office did not constitute a third ecclesiastical order. In the debate that ensued, a substitute resolution that he should retire rather than resign was proposed. The defeat of this marked the acceptance by the conference of the view of the bishop as an officer. Hamline was then received as an elder by the Ohio Conference.

After his retirement, Hamline and his wife at first remained in the East near their son (from his first marriage). During this time, Hamline donated generously from the wealth he had inherited from his first wife, focusing on the promotion of education and missions. In May 1854 he gave $25,000 to found Hamline University in St. Paul, Minnesota, and the same sum to found Mount Vernon Institute in Iowa. He bequeathed also to Methodist missions, church buildings, and societies. In April 1857 he and his wife moved to Mount Pleasant, Iowa, where Hamline, despite illness, drew up a plan of financial reorganization on behalf of Wesleyan College in Mount Pleasant.

Hamline's work as a publisher for the Methodist Episcopal church marked him as one of the church's intellectual talents. His contribution to the Bishop Andrew controversy established for him a place in the history of the development of Methodist doctrine. It is to be noted, too, that his personal popularity played no small part in the debate over the acceptance of his resignation, despite the fact that on theological issues he held forthright views, never afraid to question current thinking. He died in Mount Pleasant.

• Some of Hamline's correspondence is in the Drew University Manuscript Collection, Madison, N.J. Hamline's writings and sermons were published as *Works of Rev. Leonidas L. Hamline D.D.*, ed. F. G. Hibbard (2 vols., 1869, 1871). Biographies of Hamline are Walter C. Palmer, *Life and Letters of Leonidas L. Hamline D.D.* (1866), and Hibbard, *Biography of Rev. Leonidas L. Hamline D.D.* (1880). Biographical articles of interest are in Matthew Simpson, ed., *Cyclopaedia of Methodism* (1878), and Frederick D. Leete, *Methodist Bishops* (1948). For discussions of Hamline's contribution to the James O. Andrew debate, see Charles W. Ferguson, *Methodists and the Making of America* (1983); Marie S. White, "The Methodist Antislavery Struggle in the Land of Lincoln," *Methodist History* 10, no. 4: 33–52; Albea Godbold, "Methodist Episcopacy," *Methodist History* 11, no. 1: 15–29; and Emory Stevens Bucke, ed., *The History of American Methodism*, vol. 2 (1964), which also includes a discussion of the debate over Hamline's resignation. Contextual reference to the *Ladies Repository* and Hamline's editorship is Frederick A. Norwood, *The Story of American Methodism* (1974). His support of missions is discussed in Gerald O. McCulloh, *Ministerial Education in the American Methodist Movement* (1980). For Hamline's view on sanctification, see J. Wesley Corbin, "Christian Perfection and the Evangelical Association through 1875," *Methodist History* 7, no. 2: 28–44, and for his support of the holiness revival, see Charles Edwin Jones, *Perfectionist Persuasion* (1974).

JOANNA HAWKE

HAMMER, Armand (21 May 1898–10 Dec. 1990), entrepreneur and philanthropist, was born on the Lower East Side of New York City, the son of Russian-born Julius Hammer, a pharmacist and physician, and Rose Robinson. Hammer's childhood economic circumstances were better than those of many of his immigrant contemporaries. When he was still a child, his family moved to the Bronx, where his father balanced a quest for a medical degree with the demands of his drugstores. Hammer attended Morris High School and in 1917 registered at Columbia Heights Premedical School. Two years later he enrolled at Columbia College of Physicians and Surgeons, from which he graduated in June 1921.

Medicine, however, never captured Hammer's interest. He rarely attended lectures and did not undertake an internship upon graduation. By 1917 he was manager at his father's pharmaceutical company, Good Laboratories (subsequently Allied Drug and Chemical). Those operations made Hammer a millionaire before the age of twenty and more accurately reflected his career interests than his medical degree.

Hammer's business success, while remarkable, might have attracted little historical interest had he not sought further fortune in the Soviet Union in the 1920s. At a time when the West was ostracizing Lenin's government, Hammer saw opportunity there. With contacts provided by his uncle Alexander Gomberg, Hammer sailed for Moscow. He obtained, partly with the assistance of Lenin, an asbestos concession, the first foreign concession granted to western interests after the revolution. He simultaneously founded Alamerico Corporation to engage in barter between the Soviet Union and the West in commodities that were in short supply in Russia, such as wheat, and in high demand in the West, such as caviar. Recognizing the shortage of quality lead pencils in a society that was dedicated to universal education, Hammer established in 1925 a pencil factory in Moscow and imported skilled workers and technology from Germany and England. In the same period, he facilitated the first sales of Ford tractors in Russia.

Russia brought Hammer fortune and his first wife, Olga von Root, with whom he had his only child. He demonstrated in the Soviet Union that he was able to work with diverse political regimes, as long as they were favorable to business. When Stalin's rise, however, threatened his interests, he moved with his young family first to Paris and then to New York.

The 1930s and 1940s were eventful both personally and professionally. His first marriage ended in divorce in 1934. In 1943 he married Angela Zevely, who developed alcoholism and refused to bear children. Both facts devastated Hammer, and the marriage ended in divorce in 1956. That same year Hammer married Frances Tolman Barrett, with whom he had long shared a love of art.

Hammer's business activities in these years were eclectic. He convinced several major American department stores, most significantly Lord & Taylor's in New York City, to market the collection of czarist Russian art, jewelry, memorabilia, and artifacts that he had brought from Moscow. He established the Hammer Galleries on Fifth Avenue in the mid-1930s. He also obtained a contract to sell a substantial portion of William Randolph Hearst's art collection for the cash-starved newspaper magnate, this time in cooperation with Saks Fifth Avenue.

Hammer also found opportunities in the liquor industry. Anticipating a major demand for beer and liquor barrels after the Volstead Act was repealed, he made a timely investment in that area. By 1943 he had also moved into alcoholic beverages with the purchases of shares in American Distilling, a New England rum distillery, where he processed potatoes, and then the J. W. Dant distillery in Dant, Kentucky, producers of high-quality sour mash bourbon. In 1954 he sold Dant distilleries to Schenley's, the major multinational whiskey producer.

In 1947 Hammer shifted directions yet again. Acting on impulse, he acquired high-quality Black Angus breeding operations in the United States. In 1955 he settled with his third wife on the West Coast. He was in his late fifties, an age at which many individuals of his wealth would have considered retiring. A desire to reduce his taxable income led him into the oil industry, and once involved, his pride and business skills drove him beyond an interest in tax relief.

In 1957 Hammer acquired a controlling interest in Occidental Petroleum Company, which at that time was on the verge of financial collapse. Combining reckless financial risk and the employment of highly successful oil drilling interests, Occidental made a major natural gas strike in the Sacramento Valley. Hammer then diversified by acquiring potash, phosphate, and sulfur resources, including Best Fertilizer Company, Jefferson Lake Petro-Chemicals, and International Ore and Fertilizer Corporation, at that time the world's largest marketer of fertilizer. These holdings contributed to his conclusion of a major contract to supply the Soviet Union with chemical fertilizers. In the late 1960s he also acquired the Island Creek Coal Company and Hooker Chemical and Plastics.

In 1966 Hammer took Occidental into the international arena by successfully bidding on a concession in Libya, which was then ruled by Emir Mohammed Idris El Senussi. Once again, bravado, luck, and improved drilling technology favored Occidental, which uncovered two valuable fields of high-quality crude oil in the Libyan desert. The second strike represented the largest well in Libya, with an estimated reserve of two billion barrels. Hammer thoughtfully named it the Idris Field. Because Occidental did not possess the refineries and markets, Hammer reached an agreement with Signal Oil, which had refining, transport, and marketing facilities in Western Europe.

Hammer and Occidental survived the nationalistic policies of the post-1969 Libyan military government of Muammar al-Qaddafi. Inspired by Egyptian president Gamal Abdel Nasser's Arab nationalism, Qadaffi at first threatened nationalization of the oil industry and then settled with Hammer in 1973 for a 51 percent interest, increased royalties and taxes, and a substantial price increase for Libyan oil. The Libyan initiative was a critical development in the history of the international oil industry, reversing a downward trend in international prices and encouraging more nationalistic policies by the world's producers.

Hammer's contribution to international relations is difficult to evaluate. His own accounts of his relationship with Soviet leaders from Lenin and Trotsky to Gorbachev are exaggerated. He met Lenin only once, and then briefly. Nonetheless, a combination of his professional skills and personal charm, along with his economic contribution to the Soviet Union in the 1920s, gave him privileged entrée to Soviet officials. That access made him useful to President Franklin D. Roosevelt and New Deal administrator Harry Hopkins during the implementation of lend-lease, the prewar Roosevelt administration program that enabled the United States to supply war materiel primarily to the Soviet Union and Great Britain. His contacts with Premier Nikita Khrushchev and Deputy Premier Anastas Mikoyan made him valuable to President John F. Kennedy in early 1961, when they were seeking resolution of a trade dispute. His meetings with Premier Leonid Brezhnev in 1973 smoothed the way for President Richard Nixon's own negotiations with the Soviet leader. His meeting with Mikhail Gorbachev and subsequently with President Ronald Reagan in 1985 contributed to the Reagan-Gorbachev Geneva summit later that year. Whatever the real extent of his influence on events, Hammer was a tireless worker for international peace, who was generally free of the restraints of narrow ideology that blinded so many of his generation.

A significant philanthropist, Hammer worked to provide a team of physicians to Russia after the Chernobyl nuclear accident, to allow Soviet dissident Jews to emigrate, and to gain official and private support for cancer research in the United States. For thirty years Hammer served on the board of the Eleanor Roosevelt Cancer Foundation. In 1970 he established a cancer research center in San Diego. In a contribution to bilateral goodwill between the United States and Canada, he donated Franklin Roosevelt's island, Campobello, to the two nations for a peace park in 1963. He died in Los Angeles.

Hammer was one of the most prominent and controversial American businessmen of the twentieth century. His career was a model of the spirit of American free enterprise capitalism, unfettered by rigid ideological impediments. He will be best remembered for his seventy-year business involvement with the Soviet Union, his transformation of Occidental Petroleum Company into one of the twelve major U.S. corporations of his time, and his philanthropic endeavors.

• The corporate papers of the Occidental Petroleum Company, of which Hammer was the chairman and CEO at the time of his death, are in the company offices in Los Angeles. His autobiography is *Hammer*, with Neil Lyndon (1987). Bob Considine's journalistic overview, which was completed more than a decade before Hammer's death, is *The Remarkable Life of Dr. Armand Hammer* (1975). A later account is Steve Weinberg, *Armand Hammer: The Untold Story* (1989). On the Hammer art collection, see John Walker, *The Armand Hammer Collection* (1979). An obituary is in the *New York Times*, 11 Dec. 1990.

STEPHEN J. RANDALL

HAMMER, William Joseph (26 Feb. 1858–27 Mar. 1934), electrical engineer and scientist, was born in Cressona, Pennsylvania, the son of William Alexander Hammer, a merchant, and Martha Ann Beck. He received his early education in the private and public schools of Newark, New Jersey. These formal studies were supplemented throughout his life by self-study and attendance of lectures at the University of Berlin and the Technische Hochschule.

Hammer's career began in 1878 when he became an assistant to Edward Weston of the Weston Malleable Nickel Company in Newark. In December 1879 Hammer visited the laboratory of Thomas A. Edison in Menlo Park, New Jersey, where he obtained a position assisting with experiments on telephony, electric lighting, the phonograph, and electric traction. Hammer was eventually placed in charge of incandescent lamp testing at the Menlo Park laboratory, becoming chief electrician of the first lamp factory there in 1880. While associated with Edison, Hammer helped plan and construct several early electric power plants, including the Holborn Viaduct station in London (1882), the first commercial central-station electric power plant in the world, and the Pearl Street station in New York City (1884), the first such station in the United States.

While in London in 1882, Hammer installed an Edison Electric Lighting system at the Crystal Palace Electrical Exposition, which included the first electric sign, of his own design. Hammer supervised Edison exhibits at a number of other important expositions, including the Berlin Exposition (1883), the Franklin Institute International Electrical Exhibition (1884), and the Paris Universal Exposition (1889). His work in England brought offers to head both the French and German Edison companies. He accepted the latter, and as the company's chief engineer, designed and supervised the construction of all the installations made by the company until his return to the United States in 1884.

On his arrival in the United States, Hammer became chief inspector of central stations for the Edison Electric Illuminating Company, in charge of evaluating the various power plants operated by the company. In 1886 Hammer took the post of general manager and chief engineer of the Boston Edison Company's plant. During the next two years he filled similar positions in New York City and St. Augustine, Florida. In 1888 Hammer became the electrical engineer in charge of the Cincinnati Centennial Exposition, designing a number of novel and dramatic electric lighting effects that contributed greatly to the popularity and success of the exposition.

In 1889, as Edison's personal representative, Hammer went to the Paris Exposition, where he supervised the installation and operation of Edison's extensive exhibits. Covering an area of some 9,000 square feet, the Edison pavilion was a centerpiece of the exposition. During his stay in Paris, Hammer accompanied Edison to the German Science Congress in Heidelberg, Germany, and to Berlin, where they were received by a number of Germany's most distinguished scientists.

After returning to the United States in 1890 Hammer opened an office in New York City to practice as a consulting electrical engineer. In this capacity Hammer spent much time testing and evaluating the inventions of others and as an expert witness in patent cases involving electrical apparatus. He also served as president (1896–1906) of the National Conference on Standard Electrical Rules, which promulgated the United States' first national electrical code in 1897. In 1894 Hammer married Alice Maud White of Cleveland, Ohio, who died in 1906. The Hammers had one child.

In the summer of 1902, after visiting Marie and Pierre Curie in Paris, Hammer returned to the United States with samples of their newly discovered element radium. He then began a series of pioneering investigations that resulted in practical applications such as luminous gun sights, watch dials and instrument faces, and, most importantly, the use of radium in the treatment of cancer, which Hammer was one of the first to propose. In 1903 he wrote one of the earliest published works on the subject, *Radium and Other Radioactive Substances*, which went through several editions in the United States and Europe. Between 1902 and 1909 Hammer published numerous encyclopedia and technical journal articles on radioactivity (including "Radium and Other Radioactive Substances," *Scientific American*, 23 May 1903, and "Radium" in the *Encyclopedia Americana* [1904]) and lectured extensively on his own work and that of the Curies.

An early interest in ballooning developed into a fascination with flight and airplanes. He became acquainted with Orville and Wilbur Wright soon after their first successful flight in 1903 and later served as an incorporator and vice president of the Aeronautical Society of America. He reportedly owned the first airplane sold to an individual in the United States.

In June 1918 Hammer received a commission in the U.S. Army as a major. Shortly thereafter he was appointed to the Army War College, joining its General Staff on 13 December. During this period he rendered valuable service to the war effort by conducting scientific and technical research, much of which dealt with developing communications between aircraft and the ground and with improving the design and construction of aircraft. Hammer's War College responsibilities also included the examination of captured enemy documents for potentially useful technical information and advising the U.S. Patent Office on the confidentiality of U.S. patents that might prove useful to the enemy.

One of Hammer's most notable achievements was the creation of his incandescent lamp collection, which he began in 1879 while at the Menlo Park laboratory. This vast collection, now in the possession of the Smithsonian Institution, is the world's most important and complete accumulation of artifacts and memorabilia relating to the history of the incandescent electric lamp and the early electric power industry.

Hammer enjoyed membership in many professional organizations, including the American Institute of Electrical Engineers, the American Association for the Advancement of Science, the Agassiz Natural History Society, the Aeronautical Society of America, the American Physical Society, and the Franklin Institute. Hammer received numerous awards during his career, including a special Silver Medal at the Crystal Palace Exposition (1882), the Grand Prize of the St. Louis Exposition (1904), and the Elliott Cresson Medal (1906), all for his collection of electric lighting memorabilia. He was given the John Scott Medal (1902) for his work in telephony, and in 1925 the French Government made Hammer a chevalier of the Legion of Honor for his contributions to the Paris Exposition of 1889. Hammer died in New York City.

• Hammer's papers are in the collections of the Archives Center of the National Museum of American History, Smithsonian Institution. This large and important collection includes biographical information and material relating to his scientific and engineering interests and activities. George S. Bryan, *Edison: The Man and His Work* (1926), includes interviews with Hammer. An obituary is in the *New York Times*, 25 March 1934.

GREG L. POTTER

HAMMERSTEIN, Arthur (21 Dec. 1872–12 Oct. 1955), theatrical producer, was born in New York City, the son of Oscar Hammerstein, a cigarmaker and later an impresario, and Rosa Blau. Educated locally, Hammerstein was apprenticed as a bricklayer and plasterer, and by age sixteen he was helping to build an apartment house for his father. Like his three brothers, he was inevitably involved in the multifarious theatrical enterprises of Oscar Hammerstein. Even while conducting his successful contracting business, he also wrote vaudeville skits. In 1893 he married Jean Allison; they were divorced in 1910 and had no children.

Hammerstein helped out with the 1896 debut of the Cherry Sisters, "the worst sister act in vaudeville," by tossing vegetables from the wings. When his father's huge Olympia Music Hall failed in 1897, Hammerstein's savings helped restore Oscar's fortunes. Hammerstein was also enlisted to supervise the construction of his father's money-spinning Victoria [variety] Theatre, which opened in 1899. The elegant Victoria's white-and-gold decor was a testament to Hammerstein's frugality; the plaster was unpainted and the gold was deftly applied gilt. The much-admired lighting was built into the walls, thus eliminating the need for separate fixtures.

When Oscar Hammerstein determined to construct the world's largest opera house, he commissioned Arthur to build the 3,100-seat theater, which opened in 1906 as the Manhattan Opera House. Acquiring a reputation for building acoustically sound theaters, he also built the Philadelphia Opera House, opened by his father in 1909. The sociable Hammerstein, called by his father "my Beau Brummel son," later referred to this time as his "four years of operatic torture."

Especially good at raising money, Hammerstein was also a talent scout and deal closer, and finally, in the war of attrition between the Manhattan and Metropolitan operas, a negotiator. In 1910 Hammerstein struck a deal with the Metropolitan that brought his father $1.25 million, thus saving him from bankruptcy. In exchange, Oscar and Arthur, who had begun to imagine a producing career of his own, gave up the right to produce opera in New York, Philadelphia, Boston, and Chicago for ten years. In 1910 Hammerstein married Grace Hoagland; they had one child and were divorced five years later.

As a producer, Arthur Hammerstein launched thirty-one shows, mostly original American operetta. Initially, his profits were drained by his father's enterprises, including a doomed opera house in London. This was the case with the highly successful *Naughty Marietta* (1910), perhaps Victor Herbert's best-known work. In 1912 Hammerstein produced the first of twelve operettas by Rudolf Friml, *The Firefly*. Theatrical historian Ken Bloom wrote that a Hammerstein show was always "exquisitely designed and executed."

Although the next Friml-Hammerstein venture, *High Jinks* (1913), was destined only for brief fame, it made a great deal of money. When Hammerstein's three brothers all died in 1914, he took over management of the Victoria, by then suffering from competition with B. F. Keith's even larger Palace Theatre. The Hammersteins sold the Victoria in 1915. That same year Hammerstein married Clair Nagle, who died six years later. They had no children.

Katinka (1915) continued Hammerstein's run of successes in operetta. *Furst and Frills* (1917) included nephew Oscar Hammerstein II's first professional song. Young Oscar Hammerstein also wrote his first complete musical score for the Arthur Hammerstein production, *Always You* (1920). As the success of the smaller-scale musical comedies at the Princess Theatre began to impress Broadway, Hammerstein's American operettas began to lose favor. In 1923 he produced Vincent Youmans's operettish *Wildflower* and the musical comedy *Mary Jane McKane*, a show much more in the modern manner.

Hammerstein's greatest success came with *Rose Marie* (1924), the Friml-Hammerstein II operetta that ran 557 performances and netted its producer $2.5 million. *Rose Marie*, influenced partly by the Princess comedies, prefigured such operettic musicals as *Show Boat* (1927) and *Oklahoma!* (1943)—both with book and lyrics by Hammerstein II—by subordinating musical numbers to plot and character development. For *Rose Marie*'s star, Hammerstein lured the Metropolitan Opera's Mary Ellis from her new legitimate stage career. Ellis later called Hammerstein a "charming, elitist manager, full of ideals and ideas. He wanted to start *real* operetta, as opposed to musical comedy. He was *not* over generous—until he knew he had a success—then he shared." In 1924 Hammerstein married Dorothy Dalton; they had no children.

After moderate success with *Song of the Flame* (1925), a collaboration between George Gershwin, Herbert Stothart, Otto Harbach, and Hammerstein II, Hammerstein's producing fortunes went downhill. Flops included *The Wild Rose* (1926) and *Golden Dawn* (1927), notable mainly for opening the Oscar Hammerstein Theater—in which Hammerstein had invested $2.5 million—and a young performer named Archie Leach (Cary Grant). No more successful were *Good Boy* (1928), *Pollu* (1929), and *Sweet Adeline* (1929), although the latter's lovely score by Jerome Kern and Hammerstein II eventually redeemed it.

Two short-lived 1930 fiascos, *Luana* and *Ballyhoo*, were followed by Hammerstein's lone motion picture venture, a 1930 film musical called *The Lottery Bride*. Despite songs by Friml and Arthur Schwartz, along with stars such as Jeanette MacDonald and Joe E. Brown, the film did not succeed. One of the earliest of many depression casualties on Broadway, Hammerstein filed for bankruptcy in 1931. His last New York production, *The Man Who Lost His Head* (1932), also failed.

Hammerstein retired from the theater and, except for an inconsequential involvement in 1937, stayed retired. In 1950 Hammerstein, an amateur composer like his father, wrote a popular song, "Because of You," that reached the top of the Hit Parade. Like his father, he then turned to inventing gadgets, including a salt container that was patented in 1952. Hammerstein died in Palm Beach, Florida.

• The Billy Rose Theatre Collection at the New York Public Library for the Performing Arts, Lincoln Center, holds a large file on Hammerstein. The Hammerstein family's theatrical exploits are well documented, the best source being Vincent Sheean, *The Amazing Oscar Hammerstein* (1956). Ken Bloom, *Broadway* (1991), succinctly details each member of the clan. Obituaries are in the *New York Times*, 13 Oct. 1955, and *Variety*, 19 Oct. 1955.

JAMES ROSS MOORE

HAMMERSTEIN, Oscar (8 May 1848–1 Aug. 1919), inventor, operatic impresario, and theatrical manager, was born in Berlin, Germany (although his family lived in Stettin, Prussia), the son of Abraham Hammerstein, a well-to-do, German-Jewish merchant, and Bertha Valentine, from a musically oriented French Huguenot family. Hammerstein was educated by private tutors, but at age sixteen, after a severe and unwarranted punishment from his father, he ran away from home. He fled to England and then boarded a ship bound for America, paying for his passage by selling his violin. Arriving at New York, Hammerstein found employment filling rush orders for the U.S. Army at a Pearl Street cigar factory. Within two years he had mastered the process well enough to invent a machine that greatly improved cigar production. Patented in July 1865, the invention revolutionized cigar making but brought only about $6,000 to the young inventor. However, subsequent similar labor-saving inventions reportedly brought him more than $1 million. In 1884 he invested his first royalties in the *Unit-*

ed States Tobacco Journal, which ran successfully until he sold it in 1885. Early in his career he also invested in real estate in Harlem.

For all his business ventures, Hammerstein's great passion was music, specifically the operatic stage and the theater. This passion led Hammerstein, in 1870, to become manager of the Stadt Theatre in Harlem; he later went into theater building as a speculation, intending to give the public wholesome entertainment. In 1880 he built the Harlem Opera House, where, against the advice and counsel of friends, he produced several operas in English at a financial loss. To recoup his losses, he built the Columbia Opera House (1890), for use in producing standard theatrical fare, and the Manhattan Theatre (1892), which he leased to Koster and Bial for use as a vaudeville house. Hammerstein's other New York properties were the Olympia Music Hall (1895), built at a cost of $2.5 million, the Victoria Music Hall (1899), the Republic Theatre (1900), the H. B. Harris Theatre (1904), and the Belasco Theatre (1904). He generally supervised each part in the construction of his theaters, requiring architects and decorators to follow his instructions and concepts of improved convenience or decoration.

Hammerstein had dreamed of presenting grand opera in English at popular prices. His greatest attempt to realize this ambition was the Manhattan Opera House, constructed on Thirty-fourth Street. Hammerstein had always intended to compete with the Metropolitan Opera, and he opened his theater on 3 December 1906 with an expansive production of *I Puritani* by Bellini. Distinguishing Hammerstein's productions at the Manhattan from those at the Metropolitan was his use of better production standards for scenery, lighting, and costuming and his willingness to attempt a newer repertoire, though such productions required him to use new and sometimes younger artists. For three years the rivals engaged in a furious and expensive competition that forced the Metropolitan to improve its standards of production, broaden its repertoire, change managerial control, and hire a new conductor but that also effectively ended Hammerstein's career as a producer of grand opera in America.

The Metropolitan extended its repertoire to include new works by French and Italian composers, and Hammerstein introduced such stars as Mary Garden, Nellie Melba, Luisa Tetrazzini, Charles Dalmorès, and Giovanni Zenatello and the conductor Cleofonte Campanini. He also presented a number of new as well as neglected favorites, such as *Salome*, *Elektra*, *Thaïs*, *Pelléas et Mélisande*, *Les Contes d'Hoffmann*, *Louise*, and *Le Jongleur de Notre Dame*. One tangible result of the struggle was increased interest in producing opera in cities throughout North America. In the fall of 1908 Hammerstein opened the Philadelphia Opera House, at a cost of $1.2 million, intending to introduce opera to other cities as well. The next fall he experimented with what he called "educational grand opera" by reducing prices for those who could not afford to attend the more expensive performances. The approach was not financially successful, but the operagoing public appreciated his willingness to sacrifice profits on their behalf.

The contest between the Metropolitan and Hammerstein was unequal because Hammerstein insisted on bearing all costs himself in order to avoid any conflict over choice of artists, production, or repertoire. As a result, he became financially over-extended and entered into negotiations with the principals of the Metropolitan to end the feud. In April 1910 Hammerstein agreed to give up opera production, forfeiting most of his unpaid for or deeply mortgaged theater holdings. In addition, he agreed to sell his interests to the Metropolitan for a little more than $1.2 million and not to produce grand opera in the New York area at least until April 1920.

Hammerstein's next venture was in London, where he opened his London Opera House on 13 November 1911 with a lavish production of Nougue's panoramic *Quo Vadis?* The attempt was an artistic success, but apparently no city was large enough to support two opera companies, and he sold the property in 1913.

The outbreak of World War I nullified Hammerstein's almost completed plans for a national grand opera circuit in the United States, to consist of a cycle of grand opera performed in important cities over a long season. He had devoted almost three years to the endeavor. During the latter years of his life he seriously considered becoming involved in motion pictures.

Hammerstein was married three times. In 1868 he married Rosa Blau, who bore him five sons (one died in infancy) before her death soon after the birth of her last child in 1876. He then married Malvina Jacobi of Selma, Alabama, in 1878; they had two daughters before they were divorced in 1911. In early 1915 he married Mary Emma Miller Swift, who survived him. Two of Hammerstein's sons, William and Arthur, were in partnership with him in theatrical management. William was the father of the famous lyricist Oscar Hammerstein II.

Oscar Hammerstein I died in New York City. At his funeral Rabbi Silverman eulogized: "Oscar Hammerstein has become part of this metropolis and will be remembered for many a day. The story of the theatrical and operatic life of this city—aye, of this country—cannot be written without an important record of Oscar Hammerstein." He was indeed unique in nineteenth-century theater and one of the foremost figures of the American stage for more than a third of a century. His most important personal traits were self-reliance and cheerfulness in difficult circumstances. He fervently stated his original opinions in defense of his convictions, as for example, "Grand Opera is, I truly believe, the most elevating influence upon Modern society after religion. . . . it employs and unifies all the arts."

Hammerstein had a wide circle of friends in Europe as well as America, and he made and lost several fortunes. Money meant nothing to him, however, except as a means of presenting opportunities to develop musical taste or to exploit rare voices. For his interests in performing and producing French opera, he was made a member of the French Legion of Honor. Probably no other theatrical manager of his time spent money more lavishly in the pursuit of personal artistic ideals.

• The three volumes of the Robinson Locke Collection at the New York Public Library contain much information on Hammerstein; the library also houses two rather dry, scholarly articles on Hammerstein and scrapbooks on American theater history. The only biography, Vincent Sheean's *The Amazing Oscar Hammerstein: The Life and Exploits of an Impresario* (1956), is exceedingly well written and interesting and should be generally available. An obituary is in the *New York Times*, 5 Aug. 1919, and the *New York World*, 2 Aug. 1919.

JOHN COGDILL

HAMMERSTEIN, Oscar, II (12 July 1895–23 Aug. 1960), Broadway librettist, lyricist, and producer, was born Oscar Greeley Clendenning Hammerstein II in New York City, the son of William Hammerstein, the manager of the Victoria Theater, and Alice Nimmo. In addition to his career as a builder of New York theaters (including the Victoria), Oscar's grandfather founded and managed the Manhattan Opera Company and Opera House from 1906 until 1910, a company that successfully rivaled the Metropolitan Opera by introducing many famous European opera singers and offering the American premieres of *The Tales of Hoffmann, Salome, Electra*, and *Pelléas et Mélisande*.

After attending Hamilton Institute (1908–1912), a quasi-military academy, Hammerstein completed his education at Columbia University (1912–1916) where he took part in several Varsity Show productions, first as an actor and later as a librettist and lyricist. During summers from 1911 until 1914 Hammerstein also participated in dramatic productions at Weingart Institute in the Catskills. Against the dying wishes of his father, he left Columbia Law School (1915–1917) without a degree to pursue a life in the theater, and the same week he married Myra Finn and became a production stage manager for his uncle Arthur Hammerstein, a Broadway producer whose credits included Victor Herbert's *Naughty Marietta* and Rudolf Friml's *The Firefly*. Following his inauspicious debut as a playwright with *The Light*, which failed out of town in 1919, Hammerstein worked on a string of unsuccessful musicals with colyricist, librettist, and mentor Otto Harbach and composer Herbert Stothart (among other collaborators), beginning with *Always You* in 1920. Also during this period he worked on six amateur musical productions with composer Richard Rodgers with whom he would begin a historic professional collaboration with *Oklahoma!* in 1943.

Wildflower (1923), with Harbach and composers Stothart and Vincent Youmans, launched for Hammerstein a phenomenally successful decade as librettist, lyricist, and frequent director for many of Broadway's most popular operettas and musical comedies: *Rose-Marie* (1924) with Friml and Stothart ("Indian Love Call"); *Song of the Flame* (1925) with George Gershwin and Stothart; *Sunny* (1925) ("Who?"), *Show Boat* (1927) ("Make Believe," "Ol' Man River,"

"Can't Help Lovin' Dat Man," "You Are Love," "Why Do I Love You?" and "Bill"), *Sweet Adeline* (1929) ("Don't Ever Leave Me" and "Why Was I Born?"), and *Music in the Air* (1932) ("I've Told Ev'ry Little Star" and "The Song Is You") with Jerome Kern; and *The Desert Song* (1926) ("One Alone") and *The New Moon* (1928) ("Stouthearted Men," "One Kiss," and "Lover, Come Back to Me") with Sigmund Romberg.

Although several of these shows (for the most part traditional operettas on romantic and exotic themes) are revived and many of their songs have become standards, the outstanding legacy of this period is without a doubt *Show Boat* (based on Edna Ferber's popular novel of the same name). When creating *Show Boat* with Kern (and later in his musicals with Rodgers), Hammerstein profited from the time he allowed for the extensive preliminary planning and discussion that preceded the painstaking work of drafting a libretto and lyrics. The foundation of the modern integrated musical that would become the Broadway standard during Hammerstein's years with Rodgers (1943–1959), *Show Boat* has been assessed as "perhaps the most successful and influential Broadway musical play ever written" by no less an arbiter of historical and critical opinion than *The New Grove Dictionary of Music and Musicians* (1980). Certainly no American musical before *Show Boat* achieved both permanence in the repertoire and the critical respect due a masterpiece.

Following the success of *Music in the Air,* a series of unwise choices (both in dramatic material and collaborators) and hurried work resulted in eleven years of Broadway failures, despite the occasional success of individual songs such as "All the Things You Are" from *Very Warm for May* (1939) with Kern. Similarly, his Hollywood years in the 1930s and early 1940s yielded no original musical films of lasting value, although several songs with Hammerstein's lyrics have become standards, including "When I Grow Too Old to Dream" from *The Night Is Young* (1935) with Romberg, and a quartet of hits with Kern, "The Folks Who Live on the Hill" and "Can I Forget You?" from *High, Wide and Handsome* (1937), the Academy Award–winning "The Last Time I Saw Paris" from *Lady, Be Good* (1940), and "All Through the Day" from *Centennial Summer* (1946), that would continue even after he had begun working with Rodgers. Hammerstein also adapted the screenplay for the penultimate Fred Astaire and Ginger Rogers film, *The Story of Vernon and Irene Castle* (1939). Beginning with the first of three versions of *Show Boat* in 1929 (other versions followed in 1936 and 1951), Hollywood would more successfully adapt twenty-six of Hammerstein's Broadway shows for film.

In 1943 Hammerstein emerged from his disillusioning and failure-laden decade on Broadway and Hollywood with his auspicious first professional collaboration with Richard Rodgers, *Oklahoma!,* which launched a new era of thoughtful and convention-shattering adaptations, often on American subjects with innovative central plots, imaginative and sometimes serious subplots, credible stories populated with believable and complex characters who spoke in an authentic vernacular, and songs and ballets that advanced the action. After *Oklahoma!*—at 2,212 performances the longest-running musical until 1961—popularized the "integrated" musical, in which all of the formerly disparate dramatic elements contributed to the integrity of the whole, nearly every musical of the next two decades would be judged on how well it measured up to the Rodgers and Hammerstein model.

With the exception of *Pipe Dream* (1955), Rodgers and Hammerstein's adaptations were all major box office hits: *Oklahoma!* (1943), *Carousel* (1945), *South Pacific* (1949), *The King and I* (1951), *Flower Drum Song* (1958), and *The Sound of Music* (1959). Hammerstein's modern African-American adaptation of Bizet's *Carmen* in 1943, *Carmen Jones* (without Rodgers), also triumphed with a long Broadway run and national tour. Rodgers and Hammerstein's original efforts, *Allegro* (1947) and *Me and Juliet* (1953), fared much less well in popularity and critical acclaim. Before he shared libretto duties on *Flower Drum Song* with Joseph Fields and trusted Howard Lindsay and Russel Crouse with *The Sound of Music* Hammerstein was the sole author of all of these shows, and Rodgers and Hammerstein took an active role in casting their shows as well as in production details. The team also collaborated on one film musical, *State Fair* (1945), which produced the Academy Award–winning best song, "It Might As Well Be Spring," and a popular television musical, *Cinderella*, in 1957.

Not only were Rodgers and Hammerstein's songs thoroughly integrated into their shows, but nearly every song from their hit musicals achieved a life outside its own carefully crafted context. Even a generous list would only partially represent their achievement as songwriters: "Oh, What a Beautiful Mornin'," "The Surrey with the Fringe on Top," "I Cain't Say No," "Many a New Day," and "People Will Say We're in Love" in *Oklahoma!*; "Mister Snow," "If I Loved You," "June Is Bustin' Out All Over," "Soliloquy," "What's the Use of Wond'rin'," and "You'll Never Walk Alone" in *Carousel*; "A Cockeyed Optimist," "Some Enchanted Evening," "There Is Nothing Like a Dame," "Bali Ha'i," "I'm Gonna Wash That Man Right Outa My Hair," "A Wonderful Guy," "Younger Than Springtime," "Happy Talk," and "Carefully Taught" in *South Pacific*; "I Whistle a Happy Tune," "Hello, Young Lovers," "Getting to Know You," "We Kiss in a Shadow," "Something Wonderful," and "Shall We Dance?" in *The King and I*; "My Favorite Things," "Do-Re-Mi," "Climb Ev'ry Mountain," "Edelweiss," and the title song in *The Sound of Music.*

Starting with *South Pacific*, Rodgers and Hammerstein would produce their own shows and would control the distribution, recording, and filming of their theatrical offspring. With *Oklahoma!* the team formed a publishing company for their shows, Williamson Music (in partnership with Chappell). They also produced two major American hits by other writers and composers, John Van Druten's *I Remember Mama* (1944) and *Annie Get Your Gun* (1946) (book by Herbert and Dorothy Fields; music and lyrics by Irving Berlin). Although they ceased producing plays and musicals by other writers in New York after 1950, the team would continue to produce such work as well as their own musicals for the London stage.

In "Notes on Lyrics," published as a thoughtful foreword to a collection of lyrics in 1949 (revised and expanded in 1985), Hammerstein clearly articulated his ideas on the craft of lyric writing. In direct contrast to Rodgers's previous pyrotechnically rhyming collaborator, Lorenz Hart, Hammerstein argues that a rhyme should be unassertive, never standing out too noticeably and that in the sparsely rhymed "Ol' Man River" "brilliant and frequent rhyming would diminish its importance." Hammerstein practiced what he preached that "the most important ingredient of a good song is sincerity." In musicals like *Show Boat* and *Oklahoma!* Hammerstein brought a new kind of lyric to the Broadway stage, a lyric that Philip Furia describes as "neither the florid, elevated style of European operetta, nor the sophisticated urbanity of Hart, Gershwin, and Porter, but a style that took its cue from the regional character who voiced it."

Hammerstein's response when accused of naive and excessive sentimentality in such inspirational songs as *Carousel*'s "You'll Never Walk Alone" and *The Sound of Music*'s "Climb Ev'ry Mountain" was that his deeply felt "cockeyed optimism" was no less real than the pessimism and negativism that prevailed in many Broadway plays. As early as *Show Boat*, Hammerstein tried to portray race relations realistically and sensitively. When urged to remove the plea for racial tolerance expressed in the controversial "You've Got to Be Carefully Taught" in *South Pacific*, Hammerstein and later Rodgers stood firm. *Tales of the South Pacific* author James Michener wrote that this song "represented why they had wanted to do this play, and that even if it meant the failure of the production, it was going to stay in."

Hammerstein took an active role in many organizations, serving as president of the Author's League and as vice president of ASCAP, offered his services in the fight against the Nazis, participated enthusiastically in the World Federalism movement and in many fundraising drives. An actor himself, his empathy gave him a legendary rapport with actors. And despite the enormous power and control wielded by Rodgers and Hammerstein, Inc., Hammerstein was one of Broadway's most genuinely loved figures.

Hammerstein had a son and daughter by his first marriage, an unhappy union that ended in divorce. In 1929 he married Dorothy Blanchard, a respected professional interior decorator, and together they had one son. His sons, William and James, became musical theater managers and producers. Although after leaving Hollywood Hammerstein always kept a New York City residence, he preferred to live and work on the quiet farm he purchased in Doylestown, Pennsylvania, where he died.

Hammerstein's historical significance in American musical theater is of supreme importance. Broadway historian Ethan Mordden goes so far as to assess Hammerstein as "the single most influential figure in the American musical." More than that of any other Broadway composer, Hammerstein's career marks the transition from traditional operetta to a new genre of American vernacular operetta, the musical play. After creating two of the major operettas of the 1920s with Friml and Romberg, Hammerstein with Kern established a new standard for the Broadway musical in *Show Boat*. His musicals with Rodgers in the 1940s launched the even more influential era of the integrated musical. His inspiring tutelage of Stephen Sondheim, his Doylestown neighbor, spiritual son, and arguably the major Broadway composer-lyricist after 1960, would further ensure Hammerstein's vast historical and artistic legacy. In the words of Irving Berlin, "there's only one lyric writer that came close to being a poet and that's Oscar Hammerstein."

• The major repository of Hammerstein's lyrics and other materials for his shows is the Rodgers and Hammerstein Theatre Library in New York City. Scripts and lyrics for many Hammerstein shows are located in the New York Public Library, and numerous holograph manuscripts of songs are housed in the Music Division of the Library of Congress in Washington, D.C. A generous selection of song lyrics with Rodgers and Bizet and representative lyrics with Romberg and Kern, as well as Hammerstein's essay on lyric writing, is anthologized in *Lyrics* (1949; rev. and expanded, 1985). Librettos for all of his work with Rodgers except for *State Fair* and *Cinderella* were published by Random House. A generous portion of the *Show Boat* libretto is contained on the longer version of the London Sinfonietta and Ambrosian Chorus recording, based on the original 1927 version and orchestration, conducted by John McGlinn. Some of the most famous Hammerstein songs with Kern are anthologized in *Jerome Kern: The Man and His Music in Story, Picture and Song*, and most of his songs with Rodgers can be found in *The Rodgers and Hammerstein Song Book* (1956).

The principal compilation of factual information on Hammerstein's entire career on stage and film (including production histories, casts, act-by-act song roster, plot summaries, and excerpts from reviews) is *Rodgers and Hammerstein Fact Book*, ed. Stanley Green (1980). The most comprehensive biography is Hugh Fordin, *Getting to Know Him* (1977). Other useful biographical profiles are found in Deems Taylor, *Some Enchanted Evenings* (1953); David Ewen, *Richard Rodgers* (1957); Stanley Green, *The Rodgers and Hammerstein Story* (1963); Richard Rodgers, *Musical Stages* (1975); Frederick Nolan, *The Sound of Their Music: The Story of Rodgers and Hammerstein* (1978); and William G. Hyland, *Richard Rodgers* (1998). For critical discussions of Hammerstein's lyrics and shows, see Joseph P. Swain, *The Broadway Musical: A Critical and Musical Survey* (1990); Philip Furia, *The Poets of Tin Pan Alley* (1990); Ethan Mordden, *Rodgers & Hammerstein* (1992); and Geoffrey Block, *Enchanted Evenings: The Broadway Musical from "Show Boat" to Sondheim* (1997).

GEOFFREY BLOCK

HAMMETT, Dashiell (27 May 1894–10 Jan. 1961), writer, was born Samuel Dashiell Hammett in Saint Mary's County, Maryland, the son of Richard Hammett and Annie Bond. Struggling to make a living,

Hammett's father moved the family first to Philadelphia in 1900, and the following year to Baltimore. In 1908 young Dashiell (as he was to be known) entered high school at the Baltimore Polytechnic Institute, leaving after one semester to help with family finances. After holding a series of clerical jobs, he was hired in 1915 by the Baltimore office of the Pinkerton National Detective Agency, where he was employed first as a clerk and then as a detective, or "operative." Although he worked for the Pinkerton Agency for only slightly more than four years in several cities, he would draw on the experience throughout his career as a writer. In a series of five novels and several dozen short stories published from 1923 until 1934, he fashioned the distinctive vernacular style and the mordant, knowing attitudes of the modern American genre of private eye fiction.

Hammett joined the U.S. Army in June 1918, serving less than a year and falling victim to the great influenza epidemic of 1918–1919, which especially struck American military camps. For the rest of his life he suffered severe lung and bronchial problems. In 1920 during one of his periods of hospitalization he met his future wife, Josephine Dolan, who was a nurse. They married that year. Taking up residence in San Francisco in 1921, where briefly once again he was employed by the Pinkerton Agency, he began to write sketches and fiction, first for the sophisticated magazine *Smart Set* and then for the pulp detective magazine *Black Mask*, with which he would be principally associated for most of his writing career.

With the anonymous "Continental Op," a character he introduced into his stories beginning in 1923, Hammett began to develop possibilities for detective fiction that have been echoed and exploited ever since in popular fiction, movies, and television drama. Hammett's detective is neither a sleuth, on the model of Edgar Allan Poe's C. Auguste Dupin or Arthur Conan Doyle's Sherlock Holmes, nor merely a tough guy, on the model of Carroll John Daly's "Race Williams." In stories including "The Gutting of Couffignal" (1925) and "The Big Knock-Over" (1927), as well as the novels *Red Harvest* (1929) and *The Dain Curse* (1929), the Continental Op is a man already weary and without illusions, who regards detective work as a job to be done, although sometimes he has flashes of enthusiasm. He is thirty-five or forty, depending on the text, is 5′6″, weighs an unmuscular 180 to 190 pounds, and sometimes is called "Fat Shorty." Similarly, Hammett's other major protagonists run counter to romantic stereotype, providing an unsentimental, streetwise perspective on crime and criminals. Sam Spade in *The Maltese Falcon* (1930), with his "yellow-grey eyes," is several times referred to as a "blond satan." Ned Beaumont in *The Glass Key* (1931), a strategist for a corrupt political boss, is a former gambler who has knowledge of both human greed and human triviality. Nick Charles in *The Thin Man* (1934) is a somewhat alcoholic 41-year-old premature retiree who lives on his wife's money and does detective work only with great reluctance.

Hammett's fellow detective-story writer Raymond Chandler was to say of him that he wrote for people who "were not afraid of the seamy side of things; they lived there," adding that "he had style, but his audience didn't know it, because it was in a language not supposed to be capable of such refinements." In fact, however, Hammett was very widely admired by persons including the French novelist André Gide, who especially praised *Red Harvest* for its "implacable cynicism," and the American experimental writer Gertrude Stein, who, as she was to say in her *Everybody's Autobiography* (1937), particularly sought Hammett's acquaintance. Although he wrote primarily for a pulp-magazine audience and despite his relative lack of formal education, Hammett was indeed a man of considerable learning. It was to the Icelandic sagas, he said, that he owed his idea of tone in fiction, and he noted that study of the works of Henry James (1843–1916) brought him to his conception of literary style.

Beginning in 1934 and thereafter, Hammett worked occasionally as a Hollywood screenwriter, but his career as a publishing writer of fiction was otherwise now finished. He left his wife and two daughters in 1929, and in 1931 he entered into a relationship with the prospective playwright Lillian Hellman, which was to last until his death. According to Hellman's memoirs, during these years Hammett devoted much of his time to aiding her in her work for the stage.

In the early 1930s he became increasingly involved in political activities. He supported various causes, including the Loyalists at the time of the Spanish Civil War, the efforts of the American Communist party in 1940 to secure a place on the ballot, and, as president of the New York Civil Rights Congress, from 1946 until the mid-1950s, the rights of political dissidents. In 1942, despite his age and his health problems, he managed to enlist in the U.S. Army once again, serving in the Aleutians until his discharge in 1945. In July 1951 he was sentenced to six months in jail for contempt of court, eventually serving twenty-two weeks of that sentence. As chairman of a bail fund committee established by the Civil Rights Congress for the purpose of aiding political defendants, he had refused to answer questions by a federal court as to the identity of donors to the fund.

He had been sickly much of his adult life, and the term in prison further affected his health. Moreover, the Internal Revenue Service moved to attach all of his income in lieu of payment for back taxes. In 1953 he was called to testify before Senator Joseph R. McCarthy's Permanent Subcommittee on Investigations, and in 1955 he was subpoenaed by a New York State Joint Legislative Committee likewise engaged in displaying supposed Communist sympathizers. From 1952 until his death, he lived in Katonah, New York, rent-free, in a house belonging to a friend. He died in New York City and was buried at Arlington National Cemetery.

• Principal collections of Hammett's stories are *The Big Knockover*, ed. with an introduction by Lillian Hellman (1966), and *The Continental Op*, ed. with an introduction by

Steven Marcus (1974). The definitive bibliography, compiled by Richard Layman, is *Dashiell Hammett: A Descriptive Bibliography* (1979). Layman also has written the most substantial of the several Hammett biographies, *Shadow Man: The Life of Dashiell Hammett* (1981). Other biographies are Diane Johnson, *Dashiell Hammett: A Life* (1985); Julian Symons, *Dashiell Hammett* (1985); and William F. Nolan, *Hammett: A Life at the Edge* (1983). The memoirs of Hammett's longtime companion, Hellman, collected in *Three* (1979), contain frequent and extensive references to him. Important critical works include Sinda Gregory, *Private Investigations: The Novels of Dashiell Hammett* (1985); Dennis Dooley, *Dashiell Hammett* (1984); Peter Wolfe, *Beams Falling: The Art of Dashiell Hammett* (1980); Robert I. Edenbaum, "The Poetics of the Private-Eye: The Novels of Dashiell Hammett," in *Tough Guy Writers of the Thirties*, ed. David Madden (1968); and Raymond Chandler, "The Simple Art of Murder," published originally in 1944 and included in Chandler, *The Simple Art of Murder* (1950; repr. 1988).

MARCUS KLEIN

HAMMETT, Samuel Adams (4 Feb. 1816–24 Dec. 1865), merchant and writer, was born probably in Connecticut or New York, though the precise location remains uncertain, the son of Augustus J. Hammett, a merchant, and Mary Wright. In the fall of 1832 Hammett entered the newly formed University of the City of New York. His father's declining health and business demanded much of Hammett's time, however, and he discontinued his studies in 1835. Hammett soon left for the Southwest and arrived in present-day Texas toward the end of the year. He lived there for over a decade, as it won independence, established a republic, and eventually became a state. Hammett probably engaged in a variety of business activities during this time, most possibly land speculation or traveling sales. Either would have given him ample opportunity to observe the area's people and customs, a background he drew on for later writings. Hammett joined other businessmen and set up general stores in Galveston and Houston during 1846. Following severe financial difficulties just a year later, he closed the last shop and returned to the East.

Hammett settled in metropolitan New York and became a merchant once again. He found the city—and the nation—eager for news of Texas. He wrote articles about his experience there and sold them to a wide range of periodicals, including *Literary World, Spirit of the Times, Democratic Review*, and *Knickerbocker*.

Though Hammett claimed to have "twisted and turned" the magazine pieces, they formed the basis of *A Stray Yankee in Texas*, his first book. He used the pseudonym "Philip Paxton" for the 1853 publication, as with later works. Hammett presented *A Stray Yankee in Texas* as a work of true description, an insider's guide to one of the largest states in the nation. "The only object the author has in view is to give a correct idea of scenes and scenery, men and manners, as they exist in a section of our country of which much has been written, but little is really known." He tailored the book to readers unfamiliar with Texas, giving lengthy descriptions of cities, plants, animals, and even the weather, which he portrayed as brutal and de-

feating. Hammett also painstakingly recorded the "new expression" and the "rude, wild, and energetic" speech of the Southwest, a dialect he attributed in large part to African-American influence. Reviewers praised *A Stray Yankee in Texas* for its lighthearted authenticity, placing it in the tradition of homespun humor. The book had at least two American editions. A German publisher also included portions in a popular anthology.

Hammett's second work, *The Wonderful Adventures of Captain Priest*, appeared in 1855 to decidedly mixed reviews. Unlike *A Stray Yankee in Texas*, it was a "Down East" story of a cantankerous Long Island sailor and his family. Hammett interrupted the tale to explain his ambivalent attitude toward his free-time occupation. "I do not claim to belong regularly to the Guild. Because I may have written a book or so does not necessarily make *me* an author." The book also contained poems and short essays.

Hammett made his literary return to Texas in 1858, when *Piney Woods Tavern; or, Sam Slick in Texas* came out. It captured just one night in an East Texas bar, where a group of men had gathered to escape the rain and tell their stories around the fireplace. As with *A Stray Yankee in Texas*, many reviewers recommended the book for its amusing but realistic portrayal of Texas and its people. Other critics attacked Hammett, decrying his supposed theft of Canadian writer Thomas C. Haliburton's earlier "Sam Slick" character. Hammett actually alluded to the existence of the other Sam Slick figure in the book, but it did not defend him against the charge.

Hammett died in Brooklyn of pneumonia. He never married. Little information exists about him, and his books no longer receive even highly specialized critical attention. Entertaining and based on long-term residence, his writings introduced thousands of Americans to the people and places of Texas. The books helped cement the national perception of Texas as a country unto itself.

• A biography of Hammett is W. Stanley Hoole, *Sam Slick in Texas* (1945). Walter Blair, *Native American Humor, 1800–1900* (1937), briefly mentions Hammett as a southwestern humorist, as does Mody Boatright, *Folk Laughter of the American Frontier* (1942). Hammett's obituary is in the *New York Tribune*, 25 Dec. 1865.

MARGARET THOMPSON

HAMMON, Jupiter (11 Oct. 1711–?), poet and preacher, was born on the estate of Henry Lloyd on Long Island, New York, most probably the son of Lloyd's slaves Opium, renowned for his frequent escape attempts, and Rose. Few records remain from Hammon's early life, though correspondence of the Lloyd family indicates that in 1730 he suffered from a near-fatal case of gout. He was educated by Nehemiah Bull, a Harvard graduate, and Daniel Denton, a British missionary, on the Lloyd manor. Except for a brief period during the revolutionary war, when Joseph Lloyd removed the family to Hartford, Connecticut, Hammon lived his entire life on Long Island, in the Huntington area, serving the Lloyds as clerk and bookkeeper. There is no surviving indication that Hammon either married or had children. The precise date of his death and the location of his grave remain unknown, although it is known that he was alive in 1790 and had died by 1806.

Hammon is best known for his skill as a poet and preacher. Early in the spiritual Great Awakening of the 1730s and 1740s he was converted to a Wesleyan Christianity, and his poems and sermons reflect a Calvinist theology. Within the framework of these religious doctrines Hammon crafted a body of writing that critically investigates slavery. His first published poem, "An Evening Thought," appeared as a broadside on Christmas Day 1760. Imbedded within the religious exhortation is a subtle apocalyptic critique of slavery in which the narrator prays that Christ will free all men from imprisonment:

> Now is the Day, excepted Time;
>   The Day of Salvation;
> Increase your Faith, do not repine:
>   Awake ye every Nation.

The poem ends by calling on Jesus to "Salvation give" and to bring equality to all: "Let us with Angels share." Hammon couples a protest against earthly injustice with his religious conviction that all men are enslaved by sin.

Hammon's next publication, "An Address to Miss Phillis Wheatley," appeared in Hartford on 4 August 1778. The language of the poem offers Wheatley, then the most prominent African in America, spiritual— and thereby literary—advice. From the position of elder statesman Hammon attempts to correct what he sees as the pagan influences in Wheatley's verse:

> Thou hast left the heathen shore;
>   Thro' mercy of the Lord,
> Among the heathen live no more,
>   Come magnify thy God.
>   Psalm 34:1–3.

Typical of eighteenth-century American poetry, and primarily influenced by Michael Wigglesworth, Hammon's verse portrays America as a site for spiritual salvation since it is free of the corruption of the Old World. The poem seizes on biblical passages in order to fashion an argument that he hopes will convince Wheatley to write more religious verse. Hammon's next piece, *An Essay on the Ten Virgins*, advertised for sale in Hartford in 1779, is now lost.

Hammon exhorts his "brethren" to confess their sins and thus receive eternal salvation in his 1782 sermon *Winter Piece*. Its call to repentance and the proclamation of man's inherent sinfulness is consistent with other sermons of this era. Another prose essay, *An Evening's Improvement*, was printed in Hartford in 1783, and in it Hammon continues his protest against the institution of slavery. Published along with the sermon is Hammon's greatest poem, "A Dialogue, Entitled, the Kind Master and the Dutiful Servant," wherein he directly questions the unequal relationship

between slave and master by emphasizing that before God, only sin divides Man:

> Master
> My Servant we must all appear,
>   And follow then our King;
> For sure he'll stand where sinners are,
>   To take true converts in.

> Servant
> Dear master, now if Jesus calls,
>   And sends his summons in;
> We'll follow saints and angles all,
>   And come unto our King.

The end of the poem disrupts the dialogue structure as the voice of the servant blends into that of the poet's. In the last seven stanzas Hammon instructs all in how to attain peace and harmony:

> Believe me now my Christian friends,
>   Believe your friend call'd Hammon:
> You cannot to your God attend,
>   And serve the God of Mammon.

Here Hammon argues that materialism (Mammon), a code for economic slavery, prohibits salvation because it leads an individual away from religious contemplation.

Hammon's final and most widely read piece, *An Address to the Negroes in the State of New-York*, was first printed in 1787 and then republished by the Pennsylvania Society for Promoting Abolition in 1806. In it Hammon speaks most directly against slavery. Within the body of his address Hammon argues that young African Americans should pursue their freedom even though he, at age seventy-six, does not want to be set free. Hammon calls for gradual emancipation: "Now I acknowledge that liberty is a great thing, and worth seeking for, if we can get it honestly, and by our good conduct prevail on our masters to set us free."

Hammon argues that earthly freedom is subordinate to spiritual salvation and that the need to be born again in the spirit of Christ overpowers all else, for in death "there are but two places where all go . . . white and black, rich and poor; those places are Heaven and Hell." Eternal judgment is what ultimately matters; thus Hammon urges his fellow African Americans, in their pursuit of freedom, to seek forgiveness through repentance and to place spiritual salvation above mortal concerns.

Hammon remained unknown from the early nineteenth century until 1915, when literary critic Oscar Wegelin, who rediscovered Hammon in 1904, published the first biographical information on him as well as some of his poetry. Although Hammon apparently was not the first African-American writer (evidence suggests he was predated by one Lucy Terry poem), his canon makes him one of America's first significant African-American writers.

• Biographical information can be found in Oscar Wegelin, *Jupiter Hammon: American Negro Poet* (1915); Stanley Austin Ransom, Jr., ed., *America's First Negro Poet: The Complete*

Works of Jupiter Hammon of Long Island (1970); M. Thomas Inge et al., eds., *Black American Writers*, vol. 1 (1978); Carol Aisha Balckshire-Belay, ed., *Language and Literature in the African American Imagination* (1992); and Sondra A. O'Neale, *Jupiter Hammon and the Biblical Beginnings of African-American Literature* (1993).

DUNCAN F. FAHERTY

HAMMOND, Bray (20 Nov. 1886–20 July 1968), economic historian and banker, was born in Springfield, Missouri, the son of Harry H. Hammond, a bank cashier, and Lucy Bray. In 1907 he married Lucille Bennett; they had four children before her death in 1927. In 1912 he graduated from Stanford University and was elected Phi Beta Kappa. From 1913 through 1916 he was assistant professor of English at the State College of Washington, in Pullman. From 1917 to 1919 he served in the U.S. Army Signal Corps, Aviation Section, rising to captain rank. From 1919 to 1928 he served as personnel manager for a manufacturing firm in New Haven, Connecticut. In 1929 he was a bookkeeper for the Irving Trust Company in New York City, then in 1930 began serving on the Board of Governors for the Federal Reserve System. Hammond remained on the board until 1950, retiring after serving as its assistant secretary during the final six years of his tenure.

During the 1920s Hammond began publishing essays in magazines such as *Harper's*, *New Republic*, and the *Unpopular Review*. While serving on the board he used his writing talents to develop an intellectual framework for national banking policy. He was placed in charge of publications for the banking section of the Federal Reserve System. In this capacity he wrote the first edition of *The Federal Reserve System: Its Purposes and Functions* (1939) and the historical overview for *Banking Studies* (1941). In 1939 he married Melitta de Kern.

While at the Federal Reserve, Hammond wrote articles and reviews in scholarly journals, which provided the groundwork for his major historical work. In 1950 he retired from government service and devoted his full attention to producing a detailed examination of the issues that concerned him. Underwritten by two Guggenheim grants, in 1950 and 1955, his *Banks and Politics in America from the Revolution to the Civil War* earned the Pulitzer Prize upon its publication in 1957. In *Banks and Politics*, Hammond considers banking as an optic through which to view the monumental struggle between those who sought to modify the dislocations emanating from the mushrooming U.S. economy by establishing the second United States Bank and those who followed what the author claimed was the Jacksonian course of inept laissez-faire.

Hammond rejected the arguments of historians like James Schlesinger, Jr., who represented "the age of Jackson as one of triumphant liberalism." Instead, he claimed, it was "more an age of triumphant exploitation." He pointed out that capitalism by Jackson's reign had made a decisive break from its mercantilist past in which business was largely the exclusive domain of a selected, self-perpetuating commercial aristocracy. By the time of Jackson, "business democracy" was in full bloom and common people could engage in "free enterprise" with far less restraint than in the not-so-distant past. So then, rural capitalists and village entrepreneurs could gamble freely on the vicissitudes of the market—so freely in fact, Hammond maintains, "that the speculation which mounted in the Panic of 1837 was a great popular phenomenon."

In this freewheeling, avaricious economy, banks were blooming like ragweed, creating chaotic credit and currency practices. Hammond insisted that, far from simple country folk, those with whom Jackson aligned were eastern monied interests who wanted free reign to balloon American inflation and credit. Among Jackson's allies was Alexander Hamilton's son, who wanted to bury the United States Bank so that he and his associates would have a clear field for a big bank of their own.

Restraint upon the powerful forces that were driving the U.S. economy was deeply needed, and the United States Bank under Nicholas Biddle was attempting to apply such restraint, Hammond argued. By destroying the bank, Hammond charged, Jackson "delivered the country to the excesses of a disorderly currency and unregulated credit expansion." Far from advancing the interests of common people, Hammond asserted, Jackson destroyed the best possible vehicle to protect them from the concentration of immense wealth in the hands of a small part of the population that used elastic credit to further enrich themselves and periodically throw the nation into economic chaos.

Hammond's later work, *Sovereignty and an Empty Purse* (published posthumously in 1970) described more fully the financing of the Civil War than did *Banks and Politics*. This book did not have the same impact as his earlier assault on "Jacksonian Democracy," which drew new lines of engagement for historians.

Hammond died in Middlebury, Vermont.

• Hammond's papers are at the Dartmouth College Library. Besides works mentioned above, see Hammond's "Public Policy and National Banks," *Journal of Economic History* 16 (1956): 79–83. Reviews of his work are in *American Historical Review* 63 (1958), *Labor History* 4 (1963), and *William and Mary Quarterly* 73 (1958). An obituary is in the *New York Times*, 23 July 1968.

MICHAEL T. JOHNSON

HAMMOND, George Henry (5 May 1838–29 Dec. 1886), meatpacker, was born in Fitchburg, Massachusetts, the son of John Hammond, a carpenter and joiner, and Sarah Huston. He attended common schools but left at age ten to work, making leather pocketbooks for a Mr. Barrett in Ashburnham, Massachusetts. When Barrett became ill, he carried on the business, employing twelve girls. But steel-clasp pocketbooks soon undercut demand, so he worked briefly for a butcher, then for three years in Milton Frost's mattress and palm-leaf hat factory in Fitchburg. When

Frost moved west, Hammond, aged fifteen, bought the business. But Frost then urged him to come west, so Hammond sold out after six months, moving to Detroit, Michigan, in 1854. He again worked briefly for a butcher, then went to work for Frost, manufacturing mattresses and furniture.

In 1857 Hammond began his own business, making chairs, only to have a fire destroy it six months later, leaving him with thirteen dollars and a fifty-dollar note. Using that note as collateral, he borrowed forty dollars to open a meat store at the corner of Howard and Third streets and began attending commercial school after hours. His shop was an immediate success; he soon moved to a brick building he built across the street. He married Ellen Barry in 1857; they had eleven children. In 1865 he moved his business to Michigan Grand Avenue, where he ran a large, prosperous wholesale and retail meat business, even adding his own slaughterhouse.

After the end of the Civil War, Hammond traveled extensively in the Midwest and East; he recognized that the burgeoning industrial urban centers offered rapidly growing demand for meat while the dramatically expanding cattle herds of the Midwest had the capacity to meet that demand—if suitable transportation could be developed. Shipping live cattle would not work well: the animals needed constant tending and lost weight or died en route, leaving only about 40 percent for marketing. He found his answer at William Davis's fish market near his own store. Davis had been seeking ways to extend his market for fresh fish and thus had experimented with an "icebox on wheels." He began using his new refrigerator car for fruit, bringing fresh peaches and strawberries to Detroit from Dayton, Ohio, then shipping fruit to New York City successfully. Next he tried bringing fresh fish from Lakes Huron and Superior. He was sufficiently pleased with his design—a wooden shell lined with hair felt, with iron wedge-shaped tanks at the sides holding 6,500 pounds of crushed ice and salt—that he patented it on 16 June 1868. Hammond followed these efforts closely, and in 1868 he contracted with Davis to develop a car for dressed beef. He then ordered the car built at the Michigan Car Company. In April 1869 he accompanied a load of 16,000 pounds of dressed beef to Boston, Massachusetts. The *Boston Daily Advertiser* (22 Apr. 1869), declaring that Boston butchers found the meat "in better condition than meat received directly from our home markets," heralded the new development as promising higher quality and lower cost beef for the East. Hearing of the Boston, delivery, H. A. Botsford & Co. of Hartford, Connecticut, contracted for Hammond to dress and ship beef to them.

On 1 July 1869 Hammond bought exclusive rights to the Davis design (Davis had died the previous November). Then, with Caleb Ives, Stanley Plumer, and Marcus Towle, he organized Hammond, Plumer & Company; on 10 September 1869 the firm bought land on the Calumet River, next to the Illinois state line, not far from the stockyards in Chicago, Illinois, and near the ice-harvesting and ice houses of P. J. Smith & Co. (This was the origin of Hammond, Indiana.) In 1873, with annual sales already above $1 million, the firm changed its name to George H. Hammond & Company. By 1875 sales passed $2 million. The company began with just two refrigerator cars; in six months it began ordering more. In 1878 it owned 180; in 1885, 800. That year, Hammond was the first national packer to open a slaughterhouse in Omaha, Nebraska, beginning major development of the industry there. In 1872, with James D. Standish and his longtime clerk Stanley B. Dixon, Hammond organized his Detroit wholesale and retail activities into Hammond, Standish & Company, which built large new facilities on Twentieth Street.

Hammond's success attracted interest slowly. Only in 1874 did Nelson Morris begin to ship dressed beef east. Then, in 1875, Gustavus Swift contracted with Hammond to slaughter, dress, and ship beef to his brother's wholesale house in Clinton, Massachusetts, and his own Boston firm, Hathaway & Swift. Because the Davis design did not have proper ventilation, it did not work well in warmer weather; Hammond, rather than improve the design, simply confined shipments to colder months. After two years of using Hammond, Swift established his own Chicago firm and began experimenting with improved refrigeration so he could have year-round shipping. He soon had a superior design and in 1879 contracted with Michigan Car to build cars. Hammond tried to stop Swift with a patent infringement suit, but he lost.

Hammond made one additional significant contribution to the development of the dressed-beef trade—in exports. In September 1879 he received a patent for an onboard refrigerator room with which he began exporting dressed beef to Europe. In April 1879 the first shipment of American dressed beef arrived in good condition in Liverpool, England, aboard the SS *Minnesota*; he was soon shipping to Aberdeen, Scotland, as well.

By 1886 Hammond had fallen to fourth place among the packers. Although he had followed the standard pattern of forward and backward integration, he had been neither as innovative nor as aggressive as Swift, Armour, or Morris. Then when Hammond died, aged only forty-eight, foreign interests bought the firm and concentrated on exports; in 1901 Armour bought out the Hammond operations.

Hammond was quite wealthy and devoted to Detroit, where he kept his home despite his primary business interests in the Chicago area. He was at the time of his death possibly Detroit's largest owner of real estate. He also served as vice president and director of Commercial National Bank, served as director of Michigan Savings Bank and Detroit Fire and Marine Insurance Company, and was a founder of the Museum of Art. He died in Detroit of a heart ailment, after a two-week illness.

• Although no original sources seem to be extant, Rudolf A. Clemen's admiring biography *George H. Hammond: Pioneer in Refrigerator Transportation* (1946) quotes original letters and documents. There is substantial literature on the development of the meatpacking industry and the central role that it played in the development of refrigeration technology and its sometimes bitter relationship with railroads. See Oscar Edward Anderson, Jr., *Refrigeration in America* (1953); Rudolf A. Clemen, *The American Livestock and Meat Industry* (1923); Wilfred V. Casgrain, *Memorandum on the Life of George H. Hammond, 1838–1886* (1945); Mary Yeager Kujovich, "The Refrigerator Car and the Growth of the American Dressed Beef Industry," *Business History Review* 44, no. 4 (Winter 1970): 460–82; Jimmy M. Skaggs, *Prime Cut: Livestock Raising and Meatpacking in the United States: 1607–1983* (1986); and Mary Yeager, *Competition and Regulation: The Development of Oligopoly in the Meat Packing Industry* (1981).

FRED CARSTENSEN

HAMMOND, Jabez Delano (2 Aug. 1778–18 Aug. 1855), politician and historian, was born in New Bedford, Massachusetts, the son of Jabez Hammond and Priscilla Delano. He grew up in Woodstock, Vermont, where he was educated in the common schools. At age fifteen he began teaching school, and, after becoming eligible through a brief apprenticeship, began a medical practice in Reading, Vermont. Dissatisfied with the medical profession for unknown reasons, Hammond sought to improve his fortune in New York, moving to Newburgh and reading law in Jonathan Fiske's office while supporting himself as a schoolmaster. Admitted to the bar in 1805, the young lawyer pursued further opportunity in the Susquehanna Valley in the town of Cherry Valley, building "within a short time a reputable and profitable legal practice" and entering politics.

Since Hammond had begun his career "entirely destitute," his commitment to social, economic, and political issues—most notably evinced in his Independence Day orations—is understandable. Evidence of his business acumen was his service as DeWitt Clinton's land agent and attorney. Clinton's holdings were extensive, he had a first-rate legal mind, and he did not suffer fools, so Hammond's expertise was of necessity top-notch. In 1810 Hammond married Miranda Stoddard; they had three children, two of whom died in infancy. Miranda died in 1832, and two years later Hammond married Laura Williams; they had no children.

Hammond's brief political career consisted of a term in the Fourteenth Congress (1815–1817) and two terms as a state senator (1818–1821). By his own admission he was an ineffectual debater, but his legislative tours proved to be important educational experiences. If he "was entirely ignorant of what we call New York politics" when he entered the senate, he did not remain in that condition long. The constitution of 1777 provided that the entire state's patronage be dispensed by a state Council of Appointment consisting of four senators from designated districts and the governor. Hammond was placed on this body, and after a year on the council (senators seldom served on the council more than a year) his innocence and ignorance had been largely dispelled.

After his tenure in politics concluded, Hammond practiced law for a few years in Albany during the 1820s, but he eventually returned to Cherry Valley. He was extremely interested in education and traveled to Europe in 1831 to observe educational systems. He also served a term as Otsego County superintendent of schools, and for the last eleven years of his life he served as a regent of the University of the State of New York.

Hammond was an Otsego County judge from 1838 to 1843. He tried to influence policy through correspondence with influential men such as Martin Van Buren, New York governor William H. Seward, and abolitionist Gerrit Smith. These letters reflect Hammond's opposition to slavery and monopolies, evils that he felt obstructed the fulfillment of the American dream as he had known it. He looked upon Van Buren as an instrument in the war against the banking monopoly and held to the mistaken notion (as he later confessed) that the Democratic party would become a northern antislavery party. Hammond's opposition to banking monopolies and slavery also took the form of pamphlets, letters to the editor, and a fictional work, *The Life and Opinions of Julius Melbourn*, published anonymously in 1847 (the second edition [1851] reveals his authorship). The central character in the latter is a North Carolina born orphaned slave adopted by a well-to-do English widow. The coincidence-riddled novel describes the young man's movement through the seats of power, and in it Hammond criticizes all segments of society, from slaveholders to abolitionists.

The History of Political Parties in the State of New York (1846), however, is Hammond's lasting monument. Originally intended as a biography of DeWitt Clinton, the work took the form of a two-volume collection of biographies of American political movers from the Constitution's framing to 1840. A third volume was added in 1852, titled *The Life of Silas Wright*. Hammond sought "to exhibit all the parts of the machinery and its action and counter action and the wheels within wheels which keep it in motion," and let each participant in the political game speak for himself against another holding a contrary position. His massive chapter on the ground-breaking state constitutional convention of 1821 appears to be little more than a condensed version of the report of its debates, yet Hammond's selection of speeches not only catches the full flavor of the convention, it also leads to astute conclusions in the form of repeated rhetorical questions. As a Democrat, Hammond welcomed broadening of the suffrage; but when certain Democrats at the convention sought to prevent African Americans from voting, Hammond asks (after quoting from speeches attacking black voters for unduly influencing elections by following en masse the lead of their Federalist former masters) whether it had occurred to these opponents of African American participation "that, during the most perilous period of the late war [1812], when the country was in imminent danger, they themselves had voted for a law encouraging the enlistment of negroes, and for raising a regiment of blacks?"

Hammond's book was generally well received by contemporaries, with the notable exception of former supreme court chief justice Ambrose Spencer, who accused the historian of being unfairly critical of his former patron Clinton, and using the work as an endorsement of Van Buren in return for the county judgeship. Many modern historians find Hammond's work to be an essential source. Hammond died in Cherry Valley.

• There is a small collection of Hammond's papers at the New-York Historical Society, including an autobiographical letter to his publisher. His letters to Van Buren are found in the Martin Van Buren Papers at the Library of Congress; his letters to Gerrit Smith are at Syracuse Library; and his letters to William H. Seward are at the University of Rochester. Also see Hammond, *An Address Delivered . . . before the Otsego County Education Society, Oct. 10, 1838* (1839); *An Address Delivered at Cherry Valley on the Fourth of July, 1832* (1832); *Letters on the Repeal of the Restraining Act* (1836); "Plain Truth," *Emancipator*, 2nd. series, 20 Oct. 1835; *On the Evidence, Independent of Written Revelation, of the Immortality of the Soul* (1851); and *Letter to the Hon. John C. Calhoun on the Annexation of Texas* (1844). His early law partner Levi Beardsley has some comments on Hammond in his *Reminiscences* (1852). Spencer's critique is in the *New World*, 19 Aug. 1843. An obituary is in the *New York Tribune*, 28 Aug. 1855.

DONALD M. ROPER

HAMMOND, James Henry (15 Nov. 1807–13 Nov. 1864), U.S. senator and governor of South Carolina, was born in Newberry District, South Carolina, the son of Elisha Hammond, a struggling merchant and schoolmaster who had migrated from New England at the turn of the century, and Catherine Fox Spann. Hammond graduated from South Carolina College in 1825 determined not to repeat his father's difficult existence. After several years of teaching and preparing for the bar, he began to practice law in Columbia in 1828. The excitement of the nullification controversy over the constitutionality of the federal tariff gave Hammond his initial prominence as a strongly sectionalist editor of the *Southern Times*, a newspaper he inaugurated in January 1830. The next year Hammond married a sixteen-year-old Charleston heiress, Catherine Fitzsimons, despite the strong opposition of her family, who thought him a fortune hunter; the couple had five children who lived to adulthood. Hammond left public life to manage the Savannah River plantation and 147 slaves he acquired as a result of the union. Agriculture and slave management became central practical and intellectual concerns for the remainder of his life. Cherishing an image of himself as a concerned paternalist, Hammond strove to control a slave force that resisted his intrusive efforts to name their children, regulate their religion, and prescribe their work rhythms. In urging agricultural reform and soil improvement through use of marl, Hammond became an ally of Virginian Edmund Ruffin. Like Ruffin, he wrote extensively on agricultural topics and actively supported state and local agricultural societies. Under Hammond's direction, the property at "Silver Bluff" produced bountiful returns of cotton and corn, making him one of the South's wealthiest men and largest slave owners, with a force that numbered more than three hundred by the outbreak of the Civil War.

Hammond soon recognized that his self-conscious drive for power and achievement could not stop with plantation management, and he returned to political life. Elected to Congress, he moved to Washington in 1835. After a dramatic debut attacking the reception of abolition petitions by the House of Representatives, thereby precipitating the gag rule controversy over rights of free speech in Congress, he was stricken with an ill-defined nervous ailment and resigned his congressional seat for restorative travel in Europe.

By the end of the decade, Hammond had resumed his political career, and he experienced a painful loss in the 1840 gubernatorial contest when John C. Calhoun threw his influence behind Hammond's opponent. In 1841, however, Hammond was chosen a general of the state militia and in 1842 won the governor's chair. During his term he supported the transformation of the Citadel into a military academy, inaugurated a state agricultural survey, encouraged public education, and attacked the powers of the Bank of the State. His stance on national political questions, particularly his opposition to the tariff of 1842, gained him attention as a sectionalist even more radical than Calhoun. At the end of his gubernatorial term, a scandal over sexual improprieties with his four nieces, the daughters of the powerful Wade Hampton II (1818–1902), returned Hammond once again to his plantation, where he continued to write on agricultural and political topics, including a widely influential defense of slavery published in 1845 as two letters to English abolitionist Thomas Clarkson.

Although Hammond served in the Southern Convention that met at Nashville in 1850 to consider united sectional action in the national crisis, he was otherwise blocked from politics by Hampton and his allies until 1857, when Hampton abandoned his opposition, and Hammond was chosen for the U.S. Senate. Despite the sectional hostility he encountered in Washington, Hammond was more sanguine about the possibilities for the South in the Union than he had been at any previous time in his life, and he doubted southern readiness for secession. A radical when moderation held sway, Hammond embraced moderation as secessionists at last secured southern independence. Himself mentioned as a potential Democratic presidential candidate in 1860, Hammond supported Virginian R. M. T. Hunter and resigned from the Senate upon Abraham Lincoln's election. Embittered by the failure of Confederate leadership to seek his advice on matters of economic and political policy, Hammond criticized the government of Jefferson Davis vociferously and deplored the centralizing measures necessitated by war. His health declined throughout the war years, and he died at "Redcliffe," the plantation house he had carefully designed in the 1850s to symbolize his rise to prominence.

One of the Old South's leading intellects, Hammond is perhaps best remembered for his defenses of slavery and for his oft quoted "mud-sill" speech in the Senate in 1858, justifying hierarchy as fundamental and essential to all societies. Such a doctrine extended beyond invocation of racial difference to suggest a far broader legitimacy for slavery. Known for his physical attractiveness and brilliant mind, Hammond was an arrogant and contentious individual who quarreled regularly with both friends and family. His wife lived separately from him for several years in the 1850s, when Hammond refused to give up a slave mistress with whom he sired one or more children. His relationships with his legitimate children were difficult as well, for his offspring resented his high expectations and his constant efforts at control. Hammond died an unfulfilled and bitter man, alienated personally and politically, frustrated in the boundless ambition that had dominated his life.

• The James Henry Hammond Papers are in the Library of Congress and the South Caroliniana Library, University of South Carolina, Columbia. His views are indicated in James Henry Hammond, *Letters and Speeches of the Hon. James H. Hammond of South Carolina* (1866). See also Drew Gilpin Faust, *James Henry Hammond and the Old South: A Design for Mastery* (1982); Carol Bleser, ed., *The Hammonds of Redcliffe* (1981); and Bleser, ed., *Secret and Sacred: The Diaries of James Henry Hammond* (1988).

DREW GILPIN FAUST

HAMMOND, John (1613?–c. 1 Mar. 1663), promotion writer and lawyer, first appears in the historical records in Virginia in 1646. Nothing is known of his parentage or education. He remarked in 1654 that he had spent nineteen years in Virginia and two in Maryland, so he evidently emigrated to Virginia about 1633. He probably farmed and practiced law in Isle of Wight County, Virginia. He witnessed a deed there in 1646 and was elected a burgess in 1652, but the Puritan assembly expelled him as "a scandalous person, and a frequent disturber of the peace of the country, by libell and other illegall practices." The offended Hammond, with his wife and four children, promptly moved to Maryland, where he bought a plantation in St. Mary's County. In June 1653 he argued a case before the Maryland Provincial Court. The entrepreneurial Hammond was granted a license to sell liquor on 5 December 1654 and established an inn at Newtown. He was also given the right to provide a ferry over the Newtown River. In return, Hammond allowed the St. Mary's County Court to meet at his inn, "the most Convenient place."

During the Interregnum, Lord Baltimore's supporters (including John Hammond) and the Puritan forces fought for control of Maryland. The Puritan forces defeated Lord Baltimore's supporters in a series of skirmishes, the most decisive being the battle of Severn on 25 March 1655. After their victory, the Puritans sought to capture John Hammond, who made his wife his attorney and fled to England in disguise. Several pamphlets appeared in London, each appealing, di-

rectly or indirectly, to Cromwell to settle the dispute. Roger Heaman, a Puritan who had taken part in the battle of Severn, described it in *An Additional Brief Narrative of a Late Bloody Design against the Protestants in Ann Arundel County* (1655).

Heaman's pamphlet occasioned Hammond's first publication, *Hammond vs. Heamans or an Answer to an Audacious Pamphlet, Published by an Impudent and Ridiculous Fellow, Named Roger Heamans, Calling Himself Commander of the Ship Golden Lion, wherein He Endeavours by Lies and Holy Expressions, to Colour over His Murthers and Treacheries Committed in the Province of Maryland* (1655). Hammond shows more wit, verve, and liveliness than any other writer in the literary dispute, writing that he would "anatomize and lay him [Roger Heaman] open to the world a fool, to the State a Knave, to God a notorious offender, whose unfeigned repentance I cordially wish, and that his future portion of Grace may over-ballance his former talents of wit and honesty, in the want of which the poor man hath been too unhappy." Though the pamphlet is filled with invective, Hammond also introduces the sworn testimony of three witnesses who had been at the battle of Severn to prove that "Heamans hath abused the World with his Pamphlet, not a sillable whereof is truth."

Having discovered that he was a good writer, Hammond wrote *Leah and Rachel, or the Two Fruitful Sisters Virginia and Maryland* (1656), one of the best seventeenth-century promotion tracts. It contains an early statement of love for America and the best seventeenth-century statement, after the one by Captain John Smith (1580–1631), of the American dream. Some writers had, however, praised America too highly. Hammond ridicules the idea of America as heaven: it was "not such a Lubberland as the Fiction of the land of Ease, is reported to be, nor such a *Utopian* as *Sr. Thomas Moore* hath related to be found out." He also censures the "spirits" who lured people to the New World but assures the prospective emigrants that the life of an American indentured servant compared favorably to that of the ordinary English farmer. If he or she worked hard, the common person would find greater opportunities in America than England. Hammond contrasts New World opportunity with the life of a poor Londoner:

The other day, I saw a man heavily loaden with a burden of Faggots on his back, crying Dry Faggots, Dry Faggots; he travailed much ground, bawled frequently, and sweat with his burthen: but I saw none buy any, neer three houres I followed him . . . me thought it was a pittifull life, and I admired how he could live on it; And yet it were dangerous to advise these wretches to better their conditions by travaile, for fear of the cry of, spirit, a spirit.

Hammond assures his readers that a number of emigrants had already transformed themselves: "from being wool-hoppers and of as mean and meaner imployment in England have there grown great merchants, and attained to the most eminent advancements the

Country afforded." He says that not everyone will succeed, but persons have a better chance to do so in the New World than anywhere else. In closing, Hammond reiterates his love for America: "it is that Country in which I desire to spend the remnant of my dayes, in which I covet to make my grave."

Hammond was back in Maryland before 8 May 1661, when he served as an attorney. For the next two years, he turns up in various court records. His most interesting case was a suit he brought against Dr. Jacob Lumbrozo for slandering his wife. On 10 October 1662, Lumbrozo was found guilty and fined. Hammond witnessed a deed on 25 November 1662 and was alive in early February, but he had died (presumably in Maryland) by mid-March 1663. He was survived by his wife, Ann, and at least two children. In *Leah and Rachel*, Hammond revealed his love for, and identification with, the Chesapeake Bay colonies.

• No manuscripts of Hammond are extant. The only biography, with a bibliography of primary and secondary sources, is J. A. Leo Lemay, *Men of Letters in Colonial Maryland* (1972). For additional critical insights, see Robert D. Arner, "A Note on John Hammond's *Leah and Rachel*," *Southern Literature Journal* 6 (Fall 1973): 77–80.

J. A. Leo Lemay

HAMMOND, John Hays (31 Mar. 1855–8 June 1936), mining engineer, was born in San Francisco, California, the son of Richard Pindell Hammond, an army officer and politician, and Sara Elizabeth Hays. The scion of a moderately well-to-do family, he graduated from the Sheffield Scientific School of Yale with a Ph.B. in 1876 and then studied for three years at the Königliche Sächsische Bergakademie in Freiberg, Saxony, where a substantial number of important American mining engineers were trained in the nineteenth century. Young Hammond gained experience in jobs typical of those offered neophyte engineers: first as assayer for George Hearst, a major western mine owner, then collecting mineral statistics in California, with the U.S. Geological Survey. In 1881, in Hancock, Maryland, he married Natalie Harris, daughter of a Confederate general; the couple had four children.

Hammond spent the next eight years examining mines throughout the American West and as far afield as Central and South America for individual and corporate capitalists. This work was interrupted when he spent fifteen months as superintendent of a silver mine in Mexico. In 1885 he considerably enhanced his reputation by his skillful reopening of the North Star mine at Grass Valley in California's rich Nevada County. Four years later he took an option on the Bunker Hill & Sullivan in Idaho's Coeur d'Alene district, raised working capital through family and college friends, and took over as president of what became one of the world's most important silver-lead-zinc operations.

In 1893 he joined the growing American mining fraternity in South Africa, first as consultant to the pioneer Barnato brothers, then to Cecil Rhodes, whom he considered the "biggest man I ever met" and "the greatest Englishman of the age." He persuaded Rhodes that in the area later known as Rhodesia the older ancient mines were of great value and should be developed, which was done with dazzling success. On the Witwatersrand in the Transvaal, an incredibly rich area of quartz-pebble conglomerates in South Africa, he convinced Rhodes and others to sell their outcrop mines and develop the deep-level properties adjacent to them, a shrewd appraisal that returned millions.

Hammond described his own work as "more commercial and financial than technical." It was lucrative business, but other engineers believed that the attendant publicity made him "more reputation in So Africa than he would have made in the U.S. in twenty years." Distressed by policies of the dominant Boer minority government—policies Rhodes believed threatened effective mining operations—Hammond joined the Americans and Englishmen in South Africa who plotted an internal revolution. After the failure of Jameson's premature raid across the Transvaal border early in 1896, sixty-four planners of the Reform movement were arrested, and Hammond and three others were sentenced to death for high treason. But the sentences were soon commuted to fifteen years in prison, and Hammond was released after paying a fine of $125,000. Though his African career was over, he left as the best-known mining engineer in the world.

He continued extensive mining dealings, first from London, then from New York. He was one of several invited to survey Russian mineral resources in the winter of 1897–1898 (and again a dozen years later). With a large technical staff under his supervision, he was constantly involved in mine evaluation, sales, promotion, and financing, arguing that the mining engineer was destined to "invade the sphere now monopolized by the employer and capitalist and eventually become, in fact himself, the master." In 1903 he became consulting engineer and general manager of the Guggenheim Exploration Company, created expressly to acquire promising mining properties. In this capacity, he obtained the Utah Copper and Nevada Consolidated, two of the West's most important, new, low-grade copper operations; the Esperanza gold mine in Mexico; and the Central lead mine in Missouri, all of which added to the success of the Guggenheim's powerful American Smelting & Refining Company. Based on a percentage of profits, Hammond's compensation was said to have been $1 million a year, probably twenty to thirty times the income of the average mining engineer.

Though often labeled the "wizard of modern mining" who "could smell a gold mine a thousand miles away," Hammond was not infallible. In 1906, after he enthusiastically endorsed the Nipissing silver mine in Canada, the Guggenheims lost heavily when the property failed to live up to expectations. Pleading poor health, Hammond ended his association with the company in the following year.

While he subsequently became involved in hydroelectric, irrigation, and petroleum projects in California and Mexico, increasingly he turned to "prospecting in politics," as he called it. By his own admission, Hammond knew every president from Ulysses S. Grant to Herbert Hoover, with the exception of Chester A. Arthur, and became enough of an unofficial adviser to William Howard Taft that Colonel House (Edward M. House) could subsequently be referred to as "the John Hays Hammond of the Wilson Administration." He "enjoyed a flutter in the direction of the vice-presidency" with Taft in 1909 but turned down an appointment as minister to China, though he did serve as special ambassador at the coronation of George V in England in 1911. An ardent and active Republican, Hammond developed a strong interest in the settlement of international disputes by judicial arbitration in the pre–World War I era, but he also worked hard in favor of American preparedness and headed Warren G. Harding's commission to survey the coal industry in 1922.

He was elected president of the American Institute of Mining and Metallurgical Engineers in 1907 and was awarded its prestigious Saunders Medal in 1929. Early in the century he served as professor at Yale, where he endowed the Hammond Metallurgical Laboratory. He died at his summer home at Gloucester, Massachusetts, and was buried in Greenwood Cemetery, Brooklyn.

Hammond moved in high social circles. He was a supporter of causes and a joiner of organizations, ranging from the Episcopal church to the twenty-five private clubs to which he belonged in 1931. Ever a spokesman of American business, preaching the standard rags-to-riches message of the gospel of wealth, he also openly espoused such progressive doctrines as woman suffrage and improved labor benefits. This was something of a switch from his early days in Idaho, when he was a leader in quashing the miners' union. By World War I Samuel Gompers could call him "the most conservative, practical, radically democratic millionaire I ever met."

Despite his diminutive physical stature, Hammond was the prototype for Richard Harding Davis's swashbuckling Robert Clay in *Soldiers of Fortune* (1897). He was a model for inspirational success stories for boys: as one writer said in 1921, "As an empire-builder the name of John Hays Hammond shines with equal splendor alongside those of Henry Hudson, La Salle, and Cecil Rhodes." His flair for publicity and his lack of modesty made him less popular with many of his fellow engineers, who saw him "as a dynamic but smallish sort of man, ever anxious to appear a little bigger than he was" (quoted in Marshall Bond, Jr., *Gold Hunter* [1969], p. 214). In truth, he fell somewhere in between: he was an able mining engineer who was more publicized and successful than most. Above all, Hammond was the embodiment of the modern engineer-promoter; with ambition and vision, he understood well his own era and the systematic exploration, large-scale business consolidation, and overseas expansion that were part of it.

• The John Hays Hammond Papers are in the Sterling Library, Yale University. Comprising some 6,000 items of correspondence and printed material, this collection deals with South African mining business, the Jameson raid, and Hammond's articles and speeches (1893–1934) on many subjects. *The Autobiography of John Hays Hammond* (2 vols., 1935) is complete but uneven in quality. A sound appraisal of the African years appears in chapter 5 ("John Hays Hammond and the Jameson Raid: Engineering a Capitalist Revolution in South Africa") of Lysle E. Meyer, *The Farther Frontier: Six Case Studies of Americans and Africa, 1848–1936* (1992). Obituaries are in the *New York Times*, 9 July 1936, and Pope Yeatman, "John Hays Hammond," *Mining and Metallurgy* 17 (July 1936): 369.

CLARK C. SPENCE

HAMMOND, John Henry, Jr. (15 Dec. 1910–10 July 1987), critic and producer of jazz and popular music, was born in New York City, the son of John Henry Hammond, corporate lawyer, and Emily Vanderbilt Sloane. Born to privilege, Hammond used his wealth and position, along with considerable resourcefulness and conviction, to promote primarily black music through the 1940s in ways that profoundly influenced its development and international acceptance. He later branched out to produce important folk and rock recordings.

Hammond acquired a passion for jazz and blues as a student at Hotchkiss School. He attended Yale (1929–1931), studied briefly at the Juilliard School of Music, and furthered his musical education in frequent visits to Harlem clubs and theaters. In 1971 he said, "One reason I'm the way I am is because I got to know Harlem. Upperclass white folks went up to Harlem in the 20's, slumming. I went out of passion." After dropping out of Yale, he became a journalist and covered the Scottsboro trials for the *Nation* and *New Republic*, in part as a way of exploring the South in search of new musical talent to promote. Throughout his life he fought segregation in and out of the popular music business, doing what he could to see that blacks were hired in places hitherto closed to them: recording studios, dance halls, theaters, and clubs whose owners and patrons resisted his efforts, sometimes by pointing to his left-leaning politics. He was active in the National Association for the Advancement of Colored People, becoming a board member in 1937 and eventually vice president.

His activities did much to shape musical taste. In the thirties he was jazz critic for the *Brooklyn Daily Eagle*; *Melody News*, of which he was associate editor (1934–1935); *Down Beat*, as a columnist; and for the British publications the *Gramophone*, *Melody Maker*, and *Rhythm*. In the 1950s he wrote about jazz in the *New York Daily Compass*, the *New York Times*, and the *New York Herald Tribune*, *Hi-Fi Music at Home*, and *Gentry* as its music editor (1956–1957).

He was a tireless organizer of performances and recording sessions. In 1932 he bought a theater in lower Manhattan to stage shows starring the bands of Fletcher Henderson and Luis Russell, among others, and at the same time he worked for radio station WEVD as announcer, disk jockey, and producer of programs using integrated bands. Shortly, he convinced the English division of Columbia Records to make a session with Henderson's band—this in the midst of the depression when record sales were less than 6 percent of what they had been three years earlier. Many of these undertakings were supported by the $12,000 annual earnings from Hammond's trust fund. In the 1930s he supervised further recordings for Columbia (including Bessie Smith's last session) and for English Parlophone.

Thereafter, he was involved with record making for most of his life. He became sales manager of Columbia Masterworks in 1934, and he was associate recording director for Columbia from 1939 through 1943 and again in 1946. He served as president of Keynote Records in 1947 and was then music director at Majestic Records, becoming vice president when Mercury Records took over the two companies in the late 1940s. At Mercury, he named as head of artists and repertoire Mitch Miller, whose touch created many popular music successes. Later, Hammond produced several dozen mainstream jazz albums for Vanguard Records (1953–1958) before returning to Columbia as executive producer in 1959.

In all of these roles, Hammond was an outstanding scout and developer of talent. During the 1930s he supervised the historically important small-group recordings of Billie Holiday, one of his discoveries. In 1935 he played a key role in putting the Benny Goodman band together, and he helped engineer its phenomenal popularity. He also was largely responsible for creation of the Benny Goodman Trio, the first interracial jazz group to tour the United States. Traveling through the Midwest in 1936, Hammond heard the Count Basie band broadcasting from a Kansas City nightclub, and he subsequently helped shape the group's fortunes, Noteworthy was the historic Basie session he produced in October 1936, which featured the band's star tenor saxophonist Lester Young.

In 1938 and 1939 Hammond produced two memorable "Spirituals to Swing Concerts" at Carnegie Hall, again using black and white musicians together. During this time he helped generate interest in boogie-woogie, a form of piano blues that became an intermittent fad through the postwar years and profoundly influenced rhythm and blues and rock music. Boogie-woogie's leading practitioners, Meade Lux Lewis, Pete Johnson, and Albert Ammons, were greatly supported in their careers by Hammond's efforts. Other major jazz musicians whom Hammond assisted in bringing to light were vibraphonist Lionel Hampton, pianist Teddy Wilson, guitarist Charlie Christian, and singer Mildred Bailey.

At Columbia in the 1960s Hammond played a major role in the recording careers of rock, folk, and crossover jazz artists Aretha Franklin, Bob Dylan (known at the time as "Hammond's folly"), Bruce Springsteen, Leonard Cohen, Pete Seeger, George Benson, and Ray Bryant. Of importance were the multivolume classic jazz reissues he produced at Columbia in 1975

and 1976 (including those of legendary bluesman Robert Johnson).

An optimistic extrovert, known for his boyish appearance and perennial crew cut, Hammond was a man of strong convictions and tastes, which he made no attempt to conceal. Above all, he favored big-band swing and the blues. He was not fond of bebop, the eventually prevailing jazz style of the post–World War II era. He openly admitted some mistakes, however, such as his initial rejection of singer Ella Fitzgerald.

For all of his passion for jazz, Hammond was a proficient viola player and encouraged performances of classical music by Benny Goodman (who married Hammond's sister Alice). Hammond's first marriage ended in divorce; in 1947 he married Esmé O'Brien, who died in 1986. Their son is the blues singer John Hammond. Hammond died in New York City.

• There is oral-history material on Hammond at the New York Public Library and the Institute of Jazz Studies at Rutgers University, Newark. His autobiography, written with Irving Townsend, *John Hammond On Record*, was published in 1977. Useful articles include "Hammond, John Henry, Jr.," *Encyclopedia of Jazz* (1960) pp. 241–42; G. Graham, "Meet the A & R Man: John Hammond," *Down Beat*, Oct. 12, 1961, p. 23; P. J. Sullivan, "John Hammond," *Jazz Journal*, Sept. 1968, p. 6; J. McDonough, "John Hammond: Man for All Seasons," *Down Beat*, Mar. 4, 1971, p. 13; and "Review of *John Hammond On Record*," *Down Beat*, Jan. 12, 1978, p. 58; Leonard Feather, "John Hammond," *The Passion for Jazz* (1980), p. 176; and "John Hammond, Discoverer of Musical Talent Dies," *New York Times*, 11 July 1987.

NEIL LEONARD

HAMMOND, Percy Hunter (7 Mar. 1873–25 Apr. 1936), drama critic, was born in Cadiz, Ohio, the son of Alexander J. Hammond, a merchant, and Lottie E. F. Hunter. Hammond's fascination with the theater began at age thirteen, when he attended a tent performance of *Little Nugget* at the Cadiz fair. Thereafter, he passed out show bills for a local theater and served as an usher in exchange for free tickets. By age sixteen, without parental consent, Hammond left school and family to seek his fortune in Washington, D.C. Fortune was elusive, however, until Ohio senator John Sherman, a friend of his father, got him a job at the Government Printing Office, where he learned the skills of a compositor and became an expert typesetter. After a few years he returned home, enrolled in Franklin College, and graduated in 1896, a year that also witnessed his marriage to Florence Carnahan of Cadiz and his first newspaper job on the *Chillicothe News-Advertiser*. Two years later he became a police reporter on the *Chicago Evening Post* at a salary of eight dollars per week. Successive jobs at the paper included correspondent, editorial writer, and for the final five years, drama critic. By 1908 he had moved on to become the drama critic of the *Chicago Tribune*. Except for an assignment as a roving reporter in France during the closing days of World War I, during which he sent back vivid dispatches from the war zone, Hammond remained as the paper's drama critic, honing his already considerable writing and critical skills into a new style of dramatic criticism, described years later in his obituary in the *New York Times*: "His debut as a theatrical journalist marked the end of the old style pontifical school of play reviewing and the beginning of the modern era. Mr. Hammond practiced the 'light touch' with a pretense of Oxonian learning which seemed to be laughing at itself. He was perhaps the first of the 'sophisticates' of American journalism."

Hammond had a passion for words. He was known to carry both a notebook for jotting down new and esoteric words and Hart's *Rhetoric*; he usually had Roget's *Thesaurus* and Crabb's *English Synonyms* nearby. He avoided pretentiousness by giving his reviews a satiric or cynical turn. Hammond was a meticulous stylist, and his keen wit and sometimes caustic critiques were not always well received by theater owners, producers, and casts; not surprisingly, there were sometimes stormy confrontations. At one point Hammond was barred from Shubert theaters for two years, whereupon the *Chicago Tribune* barred all Shubert advertising from its pages, forcing the producers to sue for peace. So widespread was Hammond's reputation for incisive, acerbic reactions that when he was sent to cover the winding down of the war, a Chicago actor remarked, "Heavens! What if he doesn't like it?"

In 1921, after hesitating for several years because he feared the Broadway atmosphere and thought he would be at a disadvantage as an "immigrant" from another city (he describes his fright in a typically sly essay, "Tremors on Moving from Chicago to New York"), Hammond finally accepted the *New York Tribune*'s offer to become its drama critic. At first his reviews seemed noncommittal, prompting DeWolf Hopper to remark, "He seems to have left his stiletto in Chicago." But gradually the integrity of his criticism, even though it sometimes meant frank disapproval, won him an audience. According to the *New York Times*, "New York soon grew to know him as its most graceful and original theatrical writer. His point of view had a quality which taught Broadway something new in the vein of light criticism."

Unsparing about plays he judged immoral or salacious, Hammond voiced his disapproval of scantily clad showgirls with a typical bon mot: "The human knee is a joint, not an entertainment." Of a dull musical he wrote, "I find I have knocked everything but the chorus girls' knees, and there God anticipated me." Of a performance by actors who had appeared in a certain work too often, he quipped, "They have played it so long they can act it in their sleep, which they did yesterday afternoon."

Since his theater column was syndicated, Hammond was for some years the most influential drama critic in the nation. He also wrote occasional book reviews for the *Tribune* and a popular column of short essays for the paper titled "Oddments and Remainders," which was also syndicated. In 1927 *But—Is It Art?*, a book of his essays on the theater, was published.

An active, outspoken member of the New York Drama Critics Circle, Hammond voiced the opinion of three dissenting members when the group's 1936 Best Play award went to Maxwell Anderson's *Winterset*: "To our taste, it is spinach, smothered with music's rich gravies, but still spinach."

Three weeks later, just five months after the death of his wife of thirty-nine years, Hammond died suddenly, of pneumonia, in New York City. He was survived by a son, the couple's only child. Their admiration evident, the New York drama critics reacted publicly to the loss of their gifted colleague. Wrote Brooks Atkinson of the *New York Times*, "His epigrams were prodigal and brilliant. . . . What discouraged his colleagues on rival journals was the quiet choice of untarnished words that turned his reviews into self-disparaging fragments of literature . . ." John Mason Brown of the *New York Evening Post* wrote, "Criticism as Percy wrote it was not only about a show, it was a show in itself." Burns Mantle of the *New York Daily News* observed, "He probably was the creator of more penetrating lines that simply cried out for quotation than any dramatic writer of the last two generations." And as John Anderson of the *New York Evening Journal* described him, "He was incorrigible, wayward, often wrong-headed and stubborn but completely lovable. His enemies (and he rejoiced in many) used to say he slept through most plays.. . . . Behind his impassive mask was a brain on a flying trapeze, performing outrageous and hair-raising stunts with the most peculiar vocabulary in the world." An editorial in the *New York Herald-Tribune* of 27 April 1936 sums up Hammond's unique contribution to his profession: "He leaves a large gap in the life of New York. . . . For years he has been the dean of New York critics, their oracle and standard-bearer against every effort to cabin thought or confine criticism. Power was his and the conscience to wield it with scrupulous integrity." In 1940 Hammond's son published a posthumous collection of Hammond's reviews, essays, and commentary titled *This Atom in the Audience*.

• An excellent source of information on Hammond is the Billy Rose Theatre Collection of the New York Public Library for Performing Arts, which includes newspaper and periodical clippings, theater reviews, and photographs. William Cole, ed., *Ohio Authors and Their Books* (1962), and the *National Cyclopedia of American Biography*, vol. 27 (1939) provide important material. Franklin P. Adams et al., *Percy Hammond: A Symposium in Tribute* (1936), is very useful. Extensive obituaries appear in the *New York Times* and the *New York Herald-Tribune*, both 26 Apr. 1936.

ADELE S. PARONI

HAMMOND, William Alexander (28 Aug. 1828–5 Jan. 1900), neurologist, was born in Annapolis, Maryland, son of John Wesley Hammond, a doctor, and Sarah Pinckney. He attended St. Johns College and then the Medical College of the University of the City of New York, where he received the M.D. in 1848. After a year as resident physician at the Pennsylvania Hospital in Philadelphia, he married Helen Nisbet and enlisted as an assistant surgeon in the United States Army.

While serving at frontier posts in New Mexico and Kansas, between 1849 and 1856, Hammond collected natural history specimens for colleagues in the Academy of Natural Sciences in Philadelphia and for the Smithsonian Institution. He also earned an international reputation as a physiologist for original experiments in metabolic chemistry, mainly conducted on himself. On medical leave in Philadelphia between 1857 and 1859, he helped to organize the Philadelphia Biological Society and pursued experiments on toxicology with Silas Weir Mitchell. After a brief stint at Fort Mackinac, Michigan, he resigned from the army in the fall of 1860 to join the faculty of the medical school of the University of Maryland at Baltimore.

Hammond reenlisted six months later, at the outset of the Civil War. Still an assistant surgeon, he was soon promoted to inspector of hospitals. In April 1862 he was promoted to the post of surgeon general after intensive lobbying on his behalf by the U.S. Sanitary Commission. He gave dynamic leadership to the newly reorganized Medical Department, emphasizing centralization of authority and the pursuit of efficiency. He also used his influence to advance the cause of medical science, initiating the Army Medical Museum and the monumental *Medical and Surgical History of the War of the Rebellion* (1870–1883), and making books as well as instruments such as thermometers and microscopes available to medical officers. Other measures—such as increasingly stringent examinations for appointment to positions in the Medical Department, and the famous "Circular #6" of 1863 limiting the use of the common remedies calomel and tartar emetic—diminished Hammond's popularity among a large segment of the medical profession. The controversies thus engendered made it possible in 1864 for Secretary of War Edwin Stanton to have Hammond court-martialed on unrelated charges, found guilty of "conduct unbecoming an officer," and dismissed from the service.

Hammond continued to receive support from the scientific and professional elite of the American medical community. Friends helped him establish himself in practice in New York City, where he and his wife raised the two of their five children who ultimately survived them. Once on his feet, Hammond made the unusual choice to limit his work to a specialty and played a crucial role in the shaping of American neurology. He was one of its first full-time practitioners and a founding member of the American Neurological Association and the New York Neurological Society. He served as a professor of nervous and mental diseases at Bellevue Hospital Medical College, the Medical College of the University of the City of New York; and later the Postgraduate Medical School of New York. His influential *Treatise on Diseases of the Nervous System* (1871) remained in print through nine editions, the last revision of which appeared in 1898. He published monographs on sleep and insomnia, on sexual impotence and venereal diseases, on medico-legal themes, and against spiritualism, as well as texts on insanity and on hygiene. In addition, Hammond published some two hundred contributions to medical journals. He served as editor to the *Maryland and Virginia Medical Journal*, the *New York Medical Journal*, the *Quarterly Journal of Psychological Medicine and Medical Jurisprudence*, the *Journal of Psychological Medicine*, the *Psychological and Medico-Legal Journal*, the *Journal of Nervous and Mental Diseases*, and *Neurological Contributions*.

Hammond, an astute clinician, found in neurology the opportunity to pursue his scientific interests. He studied and treated patients with mental disorders as well as those who appeared to have functional or organic diseases of the nervous system. He also attempted to apply his results to social problems of the day, such as the "woman question," on which he was a self-proclaimed reactionary. He sought in the study of the nervous system the key to normal and abnormal psychology, and had virtually unlimited faith in the ability of science to explain even the most mysterious of phenomena. However, his own medical theories (for example, his explanation of insomnia as a symptom of "cerebral hyperemia"—excess blood circulating in the brain) and his style of scientific work increasingly came to diverge from the main scientific currents of his time.

Hammond wrote extensively on medical subjects for lay audiences and published seven novels, a volume of short stories coauthored with his daughter Clara Hammond Lanza, and (posthumously) a four-act play. He was active in New York civic, scientific, and society affairs. His extensive and lucrative practice, his commanding presence, his often idiosyncratic opinions, his wide-ranging interests, and his unshakable self-confidence all combined to make him one of the best-known (if not always best-liked) American physicians of his time. The verdict of the court-martial was overturned in 1879, Hammond's medical career having suffered no appreciable damage from the affair.

Hammond's first wife died in 1885; he was remarried, to Esther Dyer Chapin of Providence, Rhode Island, the following year. In 1888 the couple moved to Washington, D.C., where Hammond established a sanitarium for patients with nervous diseases in 1889. At this time he also involved himself in the manufacture and sale of "animal extract" remedies of the sort introduced by Charles-Edouard Brown-Séquard, a medical researcher and physician at the Collège de France. Both Hammond's scientific reputation and his financial affairs suffered setbacks from some of the business methods he employed in these last ventures. He died in his Washington home.

• For a full-length biography of Hammond, see Bonnie Ellen Blustein, *Preserve Your Love for Science: Life of William A. Hammond, Neurologist* (1991), which includes a bibliography of works by Hammond and a note on archival and manuscript sources. On Hammond's court-martial, see also Mark D. Miller, "William A. Hammond: Restoring the Reputation of a Surgeon General," *Military Medicine* 152 (1987):452–57; and Henry C. Friend, "Abraham Lincoln and the Court Martial of Surgeon General William A. Hammond," *Commercial Law Journal* 62 (1957):71–80. For an annotated bibliography of Hammond's works, see Jack D. Key and Bonnie Ellen Blustein, *William A. Hammond, M.D. (1828–1900): The Publications of an American Neurologist* (1983).

BONNIE ELLEN BLUSTEIN

HAMPDEN, Walter (30 June 1879–11 June 1955), actor, was born Walter Hampden Dougherty in Brooklyn, New York, the son of John Hampden Dougherty, a lawyer, and Alice Hill. He was one of six children raised in a household where the arts were appreciated and practiced by all. At his father's suggestion, Hampden and Clayton Hamilton, dramatic critic and Hampden's lifelong friend, had, according to Hamilton, read "nearly every Elizabethan play extant before we had reached the usual age of going to college." The two friends also acted and produced together at the Brooklyn Polytechnic Institute, where both went for high school and college; made frequent sojourns to the theaters of Manhattan; and toured to London and Paris for almost a year to absorb European culture.

After graduation in 1900 Hampden returned to Paris to study acting, dancing, singing, fencing, and cello. The following year Hampden went to England, where, with the influence of a family friend, he secured a position in the F. R. Benson acting company, which was noted as a training ground for many new actors. Hampden played larger and larger roles in Shakespearean plays, as well as other roles in the older repertory. He also met company member Mabel Moore, whom he married in 1905. They had a daughter and a son. Hampden left Benson in 1904 and until 1906 played a series of engagements in London and Glasgow under various managements in Shakespearean and modern dramas. By the time Hampden returned to his homeland, he was a classically trained and thoroughly experienced young actor.

He intended to return in the role of Manson in Charles Rann Kennedy's *The Servant in the House*. Kennedy wrote the play with Hampden in mind, and Hampden convinced American producer Henry Miller to back it. Miller was not immediately able to produce it, however. Instead he brought Hampden back to the United States in 1907 to play in support of Russian actress Alla Nazimova. Hampden first appeared in support of Nazimova as Comte Silvio in *The Comtesse Coquet*. He also played Solness to Nazimova's Hilda Wangel in the American premiere of Ibsen's *The Master Builder*. *The Servant in the House* opened in 1908 and played continually in New York and on the road for two years. Hampden played this intense "Christ-like" role for many years. As Manson, Hampden exhibited dignity, concentration, commanding presence, and the romantic style of acting in which he was trained. It was a larger-than-life, highly theatrical style that suited an older repertoire and was more popular, usually, on the road than in the big city.

Between 1910 and 1918, Hampden acted for various producers. While he was especially successful in the romantic roles available, he did not achieve great financial or artistic success in a repertory that did not really suit him. He spent many months at a time waiting for suitable work. An unusual opportunity came in the spring and summer of 1918, when Hampden played, in order, Elihu in *The Book of Job*, Marc Antony in *Julius Caesar*, Macbeth, Hamlet, Oberon in *A Midsummer Night's Dream*, Iokonan in Oscar Wilde's *Salomé*, and Siddartha in *The Light of Asia*. These were all short-run independent productions, but all were well received by critics.

In the fall of 1918 Hampden began to present matinee productions of *Hamlet* at the Plymouth Theatre in New York. Unable to secure commercial backing and to afford the theater for nighttime performances, Hampden nonetheless played Hamlet at twice-weekly matinees for a year and a half. In the winter of 1919 Hampden acquired the support of some wealthy admirers, formed a corporation bearing his own name, and initiated a plan to take his production of *Hamlet* on tour. For four years his company crossed the nation, bringing an ever larger Shakespearean repertory to appreciative audiences. Despite his great artistic and popular success, Hampden's company was usually forced to play matinees in theaters that were reserved for more commercial ventures at night. His financial success, therefore, was continually compromised. For the fall of 1923 Hampden had determined to attempt a full season in repertory at the National Theatre in New York. At the urging of his friend Hamilton, he added *Cyrano de Bergerac*, a romantic drama by Edmund Rostand. Upon its opening, Colgate Baker declared in the *New York Review* that "In an age when romance was supposed to be dead, Walter Hampden has revived romance . . . so gloriously that he has made romanticists even out of dramatic critics, and I know of no greater tribute to pay to his acting" (10 Nov. 1923). The enormous success of *Cyrano* was unexpected by Hampden, who elected to present it exclusively during the year in New York to recover the finances of his company. The following fall Hampden took *Cyrano* on a successful tour.

Hampden returned to New York in January 1924 to play Othello and to make preparations for his own theater in New York. He arranged for a lease on what was then known as the Colonial Theatre and made it the home of his company until April 1930. During these years *Cyrano* proved to be a perennial money-maker, as was a lesser-known romantic drama titled *Caponsacchi*, which featured Hampden in another romantic role. Each year his efforts sustained a company of fifty or more performers, including his wife and a small coterie of company regulars. Hampden's friend, architect Paul Bragdon, had designed most of Hampden's productions since 1921. Together they embraced the aesthetics of the "New Stagecraft" movement, which tended to use minimal, suggestive scenic elements. Hampden's standard combination of backward-looking repertory and forward-looking stagecraft was never a huge financial success. With audiences declining in the year beginning the Great Depression, Hampden elected to cease his own productions.

After 1930 Hampden performed more frequently for other producers. Between 1932 and 1936 he reorganized his company to present *Cyrano* and other romantic fare on what was to become his last series of major national tours. *Newsweek* commented on his farewell performances of *Cyrano*: "*Cyrano de Bergerac*, a gossamer wisp of comedy and tragedy, has grown cobwebby with use. Thirteen years with Hampden has taken the fluff off it. The homely lover has become a blustering pantaloon instead of the swaggering poet-swordsman Rostand wrote of. . . . But audiences, sated with sentimental remembrances of Cyrano, enjoy a lengthy five acts, for all their creakiness" (9 May 1936, p. 44). In 1940 he performed in his first film as the Archbishop in *The Hunchback of Notre Dame*.

Hampden acted in some significant Broadway productions in the 1940s and helped to organize the American Repertory Theatre, established in 1946 as an American national theater. Long associated with the Players, the theatrical confraternity of which he was president from 1927 to 1954, Hampden performed *Macbeth* in their first television production in 1949. In 1953 he was Deputy-Governor Danforth in Arthur Miller's *The Crucible* in a production that suited his vigorous acting style and proved to be a fitting vehicle for his last Broadway performance. Ready to begin his fifteenth film, the seventh in two years after *The Crucible*, he died suddenly in Hollywood. He is remembered today as the last great starring actor to maintain a company of players in a repertory of Shakespearean and romantic drama.

• A substantial collection pertaining to Hampden's career is in the Walter Hampden Memorial Library at the Players. Two works that should be consulted are E. Laurent, "Walter Hampden: Actor-Manager" (Ph.D. diss., Univ. of Illinois, 1969), and G. J. Parola, "Walter Hampden's Career as Actor-Manager" (Ph.D. diss., Indiana Univ., 1970). A more accessible overview is in William C. Young, *Famous Actors and Actresses on the American Stage*, vol. 1 (1975). An obituary is in the *New York Times*, 12 June 1955.

MAARTEN REILINGH

HAMPTON, James (8 Apr. 1909–4 Nov. 1964), artist, was born in Elloree, South Carolina, the son of James Hampton, believed to have been a gospel singer and Baptist preacher who abandoned his wife (identity unknown) and four children for his itinerant calling. A shy, thin man with little formal education, Hampton moved to Washington, D.C., around the age of nineteen. He began to have religious visions at the age of twenty-two but told few, if any, about them; nor did he belong to a congregation. Nothing is known of his activities from 1928 to 1939. He worked as a short-order cook in local cafes from 1939 to 1942, until he joined the federal labor force, then served with the 385th Aviation Squadron (a noncombatant unit) in Texas, Seattle, Hawaii, Saipan, and Guam during World War II. After receiving an honorable discharge

in 1945, he returned to Washington, D.C., where in 1946 he became a janitor for the General Services Administration. He had hoped to find a holy woman to help him with his life's ambition, but he never married.

For about fourteen years beginning in 1950, Hampton spent five or six hours every night working in an unheated, poorly lit, rented garage (originally a nineteenth-century stable) at 1133 Seventh Street, N.W., where he created an elaborate sculptural ensemble called *The Throne of the Third Heaven of the Nations' Millennium General Assembly*. (Given that his first recorded vision was in 1931, it is possible that he began the project as early as the late 1930s or early 1940s.) Hampton's mission was to build "a monument to Jesus," something he thought was lacking in the nation's capital. He wrapped and glued silver and gold aluminum foil over pieces of scavenged wood furniture, cardboard, glass, paper, and plastic and adorned their surfaces with purple kraft paper and fragments from green desk blotters. Hampton arranged these components, which resemble altars, pulpits, offertory tables, and bishop's chairs (many on rusty metal casters), on and around a platform as if they furnished a religious sanctuary. The left side of the symmetrical arrangement features objects related to the New Testament, Jesus, the Apostles, and Grace, whereas the system on the right is based on the Old Testament, Moses, the Prophets, and the Law. Hampton's reference to the third heaven is based on a scriptural hierarchy of heavens: the first is the region of clouds; the second, the planetary heavens; and the third, the heaven of heavens, that is, God's abode.

No single religious impulse seems to have driven Hampton, but in writing many of the object's labels and recording his activity in notebooks, he used a still-undeciphered, graceful script made up of letters that look similar to those of some Semitic and oriental languages. Passages in English indicate that Hampton believed God had given him a second set of commandments, a "Nations Readjustment Plan" and "Millennium Laws for Peace on Earth" to share with those who did not obey the original ten. Evidently viewing himself as a religious agent, he used the eponym St. James in authoring the notebooks. Inscriptions such as "St. James Dispensation of Counseling" and "Director, Special Projects for the State of Eternity" suggest the roles of minister, counselor, and prophet. Deeply impressed by the apocalyptic Book of Revelation, Hampton may have made the *Throne* both to ensure personal salvation and to warn and instruct others. An adage from the Book of Proverbs found on his bulletin board cautions: WHERE THERE IS NO VISION THE PEOPLE PERISH.

Cartons of incomplete parts suggest that Hampton had not finished the *Throne* when he died of cancer. Though it has since been acclaimed as a work of art, the piece is not easily categorized as sculpture, assemblage, architecture, or environmental art.

A few people and the merchant from whom Hampton rented the garage sometimes viewed the *Throne*, and the bespectacled artist occasionally took or had photographs made of it, but he seems not to have shared his creation with the public during his lifetime. The *Throne* came to the attention of the Washington art community shortly after his death in 1964. Private patrons acquired the work, stored it at the National Museum of American Art (NMAA), and later anonymously donated it to the museum in 1970. Since 1971 the ensemble has been featured in eight major exhibitions in the United States, four long-term installations at the NMAA, and numerous publications related to folk art, African-American art, modern sculpture, religion, and psychiatry. Of the original 180 objects, 110 form the centerpiece of an installation of the museum's folk art holdings, and *The Throne of the Third Heaven* continues to reach an ever-widening and diverse audience.

• Hampton's papers are in the Archives of American Art, Washington, D.C. The most significant publications on him are by Lynda Roscoe Hartigan. They include: "James Hampton's Throne," in *Naives and Visionaries* (1974), an exhibition catalog for the Walker Art Center in Minneapolis, Minn.; *James Hampton: The Throne of the Third Heaven of the Nations' Millennium General Assembly* (1976); "James Hampton: Washington's Visionary," *Washington Review of the Arts* 2, no. 1 (Spring 1976); *The Throne of the Third Heaven of the Nations' Millennium General Assembly, James Hampton* (1977); *James Hampton* (1984); and "From Garage to Gallery: James Hampton's Capital Monument," *Public Art Review* (Summer/Fall 1992).

THERESA LEININGER-MILLER

HAMPTON, Wade (1754?–4 Feb. 1835), planter, military commander, and congressman, was born (according to different sources) in either Halifax County, Virginia, or Rowan County, North Carolina, the son of Anthony Hampton, a farmer, land jobber, and trader, and Elizabeth Preston. He is often known as Wade Hampton I to distinguish him from two noted descendants of the same name. Hampton's history prior to the American Revolution is largely mysterious. He must, however, have received some sort of formal education. Early in 1774 the Hampton family followed the example set by other backcountry residents and moved to South Carolina. Wade Hampton joined several of his brothers in a mercantile enterprise before the American War of Independence intervened.

In 1776 a party of Cherokees killed Hampton's parents, a brother, and a nephew. He joined the successful expedition against the Cherokees that produced a truce in 1777, then refocused his attention on personal profit. The family commercial venture in the backcountry prospered to the extent that by 1779, the Hamptons were able to purchase a lot in Charleston, South Carolina, another at Granby in Saxe-Gotha on the Congaree River, and 545 acres at the confluence of the Broad and Saluda rivers, already the location of a thriving store. Consequently, the Hampton brothers were well able to supply patriot forces. Over the last year or two of the war, they provided 136,000 pounds of corn meal and 265 bushels of corn to the Continental Army and received 4,946.13.4 pounds (sterling) in settlement from South Carolina for unpaid bills.

Hampton also contributed politically and militarily to the war effort. He represented first the Lower District, between the Broad and Saluda rivers (including the Hampton store), in the South Carolina General Assembly, then returned to the assembly as representative of Saxe-Gotha in the sessions of 1782 and 1783. The capture of Charlestown by the British in 1780 interrupted his war experience, but his military successes, notably at the Battle of Eutaw Springs in 1781, added polish to his image; some, however, complained of irregularities committed in the confiscation of the slaves of Loyalists.

After the war Hampton returned to the General Assembly in 1784, 1785–1786, 1789, and 1791, before his election as sheriff of Camden District. He also served as a state senator for one term in 1787–1788. During these years Hampton voted against the new federal Constitution as a member of South Carolina's ratifying convention in 1788. In 1794 he joined the Representative Reform Association in its campaign for legislative reapportionment on the basis of population in order to provide more back-country representation. At the same time, he became involved in bridge-building and ferry operation.

Hampton was first elected to Congress in 1795. Some Carolinians hailed his tenure as magisterial; others claimed that Hampton's legislative agenda centered on securing federal compensation for himself and his fellow Yazoo Company land speculators following the collapse of their scandal-ridden venture in Alabama and Mississippi. Ill health and family problems prevented him from undertaking many of his responsibilities as a representative, and he declined to seek reelection. Hampton returned to the House for a second time in 1803; he supported the Louisiana Purchase, but again health difficulties limited his participation, prompting his retirement after only one term.

Hampton's final foray into public life occurred when he accepted a commission in the army in 1808. After successfully refurbishing Charleston's defenses, he replaced General James Wilkinson as commander at New Orleans in 1809. Cynics proclaimed that Hampton's presence in Louisiana furthered his interests in the state, but he did move to relieve the disease-ridden and unsanitary conditions of the army, while earning Wilkinson's enmity.

Hampton helped to suppress a Louisiana slave rebellion in 1811. When about 500 slaves revolted, he led a small force of regulars who joined with local planters in crushing the movement, to the gratification of Governor William Claiborne and the white residents of New Orleans.

In 1813, during the War of 1812, Hampton took part in a disastrous invasion of Canada. Despite his objections, he found himself under Wilkinson's command. He balked at cooperating with Wilkinson and pleaded an inadequate army and a superior enemy, while Wilkinson and Secretary of War John Armstrong dithered. Predictably, the campaign resulted in embarrassing failure, and Hampton resigned his commission with his reputation in tatters.

Hampton was best known, however, for his spectacular wealth. By 1787, thanks largely to his first marriage and the success of his business as well as his claims for war-related expenditures, he had emerged as the owner of 127 slaves (to whom he apparently was less than a model master) and 2,710 acres of land. By 1810, enriched by highly profitable speculation and cotton plantations, he owned 635 slaves. In 1811 he began his involvement in Louisiana sugar; by 1820 he had approximately 500 slaves in Louisiana and 434 in South Carolina. In 1823 Hampton reportedly had three Louisiana plantations with 300 slaves, producing 1,000 hogsheads of sugar worth $89,600 per annum. In 1835, the year of his death, his annual Louisiana income alone was estimated at $120,000.

Hampton married three times: first in 1783 to Martha Epps Goodwyn Howell, who died just one year later; second, in 1786 to Harriet Flud, with whom he had two children before her death in 1794; and third, in 1801 to Mary Cantey, with whom he had six children. He died at his Columbia residence.

Hampton's pursuit of gentlemanly status parallels the quest of many other Americans in the period after the Revolution. Unlike his Northern counterparts, however, Hampton joined other newly prosperous residents of the Southern back country in perpetuating the attitude that landed wealth, generated by staple agriculture (notably cotton) and slave labor provided the ideal socioeconomic situation for a gentleman. By virtue of his acquisitions in Louisiana and elsewhere, he helped to extend this concept westward.

• The South Caroliniana Library at the University of South Carolina holds the Hampton Family Papers. The American Antiquarian Society, the Boston Public Library, the William R. Perkins Library at Duke University, the Newberry Library, the New-York Historical Society, and the Pierpont Morgan Library hold Hampton documents. The only secondary treatment of the life of Hampton is Ronald E. Bridwell, "The South's Wealthiest Planter: Wade Hampton I of South Carolina, 1754–1835" (Ph.D. diss., Univ. of South Carolina, 1980). Rachel N. Klein, *Unification of a Slave State: The Rise of the Planter Class in the South Carolina Backcountry, 1760–1808* (1990), incorporates Hampton into its argument. See also Charles E. Cauthen, ed., *Family Letters of the Three Wade Hamptons, 1782–1801* (1953).

L. H. ROPER

HAMPTON, Wade (28 Mar. 1818–11 Apr. 1902), Confederate general, governor of South Carolina, and U.S. senator, was born in Charleston, South Carolina, the son of Wade Hampton II and Ann FitzSimons. Named after his father, an immensely wealthy South Carolina planter, Hampton was raised at "Millwood," the family estate on the Congaree River near Columbia. Privately tutored in his youth, he graduated from South Carolina College in 1836. He married Margaret Preston in 1838, and the couple settled at "Sand Hills," Hampton's estate on the outskirts of Columbia. They had four children before Margaret's death in

1855. In 1858 Hampton married Mary McDuffie, daughter of Senator George McDuffie of South Carolina; they had two children.

As the eldest son, Hampton was entrusted with the responsibility of developing the family's vast landholdings in Louisiana and Mississippi. At his father's urgings, he had studied law, and he applied his legal training to his extensive business interests in three southern states. In 1852 he embarked on a political career by winning election to the South Carolina legislature from Richland District. He was reelected twice to the South Carolina House and in 1856 entered the state senate.

Hampton was one of the wealthiest men in the late antebellum South. The annual gross income from the various plantations that he owned or administered for family members was around $200,000. Perhaps because of his great wealth, he was cautious and conservative in his politics. Although a Democrat in the one-party state of South Carolina, he did not share the extreme proslavery and states' rights views of most of his colleagues. He felt that the Union offered the greatest security for the preservation of slavery, and he strongly opposed measures, such as the attempt by southern radicals to reopen the African slave trade in the late 1850s, that he feared would culminate in the breakup of the Union. He conceded that secession was a constitutional remedy for southern grievances but insisted that remedies within the Union had not yet been exhausted. When the secession crisis erupted in the wake of Abraham Lincoln's election in 1860, he opposed any precipitous action by South Carolina. Nonetheless, when South Carolina seceded, he followed his kinsmen and his state in supporting the new Confederacy. When war broke out in April 1861, he immediately volunteered his services. Governor Francis Pickens of South Carolina commissioned him a colonel and instructed him to raise his own command.

Hampton's Legion, equipped largely at Hampton's expense, enlisted the sons of the South Carolina aristocracy. It was an elite unit consisting of companies of infantry, cavalry, and artillery. Although he had no previous military experience, Hampton soon developed into a very effective officer. He was a superb rider and marksman, skills he had honed while hunting on his family's estate in the North Carolina mountains. Tall and strapping, he was well prepared for the rigors of a field command. Commanding his infantry at First Bull Run (First Manassas) in July 1861, he was wounded while blocking a Federal flanking maneuver. He was promoted to brigadier general on 23 May 1862 and a week later was wounded in the foot at Seven Pines during the Peninsula campaign.

After a brief convalescence, Hampton received his first cavalry command in July 1862. He was assigned as senior brigadier to J. E. B. Stuart's Cavalry Corps of the Army of Northern Virginia. He participated in the Antietam campaign in September 1862, led a series of successful raids in the winter of 1862–1863, and fought at Gettysburg in July 1863, where he received saber and shrapnel wounds. Commissioned a major general on 3 September 1863, he replaced Stuart as corps commander after Stuart's death in May 1864. Hampton performed brilliantly at Trevilian Station, a battle that saved Lynchburg from a Federal advance in June 1864. He also distinguished himself in the fall of 1864 through a series of defensive actions that kept open Richmond's communications to the south and west.

Faced with a crippling shortage of horses, Hampton took part of his command out of Virginia in January 1865 and went to South Carolina in search of fresh mounts. Before he could return, he was promoted to lieutenant general on 15 February 1865 and ordered to screen General Joseph E. Johnston's retreat through the Carolinas. Hampton was forced to abandon Columbia, the state capital, on 16 February 1865, and he was subsequently blamed by General William T. Sherman, commander of the occupying Federal troops, for the fire that engulfed the city on the seventeenth. Contrary to Sherman's charge that the fire had been set by Confederates ordered by Hampton to torch bales of cotton, Hampton adamantly insisted that Sherman had deliberately destroyed the city. Johnston surrendered to Sherman on 26 April 1865, but Hampton considered himself exempt from the terms of the surrender. He wanted to escort Jefferson Davis on his retreat from Richmond, cross over the Mississippi into Texas, and continue resistance from there. Unable to catch up with Davis's retreating party, Hampton finally accepted defeat. He signed a parole and returned home.

Hampton had suffered grievous losses during the war. Sherman's troops had burned his Columbia estates, Millwood and Sand Hills; his brother Frank had been killed in Confederate service; and during the Petersburg fighting Hampton experienced the anguish of holding in his arms his mortally wounded son Preston. Whatever bitterness he may have harbored, he counseled accommodation to the northern victors. He opposed the plans of some Confederate diehards for an emigration of southern whites to Mexico or Brazil. He supported President Andrew Johnson's program for reunion and, despite the entreaties of friends, refused to run for governor of South Carolina in 1865 out of concern that his fame as a symbol of Confederate resistance might antagonize the Republicans in Washington. As the former owner of 3,000 slaves, Hampton felt that he knew and understood the freedmen, and he was confident that they would turn to their ex-masters for advice and support. Thus, unlike most white South Carolinians, he advocated a limited form of black male suffrage. The South Carolina constitutional convention of 1865, however, rejected his advice of conferring the vote upon blacks and limiting that vote through an impartial educational qualification applied to both races.

Hampton denounced the terms of congressional Reconstruction in 1867 as "illegal, unconstitutional, and ruinous." Among those terms was the imposition of unrestricted black male suffrage, and Hampton tried in vain to convince South Carolina blacks to accept the leadership of their former masters in a political alliance that would maintain the power of the state's traditional white leaders. He argued that the only true friends of the freedman were southern whites, and he promised protection of the rights of the freedmen in return for their political support. Despite his efforts, the newly enfranchised blacks enthusiastically endorsed the Republican party. After chairing the state Democratic Executive Committee during the presidential campaign of 1868, Hampton withdrew from politics for the next eight years. While the Republicans controlled South Carolina, he spent most of his time in Mississippi attending to his "Wild Woods" plantation.

In one of the most violent and notorious elections in the history of South Carolina, Hampton won the governorship in 1876 at the head of a Democratic party pledged to "redeem" the state by forcing the Republicans from office by whatever means necessary. Democrats made race the focal point of the election and organized their white followers into paramilitary political clubs known as the Red Shirts. The Hamburg massacre in July 1876, in which six blacks and one white were killed, was the worst outbreak of violence in a campaign characterized by white attempts to demoralize black voters. Although Hampton tried to moderate the violence of his supporters, he undoubtedly benefited from the terroristic tactics. Hampton won by 1,134 votes out of the 183,388 that were cast, or so the Democrats claimed. The Republican candidate, incumbent governor Daniel Chamberlain, charged that the Democrats had prevented large numbers of freedmen from voting through fraud and intimidation and refused to surrender his office. From November 1876 to April 1877 the Democrats and Republicans confronted each other in a tense standoff. President Rutherford B. Hayes broke the stalemate with his decision to remove the federal troops that provided the last prop for the Chamberlain government. Hampton had convinced Hayes that he would uphold the rights of the freedmen and maintain peace and order.

Once in office, Hampton worked to uphold the pledge he had made to Hayes. Against the opposition of most Democrats, who wanted to eliminate blacks from politics and cut funds for black education, he pursued a moderate policy in race relations. Blacks retained the right to vote, received minor political appointments, and were allotted a few places on the Democratic ticket. Largely because of Hampton's support, funding for black schools was strengthened with the passage of a constitutional amendment providing a two-mill tax for the education of both races. Nevertheless, Hampton firmly believed that blacks should accept a subordinate role in a Democratic party led and controlled by whites. Blacks still faced fraud and harassment, as well as new legal restrictions, when they tried to pursue their own interests in the Republican party.

After easily winning reelection as governor in 1878, Hampton was almost immediately elected by the legislature to represent the state in the U.S. Senate. Without a doubt, he was now the most popular political figure in South Carolina—a symbol both of the state's heroic sacrifice in the Civil War and of its salvation from Radical Reconstruction. He served continuously in the Senate through March 1891. National affairs, however, held little interest for him. With the exception of his vigorous opposition to the Force Bill, a Republican measure of 1890 that called for federal supervision of congressional elections, he did not play an active role in the Senate.

Though still the symbolic leader of the Democratic party in South Carolina, Hampton's influence declined during the 1880s. In his sixties and physically drained by the loss of a leg in a hunting accident in 1878, he felt that his life's work was done. As he wrote a sister in 1880, "Life seems closed to me, and I have nothing but duty to live for." He had neither the energy nor the vision to respond positively to the agricultural depression that settled over South Carolina in the 1880s. In 1890 he and his fellow conservatives were swept from office by the movement led by Benjamin R. Tillman, a political insurgency that fed on agrarian discontent. After serving as a U.S. railroad commissioner from 1893 to 1897, Hampton retired to Columbia, the site of his death.

• The bulk of Hampton's papers are in the South Caroliniana Library at the University of South Carolina, Columbia. The Southern Historical Collection at the University of North Carolina, Chapel Hill, has a smaller collection of his family letters. Manly Wade Wellman, *Giant in Gray* (1949), is a colorful biography, but it is thin and based too heavily on secondary sources. For Hampton's military career, Edward L. Wells, *Hampton and His Cavalry in '64* (1899), is still useful. A sympathetic treatment of Hampton's policies toward the freedmen can be found in Hampton Jarrell, *Wade Hampton and the Negro* (1950). For an excellent study of the political setting in South Carolina that molded Hampton's postwar career, see William J. Cooper, Jr., *The Conservative Regime: South Carolina, 1877–1890* (1968). An obituary is in the Charleston *News and Courier*, 12 Apr. 1902.

WILLIAM L. BARNEY

HAMTRAMCK, John Francis (19 Apr. 1798–21 Apr. 1858), soldier, mayor, and jurist, was born in Fort Wayne, Indiana, the son of John F. Hamtramck, Sr., a soldier, and Rebecca Mackenzie. When his father died in Detroit in 1803, Hamtramck fell under the guardianship of William Henry Harrison, governor of the Indiana territory, and was raised in a military environment. Army life appealed to the young man, and in 1813 he was appointed a sergeant in the First U.S. Infantry. In this capacity Hamtramck accompanied Major Zachary Taylor's Mississippi River expedition, and on 24 July 1814 he distinguished himself at the battle of Rock River. In 1815 he received appointment in the U.S. Military Academy through the influence of General Harrison and Illinois senator Jesse B. Thomas. Hamtramck graduated fifteenth in his class on 1 July 1819 and was commissioned a second lieutenant in the Corps of Artillery. He served for two years at

Fortress Monroe, Virginia, before an unsolicited transfer to the Third Artillery Regiment prompted his resignation on 1 March 1822.

Once out of the service, Hamtramck relocated to St. Louis, where he lived for several years as a planter. Previously, he had married a Miss Williamson, who died at an unknown date. They had two daughters. Hamtramck married Eliza Claggett Selby in 1825; they had six children. In 1826 President John Quincy Adams appointed him agent to the Osage Indians of Missouri, a post he held until 4 July 1831. Hamtramck then permanently relocated in Shepherdstown, Virginia (now W.Va.), his wife's hometown, where he resumed his planting activities. He also served as captain of the Potomac Rifle Company, Jefferson County, from 1835 to 1841.

When war with Mexico erupted in 1846, Governor William Smith of Virginia appointed Hamtramck to command the First Regiment of Volunteers. In February 1847 Hamtramck and his charge sailed for Texas. They landed at the mouth of the Rio Grande and marched overland to Monterrey, Mexico, as part of General Taylor's army. Several months of garrison activity ensued, during which the men endured sickness and brushes with Mexican irregulars. In June 1847 Hamtramck pushed his regiment forward and occupied the old battlefield of Buena Vista, where he subsequently obtained the command of first a brigade and then a division of infantry. The Virginia Volunteers continued performing useful service protecting Taylor's lines of communication, and on 7 March 1848 Hamtramck became military governor of Saltillo. He remained there until the advent of peace, then marched his men to the Rio Grande for transportation back to Virginia. Hamtramck arrived in Richmond on 15 July 1848 amidst fanfare and returned to Shepherdstown. Sometime previously his second wife had died, and he married her sister, Sarah Selby. He was elected mayor of Shepherdstown, serving from 1850 to 1854, and concurrently served as justice of Jefferson County. He also functioned as major of the Shepherdstown Light Infantry from 1850 until his death in that town.

Hamtramck was an accomplished soldier of two wars but was apparently comfortable in civilian life. By turns a planter, American Indian agent, politician, and judge, he never failed to distinguish himself by virtue of his intelligence, honesty, and devotion to the tasks before him. Six days after his death, his former command was renamed the Hamtramck Guards as a tribute.

• Hamtramck's official correspondence is in RG 94, Records of the Adjutant General's Office, National Archives. A letterbook of his Indian agent work is at the Perkins Library, Duke University. Printed matter is in "Documents on the Mexican War," *Southern Historical Association Publications* 9 (1905): 45–48. Useful sketches of his military career are in Lee A. Wallace, "The First Regiment of Virginia Volunteers," *Virginia Magazine of History and Biography* 77 (Jan. 1969): 48–77; E. T. Crowson, "West Virginians with General Taylor in Mexico," *West Virginia History* 35, no. 1 (1973): 56–65;

and George W. Cullum, *Biographical Register of the Officers and Graduates of the U.S. Military Academy*, vol. 1 (3 vols., 1868). See also "The Black Rose of Shepherdstown," *Magazine of the Jefferson County Historical Society* 6 (Dec. 1950): 37–39.

JOHN C. FREDRIKSEN

HANBY, Benjamin Russel (22 July 1833–18 Mar. 1867), songwriter and music educator, was born in Rushville, Ohio, the son of the Reverend William Hanby and Ann Miller. He learned music as a child by attending singing schools. The family moved to Westerville, Ohio, around 1848 in part so that the children might attend Otterbein College. Hanby entered Otterbein in 1849, but his studies were seldom full-time, for he also taught school and directed singing schools. In addition he began composing songs, generally of a type promoting social, moral, or religious betterment. In 1856 his immensely popular "Darling Nelly Gray" was published by Oliver Ditson. In keeping with Hanby's ideals, the song was sympathetic to the plight of a Kentucky slave sold away from her lover. Based on the popular song style of Stephen Foster, it was lyrical, nostalgic, and sentimental, appropriate for the minstrel show stage and the parlor. In 1858 Hanby graduated from Otterbein and two days later married Mary Katherine "Kate" Winter, also a graduate of Otterbein. There followed service as a College agent and a principalship at an academy in Seven Mile, Ohio. In 1861, shortly after the outbreak of the Civil War, he wrote "Ole Shady or the Song of the Contraband," a dialect minstrel show song about freedom coming to a slave. This was one of the first of the so-called "jubilee songs" that celebrated release from slavery.

Hanby had trained for the ministry at Otterbein and in 1862 assumed a pastorate in the United Brethren Church at Lewisburg, Ohio. During the period 1862–1865 he also worked part time for the John Church Music Company in Cincinnati. Although his primary duties were to the pulpit, Hanby continued to sing, play, and compose songs. His congregation's resentment of his secular activities led Hanby to request a transfer to a church in New Paris, Ohio, in 1863. There he continued to minister through songs, stories, and plays, but the results were the same as at Lewisburg: the congregation was suspicious of the use of secular idioms in the service of sacred dogma. Hanby withdrew from the UBC shortly after leaving the ministry in 1864, subsequently relying upon piecework for John Church and conducting singing schools. For one of the latter he composed his most enduring song, the children's Christmas song "Santa Claus, or Up on the House Top." In 1865 he accepted a position with the Chicago music publishers Root & Cady. There he edited the children's music quarterly, *Our Song Birds*, organized "monster" concerts involving up to a thousand performers, and composed more than sixty songs. By all indications the two years in Chicago were the happiest and most productive of his life. Late in the summer of 1866 he contracted tuberculosis, from which he never recovered. Shortly before he died in

Chicago, he wrote "Who Is He in Yonder Stall," another popular children's song.

Altogether Hanby wrote more than eighty songs. Some were in style much like those of Foster, to whom were attributed authorship of some of Hanby's best-known songs, mistakes only corrected in the mid-twentieth century. His songs for children established a genre with their simple, appealing lyrics and accessible melodies.

• Papers and materials relating to Benjamin Hanby are found mainly in the Otterbein College archives and in the holdings of the Hanby House Museum in Westerville, Ohio. Full-length studies of Hanby are the biography by Dacia Custer Shoemaker, *Choose You This Day: The Legacy of the Hanbys*, ed. Harold B. Hancock and Millard J. Miller (1983), and Jeanne Bilger Gross, "Benjamin Russel Hanby, Ohio Composer-Educator, 1833–1867: His Contributions to Early Music Education" (Ph.D. diss., Ohio State Univ., 1987). Both of these sources include major bibliographies of primary and secondary sources.

DALE COCKRELL

HANCOCK, John (12 Jan. 1737–8 Oct. 1793), merchant and politician, was born in Braintree (present-day Quincy), Massachusetts, the son of John Hancock, a Harvard graduate and minister, and Mary Hawke. In 1744 Hancock's father died, forcing Hancock's mother to move with her three children to Lexington to live with her father-in-law, John Hancock. In 1745 young John was sent to live with his uncle and aunt, Thomas and Lydia Hancock, in Boston. Thomas Hancock was one of the town's wealthiest merchants, and he and his wife lived in a grand mansion atop Beacon Hill.

To prepare for Harvard College, John attended the Boston Latin School, graduating in the spring of 1750. Thanks to his academic preparation, as well as to his uncle's influence, he was admitted to Harvard College with the class of 1754, the second-youngest in his class of twenty. He was ranked fifth, an indication of his family's prominence. It is impossible to determine how well Hancock did in his courses, but it really did not matter. For someone of his station, it was enough simply to acquire a socially acceptable intellectual patina. Nor is there anything to indicate that his learning ever went much beyond this level. On one occasion he ran afoul of the school authorities in a drinking incident, and another time he was fined for cutting chapel. These, however, were minor infractions. Hancock graduated in 1754 and returned to Boston to join his Uncle Thomas's business.

Hancock's return coincided with the outbreak of the French and Indian War, and for the next six years the House of Hancock was extraordinarily busy fulfilling government contracts. During this time Hancock learned a good deal about business. Although the war continued until the Peace of Paris in 1763, for all intents and purposes the American phase came to an end with the fall of Quebec in 1759. To cement business ties and introduce him to a wider world, in 1760 his uncle sent Hancock to spend nearly a year in England. On his return to Boston in the summer of 1761 he found his uncle in ill health and anxious to have his nephew take greater responsibility for the business. Hancock quickly immersed himself in exporting whale oil, loaning money, buying and selling real estate, negotiating government contracts, and general merchandising.

On 1 August 1764 Thomas Hancock died. John Hancock took charge of the business at an ill moment. Saddled by the long war with an enormous debt, the British government was desperate for new revenue sources and sought them in the American colonies. As a businessman Hancock resented the actions of the king and Parliament. Their blundering attempts at raising revenue in the colonies through the Sugar Act of 1764 and the Stamp Act of 1765 proved disastrous for his business. At the same time, as an American and a key political leader in Boston, Hancock resented what he and others saw as an abridgement of their rights as Englishmen. There is little doubt that in the turbulent 1760s and early 1770s Hancock tried to play the role of a moderate; increasingly, however, British policy made such a stance untenable, and Hancock, not surprisingly, allied himself with the patriot side. He took a prominent role in politics as a Boston selectman (1765–1774) and as a member of the General Court (1766–1774). His success at the polls was in no small measure due to his economic influence. The number of people employed in his enterprises, shipping, warehouses, and real estate, was considerable. The list of debtors was equally long, made up of those who had borrowed money from him directly as well as those who had purchased goods from him on credit. Those who supported him politically found him to be a generous and patient creditor. Those in his debt who did not support him found Hancock to be a tireless dunner.

Hancock's image as a patriot leader was further enhanced in May 1768 when customs officers seized his sloop *Liberty* on charges of smuggling Madeira wine. That Hancock was guilty was less important than that the local Whig propaganda machine could turn this event into yet another example of dreadful British tyranny. With the help of the Sons of Liberty the mob was aroused, and the customs officers were forced to flee for their lives. At the same time Hancock was portrayed as a victim of oppression and a martyr to the patriot cause.

In recognition of his role as a leader of the resistance, in March 1774 Hancock was asked to deliver the annual Massacre Day oration. Each year since its occurrence on 5 March 1770, the people of Boston had remembered that horrid event on King Street by selecting a prominent citizen to deliver an address commemorating the massacre. It was an honor Hancock relished. Before a packed house in the Old South Meeting House, Hancock delivered a stirring oration reminding his listeners of the terrible thing done by British soldiers on that day. The speech, coming so soon after the Boston Tea Party (16 Dec. 1773), created a great stir in the town.

During the spring of 1774 news arrived in Boston announcing the passage of the Intolerable Acts, a series of harsh measures intended to strengthen royal authority in the colonies and to punish Boston for its role in the Tea Party by closing the port until the townspeople paid for the destroyed tea. These actions deepened the crisis. In October the General Court, in defiance of the new royal governor, Thomas Gage, resolved itself into a Provincial Congress and elected Hancock president. In December the Congress elected him a delegate to the Second Continental Congress meeting in Philadelphia.

Mindful of his own safety, Hancock left Boston early in the spring of 1775 and took up residence in Lexington at the same parsonage where he had once lived with his grandfather. He was there with Samuel Adams on 18 April when Paul Revere arrived to warn them of the approach of British troops. Hancock and Adams escaped, and within a few days of the events at Lexington and Concord they were en route to Philadelphia to attend the Continental Congress.

The Congress convened on 10 May. One of the first orders of business was the election of a president. The president of the First Congress, Peyton Randolph of Virginia, had been summoned home to preside at a meeting of the House of Burgesses. Henry Middleton of South Carolina was elected to succeed him but then resigned because of poor health. On the third try the Congress turned to Hancock.

It was a deft political move. As a Bostonian, Hancock was closely associated with some of the most radical elements in the Congress. At the same time, however, his wealth and social standing gave him an air of conservatism and respectability. He could also point to a distinguished career in politics. His election was unanimous.

On 1 August 1775 the Congress adjourned temporarily, and Hancock returned to Massachusetts. After spending some time in Watertown, where the Provincial Congress was assembled, Hancock made preparations to return to Philadelphia. On 24 August he set off for Congress, stopping long enough in Fairfield, Connecticut, to marry Dorothy Quincy, with whom he had two children.

Hancock's presidency lasted more than two years. His authority was limited to that of a presiding officer. Most of the work of the Congress was accomplished through numerous committees, creating a confusing patchwork of enormous inefficiencies. Hancock's greatest moment came on 4 July 1776 when with characteristic flair he was the first person to sign the Declaration of Independence. Always a vain person, Hancock took his role with great seriousness and even a bit of pomp. His style annoyed many in the Congress, particularly the New England delegations whose sense of republican simplicity was offended by Hancock's extravagance. Criticism of Hancock both in the Congress and at home in Massachusetts was rising. Chief among his detractors were Samuel Adams and James Warren.

In October 1777 Hancock announced that for reasons of health he was returning to Boston. On a motion of thanks to Hancock every member of the Massachusetts delegation, save Hancock, voted no. Hancock returned briefly to the Congress in the summer of 1778. During his absence Congress had elected Henry Laurens of South Carolina as president, and because Laurens showed no signs of stepping down, Hancock lost interest in the Congress and returned to Boston.

In 1780 the people of Massachusetts approved a state constitution and by an overwhelming margin elected Hancock the first governor of the commonwealth. Governor Hancock continued to display his keen political instincts. He managed to avoid taking stands on the most controversial issues of the day and presented himself as a moderate in most matters. He was also a generous man. To be sure, his generosity often had political goals; still, he was always among the first to support widows, orphans, and those in need in Boston. This helped to account for his immense popularity among the citizens of Massachusetts, and he had no difficulty being reelected.

On 29 January 1785 Hancock shocked the commonwealth when he resigned the governorship. He gave ill health as his reason. That may well have been true, but only in part. Massachusetts was in dire financial straits, and Hancock, whose political instincts were nearly infallible, wished to avoid the rising storm. That storm came in the winter of 1785–1786 with the outbreak of Shays's Rebellion. The unhappy task of suppressing the rebellion fell to Hancock's successor and rival, Governor James Bowdoin. In the aftermath of the rebellion Hancock ran for the governorship and defeated Bowdoin handily and then wisely pardoned the Shaysites.

Hancock's reappearance as governor came at a time when a national movement was under way to replace the Articles of Confederation with a new constitution. This movement resulted in the convening of the Constitutional Convention in May 1787. When as governor Hancock received the proposed constitution for ratification, he summoned a joint session of the Massachusetts House and Senate and laid the document before it. He said nothing to indicate either his approval or disapproval. Hancock was one of the delegates elected to the state ratifying convention, and when that body met on 2 January 1788 he was named president. Again, ill health, or perhaps political expediency, kept him out of the chair for most of the sessions.

The debates were heated, and ratification was in doubt. Finally, on 31 January, Hancock attended and spoke. He favored ratification but with certain changes that would have the result of curbing some powers of the federal government. His speech was the turning point; by a vote of 187 to 168 Massachusetts ratified the Constitution. Without Hancock's support it seems unlikely that ratification would have occurred. This was Hancock's finest moment, for without the support of Massachusetts the entire constitutional effort might have failed. In the first elections of the new republic everyone agreed that George Washington was certain to be president. Hancock, however, held out some hope that he might be elected vice president. In this he was disappointed, and another Massachusetts native, John Adams, won the post instead.

Hancock continued to be reelected governor. He treated the job as something of a sinecure. The decline in his health removed him from many activities, but his popularity remained as high as ever. Hancock's last appearance before the legislature was on 18 September 1793, but his poor health left him unable to stand or speak. He died in Boston.

Hancock was a moderate man who loved to court popularity. While many saw in him nothing but pomposity and vainglory, he was nonetheless a key figure in securing independence and creating the republic. His capacity to avoid controversy made him an ideal presiding officer, a task for which he had considerable ability. He displayed this in both the Provincial Congress and the Continental Congress and in the governorship. He thus served as a center of unity around which various elements coalesced, and he played a critical role in promoting harmony among the founding fathers at important moments in the revolutionary era.

• The largest collection of the Hancock papers is located at the New England Historic Genealogical Society, Boston. For biographies of Hancock see W. T. Baxter, *The House of Hancock* (1945); Herbert S. Allan, *John Hancock, Patriot in Purple* (1953); and William M. Fowler, Jr., *The Baron of Beacon Hill: A Biography of John Hancock* (1980).

WILLIAM M. FOWLER, JR.

HANCOCK, John (24 Oct. 1824–19 July 1893), congressman, was born near Bellefonte, Jackson County, Alabama, the son of John Allen Hancock and Sarah Ryan, farmers. After attending public schools and studying for two years at the University of East Tennessee in Knoxville, he studied law in Winchester, Tennessee. Hancock was admitted to the bar in 1846 and relocated the next year to Texas, where he practiced law in Austin with Andrew Jackson Hamilton, who later was a congressman and military governor of Texas. Hancock held the office of state's attorney in 1847 and won election in 1851 as judge of the Second Judicial District of Texas. He served in this capacity until 1855, when he resigned to resume the practice of law, raise livestock, and plant crops. In 1855 he married Susan E. Richardson, with whom he raised one son.

In 1860 Hancock was elected to the Texas House of Representatives. A Unionist fiercely opposed to secession, he was expelled from the state legislature in 1861 for his refusal to take the oath of allegiance to the Confederacy when Texas left the Union. Hancock thereupon continued his law practice. Dressed in a frock coat and tall hat, his appearance suited a successful lawyer who had become familiar with the land laws of Texas. In 1864 he defended four men arrested as Unionists. After securing their release and declining to fight in the Civil War, Hancock fled to Mexico and subsequently to Kentucky and New York to avoid conscription and to await the end of the war. Following General Robert E. Lee's surrender and the conclusion of the conflict in 1865, Hancock returned to Texas, where he took an active role in Reconstruction.

Hancock assumed a moderate position as a delegate to the state constitutional convention in 1866. He worked to heal the wounds of the war while mediating disputes between radicals and conservatives. Hancock clearly defined his principles, marshaled his arguments, and sought a reasoned consensus. Many of his suggestions and amendments were adopted. A member of the Committee on General Provisions, he successfully reported an article providing that freedmen should be secure in all rights of person and property and should not be prohibited from testifying in any case affecting a person of their race. On the whole, Texas granted the former slaves substantial civil rights. Hancock was more liberal on the subject of African-American rights than most of his colleagues, pointing out from history that many ancient Britons were held in a state of servitude more degrading in some respects than that of the African-American population of the southern states in the pre–Civil War era. Noting that the fundamental principle of equal rights to all embodied in the Declaration of Independence contained no words regarding color, he reaffirmed his contention that color was a very poor criterion by which to judge the intellect and worth of an individual. Admitting that prejudices, arising from the peculiar condition and habits of the people, existed in all ranks of society, Hancock maintained that no adult male should be denied the rights of U.S. citizenship.

Defeated in 1866 in his bid to win a seat in the U.S. Senate from Texas, Hancock resumed the practice of law, continuing to earn a solid reputation as a brilliant courtroom lawyer. In 1870 he was elected to the U.S. House of Representatives, defeating Republican incumbent Edward Degener, a San Antonio businessman and Unionist who had worked with Hancock at the 1866 constitutional convention. Hancock carried the Fourth Congressional District with 17,010 votes to 12,636 for his opponent.

Hancock, a Democrat, served in the Forty-second, Forty-third, and Forty-fourth Congresses (1871–1877). Unsuccessful in his endeavor to obtain renomination in 1876, he reclaimed his House seat in 1882 and again served in Congress from 1883 to 1885, choosing not to seek reelection in 1884. During his congressional tenure, Hancock helped pass acts that changed the manner of issuing rations to Native Americans on reservations to every seventh day, prohibited Native American hunting parties unless accompanied by U.S. troops, and established a military telegraph around the frontiers of Texas. He introduced bills to provide for a public building in Austin, to ascertain losses by depredations on the Texas frontier, and to authorize appropriations for the army and for Native Americans. Hancock was interested in internal improvements, particularly the development of the railroads in Texas. In this connection, he formed a friendship with Thomas A. Scott, president of the Texas and Pacific Railroad. Hancock also fought for low taxation, tariff reform, and federal noninterference in elections.

Upon the expiration of his final congressional term in 1885, Hancock returned to his law practice. Although not a great orator, he was an able lawyer and representative who achieved local, state, and national attention. He died in Austin.

• Hancock's papers, including his diary, are in the Archives Division of the Texas State Library in Austin. Some letters are scattered in the manuscript collections of his contemporaries. His speeches are in the *Congressional Record*, 1871–1877 and 1883–1885. Hancock's published works include *To the Patriotic Citizens of the United States* (1856) and *The Great Question for the People: Essays on the Elective Franchise; or, Who Has the Right to Vote* (1865). Volumes and articles containing information about Hancock and his times are Charles William Ramsdell, *Reconstruction in Texas* (1910); Keith Ian Polakoff, *The Politics of Inertia: The Election of 1876 and the End of Reconstruction* (1973); C. Vann Woodward, *Reunion and Reaction: The Compromise of 1877 and the End of Reconstruction* (1951); Randolph B. Campbell and Richard G. Lowe, *Wealth and Power in Antebellum Texas* (1977); Alwyn Barr, *Reconstruction to Reform: Texas Politics, 1876–1906* (1971); Carl H. Moneyhon, *Republicans in Reconstruction Texas* (1980); William L. Richter, *The Army in Texas during Reconstruction* (1987); Paul L. Haworth, *Reconstruction and Union: 1865–1912* (1987); Stanley B. Hirshson, *Greenville M. Dodge* (1967); Walter L. Buenger, *Secession and the Union in Texas* (1984); Michael Les Benedict, "Southern Democrats in the Crisis of 1876–1877: A Reconsideration of *Reunion and Reaction*," *Journal of Southern History* 46 (1980): 489–524; and George C. Rable, "Southern Interests and the Election of 1876: A Reappraisal," *Civil War History* 26 (1980): 347–61. An obituary is in the *Galveston Daily News*, 20 July 1893.

LEONARD SCHLUP

HANCOCK, Joy Bright (4 May 1898–20 Aug. 1986), U.S. Navy officer, was born Joy Bright in Wildwood, New Jersey, the daughter of William Henry Bright, a banker, and Priscilla Buck. After attending high school in Wildwood, she entered the Pierce School of Business Administration in Philadelphia; in 1918 she enlisted in the U.S. Naval Reserve. As a yeoman first class, she served as a clerk and then chief yeoman at the New York Shipbuilding Corporation yards located in Camden, New Jersey, later transferring to the U.S. Naval Air Station at Cape May, New Jersey. After the end of World War I she worked at the U.S. Naval Air Station in Lakehurst, New Jersey, and the Department of the Navy in Washington.

Joy Bright married Lieutenant Charles Gray Little, a holder of the Navy Cross, in 1920, but a year later Little died in a crash of the navy's ZR-3 dirigible in England. In 1924 she married Lieutenant Commander Lewis Hancock, another naval aviator, who also died within a year and under similar circumstances: the explosion and crash in Ohio of the navy's dirigible *Shenandoah*.

Nevertheless, possessing a strong character, Hancock was determined to challenge the existing limitations on opportunities for women in the fields of aviation and the military. She earned a private pilot's license (1928), entered graduate school at George Washington University, and obtained an advanced degree in aeronautics. She then accepted a position with the navy's Bureau of Aeronautics and became special assistant to the chief of that bureau. While serving as a civilian employee with the bureau, she wrote a monograph, *Airplanes in Action* (1938).

With the outbreak of war in 1942, the Navy Department sought to alleviate the manpower shortage and expedite the war effort by recruiting women. After passage of an amendment to the 1938 Naval Reserve Act, the navy prepared to accept women into the reserves. A separate office was established for Women Accepted for Volunteer Emergency Service (WAVES) inside the Bureau of Personnel under the direction of Captain Mildred H. McAfee. In October 1942 Hancock was sworn in as a lieutenant in the Women's Reserve, U.S. Naval Reserve. Subsequently, she was transferred to the office of the deputy chief of naval operations (Air) and promoted to lieutenant commander in 1943 and commander two years later. In recognition of her outstanding service in the WAVES, Secretary of the Navy James Forrestal awarded Hancock a Letter of Commendation with Ribbon.

Commander Hancock remained in the navy at the conclusion of World War II, serving as assistant director, then director, of the Women's Reserve. The navy quickly advanced her to the rank of captain. In coordination with the integration of African Americans into the armed services in 1947, the U.S. Department of Defense moved ahead with bringing women into the regular armed forces. Accordingly, the Women's Armed Services Integration Act was signed by President Harry S. Truman on 12 June 1948. In October of that year Captain Hancock became assistant to the chief of naval personnel for women. She was one of a group of eight women sworn in as regular commissioned officers in the armed forces; in lieu of promotion, she was made a permanent lieutenant commander and temporary captain. Hancock continued to serve as director of women's affairs inside the Bureau of Personnel until she retired in 1953. In recognition of her pioneering efforts, the navy awarded her the Legion of Merit, for "exceptionally meritorious conduct" and her contributions to the successes achieved by women throughout the naval service. During her career in the navy, Hancock retained her interest in naval aviation and contributed many articles to aviation-and navy-oriented publications.

After retiring from the navy, Hancock married Vice Admiral Ralph A. Ofstie, who predeceased her in 1956. She died at the U.S. Naval Medical Center in Bethesda, Maryland.

Hancock's most effective role in the military was in directing the WAVES organization, which during World War II and the immediate post–World War II era grew to a force numbering 500 officers, 50 warrant officers, and 6,000 enlisted women. She was a pioneer in helping to open up a realm of national service previously held to be essentially the domain of men alone.

• The Department of the Navy in Washington, D.C., has on record two sources of biographical information: *Captain Joy Bright Hancock, U.S. Navy (W), Ret.* (Dec. 1960), Office of Information, Biographic Branch; and Julius Augustus Furer, *Administration of the Navy Department in World War II* (1959), Naval Historical Division. An entry on Hancock appears in *Current Biography* (1949), and an obituary is in the *New York Times*, 25 Aug. 1986.

LEO J. DAUGHERTY III

HANCOCK, Thomas (17 July 1703–1 Aug. 1764), merchant, was born in the North Precinct of Cambridge (now Lexington), Massachusetts, the son of John Hancock, a Lexington minister, and Elizabeth Clark. At age fourteen he was sent to Boston and apprenticed with Samuel Gerrish to learn the book trade. Hancock spent seven years with Gerrish and then opened his own shop in Boston's North End. Hancock prospered as a bookseller and quickly expanded his business into other areas, including publishing. His success brought him into contact with many influential people, including Daniel Henchman, a prominent Bostonian with whom Hancock went into partnership in a papermaking venture. Hancock married Henchman's daughter Lydia in 1730; they had no children.

By the early 1730s Hancock had established himself as a merchant. Among other activities he imported manufactured goods for resale at his shop. To pay for these imports he exported rum to fishermen in Newfoundland, whale oil to London, and fish to Spain and Portugal. As a demonstration of their wealth and position, Hancock and his wife built a mansion on Beacon Hill that became one of the grandest homes in Boston.

As the international situation deteriorated in the late 1730s, Hancock, who had invested a substantial portion of his capital in the overseas trade, began to retrench, fearing that war would disrupt his business. Instead, when the War of Jenkins' Ear erupted in 1740 and the British prepared to attack the Spanish in the Caribbean, Hancock played an important and profitable role in supplying the army and navy. He was also able to tap lucrative markets in the West Indies. He also engaged in illegal trade with Holland. In 1744 the war expanded to include France as an enemy. The entry of the French into what became known as King George's War made Hancock's transatlantic trade with Holland risky but at the same time opened new opportunities in America. The British hoped to defend their position in Nova Scotia while capturing the French bastion at Louisbourg on Cape Breton Island. With the help of Christopher Kilby, his friend and the Massachusetts agent in London, Hancock garnered large and profitable contracts for supplying British forces in Nova Scotia. By the end of the war in 1748, Hancock was clearly one of the richest men in Boston.

For the next six years, although he assisted in the expulsion of the Acadians from Nova Scotia, Hancock secured few government contracts. That changed quickly in 1754 when the French and Indian War erupted, bringing Hancock new contracts and greater prosperity. Although the war continued until 1763, the fall of Quebec (1759) and Montreal (1760) for all intents and purposes marked the end of the North American phase of the struggle.

Facing a decline in his government business, Hancock decided to explore new opportunities. It was in this context that in 1760 Thomas sent his nephew John to London. John's father, Thomas's brother John, had died in 1744, leaving his widow, Mary, with three children. In 1745 the eldest of these children, John, who later rose to fame during the American Revolution, was sent to live with Thomas. John graduated from Harvard in 1754 and continued to live with Thomas and Lydia.

Upon his return from London in 1761, John played an ever larger role in the business, while Thomas, because of declining health, took less and less of an interest. Hancock's wealth and considerable holdings, including real estate in Boston and northern New England, made him an important political figure. In 1758 he was elected to the Massachusetts Council. It was while entering the council chamber six years later that he collapsed and died.

Thomas Hancock was an exemplar of the Boston merchant who rose to power and wealth as a result of being favored with government business. At the same time, as an enterprising merchant he often followed his own interests at the expense of British trade policy. Although he was able to reconcile these divergent interests, those who came later would find it increasingly difficult to do so.

• The Hancock papers, including important Henchman material, are located at the Baker Library of the Harvard Business School. William T. Baxter, *The House of Hancock Business in Boston, 1724–1775* (1945), is the most complete study of Thomas Hancock. The most recent biography of his nephew, in which a good deal of material relating to Thomas may be found, is William M. Fowler, Jr., *The Baron of Beacon Hill* (1980).

WILLIAM M. FOWLER, JR.

HANCOCK, Winfield Scott (14 Feb. 1824–9 Feb. 1886), soldier and presidential candidate, was born at Montgomery Square, Pennsylvania, the son of Benjamin Franklin Hancock, a schoolteacher and later a lawyer, and Elizabeth Hoxworth, who named him in honor of a military hero of the War of 1812. Raised at Norristown, Pennsylvania, he attended the local academy, where he organized a military company before his appointment to the U.S. Military Academy at West Point. After graduating in 1844, eighteenth in a class of twenty-five (with fifty-five nongraduates), Hancock was assigned to the Sixth Infantry. He barely arrived in time for the last month of fighting in the Mexican War, winning brevet promotion to first lieutenant. While stationed at St. Louis, in 1850 he married Almira Russell; they had two children.

Following his marriage, Hancock served at several posts, including Fort Leavenworth, where his regiment calmed disorder in "Bleeding Kansas," and in Utah, where the "Mormon War" ended before the Sixth Infantry arrived. At the outbreak of the Civil War, he ranked as captain and served as chief quartermaster, Southern District of California.

Appointed brigadier general of volunteers as of 23 September 1861, Hancock served in Major General George B. McClellan's (1826–1885) Army of the Potomac. After the battle of Williamsburg (5 May 1862), the first in which Hancock fought, McClellan referred to him as "superb," bestowing a nickname that Hancock retained. At Antietam (17 Sept. 1862), Hancock commanded a division and won promotion to major general. Distinguished service at Chancellorsville (1–4 May 1863), where he conducted a stubborn rearguard action that saved a demoralized Union army from total destruction, advanced Hancock to corps command on the eve of Gettysburg. There he assumed command of the entire army late in the first day of battle before the arrival of Major General George G. Meade and placed Union forces in a strong defensive position on Cemetery Ridge. Hancock's II Corps fought valiantly on all three days (1–3 July). On the second day, Hancock redeemed the blunder of an advance by Major General Daniel Sickles and stabilized the left center before confederates could turn the Union flank. Severely wounded in the thigh on the third day, Hancock refused to leave the field until his troops had repulsed Confederate General George E. Pickett's charge. Gettysburg marked the zenith of Hancock's military career.

After six months of medical leave, Hancock commanded his corps through the spring 1864 campaign of Ulysses S. Grant from the Rapidan to Petersburg. Hancock served with distinction in the strenuous and bloody series of battles that began in the Wilderness and continued through Spotsylvania, the North Anna, and Cold Harbor to the trenches of Petersburg before his wound reopened in June. Hancock soon resumed command, traveling by ambulance, but poor health forced him back to Washington in November to organize wounded veterans for service.

Hancock remained in the postwar army as brigadier general. Promoted to major general as of 26 July 1866, he served at that rank for the rest of his life. Sent to command in the West, he campaigned on the Plains and on 29 November 1868 was assigned to the Fifth Military District (La. and Tex.) under Reconstruction legislation. His restoration of civil jurisdiction in Louisiana and refusal to use military authority to assist Republican radicals strengthened his ties to Democrats and angered Grant, who soon reassigned Hancock to New York City. Politically conservative, Hancock's view of Reconstruction too closely resembled that of President Andrew Johnson to suit Grant. When Grant entered the White House in 1869, Hancock was ordered to the Department of Dakota, an assignment he regarded as punishment for political disagreement.

As early as 1864 Democratic strategists considered Hancock a potential presidential nominee, and his name resurfaced quadrennially as the military hero who might best challenge Republican claims to a monopoly on patriotism. In 1880 Hancock finally received the nomination. Republicans nominated James A. Garfield, a longtime Ohio congressman, and attacked Hancock's complete lack of political experience and his reference to the tariff as a "local" issue, disregarding the justification for the thought and portraying Hancock as ludicrously ignorant. In fact, he meant that the tariff "affects localities differently," hardly a monumental gaffe. Neither candidate inspired voters to shift political allegiance, and the outcome hinged upon Republican organization overwhelming Democratic disharmony. Garfield's majority was less than ten thousand votes; the electoral vote (214–155) would have gone the other way had New York's Tammany Democrats, more concerned with retaining power in New York City than with gaining the White House, not betrayed Hancock at a cost of thirty-five electoral votes.

Hancock remained in the army until his death at Governors Island, New York. At his last major public appearance in 1885, he organized and led the enormous New York City funeral procession for Grant, who had made a major political speech in 1880 in behalf of Garfield, Hancock's opponent. Grant's posthumously published *Memoirs* (1885–1886) included a generous tribute to Hancock's wartime services. Hancock's presidential potential remained unknown, but as a soldier he always retained his reputation for dependability and heroism.

• Almira Russell Hancock apparently destroyed personal papers after drawing upon them for *Reminiscences of Winfield Scott Hancock by His Wife* (1887). Former aide Francis A. Walker wrote *General Hancock* (1894). A popular biography with emphasis on the Civil War is Glenn Tucker, *Hancock the Superb* (1960); the current standard biography is David M. Jordan, *Winfield Scott Hancock: A Soldier's Life* (1988). Documentary sources on Hancock's military career include *The War of the Rebellion: A Compilation of the Official Records of the Union and Confederate Armies* (128 vols., 1880–1901) and John Y. Simon, ed., *The Papers of Ulysses S. Grant* (1967–). Useful specialized studies include Edwin B. Coddington, *The Gettysburg Campaign: A Study in Command* (1968), and Herbert J. Clancy, *The Presidential Election of 1880* (1958).

JOHN Y. SIMON

HAND, Augustus Noble (26 July 1869–28 Oct. 1954), lawyer and judge, was born in Elizabethtown, New York, the son of Richard Lockhart Hand, a lawyer, and Mary Elizabeth Noble, a member of a prosperous merchant family. Hand's grandfather Augustus was a lawyer, a member of Congress, a state senator, and a judge in whose law offices Hand's father and uncles were trained. Hand's father was a leading figure in the local bar association, serving as the president of the state bar association from 1904 to 1906 and editing the *Elizabethtown Post*. Hand graduated from Phillips Exeter Academy in 1886, having been there for one year, and he graduated summa cum laude from Harvard College (1890). After spending a year working in his father's office, Hand enrolled in Harvard Law School, from which he graduated magna cum laude in 1894.

Hand's mother encouraged him to leave Elizabethtown for New York City, where he began practicing

with the law firm of Curtis, Mallet-Prevost & Colt in 1895. In 1901 he joined his uncle Clifford's law firm, Hand, Bonney & Jones. Hand married Susan Train, the daughter of a naval officer, in 1899; they had one daughter. Hand was a member of several elite associations, served as an overseer of Harvard University and as president of its alumni association, and was a vestryman at Grace Church in lower Manhattan.

Acting on the recommendation of Attorney General James McReynolds, who selected Hand as a Democrat untainted by an association with the Tammany Hall political organization, President Woodrow Wilson appointed Hand to the federal trial court in New York in 1914. President Calvin Coolidge named him to the U.S. Court of Appeals for the Second Circuit in 1927. His cousin Learned Hand preceded him on both courts, and they served together on the court of appeals until Learned Hand's retirement in 1951.

Hand enjoyed his work as a trial judge more than his appellate work, finding that it required him to exercise a wider range of legal talents—including the ability to assemble a coherent factual account out of the mass of information presented at a trial. His 1917 opinion explaining why the International News Service should be barred from copying news items posted by the Associated Press was later endorsed by the U.S. Supreme Court with opinions that have become classics in property law. Finding the time consumed by naturalization inquiries excessive, Hand successfully urged Congress to establish a system of administrative officers to conduct the hearings. He also criticized legislation that discriminated against immigrants and restricted their free-speech rights.

Hand's most famous case on the court of appeals affirmed Judge John M. Woolsey's decision overturning a ban on importing James Joyce's novel *Ulysses* because it was obscene. Hand appreciated the literary qualities of Joyce's book, although he was less certain that it was a great work. Working closely with his cousin, Hand produced an opinion, as Learned Hand wished, "without using a phrase that could be quoted on the jacket of the book" (*United States v. One Book Entitled Ulysses*, 1934).

In 1944 Hand wrote the court's opinion rejecting a challenge to segregation in the armed forces. Putting aside his privately expressed view that "many . . . cherish the illusion that black is white and white is black," which would have led him to uphold segregation as good policy, Hand denied the claim for a highly technical reason: the African-American draftee who filed the suit was complaining that segregation meant that he had not been called for service earlier, which Hand did not think was an injury that allowed him to sue (*United States ex rel. Lynn v. Downer*, 1944).

After Judge Harold Medina found the lawyers representing leaders of the Communist party in contempt of court for their actions during the trial, Hand wrote the court of appeals opinion, later affirmed by the Supreme Court, upholding the convictions even though Medina had not held a hearing on the contempt issue (*United States v. Sacher*, 1950). Hand worked hard to contain a dispute between his two colleagues on the case, Jerome Frank, who eventually agreed with Hand, and Charles Clark, who dissented.

Hand believed that his major contributions had come in ordinary lawsuits. One, a decision holding that people with antitrust complaints had to present their claims to an administrative agency before taking them to court, was deemed by the Supreme Court an "able and carefully drawn opinion" (*United States Navigation Co. v. Cunard Steamship Co.*, 1931). Another was an opinion concerning an especially complex aspect of bankruptcy law (*In re Salmon Weed & Co.*, 1931) that the leading scholar in the field, Edward Warren, called "the best opinion" among all reported cases of this nature. Among his colleagues, Hand was a mediator who strove to find the middle ground on which all could agree.

Described by Charles Wyzanski as "a nineteenth century liberal," Hand responded to the legal innovations of the New Deal with characteristic caution. He routinely affirmed expansive exercises of national power and endorsed aggressive interpretations of the antitrust laws. Writing in 1946, Hand called "average conservative[s] . . . distressingly ignorant," but said that they "can hardly be exceeded in intolerance or stupidity by that of the liberal who advocates everything that involves change." Neither side, he continued, had acted with prudence: "We are paying the price for too many follies in this country of ours—for holding back needed changes too long and then carrying them out too swiftly and with too much emotion."

Hand's opinion in the *Ulysses* case was characteristic of his work. He was a solid, hardworking judge who disciplined himself to refrain from using in his published opinions the more vivid phrases that he wrote in his informal memoranda to his colleagues. Hand's strength lay in his ability to state the relevant facts clearly, lay out the applicable law, and move straightforwardly to what he presented as the inevitable result. Experienced lawyers in the circuit court expressed their view of the Hand cousins in the affectionate aphorism, "Always quote Learned and follow Gus." Hand retired from the bench in 1953 and died in Middlebury, Vermont, while on vacation.

• Hand did not retain a collection of papers. Some letters are in the Learned Hand and Felix Frankfurter Papers at Harvard Law School and in the papers of William Howard Taft at the Library of Congress. Marcia Nelson, ed., *The Remarkable Hands: An Affectionate Portrait* (1983), contains personal recollections. Marvin Schick, *Learned Hand's Court* (1970), discusses Hand's work on the court of appeals during the 1940s. An extensive appreciation by Charles Wyzanski is in the *Harvard Law Review* 61 (Apr. 1948): 573–91. Shorter tributes by Charles E. Clark and Charles A. Horsky are in the *Harvard Law Review* 68 (May 1955): 1113–21. An obituary is in the *New York Times*, 29 Oct. 1954.

MARK V. TUSHNET

HAND, Daniel (16 July 1801–17 Dec. 1891), merchant and philanthropist, was born in East Guilford (now Madison), Connecticut, the son of Daniel Hand, a far-

mer, and Artemesia Meigs. The Hands were a distinguished family with deep roots in Calvinist New England, and Daniel was the third of that name. The first Daniel Hand was his grandfather, a captain in the revolutionary war; the second was his father, a local judge as well as a successful merchant-farmer. He was educated at home by his parents, supplemented by a few terms in the district school and a lifetime of serious reading, especially in the Bible. The scholarly John Elliott (b. 1768), a graduate of Yale and the great-great-grandson of John Eliot (1604–1690), "apostle to the Indians," was the pastor of Hand's family church through his youth. Elliott was intimately involved in the momentous redirection of Calvinism from formal observance to social activism in the Second Great Awakening. His penchant for good works, among the products of which were a public library and a Home Mission Society, could not have been lost on his young parishioner. In 1818, just sixteen, Hand left home for Augusta, Georgia, to clerk in the mercantile establishment of an uncle, Daniel Meigs, where an older brother, Augustus Hand, had gone before.

On the edge of the southern cotton belt, Augusta had direct river and railroad connections, respectively, with the major seaports of Savannah, Georgia, and Charleston, South Carolina. It was a good location for trading firms, and beginning in the 1790s aspiring entrepreneurs had moved in. Hand grew to manhood in a circle of transplanted relatives. In 1829 he married a cousin, Elizabeth Ward, of Rochester, New York, and brought her back to Augusta. They had two children, neither of whom survived into adulthood, and Elizabeth died after ten years of marriage. Hand never married again. Careful attention to business and devoted philanthropic and church work—he headed the Sunday school at Augusta First Presbyterian Church for three decades—occupied the rest of a long and useful life.

By 1822, four years after his arrival in Augusta, Hand was an entrepreneur in his own right, having succeeded to his uncle's general store through business sagacity, Meigs's retirement, and the death of Augustus. For twenty years the business grew slowly; then in 1841, the same year he was left without an immediate family, Hand began to expand his commercial range. Within a few years he placed outlets for food, hats, and leather goods in Madison, Georgia, ninety miles to the west, and Charleston, a similar distance east. The managing partner in the Charleston venture was George Walton Williams, a North Carolinian of New England stock who had appeared at Hand's door in 1838, a boy of seventeen looking for work. About this time, temperance, the first great reform movement of the century, which was a product of religious revivalism and fears about the social problems associated with alcoholic intoxication, swept up Hand and Williams. Theirs was the first wholesale grocery established upon temperance principles in Charleston.

By 1854 Hand & Williams was large enough to warrant a purchasing office in New York City, and Hand decided to take this post, leaving partners in charge of the southern outlets. Doubtless, a burgeoning section-al conflict over slavery influenced this decision. The horrors of bonded servitude had been shielded from him in Augusta, where the lash was seldom seen and slaves wore livery. Even so, he never approved of the South's "peculiar institution," for it seemed to him, like strong drink and tobacco, a moral evil, and for that reason he had been a perpetual outsider in the South. Yet he was no abolitionist. He recognized the constitutional safeguards by which slavery's existence was legalized, and because his personal, family, and business interests were national, he would do nothing to imperil the Union.

When the Civil War exploded at Charleston in April 1861, the Hand partners' enterprises had annual sales of $2 million and profits of perhaps $150,000, with the largest part generated at Charleston. Williams was firmly ensconced in the southern metropolis, an alder-man of the city and supporter of slavery, southern rights, and the southern Confederacy. However, an act of state providing for the confiscation of northern capital in the Confederacy put the Hand interests in jeopardy. At William's urging, Hand returned south in the fall of 1861 to declare his citizenship. Obliged by the war to take a circuitous route, he was arrested as a Union spy in New Orleans, menaced by a mob in transit in Augusta, and finally freed with Williams's aid in Richmond. The confiscation suit was found in his favor, but his difficulties were not over. Under or-ders not to leave the Confederacy but limited by his new notoriety where he could reside, he settled, a man without a country, in a small mountain community in North Carolina to await the end of the war.

When the end came in early 1865, Hand at sixty-four took his leave of the South and the business world, entrusting his (unspecified) share of their com-pany to Williams. In gregarious retirement in Con-necticut, he watched, bemused, as the Charleston company rose, phoenix-like, from the ruins of the Confederacy. During the war, Williams had parlayed canny timing and an earned reputation for reliability to procure hard-to-get imports on credit—coffee from Brazil and clothing from England. He kept his debts paid and turned nice profits into real estate, cotton, timberlands, and silver. Now he guided the company through good and bad times, plowing gains in cotton and fertilizers into banking. In 1881, when Hand, aged eighty and in failing health, wrote his partner asking for a final settlement, Williams pointed to secu-rities in Hand's account showing between $1.5 million and $2 million. "I always knew Mr. Williams would do the best he could," the amazed senior partner de-clared, "but this is the most extraordinary thing I ever heard of" (Dickerman, p. 61).

Hand proceeded to do something equally remarka-ble. Contemplating the proper stewardship of his es-tate, he had decided already to give it to purposes of education; now he determined to direct the whole to the benefit of one group of Americans. In October 1888, he signed over to the American Missionary As-sociation, in trust, securities worth $1 million, the in-come derived therefrom to be used for the education of needy and deserving "colored people of African de-scent, residing, or who may hereafter reside in the re-cent slave States" (Oedel, p. 35).

Hand arrived at this defining moment by an almost inevitable process. His wealth was garnered in the South. Although he had resided elsewhere since 1865, he was attached to the South through sentiment and memory, and he watched the movement of events there with engrossing interest. He wished the very best for black freedmen, beneficiaries of the northern victory at arms. He also believed with many contem-poraries (including black leaders like Booker T. Washington and white southerners like Williams) that they had not the means, were not ready, for a good life and full equality. How better to provide the means than through education, schooling in practical subjects, "civilization," and right religion? How better to reconcile the races, "bury the bloody shirt" of sec-tional antagonism, and achieve the complete unifica-tion of the American people? In his last letter to Wil-liams in 1889, Hand espoused his simple faith: "The color question will solve itself slowly, but surely, and to the advantage of all. Its security is in the Christian religion and the humanity of the people to all, for all" (Dickerman, p. 62).

He died in Guilford, Connecticut, having lived his last years in the home of a niece. The event was little noticed, and the man and his inspired gesture were never widely known. Yet the Daniel Hand Education-al Fund for Colored People, although it cannot be said to have resolved all the difficulties of race and section, exerted a continuing and salubrious influence. By 1972, income from the original grant and the $500,000 added later reached $6,319,009, a bit over $75,000 an-nually. At first judiciously applied to elementary edu-cation, especially the training of teachers, after the middle of the twentieth century most of the money was bestowed upon colleges, including Fisk and Dillard.

• The bulk of Hand's papers are in the Madison Historical Society, Madison, Conn. Williams's papers and some of Hand's are in the South Carolina Historical Society, Charles-ton. There is no full-scale biography, but the following are useful: George A. Wilcox, *A Christian Philanthropist: A Sketch of the Life of Mr. Daniel Hand and His Benefaction to the American Missionary Association for the Education of the Colored People of the Southern States of America* (1889); George Sherwood Dickerman, *Sketch of Daniel Hand* (1900); and Howard T. Oedel, *Daniel Hand of Madison, Connecticut, 1801–1891* (1973). E. Merton Coulter, *George Walton Wil-liams: The Life of a Southern Merchant and Banker* (1976), has the best treatment of one of the most remarkable partnerships in the annals of business.

LAYLON WAYNE JORDAN

HAND, Edward (31 Dec. 1744–3 Sept. 1802), medical doctor and revolutionary war soldier, was born in Cly-duff, King's County, Province of Leinster, Ireland, the son of John Hand, occupation unknown, and Dor-othy (maiden name unknown). In the 1760s he en-rolled in Trinity College, Dublin, and completed medical studies in 1766 with a good academic record. Thereupon he entered the British army as a surgeon's mate and came to Philadelphia in 1767 with the Eighteenth Royal Irish Regiment of Foot. He was ordered to Fort Pitt in western Pennsylvania, and in 1772 he purchased an ensign's commission with profits earned from land speculation. Two years later he sold his ensigncy, resigned from the army, and settled in Lancaster, Pennsylvania to practice medicine and surgery. In 1775 he married Catharine Ewing, with whom he had eight children over the next seventeen years. At the outbreak of the revolutionary war, Hand, an ardent Whig, joined his neighbors in resisting Britain. Offered a commission as a lieutenant colonel in the Continental army, he obeyed the "glorious summons" to arms and marched with Colonel William Thompson's Pennsylvania Rifle Battalion to the siege of Boston. On 1 January 1776 he was appointed lieutenant colonel of the First Continental Infantry and two months later was chosen its colonel. With this regiment, he fought in the battle of Long Island and later, at Throg's Neck delayed a British advance toward White Plains. He retreated with George Washington across New Jersey, fought at Trenton on 26 December, and served gallantly under General Hugh Mercer in the battle of Princeton on 3 January 1777. Three months later, while at Morristown, New Jersey, he was promoted to brigadier general at the early age of thirty-two.

On 10 April 1777 Hand was sent by Washington to Fort Pitt to defend the citizens of western Pennsylvania from American Indian, Loyalist, and British war parties. In the summer and fall of 1777 he attempted to organize an expedition against hostile Indians but could not get surrounding counties to provide him with the requisite manpower. Finally, in February 1778 he mounted an ineffectual expedition with 500 men but was ridiculed by western Pennsylvanians for conducting a "squaw campaign." Under suspicion of being a Tory sympathizer because of his failure, he informed Washington that he was no longer effective in his command at Fort Pitt and successfully petitioned to be relieved. In late summer he rejoined the Continental army in New York and in October was sent by Washington to command American troops to Albany. In 1779 he served with General John Sullivan in a large expedition against American Indians and Tories in New York. During this campaign, Hand's light infantry troops did invaluable duty in protecting the movements of Sullivan's main army, especially in the battle of Newtown. He rejoined the main army at Morristown in the fall of 1779, and in 1780 he sat on a court-martial that condemned Major John André, adjutant general of the British army, to death by hanging. Also in 1780 he assumed command of a brigade of light infantry in a special corps that Washington had organized. On 8 January 1781 he was appointed adjutant general, continuing in that position until hostilities ceased, despite threats to resign when Congress reduced his pay a year later. He marched with Washington to Yorktown and was with the commander in chief when Lord Cornwallis surrendered on 19 October 1781. He took his Pennsylvania troops to Philadelphia in 1782 and afterward joined Washington's army encampment at Newburg, New York. There, he took part in suppressing discontent against Congress when some of the officers threatened to become mutinous. Also, he actively promoted the formation of the Society of the Cincinnati, an organization of army officers whose purpose was to keep alive the spirit of the Revolution. In September 1783, months after the fighting had ceased, he was promoted brevet major general.

Returning to Lancaster after the revolutionary war, Hand resumed his medical practice, often providing free services to the poor. He also remained active in public life, serving in Congress, 1784–1785, and in the Pennsylvania assembly, 1785–1786. In 1789 he became an ardent Federalist, serving as a presidential elector and a burgess of Lancaster. Also in 1789–1790 he attended the Pennsylvania constitutional convention and spoke for a more conservative basic law for his state. During these years, he actively promoted Lancaster as the site for the nation's capital and continued as a member of the Society of the Cincinnati. In 1789 he was elected president of that organization. As a Federalist, he was appointed by President Washington in 1791 as inspector of customs for the Third District of Pennsylvania and served in that office for the next eleven years. That same year, Washington considered appointing Hand commander in chief of the Legion of the United States (as the army was then called) but decided to commission Anthony Wayne instead. During the Whiskey Rebellion in 1794, Hand served Washington again as adjutant general of a militia army and in 1798 was promoted major general in the regular forces. He opposed Thomas Jefferson's election in 1800, and two years later his accounts as customs collector were suddenly challenged. Charged with losses, he was compelled to battle in court against the sale of his estate, "Rock Ford," to cover these putative shortfalls. Distressed by these events, he died at Rock Ford of a stroke. He was buried at St. James Episcopal Church, Lancaster, where for many years he had been an active member.

As a doctor, both before and after the revolutionary war, Hand was widely respected by his Lancaster neighbors for his skilled and selfless practice of medicine. During the war, he proved himself a zealous soldier and was idolized by his troops and other officers for his fine horsemanship, battlefield daring, amiability, and gentleness. Washington became his friend for life, and Major General Frederick Von Steuben remarked, upon hearing of Hand's appointment as adjutant general in 1781, "Nothing has given me more pleasure," for the duties of that office "require a person of [your] ability to discharge them" (Fitzpatrick, p. 7). Hand was a good citizen and capable patriot leader at a time when such qualities were at a premium.

• The largest single collection of Hand correspondence is in the Papers of the Continental Congress, no. 159, National Archives. Other papers are scattered among a number of repositories: the Washington papers in the Library of Congress; the Lancaster County Historical Society; the Historical Society of Pennsylvania; the Pennsylvania Historical and Museum Commission; the Rockford Foundation of Lancaster, Pa.; and the New York Public Library. Some of his papers are published in "Correspondence of General Edward Hand, of the Continental Line, 1779–1781," *Pennsylvania Magazine of History and Biography* 33 (1909): 353–60. The only full-length biography, Richard R. Forry, "Edward Hand: His Role in the American Revolution" (Ph.D. diss., Duke Univ., 1976), is a good one. Shorter treatments are Paul J. Fitzpatrick, "General Edward Hand and Rock Ford," *Social Science* 44 (1969): 3–11; Charles William Heathcote, "General Edward Hand—A Capable Pennsylvania Military Officer and Colleague of Washington," *Picket Post* 69 (1960): 14–22; and Lawrence A. Orrill, "General Edward Hand," *Western Pennsylvania Historical Magazine* 25 (1942): 99–112.

PAUL DAVID NELSON

HAND, Learned (27 Jan. 1872–18 Aug. 1961), federal judge, was born Billings Learned Hand in Albany, New York, the son of Samuel Hand, a prominent attorney, and Lydia Coit Learned. Learned Hand came from a family of lawyers, including his two uncles and his paternal grandfather. His father, a refined, emotionally removed gentleman, specialized in arguing before the New York Court of Appeals, on which he served briefly as a judge. His death, when Learned was only fourteen, heightened the boy's esteem for his highly successful father but also led to unrealistic expectations that resulted in a lifelong sense of inadequacy. Hand was a studious, withdrawn boy whose primary pleasures were reading and hiking in the Adirondacks with his cousin Augustus N. Hand, who for decades would serve as his colleague on the bench.

After an unexciting education at Albany Academy, Hand entered Harvard College in 1889 and for the first time in his life encountered genuine intellectual challenges. He veered away from the usual undergraduate track focusing on the classics and mathematics and chose instead courses in the more stimulating fields of economics and philosophy. Philosophy in particular appealed to Hand, and under the tutelage of the great Harvard philosophers William James, Josiah Royce, and George Santayana, his increasingly skeptical and independent mind flourished. His growing skepticism led him, while still an undergraduate, to become an agnostic. Hand never imposed his personal religious doubts on others, however, and he nonetheless recognized the benefit of religious faith in the lives of other people.

After receiving his B.A. and M.A. degrees in 1893, Hand would have preferred to undertake graduate study in philosophy but fell prey to family pressures and entered Harvard Law School instead. As it turned out, he relished the intellectual engagement and independent thinking encouraged by Dean Christopher C. Langdell's case method of instruction, and he never lost his admiration for many of his law professors, above all James Bradley Thayer, whose emphasis on judicial self-restraint in reviewing legislation left a lasting impression. Although Hand excelled both as an undergraduate and as a law student, he was not accepted into the upper echelons of campus society, and this rejection not only bothered him throughout his life, it also made him feel awkward and out of place. After graduation in 1896, Hand dropped the use of Billings and though unsure of himself, returned to Albany to practice law. His mother wanted him there, but Hand felt hamstrung, professionally as well as intellectually. In November 1902, three weeks before his marriage to Frances Amelia Fincke, with whom he would have three daughters, he moved to New York City.

If Hand had thought that practicing law in New York would interest him more—and make him feel better about himself—than it had in Albany, he was mistaken on both counts. Fortunately New York did have its compensations. His wife, a refined, self-assured graduate of Bryn Mawr, helped to ameliorate his sense of social awkwardness and her equanimity curbed his tendency toward moodiness. In addition, although he found the practice of law dull and uninspiring, he was drawn to the subject intellectually and began to contribute articles to legal journals. His most notable, "Due Process of Law and the Eight-Hour Day" (*Harvard Law Review* 21 [May 1908]: 495–509), criticized the U.S. Supreme Court for its lack of judicial restraint in *Lochner v. New York* (1905), which struck down New York's maximum-hours law for bakers and resulted in decades of judicial curbs on progressive-minded legislation.

The principal benefit that New York offered to Hand was acceptance among the city's intellectual elite, an involvement that, as his reputation as a civic reformer grew, led him into a judicial career. In 1909, after spending only a dozen years in private practice, and at the relatively young age of thirty-seven, Hand was named a district judge by President William Howard Taft. Hand had failed two years earlier to attain a federal judgeship, and he lacked the political connections ordinarily required for such an appointment—an independent, he voted in seventeen presidential elections: eight times for a Republican, eight times for a Democrat, and once for an independent—but he had his supporters, in this case New York reformer Charles C. Burlingham, who, aware that Attorney General George W. Wickersham was counseling the new president to improve the quality of the federal bench, urged him to select Hand. Hand began his judicial career with characteristic self-doubt, questioning whether his talents were up to the challenge and feeling especially insecure because his legal experience had not exposed him to the fields in which federal courts specialized, such as bankruptcy, admiralty, patents, and copyrights. Yet his intellect and hard work were more than equal to the task: within a very few years he was recognized as the outstanding judge in each of these areas.

In his early years as a judge Hand remained actively engaged in public policy and political issues, to a degree that in the late twentieth century would have raised serious issues of propriety. He brought to Theodore Roosevelt's attention Herbert Croly's important book, *The Promise of American Life* (1909), an argument in favor of state intervention in the private sector in order to achieve social goals. Roosevelt hailed the book as a major influence on his New Nationalism, which attempted to regulate monopoly rather than break up trusts, a position that Hand also espoused. He soon became an enthusiastic supporter of and participant in Roosevelt's Bull Moose Progressive movement, contributing to the "social and industrial" planks of the party's platform in 1912 and agreeing to be the party's candidate for chief judge of New York's highest court in 1913. He also helped to formulate the *New Republic* magazine, founded by Croly in 1914, and he contributed numerous essays to it. With the conclusion of World War I, however, he decided to heed U.S. Supreme Court Justice Oliver Wendell Holmes's private advice and began to avoid public involvement in heated public disputes that were unrelated to his position on the bench. Hand adhered to this policy until the last decade of his life, when his hostility to the spread of McCarthyism prompted him to speak out repeatedly, forcefully and eloquently, and earlier than almost any other establishment figure. In 1924 he was promoted by President Calvin Coolidge to the Court of Appeals for the Second Circuit, which at that time was the leading intermediate appellate court in the country. Hand became the court's chief judge in 1939 and served in that capacity until 1951, when he retired from active service, though he continued to participate in the court's work until his death, ten years later, in New York City.

Along with Oliver Wendell Holmes, Louis D. Brandeis, and Benjamin N. Cardozo, Hand, who sat on the bench for more than fifty years and wrote nearly 4,000 opinions in every area of the law, is counted among the leading American judges of the twentieth century. Once asked who among his Supreme Court colleagues was the greatest living American jurist, Justice Cardozo, speaking of Hand, replied, "The greatest living American jurist isn't *on* the Supreme Court." Not that he was never considered for the nation's highest court. In the early 1920s Justice Holmes included Hand on his ideal Supreme Court, but he had no chance during the conservative Harding and Coolidge Administrations, in part because expresident Taft, then the chief justice, exerted his influence to block any consideration, undoubtedly still bitter over Hand's support for the insurgent Bull Moose movement that turned Taft into a one-term president. Hand's chances were stronger in 1930, when President Herbert Hoover almost nominated him, and in 1942, when President Franklin D. Roosevelt also considered him for the Court. But by then Hand was seventy, so age rather than his reputation as a political maverick became his final bar to promotion.

As a nationally renowned jurist Hand had great influence, which was felt throughout the profession. He participated in the founding of the American Law Institute (ALI) in 1923 and played a leading role in formulating the ALI's model statutes and preparing its restatements of the law. However, it is for his published opinions that Hand is best remembered. It is not customary for judges and lawyers, in referring to a precedent, to name the judge who wrote the decision—except in the case of Hand. In usual references to his opinions, the case name and page citation appear followed by—usually in parentheses—"Learned Hand, J." Most of Hand's precedent-setting opinions are in the areas of private law (judge-made common law governing disputes between private litigants, such as contract and tort law) and statutory interpretation (the judge's difficult task of determining the *meaning* of a legislative act as applied to particular circumstances), but he also played a prominent role in shaping constitutional theory, in particular in the area of free speech.

In tort law, the law of negligence illustrates an area of common law created by judges without the guidance of statutes. The determination of what constitutes "negligence"—depending on what degree of care "a reasonably prudent man" would exercise in a particular context—was an area in which Hand was an especially influential master. In *The T. J. Hooper* (1932), for example, he found that a tug owner was negligent in not having a radio receiver on his tug, even though tugs in general did not at that time make it a practice to carry such radios. And *United States v. Carroll Towing Co.* (1947) contained what Judge Richard Posner has called "Hand's famous formulation of the negligence standard—one of the few attempts to give content to the deceptively simple concept of ordinary care. In stating the factors a court should consider in determining whether the standard of 'due care' had been violated, he anticipated, perhaps unwittingly, an economic meaning of negligence that has become central in the modern law-and-economics field of legal studies."

With regard to statutory interpretation, the proliferation of congressional statutes during the days Hand served as a federal judge confronted Hand with numerous statutes in a wide range of fields, from criminal law and tax law to the law of intellectual property (copyright, patent, and trademark law), antitrust law, and immigration law. Hand's major contribution was to delineate an approach that sought to avoid the twin dangers of, on the one hand, reading laws too literally, so that the legislative purpose might be obscured, and interpreting them so broadly, on the other, that judges had too much discretion in imposing their personal views that would undermine the meaning of the word used by Congress. As Hand once put it, there was no simple absolute rule to guide judges "between a sterile literalism which loses sight of the forest for the trees" and "a proper scruple against imputing meanings for which the words give no warrant." Hand himself called the task of interpreting statutes "an act of creative imagination" and an "undertaking [of] delightful uncertainty." In setting forth so influential an approach and illustrating it repeatedly in his interpretation of particular statutes, Hand demonstrated what a fellow judge (Henry J. Friendly) called "perhaps [his] greatest mastery."

Hand's most important, and controversial, constitutional contribution was his decision in *Masses Publishing Co. v. Patten* (1917), a ruling that safeguarded the right of *The Masses*, a left-wing magazine, to publish and distribute its pacifist, socialist views, however great their perceived threat to the prevailing national sentiment favoring the war. In 1919 the U.S. Supreme Court established, in *Schenck v. United States*, the "clear and present danger" standard for determining the limits of free speech under the First Amendment. Although this standard was formulated by Justice Holmes, whom Hand greatly admired, he believed that the *Masses* decision provided greater safeguards for freedom of expression by disallowing as unconstitutional only speech that incited others to take illegal action. Hand always believed that the "clear and present danger" test was too vague and thus vulnerable to the biases of judges and juries. To Hand, the "incitement" test was "a qualitative formula, hard, conventional, difficult to evade." Hand focused entirely on the *words* the speaker had used, not on guesses about their consequences. Only if the words directly incited to illegal action would conviction be consistent with the speaker's freedom of expression. Under Holmes's "clear and present danger" standard, by contrast, the punishability of speech turned on an evaluation of its likelihood to cause forbidden consequences. In brief, it required fact finders (juries and trial judges) to *guess* about the risks created by the challenged speech. Hand thought that this aspect was too slippery, too dangerous, to free expression—too much at the mercy of fact finders reflecting majoritarian sentiments hostile to dissent. To Hand, any speech falling short of direct incitement was protected by the First Amendment. For example, he would not permit juries after the fact to guess about the probable future harms that might have resulted from the speech, for fear that emotions contemptuous of dissidents would carry the day. Moreover, by emphasizing the quality of the words, the actual words used, appellate judges could play a larger role in protecting free speech. Hand always thought that his *Masses* approach had failed, but after his death, in *Brandenburg v. Ohio* (1969), the Supreme Court adopted a new standard for First Amendment coverage: Hand's "incitement" approach combined with the best elements of Holmes's "clear and present danger" test.

Hand was also known for diluting the "clear and present danger" standard in *U.S. v. Dennis* (1950), a decision upholding the conviction of American communist Eugene Dennis for violating the Smith Act, which made it illegal to advocate the violent overthrow of the government. In *Dennis*, Hand felt bound to follow the Supreme Court's prior endorsement of "clear and present danger" and recast it—conscientiously in his view—in a rather diluted, less speech-protective way, thereby reflecting both his growing skepticism of judicial enforcement of individual rights as well as his long-maintained obedience to Supreme Court doctrine.

In May 1944, his unusual name and his eloquence now well known beyond the legal profession, Hand delivered a brief but moving speech in New York City's Central Park on the occasion of "I Am an American Day," on which Hand led 150,000 new citizens in reciting the Pledge of Allegiance. The address, which attracted widespread attention and is often compared to Lincoln's Gettysburg Address, contained an especially striking and oft-quoted passage: "The spirit of liberty is the spirit which is not too sure that it is right." By then, as Justice Lewis F. Powell, Jr., has written, Hand's "rugged square features and imposing eyebrows [had become] the public's ideal of what a judge should look like" (foreword to Gunther [1994]).

Hand's primary achievement, however, was bringing a skeptical, analytical approach to bear in dealing with thousands of everyday cases involving virtually every facet of the law and rendering opinions that were characterized by cogent, clear expression. Hand was an innovative jurist but not a crusader. That is, he always strove to uncover the order within the chaotic confines of accepted legal wisdom, but he so distrusted absolutes that he was firmly opposed to judicial activism that invalidated majoritarian results on the basis of a judge's personal values. Hand reiterated this view in his Oliver Wendell Holmes Lectures, given in 1958 and published that same year as *The Bill of Rights*.

Hand's genuine open-mindedness, his determination to hear both sides of an argument, and his ceaseless probing and questioning were not merely the products of an astute philosophical mind. Rather they were deep-seated traits of the man himself, traits that were already fully ingrained by the time he became a judge. As unconvinced of the purported value of his own work as of the permanence of truth, he nonetheless persevered in the search for answers and thereby embodied the definition of a wise judge.

• The voluminous collection of Hand's papers, especially strong in his wide-ranging personal correspondence, is in the Harvard Law School Library. Additional especially important Hand letters are in the Felix Frankfurter papers in the Library of Congress; the Bernard Berenson Archive, Villa I Tatti, the Harvard University Center for Italian Renaissance Studies, Florence, Italy; and the Walter Lippmann papers at Yale University Library. The best collections of his writings are *The Art and Craft of Judging: The Decisions of Judge Learned Hand*, ed. Hershel Shanks (1968), and *The Spirit of Liberty: Papers and Addresses of Learned Hand*, ed. Irving Dilliard (1952; 3d ed., 1960). Gerald Gunther, *Learned Hand: The Man and the Judge* (1994), is the first full-scale biography; it is also the first to rely on the rich collection of Hand papers. Further useful sources are Marvin Schick, *Learned Hand's Court* (1970); Kathryn P. Griffith, *Judge Learned Hand and the Role of the Federal Judiciary* (1973); Gunther, "Learned Hand and the Origins of Modern First Amendment Doctrine: Some Fragments of History," *Stanford Law Review* 27 (1975): 719–73; Henry J. Friendly, "Learned Hand: An Expression from the Second Circuit," *Brooklyn Law Review* 60 (1962): 6–15; and Philip Hamburger, "The Great Judge," *Life*, 4 Nov. 1946. Volume 60 of the *Harvard Law Review* contains a wide-ranging collection of articles evaluating Hand's work on the occasion of his seventy-fifth birthday. Obituaries are in the *New York Times* and *The Times* (London), both 19 Aug. 1961.

GERALD GUNTHER